HALSBURY'S
Laws of England

FIFTH EDITION
2016

Volume 102

This is volume 102 of the Fifth Edition of Halsbury's Laws of England, containing the first part of the title WILLS AND INTESTACY.

The title WILLS AND INTESTACY replaces the WILLS AND INTESTACY title contained in volumes 102 (2010) and 103 (2010). Upon receipt of volumes 102 (2016) and 103 (2016), volumes 102 (2010) and 103 (2010) may be archived.

For a full list of volumes comprised in a current set of Halsbury's Laws of England please see overleaf.

Fifth Edition volumes:

1 (2008), 2 (2008), 3 (2011), 4 (2011), 5 (2013), 6 (2011), 7 (2015), 8 (2015), 9 (2012), 10 (2012), 11 (2015), 12 (2015), 12A (2015), 13 (2009), 14 (2016), 15 (2016), 15A (2016), 16 (2011), 17 (2011), 18 (2009), 19 (2011), 20 (2014), 21 (2016), 22 (2012), 23 (2016), 24 (2010), 25 (2016), 26 (2016), 27 (2015), 28 (2015), 29 (2014), 30 (2012), 31 (2012), 32 (2012), 33 (2013), 34 (2011), 35 (2015), 36 (2015), 37 (2013), 38 (2013), 38A (2013), 39 (2014), 40 (2014), 41 (2014), 41A (2014), 42 (2011), 43 (2011), 44 (2011), 45 (2010), 46 (2010), 47 (2014), 47A (2014), 48 (2015), 49 (2015), 50 (2016), 50A (2016), 51 (2013), 52 (2014), 53 (2014), 54 (2008), 55 (2012), 56 (2011), 57 (2012), 58 (2014), 58A (2014), 59 (2014), 59A (2014), 60 (2011), 61 (2010), 62 (2012), 63 (2012), 64 (2012), 65 (2015), 66 (2015), 67 (2016), 68 (2016), 69 (2009), 70 (2012), 71 (2013), 72 (2015), 73 (2015), 74 (2011), 75 (2013), 76 (2013), 77 (2016), 78 (2010), 79 (2014), 80 (2013), 81 (2010), 82 (2010), 83 (2010), 84 (2013), 84A (2013), 85 (2012), 86 (2013), 87 (2012), 88 (2012), 88A (2013), 89 (2011), 90 (2011), 91 (2012), 92 (2015), 93 (2008), 94 (2008), 95 (2013), 96 (2012), 97 (2015), 97A (2014), 98 (2013), 99 (2012), 100 (2009), 101 (2009), 102 (2016), 103 (2016), 104 (2014)

Consolidated Index and Tables:

2016 Consolidated Index (A–E), 2016 Consolidated Index (F–O), 2016 Consolidated Index (P–Z), 2017 Consolidated Table of Statutes, 2017 Consolidated Table of Statutory Instruments, etc, 2016 Consolidated Table of Cases (A–G), 2016 Consolidated Table of Cases (H–Q), 2016 Consolidated Table of Cases (R–Z, ECJ Cases)

Updating and ancillary materials:

2016 Annual Cumulative Supplement; Monthly Current Service; Annual Abridgments 1974–2015

October 2016

HALSBURY'S
Laws of England

Volume 102

2016

Members of the LexisNexis Group worldwide

United Kingdom	RELX (UK) Ltd, trading as LexisNexis, 1–3 Strand, London WC2N 5JR and 9–10 St Andrew Square, Edinburgh EH2 2AF
Australia	Reed International Books Australia Pty Ltd trading as LexisNexis, Chatswood, New South Wales
Austria	LexisNexis Verlag ARD Orac GmbH & Co KG, Vienna
Benelux	LexisNexis Benelux, Amsterdam
Canada	LexisNexis Canada, Markham, Ontario
China	LexisNexis China, Beijing and Shanghai
France	LexisNexis SA, Paris
Germany	LexisNexis GmbH, Dusseldorf
Hong Kong	LexisNexis Hong Kong, Hong Kong
India	LexisNexis India, New Delhi
Italy	Giuffrè Editore, Milan
Japan	LexisNexis Japan, Tokyo
Malaysia	Malayan Law Journal Sdn Bhd, Kuala Lumpur
New Zealand	LexisNexis New Zealand Ltd, Wellington
Singapore	LexisNexis Singapore, Singapore
South Africa	LexisNexis, Durban
USA	LexisNexis, Dayton, Ohio

FIRST EDITION	*Published in 31 volumes between 1907 and 1917*
SECOND EDITION	*Published in 37 volumes between 1931 and 1942*
THIRD EDITION	*Published in 43 volumes between 1952 and 1964*
FOURTH EDITION	*Published in 56 volumes between 1973 and 1987, with reissues between 1988 and 2008*
FIFTH EDITION	*Published between 2008 and 2014, with reissues from 2014*

A CIP Catalogue record for this book is available from the British Library.

ISBN 978-1-4743-0579-2

9 781474 305792

ISBN for the set: 9781405734394
ISBN for this volume: 9781474305792

Typeset by LexisNexis
Printed and bound by CPI Group (UK) Ltd, Croydon, CR0 4YY

Visit LexisNexis at www.lexisnexis.co.uk

HALSBURY ADVISORY BOARD

WILLS AND INTESTACY

Consultant Editor

PROFESSOR LESLEY KING, LLB, Dip Crim,

a Solicitor of the Senior Courts of England and Wales;
Professional Development Consultant, University of Law

The law stated in this volume is in general that in force on 1 September 2016, although subsequent changes have been included wherever possible.

Any future updating material will be found in the Current Service and annual Cumulative Supplement to Halsbury's Laws of England.

TABLE OF CONTENTS

PAGE

How to use Halsbury's Laws of England 11

References and Abbreviations 13

Table of Statutes 19

Table of Statutory Instruments 25

Table of Procedure 29

Table of European Union Legislation 33

Table of Conventions 35

Table of Cases 37

Volume 102

Table of Contents 1

1. Testamentary Disposition 9

2. Types of Testamentary Disposition 109

3. Failure of Testamentary Dispositions 141

4. Construction of Wills 173

5. Construction of Particular Dispositions 251

6. Intestate Succession 435

Index 489

Volume 103

Table of Contents 1

7. Family Provision Claims 9

8. The Office of Representative 59

9. The Grant of Probate or Administration 101

10. Contentious Probate 205

11. Devolution on the Representative 247

12. The Administration of Assets 267

13. The Distribution of Assets 323

14. The Role of the Court 385

15. Personal Representatives' Liabilities 411

16. Actions by and against Personal Representatives 443

Index 463

HOW TO USE HALSBURY'S LAWS OF ENGLAND

Volumes

Each text volume of Halsbury's Laws of England contains the law on the titles contained in it as at a date stated at the front of the volume (the operative date).

Information contained in Halsbury's Laws of England may be accessed in several ways.

First, by using the tables of contents.

Each volume contains both a general Table of Contents, and a specific Table of Contents for each title contained in it. From these tables you will be directed to the relevant part of the work.

Readers should note that the current arrangement of titles can be found in the Current Service.

Secondly, by using tables of statutes, statutory instruments, cases or other materials.

If you know the name of the Act, statutory instrument or case with which your research is concerned, you should consult the Consolidated Tables of statutes, cases and so on (published as separate volumes) which will direct you to the relevant volume and paragraph.

(Each individual text volume also includes tables of those materials used as authority in that volume.)

Thirdly, by using the indexes.

If you are uncertain of the general subject area of your research, you should go to the Consolidated Index (published as separate volumes) for reference to the relevant volume(s) and paragraph(s).

(Each individual text volume also includes an index to the material contained therein.)

Updating publications

The text volumes of Halsbury's Laws should be used in conjunction with the annual Cumulative Supplement and the monthly Noter-Up.

The annual Cumulative Supplement

The Supplement gives details of all changes between the operative date of the text volume and the operative date of the Supplement. It is arranged in the same volume, title and paragraph order as the text volumes. Developments affecting particular points of law are noted to the relevant paragraph(s) of the text volumes.

For narrative treatment of material noted in the Cumulative Supplement, go to the Annual Abridgment volume for the relevant year.

Destination Tables

In certain titles in the annual *Cumulative Supplement,* reference is made to Destination Tables showing the destination of consolidated legislation. Those Destination Tables are to be found either at the end of the titles within the annual *Cumulative Supplement,* or in a separate *Destination Tables* booklet provided from time to time with the *Cumulative Supplement.*

The Noter-Up

The Noter-Up is contained in the Current Service Noter-Up booklet, issued monthly and noting changes since the publication of the annual Cumulative Supplement. Also arranged in the same volume, title and paragraph order as the text volumes, the Noter-Up follows the style of the Cumulative Supplement.

For narrative treatment of material noted in the Noter-Up, go to the relevant Monthly Review.

REFERENCES AND ABBREVIATIONS

ACT	Australian Capital Territory
A-G	Attorney General
Admin	Administrative Court
Admlty	Admiralty Court
Adv-Gen	Advocate General
affd	affirmed
affg	affirming
Alta	Alberta
App	Appendix
art	article
Aust	Australia
B	Baron
BC	British Columbia
C	Command Paper (of a series published before 1900)
c	chapter number of an Act
CA	Court of Appeal
CAC	Central Arbitration Committee
CA in Ch	Court of Appeal in Chancery
CB	Chief Baron
CCA	Court of Criminal Appeal
CCR	County Court Rules 1981 (as subsequently amended)
CCR	Court for Crown Cases Reserved
CJEU	Court of Justice of the European Union
C-MAC	Courts-Martial Appeal Court
CO	Crown Office
COD	Crown Office Digest
CPR	Civil Procedure Rules
Can	Canada
Cd	Command Paper (of the series published 1900–18)
Cf	compare
Ch	Chancery Division
ch	chapter
cl	clause
Cm	Command Paper (of the series published 1986 to date)
Cmd	Command Paper (of the series published 1919–56)
Cmnd	Command Paper (of the series published 1956–86)
Comm	Commercial Court

Comr	Commissioner
Court Forms (2nd Edn)	Atkin's Encyclopaedia of Court Forms in Civil Proceedings, 2nd Edn. See note 2 post.
CrimPR	Criminal Procedure Rules
DC...........................	Divisional Court
DPP..........................	Director of Public Prosecutions
EAT..........................	Employment Appeal Tribunal
EC	European Community
ECJ	Court of Justice of the European Community (before the Treaty of Lisbon (OJ C306, 17.12.2007, p 1) came into force on 1 December 2009); European Court of Justice (after the Treaty of Lisbon (OJ C306, 17.12.2007, p 1) came into force on 1 December 2009)
EComHR	European Commission of Human Rights
ECSC.........................	European Coal and Steel Community
ECtHR Rules of Court	Rules of Court of the European Court of Human Rights
EEC..........................	European Economic Community
EFTA	European Free Trade Association
EGC	European General Court
EWCA Civ	Official neutral citation for judgments of the Court of Appeal (Civil Division)
EWCA Crim	Official neutral citation for judgments of the Court of Appeal (Criminal Division)
EWHC	Official neutral citation for judgments of the High Court
Edn	Edition
Euratom.....................	European Atomic Energy Community
EU	European Union
Ex Ch	Court of Exchequer Chamber
ex p..........................	ex parte
Fam..........................	Family Division
Fed..........................	Federal
Forms & Precedents (5th Edn)	Encyclopaedia of Forms and Precedents other than Court Forms, 5th Edn. See note 2 post
GLC	Greater London Council
HC...........................	High Court
HC...........................	House of Commons
HK..........................	Hong Kong
HL	House of Lords
IAT	Immigration Appeal Tribunal
ILM.........................	International Legal Materials
INLR	Immigration and Nationality Law Reports

IRC .... Inland Revenue Commissioners
Ind .... India
Int Rels...................... International Relations
Ir .... Ireland
J............................... Justice
JA............................. Judge of Appeal
Kan .... Kansas
LA .... Lord Advocate
LC .... Lord Chancellor
LCC .... London County Council
LCJ .... Lord Chief Justice
LJ .... Lord Justice of Appeal
LoN........................... League of Nations
MR .... Master of the Rolls
Man .... Manitoba
n............................... note
NB............................ New Brunswick
NI............................. Northern Ireland
NS .... Nova Scotia
NSW......................... New South Wales
NY........................... New York
NZ............................ New Zealand
OHIM........................ Office for Harmonisation in the Internal Market
OJ............................ The Official Journal of the European Union
published by the Publications Office of the
European Union
Ont .... Ontario
P............................... President
PC............................ Judicial Committee of the Privy Council
PEI........................... Prince Edward Island
Pat .... Patents Court
q............................... question
QB .... Queen's Bench Division
QBD......................... Queen's Bench Division of the High Court
Qld .... Queensland
Que........................... Quebec
r............................... rule
RDC.......................... Rural District Council
RPC.......................... Restrictive Practices Court
RSC.......................... Rules of the Supreme Court 1965 (as subsequently
amended)
reg .... regulation
Res........................... Resolution
revsd......................... reversed

Rly	Railway
s	section
SA	South Africa
S Aust	South Australia
SC	Supreme Court
SI	Statutory Instruments published by authority
SR & O	Statutory Rules and Orders published by authority
SR & O Rev 1904	Revised Edition comprising all Public and General Statutory Rules and Orders in force on 31 December 1903
SR & O Rev 1948	Revised Edition comprising all Public and General Statutory Rules and Orders and Statutory Instruments in force on 31 December 1948
SRNI	Statutory Rules of Northern Ireland
STI	Simon's Tax Intelligence (1973–1995); Simon's Weekly Tax Intelligence (1996-current)
Sask	Saskatchewan
Sch	Schedule
Sess	Session
Sing	Singapore
TCC	Technology and Construction Court
TS	Treaty Series
Tanz	Tanzania
Tas	Tasmania
UDC	Urban District Council
UKHL	Official neutral citation for judgments of the House of Lords
UKPC	Official neutral citation for judgments of the Privy Council
UN	United Nations
V-C	Vice-Chancellor
Vict	Victoria
W Aust	Western Australia
Zimb	Zimbabwe

NOTE 1. A general list of the abbreviations of law reports and other sources used in this work can be found at the beginning of the Consolidated Table of Cases.

NOTE 2. Where references are made to other publications, the volume number precedes and the page number follows the name of the publication; eg the reference '12 Forms & Precedents (5th Edn) 44' refers to volume 12 of the Encyclopaedia of Forms and Precedents, page 44.

NOTE 3. An English statute is cited by short title or, where there is no short title, by regnal year and chapter number together with the name by which it is commonly known or a description of its subject matter and date. In the case of a foreign statute, the mode of citation generally follows the style of citation in use in the country concerned with the addition, where necessary, of the name of the country in parentheses.

NOTE 4. A statutory instrument is cited by short title, if any, followed by the year and number, or, if unnumbered, the date.

TABLE OF STATUTES

PARA

Administration of Estates Act 1925

s 1 (1) 831, 945
(2) 608, 831, 952
(3) 608, 831
(4) 832
(5) 834
(7) 831
2 (1) 833, 945
(2) 833, 1024
(3) 833, 945
3 (1) 833
(i), (ii) 946
(2), (3) 948
(4), (5) 917, 948
4 830
5 .... 788, 831
(ii) 689
(iii) 631
6 .... 632, 831
7 (1) 637, 638
(2) 637
(3) 640
(4)(a), (b) 641
8 (1) 629
9 (1) 644
(2)(a), (b) 644
(3) 644
11 (1) 840
(2) 839
(3)–(7) 840
15 669
18 1019
21 643
21A (1)(a), (b) 641, 643
(2) 641, 643
(3) 643
22 821
23 828
24 829
25 (a) 959
(b) 957
(c) 847
26 (4) 1034
27 (1) 856
(2) 855
28 1261
29 1270
30 (1), (2) 780
(3) 779, 782
(4) 779
32 (1) 969
(2) 970
33 (1) 479, 1021, 1135
(2) 1108, 1135
(3) 1136
(4) 1137
(5) 496, 1138
(6), (7) 1135
34 (3) 992, 993, 998–1005, 1108
35 (1) 1006, 1009
(2) 1008
(3) 1006
36 (1) 1143
(2) 1146

PARA

Administration of Estates Act 1925—
continued

s 36 (4) 1144
(5) 1147
(6) 1027
(7) 1147
(8) 1026
(9) 1147
(10) 1145
(11) 1026, 1027, 1147
(12) 1026, 1027, 1143
37 858
38 (1), (2) 970
39 (1) 1019
(i) 1021
(iii) 1021
(1A) 1019
(2) 1021
(3) 1019
40 (1) 1022
41 (1) proviso (i) 1153
(ii) 1154
(b) 1155
(iii) 1155
(iv) 1154, 1155
(v) 1155
(1A) 1155
(2) 1156
(3) 1156, 1157
(4) 1156
(5) 1153
(6) 1153, 1156
(7) 1156
(9) 1153
42 (1) 1074, 1075
(2) 1075
43 (1) 1022
(2) 1143
(3) 1022
(4) 1143
44 .... 961, 1054
45 (1)(a) 478, 563, 564
(2) 478
46 (1)(i) 485, 488, 501, 518
(ii) 500
(iii), (iv) 509
(v) 511
(vi) 512, 778, 782
(1A) 488
(2) 485, 511
(2A) 485, 488, 500, 508, 510, 770
(4)–(9) 488
46A 488
47 (1)(i) 499
(ii) 502
(iv) 505
(3) 511
(4) 485
(4A) 488, 507
(4B)–(4D) 507
48 (2) 495
49 (1)(b) 517
50 (1), (2) 344, 535

PARA

Administration of Estates Act 1925—
continued
s 50 (3) 535
  51 (1), (2) 478
     (3) 478, 534
     (4) 478
  53 (1), (2) 607
  54 .... 917, 1135
  55 (1)(via) 946
     (ix) 1003
     (xi) 608
     (xvii) 608
     (xix) 607
     (xx) 608
     (xxiv) 942
     (xxvi) 622
     (xxviii) 607
     (2) 362, 499
     (3) 955
  Sch 1 Pt II 992, 998
     para 1 .... 999, 1108
          2 1000
          3 1001
          4 1002
          5 1003
          6 1004
          7 1005
       8 (a) 993
     1A para 1 488
Administration of Estates Act 1971
s 10 (1), (2) 983
  12 (6) 983
  14 983
Administration of Estates (Small Payments) Act 1965
s 1, 2 661
  5 661
  6 (1)(a) 661
     (2) 661
     (4) 661
  Sch 1, 2 661
Administration of Justice Act 1970
s 1 (6)(b) 678
Administration of Justice Act 1982
s 20 (1), (2) 187, 741
     (3) 741
     (4)(a)–(d) 187
     (5) 187
  21 .... 138, 140
     (1)(a) 195, 219
        (b), (c) 219
     (2) 195, 219
  22 .... 369, 382
  23 (1)(a) 16
     (2), (3) 16
     (4)(a), (b) 16
     (5)(a) 15
     (6)(a) 16
  24 (1)(a), (b) 16
     (2) 16
  25 (1)(a)–(c) 16
     (2) 16
     (3)(a) 16
     (4) 16
     (7)–(9) 16
  27 (1)–(3) 14
  28 (1)–(6) 14
  50 (1)–(5) 1163

PARA

Administration of Justice Act 1982—
continued
s 73 (6)(a) 65
     (c) 167, 169, 176, 186, 195,
                              219, 369
     (7) 87, 88
  76 (5) 14, 16
     (6)(a) 16
     (b) 14
     (7), (8) 14, 16
     (11) 65, 87, 88, 167, 169, 176,
          177, 186, 187, 219, 331, 369
  Sch 2 14
Administration of Justice Act 1985
s 47 (1), (2) 1272
  48 (1), (2) 192
  49 (1)(a), (b) 885
     (2) 885
  56 885
Adoption Act 1976
s 39 (1)–(3) 357
     (5), (6) 357
  42 (1)–(4) 357
  43 (2) 357
  44 (2), (3) 357
  46 (3) 357
Adoption and Children Act 2002
s 66 (2) 357
  67 (1) 357
     (3)–(5) 357
  69 (1)–(4) 357
  70 (2) 357
  71 (2), (3) 357
  73 (4) 357
  Sch 4 para 17 357
Apportionment Act 1870
s 2 927
  4–7 927
Children Act 1989
s 3 (3) 37
Civil Partnership Act 2004
s 71 .... 369, 382
  Sch 4 para 5 382
Colonial Probates Act 1892
s 1 .... 837, 842
  1A 837
  2 (1) 837
     (2) 840
     (4) 841
     (5) 837
  3, 4 837
  6 837
Colonial Probates (Protected States and Mandated Territories) Act 1927
s 1 837
Companies Act 2006
s 773 1023
Constitutional Reform Act 2005
s 19 (5) 15
  Sch 1 para 2 (1) 685
     7 para 4 15
Consular Conventions Act 1949
s 1 (1) 802
     (2)(a), (b) 667
     (3) 667
     (4) 802

PARA

Consular Conventions Act 1949—*continued*
s 3 667

County Courts Act 1984
s 25 566
  40 (4) 1162
  82 890

Courts Act 2003
s 99 (2) 1295

Courts and Legal Services Act 1990
s 56 (1)–(4) 728

Criminal Justice Act 1988
s 133 937

Duchy of Lancaster Act 1920
s 3 (3) 782

Escheat (Procedure) Act 1887
s 2 (3)–(5) 557

Family Law Reform Act 1969
s 3 (3), (4) 79
  28 (3) 167

Family Law Reform Act 1987
s 1 (1) 356, 482
  18 (1), (2) 482
    (2ZA), (2A) 482
  19 (1), (2) 356
    (4)–(6) 356
    (7) 350, 356
  21 (1) 768
    (3) 768
  34 (2) 358
  Sch 3 para 6 1218

Finance Act 1986
s 100 (1) 1003

Finance Act 2003
Pt 4 (ss 42–124) 1151
s 125 1151
Sch 3 para 3A (1)–(3) 489, 1151
              (4) 1151
         4–20 1151

Finance Act 2008
s 99 1151
Sch 32 1151

Forfeiture Act 1982
s 1 (2) 40
  2 40
  3 39
  5 40
  7 (2) 40
    (4) 40

Gender Recognition Act 2004
s 9 (1) 300, 329
    (2), (3) 300
  12 329
  15 300
  17 (1)–(3) 329
  18 (1)–(5) 300, 329

Human Fertilisation and Embryology Act
1990
s 1 (4), (5) 359
  2 (3) 359
  28 (4) 359
    (5)(a) 359
      (c) 359
    (7) 359
    (9) 359
  49 (2) 358, 359
    (3) 359

PARA

Human Fertilisation and Embryology Act
2008
s 57 (2) 359
  68 (2) 360

Inheritance Act 1833
s 1, 2 539
  3 540
  4 542
  6 548
  7 549
  9 550

Inheritance and Trustees' Powers Act 2014
s 3 (2) 288

Inheritance (Provision for Family and
Dependants) Act 1975
s 1 567
    (1) 566, 568
    (2)(a), (aa) 569
       (b) 570
  2 591
    (4) 592
  3 (1) 571
    (a)–(c) 572
    (d) 573
    (e) 574
    (f) 575
    (g) 576
    (2) 577, 578
    (2A) 579
    (3) 580
    (4) 581
    (5) 568
    (6) 572
  4 597
  5 603
    (4) 592
  6 594
  8 (1) 583
    (2) 584
    (3) 583
  9 585
  10 (1)–(4) 586
    (5) 587
    (6) 589
    (7), (8) 586
  11 (2), (3) 588
    (4) 589
    (5) 588
  12 (1)–(3) 588
    (4) 586, 588
  13 590
    (3) 588, 589
  14, 14A 578
  16 595
  17 596
  19 (1), (2) 593
  20 (2) 603
    (3) 590
  26 (3) 565
  27 (2), (3) 566

Inheritance Tax Act 1984
s 5 (2) 955
  200 (1)(a) 608
  204 (1) 608
  272 608
  273 1003
  Sch 6 para 1 1003

PARA

Inheritance Trustees' Powers Act 2014
s 12 (4) 485, 508, 518, 519

Insolvency Act 1986
s 284, 285 988
305 (5) 981
339–344 988
346, 347 988
421 (4) 981
421A (1)–(9) 988
423–425 988

Intestates' Estates Act 1952
s 5 489
6 (2) 344
Sch 2 para 1 (1)–(3) 489
(5) 489
2 489
3 (1)(a)–(c) 489
(2) 489
(4), (5) 489
4 (1)–(5) 490
5 489
6 (1), (2) 489
7 (1) 489

Land Registration Act 2002
s 4 (1)(a)(ii) 1144
(2) 1144
11 (5) 513
27 (2) 1144

Law of Property Act 1925
s 1 (2)(e) 17
4 (3) 17
7 (1) 17
27 (2) 1032
37 393
52 (2)(a) 1144
130 121
(4) 478
132 532
175 (1), (2) 1083
177 (1), (2) 88
179 4
180 (1) 943
184 .... 33, 746
204 669
(1) 679
205 (1)(xx) 943

Law of Property (Amendment) Act 1859
s 19, 20 543

Law of Property (Amendment) Act 1924
s 9 .... 17, 478, 633
Sch 9 478
para 3 .... 17, 633

Law of Property (Amendment) Act 1926
s 3 (1), (2) 622

Law of Property (Miscellaneous Provisions) Act 1994
s 12 (3) 1144
14 (2)–(6) 644
19 (1), (2) 644
(3)(a)–(c) 644
(5) 644

Law Reform (Miscellaneous Provisions) Act 1934
s 1 (1) proviso 1277, 1278
(1A) 1277, 1278
(2)(a)(i) 1281
(c) 1280

PARA

Law Reform (Miscellaneous Provisions) Act 1934—continued
s 1 (5) 1280
(6) 981, 1277

Law Reform (Succession) Act 1995
.... 344
s 3 (2) 178

Leasehold Reform Act 1967

Legitimacy Act 1976
s 4 (1) 483
5 350
(1) 357
(3), (4) 357
(6) 357
6 (2), (3) 357
10 (1) 357
(3) 357
11 357
(1) 350
Sch 1 para 4 350
(3) 357

Limitation Act 1980
s 11 (4), (5) 1279
(7) 1279

Mental Capacity Act 2005
s 18 (2) 47

Naval Pensions Act 1884
s 2 662

Navy and Marines (Property of Deceased) Act 1865
s 6 662
8 662

Partnership Act 1890
s 9 1232

Patronage (Benefices) Measures 1986
s 21 944

Pensions and Yeomanry Pay Act 1884
s 4 662

Perpetuities and Accumulations Act 1964
s 6 182
15(5) 182

Presumption of Death Act 2013
s 1 (1)–(5) 745

Public Trustee Act 1906
s 2 (4) 1164
3 (1) 1164
(5) 1165
6 (2) 642
11 (4) 784

Regimental Debts Act 1893
s 7 662
9 662

Revenue Act 1884
s 11 665

Senior Courts Act 1981
s 25 677
51 1196
(6) 914
(7), (7A) 914
(12A) 914
(13) 914
61 (1) 185, 865
105 724
(b) 683
106 (1) 683

PARA

Senior Courts Act 1981—*continued*
s 107 683
108 (1), (2) 690
109 (1), (2) 731
110, 111 732
112 689
113 (1), (2) 616
114 (1) 611, 757
(2) 757, 775
(4), (5) 775
115 (1)(a), (b) 622
(2), (3) 622
116 (1), (2) 758
117 808
118 620
119 788
120 766
121 (1), (2) 851
(3), (4) 843
122, 123 680
124, 125 732
126 (1) 15
127 (1), (2) 685
128 .... 620, 622, 784
Sch 1 para 1 (d) 185
(h) 678, 865
3 (b)(iv) 678

South Africa Act 1962
s 2 (1) 838
Sch 2 para 1 838

Stamp Act 1815
s 37 668

Statute of Westminster the Second (13 Edw 1) (1285)
c 1 559

Taxes Management Act 1970
s 40 (1), (2) 1217

Treasury Solicitor Act 1876
s 2 .... 779, 782
4, 5 779

Tribunals, Courts and Enforcement Act 2007
s 62 (4)(a) 1295
Sch 12, 13 1295

Trustee Act 1925
s 12 (1), (2) 1031
13 (1), (2) 1032
(4) 1032
14 (1) 1032
(3) 1026
16 (2) 1022
17 1026
18 (2) 952
19 (1)–(5) 1033
26 (1), (1A) 990
(2), (3) 990
27 (1) 964
(3) 964
36 (1) 950
63 (1) 1045
63A (3)(d) 1046
68 (1) para (9) 642, 1019
(17) ... 1019, 1026, 1033, 1045
69 (1) 1019, 1031, 1033
(2) 1019, 1031

PARA

Trustee Act 2000
s 12 (1)–(4) 1049
21 (2), (3) 1049
22 (4) 1049
23 (2) 1049
25 642
35 1049
(1) 1019
40 (2) 1049
Sch 1 para 1–7 1020
3 para 2, 3 959
6 1049

Trusts (Capital and Income) Act 2013
s 1 (1) 927
(2)(c) 1127
(d) 1118
(3) 1122
(4) 927, 1118, 1122, 1127
(5) 1127

Trusts of Land and Appointment of Trustees Act 1996
s 2 (6) 387
3 (1) 1160
4 (1) 1035, 1160
(2) 1160
6 (5) 1020
11 (1), (2) 1020
25 (4) 27, 166
Sch 1 para 5 (1) 387

Wills Act 1837
s 1 27
3 .... 26, 27, 29
7 46
9 .... 72, 707
(a) 60, 62, 64
(b) 62, 66
(c) 60, 68, 70
(d) 70
11 79
13 .... 70, 113
14 78
15 .... 41, 78
16, 17 78
18 (1), (2) 87
(3) 89
(4)(a), (b) 89
18A (1)(a), (b) 177, 178
(2) 177, 178
(3) 177
18B (1), (2) 90
(3)–(6) 91
18C (1) 179
(2)(a), (b) 179
(3) 179
19 93
20 .... 93–96, 101, 104
21 .... 82, 84
22 110
23 94
24 .... 29, 282
25 183
26 291
27 170
28 376
33 170
(1) 169, 331
(2) 169, 305
(3), (4) 169

PARA

Wills Act 1837—*continued*
s 33A 169
  35 44

Wills Act 1963
s 1 12
  4 94
  6 (2) 12
  7 (2) 12

PARA

Wills Act 1968
s 1 78
  (1), (2) 44

Wills (Soldiers and Sailors) Act 1918
s 1–4 79
  5 (2) 79

TABLE
OF STATUTORY INSTRUMENTS

PARA

Access to Justice Act 1999
(Destination of Appeals) Order
2000, SI 2000/1071
art 1 (2)(a) 890
(c) 890
Administration of Estates (Small
Payments) (Increase of Limit)
Order 1984, SI 1984/539 663
Administration of Insolvent Estates of
Deceased Persons Order 1986, SI
1986/1999
art 3 1104
(1), (2) 981
4 (1)–(3) 981
5 (A1) 981
(1) 981, 1104
(2), (3) 981
Sch 1 1104
Pt II para 12 988
26–28 988
36 988
2 1104
Civil Partnership Act 2004
(Commencement No 2) Order
2005, SI 2005/3175 .... 369, 382
Civil Procedure (Amendment No 2)
Rules 2001, SI 2001/1388
r 19 860
Civil Proceedings Fees Order 2008, SI
2008/1053
art 3 (a) 686
Consular Conventions (Arab Republic
of Egypt) Order 1986, SI
1986/216 802
Consular Conventions (Czechoslovak
Socialist Republic) Order 1976, SI
1976/1216 802
Consular Conventions (Federal
Republic of Germany) Order
1957, SI 1957/2052 802
Consular Conventions (French
Republic) Order 1953, SI
1953/1455 802
Consular Conventions (Hungarian
People's Republic) Order 1971, SI
1971/1845 802
Consular Conventions (Italian
Republic) Order 1957, SI
1957/2053 802
Consular Conventions (Japan) Order
1965, SI 1965/1714 802
Consular Conventions (Kingdom of
Belgium) Order 1964, SI
1964/1399 802
Consular Conventions (Kingdom of
Denmark) Order 1963, SI
1963/370 802

PARA

Consular Conventions (Kingdom of
Greece) Order 1953, SI
1953/1454 802
Consular Conventions (Kingdom of
Norway) Order in Council 1951,
SI 1951/1165 802
Consular Conventions (Kingdom of
Sweden) Order 1952, SI
1952/1218 802
Consular Conventions (Mongolian
People's Republic) Order 1976, SI
1976/1150 802
Consular Conventions
(People's Republic of Bulgaria)
Order 1968, SI 1968/1861 802
Consular Conventions (Polish
People's Republic) Order 1971, SI
1971/1238 802
Consular Conventions (Republic of
Austria) Order 1963, SI
1963/1927 802
Consular Conventions (Socialist
Federal Republic of Yugoslavia)
Order 1966, SI 1966/443 802
Consular Conventions (Spanish State)
Order 1963, SI 1963/614 802
Consular Conventions (Union of
Soviet Socialist Republics) Order
1968, SI 1968/1378 802
Consular Conventions (United States
of Mexico) Order 1955, SI
1955/425 802
County Courts (Interest on Judgment
Debts) Order 1991, SI 1991/1184
.... 1187
Court Funds Rules 2011, SI
2011/1734
r 6 (6) 1046
24 (1) 666, 1284
(2), (3) 1284
(4) 666, 1284
(5)–(7) 1284
25 (1), (2) 1284
26 (1), (2) 1284
Estates of Deceased Persons
(Forfeiture Rule and Law of
Succession) Act 2011
(Commencement) Order 2011, SI
2011/2913
art 2 169
Family Law Reform Act 1969
(Commencement No 1) Order
1969, SI 1969/1140
art 2 167
Family Law Reform Act 1987
(Commencement No 1) Order
1988, SI 1988/425
art 2 358

PARA

Family Law Reform Act 1987
(Commencement No 1) Order 1988, SI
1988/425—*continued*
Schedule 358

Family Provision (Intestate Succession)
Order 1977, SI 1977/415 485

Family Provision (Intestate Succession)
Order 1981, SI 1981/255 485

Family Provision (Intestate Succession)
Order 1987, SI 1987/799 485

Family Provision (Intestate Succession)
Order 1993, SI 1993/2906 485

Family Provision (Intestate Succession)
Order 2009, SI 2009/135 485

Financial Collateral Arrangements (No
2) Regulations 2003, SI
2003/3226
reg 4 (1) 975

Gender Recognition Act 2004
(Commencement) Order 2005, SI
2005/54 329

Government Stock Regulations 2004,
SI 2004/1611
reg 17 (4) 663

High Court and County Courts
Jurisdiction Order 1991, SI
1991/724
art 2 (7B) 866

Human Fertilisation and Embryology
Act 1990 (Commencement No 3
and Transitional Provisions)
Order 1991, SI 1991/1400
art 2 (2) 358, 359

Human Fertilisation and Embryology
Act 2008 (Commencement No 1
and Transitional Provisions)
Order 2009, SI 2009/479 360
art 6 (1)(a) 359

Human Fertilisation and Embryology
(Parental Orders) (Consequential,
Transitional and Saving
Provisions) Order 2010, SI
2010/986
art 3 361

Inheritance and Trustees' Powers Act
2014 (Commencement) Order
2014, SI 2014/2039
art 2 .... 485, 519

Insolvency Act 2000 (Commencement
No 1 and Transitional Provisions)
Order 2001, SI 2001/766
art 2 (1)(b) 988

Insolvency Rules 1986, SI 1986/1925
r 6.96 987
6.98 (1)(e) 987
6.109 (1), (2) 987
6.115–6.118 987
11.9 (3) 987

Intestate Succession (Interest and
Capitalisation) Order 1977, SI
1977/1491
art 2 485

Land Registration Rules 2003, SI
2003/1417
r 206 1144

PARA

Land Registration Rules 2003, SI
2003/1417—*continued*
Sch 1 1144

Non–Contentious Probate Fees (Indian
Ocean Tsunami) Order 2005, SI
2005/266
art 2 686

Non–Contentious Probate Fees
(London Terrorist Bombings)
Order 2005, SI 2005/3359
art 2 686

Non–Contentious Probate Fees Order
2004, SI 2004/3120
art 2 .... 688, 690, 732
3 686
6 (1), (2) 686
7 686
Sch 1 686
Fee 1 841
4 690
5 688
7, 8 732
11 695
1A para 16 686

Non–Contentious Probate Rules 1987,
SI 1987/2024
r 2 (1) 622, 631
3 .... 685, 696
4 726
5 727
6 742
(1) 728, 738
7 742
8 (1)–(3) 728
(4) 765
9, 10 728
11 732
(2)(b) 741
(3) 741
12 733
(1) 72
13 734
14 (1) 735
(2) 83, 735
(3) 736
(4) 737
15 737
16 734
17 .... 710, 733
18 710
19 .... 706, 846
20, 21 790
22 (1) 768
(2), (3) 769
(4) 769, 770
23 685
24 769
25, 26 776
27 (1), (1A) 729
(2), (3) 729
(4)–(8) 774
28 .... 768, 774, 776
(2) 718, 844
29 822
30 (1) 844
(a), (b) 841
(2) 844
(3) 718

PARA

Non–Contentious Probate Rules 1987, SI 1987/2024—continued

r 30 (3)(a) 841
   31 (1)–(3) 800
   32 (1)–(3) 795, 799
   33 (1), (2) 798
   34 (1) 795, 798
     (2) 795
   35 (1) 804
     (2) 804, 805
     (5) 804
   36 (1)–(3) 783
     (4) 813
   37 (1), (2) 631
     (2A) 631, 632
     (3) 632
     (4) 631, 632
   38 778
   39 (1)–(6) 841
     (7) 842
   40 .... 766, 841
   43 (1)–(3) 688
   44 (1)–(4) 690
     (5) 691
     (6), (7) 692
     (8) 694
     (9), (10) 692
     (11), (12) 693
     (13), (14) 694
   45 (1), (2) 692
     (3), (4) 694
   46 (1)–(3) 695
     (4) 696
     (5) 695
     (6) 697
   47 (1), (2) 698
     (3) 699
     (4) 698, 699
     (5)(a), (b) 698
       (c) 699
     (6) 698, 699
     (7)(a), (b) 698
       (c) 699
   48 (1), (2) 700
   49 .... 690, 691, 695, 697
   50 (1), (2) 680
   51 819
   52 (a) 758
     (b) 815
   53 744
   54 730
     (2) 721
   55 741
   57 683
   58, 59 732
   60 (1) 685
     (2) 687
     (3) 685, 687
     (4) 687

PARA

Non–Contentious Probate Rules 1987, SI 1987/2024—continued

r 60 (8) 705
     (9) 687, 705
     (10) 705
     (11) 687
   61 701
     (1) 815
     (2) 753
   62, 62A 683
   63 687
   64 681
   65 705
     (1) 681
   66, 67 704
Sch 1 form 3 690
        4 691
        5 692

Police Pensions Regulations 1987, SI 1987/257
reg L4 (3) 662

Police Pensions Regulations 2006, SI 2006/3415
reg 83 (4) 662

Presumption of Death Act 2013 (Commencement and Transitional and Saving Provision) Order 2014, SI 2014/1810
art 2 745

Stamp Duty (Exempt Instruments) Regulations 1987, SI 1987/516
.... 1151

Stamp Duty Land Tax (Appointment of the Implementation Date) Order 2003, SI 2003/2899
art 2 1151

Statutory Wills Forms 1925, SR & O 1925/780 4

Treasury Solicitor (Crown's Nominee) Rules 1997, SI 1997/2870
r 3 (1), (2) 779

Trustee Act 2000 (Commencement) Order 2001, SI 2001/49 959
art 2 1049

Wills (Deposit for Safe Custody) Regulations 1978, SI 1978/1724
reg 2 (2) 15
   3 (1) 15

TABLE OF PROCEDURE

Civil Procedure

Civil Procedure Rules 1998, SI 1998/3132 (CPR)

	PARA
CPR	
Pt 1 (rr 1.1–1.4)	882
r 2.1 (2)	685
2.3 (1)	875, 890
2.4	681
3.1 (2)(f)	1177
(g)	1175
(i)	1273
3.3 (1)	1175, 1177
(2)(a)	1175
(5)(a)	1175
(7)	1175
6.37 (3), (4)	1167
6.117, 6.118	987
8.5 (4)	602
Pt 12 (rr 12.1–12.11)	876
r 15.4 (2)	873
16.2 (1)(a)	875
(3), (4)	1271
19.2 (2)	1172
19.7A (1), (2)	1172, 1271
19.8 (1)	818, 1278, 1283
(2)	818, 1278
(b)(ii)	1283
(3)–(5)	818
19.8A (1)	1172
(2)	1172, 1272
(3)–(7)	1272
(8)	1172
21.10	1043
22.1 (1)(a)	875
(4)–(6)	875
25.2 (1)	1274
26.3 (2)	877
29.2 (2)	877
29.8	877
30.2 (6)	1176
30.3 (1)	867
(2)(a)–(h)	867
30.4 (1)	1176
30.5 (1)	1176
(3)	1176
31.2	880
31.4	880
32.1–32.3	886
32.4	886
(1)	882
32.5	886
32.10	882
39.2 (1)	886
(3)(c)	886
(f)	886
44.2	1196
(1)	908
(2)(a), (b)	908
(3)(b)	908
(5)	908
44.11	914

PARA

CPR
  r 46.3 .... 909, 1196
    52.1 (3)(b), (c) 890
    Pt 57 (rr 57.1–57.23) 860
  r 57.1 (2)(a) 680
          (ii) 847
      (b) 680
      (c) 870
    57.2 (2) 865
      (3) 866
      (4) 877
    57.3 (a) 868
    57.4 (1) 869
      (2) 869, 873
      (3) 869
      (4) 873
    57.5 (1) 870
      (2)(a), (b) 870
      (3) 870
      (4) 868, 870
      (5) 870
    57.6 847
      (1) 868, 878, 888
      (2)–(4) 888
    57.7 (1), (2) 777, 875
      (3) 875, 901
      (4) 875
      (5)(a), (b) 874
    57.8 (1), (2) 873
    57.9 (1)–(5) 873
    57.10 (1) 869, 876
      (2)–(5) 869
    57.11 (1), (2) 883
    57.12 (2) 889
    57.13 (2), (3) 1163
      (5) 1163
    57.15 599
    57.16 (1)–(3) 599
      (3A), (3B) 599
      (4), (4A) 599
      (5) 599, 889
    64.1 (2) 1166, 1198
      (3) 185
    64 2 1274
      (a) 1162
      (d) 192
    64.3 .... 185, 192, 1166, 1169
    64.4 .... 191, 1274
      (1) 1166
      (c) 1172

Practice Directions supplementing CPR

PARA
CPR PD 2B: Allocation of Cases to Levels of Judiciary 1274
  para 7B.2 1180
CPR PD 2C: Starting Proceedings in the County Court
  para 3.1 (3) 861
CPR PD 3A: Striking Out a Statement of Case 884
CPR PD 6B: Service Out of the Jurisdiction
  para 3.1 (13) 1167
CPR PD 7A: How to Start Proceedings: The Claim Form
  868
  para 5.5 1283
CPR PD 15: Defence and Reply
  para 3.2 873

PARA

CPR PD 16: Statements of Case
para 8.2 875
    13.3 875
CPR PD 17: Amendments to Statements of Case 875
CPR PD 19B: Group Litigation 1283
CPR PD 21: Children and Protected Parties 1043
CPR PD 29: The Multi-Track
para 2.2 867
    2.6 867
    4.3 877
    9, 10 886
CPR PD 37: Miscellaneous Provisions about Payments into Court
para 6.1–6.3 1046
CPR PD 39A: Miscellaneous Provisions relating to Hearings
para 1.5 886
CPR PD 40A: Accounts, Inquiries etc
para 1.1 1192
    10 1192
    14 (1)–(3) 1187
    15 .... 405, 1080, 1187
CPR PD 46: Costs Special Cases
para 1.1, 1.2 1196
CPR PD 57: Probate 860
para 2.2 .... 680, 868
    2.3 .... 682, 871
    2.4 .... 682, 868
    3.1 682
    3.2, 3.3 870
    4 877
    5.1 .... 876, 884
    5.2 874
    6.1 (1) 885
      (2) 883, 885
    6.2 885
    7.1–7.4 680
    8.1–8.4 810
    8.5 811
    10.1, 10.2 889
    11 .... 682, 889
    12–14 1163
    15 599
    16 (1)–(3) 602
      (4) 602, 889
    17 600
    18.1, 18.2 602
CPR PD 64A: Estates, Trusts and Charities
para 1 (1) 1169
    (2)(b) 1030
    1A 1030, 1169
    1A.5 1030
    3.1 .... 1162, 1166, 1179
    3.2 .... 1166, 1181
    3.3 .... 1166, 1172
    3.4 1169
    6.2–6.4 1198
CPR PD: Pre-Action Conduct and Protocols
para 3 860
    18 860

TABLE OF EUROPEAN UNION LEGISLATION

Secondary Legislation

Regulations

PARA

Commission Implementing Regulation (EU) 1329/2014 (OJ L359, 16.12.2014, p 30)
.... 13
European Parliament and Council Regulation (EU) 650/2012 (OJ L201, 27.7.2012, p 107)
  recital (67) 13
       (82) 13
  art 20 13
     22 13
     62–73 13

TABLE OF CONVENTIONS

PARA

Convention on the Establishment of a Scheme of Registration of Wills (Basle,
16 May 1972; Misc 30 (1972); Cmnd 5073) 16

Convention providing a Uniform Law on the Form of an International Will (Washington,
26 October to 31 December 1974; Misc 9 (1975); Cmnd 5950)
.... 14
Annex art 1 (1), (2) 14
2 14
3 (1)–(3) 14
4 (1), (2) 14
5 (1)–(3) 14
6 (1), (2) 14
7 (1), (2) 14
8–15 14

TABLE OF CASES

PARA

A

A (child of the family), Re [1998] 1 FCR 458, [1998] 1 FLR 347, [1998] Fam Law 14, CA 567

A, B and C, X, Y and Z [2012] EWHC 2400 (COP), [2013] WTLR 187 893

AN v Barclays Private Bank and Trust (Cayman) Ltd (2006) 9 ITELR 630 .... 138, 141, 149, 190

AP, MP and TP v Switzerland (Application 19958/92) (1997) 26 EHRR 541, ECtHR 1217

ARMS (Multiple Sclerosis Research) Ltd, Re, Alleyne v A-G [1997] 2 All ER 679, [1997] 1 WLR 877, [1997] 1 BCLC 157 162

A-B v Dobbs [2010] EWHC 497 (Fam), [2010] WTLR 931 758

Abbay v Howe (1847) 1 De G & Sm 470, 11 Jur 765, 9 LTOS 392, sub nom Abbey v Howe 16 LJ Ch 437 397

Abbiss v Burney, Re Finch (1881) 17 Ch D 211, 50 LJ Ch 348, 29 WR 449, 44 LT 267, CA 246, 424

Abbot v Massie (1796) 3 Ves 148 .... 212, 1070

Abbott, Re, Public Trustee v St Dunstan's British Home and Hospital for Incurables and Trustees of Western Ophthalmic Hospital and Lady Dugan [1944] 2 All ER 457, 88 Sol Jo 406, CA 296

Abbott v Middleton (1855) 21 Beav 143; affd (1858) 7 HL Cas 68, 28 LJ Ch 110, 33 LTOS 66, 5 Jur NS 717, 11 ER 28, HL 225, 237, 242–244, 253, 260

Abbott v Parfitt (1871) LR 6 QB 346, 40 LJQB 115, 19 WR 718, 24 LT 469 1288

Abbott v Service. See Westminster Bank Ltd's Declaration of Trust, Re

Abdul Hamid Bey's Goods, Re (1898) 67 LJP 59, 78 LT 202, P, D and Admlty 800

Abdullahi v Mudashir [2003] All ER (D) 477 (Oct) 31

Aberdein, Re (1896) 41 Sol Jo 12, 13 TLR 7 973

Abraham v Alman (1826) 1 Russ 509 263

Abraham v Conyngham (1676) Freem KB 445, 3 Keb 725, 2 Lev 182, 2 Mod Rep 146, T Jo 72, 1 Vent 303, 89 ER 333 .... 671, 858

Abrahams, Re, Abrahams v Abrahams [1908] 2 Ch 69, 77 LJ Ch 578, 99 LT 240 1067

Abrahams, Re, Abrahams v Bendon [1911] 1 Ch 108, 80 LJ Ch 83, 55 Sol Jo 46, 103 LT 532 1076

Abrahams' Will Trusts, Re, Caplan v Abrahams [1969] 1 Ch 463, [1967] 2 All ER 1175, [1967] 3 WLR 1198, 111 Sol Jo 794 .... 11, 138, 140

Abram, Re [1997] 2 FCR 85, [1996] 2 FLR 379, [1996] Fam Law 666, [1997] BPIR 1 .... 568, 570, 573, 591

Abrey v Newman (1853) 16 Beav 431, 22 LJ Ch 627, 17 Jur 153, 1 WR 156 .... 395, 397

Acherley v Vernon (1739) 2 Com 513, Fortes Rep 186, Willes 153 .... 148, 414

Acheson v Fair (1843) 2 Con & Law 208, 3 Dr & War 512 467

Acheson v Russell [1951] Ch 67, 66 (pt 2) TLR 279, sub nom Manor Farm, Kytes Hardwick, Re, Acheson v Russell [1950] 2 All ER 572 .... 280, 291

Achillopoulos, Re, Johnson v Mavromichali [1928] Ch 433, 97 LJ Ch 246, [1928] All ER Rep 326, 139 LT 62 803

Ackerman v Burrows (1750) 3 Ves & B 54 395

Ackers v Phipps (1835) 9 Bli NS 430, 3 Cl & Fin 665, HL 284

Ackland v Pring (1841) 10 LJCP 231, Drinkwater 189, 2 Man & G 937, 3 Scott NR 297 942

Ackroyd v Smithson (1780) 1 Bro CC 503, [1775–1802] All ER Rep 227, 1 Wh & T 68, 28 ER 1262, sub nom Akeroid v Smithson 2 Dick 566, 3 P Wms 22n 173, 183

Adair, Re [1909] 1 IR 311 145

PARA

Adair v Maitland. *See* Maitland v Adair
Adair v Shaw (1803) 1 Sch & Lef 243 1238
Adam's Policy Trusts, Re (1883) 23 Ch D 525, 52 LJ Ch 642, 31 WR 810, 48 LT 727

.... 390
Adam's Trusts, Re (1865) 11 Jur NS 961, 14 WR 18, 13 LT 347

.... 382, 449
Adams, Re [1990] Ch 601, [1990] 2 All ER 97, [1990] 2 WLR 924, [1990] 2 FLR 519,
    [1990] Fam Law 403, 134 Sol Jo 518 105
Adams, Re (1911) 45 ILT 93 713
Adams, Re, Adams v Adams (1906) 94 LT 720, CA 334
Adams, Re, Adams v Lewis [2001] WTLR 493, [2001] All ER (D) 274 (Jan)

.... 577
Adams, Re, Gee v Barnet Group Hospital Management Committee [1968] Ch 80, [1967]
    3 All ER 285, [1967] 3 WLR 1088, 111 Sol Jo 587, CA

.... 278
Adams, Re, Verrier v Haskins [1906] WN 220, 51 Sol Jo 113

.... 1074, 1079
Adams v Adams [1892] 1 Ch 369, 61 LJ Ch 237, 40 WR 261, 36 Sol Jo 215, 66 LT 98, 8
    TLR 236, CA 190
Adams v Adams (1842) 1 Hare 537, 11 LJ Ch 305, 6 Jur 681

.... 252, 291
Adams v Cheverel (1606) Cro Jac 113 1287
Adams v Clerke (1725) 9 Med Rep 154 232
Adams v Gibney (1830) 6 Bing 656, 8 LJOSCP 242, 4 Moo & P 491

.... 1223
Adams v Jones (1852) 9 Hare 485, 21 LJ Ch 352, 16 Jur 159, 18 LTOS 326

.... 263, 272, 276
Adams v Lopdell (1890) 25 LR Ir 311 371
Adams v Peirce (1724) 3 P Wms 11 1141
Adams v Robarts (1858) 25 Beav 658 .... 427, 429
Adams v Schofield [2004] WTLR 1049, CA 598
Adams and Kensington Vestry, Re (1884) 27 Ch D 394, 54 LJ Ch 87, 32 WR 883, 51 LT
    382, CA 370
Adams' Goods, Re (1872) LR 2 P & D 367, 36 JP 407, 41 LJP & M 31, 20 WR 400, 26
    LT 526 60
Adamson, Re (1875) LR 3 P & D 253, P, D and Admlty

.... 83, 613
Adamson, Re, Public Trustee v Billing (1913) 109 LT 25, CA

.... 464
Adamson v Armitage (1815) Coop G 283, 19 Ves 416 375
Addams v Ferick (1859) 26 Beav 384, 28 LJ Ch 594, 5 Jur NS 588, 33 LTOS 252

.... 1011
Addison's Estate, Re (1964) 108 Sol Jo 504, P, D and Admlty

.... 108
Addy v Grix (1803) 8 Ves 504 74
Adkins, Re, Solomon v Catchpole (1908) 98 LT 667 293
Admiralty Comrs v SS Amerika [1917] AC 38, 86 LJP 58, 13 Asp MLC 558,
    [1916–17] All ER Rep 177, 61 Sol Jo 158, 116 LT 34, 33 TLR 135, HL

.... 1280
Adney v Greatrex (1869) 38 LJ Ch 414, 17 WR 637, 20 LT 647

.... 328
Adshead v Willetts (1861) 29 Beav 358, 9 WR 405 .... 241, 342, 375
Advocate (Lord) v Bogie [1894] AC 83, 63 LJPC 85, 6 R 98, 70 LT 533, [1891–4] All ER
    Rep Ext 1432, HL 165
Aeroflot v Berezovsky [2013] EWHC 4348 (Ch), [2014] All ER (D) 166 (Jan)

.... 1166
Agnese's Goods, Re [1900] P 60, 69 LJP 27, 82 LT 204, P, D and Admlty

.... 819
Agricultural Holdings (England) Act 1883, Re, Gough v Gough [1891] 2 QB 665, 55 JP
    807, 60 LJQB 726, 39 WR 593, 65 LT 110, 7 TLR 608, CA

.... 937
Ahluwalia v Singh [2011] EWHC 2907 (Ch), [2011] 38 LS Gaz R 18, [2011] All ER (D)
    113 (Sep) 70
Ahmed Angullia Bin Hadjee Mohamed Salleh Angullia v Estate and Trust Agencies
    (1927) Ltd [1938] AC 624, [1938] 3 All ER 106, 107 LJPC 71, 159 LT 428, 54 TLR
    831, PC 1212, 1215

PARA

Ainslie, Re, Swinburn v Ainslie (1885) 30 Ch D 485, 50 JP 180, 55 LJ Ch 615, 33 WR
910, 53 LT 645, 1 TLR 678, CA 931
Ainsworth, Re, Cockcroft v Sanderson [1895] WN 153, P, D and Admlty
.... 1173
Ainsworth, Re, Finch v Smith [1915] 2 Ch 96, 84 LJ Ch 701, 113 LT 368, 31 TLR 392
.... 1098
Ainsworth, Re, Millington v Ainsworth [1922] 1 Ch 22, 91 LJ Ch 51, [1922] B & CR 21,
66 Sol Jo 107, 126 LT 247 404
Ainsworth's Goods, Re (1870) LR 2 P & D 151, 34 JP 664, 23 LT 324
.... 65
Aird's Estate, Re, Aird v Quick (1879) 12 Ch D 291, 48 LJ Ch 631, 27 WR 882, 41 LT
180, [1874–80] All ER Rep Ext 1526 406
Aiscough, ex p (1731) 2 Eq Cas Abr 780, 2 P Wms 591, sub nom Ascough v Lady
Chaplin Cooke Pr Cas 62, sub nom ex p Ayscoughe Mos 391
.... 551
Aislabie v Rice (1818) 3 Madd 256, 8 Taunt 459, 2 Moore CP 358
.... 135
Aitken's Trustees v Aitken 1970 SC 28, HL 322
Akerman, Re, Akerman v Akerman [1891] 3 Ch 212, 61 LJ Ch 34, 40 WR 12,
[1891–4] All ER Rep 196, 65 LT 194 1067
Akeroid v Smithson. See Ackroyd v Smithson
Akeroyd's Settlement, Re, Roberts v Akeroyd [1893] 3 Ch 363, 63 LJ Ch 32, 7 R 405, 69
LT 474, CA 446
Albemarle (Earl) v Rogers (1796) 7 Bro Parl Cas 522, HL
.... 375
Alchorne, Re, Eade v Bourner (1911) 130 LT Jo 528 397
Alcock, Re, Bonser v Alcock (or Seville) [1945] Ch 264, [1945] 1 All ER 613, 114 LJ Ch
161, 89 Sol Jo 246, 173 LT 4, 61 TLR 351 .... 205, 236, 332, 396
Alcock v Ellen (1692) 2 Eq Cas Abr 290, Freem Ch 186
.... 390
Alder v Park (1836) 5 Dowl 16, 2 Har & W 78 1299
Aldersey, Re, Gibson v Hall [1905] 2 Ch 181, 74 LJ Ch 548, [1904–7] All ER Rep 644, 92
LT 826 33
Alderton, Re, Hughes v Vanderspar [1913] WN 129 326
Aldhous, Re, Noble v Treasury Solicitor [1955] 2 All ER 80, [1955] 1 WLR 459, 99 Sol Jo
276 .... 167, 484, 793, 964
Aldrich v A-G (Rogers intervening) [1968] P 281, [1968] 1 All ER 345, [1968] 2 WLR
413, 111 Sol Jo 945, P, D and Admlty 722
Aldrich v Cooper (1803) 8 Ves 382, 32 ER 402, [1803–13] All ER Rep 51
.... 1012
Aldridge v Lord Wallscourt (1810) 1 Ball & B 312 1012
Aldridge v Turner [2004] EWHC 2768 (Ch), [2004] All ER (D) 451 (Nov)
.... 155, 197
Alexander, Re, Alexander v Alexander [1919] 1 Ch 371, 88 LJ Ch 242, 120 LT 692
.... 399
Alexander, Re, Bathurst v Greenwood [1910] WN 94, CA
.... 282
Alexander v Alexander (1842) 5 Beav 518 409
Alexander v Alexander (1855) 16 CB 59, 24 LJCP 150, 1 Jur NS 598, 3 WR 450, 3 CLR
801, 25 LTOS 99 419
Alexander v Alexander (1856) 6 De GM & G 593, 3 Jur NS 28, 5 WR 28, 28 LTOS 112
.... 378
Alexander v Brame (1855) 7 De GM & G 525, 3 Eq Rep 919, 1 Jur NS 1032, 3 WR 642,
25 LTOS 298; revsd sub nom Jeffries v Alexander (1860) 24 JP 643, 8 HL Cas 594,
31 LJ Ch 9, 7 Jur NS 221, 2 LT 748 2
Alexander v Kirkpatrick (1874) LR 2 Sc & Div 397, HL
.... 107
Alexander v Sizer (1869) LR 4 Exch 102, 38 LJ Ex 59, 20 LT 38
.... 1241
Alexander's Will Trust, Re [1948] 2 All ER 111, sub nom Re Alexander, Courtauld-
Thomson v Tilney [1948] LJR 1373, 92 Sol Jo 350, 64 TLR 308
.... 234
Alford's Estate, Re (1939) 83 Sol Jo 566, P, D and Admlty
.... 8, 97, 111, 679
Alger v Parrott (1866) LR 3 Eq 328 .... 364, 377

PARA

Algermann v Ford. See Angermann v Ford

Alker v Barton (1842) 12 LJ Ch 16 397

Alkin v Raymond [2010] All ER (D) 48 (May) 1163

Allan, Re, Allan v Midland Bank Executor and Trustee Co Ltd [1954] Ch 295, [1954]
1 All ER 646, [1954] 2 WLR 512, 98 Sol Jo 193, CA 346, 493

Allan, Re, Dow v Cassaigne [1903] 1 Ch 276, 72 LJ Ch 159, 51 WR 403, 88 LT 246, CA
.... 173, 298, 410, 1115

Allan, Re, Havelock v Havelock-Allan (1896) 12 TLR 299
.... 190

Allan v Backhouse (1813) 2 Ves & B 65; affd (1821) Jac 631
.... 375

Allan v Gott (1872) 7 Ch App 439, 41 LJ Ch 571, 20 WR 427, 26 LT 412
.... 992

Allan v Morrison [1900] AC 604, 69 LJPC 141, PC 106, 716

Allanson v Clitherow (1747) 1 Ves Sen 24 473

Allen, Re (1962) 106 Sol Jo 115, P, D and Admlty 108

Allen, Re, Faith v Allen [1953] Ch 810, [1953] 2 All ER 898, [1953] 3 WLR 637, 97 Sol
Jo 606, CA 138, 140, 273

Allen, Re, Faith v Allen [1954] Ch 259, [1954] 1 All ER 526, [1954] 2 WLR 333, 98 Sol
Jo 146 .... 129, 300

Allen, Re, Hincks v Allen (1880) 49 LJ Ch 553, 28 WR 533
.... 21

Allen, Re, Lewis v Vincent (2007) 10 ITELR 506 1080

Allen, Re, Wilson v Atter (1881) 29 WR 480, 44 LT 240
.... 175

Allen v Allen (1862) 30 Beav 395, 31 LJ Ch 442, 8 Jur NS 758, 10 WR 261, 5 LT 737
.... 1008

Allen v Callow (1796) 3 Ves 289 403

Allen v Crane (1953) 89 CLR 152, [1953] ALR 959, 27 ALJ 538 (Aust HC), Aust HC
.... 335

Allen v Dundas (1789) 3 Term Rep 125, 100 ER 490, [1775–1802] All ER Rep 398
.... 670–671, 856

Allen v Emery [2005] EWHC 2389 (Ch), 8 ITELR 358, [2005] All ER (D) 175 (Oct)
.... 49

Allen v Humphrys (1882) 8 PD 16, 52 LJP 24, sub nom Humphreys v Allen 47 JP 24, 31
WR 292, sub nom Re Humphreys' Goods, Allen v Humphreys 48 LT 125, P, D and
Admlty 770

Allen v Jackson (1875) 1 Ch D 399, 40 JP 262, 45 LJ Ch 310, 24 WR 306, 33 LT 713, CA
.... 133

Allen v M'Pherson (1847) 1 HL Cas 191, 11 Jur 785 .... 58–59, 671, 892, 903, 907

Allen v Maddock (1858) 11 Moo PCC 427, 6 WR 825, 14 ER 757, [1843–60] All ER Rep
285, 31 LTOS 359, PC 201, 711

Allen v Wood (1834) 1 Bing NC 8, 3 LJCP 219, 4 Moo & S 510, 131 ER 1020
.... 246

Allen's Estate, Re, Prescott v Allen and Beaumont [1945] 2 All ER 264, 114 LJ Ch 298, 89
Sol Jo 316, 173 LT 198 239

Allen's Trusts, Re [1909] WN 181 168

Allgood v Blake (1873) LR 8 Exch 160, 42 LJ Ex 101, 21 WR 599, 29 LT 331
.... 212, 400

Allgood's Will Trusts, Re, Chatfield v Allen (18 December 1980, unreported), CA
.... 126

Allhusen v Whittell (1867) LR 4 Eq 295, 36 LJ Ch 929, [1861–73] All ER Rep 149, 16 LT
695 .... 1118–1119, 1121, 1126

Allin v Crawshay (1851) 9 Hare 382, 21 LJ Ch 873 468

Alliston v Chapple (1860) 6 Jur NS 288, 2 LT 110 284

Allnutt v Wilding [2007] EWCA Civ 412, 9 ITELR 806, [2007] WTLR 941, [2007] All ER
(D) 41 (Apr) 187

Alloway v Alloway (1843) 2 Con & Law 517, 4 Dr & War 380
.... 395

Allsop, Re, Cardinal v Warr [1968] Ch 39, [1967] 3 WLR 793, 111 Sol Jo 415, sub nom
Re Alsopp, Cardinal v Warr [1967] 2 All ER 1056, CA 244, 315–316

Allsop, Re, Whittaker v Bamford [1914] 1 Ch 1, 83 LJ Ch 42, [1911–13] All ER Rep 834,
58 Sol Jo 9, 109 LT 641, 30 TLR 18, CA 1259

Almack v Horn (1863) 1 Hem & M 630, 32 LJ Ch 304, 1 New Rep 535, 11 WR 505, 8
LT 415 .... 309, 330

Almes v Almes (1796) 2 Hag Ecc App 155 794

PARA

Almosnino's Goods, Re (1859) 23 JP 328, 29 LJP & M 46, 6 Jur NS 302, 1 Sw & Tr 508,
  2 LT 191 .... 67, 711, 725
Alsop Wilkinson (a firm) v Neary [1995] 1 All ER 431, [1996] 1 WLR 1220, [1995] NLJR
  52n 604, 1196, 1274
Alston, Re, Alston v Trollope (1866) LR 2 Eq 205, 35 Beav 466, 35 LJ Ch 846, 14 WR
  722, 14 LT 451 974
Alt v Gregory (1856) 8 De GM & G 221, 2 Jur NS 577, 4 WR 436
  .... 395, 470
A-M v A-M (divorce: jurisdiction: validity of marriage) [2001] 2 FLR 6, [2001] Fam Law
  495, [2001] All ER (D) 288 (Feb) 567
Ambler v Bolton (1872) LR 14 Eq 427, 41 LJ Ch 783, 20 WR 934
  1216
Ambrose v Hodgson. See Hodgson v Ambrose
Ames, Re, Ames v Taylor (1883) 25 Ch D 72, 32 WR 287
  652
Amherst v Lytton (1729) Mos 131, 212, 5 Bro Parl Cas 254, Fitz-G 99
  448
Amherst (Lord) v Duchess of Leeds (1842) 12 Sim 476, 6 Jur 141
  371
Amies v Skillern (1845) 14 Sim 428, 14 LJ Ch 165, 9 Jur 124, 4 LTOS 471
  393
Amirteymour, Re [1978] 3 All ER 637, [1979] 1 WLR 63, sub nom Bank Melli Iran v
  Personal Representatives of Amirteymour 122 Sol Jo 525, CA
  1278
Amiss Goods, Re (1849) 2 Rob Eccl 116, 7 Notes of Cases 274
  74
Amory, Re, Westminster Bank Ltd v British Sailors' Society Inc at Home and Abroad
  [1951] 2 All ER 947n, [1951] WN 561, 95 Sol Jo 744 .... 1017, 1203, 1209
Amos, Re, Carrier v Price [1891] 3 Ch 159, 60 LJ Ch 570, 39 WR 550, [1891–4] All ER
  Rep 320, 65 LT 69, 7 TLR 559 .... 35–36, 117
Amos v Horner (1699) 1 Eq Cas Abr 112 134
Amson v Harris (1854) 19 Beav 210 .... 396, 398
Amyot v Dwarris [1904] AC 268, 73 LJPC 40, 53 WR 16, 90 LT 102, 20 TLR 268, PC
  .... 300, 333
Ancaster v Mayer (1785) 1 Bro CC 454 1012
Anderson, Re, Halligey v Kirkley [1920] 1 Ch 175, 89 LJ Ch 81, [1918–19] All ER Rep
  975, 122 LT 261 379
Anderson, Re, Public Trustee v Bielby (1928) 44 TLR 295
  .... 156, 270
Anderson v Anderson (1872) LR 13 Eq 381, 41 LJ Ch 247, 20 WR 313, [1861–73] All ER
  Rep 161, 26 LT 12 43
Anderson v Berkley [1902] 1 Ch 936, 71 LJ Ch 444, 50 WR 684, 46 Sol Jo 450, 86 LT
  443, 18 TLR 531 .... 269, 277, 346
Anderson's Will, Re (1953) 75 WNNSW 334 79
Andree v Ward (1826) 1 Russ 260, 4 LJOS Ch 98 457
Andrew v Andrew (1845) 1 Coll 686 122
Andrew v Andrew (1875) 1 Ch D 410, 45 LJ Ch 232, 24 WR 349, 34 LT 82, CA
  .... 376, 416, 419, 473
Andrew v Master and Wardens of Merchant Taylors' Co. See A-G v Andrew
Andrew v Motley (1862) 12 CBNS 514 101
Andrew v Trinity Hall, Cambridge (1804) 9 Ves 525 153
Andrew v Wrigley (1792) 4 Bro CC 125 1023
Andrew's Estate, Re, Creasey v Graves (1902) 50 WR 471, 46 Sol Jo 450
  .... 250, 298
Andrew's Will, Re (1859) 27 Beav 608, 29 LJ Ch 291, 5 Jur NS 114, 1 LT 319
  .... 385–386, 392
Andrewes v George (1830) 3 Sim 393 405
Andrews, Re, Dunedin Corpn v Smyth (1910) 29 NZLR 43
  278
Andrews v Andrews (1885) 15 LR Ir 199, 212, Ir CA 215, 275
Andrews v Dobson (1788) 1 Cox Eq Cas 425 217
Andrews v Partington (1791) 3 Bro CC 401, 29 ER 610, [1775–1802] All ER Rep 209
  .... 181, 307–308, 310
Andrews d Jones v Fulham (1738) 2 Eq Cas Abr 294, Andr 263, 2 Stra 1092
  446

                                                                                          PARA
Andrews' Will, Re, Andrews v O'Mara (1899) 25 VLR 408
.... 293
Andros, Re, Andros v Andros (1883) 24 Ch D 637, 52 LJ Ch 793, 32 WR 30,
     [1881–5] All ER Rep 467, 49 LT 163 350
Angell v Haddon (1816) 1 Madd 529 985
Angermann v Ford (1861) 29 Beav 349, sub nom Algermann v Ford 7 Jur NS 668, 9 WR
     512, 4 LT 230 1081
Angerstein v Martin (1823) Turn & R 232, 2 LJOS Ch 88
.... 1054, 1118
Angus v Emmott [2010] EWHC 154 (Ch), [2010] All ER (D) 70 (Feb)
.... 1163
Angus Will Trusts, Re, Hall v Angus [1960] 3 All ER 835, [1960] 1 WLR 1296, 104 Sol Jo
     1034 252
Anon (1341) 35 Lib Ass, pl 14 473
Anon (1346) (Rolls Series), 20 Edw 3, Pt II 428, pl 69 2
Anon (1431) YB 9 Hen 6, fo 24b 182
Anon (1441) YB 19 Hen 6, fo 73, pl 2 473
Anon (1459) YB 37 Hen 6, fo 35, pl 23 182
Anon (1498) YB 13 Hen 7, fo 17, pl 22 469
Anon (1535) YB 27 Hen 8, fo 27, pl 11 384
Anon (1542) Bro NC pl 334 121
Anon (1548) Bro NC pl 388 121
Anon (1553) Bro NC 62 378
Anon (1567) 3 Dyer 261b, Jenk 232 210
Anon (1572) 3 Dyer 303b, pl 49 474
Anon (1578) 3 Leon 71 pl 108 383
Anon (1582) Cro Eliz 9 234
Anon (1584) 3 Leon 87 330
Anon (1590) 4 Leon 14, pl 51 474
Anon (1608) Godb 159 930
Anon (1683) 1 Vern 162 1099
Anon (1689). See Morley v Polhill
Anon (1707) 1 Salk 155 657
Anon (1710) 5 Vin Abr 292 21
Anon (1714) 1 P Wms 267 27
Anon (1718) 1 P Wms 495 1099
Anon (1744) 2 Eq Cas Abr 551, pl 33 439
Anon (circa 1660) Freem Ch 137 123
Anon (undated) (1834) 1 My & K 14 115
Anstead, Re, Gurney v Anstead [1943] Ch 161, [1943] 1 All ER 522, 87 Sol Jo 139, 168
     LT 309, 59 TLR 219, sub nom Re Anstead, Anstead v Gurney 112 LJ Ch 161
.... 1000
Anstee v Nelms (1856) 1 H & N 225, 26 LJ Ex 5, 4 WR 612, 27 LTOS 190
.... 212–213
Anstee's Goods, Re [1893] P 283, 63 LJP 61, 1 R 487, 42 WR 16, P, D and Admlty
.... 83
Anstey v Mundle [2016] EWHC 1073 (Ch) 31, 956
Anstice, Re (1856) 23 Beav 135 450
Anstruther v Chalmer (1826) 2 Sim 1, 4 LJOS Ch 123 .... 385, 800
Antaios Compania Naviera SA v Salen Rederierna AB [1985] AC 191, [1984] 3 WLR 592
.... 189
Anthony, Re, Anthony v Anthony [1892] 1 Ch 450 1007
Anthony, Re, Anthony v Anthony [1893] 3 Ch 498, 62 LJ Ch 1004, 3 R 671, 41 WR 667,
     37 Sol Jo 632, 69 LT 300 1006
Anthony v Donges [1998] 2 FLR 775, [1998] Fam Law 666
.... 262, 266
Anziani, Re, Herbert v Christopherson [1930] 1 Ch 407, 99 LJ Ch 215, 142 LT 570
.... 6
Aplin v Stone [1904] 1 Ch 543, 73 LJ Ch 456, 90 LT 284
.... 41, 181, 1115
Appelbee's Goods, Re (1828) 1 Hag Ecc 143 108
Applebee, Re, Leveson v Beales [1891] 3 Ch 422, 60 LJ Ch 793, 40 WR 90, 65 LT 406
.... 198, 222, 625
Appleton, Re, Barber v Tebbit (1885) 29 Ch D 893, 49 JP 708, 54 LJ Ch 594, 53 LT 906,
     [1881–5] All ER Rep Ext 1250, CA 1069
Apreece v Apreece (1813) 1 Ves & B 364 371
Apted's Goods, Re [1899] P 272, 68 LJP 123, 81 LT 459, P, D and Admlty
.... 730

                                                                            PARA
Arbery v Ashe (1828) 1 Hag Ecc 214 899
Arbib and Class Contract, Re [1891] 1 Ch 601, 60 LJ Ch 263, 39 WR 305, 64 LT 217,
    CA 147, 152
Arbuthnot, Re, Arbuthnot v Arbuthnot [1915] 1 Ch 422, 84 LJ Ch 424, 59 Sol Jo 398,
    112 LT 987 404
Arbuthnott v Fagan [1995] CLC 1396, [1995] 1 Lloyds Re Insurance Law Reports 135
    194
Archer, Re [1907] 14 OLR 374, 9 OWR 652 182
Archer v Jegon (1837) 8 Sim 446, 6 LJ Ch 340, Coop Pr Cas 172, 1 Jur 792
    302
Archer v Kelk (1852) 16 Jur 605, 19 LTOS 252 1175
Archer v Legg (1862) 31 Beav 187, 10 WR 703 .... 395, 397
Archer's Case, Baldwin v Smith (1597) 2 And 37, 1 Co Rep 66b, Cro Eliz 453
    339
Archibald v Hartley (1852) 21 LJ Ch 399 293
Ards v Walkin (1598) Cro Eliz 637, sub nom Ardes v Watkins Moore KB 549
    27
Aribisala v St James Homes (Grosvenor Dock) Ltd [2007] EWHC 1694 (Ch),
    [2007] All ER (D) 101 (Jun) 190
Arkitt, Re. See Rickit's Trusts, Re
Armitage v Nurse [1998] Ch 241, [1997] 2 All ER 705, [1997] 3 WLR 1046, 74 P & CR
    D13, [1997] PLR 51, CA 1196, 1238, 1246
Armitage v Williams (1859) 27 Beav 346, 7 WR 650 .... 305, 308, 396
Armstrong, Re, Ayne v Woodward (1893) 31 LR Ir 154
    403
Armstrong, Re, ex p Gilchrist (1886) 17 QBD 521, 51 JP 292, 55 LJQB 578, 34 WR 709,
    55 LT 538, 2 TLR 745, CA 378
Armstrong v Armstrong (1869) LR 7 Eq 518, 38 LJ Ch 463, 17 WR 570, 20 LT 776
    .... 390, 394
Armstrong v Armstrong (1871) LR 12 Eq 614, 19 WR 971, 25 LT 199
    .... 1068, 1178
Armstrong v Armstrong (1888) 21 LR Ir 114 .... 348, 441
Armstrong v Buckland (1854) 18 Beav 204 277
Armstrong v Burnet (1855) 20 Beav 424, 24 LJ Ch 473, 3 Eq Rep 870, 1 Jur NS 765, 3
    WR 433, 25 LTOS 209 1011
Armstrong v Clavering (1859) 27 Beav 226 366
Armstrong v Eldridge (1791) 3 Bro CC 215 .... 395, 470
Armstrong v Stockham (1843) 7 Jur 230 398
Armstrong's Will Trusts, Re, Graham v Armstrong [1943] Ch 400, [1943] 2 All ER 537,
    112 LJ Ch 335, 87 Sol Jo 310, 169 LT 268, 59 TLR 420
    126
Armytage v Wilkinson (1878) 3 App Cas 355, 47 LJPC 31, 26 WR 559, sub nom
    Armytage v Master in Equity of Supreme Court of Victoria 38 LT 185, PC
    412
Arnald v Arnald (1784) 1 Bro CC 401 157
Arnold, Re, Calvert v Whelen [1942] Ch 272, [1942] 1 All ER 501, 111 LJ Ch 147, 86 Sol
    Jo 105, 166 LT 199, 58 TLR 185 991
Arnold v Arnold (1834) 2 My & K 365, 4 LJ Ch 79, 123
    250
Arnold v Chapman (1748) 1 Ves Sen 108 184
Arnold's Estate, Re (1863) 33 Beav 163, 9 Jur NS 1186, 12 WR 4, 9 LT 530
    .... 193, 252, 412, 453, 473
Arnold's Trusts, Re (1870) LR 10 Eq 252, 39 LJ Ch 875, 18 WR 912, 23 LT 337
    317
Arnould, Re, Arnould v Lloyd [1955] 2 All ER 316, [1955] 1 WLR 539, 99 Sol Jo 338
    471
Arrow v Mellish (1847) 1 De G & Sm 355 .... 395, 397
Arrowsmith's Trust, Re (1860) 29 LJ Ch 774, 6 Jur NS 1231, 8 WR 555; on appeal (1861)
    2 De GF & J 474, 30 LJ Ch 148, 7 Jur NS 9, 9 WR 258, 3 LT 635
    451
Arthur v Bokenham (1708) 11 Mod Rep 148, Fitz-G 233
    51
Arthur v Mackinnon (1879) 11 Ch D 385, 48 LJ Ch 534, 27 WR 704, 41 LT 275
    127
Arthur v Walker [1897] 1 IR 68 473
Arthur's Goods, Re (1871) LR 2 P & D 273, 36 JP 168, 19 WR 1016, 25 LT 274
    65

PARA

Ascough v Lady Chaplin Cooke. See Aiscough, ex p

Ascough v Lady Chaplin. See Aiscough, ex p
Ashburner v Macguire (1786) 2 Bro CC 108 159
Ashburner v Wilson (1850) 17 Sim 204, 19 LJ Ch 330, 14 Jur 497

.... 265, 456
Ashburnham, Re, Gaby v Ashburnham (1912) 57 Sol Jo 28, 107 LT 601

.... 282, 296
Ashby v Ashby (1827) 7 B & C 444, 6 LJOSKB 41, 1 Man & Ry KB 180

.... 1231
Ashby v Costin (1888) 21 QBD 401, 53 JP 69, 57 LJQB 491, 37 WR 140, 59 LT 224, DC

.... 32
Ashby v Day (1885) 33 WR 631; affd (1886) 34 WR 312, 54 LT 408, 2 TLR 260, CA

.... 1236
Ashby v White (1703) 1 Bro Parl Cas 62, 2 Ld Raym 938, 956, 6 Mod Rep 45, 54, 3 Salk
  17, 1 Salk 19, Holt KB 524, 1 Smith LC 266, 14 State Tr 695, 92 ER 126

.... 191
Asher v Whitlock (1865) LR 1 QB 1, 30 JP 6, 35 LJQB 17, 11 Jur NS 925, 14 WR 26, 13
  LT 254 28
Ashford v Haines (1851) 21 LJ Ch 496, sub nom Ashford v Field 18 LTOS 115

.... 318, 395
Ashforth, Re, Sibley v Ashforth [1905] 1 Ch 535, [1904–7] All ER Rep 275, sub nom Re
  Ashforth's Trusts, Ashforth v Sibley 74 LJ Ch 361, 53 WR 328, 49 Sol Jo 350, 92 LT
  534, 21 TLR 329 117
Ashley v Ashley (1833) 6 Sim 358, 3 LJ Ch 61 .... 395, 420, 474
Ashley v Ashley (1877) 4 Ch D 757, 46 LJ Ch 322, 25 WR 356, 36 LT 200, CA

.... 986
Ashley v Waugh (1839) 9 LJ Ch 31, 4 Jur 572 115
Ashling v Knowles (1856) 3 Drew 593 322
Ashmore's Goods, Re (1843) 3 Curt 756, 7 Jur 1045, 2 Notes of Cases 465

.... 74
Ashmore's Trusts, Re (1869) LR 9 Eq 99, 39 LJ Ch 202

.... 432
Ashton, Re, Ballard v Ashton [1920] 2 Ch 481, 89 LJ Ch 583, 65 Sol Jo 44, 124 LT 374

.... 381
Ashton v Adamson (1841) 1 Dr & War 198 .... 228, 375
Ashton v Poynter (1835) 1 Cr M & R 738, 3 Dowl 465, 4 LJ Ex 71, 1 Gale 57, 5 Tyr 322

.... 1276
Ashton's Goods, Re [1892] P 83, 61 LJP 85, 67 LT 325, P, D and Admlty

.... 220
Ashworth, Re Bent v Thomas (1942) 86 Sol Jo 134 293
Askew v Askew [1961] 2 All ER 60, [1961] 1 WLR 725, 105 Sol Jo 160, P, D and Admlty

.... 591
Askew v Askew (1888) 57 LJ Ch 629, 36 WR 620, 58 LT 472

.... 316–317
Aspinall, Re, Aspinall v Aspinall [1961] Ch 526, [1961] 2 All ER 751, [1961] 3 WLR 235,
  105 Sol Jo 529 927
Aspinall v Duckworth (1866) 35 Beav 307, 14 WR 527

.... 165, 174–175,176
Aspinall v Petvin (1824) 1 Sim & St 544, 2 LJOS Ch 121

.... 469
Aspinall v Wake (1833) 10 Bing 51, 2 LJCP 227, 3 Moo & S 423

.... 1288
Astbury, Re, Astbury v Godson [1926] WN 336 390
Astbury v Astbury [1898] 2 Ch 111, 67 LJ Ch 471, 46 WR 536, 78 LT 494

.... 974
Aste, Re, Mossop v Macdonald (1918) 87 LJ Ch 660, 118 LT 433

.... 1123
Asten v Asten [1894] 3 Ch 260, 63 LJ Ch 834, 8 R 496, 71 LT 228, [1891–4] All ER Rep
  Ext 1291 .... 116, 127, 263, 266, 400
Astley v Earl of Essex (1871) 6 Ch App 898, 25 LT 470

.... 415
Astley v Earl of Essex (1874) LR 18 Eq 290, 43 LJ Ch 817, 22 WR 620, 30 LT 485

.... 145
Aston v Aston [2007] WTLR 1349 .... 572, 577
Aston v Aston (1703) 2 Vern 452, sub nom Anon 2 Eq Cas Abr 212, sub nom Ashton v
  Ashton Prec Ch 226 .... 134, 146, 149
Aston v Smallman (1706) 2 Vern 556 393

PARA

Aston v Wood (1874) 43 LJ Ch 715, 22 WR 893, 31 LT 293
..... 153
Astor, Re, Astor v Astor [1922] 1 Ch 364, 91 LJ Ch 277, CA
..... 416, 423–424
Astor's Goods, Re (1876) 1 PD 150, 40 JP 617, 45 LJP 78, 24 WR 539, 34 LT 856, P, D and Admlty 723
Astor's Settlement Trusts, Re, Astor v Scholfield [1952] Ch 534, [1952] 1 All ER 1067, 96 Sol Jo 246, [1952] 1 TLR 1003 ..... 11, 33, 150
Atcherley (or Acherley) v Vernon (1725) 1 Com 382, 3 Bro Parl Cas 85, HL
..... 113, 284
Atherton v Crowther (1854) 19 Beav 448, 2 WR 639, 24 LTOS 64
..... 364
Atherton v Pye (1792) 4 Term Rep 710 474
Atherton's Goods, Re [1892] P 104, 61 LJP 134, 66 LT 267, P, D and Admlty
..... 763
Athill, Re, Athill v Athill (1880) 16 Ch D 211, 50 LJ Ch 123, 29 WR 309, 43 LT 581, CA
..... 204, 236, 1009
Atkin's Will Trusts, Re, National Westminster Bank Ltd v Atkins [1974] 2 All ER 1, [1974] 1 WLR 761, 118 Sol Jo 391 182
Atkins, Re, ex p Edmonds (1882) 51 LJ Ch 406, 30 WR 432, 46 LT 240
..... 973
Atkins v Hiccocks (1737) 1 Atk 500, West temp Hard 114
..... 428
Atkins v Tredgold (1823) 2 B & C 23, 1 LJOSKB 228, 3 Dow & Ry KB 200
..... 976
Atkinson, Re, Atkinson v Weightman [1925] WN 30, CA
..... 231, 251
Atkinson, Re, Proctor v Atkinson [1908] 2 Ch 307, 77 LJ Ch 766, 99 LT 174, CA
..... 970
Atkinson, Re, Pybus v Boyd [1918] 2 Ch 138, 87 LJ Ch 505, [1918–19] All ER Rep 1043, 119 LT 235 331
Atkinson, Re, Webster v Walter [1930] 1 Ch 47, 99 LJ Ch 35, [1929] All ER Rep 491, 142 LT 129 ..... 994, 998–999, 1012
Atkinson, Re, Wilson v Atkinson [1892] 3 Ch 52, 61 LJ Ch 504, 40 WR 666, 36 Sol Jo 503, 66 LT 717 ..... 393, 395
Atkinson v Atkinson (1872) IR 6 Eq 184 322
Atkinson v Barton (1861) 3 De GF & J 339; revsd sub nom Atkinson v Holtby (1863) 10 HL Cas 313, 32 LJ Ch 735, 9 Jur NS 503, 11 WR 544, 8 LT 583
..... 244, 474–475
Atkinson v Bartrum (1860) 28 Beav 219 397
Atkinson v Holtby. See Atkinson v Barton
Atkinson v Hutchinson (1734) 2 Eq Cas Abr 294, 3 P Wms 258
..... 385–386, 460
Atkinson v L'Estrange (1885) 15 LR Ir 340 385
Atkinson v Morris [1897] P 40, 66 LJP 17, 45 WR 293, 41 Sol Jo 110, 75 LT 440, 13 TLR 83, CA 716
Atkinson v Paice (1781) 1 Bro CC 91 471
Atkinson v Turner (1740) 2 Atk 41, Barn Ch 74 416
Atkinson's Goods, Re (1883) 8 PD 165, 47 JP 440, 52 LJP 80, 31 WR 660, P, D and Admlty 72, 95
Atkinson's Will Trust, Re, Prescott v Child [1957] Ch 117, [1956] 3 All ER 738, [1956] 3 WLR 900, 100 Sol Jo 859 ..... 231, 410
Atkinson's Will Trusts, Re, Atkinson v Hall [1978] 1 All ER 1275, [1978] 1 WLR 586, 122 Sol Jo 148 ..... 11, 205
Atlay, Re, Atlay v Atlay (1912) 56 Sol Jo 444 211
Attenborough (George) & Son v Solomon. See Solomon v Attenborough
Atter v Atkinson (1869) LR 1 P & D 665, 33 JP 440, 20 LT 404
..... 902, 904
A-G v Alford (1855) 4 De GM & G 843, 3 Eq Rep 952, 1 Jur NS 361, 102 RR 406, 3 WR 200, 24 LTOS 265 658
A-G v Andrew (1798) 3 Ves 633; affd sub nom Andrew v Master and Wardens of Merchant Taylors' Co (1800) 7 Ves 223, HL 152
A-G v Bamfield (1703) 2 Eq Cas Abr 365, Freem Ch 268
..... 384

PARA

A-G v Brackenbury (1863) 1 H & C 782, 32 LJ Ex 108, 9 Jur NS 257, 1 New Rep 334,
11 WR 380, 8 LT 22 153
A-G v Bright (1836) 2 Keen 57, 5 LJ Ch 325 392
A-G v Bury (1701) 1 Eq Cas Abr 201 282
A-G v Canter [1939] 1 KB 318, [1939] 1 All ER 13, 22 TC 422, 108 LJKB 260, 83 Sol Jo
33, 160 LT 89, 55 TLR 280, CA 1217, 1279
A-G v Cast-Plate Glass Co (1792) 1 Anst 39 205
A-G v Chapman (1840) 3 Beav 255, 10 LJ Ch 90 1298
A-G v Christ's Hospital (1790) 3 Bro CC 165 152
A-G v Christ's Hospital (1830) Taml 393, 9 LJOS Ch 186, 1 Russ & M 626
.... 152, 154
A-G v Crispin (1784) 1 Bro CC 386 .... 301, 429
A-G v Dillon (1862) 13 I Ch R 127, 14 Ir Jur 251 252
A-G v Duke of Leeds (1833) 2 My & K 343 951
A-G v Farrell [1931] 1 KB 81, 99 LJKB 605, [1930] All ER Rep Ext 886, 143 LT 639, 46
TLR 587, CA 1174
A-G v Fletcher (1835) 5 LJ Ch 75 1052
A-G v Fletcher (1871) LR 13 Eq 128, 41 LJ Ch 167, 25 LT 892
.... 326, 395
A-G v George (1843) 12 LJ Ch 165, 7 Jur 141 403
A-G v Gill (1726) 2 P Wms 369 387
A-G v Grote (1827) 2 Russ & M 699 .... 210, 228
A-G v Harley (1819) 4 Madd 263 403
A-G v Hickman (1732) 2 Eq Cas Abr 193, Kel W 34, 2 Eq Cas Abr 193 pl 14
.... 11
A-G v Higham (1843) 2 Y & C Ch Cas 634 .... 959, 1298
A-G v Hird (1782) 1 Bro CC 170 .... 385, 461
A-G v Hodgson (1846) 10 JP 215, 15 Sim 146, 15 LJ Ch 290, 10 Jur 300, 7 LTOS 174
.... 445
A-G v Hubbuck (1884) 13 QBD 275, 53 LJQB 146, 50 LT 374, CA
.... 919
A-G v Hudson (1720) 1 P Wms 674 218
A-G v Jackson [1932] AC 365, [1932] All ER Rep 936, 76 Sol Jo 146, 48 TLR 261, sub
nom Re Cockell, Jackson v A-G 16 TC 681, 146 LT 450, sub nom Re Cockell, A-G v
Jackson 101 LJ Ch 186, [1931] B & CR 167, HL 981
A-G v Jefferys [1908] AC 411, 77 LJ Ch 685, 52 Sol Jo 660, 99 LT 737, 24 TLR 793, HL
.... 235
A-G v Jones and Bartlett (1817) 3 Price 368 1
A-G v Köhler (1861) 9 HL Cas 654, 8 Jur NS 467, 9 WR 933, 5 LT 5, HL
.... 780–781, 1256
A-G v Lloyd (1747) 3 Atk 551, 1 Ves Sen 32 .... 107, 109
A-G v Lloyds Bank Ltd [1935] AC 382, 104 LJKB 523, [1935] All ER Rep 518, 152 LT
577, HL 231
A-G v Malkin (1846) 2 Ph 64, 16 LJ Ch 99, 1 Coop temp Cott 237, 10 Jur 955, 9 LTOS
69 377
A-G v Milner (1744) 3 Atk 112; revsd sub nom Lynch v Milner (1752) 1 Hov Supp 273
.... 184
A-G v Munby (1858) 3 H & N 826 154
A-G v National Provincial and Union Bank of England [1924] AC 262, [1923] All ER Rep
123, 68 Sol Jo 235, 40 TLR 191, sub nom Tetley, Re, A-G v National Provincial and
Union Bank of England 93 LJ Ch 231, 131 LT 34, HL 11
A-G v New York Breweries Co [1898] 1 QB 205, 62 JP 132, 67 LJQB 86, 46 WR 193, 42
Sol Jo 132, 78 LT 61, 14 TLR 119, CA; affd sub nom New York Breweries Co v A-G
[1899] AC 62, 63 JP 179, 68 LJQB 135, 48 WR 32, 43 Sol Jo 111, 79 LT 568, 15
TLR 93, [1895–9] All ER Rep Ext 1696, HL 668, 1262, 1264, 1266
A-G v Norwich Corpn (1837) 1 JP 164, 2 My & Cr 406, 1 Jur 398
.... 1018
A-G v Parkin (1769) Amb 566, 1 Dick 422 159
A-G v Parsons [1956] AC 421, [1956] 1 All ER 65, [1956] 2 WLR 153, 100 Sol Jo 51, HL
.... 513
A-G v Partington (1864) 3 H & C 193, 33 LJ Ex 281, 10 Jur NS 825, 13 WR 54, 10 LT
751, Ex Ch; on appeal sub nom Partington v A-G (1869) LR 4 HL 100, 38 LJ Ex 205,
21 LT 370 .... 669, 780
A-G v Potter (1842) 5 Beav 164, 14 LJ Ch 16, 9 Jur 241
.... 1142
A-G v Rochester Corpn (1854) 5 De GM & G 797, 23 LTOS 104
.... 196

PARA

A-G v Rowsell (1844) 36 Ch D 67n, 56 LJ Ch 942n, 36 WR 378n, sub nom Rowsell,
Re 3 LTOS 105 32
A-G v Rye Corpn (1817) 7 Taunt 546, 1 Moore CP 267
.... 270
A-G v Sands (1669–1670) Freem Ch 129, Hard 488, Nels 130, 3 Rep Ch 33
.... 552–553
A-G v Sidney Sussex College (1869) 4 Ch App 722, 34 JP 52, 38 LJ Ch 656
.... 196
A-G v Solly (1829) 2 Sim 518 658
A-G v Sutton (1721) 3 Bro Parl Cas 75, 1 P Wms 754, HL
.... 457, 473
A-G v Vigor (1803) 8 Ves 256 .... 26, 284
A-G v Ward (1797) 3 Ves 327 109
A-G v Wax Chandlers' Co (1873) LR 6 HL 1, 37 JP 532, 42 LJ Ch 425, 21 WR 361, 28
LT 681 407
A-G v Williams (1794) 2 Cox Eq Cas 387, 4 Bro CC 526
.... 258
A-G for New Zealand v Brown [1917] AC 393, 86 LJPC 132, [1916–17] All ER Rep 245,
116 LT 624, 33 TLR 294, [1917] NZPCC 698, PC 11
A-G for New Zealand v New Zealand Insurance Co Ltd [1936] 3 All ER 888, 80 Sol Jo
912, 53 TLR 37, PC 11
A-G of Ontario v Mercer (1883) 8 App Cas 767, 52 LJPC 84, 49 LT 312, PC
.... 512, 552
Attree v Attree (1871) LR 11 Eq 280, 40 LJ Ch 192, 19 WR 464, 24 LT 121
.... 298
Attwater v Attwater (1853) 18 Beav 330, 23 LJ Ch 692, 18 Jur 50, 2 WR 81, 22 LTOS
150 .... 142, 271, 422, 424, 476
Attwood v Alford (1866) LR 2 Eq 479, 14 WR 956 321
Audsley v Horn (1858) 26 Beav 195, 1 F & F 135, 28 LJ Ch 293, 4 Jur NS 1267, 7 WR
125, 32 LTOS 203; affd (1859) 1 De GF & J 226, 29 LJ Ch 201, 6 Jur NS 205, 8 WR
150, 1 LT 317 .... 235, 385, 390
Auger v Beaudry [1920] AC 1010, 89 LJPC 251, 124 LT 106, PC
.... 315, 317, 460
Auldjo v Wallace (1862) 31 Beav 193 408
Aumble v Jones (1709) 1 Salk 238 241
Austen v Graham (1854) 8 Moo PCC 493, 1 Ecc & Ad 357, 24 LTOS 37
.... 49
Austen's Goods, Re (1853) 2 Rob Eccl 611, 17 Jur 284, 21 LTOS 65
.... 80
Auster v Powell (1863) 1 De GJ & Sm 99, 9 Jur NS 421, 8 LT 73
.... 404
Austin v Beddoe (1893) 3 R 580, 41 WR 619, 37 Sol Jo 456
.... 1139
Austin v Tawney (1867) 2 Ch App 143, 36 LJ Ch 339, 15 WR 463
.... 126, 148
Austin's Estate, Re (1929) 73 Sol Jo 545, P, D and Admlty
.... 910
Avard, Re, Hook v Parker [1948] Ch 43, [1947] 2 All ER 548, [1948] LJR 354, 91 Sol Jo
613, 63 TLR 567 .... 125, 145, 148–149
Avelyn v Ward (1750) 1 Ves Sen 420 .... 27, 446
Averill, Re, Salsbury v Buckle [1898] 1 Ch 523, 67 LJ Ch 233, 46 WR 460, 78 LT 320
.... 312
Avern v Lloyd (1868) LR 5 Eq 383, 37 LJ Ch 489, 16 WR 669, 18 LT 282
.... 377
Avison v Holmes (1861) 1 John & H 530, 30 LJ Ch 564, 7 Jur NS 722, 9 WR 550, 4 LT
617 463
Avison v Simpson (1859) John 43, 5 Jur NS 594, 7 WR 277, 33 LTOS 27
.... 288, 343
Awse v Melhuish (1780) 1 Bro CC 519 257
Ayles' Trusts, Re (1875) 1 Ch D 282, 40 JP 181, 45 LJ Ch 223, 24 WR 202
.... 350, 352
Aylward v Lewis [1891] 2 Ch 81, 39 WR 552, 64 LT 250
.... 818
Aylwin v Aylwin [1902] P 203, 71 LJP 130, 87 LT 142, P, D and Admlty
.... 911
Aylwin's Trusts, Re (1873) LR 16 Eq 585, 42 LJ Ch 745, 21 WR 864, 28 LT 865
.... 306

PARA

Aynsley, Re, Kyrle v Turner [1914] 2 Ch 422, 83 LJ Ch 807, 50 Sol Jo 754, 111 LT 525,
30 TLR 664; on appeal [1915] 1 Ch 172, 84 LJ Ch 211, 59 Sol Jo 128, 112 LT 433,
31 TLR 101, CA 115, 156
Ayrey v Hill (1824) 2 Add 206 48
Ayscough v Savage (1865) 13 WR 373 397

B

B, Re [1999] Ch 206, [1999] 2 All ER 425, [1999] 2 WLR 1114, [1999] 2 FCR 145,
[1999] 2 FLR 466, [1999] Fam Law 303; revsd [2000] Ch 662, [2000] 1 All ER 665,
[2000] 2 WLR 929, [2000] 1 FCR 385, [2000] NLJR 20, CA
.... 567, 581, 598
B, Re, O v D [1916] 1 IR 364 .... 352, 354
BCA Pension Plan, Re [2015] EWHC 3492 (Ch), [2016] 4 WLR 5, [2015] All ER (D) 38
(Dec) 189, 192
Bacchus v Gilbee (1863) 3 De GJ & Sm 577, 9 Jur NS 838, 2 New Rep 502, 11 WR 1049,
8 LT 714 294
Bach, Re, Lloyds Bank v Bach [1892] WN 108 1174
Bach, Re, Walker v Bach [1892] WN 108 1174
Bacharach's Will Trusts, Re, Minden v Bacharach [1959] Ch 245, [1958] 3 All ER 618,
[1959] 2 WLR 1, 103 Sol Jo 16 .... 187, 253
Backhouse, Re, Salmon v Backhouse [1916] 1 Ch 65, 85 LJ Ch 146, 60 Sol Jo 121, 114 LT
39 409
Backhouse, Re, Westminster Bank Ltd v Shaftesbury School and Ragged School Union
[1931] WN 168, 172 LT Jo 10, 71 L Jo 79 .... 151, 180
Backwell v Child (1755) Amb 260 156
Bacon, Re, Grissel v Leathes (1893) 62 LJ Ch 445, 3 R 459, 41 WR 478, 37 Sol Jo 340,
68 LT 522 1121
Bacon, Re, Toovey v Turner [1907] 1 Ch 475, 76 LJ Ch 213, 96 LT 690
.... 1052
Bacon v Bacon (1800) 5 Ves 331 1259
Bacon v Cosby (1851) 4 De G & Sm 261, 20 LJ Ch 213, 15 Jur 695, 17 LTOS 239
.... 296, 461, 473
Bacon v Proctor (1822) Turn & R 31 415
Bacon's Will, Re, Camp v Coe (1886) 31 Ch D 460, 55 LJ Ch 368, 34 WR 319, 54 LT
150, 2 TLR 278, DC 197
Baden's Deed Trusts (No 2), Re [1973] Ch 9, [1972] 2 All ER 1304, [1972] 3 WLR 250,
116 Sol Jo 356, CA 138, 348–349
Badenach's Goods, Re (1864) 28 JP 711, 33 LJPM & A 179, 10 Jur NS 521, 3 Sw & Tr
465, 11 LT 275 .... 628, 632
Badge v Floyd (1701) 1 Ld Raym 523, HL 460
Badger v Gregory (1869) LR 8 Eq 78, 17 WR 1090, 21 LT 137
.... 317
Badrick v Stevens (1792) 3 Bro CC 431 159
Bagge v Bagge [1921] 1 IR 213 1113
Bagley v Mollard (1830) 8 LJOS Ch 145, 1 Russ & M 581
.... 352
Bagnall, Re, Scale v Willett [1948] WN 324, [1949] LJR 1, 92 Sol Jo 485
.... 403
Bagot, Re, Paton v Ormerod [1893] 3 Ch 348, 62 LJ Ch 1006, 37 Sol Jo 730, 69 LT 399,
[1891–4] All ER Rep Ext 1583, CA 252, 1113
Bagot's Settlement, Re (1862) 31 LJ Ch 772, 10 WR 607, 6 LT 774
.... 156
Bagshaw v Pimm [1900] P 148, 69 LJP 45, 48 WR 422, 44 Sol Jo 313, 82 LT 175, CA
.... 909
Bagshaw v Spencer (1748) 2 Atk 579, 1 Wils 238, 1 Ves Sen 142, 95 ER 594
.... 415, 474
Bagshaw's Trusts, Re (1877) 46 LJ Ch 567, 25 WR 659, 36 LT 749, CA
.... 122, 234, 251, 369
Bagwell v Dry (1721) 2 Eq Cas Abr 344, 1 P Wms 700
.... 173, 183
Bailey, Re, Barclay's Bank Ltd v James [1945] Ch 191, [1945] 1 All ER 616, 114 LJ Ch
147, 89 Sol Jo 130, 172 LT 333, 61 TLR 256 298
Bailey, Re, Barrett v Hyder [1951] Ch 407, [1951] 1 All ER 391, 95 Sol Jo 155, CA
.... 182, 445

PARA

Bailey, Re, Tatham v Welch. See Burley, Re, Tatham v Welch
Bailey v Piper (1875) 1 Ch D 90, 45 LJ Ch 99, 24 WR 152, 33 LT 499
.... 1105
Bailey's Goods, Re (1838) 1 Curt 914 64
Bailey's Trust, Re (1854) 3 WR 31 1047
Bailie, Re (1919) 53 ILT 208 763
Bailis v Gale (1750) 2 Ves Sen 48 376
Baillie v Butterfield (1787) 1 Cox Eq Cas 392 .... 401, 403, 672
Baily v Boult (1851) 14 Beav 595, 21 LJ Ch 277, 15 Jur 1049, 18 LTOS 83
.... 1133
Bain v Brand (1876) 1 App Cas 762, HL 932
Bain v Lescher (1840) 11 Sim 397 .... 175, 390
Bainbridge v Cream (1852) 16 Beav 25, 19 LTOS 151 .... 306, 446
Bainbrigge v Blair (1845) 8 Beav 588, 1 New Pract Cas 283, 9 Jur 765, 68 RR 208,
  5 LTOS 454, sub nom Blair v Bainbrigge 14 LJ Ch 405
.... 654
Baines v Dixon (1747) 1 Ves Sen 41 375
Baird v Baird [1990] 2 AC 548, [1990] 2 All ER 300, [1990] 2 WLR 1412, [1990] ICR
  525, [1991] Fam Law 96, 134 Sol Jo 725, [1990] 23 LS Gaz R 28, PC
.... 2
Baker, Re, Baker v Baker [1904] 1 Ch 157, 73 LJ Ch 172, 52 WR 213, 48 Sol Jo 101, 89
  LT 742 462
Baker, Re, Baker v Baker [1929] 1 Ch 668, 98 LJ Ch 174, 141 LT 29
.... 97, 100, 111
Baker, Re, Baker v Public Trustee [1924] 2 Ch 271, 93 LJ Ch 599, 68 Sol Jo 645, 131 LT
  763 1126–1127
Baker, Re, Pursey v Holloway (1898) 79 LT 343 393
Baker, Re, Steadman v Dicksee [1934] WN 94, 78 Sol Jo 336, CA
.... 161
Baker v Baker [2008] EWHC 937 (Ch), 10 ITELR 897, [2008] 3 FCR 547, [2008] 2 FLR
  767, [2008] Fam Law 626, [2008] All ER (D) 179 (Mar)
.... 50, 567
Baker v Baker [2008] EWHC 977 (Ch), [2008] 2 FLR 1956, [2008] Fam Law 625,
  [2008] All ER (D) 312 (Mar) 574, 577
Baker v Baker (1847) 6 Hare 269, 11 Jur 585 .... 232, 396
Baker v Baker (1860) 24 JP 150, 29 LJPM & A 138, 2 Sw & Tr 380
.... 1188
Baker v Batt (1838) 2 Moo PCC 317, PC 903, 910
Baker v Bayldon (1862) 31 Beav 209 336
Baker v Blount [1917] 1 IR 316 375
Baker v Bolton (1808) 1 Camp 493 1280
Baker v Dening (1838) 8 Ad & El 94, 7 LJQB 137, 1 Will Woll & H 148, sub nom Taylor
  v Dening 2 Jur 775, 3 Nev & PKB 228 63
Baker v Gibson (1849) 12 Beav 101 394
Baker v Hall (1806) 12 Ves 497 184
Baker v Ker (1882) 11 LR Ir 3, 17 217
Baker v Lucas (1828) 1 Mol 481 459
Baker v Martin (1832) 5 Sim 380 1238
Baker v Martin (1836) 8 Sim 25, 5 LJ Ch 205 1070
Baker v Story (1874) 23 WR 147, 31 LT 631 107
Baker v Tucker (1850) 3 HL Cas 106, 14 Jur 771 .... 456, 473
Baker v Wall (1697) 2 Eq Cas Abr 307, 1 Ld Raym 185
.... 340, 384
Baker's Settlement Trusts, Re, Hunt v Baker [1908] WN 161
.... 239
Bakewell v Tagart (1838) 3 Y & C Ex 173, 2 Jur 699 1208
Balchin, Re, Havenhand v Perugia (1922) 67 Sol Jo 12, 38 TLR 868
.... 295
Baldwin v Rogers (1853) 3 De GM & G 649, 22 LJ Ch 665, 17 Jur 267, 22 LTOS 29,
  21 LTOS 70 .... 305, 309, 327
Baldwin's Goods, Re [1903] P 61, 72 LJP 23, 88 LT 565, P, D and Admlty
.... 820
Balfe v Halpenny [1904] 1 IR 486 223
Ball, Re [1899] 2 IR 313, 33 ILT 42, CA 1065
Ball, Re, Hand v Ball [1947] Ch 228, [1947] 1 All ER 458, [1947] LJR 513, 91 Sol Jo 220,
  176 LT 369, 63 TLR 94 348
Ball, Re, Jones v Jones [1930] WN 111, 74 Sol Jo 298 1035

PARA

Ball, Re, Lucas v Ball [1940] 4 All ER 245 1093
Ball, Re, Slattery v Ball (1888) 40 Ch D 11, 58 LJ Ch 232, 37 WR 37, 59 LT 800, CA
.... 440–441
Ball's Goods, Re (1902) 47 Sol Jo 129, P, D and Admlty
.... 556, 778
Ballance, Re, Ballance v Lanphier (1889) 42 Ch D 62, 58 LJ Ch 534, 37 WR 600, 61 LT
158 298
Ballard v Marsden (1880) 14 Ch D 374, 49 LJ Ch 614, 28 WR 914, [1874–80] All ER
Rep 999, 42 LT 763 1067
Ballingall's Goods, Re (1863) 27 JP 536, 32 LJPM & A 138, 3 Sw & Tr 441n, 11 WR
591, 9 LT 116 801
Ballman, Re, ex p Garland (1804) 1 Smith KB 220, 10 Ves 110, 32 ER 786,
[1803–13] All ER Rep 750 .... 1036, 1039–1040, 1242
Balls, Re, Trewby v Balls [1909] 1 Ch 791, 78 LJ Ch 341, 100 LT 780
.... 979, 1109
Balm v Balm (1830) 3 Sim 492 307–308
Bambridge v IRC [1955] 3 All ER 812, [1955] 1 WLR 1329, 36 TC 313, 34 ATC 281,
[1955] TR 295, 99 Sol Jo 910, L(TC) 1754, HL 2
Bamfield v Popham (1703) Holt KB 233, 2 Vern 449, 1 Eq Cas Abr 183, 1 P Wms 54,
Freem Ch 266, 90 ER 1028, sub nom Popham v Bamfield, Freem Ch 269, 2 Eq Cas
Abr 308, 1 Salk 236 .... 193, 456, 473
Bamford v Lord (1854) 14 CB 708, sub nom Bamford v Chadwick 23 LJCP 172, 1 Jur NS
139, 2 WR 531, 2 CLR 1757 460
Bancroft, Re, Bancroft v Bancroft [1928] Ch 577, 97 LJ Ch 245, 139 LT 372, 43 TLR 591
.... 158, 282
Bandon (Earl) v Moreland [1910] 1 IR 220 127
Banfield v Pickard (1881) 6 PD 33, 29 WR 613, sub nom Pickard's Goods, Re, Banfield v
Pickard 45 JP 508, 50 LJP 72, P, D and Admlty 680
Bangham's Goods, Re (1876) 1 PD 429, 24 WR 712, sub nom Re Baugham's Goods 40 JP
487, 45 LJP 80, P, D and Admlty 111
Bank Melli Iran v Personal Representatives of Amirteymour. See Amirteymour, Re
Bank of Bombay v Suleman Somji [1908–10] All ER Rep 967, 52 Sol Jo 727, 99 LT 532,
24 TLR 840, PC 1025
Bank of Credit and Commerce International SA (in liquidation) v Ali [2001] UKHL 8,
[2002] 1 AC 251, [2001] 1 All ER 961, [2001] 2 WLR 735, [2001] ICR 337, [2001]
IRLR 292, 151 NLJ 351, (2001) Times, 6 March, 145 Sol Jo LB 67, [2001] All ER
(D) 06 (Mar) 224
Bank of Ireland v McCarthy [1898] AC 181, 67 LJPC 13, 77 LT 777, HL
.... 1110
Bankes v Holme (1821) 1 Russ 394n, HL 460
Banks, Re, Banks v Busbridge [1905] 1 Ch 547, 74 LJ Ch 336, 92 LT 225
.... 1012
Banks, Re, Weldon v Banks (1912) 56 Sol Jo 362 311
Banks v Braithwaite (1863) 32 LJ Ch 198, 9 Jur NS 294, 1 New Rep 306, 11 WR 298, 8
LT 80 380
Banks v Goodfellow (1870) LR 5 QB 549, 39 LJQB 237, [1861–73] All ER Rep 47, 22 LT
813 .... 49,50, 52–53, 893, 900
Banks v National Westminster Bank plc [2005] EWHC 3479 (Ch), [2005] All ER (D) 159
(Apr) 155–157, 296
Banks v Sutton (1732) 2 P Wms 700 538
Banks' Trusts, Re, ex p Hovill (1855) 2 K & J 387 .... 382, 385
Bannatyne and Bannatyne v Bannatyne (1852) 2 Rob Eccl 472, 16 Jur 864
.... 899–900
Bannister, Re, Heys-Jones v Bannister (1921) 90 LJ Ch 415, 125 LT 54
.... 382
Bannister v Lang (1867) 17 LT 137 385
Barber, Re, Burgess v Vinicome (1886) 34 Ch D 77, 56 LJ Ch 216, 35 WR 326, 55 LT 882
.... 649, 653–655
Barber, Re, Burgess v Vinnicome (1886) 31 Ch D 665, 55 LJ Ch 373, 34 WR 395, 54 LT
375 .... 41, 652
Barber v Barber (1838) 3 My & Cr 688, 8 LJ Ch 36, 2 Jur 1029
.... 175
Barber v Wood (1877) 4 Ch D 885, 46 LJ Ch 728, 36 LT 373
.... 279, 1012

                                                                              PARA
Barber's Goods, Re (1866) LR 1 P & D 267, 36 LJP & M 19, 15 WR 231, 15 LT 192
.... 730
Barber's Goods, Re (1886) 11 PD 78, 35 WR 80, 56 LT 894, P, D and Admlty
.... 744
Barber's Trusts, Re (1863) 32 LJ Ch 709, 9 Jur NS 1098, 2 New Rep 571, 11 WR 1056, 8
    LT 825 1048
Barbour's Settlement, Re, National Westminster Bank Ltd v Barbour [1974] 1 All ER 1188,
    [1974] 1 WLR 1198, 118 Sol Jo 681 656
Barclay, Re, Barclay v Andrew [1899] 1 Ch 674, 68 LJ Ch 383, 80 LT 702
.... 1257
Barclay, Re, Gardner v Barclay, Steuart v Barclay [1929] 2 Ch 173, 98 LJ Ch 410,
    [1929] All ER Rep 272, 141 LT 447, 45 TLR 406, CA 367
Barclay v Owen (1889) 60 LT 220 1161
Barclay v Wainwright (1797) 3 Ves 462 403
Barclays Bank v Zeitline (1962) 182 Estates Gazette 291
.... 290
Barclays Bank International Ltd v Levin Bros (Bradford) Ltd [1977] QB 270, [1976]
    3 All ER 900, [1976] 3 WLR 852, [1977] 1 Lloyd's Rep 51, 120 Sol Jo 801
.... 967
Barclays Bank Trust Co Ltd v Csoti [2004] EWHC 2769 (Ch), [2004] All ER (D) 88 (Oct)
.... 186, 212–213, 285
Barder v Caluori [1988] AC 20, [1987] 2 All ER 440, [1987] 2 WLR 1350, [1987] 2 FLR
    480, [1988] Fam Law 18, 131 Sol Jo 776, [1987] LS Gaz R 2046, [1987] NLJ Rep
    497, HL 567, 1279, 1285
Barfield, Re, Goodman v Child (1901) 84 LT 28 287
Baring, Re, Jeune v Baring [1893] 1 Ch 61, 62 LJ Ch 50, 3 R 37, 41 WR 87, 67 LT 702, 9
    TLR 7 1228
Baring v Ashburton (1886) 54 LT 463 .... 239, 268, 296
Baring's Settlement Trusts, Re, Baring Bros & Co Ltd v Liddell [1940] Ch 737, [1940]
    3 All ER 20, 109 LJ Ch 337, 84 Sol Jo 382, 163 LT 403, 56 TLR 777
.... 465
Barke's Goods, Re (1845) 4 Notes of Cases 44 113–114
Barker, Re, Asquith v Saville (1882) 51 LJ Ch 835, 47 LT 38
.... 322
Barker, Re, Buxton v Campbell [1892] 2 Ch 491, 62 LJ Ch 76, 66 LT 848
.... 1150
Barker, Re, Capon v Flick (1905) 92 LT 831 308
Barker, Re, Gilbey v Barker [1918] 1 Ch 128, 87 LJ Ch 166, 62 Sol Jo 142, 118 LT 206
.... 404
Barker v Barker (1852) 5 De G & Sm 753, 21 LJ Ch 794, 17 Jur 125, 19 LTOS 268
.... 325
Barker v Barker (1870) LR 10 Eq 438, 39 LJ Ch 825 152
Barker v Cocks (1843) 6 Beav 82 450
Barker v Giles (1725) 9 Mod Rep 157, 2 P Wms 280, Cas temp King 17; on appeal (1727)
    3 Bro Parl Cas 104, HL 248, 395
Barker v Gyles (1727) 3 Bro Parl Cas 104 394–395
Barker v Lea (1814) 3 Ves & B 113 302
Barker v Lea (1823) Turn & R 413 410
Barker v Peile (1865) 2 Drew & Sm 340, 34 LJ Ch 497, 11 Jur NS 436, 5 New Rep 425,
    143 RR 150, 13 WR 573, 12 LT 50 1047
Barker v Rayner (1826) 2 Russ 122 159
Barker v Wardle (1835) 2 My & K 818 1203
Barker v Young (1864) 33 Beav 353, 33 LJ Ch 279, 10 Jur NS 163, 3 New Rep 350, 12
    WR 659, 9 LT 704; affd sub nom Earle v Barker (1865) 11 HL Cas 280, 13 LT 29
.... 254
Barker's Goods, Re [1891] P 251, 60 LJP 87, 39 WR 560, P, D and Admlty
.... 800
Barker's Trusts, Re (1883) 52 LJ Ch 565, 48 LT 573 385
Barklie, Re, McClamont v Barklie [1917] 1 IR 1 375
Barksdale v Gilliat (1818) 1 Swan 562 .... 210, 228, 1131
Barksdale v Morgan (1693) 4 Mod Rep 185 205
Barkwell v Barkwell [1928] P 91, [1927] All ER Rep 138, 72 Sol Jo 69, 44 TLR 207, sub
    nom Re Barkwell's Estate, Barkwell v Barkwell 97 LJP 53, 138 LT 526, P, D and
    Admlty 98, 716
Barkworth v Barkworth (1906) 75 LJ Ch 754 441

PARA

Barkworth v Young (1856) 4 Drew 1, 26 LJ Ch 153, 3 Jur NS 34, 113 RR 97, 5 WR 156,
28 LTOS 199 22
Barlow, Re [1933] P 184, 102 LJP 84, 77 Sol Jo 524, 149 LT 456, 49 TLR 544, P, D and
Admlty 622
Barlow v Bateman (1735) 2 Bro Parl Cas 272, [1558–1774] All ER Rep 310, 24 ER 971, 1
ER 939, HL 278
Barlow v Grant (1684) 1 Vern 255, 23 ER 451, [1558–1774] All ER Rep 198
.... 371, 1061
Barlow v Salter (1810) 17 Ves 479 459–460
Barlow's Estate, Re, Haydon v Pring [1919] P 131, 88 LJP 82, 120 LT 645, 35 TLR 326,
CA 910
Barlow's Will Trusts, Re [1979] 1 All ER 296, [1979] 1 WLR 278, 122 Sol Jo 646
.... 45, 246, 302, 348
Barnaby v Tassell (1871) LR 11 Eq 363, 19 WR 323, 24 LT 221
.... 200, 250, 306, 397–398
Barnacle v Nightingale (1845) 14 Sim 456, 9 Jur 221, 5 LTOS 18
.... 473
Barnard v Pumfrett (1841) 5 My & Cr 63, 10 LJ Ch 124
.... 1141, 1301
Barnardiston v Carter (1717) 3 Bro Parl Cas 64 415
Barnardiston v Fane (1699) 2 Vern 366 149
Barnardo's Homes v Special Income Tax Comrs [1921] 2 AC 1, 90 LJKB 545, 65 Sol Jo
433, 125 LT 250, 37 TLR 540, sub nom R v Income Tax Acts Special Purposes Comr,
ex p Dr Barnardo's Homes National Incorporated Association 7 TC 646, HL
.... 922, 1053
Barne, Re, Lee v Barne (1890) 62 LT 922 1196
Barnes, Re, Ashenden v Heath [1940] Ch 267, 109 LJ Ch 102, 84 Sol Jo 151, 162 LT 263,
56 TLR 356 32
Barnes v Allen (1782) 1 Bro CC 181 429
Barnes v Crowe (1792) 1 Ves 485, 4 Bro CC 2 113
Barnes v Grant (1856) 26 LJ Ch 92, 2 Jur NS 1127, 5 WR 14, 28 LTOS 78
.... 370
Barnes v Jennings (1866) LR 2 Eq 448, 35 LJ Ch 675, 14 WR 831
.... 247, 446
Barnes v Patch (1803) 8 Ves 604 .... 348, 396
Barnes v Rowley (1797) 3 Ves 305 1058
Barnes v Tomlinson [2006] EWHC 3115 (Ch), [2006] All ER (D) 95 (Dec)
.... 1238, 1246
Barnes Goods, Re, Hodson v Barnes (1926) 96 LJP 26, 136 LT 380, 43 TLR 71, P, D and
Admlty 60, 80
Barnes' Will Trusts, Re, Prior v Barnes [1972] 2 All ER 639, [1972] 1 WLR 587, 116 Sol
Jo 336 .... 288, 293, 298, 1113
Barnesly v Powel (1748) 1 Ves Sen 119 671
Barnet v Barnet (1861) 29 Beav 239 .... 412, 468–469
Barnett v Earl of Guildford (1855) 24 LJ Ex 281, 11 Exch 19, 1 Jur NS 1142, 3 WR 406,
3 CLR 1440, 25 LTOS 85 645
Barnett v Semenyuk [2008] EWHC 2939 (Ch), [2008] 2 P & CR D44, [2008] BPIR 1427,
[2008] All ER (D) 205 (Jul) 1242
Barnett v Sheffield (1852) 1 De GM & G 371, 21 LJ Ch 692, 16 Jur 942, 91 RR 122
.... 1071
Barnett v Tugwell (1862) 31 Beav 232, 31 LJ Ch 629, 8 Jur NS 787, 10 WR 679, 7 LT
121 354
Barnshaw's Trusts, Re (1867) 15 WR 378 431
Barnsley v Noble [2016] EWCA Civ 799 1246
Barnsley v Ward (18 January 1980, unreported), CA 592, 603
Barraclough, Re, Barraclough v Young [1967] P 1, [1965] 2 All ER 311, [1965] 3 WLR
1023, 109 Sol Jo 134, P, D and Admlty 860
Barraclough v Cooper [1908] 2 Ch 121n, 77 LJ Ch 555n, 98 LT 852, [1904–7] All ER Rep
Ext 1337, HL 235, 244, 247, 323
Barraclough v Shillito [1884] WN 158, 53 LJ Ch 841, 32 WR 875
.... 336
Barrance, Re, Barrance v Ellis [1910] 2 Ch 419, 79 LJ Ch 544, 54 Sol Jo 651, 103 LT 104
.... 669
Barrass v Harding [2001] 1 FCR 297, [2001] 1 FLR 138, [2000] Fam Law 878, CA
.... 578
Barratt, Re, Barratt v Coates (1915) 31 TLR 502, CA 296

PARA

Barratt, Re, National Provincial Bank Ltd v Barratt [1925] Ch 550, 94 LJ Ch 345,
  [1925] All ER Rep 193, 133 LT 133 1123
Barrett, Re, Whitaker v Barrett (1889) 43 Ch D 70, 59 LJ Ch 218, 38 WR 59
  1181
Barrett v Bem [2009] All ER (D) 157 (Oct) 849, 894
Barrett v Bem [2012] EWCA Civ 52, [2012] Ch 573, [2012] 2 All ER 920, [2012] 3 WLR
  330, (2012) Times, 05 March, [2012] All ER (D) 175 (Jan)
  .... 41, 56, 64, 903
Barrett v White (1855) 24 LJ Ch 724, 1 Jur NS 652, 3 WR 578
  293
Barrington v Tristram (1801) 6 Ves 345 .... 307–308, 331
Barrow v Griffith (1864) 11 Jur NS 6, 5 New Rep 6, 13 WR 41
  1028
Barrow v Methold (1855) 1 Jur NS 994, 3 WR 629, 26 LT 56
  202
Barrow v Newman (1864) 11 Jur NS 6, 5 New Rep 6, 13 WR 41
  1028
Barrs v Fewkes (1864) 2 Hem & M 60, 33 LJ Ch 484, 10 Jur NS 466, 3 New Rep 704, 12
  WR 66, 10 LT 232 370
Barrs v Jackson (1845) 1 Ph 582, 14 LJ Ch 433, 9 Jur 609, 5 LTOS 365
  670
Barry v Butlin (1838) 2 Moo PCC 480 .... 55, 899, 903–905
Barry v Crundall (1835) 7 Sim 430, 4 LJ Ch 264 409
Barry v Harding (1844) 7 I Eq R 313, 1 Jo & Lat 475 .... 294, 1011
Barry v Rush (1787) 1 Term Rep 691 1299
Bartholomew and Brown v Henley (1820) 3 Phillim 317
  54
Bartholomew's Trust, Re (1849) 19 LJ Ch 237, 1 H & Tw 565, 14 Jur 181, 1 Mac & G
  354 428
Bartleman v Murchison (1831) 9 LJOS Ch 60, 2 Russ & M 136
  304
Bartlett v Barclays Bank Trust Co Ltd [1980] Ch 515, [1980] 1 All ER 139, [1980] 2 WLR
  430, 124 Sol Jo 85 1247
Bartlett v Barclays Bank Trust Co Ltd (No 2) [1980] Ch 515, [1980] 2 All ER 92, [1980] 2
  WLR 430, 124 Sol Jo 221 .... 1080, 1257
Bartlett v Hollister (1757) Amb 334 305
Bartlett v Wood (1861) 30 LJ Ch 614, 9 WR 817, 4 LT 692
  1203
Barton, Re, Barton v Bourne (1932) 48 TLR 205 222
Barton, Re, Holland v Kersley (1912) 56 Sol Jo 380 1203
Barton v Barton (1693) 2 Vern 308 133
Barton v Cooke (1800) 5 Ves 461 1061
Barton v Hassard (1843) 3 Dr & War 461 657
Barton v London and North Western Rly Co (1889) 24 QBD 77, 59 LJQB 33, 38 WR 197,
  62 LT 164, 6 TLR 70, CA 926
Barton v North Staffordshire Rly Co (1888) 38 Ch D 458, 57 LJ Ch 800, 36 WR 754,
  [1886–90] All ER Rep 288, 58 LT 549, 4 TLR 403 926
Barton v Robins (1769) 3 Phillim 455n 892
Barton's Goods, Re [1898] P 11, 67 LJP 10, 78 LT 81, P, D and Admlty
  .... 759, 792
Barwick v Mullings (1829) 2 Hag Ecc 225 5
Basan v Brandon (1836) 8 Sim 171 156
Basham, Re [1987] 1 All ER 405, [1986] 1 WLR 1498, [1987] 2 FLR 264, [1987] Fam
  Law 310, 130 Sol Jo 986, [1987] LS Gaz R 112 .... 20, 588
Basham, Re, Hannay v Basham (1883) 23 Ch D 195, 52 LJ Ch 408, 31 WR 743, 48 LT
  476 1201
Basioli, Re, Re Depaoli, McGahey v Depaoli [1953] Ch 367, [1953] 1 All ER 301, [1953]
  2 WLR 251, 97 Sol Jo 80 168
Baskett's Goods, Re (1898) 78 LT 843, P, D and Admlty
  738
Bass v Russell (1829) Taml 18, 7 LJOS Ch 177 318
Basset v St Levan (1894) 13 R 235, 43 WR 165, 39 Sol Jo 80, 71 LT 718
  289
Bassett's Estate, Re, Perkins v Fladgate (1872) LR 14 Eq 54, 41 LJ Ch 681, 20 WR 589
  .... 255–256, 266, 274

PARA

Batard v Hawes (1853) 2 E & B 287, 22 LJQB 443, 17 Jur 1154, 1 WR 287, 386, 1 CLR
812, 818 1231
Batchelar v Evans [1939] Ch 1007, [1939] 3 All ER 606, 109 LJ Ch 34, 83 Sol Jo 639,
161 LT 160 .... 1294, 1301
Bate, Re, Bate v Bate (1890) 43 Ch D 600, 59 LJ Ch 277, 62 LT 559
.... 997
Bate, Re, Chillingworth v Bate [1947] 2 All ER 418, [1947] LJR 1409, 91 Sol Jo 560
.... 746
Bate, Re, Public Trustee v Bate [1938] 4 All ER 218 1085
Bate v Amherst and Norton (1663) 1 Eq Cas Abr 212, T Raym 82
.... 45, 265
Bate v Hooper (1855) 5 De GM & G 338, 104 RR 146, 3 WR 639
.... 1097
Bate v Robins (1863) 32 Beav 73 1246
Bateman, Re, Wallace v Mawdsley (1911) 27 TLR 313 199
Bateman v Foster (1844) 1 Coll 118, 3 LTOS 3 308
Bateman v Gray (1868) LR 6 Eq 215, 37 LJ Ch 592, 16 WR 962
.... 308
Bateman v Roach (1724) 9 Mod Rep 104 426
Bateman's Trusts, Re (1873) LR 15 Eq 355, 37 JP 484, 42 LJ Ch 553, 12 Cox CC 447, 21
WR 435, 28 LT 395 436
Bateman's Will Trusts, Re, Brierley v Perry [1970] 3 All ER 817, [1970] 1 WLR 1463, 114
Sol Jo 707 223
Bater v Bater, Greenwich London Borough Council v Bater [1999] 4 All ER 944, CA, sub
nom Bater v Greenwich London Borough Council [1999] 3 FCR 254, [1999] 2 FLR
993, [1999] Fam Law 694, 32 HLR 127, [1999] NPC 102, [1999] 33 LS Gaz R 30,
[1999] EG 111 (CS), CA 586
Bates, Re, Hodgson v Bates [1907] 1 Ch 22, [1906] WN 191, 76 LJ Ch 29,
[1904–7] All ER Rep 450, 51 Sol Jo 27, 95 LT 753, 23 TLR 15
.... 1122, 1125
Bates v Bates [1884] WN 129, 19 LJNC 67 463
Bates v Taylor (1893) 19 VLR 120, Vic Full Ct 375
Bath's (Marquis) Settlement, Re, Thynne v Stewart (1914) 58 Sol Jo 578, 111 LT 153
.... 1130
Bath and Wells Diocesan Board of Finance v Jenkinson [2002] EWHC 218 (Ch), [2003] Ch
89, [2002] 4 All ER 245, [2002] 3 WLR 202, [2002] P & CR 350, (2002) Times,
29 March, [2002] All ER (D) 355 (Feb) 27, 183
Bathe, Re, Bathe v Public Trustee [1925] Ch 377, 133 LT 132, sub nom Re Bathe, Public
Trustee v Bathe 95 LJ Ch 37 133
Bathurst v Errington (1877) 2 App Cas 698, 46 LJ Ch 748, 25 WR 908, 37 LT 338, HL
.... 243–244, 333
Batsford v Kebbell (1797) 3 Ves 363 .... 430, 433
Battan Singh v Amirchand [1948] AC 161, [1948] 1 All ER 152, [1948] LJR 827, PC
.... 49–50, 53
Batten's Will Trusts, Re (1961) 105 Sol Jo 529 39
Batterbee's Goods, Re (1889) 14 PD 39, 53 JP 231, 58 LJP 38, 37 WR 416, 60 LT 838, P,
D and Admlty 763
Battersby's Trusts [1896] 1 IR 600 .... 325–326, 348
Batthyany v Walford (1887) 36 Ch D 269, 56 LJ Ch 881, 35 WR 814, 57 LT 206, CA
.... 1237
Battie-Wrightson, Re, Cecil v Battie-Wrightson [1920] 2 Ch 330, 89 LJ Ch 550,
[1920] All ER Rep 597, 64 Sol Jo 585, 124 LT 84, 36 TLR 693
.... 200, 218, 672
Battye's Trustee v Battye 1917 SC 385 2
Battyll v Lyles and Phillips (1858) 4 Jur NS 718 106
Baudains v Richardson [1906] AC 169, 75 LJPC 57, 94 LT 290, 22 TLR 333, PC
.... 56
Baugh v Reed (1790) 1 Ves 257, 3 Bro CC 192 2
Bawden, Re, Bawden v Cresswell [1894] 1 Ch 693, 63 LJ Ch 412, 8 R 76, 42 WR 235, 70
LT 526 .... 235, 1004, 1109
Bawden, Re, National Provincial Bank of England v Cresswell [1894] 1 Ch 693, 63 LJ Ch
412, 8 R 76, 42 WR 235, 70 LT 526 .... 235, 1004, 1109
Bawden's Settlement, Re, Besant v London Hospital Board of Governors [1953] 2 All ER
1235, [1954] 1 WLR 33n, 98 Sol Jo 11 278
Baxendale, Re, Baxendale v Baxendale (1919) 148 LT Jo 139
.... 285

PARA

Baxter, Re, Baxter v Baxter (1898) 42 Sol Jo 611 1132
Baxter v Losh (1851) 14 Beav 612, 21 LJ Ch 55, 18 LTOS 181
.... 470, 475
Baxter's Trusts, Re (1864) 10 Jur NS 845, 4 New Rep 131, 10 LT 487
.... 412, 436
Bayard's Goods, Re (1849) 1 Rob Eccl 768, 13 Jur 664, 13 LTOS 448, 7 Notes of Cases
117 637
Bayles v Phillips (1854) 2 WR 331 627
Bayley v Bishop (1803) 9 Ves 6 .... 429, 438, 1058
Baylis v A-G (1741) 2 Atk 239 .... 207, 275
Baylis' Goods, Re (1862) 26 JP 599, 31 LJPM & A 119, 8 Jur NS 546, 2 Sw & Tr 613, 7
LT 251 611
Baylis Goods, Re (1865) LR 1 P & D 21, 35 LJP & M 15, 11 Jur NS 1028, 13 LT 446
.... 613
Bayliss' Trust, Re (1849) 17 Sim 178, 13 Jur 1090 247
Bayly v Stevens (1607) Cro Jac 198 564
Bayne's Goods, Re (1858) 1 Sw & Tr 132, 6 WR 815, 31 LTOS 172
.... 639
Baynes v Harrison (1856) Dea & Sw 15, 2 Jur NS 72 787
Baynes v Hedger [2008] EWHC 1587 (Ch), 11 ITELR 71, [2008] 3 FCR 151, [2008] 2
FLR 1805, [2008] Fam Law 952, [2008] Fam Law 1087, [2008] All ER (D) 175 (Jul);
affd on other grounds [2009] EWCA Civ 374, 11 ITELR 987, [2009] 2 FCR 30,
[2009] 2 FLR 767, [2009] Fam Law 666, [2009] 20 LS Gaz R 19, [2009] All ER (D)
50 (May) 219–220, 251, 567–568, 581
Baynham, Re, Hart v Mackenzie (1891) 7 TLR 587 .... 186, 200, 331
Beachcroft v Beachcroft (1816) 1 Madd 430 351
Beachcroft v Broome (1791) 4 Term Rep 441 442
Beadle, Re, Mayes v Beadle [1974] 1 All ER 493, [1974] 1 WLR 417, 118 Sol Jo 170
.... 65, 67
Beal v Wyman (1650) Sty 240 45
Beale, Re, Beale v Royal Hospital for Incurables (1890) 6 TLR 308, CA
.... 214
Beale v Beale (1713) 1 P Wms 244 333
Beale v Symonds (1853) 16 Beav 406, 22 LJ Ch 708, 1 WR 137, 22 LTOS 61
.... 555
Beales v Crisford (1843) 13 Sim 592, 13 LJ Ch 26, 7 Jur 1076, 2 LTOS 146
.... 293, 348, 390
Beamish v Beamish [1894] 1 IR 7 902
Bean's Estate, Re [1944] P 83, [1944] 2 All ER 348, 113 LJP 65, 60 TLR 418, P, D and
Admlty 67
Beaney, Re [1978] 2 All ER 595, [1978] 1 WLR 770, 121 Sol Jo 832
.... 48–49
Beard, Re, Beard v Hall [1908] 1 Ch 383, 77 LJ Ch 265, 98 LT 315, 24 TLR 225
.... 131
Beard, Re, Reversionary and General Securities Co Ltd v Hall [1908] 1 Ch 383, 77 LJ Ch
265, 98 LT 315, 24 TLR 225 131
Beard, Re, Simpson v Beard (1888) 57 LJ Ch 887, 36 WR 519, 58 LT 629
.... 287
Beardmore & Co Ltd v Barry 1928 SC 101, Ct of Sess 1230
Beardsley v Beynon (1865) 13 WR 831, 12 LT 698 .... 446, 453
Beardsley v Lacey (1897) 67 LJP 35, 78 LT 25, 14 TLR 140, P, D and Admlty
.... 93, 101, 109
Beater, Re, ex p Edmonds (1862) 4 De GF & J 488, sub nom Beater, Re, Dennant and
Russ, ex p Coster's Executors 31 LJ Bcy 15, 8 Jur NS 629, sub nom Coster, Re, Beater
& Co, ex p Coster's Executors 10 WR 372, 6 LT 199 1040–1041
Beattie v Cordner [1903] 1 IR 1, CA; affd sub nom Harrison v Kirk [1904] AC 1, 73 LJPC
35, [1900–3] All ER Rep 680, 89 LT 566, HL 985, 1099, 1101–1102
Beatty's Will Trusts, Re, Hinves v Brooke [1990] 3 All ER 844, sub nom Re Beatty, Hinves
v Brooke [1990] 1 WLR 1503 .... 11, 128, 262–263, 266, 657
Beaty v Curson (1868) LR 7 Eq 194, 38 LJ Ch 161, 17 WR 132, 20 LT 61
.... 1048
Beauclerk v Dormer (1742) 2 Atk 308 459
Beaudry v Barbeau [1900] AC 569, 69 LJPC 131, 83 LT 236, PC
.... 261
Beaufort (Duke) v Lord Dundonald (1716) 2 Vern 739 285
Beaumont, Re, Beaumont v Ewbank [1902] 1 Ch 889, 71 LJ Ch 478, 50 WR 389,
[1900–3] All ER Rep 273, 46 Sol Jo 317, 86 LT 410 921

  PARA

Beaumont, Re, Martin v Midland Bank Trust Co Ltd [1980] Ch 444, [1980] 1 All ER 266,
  [1979] 3 WLR 818, 123 Sol Jo 803 .... 567, 581
Beaumont, Re, Woods v Beaumont [1910] WN 181, 79 LJ Ch 744, 103 LT 124
  463
Beaumont v Fell (1723) 2 P Wms 141 .... 215, 270
Beaumont v Squire (1852) 17 QB 905, 21 LJQB 123, 16 Jur 591, 19 LTOS 44
  148
Beaumont's Will Trusts, Re, Walker v Lawson [1950] Ch 462, [1950] 1 All ER 802, 94 Sol
  Jo 239, 66 (pt 1) TLR 712 1108–1109
Beavan, Re, Beavan v Beavan (1885) 53 LT 245 294
Beavan, Re, Davies, Banks & Co v Beavan [1912] 1 Ch 196, 81 LJ Ch 113,
  [1911–13] All ER Rep 793, 105 LT 784 976
Beavan v Beavan (1869) 24 Ch D 649n, 52 LJ Ch 961n, 32 WR 363n, 49 LT 263n
  1127
Beavan v Lord Hastings (1856) 2 K & J 724, 2 Jur NS 1044, 4 WR 785, 27 LTOS 282
  1264
Beavan's Goods, Re (1840) 2 Curt 369 83
Beaver v Nowell (1858) 25 Beav 551 .... 385, 392, 475
Bebb v Beckwith (1839) 2 Beav 308 324
Becher, Re [1944] Ch 78, 113 LJ Ch 74, 88 Sol Jo 35, 170 LT 194, 60 TLR 187
  987
Beck v Burn (1844) 7 Beav 492, 13 LJ Ch 319, 8 Jur 348, 2 LTOS 515
  427
Beckett v Howe (1869) LR 2 P & D 1, 33 JP 807, 39 LJP & M 1, 18 WR 75, 21 LT 400
  .... 68, 70
Beckett's Settlement, Re, Re Beckett, Eden v Von Stutterheim [1940] Ch 279, 109 LJ Ch
  81, 84 Sol Jo 133, 163 LT 78, 56 TLR 342 1174
Beckford v Tobin (1749) 1 Ves Sen 308 1076–1077
Beckham v Drake (1849) 2 HL Cas 579, 13 Jur 921 1279
Beckley v Newland (1723) 2 P Wms 182 284
Beckton v Barton (1859) 27 Beav 99, 28 LJ Ch 673, 5 Jur NS 349, 33 LTOS 231
  .... 429, 450
Beckwith v Beckwith (1876) 46 LJ Ch 97, 25 WR 282, 36 LT 128, CA
  317
Beckwith's Case, Ex Ch. See Slingsby's Case
Bective v Hodgson. See Hodgson v Bective
Beddington, Re, Micholls v Samuel [1900] 1 Ch 771, 69 LJ Ch 374, 48 WR 552, 82 LT
  557, 16 TLR 291 405
Beddington v Baumann. See Moses, Re, Beddington v Beddington
Beddoe, Re, Downes v Cottam [1893] 1 Ch 547, 62 LJ Ch 233, 2 R 223, 41 WR 177, 37
  Sol Jo 99, 68 LT 595, [1891–4] All ER Rep Ext 1697, CA
  .... 1018, 1196, 1274
Bedell v Constable (1668) Vaugh 177 1073
Bedford, Re, National Provincial Bank Ltd v Aulton [1951] Ch 905, [1951] 1 All ER 1093,
  95 Sol Jo 368, [1951] 2 TLR 216 366
Bedford v Bedford (1865) 35 Beav 584 992
Bedford v Kirkpatrick (1878) 4 App Cas 96, HL 402
Bedford (Duke), Re, Russell v Bedford [1960] 3 All ER 756, 104 Sol Jo 1058
  1132
Bedson's Trusts, Re (1885) 28 Ch D 523, 54 LJ Ch 644, 33 WR 386, 52 LT 554, CA
  .... 232, 235, 306–307
Beech, Re, Saint v Beech [1920] 1 Ch 40, 89 LJ Ch 9, 122 LT 117
  .... 1126, 1257
Beech's Estate, Re, Beech v Public Trustee [1923] P 46, 92 LJP 33, [1922] All ER Rep 106,
  67 Sol Jo 145, 128 LT 616, 39 TLR 88, CA 5, 81, 227, 906
Beecham, Re, Woolley v Beecham (1919) 63 Sol Jo 430 .... 287, 1011
Beecham, Re, Woolley v Beecham (1923) 68 Sol Jo 208, 130 LT 558, CA
  1130
Beer's Goods, Re (1851) 2 Rob Eccl 349, 15 Jur 160, 16 LTOS 512
  639
Beeston v Booth (1819) 4 Madd 161 1087
Beesty's Will Trusts, Re, Farrar v Royal Alfred Merchant Seamen's Society [1966] Ch 223,
  [1964] 3 All ER 82, [1964] 3 WLR 689, 108 Sol Jo 481
  154
Beetlestone, Re, Beetlestone v Hall (1907) 122 LT Jo 367
  142

PARA

Beevor v Partridge (1840) 11 Sim 229, 10 LJ Ch 89 373
Begbie v Crook (1835) 2 Bing NC 70, 44 LJCP 264, 2 Scott 128
.... 151
Begley v Cook (1856) 3 Drew 662, 5 WR 66, 28 LTOS 138
.... 395, 470
Beirnstein, Re, Barnett v Beirnstein [1925] Ch 12, 94 LJ Ch 62, 69 Sol Jo 88, 132 LT 251
.... 115, 1008
Belaney v Belaney (1867) 2 Ch App 138, 36 LJ Ch 265, 15 WR 369, 16 LT 269
.... 195, 288
Belaney v Kelly (1871) 19 WR 1171, 24 LT 738 2
Belbin v Skeats (1858) 27 LJP & M 56, 1 Sw & Tr 148
.... 72, 894
Belcher v Belcher (1865) 2 Drew & Sm 444, 6 New Rep 314, 13 WR 913, 12 LT 792
.... 1178
Belfast Town Council, Re, ex p Sayers (1884) 13 LR Ir 169
.... 318
Belk v Slack (1836) 1 Keen 238, 44 RR 71 444
Bell, Re, Bell v Agnew (1931) 47 TLR 401 462
Bell, Re, Wright v Scrivener (1914) 58 Sol Jo 517 365
Bell v Armstrong (1822) 1 Add 365 863
Bell v Bell (1864) 15 I Ch R 517 473
Bell v Cade (1861) 2 John & H 122, 31 LJ Ch 383, 10 WR 38, 5 LT 528
.... 432
Bell v Clarke (1858) 25 Beav 437, 27 LJ Ch 674, 4 Jur NS 499, 6 WR 476, 31 LTOS 324
.... 22
Bell v Fothergill (1870) LR 2 P & D 148, 34 JP 679, 18 WR 1040, 23 LT 323
.... 103, 105, 111
Bell v Georgiou [2002] EWHC 1080 (Ch), [2002] WTLR 1105, [2002] All ER (D) 433
   (May) 187
Bell v Park [1914] 1 IR 158 403
Bell v Phyn (1802) 7 Ves 453 .... 443, 461
Bell v Timiswood (1812) 2 Phillim 22 774
Bell's Estate, Re, Bath v Bell (1878) 39 LT 422 1200
Bell's Goods, Re (1878) 4 PD 85, 40 LT 659, P, D and Admlty
.... 613
Bell's Indenture, Re, Bell v Hickley [1980] 3 All ER 425, [1980] 1 WLR 1217, 123 Sol Jo
   322 1234
Bellairs v Bellairs (1874) LR 18 Eq 510, 43 LJ Ch 669, 22 WR 942
.... 130, 132, 134, 425
Bellamy, Re, Pickard v Holroyd (1883) 48 LT 212 132
Bellamy's Goods, Re (1866) 14 WR 501 60
Bellamy's Trust, Re (1862) 1 New Rep 191 232
Bellasis v Ermine (1663) 1 Cas in Ch 22, Freem Ch 171
.... 135
Bellett, ex p (1786) 1 Cox Eq Cas 297 551
Bellew v Bellew (1865) 34 LJPM & A 125, 11 Jur NS 588, 4 Sw & Tr 58, 13 LT 247
.... 809
Belling v Ellise. See Bulling v Ellice
Belliss, Re, Polson v Parrott (1929) 73 Sol Jo 628, 141 LT 245, 45 TLR 452, P, D and
   Admlty 49
Bellman, Re [1963] P 239, [1963] 1 All ER 513, [1963] 2 WLR 314, 107 Sol Jo 16, P, D
   and Admlty 573
Bellville, Re, Westminster Bank Ltd v Walton (or Wolton) [1941] Ch 414, [1941] 2 All ER
   629, 111 LJ Ch 18, 85 Sol Jo 349, 165 LT 344, CA 301
Belshaw v Rollins [1904] 1 IR 284 125
Benbow's Goods, Re (1862) 26 JP 663, 31 LJPM & A 171, 2 Sw & Tr 488, 6 LT 659
.... 862
Bence, Re, Smith v Bence [1891] 3 Ch 242, 60 LJ Ch 636, [1891–4] All ER Rep 253, 65
   LT 530, 7 TLR 593, CA 456, 459
Bence v Gilpin (1868) LR 3 Exch 76, 37 LJ Ex 36, 16 WR 705, 17 LT 655
.... 152, 154
Benett, Re, Ward v Benett [1906] 1 Ch 216, 75 LJ Ch 122, 54 WR 237, 50 Sol Jo 125, 94
   LT 72, CA 952
Benett v Wyndham (1862) 4 De GF & J 259 1242
Benham's Will Trusts, Re, Lockhart v Harker, Read and the Royal National Lifeboat
   Institution [1995] STC 210 .... 220, 298, 1134

PARA

Benjamin, Re, Neville v Benjamin [1902] 1 Ch 723, 71 LJ Ch 319, 46 Sol Jo 266, 86 LT
   387, 18 TLR 283, [1900–3] All ER Rep Ext 1300 .... 33, 191, 484, 1106
Benjamin's Estate, Re [1934] All ER Rep 359, 150 LT 417, P, D and Admlty
   896
Benn, Re, Benn v Benn (1885) 29 Ch D 839, 34 WR 6, 53 LT 240, CA
   .... 255, 315, 317–318
Benn v Dixon (1847) 16 Sim 21, 11 Jur 812, 10 LTOS 50
   444
Benn's Goods, Re [1938] IR 313 83
Bennet v Baud (1664) 1 Sid 185 620
Bennet v Davis (1725) 2 P Wms 316 .... 199, 207
Bennet v Duke of Manchester (1854) 2 WR 644, 23 LTOS 331
   50
Bennet v Lewknor (1616) 1 Roll Rep 356 385
Bennett, Re [1907] 1 KB 149, 76 LJKB 134 1219
Bennett, Re, Bennett v Bennett [1934] WN 177, 178 LT Jo 172, 78 L Jo 231; revsd (1934)
   78 Sol Jo 876, CA 22
Bennett, Re, Midland Bank Executor and Trustee Co Ltd v Fletcher [1943] 1 All ER 467,
   87 Sol Jo 102 991
Bennett, Re, ex p Kirk (1877) 5 Ch D 800, 46 LJ Bcy 101, 25 WR 598, 36 LT 431, CA
   271
Bennett v Attkins (1835) 1 Y & C Ex 247, 4 LJ Ex Eq 35
   1202
Bennett v Baxter (1840) 10 Sim 417, 9 LJ Ch 137, 4 Jur 50
   1178
Bennett v Bennett (1864) 2 Drew & Sm 266, 34 LJ Ch 34, 10 Jur NS 1170, 13 WR 66, 62
   ER 623, [1861–73] All ER Rep 602, 11 LT 362 .... 333, 384
Bennett v Honywood (1772) Amb 708 362
Bennett v Houldsworth [1911] WN 47, 55 Sol Jo 270, 104 LT 304
   .... 336, 393
Bennett v Marshall (1856) 2 K & J 740 220
Bennett v Merriman (1843) 6 Beav 360 325
Bennett v Petit [2013] EWHC 955 (Ch), [2013] All ER (D) 37 (May)
   903
Bennett v Slater [1899] 1 QB 45, 68 LJQB 45, 47 WR 82, 43 Sol Jo 26, 79 LT 324, 15
   TLR 25, CA 32
Bennett v Wood (1837) 7 Sim 522, 6 LJ Ch 330 1208
Bennett's Trust, Re (1857) 3 K & J 280 .... 172, 325, 398, 429
Benson, Re, Elletson v Pillers [1899] 1 Ch 39, 68 LJ Ch 5, 47 WR 264, 79 LT 590
   1186
Benson v Benson (1870) LR 2 P & D 172, 34 JP 807, 40 LJP & M 1, 19 WR 190, 23 LT
   709, [1861–73] All ER Rep Ext 1707 .... 93, 101, 106
Benson v Maude (1821) 6 Madd 15 .... 1054, 1081
Benson v Whittam (1831) 5 Sim 22, 1 LJ Ch 94, 35 RR 113
   .... 370, 375
Bentham, Re, Pearce v Bentham (1906) 94 LT 307 1123
Bentinck v Duke of Portland (1877) 7 Ch D 693, 47 LJ Ch 235, 26 WR 278, 38 LT 58
   45
Bentley, Re [1930] IR 445 717
Bentley, Re, Podmore v Smith (1914) 58 Sol Jo 362, 110 LT 623
   .... 175, 1115
Bentley, Re, Public Trustee v Bentley [1914] 2 Ch 456, 84 LJ Ch 54, [1914–15] All ER Rep
   164, 111 LT 1097 1015
Bentley v Blizard (1858) 4 Jur NS 652 354
Bentley v Meech (1858) 25 Beav 197 442
Bentley v Oldfield (1854) 19 Beav 225 256
Benyon, Re, Benyon v Grieve (1884) 53 LJ Ch 1165, 32 WR 871, 51 LT 116
   .... 366, 409
Benyon v Benyon (1810) 17 Ves 34 403
Benyon v Maddison (1786) 2 Bro CC 75 429
Bercovitz, Re, Canning v Enever [1962] 1 All ER 552, [1962] 1 WLR 321, 106 Sol Jo 110,
   CA 76
Berens, Re, Re Dowdeswell, Berens-Dowdeswell v Holland-Martin [1926] Ch 596, 95 LJ
   Ch 370, 70 Sol Jo 405, 135 LT 298, 42 TLR 267, 312 143
Beresford v Browning [1875] LR 20 Eq 564, Ct of Ch; affd (1875) 1 Ch D 30, 45 LJ Ch
   36, 24 WR 120, 33 LT 524, CA 1232
Beresford v Preston (1920) 54 ILT 48 122

PARA

Beresford v Royal Insurance Co Ltd [1938] AC 586, [1938] 2 All ER 602, 107 LJKB 464,
5 LDAB 145, 82 Sol Jo 431, 158 LT 459, 54 TLR 789, HL
.... 39
Beresford's Case (1607) 7 Co Rep 41a 384
Berger, Re [1990] Ch 118, [1989] 1 All ER 591, [1989] 2 WLR 147, 133 Sol Jo 122,
[1989] 15 LS Gaz R 41, CA 2, 5, 54, 202–203, 239, 708, 711, 891
Berger v Berger [2013] EWCA Civ 1305, [2013] All ER (D) 319 (Oct)
.... 577, 597–598
Bergliter v Cohen [2006] EWHC 123 (Ch), [2006] All ER (D) 88 (Jan)
.... 290, 296, 1259
Bergman's Goods, Re (1842) 2 Notes of Cases 22 .... 848, 854
Berkeley v Berkeley [1946] AC 555, [1946] 2 All ER 154, 25 ATC 209, 115 LJ Ch 281, 90
Sol Jo 345, 175 LT 153, 62 TLR 478, HL 113–115, 240
Berkeley v Swinburne (1848) 16 Sim 275, 17 LJ Ch 416, 12 Jur 571
.... 308, 412, 436
Berkeley (Earl), Re, Inglis v Countess of Berkeley [1968] Ch 744, [1968] 3 All ER 364,
[1968] 3 WLR 253, 112 Sol Jo 601, CA 1084, 1118, 1121
Berkenshaw v Gilbert. See Burtenshaw v Gilbert
Berkley v Poulett [1977] 1 EGLR 86 932
Bernal v Bernal (1838) 3 My & Cr 559, 7 LJ Ch 115, Coop Pr Cas 55, 2 Jur 273
.... 200, 335
Bernard v Minshull (1859) John 276, 28 LJ Ch 649, 5 Jur NS 931, 70 ER 427
.... 1113
Bernard v Mountague (1816) 1 Mer 422 .... 243, 334, 415
Bernard v Walker (1921) 55 ILT 73 413
Bernard's Settlement, Re, Bernard v Jones [1916] 1 Ch 552, 85 LJ Ch 414, 60 Sol Jo 458,
114 LT 654 107
Bernasconi v Atkinson (1853) 10 Hare 345, 23 LJ Ch 184, 17 Jur 128, 1 WR 125,
20 LTOS 217 .... 199, 212, 215, 217, 220, 272, 276
Bernstein v Jacobson [2008] EWHC 3454 (Ch) 922
Berrey, Re, Lewis v Berrey [1936] Ch 274, 105 LJ Ch 38, [1935] All ER Rep 826, 154 LT
335 533
Berrey's Will Trusts, Re, Greening v Warner (or Waters) [1959] 1 All ER 15, [1959] 1 WLR
30, 103 Sol Jo 34 .... 180, 246, 993, 1108
Berry, Re [1907] 2 IR 209 820
Berry, Re, Lloyds Bank Ltd v Berry [1962] Ch 97, [1961] 1 All ER 529, [1961] 1 WLR
329, 105 Sol Jo 256 .... 1122, 1124
Berry v Berry (1861) 3 Giff 134, 7 Jur NS 752, 9 WR 889, 4 LT 635
.... 331
Berry v Child Support Agency [2016] EWHC 1418 (Ch)
.... 981, 1218
Berry v Fisher [1903] 1 IR 484 336–337
Berry v Gaukroger [1903] 2 Ch 116, 72 LJ Ch 435, 51 WR 449, [1900–3] All ER Rep
166, 47 Sol Jo 490, 88 LT 521, 19 TLR 445, CA 1132
Berry v Geen [1938] AC 575, 159 LT 122, sub nom Re Blake, Berry v Geen [1938]
2 All ER 362, 107 LJ Ch 173, 82 Sol Jo 491, 54 TLR 703, HL
.... 146, 302, 422
Berry v Gibbons (1873) 8 Ch App 747, 38 JP 4, 42 LJ Ch 89, 21 WR 754, 29 LT 88
.... 1190
Berry v IBS-STL Ltd (in liq) [2012] EWHC 666 (Ch), [2012] All ER (D) 10 (Mar)
.... 162
Berry v Usher (1805) 11 Ves 87 625
Bertie v Faulkland. See Falkland (Lord Viscount) v Bertie
Berton, Re, Vandyk v Berton [1939] Ch 200, [1938] 4 All ER 286, 108 LJ Ch 139, 82 Sol
Jo 890, 159 LT 566, 55 TLR 40 1123
Berwick-on-Tweed Corpn v Murray (1857) 7 De GM & G 497, 26 LJ Ch 201, 109 RR
218, 5 WR 208, sub nom Berwick Corpn v Murray, Berwick Corpn v Dobie 3 Jur NS
1, 847, 28 LTOS 277 1257
Besant v Cox (1877) 6 Ch D 604, 25 WR 789 450
Bescoby v Pack (1823) 1 Sim & St 500, 2 LJOS Ch 17 294
Best v Donmall (1871) 40 LJ Ch 160, 19 WR 400, 24 LT 217
.... 424
Best v Stonehewer (1865) 2 De GJ & Sm 537, 34 LJ Ch 349, 11 Jur NS 315, 5 New Rep
500, 13 WR 566, 12 LT 195 .... 175, 248, 338
Best v Williams [1890] WN 189 412

PARA

Best's Settlement Trusts, Re (1874) LR 18 Eq 686, 43 LJ Ch 545, 22 WR 599
.... 364, 377

Besterman, Re, Besterman v Grusin [1984] Ch 458, [1984] 2 All ER 656, [1984] 3 WLR
280, [1984] FLR 503, [1984] Fam Law 203, 128 Sol Jo 515, CA
.... 569, 573–574, 577, 591, 603

Beswick v Beswick [1968] AC 58, [1967] 2 All ER 1197, [1967] 3 WLR 932, 111 Sol Jo
540, HL 30

Bethell v Abraham (1873) LR 17 Eq 24, 43 LJ Ch 180, 22 WR 179, [1861–73] All ER Rep
811, 29 LT 715; affd (1874) 3 Ch D 590n, 22 WR 745, 31 LT 112
.... 1190

Bettisworth's Case, Hayward v Bettisworth (1580) 2 Co Rep 31b, sub nom Heyward v
Bettesworth Moore KB 250 286

Betts, Re, Burrell v Betts [1949] 1 All ER 568, 93 Sol Jo 164sub nom Betts, Re, Burnell v
Betts [1949] WN 91 287

Betts v Doughty (1879) 5 PD 26, 48 LJP 71, 41 LT 560, P, D and Admlty
.... 59, 679

Betts v Gannell (1903) 19 TLR 304, P, D and Admlty 70
Betts Goods, Re (1861) 25 JP 392, 30 LJPM & A 167 616
Betty, Re, Betty v A-G [1899] 1 Ch 821, 68 LJ Ch 435, 80 LT 675
.... 1228

Bevan, Re, Bevan v Houldsworth [1948] 1 All ER 271, 92 Sol Jo 140, CA
.... 809–810

Bevan v A-G (1863) 4 Giff 361, 9 Jur NS 1099, 2 New Rep 52, 9 LT 221
.... 287
Bevan v Bevan (1880) 5 LR Ir 57, Ir CA 293
Bevan v Mahon-Hagan (1892) 27 LR Ir 399; affd (1893) 31 LR Ir 342, Ir CA
.... 145

Bevan v Webb [1905] 1 Ch 620, 74 LJ Ch 300, 53 WR 651, 93 LT 298
.... 657
Bevan v White (1844) 7 I Eq R 473 230
Bevan's Trusts, Re (1887) 34 Ch D 716, 56 LJ Ch 652, 35 WR 400, [1886–90] All ER Rep
706, 56 LT 277 .... 256, 434, 437

Beverly, Re, Watson v Watson [1901] 1 Ch 681, 70 LJ Ch 295, 49 WR 343, 45 Sol Jo 259,
84 LT 296, 17 TLR 228, [1900–3] All ER Rep Ext 1519
.... 1160–1161

Bewick, Re, Ryle v Ryle [1911] 1 Ch 116, 80 LJ Ch 47, 55 Sol Jo 109, 103 LT 634
.... 415
Bewick v Whitfield (1734) 3 P Wms 267, 24 ER 1058, [1558–1774] All ER Rep 541
.... 931
Bewley's Estates, Re, Jefferys v Jefferys (1871) 19 WR 464, 24 LT 177
.... 1245
Bewsher v Williams and Ball (1861) 3 Sw & Tr 62, 11 WR 541n, 8 LT 290
.... 861, 908–909

Beyfus v Lawley. See Lawley, Re, Zaiser v Lawley (or Perkins)
Bheekhun v Williams (1998) 1 ITELR 491, [1999] 2 FLR 229, [1999] Fam Law 379, CA
.... 582
Bibbens v Potter (1879) 10 Ch D 733, 27 WR 304 382
Bibin v Walker (1768) Amb 661 252
Bick, Re, Edwards v Bush [1920] 1 Ch 488, 89 LJ Ch 335, 64 Sol Jo 359, 123 LT 49
.... 156

Bickersteth v Shanu [1936] AC 290, [1936] 1 All ER 227, 105 LJPC 53, 80 Sol Jo 164,
154 LT 360, 52 TLR 290, PC 413–414, 416, 1082
Bickerton's Settlement, Re, Shaw v Bickerton [1942] Ch 84, [1942] 1 All ER 217, 111 LJ
Ch 132, 85 Sol Jo 481, 166 LT 38 475
Bickford v Chalker (1854) 2 Drew 327, 2 WR 502 .... 232, 251, 412
Bickham v Cruttwell (1838) 3 My & Cr 763 1012
Bickley v Bickley (1867) LR 4 Eq 216, 36 LJ Ch 817 477
Biddell v Dowse. See Dowse v Coxe
Biddles v Biddles (1847) 16 Sim 1, sub nom Ward v Biddles 16 LJ Ch 455
.... 370
Biddulph v Lees (1859) EB & E 289, 306, 28 LJQB 211, 5 Jur NS 818, 7 WR 309,
32 LTOS 392, Ex Ch 387, 456
Biddulph's Trusts, Re, Re Poole's Trusts (1852) 5 De G & Sm 469
.... 1047
Bide v Harrison (1873) LR 17 Eq 76, 43 LJ Ch 86, 29 LT 451
.... 293

PARA

Bidie, Re, Bidie v General Accident Fire and Life Assurance Corpn Ltd [1949] Ch 121, [1948] 2 All ER 995, 47 LGR 465, 113 JP 22, [1949] LJR 386, 92 Sol Jo 705, 65 TLR 25, CA 565, 597

Biederman v Seymour (1841) 3 Beav 368, 10 LJ Ch 177 540

Biedermann, Re, Best v Wertheim [1922] 2 Ch 771, 91 LJ Ch 655, 127 LT 507, 38 TLR 778, CA 465

Bifield's Case. See Milliner v Robinson

Biggar v Eastwood (1884) 15 LR Ir 219 1258

Bigge v Bensley (1783) 1 Bro CC 187 .... 385, 459

Bigger, Re [1977] Fam 203, [1977] 2 All ER 644, [1977] 2 WLR 773, 121 Sol Jo 172 622

Biggs' Estate, Re [1966] P 118, [1966] 1 All ER 358, [1966] 2 WLR 536, 110 Sol Jo 173, P, D and Admlty 628, 759

Bignall v Rose (1854) 24 LJ Ch 27, 3 WR 77 375

Bilbee v Hasse & Co (1889) 5 TLR 677; affd (1890) Times, 16 January, CA 1279

Bilham, Re, Buchanan v Hill [1901] 2 Ch 169, 70 LJ Ch 518, 49 WR 483, 45 Sol Jo 537, 84 LT 499 317

Billinghurst v Vickers (formerly Leonard) (1810) 1 Phillim 187, 200 .... 50, 892

Billings v Sandom (1784) 1 Bro CC 393 449

Billingshurst v Speerman (1695) 1 Salk 297, Holt KB 306 .... 942, 1225

Billingsley v Wills (1745) 3 Atk 219 429

Bindon (Earl) v Earl of Suffolk (1707) 1 P Wms 96; revsd (1707) 4 Bro Parl Cas 574, HL 2, 395, 449

Bingham v Lord Clanmorris (1828) 2 Mol 253 151

Bingley v Broadhead (1803) 8 Ves 415 415

Binning (or Billing) v Binning (or Billing) [1895] WN 116, 13 R 654, 39 Sol Jo 622, 11 TLR 502 394

Binns, Re, Public Trustee v Ingle [1929] 1 Ch 677, 98 LJ Ch 307, [1929] All ER Rep 542, 141 LT 91 404

Biou's Goods, Re, Indigent Blind School and Westminster Hospital v Flack (1843) 3 Curt 739, 2 Notes of Cases 106 820

Birch, Re (1853) 17 Beav 358, 51 ER 1072 136

Birch, Re, Hunt v Thorn [1909] 1 Ch 787, 78 LJ Ch 385, 101 LT 101 1008

Birch v Birch [1902] P 130, 71 LJP 58, 50 WR 437, 46 Sol Jo 393, 80 LT 364, 18 TLR 485, CA 848, 884

Birch v Birch (1848) 1 Rob Eccl 675, 12 Jur 1057, 12 LTOS 334, 6 Notes of Cases 581 83

Birch v Curtis [2002] EWHC 1158 (Ch), [2002] 2 FLR 847, [2002] Fam Law 815, [2002] WTLR 965, [2002] 29 EG 139 (CS), [2002] All ER (D) 77 (Jun) 23

Birch's Estate, Re [1929] P 164, 98 LJP 66, 73 Sol Jo 221, 141 LT 32, P, D and Admlty 827

Birchall, Re, Birchall v Ashton (1889) 40 Ch D 436, 37 WR 387, 60 LT 369, CA 151

Birchall, Re, Kennedy v Birchall [1940] Ch 424, [1940] 1 All ER 545, 109 LJ Ch 129, 162 LT 261, CA 247

Birchall, Re, Wilson v Birchall (1880) 16 Ch D 41, 29 WR 27, 44 LT 113, CA 885

Bird, Re, Bird v Cross (1894) 8 R 326 143

Bird, Re, Re Evans, Dodd v Evans [1901] 1 Ch 916, 70 LJ Ch 514, 49 WR 599, 45 Sol Jo 327, 84 LT 294 1097

Bird v Bird (1842) 11 LJ Ch 390, 6 Jur 1030 419

Bird v Harris (1870) LR 9 Eq 204, 39 LJ Ch 226, 18 WR 374, 23 LT 213 407

Bird v Hunsdon (1818) 1 Wils Ch 456, 3 Swan 342 468

Bird v Luckie (1850) 8 Hare 301, 14 Jur 1015 313

Bird v Webster (1853) 1 Drew 338, 22 LJ Ch 483, 1 WR 121 .... 369, 384

Bird and Barnard's Contract, Re (1888) 59 LT 166 473

Birds v Askey (1857) 24 Beav 615 .... 415, 422

Birdsall v York (1859) 5 Jur NS 1237 .... 336, 398

                                                                        PARA
Birkby's Estate, Re (1929) 73 Sol Jo 556, P, D and Admlty
.... 911
Birkett, Re, Holland v Duncan [1950] Ch 330, [1950] 1 All ER 316, 94 Sol Jo 131, 66 (pt
  1) TLR 411 .... 236–237, 332, 396
Birkhead v Bowdoin (1842) 2 Notes of Cases 66 110
Birkhead v North (1847) 4 Dow & L 732, 16 LJQB 284, 11 Jur 436, 2 Saund & C 9,
  9 LTOS 106 1276
Birkin, Re, Heald v Millership [1949] 1 All ER 1045, [1949] LJR 1252, 93 Sol Jo 338
.... 209, 253
Birks, Re, Kenyon v Birks [1900] 1 Ch 417, 69 LJ Ch 723, 50 WR 695, 46 Sol Jo 632, 87
  LT 316, 18 TLR 710, CA 249, 334, 336
Birks v Birks (1865) 29 JP 360, 34 LJPM & A 90, 4 Sw & Tr 23, 13 WR 638, 13 LT 193
.... 95, 99
Birmingham, Re, Savage v Stannard [1959] Ch 523, [1958] 2 All ER 397, [1958] 3 WLR
  10, 102 Sol Jo 454 .... 996, 1008
Birmingham v Renfrew (1936) 57 CLR 666, 43 ALR 520, [1937] VLR 327, 11 ALJ 188,
  Aust HC 23, 588
Birmingham, Dudley and District Banking Co v Ross (1888) 38 Ch D 295, 57 LJ Ch 601,
  36 WR 914, 59 LT 609, 4 TLR 437, CA 283
Birt's Goods, Re (1871) LR 2 P & D 214, 35 JP 296, 40 LJP & M 26, 19 WR 511, 24 LT
  142, [1861–73] All ER Rep Ext 1320 83
Bischoffsheim, Re, Cassel v Grant [1948] Ch 79, [1947] 2 All ER 830, [1948] LJR 213, 92
  Sol Jo 26, 64 TLR 36 350
Bishop v Cappel (1847) 1 De G & Sm 411, 11 Jur 939, 9 LTOS 371
.... 349
Bishop v Church (1748) 3 Atk 691 1296
Bishop v Curtis (1852) 18 QB 878, 21 LJQB 391, 17 Jur 23, 19 LTOS 217
.... 27
Bishop v Elliott. See Elliott v Bishop
Bishop v Fountain (1695) 1 Eq Cas Abr 175, 3 Lev 427, 1 Roll Abr 609
.... 27
Bishop v Plumley [1991] 1 All ER 236, [1991] 1 WLR 582, [1991] 1 FLR 121, [1991] Fam
  Law 61, [1990] NLJR 1153, CA 567
Bishop and Richardson's Contract, Re [1899] 1 IR 71 384
Bishop's Goods, Re (1882) 46 JP 392, 30 WR 567, P, D and Admlty
.... 69
Biss, Re, Biss v Biss [1903] 2 Ch 40, 72 LJ Ch 473, 51 WR 504, [1900–3] All ER Rep 406,
  47 Sol Jo 383, 88 LT 403, CA 657
Biss, Re, Heasman v Biss [1956] Ch 243, [1956] 1 All ER 89, [1956] 2 WLR 94, 100 Sol
  Jo 35 1009
Biss v Smith (1857) 2 H & N 105, 26 LJ Ex 295 460
Bizzey v Flight (1876) 3 Ch D 269, 45 LJ Ch 852, 24 WR 957
.... 159
Black, Re (1953) Times, 25 March 574
Black, Re, Falls v Alford [1907] 1 IR 486 371
Black v Jobling (1869) LR 1 P & D 685, 33 JP 727, 38 LJP & M 74, 17 WR 1108, 21 LT
  298 .... 100, 106, 712
Black's Goods, Re (1887) 13 PD 5, 57 LJP 20, 36 WR 400, P, D and Admlty
.... 801
Blackborn v Edgley (1719) 1 P Wms 600, 24 ER 534, [1558–1774] All ER Rep 486
.... 286, 290, 456
Blackborough v Davis (1701) 1 Com 96, 108, 1 Ld Raym 684, 12 Mod Rep 615, 1 P Wms
  41, 1 Salk 38, 249, Holt KB 43 858
Blackburn, Re, Smiles v Blackburn (1889) 43 Ch D 75, 59 LJ Ch 208, 38 WR 140
.... 114
Blackburn v Stables (1814) 13 RR 120, 2 Ves & B 367, 35 ER 358, [1814–23] All ER Rep
  178 .... 45, 265, 368
Blackham's Case (1709) 1 Salk 290 670
Blackler v Webb (1726) 2 P Wms 383 396
Blackman, Re (1852) 16 Beav 377 .... 220, 276, 331
Blackman v Fysh [1892] 3 Ch 209, 2 R 1, 67 LT 802, CA
.... 311, 463
Blackman v Man [2007] EWHC 3162 (Ch), [2007] All ER (D) 118 (Dec)
.... 53
Blackmore v Snee (1857) 1 De G & J 455 318

PARA

Blackmore v White [1899] 1 QB 293, 68 LJQB 180, 47 WR 448, 80 LT 79
.... 152

Blackstone v Stone. See Blaxton v Stone

Blackwell, Re, Blackwell v Blackwell [1929] AC 318, 98 LJ Ch 251, 73 Sol Jo 92, 140 LT
    444, 45 TLR 208, HL 208, 283, 413–414, 416, 419

Blackwell v Bull (1836) 1 Keen 176, Donnelly 54, 5 LJ Ch 251
.... 348, 469

Blackwell v Pennant (1852) 9 Hare 551, 22 LJ Ch 155, 16 Jur 420, 19 LTOS 336
.... 212, 365–366

Blackwell's Goods, Re (1877) 2 PD 72, 41 JP 392, 46 LJP 29, 25 WR 305, 36 LT 413, P,
    D and Admlty 611

Blackwood v Damer (1783) 3 Add 239n, 3 Phillim 458n
.... 99

Blackwood v R (1882) 8 App Cas 82, 52 LJP 10, 31 WR 645, 48 LT 441, PC
.... 968

Blades v Free (1829) 9 B & C 167, 7 LJOS 211, 4 Man & Ry KB 282, 109 ER 63
.... 1279

Blades v Isaac [2016] EWHC 601 (Ch), [2016] WTLR 589
.... 1196–1197

Blagrove v Bradshaw (1858) 4 Drew 230, 27 LJ Ch 440, 4 Jur NS 107, 6 WR 266,
    30 LTOS 363 440

Blagrove v Coore (1859) 27 Beav 138 .... 285, 305

Blagrove v Hancock (1848) 16 Sim 371, 18 LJ Ch 20, 12 Jur 1081
.... 423

Blague v Gold (1637) Cro Car 473 277

Blaiberg, Re, Blaiberg and Public Trustee v De Andia Yrarrazaval and Blaiberg [1940] Ch
    385, [1940] 1 All ER 632, 109 LJ Ch 166, 84 Sol Jo 287, 162 LT 418, 56 TLR 487
.... 140

Blair v Bainbrigge. See Bainbrigge v Blair

Blair v Duncan [1902] AC 37, 71 LJPC 22, 50 WR 369, 86 LT 157, 18 TLR 194, HL
.... 11

Blake, Re [1955] IR 89 .... 121, 130–131, 1130

Blake, Re, Gawthorne v Blake [1917] 1 Ch 18, 86 LJ Ch 160, 61 Sol Jo 71, 115 LT 663
.... 157

Blake, Re, Jones v Blake (1885) 29 Ch D 913, 54 LJ Ch 880, 33 WR 886, 53 LT 302, CA
.... 1179

Blake, Re, Minahan's Petition of Right [1932] 1 Ch 54, 100 LJ Ch 251, [1931] All ER Rep
    372, 145 LT 42, 47 TLR 357 780

Blake v Blake [1923] 1 IR 88 273

Blake v Blake (1880) 15 Ch D 481, 49 LJ Ch 393, 28 WR 647, 42 LT 724
.... 94, 150

Blake v Gale (1886) 32 Ch D 571, 55 LJ Ch 559, 34 WR 555, 55 LT 234, CA
.... 1101

Blake v Gibbs (1825) 5 Russ 13n 291

Blake v Knight (1843) 3 Curt 547, 7 Jur 633, 1 LTOS 208, 2 Notes of Cases 337
.... 69, 896

Blake v Shaw (1860) John 732, 8 WR 410, 70 ER 615, [1843–60] All ER Rep 504, 2 LT
    84 287

Blake's Estate, Re (1871) 19 WR 765 333

Blake's Trust, Re (1867) LR 3 Eq 799, 36 LJ Ch 747, 16 LT 279
.... 468

Blake's Trusts, Re [1904] 1 IR 98 276

Blakemore's Settlement, Re (1855) 20 Beav 214 412–413

Blakeney v Blakeney (1833) 6 Sim 52 370

Blamford v Blamford (1615) 3 Bulst 98, sub nom Blanford v Blanford Cro Jac 394,
    Moore KB 846, sub nom Blanford's Case Godb 266, sub nom Blandford v Blandford 1
    Roll Rep 318 .... 228, 248

Blamire v Geldart (1809) 16 Ves 314 429

Blanch, Re, Blanch v Honhold [1967] 2 All ER 468, [1967] 1 WLR 987, 111 Sol Jo 258
.... 591, 602

Bland v Wilkins (1782) 1 Bro CC 61n 184

Bland v Williams (1834) 3 My & K 411, 3 LJ Ch 218 .... 436, 447

Blandy v Widmore (1715) 1 P Wms 324, 2 Vern 709 .... 491, 497

Blanford's Case. See Blamford v Blamford

Blann v Bell (1852) 2 De GM & G 775, 22 LJ Ch 236, 16 Jur 1103, 20 LTOS 162
.... 235, 375

PARA

Blann v Bell (1877) 7 Ch D 382, 47 LJ Ch 120, 26 WR 165
.... 1012
Blantern, Re, Lowe v Cooke [1891] WN 54, CA 237
Blasson v Blasson (1864) 2 De GJ & Sm 665, 36 LJ Ch 18, 10 Jur NS 1113, 5 New Rep
    65, 13 WR 113, 11 LT 353 362
Blathwayt v Baron Cawley [1976] AC 397, [1975] 3 All ER 625, [1975] 3 WLR 684, 119
    Sol Jo 795, HL 34, 131, 133, 140, 181, 204
Blathwayt's Will Trusts, Re, Blathwayt v Blathwayt [1950] 1 All ER 582, 94 Sol Jo 254, 66
    (pt 1) TLR 669   182
Blaxton v Stone (1687) 3 Mod Rep 123, sub nom Blackstone v Stone Skin 269
.... 384
Blayney's (Lord) Trust, Re (1875) IR 9 Eq 413 276
Blease v Burgh (1840) 2 Beav 221, 9 LJ Ch 226 .... 307, 428
Blech v Blech [2001] All ER (D) 141 (Dec) ... 45, 115, 194, 205–206, 212, 214, 223, 244, 246,
                                                                                315–316
Bleckley's Goods, Re (1883) 8 PD 169, 47 JP 663, 52 LJP 102, 32 WR 171, P, D and
    Admlty 100
Bleckly, Re, Bleckly v Bleckly [1951] Ch 740, [1951] 1 All ER 1064, 95 Sol Jo 335, [1951]
    1 TLR 902, CA 304, 308
Bleckly, Re, Sidebotham v Bleckly [1920] 1 Ch 450, 89 LJ Ch 290, 64 Sol Jo 306, 122 LT
    754, 36 TLR 246, CA 352
Blenkinsop v Foster (1838) 3 Y & C Ex 205, 8 LJ Ex Eq 8
.... 1186
Blewitt v Blewitt (1832) You 541 636
Blewitt v Roberts (1841) Cr & Ph 274, 10 LJ Ch 342, 5 Jur 979
.... 318
Blewitt's Goods, Re (1880) 5 PD 116, 44 JP 768, 49 LJP 31, 28 WR 520, 42 LT 329, P, D
    and Admlty 63, 74, 84
Blight, Re, Blight v Hartnall (1880) 13 Ch D 858, 49 LJ Ch 255, 28 WR 302, 41 LT 730
.... 417, 422
Blight, Re, Blight v Westminster Bank Ltd (1946) 96 LJ 233
.... 600
Blight v Hartnoll (1883) 23 Ch D 218, 52 LJ Ch 672, 31 WR 535, [1881–5] All ER Rep
    660, 48 LT 543, CA 184, 298, 415, 1113
Bliss, Re [2001] 1 WLR 1973, 145 Sol Jo LB 122, sub nom Layton v Newcombe [2002]
    WTLR 541 125–126
Blockley, Re, Blockley v Blockley (1885) 29 Ch D 250, 54 LJ Ch 722, 33 WR 777
.... 503
Blount, Re, Nayler v Blount (1879) 27 WR 865 1173
Blount v Crozier [1917] 1 IR 461 346
Blount v Hipkins (1834) 7 Sim 43, 4 LJ Ch 13 1011
Blower v Morret (1752) 2 Ves Sen 420 .... 125, 1087
Blower's Trusts, Re (1871) 6 Ch App 351, 42 LJ Ch 24, 19 WR 666, 25 LT 181
.... 328
Bloye's Trust, Re (1849) 19 LJ Ch 89, 2 H & Tw 140, 14 Jur 49, 1 Mac & G 488, 47 ER
    1630, [1843–60] All ER Rep 1092, 15 LTOS 157; affd sub nom Lewis v Hillman
    (1852) 3 HL Cas 607, 10 ER 23, [1843–60] All ER Rep 1092, 19 LTOS 329, HL
.... 1048
Bluett v Jessop (1821) Jac 240 1204
Blundell, Re, Blundell v Blundell [1906] 2 Ch 222, 75 LJ Ch 561, 94 LT 818, 22 TLR 570
.... 168
Blundell, Re, Blundell v Blundell (1888) 40 Ch D 370, 57 LJ Ch 730, 36 WR 779,
    [1886–90] All ER Rep 837, 58 LT 933, 4 TLR 506 1050
Blundell v Chapman (1864) 33 Beav 648, 33 LJ Ch 660, 10 Jur NS 332, 12 WR 540, sub
    nom Bundell v Chapman 10 LT 152 .... 254, 316
Blundell v Gladstone (1841) 11 Sim 467; on appeal (1843) 1 Ph 279, 12 LJ Ch 225, 7 Jur
    269; affd sub nom Camoys (Lord) v Blundell (1848) 1 HL Cas 778
.... 212, 214–215, 270, 276
Blundell v Gladstone (1844) 14 Sim 83, 8 Jur 301, 3 LTOS 118
.... 263
Blundell v Gladstone (1852) 3 Mac & G 692, 19 LTOS 354
.... 127
Blunt v Clark (1658) 2 Sid 61 561
Blyth v Fladgate [1891] 1 Ch 337, 60 LJ Ch 66, 39 WR 422, 63 LT 546, 7 TLR 29
.... 1237
Boam, Re, Shorthouse v Annibal (1911) 56 Sol Jo 142 172

PARA

Boardman v Stanley (1873) 21 WR 644 293

Boards, Re, Knight v Knight [1895] 1 Ch 499, 64 LJ Ch 305, 13 R 278, 43 WR 472, [1895–9] All ER Rep 994, 72 LT 220 1111

Boatwright v Boatwright (1873) LR 17 Eq 71, 38 JP 228, 43 LJ Ch 12, 22 WR 147, 29 LT 603 978

Boddicott and Hamilton v Dalzell (1756) 2 Lee 294 613

Boddington, Re, Boddington v Clairat (1883) 22 Ch D 597, 52 LJ Ch 239, 31 WR 449, 48 LT 110; on appeal (1884) 25 Ch D 685, 53 LJ Ch 475, 32 WR 448, 50 LT 761, [1881–5] All ER Rep Ext 1444, CA 58, 346–347, 375, 380, 409

Boden, Re, Boden v Boden [1907] 1 Ch 132, 76 LJ Ch 100, 95 LT 741, CA 228, 248, 409

Bodger v Arch (1854) 24 LJ Ex 19, 10 Exch 333, 2 CLR 1491, 24 LTOS 96 .... 646, 668

Bodh v Boudh [2007] EWCA Civ 1019, [2007] All ER (D) 384 (Oct) 4, 55

Bodman, Re, Bodman v Bodman [1891] 3 Ch 135, 61 LJ Ch 31, 40 WR 60, 65 LT 522 295

Boehm v Clarke (1804) 9 Ves 580 459–460

Boehm's Goods, Re [1891] P 247, 60 LJP 80, 39 WR 576, 64 LT 806, 7 TLR 368, [1891–4] All ER Rep Ext 2044, P, D and Admlty 186, 739

Bogg v Raper (1998) 1 ITELR 267, [1998] CLY 4592, (1998) Times, 22 April, CA 1246

Bogle, Re, Bogle v Yorstoun (1898) 78 LT 457 .... 378, 441

Bohrmann's Estate, Re, Caesar and Watmough v Bohrmann [1938] 1 All ER 271, 82 Sol Jo 176, 158 LT 180, P, D and Admlty 51–52

Boidell v Golightly. See Boydell v Golightly
Bold, Re, Banks v Hartland (1926) 95 LJ Ch 201, 70 Sol Jo 526, 134 LT 595 182

Boles and British Land Co's Contract, Re [1902] 1 Ch 244, 71 LJ Ch 130, 50 WR 185, 46 Sol Jo 123, 85 LT 607 657

Bolger v Mackell (1800) 5 Ves 509 .... 256, 428

Bolingbroke v Kerr (1866) LR 1 Exch 222, 35 LJ Ex 137, 14 WR 657, 14 LT 365 1288

Bolitho v Hillyar (1865) 34 Beav 180, 11 Jur NS 556, 13 WR 600 449

Bolton, Re, Brown v Bolton (1886) 31 Ch D 542, 50 JP 532, 55 LJ Ch 398, 34 WR 325, 54 LT 396, 2 TLR 303, CA 354

Bolton v Bolton (1861) 12 I Ch R 233 438

Bolton v Bolton (1870) LR 5 Exch 145, 39 LJ Ex 89, 18 WR 460, 21 LT 7793 376

Bolton's Goods, Re [1899] P 186, 68 LJP 63, 80 LT 631, P, D and Admlty 815

Bolton's Goods, Re (1887) 12 PD 202, 57 LJP 12, 36 WR 287, P, D and Admlty 723

Bon v Smith (1596) Cro Eliz 532 278

Bond, Re, Osborne v Creswell [1952] WN 534, [1952] 2 TLR 880, CA 913

Bond v Graham (1842) 1 Hare 482, 11 LJ Ch 306, 6 Jur 620 669

Bond v Seawell (1765) 3 Burr 1773, 1 Wm Bl 454n 67

Bone, Re, Bone v Midland Bank Ltd [1955] 2 All ER 555, [1955] 1 WLR 703, 99 Sol Jo 434 598

Bone v Cook (1824) M'Cle 168, 13 Price 332, 28 RR 697 165

Bone and Newsam v Spear. See Spear v Bone
Bonfield v Hassell (1863) 32 Beav 217, 32 LJ Ch 475, 9 Jur NS 453, 1 New Rep 254, 11 WR 297, 7 LT 776 463

Bonham v Fishwick [2007] EWHC 1859 (Ch) 1246

Bonnefoi, Re, Surrey v Perrin [1912] P 233, 82 LJP 17, 57 Sol Jo 62, 107 LT 512, CA 190, 239

Bonner, Re, Tucker v Good (1881) 19 Ch D 201, 51 LJ Ch 83, 30 WR 58, 45 LT 470 328

Bonser v Cox (1842) 6 Beav 84 987

Bonsor v Musicians' Union [1954] Ch 479, [1954] 1 All ER 822, 98 Sol Jo 248, CA; revsd [1956] AC 104, [1955] 3 All ER 518, [1955] 3 WLR 788, 99 Sol Jo 814, HL 125

PARA

Boocher v Samford (1588) Cro Eliz 113, sub nom Bucher v Samford Gouldsb 99
.... 286
Booker v Allen (1831) 9 LJOS Ch 130, 2 Russ & M 270
.... 115
Boon v Cornforth (1751) 2 Ves Sen 277 469
Boorer, Re, Boorer v Boorer [1908] WN 189 293
Boosey v Gardener (1854) 18 Beav 471; revsd (1854) 5 De GM & G 122
.... 243, 375, 408, 417
Booth, Re, Booth v Booth [1894] 2 Ch 282, 63 LJ Ch 560, 8 R 256, 42 WR 613
.... 237, 370
Booth, Re, Booth v Booth [1926] P 118, 95 LJP 64, [1926] All ER Rep 594, 134 LT 229,
42 TLR 454, P, D and Admlty 79, 104
Booth, Re, Hattersley v Cowgill (1917) 86 LJ Ch 270, 116 LT 465
.... 378
Booth, Re, Pickard v Booth [1900] 1 Ch 768, 69 LJ Ch 474, 48 WR 566, 44 Sol Jo 348
.... 461
Booth v Alington (1857) 27 LJ Ch 117, 3 Jur NS 835, 5 WR 811
.... 393, 395
Booth v Booth (1799) 4 Ves 399 .... 256, 413, 426, 428, 430
Booth v Booth (1838) 1 Beav 125, 8 LJ Ch 39, 2 Jur 938, 49 RR 304
.... 1253
Booth v Meyer (1877) 38 LT 125 135
Booth v Vicars (1844) 13 LJ Ch 147, 1 Coll 6, 8 Jur 76, 2 LTOS 307
.... 364, 394, 397
Booth's Will Trusts, Re, Robbins v King (1940) 84 Sol Jo 256, 163 LT 77, 56 TLR 507;
affd [1940] WN 293, CA 247, 322
Bootle v Blundell (1815) Coop G 136, 1 Mer 193, 15 RR 93, 19 Ves 494
.... 77, 1012
Bootle's Goods, Re, Heaton v Whalley (1901) 45 Sol Jo 484, 84 LT 570, 17 TLR 476, P, D
and Admlty 754
Boraston's Case (1587) 3 Co Rep 16a, 19a, [1558–1774] All ER Rep 377, 76 ER 664
.... 413, 415, 419, 422
Bordass' Estate, Re [1929] P 107, 98 LJP 65, 72 Sol Jo 826, 140 LT 120, 45 TLR 52, P, D
and Admlty 824, 827, 949
Boreham v Bignall (1850) 8 Hare 131 .... 194, 346, 432, 1210
Borlase v Borlase (1845) 4 Notes of Cases 106 93
Borman v Lel [2002] WTLR 237, [2001] All ER (D) 94 (Jun)
.... 63
Borne, Re, Bailey v Bailey [1944] Ch 190, [1944] 1 All ER 382, 113 LJ Ch 159, 88 Sol Jo
120, 171 LT 63, 60 TLR 221 156
Borrer's Trusts, Re, Dunlop v Borrer (1909) 54 Sol Jo 32
.... 156
Borrett v Hart (1863) 3 De GJ & Sm 504 475
Borthwick, Re, Borthwick v Beauvais (No 2) [1949] Ch 395, [1949] 1 All ER 472,
[1949] LJR 752, 93 Sol Jo 147 .... 574, 576–577
Bortoft v Wadsworth (1864) 12 WR 523 306
Borton v Borton (1849) 16 Sim 552, 18 LJ Ch 219, 13 Jur 247, 13 LTOS 5
.... 382
Borwick, Re, Borwick v Borwick [1933] Ch 657, 102 LJ Ch 199, [1933] All ER Rep 737,
77 Sol Jo 197, 149 LT 116, 49 TLR 288 .... 131, 140
Bosanquet, Re, Unwin v Petre (1915) 85 LJ Ch 14, 113 LT 152
.... 165, 1087
Boston's (Lord) Will Trusts, Re, Inglis v Lord Boston [1956] Ch 395, [1956] 1 All ER 593,
[1956] 2 WLR 700, 100 Sol Jo 209 1020
Bosworth, Re, Martin v Lamb (1889) 58 LJ Ch 432 1254
Bosworthick v Clegg [1929] WN 133, 45 TLR 438 .... 346, 493
Bothamley v Sherson (1875) LR 20 Eq 304, 44 LJ Ch 589, 23 WR 848, 33 LT 150, Ct of
Ch 118, 1006
Botting's Estate, Re, Botting v Botting [1951] 2 All ER 997, [1951] 2 TLR 1089, P, D and
Admlty 108
Boughey v Minor [1893] P 181, 62 LJP 104, P, D and Admlty
.... 885
Boughey v Moreton (1758) 3 Hag Ecc 191, 2 Lee 532 102
Boughton v Boughton (1750) 2 Ves Sen 12 190
Boughton v Boughton (1848) 1 HL Cas 406, 10 LTOS 497
.... 251, 302, 431, 993
Boughton v James (1848) 1 HL Cas 406, 10 LTOS 497 .... 251, 447, 993

                                                                          PARA
Boughton v Knight (1873) LR 3 P & D 64, 37 JP 598, 647, 42 LJP & M 25, 41,
    [1861–73] All ER Rep 40, 28 LT 562 .... 48–49, 52, 910
Boughton-Knight v Wilson (1915) 32 TLR 146, P, D and Admlty
    .... 5, 60, 81
Boulcott v Boulcott (1853) 2 Drew 25, 23 LJ Ch 57, 2 Eq Rep 457, 18 Jur 231, 2 WR 52,
    22 LTOS 130 110
Boulter, Re, Capital and Counties Bank v Boulter [1922] 1 Ch 75, 91 LJ Ch 250,
    [1921] All ER Rep 167, 126 LT 653, 66 Sol Jo (WR) 14
    .... 129, 131, 139
Boulton v Beard (1853) 3 De GM & G 608, 98 RR 252
    .... 303, 423, 1256
Boulton v Pilcher (1861) 29 Beav 633, 7 Jur NS 767, 9 WR 626
    429
Bourk's Will, Re, Cunningham v Rubenach [1907] VLR 171
    378
Bourke's Trusts, Re (1891) 27 LR Ir 573 369
Bourke's Will Trusts, Re, Barclays Bank Trust Co Ltd v Canada Permanent Trust Co [1980]
    1 All ER 219, [1980] 1 WLR 539, 124 Sol Jo 362   . 173, 226–227, 302, 315, 318, 320–321,
                                                                  326, 334, 336, 341
Bourn v Gibbs (1831) Taml 414, 8 LJOS Ch 151, 1 Russ & M 614
    381
Bourne, Re, Bourne v Bourne [1906] 2 Ch 427, 75 LJ Ch 779, 54 WR 559, 50 Sol Jo 575,
    95 LT 131, CA 919–920
Bourne, Re, Bourne v Brandreth (1888) 58 LT 537 296
Bourne, Re, Rymer v Harpley (1887) 56 LJ Ch 566, 35 WR 359, 56 LT 388
    424
Bouverie v Bouverie (1847) 2 Ph 349, 16 LJ Ch 411, 11 Jur 661, 9 LTOS 469
    260
Bowden's Goods, Re (1904) 21 TLR 13, P, D and Admlty
    761
Bowen, Re, Treasury Solicitor v Bowen [1949] Ch 67, [1948] 2 All ER 979, [1949] LJR
    413, 92 Sol Jo 689 445
Bowen v Lewis (1884) 9 App Cas 890, 54 LJQB 55, 52 LT 189, HL
    .... 331, 384, 456
Bowen v Phillips [1897] 1 Ch 174, 66 LJ Ch 165, 4 Mans 370, 45 WR 286, 41 Sol Jo 188,
    75 LT 628 624
Bowen v Scowcroft (1837) 2 Y & C Ex 640, 7 LJ Ex Eq 25
    389
Bowen-Buscarlet's Will Trusts, Re, Nathan v Bowen-Buscarlet [1972] Ch 463, [1971]
    3 All ER 636, [1971] 3 WLR 742, 115 Sol Jo 872 516
Bower v Turner (1863) 32 Beav 86, 32 LJ Ch 540, 9 Jur NS 267, 1 New Rep 379, 11 WR
    411, 8 LT 135 657
Bower's Settlement Trusts, Re, Bower v Ridley-Thompson [1942] Ch 197, [1942] 1 All ER
    278, 111 LJ Ch 225, 86 Sol Jo 48, 58 TLR 137 410
Bowerman, Re, Porter v Bowerman [1908] 2 Ch 340, 77 LJ Ch 594, 99 LT 7
    1007
Bowers v Bowers (1870) 5 Ch App 244, 39 LJ Ch 351, 18 WR 301, 23 LT 35
    450
Bowes, Re, Earl Strathmore v Vane [1896] 1 Ch 507, 65 LJ Ch 298, 44 WR 441, 74 LT 16
    374
Bowes, Re, Earl Strathmore v Vane, Norcliffe's Claim (1887) 37 Ch D 128,
    [1886–90] All ER Rep 693, 57 LJ Ch 455, 36 WR 393, 58 LT 309, 4 TLR 20
    1225
Bowes v Bowes (1801) 2 Bos & P 500, HL 115
Bowes v Goslett (1857) 27 LJ Ch 249, 4 Jur NS 17, 6 WR 8, 30 LTOS 268
    381
Bowker's Goods, Re [1932] P 93, 101 LJP 30, 76 Sol Jo 344, 146 LT 572, 48 TLR 332, P,
    D and Admlty 739
Bowlby, Re, Bowlby v Bowlby [1904] 2 Ch 685, 73 LJ Ch 810, 53 WR 270, 48 Sol Jo 698,
    91 LT 573, CA 1076, 1078
Bowler v John Mowlem & Co Ltd [1954] 3 All ER 556, [1954] 1 WLR 1445, [1954] 2
    Lloyd's Rep 387, 98 Sol Jo 820, CA 647
Bowles v Harvey (1832) 4 Hag Ecc 241 957
Bowles, Re; Hayward v Jackson [2003] EWHC 253 (Ch), [2003] Ch 422, [2003] 2 All ER
    387, [2003] 2 WLR 1274, 5 ITELR 666, [2003] 13 LS Gaz R 27, (2003) Times,
    27 February, [2003] All ER (D) 240 (Feb) 125, 145, 148–149

PARA

Bowman, Re, Re Lay, Whytehead v Boulton (1889) 41 Ch D 525, 37 WR 583, 60 LT 888
.... 316
Bowman v Bowman [1899] AC 518, HL 244, 318, 320
Bowman v Hodgson (1867) LR 1 P & D 362, 31 JP 678, 36 LJP & M 124, 16 LT 392
.... 894
Bowman v Milbanke (1664) 1 Lev 130 266
Bowman v Secular Society Ltd [1917] AC 406, 86 LJ Ch 568, [1916–17] All ER Rep 1, 61
    Sol Jo 478, 117 LT 161, 33 TLR 376, HL 33, 36
Bowman's Estate, Re, Bowman v Bowman (1891) 36 Sol Jo 110, 8 TLR 117
.... 210, 212
Bowring-Hanbury's Trustee v Bowring-Hanbury [1943] Ch 104, [1943] 1 All ER 48,
    112 LJ Ch 37, 87 Sol Jo 39, 168 LT 72, 59 TLR 121, CA
.... 976
Bowron's Goods, Re (1914) 84 LJP 92, [1915] HBR 78, 59 Sol Jo 108, 112 LT 478, P, D
    and Admlty 759
Bowyer v West (1871) 19 WR 598, 24 LT 414 .... 416, 432
Boxall v Boxall (1884) 27 Ch D 220, 53 LJ Ch 838, 32 WR 896, 51 LT 771
.... 671, 858
Boxer, Re, Morris v Woore [1910] 2 Ch 69, 79 LJ Ch 492, 103 LT 126
.... 1132
Boyce v Boyce (1849) 16 Sim 476, 80 RR 123 .... 127, 266
Boyce v Corbally (1834) L & G temp Plunk 102 135
Boycot v Cotton (1738) 1 Atk 552, West temp Hard 520, 25 ER 1064,
    [1558–1774] All ER Rep 313 438
Boycott v Mollekin [2005] All ER (D) 433 (Jul) 893
Boyd, Re (1912) 46 ILT 294 .... 800, 850
Boyd v Boyd (1867) LR 4 Eq 305, 36 LJ Ch 877, 15 WR 1071, 16 LT 660
.... 503
Boyd v Mathers and South Africa Ltd (1893) 9 TLR 443, CA
.... 1279
Boydell v Golightly (1844) 14 Sim 327, 9 Jur 2, sub nom Boidell v Golightly 14 LJ Ch 109
.... 341, 456
Boydell v Morland (1844) 14 Sim 327, 14 LJ Ch 109, 9 Jur 2
.... 456
Boydell v Stanton (1844) 14 Sim 327, 14 LJ Ch 109, 9 Jur 2
.... 456
Boyer, Re, Neathercoat v Lawrence [1935] Ch 382, 104 LJ Ch 171, [1935] All ER Rep
    274, 152 LT 553, 51 TLR 259 .... 339, 342
Boyes, Re, Boyes v Carritt (1884) 26 Ch D 531, 53 LJ Ch 654, 32 WR 630, 50 LT 581
.... 222–223
Boyes v Bedale (1863) 1 Hem & M 798, 33 LJ Ch 283, 10 Jur NS 196, 3 New Rep 290,
    12 WR 232, 10 LT 131 350
Boyes v Cook (1880) 14 Ch D 53, 49 LJ Ch 350, 28 WR 754, 42 LT 556, CA
.... 212
Boyle's Goods, Re (1864) 28 JP 424, 33 LJPM & A 109, 4 New Rep 120, 3 Sw & Tr 426,
    10 LT 541 .... 630, 801
Boynton v Boynton (1879) 4 App Cas 733, 27 WR 825, 41 LT 450, HL
.... 1276, 1283
Boys v Williams (1831) 2 Russ & M 689 210
Boyse v Rossborough (1857) 6 HL Cas 2, 3 Jur NS 373, 5 WR 414, 10 ER 1192,
    [1843–60] All ER Rep 610, 29 LTOS 27, HL 48, 56–57
Brace, Re, Gurton v Clements [1954] 2 All ER 354, [1954] 1 WLR 955, 98 Sol Jo 456
.... 134, 139, 298
Bracey, Re, Hull v Johns [1936] Ch 690, [1936] 2 All ER 767, 105 LJ Ch 270, 80 Sol Jo
    511, 155 LT 473 1042
Bracken, Re, Doughty v Townson (1889) 43 Ch D 1, 59 LJ Ch 18, 38 WR 48, 61 LT 531,
    6 TLR 11, CA 964
Brackenbury v Gibbons (1876) 2 Ch D 417 424
Bradberry, Re, National Provincial Bank v Bradberry [1943] Ch 35, [1942] 2 All ER 629,
    112 LJ Ch 49, 86 Sol Jo 349, 167 LT 396, 59 TLR 131
.... 1090, 1093
Bradbury, Re, Wing v Bradbury (1904) 73 LJ Ch 591, 48 Sol Jo 524, 90 LT 824, CA
.... 325, 441
Braddock's Goods, Re (1876) 1 PD 433, 40 JP 792, 45 LJP 96, 24 WR 1017, P, D and
    Admlty 73, 76
Bradfield, Re, Bradfield v Bradfield [1914] WN 423 .... 288, 293

PARA

Bradford v Foley (1779) 1 Doug KB 63 448

Bradford v Young (1884) 26 Ch D 656, 54 LJ Ch 96, 32 WR 901, 50 LT 707; on appeal
    (1885) 29 Ch D 617, 33 WR 860, 53 LT 407, CA 231, 239, 670, 678

Bradley, Re, Bradley v Barclays Bank Ltd [1956] Ch 615, [1956] 3 All ER 113, [1956] 3
    WLR 610, 100 Sol Jo 634 1171

Bradley v Cartwright (1867) LR 2 CP 511, 36 LJCP 218, 15 WR 922, 16 LT 587
    334

Bradley v Peixoto (1797) 3 Ves 324, 30 ER 1034, [1775–1802] All ER Rep 561
    142

Bradly v Heath (1830) 3 Sim 543 1240

Bradly v Westcott (1807) 13 Ves 445 383

Bradshaw, Re, Bradshaw v Bradshaw [1950] Ch 582, [1950] 1 All ER 643, 94 Sol Jo 162,
    66 (pt 1) TLR 579, CA 533

Bradshaw v Bradshaw [1908] 1 IR 288, 42 ILT 80 .... 335, 390

Bradshaw v Bradshaw (1836) 2 Y & C Ex 72, 6 LJ Ex Eq 1
    .... 186, 199, 214, 272, 276

Bradshaw v Melling (1853) 19 Beav 417, 23 LJ Ch 603
    .... 336, 397

Bradshaw v Skilbeck (1835) 2 Bing NC 182, 1 Hodg 240, 2 Scott 294
    473

Bradshaw's Goods, Re (1887) 13 PD 18, 52 JP 56, 57 LJP 12, 36 WR 848, 58 LT 58, P, D
    and Admlty 850

Bradwin v Harpur (1759) Amb 374 270

Brady, Re, Wylie v Ratcliff (1919) 147 LT Jo 235 .... 199, 211, 220

Brady v Brady [1920] 1 IR 170, Ir CA 657

Brady v Cubitt (1778) 1 Doug KB 31 284

Bragger, Re, Bragger v Bragger (1887) 56 LJ Ch 490, 56 LT 521
    428

Braham v Burchell (1826) 3 Add 243 863

Brailsford, Re, Holmes v Crompton and Evans' Union Bank [1916] 2 Ch 536, 85 LJ Ch
    709, 115 LT 343 450

Braithwaite v Britain (1836) 1 Keen 206 1232

Braithwaite v Cooksey (1790) 1 Hy Bl 465 1226

Brake's Goods, Re (1881) 6 PD 217, 50 LJP 48, 29 WR 744, 45 LT 191, P, D and Admlty
    .... 214, 220, 276, 611

Bramley v Bramley (1864) 33 LJPM & A 111n, 3 Sw & Tr 430, 12 WR 992
    911

Bramley's Goods, Re [1902] P 106, 71 LJP 32, 85 LT 645, P, D and Admlty
    293

Bramwell, Re, Campbell v Tobin [1988] 2 FLR 263, [1988] Fam Law 391
    567

Brand v Chaddock (1871) 19 WR 378, 24 LT 347 1069

Brandon v Aston (1843) 2 Y & C Ch Cas 24, 7 Jur 10 306

Brandon v Brandon (1819) 2 Wils Ch 14, 3 Swan 312 .... 343, 349

Brandt v Heatig (1818) 2 Moore CP 184 1279

Brannigan v Murphy [1896] 1 IR 418 .... 145, 205

Bransby v Grantham (1577) 2 Plowd 525 30

Branstrom v Wilkinson (1802) 7 Ves 421 .... 431, 434

Brasier v Hudson. See Brazier v Hudson

Brasier's Goods, Re [1899] P 36, 79 LT 476, sub nom Brazier's Goods, Re 68 LJP 2, 47
    WR 272, P, D and Admlty 82

Brassington's Goods, Re [1902] P 1, 71 LJP 9, 85 LT 644, 18 TLR 15, P, D and Admlty
    .... 93, 101, 730

Bravda's Estate, Re [1967] 2 All ER 1233, [1967] 1 WLR 1080, 111 Sol Jo 586, P, D and
    Admlty; on appeal [1968] 2 All ER 217, [1968] 1 WLR 479, 112 Sol Jo 137, CA
    44

Bray v Ford [1896] AC 44, [1895–99] All ER Rep 1009
    657

Brazier v Hudson (1836) 8 Sim 67, sub nom Brasier v Hudson 5 LJ Ch 296
    .... 634, 1139

Breadner v Granville Grossman [2000] All ER (D) 996 .... 1196, 1274

Breadner v Granville-Grossman [2001] Ch 523, [2000] 4 All ER 705, [2001] 2 WLR 593,
    2 ITELR 812 224

Bree v Perfect (1844) 1 Coll 128, 8 Jur 282, 2 LTOS 476
    437

Breedon v Tugman (1834) 3 My & K 289, 2 LJ Ch 169
    430

PARA

Brennan v Brennan [1894] 1 IR 69, 73 .... 430–432, 434
Brennan v Brennan (1868) IR 2 Eq 321 293
Brennan v Prior [2015] EWHC 3082 (Ch), [2015] All ER (D) 119 (Nov)
.... 875
Brennan's Goods, Re [1932] IR 633, 67 ILT 1 .... 95, 97, 99
Brereton v Hutchinson (1853) 2 I Ch R 648; affd (1854) 31 Ch R 361, CA
.... 1238
Breton v Mockett (1878) 9 Ch D 95, 47 LJ Ch 754, 26 WR 850
.... 122
Brett v Carmichael (1866) 35 Beav 340, 35 LJ Ch 369, 14 WR 507, 14 LT 247
.... 985
Brett v Cumberland (1619) 3 Bulst 163, Cro Jac 521, Godb 276, 1 Roll Rep 359, 2 Roll
Rep 63 1222
Brett v Horton (1841) 4 Beav 239, 10 LJ Ch 371, 5 Jur 696
.... 397
Brett v Rigden (1568) 1 Plowd 340, 340, 1 Co Rep 105a, 155b
.... 321
Bretton v Lethulier (1710) 2 Vern 653 411
Brewer v Westminster Bank Ltd [1952] 2 All ER 650, 6 LDAB 344, 96 Sol Jo 531, [1952]
2 TLR 568; on appeal (1953) Times, 5 February, CA 1271
Brewer's Settlement, Re, Morton v Blackmore [1896] 2 Ch 503, 65 LJ Ch 821, 45 WR 8,
75 LT 177 463
Brewster, Re, Butler v Southam [1908] 2 Ch 365, 77 LJ Ch 605, 99 LT 517
.... 1016
Brewster v Prior (1886) 35 WR 251, 55 LT 771, 3 TLR 205
.... 1298, 1301
Brewster's Goods, Re (1859) 24 JP 87, Sea & Sm 108, 29 LJPM & A 69, 6 Jur NS 56
.... 101
Brice v Smith (1737) Willes 1 473
Brice v Stokes (1805) 8 RR 164, 11 Ves 319, 2 White & Tud LC 631, 32 ER 1111,
[1803–19] All ER Rep 401 1252–1253
Bridge v Abbot (1791) 3 Bro CC 224 .... 165, 364, 537
Bridge v Yates (1842) 12 Sim 645 .... 326, 393
Bridgen, Re, Chaytor v Edwin [1938] Ch 205, [1937] 4 All ER 342, 107 LJ Ch 124, 81 Sol
Jo 922, 158 LT 238, 54 TLR 100 .... 289, 313–314, 349
Bridger, Re, Brompton Hospital for Consumption v Lewis [1894] 1 Ch 297, 63 LJ Ch 186,
42 WR 179, 38 Sol Jo 111, 70 LT 204, 10 TLR 153, CA
.... 240, 282
Bridger v Ramsey (1853) 10 Hare 320 .... 456, 473
Bridger's Goods, Re (1878) 4 PD 77, 42 JP 520, 47 LJP 46, 26 WR 535, 39 LT 123, P, D
and Admlty 639
Bridges v Bridges (1729) 8 Vin Abr, Devise (Ob) 295 pl 13
.... 250
Bridgett and Hayes' Contract, Re [1928] Ch 163, 97 LJ Ch 33, [1927] All ER Rep 191, 71
Sol Jo 910, 138 LT 106, 44 TLR 222 .... 629, 669, 679, 821, 824, 827, 858, 949
Bridgewater (Countess) v Duke of Bolton (1704) 1 Eq Cas Abr 177, 6 Mod Rep 106, 1
Salk 236, Holt KB 281 289
Bridgewater's Estate, Re [1965] 1 All ER 717, [1965] 1 WLR 416, 109 Sol Jo 13, P, D and
Admlty 101, 108
Bridgman v Dove (1744) 3 Atk 201 296
Bridgnorth Corpn v Collins (1847) 15 Sim 538 328
Bridle, Re (1879) 4 CPD 336, 41 LT 343, CPD 158–159
Brier, Re, Brier v Evison (1884) 26 Ch D 238, 33 WR 20, 51 LT 133, CA
.... 1247
Briesemann's Goods, Re [1894] P 260, 63 LJP 159, 6 R 558, 71 LT 263, P, D and Admlty
.... 720, 845
Brigg v Brigg (1885) 54 LJ Ch 464, 33 WR 454, 52 LT 753
.... 343
Briggs, Re, Richardson v Bantoft [1914] 2 Ch 413, 83 LJ Ch 874, 58 Sol Jo 722, 111 LT
939 1131–1132
Briggs v Penny (1849) 3 De G & Sm 525, 21 LJ Ch 265, 13 Jur 905, 13 LTOS 443; on
appeal (1851) 16 Jur 93, 3 Mac & G 546, 87 RR 192, 18 LTOS 101
.... 208
Briggs v Upton (1872) 7 Ch App 376, 41 LJ Ch 519, 21 WR 30, 26 LT 485
.... 364

PARA

Briggs v Wilson (1854) 5 De GM & G 12, 2 Eq Rep 153, 23 LTOS 136
.... 974
Bright v Larcher (1858) 3 De G & J 148 992
Bright v Rowe (1834) 3 My & K 316 .... 260, 410
Bright's Trusts, Re (1855) 21 Beav 67, 3 WR 544 429
Brighton's Goods, Re (1865) 29 JP 503, 34 LJPM & A 55
.... 770
Bright-Smith, Re, Bright-Smith v Bright-Smith (1886) 31 Ch D 314, 55 LJ Ch 365, 34 WR
    252, 54 LT 47, 2 TLR 230 .... 237, 255, 268, 271, 277
Brill v Proud [1984] Fam Law 59, CA 574
Brimble, Re, Brimble v Brimble (1918) 144 LT Jo 217 285
Brine v Ferrier (1835) 7 Sim 549 401–402
Brinkley's Will Trusts, Re, Westminster Bank Ltd v Brinkley [1968] Ch 407, [1967]
    3 All ER 805, [1968] 2 WLR 217, 111 Sol Jo 852 331
Brinton, Re, Brinton v Preen [1923] WN 195, 67 Sol Jo 704
.... 1080
Brisco v Baillie and Hamilton [1902] P 234, 71 LJP 121, 87 LT 746, P, D and Admlty
.... 186, 914
Briscoe, Re, Royds v Briscoe (1910) 55 Sol Jo 93 1131
Briscoe v Briscoe (1830) Hayes 34 473
Briscoe's Trusts, Re (1872) 20 WR 355, 26 LT 149 214
Bristow v Bristow (1842) 5 Beav 289 .... 262, 270, 409
Bristow v Masefield (1882) 52 LJ Ch 27, 31 WR 88 233
Bristow's Goods, Re (1891) 66 LT 60, P, D and Admlty
.... 628
British Home and Hospital for Incurables v Royal Hospital for Incurables (1904) 90 LT
    601, CA 199, 214, 272
British Mutual Investment Co v Smart (1875) 10 Ch App 567, 44 LJ Ch 695, 23 WR 800,
    32 LT 849, CA in Ch 970
Brittlebank v Goodwin (1868) LR 5 Eq 545, 37 LJ Ch 377, 16 WR 696
.... 1055, 1238
Britton v Twining (1817) 3 Mer 176 .... 382, 385
Broad v Bevan (1823) 1 Russ 511n, 1 LJOS Ch 69 263
Broadbent, Re, Imperial Cancer Research Fund v Bradley [2001] EWCA Civ 714, 3 ITELR
    787, [2001] All ER (D) 219 (May) 138, 140
Broadhurst v Morris (1831) 2 B & Ad 1, 9 LJOSKB 27
.... 389
Broadway v Fernandes [2007] EWHC 684 (Ch), [2007] All ER (D) 485 (Mar)
.... 98,106
Broadway Cottages Trust v IRC. See IRC v Broadway Cottages Trust
Broadwell, Re, Mackenzie v Readman (1912) 134 LT Jo 107
.... 253
Brock, Re, Jones v Jones (1908) 52 Sol Jo 699, 24 TLR 839, P, D and Admlty
.... 894
Brocket, Re, Dawes v Miller [1908] 1 Ch 185, 77 LJ Ch 245, 52 Sol Jo 159, 97 LT 780
.... 269, 271, 273
Brocklebank v Johnson (1855) 20 Beav 205, 24 LJ Ch 505, 1 Jur NS 318, 3 WR 341,
    25 LTOS 56 .... 232, 413, 429, 431
Brocklehurst v Flint (1852) 16 Beav 100 404
Brocksopp v Barnes (1820) 5 Madd 90 649
Brogden, Re, Billing v Brogden (1888) 38 Ch D 546, 37 WR 84, [1886–90] All ER Rep
    927, 59 LT 650, 4 TLR 521, CA 959
Bromage v Lloyd (1847) 5 Dow & L 123, 16 LJ Ex 257, 1 Exch 32, 9 LTOS 201
.... 27
Bromfield v Crowder (1805) 1 Bos & PNR 313; affd (1811) 14 East 604, HL
.... 423
Bromham's Estate, Re, Wass v Treasury Solicitor (or Solicitor-General) [1952] 1 All ER
    110n, 95 Sol Jo 804, [1951] 2 TLR 1149, P, D and Admlty
.... 108
Bromhead v Hunt (1821) 2 Jac & W 459 .... 440, 475
Bromitt v Moor (1851) 9 Hare 374, 22 LJ Ch 129 379
Bromley, Re, Wilson v Bromley (1900) 44 Sol Jo 675, 83 LT 315
.... 364
Bromley v Tryon [1952] AC 265, [1951] 2 All ER 1058, [1951] 2 TLR 1119, HL
.... 138, 141
Bromley v Wright (1849) 7 Hare 334 .... 276, 284, 428–429
Bronsdon v Winter (1738) Amb 57 .... 156, 158

                                                                          PARA
Brook v Brook (1856) 3 Sm & G 280 .... 376, 382
Brooke, Re, Brooke v Brooke [1894] 2 Ch 600, 64 LJ Ch 21, 8 R 444, 71 LT 398,
    [1891–4] All ER Rep Ext 1294 1040
Brooke, Re, Brooke v Dickson [1923] 2 Ch 265, 92 LJ Ch 504, 67 Sol Jo 594, 129 LT
    379, CA 182
Brooke, Re, Brooke v Rooke (1876) 3 Ch D 630, 45 LJ Ch 730, 24 WR 959, 35 LT 301
    1109
Brooke v Garrod (1857) 2 De G & J 62, 27 LJ Ch 226, 6 WR 121, 30 LTOS 194
    .... 125–126, 148–149
Brooke v Haymes (1868) LR 6 Eq 25 629
Brooke v Kent (1841) 3 Moo PCC 334, 1 Notes of Cases 93
    107–108
Brooke v Purton [2014] EWHC 547 (Ch), [2014] WTLR 745, [2014] All ER (D) 262
    (Mar) 188
Brooke v Turner (1836) 2 Bing NC 422, 1 Hodg 440, 2 Scott 611
    474
Brooke v Turner (1836) 7 Sim 671, Donnelly 20, 5 LJ Ch 175, 1 Hodg 440
    285
Brooke (Lord) v Earl of Warwick (1848) 2 De G & Sm 425, 12 Jur 912, 12 LTOS 41; on
    appeal (1849) 18 LJ Ch 137, 1 H & Tw 142, 13 Jur 547, 13 LTOS 5
    285
Brooke's Will Trusts, Re, Jubber v Brooke [1953] 1 All ER 668, [1953] 1 WLR 439, 97 Sol
    Jo 151 .... 322, 393, 429
Brooker, Re, Brooker v Brooker [1926] WN 93, 70 Sol Jo 526
    1123
Brookes, Re, Brookes v Taylor [1914] 1 Ch 558, 83 LJ Ch 424, 58 Sol Jo 286, 110 LT 691
    1157
Brookes v Stroud (1702) 7 Mod Rep 39, 1 Salk 3 673
Brookman v Smith (1872) LR 7 Exch 271, 41 LJ Ex 114, 20 WR 906, 26 LT 974
    445
Brookman's Trust, Re (1869) 5 Ch App 182, 39 LJ Ch 138, 18 WR 199, 22 LT 891
    .... 21–22, 161, 163
Brooks, Re, Coles v Davis (1897) 76 LT 771 1160–1161
Brooks, Re, Public Trustee v White [1928] Ch 214, 97 LJ Ch 88, 72 Sol Jo 17, 138 LT
    437, CA 364, 369, 377
Brooks v Brooks [1996] AC 375, [1995] 3 All ER 257, [1995] 3 WLR 141, [1995] 3 FCR
    214, [1995] 2 FLR 13, [1995] Fam Law 545, [1995] 31 LS Gaz R 34, [1995] NLJR
    995, 139 Sol Jo LB 165, HL 591
Brooks' Will, Re (1865) 2 Drew & Sm 362, 34 LJ Ch 616, 13 WR 573, 12 LT 172
    382
Broome v Monck (1805) 10 Ves 597, 32 ER 976, [1803–13] All ER Rep 631
    27
Brotherton v Bury (1853) 18 Beav 65, 2 WR 46, 22 LTOS 140
    450
Brotherton v IRC [1978] 2 All ER 267, [1978] 1 WLR 610, [1978] STC 201, 52 TC 137,
    [1977] TR 317, 122 Sol Jo 164, L(TC) 2667, CA 423
Brotherton's Goods, Re [1901] P 139, 70 LJP 33, 84 LT 330, P, D and Admlty
    759
Brough, Re, Currey v Brough (1888) 38 Ch D 456, 57 LJ Ch 436, 36 WR 409
    96
Brougham (Lord) v Lord Poulett (1855) 19 Beav 119, 24 LJ Ch 233, 1 Jur NS 151, 105
    RR 85, 24 LTOS 248 1013
Broughton, Re, Peat v Broughton (1887) 57 LT 8 463
Broughton v Broughton (1855) 5 De GM & G 160; 25 LJ Ch 250; 26 LTOS 54; 1 Jur NS
    965; 3 WR 602; 43 ER 831 649
Broughton v White (1855) 5 De GM & G 160, 25 LJ Ch 250, 1 Jur NS 965, 3 WR 602,
    26 LTOS 54 653
Brouncker, Re, Mairis v Mandeville [1938] WN 147, 82 Sol Jo 315
    .... 1090, 1093
Brouncker v Bagot (1816) 1 Mer 271, sub nom Browncker v Bagot 19 Ves 574
    385
Brouncker v Brouncker (1812) 2 Phillim 57 51
Brown, Re, Brown v Knowles (1955) 219 LT Jo 129, 105 L Jo 169
    573
Brown, Re, District Bank Ltd v Brown [1954] Ch 39, [1953] 2 All ER 1342, [1953] 3
    WLR 877, 97 Sol Jo 796 142

PARA

Brown, Re, Golding v Brady (1910) 54 Sol Jo 251, 26 TLR 257
.... 346
Brown, Re, Ingall v Brown [1904] 1 Ch 120, 73 LJ Ch 130, 52 WR 173, 90 LT 220
.... 136
Brown, Re, Leeds v Spencer [1917] 2 Ch 232, 86 LJ Ch 561, 61 Sol Jo 546, 117 LT 268
.... 247, 322
Brown, Re, Penrose v Manning (1890) 63 LT 159 351
Brown, Re, Turnbull v Royal Lifeboat Institution (1916) 60 Sol Jo 353
.... 1130, 1132
Brown, Re, Wace v Smith [1918] WN 118, 62 Sol Jo 487
.... 652, 1087
Brown, Re, ex p Wallop (1792) 2 Dick 767, 4 Bro CC 90
.... 551
Brown v Allen (1681) 1 Vern 31 1087–1088
Brown v Bimson [2010] All ER (D) 325 (Jul) 187
Brown v Brown (1856) 2 K & J 426, 25 LJ Ch 702, 2 Jur NS 781, 4 WR 473, 27 LTOS
259 .... 412, 433
Brown v Brown (1858) 4 K & J 704, 6 WR 613, 31 LTOS 297
.... 293, 295
Brown v Brown (1858) 8 E & B 876, 27 LJQB 173, 4 Jur NS 163, 30 LTOS 273
.... 716
Brown v Brown (1901) 1 SRNSW Eq 218 290
Brown v Burdett (1882) 21 Ch D 667, 52 LJ Ch 52, 47 LT 94
.... 33
Brown v Burdett (1888) 40 Ch D 244, 37 WR 533, 60 LT 520, 5 TLR 88, CA
.... 33, 1209
Brown v Croley. See Southgate v Crowley
Brown v Cutter. See Luxford v Cheeke
Brown v Executors of the Estate of Her Majesty Queen Elizabeth the Queen Mother [2008]
EWCA Civ 56, [2008] 1 WLR 2327, (2008) Times, 19 February, [2008] All ER (D)
118 (Feb) 660, 732
Brown v Feeney [1906] 1 KB 563, 75 LJKB 494, 54 WR 445, 50 Sol Jo 358, 94 LT 460,
22 TLR 393, [1904–7] All ER Rep Ext 1266, CA 1284
Brown v Fisher (1890) 63 LT 465, P, D and Admlty 905
Brown v Gellatly (1867) 2 Ch App 751, 15 WR 1188, 17 LT 131, [1861–73] All ER Rep
Ext 2080 .... 1123–1124, 1126
Brown v Gordon (1852) 16 Beav 302, 22 LJ Ch 65, 1 WR 2, 20 LTOS 75
.... 976, 1232
Brown v Gould [1972] Ch 53, [1971] 2 All ER 1505, [1971] 3 WLR 334, 22 P & CR 871,
115 Sol Jo 406 45
Brown v Higgs (1799) 4 RR 323, 4 Ves 708; re-heard (1800) 5 Ves 495, 31 ER 366,
[1803–13] All ER Rep 146; affd (1803) 8 Ves 561, 32 ER 473, [1803–13] All ER Rep
146; on appeal (1813) 18 Ves 192, [1803–13] All ER Rep 146, HL
.... 11, 256
Brown v Jarvis (1860) 2 De GF & J 168, 29 LJ Ch 595, 6 Jur NS 789, 8 WR 644, 2 LT
708 .... 395, 446
Brown v Jervas (1611) Cro Jac 290 473
Brown v Lake (1847) 1 De G & Sm 144 985
Brown v Langley (1731) 2 Barn KB 118 .... 207, 210
Brown v Longley (1732) 2 Eq Cas Abr 416 277
Brown v Peys (1594) 1 And 306, Cro Eliz 357 147
Brown v Skirrow [1902] P 3, 71 LJP 19, 85 LT 645, 18 TLR 59, P, D and Admlty
.... 70
Brown v Walker (1824) 2 LJOS Ch 82 443
Brown v Wildman (1859) 28 LJP & M 54 696
Brown v Wooler (1843) 2 Y & C Ch Cas 134, 7 Jur 103
.... 438
Brown's (Hope) Goods, Re [1942] P 136, 111 LJP 78, 58 TLR 338, sub nom Re
Brown's Goods [1942] 2 All ER 176, 86 Sol Jo 260, 167 LT 95, P, D and Admlty
.... 95, 108
Brown and Campbell, Re (1898) 29 OR 402 454
Brown and Sibly's Contract, Re (1876) 3 Ch D 156, 24 WR 782, 35 LT 305
.... 182
Brown's Case (1581) 4 Co Rep 21a 561
Brown's Goods, Re (1858) 27 LJP & M 20, 4 Jur NS 244, 1 Sw & Tr 32, 30 LTOS 353
.... 106, 110
Brown's Goods, Re (1872) LR 2 P & D 455 852

PARA

Brown's Goods, Re (1877) 2 PD 110, 41 JP 601, 46 LJP 31, WR 431, 36 LT 519, P, D and
Admlty 613
Brown's Goods, Re (1899) 80 LT 360, P, D and Admlty
.... 816
Brown's Goods, Re (1910) 54 Sol Jo 478, P, D and Admlty
.... 613
Brown's Goods, Re, Quincey v Quincey (1846) 11 Jur 111
.... 112
Brown's Trust, Re (1865) 13 WR 677, 12 LT 488 1072
Brown's Trust, Re (1873) LR 16 Eq 239, 38 JP 4, 43 LJ Ch 84, 21 WR 721, 28 LT 616
.... 354, 441
Brown's Trustees v Gow (1902) 40 SLR 62, 5 F 127, Ct of Sess
.... 1130
Brown's Trustees v Thom (1915) 53 SLR 59 1058
Brown's Trusts, Re (1855) 1 K & J 522, 3 WR 542 .... 183, 298
Brown's Will, Re, Re Brown's Settlement (1881) 18 Ch D 61, 50 LJ Ch 724, 30 WR 171,
44 LT 757, CA 135
Brownbridge, Re (1942) 193 LT Jo 185 573–574
Browncker v Bagot. See Brouncker v Bagot
Browne v Browne [1912] 1 IR 272 147
Browne v Browne [1919] 1 IR 251 1102
Browne v Browne (1857) 26 LJ Ch 635, 3 Jur NS 728, 3 Sm & G 568, 5 WR 777,
29 LTOS 258 .... 413, 424
Browne v Groombridge (1819) 4 Madd 495 .... 995, 1012
Browne v Hammond (1858) John 210 .... 167, 305, 311, 446
Browne v Hope (1872) LR 14 Eq 343, 41 LJ Ch 475, 20 WR 667, 26 LT 688
.... 164, 413
Browne v Lord Kenyon (1818) 3 Madd 410, 18 RR 261
.... 318, 444
Browne v Moody [1936] AC 635, [1936] 2 All ER 1695, 105 LJPC 140, 80 Sol Jo 814,
155 LT 469, 53 TLR 5, PC 429
Browne v Paull (1850) 1 Sim NS 92, 20 LJ Ch 75, 15 Jur 5, 16 LTOS 550
.... 370
Browne v Rainsford (1867) IR 1 Eq 384 317
Browne's Will Trusts, Re, Landon v Brown [1915] 1 Ch 690, 84 LJ Ch 623, 113 LT 39
.... 397, 422, 476
Browning v Reane (1812) 2 Phillim 69, 161 ER 1080, [1803–13] All ER Rep 265
.... 770
Brownlie, Re, Brownlie v Muaux [1938] 4 All ER 54 339
Brownlow (Earl), Re, Tower v Sedgwick (1924) 69 Sol Jo 176
.... 366
Brownsword v Edwards (1751) 2 Ves Sen 243, 28 ER 157, [1558–1774] All ER Rep 369
.... 442–443
Bruce, Re, Lawford v Bruce [1908] 2 Ch 682, 78 LJ Ch 56, 99 LT 704, CA
.... 1067
Bruce v Charlton (1842) 13 Sim 65, 6 Jur 594; affd (1843) 13 LJ Ch 97
.... 172, 427
Bruce v Curzon Howe (1870) 19 WR 116, sub nom Cardigan v Curzon-Howe 23 LT 642
.... 285
Brudenell-Bruce v Moore [2014] EWHC 3679 (Ch), [2015] WTLR 373, [2014] All ER (D)
113 (Nov) 656, 1163
Brudenell-Bruce, Earl of Cardigan v Moore [2012] EWHC 1024 (Ch), [2012] All ER (D)
108 (Apr) 932
Brummel v Prothero (1796) 3 Ves 111 1012
Brunning, Re, Gammon v Dale [1909] 1 Ch 276, 78 LJ Ch 75, 99 LT 918
.... 1058
Brunt v Brunt (1873) LR 3 P & D 37, 37 JP 312, 21 WR 392, 28 LT 368
.... 93, 101
Bryan v Mansion (1852) 5 De G & Sm 737, 22 LJ Ch 233, 17 Jur 202, 19 LTOS 362
.... 457, 459
Bryan v White (1850) 2 Rob Eccl 315, 14 Jur 919 .... 70, 72, 76, 78
Bryan's Estate, Re [1907] P 125, 76 LJP 30, 96 LT 584, P, D and Admlty
.... 97, 99
Bryan's Trust, Re, ex p Darnborough (1851) 2 Sim NS 103, 18 LTOS 269, sub nom ex p
Bryan's Trust 21 LJ Ch 7 346
Bryant v Easterson (1859) 5 Jur NS 166, 7 WR 298, 32 LTOS 352
.... 122

                                                                          PARA
Bryce's Goods, Re (1839) 2 Curt 325 63
Bryden v Willett (1869) LR 7 Eq 472, 20 LT 518 .... 336, 441
Brydges v Brydges (1796) 3 Ves 120, 30 ER 927, [1775–1802] All ER Rep 530
.... 544
Brydges v King (1828) 1 Hag Ecc 256 903
Bryon, Re, Drummond v Leigh (1885) 30 Ch D 110, 55 LJ Ch 30
.... 352
Bubb v Padwick (1880) 13 Ch D 517, 49 LJ Ch 178, 28 WR 382, 42 LT 116
.... 451
Bubb v Yelverton (1871) LR 13 Eq 131, 20 WR 164 1069
Buchanan v Harrison (1861) 1 John & H 662, 31 LJ Ch 74, 8 Jur NS 965, 10 WR 118
.... 288, 375, 541
Buchanan v Milton [1999] 2 FLR 844, [1999] Fam Law 692
.... 31, 759, 956
Bucher v Samford Gouldsb. See Boocher v Samford
Buck d Whalley v Nurton (1797) 1 Bos & P 53 .... 241, 286
Buckenham v Dickinson [1997] CLY 4733 4
Buckinghamshire Rly Co, Re, Tookey's Trust, Re, ex p Hooper (1852) 1 Drew 264, 21 LJ
    Ch 402 441
Buckle, Re, Williams v Marson [1894] 1 Ch 286, 63 LJ Ch 330, 7 R 72, 42 WR 229, 38
    Sol Jo 112, 70 LT 115, CA 249
Buckle v Fawcett (1845) 4 Hare 536, 9 Jur 891, 5 LTOS 236
.... 318
Buckley v Barber (1851) 20 LJ Ex 114, 6 Exch 164, 15 Jur 63, 16 LTOS 463
.... 1266
Buckley v Pirk (1710) 20 Mod Rep 12, 1 Salk 316 1225
Buckley's Trusts, Re (1883) 22 Ch D 583, 52 LJ Ch 439, 31 WR 376, 48 LT 109
.... 1082
Buckmaster's Estate, Re (1882) 47 LT 514 389
Buckton, Re, Buckton v Buckton [1907] 2 Ch 406, 76 LJ Ch 584, 97 LT 332, 23 TLR 692
.... 391, 1017, 1197
Budd v Silver (1813) 2 Phillim 115 773
Budd's Goods, Re (1862) 3 Sw & Tr 196 99
Buffar v Bradford (1741) 2 Atk 220 .... 173, 390
Bulcock, Re, Ingham v Ingham [1916] 2 Ch 495, 86 LJ Ch 82, 115 LT 299
.... 302, 343
Bulkeley v Lyne Stephens, Re Lyne Stephens (1895) 11 TLR 564
.... 932
Bulkeley v Stephens [1896] 2 Ch 241, 65 LJ Ch 597, 44 WR 490, [1895–9] All ER Rep
    196, 40 Sol Jo 458, 74 LT 409, 12 TLR 350 927
Bulkley v Wilford (1834) 8 Bli NS 111, 2 Cl & Fin 102, HL
.... 907
Bull v Comberbach (1858) 25 Beav 540, 4 Jur NS 526, 31 LTOS 324
.... 341, 385
Bull v Johns (1830) Taml 513 428
Bull v Jones (1862) 31 LJ Ch 858, 10 WR 820 453
Bull v Kingston (1816) 1 Mer 314 .... 142, 378
Bull v Pritchard (1847) 5 Hare 567, 16 LJ Ch 185, 11 Jur 34, 8 LTOS 337
.... 412, 423–424
Buller, Re, Buller v Giberne (1896) 74 LT 406 .... 293, 470
Bulley's Trust Estate, Re (1865) 11 Jur NS 847, 13 LT 264
.... 430
Bulling v Ellice (1845) 9 Jur 936, sub nom Belling v Ellise 5 LTOS 475
.... 366
Bullivant v A-G for Victoria [1901] AC 196, 70 LJKB 645, 50 WR 1, [1900–3] All ER Rep
    812, 84 LT 737, 17 TLR 457, HL 882
Bullmore v Wynter (1883) 22 Ch D 619, 47 JP 373, 31 WR 396, sub nom Bullmore, Re,
    Bullmore v Wynter 52 LJ Ch 456, 48 LT 309 346
Bulloch v Beaton (1853) 25 Sc Jur 229, 15 Dunl 373, Ct of Sess
.... 1133
Bullock v Bennett (1855) 7 De GM & G 283, 24 LJ Ch 512, 3 Eq Rep 779, 1 Jur NS 567,
    3 WR 545, 25 LTOS 230 .... 247, 300
Bullock v Downes (1860) 9 HL Cas 1, 11 ER 627, [1843–60] All ER Rep 706, 3 LT 194,
    HL 313, 395, 1097
Bulwer v Astley (1844) 1 Ph 422, 13 LJ Ch 329, 8 Jur 523, 65 RR 416
.... 1121
Bunbury v Doran (1875) IR 9 CL 284 .... 2, 143, 212

PARA

Bunbury's Trusts, Re (1876) 10 IR Eq 408 1069
Bund, Re, Cruikshank v Willis [1929] 2 Ch 455, 99 LJ Ch 4, 142 LT 39
...... 251
Bund v Green (1879) 12 Ch D 819, 28 WR 275 .... 468, 511
Bundell v Chapman. See Blundell v Chapman
Bunn, Re, Durber v Bunn [1926] All ER Rep 626, 134 LT 669, P, D and Admlty
...... 108
Bunn, Re, Isaacson v Webster (1880) 16 Ch D 47, 29 WR 348
...... 430–431
Bunn v Pettinger (1866) LR 1 Eq 510, 35 Beav 321, 35 LJ Ch 389, 14 LT 118
...... 1
Bunning, Re, Bunning v Salmon [1984] Ch 480, [1984] 3 All ER 1, [1984] 3 WLR 265,
  [1985] FLR 1, [1985] Fam Law 21, 128 Sol Jo 516 .... 569, 572, 577, 591–592
Bunter v Coke (1707) 1 Salk 237 26
Bur Singh v Uttam Singh (1911) LR 38 Ind App 13, PC
...... 56
Burbey v Burbey (1862) 9 Jur NS 96, 6 LT 573 328
Burbey v Burbey (1867) 15 WR 479, 15 LT 501 277
Burchett v Woolward (1823) Turn & R 442 366
Burden, Re, Mitchell v St Luke's Hostel Trustees [1948] Ch 160, [1948] 1 All ER 31,
  [1948] LJR 631, 92 Sol Jo 72 422
Burden v Burden (1813) 12 RR 210, 1 Ves & B 170, 35 ER 67, [1803–13] All ER Rep 573
...... 649
Burdet v Hopegood (1718) 1 P Wms 486 .... 45, 362
Burdett v Thompson (1873) LR 3 P & D 72n 48–49
Burdett's Goods, Re (1876) 1 PD 427, 40 JP 519, 45 LJP 71, 34 LT 855, P, D and Admlty
...... 787
Burdick v Garrick (1870) 5 Ch App 233, 39 LJ Ch 369, 18 WR 387
...... 658
Burge v Brutton (1843) 2 Hare 373, 12 LJ Ch 368, 7 Jur 988
...... 654
Burgess v Burgess (1844) 1 Coll 367, 8 Jur 660, 3 LTOS 452
...... 1069
Burgess v Marriott (1843) 3 Curt 424, 7 Jur 473, 2 Notes of Cases 171
...... 957
Burgess v Robinson (1817) 3 Mer 7 .... 145, 1161
Burgess v Wheate (1759) 1 Eden 177, 1 Wm Bl 123 .... 552, 554–555
Burgess Goods, Re (1863) 32 LJPM & A 158, 9 Jur NS 553, 4 Sw & Tr 188, 11 WR 687,
  9 LT 86 763
Burgoyne v Showler (1844) 1 Rob Eccl 5, 8 Jur 814, 3 Notes of Cases 201
...... 895–896
Burke, Re, King v Terry (1919) 148 LT Jo 175, 54 L Jo 430
...... 965
Burke, Re, Wood v Taylor [1914] 1 IR 81 293
Burke v Annis (1853) 11 Hare 232 376
Burke v Burke (1899) 18 NZLR 216 182
Burke v Jones (1813) 2 Ves & B 275 980
Burke v Moore, Re Moore's Goods (1875) IR 9 Eq 609
...... 62
Burke and O'Reilly v Burke and Quail. See Burke's Estate, Re, Burke v Burke
Burke's Estate, Re, Burke v Burke [1951] IR 216, sub nom Burke and O'Reilly v Burke and
  Quail 84 ILTR 70 .... 131, 141
Burke Irwin's Trusts, Barrett v Barrett [1918] 1 IR 350 180
Burkinshaw v Hodge (1874) 22 WR 484 401
Burkitt, Re, Handcock v Studdert [1915] 1 IR 205 383
Burkitt v Ransom (1846) 2 Coll 536 1205
Burleigh v Pearson (1749) 1 Ves Sen 281 254
Burleton v Humfrey (1755) Amb 256 136
Burley, Re, Tatham v Welch [1917] WN 115, sub nom Bailey, Re, Tatham v Welch 61 Sol
  Jo 398 1080
Burls v Burls (1868) LR 1 P & D 472, 36 LJP & M 125, 15 WR 1090, 16 LT 677
...... 716, 910
Burnaby v Griffin (1796) 3 Ves 266 474–475
Burnard v Burnard, Estate of Godfrey Harry Burnard Deceased, Re [2014] EWHC 340
  (Ch), [2014] All ER (D) 51 (Mar) 188
Burney v Macdonald (1845) 15 Sim 6, 9 Jur 588, 6 LTOS 1
...... 222

                                                                                    PARA
Burnham, Re, Carrick v Carrick [1918] 2 Ch 196, 87 LJ Ch 617, [1918–19] All ER Rep
    1194, 119 LT 299 334
Burnie v Getting (1845) 2 Coll 324, 9 Jur 937, 63 ER 754, 6 LTOS 97
    295
Burns v Campbell [1952] 1 KB 15, [1951] 2 All ER 965, 95 Sol Jo 743, [1951] 2 TLR
    1007, CA 835
Burnside v Burnside (1921) 56 ILT 20 296
Burnyeat v Van de Loeff [1924] AC 653, 93 LJ Ch 397, 68 Sol Jo 517, 131 LT 292, 40
    TLR 493, HL 107–108
Burrell, Re, Burrell v Smith (1870) LR 9 Eq 443, 39 LJ Ch 544, 22 LT 263
    1205
Burrell v Baskerfield (1849) 11 Beav 525, 18 LJ Ch 422, 13 Jur 311, sub nom Burrell v
    Maberley 14 LTOS 61 175
Burrell's Goods, Re (1858) 1 Sw & Tr 64, 6 WR 461, 31 LTOS 41
    806
Burridge v Bradyl (1710) 1 P Wms 127 1087
Burrow's Trusts, Re (1864) 10 LT 184 346
Burrowes v Lock (1805) 8 RR 33, 856, 10 Ves 470, 1 White & Tud LC 446, 32 ER 927,
    [1803–13] All ER Rep 477 77
Burrows, Re, Cleghorn v Burrows [1895] 2 Ch 497, 65 LJ Ch 52, 13 R 689, 43 WR 683,
    39 Sol Jo 656, 73 LT 148, 11 TLR 527 362
Burrows v Burrows (1827) 1 Hag Ecc 109 899
Burrows v Cottrell (1830) 3 Sim 375 .... 409, 1130
Burrows v HM Coroner for Preston [2008] EWHC 1387 (QB), [2008] 2 FLR 1225, [2008]
    Fam Law 951, [2008] Fam Law 984, [2008] All ER (D) 201 (May)
    .... 31, 956
Burrows v Walls (1855) 5 De GM & G 233, 3 Eq Rep 960, 104 RR 95, 3 WR 327,
    25 LTOS 18 1055
Burt v Hellyar (1872) LR 14 Eq 160, 41 LJ Ch 430, 26 LT 833
    .... 321, 348, 394
Burtenshaw v Gilbert (1774) 1 Cowp 49, sub nom Berkenshaw v Gilbert Lofft 465
    .... 93, 102
Burton v Collingwood (1832) 4 Hag Ecc 176 7
Burton v Gowell (1593) Cro Eliz 306 93
Burton v Hodsoll (1827) 2 Sim 24 429
Burton v Knowlton (1796) 3 Ves 107 1012
Burton v Newbery (1875) 1 Ch D 234, 45 LJ Ch 202, 24 WR 388, 34 LT 15
    112
Burton's Settlement Trusts, Re, Public Trustee v Montefiore [1955] Ch 348, [1955]
    1 All ER 433, [1955] 2 WLR 452, 99 Sol Jo 148, CA 231
Burton's Settlements, Re, Scott v National Provincial Bank Ltd [1955] Ch 82, [1954]
    3 All ER 193, [1954] 3 WLR 581, 98 Sol Jo 734 .... 141, 149
Burton's Will, Re, Banks v Heaven [1892] 2 Ch 38, 61 LJ Ch 702, 67 LT 221
    1083
Bush, Re, Lipton (B) Ltd v Mackintosh [1930] 2 Ch 202, 99 LJ Ch 503, [1929] B & CR
    216, [1930] All ER Rep 605, 143 LT 700 981
Bush v Allen. See South v Alleine
Bush v Jouliac [2006] EWHC 363 (Ch), [2006] All ER (D) 108 (Jan)
    .... 169, 187
Bushell's Goods, Re (1887) 13 PD 7, 51 JP 806, 57 LJP 16, 36 WR 528, 58 LT 58, P, D
    and Admlty 739
Bustard v Saunders (1843) 7 Beav 92, 7 Jur 986 .... 390, 393
Busteed v Eager (1834) Milw 345, 347 99
Butcher v Leach (1843) 5 Beav 392, 7 Jur 74 .... 416, 431
Bute (Marquess), Re, Marquess of Bute v Ryder (1884) 27 Ch D 196, 53 LJ Ch 1090, 32
    WR 996 277
Bute (Marquis) v Harman (1846) 9 Beav 320 433
Butler, ex p (1749) 1 Atk 210 923
Butler, Re, Joyce v Brew [1918] 1 IR 394 167
Butler, Re, Le Bas v Herbert [1894] 3 Ch 250, (1894) 10 WN 128, 63 LJ Ch 662, 8 R 504,
    43 WR 190, 15 NSWLR 236 .... 293, 1006, 1011, 1096
Butler v Baker and Delves Poph. See Butler and Baker's Case
Butler v Butler (1884) 28 Ch D 66, 54 LJ Ch 197, 33 WR 192, 52 LT 90
    .... 291, 917
Butler v Lowe (1839) 10 Sim 317, 3 Jur 1143 .... 301, 309

PARA

Butler v Stratton (1791) 3 Bro CC 367 .... 332, 338, 396
Butler v Trustees, Executors and Agency Co Ltd (1906) 3 CLR 435, Aust HC
.... 442
Butler and Baker's Case (1591) 1 And 348, 3 Co Rep 25a, 3 Leon 271, Moore KB 254,
    sub nom Butler v Baker and Delves Poph 87, Ex Ch 29
Butler's Goods, Re [1898] P 9, 67 LJP 15, 46 WR 445, 77 LT 376, P, D and Admlty
.... 819
Butlin's Settlement Trusts, Re, Butlin v Butlin [1976] Ch 251, [1976] 2 All ER 483, [1976]
    2 WLR 547, 119 Sol Jo 794 187
Butt v Kelson [1952] Ch 197, [1952] 1 TLR 214, sub nom Butt, Re, Butt v Kelson [1952]
    1 All ER 167, CA 1020
Butt v Thomas (1855) 11 Exch 235 473
Butter v Ommaney (1827) 4 Russ 70, 6 LJOS Ch 54 .... 322, 337, 392
Butterfield v Butterfield (1748) 1 Ves Sen 133 385
Buxton, Re, Buxton v Buxton [1930] 1 Ch 648, 99 LJ Ch 334, [1930] All ER Rep 369,
    143 LT 37 1085
Buxton v Buxton (1835) 1 My & Cr 80 961
Buzzacott, Re, Munday v King's College Hospital [1953] Ch 28, [1952] 2 All ER 1011, 96
    Sol Jo 850, [1952] 2 TLR 884 278
Byam v Sutton (1855) 19 Beav 646 818
Byles v Cox (1896) 74 LT 222, P, D and Admlty 65, 73, 895
Byne v Blackburn (1858) 26 Beav 41, 27 LJ Ch 788, 4 Jur NS 803, 6 WR 861, 32 LTOS
    34 370
Byne v Currey (1834) 2 Cr & M 603, 3 LJ Ex 177, 4 Tyr 478
.... 1130

Byng v Byng. See Webb v Byng
Byng v Lord Strafford (1843) 5 Beav 558, 12 LJ Ch 169, 7 Jur 98; affd sub nom Hoare v
    Byng (1844) 10 Cl & Fin 508, 8 Jur 563, HL 134, 142, 382
Byrchall v Bradford (1822) 6 Madd 235 1149
Byrne, Re (1910) 3 BWCC 591, 44 ILT 98 .... 759, 817, 820
Byrne, Re, Byrne v Kenny (1889) 23 LR Ir 260 431
Byrne, Re, Dowling v Lawler [1967] IR 304, Ir SC 451
Byrne's Goods (No 2), Re (1910) 44 ILT 192 .... 849, 852
Byrne's Will, Re, Byrne v Byrne (1898) 24 VLR 832 266
Byrom v Brandreth (1873) LR 16 Eq 475, 42 LJ Ch 824
.... 293
Byron's Settlement, Re, Williams v Mitchell [1891] 3 Ch 474, 60 LJ Ch 807, 40 WR 11, 65
    LT 218 11
Bythsea v Bythsea (1854) 23 LJ Ch 1004, 2 WR 677, 24 LTOS 17
.... 260, 441
Bythway, Re, Gough v Dames (1911) 80 LJ Ch 246, 55 Sol Jo 235, 104 LT 411
.... 1158
Bywater, Re, Bywater v Clarke (1881) 18 Ch D 17, 30 WR 94, CA
.... 186, 207, 232, 669

C

C, Re (1960) Times, 28 July 739
C (children) (parent: purported marriage between two women: artificial insemination by
    donor), Re [2006] EWCA Civ 551, [2006] All ER (D) 216 (May), sub nom J v C
    [2007] Fam 1, [2006] 3 WLR 876, sub nom J v C (void marriage: status of children)
    [2008] 1 FCR 368, [2006] 2 FLR 1098, [2006] Fam Law 742, (2006) Times, 1 June
.... 358–359
CA v CC. See McC's Estate, Re
CI v NS [2004] EWHC 659 (Fam), [2004] All ER (D) 30 (Apr)
.... 701, 957
Cabburn, Re, Gage v Rutland (1882) 46 LT 848 .... 369, 1200
Caborne, Re, Hodge and Nabarro v Smith [1943] Ch 224, [1943] 2 All ER 7, 112 LJ Ch
    210, 87 Sol Jo 201, 169 LT 109, 59 TLR 309 .... 131, 137
Cadbury v Smith (1869) LR 9 Eq 37, 18 WR 105, 24 LT 52
.... 1300
Cadell v Wilcocks [1898] P 21, 67 LJP 8, 46 WR 394, 78 LT 83, 14 TLR 100, P, D and
    Admlty 95, 97
Cadett v Earle (1877) 5 Ch D 710, 46 LJ Ch 798 295

PARA

Cadge's Goods, Re (1868) LR 1 P & D 543, 32 JP 198, 37 LJP & M 15, 16 WR 406, 17
    LT 484, [1861–73] All ER Rep Ext 1666 83
Cadlock v Aboagye [2006] EWHC 3654 (Ch), [2006] All ER (D) 170 (Dec)
    1219
Cadman v Cadman (1872) LR 13 Eq 470, 41 LJ Ch 468, 20 WR 356
    288
Cadogan, Re, Cadogan v Palagi (1883) 25 Ch D 154, 53 LJ Ch 207, 32 WR 57, 49 LT
    666, [1881–5] All ER Rep Ext 1527 293
Cadogan v Cadogan [1977] 3 All ER 831, [1977] 1 WLR 1041, 35 P & CR 92, 121 Sol Jo
    443, CA 1221
Cadogan (Earl) Settlements, Re, Richmond v Lambton (1911) 56 Sol Jo 11
    1131
Cadywold's Goods, Re (1890) 27 LJP & M 36, 1 Sw & Tr 34, 6 WR 375, P, D and
    Admlty 88
Cafe v Bent (1845) 5 Hare 24, 9 Jur 653 1122
Caffary v Caffary (1844) 8 Jur 329, 3 LTOS 70 390
Cage v Russel (1681) 2 Vent 352 149
Caie's Estate, Re (1927) 71 Sol Jo 898, 43 TLR 697, P, D and Admlty
    739
Cain's Will, Re, Linehan v Cain [1913] VLR 50 212
Cairnes, Re, Howard v Cairnes (1982) 4 FLR 225, 12 Fam Law 177
    582–583
Caithness (Earl), Re (1891) 7 TLR 354 111
Caithness (Earl) v Sinclair 1912 SC 79, Ct of Sess 131
Caldbeck v Caldbeck [1911] 1 IR 144 333
Caldecott v Caldecott (1842) 1 Y & C Ch Cas 312, 11 LJ Ch 158, 6 Jur 232
    1124
Caldecott v Harrison (1840) 9 Sim 457, 9 LJ Ch 331, 4 Jur 885
    328
Calder v Alexander (1900) 16 TLR 294 28
Caldwell v Cresswell (1871) 6 Ch App 278, 24 LT 564 147
Caldwell's Will Trust, Re, Jenyns v Sackville West [1971] 1 All ER 780, [1971] 1 WLR
    181, 115 Sol Jo 567 .... 253, 387
Caledon (Earl), Re, Almander v Earl Caledon [1915] 1 Ch 150, 84 LJ Ch 319, 112 LT 75
    300
Caledonian Rly Co v North British Rly Co (1881) 6 App Cas 114, 29 WR 685, HL
    241
Callaghan, Re [1985] Fam 1, [1984] 3 All ER 790, [1984] 3 WLR 1076, [1985] FLR 116,
    [1985] Fam Law 28, 128 Sol Jo 705 .... 567, 573, 580, 591
Callaway, Re, Callaway v Treasury Solicitor [1956] Ch 559, [1956] 2 All ER 451, [1956] 3
    WLR 257, 100 Sol Jo 452 .... 39, 480
Callaway's Goods, Re (1890) 15 PD 147, 59 LJP 73, 38 WR 528, 63 LT 227, P, D and
    Admlty 723
Callicott's Goods, Re [1899] P 189, 68 LJP 67, 80 LT 421, P, D and Admlty
    761
Callow v Callow (1889) 42 Ch D 550, 58 LJ Ch 698, 38 WR 104, 5 TLR 705
    294
Calow, Re, Calow v Calow [1928] Ch 710, 97 LJ Ch 253, [1928] All ER Rep 518, 72 Sol
    Jo 437, 139 LT 235 157
Calthorpe v Gough (1789) 4 Term Rep 707n, 3 Bro CC 395n
    445
Calvert v Sebbon (1841) 4 Beav 222 1069
Cambridge v Rous (1802) 6 RR 199, 8 Ves 12 .... 183, 237, 449
Cambridge v Rous (1858) 25 Beav 409 .... 319, 444
Camden v Fletcher (1838) 8 LJ Ex 17, 1 Horn & H 361, 4 M & W 378
    1263
Cameron, Re [1999] Ch 386, [1999] 2 All ER 924, [1999] 3 WLR 394, 1 ITELR 815,
    [1999] 16 LS Gaz R 35 .... 155, 158, 197, 503
Cameron v Harper (1892) 21 SCR 273 284
Cameron v Treasury Solicitor [1997] 1 FCR 188, [1996] 2 FLR 716, [1996] Fam Law 723,
    CA 578, 604
Cameron's Trustees v Mackenzie 1915 SC 313, Ct of Sess
    54
Camfield v Gilbert (1803) 3 East 516 .... 17, 288, 469
Cammell, Re, Public Trustee v A-G [1925] WN 36, 69 Sol Jo 345, DC
    382

                                                                                          PARA
Camoys (Lord) v Blundell. See Blundell v Gladstone
Campanari v Woodburn (1854) 15 CB 400, 24 LJCP 13, 1 Jur NS 17, 3 WR 59, 3 CLR
    140, 24 LTOS 95 1279
Campbell, Re, Campbell v Campbell [1893] 2 Ch 206, 62 LJ Ch 594, 3 R 331, 68 LT 851
    1008
Campbell, Re, Campbell v Campbell [1893] 3 Ch 468, 62 LJ Ch 878, 37 Sol Jo 582, 69 LT
    134 1080
Campbell, Re, Cooper v Campbell (1919) 88 LJ Ch 239, 63 Sol Jo 286, 120 LT 562
    .... 416, 432, 435, 437
Campbell, Re, M'Cabe v Campbell [1918] 1 IR 429 .... 226, 370
Campbell v Bouskell (1859) 27 Beav 325 .... 253, 328, 334, 389, 391
Campbell v Brownrigg (1843) 1 Ph 301, 13 LJ Ch 7 231
Campbell v Campbell [1976] Fam 347, [1977] 1 All ER 1, [1976] 3 WLR 572, 120 Sol Jo
    116 577
Campbell v Campbell and Davis (1895) 72 LT 294, P, D and Admlty
    464
Campbell v French (1797) 3 Ves 321 109
Campbell v Gillespie [1900] 1 Ch 225, 69 LJ Ch 223, 48 WR 151, 44 Sol Jo 90, 81 LT
    514 1179
Campbell v Harding (1831) 2 Russ & M 390; on appeal sub nom Candy v Campbell
    (1834) 8 Bli NS 469, 2 Cl & Fin 421, HL 385, 457, 459
Campbell v Hoskins. See Hoskins v Campbell
Campbell v M'Grain (1875) IR 9 Eq 397 .... 250, 288
Campbell v Prescott (1808) 15 Ves 500 288
Campbell's Estate, Re [1954] 1 All ER 448, [1954] 1 WLR 516, 98 Sol Jo 197, P, D and
    Admlty 652
Campbell's Goods, Re (1829) 2 Hag Ecc 555 816
Campbell's Trustee v Dick 1915 SC 100, Ct of Sess 325, 397
Campbell's Trustee v Welsh 1952 SC 343, 1952 SLT 352, Ct of Sess
    332
Campbell's Trusts, Re (1886) 31 Ch D 685, 55 LJ Ch 389, 34 WR 396, 54 LT 419; affd
    (1886) 33 Ch D 98, 55 LJ Ch 911, 34 WR 629, 55 LT 463, CA
    397
Campion's Goods, Re [1900] P 13, 69 LJP 19, 48 WR 288, 81 LT 790, P, D and Admlty
    763
Campsill, Re, Reading v Hinde (1910) 128 LT Jo 548 266
Cancellor v Cancellor (1862) 2 Drew & Sm 194, 32 LJ Ch 17, 8 Jur NS 1146, 1 New Rep
    12, 11 WR 16, 7 LT 307, [1861–73] All ER Rep Ext 2272
    396
Cancer Research Campaign v Ernest Brown & Co (a firm) [1997] STC 1425, [1998] PNLR
    592 1054–1055
Candler v Tillett (1855) 22 Beav 257, 25 LJ Ch 505, 111 RR 351, 4 WR 160
    1253
Candy v Campbell. See Campbell v Harding
Cane, Re, Ruff v Sivers (1890) 60 LJ Ch 36, 63 LT 746
    446
Caney v Bond (1843) 6 Beav 486, 1 LTOS 409, sub nom Carry v Bond 12 LJ Ch 484
    959
Canney's Trusts, Re, Mayers v Strover (1910) 54 Sol Jo 214, 101 LT 905
    311
Canning's Will Trusts, Re, Skues v Lyon [1936] Ch 309, 105 LJ Ch 241, 154 LT 693
    182
Cannings v Flower (1835) 7 Sim 523, 5 LJ Ch 8 1076
Cant's Estate, Re (1859) 4 De G & J 503, 28 LJ Ch 641, 5 Jur NS 829, 7 WR 624, 45 ER
    196, [1843–60] All ER Rep 542, 33 LTOS 280, CA in Ch
    126
Cantillon's Minors, Re (1864) 16 I Ch R 301 .... 428, 442
Cape v Cape (1837) 2 Y & C Ex 543, 1 Jur 307 390
Capel, Re, Arbuthnot v Capel (1914) 59 Sol Jo 177 293
Capelovitch's Estate and Will Trusts, Re, Sandelson v Capelovitch [1957] 1 All ER 33,
    [1957] 1 WLR 102, 101 Sol Jo 63 1176
Capes v Dalton (1902) 86 LT 129, CA; revsd sub nom Kekewich v Barker (1903) 88 LT
    130, HL 396–397
Caplin's Will, Re (1865) 2 Drew & Sm 527, 34 LJ Ch 578, 11 Jur NS 383, 6 New Rep 17,
    143 RR 273, 13 WR 646, 12 LT 526 349

                                                                        PARA
Car v Ellison (1744) 3 Atk 73 27
Carapeto v Good. See Good, Re, Carapeto v Good
Cardigan v Curzon-Howe. See Bruce v Curzon Howe
Careless v Careless (1816) 1 Mer 384, 19 Ves 601 .... 220, 261
Carew, Re, Carew v Carew [1896] 1 Ch 527; affd [1896] 2 Ch 311, 65 LJ Ch 686, 44 WR
    700, 74 LT 501, CA 1071
Carew, Re, Channer v Francklyn [1939] Ch 794, [1939] 3 All ER 200, 108 LJ Ch 291, 83
    Sol Jo 545, 161 LT 139, 55 TLR 875 1092
Carey, Re (1977) 121 Sol Jo 173 .... 101, 108,109
Carey, Re, Carey v Carey (1915) 49 ILT 226 974
Carey v Carey (1857) 6 I Ch R 255 320
Carey v Goodinge (1790) 3 Bro CC 110 625
Carleton, Re (1909) 28 NZLR 1066 446
Carleton's Goods, Re [1915] 2 IR 9 112
Carlisle, Re, Belfast Bank Executor and Trustee Co v Patterson [1950] NI 105
    186
Carlton v Thompson (1867) LR 1 Sc & Div 232, HL 414
Carmichael v Carmichael (1846) 2 Ph 101, 10 Jur 908, 9 LTOS 17
    1268
Carne v Long (1860) 24 JP 676, 2 De GF & J 75, 29 LJ Ch 503, 6 Jur NS 639, 8 WR
    570, 2 LT 552 36
Carolin v Carolin (1881) 17 LR Ir 25n 443
Carpenter v Bott (1847) 15 Sim 606, 16 LJ Ch 433, 11 Jur 723, 9 LTOS 333
    278
Carr v Beaven [2008] EWHC 2582 (Ch), [2008] All ER (D) 289 (Oct)
    .... 50, 53
Carr v Ingleby (1831) 1 De G & Sm 362 1091
Carr v Isard [2006] EWHC 2095 (Ch), [2006] All ER (D) 343 (Nov)
    29
Carr's Goods, Re (1867) LR 1 P & D 291, 31 JP 297, 15 WR 718, 16 LT 181
    .... 774, 794
Carr's Will, Re (1902) 27 WN 23, 2 SRNSW 1, NSW SC
    456
Carrington, Re, Ralphs v Swithenbank [1932] 1 Ch 1, 100 LJ Ch 299, [1931] All ER Rep
    658, 145 LT 284, CA 157
Carritt's Goods, Re (1892) 66 LT 379, P, D and Admlty
    112
Carry v Bond. See Caney v Bond
Carter, Re (1892) 41 WR 140 1124
Carter, Re, Dodds v Pearson [1900] 1 Ch 801, 69 LJ Ch 426, 48 WR 555, 82 LT 526
    156
Carter, Re, Walker v Litchfield (1911) 30 NZLR 707, NZ CA
    310
Carter v Bentall (1840) 2 Beav 551, 9 LJ Ch 303, 4 Jur 691
    .... 249, 334, 459
Carter v Bletsoe (1708) 2 Eq Cas Abr 540, Gilb Ch 11, Prec Ch 267, 2 Vern 617
    438
Carter v Haswell (1857) 26 LJ Ch 576, 3 Jur NS 788, 5 WR 388, 29 LTOS 398
    184
Carter v Seaton (1901) 45 Sol Jo 673, 85 LT 76, 17 TLR 671, P, D and Admlty
    71
Carter's Estate, Re (1908) 52 Sol Jo 600, P, D and Admlty
    730
Carteret v Carteret (1723) 2 P Wms 132 140
Cartwright, Re, Avis v Newman (1889) 41 Ch D 532, 58 LJ Ch 590, 37 WR 612, 60 LT
    891, 5 TLR 482 1229
Cartwright, Re, Cartwright v Smith [1939] Ch 90, [1938] 4 All ER 209, 108 LJ Ch 51, 82
    Sol Jo 930, 159 LT 538, 55 TLR 69, CA 282
Cartwright v Cartwright (1793) 1 Phillim 90, 161 ER 923, [1775–1802] All ER Rep 476;
    affd [1775–1802] All ER Rep 476n 50, 899
Cartwright v Vawdry (1800) 5 Ves 530 350
Carville, Re, Shone v Walthamstow Borough Council [1937] 4 All ER 464
    .... 11, 517
Cary v Hills (1872) LR 15 Eq 79, 42 LJ Ch 100, 21 WR 166, 28 LT 6
    636
Cary and Lott's Contract, Re [1901] 2 Ch 463, 70 LJ Ch 653, 49 WR 581, 45 Sol Jo 596,
    84 LT 859, 17 TLR 598 1145

PARA

Casamajor v Strode (1809) 19 Ves 390n 1123
Casamajor v Strode (1843) 8 Jur 14 441
Case of the Grail (1459) YB 37 Hen 6, fo 30, pl 11 .... 121, 123
Casement v Fulton (1845) 3 Moo Ind App 395, 5 Moo PCC 130, PC

.... 70
Casimir v Alexander [2001] WTLR 939 155
Casmore's Goods, Re (1869) LR 1 P & D 653, 33 JP 392, 38 LJP & M 54, 17 WR 627,
    20 LT 497, [1861–73] All ER Rep Ext 1907 65
Cassel, Re, Public Trustee v Ashley (1922) 39 TLR 75 366
Cassidy's Goods, Re (1832) 4 Hag Ecc 360 800
Casson v Dade (1781) 2 Dick 586, 1 Bro CC 99 70–71
Castiglione's Will Trusts, Re, Hunter v Mackenzie [1958] Ch 549, [1958] 1 All ER 480,
    [1958] 2 WLR 400, 102 Sol Jo 176 35
Castle, Re, Public Trustee v Floud [1949] Ch 46, [1948] 2 All ER 927, [1949] LJR 610, 64
    TLR 599 315
Castle v Eate (1844) 7 Beav 296, 8 Jur 280, 3 LTOS 2 429
Castle v Fox (1871) LR 11 Eq 542, 40 LJ Ch 302, 19 WR 840, 24 LT 536

.... 215
Castle v Torre (1837) 2 Moo PCC 133, PC 5
Castledon v Turner (1745) 3 Atk 257 .... 194, 241
Castlehow, Re, Lamonby v Carter [1903] 1 Ch 352, 72 LJ Ch 211, 88 LT 455

.... 250
Cater's Trusts (No 2), Re (1858) 25 Beav 366, 119 RR 453

.... 1047, 1057
Cathcart (Earl), Re (1912) 56 Sol Jo 271 .... 300, 341
Catlin v Cyprus Finance Corpn (London) Ltd [1983] QB 759, [1983] 1 All ER 809, [1983]
    2 WLR 566, 126 Sol Jo 744 1271
Catmull, Re, Catmull v Watts [1943] Ch 262, [1943] 2 All ER 115, 112 LJ Ch 242, 87 Sol
    Jo 112, 228, 169 LT 62, 59 TLR 192, 317 .... 572, 574
Caton v Goddard [2007] All ER (D) 370 (Oct) 893
Cator v Cator (1851) 14 Beav 463 390
Catt's Trusts, Re (1864) 2 Hem & M 46, 33 LJ Ch 495, 10 Jur NS 536, 4 New Rep 88, 12
    WR 739, 10 LT 409 .... 124, 134
Cattermole v Prisk [2006] 1 FLR 693, [2006] Fam Law 98

.... 56
Cattle v Evans [2011] EWHC 945 (Ch), [2011] 2 FLR 843, [2011] Fam Law 809, 155 Sol
    Jo (no 18) 31, 155 Sol Jo (no 19) 31, [2011] 2 P & CR DG27, [2011] All ER (D) 209
    (Apr) 568, 579
Cattley v Vincent (1852) 15 Beav 198 417
Caudle v LD Law Ltd [2008] EWHC 374 (QB), [2009] 2 All ER 1020, [2008] 1 WLR
    1540, 11 ITELR 882, [2008] All ER (D) 435 (Feb) 645–646, 680
Caulfield v Maguire (1845) 2 Jo & Lat 141 336
Cave v Cave (1762) 2 Eden 139 .... 226, 288
Cave v Harris (1887) 57 LJ Ch 62, 36 WR 182, 57 LT 768

.... 271, 279, 282
Cave v Horsell [1912] 3 KB 533, 81 LJKB 981, 107 LT 186, 28 TLR 543, CA

.... 206, 242, 245
Cavendish v Mercer (1776) 5 Ves 195n 1076
Cavendish (Lord) v Lowther. See Lowther v Cavendish
Cawthron's Goods, Re (1863) 28 JP 201, 33 LJPM & A 23, 10 Jur NS 51, 3 New Rep 93,
    3 Sw & Tr 417, 12 WR 443 7
Cayley, Re, Awdry v Cayley [1904] 2 Ch 781, 74 LJ Ch 31, 53 WR 260, 91 LT 743

.... 1133
Cazenove v Cazenove (1889) 61 LT 115 1087
Chadda v Revenue and Customs Comrs [2014] UKFTT 1061 (TC), [2015] WTLR 75

.... 29
Chadock v Cowley (1624) Cro Jac 695 .... 460, 473
Chadwick v Collinson [2014] EWHC 3055 (Ch), [2015] WTLR 25, [2014] All ER (D) 172
    (Sep) 39–40
Chadwick v Doleman (1705) 1 Eq Cas Abr 344, 2 Vern 528

.... 333
Chadwick v Greenall (1861) 3 Giff 221, 7 Jur NS 959, 5 LT 232

.... 441
Chadwick v Heatley (1845) 2 Coll 137, 9 Jur 504, 5 LTOS 303

.... 1057
Chaffe v Kelland (1637) 1 Roll Abr 929 976
Chaffers v Abell (1839) 3 Jur 577 428

PARA

Chalcraft, Re, Chalcraft v Giles [1948] P 222, [1948] 1 All ER 700, [1948] LJR 1111, 92 Sol Jo 181, 64 TLR 246, P, D and Admlty 63, 71

Chalinder and Herington, Re [1907] 1 Ch 58, 76 LJ Ch 71, 51 Sol Jo 69, 96 LT 196, 23 TLR 71 652

Challen v Shippam (1845) 4 Hare 555, 67 RR 151 962

Challenger v Shephard (1800) 8 Term Rep 597 376

Challinor v Challinor [2009] EWHC 180 (Ch) [2009] WTLR 931 .... 572–573, 575–576, 591

Chalmers, Re, Chalmers v Chalmers [1921] WN 129, 65 Sol Jo 475 1265

Chalmers v Storil (1813) 2 Ves & B 222 250

Chamber, Re, Watson v National Children's Home [2001] WTLR 1375 143

Chamberlain v Chamberlain (1675) 1 Cas in Ch 256, Freem Ch 141 1099

Chamberlain v Williamson (1814) 2 M & S 408, 105 ER 433 1279

Chamberlain's Goods, Re (1867) LR 1 P & D 316, 31 JP 247, 36 LJP & M 52, 15 WR 680, 16 LT 97, [1861–73] All ER Rep Ext 2106 .... 853, 862

Chamberlaine v Chamberlaine (1674) 1 Cas in Ch 256, Freem Ch 141 123

Chamberlaine v Turner (1628) Cro Car 129, W Jo 195 376

Chambers v Atkins (1823) 1 Sim & St 382, 1 LJOS Ch 208 370

Chambers v Bicknell (1843) 2 Hare 536, 7 Jur 167 803

Chambers v Brailsford (1816) 2 Mer 25, 19 Ves 652 253

Chambers v Goldwin [1904] 2 Ch 693, 11 Ves 1, [1803–13] All ER Rep 255 1076

Chambers v Howell (1847) 11 Beav 6, 12 Jur 905, 83 RR 104, 11 LTOS 509 1029

Chambers v Jeoffrey (1709) 2 Eq Cas Abr 541 pl 9 428

Chambers v Minchin (1802) 6 RR 111, 7 Ves 186, 32 ER 76, [1775–1802] All ER Rep 511 1253

Chambers v Randall [1923] 1 Ch 149, 92 LJ Ch 227, [1922] All ER Rep 565, 67 Sol Jo 61, 128 LT 507, 39 TLR 6 1282

Chambers v Smith (1847) 2 Coll 742, 16 LJ Ch 291, 11 Jur 359, 9 LTOS 33, sub nom Smith v Chambers 2 Ph 221 1018

Chambers v Taylor (1836) 2 My & Cr 376, 6 LJ Ch 193 340

Chamney's Goods, Re (1849) 1 Rob Eccl 757, 14 LTOS 89, 7 Notes of Cases 70 73

Champ v Champ (1892) 30 LR Ir 72 472

Champion, Re, Dudley v Champion [1893] 1 Ch 101, 62 LJ Ch 372, 2 R 162, 67 LT 694, CA 113–114, 282

Champion v Pickax (1737) 1 Atk 472 331

Chana v Chana [2001] WTLR 205 106

Chance, Re, Westminster Bank Ltd v Chance [1962] Ch 593, [1962] 1 All ER 942, [1962] 1 WLR 409, 106 Sol Jo 285 1127

Chance v Chance (1853) 16 Beav 572 .... 416, 427

Chance's Settlement Trusts, Re, Chance v Billing [1918] WN 34, 62 Sol Jo 349 377

Chancellor, Re, Chancellor v Brown (1884) 26 Ch D 42, 53 LJ Ch 443, 32 WR 465, 51 LT 33, CA 1035, 1124

Chandler v Gibson (1901) 2 OLR 442 389

Chandless v Price (1796) 3 Ves 99 .... 385, 459

Chandos (Duke) (or Chandois (Dux)) v Talbot (or Talbott) (1731) Kel W 25, 2 P Wms 601 438–439

Channon v Perkins (a firm) [2005] EWCA Civ 1808, 149 Sol Jo LB 1493, [2005] All ER (D) 30 (Dec) 77, 895

Chant, Re, Chant v Lemon [1900] 2 Ch 345, 69 LJ Ch 601, 48 WR 646, 83 LT 341, [1900–3] All ER Rep Ext 1612 .... 246, 443

Chantrell, Re, Sutleffe v Von Liverhoff [1907] WN 213 1006

Chaplin, Re, Royal Bank of Scotland v Chaplin [1950] Ch 507, [1950] 2 All ER 155, 94 Sol Jo 369, 66 (pt 1) TLR 1166 288

Chaplin v Leroux (1816) 5 M & S 14 540

PARA

Chaplin and Staffordshire Potteries Waterworks Co's Contract, Re [1922] 2 Ch 824, 92 LJ
Ch 34, 67 Sol Jo 46, 128 LT 186, 38 TLR 857, CA 1031
Chaplin's Trusts, Re (1863) 33 LJ Ch 183, 3 New Rep 192, 12 WR 147, 9 LT 475
.... 175
Chapman, Re, Charley v Lewis (1922) 56 ILT 32 311
Chapman, Re, Cocks v Chapman [1896] 2 Ch 763, 65 LJ Ch 892, 45 WR 67,
[1895–9] All ER Rep 1104, 40 Sol Jo 715, 75 LT 196, 12 TLR 625, CA
.... 959, 961
Chapman, Re, Ellick v Cox (1883) 32 WR 424, 49 LT 673
.... 349
Chapman, Re, Fardell v Chapman (1886) 54 LT 13 1186
Chapman, Re, Hales v A-G [1922] 2 Ch 479, 91 LJ Ch 527, 66 Sol Jo 522, 127 LT 616,
CA 11
Chapman v Chapman (1864) 33 Beav 556 364
Chapman v Chapman (1876) 4 Ch D 800, 46 LJ Ch 104
.... 250, 298
Chapman v Gilbert (1853) 4 De GM & G 366 232
Chapman v Hart (1749) 1 Ves Sen 271 .... 285, 291
Chapman v Mason (1879) 40 LT 678 1176
Chapman v Perkins [1905] AC 106, 74 LJ Ch 331, 53 WR 485, 92 LT 372, HL
.... 236–237, 247, 282, 411
Chapman v Reynolds (1860) 28 Beav 221, 29 LJ Ch 594, 6 Jur NS 440, 8 WR 403, 2 LT
319 293
Chapman's Case (1574) 3 Dyer 333b 348
Chapman's Goods, Re [1903] P 192, 72 LJP 62, 89 LT 308, P, D and Admlty
.... 759, 761
Chapman's Goods, Re (1844) 1 Rob Eccl 1, 8 Jur 902, 3 Notes of Cases 198
.... 112
Chapman's Settlement Trusts, Re, Jones v Chapman [1978] 1 All ER 1122, [1977] 1 WLR
1163, 121 Sol Jo 619, CA 302, 307–308
Chapman's Will, Re (1863) 32 Beav 382, 9 Jur NS 657, 11 WR 578
.... 323
Chappell v Somers & Blake (a firm) [2003] EWHC 1644 (Ch), [2004] Ch 19, [2003]
3 All ER 1076, [2003] 3 WLR 1233, (2003) Times, 2 September, 147 Sol Jo LB 1148,
[2003] All ER (D) 120 (Jul) 1288
Chappell & Co Ltd v Redwood Music Ltd [1980] 2 All ER 817, [1981] RPC 337, HL
.... 633, 1288
Chappell's Goods, Re [1894] P 98, 63 LJP 95, 6 R 576, 70 LT 245, P, D and Admlty
.... 214, 220, 276, 611
Chappell's Trusts, Re (1862) 10 WR 573, 6 LT 643 445
Chapple, Re, Newton v Chapman (1884) 27 Ch D 584, 33 WR 336, 51 LT 748
.... 652
Chard v Chard (otherwise Northcott) [1956] P 259, [1955] 3 All ER 721, [1955] 3 WLR
954, 99 Sol Jo 890, P, D and Admlty 745
Charge v Goodyer (1826) 3 Russ 140 328
Charitable Donations (Donations and Bequests) Comrs v De Clifford (1841) 1 Dr & War
245 375
Charitable Donations and Bequests Comrs v Deey (1891) 27 LR Ir 289
.... 348
Charles v Barzey [2002] UKPC 68, [2003] 1 WLR 437, [2002] All ER (D) 328 (Dec)
.... 142
Charles v Jones (1886) 33 Ch D 80, 56 LJ Ch 161, 35 WR 88, 55 LT 331, CA
.... 1211
Charlton v Earl of Durham (1869) 4 Ch App 433, 38 LJ Ch 183, 17 WR 995, 20 LT 467
.... 926, 1149
Charlton v Low (1734) 2 Eq Cas Abr 259, 462, 469, 3 P Wms 328
.... 1150
Charman, Re, Charman v Williams [1951] WN 599, [1951] 2 TLR 1095
.... 572
Chartbrook Ltd v Persimmon Homes Ltd [2009] UKHL 38, [2009] AC 1101, [2009]
4 All ER 677 189
Charter v Charter (1874) LR 7 HL 364, 43 LJP & M 73
.... 212, 217–218, 276, 611
Charteris, Re, Charteris v Biddulph [1917] 2 Ch 379, 86 LJ Ch 658, 61 Sol Jo 591, 117 LT
391, CA 1020, 1157
Chartres, Re, Farman v Barrett [1927] 1 Ch 466, 96 LJ Ch 241, [1927] All ER Rep 408,
137 LT 52 .... 304, 308

PARA

Chaston, Re, Chaston v Seago (1881) 18 Ch D 218, 50 LJ Ch 716, 29 WR 778, 45 LT 20,
[1881–5] All ER Rep Ext 1730 .... 317, 410, 451

Chatard's Settlement, Re [1899] 1 Ch 712, 68 LJ Ch 350, 47 WR 515, 80 LT 645
.... 1072

Chatham (Earl) v Tothill (1771) 7 Bro Parl Cas 453, HL
.... 385

Chatteris v Young (1827) 2 Russ 183 .... 409, 1130

Chauncy v Graydon (1743) 2 Atk 616 .... 145, 1055

Chaytor, Re, Chaytor v Horn [1905] 1 Ch 233, 74 LJ Ch 106, 53 WR 251,
[1904–7] All ER Rep 230, 92 LT 290 .... 1124, 1126

Cheadle, Re, Bishop v Holt [1900] 2 Ch 620, 69 LJ Ch 753, 49 WR 88, 44 Sol Jo 673, 83
LT 297, [1900–3] All ER Rep Ext 1614, CA 116, 127, 217, 220, 266

Cheese v Lovejoy (1877) 2 PD 251, 25 WR 853, 37 LT 295, sub nom Re Harris, Cheese v
Lovejoy 46 LJP 66, CA 93, 101

Cheetham v Ward (1797) 1 Bos & P 630, 126 ER 1102, [1775–1802] All ER Rep 211
.... 625

Chekov v Fryer [2015] EWHC 1642 (Ch), 165 NLJ 7668, [2015] All ER (D) 303 (Jun)
.... 567

Chellaram v Chellaram [1985] Ch 409, [1985] 1 All ER 1043, [1985] 2 WLR 510, 128 Sol
Jo 877 .... 960, 1075

Chellew v Martin (1873) 21 WR 671, 28 LT 662 422

Chelsea Waterworks (Governor & Co) v Cowper (1795) 1 Esp 275
.... 1245

Chelsea Yacht and Boat Co Ltd v Pope [2001] 2 All ER 409, [2000] 1 WLR 1941,
[2000] 2 EGLR 23, [2000] 22 EG 145, [2000] All ER (D) 501, CA
.... 932

Chenoweth, Re, Ward v Dwelley [1902] 2 Ch 488, 71 LJ Ch 739, 50 WR 663, 46 Sol Jo
634, 86 LT 890, 18 TLR 702 563

Chenoweth, Re, Ward v Dwelley (1901) 45 Sol Jo 520, 17 TLR 515
.... 186, 217

Cherrington, Re [1984] 2 All ER 285, [1984] 1 WLR 772, [1984] FLR 559, [1984] Fam
Law 181, 128 Sol Jo 302, [1984] CLY 3660, DC 178

Cherry v Boultbee (1839) 2 Keen 319, 4 My & Cr 442, 9 LJ Ch 118, 3 Jur 1116
.... 1067–1068, 1236

Cheslyn v Cresswell. See Cresswell v Cheslyn

Chester, Re, Ryan v Chester (1914) 49 ILT 97 .... 99, 1110

Chester, Re, Servant v Hills [1914] 2 Ch 580, 84 LJ Ch 78
.... 328

Chester v Chester (1730) Mos 313, 336, 3 P Wms 56, Fitz-G 150
.... 284

Chester v Painter (1725) 2 Eq Cas Abr 314, 2 P Wms 335, PC
.... 428

Chesterfield's (Earl) Trusts, Re (1883) 24 Ch D 643, 52 LJ Ch 958, 32 WR 361,
[1881–5] All ER Rep 737, 49 LT 261 .... 1122, 1127

Chesterfield's (Lord) Settled Estates, Re [1911] 1 Ch 237, 80 LJ Ch 186, 103 LT 823
.... 932

Cheung v Worldcup Investments Inc (2008) 11 ITELR 449
.... 1060

Chevaux v Aislabie (1842) 13 Sim 71 427–428

Cheyney's (Lord) Case (1591) 5 Co Rep 68a 45, 207, 218

Chia Khwee Eng v Chia Poh Choon [1923] AC 424, 92 LJPC 70, 128 LT 556, PC
.... 445

Chichester v Quatrefages [1895] P 186, 64 LJP 79, 11 R 605, 43 WR 667, 72 LT 475, 11
TLR 328, P, D and Admlty 97

Chichester Diocesan Fund and Board of Finance Inc v Simpson [1944] AC 341, [1944]
2 All ER 60, 113 LJ Ch 225, 88 Sol Jo 246, 171 LT 141, 60 TLR 492, HL
.... 11, 263, 266

Chief Edward Iguda Aleyideino's Estate, Re, Aleyideino v Aleyideino [2003] JRC 018, 2013
JLR Note 7, 6 ITELR 584, Royal Ct Jer 95

Chilcot v Bromley (1806) 12 Ves 114 366

Chilcott's Goods, Re [1897] P 223, 66 LJP 108, 46 WR 32, 77 LT 372, 13 TLR 378, P, D
and Admlty 95, 98, 111–112

Child v Elsworth (1852) 2 De GM & G 679 .... 200, 241

Child v Giblett (1834) 3 My & K 71, 3 LJ Ch 124 450

Childe, Re, Childe-Pemberton v Childe [1883] WN 48 384

PARA

Childs v Monins (1821) 2 Brod & Bing 460, 5 Moore CP 282
.... 1240

Chillingworth v Chambers [1896] 1 Ch 685, 65 LJ Ch 343, 44 WR 388, 40 Sol Jo 294, 74
LT 34, 12 TLR 217, CA 1250

Chinery, Re, Chinery v Hill (1888) 39 Ch D 614, 57 LJ Ch 804, 59 LT 303
.... 322–323

Chinn v Hanrieder 2009 BCSC 635, 11 ITELR 1009, BC SC
.... 221

Chinnery's Estate, Re (1877) 1 LR Ir 296 454

Chipchase v Simpson (1849) 16 Sim 485, 18 LJ Ch 145, 13 Jur 90
.... 320

Chittenden, Re, Chittenden v Doe [1970] 3 All ER 562, [1970] 1 WLR 1618, 114 Sol Jo
954 598

Chittock v Stevens [2000] WTLR 643, [2000] 16 LS Gaz R 42, 144 Sol Jo LB 166
.... 598, 741

Chitty v Chitty (1797) 3 Ves 545 445

Choa Eng Wan v Choa Giang Tee [1923] AC 469, 92 LJPC 145, 129 LT 226, PC
.... 199

Choat v Yeats (1819) 1 Jac & W 102 1012

Cholmeley v Paxton (1825) 3 Bing 207, 4 LJOSCP 41, 10 Moore CP 246; affd sub
nom Cockerell v Cholmeley (1830) 10 B & C 564, 1 Cl & F 60
.... 1031

Cholmondeley v Meyrick (1758) 1 Eden 77, 3 Bro CC 254n
.... 452

Cholmondeley (Marquis) v Lord Clinton (1821) 2 Jac & W 189n, 4 Bli 1, HL
.... 27, 340, 1144

Chorley v Loveband (1863) 33 Beav 189, 12 WR 187, 9 LT 596
.... 246

Christian v Taylor [1926] AC 773, 96 LJPC 6, 136 LT 168, 42 TLR 699, PC
.... 450

Christian's Goods, Re (1849) 2 Rob Eccl 110, 7 Notes of Cases 265
.... 74

Christie, Re, Christie v Keeble [1979] Ch 168, [1979] 1 All ER 546, [1979] 2 WLR 105,
122 Sol Jo 663 .... 570, 580, 591

Christmas and Christmas v Whinyates (1863) 27 JP 327, 32 LJPM & A 73, 9 Jur NS 283,
1 New Rep 336, 3 Sw & Tr 81, 11 WR 371, 7 LT 801 .... 85, 101, 105–106

Christophers v White (1847) 10 Beav 523, 76 RR 191 653

Christopherson v Naylor (1816) 1 Mer 320 .... 247, 305, 322

Chunilal Parvatishankar v Bai Samrath (1914) 30 TLR 407, PC
.... 441, 461

Church v Mundy (1808) 15 Ves 396 .... 241, 284

Church Property Trustees v Public Trustee (1907) 27 NZLR 354
.... 205

Churchill, Re, Hiscock v Lodder [1909] 2 Ch 431, 79 LJ Ch 10, 53 Sol Jo 697, 101 LT
380 1077

Churchill, Re, Taylor v Manchester University [1917] 1 Ch 206, 86 LJ Ch 209, 61 Sol Jo
131, 115 LT 769 109

Churchill v Dibden (1754) Keny Ch 68, 9 Sim 447n 289

Churchill v Roach [2004] 3 FCR 744, [2004] 2 FLR 989, [2003] All ER (D) 348 (Apr)
.... 567, 570, 591

Circuitt v Perry (1856) 23 Beav 275, 2 Jur NS 1157, 5 WR 15, 28 LTOS 115
.... 1113

Clache's Case (1572) 3 Dyer 330b 474

Clack v Carlon (1861) 30 LJ Ch 639, 7 Jur NS 441, 9 WR 568, sub nom Clark v Carlon 4
LT 361 653

Clack v Holland (1854) 19 Beav 262, 24 LJ Ch 13, 18 Jur 1007, 105 RR 134, 2 WR 402,
24 LTOS 49 959

Clanchy's Will Trusts, Re, Lynch v Edwards [1970] 2 All ER 489, CA
.... 313

Clancy v Clancy [2003] EWHC 1885 (Ch), [2003] 37 LS Gaz R 32, [2003] All ER (D) 536
(Jul) 48, 50

Clapham, Re, Barraclough v Mell [2005] EWHC 3387 (Ch), [2006] WTLR 203
.... 1097

Clare v Clare (1882) 21 Ch D 865, 51 LJ Ch 553, 30 WR 789, 46 LT 851
.... 1201

Claridge's Goods, Re (1879) 43 JP 161, 39 LT 612, P, D and Admlty
.... 68–69

PARA

Clark, Re (1932) 101 LJP 27, 76 Sol Jo 461, 147 LT 240, 48 TLR 544, P, D and Admlty
.... 739

Clark, Re, Clark v Clark [1926] Ch 833, 95 LJ Ch 325, [1926] B & CR 77, [1925] All ER
Rep 219, 70 Sol Jo 344, 135 LT 666 463

Clark, Re, Clark v Clark (1910) 55 Sol Jo 64 1283

Clark, Re, Clark v Randall (1885) 31 Ch D 72, 55 LJ Ch 89, 34 WR 70, 53 LT 591, 2
TLR 53 .... 41, 182

Clark, Re, Cross v Hillis [1924] WN 75, 59 L Jo 150 297

Clark, Re, Cumberland v Clark (1869) 4 Ch App 412, 17 WR 524
.... 1177

Clark, Re, McKecknie v Clark [1904] 1 Ch 294, 73 LJ Ch 188, 52 WR 212, 48 Sol Jo
130, 89 LT 736, 20 TLR 101 285

Clark v Bates (1848) 2 De G & Sm 203, 12 Jur 597, 11 LTOS 123
.... 1301

Clark v Browne (1854) 18 Jur 903, 2 Sm & G 524, 2 WR 665, 24 LTOS 3
.... 158

Clark v Carlon. See Clack v Carlon
Clark v Clark (1884) 9 App Cas 733, 53 LJPC 99, 51 LT 750, PC
.... 1030

Clark v Henry (1871) 6 Ch App 588, 40 LJ Ch 377, 19 WR 706, CA
.... 450

Clark v Hooper (1834) 10 Bing 480, 3 LJCP 159, 4 Moo & S 353
.... 646

Clark v Hougham (1823) 2 B & C 149, 1 LJOSKB 249, 3 Dow & Ry KB 322
.... 1288

Clark v London General Omnibus Co Ltd [1906] 2 KB 648, 75 LJKB 907, 50 Sol Jo 631,
95 LT 435, 22 TLR 691, CA 1280

Clark v Phillips (1854) 2 WR 331 627
Clark v Ross (1773) 2 Dick 529, 1 Bro CC 120n 438
Clark v Sewell (1744) 3 Atk 96 1081

Clark (WG) (Properties) Ltd v Dupre Properties Ltd [1992] Ch 297, [1992] 1 All ER 596,
[1991] 3 WLR 579, 63 P & CR 343, 23 HLR 544, [1991] 2 EGLR 59, [1991] 42 EG
125 926

Clark's Estate, Re (1864) 3 De GJ & Sm 111, 13 WR 115
.... 315

Clark's Goods, Re (1839) 2 Curt 239 64
Clark's Trust, Re (1875) 1 Ch D 497, 45 LJ Ch 194, 24 WR 233
.... 36

Clark's Trusts, Re (1863) 32 LJ Ch 525, 2 New Rep 386, 11 WR 871, 8 LT 571
.... 194, 474–475

Clark's Trusts, Re (1870) LR 9 Eq 378, 18 WR 446, 22 LT 151
.... 444

Clarke, Re [1991] Fam Law 364 577

Clarke, Re, Bracey v Royal National Lifeboat Institution [1923] 2 Ch 407, 92 LJ Ch 629,
[1923] All ER Rep 607, 67 Sol Jo 680, 129 LT 310, 39 TLR 433
.... 11

Clarke, Re, Clarke v Clarke [1901] 2 Ch 110, 70 LJ Ch 631, 49 WR 628, 45 Sol Jo 484,
84 LT 811, 17 TLR 479 36

Clarke, Re, Clarke v Roberts [1968] 1 All ER 451, [1968] 1 WLR 415, 112 Sol Jo 97
.... 577

Clarke, Re, Clarke v St Mary's Convalescent Home (1907) 97 LT 707
.... 1017

Clarke, Re, Sheldon v Redrup [1942] Ch 434, [1942] 2 All ER 294, 111 LJ Ch 261, 86 Sol
Jo 282, 167 LT 220, 58 TLR 366 182

Clarke v Berkeley (1716) 2 Vern 720, sub nom Clerke v Berkeley 8 Vin Abr 154
.... 135

Clarke v Bickers (1845) 14 Sim 639, 9 Jur 678 1232
Clarke v Blake (1788) 2 Bro CC 319; on appeal (1795) 2 Ves 673
.... 362

Clarke v Brothwood [2006] EWHC 2939 (Ch), [2006] All ER (D) 207 (Nov)
.... 187

Clarke v Clarke (1836) 8 Sim 59, 5 LJ Ch 286 308–309
Clarke v Clarke (1868) IR 2 CL 395 28
Clarke v Clarke (1879) 5 LR Ir 47 .... 74, 716, 895
Clarke v Clemmans (1866) 36 LJ Ch 171, 15 WR 250 .... 160, 173
Clarke v Colls (1861) 9 HL Cas 601 .... 246, 248

PARA

Clarke v Earl of Ormonde (1821) Jac 108, [1814–23] All ER Rep 329
.... 1060

Clarke v Leare and Scarwell (1791) 1 Phillim 119 899

Clarke v Lubbock (1842) 1 Y & C Ch Cas 492, 6 Jur 548
.... 444, 449

Clarke v Parker (1812) 19 Ves 1, 34 ER 419, [1803–13] All ER Rep 301
.... 135–136, 147, 149

Clarke v Scripps (1852) 2 Rob Eccl 563, 16 Jur 783, 20 LTOS 83
.... 93, 96, 101, 105

Clarke's Goods, Re [1896] P 287, 66 LJP 9, P, D and Admlty
.... 744

Clarke's Goods, Re (1858) 27 LJP & M 18, 4 Jur NS 234, 1 Sw & Tr 22, 6 WR 307,
30 LTOS 340 63

Clarke's Goods, Re (1867) 36 LJP & M 72, 15 WR 881, 16 LT 366
.... 721

Clarkington's Goods, Re (1861) 8 Jur NS 84, 2 Sw & Tr 380, 10 WR 124, 7 LT 218
.... 815

Clarkson, Re, Public Trustee v Clarkson [1915] 2 Ch 216, 84 LJ Ch 881, 59 Sol Jo 630,
113 LT 917 393

Clarkson v Clarkson (1862) 26 JP 631, 31 LJPM & A 143, 2 Sw & Tr 497, 10 WR 781, 6
LT 506 .... 93, 101, 109

Clarkson v Robinson [1900] 2 Ch 722, 69 LJ Ch 859, 48 WR 698, 83 LT 164
.... 652

Clavering v Ellison (1859) 7 HL Cas 707, 29 LJ Ch 761
.... 138, 140–141

Clay, Re, Spencer v Clay (1922) 153 LT Jo 473 173

Clay v Coles (1887) 57 LT 682 441

Clay v Pennington (1835) 7 Sim 370, 6 LJ Ch 183, sub nom Clayton v Pennington
Donnelly 165 .... 320, 337

Clayton, Re, Clayton v Howell [1966] 2 All ER 370, [1966] 1 WLR 969, 110 Sol Jo 445
.... 572, 574–575

Clayton v Gregson (1836) 5 Ad & El 302, 4 LJKB 161, 1 Har & W 159, 4 Nev & MKB
159, 6 Nev & MKB 694, 111 ER 1180, [1835–42] All ER Rep 626
.... 245

Clayton v Lord Nugent (1844) 13 LJ Ex 363, 13 M & W 200
.... 202

Clayton v Lowe (1822) 5 B & Ald 636 450

Clayton v Pennington Donnelly. See Clay v Pennington

Clayton v Ramsden [1943] AC 320, [1943] 1 All ER 16, 112 LJ Ch 22, 86 Sol Jo 384, 168
LT 113, 59 TLR 75, HL 138, 140

Clayton v Roe. See Roe d Wren v Clayton

Cleare and Forster v Cleare (1869) LR 1 P & D 655, 38 LJP & M 81, 17 WR 687, 20 LT
497 .... 11, 55, 874, 899

Cleaver, Re, Cleaver v Insley [1981] 2 All ER 1018, [1981] 1 WLR 939, 125 Sol Jo 445
.... 23, 588

Cleaver v Mutual Reserve Fund Life Association [1892] 1 QB 147, 56 JP 180, 61 LJQB
128, 40 WR 230, [1891–4] All ER Rep 335, 36 Sol Jo 106, 66 LT 220, 8 TLR 139,
CA 39

Cleaver v Spurling (1729) Mos 179, 2 P Wms 528 190

Cleaver's Estate, Re [1905] P 319, 74 LJP 164, 94 LT 99, P, D and Admlty
.... 809

Clegg v Clegg (1831) 2 Russ & M 570 22

Clegg v Rowland (1866) LR 3 Eq 368, 36 LJ Ch 137, 15 WR 251, 15 LT 385
.... 965, 1106, 1149

Clegg's Estate, Re, ex p Evans (1862) 15 Jur 27, 14 I Ch R 70
.... 442

Clements, Re [2007] WTLR 1717, SC NS 156

Clements, Re, Clements v Pearsall [1894] 1 Ch 665, 63 LJ Ch 326, 42 WR 374, 38 Sol Jo
272, 70 LT 682 1083

Clements v Paske (1784) 2 Cl & Fin 230n, 3 Doug KB 384
.... 333

Clements v Scudamore (1703) 2 Ld Raym 1024, 6 Mod Rep 120, 1 P Wms 63, 1 Salk 243,
Holt KB 124 .... 563, 564

Clements' Goods, Re [1892] P 254, 61 LJP 130, 67 LT 356, P, D and Admlty
.... 100

PARA

Clementson v Gandy (1836) 1 Keen 309, Donnelly 85, 5 LJ Ch 260
.... 193, 207
Clemow, Re, Yeo v Clemow [1900] 2 Ch 182, 69 LJ Ch 522, 48 WR 541, 44 Sol Jo 428,
82 LT 550 1013–1014
Cleoburey v Beckett (1851) 14 Beav 583 93
Clergy Society, Re (1856) 2 K & J 615, 4 WR 664 217
Clergymen's Sons Corpn v Swainson (1748) 1 Ves Sen 75
.... 1298
Clerke, Re, Clowes v Clerke [1915] 2 Ch 301, 84 LJ Ch 807, 59 Sol Jo 667, 113 LT 1105
.... 334, 342, 391, 455
Clerke v Berkeley. See Clarke v Berkeley
Clery v Barry (1887) 21 LR Ir 152 .... 68, 894–895
Cleveland's (Duke) Estate, Re, Hay v Wolmer [1895] 2 Ch 542, 65 LJ Ch 29, 13 R 715, 73
LT 313 1127
Cleveland's (Duke) Settled Estates, Re [1893] 3 Ch 244, 37 Sol Jo 630, 69 LT 735, 9 TLR
573, sub nom Re Cleveland (Duke), Barnard v Wolmer 62 LJ Ch 955, CA
.... 225
Cleverly v Brett (1772) 5 Term Rep 8n 1300
Clibborn v Clibborn (1857) 2 Ir Jur 386 1113
Cliff's Trusts, Re [1892] 2 Ch 229, 61 LJ Ch 397, 40 WR 439, 36 Sol Jo 398, 66 LT 483
.... 200, 203, 239, 672
Clifford, Re, Mallam v McFie [1912] 1 Ch 29, 81 LJ Ch 220, 56 Sol Jo 91, 106 LT 14, 28
TLR 57, [1911–13] All ER Rep Ext 1284 .... 116, 127, 156, 266, 282
Clifford v Beaumont (1828) 4 Russ 325 148
Clifford v Koe (1880) 5 App Cas 447, 28 WR 633, 43 LT 322, HL
.... 212, 249, 389
Clifford v Tanner [1987] CLY 3881 586
Clifford's Settlement Trusts, Re, Heaton v Westwater [1981] Ch 63, [1980] 1 All ER 1013,
[1980] 2 WLR 749, 124 Sol Jo 362 .... 302, 307, 309
Clifton v Crawford (1900) 27 AR 315 410
Clifton v Goodbun (1868) LR 6 Eq 278 352
Clifton's Estate, Re [1931] P 222, 100 LJP 121, 146 LT 14, 47 TLR 618, P, D and Admlty
.... 752, 807, 828
Clive v Clive (1854) Kay 600, 23 LJ Ch 981, 2 Eq Rep 913, 24 LTOS 33
.... 379, 1011
Cloberry v Lampen (1677) 2 Eq Cas Abr 539, 1 Eq Cas Abr 294, Freem Ch 24, 2 Vent
342 430
Clogstoun v Walcott (1848) 12 Jur 422, 11 LTOS 185, 5 Notes of Cases 623
.... 100, 712
Clook, Re (1890) 15 PD 132, 63 LT 536, CA 705
Clore, Re [1982] Fam 113, [1982] 2 WLR 314, 12 Fam Law 85, 126 Sol Jo 85; affd
[1982] Ch 456, [1982] 3 All ER 419, [1982] 3 WLR 228, [1982] STC 625, 126 Sol Jo
497, CA 690, 759, 815
Clough v Bond (1838) 3 My & Cr 490, 8 LJ Ch 51, 2 Jur 958, 45 RR 314, 40 ER 1159
.... 1253
Clough v Clough (1834) 3 My & K 296 156
Clough v Wynne (1817) 2 Madd 188 375
Clough-Taylor, Re, Coutts & Co v Banks [2003] WTLR 15
.... 1060
Clout and Frewer's Contract, Re [1924] 2 Ch 230, 93 LJ Ch 624, [1924] All ER Rep 798,
68 Sol Jo 738, 132 LT 483 151
Clowes, Re [1893] 1 Ch 214, 2 R 115, 41 WR 69, 37 Sol Jo 25, 68 LT 395,
[1891–4] All ER Rep Ext 1693, CA 156
Clowes v Hilliard (1876) 4 Ch D 413, 46 LJ Ch 271, 25 WR 224
.... 313, 1174
Clulow's Trust, Re (1859) 1 John & H 639, 28 LJ Ch 696, 5 Jur NS 1002, 7 WR 594,
33 LTOS 359 184
Clunies-Ross, Re, Stubbings v Clunies-Ross (1912) 56 Sol Jo 252, 106 LT 96
.... 164
Clutterbuck v Edwards (1832) 2 Russ & M 577 428
Coard v Holderness (1855) 20 Beav 147, 24 LJ Ch 388, 1 Jur NS 316, 3 WR 311,
25 LTOS 27 .... 228, 284
Coates, Re, Ramsden v Coates [1955] Ch 495, [1955] 1 All ER 26, [1954] 3 WLR 959, 98
Sol Jo 871 348
Coates v Coates (1864) 33 Beav 249, 33 LJ Ch 448, 10 Jur NS 532, 3 New Rep 355, 12
WR 634, 9 LT 795 1067

                                                                                        PARA
Coates v Hart (1863) 32 Beav 349, 55 ER 137; varied (1863) 3 De GJ & Sm 504
.... 254, 443, 475
Coates v Stevens (1834) 1 Y & C Ex 66, 160 ER 28 29
Coates Goods, Re (1898) 78 LT 820, P, D and Admlty 628
Cobban's Executors v Cobban 1915 SC 82, Ct of Sess 332
Cobbold, Re, Cobbold v Lawton [1903] 2 Ch 299, [1915] 1 Ch 847n, 72 LJ Ch 588, 88
    LT 745, [1900–3] All ER Rep Ext 1089, CA 441
Cochran v Graham (1811) 19 Ves 63 22
Cochrane v Wiltshire (1847) 16 LJ Ch 366, 11 Jur 426, sub nom Cockrane v
    Wiltshire 9 LTOS 310 429
Cock v Cock (1873) 21 WR 807, 28 LT 627 469
Cock v Cooke (1866) LR 1 P & D 241, 36 LJP & M 5, 15 WR 89, 15 LT 296,
    [1861–73] All ER Rep Ext 2002 .... 8, 54, 708
Cockayne v Harrison (1872) LR 13 Eq 432, 41 LJ Ch 509, 20 WR 504, 26 LT 385
.... 122
Cockburn v Raphael (1852) 22 LJ Ch 299 239
Cockburn's Will Trusts, Re, Cockburn v Lewis [1957] Ch 438, [1957] 2 All ER 522,
    [1957] 3 WLR212, 101 Sol Jo 534 .... 1074, 1144, 1148–1150
Cockcroft, Re, Broadbent v Groves (1883) 24 Ch D 94, 52 LJ Ch 811, 32 WR 223, 49 LT
    497 .... 27, 996, 1006
Cocke's Goods, Re [1960] 2 All ER 289, [1960] 1 WLR 491, 104 Sol Jo 389, P, D and
    Admlty 54, 95, 108
Cockerell v Cholmeley. See Cholmeley v Paxton
Cockerill, Re, Mackaness v Percival [1929] 2 Ch 131, 98 LJ Ch 281, 141 LT 198
.... 142
Cockle v Treacy [1896] 2 IR 267 1291
Cockle's Will Trusts, Re [1967] Ch 690, [1967] 1 All ER 391, [1967] 2 WLR 637, 111 Sol
    Jo 37 .... 306, 309, 398
Cockrane v Wiltshire. See Cochrane v Wiltshire
Cockrill v Pitchforth (1845) 1 Coll 626, 9 Jur 223, 4 LTOS 352
.... 408
Cocks v Manners (1871) LR 12 Eq 574, 36 JP 244, 40 LJ Ch 640, 19 WR 1055, 24 LT
    869 36
Cockshott v Cockshott (1846) 15 LJ Ch 131, 2 Coll 432, 10 Jur 41, 6 LTOS 389
.... 468–469
Cockson v Drinkwater (1783) 3 Doug KB 239 1291
Coe v Bigg (1863) 1 New Rep 536 326
Coe's Trust, Re (1858) 4 K & J 199, 4 Jur NS 158, 32 LTOS 239
.... 141, 1047
Coghill, Re, Drury v Burgess [1948] 1 All ER 254 297
Coghill v Freelove (1690) 3 Mod Rep 325, 2 Vent 209 1222
Coghlan, Re, Briscoe v Broughton [1948] 2 All ER 68, CA
.... 884, 888
Cogswell v Armstrong (1855) 2 K & J 227, 1 Jur NS 1162
.... 298
Cohen, Re, Cohen v Cohen [1915] WN 361, 60 Sol Jo 239
.... 231
Cohen, Re, National Provincial Bank Ltd v Katz [1960] Ch 179, [1959] 3 All ER 740,
    [1959] 3 WLR 916, 103 Sol Jo 961 .... 997, 1004, 1009, 1088
Cohen v Mitchell (1890) 25 QBD 262, 59 LJQB 409, 7 Morr 207, 38 WR 551, 63 LT
    206, 6 TLR 326, [1886–90] All ER Rep Ext 1172, CA 1065, 1219
Cohen's Executors and LCC, Re [1902] 1 Ch 187, 71 LJ Ch 164, 50 WR 117, 86 LT 73
.... 616, 947
Cohen's Will Trusts, Re, Cullen v Westminster Bank Ltd [1936] 1 All ER 103
.... 231, 369
Cohn, Re, National Westminster Bank Ltd v Cohn [1974] 3 All ER 928, [1974] 1 WLR
    1378, 118 Sol Jo 662, CA 429
Coke v Bullock (1604) 1 Eq Cas Abr 410, Cro Jac 49 232
Colahan, Re, Molloy v Hara Hara Shrewbridge and Hara [1967] IR 29
.... 328
Colberg's Goods, Re (1841) 2 Curt 832, 1 Notes of Cases 90
.... 103
Colborne v Wright (1678) 2 Lev 239, sub nom Coleburne v Wight T Jo 119
.... 620
Colclough's Goods, Re [1902] 2 IR 499, 36 ILTR 39 850
Coldicott v Best [1881] WN 150 429

PARA

Cole, Re, Cole v Cole [1919] 1 Ch 218, 88 LJ Ch 82, 120 LT 374, 35 TLR 183
.... 366
Cole v Fitzgerald (1823) 1 Sim & St 189; on appeal (1827) 3 Russ 301
.... 296
Cole v Goble (1853) 13 CB 445, 22 LJCP 148, 17 Jur 808, 1 WR 309, 1 CLR 228,
21 LTOS 77 459
Cole v Moore (1607) Moore KB 806 27
Cole v Muddle (1852) 10 Hare 186, 22 LJ Ch 401, 16 Jur 853, 90 RR 332, 20 LTOS 107
.... 1071
Cole v Scott (1849) 19 LJ Ch 63, 1 H & Tw 477, 14 Jur 25, 1 Mac & G 518, 14 LTOS
325 282
Cole v Sewell (1843) 4 Dr & War 1; affd (1848) 2 HL Cas 186, 12 Jur 927
.... 316, 418
Coleburne v Wight. See Colborne v Wright
Coleby v Coleby (1866) LR 2 Eq 803, 12 Jur NS 496, 14 LT 697
.... 1007
Coleman, Re, Coleman v Coleman [1976] Ch 1, [1975] 1 All ER 675, [1975] 2 WLR 213,
119 Sol Jo 86 88
Coleman, Re, Henry v Strong (1888) 39 Ch D 443, 58 LJ Ch 226, 60 LT 127, CA
.... 431
Coleman, Re, Public Trustee v Coleman [1936] Ch 528, [1936] 2 All ER 225, 105 LJ Ch
244, 155 LT 402 182
Coleman and Jarrom, Re (1876) 4 Ch D 165, 46 LJ Ch 33, 25 WR 137, 35 LT 614
.... 174, 176, 305
Coleman's Goods, Re [1920] 2 IR 332 81
Coleman's Goods, Re (1861) 25 JP 503, 2 Sw & Tr 314, 5 LT 119, sub nom
Re Colman's Goods 30 LJPM & A 170 101
Coles v Coles and Brown (1866) LR 1 P & D 70, 35 LJP & M 40, 14 WR 290, 13 LT 608
.... 894
Coles v Witt (1856) 2 Jur NS 1226 384
Coles Goods, Re (1871) LR 2 P & D 362, 36 JP 120, 41 LJP & M 21, 20 WR 214, 25 LT
852 .... 8, 708
Coles' Goods, Re, Macnin v Coles (1863) 33 LJPM & A 175, 9 Jur NS 1080, 3 Sw & Tr
181, 9 LT 519 787
Coles' Will, Re (1869) LR 8 Eq 271, 22 LT 221 1133
Coley, Re, Gibson v Gibson [1901] 1 Ch 40, 70 LJ Ch 153, 49 WR 165, 45 Sol Jo 164, 83
LT 671 326
Coley, Re, Hollinshead v Coley [1903] 2 Ch 102, 72 LJ Ch 502, 51 WR 563, 47 Sol Jo
491, 88 LT 517, [1900–3] All ER Rep Ext 1094, CA 237, 346
Collens, Re, Royal Bank of Canada (London) Ltd v Krogh [1986] Ch 505, [1986] 1 All ER
611, [1986] 2 WLR 919, 130 Sol Jo 373, [1986] LS Gaz R 1901
.... 1137
Colles' Estate, Re [1918] 1 IR 1 450
Collet v Lawrence (1791) 1 Ves 268 248
Colleton v Garth (1833) 6 Sim 19, 2 LJ Ch 75 285
Collett v Collett (1866) 35 Beav 312, 12 Jur NS 180, 14 WR 446, 14 LT 94
.... 135, 143, 442
Collett's Goods, Re (1857) Dea & Sw 274, 3 Jur NS 72, 5 WR 251, 28 LTOS 276
.... 613
Colley's Goods, Re (1879) 3 LR Ir 243 111
Collier v Rivaz (1841) 2 Curt 855 12
Colling, Re (1886) 32 Ch D 333, 55 LJ Ch 486, 34 WR 464, 54 LT 809, CA
.... 1214
Colling, Re, Lawson v von Winckler [1972] 3 All ER 729, [1972] 1 WLR 1440, 116 Sol Jo
547 70
Collings, Re, Jones v Collings [1933] Ch 920, 102 LJ Ch 337, [1933] All ER Rep 745, 150
LT 19 293
Collingwood v Pace (1664) 1 Keb 699, 1 Lev 59, 1 Sid 193, O Bridg 410, 1 Vent 413, Ex
Ch 548
Collingwood v Stanhope (1869) LR 4 HL 43, 38 LJ Ch 421, 17 WR 537
.... 333
Collins, Re [1990] Fam 56, [1990] 2 All ER 47, [1990] 2 WLR 161, [1990] FCR 433,
[1990] 2 FLR 72, [1990] Fam Law 337, 134 Sol Jo 262
.... 567, 572, 591
Collins v Carey (1839) 2 Beav 128, 50 RR 124 653
Collins v Doyle (1826) 1 Russ 135 293

PARA

Collins v Elstone [1893] P 1, 62 LJP 26, 1 R 458, 41 WR 287, 67 LT 624, 9 TLR 16, P, D
  and Admlty 187, 906
Collins v Johnson (1835) 4 LJ Ch 226, 8 sim 356n 323
Collins v Lewis (1869) LR 8 Eq 708 1003
Collins v Macpherson (1827) 2 Sim 87 452
Collins v Metcalfe (1687) 1 Vern 462 430
Collins' Trust, Re [1877] WN 87 344
Collins' Will Trusts, Re, Donne v Hewetson [1971] 1 All ER 283, [1971] 1 WLR 37, 114
  Sol Jo 936 .... 127, 288, 488, 1014, 1060
Collinson v Lister (1855) 20 Beav 356, 24 LJ Ch 762, 1 Jur NS 835, [1843–60] All ER
  Rep 1053, 26 LTOS 9, CA in Ch; on appeal (1855) 7 De GM & G 634, 25 LJ Ch 38,
  2 Jur NS 75, 4 WR 133, 44 ER 247, [1843–60] All ER Rep 1053, 26 LTOS 132
  1035
Collison, Re, Collison v Barber (1879) 12 Ch D 834, 48 LJ Ch 720, 28 WR 391, 41 LT
  175 451
Collison v Curling (1842) 9 CL & Fin 88, 6 Jur 673, HL
  156
Collison v Girling (1838) 4 My & Cr 63 284
Collyer, Re, Collyer v Back (1907) 24 TLR 117 246
Colman's Goods, Re (1842) 3 Curt 118 71
Colpoys v Colpoys (1822) Jac 451 210
Colson's Trusts, Re (1853) Kay 133, 23 LJ Ch 155, 2 Eq Rep 257, 2 WR 111, 22 LTOS
  183 374
Colston v Morris (1821) Jac 257n, 6 Madd 89 .... 131, 146
Coltman v Gregory (1870) 40 LJ Ch 352, 19 WR 122, 23 LT 583
  277
Coltsmann v Coltsmann (1868) LR 3 HL 121, 16 WR 943
  .... 229, 376, 461
Colvin v Fraser (1829) 2 Hag Ecc 266 102
Colyer, Re, Millikin v Snelling (1886) 55 LT 344, 3 TLR 7
  .... 122, 409
Colyer v Finch (1856) 5 HL Cas 905, 26 LJ Ch 65, 3 Jur NS 25, 10 ER 1159,
  [1843–60] All ER Rep 1020, 28 LTOS 27, HL 1025
Colyer's Goods, Re (1889) 14 PD 48, 53 JP 134, 37 WR 272, 60 LT 368, P, D and Admlty
  .... 3, 708
Combe v Hughes (1872) LR 14 Eq 415, 41 LJ Ch 693, 20 WR 793, 27 LT 366
  390
Comber v Graham (1830) 1 Russ & M 450 .... 378, 382
Comber v Hill (1734) 7 Mod Rep 195, Ridg temp H 35, 2 Stra 699, Lee temp Hard 22,
  sub nom Cumber v Hill 2 Barn KB 433, Kel W 188 474
Comber's Case (1721) 1 P Wms 766 .... 633, 643
Comfort v Brown (1878) 10 Ch D 146, 48 LJ Ch 318, 27 WR 226
  385
Comiskey v Bowring-Hanbury [1905] AC 84, 74 LJ Ch 263, 53 WR 402, 92 LT 241, 21
  TLR 252, HL 225, 236, 253, 382
Commercial Bank Corpn of India and the East, Re, Fernandes' Exors' Case (1870) 5 Ch
  App 314, 39 LJ Ch 497, 18 WR 411, 22 LT 219 19
Commercial Railway Act, Re, ex p Harrison (1838) 3 Y & C Ex 275, 8 LJ Ex Eq 28, 2 Jur
  1038 385
Comport v Austen (1841) 12 Sim 218 412
Compton, Re, Vaughan v Smith [1914] 2 Ch 119, 83 LJ Ch 862, 58 Sol Jo 580, 111 LT
  245 .... 150, 1088
Compton v Bloxham (1845) 14 LJ Ch 380, 2 Coll 201, 9 Jur 935, 5 LTOS 368
  .... 200, 672, 1069
Conbay's Estate, Re [1916] 1 IR 51 454
Concha v Concha (1886) 11 App Cas 541, 56 LJ Ch 257, 35 WR 477, 55 LT 522, HL
  670
Concha v Murrieta (1889) 40 Ch D 543, 60 LT 798, CA; on appeal sub nom Concha
  v Concha [1892] AC 670, 66 LT 303, 8 TLR 460, HL 1238
Congreve v Congreve (1781) 1 Bro CC 530 305
Congreve v Palmer (1853) 16 Beav 435, 23 LJ Ch 54, 1 WR 156
  .... 322, 397
Conmy v Cawley [1910] 2 IR 465, Ir CA 251
Conn, Re, Conn v Burns [1898] 1 IR 337 .... 11, 263
Connell v Connell; Connell v Findlay [2008] UKPC 44, [2009] All ER (D) 123 (Jan)
  1220

PARA

Connell's Settlement, Re, Re Benett's Trusts, Fair v Connell [1915] 1 Ch 867, 84 LJ Ch
601, 113 LT 234 231
Connell's Trustees v Milngavie District Nursing Association 1953 SC 230, 1953 SLT
(Notes) 27, Ct of Sess 278
Connington's Will, Re (1860) 2 LT 535, sub nom Re Conington's Will 24 JP 419, 6 Jur NS
992, 8 WR 444 147
Connolly, Re, Walton v Connolly (1914) 110 LT 688, CA
.... 295
Connor, Re (1845) 8 I Eq R 401, 2 Jo & Lat 456 354
Conolly v Brophy (1920) 54 ILT 41 302
Conolly v Farrell (1846) 10 Beav 142 1104
Conquest v Conquest (1868) 16 WR 453 232
Conron v Conron (1858) 7 HL Cas 168 1110
Constable v Bull (1849) 3 De G & Sm 411, 18 LJ Ch 302, 22 LJ Ch 182, 13 Jur 619
.... 382
Constable v Constable (1879) 11 Ch D 681, 48 LJ Ch 621, 40 LT 516
.... 240, 1085
Constable v Tufnell (1833) 4 Hag Ecc 465 903
Constantine, Re, Willan v Constantine (1926) 70th Report of Inland Revenue
.... 1132
Constantine v Constantine (1801) 6 Ves 100 .... 232, 248
Conyngham, Re, Conyngham v Conyngham [1921] 1 Ch 491, 90 LJ Ch 364, 65 Sol Jo
342, 125 LT 300, 37 TLR 420, CA 182
Conyngham v Tripp [1925] 1 IR 27 390
Cooch v Walden (1877) 46 LJ Ch 639 .... 277, 279
Coode's Goods, Re (1867) LR 1 P & D 449, 36 LJP & M 129, 16 LT 756
.... 722
Coogan v Hayden (1879) 4 LR Ir 585 349
Cook, Re, Beck v Grant [1948] Ch 212, [1948] 1 All ER 231, [1948] LJR 902, 92 Sol Jo
125, 64 TLR 97 .... 288, 291
Cook v Bolton (1828) 5 Russ 282 1178
Cook v Collingridge (1823) Jac 607, 1 LJOS Ch 74, 37 ER 979, [1814–23] All ER Rep 7
.... 1030
Cook v Cook (1706) 2 Vern 545, 23 ER 952, [1558–1774] All ER Rep 568
.... 311, 330, 389–390, 395
Cook v Gerrard (1668) 2 Keb 206, 224, 1 Lev 212, 1 Saund 180
.... 284, 476
Cook v Gregson (1854) 2 Drew 286, 23 LJ Ch 734, 2 Eq Rep 1132, 2 WR 401, 23 LTOS
86 968
Cook v Hutchinson (1836) 1 Keen 42, 44 RR 11 197
Cook v IRC [2002] STC (SCD) 318, [2002] WTLR 1003
.... 151–152
Cook v Lambert (1863) 27 JP 376, 32 LJPM & A 93, 9 Jur NS 258, 3 Sw & Tr 46, 11
WR 401, 8 LT 211 67
Cook v Martyn (1737) 2 Atk 2 1300
Cook v Saxlova (18 October 1988, unreported) 220
Cook (executors of Watkins) v IRC Revenue [2002] STC (SCD) 318, SCD
.... 151
Cook's Estate, Re, Murison v Cook [1960] 1 All ER 689, [1960] 1 WLR 353, 104 Sol Jo
311, P, D and Admlty 63, 75
Cook's Goods, Re [1902] P 114, 71 LJP 49, 46 Sol Jo 318, 86 LT 537, P, D and Admlty
.... 613
Cooke, Re, Randall v Cooke [1916] 1 Ch 480, 85 LJ Ch 452, 60 Sol Jo 403, 114 LT 555
.... 405
Cooke v Bowen (1840) 4 Y & C Ex 244 .... 305, 396
Cooke v Cholmondeley (1849) 19 LJ Ch 81, 2 H & Tw 162, 14 Jur 117, 2 Mac & G 18,
14 LTOS 413 190
Cooke v Cholmondeley (1854) 3 Drew 1, 3 WR 1, 24 LTOS 68
.... 375
Cooke v Cholmondeley (1858) 4 Drew 326, 27 LJ Ch 826, 4 Jur NS 827, 6 WR 802,
32 LTOS 59 152
Cooke v Cooke (1864) 4 De GJ & Sm 704, 34 LJ Ch 459, 11 Jur NS 533, 13 WR 697, 12
LT 468 128
Cooke v Farrand (1816) 7 Taunt 122, 2 Marsh 421 127
Cooke v Henry [1932] IR 574 69
Cooke v Mirehouse (1864) 34 Beav 27 442
Cooke v Stationers' Co (1831) 3 My & K 262 184

PARA

Cooke v Turner (1846) 14 Sim 493, 17 LJ Ex 106, 15 M & W 727
.... 131, 190

Cooke v Wagster (1854) 23 LJ Ch 496, 2 Eq Rep 789, 18 Jur 849, 2 Sm & G 296, 2 WR 434, 23 LTOS 293 293

Cooke's Goods, Re (1847) 5 Notes of Cases 390 101

Cooke's Settlement, Re, Tarry v Cooke [1913] 2 Ch 661, 83 LJ Ch 76, 58 Sol Jo 67, 109 LT 705 1160

Cookson v Bingham (1853) 17 Beav 262, 1 WR 459, 21 LTOS 236; affd (1853) 3 De GM & G 668 395

Cookson v Hancock (1836) 2 My & Cr 606 409

Coombs v Coombs (1866) LR 1 P & D 288, 31 JP 118, 36 LJP & M 21, 15 WR 286, 15 LT 329 787

Coombs Goods, Re (1866) LR 1 P & D 302, 31 JP 9, 36 LJP & M 25, 15 LT 363
.... 65

Cooney v Nicholls (1881) 7 LR Ir 107, 115, Ir CA 298, 375, 409, 428

Coope v Cresswell (1867) 2 Ch App 112, 36 LJ Ch 114, 15 WR 242, 11 Sol Jo 953, 15 LT 427 .... 970, 977

Cooper, Re, Cooper v Vesey (1882) 20 Ch D 611, 51 LJ Ch 862, 30 WR 648, 47 LT 89, [1881–5] All ER Rep Ext 1643, CA 1271

Cooper, Re, Le Neve-Foster v National Provincial Bank Ltd [1939] Ch 811, [1939] 3 All ER 586, 108 LJ Ch 388, 83 Sol Jo 671, 161 LT 127, CA
.... 223

Cooper, Re, Le Neve-Foster v National Provincial Bank Ltd (1939) 160 LTR 453
.... 652

Cooper, Re, Townend v Townend (1917) 86 LJ Ch 507, [1917] HBR 186, 61 Sol Jo 444, 116 LT 760 182

Cooper v Blissett (1876) 1 Ch D 691, 45 LJ Ch 272, 2 Char Pr Cas 283, 24 WR 235
.... 1173

Cooper v Bockett (1843) 3 Curt 648; revsd (1846) 4 Moo PCC 419, 10 Jur 931, 4 Notes of Cases 685 .... 70, 83, 896

Cooper v Cooper [1936] 2 All ER 542, 80 Sol Jo 510, 52 TLR 590, CA
.... 705

Cooper v Cooper (1855) 1 K & J 658, 3 WR 470 450

Cooper v Cooper (1856) 6 I Ch R 217 115

Cooper v Cooper (1861) 29 Beav 229, 7 Jur NS 178, 9 WR 354, 3 LT 800
.... 429

Cooper v Cooper (1873) 8 Ch App 813, 43 LJ Ch 158, 21 WR 921, 29 LT 321
.... 404

Cooper v Cooper (1874) LR 7 HL 53, 44 LJ Ch 6, 22 WR 713, [1874–80] All ER Rep 307, 30 LT 409 .... 477, 487, 523, 537, 922, 1053

Cooper v Day (1817) 3 Mer 154 .... 409, 1130

Cooper v Forbes (1786) 2 Bro CC 63 362

Cooper v France (1850) 19 LJ Ch 313, 14 Jur 214 .... 539, 546

Cooper v Green (1825) 2 Add 454 696

Cooper v Jarman (1866) LR 3 Eq 98, 36 LJ Ch 85, 12 Jur NS 956, 15 WR 142
.... 1215

Cooper v Macdonald (1873) LR 16 Eq 258, 42 LJ Ch 533, 21 WR 833, 28 LT 693
.... 416

Cooper v Martin (1867) 3 Ch App 47, 16 WR 234, 17 LT 587
.... 2

Cooper v Pitcher (1846) 16 LJ Ch 24 .... 472, 1210

Cooper v Thornton (1790) 3 Bro CC 96; on appeal (1790) 3 Bro CC 186
.... 37, 370, 1073

Cooper v Woolfitt (1857) 2 H & N 122, 26 LJ Ex 310, 3 Jur NS 870, 5 WR 790, 29 LTOS 212 .... 291, 368, 930

Cooper's Estate, Re, Bendall v Cooper [1946] Ch 109, [1946] 1 All ER 28, 115 LJ Ch 47, 89 Sol Jo 591, 174 LT 79, 62 TLR 65 246

Cooper's Goods, Re [1899] P 193, 68 LJP 65, 80 LT 632, P, D and Admlty
.... 738

Cooper's Goods, Re (1855) Dea & Sw 9, 4 WR 182, 26 LTOS 138
.... 7

Cooper's Trusts, Re (1853) 4 De GM & G 757, 23 LJ Ch 25, 2 Eq Rep 65, 17 Jur 1087, 2 WR 601, 22 LTOS 162 184

Coote v Boyd (1789) 2 Bro CC 521 403

Coote v Coote (1789) 2 Bro CC 521 .... 194, 197

PARA

Coote v Whittington (1873) LR 16 Eq 534, 42 LJ Ch 846, 21 WR 837, 29 LT 206
.... 636

Cope, Re, Cope v Cope (1880) 16 Ch D 49, 50 LJ Ch 13, 29 WR 98, 43 LT 566
.... 796

Cope, Re, Cross v Cross [1908] 2 Ch 1, 77 LJ Ch 558, [1908–10] All ER Rep 154, 99 LT
374, CA 236, 242, 247, 322

Cope v Wilmot (1772) Amb 704, 1 Coll 396n 264, 371

Cope's Estate, Re [1954] 1 All ER 698, [1954] 1 WLR 608, 98 Sol Jo 253, P, D and
Admlty 848

Cope's Goods, Re (1850) 2 Rob Eccl 335 75

Cope's Goods, Re (1867) 36 LJP & M 83 680

Copland's Executors v Milne (1908) 45 SLR 314, 1908 SC 426, 15 SLT 733, Ct of Sess
.... 328

Coppard's Estate, Re, Howlett v Hodson (1887) 35 Ch D 350, 56 LJ Ch 606, 35 WR 473,
56 LT 359 .... 256, 308

Coppen v Dingle [1899] 1 Ch 726, 68 LJ Ch 337, 47 WR 279, 79 LT 693
.... 152, 1067

Coppin v Coppin (1725) 2 P Wms 291, Cas temp King 28, 24 ER 735,
[1558–1774] All ER Rep 290 .... 163, 1089, 1097

Coppin v Dillon (1832) 4 Hag Ecc 361 773

Corballis v Corballis (1882) 9 LR Ir 309 267

Corbett v Bond Pearce (a firm) [2006] EWHC 909 (Ch), [2006] All ER (D) 01 (May)
.... 1017

Corbett v IRC [1938] 1 KB 567, [1937] 4 All ER 700, 21 TC 449, 107 LJKB 276, 82 Sol
Jo 34, 158 LT 98, 54 TLR 279, CA 922

Corbett v Newey [1998] Ch 57, [1996] 2 All ER 914, [1996] 3 WLR 729, [1996]
09 LS Gaz R 29, [1996] NLJR 333, 140 Sol Jo LB 65, CA
.... 7–8, 54, 60–61, 708, 891

Corbett v Palmer (1735) 2 Eq Cas Abr 548 429

Corbett's Trusts, Re (1860) John 591, 29 LJ Ch 458, 6 Jur NS 339, 8 WR 257, 2 LT 147
.... 231, 316

Corbyn v French (1799) 4 Ves 418, 31 ER 213, [1775–1802] All ER Rep 444
.... 164, 321, 364

Corcoran, Re, Corcoran v O'Kane [1913] 1 IR 1 .... 367, 407

Cordeux v Trasler (1865) 34 LJPM & A 127, 11 Jur NS 587, 4 Sw & Tr 48
.... 773

Cordwell's Estate, Re, White v Cordwell (1875) LR 20 Eq 644, 44 LJ Ch 746, 23 WR 826
.... 1067

Core v Spencer (1796) 1 Add 374 863

Corelli, Re (1925) 69 Sol Jo 525 1123

Corlass, Re (1875) 1 Ch D 460, 45 LJ Ch 118, 24 WR 204, 33 LT 630
.... 334, 337, 362

Cormack v Copous (1853) 17 Beav 397 .... 237, 389, 456

Corner v Shew (1838) 6 Dowl 584, 7 LJ Ex 105, 1 Horn & H 65, 3 M & W 350
.... 1239

Cornwall (Duchy Solicitor) v Canning (1880) 5 PD 114, sub nom Re Canning's Goods 28
WR 278, 41 LT 737, P, D and Admlty 556

Corr v Corr (1873) IR 7 Eq 397 428

Corsellis, Re, Freeborn v Napper [1906] 2 Ch 316, 75 LJ Ch 607, 54 WR 536, 50 Sol Jo
499, 95 LT 583 .... 210, 352

Corsellis, Re, Lawton v Elwes (1887) 34 Ch D 675, 51 JP 597, 56 LJ Ch 294, 35 WR 309,
56 LT 411, 3 TLR 355, CA 653–655

Corser v Cartwright (1875) LR 7 HL 731, 45 LJ Ch 605, HL
.... 1025, 1028

Cort v Winder (1844) 1 Coll 320, 3 LTOS 280 452

Cory, Re, Cory v Morel [1955] 2 All ER 630, [1955] 1 WLR 725, 99 Sol Jo 435
.... 254, 468

Cory's Goods, Re (1901) 84 LT 270, P, D and Admlty 79

Cosby's Estate, Re [1922] 1 IR 120, CA 334

Cosens Case. See Newton v Barnardine

Cosgrove's Estate, Re, Willis v Goddard (1909) Times, 3 April
.... 293

Cosh's Goods, Re (1909) 53 Sol Jo 755, 25 TLR 785, P, D and Admlty
.... 787

Cosnahan's Goods, Re (1866) LR 1 P & D 183, 35 LJP & M 76, 14 WR 969, 14 LT 337
.... 720

PARA

Cossentine, Re, Philip v Wesleyan Methodist Local Preachers' Mutual Aid Association
  Trustees [1933] Ch 119, 102 LJ Ch 78, [1932] All ER Rep 785, 76 Sol Jo 512, 148 LT
  261 .... 332, 396
Cossey v Cossey (1900) 64 JP 89, 69 LJP 17, 82 LT 203, 16 TLR 133, P, D and Admlty
  107–108
Costabadie v Costabadie (1847) 6 Hare 410, 16 LJ Ch 259, 11 Jur 345, 9 LTOS 20
  370
Coster, Re, Beater & Co, ex p Coster's Executors. See Beater, Re, ex p Edmonds
Cotton v Cotton (1839) 2 Beav 67, 8 LJ Ch 349, 3 Jur 886
  364
Cotton v Cotton (1854) 23 LJ Ch 489, 2 WR 207 450
Cotton v Scarancke (1815) 1 Madd 45 343
Cottrell, Re, Buckland v Bedingfield [1910] 1 Ch 402, 79 LJ Ch 189, [1908–10] All ER
  Rep 70, 102 LT 157 1090
Cottrell v Cottrell (1872) LR 2 P & D 397, 36 JP 567, 41 LJP & M 57, 20 WR 590, 26
  LT 527 95
Couch v Stratton (1799) 4 Ves 391 491
Coulden, Re, Coulden v Coulden [1908] 1 Ch 320, 77 LJ Ch 209, 52 Sol Jo 172, 98 LT
  389 .... 321, 391–392, 397
Coulter's Case (1598) 5 Co Rep 30a, sub nom Ireland v Coulter Cro Eliz 630, sub
  nom Colter v Ireland Moore KB 527 1266
Coulthard's Goods, Re (1865) 11 Jur NS 184 100
Coulthurst v Carter (1852) 15 Beav 421, 21 LJ Ch 555, 16 Jur 532, 20 LTOS 20
  .... 247, 322, 324
Councell's Goods, Re (1871) LR 2 P & D 314, 36 JP 89, 41 LJP & M 16, 25 LT 763
  168
Counden v Clerke (1612) Hob 29, sub nom Coronder v Clerk 1 Brownl 129, sub
  nom Cownden v Clerk Moore KB 860, sub nom Cowndon's Case Jenk 294
  .... 340, 348
Court v Despallieres, Re Ikin [2009] EWHC 3340 (Ch), [2010] 2 All ER 451, [2010] Fam
  Law 251, 154 Sol Jo (no 1) 30, [2009] All ER (D) 167 (Dec)
  .... 91, 849, 891
Courtenay, Re, Pearce v Foxwell (1905) 74 LJ Ch 654 308
Courtenay v Williams (1846) 15 LJ Ch 204, [1843–60] All ER Rep 755, 6 LTOS 517
  1067
Courtier, Re, Coles v Courtier (1886) 34 Ch D 136, 51 JP 117, 56 LJ Ch 350, 35 WR 85,
  55 LT 574, CA 1228
Courtier, Re, Courtier v Coles (1886) 34 Ch D 136, 51 JP 117, 56 LJ Ch 350, 35 WR 85,
  55 LT 574, CA 1228
Courtoy v Vincent (1823) Turn & R 433 1131
Cousen's Will Trusts, Re, Wright v Killick [1937] Ch 381, [1937] 2 All ER 276, 106 LJ Ch
  261, 81 Sol Jo 317, 157 LT 32, 53 TLR 490 .... 27, 165, 176
Couser v Couser [1996] 3 All ER 256, [1996] 1 WLR 1301, [1996] 3 FCR 745, [1996] 2
  FLR 46, [1996] Fam Law 470, [1996] 12 LS Gaz R 29, [1996] NLJR 651, 140 Sol Jo
  LB 91 .... 62, 68–71
Cousins, Re, Alexander v Cross (1885) 30 Ch D 203, CA
  125
Cousins v Paddon (1835) 2 Cr M & R 547, 4 Dowl 488, 5 LJ Ex 49, 1 Gale 305, 5 Tyr
  535 1293
Cousins v Schroder (1830) 4 Sim 23 429
Couturier, Re, Couturier v Shea [1907] 1 Ch 470, 76 LJ Ch 296, 51 Sol Jo 342, 96 LT
  560, [1904–7] All ER Rep Ext 1191 .... 146, 428–429, 1062
Couwenbergh v Valkova [2008] EWHC 2451 (Ch), [2008] All ER (D) 264 (Oct)
  875
Covell's Goods, Re (1889) 15 PD 8, 59 LJP 7, 38 WR 79, 61 LT 620, [1886–90] All ER
  Rep Ext 1346, P, D and Admlty 850
Coventry, Re, Coventry v Coventry [1980] Ch 461, [1979] 2 All ER 408, [1979] 2 WLR
  853, 123 Sol Jo 406; affd [1980] Ch 461, [1979] 3 All ER 815, [1979] 3 WLR 802,
  123 Sol Jo 606, CA 568, 570, 572–574, 580
Coventry v Coventry (1865) 34 Beav 572, 2 Drew & Sm 470, 13 WR 985, 13 LT 83
  .... 306, 308–309
Coventry v Higgins (1844) 14 Sim 30, 8 Jur 182 .... 135, 430
Coventry v Williams (1844) 3 Curt 787, 8 Jur 699, 3 LTOS 452, 3 Notes of Cases 164
  .... 5, 54

                                                                              PARA
Coverdale v Eastwood (1872) LR 15 Eq 121, 37 JP 212, 42 LJ Ch 118, 21 WR 216, 27 LT
    646 21
Cowan and Johnson v Ball [1933] NI 173 .... 83, 455
Coward, Re, Coward v Larkman (1887) 57 LT 285, CA; affd sub nom Coward v Larkman
    (1888) 60 LT 1, [1886–90] All ER Rep 896, 4 TLR 759, HL
    .... 235, 368, 379
Coward v Gregory (1866) LR 2 CP 153, 36 LJCP 1, 12 Jur NS 1000, 15 WR 170, 15 LT
    279 1270
Cowell, Re, Temple v Temple (1920) 150 LT Jo 296 .... 992, 1109
Cowell v Sikes (1827) 2 Russ 191 1232
Cowen v Truefitt Ltd [1899] 2 Ch 309, 68 LJ Ch 563, 47 WR 661, 43 Sol Jo 622, 81 LT
    104, CA 269
Cowley, Re, Souch v Cowley (1885) 53 LT 494 .... 152, 407
Cowling, Re, Jinkin v Cowling [1924] P 113, 93 LJP 43, [1924] All ER Rep 469, 131 LT
    157, 40 TLR 358, P, D and Admlty 101
Cowling v Cowling (1859) 26 Beav 449, 33 LTOS 5 293
Cowman v Harrison (1852) 10 Hare 234, 22 LJ Ch 993, 17 Jur 313, 90 RR 334, 1 WR
    96, 21 LTOS 148 370
Cowper v Mantell (1856) 22 Beav 223, 2 Jur NS 745, 4 WR 500, 27 LTOS 130
    .... 114–115, 156, 184
Cowper v Mantell (No 2) (1856) 22 Beav 231, 2 Jur NS 745, 4 WR 500, 52 ER 1097,
    27 LTOS 130 373
Cowper v Scott (1731) 3 P Wms 119 387
Cox, Re, Public Trustee v Eve [1938] Ch 556, [1938] 1 All ER 661, 108 LJ Ch 67, 82 Sol
    Jo 233, 159 LT 13, 54 TLR 527 1093
Cox v Allingham (1822) Jac 514 670
Cox v Bockett (1865) 35 Beav 48 462–463
Cox v Cox [2006] EWHC 1077 (Ch), [2006] BCC 890, [2006] All ER (D) 256 (Apr)
    1279
Cox v Godsalve (1699) 6 East 604n 930
Cox v Parker (1856) 22 Beav 168, 25 LJ Ch 873, 2 Jur NS 842, 4 WR 453, 27 LTOS 179
    .... 440, 445, 555
Cox v Sutton (1856) 25 LJ Ch 845, 2 Jur NS 733, 28 LTOS 119
    374
Coxen, Re, McCallum v Coxen [1948] Ch 747, [1948] 2 All ER 492, [1948] LJR 1590, 92
    Sol Jo 442 .... 138–140, 996
Coxwell's Trusts, Re, Kinloch-Cooke v Public Trustee [1910] 1 Ch 63, 79 LJ Ch 62, 101
    LT 627 1131
Coyne v Coyne (1876) IR 10 Eq 496 157
Coyte, Re, Coyte v Coyte (1887) 56 LT 510, 3 TLR 352
    .... 258, 406
Cozens, Re, Miles v Wilson [1903] 1 Ch 138, 72 LJ Ch 39, 51 WR 220, 47 Sol Jo 50, 87
    LT 581 .... 328, 352
Cozens v Crout (1873) 42 LJ Ch 840, 21 WR 781 44
Cracklow v Norie (1838) 7 LJ Ch 278, 2 Jur 804 349
Cradock v Cradock (1858) 4 Jur NS 626, 6 WR 710, 32 LTOS 48
    .... 232, 400
Cradock v Piper (1850) 19 LJ Ch 107, 1 H & Tw 617, 14 Jur 97, 1 Mac & G 664, 84 RR
    223, 15 LTOS 61 654
Craig v Lamoureux [1920] AC 349, 89 LJPC 22, 122 LT 208, 36 TLR 26, PC
    56
Craik v Lamb (1844) 14 LJ Ch 84, 1 Coll 489, 9 Jur 6, 4 LTOS 152
    248
Crandon's Goods, Re (1901) 84 LT 330, 17 TLR 341, P, D and Admlty
    .... 716, 730
Crane, Re, Adams v Crane [1908] 1 Ch 379, 77 LJ Ch 212, [1904–7] All ER Rep 577, 98
    LT 314 1077
Cranfield, Re, Mosse v Cranfield [1895] 1 IR 80 270
Cranley v Dixon (1857) 23 Beav 512, 26 LJ Ch 529, 3 Jur NS 531, 29 LTOS 119
    468–469
Cranmer, ex p (1806) 12 Ves 445 48
Crannis' Estate, Re, Mansell v Crannis (1978) 122 Sol Jo 489
    .... 108, 713
Cranstoun's Will Trusts, Re, Gibbs v Home of Rest for Horses [1949] Ch 523, [1949]
    1 All ER 871, [1949] LJR 1066, 93 Sol Jo 251 154

PARA

Cranswick v Pearson (1862) 31 Beav 624, 9 Jur NS 397, 11 WR 229, 9 LT 215; affd
    (1863) 9 LT 275 .... 395, 470
Craster v Thomas [1909] 2 Ch 348, 78 LJ Ch 734, 101 LT 66, 25 TLR 659, CA
    858
Crause v Cooper (1859) 1 John & H 207 325
Craven, Re (1857) 23 Beav 333 342
Craven, Re, Crewdson v Craven (1908) 99 LT 390, 24 TLR 750; affd (1909) 100 LT 284,
    CA 43, 285, 298
Craven, Re, Watson v Craven [1914] 1 Ch 358, 83 LJ Ch 403, 58 Sol Jo 138, 109 LT 846
    .... 405, 1096, 1160
Craven v Brady (1867) LR 4 Eq 209; affd (1869) 4 Ch App 296, 38 LJ Ch 345, 17 WR
    505, 23 LT 57 .... 134, 181, 463
Craw's Trustees v Blacklock (1920) 57 SLR 20, 1920 SC 22, Ct of Sess
    1113
Crawford, Re (1982) 4 FLR 273 .... 572, 585, 591
Crawford v Forshaw [1891] 2 Ch 261, 60 LJ Ch 683, 39 WR 484, 65 LT 32,
    [1891–4] All ER Rep Ext 1895, CA 1052
Crawford v Trotter (1819) 4 Madd 361 .... 385, 390
Crawford's Trustees v Fleck (1910) 47 SLR 755, 1910 SC 998, Ct of Sess
    .... 243, 256
Crawford's Trusts, Re (1854) 2 Drew 230, 23 LJ Ch 625, 2 Eq Rep 553, 18 Jur 616, 2
    WR 341 .... 241–242, 364
Crawhall's Trust, Re (1856) 8 De GM & G 480, 2 Jur NS 892, 27 LTOS 278
    .... 318, 331, 410
Crawshay, Re, Crawshay v Crawshay (1890) 43 Ch D 615, 59 LJ Ch 395, 38 WR 600,
    [1886–90] All ER Rep 724, 62 LT 489 222
Crawshay, Re, Hore-Ruthven v Public Trustee [1948] Ch 123, [1948] 1 All ER 107,
    [1948] LJR 586, 92 Sol Jo 95, 64 TLR 67, CA 251
Crawshay's Goods, Re [1893] P 108, 62 LJP 91, 1 R 477, 41 WR 303, 68 LT 260, P, D
    and Admlty 763, 788
Creagh v Blood (1845) 8 I Eq R 434, 2 Jo & Lat 509 900
Creagh v Wilson (1706) 2 Vern 572 135
Creasor v Robinson (1851) 14 Beav 589, 21 LJ Ch 64, 15 Jur 1049, 18 LTOS 82
    636
Creed v Creed [1913] 1 IR 48 643
Creeth v Wilson (1882) 9 LR Ir 216, 223 412
Cremorne v Antrobus (1829) 5 Russ 312, 7 LJOS Ch 88
    296
Creror, Re (unreported) 902
Cresswell, Re (1881) 30 WR 244, 45 LT 468 .... 37, 1073
Cresswell v Cheslyn (1762) 2 Eden 123; affd sub nom Cheslyn v Cresswell (1763) 3 Bro
    Parl Cas 246 .... 173, 175
Cresswell v Cresswell (1868) LR 6 Eq 69, 32 JP 564, 37 LJ Ch 521, 16 WR 699, 18 LT
    392 .... 41, 403
Creswick v Gaskell (1853) 16 Beav 577 452
Crichton v Grierson (1828) 3 Bli NS 424, 3 W & S 329, HL
    .... 11, 349
Crichton's Settlement, Re, Sweetman v Batty (1912) 56 Sol Jo 398, 106 LT 588
    409
Crichton's Trust, Re (1855) 24 LTOS 267 1072
Crickett v Dolby (1795) 3 Ves 10 .... 426, 1077, 1081
Crigan v Baines (1834) 7 Sim 40 449
Cringan's Goods, Re (1828) 1 Hag Ecc 548 612
Crippen's Estate, Re [1911] P 108, 80 LJP 47, [1911–13] All ER Rep 207, 55 Sol Jo 273,
    104 LT 224, 27 TLR 258, P, D and Admlty 39, 756, 759, 897
Cripps v Trustee Solutions Ltd. See Trustee Solutions Ltd v Dubery
Cripps v Wolcott (1819) 4 Madd 11 318
Crispin's Will Trusts, Re, Arkwright v Thurley [1975] Ch 245, [1974] 3 All ER 772, [1974]
    3 WLR 657, 118 Sol Jo 739, CA 288, 296, 488
Critchell v Critchell (1863) 32 LJPM & A 108, 3 Sw & Tr 41, 11 WR 401, 8 LT 173
    909
Critchett v Taynton (1830) 8 LJOS Ch 143, 1 Russ & M 541
    331
Crocker, Re, Crocker v Crocker [1916] 1 Ch 25, 85 LJ Ch 179, 114 LT 61,
    [1914–15] All ER Rep Ext 1211 405

PARA

Crockett v Crockett (1848) 2 Ph 553, 17 LJ Ch 230, 12 Jur 234, 78 RR 183, 10 LTOS
409 .... 370, 390
Croft v Croft (1865) 29 JP 168, 34 LJPM & A 44, 11 Jur NS 183, 4 Sw & Tr 10, 13 WR
526, 11 LT 781 895
Croft v Lumley (1858) 22 JP 639, 6 HL Cas 672, 27 LJQB 321, 4 Jur NS 903, 6 WR 523,
10 ER 1459, [1843–60] All ER Rep 162, 31 LTOS 382, HL
.... 463
Crofton's Goods, Re (1897) 13 TLR 374, P, D and Admlty
.... 9
Crofts v Beamish [1905] 2 IR 349, CA 142, 191, 333
Crofts Goods, Re (1900) 17 TLR 16, P, D and Admlty 730
Croggan v Allen (1882) 22 Ch D 101, 31 WR 319, 47 LT 437
.... 1203
Croker v Marquess of Hertford (1844) 4 Moo PCC 339, 8 Jur 863, 3 Notes of Cases 150,
sub nom Re Marquis of Hertford's Will 3 LTOS 257 .... 242, 711
Croly v Croly (1825) Batt 1, 2 459
Cromek v Lumb (1839) 3 Y & C Ex 565 .... 316, 433
Crommelin v Crommelin (1796) 3 Ves 227 135
Crompton v Jarratt (1885) 30 Ch D 298, 54 LJ Ch 1109, 33 WR 913, 53 LT 603, CA
.... 291
Crompton and Evans' Union Bank v Burton [1895] 2 Ch 711, 64 LJ Ch 811, 13 R 792, 44
WR 60, 73 LT 181 1186
Crone v Odell (1811) 1 Ball & B 449; affd sub nom Odell v Crone (1815) 3 Dow 61, HL
.... 304–305, 311
Crook v Brooking (1688) 2 Vern 50, 106 223
Crook v Hill (1876) 3 Ch D 773, 41 JP 228, 46 LJ Ch 119, 24 WR 876
.... 354
Crook v Whitley (1857) 7 De GM & G 490, 26 LJ Ch 350, 3 Jur NS 703, 5 WR 383
.... 214, 328
Crooke v De Vandes (1803) 9 Ves 197 .... 385, 393, 461
Croome v Croome (1889) 61 LT 814, [1886–90] All ER Rep Ext 1393, HL
.... 370
Cropton v Davies (1869) LR 4 CP 159, 38 LJCP 159, 17 WR 444, 20 LT 30
.... 471
Crosbie v Macdoual (1799) 4 Ves 610 .... 112, 114
Crosby v Noton (1867) 31 JP 407, 36 LJP & M 55, 15 WR 775, 16 LT 153
.... 754
Croskery v Ritchie [1901] 1 IR 437 145
Crosland, Re, Craig v Midgley (1886) 54 LT 238 453
Crosley v Clare (1761) Amb 397, 3 Swan 320n 339
Cross v Cross (1864) 28 JP 183, 33 LJPM & A 49, 10 Jur NS 183, 3 Sw & Tr 292, 12
WR 694, 10 LT 70 909
Cross v Cross (1877) 1 LR Ir 389 2
Cross v Kennington (1848) 11 Beav 89 1205
Cross v Sprigg (1849) 6 Hare 552, 18 LJ Ch 204, 13 Jur 785, 13 LTOS 505; affd (1850)
19 LJ Ch 528, 2 H & Tw 233, 14 Jur 634, (1850) 2 Mac & G 113, 13 LTOS 322
.... 217
Cross v Wilks (1866) 35 Beav 562 288
Crosse, Re, Crosse v Crosse [1933] WN 36, 77 Sol Jo 116
.... 317
Crosse v Eldridge (1918) 53 L Jo 52 417
Crosse v Smith (1806) 7 East 246, 3 Smith KB 203 1247
Crosse's Will, Re (1863) 32 LJ Ch 344, 9 Jur NS 429, 1 New Rep 419, 11 WR 396, 8 LT
299 260
Crosskill v Bower (1863) 32 Beav 86, 32 LJ Ch 540, 9 Jur NS 267, 1 New Rep 379, 11
WR 411, 8 LT 135 656–657
Crosthwaite v Dean [1874–80] All ER Rep 714, 40 LT 837
.... 393
Crother's Trusts, Re [1915] 1 IR 53 .... 181, 306, 463
Crother's Trusts (No 2), Re [1917] 1 IR 356 .... 426, 429
Crowder v Clowes (1794) 2 Ves 449 409
Crowder v Stone (1829) 3 Russ 217, 7 LJOS Ch 93 .... 319, 410, 452, 458
Crowe v Appleby (Inspector of Taxes) [1975] 3 All ER 529, [1975] 1 WLR 1539, [1975]
STC 502, 51 TC 457, 54 ATC 177, [1975] TR 151, 119 Sol Jo 776, L(TC) 2561; affd
[1976] 2 All ER 914, [1976] 1 WLR 885, [1976] STC 301, 51 TC 457, [1976] TR
105, L(TC) 2584, CA 1053

                                                                            PARA
Crowhurst Park, Re, Sims-Hilditch v Simmons [1974] 1 All ER 991, [1974] 1 WLR 583,
    28 P & CR 14, 118 Sol Jo 331 .... 608, 634–635, 659
Crowther, Re, Midgley v Crowther [1895] 2 Ch 56, 64 LJ Ch 537, 13 R 496, 43 WR 571,
    [1895–9] All ER Rep 1208, 72 LT 762, 11 TLR 380 1035
Croxon, Re, Croxon v Ferrers [1904] 1 Ch 252, 73 LJ Ch 170, 52 WR 343, 48 Sol Jo 191,
    89 LT 733 .... 143, 248
Crozier v Crozier (1873) LR 15 Eq 282, 21 WR 398 382
Cruikshank v Duffin (1872) LR 13 Eq 555, 36 JP 708, 41 LJ Ch 317, 20 WR 354, 26 LT
    121 1023
Crump d Woolley v Norwood (1815) 7 Taunt 362, 2 Marsh 161
    563
Crump's Goods, Re (1821) 3 Phillim 497 807
Crumpe, Re, Orpen v Moriarty [1912] 1 IR 485 145
Crumpe v Crumpe [1900] AC 127, 69 LJPC 7, 82 LT 130, HL
    .... 376, 382, 384, 467
Crunden and Meux's Contract, Re [1909] 1 Ch 690, 78 LJ Ch 396, 100 LT 472
    951
Cruse, Re, Gass v Ingham [1930] WN 206 .... 218, 295, 994
Cruse v Howell (1858) 4 Drew 215, 6 WR 271 175
Crutchley, Re, Kidson v Marsden [1912] 2 Ch 335, 81 LJ Ch 644, 107 LT 194
    442
Cruwys v Colman (1804) 9 Ves 319 348
Cuffe, Re, Fooks v Cuffe [1908] 2 Ch 500, 77 LJ Ch 776, 52 Sol Jo 661, 99 LT 267, 24
    TLR 781 479
Cull's Trusts, Re (1875) LR 20 Eq 561, 44 LJ Ch 664, 23 WR 850, 32 LT 853
    1047
Cullen v A-G for Ireland (1866) LR 1 HL 190, 12 Jur NS 531, 14 WR 869, 14 LT 644
    221
Cullen's Estate, Re [1907] 1 IR 73 385
Cullimore's Trust, Re (1891) 27 LR Ir 18 348
Cullum, Re, Mercer v Flood [1924] 1 Ch 540, 93 LJ Ch 281, 68 Sol Jo 369, 130 LT 601
    352
Culsha v Cheese (1849) 7 Hare 236 .... 160, 252
Culverhouse, Re, Cook v Culverhouse [1896] 2 Ch 251, 65 LJ Ch 484, 45 WR 10, 40 Sol
    Jo 374, 74 LT 347 1146
Cumber v Hill. See Comber v Hill
Cuming, Re (1869) 5 Ch App 72, 18 WR 157, 21 LT 739
    1214
Cummins v Cummins (1845) 72 RR 29, 8 I Eq R 723, 3 Jo & Lat 64
    .... 673, 798
Cunliffe v Fielden [2005] EWCA Civ 1508, [2006] Ch 361, [2006] 2 All ER 115, [2006] 2
    WLR 481, 8 ITELR 855, sub nom Fielden v Cunliffe [2005] 3 FCR 593, [2006] 1 FLR
    745, [2006] Fam Law 263, 150 Sol Jo LB 96, [2005] All ER (D) 80 (Dec)
    577
Cunliffe-Owen, Re, Mountain v Comber [1951] Ch 964, [1951] 2 All ER 220, 95 Sol Jo
    285, [1951] 1 TLR 1073, [1951] 2 TLR 231 1130
Cunliffe-Owen, Re, Mountain v IRC [1953] Ch 545, [1953] 2 All ER 196, [1953] 3 WLR
    120, 32 ATC 215, 46 R & IT 399, [1953] TR 209, 97 Sol Jo 436, CA
    922
Cunningham v Foot (1878) 3 App Cas 974, 26 WR 858, 38 LT 889, HL
    407
Cunningham v Murray (1847) 1 De G & Sm 366, 16 LJ Ch 484, 11 Jur 814, sub nom
    Anon 10 LTOS 34; revsd sub nom Cunningham v Murray (1848) 17 LJ Ch 407
    .... 390, 396
Cunningham's Goods, Re (1860) Sea & Sm 132, 29 LJPM & A 71, 4 Sw & Tr 194
    .... 74–75, 84
Curle's Trustees v Millar. See Lamont (or Chearnley) v Millar
Curling's Goods, Re [1928] IR 521 288
Curran v Corbet [1897] 1 IR 343 135
Currie, Re, Bjorkman v Lord Kimberley (1888) 57 LJ Ch 743, 36 WR 752, 59 LT 200,
    [1886–90] All ER Rep Ext 1521 1131
Currie's Settlement, Re, Re Rooper, Rooper v Williams [1910] 1 Ch 329, 70 LJ Ch 285,
    [1908–10] All ER Rep 274, 54 Sol Jo 270, 101 LT 899 .... 160, 164, 231
Curry v Pile (1787) 2 Bro CC 225 402
Cursham v Newland (1838) 7 LJ Ex 212, 1 Horn & H 296, 4 M & W 101
    336

PARA

Cursham v Newland (1839) 2 Beav 145 410
Curteis v Candler (1821) 6 Madd 123 1209
Curtis v Curtis (1821) 6 Madd 14 307–308
Curtis v Curtis (1825) 3 Add 33 739
Curtis v Lukin (1842) 5 Beav 147, 11 LJ Ch 380, 6 Jur 721, 49 ER 533, [1835–42] All ER
　　Rep 403 .... 263, 1062
Curtis v Vernon (1790) 3 Term Rep 587; affd sub nom Vernon v Curtis (1792) 2 Hy Bl 18
　　.. 1268
Curtis and Betts, Re [1887] WN 126, CA 818
Curtius v Caledonian Fire and Life Insurance Co (1881) 19 Ch D 534, 51 LJ Ch 80, 30
　　WR 125, 45 LT 662, CA 818
Curzon, Re, Martin v Perry (1912) 56 Sol Jo 362 306
Cust v Goring (1854) 18 Beav 383, 24 LJ Ch 308, 18 Jur 884, 2 WR 370, 23 LTOS 338
　　.. 294
Cust v Middleton (1864) 34 LJ Ch 185, 10 Jur NS 1227, 13 WR 249, 11 LT 552
　　.. 375
Cutbush v Cutbush (1839) 1 Beav 184, 8 LJ Ch 175, 3 Jur 142
　　.. 1036
Cutcliffe's Estate, Re, Le Duc v Veness [1959] P 6, [1958] 3 All ER 642, [1958] 3 WLR
　　707, 102 Sol Jo 915, CA 908, 911
Cuthbert v Lemprière (1814) 3 M & S 158 375
Cuthbert v Purrier (1822) Jac 415 .... 142, 442
Cuthbert v Robinson (1882) 51 LJ Ch 238, 30 WR 366, 46 LT 57
　　.. 256, 286
Cutto v Gilbert (1854) 9 Moo PCC 131, 1 Ecc & Ad 417, 18 Jur 560, 24 LTOS 193
　　.. 1, 95, 98
Cyganik v Agulian [2006] EWCA Civ 129, 8 ITELR 762, [2006] 1 FCR 406,
　　[2006] All ER (D) 372 (Feb) 566

D

D (a child), Re. See R (a child) (IVF: Paternity of Child), Re
D (J) v D (S). See D'Este v D'Este
DWS, Re; Re EHS; TWGS (a child) v JMG [2000] 2 All ER 83; affd [2001] Ch 568,
　　[2001] 1 All ER 97, [2000] 3 WLR 1910, [2001] 1 FCR 339, [2000] NLJR 1788, 150
　　NLJ 1788, (2000) Times, 22 November, CA 39, 151, 480
Da Costa, Re, Clarke v Church of England Collegiate School of St Peter [1912] 1 Ch 337,
　　81 LJ Ch 293, 56 Sol Jo 240, 106 LT 458, 28 TLR 189, [1911–13] All ER Rep Ext
　　1244 .... 11, 152
Da Costa v Keir (1827) 3 Russ 360, 5 LJOS Ch 161 450
Da Costa v Prudential Assurance Co (1918) 88 LJKB 884, 120 LT 353, CA
　　.. 938
Da Cunha's (Countess), Goods, Re (1828) 1 Hag Ecc 237
　　.. 720, 845
Da Silva's Goods, Re (1861) 25 JP 519, 30 LJPM & A 171, 2 Sw & Tr 315, 5 LT 140
　　.. 111
Dabbs v Chisman (1810) 1 Phillim 155 863
D'Abo v Paget [2000] All ER (D) 944 .... 45, 121, 204, 241, 331
Dack's Will Trusts, Re, Barlcays Bank Ltd v Tracey (1964) 114 L Jo 656
　　.. 114
Dacre, Re, Whitaker v Dacre [1916] 1 Ch 344, 85 LJ Ch 274, 60 Sol Jo 306, 114 LT 387,
　　CA 1067, 1071
Dacre v Patrickson (1860) 1 Drew & Sm 182, 29 LJ Ch 846, 6 Jur NS 863, 8 WR 597, 2
　　LT 500, 764 995
Dadds' Goods, Re (1857) Dea & Sw 290, 29 LTOS 99 104
Dagley v Tolferry (1715) 1 P Wms 285, sub nom Doyley v Tollferry 1 Eq Cas Abr 300, sub
　　nom Dawley v Ballfrey Gilb 103 1073
D'Aglie v Fryer (1841) 12 Sim 1; affd (1841) 12 Sim 328n
　　.. 273
D'Aguilar v Drinkwater (1813) 2 Ves & B 225 .... 136, 149
Daintree v Butcher and Fasulo (1888) 13 PD 102, 57 LJP 76, 58 LT 661, 4 TLR 445, CA
　　.. 68, 70
Daintry v Daintry (1795) 6 Term Rep 307 473
Dakin v Nicholson (1837) 6 LJ Ch 329 385
Dale, Re, Mayer v Wood [1931] 1 Ch 357, 100 LJ Ch 237, [1930] All ER Rep 10, 145 LT
　　632 332

  PARA

Dale, Re, Proctor v Dale [1994] Ch 31, [1993] 4 All ER 129, [1993] 3 WLR 652, [1994]
   Fam Law 77, [1993] 14 LS Gaz R 43, [1993] NLJR 544, 137 Sol Jo LB 83
   .... 10, 20–21, 23, 588
Daley v Desbouverie (1738) 2 Atk 261, sub nom Daly v Desbouverie West temp Hard 547
   147
Dallaway, Re [1982] 3 All ER 118, [1982] 1 WLR 756, 126 Sol Jo 314
   1018
Dalley, Re (1926) 70 Sol Jo 839, 136 LT 223, P, D and Admlty
   827
Dallmeyer, Re, Dallmeyer v Dallmeyer [1896] 1 Ch 372, 65 LJ Ch 201, 44 WR 375, 40 Sol
   Jo 151, 73 LT 671, [1895–9] All ER Rep Ext 2054, CA
   .... 125, 405
Dallow's Goods, Re (1866) LR 1 P & D 189, 35 LJP & M 81, 12 Jur NS 492, 14 WR
   902, 14 LT 573 .... 65, 611
D'Almaine v Moseley (1853) 1 Drew 629, 22 LJ Ch 971, 1 Eq Rep 252, 17 Jur 872, 1 WR
   475, 21 LTOS 297 284
Dalrymple v Hall (1881) 16 Ch D 715, 50 LJ Ch 302, 29 WR 421
   246
Dalton v Latham [2003] EWHC 796 (Ch), 147 Sol Jo LB 537, [2003] All ER (D) 305
   (Apr) 39
d'Altroy's Will Trusts, Re, Crane v Lowman [1968] 1 All ER 181, [1968] 1 WLR 120, 111
   Sol Jo 870 380
Daly v Aldworth (1863) 15 I Ch R 69 395
Dalzell v Welch (1828) 2 Sim 319 249
Dalziel, Re, Midland Bank Executor and Trustee Co Ltd v St Bartholomew's Hospital
   [1943] Ch 277, [1943] 2 All ER 656, 112 LJ Ch 353, 87 Sol Jo 281, 169 LT 168, 59
   TLR 408 298
Dancer v Crabb (1873) LR 3 P & D 98, 37 JP 663, 42 LJP & M 53, [1861–73] All ER
   Rep 692, 28 LT 914 108
Daniel, Re, Jones v Michael [1945] 2 All ER 101, 173 LT 315
   .... 332, 397
Daniel v Tee [2016] EWHC 1538 (Ch), [2016] 4 WLR 115
   1049
Daniel v Warren (1843) 2 Y & C Ch Cas 290, 7 Jur 462, 60 RR 148
   460
Daniell v Daniell (1849) 3 De G & Sm 337, 18 LJ Ch 157, 13 Jur 164, 12 LTOS 492
   .... 274, 1090
Daniels, Re, London City and Midland Executor and Trustee Co Ltd v Daniels (1918)
   87 LJ Ch 661, 118 LT 435 .... 300, 1087
Danish Bacon Co Ltd Staff Pension Fund, Re, Christensen v Arnett [1971] 1 All ER 486,
   [1971] 1 WLR 248, 115 Sol Jo 95 2
Dansereau v Berget [1954] AC 1, [1953] 2 All ER 1058, 97 Sol Jo 728, PC
   887
Dansey v Griffiths (1815) 4 M & S 61 .... 460, 473
Danvers v Earl of Clarendon (1681) 1 Vern 35 339
Daoust, Re, Dobell v Dobell [1944] 1 All ER 443, 113 LJ Ch 193, 171 LT 39
   328
Darbison v Beaumont (1714) 2 Eq Cas Abr 331, 3 Bro Parl Cas 60, 1 P Wms 229, HL
   339
Darby, Re, Russell v MacGregor [1939] Ch 905, [1939] 3 All ER 6, 108 LJ Ch 347, 83 Sol
   Jo 436, 160 LT 602, 55 TLR 792, CA 1121
D'Arcy v O'Kelly (1921) 55 ILT 48 653
Dargie, Re, Miller v Thornton-Jones [1954] Ch 16, [1953] 2 All ER 577, [1953] 1 WLR
   991, 97 Sol Jo 506 1196
Dark, Re, Glover v Dark [1954] Ch 291, [1954] 1 All ER 681, [1954] 2 WLR 509, 98 Sol
   Jo 196 825
Darke's Goods, Re (1859) 29 LJPM & A 71, 1 Sw & Tr 516, 8 WR 273, 2 LT 24
   622
Darley v Langworthy (1774) 3 Bro Parl Cas 359, HL 143–144, 388
Darley v Martin (1853) 13 CB 683, 22 LJCP 249, 17 Jur 1125, 1 CLR 729
   .... 193, 252
Darley v Perceval [1900] 1 IR 129 413
Darlington v Roscoe & Sons [1907] 1 KB 219, 76 LJKB 371, 9 WCC 1, 51 Sol Jo 130, 96
   LT 179, 23 TLR 167, CA 1279
Darlington (Earl) v Pulteney (1775) 1 Cowp 260, [1775–1802] All ER Rep 353, 98 ER
   1075 9

PARA

Darlow v Edwards (1862) 1 H & C 547, 32 LJ Ex 51, 9 Jur NS 336, 10 WR 700, 6 LT
  905, Ex Ch 366
Darnley (Earl) Re, Clifton v Darnley [1907] 1 Ch 159, 76 LJ Ch 58, 51 Sol Jo 82, 95 LT
  706, 23 TLR 93 1123
Darrel v Molesworth (1700) 2 Vern 378 .... 411, 452
Dash, Re, Darley v King (1887) 57 LT 219 463
Dashfield v Davidson [2008] EWHC 486 (Ch), [2009] 1 BCLC 220, [2008] All ER (D) 258
  (Mar) 959
Dashwood v Lord of Bulkeley (1804) 10 Ves 230, 32 ER 832
  .... 136, 149
Dashwood v Magniac [1891] 3 Ch 306, 60 LJ Ch 809, 36 Sol Jo 362, 65 LT 811, 7 TLR
  629, [1891–4] All ER Rep Ext 1906, CA 212, 931
Dashwood v Peyton (1811) 18 Ves 27, 34 ER 227, [1803–13] All ER Rep 278
  .... 252, 467, 469
Daubeny v Coghlan (1842) 12 Sim 507, 11 LJ Ch 177, 6 Jur 230
  .... 211, 268
Davall v New River Co (1849) 3 De G & Sm 394, 18 LJ Ch 299, 13 Jur 761, 13 LTOS 88
  555
Davenhill v Fletcher (1754) Amb 244 1087
Davenport v Coltman (1842) 11 LJ Ex 114, 6 Jur 381, 9 M & W 481
  476
Davenport v Coltman (1842) 12 Sim 588, 11 LJ Ch 262, 6 Jur 381
  .... 235, 298
Davenport v Hanbury (1796) 3 Ves 257 .... 320, 326, 334, 337
Davenport v National Westminster Bank plc (14 April 2005, unreported)
  157
Davenport v Stafford (1852) 2 De GM & G 901 1301
Davey, Re, Prisk v Mitchell [1915] 1 Ch 837, 84 LJ Ch 505, 113 LT 60, CA
  .... 441, 454
David v Frowd (1833) 1 My & K 200, 2 LJ Ch 68, 39 ER 657, [1824–34] All ER Rep 714
  .... 985, 1099–1100
David's Trusts, Re (1859) John 495, 29 LJ Ch 116, 6 Jur NS 94, 8 WR 39, 1 LT 130
  383
Davidson, Re, Minty v Bourne [1909] 1 Ch 567, 78 LJ Ch 437, [1908–10] All ER Rep
  140, 52 Sol Jo 622, 99 LT 222, 24 TLR 760, CA 11
Davidson, Re, National Provincial Bank Ltd v Davidson [1949] Ch 670, [1949] 2 All ER
  551, 65 TLR 574 328
Davidson v Dallas (1808) 14 Ves 576 .... 305, 307, 316
Davidson v Kimpton (1881) 18 Ch D 213, 29 WR 912, 45 LT 132
  .... 316, 375
Davidson v Proctor (1848) 19 LJ Ch 395, 14 Jur 31 438
Davie v Beardsham (1663) 1 Cas in Ch 39 27
Davies, ex p (1851) 2 Sim NS 114, 21 LJ Ch 135, 15 Jur 1102
  459
Davies, Re, Davies v Davies [1892] 3 Ch 63, 61 LJ Ch 595, 41 WR 13, [1891–4] All ER
  Rep 498, 36 Sol Jo 627, 67 LT 548, 8 TLR 673 .... 32, 1114
Davies, Re, Davies v Mackintosh [1957] 3 All ER 52, [1957] 1 WLR 922, 101 Sol Jo 611
  .... 181, 308, 403
Davies, Re, Panton v Jones, (1978) Times, 23 May 106, 851
Davies, Re, Scourfield v Davies [1925] Ch 642, 94 LJ Ch 337, [1925] All ER Rep 494, 69
  Sol Jo 744, 133 LT 460 .... 247, 282
Davies, Re, Thomas v Thomas-Davies [1928] Ch 24, 97 LJ Ch 141, 71 Sol Jo 880, 138 LT
  262 .... 107, 282
Davies v Bush (1831) You 341 1089
Davies v Davies [2016] EWCA Civ 463, Fam Law 815 20
Davies v Davies (1753) 1 Lee 444 106
Davies v Davies (1831) 1 LJ Ch 31 22
Davies v Fisher (1842) 5 Beav 201, 11 LJ Ch 338, 6 Jur 248
  .... 431, 435–436
Davies v Gregory (1873) LR 3 P & D 28, 37 JP 279, 42 LJP & M 33, 21 WR 462, 28 LT
  239, [1861–73] All ER Rep Ext 1008 911
Davies v Hood (1903) 88 LT 19, 19 TLR 158 1237
Davies v Jones [1899] P 161, 68 LJP 69, 80 LT 631, P, D and Admlty
  874
Davies v Kempe (1663) 1 Eq Cas Abr 216, Cart 2 173
Davies v Lowndes (1835) 1 Bing NC 597, 4 LJCP 214, 1 Hodg 125, 2 Scott 71; on appeal
  (1838) 4 Bing NC 478, Ex Ch 148

PARA

Davies v Nicolson (1858) 2 De G & J 693, 27 LJ Ch 719, 5 Jur NS 49, 6 WR 790,
  31 LTOS 374 1103
Davies v Ridge (1800) 3 Esp 101 1299
Davies v Sharples [2006] EWHC 362 (Ch), [2006] WTLR 839
  1150
Davies v Thorns (1849) 3 De G & Sm 347, 18 LJ Ch 212, 13 Jur 383, 12 LTOS 551
  318
Davies' Estate, Re, Russell v Delaney [1951] 1 All ER 920
  .... 70, 108
Davies' Goods, Re (1850) 2 Rob Eccl 337 68
Davies' Policy Trusts, Re [1892] 1 Ch 90, 61 LJ Ch 650, 66 LT 104
  390
Davies' Trusts, Re (1914) 59 Sol Jo 234 1047
Davies' Will, Re (1860) 29 Beav 93, 7 Jur NS 118, 9 WR 134
  332
Davis, Re [1993] 1 FCR 1002, [1993] 1 FLR 54, [1993] Fam Law 59, CA
  577
Davis, Re, Davis v Davis [1902] 2 Ch 314, 71 LJ Ch 539, 51 WR 8, 86 LT 523
  658
Davis, Re, Evans v Moore [1891] 3 Ch 119, 61 LJ Ch 85, 39 WR 627, 35 Sol Jo 624, 65
  LT 128, CA 629, 922, 1150
Davis, Re, Thomas v Davis [1923] 1 Ch 225, 92 LJ Ch 322, 67 Sol Jo 297, 128 LT 735,
  39 TLR 201 11
Davis, Re, ex p Courtenay (1835) 4 Deac & Ch 456, 2 Mont & A 227, 4 LJ Bcy 76
  1248
Davis v Angel (1862) 4 De GF & J 524, 31 LJ Ch 613, 8 Jur NS 1024, 10 WR 722, 6 LT
  880 .... 133, 414, 1174
Davis v Bennett (1861) 30 Beav 226; on appeal (1862) 4 De GF & J 327, 31 LJ Ch 337, 8
  Jur NS 269, 10 WR 275, 5 LT 815 .... 233, 395, 397
Davis v Chanter (1848) 2 Ph 545, 15 Sim 300, 17 LJ Ch 297, 10 LTOS 477
  817
Davis v Gibbs (1730) 2 Eq Cas Abr 326, 3 P Wms 26, Fitz-G 116, sub nom Gibbs v Davis
  Mos 269 291
Davis v Kirk (1856) 2 K & J 391, 2 Jur NS 857 .... 340, 541
Davis v Norton (1726) 2 P Wms 390 417
Davis v Reyner (1671) 2 Keb 744, 758, 2 Lev 3, sub nom Davis v Wright 1 Vent 120
  1240
Davis v Wright. See Davis v Reyner
Davis' Estate, Re [1906] P 330, 75 LJP 94, P, D and Admlty
  760
Davis' Estate, Re [1952] P 279, [1952] 2 All ER 509, 96 Sol Jo 514, [1952] 2 TLR 541, P,
  D and Admlty 111
Davis' Goods, Re (1843) 3 Curt 748, 2 Notes of Cases 350
  .... 69, 73
Davis' Goods, Re (1860) Sea & Sm 152, 29 LJPM & A 72, 4 Sw & Tr 213
  659
Davison, Re, Greenwell v Davison (1888) 58 LT 304, [1886–90] All ER Rep Ext 1482
  291
Davison and Torrens, Re (1865) 17 I Ch R 7 125
Davitt v Titcumb [1990] Ch 110, [1989] 3 All ER 417, [1990] 2 WLR 168, 134 Sol Jo 21,
  [1990] 1 LS Gaz R 30 39
Davoren v Wootton [1900] 1 IR 273 1277
Davy, Re, Hollingsworth v Davy [1908] 1 Ch 61, 77 LJ Ch 67, 97 LT 654, CA
  .... 405, 1127
Davy v Redington [1917] 1 IR 250, Ir CA 241, 284
Davy v Smith (1693) 12 Mod Rep 37, 3 Salk 395 71
Daw v IRC (1928) 14 TC 58, 7 ATC 238 1141
Dawes, Re, ex p Kendall (1811) 1 Rose 71, 34 ER 199, sub nom ex p Kendall 17 Ves 514,
  [1803–13] All ER Rep 295 1232
Dawes v Ferrars (1722) 2 Eq Cas Abr 331, 2 P Wms 1, Prec Ch 589
  340
Dawes' Trusts, Re (1876) 4 Ch D 210 326
Dawkins, Re, Dawkins v Judd [1986] 2 FLR 360, [1986] Fam Law 295
  574
Dawkins v Tatham (1829) 2 Sim 492 1133
Dawson, Re, Arathoon v Dawson [1906] 2 Ch 211, 75 LJ Ch 604, 54 WR 556, 94 LT 817
  1121

                                                                          PARA
Dawson v Bourne (1852) 16 Beav 29, 19 LTOS 252 390
Dawson v Hearn (1831) 9 LJOS Ch 249, 1 Russ & M 606
    1058
Dawson v Killet (1781) 1 Bro CC 119 438
Dawson v Massey (1809) 1 Ball & B 231 962
Dawson v Oliver-Massey (1876) 2 Ch D 753; revsd (1876) 2 Ch D 753, 40 JP 676, 45 LJ
    Ch 519, 24 WR 993, 34 LT 551, CA 135, 143, 147, 307, 310
Dawson v Reid (1915) 113 LT 52, HL 118, 120
Dawson v Small (1874) 9 Ch App 651 454
Dawson's Settlement, Re, Lloyds Bank Ltd v Dawson [1966] 3 All ER 68, [1966] 1 WLR
    1456, 110 Sol Jo 689 182
Dawson's Will Trusts, Re, National Provincial Bank Ltd v National Council of YMCA Inc
    [1957] 1 All ER 177, [1957] 1 WLR 391, 50 R & IT 431, 101 Sol Jo 191
    1131
Day, Re, Sprake v Day [1898] 2 Ch 510, 67 LJ Ch 619, 47 WR 238, [1895–9] All ER Rep
    453, 79 LT 436 1215
Day v Croft (1842) 4 Beav 561 409
Day v Daveron (1841) 12 Sim 200, 10 LJ Ch 349 298
Day v Day (1854) Kay 703, 18 Jur 1013, 2 WR 700, 24 LTOS 5
    443
Day v Thompson, Re Frampton's Goods (1863) 27 JP 712, 32 LJPM & A 183, 9 Jur NS
    755, 3 Sw & Tr 169, 8 LT 701 .... 787, 817
Day v Trig (1715) 2 Eq Cas Abr 323, 1 P Wms 286 .... 277, 291
Day's Estate, Re [1940] 2 All ER 544, 84 Sol Jo 274, 56 TLR 623, P, D and Admlty
    809
Day's Will Trusts, Re, Lloyds Bank Ltd v Shafe [1962] 3 All ER 699, [1962] 1 WLR 1419,
    106 Sol Jo 856 .... 153, 1215
Dayman v Dayman (1894) 71 LT 699, P, D and Admlty
    895
Dayrell, Re, Hastie v Dayrell [1904] 2 Ch 496, 73 LJ Ch 795, 91 LT 373
    .... 226, 253
Daysh, Re, Dale v Duke of Richmond and Gordon (1951) 95 Sol Jo 108, [1951] 1 TLR
    257 1017
De Beauvoir v De Beauvoir (1852) 3 HL Cas 524, 16 Jur 1147, 88 RR 191
    341
De Bode's Goods, Re (1847) 5 Notes of Cases 189 103
de Chassiron, Re, Lloyds Bank Ltd v Sharpe [1939] Ch 934, [1939] 3 All ER 321, 108 LJ
    Ch 406, 83 Sol Jo 524, 161 LT 53, 55 TLR 841 1090
De Chatelain v Pontigny (1858) 27 LJP & M 18, 1 Sw & Tr 34, 6 WR 409, 30 LTOS 353
    810
De Clifford (Lord) v Marquis of Lansdowne [1900] 2 Ch 707, 69 LJ Ch 828, 44 Sol Jo
    689, 83 LT 160, 16 TLR 547 1259
De Clifford's (Lord) Estate, Re, Lord De Clifford v Quilter [1900] 2 Ch 707, 69 LJ Ch
    828, 44 Sol Jo 689, 83 LT 160, 16 TLR 547 1259
De Cordova v De Cordova (1879) 4 App Cas 692, 28 WR 105, 41 LT 43, PC
    1044
De Crespigny, Re, De Crespigny v De Crespigny [1886] WN 24, CA
    371
De Falbe, Re, Ward v Taylor [1901] 1 Ch 523, 70 LJ Ch 286, 49 WR 455, 45 Sol Jo 294,
    84 LT 273, 17 TLR 246, CA; affd sub nom Leigh v Taylor [1902] AC 157, 71 LJ Ch
    272, 50 WR 623, [1900–3] All ER Rep 520, 46 Sol Jo 264, 86 LT 239, 18 TLR 293,
    HL 930, 932
De Garagnol v Liardet (1863) 32 Beav 608, 2 New Rep 296
    316
De Kremer's Estate, Re, Lundbeck v De Kremer (1965) 110 Sol Jo 18, P, D and Admlty
    104
De La Hunty, Re, O'Connor v Butler [1907] 1 IR 507, 41 ILT 155
    370
De la Rochefoucauld v Boustead. See Rochefoucauld v Boustead
De La Rue's Goods, Re (1890) 15 PD 185, 39 WR 64, 63 LT 253, P, D and Admlty
    723
De La Saussaye's Goods, Re (1873) LR 3 P & D 42, 37 JP 312, 42 LJP & M 47, 21 WR
    549, 28 LT 368, [1861–73] All ER Rep Ext 1143 .... 1, 95, 112, 114, 723
De La Warr (Earl) v Miles (1881) 17 Ch D 535, 50 LJ Ch 754, 29 WR 809,
    [1881–5] All ER Rep 252, 44 LT 487, CA 205

PARA

De Lisle v Hodges (1874) LR 17 Eq 440, 43 LJ Ch 385, 22 WR 363, 30 LT 158
.... 1088
De Lisle's Will Trusts, Re, White v De Lisle [1968] 1 All ER 492, [1968] 1 WLR 322,
[1968] TR 221, 111 Sol Jo 999 246
De Mora v Concha (1889) 40 Ch D 543, 60 LT 798, CA; on appeal sub nom Concha
v Concha [1892] AC 670, 66 LT 303, 8 TLR 460, HL 1238
De Quetteville v De Quetteville, Re De Quetteville (1902) 19 TLR 109; varied (1903) 19
TLR 383, CA 1179
De Rochefort v Dawes (1871) LR 12 Eq 540, 40 LJ Ch 625, 25 LT 456
.... 1009
De Rosaz, Re, Rymer v De Rosaz (1886) 2 TLR 871 1130
De Rosaz's Goods, Re (1877) 2 PD 66, 41 JP 247, 46 LJP 6, 25 WR 352, 36 LT 263, P, D
and Admlty 214, 611, 738
De Sommery, Re Coelenbier v De Sommery [1912] 2 Ch 622, 82 LJ Ch 17, 57 Sol Jo 78,
107 LT 253, 823 .... 27, 1014, 1016, 1052, 1060
De Tastet v Andrade (1817) 1 Chit 629n 1291
De Trafford v Tempest (1856) 21 Beav 564 180
De Vere's Will Trusts, Jellett v O'Brien [1961] IR 224 .... 138, 141
De Viesca v Lubbock (1840) 10 Sim 629 803
De Windt v De Windt (1866) LR 1 HL 87, 35 LJ Ch 332, 14 WR 545, 14 LT 529
.... 241, 400
De Witte v De Witte (1840) 11 Sim 41, 9 LJ Ch 270, 4 Jur 625
.... 390
Deacon's Trusts, Re, Deacon v Deacon (1906) 95 LT 701
.... 182, 444
Deacon's Trusts, Re, Hagger v Heath (1906) 95 LT 701
.... 182, 444
Deakin, Re, Starkey v Eyres [1894] 3 Ch 565, 63 LJ Ch 779, 8 R 702, 43 WR 70, 71 LT
838 350
Deakin v Garvie (1919) 36 TLR 122, CA 97, 99, 713
Dean, Re, Dean v Wright (1882) 21 Ch D 581, 31 WR 174, 47 LT 501, CA
.... 859
Dean, Re, Wollard v Dickinson [1923] WN 227, 67 Sol Jo 768
.... 336
Dean v Allen (1855) 20 Beav 1, 3 WR 294 991
Dean v Bulmer [1905] P 1, 74 LJP 12, 92 LT 426, P, D and Admlty
.... 914
Dean v Dean [1891] 3 Ch 150, 60 LJ Ch 553, 39 WR 568, 65 LT 65, 7 TLR 579
.... 424
Dean v Wiesengrund [1955] 2 QB 120, [1955] 2 All ER 432, [1955] 2 WLR 1171, 99 Sol
Jo 369, 165 Estates Gazette 568, CA 917, 1279
Deans, Re, Westminster Bank Ltd v Official Solicitor [1954] 1 All ER 496, [1954] 1 WLR
332, 6 LDAB 409, 98 Sol Jo 110 .... 644, 818
Dear, Re [1975] 2 NZLR 254, NZ CA 98, 112
Dear, Re, Helby v Dear (1889) 58 LJ Ch 659, 38 WR 31, 61 LT 432
.... 306, 446
Debac's Goods, Re, Sanger v Hart (1897) 77 LT 374, P, D and Admlty
.... 98,106
Debenham, Re [1986] 1 FLR 404, [1986] Fam Law 101
.... 573, 575, 580, 591
Debney v Eckett (1858) 4 Jur NS 805 1070
Debtor, a, (No 87 of 1999) [2000] 07 LS Gaz R 40, [2000] TLR 95, [2000] BPIR 589
.... 1294, 1296, 1298, 1300–1301
Deeley's Settlement, Re, Batchelor v Russell [1974] Ch 454, [1973] 3 All ER 1127, [1974]
2 WLR 41, 117 Sol Jo 877 .... 306, 309
Defflis v Goldschmidt (1816) 1 Mer 417, 19 Ves 566 .... 243, 301, 308
Defoe, Re (1882) 2 OR 623 152
Degazon v Barclays Bank International Ltd [1988] 1 FTLR 17, CA
.... 1265, 1268
Deichman's Goods, Re (1842) 3 Curt 123, 1 Notes of Cases 514
.... 612
Deighton's Settled Estates, Re (1876) 2 Ch D 783, 45 LJ Ch 825, 35 LT 81, CA
.... 302, 413
Del Mare v Robello (1792) Cas temp Talb 296, 1 Ves 412, 3 Bro CC 446
.... 207, 211, 265, 268
Delacour's Goods, Re (1874) 9 IR Eq 86 629
Delany, Re, Delany v Delany (1895) 39 Sol Jo 468 315

                                                                        PARA
Delany v Delany (1885) 15 LR Ir 55 287
Dellar v Zivy [2007] EWHC 2266 (Ch), [2007] All ER (D) 121 (Oct)
.... 13
Deller's Estate, Re, Warman v Greenwood [1888] WN 62
.... 287
Dellow's Will Trusts, Re, Lloyds Bank Ltd v Institute of Cancer Research [1964] 1 All ER
    771, [1964] 1 WLR 451, 108 Sol Jo 156 39
Deloitte, Re, Griffiths v Allbeury [1919] 1 Ch 209, 88 LJ Ch 112, 63 Sol Jo 178, 120 LT
    323, CA 308
Deloitte, Re, Griffiths v Deloitte [1926] Ch 56, 95 LJ Ch 154, [1925] All ER Rep 118, 70
    Sol Jo 161, 135 LT 150 302
Delves v Newington (1885) 52 LT 512 .... 1093, 1127
Dempsey v Lawson (1877) 2 PD 98, 41 JP 696, 46 LJP 23, 25 WR 629, [1874–80] All ER
    Rep 296, 36 LT 515, P, D and Admlty 95, 97,99
Dempster, Re, Borthwick v Lovell [1915] 1 Ch 795, 84 LJ Ch 597, [1914–15] All ER Rep
    998, 112 LT 1124 1090–1091
Denby, Re (1861) 3 De GF & J 350, 31 LJ Ch 184, 10 WR 115, 5 LT 514,
    [1861–73] All ER Rep Ext 1592, sub nom Re Dendy 31 LJ Ch 184
.... 1069
Dench v Dench (1877) 2 PD 60, 41 JP 328, 46 LJP 13, 25 WR 414, P, D and Admlty
.... 83
Denekin, Re, Peters v Tanchereau (1895) 13 R 294, 72 LT 220
.... 37
Denholm's Trustees v Denholm (1908) 45 SLR 32, 1908 SC 43, 15 SLT 429, Ct of Sess
.... 296
Denley's Trust Deed, Re, Holman v HH Martyn & Co Ltd [1969] 1 Ch 373, [1968]
    3 All ER 65, [1968] 3 WLR 457, 112 Sol Jo 673 .... 11, 36, 263
Denn v Spray (1786) 1 Term Rep 466 .... 562, 564
Denn d Franklin v Trout (1812) 15 East 394 469
Denn d Gaskin v Gaskin (1599) 2 Cowp 657 395
Denn d Geering v Shenton (1776) 2 Chit 662, 1 Cowp 410
.... 460, 473
Denn d Moor v Mellor (1794) 5 Term Rep 558; revsd (1796) 1 Bos & P 558; affd sub nom
    Moor v Denn (1800) 2 Bos & P 247, HL 376
Denn d Radclyffe v Bagshaw (1796) 6 Term Rep 512 321
Denn d Satterthwaite v Satterthwaite (1764) 1 Wm Bl 519
.... 419
Denn d Wilkins v Kemeys (1808) 8 East 366 .... 254, 277, 442
Denne d Briddon v Page (1783) 1 Bos & P 261n, 11 East 603n, 3 Doug KB 294
.... 456
Denning, Re, Harnett v Elliott [1958] 2 All ER 1, [1958] 1 WLR 462, 102 Sol Jo 293, P, D
    and Admlty 896
Dennis, Re, Dennis v Lloyds Bank Ltd [1981] 2 All ER 140, 124 Sol Jo 885, 131 NLJ 210
.... 568, 570, 574, 580, 598
Dennis v Frend (1863) 14 I Ch R 271 415
Dennis' Goods, Re [1891] P 326, P, D and Admlty 111
Dennis' Goods, Re [1899] P 191, 68 LJP 67, P, D and Admlty
.... 754
Denny v Barton and Rashleigh (1818) 2 Phillim 575 .... 54, 95
Dent v Bennett (1839) 4 My & Cr 269, 8 LJ Ch 125, 3 Jur 99, 48 RR 94
.... 904
Dent v Pepys (1822) 6 Madd 350 .... 186, 253
Denyssen v Hiddingh (1887) 12 App Cas 624, 56 LJPC 107, 57 LT 885, PC
.... 961
Denyssen v Mostert (1872) LR 4 PC 236, 8 Moo PCC 502, 41 LJPC 41, 20 WR 1017
.... 10
Deprez, Re, Henriques v Deprez [1917] 1 Ch 24, 86 LJ Ch 91, 61 Sol Jo 72, 115 LT 662,
    [1916–17] All ER Rep Ext 1315 .... 201, 406
Derbyshire, Re, Webb v Derbyshire [1906] 1 Ch 135, 75 LJ Ch 95, 54 WR 135, 94 LT 138
.... 168, 293
Derick v Kery Moore KB. See Kerry v Derrick
Dering, Re, Neall v Beale (1911) 105 LT 404 399
Desbody v Boyville (1729) 2 Eq Cas Abr 365, 2 P Wms 547
.... 135
Deshais' Goods, Re (1865) 29 JP 233, 34 LJPM & A 58, 4 Sw & Tr 13, 13 WR 640, 12
    LT 54, 13 LT 246 718

                                                                                                PARA
D'Este v D'Este [1973] Fam 55, [1973] 2 WLR 183, 116 Sol Jo 969, sub nom D (J) v D (S)
  [1973] 1 All ER 349 1279
Destouches v Walker (1764) 2 Eden 261 459
Detmold, Re, Detmold v Detmold (1889) 40 Ch D 585, 58 LJ Ch 495, 37 WR 442, 61 LT
  21 465
Deudon v De Massals (1854) 19 Beav 448, 2 WR 639, 24 LTOS 64
  364
Devall v Dickens (1845) 9 Jur 550 377
Devas v Mackay [2009] EWHC 1951 (Ch), [2009] All ER (D) 09 (Aug)
  .... 53, 55, 899
Devaynes v Noble, Houlton's Case (1818) 1 Mer 529, 616
  1234
Devaynes v Noble, Sleech's Case (1816) 1 Mer 529, 539
  1232
Devaynes v Robinson (1857) 24 Beav 86, 27 LJ Ch 157, 3 Jur NS 707, 5 WR 509,
  29 LTOS 244 1238
Devereux, Re, Toovey v Public Trustee [1911] 2 Ch 545, 80 LJ Ch 705, [1911–13] All ER
  Rep 641, 55 Sol Jo 715, 105 LT 407, 27 TLR 574 1164
Devillebichot (deceased), Re; Brennan v Prior [2013] EWHC 2867 (Ch), [2013] All ER (D)
  243 (Sep) 56, 60
Devisme v Mellish (1800) 5 Ves 529 349
Devisme v Mello (1782) 1 Bro CC 537 305
Devitt v Kearney (1883) 13 LR Ir 45, Ir CA 287, 1037
Devon (Duke) v Atkins (1726) 2 P Wms 381, Cas temp King 71
  1088
Dew v Clark and Clark (1826) 3 Add 79 52
Dewar v Brooke (1880) 14 Ch D 529, 49 LJ Ch 374, 28 WR 613
  432–433
Dewell, Re, Edgar v Reynolds (1858) 4 Drew 269, 27 LJ Ch 562, 4 Jur NS 399, 6 WR
  404, 62 ER 104, [1843–60] All ER Rep 859, 31 LTOS 50
  .... 780, 803
Dewell's Goods, Re (1853) 1 Ecc & Ad 103, 17 Jur 1130, 22 LTOS 124
  .... 63, 68–69, 84
Dewhirst, Re, Flower v Dewhirst [1948] Ch 198, [1948] 1 All ER 147, [1948] LJR 912, 92
  Sol Jo 84, 64 TLR 74 380
D'Eye v Avory [2001] WTLR 227 106
D'Eyncourt v Gregory (1864) 34 Beav 36, 10 Jur NS 484, 3 New Rep 628, 12 WR 679, 10
  LT 317 182
D'Eyncourt v Gregory (1866) LR 3 Eq 382, 36 LJ Ch 107, 15 WR 186
  932
Di Sora v Phillipps (1863) 10 HL Cas 624, 33 LJ Ch 129, 2 New Rep 553
  .... 190, 203, 239
Dias v De Livera (1879) 5 App Cas 123, PC 10, 309, 311
Dibbs v Goren (1849) 11 Beav 483 1098
Dick v Audsley [1908] AC 347, 77 LJPC 126, HL 11
Dick v Lacy (1845) 8 Beav 214, 14 LJ Ch 150, 9 Jur 221, 5 LTOS 70
  .... 339, 392, 398
Dick's Trustees v Dick (1911) 48 SLR 325, 1911 SLT 95
  371
Dicken v Clarke (1837) 2 Y & C Ex 572 448
Dickens, Re, Dickens v Hawksley [1935] Ch 267, 104 LJ Ch 174, 78 Sol Jo 898, 152 LT
  375, 51 TLR 181, CA 296
Dickens v Barker. See Dickin v Edwards
Dicker, Re [1947] Ch 248, [1947] 1 All ER 317, [1948] LJR 544, 91 Sol Jo 148, 177 LT
  274 .... 350, 352
Dickin v Edwards (1844) 4 Hare 273, sub nom Dickens v Barker 14 LJ Ch 22, 8 Jur 1089,
  4 LTOS 193 1112
Dickinson v Swatman (1860) 24 JP 792, 30 LJPM & A 84, 6 Jur NS 831, 4 Sw & Tr 205
  .... 108, 110
Dicks v Lambert (1799) 4 Ves 725 293–294
Dickson, Re, Dickson v Dickson (1984) [2002] WTLR 1395, [1984] 81 LS Gaz R 3012,
  CA 106
Dickson, Re, Hill v Grant (1885) 29 Ch D 331, 54 LJ Ch 510, 33 WR 511, 52 LT 707, 1
  TLR 331, CA 1077
Dickson's Trust, Re, ex p Dickson (1850) 1 Sim NS 37, 20 LJ Ch 33, 15 Jur 282, sub nom
  Re Dixon's Trusts 16 LTOS 168 .... 131, 134

                                                                                    PARA
Digby v Legard (1774) 2 Dick 500, cited in 3 P Wms at p 21
.... 173
Digg's Case (1680) (circa 1680) cited in Skin at 79 77
Dilkes v Broadmead (1860) 2 Giff 113; on appeal (1860) 2 De GF & J 566
.... 1105
Dilkes Goods, Re (1874) LR 3 P & D 164, 38 JP 329, 43 LJP & M 38, 22 WR 456, 30 LT
    305, [1874–80] All ER Rep Ext 1968 63
Dilley v Matthews (1865) 11 Jur NS 425, 13 WR 676, 12 LT 488
.... 351
Dillon, Re, Duffin v Duffin (1890) 44 Ch D 76, 59 LJ Ch 420, 38 WR 369,
    [1886–90] All ER Rep 407, 62 LT 614, 6 TLR 204, CA
.... 921
Dillon v Arkins (1885) 17 LR Ir 636, Ir CA 295–296
Dillon v Harris (1830) 4 Bli NS 321, HL 136, 201, 443
Dillon v Public Trustee of New Zealand [1941] AC 294, [1941] 2 All ER 284, 165 LT 357,
    57 TLR 425, PC 24
Dimes v Scott (1828) 4 Russ 195, 28 RR 46, 38 ER 778, [1824–34] All ER Rep 653
.... 1122, 1124, 1126
Dimmock, Re, Dimmock v Dimmock (1885) 52 LT 494
.... 1037
Dimond v Bostock (1875) 10 Ch App 358, 23 WR 554, 33 LT 217, CA in Ch
.... 174–175, 305
Dingle v Coppen [1899] 1 Ch 726, 68 LJ Ch 337, 47 WR 279, 79 LT 693
.... 152, 1067
Dingmar v Dingmar [2006] EWCA Civ 942, [2007] Ch 109, [2007] 2 All ER 382, [2006]
    3 WLR 1183, [2006] 2 FCR 595, [2007] 1 FLR 210, [2006] All ER (D) 160 (Jul)
.... 585
Dingwell v Askew (1788) 1 Cox Eq Cas 427 156
Dinshaw's Goods, Re [1930] P 180, 99 LJP 118, 74 Sol Jo 264, 142 LT 652, 46 TLR 308,
    [1930] All ER Rep Ext 913, P, D and Admlty 792
Diplock, Re, Diplock v Wintle [1948] Ch 465, [1948] 2 All ER 318, [1948] LJR 1670, 92
    Sol Jo 409, 482, CA; affd sub nom Ministry of Health v Simpson [1951] AC 251,
    [1950] 2 All ER 1137, 94 Sol Jo 777, 66 (pt 2) TLR 1015, HL
.... 780, 1096–1097, 1099–1100
Dipple v Dipple [1942] P 65, [1942] 1 All ER 234, 111 LJP 18, 86 Sol Jo 70, 166 LT 120,
    58 TLR 141, P, D and Admlty 1279
Ditmas v Robertson (1840) 4 Jur 957 451
Dix v Burford (1854) 19 Beav 409 1149
Dix v Reed (1823) 1 Sim & St 237 1069
Dixon, Re, Dixon v Charlesworth [1903] 2 Ch 458, 72 LJ Ch 642, 51 WR 652, 88 LT 862
.... 381
Dixon, Re, Dixon v Dixon (1912) 56 Sol Jo 445 382
Dixon v Nicholson (1847) 16 Sim 21, 11 Jur 812, 10 LTOS 50
.... 444
Dixon v Priestley (1847) 16 Sim 21, 11 Jur 812, 10 LTOS 50
.... 444
Dixon v Treasury Solicitor [1905] P 42, 74 LJP 33, 92 LT 427, 21 TLR 145, P, D and
    Admlty 107–108
Dobbins v Bland (1730) 2 Eq Cas Abr 545 135
Dobson v Banks (1863) 32 Beav 259 255
Dobson v Bowness (1868) LR 5 Eq 404, 37 LJ Ch 309, 16 WR 640
.... 284
Dobson v North Tyneside Health Authority [1996] 4 All ER 474, [1997] 1 WLR 596,
    [1997] 2 FCR 651, [1997] 1 FLR 598, [1997] Fam Law 326, [1996] 31 LS Gaz R 29,
    [1996] NLJR 1458, 140 Sol Jo LB 165, CA 956
Dobson's Goods, Re (1866) LR 1 P & D 88, 35 LJP & M 54, 14 WR 408, 13 LT 758
.... 7
Docker v Somes (1834) 2 My & K 655, 3 LJ Ch 200, 39 ER 1095, [1824–34] All ER Rep
    402 658
Dodd v Wake (1837) 8 Sim 615 302
Dodd's Goods, Re (1897) 77 LT 137, P, D and Admlty 744
Dodds v Dodds (1860) 11 I Ch R 374, 13 Ir Jur 75, Ir CA
.... 385, 454
Dodds v Pedley (1866) LR 2 Eq 819, 12 Jur NS 759, 14 WR 884, 14 LT 823
.... 271
Dodds v Tuke (1884) 25 Ch D 617, 53 LJ Ch 598, 32 WR 424, 50 LT 320
.... 1196

                                                                    PARA
Dodgson's Goods, Re (1859) 28 LJP & M 116, 5 Jur NS 252, 1 Sw & Tr 259
.... 817
Dodgson's Trust, Re (1853) 1 Drew 440 451
Dodson v Hay (1791) 3 Bro CC 405 .... 415, 431–432
Dodson v Sammell (1861) 25 JP 629, 1 Drew & Sm 575, 30 LJ Ch 799, 8 Jur NS 584, 9
    WR 887 991
Dodsworth v Addy (1842) 11 LJ Ch 382, 6 Jur 700 334
Doe d Allen v Allen (1840) 12 Ad & El 451, 9 LJQB 395, 4 Jur 985, 4 Per & Dav 220
.... 218
Doe d Andrew v Lainchbury (1809) 11 East 290 245
Doe d Angell v Angell (1846) 9 QB 328, 15 LJQB 193, 10 Jur 705, 6 LTOS 520
.... 262, 335, 340, 384
Doe d Annandale v Brazier (1821) 5 B & Ald 64 476
Doe d Ashforth v Bower (1832) 3 B & Ad 453, 1 LJKB 156
.... 271
Doe d Bailey v Pugh. See Goodtitle d Bailey v Pugh
Doe d Bailey v Sloggett (1850) 19 LJ Ex 220, 5 Exch 107
.... 408
Doe d Baldwin v Rawding (1819) 2 B & Ald 441 .... 248, 443
Doe d Bates v Clayton (1806) 8 East 141 256
Doe d Beach v Earl of Jersey (1818) 1 B & Ald 550; on appeal (1825) 3 B & C 870, HL
.... 215, 275, 277
Doe d Bean v Halley (1798) 8 Term Rep 5 387
Doe d Biddulph v Hole (1850) 15 QB 848, 20 LJQB 57, 15 LTOS 392
.... 115
Doe d Birtwhistle v Vardill (1835) 9 Bli NS 32, 2 Cl & Fin 571, HL
.... 548
Doe d Blackburn v Blackburn (1836) 1 Mood & R 547
.... 543
Doe d Blakiston v Haslewood (1851) 10 CB 544, 20 LJCP 89, 15 Jur 272
.... 468
Doe d Blomfield v Eyre (1848) 5 CB 713, 18 LJCP 284, 10 LTOS 525, Ex Ch
.... 182, 231
Doe d Borwell v Abey (1813) 1 M & S 428 .... 395, 470
Doe d Brodbelt v Thomson (1858) 12 Moo PCC 116, 32 LTOS 65
.... 228, 376
Doe d Brown v Brown (1809) 11 East 441 .... 199, 210, 267, 271
Doe d Browne v Greening (1814) 3 M & S 171 .... 210, 267
Doe d Burden v Burville (1801) 2 East 47n 474
Doe d Burkitt v Chapman (1789) 1 Hy Bl 223 284
Doe d Burrin v Charlton (1840) 1 Man & G 429, 1 Scott NR 290
.... 384
Doe d Burton v White (1847) 1 Exch 526; affd (1848) 18 LJ Ex 59, 2 Exch 797
.... 376
Doe d Cadogan v Ewart (1838) 7 Ad & El 636, 7 LJQB 177, 3 Nev & PKB 197, 1
    Will Woll & H 246 .... 419, 460
Doe d Calkin v Tomkinson (1813) 2 M & S 165 27
Doe d Campton v Carpenter (1850) 16 QB 181, 20 LJQB 70, 15 Jur 719, 16 LTOS 234
.... 277
Doe d Chattaway v Smith (1816) 5 M & S 126 .... 249, 348
Doe d Chichester v Oxenden (1810) 3 Taunt 147 210
Doe d Chidgey v Harris (1847) 16 M & W 517 .... 151, 154, 1141
Doe d Chillcott v White (1800) 1 East 33 .... 288, 379
Doe d Clarke v Clarke (1795) 2 Hy Bl 399 362
Doe d Clarke v Ludlam (1831) 7 Bing 275, 9 LJOSCP 74, 5 Moo & P 48
.... 235
Doe d Clements v Collins (1788) 2 Term Rep 498 290
Doe d Clift v Birkhead (1849) 18 LJ Ex 441, 4 Exch 110, 13 LTOS 529
.... 410, 474
Doe d Cock v Cooper (1801) 1 East 229 .... 249, 459
Doe d Comberbach v Perryn (1789) 3 Term Rep 484 .... 413, 456
Doe d Cross v Cross (1846) 8 QB 714, 15 LJQB 217, 10 Jur 564, 7 LTOS 61
.... 6
Doe d Crosthwaite v Dixon (1836) 5 Ad & El 834, 6 LJKB 61, 2 Har & W 364, 1 Nev &
    PKB 255 546
Doe d Dacre (Baroness) v Dowager Lady Dacre (1798) 1 Bos & P 250; affd sub nom Dacre
    (Dowager Lady) v Doe d Baroness Dacre (1799) 8 Term Rep 112
.... 420

                                                                                    PARA
Doe d Dacre (Lady) v Roper (1809) 11 East 518 376
Doe d Davy v Burnsall (1794) 6 Term Rep 30 391
Doe d Dolley v Ward (1839) 9 Ad & El 582, 8 LJQB 154, 1 Per & Dav 568
.... 423–424
Doe d Driver v Bowling (1822) 5 B & Ald 722, 1 Dow & Ry KB 367
.... 469
Doe d Dunning v Cranstoun (1840) 9 LJ Ex 294, 4 Jur 683, 7 M & W 1
.... 277
Doe d Ellis v Ellis (1808) 9 East 382 473
Doe d Ellis v Hardy (1836) 1 Mood & R 525 217
Doe d Evans v Evans (1839) 10 Ad & El 228, 8 LJQB 284, 3 Jur 844, 2 Per & Dav 378
.... 109
Doe d Everett v Cooke (1806) 7 East 269, 3 Smith KB 236
.... 443
Doe d Evers v Ward (1852) 18 QB 197, 21 LJQB 145, 16 Jur 709, 18 LTOS 317
.... 251
Doe d Gains v Rouse (1848) 5 CB 422, 17 LJCP 108, 12 Jur 99, 10 LTOS 327
.... 276–277, 346
Doe d Gallini v Gallini (1833) 5 B & Ad 621, 3 LJKB 71, 2 Nev & MKB 619; affd (1835)
    3 Ad & El 340, 4 LJ Ex 337, 4 Nev & MKB 894 384
Doe d Garner v Lawson (1803) 3 East 278 313
Doe d Gigg v Bradley (1812) 16 East 399 390
Doe d Gill v Pearson (1805) 6 East 173, 2 Smith KB 295
.... 142
Doe d Gilman v Elvey (1803) 4 East 313, 1 Smith KB 94
.... 391
Doe d Goldin v Lakeman (1831) 2 B & Ad 30, 9 LJOSKB 138
.... 375
Doe d Gord v Needs (1836) 6 LJ Ex 59, 2 Gale 245, 2 M & W 129
.... 218, 220
Doe d Gore v Langton (1831) 2 B & Ad 680 212
Doe d Gorges v Webb (1808) 1 Taunt 234 474
Doe d Gwillim v Gwillim (1833) 5 B & Ad 122, 2 LJKB 194, 2 Nev & MKB 247
.... 225
Doe d Harris v Greathed (1806) 8 East 91 267
Doe d Harris v Taylor (1847) 10 QB 718, 9 LTOS 218 473
Doe d Hatch v Bluck (1816) 6 Taunt 485, 2 Marsh 170
.... 387
Doe d Haw v Earles (1846) 16 LJ Ex 242, 15 M & W 450, 9 LTOS 538
.... 288
Doe d Hayes v Sturges (1816) 7 Taunt 217, 2 Marsh 505
.... 1142
Doe d Hayter v Joinville (1802) 3 East 172, 6 RR 585 .... 45, 217, 348
Doe d Hearle v Hicks (1832) 8 Bing 475, 6 Bli NS 37, 1 Cl & Fin 20, 1 Moo & S 759,
    HL 251, 369
Doe d Hemming v Willetts (1849) 7 CB 709, 18 LJCP 240
.... 290
Doe d Herbert v Selby (1824) 2 B & C 926, 4 Dow & Ry KB 608
.... 442
Doe d Herbert v Thomas (1835) 3 Ad & El 123, sub nom Doe d Herbert v Lewis and
    Thomas 1 Har & W 231, 4 Nev & MKB 697 382
Doe d Hick v Dring (1814) 2 M & S 448 .... 257, 288
Doe d Hiscocks v Hiscocks (1839) 9 LJ Ex 27, 2 Horn & H 54, 3 Jur 955, 5 M & W 363,
    151 ER 154, [1835–42] All ER Rep 380, Exch Ct . 192, 209, 211–212, 215, 217–218, 220,
                                                                                           272
Doe d Hornby v Glenn (1834) 1 Ad & El 49, 3 LJKB 161, 3 Nev & MKB 837
.... 645–646
Doe d Howell v Thomas (1840) 1 Man & G 335, 1 Scott NR 359
.... 284
Doe d Hubbard v Hubbard (1850) 15 QB 227, 20 LJQB 61, 14 Jur 1110, 15 LTOS 411
.... 199, 217, 267, 271
Doe d Humphreys v Roberts (1822) 5 B & Ad 407 268
Doe d Hunt v Moore (1811) 14 East 601 .... 423, 436
Doe d Hurrell v Hurrell (1821) 5 B & Ald 18 284
Doe d James v Hallett (1813) 1 M & S 124 330
Doe d Jearrad v Bannister (1840) 10 LJ Ex 33, H & W 61, 5 Jur 102, 7 M & W 292
.... 387

                                                                              PARA
Doe d Johnson v Johnson (1852) 22 LJ Ex 90, 8 Exch 81, 19 LTOS 313
.... 460
Doe d Jones v Davies (1832) 4 B & Ad 43, 1 LJKB 244, 1 Nev & MKB 654
.... 384
Doe d Jones v Owens (1830) 1 B & Ad 318, 8 LJOSKB 404
.... 460, 473
Doe d King v Frost (1820) 3 B & Ald 546 .... 339, 348, 459
Doe d Le Chevalier v Huthwaite (1820) 3 B & Ald 632
.... 212, 276
Doe d Leach v Micklem (1805) 6 East 486, sub nom Doe d Leech v Micklem 2 Smith KB
   499 .... 253, 407
Doe d Lees v Ford (1853) 2 E & B 970, 23 LJQB 53, 18 Jur 420, 2 CLR 654, 22 LTOS
   184 417
Doe d Leicester v Biggs (1809) 2 Taunt 109, 127 ER 1017, [1803–13] All ER Rep 546
.... 232
Doe d Lempriere v Martin (1777) 2 Wm Bl 1148 286
Doe d Littlewood v Green (1838) 8 LJ Ex 65, 1 Horn & H 314, 2 Jur 859, 4 M & W 229
.... 395
Doe d Liversage v Vaughan (1822) 5 B & Ald 464, 1 Dow & Ry KB 52
.... 389
Doe d Lloyd v Davies (1854) 23 LJCP 169, sub nom Lloyd v Davies 15 CB 76, 18 Jur
   1056, 2 WR 495, 2 CLR 1788, 23 LTOS 160 444
Doe d Long v Laming (1760) 2 Burr 1100, 1 Wm Bl 265
.... 237
Doe d Long v Prigg (1828) 8 B & C 231, 6 LJOSKB 296, 2 Man & Ry KB 338
.... 318
Doe d Lord and Lady Cholmondeley v Weatherby (1809) 11 East 322
.... 284
Doe d Luscombe v Yates (1822) 5 B & Ald 544, 1 Dow & Ry KB 187
.... 145
Doe d Lyde v Lyde (1787) 1 Term Rep 593 .... 385, 459
Doe d Mabberley v Mabberley (1833) 6 C & P 126 1141
Doe d Mitchinson v Carter (1798) 8 Term Rep 57, 101 ER 1264, [1775–1802] All ER Rep
   611 464
Doe d Mitchinson v Carter (1799) 8 Term Rep 300 463
Doe d Morgan v Morgan (1832) 1 Cr & M 235, 2 LJ Ex 88, 3 Tyr 179
.... 218, 220
Doe d Morris v Underdown (1741) Willes 293, Andr App 8
.... 419
Doe d Murch v Marchant (1843) 13 LJCP 59, 8 Jur 21, 6 Man & G 813, 7 Scott NR 644,
   2 LTOS 209 107
Doe d Norfolk (Duke) v Hawke (1802) 2 East 481 463
Doe d Oxenden v Chichester (1816) 4 Dow 65, HL 210
Doe d Parkin v Parkin (1814) 5 Taunt 321, 1 Marsh 61
.... 271, 277
Doe d Patrick v Royle (1849) 13 QB 100, 18 LJQB 145, 13 Jur 745, 12 LTOS 493
.... 470, 474
Doe d Pell v Jeyes (1830) 1 B & Ad 593, 9 LJOSKB 82
.... 284
Doe d Penwarden v Gilbert (1821) 3 Brod & Bing 85, 6 Moore CP 268
.... 237
Doe d Perkes v Perkes (1820) 3 B & Ald 489 103
Doe d Phillips v Aldridge (1791) 4 Term Rep 264 367
Doe d Phipps v Lord Mulgrave (1793) 5 Term Rep 320
.... 384, 400
Doe d Pilkington v Spratt (1833) 5 B & Ad 731, 3 LJKB 53, 2 Nev & MKB 524
.... 339
Doe d Planner v Scudamore (1800) 2 Bos & P 289 .... 414, 423
Doe d Preedy v Holtom (1835) 4 Ad & El 76, 5 LJKB 10, 1 Har & W 528, 5 Nev &
   MKB 391 .... 209, 217
Doe d Reed v Harris (1837) 6 Ad & El 209, 6 LJKB 84, 1 Nev & PKB 405, Will Woll &
   Dav 106, sub nom Doe d Read v Harris 1 Jur 134 101
Doe d Renow v Ashley (1847) 10 QB 663, 16 LJQB 356, 11 Jur 905
.... 271, 286
Doe d Rew v Lucraft (1832) 8 Bing 386, 1 LJCP 109, 1 Moo & S 573
.... 457

PARA

Doe d Roake v Nowell (1813) 1 M & S 327; affd sub nom Randoll v Doe d Roake (1817)
5 Dow 202, HL 423
Doe d Roberts v Polgrean (1791) 1 Hy Bl 535 121
Doe d Ryall v Bell (1800) 8 Term Rep 579 271
Doe d Saye and Lord Sele v Guy (1802) 3 East 120, 4 Esp 154
.... 634, 1146
Doe d Shallcross v Palmer (1851) 16 QB 747, 15 JP 689, 20 LJQB 367, 15 Jur 836, 117
ER 1067, [1843–60] All ER Rep 139, 17 LTOS 252 .... 83, 217, 716
Doe d Shore v Porter (1789) 3 Term Rep 13, 100 ER 429, [1775–1802] All ER Rep 575
.... 942
Doe d Simpson v Simpson (1838) 4 Bing NC 333; affd sub nom Doe d Blesard v Simpson
(1842) 3 Man & G 929, 3 Scott NR 774, Ex Ch 461, 473, 560
Doe d Smith v Fleming (1835) 2 Cr M & R 638, 5 LJ Ex 74, 1 Gale 278, 5 Tyr 1013
.... 45, 237, 299, 348
Doe d Smith v Webber (1818) 1 B & Ald 713 .... 331, 460–461
Doe d Smyth v Smyth (1826) 6 B & C 112, 5 LJOSKB 13, 9 Dow & Ry KB 136
.... 154
Doe d Southouse v Jenkins (1829) 5 Bing 469, 7 LJOSCP 182, 3 Moo & P 59
.... 474
Doe d Spearing v Buckner (1796) 6 Term Rep 610 284
Doe d Spencer v Clark (1822) 5 B & Ald 458, 1 Dow & Ry KB 44
.... 560
Doe d Spencer v Pedley (1836) 5 LJ Ex 221, 2 Gale 106, 1 M & W 662, Tyr & Gr 882
.... 232
Doe d Stevenson v Glover (1845) 1 CB 448, 14 LJCP 169, 9 Jur 493, 5 LTOS 54
.... 381
Doe d Stewart v Sheffield (1811) 13 East 526 174
Doe d Sturges v Tatchell (1832) 3 B & Ad 675, 1 LJKB 239
.... 1141–1142
Doe d Templeman v Martin (1833) 4 B & Ad 771, 1 Nev & MKB 512
.... 210, 213, 267
Doe d Thomas v Beynon (1840) 12 Ad & El 431, 9 LJQB 359, 4 Per & Dav 193
.... 214
Doe d Thwaites v Over (1808) 1 Taunt 263 311
Doe d Todd v Duesbury (1841) 10 LJ Ex 410, 8 M & W 514
.... 460
Doe d Tofield v Tofield (1809) 11 East 246 288
Doe d Tremewen v Permewen (1840) 11 Ad & El 431, 3 Per & Dav 303
.... 384
Doe d Turner v Kett (1792) 4 Term Rep 601 .... 115, 321
Doe d Tyrrell v Lyford (1816) 4 M & S 550 .... 210, 248, 267
Doe d Usher v Jessep (1810) 12 East 288 443
Doe d Vessey v Wilkinson (1788) 2 Term Rep 209 448
Doe d Wall v Langlands (1811) 14 East 370 .... 255–256, 284, 298
Doe d Watson v Shipphard (1779) 1 Doug KB 75 417
Doe d Watts v Wainwright (1793) 5 Term Rep 427 316
Doe d Wells v Scott (1814) 3 M & S 300 446
Doe d Westlake v Westlake (1820) 4 B & Ald 57 220
Doe d Westminster (Dean) v Freeman (1786) 2 Chit 498, 1 Term Rep 389
.... 369
Doe d Wheedon v Lea (1789) 3 Term Rep 41 .... 416, 419
Doe d Wightwick v Truby (1774) 2 Wm Bl 944 560
Doe d Willey v Holmes (1798) 8 Term Rep 1 376
Doe d Williams v Davies (1834) 6 C & P 614, 4 LJ Ex 10, sub nom Doe d Bridgman v
David 1 Cr M & R 405, 5 Tyr 125 923
Doe d Winter v Perratt (1826) 5 B & C 48, 4 LJOSKB 246, 7 Dow & Ry KB 733; affd
(1843) 9 Cl & Fin 606, 6 Man & G 314, 7 Scott NR 1
.... 262, 339–340
Doe d Wright v Cundall (1808) 9 East 400 471
Doe d Wright v Plumptre (1820) 3 B & Ald 474 278
Doe d Wyatt v Stagg (1839) 5 Bing NC 564, 9 LJCP 73, 3 Jur 1127, 7 Scott 690
.... 151
Doe d York v Walker (1844) 13 LJ Ex 153, 12 M & W 591, 2 LTOS 424
.... 113–114, 282
Doe d Young v Sotheron (1831) 2 B & Ad 628, 9 LJOSKB 286
.... 394
Doering v Doering (1889) 42 Ch D 203, 58 LJ Ch 553, 37 WR 796
.... 1071

PARA

Doetsch, Re, Matheson v Ludwig [1896] 2 Ch 836, 65 LJ Ch 855, 45 WR 57, 40 Sol Jo
  685, 75 LT 69 1232
Doherty v Dwyer (1890) 25 LR Ir 297 83
Doherty v Nelson [1895] 2 IR 90 1267
Doland's Will Trusts, Re, Westminster Bank Ltd v Phillips [1970] Ch 267, [1969] 3 All ER
  713, [1969] 3 WLR 614, 113 Sol Jo 798 .... 41, 181, 228, 244, 256, 1115
Domvile v Taylor (1863) 32 Beav 604, 2 New Rep 258, 11 WR 796, 8 LT 624
  285
Don's Estate, Re (1857) 21 JP 694, 4 Drew 194, 27 LJ Ch 98, 3 Jur NS 1192, 5 WR 836,
  30 LTOS 190 548
Donald, Re, Moore v Somerset [1909] 2 Ch 410, 78 LJ Ch 761, 53 Sol Jo 673, 101 LT
  377, [1908–10] All ER Rep Ext 1224 .... 115, 278
Donald, Re, Royal Exchange Assurance v Donald [1947] 1 All ER 764, 91 Sol Jo 338, CA
  247
Donaldson's Goods, Re (1840) 2 Curt 386 79
Doncaster v Doncaster (1856) 3 K & J 26, 2 Jur NS 1066
  385
Donisthorpe, Re, Churchward v Rowden and Churchward [1947] WN 226
  106
Donn, Re, Donn v Moses [1944] Ch 8, [1943] 2 All ER 564, 113 LJ Ch 61, 87 Sol Jo 406,
  169 LT 335, 60 TLR 30 140
Donn v Penny (1815) 1 Mer 20, 19 Ves 545 .... 392, 459
Donnellan v O'Neill (1870) IR 5 Eq 523 367
Donnelly v Broughton [1891] AC 435, 60 LJPC 48, 40 WR 209, 65 LT 558, PC
  903
Donner's Estate, Re (1917) 62 Sol Jo 161, 34 TLR 138, P, D and Admlty
  81
Donohoe v Donohoe (1887) 19 LR Ir 349 1072
Donovan v Needham (1846) 9 Beav 164, 15 LJ Ch 193, 10 Jur 150, 7 LTOS 107
  .... 1076, 1082
Doo v Brabant (1792) 4 Term Rep 706, 3 Bro CC 393 445
Doody, Re, Fisher v Doody [1893] 1 Ch 129, 62 LJ Ch 14, 2 R 166, 41 WR 49,
  [1891–4] All ER Rep 977, 37 Sol Jo 49, 68 LT 128, 9 TLR 77, CA
  653–654
Doody, Re, Hibbert v Lloyd [1893] 1 Ch 129, 62 LJ Ch 14, 2 R 166, 41 WR 49,
  [1891–4] All ER Rep 977, 37 Sol Jo 49, 68 LT 128, 9 TLR 77, CA
  653–654
Doody v Higgins (1852) 1 WR 30, 9 Hare App I xxxii 342
Doody v Higgins (1856) 2 K & J 729, 25 LJ Ch 773, 4 WR 737, 27 LTOS 281
  341–342
Dooley v Dooley [1927] IR 190 .... 858, 862
Dooley v Mahon (1877) IR 11 Eq 299 278
Door v Geary (1749) 1 Ves Sen 255, sub nom Dore v Geary 1 Wils 247
  277
Dorgan, Re, Dorgan v Polley [1948] Ch 366, [1948] 1 All ER 723, [1948] LJR 1217, 92
  Sol Jo 258, 64 TLR 229 594
Dorin v Dorin (1875) LR 7 HL 568, 39 JP 790, 45 LJ Ch 652, 23 WR 570,
  [1874–80] All ER Rep 71, 33 LT 281, HL 350–351
Doring, Re, Doring v Clark [1955] 3 All ER 389, [1955] 1 WLR 1217, 99 Sol Jo 796
  592
D'Orleans (Duchess) Goods, Re (1859) 28 LJP & M 129, 5 Jur NS 104, 1 Sw & Tr 253, 7
  WR 269, 32 LTOS 261 .... 720, 845
Dorman, Re [1994] 1 All ER 804, [1994] 1 WLR 282, [1994] 2 FLR 52, [1994] Fam Law
  569, [1994] 9 LS Gaz R 38 .... 156, 158, 270, 285
Dormer v Phillips (1855) 4 De GM & G 855, 3 WR 337, 25 LTOS 74
  .... 191, 339
Dornford v Dornford (1806) 12 Ves 127 .... 1246, 1257
Douglas, Re, Obert v Barrow (1886) 35 Ch D 472; affd (1887) 35 Ch D 472, 56 LJ Ch
  913, 35 WR 740, [1886–90] All ER Rep 228, 56 LT 786, 3 TLR 589, CA
  11
Douglas, Re, Wood v Douglas (1884) 28 Ch D 327, 33 WR 390, sub nom Wood v
  Douglas 54 LJ Ch 421, sub nom Re Douglas, Douglas v Wood 52 LT 131
  544
Douglas v Andrews (1851) 14 Beav 347 410
Douglas v Congreve (1838) 1 Beav 59, 8 LJ Ch 53, 3 Jur 120
  385

PARA
Douglas v Douglas (1854) Kay 400, 23 LJ Ch 732 282
Douglas v Fellows (1853) Kay 114, 23 LJ Ch 167, 2 WR 654, 24 LTOS 21
.... 217, 220, 270
Douglas v Forrest (1828) 4 Bing 686, 6 LJOSCP 157, 1 Moo & P 663
.... 636, 978
Douglas v Willes (1849) 7 Hare 318 404
Douglas (Lord) v Chalmer (1795) 2 Ves 501 .... 237, 449
Douglas Will Trusts, Re, Lloyds Bank Ltd v Nelson [1959] 2 All ER 620, [1959] 1 WLR
    744, 103 Sol Jo 657; affd [1959] 3 All ER 785, [1959] 1 WLR 1212, 104 Sol Jo 126,
    CA 294, 318, 444, 516
Douglas-Menzies v Umphelby [1908] AC 224, 77 LJPC 64, 98 LT 509, 24 TLR 344, PC
.... 1
Dove v Everard (1830) Taml 376, 32 RR 200, 1 Russ & M 231
.... 627
Dover, ex p (1834) 5 Sim 560 1149
Dover v Alexander (1843) 2 Hare 275, 12 LJ Ch 175, 7 Jur 124
.... 351
Dowdeswell v Dowdeswell (1878) 9 Ch D 294, 48 LJ Ch 23, 27 WR 241, 38 LT 828, CA
.... 636, 817, 1165, 1172
Dowding v Smith (1841) 3 Beav 541, 10 LJ Ch 235 396
Dowds' Goods, Re [1948] P 256, [1948] LJR 1887, 64 TLR 244, P, D and Admlty
.... 745
Dowling, Re [1933] IR 150 72
Dowling v Dowling [1902] 1 IR 79, 83 371
Dowling v Dowling (1866) 1 Ch App 612, 12 Jur NS 720, 14 WR 1003, 15 LT 152
.... 375, 454, 472
Down v Down (1817) 7 Taunt 343, 1 Moore CP 80 267
Downe v Sheffield (1894) 71 LT 292 217
Downer Enterprises Ltd, Re [1974] 2 All ER 1074, [1974] 1 WLR 1460, 118 Sol Jo 829
.... 1222, 1232, 1242
Downer's Goods, Re (1853) 1 Ecc & Ad 106, 18 Jur 66, 23 LTOS 11
.... 93
Downing (or Downes) v Townsend (1755) Amb 280, sub nom Downing v Bagnall Amb
    App 818 293
Downs v Collins (1848) 6 Hare 418, 12 LTOS 102 919
Downward v Dickinson, Re Chune's Goods (1864) 28 JP 825, 34 LJPM & A 4, 10 Jur NS
    1084, 3 Sw & Tr 564, 11 LT 641 787
Dowse, Re, Dowse v Dowse [1951] 1 All ER 558n, 95 Sol Jo 107, [1951] 1 TLR 444
.... 125
Dowse v Coxe (1825) 3 Bing 20, 3 LJOSCP 127, 10 Moore CP 272; revsd sub nom Biddell
    v Dowse (1827) 6 B & C 255, 9 Dow & Ry KB 404, sub nom Coxe and Biddell v
    Dowse 5 LJOSKB 128 1239
Dowse v Gorton [1891] AC 190, 60 LJ Ch 745, 40 WR 17, [1891–4] All ER Rep 1230, 64
    LT 809, HL 1039–1040
Dowset v Sweet (1753) Amb 175 .... 215, 217, 265, 275–276, 278
Dowson, Re, Dowson v Beadle [1909] WN 245, 101 LT 671
.... 328
Dowson v Gaskoin (1837) 2 Keen 14, 6 LJ Ch 295 293
Doyle v Blake (1804) 9 RR 76, 2 Sch & Lef 231 .... 627, 1256
Doyle v Foley [1903] 2 IR 95 1267
D'Oyley, Re, Swayne v D'Oyley (1921) 152 LT Jo 259 346
Doyley v Tollferry. See Dagley v Tolferry
D'Oyly, Re, Vertue v D'Oyly [1917] 1 Ch 556, 86 LJ Ch 373, 61 Sol Jo 336, 116 LT 442
.... 1130
Dracup, Re, Field v Dracup [1892] WN 43, 36 Sol Jo 327
.... 1172
Drage v Hartopp (1885) 28 Ch D 414, 54 LJ Ch 434, 33 WR 410, 51 LT 902
.... 926
Drake, Re, Drake v Drake [1971] Ch 179, [1970] 3 All ER 32, [1970] 3 WLR 228, 114
    Sol Jo 399, CA 335
Drake, Re, Drake v Green [1921] 2 Ch 99, 90 LJ Ch 381, [1921] All ER Rep 157, 65 Sol
    Jo 553, 125 LT 461 366
Drake v Collins (1869) 20 LT 970 450
Drake v Drake (1860) 8 HL Cas 172, 29 LJ Ch 850, 3 LT 193
.... 199, 207, 217, 257, 263, 276
Drake v Martin (1856) 23 Beav 89, 26 LJ Ch 786 277

PARA

Drakeford v Drakeford (1863) 33 Beav 43, 11 WR 977, 9 LT 10
.... 175
Drakeley, Re, ex p Paddy (1818) 3 Madd 241, Buck 235
.... 635
Drakeley's Estate, Re (1854) 19 Beav 395, 2 WR 613, 25 LTOS 292
.... 395, 468
Drant v Vause (1842) 1 Y & C Ch Cas 580, 11 LJ Ch 170, 6 Jur 313
.... 157
Drax, Re, Dunsany v Sawbridge (1906) 75 LJ Ch 317, 54 WR 418, 50 Sol Jo 325, 94 LT
    611, 22 TLR 343 141
Drax, Re, Savile v Yeatman (1887) 57 LT 475 366
Draycott v Wood (1856) 5 WR 158, 28 LTOS 196 412
Dresden, Re, Lindo v London Hospital (1910) Times, 22 July
.... 1130
Drew, Re, Drew v Drew [1899] 1 Ch 336, 68 LJ Ch 157, 47 WR 265, 43 Sol Jo 126, 79
    LT 656, [1895–9] All ER Rep Ext 1572 .... 346, 348
Drew, Re, Simmons and Simmons v Drew (1913) 135 LT Jo 323
.... 153, 1196
Drew v Killick (1847) 1 De G & Sm 266, 11 Jur 900, 10 LTOS 50
.... 476
Drew v Merry (1701) 1 Eq Cas Abr 175 pl 7 27
Drewett v Edwards (1877) 26 WR 122, 37 LT 622, CA
.... 1189
Drewry v Thacker (1819) 3 Swan 529 1301
Drexel Burnham Lambert UK Pension Plan, Re [1995] 1 WLR 32
.... 657
Drinkwater v Falconer (1755) 2 Ves Sen 623 115
Driver d Frank v Frank (1814) 3 M & S 25; affd (1818) 8 Taunt 468, 2 Moore CP 519, 6
    Price 41, Ex Ch 243, 413
Driver d Frank v Frank (1818) 8 Taunt 468, 2 Moore CP 519, 6 Price 41, Ex Ch
.... 413, 416
Drosier v Brereton (1851) 15 Beav 221, 92 RR 388 963
Drought's Will Trusts, Re, Public Trustee v Palmer (1967) 101 ILTR 1
.... 231
Druce v Denison (1801) 6 Ves 385 210
Druce v Young [1899] P 84, Consist Ct 881
Drumm's Goods, Re [1931] NI 12 .... 613, 725
Drummond, Re, Ashworth v Drummond [1914] 2 Ch 90, 83 LJ Ch 817, [1914–15] All ER
    Rep 223, 58 Sol Jo 472, 111 LT 156, 30 TLR 429 36
Drummond v Parish (1843) 3 Curt 522, 7 Jur 538, 163 ER 812, [1843–60] All ER Rep
    100, 1 LTOS 207, 2 Notes of Cases 318 .... 79, 81
Drummond's Goods, Re (1860) 2 Sw & Tr 8, 8 WR 476, 2 LT 391
.... 2
Drummond's Settlement, Re, Foster v Foster [1988] 1 All ER 449, [1988] 1 WLR 234, 132
    Sol Jo 192, [1988] 9 LS Gaz R 46, CA 300, 307–308
Drury v Johnston [1928] NI 25 942
Du Bochet, Re, Mansell v Allen [1901] 2 Ch 441, 70 LJ Ch 647, 49 WR 588, 84 LT 710
.... 350, 354
Du Cros' Settlement, Re, Du Cros Family Trustee Co Ltd v Du Cros [1961] 3 All ER 193,
    [1961] 1 WLR 1252, 105 Sol Jo 630 335
Du Maurier, Re, Millar v Coles (1916) 32 TLR 579 296
Duboudieu v Patterson (1919) 54 ILT 23 895
Duce and Boots Cash Chemists (Southern) Ltd's Contract, Re [1937] Ch 642, [1937]
    3 All ER 788, 106 LJ Ch 387, 81 Sol Jo 651, 157 LT 477, 53 TLR 1000
.... 1147
Ducker v Pulling [2007] EWHC 2148 (Ch), [2007] All ER (D) 488 (Jul)
.... 1290, 1296
Duckett v Gordon (1860) 11 I Ch R 181 22
Duckmanton v Duckmanton (1860) 5 H & N 219, 29 LJ Ex 132
.... 127, 400
Ducksbury, Re, Ducksbury v Ducksbury [1966] 2 All ER 374, [1966] 1 WLR 1226, 110
    Sol Jo 601 572–573
Duddell, Re, Roundway v Roundway [1932] 1 Ch 585, 101 LJ Ch 248, [1932] All ER Rep
    714, 146 LT 565 9
Duddy v Gresham (1878) 2 LR Ir 442, Ir CA 134, 141
Dudley (Lord) v Lord Warde (1751) Amb 113 932
Dufaur v Croft (1840) 3 Moo PCC 136 904

PARA

Duffield v Currie (1860) 29 Beav 284 409
Duffield v Duffield (1829) 3 Bli NS 260, 1 Dow & Cl 268, 4 ER 1334, [1824–34] All ER
    Rep 694, HL 413, 415–416, 424
Duffield v Elwes (1827) 1 Bli NS 497, 1 Dow & Cl 1, 4 ER 959, [1824–34] All ER Rep
    247, HL 921
Duffield v M'Master [1906] 1 IR 333, 352, Ir CA 260, 417
Duffill v Duffill [1903] AC 491, 72 LJPC 97, 89 LT 82, 19 TLR 600, [1900–3] All ER Rep
    Ext 1282, PC 450
Duffy v Duffy [1920] 1 IR 122, 54 ILT 187, CA 152, 1012
Duffy's Goods, Re (1871) IR 5 Eq 506 83
Dufour v Pereira (1769) 1 Dick 419, 2 Hargrave Juridical Arguments 304
    .... 20–21, 23
Dugdale v Dugdale (1849) 11 Beav 402 396
Dugdale v Dugdale (1872) LR 14 Eq 234, 41 LJ Ch 565, 27 LT 705
    1003
Duggan v Kelly (1848) 10 I Eq R 295, 473 .... 133, 140
Duggins' Goods, Re (1870) 34 JP 265, 39 LJP & M 24, 22 LT 182
    75
Duguid v Fraser (1886) 31 Ch D 449, 55 LJ Ch 285, 34 WR 267, 54 LT 70
    107
Dulson, Re (1929) 140 LT 470, 45 TLR 228, P, D and Admlty
    679
Dumble, Re, Williams v Murrell (1883) 23 Ch D 360, 52 LJ Ch 631, 31 WR 605, 48 LT
    661 1083
Dummer v Pitcher (1831) 5 Sim 35; affd (1833) 2 My & K 262, Coop temp Brough 257,
    39 ER 944 29
Dunbar v Plant [1998] Ch 412, [1997] 4 All ER 289, [1997] 3 WLR 1261, [1998] 1 FLR
    157, [1998] Fam Law 139, [1997] 36 LS Gaz R 44, CA
    .... 39–40, 480
Duncan, Re, Terry v Sweeting [1899] 1 Ch 387, 68 LJ Ch 253, 47 WR 379, 43 Sol Jo 244,
    80 LT 322, 15 TLR 185 1277
Duncan v Duncan (No 2) (1859) 27 Beav 392 .... 403, 409
Duncan v Lawson (1889) 41 Ch D 394, 53 JP 532, 58 LJ Ch 502, 37 WR 524, 60 LT 732
    845
Duncan v Watts (1852) 16 Beav 204 .... 1070, 1087
Dundas v Wolfe Murray (1863) 1 Hem & M 425, 32 LJ Ch 151, 1 New Rep 429, 11 WR
    359 .... 430, 434, 1083
Dundas Trustees v Dundas Trustees 1912 SC 375, Ct of Sess
    1133
Dundee General Hospitals Board of Management v Walker [1952] 1 All ER 896, sub nom
    Dundee General Hospitals v Bell's Trustees 1952 SC (HL) 78, 1952 SLT 270, HL
    .... 138, 140
Dundee Magistrates v Morris (1858) 3 Macq 134, sub nom, Ewan v Morgan 22 JP 607, 6
    WR 556, 32 LTOS 19, HL 263
Dunk v Fenner (1831) 2 Russ & M 557 .... 385, 993
Dunlevy's Trusts, Re (1882) 9 LR Ir 349, Ir CA 316
Dunn, Re, Brinklow v Singleton (1902) 46 Sol Jo 432 1209
Dunn's Trustees v Dunn 1924 SC 613, Ct of Sess 1130
Dunnage v White (1820) 1 Jac & W 583, 37 ER 490 284
Dunne v Byrne [1912] AC 407, 81 LJPC 202, [1911–13] All ER Rep 1105, 56 Sol Jo 324,
    106 LT 394, 28 TLR 257, PC 11
Dunne v Doran (1844) 13 I Eq R 545 1238
Dunne v Dunne (1855) 7 De GM & G 207, 3 Eq Rep 760, 1 Jur NS 1056, 3 WR 380,
    25 LTOS 60 139
Dunstan, Re, Dunstan v Dunstan [1918] 2 Ch 304, 87 LJ Ch 597, [1918–19] All ER Rep
    694, 63 Sol Jo 10, 119 LT 561 .... 172, 381
Dunster, Re, Brown v Heywood [1909] 1 Ch 103, 78 LJ Ch 138, 99 LT 921,
    [1908–10] All ER Rep Ext 1391 174–175
Duppa v Mayo (1669) 1 Wms Saund 275 113
Durance's Goods, Re (1872) LR 2 P & D 406, 36 JP 615, 41 LJP & M 60, 20 WR 759,
    26 LT 983, [1861–73] All ER Rep Ext 1211 .... 95, 707, 791
Durant v Heritage [1994] EGCS 134 20
Durham v Northen [1895] P 66, 6 R 582, 69 LT 691, 10 TLR 49, P, D and Admlty
    711
Durling and Parker v Loveland (1839) 2 Curt 225 .... 899, 903–904
Durran v Durran (1905) 91 LT 819, CA 463

PARA

Durrant v Friend (1852) 5 De G & Sm 343, 21 LJ Ch 353, 16 Jur 709, 19 LTOS 152
.... 156, 351
Dutton, Re, Herbert v Harrison (1869) 17 WR 523, 20 LT 386
.... 293
Dutton, Re, Plunkett v Simeon [1893] WN 65 274
Dutton, Re, ex p Peake (1878) 4 Ex D 54, 43 JP 6, 48 LJQB 350, 27 WR 398, 40 LT 430,
    Ex D 36
Dutton v Crowdy (1863) 33 Beav 272, 33 LJ Ch 241, 10 Jur NS 28, 3 New Rep 234, 12
    WR 222, 9 LT 630 .... 410, 474
Dutton v Dutton [2001] WTLR 552 125
Dutton-Forshaw v HMRC [2015] UKFTT 478 (TC), [2016] STI 146
.... 489
Duxbury v Duxbury [1992] Fam 62n, [1990] 2 All ER 77, [1991] 3 WLR 639n, [1987] 1
    FLR 7, [1987] Fam Law 13, CA 591
Dwyer v Lysaght (1812) 2 Ball & B 156 218
Dye's Goods, Re (1850) 2 Rob Eccl 342 850
Dyer v Dyer (1816) 1 Mer 414, 19 Ves 612 468–469
Dyet, Re, Morgan v Dyet (1902) 87 LT 744 1133
Dyke, Re. See Stedham's Goods, Re, Re Dyke's Goods
Dyke, Re, Dyke v Dyke (1881) 44 LT 568 401
Dyke v Walford (1848) 5 Moo PCC 434, 6 State Tr NS 699, 12 Jur 839, 6 Notes of Cases
    309, PC 556, 782
Dynamics Corporation of America, Re [1976] 2 All ER 669, [1976] 1 WLR 757
.... 967
Dyson v Morris (1842) 1 Hare 413, 11 LJ Ch 241, 6 Jur 297
.... 1172

                                            E

E, Re, E v E [1966] 2 All ER 44, [1966] 1 WLR 709, 110 Sol Jo 214
.... 570, 572, 574–575
Eades, Re, Eades v Eades [1920] 2 Ch 353, 89 LJ Ch 604, 123 LT 777
.... 11
Eady v Waring (1974) 43 DLR (3d) 667, [1974] 2 OR (2d) 627, Ont CA
.... 50
Eager v Furnivall (1881) 17 Ch D 115, 45 JP 603, 50 LJ Ch 537, 29 WR 649, 44 LT 464
.... 168
Eagles v Le Breton (1873) LR 15 Eq 148, 42 LJ Ch 362
.... 349, 394–395, 397
Eames v Anstee (1863) 33 Beav 264 408
Eames v Hacon (1881) 18 Ch D 347, 50 LJ Ch 740, 29 WR 877, 45 LT 196,
    [1881–5] All ER Rep Ext 1737, CA 670, 803, 968
Eardley v Owen (1847) 10 Beav 572 22
Eardley's Will, Re, Simeon v Freemantle [1920] 1 Ch 397, 89 LJ Ch 234, 122 LT 769
.... 155
Earl's Goods, Re (1867) LR 1 P & D 450, 36 LJP & M 127, 16 LT 799
.... 718, 720, 837, 845
Earl of Northumberland v Earl of Aylsford Amb. See Northumberland (Earl) v Marquis of
    Gransby
Earl Shaftsbury v Shaftsbury Gilb Ch. See Eyre v Countess of Shaftesbury
Earle v Barker. See Barker v Young
Earle v Wilson (1811) 17 Ves 528 354
Earle's Settlement Trusts, Re, Reiss v Norrie [1971] 2 All ER 1188, [1971] 1 WLR 1118,
    115 Sol Jo 529 .... 321–324, 326, 334
Early v Benbow (1846) 15 LJ Ch 169, 2 Coll 354, 10 Jur 571, 6 LTOS 498
.... 1130
Early v Benbow (1846) 2 Coll 342 1130
Earnshaw v Hartley [2000] Ch 155, [1999] 3 WLR 709, [1999] 2 EGLR 100, [1999]
    16 LS Gaz R 37, [1999] 32 EG 89, [1999] EGCS 52, 143 Sol Jo LB 129,
    [1999] All ER (D) 375, CA 1267
East, Re, London County and Westminster Banking Co Ltd v East (1914) 58 Sol Jo 513,
    111 LT 101, CA 1040
East v Twyford (1851) 9 Hare 713; affd (1853) 4 HL Cas 517, 22 LTOS 173
.... 202, 384
Eastman v Baker (1808) 1 Taunt 174 .... 376, 442

                                                                              PARA
Eastwood v Avison (1869) LR 4 Exch 141, 38 LJ Ex 74, 19 LT 834
.... 457, 473
Easum v Appleford (1840) 5 My & Cr 56, 10 LJ Ch 81, 4 Jur 981
.... 1113
Eaton, Re, Daines v Eaton [1894] WN 95, 70 LT 761, 10 TLR 594
.... 1123, 1125
Eaton v Barker (1845) 2 Coll 124, 9 Jur 822, 5 LTOS 283
.... 444
Eaton v Daines [1894] WN 32 1149–1150
Eaton v Hewitt (1862) 2 Drew & Sm 184, 8 Jur NS 1120, 1 New Rep 10, 11 WR 76, 7
   LT 496 .... 417, 446
Eaves, Re, Eaves v Eaves [1940] Ch 109, [1939] 4 All ER 260, 109 LJ Ch 97, 83 Sol Jo
   942, 162 LT 8, 56 TLR 110, CA 380
Eavestaff v Austin (1854) 19 Beav 591 182
Ebbern v Fowler [1909] 1 Ch 578, 78 LJ Ch 497, [1908–10] All ER Rep 673, 53 Sol Jo
   356, 100 LT 717, CA 350, 354
Ebden's Estate v Ebden [1910] App D 321 23
Eccard v Brooke (1790) 2 Cox Eq Cas 213 .... 254, 320, 390
Eccles v Birkett (1850) 4 De G & Sm 105, 19 LJ Ch 280, 14 Jur 800, 15 LTOS 324
.... 433
Eccles v Cheyne (1856) 2 K & J 676 170
Eccles' Goods, Re (1889) 15 PD 1, 54 JP 55, 59 LJP 5, 61 LT 652, P, D and Admlty
.... 806
Eckersley v Platt (1866) LR 1 P & D 281, 36 LJP & M 7, 15 WR 232, sub nom Ekersley v
   Platt 15 LT 327 .... 106, 108
Eddels' Trusts, Re (1871) LR 11 Eq 559, 40 LJ Ch 316, 24 LT 223, sub nom Re Eddels'
   Trusts, ex p Hemming 19 WR 815 424
Eddowes v Eddowes (1862) 30 Beav 603 311
Eden, Re, Ellis v Crampton [1957] 2 All ER 430, [1957] 1 WLR 788, 101 Sol Jo 481
.... 45
Eden v Wilson (1852) 4 HL Cas 257 .... 226, 253
Edge v Pensions Ombudsman [1998] Ch 512, [1998] 2 All ER 547, [1998] 3 WLR 466,
   [1998] PLR 15; affd [2000] Ch 602, [1999] 4 All ER 546, [2000] 3 WLR 79, [2000]
   ICR 748, [1999] PLR 215, [1999] 35 LS Gaz R 39, [1999] NLJR 1442, CA
.... 657
Edge v Salisbury (1749) Amb 70, 27 ER 42, [1558–1774] All ER Rep 628
.... 215, 275, 349
Edgeworth v Edgeworth (1869) LR 4 HL 35, 17 WR 714
.... 226, 255, 407, 422, 446
Edmonds v Edmonds [1965] 1 All ER 379n, [1965] 1 WLR 58, 108 Sol Jo 1047, P, D and
   Admlty 465
Edmonds v Fessey. See Edmunds v Fessey
Edmonds v Millett (1855) 20 Beav 54, 109 RR 341 125
Edmonds v Robinson (1885) 29 Ch D 170, 33 WR 471, 52 LT 339, sub nom Edmunds v
   Robinson 54 LJ Ch 586 1183
Edmondson v Edmondson (1901) 45 Sol Jo 395, 17 TLR 397, P, D and Admlty
.... 7
Edmondson's Estate, Re (1868) LR 5 Eq 389, 16 WR 890
.... 256, 412, 436
Edmondson's Will Trusts, Re, Baron Sandford of Banbury v Edmondson [1972] 1 All ER
   444, [1972] 1 WLR 183, 116 Sol Jo 79, CA 308–309, 311
Edmunds v Fessey (1861) 29 Beav 233, 30 LJ Ch 279, 7 Jur NS 282, 9 WR 365, sub nom
   Edmonds v Fessey 3 LT 765 352
Edmunds v Robinson. See Edmonds v Robinson
Edmunds v Waugh (1858) 4 Drew 275, 6 WR 589; on appeal (1863) 2 New Rep 408
.... 427
Edward's Will Trusts, Re, Dalgleish v Leighton [1947] 2 All ER 521, [1948] LJR 60, 91 Sol
   Jo 572; revsd sub nom Edwards' Will Trusts, Re, Dalgleish v Leighton [1948] Ch 440,
   [1948] 1 All ER 821, [1948] LJR 1364, 92 Sol Jo 297, CA 201, 246, 657
Edwards v Jones (1864) 33 Beav 348 395
Edwardes v Jones (No 2) (1866) 35 Beav 474, 14 WR 815
.... 263
Edwards, Re, Edwards v Edwards [1894] 3 Ch 644, 64 LJ Ch 179, 8 R 618, 43 WR 169
.... 204, 454

                                                                                        PARA
Edwards, Re, Edwards v Edwards [2007] EWHC 1119 (Ch), [2007] All ER (D) 46 (May)
.... 56, 58–59
Edwards, Re, Jones v Jones [1906] 1 Ch 570, 75 LJ Ch 321, 54 WR 446, 50 Sol Jo 324,
  94 LT 593, [1904–7] All ER Rep Ext 1276, CA 255, 416, 436–437, 456
Edwards, Re, Lloyd v Boyes [1910] 1 Ch 541, 79 LJ Ch 281, 54 Sol Jo 325, 102 LT 308,
  26 TLR 308 145
Edwards, Re, Lloyds Bank Ltd v Worthington [1946] 2 All ER 408, 115 LJ Ch 335, 175
  LT 231 1130
Edwards, Re, Macadam v Wright [1958] Ch 168, [1957] 2 All ER 495, [1957] 3 WLR
  131, 101 Sol Jo 515, CA 156, 282
Edwards, Re, Rowland v Edwards (1890) 63 LT 481 282
Edwards v Alliston (1827) 4 Russ 78, 6 LJOS Ch 30 474
Edwards v Bethel (1818) 1 B & Ald 254 1291
Edwards v Champion (1847) 1 De G & Sm 75 395
Edwards v Champion (1853) 3 De GM & G 202, 23 LJ Ch 123, 1 Eq Rep 419, 1 WR
  497, 21 LTOS 293 395
Edwards v Edwards (1837) 1 Jur 654 125
Edwards v Edwards (1849) 12 Beav 97 .... 249, 336
Edwards v Edwards (1852) 15 Beav 357, 21 LJ Ch 324, 16 Jur 259, 19 LTOS 483
.... 449–450
Edwards v Grace (1836) 5 Dowl 302, 6 LJ Ex 68, 2 Gale 241, 2 M & W 190
.... 1288
Edwards v Hammond (1684) 1 Bos & P 324n, 3 Lev 132, sub nom Stocker v Edwards 2
  Show 398 423
Edwards v Saloway (1848) 2 Ph 625, 17 LJ Ch 329, 12 Jur 487, 12 LTOS 101
.... 161
Edwards v Thompson (1868) 38 LJ Ch 65 250
Edwards' Will Trusts, Re, Edwards v Edwards [1982] Ch 30, [1981] 2 All ER 941, [1981]
  3 WLR 15, 125 Sol Jo 258, CA 1144
Edwards-Taylor's Goods, Re [1951] P 24, 94 Sol Jo 536, 66 (pt 2) TLR 593, sub nom
  Taylor, Re [1950] 2 All ER 446, P, D and Admlty 759
Edyvean v Archer, Re Brooke [1903] AC 379, 72 LJPC 85, 89 LT 4, 19 TLR 561,
  [1900–3] All ER Rep Ext 1285, PC 249, 334
Eeles v Lambert (1648) Aleyn 38, Sty 38, 54, 73, 2 Vern 101n
.... 989
Eeles Goods, Re (1862) 27 JP 9, 32 LJPM & A 4, 2 Sw & Tr 600, 11 WR 31, 7 LT 338
.... 103, 108
Egan, Re, Mills v Penton [1899] 1 Ch 688, 68 LJ Ch 307, 80 LT 153
.... 284, 293
Egerton v Earl Brownlow (1853) 4 HL Cas 1, 8 State Tr NS 193, 23 LJ Ch 348, 18 Jur 71,
  10 ER 359, [1843–60] All ER Rep 970, 21 LTOS 306, HL
.... 33–34, 116, 129–131, 143, 194, 258, 414, 423
Egerton v Jones (1830) 3 Sim 409 460
Egg v Devey (1847) 10 Beav 444, 16 LJ Ch 509, 11 Jur 1023, 76 RR 170, 10 LTOS 243
.... 152
Eglin v Sanderson (1862) 3 Giff 434, 8 Jur NS 329, 133 RR 156, 6 LT 151
.... 1200
Egmont's (Earl) Settled Estates, Re, Lefroy v Egmont [1912] 1 Ch 251, 81 LJ Ch 250, 106
  LT 292 1131
Eichardt, Re, Brebrer v O'Meara (1905) 25 NZLR 374 432
Eichholz, Re, Eichholz's Trustee v Eichholz [1959] Ch 708, [1959] 1 All ER 166, [1959] 2
  WLR 200, 103 Sol Jo 131 .... 988, 1221
Eilbeck, Re, ex p Good Intent Lodge, No 987 of Grand United Order of Odd Fellows
  (Trustees) [1910] 1 KB 136, 79 LJKB 265, 17 Mans 1, 54 Sol Jo 118, 101 LT 688, 26
  TLR 111 973
Eiser's Will Trusts, Re, Fogg v Eastwood [1937] 1 All ER 244
.... 625
Ekersley v Platt. See Eckersley v Platt
Eland v Eland (1830) 4 My & Cr 420, 8 LJ Ch 289, 3 Jur 474
.... 1024
Elcom, Re, Layborn v Grover Wright [1894] 1 Ch 303, 63 LJ Ch 392, 7 R 87, 42 WR
  279, [1891–4] All ER Rep 258, 38 Sol Jo 127, 70 LT 54, 10 TLR 162, CA
.... 1, 115
Elderton's Goods, Re (1832) 4 Hag Ecc 210 801

PARA

Elementary Education Acts 1870 and 1873, Re [1909] 1 Ch 55, 73 JP 22, 78 LJ Ch 281,
99 LT 862, 25 TLR 78, CA 1014

Elford, Re, Elford v Elford [1910] 1 Ch 814, 79 LJ Ch 385, 54 Sol Jo 542, 102 LT 488
.... 1124

Elitestone Ltd v Morris [1997] 2 All ER 513, [1997] 1 WLR 687, 30 HLR 266, [1997]
19 LS Gaz R 25, [1997] NLJR 721, [1997] 27 EG 116, 141 Sol Jo LB 113, HL
.... 932

Ellard v Phelan [1914] 1 IR 76 .... 17, 253, 365

Ellicombe v Gompertz (1837) 3 My & Cr 127 456

Elliot, Re, Kelly v Elliot [1896] 2 Ch 353, 65 LJ Ch 753, 44 WR 632, 40 Sol Jo 600, 75
LT 138, 12 TLR 497, [1895–9] All ER Rep Ext 1885 .... 116, 228

Elliot v Collier (1747) 3 Atk 526, 1 Wils 168, 1 Ves Sen 15
.... 503

Elliot v Jekyl (1755) 2 Ves Sen 681 249

Elliot v Joicey [1935] AC 209, 104 LJ Ch 111, [1935] All ER Rep 578, 79 Sol Jo 144, 152
LT 398, 51 TLR 261, 1935 SC (HL) 57, HL 169, 315, 362, 1210

Elliot v Merryman (1740) 2 Atk 41, Barn Ch 78 1025

Elliot's Trusts, Re (1873) LR 15 Eq 194, 42 LJ Ch 289, 21 WR 455
.... 1047, 1074

Elliott, Re (1956) Times, 18 May 572

Elliott, Re, Lloyds Bank Ltd v Burton-on-Trent Hospital Management Committee [1952]
Ch 217, [1952] 1 All ER 145, 96 Sol Jo 73, [1952] 1 TLR 298
.... 130, 143

Elliott v Bishop (1854) 19 JP 71, 24 LJ Ex 33, 10 Exch 496, 3 WR 160, 3 CLR 272,
24 LTOS 217; on appeal sub nom Bishop v Elliott (1855) 19 JP 501, 24 LJ Ex 229, 11
Exch 113, 1 Jur NS 962, 3 WR 454, 3 CLR 1337, sub nom Elliott v Bishop 25 LTOS
150 932

Elliott v Davenport (1705) 1 P Wms 83, 2 Vern 521 .... 160, 163,164, 321

Elliott v Dearsley (1880) 16 Ch D 322, 29 WR 494, 44 LT 198, CA
.... 1111

Elliott v Elliott (1841) 11 LJ Ex 3, 9 M & W 23 .... 1139, 1141

Elliott v Elliott (1841) 12 Sim 276, 10 LJ Ch 363 308

Elliott v Kemp (1840) 10 LJ Ex 321, 7 M & W 306 1161

Elliott v Simmonds [2016] EWHC 962 (Ch) 874

Elliott v Smith (1882) 22 Ch D 236, 48 LT 27, sub nom Elliott, Re, Elliott v Smith 52 LJ
Ch 222, 31 WR 336 449

Ellis, Re, Nettleton v Crimmins [1935] Ch 193, 104 LJ Ch 53, [1934] All ER Rep 58, 152
LT 370 1093

Ellis, Re, Owen v Bentley (1918) 53 ILT 6 221–223

Ellis v Bartrum (No 2) (1857) 25 Beav 109 270

Ellis v Eden (1857) 23 Beav 543, 26 LJ Ch 533, 3 Jur NS 950, 30 LTOS 60
.... 295

Ellis v Eden (No 2) (1858) 25 Beav 482 277

Ellis v Ellis [1905] 1 Ch 613, 74 LJ Ch 296, 53 WR 617, 92 LT 727
.... 646, 858

Ellis v Ellis (1802) 1 Sch & Lef 1 428

Ellis v Houston (1878) 10 Ch D 236, 27 WR 501 .... 210, 350

Ellis v Maxwell (1841) 3 Beav 587, 10 LJ Ch 266, 52 RR 235
.... 412

Ellis v Selby (1836) 1 My & Cr 286, 5 LJ Ch 214, 43 RR 188
.... 11, 250

Ellis v Smith (1754) 1 Dick 225, 1 Ves 11 63

Ellis Goods, Re (1840) 2 Curt 395 71

Ellison v Airey (1748) 1 Ves Sen 111, 27 ER 924, [1558–1774] All ER Rep 475
.... 304–305, 362

Ellison v Thomas (1862) 1 De GJ & Sm 18, 32 LJ Ch 32, 8 Jur NS 1139, 1 New Rep 37,
11 WR 56, 7 LT 342 333

Ellisons' Goods, Re [1907] 2 IR 480, 41 ILT 123 73

Elms v Elms (1858) 27 LJP & M 96, 4 Jur NS 765, 1 Sw & Tr 155, 6 WR 864, 31 LTOS
332 103

Elmsley v Young (1835) 2 My & K 780, 4 LJ Ch 200 .... 309, 343, 395

Elmsley's Goods, Re, Dyke v Williams (1871) LR 2 P & D 239, 35 JP 744, 40 LJP & M
33, 19 WR 784, 24 LT 805 908

Elsworthy v Hewett. See Elworthy v Sandford

Elton, Re, Elton v Elton [1917] 2 Ch 413, 87 LJ Ch 49, 62 Sol Jo 71, 117 LT 533
.... 384

PARA

Elton v Eason (1812) 19 Ves 73 385
Elton v Elton (1747) 3 Atk 504, 1 Wils 159, 1 Ves Sen 4
.... 135
Elton v Shephard (1781) 1 Bro CC 532 375
Elwes v Elwes (1728) 2 Lee 573 773
Elwin v Elwin (1803) 8 Ves 547 .... 243, 415
Elworthy v Sandford (1864) 3 H & C 330, 34 LJ Ex 42, 12 WR 1008, 10 LT 654, sub
    nom Elsworthy v Hewett 4 New Rep 371 1267
Ely, Re, Tottenham v Ely (1891) 65 LT 452, [1891–4] All ER Rep Ext 1931
.... 207, 217, 220
Embleton's Will Trusts, Re, Sodeau v Nelson [1965] 1 All ER 771, [1965] 1 WLR 840, 44
    ATC 69, [1965] TR 83, 109 Sol Jo 437 1130
Embrey v Martin (1754) Amb 230, 1 Keny 77 438
Embury, Re, Bowyer v Page (No 2) [1914] WN 220, 58 Sol Jo 612, 111 LT 275
.... 352
Embury, Re, Page v Bowyer (1913) 58 Sol Jo 49, 109 LT 511, [1911–13] All ER Rep Ext
    1418 336
Emeris v Woodward (1889) 43 Ch D 185, 59 LJ Ch 230, 38 WR 346, 61 LT 666
.... 1188
Emerson, Re, Morrill v Nutty [1929] 1 Ch 128, 98 LJ Ch 145, [1928] All ER Rep 386,
    140 LT 217 293
Emerson's Goods, Re (1882) 9 LR Ir 443 63
Emery, Re, Emery v Emery [1923] P 184, 92 LJP 138, 130 LT 127, 39 TLR 713, P, D and
    Admlty 915
Emery's Estate, Re, Jones v Emery (1876) 3 Ch D 300, sub nom Emery's Estate, Re, Jones v
    Ratcliffe 24 WR 917, 34 LT 846 .... 274, 362
Emes v Hancock (1743) 2 Atk 507 17
Emmerson, Re, Rawlings v Emmerson (1887) 57 LJP 1, CA
.... 680
Emmet's Estate, Re, Emmet v Emmet (1880) 13 Ch D 484, 49 LJ Ch 295, 28 WR 401,
    [1874–8] All ER Rep 576, 42 LT 4, CA 304, 307–308, 310
Emmet's Estate, Re, Emmet v Emmet (1881) 17 Ch D 142, 50 LJ Ch 341, 29 WR 464, 44
    LT 172 1257
Emmett, Re, Jenkins v Emmett (1906) 95 LT 755 976
Emperor v Rolfe (1748–9) (1748) 1 Ves Sen 208 .... 260, 452
Emson, Re, Grain v Grain (1905) 74 LJ Ch 565, 93 LT 104, 21 TLR 623
.... 414
Emuss v Smith (1848) 2 De G & Sm 722 .... 114, 157, 279, 282
Endacott, Re, Corpe v Endacott [1960] Ch 232, [1959] 3 All ER 562, [1959] 3 WLR 799,
    58 LGR 25, 103 Sol Jo 918, CA 11, 35, 263
England, Re, England v Bayles [1906] VLR 94 287
England v England (1869) 17 WR 719, 20 LT 648 332
England's Settlement Trusts, Re, Dobb v England [1918] 1 Ch 24, 87 LJ Ch 73, 117 LT
    466 .... 1018, 1274
English's Goods, Re (1864) 29 JP 72, 34 LJPM & A 5, 3 Sw & Tr 586, 13 WR 503, sub
    nom Newcombe v English, Re English's Goods 11 LT 612
.... 8, 54
Ennis v Smith (1839) Jo & Car 400 21
Eno v Eno (1847) 6 Hare 171, 16 LJ Ch 358, 11 Jur 746
.... 460
Enohin v Wylie (1862) 10 HL Cas 1, 31 LJ Ch 402, 8 Jur NS 897, 10 WR 467, 6 LT 263,
    [1861–73] All ER Rep Ext 2305 .... 12, 225, 257, 293, 718, 845
Epple v Stone (1906) 3 CLR 412, Aust HC 375
Erlanger v New Sombrero Phosphate Co (1878) 3 App Cas 1218, 27 WR 65,
    [1874–80] All ER Rep 271, 39 LT 269, sub nom New Sombrero Phosphate Co v
    Erlanger 48 LJ Ch 73, HL 1234
Ernst v Zwicker (1897) 27 SCR 594 387
Errington, Re, Gibbs v Lassam [1927] 1 Ch 421, 96 LJ Ch 345, 71 Sol Jo 309, 136 LT
    764, [1927] All ER Rep Ext 827 397
Erving v Peters (1790) 3 Term Rep 685 .... 1290, 1294
Escott's Goods, Re (1842) 1 Notes of Cases 571 86
Escritt v Escritt (1982) 3 FLR 280; affd (1982) 3 FLR 280, 131 NLJ 1266, CA
.... 598
Espinasse v Luffingham (1846) 3 Jo & Lat 186 379
Espinosa v Bourke [1999] 3 FCR 76, [1999] 1 FLR 747, [1999] Fam Law 210, CA
.... 568, 570, 572–573, 576, 580, 591, 604

PARA

Esson v Esson [2009] EWHC 3045 (Ch), [2009] All ER (D) 325 (Nov)
.... 219, 226, 228, 242
Etches v Etches (1856) 3 Drew 441, 4 WR 307 .... 324, 446
Ettricke v Ettricke (1767) Amb 656 395
Eumorfopoulos, Re, Ralli v Eumorfopoulos [1944] Ch 133, [1943] 2 All ER 719, 113 LJ
    Ch 30, 87 Sol Jo 423, 170 LT 21 .... 246, 296
Eustace, Re, Lee v McMillan [1912] 1 Ch 561, 81 LJ Ch 529, 56 Sol Jo 468, 106 LT 789
    1101
Evan's Will Trusts, Re, Pickering v Evans [1921] 2 Ch 309, 91 LJ Ch 29, 65 Sol Jo 753,
    125 LT 822 .... 1123, 1126–1127
Evans, Re, Evans v Evans (1887) 34 Ch D 597, 35 WR 586, 56 LT 768, CA
    .... 1039, 1041
Evans, Re, Evans v Powell [1909] 1 Ch 784, 78 LJ Ch 441, 100 LT 779
    .... 280, 282
Evans, Re, Evans v Westcombe [1999] 2 All ER 777, 143 Sol Jo LB 72, [1999] All ER (D)
    75 .... 964, 1013–1014, 1106, 1194, 1259
Evans, Re, Hewitt v Edwards [1940] Ch 629, 109 LJ Ch 216, 84 Sol Jo 319, 162 LT 420,
    56 TLR 630 .... 140, 247
Evans, Re, Public Trustee v Evans [1920] 2 Ch 304, 89 LJ Ch 525, 123 LT 735, 36 TLR
    674, CA 229, 462
Evans v Amicus Healthcare Ltd [2004] EWCA Civ 727, [2005] Fam 1, [2004] 3 All ER
    1025, [2004] 3 WLR 681, [2004] 2 FCR 530, [2004] 2 FLR 766, [2004] Fam Law
    647, 78 BMLR 181, (2004) Times, 30 June, 148 Sol Jo LB 823, [2004] All ER (D)
    309 (Jun) 359
Evans v Angell (1858) 26 Beav 202, 5 Jur NS 134, 32 LTOS 382
    .... 210, 271, 286
Evans v Brown (1842) 5 Beav 114, 11 LJ Ch 349, 6 Jur 380
    558
Evans v Burrell (1859) 23 JP 280, 28 LJP & M 82, 4 Sw & Tr 185
    754
Evans v Charles (1794) 1 Anst 128 537
Evans v Crosbie (1847) 15 Sim 600, 16 LJ Ch 494, 11 Jur 510, 9 LTOS 291
    298
Evans v Dallow, Re Dallow's Goods (1862) 26 JP 631, 31 LJPM & A 128
    105
Evans v Davies (1849) 7 Hare 498, 18 LJ Ch 180 350
Evans v Evans [1892] 2 Ch 173, 61 LJ Ch 456, 40 WR 465, 36 Sol Jo 425, 67 LT 152, CA
    339
Evans v Evans [1985] 3 All ER 289, [1986] 1 WLR 101, [1986] 1 FLR 319, [1986] Fam
    Law 103, 129 Sol Jo 833, [1985] LS Gaz R 3530, [1985] NLJ Rep 1008, CA
    .... 1018, 1196, 1274
Evans v Evans (1849) 17 Sim 86, 14 Jur 383 291
Evans v Evans (1858) 25 Beav 81, 53 ER 566 410
Evans v Evans (1865) 33 LJ Ch 662, 10 LT 59, CA 376, 378
Evans v Evans (1892) 67 LT 719 628
Evans v Flight (1838) 2 Jur 818 959
Evans v Harris (1842) 5 Beav 45 301
Evans v Jones (1846) 2 Coll 516 336
Evans v Massey (1819) 8 Price 22 354
Evans v Pilkington (1839) 10 Sim 412 429
Evans v Rosser (1864) 2 Hem & M 190, 10 Jur NS 385, 3 New Rep 685, 12 WR 570, sub
    nom Evans v Rossall 10 LT 159 133
Evans v Scott (1847) 1 HL Cas 43, 11 Jur 291, 9 LTOS 509
    438
Evans v Stratford (1864) 2 Hem & M 142, 10 Jur NS 861, 10 LT 713
    .... 126, 152
Evans v Tripp (1821) 6 Madd 91 268
Evans v Turner (1904) 23 NZLR 825 396
Evans v Tyler (1849) 2 Rob Eccl 128, 14 Jur 47, 13 Jur 413, 14 LTOS 450, 13 LTOS 264,
    7 Notes of Cases 296 621
Evans v Wyatt (1862) 31 Beav 217 1009
Evans and Bettell's Contract, Re [1910] 2 Ch 438, 79 LJ Ch 669, [1908–10] All ER Rep
    202, 54 Sol Jo 680, 103 LT 181 1058
Evans d Brooke v Astley (1764) 3 Burr 1570, 1 Wm Bl 499, 521
    456
Evans' Goods, Re (1923) 128 LT 669, P, D and Admlty
    .... 65, 611

PARA

Evans Goods, Re, Evans v Evans (1890) 15 PD 215, 60 LJP 18, 63 LT 254, P, D and
Admlty 809

Evans' Will Trusts, Re, Public Trustee v Gausby [1948] Ch 185, [1948] 1 All ER 381,
[1949] LJR 555, 92 Sol Jo 72 1015

Evanturel v Evanturel (1874) LR 6 PC 1, 43 LJPC 58, 23 WR 32, 31 LT 105
.... 131, 141

Eve, Re, Belton v Thompson (1905) 93 LT 235 .... 172, 427

Eve, Re, Edwards v Burns [1909] 1 Ch 796, 78 LJ Ch 388, [1908–10] All ER Rep 131,
100 LT 874 .... 212, 350–351

Eve, Re, Hall v Eve [1917] 1 Ch 562, 86 LJ Ch 396, 116 LT 682, 33 TLR 251
.... 1130

Eve, Re, National Provincial Bank Ltd v Eve [1956] Ch 479, [1956] 2 All ER 321, [1956]
3 WLR 69, 100 Sol Jo 381 .... 125, 1004

Everall v Browne (1853) 22 LJ Ch 376, 1 Sm & G 368, 1 WR 210
.... 250

Everest, Re [1975] Fam 44, [1975] 1 All ER 672, [1975] 2 WLR 333, 119 Sol Jo 86
.... 105

Everest v Gell (1791) 1 Ves 286 459

Everett, Re, Prince v Hunt [1944] Ch 176, [1944] 2 All ER 19, 113 LJ Ch 81, 170 LT 178,
60 TLR 223 295

Everett v Everett (1877) 7 Ch D 428, 47 LJ Ch 367, 26 WR 333, 38 LT 580, CA
.... 282

Evers v Challis (1859) 7 HL Cas 531, 29 LJQB 121, 5 Jur NS 825, 115 RR 257, 7 WR
622, 33 LTOS 373 446

Ewart v Cochrane (1861) 25 JP 612, 7 Jur NS 925, 10 WR 3, 5 LT 1, 4 Macq 117, HL
.... 283

Ewen v Franklin (1855) Dea & Sw 7, 1 Jur NS 1220, 4 WR 164, 26 LTOS 127
.... 63

Ewens v Addison (1858) 4 Jur NS 1034, 7 WR 23, 32 LTOS 103
.... 135

Ewer v Corbet (1723) 2 P Wms 148 .... 1023, 1025, 1028

Ewing v Orr Ewing (1883) 9 App Cas 34, 53 LJ Ch 435, 32 WR 573, 50 LT 401, HL
.... 960

Ewing v Orr Ewing (1885) 10 App Cas 453, 53 LT 826, 1 TLR 645, HL
.... 718

Ewington v Fenn (1852) 16 Jur 398 395

Exmouth (Viscount), Re, Viscount Exmouth v Praed (1883) 23 Ch D 158, 52 LJ Ch 420,
31 WR 545, [1881–5] All ER Rep 647, 48 LT 422 .... 138, 141

Experience Hendrix LLC v Purple Haze Records Ltd [2007] EWCA Civ 501, [2007] FSR
769, [2007] IP & T 920, [2008] EMLR 351, [2007] All ER (D) 430 (May)
.... 917, 1213

Eynon's Goods, Re (1873) LR 3 P & D 92, 37 JP 616, 42 LJP & M 52, 21 WR 856, 29
LT 45 75

Eyre, Re, Johnson v Williams [1917] 1 Ch 351, 86 LJ Ch 257, 61 Sol Jo 336, 116 LT 469
.... 1076, 1083

Eyre v Countess of Shaftesbury (1722) 2 Eq Cas Abr 710, 755, 2 P Wms 103,
[1558–1774] All ER Rep 129, sub nom Earl Shaftsbury v Shaftsbury Gilb Ch 172, 24
ER 659 637

Eyre v Eyre [1903] P 131, 72 LJP 45, 51 WR 701, 88 LT 567, 19 TLR 380, P, D and
Admlty 711, 716

Eyre v Eyre [1968] 1 All ER 968, sub nom Re Eyre [1968] 1 WLR 530, 112 Sol Jo 273, P,
D and Admlty 591

Eyre v Marsden (1839) 4 My & Cr 231, 3 Jur 450 410

Eyre v Monro (1857) 3 K & J 305, 26 LJ Ch 757, 3 Jur NS 584, 5 WR 870, 30 LTOS 61
.... 21

Eyre's Goods, Re [1905] 2 IR 540 95

Ezekiel's Settlement Trusts, Re, National Provincial Bank Ltd v Hyam [1942] Ch 230,
[1942] 2 All ER 224, 111 LJ Ch 41; affd [1942] Ch 230, [1942] 2 All ER 224, 111 LJ
Ch 155, 86 Sol Jo 76, 166 LT 137, CA 1043

F

F, Re (1965) Times, 26 February 591
Fagg's Trust, Re (1850) 19 LJ Ch 175 1047

PARA

Fairchild v Glenhaven Funeral Services Ltd [2002] UKHL 22, [2003] 1 AC 32, [2002] 3 All ER 305, [2002] ICR 798, [2002] IRLR 533, 67 BMLR 90, [2002] NLJR 998, (2002) Times, 21 June, [2003] 1 LRC 674, [2002] All ER (D) 139 (Jun) 1280
Fairfield v Bushell (1863) 32 Beav 158 336
Fairfield v Morgan (1805) 2 Bos & PNR 38, HL 442
Fairman v Green (1804) 10 Ves 45 1076
Fairtlough v Johnstone (1865) 16 I Ch R 442 153
Fairweather's Goods, Re (1862) 2 Sw & Tr 588, 10 WR 862, 6 LT 788 761
Falkiner, Re, Mead v Smith [1924] 1 Ch 88, 93 LJ Ch 76, [1923] All ER Rep 681, 68 Sol Jo 101, 130 LT 405 .... 222, 370, 1069
Falkiner v Hornidge (1858) 8 I Ch R 184 459
Falkland (Lord Viscount) v Bertie (1698) 2 Vern 333, [1558–1774] All ER Rep 396, Holt KB 230, sub nom Bertie v Faulkland 1 Eq Cas Abr 110, 3 Cas in Ch 129, Freem Ch 220, 12 Mod Rep 182, 1 Salk 231, 23 ER 814; on appeal sub nom Bertie v Viscount Falkland (1698) Colles 10, HL 133, 146, 149, 199, 207, 246
Falkner v Butler (1765) Amb 514 328
Falle v Godfray (1888) 14 App Cas 70, 58 LJPC 61, 60 LT 120, PC 1
Fane, Re, Fane v Fane (1886) 2 TLR 510 201
Fane v Fane (1681) 1 Vern 30 232
Fanshaw, Re, Harari v Rollo (1983) Times, 17 November, CA 911
Farhall v Farhall (1871) 7 Ch App 123, 41 LJ Ch 146, 20 WR 157, 25 LT 685 .... 1041, 1239
Faris, Re, Goddard v Overend [1911] 1 IR 165 156
Faris, Re, Goddard v Overend (No 2) [1911] 1 IR 469 109
Farley v Briant (1835–7) (1835) 3 Ad & El 839, 4 LJKB 246, 5 LJKB 132, 6 LJKB 87, 1 Har & W 299, 775, 5 Nev & MKB 42 1276
Farley v Westminster Bank [1939] AC 430, [1939] 3 All ER 491, 108 LJ Ch 307, 161 LT 103, 55 TLR 943, HL 11
Farmer, Re, Nightingale v Whybrow [1939] Ch 573, [1939] 1 All ER 319, 108 LJ Ch 197, 2 Sol Jo 1050, 160 LT 59 1092
Farmer v Francis (1824) 2 Bing 151 423–424
Farmer v Francis (1826) 2 Sim & St 505, 4 LJOS Ch 154 .... 423–425, 428
Farncombe's Trusts, Re (1878) 9 Ch D 652, 47 LJ Ch 328 174
Farquhar v Hadden (1871) 7 Ch App 1, 41 LJ Ch 260, 20 WR 46, 25 LT 717 287
Farquharson v Floyer (1876) 3 Ch D 109, 45 LJ Ch 750, 35 LT 355 1003
Farr v Hennis (1881) 44 LT 202, CA 370
Farr v Newman (1792) 4 Term Rep 621 924
Farrant v Nichols (1846) 9 Beav 327, 15 LJ Ch 259 .... 260, 336
Farrar v Lord Winterton (1842) 5 Beav 1, 6 Jur 204 156
Farrelly v Corrigan [1899] AC 563, 68 LJPC 133, PC 892
Farrer v Barker (1852) 9 Hare 737 260
Farrer v St Catherine's College, Cambridge (1873) LR 16 Eq 19, 42 LJ Ch 809, 21 WR 643, 28 LT 800, [1861–73] All ER Rep Ext 1108 .... 100, 217, 252, 276
Farrer's Estate, Re (1858) 8 ICLR 370 .... 115, 282
Farrington v Knightly (1721) 1 P Wms 544 606
Farrow, Re [1987] 1 FLR 205, [1987] Fam Law 14 .... 574, 577, 591
Farrow v Wilson (1869) LR 4 CP 744, 38 LJCP 326, 18 WR 43, [1861–73] All ER Rep 846, 20 LT 810 .... 1213, 1279
Faulding's Trust, Re (1858) 26 Beav 263, 28 LJ Ch 217, 4 Jur NS 1289, 7 WR 74, 32 LTOS 154 .... 322, 324
Faulds v Jackson (1845) 6 Notes of Cases Supp i, PC 69–70
Faulkner v Daniel (1843) 3 Hare 199, 8 Jur 29 817
Faulkner v Hollingsworth (1784) 8 Ves 558 451
Faux, Re, Taylor v Faux [1915] WN 135, 84 LJ Ch 873, 59 Sol Jo 457, 113 LT 81, 31 TLR 289 .... 308, 312
Fawcet v Lowther (1751) 2 Ves Sen 300 561
Fawcett, Re, Public Trustee v Dugdale [1940] Ch 402, 109 LJ Ch 124, 84 Sol Jo 186, 162 LT 250, 56 TLR 468 1126
Fawcett v Jones (1813) 2 Ves & B 313 446

PARA

Fawcett v Jones, Codrington and Pulteney (1810) 3 Phillim 434; on appeal (1810) 3 Phillim
490 99
Fawcett's Estate, Re [1941] P 85, [1941] 2 All ER 341, 110 LJP 33, 165 LT 350, 57 TLR
541, P, D and Admlty 97, 679
Fawcett Properties Ltd v Buckingham County Council [1961] AC 636, [1960] 3 All ER
503, [1960] 3 WLR 831, 59 LGR 69, 12 P & CR 1, 125 JP 8, 104 Sol Jo 912, 176
Estates Gazette 1115, HL 138
Fawkes v Gray (1811) 18 Ves 131 146
Fawlkner v Fawlkner (1681) 1 Eq Cas Abr 119, 1 Vern 21
.... 469
Fay v Fay (1880) 5 LR Ir 274 .... 256, 455
Fazakerley v Gillibrand (1834) 6 Sim 591 404
Fazio v Rush [2002] EWHC 1742 (Ch) 657
Feakes v Standley (1857) 24 Beav 485, 30 LTOS 182 460
Fearn's Will, Re (1879) 27 WR 392 214
Feather, Re, Harrison v Tapsell [1945] Ch 343, [1945] 1 All ER 552, 115 LJ Ch 6, 89 Sol
Jo 235, 172 LT 308 .... 284, 328, 366
Featherstone's Trusts, Re (1882) 22 Ch D 111, 52 LJ Ch 75, 31 WR 89, 47 LT 538
.... 173, 175, 332, 412
Fegan, Re, Fegan v Fegan [1928] Ch 45, 97 LJ Ch 36, [1927] All ER Rep 606, 71 Sol Jo
866, 138 LT 265 1008
Feis, Re, Guillaume v Ritz-Remorf [1964] Ch 106, [1963] 3 All ER 303, [1963] 3 WLR
451, 107 Sol Jo 555 .... 107–109, 993, 999
Fell v Biddolph (1875) LR 10 CP 701, 44 LJPC 402, 23 WR 913, 32 LT 864
.... 174, 305
Feltham's Will Trusts, Re (1855) 1 K & J 528 .... 199, 214–215, 276
Femings v Jarrat (1795) 1 Esp 335 1262
Fendall v Nash (1779) 5 Ves 197n 1076
Fender v St John-Mildmay [1938] AC 1, 81 Sol Jo 549, 53 TLR 885, sub nom Fender v
Mildmay [1937] 3 All ER 402, 106 LJKB 641, 157 LT 340, HL
.... 131
Fenn v Death (1856) 23 Beav 73, 2 Jur NS 700, 4 WR 828
.... 331
Fenny d Collings v Ewestace (1815) 4 M & S 58 241
Fentem, Re, Cockerton v Fentem [1950] 2 All ER 1073, 94 Sol Jo 779
.... 132–133, 247
Fenton v Clegg (1854) 23 LJ Ex 197, 9 Exch 680, 2 CLR 1014
.... 1142
Fenton v Farington (1856) 2 Jur NS 1120 409
Fenton's Goods, Re (1825) 3 Add 35 630
Fenwick, Re, Lloyds Bank Ltd v Fenwick [1922] 2 Ch 775, 92 LJ Ch 97, 66 Sol Jo 631,
128 LT 191 1130
Fenwick's Goods, Re (1867) LR 1 P & D 319, 31 JP 359, 36 LJP & M 54, 16 LT 124
.... 99
Fenwick's Will Trusts, Re, Fenwick v Stewart [1936] Ch 720, [1936] 2 All ER 1096,
105 LJ Ch 351, 80 Sol Jo 553, 155 LT 199 .... 1118, 1121, 1123
Fenwicke v Clarke (1862) 4 De GF & J 240, 31 LJ Ch 728, 10 WR 636, 6 LT 593
.... 962, 1099
Fereyes v Robertson (1731) Bunb 301 392
Ferguson, Re, Curry v Bell (1915) 49 ILT 110 1078
Ferguson v Ferguson (1872) IR 6 Eq 199 282
Ferguson v Ferguson (1886) 17 LR Ir 552 424
Ferguson v Ogilby (1862) 12 I Ch R 411 1131
Ferguson's Trust, Re (1874) 22 WR 762 1072
Ferguson-Davie v Ferguson-Davie (1890) 15 PD 109, 59 LJP 70, 62 LT 703, P, D and
Admlty 54, 708
Fergusson's Will, Re [1902] 1 Ch 483, 71 LJ Ch 360, 50 WR 312, 46 Sol Jo 247
.... 343
Ferman v Ryan [1912] QSR 145 293
Ferneley v Napier [2010] EWHC 3345 (Ch), [2010] All ER (D) 234 (Dec)
.... 716
Fernie's Goods, Re (1849) 13 Jur 216, 12 LTOS 559, 6 Notes of Cases 657
.... 623
Ferns v Carr (1885) 28 Ch D 409, 49 JP 503, 54 LJ Ch 478, 33 WR 363, [1881–5] All ER
Rep 1033, 52 LT 348, 1 TLR 220 1213
Ferrey v King (1861) 26 JP 88, 31 LJPM & A 120, 3 Sw & Tr 51, 7 LT 219
.... 911

PARA

Ferrier's Goods, Re (1828) 1 Hag Ecc 241 .... 850, 852
Fessi v Whitmore [1999] 1 FLR 767, [1999] Fam Law 221
.... 956
Festing v Allen (1843) 13 LJ Ex 74, 12 M & W 279, 2 LTOS 150
.... 424
Festing v Allen (1844) 5 Hare 573 436
Fetherston v Fetherston (1835) 3 Cl & Fin 67, sub nom Jack v Fetherston 9 Bli NS 237,
    HL 369, 382, 391
Fetherston-Haugh-Whitney's Estate, Re [1924] 1 IR 153, Ir CA
.... 284, 298
Fewster, Re, Herdman v Fewster [1901] 1 Ch 447, 70 LJ Ch 254, 45 Sol Jo 240, 84 LT 45,
    17 TLR 205 1186
Ffinch v Combe [1894] P 191, 63 LJP 113, 6 R 545, 70 LT 695, 10 TLR 358, P, D and
    Admlty 82, 735
Fickus, Re, Farina v Fickus [1900] 1 Ch 331, 69 LJ Ch 161, 48 WR 250, 44 Sol Jo 157,
    81 LT 749 21–22
Field, Re, Sanderson v Young [1925] Ch 636, 94 LJ Ch 322, [1925] All ER Rep 712, 69
    Sol Jo 661, 133 LT 463 1228–1229
Field v Field [1877] WN 98 1176
Field v Peckett (No 2) (1861) 29 Beav 573, 30 LJ Ch 813, 7 Jur NS 983, 9 WR 526, 4 LT
    459 296
Field v Seward (1877) 5 Ch D 538 405
Field's Will Trusts, Re, Parry-Jones v Hillman [1950] Ch 520, [1950] 2 All ER 188, 66 (pt
    1) TLR 1221 139
Fielden v Ashworth (1875) LR 20 Eq 410, 33 LT 197, Ct of Ch
.... 314, 349, 395
Fielden v Cunliffe. See Cunliffe v Fielden
Fielding v Cronin (1885) 16 LR Ir 379, CA 1224
Fielding v Preston (1857) 1 De G & J 438, 5 WR 851, 29 LTOS 337
.... 1004
Fielding v Walshaw, Re Walshaw's Goods (1879) 43 JP 463, 48 LJP 27, 27 WR 492, 40 LT
    103, P, D and Admlty 3
Figg v Clarke (Inspector of Taxes) [1997] 1 WLR 603, [1997] STC 247, 68 TC 645, [1996]
    10 LS Gaz R 21, 140 Sol Jo LB 66 302
Figgis, Re, Roberts v MacLaren [1969] 1 Ch 123, [1968] 1 All ER 999, [1968] 2 WLR
    1173, 112 Sol Jo 156 .... 148, 246, 1130
Filingham v Bromley (1823) Turn & R 530, 37 ER 1204, [1814–23] All ER Rep 710
.... 138–139
Finch v Finch (1867) LR 1 P & D 371, 31 JP 647, 36 LJP & M 78, 15 WR 797, 16 LT
    268 106
Finch v Finch (1876) 45 LJ Ch 816, 35 LT 235, [1874–80] All ER Rep Ext 1861
.... 286
Finch v Lane (1870) LR 10 Eq 501 .... 421, 423
Finch v Pescott (1874) LR 17 Eq 554, 43 LJ Ch 728, 22 WR 437, 30 LT 156
.... 1042, 1258
Finden v Stephens (1846) 2 Ph 142, 16 LJ Ch 63, 1 Coop temp Cott 318, 10 Jur 1019,
    8 LTOS 249; on appeal (1848) 17 LJ Ch 342, 11 LTOS 325
.... 2, 1049
Findlater v Lowe [1904] 1 IR 519, 38 ILT 127 .... 215, 279
Fingal (Earl) v Blake (1829) 2 Mol 50, 80 131
Finger's Will Trusts, Re, Turner v Ministry of Health [1972] Ch 286, [1971] 3 All ER
    1050, [1971] 3 WLR 775, 115 Sol Jo 790 35–36
Finlason v Tatlock (1870) LR 9 Eq 258, 39 LJ Ch 422, 18 WR 332, 22 LT 3
.... 326, 342
Finlay, Re, Dinamore v Finlay [1932] NI 89 148
Finlay's Estate, Re [1913] 1 IR 143 384
Finn's Estate, Re (1935) 105 LJP 36, [1935] All ER Rep 419, 80 Sol Jo 56, 154 LT 242, 52
    TLR 153, P, D and Admlty 63
Finnegan v Cementation Co Ltd [1953] 1 QB 688, [1953] 1 All ER 1130, [1953] 2 WLR
    1015, 97 Sol Jo 332, CA 647
Finnemore, Re [1992] 1 All ER 800, [1991] 1 WLR 793
.... 8, 41–42, 96–97, 107–109, 185, 708, 865
Finney v Grice (1878) 10 Ch D 13, 48 LJ Ch 247, 27 WR 147
.... 296, 932
Finny v Govett (1908) 25 TLR 186, CA 905

PARA
Finucane v Daly [1919] 1 IR 284 384
Firstpost Homes Ltd v Johnson [1995] 4 All ER 355, [1995] 1 WLR 1567, [1995] NPC
    135, [1996] 1 EGLR 175, [1995] 28 LS Gaz R 30, [1996] 13 EG 125, 139 Sol Jo LB
    187, CA; on appeal [1996] 1 WLR 67, HL 1214
Firth, Re, Loveridge v Firth [1914] 2 Ch 386, 83 LJ Ch 901, 111 LT 332
    440
Firth, Re, Sykes v Ball [1938] Ch 517, [1938] 2 All ER 217, 107 LJ Ch 251, 82 Sol Jo
    332, 158 LT 489, 54 TLR 633 927
Firth v Fielden (1874) 22 WR 622 346
Fischer v Diffley [2013] EWHC 4567 (Ch), [2014] WTLR 757
    899
Fischer v Popham (1875) LR 3 P & D 246, 39 JP 728, 44 LJP & M 47, 23 WR 683, 33
    LT 231, P, D and Admlty 69
Fish, Re, Bennett v Bennett [1893] 2 Ch 413, 62 LJ Ch 977, 2 R 467, 69 LT 233, CA
    .... 652, 1044
Fish, Re, Ingham v Rayner [1894] 2 Ch 83, 63 LJ Ch 437, 7 R 434, 42 WR 520, 38 Sol Jo
    307, 70 LT 825, CA 210, 220, 350
Fisher, Re, Harris v Fisher [1943] Ch 377, [1943] 2 All ER 615, 113 LJ Ch 17, 87 Sol Jo
    372, 169 LT 289, 59 TLR 446 .... 496, 1127, 1138
Fisher, Re, Robinson v Eardley [1915] 1 Ch 302, 84 LJ Ch 342, 59 Sol Jo 318, 112 LT 548
    .... 320, 393, 449
Fisher v Anderson (1879) 4 SCR 406 393
Fisher v Brierley (No 2) (1861) 30 Beav 267 1130
Fisher v Dixon (1845) 12 Cl & Fin 312, 9 Jur 883, HL
    932
Fisher v Fisher (1878) 4 PD 231, 48 LJP 69, P, D and Admlty
    913
Fisher v Goode (1875) 23 WR 225, Ct of Ch 1178
Fisher v Hepburn (1851) 14 Beav 626 250
Fisher v Webster (1872) LR 14 Eq 283, 42 LJ Ch 156, 20 WR 765
    459
Fisher v Wigg (1701) 2 Eq Cas Abr 535, 1 Com 92, 1 Ld Raym 622, 12 Mod Rep 296, 1
    P Wms 14, 1 Salk 391, Holt KB 369 473
Fisher & Sons, Re [1912] 2 KB 491, 81 LJKB 1246, 19 Mans 332, 56 Sol Jo 553, 106 LT
    814 1039
Fisher's Goods, Re (1869) 33 JP 503, 20 LT 684 5
Fison's Will Trusts, Re, Fison v Fison [1950] Ch 394, [1950] 1 All ER 501, 94 Sol Jo 238,
    66 (pt 1) TLR 475 .... 125–126, 284
Fitchet v Adams (1740) 2 Stra 1128 132
Fittock's Goods, Re (1863) 32 LJPM & A 157, 9 Jur NS 311
    754
Fitzgerald, Re (1889) 58 LJ Ch 662, 37 WR 552, 61 LT 221
    344
Fitzgerald v Jervoise (1820) 5 Madd 25 1123
Fitzgerald v Ryan [1899] 2 IR 637 .... 148, 212, 414
FitzGibbon v M'Neill [1908] 1 IR 1 231
Fitzhardinge (Lord), Re, Lord Fitzhardinge v Jenkinson (1899) 43 Sol Jo 296, 80 LT 376,
    15 TLR 225, CA 1131
Fitzhenry v Bonner (1853) 2 Drew 36, 2 Eq Rep 454, 2 WR 30, 22 LTOS 152
    471
Fitzpatrick, Re, Bennett v Bennett [1952] Ch 86, [1951] 2 All ER 949, 95 Sol Jo 744,
    [1951] 2 TLR 995 .... 1013–1014, 1060
Fitzpatrick, Re, Deane v De Valera (1934) 78 Sol Jo 735
    288
Fitzpatrick's Goods, Re (1892) 29 LR Ir 328 .... 628, 1263
Fitzwilliams v Kelly (1852) 10 Hare 266, 22 LJ Ch 1016, 17 Jur 249
    1011
Flanders v Clark (1747) 3 Atk 509, 1 Ves Sen 9 637
Flavel's Will Trusts, Re, Coleman v Flavel [1969] 2 All ER 232, [1969] 1 WLR 444, 113
    Sol Jo 189 194
Flavell, Re, Murray v Flavell (1883) 25 Ch D 89, 53 LJ Ch 185, 32 WR 102,
    [1881–5] All ER Rep 267, 49 LT 690, CA 32
Flecher, Re, King v King (1918) 62 Sol Jo 740 .... 1017, 1197
Fleck, Re, Colston v Roberts (1888) 37 Ch D 677, 36 WR 663, sub nom Re Fleck, Colton
    v Roberts 57 LJ Ch 943, sub nom Re Fleck, Carlton v Roberts 58 LT 624
    1008

                                                                        PARA
Fleetwood, Re, Sidgreaves v Brewer (1880) 15 Ch D 594, 49 LJ Ch 514, 29 WR 45
.... 41–43, 107, 221, 223, 250
Fleming v Brook (1804) 1 Sch & Lef 318 285
Fleming v Buchanan (1853) 3 De GM & G 976, 22 LJ Ch 886, 1 Eq Rep 186, 22 LTOS 8
.... 1005, 1012
Fleming v Burrows (1826) 1 Russ 276, 4 LJOS Ch 115 298
Fleming v Fleming (1862) 1 H & C 242, 31 LJ Ex 419, 8 Jur NS 1042, 10 WR 778, 6 LT
   896 218
Fleming's Will Trust, Re, Ennion v Hampstead Old People's Housing Trust Ltd [1974]
   3 All ER 323, [1974] 1 WLR 1552, 118 Sol Jo 850 .... 279, 282
Fletcher, Re, Barclays Bank Ltd v Ewing [1949] Ch 473, [1949] 1 All ER 732, [1949] LJR
   1255, 93 Sol Jo 301 .... 215, 331
Fletcher, Re, Doré v Fletcher (1885) 34 WR 29, 53 LT 813
.... 416
Fletcher v Collis [1905] 2 Ch 24, 74 LJ Ch 502, 53 WR 516, 49 Sol Jo 499, 92 LT 749,
   CA 1250, 1260
Fletcher v Fletcher (1844) 4 Hare 67, 14 LJ Ch 66, 8 Jur 1040, 67 RR 6
.... 2
Fletcher v Stevenson (1844) 3 Hare 360, 13 LJ Ch 202, 8 Jur 307
.... 991
Fletcher v Walker (1818) 3 Madd 73 962
Fletcher's Goods, Re (1883) 11 LR Ir 359 9
Flinn v Jenkins (1844) 1 Coll 365, 8 Jur 661, 3 LTOS 320
.... 397
Flint v Warren (1847) 15 Sim 626, 16 LJ Ch 441, 11 Jur 665, 9 LTOS 351
.... 45, 320
Flood v Flood [1902] 1 IR 538 279
Flood v Patterson (1861) 29 Beav 295, 30 LJ Ch 486, 7 Jur NS 324, 9 WR 294, 4 LT 78
.... 978
Florence, Re, Lydall v Haberdashers' Co (1917) 87 LJ Ch 86, 62 Sol Jo 87, 117 LT 701
.... 251
Flower, Re, Matheson v Goodwyn (1890) 62 LT 216; revsd (1890) 63 LT 201, CA
.... 339
Flower v Prechtel [1934] All ER Rep 810, 150 LT 491, CA
.... 1242
Flower's Settlement Trusts, Re, Flower v IRC [1957] 1 All ER 462, [1957] 1 WLR 401, 36
   ATC 22, 50 R & IT 150, [1957] TR 29, 101 Sol Jo 189, CA
.... 182
Floyer v Bankes (1863) 27 JP 743, 3 De GJ & Sm 306, 33 LJ Ch 1, 9 Jur NS 1255, 3 New
   Rep 16, 12 WR 28, 9 LT 353 1131
Fludyer, Re, Wingfield v Erskine [1898] 2 Ch 562, 67 LJ Ch 620, 47 WR 5, 79 LT 298
.... 1245
Flynn, Re, Flynn v Flynn [1982] 1 All ER 882, [1982] 1 WLR 310, 126 Sol Jo 189
.... 884
Flynn, Re, Guy v M'Carthy (1886) 17 LR Ir 457 1205
Folds v Abrahart [2003] EWHC 2550 (Ch), [2004] WTLR 327, [2003] All ER (D) 322
   (Jul) 7
Foley v Burnell (1783) 1 Bro CC 274; affd (1558) 4 Bro Parl Cas 319, Rom 1, 2 ER 216,
   [1558–1774] All ER Rep 123, HL 228, 386
Foley v Burnell (1789) 4 Bro Parl Cas 34, HL 123
Foley v Foley [1981] Fam 160, [1981] 2 All ER 857, [1981] 3 WLR 284, 2 FLR 215, 125
   Sol Jo 442, CA 577
Folkes v Western (1804) 9 Ves 456 395
Follett, Re, Barclays Bank Ltd v Dovell [1955] 2 All ER 22, [1955] 1 WLR 429, 99 Sol Jo
   275, CA 236, 253, 466
Follett v Pettman (1883) 23 Ch D 337, 52 LJ Ch 521, 31 WR 779, 48 LT 865,
   [1881–5] All ER Rep Ext 1564 .... 95, 99–100, 114
Fonnereau v Fonnereau (1745) 3 Atk 315 .... 446, 471
Fonnereau v Fonnereau (1748) 3 Atk 645, 1 Ves Sen 118
.... 430
Fonnereau v Poyntz (1785) 1 Bro CC 472 210
Fontaine v Tyler (1821) 9 Price 94 119
Foord, Re, Foord v Conder [1922] 2 Ch 519, 92 LJ Ch 46, [1922] All ER Rep 166, 128
   LT 501 370
Foord v Foord (1730) 3 Bro Parl Cas 124, HL 384

PARA

Foot v Stanton (1856) Dea & Sw 19, 2 Jur NS 380, 26 LTOS 288
.... 48

Forbes, Re, Public Trustee v Hadlow (1934) 78 Sol Jo 336
.... 366

Forbes v Lawrence (1844) 1 Coll 495 403
Forbes v Peacock (1846) 1 Ph 717, 15 LJ Ch 371 1024

Ford, Re, Ford v Ford [1902] 2 Ch 605, 71 LJ Ch 778, 51 WR 20, 46 Sol Jo 715, 87 LT
    113, 18 TLR 809, CA 477, 479, 504
Ford, Re, Myers v Molesworth [1911] 1 Ch 455, 80 LJ Ch 355, 104 LT 245
.... 296

Ford, Re, Patten v Sparks (1895) 72 LT 5, CA 313
Ford v Batley (1852) 17 Beav 303, 23 LJ Ch 225, 227 276–277
Ford v De Pontés (1861) 30 Beav 572, 31 LJ Ch 185, 8 Jur NS 323, 10 WR 69, 5 LT 515
.... 94

Ford v Earl of Chesterfield (No 3) (1856) 21 Beav 426 1203
Ford v Ford (1848) 6 Hare 486 284
Ford v Fowler (1840) 3 Beav 146, 9 LJ Ch 352, 4 Jur 958
.... 370

Ford v Ossulton. See Ossulston's (Lord) Case
Ford v Rawlins (1823) 1 Sim & St 328, 1 LJOS Ch 170
.... 429

Ford v Ruxton (1844) 1 Coll 403 .... 402, 1131
Ford v Tynte (1861) 26 JP 228, 2 John & H 150, 31 LJ Ch 177
.... 928

Fordyce v Ford (1795) 2 Ves 536 386
Forest and Hemburg's Case (1588) 4 Co Rep 606 93
Forest's Goods, Re (1861) 31 LJPM & A 200, 2 Sw & Tr 334, 5 LT 689
.... 44

Formaniuk Estate, Re, Pitz v Kasjan (1963) 42 DLR (2d) 78, 44 WWR 686, Man CA
.... 110

Formby v Barker [1903] 2 Ch 539, 72 LJ Ch 716, 51 WR 646, [1900–3] All ER Rep 445,
    47 Sol Jo 690, 89 LT 249, CA 1282
Forrest, Re, Bubb v Newcomb [1916] 2 Ch 386, 85 LJ Ch 784, [1916–17] All ER Rep
    767, 60 Sol Jo 655, 115 LT 476, 32 TLR 656 366
Forrest, Re, Carr v Forrest [1931] 1 Ch 162, 100 LJ Ch 122, 144 LT 297
.... 173, 1115

Forrest v Prescott (1870) LR 10 Eq 545, 18 WR 1065 1012
Forrest v Whiteway (1849) 18 LJ Ex 207, 3 Exch 367, 12 LTOS 380
.... 395

Forsbrook v Forsbrook (1867) 3 Ch App 93, 16 WR 290
.... 384, 391

Forse and Hembling's Case (1588) 4 Co Rep 60b, sub nom Anon 1 And 181, Gouldsb 109
.... 2

Forster v Forster (1864) 28 JP 376, 33 LJPM & A 113, 10 Jur NS 594, 4 New Rep 252
.... 894

Forster v Ridley (1864) 4 De GJ & Sm 452, 4 New Rep 417, sub nom Foster v Ridley 11
    LT 200 656
Forster-Brown, Re, Barry v Forster-Brown [1914] 2 Ch 584, 84 LJ Ch 361, 112 LT 681
.... 405

Fortescue v Hennah (1812) 19 Ves 67 22
Forth v Chapman (1720) 2 Eq Cas Abr 292, 359, 1 P Wms 663, 24 ER 559, Ct of Ch
.... 226, 249, 385–386, 460
Fortlage, Re, Ross v Fortlage (1916) 60 Sol Jo 527 296
Fosbrooke v Balguy (1833) 1 My & K 226, 2 LJ Ch 135
.... 657

Foster, Re, Coomber v Hospital for the Maintenance and Education of Exposed and
    Deserted Young Children (Governors and Guardians) [1946] Ch 135, [1946] 1 All ER
    333, 115 LJ Ch 251, 90 Sol Jo 116, 174 LT 392, 62 TLR 152
.... 397, 470

Foster, Re, Hunt v Foster [1920] 1 Ch 391, 89 LJ Ch 206, 122 LT 585
.... 405

Foster v Bates (1843) 1 Dow & L 400, 13 LJ Ex 88, 7 Jur 1093, 12 M & W 226, 2 LTOS
    150 .... 645–646, 1279
Foster v Blakelock (1826) 5 B & C 328, 4 LJOSKB 170, 8 Dow & Ry KB 48
.... 1290

Foster v Cook (1791) 3 Bro CC 347 446
Foster v Earl of Romney (1809) 11 East 594 .... 230, 456

PARA

Foster v Elsley (1881) 19 Ch D 518, 51 LJ Ch 275, 30 WR 596
.... 2, 1049
Foster v Foster (1789) 2 Bro CC 616 1301
Foster v Hayes (1855) 4 E & B 717, 24 LJQB 161, 1 Jur NS 515, 3 WR 168, 119 ER 265,
    3 CLR 576, 24 LTOS 312, Ex Ch 456, 473
Foster v Ridley. See Forster v Ridley
Foster v Spencer [1996] 2 All ER 672, (1995) Times, 14 June
.... 656
Foster v Wybrants (1874) IR 11 Eq 40 385
Foster's Estate, Re, Foster v Foster (1922) 67 Sol Jo 199, P, D and Admlty
.... 5
Foster's Goods, Re (1871) LR 2 P & D 304, 36 JP 24, 41 LJP & M 18, 20 WR 302, 25 LT
    763 .... 616, 752
Foster's Will Trusts, Re, Smith v Foster (1967) 111 Sol Jo 685
.... 332
Fothergill, Re, Horwood v Fothergill (1916) 51 L Jo 169
.... 296
Fothergill's Estate, Re, Price-Fothergill v Price [1903] 1 Ch 149, 72 LJ Ch 164, 51 WR
    203, 87 LT 677 246
Foulkes v Metropolitan District Rly Co (1880) 5 CPD 157, 44 JP 568, 49 LJQB 361, 28
    WR 526, 42 LT 345, CA 153
Foundling Hospital (Governors and Guardians) v Crane [1911] 2 KB 367, 80 LJKB 853,
    105 LT 187, [1911–13] All ER Rep Ext 1567, CA 3, 708
Fountain Forestry Ltd v Edwards [1975] Ch 1, [1974] 2 All ER 280, [1974] 2 WLR 767,
    118 Sol Jo 367 .... 926, 1023, 1043, 1246, 1253
Fourdrin v Gowdey (1834) 3 My & K 383, 3 LJ Ch 171
.... 992
Fowkes v Pascoe (1875) 10 Ch App 343, 44 LJ Ch 367, 23 WR 538, [1874–80] All ER
    Rep 521, 32 LT 545, CA 197
Fowler, Re, Fowler v Booth (1914) 31 TLR 102, CA 367
Fowler, Re, Fowler v Odell (1881) 16 Ch D 723, 29 WR 891, 44 LT 99
.... 1228
Fowler, Re, Fowler v Wittingham (1915) 139 LT Jo 183
.... 282, 1109
Fowler v James (1847) 1 Ph 803, 16 LJ Ch 266, 1 Coop temp Cott 290
.... 1174
Fowler v Willoughby (1825) 2 Sim & St 354, 4 LJOS Ch 72
.... 120, 1088
Fowler's Goods, Re (1852) 16 Jur 894 787
Fox, Re (1865) 35 Beav 163, 11 Jur NS 735, 6 New Rep 374, 13 WR 1013
.... 396
Fox v Collins (1761) 2 Eden 107 .... 220, 241
Fox v Fisher (1819) 3 B & Ald 135 923
Fox v Fox (1870) LR 11 Eq 142, 40 LJ Ch 182, 19 WR 151, 23 LT 584
.... 404
Fox v Fox (1875) LR 19 Eq 286, 23 WR 314, Ct of Ch
.... 431–432, 436
Fox's Estate, Re, Dawes v Druitt [1937] 4 All ER 664, 82 Sol Jo 74, CA
.... 160, 182, 289, 445–446
Foxwell v Van Grutten [1897] AC 658, 66 LJQB 745, 46 WR 426, 77 LT 170, HL243,
    242, 243, 339, 384, 474
Foxwell v Van Grutten (1900) 48 WR 653, 82 LT 272, 16 TLR 259, HL
.... 248
Foxwist v Tremain (or Tremayn) (1670) 2 Keb 698, 1 Lev 299, 1 Mod Rep 47, 1 Sid 449,
    T Raym 198, 1 Vent 102, 2 Saund 212 620
Foy v Foy (1785) 1 Cox Eq Cas 163 403
Frame, Re, Edwards v Taylor [1939] Ch 700, [1939] 2 All ER 865, 108 LJ Ch 217, 83 Sol
    Jo 438, 160 LT 620, 55 TLR 746 .... 128, 407
Framlingham v Brand (1746) 3 Atk 390, 1 Wils 140 443
Francis, Re, Francis v Francis [1905] 2 Ch 295, 74 LJ Ch 487, 53 WR 571, 49 Sol Jo 536,
    93 LT 132 .... 416, 419
Franco v Alvares (1746) 3 Atk 342 .... 143, 147
Franguesco v Shaw [1977] 1 NSWLR 660, NSW SC 119
Franklin v Lay (1820) 6 Madd 258, 2 Bli 59n 460
Franklyn, Re, Franklyn v Franklyn (1913) 30 TLR 187, CA
.... 1238

PARA

Franks, Re, Franks v Franks [1948] Ch 62, [1947] 2 All ER 638, [1948] LJR 345, 91 Sol
  Jo 638, 63 TLR 583 .... 568, 592
Franks v Brooker (1860) 27 Beav 635, 29 LJ Ch 292, 6 Jur NS 87, 8 WR 205, 1 LT 426
  346
Franks v Price (1838) 5 Bing NC 37, 1 LT 426 .... 422, 457
Franks v Price (1840) 3 Beav 182, 9 LJ Ch 383, 4 Jur 909, 49 ER 72
  .... 457, 473
Franks v Sinclair [2006] EWHC 3365 (Ch), [2006] All ER (D) 340 (Dec)
  901–905
Fraser, Re, Lowther v Fraser [1904] 1 Ch 726, 73 LJ Ch 481, 52 WR 516,
  [1904–7] All ER Rep 177, 48 Sol Jo 383, 91 LT 48, 20 TLR 414, CA
  .... 114, 160, 1006
Fraser v Byng (1829) 1 Russ & M 90 403
Fraser v Croft (1898) 25 R 496 1132
Fraser v Fraser (1863) 1 New Rep 430, 8 LT 20 246
Fraser v Murdoch (1881) 6 App Cas 855, sub nom Robinson v Murdock 30 WR 162, 45
  LT 417, HL 1036, 1039, 1096, 1160
Fraser's Goods, Re [1891] P 285, 60 LJP 93, 64 LT 808, P, D and Admlty
  723
Fraser's Goods, Re (1869) LR 2 P & D 40, 34 JP 264, 39 LJP & M 20, 18 WR 263, 21 LT
  680 .... 95, 707
Fraser's Goods, Re (1870) LR 2 P & D 183, 35 JP 24, 40 LJP & M 9, 19 WR 333, 24 LT
  72 .... 613, 725
Fraunces Case(1609) 8 Co Rep 89b, sub nom Miller v Francis Brownl 277
  440
Freakley v Fox (1829) 9 B & C 130, 7 LJOSKB 148, 4 Man & Ry KB 18
  625
Frear v Frear [2008] EWCA Civ 1320, [2009] 2 FCR 727, [2009] 1 FLR 391, [2009] Fam
  Law 198, [2008] 49 EG 77 (CS), 152 Sol Jo (no 47) 33, [2008] All ER (D) 24 (Dec)
  .... 150, 284
Freel v Robinson (1909) 18 OLR 651, 13 OWR 1164 107
Freeland, Re, Jackson v Rodgers [1952] Ch 110, 95 Sol Jo 802, sub nom Jackson v Rodger
  [1952] 1 All ER 16, [1951] 2 TLR 1076, CA 626
Freeland v Pearson (1867) LR 3 Eq 658, 36 LJ Ch 374, 15 WR 419
  .... 161, 170
Freeman, Re [1984] 3 All ER 906, [1984] 1 WLR 1419, [1985] FLR 543, [1985] Fam Law
  256, 128 Sol Jo 769, [1984] LS Gaz R 3254 597
Freeman, Re, Hope v Freeman [1910] 1 Ch 681, 79 LJ Ch 678, 54 Sol Jo 443, 102 LT
  516, CA 96, 369
Freeman, Re, Shilton v Freeman [1908] 1 Ch 720, 77 LJ Ch 401, 52 Sol Jo 262, 98 LT
  429, 24 TLR 300, CA 11
Freeman v Cox (1878) 8 Ch D 148, 47 LJ Ch 560, 26 WR 689
  1186
Freeman v Fairlie (1812) 3 Mer 29 1254
Freeman v Freeman (1854) 5 De GM & G 704, 23 LJ Ch 838, 2 Eq Rep 970, 2 WR 658,
  23 LTOS 317 .... 1, 95
Freeman v Lomas (1851) 9 Hare 109, 20 LJ Ch 564, 15 Jur 648, 68 ER 435, 17 LTOS
  252 1296
Freeman v Parsley (1797) 3 Ves 421 334
Freeman's Estate, Re (1931) 75 Sol Jo 764, 146 LT 143, sub nom Re Freeman's Goods 48
  TLR 1, P, D and Admlty 616, 752
Freeman's Settlement Trusts, Re (1887) 37 Ch D 148, 57 LJ Ch 160, 36 WR 71, 57 LT
  798 656
Freeman's Will Trusts, Re (10 July 1987, unreported) 220
Freemantle v Freemantle (1786) 1 Cox Eq Cas 248 362
Freer v Peacocke. See Frere v Peacocke
Freke v Lord Carbery (1873) LR 16 Eq 461, 21 WR 835
  13
Freme's Contract, Re [1895] 2 Ch 778, 64 LJ Ch 862, 44 WR 164, 73 LT 366, CA
  409
French v Caddell (1765) 3 Bro Parl Cas 257, HL 460
French v Chichester (1706) 2 Eq Cas Abr 493, 3 Bro Parl Cas 16, 2 Vern 568
  1012
French v French [1902] 1 IR 172, HL 222
French v French [1902] 1 IR 230 222
French v French (1755) 1 Dick 268 670

                                                                                          PARA
French v French (1840) 11 Sim 257 390
French v Hoey [1899] 2 IR 472 112
French's Case (1587) 1 Roll Abr 614 107
French's Estate, Re [1910] P 169, 79 LJP 56, 54 Sol Jo 361, 26 TLR 374, P, D and Admlty
.... 793, 850
Frengley, Re [1915] 2 IR 1 640
Frere v Peacocke (1846) 1 Rob Eccl 442, sub nom Freer v Peacocke 11 Jur 247
.... 49
Fretwell v Stacy (1702) 2 Vern 434 1070
Frewen, Re, Frewen v Frewen [1889] WN 109, 60 LT 953
.... 1106
Frewen v Frewen (1875) 10 Ch App 610, 23 WR 864, 33 LT 43, CA in Ch
.... 156
Frewen v Law Life Assurance Society [1896] 2 Ch 511, 65 LJ Ch 787, 44 WR 682, 40 Sol
    Jo 621, 75 LT 17 153
Fricker v Fricker's Personal Representatives (1981) 3 FLR 228, 11 Fam Law 188
.... 594
Friedman, Re, Friedman v Friedman (1908) 25 WN 49, 8 SRNSW 127, NSW SC
.... 293
Friend, Re, Friend v Young (No 2) (1898) 78 LT 222 1058
Friend v Young [1897] 2 Ch 421, sub nom Re Friend, Friend v Friend 66 LJ Ch 737, 46
    WR 139, 41 Sol Jo 607, 77 LT 50 .... 1232, 1234, 1279
Friend's Settlement, Re, Cole v Allcot [1906] 1 Ch 47, 75 LJ Ch 14, 54 WR 295, 93 LT
    739 316
Frith, Re, Hindson v Wood (1901) 46 Sol Jo 15, 85 LT 455
.... 339
Frith, Re, Newton v Rolfe [1902] 1 Ch 342, 71 LJ Ch 199, 86 LT 212
.... 1041
Frith's Goods, Re (1858) 27 LJP & M 6, 4 Jur NS 288, 1 Sw & Tr 8, 6 WR 262, 30 LTOS
    295 75
Froggatt v Wardell (1850) 3 De G & Sm 685, 14 Jur 1101, 15 LTOS 21
.... 390
Frogley v Phillips (1861) 3 De GF & J 466, 7 Jur NS 349, 3 LT 718
.... 328
Frogley's Estate, Re [1905] P 137, 74 LJP 72, 54 WR 48, 92 LT 429, 21 TLR 341, P, D
    and Admlty 351
Frogmorton d Bramstone v Holyday (1765) 3 Burr 1618, 1 Wm Bl 535
.... 446
Frost v Ward (1864) 2 De GJ & Sm 70, 3 New Rep 348, 12 WR 285, 9 LT 668
.... 1178
Froy, Re, Froy v Froy [1938] Ch 566, [1938] 2 All ER 316, 107 LJ Ch 342, 82 Sol Jo 273,
    158 LT 518, 54 TLR 613 393
Fry, Re, Reynolds v Denne [1945] Ch 348, [1945] 2 All ER 205, 115 LJ Ch 3, 89 Sol Jo
    349, 173 LT 282, 61 TLR 449 141–142
Fry v Densham-Smith [2010] EWCA Civ 1410, [2010] All ER (D) 136 (Dec)
.... 10
Fry v Fry (1859) 27 Beav 144, 28 LJ Ch 591, 5 Jur NS 1047, 122 RR 354, 34 LTOS 51
.... 961
Fry v Porter (1670) 1 Eq Cas Abr 111, 1 Cas in Ch 137, 1 Mod Rep 300, 2 Rep Ch 26
.... 145
Fry's (Lady Anne) Case (1674) 1 Vent 199, sub nom Porter v Frye Freem KB 31, sub nom
    Williams v Fry 3 Keb 19, 2 Lev 21, T Raym 236, sub nom Williams d Porter v Fry 1
    Mod Rep 86 145
Fry's Estate, Re, Matthews v Greenman (1874) 22 WR 813, 31 LT 8, CA
.... 276
Fryer v Buttar (1837) 8 Sim 442 1122
Fryer v Morris (1804) 9 Ves 360 159
Fryer v Ranken (1840) 11 Sim 55, 9 LJ Ch 337 293
Fuld, Re, Hartley v Fuld (Fuld intervening) [1965] P 405, [1965] 3 WLR 162, 63 LGR
    482, 109 Sol Jo 394, sub nom Fuld (No 2), Re, Hartley v Fuld (Fuld intervening)
    [1965] 2 All ER 657 894
Fuld's Estate (No 3), Re, Hartley v Fuld [1968] P 675, [1965] 3 All ER 776, [1966] 2 WLR
    717, 110 Sol Jo 133, P, D and Admlty 875, 909
Fulford, Re, Fulford v Hyslop [1930] 1 Ch 71, 8 ATC 588, 99 LJ Ch 80, 142 LT 185
.... 283

PARA

Fulford v Fulford. See Fullford v Fullford
Fullard, Re, Fullard v King [1982] Fam 42, [1981] 2 All ER 796, [1981] 3 WLR 743, 11
   Fam Law 116, 125 Sol Jo 747, CA 573–574, 576–578
Fuller, Re, Arnold v Chandler (1915) 59 Sol Jo 304 290
Fuller v Fuller (1595) Cro Eliz 422, Moore KB 353 .... 181, 321
Fuller v Green (1857) 24 Beav 217 1204
Fuller v Redman (No 2) (1859) 26 Beav 614 974
Fuller v Strum [2001] EWCA Civ 1879, [2002] 2 All ER 87, [2002] 1 WLR 1097,
   4 ITELR 454, [2002] 1 FCR 608, (2002) Times, 22 January, [2001] All ER (D) 92
   (Dec) 55, 892, 903, 905–906
Fuller's Contract, Re [1933] Ch 652, 102 LJ Ch 255, 149 LT 237
   919
Fuller's Goods, Re [1892] P 377, 56 JP 713, 62 LJP 40, 1 R 453, 67 LT 501, P, D and
   Admlty 73
Fullerton v Martin (1853) 22 LJ Ch 893, 1 Eq Rep 224, 17 Jur 778, 1 WR 379
   .... 284, 289
Fullford v Fullford (1853) 16 Beav 565, 1 WR 315, sub nom Fulford v Fulford 21 LTOS
   205 167
Fulton v Andrew (1875) LR 7 HL 448, 44 LJP 17, 23 WR 566, [1874–80] All ER Rep
   1240, 32 LT 209, HL 892, 902–905
Fulton v Kee [1961] NI 1, CA 63
Funnell v Stewart. See Le Cren Clarke, Re, Funnell v Stewart
Furley v Hyder (1873) 42 LJ Ch 626 .... 1124, 1126
Furness (Viscount) Re, Wilson v Kenmare [1943] Ch 415, [1944] 1 All ER 66, 112 LJ Ch
   317, 87 Sol Jo 390, 169 LT 314, 59 TLR 418 1190
Fussell v Dowding (1884) 27 Ch D 237, 53 LJ Ch 924, 32 WR 790, 51 LT 332
   1174
Fyfe v Irwin [1939] 2 All ER 271, 83 Sol Jo 454, HL 231
Fyson v Chambers (1842) 11 LJ Ex 190, 9 M & W 460
   .... 928, 1267

G

GHR Co Ltd v IRC [1943] KB 303, [1943] 1 All ER 424, 112 LJKB 311, 169 LT 206, 59
   TLR 211 .... 1143, 1151
Gage, Re, Crozier v Gutheridge [1934] Ch 536, 103 LJ Ch 241, [1934] All ER Rep 610,
   151 LT 240 .... 119, 156
Gainsford v Dunn (1874) LR 17 Eq 405, 43 LJ Ch 403, 22 WR 499, 30 LT 283
   1111
Gaitskell's Trusts, Re (1873) LR 15 Eq 386, 21 WR 768, 28 LT 760
   411
Galbraith's Goods, Re [1951] P 422, [1951] 2 All ER 470n, 95 Sol Jo 548, [1951] 2 TLR
   412, P, D and Admlty 850
Gale, Re, Gale v Gale [1941] Ch 209, [1941] 1 All ER 329, 110 LJ Ch 69, 85 Sol Jo 118,
   165 LT 224, 57 TLR 320 347
Gale, Re, Gale v Gale [1966] Ch 236, [1966] 1 All ER 945, [1966] 2 WLR 571, 110 Sol Jo
   148, CA 594
Gale v Bennett (1768) Amb 681 331
Gale v Gale [2010] EWHC 1575 (Ch), [2010] All ER (D) 234 (Jun)
   59
Gale v Gale (1856) 21 Beav 349, 4 WR 277 94
Gale v Luttrell (1824) 2 Add 234 957
Gallagher v Kennedy [1931] NI 207 .... 59, 671
Galland v Leonard (1818) 1 Wils Ch 129, 1 Swan 161 449–450
Gallini v Noble (1810) 3 Mer 691 293
Galsworthy, Re, Galsworthy v Galsworthy [1922] 2 Ch 558, 91 LJ Ch 534, 127 LT 458
   462
Galway Incorporated Cripples' Institute, People's Palace and Homes of Rest, Re [1944]
   NI 28 180
Galway's Will Trusts, Re, Lowther v Viscount Galway [1950] Ch 1, [1949] 2 All ER 419,
   [1949] LJR 1531, 93 Sol Jo 525, 65 TLR 499 .... 115, 150, 156–157
Galwey v Barden [1899] 1 IR 508 .... 34, 147
Gamboa's Trusts, Re (1858) 4 K & J 756 341
Game, Re, Game v Young [1897] 1 Ch 881, 66 LJ Ch 505, 45 WR 472, 41 Sol Jo 438, 76
   LT 450 1123

PARA

Gammon, Re, Shelton v Williams [1986] CLY 3547 293
Ganapathy Pillay v Alamaloo [1929] AC 462, 98 LJPC 109, 141 LT 43, PC
.... 410
Gandhi v Patel [2002] 1 FLR 603, [2002] Fam Law 262, [2001] All ER (D) 436 (Jul)
.... 567
Gann v Gregory (1854) 3 De GM & G 777, 2 Eq Rep 605, 18 Jur 1063, 2 WR 484,
  23 LTOS 136 .... 83, 200, 672
Gannon, Re, Spence v Martin [1914] 1 IR 86 376
Gansloser's Will Trusts, Re, Chartered Bank of India, Australia and China v Chillingworth
  [1952] Ch 30, [1951] 2 All ER 936, CA 246, 349, 397, 535
Gant v Laurence (1811) Wight 395 395
Gape, Re, Verey v Gape [1952] Ch 743, 96 Sol Jo 595, [1952] TLR 477, sub nom
  Gape's Will Trusts, Re, Verey v Gape [1952] 2 All ER 579, CA
.... 139
Garbrand v Mayot (1689) 2 Vern 105 301
Garbut v Hilton (1739) 1 Atk 381, 9 Mod Rep 210 135
Garden v Pulteney (1765) 2 Eden 323 390
Gardiner v But (1818) 3 Madd 425 430
Gardiner v Courthope (1886) 12 PD 14, 50 JP 791, 56 LJP 55, 35 WR 352, 57 LT 280, P,
  D and Admlty 100, 106, 712
Gardiner v Slater (1858) 25 Beav 509 .... 134–135, 427
Gardiner v Stevens (1860) 30 LJ Ch 199, 7 Jur NS 307, 9 WR 138
.... 471
Gardiner (W) & Co Ltd v Dessaix [1915] AC 1096, 84 LJPC 231, 113 LT 933, PC
.... 334, 384, 391
Gardner, Re, Ellis v Ellis [1924] 2 Ch 243, 93 LJ Ch 486, 68 Sol Jo 595, 131 LT 530
.... 393
Gardner, Re, Huey v Cunningham [1923] 2 Ch 230, 92 LJ Ch 569, 67 Sol Jo 517, 129 LT
  206 221
Gardner, Re, Huey v Cunnington [1920] 2 Ch 523, 89 LJ Ch 649, [1920] All ER Rep 723,
  64 Sol Jo 650, 124 LT 49, 36 TLR 784, CA 222, 370
Gardner, Re, Long v Gardner (1892) 3 R 96, 41 WR 203, 37 Sol Jo 67, 67 LT 552
.... 1081
Gardner, Re, Roberts v Fry [1911] WN 155 1200
Gardner v Gardner (1837) 1 Jur 402 959
Gardner v Hatton (1833) 6 Sim 93 159
Gardner v James (1843) 6 Beav 170 .... 306, 308
Gardner v Sheldon (1671) 1 Eq Cas Abr 197, Freem KB 11, 2 Keb 781, Vaugh 259
.... 469
Gare, Re, Filmer v Carter [1952] Ch 80, [1951] 2 All ER 863, 95 Sol Jo 744, [1951] 2
  TLR 1003 .... 96, 200, 232–233
Gargan, Governor & Co of Bank of Ireland v A-G [1962] IR 264
.... 315
Garland, Re, Eve v Garland [1934] Ch 620, 103 LJ Ch 287, [1934] All ER Rep 605, 78
  Sol Jo 519, 151 LT 326 291
Garland v Beverley (1878) 9 Ch D 213, 26 WR 718, 38 LT 911, sub nom Re Garland,
  Garland v Beverley 47 LJ Ch 711 .... 276, 340, 563
Garland v Morris [2007] EWHC 2 (Ch), [2007] 2 FLR 528, [2007] Fam Law 585, [2007]
  WTLR 797, [2007] All ER (D) 11 (Jan) 572–573, 576, 580
Garland v Smyth [1904] 1 IR 35, 41, Ir CA 316
Garner v Garner (1860) 29 Beav 114, 7 LT 182, 3 LT 396
.... 220, 276
Garnett's Goods, Re [1894] P 90, 63 LJP 82, 6 R 579, 70 LT 37, P, D and Admlty
.... 711
Garnett-Botfield v Garnett-Botfield [1901] P 335, 71 LJP 1, 85 LT 641, P, D and Admlty
.... 902
Garrard v Garrard (1871) LR 2 P & D 238, 35 JP 647, 19 WR 569, 25 LT 162
.... 788
Garratt v Niblock (1830) 1 Russ & M 629 346
Garratt's Trust, Re (1870) 18 WR 684 975
Garret v Pritty (1693) 2 Vern 293 135
Garrett v Noble (1834) 6 Sim 504, 3 LJ Ch 159 1035
Garrick v Lord Camden (1807) 14 Ves 372 344
Garth v Baldwin (1755) 2 Ves Sen 646 385
Garth v Meyrick (1779) 1 Bro CC 30 .... 274, 276, 402
Garthshore v Chalie (1804) 10 Ves 1, 32 ER 743, [1803–13] All ER Rep 239
.... 491, 498, 1054

PARA

Garvey v Hibbert (1812) 19 Ves 125 274
Gaskell v Harman (1801) 6 Ves 159; on appeal (1805) 11 Ves 489
    .... 243, 415, 451
Gaskell v Holmes (1844) 3 Hare 438, 8 Jur 396, 3 LTOS 5
    .... 302, 324
Gaskell v Marshall (1831) 5 C & P 31, 1 Mood & R 132
    924
Gaskin v Rogers (1866) LR 2 Eq 284, 14 WR 707 43
Gasquoine, Re, Gasquoine v Gasquoine [1894] 1 Ch 470, 63 LJ Ch 377, 7 R 449, 70 LT
    196, 10 TLR 220, CA 1253
Gassiot, Re, Fladgate v Vintners' Co (1901) 70 LJ Ch 242, 17 TLR 216
    130
Gates, Re, Arnold v Gates [1933] Ch 913, 102 LJ Ch 369, [1933] All ER Rep 546, 149 LT
    521 653
Gates, Re, Gates v Cabell [1929] 2 Ch 420, 98 LJ Ch 360, [1929] All ER Rep 379, 73 Sol
    Jo 429, 141 LT 392, 45 TLR 522, CA 679
Gates, Re, Gates v Gates [1930] 1 Ch 199, 99 LJ Ch 161, [1929] All ER Rep 338, 142 LT
    327 533
Gates Goods, Re [1928] P 128, 97 LJP 76, 72 Sol Jo 172, 138 LT 714, 44 TLR 353, P, D
    and Admlty; varied [1928] P 178, CA 679
Gath v Burton (1839) 1 Beav 478, 3 Jur 817 143–144
Gatti's Voluntary Settlement Trusts, Re, De Ville v Gatti [1936] 2 All ER 1489, 80 Sol Jo
    704, 52 TLR 674 231
Gattward v Knee [1902] P 99, 71 LJP 34, [1900–3] All ER Rep 151, 18 TLR 163, sub
    nom Knee's Goods, Re, Gattward v Knee 46 Sol Jo 123, 86 LT 119, P, D and Admlty
    79
Gault's Estate, Re [1922] P 195, 91 LJP 144, 127 LT 402, 38 TLR 499, P, D and Admlty
    832
Gaunt v Taylor (1843) 2 Hare 413 1196
Gauntlett v Carter (1853) 17 Beav 586, 23 LJ Ch 219, 17 Jur 981, 1 WR 500
    .... 226, 277
Gaussen's Goods, Re (1867) 32 JP 104, 16 WR 212, 17 LT 354
    83
Gawler v Cadby (1821) Jac 346 .... 390, 449, 459
Gawler v Standerwick (1788) 2 Cox Eq Cas 15 438
Gaynor's Goods, Re (1869) LR 1 P & D 723, 33 JP 762, 38 LJP & M 79, 17 WR 1062,
    21 LT 367 .... 637, 793
Gayre v Gayre (1705) 2 Vern 538 285
Gaze v Gaze (1843) 3 Curt 451, 7 Jur 803, 2 Notes of Cases 224
    69
Geale's Goods, Re (1864) 28 JP 630, 33 LJPM & A 125, 4 New Rep 349, 3 Sw & Tr 431,
    12 WR 1027 48
Geary v Beaumont (1817) 3 Mer 431 1071
Gee v Liddell (1866) LR 2 Eq 341, 35 Beav 658, 35 LJ Ch 640, 12 Jur NS 541, 14 WR
    853 .... 315, 459
Gee v Liddell (No 2) (1866) 35 Beav 629 1067
Gee v Manchester Corpn (1852) 17 QB 737, 12 LJQB 242, 16 Jur 758, 18 LTOS 236
    450
Gee's Goods, Re (1898) 78 LT 843, P, D and Admlty 83
Geering, Re, Gulliver v Geering [1964] Ch 136, [1962] 3 All ER 1043, [1962] 3 WLR
    1541, 106 Sol Jo 919 .... 180, 257, 422, 466, 1080
Genery v Fitzgerald (1822) Jac 468, 23 RR 121 1083
Gennings v Lake (1629) Cro Car 168 286
Gent and Eason's Contract, Re [1905] 1 Ch 386, 74 LJ Ch 333, 53 WR 330, 92 LT 356
    294
George, Re (1877) 5 Ch D 837, 47 LJ Ch 118, 26 WR 65, 37 LT 204, CA
    1076
Gerahty v Baines & Co (1903) 19 TLR 554 1279
Gess, Re, Gess v Royal Exchange Assurance [1942] Ch 37, 111 LJ Ch 117
    .... 964, 1106
Gether v Capper (1855) 24 LJCP 69, 15 CB 696, 139 ER 599; affd (1856) 25 LJCP 260,
    27 LTOS 298, 18 CB 866, 139 ER 1613, Ex Ch 241
Gethin v Allen (1888) 23 LR Ir 236 298
Ghafoor v Cliff [2006] EWHC 825 (Ch), [2006] 2 All ER 1079, [2006] 1 WLR 3020,
    [2006] All ER (D) 165 (Apr) 701, 742, 774, 815

PARA

Ghaidan v Godin-Mendoza [2004] UKHL 30, [2004] 2 AC 557, [2004] 3 WLR 113,
[2004] 2 FCR 481, [2004] 2 FLR 600, [2004] Fam Law 641, [2004] HLR 827,
[2004] 2 EGLR 132, [2004] 27 LS Gaz R 30, [2004] NLJR 1013, (2004) Times,
24 June, 148 Sol Jo LB 792, [2004] All ER (D) 210 (Jun), sub nom Ghaidan v
Mendoza [2004] 3 All ER 411, [2005] 1 LRC 449 567

Gibbard, Re, Public Trustee v Davis [1966] 1 All ER 273, [1967] 1 WLR 42, 110 Sol Jo
871 348

Gibbings Estates, Re [1928] P 28, 97 LJP 4, 71 Sol Jo 911, 138 LT 272, 44 TLR 230, P, D
and Admlty 825

Gibbon v Campbell (1864) 2 Hem & M 43, 12 WR 546, sub nom Gibson v Campbell 10
LT 93 1177

Gibbon v Warner (1585) 14 Vin Abr 484 395

Gibbons, Re, Gibbons v Gibbons [1920] 1 Ch 372, 89 LJ Ch 148, 64 Sol Jo 274, 122 LT
710, 36 TLR 203, CA 379

Gibbons v Gibbons (1881) 6 App Cas 471, 50 LJPC 45, 45 LT 177, PC
.... 228, 241

Gibbons v Langdon (1833) 6 Sim 260 410

Gibbons v Nelsons (2000) Times, 21 April, [2000] All ER (D) 479
.... 1114

Gibbs, Re, Martin v Harding [1907] 1 Ch 465, 76 LJ Ch 238, 96 LT 423
.... 212, 298

Gibbs, Re, Midland Bank Executor and Trustee Co Ltd v IRC [1951] Ch 933, [1951]
2 All ER 196, 30 ATC 129, [1951] TR 113 .... 922, 1149

Gibbs v Davis Mos. See Davis v Gibbs

Gibbs v Lawrence (1860) 30 LJ Ch 170, 7 Jur NS 137, 9 WR 93, sub nom Gibson v
Lawrence 3 LT 367 .... 250, 288

Gibbs v Rumsey (1813) 13 RR 88, 2 Ves & B 294, 35 ER 331, [1803–13] All ER Rep 701
.... 11

Gibson, Re [1949] P 434, [1949] 2 All ER 90, [1949] LJR 1260, 93 Sol Jo 376, 65 TLR
395, P, D and Admlty 70, 78

Gibson, Re, Mathews v Foulsham (1866) LR 2 Eq 669, 35 LJ Ch 596, 14 WR 818
.... 282

Gibson v Bott (1802) 7 Ves 89 .... 1058, 1122, 1124

Gibson v Campbell. See Gibbon v Campbell

Gibson v Fisher (1867) LR 5 Eq 51, 37 LJ Ch 67, 16 WR 115
.... 345, 398–399

Gibson v Lawrence. See Gibbs v Lawrence

Gibson v Lord Montfort (1750) Amb 93, 1 Ves Sen 485
.... 27

Gibson v Wells (1805) 1 Bos & PNR 290, 2 Smith KB 677
.... 1229

Gibson's Trusts, Re (1861) 2 John & H 656, 31 LJ Ch 231
.... 175, 409

Giesler v Jones (1858) 25 Beav 418 409

Gifford, Re, Gifford v Seaman [1944] Ch 186, [1944] 1 All ER 268, 113 LJ Ch 94, 88 Sol
Jo 76, 170 LT 267, 60 TLR 202 .... 269–270, 279, 295

Gilbert, Re [1911] 2 IR 36 754

Gilbert, Re, Daniel v Matthews (1886) 34 WR 577, 54 LT 752
.... 322, 326

Gilbert, Re, Gilbert v Gilbert [1908] WN 63 405

Gilbert v Boorman (1805) 11 Ves 238 309

Gilbert's Goods, Re [1893] P 183, 62 LJP 111, 1 R 478, 68 LT 461, P, D and Admlty
.... 108, 735

Gilbertson v Gilbertson (1865) 34 Beav 354, 6 New Rep 78, 13 WR 765, 12 LT 816
.... 1012

Giles, Re (1886) 55 LJ Ch 695, 34 WR 712, 55 LT 51 1047

Giles, Re, Giles v Giles [1972] Ch 544, [1971] 3 All ER 1141, [1971] 3 WLR 640, 115 Sol
Jo 428 .... 39–40, 480

Giles v Dyson (1815) 1 Stark 32 1290

Giles v Giles (1836) 1 Keen 685, sub nom Penfold v Giles 6 LJ Ch 4
.... 59, 276, 346

Giles v Giles (1837) 8 Sim 360, 6 LJ Ch 176, 1 Jur 234
.... 324

Giles v Melsom (1873) LR 6 HL 24, 42 LJCP 122, 21 WR 417, 28 LT 789
.... 228, 241, 248, 410

PARA

Giles v The Royal National Institute for the Blind [2014] EWHC 1373 (Ch), [2014] STC
1631, 17 ITELR 170, 164 NLJ 7605, [2014] WTLR 1347, [2014] All ER (D) 36
(May) 187
Giles v Warren (1872) LR 2 P & D 401, 36 JP 663, 41 LJP & M 59, 20 WR 827, 26 LT
780 .... 93, 101, 109
Gilfoyle v Wood-Martin [1921] 1 IR 105 156
Gill v Barrett (1860) 29 Beav 372 249
Gill v Gill [1909] P 157, 78 LJP 60, 53 Sol Jo 359, 100 LT 861, 25 TLR 400, P, D and
Admlty 104, 717
Gill v Shelley (1831) 9 LJOS Ch 68, 2 Russ & M 336 352
Gill v Woodall [2009] EWHC 3778 (Ch), [2010] All ER (D) 60 (Jan)
.... 20, 56, 903
Gill v Woodall [2010] EWCA Civ 1430, [2011] Ch 380, [2011] 3 WLR 85, (2011) Times,
01 February, [2010] All ER (D) 167 (Dec) 55, 902
Gill's Goods, Re (1873) LR 3 P & D 113 631–632
Gillespie, Re, Gillespie v Gillespie (1902) 22 NZLR 74, NZ CA
.... 127
Gillespie v Alexander (1824) 2 Sim & St 145, 3 LJOS Ch 52
.... 403
Gillespie v Alexander (1827) 3 Russ 130 1102
Gillet v Wray (1715) 1 P Wms 284 135
Gillett v Gane (1870) LR 10 Eq 29, 39 LJ Ch 818, 18 WR 423, 22 LT 58
.... 276
Gillett v Holt [2001] Ch 210, [2000] 2 All ER 289, [2000] 3 WLR 815, [2000] 1 FCR
705, [2000] FLR 266, [2000] Fam Law 714, [2000] 12 LS Gaz R 40, CA
.... 20
Gillett's Will Trusts, Re, Barclays Bank Ltd v Gillett [1950] Ch 102, [1949] 2 All ER 893,
93 Sol Jo 742, 65 TLR 727 .... 422, 1080, 1082, 1108
Gilliat v Gilliat (1860) 28 Beav 481 271
Gilliat v Gilliat and Hatfield (1820) 3 Phillim 222 707
Gillic v Smyth (1914) 49 ILT 36 68
Gilligan, Re [1950] P 32, [1949] 2 All ER 401, [1949] LJR 1592, 93 Sol Jo 563, 65 TLR
651, P, D and Admlty 344
Gillins, Re, Inglis v Gillins [1909] 1 Ch 345, 78 LJ Ch 244, 15 Mans 74, 100 LT 226,
[1908–10] All ER Rep Ext 1288 282
Gillman v Daunt (1856) 3 K & J 48 307
Gillow and Orrell v Bourne (1831) 4 Hag Ecc 192 5
Gillson, Re, Ellis v Leader [1949] Ch 99, [1948] 2 All ER 990, [1949] LJR 620, 92 Sol Jo
674, 65 TLR 54, CA 296
Gilmore v Severn (1785) 1 Bro CC 582 307
Gilmour v MacPhillamy [1930] AC 712, 143 LT 606, sub nom MacPhillamy, Re, Gilmour
v MacPhillamy 99 LJPC 199, PC 315, 317
Gilpin, Re, Hutchinson v Gilpin [1954] Ch 1, [1953] 2 All ER 1218, [1953] 3 WLR 746,
97 Sol Jo 763 331
Gilroy v Stephens (1882) 51 LJ Ch 834, 30 WR 745, 46 LT 761
.... 1257
Gimblett v Purton (1871) LR 12 Eq 427, 40 LJ Ch 556, 24 LT 793
.... 299, 308–309
Gingell v Horne (1839) 9 Sim 539, 3 Jur 194 671
Ginger, Re, Wood Roberts v Westminster Hospital Board of Governors [1951] Ch 458, 95
Sol Jo 76, [1951] 1 TLR 750, sub nom Re Ginger, Roberts v Westminster Hospital
Governors [1951] 1 All ER 422 278
Ginger d White v White (1742) Willes 348 .... 230, 389
Girdlestone v Creed (1853) 10 Hare 480, 1 WR 228, 21 LTOS 124
.... 277
Girdlestone v Doe (1828) 2 Sim 225 .... 320, 342
Gittings v M'Dermott (1834) 2 My & K 69, 2 LJ Ch 212
.... 321, 341
Gittins v Steele (1818) 1 Swan 199 1097
Givan v Massey (1892) 31 LR Ir 126 125
Gjers, Re, Cooper v Gjers [1899] 2 Ch 54, 68 LJ Ch 442, 47 WR 535, 43 Sol Jo 497, 80
LT 689 1228
Gladdon v Stoneman (1808) 1 Madd 143n 624
Gladstone v Tempest (1840) 2 Curt 650 95
Glanvill v Glanvill (1816) 2 Mer 38 412

PARA

Glanville v Glanville (1863) 33 Beav 302, 33 LJ Ch 317, 9 Jur NS 1189, 3 New Rep 58,
12 WR 92, 9 LT 470 273

Glass, Re, Public Trustee v South-West Middlesex Hospital Management Committee [1950]
Ch 643n, [1950] 2 All ER 953n 278

Glassington, Re, Glassington v Follett [1906] 2 Ch 305, 75 LJ Ch 670, 95 LT 100,
[1904–7] All ER Rep Ext 1227 .... 193, 212, 270, 291

Gledhill v Arnold [2015] EWHC 2939 (Ch), [2016] WTLR 653
.... 188, 236, 253

Glendening v Glendening (1846) 9 Beav 324, 7 LTOS 134
.... 232

Glendinning, Re, Steel v Glendinning (1918) 88 LJ Ch 87, 63 Sol Jo 156, 120 LT 222
.... 293

Glenister v Moody [2003] EWHC 3155 (Ch), [2005] WTLR 1205, [2003] All ER (D) 242
(Nov) 652
Glover v Hall (1849) 16 Sim 568, 18 LJ Ch 305 378
Glover v Monckton (1825) 3 Bing 13, 3 LJOSCP 189, 10 Moore CP 453
.... 460

Glover v Smith (1886) 50 JP 456, 57 LT 60, P, D and Admlty
.... 895
Glover v Spendlove (1793) 4 Bro CC 337 284

Glover v Staffordshire Police Authority [2006] EWHC 2414 (Admin), [2007] ICR 661,
(2006) Times, 24 October, [2006] All ER (D) 77 (Oct) 39
Glover v Strothoff (1786) 2 Bro CC 33 .... 385, 459
Glover's Goods, Re (1847) 11 Jur 1022, 10 LTOS 118, 5 Notes of Cases 553
.... 63

Glubb, Re, Bamfield v Rogers [1900] 1 Ch 354, 69 LJ Ch 278, 82 LT 412, CA
.... 148

Glyn v Glyn (1857) 26 LJ Ch 409, 3 Jur NS 179, 5 WR 241
.... 444
Goblet v Beechey (1831) 2 Russ & M 624 202
Goddard v Norton (1846) 10 Jur 1064, 8 LTOS 216, 5 Notes of Cases 76
.... 863

Godfree, Re, Godfree v Godfree [1914] 2 Ch 110, 83 LJ Ch 734
.... 1124
Godfrey v Davis (1901) 6 Ves 43 352
Godfrey v Hughes (1847) 1 Rob Eccl 593, 5 Notes of Cases 499
.... 137

Godfrey's Goods, Re (1861) 2 Sw & Tr 133, 9 WR 499, 3 LT 895
.... 787
Godfrey's Goods, Re (1893) 1 R 484, 69 LT 22, P, D and Admlty
.... 105

Godman v Godman [1920] P 261, 89 LJP 193, 123 LT 274, sub nom Re Godman,
Godman v Godman 64 Sol Jo 424, 36 TLR 434, CA 79, 81, 708
Godson v Freeman (1835) 2 Cr M & R 585, 5 LJ Ex 41, 1 Gale 329, Tyr & Gr 35
.... 1276

Godwin, Re, Coutts & Co v Godwin [1938] Ch 341, [1938] 1 All ER 287, 107 LJ Ch 166,
82 Sol Jo 113, 158 LT 166, 54 TLR 339 1015
Godwin v Munday (1783) 2 Dick 551, 1 Bro CC 191 438

Goenka v Goenka [2014] EWHC 2966 (Ch), [2016] Ch 267, [2015] 4 All ER 123, [2016]
2 WLR 170, [2015] 3 FCR 207, [2016] WTLR 417, [2014] All ER (D) 312 (Jul)
.... 577, 583

Goetze, Re, National Provincial Bank Ltd v Mond [1953] Ch 96, [1953] 1 All ER 76,
[1953] 2 WLR 26, 31 ATC 551, [1952] TR 511, 97 Sol Jo 28, CA
.... 1130

Goff, Re, Featherstonehaugh v Murphy (1914) 58 Sol Jo 535, 111 LT 34
.... 198, 625

Goilmere v Battison (1682) 1 Eq Cas Abr 17, 1 Vern 48, sub nom Goylmer v Paddiston 2
Vent 353 21
Golay, Re, Morris v Bridgewater [1965] 2 All ER 660, [1965] 1 WLR 969, 109 Sol Jo 517
.... 263, 266
Gold, Re, Gold v Curtis [2005] WTLR 673 .... 568, 572–575, 580, 591

Gold v Hill (1998) 1 ITELR 27, [1999] 1 FLR 54, [1998] Fam Law 664, 142 Sol Jo LB
226 221

Goldie v Adam [1938] P 85, 107 LJP 106, 158 LT 359, 54 TLR 422, sub nom
Taylor's Estate, Re, Goldie v Adam [1938] 1 All ER 586, 82 Sol Jo 236, P, D and
Admlty 111–112

PARA

Goldie v Greaves (1844) 14 Sim 348 336
Goldney, Re, Re Dighton, Clarke v Dighton (1911) 130 LT Jo 484
.... 441
Goldney v Crabb (1854) 19 Beav 338, 2 WR 579 385
Golds v Greenfield (1854) 23 LJ Ch 639, 2 Eq Rep 793, 2 Sm & G 476, 2 WR 583
.... 404
Goldschmidt's Goods, Re (1898) 78 LT 763, P, D and Admlty
.... 807
Goldsmith v Goldsmith (1815) Coop G 225, 19 Ves 368
.... 135
Goldsmith v Russell (1855) 5 De GM & G 547, 25 LJ Ch 232, 1 Jur NS 985, 3 WR 218,
24 LTOS 285 1205
Goldsmith's Will Trusts, Re, Brett v Bingham [1947] Ch 339, [1947] 1 All ER 451,
[1947] LJR 775, 91 Sol Jo 131, 176 LT 321 148–149
Gollin's Declaration of Trust, Re, Turner v Williams [1969] 3 All ER 1591, [1969] 1 WLR
1858, 113 Sol Jo 904 1158
Gompertz v Gompertz (1846) 2 Ph 107, 16 LJ Ch 23, 10 Jur 937, 78 RR 43
.... 231
Gompertz's Estate, Re, Parker v Gompertz (1910) 55 Sol Jo 76
.... 1074, 1149
Gonin, Re [1979] Ch 16, [1977] 3 WLR 379, 121 Sol Jo 558, sub nom Re Gonin, Gonin v
Garmeson [1977] 2 All ER 720 .... 198, 598, 626
Gooch v Gooch (1853) 3 De GM & G 366, 22 LJ Ch 1089, 1 WR 397, 21 LTOS 249
.... 311
Good, Re, Carapeto v Good [2002] EWHC 640 (Ch), (2002) Times, 22 May,
[2002] All ER (D) 141 (Apr); affd sub nom Carapeto v Good [2002] EWCA Civ 944
.... 55, 57
Good v Good (1857) 7 E & B 295, 3 Jur NS 536, 28 LTOS 266
.... 376, 384
Goodale v Gawthorne (1854) 23 LJ Ch 878, 2 Eq Rep 936, 18 Jur 927, 2 Sm & G 375, 2
WR 680, 24 LTOS 14 551
Goodburn v Bainbridge (1860) 29 LJPM & A 163, 2 Sw & Tr 4, 8 WR 504, 2 LT 439
.... 696
Goodchild, Re, Goodchild v Goodchild [1996] 1 All ER 670, [1996] 1 WLR 694, [1997] 1
FCR 45, [1996] 1 FLR 591, [1996] Fam Law 209; affd [1997] 3 All ER 63, [1997] 1
WLR 1216, [1997] 3 FCR 601, [1997] 2 FLR 644, [1997] NLJR 758, CA
.... 10, 21, 23, 87, 570, 573, 580, 588, 714
Goodenough, Re, Marland v Williams [1895] 2 Ch 537, 65 LJ Ch 71, 13 R 454, 44 WR
44, 39 Sol Jo 656, 73 LT 152 .... 1127, 1257
Goodfellow v Goodfellow (1854) 18 Beav 356, 2 WR 360, 23 LTOS 46
.... 468
Goodinge v Goodinge (1749) 1 Ves Sen 231 .... 214–215, 275, 349
Goodisson v Goodisson [1913] 1 IR 31; on appeal [1913] 1 IR 218, CA
.... 895
Goodlad v Burnett (1855) 1 K & J 341 282
Goodman v Drury (1852) 21 LJ Ch 680, 20 LTOS 6 438
Goodman v Edwards (1833) 2 My & K 759 291
Goodman v Goodman [2013] EWHC 758 (Ch), [2014] Ch 186, [2013] 3 All ER 490,
[2013] 3 WLR 1551, [2013] All ER (D) 118 (Jan) 1163
Goodman v Goodman (1847) 1 De G & Sm 695, 17 LJ Ch 103, 12 Jur 258, 10 LTOS 322
.... 256, 409–410
Goodman v Saltash Corpn (1882) 7 App Cas 633, 47 JP 276, 52 LJQB 193, 31 WR 293,
[1881–5] All ER Rep 1076, 48 LT 239, HL 128
Goodman's Trusts, Re (1881) 17 Ch D 266, 50 LJ Ch 425, 29 WR 586, [1881–5] All ER
Rep 1138, 44 LT 527, CA 350
Goodright v Dunham (1779) 1 Doug KB 264 456
Goodright v Wright (1717) 1 P Wms 397, 1 Stra 25, sub nom Woodright v Wright 10 Mod
Rep 370 164
Goodright d Baker v Stocker (1792) 5 Term Rep 13 256
Goodright d Brooking v White (1775) 2 Wm Bl 1010 339
Goodright d Hoskins v Hoskins (1808) 9 East 306 471
Goodright d Lamb v Pears (1809) 11 East 58 269
Goodright d Lloyd v Jones (1815) 4 M & S 88 420
Goodright d Revell v Parker (1813) 1 M & S 692 419
Goodright d Rolfe v Harwood (1775) 7 Bro Parl Cas 489, HL
.... 98, 110

PARA

Goodtitle d Bailey v Pugh (1787) 2 Jac & W 102, sub nom Pugh v Goodtitle 3 Bro Parl
Cas 454, sub nom Doe d Bailey v Pugh 2 Mer 348, HL
.... 339
Goodtitle d Cross v Wodhull (1745) Willes 592 369
Goodtitle d Daniel v Miles (1805) 6 East 494, 2 Smith KB 467
.... 284
Goodtitle d Hayward v Whitby (1757) 1 Burr 228, 1 Keny 506
.... 419
Goodtitle d Newman v Newman (1774) 3 Wils 516, 2 Wm Bl 938
.... 539
Goodtitle d Paul v Paul (1760) 2 Burr 1089, sub nom Paul v Paul 1 Wm Bl 255
.... 277
Goodtitle d Peake v Pegden (1788) 2 Term Rep 721 460
Goodtitle d Pearson v Otway (1753) 2 Wils 6 .... 378, 383
Goodtitle d Radford v Southern (1813) 1 M & S 299, 105 ER 112, [1803–13] All ER Rep
195 .... 212, 277
Goodtitle d Sweet v Herring (1801) 1 East 264 456
Goodtitle d Weston v Burtenshaw (1772) 1 Fearne on Contingent Remainders 10th ed App
I 570 340
Goodtitle d Woodhouse v Meredith (1813) 2 M & S 5 115
Goodwin, Re, Ainslie v Goodwin [1924] 2 Ch 26, 93 LJ Ch 331, [1924] All ER Rep 180,
68 Sol Jo 478, 130 LT 822 .... 148, 933
Goodwin, Re, Goodwin v Goodwin [1969] 1 Ch 283, [1968] 3 All ER 12, [1968] 3 WLR
558, 112 Sol Jo 691 .... 568, 591
Goodwin v Curtiss [1998] STC 475, 70 TC 478 489
Goodwin v Finlayson (1858) 25 Beav 65 .... 251, 410
Goold v Teague (1858) 5 Jur NS 116, 7 WR 84, 32 LTOS 251
.... 294
Goold's Will Trusts, Re, Lloyd's Bank Ltd v Goold [1967] 3 All ER 652, 111 Sol Jo 812
.... 231
Goolding v Haverfield (1824) 13 Price 593 404
Goonewardene v Goonewardene [1931] AC 647, 100 LJPC 145, 145 LT 7, PC
.... 114
Gorbell v Davison (1854) 18 Beav 556 313
Gorbell v Forrest (1854) 18 Beav 556 313
Gordon, Re, Public Trustee v Bland [1942] Ch 131, [1942] 1 All ER 59, 111 LJ Ch 114,
86 Sol Jo 21, 166 LT 102, 58 TLR 112 404
Gordon, Re, Watts v Rationalist Press Association Ltd [1940] Ch 769, [1940] 3 All ER
205, 109 LJ Ch 289, 84 Sol Jo 415, 163 LT 308, 56 TLR 860
.... 184, 994
Gordon v Adolphus (1769) 3 Bro Parl Cas 306, HL 446, 460
Gordon v Anderson (1858) 4 Jur NS 1097, 32 LTOS 119
.... 402
Gordon v Atkinson (1847) 1 De G & Sm 478 395
Gordon v Gordon (1816) 1 Mer 141 354
Gordon v Gordon (1871) LR 5 HL 254 .... 194, 226, 241, 244, 408
Gordon v Hoffmann (1834) 7 Sim 29 252
Gordon v Hope (1849) 3 De G & Sm 351, 18 LJ Ch 228, 13 Jur 382, 12 LTOS 551
.... 440
Gordon v Raynes (1732) 3 P Wms 134 438
Gordon v Scott (1844) 3 Hare 459n 1301
Gordon v Trail (1820) 8 Price 416 1258
Gordon v Whieldon (1848) 11 Beav 170, 18 LJ Ch 5, 12 Jur 988, 12 LTOS 63
.... 390
Gordon's (Lady Isabella) Goods, Re [1892] P 228, 61 LJP 132, 67 LT 328, P, D and
Admlty 112
Gornall v Mason (1887) 12 PD 142, 51 JP 663, 56 LJP 86, 35 WR 672, 57 LT 601, P, D
and Admlty 894
Gorringe v Mahlstedt [1907] AC 225, 76 LJ Ch 527, 51 Sol Jo 497, 97 LT 111,
[1904–7] All ER Rep Ext 1110, HL 226, 236, 241, 247, 322–323
Gorst v Lowndes (1841) 11 Sim 434, 10 LJ Ch 161, 5 Jur 457
.... 148
Gorton v Gregory (1862) 3 B & S 90, 6 LT 656, sub nom Garton v Gregory 31 LJQB 302,
sub nom Gregory v Gorton 10 WR 713, Ex Ch 1293
Gosden v Dotterill (1832) 1 My & K 56, 2 LJ Ch 15 1131
Gosling v Gosling (1859) John 265, 5 Jur NS 910, 123 RR 107
.... 146, 256, 372, 1062

PARA

Gosling v Townsend (1853) 17 Beav 245, 2 WR 23, 22 LTOS 125
.... 450

Gosling's Goods, Re (1886) 11 PD 79, 50 JP 263, 55 LJP 27, 34 WR 492, 2 TLR 476, P,
D and Admlty 95

Gosman, Re (1881) 17 Ch D 771, 50 LJ Ch 624, 29 WR 793, 45 LT 267, CA
.... 780

Gossage's Estate, Re, Wood v Gossage [1921] P 194, 90 LJP 201, [1921] All ER Rep 107,
65 Sol Jo 274, 124 LT 770, 37 TLR 302, CA 79, 81, 94–95, 101

Gosset's Settlement, Re, Gribble v Lloyds Bank Ltd [1943] Ch 351, [1943] 2 All ER 515,
112 LJ Ch 291, 87 Sol Jo 282, 169 LT 172, 59 TLR 386
.... 400

Gossling, Re, Gossling v Elcock [1903] 1 Ch 448, 72 LJ Ch 433, 88 LT 279,
[1900–3] All ER Rep Ext 1156, CA 431

Gott, Re, Glazebrook v Leeds University [1944] Ch 193, [1944] 1 All ER 293, 113 LJ Ch
124, 88 Sol Jo 103, 170 LT 210, 60 TLR 214 140

Gough, Re, Phillips v Simpson [1957] Ch 323, [1957] 2 All ER 193, [1957] 2 WLR 961,
101 Sol Jo 409 1123

Gough v Bult (1847) 16 Sim 45, 17 LJ Ch 10, 80 RR 19; affd (1848) 16 Sim 50, 17 LJ Ch
401, 12 Jur 859, 80 RR 80, 13 LTOS 86 .... 264, 371, 373

Gouk, Re, Allen v Allen [1957] 1 All ER 469, [1957] 1 WLR 493, 101 Sol Jo 265
.... 382, 449

Goulbourn v Brooks (1837) 2 Y & C Ex 539, 7 LJ Ex Eq 33, 1 Jur 354
.... 438

Gould, Re, ex p Official Receiver (1887) 19 QBD 92, 56 LJQB 333, 4 Morr 202, 35 WR
569, 56 LT 806, 3 TLR 605, [1886–90] All ER Rep Ext 1831, CA
.... 988

Gould v Lakes (1880) 6 PD 1, 44 JP 698, 49 LJP 59, 29 WR 155, 43 LT 382, P, D and
Admlty 8, 67, 716

Goulder, Re, Goulder v Goulder [1905] 2 Ch 100, 74 LJ Ch 552, 53 WR 531, 49 Sol Jo
481, 93 LT 163, [1904–7] All ER Rep Ext 1361 451

Goulding v James [1997] 2 All ER 239, CA 146

Gourju's Will Trusts, Re, Starling v Custodian of Enemy Property [1943] Ch 24, [1942]
2 All ER 605, 112 LJ Ch 75, 86 Sol Jo 367, 168 LT 1, 59 TLR 47
.... 465

Govier, Re [1950] P 237, 66 (pt 1) TLR 1042, P, D and Admlty
.... 7

Gowenlock, Re, Public Trustee v Gowenlock (1934) 177 LT Jo 95
.... 220

Gower v Mainwaring (1750) 2 Ves Sen 87 349

Gowling v Thompson (1868) 16 WR 1131, 19 LT 242, LR 11 Eq 366n
.... 305, 397–398

Goylmer v Paddiston. See Goilmere v Battison

Grace v Webb. See Webb v Grace

Graham, Re, Graham v Graham [1929] 2 Ch 127, 98 LJ Ch 291, [1929] All ER Rep 433,
141 LT 197 .... 182, 445

Graham v Drummond [1896] 1 Ch 968, 65 LJ Ch 472, 44 WR 596, 74 LT 417, 12 TLR
319 1025

Graham v Jackson (1845) 6 QB 811, 14 LJQB 129, 9 Jur 275, 4 LTOS 331
.... 792

Graham v Lee (1857) 23 Beav 388, 26 LJ Ch 395, 3 Jur NS 550, 4 WR 328, 29 LTOS 46
.... 464

Graham v McCashin [1901] 1 IR 404, 35 ILT 169 .... 909, 1018, 1043

Graham v Murphy [1997] 2 FCR 441, [1997] 1 FLR 860, [1997] Fam Law 393
.... 567, 577, 604

Graham v Wickham (1862) 31 Beav 447; affd (1863) 1 De GJ & Sm 474
.... 21

Grainger, Re, Dawson v Higgins [1900] 2 Ch 756, 69 LJ Ch 789, 48 WR 673, 83 LT 209,
CA; revsd sub nom Higgins v Dawson [1902] AC 1, 71 LJ Ch 132, 50 WR 337, 85
LT 763, [1900–3] All ER Rep Ext 1470, HL 193, 195, 210, 212, 241, 258, 279, 282

Grant, Re, Grant v Grant (1920) 150 LT Jo 296 1123

Grant, Re, Nevinson v United Kingdom Temperance and General Provident Institution
(1915) 85 LJ Ch 31, 59 Sol Jo 1316, 112 LT 1126, 31 TLR 235
.... 1131

Grant v Bridger (1866) LR 3 Eq 347, 36 LJ Ch 377, 15 WR 610
.... 150

PARA

Grant v Dyer (1813) 2 Dow 73, HL 442
Grant v Edmondson [1931] 1 Ch 1, 100 LJ Ch 1, [1930] All ER Rep 48, 143 LT 749, CA
.... 156
Grant v Fuller (1902) 33 SCR 34, Can SC 389
Grant v Grant (1869) LR 2 P & D 8, 34 JP 23, 39 LJP & M 17, 18 WR 230, 21 LT 645
.... 611
Grant v Grant (1870) LR 5 CP 380; on appeal (1861) LR 5 CP 727, 39 LJCP 272, 18 WR
    951, [1861–73] All ER Rep 308, 22 LT 829, Ex Ch 210, 212, 220, 328
Grant v Knaresborough UDC [1928] Ch 310, 26 LGR 165, 92 JP 30, (1926–31) 1 BRA
    238, 97 LJ Ch 106, 138 LT 488, 44 TLR 224 912
Grant v Leslie (1819) 3 Phillim 116 613
Grant v Lynam (1828) 4 Russ 292, 6 LJOS Ch 129, 38 ER 815, [1824–34] All ER Rep
    522 348
Grant's Case (1588) 10 Co Rep 50a, sub nom Johnson v Gabriel and Bellamy Cro
    Eliz 122, sub nom Johnson and Bellamy's Case 2 Leon 36
.... 416
Grant's Will Trusts, Re, Harris v Anderson [1979] 3 All ER 359, [1980] 1 WLR 360, 124
    Sol Jo 84 .... 11, 36
Grantham v Hawley (1615) Hob 132 930
Grassi, Re, Stubberfield v Grassi [1905] 1 Ch 584, 74 LJ Ch 341, 53 WR 396,
    [1904–7] All ER Rep 845, 49 Sol Jo 366, 92 LT 455, 21 TLR 343
.... 282
Gratrix v Chambers (1860) 2 Giff 321, 7 Jur NS 960 1091
Grattan, Re, Grattan v McNaughton [2001] WTLR 1305
.... 187
Gratton v Langdale (1883) 11 LR Ir 473 333
Gravenor v Hallum (1767) Amb 643, 27 ER 417, [1558–1774] All ER Rep 444
.... 184
Gravenor v Watkins (1871) LR 6 CP 500, 40 LJCP 220, 19 WR 978, 24 LT 802, Ex Ch
.... 234, 376
Graves v Bainbrigge (1792) 1 Ves 562 .... 237, 243
Graves v Cohen (1929) 46 TLR 121 .... 1213, 1279
Graves v Waters (1847) 10 I Eq R 234 475
Gray, Re, Allardyce v Roebuck [2004] EWHC 1538 (Ch), [2004] 3 All ER 754, 7 ITELR
    232, [2004] WTLR 779, [2004] All ER (D) 34 (Jul) 124, 126, 145, 148–149, 1214
Gray v Barr [1970] 2 QB 626, [1970] 2 All ER 702, [1970] 3 WLR 108, [1970] 2
    Lloyd's Rep 69, 114 Sol Jo 413; on appeal [1971] 2 QB 554, [1971] 2 All ER 949,
    [1971] 2 WLR 1334, [1971] 2 Lloyd's Rep 1, 115 Sol Jo 364, CA
.... 39
Gray v Garman (1843) 2 Hare 268, 12 LJ Ch 259, 7 Jur 275
.... 322, 327
Gray v Golding (1860) 6 Jur NS 474, 8 WR 371, 2 LT 198, HL
.... 417
Gray v Gray [1915] 1 IR 261 .... 342, 384
Gray v Gray (1889) 23 LR Ir 399 134–135
Gray v Perpetual Trustee Co Ltd [1928] AC 391, 97 LJPC 85, [1928] All ER Rep 758, 139
    LT 469, 44 TLR 654, PC 10, 21, 23
Gray v Richards Butler [1996] 29 LS Gaz R 29, 140 Sol Jo LB 194, Times, 23 July
.... 652
Gray v Shawne (1758) 1 Eden 153 459
Gray v Siggers (1880) 15 Ch D 74, 49 LJ Ch 819, 29 WR 13
.... 1125
Gray's Settlement, Re, Akers v Sears [1896] 2 Ch 802, 65 LJ Ch 858, 40 Sol Jo 702, 75 LT
    407 395
Grayburn v Clarkson (1868) 3 Ch App 605, 37 LJ Ch 550, 16 WR 716, 18 LT 494
.... 961, 966, 1238
Graydon v Hicks (1739) 2 Atk 16, 9 Mod Rep 215 .... 135, 143
Graysbrook v Fox (1564) 1 Plowd 275 .... 789, 858
Grayson v Atkinson (1752) 2 Ves Sen 454, sub nom Grayson v Wilkinson 1 Dick 158
.... 63
Grealey v Sampson [1917] 1 IR 286, Ir CA 113, 115, 210, 403
Greally, Re, Travers v O'Donoghue [1910] 1 IR 239 298
Greata's Goods, Re (1856) Dea & Sw 266, 2 Jur NS 1172, 5 WR 42, 28 LTOS 107
.... 65
Greated v Greated (1859) 26 Beav 621, 28 LJ Ch 756, 5 Jur NS 454, 7 WR 367, 33 LTOS
    176 .... 183, 442

PARA

Greaves, Re, Bray v Tofield (1881) 18 Ch D 551, 50 LJ Ch 817, 30 WR 55, 45 LT 464
.... 1172–1173, 1191
Greaves, Re, Greaves v Greaves [1954] 2 All ER 109, [1954] 1 WLR 760, 98 Sol Jo 337
.... 598
Greaves v Greenwood (1877) 2 Ex D 289, 46 LJQB 252, 25 WR 639, 36 LT 1, CA
.... 549
Green, Re, Baldock v Green (1888) 40 Ch D 610, 58 LJ Ch 157, 37 WR 300, 60 LT 225
.... 375
Green, Re, Bath v Cannon [1914] 1 Ch 134, 83 LJ Ch 248, 58 Sol Jo 185, 110 LT 58,
  [1911–13] All ER Rep Ext 1358 328
Green, Re, Fitzwilliam v Green (1916) 50 ILT 179 400
Green, Re, Lindner v Green [1951] Ch 148, [1950] 2 All ER 913, 94 Sol Jo 742, 66 (pt 2)
  TLR 819 .... 10, 20, 23, 714
Green, Re, Walsh v Green (1893) 31 LR Ir 338 284
Green v Barrow (1853) 10 Hare 459, 1 WR 197, 21 LTOS 33
.... 449
Green v Belchier (1737) 1 Atk 505, West temp Hard 217
.... 1076
Green v Briscoe [2005] All ER (D) 96 (May) 883
Green v Britten (1863) 1 De GJ & Sm 649 1126
Green v Britten (1872) 42 LJ Ch 187, 27 LT 811 153
Green v Dunn (1855) 20 Beav 6, 24 LJ Ch 577, 3 WR 277, 25 LTOS 154
.... 180
Green v Ekins (1742) 2 Atk 473, 3 P Wms 306n 1083
Green v Froud (1674) 3 Keb 310, sub nom Green v Proude 1 Mod Rep 117, sub nom
  Anon (ancient demesne) 1 Vent 257 54
Green v Giles (1855) 5 I Ch R 25, 8 Ir Jur 90 455
Green v Green (1845) 2 Jo & Lat 529 135
Green v Green (1849) 3 De G & Sm 480, 18 LJ Ch 465, 14 Jur 74, 14 LTOS 3
.... 454–455
Green v Harvey (1842) 1 Hare 428, 11 LJ Ch 290, 6 Jur 704
.... 254, 442
Green v Howard (1779) 1 Bro CC 31 .... 210, 349
Green v Marsden (1853) 1 Drew 646, 22 LJ Ch 1092, 1 Eq Rep 437, 54 RR 789, 1 WR
  511, 22 LTOS 17 348
Green v Pertwee (1846) 5 Hare 249, 15 LJ Ch 372, 10 Jur 538, 7 LTOS 405
.... 1115
Green v Pigot (1781) 2 Dick 585, 1 Bro CC 103 .... 430, 1159
Green v Proude. See Green v Froud
Green v Skipworth (1809) 1 Phillim 53 903
Green v Stephens (1810) 17 Ves 64 474
Green v Symonds (1730) 1 Bro CC 129n 285
Green v Tribe (1878) 9 Ch D 231, 27 WR 39, 38 LT 914, sub nom Love, Re, Green v
  Tribe 47 LJ Ch 783 .... 1, 100, 112, 114, 181
Green v Walkling [2007] EWHC 3251 (Ch), [2008] 2 BCLC 332, [2007] All ER (D) 299
  (Dec), sub nom Ortega Associates Ltd, Re; Green v Walkling [2008] BCC 256
.... 1259
Green v Whitehead [1930] 1 Ch 38, 99 LJ Ch 153, 4 LDAB 228, 142 LT 1, 46 TLR 11,
  CA 919
Green's Estate, Re (1860) 1 Drew & Sm 68, 29 LJ Ch 716, 6 Jur NS 479, 8 WR 403, 2 LT
  791 .... 165, 172, 446
Green's Estate, Re, Ward v Bond (1962) 106 Sol Jo 1034, P, D and Admlty
.... 105
Green's Goods, Re (1899) 79 LT 738, P, D and Admlty 723
Green's Will, Re, Crowson v Wild [1907] VLR 284 408
Green's Will Trusts, Re, Fitzgerald-Hart v A-G [1985] 3 All ER 455
.... 33
Greenberry, Re, Hops v Daniell (1911) 55 Sol Jo 633 156
Greene, Re, Greene v Greene [1949] Ch 333, [1949] 1 All ER 167, 93 Sol Jo 27
.... 32, 626
Greene, Re, Greene v Kirkwood [1895] 1 IR 130, 142 133
Greene v Flood (1885) 15 LR Ir 450 469
Greene v Greene (1819) 4 Madd 148 1012
Greene v Potter (1843) 2 Y & C Ch Cas 517, 7 Jur 736
.... 419
Greenhill v Greenhill (1711) Gilb Ch 77, Prec Ch 320, 2 Vern 679, 1 Eq Cas Abr 174 pl 4
.... 27, 284

PARA

Greenough v Martin (1824) 2 Add 239 .... 99, 114, 185, 193, 611, 708
Greenstreet's Estate, Re (1930) 74 Sol Jo 188, P, D and Admlty
.... 101
Greenway v Greenway (1860) 2 De GF & J 128, 29 LJ Ch 601, 129 RR 41
.... 254, 342, 455, 460
Greenwich Hospital Improvement Act, Re (1855) 20 Beav 458
.... 284, 298
Greenwood, Re, Goodhart v Woodhead [1902] 2 Ch 198, 71 LJ Ch 579, 86 LT 500, 18
    TLR 530; revsd [1903] 1 Ch 749, 72 LJ Ch 281, 51 WR 358, [1900–3] All ER Rep
    332, 47 Sol Jo 238, 88 LT 212, 19 TLR 180, CA 143, 148, 414
Greenwood, Re, Greenwood v Firth (1911) 105 LT 509, [1911–13] All ER Rep Ext 1577
.... 959
Greenwood, Re, Greenwood v Greenwood [1892] 2 Ch 295, 61 LJ Ch 558, 40 WR 681,
    36 Sol Jo 608, 67 LT 76, 8 TLR 659 1087
Greenwood, Re, Greenwood v Sutcliffe [1912] 1 Ch 392, 81 LJ Ch 298, 56 Sol Jo 443,
    106 LT 424 .... 27, 164, 176
Greenwood, Re, Sutcliffe v Gledhill [1901] 1 Ch 887, 70 LJ Ch 326, 49 WR 461,
    [1900–3] All ER Rep 97, 84 LT 118 463
Greenwood v Greenwood (1776) 1 Bro CC 31n 402
Greenwood v Greenwood (1877) 5 Ch D 954, 47 LJ Ch 298, 26 WR 5, 21 Sol Jo 630, 37
    LT 305, CA 467
Greenwood v Greenwood (1939) 55 TLR 607, [1939] 2 All ER 150n, PC
.... 429
Greenwood v Percy (1859) 26 Beav 572 316
Greenwood v Verdon (1854) 1 K & J 74, 24 LJ Ch 65, 3 Eq Rep 181, 3 WR 124
.... 460
Greenwood's Goods, Re [1892] P 7, 61 LJP 56, 66 LT 61, P, D and Admlty
.... 83, 105
Greenwood's Will, Re (1861) 3 Giff 390, 31 LJ Ch 119, 8 Jur NS 907, 10 WR 117, 5 LT
    487 395
Greer, Re (1929) 73 Sol Jo 349, 45 TLR 362, P, D and Admlty
.... 732
Greet v Greet (1842) 5 Beav 123 434
Greg, Re, Fordham v Greg [1921] 2 Ch 243, 91 LJ Ch 48, 125 LT 825
.... 625
Gregg v Coates (1856) 23 Beav 33, 2 Jur NS 964, 4 WR 735
.... 152, 1229
Gregg v Pigott [2012] EWHC 732 (Ch), [2012] 3 WLR 913
.... 345
Gregory, Re, Gregory v Goodenough [1971] 1 All ER 497, [1970] 1 WLR 1455, 114 Sol
    Jo 532, CA 568, 574, 577
Gregory, Re, How v Charrington (1935) 79 Sol Jo 880, 52 TLR 130
.... 407
Gregory v Queen's Proctor (1846) 7 LTOS 470, 4 Notes of Cases 620
.... 67
Gregory v Smith (1852) 9 Hare 708 .... 214, 348, 394
Gregory's Settlement and Will, Re (1865) 34 Beav 600, 11 Jur NS 634, 6 New Rep 282, 13
    WR 828 .... 214, 261
Gregson, Re, Christison v Bolam (1887) 36 Ch D 223, 57 LJ Ch 221, 35 WR 803, 57 LT
    250 1296
Gregson v Taylor [1917] P 256, 86 LJP 124, sub nom Re Philpot, Gregson v Taylor 61 Sol
    Jo 578, 117 LT 318, 33 TLR 402, P, D and Admlty 902, 906
Gregson's Trusts, Re (1864) 2 Hem & M 504, 33 LJ Ch 531, 10 Jur NS 696, 4 New Rep
    222, 12 WR 935, 10 LT 642; on appeal (1864) 2 De GJ & Sm 428, 34 LJ Ch 41, 10
    Jur NS 1138, 5 New Rep 99, 13 WR 193, 46 ER 441, [1861–73] All ER Rep 967, 11
    LT 460, CA in Ch 214, 318
Greig v Merchant Co of Edinburgh 1921 SC 76, Ct of Sess
.... 745
Greig v Somerville (1830) 1 Russ & M 338 1102
Greig's Goods, Re (1866) LR 1 P & D 72, 35 LJP & M 113, 14 WR 349, 13 LT 681
.... 816
Gresham v Price (1865) 35 Beav 47 1200
Gresley v Mousley (1859) 4 De G & J 78, 28 LJ Ch 620, 5 Jur NS 583, 124 RR 164, 7
    WR 427, 33 LTOS 154 28
Gresley's Settlement, Re, Willoughby v Drummond [1911] 1 Ch 358, 80 LJ Ch 255, 104
    LT 244 .... 164, 167

PARA

Greville v Browne (1859) 7 HL Cas 689, 5 Jur NS 849, 7 WR 673, 11 ER 275,
  [1843–60] All ER Rep 888, 34 LTOS 8, HL 235, 1109
Greville v Tylee (1851) 7 Moo PCC 320 .... 83, 904
Grewe's Goods, Re (1922) 127 LT 371, [1922] All ER Rep 779, 38 TLR 440
  720
Grey v Montagu (1770) 3 Bro Parl Cas 314 459
Grey v Pearson. See Pearson v Rutter
Grey's Estate, Re [1922] P 140, 91 LJP 111, [1922] All ER Rep 124, 126 LT 799, 38 TLR
  401, P, D and Admlty 79
Grey's Trusts, Re, Grey v Stamford [1892] 3 Ch 88, 61 LJ Ch 622, 41 WR 60, 36 Sol Jo
  523 350
Grieve v Grieve (1867) LR 4 Eq 180, 36 LJ Ch 932, 15 WR 577, 16 LT 201
  389
Grieves v Rawley (1852) 10 Hare 63, 22 LJ Ch 625 .... 205, 328
Griffin, Re (1910) 54 Sol Jo 378, P, D and Admlty 751–753
Griffin, Re, Griffin v Ackroyd [1925] P 38, 94 LJP 32, 132 LT 494, 41 TLR 191, P, D and
  Admlty 810
Griffin v McCabe (1918) 52 ILT 134 122
Griffin and Amos v Ferard (1835) 1 Curt 97 54
Griffith, Re, Jones v Owen [1904] 1 Ch 807, 73 LJ Ch 464, 90 LT 639
  1196
Griffith v Blunt (1841) 4 Beav 248, 10 LJ Ch 372 412
Griffith v Hughes [1892] 3 Ch 105, 62 LJ Ch 135, 40 WR 524, 36 Sol Jo 504, 66 LT 760
  1260
Griffith v Killingley (1931) unreported 1293
Griffith's Goods, Re (1872) LR 2 P & D 457, 36 JP 424, 20 WR 495, 26 LT 780
  99
Griffiths v Evan (1842) 5 Beav 241, 11 LJ Ch 219 348
Griffiths v Gale (1844) 12 Sim 327, 353, 13 LJ Ch 286, 8 Jur 235, 3 LTOS 17
  170
Griffiths v Griffiths (1871) LR 2 P & D 300, 36 JP 8, 41 LJP & M 14, 20 WR 192, 25 LT
  574 .... 70, 76
Griffiths v Hamilton (1806) 12 Ves 298 659
Griffiths v Pruen (1840) 11 Sim 202 1069
Griffiths v Robins (1818) 3 Madd 191 .... 48, 903
Griffiths v Smith (1790) 1 Ves 97 146
Griffiths Estate, Re, Morgan v Stephens [1917] P 59, 86 LJP 42, 116 LT 382, P, D and
  Admlty 446, 794
Griffiths' Policy, Re [1903] 1 Ch 739, 72 LJ Ch 330, 88 LT 547, [1900–3] All ER Rep Ext
  1101 346
Griggs, Re, ex p London School Board [1914] 2 Ch 547, 13 LGR 27, 80 JP 35, 83 LJ Ch
  835, 58 Sol Jo 796, 111 LT 931, CA 945
Griggs v Gibson, ex p Maynard (No 2) (1866) 35 LJ Ch 458, 14 WR 538
  .... 161, 170
Grimond v Grimond [1905] AC 124, 74 LJPC 35, 92 LT 477, 21 TLR 323, HL
  11
Grimshaw's Trusts, Re (1879) 11 Ch D 406, 48 LJ Ch 399, 27 WR 544
  432
Grimshawe v Pickup (1839) 9 Sim 591, 3 Jur 286 442
Grimston v Lord Bruce (1707) 1 Salk 156, 2 Vern 594 149
Grimwood, Re, Trewhella v Grimwood [1946] Ch 54, [1945] 2 All ER 686, 115 LJ Ch 21,
  89 Sol Jo 579, 174 LT 76, 62 TLR 40 296
Grimwood v Cozens (1860) 5 Jur NS 497, 2 Sw & Tr 364
  .... 100, 712
Grindey, Re, Clews v Grindey [1898] 2 Ch 593, 67 LJ Ch 624, 47 WR 53, 79 LT 105, 14
  TLR 555, [1895–9] All ER Rep Ext 1628, CA 1259
Grobelaar v News Group Newspapers Ltd (1999) Times, 12 August, CA
  882
Groffman, Re, Groffman and Block v Groffman [1969] 2 All ER 108, [1969] 1 WLR 733,
  113 Sol Jo 58, P, D and Admlty 70
Groom, Re, Booty v Groom [1897] 2 Ch 407, 66 LJ Ch 778, 77 LT 154
  .... 274, 1017, 1208
Groom v Thomas (1829) 2 Hag Ecc 433 899–900
Groos' Estate, Re [1904] P 269, 73 LJP 82, 91 LT 322, P, D and Admlty
  94

PARA

Grosvenor, Re, Grosvenor v Grosvenor [1916] 2 Ch 375, 85 LJ Ch 735, 60 Sol Jo 681,
115 LT 298, [1916–17] All ER Rep Ext 1364 .... 1014, 1060, 1152

Grosvenor v Durston (1858) 25 Beav 97 .... 29, 293

Grotrian, Re, Cox v Grotrian [1955] Ch 501, [1955] 1 All ER 788, [1955] 2 WLR 695, 99
Sol Jo 220 147

Grove, Re, Public Trustee v Dixon [1919] 1 Ch 249, 88 LJ Ch 96, 63 Sol Jo 213, 120 LT
382 144

Grove v Banson (1669) 1 Cas in Ch 148 1099

Grove's Trusts, Re (1862) 3 Giff 575, 9 Jur NS 38, 6 LT 376
.... 429

Grover v Burningham (1850) 5 Exch 184 225

Grover v Raper (1856) 5 WR 134, 28 LTOS 215 .... 193, 252

Grover's Will Trusts, Re, National Provincial Bank Ltd v Clarke [1971] Ch 168, [1970]
1 All ER 1185, [1970] 2 WLR 574, 114 Sol Jo 207 .... 502, 515

Groves v Lane (1852) 16 Jur 1061, 1 WR 31 817

Groves v Wright (1856) 2 K & J 347, 2 Jur NS 277 122

Grundy v Ottey [2003] EWCA Civ 1176, [2003] WTLR 1253, sub nom Ottey v Grundy
[2003] All ER (D) 05 (Aug) 20

Grundy's Goods, Re (1868) LR 1 P & D 459, 32 JP 168, 37 LJP & M 21, 16 WR 406, 17
LT 451 759

Grylls' Trusts, Re (1868) LR 6 Eq 589 246

Guardhouse v Blackburn (1866) LR 1 P & D 109, 35 LJP & M 116, 12 Jur NS 278, 14
WR 463, [1861–73] All ER Rep 680, 14 LT 69 .... 55, 59, 193, 902

Guardian Trust and Executors Co of New Zealand Ltd v Public Trustee of New Zealand
[1942] AC 115, [1942] 1 All ER 598, 111 LJPC 119, 167 LT 162, 58 TLR 132,
[1942] NZLR 294, sub nom Public Trustee of New Zealand v Guardian Trust and
Executors Co of New Zealand Ltd [1942] 2 WWR 289, PC
.... 965

Gudavdze v Kay [2012] EWHC 1683 (Ch) 758

Gude v Mumford (1837) 2 Y & C Ex 445 .... 1129, 1133

Gude v Worthington (1849) 3 De G & Sm 389, 18 LJ Ch 303, 13 Jur 847, 13 LTOS 88
.... 373

Gudolle's Goods, Re (1835) 3 Sw & Tr 22 815

Gue, Re, Smith v Gue [1892] WN 88, 61 LJ Ch 510, 40 WR 552, 36 Sol Jo 503, 67 LT
823; affd [1892] WN 132, 36 Sol Jo 698, CA 328

Guedalla, Re, Lee v Guedalla's Trustee [1905] 2 Ch 331, 75 LJ Ch 52, 12 Mans 392, 54
WR 77, [1904–7] All ER Rep 1012, 94 LT 94 955

Guggenheim Estate, Re (1941) Times, 20 June 746

Guinee, Re (1929) 73 Sol Jo 569 732

Guinness Settlement, Re, Guinness v SG Warburg (Executor and Trustee) Ltd [1966]
2 All ER 497, [1966] 1 WLR 1355, 110 Sol Jo 636 1127

Gulbenkian's Settlement Trusts (No 2), Re, Stevens v Maun [1970] Ch 408, [1969]
2 All ER 1173, [1969] 3 WLR 450, 113 Sol Jo 758 151

Gullan v Grove (1858) 26 Beav 64 105

Gullan's Goods, Re (1858) 27 LJP & M 15, 4 Jur NS 196, 1 Sw & Tr 23, 5 WR 307,
30 LTOS 326 105

Gulliver v Vaux (1746) 8 De GM & G 167n, 114 RR 83
.... 142, 381

Gulliver v Wickett (1745) 1 Wils 105 446

Gulliver d Corrie v Ashby (1766) 4 Burr 1929, 1 Wm Bl 607
.... 129

Gulliver d Jeffereys v Poyntz (1770) 3 Wils 141, 2 Wm Bl 726
.... 290

Gully v Davis (1870) LR 10 Eq 562, 39 LJ Ch 684, 19 WR 265
.... 291

Gully v Dix [2004] EWCA Civ 139, [2004] 1 FCR 453, [2004] 1 FLR 918, [2004] Fam
Law 334, [2004] 06 LS Gaz R 32, (2004) Times, 28 January, [2004] All ER (D) 162
(Jan), sub nom Dix, Re [2004] 1 WLR 1399 .... 567, 579

Gundry v Pinniger (1852) 1 De GM & G 502, 21 LJ Ch 405, 16 Jur 488, 42 ER 647,
[1843–60] All ER Rep 403, 18 LTOS 325, CA in Ch 313

Gunn, Re, Harvey v Gunn [1916] WN 283, 51 L Jo 387
.... 1130

Gunning's Estate, Re (1884) 13 LR Ir 203 435–436

PARA

Gunstan's (or Gunston) Goods, Re, Blake v Blake (1882) 7 PD 102, 51 LJ Ch 377, 51 LJP
36, 30 WR 505, [1881–5] All ER Rep 870, 46 LT 641, CA
.... 68, 70, 78, 896
Gunther's Will Trusts, Re, Alexander v Gunther [1939] Ch 985, [1939] 3 All ER 291,
108 LJ Ch 395, 83 Sol Jo 545, 161 LT 156, 55 TLR 890
.... 405, 1117
Gurney v Gurney (1855) 3 Drew 208, 24 LJ Ch 656, 3 Eq Rep 569, 1 Jur NS 298, 3 WR
353, 25 LTOS 30 43
Guthrie v Walrond (1883) 22 Ch D 573, 52 LJ Ch 165, 31 WR 285, 47 LT 614
.... 153, 285, 1083, 1085
Guy v Sharp (1833) 1 My & K 589, Coop temp Brough 80
.... 401
Guyton and Rosenberg's Contract, Re [1901] 2 Ch 591, 70 LJ Ch 751, 50 WR 38, 85 LT
66 291
Gwillim v Gwillim (1859) 23 JP 825, Sea & Sm 26, 29 LJP & M 31, 3 Sw & Tr 200
.... 68, 70, 896
Gwyer v Peterson (1858) 26 Beav 83 1177
Gwynne v Berry (1875) IR 9 CL 494 .... 454, 460
Gwynne v Muddock (1808) 14 Ves 488 341
Gyett v Williams (1862) 2 John & H 429, 6 LT 279 284
Gyhon, Re, Allen v Taylor (1885) 29 Ch D 834, 54 LJ Ch 945, 33 WR 620, 53 LT 539,
CA 1179
Gyles, Re (1863) 14 I Ch R 311, 15 Ir Jur 315 298
Gyles, Re, Gibbon v Chaytor [1907] 1 IR 65 1082
Gynes v Kemsley (1677) Freem KB 293 275

H

H, Re [1990] 1 FLR 441, [1990] Fam Law 175 39–40
H v Mitson [2009] EWHC 3114 (Fam), sub nom H v J's Personal Representatives [2010]
Fam Law 343 .... 568, 571, 573, 576, 580
Haarbleicher and Schumann v Baerselman (1914) 137 LT Jo 564
.... 351
Haas v Atlas Assurance Co Ltd [1913] 2 KB 209, 82 LJKB 506, 6 BWCCN 87, 57 Sol Jo
446, 108 LT 373, 29 TLR 307 665
Habergham v Ridehalgh (1870) LR 9 Eq 395, 39 LJ Ch 545, 18 WR 427, 23 LT 214
.... 172, 323
Habergham v Vincent (1793) 2 Ves 204, 4 Bro CC 353 .... 54, 201, 708
Hack, Re (1930) 169 LT Jo 285, P, D and Admlty 9
Hack, Re, Beadman v Beadman [1925] Ch 633, 94 LJ Ch 343, 69 Sol Jo 662, 133 LT 134
.... 387
Hack v London Provident Building Society (1883) 23 Ch D 103, 52 LJ Ch 541, 31 WR
392, 48 LT 247, CA 237
Hackett's Goods, Re (1859) 23 JP 152, 28 LJP & M 42, 4 Sw & Tr 220
.... 710
Hackney London Borough Council v Driscoll [2003] EWCA Civ 1037, [2003] 4 All ER
1205, [2003] 1 WLR 2602, [2004] HLR 80, [2003] 35 LS Gaz R 38, (2003) Times,
29 August, [2003] All ER (D) 280 (Jul) 860
Haddelsey v Adams (1856) 22 Beav 266, 25 LJ Ch 826, 2 Jur NS 724, 27 LTOS 148
.... 395
Hadler's Estate, Re, Goodall v Hadler (1960) Times, 20 October
.... 68
Hadow v Hadow (1838) 9 Sim 438 370
Hagen's Trusts, Re (1877) 46 LJ Ch 665 317
Hagger, Re, Freeman v Arscott [1930] 2 Ch 190, 99 LJ Ch 492, [1930] All ER Rep 620,
143 LT 610 .... 9–10, 20, 23
Hagger v Payne (1857) 23 Beav 474, 26 LJ Ch 617, 3 Jur NS 479, 29 LTOS 47
.... 306, 308
Hagger's Goods, Re (1863) 32 LJPM & A 96, 9 Jur NS 386, 3 Sw & Tr 65, 11 WR 540, 8
LT 470 763
Haig, Re, Powers v Haig [1979] LS Gaz R 476, 129 NLJ 420
.... 592
Haig v Swiney (1823) 1 Sim & St 487, 2 LJOS Ch 26 375
Haigh's Estate, Re, Haigh v Haigh (1907) 51 Sol Jo 343
.... 287
Hains Goods, Re (1847) 5 Notes of Cases 621 102

PARA

Haldenby v Spofforth (1846) 9 Beav 195, 15 LJ Ch 328, 7 LTOS 155
.... 1201
Hale v Beck (1764) 2 Eden 229 471
Hale v Hale [1975] 2 All ER 1090, [1975] 1 WLR 931, 30 P & CR 98, 119 Sol Jo 256,
   CA 591
Hale v Hale (1692) Prec Ch 50 362
Hale v Hale (1876) 3 Ch D 643, 24 WR 1065, 35 LT 933
.... 412
Hale v Tokelove (1850) 2 Rob Eccl 318, 14 Jur 817, 16 LTOS 85
.... 110
Hale's Goods, Re [1915] 2 IR 362 80
Hale's Goods, Re (1874) LR 3 P & D 207, 44 LJP & M 45, 31 LT 799
.... 759
Hales v Margerum (1796) 3 Ves 299 382
Haley v Bannister (1857) 23 Beav 336 409
Halford v Halford [1897] P 36, 66 LJP 29, 75 LT 520, 13 TLR 69, P, D and Admlty
.... 7
Hall, Re [1943] 1 All ER 159 739
Hall, Re [1950] P 156, [1950] 1 All ER 718, 94 Sol Jo 195, 66 (pt 1) TLR 416, P, D and
   Admlty 761, 775
Hall, Re (1918) 53 ILT 11 407
Hall, Re, Barclays Bank Ltd v Hall [1951] 1 All ER 1073, 95 Sol Jo 300, [1951] 1 TLR
   850 .... 1080, 1085
Hall, Re, Branston v Weightman (1887) 35 Ch D 551, 56 LJ Ch 780, 35 WR 797, 57 LT
   42 352
Hall, Re, Foster v Metcalfe [1903] 2 Ch 226, 72 LJ Ch 554, 51 WR 529, [1900–3] All ER
   Rep 371, 42 Sol Jo 514, 88 LT 619, CA 1059, 1158–1159, 1161
Hall, Re, Hall v Hall [1932] 1 Ch 262, 101 LJ Ch 129, [1931] All ER Rep 88, 147 LT 33
.... 328, 331, 350
Hall, Re, Parker v Knight [1948] Ch 437, [1948] LJR 1430, 92 Sol Jo 310, 64 TLR 243
.... 332, 396
Hall, Re, Public Trustee v Montgomery [1944] Ch 46, [1943] 2 All ER 753, 113 LJ Ch 67,
   87 Sol Jo 423, 169 LT 387, 60 TLR 84 465
Hall v Andrews (1872) 20 WR 799, 27 LT 195 1025
Hall v Elliot (1791) Peake 86 1264
Hall v Fennell (1875) IR 9 Eq 615, 10 ILT 1 287
Hall v Fisher (1844) 1 Coll 47, 8 Jur 119 271
Hall v Hall [1891] 3 Ch 389, 60 LJ Ch 802, 40 WR 138, 35 Sol Jo 695, 65 LT 643; affd
   [1892] 1 Ch 361, 61 LJ Ch 289, 40 WR 277, 36 Sol Jo 200, 66 LT 206, CA
.... 17, 256, 288
Hall v Hall (1868) LR 1 P & D 481, 32 JP 503, 37 LJP & M 40, 16 WR 544, 18 LT 152
.... 56
Hall v Hallet (1784) 1 RR 3, 1 Cox Eq Cas 134 .... 657, 966, 1030, 1246
Hall v Hill (1841) 4 I Eq R 27, 1 Con & Law 120, 1 Dr & War 94
.... 197
Hall v Nalder (1852) 22 LJ Ch 242, 20 LTOS 153 334
Hall v Robertson (1853) 4 De GM & G 781, 23 LJ Ch 241, 2 Eq Rep 15, 18 Jur 635, 1
   WR 464 .... 246, 305
Hall v Terry (1738) 1 Atk 502, West temp Hard 500 438
Hall v Turner (1880) 14 Ch D 829, 44 JP 734, 28 WR 859, 42 LT 495, [1874–80] All ER
   Rep Ext 1448 28
Hall v Warren. See Warren v Rudall
Hall v Wright (1859) EB & E 765, 29 LJQB 43, 6 Jur NS 193, 8 WR 160, 120 ER 695,
   [1943–60] All ER Rep 734, 1 LT 230, Ex Ch 1213
Hall (Arthur J S) & Co (a firm) v Simons [1999] 3 WLR 873, [1999] 2 FCR 193, [1999] 1
   FLR 536, [1999] Fam Law 215, [1999] PNLR 374, CA; affd [2002] 1 AC 615, [2000]
   3 All ER 673, [2000] 3 WLR 543, [2000] 2 FCR 673, [2000] 2 FLR 545, [2000] Fam
   Law 806, [2000] 32 LS Gaz R 38, [2000] NLJR 1147, [2000] BLR 407, [2000] EGCS
   99, 144 Sol Jo LB 238, [2001] 3 LRC 117, [2000] All ER (D) 1027, HL
.... 1279
Hall's Estate, Re, Hall v Knight and Baxter [1914] P 1, 83 LJP 1, [1911–13] All ER Rep
   381, 58 Sol Jo 30, 109 LT 587, 30 TLR 1, CA 39–40, 756, 759
Hall's Goods, Re (1871) LR 2 P & D 256, 35 JP 808, 40 LJP & M 37, 19 WR 897, 25 LT
   384 .... 60, 85
Hall's Will, Re (1855) 1 Jur NS 974 122

                                                                                          PARA
Hall-Dare, Re, Le Marchant v Lee Warner [1916] 1 Ch 272, 85 LJ Ch 365, 114 LT 559
.... 246, 911, 1017, 1060, 1208
Hallett, Re, Hallett v Hallett [1892] WN 148 362
Hallett v Hallett (1898) 14 TLR 420, CA 271
Halley v O'Brien [1920] 1 IR 330 1190
Hallifax v Wilson (1812) 16 Ves 168 .... 260, 429, 452
Halliwell v Tanner (1830) 1 Russ & M 633 1011
Hallyburton's Goods, Re (1866) LR 1 P & D 90, 35 LJP & M 122, 12 Jur NS 416, 14 LT
   136 789
Halpin's Goods, Re (1873) 8 IR Eq 567 2
Halston, Re, Ewen v Halston [1912] 1 Ch 435, 81 LJ Ch 265, [1911–13] All ER Rep 667,
   56 Sol Jo 311, 106 LT 182 .... 211, 220, 1197
Halton v Foster (1868) 3 Ch App 505, 37 LJ Ch 547, 16 WR 683, 18 LT 623
.... 343
Haly v Barry (1868) 3 Ch App 452, 37 LJ Ch 723, 16 WR 654, 18 LT 491
.... 1176
Hambleton, Re, Hamilton v Hambleton [1884] WN 157
.... 441
Hamblett, Re, McGowan v Hamblett (2006) 8 ITELR 943
.... 13
Hambly v Trott (1776) 1 Cowp 371 1212
Hambro v Hambro [1894] 2 Ch 564, 63 LJ Ch 627, 8 R 413, 43 WR 92, 70 LT 684
.... 375
Hamer's Estate, Re (1943) 113 LJP 31, 60 TLR 168, P, D and Admlty
.... 82, 108
Hamilton v Buckmaster (1866) LR 3 Eq 323, 36 LJ Ch 58, 12 Jur NS 986, 15 WR 149, 15
   LT 177 284
Hamilton v Carroll (1839) 1 I Eq R 175 114
Hamilton v Mills (1861) 29 Beav 193, 13 LT 766 341,343
Hamilton v Ritchie [1894] AC 310, HL 241, 413
Hamilton v West (1846) 10 I Eq R 75 473
Hamilton Corpn v Hodsdon (1847) 6 Moo PCC 76, 11 Jur 193
.... 289
Hamlet, Re, Stephen v Cunningham (1888) 38 Ch D 183, sub nom Hamlet, Re,
   Cunningham v Graham 57 LJ Ch 1007; affd sub nom Hamlet, Re, Stephen v
   Cunningham (1888) 39 Ch D 426, 58 LJ Ch 242, 37 WR 245, 59 LT 745, 4 TLR
   752, [1886–90] All ER Rep Ext 1599, CA 235, 243, 260, 441
Hamley v Gilbert (1821) Jac 354 370
Hammersley, Re, Foster v Hammersley [1965] Ch 481, [1965] 2 All ER 24, [1965] 2 WLR
   938, 109 Sol Jo 198 .... 125, 182
Hammersley, Re, Heasman v Hammersley (1899) 81 LT 150
.... 288, 296
Hammersley, Re, Kitchen v Myers (1886) 2 TLR 459 328
Hammersley v Baron de Biel (1845) 12 Cl & Fin 45, 69 RR 18, HL
.... 21
Hammond, Re, Burniston v White [1911] 2 Ch 342, 80 LJ Ch 690, 55 Sol Jo 649, 105 LT
   302, 27 TLR 522 346–347
Hammond, Re, Hammond v Treharne [1938] 3 All ER 308, 82 Sol Jo 523, 54 TLR 903
.... 232
Hammond, Re, Parry v Hammond [1924] 2 Ch 276, 93 LJ Ch 620, [1924] All ER Rep
   183, 68 Sol Jo 706, 131 LT 632 .... 321, 384, 391–392
Hammond v Maule (1844) 13 LJ Ch 386, 1 Coll 281, 8 Jur 568, 3 LTOS 261
.... 430
Hammond v Neame (1818) 1 Wils Ch 9, 1 Swan 35, 36 ER 287, [1814–23] All ER Rep
   543 371
Hampden v Brewer (1666) 1 Cas in Ch 77 133
Hampshire v Peirce (1751) 2 Ves Sen 216 .... 193, 207, 265, 274
Hampshire's Estate, Re [1951] WN 174, P, D and Admlty
.... 98
Hampson v Brandwood (1858) 1 Madd 381 336
Hampton, Re, Hampton v Mawer (1918) 62 Sol Jo 585
.... 248
Hanbury v Hanbury [1999] 3 FCR 217, [1999] 2 FLR 255, [1999] Fam Law 447, Cty Ct
.... 572, 586
Hanbury v Spooner (1843) 5 Beav 630, 12 LJ Ch 434 1070

PARA

Hanchett-Stamford v A-G [2008] EWHC 330 (Ch), [2009] Ch 173, [2008] 4 All ER 323,
[2009] 2 WLR 405, [2008] 2 P & CR 102, [2009] PTSR 1, [2008] NLJR 371,
[2008] All ER (D) 391 (Feb) 36
Hancock, Re [1999] 1 FCR 500, [1998] 2 FLR 346, [1998] Fam Law 520, CA
.... 568, 573–574, 576, 580
Hancock, Re, Malcolm v Burford-Hancock [1896] 2 Ch 173, 65 LJ Ch 690, 44 WR 545,
40 Sol Jo 498, 74 LT 658, CA 346
Hancock v Clavey (1871) 19 WR 1044, 25 LT 323 387
Hancock v Watson [1902] AC 14, 71 LJ Ch 149, 50 WR 321, [1900–3] All ER Rep 87, 85
LT 729, HL 231, 446
Hand v North (1863) 33 LJ Ch 556, 10 Jur NS 7, 3 New Rep 239, 12 WR 229, 9 LT 634
.... 395
Handford v Storie (1825) 2 Sim & St 196 1173
Hanlon, Re, Heads v Hanlon [1933] Ch 254, 102 LJ Ch 62, [1932] All ER Rep 851, 76
Sol Jo 868, 148 LT 448 .... 133–134, 138, 141
Hannaford v Hannaford (1871) LR 7 QB 116, 41 LJQB 62, 20 WR 292, 25 LT 820
.... 474
Hannam, Re, Haddelsey v Hannam [1897] 2 Ch 39, 66 LJ Ch 471, 45 WR 613, 76 LT
681 .... 260, 302, 305, 322–323
Hannam v Sims (1858) 2 De G & J 151, 27 LJ Ch 251, 4 Jur NS 863, 6 WR 347,
30 LTOS 358 .... 322, 445
Hannigan v Hannigan [2000] 2 FCR 650, [2006] WTLR 597, [2000] All ER (D) 693, CA
.... 598
Hanson v Graham (1801) 6 Ves 239, 31 ER 1030, [1775–1802] All ER Rep 433
.... 238, 416, 426, 430–431
Haq v Singh [2001] EWCA Civ 957, [2001] 1 WLR 1594, (2001) Times, 10 July, [2001]
BPIR 1002, [2001] All ER (D) 394 (May) 647
Harbin v Masterman [1894] 2 Ch 184, 63 LJ Ch 388, 7 R 159, 38 Sol Jo 306, 70 LT 357,
10 TLR 340, CA; affd sub nom Wharton v Masterman [1895] AC 186, 64 LJ Ch 369,
11 R 169, 43 WR 449, [1895–9] All ER Rep 687, 72 LT 431, 11 TLR 301, HL
.... 146, 1062
Harbin v Masterman [1896] 1 Ch 351, 65 LJ Ch 195, 44 WR 421, [1895–9] All ER Rep
695, 40 Sol Jo 129, 73 LT 591, 12 TLR 105, CA 1058
Harbison, Re, Morris v Larkin [1902] 1 IR 103 371
Harby v Moore (1860) 6 Jur NS 883, 3 LT 209 127
Harcourt, Re, Fitzwilliam v Portman [1920] 1 Ch 492, 89 LJ Ch 655, 123 LT 36
.... 400
Hardcastle v Dennison (1861) 10 CBNS 606, 4 LT 707 560
Hardcastle v Hardcastle (1862) 1 Hem & M 405, 1 New Rep 83, 7 LT 503
.... 432, 435–436
Harding, Re, Drew v St Thomas Hospital (1910) 55 Sol Jo 93, 27 TLR 102
.... 293
Harding, Re, Gibbs v Harding [2007] EWHC 3 (Ch), [2008] Ch 235, [2007] 1 All ER 747,
[2008] 2 WLR 361, 9 ITELR 563, [2007] All ER (D) 28 (Jan)
.... 128, 131, 140, 206, 259
Harding, Re, Westminster Bank Ltd v Laver [1934] Ch 271, 103 LJ Ch 121, 77 Sol Jo 853,
150 LT 277 533
Harding v Metropolitan Rly Co (1872) 7 Ch App 154, 36 JP 340, 41 LJ Ch 371, 20 WR
321, 26 LT 109 157
Harding v Nott (1857) 7 E & B 650, 26 LJQB 244, 3 Jur NS 1020, 5 WR 574, 29 LTOS
179 194
Hardwick v Hardwick (1873) LR 16 Eq 168, 42 LJ Ch 636, 21 WR 719
.... 267–268, 271, 273, 277
Hardwick v Thurston (1828) 4 Russ 380, 6 LJOS Ch 124
.... 161
Hardwicke (Earl) v Douglas (1840) 7 Cl & Fin 795, West 555, HL
.... 96, 233, 251
Hardy, Re, Wells v Borwick (1881) 17 Ch D 798, 50 LJ Ch 241, 29 WR 834, 41 LT 49
.... 1087
Hardyman, Re, Teesdale v McClintock [1925] Ch 287, 94 LJ Ch 204, [1925] All ER Rep
83, 133 LT 175 .... 114–115, 346
Hare v Cartridge (1842) 13 Sim 165 274
Hare v Hill (1841) 3 Beav 450 403
Hare v Roberts (1859) 7 HL Cas 429, 28 LJ Ch 948, 5 Jur NS 1031, 7 WR 563, 33 LTOS
379 .... 226, 242, 244, 333
Harford v Browning (1787) 1 Cox Eq Cas 302 1070

PARA

Hargreaves, Re, Dicks v Hare (1890) 44 Ch D 236, 59 LJ Ch 375, [1886–90] All ER Rep
1017, 62 LT 819, 6 TLR 264, CA 989, 991, 1174

Hargreaves, Re, Hargreaves v Hargreaves (1902) 86 LT 43; varied [1900–3] All ER Rep
80, 88 LT 100, CA 405

Hargreaves v Pennington (1864) 34 LJ Ch 180, 10 Jur NS 834, 12 WR 1047, 10 LT 857
.... 409

Hargthorpe v Milforth (1594) Cro Eliz 318 1252

Harker's Will Trusts, Re, Kean v Harker [1969] 3 All ER 1, [1969] 1 WLR 1124, 113 Sol
Jo 588 .... 181, 308

Harker-Thomas, Re [1969] P 28, [1968] 3 All ER 17, [1968] 3 WLR 1267, 112 Sol Jo
522, CA 576

Harkness v Harkness (1905) 9 OLR 705, 6 OWR 122 348

Harland v Trigg (1782) 1 Bro CC 142 348

Harland-Peck, Re, Hercy v Mayglothing [1941] Ch 182, [1940] 4 All ER 347, 110 LJ Ch
81, 84 Sol Jo 717, 164 LT 215, 57 TLR 118, CA 287, 994

Harling's Goods, Re [1900] P 59, 69 LJP 32, 81 LT 791, P, D and Admlty
.... 761

Harloe v Harloe (1875) LR 20 Eq 471, 44 LJ Ch 512, 23 WR 789, 33 LT 247,
[1874–80] All ER Rep Ext 2260, Ct of Ch 1017, 1199

Harman, Re, Lloyd v Tardy [1894] 3 Ch 607, 63 LJ Ch 822, 8 R 549, 71 LT 401
.... 239

Harman v Dickenson (1781) 1 Bro CC 91 448

Harman v Gurner (1866) 35 Beav 478 277

Harman v Harman (1686) Comb 35, 3 Mod Rep 115, 2 Show 492
.... 1245

Harmer, Re (1964) 42 DLR (2d) 321, [1964] 1 OR 367, Ont CA; affd sub nom Kilby v
Meyers [1965] SCR 24, Can SC 246

Harmes v Hinkson [1946] WN 118, 62 TLR 445, [1946] 3 DLR 497, PC
.... 905

Harmood v Oglander (1803) 8 Ves 106 1012

Harney v Towell. See Harvey v Towell

Harper, Re (1843) 6 Man & G 732, 7 Scott NR 431 48

Harper, Re, Plowman v Harper [1914] 1 Ch 70, 83 LJ Ch 157, 58 Sol Jo 120, 109 LT 925,
[1911–13] All ER Rep Ext 1453 .... 332, 396

Harper's Goods, Re [1899] P 59, 68 LJP 48, 80 LT 294, P, D and Admlty
.... 695

Harper's Goods, Re (1849) 7 Notes of Cases 44 111

Harper's Trustee v Bain (1903) 40 SLR 476, 5 F 716, 10 SLT 758, Ct of Sess
.... 293

Harpur's Will Trusts, Re, Haller v A-G [1962] Ch 78, [1961] 3 All ER 588, [1961] 3 WLR
924, 105 Sol Jo 609, CA 225

Harrell v Wilts and Humbley. See Horrell v Witts and Plumley

Harrington, Re, Wilder v Turner [1908] 2 Ch 687, 72 JP 501, 78 LJ Ch 27, 21 Cox CC
709, [1908–10] All ER Rep 235, 52 Sol Jo 855, 99 LT 723, 25 TLR 3
.... 1218

Harrington v Bowyer (1871) LR 2 P & D 264, 36 JP 184, 41 LJP & M 17, 19 WR 982,
25 LT 385 874

Harrington v Butt [1905] P 3n, 74 LJP 13n, P, D and Admlty
.... 914

Harrington v Gill (1983) 4 FLR 265, CA 567, 572, 591

Harris, Re, Cope v Evans [1945] Ch 316, [1945] 1 All ER 702, 114 LJ Ch 302, 89 Sol Jo
282, 173 LT 284, 61 TLR 364 465

Harris, Re, Harris v Harris [1912] 2 Ch 241, 81 LJ Ch 512, 106 LT 755
.... 1087

Harris, Re, Murray v Everard [1952] P 319, [1952] 2 All ER 409, 96 Sol Jo 563, [1952] 2
TLR 585, P, D and Admlty 65

Harris v Beneficiaries of the Estate of Margaret Alice Cooper [2010] All ER (D) 64 (Jan)
.... 195, 212, 214, 256, 349

Harris v Berrall (1858) 1 Sw & Tr 153, 7 WR 19 .... 93, 106

Harris v Cave (1887) 57 LJ Ch 62, 36 WR 182, 57 LT 768
.... 271, 279, 282

Harris v Davis (1844) 1 Coll 416, 9 Jur 269 .... 173, 342, 387, 454

Harris v Earwicker [2015] EWHC 1915 (Ch) 1163

Harris v Farwell (1846) 13 Beav 403, 15 LJ Ch 185, 7 LTOS 426
.... 1233

PARA

Harris v Gandy (1859) 1 De GF & J 13, 29 LJ Ch 38, 8 WR 32
.... 1177
Harris v Harris [1942] LJNCCR 119 1144
Harris v Harris (1861) 10 WR 31 1177
Harris v Harris (1861) 29 Beav 107, 7 Jur NS 955, 131 RR 475, 9 WR 444
.... 294
Harris v Harris (1869) 17 WR 790 1113
Harris v Ingledew (1730) 2 Eq Cas Abr 255, 461, 3 P Wms 91
.... 899
Harris v Knight (1890) 15 PD 170, 62 LT 507, 6 TLR 234, CA
.... 716, 895
Harris v Lightfoot (1861) 10 WR 31 1177
Harris v Lloyd (1823) Turn & R 310 305
Harris v Moat Housing Group South Ltd [2007] EWHC 3092 (QB), [2008] 1 WLR 1578,
    [2008] NLJR 67, [2008] 2 Costs LR 294, [2007] All ER (D) 323 (Dec)
.... 908
Harris v Newton (1877) 46 LJ Ch 268, 25 WR 228, 36 LT 173
.... 343
Harris v Poyner (1852) 1 Drew 174, 21 LJ Ch 915, 16 Jur 880
.... 1011
Harris' Goods, Re (1860) 29 LJPM & A 79, 1 Sw & Tr 536, 8 WR 368, 2 LT 118
.... 108
Harris Goods, Re (1870) LR 2 P & D 83, 34 JP 455, 39 LJP & M 48, 18 WR 901, 22 LT
    630, [1861–73] All ER Rep Ext 1692 .... 616, 723
Harris' Trusts, Re (1854) 2 Eq Rep 1110, 2 WR 689, 23 LTOS 344
.... 333
Harrison, Re, Harrison v A-G (1915) 85 LJ Ch 77, 113 LT 308, 31 TLR 398
.... 152
Harrison, Re, Harrison v Gibson [2005] EWHC 2957 (Ch), [2006] 1 All ER 858, 8 ITELR
    588, (2006) Times, 25 January, [2005] All ER (D) 345 (Dec), sub nom Harrison v
    Gibson [2006] 1 WLR 1212 382
Harrison, Re, Harrison v Higson [1894] 1 Ch 561, 63 LJ Ch 385, 70 LT 868
.... 352
Harrison, Re, Hunter v Bush [1918] 2 Ch 59, 87 LJ Ch 433, [1918–19] All ER Rep 785,
    62 Sol Jo 568, 118 LT 756 231
Harrison, Re, Smith v Allen [1891] 2 Ch 349, 60 LJ Ch 287, 64 LT 442
.... 1238
Harrison, Re, Townson v Harrison (1889) 43 Ch D 55, 59 LJ Ch 169, 38 WR 265, 61 LT
    762 1121
Harrison, Re, Turner v Hellard (1885) 30 Ch D 390, 55 LJ Ch 799, 34 WR 420, 53 LT
    799, CA 60, 200, 241, 255, 263, 672
Harrison v Asher (1848) 2 De G & Sm 436, 17 LJ Ch 452, 12 Jur 833, 12 LTOS 25
.... 156
Harrison v Buckle (1719) 1 Stra 238 430
Harrison v Elvin (1842) 3 QB 117, 11 LJQB 197, 2 Gal & Dav 769, 6 Jur 849
.... 75
Harrison v Foreman (1800) 5 Ves 207 .... 395, 444
Harrison v Grimwood (1849) 12 Beav 192, 18 LJ Ch 485, 13 Jur 864, 14 LTOS 502
.... 431–432, 436, 447
Harrison v Harrison [1901] 2 Ch 136, 70 LJ Ch 551, 49 WR 613, 45 Sol Jo 484, 85 LT
    39 316
Harrison v Harrison (1803) 8 Ves 185 74
Harrison v Harrison (1829) Taml 273, 1 Russ & M 71 274
Harrison v Harrison (1860) 28 Beav 21 313
Harrison v Harrison (1904) 7 OLR 297, 3 OWR 247, 24 CLT 222
.... 190
Harrison v Hyde (1859) 4 H & N 805, 29 LJ Ex 119 277
Harrison v Jackson (1877) 7 Ch D 339 .... 156, 158, 293
Harrison v Kirk. See Beattie v Cordner
Harrison v Mitchell (1731) 2 Barn KB 20, Fitz-G 303, sub nom Harrison v Weldon 2 Stra
    911 848
Harrison v Naylor (1790) 2 Cox Eq Cas 247, 3 Bro CC 108
.... 438
Harrison v Rowley (1798) 4 Ves 212 .... 1070, 1263
Harrison v Tucker [2003] EWHC 1168 (Ch), [2003] WTLR 883, 147 Sol Jo LB 692,
    [2003] All ER (D) 341 (May) 430, 433

PARA

Harrison v Weldon. See Harrison v Mitchell

Harrison (Inspector of Taxes) v Willis Bros (Willis and Executors of Willis) [1966] Ch 619, [1965] 3 All ER 753, [1966] 2 WLR 183, 43 TC 61, 109 Sol Jo 875, sub nom Willis and Willis Executors v Harrison 44 ATC 343, [1965] TR 345, CA

.... 1231

Harrison's Estate, Re (1870) 5 Ch App 408 471

Harrison's Estate, Re (1879) 3 LR Ir 114 336

Harrison's Goods, Re (1841) 2 Curt 863, 5 Jur 1017, 1 Notes of Cases 168

.... 68

Harrowby (Earl) v Snelson [1951] 1 All ER 140, 95 Sol Jo 108

.... 644

Hart, Re, Hart v Arnold (1912) 107 LT 757 405

Hart v Durand (1796) 3 Anst 684 352

Hart v Hernandez (1885) 52 LT 217 293

Hart v Tribe (1854) 18 Beav 215, 23 LJ Ch 462, 2 WR 289, 23 LTOS 124

.... 370

Hart v Tribe (1863) 32 Beav 279 390

Hart v Tulk (1852) 2 De GM & G 300, 22 LJ Ch 649, 21 LTOS 174

.... 241, 243, 246, 253

Hart's Trusts, Re, ex p Block (1858) 3 De G & J 195, 28 LJ Ch 7, 4 Jur NS 1264, 7 WR 28, 32 LTOS 98 .... 425, 430–431

Hart's Will Trusts, Re, Public Trustee v Barclays Bank Ltd [1950] Ch 84, [1949] 2 All ER 898, 93 Sol Jo 791, 65 TLR 742 475

Harte, Re [2015] EWHC 2351 (Ch), [2015] WTLR 1735

.... 268, 270

Harter v Harter (1873) LR 3 P & D 11, 37 JP 583, 42 LJP & M 1, 21 WR 341, 27 LT 858 .... 187, 906

Hartley, Re [1899] P 40, 68 LJP 16, 47 WR 287, P, D and Admlty

.... 556

Hartley, Re, Stedman v Dunster (1887) 34 Ch D 742, 56 LJ Ch 564, 35 WR 624, 56 LT 565 147

Hartley v Hurle (1800) 5 Ves 540 291

Hartley v Tribber (1853) 16 Beav 510, sub nom Hart v Tribe 22 LJ Ch 890, 21 LTOS 29

.... 193

Hartley's Goods, Re (1880) 50 LJP 1, 29 WR 356, P, D and Admlty

.... 99

Hartley's Trusts, Re (1878) 47 LJ Ch 610, 26 WR 590 366

Hartopp's Case (1591) Cro Eliz 243, 1 Leon 253 321

Hartshorne v Gardner [2008] 2 FLR 1681, [2008] Fam Law 985

.... 31, 956

Harvell v Foster [1954] 2 QB 367, [1954] 2 All ER 736, [1954] 3 WLR 351, 98 Sol Jo 540, CA 1144, 1148–1150

Harver's Goods, Re, Harver v Harver (1889) 14 PD 81, 58 LJP 72, 37 WR 768, 61 LT 338, P, D and Admlty 809

Harvey, Re, Harvey v Lambert (1888) 58 LT 449 1030

Harvey, Re, Public Trustee v Hoskin [1947] Ch 285, [1947] 1 All ER 349, [1947] LJR 1015, 91 Sol Jo 148, 177 LT 133 156

Harvey, Re, Wright v Woods (1884) 26 Ch D 179, 53 LJ Ch 544, 32 WR 765, 50 LT 554

.... 1205

Harvey v Coxwell (1875) 32 LT 52, Ct of Ch 1177

Harvey v Harvey (1722) 2 P Wms 21, 2 Eq Cas Abr 566 pl 10

.... 1077

Harvey v Harvey (1842) 5 Beav 134, 49 ER 528, [1835–42] All ER Rep 544

.... 375, 383

Harvey v Lady Aston (1737) 2 Eq Cas Abr 539, 1 Atk 361, 2 Com 726, sub nom Hervey v Aston West temp Hard 350 .... 130, 134–135

Harvey v RG O'Dell Ltd [1958] 2 QB 78, [1958] 1 All ER 657, [1958] 2 WLR 473, [1958] 1 Lloyd's Rep 273, 102 Sol Jo 196 1279

Harvey v Stracey (1852) 1 Drew 73, 22 LJ Ch 13, 16 Jur 771, 20 LTOS 61

.... 306

Harvey v Towell (1847) 7 Hare 231, 17 LJ Ch 217, 68 ER 94, sub nom Harney v Towell 12 Jur 241 .... 384–385, 387

Harvey's Estate, Re [1907] P 239, 76 LJP 61, 51 Sol Jo 357, 23 TLR 433, P, D and Admlty

.... 680

                                                                          PARA
Harvey's Estate, Re, Harvey v Gillow [1893] 1 Ch 567, 62 LJ Ch 328, 3 R 247, 41 WR
  293, 37 Sol Jo 212, 68 LT 562, 9 TLR 187, [1891–4] All ER Rep Ext 1648
  .... 167, 305
Harvy v Aston (1740) Com 726 129
Harward, Re, Newton v Bankes [1938] Ch 632, [1938] 2 All ER 804, 107 LJ Ch 307, 159
  LT 354, 54 TLR 784 171
Harwood v Baker (1840) 3 Moo PCC 282 .... 49, 899, 903
Harwood v Harwood [2005] EWHC 3019 (Ch), [2005] All ER (D) 121 (Nov)
  .... 230, 282
Harwood and Higham's Case (1586) Godb 40 286
Haseldine, Re, Grange v Sturdy (1886) 31 Ch D 511, 50 JP 390, 34 WR 327, 54 LT 322, 2
  TLR 256, CA 351
Hasker v Sutton (1824) 1 Bing 500, 2 LJOSCP 68, 9 Moore CP 2
  442
Haslewood v Pope (1734) 3 P Wms 322 1012
Haslip, Re [1958] 2 All ER 275n, [1958] 1 WLR 583, 102 Sol Jo 366, P, D and Admlty
  .... 775, 808
Hasluck v Pedley (1874) LR 19 Eq 271, 44 LJ Ch 143, 23 WR 155
  .... 240, 1085
Hassan, Re [1981] 78 LS Gaz R 842 884
Hastead v Searle (1679) 1 Ld Raym 728 277
Hastie's Trusts, Re (1887) 35 Ch D 728, 56 LJ Ch 792, 35 WR 692, 57 LT 168
  .... 352, 354
Hastilow v Stobie (1865) LR 1 P & D 64, 35 LJP & M 18, 11 Jur NS 1039, 14 WR 211,
  13 LT 473 .... 11, 48, 55
Hastings v Hane (1833) 6 Sim 67 248
Hastings (Lord) v Douglas (1634) Cro Car 343, W Jo 332, 79 ER 901,
  [1558–1774] All ER Rep 576 .... 30, 121
Hastings' Goods, Re (1877) 4 PD 73, 42 JP 185, 47 LJP 30, 39 LT 45, P, D and Admlty
  805
Hatch, Re, Hatch v Hatch (1916) 86 LJ Ch 454, 60 Sol Jo 567, 115 LT 472
  1130
Hatch, Re, Public Trustee v Hatch [1948] Ch 592, [1948] 2 All ER 288, [1948] LJR 1393,
  92 Sol Jo 456 465
Hatch v Hatch (1855) 20 Beav 105, 3 WR 354 320
Hatch v Mills (1759) 1 Eden 342 429
Hatfeild v Minet (1878) 8 Ch D 136, 47 LJ Ch 612, 26 WR 701, 38 LT 629, CA
  503
Hatfeild's Will Trusts, Re, Hatfeild v Hatfeild [1958] Ch 469, [1957] 2 All ER 261, [1957]
  3 WLR 28, 101 Sol Jo 480 182
Hattatt v Hattatt (1832) 4 Hag Ecc 211 5
Hatton v Finch (1841) 4 Beav 186, 5 Jur 548 395
Hatton v Hooley Lofft. See Hooley v Hatton
Haughton v Harrison (1742) 2 Atk 329 1077
Haughton v Haughton (1824) 1 Mol 611 133
Haverd v Church (1851) 61 LJ Ch 601, 16 Jur 181, 3 Mac & G 622, 19 LTOS 13
  381
Havergal v Harrison (1843) 7 Beav 49, 13 LJ Ch 36, 7 Jur 1100
  .... 173, 672
Haverty v Curtis [1895] 1 IR 23 438
Hawes v Hawes (1880) 14 Ch D 614, 43 LT 280 .... 332, 563
Hawes v Hawes. See Haws v Haws
Hawes v Leader (1611) 1 Brownl 111, Cro Jac 270, Yelv 196
  1261
Hawes v Smith (1675) 2 Lev 122, 1 Vent 268, sub nom Smith v Haws 3 Keb 336, 416
  1240
Hawkes, Re, Reeve v Hawkes [1912] 2 Ch 251, 81 LJ Ch 641, 106 LT 1014
  1006
Hawkes v Baldwin (1838) 9 Sim 355, 7 LJ Ch 297, 2 Jur 698
  145
Hawkes v Barrett (1820) 5 Madd 17 1178
Hawkesley v May [1956] 1 QB 304, [1955] 3 All ER 353, [1955] 3 WLR 569, 99 Sol Jo
  781 1055
Hawkin's Trusts, Re (1864) 33 Beav 570, 34 LJ Ch 80, 10 Jur NS 922, 12 WR 945, 10 LT
  557 1070
Hawkins, ex p (1843) 13 Sim 569, 2 LTOS 94 156
Hawkins, Re, Hawkins v Argent (1913) 109 LT 969 287

PARA

Hawkins, Re, Public Trustee v Shaw [1922] 2 Ch 569, 91 LJ Ch 486, 66 Sol Jo 612, 127
  LT 488 119
Hawkins v Hamerton (1848) 16 Sim 410, 13 JR 2 .... 395, 460, 470
Hawkins v Hawkins (1880) 13 Ch D 470, CA 153
Hawks v Longridge (1873) 29 LT 449 1113
Hawksley's Settlement, Re, Black v Tidy [1934] Ch 384, 50 TR 231, [1934] All ER Rep
  94, 151 LT 299 .... 95, 97, 107–108, 193, 223, 298, 670, 679, 713
Hawksworth v Hawksworth (1858) 27 Beav 1 .... 254, 289
Haws v Haws (1747) 3 Atk 524, 1 Ves Sen 13, sub nom Hawes v Hawes 1 Wils 165
  .... 249, 253, 256, 395
Hawthorn v Shedden (1856) 25 LJ Ch 833, 2 Jur NS 749, 3 Sm & G 293, 27 LTOS 304
  1114
Hay, Re, Kerr v Stinnear [1904] 1 Ch 317, 73 LJ Ch 33, 52 WR 92, 48 Sol Jo 15
  85
Hay, Re, Leech v Hay [1932] NI 215 182
Hay v Earl of Coventry (1789) 3 Term Rep 83 456
Hay Drummond, Re, Halsey v Pechell [1922] All ER Rep 330, 67 Sol Jo 247, 128 LT 621,
  39 TLR 144 294
Hay's Goods, Re (1865) LR 1 P & D 51, 35 LJP & M 3, 11 Jur NS 936, 14 WR 147, 13
  LT 335 770
Hay's Settlement Trusts, Re [1981] 3 All ER 786, [1982] 1 WLR 202, 125 Sol Jo 866
  11
Hayden, Re, Pask v Perry [1931] 2 Ch 333, 100 LJ Ch 381, [1931] All ER Rep 139, 146
  LT 303 .... 254, 320, 334, 342, 391
Haydon v Rose (1870) LR 10 Eq 224, 39 LJ Ch 688, 18 WR 1146, 23 LT 334
  452
Haydon v Wilshire (1789) 3 Term Rep 372 .... 334, 336
Hayes v Hayes [1917] 1 IR 194 410
Hayes v Hayes (1674) 1 Eq Cas Abr 78, Cas temp Finch 231, 1 Cas in Ch 223, Freem Ch
  138 149
Hayes v Hayes (1836) 1 Keen 97, 5 LJ Ch 243 .... 156, 369
Hayes v Willis (1906) 75 LJP 86, P, D and Admlty 894
Hayes Goods, Re (1839) 2 Curt 338 79–80
Hayes' Will Trusts, Re, Dobie v National Hospital Board of Governors [1953] 2 All ER
  1242, [1954] 1 WLR 22, 98 Sol Jo 11 278
Hayes Will Trusts, Re, Pattinson v Hayes [1971] 2 All ER 341, [1971] 1 WLR 758, 115
  Sol Jo 310, 219 Estates Gazette 1181 .... 125, 1020
Haygarth, Re, Wickham v Haygarth [1913] 2 Ch 9, 82 LJ Ch 328, 108 LT 756,
  [1911–13] All ER Rep Ext 1473 .... 253, 404
Haynes v Haynes (1853) 3 De GM & G 590 1133
Haynes v Haynes (1861) 1 Drew & Sm 426, 30 LJ Ch 578, 7 Jur NS 595, 9 WR 497, 4
  LT 199 157
Haynes' Goods, Re (1842) 3 Curt 75, 1 Notes of Cases 402
  622
Hayter, Re, Hayter v Wells (1883) 32 WR 26 1200
Hayton's Trusts, Re (1864) 4 New Rep 55, 10 LT 336 472
Hayward, Re, Creery v Lingwood (1882) 19 Ch D 470, 51 LJ Ch 513, 30 WR 315, 45 LT
  790 .... 322, 450
Hayward, Re, Kerrod v Hayward [1957] Ch 528, [1957] 2 All ER 474, [1957] 3 WLR 50,
  101 Sol Jo 502, CA 502–503
Hayward v Angell (1683) 1 Vern 222 149
Hayward v James (1860) 28 Beav 523, 29 LJ Ch 822, 6 Jur NS 689, 8 WR 676, 2 LT 452
  452
Hayward v Kinsey. See Kinsey v Hayward
Hazeldine, Re, Public Trustee v Hazeldine [1918] 1 Ch 433, 87 LJ Ch 303, 62 Sol Jo 350,
  118 LT 437 1126
Hazlette, Re [1915] 1 IR 285 407
Heach v Prichard [1882] WN 140 290
Head, Re, Head v Head [1893] 3 Ch 426, 63 LJ Ch 35, 3 R 712, 42 WR 55, 69 LT 753
  1233
Head, Re, Head v Head (No 2) [1894] 2 Ch 236, 63 LJ Ch 549, 7 R 167, 42 WR 419, 38
  Sol Jo 385, 70 LT 608, [1891–4] All ER Rep Ext 1451, CA
  1233
Head v Randall (1843) 2 Y & C Ch Cas 231, 7 Jur 298
  .... 249, 334
Headington v Holloway (1830) 3 Hag Ecc 280 909

PARA

Healey v Brown [2002] EWHC 1405 (Ch), 4 ITELR 894, [2002] WTLR 849,
[2002] All ER (D) 249 (Apr) 20–21, 23, 221
Healy v Healy (1875) IR 9 Eq 418 .... 218, 220
Hearn v Allen (1627) Cro Car 57, Hut 85 286
Hearn v Baker (1856) 2 K & J 383 318
Heasman v Pearse (1870) LR 11 Eq 522, 40 LJ Ch 258, 19 WR 673, 24 LT 864; affd
(1871) 7 Ch App 275, 41 LJ Ch 705, 20 WR 271, 26 LT 299
.... 248, 258, 261, 324–326, 336
Heath, Re, Jackson v Norman (1904) 48 Sol Jo 416 315
Heath, Re, Public Trustee v Heath [1936] Ch 259, 105 LJ Ch 29, [1935] All ER Rep 677,
154 LT 536, 52 TLR 54 .... 235, 422–423, 436
Heath v Chilton (1844) 13 LJ Ex 225, 12 M & W 632, 2 LTOS 424
.... 1288
Heath v Dendy (1826) 1 Russ 543, 5 LJOS Ch 59 1087
Heath v Lewis (1853) 3 De GM & G 954, 22 LJ Ch 721, 1 Eq Rep 55, 17 Jur 443, 98 RR
386, 1 WR 314, 21 LTOS 135 137
Heath v Nugent (1860) 29 Beav 226 1093
Heath v Perry (1744) 3 Atk 101 428
Heath's Goods, Re [1892] P 253, 61 LJP 131, 67 LT 356, P, D and Admlty
.... 83, 85
Heath's Settlement, Re (1856) 23 Beav 193 441
Heath's Will Trusts, Re, Hamilton v Lloyds Bank Ltd [1949] Ch 170, [1949] 1 All ER 199,
[1949] LJR 641, 93 Sol Jo 59 115
Heathcote's Estate, Re [1913] P 42, 82 LJP 40, 57 Sol Jo 266, 108 LT 122, 29 TLR 268, P,
D and Admlty 632
Heathe v Heathe (1741) 2 Atk 121 395
Heather v Winder (1835) 5 LJ Ch 41 460
Hebblethwaite v Cartwright (1734) 2 Barn KB 438, Cas temp Talb 31
.... 330
Hedgely, Re, Small v Hedgely (1886) 34 Ch D 379, 56 LJ Ch 360, 35 WR 472, 56 LT 19
.... 970
Hedges v Blick (1858) 3 De G & J 129, 27 LJ Ch 742, 4 Jur NS 1209, 6 WR 842,
32 LTOS 67 441
Hedges v Harpur (1846) 9 Beav 479; on appeal (1858) 3 De G & J 129, 27 LJ Ch 742, 4
Jur NS 1209, 6 WR 842, 32 LTOS 67 .... 249, 441
Hedley's Trusts, Re (1877) 25 WR 529 471
Heerman's Estate, Re [1910] P 357, 80 LJP 7, 55 Sol Jo 30, 103 LT 816, 27 TLR 51, P, D
and Admlty 763, 786
Heighington v Grant (1840) 5 My & Cr 258, 10 LJ Ch 12, 4 Jur 1052, 41 ER 369
.... 649
Heighington v Grant (1845) 1 Ph 600, 10 Jur 21 1202
Heilbronner, Re, Nathan v Kenny [1953] 2 All ER 1016, [1953] 1 WLR 1254, 97 Sol Jo
729 .... 285, 293
Heinke, Re, Westminster Bank Ltd v Massey (1959) Times, 21 January
.... 48, 903
Hele v Gilbert (1752) 2 Ves Sen 430 296
Helier v Casebert (1665) 1 Keb 839, 923, 1 Lev 127, sub nom Hellier v Casbard 1 Sid 240,
263 1222
Hellier v Hellier (1884) 9 PD 237, 49 JP 8, 53 LJP 105, 33 WR 324, P, D and Admlty
.... 98
Helliwell, Re, Pickles v Helliwell [1916] 2 Ch 580, 86 LJ Ch 45, 60 Sol Jo 619, 115 LT
478 352
Hellmann's Will, Re (1866) LR 2 Eq 363, 14 WR 682 1072
Helsby, Re, Neate v Bozie (1914) 84 LJ Ch 682, 112 LT 539
.... 302, 313
Heming v Clutterbuck (1827) 1 Bli NS 479, sub nom Hemming v Gurrey 1 Dow & Cl 35,
HL 402
Heming's Trust, Re (1856) 3 K & J 40, 26 LJ Ch 106, 2 Jur NS 1186, 5 WR 33, 28 LTOS
99 1074
Hemings v Munckley (1783) 1 Cox Eq Cas 38, sub nom Hemmings v Munckley 1 Bro CC
304 135
Hemingway, Re, James v Dawson (1890) 45 Ch D 453, 60 LJ Ch 85, 39 WR 4, 63 LT 218
.... 441

PARA

Hemming, Re, Raymond Saul & Co (a firm) v Holden [2008] EWHC 2731 (Ch), [2009]
   Ch 313, [2009] 2 WLR 1257, (2008) Times, 9 December, [2009] BPIR 50,
   [2008] All ER (D) 176 (Nov) 32, 150, 922, 1053, 1218–1219
Hemming v Gurrey. See Heming v Clutterbuck
Hemming v Whittam (1831) 5 Sim 22, 1 LJ Ch 94 .... 370, 375
Hemmings v Munckley. See Hemings v Munckley
Henchman v A-G (1834) 3 My & K 485 555
Hender v Rose (1718) 2 Eq Cas Abr 265 503
Henderson, Re, Public Trustee v Reddie [1940] Ch 368, [1940] 1 All ER 623, 109 LJ Ch
   169, 84 Sol Jo 255, 162 LT 376, 56 TLR 423 .... 927, 1118
Henderson v Cross (1861) 29 Beav 216, 7 Jur NS 177, 9 WR 263
   .... 381, 383
Henderson v Dodds (1866) LR 2 Eq 532, 14 WR 908, 14 LT 752
   1205
Henderson v Farbridge (1826) 1 Russ 479, 4 LJOS Ch 209
   288
Henderson v Henderson [1905] 1 IR 353 220
Henderson's Trusts, Re, Schreiber v Baring [1969] 3 All ER 769, [1969] 1 WLR 651, 113
   Sol Jo 328, CA 308
Hendy's Will, Re, Hayes v Hendy [1913] VLR 559 146
Henfrey v Henfrey (1842) 4 Moo PCC 29, 6 Jur 355, 1 Notes of Cases 356, PC
   97
Hengler, Re, Frowde v Hengler [1893] 1 Ch 586, 62 LJ Ch 383, 3 R 207, 41 WR 491, 68
   LT 84 1127
Hennessey v Bray (1863) 33 Beav 96, 9 Jur NS 1065, 11 WR 1053, 9 LT 41
   230
Hennessy (Richard B), Re (1963) 98 ILTR 39 .... 141–142, 182
Henrique's Trusts, Re [1875] WN 187 410
Henry, Re, Gordon v Gordon [1907] 1 Ch 30, 76 LJ Ch 74, 95 LT 776
   1121
Henry v Henry [2010] UKPC 3, [2010] 1 All ER 988, 75 WIR 254, [2010] 4 LRC 643,
   [2010] 2 P & CR D17, [2010] All ER (D) 288 (Feb) 20
Henry Will Trust, Re, Mussett v Smith (or Henry) [1953] 1 All ER 531, [1953] 1 WLR
   376, 97 Sol Jo 133 375
Hensler, Re, Jones v Hensler (1881) 19 Ch D 612, 51 LJ Ch 303, 30 WR 482, 45 LT 672
   168
Hensloe's Case (1600) 9 Co Rep 36b 349
Hensman v Fryer (1867) 3 Ch App 420, 37 LJ Ch 97, 16 WR 162, 17 LT 394
   .... 119, 195, 210
Henson, Re, Chester v Henson [1908] 2 Ch 356, 77 LJ Ch 598, 99 LT 336
   1024–1025
Henton, Re, Henton v Henton (1882) 30 WR 702 .... 255, 287
Hepburn, Re, ex p Smith (1884) 14 QBD 394, 54 LJQB 422
   979
Hepburn v Skirving (1858) 4 Jur NS 651, 32 LTOS 26 282
Hepplewhite's Will Trusts, Re [1977] CLY 2710 131
Heptinstall v Gott (1862) 2 John & H 449, 31 LJ Ch 776, 8 Jur NS 1091, 10 WR 708, 7
   LT 92 184
Hepworth, Re, Rastall v Hepworth [1936] Ch 750, [1936] 2 All ER 1159, 105 LJ Ch 380,
   80 Sol Jo 672, 155 LT 250, 52 TLR 694 350
Hepworth v Heslop (1849) 6 Hare 561, 18 LJ Ch 352, 13 Jur 166
   1029
Hepworth v Hill (1862) 30 Beav 476, 31 LJ Ch 569, 8 Jur NS 960, 10 WR 477, 6 LT 403
   1007
Hepworth v Scale (1855) 1 Jur NS 698, 25 LTOS 328 423
Herbert, Re [1926] P 109, sub nom Re Herbert's Goods 95 LJP 53, 135 LT 123, 42 TLR
   469, P, D and Admlty 775
Herbert v Badgery (1894) 10 WN 128, 15 NSWLR 236
   1096
Herbert v Blunden (1837) 1 Dr & Wal 78 384
Herbert v Reid (1810) 16 Ves 481 .... 199, 366
Herbert's Trusts, Re (1860) 1 John & H 121, 29 LJ Ch 870, 6 Jur NS 1027, 8 WR 660, 2
   LT 743 .... 214, 352
Herlakenden's Case (1589) 4 Co Rep 62a, 76 ER 1025, [1558–1774] All ER Rep 374
   931
Herne v Bembow (1813) 4 Taunt 764 1229

PARA

Heron v Stokes (1842) 2 Dr & War 89; revsd sub nom Stokes v Heron (1845) 12 Cl & Fin
  161, 9 Jur 563, HL 385, 390
Herring, Re, Murray v Herring [1908] 2 Ch 493, 77 LJ Ch 665, 99 LT 144, 24 TLR 747
  .... 156, 205, 296
Hertford (Marquis) v Lord Lowther (1843) 7 Beav 1, 13 LJ Ch 41, 7 Jur 1167
  .... 250, 285
Hertford (Marquis) v Lord Lowther (1845) 4 LTOS 450
  403
Hervey v Aston (1738) Willes 83 134
Hervey v Aston West temp Hard. See Harvey v Lady Aston
Hervey v M'Laughlin (1815) 1 Price 264 449
Hervey-Bathurst v Stanley (1876) 4 Ch D 251, 46 LJ Ch 162, 25 WR 482, 35 LT 709, CA
  147
Herwin, Re, Herwin v Herwin [1953] Ch 701, [1953] 2 All ER 782, [1953] 3 WLR 530,
  97 Sol Jo 570, CA 212, 214, 351
Heseltine v Heseltine (1818) 3 Madd 276 285
Hesketh v Magennis (1859) 27 Beav 395 318
Heslop's Goods, Re (1846) 1 Rob Eccl 457, 10 Jur 953, 8 LTOS 348, 5 Notes of Cases 2
  850
Hester v Trustees, Executors and Agency Co Ltd (1892) 18 VLR 509
  291
Hetherington, Re [1990] Ch 1, [1989] 2 WLR 1094, sub nom Re Hetherington, Gibbs v
  McDonnell [1989] 2 All ER 129, 133 Sol Jo 457 .... 150, 259, 298
Hetley, Re, Hetley v Hetley [1902] 2 Ch 866, 71 LJ Ch 769, 51 WR 202, [1900–3] All ER
  Rep 292, 87 LT 265 208
Heugh v Scard (1875) 24 WR 51, 33 LT 659 1200
Hewet v Ireland (1718) Gilb Ch 145, 1 P Wms 426, sub nom Hewitt v Ireland Prec Ch
  489, 2 Eq Cas Abr 139, pl 9 .... 247, 261, 330
Hewett, Re, Eldridge v Hewett (1920) 90 LJ Ch 126, 65 Sol Jo 116
  1060
Hewett, Re, Eldridge v Iles [1918] 1 Ch 458, [1918–19] All ER Rep 530, 118 LT 524, sub
  nom Re Hewitt, Eldridge v Iles 87 LJ Ch 209 .... 132, 137
Hewett v Foster (1844) 7 Beav 348, 8 Jur 769 1200
Hewett v Snare (1847) 1 De G & Sm 333 1012
Hewitson v Todhunter (1852) 22 LJ Ch 76, 1 WR 78, 20 LTOS 153
  165
Hewitt, Re, Hewitt v Hewitt [1926] Ch 740, 95 LJ Ch 300, [1926] All ER Rep 628, 70 Sol
  Jo 607, 135 LT 319 247
Hewitt v Ireland. See Hewet v Ireland
Hewitt v Jardine (1872) LR 14 Eq 58, 26 LT 546 404
Hewitt v Morris (1824) Turn & R 241, 2 LJOS Ch 87 1118
Hewitt's Estate, Re, Gateshead Corpn v Hudspeth (1883) 53 LJ Ch 132, 49 LT 587
  11
Hewitt's Settlement, Re, Hewitt v Hewitt [1915] 1 Ch 228, 84 LJ Ch 358, 59 Sol Jo 177,
  112 LT 287, 31 TLR 81 785
Hewson v Shelley [1914] 2 Ch 13, 83 LJ Ch 607, 58 Sol Jo 397, 10 LT 785, 30 TLR 402,
  CA 605, 669, 858
Hey's Estate, Re, Walker v Gaskill [1914] P 192, 83 LJP 152, 59 Sol Jo 45, 111 LT 941, 30
  TLR 637, P, D and Admlty 2, 9–10, 23, 679
Hey's Settlement Trusts and Will Trusts, Re, Hey v Nickell-Lean [1945] Ch 294, [1945]
  1 All ER 618, 114 LJ Ch 278, 89 Sol Jo 269, 172 LT 396, 61 TLR 334
  .... 288, 470, 1122, 1124, 1127
Heyman v Dobson [2007] EWHC 3503 (Ch), [2007] All ER (D) 275 (Dec)
  1163
Heyward v Bettesworth. See Bettisworth's Case, Hayward v Bettisworth
Heywood v Heywood (1860) 29 Beav 9, 30 LJ Ch 155, 7 Jur NS 228, 9 WR 62, 3 LT 429
  246
Heywood v Heywood (1865) 34 Beav 317, 34 LJ Ch 317, 11 Jur NS 633, 5 New Rep 441,
  13 WR 514, 12 LT 168 541
Heywood's Estate, Re [1916] P 47, 85 LJP 24, 60 Sol Jo 239, 114 LT 375, P, D and
  Admlty 710, 739
Hibbert v Hibbert (1808) 3 Mer 681 2
Hibbert v Hibbert (1873) LR 15 Eq 372, 42 LJ Ch 383, 21 WR 506, 28 LT 397
  349
Hibernian Bank v Lauder [1898] 1 IR 262 1204

PARA

Hibon v Hibon (1863) 32 LJ Ch 374, 9 Jur NS 511, 1 New Rep 532, 11 WR 455, 8 LT
  195 290
Hickey, Re, Beddoes v Hodgson [1917] 1 Ch 601, 86 LJ Ch 385, 61 Sol Jo 368, 116 LT
  556 .... 323, 338, 397
Hickey, Re, Hickey v Hickey [1913] 1 IR 390 370
Hicklin, Re, Public Trustee v Hoare [1917] 2 Ch 278, 86 LJ Ch 740, [1916–17] All ER
  Rep 658, 61 Sol Jo 630, 117 LT 403, 33 TLR 478 1015
Hickling v Boyer (1851) 21 LJ Ch 388, 16 Jur 137, 3 Mac & G 635, 20 LTOS 33
  .... 152, 1011
Hickling v Fair [1899] AC 15, 68 LJPC 12, HL 238, 243, 303, 305, 413–414, 429
Hickman v Peacey [1945] AC 304, [1945] 2 All ER 215, 114 LJ Ch 225, 89 Sol Jo 339,
  173 LT 89, 61 TLR 489, HL 33, 246, 746
Hickman's Will Trusts, Re, Hickman v Hickman [1948] Ch 624, [1948] 2 All ER 303,
  [1948] LJR 1500, 64 TLR 420 .... 300, 346
Hicks, Re, Bach v Cockburn [1933] 1 Ch 335, 102 LJ Ch 177, 148 LT 466
  1130
Hicks v Chief Constable of the South Yorkshire Police [1992] 2 All ER 65, 8 BMLR 70,
  [1992] PIQR P433, HL 1279
Hicks v Sallitt (1854) 3 De GM & G 782, 23 LJ Ch 571, 2 Eq Rep 818, 18 Jur 915, 2 WR
  173, 22 LTOS 322 .... 242, 248
Hicks' Goods, Re (1869) LR 1 P & D 683, 33 JP 711, 38 LJP & M 65, 21 LT 300
  .... 95, 707
Hiddingh (Heirs) v De Villiers Denyssen (1887) 12 App Cas 624, 56 LJPC 107, 57 LT 885,
  PC 961
Hide v Mason (1734) 2 Eq Cas Abr 776, 8 Vin Abr 140
  108
Higgins, Re, Day v Turnell (1885) 31 Ch D 142, 55 LJ Ch 235, 34 WR 81, 54 LT 199, CA
  1131
Higgins' Trusts, Re (1861) 2 Giff 562, 30 LJ Ch 405, 7 Jur NS 403, 3 LT 803
  1294
Higham, Re, Higham v Higham [1937] 2 All ER 17 .... 340, 533
Higham v Baker (1583) Cro Eliz 15 .... 271, 469
Higstrim v Ray (1895) 16 NSWLR Eq 1 209
Hildick, Re, Hipkins v Hildick (1881) 29 WR 733, 44 LT 547
  982
Hill, Re, Claremont v Hill [1934] Ch 623, 103 LJ Ch 289, [1934] All ER Rep 617, 78 Sol
  Jo 446, 151 LT 416, 50 TLR 487, CA 653
Hill, Re, Fettes v Hill [1914] WN 132, 58 Sol Jo 399 295
Hill, Re, Public Trustee v O'Donnell [1923] 2 Ch 259, 93 LJ Ch 13, 129 LT 824
  370
Hill, Re, Westminster Bank Ltd v Wilson [1944] Ch 270, [1944] 1 All ER 502, 113 LJ Ch
  241, 88 Sol Jo 179, 170 LT 317, 60 TLR 358, CA 1090
Hill v Bonner (1858) 26 Beav 372, 7 WR 81 818
Hill v Brown [1894] AC 125, 63 LJPC 46, 6 R 440, 70 LT 175, PC
  376
Hill v Chapman (1791) 1 Ves 405, 3 Bro CC 391 305–306
Hill v Crook (1873) LR 6 HL 265, 42 LJ Ch 702, 22 WR 137, [1874–80] All ER Rep 62
  .... 2331, 351–352, 354, 466, 482
Hill v Curtis (1865) LR 1 Eq 90, 35 LJ Ch 133, 12 Jur NS 4, 14 WR 125, 13 LT 584
  .... 646, 1264, 1268
Hill v Gomme (1839) 1 Beav 540, 8 LJ Ch 350, 3 Jur 744; affd (1839) 5 My & Cr 250,
  9 LJ Ch 54, 4 Jur 165, 41 ER 366, [1835–42] All ER Rep 118
  1245
Hill v Grange (1555) 2 Dyer 130b, 1 Plowd 164 .... 225, 286
Hill v Hill (1814) 3 Ves & B 183 1077
Hill v Hill (1860) 8 WR 536, 2 LT 792 417
Hill v Jones (1868) 37 LJ Ch 465 409
Hill v Mills (1691) Comb 185, 12 Mod Rep 9, 1 Salk 36, 1 Show 293, Holt KB 305, sub
  nom Mill's Case Skin 299 624
Hill v Nalder (1852) 17 Jur 224 394
Hill v St John (1775) 3 Bro Parl Cas 375 277
Hill v Simpson (1802) 7 Ves 152 .... 1023, 1028
Hill v Spread Trustee Co Ltd [2006] EWCA Civ 542, [2007] 1 All ER 1106, [2007] 1
  WLR 2404, [2007] Bus LR 1213, [2007] 1 BCLC 450, [2006] BCC 646, (2006)
  Times, 10 July, [2006] BPIR 789, [2006] All ER (D) 202 (May)
  1221

PARA

Hill v Walker (1858) 4 K & J 166, 32 LTOS 71 974

Hill (Viscount) v Bullock [1897] 2 Ch 482, 66 LJ Ch 705, 46 WR 84, 41 Sol Jo 696, 77 LT 240, 13 TLR 554, CA 932

Hill (Viscount) v Dowager Viscountess Hill [1897] 1 QB 483, 66 LJQB 329, 45 WR 371, 41 Sol Jo 292, 76 LT 103, 13 TLR 227, CA 928

Hill's Goods, Re (1845) 1 Rob Eccl 276, 4 Notes of Cases 174
.... 79

Hill's Goods, Re (1870) LR 2 P & D 89, 34 JP 567, 39 LJP & M 52, 18 WR 1005, 23 LT 167 720

Hillas v Hillas (1847) 10 I Eq R 134 298

Hillas-Drake, Re, National Provincial Bank Ltd v Liddell [1944] Ch 235, [1944] 1 All ER 375, 113 LJ Ch 137, 88 Sol Jo 103, 170 LT 240, 60 TLR 261
.... 405, 1117

Hillersdon v Lowe (1843) 2 Hare 355, 12 LJ Ch 321, 7 Jur 482
.... 244, 422

Hilliard v Fulford (1876) 4 Ch D 389, 46 LJ Ch 43, 25 WR 161, [1874–80] All ER Rep 247, 35 LT 750 .... 1096, 1207

Hillingdon Estates Co v Stonefield Estates Ltd [1952] Ch 627, [1952] 1 All ER 853, 50 LGR 587, 2 P & CR 415, [1952] 1 TLR 1099 157

Hills v Wirley (1743) 2 Atk 605 185

Hilton v Hilton (1866) 15 WR 193 322

Hilton v Hilton (1872) LR 14 Eq 468 404–405

Hilton v Sutton Steam Laundry [1946] KB 65, [1945] 2 All ER 425, 115 LJKB 33, 174 LT 31, CA 647

Hinchliffe v Westwood (1848) 2 De G & Sm 216, 17 LJ Ch 167, 12 Jur 618, 11 LTOS 123
.... 165, 364

Hinckley v Simmons (1798) 4 Ves 160 .... 237, 449

Hindle, Re, Megson v Hindle. See Megson v Hindle

Hindmarch's Goods, Re (1866) LR 1 P & D 307, 31 JP 41, 36 LJP & M 24, 15 LT 391, [1861–73] All ER Rep Ext 2005 83

Hindmarsh v Charlton (1861) 25 JP 339, 8 HL Cas 160, 7 Jur NS 611, 9 WR 521, [1861–73] All ER Rep 63, 4 LT 125, HL 63, 70, 74–75

Hine's Goods, Re [1893] P 282, 63 LJP 45, 6 R 573, 69 LT 458, P, D and Admlty
.... 93, 106

Hipwell, Re, Hipwell v Hewitt [1945] 2 All ER 476, 89 Sol Jo 487, 173 LT 192, CA
.... 336

Hirst v Tolson (1850) 19 LJ Ch 441, 2 H & Tw 359, 14 Jur 559, 2 Mac & G 134
.... 1213

Hiscock's Goods, Re [1901] P 78, 70 LJP 22, [1900–3] All ER Rep 63, 84 LT 61, 17 TLR 110, P, D and Admlty 79

Hiscoe, Re, Hiscoe v Waite [1902] WN 49, 71 LJ Ch 347
.... 1084

Hiscoe, Re, Hiscoe v Waite (1883) 48 LT 510 306

Hitchins v Basset. See Nosworthy v Basset

Hixon v Oliver (1806) 13 Ves 108 378

Hixon v Wytham (1675) 1 Cas in Ch 248, sub nom Hickson v Witham Cas temp Finch 195, Freem Ch 305, Freem KB 305 .... 3, 5

Hoare v Byng. See Byng v Lord Strafford

Hoare v Osborne (1864) 33 LJ Ch 586, 10 Jur NS 383, 12 WR 397, 10 LT 20
.... 175

Hoare v Parker (1788) 2 Term Rep 376 121

Hoare's Goods, Re (1833) 2 Sw & Tr 361n 850

Hoare Trustees v Jaques [2008] EWHC 2022 (Ch), [2008] All ER (D) 68 (Feb)
.... 95, 97, 100, 110–112

Hoath v Hoath (1785) 2 Bro CC 3 431

Hoban, Re, Lonergan v Hoban [1896] 1 IR 401 1190

Hobart v Hobart [2006] EWHC 1784 (Ch), [2006] All ER (D) 295 (May)
.... 187

Hobbs, Re, Hobbs v Hobbs [1917] 1 Ch 569, 86 LJ Ch 409, 116 LT 270; affd [1917] 1 Ch 569, CA 334, 336, 384, 386

Hobbs v Knight (1838) 1 Curt 768 .... 101, 105

Hobgen v Neale (1870) LR 11 Eq 48, 40 LJ Ch 36, 19 WR 144, 23 LT 681
.... 326, 337, 394–395

Hobley, Re (1997) Times, 16 June 23

PARA

Hobson, Re, Barwick v Holt [1912] 1 Ch 626, [1911–13] All ER Rep 257, 56 Sol Jo 400,
106 LT 507 .... 257, 316–317, 470
Hobson, Re, Walter v Appach (1885) 55 LJ Ch 422, 34 WR 70, 53 LT 627
.... 1127
Hobson v Blackburn (1833) 1 My & K 571, 2 LJ Ch 168
.... 127, 284, 286
Hobson v Blackburn and Blackburn (1822) 1 Add 274 9
Hobson's Estate, Re, Hobson v Sharp [1907] VLR 724 308
Hockin, Re (1895) 59 JP 472, 73 LT 316, P, D and Admlty
.... 759
Hockley v Mawbey (1790) 1 Ves 143, 3 Bro CC 82, 29 ER 420
.... 334, 457
Hoddle v CCF Construction Ltd [1992] 2 All ER 550 1211
Hodge, Re, Hodge v Griffiths [1940] Ch 260, 109 LJ Ch 185, 84 Sol Jo 113, 162 LT 155,
56 TLR 327 .... 152, 1144
Hodge, Re, Midland Bank Executor and Trustee Co Ltd v Morrison [1943] Ch 300, [1943]
2 All ER 304, 112 LJ Ch 241, 87 Sol Jo 274, 169 LT 155, 59 TLR 373
.... 182
Hodge v Churchward (1847) 16 Sim 71 407
Hodge v Foot (1865) 34 Beav 349 316
Hodges, Re (1855) 4 De GM & G 491 1047
Hodges, Re, Hodges v Hodges [1899] 1 IR 480 1040–1041
Hodges v Grant (1867) LR 4 Eq 140, 36 LJ Ch 935, 15 WR 607
.... 326
Hodges v Smith [1950] WN 455 1247
Hodges' Legacy, Re (1873) LR 16 Eq 92, 42 LJ Ch 452, 21 WR 558, 28 LT 624
.... 145
Hodgeson v Bussey (1740) 2 Atk 89, Barn Ch 195, 9 Mod Rep 236
.... 385
Hodgkinson, Re, Hodgkinson v Hodgkinson [1895] 2 Ch 190, 64 LJ Ch 663, 12 R 297,
43 WR 594, 39 Sol Jo 468, 72 LT 617, [1895–9] All ER Rep Ext 2136, CA
.... 1211
Hodgkinson's Goods, Re [1893] P 339, 62 LJP 116, 37 Sol Jo 700, 69 LT 540, 9 TLR 650,
CA 110
Hodgson, Re, Beckett v Ramsdale (1885) 31 Ch D 177, 55 LJ Ch 241, 34 WR 127,
[1881–5] All ER Rep 931, 54 LT 222, 2 TLR 73, CA 1232–1233
Hodgson, Re, Darley v Hodgson [1899] 1 Ch 666, 68 LJ Ch 313, 47 WR 443, 80 LT 276
.... 277
Hodgson, Re, Hodgson v Fox (1878) 9 Ch D 673, 48 LJ Ch 52, 27 WR 38
.... 1068
Hodgson, Re, Hodgson v Gillett [1952] 1 All ER 769, 96 Sol Jo 262
.... 315
Hodgson, Re, Nowell v Flannery [1936] Ch 203, 105 LJ Ch 51, [1935] All ER Rep 161,
79 Sol Jo 880, 154 LT 338, 52 TLR 88 193
Hodgson, Re, Taylor v Hodgson [1898] 2 Ch 545, 67 LJ Ch 591, 47 WR 44, 79 LT 345
.... 291
Hodgson, Re, Weston v Hodgson [1913] 1 Ch 34, 82 LJ Ch 31, 57 Sol Jo 112, 107 LT 607
.... 462
Hodgson v Ambrose (1780) 1 Doug KB 337; affd sub nom Ambrose v Hodgson (1781) 3
Bro Parl Cas 416, HL 245
Hodgson v Bective (1863) 1 Hem & M 376; varied sub nom Bective v Hodgson (1864) 10
HL Cas 656, 33 LJ Ch 601, 10 Jur NS 373, 3 New Rep 654, 138 RR 350, 12 WR
625, 10 LT 202, HL 1083
Hodgson v Clarke (1860) 1 De GF & J 394 .... 214, 276
Hodgson v Coates (1856) 23 Beav 33, 2 Jur NS 964, 4 WR 735
.... 152, 1229
Hodgson v Green (1842) 11 LJ Ch 312, 6 Jur 819 370
Hodgson v Halford (1879) 11 Ch D 959, 48 LJ Ch 548, 27 WR 545
.... 131, 133, 140
Hodgson v Jex (1876) 2 Ch D 122, 45 LJ Ch 388 .... 250, 288
Hodgson v Lakeman [1943] KB 15, 41 LGR 203, 107 JP 27, 112 LJKB 162, 87 Sol Jo
103, 168 LT 78, DC 1277, 1286
Hodgson v Smithson (1856) 8 De GM & G 604, 26 LJ Ch 110, 2 Jur NS 1199, 111 RR
120, 5 WR 3, 28 LTOS 73 .... 322, 449
Hodgson's Trust, Re (1854) 1 K & J 178, 2 Eq Rep 1083, 18 Jur 786, 2 WR 539
.... 326, 395

PARA

Hodson, Re, ex p Richardson (1818) 3 Madd 138, Buck 202; affd (1819) Buck 421
.... 1036, 1039
Hodson v Micklethwaite (1854) 2 Drew 294, 23 LJ Ch 719, 2 Eq Rep 1157, 2 WR 440
.... 302
Hoff v Atherton [2004] EWCA Civ 1554, [2004] All ER (D) 314 (Nov)
.... 48–49, 55, 891
Hogan v Byrne (1862) 13 ICLR 166, 14 Ir Jur 223 36
Hogg v Cook (1863) 32 Beav 641 328
Hogg v Graham (1811) 4 Taunt 135 1291
Hoggins v Paull (1850) 1 Sim NS 92, 20 LJ Ch 75, 15 Jur 5, 16 LTOS 550
.... 370
Hoghton, Re, Hoghton v Fiddey (1874) LR 18 Eq 573, 43 LJ Ch 758, 22 WR 854
.... 1183
Holden, Re (1903) 5 OLR 156, 2 OWR 11, 23 CLT 52
.... 296
Holden, Re, Holden v Smith (1888) 57 LJ Ch 648, 59 LT 358
.... 382
Holden, Re, Isaacson v Holden [1935] WN 52, 179 LT Jo 235
.... 803, 965
Holden v Ramsbottom (1863) 4 Giff 205, 9 Jur NS 350, 1 New Rep 307, 354, 11 WR
    302, 66 ER 680, 7 LT 735 296
Holder, Re, National Provincial Bank Ltd v Holder [1953] Ch 468, [1953] 2 All ER 1,
    [1953] 2 WLR 1079, 97 Sol Jo 353 283
Holder v Holder [1968] Ch 353, [1968] 1 All ER 665, [1968] 2 WLR 237, 112 Sol Jo 17,
    205 Estates Gazette 211, CA 627, 657
Holder v Howell (1803) 8 Ves 97 96
Holding and Management Ltd v Property Holding and Investment Trust plc [1988]
    2 All ER 702, [1988] 1 WLR 644, 132 Sol Jo 626, [1988] 11 LS Gaz R 43; affd
    [1990] 1 All ER 938, [1989] 1 WLR 1313, 21 HLR 596, 134 Sol Jo 262,
    [1990] 1 EGLR 65, [1990] 05 EG 75, CA 1196
Holford, Re, Holford v Holford [1894] 3 Ch 30, 63 LJ Ch 637, 7 R 304, 42 WR 563, 38
    Sol Jo 512, 70 LT 777, 10 TLR 496, CA 312
Holford v Wood (1798) 4 Ves 76 402
Holland, Re, Brettell v Holland [1907] 2 Ch 88, 76 LJ Ch 449, 97 LT 49
.... 287
Holland v Allsop (1861) 29 Beav 498, Jur NS 856, 9 WR 683
.... 317
Holland v Clark (1843) 2 Y & C Ch Cas 319, 7 Jur 213
.... 1298
Holland v Hodgson (1872) LR 7 CP 328, 41 LJCP 146, 20 WR 990, [1861–73] All ER
    Rep 237, 26 LT 709, Ex Ch 932
Holland v Wood (1870) LR 11 Eq 91 .... 311, 320
Holland's Estate, Re [1936] 3 All ER 13, 105 LJP 113, 80 Sol Jo 838, 155 LT 417, 53
    TLR 3, P, D and Admlty 611
Hollebone, Re, Hollebone v Hollebone [1919] 2 Ch 93, 88 LJ Ch 386, [1918–19] All ER
    Rep 323, 63 Sol Jo 553, 121 LT 116 1127
Holliday, Re [1922] 2 Ch 698, 92 LJ Ch 55, 127 LT 585, 38 TLR 709
.... 556
Holliday, Re, Houghton v Adlard [1947] Ch 402, [1947] 1 All ER 695, [1947] LJR 1086,
    91 Sol Jo 278, 76 LT 478, 63 TLR 255 1127
Holliday v Musa [2010] EWCA Civ 335, [2010] All ER (D) 288 (Mar)
.... 566
Hollingshead, Re, Hollingshead v Webster (1888) 37 Ch D 651, 57 LJ Ch 400, 36 WR
    660, 58 LT 758, 4 TLR 275 977
Hollinrake v Lister (1826) 1 Russ 500 149
Hollis v Smith (1808) 10 East 293 1287
Hollis' Hospital Trustees and Hague's Contract, Re [1899] 2 Ch 540, 68 LJ Ch 673, 47
    WR 691, [1895–9] All ER Rep 643, 43 Sol Jo 644, 81 LT 90
.... 143
Holloway, Re, Young v Holloway (1887) 12 PD 167, 56 LJP 81, 35 WR 751, 57 LT 515, 3
    TLR 616, sub nom Young v Holloway 56 LJP 81, CA 879
Holloway v Clarkson (1843) 2 Hare 521 377
Holloway v Collins (1675) 1 Eq Cas Abr 300, 1 Cas in Ch 245
.... 1073
Holloway v Radcliffe (1857) 23 Beav 163, 26 LJ Ch 401, 5 WR 271, 28 LTOS 301
.... 314, 364

                                                                                            PARA
Holme v Hammond (1872) LR 7 Exch 218, 41 LJ Ex 157, 20 WR 747
.... 1239
Holmes, Re, Holmes v Holmes (1890) 62 LT 383 .... 468, 511
Holmes, Re, Villiers v Holmes [1917] 1 IR 165 .... 295, 922
Holmes v Barker (1816) 2 Madd 462 284
Holmes v Coghill (1802) 6 RR 166, 7 Ves 499; affd (1806) 8 RR 323, 12 Ves 206
.... 1005
Holmes v Custance (1806) 12 Ves 279 210
Holmes v Dring (1788) 2 Cox Eq Cas 1 963
Holmes v Godson (1856) 8 De GM & G 152, 25 LJ Ch 317, 2 Jur NS 383, 114 RR 73, 4
    WR 415, 27 LTOS 8 .... 142, 381
Holmes v Lysaght (1733) 2 Bro Parl Cas 261 135
Holmes v Meynel, T Jo. See Holmes v Willett
Holmes v Milward (1878) 47 LJ Ch 522, sub nom Holmes v Sayer-Milward 26 WR 608,
    38 LT 381 291
Holmes v Prescott (1864) 33 LJ Ch 264, 10 Jur NS 507, 3 New Rep 559, 12 WR 636, 11
    LT 38 .... 237, 424–425
Holmes v Sayer-Milward. See Holmes v Milward
Holmes v Willett (1681) Freem KB 483, sub nom Holmes v Meynel 2 Show 136, T Jo 172,
    T Raym 452 473–474
Holmes' Trusts, Re (1853) 1 Drew 321, 22 LJ Ch 393 276
Holt, Re, Holt v Holt [1921] 2 Ch 17, 90 LJ Ch 410, 65 Sol Jo 293, 125 LT 478
.... 291
Holt, Re, Holt v Holt (1916) 85 LJ Ch 779, 60 Sol Jo 640, 115 LT 73
.... 1010
Holt v Frederick (1726) 2 P Wms 356 504
Holt v Holt (1694) 2 Vern 322, 1 Eq Cas Abr 274 pl 11
.... 1215
Holt v Sindrey (1868) LR 7 Eq 170, 33 JP 260, 38 LJ Ch 126, 17 WR 249, 19 LT 669
.... 352, 354
Holt's Estate, Re, Bolding v Strugnell (1876) 45 LJ Ch 208, 24 WR 339
.... 430–431
Holtam's Estate, Re, Gillett v Rogers (1913) 108 LT 732, P, D and Admlty
.... 63
Holton v Lloyd (1827) 1 Mol 30 136
Holyland, ex p (1805) 11 Ves 10 900
Holyland v Lewin (1884) 26 Ch D 266, 53 LJ Ch 530, 32 WR 443, 51 LT 14, CA
.... 170
Home v Pillans (1833) 2 My & K 15, 4 LJ Ch 2, Coop temp Brough 198
.... 382, 449–450
Homer, Re, Cowlishaw v Rendell (1916) 86 LJ Ch 324, 115 LT 703
.... 354
Homer v Homer (1878) 8 Ch D 758, 47 LJ Ch 635, 27 WR 101, 39 LT 3, CA
.... 210, 267, 271, 277
Hone's Trusts, Re (1883) 22 Ch D 663, 52 LJ Ch 295, 31 WR 379, 48 LT 266
.... 168
Honywood v Honywood (1874) LR 18 Eq 306, 43 LJ Ch 652, 22 WR 749, 30 LT 671,
    [1874–80] All ER Rep Ext 1946 931
Honywood v Honywood (1905) 92 LT 814, HL 400
Honywood's Goods, Re (1871) LR 2 P & D 251, 35 JP 600, 40 LJP & M 35, 19 WR 760,
    25 LT 164, [1861–73] All ER Rep Ext 1355 739
Hood v Clapham (1854) 19 Beav 90, 24 LJ Ch 193, 1 Jur NS 78, 105 RR 67, 3 WR 78,
    24 LTOS 206 237
Hood v Wilson (1831) 2 Russ & M 687 1205
Hook v Hook (1862) 1 Hem & M 43, 32 LJ Ch 14, 9 Jur NS 42, 1 New Rep 85, 11 WR
    105, 7 LT 501 .... 561, 563
Hook v Taylor (1706) 2 Vern 561 419
Hooley v Hatton (1773) 2 Dick 461, 1 Bro CC 390n, sub nom Hatton v Hooley Lofft 122
.... 402–403
Hooper, Re, Hooper v Carpenter [1936] Ch 442, [1936] 1 All ER 277, 105 LJ Ch 298, 80
    Sol Jo 205, 154 LT 677, CA 339
Hooper, Re, Hooper v Warner (1902) 51 WR 153, 47 Sol Jo 30, 88 LT 160
.... 272, 276–277
Hooper, Re, Parker v Ward [1932] 1 Ch 38, 101 LJ Ch 61, [1931] All ER Rep 129, 146
    LT 208 150

PARA

Hooper v Smart (1875) 1 Ch D 90, 45 LJ Ch 99, 24 WR 152, 33 LT 499
.... 1105
Hooper v Summersett (1810) Wight 16 1262
Hooper's Settlement, Re, Phillips v Lake [1943] Ch 116, [1943] 1 All ER 173, 112 LJ Ch
  135, 87 Sol Jo 83, 168 LT 165, 59 TLR 182, CA 344
Hooper's Settlement Trusts, Re, Bosman v Hooper [1948] Ch 586, [1948] 2 All ER 261,
  [1948] LJR 1455, 92 Sol Jo 362 324
Hope v Campbell [1899] AC 1, HL 49
Hope v d'Hedouville [1893] 2 Ch 361, 62 LJ Ch 589, 3 R 348, 41 WR 330, 68 LT 516
.... 1123
Hope v Knight [2010] EWHC 3443 (Ch), [2011] WTLR 583
.... 573, 577
Hope v Lord Clifden (1801) 6 Ves 499 452
Hope v Potter (1857) 3 K & J 206, 5 WR 389 .... 253, 407
Hope d Brown v Taylor (1757) 1 Burr 268, 2 Keny 9 284
Hope's Will Trust, Re, Hope v Thorp [1929] 2 Ch 136, 98 LJ Ch 249, [1929] All ER Rep
  561, 141 LT 509 385
Hopewell v Ackland (1710) 1 Salk 239 17
Hopkins, Re, Dowd v Hawtin (1881) 19 Ch D 61, 30 WR 601, CA
.... 624
Hopkins, Re, Williams v Hopkins (1881) 18 Ch D 370, 29 WR 767, 45 LT 117, CA
.... 982
Hopkins v Abbott (1875) LR 19 Eq 222, 44 LJ Ch 316, 23 WR 227, 31 LT 820, Ct of Ch
.... 294
Hopkins Goods, Re (1875) LR 3 P & D 235, 39 JP 696, 44 LJP & M 42, 33 LT 320, P, D
  and Admlty 759
Hopkins' Trusts, Re (1878) 9 Ch D 131, 47 LJ Ch 672, 26 WR 629
.... 336
Hopkinson, Re, Dyson v Hopkinson [1922] 1 Ch 65, 91 LJ Ch 128, 126 LT 649, 66 Sol Jo
  (WR) 18 180
Hopkinson v Ellis (1842) 5 Beav 34 270
Hopkinson v Ellis (1846) 10 Beav 169, 16 LJ Ch 59, 8 LTOS 490
.... 232
Hopwood v Hopwood (1859) 7 HL Cas 728, 29 LJ Ch 747, 5 Jur NS 897, 34 LTOS 56
.... 115
Hopwood v Whaley (1848) 6 CB 744, 6 Dow & L 342, 18 LJCP 43, 12 Jur 1088
.... 1225
Hordern v Hordern [1909] AC 210, 78 LJPC 49, 100 LT 52, 25 TLR 185, PC
.... 450
Hordern v Hordern [1910] AC 465, 80 LJPC 15, 102 LT 867, 26 TLR 524, PC
.... 1030
Horgan, Re [1971] P 50, [1969] 3 All ER 1570, [1970] 2 WLR 393, 113 Sol Jo 878, P, D
  and Admlty 611, 623
Horley Town Football Club, Re; Hunt v McLaren [2006] EWHC 2386 (Ch), [2006] All ER
  (D) 34 (Oct) 36
Horn, Re, Westminster Bank Ltd v Horn [1946] Ch 254, [1946] 2 All ER 118, 115 LJ Ch
  271, 90 Sol Jo 307, 175 LT 194, 62 TLR 408, CA 404
Horn v Coleman (1853) 22 LJ Ch 779, 17 Jur 408, 1 Sm & G 169, 1 WR 194, 20 LTOS
  290 395
Horn v Horn (1825) 2 Sim & St 448, 4 LJOS Ch 52 1024
Hornbuckle's Goods, Re (1890) 15 PD 149, 59 LJP 78, 39 WR 80, 63 LT 464, P, D and
  Admlty 707
Hornby, Re [1946] P 171, [1946] 2 All ER 150, 90 Sol Jo 249, 175 LT 161, 62 TLR 348,
  P, D and Admlty 65
Hornby's Will, Re (1859) 7 WR 729, 34 LTOS 6 .... 173, 175, 302
Horne, Re, Wilson v Cox Sinclair [1905] 1 Ch 76, 74 LJ Ch 25, 53 WR 317, 92 LT 263
.... 1098
Horne v Barton (1815) Coop G 257, 19 Ves 398 475
Horne v Featherstone (1895) 73 LT 32, P, D and Admlty
.... 75
Horner, Re, Eagleton v Horner (1887) 37 Ch D 695, 57 LJ Ch 211, 36 WR 348, 58 LT
  103, 4 TLR 100 .... 326, 352, 364
Horner's Estate, Re, Pomfret v Graham (1881) 19 Ch D 186, 51 LJ Ch 43, 45 LT 670
.... 316

PARA

Horrell v Witts and Plumley (1866) LR 1 P & D 103, 35 LJP & M 55, 14 WR 515, sub
  nom Harrell v Wilts and Humbley 12 Jur NS 673, 14 LT 137
  809
Horridge v Ferguson (1822) Jac 583 .... 254, 320
Horrigan v Horrigan [1904] 1 IR 29; on appeal [1904] 1 IR 271, CA
  414
Horrocks, Re, Taylor v Kershaw [1939] P 198, [1939] 1 All ER 579, 108 LJP 86, 83 Sol Jo
  214, 160 LT 324, 55 TLR 444, CA 54–55, 187, 739
Horsepool v Watson (1797) 3 Ves 383 364
Horsford's Goods, Re (1874) LR 3 P & D 211, 44 LJP & M 9, 23 WR 211,
  [1874–80] All ER Rep 732, 31 LT 553 .... 65, 67, 82, 108
Horsley v Chaloner (1750) 2 Ves Sen 83 1301
Horton, Re, Lloyd v Hatchett [1920] 2 Ch 1, 89 LJ Ch 297, 64 Sol Jo 425, 123 LT 262
  282
Horton v Horton (1604) Cro Jac 74 469
Horton v Whittaker (1786) 1 Term Rep 346 .... 417, 448
Horwood v Griffith (1853) 4 De GM & G 700, 23 LJ Ch 465, 2 Eq Rep 158, 2 WR 71
  210
Hoskin's Trusts, Re (1877) 6 Ch D 281, 46 LJ Ch 817, 25 WR 779, CA
  .... 955, 1057
Hoskins v Campbell (1864) 2 Hem & M 43, 12 WR 546, sub nom Campbell v Hoskins 10
  LT 93 1177
Hoste v Pratt (1798) 3 Ves 730 .... 307, 310
Hotchkiss Trusts, Re (1869) LR 8 Eq 643, 38 LJ Ch 631
  322
Hotchkys, Re, Freke v Calmady (1886) 32 Ch D 408, 55 LJ Ch 546, 34 WR 569,
  [1886–90] All ER Rep 1104, 55 LT 110, CA 153
Houghton, Re, Hawley v Blake [1904] 1 Ch 622, 73 LJ Ch 317, 52 WR 505,
  [1904–7] All ER Rep 486, 48 Sol Jo 312, 90 LT 252, 20 TLR 276
  1043–1044
Houghton, Re, Houghton v Brown (1884) 53 LJ Ch 1018, 50 LT 529
  369
Houghton, Re, Houghton v Houghton [1915] 2 Ch 173, 84 LJ Ch 726, 59 Sol Jo 562, 113
  LT 422, 31 TLR 427 39
Houghton v Bell (1892) 23 SCR 498, 508 152
Houghton v Franklin (1823) 1 Sim & St 390, 1 LJOS Ch 231
  1058
Houlding v Cross (1855) 1 Jur NS 250, 3 WR 334, 25 LTOS 29
  285
Hounsell v Dunning [1902] 1 Ch 512, 71 LJ Ch 259, 86 LT 382
  289
Houseman v Houseman (1876) 1 Ch D 535, 24 WR 592, 34 LT 633, CA
  859
Houston v Burns [1918] AC 337, 87 LJPC 99, [1918–19] All ER Rep 817, 118 LT 462, 34
  TLR 219, HL 11, 200, 248
Hovey v Blakeman (1799) 4 Ves 596 1301
How, Re, How v How [1930] 1 Ch 66, 99 LJ Ch 1, [1929] All ER Rep 354, 12 LT 86
  205
Howard, Re, Howard v Treasury Solicitor [1944] P 39, 113 LJP 39, 171 LT 376, 60 TLR
  248, P, D and Admlty 97, 110
Howard, Re, Taylor v Howard [1901] 1 Ch 412, 70 LJ Ch 317, 84 LT 296
  375
Howard v Braithwaite (1812) 1 Ves & B 202 77
Howard v Chaffers (1863) 2 Drew & Sm 236, 32 LJ Ch 686, 9 Jur NS 767, 2 New Rep
  381, 11 WR 1057, 9 LT 243 1109
Howard v Collins (1868) LR 5 Eq 349 318
Howard v Howard (1856) 21 Beav 550 .... 318, 449
Howard v Kay (1858) 27 LJ Ch 448, 6 WR 361 295
Howard v Papera (1815) 1 Madd 142 624
Howard v Robinson (1863) 2 Drew & Sm 236, 32 LJ Ch 686, 9 Jur NS 767, 2 New Rep
  381, 11 WR 1057, 9 LT 243 1109
Howard v Wilson (1832) 4 Hag Ecc 107 366
Howard and Crowley v Hennessey and O'Leaky [1947] IR 336
  6
Howard's Goods, Re (1869) LR 1 P & D 636, 33 JP 280, 38 LJP & M 32, 20 LT 230
  95

PARA

Howard's Will Trusts, Re, Levin v Bradley [1961] Ch 507, [1961] 2 All ER 413, [1961] 2
WLR 821, 105 Sol Jo 347 .... 131, 141

Howarth, Re, Macqueen v Kirby [1916] WN 50, 60 Sol Jo 307
.... 384

Howarth v Mills (1866) LR 2 Eq 389, 30 JP 759, 12 Jur NS 794, 14 LT 544
.... 354

Howden's (Lord) Goods, Re (1874) 38 JP 663, 43 LJP 26, 22 WR 711, 30 LT 768
.... 723

Howe, Re, Ferniehough v Wilkinson [1908] WN 223 296

Howe, Re, Wilkinson v Ferniehough (1910) 54 Sol Jo 704, 103 LT 185
.... 409

Howe v Countess of Aylesbury (1802) 7 Ves 137, [1775–1802] All ER Rep 24, 6 RR 96, 1
White & Tud LC 68, 32 ER 56 122

Howe v Earl of Dartmouth (1802) 7 Ves 137, [1775–1802] All ER Rep 24, 6 RR 96, 1
White & Tud LC 68, 32 ER 56 .... 122, 1122

Howell, Re, Drury v Fletcher [1952] Ch 264, [1952] 1 All ER 363, 31 ATC 115, [1952]
TR 65, 96 Sol Jo 104, [1952] 1 TLR 371 1130

Howell v Gayler (1842) 5 Beav 157, 11 LJ Ch 398 293

Howell's Trusts, Re, Barclays Bank Ltd v Simmons [1937] 3 All ER 647
.... 365

Howgrave v Cartier (1814) Coop G 66, 3 Ves & B 79 260

Howlett, Re, Howlett v Howlett [1950] P 177, [1950] 1 All ER 485, 94 Sol Jo 195, 66 (pt
1) TLR 502, P, D and Admlty 913

Howorth v Dewell (1860) 29 Beav 18, 6 Jur NS 1360, 9 WR 27
.... 382

Howston v Ives (1764) 2 Eden 216 .... 392, 459

Hoy v Master (1834) 6 Sim 568, 3 LJ Ch 134, 38 RR 176
.... 383

Hoyle, Re, Hoyle v Hoyle [1893] 1 Ch 84, 62 LJ Ch 182, 2 R 145, 41 WR 81, 37 Sol Jo
46, 67 LT 674, [1891–4] All ER Rep Ext 1800, CA 6

Hoyles, Re, Row v Jagg (No 2) [1912] 1 Ch 67, 81 LJ Ch 163, 56 Sol Jo 11, 105 LT 663
.... 1126

Hubbard v Alexander (1876) 3 Ch D 738, 45 LJ Ch 740, 24 WR 1058, 35 LT 52
.... 197, 200, 403, 672

Hubbard's Goods, Re (1865) LR 1 P & D 53, 35 LJP & M 27
.... 95, 707

Hubbard's Will Trusts, Re, Marston v Angier [1963] Ch 275, [1962] 2 All ER 917, [1962]
3 WLR 682, 106 Sol Jo 705 320

Hubbuck, Re, Hart v Stone [1896] 1 Ch 754, 65 LJ Ch 271, 44 WR 289, 40 Sol Jo 257,
73 LT 738, CA 1123

Hubbuck's Estate, Re [1905] P 129, 74 LJP 58, 54 WR 16, 92 LT 665, 21 TLR 333, P, D
and Admlty 199, 220, 611

Huber's Goods, Re [1896] P 209, 65 LJP 119, 75 LT 453, 12 TLR 499, P, D and Admlty
.... 789

Hubert v Parsons (1751) 2 Ves Sen 261 430

Huckstep v Mathews (1685) 1 Vern 362 .... 45, 126, 148

Huckvale's Goods, Re (1867) LR 1 P & D 375, 36 LJP & M 84, 16 WR 64, 16 LT 434
.... 65

Huddleston's Goods, Re (1890) 63 LT 255, P, D and Admlty
.... 739

Hudleston v Gouldsbury (1847) 10 Beav 547, 11 Jur 464, 9 LTOS 531
.... 294

Hudson, Re [1912] VLR 140 451

Hudson, Re, Cassels v Hudson [1908] 1 Ch 655, 77 LJ Ch 305, 98 LT 567, 24 TLR 333
.... 561, 953

Hudson, Re, Creed v Henderson (1885) 54 LJ Ch 811, 33 WR 319, 1 TLR 447
.... 21

Hudson, Re, Hudson v Hudson (1882) 20 Ch D 406, 51 LJ Ch 455, 30 WR 487, 46 LT 93
.... 244, 475

Hudson, Re, Nicholls v Hudson [2006] EWHC 3006 (Ch), 150 Sol Jo LB 1333,
[2006] All ER (D) 60 (Oct) 106

Hudson, Re, Spencer v Turner [1911] 1 Ch 206, 80 LJ Ch 129, 103 LT 718
.... 921, 1128, 1130

Hudson v Bryant (1845) 1 Coll 681 253

Hudson v Forster (1841) 2 Mont D & De G 177, sub nom Re Forster 10 LJ Ch 340
.... 438

PARA

Hudson v Hudson (1737) 1 Atk 460, West temp Hard 155
.... 926
Hudson v Parker (1844) 1 Rob Eccl 14, 8 Jur 786, 3 Notes of Cases 236
.... 68, 70, 78
Hudson's Case (1682) Skin 79 77
Hudson's Minors, Re (1843) Drury temp Sug 6 .... 425, 438–439
Hughes, Re, Hughes v Footner [1921] 2 Ch 208, 91 LJ Ch 10, [1921] All ER Rep 310,
    127 LT 117 11
Hughes, Re, Loddiges v Jones [1916] 1 Ch 493, 85 LJ Ch 476, 60 Sol Jo 418, 114 LT 845
.... 535
Hughes, Re, Rea v Black [1943] Ch 296, [1943] 2 All ER 269, 112 LJ Ch 234, 87 Sol Jo
    265, 169 LT 140, 59 TLR 375 145
Hughes v Empson (1856) 22 Beav 181, 111 RR 321 961
Hughes v Hughes (1807) 14 Ves 256 302
Hughes v Jones (1863) 1 Hem & M 765, 32 LJ Ch 487, 2 New Rep 417, 11 WR 898, 71
    ER 335, 9 LT 143 282
Hughes v Kelly (1843) 61 RR 109, 5 I Eq R 286, 2 Con & Law 223, 3 Dr & War 482
.... 407
Hughes v McNaull [1923] 1 IR 78, Ir CA 180, 231
Hughes v Pritchard (1877) 6 Ch D 24, 46 LJ Ch 840, 25 WR 761, 37 LT 259, CA
.... 256, 298
Hughes v Sayer (1718) 1 P Wms 534 460–461
Hughes v Turner (1835) 3 My & K 666, 4 LJ Ch 141 .... 115, 199
Hughes v Wells (1852) 9 Hare 749, 16 Jur 927, 89 RR 651, 68 ER 717, 20 LTOS 136
.... 558
Hughes Goods, Re (1860) 24 JP 664, 29 LJPM & A 165, 4 Sw & Tr 209
.... 639
Hughes Goods, Re (1887) 12 PD 107, 56 LJP 71, 35 WR 568, 57 LT 495, P, D and
    Admlty 65
Hugo's Goods, Re (1877) 2 PD 73, 41 JP 632, 46 LJP 21, 25 WR 396, 36 LT 518, P, D
    and Admlty 7
Huguenin v Baseley (1807) 9 RR 276, 14 Ves 273, 1 White & Tud LC 259, 33 ER 526,
    [1803–13] All ER Rep 1 904
Hulbert and Crowe v Cathcart [1894] 1 QB 244, 63 LJQB 121, 70 LT 558, DC; on appeal
    [1896] AC 470, 65 LJQB 644, 75 LT 302, 12 TLR 379, HL
.... 1189
Hulkes, Re, Powell v Hulkes (1886) 33 Ch D 552, 55 LJ Ch 846, 34 WR 733, 35 WR
    194, [1886–90] All ER Rep 659, 55 LT 209 1256
Hull v Falkoner (1865) 11 Jur NS 151, 5 New Rep 266, 11 LT 761
.... 985
Hull's Estate, Re (1855) 21 Beav 314, 4 WR 194 175
Hulme v Hulme (1839) 9 Sim 644 231
Hulse, Re, Beattie v Hulse [1905] 1 Ch 406, 74 LJ Ch 246, 92 LT 232, [1904–7] All ER
    Rep Ext 1629 932
Hulton, Re, Midland Bank Executor and Trustee Co Ltd v Thompson [1936] Ch 536,
    [1936] 2 All ER 207, 105 LJ Ch 273, 80 Sol Jo 386, 155 LT 226, 52 TLR 507
.... 1015
Humberstone v Stanton (1813) 1 Ves & B 385 .... 445, 452
Humble v Humble (1838) 2 Jur 696 1109
Humble v Shore (1847) 7 Hare 247, 1 Hem & M 550n, 33 LJ Ch 188n, 10 Jur NS 308n,
    12 WR 149n; affd (1874) 7 Hare 249 .... 173, 1115
Hume, Re, Public Trustee v Mabey [1912] 1 Ch 693, 81 LJ Ch 382, 56 Sol Jo 414, 106 LT
    335, [1911–13] All ER Rep Ext 1248 .... 258, 424, 432–433
Hume v Richardson (1862) 4 De GF & J 29, 31 LJ Ch 713, 8 Jur NS 686, 135 RR 18, 10
    WR 528, 6 LT 624 1126
Humphrey v Humphrey (1851) 1 Sim NS 536, 20 LJ Ch 425
.... 375
Humphrey v Tayleur (1752) Amb 136, 1 Dick 161 173
Humphrey's Estate, Re [1916] 1 IR 21 382
Humphreys, Re, Wren v Ward (1915) 60 Sol Jo 105, 114 LT 230
.... 156, 295
Humphreys v Allen. See Allen v Humphrys
Humphreys v Green (1882) 10 QBD 148, 47 JP 244, 52 LJQB 140, 48 LT 60, CA
.... 21
Humphreys v Howes (1830) Taml 497, 8 LJOS Ch 165, 1 Russ & M 639
.... 411, 452

PARA

Humphreys v Humphreys (1789) 2 Cox Eq Cas 184 .... 156, 274
Humphreys v Humphreys (1867) LR 4 Eq 475, 15 WR 391, 15 LT 557
.... 469
Humphries, Re, Smith v Millidge (1883) 24 Ch D 691, 49 LT 594
.... 352
Humphries Estate, Re [1934] P 78, 103 LJP 31, 78 Sol Jo 83, 150 LT 220, 50 TLR 126, P,
D and Admlty 720, 845
Hungerford v Nosworthy. See Nosworthy v Basset
Hunt, Re, Davies v Hetherington (1890) 62 LT 753 253
Hunt v Dorsett (1855) 5 De GM & G 570, 1 Jur NS 1053, 26 LTOS 113
.... 397
Hunt v Hort (1791) 3 Bro CC 311 207
Hunt v Hunt (1902) 19 WN 96, 2 SRNSW (Eq) 72 451
Hunt's Goods, Re [1896] P 288, 66 LJP 8, 45 WR 236, P, D and Admlty
.... 622
Hunt's Goods, Re (1853) 2 Rob Eccl 622, 17 Jur 720, 21 LTOS 292
.... 711
Hunt's Goods, Re (1875) LR 3 P & D 250, 39 JP 744, 44 LJP & M 43, 23 WR 553, 33
LT 321, P, D and Admlty 55
Hunter, Re, Lloyds Bank Ltd v Girton College, Cambridge (Mistress and Governors) [1951]
Ch 190, [1951] 1 All ER 58, 95 Sol Jo 61, 66 (pt 2) TLR 1108
.... 278
Hunter, Re, Northey v Northey (1908) 25 TLR 19 285
Hunter v A-G [1899] AC 309, 68 LJ Ch 449, 47 WR 673, [1895–9] All ER Rep 558, 43
Sol Jo 530, 80 LT 732, 15 TLR 384, HL 11, 229
Hunter v Judd (1833) 4 Sim 455 .... 416, 428, 447
Hunter v Moss [1993] 1 WLR 934; affd [1994] 3 All ER 215, [1994] 1 WLR 452, [1994]
8 LS Gaz R 38, 138 Sol Jo LB 25, CA 116, 127, 266
Hunter v Pugh (1839) 1 Hare 308n, 9 LJ Ch 62, 4 Jur 571
.... 284
Hunter v Young (1879) 4 Ex D 256, 48 LJQB 689, 27 WR 637, 41 LT 142, CA
.... 1106
Hunter's Executors, Petitioners, Re 1992 SC 474, 1992 SLT 1141, HC of Justiciary (Sc)
.... 39, 180, 445
Hunter's Settlement Trust, Re, Elliott v Hunter (1939) 83 Sol Jo 339
.... 263
Hunter's Trusts, Re (1865) LR 1 Eq 295 .... 429, 432
Huntingdon's Settlement Trusts, Re, Struthers v Mayne [1949] Ch 414, [1949] 1 All ER
674, [1949] LJR 1185, 93 Sol Jo 217, 65 TLR 249 410
Huntley's Case (1574) 3 Dyer 326a 395, 474
Hurd, Re, Stott v Stott [1941] Ch 196, [1941] 1 All ER 238, 110 LJ Ch 67, 85 Sol Jo 70,
164 LT 296, 57 TLR 287 168
Hurd v Lenthall (1649) Sty 211 395
Hurdle, Re, Blakeney v Hurdle [1936] 3 All ER 810 201
Hurlston's Goods, Re [1898] P 27, 67 LJP 69, P, D and Admlty
.... 744
Hurry v Hurry (1870) LR 10 Eq 346, 39 LJ Ch 824, 18 WR 829
.... 321
Hurry v Morgan (1866) LR 3 Eq 152, 36 LJ Ch 105, 15 WR 87
.... 317
Hursell v Bird [1891–4] All ER Rep 919, 65 LT 709, 8 TLR 8, DC
.... 1264
Hurst, Re, Addison v Topp (1892) 67 LT 96, 8 TLR 528, CA
.... 962
Hurst v Beach (1821) 5 Madd 351, 56 ER 929, [1814–23] All ER Rep 523
.... 197, 403
Hurst v Hurst (1882) 21 Ch D 278, 51 LJ Ch 729, 31 WR 327, [1881–5] All ER Rep 903,
46 LT 899, CA 182, 462
Hussey v Berkeley (1763) 2 Eden 194, sub nom Hussey v Lady Dillon Amb 603
.... 328
Hussey and Green's Contract, Re, Re Hussey, Hussey v Simper [1921] 1 Ch 566, 90 LJ Ch
253, 65 Sol Jo 357, 124 LT 783, 37 TLR 407 .... 339, 387
Hutcheon v Mannington (1791) 1 Ves 366, 4 Bro CC 491n
.... 451
Hutcheson v Hammond (1790) 3 Bro CC 128 .... 115, 160
Hutcheson v Jones (1817) 2 Madd 124 305

                                                                                    PARA
Hutchinson, Re, Crispin v Hadden (1919) 88 LJ Ch 352, [1918–19] All ER Rep 1174, 121
    LT 239   294
Hutchinson, Re, Holt v Hutchinson [1955] Ch 255, [1955] 1 All ER 689, [1955] 2 WLR
    586, 99 Sol Jo 185 .... 288, 488
Hutchinson v Barrow (1861) 6 H & N 583, 30 LJ Ex 280, 9 WR 538, 4 LT 554
      282
Hutchinson v National Refuges for Homeless and Destitute Children [1920] AC 795, 89 LJ
    Ch 469, [1920] All ER Rep 701, 64 Sol Jo 496, 123 LT 439, HL
    .... 302, 313
Hutchinson v Rough (1879) 40 LT 289   371
Hutchinson v Smith (1863) 1 New Rep 513, 11 WR 417, 8 LT 602
      296
Hutchinson v Tottenham [1898] 1 IR 403; affd [1899] 1 IR 344, CA
      457
Hutchinson and Tenant, Re (1878) 8 Ch D 540, 26 WR 904, 39 LT 86, [1874–80] All ER
    Rep Ext 1620 .... 348, 382
Hutchinson's Trusts, Re (1882) 21 Ch D 811, 51 LJ Ch 924, 47 LT 573, [1881–5] All ER
    Rep Ext 1624 .... 395, 397
Hutchison's Goods, Re (1902) 18 TLR 706, P, D and Admlty
      67
Hutley v Grimstone (1879) 5 PD 24, 48 LJP 68, 41 LT 531, P, D and Admlty
      56
Hutley's Goods, Re (1869) LR 1 P & D 596, 33 JP 167, 38 LJP & M 27, 19 LT 704
      695
Hutton v Rossiter (1855) 7 De GM & G 9, 24 LJ Ch 106, 3 Eq Rep 589, 3 WR 387,
    25 LTOS 61   1298
Hutton v Simpson (1716) 2 Vern 722, sub nom Sympson v Hutton 2 Eq Cas Abr 439, sub
    nom Simpson v Hornby Gilb Ch 120, sub nom Sympson v Hornsby Prec Ch 452
    .... 164, 321
Huxtable, Re, Huxtable v Crawfurd [1902] 2 Ch 793, 71 LJ Ch 876, 51 WR 282,
    [1900–3] All ER Rep 799, 87 LT 415, CA 207, 222–223
Huxtep v Brooman (1785) 1 Bro CC 437   298
Hyde, Re, Smith v Jack [1932] 1 Ch 95, 101 LJ Ch 95, [1931] All ER Rep 52, 75 Sol Jo
    781, 146 LT 255   354
Hyde v Hyde (1708) 1 Eq Cas Abr 409, 3 Rep Ch 155   108
Hyde v Skinner (1723) 2 P Wms 196   1212
Hyndman v Hyndman [1895] 1 IR 179   382
Hynes, Re, Knapp v Hynes [1950] 2 All ER 879, 94 Sol Jo 687, 66 (pt 2) TLR 795, CA
    .... 209, 246, 288
Hyslop, Re, Hyslop v Chamberlain [1894] 3 Ch 522, 64 LJ Ch 168, 8 R 680, 43 WR 6, 38
    Sol Jo 663, 71 LT 373 .... 201, 625

I

Ibbetson, Re, Ibbetson v Ibbetson (1903) 88 LT 461 .... 322, 342
Ibbetson v Beckwith (1735) Cas temp Talb 157, 2 P Wms 337n
    255–256
Ibbetson's Goods, Re (1839) 2 Curt 337 82–83
Ibuna v Arroyo [2012] EWHC 428 (Ch), [2012] 12 LS Gaz R 22, [2012] NLJR 392,
    [2012] All ER (D) 36 (Mar)   956
Iggulden v Terson (1834) 2 Dowl 277, 4 Tyr 309   1291
Ihler's Goods, Re (1873) LR 3 P & D 50, 37 JP 425, 42 LJP & M 18, 21 WR 550, 28 LT
    479   491
Ilchester (Earl), ex p (1803) 7 Ves 348, 32 ER 142, [1803–13] All ER Rep 310
    .... 107,108, 331
Illidge, Re, Davidson v Illidge (1884) 27 Ch D 478, 53 LJ Ch 991, 33 WR 18, 51 LT 523,
    CA   970
Iliffe v Trafford [2002] WTLR 507; [2002] NPC 3   1183
Ilott v Genge (1842) 3 Curt 160, 1 Notes of Cases 572; affd (1844) 4 Moo PCC 265, PC
      69
Ilott v Mitson [2011] EWCA Civ 346, [2011] 2 FCR 1, [2012] 2 FLR 170, [2011] Fam
    Law 798, 155 Sol Jo (no 14) 30, [2011] All ER (D) 37 (Apr)
    .... 568, 572, 576
Ilott v Mitson [2015] EWCA Civ 797, [2016] 1 All ER 932, [2015] 2 FCR 547
    .... 568, 570, 572–573, 576, 580

PARA

Imray v Imeson (1872) 26 LT 93 442

Ince's Goods, Re (1877) 2 PD 111, 41 JP 425, 46 LJP 30, 25 WR 396, 36 LT 519, P, D
and Admlty 112

Inchiquin (Lord) v French (1744) Amb 33, 1 Cox Eq Cas 1, sub nom O'Brien v
Lord Inchiquin Ridg temp H 230 210

Inchley v Robinson (1587) 3 Leon 165 291

Incorporated Society in Dublin v Richards (1841) 4 I Eq R 177, 1 Con & Law 58, 1 Dr &
War 258 .... 284, 442

Inderwick v Inderwick [1901] 2 Ch 738, CA; affd sub nom Inderwick v Tatchell [1903] AC
120, [1900–3] All ER Rep Ext 1104, 72 LJ Ch 393, 88 LT 399, HL
.... 316

Inderwick v Inderwick (1844) 13 Sim 652, 8 Jur 53 370

Inderwick v Tatchell [1901] 2 Ch 738, CA; affd [1903] AC 120, [1900–3] All ER Rep Ext
1104, 72 LJ Ch 393, 88 LT 399, HL 228–229, 236, 243, 315–316

ING Bank NV v Ros Roca SA [2011] EWCA Civ 353, [2012] 1 WLR 472
.... 189

Ingall v Moran [1944] KB 160, [1944] 1 All ER 97, 113 LJKB 298, 88 Sol Jo 68, 170 LT
57, 60 TLR 120, CA 647

Inge v Kenny (1845) 4 Hare 452, 14 LJ Ch 325, 9 Jur 344
.... 1301

Ingilby v Amcotts (1856) 21 Beav 585, 25 LJ Ch 769, 2 Jur NS 556, 4 WR 433, 27 LTOS
94 284

Ingle v Richards (No 2) (1860) 25 JP 323, 28 Beav 366, 6 Jur NS 1178, 8 WR 697, 3 LT
46 625

Ingle's Trusts, Re (1871) LR 11 Eq 578, 40 LJ Ch 310, 19 WR 676, 24 LT 315
.... 217, 237, 277, 332

Ingleby and Boak and Norwich Union Insurance Co, Re (1883) 13 LR Ir 326
.... 951

Inglefield v Coghlan (1845) 2 Coll 247 402

Inglesant v Inglesant (1874) LR 3 P & D 172, 38 JP 584, 43 LJP & M 43, 22 WR 741, 30
LT 909 69

Inglewood Investment Co Ltd v Forestry Commission [1989] 1 All ER 1, [1988] 1 WLR
1278, CA 928

Ingram v Soutten (1874) LR 7 HL 408, 44 LJ Ch 55, 23 WR 363, 31 LT 215
.... 450

Ingram v Suckling (1859) 7 WR 386, 33 LTOS 89 .... 425, 437

Ingram v Wyatt (1828) 1 Hag Ecc 384; on appeal sub nom Wyatt v Ingram (1832) 3 Hag
Ecc 466, sub nom Ingram v Wyatt 1 LJ Ch 135 .... 48, 903–904

IRC v Bernstein [1960] Ch 444, [1960] 1 All ER 697, [1960] 2 WLR 554, 39 TC 391, 39
ATC 117, 53 R & IT 301, [1960] TR 21, 104 Sol Jo 250; affd [1961] Ch 399, [1961]
1 All ER 320, [1961] 2 WLR 143, 39 TC 391, 39 ATC 415, [1960] TR 369, 105 Sol
Jo 128, CA 302

IRC v Broadway Cottages Trust [1955] Ch 20, [1954] 3 All ER 120, [1954] 3 WLR 438,
35 TC 577, 98 Sol Jo 588, L(TC) 1703, sub nom Broadway Cottages Trust v IRC 33
ATC 305, 47 R & IT 574, [1954] TR 295, CA 11

IRC v Hawley [1928] 1 KB 578, 13 TC 327, 6 ATC 1021, 97 LJKB 191, 138 LT 710
.... 1060, 1146

IRC v Lady Castlemaine [1943] 2 All ER 471, 25 TC 408, 22 ATC 206, 112 LJKB 508, 87
Sol Jo 354, 169 LT 338, 60 TLR 2 1090

IRC v Smith [1930] 1 KB 713, 15 TC 661, 99 LJKB 361, 142 LT 517, CA
.... 922, 1141

IRC v Stype Investments (Jersey) Ltd [1982] Ch 456, [1982] 3 All ER 419, [1982] 3 WLR
228, [1982] STC 625, 126 Sol Jo 497, CA 759, 815, 1264, 1266

Inman, Re, Inman v Inman [1915] 1 Ch 187, 84 LJ Ch 309, 59 Sol Jo 161, 112 LT 240
.... 295, 1123–1124

Inman, Re, Inman v Rolls [1893] 3 Ch 518, 62 LJ Ch 940, 8 R 293, 42 WR 156, 69 LT
374, [1891–4] All ER Rep Ext 1576 .... 235, 1083

Innes, Re, Innes v Innes [1910] 1 Ch 188, 79 LJ Ch 174, [1908–10] All ER Rep 270, 101
LT 633 626

Innes v Mitchell (1846) 1 Ph 710 1094

Innes v Mitchell (1847) 2 Ph 346, 16 LJ Ch 415 1090

Innes v Sayer (1849) 7 Hare 377, 13 Jur 402; on appeal (1851) 21 LJ Ch 190, 16 Jur 21, 3
Mac & G 606, 18 LTOS 129 209

Inns, Re, Inns v Wallace [1947] Ch 576, [1947] 2 All ER 308, [1947] LJR 1207, 91 Sol Jo
468, 177 LT 165, 63 TLR 439 574

PARA

Investors Compensation Scheme Ltd v West Bromwich Building Society [1998] 1 All ER
    98, [1998] 1 WLR 896, [1998] 1 BCLC 493, [1997] NLJR 989, [1997] CLC 1243,
    [1997] PNLR 541, HL 189, 201, 223, 304
Ionides, Re, London County Westminster and Parr's Bank Ltd v Craies [1922] WN 46, 66
    Sol Jo 315, 38 TLR 269 .... 242, 270, 295
Iqbal v Ahmed [2011] EWCA Civ 900, [2011] 3 FCR 1, [2012] 1 FLR 31, [2011] Fam
    Law 1199, [2011] All ER (D) 32 (Aug) 577
Irby v Irby (No 3) (1858) 25 Beav 632, 4 Jur NS 989, 119 RR 577, 6 WR 853, 32 LTOS
    141 1071
Iredale v Ford and Bramworth (1859) 23 JP 263, 5 Jur NS 474, 1 Sw & Tr 305, 7 WR
    462, 33 LTOS 78 774
Iredell v Iredell (1858) 25 Beav 485 308
Ireland v Coulter. See Coulter's Case
Ireland v Rendall (1866) LR 1 P & D 194, 30 JP 647, 35 LJP & M 79, 14 LT 574
    874
Irvin v Ironmonger (1831) 2 Russ & M 531 1058
Irvin's Estate, Re (1908) 25 TLR 41, P, D and Admlty 108
Irvine v Sullivan (1869) LR 8 Eq 673, 38 LJ Ch 635, 17 WR 1083
    .... 207–208, 370
Irvine's Goods, Re [1919] 2 IR 485 .... 108, 707, 791
Irwin v Caruth. See Millar's Estate, Re, Irwin v Caruth
Isaac, Re, Harrison v Isaac [1905] 1 Ch 427, 74 LJ Ch 277, 92 LT 227
    233
Isaacs, Re, Isaacs v Reginall [1894] 3 Ch 506, 63 LJ Ch 815, 8 R 660, 42 WR 685, 38 Sol
    Jo 662, 71 LT 386 157
Isaacson v Van Goor (1872) 42 LJ Ch 193, 21 WR 156, 27 LT 752
    468
Isherwood v Payne (1800) 5 Ves 677 371
Itter, Re, Dedman v Godfrey [1948] 2 All ER 1052, P, D and Admlty
    .... 108, 735
Itter, Re, Dedman v Godfrey [1950] P 130, [1950] 1 All ER 68, 93 Sol Jo 805, 66 (pt 1)
    TLR 45, P, D and Admlty 82, 108, 735
Ive v King (1852) 16 Beav 46, 21 LJ Ch 560, 16 Jur 489, 20 LTOS 5
    .... 322, 326, 411, 452
Ives v Brown [1919] 2 Ch 314, 88 LJ Ch 373, 122 LT 267
    1282
Ives v Dodgson (1870) LR 9 Eq 401, 39 LJ Ch 693, 23 LT 215
    252
Ives v Legge (1743) 3 Term Rep 488n, sub nom Jones v Legg 9 Mod Rep 461
    413
Ivory, Re, Hankin v Turner (1878) 10 Ch D 372, CA 670
Izard v Hurst (1698) Freem Ch 224 115
Izard v Tamahau Mahupuka (1902) 22 NZLR 418 27
Izon v Butler (1815) 2 Price 34 163

J

J v C. See C (children) (parent: purported marriage between two women: artificial
    insemination by donor), Re
JH, Re (1911) 25 OLR 132 294
Jack v Fetherston. See Fetherston v Fetherston
Jackson, Re, Beattie v Murphy [1933] Ch 237, 102 LJ Ch 1, [1932] All ER Rep 696, 76
    Sol Jo 779, 148 LT 238, 49 TLR 5 .... 218, 220, 350
Jackson, Re, Holliday v Jackson [1944] WN 26, 113 LJ Ch 78, 88 Sol Jo 17, 170 LT 244,
    60 TLR 157 535
Jackson, Re, Jackson v Hamilton [1923] 2 Ch 365, 92 LJ Ch 622, 67 Sol Jo 481, 129 LT
    307, 39 TLR 400, CA 366
Jackson, Re, Jackson v Nottidge [1952] WN 352, [1952] 2 TLR 90
    592
Jackson, Re, Midland Bank Executor and Trustee Co Ltd v Archbishop of Wales [1930] 2
    Ch 389, 99 LJ Ch 450, 144 LT 102, 46 TLR 558 11
Jackson, Re, Shiers v Ashworth (1883) 25 Ch D 162, 53 LJ Ch 180, 32 WR 194, 50 LT 18
    .... 167, 174–175
Jackson v Calvert (1860) 1 John & H 235 385

PARA

Jackson v Craig (1851) 20 LJ Ch 204, 15 Jur 811, 17 LTOS 207
.... 255
Jackson v Dover (1864) 2 Hem & M 209, 10 Jur NS 631, 4 New Rep 136, 12 WR 855,
10 LT 489 260
Jackson v Hamilton (1846) 9 I Eq R 430, 3 Jo & Lat 702
.... 263
Jackson v Hogan (1776) 3 Bro Parl Cas 388, HL 256, 288
Jackson v Hurlock (1764) Amb 487, 2 Eden 263 184
Jackson v Jackson (1749) 1 Ves Sen 217 .... 254, 428
Jackson v Jackson (1788) 2 Cox Eq Cas 35 403
Jackson v Jackson (1869) 17 WR 547, 20 LT 354 1126
Jackson v Marjoribanks (1841) 12 Sim 93, 5 Jur 885 .... 419, 422
Jackson v Noble (1838) 2 Keen 590, 7 LJ Ch 133, 2 Jur 251
.... 182
Jackson v Pease (1874) LR 19 Eq 96, 23 WR 43 1012
Jackson v Rodger. See Freeland, Re, Jackson v Rodgers
Jackson v Watson & Sons [1909] 2 KB 193, 78 LJKB 587, 53 Sol Jo 447, 100 LT 799, 25
TLR 454, CA 1280
Jackson v White [1967] 2 Lloyd's Rep 68 1271
Jackson v Yates [1912] 1 IR 267 1067
Jackson and Gill v Paulet (1851) 2 Rob Eccl 344 612
Jackson and Wallington v Whitehead (1821) 3 Phillim 577
.... 627
Jackson's Goods, Re [1892] P 257, 56 JP 457, 61 LJP 126, 67 LT 327, P, D and Admlty
.... 759
Jackson's Goods, Re (1902) 47 Sol Jo 93, 87 LT 747, 19 TLR 74, P, D and Admlty
.... 744, 761
Jackson's Will, Re (1879) 13 Ch D 189, 49 LJ Ch 82, 28 WR 209, 41 LT 499
.... 237, 441
Jacob, Re, M'Coy v Jacob [1919] 1 IR 134 1085
Jacob v Catling [1881] WN 105 175
Jacob's Will, Re (1861) 29 Beav 402, 7 Jur NS 302, 9 WR 474, 4 LT 104
.... 430, 447
Jacobs v Jacobs (1853) 16 Beav 557, 22 LJ Ch 668, 17 Jur 293, 1 WR 238, 51 ER 895,
21 LTOS 97 .... 313, 342
Jacomb v Harwood (1751) 2 Ves Sen 265 .... 926, 1023, 1233
Jacques v Chambers (1846) 4 Ry & Can Cas 205, sub nom Jaques v Chambers 4 Ry &
Can Cas 499, 16 LJ Ch 243, sub nom Jacques v Chambers 2 Coll 435, 10 Jur 151,
sub nom Jaques v Chambers 11 Jur 295, sub nom Jacques v Chambers 6 LTOS 429
.... 127, 1011
Jacquet v Jacquet (1859) 27 Beav 332, 7 WR 543 407
Jacubs v Rylance (1874) LR 17 Eq 341, 43 LJ Ch 280 1071
Jaffray v Marshall [1994] 1 All ER 143, [1993] 1 WLR 1285, [1993] 15 LS Gaz R 39
.... 1257
James, ex p (1803) 8 Ves 337, 32 ER 385, [1803–13] All ER Rep 78
.... 657
James, Re, Clutterbuck v James (1890) 62 LT 545, 6 TLR 240
.... 465
James, Re, Hole v Bethune [1910] 1 Ch 157, 79 LJ Ch 45, 101 LT 625
.... 282
James, Re, James v James [1935] Ch 449, 104 LJ Ch 247, [1935] All ER Rep 235, 153 LT
277 .... 198, 626
James, Re, James v Jones [1911] 2 Ch 348, 80 LJ Ch 681, 106 LT 214
.... 969
James, Re, Lloyds Bank Ltd v Atkins [1947] Ch 256, [1947] 1 All ER 402, [1947] LJR
735, 91 Sol Jo 236, 176 LT 370, 63 TLR 246 994
James v Allen (1817) 3 Mer 17, 17 RR 4, 36 ER 7, [1814–23] All ER Rep 578
.... 11
James v Buena Ventura Nitrate Grounds Syndicate Ltd [1896] 1 Ch 456, 65 LJ Ch 284, 44
WR 372, 40 Sol Jo 238, 74 LT 1, 12 TLR 176, [1895–9] All ER Rep Ext 1968, CA
.... 936
James v Dean (1805) 11 Ves 383 942
James v Lord Wynford (1852) 22 LJ Ch 450, 17 Jur 17, 1 Sm & G 40, 1 WR 61, 65 ER
18, 20 LTOS 273 .... 419, 425
James v Lord Wynford (1854) 23 LJ Ch 767, 18 Jur 868, 2 Sm & G 350, 2 WR 607,
23 LTOS 320 348

PARA

James v Richardson (1677) 3 Keb 832, 2 Lev 232, Poll 457, T Jo 99, 1 Vent 334, 1 Eq Cas
	Abr 214 pl 11, Freem KB 472; affd (1678) Freem KB 472n, HL
	.... 302, 339
James v Shannon (1868) IR 2 Eq 118 471
James v Shrimpton (1876) 1 PD 431, 45 LJP 85, P, D and Admlty
	.... 93, 109
James v Smith (1844) 14 Sim 214, 13 LJ Ch 376, 8 Jur 594, 3 LTOS 297
	 328
James v Williams [2000] Ch 1, [1999] 3 All ER 309, [1999] 3 WLR 451, 79 P & CR 421,
	1 ITELR 643, [1999] 2 FCR 498, [1999] 15 LS Gaz R 30, CA
	.... 1261–1262, 1264, 1267, 1270
James and Thoroughgood v Collins Het. See Thorowood v Collins
James Goods, Re (1858) 1 Sw & Tr 238 83
James' Settled Estates, Re (1884) 32 WR 898, 51 LT 596
	.... 416, 419
James Will Trusts, Re, Peard v James [1962] Ch 226, [1960] 3 All ER 744, [1960] 3 WLR
	1031, 104 Sol Jo 1077 .... 225, 315–317
Jameson, Re, King v Winn [1908] 2 Ch 111, 77 LJ Ch 729, 98 LT 745
	.... 211, 279
Jane v Jane (1917) 33 TLR 389, P, D and Admlty 112, 739
Jaques, Re, Hodgson v Braisby [1903] 1 Ch 267, 72 LJ Ch 197, 51 WR 229, 47 Sol Jo
	145, 88 LT 210, CA 404
Jardine, Re, ex p Fleet (1850) 4 De G & Sm 52, 19 LJ Bcy 10, 14 Jur 685, 15 LTOS 435
	 973
Jarman v Vye (1866) LR 2 Eq 784, 35 LJ Ch 821, 14 WR 1011
	 458
Jarman's Estate, Re, Leavers v Clayton (1878) 8 Ch D 584, 42 JP 662, 47 LJ Ch 675, 26
	WR 907, 39 LT 89 11
Jarman's Trusts, Re (1865) LR 1 Eq 71 410
Jarrett, Re, Re Vrenegroor, Bird v Green [1919] 1 Ch 366, 88 LJ Ch 150,
	[1918–19] All ER Rep 388, 63 Sol Jo 353, 121 LT 119 1114
Jarvis, Re, Edge v Jarvis [1958] 2 All ER 336, [1958] 1 WLR 815, 102 Sol Jo 546
	.... 287, 656–657
Jarvis v Duke (1681) 1 Vern 19 133–134
Jarvis v Pond (1839) 9 Sim 549, 8 LJ Ch 167 323
Jay v Jay [1924] 1 KB 826, 93 LJKB 280, 130 LT 667, DC
	.... 152, 1229, 1278
Jeaffreson's Trusts, Re (1866) LR 2 Eq 276, 35 LJ Ch 622, 12 Jur NS 660, 14 WR 759
	 385
Jeale v Titchener (1771) Amb 703, 1 Bro CC 120n, sub nom Seal v Tichener 2 Dick 444
	 438
Jeans, Re, Upton v Jeans (1895) 13 R 627, 72 LT 835 331
Jebb, Re, Ward-Smith v Jebb [1966] Ch 666, [1965] 3 All ER 358, [1965] 3 WLR 810,
	109 Sol Jo 613, CA 331
Jee v Audley (1787) 1 Cox Eq Cas 324 302
Jeeves, Re, Morris-Williams v Haylett [1949] Ch 49, [1948] 2 All ER 961, [1949] LJR 317,
	92 Sol Jo 675 332
Jeffereys v Small (1683) 1 Eq Cas Abr 290, 1 Vern 217 919
Jeffery, Re, Arnold v Burt [1895] 2 Ch 577, 64 LJ Ch 830, 13 R 857, 44 WR 61, 73 LT
	332 312
Jeffery, Re, Nussey v Jeffery [1914] 1 Ch 375, 83 LJ Ch 251, 58 Sol Jo 120, 110 LT 11
	.... 214, 218, 393
Jeffery v De Vitre (1857) 24 Beav 296 390
Jeffery v Honywood (1819) 4 Madd 398 389
Jeffery v Sprigge (1784) 1 Cox Eq Cas 62 459
Jeffery's Trusts, Re (1866) LR 2 Eq 68, 35 LJ Ch 426 1085
Jeffrey, Re, Welch v Jeffrey [1948] 2 All ER 131, 92 Sol Jo 377
	.... 200, 332
Jeffrey v Scott (1879) 27 Grant (Ontario) 314 126
Jeffreys v Conner (1860) 28 Beav 328, 6 Jur NS 986, 8 WR 572, 3 LT 45
	 461
Jeffreys v Jeffreys (1901) 84 LT 417, 17 TLR 356 141
Jeffries, Re, Hill v Jeffries (1916) 33 TLR 80, CA 910
Jeffries v Alexander. See Alexander v Brame
Jeffs v Wood (1723) 2 P Wms 128, 24 ER 668, 2 Eq Cas Abr 10 pl 9
	 1301

PARA

Jelley v Iliffe [1981] Fam 128, [1981] 2 All ER 29, [1981] 2 WLR 801, 125 Sol Jo 355, CA
.... 567, 573
Jenings v Baily (1853) 17 Beav 118, 22 LJ Ch 977, 17 Jur 433, 21 LTOS 112
.... 375
Jenkins, Re, Jenkins v Davies [1931] 2 Ch 218, 100 LJ Ch 265, [1931] All ER Rep 382,
  145 LT 184, 47 TLR 379, CA 156
Jenkins, Re, Williams v Jenkins [1915] 1 Ch 46, 84 LJ Ch 349
.... 463
Jenkins v Gaisford and Thring, Re Jenkins Goods (1863) 27 JP 504, 32 LJPM & A 122, 9
  Jur NS 630, 2 New Rep 401, 3 Sw & Tr 93, 11 WR 854, 8 LT 517, [1861–73] All ER
  Rep Ext 1567 63–64
Jenkins v Gower (1846) 2 Coll 537, 10 Jur 702, 7 LTOS 449
.... 344
Jenkins v Herries (1819) 4 Madd 67; on appeal (1823) 55 Lords Journals 517, HL
.... 244, 387
Jenkins v Hughes (1860) 8 HL Cas 571, 30 LJ Ch 870, 6 Jur NS 1043, 8 WR 667, 3 LT
  106 .... 229, 237, 243–244, 261, 387, 391, 473
Jenkins v Jenkins [1928] 2 KB 501, 97 LJKB 400, [1928] All ER Rep 546, 72 Sol Jo 319,
  139 LT 119, 44 TLR 483 625
Jenkins v Jones (1866) LR 2 Eq 323, sub nom Re Jones, Jenkins v Jones 35 LJ Ch 520, 12
  Jur NS 368, 14 WR 665, 14 LT 540 156
Jenkins v Morris (1880) 14 Ch D 674, 49 LJ Ch 392, 42 LT 817, CA
.... 52
Jenkins Goods, Re (1819) 3 Phillim 33 850
Jennens v Lord Beauchamp (1810) 1 Phillim 155 863
Jenner v Ffinch (1879) 5 PD 106, 49 LJP 25, 28 WR 520, 42 LT 327, P, D and Admlty
.... 71, 99, 200, 911
Jenner v Turner (1880) 16 Ch D 188, 45 JP 124, 50 LJ Ch 161, 29 WR 99, 43 LT 468
.... 133–134
Jennery, Re, Jennery v Jennery [1967] Ch 280, [1967] 1 All ER 691, [1967] 2 WLR 201,
  110 Sol Jo 910, CA 591
Jennings, Re [1994] Ch 286, [1994] 3 All ER 27, [1994] 3 WLR 67, [1995] 1 FCR 257,
  sub nom Jennings, Re, Harlow v National Westminster Bank plc [1994] 1 FLR 536,
  [1994] Fam Law 439, CA 568, 570, 572–573, 580
Jennings, Re, Caldbeck v Stafford and Lindemere [1930] 1 IR 196
.... 293
Jennings v Hanna [1904] 1 IR 540 .... 470, 475
Jennings v Jennings (1877) 1 LR Ir 552 215
Jennings v Looks (1725) 2 P Wms 276, sub nom Anon 2 Eq Cas Abr 488
.... 438
Jennings v Newman (1839) 10 Sim 219, 3 Jur 748; varied (1839) 3 Jur 1068
.... 302
Jennings v Rice [2002] EWCA Civ 159, [2003] 1 P & CR 100, [2003] 1 FCR 501, [2002]
  NPC 28, [2002] WTLR 367, [2002] All ER (D) 324 (Feb)
.... 20
Jenour v Jenour (1805) 10 Ves 562 318
Jermingham Trusts, Re, Gormanstown v Nicholl [1922] 1 IR 115
.... 182
Jerningham v Herbert (1829) 4 Russ 388, Taml 103, 6 LJOS Ch 134
.... 266
Jersey Society for the Prevention of Cruelty to Animals v Rees 2001 JLR 506,
  (2001) 4 ITELR 294, Royal Ct Jer 106
Jervis v Wolferstan (1874) LR 18 Eq 18, 43 LJ Ch 809, 30 LT 452, [1874–80] All ER Rep
  Ext 1933 .... 21, 1097
Jesson v Wright (1820) 2 Bli 1, HL 230, 235, 241, 248
Jessop, Re [1924] P 221, 93 LJP 135, [1924] All ER Rep 692, 132 LT 31, 40 TLR 800, P,
  D and Admlty 83
Jessop, Re (1859) 11 I Ch R 424 233
Jessop v Jessop [1992] 1 FCR 253, [1992] 1 FLR 591, [1992] Fam Law 328, CA
.... 568–569, 572–573, 577, 582, 585, 591
Jewis v Lawrence (1869) LR 8 Eq 345, 33 JP 776 1069
Jeyes v Savage (1875) 10 Ch App 555, 44 LJ Ch 706, 23 WR 764, 33 LT 139, CA in Ch
.... 441
Jickling v Bircham (1843) 2 Notes of Cases 463 957
Jillard v Edgar (1849) 3 De G & Sm 502, 13 Jur 1114, 14 LTOS 63
.... 152
Job v Job (1877) 6 Ch D 562, 26 WR 206 1247

PARA

Jobson, Re, Jobson v Richardson (1889) 44 Ch D 154, 59 LJ Ch 245, 62 LT 148
.... 419, 433
Jobson's Case (1597) Cro Eliz 576 278
Jodrell, Re, Jodrell v Seale (1890) 44 Ch D 590, 59 LJ Ch 538, 38 WR 721, 63 LT 15, CA;
on appeal sub nom Seale-Hayne v Jodrell [1891] AC 304, 61 LJ Ch 70,
[1891–4] All ER Rep 477, 65 LT 57, HL 235, 237, 241, 245, 260, 276, 352
Joel, Re, Rogerson v Joel [1943] Ch 311, [1943] 2 All ER 263, 112 LJ Ch 282, 87 Sol Jo
353, 169 LT 247, 59 TLR 355, CA 151, 153
Joel's Will Trusts, Re, Rogerson v Brudenell-Bruce [1967] Ch 14, [1966] 2 All ER 482,
[1966] 3 WLR 209, 110 Sol Jo 570 312
John, Re, Jones v John [1933] Ch 370, 102 LJ Ch 72, [1932] All ER Rep 556, 148 LT 450
.... 1004
John v John [1898] 2 Ch 573, 67 LJ Ch 616, 47 WR 52, 42 Sol Jo 731, 79 LT 362, 14
TLR 583, CA 945
Johns v Pink [1900] 1 Ch 296, 69 LJ Ch 98, 48 WR 247, 81 LT 712, 16 TLR 70
.... 17
Johns v Wilson [1900] 1 IR 342 233
Johnson, Re [1987] CLY 3882 597
Johnson, Re (1912) 27 OLR 472 375
Johnson, Re, Cockerell v Earl of Essex (1884) 26 Ch D 538, 53 LJ Ch 645, 32 WR 634,
52 LT 44 285
Johnson, Re, Danily v Johnson (1893) 3 R 308, 68 LT 20
.... 181, 311
Johnson, Re, Greenwood v Greenwood and Robinson (1903) 89 LT 520, CA
.... 294
Johnson, Re, Johnson v King Edward Hospital Fund for London [1940] WN 195
.... 991
Johnson, Re, Pitt v Johnson (1913) 58 Sol Jo 219, 30 TLR 200; affd (1914) 111 LT 130,
30 TLR 505, CA 336
Johnson, Re, Public Trustee v Calvert [1939] 2 All ER 458
.... 382
Johnson, Re, Sandy v Reilly [1904–7] All ER Rep 539, 49 Sol Jo 314, 92 LT 357
.... 296, 298
Johnson, Re, Shearman v Robinson (1880) 15 Ch D 548, 49 LJ Ch 745, 29 WR 168,
[1874–80] All ER Rep 1155, 43 LT 372 1041
Johnson v Arnold (1748) 1 Ves Sen 169 375
Johnson v Aston (1822) 1 Sim & St 73 1186
Johnson v Ball (1851) 5 De G & Sm 85, 16 Jur 538, 18 LTOS 182
.... 201, 223
Johnson v Burgess (1873) LR 15 Eq 398, 42 LJ Ch 400, 21 WR 453, 28 LT 188
.... 1188
Johnson v Clarke [1928] Ch 847, 97 LJ Ch 337, 72 Sol Jo 556, 139 LT 552
.... 1024
Johnson v Crook (1879) 12 Ch D 639, 48 LJ Ch 777, 28 WR 12, 41 LT 400,
[1874–80] All ER Rep Ext 1469 451
Johnson v Foulds (1868) LR 5 Eq 268, 37 LJ Ch 260 416
Johnson v Gabriel and Bellamy Cro Eliz. See Grant's Case
Johnson v Johnson (1841) 4 Beav 318 .... 468, 511
Johnson v Johnson (1843) 3 Hare 157, 13 LJ Ch 79, 8 Jur 77, 2 LTOS 118
.... 27, 167–168
Johnson v Kennett (1835) 3 My & K 624, 6 Sim 384 1024
Johnson v Mills (1749) 1 Ves Sen 282 1158
Johnson v Newton (1853) 11 Hare 160, 22 LJ Ch 1039, 1 Eq Rep 511, 17 Jur 825
.... 962
Johnson v Routh (1857) 27 LJ Ch 305, 3 Jur NS 1048, 6 WR 6, 30 LTOS 111
.... 1126
Johnson v Simcock (1861) 7 H & N 344, 31 LJ Ex 38, 8 Jur NS 284, 9 WR 895, sub nom
Jackson and Simcock v Johnson 4 LT 836, Ex Ch 442
Johnson v Warwick (1856) 17 CB 516, 25 LJCP 102, 26 LTOS 220
.... 634, 1139
Johnson v Weldy (1861) 2 Sw & Tr 313 696
Johnson's Goods, Re (1858) 27 LJP & M 9, 1 Sw & Tr 17, 6 WR 275, 30 LTOS 295
.... 616
Johnson's Goods, Re (1862) 2 Sw & Tr 595, 7 LT 337 759
Johnson's Trusts, Re (1866) LR 2 Eq 716, 12 Jur NS 616
.... 386, 459

PARA

Johnson's Will Trusts, Re, National Provincial Bank Ltd v Jeffrey [1967] Ch 387, [1967]
  1 All ER 553, [1967] 2 WLR 152, 110 Sol Jo 811 .... 131, 137
Johnston, Re, Mills v Johnston [1894] 3 Ch 204, 63 LJ Ch 753, 8 R 563, 42 WR 616, 38
  Sol Jo 564, 71 LT 392 .... 372–373, 1062
Johnston v Antrobus (1856) 21 Beav 556 .... 369, 450
Johnston v O'Neill (1879) 3 LR Ir 476 427
Johnston v Rowlands (1848) 2 De G & Sm 356, 17 LJ Ch 438, 12 Jur 769, 11 LTOS 511
  378
Johnston v Todd (1845) 8 Beav 489 1210
Johnston and Smith, Re ((1906) 12 OLR 262 461
Johnstone v Earl of Harrowby (1859) 1 De GF & J 183, 29 LJ Ch 145, 6 Jur NS 153, 8
  WR 105, 1 LT 390 .... 403, 409
Johnstone's Settlement, Re (1880) 14 Ch D 162, 49 LJ Ch 596, 28 WR 593
  158
Joliffe v Twyford (1858) 26 Beav 227, 28 LJ Ch 93, 4 Jur NS 1165, 32 LTOS 141
  152
Jolley, Re, Jolley v Jarvis [1964] P 262, [1964] 1 All ER 596, [1964] 2 WLR 556, 108 Sol
  Jo 115, CA 700, 863
Jolley, Re, Neal v Jolley (1901) 17 TLR 244 1132
Jolliffe, ex p (1845) 8 Beav 168, 10 Jur 813, 4 LTOS 309, sub nom Joliffe, ex p 14 LJ Ch
  134 670
Jolliffe v East (1789) 3 Bro CC 25 .... 393, 395
Jolliffe v Pitt (1715) 2 Vern 694 978
Jolly, Re, Gathercole v Norfolk [1900] 2 Ch 616, 69 LJ Ch 661, 48 WR 657,
  [1900–3] All ER Rep 286, 44 Sol Jo 642, 83 LT 118, 16 TLR 521, CA
  404
Jones, Re [1981] Fam 7, [1981] 1 All ER 1, [1981] 1 WLR 106, 124 Sol Jo 545
  79
Jones, Re (1857) 3 Drew 679, 5 WR 336 1047
Jones, Re (1904) 74 LJP 27, P, D and Admlty 770
Jones, Re, Christmas v Jones [1897] 2 Ch 190, 66 LJ Ch 439, 45 WR 598,
  [1895–9] All ER Rep 1084, 76 LT 454 .... 1202, 1256
Jones, Re, Evans v Harries [1976] Ch 200, [1976] 1 All ER 593, [1976] 2 WLR 437, 120
  Sol Jo 10, CA 93, 105, 108
Jones, Re, Jones v Midland Bank Trust Co Ltd [1997] 3 FCR 697, [1998] 1 FLR 246, CA
  .... 39, 180, 445
Jones, Re, Jones v Searle (1883) 49 LT 91 1257
Jones, Re, Lambert v Colbourn [1928] WN 227 1130
Jones, Re, Last v Dobson [1915] 1 Ch 246, 84 LJ Ch 222, 59 Sol Jo 218, 112 LT 409
  .... 246, 443
Jones, Re, Lewis v Lewis [1910] 1 Ch 167, 79 LJ Ch 34, 101 LT 549
  .... 244, 389–390
Jones, Re, Meacock v Jones [1932] 1 Ch 642, 101 LJ Ch 307, [1932] All ER Rep 804, 147
  LT 137 1076
Jones, Re, Midland Bank Executor and Trustee Co Ltd v Jones [1953] Ch 125, [1953]
  1 All ER 357, [1953] 2 WLR 283, 97 Sol Jo 96 .... 138, 141
Jones, Re, Midland Bank Exor and Trustee Co Ltd v League of Welldoers [1950] 2 All ER
  239, 94 Sol Jo 405, 66 (pt 2) TLR 51 451
Jones, Re, Peak v Jones [1914] 1 Ch 742, 83 LJ Ch 568, 58 Sol Jo 579
  1029
Jones, Re, Public Trustee v Jones [1945] Ch 105, 115 LJ Ch 33, 89 Sol Jo 22, 173 LT 357,
  61 TLR 120 11
Jones, Re, Richards v Jones [1898] 1 Ch 438, 67 LJ Ch 211, 46 WR 313, 42 Sol Jo 269,
  78 LT 74 381
Jones, Re, Williams v A-G (1912) 106 LT 941, CA 365
Jones, Re, Williams v Rowlands [1948] Ch 67, [1947] 2 All ER 716, [1948] LJR 431, 91
  Sol Jo 678 .... 143, 149
Jones v Ashburnham (1804) 4 East 455, 1 Smith KB 188, 102 ER 905, [1803–13] All ER
  Rep 416 1240
Jones v Badley (1868) 3 Ch App 362, 16 WR 713, 19 LT 106, CA
  221
Jones v Bromley (1821) 6 Madd 137 131
Jones v Cherney (1680) Freem KB 530 933
Jones v Davies (1880) 28 WR 455 .... 182, 416, 444
Jones v Earl of Strafford (1730) 2 Eq Cas Abr 427, 3 P Wms 79
  796

PARA

Jones v Foxall (1852) 15 Beav 388, 21 LJ Ch 725, 92 RR 473
.... 658

Jones v Frewin (1864) 3 New Rep 415, 12 WR 369, 10 LT 330
.... 322

Jones v Hall (1849) 16 Sim 500 410

Jones v Harding (1887) 52 JP 71, 58 LT 60, P, D and Admlty
.... 102

Jones v Henley (1685) 2 Rep Ch 361 365

Jones v How (1850) 7 Hare 267 21–22

Jones v Jones (1843) 13 Sim 561, 13 LJ Ch 16, 7 Jur 986
.... 429

Jones v Jones (1876) 1 QBD 279, 45 LJQB 166, 24 WR 274, 34 LT 243,
[1874–80] All ER Rep Ext 1857 .... 130, 132

Jones v Jones (1881) 29 WR 786, 44 LT 642, DC 395

Jones v King. See King v Jones

Jones v Legg. See Ives v Legge

Jones v Lewis (1751) 2 Ves Sen 240 1247

Jones v Lord Sefton (1798) 4 Ves 166 285

Jones v Mackilwain (1826) 1 Russ 220 .... 430, 432

Jones v Martin (1798) 6 Bro Parl Cas 437, 8 Bro Parl Cas App I 242, 5 Ves 266n
.... 22

Jones v Morgan (1774) 3 Bro Parl Cas 323, HL 460

Jones v Morrall (1852) 2 Sim NS 241, 21 LJ Ch 630, 20 LTOS 30
.... 1256

Jones v Morris (1922) 91 LJ Ch 495, 127 LT 94 449

Jones v Newman (1750) 1 Wm Bl 60 218

Jones v Nicolay (1850) 2 Rob Eccl 288, 14 Jur 675, 15 LTOS 328, 7 Notes of Cases 564
.... 54

Jones v Noyes and Allen (1858) 28 LJ Ch 47, 4 Jur NS 1033, 7 WR 21, 32 LTOS 102
.... 970

Jones v Ogle (1872) 8 Ch App 192, 42 LJ Ch 334, 21 WR 236, [1861–73] All ER Rep
919, 28 LT 245, CA in Ch 240

Jones v Price (1841) 11 Sim 557, 10 LJ Ch 195, 5 Jur 719
.... 226, 253

Jones v Roberts [1995] 2 FLR 422, [1995] Fam Law 673
.... 39

Jones v Roe. See Roe d Perry v Jones

Jones v Scott. See Scott v Jones

Jones v Simes (1890) 43 Ch D 607, 59 LJ Ch 351, 62 LT 447
.... 1277, 1283

Jones v Skinner (1835) 5 LJ Ch 87 284

Jones v Southall (No 2) (1862) 32 Beav 31, 32 LJ Ch 130, 9 Jur NS 93, 1 New Rep 152,
11 WR 247, 8 LT 103 .... 156, 161

Jones v Tanner (1827) 7 B & C 542, 6 LJOS 71, 1 Man & Ry KB 420
.... 1146, 1240

Jones v Torin (1833) 6 Sim 255 .... 320, 338

Jones v Treasury Solicitor (1932) 76 Sol Jo 690, 147 LT 340, 48 TLR 615, P, D and
Admlty; affd (1932) 49 TLR 75, CA 97, 778

Jones v Westcomb (1711) 1 Eq Cas Abr 245, Gilb Ch 74, Prec Ch 316
.... 182, 445–446

Jones d Henry v Hancock (1816) 4 Dow 145, HL 266

Jones' Estate, Re (1927) 43 TLR 324, P, D and Admlty 300, 611, 679

Jones Estate, Re, Hume v Lloyd (1878) 47 LJ Ch 775, 26 WR 828
.... 326

Jones Goods, Re (1842) 1 Notes of Cases 396 73

Jones Goods, Re (1861) 31 LJPM & A 199, 2 Sw & Tr 155, 4 LT 477, [1861–73] All ER
Rep Ext 1629 613

Jones' Goods, Re (1865) 29 JP 104, 34 LJPM & A 41, 11 Jur NS 118, 4 Sw & Tr 1, 13
WR 414, 13 LT 210 65

Jones' Goods, Re (1920) 123 LT 202, 36 TLR 294, P, D and Admlty
.... 711

Jones' Trusts, Re (1857) 23 Beav 242 .... 334, 337

Jones Will Trusts, Re, Jones v Hawtin Squire [1965] Ch 1124, [1965] 2 All ER 828, [1965]
3 WLR 506, 109 Sol Jo 476 331

Jones' Will Trusts, Re, Jones v Jones [1942] Ch 328, [1942] 1 All ER 642, 111 LJ Ch 193,
86 Sol Jo 174, 167 LT 84, 58 TLR 403 201

PARA

Jongsma v Jongsma (1787) 1 Cox Eq Cas 362 289
Jopling v IRC [1940] 2 KB 282, [1940] 3 All ER 279, 109 LJKB 734, 84 Sol Jo 525, 163
  LT 361, 56 TLR 877 1151
Jopling v Jopling (1909) 8 CLR 33, Aust HC 21
Jopp v Wood (1865) 2 De GJ & Sm 323, 34 LJ Ch 625, 11 Jur NS 833, 6 New Rep 359,
  13 WR 954, 12 LT 689 453
Jordan, Re, Hayward v Hamilton [1904] 1 Ch 260, 73 LJ Ch 128, 52 WR 150, 48 Sol Jo
  142, 90 LT 223 1238
Jordan v Fortescue (1847) 10 Beav 259, 16 LJ Ch 332, 11 Jur 549, 9 LTOS 290
  252
Jordan v Holkham (1753) Amb 209 .... 380, 446
Jordan v Lowe (1843) 6 Beav 350 392
Jordan's Goods, Re (1868) LR 1 P & D 555, 32 JP 631, 37 LJP & M 22, 16 WR 407
  707
Jordan's Trusts, Re (1863) 2 New Rep 57, 8 LT 307 324–325
Jorden v Jorden (1843) 2 Notes of Cases 388 110
Joseph, Re, Pain v Joseph [1908] 2 Ch 507, 77 LJ Ch 832, 99 LT 539, 24 TLR 770, CA
  409
Joseph v Goode (1875) 23 WR 225, Ct of Ch 1178
Joseph v Phillips [1934] AC 348, 103 LJPC 79, [1934] All ER Rep 685, 78 Sol Jo 317, 151
  LT 51, 50 TLR 385, PC 285, 288
Joslin, Re, Joslin v Murch [1941] Ch 200, [1941] 1 All ER 302, 110 LJ Ch 65, 85 Sol Jo
  105, 165 LT 171, 57 TLR 293 573–574
Joslin v Hammond (1834) 3 My & K 110, 3 LJ Ch 148
  369
Josselyn v Josselyn (1837) 9 Sim 63 .... 428, 1062
Joy, Re, Purday v Johnson [1886–90] All ER Rep 1111, 60 LT 175, 5 TLR 117
  278
Joyner v Watts. See Taylor v Watts
Joys, Re (1860) 30 LJPM & A 169, 4 Sw & Tr 214 95
Jubber v Jubber (1839) 9 Sim 503 .... 246, 266, 305, 370, 390, 1069
Judd v Judd (1830) 3 Sim 525, sub nom Judd v Hobbs 8 LJOS Ch 119
  .... 416, 428, 447
Judd's Trusts, Re [1884] WN 206 336
Judkin's Trusts, Re (1884) 25 Ch D 743, 53 LJ Ch 496, 32 WR 407, [1881–5] All ER Rep
  979, 50 LT 200 .... 1083, 1115
Julian, Re, O'Brien v Missions to Seamen's Trust Corpn Ltd [1950] IR 57
  214
Jull v Jacobs (1876) 3 Ch D 703, 24 WR 947, 35 LT 153
  .... 41, 181, 1115
Jupp, Re, Gladman v Jupp (1903) 87 LT 739 184
Jury v Jury (1882) 9 LR Ir 207 .... 227, 394–395

K

K, Re [1985] Ch 85, [1985] 1 All ER 403, [1985] 2 WLR 262, [1985] FLR 558, [1985]
  Fam Law 129, 129 Sol Jo 132, [1985] LS Gaz R 1335; affd [1986] Ch 180, [1985]
  2 All ER 833, [1985] 3 WLR 234, [1986] 1 FLR 79, [1985] Fam Law 19, 129 Sol Jo
  364, [1985] LS Gaz R 2242, [1985] NLJ Rep 655, CA 39–40, 566
K, Re [2007] EWHC 622 (Ch), 9 ITELR 759, [2007] WTLR 1007, (2007) Times, 16 April,
  [2007] All ER (D) 473 (Mar) 991, 1290
K v K. See Kokosinski v Kokosinski
Kane v Radley-Kane [1999] Ch 274, [1998] 3 All ER 753, [1998] 3 WLR 617, 1 ITELR
  229, [1998] 3 FCR 502, [1998] 24 LS Gaz R 33, 142 Sol Jo LB 189, sub nom Radley-
  Kane, Re [1998] 2 FLR 585, [1998] Fam Law 525 .... 657, 1153, 1158
Karsten, Re, Edwards v Moore [1953] NZLR 456, NZ CA
  .... 221, 223
Kasperbauer v Griffith [2000] WTLR 333, CA 221
Kaufman's Goods, Re [1952] P 325, [1952] 2 All ER 261, 96 Sol Jo 562, P, D and Admlty
  845
Kaur v Dhaliwal [2014] EWHC 1991 (Ch), [2015] 2 FCR 40, [2014] Fam Law 1241,
  [2014] WTLR 1381, [2014] All ER (D) 164 (Jun) 567, 579
Kavanagh, Re, Murphy v Border (1874) IR 9 CL 123 414
Kavanagh, Re, Murphy v Doyle (1892) 29 LR Ir 333, 29 LR Ir 333, Ir CA
  294
Kavanagh v Best [1971] NI 89 1060

PARA

Kavanagh v Fegan [1932] IR 566 68–69
Kavanagh v Morland (1853) Kay 16, 23 LJ Ch 41, 2 Eq Rep 771, 18 Jur 185, 2 WR 8,
   22 LTOS 143 334
Kay, Re, Mosley v Kay [1897] 2 Ch 518, 46 WR 74, 13 TLR 582, sub nom Kay, Re,
   Mosley v Keyworth 66 LJ Ch 759 .... 964, 1259
Kay v Crook (1857) 3 Jur NS 104, 3 Sm & G 407, 5 WR 220, 29 LTOS 10
   21
Kay v Tibbs [2007] All ER (D) 31 (Feb) 883, 1261
Kaye v Laxon (1780) 1 Bro CC 76 375
Kaye v Zeital [2010] EWCA Civ 159, [2010] All ER (D) 49 (D) (Mar)
   1220
Keane v Dee (1821) Alc & N 496n 646
Keane v Robarts (1819) 4 Madd 332 1025
Keane's (Baron) Estate, Re [1903] 1 IR 215 241
Kearney v Kearney [1911] 1 IR 137, CA 41, 182
Keay v Boulton (1883) 25 Ch D 212, 54 LJ Ch 48, 32 WR 591, 49 LT 631
   341
Keays v M'Donnell (1872) IR 6 Eq 611 899
Kebbeh v Farmer [2015] EWHC 3927 (Ch) 566
Kebty-Fletcher's Will Trusts, Re, Public Trustee v Swan and Snowden [1969] 1 Ch 339,
   [1967] 3 All ER 1076, [1968] 2 WLR 34, 111 Sol Jo 892
   .... 181, 308
Keech v Sandford (1726) 2 Eq Cas Abr 741, Sel Cas Ch 61, Cas temp King 61, 25 ER 223,
   [1558–1774] All ER Rep 230 657
Keele Estates (No 2), Re, Aveling v Sneyd [1952] Ch 603, [1952] 2 All ER 164, 31 ATC
   314, [1952] TR 293, [1952] 2 TLR 149, CA 1131
Keen, Re, Evershed v Griffiths [1937] Ch 236, [1937] 1 All ER 452, 106 LJ Ch 177, 81 Sol
   Jo 97, 156 LT 207, 53 TLR 320, CA 207, 222–223
Keen v Keen (1873) LR 3 P & D 105, 37 JP 696, 42 LJP & M 61, 29 LT 247
   .... 101, 106
Keep's Will, Re (1863) 32 Beav 122 317
Kehr, Re, Martin v Foges [1952] Ch 26, [1951] 2 All ER 812, 95 Sol Jo 711, [1951] 2 TLR
   788 1075
Keighley, Re, Keighley v Keighley [1919] 2 Ch 388, 88 LJ Ch 445, 63 Sol Jo 643, 121 LT
   465, 35 TLR 491 348
Keigwin v Keigwin (1843) 3 Curt 607, 7 Jur 840 69
Keily v Monck (1795) 3 Ridg Parl Rep 205 .... 133, 430
Kekewich v Barker. See Capes v Dalton
Kekewich v Kekewich (1909) 101 LT 887 1132
Kelk v Archer (1852) 16 Jur 605, 19 LTOS 252 1175
Kell v Charmer (1856) 23 Beav 195, 4 WR 787 .... 60, 202
Kellett v Kellett (1811) 1 Ball & B 533; affd (1815) 3 Dow 248, HL
   .... 210, 298
Kellett v Kellett (1868) LR 3 HL 160 .... 96, 231, 378
Kellett v Kellett (1871) IR 5 Eq 298 .... 161, 168, 445
Kellow v Westcombe (1673) Freem KB 122, 3 Keb 202 1267
Kelly v Hammond (1858) 26 Beav 36 352
Kelly v Keatinge (1871) IR 5 Eq 174 68
Kelly v Kelly (1874) 8 IR Eq 403 657
Kelly v O'Connor [1917] 1 IR 312, 51 ILTR 60 910
Kelly v Powlet (1763) Amb 605, 1 Dick 359 296
Kelly's Settlement, Re, West v Turner (1888) 59 LT 494
   464
Kelsey, Re, Woolley v Kelsey [1905] 2 Ch 465, 74 LJ Ch 701, 54 WR 136, 49 Sol Jo 701,
   93 LT 662 406
Kelsey v Ellis (1878) 38 LT 471 .... 33, 322
Kelsey v Kelsey (1922) 91 LJ Ch 382, [1922] All ER Rep 536, 127 LT 86
   634
Kemmis v Kemmis (Welland intervening) [1988] 1 WLR 1307, [1988] 2 FLR 223, [1989]
   3 LS Gaz R 43, CA 586
Kemnal and Still's Contract, Re [1923] 1 Ch 293, 92 LJ Ch 298, 67 Sol Jo 364, 129 LT
   12, 39 TLR 285, [1923] All ER Rep Ext 723, CA 1028
Kemp v Burn (1863) 4 Giff 348, 9 Jur NS 375, 1 New Rep 257, 11 WR 278, 7 LT 666
   1200
Kemp v Davy (1774) 1 Bro CC 120n 438

PARA

Kempster, Re, Kempster v Kempster [1906] 1 Ch 446, 75 LJ Ch 286, 54 WR 385, 50 Sol Jo 271, 94 LT 248, [1904–7] All ER Rep Ext 1304 .... 997, 1002

Kempthorne, Re, Charles v Kempthorne [1930] 1 Ch 268, 99 LJ Ch 177, [1929] All ER Rep 495, 142 LT 111, 46 TLR 15, CA 156, 288, 291, 993–994, 1001–1002

Kendall v Hamilton (1879) 4 App Cas 504, 48 LJQB 705, 28 WR 97, [1874–80] All ER Rep 932, 41 LT 418, HL 1232

Kendall v Kendall (1828) 4 Russ 360, 6 LJOS Ch 111 .... 250, 288, 293

Kendall's Trust, Re (1851) 14 Beav 608, 18 LTOS 116 250

Kendrew, Re, Hird v Kendrew [1953] Ch 291, [1953] 1 All ER 551, [1953] 2 WLR 550, 97 Sol Jo 169, CA 147

Kennedy, Re, Corbould v Kennedy [1917] 1 Ch 9, 86 LJ Ch 40, 61 Sol Jo 55, 115 LT 690, 33 TLR 44, CA 284

Kennedy, Re, Kennedy v Official Solicitor of the Supreme Court [1980] CLY 2820 586

Kennedy v Kennedy [1914] AC 215, 83 LJPC 63, 51 SLR 581, 109 LT 833, PC 374

Kennedy v Kennedy (1853) 10 Hare 438, 1 WR 177 127

Kennedy v Kingston (1821) 2 Jac & W 431 161

Kennedy v Sedgwick (1857) 3 K & J 540 .... 416, 429, 441

Kennell v Abbott (1799) 4 Ves 802, 31 ER 416 .... 58, 184, 276

Kennett's Goods, Re (1863) 2 New Rep 461 103

Kennewell v Dye [1949] Ch 517, [1949] 1 All ER 881, [1949] LJR 1250, 93 Sol Jo 250 .... 1212, 1214

Kensington (Baron), Re, Longford (Earl) v Baron Kensington [1902] 1 Ch 203, 71 LJ Ch 170, 50 WR 201, 46 Sol Jo 176, 85 LT 577, 18 TLR 89 .... 153, 1010

Kentfield v Wright [2010] EWHC 1607 (Ch), [2010] All ER (D) 07 (Jul) 77

Kenward v Adams (1975) Times, 29 November 4

Kenworthy v Ward (1853) 11 Hare 196, 1 Eq Rep 389, 17 Jur 1047, 1 WR 493, 22 LTOS 92 394

Kenyon v Kenyon (1866) 35 Beav 300 1177

Kenyon's Estate, Re, Mann v Knap (1887) 56 LT 626 158

K'Eogh v K'Eogh [1911] 1 IR 396 370

Keogh v Keogh (1874) IR 8 Eq 179 271

Kerr v Baroness Clinton (1869) LR 8 Eq 462, 17 WR 980 .... 232, 251

Kerr's Estate, Re [1913] 1 IR 214 .... 444, 449

Kerry, Re, Bocock v Kerry, Arnull v Kerry [1889] WN 3, 5 TLR 178 126

Kerry v Derrick (1605) Cro Jac 104, Moore KB 771, sub nom Derick v Kery Moore KB 640 375

Kersey, Re, Alington v Alington [1952] WN 541, 96 Sol Jo 851 141

Kershaw v Kershaw (1854) 3 E & B 845 230

Kershaw v Micklethwaite [2010] EWHC 506 (Ch) 1163

Kettlewell, Re, Jones v Kettlewell (1907) 98 LT 23 347

Kevern v Williams (1832) 5 Sim 171 308

Kevil v Lynch (1874) IR 9 Eq 249 63

Kew v Rouse (1685) 1 Vern 353 395

Key v Key [2010] EWHC 408 (Ch), [2010] All ER (D) 155 (Apr) 49, 55, 893, 897, 903

Key v Key (1853) 4 De GM & G 73, 22 LJ Ch 641, 1 Eq Rep 82, 17 Jur 769, 22 LTOS 67 .... 228, 238, 242, 422, 457, 473

Key v Key (1855) 1 Jur NS 372 443

Kiallmark v Kiallmark (1856) 26 LJ Ch 1 440

Kicks v Leigh [2014] EWHC 3926 (Ch), [2015] 4 All ER 329, [2015] WTLR 579, [2014] All ER (D) 295 (Nov) 47, 899

Kidd, Re, Brooman v Withall [1894] 3 Ch 558, 63 LJ Ch 855, 13 R 101, 43 WR 51, 71 LT 481 .... 27, 996

Kidd, Re, Kidd v Kidd (1894) 8 R 261, 42 WR 571, 70 LT 648 1041

Kidd v North (1846) 2 Ph 91, 16 LJ Ch 116, 10 Jur 995, sub nom Tidd v North 8 LTOS 289 .... 401, 403

Kiddle, Re, Gent v Kiddle (1905) 53 WR 616, 49 Sol Jo 481, 92 LT 724, [1904–7] All ER Rep Ext 1655 352

PARA

Kidman v Kidman (1871) 40 LJ Ch 359 .... 437, 456, 1083
Kidney v Coussmaker (1797) 7 Bro Parl Cas 573, HL 992
Kieran, Re [1933] IR 222 63
Kiersey v Flahavan [1905] 1 IR 45 .... 133, 414
Kilby v Meyers. See Harmer, Re
Killick, Re, Killick v Pountney (1999) Times, 30 April, [1999] All ER (D) 365
.... 56
Kilpatrick's Policies Trusts, Re, Kilpatrick v IRC [1966] Ch 730, [1965] 2 All ER 673,
    [1966] 2 WLR 1346, 44 ATC 170, [1965] TR 173, 109 Sol Jo 417; affd [1966] Ch
    730, [1966] 2 All ER 149, [1966] 2 WLR 1346, 110 Sol Jo 232, CA
.... 423
Kilvert, Re, Midland Bank Executor and Trustee Co Ltd v Kilvert [1957] Ch 388, [1957]
    2 All ER 196, [1957] 2 WLR 854, 101 Sol Jo 372 .... 313, 349, 394, 397
Kilvert's Trusts, Re (1871) 7 Ch App 170, 41 LJ Ch 351, 20 WR 225, 26 LT 221
.... 214, 218
Kilvington v Gray (1825) 2 Sim & St 396, 4 LJOS Ch 80
.... 1123
Kilvington v Parker (1872) 21 WR 121 233
Kimberley v Tew (1843) 4 Dr & War 139 1161
Kinch v Ward (1825) 2 Sim & St 409, 4 LJOS Ch 28 385
Kinchella's Goods, Re [1894] P 264, 63 LJP 162, 6 R 556, 71 LT 263, P, D and Admlty
.... 774
Kinderley v Jervis (1856) 22 Beav 1, 25 LJ Ch 538, 2 Jur NS 602, 4 WR 579, 27 LTOS
    245 .... 924, 972
King, Re, Barclays Bank Ltd v King [1942] Ch 413, [1942] 2 All ER 182, 111 LJ Ch 289,
    86 Sol Jo 252, 167 LT 129, CA 1130
King, Re, Jackson v A-G [1917] 2 Ch 420, 87 LJ Ch 3, [1916–17] All ER Rep 786, 62 Sol
    Jo 9, 117 LT 529, 33 TLR 535 .... 366, 885
King, Re, Mellor v South Australian Land Mortgage and Agency Co [1907] 1 Ch 72, 76 LJ
    Ch 44, 51 Sol Jo 48, 95 LT 724 991
King, Re, Public Trustee v Aldridge [1928] Ch 330, 97 LJ Ch 172, [1927] All ER Rep 214,
    138 LT 641 312
King, Re, Salisbury v Ridley (1890) 62 LT 789, 6 TLR 320
.... 443
King v Badeley (1834) 3 My & K 417, 3 LJ Ch 206 202
King v Bennett (1838) 7 LJ Ex 242, 1 Horn & H 289, 4 M & W 36
.... 333
King v Bryant (1841) 4 Beav 460, sub nom King v Hammett 11 LJ Ch 14, 5 Jur 1052
.... 1204
King v Burchall (or Burchell) (1759) Amb 379, 2 Burr 1103, 1 Eden 424, 4 Term Rep 296n
.... 248
King v Cleaveland (1858) 26 Beav 26, 4 Jur NS 702; affd (1859) 4 De G & J 477, 28 LJ
    Ch 835, 7 WR 602, 33 LTOS 340 .... 248, 322, 364
King v Cullen (1848) 2 De G & Sm 252 453
King v Denison (1813) 12 RR 227, 1 Ves & B 260 .... 184, 370
King v Dubrey [2015] EWCA Civ 581, [2016] Ch 221, [2016] 2 WLR 1, sub nom King v
    Chiltern Dog Rescue [2015] All ER (D) 105 (Jun) 921
King v Farley (1828) 1 Hag Ecc 502 903
King v Frost (1890) 15 App Cas 548, 60 LJPC 15, 63 LT 422, 6 TLR 443, PC
.... 316–317
King v George (1877) 5 Ch D 627, 36 LT 759, [1874–80] All ER Rep Ext 1705, sub nom
    Re George's Estate, King v George 46 LJ Ch 670, 25 WR 638, CA
.... 250
King v Hammett. See King v Bryant
King v Jones (1814) 5 Taunt 418, 1 Marsh 107; affd sub nom Jones v King (1815) 4 M &
    S 188 1282
King v King (1885) 13 LR Ir 531 210
King v Malcott (1852) 9 Hare 692, 22 LJ Ch 157, 16 Jur 237, 19 LTOS 19
.... 991, 1059, 1159
King v Melling (1671) 1 Vent 225; on appeal (1671) 1 Vent 232, Ex Ch
.... 334
King v Mullins (1852) 1 Drew 308, 20 LTOS 178 1057
King v Taylor (1801) 5 Ves 806 449
King v Thom (1786) 1 Term Rep 487 1241
King v Tootel (1858) 25 Beav 23 .... 309, 409

PARA

King v Withers (1735) Cas temp Talb 117, 3 P Wms 414; affd sub nom Wither v King
   (1735) 3 Bro Parl Cas 135, HL 427, 438, 459
King v Wright (1845) 14 Sim 400, 14 LJ Ch 214 279
King's College Hospital v Wheildon (1854) 18 Beav 30, 23 LJ Ch 537, 2 WR 202
   214
King George III, His Late Majesty's Goods, Re (1822) 1 Add 255, 1 State Tr NS 1273
   660
King George III, His Late Majesty's Goods, Re (1862) 27 JP 137, 32 LJPM & A 15, 8 Jur
   NS 1134, 1 New Rep 69, 3 Sw & Tr 199, 11 WR 190 660
King's Goods, Re (1851) 2 Rob Eccl 403 101
King's Proctor v Daines (1830) 3 Hag Ecc 218 .... 3, 54
King's Trusts, Re (1892) 29 LR Ir 401 .... 137, 284
King's Will Trusts, Re, Assheton v Boyne [1964] Ch 542, [1964] 1 All ER 833, [1964] 2
   WLR 913, 108 Sol Jo 335, 189 Estates Gazette 879 1144
Kingdon, Re, Wilkins v Pryer (1886) 32 Ch D 604, 55 LJ Ch 598, 34 WR 634, 54 LT 753
   95
Kingdon v Nottle (1813) 1 M & S 355 1282
Kingham, Re, Kingham v Kingham [1897] 1 IR 170 1228
Kingsbury v Walter [1901] AC 187, 70 LJ Ch 546, 84 LT 697, [1900–3] All ER Rep Ext
   1531, HL 175, 212, 235, 302
Kingsman v Kingsman (1706) 2 Vern 559 141
Kingston (Earl) v Lady Elizabeth Pierepont (1681) 1 Vern 5
   131
Kingwell's Goods, Re (1899) 81 LT 461, P, D and Admlty
   819–820
Kinleside v Harrison (1818) 2 Phillim 449 .... 77, 903
Kinnear, Re, Kinnear v Barnett (1904) 90 LT 537 305
Kinsella v Caffrey (1860) 11 I Ch R 154; affd (1860) 13 Ir Jur 277
   472
Kinsey v Hayward (1701) 1 Ld Raym 432, 1 Lut 256, sub nom Hayward v Kinsey 12 Mod
   Rep 568 1246
Kirin-Amgen Inc v Hoechst Marion Roussel Ltd [2004] UKHL 46
   194
Kipping, Re, Kipping v Kipping [1914] 1 Ch 62, 83 LJ Ch 218, 109 LT 919,
   [1911–13] All ER Rep Ext 1422, CA 308
Kirby's Goods, Re [1902] P 188, 71 LJP 116, 87 LT 141, P, D and Admlty
   613
Kirby-Smith v Parnell [1903] 1 Ch 483, 72 LJ Ch 468, 51 WR 493, 47 Sol Jo 279
   .... 235, 255, 284
Kircudbright (Lord) v Lady Kircudbright (1802) 8 Ves 51
   503–504
Kirk, Re, Kirk v Kirk (1882) 21 Ch D 431, 31 WR 94, 47 LT 36, CA
   .... 184, 407
Kirk, Re, Nicholson v Kirk (1885) 52 LT 346 331
Kirk, Re, Wethey v Kirk (1915) 85 LJ Ch 182, 113 LT 1204
   .... 247, 323
Kirk v Eddowes (1844) 3 Hare 509, 13 LJ Ch 402, 8 Jur 530
   .... 197, 406
Kirk v Todd (1882) 21 Ch D 484, 52 LJ Ch 224, 31 WR 69, 47 LT 676, CA
   1277
Kirkbride's Trusts, Re (1866) LR 2 Eq 400, 14 WR 728, 15 LT 51
   .... 248, 440, 443
Kirke v Kirke (1828) 4 Russ 435, 6 LJOS Ch 143 108
Kirkley, Re, Halligey v Kirkley (1918) 87 LJ Ch 247, 62 Sol Jo 364, 119 LT 304
   .... 415–416, 430
Kirkman v Booth (1848) 11 Beav 273, 18 LJ Ch 25, 13 Jur 525, 83 RR 158, 13 LTOS 482
   .... 649, 1035
Kirkman v Siboni. See Siboni v Kirkman
Kirkman's Trust, Re (1859) 3 De G & J 558 325
Kirkpatrick v Bedford (1878) 4 App Cas 96, HL 402
Kitcat v King [1930] P 266, 99 LJP 126, 74 Sol Jo 488, 143 LT 408, 46 TLR 617, P, D
   and Admlty 44, 95, 739
Kitchen, Re, Kitchen v Allman (1919) 35 TLR 612, P, D and Admlty
   79
Kitchen v Ibbetson (1873) LR 17 Eq 46, 38 JP 212, 43 LJ Ch 52, 22 WR 68, 29 LT 450
   923
Kitto, Re, Kitto v Luke (1879) 28 WR 411 1201

                                                                                                              PARA
Kleinwort Benson Ltd v Lincoln City Council [1999] 2 AC 349, [1998] 4 All ER 513,
    [1998] 3 WLR 1095, [1999] LGR 1, 14 LDAB 353, [1998] NLJR 1674, [1998] RVR
    315, 142 Sol Jo LB 279, [1999] 3 LRC 219, [1998] All ER (D) 518, HL
    .... 1097, 1099
Kloebe, Re, Kannreuther v Geiselbrecht (1884) 28 Ch D 175, 54 LJ Ch 297, 33 WR 391,
    [1881–5] All ER Rep 1120, 52 LT 19, 1 TLR 139 968
Knapman, Re, Knapman v Wreford (1881) 18 Ch D 300, 50 LJ Ch 629, 30 WR 395, 45
    LT 102, [1881–5] All ER Rep Ext 1758, CA 1067
Knapp v Noyes (1768) Amb 662 135
Knapp's Settlement, Re, Knapp v Vassall [1895] 1 Ch 91, 64 LJ Ch 112, 13 R 147, 43 WR
    279, 71 LT 625, [1891–4] All ER Rep Ext 1343 306–308
Knapton, Re, Knapton v Hindle [1941] Ch 428, [1941] 2 All ER 573, 110 LJ Ch 177, 85
    Sol Jo 322, 166 LT 37 127
Knee's Goods, Re, Gattward v Knee. See Gattward v Knee
Knibbs' Estate, Re, Flay v Trueman (Hoskins cited) [1962] 2 All ER 829, [1962] 1 WLR
    852, 106 Sol Jo 454, P, D and Admlty 81
Knight, Re (1944) unreported 88
Knight, Re, Knight v Burgess (1887) 34 Ch D 518, 56 LJ Ch 770, 35 WR 536, 56 LT 630,
    3 TLR 387 279
Knight v Burgess (1864) 33 LJ Ch 727, 10 Jur NS 166, 10 LT 90
    1279
Knight v Cameron (1807) 14 Ves 389 .... 135, 428
Knight v Davis (1833) 3 My & K 358, 3 LJ Ch 81 1006
Knight v Edonya [2009] EWHC 2181 (Ch), [2009] All ER (D) 207 (Aug)
    .... 903, 905
Knight v Ellis (1789) 2 Bro CC 570 385
Knight v Gould (1833) 2 My & K 295, Coop temp Brough 240
    175
Knight v Knight (1826) 2 Sim & St 490 430
Knight v Knight (1912) 14 CLR 86, Aust HC 315
Knight's Goods, Re [1939] 3 All ER 928, 83 Sol Jo 733, 55 TLR 992, P, D and Admlty
    .... 759, 817–818
Knight's Will, Re (1884) 26 Ch D 82, 63 LJ Ch 223, 32 WR 417, 50 LT 550, CA
    952
Knights v Quarles (1820) 2 Brod & Bing 102, 4 Moore CP 532
    1237
Knott v Cottee (1852) 16 Beav 77, 16 Jur 752 1257
Knowles, Re, Knowles v Birtwell (or Britwell) [1966] Ch 386, [1966] 2 All ER 480n,
    [1966] 3 WLR 51, 110 Sol Jo 549 600
Knowles, Re, Nottage v Buxton (1882) 21 Ch D 806, 51 LJ Ch 851, 31 WR 182, 47 LT
    161, [1881–5] All ER Rep Ext 1615 .... 260, 299
Knowles, Re, Rainford v Knowles (1888) 59 LT 359 364
Knowles v A-G [1951] P 54, [1950] 2 All ER 6, 94 Sol Jo 421, 66 (pt 1) TLR 1188, P, D
    and Admlty 679
Knox, Re, Von Scheffler v Shuldham [1912] 1 IR 288 .... 142–143, 148
Knox v Lord Hotham (1845) 15 Sim 82 .... 371, 1061
Knox v Wells (1864) 2 Hem & M 674, 34 LJ Ch 150, 10 Jur NS 1252, 13 WR 228, 11 LT
    666 429
Knox's Goods, Re (1889) 23 LR Ir 542 .... 133, 140
Koeppler Will Trusts, Re, Barclays Bank Trust Co Ltd v Slack [1984] Ch 243, [1984]
    2 All ER 111, [1984] 2 WLR 973, 128 Sol Jo 398, [1984] LS Gaz R 1843; revsd
    [1986] Ch 423, [1985] 2 All ER 869, [1985] 3 WLR 765, 129 Sol Jo 670, [1985] NLJ
    Rep 531, CA 206, 445
Kokosinski v Kokosinski [1980] Fam 72, [1980] 1 All ER 1106, [1980] 3 WLR 55, 1 FLR
    205, 124 Sol Jo 16, sub nom K v K 10 Fam Law 91 577
Kolb's Will Trusts, Re, Lloyd's Bank Ltd v Ullman [1962] Ch 531, [1961] 3 All ER 811,
    [1961] 3 WLR 1034, 105 Sol Jo 888; on appeal (1962) 106 Sol Jo 669, CA
    295
Korda, Re (1958) Times, 19 July, CA 959
Kosa v Nesheim [2006] EWHC 2710 (Ch), [2007] Fam Law 1132, [2006] All ER (D) 40
    (Oct) 868
Kostic v Chaplin [2007] EWHC 2298 (Ch), 10 ITELR 364, [2007] All ER (D) 203 (Oct)
    .... 49, 52
Kostic v Chaplin [2007] EWHC 2909 (Ch), [2008] 2 Costs LR 271, [2007] All ER (D) 119
    (Dec) 908, 911, 913

PARA

Kotke v Saffarini [2005] EWCA Civ 221, [2005] 1 FCR 642, [2005] 2 FLR 517, [2005] Fam Law 535, [2005] NLJR 414, [2005] All ER (D) 145 (Mar) 567

Kourkgy v Lusher (1981) 4 FLR 65, 12 Fam Law 86 .... 567, 581, 585

Krawitz's Will Trusts, Re, Krawitz v Crawford [1959] 3 All ER 793, [1959] 1 WLR 1192, 103 Sol Jo 1004 .... 140, 313–314, 344

Krehl v Park (1875) 10 Ch App 334, 44 LJ Ch 286, 23 WR 475, 33 LT 83, DC 1203

Krubert, Re [1997] Ch 97, [1996] 3 WLR 959, [1996] 3 FCR 281, [1997] 1 FLR 42, [1997] Fam Law 165, [1996] 27 LS Gaz R 28, 140 Sol Jo LB 167, CA 569, 577

Kurtz, Re, Emerson v Henderson (1904) 90 LT 12 1183

Kusminow v Barclays Bank Trust Co Ltd and Sokolow and Sitnikova [1989] Fam Law 66 577

Kuypers, Re, Kuypers v Kuypers [1925] Ch 244, 94 LJ Ch 253, [1925] All ER Rep 343, 69 Sol Jo 366, 133 LT 468 156

Kynnaird v Leslie (1866) LR 1 CP 389, 35 LJCP 226, Har & Ruth 521, 12 Jur NS 468, 14 WR 761, 14 LT 756 548

L

La Terriere v Bulmer (1827) 2 Sim 18 1118

Labouchere v Tupper (1857) 11 Moo PCC 198, 5 WR 797, 14 ER 670, [1843–60] All ER Rep 937, 29 LTOS 357, PC 1039

Lachlan v Reynolds (1852) 9 Hare 796 .... 254, 256, 341–342

Lacons v Warmoll [1907] 2 KB 350, 76 LJKB 914, 97 LT 379, 23 TLR 495, CA 1172, 1294

Ladd, Re, Henderson v Porter [1932] 2 Ch 219, 101 LJ Ch 392, 147 LT 433 164

Laffan and Downes Contract, Re [1897] 1 IR 469 .... 300, 309

Lafone v Griffin (1909) 25 TLR 308, P, D and Admlty 730

Laidlaw, Re, Wilkinson v Lyde [1930] 2 Ch 392, 99 LJ Ch 463, [1930] All ER Rep 252, 143 LT 761 1130

Laing, Re, Laing v Morrison [1912] 2 Ch 386, 81 LJ Ch 686, 57 Sol Jo 80, 107 LT 822 .... 172, 416

Lainson v Lainson (1854) 5 De GM & G 754, 24 LJ Ch 46, 3 Eq Rep 43, 1 Jur NS 49, 3 WR 31, 24 LTOS 85 182

Laird's Goods, Re [1892] P 380, 62 LJP 15, 1 R 456, 67 LT 504, P, D and Admlty 613

Laker v Hordern (1876) 1 Ch D 644, 45 LJ Ch 315, 24 WR 543, 34 LT 88 .... 351, 353

Lamb, Re, Marston v Chauvet (1933) 77 Sol Jo 503, 49 TLR 541 .... 270, 295

Lamb, Re, Vipond v Lamb [1929] 1 Ch 722, 98 LJ Ch 305, [1929] All ER Rep 82, 73 Sol Jo 77, 141 LT 60, 45 TLR 190 .... 994, 999

Lambe v Eames (1871) 6 Ch App 597, 40 LJ Ch 447, 19 WR 659, 25 LT 174, [1861–73] All ER Rep Ext 1322 .... 348, 370, 382

Lambell v Lambell (1831) 3 Hag Ecc 568 106

Lambert, Re, Corns v Harrison [1908] 2 Ch 117, 77 LJ Ch 553, [1908–10] All ER Rep 521, 98 LT 851 .... 247, 323

Lambert, Re, Lambert v Lambert (1892) 36 Sol Jo 327 1126

Lambert, Re, Middleton v Moore [1897] 2 Ch 169, 66 LJ Ch 624, 45 WR 661, 41 Sol Jo 560, 76 LT 752 .... 405, 1257

Lambert v Overton (1864) 13 WR 227, 11 LT 503 271

Lambert v Rendle (1863) 3 New Rep 247 1035

Laming v Gee (1878) 10 Ch D 715, 48 LJ Ch 196, 27 WR 227, 40 LT 33 1183

Lamont (or Chearnley) v Millar [1921] WN 334, 152 LT Jo 417, sub nom Curle's Trustees v Millar 59 SLR 21, 1922 SC (HL) 15, HL 317

Lamothe v Lamothe [2006] EWHC 1387 (Ch), [2006] WTLR 1431, [2006] All ER (D) 153 (Jun) 8, 93, 95–96, 185, 187, 708

Lampet's Case (1612) 10 Co Rep 46b 416

Lamphier v Buck. See Lanphier v Buck

Lamphier v Despard (1842) 2 Dr & War 59 .... 250, 288

Lampley v Blower (1746) 3 Atk 396 .... 389, 460

PARA

Lancaster v Varty (1826) 5 LJOS Ch 41 369
Lance v Aglionby (1859) 27 Beav 65, 5 Jur NS 561, 34 LTOS 69
  1012
Lancefield v Iggulden (1874) 10 Ch App 136, 44 LJ Ch 203, 23 WR 223,
   [1874–80] All ER Rep 910, 31 LT 813 119
Land, Re, Land v Land [2006] EWHC 2069 (Ch), [2007] 1 All ER 324, [2007] 1 WLR
   1009, [2006] All ER (D) 71 (Oct) 39–40, 566, 576
Land v Devaynes (1794) 4 Bro CC 537 285
Land v Land (1874) 43 LJ Ch 311 1035
Land Credit Co of Ireland, Re, Markwell's Case (1872) 21 WR 135
  965
Lander, Re, Lander v Lander [1951] Ch 546, [1951] 1 All ER 622, 30 ATC 93, [1951] TR
   93, [1951] 1 TLR 456 125
Landon's Trusts, Re (1871) 40 LJ Ch 370 1047
Lane, Re, Luard v Lane (1880) 14 Ch D 856, 49 LJ Ch 768, 28 WR 764, 43 LT 87
  .... 156, 296
Lane, Re, Meagher v National Gallery for Ireland (1917) 33 TLR 418
  296
Lane v Goudge (1803) 9 Ves 225 429–431
Lane v Green (1851) 4 De G & Sm 239, 15 Jur 763, 17 LTOS 1
  274
Lane v Sewell (1874) 43 LJ Ch 378 285
Lane's Estate, Re, Meagher v National Gallery of Ireland (Governors and Guardians) and
   Heaven [1946] 1 All ER 735, 115 LJ Ch 195, 175 LT 50
  471
Lane's Goods, Re (1864) 33 LJPM & A 185, 4 New Rep 253
  616
Lanesborough (Lady) v Fox (1733) Cas temp Talb 262, 3 Bro Parl Cas 130, HL
  459–460
Lang v Lang (1837) 8 Sim 451, 6 LJ Ch 324, 1 Jur 472
  497–498
Lang v Pugh (1842) 1 Y & C Ch Cas 718, 6 Jur 939 .... 226, 427
Langdale v Whitfeld (1858) 4 K & J 426, 27 LJ Ch 795, 4 Jur NS 706, 6 WR 862,
   32 LTOS 18 293
Langdale (Lady) v Briggs, ex p Lady Bacon, ex p Martineau (1873) 28 LT 467; affd sub
   nom Martineau v Briggs (1875) 45 LJ Ch 674, 23 WR 889, HL
  .... 243, 253, 388
Langdale (Lady) v Briggs (1855) 25 LJ Ch 100, 2 Jur NS 35, 3 Sm & G 246, 4 WR 144,
   26 LTOS 306; on appeal (1856) 8 De GM & G 391 .... 114, 195, 228, 282, 414, 440
Langdon v Rooke. See Thorne v Rooke
Langford v Gascoyne (1805) 11 Ves 333 1253
Langford's Goods, Re (1867) LR 1 P & D 458, 32 JP 104, 37 LJP & M 20, 17 LT 415
  616
Langham v Peterson (1903) 67 JP 75, 87 LT 744, 19 TLR 157
  .... 11, 36
Langham v Sanford (1816) 2 Mer 6, 19 Ves 641 .... 207, 218
Langlands, Re, Langlands v Langlands (1917) 87 LJ Ch 1, 117 LT 11
  .... 325, 336
Langley v Baldwin (1707) 1 Eq Cas Abr 185 .... 457, 473
Langley v Earl of Oxford (1748) Amb 795, 2 Hov Supp 98
  1023
Langley v Hawk (1820) 5 Madd 46 624
Langley v Oates (1708) 2 Eq Cas Abr 541 438
Langley's Goods, Re (1851) 2 Rob Eccl 407 848
Langley's Settlement Trusts, Re, Lloyds Bank Ltd v Langley [1962] Ch 541, [1961]
   3 All ER 803, [1961] 3 WLR 1169, 105 Sol Jo 866, CA
  34
Langmead's Trusts, Re (1855) 20 Beav 20, 24 LJ Ch 237, 1 Jur NS 198, 3 WR 260,
   24 LTOS 330; affd (1855) 7 De GM & G 353 920
Langston v Langston (1834) 8 Bli NS 167, 2 Cl & Fin 194, 6 ER 1128, [1824–34] All ER
   Rep 598, HL 186, 207, 227, 253, 333
Langston's Estate, Re [1953] P 100, [1953] 1 All ER 928, [1953] 1 WLR 581, 97 Sol Jo
   249, P, D and Admlty 88
Langton's Estate, Re [1964] P 163, [1964] 2 WLR 585, sub nom Langton, Re, Langton v
   Lloyds Bank Ltd [1964] 1 All ER 749, 108 Sol Jo 96, CA
  .... 669, 853, 884, 887–888

PARA

Lannoy v Lannoy (1725) Cas temp King 48 29

Lanphier v Buck (1865) 2 Drew & Sm 484, 34 LJ Ch 650, 11 Jur NS 837, 112 LT 660,
sub nom Lamphier v Buck 6 New Rep 196, 13 WR 767
.... 321–322, 325–326, 336, 393, 446

Lansdown's (Lord) Case (1712) 10 Mod Rep 96 218

Lanyon, Re, Lanyon v Lanyon [1927] 2 Ch 264, 96 LJ Ch 487, [1927] All ER Rep 61, 71
Sol Jo 865, 137 LT 806, 43 TLR 714 133

Larke v Nugus (1979) 123 Sol Jo 337, [2000] WTLR 1033, CA
.... 860, 882, 911

Larking, Re, Larking v Larking (1887) 37 Ch D 310, 57 LJ Ch 282
.... 156

Larkins v Paxton (1835) 2 My & K 320 1203

Lashbrook v Cock (1816) 2 Mer 70 395

Lashley v Hogg (1805) 11 Ves 602 985

Lassence v Tierney (1849) 2 H & Tw 115, 14 Jur 182, 1 Mac & G 551, 84 RR 158, 41
ER 1379, [1843–60] All ER Rep 47, 15 LTOS 557 .... 231, 369, 378, 410, 1061

Lasseur v Tyrconnel (1846) 10 Beav 28, 8 LTOS 153 669

Last, Re [1958] P 137, [1958] 1 All ER 316, [1958] 2 WLR 186, 102 Sol Jo 89, P, D and
Admlty 382

Latch v Latch (1875) 10 Ch App 464, 44 LJ Ch 445, 23 WR 686, CA in Ch
.... 1172

Latham's Trusts, Re, Seymour v Bolton [1901] WN 248, 46 Sol Jo 136
.... 310

Laver v Fielder (1862) 32 Beav 1, 32 LJ Ch 365, 9 Jur NS 190, 1 New Rep 188, 11 WR
245, 7 LT 602 21

Laverick's Estate, Re, Re Whitby Improvement Act (1853) 18 Jur 304, 2 WR 113,
22 LTOS 168 395

Law v Thompson (1827) 4 Russ 92, 6 LJOS Ch 56 451

Law v Thorp (1858) 27 LJ Ch 649, 4 Jur NS 447, 6 WR 480, 31 LTOS 378
.... 337, 392

Law Society Practice Note (Disputed Wills) (16 April 2009)
.... 860, 882

Law's Trustees v Gray 1921 SC 455, Ct of Sess 252

Law Union and Crown Insurance Co v Hill [1902] AC 263, 71 LJ Ch 602, 86 LT 773, HL
.... 229

Lawes v Bennett (1785) 1 Cox Eq Cas 167 157

Lawes-Wittewronge, Re, Maurice v Bennett [1915] 1 Ch 408, 84 LJ Ch 472,
[1914–15] All ER Rep 502, 112 LT 931 .... 287, 375

Lawley, Re, Jackson v Leighton [1911] 2 Ch 530, 81 LJ Ch 97, 56 Sol Jo 13, 105 LT 571
.... 990

Lawley, Re, Zaiser v Lawley (or Perkins) [1902] 2 Ch 799, 71 LJ Ch 895, 51 WR 150, 47
Sol Jo 29, 87 LT 536, 19 TLR 8, CA; affd sub nom Beyfus v Lawley [1903] AC 411,
72 LJ Ch 781, [1900–3] All ER Rep 796, 89 LT 309, HL
.... 969, 1005, 1012, 1089

Lawrance v Galsworthy (1857) 3 Jur NS 1049, 30 LTOS 112
.... 294

Lawrence v Dodwell (1699) 1 Ld Raym 438, Lut 734 207

Lawrence (Lord), Re, Lawrence v Lawrence [1915] 1 Ch 129, 84 LJ Ch 273, 59 Sol Jo
127, 117 LT 195, CA 384, 391

Lawrence's Will Trusts, Re, Public Trustee v Lawrence [1972] Ch 418, [1971] 3 All ER
433, [1972] 3 All ER 433, [1971] 3 WLR 188, 115 Sol Jo 550
.... 96, 248, 251

Laws Goods, Re (1872) LR 2 P & D 458, 36 JP 503, 41 LJP & M 41, 20 WR 572, 26 LT
530 680

Lawson, Re, Wardley v Bringloe [1914] 1 Ch 682, 83 LJ Ch 519, [1914–15] All ER Rep
206, 58 Sol Jo 320, 110 LT 573, 30 TLR 335 366

Lawson v Stitch (1738) 1 Atk 507, West temp Hard 325
.... 118

Lawton v Lawton (1743) 3 Atk 13 .... 930, 932

Lawton v Salmon (1782) 1 Hy Bl 260n 932

Layard, Re, Layard v Earl of Bessborough (1916) 85 LJ Ch 505, 115 LT 15, 32 TLR 517,
CA; on appeal (1917) 33 TLR 261, HL 250, 296

Laye, Re, Turnbull v Laye [1913] 1 Ch 298, 82 LJ Ch 218, 20 Mans 124, 57 Sol Jo 284,
108 LT 324 465

Layfield v Layfield (1834) 7 Sim 172, 4 LJ Ch 2 1268

PARA

Layton v Martin [1986] 2 FLR 227, [1986] Fam Law 212
.... 567

Layton v Newcombe. See Bliss, Re

Lazarus v Lazarus (1919) 88 LJ Ch 525, sub nom Lazarus, Re, Lazarus v Lazarus 121 LT
    491, CA 285

Lazonby v Rawson (1854) 4 De GM & G 556, 24 LJ Ch 482, 3 Eq Rep 89, 1 Jur NS 289,
    3 WR 34, 24 LTOS 175 .... 1290, 1298

Le Cras v Perpetual Trustee Co Ltd. See Resch's Will Trusts, Re, Le Cras v Perpetual
    Trustee Co Ltd

Le Cren Clarke, Re, Funnell v Stewart [1996] 1 All ER 715, sub nom Funnell v Stewart
    [1996] 1 WLR 288 .... 256, 259, 263
Le Grice v Finch (1817) 3 Mer 50 158
Le Jeune v Budd (1834) 6 Sim 441 136
Le Jeune v Le Jeune (1837) 2 Keen 701, 1 Jur 235 .... 322, 449
Le Page v Gardom [1915] WN 216, 84 LJ Ch 749, 59 Sol Jo 599, 113 LT 475, HL
.... 222–223
Lea, Re, Wells v Holt (1911) 104 LT 253 285
Lea v Grundy (1855) 1 Jur NS 951, 25 LTOS 287 298
Leach, Re, Leach v Leach [1912] 2 Ch 422, 81 LJ Ch 683, 56 Sol Jo 649, 106 LT 1003
.... 454, 461
Leach, Re, Leach v Lindeman [1986] Ch 226, [1985] 2 All ER 754, [1985] 3 WLR 413,
    [1985] FLR 1120, [1985] Fam Law 319, 129 Sol Jo 318, CA
.... 567, 573, 580
Leach, Re, Milne v Daubeny [1923] 1 Ch 161, 92 LJ Ch 225, [1922] All ER Rep 714, 67
    Sol Jo 198, 128 LT 525 .... 1014, 1060, 1087
Leach v Jay (1878) 9 Ch D 42, 47 LJ Ch 876, 27 WR 99, 39 LT 242, CA
.... 204
Leach v Leach [1878] WN 79 286
Leach v Leach (1843) 13 Sim 304, 7 Jur 273 370
Leach v Leach (1843) 2 Y & C Ch Cas 495 259
Leach v Leach (1866) 35 Beav 185 165
Leach's Goods, Re (1890) 63 LT 111, P, D and Admlty 105
Leach's Will Trusts, Re, Chatterton v Leach [1948] Ch 232, [1948] 1 All ER 383,
    [1948] LJR 990, 92 Sol Jo 167, 64 TLR 175 .... 163, 246
Leacroft v Maynard (1791) 1 Ves 279, 3 Bro CC 233 409
Leadbetter v Cross (1876) 2 QBD 18, 46 LJQB 31, 25 WR 96
.... 420, 422
Leader v Duffey (1888) 13 App Cas 294, 58 LJPC 13, 59 LT 9, HL
.... 236
Leahy v A-G for New South Wales [1959] AC 457, [1959] 2 All ER 300, [1959] 2 WLR
    722, 103 Sol Jo 391, 33 ALJR 105, PC 11, 36–37
Leak v Macdowall (No 2) (1863) 33 Beav 238, 3 New Rep 185
.... 363
Leake v Leake (1805) 10 Ves 477 404
Leake v Robinson (1817) 2 Mer 363, [1814–23] All ER Rep 363
.... 256, 304–305, 316, 416, 427, 431, 433
Lean v Alston [1947] KB 467, [1947] 1 All ER 261, [1947] LJR 559, CA
.... 818
Lean v Viner (1864) 33 LJPM & A 88, 3 Sw & Tr 469 696
Lechmere and Lloyd, Re (1881) 18 Ch D 524, 45 LT 551
.... 424
Lecoche, Re, Lecoche v Barclays Bank Ltd (1967) 111 Sol Jo 136
.... 591
Leconfield, Re, Wyndham v Leconfield (1904) 90 LT 399, 20 TLR 347, CA
.... 1132
Ledger v Wootton [2007] EWHC 90 (Ch), [2007] All ER (D) 99 (Oct)
.... 52, 893, 897, 899
Ledsome v Hickman (1708) 2 Vern 611 411
Ledward v Hassells (1856) 2 K & J 370, 25 LJ Ch 311, 2 Jur NS 277, 4 WR 315
.... 145, 147
Lee, Re, Gibbon v Peele (1910) 103 LT 103 252
Lee, Re, ex p Good (1880) 14 Ch D 82, 49 LJ Bcy 49, 28 WR 553, 42 LT 450, CA
.... 987
Lee v Busk (1852) 2 De GM & G 810, 22 LJ Ch 97, 16 Jur 1057, 20 LTOS 173
.... 472
Lee v Cox and D'Aranda (1746–7) (1746) 3 Atk 419, sub nom Lee v D'Aranda 1 Ves Sen
    1 497

PARA

Lee v Delane (1850) 4 De G & Sm 1, 14 Jur 861, 16 LTOS 102
.... 1210
Lee v Flinn (1833) Alc & N 418 459
Lee v Lee (1858) 27 LJ Ch 824, 6 WR 846, 32 LTOS 59
.... 156, 158
Lee v Lee (1860) 1 Drew & Sm 85, 29 LJ Ch 788, 6 Jur NS 621, 8 WR 443, 2 LT 532
.... 260, 305, 313–314, 344
Lee v Lee (1864) 10 Jur NS 1041 274
Lee v Pain (1844) 4 Hare 201, 8 Jur 705 .... 174, 197, 215, 227, 235, 270, 274–275, 302, 305,
403
Lee (George) & Sons (Builders) Ltd v Olink [1972] 1 All ER 359, [1972] 1 WLR 214, 116
Sol Jo 102, CA 966
Lee's Case (1584) 1 Leon 285, 3 Leon 106, sub nom Lee v Vincent Cro Eliz 26, sub nom
Vincent v Lee Moore KB 147 459
Leeder v Ellis [1953] AC 52, [1952] 2 All ER 814, [1952] 2 TLR 577, PC
.... 984
Leeds (Duke) v Lord Amherst (1844) 13 Sim 459, 14 LJ Ch 73, 9 Jur 359
.... 199
Leek, Re, Darwen v Leek [1969] 1 Ch 563, [1968] 1 All ER 793, [1968] 2 WLR 1385, 47
ATC 28, [1967] TR 375, 112 Sol Jo 444, CA 231, 348
Leeming, Re, Turner v Leeming [1912] 1 Ch 828, 81 LJ Ch 453, 106 LT 793,
[1911–13] All ER Rep Ext 1292 156
Leeming v Sherratt (1842) 2 Hare 14, 11 LJ Ch 423, 6 Jur 663, 67 ER 6,
[1835–42] All ER Rep 458 .... 238, 249, 316, 410, 426–429, 456–457
Lees v Sanderson (1830) 4 Sim 28 1253
Leese's Goods, Re (1862) 26 JP 232, 31 LJPM & A 169, 2 Sw & Tr 442, 5 LT 848
.... 707
Leeson's Goods, Re (1859) 23 JP 809, Sea & Sm 31, 29 LJP & M 19, 5 Jur NS 1270, 1
Sw & Tr 463, 1 LT 74 801
Legard v Haworth (1800) 1 East 120 339
Legg v Mackrell (1860) 2 De GF & J 551, 4 LT 568 952
Legge v Asgill (1818) Turn & R 265n, Turn & R 265n 293
Legh's Settlement Trusts, Re, Public Trustee v Legh [1938] Ch 39, [1937] 3 All ER 823,
107 LJ Ch 6, 81 Sol Jo 701, 157 LT 270, 53 TLR 1036, CA
.... 416
Leguia's Estate, Re (1936) 105 LJP 72, 155 LT 270, CA
.... 759
Leguia's Estate, Re, ex p Ashworth [1934] P 80, 103 LJP 34, 78 Sol Jo 136, 150 LT 339,
50 TLR 177, P, D and Admlty 759, 763, 788
Lehman Bros International (Europe) (in administration) (No 4), Re [2015] EWCA Civ 485,
[2016] Ch 50 967
Leigh v Byron (1853) 22 LJ Ch 1064, 1 Eq Rep 519, 17 Jur 822, 1 Sm & G 486, 1 WR
407, 22 LTOS 32 352
Leigh v Leigh (1808) 15 Ves 92 278
Leigh v Leigh (1848) 12 Jur 907 370
Leigh v Leigh (1854) 17 Beav 605, 23 LJ Ch 287, 18 Jur 115, 2 WR 205, 22 LTOS 279
.... 174, 302, 305
Leigh v Mosley (1851) 14 Beav 605, 18 LTOS 84 410
Leigh v Norbury (1807) 13 Ves 340, CA 334
Leigh v Taylor. See De Falbe, Re, Ward v Taylor
Leigh's Goods, Re [1892] P 82, 61 LJP 124, 66 LT 379, 8 TLR 210, P, D and Admlty
.... 717
Leigh's Will Trusts, Re, Handyside v Durbridge [1970] Ch 277, [1969] 3 All ER 432,
[1969] 3 WLR 649, 113 Sol Jo 758 .... 27, 295, 922, 1139
Lemage v Goodban (1865) LR 1 P & D 57, 35 LJP & M 28, 12 Jur NS 32, 13 LT 508,
[1861–73] All ER Rep Ext 1364 .... 1, 95, 97, 99, 713, 911
Lemaine v Staneley (1681) Freem KB 538, 3 Lev 1 63
Lemme's Goods, Re [1892] P 89, 61 LJP 123, 66 LT 592, P, D and Admlty
.... 721, 750
Lemon's Estate, Re, Winwood v Lemon (1961) 105 Sol Jo 1107, P, D and Admlty
.... 78
Lenden v Blackmore (1840) 10 Sim 626 .... 390, 396
Leng, Re, Tarn v Emmerson [1895] 1 Ch 652, 64 LJ Ch 468, 12 R 202, 43 WR 406,
[1895–9] All ER Rep 1210, 39 Sol Jo 329, 72 LT 407, 11 TLR 286, CA
.... 982

PARA

Lenox v Lenox (1839) 10 Sim 400, 9 LJ Ch 83, 4 Jur 5
.... 445
Leonard v Earl of Sussex (1705) 2 Vern 526 194
Leonard v Leonard [1902] P 243, 71 LJP 117, 46 Sol Jo 666, 87 LT 145, 18 TLR 747, P,
  D and Admlty 96, 105
Leonard v Simpson (1835) 2 Bing NC 176, 4 LJCP 302, 1 Hodg 251, 2 Scott 335
.... 1294, 1301
Leong v Lim Beng Chye [1955] AC 648, [1955] 2 All ER 903, [1955] 3 WLR 303, 99 Sol
  Jo 524, PC 133–134
Leonino v Leonino (1879) 10 Ch D 460, 48 LJ Ch 217, 27 WR 388, 40 LT 359
.... 1009
Lepard v Vernon (1813) 2 Ves & B 51 926
Lepine, Re, Dowsett v Culver [1892] 1 Ch 210, 61 LJ Ch 153, [1891–4] All ER Rep 945,
  66 LT 360, CA 1020, 1158, 1161
Lepine v Bean (1870) LR 10 Eq 160, 39 LJ Ch 847, 18 WR 797, 22 LT 833
.... 352
Lepine v Ferard (1831) 1 LJ Ch 150, 2 Russ & M 378 459–460
Leslie v Earl of Rothes [1894] 2 Ch 499, 63 LJ Ch 617, 7 R 600, 71 LT 134, CA
.... 195, 369
Leslie v Leslie (1835) L & G temp Sugd 1 1077
Leslie v Leslie (1872) IR 6 Eq 332 95
Lester, Re, Burton v Lester (1906) 23 WN 240, 7 SRNSW 58, NSW SC
.... 146
Lester, Re, Lester v Lester [1942] Ch 324, [1942] 1 All ER 646, 111 LJ Ch 197, 86 Sol Jo
  168, 58 TLR 250 .... 152, 407
Lester v Garland (1808) 15 Ves 248, 33 ER 748, [1803–13] All ER Rep 436
.... 133, 148
L'Estrange v L'Estrange (1890) 25 LR Ir 399 424
Lethbridge v Lethbridge (1862) 4 De GF & J 35, 31 LJ Ch 737, 8 Jur NS 836, 10 WR
  449, 6 LT 727 290
Letherbrow, Re, Hopp v Dean [1935] WN 34, 179 LT Jo 161
.... 965
Lethieullier v Tracey (1754) Amb 220, 3 Atk 784, 1 Keny 56
.... 473
Lethieullier v Tracy (1753) 3 Atk 774, Keny Ch 40, Amb 204
.... 417
Lett v Randall (1855) 24 LJ Ch 708, 3 Eq Rep 1034, 1 Jur NS 747, 3 Sm & G 83, 3 WR
  564, 25 LTOS 244; affd (1860) 2 De GF & J 388, 30 LJ Ch 110, 6 Jur NS 1359, 9
  WR 130, 3 LT 455 .... 468, 498
Letterstedt v Broers (1884) 9 App Cas 371, 53 LJPC 44, [1881–5] All ER Rep 882, 51 LT
  169, PC 1163
Leven and Melville's (Earl) Goods, Re (1889) 15 PD 22, 59 LJP 35, P, D and Admlty
.... 613
Leventhorpe v Ashbie (1635) 1 Roll Abr 831 385
Lever's Estate, Re (1935) 105 LJP 9, [1935] All ER Rep 455, 79 Sol Jo 861, 154 LT 270,
  52 TLR 97, P, D and Admlty 744
Leverhulme, Re, Cooper v Leverhulme (No 2) [1943] 2 All ER 274, 169 LT 294
.... 266
Leverington's Goods, Re (1886) 11 PD 80, 55 LJP 62, P, D and Admlty
.... 75
Levinstein, Re, Levinstein v Levinstein [1921] 2 Ch 251, 91 LJ Ch 32, 65 Sol Jo 767, 126
  LT 177 465
Levy, Re, Barclays Bank Ltd v Board of Guardians and Trustees for the Relief of the Jewish
  Poor [1960] Ch 346, [1960] 1 All ER 42, [1960] 2 WLR 278, 104 Sol Jo 86, CA
.... 375
Levy, Re, Cohen v Cohen (1907) 24 WN 211, 7 SRNSW 885, NSW SC
.... 432
Levy, Re, ex p Walton (1881) 17 Ch D 746, 50 LJ Ch 657, 30 WR 395, [1881–5] All ER
  Rep 548, 45 LT 1, CA 241
Levy v Leo (1909) 25 TLR 717, P, D and Admlty 911
Levy v Lindo (1817) 3 Mer 81 899
Levy's Estate, Re [1908] P 108, 77 LJP 57, 52 Sol Jo 193, P, D and Admlty
.... 720
Levy Estate Trust, Re [2000] CLY 5363 302

PARA

Lewen v Cox (1599) Cro Eliz 695, sub nom Lewen v Dodd Cro Eliz 443, sub nom Lowen
v Cocks Het 63, sub nom Lewin v Cox Moore KB 558; affd sub nom Lowen v Cocks
(1657) Cro Eliz 696, Ex Ch 395
Lewes v Lewes (1848) 16 Sim 266, 17 LJ Ch 425 371
Lewes' Trusts, Re (1871) 6 Ch App 356, 35 JP 357, 40 LJ Ch 602, 19 WR 617, 24 LT 533
.... 33
Lewin v Killey (1888) 13 App Cas 783, 59 LT 675, PC 450
Lewin v Lewin (1752) 2 Ves Sen 415 1087
Lewis, Re (1860) 25 JP 280, 7 Jur NS 220 .... 98, 112
Lewis, Re, Goronwy v Richards [1942] Ch 424, [1942] 2 All ER 364, 111 LJ Ch 256, 86
Sol Jo 253, 167 LT 235 320
Lewis, Re, Jennings v Hemsley [1939] Ch 232, [1939] 3 All ER 269, 108 LJ Ch 177, 82
Sol Jo 931, 159 LT 600, 55 TLR 53 991
Lewis, Re, Lewis v Lewis [1904] 2 Ch 656, 73 LJ Ch 748, 53 WR 393, 91 LT 242, CA
.... 145, 1055
Lewis, Re, Lewis v Lewis [1910] WN 217, [1908–10] All ER Rep 281, 55 Sol Jo 29, 103
LT 495 1030
Lewis, Re, Lewis v Smith [1900] 2 Ch 176, 69 LJ Ch 406, 48 WR 426, 44 Sol Jo 347, 82
LT 291 1133
Lewis, Re, Prothero v Lewis (1909) 26 TLR 145 296
Lewis v Cotton [2000] NZCA 399, [2001] WTLR 1117, 3 ITELR 447, NZ CA
.... 23
Lewis v Hillman. See Bloye's Trust, Re
Lewis v Lewis [1908] P 1, 77 LJP 7, 52 Sol Jo 31, 98 LT 58, 24 TLR 45, P, D and Admlty
.... 63, 65, 67
Lewis v Lewis (1850) 13 Beav 82 1258
Lewis v Madocks (1803) 8 Ves 150, 32 ER 310, [1803–13] All ER Rep 527
.... 22
Lewis v Mathews (1869) LR 8 Eq 277, 33 JP 775, 38 LJ Ch 510, 17 WR 841, 20 LT 905
.... 1070
Lewis v Morris (1854) 19 Beav 34 397
Lewis v Nobbs (1878) 8 Ch D 591, 47 LJ Ch 662, 26 WR 631
.... 600, 1253
Lewis v Puxley (1847) 16 LJ Ex 216, 16 M & W 733, 9 LTOS 104
.... 384
Lewis v Rees (1856) 3 K & J 132, 26 LJ Ch 101, 3 Jur NS 12, 5 WR 96, 28 LTOS 229
.... 226
Lewis v Templer (1864) 33 Beav 625, 12 WR 928, 10 LT 638
.... 460
Lewis v Trask (1882) 21 Ch D 862 1201
Lewis v Warner [2016] EWHC 1787 (Ch), [2016] All ER (D) 104 (Jul)
.... 570
Lewis d Ormond v Waters (1805) 6 East 336 .... 400, 420, 456
Lewis Declaration of Trust, Re, Lewis v Lewis, Re Lewis Declaration of Trust, Lewis v
Ryder. See Loudon v Ryder (No 2)
Lewis Goods, Re (1858) 27 LJP & M 31, 4 Jur NS 243, 1 Sw & Tr 31, 30 LTOS 353
.... 105–106
Lewis Goods, Re (1861) 31 LJPM & A 153, 7 Jur NS 688, sub nom Lewis v Lewis 26 JP
88, 2 Sw & Tr 153, 4 LT 583 75
Lewis' Will Trust, Re, Whitelaw v Beaumont [1951] WN 591, 95 Sol Jo 789, [1951] 2 TLR
1032 141
Lewis Will Trusts, Re, Lewis v Williams [1984] 3 All ER 930, [1985] 1 WLR 102, 128 Sol
Jo 385 .... 156, 270, 279, 291
Lewis Will Trusts, Re, O'sullivan v Robbins [1937] Ch 118, [1937] 1 All ER 227, 106 LJ
Ch 90, 80 Sol Jo 1035, 156 LT 235, 53 TLR 132 .... 158, 293
Lewis Will Trusts, Re, Phillips v Bowkett [1937] 1 All ER 556, 81 Sol Jo 179
.... 332
Lewisham Hospital NHS Trust v Hamuth [2006] EWHC 1609 (Ch), 150 Sol Jo LB 168,
[2006] All ER (D) 145 (Jan) 31, 956
Ley v Ley (1841) 10 LJCP 222, 2 Man & G 780, 3 Scott NR 161
.... 382
L'Herminier, Re, Mounsey v Buston [1894] 1 Ch 675, 63 LJ Ch 496, 8 R 598, 70 LT 727
.... 375
Lichfield v Mouchett (1821) Madd & G 216 95

PARA

Lidington, Re, Lidington v Thomas [1940] Ch 927, [1940] 3 All ER 600, [1940] WN 279,
    109 LJ Ch 421, 84 Sol Jo 525, 163 LT 280, 56 TLR 951
    600
Liebeskind, Re [1952] CLY 1349 745
Life Association of Scotland v Douglas (1886) 13 R 910, Ct of Sess
    792
Lightburne v Gill (1764) 3 Bro Parl Cas 250, HL 381
Lightfoot v Burstall (1863) 1 Hem & M 546, 33 LJ Ch 188, 10 Jur NS 308, 3 New Rep
    112, 12 WR 148, 9 LT 711 237
Lightfoot v Maybery. See Watkins, Re, Maybery v Lightfoot
Lighton's Goods, Re (1828) 1 Hag Ecc 235 616
Lilford (Lord) v Keck (1862) 30 Beav 295 126
Lill v Lill (1857) 23 Beav 446, 5 WR 390 .... 395, 476
Lilleyman v Lilleyman [2012] EWHC 821 (Ch), [2013] Ch 1, [2013] 1 All ER 302
    578
Lilleyman v Lilleyman [2012] EWHC 1056 (Ch), [2013] 1 Costs LR 25, [2013] 1 All ER
    325 604
Lillie v Lillie (1829) 3 Hag Ecc 184 106
Lillie v Willis (1899) 31 OR 198 443
Lilly's Will Trusts, Re, Public Trustee v Johnstone [1948] 2 All ER 906, [1949] LJR 270,
    92 Sol Jo 705 294
Lim (an infant) v Walia [2014] EWCA Civ 1076, [2015] Ch 375, [2015] 1 All ER 902,
    [2015] 2 WLR 583, [2014] 3 FCR 284, [2015] 2 FLR 339, [2014] Fam Law 1517,
    164 NLJ 7622, [2015] WTLR 69, [2014] All ER (D) 55 (Aug)
    585
Limond, Re, Limond v Cunliffe [1915] 2 Ch 240, 84 LJ Ch 833, [1914–15] All ER Rep
    214, 59 Sol Jo 613, 113 LT 815 .... 44, 79
Limpus v Arnold (1884) 15 QBD 300, 54 LJQB 85, 33 WR 537, CA
    235
Lincoln v Windsor (1851) 9 Hare 158, 20 LJ Ch 531, 15 Jur 765, 18 LTOS 39
    653
Lincoln v Wright (1841) 4 Beav 427 .... 1253, 1301
Lincoln (Lady) v Pelham (1804) 10 Ves 166 396
Lindgren v Lindgren (1846) 9 Beav 358, 15 LJ Ch 428, 10 Jur 674
    .... 215, 279
Lindley's Goods, Re, Lindley v Lindley [1953] P 203, [1953] 2 All ER 319, [1953] 3 WLR
    168, 97 Sol Jo 439, P, D and Admlty 775, 808
Lindop, Re, Lee-Barber v Reynolds [1942] Ch 377, [1942] 2 All ER 46, 111 LJ Ch 226, 86
    Sol Jo 242, 167 LT 235, 58 TLR 291 .... 33, 746
Lindop v Agus [2009] EWHC 1795 (Ch), [2009] WTLR 1175
    567
Lindsay, Re (1852) 5 Ir Jur 97 468
Lindsay, Re (1892) 8 TLR 507, P, D and Admlty 110
Lindsay v Ellicott (1876) 46 LJ Ch 878 314
Lindsay v Lindsay (1872) LR 2 P & D 459, 36 JP 808, 27 LT 322
    7
Lines v Lines (1869) 17 WR 1004, 22 LT 400 288
Lines Bros Ltd, Re [1983] Ch 1, [1982] 2 All ER 183, [1982] 2 WLR 1010, CA
    967
Ling v Ling [2001] All ER (D) 322 (Nov) 167, 169, 175, 303, 305, 328, 331
Lipinski's Will Trusts, Re, Gosschalk v Levy [1976] Ch 235, [1977] 1 All ER 33, [1976] 3
    WLR 522, 120 Sol Jo 473 36
Lipkin Gorman (a firm) v Karpnale Ltd [1991] 2 AC 548, [1992] 4 All ER 512, [1991] 3
    WLR 10, 12 LDAB 73, [1991] NLJR 815, 135 Sol Jo LB 36, HL
    .... 1097, 1099
Lipscomb v Lipscomb (1868) LR 7 Eq 501, 38 LJ Ch 90, 17 WR 252, 19 LT 342
    1009
Lister v Bradley (1841) 1 Hare 10, 11 LJ Ch 49, 5 Jur 1034
    .... 428, 431, 434
Lister v Pickford (1865) 34 Beav 576, 34 LJ Ch 582, 11 Jur NS 649, 6 New Rep 243, 13
    WR 827, [1861–73] All ER Rep 374, 12 LT 587 286
Lister v Smith (1863) 28 JP 40, 33 LJPM & A 29, 10 Jur NS 107, 3 Sw & Tr 282, 12 WR
    319, 9 LT 578, [1861–73] All ER Rep Ext 1521 54
Lister v Tidd (1861) 29 Beav 618 335
Lister's Goods, Re (1894) 58 JP 481, 70 LT 812, P, D and Admlty
    628

PARA

Litchfield, Re, Horton v Jones (1911) 104 LT 631 407

Litt's Will Trusts, Re, Parry v Cooper [1946] Ch 154, [1946] 1 All ER 314, 115 LJ Ch
114, 90 Sol Jo 116, 174 LT 184, 62 TLR 303, CA 231

Little, Re, Barclays Bank Ltd v Bournemouth and East Dorset Hospital
Management Committee [1953] 2 All ER 852, [1953] 1 WLR 1132, 97 Sol Jo 574
.... 278

Little, Re, Foster v Cooper [1960] 1 All ER 387, [1960] 1 WLR 495, 104 Sol Jo 369, P, D
and Admlty 65, 67

Little v Governors of County Down Infirmary [1918] 1 IR 221
.... 1247

Littledale v Bickersteth (1876) 24 WR 507 127

Littlejohns v Household (1855) 21 Beav 29 444

Littlewood, Re, Clark v Littlewood [1931] 1 Ch 443, 100 LJ Ch 243, [1930] All ER Rep
151, 144 LT 718, 47 TLR 79 .... 994, 1012

Littras v Littras [1995] 2 VR 283, Vict SC 131, 141

Liver, Re, Scott v Woods (1956) 106 L Jo 75 .... 903, 905

Liverpool Borough Bank v Walker (1859) 4 De G & J 24
.... 1039

Liverpool Dock Acts, Re, Re Colshead's Will Trusts (1852) 2 De G & J 690
.... 256, 408

Livesey v Harding (1830) Taml 460, 1 Russ & M 636 474

Livesey v Livesey (1827) 3 Russ 287, 6 LJOS Ch 13 1098

Livesey v Livesey (1849) 2 HL Cas 419, 13 Jur 371, 13 LTOS 153
.... 225, 242

Livesey's Settlement Trusts, Re, Livesey v Livesey [1953] 2 All ER 723, [1953] 1 WLR
1114, 97 Sol Jo 572 404

Livingston, Re (1907) 14 OLR 161 431

Livingstone, Re, Livingstone v Durell (1917) 61 Sol Jo 384
.... 283

Llangattock (Lord), Re, Johnson v Central Board of Finance of Church of England (1918)
34 TLR 341 .... 370, 1054

Llanover (Baroness), Re, Herbert v Freshfield (No 2) [1903] 2 Ch 330, 72 LJ Ch 729, 51
WR 615, 88 LT 856, 19 TLR 524 .... 2, 240

Llewellin's Will Trusts, Re, Griffiths v Wilcox [1949] Ch 225, [1949] 1 All ER 487,
[1949] LJR 724, 93 Sol Jo 148 649

Llewellyn v Earl of Jersey (1843) 12 LJ Ex 243, 11 M & W 183
.... 269

Llewellyn's Trust, Re (1861) 29 Beav 171, 54 ER 592 .... 1123, 1126

Lloyd v Branton (1817) 3 Mer 108 134–135

Lloyd v Coote and Ball [1915] 1 KB 242, 84 LJKB 567, 112 LT 344
.... 976

Lloyd v Davies. See Doe d Lloyd v Davies

Lloyd v Jackson (1867) LR 2 QB 269, 7 B & S 683, 36 LJQB 169, 15 WR 408, Ex Ch
.... 376

Lloyd v Lloyd (1841) 4 Beav 231, 10 LJ Ch 327, 5 Jur 673
.... 1115

Lloyd v Lloyd (1852) 2 Sim NS 255, 21 LJ Ch 596, 16 Jur 306, 19 LTOS 84
.... 128, 132, 134

Lloyd v Lloyd (1856) 3 K & J 20 .... 429, 432

Lloyd v Lloyd (1869) LR 7 Eq 458, 38 LJ Ch 458, 17 WR 702, 20 LT 898
.... 284

Lloyd v Lloyd (1875) 23 WR 787, Ct of Ch 1245

Lloyd v Lloyd (1886) 34 WR 608, 54 LT 841 293

Lloyd v Roberts (1858) 12 Moo PCC 158, PC 895–896

Lloyd v Tweedy [1898] 1 IR 5 .... 381, 449

Lloyd's Trust Instruments, Re (24 June 1970, unreported)
.... 45

Lloyds Bank Ltd v Jones [1955] 2 QB 298, [1955] 3 WLR 5, 53 LGR 433, 99 Sol Jo 398,
165 Estates Gazette 537, sub nom Lower Onibury Farm, Onibury, Shropshire, Re,
Lloyds Bank Ltd v Jones [1955] 2 All ER 409, CA 942, 1224

Lloyds Bank plc v Duker [1987] 3 All ER 193, [1987] 1 WLR 1324, 131 Sol Jo 1358,
[1987] LS Gaz R 3254 1053

Lobley v Stocks (1854) 19 Beav 392 403

Locke v Dunlop (1888) 39 Ch D 387, 57 LJ Ch 1010, 59 LT 683, 4 TLR 712, CA
.... 244, 330, 333

Locke v James (1843) 13 LJ Ex 186, 11 M & W 901, 1 LTOS 387
.... 108

PARA

Locke v Lamb (1867) LR 4 Eq 372, 15 WR 1010, 16 LT 616
.... 308, 427–428, 430, 433
Locker v Bradley (1842) 5 Beav 593, 6 Jur 1098 305
Lockhart v Hardy (1846) 9 Beav 379, 10 Jur 728 371
Lockhart v Reilly (1857) 1 De G & J 464, 27 LJ Ch 54
.... 963
Lockwood v Sikes (1884) 51 LT 562 463
Lodwig, Re, Lodwig v Evans [1916] 2 Ch 26, 85 LJ Ch 585, 60 Sol Jo 494, 114 LT 881,
 32 TLR 491, [1916–17] All ER Rep Ext 1425, CA 429
Loftus, Re, Green v Gaul [2006] EWCA Civ 1124, [2006] 4 All ER 1110, [2007] 1 WLR
 591, 9 ITELR 107, [2006] NLJR 1365, (2006) Times, 1 September, [2007] 1 P & CR
 D30, [2006] All ER (D) 454 (Jul) 1163, 1185
Loftus v Stoney (1867) 15 WR 550, 17 I Ch R 178 .... 95, 97
Logan v Fairlie (1825) 2 Sim & St 284, 3 LJOS Ch 152; revsd (1835) 1 My & Cr 59
.... 669
Logan v Wienholt (1833) 7 Bli NS 1, 1 Cl & Fin 611, 5 ER 674, [1824–34] All ER Rep
 281, sub nom Wienholt v Logan 3 Sim 141, HL 22
Loir's Policies, Re [1916] WN 87 665
Lomax v Holmden (1749) 1 Ves Sen 290 300
Lomax v Lomax (1849) 12 Beav 285, 19 LJ Ch 137, 13 Jur 1064, 14 LTOS 482
.... 1012
Lombe v Stoughton (1849) 17 Sim 84, 18 LJ Ch 400, 13 LTOS 398
.... 290
Lomer, Re, Public Trustee v Victoria Hospital for Children [1929] 1 Ch 731, 98 LJ Ch 201,
 140 LT 687 1130
Londesborough, Re, Bridgeman v Fitzgerald (1880) 50 LJ Ch 9, 43 LT 408
.... 250, 296
London City v Garway (1706) 2 Vern 571, 23 ER 972 469
London Wine Co (Shippers) Ltd, Re [1986] PCC 121 116
Londonderry's Settlement, Re, Peat v Walsh [1965] Ch 918, [1964] 3 All ER 855, [1965] 2
 WLR 229, 108 Sol Jo 896, CA 1196, 1210
Long v Blackall (1799) 3 Ves 486, 30 ER 1119 364
Long v Dennis (1767) 4 Burr 2052, 1 Wm Bl 630 132
Long v Hebb (1652) Sty 341 645
Long v Hughes (1831) 1 De G & Sm 364, 7 LJOS Ch 105
.... 1090
Long v Kent (1865) 11 Jur NS 724, 6 New Rep 354, 13 WR 961, 12 LT 794
.... 153
Long v Lane (1885) 17 LR Ir 11; on appeal (1885) 17 LR Ir 24, CA
.... 242, 443
Long v Overden (1881) 16 Ch D 691, 50 LJ Ch 314, 29 WR 709, 44 LT 462
.... 1085
Long v Wakeling (1839) 1 Beav 400 670
Long v Watkinson (1852) 17 Beav 471, 21 LJ Ch 844, 16 Jur 235, 19 LTOS 309
.... 27, 165, 363
Long (Fred) & Son Ltd v Burgess [1950] 1 KB 115, [1949] 2 All ER 484, 93 Sol Jo 631,
 65 TLR 606, CA 644–645
Long and Feaver v Symes and Hannam (1832) 3 Hag Ecc 771
.... 627–628, 1263
Longford v Eyre (1721) 1 P Wms 740 71
Longford (Earl) v Purdon (1877) 1 LR Ir 75 899
Longley, Re, Longley and Longley v Longley [1981] CLY 2885
.... 598
Longley v Longley (1871) LR 13 Eq 133, 41 LJ Ch 168, 20 WR 227, 25 LT 736
.... 284
Longman, Re, Westminster Bank Ltd v Hatton [1955] 1 All ER 455, [1955] 1 WLR 197,
 99 Sol Jo 169 465
Longmore v Broom (1802) 7 Ves 124 .... 254, 320
Longmore v Elcum (1843) 2 Y & C Ch Cas 363, 12 LJ Ch 469, 1 LTOS 311
.... 370
Long-Sutton's Estate, Re [1912] P 97, 81 LJP 28, 56 Sol Jo 293, 106 LT 643, P, D and
 Admlty 743, 745
Longton v Wilsby (1897) 76 LT 770 657
Longworth, Re, Longworth v Campbell [1910] 1 IR 23 .... 385, 392
Longworth v Bellamy (1871) 40 LJ Ch 513 346
Lonsdale (Earl) v Countess of Berchtoldt (1854) Kay 646, 23 LJ Ch 816, 18 Jur 811,
 24 LTOS 51 .... 369, 382

PARA

Lonsdale (Earl) v Countess of Berchtoldt (1857) 3 K & J 185, 3 Jur NS 328
.... 154, 374

Lonsdale's Will Trusts, Re, Lowther v Lowther [1960] Ch 288, [1959] 3 All ER 679, [1959] 3 WLR 879, 38 ATC 331, [1959] TR 335, 103 Sol Jo 939, CA
.... 1131

Loom, Re, Fulford v Reversionary Interest Society Ltd [1910] 2 Ch 230, 79 LJ Ch 704, 54 Sol Jo 583, 102 LT 907 152–153

Loomes v Stotherd (1823) 1 Sim & St 458, 1 LJOS Ch 220
.... 1203

Lord's Estate, Re, Lord v Lord (1867) 2 Ch App 782, 36 LJ Ch 533, 15 WR 1118, 17 LT 105 1080

Lord Fermoy, Re (1890) MacCarthy's Leading Cases in Land Purchase Law 55
.... 1133

Lord's Settlement, Re, Martins Bank Ltd v Lord [1947] 2 All ER 685, [1948] LJR 207, 91 Sol Jo 654 324

Lorillard, Re, Griffiths v Catforth [1922] 2 Ch 638, 92 LJ Ch 148, [1922] All ER Rep 500, 127 LT 613, 38 TLR 666, CA 803, 865, 960, 968

Loring v Thomas (1861) 1 Drew & Sm 497, 30 LJ Ch 789, 7 Jur NS 1116, 9 WR 919, 62 ER 469, [1861–73] All ER Rep 620, 5 LT 269 .... 247, 293, 323, 331

Loring v Woodland Trust [2014] EWCA Civ 1314, [2015] 1 WLR 3238, [2014] All ER (D) 198 Oct 657

Lory, Re (1891) 7 TLR 419 346

Lory's Will Trusts, Re, Lambrick v Public Trustee of Colony and Protectorate of Kenya [1950] 1 All ER 349, 94 Sol Jo 98, 66 (pt 1) TLR 330 291

Lothian's Trustees v Back 1918 SC 401, Ct of Sess 111

Louch v Peters (1834) 1 My & K 489, 3 LJ Ch 167 1133

Loudon v Ryder (No 2) [1953] Ch 423, [1953] 2 WLR 863, 97 Sol Jo 299, sub nom Lewis Declaration of Trust, Re, Lewis v Lewis, Re Lewis Declaration of Trust, Lewis v Ryder [1953] 1 All ER 1005 647

Loughhead, Re, Hamilton v Loughhead [1918] 1 IR 227
.... 386

Loughlin's Will, Re, Acheson v O'Meara [1906] VLR 597
.... 220

Louis, Re, Louis v Treloar (1916) 32 TLR 313 .... 201, 222

Louis v Louis (1863) 9 Jur NS 244, 7 LT 666 334

Love, Re, Hill v Spurgeon (1885) 29 Ch D 348, 54 LJ Ch 816, 33 WR 449, 52 LT 398, CA 1196

Love v Honeybourne (1824) 4 Dow & Ry KB 814 1299

Love v L'Estrange (1727) 5 Bro Parl Cas 59, HL 413

Love v Love (1881) 7 LR Ir 306 416

Love's Goods, Re (1881) 7 LR Ir 178 613

Love's Goods, Re (1901) 17 TLR 721, P, D and Admlty
.... 761

Loveacres d Mudge v Blight (1775) 1 Cowp 352 .... 379, 395

Loveday v Hopkins (1755) Amb 273 341

Loveday's Goods, Re [1900] P 154, 69 LJP 48, 82 LT 692, P, D and Admlty
.... 850

Lovegrove's Goods, Re (1862) 26 JP 375, 31 LJPM & A 87, 8 Jur NS 442, 2 Sw & Tr 453, 6 LT 131 9

Lovejoy v Crafter (1865) 35 Beav 149 331

Lovelace v Lovelace (1585) 1 And 132, Cro Eliz 40, sub nom Lovelace's Case 2 Leon 35, Sav 75 334

Loveland, Re, Loveland v Loveland [1906] 1 Ch 542, 75 LJ Ch 314, 94 LT 336, 22 TLR 321 354

Lovell, Re, Sparks v Southall [1920] 1 Ch 122, 88 LJ Ch 540, 64 Sol Jo 35, 122 LT 26, 35 TLR 715 .... 121, 131

Lovett, Re, Ambler v Lindsay (1876) 3 Ch D 198, 45 LJ Ch 768, 23 WR 982, 35 LT 93 .... 636, 978, 1172

Lovibond (John) & Sons Ltd v Vincent [1929] 1 KB 687, 27 LGR 471, 93 JP 161, 98 LJKB 402, [1929] All ER Rep 59, 73 Sol Jo 252, 141 LT 116, 45 TLR 383, CA
.... 942

Low v Burron (1734) 3 P Wms 262 459

Low v Carter (1839) 1 Beav 426, 48 ER 1005 379

Low v Guthrie [1909] AC 278, 78 LJPC 126, HL 905

Low v Smith (1856) 25 LJ Ch 503, 2 Jur NS 344, 4 WR 429
.... 341

PARA

Lowe v Lord Huntingtower (1824) 4 Russ 532n, 2 LJOSKB 164
.... 212
Lowe v Shields [1902] 1 IR 320, CA 1253
Lowe v Thomas (1854) Kay 369; on appeal (1854) 5 De GM & G 315, 23 LJ Ch 616, 2
    Eq Rep 742, 18 Jur 563, 2 WR 499, 23 LTOS 238 .... 241, 293
Lowe's Estate, Re, Swann v Rockley [1938] 2 All ER 774, 82 Sol Jo 454
.... 293
Lowe's Goods, Re (1898) 78 LT 566, P, D and Admlty 787, 820
Lowe's Will Trusts, Re, More v A-G [1973] 2 All ER 1136, [1973] 1 WLR 882, 117 Sol Jo
    489, CA 555
Lowfield v Stoneham (1746) 2 Stra 1261 207
Lowman, Re, Devenish v Pester [1895] 2 Ch 348, 64 LJ Ch 567, 12 R 362, 72 LT 816, 11
    TLR 396, CA 172, 291, 385–386
Lowndes v Stone (1799) 4 Ves 649 .... 320, 341
Lowry v Fulton (1839) 9 Sim 115, 8 LJ Ch 314, 3 Jur 454
.... 1267
Lowry v Patterson (1874) IR 8 Eq 372, 8 LR Ir 372 135
Lowry's Goods, Re (1874) LR 3 P & D 157, 38 JP 631, 43 LJP & M 34, 22 WR 352, 30
    LT 695 613
Lowry's Will Trusts, Re, Barclays Bank Ltd v United Newcastle-upon-Tyne Hospitals Board
    of Governors [1967] Ch 638, [1966] 3 All ER 955, 110 Sol Jo 871
.... 138, 407, 414, 416, 422
Lowson v Copeland (1787) 2 Bro CC 156 959
Lowther v Cavendish (1758) 1 Eden 99, Amb 356; affd sub nom Cavendish (Lord) v
    Lowther (1759) 3 Bro Parl Cas 186, HL 143
Lowther v Condon (1741) 2 Atk 127, Barn Ch 327 438
Lowthorpe-Lutwidge v Lowthorpe-Lutwidge [1935] P 151, 104 LJKB 71, [1935] All ER
    Rep 338, 153 LT 103, P, D and Admlty 95
Loyd v Finlayson (1797) 2 Esp 564 670
Lucas v Carline (1840) 2 Beav 367 428
Lucas v Goldsmid (1861) 29 Beav 657, 30 LJ Ch 935, 7 Jur NS 719, 9 WR 759, 4 LT 632
.... 348, 384, 395
Lucas v Jenner (1833) 1 Cr & M 597, 2 Dowl 64, 3 Tyr 564
.... 1291
Lucas v Williams (No 2) (1862) 4 De GF & J 439, 10 WR 677
.... 1040
Lucas-Tooth, Re, Lucas-Tooth v Public Trustee (1923) 156 LT Jo 382
.... 284
Lucas-Tooth v Lucas-Tooth [1921] 1 AC 594, 90 LJ Ch 347, 65 Sol Jo 377, 125 LT 225,
    HL 339
Lucena v Lucena (1876) 7 Ch D 255, 36 LT 87, CA; on appeal (1877) 7 Ch D 266, 47 LJ
    Ch 203, 26 WR 254, 37 LT 420, CA 317
Luckcraft v Pridham (1879) 48 LJ Ch 636 992
Lucking's Will Trusts, Re, Renwick v Lucking [1967] 3 All ER 726, [1968] 1 WLR 866,
    112 Sol Jo 444 1252
Luddy, Re, Peard v Morton (1883) 25 Ch D 394, 53 LJ Ch 21, 32 WR 272, 49 LT 706
.... 444, 450
Ludlow, Re, Bence-Jones v A-G (1923) 93 LJ Ch 30, CA
.... 11
Lugar v Harman (1786) 1 Cox Eq Cas 250 .... 332, 396
Lumley v Robbins (1853) 10 Hare 621, 22 LJ Ch 869, 1 Eq Rep 129, 17 Jur 410, 1 WR
    285, 22 LTOS 40 408
Lundy v Lundy (1895) 24 SCR 650 39
Lunn v Osborne (1834) 7 Sim 56, 3 LJ Ch 233 .... 200, 407
Lupton's Estate, Re [1905] P 321, 74 LJP 162, 94 LT 100, P, D and Admlty
.... 369
Lush's Goods, Re (1887) 13 PD 20, 52 JP 199, 57 LJP 23, 36 WR 847, 58 LT 684, P, D
    and Admlty 613
Lushington v Boldero (1851) 15 Beav 1, 21 LJ Ch 49, 16 Jur 140, 18 LTOS 151
.... 931
Lushington v Onslow (1848) 12 Jur 465, 11 LTOS 206, 6 Notes of Cases 183
.... 85
Lushington v Penrice (1868) 16 WR 836, 18 LT 597 412
Lusternik v Lusternik [1972] Fam 125, [1972] 1 All ER 592, [1972] 2 WLR 203, 116 Sol
    Jo 98, CA 591

                                                                                          PARA
Lutwyche v Lutwyche (1735) 2 Eq Cas Abr 448, Cas temp Talb 276
.... 564
Luxford v Cheeke (1683) 3 Lev 125, sub nom Brown v Cutter 2 Show 152, T Raym 427
.... 253, 306, 446
Lybbe's Will Trusts, Re, Kildahl v Bowker [1954] 1 All ER 487, [1954] 1 WLR 573, 98 Sol
    Jo 215 410
Lyddon v Ellison (1854) 19 Beav 565, 18 Jur 1006, 2 WR 690, 24 LTOS 123
.... 333
Lynch, Re, Lynch v Lynch [1943] 1 All ER 168, 87 Sol Jo 48, 168 LT 189, 59 TLR 130
.... 346
Lynch v Bellew and Fallon (1820) 3 Phillim 424 615
Lynch v Milner. See A-G v Milner
Lynch Blosse, Re, Richards v Lynch Blosse [1899] WN 27, 43 Sol Jo 297
.... 1126
Lyne's Settlement Trusts, Re, Re Gibbs, Lyne v Gibbs [1919] 1 Ch 80, 88 LJ Ch 1,
    [1918–19] All ER Rep 419, 63 Sol Jo 53, 120 LT 81, 35 TLR 44, CA
.... 282
Lyne Stephens v Lubbock, Re Lyne Stephens (1895) 11 TLR 564
.... 932
Lyne's Trust, Re (1869) LR 8 Eq 65, 38 LJ Ch 471, 20 LT 735
.... 346
Lynn v Beaver (1823) Turn & R 63, 23 RR 185 200
Lynn v Kerridge (1737) West temp Hard 172 293
Lyon v Coward (1846) 15 Sim 287, 15 LJ Ch 460, 10 Jur 486, 7 LTOS 385
.... 325–326
Lyon v Geddes (1807) 9 East 170 407
Lyon v Mitchell (1816) 1 Madd 467 392
Lyon's Trusts, Re (1879) 48 LJ Ch 245 276
Lysaght v Edwards (1876) 2 Ch D 499, 45 LJ Ch 554, 3 Char Pr Cas 243, 24 WR 778, 34
    LT 787 .... 282, 996
Lytton v Lytton (1793) 4 Bro CC 441 460
Lywood v Kimber (1860) 29 Beav 38, sub nom Lywood v Warwick 30 LJ Ch 507, 7 Jur
    NS 507, 9 WR 88 335

M

M (vulnerable adult) (testamentary capacity), Re [2009] EWHC 2525 (Fam), [2010]
    3 All ER 682, [2009] All ER (D) 314 (Oct) 47
MCP Pension Trustees Ltd v AON Pension Trustees Ltd [2009] EWHC 1351 (Ch), [2010]
    1 All ER (Comm) 323, [2010] 2 WLR 268, [2009] ALL ER (D) 222 (Jul)
.... 965
Mabank v Brooks (1780) 2 Dick 577, sub nom Maybank v Brooks 1 Bro CC 84
.... 160, 164
Maber, Re, Ward v Maber [1928] Ch 88, 97 LJ Ch 101, 138 LT 318
.... 312
Maberley v Strode (1797) 3 Ves 450 443
Macadam, Re, Dallow and Moscrop v Codd [1946] Ch 73, [1945] 2 All ER 664, 115 LJ
    Ch 14, 89 Sol Jo 531, 173 LT 395, 62 TLR 48 .... 656, 1030
M'Afee, Re, Mack v Quirey [1909] 1 IR 124 282
McAfee v Kerr (1918) 52 ILT 178 285
M'Alpine v Studholme (1883) 10 R 837, 20 SLR 551, Ct of Sess
.... 1130
Macandrew's Will Trusts, Re, Stephens v Barclays Bank Ltd [1964] Ch 704, [1963]
    2 All ER 919, [1963] 3 WLR 822, 107 Sol Jo 910 .... 228, 253, 441, 453
M'Ara v M'Cay (1889) 23 LR Ir 138 97
Macartney, Re, Brookhouse v Barman (1920) 36 TLR 394
.... 156
Macaulay's Estate, Re, Macaulay v O'Donnell [1943] Ch 435n, HL
.... 36
McBroom, Re [1992] 2 FLR 49, [1992] Fam Law 376 597
McC's Estate, Re (1978) 9 Fam Law 26, sub nom CA v CC (1978) Times, 18 November
.... 580
MacCabe v Hussey (1831) 5 Bli NS 715, 2 Dow & Cl 440, HL
.... 904
M'Cabe's Goods, Re (1862) 26 JP 744, 31 LJPM & A 190, 2 Sw & Tr 474, 10 WR 848, 6
    LT 474 112

PARA

McCabe's Goods, Re (1873) LR 3 P & D 94, 38 JP 9, 42 LJP & M 79, 29 LT 250
.... 82, 108

McCalmont, Re, Rooper v McCalmont (1903) 19 TLR 490
.... 286

M'Cann, Re, Donnelly v Moore [1916] 1 IR 255 348

McCarthy, Re, National Bank Ltd v Archbishop of Dublin [1958] IR 311
.... 1087

M'Carthy v M'Carthy (1878) 1 LR Ir 189, 3 LR Ir 317
.... 182

McCausland v Young [1949] NI 49, CA 140

McClean v Kennard (1874) 9 Ch App 336, 43 LJ Ch 323, 22 WR 382, 30 LT 186,
[1874–80] All ER Rep Ext 2058 1216

M'Cleary, Re, Moffat v M'Cleary [1932] 1 IR 16 139

M'Cleland v Shaw (1805) 2 Sch & Lef 538 1012

McClellan, Re, McClellan v McClellan (1885) 29 Ch D 495, 54 LJ Ch 659, 33 WR 888,
52 LT 741, 1 TLR 400, CA 1203

McClement's Trustees v Campbell 1951 SC 167, Ct of Sess
.... 278

M'Clure v Evans (or Dawson) (1861) 29 Beav 422, 30 LJ Ch 295, 7 Jur NS 204, 9 WR
428, 3 LT 870 .... 217, 404

McClymont v Hooper (1973) 47 ALJR 222, Aust HC 471

McCormick v Grogan (1869) 4 App Cas 82, LR 4 HL 82, 17 WR 961, HL
.... 221

McCormick v Simpson [1907] AC 494, 77 LJPC 12, 97 LT 616, PC
.... 450

M'Creight v M'Creight (1849) 13 I Eq R 314, 2 Ir Jur 17
.... 37, 1073

Macculloch v Anderson [1904] AC 55, HL 236, 308

M'Culloch v Dawes (1826) 5 LJOSKB 56, 9 Dow & Ry KB 40
.... 974, 976

M'Cutcheon v Allen (1880) 5 LR Ir 268 428

M'Dermott v Wallace (1842) 5 Beav 142, 6 Jur 547 395

McDonald, Re (1903) 20 WR 968, 6 OLR 478, 23 CLT 326
.... 387

McDonald, Re (1911) 30 NZLR 896 .... 2, 6

Macdonald, Re, Dick v Fraser [1897] 2 Ch 181, 66 LJ Ch 630, 45 WR 628, 76 LT 713
.... 976–977

Macdonald, Re, McAlpin v Macdonald (1889) 59 LJ Ch 231, 62 LT 541
.... 986

M'Donald v Bryce (1853) 16 Beav 581, 22 LJ Ch 779, 17 Jur 335, 1 WR 261, 21 LTOS
54 318

McDonald v Horn [1995] 1 All ER 961, [1995] ICR 685, [1994] NLJR 1515, CA
.... 1196, 1274

Macdonald v Irvine (1878) 8 Ch D 101, 47 LJ Ch 494, 26 WR 381, 38 LT 155, CA
.... 114, 156, 1122–1123

Macdonald v Richardson (1858) 1 Giff 81, 5 Jur NS 9, 32 LTOS 237
.... 658

McDonald v Trustees, Executors and Agency Co Ltd (1902) 28 VLR 442
.... 131

M'Donnell v Jebb (1865) 16 I Ch R 359 393

McDonnell v Morrow (1889) 23 LR Ir 591 294

McDonnell v Neil [1951] AC 342, 95 Sol Jo 298, [1951] 1 TLR 642, PC
.... 397

M'Donnell v Prendergast (1830) 3 Hag Ecc 212 627

Macduff, Re, Macduff v Macduff [1896] 2 Ch 451, 65 LJ Ch 700, 45 WR 154,
[1895–9] All ER Rep 154, 40 Sol Jo 651, 74 LT 706, 12 TLR 452, CA
.... 11

McElligott, Re, Grant v McElligott [1944] Ch 216, [1944] 1 All ER 441, 113 LJ Ch 277,
88 Sol Jo 170, 171 LT 10, 60 TLR 246 .... 377, 385

McEuen, Re, McEuen v Phelps [1913] 2 Ch 704, 83 LJ Ch 66, 30 TLR 44, sub nom Re
McEwen, McEwen v Phelps [1911–13] All ER Rep 176, 58 Sol Jo 82, 109 LT 701, CA
.... 1093, 1118

McEwan v Crombie (1883) 25 Ch D 175, 53 LJ Ch 24, 32 WR 115, 49 LT 499
.... 1201

McFee, Re, McFee v Toner (1910) 79 LJ Ch 676, 103 LT 210
.... 313

McGarrity, Re, Ballance and Benson v McGarrity (1912) 46 ILT 175
.... 408, 435

PARA

McGeorge, Re, Ratcliff v McGeorge [1963] Ch 544, [1963] 1 All ER 519, [1963] 2 WLR 767, 107 Sol Jo 253 .... 415–416, 1082–1083

MacGillivray's Estate, Re [1946] 2 All ER 301, 90 Sol Jo 488, 175 LT 383, 62 TLR 538, CA 81, 716

McGovern v A-G [1982] Ch 321, [1981] 3 All ER 493, [1982] 2 WLR 222, [1981] TR 157, 125 Sol Jo 255 258–259

McGowan v Grimes (1921) 55 ILT 208 142

McGrane, Re, McGrane v McGrane (1964) 98 ILTR 95
.... 450

McGredy v IRC [1951] NI 155 423

Macgregor v Macgregor (1845) 2 Coll 192 325

M'Gregor v M'Gregor (1859) 1 De GF & J 63 .... 326, 334, 336, 395

M'Gregor v Topham (1850) 3 HL Cas 132 895

Machell v Weeding (1836) 8 Sim 4, Donnelly 26, 5 LJ Ch 182
.... 473

Machu, Re (1882) 21 Ch D 838 142

M'Hugh v M'Hugh [1908] 1 IR 155 .... 205, 217, 328

M'Intyre v Miller (1845) 2 Dow & L 708, 14 LJ Ex 180, 13 M & W 725, 4 LTOS 338, 357 1232

McIsaac v Beaton (1905) 37 SCR 143, 38 NSR 60 370

M'Kane's Goods, Re (1887) 21 LR Ir 1 613

Mackay, Re, Mackay v Gould [1906] 1 Ch 25, 75 LJ Ch 47, 54 WR 88, 50 Sol Jo 43, 93 LT 694 1055

M'Kay v M'Alister (1912) 46 ILT 88 461

M'Kay v M'Kay [1900] 1 IR 213 .... 174, 298

M'Kay v M'Kay [1901] 1 IR 109, 120 422

Mackay v Rawlinson (1919) 63 Sol Jo 229, 35 TLR 223, P, D and Admlty
.... 70, 894

Mckechnie v Vaughan (1873) LR 15 Eq 289, 21 WR 399, 28 LT 263
.... 274

MacKechnie's Trustees v Macadam 1912 SC 1059, Ct of Sess
.... 1038

McKee, Re, Public Trustee v McKee [1931] 2 Ch 145, 100 LJ Ch 325, 75 Sol Jo 442, 145 LT 605, 47 TLR 424, CA 478–479, 516

Mackell v Winter (1797) 3 Ves 536 .... 428, 475

McKendrick v Winter (1889) 15 VLR 450, Vic Full Ct 125

M'Kenna v Everitt (1838) 1 Beav 134 58

McKenna v McCarten [1915] 1 IR 282 .... 231, 382

McKenna's Will Trusts, Re, Higgins v Bank of Ireland and McKenna [1947] IR 277
.... 140

Mackenzie v Bradbury (1865) 35 Beav 617, 34 LJ Ch 627, 11 Jur NS 650, 6 New Rep 283
.... 252

Mackenzie v Handasyde (1829) 2 Hag Ecc 211 903

Mackenzie v King (1848) 17 LJ Ch 448, 12 Jur 787, 12 LTOS 4
.... 443

Mackenzie v Mackenzie (1826) 2 Russ 262 403

Mackenzie v Taylor (1844) 7 Beav 467 1207

Mackenzie's Estate, Re [1909] P 305, 79 LJP 4, 26 TLR 39, P, D and Admlty
.... 106, 613

McKeown, Re (1874) 22 WR 292 1173

Mackett v Mackett (1872) LR 14 Eq 49, 41 LJ Ch 704, 20 WR 860
.... 370

M'Key's Goods, Re (1876) 11 IR Eq 220 67

Mackie v Mackie (1845) 5 Hare 70, 9 Jur 753 1124

Mackinlay, Re, Scrimgeour v Mackinlay (1911) 56 Sol Jo 142
.... 450

Mackinley v Sison (1837) 8 Sim 561, 1 Jur 558 277

Mackinnon v Peach (1833) 2 My & K 202 446

Mackinnon v Peach (1838) 2 Keen 555, 7 LJ Ch 211 .... 402, 411

M'Kinnon's Trustees v Brownlie. See Mackintosh (or Miller) v Gerrard

Mackintosh v Barber (1822) 1 Bing 50, 7 Moore CP 315
.... 1030

Mackintosh (or Miller) v Gerrard [1947] AC 461, [1948] LJR 692, 176 LT 262, 63 TLR 265, sub nom M'Kinnon's Trustees v Brownlie 1947 SC 27, HL
.... 247, 322

Mackworth v Hinxman (1836) 2 Keen 658, Donnelly 29, 5 LJ Ch 127
.... 375

PARA

Maclachlan, Re, Maclachlan v Campbell (1900) 26 VLR 548
.... 122

M'Lachlan v Taitt (1860) 28 Beav 407, 2 De GF & J 449, 30 LJ Ch 276, 6 Jur NS 1269, 9
WR 152, 3 LT 492 .... 248, 303, 413, 415

Maclaren v Stainton (1858) 27 LJ Ch 442, 4 Jur NS 199, 30 LTOS 331
.... 379

McLaughlin, Re [1922] P 235, 66 Sol Jo 578, 127 LT 527, 38 TLR 622, sub nom
McLaughlin v McLaughlin 91 LJP 205, P, D and Admlty
.... 841

McLean, Re, Lockhart v McLean [1950] IR 180 68

Maclean, Re, Williams v Nelson (1894) 11 TLR 82 293

M'Lean v Simpson (1887) 19 LR Ir 528 472

Macleay, Re (1875) LR 20 Eq 186, 44 LJ Ch 441, 23 WR 718, 32 LT 682
.... 142, 348

M'Leod v Drummond (1807) 14 Ves 353; on appeal (1810) 17 Ves 152
.... 924, 1023, 1025

McLeod v McNab [1891] AC 471, 60 LJP 70, 65 LT 266, PC
.... 111–112, 114

MacLeroth v Bacon (1799) 5 Ves 159 348

Macleur v Macleur (1868) LR 1 P & D 604, 37 LJP & M 68
.... 867

M'Loughlin's Estate, Re (1878) 1 LR Ir 421, Ir CA 137, 246

McLoughlin's Goods, Re [1936] IR 223 64

M'Mahon, Re, M'Mahon v M'Mahon [1901] 1 IR 489, 35 ILTR 10, Ir CA
.... 152, 414

M'Mahon v Rawlings (1848) 16 Sim 429 669

McMurdo, Re, Penfield v McMurdo [1902] 2 Ch 684, 71 LJ Ch 691, 50 WR 644, 46 Sol
Jo 550, 86 LT 814, [1900–3] All ER Rep Ext 1350, CA
.... 985, 987

M'Murdo's Goods, Re (1868) LR 1 P & D 540, 32 JP 72, 37 LJP & M 14, 3 Mar LC 37,
16 WR 283, 17 LT 393 80

Macnamara, Re, Hewitt v Jeans (1911) 104 LT 771 .... 147, 204

McNare, Re, McNare v McNare [1964] 3 All ER 373, [1964] 1 WLR 1255, 108 Sol Jo
839 598

McNeill, Re, Royal Bank of Scotland v MacPherson [1958] Ch 259, [1957] 3 All ER 508,
[1957] 3 WLR 1007, 36 ATC 301, [1957] TR 313, 101 Sol Jo 958, CA
.... 1129

McNeill, Re, Wright v Johnstone (1909) 26 WN 45, 9 SRNSW 220, NSW SC
.... 274

M'Neillie v Acton (1853) 4 De GM & G 744, 23 LJ Ch 11, 2 Eq Rep 21, 17 Jur 1041,
22 LTOS 111 1037

McNulty v McNulty [2002] EWHC 123 (Ch), [2002] WTLR 737
.... 574, 598

McParland v Coulson [1930] NI 138, CA 858

McPhail v Doulton [1971] AC 424, [1970] 2 All ER 228, [1970] 2 WLR 1110, 114 Sol Jo
375, HL 11, 33

MacPhail v Phillips [1904] 1 IR 155 .... 250, 288, 296

Macpherson v Macpherson (1852) 16 Jur 847, 1 WR 8, 19 LTOS 221, 1 Macq 243, HL
.... 225, 1123

McPhilemy v Times Newspapers Ltd [1999] 3 All ER 775, [1999] EMLR 751, CA
.... 875

McRae, Re, Forster v Davis (1883) 25 Ch D 16, 53 LJ Ch 1132, 32 WR 304, 49 LT 544,
CA 1178

McRae, Re, Norden v McRae (1883) 25 Ch D 16, 53 LJ Ch 1132, 32 WR 304, 49 LT
544, CA 1178

McRea, Re, Norden v McRea (1886) 32 Ch D 613, 55 LJ Ch 708, sub nom Re McRea,
Narden v McRea 54 LT 728 1205

M'Sweeney v Murphy [1919] 1 IR 16 1172

Madden's Goods, Re [1905] 2 IR 612, 39 ILT 205 67

Maddison v Alderson (1883) 8 App Cas 467, 47 JP 821, 52 LJQB 737, 31 WR 820,
[1881–5] All ER Rep 742, 49 LT 303, HL 21, 1221

Maddison v Andrew (1747) 1 Ves Sen 57, 27 ER 889, [1558–1774] All ER Rep 524
.... 426, 428

Maddison v Chapman (1858) 4 K & J 709; affd (1859) 3 De G & J 536
.... 410, 422, 440

PARA

Maddison v Chapman (1861) 1 John & H 470, 70 ER 831
.... 444
Maddock, Re, Llewelyn v Washington [1902] 2 Ch 220, 71 LJ Ch 567, 50 WR 598, 86 LT
  644, CA 221–222
Maddock v Legg (1858) 25 Beav 531 336
Maddock's Goods, Re (1874) LR 3 P & D 169, 38 JP 631, 43 LJP & M 29, 22 WR 741,
  [1874–80] All ER Rep 367, 30 LT 696 .... 63, 75
Maddy's Estate, Re, Maddy v Maddy [1901] 2 Ch 820, 71 LJ Ch 18, 45 Sol Jo 673, 85 LT
  341 204
Maden v Taylor (1876) 45 LJ Ch 569 .... 316, 474
Madge, Re, Pridie v Bellamy (1928) 72 Sol Jo 284, 44 TLR 372
.... 127
Madill v Madill (1907) 26 NZLR 737, NZ CA 146
Magee v Lavell (1874) LR 9 CP 107, 38 JP 344, 43 LJCP 131, 22 WR 334, 30 LT 169
.... 282
Magee v Magee [1936] 3 All ER 15, PC 45
Magee v Martin [1902] 1 IR 367, 36 ILT 62, 110 382
Magnesi v Hazelton (1881) 45 JP 816, 44 LT 586, P, D and Admlty
.... 103, 106
Mahaffy v Rooney (1853) 5 Ir Jur 245 442
Maher, Re Maher v Toppin [1909] 1 IR 70, 76, 41 ILT 232, Ir CA
.... 278, 313, 339
Maher v Maher (1877) 1 LR Ir 22 428
Mahon v Quinn [1904] 2 IR 267 .... 884, 888
Mahony v Donovan (1863) 14 I Ch R 262; on appeal (1863) 14 I Ch R 388, Ir CA
.... 285
Main, Re, Official Solicitor v Main [1947] 1 All ER 255, [1947] LJR 548, 91 Sol Jo 160,
  176 LT 191 446
Mainwaring v Beevor (1849) 8 Hare 44, 19 LJ Ch 396, 14 Jur 58
.... 258, 308–309
Mair, Re, Richards v Doxat [1935] Ch 562, 104 LJ Ch 258, [1935] All ER Rep 736, 153
  LT 145 464
Mair, Re, Williamson v French [1909] 2 Ch 280, 78 LJ Ch 711, 101 LT 70
.... 462
Mair v Quilter (1843) 2 Y & C Ch Cas 465 416
Maitland, Re, Chitty v Maitland (1896) 74 LT 274 294
Maitland v Adair (1796) 3 Ves 231; affd sub nom Adair v Maitland (1798) 7 Bro Parl Cas
  587 163
Maitland v Chalie (1822) 6 Madd 243 441
Major, Re, Taylor v Major [1914] 1 Ch 278, 83 LJ Ch 461, 58 Sol Jo 286, 110 LT 422
.... 1008–1009
Major v Major (1854) 2 Drew 281, 23 LJ Ch 718, 2 Eq Rep 1155, 2 WR 382, 23 LTOS
  340 914
Major and Mundy v Williams and Iles (1843) 3 Curt 432, 7 Jur 219, 2 Notes of Cases 196
.... 110
Makein, Re, Makein v Makein [1955] Ch 194, [1955] 1 All ER 57, [1955] 2 WLR 43, 99
  Sol Jo 44 482
Makin (William) & Sons Ltd, Re [1992] PLR 177, [1993] BCC 453, [1993] OPLR 171
.... 657
Malcolm, Re, Marjoribanks v Malcolm (1923) 156 LT Jo 361
.... 114, 155
Malcolm v Malcolm (1856) 21 Beav 225 .... 384, 443
Malcolm v Martin (1790) 3 Bro CC 50 .... 395, 470
Malcolm v O'Callaghan (1817) 2 Madd 349 .... 134, 136, 435
Malcolm v O'Callaghan (1833) Coop temp Brough 73 .... 435, 442
Malcolm v Taylor (1831) 2 Russ & M 416 .... 180, 456
Malden v Maine (1855) 2 Jur NS 206 254
Maldonado, Re, State of Spain v Treasury Solicitor [1954] P 223, [1953] 2 All ER 1579,
  [1954] 2 WLR 64, 98 Sol Jo 27, CA 767
Maley's Goods, Re (1887) 12 PD 134, 51 JP 423, 56 LJP 112, 35 WR 764, 57 LT 500, P,
  D and Admlty 101, 105
Malins Goods, Re (1887) 19 LR Ir 231 896
Mallinson v Siddle (1870) 39 LJ Ch 426, 18 WR 569 561
Mallinson Consolidated Trusts, Re, Mallinson v Gooley [1974] 2 All ER 530, [1974] 1
  WLR 1120, 118 Sol Jo 549 .... 281, 423, 436
Mallott v Wilson [1903] 2 Ch 494, 72 LJ Ch 664, [1900–3] All ER Rep 326, 89 LT 522
.... 151

PARA

Malmesbury v Malmesbury (1862) 31 Beav 407 254
Malone v Harrison [1979] 1 WLR 1353, 123 Sol Jo 804
.... 567, 570, 574, 576, 591,592
Malone v Malone [1925] 1 IR 140, Ir CA 250, 288
Malpass, Re, Lloyds Bank plc v Malpass [1985] Ch 42, [1984] 2 All ER 313, [1984] 3
    WLR 372, 128 Sol Jo 334, [1984] LS Gaz R 1916 .... 125, 262–263
Manby v Manby. See Maundy v Maundy
Manchester and Southport Rly Co, Re (1854) 19 Beav 365
.... 156
Manchester Corpn v Manchester Palace of Varieties Ltd [1955] P 133, [1955] 1 All ER
    387, [1955] 2 WLR 440, 53 LGR 269, 119 JP 191, 99 Sol Jo 150
.... 917
Mandeville v Carrick (1795) 3 Ridg Parl Rep 352 384
Mandeville v Duncan 1965 SLT 246, Ct of Sess 287
Mandeville v Mandeville (1888) 23 LR Ir 339 1171
Mandeville's Case (1328) Co Litt 26b 339, 384
Mangin v Mangin (1852) 16 Beav 300 295
Manifold, Re, Slater v Chryssaffinis [1962] Ch 1, [1961] 1 All ER 710, [1961] 2 WLR 456,
    105 Sol Jo 321 .... 803, 865, 960
Manisty's Settlement, Re, Manisty v Manisty [1974] Ch 17, [1973] 2 All ER 1203, [1973]
    3 WLR 341, 117 Sol Jo 665 11
Manley's Will Trusts (No 2), Re, Tickle v Manly [1976] 1 All ER 673
.... 323, 327, 336, 338, 395
Manly's Goods, Re (1862) 27 JP 9, 31 LJPM & A 198, 8 Jur NS 493, 3 Sw & Tr 56, 7 LT
    220 .... 613, 725
Manly's Will Trusts, Re (or Re Manly), Burton v Williams [1969] 3 All ER 1011, [1969] 1
    WLR 1818, 113 Sol Jo 941 .... 322, 325–327, 336, 395
Mann, Re, Ford v Ward (or Mann) [1912] 1 Ch 388, 81 LJ Ch 217, 56 Sol Jo 272, 106 LT
    64 293
Mann v Copland (1817) 2 Madd 223 .... 120, 1088
Mann v Fuller (1854) Kay 624, 23 LJ Ch 543, 2 Eq Rep 1085, 2 WR 510, 24 LTOS 34
.... 252, 409
Mann v Lang (1835) 3 Ad & El 699, 4 LJKB 210, 1 Har & W 441, 5 Nev & MKB 202
.... 1290
Mann v Thompson (1854) Kay 628, 18 Jur 826, 2 WR 582, 23 LTOS 345
.... 301, 308, 316
Mann's Goods, Re [1942] P 146, [1942] 2 All ER 193, 111 JP 86, 86 Sol Jo 254, 167 LT
    189, 58 TLR 400, P, D and Admlty 67
Mann's Goods, Re (1858) 28 LJP & M 19 65
Mannai Investment Co Ltd v Eagle Star Life Assurance Co Ltd [1997] AC 749, [1997]
    3 All ER 352, [1997] 2 WLR 945, [1997] 1 EGLR 57, [1997] 30 LS Gaz R 30, [1997]
    NLJR 846, [1997] 24 EG 122, 141 Sol Jo LB 130, HL 188, 224
Manners, Re, Manners v Manners [1923] 1 Ch 220, 92 LJ Ch 249, 67 Sol Jo 262, 128 LT
    564 .... 203, 296
Manners, Re, Public Trustee v Manners [1955] 3 All ER 83, [1955] 1 WLR 1096, 99 Sol
    Jo 726 .... 235, 308
Manning v Chambers (1847) 1 De G & Sm 282, 16 LJ Ch 245, 11 Jur 466, 9 LTOS 146
.... 247
Manning v Herbert (1769) Amb 575 438
Manning v Moore (1832) Alc & N 96 459
Manning v Purcell (1855) 7 De GM & G 55, 24 LJ Ch 522, 3 Eq Rep 387, 3 WR 273,
    24 LTOS 317 .... 122, 200, 293, 296, 672
Manning v Spooner (1796) 3 Ves 114 1012
Manning v Thesiger (1835) 3 My & K 29, 4 LJ Ch 285
.... 402
Manning's Case (1609) 8 Co Rep 94b 123
Mannox v Greener (1872) LR 14 Eq 456, 27 LT 408 .... 375, 379
Manor Farm, Kytes Hardwick, Re, Acheson v Russell. See Acheson v Russell
Mansel, Re, Smith v Mansel [1930] 1 Ch 352, 99 LJ Ch 128, [1929] All ER Rep 189, 142
    LT 281 .... 405, 1117
Mansell v Grove (1843) 2 Y & C Ch Cas 484, 7 Jur 666, 1 LTOS 410
.... 460
Mansfield v Dugard (1713) 1 Eq Cas Abr 195, sub nom Mansfield v Mansfield 2 Eq Cas
    Abr 363, sub nom Manfield v Dugard Gilb Ch 36 419

PARA

Manton v Tabois (1885) 30 Ch D 92, 54 LJ Ch 1008, 33 WR 832, 53 LT 289, [1881–5] All ER Rep Ext 1227 .... 156–157, 288

March, Re, Mander v Harris (1884) 27 Ch D 166, 54 LJ Ch 143, 32 WR 941, 51 LT 380, [1881–5] All ER Rep Ext 1346, CA 240

March v Russell (1837) 3 My & Cr 31, 6 LJ Ch 303, 1 Jur 588, 45 RR 196, 40 ER 836, [1835–42] All ER Rep 501 .... 1101, 1103

Marcon's Estate, Re, Finch v Marcon (1871) 40 LJ Ch 537 962

Marcus, Re, Marcus v Marcus (1887) 56 LJ Ch 830, 57 LT 399, 3 TLR 816 .... 43, 365

Mardon's Estate, Re [1944] P 109, [1944] 2 All ER 397, 113 LJP 67, 171 LT 276, 60 TLR 539, P, D and Admlty 110, 112, 711

Margary v Robinson (1886) 12 PD 8, 51 JP 407, 56 LJP 42, 35 WR 350, 57 LT 281, P, D and Admlty 65, 105

Margitson, Re, Haggard v Haggard (1882) 31 WR 257, 48 LT 172, CA 252

Margitson v Hall (1864) 10 Jur NS 89, 12 WR 334, 9 LT 755 320

Margulies v Margulies (2000) 2 ITELR 641, [2000] All ER (D) 344, CA 221–222

Marhant v Twisden (1711) Gilb Ch 30 289

Marie of Roumania (Queen), Re [1950] WN 457, 94 Sol Jo 673, P, D and Admlty 716

Marjoribanks, Re, Marjoribanks v Dansey [1923] 2 Ch 307, 92 LJ Ch 609, 67 Sol Jo 659, 129 LT 669 283

Marjoribanks v Hovenden (1843) Drury temp Sug 11 2–3

Mark v Mark [2005] UKHL 42, [2006] 1 AC 98, [2005] 3 All ER 912, [2005] 3 WLR 111, [2005] 2 FCR 467, [2005] 2 FLR 1193, [2005] Fam Law 857, [2005] 28 LS Gaz R 32, (2005) Times, 5 July, [2005] All ER (D) 370 (Jun) 566

Markham v Ivatt (1855) 20 Beav 579 313

Marklew v Turner (1900) 17 TLR 10, P, D and Admlty 95

Marks v Marks (1908) 40 SCR 210, Can SC 210

Marks v Solomons (1849) 18 LJ Ch 234; revsd (1850) 19 LJ Ch 555, 2 H & Tw 323 232

Marlborough (Duke) v Lord Godolphin (1750) 2 Ves Sen 61, 28 ER 41, [1558–1774] All ER Rep 264 .... 161, 253

Marley v Mutual Security Merchant Bank and Trust Co Ltd [1991] 3 All ER 198, PC 1168

Marley v Rawlings [2014] UKSC 2, [2015] AC 129, [2014] 1 All ER 807, [2014] 2 WLR 213, 16 ITELR 642, [2015] 1 FCR 187, [2014] 2 FLR 555, [2014] Fam Law 466, 164 NLJ 7592, (2014) Times, 28 January, [2014] All ER (D) 132 (Jan) 187–189, 194, 212, 224–230, 232, 235–239, 241–245, 248, 260, 262–263, 265–266, 281, 304, 323, 741

Marples v Bainbridge (1816) 1 Madd 590, 16 RR 271 134

Marriot v Marriot (1725) Gilb Ch 203, 1 Stra 666 670

Marriott v Abell (1869) LR 7 Eq 478, 38 LJ Ch 451, 17 WR 569, 20 LT 690 444

Marryat, Re, Westminster Bank Ltd v Hobcroft [1948] Ch 298, [1948] 1 All ER 796, [1918] LJR 1237, 92 Sol Jo 283, 64 TLR 125 .... 278, 366

Marryat v Townly (1748) 1 Ves Sen 102 395

Marsden, Re, Bowden v Layland (1884) 26 Ch D 783, 54 LJ Ch 640, 33 WR 28, [1881–5] All ER Rep 993, 51 LT 417 .... 629, 1244

Marsden v Kent (1877) 5 Ch D 598, 46 LJ Ch 497, 25 WR 522, 37 LT 49, CA 961

Marsden v Regan [1954] 1 All ER 475, [1954] 1 WLR 423, 98 Sol Jo 144, CA 1256, 1259, 1294, 1298, 1301

Marsden's Goods, Re (1860) 6 Jur NS 405, 1 Sw & Tr 542, 2 LT 87 54

Marsh v Evans (1720) 2 Eq Cas Abr 556, 1 P Wms 668 1087

Marsh v Kirby (1634) 1 Rep Ch 76 45

Marsh v Marsh (1860) 24 JP 311, 30 LJPM & A 77, 6 Jur NS 380, 1 Sw & Tr 528, 1 LT 523 .... 67, 111, 739

PARA

Marsh v Tyrrell and Harding (1828) 2 Hag Ecc 84; on appeal (1832) 3 Hag Ecc 471
.... 59, 903
Marshal's Case (1598) 3 Dyer 281a, n 127
Marshall, Re, Barclays Bank Ltd v Marshall [1957] Ch 507, [1957] 3 All ER 172, 101 Sol
Jo 664, CA 331
Marshall, Re, Marshall v Marshall [1914] 1 Ch 192, 83 LJ Ch 307, [1911–13] All ER Rep
671, 58 Sol Jo 118, 109 LT 835, CA 1053, 1062
Marshall, Re, Marshall v Whateley [1920] 1 Ch 284, 89 LJ Ch 204, [1920] All ER Rep
190, 64 Sol Jo 241, 122 LT 673 464
Marshall v Blew (1741) 2 Atk 217 379
Marshall v Bousfield (1817) 2 Madd 166 305
Marshall v Broadhurst (1831) 1 Cr & J 403, 9 LJOS Ex 105, 1 Tyr 348
.... 1035, 1216
Marshall v Crowther (1874) 2 Ch D 199, 23 WR 210 1120
Marshall v Hill [2003] All ER (D) 304 (Mar) 305, 315–316
Marshall v Hill (1814) 2 M & S 608 441
Marshall v Holloway (1820) 19 RR 94, 2 Swan 432, 36 ER 681, [1814–23] All ER Rep
395 .... 415, 656
Marshall v Hopkins (1812) 15 East 309 .... 253, 277
Marshall v Wilder (1829) 9 B & C 655, 7 LJOS 325, 4 Man & Ry KB 607
.... 1292
Marshall (Inspector of Taxes) v Kerr [1995] 1 AC 148, [1994] 3 All ER 106, [1994] 3
WLR 299, [1994] STC 638, 67 TC 56, 138 Sol Jo LB 155, HL
.... 922
Marshall's Goods, Re (1866) 13 LT 643 64
Marshman v Brookes (1863) 32 LJPM & A 95, 11 WR 549
.... 1188
Marsland, Re, Lloyds Bank Ltd v Marsland [1939] Ch 820, [1939] 3 All ER 148, 108 LJ
Ch 344, 83 Sol Jo 564, 161 LT 1, 55 TLR 819, CA 21, 23
Martelli v Holloway (1872) LR 5 HL 532, 42 LJ Ch 26
.... 259
Marten, Re, Shaw v Marten [1901] 1 Ch 370, 70 LJ Ch 354, 85 LT 704; revsd [1902] 1
Ch 314, 71 LJ Ch 203, 50 WR 209, 46 Sol Jo 163, 85 LT 704, CA
.... 1085
Martin, Re, Martin v Martin [1892] WN 120 .... 287, 375
Martin, Re, Midland Bank Executor and Trustee Co Ltd v Marfleet [1955] Ch 698, [1955]
1 All ER 865, [1955] 2 WLR 1029, 99 Sol Jo 318 .... 992, 994, 1108
Martin, Re, Smith v Martin (1885) 54 LJ Ch 1071, 53 LT 34
.... 422
Martin, Re, Tuke v Gilbert (1887) 57 LT 471 432
Martin v Browne [2008] EWCA Civ 712, [2008] All ER (D) 320 (Oct)
.... 884
Martin v Drinkwater (1840) 2 Beav 215, 9 LJ Ch 247 .... 217, 409
Martin v Glover (1844) 1 Coll 269, 8 Jur 640 .... 314, 344
Martin v Hobson (1873) 8 Ch App 401, 42 LJ Ch 342, 21 WR 376, 28 LT 427
.... 293
Martin v Holgate (1866) LR 1 HL 175, 35 LJ Ch 789, 15 WR 135
.... 229, 243, 248, 321, 325, 336
Martin v Lee (1861) 14 Moo PCC 142, 9 WR 522, 4 LT 657
.... 225
Martin v Long (1690) 1 Eq Cas Abr 193, Prec Ch 15, 2 Vern 151
.... 460
Martin v Martin (1842) 12 Sim 579, 11 LJ Ch 291, 6 Jur 360
.... 375
Martin v Martin (1866) LR 2 Eq 404, 35 LJ Ch 679, 12 Jur NS 889, 14 WR 986, 15 LT
99 451
Martin v Myers [2004] EWHC 1947 (Ch), [2004] All ER (D) 396 (Jul)
.... 1261, 1267, 1270
Martin v Swannell (1840) 2 Beav 249, 9 LJ Ch 174 391
Martin v Toleman (1897) 77 LT 138, P, D and Admlty 812
Martin v Welstead (1848) 18 LJ Ch 1, 12 LTOS 286 227
Martin's Goods, Re (1849) 1 Rob Eccl 712, 6 Notes of Cases 694
.... 74, 76, 83
Martin's Goods, Re (1862) 27 JP 137, 32 LJPM & A 5, 8 Jur NS 1134, 3 Sw & Tr 1, 11
WR 191, 7 LT 756 639
Martin's Goods, Re (1867) LR 1 P & D 380, 31 JP 727, 36 LJP & M 116, 17 LT 32
.... 7

PARA

Martin's Goods, Re (1904) 90 LT 264, 20 TLR 257, P, D and Admlty
.... 622

Martineau v Briggs. See Langdale (Lady) v Briggs, ex p Lady Bacon, ex p Martineau

Martineau v Rogers (1856) 8 De GM & G 328, 25 LJ Ch 398, 4 WR 502, 27 LTOS 129
.... 444

Marvin, Re, Crawter v Marvin [1905] 2 Ch 490, 74 LJ Ch 699, 54 WR 74, 93 LT 599, 21
    TLR 765 .... 1294, 1298

Maryon-Wilson, Re Maryon-Wilson v Maryon-Wilson [1900] 1 Ch 565, 68 LJ Ch 310, 48
    WR 338, 44 Sol Jo 312, 82 LT 171, 16 TLR 256, CA 1131

Maskelyn v Maskelyn (1775) Amb 750 382

Mason, Re [1928] Ch 385, 97 LJ Ch 321, 139 LT 477, 44 TLR 225; affd [1929] 1 Ch 1,
    97 LJ Ch 321, 72 Sol Jo 545, 139 LT 477, 44 TLR 603, CA
    780–781

Mason, Re, Mason v Mason [1910] 1 Ch 695, 79 LJ Ch 605, 54 Sol Jo 425, 102 LT 514,
    [1908–10] All ER Rep Ext 1184, CA 137, 375, 380, 446

Mason, Re, Mason v Mason (1975) 5 Fam Law 124 591–592

Mason v A-G of Jamaica (1843) 4 Moo PCC 228, 7 Jur 1071, PC
    557

Mason v Baker (1856) 2 K & J 567, sub nom Re Lloyd's Estate, Baker v Mason 2 Jur NS
    539 .... 253, 332, 396

Mason v Bishop (1883) Cab & El 21 .... 72, 76

Mason v Clarke (1853) 17 Beav 126, 22 LJ Ch 956, 17 Jur 479, 1 WR 297, 21 LTOS 122
    .... 362, 390, 394

Mason v Farnell (1844) 1 Dow & L 576, 13 LJ Ex 142, 12 M & W 674, 2 LTOS 424
    1141

Mason v Mason (1816) 1 Mer 308 33

Mason v Ogden [1903] AC 1, 72 LJ Ch 152, 51 WR 560, 87 LT 622, HL
    .... 183, 298

Mason v Robinson (1825) 2 Sim & St 295 .... 243, 262

Mason's Will, Re (1865) 34 Beav 494, 34 LJ Ch 603, 11 Jur NS 835, 6 New Rep 193, 13
    WR 799 .... 167, 294

Masonic and General Life Assurance Co, Re (1885) 32 Ch D 373, 55 LJ Ch 666, 34 WR
    739 635

Massey, Re, Ram v Massey (1920) 90 LJ Ch 40, 64 Sol Jo 308, 122 LT 676
    1132

Massey v Hudson (1817) 2 Mer 130 .... 422, 428, 460

Massey's Goods, Re [1899] P 270, 68 LJP 127, 81 LT 493, P, D and Admlty
    788

Masson, Re, Morton v Masson (1917) 86 LJ Ch 753, 61 Sol Jo 676, 117 LT 548, 33 TLR
    527, CA 237, 284, 296

Masson v Smellie (1903) 41 SLR 104, 6 F 148, 11 SLT 450, Ct of Sess
    293

Massy v Gahan (1889) 23 LR Ir 518 1119

Massy v Rogers (1883) 11 LR Ir 409 190

Massy v Rowen (1869) LR 4 HL 288 248

Mastaka v Midland Bank Executor and Trustee Co Ltd [1941] Ch 192, sub nom White,
    Re, Mastaka v Midland Bank Executor and Trustee Co Ltd [1941] 1 All ER 236,
    110 LJ Ch 49, 85 Sol Jo 56, 164 LT 282, 57 TLR 279 .... 566, 576

Master v Willoughby (1705) 2 Bro Parl Cas 244, HL 126

Masterman v Maberly (1829) 2 Hag Ecc 235 .... 3, 5, 54, 708

Masterman-Lister v Brutton & Co; Masterman-Lister v Jewell [2002] EWCA Civ 1889,
    [2003] 3 All ER 162, [2003] 1 WLR 1511, 73 BMLR 1, (2002) Times, 28 December,
    147 Sol Jo LB 60, [2002] All ER (D) 297 (Dec) 900

Masters, Re, Coutts & Co v Masters [1953] 1 All ER 19, [1953] 1 WLR 81, 97 Sol Jo 10
    656

Masters v Hooper (1793) 4 Bro CC 207 349

Masters v Masters (1718) 1 P Wms 421, 24 ER 454, [1558–1774] All ER Rep 483, 2 Eq
    Cas Abr 352 pl 12, 8 Vin Abr 312 pl 29 .... 202, 270, 403

Masters v Scales (1850) 13 Beav 60, 15 LTOS 452 325

Masterson, Re, Trevanion v Dumas [1902] WN 192, CA
    .... 165, 342

Mather, Re, Mather v Mather [1927] WN 13, 71 Sol Jo 142, 163 LT Jo 52, 63 L Jo 82
    284

Mathew, Re [1984] 2 All ER 396, [1984] 1 WLR 1011, [1984] FLR 676, [1984] Fam Law
    246, 128 Sol Jo 533, [1984] LS Gaz R 1361 .... 681, 758, 760, 847

Mathew v Warner (1799) 5 Ves 23 5

PARA

Mathews v Mathews (1867) LR 4 Eq 278, 15 WR 761 .... 271, 291

Mathison v Clark. See Matthison v Clarke

Matson, Re, James v Dickinson [1897] 2 Ch 509, 66 LJ Ch 695, 77 LT 69
.... 539, 546

Matthews v Foulsham (or Foulshaw) (1864) 4 New Rep 500, 12 WR 1141, 11 LT 82
.... 274

Matthews v Gardiner (1853) 17 Beav 254, 21 LTOS 236
.... 384, 461, 473

Matthews v Matthews (1876) 45 LJ Ch 711, 2 Char Pr Cas 149, 34 LT 718
.... 1178

Matthews v Maude (1830) 8 LJOS Ch 106, 1 Russ & M 397
.... 273

Matthews v Palmer (1863) 11 WR 610 1177

Matthews v Paul (1819) 2 Wils Ch 64, 3 Swan 328 333

Matthews v Warner (1798) 4 Ves 186 5

Matthews Goods, Re [1898] P 17, 67 LJP 11, 77 LT 630, P, D and Admlty
.... 745

Matthews Will Trusts, Re, Bristow v Matthews [1961] 3 All ER 869, [1961] 1 WLR 1415,
[1961] TR 345, 105 Sol Jo 888 .... 246, 997, 1013, 1016

Matthison v Clarke (1854) 3 Drew 3, sub nom Mathison v Clark 24 LJ Ch 202, 3 Eq Rep
127, 18 Jur 1020, 3 WR 2, 24 LTOS 105 653

Mattison v Tanfield (1840) 3 Beav 131, 4 Jur 933 .... 314, 397

Maud v Maud (1860) 27 Beav 615, 29 LJ Ch 312 141

Maude v Maude (1856) 22 Beav 290 254

Maunder, Re, Maunder v Maunder [1902] 2 Ch 875, 71 LJ Ch 815, 51 WR 31, 87 LT
262; affd [1903] 1 Ch 451, 72 LJ Ch 367, 51 WR 549, 88 LT 280, CA
.... 453

Maundy v Maundy (1734) 2 Stra 1020, sub nom Manby v Manby 2 Barn KB 202, sub
nom Mandy v Mandy Kel W 297, Fitz-G 70, sub nom Maudy v Maudy Lee temp
Hard 142 375

Maunsell v White (1854) 4 HL Cas 1039, 22 LTOS 293
.... 21

Maurice, Re, Brown v Maurice (1896) 75 LT 415, 13 TLR 36
.... 392

Mausner v Mincher [2006] EWHC 1283 (Ch), [2006] All ER (D) 240 (Apr)
.... 12

Maxton, Re (1858) 4 Jur NS 407 348

Maxwell, Re (1929) 140 LT 471, [1929] All ER Rep 341, 73 Sol Jo 159, 45 TLR 215
.... 739

Maxwell, Re, Eivers v Curry [1906] 1 IR 386, CA 1069

Maxwell, Re, Stirling-Maxwell v Cartwright (1879) 9 Ch D 173; on appeal (1879) 11 Ch
D 522, 48 LJ Ch 562, 27 WR 850, 40 LT 669, CA 960, 1182

Maxwell v Maxwell (1852) 16 Beav 106, 2 De GM & G 705, 22 LJ Ch 43, 16 Jur 982, 1
WR 2, 20 LTOS 86 268

Maxwell v Maxwell (1868) IR 2 Eq 478 165

Maxwell v Viscount Wolseley [1907] 1 KB 274, 76 LJKB 163, 51 Sol Jo 130, 96 LT 4, 23
TLR 157, CA 1284

Maxwell's Will, Re (1857) 24 Beav 246, 26 LJ Ch 854, 3 Jur NS 902, 30 LTOS 49
.... 378, 383

May, Re, Eggar v May [1917] 2 Ch 126, 86 LJ Ch 698, 61 Sol Jo 577, 117 LT 401, 33
TLR 419 .... 34, 131, 140, 407

May, Re, Eggar v May [1932] 1 Ch 99, 101 LJ Ch 12, [1931] All ER Rep 558, 75 Sol Jo
741, 146 LT 56, 48 TLR 3, CA 131, 140, 407

May v Grave (1849) 3 De G & Sm 462, 18 LJ Ch 401, 13 Jur 1021, 13 LTOS 463
.... 293

May v May [1902] P 103n, 71 LJP 35, 18 TLR 184, sub nom May's Goods, Re, May v
May 86 LT 120, P, D and Admlty 79

May v May (1881) 44 LT 412 379

May v Wood (1792) 3 Bro CC 471 .... 426, 430

May and Bannister v Street (1588) Cro Eliz 120 552

May's Will Trusts, Re, Cockerton v Jones [1944] Ch 1, [1943] 2 All ER 604, 113 LJ Ch
73, 87 Sol Jo 399, 169 LT 386, 60 TLR 43 445

Maybank v Brooks. See Mabank v Brooks

Maybee, Re (1904) 8 OLR 601, 4 OWR 421, 24 CLT 399
.... 182

PARA

Maybery v Brooking (1855) 7 De GM & G 673, 25 LJ Ch 87, 2 Jur NS 76, 4 WR 155,
  26 LTOS 162 277
Mayd's Goods, Re (1880) 6 PD 17, 45 JP 8, 50 LJP 7, 29 WR 214, P, D and Admlty
  7
Mayell, Re, Foley v Wood [1913] 2 Ch 488, 83 LJ Ch 40, 109 LT 40
  277
Mayer v Townsend (1841) 3 Beav 443, 10 LJ Ch 216, 5 Jur 91
  231
Mayer's Goods, Re (1873) LR 3 P & D 39, 37 JP 696, 42 LJP & M 57, 29 LT 247
  759
Mayhew, Re, Rowles v Mayhew (1877) 5 Ch D 596, 46 LJ Ch 552, 25 WR 521, 37 LT
  48, CA 914
Maynard, Re, Pearce v Pearce [1930] WN 127, 169 LT Jo 519, 69 L Jo 440
  174–175
Maynard v Gibson, ex p Maynard (No 2) (1866) 35 LJ Ch 458, 14 WR 538
  .... 161, 170
Maynard v Gibson [1876] WN 204 122
Maynard v Wright (1858) 26 Beav 285 .... 254, 321, 336
Mayne, Re, Stoneham v Woods [1914] 2 Ch 115, [1914] WN 202, 83 LJ Ch 815, 58 Sol
  Jo 579 294
Mayne v Mayne [1897] 1 IR 324, 35 ILT 35 293
Mayo, Re, Chester v Keirl [1901] 1 Ch 404, 70 LJ Ch 261, 45 Sol Jo 219, 84 LT 117
  .... 193, 274
Mayott v Mayott (1786) 2 Bro CC 125 328
Mead v Lord Orrery (1745) 3 Atk 235 .... 1023, 1025, 1028
Meadows v Duchess of Kingston (1775) Amb 756 671
Meadows v Parry (1812) 1 Ves & B 124 446
Meagher, Re, Trustees, Executors and Agency Co Ltd v Meagher [1910] VLR 407
  134
Mears, Re, Parkers v Mears [1914] 1 Ch 694, 83 LJ Ch 450, 110 LT 686
  475
Meatyard's Goods, Re [1903] P 125, 72 LJP 25, 89 LT 70, P, D and Admlty
  .... 720, 845
Mecredy v Brown [1906] 2 IR 437, CA 887
Medland, Re, Eland v Medland (1889) 41 Ch D 476, 58 LJ Ch 572, 37 WR 753, 60 LT
  851, 5 TLR 523, CA 959, 1196
Medlicot v Bowes (1749) 1 Ves Sen 207, 27 ER 985 429
Medlock, Re, Ruffle v Medlock (1886) 55 LJ Ch 738, 54 LT 828
  .... 1076, 1083
Medworth v Pope (1859) 27 Beav 71, 28 LJ Ch 905, 5 Jur NS 996
  354
Meeds v Wood (1854) 19 Beav 215 .... 289, 369, 446
Meek and Donald v Curtis (1827) 1 Hag Ecc 127 850
Meere, Re, Kilford v Blaney (1885) 31 Ch D 56, 55 LJ Ch 185, 34 WR 109, 54 LT 287,
  CA 995, 1012
Megit v Johnson (1780) 2 Doug KB 542 .... 556, 778
Megson v Hindle (1880) 15 Ch D 198, sub nom Hindle, Re, Megson v Hindle 28 WR 866,
  43 LT 551, CA 352
Megson's Goods, Re (1899) 80 LT 295, P, D and Admlty
  770
Mehrtens v Andrews (1839) 3 Beav 72 1126
Meinertzagen v Walters (1872) 7 Ch App 670, 41 LJ Ch 801, 20 WR 918, 27 LT 326,
  [1861–73] All ER Rep Ext 1255, CA 404
Meldrum, Re, Swinson v Meldrum [1952] Ch 208, [1952] 1 All ER 274, [1952] 1 TLR 92
  .... 184, 994
Mellish, Re, Day v Withers [1916] 1 Ch 562, 85 LJ Ch 433, [1916–17] All ER Rep 634,
  114 LT 991 .... 302, 313
Mellish v Mellish (1798) 4 Ves 45 .... 186, 228
Mellish v Mellish (1824) 2 B & C 520, 2 LJOSKB 45, 3 Dow & Ry KB 804
  384
Mellor, Re, Alvarez v Dodgson [1922] 1 Ch 312, 91 LJ Ch 393, [1922] All ER Rep 735,
  66 Sol Jo 249, 126 LT 562, CA 283, 1083
Mellor, Re, Dodgson v Ashworth (1912) 56 Sol Jo 596, 28 TLR 473
  .... 114, 367
Mellor, Re, Porter v Hindsley [1929] 1 Ch 446, 98 LJ Ch 209, 140 LT 469
  293

PARA

Mellor v Daintree (1886) 33 Ch D 198, 56 LJ Ch 33, [1886–90] All ER Rep 343, 55 LT
   175 .... 253, 315, 466–467
Meluish v Milton (1876) 3 Ch D 27, 45 LJ Ch 836, 24 WR 892, 35 LT 82, CA
   .... 58, 671, 907
Melville v Ancketill (1909) 25 TLR 655, CA 632
Mence v Bagster (1850) 4 De G & Sm 162 394
Mendham v Williams (1866) LR 2 Eq 396, 15 LT 130 429
Mengel's Will Trusts, Re, Westminster Bank Ltd v Mengel [1962] Ch 791, [1962] 2 All ER
   490, [1962] 3 WLR 311, 106 Sol Jo 510 .... 284, 296
Menzies v Pulbrook and Ker (1841) 2 Curt 845, 1 Notes of Cases 132
   863
Mercer v Hall (1793) 4 Bro CC 326 135–136
Mercer's Goods, Re (1870) LR 2 P & D 91, 34 JP 551, 39 LJP & M 43, 18 WR 1040, 23
   LT 195 723
Merceron's Trusts, Re, Davies v Merceron (1876) 4 Ch D 182, 35 LT 701
   456–457
Merchant Taylors' Co v A-G (1871) 6 Ch App 512, 35 JP 774, 40 LJ Ch 545, 19 WR 641,
   25 LT 109 194
Merchants Bank of Canada v Keefer (1885) 13 SCR 515
   422
Meredith, Re, Davies v Davies [1924] 2 Ch 552, 94 LJ Ch 87, [1924] All ER Rep 409, 131
   LT 800 167
Meredith v Farr (1843) 2 Y & C Ch Cas 525, 7 Jur 797
   352
Meredith v Treffry (1879) 12 Ch D 170, 48 LJ Ch 337, 27 WR 406
   333
Merlin v Blagrave (1858) 25 Beav 125, 119 RR 356 .... 416, 430, 1210
Merricks' Trusts, Re (1866) LR 1 Eq 551, 35 LJ Ch 418, 12 Jur NS 245, 14 WR 473, 14
   LT 130 .... 321, 325, 413
Merrill v Morton (1881) 17 Ch D 382, 50 LJ Ch 249, 29 WR 394, 43 LT 750
   .... 220, 328
Merritt's Goods, Re (1858) 4 Jur NS 1192, 1 Sw & Tr 112, 32 LTOS 78
   95
Merry v Hill (1869) LR 8 Eq 619, 17 WR 985 .... 428, 433
Merry v Ryves (1757) 1 Eden 1, 28 ER 584 136
Merryweather v Turner (1844) 3 Curt 802, 8 Jur 295, sub nom Meryweather v
   Turner 3 LTOS 6, 3 Notes of Cases 55 863
Mervin, Re, Mervin v Crossman [1891] 3 Ch 197, 60 LJ Ch 671, 39 WR 697, 65 LT 186
   .... 175, 307–308, 310, 432
Meryweather v Turner. See Merryweather v Turner
Mesgrett v Mesgrett (1706) 2 Vern 580 146
Messenger v Andrews (1828) 4 Russ 478, 38 ER 885, [1824–34] All ER Rep 651
   .... 152, 1229
Messenger's Estate, Re, Chaplin v Ruane [1937] 1 All ER 355, 81 Sol Jo 138
   .... 255–256, 266
Metcalf, Re, Metcalf v Blencowe [1903] 2 Ch 424, 72 LJ Ch 786, 51 WR 650,
   [1900–3] All ER Rep 986, 88 LT 727 1093–1094
Metcalfe, Re, Hicks v May (1879) 13 Ch D 236, 49 LJ Ch 192, 28 WR 499, 41 LT 572,
   42 LT 383, CA 985
Metcalfe, Re, Metcalfe v Earle [1909] 1 Ch 424, 78 LJ Ch 303, 100 LT 222
   323
Metcalfe, Re, Metcalfe v Metcalfe (1900) 32 OR 103 443
Metcalfe v Hutchinson (1875) 1 Ch D 591, 45 LJ Ch 210
   375
Metcalfe v O'Kennedy (1904) 1 CLR 421, 4 SRNSW 175, Aust HC
   378
Metcalfe's Goods, Re (1822) 1 Add 343 816
Metcalfe's Trusts, Re (1864) 28 JP 260, 2 De GJ & Sm 122, 33 LJ Ch 308, 10 Jur NS 287,
   3 New Rep 657, 12 WR 538, 10 LT 78 34
Metham v Duke of Devon (1718) 1 P Wms 529 354
Methuen v Methuen (1817) 2 Phillim 416 .... 99, 185, 193, 708
Methuen and Blore's Contract, Re (1881) 16 Ch D 696, 50 LJ Ch 464, 29 WR 656, 44 LT
   332 .... 256, 298
Methuen-Campbell v Walters [1979] QB 525, [1979] 1 All ER 606, [1979] 2 WLR 113, 38
   P & CR 693, 122 Sol Jo 610, 245 Estates Gazette 899, CA
   286

                                                                        PARA
Mette v Mette (1859) 28 LJP & M 117, 1 Sw & Tr 416, 7 WR 543, 33 LTOS 139
.... 87
Metters v Brown (1863) 1 H & C 686, 32 LJ Ex 138, 9 Jur NS 416, 1 New Rep 367, 11
  WR 429, 7 LT 795 645–646
Mexborough (Earl) v Savile (1903) 88 LT 131, 19 TLR 287, HL
.... 371
Meyappa Chetty v Supramanian Chetty [1916] 1 AC 603, LR 43 Ind App 113, 85 LJPC
  179, 114 LT 1002, PC 633, 635
Meyer v Simonsen (1852) 5 De G & Sm 723, 21 LJ Ch 678, 90 RR 204, 19 LTOS 337
.... 1125–1126
Meyer's Estate, Re [1908] P 353, 77 LJP 150, 52 Sol Jo 716, 99 LT 881, P, D and Admlty
.... 10, 55, 906
Meyers, Re, London Life Association v St George's Hospital [1951] Ch 534, [1951]
  1 All ER 538, [1951] 1 TLR 435 .... 33, 37, 267, 278
Meyrick v Anderson (1850) 14 QB 719, 19 LJQB 231, 14 Jur 457, 15 LTOS 24
.... 1269
Michell, Re, Thomas v Hoskins [1929] 1 Ch 552, 98 LJ Ch 197, 140 LT 686, 45 TLR 243
.... 403
Michell v Michell (1820) 5 Madd 69 .... 288, 1012
Michie's Executors v Michie (1905) 42 SLR 386, 7 F 509, 12 SLT 738, Ct of Sess
.... 1132
Mid Kent Railway Act 1856, Re, ex p Styan (1859) John 387
.... 424
Middleton v Chichester (1871) 6 Ch App 152, 40 LJ Ch 237, 19 WR 369, 24 LT 173
.... 1186
Middleton v Forbes (1787) 1 Hag Ecc 395 903
Middleton v Messenger (1799) 5 Ves 136 305–306
Middleton v Sherburne (1841) 4 Y & C Ex 358, 10 LJ Ex Eq 75; on appeal sub nom
  Sherburne v Middleton (1842) 9 Cl & Fin 72, HL 904
Middleton's Goods, Re (1864) 34 LJPM & A 16, 10 Jur NS 1109, 3 Sw & Tr 583, 11 LT
  684 109
Midgley, Re, Barclays Bank Ltd v Midgley [1955] Ch 576, [1955] 2 All ER 625, [1955] 3
  WLR 119, 99 Sol Jo 434 .... 173, 183, 1108–1109
Midgley, Re, Midgley v Midgley [1893] 3 Ch 282, 62 LJ Ch 905, 2 R 561, 41 WR 659, 37
  Sol Jo 616, 69 LT 241, 9 TLR 565, CA 974, 976, 1245
Mid-Kent Railway Act 1856, Re, ex p Bate (1863) 1 New Rep 470, 11 WR 417
.... 454
Midland Bank Executor and Trustee Co Ltd v IRC [1959] Ch 277, [1959] 1 All ER 180,
  [1959] 2 WLR 77, 103 Sol Jo 75, CA 182
Midland Bank Executor and Trustee Co Ltd v Yarners Coffee Ltd [1937] 2 All ER 54, 81
  Sol Jo 237, 156 LT 274, 53 TLR 403 297
Midland Bank Trust Co Ltd v Green [1980] Ch 590, [1978] 3 All ER 555, [1978] 3 WLR
  149, 121 Sol Jo 794; revsd [1980] Ch 590, [1979] 3 All ER 28, [1979] 3 WLR 167,
  39 P & CR 265, 123 Sol Jo 388, CA; revsd [1981] AC 513, [1981] 1 All ER 153,
  [1981] 2 WLR 28, 42 P & CR 201, 125 Sol Jo 33, HL 1274
Midland Bank Trust Co Ltd v Green (No 2) [1979] 1 All ER 726, [1979] 1 WLR 460, 123
  Sol Jo 142 1294
Midland Counties Rly Co v Oswin (1844) 3 Ry & Can Cas 497, 13 LJ Ch 209, 1 Coll 74,
  8 Jur 138, 2 LTOS 399 .... 257, 289
Midland Rly Co, Re, Re Otley and Ilkey Branch (1865) 34 Beav 525, 34 LJ Ch 596, 11 Jur
  NS 818, 6 New Rep 244, 13 WR 851, 12 LT 659 282
Midleton's Will Trusts, Re, Whitehead v Earl of Midleton [1969] 1 Ch 600, [1967]
  2 All ER 834, [1967] 3 WLR 965, 111 Sol Jo 637 27
Miesegaes Estate, Re, Misegaes v Misegaes [1950] WN 232, P, D and Admlty
.... 808
Miles, Re, Miles v Miles (1889) 61 LT 359 .... 305, 326
Miles v Durnford (1852) 2 De GM & G 641, 21 LJ Ch 667, 19 LTOS 369
.... 1028
Miles v Dyer (1832) 5 Sim 435 442
Miles v Dyer (1837) 8 Sim 330 442
Miles v Harford (1879) 12 Ch D 691, 41 LT 378, [1874–80] All ER Rep Ext 1495
.... 237
Miles v Harrison (1874) 9 Ch App 316, 43 LJ Ch 585, 22 WR 441, 30 LT 190
.... 1017, 1199
Miles v Jarvis (1883) 24 Ch D 633, 52 LJ Ch 796, 49 LT 162
.... 424

PARA

Miliangos v George Frank (Textiles) Ltd [1976] AC 443, [1975] 3 All ER 801, [1975] 3
    WLR 758, [1975] 2 CMLR 585, [1976] 1 Lloyd's Rep 201, 9 LDAB 408, 119 Sol Jo
    774, HL 967
Millar, Re, Barnard v Mahoney (1898) 17 NZLR 160 210
Millar v Sinclair [1903] 1 IR 150 990
Millar v Turner (1748) 1 Ves Sen 85 362
Millar v Woodside (1872) IR 6 Eq 546 .... 268, 271
Millar & Co v Keane (1889) 24 LR Ir 49 1291
Millar's Estate, Re, Irwin v Caruth [1916] P 23, 60 Sol Jo 210, 114 LT 373, sub nom Irwin
    v Caruth 85 LJP 25, 32 TLR 193 836
Millard, Re, ex p Yates (1895) 2 Mans 56, 72 LT 823, [1895–9] All ER Rep Ext 2149, CA
    1039–1040
Millard v Bailey (1866) LR 1 Eq 378, 35 LJ Ch 312, 14 WR 385, 13 LT 751,
    [1861–73] All ER Rep Ext 2237 .... 127, 210
Millbank v Millbank [1982] 79 LS Gaz R 1291 307
Miller, Re, Daniel v Daniel (1889) 61 LT 365, 5 TLR 711
    .... 250, 288
Miller, Re, Galloway v Miller (1913) 135 LT Jo 10 365
Miller, Re, Miller v de Courcey [1968] 3 All ER 844, [1969] 1 WLR 583, 113 Sol Jo 246
    597
Miller, Re, ex p Official Receiver [1893] 1 QB 327, 57 JP 469, 62 LJQB 324, 10 Morr 21,
    4 R 256, 41 WR 243, 37 Sol Jo 404, 68 LT 367, 9 TLR 194, CA
    973
Miller v Callender (1993) Times, 4 February, HL 240
Miller v Huddlestone (1851) 21 LJ Ch 1, 15 Jur 1043, 3 Mac & G 513, 87 RR 171,
    18 LTOS 147 .... 1087, 1090
Miller v James (1872) LR 3 P & D 4, 37 JP 488, 42 LJP & M 21, 21 WR 272, 27 LT 862,
    [1861–73] All ER Rep Ext 1247 718
Miller v Travers (1832) 8 Bing 244, 1 LJ Ch 157, 1 Moo & S 342, 131 ER 395,
    [1824–34] All ER Rep 233 .... 186, 199, 210–211, 215, 267
Miller v Warren (1690) 2 Vern 207 452
Miller v Wheatley (1891) 28 LR Ir 144 148
Miller and Pickersgill's Contract, Re [1931] 1 Ch 511, 100 LJ Ch 257, [1931] All ER Rep
    531, 144 LT 635 .... 633, 1147
Milligan's Goods, Re (1849) 2 Rob Eccl 108, 13 Jur 1011, 14 LTOS 294, 7 Notes of Cases
    271 80
Milliner v Robinson (1600) Moore KB 682, sub nom Bifield's Case 1 Vent 231
    .... 384, 461, 473
Milling's Settlement, Re, Peake v Thom [1944] Ch 263, [1944] 1 All ER 541, 113 LJ Ch
    167, 88 Sol Jo 179, 171 LT 92, 60 TLR 317 441
Millington v Thompson (1852) 3 I Ch R 236 6
Mills, Re, Midland Bank Executor and Trustee Co Ltd v United Birmingham Hospitals
    Board of Governors [1953] 1 All ER 835, [1953] 1 WLR 554, 97 Sol Jo 229
    .... 263, 278
Mills, Re, Mills v Mills [1884] WN 21 1181
Mills, Re, Mills v Mills (1902) 22 NZLR 425 390
Mills v Anderson [1984] QB 704, [1984] 2 All ER 538, [1984] 3 WLR 481, 128 Sol Jo
    550 645–646
Mills v Boyd (1842) 6 Jur 943 1232
Mills v Millward (1889) 15 PD 20, 59 LJP 23, 61 LT 651, P, D and Admlty
    104
Mills v Norris (1800) 5 Ves 335 312
Mills v Robarts (1830) Taml 476, 8 LJOS 141, 1 Russ & M 555
    430
Mills' Will Trusts, Re, Marriott v Mills [1937] 1 All ER 142, 106 LJ Ch 159, 80 Sol Jo
    975, 156 LT 190, 53 TLR 139 288
Mills' Will Trusts, Re, Yorkshire Insurance Co Ltd v Coward [1967] 2 All ER 193, [1967]
    1 WLR 837, 111 Sol Jo 522 140
Millward v Shenton [1972] 2 All ER 1025, [1972] 1 WLR 711, 116 Sol Jo 355, CA
    .... 568, 570, 575, 580, 604
Milman v Lane [1901] 2 KB 745, 70 LJKB 731, 49 WR 545, 85 LT 180, 17 TLR 542, CA
    376
Milne, Re, Grant v Heysham (1887) 56 LJ Ch 543, 56 LT 852; affd (1887) 57 LT 828, CA
    302
Milne v Gilbart (1852) 2 De GM & G 715 344
Milne v Milne (1852) 2 De GM & G 715 344

PARA

Milne v Walker (1852) 2 De GM & G 715 344

Milner v Milner (1748) 1 Ves Sen 106 .... 252, 371

Milner's Safe Co Ltd v Great Northern and City Rly Co [1907] 1 Ch 208, 75 LJ Ch 807, 50 Sol Jo 668, 95 LT 321, 22 TLR 706; on appeal [1907] 1 Ch 229, 76 LJ Ch 99, 23 TLR 88, CA 283

Milner-Gibson-Cullum, Re, Cust v A-G [1924] 1 Ch 456, 93 LJ Ch 196, 68 Sol Jo 383, 131 LT 555, 40 TLR 298 270

Milnes, Re, Milnes v Sherwin (1885) 33 WR 927, 53 LT 534 1067

Milnes v Foden (1890) 15 PD 105, 59 LJP 62, 62 LT 498, P, D and Admlty 54, 708

Milnes v Slater (1803) 8 Ves 295 1012

Milroy v Milroy (1844) 14 Sim 48, 13 LJ Ch 266, 8 Jur 234, 2 LTOS 456 .... 246, 419, 431

Milsome v Long (1857) 3 Jur NS 1073 .... 200, 288

Milson v Awdry (1800) 5 Ves 465 .... 248, 256, 408, 410

Milward's Estate, Re, ex p Midland Rly Co [1940] Ch 698, 109 LJ Ch 274, 84 Sol Jo 393, 163 LT 108, 56 TLR 849 .... 331, 461

Minchell's Will Trusts, Re [1964] 2 All ER 47 382–383

Ministry of Health v Simpson. See Diplock, Re, Diplock v Wintle

Minors v Battison (1876) 1 App Cas 428, 46 LJ Ch 2, 25 WR 27, [1874–80] All ER Rep 1069, 35 LT 1, HL 440, 451, 1190

Minshull's Goods, Re (1889) 14 PD 151, 58 LJP 69, 38 WR 80, 61 LT 257, P, D and Admlty 759–760

Miskelly's Goods, Re (1869) 4 IR Eq 62 9

Mitchel v Reynolds (1711) Fortes Rep 296, 10 Mod Rep 130, 1 P Wms 181, 24 ER 347, [1558–1774] All ER Rep 26 131

Mitchell, Re, Freelove v Mitchell [1913] 1 Ch 201, 82 LJ Ch 121, [1911–13] All ER Rep 187, 57 Sol Jo 213, 108 LT 34 .... 118, 282

Mitchell, Re, Hatton v Jones [1954] Ch 525, [1954] 2 All ER 246, [1954] 2 WLR 1114, 98 Sol Jo 373 .... 313, 512, 981

Mitchell, Re, Mitchell v Mitchell (1913) 57 Sol Jo 339, 108 LT 180 .... 253, 382, 450

Mitchell v Halliwell [2005] EWHC 937 (Ch), [2005] All ER (D) 210 (May) 1250, 1259

Mitchell v James [2002] EWCA Civ 997, [2003] 2 All ER 1064, [2004] 1 WLR 158, [2002] 36 LS Gaz R 38, (2002) Times, 20 July, [2002] All ER (D) 200 (Jul) 908

Mitchell and Mitchell v Gard and Kingwell (1863) 28 JP 104, 33 LJPM & A 7, 10 Jur NS 51, 3 Sw & Tr 275, 12 WR 255, 9 LT 491 911

Mitchell's Goods, Re (1841) 2 Curt 916 44

Mitchell's Trustees v Aspin 1971 SLT 166, HL 228

Mitchell's Trustees v Fraser 1915 SC 350 45

Mitchelson v Piper (1836) 8 Sim 64, Donnelly 89, 5 LJ Ch 294, 42 RR 104 1190

Mitcheson's Goods, Re (1863) 32 LJPM & A 202, 9 Jur NS 360 108

Moase v White (1876) 3 Ch D 763, 24 WR 1038 291

Mocatta v Mocatta (1883) 32 WR 477, 49 LT 629 290

Moffatt v Burnie (1853) 18 Beav 211, 23 LJ Ch 591, 18 Jur 32, 2 WR 83, 22 LTOS 218 .... 305, 470

Moffatt's Goods, Re [1900] P 152, 69 LJP 98, P, D and Admlty 763

Moffett v Bates (1857) 26 LJ Ch 465, 3 Jur NS 200, 3 Sm & G 468, 5 WR 338, 28 LTOS 352 153

Mogg v Mogg (1815) 1 Mer 654, 35 ER 811, [1814–23] All ER Rep 314 .... 45, 310–311, 362

Moggridge v Thackwell (1803) 7 Ves 36, 32 ER 15, [1803–13] All ER Rep 754; affd (1807) 13 Ves 416, [1803–13] All ER Rep 754n, HL 11, 403, 557

Mohamidu Mohideen Hadjiar v Pitchey [1894] AC 437, 63 LJPC 90, 6 R 510, 71 LT 99, PC 627

Mohan v Broughton [1899] P 211, 68 LJP 91, 81 LT 57, P, D and Admlty; affd [1900] P 56, 69 LJP 20, 48 WR 371, 44 Sol Jo 210, 82 LT 29, CA 670, 884, 888

Mohun v Mohun (1818) 1 Wils Ch 151, 1 Swan 201 266

PARA

Mohun (Lord) v Duke of Hamilton (1703) 2 Bro Parl Cas 239, HL
.... 147
Moir, Re, Warner v Moir (1884) 25 Ch D 605, 53 LJ Ch 474, 32 WR 377, 50 LT 10
.... 139, 147
Moir's Estate, Re, Moir v Warner [1882] WN 139 .... 122, 284
Molesworth v Molesworth (1793) 4 Bro CC 408 429
Mollison's Trustees v Aberdeen General Hospitals Board of Management 1953 SC 264,
   1953 SLT 233, Ct of Sess 278
Molyneux v Rowe (1856) 8 De GM & G 368, 25 LJ Ch 570, 2 Jur NS 769, 4 WR 539,
   27 LTOS 179 289
Monck v Lord Monck (1810) 1 Ball & B 298 115
Monck's (Lady) Will, Re, Monck v Croker [1900] 1 IR 56, Ir CA
.... 255, 369, 449
Moncrieff v Jamieson [2007] UKHL 42, [2008] 4 All ER 752, [2007] 1 WLR 2620, [2008]
   1 P & CR 349, [2007] 43 EG 200 (CS), 2008 SC (HL) 1, 2007 SLT 989, 2007 SCLR
   790, 151 Sol Jo LB 1368, 2007 Scot (D) 1/9 283
Monk v Mawdsley (1827) 1 Sim 286, 5 LJOS Ch 149 248
Monkhouse v Holme (1783) 1 Bro CC 298 .... 238, 426, 429
Monkhouse v Monkhouse (1829) 3 Sim 119 442
Monsell v Armstrong (1872) LR 14 Eq 423, 41 LJ Ch 715, 20 WR 921, 27 LT 407
.... 796
Montagu v Earl of Sandwich (1863) 33 Beav 324, 10 Jur NS 61, 3 New Rep 186, 12 WR
   236, 9 LT 632 293
Montagu v Nucella (1826) 1 Russ 165 320
Montague v Montague (1852) 15 Beav 565 115
Montfort (Lord) v Lord Cadogan (1810) 13 RR 270, 17 Ves 485, 34 ER 188,
   [1803–13] All ER Rep 482; varied (1816) 2 Mer 3, 19 Ves 635, [1803–13] All ER Rep
   482 1238
Montgomerie v Woodley (1800) 5 Ves 522 .... 256, 415
Montgomery's Goods, Re (1846) 10 Jur 1063, 8 LTOS 294, 5 Notes of Cases 99
.... 613
Montresor v Montresor (1845) 1 Coll 693 .... 122, 379
Monypenny v Bristow (1832) 1 LJ Ch 88, 2 Russ & M 117
.... 115
Monypenny v Dering (1852) 2 De GM & G 145, 22 LJ Ch 313, 17 Jur 467, 42 ER 826,
   [1843–60] All ER Rep 1098, 19 LTOS 320, CA in Ch 466
Moodie v Bannister (1859) 4 Drew 432, 28 LJ Ch 881, 5 Jur NS 402, 7 WR 278, 316,
   32 LTOS 376 974
Moodie v Hosegood [1952] AC 61, [1951] 2 All ER 582, 95 Sol Jo 499, [1951] 2 TLR
   455, HL 644
Moody, Re, Woodroffe v Moody [1895] 1 Ch 101, 64 LJ Ch 174, 13 R 13, 43 WR 462,
   72 LT 190 1076
Moody v Stevenson [1992] Ch 486, [1992] 2 WLR 640, [1992] 1 FCR 107, [1992] 1 FLR
   494, [1992] Fam Law 284, 135 Sol Jo LB 84, sub nom Moody, Re, Moody
   v Stevenson [1992] 2 All ER 524, CA 565, 568, 577, 591
Moon, Re, Holmes v Holmes [1907] 2 Ch 304, 76 LJ Ch 535, 51 Sol Jo 552, 97 LT 748
.... 979
Moon, Re, ex p Dawes (1886) 17 QBD 275, 3 Morr 105, 34 WR 752, [1886–90] All ER
   Rep 479, 55 LT 114, 2 TLR 506, CA 465
Moons v De Bernales (1826) 1 Russ 301 670
Moor v Denn. See Denn d Moor v Mellor
Moor v Hawkins (1765) 2 Eden 342 27
Moor v Raisbeck (1841) 12 Sim 123, 59 ER 1078, [1835–42] All ER Rep 516
.... 94, 150, 156, 331
Moore, Re (1885) 17 LR Ir 549 465
Moore, Re, Long v Moore [1907] 1 IR 315, 41 ILT 150
.... 115
Moore, Re, Moore v Pope Benedict XV [1919] 1 IR 316, 53 ILT 217
.... 11
Moore, Re, Prior v Moore [1901] 1 Ch 936, 70 LJ Ch 358, 49 WR 484, [1900–3] All ER
   Rep 140, 84 LT 501, 17 TLR 356 266
Moore, Re, Trafford v Maconochie (1888) 39 Ch D 116, 52 JP 596, 57 LJ Ch 936, 37 WR
   83, [1886–90] All ER Rep 187, 59 LT 681, 4 TLR 591, CA
.... 121, 130, 137, 143
Moore v Cleghorn (1847) 10 Beav 423, 16 LJ Ch 469, 11 Jur 958; affd (1848) 17 LJ Ch
   400, 12 Jur 591, 12 LTOS 265 395

PARA

Moore v Holdsworth [2010] EWHC 683 (Ch), [2010] All ER (D) 87 (Jun)
.... 569
Moore v King (1842) 3 Curt 243, 7 Jur 205, 2 Notes of Cases 45
.... 70
Moore v M'Glynn [1904] 1 IR 334 1041
Moore v Moore (1781) 1 Bro CC 127 285
Moore v Moore (1860) 29 Beav 496 158
Moore v Moore (1872) IR 6 Eq 166 83
Moore v Phelan [1920] 1 IR 232 273
Moore v Simkin (1885) 31 Ch D 95, 55 LJ Ch 305, 34 WR 254, 53 LT 815
.... 384, 542
Moore's Goods, Re [1892] P 145, 61 LJP 119, P, D and Admlty
.... 759
Moore's Goods, Re [1892] P 378, 62 LJP 9, 1 R 454, P, D and Admlty
.... 60, 95, 739
Moore's Goods, Re [1901] P 44, 70 LJP 16, 84 LT 60, P, D and Admlty
.... 895–896
Moore's Goods, Re (1845) 3 Notes of Cases 601 848
Moore's Settlement Trusts, Re (1862) 31 LJ Ch 368, 10 WR 315, 6 LT 43
.... 395
Moore's Trusts, Re, Lewis v Moore (1906) 96 LT 44 141
Moors v Marriott (1878) 7 Ch D 543, 42 JP 452, 26 WR 626, sub nom Re Marriott,
     Moors v Marriott 47 LJ Ch 331 973
Moran v Place [1896] P 214, 65 LJP 83, 44 WR 593, 40 Sol Jo 514, 74 LT 661, 12 TLR
     407, CA 694, 741
Morant's Goods, Re (1874) LR 3 P & D 151, 38 JP 168, 43 LJP & M 16, 22 WR 267, 30
     LT 74 630
Mordaunt, Re, Mordaunt v Mordaunt (1914) 49 L Jo 225
.... 463
Mordaunt v Clarke (1868) LR 1 P & D 592, 33 JP 135, 38 LJP & M 45, 19 LT 610
.... 628
Moreland (formerly Pittaway) v Draffen [1967] Ch 690, [1967] 1 All ER 391, [1967] 2
     WLR 637, 111 Sol Jo 37 .... 306, 309, 398
Morelle Ltd v Wakeling [1955] 2 QB 379, [1955] 1 All ER 708, [1955] 2 WLR 672, 99
     Sol Jo 218, CA 513
Mores' Trust, Re (1851) 10 Hare 171 .... 167, 169, 409
Morewood v Currey (1879) 28 WR 213 1300
Morgan, Re (1883) 24 Ch D 114, 53 LJ Ch 85, 31 WR 948, 48 LT 964
.... 460
Morgan, Re, Dowson v Davey (1910) 26 TLR 398 131
Morgan, Re, Morgan v Morgan [1893] 3 Ch 222, 62 LJ Ch 789, [1891–4] All ER Rep
     1082, 37 Sol Jo 581, 69 LT 407, CA 236–237, 338, 375
Morgan, Re, Morgan v Morgan [1920] 1 Ch 196, 89 LJ Ch 97, [1918–19] All ER Rep
     317, 63 Sol Jo 759, 121 LT 573 .... 343, 535
Morgan, Re, Pillgrem v Pillgrem (1881) 18 Ch D 93, 50 LJ Ch 834, 30 WR 223, 45 LT
     183, CA 924, 1028, 1039
Morgan v Blyth [1891] 1 Ch 337, 60 LJ Ch 66, 39 WR 422, 63 LT 546, 7 TLR 29
.... 1237
Morgan v Cilento [2004] EWHC 188 (Ch), [2004] WTLR 457, [2004] All ER (D) 122
     (Feb) 566
Morgan v Earl of Abergavenny (1849) 8 CB 768, 14 LTOS 328
.... 928
Morgan v Griffiths (1775) 1 Cowp 234 387
Morgan v Holford (1852) 17 Jur 225, 1 Sm & G 101, 1 WR 101, 20 LTOS 177
.... 27
Morgan v Morgan (1851) 14 Beav 72 .... 1123, 1125–1126
Morgan v Morgan (1851) 4 De G & Sm 164, 20 LJ Ch 109, 15 Jur 319, 64 ER 781,
     17 LTOS 114 .... 427–428, 430
Morgan v Morgan (1870) LR 10 Eq 99, 39 LJ Ch 493, 18 WR 744, 22 LT 595
.... 473
Morgan v Ravey (1861) 25 JP 376, 6 H & N 265, 30 LJ Ex 131, 9 WR 376, 158 ER 109,
     3 LT 784 1237
Morgan v Thomas (1853) 22 LJ Ex 152, 8 Exch 302, 17 Jur 283, 20 LTOS 225
.... 646
Morgan v Thomas (1877) 6 Ch D 176, 46 LJ Ch 775, 25 WR 750, 36 LT 689
.... 158, 293

PARA

Morgan v Thomas (1882) 9 QBD 643, 51 LJQB 556, 31 WR 106, 47 LT 281, CA
.... 186, 237
Morgan d Surman v Surman (1808) 1 Taunt 289 284
Morgan's Goods, Re (1866) LR 1 P & D 214, 30 JP 679, 35 LJP & M 98, 14 WR 1022,
14 LT 894 .... 3, 54
Morgan's Goods, Re (1867) LR 1 P & D 323, 36 LJP & M 64, 16 LT 181
.... 713
Morgan's Will Trusts, Re, Lewarne v Ministry of Health or Minister of Health [1950] Ch
637, [1950] 1 All ER 1097, 94 Sol Jo 368, 66 (pt 1) TLR 1037
.... 278
Morgans, Re [1931] All ER Rep 440, 145 LT 392, 47 TLR 452, P, D and Admlty
.... 759, 773
Morice v Bishop of Durham (1805) 10 Ves 522 .... 11, 33
Morison v Moat (1851) 9 Hare 241, 20 LJ Ch 513, 15 Jur 787, 18 LTOS 28; affd (1852)
21 LJ Ch 248, 16 Jur 321 1279
Morley, Re, Morley v Haig [1895] 2 Ch 738, 64 LJ Ch 727, 13 R 680, 44 WR 140, 73 LT
151, [1895–9] All ER Rep Ext 2027 1127
Morley v Bird (1798) 3 Ves 629, 30 ER 1192, [1775–1802] All ER Rep 108
.... 173, 393
Morley v Linkson (1843) 2 Hare 570, 12 LJ Ch 372, 7 Jur 938, 1 LTOS 12
.... 132–134
Morley v Polhill (1689) 2 Vent 56, sub nom Anon 3 Salk 109 pl 10
.... 1282
Morley v Rennoldson [1895] 1 Ch 449, 64 LJ Ch 485, 12 R 158, 43 WR 518, 39 Sol Jo
283, 72 LT 308, CA 107
Morley v Rennoldson (1843) 2 Hare 570, 12 LJ Ch 372, 7 Jur 938, 62 RR 236, 1 LTOS
12 132–134
Morley's Estate, Re, Hollenden v Morley [1937] Ch 491, [1937] 3 All ER 204, 107 LJ Ch
18, 81 Sol Jo 458, 157 LT 547, 53 TLR 768 1086
Morrall v Sutton (1842) 5 Beav 100, 14 LJ Ch 266; on appeal (1845) 1 Ph 533, 9 Jur 697,
5 LTOS 1 369
Morrall v Sutton (1845) 1 Ph 533, 14 LJ Ch 266, 9 Jur 697, 5 LTOS 1
.... 228, 232, 235, 248
Morrell v Fisher (1849) 19 LJ Ex 273, 4 Exch 591, 14 LTOS 398
.... 269, 271
Morrell v Fisher (1851) 4 De G & Sm 422 1017
Morrell v Morrell (1827) 1 Hag Ecc 51 80–81
Morrell v Morrell (1882) 7 PD 68, 46 JP 328, 51 LJP 49, 30 WR 491, [1881–5] All ER
Rep 642, 46 LT 485, P, D and Admlty 739
Morrice v Aylmer (1875) LR 7 HL 717, 45 LJ Ch 614, 24 WR 587, [1874–80] All ER Rep
914, 34 LT 218, HL 295
Morrieson, Re, Hitchins v Morrieson (1888) 40 Ch D 30, 58 LJ Ch 80, 37 WR 91, 59 LT
847 .... 346, 493
Morris, Re (1889) 23 LR Ir 333 1041
Morris, Re [1967] CLY 4114 576
Morris, Re [1971] P 62, [1970] 1 All ER 1057, [1970] 2 WLR 865
.... 185, 902
Morris, Re, Corfield v Waller (1916) 86 LJ Ch 456, 115 LT 915
.... 167, 410
Morris, Re, Griffiths, Morris v Morris (1908) 124 LT Jo 315
.... 1246
Morris, Re, Lloyds Bank Ltd v Peake (Hurdwell cited) [1971] P 62, [1970] 1 All ER 1057,
[1970] 2 WLR 865, 113 Sol Jo 923, P, D and Admlty 11, 54, 95, 187, 739
Morris, Re, Morris v Atherden (1894) 71 LT 179 298
Morris, Re, Salter v A-G (1885) 33 WR 895, 52 LT 840
.... 432
Morris v Burroughs (1737) 1 Atk 399, West temp Hard 242, 2 Eq Cas Abr 272 pl 39
.... 190
Morris v Davies [2012] EWHC 1981 (Ch), [2012] All ER (D) 275 (Jul)
.... 908
Morris v Hunt & Co (1896) 12 TLR 187 1279
Morris v Livie (1842) 1 Y & C Ch Cas 380, 11 LJ Ch 172, 57 RR 391, 62 ER 934,
[1835–42] All ER Rep 77 1071
Morris v Morris (1847) 15 Sim 505, 16 LJ Ch 201, 11 Jur 178; affd (1847) 11 Jur 196
.... 450

PARA

Morris v Morris (1853) 17 Beav 198, 1 Eq Rep 167, 17 Jur 966, 1 WR 377, 21 LTOS 190
.... 442, 454, 460
Morris Goods, Re (1862) 26 JP 263, 31 LJPM & A 80, 2 Sw & Tr 360, 5 LT 768
.... 848
Morrison, Re [1913] VLR 348 324
Morrison v Hoppe (1851) 4 De G & Sm 234, 15 Jur 737, 17 LTOS 1
.... 284
Morrison v M'Ferran [1901] 1 IR 360 222
Morrison v Martin (1846) 5 Hare 507, 7 LTOS 320 274
Morrison's Goods, Re (1861) 2 Sw & Tr 129, 9 WR 518, 3 LT 786
.... 632
Morrison's Will Trusts, Re, Walsingham v Blathwayt [1940] Ch 102, [1939] 4 All ER 332,
  109 LJ Ch 25, 83 Sol Jo 908, 162 LT 45, 56 TLR 99 140
Morritt v Douglas (1872) LR 3 P & D 1, 37 JP 24, 42 LJP & M 10, 21 WR 162, 27 LT
  591 69
Morse v Lord Ormonde (1826) 1 Russ 382, 4 LJOS Ch 158
.... 460
Morse v Morse (1829) 2 Sim 485 390
Morse's Settlement, Re (1855) 21 Beav 174, 25 LJ Ch 192, 2 Jur NS 6, 4 WR 148,
  26 LTOS 163 412
Morshead v Reynolds (1856) 21 Beav 638 1204
Mort, Re, Perpetual Trustee Co Ltd v Bisdee (1904) 21 WN 259, 4 SRNSW 760, NSW SC
.... 294
Mortifee's Estate, Re [1948] P 274, [1948] LJR 1886, P, D and Admlty
.... 827
Mortimer, Re, Gray v Gray [1905] 2 Ch 502, 74 LJ Ch 745, 93 LT 459, CA
.... 259, 466
Mortimer, Re, Griffiths v Mortimer (1885) 54 LJ Ch 414, 33 WR 441, 52 LT 383
.... 316
Mortimer v Hartley (1848) 6 CB 819 442
Mortimer v Hartley (1851) 3 De G & Sm 316 442
Mortimer v Hartley (1851) 3 De G & Sm 328n, 20 LJ Ex 129, 6 Exch 47, 16 LTOS 551
.... 382, 442
Mortimer v Paull (1870) LR 2 P & D 85, 34 JP 487, 39 LJP & M 47, 18 WR 901, 22 LT
  631 809
Mortimer v West (1827) 3 Russ 370, 5 LJOS Ch 181 352
Mortimore v Mortimore (1879) 4 App Cas 448, 48 LJ Ch 470, 27 WR 601, 40 LT 696,
  [1874–80] All ER Rep Ext 1592, HL 313
Mortlock's Trusts, Re (1857) 3 K & J 456, 26 LJ Ch 671, 112 RR 230, 5 WR 748,
  30 LTOS 90 382
Morton, Re, M'Auley v Harvey (1919) 53 ILT 105 .... 137, 466
Morton, Re, Morton v Warham [1956] Ch 644, [1956] 3 All ER 259, [1956] 3 WLR 663,
  100 Sol Jo 650 .... 514–515, 1117
Morton v Tewart (1842) 2 Y & C Ch Cas 67, 60 RR 35
.... 348
Morton's Goods, Re (1864) 33 LJPM & A 87, 3 Sw & Tr 422, 12 WR 320, 9 LT 809
.... 707
Morton's Goods, Re (1887) 12 PD 141, 51 JP 680, 56 LJP 96, 35 WR 735, 57 LT 501, 3
  TLR 577, P, D and Admlty 105
Morton's Goods, Re, Morton v Thorpe (1863) 27 JP 679, 32 LJPM & A 174, 9 Jur NS
  728, 3 Sw & Tr 179, 9 LT 300, [1861–73] All ER Rep Ext 1536
.... 754
Moryoseph v Moryoseph [1920] 2 Ch 33, 89 LJ Ch 376, [1920] All ER Rep 216, 64 Sol
  Jo 497, 123 LT 569 .... 231, 1061
Moseley v Rendell (1871) LR 6 QB 338, 40 LJQB 111, 19 WR 619, 23 LT 774
.... 1216, 1289
Moser v Platt (1844) 14 Sim 95, 8 Jur 389, 3 LTOS 217
.... 271
Moses, Re, Beddington v Beddington [1902] 1 Ch 100, 71 LJ Ch 101, 85 LT 596, 18 TLR
  147, CA; affd sub nom Beddington v Baumann [1903] AC 13, 72 LJ Ch 155, 51 WR
  383, 47 Sol Jo 90, 87 LT 658, 19 TLR 58, HL 2, 158
Moses, Re, Moses v Valentine [1908] 2 Ch 235, 77 LJ Ch 783, [1908–10] All ER Rep 313,
  99 LT 519 1123
Moses v Levi (1839) 3 Y & C Ex 359 1253
Moss v Cooper (1861) 1 John & H 352, 128 RR 410, 4 LT 790
.... 59, 222

PARA

Moss v Dunlop (1859) John 490 313

Moss Trusts, Re, Moss v Allen [1945] 1 All ER 207, 114 LJ Ch 152, 89 Sol Jo 69, 172 LT
196, 61 TLR 147 140

Mostyn v Mostyn (1854) 5 HL Cas 155, 23 LJ Ch 925, 24 LTOS 175
.... 215, 276

Motherwell, Re, Keane v Motherwell [1910] 1 IR 249, 44 ILT 148
.... 476

Mottram, Re (1864) 10 Jur NS 915, 10 LT 866 419
Mounsey v Blamire (1828) 4 Russ 384 341
Mountain v Bennet (1787) 1 Cox Eq Cas 353 .... 56, 903
Mountcashell (Earl) v Smyth [1895] 1 IR 346 115
Mountford v Gibson (1804) 4 East 441, 1 Smith KB 129
.... 1266–1267

Mousley v Carr (1841) 4 Beav 49, 10 LJ Ch 260, 55 RR 13
.... 1257

Mower v Orr (1849) 7 Hare 473, 13 Jur 421, 82 RR 191, 13 LTOS 184, sub nom Mower
v Orr, Mower v Mower 18 LJ Ch 361 .... 167, 308

Mowlem, Re (1874) LR 18 Eq 9, 43 LJ Ch 353, 22 WR 398
.... 551

Moyle v Moyle (1831) 34 RR 186, 2 Russ & M 710 962
Moyles' Estate, Re (1878) 1 LR Ir 155, Ir CA 389
Mucklow v Fuller (1821) Jac 198, 23 RR 186 629

Muffett, Re, Jones v Mason (1886) 55 LT 671, 3 TLR 126; on appeal (1887) 56 LJ Ch
600, CA 348

Muffett, Re, Jones v Mason (1888) 39 Ch D 534, 57 LJ Ch 1017, 37 WR 9, 59 LT 499, 4
TLR 738 1121

Muggleton v Barnett (1857) 2 H & N 653, 27 LJ Ex 125, 4 Jur NS 139, 6 WR 182,
30 LTOS 247, Ex Ch 562, 564

Muir (or Williams) v Muir [1943] AC 468, 112 LJPC 39, 1943 SC (HL) 47, 1944 SLT 67,
HL 161, 1130

Muirhead, Re, Muirhead v Hill [1916] 2 Ch 181, 85 LJ Ch 598, [1916–17] All ER Rep
771, 115 LT 65 927

Muirhead's Estate, Re [1971] P 263, [1971] 2 WLR 369, 115 Sol Jo 128, sub nom
Muirhead, Re [1971] 1 All ER 609, P, D and Admlty 862

Mulcair, Re, McCarthy v Mulcair [1960] IR 321, 94 ILTR 126
.... 184

Mulder, Re, Westminster Bank Ltd v Mulder [1943] 2 All ER 150, CA
.... 268, 270

Mulholland's Will Trusts, Re, Bryan v Westminster Bank Ltd [1949] 1 All ER 460,
[1949] LJR 1078, 93 Sol Jo 148 1030

Mullins v Smith (1860) 1 Drew & Sm 204, 8 WR 739 .... 120, 250, 1088
Mulock's Goods, Re [1933] IR 171 110–112
Mulqueen's Trusts, Re (1881) 7 LR Ir 127 348
Munday, Re, Wong v Wong [2003] WTLR 1161 187

Mundy's Goods, Re (1860) 25 JP 151, 30 LJPM & A 85, 7 Jur NS 52, 2 Sw & Tr 119, 9
WR 171, 3 LT 380 54

Munro v Fitzgerald (1844) 3 LTOS 3 1056
Munro v Henderson [1907] 1 IR 440; affd [1908] 1 IR 260, Ir CA
.... 200, 232, 253

Munton, Re, Munton v West [1927] 1 Ch 262, 96 LJ Ch 151, 136 LT 661, [1926] All ER
Rep Ext 728, CA 1252

Murdoch v Brass (1904) 41 SLR 666, 6 F 841, 12 SLT 208, Ct of Sess
.... 45, 252

Murfett v Smith (1887) 12 PD 116, 51 JP 374, 57 LT 498, DC
.... 52

Murguia's Goods, Re (1884) 9 PD 236, 48 JP 711, 53 LJP 47, 2 WR 799, P, D and Admlty
.... 637

Murkin v Phillipson (1834) 3 My & K 257, 3 LJ Ch 143
.... 438

Murphy, Re, Dalton v Latham [2003] EWHC 796 (Ch), 147 Sol Jo LB 537, [2003] WTLR
687, [2003] All ER (D) 305 (Apr) 39–40

Murphy, Re, Murphy v Murphy and Byrne [1964] IR 308
.... 424

Murphy v Burrows [2004] EWHC 1900 (Ch), 7 ITELR 116, [2004] All ER (D) 572 (Jul)
.... 20

PARA

Murphy v Murphy [2003] EWCA Civ 1862, [2004] Lloyd's Rep IR 744, [2004] 1 FCR 1,
　[2003] All ER (D) 410 (Dec) 585
Murphy's Goods, Re (1873) 8 IR Eq 300 .... 44, 76
Murphy's Trusts, Re [1900] 1 IR 145 1047
Murray, Re, Martins Bank Ltd v Dill [1955] Ch 69, [1954] 3 All ER 129, [1954] 3 WLR
　521, 98 Sol Jo 716, CA 138, 141, 253
Murray, Re, Murray v Murray [1956] 2 All ER 353, [1956] 1 WLR 605, 100 Sol Jo 420
　.. 107
Murray, Re, Woods v Greenwell (1882) 30 WR 283, 45 LT 707
　.. 982
Murray v Addenbrook (1830) 4 Russ 407, 8 LJOS Ch 79
　.. 460
Murray v Champernowne [1901] 2 IR 232, 35 ILT 68 819
Murray v Nisbett (1799) 5 Ves 149 285
Murray v Tancred (1840) 10 Sim 465 427
Murray's Goods, Re [1896] P 65, 65 LJP 49, 44 WR 414, 12 TLR 143, P, D and Admlty
　.. 722–723
Murry v Jones (1813) 2 Ves & B 313 446
Murthwaite v Jenkinson (1824) 2 B & C 357, 3 Dow & Ry KB 764
　.. 375
Muschamp v Bluet (1617) J Bridg 132 .... 142, 382
Musgrave v Brooke (1884) 26 Ch D 792, sub nom Re Brooke, Musgrave v Brooke 54 LJ
　Ch 102, 33 WR 211 124
Musgrave v Parry (1715) 2 Vern 710 362
Musgrove's Estate, Re, Davis v Mayhew [1927] P 264, 96 LJP 140, 71 Sol Jo 542, 137 LT
　612, 43 TLR 648, CA 894–895, 901
Muskett v Eaton (1875) 1 Ch D 435, 45 LJ Ch 22, 24 WR 52, 33 LT 716
　.. 424
Musther, Re, Groves v Musther (1890) 43 Ch D 569, 59 LJ Ch 296, CA
　.. 322
Myddleton v Rushout (1797) 1 Phillim 244 957
Myers, Re, Myers v Myers [2004] EWHC 1944 (Fam) [2005] WTLR 851
　.. 568, 572–574, 580, 591
Myers v Washbrook [1901] 1 KB 360, 70 LJKB 357, 83 LT 633, [1900–3] All ER Rep Ext
　1592, DC 122
Mynn v Robinson (1828) 2 Hag Ecc 169 903
Mytton v Boodle (1834) 6 Sim 457 .... 436, 442

N

NS v MI [2006] EWHC 1646 (Fam), [2007] 2 FCR 748, [2007] 1 FLR 444, [2006] Fam
　Law 839, [2006] All ER (D) 48 (Jul) 136
Nanfan v Legh (1816) 7 Taunt 85, 2 Marsh 107 384
Nanson v Barnes (1869) LR 7 Eq 250, 17 WR 429, 20 LT 154
　.. 561
Napier's Goods, Re (1809) 1 Phillim 83 848
Napper v Napper (1846) 10 Jur 342 54
Napper v Sanders (1632) Hut 118 417
Nares Goods, Re (1888) 13 PD 35, 52 JP 231, 57 LJP 19, 36 WR 528, 58 LT 529, P, D
　and Admlty 770
Nash, Re, Miller v Allen [1965] 1 All ER 51, [1965] 1 WLR 221, 109 Sol Jo 94
　.. 180, 422
Nash, Re, Prall v Bevan (1894) 38 Sol Jo 513, 71 LT 5, CA
　.. 313
Nash v Allen (1889) 42 Ch D 54, 58 LJ Ch 754, 37 WR 646, 61 LT 193
　.. 331, 346
Nash v Yelloly (1862) 1 New Rep 69, 3 Sw & Tr 59, 11 WR 541, 8 LT 290
　.. 909
Natal Bank Ltd v Rood [1910] AC 570, 80 LJPC 22, 103 LT 229, 26 TLR 622, PC
　.. 10
Naters, Re, Ainger v Naters (1919) 83 JP 266, 88 LJ Ch 521, 63 Sol Jo 800, 122 LT 154
　.. 1174
Nathan v Leonard [2002] EWHC 1701 (Ch), [2003] 4 All ER 198, [2003] 1 WLR 827,
　4 ITELR 909, [2002] 28 LS Gaz R 32, (2002) Times, 4 June, 146 Sol Jo LB 160,
　[2002] All ER (D) 432 (May) 34, 131, 138, 142, 149, 182, 190, 195, 242, 262
Nation v Tozer (1834) 1 Cr M & R 172, 3 LJ Ex 234, 4 Tyr 561
　.. 1224

                                                                                            PARA
National Assurance Co v Scott [1909] 1 IR 325 1101
National Provincial Bank Ltd v Moore (1967) 111 Sol Jo 357
.... 21
National Society for the Prevention of Cruelty to Children v Scottish National Society for
    the Prevention of Cruelty to Children [1915] AC 207, 84 LJPC 29, 58 Sol Jo 720, 111
    LT 869, 30 TLR 657, HL 214, 267
National Trust for Places of Historic Interest and Natural Beauty v Royal National Institute
    for the Blind [1999] All ER (D) 81, sub nom Re Chapman (1999) 1 ITELR 863
    .... 5, 54, 62, 77, 895
National Trustees Co of Australasia v General Finance Co of Australasia [1905] AC 373,
    74 LJPC 73, 54 WR 1, 92 LT 736, 21 TLR 522, [1904–7] All ER Rep Ext 1650, PC
    .... 1244, 1256
National Trustees, Executors and Agency Co Ltd v Keast (1896) 22 VLR 447, Vic Full Ct
    379
National Westminster Bank plc v Lucas, Estate of Jimmy Savile (deceased), Re [2014]
    EWHC 653 (Ch), [2014] BPIR 551, [2014] WTLR 637, [2014] All ER (D) 92 (Mar);
    sub nom Estate of Jimmy Savile, Re, National Westminster Bank plc v Lucas [2014]
    EWCA Civ 1632, 165 NLJ 7637, [2015] BPIR 450, [2015] WTLR 635, [2014] All ER
    (D) 190 (Dec) 982, 1163
Natt, Re, Walker v Gammage (1888) 37 Ch D 517, 57 LJ Ch 797, 36 WR 548, 58 LT 722
    537
Nayler v Yearsley (1860) 2 F & F 41 1279
Naylor v Robson (1865) 34 Beav 571 318
Neal v Barrett [1887] WN 88 818
Neal v Denston (1932) 76 Sol Jo 691, 147 LT 460, 48 TLR 637, P, D and Admlty
    .... 716, 894–896
Neary's Estate, Re (1881) 7 LR Ir 311 449
Neate v Pickard (1843) 2 Notes of Cases 406 110–111
Neathway v Reed (1853) 3 De GM & G 18, 22 LJ Ch 809, 17 Jur 169
    .... 248–249, 318
Neave, Re, Neave v Neave [1938] Ch 793, [1938] 3 All ER 220, 107 LJ Ch 395, 82 Sol Jo
    546, 159 LT 210, 54 TLR 921 .... 128, 407
Nedham's Case (1610) 8 Co Rep 135a 625
Needham v Kirkman (1820) 3 B & Ald 531 22
Needham v Smith (1828) 4 Russ 318, 6 LJOS Ch 107 22
Neeld, Re, Carpenter v Inigo-Jones [1962] Ch 643, [1962] 2 All ER 335, [1962] 2 WLR
    1097, 106 Sol Jo 449, CA 131, 138, 141, 148, 253, 1009, 1060
Neeld, Re, Carpenter v Inigo-Jones [1964] 2 All ER 952n, [1965] 1 WLR 73n, 43 ATC
    397, [1964] TR 437, CA 1130, 1132
Neeld, Re, Inigo-Jones v Inigo-Jones (No 3) [1969] 2 All ER 1025, [1969] 1 WLR 988,
    113 Sol Jo 527 278
Negus v Bahouse [2007] EWHC 2628 (Ch), [2008] 1 FCR 768, [2008] 1 FLR 381, [2008]
    Fam Law 208, [2007] Fam Law 1132, [2007] All ER (D) 353 (Oct)
    .... 570, 579
Neighbour v Thurlow (1860) 28 Beav 33 472
Neilson, Re, Cumming v Clyde (1929) 73 Sol Jo 765 285
Neilson v Monro (1879) 27 WR 936, 41 LT 209 322
Nelson v Hopkins (1851) 21 LJ Ch 410 277
Nelson v Oldfield (1688) 2 Vern 76 907
Nelson v Serle. See Serle v Waterworth
Nelson's Goods, Re (1872) IR 6 Eq 569 .... 105, 108
Nesbitt v Nicholson; Boyes, Re [2013] EWHC 4027 (Ch), [2014] All ER (D) 102 (Jan)
    59
Nesbitt's Will Trusts, Re, Dr Barnardo's Homes National Inc Association v Board of
    Governors of United Newcastle-upon-Tyne Hospitals [1953] 1 All ER 936, [1953] 1
    WLR 595, 32 ATC 101, 46 R & IT 332, [1953] TR 111, 97 Sol Jo 264
    199
Nesfield, Re, Barber v Cooper (1914) 59 Sol Jo 44, 110 LT 970
    1131
Nettleingham & Co Ltd v Powell & Co [1913] 3 KB 209, 82 LJKB 911, 57 Sol Jo 593,
    108 LT 912, 29 TLR 577, 6 BWCC 478, CA 665
Nettleton v Stephenson (1849) 3 De G & Sm 366, 18 LJ Ch 191, 13 Jur 618, 13 LTOS 42
    397
Nevill v Boddam (1860) 28 Beav 554, 29 LJ Ch 738, 6 Jur NS 573, 8 WR 490, 2 LT 273
    .... 107, 316
Nevill v Nevill (1701) 2 Vern 431 1061

PARA

Neville, Re, Neville v First Garden City Ltd [1925] Ch 44, 94 LJ Ch 130, [1924] All ER
    Rep 377, 69 Sol Jo 125, 132 LT 602, 41 TLR 2 297
Neville v Matthewman [1894] 3 Ch 345, 63 LJ Ch 734, 7 R 511, 42 WR 675, 38 Sol Jo
    694, 71 LT 282, CA 1186
Neville v Thacker (1888) 23 LR Ir 344, 358 .... 454–455, 473
Neville Estates Ltd v Madden [1962] Ch 832, [1961] 3 All ER 769, [1961] 3 WLR 999,
    105 Sol Jo 806 .... 11, 36
Neville's Goods, Re (1859) 28 LJP & M 52, 4 Sw & Tr 218
    710
Nevinson v Lady Lennard (1865) 34 Beav 487 293
New Sombrero Phosphate Co v Erlanger. See Erlanger v New Sombrero Phosphate Co
New South Wales Stamp Duties Comr v Pearse [1954] AC 91, [1954] 1 All ER 19, [1954]
    2 WLR 5, 98 Sol Jo 8, 89 CLR 51, 27 ALJ 616, PC 652
New York Breweries Co v A-G. See A-G v New York Breweries Co
New Zealand Midland Rly Co, Re, Smith v Lubbock [1901] 2 Ch 357, 70 LJ Ch 595,
    8 Mans 363, 49 WR 529, 45 Sol Jo 519, 84 LT 852, CA
    1205
Newbegin v Bell (1857) 23 Beav 386 1012
Newbolt v Pryce (1844) 14 Sim 354, 8 Jur 1112, 4 LTOS 272
    276
Newburgh v Newburgh (1820) 5 Madd 364 .... 186, 207
Newburgh v Newburgh (1825) Sugden's Law of Property 367, HL
    253
Newcastle Diocese (Church Property Trustee) v Ebbeck (1960) 104 CLR 394, [1961] ALR
    339, 34 ALJR 413, Aust HC 140
Newcoman v Bethlem Hospital (1741) Amb 8 App 785
    340
Newcombe v Beloe (1867) LR 1 P & D 314, 31 JP 168, 36 LJP & M 37, 16 LT 33
    787
Newell v Weeks (1814) 2 Phillim 224 .... 863, 887
Newill v Newill (1872) 7 Ch App 253, 41 LJ Ch 432, 20 WR 308, 26 LT 175,
    [1861–73] All ER Rep Ext 1259 390
Newland, Re, Bush v Summers [1904] WN 181, 49 Sol Jo 14
    1184
Newland v Marjoribanks (1813) 5 Taunt 268, 1 Marsh 44
    284
Newland v Shephard (1723) 9 Mod Rep 57, 2 P Wms 194, 2 Eq Cas Abr 329 pl 4
    471
Newland's Goods, Re [1952] P 71, [1952] 1 All ER 841, [1952] 1 Lloyd's Rep 280, 96 Sol
    Jo 230, [1952] 1 TLR 896, P, D and Admlty 95
Newman, Re, Slater v Newman [1930] 2 Ch 409, 99 LJ Ch 427, [1930] All ER Rep 617,
    143 LT 676 .... 156, 288, 291
Newman v Barton (1690) 2 Vern 205 .... 1096, 1099
Newman v Newman (1839) 10 Sim 51, 8 LJ Ch 354 416
Newman v Newman (1858) 26 Beav 218, 4 Jur NS 1030, 7 WR 6, 32 LTOS 83
    293
Newman v Nightingale (1787) 1 Cox Eq Cas 341 390
Newman v Piercey (1876) 4 Ch D 41, 46 LJ Ch 36, 25 WR 37, 35 LT 461
    274
Newman's Goods, Re (1838) 1 Curt 914 71
Newmarch, Re, Newmarch v Storr (1878) 9 Ch D 12, 48 LJ Ch 28, 27 WR 104, 39 LT
    146, CA 1009
Newns Goods, Re (1861) 7 Jur NS 688 18
Newsham's Estate, Re [1967] P 230, [1966] 3 All ER 681, [1966] 3 WLR 1207, 110 Sol Jo
    621, P, D and Admlty 759, 819–820
Newson-Smith's Settlement, Re, Grice v Newson-Smith [1962] 3 All ER 963n, [1962] 1
    WLR 1478 33
Newton v Barnardine (1587) Moore KB 127, sub nom Cosens Case 1 Eq Cas Abr 179,
    Owen 29 459
Newton v Lucas (1836) 1 My & Cr 391 277
Newton v Marsden (1862) 2 John & H 356, 31 LJ Ch 690, 8 Jur NS 1034, 10 WR 438, 6
    LT 155 133
Newton v Metropolitan Rly Co (1861) 1 Drew & Sm 583, 8 Jur NS 738, 10 WR 102, 5
    LT 542 634–635
Newton v Newton (1861) 12 I Ch R 118 .... 107, 110

PARA

Newton v Sherry (1876) 1 CPD 246, 40 JP 584, 45 LJQB 257, 24 WR 371, 34 LT 251,
[1874–80] All ER Rep Ext 1846, CPD 964
Newton's Goods, Re (1843) 3 Curt 428, 7 Jur 219 807
Newton's Trusts, Re (1867) LR 4 Eq 171, 37 LJ Ch 23 .... 165, 341
Nicholl, Re, Re Perkins, Nicholl v Perkins (1920) 65 Sol Jo 8, 125 LT 62
.... 215, 270
Nicholls, Re, Hunter v Nicholls [1921] 2 Ch 11, 90 LJ Ch 379, 65 Sol Jo 533, 125 LT 55
.... 67, 711
Nicholls v Osborn (1727) 2 P Wms 419 296
Nichols v Haviland (1855) 1 K & J 504, 1 Jur NS 891, 26 LTOS 52
.... 161
Nichols v Hawkes (1853) 10 Hare 342, 22 LJ Ch 255, 1 WR 124, 20 LTOS 257
.... 376
Nichols v Hooper (1712) 1 P Wms 198, 2 Vern 686; revsd (1712) 1 P Wms 200n, HL
.... 460
Nichols v Nichols (1814) 2 Phillim 180 .... 54, 708
Nichols v Tolley (1700) 2 Vern 388 254
Nichols and Freeman v Binns (1858) 1 Sw & Tr 239, 32 LTOS 50
.... 900
Nicholson, Re, Chadwyck-Healey v Crawford [1938] 3 All ER 270, 82 Sol Jo 624
.... 1092
Nicholson, Re, Eade v Nicholson [1909] 2 Ch 111, 78 LJ Ch 516, [1908–10] All ER Rep
669, 100 LT 877 1125
Nicholson, Re, Nicholson v Boulton [1923] WN 251, 68 Sol Jo 84
.... 1008
Nicholson, Re, Stace v Nicholson (1904) 24 NZLR 633
.... 429
Nicholson v Patrickson (1861) 3 Giff 209, 7 Jur NS 987, 5 LT 202
.... 175
Nicholson v Revill (1836) 4 Ad & El 675, 5 LJKB 129, 1 Har & W 756,
[1835–42] All ER Rep 148, sub nom Nicolson v Revell 6 Nev & MKB 192
.... 625
Nicholson v Tutin (No 2) (1857) 3 K & J 159, 3 Jur NS 235
.... 649
Nickels, Re, Nickels v Nickels [1898] 1 Ch 630, 67 LJ Ch 406, 46 WR 422,
[1895–9] All ER Rep 783, 42 Sol Jo 414, 78 LT 379 1160–1161
Nicloson v Wordsworth (1818) 19 RR 86, 2 Swan 365 151
Nicol v Askew (1837) 2 Moo PCC 88, PC 853
Nicolson v Revell. See Nicholson v Revill
Nightingale, Re, Bowden v Griffiths [1909] 1 Ch 385, 78 LJ Ch 196, [1908–10] All ER
Rep 237, 100 LT 292 535
Nightingall v Smith (1848) 1 Exch 879 .... 271, 277
Nisbett v Murray (1799) 5 Ves 149 285
Nixon, Re, Askew v Briggs (1965) 109 Sol Jo 757 .... 96, 403
Nixon, Re, Gray v Bell [1904] 1 Ch 638, 73 LJ Ch 446, 48 Sol Jo 396
.... 991
Nixon v Prince (1918) 34 TLR 444, P, D and Admlty 7, 713
Noad, Re, Midland Bank Exor and Trustee Co Ltd v Noad [1944] 2 All ER 470, CA
.... 246
Noad, Re, Noad v Noad [1951] Ch 553, [1951] 1 All ER 467, 95 Sol Jo 188, [1951] 1
TLR 703 .... 334, 336
Noble v Brett (1858) 24 Beav 499, 27 LJ Ch 516, 4 Jur NS 623, 6 WR 219, 31 LTOS 228
.... 1105
Noble v Stow (1859) 29 Beav 409, 5 Jur NS 1115, 7 WR 709
.... 394
Noble's Trusts, Re (1870) IR 5 Eq 140 214
Nockolds v Locke (1856) 3 K & J 6, 2 Jur NS 1064, 5 WR 3
.... 397
Noddings Goods, Re (1860) 2 Sw & Tr 15, 9 WR 40, 3 LT 178
.... 638
Noel v Jones (1848) 16 Sim 309, 17 LJ Ch 470, 12 Jur 906
.... 371
Noel v Robinson (1682) 1 Vern 90, 94n, 452, 459, 468, sub nom Noell v Robinson 2 Rep
Ch 248, 250, 2 Vent 358 .... 1099, 1101, 1146
Noel v Weston (1813) 2 Ves & B 269 992
Nolan, Re, Sheridan v Nolan [1912] 1 IR 416 .... 237, 370

PARA

Norbury, Re, Norbury v Fanland [1939] Ch 528, [1939] 2 All ER 625, 108 LJ Ch 219, 83
Sol Jo 359, 160 LT 572, 55 TLR 589 1130
Nordenfelt v Maxim Nordenfelt Guns and Ammunition Co Ltd [1894] AC 535, 63 LJ Ch
908, 11 R 1, [1891–4] All ER Rep 1, 71 LT 489, 10 TLR 636, HL
.... 131
Norfolk's (Duke) Settlement Trusts, Re, Earl of Perth v Fitzalan-Howard [1982] Ch 61,
[1981] 3 All ER 220, [1981] 3 WLR 455, 125 Sol Jo 554, CA
.... 656, 1247
Norman v Baldry (1834) 6 Sim 621 1245
Norman v Norman [1919] 1 Ch 297, 88 LJ Ch 109, 120 LT 379, 35 TLR 181
.... 271, 273, 277
Norman v Strains (1880) 6 PD 219, 50 LJP 39, 29 WR 744, 45 LT 191, P, D and Admlty
.... 885
Norman's Trust, Re (1853) 3 De GM & G 965, 22 LJ Ch 720, 1 Eq Rep 53, 17 Jur 444, 1
WR 220, 21 LTOS 97 226
Norreys v Franks (1875) IR 9 Eq 18 285
Norrington, Re, Brindley v Partridge (1879) 13 Ch D 654, 44 JP 474, 28 WR 711, CA
.... 961, 1030
Norrington, Re, Norrington v Norrington (1923) 40 TLR 96
.... 387
Norris v Allen (1862) 27 JP 9, 32 LJPM & A 3, 1 New Rep 34, 2 Sw & Tr 601, 11 WR
32, 7 LT 338 867
Norris v Norris (1846) 15 LJ Ch 420, 2 Coll 719, 10 Jur 629, 7 LTOS 508
.... 285
Norris v Wright (1851) 14 Beav 291 963
North, Re, North v Cusden [1952] Ch 397, [1952] 1 All ER 609, 96 Sol Jo 181, [1952] 1
TLR 674 .... 393, 395
North v North (1909) 25 TLR 322, P, D and Admlty 93
North v Wakefield (1849) 13 QB 536, 18 LJQB 214, 13 Jur 731, 13 LTOS 115
.... 625
North's Goods, Re (1842) 6 Jur 564 86
Northcliffe, Re, Arnholz v Hudson [1925] Ch 651, 95 LJ Ch 41, 133 LT 466
.... 2, 199
Northcliffe, Re, Arnholz v Hudson [1929] 1 Ch 327, 98 LJ Ch 65, [1928] All ER Rep 310,
140 LT 300 1130
Northcote's Will Trusts, Re, Northcote v Northcote [1949] 1 All ER 442, [1949] WN 69
.... 649, 657
Northen's Estate, Re, Salt v Pym (1884) 28 Ch D 153, 54 LJ Ch 273, 33 WR 336, 52 LT
173 .... 253, 256
Northey v Cock (1822) 1 Add 326 810
Northey v Paxton (1888) 60 LT 30 .... 250, 296
Northey v Strange (1716) 1 P Wms 340 .... 362, 396, 411
Northumberland (Earl) v Marquis of Gransby (1760) 1 Eden 489, sub nom Earl of
Northumberland v Earl of Aylsford Amb 540; affd sub nom Northumberland (Duke) v
Lord Egremont (1768) Amb 657 152
Northumberland's (Earl) Case (1584) Owen 124 928
Norton v Dashwood [1896] 2 Ch 497, 65 LJ Ch 737, 44 WR 680, 40 Sol Jo 635, 75 LT
205, 12 TLR 512 932
Norton v Turvill (1723) 35 Ch D 99, 2 Eq Cas Abr 152, 2 P Wms 144, 24 ER 674
.... 1301
Norwood and Blake's Contract, Re [1905] 1 IR 172 1021
Nosworthy v Basset (1688) Comb 90, 90 ER 362, sub nom Hitchins v Basset 2 Salk 592;
affd sub nom Hungerford v Nosworthy (1694) Show Parl Cas 146, HL
.... 98
Nosworthy's Goods, Re (1865) 34 LJPM & A 145, 11 Jur NS 570, 4 Sw & Tr 44
.... 8, 54
Note: Inherited National Savings [1954] 1 All ER 519n 118, 1141
Nottage, Re, Jones v Palmer (No 2) [1895] 2 Ch 657, 64 LJ Ch 695, 12 R 571, 44 WR 22,
sub nom Nottage, Re, Nottage v Palmer 73 LT 265, CA
.... 296
Nottingham v Jennings (1700) 2 Eq Cas Abr 308, 1 Com 82, 1 Ld Raym 568, 1 P Wms
23, 1 Salk 233, Willes 166n 387, 461
Nourse, Re, Hampton v Nourse [1899] 1 Ch 63, 68 LJ Ch 15, 47 WR 116, 43 Sol Jo 29,
79 LT 376 135

PARA

Novello & Co Ltd v Keith Prowse Music Publishing Co Ltd [2004] EWCA Civ 1776,
    [2005] RPC 578, [2005] IP & T 576, (2005) Times, 10 January, [2004] All ER (D)
    198 (Dec) 1288
Nowlan v Nelligan (1785) 1 Bro CC 489 449
Nowlan v Walsh (1851) 4 De G & Sm 584, 17 LTOS 292
    .... 378, 383
Nowlan v Wilde (1851) 4 De G & Sm 584, 17 LTOS 292
    .... 378, 383
Noyce, Re, Brown v Rigg (1885) 31 Ch D 75, 55 LJ Ch 114, 34 WR 147, 53 LT 688
    453
Nugee v Chapman (1860) 29 Beav 288 404
Nugent v Gifford (1738) 1 Atk 463, West temp Hard 494
    1025
Nulty v Fagan (1888) 22 LR Ir 604 1262
Nunburnholme (Lord), Re, Wilson v Nunburnholme [1912] 1 Ch 489, 81 LJ Ch 347, 56
    Sol Jo 343, 106 LT 361, CA 433–434
Nunn v Hancock (1868) 16 WR 818 258
Nunn v Wilsmore (1800) 8 Term Rep 521 1261
Nunn's Estate, Re [1936] 1 All ER 555, 105 LJP 57, 80 Sol Jo 267, 154 LT 498, 52 TLR
    322, P, D and Admlty 105
Nunn's Trusts, Re (1875) LR 19 Eq 331, 44 LJ Ch 255, 23 WR 376, Ct of Ch
    276
Nussey's Goods, Re (1898) 78 LT 169, P, D and Admlty
    613
Nutt v Burrell (1724) Cas temp King 1 190
Nuttall's Estate, Re [1955] 2 All ER 921n, [1955] 1 WLR 847, 99 Sol Jo 493, P, D and
    Admlty 730
Nutter v Holland [1894] 3 Ch 408, 63 LJ Ch 932, 7 R 491, 43 WR 18, 38 Sol Jo 707, 71
    LT 508, CA 1186

O

Oakes v Oakes (1852) 9 Hare 666 .... 156, 295
Oakes v Uzzell [1932] P 19, 100 LJP 99, 75 Sol Jo 543, 146 LT 95, 47 TLR 573, P, D and
    Admlty 894
Oakey & Sons v Dalton (1887) 35 Ch D 700, 56 LJ Ch 823, 35 WR 709, 57 LT 18, 3
    TLR 701 1279
Oakley v Wood (1867) 37 LJ Ch 28, 15 WR 862, 16 LT 450
    395
Oates d Hatterley v Jackson (1742) 7 Mod Rep 439, 2 Stra 1172
    .... 389, 394
Oates Estate, Re, Callow v Sutton [1946] 2 All ER 735, 63 TLR 83, P, D and Admlty
    83
Obee v Bishop (1859) 1 De GF & J 137, 29 LJ Ch 148, 6 Jur NS 132, 8 WR 102, 1 LT
    151 1238
O'Bierne, Re [1844] 1 Jo & Lat 352 455
O'Brien, Re, Little v O'Brien (1946) 115 LJ Ch 340, 90 Sol Jo 528, 175 LT 406, 62 TLR
    594 156
O'Brien, Re, O'Brien v O'Brien [1906] 1 IR 649, 40 ILT 93, Ir CA
    .... 250, 285
O'Brien v Condon [1905] 1 IR 51, 38 ILT 252 .... 42, 221
O'Brien v Lord Inchiquin Ridg temp H. See Inchiquin (Lord) v French
O'Brien v O'Brien [1896] 2 IR 459, Ir CA 316,319
O'Brien v Seagrave [2007] EWHC 1247 (Ch), [2007] 3 All ER 633, [2007] 1 WLR 2002,
    (2007) Times, 2 May, [2007] All ER (D) 56 (Apr) 863, 875
O'Brien's Goods, Re [1900] P 208, 69 LJP 55, P, D and Admlty
    .... 67, 82
Occleston v Fullalove (1874) 9 Ch App 147, 38 JP 196, 43 LJ Ch 297, 22 WR 305, 29 LT
    785 .... 243, 354
O'Connor, Re, M'Dermott v A-G (No 2) [1923] 1 IR 142, 57 ILT 158
    181
O'Connor, Re, Westminster Bank Ltd v O'Connor [1948] Ch 628, [1948] 2 All ER 270,
    [1948] LJR 1606, 92 Sol Jo 441 119
O'Connor v O'Connor [1911] 1 IR 263, 45 ILT 94 293
O'Connor v O'Connor (1870) IR 4 Eq 483 271

PARA

O'Connor's Estate, Re [1942] 1 All ER 546, 86 Sol Jo 106, 166 LT 222, P, D and Admlty
.... 7, 9, 95
O'Connor's Goods, Re (1884) 13 LR Ir 406 95
Oddie v Brown (1859) 4 De G & J 179, 28 LJ Ch 542, 5 Jur NS 635, 7 WR 472,
33 LTOS 174 .... 263, 407, 413
Oddie v Woodford (1821) 3 My & Cr 584; on appeal (1825) 3 My & Cr 625, HL
.... 248, 262, 335, 338
Oddy, Re, Major v Harness [1906] 1 Ch 93, 75 LJ Ch 141, 54 WR 291, 50 Sol Jo 155, 94
LT 146, CA 1189
Odell v Crone. See Crone v Odell
O'Donnell, Re [1905] 1 IR 406, CA 1021
O'Donnell v O'Donnell (1878) 1 LR Ir 284 205
O'Donnell v Welsh [1903] 1 IR 115 127
O'Donoghue v O'Donoghue [1906] 1 IR 482 446
Offiler, Re, Offiler v Offiler (1901) 83 LT 758 322
Offley v Best (1666) 2 Keb 392, 419, 1 Lev 186, 1 Sid 370
.... 849
Ofner, Re, Samuel v Ofner [1909] 1 Ch 60, 78 LJ Ch 50, [1908–10] All ER Rep 851, 99
LT 813, CA 199, 215, 220, 268
Ogden, Re, Brydon v Samuel [1933] Ch 678, 102 LJ Ch 226, [1933] All ER Rep 720, 77
Sol Jo 216, 149 LT 162, 49 TLR 341 .... 36, 45
Ogden, Re, Taylor v Sharp (1909) 25 TLR 382, CA 11
Ogilby, Re, Cochrane v Ogilby [1903] 1 IR 525 366
Ogilby, Re, Ogilby v Wentworth-Stanley [1942] Ch 288, [1942] 1 All ER 524, 111 LJ Ch
169, 86 Sol Jo 132, 167 LT 65, 58 TLR 209 488
Ogilvie, Re, Ogilvie v Ogilvie [1918] 1 Ch 492, 87 LJ Ch 363, 118 LT 749
.... 190
Ogilvie-Forbes' Trustees v Ogilvie-Forbes 1955 SC 405, 1955 SLT 121, Ct of Sess
.... 156
Ogle v Knipe (1869) LR 8 Eq 434, 38 LJ Ch 692, 17 WR 1090, 20 LT 867
.... 293–294
Ogle v Morgan (1852) 1 De GM & G 359 366
O'Grady v Wilmot [1916] 2 AC 231, 85 LJ Ch 386, 60 Sol Jo 456, 114 LT 1097, 32 TLR
456, [1916–17] All ER Rep Ext 1385, HL 917, 955, 1128, 1130
O'Hanlon v Unthank (1872) IR 7 Eq 68 387
O'Hare, Re, Madden v M'Givern [1918] 1 IR 160 381
O'Higgins v Walsh [1918] 1 IR 126 1087
Oke v Heath (1748) 1 Ves Sen 135 185
O'Kean, Re, Ferris v O'Kean [1907] 1 IR 223, 225, 41 ILT 8
.... 1201
Okeden v Clifden (1826) 2 Russ 309 .... 212, 267
O'Kelly, Re, Burke v Whelan [1920] 1 IR 200 1041
Oldcorn v Tenniswood (1909) 25 TLR 825, P, D and Admlty
.... 911
Oldham, Re, Hadwen v Myles [1925] Ch 75, 95 LJ Ch 148, [1924] All ER Rep 288, 69
Sol Jo 193, 132 LT 658 .... 10, 21, 23
Oldham, Re, Oldham v Myles [1927] WN 113, 71 Sol Jo 491
.... 1118
Oldham v Oldham (1867) LR 3 Eq 404, 36 LJ Ch 205, 15 WR 300
.... 463
Oldroyd v Harvey [1907] P 326, 76 LJP 161, 98 LT 56, 23 TLR 729, P, D and Admlty
.... 5, 85
O'Leary v Douglass (1878) 1 LR Ir 45; revsd (1879) 3 LR Ir 323, CA
.... 95, 97
Olins v Walters [2007] EWCA Civ 1347, [2007] All ER (D) 488 (Oct)
.... 714
Olins v Walters [2007] EWHC 3060 (Ch), [2008] WTLR 339, [2007] All ER (D) 291
(Dec); affd [2008] EWCA Civ 782, [2009] Ch 212, [2009] 2 WLR 1, [2008] WTLR
1449, [2008] All ER (D) 58 (Jul) 10, 20–21, 23
Oliphant's Goods, Re (1860) 24 JP 231, 30 LJPM & A 82, 6 Jur NS 256, 1 Sw & Tr 525,
1 LT 446 613
Olivant v Wright (1875) 1 Ch D 346, 45 LJ Ch 1, 24 WR 84, 33 LT 457, CA
.... 450
Olivant v Wright (1878) 9 Ch D 646, 47 LJ Ch 664, 27 WR 284, 38 LT 677
.... 2, 473
Olive, Re, Olive v Westerman (1884) 53 LJ Ch 525, 32 WR 608, 50 LT 355
.... 1082

                                                                                        PARA
Oliver, Re, Newbald v Beckitt [1886–90] All ER Rep 810, 62 LT 533
.... 152, 407
Oliver, Re, Theobald v Oliver [1927] 2 Ch 323, 96 LJ Ch 496, 71 Sol Jo 710, 137 LT 788
.... 1150
Oliver, Re, Watkins v Fitton [1947] 2 All ER 162, [1947] LJR 1400, 91 Sol Jo 421, 177 LT
   308 1080
Oliver, Re, Wilson v Oliver [1908] 2 Ch 74, 77 LJ Ch 547, 99 LT 241, [1908–10] All ER
   Rep Ext 1377   1123
Oliver v Brickland (1732) 3 Atk 420, 422 497
Olliver's Goods, Re (1854) 2 Ecc & Ad 57 75
Olney v Bates (1855) 3 Drew 319, 3 WR 606, 26 LTOS 35
.... 167, 305
O'Loughlin v Bellew [1906] 1 IR 487 .... 351, 354
O'Loughlin's Goods, Re (1870) LR 2 P & D 102, 39 LJP & M 53, 18 WR 902
.... 288
Olphert v Olphert [1903] 1 IR 325 316
Olszanecki v Hillocks [2002] EWHC 1997 (Ch), [2004] WTLR 975, [2002] All ER (D) 68
   (Aug) 128, 407
O'Mahoney v Burdett (1874) LR 7 HL 388, 44 LJ Ch 56n, 23 WR 361, 31 LT 705,
   [1874–80] All ER Rep Ext 1989 .... 182, 444, 449–450
O'Meagher v O'Meagher (1883) 11 LR Ir 117 .... 68, 70, 895
Ommaney v Bevan (1811) 18 Ves 291 449
O'Neill v M'Grorty [1915] 1 IR 1   1040, 1102
O'Neill v Montgomery (1861) 12 I Ch R 163, 13 Ir Jur 351
.... 454
O'Neill's Goods, Re (1916) 50 ILT 180 65
Ongley v Chambers (1824) 1 Bing 483, 2 LJOSCP 49, 8 Moore CP 665
.... 225, 286
Ongley v Peale. See Ungly v Peale
Onions v Tyrer. See Onyons v Tryers
Onslow v Corrie (1817) 2 Madd 330 1223
Onslow v Michell (1812) 18 Ves 490 404
Onyons v Tryers (1716) Gilb Ch 130, Prec Ch 459, sub nom Onions v Tyrer 1 P Wms 343,
   2 Vern 741 .... 93, 102, 107–108
Opanubi v Daley [2002] EWHC 1596 (Ch), [2002] All ER (D) 411 (Jul)
.... 1261, 1266–1267
Oppenheim, Re, Oppenheim v Oppenheim (1914) 58 Sol Jo 723, 111 LT 937
.... 285
Oppenheim v Henry (1853) 10 Hare 441, 9 Hare 803n, sub nom Openheim v Henry 1 WR
   126, 20 LTOS 291 .... 186, 200, 305, 428
Oppenheim v Henry (1853) 9 Hare 802n, 1 WR 126, 20 LTOS 291
.... 186, 672
Oppenheim's Will Trusts, Re, Westminster Bank Ltd v Oppenheim [1950] Ch 633, [1950]
   2 All ER 86, 66 (pt 1) TLR 1040 465
Oppenheimer, Re, Tyser v Oppenheimer [1948] Ch 721, [1948] LJR 1553, 92 Sol Jo 442
.... 1132
Oram, Re, Oram v Oram [1940] Ch 1001, [1940] 4 All ER 161, 109 LJ Ch 427, 84 Sol Jo
   549, 164 LT 264 .... 405, 1117
Orchard, Re, Carpenter v Lauer [1948] 1 All ER 203, 92 Sol Jo 97, 64 TLR 144
.... 246
Ord, Re, Dickinson v Dickinson (1879) 12 Ch D 22, 28 WR 141, 41 LT 13,
   [1874–80] All ER Rep Ext 1518, CA 282
Ord v Ord (1866) LR 2 Eq 393, 15 LT 51 408
O'Reilly v Prudential Assurance Co Ltd [1934] Ch 519, 103 LJ Ch 323, [1934] All ER Rep
   672, 78 Sol Jo 349, 151 LT 215, 50 TLR 359, CA 938
O'Reilly v Smith (1851) 17 LTOS 280 284
O'Reilly v Walsh (1872) 6 IR Eq 555; affd (1872) 7 IR Eq 167
.... 436, 1149
O'Reilly's Goods, Re (1873) 38 JP 24, 43 LJP & M 5, 22 WR 224, 29 LT 546
.... 611
Orford (Earl) v Churchill (1814) 3 Ves & B 59 328
Ormiston's Executor v Laws 1966 SC 47, 1966 SLT 110, Ct of Sess
.... 276
Ormond (Marquis) v Kynnersley (1829) 15 Beav 10, 7 LJOS Ch 150, 8 LJOS Ch 67
.... 931
Ormond's Goods, Re (1828) 1 Hag Ecc 145 801

PARA

Orr, Re, M'Dermott v Anderson [1915] 1 IR 191 .... 231, 375
Orr v Kaines (1750) 2 Ves Sen 194 1096–1097
Orr v Newton (1791) 2 Cox Eq Cas 274, PC 627
Ortega Associates Ltd, Re; Green v Walkling. See Green v Walkling
Orton v Smith (1873) LR 3 P & D 23, 37 JP 503, 42 LJP & M 50, 28 LT 712
.... 911
Orton's Trust, Re (1866) LR 3 Eq 375, 36 LJ Ch 279, 15 WR 251, 16 LT 146
.... 398
Orwell's Will Trusts, Re, Dixon v Blair [1982] 3 All ER 177, [1982] 1 WLR 1337, 126 Sol
    Jo 593 652
Osborn v Gillett (1873) LR 8 Exch 88, 42 LJ Ex 53, 21 WR 409, [1861–73] All ER Rep
    923, 28 LT 197, Exch Ct 1280
Osborne v Duke of Leeds (1800) 5 Ves 369 403
Osburn, Re (1969) 113 Sol Jo 387, CA 245, 711
Oseland v Oseland (1795) 3 Anst 628 428
Osment's Estate, Re, Child and Jarvis v Osment [1914] P 129, 83 LJP 72, 58 Sol Jo 596,
    110 LT 990, P, D and Admlty 910, 914
Osmond, Re, Cummings v Galaway (1910) 30 NZLR 65
.... 429
Osoba, Re, Osoba v Osoba [1979] 2 All ER 393, [1979] 1 WLR 247, 123 Sol Jo 35, CA
.... 171, 173, 175, 371, 393, 1061
Ossulston's (Lord) Case (1708) 3 Salk 336, sub nom Ford v Ossulton 11 Mod Rep 189
.... 384
Oswald, Re, Oswald v Oswald (1919) 64 Sol Jo 242 .... 1059, 1159
Oswald's Goods, Re (1874) LR 3 P & D 162, 38 JP 425, 43 LJP & M 24, 30 LT 344
.... 95, 739
O'Toole v Browne (1854) 3 E & B 572, 23 LJQB 282, 18 Jur 1113, 2 WR 430, 2 CLR
    1701, 23 LTOS 111 .... 256, 284, 289
Ottaway v Norman [1972] Ch 698, [1971] 3 All ER 1325, [1972] 2 WLR 50, 116 Sol Jo
    38, 221 Estates Gazette 1434 .... 20, 23, 221–222
Otter v Church, Adams, Tatham & Co [1953] Ch 280, [1953] 1 All ER 168, [1953] 1
    WLR 156, 97 Sol Jo 48 1279
Ottey v Grundy [2003] EWCA Civ 1176, [2003] WTLR 1253, [2003] All ER (D) 05 (Aug)
.... 567, 581
Ottley v Gilby (1845) 8 Beav 602, 14 LJ Ch 177, 68 RR 218, 4 LTOS 411
.... 1254
Otuka v Alozie [2006] EWHC 3493 (Ch), [2005] All ER (D) 265 (Dec)
.... 50, 77, 895
Otway v Sadleir (1858) 33 LTOS 46, 4 Ir Jur NS 97 88
Oughton v Seppings (1830) 1 B & Ad 241, 8 LJOS 394, 109 ER 776, [1824–34] All ER
    Rep 376 635
O'sullivan v National Trustees, Executors and Agency Co of Australia Ltd [1913] VLR 173
.... 21
Ousby v Harvey (1848) 17 LJ Ch 160 385
Ouseley v Anstruther (1847) 10 Beav 453 296
Outerbridge v Hollis [1951] WN 318, PC 318
Overend v Gurney (1834) 7 Sim 128 409
Overhill's Trusts, Re, Re Trustee Relief Act (1853) 22 LJ Ch 485, 17 Jur 342, 1 Sm & G
    362, 1 WR 208, 20 LTOS 290 .... 210, 212
Overton v Banister (1841) 4 Beav 205 397
Ovey, Re, Broadbent v Barrow (1885) 31 Ch D 113, 55 LJ Ch 103, 34 WR 100, 53 LT
    723 1109
Owen, Re, Frisby, Dyke & Co v Owen [1891–4] All ER Rep 917, 36 Sol Jo 504, 66 LT
    718 1042
Owen, Re, Hodgson v Clare [2002] WTLR 619, sub nom Hodgson v Clare [1999] All ER
    (D) 359 .... 194, 220, 229, 235–236, 242–243, 255
Owen, Re, Peat v Owen (1898) 78 LT 643 296
Owen, Re, Slater v Owen [1912] 1 Ch 519, 81 LJ Ch 337, [1911–1913] All ER Rep 261,
    56 Sol Jo 381, 106 LT 671 1126
Owen v Bryant (1852) 2 De GM & G 697, 21 LJ Ch 860, 16 Jur 877, 20 LTOS 45
.... 350
Owen v Delamere (1872) LR 15 Eq 134, 42 LJ Ch 232, 21 WR 218, 27 LT 647
.... 1039, 1041
Owen v Gibbons [1902] 1 Ch 636, 71 LJ Ch 338, 86 LT 571, 18 TLR 347, CA
.... 540
Owen v Owen (1738) 1 Atk 494 173

PARA

Owen v Penny (1850) 14 Jur 359 348
Owen's Trusts, Re (1871) LR 12 Eq 316, 25 LT 489 390
Owens v Bean (1678) Cas temp Finch 395 277
Owers, Re, Public Trustee v Death [1941] Ch 17, [1940] 4 All ER 225, 110 LJ Ch 22, 84
    Sol Jo 633, 164 LT 337, 57 TLR 80, CA 1111
Owers, Re, Public Trustee v Death [1941] Ch 389, [1941] 2 All ER 589, 110 LJ Ch 157,
    85 Sol Jo 341, 165 LT 94 .... 990–991, 1224
Owston's Goods, Re (1862) 26 JP 728, 31 LJPM & A 177, 2 Sw & Tr 461, 10 WR 410, 6
    LT 368 .... 48, 68
Oxenham v Clapp (1831) 2 B & Ad 309, 9 LJOSKB 229
    1268
Oxley, Re, John Hornby & Sons v Oxley [1914] 1 Ch 604, 83 LJ Ch 442, 58 Sol Jo 319,
    110 LT 626, 30 TLR 327, sub nom Oxley, Re, John Hornby [1914–15] All ER Rep
    505, CA 1040

P

P, Re [2009] EWHC 163 (Ch), [2010] Ch 33, [2009] 2 All ER 1198, [2009] All ER (D)
    160 (Feb) 47
P v G (family provision: relevance of divorce provision) [2004] EWHC 2944 (Fam), [2006]
    1 FLR 431, [2006] Fam Law 178 577
Packard, Re, Packard v Waters [1920] 1 Ch 596, 89 LJ Ch 301, [1918–19] All ER Rep
    365, 123 LT 401 148–149
Packham v Gregory (1845) 4 Hare 396, 14 LJ Ch 191, 9 Jur 175
    429
Packman's Case (1596) 6 Co Rep 18b, sub nom Wilson v Packman Cro Eliz 459, sub nom
    Anon 3 Salk 22, sub nom Wilson v Pateman Moore KB 396
    858
Padget v Priest (1787) 2 Term Rep 97 .... 1265, 1267–1268
Page, Re, Jones v Morgan [1893] 1 Ch 304, 62 LJ Ch 592, 3 R 171, 41 WR 357
    1150
Page v Adam (1841) 4 Beav 269, 10 LJ Ch 407, 5 Jur 793
    1024
Page v Cox (1852) 10 Hare 163, 90 RR 314 .... 30, 32
Page v Hayward (1705) 2 Eq Cas Abr 362, 11 Mod Rep 61, 2 Salk 570, Holt KB 618
    .... 129, 407
Page v Leapingwell (1812) 18 Ves 463 .... 375, 1088
Page v May (1857) 24 Beav 323, 27 LJ Ch 242, 3 Jur NS 1047, 5 WR 840, 30 LTOS 84
    444
Page v Page (1728) Mos 42, 2 P Wms 489, 2 Stra 820 .... 173, 183
Page v Soper (1853) 11 Hare 321, 22 LJ Ch 1044, 1 Eq Rep 540, 17 Jur 851, 1 WR 518
    377
Page v Williamson (1902) 87 LT 146, 18 TLR 770, P, D and Admlty
    .... 908, 910
Paget v Huish (1863) 1 Hem & M 663, 32 LJ Ch 468, 9 Jur NS 906, 2 New Rep 104, 11
    WR 636, 8 LT 445 1088
Paget's Goods, Re (1913) 47 ILT 284 106
Paice v Archbishop of Canterbury (1807) 14 Ves 364 371
Paige v Brooks (1896) 75 LT 455, P, D and Admlty 102
Pain v Benson (1744) 3 Atk 78 410
Paine v Countess of Warwick [1914] 2 KB 486, sub nom White v Paine 83 LJKB 895, 58
    Sol Jo 381, 30 TLR 347 122
Paine v Hyde (1841) 4 Beav 468 149
Paine v Wagner (1841) 12 Sim 184 .... 390, 396
Painton v Berry, etc (Administrators of Thornton). See Peyton v Bury
Palfreeman, Re, Public Trustee v Palfreeman [1914] 1 Ch 877, 83 LJ Ch 702, 58 Sol Jo
    456, 110 LT 972, [1914–15] All ER Rep Ext 1541 .... 430, 1081
Palmer, ex p (1852) 5 De G & Sm 649, 17 Jur 108 146
Palmer, Re, Leventhorpe v Palmer (1912) 106 LT 319, [1911–13] All ER Rep Ext 1270,
    CA 1131
Palmer, Re, Palmer v Answorth [1893] 3 Ch 369, 62 LJ Ch 988, 2 R 619, 42 WR 151, 37
    Sol Jo 701, 69 LT 477, CA 173, 236, 298, 1115
Palmer, Re, Palmer v Palmer [1916] 2 Ch 391, 85 LJ Ch 577, [1916–17] All ER Rep 892,
    60 Sol Jo 565, 115 LT 57, CA 1130–1131

PARA

Palmer (a debtor), Re [1994] Ch 316, [1994] 3 All ER 835, [1994] 3 WLR 420, [1995] 1
  FCR 320, [1994] 2 FLR 609, [1994] Fam Law 566, 138 Sol Jo LB 72, CA
  988
Palmer v Craufurd (1819) 2 Wils Ch 79, 3 Swan 483 1058
Palmer v Crutwell (1862) 8 Jur NS 479 397
Palmer v Fleshees (1663) 1 Keb 625, 1 Sid 167, sub nom Palmer v Fletcher 1 Lev 122
  283
Palmer v Flower (1871) LR 13 Eq 250, 41 LJ Ch 193, 20 WR 174, 25 LT 816
  371
Palmer v Jones (1874) 43 LJ Ch 349 1201
Palmer v O'Connor [2006] EWHC 1589 (Ch), [2006] All ER (D) 278 (Mar)
  694
Palmer v Orpen [1894] 1 IR 32 .... 248, 302
Palmer v Waller (1836) 5 Dowl 172, 5 LJ Ex 246, 2 Gale 105, 1 M & W 689, Tyr & Gr
  1014 1294
Palmer's Goods, Re, Palmer v Peat (1889) 58 LJP 44, P, D and Admlty
  97
Panter, Re, Panter-Downes v Bally (1906) 22 TLR 431 415
Papillon, Re, Murrin v Matthews [2006] EWHC 3419 (Ch), [2006] All ER (D) 297 (Dec)
  .... 718, 845
Papouis v West [2004] EWHC 396 (Ch), sub nom Papouis v Gibson-West [2004] All ER
  (D) 98 (Mar), sub nom Re Bennett, Papouis v Gibson-West [2004] WTLR 485
  56
Paradise Motor Co Ltd, Re [1968] 2 All ER 625, [1968] 1 WLR 1125, 112 Sol Jo 271, CA
  154
Paramour v Yardley (1579) 2 Plowd 539 .... 121, 232, 234, 379, 1141
Parfitt v Lawless (1872) LR 2 P & D 462, 36 JP 822, 41 LJP & M 68, 21 WR 200, 27 LT
  215 .... 56–57, 904
Park, Re, Bott v Chester [1910] 2 Ch 322, 79 LJ Ch 502, 54 Sol Jo 563, 102 LT 725
  .... 115, 135, 144
Park, Re, Public Trustee v Armstrong [1932] 1 Ch 580, 101 LJ Ch 295, [1931] All ER Rep
  633, 147 LT 118 11
Park's Estate, Re, Park v Park [1954] P 112, [1953] 2 All ER 1411, [1953] 3 WLR 1012,
  97 Sol Jo 830, CA 49
Parker, Re, Barker v Barker (1880) 16 Ch D 44 431–432
Parker, Re, Bentham v Wilson (1881) 17 Ch D 262, 50 LJ Ch 639, 29 WR 855, 44 LT
  885, CA 210, 328
Parker, Re, Cash v Parker (1879) 12 Ch D 293, 48 LJ Ch 691, 27 WR 835, 40 LT 878
  1283
Parker, Re, Parker v Osborne [1897] 2 Ch 208, 66 LJ Ch 509, 45 WR 536, 76 LT 421,
  [1895–9] All ER Rep Ext 1822 352
Parker, Re, Stephenson v Parker [1901] 1 Ch 408, 70 LJ Ch 170, 49 WR 215, 45 Sol Jo
  219, 84 LT 116 .... 474, 1115
Parker, Re, White v Stewart (1917) 86 LJ Ch 766, 117 LT 422, 33 TLR 501, CA
  1130
Parker v Birks (1854) 1 K & J 156, 24 LJ Ch 117, 3 WR 102
  461
Parker v Clark [1960] 1 All ER 93, [1960] 1 WLR 286, 104 Sol Jo 251
  21
Parker v Felgate (1883) 8 PD 171, 47 JP 808, 52 LJP 95, 32 WR 186, P, D and Admlty
  .... 48, 50, 892, 901
Parker v Golding (1843) 13 Sim 418 432
Parker v Hodgson (1861) 1 Drew & Sm 568, 30 LJ Ch 590, 7 Jur NS 750, 9 WR 607, 4
  LT 762 438–439
Parker v Judkin [1931] 1 Ch 475, 100 LJ Ch 159, [1931] All ER Rep 222, 144 LT 662,
  CA 1024–1025, 1145
Parker v Kett (1701) 1 Com 84, 1 Ld Raym 658, 12 Mod Rep 467, 1 Salk 95, Holt KB
  221, 91 ER 88, [1558–1774] All ER Rep 199 1266
Parker v Marchant (1842) 1 Y & C Ch Cas 290, 11 LJ Ch 223, 6 Jur 292,
  [1843–60] All ER Rep 1061; affd (1843) 1 Ph 356, 12 LJ Ch 385, 62 ER 893,
  [1843–60] All ER Rep 1061 .... 205, 238, 250, 288, 293, 365
Parker v Marchant (1843) 5 Man & G 498 291
Parker v Nickson (1863) 1 De GJ & Sm 177, 32 LJ Ch 397, 9 Jur NS 451, 1 New Rep
  298, 11 WR 533, 7 LT 813 387
Parker v Parker (1841) Milw 541 .... 64, 68
Parker v Parker (1863) 1 New Rep 508 379

PARA

Parker v Sowerby (1853) 1 Drew 488, 22 LJ Ch 942, 1 Eq Rep 217, 17 Jur 752, 1 WR
    404; affd (1854) 4 De GM & G 321, 23 LJ Ch 623, 2 Eq Rep 664, 18 Jur 523, 2 WR
    547 .... 415, 429
Parker v Tootal (1865) 11 HL Cas 143, 34 LJ Ex 198, 11 Jur NS 185, 5 New Rep 378, 13
    WR 442, 12 LT 89 .... 248, 253, 456, 466, 473
Parker d Walker v Constable (1769) 3 Wils 25 942
Parker's Goods, Re (1859) 23 JP 360, 28 LJP & M 91, 5 Jur NS 553, 2 Sw & Tr 375
    80
Parker's Goods, Re (1860) 24 JP 199, 31 LJPM & A 8, 6 Jur NS 354, 1 Sw & Tr 523, 1
    LT 447 167
Parker's Trusts, Re [1894] 1 Ch 707, 63 LJ Ch 316, 70 LT 165
    615–616
Parker's Will, Re (1888) 39 Ch D 303, 58 LJ Ch 23, 37 WR 313, 60 LT 83, 4 TLR 740,
    CA 1047–1048, 1065
Parker's Will, Re, Kilroy and Callan v Parker and McGauran [1966] IR 309
    45
Parker-Jervis, Re, Salt v Locker [1898] 2 Ch 643, 67 LJ Ch 682, 47 WR 147,
    [1895–9] All ER Rep 439, 79 LT 403 1131
Parkes (or Keswick) v Parkes (or Keswick) [1936] 3 All ER 653, HL
    412–413
Parkin v Hodgkinson (1846) 15 Sim 293 453
Parkin v Knight (1846) 15 Sim 83, 15 LJ Ch 209, 10 Jur 23, 6 LTOS 450
    .... 254, 320, 392, 419
Parkinson, Re (1975) Times, 4 October, CA 574
Parkinson v Fawdon [2009] EWHC 1953 (Ch), [2009] All ER (D) 322 (Jul)
    .... 8, 611, 670, 708
Parkinson v Thornton (1867) 37 LJP & M 3 680
Parkinson's Trust, Re, ex p Thompson (1851) 1 Sim NS 242, 20 LJ Ch 224, 15 Jur 165
    348
Parks v Clout [2002] EWHC 1843 (Ch), [2002] All ER (D) 26 (Sep); affd [2003] EWCA
    Civ 982, [2003] All ER (D) 105 (Jun) 3, 106
Parnall, Re, Parnall v Hurst [2003] WTLR 997 .... 598, 690
Parnall's Estate, Re [1936] P 47, 105 LJP 20, 80 Sol Jo 94, 154 LT 374, 52 TLR 160, P, D
    and Admlty 759, 761
Parnell, Re, Ranks v Holmes [1944] Ch 107, 113 LJ Ch 92, 88 Sol Jo 25, 170 LT 40, 60
    TLR 154 298
Parnell v Boyd [1896] 2 IR 571 .... 153–154, 369, 378
Parnell v Lyon (1813) 1 Ves & B 479 135
Parr v Parr (1833) 1 My & K 647, 2 LJ Ch 167 .... 205, 305, 916
Parr v Swindels (1828) 4 Russ 283, 6 LJOS Ch 99 .... 457, 473
Parr's Goods, Re (1859) Sea & Sm 146, 29 LJPM & A 70, 6 Jur NS 56
    108
Parr's Trusts, Re (1871) 41 LJ Ch 170 412
Parrish v Sharman [2001] WTLR 593, CA 577
Parrott, Re, Cox v Parrott [1946] Ch 183, [1946] 1 All ER 321, 115 LJ Ch 211, 90 Sol Jo
    139, 175 LT 190, 62 TLR 189 143
Parrott, Re, Parrott v Parrott (1885) 53 LT 12 250
Parrott, Re, Walter v Parrott (1886) 33 Ch D 274, 34 WR 553, 55 LT 132, CA
    331
Parry, Re (1956) Times, 19 April 574
Parry, Re, Brown v Parry [1947] Ch 23, [1946] 2 All ER 412, [1947] LJR 81, 90 Sol Jo
    478, 175 LT 395, 62 TLR 543 .... 1124, 1126, 1257
Parry, Re, Dalton v Cooke [1969] 2 All ER 512, [1969] 1 WLR 614, 113 Sol Jo 228
    1070
Parry, Re, Leak v Scott [1888] WN 179, 4 TLR 696 344
Parry, Re, Scott v Leak (1889) 42 Ch D 570, 38 WR 226, 61 LT 380
    1058
Parry v Huddleton (1854) 18 Jur 992 1298
Parry v Roberts (1871) 19 WR 1000, 25 LT 371 145
Parry and Daggs, Re (1885) 31 Ch D 130, 55 LJ Ch 237, 34 WR 353, 54 LT 229, CA
    450
Parry and Hopkin, Re [1900] 1 Ch 160, 64 JP 137, 69 LJ Ch 190, 48 WR 345, 81 LT 807
    1228
Parry's Estate, Re, Parry v Fraser [1977] 1 All ER 309, [1977] 1 WLR 93n, 121 Sol Jo 70
    56
Parslow, Re, Parslow v Parslow (1959) Times, 3 December
    .... 77, 895

PARA
Parsons, Re, Blaber v Parsons (1894) 8 R 430 323
Parsons, Re, Parsons v A-G [1943] Ch 12, [1942] 2 All ER 496, 86 Sol Jo 359, 167 LT
384, 59 TLR 19, CA 151, 1060
Parsons, Re, Stockley v Parsons (1890) 45 Ch D 51, 59 LJ Ch 666, 38 WR 712, 62 LT 929
.... 27
Parsons v Coke (1858) 27 LJ Ch 828, 6 WR 715 371
Parsons v Coke (1858) 4 Drew 296 .... 320, 336, 390, 392
Parsons v Hancock (1829) Mood & M 330 1293
Parsons v Lanoe (1748) Amb 557, 1 Wils 243, 1 Ves Sen 189
.... 7
Parsons v Parsons (1791) 1 Ves 266 .... 215, 275
Parsons v Peters (1864) 11 Jur NS 150, 13 WR 214, 11 LT 501
.... 434
Parsons v Saffery (1821) 9 Price 578 175
Partington v A-G. See A-G v Partington
Parton, Re, Parton v Parton (1911) 131 LT Jo 106 1208
Partridge v Baylis (1881) 17 Ch D 835, 29 WR 820, 44 LT 737
.... 452
Partridge v Foster (No 2) (1866) 35 Beav 545 417
Partridge v Partridge [1894] 1 Ch 351, 63 LJ Ch 122, 70 LT 261
.... 145
Partridge v Partridge (1736) 2 Eq Cas Abr 570, Cas temp Talb 226, 9 Mod Rep 269
.... 156
Pascoe v Smart (1901) 17 TLR 595, P, D and Admlty 68
Paske v Ollat (1815) 2 Phillim 323 903
Paskins' Will Trusts, Re, Paskins v Underwood [1948] 2 All ER 156, 92 Sol Jo 377
.... 139
Pasmore v Huggins (1855) 21 Beav 103, 25 LJ Ch 251, 1 Jur NS 1060, 4 WR 33,
26 LTOS 66 .... 253, 331
Passmore v Passmore (1811) 1 Phillim 216 54
Patch v Shore (1862) 2 Drew & Sm 589, 32 LJ Ch 185, 9 Jur NS 63, 1 New Rep 157, 11
WR 142, 7 LT 554 2–3
Patching v Barnett [1907] 2 Ch 154n, 51 LJ Ch 74, 45 LT 292, [1881–5] All ER Rep Ext
1761, CA 148
Patching v Dubbins (1853) Kay 1, 23 LJ Ch 45, 17 Jur 1113, 2 WR 2, 22 LTOS 116; on
appeal (1853) 23 LJ Ch 49, 2 Eq Rep 71 368
Patel v Patel [2007] EWCA Civ 1520, [2007] All ER (D) 276 (Dec)
.... 1232, 1235
Paterson v Mills (1850) 19 LJ Ch 310, 15 Jur 1, 16 LTOS 122
.... 546
Paterson v Rolland (1860) 28 Beav 347 395
Paterson's Will Trusts, Re, Lawson v Payn [1963] 1 All ER 114, [1963] 1 WLR 623, 41
ATC 412, [1962] TR 389, 107 Sol Jo 631 1130
Paton v Ormerod [1892] P 247, 61 LJP 120, 66 LT 381, P, D and Admlty
.... 99, 112, 217, 711
Patrick v Hevercroft (1920) 123 LT 201, 36 TLR 290, P, D and Admlty
.... 874
Patten v Patten (1833) Alc & N 493 646
Patten v Poulton (1858) 22 JP 180, 27 LJP & M 41, 4 Jur NS 341, 1 Sw & Tr 55, 6 WR
458, 31 LTOS 40 106
Patterson v Huddart (1853) 17 Beav 210, 1 WR 423 289
Patterson's Goods, Re (1898) 79 LT 123, P, D and Admlty
.... 80
Pattison v Pattison (1832) 1 My & K 12, 2 LJ Ch 15 114
Pattison v Pattison (1855) 19 Beav 638 .... 305, 396
Pattison's Goods, Re, Henderson v Priestman [1918] 2 IR 90
.... 68–69
Patton v Jones (1807) 14 Ves 372 344
Patton v Toronto General Trusts Corpn [1930] AC 629, 143 LT 572, sub nom Re Patton,
Patton v Toronto General Trusts Corpn 99 LJPC 213, PC
.... 131, 140, 407
Paul v Children (1871) LR 12 Eq 16, 19 WR 941, 25 LT 82
.... 351
Paul v Paul (1760) 1 Wm Bl 255, sub nom Goodtitle d Paul v Paul 2 Burr 1089
.... 271
Paul's Estate, Re, Gilmer v Overman (1907) 23 TLR 716, P, D and Admlty
.... 723

PARA

Paul's Settlement Trusts, Re, Paul v Nelson [1920] 1 Ch 99, 88 LJ Ch 530, 63 Sol Jo 724,
121 LT 544 308

Paulett's (Lord) Case. See Poulet (Lady) v Lord Poulet

Pauling's Settlement Trusts, Re, Younghusband v Coutts & Co [1961] 3 All ER 713, [1962]
1 WLR 86, 106 Sol Jo 135; on appeal [1964] Ch 303, [1963] 3 All ER 1, [1963] 3
WLR 742, 107 Sol Jo 492, CA 1250, 1259

Paull v Simpson (1846) 9 QB 365, 15 LJQB 382, 11 Jur 13
.... 1262, 1264

Pawle's Estate, Re, Winter v Pawle (1918) 34 TLR 437, P, D and Admlty
.... 7, 713

Pawlet v Dogget (1688) 2 Vern 86 460

Pawley and London and Provincial Bank, Re [1900] 1 Ch 58, 69 LJ Ch 6, 48 WR 107, 44
Sol Jo 25, 81 LT 507 .... 633, 635, 945

Paylor v Pegg (1857) 24 Beav 105 .... 408, 417, 471

Payne, Re (1858) 25 Beav 556 299

Payne, Re, Taylor v Payne [1927] 2 Ch 1, 96 LJ Ch 291, [1927] All ER Rep 223, 137 LT
117 231

Payne, Re, Westminster Bank Ltd v Payne [1943] 2 All ER 675, 113 LJ Ch 46, 87 Sol Jo
406, 169 LT 365, 60 TLR 49 1127

Payne v Barker (1662) O Bridg 18, sub nom Hale v - 2 Ld Raym 1025, 1 P Wms 66, sub
nom Fane v Barr 6 Mod Rep 121, 1 Salk 243 561

Payne v Haine (1847) 11 JP 462, 16 LJ Ex 130, 16 M & W 541, 8 LTOS 414
.... 152

Payne v Hornby (1858) 25 Beav 280, 27 LJ Ch 689, 4 Jur NS 446, 31 LTOS 309
.... 920

Payne v Little (1853) 13 Beav 114 600

Payne v Little (1856) 22 Beav 69 1301

Payne v Little (1859) 27 Beav 83 1018

Payne v Tanner (1886) 55 LJ Ch 611, 34 WR 714, 55 LT 258
.... 1301

Payne v Webb (1874) LR 19 Eq 26, 23 WR 43, 31 LT 637, [1874–80] All ER Rep Ext
1977 395–396

Payne and Meredith v Trappes (1847) 1 Rob Eccl 583, 11 Jur 854, 10 LTOS 36, 5 Notes
of Cases 478 112

Peace v Hains (1853) 11 Hare 151, 17 Jur 1091 217

Peacock, Re, Midland Bank Executor and Trustee Co Ltd v Peacock [1957] Ch 310, [1957]
2 All ER 98, [1957] 2 WLR 793, 101 Sol Jo 339 .... 39–40, 173–175

Peacock, Re, Public Trustee v Birchenough [1929] WN 76, 73 Sol Jo 220, 45 TLR 301
.... 296

Peacock v Colling (1885) 54 LJ Ch 743, 33 WR 528, 53 LT 620, CA
.... 1174

Peacock v Lowe (1867) LR 1 P & D 311, P, D and Admlty
.... 870

Peacock v Stockford (1853) 3 De GM & G 73 .... 253, 332

Peacock's Settlement, Re, Kelcey v Harrison [1902] 1 Ch 552, 71 LJ Ch 325, 50 WR 473,
46 Sol Jo 297, 86 LT 414 955

Pearce, Re, Alliance Assurance Co Ltd v Francis [1913] 2 Ch 674, 109 LT 514; affd [1914]
1 Ch 254, 83 LJ Ch 266, [1911–13] All ER Rep 1067, 58 Sol Jo 197, 110 LT 168, CA
.... 350–352, 354

Pearce, Re, Crutchley v Wells [1909] 1 Ch 819, 78 LJ Ch 484, 53 Sol Jo 419, 100 LT 699,
25 TLR 497, [1908–10] All ER Rep Ext 1323 .... 1014, 1060

Pearce, Re, Eastwood v Pearce (1912) 56 Sol Jo 686, CA
.... 320

Pearce, Re, Pearce v Davis Pearce [1999] 2 FCR 179, [1998] 2 FLR 705, [1998] Fam Law
588, CA 570, 573, 580

Pearce, Re, Roberts v Stephens (1894) 8 R 805 156

Pearce v Carrington (1873) 8 Ch App 969, 42 LJ Ch 900, 22 WR 41, 29 LT 706
.... 362

Pearce v Edmeades (1838) 3 Y & C Ex 246, 8 LJ Ex Eq 61, 3 Jur 245
.... 395, 397, 470

Pearce v Graham (1863) 32 LJ Ch 359, 9 Jur NS 568, 1 New Rep 507, 11 WR 415, 8 LT
378 168

Pearce v Loman (1796) 3 Ves 135 438

Pearce v Taylor (1796) 3 Ves 135 438

Pearce v Vincent (1836) 2 Keen 230, Donnelly 128, 7 LJ Ch 285
.... 349

PARA

Peard v Kekewich (1852) 15 Beav 166, 21 LJ Ch 456, 19 LTOS 360
.... 415
Peareth v Marriott (1882) 22 Ch D 182, 52 LJ Ch 221, 31 WR 68, 48 LT 170, CA
.... 1131
Pearks v Moseley (1880) 5 App Cas 714, 50 LJ Ch 57, 21 WR 1, 43 LT 449,
 [1874–80] All ER Rep Ext 1352, HL 175, 258–259, 413, 418, 423–424
Pearman v Pearman (1864) 33 Beav 394 .... 413, 431
Pearn's Goods, Re (1875) 1 PD 70, 39 JP 824, 45 LJP 31, 24 WR 143, 33 LT 705, P, D
 and Admlty 65
Pearsall v Simpson (1808) 15 Ves 29 422
Pearse v Green (1819) 1 Jac & W 135, 20 RR 25, 37 ER 327, [1814–23] All ER Rep 405
.... 1254
Pearson, Re, Rowling v Crowther [1963] 3 All ER 763, [1963] 1 WLR 1358, 107 Sol Jo
 872 .... 97, 100, 110–111
Pearson, Re, Smith v Pearson [1920] 1 Ch 247, 89 LJ Ch 123, [1920] B & CR 38,
 [1918–19] All ER Rep 390, 64 Sol Jo 83, 122 LT 515 167
Pearson v Cranswick (1862) 31 Beav 624, 9 Jur NS 397, 11 WR 229, 9 LT 215; affd
 (1863) 9 LT 275 .... 395, 470
Pearson v Dolman (1866) LR 3 Eq 315, 36 LJ Ch 258, 15 WR 120
.... 431
Pearson v Henry (1792) 5 Term Rep 6 1299
Pearson v Pearson (1802) 1 Sch & Lef 10 .... 1054, 1081
Pearson v Pearson (1871) LR 2 P & D 451, 40 LJP & M 53, 19 WR 1014, 24 LT 917
.... 69
Pearson v Rutter (1853) 3 De GM & G 398; affd sub nom Grey v Pearson (1857) 6 HL
 Cas 61, 26 LJ Ch 473, 3 Jur NS 823, 5 WR 454, 10 ER 1216, [1843–60] All ER Rep
 21, 29 LTOS 67, HL 194, 225, 235, 237, 242, 256, 417, 442–443
Pearson v Spencer (1863) 3 B & S 761, 11 WR 471, 8 LT 166, sub nom R v Pearson 1
 New Rep 373, Ex Ch 283
Pearson v Stephen (1831) 5 Bli NS 203, 2 Dow & Cl 328
.... 392, 398
Pearson's Goods, Re [1896] P 289, 66 LJP 8, 45 WR 143, P, D and Admlty
.... 730
Pearson-Gregory, Re (1957) Times, 11 October 572
Peasley v Governors of Haileybury and Imperial Service College [2001] WTLR 1365
.... 346
Peat v Chapman (1750) 1 Ves Sen 542 .... 173, 395
Peat v Gott [1885] WN 46 818
Peat v Powell (1760) Amb 387, 1 Eden 479 471
Peck v Halsey (1726) 2 P Wms 387 266
Peck's Goods, Re (1860) 29 LJPM & A 95, 2 Sw & Tr 506, 2 LT 159
.... 761
Pedley v Dodds (1866) LR 2 Eq 819, 12 Jur NS 759, 14 WR 884, 14 LT 823
.... 271
Peebles v Oswaldtwistle UDC [1896] 2 QB 159, 65 LJQB 499, 44 WR 513, 74 LT 721,
 CA 1279
Peek v Gurney (1873) LR 6 HL 377, 43 LJ Ch 19, 22 WR 29, [1861–73] All ER Rep 116,
 HL 1277
Peek's Trusts, Re (1873) LR 16 Eq 221, 42 LJ Ch 422, 21 WR 820
.... 430
Peel v Catlow (1838) 9 Sim 372, 7 LJ Ch 273, 2 Jur 759
.... 336
Peel's Goods, Re (1870) LR 2 P & D 46, 34 JP 392, 39 LJP & M 36, 22 LT 417
.... 611
Peerless, Re, Peerless v Smith [1901] WN 151, 45 Sol Jo 670
.... 167, 1104
Pegg v Chamberlain (1860) 1 Sw & Tr 527, 8 WR 273, 2 LT 25
.... 819
Peirson v Vickers. See Pierson v Vickers
Pelham-Clinton v Duke of Newcastle [1902] 1 Ch 34, 69 LJ Ch 875, 49 WR 12, 83 LT
 627, 16 TLR 543; on appeal [1902] 1 Ch 34, 71 LJ Ch 53, 50 WR 83, 18 TLR 7, CA;
 affd [1903] AC 111, 72 LJ Ch 424, 51 WR 608, 88 LT 273, 19 TLR 275, HL
.... 129, 376, 407
Pell's Trust, Re (1861) 3 De GF & J 291 325
Pellew v Horsford (1856) 25 LJ Ch 352, 2 Jur NS 514, 4 WR 442, 27 LTOS 134
.... 296

PARA

Pells v Brown (1620) Cro Jac 590, 3 Dyer 354a, Godb 282, Palm 131, 2 Roll Rep 217, 79
  ER 504, [1558–1774] All ER Rep 531, J Bridg 1 460
Pemberton v Barnes [1899] 1 Ch 544, 68 LJ Ch 192, 47 WR 444, 80 LT 181
  27
Pemberton v Pemberton (1807) 13 Ves 290 102
Penfold v Penfold (1836) 1 Keen 685, sub nom Penfold v Giles 6 LJ Ch 4
  .... 58, 276, 346
Pengelly v Pengelly [2007] EWHC 3227 (Ch), [2008] Ch 375, [2008] 3 WLR 66
  .... 187, 194
Penley v Penley (1850) 12 Beav 547 .... 254, 320
Pennant v Kingscote (1843) 3 Curt 642, 7 Jur 754, 2 Notes of Cases 405n, sub nom
  Pennant v Sedgwick 1 LTOS 412 .... 70, 77
Pennefather, Re, Savile v Savile [1896] 1 IR 249 .... 230, 376, 384
Pennefather v Lloyd [1917] 1 IR 337 .... 96, 233, 251
Pennington v Waine [2002] EWCA Civ 227, [2002] 4 All ER 215, [2002] 1 WLR 2075,
  [2002] 2 BCLC 448, [2002] All ER (D) 24 (Mar), sub nom Pennington v Crampton
  (2002) Times, 1 April 156–157
Pennock v Pennock (1871) LR 13 Eq 144, LJ Ch 141, 20 WR 141, [1861–73] All ER Rep
  611, 25 LT 691 383
Penny v Avison (1861) 1 John & H 530, 30 LJ Ch 564, 7 Jur NS 722, 9 WR 550, 4 LT
  617 463
Penny v Clarke (1860) 1 De GF & J 425, 29 LJ Ch 370, 6 Jur NS 307, 8 WR 286, 1 LT
  537 .... 326, 393
Penny v Francis (1860) 30 LJ Ch 185, 7 Jur NS 248, 9 WR 8
  1175
Penny v Penny (1879) 11 Ch D 440, 48 LJ Ch 691, 40 LT 393, [1874–80] All ER Rep Ext
  1516 .... 1017, 1199
Penny v Railways Comr [1900] AC 628, 69 LJPC 113, 83 LT 182, PC
  .... 444, 449
Penny v Turner (1846) 15 Sim 368; on appeal (1848) 2 Ph 493, 17 LJ Ch 133
  .... 254, 320
Penny v Watts (1846) 2 Ph 149, 16 LJ Ch 146 636
Penny's Goods, Re (1846) 1 Rob Eccl 426, 4 Notes of Cases 659
  806
Penrice v Lushington (1868) 16 WR 836, 18 LT 597 412
Penton's Settlements, Re, Humphreys v Birch-Reynardson [1968] 1 All ER 36, [1968] 1
  WLR 248, 112 Sol Jo 114 423
Pepin v Bruyère [1902] 1 Ch 24, 71 LJ Ch 39, 50 WR 34, 46 Sol Jo 29, 85 LT 461, CA
  845
Pepper v Pepper (1870) IR 5 Eq 85 .... 95, 97
Peppin v Bickford (1797) 3 Ves 570 346
Perceval v Perceval (1870) LR 9 Eq 386 424
Percival, Re, Boote v Dutton (1888) 59 LT 21, CA 96
Percy, Re, Percy v Percy (1883) 24 Ch D 616, 53 LJ Ch 143, 49 LT 554
  382
Percy's Goods, Re, Fairland v Percy (1875) LR 3 P & D 217, 44 LJP & M 11, 39 LJP 632,
  23 WR 597, 32 LT 405, P, D and Admlty 787, 1039
Perdoni v Curati [2011] EWHC 3442 (Ch), [2012] WTLR 505, 14 ITELR 725; affd [2012]
  EWCA Civ 1381, [2013] WTLR 63, 15 ITELR 480 .... 95, 97
Pereira, Re, Worsley v Society for Propagation of Gospel in Foreign Parts (1912) 56 Sol Jo
  614, 28 TLR 479 .... 96, 298
Perera v Perera [1901] AC 354, 70 LJPC 46, 84 LT 371, 17 TLR 389, PC
  50
Perkins, Re, Brown v Perkins [1907] 2 Ch 596, 77 LJ Ch 16, [1904–7] All ER Rep 273, 97
  LT 706 .... 1118, 1121
Perkins v Goodwin [1877] WN 111 354
Perkins v Micklethwaite (1714) 1 P Wms 274 .... 115, 410–411
Perotti v Watson [2001] All ER (D) 73 (Jul); revsd in part [2002] EWCA Civ 771,
  [2002] All ER (D) 247 (Apr) 656, 1247
Perrin v Lyon (1807) 9 East 170 .... 133, 407
Perrin v Morgan [1943] AC 399, [1943] 1 All ER 187, 112 LJ Ch 81, 87 Sol Jo 47, 168
  LT 177, 59 TLR 134, HL 206, 212, 226, 235–237, 241, 245, 293
Perrins, Re, Perrins v Holland, Perrins v Dooney [2009] EWHC 1945 (Ch), [2009] WTLR
  1387, [2009] All ER (D) 30 (Aug); affd [2010] EWCA Civ 840, [2010] All ER (D) 210
  (Jul) 48, 50, 63, 901

                                                                                          PARA
Perrins v Bellamy [1899] 1 Ch 797, 68 LJ Ch 397, 47 WR 417, 43 Sol Jo 437, 80 LT 478,
   CA   1244
Perrins v Holland (as executor of the estate of Perrins) [2009] EWHC 2558 (Ch), 153 Sol
   Jo (no 41) 30, [2009] All ER (D) 124 (Nov)   911
Perrott v Davies (1877) 38 LT 52   432
Perrott v Perrott (1811) 14 East 423   109
Perry v Dixon (1899) 80 LT 297, P, D and Admlty   874
Perry v Meddowcroft (1841) 4 Beav 197; affd (1842) 12 LJ Ch 104
   ....   27, 1060
Perry v Merritt (1874) LR 18 Eq 152, 43 LJ Ch 608, 22 WR 600
     381
Perry v Phelips (1790) 1 Ves 251   27
Perry v Phelips (1810) 17 Ves 173   27
Perry v Woods (1796) 3 Ves 204   395
Perry's Goods, Re (1840) 2 Curt 655   629
Persse's Estate, Re, O'Donnell v Bruce and Dawson (1962) 106 Sol Jo 432, P, D and
   Admlty   910
Pery v White (1778) 2 Cowp 777   474
Pesca's Estate, Re (1930) 74 Sol Jo 59, P, D and Admlty
     679
Petchell's Goods, Re (1874) LR 3 P & D 153, 38 JP 824, 43 LJP & M 22, 22 WR 353, 30
   LT 74 ....   95, 97, 99
Peters v Dipple (1841) 12 Sim 101   444
Peters v Leeder (1878) 43 JP 37, 47 LJQB 573   1262
Peters v Tilly (1886) 11 PD 145, 55 LJP 75, 35 WR 183, P, D and Admlty
   ....   884, 888
Peterson v Peterson (1858) 26 Beav 83   1177
Peterson v Peterson (1866) LR 3 Eq 111, 36 LJ Ch 101, 15 WR 164
     1099
Petre v Ferrers (1891) 61 LJ Ch 426, 36 Sol Jo 28, 65 LT 568, 8 TLR 17
     296
Petre v Petre (1851) 14 Beav 197, 15 Jur 693, 18 LTOS 14
     1088
Petrie, Re, Lloyds Bank Ltd v Royal National Institute for the Blind [1962] Ch 355, [1961]
   3 All ER 1067, [1961] 3 WLR 1348, 105 Sol Jo 966, CA
     451
Pett v Fellows (1733) 1 Swan 561n   1077
Pettifer, Re, Pettifer v Pettifer [1900] WN 182, 44 Sol Jo 698
     134
Pettifor's Will Trusts, Re, Roberts v Roberts [1966] Ch 257, [1966] 1 All ER 913, [1966] 2
   WLR 778, 110 Sol Jo 191   302
Pettinger v Ambler (1866) LR 1 Eq 510, 35 Beav 321, 35 LJ Ch 389, 14 LT 118
     1
Petts, Re (1859) 27 Beav 576, sub nom Pitts, Re 29 LJ Ch 168, 5 Jur NS 1235, 8 WR 157,
   1 LT 153 ....   58, 346
Petty, Re, Holliday v Petty [1929] 1 Ch 726, 98 LJ Ch 207, [1929] All ER Rep 493, 141
   LT 31 ....   992, 999
Petty v Willson (1869) 4 Ch App 574, 17 WR 778   293
Peverett's Goods, Re [1902] P 205, 71 LJP 114, 87 LT 143, P, D and Admlty
     896
Peynel v Peynel (1373) YB 47 Edw 3, 16b, pl 29   218
Peyton v Bury (1731) 2 P Wms 626; on appeal sub nom Painton v Berry, etc
   (Administrators of Thornton) (1732) Kel W 37   135
Peyton v Lambert (1858) 8 ICLR 485   473
Phelan, Re [1972] Fam 33, [1971] 3 All ER 1256, [1971] 3 WLR 888, 115 Sol Jo 710, P,
   D and Admlty 11, 54, 95, 187, 713, 739, 902
Phelan v Slattery (1887) 19 LR Ir 177 ....   214, 218, 220
Phelps, Re, Wells v Phelps [1980] Ch 275, [1979] 3 All ER 373, [1980] 2 WLR 277, 124
   Sol Jo 85, CA 489, 1153
Phené's Trusts, Re (1870) 5 Ch App 139, 39 LJ Ch 316, 18 WR 303, [1861–73] All ER
   Rep 514, 22 LT 111, CA in Ch   33
Pheysey v Vicary (1847) 16 M & W 484, 8 LTOS 451 ....   283, 286
Phibbs' Estate, Re [1917] P 93, 86 LJP 81, 116 LT 575, 33 TLR 214, [1916–17] All ER
   Rep Ext 1241, P, D and Admlty 716, 895–896
Philanthropic Society v Hobson (1833) 2 My & K 357, 3 LJ Ch 97
     1301

PARA

Philipps v Chamberlaine (1798) 4 Ves 51 .... 186, 200, 256, 375

Philips v Bury (1694) Comb 265, 312, 1 Ld Raym 5, 4 Mod Rep 106, Show Parl Cas 35, 1
  Show 360, Skin 447, 2 Term Rep 346, 100 ER 186, [1558–1774] All ER Rep 53,
  Carth 180, 317, Holt KB 715 190

Philips v Philips (1701) Freem Ch 11, 245, 1 Ld Raym 721, 1 P Wms 34, Prec Ch 167, 2
  Vern 430, 1 Eq Cas Abr 292 pl 6 395

Philips v Philips (1844) 3 Hare 281, 13 LJ Ch 445 163

Philips v Walter (1720) 2 Bro Parl Cas 250 145

Philipson-Stow v IRC [1961] AC 727, [1960] 3 All ER 814, [1960] 3 WLR 1008, 39 ATC
  394, [1960] TR 333, 104 Sol Jo 1055, HL 12–13

Phillip's Estate, Re, Boyle v Thompson (1918) 34 TLR 256
  711

Phillipo v Munnings (1837) 2 My & Cr 309 1149

Phillips, Re (1921) 151 LT Jo 162 318

Phillips v Alhambra Palace Co [1901] 1 KB 59, 70 LJQB 26, 49 WR 223, 45 Sol Jo 81, 83
  LT 431, 17 TLR 40, DC 1279

Phillips v Barker (1853) 23 LJ Ch 44, 2 Eq Rep 795, 17 Jur 1146, 1 Sm & G 583, 2 WR
  110, 22 LTOS 168 263

Phillips v Beal (1858) 25 Beav 25 .... 17, 288

Phillips v Beal (1862) 32 Beav 25 122

Phillips v Beal (No 2) (1863) 32 Beav 26 1190

Phillips v Bignell (1811) 1 Phillim 239 957

Phillips v Cayley (1889) 43 Ch D 222, 59 LJ Ch 177, 38 WR 241, 62 LT 86, 6 TLR 128,
  CA 32, 1114

Phillips v Eastwood (1835) L & G temp Sugd 270 .... 296, 375

Phillips v Everard (1831) 5 Sim 102 1227

Phillips v Fothergill. See Phillips v Homfray

Phillips v Gutteridge (1862) 3 De GJ & Sm 332, 32 LJ Ch 1, 8 Jur NS 1196, 1 New Rep
  3, 11 WR 12, 7 LT 402 375

Phillips v Homfray (1883) 24 Ch D 439, 52 LJ Ch 833, 32 WR 6, 49 LT 5, CA; on appeal
  sub nom Phillips v Fothergill (1886) 11 App Cas 466, HL
  .... 1229, 1277

Phillips v Jones (1888) 4 TLR 401 1279

Phillips v Low [1892] 1 Ch 47, 61 LJ Ch 44, 65 LT 552, 8 TLR 23
  283

Phillips v Phillips [1877] WN 260 190

Phillips v Phillips (1885) 29 Ch D 673, 54 LJ Ch 943, 33 WR 863, 53 LT 403, CA
  657

Phillips v Rail (1906) 54 WR 517 .... 254, 467

Phillips' Insurance, Re (1883) 23 Ch D 235, 52 LJ Ch 441, 31 WR 511, 48 LT 81, CA
  .... 27, 32

Phillipson v Turner (1862) 31 Beav 407 254

Philpott v St George's Hospital (1855) 21 Beav 134; revsd sub nom Philpott v President
  and Governors of St George's Hospital (1857) 21 JP 691, 6 HL Cas 338, 27 LJ Ch 70,
  3 Jur NS 1269, 5 WR 845, 30 LTOS 15 445

Philps v Evans (1850) 4 De G & Sm 188, 15 Jur 809, 17 LTOS 87
  313

Philps' Will, Re (1868) LR 7 Eq 151, 19 LT 713 .... 313, 322, 326, 341–342

Phipard v Mansfield (1778) 2 Cowp 797, 1 Doug KB 53n
  474

Phipps v Ackers (1835) 3 Cl & Fin 702, HL 423

Phipps v Ackers (1842) 9 Cl & Fin 583, 6 Jur 745, 4 Man & G 1107, 5 Scott NR 955,
  134 ER 453, [1558–1774] All ER Rep 381, HL 416, 419, 422–423, 436

Phipps v Annesley (1740) 2 Atk 57 1158

Phipps v Earl of Anglesey (1751) 7 Bro Parl Cas 443, HL
  .... 97, 232, 713

Phipps v Hale (1874) LR 3 P & D 166, 22 WR 742 63

Phipps v Lord Mulgrave (1798) 3 Ves 613 438

Phipps Goods, Re (1840) 2 Curt 368 79

Phuler's Will Trusts, Re, Midland Bank Executor and Trustee Co Ltd v Logan [1964]
  2 All ER 948, [1965] 1 WLR 68, 43 ATC 400, [1964] TR 441, 108 Sol Jo 710
  .... 1130, 1132

Piazzi-Smyth's Goods, Re [1898] P 7, 46 WR 426, 77 LT 375, sub nom Re Smyth's Goods
  67 LJP 4, P, D and Admlty 9, 714

PARA

Pibus v Mitford. See Pybus v Mitford

Pickard's Goods, Re, Banfield v Pickard. See Banfield v Pickard

Picken v Matthews (1878) 10 Ch D 264, 39 LT 531, sub nom Re Hoof, Picken v Matthews
48 LJ Ch 150 307

Pickering v Lord Stamford (1797) 3 Ves 332; on appeal (1797) 3 Ves 492
.... 498

Pickering v Pickering (1839) 4 My & Cr 289, 8 LJ Ch 336, 3 Jur 743, 41 ER 113,
[1835–42] All ER Rep 534 1122

Pickering v Towers (1758) Amb 363, 1 Eden 142 387

Pickersgill v Rodger (1876) 5 Ch D 163 168

Pickford v Brown (1856) 2 K & J 426, 25 LJ Ch 702, 2 Jur NS 781, 4 WR 473, 27 LTOS
259 .... 412, 433

Pickford v Hunter (1831) 5 Sim 122 1177

Pickup v Atkinson (1846) 4 Hare 624, 15 LJ Ch 213, 10 Jur 303
.... 1122

Pickup's Trusts, Re (1861) 1 John & H 389, 30 LJ Ch 278, 9 WR 251, 4 LT 85
.... 331

Pickwick v Gibbes (1839) 1 Beav 271, 3 Jur 101 430

Pickworth, Re, Snaith v Parkinson [1899] 1 Ch 642, 68 LJ Ch 324, 80 LT 212, CA
.... 319, 440, 444

Picton, Re, Porter v Jones [1944] Ch 303, 113 LJ Ch 177, 88 Sol Jo 224, 171 LT 27, 60
TLR 378 114

Pierson v Garnet (1786) 2 Bro CC 38, 29 ER 20, [1775–1802] All ER Rep 487; affd
(1787) 2 Bro CC 226, 29 ER 126, [1775–1802] All ER Rep 487
.... 333, 338, 362

Pierson v Vickers (1804) 5 East 548, sub nom Peirson v Vickers 2 Smith KB 160
.... 384

Piety v Stace (1799) 4 Ves 620 1257

Piffard v Vanrenen (1865) 5 New Rep 399, 13 WR 425, 11 LT 766
.... 1177

Pigg v Clarke (1876) 3 Ch D 672, 45 LJ Ch 849, 24 WR 1014
.... 206, 348

Piggott v Aulton [2003] EWCA Civ 24, [2003] RTR 540, [2003] 12 LS Gaz R 32, [2003]
PIQR P22, (2003) Times, 19 February, 147 Sol Jo LB 145, [2003] All ER (D) 271
(Jan) 818, 1278

Piggott v Green (1833) 6 Sim 72 1069

Pigot v Gascoin (1616) 1 Brownl 46 620

Pigott v Waller (1802) 7 Ves 98 113

Pigott v Wilder (1858) 26 Beav 90 408

Pile v Salter (1832) 5 Sim 411 446

Pilkington, Re, Pilkington v Pilkington (1892) 29 LR Ir 370
.... 308

Pilkington v Gray [1899] AC 401, 68 LJPC 63, PC 49, 895

Pilkington's Trusts, Re (1865) 6 New Rep 246, 13 LT 35
.... 156

Pilling's Trusts, Re (1884) 26 Ch D 432, 53 LJ Ch 1052, 32 WR 853
.... 951

Pilot v Gainfort [1931] P 103, 100 LJP 60, 75 Sol Jo 490, 145 LT 22, 47 TLR 376, P, D
and Admlty 88

Pimm, Re, Malkin v Pimm (No 2) [1916] WN 202, 60 Sol Jo 527, CA
.... 1176

Pimm, Re, Sharpe v Hodgson [1904] 2 Ch 345, 73 LJ Ch 627, 52 WR 648, 48 Sol Jo 588,
91 LT 190 1131–1132

Pimm, Re, Steward v Sharpe (No 2) [1916] WN 202, 60 Sol Jo 527, CA
.... 1176

Pinbury v Elkin (1719) 1 P Wms 563, Prec Ch 483, 2 Vern 758
.... 459

Pinhorne, Re, Moreton v Hughes [1894] 2 Ch 276, 63 LJ Ch 607, 8 R 264, 42 WR 438,
38 Sol Jo 400, 70 LT 901 171

Pink, Re, Elvin v Nightingale [1927] 1 Ch 237, 96 LJ Ch 202, 70 Sol Jo 1090, 136 LT 399
.... 981–982

Pink, Re, Pink v Pink [1912] 2 Ch 528, 81 LJ Ch 753, [1911–13] All ER Rep 1037, 56 Sol
Jo 668, 107 LT 338, 28 TLR 528, CA 198, 625

Pinnell v Annison [2005] EWHC 1421 (Ch), [2005] All ER (D) 458 (May)
.... 209–211, 214, 217, 220, 262, 267–268, 272, 276, 328

Pinney v Hunt (1877) 6 Ch D 98, 26 WR 69 .... 635, 670, 678

PARA
Pinney v Marriott (1863) 32 Beav 643 255
Pinney v Pinney (1828) 8 B & C 335, 6 LJOSKB 353, 2 Man & Ry KB 436
.... 635, 670
Piper, Re, Dodd v Piper [1946] 2 All ER 503, 90 Sol Jo 528, 175 LT 426, 62 TLR 618
.... 130–131
Piper v Piper (1875) 1 Ch D 90, 45 LJ Ch 99, 24 WR 152, 33 LT 499
.... 1105
Pitcairn, Re, Brandreth v Colvin [1896] 2 Ch 199, 65 LJ Ch 120, 44 WR 200,
    [1895–9] All ER Rep 1244, 73 LT 430 1123
Pitcairne v Brase (1679) Cas temp Finch 403 276
Pitcher v Tovey (1692) 12 Mod Rep 23, 4 Mod Rep 71, 1 Salk 81, 1 Show 340, Holt KB
    73, sub nom Tongue v Pitcher 3 Lev 295, sub nom Tovey v Pitcher 2 Vent 234, Carth
    177 1222
Pitman v Crum Ewing [1911] AC 217, 80 LJPC 175, 104 LT 611, HL
.... 152
Pitman v Stevens (1812) 15 East 505 298
Pitt, Re, Pitt v Mann (1928) 44 TLR 371 .... 1144, 1150
Pitt v Woodham (1828) 1 Hag Ecc 247 957
Pitt Rivers, Re, Scott v Pitt Rivers [1902] 1 Ch 403, 66 JP 275, 71 LJ Ch 225, 50 WR 342,
    46 Sol Jo 246, 86 LT 6, 18 TLR 272, CA 221–222
Pittaway, Re [1967] Ch 690, [1967] 1 All ER 391, [1967] 2 WLR 637, 111 Sol Jo 37
.... 306, 309, 398
Pitts, Re. See Petts, Re
Pitts, Re, Cox v Kilsby [1931] 1 Ch 546, 100 LJ Ch 284, [1931] All ER Rep 645, 145 LT
    116, 47 TLR 293 39
Plant, Re, Griffith v Hill (1898) 47 WR 183, 43 Sol Jo 63
.... 352
Plant, Re, Johnson v Hardwicke [1952] Ch 298, [1952] 1 All ER 78n, [1952] 1 TLR 1
.... 232, 401, 403
Plant's Estate, Re, Wild v Plant [1926] P 139, [1926] All ER Rep Ext 751, sub nom Plant,
    Re, Wild v Plant 95 LJP 87, 70 Sol Jo 605, 135 LT 238, 42 TLR 443, CA
.... 909–910
Platon Elenin (aka Boris Abramovich Berezovsky), Re, Lockston Group Inc v Wood [2015]
    EWHC 2962 (Ch), [2016] 1 WLR 2091, [2016] BPIR 94, [2015] All ER (D) 231 (Oct)
.... 967
Playfair, Re, Palmer v Playfair [1951] Ch 4, 66 (pt 1) TLR 1203, sub nom Re
    Hickman's Will Trusts, Re Playfair, Palmer v Playfair [1950] 2 All ER 285
.... 33, 160
Playne v Scriven (1849) 1 Rob Eccl 772, 13 Jur 712, 13 LTOS 405, 7 Notes of Cases 122
.... 63, 75
Plenty v West (1848) 6 CB 201 375
Plenty v West and Budd (1845) 1 Rob Eccl 264, 9 Jur 458, 4 Notes of Cases 103
.... 95
Pleydell v Pleydell (1721) 1 P Wms 748 461
Plomley v Frost (1890) 15 App Cas 548, 60 LJPC 15, 63 LT 422, 6 TLR 443, PC
.... 317
Plowman, Re, Westminster Bank Ltd v Plowman [1943] Ch 269, [1943] 2 All ER 532,
    112 LJ Ch 229, 87 Sol Jo 248, 169 LT 118, 59 TLR 335
.... 479
Plowright v Smith [2006] All ER (D) 234 (Jul) 893
Plume v Beale (1717) 1 P Wms 388, 24 ER 438, Ct of Ch
.... 59
Plunkett Will Trusts, Re, McCarthy v Dillon [1964] IR 259
.... 109
Pocock v Bishop of Lincoln (1821) 3 Brod & Bing 27, 6 Moore CP 159
.... 256
Podmore v Gunning (1836) 7 Sim 644, Donnelly 74, 5 LJ Ch 266
.... 222
Pogson v Thomas (1840) 6 Bing NC 337, 8 Scott 621 284
Pointer, Re, Pointer and Shonfeld v Edwards [1941] Ch 60, [1940] 4 All ER 372, 110 LJ
    Ch 33, 84 Sol Jo 658, 165 LT 3, 57 TLR 83 592
Pollard's Estate, Re (1863) 3 De GJ & Sm 541, 32 LJ Ch 657, 2 New Rep 404, 11 WR
    1083, 8 LT 710 .... 243, 376
Polley v Polley (1861) 29 Beav 134 .... 342, 461
Polley v Polley (No 2) (1862) 31 Beav 363 .... 340, 563–564

PARA

Pollock, Re, Pollock v Pollock [1941] Ch 219, [1941] 1 All ER 360, 110 LJ Ch 97, 85 Sol
    Jo 130, 165 LT 152, 57 TLR 359 39
Pollock, Re, Pugsley v Pollock [1943] Ch 338, [1943] 2 All ER 443, 112 LJ Ch 345, 87 Sol
    Jo 373, 169 LT 282, 59 TLR 456 .... 1076, 1081
Pollock v Croft (1816) 1 Mer 181 136
Pollock v Pollock (1874) LR 18 Eq 329, 44 LJ Ch 168, 22 WR 724, 30 LT 779
    1085
Polson v Polson (1900) 21 NSWLR Eq 90 146
Ponder, Re, Ponder v Ponder [1921] 2 Ch 59, 90 LJ Ch 426, [1921] All ER Rep 164, 65
    Sol Jo 455, 125 LT 568 .... 1074, 1144, 1148–1150
Pool v Pool (1889) 58 LJP 67, 61 LT 401, P, D and Admlty
    1279
Poole v Bott (1853) 11 Hare 33, 22 LJ Ch 1042, 1 Eq Rep 21, 17 Jur 688, 1 WR 276,
    21 LTOS 262 .... 128, 412
Poole v Poole (1804) 3 Bos & P 620 241
Poole v Poole (1871) 7 Ch App 17, 20 WR 133, 25 LT 771
    404
Poole v Terry (1831) 4 Sim 294 438
Poole's Estate, Re, Poole v Poole [1919] P 10, 88 LJP 77, 63 Sol Jo 179, 35 TLR 143, P, D
    and Admlty 749, 789
Pooley, Re (1888) 40 Ch D 1, 58 LJ Ch 1, 37 WR 17, [1886–90] All ER Rep 157, 60 LT
    73, 5 TLR 21, CA 41, 652
Pope v Energem Resources Ltd [2009] EWCA Civ 1086
    1296
Pope v Pope (1851) 14 Beav 591, 21 LJ Ch 276, 18 LTOS 83
    336
Pope v Whitcombe (1827) 3 Russ 124, 6 LJOS Ch 53 305
Popham, Re, Butler v Popham [1914] WN 257, 58 Sol Jo 673, 111 LT 524
    1121
Popham v Bampfeild (1682) 1 Vern 79 147
Popham v Brooke (1828) 5 Russ 8, 6 LJOS 184 904
Popham v Lady Aylesbury (1748) Amb 68 285
Poplar and Blackwall Free School, Re (1878) 8 Ch D 543, 42 JP 678, 26 WR 827, 39 LT
    88 1047
Pople v Evans [1969] 2 Ch 255, [1968] 2 All ER 743, [1968] 3 WLR 97, 112 Sol Jo 441
    .... 860, 1294
Portal and Lamb, Re (1885) 30 Ch D 50, 54 LJ Ch 1012, 33 WR 859, 53 LT 650, CA
    .... 49, 279, 282
Porter, Re, Coulson v Capper [1892] 3 Ch 481, 61 LJ Ch 688, 3 R 19, 41 WR 38, 36 Sol
    Jo 626, 67 LT 823, [1891–4] All ER Rep Ext 1766 .... 462, 464
Porter, Re, Porter v Porter [1925] Ch 746, 95 LJ Ch 46, [1925] All ER Rep 179, 133 LT
    812 266
Porter v Baddeley (1877) 5 Ch D 542 1125
Porter v Bradley (1789) 3 Term Rep 143 460
Porter v Fox (1834) 6 Sim 485 416
Porter v Frye. See Fry's (Lady Anne) Case
Porter v Tournay (1797) 3 Ves 311 .... 122, 284, 296
Porter's Goods, Re (1869) LR 2 P & D 22, 34 JP 247, 39 LJP & M 12, 18 WR 231, 21 LT
    680, [1861–73] All ER Rep Ext 1886 7
Porter's Trust, Re (1857) 4 K & J 188, 27 LJ Ch 196, 4 Jur NS 20, 6 WR 187, 32 LTOS
    86 .... 164–165, 320–322
Posner, Re, Posner v Miller [1953] P 277, [1953] 1 All ER 1123, [1953] 2 WLR 1149, 97
    Sol Jo 390, P, D and Admlty 58, 276
Post Office v Official Solicitor [1951] 1 All ER 522, 95 Sol Jo 173, [1951] 1 TLR 333
    1279
Postlethwaite v Mounsey (1842) 6 Hare 33n 1300
Pothecary v Pothecary (1848) 2 De G & Sm 738, 18 LJ Ch 48, 12 Jur 1016, 12 LTOS 240
    1065
Potter, Re, Stevens v Potter (1900) 83 LT 405 279
Potter v Potter (1750) 1 Ves Sen 437 .... 110, 113
Potter v Richards (1855) 24 LJ Ch 488, 1 Jur NS 462, 3 WR 266
    .... 128, 137
Potter's Goods, Re, Potter v Potter [1899] P 265, 68 LJP 97, 81 LT 234, P, D and Admlty
    759–760
Potter's Will Trusts, Re [1944] Ch 70, [1943] 2 All ER 805, 113 LJ Ch 173, 170 LT 26, 60
    TLR 155, CA 331

PARA

Potticary's Estate, Re [1927] P 202, 96 LJP 94, 137 LT 256, P, D and Admlty
.... 759
Potts v Atherton (1859) 28 LJ Ch 486, 7 WR 331 .... 430, 440
Potts v Smith (1869) LR 8 Eq 683, 39 LJ Ch 131, 17 WR 1083, 21 LT 54
.... 1093–1094
Poulet (Lady) v Lord Poulet (1685) 1 Vern 204, sub nom Paulett's (Lord) Case Freem Ch
 93, 2 Vent 366, sub nom Pawlett v Pawlett 1 Eq Cas Abr 267, 2 Rep Ch 286, 1 Vern
 321; affd sub nom Paulett's (Lord) Case (1685) 14 Lords Journals 87, HL
.... 438
Poulson v Wellington (1729) 2 P Wms 533 252
Poultney, Re, Poultney v Poultney [1912] 2 Ch 541, 81 LJ Ch 748, 56 Sol Jo 667, 107 LT
 1, CA 318
Poulton's Will Trusts, Re, Smail v Litchfield [1987] 1 All ER 1068, [1987] 1 WLR 795,
 131 Sol Jo 412, [1987] LS Gaz R 981 .... 313, 349
Pounder, Re, Williams v Pounder (1886) 56 LJ Ch 113, 56 LT 104
.... 259, 382
Powell, Re, Bodvel-Roberts v Poole [1918] 1 Ch 407, 87 LJ Ch 237, 65 Sol Jo 330, 118 LT
 567 255
Powell, Re, Campbell v Campbell [1900] 2 Ch 525, 69 LJ Ch 788, 83 LT 24
.... 171
Powell, Re, Crosland v Holliday [1898] 1 Ch 227, 67 LJ Ch 148, 46 WR 231, 42 Sol Jo
 150, 77 LT 649 .... 304, 310–311
Powell, Re, Dodd v Williams [1921] 1 Ch 178, 90 LJ Ch 161, 125 LT 603
.... 122
Powell, Re, Public Trustee v Bailey (1982) 31 SASR 361
.... 291
Powell v Boggis (1866) 35 Beav 535, 35 LJ Ch 472, 14 WR 670
.... 377
Powell v Davies (1839) 1 Beav 532, 3 Jur 839 265
Powell v Evans (1801) 5 Ves 839 959
Powell v Graham (1817) 7 Taunt 580, 1 Moore CP 305
.... 1239
Powell v Hellicar [1919] 1 Ch 138, 88 LJ Ch 68, 63 Sol Jo 116, 120 LT 218,
 [1918–19] All ER Rep Ext 1332 316–317
Powell v Howells (1868) LR 3 QB 654, 9 B & S 704, 37 LJQB 294, 16 WR 1116, 19 LT
 201 474
Powell v Morgan (1688) 2 Vern 90 190
Powell v Mouchett (1821) Madd & G 216 95
Powell v Osbourne [1993] 1 FCR 797, [1993] 1 FLR 1001, [1993] Fam Law 287, CA
.... 585–586
Powell v Powell [1900] 1 Ch 243, 69 LJ Ch 164, 44 Sol Jo 134, 82 LT 84
.... 657, 904
Powell v Powell (1866) LR 1 P & D 209, 35 LJP & M 100, [1861–73] All ER Rep 362,
 14 LT 800 .... 101, 107–108, 110
Powell v Rawle (1874) LR 18 Eq 243, 22 WR 629 145
Powell v Riley (1871) LR 12 Eq 175, 40 LJ Ch 533, 19 WR 869
.... 1012
Powell's Trust, Re (1858) John 49, 5 Jur NS 331, 7 WR 138, 32 LTOS 252
.... 293
Power v Lencham (1838) 2 Jo Ex Ir 728 277
Powis v Burdett (1804) 9 Ves 428 452
Powys v Blagrave (1854) 4 De GM & G 448, 24 LJ Ch 142, 2 Eq Rep 1204, 2 WR 700,
 24 LTOS 17 1229
Powys v Mansfield (1837) 3 My & Cr 359, 7 LJ Ch 9, 1 Jur 861
.... 115, 156
Poyser, Re, Landon v Poyser [1908] 1 Ch 828, 77 LJ Ch 482, 99 LT 50, [1908–10] All ER
 Rep Ext 1381 405
Poyser, Re, Landon v Poyser [1910] 2 Ch 444, 79 LJ Ch 748, [1908–10] All ER Rep 374,
 103 LT 134 .... 1118, 1121
Pozot's Settlement Trusts, Re, Westminster Bank Ltd v Guerbois [1952] Ch 427, [1952]
 1 All ER 1107, [1952] 1 TLR 1042, CA 463–465
Prater, Re, Desinge v Beare (1888) 37 Ch D 481, 57 LJ Ch 342, 36 WR 561, 58 LT 784, 4
 TLR 249, CA 285
Pratt v Jackson (1726) 1 Bro Parl Cas 222 296
Pratt v London Passenger Transport Board [1937] 1 All ER 473, 81 Sol Jo 79, 156 LT 265,
 53 TLR 355, CA 818

PARA

Pratt v Mathew (1856) 22 Beav 328, 25 LJ Ch 409, 2 Jur NS 364, 4 WR 418, 27 LTOS
    74; on appeal (1856) 8 De GM & G 522, 25 LJ Ch 686, 2 Jur NS 1055, 4 WR 772,
    27 LTOS 267, CA 59, 246, 346, 354
Pratt v Pratt (1844) 14 Sim 129, 8 Jur 507, 3 LTOS 466
    .... 100, 251
Pratt's Settlement Trusts, Re, McCullum v Phipps-Hornby [1943] Ch 356, [1943] 2 All ER
    458, 112 LJ Ch 251, 87 Sol Jo 265, 169 LT 181, 59 TLR 352
    182
Prescott v Barker (1874) 9 Ch App 174, 43 LJ Ch 498, 22 WR 423, 30 LT 149
    .... 228, 284, 291
Prescott v Long (1795) 2 Ves 690 307–308
Press v Parker (1825) 2 Bing 456, 3 LJOSCP 96, 10 Moore CP 158
    232
Preston, Re, Preston v Hoggarth [1969] 2 All ER 961, [1969] 1 WLR 317, 113 Sol Jo 208
    592
Preston v Funnell (1739) 7 Mod Rep 296, Willes 164 387
Preston's Estate, Re, Raby v Port of Hull Society's Sailors' Orphans' Homes [1951] Ch 878,
    [1951] 2 All ER 421, 95 Sol Jo 595, [1951] 2 TLR 258
    1017
Prestwidge v Groombridge (1833) 6 Sim 171 445
Previté, Re, Sturges v Previté [1931] 1 Ch 447, 100 LJ Ch 286, 145 LT 40
    1131–1132
Prevost, Re, Lloyds Bank Ltd v Barclays Bank Ltd [1930] 2 Ch 383, 99 LJ Ch 425, 74 Sol
    Jo 488, 143 LT 743, 46 TLR 557 36
Price, Re [1928] Ch 579, 97 LJ Ch 423, 139 LT 339 .... 478, 563
Price, Re, Midland Bank Executor and Trustee Co Ltd v Harwood [1943] Ch 422, [1943]
    2 All ER 505, 112 LJ Ch 273, 87 Sol Jo 282, 169 LT 121, 59 TLR 367
    36
Price, Re, Price v Newton [1905] 2 Ch 55, 74 LJ Ch 437, 53 WR 600, [1904–7] All ER
    Rep 448, 93 LT 44 .... 212, 257, 261, 293
Price, Re, Tomlin v Latter [1900] 1 Ch 442, 69 LJ Ch 225, 48 WR 373, 44 Sol Jo 242, 82
    LT 79, 16 TLR 189 239
Price, Re, Trumper v Price [1932] 2 Ch 54, 101 LJ Ch 278, 76 Sol Jo 217, 147 LT 351, 48
    TLR 318 .... 269–270, 295
Price, Re, Wasley v Price [1950] Ch 242, [1950] 1 All ER 338, 94 Sol Jo 146, 66 (pt 1)
    TLR 291 .... 209, 246, 284, 288
Price, Re, Williams v Jenkins (1886) 31 Ch D 485, 55 LJ Ch 501, 34 WR 291, 54 LT 416
    .... 909, 1018
Price v Craig [2006] EWHC 2561 (Ch), 9 ITELR 393, [2006] All ER (D) 249 (Oct)
    .... 95, 187, 194
Price v Dewhurst (1838) 4 My & Cr 76, 8 LJ Ch 57, 2 Jur 1006, [1835–42] All ER Rep
    442 669
Price v Frost (1890) 15 App Cas 548, 60 LJPC 15, 63 LT 422, 6 TLR 443, PC
    317
Price v Gorsuch (1789) 2 Cox Eq Cas 187 .... 339, 397
Price v Hall (1868) LR 5 Eq 399, 37 LJ Ch 191, 16 WR 642
    424
Price v Hartwell [1996] EGCS 98, CA 20
Price v Hunt (1684) Poll 645 442
Price v Page (1799) 4 Ves 680 .... 212, 220, 263
Price v Price (1858) 27 LJ Ex 409, 6 WR 597, 31 LTOS 204, sub nom Price v Powell 3 H
    & N 341 105
Price v Price (1887) 35 Ch D 297, 56 LJ Ch 530, 35 WR 386, 56 LT 842, 3 TLR 453
    971
Price v Strange (1820) 6 Madd 159 .... 364, 537
Prichard v Prichard (1870) LR 11 Eq 232, 40 LJ Ch 92, 19 WR 226, 24 LT 259
    293
Pride v Fooks (1858) 3 De G & J 252, 28 LJ Ch 81, 5 Jur NS 158, 7 WR 109, 32 LTOS
    358 .... 242, 331, 441, 445, 456–457
Pridham's Goods, Re (1889) 61 LT 302, P, D and Admlty
    761
Priest, Re, Belfield v Duncan [1944] Ch 58, [1944] 1 All ER 51, 113 LJ Ch 145, 88 Sol Jo
    43, 170 LT 159, 60 TLR 145 44
Priestley v Holgate (1857) 3 K & J 286, 26 LJ Ch 448, 3 Jur NS 486, 5 WR 445, 30 LTOS
    30 .... 143, 147, 149

PARA

Priestley's Will Trusts, Re, Hambros Bank Executor and Trustee Co Ltd v Rabagliati [1971]
    Ch 858, [1971] 2 All ER 817, [1971] 2 WLR 1119, 115 Sol Jo 350, CA
    248
Priestman v Thomas (1884) 9 PD 70; on appeal (1884) 9 PD 210, 53 LJP 109, 32 WR
    842, [1881–5] All ER Rep 287, 51 LT 843, CA 671, 678
Prince, Re, Hardman v Willis (1935) 51 TLR 526 1086
Prince of Wales etc Association Co v Palmer (1858) 25 Beav 605
    818
Pringle, Re, Baker v Matheson [1946] Ch 124, [1946] 1 All ER 88, 115 LJ Ch 92, 90 Sol
    Jo 9, 174 LT 115, 62 TLR 147 .... 246, 470, 746
Pringle, Re, Walker v Stewart (1881) 17 Ch D 819, 50 LJ Ch 689, 30 WR 44, 45 LT 11
    293
Prior v Hembrow (1841) 10 LJ Ex 371, 8 M & W 873 1231
Pritchard v Briggs [1980] Ch 338, [1980] 1 All ER 294, [1979] 3 WLR 868, 40 P & CR 1,
    123 Sol Jo 705, CA 1214
Pritchard v Palmer (1863) 11 WR 610 1177
Pritchard's Trusts, Re (1855) 3 Drew 163 318
Procedure Direction [1951] WN 167 845
Proctor v Bishop of Bath and Wells (1794) 2 Hy Bl 358
    416
Proctor v Upton (1739) West temp Hard 570, 5 De GM & G 199n
    382
Prosser, Re, Prosser v Griffith [1929] WN 85, 167 LT Jo 307, 67 L Jo 346
    .... 261, 332
Protheroe v Protheroe [1968] 1 All ER 1111, [1968] 1 WLR 519, 19 P & CR 396, 112 Sol
    Jo 151, 206 Estates Gazette 889, CA 657
Proud v Proud (1862) 32 Beav 234, 32 LJ Ch 125, 11 WR 101, 7 LT 553
    407
Prowse v Abingdon (1738) 2 Eq Cas Abr 464n, 1 Atk 482, West temp Hard 312
    439
Prowse v Spurgin (1868) LR 5 Eq 99, 37 LJ Ch 251, 16 WR 413, 17 LT 590
    1099
Pruen v Osborne (1834) 7 Sim 56, 3 LJ Ch 233 407
Pruen v Osborne (1840) 11 Sim 132 336
Pryor v Pryor (1860) 23 JP 712, 29 LJPM & A 114 75
Pryse's Goods, Re [1904] P 301, 73 LJP 84, 48 Sol Jo 474, 90 LT 747, CA
    .... 613, 645
Public Trustee v Edmond (1912) 32 NZLR 202 379
Puddephatt's Goods, Re (1870) LR 2 P & D 97, 39 LJP & M 84
    65
Pugh, Re, Pugh v Pugh [1943] Ch 387, [1943] 2 All ER 361, 112 LJ Ch 311, 87 Sol Jo
    363, 169 LT 284, 59 TLR 430 568
Pugh v Goodtitle. See Goodtitle d Bailey v Pugh
Pugh's Will Trusts, Re, Marten v Pugh [1967] 3 All ER 337, [1967] 1 WLR 1262, 111 Sol
    Jo 480 .... 221, 905, 1069
Pullan v Wilson [2014] EWHC 126 (Ch), [2014] All ER (D) 108 (Mar)
    651
Pullen v Ready (1743) 2 Atk 587, 1 Wils 21, 26 ER 751, [1558–1774] All ER Rep 502
    134–135
Pullin v Pullin (1825) 3 Bing 47, 3 LJOSCP 193, 10 Moore CP 464
    .... 252, 267
Pulling v Great Eastern Rly Co (1882) 9 QBD 110, 46 JP 617, 51 LJQB 453, 30 WR 798
    1277
Pulsford v Hunter (1792) 3 Bro CC 416 431
Punchard's Goods, Re (1872) LR 2 P & D 369, 36 JP 296, 41 LJP & M 25, 20 WR 446,
    26 LT 526, [1861–73] All ER Rep Ext 1192 613
Purcell v Purcell (1840) 2 Dr & War 219n 230
Purfry v Rogers (1671) 3 Keb 11, sub nom Purefoy v Rogers 2 Lev 39, 2 Wms Saund 380
    418
Purnchard's Will Trusts, Re, Public Trustee v Pelly [1948] Ch 312, [1948] 1 All ER 790,
    [1948] LJR 1274, 92 Sol Jo 245 295
Purse v Purse [1981] Fam 143, [1981] 2 All ER 465, [1981] 2 WLR 759, 11 Fam Law
    144, 125 Sol Jo 115, CA 1285
Purssglove's Goods, Re (1872) 26 LT 405 76
Pusey v Desbouvrie (1734) 2 Eq Cas Abr 270, 3 P Wms 315, 24 ER 1081,
    [1558–1774] All ER Rep 425 503

PARA

Pusey v Pusey (1684) 1 Vern 273 .... 30, 928
Pybus v Mitford (1674) 3 Keb 338, 2 Lev 75, 1 Mod Rep 159, 1 Mod Rep 98, Freem KB
    369, sub nom Pibus v Mitford 3 Salk 337, 1 Vent 372 540
Pycroft v Gregory (1829) 4 Russ 526, 6 LJOS Ch 121 343
Pye v Linwood (1842) 6 Jur 618 459
Pyle, Re, Pyle v Pyle [1895] 1 Ch 724, 64 LJ Ch 477, 13 R 396, 43 WR 420, 39 Sol Jo
    346, 72 LT 327, [1895–9] All ER Rep Ext 2173 .... 114, 157
Pyle v Price (1802) 6 Ves 779 133
Pyne v Franklin (1832) 5 Sim 458, 2 LJ Ch 41 390
Pyot v Pyot (1749) 1 Ves Sen 335, Belt's Sup 161 .... 45, 278
Python (Monty) Pictures Ltd v Paragon Entertainment Corpn [1998] EMLR 640
    1288
Pytt v Fendall (1754) 1 Lee 553 627

                                         Q

Quarm v Quarm [1892] 1 QB 184, 61 LJQB 154, 40 WR 302, 66 LT 418, DC
    .... 248, 376, 394
Quarrell v Beckford (1816) 1 Madd 269, 56 ER 100, [1814–23] All ER Rep 618
    1203
Queen's College, Oxford v Sutton (1842) 12 Sim 521, 11 LJ Ch 198, 6 Jur 906
    270
Quennell v Turner (1851) 13 Beav 240, 20 LJ Ch 237, 15 Jur 547, 17 LTOS 101
    .... 271, 277
Quibell's Will Trusts, Re, White v Reichert [1956] 3 All ER 679, [1957] 1 WLR 186, 101
    Sol Jo 131 .... 278–279, 282, 295
Quick v Quick and Quick (1864) 28 JP 455, 33 LJPM & A 146, 10 Jur NS 682, 4 New
    Rep 347, 3 Sw & Tr 442, 12 WR 1119, 10 LT 619 716
Quick v Staines (1798) 1 Bos & P 293, 2 Esp 657 924
Quick and Harris v Ludborrow (1615) 3 Bulst 29, 1 Roll Rep 196
    1216
Quick's Goods, Re, Quick v Quick [1899] P 187, 68 LJP 64, 80 LT 808, P, D and Admlty
    754
Quicke v Leach (1844) 13 LJ Ex 348, 13 M & W 218 417
Quihampton v Going (1876) 24 WR 917 .... 201, 406
Quinn v Butler (1868) LR 6 Eq 225 107
Quintin Dick, Re, Lord Cloncurry v Fenton [1926] Ch 992, 96 LJ Ch 9, [1926] All ER
    Rep 644, 70 Sol Jo 876, 136 LT 23, 42 TLR 681 145
Quirk, Re, Public Trustee v Quirk [1941] Ch 46, 110 LJ Ch 4, 84 Sol Jo 514, 164 LT 333,
    56 TLR 983 1130

                                         R

R, Re [1951] P 10, [1950] 2 All ER 117, 94 Sol Jo 386, 66 (pt 2) TLR 26, P, D and
    Admlty 55, 901
R (a child) (IVF: paternity of child), Re [2005] UKHL 33, [2005] 2 AC 621, [2005] 2 WLR
    1158, [2005] 2 FLR 843, (2005) Times, 13 May, sub nom D (a child), Re [2005] 2
    FCR 223, [2005] NLJR 797, [2005] All ER (D) 164 (May), sub nom R (a child), Re
    [2005] 4 All ER 433 359
R v Bentley [2001] 1 Cr App Rep 307, [1999] Crim LR 330, (1998) Times, July 31, CA
    .... 1277, 1286
R v Buttery and Macnamara (1818) Russ & Ry 342, CCR
    671
R v Chief National Insurance Comr, ex p Connor [1981] QB 758, [1981] 1 All ER 769,
    [1981] 2 WLR 412, [1980] Crim LR 579, 124 Sol Jo 478
    39–40
R v Collector of Customs, Liverpool (1813) 2 M & S 223
    919
R v Eatington Inhabitants (1791) 2 Bott 515, 4 Term Rep 177
    379
R v Fane (1589) 4 Leon 107 944
R v Gibson (1802) cited in Russ & Ry 343n 671
R v Horsley Inhabitants (1807) 8 East 405 645
R v Hunter [1974] QB 95, [1973] 3 All ER 286, [1973] 3 WLR 374, 57 Cr App Rep 772,
    137 JP 774, [1973] Crim LR 514, 117 Sol Jo 430, CA 956

PARA

R v Income Tax Acts Special Purposes Comr, ex p Dr Barnardo's Homes
    National Incorporated Association. See Barnardo's Homes v Special Income Tax Comrs
R v Jefferies [1969] 1 QB 120, [1968] 3 All ER 238, [1968] 3 WLR 830, 52 Cr App Rep
    654, 112 Sol Jo 783, CA 1277, 1286
R v Kearley (No 2) [1994] 2 AC 414, [1994] 3 All ER 246, [1994] 3 WLR 413, [1994]
    Crim LR 854, [1994] 37 LS Gaz R 49, [1994] NLJR 1007, 138 Sol Jo LB 177, HL
    .... 1277, 1286
R v Marquis of Stafford (1806) 7 East 521 456
R v Matthew [2010] EWCA Civ 29 1277
R v Netherseal Inhabitants (1791) 4 Term Rep 258 635
R v Pearson. See Pearson v Spencer
R v Peck (1698) 1 Salk 66 1213
R v Raines (1698) 1 Ld Raym 361, 12 Mod Rep 205, 1 Salk 299
    624
R v Ringstead Inhabitants (1829) 9 B & C 218, 7 LJOSMC 103, 2 Man & Ry MC 71,
    4 Man & Ry KB 67 .... 466, 469, 476
R v Rowe [1955] 1 QB 573, [1955] 2 All ER 234, [1955] 2 WLR 1056, 39 Cr App Rep
    57, 119 JP 349, 99 Sol Jo 339, CCA 1277, 1286
R v Simpson (1764) 3 Burr 1463, 1 Wm Bl 456 624
R v Skidmore [2008] EWCA Crim 1464, [2009] Crim LR 42, [2008] All ER (D) 146 (Jul)
    956
R v Sutton (1670) 1 Wms Saund 271b 778
R v Sutton (1835) 3 Ad & El 597, 4 LJKB 215, 1 Har & W 428, 5 Nev & MKB 353
    539
R v Tristram [1898] 2 QB 371, 67 LJQB 857, 46 WR 653, 42 Sol Jo 510, 79 LT 74, DC
    881
R v Vincent (1721) 1 Stra 481 671
R v Warrington [2010] EWCA Civ 29 1277
R v Westminster Betting Licensing Committee, ex p Peabody Donation Fund [1963] 2 QB
    750, [1963] 2 All ER 544, [1963] 2 WLR 1402, 61 LGR 448, 127 JP 408, 107 Sol Jo
    375, DC 964
Rabbeth v Squire (1859) 4 De G & J 406, 28 LJ Ch 565, 7 WR 657, 34 LTOS 40
    .... 379, 475
Rabbeth v Squire (No 2) (1854) 19 Beav 77; on appeal (1859) 4 De G & J 406, 28 LJ Ch
    565, 34 LTOS 40 474
Racal Group Services Ltd v Ashmore [1995] STC 1151, 68 TC 86, CA
    187
Race v Race [2002] EWHC 1868 (Ch) [2002] WTLR 1193
    155
Rackham v De La Mare (1864) 2 De GJ & Sm 74, 10 Jur NS 190, 3 New Rep 398, 12
    WR 363, 9 LT 699 .... 172, 411
Rackstraw v Vile (1824) 1 Sim & St 604, 2 LJOS Ch 102
    459
Radburn v Jervis (1841) 3 Beav 450 403
Radcliffe, Re, Radcliffe v Bewes, [1892] 1 Ch 227, 61 LJ Ch 186, 40 WR 323, 36 Sol Jo
    151, 66 LT 363, CA 925
Radcliffe, Re, Young v Beale (1903) 51 WR 409 173
Radcliffe v Buckley (1804) 10 Ves 195 331
Radclyffe, Re, Pearce v Radclyffe (1881) 50 LJ Ch 317, 29 WR 420, 44 LT 96
    .... 1196, 1200
Radford, Re, Jones v Radford (1918) 62 Sol Jo 604 .... 419, 429
Radford v Radford (1836) 1 Keen 486, 6 LJ Ch 138 460
Radford v Risdon (1912) 56 Sol Jo 416, 28 TLR 342, P, D and Admlty
    56
Radford v Willis (1871) 7 Ch App 7, 41 LJ Ch 19, 20 WR 132, 25 LT 720
    .... 299–300, 346
Radley-Kane, Re. See Kane v Radley-Kane
Radnall's Goods, Re (1824) 2 Add 232 815
Radnor (Earl) v Shafto (1805) 11 Ves 448 125
Rae's Goods, Re (1891) 27 LR Ir 116 80
Ragdale, Re, Public Trustee v Tuffill [1934] Ch 352, 103 LJ Ch 181, [1933] All ER Rep
    284, 78 Sol Jo 48, 150 LT 459, 50 TLR 159 .... 397, 466, 470
Ragg v Wells (1817) 8 Taunt 129 1291
Raggett v Beaty (1828) 5 Bing 243, 7 LJOSCP 9, 2 Moo & P 512
    473

                                                                            PARA
Raggi, Re, Brass v H Young & Co Ltd [1913] 2 Ch 206, 82 LJ Ch 396, 108 LT 917
.... 979
Raikes v Boulton (1860) 29 Beav 41 1004
Raikes v Ward (1842) 1 Hare 445, 11 LJ Ch 276, 6 Jur 530
.... 370
Rainbird v Smith [2012] EWHC 4276 (Ch), 156 Sol Jo (no 22) 31
.... 167, 169, 328, 331
Raine, Re, Tyerman v Stansfield [1929] 1 Ch 716, 98 LJ Ch 244, 141 LT 25
.... 1083
Raine's Goods, Re (1858) 1 Sw & Tr 144, 6 WR 816, 31 LTOS 284
.... 9
Raine's Goods, Re (1865) 34 LJPM & A 125, 11 Jur NS 587
.... 44
Rajabally v Rajabally [1987] 2 FLR 390, [1987] Fam Law 314, CA
.... 591–592
Ralph v Carrick (1877) 5 Ch D 984, 46 LJ Ch 530, 25 WR 530, 37 LT 112; on appeal
    (1879) 11 Ch D 873, 48 LJ Ch 801, 28 WR 67, [1874–80] All ER Rep 1054, 40 LT
    505, CA 226, 334, 336, 338, 345, 447, 468–469
Ralph v Watson (1840) 9 LJ Ch 328 252
Ralphs, Re, Ralphs v District Bank Ltd [1968] 3 All ER 285, [1968] 1 WLR 1522, 112 Sol
    Jo 787 .... 592, 603, 1064
Ramadge, Re [1969] NI 71 .... 175, 237
Rammell v Gillow (1845) 15 LJ Ch 35, 9 Jur 704 451–452
Ramsay, Re, Thorpe v Ramsay [1917] 2 Ch 64, 86 LJ Ch 514, 117 LT 117
.... 1077
Ramsay v Lowther (1912) 16 CLR 1, Aust HC 375
Ramsay v Shelmerdine (1865) LR 1 Eq 129, 11 Jur NS 903, 14 WR 46, 13 LT 393
.... 173, 175
Ramsden v Hassard (1791) 3 Bro CC 236 467
Ramsden v Jackson (1737) 1 Atk 292, sub nom Richardson v Jackson West temp Hard 237
.... 1294
Ramsey v Ramsay [2015] All ER (D) 32 (Sep) 52
Randal v Payne (1779) 1 Bro CC 55 .... 148, 414
Randall v Daniel (1857) 24 Beav 193 199
Randall v Randall [2016] EWCA Civ 494, (2016) Times, 28 June
.... 863
Randall v Russell (1817) 3 Mer 190, 17 RR 56, 136 ER 73, [1814–23] All ER Rep 427
.... 122, 657
Randfield v Randfield (1860) 8 HL Cas 225, 30 LJ Ch 177
.... 44, 122, 369, 382, 450
Randoll v Doe d Roake. See Doe d Roake v Nowell
Ranelagh v Ranelagh (1834) 2 My & K 441 460
Ranelagh v Ranelagh (1841) 4 Beav 419 410
Ranelagh v Ranelagh (1849) 12 Beav 200, 19 LJ Ch 39, 14 LTOS 434
.... 472
Ranking's Settlement Trusts, Re (1868) LR 6 Eq 601 395
Rann v Hughes (1778) 4 Bro Parl Cas 27, 7 Term Rep 350n, HL
.... 1240
Ransome, Re, Moberley v Ransome [1957] Ch 348, [1957] 2 WLR 556, 101 Sol Jo 302,
    sub nom Ransome's Will Trusts, Re [1957] 1 All ER 690
.... 308, 312, 413
Raphael, Re, Permanent Trustee Co of NSW Ltd v Lee (1903) 3 SRNSW 196, 20 WNNSW
    84, NSW SC 461
Raphael, Re, Warburg v Raphael (1916) 61 Sol Jo 99 818
Raphael v Boehm (1805) 8 RR 95, 11 Ves 92, [1903–13] All ER Rep 669; affd (1807) 13
    Ves 407 1257
Raphael v Boehm (1852) 22 LJ Ch 299 239
Rapley and Chaplein's Case (1610) Godb 166, sub nom Ratcliffe and Chaplin's Case 4
    Leon 242 564
Rapley's Estate, Re, Rapley v Rapley [1983] 3 All ER 248, [1983] 1 WLR 1069, [1984]
    FLR 173, 127 Sol Jo 394 80
Ratcliff, Re [1898] 2 Ch 352, 67 LJ Ch 562, 42 Sol Jo 654, 78 LT 834
.... 656
Ratcliffe, Re, Holmes v McMullan [1999] STC 262, [1999] 11 LS Gaz R 70, 143 Sol Jo LB
    82, [1999] All ER (D) 167 .... 298, 1134
Ratcliffe v Barnes (1862) 26 JP 232, 31 LJPM & A 61, 8 Jur NS 313, [1862] 2 Sw & Tr
    486, 6 LT 658 887

PARA

Ratcliffe's Goods, Re [1899] P 110, 68 LJP 47, 80 LT 170, P, D and Admlty
.... 819

Rathbone v Bundock [1962] 2 QB 260, [1962] 2 All ER 257, [1962] 2 WLR 1066, 60
LGR 221, 126 JP 328, 106 Sol Jo 245, DC 583

Raven, Re, Spencer v National Association for the Prevention of Consumption and Other
Forms of Tuberculosis [1915] 1 Ch 673, 84 LJ Ch 489, [1914–15] All ER Rep 353,
113 LT 131 190

Raven, Re, Spencer v Raven (1914) 111 LT 938 295

Raven v Waite (1818) 1 Wils Ch 204, 1 Swan 553 .... 1077, 1081

Ravensworth, Re, Ravensworth v Tindale [1905] 2 Ch 1, 74 LJ Ch 353, 92 LT 490, 21
TLR 357, CA 365

Raw, Re, Morris v Griffiths (1884) 26 Ch D 601, 53 LJ Ch 1051, 32 WR 986, 51 LT 283
.... 415

Rawlings v Jennings (1806) 13 Ves 39, 33 ER 209, [1803–13] All ER Rep 464
.... 288

Rawlins v Goldfrap (1800) 5 Ves 440 459

Rawlins v McMahon (1852) 1 Drew 225, 9 Hare App II lxxxiin
.... 818

Rawlins v Rawlins (1796) 2 Cox Eq Cas 425 .... 362, 1077

Rawlins' Trusts, Re (1890) 45 Ch D 299, CA; affd sub nom Scalé v Rawlins [1892] AC
342, 61 LJ Ch 421, 66 LT 542, 8 TLR 558, [1891–4] All ER Rep Ext 1872, HL
.... 225, 375, 466, 472

Rawlinson, Re, Hill v Withall [1909] 2 Ch 36, 78 LJ Ch 443, 100 LT 509
.... 339, 345, 398, 447

Rawlinson v Rawlinson (1876) 3 Ch D 302, 24 WR 946, 34 LT 848
.... 285

Rawlinson v Wass (1852) 9 Hare 673, 16 Jur 282 339

Raworth v Marriott (1833) 1 My & K 643 904

Rawson, Re, Rigby v Rawson (1920) 90 LJ Ch 304, 65 Sol Jo 204, 124 LT 498
.... 33, 447

Rawstron (Executrices of the Estate of Lucian Freud) v Freud [2014] EWHC 2577 (Ch),
17 ITELR 479, [2014] WTLR 1453, [2015] 1 P & CR D13, [2014] All ER (D) 14
(Aug) 188, 221–222

Ray, Re, Cant v Johnstone [1916] 1 Ch 461, 85 LJ Ch 781, 114 LT 688
.... 211–212, 215, 218, 220, 276

Ray v Ray (1815) Coop G 264 924

Ray's Goods, Re (1926) 96 LJP 37, 136 LT 640, P, D and Admlty
.... 759

Ray's Will Trusts, Re, Public Trustee v Barry [1936] Ch 520, [1936] 2 All ER 93, 105 LJ
Ch 257, 80 Sol Jo 406, 155 LT 405, 52 TLR 446 .... 36, 41, 221, 367

Raybould, Re, Raybould v Turner [1900] 1 Ch 199, 69 LJ Ch 249, 48 WR 301, 82 LT 46
.... 1242

Rayer, Re, Rayer v Rayer [1903] 1 Ch 685, 72 LJ Ch 230, 51 WR 538, [1900–3] All ER
Rep 104, 87 LT 712 .... 114–115, 240, 269, 1131

Rayman v Gold (1591) Moore KB 635 .... 375, 469

Raymond v Fitch (1835) 2 Cr M & R 588, 5 LJ Ex 45, 1 Gale 337, 5 Tyr 985
.... 1282

Raymond Saul & Co (a firm) v Holden (as personal representative of Hemming) [2008]
EWHC 8565 (Ch), [2008] All ER (D) 168 (Dec) 1196, 1274, 1276

Rayner, Re, Couch v Warner [1925] All ER Rep 484, 134 LT 141
.... 247, 307

Rayner, Re, Rayner v Rayner [1904] 1 Ch 176, 73 LJ Ch 111, 52 WR 273,
[1900–3] All ER Rep 107, 48 Sol Jo 178, 89 LT 681, CA
.... 202, 205–206, 236, 294

Rayner v Green (1839) 2 Curt 248 627

Rayner v Koehler (1872) LR 14 Eq 262, 41 LJ Ch 697, 20 WR 859, 27 LT 506
.... 636

Rayner v Mowbray (1791) 3 Bro CC 234 349

Rayner's Goods, Re (1908) 52 Sol Jo 226, P, D and Admlty
.... 631

Read v Blunt (1832) 5 Sim 567 989

Read v Price [1909] 1 KB 577, 78 LJKB 504, 100 LT 457, 25 TLR 283; affd [1909] 2 KB
724, 78 LJKB 1137, [1908–10] All ER Rep 599, 101 LT 60, 25 TLR 701, CA
.... 976, 1231

Read v Read [2009] EWCA Civ 739 1254

Read v Read (1866) 15 WR 165 290

Read v Snell (1743) 2 Atk 642 .... 254, 342

PARA

Read v Truelove (1762) Amb 417 628
Read v Wills (1844) 1 Coll 86, 8 Jur 165, 2 LTOS 438 390
Read's Case (1604) 5 Co Rep 33b 1262
Reade's Goods, Re [1902] P 75, 71 LJP 45, 86 LT 258, P, D and Admlty
.... 110, 739
Reade-Revell, Re, Crellin v Melling [1930] 1 Ch 52, 99 LJ Ch 136, [1929] All ER Rep
506, 142 LT 177 1077
Reading, Re, Edmands v Reading [1916] WN 262, 60 Sol Jo 655
.... 1098
Reading v Reading [2015] EWHC 946 (Ch), [2015] WTLR 1245, [2015] All ER (D) 64
(Feb) 187–188, 202, 219–220, 242, 328, 331, 334
Reay v Rawlinson (1860) 29 Beav 88, 30 LJ Ch 330, 7 Jur NS 118, 9 WR 134
.... 309, 348, 379
Rebbeck, Re, Bennett v Rebbeck (1894) 63 LJ Ch 596, 8 R 376, 42 WR 473, 38 Sol Jo
399, 71 LT 74 1024
Recher's Will Trusts, Re, National Westminster Bank Ltd v National Anti-Vivisection
Society Ltd [1972] Ch 526, [1971] 3 All ER 401, [1971] 3 WLR 321, 115 Sol Jo 448
.... 36
Recknell, Re, White v Carter [1936] 2 All ER 36, 80 Sol Jo 406
.... 250, 293
Redding, Re, Thompson v Redding [1897] 1 Ch 876, 66 LJ Ch 460, 45 WR 457, 41 Sol Jo
405, 76 LT 339 1228
Redding's (otherwise Higgins') Goods, Re (1850) 2 Rob Eccl 339, 14 Jur 1052, 16 LTOS
177 63
Redfern, Re, Redfern v Bryning (1877) 6 Ch D 133, 47 LJ Ch 17, 25 WR 902, sub nom
Redfern v Hall 37 LT 241 .... 242, 255,256, 466
Redmayne v Moon (1856) 25 LJQB 311, 2 Jur NS 691, 27 LTOS 191
.... 1276
Redwood Music Ltd v Chappell & Co Ltd [1982] RPC 1
.... 633
Reech v Kennigate (1748) Amb 67, 1 Wils 227, 1 Ves Sen 123
.... 1240
Reed, Re (1888) 57 LJ Ch 790, 36 WR 682 328
Reed v Braithwaite (1871) LR 11 Eq 514, 40 LJ Ch 355, 19 WR 697, 24 LT 351
.... 336, 443
Reed's Goods, Re (1864) 4 New Rep 301, 3 Sw & Tr 439
.... 801
Reed's Goods, Re (1874) 38 JP 169, 29 LT 932 761
Rees, Re, Lloyds Bank Ltd v Rees [1954] Ch 202, [1954] 2 WLR 59, 98 Sol Jo 28, sub
nom Rees' Will Trusts, Re, Lloyds Bank Ltd v Rees [1954] 1 All ER 7
.... 462
Rees, Re, Rees v George (1881) 17 Ch D 701, 50 LJ Ch 328, 29 WR 301, 44 LT 241
.... 405
Rees, Re, Rees v Rees (1889) 60 LT 260 1067
Rees, Re, Williams v Davies (1890) 44 Ch D 484, 59 LJ Ch 305, 38 WR 523, 62 LT 362
.... 313
Rees, Re, Williams v Hopkins [1950] Ch 204, [1949] 2 All ER 1003, 66 (pt 1) TLR 23,
CA 207, 221–222, 370, 1069
Rees v Engelback (1871) LR 12 Eq 225, 40 LJ Ch 382, 19 WR 809, 24 LT 417
.... 152
Rees v Newbery and Institute of Cancer Research [1998] 1 FLR 1041, [1998] Fam Law
320 .... 567–568, 573
Rees v Rees (1873) LR 3 P & D 84, 37 JP 760, 29 LT 375
.... 67
Rees d Mears v Perrot (1830) 4 C & P 230 644
Rees Goods, Re (1865) 29 JP 296, 34 LJPM & A 56 .... 68, 895
Reeve, Re, Reeve v Reeve [1935] Ch 110, 104 LJ Ch 101, [1934] All ER Rep 21, 152 LT
254 502
Reeve v Malster W Jo. See Reve v Malster and Barrow
Reeve's Trusts, Re (1877) 4 Ch D 841, 46 LJ Ch 412, 25 WR 628, 36 LT 906
.... 1069
Reeves, Re, Edwards v Reeves-Hughes (1907) 51 Sol Jo 325
.... 449
Reeves, Re, Reeves v Pawson [1928] Ch 351, 97 LJ Ch 211, [1928] All ER Rep 342, 72
Sol Jo 121, 139 LT 66 .... 114, 279

PARA

Reeves v Baker (1854) 18 Beav 372, 23 LJ Ch 599, 2 Eq Rep 476, 18 Jur 588, 2 WR 354,
  23 LTOS 54 273
Reeves v Brymer (1799) 4 Ves 692 .... 248, 331
Reeves v Grainger (1908) 52 Sol Jo 355, P, D and Admlty
  68
Reeves v Reeves [1909] 2 IR 521 .... 97, 672
Reffell v Reffell (1866) LR 1 P & D 139, 35 LJP & M 121, 12 Jur NS 910, 14 WR 647,
  14 LT 705 193
Regan's Goods, Re (1838) 1 Curt 908 68
Reich, Re, Public Trustee v Guthrie (1924) 40 TLR 398
  .... 131, 141
Reid v Carleton [1905] 1 IR 147 .... 378, 383
Reid v Lord Tenterden (1833) 4 Tyr 111 .... 1212, 1223
Reid v Reid (1858) 25 Beav 469 161
Reid's Goods, Re [1896] P 129, 65 LJP 60, 74 LT 462, P, D and Admlty
  638
Reid's Goods, Re (1866) LR 1 P & D 74, 35 LJP & M 43, 12 Jur NS 300, 14 WR 316, 13
  LT 681 94
Reid's Goods, Re (1868) 33 JP 7, 38 LJP & M 1, 19 LT 265
  711
Reid's Goods, Re (1886) 11 PD 70, 55 LJP 75, 34 WR 577, 54 LT 590, CA
  850
Reid's Trustees v M'George 1929 SLT 608, Ct of Sess 11
Reigh v Kearney [1936] 1 IR 138 378
Reilly v Stoney (1865) 16 I Ch R 295 293
Reilly and Brady's Contract, Re [1910] 1 IR 258, 43 ILT 117
  2
Reith v Seymour (1828) 4 Russ 263, 6 LJOS Ch 97 383
Remnant v Bremridge (1818) 8 Taunt 191, 2 Moore CP 94
  1225
Remnant v Hood (1860) 2 De GF & J 396, 30 LJ Ch 71, 6 Jur NS 1173, 3 LT 485
  438
Renaud v Lamothe (1902) 32 SCR 357 133
Rendall v Andreae (1892) 61 LJQB 630, 8 TLR 615 1224–1225
Rendell, Re, Wood v Rendell [1901] 1 Ch 230, 70 LJ Ch 265, 49 WR 131, 45 Sol Jo 78,
  83 LT 625 .... 800, 803
Rendle's Goods, Re (1899) 68 LJP 125, P, D and Admlty
  114
Rennie v Massie (1866) LR 1 P & D 118, 35 LJP & M 124, 14 WR 516, 14 LT 188
  910
Repington v Governors of Tamworth School (1763) 2 Wils 150
  944
Resch's Will Trusts, Re, Far West Children's Health Scheme v Perpetual Trustee Co Ltd
  [1969] 1 AC 514, [1968] 3 WLR 1153, [1968] ALR 161, [1967] 2 NSWR 706, sub
  nom Far West Children's Health Scheme v Perpetual Trustee Co Ltd [1967] 3 All ER
  915, PC 97, 100, 107, 185, 192, 217, 250, 403, 611, 670, 708
Resch's Will Trusts, Re, Le Cras v Perpetual Trustee Co Ltd [1969] 1 AC 514, [1968] 3
  WLR 1153, [1968] ALR 161, [1967] 2 NSWR 706, sub nom Le Cras v Perpetual
  Trustee Co Ltd [1967] 3 All ER 915, PC . 97, 100, 107, 185, 193, 217, 250, 403, 670, 708
Reve v Malster and Barrow (1635) Cro Car 410, sub nom Reeve v Malster W Jo 361
  564
Reynette-James, Re, Wightman v Reynette-James [1975] 3 All ER 1037, [1976] 1 WLR
  161, 119 Sol Jo 682 .... 11, 187, 253
Reynish v Martin (1746) 3 Atk 330, sub nom Rhenish v Martin 1 Wils 130
  .... 129–130, 134, 136
Reynolds v Kortright (1854) 18 Beav 417, 2 Eq Rep 784, 2 WR 445, 24 LTOS 40
  .... 201, 203, 239
Reynolds v Reynolds [2005] EWHC 6 (Ch), [2005] All ER (D) 70 (Jan)
  .... 55, 63
Reynolds Goods, Re (1873) LR 3 P & D 35, 37 JP 215, 42 LJP & M 20, 21 WR 512, 28
  LT 144 .... 97, 111–112
Reynolds' Will Trusts, Re, Dove v Reynolds [1965] 3 All ER 686, [1966] 1 WLR 19, 109
  Sol Jo 903 488
Rhagg, Re, Easten v Boyd [1938] Ch 828, [1938] 3 All ER 314, 107 LJ Ch 436, 82 Sol Jo
  546, 159 LT 434, 54 TLR 990 287
Rheeder v Ower (1791) 3 Bro CC 240 411

PARA

Rhenish v Martin. See Reynish v Martin

Rhoades Goods, Re (1866) LR 1 P & D 119, 35 LJP & M 125
.... 778

Rhodes v Barret, ex p Singleton (1871) LR 12 Eq 479, 41 LJ Ch 103, 19 WR 871, 24 LT
654 1177–1178

Rhodes v Dean [1996] CLY 5555, CA 573

Rhodes v Muswell Hill Land Co (1861) 29 Beav 560, 30 LJ Ch 509, 7 Jur NS 178, 9 WR
472, 4 LT 229 .... 142, 190, 242

Rhodes v Rhodes (1859) 27 Beav 413 .... 249, 334

Rhodes v Rhodes (1874) 22 WR 835 285

Rhodes v Rhodes (1882) 7 App Cas 192, 51 LJPC 53, 30 WR 709, 46 LT 463,
[1881–5] All ER Rep Ext 1675, PC 56, 237, 242, 408, 413, 476, 739, 892, 906

Rhodes v Rudge (1826) 1 Sim 79, 5 LJOS Ch 17 1012

Rhodes v Whitehead (1865) 2 Drew & Sm 532, 13 WR 800, 12 LT 601
.... 424

Rhodesia Goldfields Ltd, Re, Partridge v Rhodesia Goldfields Ltd [1910] 1 Ch 239, 79 LJ
Ch 133, 17 Mans 23, 54 Sol Jo 135, 102 LT 126 1067

Riall, Re, Westminster Bank Ltd v Harrison [1939] 3 All ER 657
.... 475

Ricabe v Garwood. See Rickabe v Garwood

Rice v Gordon (1848) 11 Beav 265 1028

Rich v Wilson (1728) Mos 68 438

Rich's Goods, Re [1892] P 143, 55 JP 760, 61 LJP 94, 65 LT 352, P, D and Admlty
.... 51

Richards, Re (1869) LR 8 Eq 119 .... 1047, 1077

Richards, Re, Cawley v Dacey (1940) 84 Sol Jo 43, 162 LT 47
.... 328

Richards, Re, Davies v Edwards [1910] 2 Ch 74, 79 LJ Ch 500, 103 LT 130
.... 314, 395

Richards, Re, Jones v Rebbeck [1921] 1 Ch 513, 90 LJ Ch 300, 124 LT 597
.... 156, 921

Richards, Re, Uglow v Richards [1902] 1 Ch 76, 71 LJ Ch 66, 50 WR 90,
[1900–3] All ER Rep 146, 46 Sol Jo 50, 85 LT 452 383

Richards, Re, Williams v Gorvin (1883) 50 LT 22, [1881–5] All ER Rep Ext 1454
.... 231

Richards v Browne (1837) 3 Bing NC 493, 6 LJCP 95, 3 Hodg 27, 4 Scott 262
.... 1142

Richards v Davies (1862) 13 CBNS 69, 32 LJCP 3, 1 New Rep 62, 11 WR 38, 7 LT 357;
affd (1863) 13 CBNS 861, Ex Ch 226, 460–461

Richards v Lady Bergavenny (1695) 2 Vern 324 385

Richards v Richards (1860) John 754, 29 LJ Ch 836, 6 Jur NS 1145
.... 551

Richards Goods, Re (1866) LR 1 P & D 156, 35 LJP & M 44, 13 LT 757
.... 639

Richardson, Re, Mahoney v Treacy [1915] 1 IR 39 1091

Richardson, Re, Morgan v Richardson [1896] 1 Ch 512, 65 LJ Ch 512, 44 WR 279, 40
Sol Jo 225, 74 LT 12, [1895–9] All ER Rep Ext 2000 .... 1153, 1158, 1160–1161

Richardson, Re, Pole v Pattenden [1920] 1 Ch 423, 89 LJ Ch 258, 64 Sol Jo 290, 122 LT
714, 36 TLR 205, CA 1150

Richardson, Re, Richardson v Richardson [1915] 1 Ch 353, 84 LJ Ch 438,
[1914–15] All ER Rep 484, 112 LT 554 1090

Richardson, Re, Richardson v Richardson (1880) 14 Ch D 611, 49 LJ Ch 612, 28 WR
942, 43 LT 279 1205

Richardson v Bank of England (1838) 4 My & Cr 165, 8 LJ Ch 1
.... 1298

Richardson v Greese (1743) 3 Atk 65 .... 365, 439

Richardson v Marten (1858) 1 Giff 81, 5 Jur NS 9, 32 LTOS 237
.... 658

Richardson v Morton (1871) LR 13 Eq 123, 41 LJ Ch 8
.... 1109

Richardson v Power (1865) 19 CBNS 780, 35 LJCP 44, 11 Jur NS 739, 13 WR 1104, Ex
Ch 412, 453

Richardson v Richardson (1845) 14 Sim 526, 9 Jur 322, 5 LTOS 142
.... 395

Richardson v Smallwood (1822) Jac 552 1221

PARA

Richardson v Spraag (1718) 1 P Wms 434, 2 Eq Cas Abr 368 pl 1
.... 320
Richardson v Watson (1833) 4 B & Ad 787, 2 LJKB 134, 1 Nev & MKB 567, 110 ER
   652, [1824–34] All ER Rep 572 .... 127, 199, 217, 263, 266
Richardson's Goods, Re (1859) 6 Jur NS 326, 1 Sw & Tr 515, 1 LT 448
.... 632
Richardson's Goods, Re (1871) LR 2 P & D 244, 35 JP 792, 40 LJP & M 36, 19 WR 979,
   25 LT 384, [1861–73] All ER Rep Ext 1287 759
Richardson's Trusts, Re [1896] 1 IR 295   450
Richardson's Will Trusts, Re, Public Trustee v Llewellyn-Evans' Trustee [1958] Ch 504,
   [1958] 1 All ER 538, [1958] 2 WLR 414, 102 Sol Jo 176
.... 465
Richerson, Re, Scales v Heyhoe (No 2) [1893] 3 Ch 146, 62 LJ Ch 708, 41 WR 583,
   [1891–4] All ER Rep 593, 69 LT 590 470
Richie, Re, Ritchie v Joslin [2009] EWHC 709 (Ch), [2009] All ER (D) 59 (Apr)
.... 893
Rickabe v Garwood (1845) 8 Beav 579, sub nom Ricabe v Garwood 5 LTOS 515
.... 396
Rickards v Mumford (1812) 2 Phillim 23 102
Rickerby v Nicolson [1912] 1 IR 343 248
Rickett v Guillemard (1841) 12 Sim 88, 5 Jur 818 410
Ricketts, Re, Ricketts v Ricketts (1910) 103 LT 278 .... 432–433, 437
Ricketts v Carpenter (1858) 7 HL Cas 68, 28 LJ Ch 110, 5 Jur NS 717, 11 ER 28,
   [1843–60] All ER Rep 482, 33 LTOS 66 .... 225, 242–244, 253, 260, 382
Ricketts v Lewis (1882) 20 Ch D 745, 51 LJ Ch 837, 30 WR 609, 46 LT 368
.... 1028
Ricketts v Turquand (1848) 1 HL Cas 472 215
Rickit's Trusts, Re (1853) 11 Hare 299, 22 LJ Ch 1044, 1 Eq Rep 251, 17 Jur 664, 1 WR
   492, 21 LTOS 334, sub nom Arkitt, Re 21 LTOS 219 .... 277, 328
Rickless v United Artists Corpn [1988] QB 40, [1987] 1 All ER 679, [1987] 2 WLR 945,
   131 Sol Jo 362, [1987] LS Gaz R 654, CA 917
Riddell, Re, Public Trustee v Riddell [1936] Ch 747, [1936] 2 All ER 1600, 105 LJ Ch
   378, 80 Sol Jo 595, 155 LT 247, 52 TLR 675 .... 1006, 1015, 1081
Riddell v Sutton (1828) 5 Bing 200, 7 LJOSCP 60, 2 Moo & P 345
.... 1299
Rider v Wager (1725) 2 Eq Cas Abr 569, 2 P Wms 329
.... 159
Rider v Wood (1855) 1 K & J 644, 24 LJ Ch 737, 3 Eq Rep 1064
.... 561
Ridge, Re, Hancock v Dutton [1933] All ER Rep 449, 149 LT 266, CA
.... 328
Ridge v Newton (1842) 4 I Eq R 389, 1 Con & Law 381, 2 Dr & War 239
.... 271, 295
Ridge's Trusts, Re (1872) 7 Ch App 665, 41 LJ Ch 787, 20 WR 878, 27 LT 141,
   [1861–73] All ER Rep Ext 1243 475
Ridges v Morrison (1784) 1 Bro CC 389 403
Ridgeway v Darwin (1802) 8 Ves 65 48
Ridgeway v Munkittrick (1841) 1 Dr & War 84 .... 249, 336
Ridgway v Newstead (1860) 2 Giff 492, 6 Jur NS 1185, 9 WR 31, 3 LT 360; on appeal
   (1861) 3 De GF & J 474, 30 LJ Ch 889, 7 Jur NS 451, 9 WR 401, 4 LT 6492
.... 1101
Ridgway v Ridgway (1851) 4 De G & Sm 271, 20 LJ Ch 256, 15 Jur 960, 17 LTOS 239
.... 436
Ridgway v Woodhouse (1844) 7 Beav 437, 3 LTOS 19 .... 131, 231
Ridley, Re, Nicholson v Nicholson [1950] Ch 415, [1950] 2 All ER 1, 94 Sol Jo 338, 66
   (pt 1) TLR 981 994
Ridley, Re, Ridley v Ridley [1904] 2 Ch 774, 48 Sol Jo 641, 91 LT 189, sub nom
   Ridley's Trusts, Re 73 LJ Ch 696 952
Ridout v Bristow (1830) 1 Cr & J 231, 9 LJOS Ex 48, 1 Tyr 84
.... 1240
Ridout v Pain (or Payne) (1747) 3 Atk 486, 1 Ves Sen 10
.... 190, 234, 284
Rigby v Strangways (1846) 2 Ph 175, 10 Jur 998 1177
Rigden v Vallier (1751) 3 Atk 731, 2 Ves Sen 252, 26 ER 1219, [1558–1774] All ER Rep
   510 .... 3, 54
Riggall, Re, Wildash v Riggall [1949] WN 491 .... 182, 445–446

                                                                                    PARA
Right v Price (1779) 1 Doug KB 241 71
Right d Compton v Compton (1808) 9 East 267 249
Right d Day v Day (1812) 16 East 67 .... 442, 460
Riland's Estate, Re, Phillips v Robinson [1881] WN 173
  11
Riley v Garnett (1849) 3 De G & Sm 629, 19 LJ Ch 146, 14 Jur 236, 14 LTOS 289
  424
Riley's Will Trusts, Re, Barclays Bank Ltd v Riley (1964) 108 Sol Jo 174, CA
  315
Riley's Will Trusts, Re, Riley v Riley [1962] 1 All ER 513, [1962] 1 WLR 344, 106 Sol Jo
  285 .... 254, 468
Ring v Hardwick (1840) 2 Beav 352, 4 Jur 242 412
Ringrose v Bramham (1794) 2 Cox Eq Cas 384 301
Ripley's Goods, Re (1858) 4 Jur NS 342, 1 Sw & Tr 68, 6 WR 460, 31 LTOS 26
  716
Rippon's Estate, Re [1943] P 61, [1943] 1 All ER 676, 112 LJP 65, 87 Sol Jo 175, 168 LT
  357, 59 TLR 285, P, D and Admlty 79
Risdon v Public Trustee [1967] Ch 690, [1967] 1 All ER 391, [1967] 2 WLR 637, 111 Sol
  Jo 37 .... 306, 309, 398
Rishton, Re [1921] WN 226, 90 LJP 374, 125 LT 863, 37 TLR 798, P, D and Admlty
  .... 745, 761
Rishton v Cobb (1839) 5 My & Cr 145, 9 LJ Ch 110, 4 Jur 2, 41 ER 326,
  [1835–42] All ER Rep 398 .... 58, 375
Rising, Re, Rising v Rising [1904] 1 Ch 533, 73 LJ Ch 455, 90 LT 504
  466
Ritchie v Rees and Rees (1822) 1 Add 144 957
Ritchie (costs), Re; Ritchie v Joslin (costs) [2009] WTLR 885, [2009] All ER (D) 78 (Apr)
  .... 911, 1276
Ritchie's Trustees v M'Donald 1915 SC 501, Ct of Sess 116, 393
Ritson, Re, Ritson v Ritson [1899] 1 Ch 128, 68 LJ Ch 77, 47 WR 213, 43 Sol Jo 95, 79
  LT 455, 15 TLR 76, CA 1006
River's Case (1737) 1 Atk 410 .... 275, 354
River Wear Comrs v Adamson (1877) 2 App Cas 743, 42 JP 244, 47 LJQB 193, 3 Asp
  MLC 521, 26 WR 217, [1874–80] All ER Rep 1, 37 LT 543, HL
  .... 212, 237
Rivers, Re, Pullen v Rivers [1920] 1 Ch 320, 88 LJ Ch 462, [1918–19] All ER Rep 273, 63
  Sol Jo 534, 121 LT 57 .... 1099, 1159
Rix, Re, Steward v Lonsdale (1921) 90 LJ Ch 474, 65 Sol Jo 513, 125 LT 216
  156
Robb, Re, Marshall v Marshall [1953] Ch 459, [1953] 2 WLR 819, 97 Sol Jo 263, sub
  nom Robb's Will Trusts, Re, Marshall v Marshall [1953] 1 All ER 920
  422
Robbins, Re, Robbins v Legge [1907] 2 Ch 8, 76 LJ Ch 531, 51 Sol Jo 445, 96 LT 755,
  CA 1058
Robe, Re, Slade v Walpole (1889) 61 LT 497 293
Roberson, Re, Campkin v Barton [1883] WN 110 963
Roberts, Re, Kiff v Roberts (1886) 33 Ch D 265, 35 WR 176, 55 LT 498, CA
  273
Roberts, Re, Knight v Roberts (1897) 41 Sol Jo 468, 76 LT 479, CA
  .... 959, 1259
Roberts, Re, Percival v Roberts [1903] 2 Ch 200, 72 LJ Ch 597, 88 LT 505
  .... 194, 260, 305, 369, 440
Roberts, Re, Repington v Roberts-Gawen (1881) 19 Ch D 520, 45 LT 450, CA
  .... 262, 304–306, 338, 400
Roberts, Re, Roberts v Morgan [1916] 2 Ch 42, 85 LJ Ch 713, 114 LT 1119
  450
Roberts, Re, Roberts v Roberts [1902] 2 Ch 834, 72 LJ Ch 38, 51 WR 89, 47 Sol Jo 30,
  87 LT 523 .... 997, 1002
Roberts, Re, Roberts v Roberts [1978] 3 All ER 225, [1978] 1 WLR 653, 122 Sol Jo 264,
  CA 87
Roberts, Re, Tarleton v Bruton (1885) 30 Ch D 234, 53 LT 432, CA
  171
Roberts v Bishop of Kilmore [1902] 1 IR 333 .... 248, 347, 443

PARA

Roberts v Dixwell (1738) 1 Atk 607, 8 Bac Abr 302, sub nom Sands v Dixwell 2 Ves Sen
234, 652, sub nom Roberts v Dixwell, Sandys v Dixwell, Pyott v Dixwell West temp
Hard 536, sub nom Roberts v Dixall 2 Eq Cas Abr 668 pl 19
.... 385, 561
Roberts v Kuffin (1741) 2 Atk 112, Barn Ch 259 285
Roberts v Phillips (1855) 4 E & B 450, 24 LJQB 171, 1 Jur NS 444, 3 CLR 513, 24 LTOS
337 73
Roberts v Pocock (1798) 4 Ves 150 .... 120, 1088
Roberts v Roberts [1964] 3 All ER 503, [1965] 1 WLR 560, 108 Sol Jo 545, P, D and
Admlty 573
Roberts v Roberts (1848) 2 Ph 534, 17 LJ Ch 174, 12 Jur 148, 11 LTOS 285
.... 1174
Roberts v Roberts (1862) 26 JP 168, 31 LJPM & A 46, 8 Jur NS 220, 2 Sw & Tr 337, 5
LT 689 7
Roberts v Thorp (1911) 56 Sol Jo 13 .... 273, 382
Roberts v Walker (1830) 39 ER 288, [1824–34] All ER Rep 723, 1 Russ & M 752
.... 992
Roberts v Youle (1880) 49 LJ Ch 744 451
Roberts Estate, Re [1934] P 102, 103 LJP 61, [1934] All ER Rep 62, 78 Sol Jo 319, 51 LT
79, 50 TLR 321, P, D and Admlty 65
Roberts' Goods, Re [1898] P 149, 67 LJP 71, 78 LT 390, P, D and Admlty
.... 815
Roberts Goods, Re (1858) 1 Sw & Tr 64, 6 WR 460, 31 LTOS 41
.... 760
Roberts' Trusts, Re (1869) 38 LJ Ch 708, 17 WR 639 .... 1047, 1056
Roberts' Will Trusts, Re, Younger v Lewins [1937] Ch 274, [1937] 1 All ER 518, 106 LJ
Ch 232, 81 Sol Jo 199, 156 LT 213, 53 TLR 358 1015
Robertson v Broadbent (1883) 8 App Cas 812, 53 LJ Ch 266, 32 WR 205, 50 LT 243, HL
.... 118, 1109
Robertson v Flynn [1920] 1 IR 78, Ir CA 218
Robertson v Fraser (1871) 6 Ch App 696, 40 LJ Ch 776, 19 WR 989
.... 393, 395
Robertson v Junkin (1896) 26 SCR 192 152
Robertson v Quiddington (1860) 28 Beav 529 27
Robertson v Robertson 136 Am St R 589 (1909) 10
Robertson v Smith (1870) LR 2 P & D 43, 34 JP 377, 39 LJP & M 41, 22 LT 417
.... 8, 54, 708
Robertson's Estate, Re, Marsden v Marsden (1963) 107 Sol Jo 318, P, D and Admlty
.... 39, 180, 445
Robertson's Goods, Re [1896] P 8, 65 LJP 16, P, D and Admlty
.... 744
Robertson's Trust, Re (1858) 6 WR 405 370
Robey v Arnold (1898) 14 TLR 220, CA 1279
Robins, Re, Nelson v Robins (1888) 58 LT 382 1133
Robins v National Trust Co [1927] AC 515, 96 LJPC 84, [1927] All ER Rep 73, 71 Sol Jo
158, 137 LT 1, 43 TLR 243, PC 905
Robinson, Re, Lamb v Robinson [1930] 2 Ch 332, 99 LJ Ch 431, [1930] All ER Rep 658,
143 LT 593, 46 TLR 542 107
Robinson, Re, Wright v Tugwell [1892] 1 Ch 95, 40 WR 137, 66 LT 81; on appeal [1897]
1 Ch 85, 61 JP 132, 66 LJ Ch 97, 45 WR 181, 41 Sol Jo 96, 76 LT 95, 13 TLR 72,
CA 152
Robinson v Addison (1840) 2 Beav 515, 9 LJ Ch 369, 4 Jur 647
.... 156
Robinson v Collins [1975] 1 All ER 321, sub nom Re Collins, Robinson v Collins [1975] 1
WLR 309, 119 Sol Jo 66 .... 489, 1157
Robinson v Comyns (1736) Cas temp Talb 164 414
Robinson v Dusgate (1690) 2 Vern 181 378
Robinson v Fernsby [2003] EWCA Civ 1820, [2004] WTLR 257, 148 Sol Jo LB 59,
[2003] All ER (D) 414 (Dec) 568, 572, 575–576, 580, 591
Robinson v Fitzherbert (1786) 2 Bro CC 127 385
Robinson v Hicks. See Robinson v Robinson
Robinson v Hunt (1841) 4 Beav 450 .... 456, 473
Robinson v Lorkin. See Robinson v Pett
Robinson v Murdock. See Fraser v Murdoch
Robinson v Ommanney (1883) 23 Ch D 285, 52 LJ Ch 440, 31 WR 525, [1881–5] All ER
Rep 265, 49 LT 19, CA 21

                                                                          PARA
Robinson v Pett (1734) 2 Eq Cas Abr 454, 3 P Wms 249, sub nom Robinson v Lorkin 2
Barn KB 435 649
Robinson v Robinson (1756) 1 Burr 38, 1 Keny 298; affd sub nom Robinson v Hicks
(1758) 3 Bro Parl Cas 180 384
Robinson v Robinson (1851) 1 De GM & G 247, 21 LJ Ch 111, 16 Jur 255, 91 RR 73,
18 LTOS 293 294
Robinson v Shepherd (1863) 4 De GJ & Sm 129, 10 Jur NS 53, 12 WR 234, 9 LT 527
.... 399
Robinson v Smith (1833) 6 Sim 47, 2 LJ Ch 76 364
Robinson v Tickell (1803) 8 Ves 142 370
Robinson v Waddelow (1836) 8 Sim 134, Donnelly 108, 5 LJ Ch 350
.... 348
Robinson v Wood (1858) 27 LJ Ch 726, 4 Jur NS 625, 6 WR 728, [1843–60] All ER Rep
318, 31 LTOS 311 .... 182, 231
Robinson's Goods, Re (1867) LR 1 P & D 384, 31 JP 743, 36 LJP & M 93, 17 LT 19
.... 2, 6
Robinson's Goods, Re (1870) LR 2 P & D 171, 34 JP 775, 40 LJP & M 16, 19 WR 135,
23 LT 397 7
Robley v Ridings (1847) 16 LJ Ch 344, 11 Jur 813, 9 LTOS 217
.... 307–308
Robley v Robley (1839) 2 Beav 95, 3 Jur 694 403
Robson, Re, Robson v Hamilton [1891] 2 Ch 559, 60 LJ Ch 851, 65 LT 173, 7 TLR 512
.... 27, 285, 288
Robson v — (1813) 2 Rose 50 1299
Robson v Flight (1865) 4 De GJ & Sm 608, 34 LJ Ch 226, 11 Jur NS 147, 5 New Rep
344, 146 RR 478, 13 WR 393, 11 LT 725 151
Robson v Ibbs (1837) Donnelly 226, 6 LJ Ch 213 343
Roby, Re, Howlett v Newington [1908] 1 Ch 71, 77 LJ Ch 169, 97 LT 773, CA
.... 479, 514
Roby, Re, Sherbrooke v Taylor (1916) 60 Sol Jo 291 1203
Roch v Callen (1848) 6 Hare 531, 17 LJ Ch 144, 12 Jur 112
.... 403
Roche v M'Dermott [1901] 1 IR 394, 35 ILT 238 .... 128, 146
Rochefoucauld v Boustead [1896] WN 74, 65 LJ Ch 794, 74 LT 783; revsd [1897] 1 Ch
196, 66 LJ Ch 74, sub nom De la Rochefoucauld v Boustead 45 WR 272, 41 Sol Jo
156, 75 LT 502, 13 TLR 118, [1895–9] All ER Rep Ext 1911, CA
.... 882
Rochford v Hackman (1852) 9 Hare 475, 21 LJ Ch 511, 16 Jur 212, 19 LTOS 5
.... 134
Rock v Hardman (1819) 4 Madd 253 1161
Rock v Leighton (1700) 1 Com 87, 1 Ld Raym 589, 1 Salk 310
.... 1294, 1298
Rocke v Hart (1805) 11 Ves 58 1257
Rocke v Rocke (1845) 9 Beav 66 1062
Roddy v Fitzgerald (1858) 6 HL Cas 823 .... 195, 225, 235, 237, 241–242, 248, 334, 391
Roden v Smith (1744) Amb 588 428
Rodmell, Re, Safford v Safford (1913) 57 Sol Jo 284, 108 LT 184
.... 293
Roe, Re, Roe v Squire (1911) 45 ILT 144 1171
Roe v Scott and Smart (1787) 1 Fearne on Contingent Remainders 10th ed 473n
.... 473
Roe d Bendall v Summerset (1770) 2 Wm Bl 692, 5 Burr 2608
.... 466, 468–469, 634
Roe d Conolly v Vernon and Vyse (1804) 5 East 51, 1 Smith KB 318, 102 ER 988,
[1803–13] All ER Rep 426 271
Roe d Dodson v Grew (1767) 2 Wils 322, Wilm 272 .... 116, 237
Roe d Fulham v Wickett (1741) Willes 303, sub nom Roe d Gulliver v Wickett Andr App 1
.... 446
Roe d James v Avis (1792) 4 Term Rep 605 387
Roe d Noden v Griffiths (1766) 1 Wm Bl 605 27
Roe d Perry v Jones (1788) 1 Hy Bl 30; affd sub nom Jones v Roe (1789) 3 Term Rep 88
.... 27
Roe d Sheers v Jeffrey (1798) 7 Term Rep 589 460
Roe d Snape v Nevill (1848) 11 QB 466, sub nom Doe d Snape v Nevell 17 LJQB 119, 12
Jur 181, 10 LTOS 391 232
Roe d Wren v Clayton (1805) 6 East 628; affd sub nom Clayton v Roe (1813) 1 Dow 384,
HL 475

PARA

Roebuck v Dean (1793) 2 Ves 265, 4 Bro CC 403 429
Roffey v Bent (1867) LR 3 Eq 759 465
Rogers, ex p (1816) 2 Madd 449 472
Rogers, Re [2006] EWHC 753 (Ch), [2006] 2 All ER 792, [2006] 1 WLR 1577, 8 ITELR
    886, [2006] NLJR 644, (2006) Times, 3 May, [2006] All ER (D) 68 (Apr)
    .... 623, 729, 813
Rogers, Re, Lloyds Bank Ltd v Lory [1944] Ch 297, [1944] 2 All ER 1, 113 LJ Ch 287, 88
    Sol Jo 246, 171 LT 65, 60 TLR 406, CA 433
Rogers, Re, Public Trustee v Rogers [1915] 2 Ch 437, 84 LJ Ch 837, 60 Sol Jo 27, 113 LT
    916 1124
Rogers v Frank (1827) 1 Y & J 409 .... 606, 628
Rogers v Ingham (1876) 3 Ch D 351, 25 WR 338, [1874–80] All ER Rep 209, 35 LT 677,
    CA 1099
Rogers v James (1816) 7 Taunt 147, 2 Marsh 425 635
Rogers v Le Cocq (1896) 65 LJP 68, 12 TLR 209, P, D and Admlty
    910
Rogers v Maule (1841) 1 Y & C Ch Cas 4 555
Rogers v Mutch (1878) 10 Ch D 25, 48 LJ Ch 133, 27 WR 131
    301
Rogers v Rogers (1910) 11 SRNSW 38, 28 WNNSW 38, NSW SC
    287
Rogers v Soutten (1838) 2 Keen 598, 7 LJ Ch 118, Coop Pr Cas 96
    1301
Rogers v Thomas (1837) 2 Keen 8 293
Rogers v Towsey (1845) 9 Jur 575, 2 Holt Eq 270 318
Rogers and Andrews v Goodenough and Rogers (1862) 26 JP 119, 31 LJPM & A 49, 8 Jur
    NS 391, 2 Sw & Tr 342, 5 LT 719 110
Rogers and Browning v Pittis (1822) 1 Add 30 114
Rogerson, Re, Bird v Lee [1901] 1 Ch 715, 70 LJ Ch 444, 84 LT 200, [1900–3] All ER
    Rep Ext 1552 184
Rolfe v Perry (1863) 3 De GJ & Sm 481, 32 LJ Ch 471, 9 Jur NS 853, 11 WR 674, 8 LT
    441 115
Rolfe v Perry (1863) 32 LJ Ch 149, 9 Jur NS 491, 1 New Rep 428, 11 WR 357
    491
Rolfe's Goods, Re (1846) 4 Notes of Cases 406 86
Rolleston v Sinclair [1924] 2 IR 157 .... 70, 896
Rook v A-G (1862) 31 Beav 313, 31 LJ Ch 791, 9 Jur NS 9, 10 WR 745
    396
Rooke, Re, Jeans v Gatehouse [1933] Ch 970, 102 LJ Ch 371, [1933] All ER Rep 978,
    149 LT 445 1060
Rooke's Will Trusts, Re, Taylor v Rooke [1953] Ch 716, [1953] 2 All ER 110, [1953] 2
    WLR 1176, 97 Sol Jo 388 .... 182, 1035
Rooney v Cardona [1999] 1 WLR 1388, [1999] 2 FLR 1148, [1999] Fam Law 542, [1999]
    BPIR 291, [1999] All ER (D) 124, CA 1219
Rooper v Radcliffe (1714) 5 Bro Parl Cas 360, sub nom Roper v Radcliffe 10 Mod Rep
    230, 9 Mod Rep 167, HL 107
Roose, Re, Evans v Williamson (1880) 17 Ch D 696, 45 JP 343, 50 LJ Ch 197, 29 WR
    230, 43 LT 719 930
Rootes, Re (1860) 1 Drew & Sm 228, 29 LJ Ch 868, 8 WR 625
    341
Roper v Roper (1867) LR 3 CP 32, 37 LJCP 7, 16 WR 253, 17 LT 286, Ex Ch
    .... 362, 389
Roper v Roper (1876) 3 Ch D 714, 24 WR 1013, 35 LT 155
    1087
Roper's Estate, Re, Morrell v Gissing (1889) 41 Ch D 409, 58 LJ Ch 439, 37 WR 731, 61
    LT 42, 5 TLR 364 316
Rose, Re, Midland Bank Executor and Trustee Co Ltd v Rose [1949] Ch 78, [1948]
    2 All ER 971, [1949] LJR 208, 92 Sol Jo 661 .... 118, 156–157
Rose v Bartlett (1633) Cro Car 292 .... 291, 616
Rose v Epstein [1974] 2 All ER 1065, 118 Sol Jo 645; affd [1974] 3 All ER 745, [1974] 1
    WLR 1565, 118 Sol Jo 757, CA 915
Rose v Rose [1897] 1 IR 9 225
Rose v Sowerby (1830) Taml 376 430–431
Rose d Vere v Hill (1766) 3 Burr 1881 .... 318, 376
Rose's Goods, Re (1845) 4 Notes of Cases 101 101
Rosenberg v Scraggs (1900) 19 NZLR 196 383

PARA

Rosenthal, Re, Schwarz v Bernstein [1972] 3 All ER 552, [1972] 1 WLR 1273, 51 ATC
371, [1972] TR 329, 116 Sol Jo 666 .... 1132, 1245
Rosher, Re, Rosher v Rosher (1884) 26 Ch D 801, 53 LJ Ch 722, 32 WR 821, 51 LT 785,
[1881–5] All ER Rep Ext 1301 142
Ross, Re (1901) 1 SRNSW 1, 18 NSWWN 40, NSW SC
.... 454
Ross, Re [2013] EWHC 2724 (Ch), [2014] WTLR 321, [2013] All ER (D) 221 (Sep)
.... 997–998, 1004, 1008
Ross, Re, Ashton v Ross [1900] 1 Ch 162, 69 LJ Ch 192, 48 WR 264, 81 LT 578
.... 1090
Ross, Re, Wingfield v Blair [1907] 1 Ch 482, 76 LJ Ch 302, 96 LT 814
.... 1178
Ross v Caunters [1980] Ch 297, [1979] 3 All ER 580, [1979] 3 WLR 605, 123 Sol Jo 605
.... 41
Ross v Perrin-Hughes [2004] EWHC 2559 (Ch), 7 ITELR 405, [2004] All ER (D) 159
(Nov) 204–205, 211–212, 219, 290, 1008
Ross v Ross (1819) 1 Jac & W 154 381
Ross v Ross (1845) 2 Coll 269, 9 Jur 795, 5 LTOS 430
.... 408
Ross v Ross (1855) 20 Beav 645 .... 334, 336, 398
Ross v Veal (1855) 1 Jur NS 751, 3 WR 652 290
Ross Trusts, Re (1871) LR 13 Eq 286, 41 LJ Ch 130, 20 WR 231, 25 LT 817
.... 537
Ross, Re, Petterson v Ross [2013] EWHC 2724 (Ch), [2013] All ER (D) 221 (Sep)
.... 997
Rosse (Countess), Re, Parsons v Earl of Rosse (1923) 93 LJ Ch 8, [1923] All ER Rep 634,
67 Sol Jo 638, 129 LT 592, CA 366
Rosser's Goods, Re (1864) 28 JP 583, 33 LJPM & A 155, 3 Sw & Tr 490, 12 WR 1014,
10 LT 695 630
Rotherham v Fanshaw (1748) 3 Atk 628 1073
Rothermere (Viscount), Re, Mellors Basden & Co v Coutts & Co [1945] Ch 72, [1944]
2 All ER 593, 115 LJ Ch 34, 88 Sol Jo 437, 172 LT 98, 61 TLR 69
.... 1093
Rothwell v Chemical and Insulating Co Ltd [2007] UKHL 39, [2007] 4 All ER 1047,
[2007] 3 WLR 876, [2007] ICR 1745, 99 BMLR 139, [2007] NLJR 1542, (2007)
Times, 24 October, 151 Sol Jo LB 1366, [2007] All ER (D) 224 (Oct), sub nom
Grieves v FT Everard & Sons Ltd [2008] PIQR P95 1279–1280
Rothwell v Rothwell (1825) 2 Sim & St 217 .... 1186, 1298
Round v Pickett (1878) 47 LJ Ch 631, 26 WR 493 .... 468, 476
Roundel v Currer (1786) 2 Bro CC 67 147
Rouse's Estate, Re (1852) 9 Hare 649 .... 430–431, 1076
Routledge's Trusts, Re, Routledge v Saul [1909] 1 Ch 280, 99 LT 919, sub nom Routledge,
Re, Saul v Routledge 78 LJ Ch 136 951
Row's Estate, Re (1874) 43 LJ Ch 347, 29 LT 824 317
Rowan v Chute (1861) 13 I Ch R 169 21
Rowe, Re, Bennetts v Eddy [1941] Ch 343, [1941] 2 All ER 330, 110 LJ Ch 145, 85 Sol Jo
264, 165 LT 76, 57 TLR 592 1108–1109
Rowe, Re, Jacobs v Hind (1889) 58 LJ Ch 703, 61 LT 581, CA
.... 1149
Rowe, Re, Merchant Taylors' Co v London Corpn (1914) 30 TLR 528
.... 11
Rowe, Re, Pike v Hamlyn [1898] 1 Ch 153, 67 LJ Ch 87, 46 WR 357, 42 Sol Jo 96, 77 LT
475, CA 252, 270
Rowe v Clarke [2005] EWHC 3068 (Ch), 149 Sol Jo LB 1450, [2005] All ER (D) 368
(Oct) 106
Rowe v Clarke [2006] EWHC 1292 (Ch), [2006] All ER (D) 124 (May)
.... 911
Rowland, Re, Jones v Rowland (1902) 86 LT 78 .... 375, 383
Rowland, Re, Smith v Russell [1963] Ch 1, [1962] 2 All ER 837, [1962] 3 WLR 637, 106
Sol Jo 450, CA 7, 225, 246, 746
Rowland v Gorsuch (1789) 2 Cox Eq Cas 187 .... 339, 397
Rowland v Tawney (1858) 26 Beav 67 412
Rowlands, Re [1984] FLR 813; affd [1984] FLR 813, [1984] Fam Law 280, CA
.... 573–574, 577
Rowlatt v Easton (1863) 2 New Rep 262, 11 WR 767 .... 272, 277

PARA

Rowley v Adams (1839) 4 My & Cr 534, 9 LJ Ch 34, 3 Jur 1069
.... 1223
Rowley v Eyton (1817) 2 Mer 128 113
Rowlls v Bebb [1900] 2 Ch 107, 69 LJ Ch 562, 48 WR 562, [1900–3] All ER Rep 756, 44
Sol Jo 448, 82 LT 633, CA 1124, 1127, 1257
Rownson, Re, Field v White (1885) 29 Ch D 358, 49 JP 759, 54 LJ Ch 950, 33 WR 604,
52 LT 825, CA 975
Rowsell, Re. See A-G v Rowsell
Rowsell v Morris (1873) LR 17 Eq 20, 43 LJ Ch 97, 22 WR 67, 29 LT 446
.... 636, 1165, 1172
Rowson's Estate, Re [1944] 2 All ER 36, 88 Sol Jo 232, 171 LT 70, P, D and Admlty
.... 79
Roxburgh v Lambert (1829) 2 Hag Ecc 557 787
Royal National Lifeboat Institution v Headley [2016] EWHC 1948 (Ch)
.... 1196, 1256
Royal Society v Robinson [2015] EWHC 3442 (Ch) 236
Royce's Will Trusts, Re, Tildesley v Tildesley [1959] Ch 626, [1959] 3 All ER 278, [1959]
3 WLR 254, 103 Sol Jo 675, CA 42
Royle, Re, Fryer v Royle (1877) 5 Ch D 540, 25 WR 528, 36 LT 441
.... 1173
Royle v Hamilton (1799) 4 Ves 437 .... 255, 331
Royse, Re, Royse v Royse [1985] Ch 22, [1984] 3 All ER 339, [1984] 3 WLR 784, [1985]
FLR 196, [1984] Fam Law 156, 128 Sol Jo 665, [1984] LS Gaz R 2543, CA
.... 39–40, 566
Rubbins, Re, Gill v Worrall (1898) 79 LT 313, CA 316
Rubery v Stevens (1832) 4 B & Ad 241, 2 LJKB 46, 1 Nev & MKB 183
.... 1223, 1225
Rudge v Barker (1735) Cas temp Talb 124 410
Rudge v Winnall (1849) 12 Beav 357, 18 LJ Ch 469, 13 Jur 737, 14 LTOS 325
.... 291, 431
Rufenack v Hope Mission 2000 ABQB 1055, (2002) 6 ITELR 1
.... 221
Rule's Goods, Re (1878) 4 PD 76, 42 LJP 776, 47 LJP 32, 26 WR 357, 39 LT 123, P, D
and Admlty 721
Rumball, Re, Sherlock v Allan [1956] Ch 105, [1955] 3 All ER 71, [1955] 1 WLR 1037,
48 R & IT 672, 99 Sol Jo 579, CA 1132
Rushbrook's Will Trusts, Re, Allwood v Norwich Diocesan Fund and Board of Finance
[1948] Ch 421, [1948] 1 All ER 932, [1948] LJR 1291, 92 Sol Jo 271, 64 TLR 301
.... 1212, 1215
Russel v Buchanan (1836) 7 Sim 628, 5 LJ Ch 122 .... 412, 423
Russel v Prat (1584) 1 And 177, sub nom Russel's Case 5 Co Rep 27a, Moore KB 146; on
appeal sub nom Russell and Prat's Case (1589) 1 Leon 193, 74 ER 178, Ex Ch
.... 798
Russel v Prat. See Russel's Case
Russell, Re (1885) 52 LT 559, CA 369, 377
Russell, Re, Public Trustee v Campbell (1912) 56 Sol Jo 651
.... 1070
Russell, Re, Russell v Chell (1882) 19 Ch D 432, 51 LJ Ch 401, 30 WR 454, 46 LT 336
.... 282
Russell v Dickson (1842) 2 Dr & War 133; affd (1853) 4 HL Cas 293, 17 Jur 307,
21 LTOS 161 403
Russell v IRC [1988] 2 All ER 405, [1988] 1 WLR 834, [1988] STC 195, 132 Sol Jo 659,
[1988] 16 LS Gaz R 44 120
Russell v Jackson (1851) 9 Hare 387, 21 LJ Ch 146, 15 Jur 1117, 18 LTOS 166
.... 882
Russell v Jackson (1852) 10 Hare 204, 90 RR 336 .... 207, 221–222
Russell v Long (1799) 4 Ves 551 395
Russell v Plaice (1854) 18 Beav 21, 23 LJ Ch 441, 2 Eq Rep 1149, 18 Jur 254, 2 WR 243,
22 LTOS 326 1023
Russell v Russell [1903] 1 IR 168, 36 ILT 207 433
Russell's Goods, Re [1892] P 380, 62 LJP 15, 1 R 456, 67 LT 504, P, D and Admlty
.... 613
Russell's Goods, Re (1890) 15 PD 111, 59 LJP 80, 62 LT 644, P, D and Admlty
.... 87, 90, 749
Rust v Baker (1837) 8 Sim 443 324
Rutherford v Maule (1832) 4 Hag Ecc 213 899

PARA

Rutter, Re, Donaldson v Rutter [1907] 2 Ch 592, 77 LJ Ch 34, 97 LT 883, 24 TLR 12
.... 133
Ruttie, Re, Ruttie v Saul [1969] 3 All ER 1633, [1970] 1 WLR 89, 113 Sol Jo 903
.... 598
Ryall v Hannam (1847) 10 Beav 536, 16 LJ Ch 491, 11 Jur 761, 10 LTOS 126
.... 277
Ryan, Re (1887) 19 LR Ir 24 465
Ryan, Re, Kenny v Ryan [1897] 1 IR 513 1269
Ryan v Cowley (1835) L & G temp Sugd 7 456–457
Ryder, Re, Burton v Kearsley [1914] 1 Ch 865, 83 LJ Ch 653, [1914–15] All ER Rep 144,
    58 Sol Jo 556, 110 LT 970, CA 383
Ryder's Goods, Re (1861) 31 LJPM & A 215, 7 Jur NS 196, 2 Sw & Tr 127, 3 LT 756
.... 612
Rye's Settlement, Re (1852) 10 Hare 106, 22 LJ Ch 345, 16 Jur 1128, 1 WR 29, 21 LTOS
    55 .... 2, 459
Rymes v Clarkson (1809) 1 Phillim 22 60
Ryves v Ryves (1871) LR 11 Eq 539, 40 LJ Ch 252 .... 395, 1012

S

S, Re [1996] 1 WLR 235, [1996] 3 FCR 357, [1996] 1 FLR 910, [1996] Fam Law 352
.... 39–40, 566
S v T1 [2006] WTLR 1461 357
SSSL Realisations (2002) Ltd (in liquidation), Re [2006] EWCA Civ 7, [2006] Ch 610,
    [2006] 2 WLR 1369, [2007] 1 BCLC 29, [2006] BPIR 457, (2006) Times, 20 January,
    [2006] All ER (D) 98 (Jan), sub nom Squires (liquidators of SSSL Realisations
    (2002) Ltd) v AIG Europe (UK) Ltd [2006] BCC 233 1236
S Estate, Re [1968] P 302, [1967] 2 All ER 150, [1967] 3 WLR 325, 110 Sol Jo 911, P, D
    and Admlty 619, 759
S-'s Goods, Re (1850) 15 LTOS 71 10
Sabatini, Re (1969) 114 Sol Jo 35, P, D and Admlty 93, 101
Sabbarton v Sabbarton (1738) 2 Eq Cas Abr 245, Andr 333, Cas temp Talb 245, Lee temp
    Hard 413 460
Saberton v Skeels (1830) Taml 383, 1 Russ & M 587 .... 364, 377
Sackville-West v Viscount Holmesdale (1870) LR 4 HL 543, 39 LJ Ch 505
.... 194, 228
Sadler, Re, Furniss v Cooper (1915) 60 Sol Jo 89 .... 315, 317, 410
Sage, Re, Lloyds Bank Ltd v Holland [1946] Ch 332, [1946] 2 All ER 298, 115 LJ Ch 305,
    90 Sol Jo 418, 175 LT 175, 62 TLR 508 149
Sahal's Will Trusts, Re, Alliance Assurance Co Ltd v A-G [1958] 3 All ER 428, [1958] 1
    WLR 1243, 123 JP 73, 102 Sol Jo 877 320
St Albans (Duke) v Beauclerk (1743) 2 Atk 636 403
St Albans' Will Trusts, Re, Coutts & Co v Beauclerk [1963] Ch 365, [1962] 2 All ER 402,
    [1962] 3 WLR 206, 106 Sol Jo 509 27
Saker's Estate, Re [1909] P 233, 78 LJP 85, 53 Sol Jo 562, 101 LT 400, P, D and Admlty
.... 793
Salaman, Re, De Pass v Sonnenthal [1907] 2 Ch 46, 76 LJ Ch 419, 96 LT 809; revsd
    [1908] 1 Ch 4, 77 LJ Ch 60, 98 LT 255, CA 362, 1045, 1158
Sales, Re, Powsland v Roberts [1920] WN 54, 64 Sol Jo 308
.... 991
Salisbury v Petty (1843) 3 Hare 86, 7 Jur 1011 .... 320, 326–327
Salisbury v Salisbury (1848) 6 Hare 526, 17 LJ Ch 480, 12 Jur 671
.... 491
Salisbury (Earl) v Lambe (1759) Amb 383, 1 Eden 465 452
Salkeld v Salkeld (1758) 1 Eden 64 .... 456, 459
Salkeld v Vernon (1758) 1 Eden 64 .... 456, 459
Sallery, Re (1861) 11 I Ch R 236 .... 385, 454
Sallis v Jones [1936] P 43, 105 LJP 17, [1935] All ER Rep 872, 79 Sol Jo 880, 154 LT
    112, 52 TLR 113, P, D and Admlty 88
Salmen, Re, Salmen v Bernstein (1912) 56 Sol Jo 632, 107 LT 108, CA
.... 652, 656
Salmon, Re, Coard v National Westminster Bank Ltd [1981] Ch 167, [1980] 3 All ER 532,
    [1980] 3 WLR 748, 124 Sol Jo 813 598
Salmon v Green (1849) 11 Beav 453, 18 LJ Ch 166, 13 Jur 272, 617, 13 LTOS 87
.... 305
Salmon v Tidmarsh (1859) 5 Jur NS 1380 390

PARA

Salmonsen, Re, National Provincial Bank Ltd v Salmonsen (1965) 109 Sol Jo 477
.... 182

Salomon v Brownfield and Brownfield Guild Pottery Society Ltd (1896) 12 TLR 239
.... 1279

Salomons, Re, Public Trustee v Wortley [1920] 1 Ch 290, 89 LJ Ch 222, [1920] All ER
  Rep 768, 64 Sol Jo 241, 122 LT 670, 36 TLR 212 .... 1074, 1158

Salt, Re, Brothwood v Keeling [1895] 2 Ch 203, 64 LJ Ch 494, 13 R 499, 43 WR 500, 39
  Sol Jo 468 .... 997, 1002

Salt v Chattaway (1841) 3 Beav 576, 10 LJ Ch 234, 49 ER 227
.... 992

Salter, Re, Farrant v Carter (1881) 44 LT 603 .... 255, 298

Salter v Salter [1896] P 291, 65 LJP 117, 12 WR 512, 45 WR 7, 40 Sol Jo 635, 75 LT 7,
  CA 694, 741, 809

Salting, Re, Baillie-Hamilton v Morgan [1932] 2 Ch 57, 101 LJ Ch 305, [1932] All ER
  Rep 857, 76 Sol Jo 344, 147 LT 432 464

Saltmarsh v Barrett (No 2) (1862) 31 Beav 349, 31 LJ Ch 783, 8 Jur NS 737, 10 WR 640,
  7 LT 87 1256

Salusbury v Denton (1857) 21 JP 726, 3 K & J 529, 26 LJ Ch 851, 3 Jur NS 740, 5 WR
  865, 30 LTOS 63 254

Sammut v Manzi [2008] UKPC 58, [2009] 2 All ER 234, [2009] 1 WLR 1834, 11 ITELR
  806, [2009] NLJR 35, 74 WIR 44, [2008] All ER (D) 79 (Dec)
  .... 174–175, 204, 220, 228, 235–236, 239, 246, 248, 302, 345, 672

Sampson, Re, Sampson v Sampson [1896] 1 Ch 630, 65 LJ Ch 406, 44 WR 557, 40 Sol Jo
  353, 74 LT 246 .... 451, 463

Sampson, Re, Sampson v Sampson [1906] 1 Ch 435, 75 LJ Ch 302, 54 WR 342, 50 Sol Jo
  239, 94 LT 241 950

Samson's Goods, Re (1873) LR 3 P & D 48, 37 JP 425, 42 LJP & M 59, 21 WR 568, 28
  LT 478 763

Samuel v Jones (1843) 2 Hare 246, 12 LJ Ch 496, 7 Jur 845
.... 1201

Samuel v Samuel (1845) 14 LJ Ch 222, 2 Coop temp Cott 119, 9 Jur 222, 5 LTOS 34
.... 392

Sandbrook, Re, Noel v Sandbrook [1912] 2 Ch 471, 81 LJ Ch 800, [1911–13] All ER Rep
  559, 56 Sol Jo 721, 107 LT 148 .... 131, 138, 140–141

Sandeman's Will Trusts, Re, Sandeman v Hayne [1937] 1 All ER 368, 81 Sol Jo 137
.... 1053

Sanders v Ashford (1860) 28 Beav 609 .... 175, 302, 457, 473

Sanders v Franks (1817) 2 Madd 147 363

Sanders Goods, Re [1900] P 292, 69 LJP 121, 83 LT 716, P, D and Admlty
.... 841

Sanders' Trusts, Re (1866) LR 1 Eq 675, 12 Jur NS 351, 14 WR 576
.... 246, 256, 443, 456

Sanderson v Bayley (1838) 4 My & Cr 56, sub nom Saunderson v Bailey 8 LJ Ch 18, 2 Jur
  958 328

Sanderson v Stoddart (1863) 32 Beav 155, 9 Jur NS 1216, 11 WR 275, 7 LT 662
.... 1196

Sanderson's Trust, Re (1857) 3 K & J 497, 26 LJ Ch 804, 3 Jur NS 658, 112 RR 357, 5
  WR 864, 30 LTOS 140 .... 371, 373, 431

Sandes v Cooke (1888) 21 LR Ir 445 334

Sandover v Brown [2004] EWHC 1307 (Ch), [2004] All ER (D) 53 (May)
.... 212–213, 215, 272, 275, 285, 290

Sands v Dixwell. See Roberts v Dixwell

Sandys' Will Trust, Re, Sandys v Kirton [1947] 2 All ER 302, CA
.... 239

Sanford, Re, Sanford v Sanford [1901] 1 Ch 939, 70 LJ Ch 591, 84 LT 456
.... 237, 248, 259, 369, 376, 382

Sanford v Irby (1820) 3 B & Ald 654 460

Sanford v Raikes (1816) 1 Mer 646 .... 209, 212, 226

Sanforth's Will, Re [1901] WN 152 422

Sanger, Re, Taylor v North [1939] Ch 238, [1938] 4 All ER 417, 108 LJ Ch 165, 82 Sol Jo
  950, 159 LT 603, 55 TLR 109 .... 994, 999, 1108

Sanpietro's Estate, Re, Re Van Tuyll van Serooskerken's Estate [1941] P 16, [1940]
  4 All ER 482, 110 LJP 23, 84 Sol Jo 705, 57 TLR 137, P, D and Admlty
.... 815

Sansbury v Read (1805) 12 Ves 75 375

PARA

Sarat Kumari Debi v Sakhi Chand (1928) LR 56 Ind App 62
.... 892
Sarel v Sarel (1856) 23 Beav 87 .... 395, 476
Sargeant v National Westminster Bank plc (1991) 61 P & CR 518, [1990] EG 62 (CS), CA
.... 657, 1030
Sarson, Re, Public Trustee v Sarson [1925] 1 Ch 31, 94 LJ Ch 155, 69 Sol Jo 105, 132 LT
339 1130
Sartoris' Estate, Re, Sartoris v Sartoris [1892] 1 Ch 11, 60 LJ Ch 634, 64 LT 730, CA; on
appeal [1892] 1 Ch 11, 61 LJ Ch 1, 40 WR 82, [1891–4] All ER Rep 193, 36 Sol Jo
41, 65 LT 544, 8 TLR 51, CA 465
Satterthwaite's Will Trusts, Re, Midland Bank Executor and Trustee Co Ltd v Royal
Veterinary College [1966] 1 All ER 919, [1966] 1 WLR 277, 110 Sol Jo 92, CA
.... 267
Saul's Goods, Re [1896] P 151, 65 LJP 101, P, D and Admlty
.... 744
Saumarez v Saumarez (1839) 4 My & Cr 331 284
Saumarez v Saumarez (1865) 34 Beav 432 428
Saunders, Re, Public Trustee v Saunders [1929] 1 Ch 674, 98 LJ Ch 303, 141 LT 27, 45
TLR 283 .... 485, 521
Saunders, Re, Saunders v Gore [1898] 1 Ch 17, 67 LJ Ch 55, 46 WR 180,
[1895–9] All ER Rep 461, 42 Sol Jo 65, 77 LT 450, CA
.... 1131
Saunders v Garrett [2005] WTLR 749 567
Saunders v Lowe (1775) 2 Wm Bl 1014 466
Saunders v Saunders (1848) 6 Notes of Cases 518 106
Saunders v Vautier (1841) 4 Beav 115, 49 ER 282; affd (1841) Cr & Ph 240, 10 LJ Ch
354, 54 RR 286, 41 ER 482, [1835–42] All ER Rep 58
.... 146, 372, 428, 430, 434, 1062
Saunders' Case (1599) 1 Brownl 241, Cro Eliz 683, 5 Co Rep 12a
.... 1146
Saunders' Goods, Re (1865) LR 1 P & D 16, 35 LJP & M 26, 11 Jur NS 1027, 14 WR
148, 13 LT 411 80
Saunders-Davies, Re, Saunders-Davies v Saunders-Davies (1887) 34 Ch D 482, 56 LJ Ch
492, 35 WR 493, 56 LT 153 1004
Saunderson v Bailey. See Sanderson v Bayley
Savage, Re, Cull v Howard [1918] 2 Ch 146, 87 LJ Ch 599, [1918–19] All ER Rep 700,
65 Sol Jo 620, 119 LT 337 1067
Savage v Blythe (1796) 2 Hag Ecc App 150 794
Savage v Lane (1847) 6 Hare 32, 17 LJ Ch 89, 11 Jur 1053
.... 1300
Savage v Robertson (1868) LR 7 Eq 176 351–352
Savage v Tyers (1872) 7 Ch App 356, 41 LJ Ch 815, 20 WR 817
.... 231, 471
Savage's Goods, Re (1870) LR 2 P & D 78, 34 JP 359, 39 LJP & M 25, 17 WR 766, 22
LT 375 .... 100, 712
Savile v Blacket (1722) 1 P Wms 777 1112
Savile v Kinnaird (1865) 11 Jur NS 195, 13 WR 308, 11 LT 687
.... 252
Savile (Jimmy), Re, National Westminster Bank plc v Lucas. See National Westminster
Bank plc v Lucas, Estate of Jimmy Savile (deceased), Re
Savory's Goods, Re (1851) 15 Jur 1042, 18 LTOS 280 63
Sawrey v Rumney (1852) 5 De G & Sm 698, 17 Jur 83, 19 LTOS 337
.... 403
Sawyer v Birchmore (1837) 1 Keen 825, 2 My & Cr 611, 6 LJ Ch 277
.... 1100
Sax, Re, Barned v Sax [1893] WN 104, 62 LJ Ch 688, 3 R 638, 41 WR 584, 37 Sol Jo
560, 68 LT 849 .... 142, 147
Saxby, Re, Saxby v Kiddell [1890] WN 171 293
Saxone Shoe Co Ltd's Trust Deed, Re, Re Abbott's Will Trusts, Abbott v Pearson [1962]
2 All ER 904, [1962] 1 WLR 943, 106 Sol Jo 687 348
Saxton v Saxton (1879) 13 Ch D 359, 49 LJ Ch 128, 28 WR 294, 41 LT 648
.... 277, 279, 282
Saxton's Estate, Re, Barclays Bank Ltd v Treasury Solicitor [1939] 2 All ER 418, 83 Sol Jo
341, P, D and Admlty 711
Say v Creed (1844) 3 Hare 455, 8 Jur 893 1301

PARA

Say v Creed (1847) 5 Hare 580, 16 LJ Ch 361, 11 Jur 603
.... 313
Sayer, Re, McClellan v Clark (1884) 53 LJ Ch 832, 50 LT 616
.... 293
Sayer v Bradly (1856) 5 HL Cas 873, 2 Jur NS 887, 4 WR 808, 28 LTOS 59, sub nom
    Sayer v Boys 25 LJ Ch 593 .... 237, 248, 335, 343
Sayer v Sayer (1714) Gilb Ch 87, Prec Ch 392, 2 Vern 688
.... 285
Sayer v Sayer (1849) 7 Hare 377, 13 Jur 402; on appeal (1851) 21 LJ Ch 190, 16 Jur 21, 3
    Mac & G 606, 18 LTOS 129 209
Sayer Trust, Re, MacGregor v Sayer [1957] Ch 423, [1956] 3 All ER 600, [1957] 2 WLR
    261, 101 Sol Jo 130 348
Scaife, Re, ex p West (1784) 1 P Wms 275n, 1 Bro CC 575
.... 410
Scalé v Rawlins. See Rawlins' Trusts, Re
Scammell v Farmer [2008] EWHC 1100 (Ch), [2008] WTLR 1261, 152 (No 23) Sol Jo LB
    31, [2008] All ER (D) 296 (May) 47, 50, 55, 64, 893, 899
Scarborough v Scarborough (1888) 58 LT 851, [1886–90] All ER Rep Ext 1485
.... 446
Scarborough (Earl) v Doe d Savile (1836) 3 Ad & El 897, 6 LJ Ex 270, 6 Nev & MKB
    884, Ex Ch 229
Scarfe v Matthews [2012] EWHC 3071 (Ch), [2012] STC 2487, 15 ITELR 321, [2012]
    35 LS Gaz R 20, [2012] SWTI 2926, [2012] All ER (D) 25 (Sep)
.... 1016
Scarff v Scarff [1927] 1 IR 13 895–896
Scarisbrick, Re, Cockshott v Public Trustee [1951] Ch 622, [1951] 1 All ER 822, 95 Sol Jo
    299, [1951] 1 TLR 989, CA 273
Scarlett v Lord Abinger (1865) 34 Beav 338 147
Scatterwood (or Scattergood) v Edge (1699) 1 Eq Cas Abr 190, 12 Mod Rep 278, 1 Salk
    229 446
Scawen v Blunt (1802) 7 Ves 294 27
Scawin v Watson (1847) 10 Beav 200, 16 LJ Ch 404, 11 Jur 576
.... 231
Schaefer v Schuhmann [1972] AC 572, [1972] 1 All ER 621, [1972] 2 WLR 481, 116 Sol
    Jo 121, [1972–73] ALR 501, PC 21, 24, 1221
Schar, Re, Midland Bank Executor and Trustee Co Ltd v Damer [1951] Ch 280, [1950]
    2 All ER 1069, 94 Sol Jo 804, 66 (pt 2) TLR 1131 151
Schenck v Legh (1803) 9 Ves 300 452
Schenk v Agnew (1858) 4 K & J 405 449
Schenley's Goods, Re (1903) 20 TLR 127, P, D and Admlty
.... 723
Scherer v Counting Instruments Ltd [1986] 2 All ER 529, [1986] 1 WLR 615n, [1977] FSR
    569, CA 1211
Schiff, Re, Henderson v Schiff [1921] 1 Ch 149, 90 LJ Ch 82, 65 Sol Jo 174, 124 LT 266,
    37 TLR 31 131
Schintz's Will Trusts, Re, Lloyds Bank Ltd v Moreton [1951] Ch 870, [1951] 1 All ER
    1095, 95 Sol Jo 369 201
Schnadhorst, Re, Sandkuhl v Schnadhorst [1901] 2 Ch 338, 70 LJ Ch 583, 84 LT 587; affd
    [1902] 2 Ch 234, 71 LJ Ch 454, 50 WR 485, 46 Sol Jo 431, 86 LT 426,
    [1900–3] All ER Rep Ext 1371, CA 450
Schnapper, Re [1928] Ch 420, 97 LJ Ch 237, [1928] All ER Rep 528, 72 Sol Jo 137, 139
    LT 42 1072
Schneider, Re, Kirby v Schneider (1906) 22 TLR 223 1300
Schnell v Tyrrell (1834) 7 Sim 86 147
Scholey v Walton (1844) 13 LJ Ex 122, 8 Jur 319, 12 M & W 510, 2 LTOS 331
.... 976
Scholfield's Will's Trusts, Re, Scholfield v Scholfield [1949] Ch 341, [1949] 1 All ER 490,
    [1949] LJR 757, 93 Sol Jo 149, 65 TLR 156 .... 18, 1122
Schomberg v Taylor [2013] EWHC 2269 (Ch), [2013] All ER (D) 74 (Jan)
.... 56
Schott's Goods, Re [1901] P 190, 70 LJP 46, 84 LT 571, 17 TLR 476, P, D and Admlty
.... 739
Schott's Will Trust, Re, Prause v Malmcrantz (1968) 112 Sol Jo 335, 207 Estates Gazette
    538 288

PARA

Schrader v Schrader [2013] EWHC 466 (Ch), 157 Sol Jo (no 11) 31, [2013] All ER (D) 89
    (Mar) 56
Schulhof's Goods, Re, Re Wolf's Goods [1948] P 66, [1947] 2 All ER 841, [1948] LJR
    910, 64 TLR 46, P, D and Admlty 745
Schwabacher, Re, Stern v Schwabacher [1907] 1 Ch 719, 76 LJ Ch 399, 51 Sol Jo 326, 96
    LT 564 1192
Schweder's Estate, Re, Oppenheim v Schweder [1891] 3 Ch 44, 60 LJ Ch 656, 39 WR 588,
    65 LT 64, [1891–4] All ER Rep Ext 1972 1087
Schwerdtfeger's Goods, Re (1876) 1 PD 424, 40 JP 136, 45 LJP 46, 24 WR 298, 34 LT 72,
    P, D and Admlty 815
Score, Re, Tolman v Score (1887) 57 LT 40 385
Scorer, Re, Burt (or Burtt) v Harrison (1924) 94 LJ Ch 196, [1924] All ER Rep 330, 132
    LT 529 294
Scorey v Harrison (1852) 16 Jur 1130, 1 WR 99, 20 LTOS 302
    285
Scotching v Birch [2008] EWHC 844 (Ch), [2008] All ER (D) 265 (Mar)
    .... 756, 759, 956
Scotney v Lomer (1886) 31 Ch D 380, 55 LJ Ch 443, 34 WR 407, 54 LT 194, CA
    430
Scott, Re [1901] 1 KB 228, 65 JP 84, 70 LJQB 66, 49 WR 178, 83 LT 613, 17 TLR 148,
    CA 27, 164, 167
Scott, Re, Huggett v Reichman (1966) 110 Sol Jo 852, P, D and Admlty
    910
Scott, Re, Langton v Scott [1903] 1 Ch 1, 72 LJ Ch 20, 51 WR 182, [1900–3] All ER Rep
    221, 47 Sol Jo 70, 87 LT 574, CA 503
Scott, Re, Scott v Scott [1911] 2 Ch 374, 80 LJ Ch 750, 105 LT 577
    182
Scott, Re, Scott v Scott [1914] 1 Ch 847, 83 LJ Ch 694, 110 LT 809, 30 TLR 345; on
    appeal [1915] 1 Ch 592, 84 LJ Ch 366, [1914–15] All ER Rep 270, 112 LT 1057, 31
    TLR 227, CA 932, 1014, 1016, 1060
Scott, Re, Scott v Scott (No 2) (1915) 31 TLR 505 .... 296, 407
Scott, Re, Widdows v Friends of the Clergy Corpn [1975] 2 All ER 1033, [1975] 1 WLR
    1260, 119 Sol Jo 508 .... 151, 175, 181, 480
Scott v Bargeman (1722) 2 Eq Cas Abr 542, 2 P Wms 68
    .... 435, 475
Scott v Brownrigg (1881) 9 LR Ir 246 223
Scott v Earl Scarborough (1838) 1 Beav 154, 8 LJ Ch 65
    .... 302, 309, 312
Scott v Fenoulhett (1784) 1 Cox Eq Cas 79 274
Scott v Harwood (1821) 5 Madd 332 311
Scott v Jones (1838) 4 Cl & Fin 382, sub nom Jones v Scott 7 LJ Ch 242, HL
    979
Scott v Josselyn (1859) 26 Beav 174, 28 LJ Ch 297, 32 LJOS 250, 5 Jur NS 560
    383
Scott v Key (1865) 35 Beav 291, 11 Jur NS 819, 6 New Rep 349, 13 WR 1030
    370
Scott v Salmond (1833) 1 My & K 363, Coop temp Brough 46
    184
Scott v Scott (1845) 15 Sim 47, 14 LJ Ch 439, 9 Jur 589
    390
Scott v Scott (1859) 5 Jur NS 228, 1 Sw & Tr 258 .... 93, 109
Scott v Streatham and General Estates Co Ltd [1891] WN 153
    818
Scott v Tyler (1788) 2 Dick 712, 2 Bro CC 431, 29 ER 241, [1775–1802] All ER Rep 237,
    Ct of Ch 133, 135, 1023, 1025, 1028
Scott's Estate, Re, Scott v Padwick (1876) 2 Ch D 736, 45 LJ Ch 350, 3 Char Pr Cas 107,
    24 WR 723 1273
Scott's Goods, Re [1903] P 243, 73 LJP 17, 47 Sol Jo 728, 89 LT 588, P, D and Admlty
    81
Scott's Trustees v Duke 1916 SC 732, 1916 SLT 409, Ct of Sess
    100
Scowby, Re, Scowby v Scowby [1897] 1 Ch 741, 66 LJ Ch 327, 41 Sol Jo 330, 76 LT 363,
    CA 1209
Scruby and Finch v Fordham (1822) 1 Add 74 93
Scull, Re, Scott v Morris (1917) 87 LJ Ch 59, 118 LT 7, CA
    1016

PARA

Sculthorpe v Tipper (1871) LR 13 Eq 232, 41 LJ Ch 266, 20 WR 276, 26 LT 119
.... 961
Scurfield v Howes (1790) 3 Bro CC 90 444
Scurrah v Scurrah (1841) 2 Curt 919, 1 Notes of Cases 248
.... 957
Seabrook, Re, Gray v Baddeley [1911] 1 Ch 151, 80 LJ Ch 61, 103 LT 587
.... 1114
Seaford, Re, Seaford v Seifert [1968] P 53, [1968] 1 All ER 482, [1968] 2 WLR 155, 111
     Sol Jo 981, CA 493
Seagood v Hone (1634) Cro Car 366, W Jo 342 473
Seagram v Knight (1867) 2 Ch App 628, 36 LJ Ch 918, 15 WR 1152, 17 LT 47,
     [1861–73] All ER Rep Ext 2101, CA 643
Seal, Re, Seal v Taylor [1894] 1 Ch 316, 63 LJ Ch 275, 70 LT 329, CA
     .... 209–210, 243, 267, 271, 290
Seal v Tichener. See Jeale v Titchener
Seale v Barter (1801) 2 Bos & P 485 389
Seale v Seale (1715) Gilb Ch 105, 1 P Wms 290, Prec Ch 421
     .... 264, 385
Seale-Hayne v Jodrell. See Jodrell, Re, Jodrell v Seale
Seally v Powis (1835) 4 LJKB 107, 1 Har & W 2 1261
Sealy v Stawell (1868) IR 2 Eq 326 .... 277, 284, 293, 460
Sealy, Re; Tomkins v Tucker (1901) 85 LT 451, [1900–3] All ER Rep Ext 1440
     1130
Searle, Re, Searle v Baker [1900] 2 Ch 829, 69 LJ Ch 712, 49 WR 44, 44 Sol Jo 716, 83
     LT 364 1123
Searle, Re, Searle v Searle [1905] WN 86 440
Searle, Re, Searle v Siems [1949] Ch 73, [1948] 2 All ER 426, [1948] LJR 1843, 92 Sol Jo
     456, 64 TLR 397 .... 568, 597
Seaton, Re, Ellis v Seaton [1913] 2 Ch 614, 83 LJ Ch 124, 107 LT 192, [1911–13] All ER
     Rep Ext 1189 446
Sebag-Montefiore, Re, Sebag-Montefiore v Alliance Assurance Co Ltd [1944] Ch 331,
     [1944] 1 All ER 672, 113 LJ Ch 280, 88 Sol Jo 238, 170 LT 395, 60 TLR 401, CA
     115
Sebba, Re, Lloyds Bank Ltd v Hutson [1959] Ch 166, [1958] 3 All ER 393, [1958] 3 WLR
     605, 37 ATC 325, [1958] TR 329, 102 Sol Jo 810 .... 1016, 1130
Seccombe v Edwards (1860) 28 Beav 440, 6 Jur NS 642, 8 WR 595, 2 LT 622
     254
See's Goods, Re (1879) 4 PD 86, 48 LJP 70, 27 WR 665, 40 LT 658, P, D and Admlty
     763
Seers v Hind (1791) 1 Hov Supp 128, 1 Ves 294 942
Sefton (Earl), Re [1898] 2 Ch 378, 67 LJ Ch 518, 47 WR 49, 42 Sol Jo 570, 78 LT 765,
     14 TLR 466, CA 145
Segalov's Estates, Re, Hyman and Teff v Segalov [1952] P 241, [1952] 2 All ER 107, 96
     Sol Jo 362, [1952] 1 TLR 1540, P, D and Admlty 908
Segbedzi v Segbedzi (13 May 1999, unreported), CA 1242, 1244, 1246, 1253, 1259
Segelcke, Re, Ziegler v Nicol [1906] 2 Ch 301, 75 LJ Ch 494, 54 WR 624, 95 LT 708
     .... 371, 401
Segelman, Re [1996] Ch 171, [1995] 3 All ER 676, [1996] 2 WLR 173
     .... 187, 243, 253, 273, 466
Segrave v Kirwan (1828) Beat 157 .... 903–904, 907
Sehota, Re, Surjit Kaur v Gian Kaur [1978] 3 All ER 385, [1978] 1 WLR 1506, 122 Sol Jo
     844 567
Seifferth v Badham (1846) 9 Beav 370, 15 LJ Ch 345, 10 Jur 892
     313
Selangor United Rubber Estates Ltd v Cradock (a bankrupt) (No 4) [1969] 3 All ER 965,
     [1969] 1 WLR 1773, 113 Sol Jo 894 1067
Selby v Whittaker (1877) 6 Ch D 239, 47 LJ Ch 121, 26 WR 117, 37 LT 514, CA
     .... 237, 243–244, 261, 303, 413
Selby's Will Trusts, Re, Donn v Selby [1965] 3 All ER 386, [1966] 1 WLR 43, 110 Sol Jo
     74 .... 138, 140
Selby-Bigge, Re [1950] 1 All ER 1009, 94 Sol Jo 287, 66 (pt 1) TLR 993, P, D and Admlty
     72
Selby-Walker, Re, Public Trustee v Selby-Walker [1949] 2 All ER 178
     1077
Selinger's Will Trusts, Re, Midland Bank Executor and Trustee Co Ltd v Levy [1959]
     1 All ER 407, [1959] 1 WLR 217, 103 Sol Jo 178 147–149

PARA

Sellwood's Estate, Re, Heynes v Sellwood (1964) 108 Sol Jo 523, P, D and Admlty
.... 72
Selot's Trust, Re [1902] 1 Ch 488, 71 LJ Ch 192, 46 Sol Jo 280
.... 34
Selsey (Lord) v Lord Lake (1839) 1 Beav 146, 8 LJ Ch 233
.... 274
Selway v Clemmans (1866) 36 LJ Ch 171, 15 WR 250 .... 160, 173
Selwin v Brown (1735) 3 Bro Parl Cas 607, HL 207, 625
Selwood v Mildmay (1797) 3 Ves 306 .... 215, 279
Selwood v Selwood [1920] All ER Rep 413, 125 LT 26, P, D and Admlty
.... 910
Selwood v Selwood (1920) 125 LT 26, [1920] All ER Rep 413
.... 81, 708
Selwyn v Selwyn (1761) 2 Burr 1131 27
Semphill v Bayly (1721) 2 Eq Cas Abr 213, Prec Ch 562
.... 134–135
Sergeant, Re, Mertens v Walley (1884) 26 Ch D 575, 54 LJ Ch 159, 32 WR 987
.... 246
Serle v Waterworth (1838) 6 Dowl 684, 7 LJ Ex 202, 1 Horn & H 281, 2 Jur 745, 4 M &
   W 9; revsd sub nom Nelson v Serle (1839) 8 LJ Ex 305, 1 Horn & H 456, 3 Jur 290,
   4 M & W 795, Ex Ch 1240, 1262
Serocold v Hemming (1758) 2 Lee 490 113
Serres Estate, Re, Venes v Marriott (1862) 26 JP 709, 31 LJ Ch 519, 8 Jur NS 882, 10 WR
   751, 6 LT 892 366
Servoz-Gavin, Re, Ayling v Summers [2009] EWHC 3168 (Ch), [2011] Ch 162, [2010]
   1 All ER 410 80
Seton-Smith, Re, Burnand v Waite [1902] 1 Ch 717, 71 LJ Ch 386, 50 WR 456,
   [1900–3] All ER Rep 144, 86 LT 322 .... 296, 932
Severs v Severs (1853) 17 Jur 706, 1 Sm & G 400, 1 WR 320, 21 LTOS 85
.... 1298
Sewell, Re, White v Sewell [1909] 1 Ch 806, 78 LJ Ch 432, 16 Mans 113, 100 LT 883
.... 1071
Seymour v Kilbee (1879) 3 LR Ir 33 472
Seymour's Trusts, Re (1859) John 472, 28 LJ Ch 765, 5 Jur NS 1049, 7 WR 609, 33 LTOS
   314 165
Seyton, Re, Seyton v Satterthwaite (1887) 34 Ch D 511, 56 LJ Ch 775, 35 WR 373, 56 LT
   479, 3 TLR 377 390
Shacklock v Jarvis (1872) 26 LT 682 375
Shaftesbury (Earl) v Duke of Marlborough (1835) 7 Sim 237
.... 409, 1130
Shafto's Trusts, Re (1885) 29 Ch D 247, 54 LJ Ch 885, 33 WR 728, 53 LT 261
.... 950
Shaftsbury (Earl) v Countess of Shaftsbury (1716) 1 Eq Cas Abr 201, 2 Vern 747
.... 156, 285
Shallcross v Wright (1850) 12 Beav 558, 19 LJ Ch 443, 14 Jur 1037, 16 LTOS 257
.... 1245
Shanahan, Re, De Winter (formerly Shanahan) v Legal personal representatives of Shanahan
   [1973] Fam 1, [1971] 3 All ER 873, [1972] 2 WLR 63, 115 Sol Jo 687, P, D and
   Admlty 568
Shand v Kidd (1854) 19 Beav 310 .... 254, 397
Shand v Robinson (1898) 19 NSW Eq 85, 14 WNNSW 214
.... 454
Shanley v Baker (1799) 4 Ves 732 408
Shannon v Good (1884) 15 LR Ir 284 384
Sharland, Re, Kemp v Rozey [1896] 1 Ch 517, 65 LJ Ch 280, 74 LT 20, [1895–9] All ER
   Rep Ext 2004 365
Sharland, Re, Kemp v Rozey (No 2) (1896) 40 Sol Jo 514, 74 LT 664, CA
.... 127
Sharland, Re, Windeatt v Sharland (1871) LR 2 P & D 266, 35 JP 808, 41 LJP & M 9, 20
   WR 211, 25 LT 574, P, D and Admlty 806
Sharland v Loosemore (1846) 5 Hare 469, 15 LJ Ch 434, 10 Jur 771, 7 LTOS 223
.... 1268
Sharland v Mildon (1846) 5 Hare 469, 15 LJ Ch 434, 10 Jur 771, 7 LTOS 223
.... 1268
Sharland's Goods, Re (1892) 56 JP 682, 67 LT 501, P, D and Admlty
.... 759

PARA

Sharman, Re, Wright v Sharman [1901] 2 Ch 280, 70 LJ Ch 671, 49 WR 555, 45 Sol Jo
    576, 84 LT 859 1132
Sharman's Goods, Re (1869) LR 1 P & D 661, 33 JP 695, 38 LJP & M 47, 17 WR 687,
    20 LT 683 .... 44, 76, 739
Sharman's Will Trusts, Re, Public Trustee v Sharman [1942] Ch 311, [1942] 2 All ER 74,
    111 LJ Ch 257, 86 Sol Jo 174, 167 LT 285 .... 629, 1070
Sharon and Stuart, Re (1906) 12 OLR 605, 8 OWR 625
    389
Sharp, Re, Maddison v Gill [1908] 1 Ch 372, 77 LJ Ch 251, 98 LT 234; on appeal [1908]
    2 Ch 190, 77 LJ Ch 724, 99 LT 129, CA 173, 274
Sharp v Adam [2006] EWCA Civ 449, 10 ITELR 419, [2006] All ER (D) 277 (Apr)
    .... 49, 243, 890, 893
Sharp v Hutchins [2015] EWHC 1240 (Ch), [2015] WTLR 1269
    902
Sharp v Lush (1879) 10 Ch D 468, 48 LJ Ch 231, 27 WR 528
    .... 246, 1013–1014, 1060
Sharpe, Re, Scott v Sharpe [1884] WN 28 1176
Sharpe v Adam [2006] EWCA Civ 449, [2006] WTLR 1059, (2007–08) 10 ITELR 419
    899
Sharpe v M'Call [1903] 1 IR 179 161
Sharpe v Stallwood. See Tharpe v Stallwood
Sharrard v Lord Harborough (1753) Amb 165 375
Shaw, Re, Bridges v Shaw [1894] 3 Ch 615, 64 LJ Ch 47, 8 R 555, 43 WR 159, 71 LT 515
    914
Shaw, Re, Mountain v Mountain [1929] WN 246, 168 LT Jo 371, 68 L Jo 334
    293
Shaw, Re, Robinson v Shaw [1894] 2 Ch 573, 63 LJ Ch 770, 8 R 421, 43 WR 43, 38 Sol
    Jo 513, 71 LT 79 354
Shaw, Re, Williams v Pledger (1912) 56 Sol Jo 380 305
Shaw v Ford (1877) 7 Ch D 669, 47 LJ Ch 531, 26 WR 235, 37 LT 749
    .... 124, 142, 381
Shaw v Lawless (1838) 5 Cl & Fin 129, 47 RR 41, 1 Dr & Wal 512, HL
    .... 2, 1049
Shaw v M'Mahon (1843) 4 Dr & War 431 173–175
Shaw's Estate, Re [1905] P 92, 74 LJP 39, 92 LT 428, P, D and Admlty
    807
Shaw's Goods, Re (1838) 1 Curt 905 93
Shaw's Goods, Re (1858) 1 Sw & Tr 62, 31 LTOS 41 106
Shaw's Goods, Re (1895) 73 LT 192, P, D and Admlty 613
Shaw's Settlement, Re, Shaw v Shaw [1951] Ch 833, [1951] 1 All ER 656, [1951] 1 TLR
    470 462
Shea v Boschetti (1854) 18 Beav 321, 23 LJ Ch 652, 2 Eq Rep 608, 18 Jur 614, 2 WR
    281, 23 LTOS 137 .... 200, 672
Shearer v Hogg (1912) 46 SCR 492, Can SC 382
Shearn's Goods, Re (1880) 45 JP 303, 50 LJP 15, 29 WR 445, 43 LT 736, P, D and
    Admlty 74, 76, 84
Shee, Re, Taylor v Stoger [1934] Ch 345, 103 LJ Ch 183, [1934] All ER Rep 623, 150 LT
    451 .... 1118, 1121
Sheers Case. See Shires v Glascock
Sheffield v Earl of Coventry (1852) 2 De GM & G 551, 22 LJ Ch 498, 17 Jur 289,
    20 LTOS 193 417
Sheffield v Kennett (1859) 27 Beav 207; affd (1859) 4 De G & J 593
    .... 303, 412, 441
Sheffield v Lord Orrery (1745) 3 Atk 282 .... 446, 448, 460
Sheffield (Earl), Re, Ryde v Bristow [1911] 2 Ch 267, 80 LJ Ch 521, 105 LT 236, CA
    365
Sheldon, Re, Nixon v Sheldon (1888) 39 Ch D 50, 58 LJ Ch 25, 37 WR 26, 59 LT 133
    1125
Sheldon v Sheldon (1739) 9 Mod Rep 211 428
Sheldon and Kemble, Re (1885) 53 LT 527 382
Shelley v Bryer (1821) Jac 207 328
Shelley v New South Wales Institution for Deaf and Dumb and Blind [1919] AC 650, PC
    1016
Shelley's Case, Wolfe v Shelley (1581) 1 And 69, 3 Dyer 373b, Moore KB 136, Jenk 249,
    1 Co Rep 93b 334, 384–385, 387

PARA

Shelton's Settled Estate (or Estates), Re, Shelton v Shelton [1945] Ch 158, [1945] 1 All ER 283, 114 LJ Ch 198, 89 Sol Jo 152, 172 LT 237, 61 TLR 220 33

Shephard v Wheeler (2000) Times, 15 February, [2000] All ER (D) 19 .... 758, 786

Shepherd, Re, Harris v Shepherd [1943] Ch 8, [1942] 2 All ER 584, 112 LJ Ch 133, 86 Sol Jo 385, 168 LT 187, 59 TLR 50 154

Shepherd, Re, Mitchell v Loram [1914] WN 65, 58 Sol Jo 304 .... 266, 284

Shepherd, Re, Public Trustees v Henderson [1949] Ch 116, [1948] 2 All ER 932, 27 ATC 350, [1949] LJR 205, 92 Sol Jo 661 1130

Shepherd v Ingram (1764) Amb 448 .... 305, 311–312, 435

Shepherd's Goods, Re [1891] P 323, 60 LJP 102, P, D and Admlty 680, 881

Shepherdson v Dale (1866) 12 Jur NS 156, 13 LT 699 326

Sheppard v Gibbons (1742) 2 Atk 441 395

Sheppard v Lessingham (1751) Amb 122 460

Sheppard's Trust, Re (1855) 1 K & J 269 446

Sherburne v Middleton. See Middleton v Sherburne

Sherer v Bishop (1792) 4 Bro CC 55 274

Shergold v Boone (1807) 13 Ves 370 186

Sheridan v O'Reilly [1900] 1 IR 386 .... 317, 334, 375

Sherman, Re, Re Walters, Trevenen v Pearce [1954] Ch 653, sub nom Re Sherman, Trevenen v Pearce [1954] 1 All ER 893, [1954] 2 WLR 903, 98 Sol Jo 302 .... 28, 118

Sherman v Collins (1745) 3 Atk 319, 1 Ves Sen 45 17

Sherratt v Bentley (1834) 2 My & K 149, 39 ER 901, [1824–34] All ER Rep 613 .... 232, 234, 253, 369

Sherratt v Mountford (1873) 8 Ch App 928, 42 LJ Ch 688, 21 WR 818, 29 LT 284, CA 209, 215–216, 328

Sherrington v Sherrington [2005] EWCA Civ 326, 7 ITELR 711, [2005] 3 FCR 538, [2005] WTLR 587, (2005) Times, 24 March, [2005] All ER (D) 359 (Mar) 68–70, 76–77, 890, 895

Sherry, Re, Sherry v Sherry [1913] 2 Ch 508, 83 LJ Ch 126, 109 LT 474 1124

Sherwood, Re (1840) 3 Beav 338, 10 LJ Ch 2, 4 Jur 982, 52 RR 146 652

Sherwood v Sanderson (1815) Coop G 108, 19 Ves 280 48

Sheward, Re, Sheward v Brown [1893] 3 Ch 502, 3 R 667, 41 WR 685, 69 LT 302 .... 462, 464

Shewell v Dwarris (1858) John 172 131

Shewen v Vanderhorst (1830) 2 Russ & M 75; on appeal (1831) 1 LJ Ch 107, 1 Russ & M 347 .... 974, 1190

Shield's Will Trusts, Re, Bache v Shield [1974] Ch 373, [1974] 2 All ER 274, [1974] 2 WLR 885, 118 Sol Jo 406 313

Shields, Re, Corbould-Ellis v Dales [1912] 1 Ch 591, 81 LJ Ch 370, 106 LT 748 .... 197, 222

Shields v Shields [1910] 1 IR 116 232

Shipbrook (Lord) v Lord Hinchinbrook (1810) 8 RR 138, 16 Ves 477 1253

Shipman v Thompson (1738) Cooke Pr Cas 151, 7 Mod Rep 246, Willes 103 1279

Shires v Glascock (1685) 1 Eq Cas Abr 403, 2 Salk 688, sub nom Sheers Case Carth 81 71

Shirinbai v Ratanbai (1921) LR 48 Ind App 69 208

Shirley's Trusts (1863) 32 Beav 394 408

Shirt v Westby (1808) 16 Ves 393 1081

Shore v Wilson, Lady Hewley's Charities (1842) 9 Cl & Fin 355, 11 Sim 615n, 7 Jur 787n, 5 Scott NR 958, 4 State Tr NS App A 1370, HL 199, 202, 205–206, 210, 212, 242

Shore (Lady) v Billingsly (1687) 1 Vern 482 393

Shorey, Re, Smith v Shorey (1898) 47 WR 188, 43 Sol Jo 29, 79 LT 349 .... 1042, 1174

Short d Gastrell v Smith (1803) 4 East 419, 1 Smith KB 96 108

Shorter's Goods, Re, Shorter v Shorter [1911] P 184, 80 LJP 120, 105 LT 382, 27 TLR 522, P, D and Admlty 810

PARA

Shortts, Re [1954] 2 DLR 817, OWN 481, Ont HC 159

Shrimpton v Shrimpton (1862) 31 Beav 425, 11 WR 61 .... 428, 431

Shuckburgh's Settlement, Re, Robertson v Shuckburgh [1901] 2 Ch 794, 71 LJ Ch 32, 50 WR 133, [1900–3] All ER Rep 101, 46 Sol Jo 13, 85 LT 406 .... 180, 422

Shuldham v Smith (1818) 6 Dow 22, HL 448

Shum v Hobbs (1855) 3 Drew 93, 24 LJ Ch 377, 3 WR 221 428

Shurey, Re, Savory v Shurey [1918] 1 Ch 263, 87 LJ Ch 245, 62 Sol Jo 246, 118 LT 355, 34 TLR 171 416

Shuttleworth, Re, Lilley v Moore (1911) 55 Sol Jo 366 652

Shuttleworth v Greaves (1838) 4 My & Cr 35, 8 LJ Ch 7, 2 Jur 957 174

Sibley v Cook (1747) 3 Atk 572 164–165

Sibley v Perry (1802) 7 Ves 522 .... 336, 338

Sibley's Trusts, Re (1877) 5 Ch D 494, 46 LJ Ch 387, [1874–80] All ER Rep 250, 37 LT 180 .... 193, 320, 323, 326, 393, 397–398

Siboni v Kirkman (1836) 1 M & W 418; affd sub nom Kirkman v Siboni (1838) 8 LJ Ex 304, 4 M & W 339 .... 1213, 1216

Sibthorp v Moxom (1747) 3 Atk 580, 1 Wils 178, 1 Ves Sen 49 1139

Sidebotham v Watson (1853) 11 Hare 170, 1 WR 303 158

Sidey v Perpetual Trustees Estate and Agency Co of New Zealand Ltd [1944] AC 194, [1944] 2 All ER 225, 113 LJPC 91, 171 LT 309, 60 TLR 507, PC 399

Sidney, Re, Hingeston v Sidney [1908] 1 Ch 488, 77 LJ Ch 296, 52 Sol Jo 262, 98 LT 625, [1908–10] All ER Rep Ext 1430, CA 11

Sidney v Shelley (1815) 19 Ves 352, sub nom Sidney v Miller Coop G 206 184

Sidney v Sidney (1873) LR 17 Eq 65, 43 LJ Ch 15, 22 WR 101, 29 LT 569 .... 115, 159

Sidney v Vaughan (1721) 2 Eq Cas Abr 211, 2 Bro Parl Cas 254 428

Sidney v Wilmer (1863) 4 De GJ & Sm 84, 10 Jur NS 217, 3 New Rep 180, 9 LT 737 244

Sienkiewicz v Greif (UK) Ltd [2009] EWCA Civ 1159, [2010] 2 WLR 951, (2009) Times, 13 November, 153 Sol Jo (no 44) 34, [2009] All ER (D) 84 (Nov) 1279–1280

Sifri v Clough & Willis (a firm) [2007] EWHC 985 (Ch), [2007] WTLR 1453 909

Sifton v Sifton [1938] AC 656, [1938] 3 All ER 435, 107 LJPC 97, 82 Sol Jo 680, 159 LT 289, 54 TLR 969, PC 129, 138–139, 414

Sigsworth, Re, Bedford v Bedford [1935] Ch 89, 104 LJ Ch 46, [1934] All ER Rep 113, 78 Sol Jo 735, 152 LT 329, 51 TLR 9 39

Sikes, Re, Moxon v Crossley [1927] 1 Ch 364, 96 LJ Ch 263, 70 Sol Jo 1197, 136 LT 666, 43 TLR 57 282

Silcocks v Silcocks [1916] 2 Ch 161, 85 LJ Ch 464, 60 Sol Jo 445, 114 LT 843 384

Silcox v Bell (1823) 1 Sim & St 301, 1 LJOS Ch 137 328

Sillett v Meek [2007] EWHC 1169 (Ch), 10 ITELR 617, [2007] All ER (D) 248 (May) 917

Sillick v Booth (1842) 1 Y & C Ch Cas 117, 11 LJ Ch 41, 123, 5 Jur 1151, 6 Jur 142 .... 410, 453

Silver v Stein (1852) 1 Drew 295, 21 LJ Ch 312 818

Silverside v Silverside (1858) 25 Beav 340 404

Silverston, Re, Westminster Bank Ltd v Kohler [1949] Ch 270, [1949] 1 All ER 641, [1949] LJR 961, 93 Sol Jo 250 366

Simcoe, Re, Vowler-Simcoe v Vowler [1913] 1 Ch 552, 82 LJ Ch 270, 57 Sol Jo 533, 108 LT 891 .... 241, 334

Simmonds v Cock (1861) 29 Beav 455, 7 Jur NS 718, 9 WR 517 419

Simmons v Dean (1858) 27 LJP & M 103 680

Simmons v Pitt (1873) 8 Ch App 978, 43 LJ Ch 267, 21 WR 860, 29 LT 320 184

                                                                                                PARA
Simmons v Rose (1856) 6 De GM & G 411, 25 LJ Ch 615, 2 Jur NS 73, 4 WR 225,
   26 LTOS 265 992
Simmons v Rudall (1851) 1 Sim NS 115, 15 Jur 162 83
Simmons v Simmons (1836) 8 Sim 22, 5 LJ Ch 198 .... 385, 473
Simmons v Vallance (1793) 4 Bro CC 345 305
Simon v Barber (1829) 3 Hare 195n, Taml 14 403
Simon v Byford [2014] EWCA Civ 280, 17 ITELR 536, [2014] WTLR 1097,
   [2014] All ER (D) 154 (Mar) 47, 49, 53, 893, 902
Simpson, Re, Schaniel v Simpson (1977) 121 Sol Jo 224, [1977] LS Gaz R 187, 127 NLJ
   487 4
Simpson v Ashworth (1843) 6 Beav 412, 7 Jur 410 .... 384, 387
Simpson v Foxon [1907] P 54, 76 LJP 7, 96 LT 473, 23 TLR 150, P, D and Admlty
   .... 1, 95, 97, 225
Simpson v Gutteridge (1816) 1 Madd 609 1023
Simpson v Hornby (1716) Gilb Ch 120, sub nom Sympson v Hornsby Prec Ch 452, sub
   nom Sympson v Hutton 2 Eq Cas Abr 439, sub nom Hutton v Simpson 2 Vern 722
   476
Simpson v Lester (1858) 4 Jur NS 1269, [1843–60] All ER Rep 690, 33 LTOS 6
   1123
Simpson v Margitson (1847) 11 QB 23, 17 LJQB 81, 12 Jur 155
   205
Simpson v Peach (1873) LR 16 Eq 208, 42 LJ Ch 816, 21 WR 728, 28 LT 731
   412
Simpson v Vickers (1807) 14 Ves 341, 33 ER 552, [1803–13] All ER Rep 178
   .... 146, 148–149
Simpson's Estate, Re, Re Gunning's Estate [1936] P 40, 105 LJP 7, [1935] All ER Rep 84,
   79 Sol Jo 861, 154 LT 136, 52 TLR 117, P, D and Admlty
   .... 759, 817
Simpson's Goods, Re (1859) 5 Jur NS 1366 105
Sims v Doughty (1800) 5 Ves 243 .... 232, 253
Sims v Ridge (1817) 3 Mer 458 1178
Simson, Re, Fowler v Tinley [1946] Ch 299, [1946] 2 All ER 220, [1947] LJR 183, 90 Sol
   Jo 418, 175 LT 314, 62 TLR 498 11
Simson, Re, Simson v National Provincial Bank Ltd [1950] Ch 38, [1949] 2 All ER 826, 93
   Sol Jo 822, 65 TLR 721 .... 573, 592, 1064
Sinclair, Re, Allen v Sinclair [1897] 1 Ch 921, 66 LJ Ch 514, 45 WR 596, 76 LT 452
   1091
Sinclair, Re, Hodgkins v Sinclair [1897] 1 Ch 921, 66 LJ Ch 514, 45 WR 596, 76 LT 452
   1091
Sinclair, Re, Lloyds Bank plc v Imperial Cancer Research Fund [1985] Ch 446, [1985]
   1 All ER 1066, [1985] 2 WLR 795, [1985] FLR 965, [1985] Fam Law 227, 129 Sol Jo
   206, [1985] LS Gaz R 1567, CA 160, 177–178, 181, 445
Sinclair v Sinclair [2009] EWHC 926 (Ch), [2009] 2 P & CR D40, [2009] All ER (D) 17
   (May) 20
Sing, Re, Sing v Mills [1914] WN 90 315
Singe v Isaac [2001] WTLR 1045 568
Singellos v Singellos [2010] EWHC 2353 (Ch), [2011] Ch 324, [2011] 2 WLR 1111,
   (2010) Times, 22 December, [2010] All ER (D) 130 (Sep)
   50
Singh, Re [2011] EWHC 2907 (Ch) 895
Singh v Bhasin (1998) Times, 21 August 1196, 1274
Singleton v Gilbert (1784) 1 Cox Eq Cas 68 .... 305–306, 311
Singleton v Tomlinson (1878) 3 App Cas 404, 26 WR 722, 38 LT 653, HL
   .... 201, 235, 237, 298, 711
Sinnott v Walsh (1880) 5 LR Ir 27, CA 348
Sitwell v Bernard (1801) 5 RR 374, 6 Ves 520, 31 ER 1174, [1775–1802] All ER Rep 308
   .... 415, 1080–1081, 1123
Sivewright, Re, Law v Fenwick [1922] WN 338, 67 Sol Jo 168, 128 LT 416, CA
   .... 1014, 1060
Sivewright v Sivewright's Trustees 1920 SC (HL) 63, 1919 2 SLT 261, HL
   52
Sivyer v Sivyer [1967] 3 All ER 429, [1967] 1 WLR 1482, 111 Sol Jo 587
   573
Skeats, Re, Thain v Gibbs [1936] Ch 683, [1936] 2 All ER 298, 105 LJ Ch 262, 80 Sol Jo
   406, 155 LT 451, 52 TLR 558 .... 479, 517
Skelton v Hawling (1749) 1 Wils 258 .... 1294, 1298

PARA

Skelton v Younghouse [1942] AC 571, [1942] 1 All ER 650, 111 LJ Ch 185, 86 Sol Jo
  273, 167 LT 325, 58 TLR 258, HL 125, 127
Skerratt v Oakley (1798) 7 Term Rep 492 193
Skey v Barnes (1816) 3 Mer 335 .... 428, 435, 474–475
Skillen, Re, Charles v Charles [1916] 1 Ch 518, 85 LJ Ch 383, 60 Sol Jo 387, 114 LT 692
  .... 210, 293
Skingley, Re (1851) 20 LJ Ch 142, 15 Jur 958, 3 Mac & G 221, 16 LTOS 405
  152
Skinner, Re [1958] 3 All ER 273, [1958] 1 WLR 1043, 102 Sol Jo 759, P, D and Admlty
  .... 622, 628, 642
Skinner, Re, Cooper v Skinner [1904] 1 Ch 289, 73 LJ Ch 94, 52 WR 346, 89 LT 663
  1200
Skinner v Geary [1931] 2 KB 546, 29 LGR 599, 95 JP 194, 100 LJKB 718, [1931] All ER
  Rep 302, 145 LT 675, 47 TLR 597, CA 942
Skinner v Gumbleton [1903] 1 IR 36, 37 ILT 126 .... 339, 341
Skinner v Ogle (1845) 1 Rob Eccl 363, 9 Jur 432, 4 Notes of Cases 74
  .... 113, 167
Skinner's Trusts, Re (1860) 1 John & H 102, 8 WR 605, 3 LT 177
  .... 371, 372, 1061
Skottowe v Young (1871) LR 11 Eq 474, 40 LJ Ch 366, 19 WR 583, 24 LT 220
  350
Skrymsher v Northcote (1818) 1 Wils Ch 248, 1 Swan 566
  1115
Slade, Re, Witham v Watson (1919) 89 LJ Ch 412, 122 LT 321, HL
  33
Slade v Fooks (1838) 9 Sim 386, 8 LJ Ch 41, 2 Jur 961
  328
Slade v Milner (1819) 4 Madd 144 449
Slade v Parr (1842) 1 Y & C Ch Cas 565, 7 Jur 102 317
Slade's (Lady) Goods, Re (1869) 33 JP 311, 20 LT 330 102
Sladen v Sladen (1862) 2 John & H 369, 31 LJ Ch 775, 8 Jur NS 1075, 10 WR 597, 7 LT
  63 .... 340, 563
Slaney v Slaney (1864) 33 Beav 631 450
Slaney v Watney (1866) LR 2 Eq 418, 35 LJ Ch 783, 14 WR 818, 14 LT 657
  1069–1070
Slater, Re, Slater v Jonas (1915) 85 LJ Ch 432, 113 LT 691
  1123–1124
Slater, Re, Slater v Slater [1907] 1 Ch 665, 76 LJ Ch 472, 51 Sol Jo 426, 97 LT 74,
  [1904–7] All ER Rep Ext 1157, CA 156, 158, 282, 293
Slater v Dangerfield (1846) 16 LJ Ex 51, 15 M & W 263, 7 LTOS 113
  .... 334, 391
Slater v Lawson (1830) 1 B & Ad 396, 9 LJOSKB 4 1231
Slater v Spreag [1936] 1 KB 83, 105 LJKB 17, [1935] All ER Rep 900, 79 Sol Jo 657, 153
  LT 297, 51 TLR 577 1279
Slatter v Slatter (1834) 1 Y & C Ex 28, 160 ER 12, 4 Y & C Ex App 561
  491
Slattery v Jagger [2015] EWHC 3976 (Ch), [2016] All ER (D) 102 (Mar)
  188
Slaughter, Re, Trustees Corpn Ltd v Slaughter [1945] Ch 355, [1945] 2 All ER 214, 115 LJ
  Ch 1, 89 Sol Jo 350, 173 LT 81, 61 TLR 453 .... 346, 493
Slavinsky's Estate, Re (1989) 53 SASR 221 60
Sleap v Newman (1862) 12 CBNS 116, 6 LT 386 1225
Slee, Re, Midland Bank Executor and Trustee Co Ltd v Slee [1962] 1 All ER 542, [1962] 1
  WLR 496, 106 Sol Jo 352 .... 405, 1117
Sleech v Thorington (1754) 2 Ves Sen 560 .... 274, 366, 1085
Sleeman, Re, Cragoe v Goodman [1929] WN 16 384
Slingsby v Grainger (1859) 7 HL Cas 273, 28 LJ Ch 616, 5 Jur NS 1111
  .... 212, 237, 242, 267, 271, 295
Slingsby's Case (1587) 5 Co Rep 18b, 77 ER 77, [1558–1774] All ER Rep 423, Jenk 262,
  sub nom Beckwith's Case 3 Leon 160, Ex Ch 393
Slinn's Goods, Re (1890) 15 PD 156, 59 LJP 82, 39 WR 175, 63 LT 229, P, D and Admlty
  .... 3, 8, 54, 708
Smaling, Re, Johnson v Smaling (1877) 26 WR 231, 37 LT 392
  450
Small v Wing (1730) 5 Bro Parl Cas 66, 2 ER 537, HL 415, 1258
Smalley, Re, Smalley v Scotton [1929] 2 Ch 112, 98 LJ Ch 300, 73 Sol Jo 234, 141 LT
  158, 45 TLR 396, CA 346

PARA

Smalley, Re, Smalley v Smalley (1883) 49 LT 662 288

Smallwood, Re, Smallwood v Martins Bank Ltd [1951] Ch 369, [1951] 1 All ER 372, 95
Sol Jo 108, [1951] 1 TLR 331 568

Smart, Re, Smart v Smart (1881) 18 Ch D 165, 30 WR 43
.... 562, 564

Smart v Clark (1827) 3 Russ 365, 5 LJOS Ch 111 449

Smart v Prujean (1801) 6 Ves 560 367

Smart's Goods, Re [1902] P 238, 71 LJP 123, 46 Sol Jo 587, 87 LT 142, 18 TLR 663, P, D
and Admlty 711

Smee v Smee (1879) 5 PD 84, 44 JP 220, 49 LJP 8, 28 WR 703, P, D and Admlty
.... 52, 899–900

Smell v Dee (1707) 2 Salk 415 .... 172, 427

Smethurst v Tomlin and Bankes (1861) 25 JP 777, 30 LJPM & A 269, 7 Jur NS 763, 2 Sw
& Tr 143, 4 LT 712 619

Smidmore v Smidmore (1905) 3 CLR 344, Aust HC 253

Smiley, Re (1908) 28 NZLR 1 274

Smilter, Re, Bedford v Hughes [1903] 1 Ch 198, 72 LJ Ch 102, 51 WR 231, 47 Sol Jo 146,
87 LT 644 352

Smith, Re (1862) 2 John & H 594 .... 193, 252, 306, 409

Smith, Re, Arnold v Smith [1896] 1 Ch 171, 65 LJ Ch 269, [1895–9] All ER Rep 1175, 74
LT 14 1035

Smith, Re, Bilke v Roper (1890) 45 Ch D 632, 60 LJ Ch 57, 39 WR 93, [1886–90] All ER
Rep 503, 63 LT 448, 6 TLR 484 113

Smith, Re, Bull v Smith [1933] Ch 847, 102 LJ Ch 359, [1933] All ER Rep 981, 149 LT
382 339–340

Smith, Re, Dowzer v Dowzer (1914) 48 ILT 236 1054

Smith, Re, Eastick v Smith [1904] 1 Ch 139, 73 LJ Ch 74, 52 WR 104, 89 LT 604, 20
TLR 66, [1900–3] All ER Rep Ext 1056 1052

Smith, Re, Green v Smith (1883) 22 Ch D 586, 52 LJ Ch 411, 31 WR 413, 48 LT 254
.... 982

Smith, Re, Henderson-Roe v Hitchins (1889) 42 Ch D 302, 58 LJ Ch 860, 37 WR 705, 61
LT 363 .... 293, 1074, 1079, 1149

Smith, Re, Johnson v Bright-Smith [1914] 1 Ch 937, 83 LJ Ch 687, 58 Sol Jo 494, 110 LT
898, 30 TLR 411, [1914–15] All ER Rep Ext 1543 .... 33, 35–36, 263, 309

Smith, Re, Keeling v Smith (1890) 44 Ch D 654, 59 LJ Ch 284, 38 WR 380, 62 LT 181, 6
TLR 183 .... 136, 147

Smith, Re, Lord v Hayward (1887) 35 Ch D 558, 56 LJ Ch 771, 35 WR 663, 56 LT 878
.... 331

Smith, Re, Phillips v Smith [1915] WN 12 296

Smith, Re, Prada v Vandroy [1916] 2 Ch 368, 85 LJ Ch 657, 60 Sol Jo 603, 115 LT 161,
CA 1, 160, 165, 1132

Smith, Re, Public Trustee v Smith [1932] 1 Ch 153, 100 LJ Ch 409, [1931] All ER Rep
617, 75 Sol Jo 780, 146 LT 145, 48 TLR 44, CA 259

Smith, Re, Smith v Johnson (1904) 20 TLR 287 199

Smith, Re, Smith v Smith [1899] 1 Ch 365, 68 LJ Ch 333, 47 WR 223, 80 LT 113
.... 1004, 1109

Smith, Re, Smith v Smith [1913] 2 Ch 216, 83 LJ Ch 13, 108 LT 952
.... 992, 1012

Smith, Re, Smith v Smith [2001] 3 All ER 552, [2001] 1 WLR 1937, [2001] 28 LS Gaz R
43, [2001] NLJR 784, (2001) Independent, 25 June, [2001] All ER (D) 112 (May)
.... 151, 154

Smith, Re, Smith v Thompson [1896] 1 Ch 71, 65 LJ Ch 159, 44 WR 270, 73 LT 604
.... 961

Smith, Re, Veasey v Smith [1948] Ch 49, [1947] 2 All ER 708, [1949] LJR 765, 91 Sol Jo
664, 63 TLR 608 .... 466, 468

Smith v Anderson (1828) 4 Russ 352, 6 LJOS Ch 105 .... 1131, 1133

Smith v Attersoll (1826) 1 Russ 266 223

Smith v Baker (1737) 1 Atk 385, West temp Hard 98 291

Smith v Blyth [1891] 1 Ch 337, 60 LJ Ch 66, 39 WR 422, 63 LT 546, 7 TLR 29
.... 1237

Smith v Butcher (1878) 10 Ch D 113, 48 LJ Ch 136, 27 WR 281
.... 241, 341

Smith v Butler (1846) 3 Jo & Lat 565 293

Smith v Campbell (1815) Coop G 275, 19 Ves 400 349

  PARA

Smith v Chambers. See Chambers v Smith
Smith v Clerical Medical and General Life Assurance Society [1992] 1 FCR 262, [1993] 1
  FLR 47, [1993] Fam Law 117, CA 1008
Smith v Coffin (1795) 2 Hy Bl 444 237
Smith v Conder (1878) 9 Ch D 170, 47 LJ Ch 878, 27 WR 149
  406
Smith v Coney (1801) 6 Ves 42 276
Smith v Cotton's Trustees 1956 SC 338, 1956 SLT 177, Ct of Sess
  125
Smith v Cowdery (1825) 2 Sim & St 358, 3 LJOS Ch 205
  144
Smith v Crabtree (1877) 6 Ch D 591, 25 WR 824 .... 253, 404
Smith v Cremer (1875) 24 WR 51 1202
Smith v Cunningham (1823) 1 Add 448 114
Smith v Dale (1881) 18 Ch D 516, 50 LJ Ch 352, 29 WR 330, 44 LT 460
  1201
Smith v Davis (1866) 35 LJ Ch 874, 14 WR 942, CA 250
Smith v Day (1837) 6 LJ Ex 219, 2 M & W 684, Murp & H 185, [1835–42] All ER Rep
  521, Exch Ct 1245
Smith v Evans (1751) 1 Wils 313 63
Smith v Everett (1859) 27 Beav 446, 29 LJ Ch 236, 5 Jur NS 1332, 7 WR 605, 34 LTOS
  58 .... 926, 1023, 1043
Smith v Farr (1839) 3 Y & C Ex 328, 8 LJ Ex Eq 46 322
Smith v Fitzgerald (1814) 3 Ves & B 2 252
Smith v Harris (1845) 1 Rob Eccl 262, 9 Jur 406, 4 Notes of Cases 48
  64
Smith v Haws. See Hawes v Smith
Smith v Horsfall (1858) 25 Beav 628 336
Smith v Jackson (1823) 1 LJOS Ch 231 308
Smith v Jobson (1888) 59 LT 397, [1886–90] All ER Rep 1024
  350
Smith v Langford (1840) 2 Beav 362 657
Smith v Lidiard (1857) 3 K & J 252 328
Smith v Martin (1672) 2 Wms Saund 394 290
Smith v Mather [1948] 2 KB 212, [1948] 1 All ER 704, [1948] LJR 1209, 92 Sol Jo 231,
  64 TLR 251, CA 644
Smith v Milles (1786) 1 Term Rep 475 633
Smith v Oliver (1848) 11 Beav 494 165
Smith v Osborne (1857) 6 HL Cas 375, 3 Jur NS 1181, 6 WR 21, 30 LTOS 57
  316
Smith v Palmer (1848) 7 Hare 225 .... 325, 364
Smith v Pepper (1859) 27 Beav 86 339
Smith v Perpetual Trustee Co Ltd and Delohery (1910) 11 CLR 148, Aust HC
  463
Smith v Poole (1841) 12 Sim 17, 10 LJ Ch 192 976
Smith v Pybus (1804) 9 Ves 566 .... 232, 253
Smith v Ridgway (1866) LR 1 Exch 331, 35 LJ Ex 198, 12 Jur NS 742, 14 WR 868, 14 LT
  632 .... 271, 286, 290
Smith v Simonds (1687) Comb 64 1282
Smith v Smith [2011] EWHC 2133 (Ch), [2011] 3 FCR 614, [2012] 2 FLR 230, [2011]
  Fam Law 1200, [2011] All ER (D) 80 (Jul) 603
Smith v Smith (1688) 2 Vern 92 438
Smith v Smith (1801) 5 Ves 721 537
Smith v Smith (1837) 8 Sim 353, 6 LJ Ch 175 302
Smith v Smith (1861) 11 CBNS 121, 8 Jur NS 459, 5 LT 447
  376
Smith v Smith (1861) 25 JP 516, 1 Drew & Sm 384, 7 Jur NS 652, 9 WR 406, 4 LT 44
  991
Smith v Smith (1865) 29 JP 119, 34 LJPM & A 57, 11 Jur NS 143, 4 Sw & Tr 3, 13 WR
  504 911
Smith v Smith (1866) LR 1 P & D 143, 35 LJP & M 65, 12 Jur NS 674, 14 WR 648, 14
  LT 417 70
Smith v Smith (Smith intervening) [1992] Fam 69, [1991] 2 All ER 306, [1991] 3 WLR
  646, [1991] FCR 791, [1991] 2 FLR 432, [1991] Fam Law 412, CA
  567
Smith v Spencer (1856) 6 De GM & G 631, 3 Jur NS 193, 5 WR 136, 29 LTOS 59
  450

PARA

Smith v Springford [2008] All ER (D) 59 (Feb) 883, 910

Smith v Stewart (1851) 4 De G & Sm 253, 20 LJ Ch 205, 15 Jur 834, 17 LTOS 195
.... 450

Smith v Stothard (1837) 1 Jur 540 1298

Smith v Streatfield (1816) 1 Mer 358 .... 243, 397

Smith v Tateham (1848) 5 Dow & L 732, 17 LJ Ex 198, 2 Exch 205, 11 LTOS 128
.... 1291

Smith v Tebbitt (1867) LR 1 P & D 398, 36 LJP & M 97, 16 WR 18, 16 LT 841
.... 52, 893, 899

Smith v Thompson (1931) 75 Sol Jo 555, 146 LT 14, 47 TLR 603, P, D and Admlty
.... 95

Smith (Surveyor of Taxes) v Williams [1922] 1 KB 158, 8 TC 321, 91 LJKB 156, 126 LT
410, 38 TLR 116, [1921] All ER Rep Ext 749, [1921] All ER Rep Ext 1440, CA
.... 1283

Smith's Estate, Re, McMurray v Mathew (1876) 33 LT 804
.... 1178

Smith's Estate, Re, Mathew v Mathew (1876) 33 LT 804
.... 1178

Smith's Goods, Re [1904] P 114, 73 LJP 28, 90 LT 169, 20 TLR 119, P, D and Admlty
.... 837, 841

Smith's Goods, Re (1858) 27 LJP & M 105 761

Smith's Goods, Re (1869) LR 1 P & D 717, 33 JP 712, 38 LJP & M 85, 17 WR 1110, 21
LT 340 .... 7, 11

Smith's Goods, Re (1889) 15 PD 2, 54 JP 183, 59 LJP 5, 38 WR 384, 62 LT 183, P, D and
Admlty 44, 739

Smith's Trusts, Re (1865) LR 1 Eq 79 .... 422, 446, 468

Smith's Trusts, Re (1878) 9 Ch D 117, 27 WR 132, 38 LT 905
.... 175

Smith's Will, Re (1855) 20 Beav 197, 24 LJ Ch 466, 1 Jur NS 220, 3 WR 277, 24 LTOS
322 429

Smith-Bosanquet, Re, Smith v Smith-Bosanquet [1940] Ch 954, [1940] 3 All ER 519,
109 LJCh 440, 164 LT 267 1131

Smithers, Re, Watts v Smithers [1939] Ch 1015, [1939] 3 All ER 689, 108 LJ Ch 369, 83
Sol Jo 689, 161 LT 193 .... 60, 294

Smithley v Chomeley (1556) 2 Dyer 135a 634

Smithwick v Hayden (1887) 19 LR Ir 490 45

Smyth v Power (1876) IR 10 Eq 192 .... 456, 473

Smyth v Smyth (1855) 3 WR 189 470

Smyth v Smyth (1878) 8 Ch D 561, 26 WR 736, 38 LT 633
.... 298

Smyth's Goods, Re (1915) 49 ILT 223 70

Smythe, Re, Guinness v Smythe [1932] IR 136 397

Snape, Re, Elam v Phillips [1915] 2 Ch 179, 84 LJ Ch 803, 59 Sol Jo 562, 113 LT 439
.... 1130

Sneesby v Thorne (1855) 7 De GM & G 399, 3 Eq Rep 849, 1 Jur NS 1058, 3 WR 605,
25 LTOS 250 .... 926, 1023

Snoek, Re (1983) 13 Fam Law 18 576

Snook v Watts (1848) 11 Beav 105, 12 Jur 444, 12 LTOS 1
.... 899

Snow v Poulden (1836) 1 Keen 186 .... 415, 422

Snow v Teed (1870) LR 9 Eq 622, 39 LJ Ch 420, 18 WR 623, sub nom Sum v Teed 23 LT
303 348

Snowball v Procter (1843) 2 Y & C Ch Cas 478, 7 Jur 619
.... 391

Snowden, Re, Smith v Spowage [1979] Ch 528, [1979] 2 All ER 172, [1979] 2 WLR 654,
123 Sol Jo 323 221–222

Snowden's Goods, Re (1896) 75 LT 279, P, D and Admlty
.... 112

Soar v Dolman, Re Rippin's Goods (1842) 3 Curt 121, 6 Jur 512, 1 Notes of Cases 513
.... 108

Solicitor, A, Re [1975] QB 475, [1974] 3 All ER 853, [1975] 2 WLR 105, 118 Sol Jo 737
.... 903

Solly v Solly (1858) 5 Jur NS 36, 32 LTOS 293 320

Solomon v Attenborough [1912] 1 Ch 451, CA; on appeal sub nom Attenborough (George)
& Son v Solomon [1913] AC 76, 82 LJ Ch 178, [1911–13] All ER Rep 155, 57 Sol Jo
76, 107 LT 833, 29 TLR 79, HL 922, 1025, 1028, 1141, 1146, 1149

PARA

Somech, Re, Westminster Bank Ltd v Phillips [1957] Ch 165, [1956] 3 All ER 523, [1956]
   3 WLR 763, 100 Sol Jo 801 .... 37, 1072, 1168
Somerset, Re, Somerset v Earl Poulett [1894] 1 Ch 231, 63 LJ Ch 41, 7 R 34, 42 WR 145,
   38 Sol Jo 39, 69 LT 744, 10 TLR 46, CA 1250, 1260
Somerset's (Lady) Goods, Re (1867) LR 1 P & D 350 820
Sonday's Case (1611) 9 Co Rep 127b 384, 473
Soper, Re, Naylor v Kettle [1912] 2 Ch 467, 81 LJ Ch 826, 107 LT 525
   343
Sotheran v Dening (1881) 20 Ch D 99, CA 95
Soule v Gerrard (1596) Cro Eliz 525, sub nom Sowell v Garret Moore KB 422
   .... 442, 473
Soulsbury v Soulsbury [2007] EWCA Civ 969, [2008] Fam 1, [2008] 2 WLR 834, [2007] 3
   FCR 811, [2008] 1 FLR 90, (2007) Times, 14 November, [2007] All ER (D) 132 (Oct)
   .... 588, 1279
South v Alleine (1695) Comb 375, 5 Mod Rep 98, 1 Salk 228, sub nom Bush v Allen 5
   Mod Rep 63 375
South v Williams (1842) 12 Sim 566, 11 LJ Ch 410, 6 Jur 332
   163
Southcot v Watson (1745) 3 Atk 226 294
Southcote v Earl of Bath (1765) 2 Eden 323 390
Southcote v Hoare (1810) 3 Taunt 87, 128 ER 36, [1803–13] All ER Rep 494
   .... 917, 934
Southerden's Estate, Re, Adams v Southerden [1925] P 177, 95 LJP 1, [1925] All ER Rep
   398, 69 Sol Jo 723, 133 LT 505, 41 TLR 539, CA 101, 108–109
Southern v Wollaston (1852) 16 Beav 166, 1 WR 86 432–433
Southgate v Clinch (1858) 27 LJ Ch 651, 4 Jur NS 428, 6 WR 489, 31 LTOS 263
   .... 241, 341
Southgate v Crowley (1835) 1 Bing NC 518, 4 LJCP 102, 1 Hodg 1, 1 Scott 374, sub nom
   Brown v Croley 3 Dowl 386 1276
Southouse v Bate (1851) 16 Beav 132, 18 LTOS 218 375
Sowell v Garret (1596) Moore KB 422, sub nom Soule v Gerrard Cro Eliz 525
   .... 116, 442
Sowerby's Trusts, Re (1856) 2 K & J 630 163
Spackman v Holbrook (1860) 2 Giff 198, 6 Jur NS 881, 2 LT 367
   1258
Spackman v Timbrell (1837) 8 Sim 253, Donnelly 171, 210, 6 LJ Ch 147
   1105
Spain, Re (1915) 31 TLR 435, P, D and Admlty 716, 895
Spalding v Spalding (1630) Cro Car 185 253
Spark's Estate, Re [1941] P 115, [1941] 2 All ER 782, 110 LJP 71, 85 Sol Jo 370, 165 LT
   234, 57 TLR 643, P, D and Admlty 79
Sparkes, Re, Kemp-Welch v Kemp-Welch (1911) 56 Sol Jo 90
   404
Sparks v Restal (1857) 24 Beav 218 .... 320, 472
Speak, Re, Speak v Speak (1912) 56 Sol Jo 273 317
Speaker's Executor v Spicker 1969 SLT (Notes) 7, Ct of Sess
   285
Speakman, Re, Unsworth v Speakman (1876) 4 Ch D 620, 46 LJ Ch 608, 25 WR 225, 35
   LT 731 .... 171, 226
Speakman v Speakman (1850) 8 Hare 180 .... 258, 320, 341
Spear v Bone (1816) 5 Ad & El 709, sub nom Bone and Newsam v Spear 1 Phillim 345
   5
Spearing v Hawkes (1857) 6 I Ch R 297 296
Speir, Re, Holt v Speir [1924] 1 Ch 359, 93 LJ Ch 225, [1923] All ER Rep 640, 68 Sol Jo
   251, 130 LT 564, CA 295
Speke's Estate, Re, Speke v Deakin (1913) 58 Sol Jo 99, 109 LT 719, 30 TLR 73, P, D and
   Admlty 861, 910
Spence, Re [1990] Ch 197, [1989] 3 WLR 834, [1990] 1 FLR 286, [1990] Fam Law 140,
   133 Sol Jo 1513, sub nom Re Spence, Spence v Dennis [1989] 2 All ER 679, [1989]
   FCR 651; affd sub nom Spence, Re, Spence v Dennis [1990] Ch 652, [1990] 2 All ER
   827, [1990] 2 WLR 1430, [1990] FCR 983, [1990] 2 FLR 278, [1990] Fam Law 475,
   CA 350
Spence, Re, Ogden v Shackleton [1979] Ch 483, [1978] 3 WLR 483, 122 Sol Jo 574, sub
   nom Re Spence's Will Trusts, Ogden v Shackleton [1978] 3 All ER 92
   .... 250, 268, 278
Spence, Re, Quick v Ackner [1949] WN 237 222

PARA

Spence v Handford (1858) 27 LJ Ch 767, 4 Jur NS 987, 31 LTOS 244
.... 471
Spenceley's Goods, Re [1892] P 255, 61 LJP 133, P, D and Admlty
.... 745
Spencer, Re, Hart v Manston (1886) 34 WR 527, 54 LT 597
.... 60, 233
Spencer v Metropolitan Board of Works (1882) 22 Ch D 142, 52 LJ Ch 249, 31 WR 347,
47 LT 459, CA 241
Spencer v Spencer (1856) 21 Beav 548 285
Spencer v Ward (1870) LR 9 Eq 507, 18 WR 858, 22 LT 702
.... 274
Spencer v Wilson (1873) LR 16 Eq 501, 42 LJ Ch 754, 21 WR 838, 29 LT 19
.... 175, 430
Spencer and Hauser's Contract, Re [1928] Ch 598, 97 LJ Ch 335, [1928] All ER Rep 514,
72 Sol Jo 336, 139 LT 287 1026
Spencer's Case (1622) Win 51 291
Spencer Cooper, Re, Poë v Spencer Cooper [1908] 1 Ch 130, 77 LJ Ch 64, 98 LT 344
.... 1111, 1132
Spencer's Will, Re (1887) 57 LT 519, 3 TLR 822, CA 207, 221–222
Spensley's Estate, Re, Spensley v Harrison (1872) LR 15 Eq 16, 21 WR 95, sub nom Re
Spensley's Estate, Harrison v Spensley 42 LJ Ch 21, 27 LT 600
.... 1196
Spensley's Will Trusts, Re, Barclays Bank Ltd v Staughton [1952] Ch 886, [1952] 2 All ER
49, 96 Sol Jo 412, [1952] 1 TLR 1435; on appeal [1954] Ch 233, [1954] 1 All ER
178, [1954] 2 WLR 145, 98 Sol Jo 77, CA 96
Sperling's Goods, Re (1863) 27 JP 777, 33 LJPM & A 25, 9 Jur NS 1205, 3 Sw & Tr 272,
12 WR 354, 9 LT 348 75
Spicer, Re, Spicer v Richardson [1949] P 441, [1949] 2 All ER 659, [1949] LJR 1588, 93
Sol Jo 679, 65 TLR 590, P, D and Admlty 81
Spicer, Re, Spicer v Spicer [1899] P 38, 68 LJP 19, 47 WR 271, 79 LT 707, 15 TLR 40, P,
D and Admlty 874
Spiers v English [1907] P 122, 76 LJP 28, 96 LT 582, P, D and Admlty
.... 905, 908, 911
Spiller, Re, Spiller v Madge (1881) 18 Ch D 614, 50 LJ Ch 750, 29 WR 782, 45 LT 41
.... 173, 175
Spink v Lewis (1791) 3 Bro CC 355 313
Spitzel's Will Trusts, Re, Spitzel v Spitzel [1939] 2 All ER 266, 83 Sol Jo 378
.... 128
Spollan v Magan (1851) 18 LTOS 200, 1 ICLR 691 976
Spong v Spong (1829) 3 Bli NS 84, 1 Dow & Cl 365, HL
.... 1110
Spracklan's Estate, Re [1938] 2 All ER 345, 82 Sol Jo 373, CA
.... 95
Sprackling v Ranier (1761) 1 Dick 344 309
Spratt's Goods, Re [1897] P 28, 66 LJP 25, 45 WR 159, 75 LT 518, P, D and Admlty
.... 7–8
Spread Trustee Co Ltd v Hutcheson [2011] UKPC 13, [2012] 2 AC 194, [2012] 1 All ER
251, [2012] 2 WLR 1360, 14 ITELR 37, [2012] 1 LRC 102, [2011] All ER (D) 51
(Jul) 1238, 1246
Sprigge v Sprigge (1868) LR 1 P & D 608, 33 JP 104, 38 LJP & M 4, 17 WR 80, 19 LT
462 .... 93, 106
Springett v Jenings (1871) 6 Ch App 333, 40 LJ Ch 348, 19 WR 575, 24 LT 643
.... 183, 298
Sproule, Re, Chambers v Chambers (1915) 49 ILT 96 390
Spurrell v Spurrell (1853) 11 Hare 54, 22 LJ Ch 1076, 1 Eq Rep 192, 17 Jur 755, 1 WR
322, 22 LTOS 32 318
Spurway v Glynn (1804) 9 Ves 483 1112
Squire v Arnison (1884) 48 JP 758, Cab & El 365, 1 TLR 67
.... 1292
Stable, Re, Dalrymple v Campbell [1919] P 7, 88 LJP 32, [1918–19] All ER Rep 299, 120
LT 160, P, D and Admlty 81
Stacey v Elph (1833) 1 My & K 195, 2 LJ Ch 50, 36 RR 306, 39 ER 655,
[1824–34] All ER Rep 97 .... 151–152, 627
Stackpole v Beaumont (1796) 3 Ves 89 133
Staffordshire County Council v B [1999] 2 FCR 333, [1998] 1 FLR 261, [1998] Fam Law
8 357

PARA

Stahlschmidt v Lett (1853) 1 Sm & G 415; on appeal (1853) 1 Eq Rep 407, 1 Sm & G
421, 21 LTOS 208 974
Staines v Maddock (1728) 3 Bro Parl Cas 108, HL 456
Stainham v Bell Lofft. See Statham v Bell
Stainland v Willott. See Staniland v Willott
Stainton v Carron Co (1854) 18 Beav 146, 23 LJ Ch 299, 2 Eq Rep 466, 18 Jur 137, 2
WR 176, 22 LTOS 299 624
Stamford v White [1901] P 46, 70 LJP 9, 84 LT 269, P, D and Admlty
.... 105, 109
Stamford (Earl), Re, Hall v Lambert (1906) 22 TLR 632, CA
.... 285
Stamford (Earl), Re, Payne v Stamford [1896] 1 Ch 288, 65 LJ Ch 134, 44 WR 249, 40
Sol Jo 114, 73 LT 559, 12 TLR 78 1149
Stamford and Warrington (Earl), Re, Payne v Grey [1912] 1 Ch 343, 81 LJ Ch 302, 56 Sol
Jo 204, 105 LT 913, 28 TLR 159, CA 259
Stamford, Spalding and Boston Banking Co v Smith [1892] 1 QB 765, 56 JP 229, 61 LJQB
405, 40 WR 355, [1891–4] All ER Rep 949, 36 Sol Jo 270, 66 LT 306, 8 TLR 336,
CA 646
Stammers v Elliott (1868) 3 Ch App 195, 37 LJ Ch 353, 16 WR 489, 18 LT 1
.... 1068
Stamp Duties Comr v Bone [1977] AC 511, [1976] 2 All ER 354, [1976] 2 WLR 968,
[1976] STC 145, [1976] TR 117, 120 Sol Jo 421, PC 625
Stamp Duties Comr (Queensland) v Livingston [1965] AC 694, [1964] 3 All ER 692,
[1964] 3 WLR 963, 43 ATC 325, [1964] TR 351, 108 Sol Jo 820, PC
.... 922
Stamper v Pickering (1838) 9 Sim 176 1058
Standley's Goods, Re (1849) 1 Rob Eccl 755, 7 Notes of Cases 69
.... 65
Stanford v Stanford (1886) 34 Ch D 362, 35 WR 191, sub nom Stanford, Re, Stanford
v Stanford 56 LJ Ch 273, 55 LT 765, [1886–90] All ER Rep Ext 1639
.... 306, 446
Stanger v Nelson (1855) 6 De GM & G 68, 25 LJ Ch 116, 2 Jur NS 27, 4 WR 109,
26 LTOS 210 328
Stanhope's Trusts, Re (1859) 27 Beav 201 .... 175, 392
Stanhouse v Gaskell (1852) 17 Jur 157, 1 WR 77, 20 LTOS 139
.... 473
Staniar v Evans (1886) 34 Ch D 470, 56 LJ Ch 581, 35 WR 286, 56 LT 87, 3 TLR 215
.... 1050
Stanier v Hodgkinson (1903) 73 LJ Ch 179, 52 WR 260, 48 Sol Jo 143
.... 446, 1123
Staniforth's Estate, Re, Gilbert v Heining (1965) 109 Sol Jo 112, P, D and Admlty
.... 68
Staniland v Willott (1852) 3 Mac & G 664, sub nom Stainland v Willott 18 LTOS 338
.... 921
Stanley, Re, Tennant v Stanley [1906] 1 Ch 131, 75 LJ Ch 56, 54 WR 103, 93 LT 661
.... 250
Stanley v Bernes (1828) 1 Hag Ecc 221 926
Stanley v Bond [1913] 1 IR 170 317
Stanley v Lennard (1758) Amb 355, 1 Eden 87 .... 457, 473
Stanley v Potter (1789) 2 Cox Eq Cas 180 159
Stanley v Stanley (1809) 16 Ves 491 .... 419, 423
Stanley v Stanley (1862) 2 John & H 491, 10 WR 857, 7 LT 136
.... 267, 273
Stanley v Wise (1788) 1 Cox Eq Cas 432 305
Stanley's Estate, Re [1916] P 192, 85 LJP 222, [1916–17] All ER Rep 352, 60 Sol Jo 604,
114 LT 1182, 32 TLR 643, P, D and Admlty 79, 613
Stanley's Settlement, Re, Maddocks v Andrews [1916] 2 Ch 50, 85 LJ Ch 809,
[1916–17] All ER Rep 342, 60 Sol Jo 478, 114 LT 933 .... 468, 470
Stansfield, Re, Stansfield v Stansfield (1880) 15 Ch D 84, 49 LJ Ch 750, 29 WR 72, 43 LT
310 .... 167, 175
Stanton v Hatfield (1836) 1 Keen 358, 5 LJ Ch 301 1205
Stapleton v Cheales (1711) 1 Eq Cas Abr 295, Gilb Ch 76, Prec Ch 317, 2 Vern 673
.... 416, 427–428
Stapleton v Conway (1750) 3 Atk 727, 1 Ves Sen 427 296
Stapleton v D'Alton (1914) 49 ILT 62 273
Stapleton v Palmer (1794) 4 Bro CC 490 415

PARA

Stapleton v Stapleton (1852) 2 Sim NS 212, 21 LJ Ch 434
.... 254
Stares v Penton (1867) LR 4 Eq 40 404
Stark v Dennison [1973] 1 WWR 368 905
Starkey v Starkey (1746) 8 Bac Abr 302, Co Litt 24b, n 3
.... 561
Statham v Bell (1774) 1 Cowp 40, 1 Doug KB 66n, sub nom Stainham v Bell Lofft 455
.... 446
Stavers v Barnard (1843) 2 Y & C Ch Cas 539, 7 Jur 1080, 2 LTOS 95
.... 331
Stead, Re, Witham v Andrew [1900] 1 Ch 237, 69 LJ Ch 49, 48 WR 221, 44 Sol Jo 146,
    81 LT 751 221
Stead v Hardaker (1873) LR 15 Eq 175, 42 LJ Ch 317, 21 WR 258
.... 1012
Stead v Platt (1853) 18 Beav 50 316
Stead v Stead [1985] FLR 16, [1985] Fam Law 154, CA
.... 577, 591
Steadman's Goods, Re (1828) 2 Hag Ecc 59 820
Stearn v Mills (1833) 4 B & Ad 657, 1 Nev & MKB 436, sub nom Steen v Mills and
    Wright 2 LJKB 106 1290
Stebbing v Walkey (1786) 1 Cox Eq Cas 250, 2 Bro CC 85
.... 274
Stebbings v Holst & Co Ltd [1953] 1 All ER 925, [1953] 1 WLR 603, 97 Sol Jo 264
.... 647
Stedham's Goods, Re, Re Dyke's Goods (1881) 6 PD 205, 45 JP 784, 46 JP 40, 50 LJP 75,
    29 WR 743, [1881–5] All ER Rep 410, 45 LT 192, P, D and Admlty
.... 97, 111–112
Steed v Calley (1836) 1 Keen 620 899
Steed v Preece (1874) LR 18 Eq 192, 43 LJ Ch 687, 22 WR 432
.... 918
Steel, Re, Public Trustee v Christian Aid Society [1979] Ch 218, [1978] 2 All ER 1026,
    [1978] 2 WLR 950, 122 Sol Jo 148 .... 200, 207, 217, 220, 410
Steel, Re, Wappett v Robinson [1903] 1 Ch 135, 72 LJ Ch 42, 51 WR 252, 47 Sol Jo 31,
    87 LT 548 .... 205, 277
Steele, Re, Steele v Steele [1913] 1 IR 292 114
Steele's (or Steel) Goods, Re, Re May's Goods, Re Wilson's Goods (1868) LR 1 P & D
    575, 32 JP 791, 37 LJP & M 68, 72, 17 WR 15, [1861–73] All ER Rep 209, 19 LT
    91 110–112
Steen v Mills and Wright. See Stearn v Mills
Steignes v Steignes (1730) Mos 296 250
Stein v Ritherdon (1868) 37 LJ Ch 369, 16 WR 477, 19 LT 184
.... 284, 289, 293, 376
Steinorth's Goods, Re (1856) Dea & Sw 270, 3 Jur NS 72, 5 WR 123, 28 LTOS 148
.... 778
Stekl, Re (1973) 40 DLR (3d) 407, [1973] 6 WWR 249, BC SC, BC SC; revsd (1974) 47
    DLR (3d) 286, [1974] 6 WWR 490, BCCA, BC CA 1035
Stent v Robinson (1806) 12 Ves 461 1081
Stephanides v Cohen [2002] EWHC 1869 (Fam), [2002] WTLR 1373
.... 573, 576–577
Stephen, Re, Stephen v Stephen [1913] WN 210 .... 212, 298
Stephens, Re, Kilby v Betts [1904] 1 Ch 322, 73 LJ Ch 3, 52 WR 89, 48 Sol Jo 15, 91 LT
    167 .... 308, 310
Stephens, Re, Tomalin v Tomalin's Trustee [1927] 1 Ch 1, 95 LJ Ch 493, 135 LT 503, CA
.... 305, 440
Stephens, Re, Warburton v Stephens (1889) 43 Ch D 39, 59 LJ Ch 109, 61 LT 609
.... 979
Stephens v Hide (1734) Cas temp Talb 27 .... 395, 397
Stephens v Hotham (1855) 1 K & J 571, 24 LJ Ch 665, 3 Eq Rep 571, 1 Jur NS 842, 3
    WR 340, 26 LTOS 37 1227
Stephens v Powys (1857) 1 De G & J 24 262
Stephens v Stephens (1736) 2 Barn KB 375, Cas temp Talb 228
.... 416
Stephens v Stephens (1886) 19 LR Ir 190 22
Stephens v Taprell (1840) 2 Curt 458 101
Stephenson, Re, Donaldson v Bamber [1897] 1 Ch 75, 66 LJ Ch 93, 45 WR 162, 41 Sol Jo
    96, 75 LT 495, 13 TLR 67, CA 45, 217, 263, 274

PARA

Stephenson v Dowson (1840) 3 Beav 342, 10 LJ Ch 93, 4 Jur 1152
.... 119, 293, 375
Stephenson v Stephenson (1885) 52 LT 576 182
Stephenson (Inspector of Taxes) v Barclays Bank Trust Co Ltd [1975] 1 All ER 625, [1975]
    1 WLR 882, [1975] STC 151, 50 TC 374, 53 ATC 357, [1974] TR 343, 119 Sol Jo
    169 1053
Stephenson's Trusts, Re (1870) 18 WR 1066 136
Stern's Will Trusts, Re, Bartlett v Stern [1962] Ch 732, [1961] 3 All ER 1129, [1962] 2
    WLR 161, 106 Sol Jo 36 362
Sterndale v Hankinson (1827) 1 Sim 393 1191
Stevens, Re, Clark v Stevens (1896) 40 Sol Jo 296 308
Stevens, Re, Cooke v Stevens [1897] 1 Ch 422, 66 LJ Ch 155, 45 WR 284, 76 LT 18; affd
    [1898] 1 Ch 162, 67 LJ Ch 118, 46 WR 177, 42 Sol Jo 113, 77 LT 508, 14 TLR 111,
    CA 627–628, 634, 659, 1246
Stevens, Re, Pateman v James [1952] Ch 323, [1952] 1 All ER 674, 96 Sol Jo 182, [1952]
    1 TLR 590 200
Stevens, Re, Stevens v Keily [1888] WN 110 .... 284, 287
Stevens, Re, Stevens v Stevens [1915] 1 Ch 429, 84 LJ Ch 432, 59 Sol Jo 441, 112 LT 982
    312
Stevens, Re, Trustees, Executors and Agency Co Ltd v Teague [1912] VLR 194
    308
Stevens v Hale (1862) 2 Drew & Sm 22, 10 WR 418, 6 LT 453
    469
Stevens v King [1904] 2 Ch 30, 73 LJ Ch 535, 52 WR 443, [1904–7] All ER Rep 951, 90
    LT 665 163
Stevens v Lawton (1588) Cro Eliz 121 389
Stevens v Phelips (1875) 10 Ch App 417, 44 LJ Ch 689, 23 WR 716, CA in Ch
    1045
Stevens v Pyle (1860) 28 Beav 388 476
Stevens v Pyle (1861) 30 Beav 284 333
Stevens' Trusts, Re (1872) LR 15 Eq 110, 21 WR 119, 27 LT 480
    341
Stevenson v Abington (1862) 31 Beav 305, 8 Jur NS 811, 10 WR 591, 6 LT 345
    .... 328, 336
Stevenson v Abington (1863) 9 Jur NS 1063, 11 WR 935, 9 LT 74
    190
Stevenson v Gullan (1854) 18 Beav 590 397
Stevenson v Liverpool Corpn (1874) LR 10 QB 81, 44 LJQB 34, 23 WR 346, 31 LT 673
    .... 123, 1141
Steward v Cotton (1777) 5 Russ 17n 122
Stewart, Re, Stewart v Bosanquet (1913) 57 Sol Jo 646 1076
Stewart, Re, Stewart v Hislop (1905) 23 NZLR 797 379
Stewart, Re, Stewart v McLaughlin [1908] 2 Ch 251, 77 LJ Ch 525, [1908–10] All ER Rep
    133, 99 LT 106, 24 TLR 679 626
Stewart v Garnett (1830) 3 Sim 398 375
Stewart v Jones (1859) 3 De G & J 532, 5 Jur NS 229, 7 WR 184, 33 LTOS 114
    171
Stewart v Mclaren (1920) 57 SLR 148, HL 111
Stewart v MacLaren (1920) 57 SLR 531, 1920 SC (HL) 148, 1920 SLT 134
    .... 112, 251
Stewart v Murdoch [1969] NI 78 .... 237, 375, 445–446
Stewart v Stewart (1880) 15 Ch D 539, 49 LJ Ch 763, 29 WR 275, 43 LT 370
    .... 404–405, 504
Stewart's Goods, Re (1863) 27 JP 376, 32 LJPM & A 94, 9 Jur NS 417, 3 Sw & Tr 192, 4
    Sw & Tr 211, 11 WR 540 711
Stewart's Goods, Re (1875) LR 3 P & D 244, 44 LJP & M 37, 23 WR 683, sub nom
    Re Stuart's Goods 39 JP 679, 33 LT 72, P, D and Admlty
    .... 759, 795, 848
Stickney v Sewell (1835) 1 My & Cr 8, 43 RR 129 963
Stiles v Guy (1832) 4 Y & C Ex 571 .... 294, 629
Stiles v Guy (1849) 19 LJ Ch 185, 1 H & Tw 523, 84 RR 111, 14 LTOS 305, sub
    nom Styles v Guy 14 Jur 355, 1 Mac & G 422 .... 959, 1252–1253
Stiles Goods, Re [1898] P 12, 67 LJP 23, 46 WR 444, 78 LT 82, 14 TLR 61, P, D and
    Admlty 632
Still v Hoste (1821) 6 Madd 192 220
Stilwell v Mellersh (1851) 20 LJ Ch 356 115

PARA

Stimpson's Trusts, Re, Stimpson v Stimpson [1931] 2 Ch 77, 100 LJ Ch 312, [1931] All ER
    Rep 809, 145 LT 249 462
Stirling, Re, Union Bank of Scotland Ltd v Stirling [1954] 2 All ER 113, [1954] 1 WLR
    763, 98 Sol Jo 337 .... 222, 370, 1069
Stirrup's Contract, Re [1961] 1 All ER 805, [1961] 1 WLR 449, 105 Sol Jo 206
    1143–1144
Stjerna v Finland (Application 18131/91) (1994) 24 EHRR 195, ECtHR
    141
Stoakes Goods, Re (1874) 39 JP 25, 23 WR 62, 31 LT 552
    65
Stock v Brown [1994] 2 FCR 1125, [1994] 1 FLR 840, [1994] Fam Law 254
    .... 568, 598
Stockdale v Bushby (1815) Coop G 229, 19 Ves 381 276
Stockdale v Nicholson (1867) LR 4 Eq 359, 36 LJ Ch 793, 15 WR 986, 16 LT 767
    .... 364, 394
Stocken, Re, Jones v Hawkins (1888) 38 Ch D 319, 57 LJ Ch 746, 59 LT 425, CA
    .... 2, 1179
Stocken v Dawson (1843) 6 Beav 371, 63 RR 116, 1 LTOS 455
    649
Stocken v Stocken (1838) 4 My & Cr 95, 7 LJ Ch 305, 2 Jur 693, 41 ER 38
    22
Stocker v Edwards. See Edwards v Hammond
Stocker v Harbin (1841) 3 Beav 479 992
Stocks v Barre (1859) John 54, 33 LJOS 8, 5 Jur NS 537, 7 WR 247
    293
Stocks v Dodsley (1836) 1 Keen 325 363
Stockwell v Ritherdon (1848) 1 Rob Eccl 661, 12 Jur 779, 12 LTOS 107, 6 Notes of Cases
    409 94
Stoddart, Re, Bird v Grainger [1916] 2 Ch 444, 86 LJ Ch 29, 60 Sol Jo 586, 115 LT 540
    1130
Stoddart v Grant (1852) 19 LTOS 305, 1 Macq 163, HL
    .... 1, 95
Stoddart v Nelson (1855) 6 De GM & G 68, 25 LJ Ch 116, 2 Jur NS 27, 4 WR 109,
    26 LTOS 210 328
Stodden v Harvey (1608) Cro Jac 204 958
Stokes, Re, Barlow v Bullock (1907) 52 Sol Jo 11 323
Stokes, Re, Bowen v Davidson [1928] Ch 716, 97 LJ Ch 273, [1928] All ER Rep 406, 72
    Sol Jo 384, 139 LT 331 1076–1077
Stokes, Re, Parsons v Miller (1892) 67 LT 223 .... 997, 1012
Stokes v Heron. See Heron v Stokes
Stokes v Porter (1558) 1 And 11, 2 Dyer 166b 1267
Stokes v Salomons (1851) 9 Hare 75, 20 LJ Ch 343, 15 Jur 483, 17 LTOS 209
    284
Stone, Re 114 Sol Jo 36, CA 598
Stone, Re, Baker v Stone [1895] 2 Ch 196, 64 LJ Ch 637, 12 R 415, 44 WR 235, 72 LT
    815, CA 235, 396–397
Stone v Evans (1740) 2 Atk 86 164
Stone v Greening (1843) 13 Sim 390 271
Stone v Harrison (1846) 15 LJ Ch 421, 2 Coll 715, 10 Jur 609, 7 LTOS 508
    312
Stone v Hoskins [1905] P 194, 74 LJP 110, 54 WR 64, 93 LT 441, 21 TLR 528,
    [1904–7] All ER Rep Ext 1406, P, D and Admlty 10, 20–21, 23, 679
Stone v Maule (1829) 2 Sim 490 461
Stone v Parker (1860) 1 Drew & Sm 212, 29 LJ Ch 874, 8 WR 722, 3 LT 79
    .... 296, 379
Stone's Trusts, Re (1866) 12 Jur NS 447, 14 LT 542 147
Stoneham, Re, Stoneham v Stoneham [1919] 1 Ch 149, 88 LJ Ch 77, [1918–19] All ER
    Rep 1051, 63 Sol Jo 192, 120 LT 341 626
Stonham, Re, Lloyds Bank Ltd v Maynard [1963] 1 All ER 377, [1963] 1 WLR 238, 107
    Sol Jo 74 293
Stoodley, Re, Hooson v Locock [1916] 1 Ch 242, [1916–17] All ER Rep 761, 114 LT 445,
    sub nom Re Stoodley, Hooson v Stoodley 85 LJ Ch 226, 60 Sol Jo 221, CA
    .... 96, 233
Stooke v Stooke (1866) 35 Beav 396, 14 WR 564 293
Stopford v Chaworth (1845) 8 Beav 331, 9 Jur 363, 5 LTOS 142
    331

PARA

Stopford v Stopford (1903) 19 TLR 185, P, D and Admlty
.... 79

Storrs v Benbow (1833) 2 My & K 46, 2 LJ Ch 201; revsd (1853) 3 De GM & G 390,
22 LJ Ch 823, 17 Jur 821, 1 WR 420, 21 LTOS 189 .... 301, 309, 362

Storrs v Benbow (1853) 3 De GM & G 390, 22 LJ Ch 823, 17 Jur 821, 1 WR 420,
21 LTOS 189 362

Storry v Walsh (1854) 18 Beav 559, 27 LJ Ch 338, 18 Jur 503, 2 WR 300, 23 LTOS 35
.... 1025

Story v Gape (1856) 2 Jur NS 706, 106 RR 974 1238

Story v Sheard [1892] 2 QB 515, 56 JP 760, 61 LJMC 178, 41 WR 31, 36 Sol Jo 559, 67
LT 423, DC 1277

Stott, Re, Klouda v Lloyds Bank Ltd [1980] 1 All ER 259, [1980] 1 WLR 246, 123 Sol Jo
422 875

Stott v Meanock (1862) 31 LJ Ch 746, 10 WR 605, 6 LT 592
.... 1267

Stott v Milne (1884) 25 Ch D 710, 50 LT 742, CA 1018

Stow v Davenport (1833) 5 B & Ad 359, 2 Nev & MKB 805
.... 1133

Stracey's Goods, Re (1855) Dea & Sw 6, 1 Jur NS 1177, 4 WR 164, 26 LTOS 127
.... 9

Strafford (Earl), Re, Royal Bank of Scotland Ltd v Byng [1980] Ch 28, [1978] 3 All ER 18,
[1978] 3 WLR 223, 122 Sol Jo 472; affd [1980] Ch 28, [1979] 1 All ER 513, [1979] 2
WLR 459, 123 Sol Jo 50, CA 121, 1043

Strahan, Re [1907] 2 IR 484 713

Strakosch, Re, Temperley v A-G [1949] Ch 529, [1949] 2 All ER 6, [1949] LJR 1477, 93
Sol Jo 372, 65 TLR 383, CA 11

Strange v Harris (1791) 3 Bro CC 365 1186

Strange (Lord) v Smith (1755) Amb 263 136

Stratford v Powell (1807) 1 Ball & B 1 400

Stratford-upon-Avon Corpn v Parker [1914] 2 KB 562, 83 LJKB 1309, [1914–15] All ER
Rep 275, 58 Sol Jo 473, 110 LT 1004 .... 1224, 1262

Stratton, Re, Knapman v A-G [1931] 1 Ch 197, 100 LJ Ch 62, [1930] All ER Rep 255, 74
Sol Jo 787, 144 LT 169, 47 TLR 32, CA 11

Stratton v Ford (1754) 2 Lee 49 810

Stratton v Grymes (1698) 2 Vern 357 134

Stratton v Payne (1726) 3 Bro Parl Cas 99, HL 385

Stratton's Disclaimer, Re, Stratton v IRC [1958] Ch 42, [1957] 2 All ER 594, [1957] 3
WLR 199, 36 ATC 145, [1957] TR 161, 101 Sol Jo 533, CA
.... 151–152, 1060

Strauss v Schmidt (1820) 3 Phillim 209 7

Streatfeild v Cooper (1859) 27 Beav 338 284

Streatley's Goods, Re [1891] P 172, 60 LJP 56, 39 WR 432, P, D and Admlty
.... 73, 76

Stretch v Watkins (1816) 1 Madd 253 .... 375, 428

Stretton v Fitzgerald (1889) 23 LR Ir 466 442

Strickland v Strickland (1839) 10 Sim 374, 9 LJ Ch 60 540

Strickland v Strickland (1842) 12 Sim 463, 11 LJ Ch 197
.... 1172

Strickland v Symons (1883) 22 Ch D 666; on appeal (1884) 26 Ch D 245, 53 LJ Ch 582,
32 WR 889, 51 LT 406, CA 1035

Stride v Cooper (1811) 1 Phillim 334 93

Stride v Sandford (1853) 17 Jur 263, 21 LTOS 24 110

Stringer v Gardiner (1859) 27 Beav 35, 4 De G & J 468, 7 WR 602, 33 LTOS 295
.... 211, 214, 277, 328

Stringer v Phillips (1730) 1 Eq Cas Abr 292 318

Stringer's Estate, Re, Shaw v Jones-Ford (1877) 6 Ch D 1, 46 LJ Ch 633, 25 WR 815, 37
LT 233, CA 382–383

Strode (Sir Litton) v Lady Russel and Lady Falkland (1707) 3 Rep Ch 169, 2 Vern 621; on
appeal sub nom Viscountess Falkland v Lytton (1708) 3 Bro Parl Cas 24, HL
.... 45, 199, 220

Strong v Bird (1874) LR 18 Eq 315, 43 LJ Ch 814, 22 R 788, [1874–80] All ER Rep 230,
30 LT 745 .... 198, 625–626

Strong v Ingram (1833) 6 Sim 197 402

Strong d Cummin v Cummin (1759) 2 Burr 767, 2 Keny 489
.... 226

PARA

Strong's Estate, Re, Strong v Hadden [1915] P 211, 84 LJP 188, 112 LT 997, 31 TLR 256,
  P, D and Admlty 896
Strother v Dutton (1857) 1 De G & J 675 .... 327, 429, 434
Stroughill v Anstey (1852) 1 De GM & G 635, 22 LJ Ch 130, 16 Jur 671, 19 LTOS 367
  1024
Stuart, Re, Johnson v Williams [1940] 4 All ER 80, 84 Sol Jo 524, CA
  1210
Stuart, Re, Smith v Stuart (1896) 74 LT 546 1184
Stuart v Bruce (1798) 3 Ves 632 393
Stuart v Cockerell (1870) 5 Ch App 713, 39 LJ Ch 729, 18 WR 1057, 23 LT 442, CA
  302
Stuart v Marquis of Bute (1813) 1 Dow 73, HL 250, 285, 287–288
Stuart's Goods, Re (1888) 21 LR Ir 105 7
Stubbings v Clunies-Ross (1911) 27 TLR 361, P, D and Admlty
  722
Stubbs v Holywell Rly Co (1867) LR 2 Exch 311, 36 LJ Ex 166, 15 WR 769, 16 LT 631
  .... 1213, 1279
Stubbs v Sargon (1837) 2 Keen 255, 6 LJ Ch 254; on appeal (1838) 3 My & Cr 507, 7 LJ
  Ch 95, 2 Jur 150, 44 RR 241 .... 45, 256
Studd v Cook (1883) 8 App Cas 577, 10 R 53, 20 SLR 566, HL
  239
Studdert v Von Steiglitz (1889) 23 LR Ir 564 230
Studholme v Hodgson (1734) 3 P Wms 300 461
Stulz's Trusts, Re, ex p Kingsford and Stulz (1853) 4 De GM & G 404, 22 LJ Ch 917, 1
  Eq Rep 334, 17 Jur 749, 1 WR 499, 22 LTOS 9 463
Stummvoli v Hales (1864) 34 Beav 124, 10 Jur NS 716, 4 New Rep 473, 12 WR 1137,
  sub nom Stammvoll v Hales, Re Johnstone 10 LT 807 332
Stump v Gaby (1852) 2 De GM & G 623, 22 LJ Ch 352, 17 Jur 5, 1 WR 85, 20 LTOS
  213 28
Sturge and Great Western Rly Co (1881) 19 Ch D 444, 51 LJ Ch 185, 30 WR 456, sub
  nom Sturge v Sturge, Sturge to Great Western Rly Co, Re Vendor and Purchaser Act
  1874 45 LT 787 313
Sturgess v Pearson (1819) 4 Madd 411, 20 RR 316 444
Sturrock v Sturrock [1900] AC 225, 69 LJPC 29, 82 LT 97, PC
  232
Sturton v Whellock (1883) 47 JP 232, 52 LJP 29, 31 WR 382, 48 LT 237, P, D and
  Admlty 108
Styler, Re, Styler v Griffith [1942] Ch 387, [1942] 2 All ER 201, 111 LJ Ch 263, 86 Sol Jo
  234, 167 LT 295 573
Styles v Guy. See Stiles v Guy
Styth v Monro (1834) 6 Sim 49 364
Suarez (No 2), Re [1924] 2 Ch 19, 93 LJ Ch 483, 68 Sol Jo 419, 130 LT 800
  .... 513, 556
Sudeley (Lord) v A-G [1897] AC 11, 61 JP 420, 66 LJQB 21, 45 WR 305, 75 LT 398, 13
  TLR 38, [1895–9] All ER Rep Ext 1904, HL 922, 1053
Sudlow, Re, Smith v Sudlow [1914] WN 424, 59 Sol Jo 162
  293
Sugden v Crossland (1856) 25 LJ Ch 563, 2 Jur NS 318, 107 RR 73, 3 Sm & G 192, 4
  WR 343, 26 LTOS 307 657
Sugden v Lord St Leonards (1876) 1 PD 154, 45 LJP 49, 2 Char Pr Cas 160, 24 WR 479,
  860, [1874–80] All ER Rep 21, 34 LT 369, 371, CA 106, 716, 730
Suisse v Lord Lowther (1843) 2 Hare 424, 12 LJ Ch 315, 7 Jur 252, 366
  403
Sullivan, Re, Dunkley v Sullivan [1930] 1 Ch 84, 99 LJ Ch 42, [1929] All ER Rep 564,
  142 LT 187, 45 TLR 590 .... 496, 517, 1138
Sullivan v Bevan (1855) 20 Beav 399 1204
Sullivan v Sullivan [1903] 1 IR 193 .... 42, 222
Sullivan v Sullivan (1870) IR 4 Eq 457 217
Sullivan v Sullivan (1879) 3 LR Ir 299 70
Sum v Teed. See Snow v Teed
Summers Goods, Re (1901) 45 Sol Jo 327, 84 LT 271, 17 TLR 325, P, D and Admlty
  97
Sumner's Will Trusts, Re, Midland Bank Executor and Trustee Co Ltd v Sumner [1969]
  1 All ER 779, [1969] 1 WLR 373, 113 Sol Jo 209 246

PARA

Sumption v Greenwich London Borough Council [2007] EWHC 2776 (Admin), [2008] 1 P
   & CR 336, [2007] All ER (D) 482 (Nov) 286
Sunderland's Goods, Re (1866) LR 1 P & D 198, 35 LJP & M 82, 14 WR 971, 14 LT 741
   711
Supple v Lowson (1773) Amb 729 349
Surridge v Clarkson (1866) 14 WR 979 .... 321, 334, 337
Surtees v Surtees (1871) LR 12 Eq 400, 19 WR 1043, 25 LT 288
   400
Susanni's Trusts, Re (1877) 47 LJ Ch 65, 26 WR 93 161
Sutcliffe, Re, Alison v Alison [1934] Ch 219, 103 LJ Ch 154, [1933] All ER Rep 773, 150
   LT 391 .... 303, 334
Sutcliffe, Re, Sutcliffe v Robertshaw [1929] 1 Ch 123, 98 LJ Ch 33, 72 Sol Jo 384, 140 LT
   135 .... 344, 535
Sutcliffe v Cole (1855) 3 Drew 135, 24 LJ Ch 486, 3 WR 265
   184
Sutcliffe v Richardson (1872) LR 13 Eq 606, 41 LJ Ch 552, 20 WR 505, 26 LT 495
   380
Sutcliffe v Sutcliffe [2005] EWHC 3058 (Ch), [2005] All ER (D) 116 (Jul)
   1254
Sutherland (Duke), Re, Chaplin v Leveson-Gower [1922] 2 Ch 782, 92 LJ Ch 113, 67 Sol
   Jo 11, 128 LT 246 1130
Sutton, Re, Evans v Oliver [1934] Ch 209, 103 LJ Ch 127, [1933] All ER Rep 671, 150 LT
   453, 50 TLR 189 .... 344, 535
Sutton v Drax (1815) 2 Phillim 323 909
Sutton v Sadler (1857) 3 CBNS 87, 26 LJCP 284, 3 Jur NS 1150, 5 WR 880, 30 LTOS 65
   .... 897, 899
Sutton v Sutton (1892) 30 LR Ir 251, CA 410, 475
Sutton v Torre (1842) 11 LJ Ch 255, 6 Jur 234 390
Sutton, Carden & Co v Goodrich (1899) 80 LT 765, 15 TLR 397
   463
Swabey v Goldie (1875) 1 Ch D 380, 34 LT 306, CA 397
Swain, Re, Brett v Ward [1918] 1 Ch 399, 87 LJ Ch 305, 62 Sol Jo 308, 118 LT 439; on
   appeal [1918] 1 Ch 574, CA 336, 447
Swain, Re, Swain v Bringeman [1891] 3 Ch 233, 61 LJ Ch 20, 65 LT 296
   1150
Swaine v Kennerley (1813) 1 Ves & B 469 .... 350, 354
Swale v Milner (1834) 6 Sim 572 1196
Swan, Re, Witham v Swan [1915] 1 Ch 829, 84 LJ Ch 590, 113 LT 42, 31 TLR 266
   .... 121, 123
Swan v Bowden (1842) 11 LJ Ch 155 305
Swan v Holmes (1854) 19 Beav 471 .... 395, 468, 476
Swannell, Re, Morice v Swannell (1909) 101 LT 76 463
Swaythling (Lord), Re, Samuel v Swaythling (1912) 57 Sol Jo 173, 29 TLR 88
   1132
Sweeney v MacMillan Publishers Ltd [2001] All ER (D) 332 (Nov)
   1279
Sweeny v Sweeny (1876) IR 10 CL 375 644
Sweetapple v Bindon (1705) 2 Vern 536 389
Sweeting, Re, Sweeting v Sweeting [1988] 1 All ER 1016
   156–157
Sweeting v Prideaux (1876) 2 Ch D 413, 45 LJ Ch 378, 24 WR 776, 34 LT 240,
   [1874–80] All ER Rep Ext 2153 466
Sweetland v Sweetland (1865) 29 JP 168, 34 LJPM & A 42, 11 Jur NS 182, 4 Sw & Tr 6,
   13 WR 504, 11 LT 749 63
Swetenham v Walkley [2014] WTLR 845 579
Swift v Swift (1859) 1 De GF & J 160, 29 LJ Ch 121, 8 WR 100, 1 LT 150
   291
Swift v Swift (1863) 32 LJ Ch 479, 1 New Rep 353, 11 WR 334
   .... 261, 408
Swift d Neale v Roberts (1764) Amb 617, 3 Burr 1488, 1 Wm Bl 476
   29
Swift's Goods, Re (1900) 17 TLR 16, P, D and Admlty 70
Swindell v Bulkeley (1886) 18 QBD 250, 56 LJQB 613, 35 WR 189, 56 LT 38, 3 TLR
   183, CA 1283
Swinfen v Swinfen (No 4) (1860) 29 Beav 207, 7 Jur NS 89, 9 WR 175, 4 LT 194
   .... 250, 285
Swinfen v Swinfen (No 5) (1860) 29 Beav 211 962

PARA

Swinford's Goods, Re (1869) LR 1 P & D 630, 33 JP 231, 38 LJP & M 38, 17 WR 536,
20 LT 87 69
Swire, Re, Mellor v Swire (1882) 21 Ch D 647, 30 WR 525, 46 LT 437, CA
.... 1178
Swords' Goods, Re [1952] P 368, [1952] 2 All ER 281, P, D and Admlty
.... 54, 739
Sydall v Castings Ltd [1967] 1 QB 302, [1966] 3 All ER 770, [1966] 3 WLR 1126, 110
Sol Jo 790, CA 339, 350
Syer v Gladstone (1885) 30 Ch D 614, 34 WR 565 .... 153, 1006
Sykes, Re, Drake v Sykes (1907) 23 TLR 747, CA 106
Sykes, Re, Skelton and Dyson v Sykes [1940] 4 All ER 10
.... 209, 212, 296
Sykes, Re, Sykes v Sykes [1909] 2 Ch 241, 78 LJ Ch 609, 101 LT 1, [1908–10] All ER Rep
Ext 1236, CA 212, 657
Sykes v Sykes (1867) LR 4 Eq 200; affd (1868) 3 Ch App 301, 37 LJ Ch 367, 16 WR 545
.... 173, 175
Sykes v Sykes (1868) 3 Ch App 301, 37 LJ Ch 367, 16 WR 545
.... 183, 1115
Sykes v Sykes (1870) LR 5 CP 113, 39 LJCP 179, 18 WR 551, 22 LT 236
.... 1264
Sykes' Goods, Re (1873) LR 3 P & D 26, 37 JP 183, 42 LJP & M 17, 21 WR 416, 28 LT
142 .... 83, 85
Symers v Jobson (1848) 16 Sim 267 .... 341, 385
Symes v Green (1859) 28 LJP & M 83, 5 Jur NS 742, 1 Sw & Tr 401, 33 LTOS 168
.... 897, 899
Symes v Symes [1896] 1 Ch 272, 65 LJ Ch 265, 44 WR 521, 73 LT 684
.... 424
Symm's Will Trusts, Re, Public Trustee v Shaw [1936] 3 All ER 236, 80 Sol Jo 994
.... 1052
Symons, Re, Luke v Tonkin (1882) 21 Ch D 757, 52 LJ Ch 709, 30 WR 874, 46 LT 684
.... 1183
Sympson v Hornsby. See Simpson v Hornby
Sympson v Hutton. See Hutton v Simpson
Synge v Synge [1894] 1 QB 466, 58 JP 396, 63 LJQB 202, 9 R 265, 42 WR 309,
[1891–4] All ER Rep 1164, 70 LT 221, 10 TLR 194, CA
.... 21
Synge's Trusts, Re (1854) 3 I Ch R 379 .... 331, 460–461
Szabo v Boros [2002] WTLR 1389, (1966) 64 DLR (2d) 48, 60 WWR 754, BC SC
.... 23

T

T, Re (1961) 105 Sol Jo 325 739
Taaffe v Conmee (1862) 10 HL Cas 64, 8 Jur NS 919, 6 LT 666
.... 318, 395, 474
Taber, Re, Arnold v Kayess (1882) 51 LJ Ch 721, 30 WR 883, 46 LT 805
.... 1131
Tabuteau v Nixon (1899) 15 TLR 485 335
Tait v Lord Northwick (1799) 4 Ves 816 1012
Talbot, Re. See Talbot v Talbot
Talbot v Earl Radnor (1834) 3 My & K 252, 41 RR 64
.... 153
Talbot v Jevers [1917] 2 Ch 363, 86 LJ Ch 731, 117 LT 430, CA
.... 555
Talbot v Talbot [1962] 3 All ER 174, 106 Sol Jo 613, sub nom Talbot, Re [1962] 1 WLR
1113, P, D and Admlty 573
Talbot v Talbot [1968] Ch 1, [1967] 2 All ER 920, [1967] 3 WLR 438, 111 Sol Jo 278,
CA 125
Talbot-Ponsonby's Estate, Re, Talbot-Ponsonby v Talbot-Ponsonby [1937] 4 All ER 309, 81
Sol Jo 883, 54 TLR 33 141
Tamplin's Goods, Re [1894] P 39, 63 LJP 75, 6 R 533, 42 WR 287, P, D and Admlty
.... 722
Tancred's Settlement, Re, Somerville v Tancred [1903] 1 Ch 715, 72 LJ Ch 324, 51 WR
510, [1900–3] All ER Rep 251, 47 Sol Jo 319, 88 LT 164
.... 463

PARA

Taniere v Pearkes (1825) 2 Sim & St 383, 4 LJOS Ch 81
.... 397

Tankard, Re, Tankard v Midland Bank Executor and Trustee Co Ltd [1942] Ch 69, [1941]
3 All ER 458, 111 LJ Ch 70, 85 Sol Jo 475, 166 LT 65, 58 TLR 56
.... 966, 1053

Tann, Re, Gravatt v Tann (No 2) (1869) LR 7 Eq 436, 38 LJ Ch 459
.... 1207

Tann, Re, Tann v Tann (No 2) (1869) LR 7 Eq 436, 38 LJ Ch 459
.... 1207

Tann v Tann (1863) 2 New Rep 412 277
Tanner v Dancey (1846) 9 Beav 339 1196
Tanner v Public Trustee [1973] 1 NZLR 68, NZ CA 903
Tanner v Tebbutt (1843) 2 Y & C Ch Cas 225, 12 LJ Ch 216, 7 Jur 339
.... 147

Tanqueray-Willaume and Landau, Re (1882) 20 Ch D 465, 51 LJ Ch 434, 30 WR 801, 46
LT 542, CA 204

Taplen v Taplen and Cowen [1891] P 283, 60 LJP 88, 64 LT 870, 7 TLR 508, P, D and
Admlty 723
Tapley v Eagleton (1879) 12 Ch D 683, 28 WR 239 127
Tapscott v Newcombe (1842) 6 Jur 755 425
Tarbuck v Tarbuck (1835) 4 LJ Ch 129 .... 440, 445
Tarbutt v Nicholson (1920) 89 LJPC 127, 123 LT 638, PC
.... 241

Target v Gaunt (1718) 1 Eq Cas Abr 193, Gilb Ch 149, 10 Mod Rep 402, 1 P Wms 432
.... 457

Tarn v Commercial Banking Co of Sydney (1884) 12 QBD 294, 32 WR 492, 50 LT 365
.... 635

Tarnpolsk, Re, Barclays Bank Ltd v Hyer [1958] 3 All ER 479, [1958] 1 WLR 1157, 102
Sol Jo 857 .... 138, 140
Tasker v Shepherd (1861) 6 H & N 575, 30 LJ Ex 207, 9 WR 476, 4 LT 19
.... 1279

Tatchell v Tatchell [1901] 2 Ch 738, CA; affd sub nom Inderwick v Tatchell [1903] AC
120, [1900–3] All ER Rep Ext 1104, 72 LJ Ch 393, 88 LT 399, HL
.... 316

Tate, Re, Williamson v Gilpin [1914] 2 Ch 182, 83 LJ Ch 593, 58 Sol Jo 119, 109 LT 621
.... 470
Tate v Clarke (1838) 1 Beav 100, 8 LJ Ch 60 .... 385, 391–392
Tate v Hilbert (1793) 2 Ves 111, 4 Bro CC 286, 30 ER 548, [1775–1802] All ER Rep 377
.... 921
Tate v Leithead (1854) Kay 658, 23 LJ Ch 736, 2 Eq Rep 1105, 2 WR 630, 23 LTOS 252
.... 921, 969

Tatham v Drummond (1864) 4 De GJ & Sm 484, 34 LJ Ch 1, 10 Jur NS 1087, 5 New Rep
24, 13 WR 61, 11 LT 324 .... 258, 403
Tatham v Vernon (1861) 29 Beav 604, 7 Jur NS 814, 9 WR 822, 4 LT 531
.... 336, 419, 431

Tatlock v Jenkins (1854) Kay 654, 23 LJ Ch 767, 18 Jur 891, 24 LTOS 42
.... 992
Tattersall v Howell (1816) 2 Mer 26 141
Tavernor v Grindley (1875) 32 LT 424, Ct of Ch 333
Tawney v Ward (1839) 1 Beav 563, 8 LJ Ch 319 .... 375, 431
Taws v Knowles [1891] 2 QB 564, 56 JP 68, 60 LJQB 641, 39 WR 675, 65 LT 124, CA
.... 283
Taylor, Re, Barber v Smith (1919) 147 LT Jo 253 .... 250, 288
Taylor, Re, Cloak v Hammond (1886) 34 Ch D 255, 56 LJ Ch 171, 35 WR 186, 55 LT
649, 3 TLR 178, CA 214, 217, 276, 328
Taylor, Re, Dale v Dale [1909] WN 59 114–115
Taylor, Re, Hockley v O'Neal [1925] Ch 739, 95 LJ Ch 43, [1925] All ER Rep 662, 133
LT 602 352
Taylor, Re, Lloyds Bank Ltd v Jones [1957] 3 All ER 56, [1957] 1 WLR 1043, 101 Sol Jo
816 182
Taylor, Re, Martin v Freeman (1888) 58 LT 538, 4 TLR 302
.... 230

Taylor, Re, Midland Bank Executor and Trustee Co Ltd v Smith [1940] Ch 481, [1940]
2 All ER 637, 109 LJ Ch 188, 84 Sol Jo 289, 163 LT 51, 56 TLR 588; affd [1940] Ch
834, CA 36
Taylor, Re, Pullan v Taylor [1931] 2 Ch 242, 100 LJ Ch 374, [1931] All ER Rep 387, 145
LT 417 534

                                                                                 PARA
Taylor, Re, Sewell v Ransford (1873) 21 WR 244 797
Taylor, Re, Shaw v Shaw [1914] 1 IR 111 384
Taylor, Re, Smart v Taylor [1901] 2 Ch 134, 70 LJ Ch 535, 49 WR 615, 84 LT 758
       1083
Taylor, Re, Taylor v Ley (1885) 52 LT 839, CA 314
Taylor, Re, Taylor v Taylor [1931] 2 Ch 237, 100 LJ Ch 309, 75 Sol Jo 393, 145 LT 443
       .... 171, 173
Taylor, Re, Taylor v Tweedie [1923] 1 Ch 99, 91 LJ Ch 801, 66 Sol Jo 693, 127 LT 684,
       38 TLR 850, [1922] All ER Rep Ext 832, CA 226
Taylor, Re, Taylor v Wade [1894] 1 Ch 671, 63 LJ Ch 424, 8 R 186, 42 WR 373, 38 Sol
       Jo 288, 70 LT 556 1067
Taylor, Re, Taylor v White (1911) 56 Sol Jo 175 323
Taylor, Re, Whitby v Highton (1888) 57 LJ Ch 430, 36 WR 683, 58 LT 842
       .... 113, 115
Taylor v Bacon (1836) 8 Sim 100 432
Taylor v Beverley (1844) 13 LJ Ch 240, 1 Coll 108, 8 Jur 265, 2 LTOS 516
       .... 248, 318
Taylor v Clark (1841) 1 Hare 161, 11 LJ Ch 189, 6 Jur 76
       1125–1126
Taylor v Clarke (1763) 2 Eden 202 460
Taylor v Cooper (1846) 10 Jur 1078, 8 LTOS 134 125
Taylor v Creagh (1858) 8 I Ch R 281 186
Taylor v Crotty [2006] EWCA Civ 1364, [2007] P & CR D22, 150 Sol Jo LB 1330,
       [2006] All ER (D) 32 (Oct) 1214
Taylor v Dening. See Baker v Dening
Taylor v Dickens [1998] 3 FCR 455, [1998] 1 FLR 806, [1998] Fam Law 191
       20–21
Taylor v Frobisher (1852) 5 De G & Sm 191, 21 LJ Ch 605, 16 Jur 283, 19 LTOS 242
       .... 256, 258, 412, 436
Taylor v Graham (1878) 3 App Cas 1287, HL 238, 413
Taylor v Hawkins (1803) 8 Ves 209 1025
Taylor v Haygarth (1844) 14 Sim 8, 8 Jur 135, 2 LTOS 437
       555
Taylor v Lambert (1876) 2 Ch D 177, 45 LJ Ch 418, 24 WR 691, 34 LT 567
       438
Taylor v Newton (1752) 1 Lee 15 .... 753, 797
Taylor v Popham (1782) 1 Bro CC 168 149
Taylor v Richardson (1853) 2 Drew 16, 23 LJ Ch 9, 2 Eq Rep 332, 2 WR 29, 22 LTOS 95
       207
Taylor v St Helens Corpn (1877) 6 Ch D 264, 46 LJ Ch 857, 25 WR 885, 37 LT 253, CA
       368
Taylor v Shaw, Re Jones (1920) 89 LJPC 124, 123 LT 643, PC
       226
Taylor v Shum (1797) 1 Bos & P 21 1223
Taylor v Southgate (1839) 4 My & Cr 203, 8 LJ Ch 137, 3 Jur 214
       1177
Taylor v Stainton (1856) 2 Jur NS 634, 4 WR 588 449
Taylor v Sturrock [1900] AC 225, 69 LJPC 29, 82 LT 97, PC
       232
Taylor v Tabrum (1833) 6 Sim 281, 1 LJ Ch 189 961
Taylor v Taylor (1837) 1 Jur 401 293
Taylor v Taylor (1870) LR 10 Eq 477, 39 LJ Ch 676, 18 WR 1102, 23 LT 134
       .... 989, 1245
Taylor v Taylor (1875) LR 20 Eq 155, 44 LJ Ch 718, 23 WR 719
       503
Taylor v Watts (1676) Freem KB 425, sub nom Joyner v Watts 3 Keb 607, 643, T Jo 48
       620
Taylor d Smith v Biddall (1677) 2 Eq Cas Abr 335, Freem KB 243, 2 Mod Rep 289
       419
Taylor's Estate, Re [1929] P 260, 98 LJP 145, 73 Sol Jo 385, 141 LT 200, 45 TLR 481, P,
       D and Admlty 824, 949
Taylor's Estate, Re, National and Provincial and Union Bank of England v Taylor (1919)
       64 Sol Jo 148, P, D and Admlty 93, 106
Taylor's Estate, Re, Tomlin v Underhay (1881) 22 Ch D 495, 48 LT 552, CA
       406
Taylor's Estate and Will Trusts, Re, Taylor v Taylor [1969] 2 Ch 245, [1969] 1 All ER 113,
       [1969] 2 WLR 1371, 113 Sol Jo 208 .... 992, 1108

PARA

Taylor's Goods, Re (1890) 63 LT 230, 6 TLR 375, P, D and Admlty
.... 105
Taylor's Trusts, Re, Taylor v Blake [1912] 1 IR 1 .... 337, 392
Taynton v Hannay (1802) 3 Bos & P 26 801
Teague and Ashdown v Wharton, Re Jeffries Goods (1871) LR 2 P & D 360, 36 JP 24,
    41 LJP & M 13, 20 WR 214, 25 LT 764 759–760
Teale, Re, Teale v Teale (1885) 34 WR 248, 53 LT 936 .... 440, 451
Teatt v Strong (1760) 3 Bro Parl Cas 219, HL 284
Tebbs, Re, Redfern v Tebbs [1976] 2 All ER 858, [1976] 1 WLR 924, 120 Sol Jo 525
.... 1183
Tebbs v Carpenter (1816) 1 Madd 290, 16 RR 224, 56 ER 107, [1814–23] All ER Rep
    561 .... 305, 658, 959, 1257
Tegg, Re, Public Trustee v Bryant [1936] 2 All ER 878, 80 Sol Jo 552
.... 131, 140
Tegg's Goods, Re (1846) 4 Notes of Cases 531 114
Telfair, Re, Garrioch v Barclay [1900–3] All ER Rep 95, 86 LT 496
.... 397, 470
Tempest v Tempest (1856) 2 K & J 635; on appeal (1857) 7 De GM & G 470
.... 43, 296
Temple, Re, ex p Thistlewood (1812) 1 Rose 290, sub nom Thistlewood, ex p 19 Ves 236
.... 1093
Templeman v Warrington (1842) 13 Sim 267 440
Templemore's Estate, Re (1925) 69 Sol Jo 382, P, D and Admlty
.... 101
Tench v Cheese (1855) 6 De GM & G 453, 24 LJ Ch 716, 3 Eq Rep 971, 1 Jur NS 689, 3
    WR 500, 582, 25 LTOS 189, 261 992
Tennent v Tennent (1844) 1 Jo & Lat 379 284
Tenny d Agar v Agar (1810) 12 East 253 .... 460, 473
Tepper's Will Trusts, Re, Kramer v Ruda [1987] Ch 358, [1987] 1 All ER 970, [1987] 2
    WLR 729, [1987] 2 FLR 439, [1987] Fam Law 379, 131 Sol Jo 327, [1987] LS Gaz R
    1057 .... 129, 131, 138, 140
Terrell v Matthews (1841) 11 LJ Ch 31, 5 Jur 1074, 1 Mac & G 433n
.... 1253
Terrible's Goods, Re (1858) 1 Sw & Tr 140, 6 WR 816, 31 LTOS 318
.... 111
Terry's Will, Re (1854) 19 Beav 580 348
Tetley, Re, A-G v National Provincial and Union Bank of England. See A-G v National
    Provincial and Union Bank of England
Tetlow v Ashton (1850) 20 LJ Ch 53, 15 Jur 213, 16 LTOS 359
.... 341
Tetsall, Re, Foyster v Tetsall [1961] 2 All ER 801, [1961] 1 WLR 938, 105 Sol Jo 444
.... 156, 199
Teulon v Teulon (1852) 22 LJ Ch 243, 1 WR 97 .... 402, 442
Tew v Earl of Winterton (1792) 1 Ves 451, 3 Bro CC 489
.... 1301
Tewart v Lawson (1874) LR 18 Eq 490, 43 LJ Ch 673, 22 WR 822
.... 415
Thacker's Goods, Re [1900] P 15, 69 LJP 1, 81 LT 790, P, D and Admlty
.... 632, 850
Thackeray v Hampson (1825) 2 Sim & St 214, sub nom Thackeray v Dorrien 3 LJOS Ch
    89 442
Thakeham Sequestration Moneys, Re (1871) LR 12 Eq 494, 19 WR 1001, 24 LT 902
.... 1047
Tharp, Re, Tharp v Macdonald (1878) 3 PD 76, 26 WR 770, 38 LT 867, CA
.... 679
Tharp v Tharp [1916] 1 Ch 142, 85 LJ Ch 162, 60 Sol Jo 176, 114 LT 495; on appeal
    [1916] 2 Ch 205, CA 221
Tharp's Estate, Re (1863) 1 De GJ & Sm 453, 33 LJ Ch 59, 2 New Rep 253, 11 WR 763,
    8 LT 559 .... 316, 474
Tharpe v Stallwood (1843) 7 JP 400, 1 Dow & L 24, 12 LJCP 241, 7 Jur 492, 5 Man &
    G 760, 6 Scott NR 715, sub nom Sharpe v Stallwood 1 LTOS 110
.... 645
Thatcher's Trusts, Re (1859) 26 Beav 365 .... 412, 433
Theaker's Case (1624) Cro Jac 686 551
Theebridge v Kilburne (1751) 2 Ves Sen 233 .... 385, 459
Thellusson v Lord Rendlesham (1859) 7 HL Cas 429, 28 LJ Ch 948, 5 Jur NS 1031, 7 WR
    563, 33 LTOS 379 .... 226, 242, 244, 333

                                                                              PARA
Thellusson v Thellusson (1859) 7 HL Cas 429, 28 LJ Ch 948, 5 Jur NS 1031, 7 WR 563,
    33 LTOS 379 .... 226, 242, 244, 333
Thellusson v Woodford (1799) 4 Ves 227; affd (1805) 1 Bos & PNR 357,
    [1803–13] All ER Rep 30, 8 RR 104, 11 Ves 112, 32 ER 1030, HL
    .... 34, 200, 241, 248, 258
Thellusson v Woodford (1829) 5 Russ 100 331
Thetford School Case (1609) 8 Co Rep 130b 407
Thicknesse v Liege (1775) 3 Bro Parl Cas 365, HL 461
Thistlethwayte's Trust, Re (1855) 24 LJ Ch 712, 1 Jur NS 881, 3 WR 629, 25 LTOS 293
    246
Thomas, Re [1956] 3 All ER 897n, [1956] 1 WLR 1516, 100 Sol Jo 929
    753
Thomas, Re, Public Trustee v Falconer [1946] Ch 36, [1945] 2 All ER 586, 115 LJ Ch 145,
    89 Sol Jo 565, 173 LT 365, 62 TLR 23 1092
Thomas, Re, Thomas v Howell (1886) 34 Ch D 166, 56 LJ Ch 9, 55 LT 629
    156
Thomas, Re, Thomas v Thomas [1921] 1 Ch 306, 90 LJ Ch 113, 125 LT 606
    .... 454–455, 460
Thomas, Re, Vivian v Vivian [1920] 1 Ch 515, 89 LJ Ch 251, 64 Sol Jo 359, 123 LT 40
    461
Thomas, Re, Wood v Thomas [1891] 3 Ch 482, 60 LJ Ch 781, 40 WR 75,
    [1891–4] All ER Rep 471, 65 LT 142 1124
Thomas, Re, ex p Thomas (1842) 3 Mont D & De G 40, 1 Ph 159, 12 LJ Ch 59, 6 Jur
    979 923
Thomas v A-G (1837) 2 Y & C Ex 525 1082
Thomas v Hole (1728) 2 Eq Cas Abr 368, Cas temp Talb 251, 1 Dick 50
    349
Thomas v Howell (1692) 2 Eq Cas Abr 360, 4 Mod Rep 66, 1 Salk 170, Holt KB 225,
    Skin 301 143
Thomas v Howell (1874) LR 18 Eq 198, 43 LJ Ch 511 109
Thomas v Jones [1928] P 162, [1928] All ER Rep 704, 72 Sol Jo 255, 139 LT 214, 44
    TLR 467, sub nom Jones Estate, Re, Thomas v Jones 97 LJP 81, P, D and Admlty
    .... 50, 910
Thomas v Jones (1860) 1 Drew & Sm 134, 29 LJ Ch 570, 6 Jur NS 391, 8 WR 328, 2 LT
    77 1205
Thomas v Kent [2006] EWCA Civ 1485, [2006] All ER (D) 57 (May)
    .... 261, 304–306, 321–322, 324, 326
Thomas v Montgomery (1830) 1 Russ & M 729 1086
Thomas v Phelps (1828) 4 Russ 348, 6 LJOS Ch 110 .... 284, 379
Thomas v Thomas (1859) 27 Beav 537, 29 LJ Ch 281, 5 Jur NS 1237, 8 WR 71, 1 LT 208
    284
Thomas v Wilberforce (1862) 31 Beav 299 .... 416, 431
Thomas and Agnes Carvel Foundation v Carvel [2007] EWHC 1314 (Ch), [2008] Ch 395,
    [2007] 4 All ER 81, [2008] 2 WLR 1234, 10 ITELR 455, [2007] All ER (D) 76 (Jun)
    .... 10, 714, 1163
Thomas d Evans v Thomas (1796) 3 RR 306, 6 Term Rep 671
    .... 217, 263, 269
Thomas d Jones v Evans (1802) 2 East 488 .... 1, 93
Thomas Estate, Re [1912] P 177, 81 LJP 91, 107 LT 201, P, D and Admlty
    850
Thomas Estate, Re, Public Trustee v Davies [1939] 2 All ER 567, P, D and Admlty
    .... 8, 679, 707, 722
Thomas Goods, Re (1859) 23 JP 72, 28 LJP & M 33, 5 Jur NS 104, 1 Sw & Tr 255, 7
    WR 270, 32 LTOS 261 895
Thomas Will Trusts, Re, Powell v Thomas [1930] 2 Ch 67, 99 LJ Ch 286, 74 Sol Jo 201,
    144 LT 64 143
Thomason v Moses (1842) 5 Beav 77, 6 Jur 403, 59 RR 421
    1210
Thomond (Earl) v Earl of Suffolk (1718) 2 Eq Cas Abr 567, 1 P Wms 461
    158–159
Thompson, Re, Griffith v Thompson (1896) 44 WR 582, 40 Sol Jo 544
    .... 142, 146, 428
Thompson, Re, Lloyds Bank Ltd v George [1939] 1 All ER 681, 83 Sol Jo 317
    131
Thompson, Re, Machell v Newman (1886) 55 LT 85 364

PARA

Thompson, Re, Public Trustee v Husband [1936] Ch 676, [1936] 2 All ER 141, 105 LJ Ch
   289, 80 Sol Jo 466, 155 LT 474 .... 1108–1109, 1111
Thompson, Re, Thompson v Thompson [1906] 2 Ch 199, 75 LJ Ch 599, 54 WR 613, 95
   LT 97, [1904–7] All ER Rep Ext 1238 2
Thompson, Re, Thompson v Watkins [1908] WN 195 1121
Thompson, Re, ex p Thompson (1864) 16 I Ch R 228, CA
   387
Thompson v Beasley (1854) 3 Drew 7, 24 LJ Ch 327, 3 Eq Rep 59, 18 Jur 973
   335
Thompson v Clive (1857) 23 Beav 282 325
Thompson v Dunn (1870) 5 Ch App 573, 18 WR 854 1254
Thompson v Lady Lawley (1800) 2 Bos & P 303 291
Thompson v Leach (1690) Comb 468, 1 Com 45, 3 Lev 284, 1 Ld Raym 313, 12 Mod
   Rep 173, 3 Mod Rep 301, 2 Salk 427, 576, 618, 675, 3 Salk 300, Holt KB 357, 2
   Vent 198, [1558–1774] All ER Rep 39, Carth 435, sub nom Leech's Case Freem KB
   502, sub nom Leach v Thompson 1 Show 296, 87 ER 199; on appeal (1698) Show
   Parl Cas 150, sub nom Thompson v Leach 2 Vent 208, HL
   152
Thompson v Percival (1834) 5 B & Ad 925, 3 LJKB 98, 3 Nev & MKB 167
   1233
Thompson v Reynolds (1827) 3 C & P 123 635
Thompson v Robinson (1859) 27 Beav 486, 29 LJ Ch 280, 5 Jur NS 1196, 8 WR 34, 1 LT
   121 328
Thompson v Teulon (1852) 22 LJ Ch 243, 1 WR 97 .... 402, 442
Thompson v Thompson [1976] Fam 25, [1975] 2 All ER 208, [1975] 2 WLR 868, 73 LGR
   488, 30 P & CR 91, 119 Sol Jo 255, CA 591
Thompson v Thompson (1844) 13 LJ Ch 455, 1 Coll 381, 8 Jur 839, 3 LTOS 452
   .... 264, 300
Thompson v Tomkins (1862) 2 Drew & Sm 8, 31 LJ Ch 633, 8 Jur NS 185, 10 WR 310, 6
   LT 305 1047
Thompson v Waithman (1856) 3 Drew 628, 26 LJ Ch 134, 2 Jur NS 1080, 5 WR 30,
   28 LTOS 95 976
Thompson v Whitelock (1859) 4 De G & J 490, 28 LJ Ch 793, 5 Jur NS 991, 7 WR 625,
   33 LTOS 339 .... 186, 200, 252, 321
Thompson and M'Williams' Contract, Re [1896] 1 IR 356
   796
Thompson & Sons v Clarke (1901) 17 TLR 455 .... 1294, 1298
Thompson's Settlement, Re, Thompson v Thompson [1986] Ch 99, [1985] 2 All ER 720,
   [1985] 3 WLR 486, 129 Sol Jo 575 .... 657, 1153
Thompson's Trust, Re, ex p Oliver (1852) 5 De G & Sm 667, 22 LJ Ch 273, 17 Jur 16,
   20 LTOS 289 441
Thompson's Trusts, Re (1878) 9 Ch D 607, 48 LJ Ch 135, 27 WR 378
   .... 320, 341
Thompson's Trusts, Re, ex p Tunstall (1854) 5 De GM & G 280, 2 WR 218, 444,
   23 LTOS 215 324
Thompson's Will, Re, Brahe v Mason [1910] VLR 251 .... 190, 301
Thomson v Eastwood (1877) 2 App Cas 215, HL 277
Thomson v Hall (1852) 2 Rob Eccl 426, 16 Jur 1144, 21 LTOS 291
   896
Thomson v Harding (1853) 2 E & B 630, 22 LJQB 448, 18 Jur 58, 1 WR 468, 1 CLR
   887, 21 LTOS 305 1266–1267
Thomson and Baxter v Hempenstall (1849) 1 Rob Eccl 783, 13 Jur 814, 13 LTOS 449, 7
   Notes of Cases 141 212
Thomson's Estate, Re, Herring v Barrow (1880) 14 Ch D 263, 49 LJ Ch 622, 28 WR 802,
   43 LT 35, CA 382–383
Thomson Settlement Trusts, Re, Robertson v Makepeace [1953] Ch 414, [1953] 1 All ER
   1139, 97 Sol Jo 334 404
Thomson's Trustess v Leith Hospital 1951 SC 533, 1952 SLT 10, Ct of Sess
   278
Thomson's Trusts, Re (1870) LR 11 Eq 146, 19 WR 196, 23 LT 693
   .... 435, 471
Thorley, Re, Thorley v Massam [1891] 2 Ch 613, 60 LJ Ch 537, 39 WR 565, 64 LT 515,
   7 TLR 479, [1891–4] All ER Rep Ext 2074, CA 652, 1070
Thorn v Dickens [1906] WN 54 215

PARA

Thornber, Re, Crabtree v Thornber [1937] Ch 29, [1936] 2 All ER 1594, 106 LJ Ch 7, 80
   Sol Jo 689, 155 LT 223, CA 143, 283, 479, 517, 1123
Thorncroft and Clarke v Lashmar (1862) 26 JP 567, 31 LJPM & A 150, 8 Jur NS 595, 2
   Sw & Tr 479, 10 WR 783, 6 LT 476 2–3
Thorne v Rooke (1841) 2 Curt 799, sub nom Langdon v Rooke 1 Notes of Cases 254
   99
Thorne v Thorne [1893] 3 Ch 196, 63 LJ Ch 38, 8 R 282, 42 WR 282, 69 LT 378
   .... 1023, 1141
Thorne v Thorne (1903) 33 SCR 309, Can SC 285
Thorne's Goods, Re (1865) 34 LJPM & A 131, 11 Jur NS 569, 4 Sw & Tr 36, 121 LT 639
   .... 7, 710
Thorner v Major [2009] UKHL 18, [2009] 3 All ER 945, [2009] 1 WLR 776, 12 ITELR
   62, [2009] 3 FCR 123, [2009] 2 FLR 405, [2009] Fam Law 583, [2009] NLJR 514,
   [2009] 13 EG 142 (CS), (2009) Times, 26 March, 153 Sol Jo (no 12) 30, [2009] 2 P &
   CR D5, [2009] All ER (D) 257 (Mar), sub nom Thorner v Curtis [2009] 2 P & CR
   269 20
Thornhill v Hall (1834) 8 Bli NS 88, 2 Cl & Fin 22, HL
   .... 369, 382
Thornhill v Thornhill (1819) 4 Madd 377 322
Thornley v Palmer [1969] 3 All ER 31, [1969] 1 WLR 1037, 113 Sol Jo 547, CA
   .... 573, 576–577
Thornton's Goods, Re (1889) 14 PD 82, 53 JP 407, 58 LJP 82, 61 LT 200, P, D and
   Admlty 93, 101, 109
Thorold v Thorold (1809) 1 Phillim 1 54
Thorowood v Collins (1627) Cro Car 75, sub nom James and Thoroughgood v Collins Het
   29, sub nom Jaques and Throughgood v Collins Litt 46
   395
Thorp v Owen (1843) 2 Hare 607, 12 LJ Ch 417, 7 Jur 894, 1 LTOS 286
   370
Thorp v Owen (1854) 23 LJ Ch 286, 2 Eq Rep 392, 18 Jur 641, 2 Sm & G 90, 2 WR 208
   .... 340, 563
Thorp v Tomson (1588) 2 Leon 120 .... 19, 277
Thorpe v Bestwick (1881) 6 QBD 311, 45 JP 440, 50 LJQB 320, 29 WR 631, 44 LT 180
   42–43
Thorpe v Jackson (1837) 2 Y & C Ex 553, 160 ER 515, [1835–42] All ER Rep 541, Exch
   Ct 1232
Thorpe v Thorpe (1862) 1 H & C 326, 32 LJ Ex 79, 8 Jur NS 871, 10 WR 778
   .... 237, 340
Throckmorton, Re, ex p Eyston (1877) 7 Ch D 145, 47 LJ Bcy 62, 26 WR 181, 37 LT
   447, CA 465
Thrupp v Collett (No 2) (1858) 26 Beav 147, 5 Jur NS 111
   366
Thruston's Will Trusts, Re (1849) 17 Sim 21, 18 LJ Ch 437
   .... 412, 430
Thurlow, Re, Riddick v Kennard [1972] Ch 379, [1972] 1 All ER 10, [1971] 3 WLR 881,
   115 Sol Jo 813 .... 262, 338
Thurston v Essington (1727) Jac 361n 370
Thwaite v Thwaite [1982] Fam 1, [1981] 2 All ER 789, [1981] 3 WLR 96, 2 FLR 280, 11
   Fam Law 181, 125 Sol Jo 307, CA 1279
Thwaites v Forman (1844) 1 Coll 409, 10 Jur 483; on appeal (1846) 15 LJ Ch 397
   1087
Thynne, Re, Thynne v Grey [1911] 1 Ch 282, 80 LJ Ch 205, 18 Mans 34, 104 LT 19
   121
Thynne (Lord John) v Stanhope (1822) 1 Add 52 109
Tibbs v Elliott (1865) 34 Beav 424 409
Tichborne v Tichborne, ex p Norris (1869) LR 1 P & D 730, 38 LJP & M 55, 17 WR
   832, 20 LT 820 809
Tichborne v Tichborne (1870) LR 2 P & D 41, 34 JP 183, 39 LJP & M 22, 22 LT 42
   812
Tidd v North. See Kidd v North
Tidwell v Ariel (1818) 3 Madd 403 .... 165, 321
Tiffin v Longman (1852) 15 Beav 275, 20 LTOS 13 .... 349, 395
Tiger v Barclays Bank Ltd [1951] 2 KB 556, [1951] 2 All ER 262, 95 Sol Jo 400, [1951] 2
   TLR 102; affd [1952] 1 All ER 85, CA 631, 1057
Tilburgh v Barbut (1748) 1 Ves Sen 89 387

PARA

Tilden, Re, Coubrough v Royal Society of London (1938) 82 Sol Jo 334
.... 184
Tilley v Simpson (1746) 2 Term Rep 659n 17
Tilly v Tilly (1874) unreported, cited in Dashwood v Peyton (1811) 18 Ves 27 at 43
.... 467
Tilson v Jones (1830) 1 Russ & M 553 449
Tilson v Thornton (1830) 1 Russ & M 553 449
Timberlake, Re, Archer v Timberlake (1919) 63 Sol Jo 286
.... 287, 1011
Timewell v Perkins (1740) 2 Atk 102 .... 250, 376
Timins v Stackhouse (1858) 27 Beav 434 397
Timmis, Re, Nixon v Smith [1902] 1 Ch 176, 71 LJ Ch 118, 50 WR 164, 46 Sol Jo 122,
    85 LT 672 1148–1150
Timson, Re, Harper v Timson [1953] 2 All ER 1252, [1953] 1 WLR 1361, 97 Sol Jo 780
.... 992
Timson, Re, Smiles v Timson [1916] 2 Ch 362, 85 LJ Ch 561, 60 Sol Jo 526, 115 LT 55,
    CA 336
Tinkler, Re, Loyd v Allen [1917] 1 Ch 242, 86 LJ Ch 177, 61 Sol Jo 170, 115 LT 710
.... 1130
Tinkler v Hindmarsh (1840) 2 Beav 348 1041
Tinline, Re, Elder v Tinline (1912) 56 Sol Jo 310 217
Tippett v Tippett (1865) LR 1 P & D 54, 35 LJP & M 41
.... 911
Titchfield (Marquis) v Horncastle (1838) 7 LJ Ch 279, 2 Jur 610
.... 288
Titcomb v Butler (1830) 3 Sim 417 307–308
Tito v Waddell (No 2), Tito v A-G [1977] Ch 106, [1977] 2 WLR 496
.... 1030
Tiverton Market Act, Re, ex p Tanner (1855) 20 Beav 374, 24 LJ Ch 657, 1 Jur NS 487,
    25 LT 76 395
Tod, Re, Bradshaw v Turner [1916] 1 Ch 567, 85 LJ Ch 668, [1916–17] All ER Rep 1054,
    60 Sol Jo 403, 114 LT 839, 32 TLR 344 405
Tod v Barton [2002] EWHC 265 (Ch), 4 ITELR 715, [2002] All ER (D) 265 (Feb)
.... 13, 142, 146
Tod v Earl of Winchelsea (1826) 2 C & P 488, Mood & M 12
.... 71
Todd v Bielby (1859) 27 Beav 353 1093
Todd's Estate, Re [1926] P 173, 95 LJP 105, [1926] All ER Rep 657, 70 Sol Jo 671, 135
    LT 381, 42 TLR 545, P, D and Admlty 723
Todd's Trustees v Todd's Executrix 1922 SC 1, Ct of Sess
.... 325
Toldervy v Colt (1836) 1 Y & C Ex 621 417
Toleman, Re, Westwood v Booker [1897] 1 Ch 866, 66 LJ Ch 452, 45 WR 548, 76 LT 381
.... 812
Tollemache, Re, Forbes v Public Trustee [1930] WN 138, 169 LT Jo 519, 69 L Jo 423
.... 405, 1117
Tollemache's Estate, Re [1917] P 246, 86 LJP 154, 61 Sol Jo 696, 116 LT 762, 33 TLR
    505, P, D and Admlty 79
Tollner v Marriott (1830) 4 Sim 19, sub nom Tolner v Marriott 9 LJOS Ch 14
.... 147
Tom's Settlement, Re, Rose v Evans [1987] 1 All ER 1081, [1987] 1 WLR 1021, 131 Sol Jo
    916, [1987] LS Gaz R 2045 307–308
Tomalin v Smart [1904] P 141, 73 LJP 37, 90 LT 171, 20 TLR 197, P, D and Admlty
.... 874
Tomkins v Colthurst (1875) 1 Ch D 626, 24 WR 267, 33 LT 591
.... 1003
Tomkins v Tomkins (1743) 2 Hov Supp 456, 19 Ves 126n, cited in 1 Burr 234
.... 274, 471
Tomlin v Hatfeild (1841) 12 Sim 167 396
Tomline's Will Trusts, Re, Pretyman v Pretyman [1931] 1 Ch 521, 100 LJ Ch 156,
    [1931] All ER Rep 713, 144 LT 592, 47 TLR 274 296
Tomlinson, Re, Tomlinson v Andrew [1898] 1 Ch 232, 67 LJ Ch 97, 46 WR 299, 42 Sol Jo
    114, 78 LT 12 1228
Tompson v Browne (1835) 3 My & K 32, 5 LJ Ch 64 2
Tong, Re, Hilton v Bradbury [1931] 1 Ch 202, 100 LJ Ch 132, [1930] All ER Rep 262,
    144 LT 260, CA 994, 998–999
Tonge's Goods, Re (1891) 66 LT 60, P, D and Admlty 60, 83

PARA

Tongue v Pitcher. See Pitcher v Tovey
Toole, Re [1913] 2 IR 188 774
Toole v Hamilton [1901] 1 IR 383 156
Toomer v Sobinska [1907] P 106, 76 LJP 19, 96 LT 475, P, D and Admlty
.... 93, 707, 791
Toomy's Goods, Re (1864) 28 JP 824, 34 LJPM & A 3, 3 Sw & Tr 562, 13 WR 106
.... 613
Tootal v Spicer (1831) 4 Sim 510 1205
Toovey v Bassett (1809) 10 East 460 460
Toplis v Baker (1787) 2 Cox Eq Cas 118 163
Toronto General Trusts Co v Irwin (1896) 27 OLR 491
.... 181
Torre v Browne (1855) 5 HL Cas 555, 24 LJ Ch 757, 26 LTOS 129
.... 1084
Torre's Goods, Re (1862) 8 Jur NS 494 65
Torrington (Lord) v Bowman (1852) 22 LJ Ch 236, 20 LTOS 153
.... 288
Toscani's Estate, Re [1912] P 1, 81 LJP 15, 56 Sol Jo 93, 105 LT 911, 28 TLR 84, P, D
and Admlty 631
Tothill v Pitt (1766) 1 Madd 488; revsd (1770) 2 Dick 431; restored sub nom Chatham
(Earl) v Tothill (1771) 7 Bro Parl Cas 453, cited in 5 De GM & G at 206, HL
.... 385
Tottenham, Re, Tottenham v Tottenham [1896] 1 Ch 628, 65 LJ Ch 549, 44 WR 539, 74
LT 376 1173
Tourton v Flower (1735) 3 P Wms 369 669
Tower v Lord Rous (1811) 18 Ves 132 1012
Towers v Hogan (1889) 23 LR Ir 53 2
Towers v Moor (1689) 2 Vern 98 199
Townend, Re, Knowles v Jessop [1914] WN 145 1060
Townend v Townend (1859) 1 Giff 201, 5 Jur NS 506, 114 RR 405, 7 WR 529, 33 LTOS
143 .... 658, 1298
Townley, Re, Public Trustee v Allder [1922] 1 Ch 154, 91 LJ Ch 258, [1921] All ER Rep
586, 66 Sol Jo 157, 126 LT 591 997
Townley, Re, Townley v Townley (1884) 53 LJ Ch 516, 32 WR 549, 50 LT 394
.... 193, 293
Townley v Bolton (1832) 1 My & K 148, 2 LJ Ch 25 .... 395, 468, 470
Townley v Watson (1844) 3 Curt 761, 8 Jur 111, 2 LTOS 376, 3 Notes of Cases 17
.... 82, 735
Towns v Wentworth (1858) 11 Moo PCC 526, 6 WR 397, 31 LTOS 274
.... 253, 456, 466, 473
Townsend v Barber (1763) 1 Dick 356 1253
Townsend v Early (1860) 3 De GF & J 1 301
Townsend v Moore [1905] P 66, 74 LJP 17, 53 WR 338, 49 Sol Jo 146, 92 LT 335, CA
.... 8, 97, 99, 185, 713
Townsend v Townsend (1883) 23 Ch D 100, 31 WR 735, 48 LT 694, CA
.... 1178
Townsend's Estate, Re, Townsend v Townsend (1886) 34 Ch D 357, 56 LJ Ch 227, 35 WR
153, 55 LT 674, 3 TLR 204 .... 41, 182
Townshend v Mostyn (1858) 26 Beav 72 403
Townshend v Windham and Robinson (1706) 2 Vern 546
.... 366
Townson v Tickell (1819) 3 B & Ald 31, 22 RR 291, 106 ER 575, [1814–23] All ER Rep
164 .... 151–152, 1139
Towry's Settled Estate, Re, Dallas v Towry (1889) 41 Ch D 64, 58 LJ Ch 593, sub nom
Towry, Re, Dallas v Law 37 WR 417, 60 LT 715, CA 388
Tracy v Butcher (1857) 24 Beav 438 432
Trafford v Ashton (1710) 2 Vern 660, 1 Eq Cas Abr 213 pl 8
.... 333
Trafford v Berrige (1729) 1 Eq Cas Abr 201 250
Trafford v Boehm (1746) 3 Atk 440, 26 ER 1054, [1558–1774] All ER Rep 470
.... 460
Trail v Bull (1853) 22 LJ Ch 1082, 1 Eq Rep 9, 21 LTOS 146
.... 1142
Trash v Wood (1839) 4 My & Cr 324, 9 LJ Ch 105, 4 Jur 669
.... 391, 538, 561, 953
Travers, Re, Hurmson v Carr (1916) 86 LJ Ch 123, [1916–17] All ER Rep 904, 61 Sol Jo
56, 115 LT 604, 33 TLR 17 366

PARA

Travers v Blundell (1877) 6 Ch D 436, 36 LT 341, CA 269, 273
Travers v Townsend (1828) 1 Mod 496 1202
Treasury v Harris [1957] 2 QB 516, [1957] 2 All ER 455, [1957] 3 WLR 12, 41 Cr App
    Rep 146, 101 Sol Jo 465, DC 1218
Tredegar (Lord) v Roberts [1914] 1 KB 283, 83 LJKB 159, 58 Sol Jo 118, 109 LT 731, CA
    1273
Tredennick v Tredennick [1900] 1 IR 354 375
Tredgold, Re, Midland Bank Executor and Trustee Co Ltd v Tredgold [1943] Ch 69,
    [1943] 1 All ER 120, 112 LJ Ch 68, 87 Sol Jo 30, 168 LT 135, 59 TLR 99
    114
Tredwell, Re, Jeffray v Tredwell [1891] 2 Ch 640, 65 LT 399, [1891–4] All ER Rep Ext
    1984, sub nom Tredwell, Re, Jaffray v Tredwell 60 LJ Ch 657, CA
    .... 236–237, 445–446
Treeby's Goods, Re (1875) LR 3 P & D 242, 44 LJP & M 44, P, D and Admlty
    83–84
Tréfond's Goods, Re [1899] P 247, 68 LJP 82, 81 LT 56, P, D and Admlty
    789
Tregonwell v Sydenham (1815) 3 Dow 194, 15 RR 40, 3 ER 1035, [1814–23] All ER Rep
    321 184
Treharne v Layton (1875) LR 10 QB 459, 44 LJQB 202, 23 WR 799, 33 LT 327,
    [1874–80] All ER Rep Ext 2174, Ex Ch 441
Trelawney v Molesworth (1701) Colles 163, HL 305
Treloar v Lean (1889) 14 PD 49, 58 LJP 39, 37 WR 560, 60 LT 512, P, D and Admlty
    105
Tremeere v Morison (1834) 1 Bing NC 89, 3 LJCP 260, 4 Moo & S 603
    1225
Trestrail v Mason (1878) 7 Ch D 655, 47 LJ Ch 249, 26 WR 260
    1009
Trethewy v Helyar (1876) 4 Ch D 53, 46 LJ Ch 125 .... 165, 363
Trevanion's Goods, Re (1850) 2 Rob Eccl 311 75
Trevelyan v Trevelyan (1810) 1 Phillim 149 54
Treves v Townshend (1783) 1 Cox Eq Cas 50, 1 Bro CC 384
    1257
Trevor v Trevor (1847) 1 HL Cas 239, 73 RR 58 .... 241, 335, 389, 391
Tribe, Re, Tribe v Dean and Chapter of Truro Cathedral (1915) 85 LJ Ch 79, 59 Sol Jo
    509, 113 LT 313 293
Tribe v Tribe (1849) 1 Rob Eccl 775, 13 Jur 793, 13 LTOS 449, 7 Notes of Cases 132
    71
Trickey v Trickey (1832) 3 My & K 560 410
Trigg's Goods, Re [1901] P 42, 69 LJP 47, 44 Sol Jo 329, 82 LT 626, P, D and Admlty
    759
Trimble, Re, Wilson v Turton [1931] 1 Ch 369, 100 LJ Ch 73, 144 LT 612
    1130
Trimlestown (Lord) v Lady Trimlestown (1830) 3 Hag Ecc 243
    848
Trimmer, Re, Crundwell v Trimmer (1904) 91 LT 26 210
Trimmer v Bayne (1802) 7 Ves 508, 32 ER 205, [1775–1802] All ER Rep 515
    197
Trinder, Re, Sheppard v Prance (1911) 56 Sol Jo 74 1130
Trinder v Trinder (1866) LR 1 Eq 695, 14 WR 557 282
Tritton, Re, ex p Singleton (1889) 6 Morr 250, 61 LT 301, 5 TLR 687
    121
Trollope, Re, Game v Trollope [1915] 1 Ch 853, 84 LJ Ch 553, 113 LT 153
    404
Trollope's Will Trusts, Re, Public Trustee v Trollope [1927] 1 Ch 596, 96 LJ Ch 340,
    [1927] All ER Rep 365, 71 Sol Jo 310, 137 LT 375 .... 1019, 1021, 1123, 1149–1150
Trott, Re, Trott v Miles [1958] 2 All ER 296, [1958] 1 WLR 604, 102 Sol Jo 401
    597–598
Trott v Buchanan (1885) 28 Ch D 446, 54 LJ Ch 678, 33 WR 339, 52 LT 248
    1012
Trott v Skidmore (1860) 24 JP 423, 6 Jur NS 760, 2 Sw & Tr 12, 8 WR 590, 2 LT 519,
    sub nom Trott v Trott 29 LJPM & A 156 .... 65, 896
Trotter, Re, Trotter v Trotter [1899] 1 Ch 764, 68 LJ Ch 363, 47 WR 477, 80 LT 647, 15
    TLR 287 43
Trotter v Oswald (1787) 1 Cox Eq Cas 317 .... 306, 459
Trower v Butts (1823) 1 Sim & St 181, 1 LJOS Ch 115
    362

PARA

Trundle, Re, Emanuel v Trundle [1961] 1 All ER 103, [1960] 1 WLR 1388, 104 Sol Jo
  1094 293
Truro's (Lady) Goods, Re (1866) LR 1 P & D 201, 35 LJP & M 89, 14 WR 976, 14 LT
  893 711
Trustee Solutions Ltd v Dubery [2006] EWHC 1426 (Ch), [2007] 1 All ER 308, [2007]
  ICR 412, (2006) Times, 7 August, [2006] All ER (D) 233 (Jun); revsd [2007] EWCA
  Civ 771, [2008] 1 All ER 826, [2008] ICR 101, (2007) Times, 17 August, sub nom
  Cripps v Trustee Solutions Ltd [2008] 1 CMLR 1174, [2007] NLJR 1354,
  [2007] All ER (D) 416 (Jul) 205–206, 238, 246
Trustees of the Christian Brothers in Western Australia Inc v A-G of Western Australia
  [2007] WTLR 1375, [2006] WASC 191, 9 ITELR 212 11
Trustees, Executors and Agency Co Ltd v Scott (1898) 24 VLR 522
  156
Trustees, Executors and Agency Co Ltd v Sleeman (1899) 25 VLR 187
  307
Tuck's Settlement Trusts, Re, Public Trustee v Tuck [1978] Ch 49, [1978] 1 All ER 1047,
  [1978] 2 WLR 411, 121 Sol Jo 796, CA 131, 138, 140, 263
Tucker, Re, Bowchier v Gordon (1887) 56 LJ Ch 449, 35 WR 344, 56 LT 118
  306
Tucker, Re, Tucker v Tucker [1894] 3 Ch 429, 63 LJ Ch 737, 12 R 141, 71 LT 453, CA
  976
Tucker v Billing (1856) 2 Jur NS 483, 27 LTOS 132 339
Tucker v Boswell (1843) 5 Beav 607 1123
Tucker v Harris (1832) 5 Sim 538, 2 LJ Ch 18 260
Tucker v Kayess (1858) 4 K & J 339 184
Tucker's Goods, Re (1864) 34 LJPM & A 29, 3 Sw & Tr 585
  .... 722, 754
Tuckerman v Jefferies (1706) 11 Mod Rep 108, sub nom Turkerman v Jeoffrys Holt KB
  370 470
Tuckett's Will Trusts, Re, Williams v National Provincial Bank Ltd (1967) 111 Sol Jo 811
  .... 313, 343
Tuckey v Henderson (1863) 33 Beav 174, 9 Jur NS 1306, 11 WR 1013
  .... 232, 403
Tufnell v Borrell (1875) LR 20 Eq 194, 44 LJ Ch 756, 23 WR 717
  384
Tugwell v Scott (1857) 24 Beav 141, 3 Jur NS 633 352
Tuite v Bermingham (1875) LR 7 HL 634, 24 WR 540, HL
  333
Tulk v Houlditch (1813) 1 Ves & B 248 147
Tullock v Dunn, etc (Exors of Hanley) (1826) Ry & M 416
  976
Tully, Re, Toolan v Costello [1941] IR 66 328
Tunaley v Roch (1857) 3 Drew 720, 5 WR 515, 29 LTOS 192
  .... 228, 467
Tunno, Re, Raikes v Raikes (1890) 45 Ch D 66, 59 LJ Ch 573, 38 WR 636, 63 LT 23
  1088
Tunstall v Brachen (1753) Amb 167, 1 Bro CC 124n 438
Tupper v Tupper (1855) 1 K & J 665, 1 Jur NS 917, 3 WR 616, 26 LTOS 47
  107
Turke v Frencham (1559) 2 Dyer 171a, sub nom Buck v Frencham 1 And 8, sub nom Tuck
  v Frencham Ben 68, Moore KB 13 384
Turkington, Re, Owen v Benson [1937] 4 All ER 501, 81 Sol Jo 1041
  36
Turnbull, Re, Skipper v Wade [1905] 1 Ch 726, 74 LJ Ch 438, 53 WR 440, 49 Sol Jo 417
  .... 240, 1087, 1090, 1133
Turner, Re (1865) 2 Drew & Sm 501, 34 LJ Ch 660, 13 WR 770, 12 LT 695
  .... 321, 325, 364
Turner, Re, Barker v Ivimey [1897] 1 Ch 536, 66 LJ Ch 282, 45 WR 495, 41 Sol Jo 313,
  76 LT 116, 13 TLR 249 1259
Turner, Re, Carpenter v Staveley [1949] 2 All ER 935, 94 Sol Jo 114
  .... 255–256, 266
Turner, Re, Hudson v Turner [1932] 1 Ch 31, 101 LJ Ch 49, [1931] All ER Rep 783, 146
  LT 209 .... 161, 174
Turner, Re, Klaftenberger v Groombridge [1917] 1 Ch 422, 86 LJ Ch 290,
  [1916–17] All ER Rep 337, 61 Sol Jo 300, 116 LT 278 974
Turner, Re, Tennant v Turner [1938] Ch 593, [1938] 2 All ER 560, 107 LJ Ch 326, 82 Sol
  Jo 295, 159 LT 246, 54 TLR 697 1006

PARA

Turner, Re, Turner v Turner (1902) 4 OLR 578, 22 CLT 389
.... 20
Turner v A-G (1876) IR 10 Eq 386 29
Turner v Brittain (1863) 3 New Rep 21 .... 58, 346
Turner v Buck (1874) LR 18 Eq 301, 43 LJ Ch 583, 22 WR 748
.... 1081
Turner v Frampton (1846) 2 Coll 331, 10 Jur 24, 6 LTOS 314
.... 460, 1203
Turner v Gosset (1865) 34 Beav 593 453
Turner v Hancock (1882) 20 Ch D 303, 51 LJ Ch 517, 30 WR 480, 46 LT 750, CA
.... 910, 1196, 1202
Turner v Hardey (1842) 1 Dowl NS 954, 11 LJ Ex 277, 9 M & W 770
.... 1023
Turner v Hudson (1847) 10 Beav 222, 16 LJ Ch 180, 9 LTOS 215
.... 302, 396
Turner v Jacob [2006] EWHC 1317 (Ch), [2006] All ER (D) 39 (Jun)
.... 20
Turner v Martin (1857) 7 De GM & G 429, 26 LJ Ch 216, 3 Jur NS 397, 5 WR 277,
28 LTOS 349 163
Turner v Moor (1801) 6 Ves 557 .... 320, 449
Turner v Newport (1846) 2 Ph 14, 1 Coop temp Cott 147, 9 LTOS 213
.... 1127
Turner v Turner [1911] 1 Ch 716, 80 LJ Ch 473, [1911–13] All ER Rep 962, 104 LT 901,
CA 1067
Turner v Turner (1783) Amb 776, 1 Bro CC 316 385
Turner v Turner (1852) 21 LJ Ch 843, 20 LTOS 30 .... 291, 294
Turner v Turner (1880) 14 Ch D 829, 44 JP 734, 28 WR 859, 42 LT 495,
[1874–80] All ER Rep Ext 1448 28
Turner v Whittaker (1856) 23 Beav 196, 2 Jur NS 848, 4 WR 689, 27 LTOS 270
.... 395, 397
Turner's Estate, Re [2003] BCSC 1226, [2004] WTLR 1467, BC Sup Ct
.... 113
Turner's Goods, Re (1872) LR 2 P & D 403, 36 JP 808, 21 WR 38, 27 LT 322
.... 100, 106, 712
Turner's Goods, Re (1886) 12 PD 18, 56 LJP 41, 35 WR 384, 57 LT 372, P, D and Admlty
.... 770
Turner's Goods, Re (1891) 64 LT 805, P, D and Admlty
.... 112
Turner's Will Trusts, Re, Westminster Bank Ltd v Turner [1968] 1 All ER 321, [1968] 1
WLR 227, 111 Sol Jo 913 1117
Turney, Re, Turney v Turney [1899] 2 Ch 739, 69 LJ Ch 1, 48 WR 97, 81 LT 548, CA
.... 320, 432, 436, 447
Turnour's Goods, Re (1886) 50 JP 344, 56 LT 671, P, D and Admlty
.... 97
Turton, Re, Whittington v Turton [1926] Ch 96, 95 LJ Ch 136, [1925] All ER Rep 340,
134 LT 439 .... 130, 144
Tussaud's Estate, Re, Tussaud v Tussaud (1878) 9 Ch D 363, 47 LJ Ch 849, 26 WR 874,
39 LT 113, CA 197
Tuthill v Rogers (1844) 6 I Eq R 429, 1 Jo & Lat 36 556
Tuttesham v Roberts (1603) Cro Jac 22 473
Tweedale v Tweedale (1840) 10 Sim 453, 9 LJ Ch 147, 4 Jur 263
.... 403
Tweedale v Tweedale (1878) 7 Ch D 633, 47 LJ Ch 530, 26 WR 457, 38 LT 137
.... 135
Tweedale's Goods, Re (1874) LR 3 P & D 204, 39 JP 152, 44 LJP & M 35, 31 LT 799
.... 710
Twining v Powell (1845) 2 Coll 262, 5 LTOS 474 250
Twisden v Twisden (1804) 9 Ves 413 404
Twiss, Re, Barclays Bank Ltd v Pratt [1941] Ch 141, [1941] 1 All ER 93, 84 Sol Jo 719,
57 TLR 16 1093
Twist v Tye [1902] P 92, 71 LJP 47, 46 Sol Jo 177, 86 LT 259, 18 TLR 211,
[1900–3] All ER Rep Ext 1410, P, D and Admlty 908
Twohill's Goods, Re (1879) 3 LR Ir 21 .... 214, 611
Twycross v Grant (1878) 4 CPD 40, 48 LJQB 1, 27 WR 87, 39 LT 618, CA
.... 1277
Twyford v Trail (1834) 7 Sim 92, 58 ER 771, [1824–34] All ER Rep 717
.... 637

PARA

Tyler, Re, Tyler v Tyler [1891] 3 Ch 252, 60 LJ Ch 686, 40 WR 7, 65 LT 367, 7 TLR 654,
[1891–4] All ER Rep Ext 1996, CA 152
Tyler v Bell (1837) 2 My & Cr 89, Donnelly 190, 6 LJ Ch 169
.... 669
Tyler v Merchant Taylors' Co (1890) 15 PD 216, 60 LJP 86, 63 LT 779, P, D and Admlty
.... 83, 85
Tylor, Re, Barclays Bank Ltd v Norris (1968) 112 Sol Jo 486
.... 328
Tyndale v Wilkinson (1856) 23 Beav 74, 2 Jur NS 963, 4 WR 695
.... 396
Tyrone (Earl) v Marquis of Waterford (1860) 1 De GF & J 613, 29 LJ Ch 486, 6 Jur NS
567, 8 WR 454, 2 LT 397 .... 230, 285, 384–385, 389, 400
Tyrrell v Clark (1854) 2 Drew 86, 23 LJ Ch 283, 2 Eq Rep 333, 18 Jur 323, 2 WR 152,
22 LTOS 313 375
Tyrrell v Painton [1894] P 151, 6 R 540, 42 WR 343, [1891–4] All ER Rep 1120, 70 LT
453, CA 55, 903, 905, 911
Tyson v Kendall (1850) 19 LJQB 434, 14 Jur 1044 1290
Tyte v Willis (1733) Cas temp Talbot 1 387
Tytherleigh v Harbin (1835) 6 Sim 329, 5 LJ Ch 15 324

U

UCB Corporate Services Ltd v Kohli [2004] EWHC 1126 (Ch), [2004] 2 All ER (Comm)
422, [2004] All ER (D) 205 (May) 976–977
Uglow v Uglow [2004] EWCA Civ 987, [2004] All ER (D) 472 (Jul)
.... 20
Ullswater, Re, Barclays Bank Ltd v Lowther [1952] Ch 105, [1951] 2 All ER 989, [1951] 2
TLR 1024 .... 496, 1118
Ulrich v Litchfield (1742) 2 Atk 372 .... 207, 232
Ulrich v Treasury Solicitor [2005] EWHC 67 (Ch), [2005] 1 All ER 1059, [2006] 1 WLR
33, 7 ITELR 552, (2005) Times, 23 March, [2005] All ER (D) 288 (Jan)
.... 150
Umbers v Jaggard (1870) LR 9 Eq 200, 18 WR 283 246
Underhill v Roden (1876) 2 Ch D 494, 45 LJ Ch 266, 24 WR 574, 34 LT 227,
[1874–80] All ER Rep Ext 2149 .... 389, 391, 446
Underwood v Frost (1890) 15 App Cas 548, 60 LJPC 15, 63 LT 422, 6 TLR 443, PC
.... 317
Underwood v Jee (1849) 19 LJ Ch 171, 1 H & Tw 379, 1 Mac & G 276, 14 LTOS 123
.... 1177
Underwood v Morris (1741) 2 Atk 184 135
Underwood v Stevens (1816) 1 Mer 712 1253
Underwood v Swain (1649) 1 Rep Ch 161 149
Underwood v Wing (1855) 4 De GM & G 633, 24 LJ Ch 293, 3 Eq Rep 794, 1 Jur NS
169, 3 WR 228, 24 LTOS 304; on appeal sub nom Wing v Angrave (1860) 8 HL Cas
183, 30 LJ Ch 65 .... 33, 164, 445–446
Ungly v Peale (1712) 2 Eq Cas Abr 358, sub nom Ongley v Peale 2 Ld Raym 1312, 10
Mod Rep 103 400
United Collieries Ltd v Simpson [1909] AC 383, 78 LJPC 129, 2 BWCC 308, 53 Sol Jo
630, 101 LT 129, 25 TLR 678, HL 1279
United Kingdom Electric Telegraph Co Ltd, Re (1881) 29 WR 332
.... 1176
University College of North Wales v Taylor [1908] P 140, 77 LJP 20, 52 Sol Jo 44, 98 LT
472, 24 TLR 29, CA 711
Uppington v Bullen (1842) 2 Dr & War 184 28
Upton, Re, Barclays Bank Ltd v Upton (1965) 109 Sol Jo 236, CA
.... 396, 399
Upton v Hardman (1874) IR 9 Eq 157 454
Upton v Lord Ferrers (1801) 5 Ves 801 466
Upton v National Westminster Bank plc [2004] EWHC 1962 (Ch), [2004] WTLR 1339
.... 331, 350, 482
Upwell v Halsey (1720) 10 Mod Rep 441, 1 P Wms 651
.... 382
Urquhart v Butterfield (1887) 37 Ch D 357, 57 LJ Ch 521, 36 WR 376, 385n, 57 LT 780,
4 TLR 161, CA 32
Usborne's Goods, Re (1909) 25 TLR 519, P, D and Admlty
.... 60, 65

PARA

Ussher, Re, Foster and Ussher [1922] 2 Ch 321, 91 LJ Ch 521, 127 LT 453
.... 431–432, 445
Usticke, Re (1866) 35 Beav 338, 14 WR 447 316
Usticke v Bawden (1824) 2 Add 116 110
Uttermare, Re, Leeson v Foulis [1893] WN 158 291
Utterson v Mair (1793) 2 Ves 95, 4 Bro CC 270 624

V

Vachell v Jefferys (1701) Prec Ch 170; revsd sub nom Vachell v Breton (1706) 2 Eq Cas
   Abr 437, 5 Bro Parl Cas 51, HL 479
Vacher & Sons Ltd v London Society of Compositors [1913] AC 107, 82 LJKB 232,
   [1911–13] All ER Rep 241, 57 Sol Jo 75, 107 LT 722, 29 TLR 73, HL
   242
Vaisey v Reynolds (1828) 5 Russ 12, 6 LJOS Ch 172 .... 293–294, 930
Valdez's Trusts, Re (1888) 40 Ch D 159, 58 LJ Ch 861, 37 WR 162, 60 LT 42
   .... 363, 449
Valentine, Re, Kennedy v Birchall [1940] Ch 424, [1940] 1 All ER 545, 109 LJ Ch 129,
   162 LT 261, CA 247
Valentine's Settlement, Re, Valentine v Valentine [1965] Ch 831, [1965] 2 All ER 226,
   [1965] 2 WLR 1015, 109 Sol Jo 237, CA 483
Valpy, Re, Valpy v Valpy [1906] 1 Ch 531, 75 LJ Ch 301, 54 WR 401, 50 Sol Jo 272, 94
   LT 472 1008
Van v Clarke (1739) 1 Atk 510, West temp Hard 699 439
Van Custem's Goods, Re (1890) 63 LT 252, P, D and Admlty
   111
Van Den Bok Will Trusts (1960) unreported, referred to in Riley's Will Trusts, Re, Riley v
   Riley 468
Van Grutten v Foxwell [1897] AC 658, 66 LJQB 745, 46 WR 426, 77 LT 170, HL
   .... 241, 243, 339, 384, 474
Van Hoorn v Van Hoorn (1978) 123 Sol Jo 65 758
Van Lessen, Re, National Provincial Bank Ltd v Beamont [1955] 3 All ER 691, [1955] 1
   WLR 1326, 99 Sol Jo 912 .... 205, 284
Van Oppen, Re, Roberts v Gray [1935] WN 51, 179 LT Jo 255
   1171
Van Straubenzee, Re, Boustead v Cooper [1901] 2 Ch 779, 70 LJ Ch 825, 45 Sol Jo 738,
   85 LT 541, 17 TLR 755 1122
Van Tassel v Frederick (1896) 27 OR 646 460
Vandeleur v Sloane [1919] 1 IR 116 152
Vander Byl, Re, Fladgate v Gore [1931] 1 Ch 216, 100 LJ Ch 108, [1930] All ER Rep 696,
   74 Sol Jo 770, 144 LT 401 344
Vandergucht v Blake (1795) 2 Ves 534 456
Vanderplank v King (1843) 3 Hare 1, 12 LJ Ch 497, 7 Jur 548
   .... 395, 474
Vane (Earl) v Rigden (1870) 5 Ch App 663, 39 LJ Ch 797, 18 WR 1092
   .... 1023, 1028–1029
Vanneck v Benham [1917] 1 Ch 60, 86 LJ Ch 7, [1916–17] All ER Rep 741, 115 LT 588
   .... 922, 1053
Vannini's Goods, Re [1901] P 330, 71 LJP 7, 85 LT 639, P, D and Admlty
   789
Vanrenen v Piffard (1865) 5 New Rep 399, 13 WR 425, 11 LT 766
   1177
Vardy v Smith (otherwise Vardy) (1932) 48 TLR 661, P, D and Admlty; affd (1932) 148 LT
   124, 49 TLR 36, CA 670, 679
Varley, Re, Thornton v Varley (1893) 62 LJ Ch 652, 68 LT 665
   379
Varley v Winn (1856) 2 K & J 700, 25 LJ Ch 831, 2 Jur NS 661, 4 WR 792, 28 LTOS 80
   .... 243, 411, 1082
Vauchamp v Bell (1822) 6 Madd 343 .... 242, 255
Vaudrey v Howard (1853) 2 WR 32 173
Vaughan, Re, Scott v British and Foreign School Society (1901) 17 TLR 278
   212
Vaughan v Booth (1852) 16 Jur 808 366
Vaughan v Burslem (1790) 3 Bro CC 101 386
Vaughan v Marquis of Headfort (1840) 10 Sim 639, 9 LJ Ch 271, 4 Jur 649
   390

PARA

Vautier's Estate, Re 2000 JLR 251, (2000) 3 ITELR 566, Royal Ct Jer
.... 187

Vaux, Re, Nicholson v Vaux [1939] Ch 465, [1938] 4 All ER 297, 703, 108 LJ Ch 60,
211, 82 Sol Jo 949, 1048, 160 LT 65, 74, 55 TLR 92, 230, CA
.... 155

Vaux v Henderson (1806) 1 Jac & W 388 341

Vavasseur v Vavasseur (1909) 25 TLR 250 626

Vawdry v Geddes (1830) Taml 361, 8 LJOS Ch 63, 1 Russ & M 203
.... 430, 432, 436

Veale's Trusts, Re (1876) 4 Ch D 61; on appeal (1877) 5 Ch D 622, 46 LJ Ch 799, 36 LT
346, CA 237

Vear, Re, Vear v Vear (1917) 62 Sol Jo 159 .... 212–213, 215, 270, 293

Veiga's Goods, Re (1862) 27 JP 41, 32 LJPM & A 9, 3 Sw & Tr 13, 11 WR 84, 7 LT 644,
sub nom Re Vega's Goods 1 New Rep 34 628

Veizy v Pinwell (1641) Poll 44 27

Velho v Leite (1864) 33 LJPM & A 107, 3 Sw & Tr 456
.... 616

Vencatanarayana Pillay v Subammal (1915) 32 TLR 118, PC
.... 107

Venn, Re, Lindon v Ingram [1904] 2 Ch 52, 73 LJ Ch 507, 52 WR 603, 90 LT 502
.... 175, 193, 252

Venn and Furze's Contract, Re [1894] 2 Ch 101, 63 LJ Ch 303, 8 R 220, 42 WR 440, 38
Sol Jo 273, 70 LT 312 1025

Vere-Wardale, Re, Vere-Wardale v Johnson [1949] P 395, [1949] 2 All ER 250, [1949] LJR
1494, 93 Sol Jo 553, 65 TLR 493, P, D and Admlty 894

Vernon, Re, Garland v Shaw (1906) 95 LT 48 182

Vernon v Curtis. See Curtis v Vernon

Vernon v Wright (1858) 7 HL Cas 35, 28 LJ Ch 198, 4 Jur NS 1113, 32 LTOS 11
.... 376, 384

Vernon's Case, Re (1572) 4 Co Rep 1a, 76 ER 845 207

Vernon's Estate, Re (1916) 33 TLR 11, P, D and Admlty
.... 81

Vernon's Will Trusts, Re, Lloyds Bank Ltd v Group 20, Hospital Management Committee
(Coventry) [1972] Ch 300n, [1971] 3 All ER 1061n, [1971] 3 WLR 796n
.... 35

Verrell's Contract, Re [1903] 1 Ch 65, 72 LJ Ch 44, 51 WR 73, 47 Sol Jo 71, 87 LT 521
.... 1028

Vertannes v Robinson (1827) LR 54 Ind App 276, PC 288

Verulam (Earl) v Bathurst (1843) 13 Sim 374, 12 LJ Ch 359, 7 Jur 295
.... 385

Vestey v IRC (No 2) [1980] AC 1148, [1979] 3 All ER 976, [1979] 3 WLR 915, [1980]
STC 10, 54 TC 503, [1979] TR 381, 123 Sol Jo 826, HL
.... 2

Vezey v Jamson (1822) 1 Sim & St 69 11

Vick v Edwards (1735) 2 Eq Cas Abr 473, 3 P Wms 372
.... 394

Vickers, Re, Vickers v Mellor (1899) 44 Sol Jo 90, 81 LT 719
.... 156

Vickers v Bell (1864) 4 De GJ & Sm 274, 10 Jur NS 376, 3 New Rep 624, 12 WR 589, 10
LT 77 .... 627, 636, 1172

Vickers v Pound (1858) 6 HL Cas 885, 28 LJ Ch 16, 4 Jur NS 543, 6 WR 580, 31 LTOS
372 .... 237, 244

Vickers' Estate, Re 2001 JLR 7812, (2001) 4 ITELR 584, Royal Ct Jer
.... 95

Vickers Will, Re [1912] VLR 385 471

Vickerstaff, Re, Vickerstaff v Chadwick [1906] 1 Ch 762, 75 LJ Ch 419, 54 WR 414, 50
Sol Jo 360, 94 LT 463 914

Viertel, Re [1996] QSC 66, [2003] WTLR 1075, Qld SC
.... 156–157

Villar, Re, Public Trustee v Villar [1929] 1 Ch 243, 98 LJ Ch 223, [1928] All ER Rep 535,
72 Sol Jo 761, 140 LT 90, 45 TLR 13, CA 266

Villar v Sir Walter Gilbey [1907] AC 139, 76 LJ Ch 339, [1904–7] All ER Rep 779, 51 Sol
Jo 341, 96 LT 511, 23 TLR 392, HL 204, 241, 362

Vincent, Re, Public Trustee v Vincent [1926] WN 307, 70 Sol Jo 1220, 162 LT Jo 451, 62
L Jo 422 328

PARA

Vincent, Re, Rohde v Palin [1909] 1 Ch 810, 78 LJ Ch 455, 100 LT 957
.... 1017, 1060
Vincent v Vincent (1887) 56 LT 243, CA 21
Vine v Joyce (1963) Times, 24 October 23
Viner v Francis (1789) 2 Cox Eq Cas 190, 2 Bro CC 658
.... 174–175, 302, 305, 309
Vines' Estate, Re, Vines v Vines [1910] P 147, 79 LJP 25, 54 Sol Jo 272, 102 LT 141, 26
TLR 257, P, D and Admlty 8
Vinnicombe v Butler (1864) 29 JP 56, 34 LJPM & A 18, 10 Jur NS 1109, 3 Sw & Tr 580,
13 WR 392 895
Violett v Brookman (1857) 26 LJ Ch 308, 5 WR 342, 29 LTOS 104
.... 115, 144, 190
Vipont v Butler [1893] WN 64 653
Virtue v Miller (1871) 19 WR 406 1177
Viscountess Falkland v Lytton. See Strode (Sir Litton) v Lady Russel and Lady Falkland
Vivian, Re, Vivian v Swansea (1920) 36 TLR 222; affd (1920) 36 TLR 657, CA
.... 139
Vivian v Mills (1839) 1 Beav 315, 8 LJ Ch 239 .... 428, 447
Vize v Stoney (1841) 1 Dr & War 337 .... 428, 430, 475
Voller v Carter (1854) 4 E & B 173, 24 LJQB 56, 1 Jur NS 278, 3 WR 22, 24 LTOS 93
.... 384
Von Brentano's Estate, Re [1911] P 172, 105 LT 78, 27 TLR 395, sub nom Re
Brentano's Goods 80 LJP 80, P, D and Admlty 722
Von Brockdorff v Malcolm (1885) 30 Ch D 172, 55 LJ Ch 121, 33 WR 934,
[1881–5] All ER Rep 1068, 53 LT 263 259
Von Faber's Goods, Re (1904) 20 TLR 640, P, D and Admlty
.... 721
Von Linden's Goods, Re [1896] P 148, 65 LJP 87, 44 WR 448, P, D and Admlty
.... 720–721
Vorley v Richardson (1856) 8 De GM & G 126, 25 LJ Ch 335, 2 Jur NS 362, 4 WR 397,
27 LTOS 22 318
Vos, Re, Dick v Kendall Freeman [2006] BPIR 348, [2005] WTLR 1619
.... 981–982
Vowles, Re, O'Donoghue v Vowles (1886) 32 Ch D 243, 55 LJ Ch 661, 34 WR 639, 54 LT
846 1201
Vrint, Re, Vrint v Swain [1940] Ch 920, [1940] 3 All ER 470, 109 LJ Ch 431, 84 Sol Jo
501, 163 LT 306, 56 TLR 953 .... 574, 602
Vulliamy v Huskisson (1838) 3 Y & C Ex 80, 2 Jur 656
.... 444
Vulliamy v Noble (1817) 3 Mer 593, 36 ER 228, [1814–23] All ER Rep 597
.... 1232
Vynior's Case (1609) 8 Co Rep 81b 2, 92
Vyse v Foster (1872) 8 Ch App 309, 42 LJ Ch 245, 21 WR 207, 27 LT 774,
[1874–80] All ER Rep Ext 2037; affd (1874) LR 7 HL 318, 44 LJ Ch 37, 23 WR 355,
31 LT 177 .... 658, 1030

W

W, Re (1975) 119 Sol Jo 439, (1975) Times, 22 April 576
W (a minor) (claim from deceased's estate), Re [1995] 2 FCR 689, sub nom C (leave to
apply for provision), Re [1995] 2 FLR 24, [1995] Fam Law 479
.... 580, 597–598
W— v B— (1849) 11 Beav 621 128
Wadley v North (1797) 3 Ves 364 428
Wagstaff, Re, Wagstaff v Jalland [1908] 1 Ch 162, 77 LJ Ch 190, 98 LT 149, 24 TLR 136,
[1904–7] All ER Rep Ext 1093, CA 346–347
Wagstaff v Crosby (1846) 2 Coll 746 444
Wagstaff v Wagstaff (1869) LR 8 Eq 229, 38 LJ Ch 528
.... 282
Wainewright v Wainewright (1797) 3 Ves 558 471
Wainford v Heyl (1875) LR 20 Eq 321, 39 JP 709, 23 WR 848, 33 LT 155, sub nom
Waynford v Heyl 44 LJ Ch 567, 23 WR 849 370
Wainman v Field (1854) Kay 507 185
Wainwright v Miller [1897] 2 Ch 255, 66 LJ Ch 616, 45 WR 652, [1895–9] All ER Rep
457, 41 Sol Jo 561, 76 LT 718 131
Wainwright v Wilson [2006] All ER (D) 180 (Nov) 49

PARA

Waite, Re, Barron v Woodhead [2008] EWHC 810 (Ch), [2009] 2 FCR 631, [2009] 1 FLR
747, [2008] Fam Law 844 576–577
Waite v Combes (1852) 5 De G & Sm 676, 21 LJ Ch 814, 17 Jur 155, 20 LTOS 40
.... 293
Waite v Littlewood (1872) 8 Ch App 70, 42 LJ Ch 216, 21 WR 131, 28 LT 123
.... 237, 316–317
Waite v Morland (1866) 12 Jur NS 763, 14 WR 746, 14 LT 649
.... 125
Wake v Varah (1876) 2 Ch D 348, 45 LJ Ch 533, 24 WR 621, 34 LT 437, CA
.... 235, 315, 317
Wakefield, Re, Gordon v Wakefield [1943] 2 All ER 29, 87 Sol Jo 371, CA
.... 1008
Wakefield v Dyott (1858) 4 Jur NS 1098, 7 WR 31, 32 LTOS 121
.... 412
Wakefield v Maffet (1885) 10 App Cas 422, 55 LJ Ch 4, 53 LT 169, HL
.... 452
Wakeham v Mackenzie [1968] 2 All ER 783, [1968] 1 WLR 1175, 19 P & CR 565, 112
Sol Jo 504 21
Wakeham's Goods, Re (1872) LR 2 P & D 395, 36 JP 807, 41 LJP & M 46, 20 WR 685,
27 LT 214 616
Wakley, Re, Wakley v Vachell [1920] 2 Ch 205, 89 LJ Ch 321, [1920] All ER Rep 749, 64
Sol Jo 357, 123 LT 150, 36 TLR 325, CA 295
Walbran, Re, Milner v Walbran [1906] 1 Ch 64, 75 LJ Ch 105, 54 WR 167,
[1904–7] All ER Rep 360, 93 LT 745 332
Walcot v Botfield (1854) Kay 534, 2 Eq Rep 758, 18 Jur 570, 2 WR 393, 23 LTOS 127
.... 139
Walcott v Hall (1788) 2 Bro CC 305, 29 ER 167, [1775–1802] All ER Rep 168
.... 431, 1099
Waldron v Boulter (1856) 22 Beav 284 .... 334, 337, 385, 397
Walford v Walford [1912] AC 658, 81 LJ Ch 828, [1911–13] All ER Rep 950, 56 Sol Jo
631, 107 LT 657, HL 120, 228, 237, 1080
Walker, Re (1871) 7 Ch App 120, 41 LJ Ch 219, 20 WR 171, 25 LT 775
.... 33
Walker, Re, Dunkerly v Hewerdine [1917] 1 Ch 38, 86 LJ Ch 196, 115 LT 708
.... 303, 305
Walker, Re, Goodwin v Scott [1921] 2 Ch 63, 90 LJ Ch 433, [1921] All ER Rep 163, 65
Sol Jo 534, 125 LT 764 155
Walker, Re, Public Trustee v Walker [1939] Ch 974, [1939] 3 All ER 902, 109 LJ Ch 1, 83
Sol Jo 731, 161 LT 223, 55 TLR 1092 462
Walker, Re, Walker v Lutyens [1897] 2 Ch 238, 66 LJ Ch 622, 45 WR 647, 41 Sol Jo 622,
77 LT 94, 13 TLR 499 352
Walker, Re, Walker v Patterson [1934] WN 104, 177 LT Jo 325
.... 927
Walker, Re, Walker v Walker [1930] 1 Ch 469, 90 LJ Ch 225, [1930] All ER Rep 392, 74
Sol Jo 106, 142 LT 472, CA 247, 307
Walker v Badmin [2014] EWHC 71 (Ch), [2014] All ER (D) 258 (Nov)
.... 899
Walker v Claridge (1968) 207 Estates Gazette 341 21
Walker v Cusin [1917] 1 IR 63 .... 342, 344
Walker v Denne (1793) 2 Ves 170, 30 ER 577, [1775–1802] All ER Rep 245
.... 555–556
Walker v Geo H Medlicott & Son [1999] 1 All ER 685, [1999] 1 WLR 727, 1 ITELR 413,
[1999] 1 FLR 1095, [1999] Fam Law 214, [1999] 01 LS Gaz R 24, [1998] All ER (D)
615, CA 187
Walker v Jackson (1743) 2 Atk 624, Bunb 302n, 1 Wils 24
.... 1012
Walker v M'Kay [1917] 1 IR 278, CA 1012
Walker v Main (1819) 1 Jac & W 1 .... 411, 429, 452
Walker v Marquis of Camden (1848) 16 Sim 329, 17 LJ Ch 448, 12 Jur 932
.... 364, 394
Walker v Mower (1852) 16 Beav 365 .... 407, 416, 437, 447
Walker v Petchell (1845) 1 CB 652, 14 LJCP 211, 5 LTOS 126
.... 456
Walker v Shore (1808) 15 Ves 122 305–306
Walker v Shore (1815) 19 Ves 387 375
Walker v Simpson (1855) 1 K & J 713, 1 Jur NS 637 447

                                                                                                    PARA
Walker v Symonds (1818) 19 RR 155, 3 Swan 1, 36 ER 751, [1814–23] All ER Rep 71
.... 963, 1250
Walker v Taylor (1861) 8 Jur NS 681, 4 LT 845, HL 1028
Walker v Walker (1860) 2 De GF & J 255, 29 LJ Ch 856
.... 143–144
Walker v Walker [2007] EWHC 597 (Ch), [2007] All ER (D) 418 (Mar)
.... 1183
Walker v Woodward (1826) 1 Russ 107 658
Walker's Estate, Re [1909] P 115, 78 LJP 50, 25 TLR 278, P, D and Admlty
.... 744
Walker's Estate, Re, Watson v Treasury Solicitor (1912) 28 TLR 466, P, D and Admlty
.... 900
Walker's Goods, Re (1862) 26 JP 168, 31 LJPM & A 62, 8 Jur NS 314, 2 Sw & Tr 354, 5
    LT 766, [1861–73] All ER Rep Ext 2342 .... 62, 65
Wall v Tomlinson (1810) 16 Ves 413 461
Wall v Wall (1847) 15 Sim 513, 16 LJ Ch 305, 11 Jur 403
.... 1081
Wallace, Re, Champion v Wallace [1920] 2 Ch 274, 89 LJ Ch 450, 64 Sol Jo 478, 123 LT
    343, 36 TLR 481, CA 34, 131
Wallace v Seymour (1872) 20 WR 634, IR 6 CL 219 251
Wallace v Wallace (1898) 24 VLR 859 190
Wallace's Estate, Re, Solicitor of Duchy of Cornwall v Batten [1952] 2 TLR 925
.... 50
Wallas Estate, Re [1905] P 326, 75 LJP 8, 54 WR 172, 94 LT 102, P, D and Admlty
.... 770
Waller, Re, Margarison v Waller [1916] 1 Ch 153, 85 LJ Ch 188, 114 LT 42
.... 1133
Waller, Re, White v Scoles (1899) 68 LJ Ch 526, 47 WR 563, 43 Sol Jo 569, 80 LT 701,
    CA 199, 212, 270
Waller v Barrett (1857) 24 Beav 413, 27 LJ Ch 214, 4 Jur NS 128, 30 LTOS 216
.... 991
Wallersteiner v Moir [1974] 3 All ER 217, [1974] 1 WLR 991, 118 Sol Jo 464, CA
.... 912
Wallett, Re, Hayter v Wells (1883) 32 WR 26 1196
Walley, Re, National Westminster Bank Ltd v Williams [1972] 1 All ER 222, [1972] 1
    WLR 257, 51 ATC 247, [1972] TR 213, 116 Sol Jo 146
.... 1130–1131
Wallis v Crimes (1667) 1 Cas in Ch 89 149
Wallis v Hodgeson (1740) 2 Atk 56 899
Wallis v Hodson (1740) 2 Atk 114, Barn Ch 272 .... 362, 499
Wallis v Taylor (1836) 8 Sim 241, Donnelly 162, 6 LJ Ch 68
.... 363
Wallop v Darby (1612) Yelv 209 387
Walmsley v Foxhall (1863) 1 De GJ & Sm 451, 32 LJ Ch 672, 2 New Rep 252, 11 WR
    792, 8 LT 559 320
Walmsley v Foxhall (1863) 1 De GJ & Sm 605 393
Walmsley's Settled Estates, Re (1911) 55 Sol Jo 600, 105 LT 332
.... 312
Walpole, Re, Public Trustee v Canterbury [1933] Ch 431, 102 LJ Ch 209, [1933] All ER
    Rep 988, 148 LT 526 478
Walpole v Laslett (1862) 1 New Rep 180, 7 LT 526 446
Walpole (Lord) v Earl of Cholmondeley (1797) 7 Term Rep 138
.... 1–2
Walrond v Walrond (1861) 29 Beav 586 658
Walsh, Re, Keenan v Brown (1911) 30 NZLR 1166 201
Walsh, Re, Public Trustee v Walsh [1936] 1 All ER 327, 80 Sol Jo 264, CA
.... 344, 535
Walsh, Re, Walsh v Walsh [1953] Ch 473, [1953] 1 All ER 982, [1953] 2 WLR 686, 97
    Sol Jo 228 296
Walsh v Johnston [1899] 1 IR 501 334
Walsh's Goods, Re [1892] P 230, sub nom Re Wash's Goods 61 LJP 123, 67 LT 355, P, D
    and Admlty 759
Walsham v Stainton (1863) 1 De GJ & Sm 678, 33 LJ Ch 68, 9 Jur NS 1261, 3 New Rep
    56, 12 WR 63, 9 LT 357 1238
Walter, Re, Turner v Walter (No 2) (1912) 56 Sol Jo 632, CA
.... 171
Walter v Drew (1723) 1 Com 373 459–460

                                                                                              PARA
Walter v Makin (1833) 6 Sim 148, 2 LJ Ch 173 364
Walter v Maunde (1815) 19 Ves 424 .... 349, 1052
Walter's Will Trusts, Re, National Provincial Bank Ltd v Board of Guardians and Trustees
     for Relief of Jewish Poor, Registered (1962) 106 Sol Jo 221
     .... 45, 138, 140
Walter's Will's Trusts, Re, Stuart v Pitman [1949] Ch 91, [1948] 2 All ER 955, [1949] LJR
     225, 92 Sol Jo 674 410
Walters v Pfeil (1829) Mood & M 362 673
Walters v Smee [2008] EWHC 2902 (Ch), [2008] All ER (D) 30 (Dec)
     911
Walton's Estate, Re (1856) 8 De GM & G 173, 25 LJ Ch 569, 2 Jur NS 363, 4 WR 416,
     27 LTOS 22 .... 190, 248, 342
Wand, Re, Escritt v Wand [1907] 1 Ch 391, 76 LJ Ch 253, 96 LT 424
     .... 173, 298
Wankford v Wankford (1704) 3 Salk 162, 1 Salk 299, Holt KB 311, sub nom Wangford v
     Wangford Freem KB 520, 11 Mod Rep 38 .... 625, 634–635, 643, 725, 793, 945
Wansborough, Re, Wansborough v Dyer (1815) 2 Chit 40
     1299
Warbrick v Varley (1861) 30 Beav 241 1131
Warbrick v Varley (No 2) (1861) 30 Beav 347 190
Warburton v Loveland d Ivie (1828) 1 Hud & B 623, Ex Ch; affd (1832) 2 Dow & Cl
     480, 6 Bli NS 1, HL 242
Ward, Re, Bemment v Balls (1878) 47 LJ Ch 781 1173
Ward, Re, National Westminster Bank Ltd v Ward [1971] 2 All ER 1249, [1971] 1 WLR
     1376, 115 Sol Jo 529 .... 670, 848
Ward, Re, Partridge v Hoare-Ward [1920] 1 Ch 334, 89 LJ Ch 181, 64 Sol Jo 115, 122 LT
     336 395
Ward, Re, Ward v Ward [1965] Ch 856, [1964] 3 WLR 957, 108 Sol Jo 801, sub nom
     Ward's Will Trusts, Re, Ward v Ward [1964] 3 All ER 442
     310
Ward v Biddles. See Biddles v Biddles
Ward v Brown [1916] 2 AC 121, 85 LJPC 183, 113 LT 929, 31 TLR 545, PC
     .... 413, 444
Ward v Butler (1824) 2 Mol 533 629
Ward v Grey (1859) 26 Beav 485, 29 LJ Ch 74, 5 Jur NS 948, 7 WR 569, 34 LTOS 50
     .... 284, 390
Ward v Van der Loeff [1924] AC 653, 93 LJ Ch 397, [1924] All ER Rep 542, 69 Sol Jo
     517, 131 LT 292, 40 TLR 493, HL 107–108, 328
Ward v Ward [1921] 1 IR 117 389
Ward's Trusts, Re (1872) 7 Ch App 727, 42 LJ Ch 4, 20 WR 1024, 27 LT 668
     371
Warde, Re, Warde v Ridgway (1914) 58 Sol Jo 472, 111 LT 35
     404
Warden, Re Midland Bank Executor and Trustee Co Ltd v Warden (1962) Times,
     12 December 352
Wardrop's Estate, Re [1917] P 54, 86 LJP 37, 61 Sol Jo 171, 115 LT 720, 33 TLR 133, P,
     D and Admlty 81, 87
Wardroper v Cutfield (1864) 33 LJ Ch 605, 10 Jur NS 194, 12 WR 458, 10 LT 19
     446
Ware, Re, Cumberlege v Cumberlege-Ware (1890) 45 Ch D 269, 59 LJ Ch 717, 38 WR
     767, 63 LT 52, 6 TLR 388 364
Ware v Cann (1830) 10 B & C 433, 8 LJOSKB 164, 5 Man & Ry KB 341, 34 RR 469
     142
Ware v Rowland (1848) 2 Ph 635, 17 LJ Ch 147, 12 Jur 165, 11 LTOS 305
     313
Ware v Watson (1855) 7 De GM & G 248, 3 WR 496 .... 242, 320, 410
Wareham, Re, Wareham v Brewin [1912] 2 Ch 312, 81 LJ Ch 578, 56 Sol Jo 613, 107 LT
     80, CA 1123, 1126
Waring v Currey (1873) 22 WR 150 237
Waring v Dewberry (1718) Fortes Rep 360, 1 Stra 97 645
Waring v Waring (1848) 6 Moo PCC 341, 12 Jur 947, 6 Notes of Cases 388
     .... 52, 899
Warner, Re, Watts v Silvey [1918] 1 Ch 368, 87 LJ Ch 234, 62 Sol Jo 159, 118 LT 353, 34
     TLR 130 .... 306, 446

PARA

Warner v Sampson [1958] 1 QB 404, [1958] 1 All ER 44, [1958] 2 WLR 212, 102 Sol Jo
  107, 170 Estates Gazette 740; revsd [1959] 1 QB 297, [1959] 1 All ER 120, [1959] 2
  WLR 109, 103 Sol Jo 91, 173 Estates Gazette 43, CA 926
Warner v Warner (1850) 20 LJ Ch 273, 15 Jur 141, 16 LTOS 320
  .... 350, 352–353
Warner v White. See White d White v Warner
Warner Engineering Co Ltd v Brennan (1913) 30 TLR 191, DC
  1230
Warren, Re, Warren v Warren [1932] 1 Ch 42, 101 LJ Ch 85, [1931] All ER Rep 702, 146
  LT 224 .... 115, 156
Warren, Re, Weedon v Reading (1884) 53 LJ Ch 1016, 32 WR 916, 51 LT 561
  1043
Warren v Kelson (1859) 28 LJP & M 122, 5 Jur NS 415, 1 Sw & Tr 290, 7 WR 348,
  33 LTOS 12 .... 679, 848
Warren v Newton (1844) Drury temp Sugd 464 298
Warren v Rudall, ex p Godfrey (1860) 1 John & H 1, 29 LJ Ch 543, 6 Jur NS 395, 8 WR
  331, 2 LT 693 153
Warren v Rudall (1858) 4 K & J 603; varied sub nom Hall v Warren (1861) 9 HL Cas
  420, 7 Jur NS 1089, 10 WR 66, 5 LT 190, [1861–73] All ER Rep Ext 2372
  .... 226, 257, 445
Warren's Trusts, Re (1884) 26 Ch D 208, 53 LJ Ch 787, 32 WR 641, 50 LT 454
  .... 226, 249, 334
Warter v Hutchinson (1823) 1 B & C 721, 3 Dow & Ry KB 58
  419
Warter v Warter (1820) 2 Brod & Bing 349, sub nom Warter v Hutchinson 5 Moore CP
  143 419
Warter v Warter (1890) 15 PD 152, 54 JP 631, 59 LJP 87, 63 LT 250, 6 TLR 391,
  [1886–90] All ER Rep Ext 1223, P, D and Admlty 87
Warter v Warter (1890) 15 PD 35, 59 LJP 45, 62 LT 328, P, D and Admlty
  .... 679, 777
Wartnaby's Goods, Re (1846) 1 Rob Eccl 423, 4 Notes of Cases 476
  739
Warwick v Greville (1809) 1 Phillim 123 .... 773, 926
Warwick v Hawkins (1852) 5 De G & Sm 481, 21 LJ Ch 796, 16 Jur 902, 19 LTOS 243
  409
Warwick v Warwick (1918) 34 TLR 475, CA 54, 708
Wass, Re, Re Clarke (1906) 95 LT 758 288
Wassell, Re, Wassell v Leggatt [1896] 1 Ch 554, 65 LJ Ch 240, 44 WR 298, 40 Sol Jo 276,
  74 LT 99, 12 TLR 208 1238
Waterer v Waterer (1873) LR 15 Eq 402, 21 WR 508 919
Waterman's Will Trusts, Re, Lloyds Bank Ltd v Sutton [1952] 2 All ER 1054, 6 LDAB 353,
  96 Sol Jo 850, [1952] 2 TLR 877 .... 649, 658, 962, 1247
Waters, Re, Preston v Waters [1889] WN 39 1160–1161
Waters, Re, Waters v Boxer (1889) 42 Ch D 517, 58 LJ Ch 750, 38 WR 57, 61 LT 431
  1081
Waters v Waters (1857) 26 LJ Ch 624, 3 Jur NS 654, 112 RR 434, 29 LTOS 310
  382
Waters v Wood (1852) 5 De G & Sm 717, 22 LJ Ch 206, 17 Jur 33, 20 LTOS 76
  268
Waterson's Trustees v St Giles Boys' Club 1943 SC 369 238
Wathen v Smith (1819) 4 Madd 325 21
Watkins, Re, Hayward v Chatterton [1949] 1 All ER 695, [1949] WN 125, 93 Sol Jo 217,
  65 TLR 410 .... 572, 575
Watkins, Re, Maybery v Lightfoot [1913] 1 Ch 376, 82 LJ Ch 240, 108 LT 237, CA; revsd
  sub nom Lightfoot v Maybery [1914] AC 782, 83 LJ Ch 627, 58 Sol Jo 609, 111 LT
  300, HL 339–340, 413
Watkins v Brent (1835) 7 Sim 512; on appeal (1835) 1 My & Cr 97, 5 LJ Ch 49
  673
Watkins v Cheek (1825) 2 Sim & St 199 .... 438, 1025, 1028
Watkins v Frederick (1865) 11 HL Cas 358 .... 230, 466
Watkins v Weston (1863) 3 De GJ & Sm 434, 32 LJ Ch 609, 11 WR 408, 8 LT 406
  .... 369, 375
Watkins v Williams (1851) 21 LJ Ch 601, 16 Jur 181, 3 Mac & G 622, 87 RR 228,
  19 LTOS 13 381
Watney, Re, Watney v Gold (1911) 56 Sol Jo 109 404

PARA

Watson, Re [1999] 3 FCR 595, [1999] 1 FLR 878, [1999] Fam Law 211, [1999]
02 LS Gaz R 28, 143 Sol Jo LB 51 .... 567, 573, 575, 579–580
Watson, Re (1887) 13 VLR 599 110
Watson, Re, Culme-Seymour v Brand [1930] 2 Ch 344, 99 LJ Ch 452, 143 LT 764
.... 362, 369
Watson, Re, Turner v Watson [1896] 1 Ch 925, 65 LJ Ch 553, 44 WR 571, 74 LT 453
.... 1068
Watson v Arundel (1876) IR 10 Eq 299 288
Watson v Arundell (1876) IR 11 Eq 53, Ir CA 210
Watson v Donaldson [1915] 1 IR 63, Ir CA 173–174, 305
Watson v Foxon (1801) 2 East 36 474
Watson v Hayes (1839) 5 My & Cr 125, 9 LJ Ch 49, 4 Jur 186, 48 RR 249
.... 430–431
Watson v Holland (Inspector of Taxes) [1985] 1 All ER 290, [1984] STC 372
.... 231
Watson v National Children's Home [1995] 37 LS Gaz R 24
.... 143, 220
Watson v Row (1874) LR 18 Eq 680, 43 LJ Ch 664, 22 WR 793
.... 1201
Watson v Watson (1840) 11 Sim 73 305–306
Watson v Watson (1864) 33 Beav 574 503
Watson v Watson (1881) 7 PD 10, 47 JP 168, 51 LJP 13, sub nom Watson v Watson, Re
Clarke's Goods 30 WR 275, 47 LT 24, P, D and Admlty
.... 449
Watson v Young (1885) 28 Ch D 436, 54 LJ Ch 502, 33 WR 637
.... 308
Watson's Trusts, Re (1870) LR 10 Eq 36, 39 LJ Ch 770, 18 WR 642
.... 303, 441
Watt's Will Trusts, Re, Watt v Watt [1936] 2 All ER 1555
.... 308
Watts, Re, Smith v Watts (1882) 22 Ch D 5, 52 LJ Ch 209, 31 WR 262, 48 LT 167, CA
.... 1173
Watts v Eden [2001] All ER (D) 261 (Oct) 107
Watts v Official Solicitor [1936] 1 All ER 249, 80 Sol Jo 204, CA
.... 818
Watts v Watts (1873) LR 17 Eq 217, 43 LJ Ch 77, 22 WR 105, 29 LT 671,
[1861–73] All ER Rep Ext 1082 156
Watts Goods, Re (1837) 1 Curt 594 899–900
Watts' Goods, Re (1860) 24 JP 519, 29 LJPM & A 108, 1 Sw & Tr 538, 8 WR 340
.... 820
Waugh, Re, Waugh v Cripps [1903] 1 Ch 744, 72 LJ Ch 586, 51 WR 461, 88 LT 54, 19
TLR 283 .... 387, 473
Waugh v Waugh (1833) 2 My & K 41 324
Wavertree of Delamere (Baron), Re, Rutherford v Hall-Walker [1933] Ch 837, 102 LJ Ch
367, [1933] All ER Rep 837, 77 Sol Jo 468, 149 LT 418, 49 TLR 515
.... 127, 296
Way v Bassett (1845) 5 Hare 55, 15 LJ Ch 1, 10 Jur 89, 6 LTOS 118
.... 1232
Way's Goods, Re [1901] P 345, 71 LJP 13, 85 LT 643, 17 TLR 758, P, D and Admlty
.... 613
Wayland's Estate, Re [1951] 2 All ER 1041, 95 Sol Jo 804, P, D and Admlty
.... 95, 722
Wayling v Jones (1993) 69 P & CR 170, [1996] 2 FCR 41, [1995] 2 FLR 1029, [1996]
Fam Law 88, [1995] Conv 409, CA 20, 567
Waynford v Heyl. See Wainford v Heyl
Weakley d Knight v Rugg (1797) 7 Term Rep 322 461
Weale v Ollive (No 2) (1863) 32 Beav 421 .... 226, 378
Weall, Re, Andrews v Weall (1889) 42 Ch D 674, 58 LJ Ch 713, 37 WR 779, 61 LT 238,
5 TLR 681 1050
Weare v Brimsdown Lead Co Ltd (1910) 103 LT 429, DC
.... 1279
Weatherall v Thornburgh (1878) 8 Ch D 261, 47 LJ Ch 658, 26 WR 593,
[1874–80] All ER Rep 382, 39 LT 9, CA 422
Weatherhill v Pearce [1995] 2 All ER 492, [1995] 1 WLR 592
.... 62–63, 68–69, 77, 895–896
Weaver v Maule (1830) 2 Russ & M 97 951

                                                                                      PARA
Weaver's Goods, Re (1866) 36 LJP & M 41, 15 WR 199, 15 LT 331
.... 767
Webb, Re, Smith v Johnston [1964] 2 All ER 91, [1964] 1 WLR 509, 108 Sol Jo 139, P, D
    and Admlty 716, 895
Webb v Adkins (1854) 14 CB 401, 23 LJCP 96, 2 WR 225, 2 CLR 702, 22 LTOS 260
.... 635
Webb v Byng (1855) 1 K & J 580, 1 Jur NS 696 .... 215–216, 279
Webb v Byng (1856) 2 K & J 669, 4 WR 657, 6 LTOS 133; on appeal (1856) 8 De GM &
    G 633; affd sub nom Byng v Byng (1862) 10 HL Cas 171, 31 LJ Ch 470, 8 Jur NS
    1135, 10 WR 633, 7 LT 1 .... 292, 389
Webb v Grace (1848) 2 Ph 701, 41 ER 1114, sub nom Grace v Webb 18 LJ Ch 13, 12 Jur
    987 137
Webb v Hearing (1617) 3 Bulst 192, Cro Jac 415, 1 Roll Rep 436, J Bridg 84, sub nom
    Anon Moore KB 852 .... 422, 473
Webb v Jonas (1888) 39 Ch D 660, 57 LJ Ch 671, 36 WR 666, 58 LT 882, 4 TLR 508,
    [1886–90] All ER Rep Ext 1509 963
Webb v Kirby (1856) 7 De GM & G 376, 26 LJ Ch 145, 3 Jur NS 73, 5 WR 189,
    28 LTOS 314 801
Webb v Needham (1823) 1 Add 494 774
Webb v Sadler (1873) 8 Ch App 419, 42 LJ Ch 498, 21 WR 394, [1861–73] All ER Rep
    569, 28 LT 388, CA in Ch 377
Webb's Case (1607) 1 Roll Abr 609 45
Webb's Goods, Re (1855) Dea & Sw 1, 1 Jur NS 1096, 4 WR 92, 26 LTOS 111
.... 70
Webb's Goods, Re (1864) 28 JP 696, 33 LJPM & A 182, 10 Jur NS 709, 4 New Rep 486,
    3 Sw & Tr 482, 11 LT 277 54
Webb's Goods, Re (1888) 13 PD 71, 52 JP 231, 57 LJP 36, 36 WR 847, 58 LT 683, P, D
    and Admlty 763
Webber v Corbett (1873) LR 16 Eq 515, 43 LJ Ch 164, 29 LT 365
.... 220
Webber v Stanley (1864) 16 CBNS 698, 33 LJCP 217, 10 Jur NS 657, 4 New Rep 192, 12
    WR 833, 10 LT 417 .... 255, 267, 271
Webber v Webber (1823) 1 Sim & St 311, 1 LJOS Ch 219
.... 427, 1059, 1159
Webster, Re, Goss v Webster [1937] 1 All ER 602, 156 LT 128, CA
.... 118, 120
Webster, Re, Webster v Webster [1974] 3 All ER 822n, [1974] 1 WLR 1641, 118 Sol Jo
    600 894
Webster v Boddington (1858) 26 Beav 128 424
Webster v Hale (1803) 8 Ves 410 .... 449, 1081
Webster v Milford (1708) 2 Eq Cas Abr 362, 1 Swan 449
.... 22
Webster v Parr (1858) 26 Beav 236 .... 385, 472
Webster v Spencer (1820) 3 B & Ald 360 .... 673, 1288
Webster v Webster [2008] EWHC 31 (Ch), [2009] 1 FLR 1240, [2009] Fam Law 286,
    [2009] 03 EG 102 (CS) 570
Webster v Webster (1804) 10 Ves 93 .... 636, 978, 1267
Webster's Estate, Re, Widgen v Mello (1883) 23 Ch D 737, 52 LJ Ch 767, 49 LT 585
.... 322
Weddell v Mundy (1801) 6 Ves 341 442
Wedderburn v Wedderburn (1838) 4 My & Cr 41, 8 LJ Ch 177, 3 Jur 596
.... 658
Wedgwood, Re, Allen v Public Trustee [1921] 1 Ch 601, 90 LJ Ch 322, [1921] All ER Rep
    545, 125 LT 146, CA 1130
Wedgwood, Re, Sweet v Cotton [1914] 2 Ch 245, 83 LJ Ch 731, 58 Sol Jo 595, 111 LT
    436, 30 TLR 527 .... 278, 370
Wedgwood v Adams (1844) 8 Beav 103 1210
Wedgwood v Denton (1871) LR 12 Eq 290, 40 LJ Ch 526, 25 LT 379
.... 115, 144
Wedgwood Museum Trust Ltd (in admin), Re; Young v Attorney General [2011] EWHC
    3782 (Ch), [2011] All ER (D) 204 (Dec) 162
Wedmore, Re, Wedmore v Wedmore [1907] 2 Ch 277, 76 LJ Ch 486, 97 LT 26, 23 TLR
    547 .... 118, 1089
Weeding, Re, Armstrong v Wilkin [1896] 2 Ch 364, 65 LJ Ch 743, 44 WR 556, 40 Sol Jo
    565, 74 LT 651 .... 270, 295

PARA

Weeding v Weeding (1861) 1 John & H 424, 30 LJ Ch 680, 7 Jur NS 908, 9 WR 431, 4
LT 616 157
Weeds v Bristow (1866) LR 2 Eq 333, 35 LJ Ch 839, 12 Jur NS 446, 14 WR 726, 14 LT
587 328
Weiner's Will Trusts, Re, Wyner v Braithwaite [1956] 2 All ER 482, [1956] 1 WLR 579,
100 Sol Jo 400 1053
Weir, Re [1993] 2 NIJB 45 586
Weiss' Estate, Re [1962] P 136, [1962] 1 All ER 308, [1962] 2 WLR 353, 106 Sol Jo 37, P,
D and Admlty 803, 960
Wekett v Raby (1724) 2 Bro Parl Cas 386 222
Welby v Rockcliffe (1830) 8 LJOS Ch 142, 1 Russ & M 571
.... 152, 1112
Welby v Welby (1813) 2 Ves & B 187 277
Welcden v Elkington (1576) 3 Dyer 358b, 2 Plowd 516 .... 121, 379
Welch, Re, Mitchell v Willders [1916] 1 Ch 375, 85 LJ Ch 500, 60 Sol Jo 368, 114 LT
685, 32 TLR 314 979
Welch v Bank of England [1955] Ch 508 1271
Welch v Phillips (1836) 1 Moo PCC 299 106
Welch and Freeman v Gardner (1887) 51 JP 760, P, D and Admlty
.... 108
Weld v Bradbury (1715) 2 Vern 705, 1 Eq Cas Abr 203 pl 25
.... 305, 311, 396
Weldon v Hoyland (1862) 4 De GF & J 564, 6 LT 96, [1861–73] All ER Rep Ext 2320
.... 337, 396
Weldon v Weldon [1911] 1 IR 177 455
Welland v Townsend [1910] 1 IR 177 227
Wellington v Wellington (1768) 4 Burr 2165, 1 Wm Bl 645
.... 460
Wellington (Duke), Re, Glentanar v Wellington [1947] Ch 506, [1947] 2 All ER 854,
[1947] LJR 1451, 91 Sol Jo 369, 63 TLR 295; affd [1948] Ch 118, [1947] 2 All ER
854, [1949] LJR 612, 92 Sol Jo 11, 64 TLR 54, CA 180
Wells v Row (1879) 48 LJ Ch 476, 40 LT 715 992
Wells v Wells (1874) LR 18 Eq 504, 43 LJ Ch 681, 22 WR 893, 31 LT 16,
[1874–80] All ER Rep Ext 1949 .... 220, 328
Wells' Estate, Re (1868) LR 6 Eq 599, 37 LJ Ch 553, 16 WR 784, 18 LT 462
.... 350, 352
Wells' Trusts, Re, Hardisty v Wells (1889) 42 Ch D 646, 58 LJ Ch 835, 38 WR 229, 61 LT
588 93
Welstead, Re (1858) 25 Beav 612 414
Wenger's Settlement, Re, Wenger v Baldwin (1963) 107 Sol Jo 981
.... 142, 145
Wenham, Re, Hunt v Wenham [1892] 3 Ch 59, 61 LJ Ch 565, 40 WR 636, 36 Sol Jo 540,
67 LT 648, [1891–4] All ER Rep Ext 1783 974
Wenmoth's Estate, Re, Wenmoth v Wenmoth (1887) 37 Ch D 266, 57 LJ Ch 649, 36 WR
409, [1886–90] All ER Rep 591, 57 LT 709, 4 TLR 74 .... 256, 308, 310
Wentworth v Cox (1882) 6 Madd 363 268
Wentworth v Wentworth [1900] AC 163, 69 LJPC 13, 81 LT 682, 16 TLR 81, PC
.... 1080, 1124
Wernher, Re, Wernher v Beit [1918] 1 Ch 339, 87 LJ Ch 255, 62 Sol Jo 268, 117 LT 801;
on appeal [1918] 2 Ch 82, 87 LJ Ch 372, 62 Sol Jo 503, 118 LT 388, 34 TLR 391,
CA 669
Wernher's Settlement Trusts, Re, Lloyds Bank Ltd v Mountbatten [1961] 1 All ER 184,
[1961] 1 WLR 136, 105 Sol Jo 88 .... 304, 308–309
Wertheimer, Re, Groves v Read (1912) 106 LT 590, 28 TLR 337
.... 652
Wesslbenyi v Jamieson [1907] AC 440, HL 339
West, Re, Barclays Bank Ltd v Handley [1947] WN 2, 63 TLR 745
.... 669
West, Re, Denton v West [1921] 1 Ch 533, 90 LJ Ch 342, [1921] All ER Rep 152, 65 Sol
Jo 379, 125 LT 117, 37 TLR 433 404
West, Re, George v Grose [1900] 1 Ch 84, 69 LJ Ch 71, 48 WR 138, 44 Sol Jo 89, 81 LT
720 370
West, Re, West v Roberts [1909] 2 Ch 180, 78 LJ Ch 559, 101 LT 375
.... 1146
West, Re, Westhead v Aspland [1913] 2 Ch 345, 82 LJ Ch 488, [1911–13] All ER Rep
692, 109 LT 39 1076

PARA

West, Re, ex p Turner (1842) 2 Mont D & De G 613, 6 Jur 840
.... 1248–1249
West v Lawday (1865) 11 HL Cas 375, 13 LT 171 .... 273, 291
West v Moore (1807) 8 East 339 930
West v West [1921] 2 IR 34 108
West v West [2003] All ER (D) 17 (Jun) 1256–1257
West v West (1863) 4 Giff 198, 32 LJ Ch 240, 9 Jur NS 400, 1 New Rep 258, 7 LT 779
.... 135, 413
West's Goods, Re (1863) 28 JP 9, 32 LJPM & A 182, 9 Jur NS 1158, 12 WR 89
.... 67
Westby, Re [1946] WN 141, 90 Sol Jo 405, 62 TLR 458
.... 592
Westcott v Culliford (1844) 3 Hare 265, 13 LJ Ch 136, 8 Jur 166
.... 1210
Westdeutsche Landesbank Girozentrale v Islington London Borough Council [1996] AC
    669, [1996] 2 All ER 961, [1996] 2 WLR 802, 95 LGR 1, 13 LDAB 444, [1996]
    NLJR 877, 140 Sol Jo LB 136, HL 1097
Westdock Realisations Ltd, Re [1988] BCLC 354, 4 BCC 192
.... 1196
Westendorp v Warwick [2006] EWHC 915 (Ch), [2006] All ER (D) 248 (Apr)
.... 55, 891
Western's Goods, Re (1898) 78 LT 49, P, D and Admlty
.... 723
Westfaling v Westfaling (1746) 3 Atk 460 291
Westland v Lillis [2003] EWHC 1669 (Ch), [2003] All ER (D) 128 (Jun)
.... 254–255, 320
Westminster Bank Ltd v Lee [1956] Ch 7, [1955] 2 All ER 883, [1955] 3 WLR 376, 99 Sol
    Jo 562 490
Westminster Bank Ltd's Declaration of Trust, Re [1963] 2 All ER 400n, [1963] 1 WLR
    820, sub nom Abbott v Service 107 Sol Jo 681 302
Weston v Clowes (1847) 15 Sim 610 1205
Weston's Goods, Re (1869) LR 1 P & D 633, 33 JP 312, 38 LJP & M 53,
    [1861–73] All ER Rep 364, 20 LT 330 108
Westover v Chapman (1844) 1 Coll 177 1257
Westropp, Re (1903) 37 ILT 183 404
Westwood v Southey (1852) 2 Sim NS 192, 21 LJ Ch 473, 16 Jur 400, 20 LTOS 7
.... 456, 460
Wetenhall v Dennis (1863) 33 Beav 285, 9 Jur NS 1216, 12 WR 66, 9 LT 361
.... 1205
Wetherell v Wetherell (1862) 4 Giff 51, 8 Jur NS 814, 10 WR 818, 7 LT 89; on appeal
    (1863) 1 De GJ & Sm 134, 32 LJ Ch 476, 9 Jur NS 368, 11 WR 274, 8 LT 39
.... 472
Wetherell v Wetherell (1863) 1 De GJ & Sm 134, 32 LJ Ch 476, 9 Jur NS 368, 11 WR
    274, 8 LT 39 .... 309, 436
Wetherell v Wilson (1836) 1 Keen 80, Donnelly 4, 5 LJ Ch 235
.... 370
Weyland v Weyland (1742) 2 Atk 632 503
Whale v Booth (1784) 4 Term Rep 625n, 4 Doug KB 36
.... 1025, 1028
Whaley, Re, Whaley v Roehrich [1908] 1 Ch 615, 77 LJ Ch 367, 98 LT 556
.... 290, 932
Wharton v Bancroft [2011] EWHC 3250 (Ch), [2012] WTLR 693
.... 902
Wharton v Barker (1858) 4 K & J 483, 4 Jur NS 553, 6 WR 534
.... 243, 313
Wharton v Gresham (1776) 2 Wm Bl 1083 389
Wharton v Masterman. See Harbin v Masterman
Whateley v Spooner (1857) 3 K & J 542 406
Whatford v Moore (1837) 3 My & Cr 270, 6 LJ Ch 378
.... 452
Whatman's Goods, Re (1864) 34 LJPM & A 17, 10 Jur NS 1242
.... 112
Wheatly v Davies (1876) 24 WR 818, 35 LT 306 1084
Wheddon v Oxenham (1731) 2 Eq Cas Abr 546 414
Wheeler, Re, Hankinson v Hayter [1904] 2 Ch 66, 73 LJ Ch 576, 52 WR 586, 48 Sol Jo
    493, 91 LT 227 293

PARA

Wheeler, Re, Jameson v Cotter [1929] 2 KB 81n, [1928] WN 225, [1928] All ER Rep 510,
141 LT 322 156
Wheeler v Bingham (1746) 3 Atk 364, 1 Wils 135 134
Wheeler v Humphreys [1898] AC 506, 67 LJ Ch 499, 47 WR 17, [1895–9] All ER Rep
362, 78 LT 799, HL 404
Wheeler v Walroone (1647) Aleyn 28 284
Wheeler v Warner (1823) 1 Sim & St 304, 24 RR 176 135
Wheeler and Batsford v Alderson (1831) 3 Hag Ecc 574
.... 899
Wheeler's Goods, Re (1879) 44 JP 285, 49 LJP 29, 28 WR 476, 42 LT 60, P, D and
Admlty 105
Wheelwright's Goods, Re (1878) 3 PD 71, 42 JP 680, 47 LJP 87, 27 WR 139, 39 LT 127,
P, D and Admlty 631
Whelan, Re [2015] EWHC 3301 (Ch) 77, 895
Whelan, Re, Doyle v Woodliff (1922) 153 LT Jo 47 296
Whichelow, Re, Bradshaw v Orpen [1953] 2 All ER 1558, [1954] 1 WLR 5, 98 Sol Jo 12
.... 1020
Whicker v Hume (1851) 14 Beav 509; affd (1858) 22 JP 591, 7 HL Cas 124, 28 LJ Ch
396, 4 Jur NS 933, 6 WR 813, 11 ER 50, [1843–60] All ER Rep 450, 31 LTOS 319,
HL 284, 669–670
Whincup v Hughes (1871) LR 6 CP 78, 40 LJCP 104, 19 WR 439, 24 LT 76
.... 1213
Whishaw v Stephens [1970] AC 508, [1968] 3 WLR 1127, 112 Sol Jo 882, sub nom Re
Gulbenkian's Settlement Trusts, Whishaw v Stephens [1968] 3 All ER 785, HL
.... 11
Whiskon and Cleytons Case (1588) 1 Leon 156 378
Whiston, Re, Whiston v Woolley [1924] 1 Ch 122, 93 LJ Ch 113, 68 Sol Jo 116, 130 LT
437, CA 173, 175, 274, 412
Whitaker, Re, Denison-Pender v Evans [1911] 1 Ch 214, 80 LJ Ch 63, 103 LT 657
.... 1060, 1208
Whitaker, Re, Whitaker v Palmer [1901] 1 Ch 9, 70 LJ Ch 6, 49 WR 106, 45 Sol Jo 43, 83
LT 449, 17 TLR 24, CA 981
Whitaker v Robinson [1877] WN 201 1176
Whitbread v Lord St John (1804) 10 Ves 152 .... 307, 309
Whitburn, Re, Whitburn v Christie [1923] 1 Ch 332, 92 LJ Ch 362, [1923] All ER Rep
574, 67 Sol Jo 276, 129 LT 449, 39 TLR 170 .... 155, 388
Whitby, Re, Public Trustee v Whitby [1944] Ch 210, [1944] 1 All ER 299, 113 LJ Ch 170,
88 Sol Jo 111, 170 LT 176, 60 TLR 224, CA 296, 488
Whitby v Von Luedecke [1906] 1 Ch 783, 75 LJ Ch 359, 54 WR 415, 94 LT 432
.... 416
Whitcher v Penley (1846) 9 Beav 477, 7 LTOS 488 .... 254, 320
White, Re [1928] P 75, 96 LJP 157, 71 Sol Jo 603, 138 LT 68, 43 TLR 729, CA
.... 775
White, Re (1987) 38 DLR (4th) 631, Ont HC 3
White, Re, Barker v Gribble [1991] Ch 1, [1990] 3 All ER 1, [1990] 3 WLR 187, [1991] 1
FLR 112, [1991] Fam Law 60 .... 63, 68–69, 74, 76, 82, 84
White, Re, Knight v Briggs [1925] Ch 179, 94 LJ Ch 211, [1924] All ER Rep 630, 69 Sol
Jo 213, 132 LT 481 201
White, Re, McCann v Hull [1958] Ch 762, [1958] 1 All ER 379, [1958] 2 WLR 464, 102
Sol Jo 195 287
White, Re, Mastaka v Midland Bank Executor and Trustee Co Ltd. See Mastaka v Midland
Bank Executor and Trustee Co Ltd
White, Re, Pennell v Franklin [1898] 2 Ch 217, 67 LJ Ch 502, 46 WR 676,
[1895–9] All ER Rep 229, 42 Sol Jo 635, 78 LT 770, 14 TLR 503, CA
.... 652, 656
White, Re, Theobald v White [1913] 1 Ch 231, 82 LJ Ch 149, 57 Sol Jo 212, 108 LT 319
.... 32
White, Re, White v Minnis [1999] 2 All ER 663, [1999] 1 WLR 2079; revsd sub nom Re
White, White v Minnis [2001] Ch 393, [2000] 3 All ER 618, [2000] 3 WLR 885,
[2000] NLJR 682, CA 1298
White, Re, White v Shenton (1909) 101 LT 780 1082
White, Re, White v White [1893] 2 Ch 41, 62 LJ Ch 342, 2 R 380, 41 WR 683,
[1891–4] All ER Rep 242, 37 Sol Jo 249, 68 LT 187, CA
.... 11

PARA

White, Re, White v White [1916] 1 Ch 172, 85 LJ Ch 368, 60 Sol Jo 210, 114 LT 353 296
White v Baker (1860) 2 De GF & J 55, 29 LJ Ch 577, 6 Jur NS 591, 8 WR 533, 2 LT 583 .... 318,321, 444
White v Barber (1771) Amb 701, 5 Burr 2703 468
White v Birch (1867) 36 LJ Ch 174, 15 WR 305, 15 LT 605 277
White v Briggs (1848) 2 Ph 583, 15 Sim 300, 17 LJ Ch 196, 78 RR 203 348
White v Hight (1879) 12 Ch D 751, 41 LT 17 441
White v Hill (1867) LR 4 Eq 265, 16 LT 826 .... 260, 441
White v Jackson (1852) 15 Beav 191 1202
White v Lake (1868) LR 6 Eq 188 284
White v Paine. See Paine v Countess of Warwick
White v Parker (1835) 1 Bing NC 573, 4 LJCP 178, 1 Hodg 112, 1 Scott 542 232
White v Repton (1844) 3 Curt 818, 8 Jur 562, 3 LTOS 322, sub nom Whyte v Repton 3 Notes of Cases 97 79
White v Springett (1869) 4 Ch App 300, 38 LJ Ch 388, 17 WR 336, 20 LT 502 314
White v Summers [1908] 2 Ch 256, 77 LJ Ch 506, 98 LT 845, 24 TLR 552 .... 418, 420, 424
White v Turner (1858) 25 Beav 505 404
White v Vitty (1826) 2 Russ 484 271
White v White [2001] 1 AC 596, [2001] 1 All ER 1, [2000] 3 WLR 1571, [2000] 3 FCR 555, [2000] 2 FLR 981, [2001] Fam Law 12, [2000] 43 LS Gaz R 38, [2000] NLJR 1716, 144 Sol Jo LB 266, HL 577
White v White (1778) 1 Bro CC 12 11
White v White (1908) 28 NZLR 129 266
White d White v Warner (1728) 11 East 552n, 3 Doug KB 4, sub nom Warner v White 3 Bro Parl Cas 435, 1 Bro CC 219n, HL 321
White's Estate, Re [1914] P 153, 58 Sol Jo 534, 111 LT 413, 30 TLR 536, sub nom Re AB's Goods 83 LJP 67, P, D and Admlty 739
White's Goods, Re [1896] 1 IR 269 .... 65, 83
White's Goods, Re (1843) 7 Jur 1045, 2 Notes of Cases 461 75
White's Goods, Re (1860) 24 JP 792, 30 LJPM & A 55, 6 Jur NS 808 83
White's Goods, Re (1879) 3 LR Ir 413 .... 96, 105
White's Goods, Re (1882) 7 PD 65, 46 JP 424, 51 LJP 40, 30 WR 660, 46 LT 695, P, D and Admlty 293
White's Trusts, Re (1860) John 656 .... 254, 320
Whiteford, Re, Inglis v Whiteford [1903] 1 Ch 889, 72 LJ Ch 540, 51 WR 491, 47 Sol Jo 336 .... 306, 404–405, 1257
Whitehall v Squire (1703) 3 Mod Rep 276, 1 Salk 295, 3 Salk 161, Holt KB 45, Skin 274, Carth 103 .... 646, 1267
Whitehead, Re, Whitehead v Hemsley [1920] 1 Ch 298, 89 LJ Ch 155, [1918–19] All ER Rep 1170, 122 LT 767, 36 TLR 129 342
Whitehead, Re, Whitehead v Street [1913] 2 Ch 56, 82 LJ Ch 302, 57 Sol Jo 323, 108 LT 368 1087
Whitehead v Palmer [1908] 1 KB 151, 77 LJKB 60, 52 Sol Jo 45, 97 LT 909, 24 TLR 41 .... 815, 1225
Whitehead v Taylor (1839) 10 Ad & El 210, 9 LJQB 65, 4 Jur 247, 2 Per & Dav 367 633–634
Whitehorne, Re, Whitehorne v Best [1906] 2 Ch 121, 75 LJ Ch 537, 54 WR 580, 94 LT 698 182
Whitehouse, Re, Whitehouse v Edwards (1887) 37 Ch D 683, 57 LJ Ch 161, 36 WR 181, 57 LT 761 404
Whiteley, Re, London (Bishop) v Whiteley [1910] 1 Ch 600, 79 LJ Ch 405, 55 Sol Jo 291, 102 LT 313, 26 TLR 309 228
Whiteley, Re, Whiteley v Bishop of London (1909) 101 LT 508, 26 TLR 16, CA 1080
Whiteley v King (1864) 17 CBNS 756, 10 Jur NS 1079, 5 New Rep 12, 13 WR 83, 11 LT 342 106
Whitelock v Heddon (1798) 1 Bos & P 243 362
Whiter, Re, Windsor v Jones (1911) 105 LT 749 .... 246, 453

                                                                                                    PARA
Whiteway v Fisher (1861) 9 WR 433 157
Whitfield v Langdale (1875) 1 Ch D 61, 45 LJ Ch 177, 24 WR 313, 33 LT 592
   .... 267, 271, 277
Whitfield v Prickett (1838) 2 Keen 608, 7 LJ Ch 187, 2 Jur 344
   464
Whitham's Goods, Re (1866) LR 1 P & D 303, 31 JP 215, 36 LJP & M 26, 15 WR 560,
   15 LT 447 632
Whithorne v Harris (1754) 2 Ves Sen 527 349
Whiting, Re, Ormond v De Launay [1913] 2 Ch 1, 82 LJ Ch 309, 57 Sol Jo 461, 108 LT
   629 173
Whiting v Force (1840) 2 Beav 571, 9 LJ Ch 345 451
Whiting v Turner (1903) 47 Sol Jo 470, 89 LT 71, P, D and Admlty
   .... 68, 895
Whiting v Whiting [1988] 2 All ER 275, [1988] 1 WLR 565, [1988] FCR 569, [1988] 2
   FLR 189, [1988] Fam Law 429, 132 Sol Jo 658, [1988] NLJR 39, CA
   577
Whiting's Settlement, Re, Whiting v De Rutzen [1905] 1 Ch 96, 74 LJ Ch 207, 53 WR
   293, 49 Sol Jo 83, 91 LT 821, 21 TLR 83, CA 134
Whitman v Aitken (1866) LR 2 Eq 414, 12 Jur NS 350, 14 LT 248
   452
Whitmore, Re, Walters v Harrison [1902] 2 Ch 66, 71 LJ Ch 673, 87 LT 210, CA
   .... 171, 243–244
Whitmore v Lambert [1955] 2 All ER 147, [1955] 1 WLR 495, 99 Sol Jo 316, CA
   633
Whitmore v Weld (1685) 2 Rep Ch 383, 2 Vent 367, 1 Vern 326sub nom Whitmore v Lord
   Craven (1685) 2 Cas in Ch 167, sub nom Whitmore v Weld 1 Vern 347
   .... 385, 798
Whitrick, Re, Sutcliffe v Sutcliffe [1957] 2 All ER 467, [1957] 1 WLR 884, 101 Sol Jo 574,
   CA 253, 466
Whitrod, Re, Burrows v Base [1926] Ch 118, 95 LJ Ch 205, 70 Sol Jo 209, 134 LT 627
   .... 298, 1113, 1115
Whittaker, Re, Whittaker v Whittaker (1882) 21 Ch D 657, 51 LJ Ch 737, 30 WR 787, 46
   LT 802 1081
Whittaker v Kershaw (1890) 45 Ch D 320, sub nom Kershaw, Re, Whittaker v Kershaw
   60 LJ Ch 9, 39 WR 22, 63 LT 203, CA 1097
Whittaker v Whittaker (1792) 4 Bro CC 31 27
Whittell v Dudin (1820) 2 Jac & W 279 231
Whitter v Bremridge (1866) LR 2 Eq 736, 35 LJ Ch 807, 14 WR 912
   .... 421, 423, 436
Whittingham's Case (1603) 8 Co Rep 42b 145
Whittle v Henning (1840) 2 Beav 396 1298
Whittle v Keats (1866) 35 LJP & M 54 809–810
Whittome v Lamb (1844) 13 LJ Ex 205, 12 M & W 813, 3 LTOS 104
   379
Whitton v Field (1846) 9 Beav 368 318
Whitton v Russell (1739) 1 Atk 448 207
Whitty, Re, Evans v Evans (1881) 43 LT 692 370
Whitworth v Walker (1915) 32 TLR 195, HL 70
Whorwood, Re, Ogle v Lord Sherborne (1887) 34 Ch D 446, 56 LJ Ch 340, 35 WR 342,
   56 LT 71, 3 TLR 307, [1886–90] All ER Rep Ext 1847, CA
   .... 214, 217, 300
Whyte v Kearney (1827) 3 Russ 208, 6 LJOS Ch 22 402
Whyte v Pollok (1882) 7 App Cas 400, 47 JP 340, 47 LT 356, HL
   5
Whyte v Repton. See White v Repton
Whyte v Rose (1842) 3 QB 493, 11 LJ Ex 457, 2 Gal & Dav 312, 4 Jur 986, 4 Per & Dav
   199, Ex Ch 669
Whyte v Whyte (1873) LR 17 Eq 50, 43 LJ Ch 104, 22 WR 180
   .... 403, 672
Whytte (or Whyte) v Ticehurst [1986] Fam 64, [1986] 2 All ER 158, [1986] 2 WLR 700,
   [1986] 2 FLR 83, [1986] Fam Law 192, 130 Sol Jo 185, [1986] LS Gaz R 875
   .... 567, 1279
Wicker v Mitford (1782) 3 Bro Parl Cas 442, HL 332
Widdicombe v Muller (1853) 1 Drew 443, 22 LJ Ch 614, 1 WR 223
   302
Widdison v Hodgkin (1823) 2 LJOS Ch 9 385

                                                                                    PARA
Widdowson v Duck (1817) 2 Mer 494 1190
Wieland's Goods, Re, Wieland v Bird [1894] P 262, 63 LJP 162, 6 R 574, 71 LT 267, P, D
    and Admlty 811
Wienholt v Logan. See Logan v Wienholt
Wigan v Rowland (1853) 11 Hare 157, 23 LJ Ch 69, 1 Eq Rep 213, 17 Jur 910, 1 WR
    383, 21 LTOS 150 44
Wigg v Wigg (1739) 1 Atk 382, West temp Hard 677 .... 17, 184
Wiggins v Wiggins (1852) 2 Sim NS 226, 21 LJ Ch 742
                                                                                      256
Wight v Leigh (1809) 15 Ves 564 .... 384, 473
Wightman v Cousins [1931] NI 138; affd [1932] NI 61, CA
    679
Wightwick v Lord (1857) 6 HL Cas 217, 28 LJ Ch 825, 3 Jur NS 699, 5 WR 713,
    29 LTOS 303 .... 1053, 1116, 1122
Wightwick's Will Trusts, Re, Official Trustees of Charitable Funds v Fielding-Ould [1950]
    Ch 260, [1950] 1 All ER 689, 94 Sol Jo 239, 66 (pt 1) TLR 592
    1259
Wilbraham v Scarisbrick (1847) 1 HL Cas 167 333
Wilce v Wilce (1831) 7 Bing 664, 9 LJOSCP 197, 5 Moo & P 682
    .... 257, 298
Wilcock, Re, Kay v Dewhirst [1898] 1 Ch 95, 67 LJ Ch 154, 46 WR 153, 42 Sol Jo 115,
    77 LT 679 .... 96, 231
Wilcocks v Wilcocks (1706) 2 Vern 558 491
Wilcocks' Settlement, Re (1875) 1 Ch D 229, 45 LJ Ch 163, 24 WR 290, 33 LT 719
    142
Wild's Case (1599) 6 Co Rep 16b 334, 384, 389–391
Wilday v Sandys (1869) LR 7 Eq 455, 17 WR 603, 20 LT 861
                                                                                      295
Wilder's Trusts, Re (1859) 27 Beav 418 .... 165, 395, 408
Wildes v Davies (1853) 22 LJ Ch 495, 1 Sm & G 475, 1 WR 253, 21 LTOS 206
    .... 298, 402, 1069
Wildman's Trusts, Re (1860) 1 John & H 299, 30 LJ Ch 174, 7 Jur NS 121
                                                                                      325
Wiley v Chanteperdrix [1894] 1 IR 209 .... 318, 375, 395, 444
Wilford's Estate, Re, Taylor v Taylor (1879) 11 Ch D 207, 48 LJ Ch 243, 27 WR 455
    23
Wilkes v Collin (1869) LR 8 Eq 338, 17 WR 878 293
Wilkins, Re, Emsley v Wilkins (1901) 46 Sol Jo 14 1186
Wilkins, Re, Spencer v Duckworth (1881) 18 Ch D 634, 50 LJ Ch 774, 29 WR 911, 45 LT
    224 451
Wilkins, Re, Wilkins v Rotherham (1884) 27 Ch D 703, 54 LJ Ch 188, 33 WR 42
    .... 1093, 1205
Wilkins, Re, Wilkins v Wilkins [1920] 2 Ch 63, 89 LJ Ch 507, 64 Sol Jo 530, 123 LT 571
                                                                                      173
Wilkins v Jodrell (1863) 11 WR 588 285
Wilkins v Jodrell (1879) 13 Ch D 564, 49 LJ Ch 26, 28 WR 224, 41 LT 649,
    [1874–80] All ER Rep Ext 1549 449
Wilkinson, Re, Neale v Newell [1978] Fam 22, [1978] 1 All ER 221, [1977] 3 WLR 514, 7
    Fam Law 176, 121 Sol Jo 375 .... 567, 581
Wilkinson, Re, Page v Public Trustee [1926] Ch 842, 95 LJ Ch 528, [1926] All ER Rep
    357, 135 LT 736 .... 129, 139, 145
Wilkinson v Adam (1813) 1 Ves & B 422; affd (1823) 12 Price 470, 147 ER 780,
    [1814–23] All ER Rep 688, HL 350, 353–354, 466
Wilkinson v Bewicke (1853) 3 De GM & G 937, 22 LJ Ch 781, 1 Eq Rep 12
    271
Wilkinson v Cawood (1797) 3 Anst 905 1212
Wilkinson v Corfield (1881) 6 PD 27, 45 JP 440, 50 LJP 44, 29 WR 613, P, D and Admlty
    909
Wilkinson v Duncan (1857) 23 Beav 469, 26 LJ Ch 495, 3 Jur NS 530, 113 RR 228, 5
    WR 398, 29 LTOS 35 1126–1127
Wilkinson v Dyson (1862) 10 WR 681 190
Wilkinson v Henderson (1833) 1 My & K 582, 2 LJ Ch 190
    1232
Wilkinson v Joughin (1866) LR 2 Eq 319, 30 JP 452, 35 LJ Ch 684, 12 Jur NS 330, 14 LT
    394 .... 58, 276
Wilkinson v South (1798) 7 Term Rep 555 .... 385, 459

PARA

Wilkinson v Spearman (undated) (1706) 2 Vern 545, HL
.... 395
Wilkinson v Wilkinson (1819) 2 Wils Ch 47, 3 Swan 515
.... 463–464
Wilkinson v Wilkinson (1871) LR 12 Eq 604, 40 LJ Ch 242, 19 WR 558, 24 LT 314
.... 145
Wilkinson's Goods, Re [1892] P 227, 61 LJP 134, 67 LT 328, P, D and Admlty
.... 613
Wilkinson's Goods, Re (1881) 6 PD 100, 45 JP 716, 29 WR 896, P, D and Admlty
.... 84
Wilks, Re, Keefer v Wilks [1935] Ch 645, 104 LJ Ch 297, [1935] All ER Rep 787, 153 LT
255, 51 TLR 489 .... 1075, 1150
Wilks v Bannister (1885) 30 Ch D 512, 54 LJ Ch 1139, 33 WR 922, 53 LT 247, 1 TLR
680 .... 328, 451
Wilks v Groom (1856) 3 Drew 584, 25 LJ Ch 724, 2 Jur NS 681, 4 WR 697, 27 LTOS
270 .... 962, 1133
Wilks v Williams (1861) 2 John & H 125, 10 WR 55, 5 LT 445, [1861–73] All ER Rep
Ext 2398 471
Willaims v Willaims (1841) 3 Beav 547 203
Willatts, Re, Willatts v Artley [1905] 1 Ch 378, 74 LJ Ch 269, 92 LT 195, 21 TLR 194; on
appeal [1905] 2 Ch 135, 74 LJ Ch 564, 93 LT 256, 21 TLR 571, CA
.... 469
Willcocks, Re, Warwick v Willcocks [1921] 2 Ch 327, 91 LJ Ch 27, [1921] All ER Rep
161, 65 Sol Jo 793, 126 LT 86 .... 119, 156
Willes v Douglas (1847) 10 Beav 47, 11 Jur 702, 9 LTOS 331
.... 395, 397
Willett v Finlay (1892) 29 LR Ir 156; affd (1892) 29 LR Ir 497, CA
.... 158
Willetts v Willetts (1848) 7 Hare 38, 17 LJ Ch 457, 12 Jur 670
.... 316
Willey, Re [1890] WN 1, CA 1149–1150
Willey, Re, Goulding v Shirtcliffe (1929) 45 TLR 327 296
Williames, Re, Andrew v Williames (1884) 52 LT 41; affd (1885) 54 LT 105, CA
.... 152, 1229, 1278
Williams, Re [1918] P 122, 87 LJP 56, 62 Sol Jo 309, 119 LT 494, P, D and Admlty
.... 788
Williams, Re (1849) 12 Beav 317, 19 LJ Ch 46, 13 Jur 1110, 14 LTOS 393
.... 452
Williams, Re, Cunliffe v Williams [1915] 1 Ch 450, 84 LJ Ch 578, 110 LT 569
.... 998, 1006
Williams, Re, Gregory v Muirhead (1913) 134 LT Jo 619, HC
.... 210, 241
Williams, Re, James v Williams (1910) 26 TLR 307 282
Williams, Re, Jones v Williams [1916] 2 Ch 38, 85 LJ Ch 498, [1916–17] All ER Rep 833,
60 Sol Jo 495, 114 LT 992 1185
Williams, Re, Metcalf v Williams [1914] 1 Ch 219, 83 LJ Ch 255, 58 Sol Jo 198, 110 LT
60; affd [1914] 2 Ch 61, 83 LJ Ch 570, 58 Sol Jo 470, 110 LT 923, CA
.... 237, 247, 323
Williams, Re, Spencer v Brighouse (1886) 54 LT 831 .... 416, 419, 424
Williams, Re, Taylor v University of Wales (1908) 24 TLR 716
.... 128, 143
Williams, Re, Wiles v Madgin [1985] 1 All ER 964, [1985] 1 WLR 905, 129 Sol Jo 469,
[1985] LS Gaz R 2996 .... 187, 195, 199, 207, 217, 220, 225
Williams, Re, Williams v All Souls, Hastings (Parochial Church Council) [1933] Ch 244,
102 LJ Ch 58, [1932] All ER Rep 724, 148 LT 310 .... 222, 370
Williams, Re, Williams v Ball [1917] 1 Ch 1, 86 LJ Ch 36, [1916–17] All ER Rep 354, 61
Sol Jo 42, 115 LT 689, CA 54
Williams, Re, Williams v Williams [1897] 2 Ch 12, 66 LJ Ch 485, 45 WR 519, 41 Sol Jo
452, 76 LT 600, [1895–9] All ER Rep Ext 1764, CA 407
Williams, Re, Williams v Williams [1907] 1 Ch 180, 76 LJ Ch 41, 51 Sol Jo 68, 95 LT 759
.... 431
Williams, Re, Williams v Williams [1912] 1 Ch 399, 81 LJ Ch 296, 56 Sol Jo 325, 106 LT
584 190
Williams, Re, Williams and Glyn's Trust Co Ltd v Williams [1974] 1 All ER 787, [1974] 1
WLR 754, [1974] STC 123, 118 Sol Jo 390, sub nom Williams' Executor v Williams
52 ATC 409, [1973] TR 339 1130–1131

PARA

Williams v Allen (1862) 4 De GF & J 71, 31 LJ Ch 550, 10 WR 512, 5 LT 313
.... 817

Williams v Arkle (1875) LR 7 HL 606, 45 LJ Ch 590, 33 LT 187, HL
.... 197

Williams v Ashton (1860) 1 John & H 115, 3 LT 148 .... 83, 343

Williams v Browne (1734) 2 Barn KB 231, 2 Stra 996 474

Williams v Burrell (1845) 1 CB 402, 14 LJCP 98, 9 Jur 282, 4 LTOS 415
.... 1223

Williams v Chitty (1797) 3 Ves 545 445

Williams v Clark (1851) 4 De G & Sm 472 428

Williams v Evans [1911] P 175, 80 LJP 115, [1911–13] All ER Rep 957, 105 LT 79, 27
TLR 506, P, D and Admlty 853, 862

Williams v Evans (1853) 1 E & B 727, 22 LJQB 241, 17 Jur 1093, 21 LTOS 150
.... 251

Williams v Goude (1828) 1 Hag Ecc 577 .... 56, 899

Williams v Haythorne (1871) 6 Ch App 782 .... 260, 299, 412

Williams v Heales (1874) LR 9 CP 177, 43 LJCP 80, 22 WR 317, [1874–80] All ER Rep
364, 30 LT 20 1262

Williams v Hensman (1861) 1 John & H 546, 30 LJ Ch 878, 7 Jur NS 771, 5 LT 203
.... 29

Williams v Holland [1965] 2 All ER 157, [1965] 1 WLR 739, 109 Sol Jo 237, 193 Estates
Gazette 1033, CA 1145

Williams v Hughes (1857) 24 Beav 474, 27 LJ Ch 218, 4 Jur NS 42, 6 WR 94, 30 LTOS
215 .... 1112, 1130

Williams v Jekyl (1755) 2 Ves Sen 681 249

Williams v Johns [1988] 2 FLR 475, [1988] Fam Law 257
.... 568, 576, 580, 602

Williams v Jones, Re Hartley [1900] 1 Ch 152, 69 LJ Ch 79, 48 WR 245, 81 LT 804
.... 1005, 1012

Williams v Jones (1826) 1 Russ 517 172

Williams v Jones (1886) 34 Ch D 120, 56 LJ Ch 1014, 56 LT 68, CA
.... 1209

Williams v Jukes (1864) 34 LJPM & A 60 787

Williams v Kershaw (1835) 5 Cl & Fin 111n, 1 Keen 274n, 5 LJ Ch 84
.... 11

Williams v Lee (1745) 3 Atk 223 1146

Williams v Lewis (1859) 6 HL Cas 1013, 28 LJ Ch 505, 5 Jur NS 323, 7 WR 349, 10 ER
1594, 33 LTOS 23 .... 241, 385

Williams v Nixon (1840) 2 Beav 472, 9 LJ Ch 269 1253

Williams v Owen (1863) 2 New Rep 585, 9 LT 200 282

Williams v Powell (1852) 15 Beav 461, 16 Jur 393 658

Williams v Russell (1863) 10 Jur NS 168 .... 299, 412

Williams v Teale (1847) 6 Hare 239, 77 RR 100 249

Williams v Tyley (1858) John 530, 5 Jur NS 35, 7 WR 116, 32 LTOS 194
.... 105

Williams v Wilkins (1812) 2 Phillim 100 773

Williams v Williams, Re Hartley [1900] 1 Ch 152, 69 LJ Ch 79, 48 WR 245, 81 LT 804
.... 1005, 1012

Williams v Williams (1786) 2 Bro CC 87 277

Williams v Williams (1851) 1 Sim NS 358, 20 LJ Ch 280, 15 Jur 715
.... 348

Williams v Williams (1871) 6 Ch App 782 .... 260, 299, 412

Williams v Williams (1878) 8 Ch D 789, 47 LJ Ch 857, 27 WR 100, 39 LT 180, CA
.... 293

Williams v Williams (1882) 20 Ch D 659, 46 JP 726, 51 LJ Ch 385, 15 Cox CC 39, 30
WR 438, [1881–5] All ER Rep 840, 46 LT 275 .... 31, 956

Williams Goods, Re (1830) 3 Hag Ecc 217 805

Williams Goods, Re (1859) 23 JP 519 820

Williams' Goods, Re (1865) LR 1 P & D 4, 35 LJP & M 2, 11 Jur NS 982, 14 WR 111,
13 LT 304 65

Williams' Settlement, Re (1858) 4 K & J 87, 116 RR 266, 6 WR 218, 32 LTOS 9
.... 1047

Williams' Settlement, Re, Greenwell v Humphries [1929] 2 Ch 361, 98 LJ Ch 358,
[1929] All ER Rep 632, 73 Sol Jo 384, 141 LT 579, 45 TLR 541, CA
.... 346, 493

Williams' Settlement, Re, Williams v Williams [1911] 1 Ch 441, 80 LJ Ch 249, 55 Sol Jo
236, 104 LT 310 305

PARA

Williams' Will Trusts, Re, Chartered Bank of India, Australia and China v Williams [1953] Ch 138, [1953] 1 All ER 536, [1953] 2 WLR 418, 97 Sol Jo 133
.... 246, 287
Williams' Will Trusts, Re, Rees v Williams [1949] 2 All ER 11, [1949] LJR 1234, 93 Sol Jo 319, 65 TLR 322 450
Williamson, Re, Murray v Williamson (1906) 94 LT 813
.... 379
Williamson v Moore (1862) 8 Jur NS 875, 10 WR 536 .... 328, 338
Williamson v Naylor (1838) 3 Y & C Ex 208 163
Willing v Baine (1731) Kel W 12, 3 P Wms 113 .... 116, 173, 411, 452
Willis, Re (1960) Times, 5 April 895
Willis, Re, Crossman v Kirkaldy [1917] 1 Ch 365, 86 LJ Ch 336, 61 Sol Jo 233, 115 LT 916 182
Willis, Re, Shaw v Willis [1921] 1 Ch 44, 90 LJ Ch 94, 65 Sol Jo 43, 124 LT 290, 37 TLR 43, [1920] All ER Rep Ext 794, CA 11
Willis, Re, Spencer v Willis [1911] 2 Ch 563, 81 LJ Ch 8, 55 Sol Jo 598, 105 LT 295
.... 279, 282, 290, 295
Willis v Barron [1902] AC 271, 71 LJ Ch 609, [1900–3] All ER Rep 876, 86 LT 806, 18 TLR 602, HL 904
Willis v Black (1824) 1 Sim & St 525, 2 LJOS Ch 131 22
Willis v Earl Beauchamp (1886) 11 PD 59, 55 LJP 17, 34 WR 357, [1886–90] All ER Rep 515, 54 LT 185, 2 TLR 270, CA 884, 888
Willis v Kibble (1839) 1 Beav 559, 49 RR 452 652
Willis v Lucas (1718) 2 Eq Cas Abr 363, 10 Mod Rep 416, 1 P Wms 472
.... 217, 469
Willis v Plaskett (1841) 4 Beav 208, 5 Jur 572 .... 293, 429, 444
Willis v Willis (1796) 3 Ves 51 452
Willock v Noble (1875) LR 7 HL 580, HL 51
Willoughby, Re, Willoughby v Decies [1911] 2 Ch 581, 80 LJ Ch 562, 104 LT 907, CA
.... 405
Willoughby's Case (1597) Cro Eliz 566 551
Wills, Re, Dulverton v Macleod [1939] Ch 705, [1939] 2 All ER 775, 108 LJ Ch 286, 83 Sol Jo 438, 160 LT 635, 55 TLR 822 .... 405, 1117
Wills, Re, Wills v Hamilton [1915] 1 Ch 769, 84 LJ Ch 580, [1914–15] All ER Rep 289, 59 Sol Jo 477, 113 LT 138 .... 496, 1118
Wills, Re, Wills v Wills [1909] 1 IR 268 212
Wills v Gandy (1859) 1 De GF & J 13, 29 LJ Ch 38, 8 WR 32
.... 1177
Wills v Palmer (1770) 5 Burr 2615, 2 Wm Bl 687 340
Wills v Rich (1742) 2 Atk 285 634–635
Wills v Wills (1841) 1 Dr & War 439 298
Wills v Wills (1875) LR 20 Eq 342, 44 LJ Ch 582, 23 WR 784, Ct of Ch
.... 253, 395, 397
Willyams v Matthews (1876) 45 LJ Ch 711, 2 Char Pr Cas 149, 34 LT 718
.... 1178
Wilmer v Currey (1848) 2 De G & Sm 347, 12 Jur 847, 11 LTOS 491
.... 1232
Wilmer's Trusts, Re, Moore v Wingfield [1903] 1 Ch 874, 72 LJ Ch 378, 51 WR 395, 47 Sol Jo 336, 88 LT 379; affd [1903] 2 Ch 411, 72 LJ Ch 670, 51 WR 609, [1900–3] All ER Rep 776, 47 Sol Jo 602, 89 LT 148, CA
.... 551
Wilmot, Re, Wilmot v Betterton (1897) 45 WR 492, 76 LT 415
.... 390–391, 393
Wilmot v Flewitt (1865) 11 Jur NS 820, 13 WR 856, 13 LT 90
.... 410
Wilmot v Wilmot (1802) 8 Ves 10 316
Wilson, Re. See Steele's (or Steel) Goods, Re, Re May's Goods, Re Wilson's Goods
Wilson, Re, Alexander v Calder (1885) 28 Ch D 457, 54 LJ Ch 487, 33 WR 579
.... 1179
Wilson, Re, Hartley v Marie Curie Hospital [1940] Ch 966, sub nom Re Wilson, Hurtley v Marie Curie Hospital [1940] 4 All ER 57, 109 LJ Ch 413, 84 Sol Jo 537, 164 LT 245, 57 TLR 8 1092
Wilson, Re, Lothian v Wilson (1920) 89 LJ Ch 216, 64 Sol Jo 389, 123 LT 165
.... 167
Wilson, Re, Parker v Winder (1883) 24 Ch D 664, 53 LJ Ch 130
.... 399

PARA

Wilson, Re, Wilson v Batchelor [1907] 1 Ch 450, 76 LJ Ch 228, 96 LT 392; affd [1907] 2
Ch 572, 77 LJ Ch 13, 52 Sol Jo 11, 97 LT 656, [1904–7] All ER Rep Ext 1118, CA
.... 313
Wilson, Re, Wilson v Mackay [1967] Ch 53, [1966] 2 All ER 867, [1966] 3 WLR 365,
110 Sol Jo 605 .... 119, 993, 1000, 1060, 1108
Wilson, Re, Wilson v Wilson [1908] 1 Ch 839, 77 LJ Ch 564, 98 LT 828,
[1908–10] All ER Rep Ext 1451 125
Wilson, Re, Wilson v Wilson (1916) 142 LT Jo 41 382
Wilson v Bassil [1903] P 239, 72 LJP 89, 52 WR 271, 89 LT 586, [1900–3] All ER Rep
Ext 1047, P, D and Admlty 911
Wilson v Bayly (1760) 3 Bro Parl Cas 195, HL 318
Wilson v Beddard (1841) 12 Sim 28, 10 LJ Ch 305, 5 Jur 624
.... 63, 895
Wilson v Coxwell (1875) 32 LT 52, Ct of Ch 1177
Wilson v Eden (1850) 20 LJ Ex 73, 5 Exch 752, 16 LTOS 152; on appeal (1852) 16 Beav
153, 20 LTOS 13 291
Wilson v Harper [1908] 2 Ch 370, 77 LJ Ch 607, 99 LT 391, sub nom Wilson v Harper,
Son [1908–10] All ER Rep 239 .... 1213, 1279
Wilson v Hodson (1872) LR 7 Exch 84, 36 JP 344, 41 LJ Ex 49, 20 WR 438
.... 1249, 1270
Wilson v Knox (1884) 13 LR Ir 349 431–433
Wilson v Maddison (1843) 2 Y & C Ch Cas 372, 12 LJ Ch 420, 7 Jur 572, 1 LTOS 336
.... 370, 1076
Wilson v Moore (1834) 1 My & K 337, 36 RR 272, [1824–34] All ER Rep 508
.... 1028
Wilson v Morley (1877) 5 Ch D 776, 46 LJ Ch 790, 25 WR 690, 36 LT 731
.... 277
Wilson v Mount (1840) 2 Beav 397, 4 Jur 262 446
Wilson v Mount (1854) 19 Beav 292, 2 WR 448 303
Wilson v O'Leary (1872) 7 Ch App 448, 41 LJ Ch 342, 20 WR 501, 26 LT 463, CA
.... 197, 225, 403
Wilson v Packman. See Packman's Case
Wilson v Piggott (1794) 2 Ves 351, 30 ER 668, [1775–1802] All ER Rep 539
.... 252
Wilson v Squire (1842) 1 Y & C Ch Cas 654 .... 210, 214
Wilson v Tucker (1822) 3 Stark 154, Dow & Ry NP 30
.... 1237
Wilson v Vansittart (1770) Amb 562 .... 341, 385
Wilson v Wilson (1847) 1 De G & Sm 152, 11 Jur 793, 9 LTOS 291
.... 127, 151
Wilson's Goods, Re (1866) LR 1 P & D 269, 36 LJP & M 1, 15 WR 229, 15 LT 191
.... 76
Wiltshire, Re, Eldred v Comport (1916) 142 LT Jo 57 380
Wimperis, Re, Wicken v Wilson [1914] 1 Ch 502, 83 LJ Ch 511, 58 Sol Jo 304, 110 LT
477 .... 151, 154
Winchester's (Marquess) Case (1598) 6 Co Rep 23a 48
Wind v Jekyl (1719) 1 P Wms 572 17
Windsor, Re, Public Trustee v Windsor (1913) 57 Sol Jo 555, 108 LT 947, 29 TLR 562
.... 293
Windus v Windus (1856) 6 De GM & G 549, 26 LJ Ch 185, 2 Jur NS 1101, 28 LTOS 31
.... 284, 298
Wing v Angrave. See Underwood v Wing
Wing v Wing (1876) 24 WR 878, 34 LT 941 377
Wingfield v Wingfield (1878) 9 Ch D 658, 47 LJ Ch 768, 26 WR 711, 39 LT 227
.... 321, 326, 341–342
Wingham, Re, Andrews v Wingham [1949] P 187, [1948] 2 All ER 908, [1949] LJR 695,
92 Sol Jo 660, 64 TLR 594, CA 79
Wingrove v Thompson (1879) 11 Ch D 419, 27 WR 910
.... 818
Wingrove v Wingrove (1885) 11 PD 81, 50 JP 56, 55 LJP 7, 34 WR 260, P, D and Admlty
.... 56
Winn, Re, Brook v Whitton [1910] 1 Ch 278, 79 LJ Ch 165, [1908–10] All ER Rep 593,
101 LT 737 .... 305, 313
Winn, Re, Burgess v Winn (1916) 86 LJ Ch 124, [1916–17] All ER Rep 758, 61 Sol Jo 99,
115 LT 698 328
Winn v Littleton (1681) 2 Cas in Ch 51, 1 Vern 3 207

PARA

Winn's Goods, Re (1861) 7 Jur NS 764, 2 Sw & Tr 147, 9 WR 852, 4 LT 655
.... 7

Winslow, Re, Frere v Winslow (1890) 45 Ch D 249, 60 LJ Ch 20, 39 WR 120, 63 LT 485
.... 1099, 1206

Winsor v Pratt (1821) 2 Brod & Bing 650, 5 Moore CP 484
.... 108

Winsor (Dean and Canons) and Webb's Case (1613) Godb 211
.... 553

Winstone's Goods, Re [1898] P 143, 67 LJP 76, 78 LT 535, P, D and Admlty
.... 745, 820

Winter v Innes (1838) 4 My & Cr 101, 2 Jur 981 1232–1233

Winter v Winter (1846) 5 Hare 306, 16 LJ Ch 111, 11 Jur 10, 8 LTOS 252, 5 Notes of
Cases 2n 27, 114–115, 167

Winterstoke's Will Trusts, Re, Gunn v Richardson [1938] Ch 158, [1937] 4 All ER 63,
107 LJ Ch 122, 81 Sol Jo 882, 158 LT 404, 54 TLR 20
.... 927

Winterton v Crawfurd (1830) 8 LJOS Ch 134, 1 Russ & M 407
.... 316

Wintle, Re, Tucker v Wintle [1896] 2 Ch 711, 65 LJ Ch 863, 45 WR 91, 75 LT 207
.... 432–433

Wintle v Nye [1959] 1 All ER 552, [1959] 1 WLR 284, 103 Sol Jo 220, HL
.... 4, 55, 875, 894, 903–904

Wipperman, Re, Wissler v Wipperman [1955] P 59, [1953] 1 All ER 764, [1953] 2 WLR
706, 97 Sol Jo 231, P, D and Admlty 716

Wisden v Wisden (1854) 18 Jur 1090, 2 Sm & G 396, 2 WR 616, 24 LTOS 250
.... 167, 376, 395

Wise v Whitburn [1924] 1 Ch 460, 93 LJ Ch 235, 68 Sol Jo 302, 130 LT 655
.... 1028, 1141, 1146, 1149

Wiseman v Wiseman (1866) LR 1 P & D 351, 31 JP 40, 35 LJP & M 22, 15 LT 415
.... 777

Witham v Witham (1861) 3 De GF & J 758, 30 LJ Ch 888, 9 WR 854, 5 LT 133
.... 444

Wither v King. See King v Withers

Withy v Mangles (1843) 10 Cl & Fin 215, 8 Jur 69, HL
.... 343, 395

Witkowska v Kaminski [2006] EWHC 1940 (Ch), [2006] 3 FCR 250, [2007] 1 FLR 1547,
[2006] All ER (D) 357 (Jul) 567

Wohlgemuth, Re, Public Trustee v Wohlgemuth [1949] Ch 12, [1948] 2 All ER 882,
[1949] LJR 231, 92 Sol Jo 660, 64 TLR 587 .... 214, 351

Wolfe v Wolfe [1902] 2 IR 246 6

Wolfe's Goods, Re [1919] 2 IR 491 288

Wolffe's Will Trusts, Re, Shapley v Wolffe [1953] 2 All ER 697, [1953] 1 WLR 1211, 97
Sol Jo 539 .... 129–130, 137, 140, 143

Wollaston v Hakewill (1841) 10 LJCP 303, 3 Man & G 297, 3 Scott NR 593
.... 1224

Wollen v Andrewes (1824) 2 Bing 126, 2 LJOSCP 145, 9 Moore CP 248
.... 391, 460

Wolson, Re, Wolson v Jackson [1939] Ch 780, [1939] 3 All ER 852, 108 LJ Ch 399, 83
Sol Jo 605, 161 LT 168, 55 TLR 923 167

Wolverton Mortgaged Estates, Re (1877) 7 Ch D 197, sub nom Re Woolverton Mortgaged
Estates 47 LJ Ch 127, 26 WR 138, 37 LT 573 220

Womersley, Re, Etheridge v Womersley (1885) 29 Ch D 557, 54 LJ Ch 965, 33 WR 935,
53 LT 260 1176

Wood, Re, A-G v Anderson [1896] 2 Ch 596, 65 LJ Ch 814, 44 WR 685, 40 Sol Jo 654,
75 LT 28, 12 TLR 522 555

Wood, Re, Barton v Chilcott [1949] Ch 498, [1949] 1 All ER 1100, [1949] LJR 1509, 93
Sol Jo 357 11

Wood, Re, Hardy v Hull (1923) 68 Sol Jo 186, 130 LT 408
.... 318–319, 444

Wood, Re, Moore v Bailey (1880) 29 WR 171, 43 LT 730
.... 305, 440

Wood, Re, Tullett v Colville [1894] 3 Ch 381, 63 LJ Ch 790, 7 R 495, 71 LT 413, CA
.... 322

Wood, Re, Walker v Carlile (1920) 36 TLR 560 131

Wood, Re, Ward v Wood (1886) 32 Ch D 517, 55 LJ Ch 720, 34 WR 788, sub nom Re
Wood's Estate, Wood v Ward 54 LT 932 406

PARA

Wood, Re, Wood v Wood [1902] 2 Ch 542, 71 LJ Ch 723, 50 WR 695, 46 Sol Jo 632, 87
LT 316, 18 TLR 710, CA 352
Wood, Re, Wood v Wood [1982] LS Gaz R 774 575
Wood v Baron (1801) 1 East 259 389
Wood v Douglas. See Douglas, Re, Wood v Douglas
Wood v Penoyre (1807) 13 Ves 325 .... 1054, 1081
Wood v Richardson (1840) 4 Beav 174, 5 Jur 623 370
Wood v Smith [1993] Ch 90, [1992] 3 All ER 556, [1992] 3 WLR 583, [1992] 17 LS Gaz
R 43, 136 Sol Jo LB 99, CA 62–63, 68, 82
Wood v Weightman (1872) LR 13 Eq 434, 20 WR 459, 26 LT 385
.... 964
Wood v Westall (1831) You 305 1173
Wood v Wood (1811) 1 Phillim 357 50
Wood v Wood (1843) 3 Hare 65, 1 LTOS 76 .... 348, 394
Wood v Wood (1866) 35 Beav 587 450
Wood (alias Cranmer) v Duke of Southampton (1692) Show Parl Cas 83, HL
.... 129
Wood (Sir Caesar) (alias Cranmer) v Webb (1695) Show Parl Cas 87, HL
.... 129
Wood's Will, Re (1861) 29 Beav 236 .... 173, 1115
Wood's Will, Re (1862) 31 Beav 323 .... 175, 322
Woodburne v Woodburne (1850) 3 De G & Sm 643, 19 LJ Ch 88, 14 Jur 565, 15 LTOS
21 444
Woodburne v Woodburne (1853) 23 LJ Ch 336, 18 Jur 184, 2 WR 131, 22 LTOS 314
.... 450
Woodden v Osbourn (1599) Cro Eliz 674 210
Woodford v Thellusson (1799) 4 Ves 227; affd (1805) 1 Bos & PNR 357, 8 RR 104, 11
Ves 112, 32 ER 1030, [1803–13] All ER Rep 30, HL 34
Woodgate, Re (1886) 2 TLR 674 11
Woodgate v Atkins. See Woodgate v Unwin
Woodgate v Field (1842) 2 Hare 211, 11 LJ Ch 321, 6 Jur 871
.... 1173, 1301
Woodgate v Unwin (1831) 4 Sim 129, sub nom Woodgate v Atkins 9 LJOS Ch 166
.... 395
Woodhouse, Re, Public Trustee v Woodhouse [1941] Ch 332, [1941] 2 All ER 265, 110 LJ
Ch 214, 85 Sol Jo 367, 165 LT 368, 57 TLR 598 .... 1123, 1127
Woodhouse v Balfour (1887) 13 PD 2, 52 JP 7, 57 LJP 22, 36 WR 368, 58 LT 59, P, D
and Admlty 68, 895–896
Woodhouse v Herrick (1855) 1 K & J 352, 24 LJ Ch 649, 3 Eq Rep 817, 3 WR 303
.... 311, 414
Woodhouse v Spurgeon (1883) 52 LJ Ch 825, 32 WR 225, 49 LT 97
.... 469
Woodhouse v Walker (1880) 5 QBD 404, 44 JP 666, 49 LJQB 609, 28 WR 765, 42 LT
770 .... 152, 1229
Woodhouselee (Lord) v Dalrymple (1817) 2 Mer 419 351
Woodin, Re, Woodin v Glass [1895] 2 Ch 309, 64 LJ Ch 501, 12 R 302, 43 WR 615, 39
Sol Jo 558, 72 LT 740, CA 1083
Woodiwiss' Will Trusts, Robotham v Burn (1959) 109 L Jo 154
.... 312
Woodley's Goods, Re (1864) 28 JP 599, 33 LJPM & A 154, 4 New Rep 72, 3 Sw & Tr
429 65
Woodman v Blake (1691) 2 Vern 222 149
Woodright v Wright. See Goodright v Wright
Woodroofe v Woodroofe [1894] 1 IR 299, 28 ILT 304 449–450
Woods, Re, Gabellini v Woods [1904] 2 Ch 4, 73 LJ Ch 204, 48 Sol Jo 207, 90 LT 8
.... 1124, 1126
Woods, Re, Woods v Creagh [1931] 2 Ch 138, 100 LJ Ch 385, [1931] All ER Rep 696,
145 LT 206 .... 173, 175
Woods v Townley (1853) 11 Hare 314, 23 LJ Ch 281, 1 WR 504, 22 LTOS 75
.... 145
Woods v Woods (1836) 1 My & Cr 401, Donnelly 61, 43 RR 214
.... 348
Woods' Goods, Re (1868) LR 1 P & D 556, 32 JP 168, 37 LJP & M 23, 16 WR 407, 17
LT 583 .... 65, 611
Woodward v Glasbrook (1700) 2 Vern 388 .... 410, 442

PARA

Woodward v Goulstone (1886) 11 App Cas 469, 51 JP 307, 56 LJP 1, 35 WR 337,
[1886–90] All ER Rep 234, 55 LT 790, HL 716
Woodward's Goods, Re (1871) LR 2 P & D 206, 35 JP 216, 40 LJP & M 17, 19 WR 448,
24 LT 40 .... 96, 105
Woolcomb v Woolcomb (1731) 2 Eq Cas Abr 326, 3 P Wms 112
.... 250
Wooldridge v Norris (1868) LR 6 Eq 410, 37 LJ Ch 640, 16 WR 965, 19 LT 144
.... 1173
Woolf, Re, Public Trustee v Lazarus [1920] 1 Ch 184, 89 LJ Ch 11, 122 LT 457
.... 283, 431, 445
Woolf's Estate, Re (1918) 62 Sol Jo 621, 34 TLR 477, P, D and Admlty
.... 759
Woolgar, Re, Woolgar v Hopkins [1942] Ch 318, [1942] 1 All ER 583, 111 LJ Ch 209, 86
Sol Jo 161, 167 LT 60, 58 TLR 252 1174
Woolley, Re, Cathcart v Eyskens [1918] 1 Ch 33, 87 LJ Ch 169, 117 LT 511
.... 293
Woolley, Re, Wormald v Woolley [1903] 2 Ch 206, 72 LJ Ch 602, 89 LT 16
.... 254, 321, 325, 393
Woolley v Clark (1822) 5 B & Ald 744, 1 Dow & Ry KB 409, 106 ER 1363,
[1814–23] All ER Rep 584 .... 633, 643, 858, 1267
Woolley and Gordon v Green (1820) 3 Phillim 314 817
Woolnough, Re Perkins & Borden [2002] WTLR 595 29
Woolrich, Re, Harris v Harris (1879) 11 Ch D 663, 48 LJ Ch 321, 27 WR 429, 41 LT 309
.... 323
Worby v Rosser (1999) 2 ITELR 59, [1999] 04 LS Gaz R 39, Times, 9 June, [1999] All ER
(D) 571, CA 909
Wordingham v Royal Exchange Trust Co Ltd [1992] Ch 412, [1992] 3 All ER 204, [1992]
2 WLR 496, [1992] 17 LS Gaz R 44 187
Wordsworth v Wood (1847) 1 HL Cas 129, 11 Jur 593, 9 LTOS 489
.... 200, 318
Worlidge v Churchill (1792) Cas temp Talb 295, 3 Bro CC 465
.... 410
Wormald, Re, Frank v Muzeen (1890) 43 Ch D 630, 59 LJ Ch 404, 38 WR 425, 62 LT
423 464
Worman, Re (1859) 29 LJPM & A 164, 5 Jur NS 687, 1 Sw & Tr 513
.... 770
Worms v De Valdor (1880) 49 LJ Ch 261, 28 WR 346, 41 LT 791
.... 34
Worraker v Pryer (1876) 2 Ch D 109, 45 LJ Ch 273, 2 Char Pr Cas 284, 24 WR 269
.... 1173
Worsley v Wood (1796) 6 Term Rep 710, 101 ER 785, [1775–1802] All ER Rep 59
.... 147
Worthington, Re, Nichols v Hart [1933] Ch 771, 102 LJ Ch 273, [1933] All ER Rep 189,
77 Sol Jo 371, 149 LT 296, 49 TLR 444, CA 994, 999, 1108
Worthington, Re, ex p Leighton v MacLeod [1954] 1 All ER 677, [1954] 1 WLR 526, 98
Sol Jo 196 .... 652–653, 656
Worthington, Re, ex p Pathé Frères [1914] 2 KB 299, 83 LJKB 885, 21 Mans 119, 110 LT
599, CA 1230
Worthington v Barlow (1797) 7 Term Rep 453 1299
Worthington v Evans (1823) 1 Sim & St 165, 1 LJOS Ch 126
.... 135–136
Worthington & Co Ltd v Abbott [1910] 1 Ch 588, 79 LJ Ch 252, 54 Sol Jo 83, 101 LT
895 970
Worts v Cubitt (1854) 19 Beav 421, 2 WR 633 352
Wragg, Re, Hollingsworth v Wragg [1959] 2 All ER 717, [1959] 1 WLR 922, 103 Sol Jo
716, CA 180, 255, 419, 422
Wragg, Re, Wragg v Palmer [1919] 2 Ch 58, 88 LJ Ch 269, [1918–19] All ER Rep 233, 63
Sol Jo 535, 121 LT 78 1160
Wrangham's Trust, Re (1860) 1 Drew & Sm 358, 30 LJ Ch 258, 7 Jur NS 15, 9 WR 156,
3 LT 722 .... 427, 437
Wray, Re, Wray v Wray [1951] Ch 425, [1951] 1 All ER 375, 95 Sol Jo 107, CA
.... 27, 96, 165
Wray v Field (1822) 6 Madd 300; affd (1826) 2 Russ 257
.... 403
Wren v Wren [2006] EWHC 2243 (Ch), 9 ITELR 223, [2006] 3 FCR 18, [2006] All ER
(D) 30 (Sep) 106, 716

PARA
Wrench v Jutting (1841) 3 Beav 521, 5 Jur 145 250
Wrey, Re, Stuart v Wrey (1885) 30 Ch D 507, 24 LJ Ch 1098, 53 LT 334
.... 428, 430, 434
Wrey v Smith (1844) 14 Sim 202 1124
Wright, Re (1910) 44 ILT 137 717
Wright, Re, Blizard v Lockhart [1954] Ch 347, [1954] 1 All ER 864, [1954] 2 WLR 481,
   98 Sol Jo 691; affd [1954] Ch 347, [1954] 2 All ER 98, [1954] 2 WLR 972, 98 Sol Jo
   336, CA 1190
Wright, Re, Mott v Issott [1907] 1 Ch 231, 76 LJ Ch 89, [1904–7] All ER Rep 169, 51 Sol
   Jo 47, 95 LT 697 .... 132, 139
Wright, Re, Public Trustee v Wright (1937) 81 Sol Jo 1022, 158 LT 368, 54 TLR 153
.... 131, 140
Wright v Atkyns (1810) 17 Ves 255; on appeal (1814) Coop G 111, 1 Ves & B 313, 19 Ves
   299; revsd (1823) Turn & R 143, Turn & R 145, HL 348, 384
Wright v Callender (1852) 2 De GM & G 652, 21 LJ Ch 787, 16 Jur 647, 42 ER 1027,
   [1843–60] All ER Rep 508, 19 LTOS 308, CA in Ch 1090
Wright v Carter [1903] 1 Ch 27, 72 LJ Ch 138, 51 WR 196, [1900–3] All ER Rep 706, 87
   LT 624, 19 TLR 29, CA 904
Wright v Englefield (1764) Amb 468, sub nom Wright v Lord Cadogan 2 Eden 239; affd
   (1766) 1 ER 707, 1 Bro Parl Cas 486, HL 474
Wright v Holford (1774) 1 Cowp 31, Lofft 443 474
Wright v Lambert (1877) 6 Ch D 649, 26 WR 206 1127
Wright v Lord Cadogan. See Wright v Englefield
Wright v Marsom [1895] WN 148, 40 Sol Jo 67 442
Wright v Rogers (1869) LR 1 P & D 678, 33 JP 711, 38 LJP & M 67, 17 WR 833, 27 LT
   156 .... 77, 895
Wright v Row (1779) 1 Bro CC 61 184
Wright v Sanderson (1884) 9 PD 149, 48 JP 180, 53 LJP 49, 32 WR 560, 50 LT 769,
   [1881–5] All ER Rep Ext 1373, CA 68–69, 895–896
Wright v Wakeford (1811) 17 Ves 454, 34 ER 176, [1803–13] All ER Rep 589
.... 63
Wright v Waters [2014] EWHC 3614 (Ch), [2015] WTLR 353, [2014] All ER (D) 85
   (Nov) 573, 575–576
Wright v Wilkin (1860) 2 B & S 232, 31 LJQB 7, 7 Jur NS 441, 10 WR 403, 6 LT 220;
   affd (1860) 2 B & S 259, 31 LJQB 196, 9 Jur NS 715, 11 WR 101, 6 LT 221
.... 152, 407
Wright v Wright (1750) 1 Ves Sen 409, 27 ER 1111, [1558–1774] All ER Rep 528
.... 342
Wright v Wright (1852) 21 LJ Ch 775, 19 LTOS 311 428
Wright d Burrill v Kemp (1789) 3 Term Rep 470 442
Wright's Goods, Re [1893] P 21, 62 LJP 31, 41 WR 318, 68 LT 25, P, D and Admlty
.... 816
Wright's Goods, Re (1865) 29 JP 504, 34 LJPM & A 104, 4 Sw & Tr 35, 13 LT 195
.... 65
Wright's Goods, Re (1898) 79 LT 473, P, D and Admlty
.... 788
Wright's Goods, Re (1908) 25 TLR 15, P, D and Admlty
.... 613
Wrightson, Re, Battie-Wrightson v Thomas [1904] 2 Ch 95, 73 LJ Ch 742, 90 LT 748, CA
.... 412–413
Wrightson v Calvert (1860) 1 John & H 250 .... 271, 274
Wrightson v Macaulay (1845) 15 LJ Ex 121, 14 M & W 214, 5 LTOS 218
.... 340
Wroe, Re, Frith v Wilson (1896) 74 LT 302 253
Wroe v Seed (1863) 4 Giff 425, 9 Jur NS 1122, 9 LT 254
.... 1055, 1254
Wroughton v Colquhoun (1847) 1 De G & Sm 357, 11 Jur 940
.... 1090
Wyatt, Re [1952] 1 All ER 1030, 96 Sol Jo 362, [1952] 1 TLR 1294, P, D and Admlty
.... 98
Wyatt, Re, Furniss v Phear (1888) 36 WR 521, 4 TLR 245
.... 214, 263
Wyatt, Re, Gowan v Wyatt (1889) 60 LT 920 446
Wyatt v Berry [1893] P 5, 62 LJP 28, 1 R 462, 68 LT 416, 9 TLR 36, P, D and Admlty
.... 70

PARA

Wyatt v Ingram. See Ingram v Wyatt
Wyatt's Goods, Re [1898] P 15, 67 LJP 7, 46 WR 425, 78 LT 80, P, D and Admlty
.... 680
Wyckoff's Goods, Re (1862) 32 LJPM & A 214, 9 Jur NS 84, 1 New Rep 131, 169, 3 Sw
   & Tr 20, 11 WR 218, 7 LT 565 814
Wyld v Lewis (1738) 1 Atk 432, West temp Hard 308 .... 384, 473
Wylde v Culver [2006] EWHC 923 (Ch), [2006] 4 All ER 345, [2006] 1 WLR 2674,
   [2006] All ER (D) 172 (Apr) 883
Wyles, Re, Foster v Wyles [1938] Ch 313, [1938] 1 All ER 347, 107 LJ Ch 164, 82 Sol Jo
   95, 54 TLR 336, sub nom Re Wyles, Porter v Wyles 158 LT 147
.... 1080
Wylie's Trustees v Bruce (1919) 56 SLR 156, 1919 SC 211, 1919 1 SLT 41, Ct of Sess
.... 302
Wylly's Trust, Re (1860) 25 JP 84, 28 Beav 458, 6 Jur NS 906, 126 RR 217, 8 WR 645, 2
   LT 788 1047
Wyman v Paterson [1900] AC 271, 69 LJPC 32, 82 LT 473, 16 TLR 270, HL
.... 1257
Wynch v Wynch (1788) 1 Cox Eq Cas 433 430
Wynch's Trusts, Re, ex p Wynch (1854) 5 De GM & G 188, 23 LJ Ch 930, 2 Eq Rep
   1025, 18 Jur 659, 2 WR 570, 23 LTOS 259 .... 384–386, 392
Wyndham's Trusts, Re (1865) LR 1 Eq 290 .... 364, 456
Wyniczenko v Plucinska-Surowka [2005] EWHC 2794 (Ch), 8 ITELR 385, [2005] All ER
   (D) 245 (Nov) 55
Wynn, Re, Landolt v Wynn [1983] 3 All ER 310, [1984] 1 WLR 237, 128 Sol Jo 34
.... 257, 468
Wynn's Will Trusts, Re, Public Trustee v Newborough [1952] Ch 271, [1952] 1 All ER
   341, 96 Sol Jo 120, [1952] 1 TLR 278 .... 190, 1168
Wynne v Fletcher (1857) 24 Beav 430 139
Wynne v Hughes (1859) 26 Beav 377, 28 LJ Ch 283, 5 Jur NS 165, 7 WR 197, 32 LTOS
   329; on appeal (1859) 28 LJ Ch 485 1177
Wynne v Wynne (1837) 2 Keen 778, 7 LJ Ch 45 375
Wythe v Thurlston (1749) Amb 555, sub nom Wyth v Blackman 1 Ves Sen 196
.... 334

X

X v A [2000] 1 All ER 490, [2000] 1 EGLR 19, [1999] 39 LS Gaz R 38, [2000] 01 EG 94,
   143 Sol Jo LB 239, [2000] Env LR 104 989
Xydhias v Xydhias [1999] 2 All ER 386, [1999] 1 FCR 289, [1999] 1 FLR 683, [1999]
   Fam Law 301, [1999] NLJR 52, CA 1279

Y

Yahuda's Estate, Re [1956] P 388, [1956] 2 All ER 262, [1956] 3 WLR 20, 100 Sol Jo
   382, P, D and Admlty 718
Yalden, Re (1851) 1 De GM & G 53 381
Yardley v Arnold (1842) Car & M 434, 2 Dowl NS 311, 11 LJ Ex 413, 6 Jur 718, 10 M
   & W 141 1267,1270
Yardley v Yardley (1858) 26 Beav 38 408
Yarnold v Wallis (1840) 4 Y & C Ex 160 113
Yarrow v Knightly (1878) 8 Ch D 736, 47 LJ Ch 874, 26 WR 704, 39 LT 238, CA
.... 376, 395
Yates, ex p (1869) 17 WR 872, 20 LT 940 288
Yates, Re, Bostock v D'Eyncourt [1891] 3 Ch 53, 39 WR 573, 64 LT 819
.... 326
Yates, Re, Singleton v Povah [1922] All ER Rep 328, 66 Sol Jo 523, 128 LT 619
.... 114, 252
Yates, Re, Throckmorton v Pike (1907) 96 LT 758, CA 1080
Yates v Clincard (1599) Cro Eliz 704 286
Yates v Compton (1725) 2 Eq Cas Abr 457, 2 P Wms 308, Cas temp King 54
.... 1058
Yates v Phettiplace (1700) Freem Ch 243, 1 Ld Raym 508, 12 Mod Rep 276, Prec Ch 140,
   2 Vern 416 438
Yates v University College, London (1873) 8 Ch App 454; on appeal (1875) LR 7 HL 438,
   45 LJ Ch 137, 23 WR 408, 32 LT 43, HL 143

PARA

Yates v Yates (1860) 28 Beav 637, 29 LJ Ch 872, 6 Jur NS 1023, 3 LT 9
.... 1121, 1123, 1126
Yates v Yates (1905) 25 NZLR 263 383
Yates Estate, Re [1919] P 93, 88 LJP 92, 63 Sol Jo 355, 120 LT 671, 35 TLR 301, P, D
and Admlty 79, 240
Yates Trust, Re (1851) 21 LJ Ch 281, 16 Jur 78, 18 LTOS 298
.... 453
Yeap Cheah Neo v Ong Cheng Neo (1875) LR 6 PC 381, PC
.... 348
Yeates v Groves (1791) 1 Ves 280 409
Yeats v Yeats (1852) 16 Beav 170 274
Yelland, Re, Broadbent v Francis (1975) 119 Sol Jo 562
.... 106, 716, 894–895
Yellowly v Gower (1855) 24 LJ Ex 289, 11 Exch 274 1229
Yeoman's Row Management Ltd v Cobbe [2008] UKHL 55, [2008] 4 All ER 713, [2009]
1 All ER (Comm) 205, [2008] 1 WLR 1752, 11 ITELR 530, [2008] 35 EG 142,
[2008] 36 EG 142, (2008) Times, 8 September, 152 Sol Jo (no 31) 31, [2008] All ER
(D) 419 (Jul) 20
Yerburgh, Re, Yerburgh v Yerburgh [1928] WN 208 .... 1075, 1144, 1149
Yockney v Hansard (1844) 3 Hare 620, 8 Jur 822 402
Yorke, Re, Stone v Chataway [1997] 4 All ER 907, [1997] 33 LS Gaz R 26
.... 991, 1169–1170, 1245, 1290
Young, Re, Brown v Hodgson [1912] 2 Ch 479, 81 LJ Ch 817, 107 LT 380
.... 375
Young, Re, Fraser v Young [1913] 1 Ch 272, 82 LJ Ch 171, 57 Sol Jo 265, 108 LT 292, 29
TLR 224 .... 154, 182
Young, Re, Young v Dolman (1881) 44 LT 499, CA 1017
Young, Re, Young v Young [1914] 1 Ch 581; affd [1914] 1 Ch 976, 83 LJ Ch 453, 111 LT
265, CA 404
Young, Re, Young v Young [1951] Ch 185, 94 Sol Jo 762, sub nom Young's Will Trusts,
Re, Young v Young [1950] 2 All ER 1040 514–515
Young, Re, Young v Young [1951] Ch 344, [1950] 2 All ER 1245, 94 Sol Jo 839, [1951] 1
TLR 262 .... 42, 208, 221
Young v Bain, Re Young (1902) 21 NZLR 503 285
Young v Burdett (1724) 5 Bro Parl Cas 54, HL 232
Young v Davies (1863) 2 Drew & Sm 167, 32 LJ Ch 372, 9 Jur NS 399, 1 New Rep 419,
11 WR 452, 8 LT 80 .... 41, 174, 318, 335, 384–385
Young v Hassard (1841) 1 Dr & War 638 251
Young v Holloway [1895] P 87, 64 LJP 55, 11 R 596, 43 WR 429, 72 LT 118, 11 TLR
128, [1891–4] All ER Rep Ext 1478, P, D and Admlty 887–888
Young v Holmes (1717) 1 Stra 70 1141
Young v Richards (1839) 2 Curt 371 77
Young v Robertson (1862) 8 Jur NS 825, 4 Macq 314, HL
.... 238, 318, 453
Young v Sheppard (1847) 10 Beav 207, 16 LJ Ch 247, 9 LTOS 331
.... 400
Young v Turner (1861) 1 B & S 550, 30 LJQB 268, 8 Jur 52, 5 LT 56
.... 441
Young v Young (1918) 52 ILT 40 390
Young (otherwise Mearing) v Brown (1827) 1 Hag Ecc 53
.... 810
Young's Estate, Re (1934) 103 LJP 75, 78 Sol Jo 431, 151 LT 221, 50 TLR 424, P, D and
Admlty 656
Young's Settlement Trusts, Re, Royal Exchange Assurance v Taylor-Young [1959] 2 All ER
74, [1959] 1 WLR 457, 103 Sol Jo 328 182
Young's Trustees v Young 1927 SC (HL) 6, HL 318, 444
Younge v Furse (1857) 8 De GM & G 756, sub nom Yonge v Furse 26 LJ Ch 352, 3 Jur
NS 603, 5 WR 394, 29 LTOS 34 .... 133, 408
Younger v Saner [2002] EWCA Civ 1077, [2002] All ER (D) 372 (Jul)
.... 1244, 1265
Youngmin v Heath [1974] 1 All ER 461, [1974] 1 WLR 135, 26 P & CR 570, 117 Sol Jo
795, CA 1222
Youngs, Re, Doggett v Revett (1885) 30 Ch D 421, 33 WR 880, 53 LT 682, CA
.... 1173
Youngs, Re, Vollum v Revett (1885) 30 Ch D 421, 33 WR 880, 53 LT 682, CA
.... 1173

PARA
Yule's Trustees v Deans 1919 SC 570, Ct of Sess 413, 422

Z

Zaman v Zoha [2006] EWCA Civ 770, [2006] All ER (D) 350 (Mar)
.... 1232
Zambaco v Cassavetti (1871) LR 11 Eq 439, 24 LT 770
.... 1177–1178
Zealley v Veryard (1866) LR 1 P & D 195, 30 JP 663, 35 LJP & M 127, 14 WR 970, 14
	LT 769 867
Zerny's Will Trusts, Re, Symons v Zerny [1968] Ch 415, [1968] 1 All ER 686, [1968] 2
	WLR 1066, 111 Sol Jo 927, CA 125
Zetland (Earl) v Lord Advocate (1878) 3 App Cas 505, 26 WR 725, 38 LT 297, HL
.... 916
Zielinski, Re Korab-Karpinski v Lucas-Gardiner [2007] WTLR 1655
.... 106
Zimmer's Estate, Re (1924) 40 TLR 502 108
Zouche (Baroness), Re, Dugdale v Baroness Zouche [1919] 2 Ch 178, 88 LJ Ch 274, 63
	Sol Jo 554, 121 LT 82 .... 285, 296

WILLS AND INTESTACY

Volume 102

		PARA
1.	**TESTAMENTARY DISPOSITION**	**1**
(1)	Form and Effect of Testamentary Instruments	1
	(i) Nature and Characteristics of Testamentary Instruments	1
	(ii) Restrictions on Freedom of Testamentary Disposition	20
(2)	Property Capable of Disposition by Will	25
	(i) English Property disposable by Will	25
	(ii) Things not disposable by Will	30
(3)	Donees	33
	(i) Capacity to Benefit	33
	(ii) Disqualification for Benefiting from Will	38
	A. Wrongful Act of Donee	38
	B. Donee or Spouse an Attesting Witness	41
	(iii) Uncertainty as to Donee	45
(4)	Requirements for a Valid Will: Mental Element	46
	(i) Testamentary Capacity	46
	A. General Testamentary Capacity	46
	B. Mental Disability	47
	(ii) Knowledge and Approval of Testator	54
	(iii) Effect of Undue Influence, Force and Fraud	56
(5)	Requirements for a Valid Will: Formalities	60
	(i) Writing	60
	(ii) Date	61
	(iii) Signature	62
	(iv) Attestation	70
	(v) Privileged Wills	79
(6)	Alterations and Erasures in Will	82
(7)	Revocation of Will	87
	(i) Revocation by Marriage	87
	(ii) Revocation by Civil Partnership	90
	(iii) Voluntary Revocation	92
	A. Requisites for Revocation	92
	B. Revocation by Later Instrument	95
	C. Revocation by Destruction	101
	D. Conditional Revocation	107
(8)	Revival of Will	110
(9)	Republication of Will	113
2.	**TYPES OF TESTAMENTARY DISPOSITION**	**116**
(1)	Interests which may be Disposed of by Will	116
(2)	Interests which may be Completed by Will	121
(3)	Conditions Attached to Gifts by Will	128
3.	**FAILURE OF TESTAMENTARY DISPOSITIONS**	**150**
(1)	Circumstances Giving Rise to Failure	150

PARA

(2)   Disclaimer 151

(3)   Ademption... 155

(4)   Doctrine of Lapse 160

    (i)   Meaning and Application of Lapse 160

    (ii)   Exceptions from Lapse 163

(5)   Dissolution or Annulment of Marriage or Civil Partnership 177

(6)   Effect of Failure and Lapse 180

4.   CONSTRUCTION OF WILLS 185

(1)   Courts of Construction 185

(2)   Admissibility of Evidence 193

    (i)   Evidence of Testator's Intentions....................................... 193

    (ii)   Evidence of Language and its Meaning................................. 200

    (iii)   Evidence for Purposes of Identification 209

    (iv)   Evidence of Secret Trusts 221

(3)   Principles of Construction of Wills.. 224

    (i)   Application of Principles of Construction 224

       A.   Ascertainment of Intention... 224

       B.   Application of Rules of Construction 235

    (ii)   Context, Meaning and Effect of Words................................. 241

    (iii)   Presumptions... 255

       A.   Presumption against Intestacy 255

       B.   Presumptions of Legality and of Knowledge of the Testator ... 258

       C.   Presumption Favouring Relatives or Persons Having a Claim on the Testator 260

    (iv)   Uncertainty... 262

    (v)   Misdescription of Property or Persons.................................. 267

5.   CONSTRUCTION OF PARTICULAR DISPOSITIONS 281

(1)   Application of Rules of Construction of Particular Dispositions 281

(2)   Property Passing... 282

    (i)   General Effect of Property Passing..................................... 282

    (ii)   Effect of Description by Locality....................................... 285

    (iii)   Effect of Particular Words.. 286

(3)   Persons Entitled to Take 299

    (i)   Time of Ascertainment of Donees...................................... 299

       A.   Identifying Donees.. 299

       B.   Class Gifts 302

       C.   Survivorship 315

       D.   Alternative Gifts.. 320

    (ii)   Identification of Donees 328

       A.   Identification by Reference to Relationships 328

          (A)   General Rule and Particular Descriptions 328

          (B)   Relations through Illegitimacy; Dispositions made before 1970... 350

          (C)   Relations through Illegitimacy; Dispositions made after 31 December 1969 and before 4 April 1988.......... 355

          (D)   Relations through Illegitimacy; Dispositions made on or after 4 April 1988................................. 356

                                                                    PARA
              (E)   Adopted and Legitimated Children; Testator dying
                       after 1975.. 357
              (F)   Artificial Insemination and In Vitro Fertilisation....... 358
              (G)   Rights of a Person en Ventre sa Mère 362
        B.   Identification by Reference to Office or Employment.......... 363
(4)   Quantity of Interest Taken... 368
       (i)   General Principles as to Quantity of Interest Taken.................... 368
       (ii)   Absolute and Life Interests 375
               A.   Absolute Interests 375
               B.   Life Interests..................................... 379
               C.   Absolute Interest Reduced to Life Interest 381
               D.   Life Interest Enlarged to Absolute Interest 383
       (iii)   Estates Tail.. 384
       (iv)   Gifts to a Person and his Children or Issue 389
       (v)   Concurrent Gifts...................................... 393
               A.   Joint Tenancy and Tenancy in Common 393
               B.   Distribution Per Capita and Per Stirpes 396
       (vi)   Cumulative and Substitutional Gifts 401
       (vii)   Hotchpot Clauses....................................... 404
(5)   Conditional Gifts.. 407
       (i)   General Provisions relating to Conditional Gifts........................ 407
       (ii)   Vesting 412
               A.   Presumption as to Vesting 412
               B.   Circumstances Affecting Vesting................. 415
               C.   Vesting of Remainders 418
               D.   Effect of Gift over on Vesting of Prior Gift 423
               E.   Gifts out of Personal Estate..................... 425
                      (A)   In general 425
                      (B)   Direction as to Payment............................. 427
                      (C)   Direction as to Maintenance 430
                      (D)   Severance from the Estate............................ 434
                      (E)   Effect of Gift Over 435
               F.   Legacies Charged on Real Estate or a Mixed Fund............. 438
       (iii)   Divesting 440
       (iv)   Gifts over by Inference 445
       (v)   Particular Conditions....................................... 449
               A.   Gifts Over in the Event of Death 449
               B.   Limitations on Failure of Issue 454
               C.   Forfeiture on Alienation.............................. 462
(6)   Implied Gifts 466

6.   INTESTATE SUCCESSION 477
(1)   Legal Framework relating to Intestate Succession 477
(2)   Capacity to Take under an Intestacy............................... 480
(3)   Deaths Intestate after 1952....................................... 485
       (i)   Right of Surviving Spouse or Civil Partner 485
       (ii)   Rights of Issue under the Statutory Trusts........................ 499
       (iii)   Rights of Relatives Other than Issue, Spouse or Civil Partner of

            Deceased 507
    (iv)   Rights of the Crown and the Duchies 512
    (v)   Partial Intestacy 514
    (vi)   Summary of Distribution on Intestacy 518
(4) Deaths Intestate after 1925 and before 1953 521
(5) Deaths Intestate before 1926 531
    (i)   Application of Old Rules in respect of Deaths after 1926 531
    (ii)   The Old Rules: Distribution of Personal Estate 536
    (iii)   The Old Rules: Descent of Real Estate 538

Volume 103

                                                                          PARA

7.   FAMILY PROVISION CLAIMS 565
(1) Requirement for Financial Provision 565
(2) Reasonable Financial Provision 568
(3) Matters which the Court Must Take into Account 571
     (i)   Guidelines Applicable to All Cases 571
     (ii)   Guidelines Applicable to Particular Applicants 577
(4) Property Available for Financial Provision 582
     (i)   Property Always Available 582
     (ii)   Property Available if the Court so Orders 585
(5) Order for Financial Provision 591
(6) Procedure 597

8.   THE OFFICE OF REPRESENTATIVE 605
(1) Representatives Generally 605
(2) The Executor 610
     (i)   Appointment of Executors 610
     (ii)   Persons Eligible for Appointment as Executor 619
     (iii) Acceptance of the Office of Executor 627
     (iv)   Renunciation of the Office of Executor 630
     (v)   Executor's Acts before Grant 633
(3) The Chain of Representation 637
     (i)   Devolution on Death 637
     (ii)   Devolution Otherwise than on Death 642
(4) The Administrator 643
     (i)   Administrator's Acts before Grant 643
     (ii)   The Doctrine of Relation Back 645
(5) Personal Representatives' Remuneration 648
(6) The Need for a Grant of Probate or Administration 659
     (i)   Need for a Grant Generally 659
     (ii)   Estates Exempt from Necessity for Grant of Probate or Administration. 660
(7) Effect of a Grant of Probate or Letters of Administration 669

9.   THE GRANT OF PROBATE OR ADMINISTRATION 676
(1) The High Court 676
     (i)   Jurisdiction 676
     (ii)   Practice and Procedure 685

			PARA
(2)	Instruments Entitled to Probate		707
	(i)	Wills in England and Wales	707
	(ii)	Foreigners' Wills	718
	(iii)	Wills disposing of Property Abroad	722
(3)	Probate in Common Form		724
	(i)	How and by whom Obtained	724
	(ii)	Limited Probates	747
	(iii)	Double and Cessate Grants	751
(4)	General Grants of Administration		754
(5)	Administration Simple		767
	(i)	Grants of Administration	767
	(ii)	Surviving Spouse or Civil Partner	770
	(iii)	Next of Kin	773
	(iv)	The Crown and the Duchies	778
	(v)	Trust Corporations and the Public Trustee	783
	(vi)	Creditors	786
(6)	Administration with the Will Annexed		788
(7)	Special and Limited Grants of Administration		793
	(i)	Unadministered Estate	793
	(ii)	Administration during Minority of Person Entitled	795
	(iii)	Administration by Attorneys and Consular Officers	800
	(iv)	Administration during Incapacity of Person Entitled	804
	(v)	Administration pending Determination of a Probate Claim	808
	(vi)	Miscellaneous Limited Grants	813
(8)	Settled Land Grants		821
(9)	Recognition and Resealing		830
	(i)	Scottish Confirmations and Northern Irish Grants	830
	(ii)	Sealing of Commonwealth and Colonial Grants	835
(10)	Foreign Domicile Grants		844
(11)	Revocation of Grants		847
	(i)	When and How a Grant may be Revoked	847
	(ii)	Effect of Revocation	855

10.	**CONTENTIOUS PROBATE**		**860**
(1)	When Probate in Solemn Form is Necessary		860
(2)	Jurisdiction		865
(3)	Procedure		868
(4)	Grounds for Opposing Probate		891
	(i)	In General	891
	(ii)	Want of Due Execution	894
	(iii)	Want of Sound Disposing Mind	897
		A. Testamentary Capacity in General	897
		B. Necessity for Sound Disposing Mind	899
	(iv)	Want of Knowledge and Approval	901
(5)	Cost of Probate Proceedings		908

11.	**DEVOLUTION ON THE REPRESENTATIVE**		**916**
(1)	Property which Devolves		916

PARA

(2) Personal Representatives' Interest in Devolved Property 922
(3) Devolution of Chattels 928
(4) Devolution of Choses in Action 934
(5) Devolution of Leases and Other Chattels Real 942
(6) Devolution of Real Estate 945
(7) Devolution of Trust and Mortgage Estates 950
(8) Devolution of Property Subject to a General Power of Appointment 954

12. THE ADMINISTRATION OF ASSETS 956
(1) The Representative's First Duties 956
    (i) Funeral and Inventory 956
    (ii) Getting in and Investing the Property 959
    (iii) Notices for Claims 964
(2) Payment of Debts Presently Due 966
    (i) Solvent Estates 966
    (ii) Insolvent Estates 981
(3) Discharge of Liabilities Not Presently Due 989
(4) Order of Application of Assets in Administration 992
    (i) General Rules for Order of Application of Assets 992
    (ii) Order in Payment of Debts and Liabilities 998
    (iii) Testamentary and Administration Expenses 1013
(5) Trusts and Powers of the Representative 1019
    (i) Trusts and Powers Generally 1019
    (ii) Power to Alienate and Charge 1021
    (iii) Power to Carry on the Deceased's Business 1035
    (iv) Power to Compromise 1043
    (v) Power to Pay into Court 1045
    (vi) Power to Employ Agents, Nominees and Custodians 1049
    (vii) Survivorship of Powers 1051

13. THE DISTRIBUTION OF ASSETS 1053
(1) Legacies and Annuities 1053
    (i) Obligation to Distribute to those Entitled 1053
    (ii) Payment of Legacies 1056
    (iii) Legacies to Debtors 1067
    (iv) Legacies to Executors 1069
    (v) Legacies to Minors 1072
    (vi) Interest and Accretions 1080
    (vii) Abatement of Legacies and Annuities 1087
    (viii) Refunding 1095
(2) Order of Application of Assets on Payment of Pecuniary Legacies 1107
(3) The Residuary Estate under a Will 1113
    (i) Residuary Estate Given Absolutely 1113
    (ii) Residuary Estate Settled 1118
    (iii) Incidence of Death Duties 1128
(4) The Residuary Estate on Intestacy 1135
(5) Assents 1139
    (i) Personal Estate 1139

PARA

(ii)   Real Estate 1143

(iii)   Effect of Assent; Stamp Duties and Costs 1146

(6) Appropriation 1153

(i)   Statutory Power...1153

(ii)   Common Law Powers 1158

14. THE ROLE OF THE COURT 1162

(1) Administration and Other Remedies 1162

(2) Determination of Questions 1168

(3) Parties 1171

(4) Consolidation and Transfer..1175

(5) The Judgment or Order...1179

(6) Proceedings under Judgment 1192

(7) Costs..1196

15. PERSONAL REPRESENTATIVES' LIABILITIES.......................1212

(1) Liability for Deceased's Obligations..1212

(2) Liability for Personal Representative's Own Acts...............................1239

(i)   Liability to Third Parties 1239

(ii)   Liability to Beneficiaries on a Devastavit 1244

(3) Liability for Acts of Third Parties and Co-executors...........................1251

(4) Liability to Account...1254

(5) Relief from Liability 1259

(6) The Executor De Son Tort...1261

(i)   Intermeddling with the Estate 1261

(ii)   Effect of Acts of Executor De Son Tort...............................1266

(iii)   Liabilities and Rights of Executor De Son Tort 1267

16. ACTIONS BY AND AGAINST PERSONAL REPRESENTATIVES....1271

(1) Practice and Procedure...1271

(2) Accrual of Causes of Action..1277

(i)   Survival of Causes of Action 1277

(ii)   Causes of Action Arising after Death................................1287

(3) Actions against Personal Representatives 1290

(i)   Defences and Judgments..................................1290

(ii)   Admission of Assets 1298

1. TESTAMENTARY DISPOSITION

(1) FORM AND EFFECT OF TESTAMENTARY INSTRUMENTS

(i) Nature and Characteristics of Testamentary Instruments

1. Meaning of 'will' and 'codicil'. A will or testament[1] is the declaration in a prescribed manner[2] of the intention of the person making it with regard to matters which he wishes to take effect on or after his death[3]. A codicil is of similar nature to a will as regards both its purposes and the formalities relating to it, but in general it is supplemental to and considered as annexed to a will previously made, being executed for the purpose of adding to, varying or revoking the provisions of that will[4]. A codicil is nevertheless capable of independent existence, so that the revocation of a will, or a part of a will[5], does not necessarily effect the revocation of a codicil to it[6]. The word 'will'[7], although commonly used to describe one of a series of instruments expressing testamentary intentions, denotes the aggregate formal expression of such intentions of the testator[8] existing at his death[9]. However, although all wills and codicils subsisting at the testator's death are construed together as one testamentary disposition, they are not construed as one document[10].

1   It has been said that the expressions 'will' and 'testament' are synonyms and freely used in our law, although by the civil law an instrument was only said to be a testament where an executor was appointed, and, when there was none, a codicil; and, by the common law, where land or tenements were devised in writing, albeit there was no executor named, the instrument was properly called a last will, and, where it only concerned chattels, a testament: see Shep Touch (8th Edn, 1826) p 399. See also Bac Abr, Wills and Testaments (A); Swinburne *A Treatise of Testaments and Last Wills* (7th Edn, 1793) Pt I ss 1, 2; Littleton's Tenures s 167. As early as 1540 the terms appear to be used interchangeably in statutes: see eg 32 Hen 8 c 1 (Wills) (1540) and 34 & 35 Hen 8 c 5 (Wills) (1542–43) (both repealed). See now note 7.
2   As to formalities see PARA 60 et seq.
3   Shep Touch (8th Edn, 1826) p 399; Termes de la Ley, s v Testament; 2 Bl Com (14th Edn) 499, explaining the definition of the civil law ('voluntatis nostrae justa sententia de eo quod quis post mortem suam fieri velit'), adopted in *A-G v Jones and Bartlett* (1817) 3 Price 368 at 391. The definition is from Modestinus in Inst XXVIII 1.1; and see II, 10. As to intestacy see PARA 477 et seq.
4   2 Bl Com (14th Edn) 500.
5   *Re De La Saussaye's Goods* (1873) LR 3 P&D 42, 37 JP 312 (codicil, found to be testator's 'last and deliberate will' and which confirmed earlier will 'in whatever does not clash or interfere' with the codicil; held not to revoke intermediate codicils).
6   As to the methods by which a codicil may be revoked see the Wills Act 1837 s 20; and PARA 94. As to the general principle that revocation of a will does not revoke a codicil by implication see PARA 100. See also *Falle v Godfray* (1888) 14 App Cas 70 at 76, PC.
7   For the purposes of the Wills Act 1837, 'will' includes a will or testament, a codicil and an appointment by will or by writing in the nature of a will in exercise of a power, an appointment by will of a guardian of a child and also to an appointment by will of a representative under the Human Tissue Act 2004 s 4 or the Human Transplantation (Wales) Act 2013 s 8 (see MEDICAL PROFESSIONS vol 74 (2011) PARAS 80, 82A) and any other testamentary disposition: see the Wills Act 1837 s 1 (amended by the Children Act 1989 Sch 13 para 1; the Human Tissue Act 2004 Sch 6 para 1; and the Human Transplantation (Wales) Act 2013 s 17). For the purposes of the Law of Property Act 1925 and of the Administration of Estates Act 1925, 'will' includes 'codicil': see the Law of Property Act 1925 s 205(1)(xxxi); and the Administration of Estates Act 1925 s 55(1)(xxviii). As to the appointment by will of guardians of minor children see CHILDREN AND YOUNG PERSONS vol 9 (2012) PARA 166; and as to the exercise of powers by will see TRUSTS AND POWERS vol 98 (2013) PARA 564 et seq.
8   'Testator' is used in this title whatever may be the contents of the will, and whether the will disposes of property or not. The terms 'testate', 'intestate', 'testacy' and 'intestacy' in their ordinary

sense are associated with the question of how far the testator's property is disposed of by the will, whether completely, incompletely or not at all: see PARA 479. In a technical sense, adopted in a court of probate, these terms may be used with reference to the question whether an executor is in existence: see PARA 605.

9   *Lemage v Goodban* (1865) LR 1 P & D 57 at 62 per Sir J P Wilde; *Green v Tribe* (1878) 9 ChD 231 at 234 per Fry J; *Re Elcom, Layborn v Grover Wright* [1894] 1 Ch 303 at 314, CA, per A L Smith LJ; *Douglas-Menzies v Umphelby* [1908] AC 224 at 233, PC (separate Scots and Australian wills to be construed according to the law of those countries respectively); *Re Smith, Prada v Vandroy* [1916] 2 Ch 368, CA ('by this my will' held not to exclude codicils). See also *Lord Walpole v Earl of Cholmondeley* (1797) 7 Term Rep 138 at 146, 150; *Thomas d Jones v Evans* (1802) 2 East 488 at 496; *Stoddart v Grant* (1852) 1 Macq 163 at 171, HL. The phrase 'last will', without more, does not revoke an earlier document: *Cutto v Gilbert* (1854) 9 Moo PCC 131; *Freeman v Freeman* (1854) 5 De GM & G 704; *Pettinger v Ambler, Bunn v Pettinger* (1866) LR 1 Eq 510; *Re De la Saussaye* (1873) LR 3 P & D 42 at 44 per Sir J Hannen ('last and deliberate will'); *Simpson v Foxon* [1907] P 54 ('last and only will'). As to words of revocation see PARA 95. As to probate of concurrent wills dealing with the testator's properties in different countries see PARA 723.

10 As to the construction of wills see PARA 185 et seq.

2. Essential characteristics of a will or testament.

A will is normally made for the purpose of making dispositions of property to take effect on or after the testator's death[1], but it may also be made for the purpose of appointing executors[2] or other persons whom the testator wishes to manage or assist in managing any part of his estate[3], for appointing guardians of his minor children after his death[4], for exercising any power exercisable by him by will[5], for revoking or altering any previous will of his[6], or for any similar purpose[7] taking effect on or after his death[8]. Every will, however, has this essential characteristic, that during the life of the testator it is a mere declaration of his intention and may be freely revoked or altered in a prescribed manner[9]. Until his death the will is ambulatory, or without a fixed effect, and capable of operating on property which is acquired by the testator after the will is made[10]. On his death it crystallizes and takes effect as an appointment, disposition or otherwise, according to its tenor[11]. A gift by will may constitute an associated operation[12] within the meaning of the Income Tax Act 2007[13]. The making of a will may amount to an 'operation' for the purposes of associated operations within the meaning of the Inheritance tax Act 1984[14].

A will must be distinguished from a disposition made inter vivos, such as a donatio mortis causa which is made in contemplation of the death of the donor in circumstances which show that it is to take effect only in that event[15], or a voluntary settlement with a power of revocation[16], or an instrument which is final on execution by the maker, although intended to take effect on some future event[17], or a nomination of a beneficiary under the trust deed and rules of a pension scheme operating by reason of the force of that deed and rules[18]. A fortiori, an instrument which is not revocable and which comes into operation in the settlor's lifetime is not testamentary[19].

An attempted testamentary disposition cannot be enforced as a declaration of trust[20]. The revocable nature of a will cannot be lost, even by a declaration that it is irrevocable[21], or by a covenant or contract not to revoke it[22]. After revocation[23] the will may, however, be revived in the prescribed manner[24].

1   As to the effect of a will on the property disposed of see PARA 18. As to the appointment of trustees for any purpose see TRUSTS AND POWERS vol 98 (2013) PARA 244 et seq; and as to their appointment for the purposes of the Settled Land Act 1925, in relation to settlements created before 1 January 1997 or subsequent settlements derived from settlements made before that date, see SETTLEMENTS vol 91 (2012) PARA 651 et seq. Subject to certain exceptions, new settlements created on or after 1 January 1997 are not settlements for the purposes of the Settled Land Act 1925: see the Trusts of Land and Appointment of Trustees Act 1996 s 2; and REAL PROPERTY AND REGISTRATION vol 87 (2012) PARA 104; SETTLEMENTS vol 91 (2012) PARA 577.

2   Before the Land Transfer Act 1897, a will which did not dispose of personalty and contained no
    appointment of executors could not be admitted to probate: *Re Drummond* (1860) 2 Sw & Tr 8.
3   The mere appointment of any assistants or coadjutors to the executors, trustees or persons
    beneficially entitled has no effect either on the vesting of the property in the executors alone (*Anon*
    (1346) YB (Rolls Series), 20 Edw 3, Pt II, 428, pl 69), or as imposing on the executors, trustees or
    persons entitled beneficially under the will a trust or duty to employ the named persons in the
    specified manner (*Shaw v Lawless* (1838) 5 Cl & Fin 129, HL (appointment of tenant for
    life's land agent); *Finden v Stephens* (1846) 2 Ph 142 (appointment of trustees' receiver and
    manager); *Belaney v Kelly* (1871) 24 LT 738; *Foster v Elsley* (1881) 19 ChD 518 (appointment of
    trustees' solicitor); and see TRUSTS AND POWERS vol 98 (2013) PARA 439 et seq); but they, or
    the court in an administration action, may give effect to such directions (*Hibbert v Hibbert* (1808)
    3 Mer 681).
4   As to the appointment by will of guardians of minor children see CHILDREN AND YOUNG
    PERSONS vol 9 (2012) PARA 166.
5   As to the exercise of powers by will see TRUSTS AND POWERS vol 98 (2013) PARA 564 et seq. A
    will may operate as a revocation of an appointment made by deed: *Re Reilly and Brady's Contract*
    [1910] 1 IR 258. A residuary gift in a will may operate so as to exercise a general power of
    appointment (where no contrary intention is expressed): see the Wills Act 1837 s 27; PARA 1114;
    and TRUSTS AND POWERS vol 98 (2013) PARA 577.
6   As to alterations see PARA 82 et seq; and as to revocation see PARA 92 et seq.
7   Eg a direction to begin proceedings to administer the estate. As to beginning proceedings to
    administer an estate see PARA 1162.
8   A direction to begin proceedings to administer the estate in court does not make it imperative on
    the court to make the order for administration: *Re Stocken, Jones v Hawkins* (1888) 38 ChD 319,
    CA. Indeed a court would not now make an order for administration unless it was shown to be
    desirable for the proper administration of the estate. As to directions as to the disposal of the
    testator's body see PARA 31.
9   See PARA 1. As to the required testamentary intention see PARA 54; as to revocation see PARA 92
    et seq. As to the incorporation of other documents in a will see PARAS 201, 711. Although a will
    is revocable, any clause in it may be referred to in order to prove a fact: *Re Northcliffe, Arnholz
    v Hudson* [1925] Ch 651 at 654 per Russell J. As to the restrictions on testamentary disposition
    or on revocation where a testator has made a binding agreement see PARA 20 et seq; and see also
    PARA 26.
10 Co Litt 112b; Pollock and Maitland's History of English Law (2nd Edn) 315; *Baugh v Read* (1790)
    1 Ves 257 at 260; *Lord Walpole v Earl of Cholmondeley* (1797) 7 Term Rep 138 at 149;
    Beddington v Baumann [1903] AC 13 at 19, HL, per Lord Davey; *Re Baroness Llanover, Herbert
    v Freshfield (No 2)* [1903] 2 Ch 330 at 335 per Farwell J; *Re Thompson, Thompson v Thompson*
    [1906] 2 Ch 199 at 205 per Joyce J; *Re Berger* [1990] Ch 118 at 129, [1989] 1 All ER 591 at 599,
    CA, per Mustill LJ. Before the Wills Act 1837, a will did not operate on realty acquired after the
    will had been made; see now the Wills Act 1837 s 24; PARA 282. Although a will is ambulatory
    and revocable, it must, when executed, be intended to have immediate effect and cannot be
    executed conditionally on a future event happening: see PARAS 7, 54.
11 *Forse and Hembling's Case* (1588) 4 Co Rep 60b; *Re Rye's Settlement* (1852) 10 Hare 106 at 112;
    Cooper v Martin (1867) 3 Ch App 47; *Re Robinson* (1867) LR 1 P & D 384 at 387; *Olivant v
    Wright* (1878) 9 ChD 646 at 650 per Bacon VC; *Beddington v Baumann* [1903] AC 13 at 19, HL,
    per Lord Davey; 2 Bl Com (14th Edn) 502; Shep Touch (8th Edn, 1826) p 401. See also *Lord
    Bindon v Earl of Suffolk* (1707) 1 P Wms 96 at 97 per Lord Cowper LC; *Bunbury v Doran* (1875)
    IR 9 CL 284 at 286, Ex Ch.
12 As to the meaning of 'associated operation' see INCOME TAXATION vol 58 (2014) PARA 607.
13 See the Income Tax Act 2007 s 719; INCOME TAXATION vol 58 (2014) PARA 607; and *Bambridge
    v IRC* [1955] 3 All ER 812, [1955] 1 WLR 1329, HL (overruled, without affecting this point, by
    Vestey v IRC (No's 1 and 2) [1980] AC 1148, [1979] 3 All ER 976, HL).
14 See the Inheritance Tax Act 1984 s 268(1): and INHERITANCE TAXATION vol 59A (2014)
    PARA 17.
15 See GIFTS vol 52 (2014) PARA 271 et seq.
16 *Tompson v Browne* (1835) 3 My & K 32; *Patch v Shore* (1862) 2 Drew & Sm 589. See also
    Alexander v Brame (1855) 7 De GM & G 525 at 530; on appeal sub nom *Jeffries v Alexander*
    (1860) 8 HL Cas 594.
17 *Marjoribanks v Hovenden* (1843) Drury temp Sug 11 (appointment on death without issue);
    Fletcher v Fletcher (1844) 4 Hare 67 at 79 per Sir James Wigram VC (deed of covenant).
18 *Re Danish Bacon Co Ltd Staff Pension Fund, Christensen v Arnett* [1971] 1 All ER 486, [1971]
    1 WLR 248; *Baird v Baird* [1990] 2 AC 548, [1990] 2 All ER 300, PC.
19 *Thorncroft and Clarke v Lashmar* (1862) 2 Sw & Tr 479; *Re Robinson* (1867) LR 1 P & D 384;
    Re Halpin (1873) IR 8 Eq 567. The Wills Act 1837 applies only to a will or testament in the

ordinary meaning of these terms; thus a marriage contract containing a clause which is in reality contractual, although with testamentary effect, is not a 'will' in the sense of that Act: *Battye's Trustee v Battye* 1917 SC 385 at 399.

20 *Cross v Cross* (1877) 1 LR Ir 389; *Towers v Hogan* (1889) 23 LR Ir 53.
21 Bacon's Maxims reg 19; *Vynior's Case* (1609) 8 Co Rep 81b at 82a; *Re McDonald* (1911) 30 NZLR 896. See also PARA 92.
22 *Re Heys, Walker v Gaskill* [1914] P 192. As to the effect of such a covenant or contract, which can include raising a trust enforceable against the persons deriving title under a later will of the covenantor or on his intestacy see PARA 21; and as to the position in equity where mutual wills are made see PARA 23.
23 As to revocation see PARA 92 et seq.
24 As to revival see PARAS 110–112.

3. Will in form of deed. If a document bears on its face a testamentary intention, it is not to be considered as a deed merely because it bears a seal or is in other respects in the form of a deed[1]; and a deed not intended to have any operation or effect until the grantor's death is testamentary[2]. An instrument which, although in form a conveyance, is made on condition that it is to take effect only on the death of the conveying party is often testamentary in character[3]. Conversely, the mere fact that a document is executed as a will does not necessarily make it a will[4].

1 *Marjoribanks v Hovenden* (1843) Drury *temp* Sug 11 at 27. See also *Hickson v Witham* (1675) Cas *temp* Finch 195. As to the meaning of 'deed' see DEEDS AND OTHER INSTRUMENTS vol 32 (2012) PARA 201. Any rule of law which required a seal for the valid execution of an instrument as a deed by an individual has, except in relation to a corporation sole, been abolished: see the Law of Property (Miscellaneous Provisions) Act 1989 s 1(1)(b), (10); and DEEDS AND OTHER INSTRUMENTS vol 32 (2012) PARA 207 et seq.
2 *Foundling Hospital (Governors and Guardians) v Crane* [1911] 2 KB 367, CA. See also *Rigden v Vallier* (1751) 2 Ves Sen 252 at 258; *Masterman v Maberly* (1829) 2 Hag Ecc 235 at 247; *King's Proctor v Daines* (1830) 3 Hag Ecc 218 at 221; *Re Morgan* (1866) LR 1 P & D 214; *Fielding v Walshaw* (1879) 27 WR 492; *Re Colyer* (1889) 14 PD 48; *Re Slinn* (1890) 15 PD 156; *Re White* (1987) 38 DLR (4th) 631, Ont HC.
3 *Patch v Shore* (1862) 2 Drew & Sm 589 at 598; cf *Parks v Clout* [2002] EWHC 1843 (Ch), [2002] All ER (D) 26 (Sep) (conveyance showing existence of tenancy in common was not evidence of testamentary intention and was not a document executed as a will). See also PARA 708.
4 *Thorncroft and Clarke v Lashmar* (1862) 2 Sw & Tr 479. See also *King's Proctor v Daines* (1830) 3 Hag Ecc 218.

4. Matters with which the will may deal. It is desirable that a will, having regard to the purposes for which it may be made[1], should make provision in an orderly manner not only for the disposition of the testator's property but also for all other matters in relation to his affairs which he wishes to take effect after his death[2]. Thus it should provide for the appointment of executors[3], and, if the testator has children who are minors, it may be appropriate to provide for their guardianship[4]. If the testator desires that the statutory order[5] in which assets are applied for the payment of his debts and liabilities be varied, the will should make express provision accordingly[6]. Subject to statutory restriction, he may alter the normal rules for the incidence of inheritance tax[7]. It is essential, where property is settled, to guard against any infringement of the rule against perpetuities or accumulations[8]. The testator should be aware that after his death a spouse, former spouse, civil partner, former civil partner, child or dependant or cohabitee[9] for whom reasonable financial provision has not been made may apply to the court under the Inheritance (Provision for Family and Dependants) Act 1975 for an order for such provision to be made from the testator's estate[10].

It must be ensured that the will as prepared has in all respects the knowledge and approval of the testator, as these are essential to validity[11]. If he proposes to benefit the person who draws up the will, that person should guard against suggestions of advantage taken or undue influence exercised in the preparation of the will[12]. If the testator has been suffering from a mental disorder, it is well to bear in mind that the person who will in due course obtain probate may have the burden of proving that the testator had capacity to make the will[13].

For purposes of probate, it is desirable to prepare a will in such a form that it can be easily photographed[14].

1   See PARA 2.
2   Under the Law of Property Act 1925 the Lord Chancellor may prescribe forms which may be incorporated in a will: see s 179; and the Statutory Wills Forms 1925, SR & O 1925/780.
3   See PARA 610 et seq.
4   See CHILDREN AND YOUNG PERSONS vol 9 (2012) PARA 166 et seq.
5   Ie the order set out in the Administration of Estates Act 1925 s 34(3), Sch 1 Pt II (see PARA 998 et seq).
6   See PARA 993 et seq.
7   In the absence of express provision, the inheritance tax on United Kingdom free estate vesting in the personal representatives is paid out of residue: see the Inheritance Tax Act 1984 s 211; and INHERITANCE TAXATION vol 59A (2014) PARA 271. The power to alter the incidence of inheritance tax is restricted by the rule that inheritance tax cannot be made payable out of an exempt gift: see s 41; and INHERITANCE TAXATION vol 59A (2014) PARA 147. 'United Kingdom' means Great Britain and Northern Ireland: Interpretation Act 1978 s 5, Sch 1. 'Great Britain' means England, Scotland and Wales: Union with Scotland Act 1706, preamble art I; Interpretation Act 1978 s 22(1), Sch 2 para 5(a). Except where statute otherwise provides, neither the Channel Islands nor the Isle of Man are within the United Kingdom. See further CONSTITUTIONAL AND ADMINISTRATIVE LAW vol 20 (2014) PARA 3.
8   See generally PERPETUITIES AND ACCUMULATIONS vol 80 (2013) PARA 1 et seq.
9   As to the persons for whom provision may be made under the Inheritance (Provision for Family and Dependants) Act 1975 see PARA 567. The category of cohabitee (ie someone who, during the whole of the period of two years ending immediately before the date when the deceased died, was living in the same household as the deceased and as the husband or wife of the deceased) was introduced in relation to persons dying on or after 1 January 1996 by the Law Reform (Succession) Act 1995 s 2, amending the Inheritance (Provision for Family and Dependants) Act 1975 s 1. As from 5 December 2005 s 1 was extended by the Civil Partnership Act 2004 Sch 4 para 15 to include someone living in the same household as the deceased as the civil partner of the deceased. As to civil partnerships see PARAS 90 et seq, 179. 'Spouse' includes a person who is married to a person of the same sex: see the Marriage (Same Sex Couples) Act 2013 Sch 3 para 1(1)(c), (2), (3); and MATRIMONIAL AND CIVIL PARTNERSHIP LAW vol 72 (2015) PARAS 1–2.
10   See PARA 565 et seq. On such an application the court must have regard to the various factors set out in the Inheritance (Provision for Family and Dependants) Act 1975 s 3 which include the applicant's conduct or any other matter which it considers relevant: see PARA 576.
11   See PARAS 47 et seq, 901.
12   See *Wintle v Nye* [1959] 1 All ER 552, [1959] 1 WLR 284, HL; and LEGAL PROFESSIONS vol 66 (2015) PARA 608. See also *Bodh v Boudh* [2007] EWCA Civ 1019,[2007] All ER (D) 384 (Oct) and PARA 901.
13   See PARA 900. A statutory declaration could be made to support a will made in a lucid interval. Templeman J (as he then was) said in *Kenward v Adams* [1975] CLY 3591, (1975) Times, 29 November: 'in the case of an aged testator or a testator who has suffered a serious illness, there is one golden rule which should always be observed, however straightforward matters appear, and however difficult or tactless it may be to suggest that precautions should be taken. The making of a will by such a testator ought to be witnessed or approved by a medical practitioner who satisfies himself of the capacity and understanding of the testator, and records and preserves his examinations and findings'; approved in *Re Simpson, Schaniel v Simpson* (1977) 121 Sol Jo 224, (1977) NLJ 487; *Buckenham v Dickinson* [1997] CLY 4733. It is probably more useful to have a statement as to the mental capacity of the testator from a qualified medical practitioner rather than to have such a person witness the will. Where there is any doubt as to a testator's capacity the person preparing a will should make a detailed note of the discussions leading to the making of the will.
14   53 Law Society's Gazette 81. The will should be typed in black on white paper, and should be on foolscap or A4 paper; but size of type is not of itself important, provided that the will is the above size, as a copy of a will clearly typed and reproduced life-size will always be legible: see (1974) 124 NLJ 1101.

5. Testamentary form unnecessary.

While the desirability and advantages of a professionally drawn will are obvious, testamentary form is not necessary to constitute a valid will, provided that the document is executed in accordance with the appropriate legal requirements[1] and with the requisite intention[2]. Thus an instrument duly executed, although apparently intended as preliminary to a more formal document, may be admitted to probate if there is evidence that the testator had the lasting intention that the document should be dispositive and operate provisionally until a more formal will was prepared[3], as may a document not intended to be admitted to probate but intended to operate in parallel with a formal will[4]. A memorandum which is merely deliberative or initiatory and does not show the testator's final intention will not, however, be admitted to probate[5]; and a paper which merely expresses an intention to instruct a solicitor to prepare a will for the purpose of leaving a certain legacy is not testamentary[6].

1   *Whyte v Pollok* (1882) 7 App Cas 400 at 409 per Lord Selborne LC. See also *Masterman v Maberly* (1829) 2 Hag Ecc 235 at 248; *Oldroyd v Harvey* [1907] P 326; *Re Beech, Beech v Public Trustee* [1923] P 46, CA. The presumption of due execution applies to wills: see PARAS 77, 895. The validity of a will as regards movables depends on the law of the testator's domicile, and as regards immovables on the lex situs: see PARA 12; and CONFLICT OF LAWS vol 19 (2011) PARA 753. As to forms of will see PARA 4 note 2.
2   See PARA 54.
3   *Bone and Newsam v Spear* (1811) 1 Phillim 345 ('heads of a will'); *Barwick v Mullings* (1829) 2 Hag Ecc 225 (instructions for will, duly executed); *Hattatt v Hattatt* (1832) 4 Hag Ecc 211 ('memorandum of my intended will'); *Castle v Torre* (1837) 2 Moo PCC 133; *Re Fisher* (1869) 20 LT 684; *Whyte v Pollok* (1882) 7 App Cas 400 (notes for an intended settlement); *National Trust for Places of Historic Interest and Natural Beauty v Royal National Institute for the Blind* [1999] All ER (D) 81, sub nom *Re Chapman* (1998–99) 1 ITELR 863 (outline will provisions summarising the testator's incomplete instructions for an intended will). See also *Re Foster, Foster v Foster* (1922) 67 Sol Jo 199 (pencil notes on the epitome of a will).
4   *Re Berger* [1990] Ch 118, [1989] 1 All ER 591, CA (Hebrew will or zavah intended by the deceased to be given effect by Jewish religious courts).
5   *Matthews v Warner* (1798) 4 Ves 186; *Mathew v Warner* (1799) 5 Ves 23 ('plan of a will'); *Gillow and Orrell v Bourne* (1831) 4 Hag Ecc 192 (intention abandoned); *Boughton-Knight v Wilson* (1915) 32 TLR 146 (holograph document, not intended to be testamentary, but only a draft in alternative form).
6   *Coventry v Williams* (1844) 3 Curt 787. See also *Hixon v Wytham* (1675) 1 Cas in Ch 248.

6.   Instruments only partly testamentary. An instrument may be partly testamentary and partly intended to take effect during the life of the person making it[1]. Even apart from the testator's intention, a will may have an effect other than testamentary, for example as a memorandum of a contract[2] under the Statute of Frauds[3] or an acknowledgment of a statute-barred debt[4].

1   *Re Anziani, Herbert v Christopherson* [1930] 1 Ch 407 at 424. See also *Doe d Cross v Cross* (1846) 8 QB 714 (power of attorney intended to be partly testamentary); *Re Robinson* (1867) LR 1 P & D 384 at 387 (lease with a direction to lessor's executors to sell at end of term, not intended to be testamentary); *Wolfe v Wolfe* [1902] 2 IR 246; *Re McDonald* (1911) 30 NZLR 896 (power of attorney).
2   *Re Hoyle, Hoyle v Hoyle* [1893] 1 Ch 84, CA (recital in will of a guarantee).
3   See the Statute of Frauds (1677) s 4; and CONTRACT vol 22 (2012) PARA 222; FINANCIAL INSTRUMENTS AND TRANSACTIONS vol 49 (2015) PARA 677. A will can have effect as a memorandum of a contract for the sale of land only if the contract was made before 27 September 1989, the Law of Property Act 1925 s 40 having been repealed in respect of contracts made on or after that date by the Law of Property (Miscellaneous Provisions) Act 1989 ss 4, 5(3), (4)(b), Sch 2: see CONVEYANCING vol 23 (2016) PARA 27.
4   *Millington v Thompson* (1852) 3 I Ch R 236; *Howard and Crowley v Hennessey and O'Leaky* [1947] IR 336. See also LIMITATION PERIODS vol 68 (2016) PARAS 1183, 1190.

7.   Instruments conditionally testamentary. An instrument may be conditionally testamentary[1]. Thus a testator may refer in his will to some contingency, such as an impending journey by him or his possible death while abroad, or other event, in terms which make the will conditional or limited in operation[2]. The terms may, however, merely import that the contingency is a reason for making the will, in which case the will is not conditional[3]. If the contingency is coincident with a period of danger to the testator, there is a ground for supposing that the danger was regarded by him only as a reason for making a will[4]. A conditional will is of no effect if the contingency fails[5], but may take effect free from the contingency in question if re-executed or republished after the contingency has passed[6]. A will can be valid as a conditional will only if the condition appears in the will itself[7].

1   Eg an instrument may be conditional on the consent of another person: see *Re Smith* (1869) LR 1 P & D 717 (where there was an option to the wife to add a codicil to the will or not).
2   *Parsons v Lanoe* (1748) 1 Ves Sen 189 ('if I die before my return'); *Re Winn* (1861) 2 Sw & Tr 147 ('in case of my decease during my absence'); *Roberts v Roberts* (1862) 2 Sw & Tr 337 ('should anything happen to me on my passage'); *Re Porter* (1869) LR 2 P & D 22 ('should anything happen to me while abroad'); *Re Robinson* (1870) LR 2 P & D 171; *Lindsay v Lindsay* (1872) LR 2 P & D 459; *Re Hugo* (1877) 2 PD 73; *Edmondson v Edmondson* (1901) 17 TLR 397 ('in case I should not return home owing to death'); *Re O'Connor* [1942] 1 All ER 546 (testatrix's will conditional on her predeceasing sister; the condition was here inferred from the wording and surrounding circumstances); *Re Govier* [1950] P 237 (joint will; the phrase 'in the event of our two deaths' held to confine operation of will to simultaneous death by enemy action); *Folds v Abrahart* [2003] EWHC 2550 (Ch), [2003] All ER (D) 322 (Jul), [2004] WTLR 327 (last will of testator if he and his wife 'should die together'; no gift to his wife; the will was held to be conditional on a condition not satisfied). See also *Re Rowland, Smith v Russell* [1963] Ch 1, [1962] 2 All ER 837, CA.
3   *Re Spratt* [1897] P 28. See also *Strauss v Schmidt* (1820) 3 Phillim 209 ('in case I should die'); *Burton v Collingwood* (1832) 4 Hag Ecc 176 ('lest I should die before the next sun'); *Re Thorne* (1865) 4 Sw & Tr 36; *Re Dobson* (1866) LR 1 P & D 88 ('in case of any fatal accident, being about to travel' etc); *Re Martin* (1867) LR 1 P & D 380 ('in the event of my death during a time of removal to hospital ship'); *Re Mayd* (1880) 6 PD 17; *Re Stuart* (1888) 21 LR Ir 105 at 108; *Halford v Halford* [1897] P 36.
4   *Re Spratt* [1897] P 28. See also *Re Pawle, Winter v Pawle* (1918) 34 TLR 437; *Nixon v Prince* (1918) 34 TLR 444 (informal will by soldier on active service admitted to probate with formal will).
5   *Parsons v Lanoe* (1748) 1 Ves Sen 189; *Re Winn* (1861) 2 Sw & Tr 147; *Roberts v Roberts* (1862) 2 Sw & Tr 337; *Re Robinson* (1870) LR 2 P & D 171. For a case where the contingency could still arise when the testator died see *Re Cooper* (1855) Dea & Sw 9.
6   *Parsons v Lanoe* (1748) 1 Ves Sen 189 at 191; *Re Cawthron* (1863) 3 Sw & Tr 417. As to republication of a will see PARA 113 et seq.
7   There is an important distinction between the conditional execution of a document described as a will (which is not authorised by the Wills Act 1837) and the unconditional execution of a will which in accordance with its terms is conditional in its operation (which is so authorised). A will cannot be executed in escrow: *Corbett v Newey* [1998] Ch 57, [1996] 2 All ER 914, CA, at 69–70 and 925 per Morritt LJ (will invalid because conditionally executed). See also PARA 54.

8.   Evidence of nature of instrument. In considering whether an instrument is of a testamentary character[1] or is conditionally or unconditionally testamentary, the probate court[2] construes the will in the manner of a court of construction[3], and may receive evidence accordingly[4]. Further the court may receive extrinsic evidence of the intention of the alleged testator with regard to the character of the instrument[5] and, also, of the true identity of the person intended by the testator to act as executor, where the will misdescribes him[6].

1   As to the grounds on which probate may be refused, and as to the evidence admissible on such questions, see PARA 891 et seq.
2   In this title the term 'probate court' is used of any court entertaining, within the scope of its jurisdiction, the grant of probate of a will or of letters of administration with the will annexed, or any question relating to the character of the instrument alleged to be testamentary, or as to the testamentary capacity of a testator, or as to the validity of a will generally, for the purposes of the will being admitted to probate, and such a grant is called the 'probate'. As to the grant of probate or letters of administration generally, including the respective jurisdictions of the Chancery Division and the Family Division in probate matters, and as to the jurisdiction of county courts in contentious probate matters, see PARAS 676 et seq, 865–866. The probate court may have to construe documents for the purpose of deciding which are to be admitted to probate: *Re Thomas, Public Trustee v Davies* [1939] 2 All ER 567; *Re Alford* (1939) 83 Sol Jo 566. Where the question of what instruments should be admitted to probate is a question of construction, it may be possible to have it determined by construction proceedings instead of by probate proceedings: *Re*

Finnemore [1992] 1 All ER 800, [1991] 1 WLR 793. See also PARA 707 et seq. As to the separation of the functions of the probate court and a court of construction see *Townsend v Moore* [1905] P 66 at 84, 86, 88, CA. See also *Lamothe v Lamothe* [2006] EWHC 1387 (Ch), [2006] WTLR 1431, [2006] All ER (D) 153 (Jun), where the relationship was examined between the separate probate and construction functions of the court and, also, the proper use of extrinsic evidence (which seems to be unaffected by the Administration of Justice Act 1982 s 21 (see PARA 219)), in ascertaining whether revocation was intended and which will or wills of a testator should be admitted to probate. As to the meaning of 'court of construction' see PARA 185. As to the construction of wills see PARA 185 et seq.

3 The court considers the whole language of the will and the surrounding circumstances: *Re Spratt* [1897] P 28 at 30 per Jeune P; *Re Vines, Vines v Vines* [1910] P 147. See also PARAS 193 et seq, 713.

4 As to the evidence receivable in a court of construction see PARA 193 et seq.

5 *Re English* (1864) 3 Sw & Tr 586; *Cock v Cooke* (1866) LR 1 P & D 241; *Robertson v Smith* (1870) LR 2 P & D 43; *Re Coles* (1871) LR 2 P & D 362; *Re Slinn* (1890) 15 PD 156; *Re Spratt* [1897] P 28; *Re Vines, Vines v Vines* [1910] P 147 (conditional wills); *Corbett v Newey* [1998] Ch 57, [1996] 2 All ER 914, CA (conditionally executed will). See also *Re Nosworthy* (1865) 4 Sw & Tr 44; *Gould v Lakes* (1880) 6 PD 1; and PARAS 54, 67. As to evidence of the contents of a lost will in a court of probate see PARA 716.

6 It seems the court may receive as evidence of the testator's intentions: (1) evidence of all the persons known to the deceased at the time of making the will; and (2) documents, substantially contemporaneous with the will, which are of important character and which showed who the testator had in mind by the misdescription: see the approach followed by Norris J to determine to whom grant of representation should issue in *Parkinson v Fawdon* [2009] EWHC 1953 (Ch) at [8], [2009] All ER (D) 322 (Jul).

9. Joint wills. A joint will is a will made by two or more testators contained in a single document, duly executed by each testator, and disposing either of their separate properties[1] or of their joint property[2]. It is not, however, recognised in English law as a single will[3]. It is in effect two or more wills, and it operates on the death of each testator as his will disposing of his own separate property; on the death of the first to die it is admitted to probate as his own will and on the death of the survivor, if no fresh will has been made, it is admitted to probate as the disposition of the property of the survivor[4]. Joint wills are now rarely, if ever, made.

1 *Re Piazzi-Smyth* [1898] P 7; *Re Hagger, Freeman v Arscott* [1930] 2 Ch 190; *Re Hack* (1930) 169 LT Jo 285; *Re O'Connor* [1942] 1 All ER 546. In *Re Stracey* (1855) Dea & Sw 6, a joint will made by husband and wife operated as an exercise of the wife's power of appointment.

2 *Re Raine* (1858) 1 Sw & Tr 144; *Re Lovegrove* (1862) 2 Sw & Tr 453. A dictum by Lord Mansfield in *Earl of Darlington v Pulteney* (1775) 1 Cowp 260 at 268, that there could not be a joint will, cannot be supported. A joint power of appointment by will may be exercised by a joint will and becomes effective on the death of the survivor, provided that at that time the will remains unaltered: *Re Duddell, Roundway v Roundway* [1932] 1 Ch 585.

3 *Hobson v Blackburn and Blackburn* (1822) 1 Add 274.

4 *Re Duddell, Roundway v Roundway* [1932] 1 Ch 585. See also *Re Stracey* (1855) Dea & Sw 6; *Re Lovegrove* (1862) 2 Sw & Tr 453; *Re Miskelly* (1869) IR 4 Eq 62; *Re Fletcher* (1883) 11 LR Ir 359 (where there was a separate will following and recognising a joint will); *Re Crofton* (1897) 13 TLR 374 (where there was a joint codicil to separate wills); *Re Piazzi-Smyth* [1898] P 7; *Re Heys, Walker v Gaskill* [1914] P 192 at 196.

10. Mutual wills. Wills are mutual when the testators confer on each other reciprocal benefits, which may be absolute benefits in each other's property[1], or life interests with the same ultimate disposition of each estate on the death of the survivor[2]. Apparently, a mutual will in the strict sense of the term is a joint will[3], but, where by agreement or arrangement similar provisions are made by separate wills, these are also conveniently known as mutual wills[4]. Wills which by agreement confer benefit on persons other than the testators, without the testators conferring benefits on each other, can also be mutual wills[5]. Where there is an agreement not to revoke mutual wills and one party dies having stood by the agreement, a survivor is bound by it[6].

The doctrine of mutual wills has been said to be anomalous and unprincipled, so that the authorities do not always speak with one voice on what is truly essential to the doctrine or as to the mechanisms by which it operates or as to the consequences of its application[7]. However it has been held that there is at least clear guidance on what must be established before the doctrine can be invoked[8] in that there must be an irreducible core of a contract between T1 and T2 that in return for T1 agreeing to make a will in form X and not to revoke it without notice to T2, then T2 will make a will in form Y and agree not to revoke it without notice to T1[9]. It seems that the precise form and terms of the underlying contract do not have as great a significance as the finding that such a contract actually exists and was entered into[10].

It appears that where it is established that there is a clear agreement, in the mutual wills or elsewhere, that the wills are to be mutually binding (whether or not expressed in language of revocation) the law will give effect to that intention by way of a 'floating trust' and the trust so created is not destroyed by the remarriage of the second testator after the death of the first[11].

1   *Stone v Hoskins* [1905] P 194. There may, however, be alternative provisions in case of lapse: *Re Oldham, Hadwen v Myles* [1925] Ch 75. See also *Re Heys, Walker v Gaskill* [1914] P 192.
2   *Gray v Perpetual Trustee Co Ltd* [1928] AC 391, PC; *Re Hagger, Freeman v Arscott* [1930] 2 Ch 190; *Re Green, Lindner v Green* [1951] Ch 148, [1950] 2 All ER 913.
3   As to joint wills see PARA 9.
4   See *Re Heys, Walker v Gaskill* [1914] P 192 at 196. If each party by mistake executed the wrong will, it was formerly the case that the court would not rectify the error: *Re S —* (1850) 15 LTOS 71; *Re Meyer* [1908] P 353. However, the wills of testators who die on or after 1 January 1983 may now be rectified: see the Administration of Justice Act 1982 s 20; and PARA 23. As to joint and mutual wills generally see the full note with references to the American authorities in *Robertson v Robertson* 136 Am St R 589 at 592n (1909); and for cases of mutual wills under community of goods in Roman-Dutch law see *Denyssen v Mostert* (1872) LR 4 PC 236 (South Africa); *Dias v De Livera* (1879) 5 App Cas 123, PC (Ceylon); *Natal Bank Ltd v Rood* [1910] AC 570, PC (South Africa).
5   *Re Dale, Proctor v Dale* [1994] Ch 31, [1993] 4 All ER 129. See also *Olins v Walters* [2007] EWHC 3060 (Ch), [2008] WTLR 339, [2007] All ER (D) 291 (Dec); affd [2008] EWCA Civ 782, [2008] Ch 212, [2008] All ER (D) 58 (Jul).
6   See PARA 23. See also *Olins v Walters* [2007] EWHC 3060, (Ch), [2008] WTLR 339, [2007] All ER (D) 291 (Dec), affd [2008] EWCA Civ 782, [2008] Ch 212, [2008] All ER (D) 58 (Jul). See also *Thomas and Agnes Carvel Foundation v Carvel* [2007] EWHC 1314 (Ch), [2008] Ch 395, [2007] 4 All ER 81 (where the survivor of two people who made mutual wills, and his personal representative, were 'trustees' for the purposes of Judicial Trustees Act 1896 s 1, and a person entitled to enforce the trust arising under the will of the first to die was a 'beneficiary', for those purposes); and *Fry v Densham-Smith* [2010] EWCA Civ 1410, [2011] WTLR 387, [2010] All ER (D) 136 (Dec) (finding of existence of mutual wills agreement upheld on appeal).
7   See *Olins v Walters* [2007] EWHC 3060 (Ch) at [8], [2008] WTLR 339, [2007] All ER (D) 291 (Dec) per Norris J, adopting the words of Rimer LJ ('anomalous and unprincipled') in an earlier interlocutory appeal in the same case and adding his own reasoning thereto. This reasoning and result affirmed at [2008] EWCA Civ 782, [2008] Ch 212, [2008] All ER (D) 58 (Jul).
8   See *Olins v Walters* [2007] EWHC 3060 (Ch) at [9], [2008] WTLR 339, [2007] All ER (D) 291 (Dec) per Norris J.
9   See *Olins v Walters* [2007] EWHC 3060 (Ch) at [9], [2008] WTLR 339, [2007] All ER (D) 291 (Dec) per Norris J.
10 See Mummery LJ in *Olins v Walters* [2008] EWCA Civ 782, [2009] Ch 212, [2008] All ER (D) 58 (Jul) (submissions based on insufficiency of terms and uncertainty in the underlying contract were held to be misconceived; the obligation on the surviving testator is equitable and arises by operation of law on the death of the first testator to die).
11 Per Carnwath J in *Re Goodchild, Goodchild v Goodchild* [1996] 1 All ER 670 at 676, 677; affd at [1997] 3 All ER 63 (although no agreement was established on the facts in that case).

11.   Delegation of will-making power. Although a testator may properly make a will or codicil conditional on the assent of a third person to its taking effect as a testamentary document[1], he may not delegate his will-making power to any other person[2]. Accordingly, if a testator signs a document prepared by another person without knowledge of its contents[3], or a document which includes a phrase or even a word inserted by another of which he has no knowledge[4], then either the document is not a valid will or the phrase or word forms no part of an otherwise valid will, as the case may be.

There is, however, no objection to the testator by his will conferring on his executors either a special[5] or a general[6] power, or indeed a certain power of any other description[7], to select his beneficiaries[8]. Furthermore, since it has now been established that there is in this regard no difference between a power and a trust[9], there is no objection to a trust to distribute between individuals and corporations, however numerous, indicated by the testator provided that the terms of the trust are conceptually certain[10]. A power which would satisfy the requirement of certainty, and thus be valid, if created by deed is valid when created by a will[11].

Where, however, the intention of the testator is not to benefit individuals, or corporations with separate legal existence, or unincorporated associations in those cases where this may properly be done[12], whom he defines with sufficient precision, but to forward some particular purpose, the situation is different. Where the estate is to be applied for charitable purposes, then, provided that the intention to benefit charity is apparent, the testator may validly leave it to his executors to determine to which particular charities his bounty is to be distributed[13]. If, however, the will provides that the estate, or a defined portion of it, is to be applied for non-charitable purposes, whether to be selected by his executors or not, such a provision is invalid[14], and cannot be validated by the fact that the executors have a discretion to devote the gift to such purposes or to such charitable purposes as they think fit[15]. The court does not wait to see whether the executors apply the fund to charitable objects, or partly to charitable objects, or not, but looks at the will as at the date of death and decides at once whether the gift is definite or indefinite, and, if it is indefinite, the gift is inoperative[16]. The reason for the failure of such a gift is that a gift for a purpose can take effect only by means of a trust, and such trusts are of imperfect obligation, for by their nature they cannot be enforced by or on behalf of any particular beneficiary. Where the testator has failed to create an enforceable trust, his executors cannot do on his behalf what they themselves as individuals would be perfectly free to do[17].

1 *Re Smith* (1869) LR 1 P & D 717 (cited in PARA 7 note 1).
2 *Grimond v Grimond* [1905] AC 124 at 126, HL, per Earl of Halsbury LC; *Houston v Burns* [1918] AC 337 at 342, HL, per Viscount Haldane; *A-G v National Provincial and Union Bank of England* [1924] AC 262 at 268, HL, per Viscount Haldane; *Chichester Diocesan Fund and Board of Finance Inc v Simpson* [1944] AC 341 at 348, [1944] 2 All ER 60 at 62, HL, per Viscount Simon LC, at 349 and 62 per Lord Macmillan, at 364 and 70 per Lord Porter, and at 371 and 74 per Lord Simonds. The mere delegation to executors, or to a third person, of the application of a formula laid down by the testator for the ascertainment of his estate does not offend this principle; it is merely a question of 'id certum est quod certum reddi potest': *Re Conn, Conn v Burns* [1898] 1 IR 337 (where a portion was to be determined by a wife and executors according to the value of the services the daughters might have rendered the family and, in the case of marriage portions, according to the match made). See also PARA 263.
3 *Hastilow v Stobie* (1865) LR 1 P & D 64; *Cleare and Foster v Cleare* (1869) LR 1 P & D 655 at 657 per Lord Penzance.
4 *Re Morris, Lloyds Bank Ltd v Peake* [1971] P 62, [1970] 1 All ER 1057; *Re Phelan* [1972] Fam 33, [1971] 3 All ER 1256; *Re Reynette-James, Wightman v Reynette-James* [1975] 3 All ER 1037, [1976] 1 WLR 161.
5 *Brown v Higgs* (1803) 8 Ves 561 (affd (1813) 18 Ves 192, HL); *Re Hughes, Hughes v Footner* [1921] 2 Ch 208; *Re Abrahams' Will Trusts, Caplan v Abrahams* [1969] 1 Ch 463, [1967] 2 All ER 1175.
6 *Gibbs v Rumsey* (1813) 2 Ves & B 294; *Re Hughes, Hughes v Footner* [1921] 2 Ch 208 at 212 per Sargant J.

7   *Re Park, Public Trustee v Armstrong* [1932] 1 Ch 580; *Re Jones, Public Trustee v Jones* [1945] Ch
    105. See also *Re Byron's Settlement, Williams v Mitchell* [1891] 3 Ch 474; *Re
    Manisty's Settlement, Manisty v Manisty* [1974] Ch 17, [1973] 2 All ER 1203; *Re
    Hay's Settlement Trusts* [1981] 3 All ER 786, [1982] 1 WLR 202; *Re Beatty's Will Trusts, Hinves
    v Brooke* [1990] 3 All ER 844, [1990] 1 WLR 1503.
8   See TRUSTS AND POWERS vol 98 (2013) PARA 103.
9   *McPhail v Doulton* [1971] AC 424, [1970] 2 All ER 228, HL (overruling *IRC v
    Broadway Cottages Trust* [1955] Ch 20, [1954] 3 All ER 120, CA; and applying the tests already
    laid down for powers in *Wishaw v Stephens* [1970] AC 508, sub nom *Re Gulbenkian's Settlement
    Trusts, Whishaw v Stephens* [1968] 3 All ER 785, HL). See also TRUSTS AND POWERS vol 98
    (2013) PARA 70.
10 As to certainty see TRUSTS AND POWERS vol 98 (2013) PARA 103; TRUSTS AND POWERS vol 98
    (2013) PARA 70. As to the liberal view of fiduciary powers for very wide classes of beneficiaries
    which has in recent years prevailed see *Re Hay's Settlement Trusts* [1981] 3 All ER 786, [1982]
    1 WLR 202; *Re Beatty's Will Trusts, Hinves v Brooke* [1990] 3 All ER 844, [1990] 1 WLR 1503.
    It seems that *Re Carville, Shone v Walthamstow Borough Council* [1937] 4 All ER 464, where it
    was held that a provision that the residue should be disposed of 'as my executors think fit' did not
    create a valid power, is now of questionable authority in view of the decision in *Re
    Beatty's Will Trusts, Hinves v Brooke*.
11 *Re Beatty's Will Trusts, Hinves v Brooke* [1990] 3 All ER 844, [1990] 1 WLR 1503. The idea that
    there might be a common law rule against testamentary delegation, in the sense of a restriction on
    the scope of testamentary powers, is a chimera, a shadow cast by the rule of certainty, having no
    independent existence: *Re Beatty's Will Trusts, Hinves v Brooke* at 849 and 1509 per Hoffmann J.
12 As to gifts to non-charitable societies see PARA 36; and TRUSTS AND POWERS vol 98 (2013)
    PARA 37.
13 *Dick v Audsley* [1908] AC 347, HL. See also *A-G v Hickman* (1732) Kel W 34; *White v White*
    (1778) 1 Bro CC 12; *Moggridge v Thackwell* (1803) 7 Ves 36 (affd (1807) 13 Ves 416, HL); *Re
    Douglas, Obert v Barrow* (1887) 35 ChD 472, CA; *Re White, White v White* [1893] 2 Ch 41, CA;
    Re Willis, Shaw v Willis [1921] 1 Ch 44, CA; *Re Ludlow, Bence-Jones v A-G* (1923) 93 LJ Ch 30,
    CA. See also *Re Trustees of Christian Brothers in Western Australia Inc* [2007] WTLR 1375 (court
    granting leave to intervene in cy-près application on basis that former members of agricultural
    college were identifiable members of class that testatrix intended to benefit). See also CHARITIES
    vol 8 (2015) PARA 124.
14 *Hunter v A-G* [1899] AC 309, HL (trust to purchase advowsons); *Dunne v Byrne* [1912] AC 407,
    PC (money to be used wholly or in part as most conducive to the good of religion in a diocese);
    A-G of New Zealand v New Zealand Insurance Co Ltd [1936] 3 All ER 888, PC (benevolent
    purposes); *Farley v Westminster Bank Ltd* [1939] AC 430, [1939] 3 All ER 491, HL (parish work).
    See also *Morice v Bishop of Durham* (1805) 10 Ves 522 (objects of benevolence and liberality);
    James v Allen (1817) 3 Mer 17 (benevolent purposes); *Re Riland's Estate, Phillips v Robinson*
    [1881] WN 173 (as trustees may think proper); *Re Freeman, Shilton v Freeman* [1908] 1 Ch 720,
    CA (societies which were in most need of help); *Re Ogden, Taylor v Sharp* (1909) 25 TLR 382,
    CA (to encourage artistic pursuits or assisting needy students in art); *Re Da Costa, Clarke v
    Church of England Collegiate School of St Peter* [1912] 1 Ch 337; *Re Rowe, Merchant
    Taylors' Co v London Corpn* (1914) 30 TLR 528 (complete discretion in trustees); *Re Moore,
    Moore v Pope Benedict XV* [1919] 1 IR 316 (to use and apply at the Pope's discretion in the
    carrying out of the sacred office); *Re Jackson, Midland Bank Executor and Trustee Co Ltd v
    Archbishop of Wales* [1930] 2 Ch 389; *Re Stratton, Knapman v Stratton* [1931] 1 Ch 197, CA
    (parochial institutions or purposes); *Re Simson, Fowler v Tinley* [1946] Ch 299, [1946] 2 All ER
    220 (benevolent work); *Re Strakosch, Temperley v A-G* [1949] Ch 529, [1949] 2 All ER 6, CA
    (trust to strengthen bonds of unity between Union of South Africa and the mother country); *Re
    Endacott, Corpe v Endacott* [1960] Ch 232, [1959] 3 All ER 562, CA ('for the purpose of
    providing some useful memorial to myself'); *Re Atkinson's Will Trusts, Atkinson v Hall* [1978]
    1 All ER 1275, [1978] 1 WLR 586 (worthy causes).
15 *Blair v Duncan* [1902] AC 37, HL (charitable or public); *Grimond v Grimond* [1905] AC 124, HL
    (charitable or religious institutions and societies); *A-G for New Zealand v Brown* [1917] AC 393,
    PC (charitable, benevolent, religious and educational institutions, societies, associations and
    objects); *Houston v Burns* [1918] AC 337, HL (public, benevolent or charitable); *A-G v National
    Provincial and Union Bank of England* [1924] AC 262, HL (patriotic purposes or objects and
    charitable institutions or objects); *Chichester Diocesan Fund and Board of Finance Inc v Simpson*
    [1944] AC 341, [1944] 2 All ER 60, HL (charitable or benevolent). See also *Vezey v Jamson*
    (1822) 1 Sim & St 69 (charitable or public); *Williams v Kershaw* (1835) 5 Cl & Fin 111n
    (benevolent, charitable and religious purposes); *Ellis v Selby* (1836) 1 My & Cr 286 (charitable or
    other); *Re Jarman's Estate, Leavers v Clayton* (1878) 8 ChD 584 (charitable or benevolent); *Re*

Hewitt's Estate, Gateshead Corpn v Hudspeth (1883) 53 LJ Ch 132 (acts of hospitality or charity); *Re Woodgate* (1886) 2 TLR 674 (sick and poor or other utilitarian purposes); *Re Macduff, Macduff v Macduff* [1896] 2 Ch 451, CA (charitable or philanthropic); *Langham v Peterson* (1903) 87 LT 744 (charity or works of public utility); *Re Sidney, Hingeston v Sidney* [1908] 1 Ch 488, CA (charitable or emigration uses); *Re Davidson, Minty v Bourne* [1909] 1 Ch 567, CA (charitable, religious or other societies in connection with the Roman Catholic faith); *Re Eades, Eades v Eades* [1920] 2 Ch 353 (religious, charitable and philanthropic objects); *Re Chapman, Hales v A-G* [1922] 2 Ch 479, CA (charitable or other objects and purposes); *Re Davis, Thomas v Davis* [1923] 1 Ch 225 (charitable or public institutions); *Re Clarke, Bracey v Royal National Lifeboat Institution* [1923] 2 Ch 407 (such other funds, charities and institutions as the executors thought fit); *Reid's Trustees v M'George* 1929 SLT 608, Ct of Sess (charitable, educational or benevolent societies or public institutions); *Re Wood, Barton v Chilcott* [1949] Ch 498, [1949] 1 All ER 1100 (objects of broadcast appeals, of which only some were charitable). See further CHARITIES vol 8 (2015) PARAS 59–67. For a case where the objects were a mixture of charitable purposes and individuals, and the gift was held valid see *Crichton v Grierson* (1828) 3 Bli NS 424, HL; and for a case where a mixture of charitable purposes and named non-charitable institutions were held to be valid objects of a power see *Re Douglas, Obert v Barrow* (1886) 35 ChD 472 (affd (1887) 35 ChD 472 at 480, CA).

16 *Re Jarman's Estate, Leavers v Clayton* (1878) 8 ChD 584 at 587 per Hall V-C.

17 *Leahy v A-G for New South Wales* [1959] AC 457 at 478, [1959] 2 All ER 300 at 307, PC. See also *Re Wood, Barton v Chilcott* [1949] Ch 498, [1949] 1 All ER 1100; *Re Astor's Settlement Trusts, Astor v Scholfield* [1952] Ch 534, [1952] 1 All ER 1067; *Re Endacott, Corpe v Endacott* [1960] Ch 232, [1959] 3 All ER 562, CA; *Neville Estates Ltd v Madden* [1962] Ch 832, [1961] 3 All ER 769; *Re Denley's Trust Deed, Holman v HH Martyn & Co Ltd* [1969] 1 Ch 373, [1968] 3 All ER 65; *Re Grant's Will Trusts, Harris v Anderson* [1979] 3 All ER 359, [1980] 1 WLR 360.

12. Foreign element in wills; formal validity. A will, other than a valid international will[1], may be regarded as properly executed either as a result of statute or by common law. By statute, if the execution of a will made on or after 1 January 1964[2] conforms to the internal law[3] in force:

(1)   in the territory where it was executed; or

(2)   in the territory where either at the time of its execution or of the testator's death he was domiciled[4] or had his habitual residence[5]; or

(3)   in a state[6] of which, at either of those times, he was a national,

the will is to be treated as properly executed[7].

At common law, a will of movables is properly executed if its execution complies with the formalities prescribed by the law of the testator's domicile at the time of his death[8]. Compliance with either the internal law of the domicile or the internal law of any system of law referred to by the law of the domicile is sufficient[9]. Similarly, at common law a will of immovables is properly executed if its execution complies with the formal requirements of the lex situs[10]. Compliance with any system of law referred to by the lex situs is probably sufficient[11].

1 As to international wills see PARA 14.

2 Ie the date of the coming into operation of the Wills Act 1963: see s 7(2).

3 In relation to any territory or state, 'internal law' means the law which would apply in a case where no question of the law in force in any other territory or state arose: Wills Act 1963 s 6(1). As to the meaning of 'state' see note 6. As to cases where there is more than one system of law in any territory or state see s 6(2); and CONFLICT OF LAWS vol 19 (2011) PARA 748. As to subsequent changes in the law see s 6(3); and CONFLICT OF LAWS vol 19 (2011) PARA 742.

4 As to domicile see CONFLICT OF LAWS vol 19 (2011) PARA 336 et seq.

5 As to residence see CONFLICT OF LAWS vol 19 (2011) PARA 358 et seq.

6 For these purposes, 'state' means a territory or group of territories having its own law of nationality: Wills Act 1963 s 6(1).

7 Wills Act 1963 s 1. For these purposes, 'will' includes any testamentary instrument or act; and 'testator' is to be construed accordingly: s 6(1). As to revocation of wills with a foreign element see CONFLICT OF LAWS vol 19 (2011) PARA 756. As to the construction of wills written in a foreign language see PARA 203; and CONFLICT OF LAWS vol 19 (2011) PARA 751. See also *Mausner v Mincher* [2006] EWHC 1283 (Ch), [2006] All ER (D) 240 (Apr) (unsuccessful challenge to will

written in Dutch for non-Dutch-speaking testator; will indorsed by Dutch civil law notary to show that will was explained to testator in English immediately before execution and witnessed in accordance with both Dutch and English law).
8   *Enohin v Wylie* (1862) 10 HL Cas 1. See also CONFLICT OF LAWS vol 19 (2011) PARA 747.
9   *Collier v Rivaz* (1841) 2 Curt 855. See also CONFLICT OF LAWS vol 19 (2011) PARA 747.
10   *Philipson-Stow v IRC* [1961] AC 727, [1960] 3 All ER 814, HL. Cf the Wills Act 1963 s 2(1)(b), which restates the common law rule: see CONFLICT OF LAWS vol 19 (2011) PARA 748. As to the application of the lex situs to immovables generally see CONFLICT OF LAWS vol 19 (2011) PARAS 695–700.
11   See CONFLICT OF LAWS vol 19 (2011) PARA 747.

13. Foreign element in wills; essential validity.

The material or essential validity of a will of movables is governed by the law of the testator's domicile at the date of his death[1], and that of a will of immovables by the lex situs[2]. There may be circumstances where the validity and effect of a trust is governed by the express choice of law of the settlor or testator[3].

In this title it is assumed, unless otherwise stated, that there is no foreign element to consider, and the law stated is the law of England and Wales.

Probate will normally be refused of a will which disposes of property situated entirely abroad[4].

European Union ('EU') legislation makes provision by regulation[5] for a person to choose the law of the state whose nationality he possesses, either at the time of making the choice or at the time of death, as the law to govern his succession as a whole[6]. The law selected is applied whether or not it is the law of a member state[7]. The legislation also makes provision in respect of the creation of a European certificate of succession, applying to the succession of persons who die on or after 17 August 2015[8]. The United Kingdom[9] is not taking part in the adoption of this regulation and is not therefore bound by it or subject to its application[10].

1   *Philipson-Stow v IRC* [1961] AC 727, [1960] 3 All ER 814, HL. For a discussion of this case see *Dellar v Zivy* [2007] EWHC 2266 (Ch), [2007] All ER (D) 121 (Oct), drawing the distinction between the question of the validity of a will with a foreign element and its interpretation. See CONFLICT OF LAWS vol 19 (2011) PARA 753.
2   *Freke v Lord Carbery* (1873) LR 16 Eq 461. See *Re Hamblett, McGown v Hamblett* (2006) 8 ITELR 943, NZHC. See also CONFLICT OF LAWS vol 19 (2011) PARA 695.
3   See *Tod v Barton* [2002] EWHC 265 (Ch), 4 ITELR 715, [2002] All ER (D) 265 (Feb) (Texas-domiciled testator's trust was governed by English law under the Recognition of Trusts Act 1987 (see CONFLICT OF LAWS vol 19 (2011) PARA 721 et seq), by reason of his express choice of law clause, rather than by Texas law).
4   See PARA 722.
5   See European Parliament and Council Regulation (EU) 650/2012 (OJ L201, 27.7.2012, p 107) (corrected in OJ L344, 14.12.2012, p 3; OJ L60, 2.3.2013, p 140) on jurisdiction, applicable law, recognition and enforcement of decisions and acceptance and enforcement of authentic instruments in matters of succession and on the creation of a European certificate of succession, applying to the succession of persons who die on or after 17 August 2015; and Commission Implementing Regulation (EU) 1329/2014 (OJ L359, 16.12.2014, p 30) establishing the forms referred to in Regulation 650/2012 (corrected in OJ L9, 14.1.2016, p 14).
6   See European Parliament and Council Regulation (EU) 650/2012 (OJ L201, 27.7.2012, p 107), art 22. The doctrine of renvoi may thus be excluded: see art 34. As to renvoi see CONFLICT OF LAWS vol 19 (2011) PARAS 308–310.
7   See European Parliament and Council Regulation (EU) 650/2012 (OJ L201, 27.7.2012, p 107), art 20.
8   See European Parliament and Council Regulation (EU) 650/2012 (OJ L201, 27.7.2012, p 107), arts 62–73. The European certificate of succession enables the heirs, legatees, executors of the will or administrators of the estate to demonstrate easily their status, rights and powers in another member state, for instance in a member state in which succession property is located: see recital (67). See also PARA 718.
9   As to the meaning of 'United Kingdom' see PARA 4 note 7.

10 See European Parliament and Council Regulation (EU) 650/2012 (OJ L201, 27.7.2012, p 107), recital (82).

14.   International wills. An international will is one made in accordance with the requirements of the Annex to the Convention on International Wills[1], which will have the force of law in the United Kingdom when the relevant statutory provisions are brought into force[2].

A will made in accordance with the requirements of the Annex to the Convention on International Wills is valid as regards form, irrespective particularly of the place where it is made, of the location of the assets and of the nationality, domicile[3] or residence[4] of the testator, if it complies with the provisions set out below[5]. The invalidity of a will as an international will does not, however, affect its formal validity as a will of another kind[6]. These provisions do not, in any event, apply to the form of testamentary dispositions made by two or more persons in one instrument[7].

The will must be made in writing[8], and it may be written in any language, by hand or any other means[9], but it need not be written by the testator himself[10]. The testator must declare in the presence of two witnesses and of a person authorised to act in connection with international wills[11] that the document is his will, and that he knows its contents[12]. He need not inform the witnesses, or the authorised person, of the contents of the will[13].

The testator must sign the will, or, if he has previously signed it, must acknowledge his signature, in the presence of the witnesses and of the authorised person[14]. When the testator is unable to sign, he must indicate the reason to the authorised person who must make note of this on the will[15]. Moreover, the testator may be authorised by the law under which the authorised person was designated to direct another person to sign on his behalf[16]. The witnesses and the authorised person must there and then attest the will by signing in the presence of the testator[17]. The signatures must be placed at the end of the will[18]. If the will consists of several sheets, each sheet must be signed by the testator or, if he is unable to sign, by the person signing on his behalf or, if there is no such person, by the authorised person; and each sheet must be numbered[19].

The date of the will is the date of its signature by the authorised person[20], and he must note that date at the end of the will[21]. In the absence of any mandatory rule pertaining to the safe-keeping of the will, the authorised person must ask the testator whether he wishes to make a declaration concerning the safe-keeping of his will. If so, and at the express request of the testator, the place where he intends to have his will kept must be mentioned in the prescribed certificate[22].

The authorised person must attach to the will a certificate in the prescribed form[23] establishing that the above obligations have been complied with[24]. He must keep a copy of this certificate, and deliver another to the testator[25]. In the absence of evidence to the contrary, the certificate is conclusive of the formal validity of the instrument as a will in accordance with these provisions[26]. The absence or irregularity of a certificate does not, however, affect the formal validity of a will made under these provisions[27].

An international will certified by virtue of these provisions may be deposited in a depository provided[28] by the registering authority[29].

An international will is subject to the ordinary rules relating to revocation of wills[30].

In interpreting and applying these provisions, regard must be had to their international origin and to the need for uniformity in their interpretation[31].

1   Administration of Justice Act 1982 s 27(3). 'Convention on International Wills' means the Convention providing a Uniform Law on the Form of an International Will (Washington, 26 October to 31 December 1974; Misc 9 (1975); Cmnd 5950): Administration of Justice Act 1982 s 27(3). The Annex to that Convention is set out in the Administration of Justice Act 1982 Sch 2: s 27(2). Sections 27, 28 and Sch 2 are to come into operation on such day as the Lord Chancellor and the Secretary of State may by order jointly appoint: s 76(5), (6)(b). Such an order must be made by statutory instrument (s 76(7)); and may appoint different days for different provisions and for different purposes (s 76(8)). At the date at which this volume states the law, no such order had been made. As to the meaning of 'United Kingdom' see PARA 4 note 7. As to the Lord Chancellor see CONSTITUTIONAL AND ADMINISTRATIVE LAW vol 20 (2014) PARA 255 et seq. In any enactment, 'Secretary of State' means one of Her Majesty's principal Secretaries of State: see the Interpretation Act 1978 s 5, Sch 1. As to the office of Secretary of State see CONSTITUTIONAL AND ADMINISTRATIVE LAW vol 20 (2014) PARA 153.
2   Administration of Justice Act 1982 s 27(1).
3   As to domicile see CONFLICT OF LAWS vol 19 (2011) PARA 336 et seq.
4   As to residence see CONFLICT OF LAWS vol 19 (2011) PARA 358 et seq.
5   Convention on International Wills Annex art 1(1).
6   Convention on International Wills Annex art 1(2). As to the formal validity of foreign wills see PARA 12.
7   Convention on International Wills Annex art 2. As to joint wills see PARA 9.
8   Convention on International Wills Annex art 3(1).
9   Convention on International Wills Annex art 3(3).
10 Convention on International Wills Annex art 3(2).
11 The persons authorised to act in the United Kingdom in connection with international wills are solicitors and notaries public: Administration of Justice Act 1982 s 28(1). A person authorised to do notarial acts in any foreign country or place (ie under the Commissioners for Oaths Act 1889 s 6(1): see CIVIL PROCEDURE vol 12 (2015) PARA 830) is authorised to act there in connection with international wills: Administration of Justice Act 1982 s 28(2). A diplomatic agent or consular officer of any state may, if authorised to do so under the laws of that state, administer oaths and take affidavits and do notarial acts in connection with an international will: Consular Relations Act 1968 s 10(1)(c), (4) (prospectively amended by the Administration of Justice Act 1982 s 28(7)). As to the commencement of these provisions see note 1.
12 Convention on International Wills Annex art 4(1).
13 Convention on International Wills Annex art 4(2).
14 Convention on International Wills Annex art 5(1).
15 Convention on International Wills Annex art 5(2).
16 Convention on International Wills Annex art 5(2). As to the signing of a will on behalf of the testator see PARA 64.
17 Convention on International Wills Annex art 5(3).
18 Convention on International Wills Annex art 6(1). Cf, however, art 15 (see the text to note 31).
19 Convention on International Wills Annex art 6(2). Presumably the numbering must be consecutive, commencing with the number 1.
20 Convention on International Wills Annex art 7(1).
21 Convention on International Wills Annex art 7(2).
22 Convention on International Wills Annex art 8. As to the certificate see the text to notes 23–27. As to the provision of official depositories for wills see PARA 16. See also the text and notes 28–29.
23 The certificate drawn up by the authorised person must be in the form set out in the Convention on International Wills Annex art 10 or in a substantially similar form: art 10. In addition to certifying compliance with these requirements, it also certifies that the maker of the certificate has satisfied himself as to the identity of the testator and the witnesses, and that those witnesses meet the conditions requisite for acting as such according to the law under which the maker of the certificate is acting. As to the capacity of witnesses under English law see PARA 78.
24 Convention on International Wills Annex art 9.
25 Convention on International Wills Annex art 11.
26 Convention on International Wills Annex art 12.
27 Convention on International Wills Annex art 13.
28 Ie a depository maintained under the Administration of Justice Act 1982 s 23 (see PARA 16). Section 23 accordingly has effect in relation to international wills: s 28(4). Regulations under s 25 (see PARA 16) have effect in relation to such international wills as they have effect in relation to wills deposited under s 23 (see PARA 16) (s 28(5)); but, without prejudice to the generality of s 25, regulations under s 25 may make special provision with regard to such international wills (s 28(6)).

29 Administration of Justice Act 1982 s 28(3). As to the registering authority see PARA 16.
30 Convention on International Wills Annex art 14. As to rules relating to revocation of wills with a foreign element see CONFLICT OF LAWS vol 19 (2011) PARAS 756–757. As to revocation generally see PARA 87 et seq.
31 Convention on International Wills Annex art 15.

15. Safe-keeping of wills; existing provisions. Safe and convenient depositories for the custody of the wills of living persons are required to be provided under the control and direction of the High Court; and any person may deposit his will in such a depository on payment of the prescribed fee[1] and subject to such conditions as may from time to time be prescribed by regulations[2] made by the President of the Family Division with the concurrence of the Lord Chancellor[3].

As from a day to be appointed this system of registration is to be replaced[4] and any will already deposited in accordance with this system[5] will be treated as if it has been deposited under the new provisions[6].

The safety of wills is protected by the criminal law[7].

1 Ie the fee prescribed by an order under the Courts Act 2003 s 92 (see CIVIL PROCEDURE vol 11 (2015) PARA 68): Senior Courts Act 1981 s 126(1) (amended by the Courts Act 2003 Sch 8 para 262(b)). As from a day to be appointed, the Senior Courts Act 1981 s 126 is repealed by the Administration of Justice Act 1982 Sch 9 Pt I. At the date at which this volume states the law, no such day had been appointed.
2 At the date at which this volume states the law no such regulations had been made but, by virtue of the Interpretation Act 1978 s 17(2)(b), the Wills (Deposit for Safe Custody) Regulations 1978, SI 1978/1724, have effect as if so made. The Principal Registry of the Family Division is the depository: regs 2(2), 3(1). As to the custody of wills by the Public Trustee on his appointment as custodian trustee see TRUSTS AND POWERS vol 98 (2013) PARA 232 et seq. As to the powers of the Court of Protection in relation to testamentary papers of a person suffering from mental disorder, see PARA 51 text and notes 4, 6; and see also MENTAL HEALTH AND CAPACITY vol 75 (2013) PARA 720 et seq. As to the Lord Chancellor see CONSTITUTIONAL AND ADMINISTRATIVE LAW vol 20 (2014) PARA 255 et seq.
3 Senior Courts Act 1981 s 126(1) (prospectively repealed: see note 1). The Lord Chancellor's function under s 126 is a protected function for the purposes of the Constitutional Reform Act 2005 s 19: see s 19(5), Sch 7 para 4; and CONSTITUTIONAL AND ADMINISTRATIVE LAW vol 20 (2014) PARAS 259, 261.
4 See note 1; and PARA 16.
5 Ie any will deposited under the Supreme Court of Judicature (Consolidation) Act 1925 s 172 (repealed), or under the Senior Courts Act 1981 s 126 (prospectively repealed).
6 Administration of Justice Act 1982 s 23(5)(a) (not yet in force). At the date at which this volume states the law, no day had been appointed for the commencement of this provision.
7 As to offences of destroying, defacing or concealing a will see CRIMINAL LAW vol 25 (2016) PARA 355. As to the offence of forgery see the Forgery and Counterfeiting Act 1981 s 1; and CRIMINAL LAW vol 25 (2016) PARA 404 et seq.

16. Safe-keeping of wills; new provisions. As from a day to be appointed[1], the Principal Registry of the Family Division of the High Court of Justice is to be the registering authority[2] charged with the duty of providing and maintaining safe and convenient depositories for the custody of wills of living persons[3], in which any person may deposit his will in accordance with the appropriate regulations[4] and on payment of the prescribed fee[5].

It is the duty of the registering authority to register in accordance with such regulations any will deposited in a depository maintained by it[6], and any other will whose registration is requested under the Registration Convention[7].

The Principal Registry of the Family Division is to be the national body for the purposes of the Registration Convention[8].

Regulations[9] may make provision:
(1)   as to the conditions for the deposit of a will[10];

(2)   as to the manner of and procedure for the deposit and registration of a will, the withdrawal of a will which has been deposited, and the cancellation of the registration of a will[11]; and

(3)   as to the manner in which the registering authority is to perform its functions as the national body under the Registration Convention[12].

Such regulations may contain such incidental or supplementary provisions as the authority making the regulations considers appropriate[13].

1   The Administration of Justice Act 1982 ss 23–25 are to come into operation on such day as the Lord Chancellor and the Secretary of State may by order jointly appoint: s 76(5), (6)(a). Such an order must be made by statutory instrument (s 76(7)); and may appoint different days for different provisions and for different purposes (s 76(8)). At the date at which this volume states the law, no such order had been made. As to the Lord Chancellor see CONSTITUTIONAL AND ADMINISTRATIVE LAW vol 20 (2014) PARA 255 et seq. As to the Secretary of State see PARA 14 note 1.

2   Administration of Justice Act 1982 s 23(1)(a).

3   Administration of Justice Act 1982 s 23(2). As to the treatment of wills deposited under earlier enactments see PARA 15.

4   Ie regulations made under the Administration of Justice Act 1982 s 25 (see the text and notes 9–13).

5   Administration of Justice Act 1982 s 23(3). For these purposes, 'prescribed' means prescribed by an order under the Courts Act 2003 s 92 (see CIVIL PROCEDURE vol 11 (2015) PARA 68): Administration of Justice Act 1982 s 23(6)(a) (amended by the Courts Act 2003 s 109(1), Sch 8 para 270).

6   Administration of Justice Act 1982 s 23(4)(a).

7   Administration of Justice Act 1982 s 23(4)(b). The registration may be requested under the Registration Convention art 6. 'Registration Convention' means the Convention on the Establishment of a Scheme of Registration of Wills (Basle, 16 May 1972; Misc 30 (1972); Cmnd 5073): Administration of Justice Act 1982 s 24(2).

8   Administration of Justice Act 1982 s 24(1). Accordingly, the Principal Registry of the Family Division is to have the functions assigned to the national body by the Registration Convention and, without prejudice to those general functions, the functions of arranging for the registration of wills in other contracting states, and of receiving and answering requests for information arising from the national bodies of other contracting states: Administration of Justice Act 1982 s 24(1)(a), (b).

9   The regulations are to be made by the President of the Family Division, with the concurrence of the Lord Chancellor: Administration of Justice Act 1982 s 25(3)(a). See, however note 12. The Lord Chancellor's function under s 25(3)(a) is a protected function for the purposes of the Constitutional Reform Act 2005 s 19: see s 19(5), Sch 7 para 4; and CONSTITUTIONAL AND ADMINISTRATIVE LAW vol 20 (2014) PARAS 259, 261. The Statutory Instruments Act 1946 (see STATUTES AND LEGISLATIVE PROCESS vol 96 (2012) PARA 1032 et seq) applies to a statutory instrument containing regulations made in accordance with the Administration of Justice Act 1982 s 25(3)(a) as if the regulations had been made by a Minister of the Crown: s 25(7). Any regulations made under the Supreme Court of Judicature (Consolidation) Act 1925 s 172 (repealed) or the Senior Courts Act 1981 s 126 (see eg the Wills (Deposit for Safe Custody) Regulations 1978, SI 1978/1724, which have effect as if so made) are to have effect for the purposes of the Administration of Justice Act 1982 Pt IV (ss 17–28) as they have effect for the purposes of the enactment under which they were made: s 25(8).

10   Administration of Justice Act 1982 s 25(1)(a).

11   Administration of Justice Act 1982 s 25(1)(b).

12   Administration of Justice Act 1982 s 25(1)(c). Regulations made by virtue of s 25(1)(c) are to be made by the Lord Chancellor after consulting the Lord Chief Justice of England and Wales: s 25(4) (amended by the Constitutional Reform Act 2005 Sch 4 para 148(2)). The Lord Chief Justice may nominate a judicial office holder (as defined in s 109(4)) to exercise his functions under the Administration of Justice Act 1982 s 25(4): s 25(9) (added by the Constitutional Reform Act 2005 Sch 4 para 148(3)).

13   Administration of Justice Act 1982 s 25(2).

17. Personal representatives have legal title. English law has adopted generally, in relation to wills, the distinction between the legal and equitable title to the property of the testator. At law the sole legal title to the testator's property, both real[1] and personal[2], devolves, notwithstanding his testamentary dispositions[3], on his personal representatives for the purpose of administration of his estate[4]. The dispositions contained in the will take effect in equity only, that is to say that the devisees or legatees only have rights, enforceable in a court of equity, against the personal representatives as legal owners[5]. Realty devised by the will requires an assent or conveyance by the personal representatives to vest it in the devisee, and personalty bequeathed by the will requires their assent to vest it in the legatee[6].

1 Before 1 January 1898, when the Land Transfer Act 1897 s 1 (now replaced in an extended form by the Administration of Estates Act 1925 s 1(1)) came into force, realty passed directly to the devisee, or, in the case of intestacy, to the heir: see PARA 945.
2 This includes leaseholds ('chattels real'): see *Wind v Jekyl* (1719) 1 P Wms 572.
3 It is the practice to use 'devise' to denote a gift of realty and 'bequest' or 'legacy' to denote a gift of personalty, the person or other object taking a benefit under a gift of realty or personalty being called respectively a 'devisee' or a 'legatee' (see eg *Ellard v Phelan* [1914] 1 IR 76); but 'devise' was formerly often used with respect to gifts by will of leaseholds ('chattels real') and other personalty (see eg *Hopewell v Ackland* (1710) 1 Salk 239; *Tilley v Simpson* (1746) 2 Term Rep 659n), and its use in a will is not in itself conclusive to show that the testator is dealing with realty (*Camfield v Gilbert* (1803) 3 East 516 at 521; *Hall v Hall* [1891] 3 Ch 389 at 393 (affd [1892] 1 Ch 361, CA)), although that prima facie is its meaning (*Phillips v Beal* (1858) 25 Beav 25). It is often used of leaseholds. Conversely, 'bequest' or 'legacy' may in a proper context carry realty: see PARA 284. As to the origin of the term 'bequest' see 2 Pollock and Maitland's History of English Law (2nd Edn) 338. 'Gift' includes devise and bequest, and 'donee' includes devisee and legatee, or other object of the testator's bounty in any kind of property. The term 'gift over' is commonly used to describe a gift in succession to a prior gift, especially by way of executory devise or bequest: see PARA 445 et seq. 'Limitation' is commonly used to describe a gift of a limited interest, or one of a series of gifts of the same property to persons in succession.
4 See PARA 917 et seq.
5 The Wills Act 1837 takes effect to enable equitable interests to be disposed of subject, and without prejudice, to the estate and powers of a personal representative: Law of Property (Amendment) Act 1924 s 9, Sch 9 para 3. While the estate of a deceased person is in the course of administration, the beneficiaries interested in the residuary estate have a right to have the estate properly administered, but do not have equitable interests in the assets comprised in the estate: see PARA 922. As to the payment of inheritance tax see INHERITANCE TAXATION vol 59A (2014) PARA 1 et seq. As to property appointed by will which devolves on the personal representatives see PARAS 954–955.
6 See PARA 1139 et seq. As to an assent or conveyance in regard to realty see the Administration of Estates Act 1925 s 36; and PARA 1143 et seq. It seems that a devise conditional on the payment of a legacy, the legatee having an express right of entry to secure the payment (a right formerly said to be in the nature of a tenancy by elegit: see *Johns v Pink* [1900] 1 Ch 296; *Wigg v Wigg* (1739) 1 Atk 382 at 383; *Emes v Hancock* (1743) 2 Atk 507 at 508; *Sherman v Collins* (1745) 3 Atk 319 at 322), would be effected by the executor making the assent subject to an equitable right of entry by the legatee: see the Law of Property Act 1925 ss 1(2)(e), 4(3). This would not prevent the devisee from obtaining a fee simple absolute, so as to have the legal estate: see s 7(1) (amended by the Law of Property (Amendment) Act 1926 s 7, Schedule). As to the limitation of actions against personal representatives to recover benefits given by will see LIMITATION PERIODS vol 68 (2016) PARA 1159.

18. Date from which will takes effect. As a disposition of his property, a will is subject to any subsequent disposition inter vivos by the testator in his lifetime[1], and to any order made by the court in favour of a successful applicant for reasonable financial provision[2]. A disposition made by a will need not come into operation immediately on the testator's death, but, to the extent that such dispositions are allowed, may take effect at a future time[3]. The dispositions in the will take effect subject to the rules as to payment of debts and liabilities[4] and the presumptions as to the order of payment of legacies and the construction of expressions giving legacies priority[5], or affecting the order of application of assets in the payment of debts or legacies[6], or charging annuities on capital or income[7]. The usual rules and presumptions may, however, be displaced if the testator shows an intention to displace them[8].

1 As to ademption see PARAS 155–159.
2 Ie under the Inheritance (Provision for Family and Dependants) Act 1975 (see PARA 565 et seq).

3   See *Re Newns* (1861) 7 Jur NS 688 (where a disposition by writing to take effect two years after the death of the testator's wife was held testamentary). As to executory devises see REAL PROPERTY AND REGISTRATION vol 87 (2012) PARAS 168–173; and as to executory bequests see PARAS 117–121. As to the rule against perpetuities see PERPETUITIES AND ACCUMULATIONS vol 80 (2013) PARA 9 et seq.
4   As to the payment of debts by the personal representatives see PARA 966 et seq.
5   As to the priority of legacies etc see PARA 1087 et seq; and PERSONAL AND OCCUPATIONAL PENSIONS vol 80 (2013) PARA 694.
6   As to the exclusion of the statutory order for payment of debts see PARAS 993–994; as to secured and unsecured debts see PARAS 996; as to the order in payment of debts see PARA 998 et seq; and as to the order of application of assets see PARA 1107 et seq.
7   See PERSONAL AND OCCUPATIONAL PENSIONS vol 80 (2013) PARA 675 et seq.
8   See PARAS 966, 993–994. See also eg *Re Scholfield's Will's Trusts, Scholfield v Scholfield* [1949] Ch 341, [1949] 1 All ER 490 (treatment of war damage value payments as capital or income). As to administration of the assets generally see PARA 956 et seq.

19.   Conditions necessary for gift by will to take effect. The following are necessary conditions that a gift by will may be effectual to confer a title to the property given on the donee[1]:

(1)   the testator must be dead[2];

(2)   the testator must have been a person who at the date of the will had the legal capacity to make a will[3];

(3)   at the time of making the will the testator must have had the intention to make it, so as to take effect on his death[4], the gift being defeated if the testator's mind was not free and unaffected by fear, fraud or undue influence, or want of knowledge and approval, or by any other matters which by law vitiate his intention[5];

(4)   the will must be made in the form and manner required by law[6];

(5)   the gift must not have been revoked[7] or altered[8], or nullified by divorce, dissolution or annulment[9], or, if revoked, must have been revived before the death of the testator[10];

(6)   probate of the will or letters of administration with the will annexed must be obtained[11];

(7)   the words used by the testator in making the gift must be sufficient to make his intention capable of being ascertained[12];

(8)   the subject matter of the gift described by the testator must be ascertainable and capable of being disposed of by the will of the testator[13], or, if not, the gift must be validated under the equitable doctrine of election[14], or otherwise;

(9)   the donee described by the testator must be ascertainable and capable by law of taking the benefit of the gift[15];

(10)   the gift so intended must be consistent with law[16], or must be capable of being effectuated in a manner consistent with the law[17];

(11)   the gift must be assented to or given effect to by the personal representatives of the testator[18];

(12)   all other conditions precedent imposed by the testator or by law must be performed[19].

1   See Shep Touch (8th Edn, 1826) p 413. As to the failure of a gift on other grounds see PARA 150 et seq. As to the meanings of 'gift' and 'donee' see PARA 17 note 3.
2   *Thorp v Tomson* (1588) 2 Leon 120. See also PARA 2.
3   As to the legal capacity to make a will see PARAS 46 et seq, 897.
4   See PARA 54. As to the effect of the will being read over to the testator see PARAS 902, 903.
5   As to want of knowledge and approval see PARAS 55, 901; and as to gifts obtained by undue influence or fraud see PARAS 38, 904. Such matters are grounds for refusing probate: see PARA 891 et seq.

6   As to the form of wills made in England and Wales see PARA 5; and as to the form of wills made abroad see PARA 12.
7   As to revocation see PARA 87 et seq.
8   As to the effect of codicils see PARA 1; and as to alterations and erasures see PARA 82 et seq.
9   As to the effect of divorce and annulment of marriages see PARAS 177–178. As to dissolution or annulment of civil partnerships see PARAS 90, 179.
10 See PARA 110 et seq.
11 As to probate generally see PARA 707 et seq. Statutory penalties are imposed on any person who takes possession of and in any way administers the testator's property without obtaining a grant (although no penalty is in practice exacted unless there is a liability to inheritance tax): see *Re Commercial Bank Corpn of India and the East, Fernandes' Executors Case* (1870) 5 Ch App 314 at 317; and PARA 668. As to inheritance tax see INHERITANCE TAXATION vol 59A (2014) PARA 1 et seq.
12 As to the construction of wills generally see PARA 185 et seq.
13 As to property capable of being disposed of see PARA 25 et seq; and as to the interests which may be created see PARA 117 et seq.
14 See EQUITABLE JURISDICTION vol 47 (2014) PARA 161 et seq.
15 As to the capacity to benefit under a will see PARA 33 et seq.
16 As to the interests created see PARA 116. As to the legal incidents of a gift, and as to the necessity for an assent, see generally PARA 1139 et seq. As to settled gifts see SETTLEMENTS vol 91 (2012) PARA 531.
17 As to the cy-près doctrine and similar rules see PARA 230 et seq.
18 As to the effect of a will in passing the property to the personal representatives see PARA 17; and as to executory trusts see TRUSTS AND POWERS vol 98 (2013) PARAS 84–86.
19 As to vesting of conditional interests see PARA 412 et seq. As to the entitlement to registration of a personal representative on the death of the proprietor of registered land see REAL PROPERTY AND REGISTRATION vol 87 (2012) PARA 440. Certain types of property may be subject to additional legal requirements: see eg MINES, MINERALS AND QUARRIES vol 76 (2013) PARA 609 (lead mines in Derbyshire).

(ii) Restrictions on Freedom of Testamentary Disposition

20. Restriction by contract, trust or estoppel. Although a will is always revocable[1], and the last will of a testator, notwithstanding any agreement, always remains his will, he may nevertheless bind himself personally by an agreement as to the contents of his will, and may so bind his assets by that agreement that a person deriving title under his will or intestacy is a trustee for the performance of that agreement[2]. The same may come about through accepting a gift of property subject to a trust to make a testamentary disposition of it in a particular way[3], or by acting in such a way as to confer other rights under the doctrine of proprietary estoppel[4]. For a restriction to arise under the doctrine of proprietary estoppel, there must be clarity as to what it was that the object of the estoppel was to be estopped from denying, or asserting, and clarity as to the interest in the property in question that that denial, or assertion, would otherwise defeat[5]. The extent of an estoppel-based restriction will usually depend upon what is the minimum equity necessary to do justice to the claimant and to avoid an unconscionable and disproportionate result[6]. Proportionality lies at the heart of the doctrine of proprietary estoppel and permeates its every application[7]. This does not mean that the court should abandon expectations and seek only to compensate detrimental reliance, but if the expectation is disproportionate to the detriment, the court should satisfy the equity in a more limited way[8].

1   See PARA 2. As to revocation see PARA 87 et seq.
2   *Dufour v Pereira* (1769) 1 Dick 419, as reported sub nom *Durour v Perraro* 2 Hargrave's Juridical Arguments 304 at 309 (cited in *Stone v Hoskins* [1905] P 194 at 196–197 and in *Re Dale, Proctor v Dale* [1994] Ch 31 at 40, [1993] 4 All ER 129 at 135). See also *Re Green, Lindner v Green* [1951] Ch 148, [1950] 2 All ER 913.
    As to a covenant not to revoke a will see PARA 21. Cf *Re Turner, Turner v Turner* (1902) 4 OLR 578 (where there was a devise on condition that the devisee made a will in favour of the

testator's children). See also *Re Hagger, Freeman v Arscott* [1930] 2 Ch 190. As to mutual wills see PARA 10; and *Olins v Walters* [2007] EWHC 3060 (Ch), [2008] WTLR 339, [2007] All ER (D) 291 (Dec); affd [2008] EWCA Civ 782, [2009] Ch 212, [2008] All ER (D) 58 (Jul).

3   *Ottaway v Norman* [1972] Ch 698, [1971] 3 All ER 1325; *Healey v Brown* [2002] All ER (D) 249 (Apr), [2002] WTLR 849. For a case where the testatrix's lifetime intention to transfer the equitable interest in property to her daughter was in issue see *Turner v Jacob* [2006] EWHC 1317 (Ch), [2006] All ER (D) 39 (Jun) (claim that donee took subject to common intention constructive trust for T's daughter failed for want of evidence of such intention).

4   *Re Basham* [1987] 1 All ER 405, [1986] 1 WLR 1498; *Wayling v Jones* (1993) 69 P & CR 170, CA; *Durant v Heritage* [1994] EGCS 134; *Price v Hartwell* [1996] EGCS 98, CA; but cf *Taylor v Dickens* [1998] 1 FLR 806, [1998] Fam Law 191 (cited in PARA 21 note 1); *Gillett v Holt* [2001] Ch 210, [2000] 2 All ER 289, CA; *Jennings v Rice* [2002] EWCA Civ 159, [2002] WTLR 367, [2002] All ER (D) 324 (Feb); *Grundy v Ottey* [2003] EWCA Civ 1176, [2003] WTLR 1253, sub nom *Ottey v Grundy* [2003] All ER (D) 05 (Aug); *Uglow v Uglow* [2004] EWCA Civ 987, [2004] All ER (D) 472 (Jul). As to proprietary estoppel see ESTOPPEL vol 47 (2014) PARA 309.

5   See *Yeoman's Row Management Ltd v Cobbe* [2008] UKHL 55 at [28], [2008] 4 All ER 713, [2008] 1 WLR 1752 per Lord Scott. See also *Thorner v Majors* [2009] UKHL 18, sub nom *Thorner v Major* [2009] 3 All ER 945, where the House of Lords distinguished *Yeoman's Row Management Ltd v Cobbe* in deciding that the Court of Appeal had given insufficient weight to the advantage of the judge in seeing and hearing the witnesses; the assurance given had clearly related to identified property, comprising whatever it did at the date of the death of the person making the assurance. See also *Davies v Davies* [2016] EWCA Civ 463, Fam Law 815 (award made took into account the fact that expectations and representations had varied over time); *Sinclair v Sinclair* [2009] EWHC 926 (Ch), [2009] 2 P & CR 40, [2009] All ER (D) 17 (May) (dependent on the facts, a trustee might acquire an estoppel interest as against the beneficiaries, but their knowledge became of particular importance where the claimant was in breach of trust; held that beneficiaries had insufficient knowledge and had not given estoppel claimant permission to occupy; no interest acquired); *Murphy v Burrows* [2004] EWHC 1900 (Ch), 7 ITELR 116, [2004] All ER (D) 572 (Jul) (vague assurances, but capable of founding an estoppel made by testator and were relied upon by claimant, but testator had not acted unconscionably in leaving the property elsewhere; the quality of the assurances impacted upon unconscionability, when looked at in the round). A similar view is found in *Gillett v Holt* [2001] Ch 210 at 225, [2000] 2 All ER 289 at 301, per Robert Walker LJ (the quality of the assurances could influence the issue of reliance, which was often intertwined with detriment).

6   *Uglow v Uglow* [2004] EWCA Civ 987, [2004] All ER (D) 472 (Jul). See also *Gill v Woodall* [2009] EWHC 3778 (Ch), [2010] All ER (D) 60 (Jan) (claimant, in reliance on an expectation, had foregone a career in industry and adopted an academic career to have significant amounts of time to spend on farming activity, which also reduced her academic research activities; the award of the farm to the claimant was not disproportionate in all the circumstances).

7   *Henry v Henry* [2010] UKPC 3 at [65], [2010] 1 All ER 988. In particular, there must be proportionality between the remedy and the detriment which is its purpose to avoid: *Jennings v Rice* [2002] EWCA Civ 159 at [28] (citing from earlier cases) and at [56], [2002] WTLR 367, [2002] All ER (D) 324 (Feb) per Aldous LJ.

8   *Davies v Davies* [2016] EWCA Civ 463 at [38], [2016] All ER (D) 09 (Jun) (citing *Jennings v Rice* [2002] EWCA Civ 159, [2002] WTLR 367, [2002] All ER (D) 324 (Feb)) and at [70]–[71] per Lewison LJ.

21. Enforceability of restrictions on testamentary freedom. As against persons deriving title as volunteers under the testator the court may order specific performance of a contract duly put into writing (if of a kind where writing is required)[1] to make an ascertainable gift[2] by will, if valuable consideration was given and specific performance is in the circumstances an appropriate remedy[3]. If the interest given is an interest in land, the court may order the personal representatives to convey the property according to the contract, and, under the Trustee Act 1925, may make a vesting order[4], or, if it is more convenient to do so, appoint a person to convey the property[5]. The court also has power to award damages, and may do so even during the lifetime of the testator, where there has been an anticipatory breach and he has put it out of his power to perform the agreement[6]. A mere representation of intention to leave property by will, not amounting to a contract, is not enforceable[7], unless it gives rise to rights under the doctrine of proprietary estoppel[8].

A covenant not to revoke a will is not normally[9] enforceable where the breach is occasioned by the marriage of the covenantor since the covenant does not extend to a case where revocation results as a matter of law[10], but in other respects there is no difference between such a contract and other agreements relating to wills as regards their binding effect[11], although the underlying contractual basis for mutual wills and the effects of the subsequent marriage of a party to such an agreement are dealt with in a manner, peculiar to such situations, as developed by the case law[12]. The covenantor's estate is not liable in damages if the provision made by him in pursuance of the contract is defeated by circumstances over which he has no control[13].

A covenant to bequeath a specific sum or devise or bequeath a specific property constitutes a debt against the covenantor's estate[14], but a covenant to bequeath a share of the estate is satisfied by a bequest of a share of residue to the covenantee, who is then in the same position as any other legatee as regards debts and lapse[15].

If there is an application under the Inheritance (Provision for Family and Dependants) Act 1975 in relation to a deceased person's estate, the court has power to reduce or nullify the effect of any contract by the deceased to leave property by will which was intended to defeat an application under that Act[16].

1   If the contract is to give land or an interest in land by will, and was made before 27 September 1989, the contract must be evidenced in writing under the Law of Property Act 1925 s 40 (repealed by the Law of Property (Miscellaneous Provisions) Act 1989 ss 4, 5(3), (4)(b), Sch 2), subject to the equitable doctrine of part performance: *Humphreys v Green* (1882) 10 QBD 148, CA; *Maddison v Alderson* (1883) 8 App Cas 467, HL; *Parker v Clark* [1960] 1 All ER 93, [1960] 1 WLR 286 (letter constituting offer and oral acceptance sufficient); *National Provincial Bank Ltd v Moore* (1967) 111 Sol Jo 357 (no writing so claim failed); *Schaefer v Schuhmann* [1972] AC 572, [1972] 1 All ER 621, PC (codicil constituted a written memorandum). See further CONTRACT vol 22 (2012) PARA 223; CONVEYANCING vol 23 (2016) PARA 27 et seq.
    In relation to any contract to give land or an interest in land by will made on or after 27 September 1989, the Law of Property (Miscellaneous Provisions) Act 1989 s 2 applies instead of the Law of Property Act 1925 s 40 (repealed). The Law of Property (Miscellaneous Provisions) Act 1989 s 2 requires such a contract to be in writing, to contain all the terms which have been agreed (but this can be by reference to another document), and to be signed by or on behalf of all parties (unless there is exchange of copies signed by the respective parties): see CONVEYANCING vol 23 (2016) PARA 27. See also *Taylor v Dickens* [1998] [1998] 1 FLR 806, [1998] Fam Law 191 (attempt to enforce contract to make a will failed for (among other reasons) lack of compliance with the Law of Property (Miscellaneous Provisions) Act 1989 s 2); *Healey v Brown* [2002] All ER (D) 249 (Apr), [2002] WTLR 849 (wills disposing of land and expressed to be mutual wills were held not effective as such because the requirements of the Law of Property (Miscellaneous Provisions) Act 1989 s 2 were not complied with; although partly effective as giving rise to a constructive trust).
2   See *Hammersley v Baron De Biel* (1845) 12 Cl & Fin 45; *Maunsell v White* (1854) 4 HL Cas 1039; *Laver v Fielder* (1862) 32 Beav 1; *Coverdale v Eastwood* (1872) LR 15 Eq 121; *Re Allen, Hincks v Allen* (1880) 49 LJ Ch 553; *Maddison v Alderson* (1883) 8 App Cas 467, HL; *Re Hudson, Creed v Henderson* (1885) 54 LJ Ch 811; *Vincent v Vincent* (1887) 56 LT 243, CA; *Synge v Synge* [1894] 1 QB 466, CA; *Re Fickus, Farina v Fickus* [1900] 1 Ch 331; *Parker v Clark* [1960] 1 All ER 93, [1960] 1 WLR 286; *Wakeham v Mackenzie* [1968] 2 All ER 783, [1968] 1 WLR 1175; *Walker v Claridge* (1968) 207 Estates Gazette 341; *Schaefer v Schuhmann* [1972] AC 572, [1972] 1 All ER 621, PC. In *O'Sullivan v National Trustees, Executors and Agency Co of Australasia Ltd* [1913] VLR 173, an agreement to provide for the donee so that she would have to work no more was held sufficiently certain. Cf *Kay v Crook* (1857) 3 Sm & G 407 (where an agreement to recognise a son in common with the rest of the family was held uncertain). In *Taylor v Dickens* [1998] 1 FLR 806, [1998] Fam Law 191, it was held that what must be shown is not only a contract to make a will but also a contract not to revoke it; but cf *Schaefer v Schuhmann* above at 587–593 and 628–633.
3   See SPECIFIC PERFORMANCE vol 95 (2013) PARA 337. Such contracts, if purely voluntary, are not as a rule enforceable in equity: see DEEDS AND OTHER INSTRUMENTS vol 32 (2012) PARA 259; EQUITABLE JURISDICTION. As to a contract by a married woman to exercise a general power of appointment by will see MATRIMONIAL AND CIVIL PARTNERSHIP LAW vol 72 (2015) PARA 277; and as to covenants to appoint by will in exercise of a power see TRUSTS AND POWERS vol 98 (2013) PARA 551.

4　See the Trustee Act 1925 ss 48, 49; and TRUSTS AND POWERS vol 98 (2013) PARAS 317, 323.
5　See the Trustee Act 1925 s 50; and TRUSTS AND POWERS vol 98 (2013) PARA 319.
6　*Synge v Synge* [1894] 1 QB 466 at 470, CA; *Parker v Clark* [1960] 1 All ER 93, [1960] 1 WLR 286 (damages for breach of agreement to allow plaintiffs to live rent-free in defendant's house during life of defendant and to leave house to female plaintiff and her sister and daughter). See also *Goilmere v Battison* (1682) 1 Vern 48, sub nom *Goylmer v Paddiston* (1682) 2 Vent 353; *Anon* (1710) 5 Vin Abr 292, Condition (Ed) 38; *Schaefer v Schuhmann* [1972] AC 572, [1972] 1 All ER 621, PC. As to remedies for anticipatory breach of contract generally see CONTRACT vol 22 (2012) PARA 568.
7　*Re Fickus, Farina v Fickus* [1900] 1 Ch 331 at 334. See also SETTLEMENTS vol 91 (2012) PARA 538.
8　See PARA 20 text and notes 4–5.
9　Such a covenant may be enforceable against personal representatives as a trust: see PARA 23.
10　*Re Marsland, Lloyds Bank Ltd v Marsland* [1939] Ch 820, [1939] 3 All ER 148, CA. In *Robinson v Ommanney* (1883) 23 ChD 285 at 286–287, CA, such a covenant was said to be bad in so far as it was in restraint of marriage, although it was divisible and enforceable as regards revocation by other means. It is not necessary, however, to rely on this ground: see *Re Marsland, Lloyds Bank Ltd v Marsland* above. In *Re Goodchild, Goodchild v Goodchild* [1996] 1 All ER 670, [1996] 1 WLR 694 (the point not being considered on appeal at [1997] 3 All ER 63, [1997] 1 WLR 1216, CA), it was held that *Re Marsland, Lloyds Bank Ltd v Marsland* above did not apply to an agreement to make mutual wills, with the consequence that marriage of the surviving party to such an agreement does not make it cease to be legally binding. Revocation of a will is not necessarily effected by marriage: see PARAS 88–89.
11　*Dufour v Pereira* (1769) 1 Dick 419, as reported sub nom *Durour v Perraro* 2 Hargrave's Juridical Arguments 304 at 309 per Lord Camden LC (cited in *Stone v Hoskins* [1905] P 194 at 196–197); *Re Oldham, Hadwen v Myles* [1925] Ch 75 at 84; *Gray v Perpetual Trustee Co Ltd* [1928] AC 391 at 399, PC; *Re Dale, Proctor v Dale* [1994] Ch 31 at 40, [1993] 4 All ER 129 at 135. See also *Robinson v Ommanney* (1883) 23 ChD 285, CA; *Jopling v Jopling* (1909) 8 CLR 33, Aust HC.
12　See *Olins v Walters* [2007] EWHC 3060 (Ch), [2008] WTLR 339, [2007] All ER (D) 291 (Dec); affd [2008] EWCA Civ 782, [2009] Ch 212, [2008] All ER (D) 58 (Jul) for discussion of the nature of the underlying contract in a mutual wills situation. See *Re Goodchild, Goodchild v Goodchild* [1996] 1 All ER 670, [1996] 1 WLR 694 in note 10 for the effect of a subsequent marriage by the surviving testator. See also PARA 10 note 11.
13　Eg by lapse: see *Re Brookman's Trust* (1869) 5 Ch App 182; *Jervis v Wolferstan* (1874) LR 18 Eq 18 (liability to refund to meet liabilities). See also *Jones v How* (1850) 7 Hare 267; and PARA 22.
14　*Eyre v Monro* (1857) 3 K & J 305; *Graham v Wickham* (1862) 31 Beav 447; *Schaefer v Schuhmann* [1972] AC 572, [1972] 1 All ER 621, PC.
15　*Ennis v Smith* (1839) Jo & Car 400; *Rowan v Chute* (1861) 13 I Ch R 169; *Re Brookman's Trust* (1869) 5 Ch App 182; *Jervis v Wolferstan* (1874) LR 18 Eq 18. Cf *Wathen v Smith* (1819) 4 Madd 325.
16　See the Inheritance (Provision for Family and Dependants) Act 1975 ss 11, 12; PARAS 24, 588.

22. Effect of particular covenants making provision for family members. A covenant by a father, for example in a marriage settlement, to leave his property in a specified way among his children does not deprive him of the right of expenditure, but he cannot evade his obligation by disposing of his property during his life, in a manner inconsistent with his contract, by any instrument[1] having the same effect as a testamentary disposition[2], or by purposely altering the nature of the property[3]; nor can he cut down the interest which he has covenanted to give[4].

Similarly, a covenant to leave a child all or an aliquot share[5] of the parent's property at death does not interfere with the covenantor's power to dispose of the property in his lifetime[6]. If the covenant is to make provision for children or grandchildren by deed or will, the covenantor is not bound to make provision for children who die in his lifetime[7]. Where, however, a father covenanted to leave to his daughter an equal share of his property with his other children, and the daughter predeceased him leaving children who survived him, it was held that the covenant could be performed[8].

1　Eg an instrument by which he reserved himself an interest for his life.

2 *Jones v Martin* (1798) 5 Ves 266n, HL; *Fortescue v Hennah* (1812) 19 Ves 67; *Logan v Wienholt* (1833) 1 Cl & Fin 611, HL. Cf *Webster v Milford* (1708) 2 Eq Cas Abr 362. See also *Re Bennett, Bennett v Bennett* [1934] WN 177; revsd on the facts (1934) 78 Sol Jo 876, CA.

3 Thus if the covenant affects personal property, the covenantor cannot evade his obligation by turning it into land: *Lewis v Madocks* (1803) 8 Ves 150; *Cochran v Graham* (1811) 19 Ves 63 at 66; *Logan v Wienholt* (1833) 1 Cl & Fin 611, HL. As to the performance of such a covenant by intestacy see EQUITABLE JURISDICTION vol 47 (2014) PARA 193; and as to election see EQUITABLE JURISDICTION vol 47 (2014) PARA 161 et seq.

4 *Davies v Davies* (1831) 1 LJ Ch 31. A covenant to settle property subject, and without prejudice, to any dispositions made by the covenantor's will is only a provision against intestacy, and does not prevent him from disposing of the property by will: see *Stocken v Stocken* (1838) 4 My & Cr 95.

5 A covenant to bequeath a fourth part of whatsoever estate the covenantor should die possessed of means a one-fourth share in value and not in specie (*Bell v Clarke* (1858) 25 Beav 437), and a covenant to leave a daughter 'her share' has been held to mean an equal share with the other children in the covenantor's residuary personal estate (*Laver v Fielder* (1862) 32 Beav 1; *Duckett v Gordon* (1860) 11 I Ch R 181), but a covenant to leave a share means only some share and may be satisfied by a legacy (*Re Fickus, Farina v Fickus* [1900] 1 Ch 331). Where the covenant was to leave a daughter an equal share with the covenantor's other five daughters, it was satisfied by an absolute bequest of a one-sixth share of the covenantor's estate, the shares of the other five daughters being settled on them for life with remainders to their issue and gifts over to the other four in the event of any one dying without issue, and the covenantee was not entitled to claim any further provision in respect of the benefit derived by the four daughters from the share of the fifth daughter who died without issue: *Clegg v Clegg* (1831) 2 Russ & M 570. See also *Stephens v Stephens* (1886) 19 LR Ir 190, where advancements to other children were not taken into consideration. A gift of a life interest to one daughter is, however, a portion to that daughter, and a covenantee is entitled to receive an equivalent in value under a covenant to give her an equal portion with her sister: *Eardley v Owen* (1847) 10 Beav 572. As to satisfaction generally see EQUITABLE JURISDICTION vol 47 (2014) PARA 176 et seq.

6 *Needham v Kirkman* (1820) 3 B & Ald 531; *Needham v Smith* (1828) 4 Russ 318. See also *Cochran v Graham* (1811) 19 Ves 63; *Willis v Black* (1824) 1 Sim & St 525.

7 *Needham v Smith* (1828) 4 Russ 318; *Jones v How* (1850) 7 Hare 267; *Re Brookman's Trust* (1869) 5 Ch App 182.

8 *Barkworth v Young* (1856) 4 Drew 1. As to gifts to a testator's issue who predecease the testator see the Wills Act 1837 s 33; and PARAS 167, 169.

23. Restrictions under an agreement to make mutual wills. Mutual wills may be made, either by a joint will or by separate wills, in pursuance of an agreement that they are not to be revoked[1]. Such an agreement may appear from the wills[2], or may be proved outside the wills[3], but it must be a legally binding contract[4]; and such a contract is not established by the mere fact that the wills are in identical terms[5]. If no such agreement is shown, each party remains free to revoke his will, if there are separate wills, or to revoke the joint will, so far as it disposes of his property, and the fact that one party has died without revoking the disposition of his property does not prevent the survivor from revoking the disposition which he has made, notwithstanding that he has received benefits out of the estate of the deceased party[6]. Even when there is such an agreement and one party has died after departing from it by revoking or altering the will, the survivor having notice of the breach cannot claim to have the other's revocation or alteration of his will set aside, since the notice gives him the chance of altering his own will as regards his own property; and the death of the deceased party is itself sufficient notice for this purpose[7]. Even a fairly minor departure by the first to die from the agreed dispositions, without the survivor's knowledge or agreement, will release the survivor from the agreement[8]. If, however, the party who has died has stood by the agreement and not revoked or altered his will, the survivor is bound by it; and although probate will be granted of a later will made by the survivor in breach of the agreement, since a court of probate is only concerned with the last will[9], the personal representatives of the survivor nevertheless hold his estate in trust to give effect to the provisions of the mutual wills[10]. Effect is given to the obligation by a floating, constructive trust which crystallizes on the death of the survivor[11].

Where mutual wills, whether contained in a joint will or in separate documents, relate to joint property, the agreement to make the mutual wills, and the making of the dispositions in pursuance of the agreement, sever the joint tenancy and convert it into a tenancy in common[12].

1 As to joint wills see PARA 9; and as to mutual wills see PARA 10.
2 *Dufour v Pereira* (1769) 1 Dick 419, as reported sub nom *Durour v Perraro* 2 Hargrave's Juridical Arguments 304; *Re Oldham, Hadwen v Myles* [1925] Ch 75 at 84.
3 *Re Heys, Walker v Gaskill* [1914] P 192 at 194; *Birmingham v Renfrew* (1936) 57 CLR 666, 43 ALR 520, Aust HC; *Re Cleaver, Cleaver v Insley* [1981] 2 All ER 1018, [1981] 1 WLR 939.
4 *Re Goodchild, Goodchild v Goodchild* [1997] 3 All ER 63 at 70–71, [1997] 1 WLR 1216 at 1224–1225, CA, per Leggatt LJ, and at 75 and 1229 per Morritt LJ; *Birch v Curtis* [2002] EWHC 1158 (Ch), [2002] 2 FLR 847, [2002] WTLR 965; *Lewis v Cotton* [2001] WTLR 1117, NZ CA; *Healey v Brown* [2002] All ER (D) 249 (Apr), [2002] WTLR 849 (the wills were expressed to be mutual wills but there was no binding contract because the Law of Property (Miscellaneous Provisions) Act 1989 s 2 was not satisfied (see PARA 21 note 1)). But see *Olins v Walters* [2007] EWHC 3060 (Ch), [2008] WTLR 339, [2007] All ER (D) 291 (Dec); affd [2008] EWCA Civ 782, [2009] Ch 212, [2008] All ER (D) 58 (Jul) (where the Law of Property (Miscellaneous Provisions) Act 1989 was held not to be relevant where land was passing as part of a gift of residue which the personal representatives were instructed to convert). See also PARA 10 text and notes 5–10.
    What is required is a mutual intention that both wills should remain unaltered and that the survivor should be bound to leave the combined estates to the agreed ultimate beneficiary: see *Re Goodchild, Goodchild v Goodchild* above at 71 and 1225–1226 per Leggatt LJ. It is a more stringent requirement than in the case of a secret trust of property inherited from another subject to an agreement as to how it will be disposed of on the donee's death (such as in *Ottaway v Norman* [1972] Ch 698, [1971] 3 All ER 1325; *Healey v Brown* above), because an agreement to make mutual wills binds the survivor's own property as well as any which he inherits from the other person: *Re Goodchild, Goodchild v Goodchild* above at 70 and 1224 per Leggatt LJ, and at 75 and 1229 per Morritt LJ. For an agreement to make mutual wills to create a binding obligation on the survivor of the testators, it is not necessary for it to be an agreement under which the will of the first to die confers a benefit on the survivor: see *Re Dale, Proctor v Dale* [1994] Ch 31, [1993] 4 All ER 129.
5 *Re Oldham, Hadwen v Myles* [1925] Ch 75 at 87; *Gray v Perpetual Trustee Co Ltd* [1928] AC 391 at 400, PC; *Vine v Joyce* (1963) Times, 24 October; *Re Cleaver, Cleaver v Insley* [1981] 2 All ER 1018, [1981] 1 WLR 939; *Re Goodchild, Goodchild v Goodchild* [1997] 3 All ER 63, [1997] 1 WLR 1216, CA; *Birch v Curtis* [2002] EWHC 1158 (Ch), [2002] 2 FLR 847; *Lewis v Cotton* [2001] WTLR 1117, NZ CA.
6 See note 5.
7 *Stone v Hoskins* [1905] P 194 at 197.
8 *Re Hobley* (1997) Times, 16 June.
9 *Re Heys, Walker v Gaskill* [1914] P 192 at 200.
10 *Dufour v Pereira* (1769) 1 Dick 419, as reported sub nom *Durour v Perraro* 2 Hargrave's Juridical Arguments 304; *Stone v Hoskins* [1905] P 194; *Re Hagger, Freeman v Arscott* [1930] 2 Ch 190; *Re Green, Lindner v Green* [1951] Ch 148, [1950] 2 All ER 913; *Re Cleaver, Cleaver v Insley* [1981] 2 All ER 1018, [1981] 1 WLR 939. Marriage of the survivor, after the death of the first party to the agreement to make mutual wills to die, will not affect this obligation: *Re Goodchild, Goodchild v Goodchild* [1996] 1 All ER 670, [1996] 1 WLR 694 (the point not being considered on appeal at [1997] 3 All ER 63, [1997] 1 WLR 1216, CA), distinguishing *Re Marsland, Lloyds Bank Ltd v Marsland* [1939] Ch 820, [1939] 3 All ER 148, CA. As to the effects of contracts relating to wills generally see PARAS 20–21. See also *Ebden's Estate v Ebden* [1910] App D 321.
11 *Re Cleaver, Cleaver v Insley* [1981] 2 All ER 1018, [1981] 1 WLR 939. The survivor may spend on himself assets subject to the mutual wills agreement in which (apart from the mutual wills agreement) he has an absolute interest, but he cannot make substantial lifetime or testamentary gifts so as to defeat the mutual wills agreement: see *Re Cleaver, Cleaver v Insley* at 1024–1025 and at 946–947 per Nourse J, citing passages from *Birmingham v Renfrew* (1936) 57 CLR 666, 43 ALR 520, Aust HC.
    See *Olins v Walters* [2007] EWHC 3060 (Ch), [2008] WTLR 339, [2007] All ER (D) 291 (Dec) (affd [2008] EWCA Civ 782, [2009] Ch 212, [2008] All ER (D) 58 (Jul)), where Norris J granted a declaration that codicils took effect as valid and effective mutual wills so as to bind the deceased's estate, but would make no findings or holdings as to the scope of the agreement under

which the mutual wills arose. This, and the effect upon the survivor's estate, were neither raised in the pleadings nor in the submissions of the parties.

12 *Re Wilford's Estate, Taylor v Taylor* (1879) 11 ChD 267; *Re Heys, Walker v Gaskill* [1914] P 192 at 195; *Szabo v Boros* [2002] WTLR 1389, (1966) 64 DLR (2d) 48, BC CA. A tenancy in common in land can now exist only in equity: see REAL PROPERTY AND REGISTRATION vol 87 (2012) PARA 215.

24. Restriction by statute and the rule against perpetuities. Where the court is of opinion that the disposition of the testator's estate is not such as to make reasonable provision for the maintenance of a surviving spouse[1] (including a former spouse who has not remarried), civil partner (including a former civil partner who has not formed a subsequent marriage or civil partnership), cohabitee, child or dependant of his who applies to the court under the Inheritance (Provision for Family and Dependants) Act 1975[2], the court may order reasonable provision for the maintenance of the applicant to be made out of the testator's net estate[3]. The court may not make such an order if the result would be that a contract for full consideration entered into by the testator as to the disposition of his estate could not be enforced[4], but, where an agreement is made on or after 1 April 1976 otherwise than for full consideration and with a view to defeating an application under the Inheritance (Provision for Family and Dependants) Act 1975, the court has power, on an application under that Act, to order that such sum of money or property as may be specified in the order be returned or retained to be made available for the provision of maintenance[5].

A provision in a will settling property on such trusts that it may vest outside the perpetuity period is, if in the event this proves to be the case, void[6]. A provision which directs accumulation of income[7] outside the time for accumulation allowed by law is void[8].

1 'Spouse' includes a person who is married to a person of the same sex: see the Marriage (Same Sex Couples) Act 2013 Sch 3 para 1(1)(c), (2), (3); and MATRIMONIAL AND CIVIL PARTNERSHIP LAW vol 72 (2015) PARAS 1–2.
2 As to the restrictions contained in the Inheritance (Provision for Family and Dependants) Act 1975 see PARA 565 et seq. The category of cohabitee (ie someone who, during the whole of the period of two years ending immediately before the date when the deceased died, was living in the same household as the deceased and as the husband or wife of the deceased) was introduced in relation to persons dying on or after 1 January 1996 by the Law Reform (Succession) Act 1995 s 2, amending the Inheritance (Provision for Family and Dependants) Act 1975 s 1. A person living in the same household and as a civil partner is added to the category of cohabitees by the Inheritance Act (Provision for Family and Dependants) Act 1975 s 1B; this change operates because as from 5 December 2005, general provision is made for applications under the Inheritance (Provision for Family and Dependants) Act 1975 by a civil partner, a former civil partner and a child treated as a child of the family, in relation to a civil partnership: see s 1B (added by the Civil Partnership Act 2004 s 71, Sch 4 Pt 2). See note 1. As to civil partnerships see PARAS 90, 179.
3 See PARA 565 et seq.
4 *Schaefer v Schuhmann* [1972] AC 572, [1972] 1 All ER 621, PC (not following *Dillon v Public Trustee of New Zealand* [1941] AC 294, [1941] 2 All ER 284, PC).
5 See PARA 591.
6 See PERPETUITIES AND ACCUMULATIONS vol 80 (2013) PARA 77 et seq.
7 As to what gifts carry intermediate income see PARA 1080 et seq.
8 See PERPETUITIES AND ACCUMULATIONS vol 80 (2013) PARA 129 et seq.

(2) PROPERTY CAPABLE OF DISPOSITION BY WILL

(i) English Property disposable by Will

25. Immovables and movables. The extent to which a person may dispose by will of property belonging to him[1] depends, in the case of immovables, on the lex situs[2], and, in the case of movables, on the law of the domicile of the testator at his death[3]. The court will, however, need to distinguish between the question of the validity of the will to make such dispositions and questions concerning the construction of the dispositive language used[4]. In this title it is assumed in both property types that there is no foreign element to consider, and the law of England and Wales only is stated.

1   As to the exercise of general and special powers see TRUSTS AND POWERS vol 98 (2013) PARA 527 et seq.
2   However, states which have adopted European Parliament and Council Regulation (EU) 650/2012 (OJ L201, 27.7.2012, p 107) cannot accept a renvoi where a testator has chosen the law of his nationality to apply: see art 3; and PARA 13 note 6. As to renvoi see CONFLICT OF LAWS vol 19 (2011) PARAS 308–310.
3   See PARA 13; and CONFLICT OF LAWS vol 19 (2011) PARA 695 et seq.
4   *Dellar v Zivy* [2007] EWHC 2266 (Ch), [2007] All ER (D) 121 (Oct) (the will must be interpreted according to the law intended by the testator),

26. Property passing under a will. A testator of full capacity[1] may dispose by will of all real estate and all personal estate[2] to which he is entitled, either at law or in equity, at the time of his death, which, if not so disposed of, would have devolved on his executor or administrator[3]. The freedom of a testator to dispose of his estate to the exclusion of a surviving spouse[4] or former spouse, a surviving civil partner or former civil partner, a cohabitee or a surviving child or dependant of his, is restricted by statute[5]. Moreover, his freedom of testamentary disposition may be restricted by an agreement entered into by him as to the contents of his will[6].

1   As to testamentary capacity see PARA 46 et seq.
2   As to the meaning of 'real estate' see PARA 282 note 3; and as to the meaning of 'personal estate' see PARA 282 note 4. The law as to realty and personalty was assimilated as regards testamentary disposition as from 1 January 1838 by the Wills Act 1837 s 3.
3   See Wills Act 1837 s 3 (amended by the Statute Law Revision (No 2) Act 1888; and the Statute Law (Repeals) Act 1969). The Law of Property Act 1925 s 178 (repealed) provided that the Wills Act 1837 s 3 should authorise and be deemed always to have authorised any person to dispose of real property or chattels real by will, notwithstanding that, by reason of illegitimacy or otherwise, he did not leave an heir or next of kin surviving him. As to devolution see PARA 917 et seq. Before the Wills Act 1837, the will of a testator disposing of all his real estate operated only as a conveyance of specific hereditaments and did not carry land acquired between the date of the will and the date of death (*A-G v Vigor* (1803) 8 Ves 256 at 283), although it might comprise after-acquired interests which before the death had become merged in the interests belonging to the testator at the date of the will (see eg *Bunter v Coke* (1707) 1 Salk 237). Personalty belonging to the testator at the date of his death but not at the date of the will might, however, pass by the will even before the Wills Act 1837: see *Bunter v Coke*. As to the abolition of the heir-at-law or customary heir see PARA 478. Realty as well as personalty now passes to the testator's personal representatives: see the Administration of Estates Act 1925 s 1; PARA 17; and PARA 917 et seq. The Wills Act 1837 takes effect only to enable equitable interests to be disposed of subject and without prejudice to the estate and powers of the personal representatives: Law of Property (Amendment) Act 1924 s 9, Sch 9 para 3.
4   'Spouse' includes a person who is married to a person of the same sex: see the Marriage (Same Sex Couples) Act 2013 Sch 3 para 1(1)(c), (2), (3); and MATRIMONIAL AND CIVIL PARTNERSHIP LAW vol 72 (2015) PARAS 1–2.
5   See PARA 24. As to the former rule against disinheriting the heir etc except expressly or by necessary implication see PARA 257.
6   See PARAS 20–22. As to the effect of taking a benefit under a mutual will see PARA 23.

27. Examples of property which may be disposed of. The following are examples of particular kinds of property[1] which may be disposed of by will:

(1)   the legal or equitable estate or interest in freeholds[2] or in personal property, other than an interest ceasing with the life of the testator[3], but including entailed interests in the case of wills executed after 31 December 1925 or confirmed or republished by codicil executed after that date[4];

(2)   incorporeal hereditaments[5], including easements[6], profits à prendre, rentcharges[7] and advowsons[8] held for an interest not ceasing on death;

(3)   personal chattels within the meaning of the Administration of Estates Act 1925[9];

(4)   all contingent, executory or other future interests in any real or personal estate[10], whether the testator may or may not be ascertained as the person or one of the persons in whom the interests respectively may become vested[11], and whether he may be entitled to them under the instrument by which they were created or under any disposition of them by deed or will or under an intestacy[12]; in this class are included rights described as possibilities coupled with an interest[13] and assets comprised in an unadministered residuary estate[14]; a 'bare' possibility, such as the expectation of an heir or the next of kin of a living person, is not a title to property in English law[15], but such a possibility may be devised so as to pass on the death of the testator if it has already before his death ripened into an interest by the death of the named person[16];

(5)   rights of entry for conditions broken, and other rights of entry, and rights of reverter[17];

(6)   property given to the testator by the will of a person who survived him, in cases where such gift does not lapse; into this class comes a gift made to the testator and in the case of his death to his personal representative[18]; and a devise to the testator of an estate tail by a person who survives the testator, if the testator leaves issue, living at the death of the devisor, who would be inheritable under the entail, unless a contrary intention appears by the devisor's will[19];

(7)   the rent reserved by a lease, which may, it seems, be devised apart from the reversion[20];

(8)   certain choses (or things) in action[21], for example rights of action for damages or other matters which devolve on the personal representative[22], copyright for the full extent of the term of the right and many other forms of intellectual property right[23], or a debt or bond[24]; but a bequest of a debt or bond does not of itself enable a legatee who is not also an executor to sue in his own name and to oust the executor's right to sue[25]; prima facie, the money payable under a policy of assurance which a person effects on his own life is his own and he can dispose of it by will, but the conditions under which the assurance is effected may provide otherwise[26];

(9)   digital assets capable of transmission[27].

A testator may dispose of an interest which arises by way of trust and is merely equitable[28], such as his interest in property which he has agreed to purchase[29].

1   As to the meaning of 'property' see REAL PROPERTY AND REGISTRATION vol 87 (2012) PARA 1.
2   At common law, under the feudal system, land or tenements of freehold tenure were not devisable by will except, by custom, in some boroughs and in Kent (Littleton's Tenures s 167; Co Litt 111b; Shep Touch (8th Edn 1826) pp 399, 420), but until the Statute of Uses (1535) (repealed) the difficulty could be obviated by resort to the doctrine of uses. Express powers to devise freehold land were given by the Statutes of Wills (ie 32 Hen 8 c 1 (1540) and 34 & 35 Hen 8 c 5 (1542) (both repealed)), by virtue of which all land of common socage tenure and two-thirds of land of

tenure in chivalry held for an estate of inheritance might be devised. The Tenures Abolition Act 1660 s 4, by converting tenure in chivalry into common socage, extended the power of disposition. Copyholds could be devised, but a surrender made after admittance to the use of the will was required until 1815, when by statute this was made unnecessary (55 Geo 3 c 192 (Disposition of Copyhold Estates by Will) (1815) (repealed and substantially re-enacted by the Wills Act 1837 s 3, the relevant parts of which have been repealed by the Statute Law (Repeals) Act 1969 s 1, Schedule Pt III)). See generally CUSTOM AND USAGE vol 32 (2012) PARA 1 et seq.

3   Thus a life interest under a trust, or an interest as a joint tenant, will not pass by will, but a joint tenancy can be severed (other than by will) so as to change the interest to an undivided share which can be disposed of by will: see PARA 29.

4   See the Law of Property Act 1925 s 176; and PARA 954; REAL PROPERTY AND REGISTRATION vol 87 (2012) PARA 136. Entailed interests cannot be created by instruments coming into operation on or after 1 January 1997 (see the Trusts of Land and Appointment of Trustees Act 1996 s 2(6), Sch 1 para 5; PARA 387; and REAL PROPERTY AND REGISTRATION vol 87 (2012) PARA 114) but the statutory power of disposition of entailed property continues in relation to entails created before that date (see PARA 387).

5   See the Wills Act 1837 s 1. See also 34 & 35 Hen 8 c 5 (Wills) (1542) s 4 (repealed). Examples of devisable incorporeal hereditaments are a seignory (Shep Touch (8th Edn, 1826) p 429) and gales (ie grants of mining rights) in the Forest of Dean (see MINES, MINERALS AND QUARRIES vol 76 (2013) PARA 618).

6   As to the transfer of easements by deed or will see REAL PROPERTY AND REGISTRATION vol 87 (2012) PARA 912.

7   As to rentcharges see REAL PROPERTY AND REGISTRATION vol 87 (2012) PARA 1104 et seq. As to the statutory extinguishment of rentcharges under the Rentcharges Act 1977 see REAL PROPERTY AND REGISTRATION vol 87 (2012) PARA 1168.

8   As to advowsons see ECCLESIASTICAL LAW vol 34 (2011) PARA 550.

9   See the Administration of Estates Act 1925 s 55(1)(x); and PARA 485.

10   As to the creation of these interests generally see PERSONAL PROPERTY vol 80 (2013) PARA 814 et seq; REAL PROPERTY AND REGISTRATION vol 87 (2012) PARA 157 et seq; SETTLEMENTS vol 91 (2012) PARA 616 et seq. In the case of real estate these interests can now be only equitable: see REAL PROPERTY AND REGISTRATION vol 87 (2012) PARA 160.

11   Prior to the Wills Act 1837, a contingent or executory interest could not be devised unless the testator was ascertained as the person in whom the interest must vest: *Doe d Calkin v Tomkinson* (1813) 2 M & S 165 at 170.

12   See the Wills Act 1837 s 3 (amended by the Statute Law Revision (No 2) Act 1888; and the Statute Law (Repeals) Act 1969).

13   *Selwyn v Selwyn* (1761) 2 Burr 1131 (remainder) (explained in *Jones v Roe* (1789) 3 Term Rep 88 at 94 per Kenyon CJ, and at 96 per Buller J); *Moor v Hawkins* (1765) 2 Eden 342 (equitable executory interest); *Roe d Noden v Griffiths* (1766) 1 Wm Bl 605 per Dennison J; *Roe d Perry v Jones* (1788) 1 Hy Bl 30 (affd sub nom *Jones v Roe* above); *Scawen v Blunt* (1802) 7 Ves 294 at 300 per Grant MR (not following *Bishop v Fountain* (1695) 3 Lev 427 and 1 Roll Abr 609); *Perry v Phelips* (1810) 17 Ves 173 at 182. Executory interests in terms of years were held to be devisable at an early period: *Cole v Moore* (1607) Moore KB 806; *Veizy v Pinwell* (1641) Poll 44.

14   *Re Leigh's Will Trusts, Handyside v Durbridge* [1970] Ch 277, [1969] 3 All ER 432.

15   *Jones v Roe* (1789) 3 Term Rep 88 at 93. See CHOSES IN ACTION vol 13 (2009) PARA 30; REAL PROPERTY AND REGISTRATION vol 87 (2012) PARA 178.

16   See the Wills Act 1837 s 3 (as amended: see note 12). See also *Re Parsons, Stockley v Parsons* (1890) 45 ChD 51; followed in *Re Earl Midleton's Will Trusts, Whitehead v Earl of Midleton* [1969] 1 Ch 600, [1967] 2 All ER 834 (not following *Re Duke of St Albans' Will Trusts, Coutts & Co v Beauclerk* [1963] Ch 365, [1962] 2 All ER 402). Cf *Izard v Tamahau Mahupuku* (1902) 22 NZLR 418. See also head (6) in the text.

17   Wills Act 1837 s 3 (as amended: see note 12). A right of re-entry may arise where an estate in fee simple is limited upon condition. Formerly the benefit of such a right was not devisable and could be exercised only by the grantor or his heir-at-law (*Avelyn v Ward* (1750) 1 Ves Sen 420 at 422–423), but now it may be made exercisable by any person and the persons deriving title under him (see the Law of Property Act 1925 s 4(3); and REAL PROPERTY AND REGISTRATION vol 87 (2012) PARA 73). The interest of the grantor and his successors in title is a possibility of reverter, and is within the express words of the Wills Act 1837 s 3: *Pemberton v Barnes* [1899] 1 Ch 544 at 549. A right of re-entry may also arise in the case of a determinable fee, and here also it exists as a possibility of reverter (see REAL PROPERTY AND REGISTRATION vol 87 (2012) PARAS 109–111, 157), and appears to be within the words 'other rights of entry' (see Challis's Law of Real Property (3rd Edn) p 228). A right of reverter under the School Sites Act 1841 can be given

by will under the Wills Act 1837 s 3: *Bath and Wells Diocesan Finance Board v Jenkinson* [2002] EWHC 218 (Ch), [2003] Ch 89, [2002] 4 All ER 245.

18 *Long v Watkinson* (1852) 17 Beav 471. Where property is given to the testator or to his personal representatives, then, although it is directed to 'form part of his estate', a person specified by the testator must, in order to take any benefit, survive the donor, for such person takes as direct beneficiary of the donor, and, if the testator's universal legatee predeceases the donor, there will be a lapse of the gift: see *Re Greenwood, Greenwood v Sutcliffe* [1912] 1 Ch 392 at 397; *Re Cousen's Will Trusts, Wright v Killick* [1937] Ch 381, [1937] 2 All ER 276; *Re Wray, Wray v Wray* [1951] Ch 425 at 428, [1951] 1 All ER 375 at 428, CA, per Sir Raymond Evershed MR. See further PARA 165.

Lapse was also prevented where a gift was made to the testator by will by an ancestor who survived him but died before 1 January 1983, if the testator left issue living at the death of the ancestor, unless a contrary intention appeared by the ancestor's will: see the Wills Act 1837 s 33 (as originally enacted); and PARA 167. This provision has been replaced in relation to persons dying on or after 1 January 1983: see the Administration of Justice Act 1982 ss 19, 73(6), 76(11); and PARA 169. As to the former position see *Johnson v Johnson* (1843) 3 Hare 157; *Winter v Winter* (1846) 5 Hare 306; *Re Scott* [1901] 1 KB 228, CA; and PARA 167.

19 Wills Act 1837 s 32 (repealed by the Trusts of Land and Appointment of Trustees Act 1996 s 25(2), Sch 4). The repeal of the Wills Act 1837 s 32 does not, however, affect any entailed interests created before 1 January 1997: Trusts of Land and Appointment of Trustees Act 1996 s 25(4). Entailed interests cannot be created by instruments coming into operation on or after 1 January 1997: see s 2, Sch 1 para 5; PARA 387; and REAL PROPERTY AND REGISTRATION vol 87 (2012) PARA 114. See also PARA 166.

20 *Ards v Watkin* (1598) Cro Eliz 637, 651. Cf PARA 659.

21 As to choses (or things) in action which are not disposable see PARA 32.

22 Shep Touch (8th Edn, 1826) p 431 (actions for goods or for an account); *Drew v Merry* (1701) 1 Eq Cas Abr 175 pl 7 (right to set aside a release). As to causes of action which survive for the benefit of the estate see PARA 1277 et seq. As to the benefit of restrictive covenants relating to user of land see CONVEYANCING vol 23 (2016) PARA 77 et seq; REAL PROPERTY AND REGISTRATION vol 87 (2012) PARA 1076 et seq.

23 See the Copyright, Designs and Patents Act 1988 s 90(1); and COPYRIGHT vol 23 (2016) PARAS 639, 653. A gift of copyright may be partial, that is, limited so as to apply to one or more, but not all, of the things which the copyright owner has the exclusive right to do, or to part, but not the whole, of the period for which the copyright is to subsist: see s 90(2); and COPYRIGHT vol 23 (2016) PARA 642. Where under a bequest (whether specific or general) a person is entitled, beneficially or otherwise, to: (1) an original document or other material thing recording or embodying a literary, dramatic, musical or artistic work which was not published before the death of the testator; or (2) an original material thing containing a sound recording or film which was not published before the death of the testator, the bequest is, unless a contrary intention is indicated in the testator's will or a codicil to it, to be construed as including the copyright in the work in so far as the testator was the owner of the copyright immediately before his death: see s 93; and COPYRIGHT vol 23 (2016) PARA 653. The following intellectual property rights are also transmissible by testamentary disposition: (a) database right (see the Copyright and Rights in Databases Regulations 1997, SI 1997/3032, reg 23; and INFORMATION TECHNOLOGY LAW vol 57 (2012) PARAS 546, 581); (b) moral rights (see the Copyright, Designs and Patents Act 1988 s 95; and COPYRIGHT vol 23 (2016) PARA 894); (c) a performer's property and non-property rights (see ss 191B, 192A; and COPYRIGHT vol 23 (2016) PARAS 958, 972); (d) design rights (see the Copyright, Designs and Patents Act 1988 s 222; the Registered Design Act 1949; and COPYRIGHT vol 23 (2016) PARA 1119); (e) patents (see the Patents Act 1977 s 30; and PATENTS AND REGISTERED DESIGNS vol 79 (2014) PARA 372); (f) publication right (see the Copyright and Related Rights Regulations 1996, SI 1996/2967, reg 17(1); and COPYRIGHT vol 23 (2016) PARA 635); and trade marks (see the Trade Marks Act 1994 s 24; and TRADE MARKS AND TRADE NAMES vol 97A (2014) PARA 297). See also the Artist's Resale Right Regulations 2006, SI 2006/346 (amended by SI 2009/2792) which create a transmissible entitlement to a royalty on certain sales of graphic or plastic art such as a picture, a collage, a painting, a drawing, an engraving, a print, a lithograph, a sculpture, a tapestry, a ceramic, an item of glassware or a photograph. See further COPYRIGHT vol 23 (2016) PARA 696 et seq.

24 *Anon* (1714) 1 P Wms 267; Shep Touch (8th Edn, 1826) p 430.

25 *Bishop v Curtis* (1852) 18 QB 878; *Robertson v Quiddington* (1860) 28 Beav 529 (bequest of share of testator's interest in goodwill of a partnership). See also PARTNERSHIP vol 79 (2014) PARA 171. The will may make the legatee a special executor with regard to the debt so as to be able to sue in his own name; and, in any event, the legatee may compel the executor to sue: Shep Touch (8th Edn, 1826) p 430. In the case of negotiable instruments payable to the testator's order, the executors, subject to administration of the estate, are bound to indorse them, or to allow one

of their number to indorse them, and to deliver them to the legatee in order to enable him to sue: *Re Robson, Robson v Hamilton* [1891] 2 Ch 559 at 563–564. Mere delivery by the executors after indorsement by the testator himself is not generally sufficient: *Bromage v Lloyd* (1847) 1 Exch 32. See also FINANCIAL INSTRUMENTS AND TRANSACTIONS vol 49 (2015) PARA 226. As to the costs of recovering a specifically bequeathed debt see *Re De Sommery, Coelenbier v De Sommery* [1912] 2 Ch 622 at 628, discussing *Perry v Meddowcroft* (1841) 4 Beav 197; and PARA 1060.

26 *Re Phillips' Insurance* (1883) 23 ChD 235 at 247, CA, per Lindley LJ. See further INSURANCE vol 60 (2011) PARAS 507–511.

27 Eg online bank accounts and investment accounts; accounts used for online gambling or auction selling and store cards which may have a credit (or debit) balance which can be transferred in the same way as conventional accounts; Bitcoin; online facilities or platforms which may hold something of value to a third party such as intellectual property rights or commercially sensitive information; and ownership of a domain name or website. Whether or not such items can be transferred will depend on the terms of the original agreement by which they were acquired. As to electronic money see FINANCIAL INSTRUMENTS AND TRANSACTIONS vol 49 (2015) PARA 29 et seq. As to online gambling see INFORMATION TECHNOLOGY LAW vol 57 (2012) PARAS 601–605. As to online auctions see AUCTION vol 4 (2011) PARA 57; INFORMATION TECHNOLOGY LAW vol 57 (2012) PARA 599. As to intellectual property rights held online see INFORMATION TECHNOLOGY LAW vol 57 (2012) PARA 513 et seq. As to informational privacy see CONFIDENCE AND INFORMATIONAL PRIVACY vol 19 (2011) PARA 1 et seq; INFORMATION TECHNOLOGY LAW vol 57 (2012) PARA 671 et seq. See also PARA 941.

28 *Car v Ellison* (1744) 3 Atk 73 (equitable interest in copyhold, under devise of real estate); *Perry v Phelips* (1790) 1 Ves 251 at 254; *Marquis of Cholmondeley v Lord Clinton* (1821) 4 Bli 1 at 80, HL. As to gifts of assets comprised in the unadministered residuary estate of a deceased person see *Re Leigh's Will Trusts, Handyside v Durbridge* [1970] Ch 277, [1969] 3 All ER 432.

29 *Davie v Beardsham* (1663) 1 Cas in Ch 39; *Greenhill v Greenhill* (1711) 2 Vern 679; *Gibson v Lord Montford* (1750) 1 Ves Sen 485; *Perry v Phelips* (1790) 1 Ves 251 at 254; *Morgan v Holford* (1852) 1 Sm & G 101. As to the rights of the devisees of land subject to contract to purchase by the testator see *Whittaker v Whittaker* (1792) 4 Bro CC 31; *Broome v Monck* (1805) 10 Ves 597 at 605; *Re Cockcroft, Broadbent v Groves* (1883) 24 ChD 94; *Re Kidd, Brooman v Withall* [1894] 3 Ch 558; and PARA 156.

28.   State of testator's title.

28.   State of testator's title. The title of the testator need not be a good title[1]. A devise or bequest of a mere possessory interest is valid[2], subject to the paramount rights of the persons dispossessed[3]. A testator who has sold property in circumstances entitling him to have the sale set aside has a devisable interest[4]. If a trustee specifically devises property which he has purchased from himself and the purchase is set aside, the specific devisee, not the residuary legatee, is entitled to the repaid purchase money[5].

1   As to estoppel of a beneficiary taking possession of any property under the terms of the will generally see ESTOPPEL vol 47 (2014) PARA 344.

2   *Asher v Whitlock* (1865) LR 1 QB 1; *Clarke v Clarke* (1868) IR 2 CL 395; *Calder v Alexander* (1900) 16 TLR 294.

3   Shep Touch (8th Edn, 1826) p 428.

4   *Gresley v Mousley* (1859) 4 De G & J 78 at 89, 92 (following *Uppington v Bullen* (1842) 2 Dr & War 184; and *Stump v Gaby* (1852) 2 De GM & G 623 at 630); *Turner v Turner, Hall v Turner* (1880) 14 ChD 829.

5   *Re Sherman, Re Walters, Trevenen v Pearce* [1954] Ch 653, [1954] 1 All ER 893.

29.   Co-owners.

29.   Co-owners. By will, tenants in common may dispose of their shares in equity of the property held in common[1]. As regards joint tenants, a gift by the will of one of them of his share in the property does not sever the joint tenancy[2], and does not affect the contingent paramount title of the other joint tenant to take by survivorship[3], but a gift of his interest in the property made by the will of one joint tenant during the joint tenancy may, in the event of the testator becoming before his death the surviving owner, be effectual to pass the property[4].

1   A tenancy in common of land cannot now exist at law but only in equity. Between 1 January 1926 and 31 December 1996 inclusive a tenancy in common of land could only exist behind a trust for sale, ie the owner of the undivided share had no estate in the land itself, but he had an interest in the proceeds of sale of the land and in the income of the land until sale: see REAL PROPERTY AND

REGISTRATION vol 87 (2012) PARAS 103, 215 et seq. On and after 1 January 1997 all trusts for sale formerly imposed by statute have become trusts of land (without a duty to sell) and land formerly held on such statutorily imposed trusts for sale is now held in trust for the persons interested in the land, so that the owner of each undivided share will now have an interest in land: see the Trusts of Land and Appointment of Trustees Act 1996 ss 1, 5, Sch 2 paras 2–5, 7 (amending the Law of Property Act 1925 ss 32, 34, 36 and the Administration of Estates Act 1925 s 33); and REAL PROPERTY AND REGISTRATION vol 87 (2012) PARA 105. Where trusts for sale are imposed expressly by the trust instrument, then, unless the trust was created by the will of a testator who died before 1 January 1997, the existence of the duty to sell no longer means that the land is to be regarded as personal property: see the Trusts of Land and Appointment of Trustees Act 1996 s 3; and REAL PROPERTY AND REGISTRATION vol 87 (2012) PARA 191. The doctrine of conversion is not wholly abolished by s 3 and will still apply to eg uncompleted agreements for the sale of land. As to the doctrine of conversion see further EQUITABLE JURISDICTION vol 47 (2014) PARA 138 et seq.

2 2 Bl Com (14th Edn) 186; Bac Abr, Joint Tenants (I) 3; Shep Touch (8th Edn, 1826) pp 414, 431. See also REAL PROPERTY AND REGISTRATION vol 87 (2012) PARA 212. As to an agreement by a joint tenant to devise his share see PARA 23 text and note 12. As to joint owners generally see PERSONAL PROPERTY vol 80 (2013) PARA 828 et seq; REAL PROPERTY AND REGISTRATION vol 87 (2012) PARA 192 et seq.

3 Littleton's Tenures s 287; Doctor and Student by Saint-German (18th Edn) 185; *Butler and Baker's Case* (1591) 3 Co Rep 25a at 30b, Ex Ch; *Lannoy v Lannoy* (1725) Cas *temp* King 48; *Turner v A-G* (1876) IR 10 Eq 386 at 392. The share would not, in default of disposition, devolve on the executor within the meaning of the Wills Act 1837 s 3: see PARA 27. Questions may arise, however, whether the surviving joint tenant is bound under the doctrine of election: *Dummer v Pitcher* (1831) 5 Sim 35 (affd (1833) 2 My & K 262); *Coates v Stevens* (1834) 1 Y & C Ex 66; *Grosvenor v Durston* (1858) 25 Beav 97; and see EQUITABLE JURISDICTION vol 47 (2014) PARA 167. As to the doctrine of election see EQUITABLE JURISDICTION vol 47 (2014) PARA 161 et seq. Where beneficial joint tenants each make wills dealing with their own interest, it may indicate an earlier equitable severance of the beneficial joint tenancy: see *Williams v Hensman* (1861) 1 J & Hem 546; *Re Woolnough, Perkins & Borden* [2002] WTLR 595; *Carr v Isard* [2007] WTLR 409; *Chadda v RCC* [2014] UKFTT 1061 (TC).

4 See the Wills Act 1837 ss 3, 24 (s 3 amended by the Statute Law Revision (No 2) Act 1888; and the Statute Law (Repeals) Act 1969). Before the Wills Act 1837, a will of a joint tenant of real property, made during the joint tenancy, did not operate even to pass his share to which he became entitled in severalty on a subsequent partition, unless the will was republished: *Swift d Neale v Roberts* (1746) 3 Burr 1488, explaining Perkins, Laws of England s 500. The law concerning personal property before the Wills Act 1837 was, however, similar to that stated in the text: see Shep Touch (8th Edn, 1826) p 430. As to the construction of a will in this respect see PARA 282.

(ii) Things not disposable by Will

30. Property not belonging to the testator. Apart from the execution by will of a power[1], a testator cannot effectually dispose by will of property which is not his own[2], or which he holds in a representative or official capacity[3], for example heirlooms, which are such by custom[4], or property bound by the covenant of the testator to devolve in some other manner[5]. Trust or mortgage estates devolve, notwithstanding any testamentary disposition, on the personal representative of the deceased[6]. Where a contract (such as a life insurance policy) has been entered into by the testator whereby the other party to the contract has agreed to confer a benefit on someone who is not a party to the contract (without any trust for the non-party being created), the testator does not have any interest or right of more than nominal value under the contract which he can dispose of by will[7].

1 See TRUSTS AND POWERS vol 98 (2013) PARA 564 et seq.
2 Such a disposition may, however, raise a question of election: see EQUITABLE JURISDICTION vol 47 (2014) PARA 161.
3 See Shep Touch (8th Edn, 1826) pp 431–432, giving as examples the masters and governors of colleges and hospitals in respect of the property of those institutions; mayors or other heads of corporations in respect of corporate property; and churchwardens in respect of church property. 'No man can devise anything but what he has to his own use': *Bransby v Grantham* (1577) 2 Plowd 525 at 526; *Lord Hastings v Douglas* (1634) Cro Car 343 at 345.

4 Co Litt 18b (Crown jewels), 185b; *Pusey v Pusey* (1684) 1 Vern 273. As to heirlooms see REAL
   PROPERTY AND REGISTRATION vol 87 (2012) PARA 17.
5 *Page v Cox* (1852) 10 Hare 163 (covenant in partnership agreement). As to the effect of covenants
   to leave property by will see PARA 20 et seq.
6 See the Administration of Estates Act 1925 ss 1(1), 3(1)(ii); and PARAS 950–953.
7 Where such a contract was made before 11 November 1999 only the executor could enforce it:
   Beswick v Beswick [1968] AC 58, [1967] 2 All ER 1197, HL. Where such a contract was made
   on or after 11 November 1999 it may also be enforceable by the non-party (although this is only
   so in relation to contracts made within the period of six months after 11 November 1999 if the
   contract expressly provides for the application of the Contracts (Rights of Third Parties) Act
   1999): see ss 1, 10; and CONTRACT vol 22 (2012) PARAS 342, 343. See also PERSONAL
   PROPERTY vol 80 (2013) PARA 874.

31. Testator's body. No person can make a binding disposition of his own dead
body, so as to oust the executors' right to the custody and possession of it and
their duties relating to disposal of it[1]. However, by statute, a direction for the
anatomical examination of a person's body after death and the removal of parts
of it for medical purposes may in certain cases be effective[2]. It appears that where
a claimant is in lawful possession of a dead body and there being no way of
resolving a dispute about the entitlement of a defendant to act as an executor
within an acceptable time period, the court may grant declaratory relief to the
claimant to allow him to take the decision as to the appropriate arrangements for
disposal of the body[3].

1 *Williams v Williams* (1882) 20 ChD 659. As to the executors' rights and duties see PARA 956. As
   to burial expenses see CREMATION AND BURIAL vol 24 (2010) PARA 1136 et seq.
2 See the Human Tissue Act 2004 ss 1, 57, 59, Sch 7 Pt 1; and MEDICAL PROFESSIONS vol 74
   (2011) PARA 54 et seq.
3 *University Hospital Lewisham NHS Trust v Hamuth* [2006] EWHC 1609 (Ch), 150 Sol Jo LB
   168, [2006] All ER (D) 145 (Jan). As to conflicting claims in respect of funeral arrangements see
   Buchanan v Milton [1999] 2 FLR 844; *Burrows v HM Coroner for Preston* [2008] EWHC 1387
   (QB), [2008] 2 FLR 1225, [2008] All ER (D) 201 (May); *Hartshorne v Gardner* [2008] EWHC
   3675 (Ch); [2008] 2 FLR 1681; *Anstey v Mundle* [2016] EWHC 1073 (Ch); and PARA 956. See
   also *Abdullahi v Mudashir* [2003] All ER (D) 477 (Oct) (injunction against wife of deceased
   obtained by persons named by will as trustees and instructing them to arrange funeral was
   discharged due to material non-disclosure and misrepresentations inter alia that they had already
   been appointed).

32. Choses (or things) in action which are not disposable. Those rights of action
which do not on death devolve on the personal representative, or which come to
an end with the life of the owner, cannot be disposed of by will[1].

The powers of nomination conferred by the rules of a friendly or other society
over the sums payable on death of a member operate as powers of appointment
and may give the member no right of property in the sum assured[2], but such a
power is testamentary and subject, for example, to the doctrine of lapse[3]. By the
terms of a policy of assurance the money payable under it may not be subject to
the right of disposition by the assured's will[4]. Such a limitation of a
testator's power of disposition by will is valid not only against persons claiming
under the will[5], but also against creditors[6].

Similarly, although shares held by the testator in a company regulated by
the Companies Act 1985 vest on his death in his personal representative[7], he may
have no right, or only a restricted right, to dispose of them, for other shareholders
may have the right to buy them from the personal representatives[8]. A similar
restriction on the personal representative may arise where a gift is made to a donee
whose estate is subject to the effects of insolvency legislation[9].

A covenant against assignment in a lease is not in general construed so as to forbid a disposition of the term by the will of the tenant[10].

1 As to such rights see PARA 1277 et seq. As to assignment of rights and liabilities under contract see CONTRACT vol 22 (2012) PARA 335 et seq; and as to assignment of rights and liabilities in respect of torts see TORT vol 97 (2015) PARA 442. See generally CHOSES IN ACTION vol 13 (2009) PARA 14 et seq.
2 See *A-G v Rowsell* (1844) 36 ChD 67n; *Re Phillips' Insurance* (1883) 23 ChD 235, CA; *Urquhart v Butterfield* (1887) 37 ChD 357, CA. As to payments under a nomination see FINANCIAL INSTITUTIONS vol 48 (2015) PARAS 703 et seq, 992 et seq; EMPLOYMENT vol 41 (2014) PARA 924.
3 *Re Barnes, Ashenden v Heath* [1940] Ch 267. As to the doctrine of lapse see PARA 160 et seq.
4 See PARA 27 head (8).
5 *Re Davies, Davies v Davies* [1892] 3 Ch 63 at 69 per North J. See also *Page v Cox* (1852) 10 Hare 163; *Ashby v Costin* (1888) 21 QBD 401, DC; *Phillips v Cayley* (1889) 43 ChD 222, CA. The nomination in such a case is not revocable by will: *Bennett v Slater* [1899] 1 QB 45, CA.
6 *Re Flavell, Murray v Flavell* (1883) 25 ChD 89, CA.
7 *Re Greene, Greene v Greene* [1949] Ch 333, [1949] 1 All ER 167.
8 *Re White, Theobald v White* [1913] 1 Ch 231. As to restrictions on transfer of shares in a company see COMPANIES vol 14 (2016) PARA 403.
9 *Re Hemming, Raymond Saul & Co (a Firm) v Holden* [2008] EWHC 2731 (Ch), [2008] All ER (D) 176 (Nov) (the residuary legatee's immediate entitlement to future payment (if any property remained to form the residue) was a chose in action which vested in his trustee in bankruptcy in priority to both the legatee and the executor).
10 See LANDLORD AND TENANT vol 62 (2012) PARA 632.

(3) DONEES

(i) Capacity to Benefit

33. Who can benefit under will. As a general rule, any person who may be a grantee under a gift inter vivos may be a donee under a will[1].

A testator must dispose of his property among persons or bodies who, whether or not in existence at the date of the will or of the death, are ascertainable within the period allowed by the rules against remoteness; the principle is that, apart from charitable gifts, there must normally be a donee capable of enforcing the gift or trust in the will[2]. Gifts for non-charitable purposes which are not for the benefit of ascertainable beneficiaries are in general invalid, and purposeless directions are void[3]. In general, a gift by will cannot be made to a person who is dead at the date of the will[4]. Even if the donee was alive at the date of the will, the gift generally fails if he is dead at the death of the testator, and his personal representatives take no interest under the gift[5]. A gift may, however, be made to the personal representatives of a deceased person[6]. Formerly, by statute, property given to a donee who predeceased the testator in certain cases passed as if the donee had survived the testator[7], and there remain cases where property given to a donee who predeceases the testator passes to the donee's issue[8]. The burden of proving that the donee was alive at the death of the testator so as to be capable of taking benefit under the will is on those deriving title under the donee[9].

The donee must always be described with certainty or be capable of being ascertained on evidence which is admissible[10]. He must also be capable of benefiting under the particular will[11], but inability to give a receipt for what is given is different from disqualification from taking[12]. The unmeritorious character of a donee, as distinct from some invalidity in the intention of the testator, gives rise to neither incapacity nor disqualification[13].

1   Shep Touch (8th Edn, 1826) p 414. As to competency to take a gift inter vivos see GIFTS vol 52 (2014) PARA 218 et seq. See also *Re Smith, Johnson v Bright-Smith* [1914] 1 Ch 937 at 948 per Joyce J ('. . . excluding cases of charitable bequests, a legatee must be either a natural person or a corporation'). Where, on or after 1 January 1997, a testator dies having made a gift of a legal estate by will to a minor, the gift operates as a declaration that the estate is to be held on trust for the minor until he attains the age of 18: see the Trusts of Land and Appointment of Trustees Act 1996 s 2(6), Sch 1 paras 1, 2; and CHILDREN AND YOUNG PERSONS vol 9 (2012) PARA 31.

2   *Bowman v Secular Society Ltd* [1917] AC 406, HL; *Re Astor's Settlement Trusts, Astor v Scholfield* [1952] Ch 534, [1952] 1 All ER 1067. See also TRUSTS AND POWERS vol 98 (2013) PARA 8.

3   As to the necessity for certainty of objects of a trust see generally *Morice v Bishop of Durham* (1805) 10 Ves 522; *McPhail v Doulton* [1971] AC 424, [1970] 2 All ER 228, HL; and TRUSTS AND POWERS vol 98 (2013) PARAS 8–9. A direction to shut up a house for 20 years, and subject to that to a devisee in fee, is void so far as the 20-year term is concerned if during that period the house devolves on an intestacy: *Brown v Burdett* (1882) 21 ChD 667. See also *Brown v Burdett* (1888) 40 ChD 244 at 256, CA, per Kay J. Gifts to non-existent persons, including corporations, by name or description are void for want of proper objects: 1 Preston's Abstracts of Title 128; *Egerton v Earl Brownlow* (1853) 4 HL Cas 1 at 122. A gift to the trustees of a settlement on its trusts failed because the settlement was no longer subsisting and there were no longer trustees to receive the property: *Re Slade, Witham v Watson* (1919) 89 LJ Ch 412, HL. Cf *Re Shelton's Settled Estates, Shelton v Shelton* [1945] Ch 158, [1945] 1 All ER 283; *Re Playfair, Palmer v Playfair* [1951] Ch 4, [1950] 2 All ER 285. Gifts to trustees for the benefit of animals or the maintenance of inanimate objects are in some cases valid: see CHARITIES vol 8 (2015) PARA 44; PERPETUITIES AND ACCUMULATIONS vol 80 (2013) PARA 5; TRUSTS AND POWERS vol 98 (2013) PARA 8. As to gifts to non-charitable societies see PARA 36. A fiduciary dispositive power may be conferred on trustees or executors, which must satisfy the requirements of certainty under the general law for powers, but those requirements are now such that it is possible to confer extremely wide powers: see PARA 11; and TRUSTS AND POWERS vol 98 (2013) PARAS 28, 70.

4   *Kelsey v Ellis* (1878) 38 LT 471 at 473.

5   As to lapse see PARA 160 et seq.

6   See PARA 165.

7   Ie under the Wills Act 1837 s 32 (repealed by the Trusts of Land and Appointment of Trustees Act 1996 s 25(2), Sch 4, with effect from 1 January 1997) (see PARA 166) and the Wills Act 1837 s 33 (repealed and replaced in relation to testators dying on or after 1 January 1983 by the Administration of Justice Act 1982 s 19) (see PARA 167).

8   Ie under the Wills Act 1837 s 33 (repealed and replaced in relation to testators dying on or after 1 January 1983 by the Administration of Justice Act 1982 s 19) (see PARA 169).

9   *Wing v Angrave* (1860) 8 HL Cas 183; *Re Phené's Trusts* (1870) 5 Ch App 139, CA; *Re Lewes' Trusts* (1871) 6 Ch App 356; *Re Walker* (1871) 7 Ch App 120; *Re Benjamin, Neville v Benjamin* [1902] 1 Ch 723; *Re Aldersey, Gibson v Hall* [1905] 2 Ch 181. See also *Mason v Mason* (1816) 1 Mer 308. The difficulty which arose in *Wing v Angrave* with regard to survivorship as between two persons dying on the same occasion is now met (subject to any order of the court) by the presumption that death occurred in order of seniority and accordingly the younger is deemed to have survived the elder: Law of Property Act 1925 s 184. For the settled construction of the statutory presumption see *Hickman v Peacey* [1945] AC 304, [1945] 2 All ER 215, HL. See also *Re Lindop, Lee-Barber v Reynolds* [1942] Ch 377, [1942] 2 All ER 46; and PARA 746. As to the construction of expressions such as 'simultaneous death' when used in wills see PARA 246. As to the presumption of the fact of death from absence without being heard of for seven years see CIVIL PROCEDURE vol 12 (2015) PARA 759. See also *Re Rawson, Rigby v Rawson* (1920) 90 LJ Ch 304 (direction for presuming death of missing legatee). In the absence of evidence of the continuance of life, the court will direct a share to be dealt with on the footing that the person to whom the share is given died at the date he was last heard of: *Re Benjamin, Neville v Benjamin* above; *Re Newson-Smith's Settlement, Grice v Newson-Smith* [1962] 3 All ER 963n, [1962] 1 WLR 1478; *Re Green, Fitzgerald-Hart v A-G* [1985] 3 All ER 455.

10   See PARA 45.

11   See PARA 34.

12   See PARA 37. See also *Re Meyers, London Life Association v St George's Hospital* [1951] Ch 534, [1951] 1 All ER 538.

13   *Thellusson v Woodford, Woodford v Thellusson* (1799) 4 Ves 227 at 312, 329 (a will is not affected on account of the unmeritorious object in the view of the testator); affd (1805) 11 Ves 112 at 145, HL (regret that such a will should be maintained goes no further than as a motive to see whether it is an attempt to make an illegal disposition).

34.   Persons incapable of taking. A testator cannot make a valid disposition of property by will to any person for any purpose, forbidden by statute or contrary to public policy[1], although where an illegal or impermissible purpose is sought to be achieved by way of a condition attaching to the disposition, the donee might take a valid gift with the condition being declared void[2].

Formerly, at common law, an alien could not take a devise of land, but this disability has been removed by statute[3]. Disability to receive a gift arising from the principles or custom or positive law of a foreign country, especially of a penal nature, is not regarded by the English court[4].

The fact that the donee is a member of a religious order or belongs to any society under vows as to the property of its members does not affect his right to take a benefit[5].

1   *Egerton v Earl Brownlow* (1853) 4 HL Cas 1 at 241–242 per Lord St Leonards. Cf *Re Wallace, Champion v Wallace* [1920] 2 Ch 274, CA. On and after 1 January 1970 gifts to future illegitimate children have been valid: see PARAS 355–356.
2   For examples of gifts against public policy see CHARITIES vol 8 (2015) PARA 66. As to public policy in relation to conditions see PARA 131 et seq; see also *Nathan v Leonard* [2002] EWHC 1701 (Ch), [2003] 4 All ER 198, [2003] 1 WLR 827 (argument that a testamentary restriction on challenges to the will was contrary to public policy rejected); and as to disqualification for benefiting see PARAS 38–39.
3   See BRITISH NATIONALITY vol 4 (2011) PARA 411.
4   *Worms v De Valdor* (1880) 49 LJ Ch 261; followed in *Re Selot's Trust* [1902] 1 Ch 488 (both cases as to the appointment of a conseil judiciaire of a French prodigue, where, however, the foreign law did not vest the property of the prodigue in the conseil judiciaire). See CONFLICT OF LAWS vol 19 (2011) PARA 332. See also *Re Langley's Settlement Trusts, Lloyds Bank Ltd v Langley* [1962] Ch 541, [1961] 3 All ER 803, CA.
5   *Re Metcalfe's Trusts* (1864) 10 LT 78; *Galwey v Barden* [1899] 1 IR 508. The disability of individual Roman Catholics to take gifts was removed by the Roman Catholic Relief Act 1829 s 23 (repealed): see ECCLESIASTICAL LAW. A condition disqualifying a legatee if a Roman Catholic may, however, still be imposed: *Re May, Eggar v May* [1917] 2 Ch 126; *Blathwayt v Baron Cawley* [1976] AC 397, [1975] 3 All ER 625, HL. As to the removal of the restrictions on gifts to superstitious uses see CHARITIES vol 8 (2015) PARA 63.

35.   Gifts to corporate bodies. Corporate bodies[1] may be the subject of testamentary bounty in the same way as individuals[2]. If, however, on the true construction of the gift, it is made to the corporate body not beneficially but on trust, the trust and hence the gift may be invalid[3].

A company regulated by the Companies Act 2006 can register itself as the holder of its own shares bequeathed to it if the shares are fully paid[4].

1   As to corporations generally see CORPORATIONS vol 24 (2010) PARA 301 et seq. The position of quasi corporations (see CORPORATIONS vol 24 (2010) PARAS 301–302) depends in every case on the relevant legislation affecting them: see *Re Amos, Carrier v Price* [1891] 3 Ch 159. As to the position of trade unions see EMPLOYMENT vol 41 (2014) PARA 891 et seq.
2   *Re Smith, Johnson v Bright-Smith* [1914] 1 Ch 937 at 948 per Joyce J. A testamentary gift to an incorporated body, including a company with charitable objects, prima facie takes effect as a gift to that body beneficially as part of its general funds and without imposition of any trust: *Re Finger's Will Trusts, Turner v Ministry of Health* [1972] Ch 286, [1971] 3 All ER 1050; *Re Vernon's Will Trusts, Lloyds Bank Ltd v Group 20, Hospital Management Committee (Coventry)* [1972] Ch 300n, [1971] 3 All ER 1061n.
3   It might be invalid because of uncertainty of objects or lack of identifiable beneficiaries who can enforce the trust. As to the validation of certain trusts contained in instruments taking effect before 16 December 1952 which would otherwise have failed because the trust property was not exclusively applicable to charitable purposes see CHARITIES vol 8 (2015) PARAS 98–103. A gift to a parish council 'for the purpose of providing some useful memorial to myself' was held not to be a beneficial gift, as the words quoted were not merely expository, but were intended to impose an obligation in the nature of a trust, the gift accordingly being void: *Re Endacott, Corpe v Endacott* [1960] Ch 232, [1959] 3 All ER 562, CA.
4   A company limited by shares may acquire any of its own fully paid shares otherwise than for valuable consideration: see Companies Act 2006 s 659(1); and COMPANIES vol 14 (2016)

PARA 334. Before 22 December 1980, when the predecessor of this provision came into force (see the Companies Act 1980 s 35(2); and the Companies Act 1980 (Commencement No 2) Order 1980, SI 1980/1785), a company could not hold in its own name shares in itself which were bequeathed to it, but had to have them vested in a nominee for it: *Re Castiglione's Will Trusts, Hunter v Mackenzie* [1958] Ch 549, [1958] 1 All ER 480.

36. Gifts to non-charitable societies or for non-charitable purposes. A gift to a non-charitable unincorporated association may be intended to take effect in one or other of three different ways[1].

First, it may be a gift to the members of the association at the relevant date as joint tenants[2], so that any member can sever his share and claim it, whether he continues to be a member of the association or not. Such a gift is clearly valid[3].

Secondly, it may be a gift to the existing members, not as joint tenants but subject to their respective contractual rights and liabilities towards one another as members of the association. If this is the effect of the gift, it will not be open to objection on the ground of perpetuity or uncertainty[4] unless there is something in its terms or circumstances or in the rules of the association which precludes the members at any given time from dividing the subject matter of the gift between them on the footing that they are solely entitled to it in equity[5]. It is a necessary characteristic of any gift within this category that the members of the association can, by an appropriate majority if the rules so provide, or acting unanimously if not, alter their rules so as to provide that the funds should be applied for some new purpose or even distributed among the members for their own benefit, notwithstanding that the testator has obviously contemplated that the money would be applied in furthering the aims, or a particular purpose, of the society in perpetuity[6].

Thirdly, the terms or circumstances of the gift or the rules of the association may show that the property in question is not to be at the disposal of the members for the time being, but is to be held on trust or applied for the purposes of the association as a quasi corporate entity. In this case the gift will fail[7], but the common phrase 'for the purposes of the association' does not by itself import such a trust[8].

If the gift is expressed as a trust for a non-charitable purpose[9], it may fail on the grounds of uncertainty or for lack of beneficiaries capable of enforcing it[10]. If, however, the trust, although so expressed, is directly or indirectly for the benefit of an ascertained individual or individuals, it is not open to objection merely on the last of these grounds[11].

1   See *Neville Estates Ltd v Madden* [1962] Ch 832 at 849, [1961] 3 All ER 769 at 778–779 per Cross J. It may, however, be open to doubt whether there should be any distinction between the first and second of the class of cases mentioned, the second class being only a gift to the members by their collective name: see *Leahy v A-G for New South Wales* [1959] AC 457 at 483–484, [1959] 2 All ER 300 at 310, PC, quoting and approving Lord Hanworth MR in *Re Macaulay's Estate, Macaulay v O'Donnell* [1943] Ch 435n, HL. As to gifts to charitable societies see *Re Finger's Will Trusts, Turner v Ministry of Health* [1972] Ch 286, [1971] 3 All ER 1050; *Re Vernon's Will Trusts, Lloyds Bank Ltd v Group 20, Hospital Management Committee (Coventry)* [1972] Ch 300n, [1971] 3 All ER 1061n.
2   In *Re Recher's Will Trusts, National Westminster Bank Ltd v National Anti-Vivisection Society Ltd* [1972] Ch 526 at 540, [1971] 3 All ER 401 at 408, Brightman J envisaged that the gift might possibly be to the members as tenants in common, but it is difficult to see how words of severance could be introduced into such a gift.
3   *Bowman v Secular Society Ltd* [1917] AC 406 at 442, HL, per Lord Parker; *Re Smith, Johnson v Bright-Smith* [1914] 1 Ch 937; *Re Ogden, Brydon v Samuel* [1933] Ch 678. The number of the members so benefited may be material in deciding whether this is the true construction of the gift: *Hogan v Byrne* (1862) 13 ICLR 166.
4   *Cocks v Manners* (1871) LR 12 Eq 574; *Re Clarke, Clarke v Clarke* [1901] 2 Ch 110; *Re Prevost, Lloyds Bank Ltd v Barclays Bank Ltd* [1930] 2 Ch 383; *Re Ray's Will Trusts, Re Ray's Estate,*

Public Trustee v Barry [1936] Ch 520, [1936] 2 All ER 93; *Re Taylor, Midland Bank Executor and Trustee Co Ltd v Smith* [1940] Ch 481, [1940] 2 All ER 637; *Re Denley's Trust Deed, Holman v HH Martyn & Co Ltd* [1969] 1 Ch 373, [1968] 3 All ER 65; *Re Recher's Will Trusts, National Westminster Bank Ltd v National Anti-Vivisection Society Ltd* [1972] Ch 526, [1971] 3 All ER 401 (where, however, the gift could not be supported as the society had ceased to exist before the date of the will and the gift could not be construed as a gift to the members of a different association subject to a different contract); *Re Lipinski's Will Trusts, Gosschalk v Levy* [1976] Ch 235, [1977] 1 All ER 33. As to the validity of gifts where the recipients can deal freely with the subject matter see CHARITIES vol 8 (2015) PARAS 60, 62; PERPETUITIES AND ACCUMULATIONS vol 80 (2013) PARA 5.

5   See eg *Re Clark's Trust* (1875) 1 ChD 497 (where, as the gift was a gift of the income of a fund in aid of the funds of a society, and the members at any time could not dispose of the capital, the gift failed).

6   *Langham v Peterson* (1903) 87 LT 744 (revenue of a sum of money to be expended 'for the benefit or hospitality of the company'); *Re Clarke, Clarke v Clarke* [1901] 2 Ch 110 (to the committee of the Corps of Commissionaires 'to aid in the purchase of their barracks'); *Re Turkington, Owen v Benson* [1937] 4 All ER 501 (to a masonic lodge 'as a fund to build a suitable temple'); *Re Lipinski's Will Trusts, Gosschalk v Levy* [1976] Ch 235, [1977] 1 All ER 33 (to be used 'solely' in constructing and improving new buildings for an association). See *Re Horley Town Football Club, Hunt v McLaren* [2006] EWHC 2386 (Ch),[2006] All ER (D) 34 (Oct) (gift of land on trust for purpose of providing permanent ground for club construed as gift to the club and its members for the time being, subject to their current rules). See also *Hanchett-Stamford v A-G* [2008] EWHC 330 (Ch), [2009] Ch 173, [2008] 4 All ER 323, for further judicial analysis of the nature of such non-charitable unincorporated associations and for a discussion of the devolution of the assets of a non-charitable association, where the last two members were husband and wife.

7   *Leahy v A-G for New South Wales* [1959] AC 457, [1959] 2 All ER 300, PC. See also *Carne v Long* (1860) 2 De GF & J 75; *Re Dutton, ex p Peake* (1878) 4 ExD 54; *Re Amos, Carrier v Price* [1891] 3 Ch 159; *Re Grant's Will Trusts* [1979] 3 All ER 359, [1980] 1 WLR 360 (doubting *Re Drummond, Ashworth v Drummond* [1914] 2 Ch 90; *Re Price, Midland Bank Executor and Trustee Co Ltd v Harwood* [1943] Ch 422, [1943] 2 All ER 505).

8   See *Leahy v A-G for New South Wales* [1959] AC 457 at 478, [1959] 2 All ER 300 at 307, PC.

9   As to the validation of certain trusts contained in instruments taking effect before 16 December 1952 which would otherwise have failed because the trust property was not exclusively applicable to charitable purposes see CHARITIES vol 8 (2015) PARAS 98–103.

10 See TRUSTS AND POWERS vol 98 (2013) PARA 8.

11 *Re Denley's Trust Deed, Holman v HH Martyn & Co Ltd* [1969] 1 Ch 373 at 383, [1968] 3 All ER 65 at 69 per Goff J; approved in *Re Lipinski's Will Trusts, Gosschalk v Levy* [1976] Ch 235 at 248, [1977] 1 All ER 33 at 44 per Oliver J.

37.   Giving of receipts.

Although a minor is capable of being a donee under a will, he cannot give the personal representatives a valid receipt for the gift except where he is expressly or impliedly authorised to do so by the testator[1] or, in respect of income, when he is married[2]. However, a parent or guardian of a minor who has parental responsibility[3] for the minor has the right to receive or recover in his own name, for the benefit of the minor, any property which the minor is entitled to receive or recover[4]. A person suffering from mental disorder may be a donee[5], but, while so suffering, cannot give the personal representatives a valid receipt[6]. In the case of a gift to a charity or a non-charitable society[7] it is prudent to provide that the receipt of the treasurer or other proper officer is to be sufficient discharge to the executors[8].

1   See PARA 505. An authority to give a receipt will be implied from a gift to be paid to a legatee on his attaining some age less than 18 (see the Family Law Reform Act 1969 s 1; and CHILDREN AND YOUNG PERSONS vol 9 (2012) PARA 1), or on marriage (*Cooper v Thornton* (1790) 3 Bro CC 96 at 97 note (2) (affd 3 Bro CC 186); *Re Denekin, Peters v Tanchereau* (1895) 72 LT 220; *Re Somech, Westminster Bank Ltd v Phillips* [1957] Ch 165, [1956] 3 All ER 523). In such a case a trustee has a discretion whether or not to transfer capital, and so the court, if discretion is surrendered to it, has inherent jurisdiction with regard to the minor's property enabling it to inquire whether the proposed transaction is for the minor's benefit or would be improvident: *Re Somech, Westminster Bank Ltd v Phillips*.

2   See the Law of Property Act 1925 s 21; and CHILDREN AND YOUNG PERSONS vol 9 (2012) PARA 40.

3   As to parental responsibility see the Children Act 1989 ss 2–4A; and CHILDREN AND YOUNG
     PERSONS vol 9 (2012) PARA 150 et seq.
4   Children Act 1989 s 3(3). Before 14 October 1991 (ie the date on which s 3 came into force), a
     guardian had such a power (see the Guardianship Act 1973 s 7(1) (repealed), replacing the Tenures
     Abolition Act 1660 s 9 (repealed)) but a parent did not have such a power. As to the power of a
     guardian or minor under the former law to give a receipt for the minor's property see *M'Creight
     v M'Creight* (1849) 13 I Eq R 314; *Re Cresswell* (1881) 45 LT 468.
5   The Court of Protection has jurisdiction with respect to the property of person lacking mental
     capacity: see the Mental Capacity Act 2005; see PARA 51; and MENTAL HEALTH AND CAPACITY
     vol 75 (2013) PARA 727 et seq.
6   See PARA 1065.
7   As to gifts to non-charitable societies see PARA 36.
8   See *Leahy v A-G for New South Wales* [1959] AC 457 at 477, [1959] 2 All ER 300 at 306, PC.
     See also *Re Meyers, London Life Association v St George's Hospital* [1951] Ch 534, [1951]
     1 All ER 538 (the non-existence of the designated persons enabled to give a good receipt did not
     cause charitable gifts to fail; it seems unlikely that the non-existence at the particular time of such
     persons would ever cause the failure of a gift to charity).

(ii) Disqualification for Benefiting from Will

A.   WRONGFUL ACT OF DONEE

38.   Undue influence or fraud. A gift by will which has been obtained by undue
influence is liable to be set aside[1], as also is a gift obtained fraudulently, whether
the fraud was practised on the testator in his lifetime or by forgery after his death[2].
Thus a donee will not be allowed to avail himself of a legacy which has been given
to him under a particular character which he has falsely assumed for the purpose
of obtaining the benefit, and which is shown or is inferred to be the only motive
for it[3]. Questions of undue influence or fraud must be raised in the court of
probate[4].

1   See PARA 56; and LEGAL PROFESSIONS vol 66 (2015) PARA 599; MISREPRESENTATION vol 76
     (2013) PARA 836 et seq.
2   See PARAS 58–59.
3   See PARA 58.
4   See PARA 58. As to the probate court see PARA 678. As to secret trusts see PARAS 221–223; and
     TRUSTS AND POWERS vol 98 (2013) PARA 87 et seq.

39.   Murder and manslaughter. It is contrary to public policy that a person
should be allowed to claim a benefit resulting from his own crime[1]. Accordingly,
a donee who is shown to the satisfaction of the court[2] to be guilty of the murder
or manslaughter of the testator, or of any other serious criminal act which resulted
in the testator's death, cannot take any benefit under his will[3], except in so far as
this rule can be and is modified by the court in exercise of its powers under the
Forfeiture Act 1982. The Act confers on the court a discretionary power in a case
of manslaughter or other criminal act resulting in death (but not where the donee
stands convicted of murder[4]) to modify the effect of the rule of public policy in
certain circumstances[5].

If the death is before 1 February 2012[6], the person precluded from acquiring
the benefit under a will or the intestacy rules is not treated as having predeceased
the testator or intestate and hence the substitutional provisions applying to gifts
by will to the beneficiary's issue[7] and those applying to the statutory trusts under
the intestacy rules[8], do not apply. If a gift is by will to a class[9], the property goes
to the other persons entitled; if the exclusion of the donee effects an intestacy as
to the property in question, to the persons, other than the donee[10], entitled on
intestacy[11], and not to the Crown as bona vacantia, save in so far as the Crown
may be entitled under the intestacy provisions in the ordinary way[12].

For deaths on or after 1 February 2012[13], unless the will provides otherwise, the person precluded from acquiring a benefit will be treated for the purposes of the Wills Act 1837[14] and the intestacy rules[15] as having died immediately before the testator.

It appears that the donee is entitled to the property if the will is made in the interval between the wound and the death[16].

A person suffering from mental disorder is not debarred from taking a benefit under the will of a person whom he has killed while so suffering[17].

The application of the forfeiture rule against a person does not, it seems, preclude that person making an application under the Inheritance (Provision for Family and Dependants) Act 1975, or the making of an order under that Act[18]. The court may make an order under the 1975 Act even though it is the forfeiture rule and not the terms of the will (or, presumably, the effect of the Intestacy Rules) that means provision has not been made for the claimant[19].

1   *Cleaver v Mutual Reserve Fund Life Association* [1892] 1 QB 147 at 156, CA, per Fry LJ. See also *Beresford v Royal Insurance Co Ltd* [1938] AC 586 at 596–599, [1938] 2 All ER 602 at 605–607, HL; and INSURANCE vol 60 (2011) PARA 480. The rule laid down in *Cleaver v Mutual Reserve Fund Life Association* is, it appears, restricted to the assertion of a claim by the criminal or his representatives, and third persons acquiring a title in good faith to personal property through the criminal may in some cases have protection: see FINANCIAL INSTRUMENTS AND TRANSACTIONS vol 49 (2015) PARA 270; PERSONAL PROPERTY vol 80 (2013) PARAS 845–847. An assignee of the offender's interest in an insurance policy, such as a mortgagee, may obtain payment under it (see eg *Davitt v Titcumb* [1990] Ch 110, [1989] 3 All ER 417; *Dunbar v Plant* [1998] Ch 412, CA, sub nom *Dunbar (administrator of the estate of Dunbar) v Plant* [1997] 4 All ER 289, CA); but the offender cannot benefit from this (*Davitt v Titcumb*).

2   In civil proceedings the certificate of a conviction for murder or manslaughter is evidence of the commission of the crime: see the Civil Evidence Act 1968 s 11(1); and CIVIL PROCEDURE vol 12A (2015) PARA 1644. As to the standard of proof required in other cases see eg *Re Dellow's Will Trusts, Lloyds Bank Ltd v Institute of Cancer Research* [1964] 1 All ER 771, [1964] 1 WLR 451 (where the testator and the beneficiary died on the same occasion in circumstances suggesting the unlawful killing of the testator by the beneficiary); *Dunbar v Plant* [1998] Ch 412, CA, sub nom *Dunbar (administrator of the estate of Dunbar) v Plant* [1997] 4 All ER 289, CA (where no criminal proceedings had been brought but the court was satisfied, on applying the civil burden of proof, that the donee had committed a criminal offence in relation to the victim's death). See also PARA 756. If it is proved by admissible evidence that the donee killed the testator, the burden is on the donee or the persons claiming through him to show that the act was not criminal: *Re Pollock, Pollock v Pollock* [1941] Ch 219, [1941] 1 All ER 360. See also *Re Callaway, Callaway v Treasury Solicitor* [1956] Ch 559 at 562, [1956] 2 All ER 451 at 452.

3   *Re Hall, Hall v Knight and Baxter* [1914] P 1, CA (manslaughter); *Re Callaway, Callaway v Treasury Solicitor* [1956] Ch 559, [1956] 2 All ER 451; *Re Giles, Giles v Giles* [1972] Ch 544, [1971] 3 All ER 1141 (manslaughter; diminished responsibility); *Re Royse, Royse v Royse* [1985] Ch 22, [1984] 3 All ER 339, CA (manslaughter; diminished responsibility); *Re K* [1985] Ch 85, [1985] 1 All ER 403 (affd [1986] Ch 180, [1985] 2 All ER 833, CA) (manslaughter); *Re Murphy, Dalton v Latham* [2003] EWHC 796 (Ch), 147 Sol Jo LB 537, [2003] All ER (D) 305 (Apr) (manslaughter; diminished responsibility); *Chadwick v Collinson* [2014] EWHC 3055 (Ch), [2015] WTLR 39, [2014] All ER (D) 172 (Sep) (manslaughter; diminished responsibility). As to a verdict of 'guilty but insane' which amounts to an acquittal see PARA 480.

    The rule also applies to aiding and abetting suicide: *Dunbar v Plant* [1998] Ch 412, CA, sub nom *Dunbar (administrator of the estate of Dunbar) v Plant* [1997] 4 All ER 289, CA.

    The motives and degree of culpability do not affect the application of the rule: *Re Hall, Hall v Knight and Baxter* above at 7 per Hamilton LJ; *Dunbar v Plant* above at 307–311 and 1280–1284 per Phillips LJ (disapproving the opinions expressed in *Gray v Barr (Prudential Assurance Co Ltd, third party)* [1970] 2 QB 626, [1970] 2 All ER 702 and *R v Chief National Insurance Comr, ex p Connor* [1981] QB 758, [1981] 1 All ER 769, DC, and the decision in *Re H* [1990] 1 FLR 441, that the rule might not apply to the less culpable categories of manslaughter). However, the rule does not apply in cases of manslaughter by reckless or drunken driving, mainly for policy reasons to do with making insurance available to the victim: see *Dunbar (administrator of the estate of Dunbar) v Plant* above at 307 and 1279–1280 per Phillips LJ. As to murder, manslaughter and diminished responsibility see CRIMINAL LAW vol 25 (2016) PARA 97 et seq.

    As to the application of the rule to interests arising other than under a will see *Re Sigsworth, Bedford v Bedford* [1935] Ch 89 (intestacy); *R v Chief National Insurance Comr, ex p Connor* above (widow's allowance); *Re K* above (joint property); *Davitt v Titcumb* [1990] Ch 110, [1989] 3 All ER 417 (increase in value of equity of redemption as a result of mortgage being paid off out of joint life policy); *Jones v Roberts* [1995] 2 FLR 422 (intestacy); *Re S* [1996] 1 WLR 235, [1996] 3 FCR 357 (joint life policy); *Dunbar (administrator of the estate of Dunbar) v Plant* above (joint property and a trust of an insurance policy); *Re DWS* [2001] Ch 568, [2001] 1 All ER 97, CA (intestacy); *Glover v Staffordshire Police Authority* [2006] EWHC 2414 (Admin), [2007] ICR 661, [2006] All ER (D) 77 (Oct) (pension to policeman's widow).

4 See the Forfeiture Act 1982 s 5; and PARA 40.

5 See the Forfeiture Act 1982 ss 1, 2; and PARA 40. The Forfeiture Act 1982 came into force on 13 October 1982: see s 7(2); and PARA 40 note 1. Before that date the court had no power to mitigate the effect of the rule of public policy.

    In *Glover v Staffordshire Police Authority* [2006] EWHC 2414 Admin, [2007] ICR 661, [2006] All ER (D) 77 (Oct), the court considered the interplay between The Forfeiture Act 1982 and a statutory pension scheme under Police Pensions Act 1976. See also *Dalton v Latham* [2003] EWHC 796 (Ch), [2003] All ER (D) 305 (Apr) (relief from forfeiture refused on consideration of all relevant circumstances, including position of deceased's family).

    See further Sukhninder Panesar 'Forfeiture Act 1982' (2016) 180 JPN 27; and Lesley King 'Relief from Forfeiture' (2016) LS Gaz, 11 Jan, 20.

6 Ie the date the Estates of Deceased Persons (Forfeiture Rule and Law of Succession) Act 2011 came into effect.

7 See the Wills Act 1837 s 33; and PARA 169.

8 See the Administration of Estates Act 1925 s 46; and PARA 485.

9 *Re Peacock, Midland Bank Executor and Trustee Co Ltd v Peacock* [1957] Ch 310, [1957] 2 All ER 98.

10 A donee can no more benefit under the intestacy of a person whose death he has caused than he can under that person's will: *Re Sigsworth, Bedford v Bedford* [1935] Ch 89. See also *Re Crippen* [1911] P 108 and *Re DWS, Re EHS, TWGS (a child) v JMG* [2000] 2 All ER 83; affd [2001] Ch 568, [2001] 1 All ER 97. Others may, however, benefit under an intestacy which might not have occurred but for the killing: see *Re Robertson, Marsden v Marsden* (1963) 107 Sol Jo 318; *Re Hunter's Executors, Petitioners* 1992 SLT 1141; *Re Jones, Jones v Midland Bank Trust Co Ltd* [1998] 1 FLR 246, CA (where in all three cases a gift over in the event of the killer of the testator predeceasing the testator did not take effect).

11 See *Re DWS, Re EHS, TWGS v JMG* [2000] 2 All ER 83; affd [2001] Ch 568, [2001] 1 All ER 97 (issue of a child of an intestate, that child having murdered the intestate and forfeited interest, cannot take under intestacy unless the murderer happens to predecease the intestate: Administration of Estates Act 1925 s 47(1)(i) is construed so that issue of children of intestates cannot take in preference to its or their parent). As to the persons entitled on intestacy see PARA 477 et seq.

12 *Re Sigsworth, Bedford v Bedford* [1935] Ch 89; *Re Callaway, Callaway v Treasury Solicitor* [1956] Ch 559, [1956] 2 All ER 451. As to the intestacy provisions see PARA 479 et seq. As to bona vacantia see PARAS 512–513; and COMPANY AND PARTNERSHIP INSOLVENCY vol 17 (2011) PARA 892 et seq; CROWN AND CROWN PROCEEDINGS vol 29 (2014) PARA 145 et seq.

13 See note 6.

14 See the Wills Act 1837 s 33A; and PARA 169.

15 See the Administration of Estates Act 1925 s 46A; and PARA 488.

16 See *Lundy v Lundy* (1895) 24 SCR 650 at 653 per Taschereau J (a Canadian case). It seems that the effect of revival of the will (see PARA 110) or republication (see PARA 113) after the wound would be the same. In other cases, eg poisoning, the outcome might well depend on the testator's knowledge of the act.

17 *Re Batten's Will Trusts* (1961) 105 Sol Jo 529. Similarly, he is not debarred from taking under the intestacy of a person whom he has killed: *Re Houghton, Houghton v Houghton* [1915] 2 Ch 173; *Re Pitts, Cox v Kilsby* [1931] 1 Ch 546. As to the burden of proving that a killing was not criminal see note 2. As to diminished responsibility, which in general does not prevent the rule from applying see *Re Giles, Giles v Giles* [1972] Ch 544, [1971] 3 All ER 1141; *Re Royse, Royse v Royse* [1985] Ch 22, [1984] 3 All ER 339, CA; *Re H* [1990] 1 FLR 441 (the decision in this case, that the rule did not apply, was disapproved in *Dunbar v Plant* [1998] Ch 412, CA, sub nom *Dunbar (administrator of the estate of Dunbar) v Plant* [1997] 4 All ER 289, CA); *Re S* [1996] 1 WLR 235, [1996] 3 FCR 357; *Jones v Roberts* [1995] 2 FLR 422.

18 See the Forfeiture Act 1982 s 3; and *Re Land, Land v Land* [2006] EWHC 2069 (Ch), [2007] 1 All ER 324, [2007] 1 WLR 1009.

19 See the Forfeiture Act 1982 s 3; and *Re Land, Land v Land* [2006] EWHC 2069 (Ch), [2007] 1 All ER 324, [2007] 1 WLR 1009in which dicta of the Court of Appeal in *Re Royse, Royse v*

Royse [1985] Ch 22, [1984] 3 All ER 339 were considered but not followed; on the facts, the forfeiture rule did not serve the public interest.

40. Unlawful killing; modification of forfeiture rule. Before 13 October 1982[1] the rule of public policy preventing a murderer from claiming a benefit from his own crime[2] applied inflexibly in relation to manslaughter also[3], but on and after that date a court may make an order modifying the effect of the rule in a case of unlawful killing, except where the perpetrator stands convicted of murder[4]. The court may not make such an order unless it is satisfied that, having regard to the conduct of the offender and of the deceased and such other circumstances as appear to the court to be material, the justice of the case requires the effect of the rule to be modified in that case[5]. Such an order may modify the effect of the rule in respect of any interest in property to which the court's determination relates[6] which the offender would otherwise have acquired either, where there is more than one such interest, by excluding the application of the rule in respect of any (but not all) of those interests[7], or, in the case of any such interest in property, by excluding the application of the rule in respect of part of the property[8]. These words are an extension, not a restriction, of the court's power to modify the effect of the rule, which includes power to relieve the offender wholly from the effect of the rule in an appropriate case[9]. On the making of an order modifying the effect of the rule, the rule has effect for all purposes (including purposes relating to anything done before the order is made) subject to the modifications made by the order[10].

Where a person stands convicted of an offence of which unlawful killing is an element, the court may not make an order modifying the effect of the rule in that case unless proceedings for the purpose are brought before the expiry of the period of three months beginning with his conviction[11]. The Forfeiture Act 1982 is concerned with the adjustment of property rights and confers upon an individual the right to apply to the court within a defined period; the Act gives the court no discretion to extend the time for the commencement of the action[12].

1   Ie the date on which the Forfeiture Act 1982 came into operation: see s 7(2). The court may not make an order under s 2 (see the text and note 4) modifying the effect of the forfeiture rule in respect of any interest in property which, in consequence of the rule of public policy preventing a murderer from claiming a benefit from his own crime (see the text and note 2), had been acquired before 13 October 1982 by a person other than the offender or a person claiming through him: s 2(7). 'Acquired' in s 2(7) denotes property which has actually been transferred to the person entitled to it as a result of the rule, or in respect of which he has acquired an indefeasible right to have it transferred, and does not extend to property which, when s 2 came into force, was still in the hands of personal representatives dealing with the administration of the estate: *Re K* [1986] Ch 180, [1985] 2 All ER 833, CA. Subject to the Forfeiture Act 1982 s 2(7), an order under s 2 may be made whether the unlawful killing occurred before, on or after 13 October 1982: s 7(4).

2   As to this rule see PARA 39. The rule is referred to in the Forfeiture Act 1982 as the 'forfeiture rule': see s 1(1).

3   *Re Hall, Hall v Knight and Baxter* [1914] P 1, CA; *Re Peacock, Midland Bank Executor and Trustee Co Ltd v Peacock* [1957] Ch 310, [1957] 2 All ER 98; *Re Giles, Giles v Giles* [1972] Ch 544, [1971] 3 All ER 1141; *R v Chief National Insurance Comr, ex p Connor* [1981] QB 758, [1981] 1 All ER 769, DC; *Re Royse, Royse v Royse* [1985] Ch 22, [1984] 3 All ER 339, CA. See also PARA 39 note 3.

4   See the Forfeiture Act 1982 ss 2(1), 5 (amended by the Social Security Act 1986 s 76(1), (4)). Reference in the Forfeiture Act 1982 to a person who has unlawfully killed another includes a reference to a person who has unlawfully aided, abetted, counselled or procured the death of that other; and references in that Act to unlawful killing are to be interpreted accordingly: s 1(2). See also *Dunbar v Plant* [1998] Ch 412, CA, sub nom *Dunbar (administrator of the estate of Dunbar) v Plant* [1997] 4 All ER 289, CA (court's powers exercised in a case of aiding and abetting suicide).

5   Forfeiture Act 1982 s 2(2). The court is not limited to allowing the applicant what he might have obtained on an application under the Inheritance (Provision for Family and Dependants) Act 1975 (see PARA 565 et seq): *Re K* [1986] Ch 180, [1985] 2 All ER 833, CA. The first and paramount

consideration must be whether the culpability attending the beneficiary's criminal conduct was such as to justify the application of the forfeiture rule at all: *Dunbar v Plant* [1998] Ch 412 at 438, sub nom *Dunbar (administrator of the estate of Dunbar) v Plant* [1997] 4 All ER 289 at 312, CA, per Phillips LJ. As to decisions that forfeiture should be relieved see *Re K* [1985] Ch 85, [1985] 1 All ER 403 (affd [1986] Ch 180, [1985] 2 All ER 833, CA); *Re H* [1990] 1 FLR 441; *Re S* [1996] 1 WLR 235, [1996] 3 FCR 357; *Dunbar (administrator of the estate of Dunbar) v Plant* above. Contrast *Re Murphy, Dalton v Latham* [2003] EWHC 796 (Ch), [2003] All ER (D) 305 (Apr), [2003] WTLR 687, where relief was refused; *Re Land, Land v Land* [2006] All ER (D) 71 (Oct); *Meeking v Meeking* [2013] All ER (D) 250 (May) (degree of claimant's responsibility for death of husband considered together with her grief and genuine remorse and circumstances in which she was placed brought her within discretion for grant of relief). For a decision that forfeiture should not be relieved see *Chadwick v Collinson* [2014] EWHC 3055 (Ch), [2015] WTLR 39, [2014] All ER (D) 172 (Sep) (see PARA 39).

6   For these purposes, 'property' includes any chose (or thing) in action or incorporeal movable property: Forfeiture Act 1982 s 2(8). The interests in property which may be made the subject of an order under s 2 are:

    (1)   any beneficial interest in property which (apart from the forfeiture rule) the offender would have acquired:

        (a)   under the deceased's will or the law relating to intestacy (see s 2(1), (4)(a)(i));

        (b)   on the nomination of the deceased in accordance with the provisions of any enactment (see s 2(1), (4)(a)(ii)); or

        (c)   as a donatio mortis causa made by the deceased (see s 2(1), (4)(a)(iii));

        (d)   under a special destination (whether relating to heritable or moveable property) (see s 2(1), (4)(a)(iv)); or

    (2)   any beneficial interest in property which (apart from the forfeiture rule) the offender would have acquired in consequence of the death of the deceased, being property which, before the death, was held on trust for any person (see s 2(1), (4)(b)).

As to donationes mortis causa see PARA 921; GIFTS vol 52 (2014) PARA 271 et seq.

7   Forfeiture Act 1982 s 2(5)(a).

8   Forfeiture Act 1982 s 2(5)(b).

9   *Re K* [1985] Ch 85, [1985] 1 All ER 403 (affd [1986] Ch 180, [1985] 2 All ER 833, CA); *Dunbar v Plant* [1998] Ch 412 at 436–437, sub nom *Dunbar (administrator of the estate of Dunbar) v Plant* [1997] 4 All ER 289 at 310–311, CA, per Phillips LJ.

10   Forfeiture Act 1982 s 2(6).

11   Forfeiture Act 1982 s 2(3).

12   *Re Land, Land v Land* [2006] EWHC 2069 (Ch) at [10], [2007] 1 All ER 324, [2007] 1 WLR 1009 per Judge Alasdair Norris QC.

B.   DONEE OR SPOUSE AN ATTESTING WITNESS

41. Gift to witnesses. Any beneficial devise, legacy, estate, interest, gift or appointment, other than charges or directions for the payment of debts, so far as it concerns any person (other than one whose attestation is superfluous[1]) attesting the execution of any will[2] by which it is given, or the wife or husband or civil partner of that person, or any person claiming under that person or the wife or husband or civil partner, is null and void[3]. A power in a will enabling a solicitor-trustee to charge profit costs against the estate in the will of a person who died before 1 February 2001 is such a beneficial interest[4], but is treated as remuneration for services and not as a gift in relation to wills of persons dying on or after that date[5]. Where there is a joint tenancy under a will and one of the joint tenants attests the will, the other takes the whole[6]. A gift to a witness merely as trustee is valid[7].

1   See PARA 44.

2   As to wills of members of the armed forces on actual military service and mariners and seamen at sea, however, see PARAS 79–80.

3   Wills Act 1837 s 15 (amended by virtue of the Civil Partnership Act 2004 s 71, Sch 4 para 3). The terms 'wife' and 'husband' include a person who is married to a person of the same sex: see the Marriage (Same Sex Couples) Act 2013 Sch 3 para 1(1)(c), (2), (3); and MATRIMONIAL AND CIVIL PARTNERSHIP LAW vol 72 (2015) PARAS 1–2. As to civil partnerships see PARAS 90, 179. Before the Wills Act 1837 s 15 is applied, the will must be construed. Thus in the case of a bequest by the testator to a daughter who attests the will, with remainder to her children, where there are

children in existence at the testator's death, the effect of the failure of the gift to the daughter is to accelerate the gift to her children: *Jull v Jacobs* (1876) 3 ChD 703; *Re Clark, Clark v Randall* (1885) 31 ChD 72. If there are no children then in existence, there can be no acceleration, and there is an intestacy until the birth of children: *Re Townsend's Estate, Townsend v Townsend* (1886) 34 ChD 357; and see *Kearney v Kearney* [1911] 1 IR 137, Ir CA. If, however, the gift is to the daughter or her children, so that the gift to the children is substitutional, it fails with the gift to the daughter: *Aplin v Stone* [1904] 1 Ch 543; *Re Doland's Will Trusts, Westminster Bank Ltd v Phillips* [1970] Ch 267, [1969] 3 All ER 713. As to the acceleration of subsequent interests see PARA 181. Although the gift is null and void, that does not preclude the court from looking at the words of gift for the purposes of ascertaining the testator's intention when he made the document in which the gift is contained: *Re Finnemore* [1992] 1 All ER 800, [1991] 1 WLR 793. See also *Barrett v Bem* [2012] EWCA Civ 52, [2012] Ch 573, [2012] 2 All ER 920 (beneficiary of will signing it on testator's behalf). As to the liability of solicitors who fail to notice that a will has been attested by a beneficiary's husband see *Ross v Caunters* [1980] Ch 297, [1979] 3 All ER 580; and LEGAL PROFESSIONS vol 66 (2015) PARA 618.

4 *Re Barber, Burgess v Vinnicome* (1886) 31 ChD 665; *Re Pooley* (1888) 40 ChD 1, CA. As to the right of a solicitor to charge profit costs generally see LEGAL PROFESSIONS vol 66 (2015) PARA 611.

5 Trustee Act 2000 ss 28(4)(a), 33(2); Trustee Act 2000 (Commencement) Order 2001, SI 2001/49.

6 *Young v Davies* (1863) 2 Drew & Sm 167. See also *Re Fleetwood, Sidgreaves v Brewer* (1880) 15 ChD 594.

7 *Cresswell v Cresswell* (1868) LR 6 Eq 69. See also *Re Ray's Will Trusts, Re Ray's Estate, Public Trustee v Barry* [1936] Ch 520, [1936] 2 All ER 93 (where a gift to the person who should be abbess of a convent at the time of the death of the testatrix was a gift in trust for the convent, and hence was not invalidated by reason of one of two nuns who witnessed the will afterwards becoming abbess and being abbess at the death of the testatrix).

42. Exceptions to general rule for an attesting witness. Where, by means of an oral trust, a beneficial interest is conferred on an attesting witness who is, at the time of attestation, unaware of the secret trust in his favour, the gift is valid[1]. The marriage of a donee to an attesting witness after attestation does not affect the validity of the gift[2]. A beneficiary's interest is not rendered void if it could not be predicted at the time when the will was attested that he would be a donee[3]. A beneficiary who and whose spouse[4] did not witness an earlier will containing a gift to him, but who or whose spouse witnesses a later will repeating the gift to him and purporting to revoke the earlier will, may still be able to take the gift under the earlier will[5].

1 See *Re Young, Young v Young* [1951] Ch 344, [1950] 2 All ER 1245 (following *O'Brien v Condon* [1905] 1 IR 51; and not following *Re Fleetwood, Sidgreaves v Brewer* (1880) 15 ChD 594). See also *Sullivan v Sullivan* [1903] 1 IR 193.

2 *Thorpe v Bestwick* (1881) 6 QBD 311. Presumably, the same result would now follow where a donee enters a civil partnership with an attesting witness after attestation. 'Marriage' includes marriage of a same sex couple: see the Marriage (Same Sex Couples) Act 2013 Sch 3 para 1(1)(a), (2), (3); and MATRIMONIAL AND CIVIL PARTNERSHIP LAW vol 72 (2015) PARAS 1–2.

3 *Re Royce's Will Trusts, Tildesley v Tildesley* [1959] Ch 626, [1959] 3 All ER 278, CA (where it was held that a solicitor who is not appointed as an executor or original trustee is not, on subsequently being appointed a trustee, prevented from relying on a charging clause in the will or taking the trustee's remuneration provided by the will, even though he was an attesting witness).

4 See PARA 41, text and note 3; see also note 2. It seems likely that the same principle would apply where a civil partner of a beneficiary under both wills is involved, instead of a spouse.

5 *Re Finnemore* [1992] 1 All ER 800, [1991] 1 WLR 793 (where it was held that the revocation of the earlier will was conditional on the repeated gift in the later will being effective). See also PARA 108.

43. Beneficiary witnessing one of a number of testamentary instruments. A gift by will to a legatee is not forfeited by his attesting a codicil confirming the will[1], unless he receives a benefit by the codicil, as, for example, where the codicil makes a contingent gift absolute[2]; but the fact that the codicil, by revoking gifts in the will, increases the residue of which he gets a share is not such a benefit[3]. Conversely, a codicil duly executed confirming a will containing a gift to an attesting witness to the will renders the gift valid[4], and the validity so acquired is not destroyed by the legatee's attesting a subsequent codicil[5]. The gift is avoided only where the witness has attested the instrument under which he takes[6], and a gift in a will consisting of separate sheets of paper separately attested may be valid if the legatee has not attested the sheet on which his gift appears[7].

1   *Re Fleetwood, Sidgreaves v Brewer* (1880) 15 ChD 594; *Gurney v Gurney* (1855) 3 Drew 208. See also *Tempest v Tempest* (1856) 2 K & J 635 at 643; *Re Marcus, Marcus v Marcus* (1887) 57 LT 399.
2   *Gaskin v Rogers* (1866) LR 2 Eq 284.
3   *Gurney v Gurney* (1855) 3 Drew 208.
4   *Anderson v Anderson* (1872) LR 13 Eq 381; *Re Trotter, Trotter v Trotter* [1899] 1 Ch 764.
5   *Thorpe v Bestwick* (1881) 6 QBD 311; *Re Trotter, Trotter v Trotter* [1899] 1 Ch 764.
6   *Re Trotter, Trotter v Trotter* [1899] 1 Ch 764.
7   *Re Craven, Crewdson v Craven* (1908) 24 TLR 750.

44. Superfluous attestation. If more persons than are necessary sign their names to a will, then, in applying the provisions relating to gifts to witnesses[1], the attestation by a person to whom or to whose spouse or civil partner there is given or made any such disposition must be disregarded if the will is duly executed without his attestation and without that of any other such person[2]. This applies to the will of any person dying after 30 May 1968, whenever the will was executed[3]. In the case of a person who died before that date, the presumption was that all such persons signed as witnesses, and consequently legacies given to them or their spouses by the will were void; if more than two persons appeared to be attesting witnesses, some of them being legatees, all the names would be included in the probate, so that the question whether the legatees did or did not sign as witnesses might be decided in a court of equity[4]. In some cases, however, the court of probate itself dealt with this question, and omitted the names from the probate. If, after execution was complete, a third person added his name, the court did not without cogent evidence conclude that the third person signed as a witness[5].

If the testator is domiciled in England or Wales but makes his will elsewhere, then, even though by the joint effect of the Wills Act 1963[6] and the law of the foreign country no witnesses are necessary, a gift to a witness is nevertheless void unless the evidence shows that the testator intended to make an unattested will[7]. A gift made by the will of a member of the royal forces on actual military service, or any mariner or seaman being at sea, to a witness attesting the will is, however, valid, for the Wills Act 1837[8] exempts such a will from the requirement of attestation[9].

1   See PARAS 41–43.
2   Wills Act 1968 s 1(1) (amended by virtue of the Civil Partnership Act 2004 s 71, Sch 4 para 3(b)). This abrogates the previous rule as set out in *Re Bravda* [1967] 2 All ER 1233, [1967] 1 WLR 1080 (revsd on appeal [1968] 2 All ER 217, [1968] 1 WLR 479, CA). As to civil partnerships see PARAS 90, 179.
3   Wills Act 1968 s 1(2).
4   *Wigan v Rowland* (1853) 11 Hare 157; *Cozens v Crout* (1873) 42 LJ Ch 840. See also *Re Mitchell* (1841) 2 Curt 916; *Re Forest* (1861) 2 Sw & Tr 334; *Re Raine* (1865) 11 Jur NS 587.
5   *Randfield v Randfield* (1860) 8 HL Cas 225 at 228 note (c); *Re Sharman* (1869) LR 1 P & D 661; *Re Murphy* (1873) IR 8 Eq 300; *Re Smith* (1889) 15 PD 2; *Kitcat v King* [1930] P 266.
6   See the Wills Act 1963 s 1; and PARA 12.
7   *Re Priest, Belfield v Duncan* [1944] Ch 58, [1944] 1 All ER 51 (holograph will made in Scotland). Although the Wills Act 1837 does not apply to Scotland (see s 35), it does apply to a will, although made in Scotland, of a testator domiciled in England or Wales. The essential validity of testamentary gifts is governed by the law of the testator's domicile in the case of a will of movables and by the lex situs in the case of a will of immovables: see CONFLICT OF LAWS vol 19 (2011) PARA 753.
8   See the Wills Act 1837 s 11; and PARAS 79–80.
9   *Re Limond, Limond v Cunliffe* [1915] 2 Ch 240.

(iii) Uncertainty as to Donee

45. Donee must be identifiable. In order to be a donee under a will, a person must be so named or described that his identity can be established with certainty; otherwise the gift is void[1]. Difficulty of ascertainment is not in itself fatal to the validity of the gift; it is a matter of degree, and it is only when, on the evidence[2], the gift is so vague, or the difficulty is so great, that it must be treated as virtually incapable of resolution, that the gift is void for uncertainty[3].

If the will requires or allows, the description may be acquired by the donee after the date of the will on any future event and contingency, or, it seems, by the testator's own act in the ordinary course of his affairs or in the management of his property, or by the acts of third persons[4], or by reference to some hypothetical formula or possibility[5], although, if the act is testamentary in character, the proper formalities must be observed[6]. There may thus be a gift to a child en ventre sa mère[7], or other persons unborn or not ascertained at the date of the will[8], or to a class, that is to say to persons who are intended to be ascertained as those composing a described fluctuating body of persons at a particular future time, and are to take one divisible subject in certain proportionate shares, the amount of which depends on the ascertainment of all those persons[9]. In the case, however, of such gifts to take effect in the future, the rules of law designed to prevent perpetuity must be observed[10].

1   For examples of gifts void for uncertainty in this respect see *Lord Cheyney's Case* (1591) 5 Co Rep 68a at 68b; *Webb's Case* (1607) 1 Roll Abr 609 (20 of the poorest of the testator's kindred); *Beal v Wyman* (1650) Sty 240 (the heirs male of any of the testator's sons or next of kin); *Bate v Amherst* (1663) T Raym 82; *Doe d Hayter v Joinville* (1802) 3 East 172 (to A's family, where no certain meaning could be given to the words); *Doe d Smith v Fleming* (1835) 2 Cr M & R 638 (to the younger branches of the family of W, where several interpretations were equally possible); *Smithwick v Hayden* (1887) 19 LR Ir 490, Ir CA ('any female niece or female relative of A provided she marries a person of the name of B, residing in C, and . . . a Roman Catholic'); *Re Stephenson, Donaldson v Bamber* [1897] 1 Ch 75, CA (gift to 'the children of the deceased son (named B) of my father's sister'; there were three such sons; no evidence to clear up the ambiguity appears to have been tendered); *Re Walter's Will Trusts, National Provincial Bank Ltd v Board of Guardians and Trustees for Relief of Jewish Poor, Registered* (1962) 106 Sol Jo 221 (bequest to each of 'my daughters who shall marry in the Jewish faith'; bequest void). Cf PARA 140 note 7. See also *Sir Litton Strode v Lady Russel* (1707) 2 Vern 621 at 624 per Tracy J; *Pyot v Pyot* (1749) 1 Ves Sen 335 at 337 (citing *Huckstep v Mathews* (1685) 1 Vern 362); *Flint v Warren* (1847) 15 Sim 626; *Murdoch v Brass* (1904) 6 F 841. A direction to trustees to make payments to such of the testator's children and grandchildren as they should think most deserving was held not void for uncertainty (*Mitchell's Trustees v Fraser* 1915 SC 350); nor was a direction to make payments to such of the testator's children as appeared to be most in need (*Magee v Magee* [1936] 3 All ER 15, PC), nor one to make payments to necessitous nieces and nephews (*Re Parker's Will, Kilroy and Callan v Parker and McGauran* [1966] IR 309); nor was a trust for distribution among political bodies in the United Kingdom void, all the bodies in the class being capable of ascertainment (*Re Ogden, Brydon v Samuel* [1933] Ch 678). Where it is not necessary for the whole class to be ascertained for the gift to take effect, a gift to 'any members of my family and any friends of mine' may be valid: *Re Barlow's Will Trusts* [1979] 1 All ER 296, [1979] 1 WLR 278. However, it is otherwise if the whole class has to be ascertained: *Re Lloyd's Trust Instruments* (24 June 1970, unreported), referred to in *Brown v Gould* [1972] Ch 53 at 56–57, [1971] 2 All ER 1505 at 1507. Cf the cases referred to in PARA 11 note 9. Where there is a power or a discretionary trust, certainty as to all the objects is not, in general, essential: see TRUSTS AND POWERS vol 98 (2013) PARAS 28, 94.
2   In the case of a testator dying on or after 1 January 1983, evidence of his intention may be admitted in certain circumstances: see PARA 195.
3   *Re Eden, Ellis v Crampton* [1957] 2 All ER 430, [1957] 1 WLR 788. As to uncertainty in relation to construction generally see PARA 262 et seq.
4   *Stubbs v Sargon* (1837) 2 Keen 255 at 269 per Lord Langdale MR; on appeal (1838) 3 My & Cr 507 at 511 per Lord Cottenham LC (partners, or the person to whom the testatrix might have disposed of her business).

5   See *D'Abo v Paget* [2000] All ER (D) 944 (hypothetical strict settlement formulated by will; '. . . on death of M . . . first to have become entitled in tail in possession of said property.' Two children of testator but only the elder could have been intended).

6   See PARA 60 et seq.

7   *Marsh v Kirby* (1634) 1 Rep Ch 76; *Burdet v Hopegood* (1718) 1 P Wms 486 at 487 (gift over in case testator should leave no son at the time of his death; held not to have taken effect owing to birth of posthumous son); *Mogg v Mogg* (1815) 1 Mer 654 at 705; *Blackburn v Stables* (1814) 2 Ves & B 367. As to the construction of certain gifts under which a child en ventre sa mère is considered as living see PARA 362.

8   *Blech v Blech* [2001] All ER (D) 141 (Dec). The court construed 'such of the children of my said son . . . as shall survive me' as including children conceived and born after death of the testatrix.

9   *Bentinck v Duke of Portland* (1877) 7 ChD 693 at 698. As to class gifts see PARA 302 et seq.

10   See PERPETUITIES AND ACCUMULATIONS vol 80 (2013) PARA 81 et seq.

(4) REQUIREMENTS FOR A VALID WILL: MENTAL ELEMENT

(i) Testamentary Capacity

A.   GENERAL TESTAMENTARY CAPACITY

46. Persons capable of making a valid will. A person aged 18 years or over and of sound mind[1] may make a valid will; but, except in specified cases[2], no will made by a person under the age of 18 years is valid[3].

A married woman is under no disability in disposing by will of her property[4]; and there is now no restriction on the testamentary capacity of persons convicted of crimes, and virtually no restriction on the testamentary capacity of aliens as such[5].

1   As to soundness of mind see PARA 48.

2   Ie in the case of a soldier, sailor or airman who is a minor (see PARAS 79–80, 898).

3   Wills Act 1837 s 7 (amended by the Family Law Reform Act 1969 s 3(1)(a)). As to when a person attains full age see CHILDREN AND YOUNG PERSONS vol 9 (2012) PARA 1. A will is to be construed to speak and take effect as if it had been executed immediately before the death of the testator (see the Wills Act 1837 s 24; and PARA 282); but this provision does not enlarge the testator's capacity to make a will; and a will made by a minor does not become valid by reason of his attaining the age of majority before his death. It seems that the Wills Act 1837 s 7 does not bind the Sovereign, who in legal contemplation is never a minor: see CHILDREN AND YOUNG PERSONS vol 9 (2012) PARA 2.

4   See the Law Reform (Married Women and Tortfeasors) Act 1935 ss 1, 2(1); and MATRIMONIAL AND CIVIL PARTNERSHIP LAW vol 72 (2015) PARA 252.

5   See PARA 897.

B.   MENTAL DISABILITY

47. Provision for persons who lack capacity. The Mental Capacity Act 2005 makes provision for when a person lacks capacity in relation to a matter or matters concerning his personal welfare or his property and affairs[1]. The Court of Protection[2] may, by making an order, make decisions about such matters on such a person's behalf, or appoint a person to make such decisions[3]. The scope of the court's power includes the execution of a will, where a person lacks the capacity to execute the will himself[4]. Guidance given under the Mental Health Acts 1959 and 1983 about making settlements or wills for a person lacking mental capacity can no longer be applied to decisions made under the Mental Capacity Act 2005[5].

The provisions of the Mental Capacity Act 2005 have no application to the question of whether a particular person had the requisite capacity to make a valid will at the time that he made it; that matter still remains to be decided according to established common law principles[6].

1   See the Mental Capacity Act 2005 ss 1–4; and MENTAL HEALTH AND CAPACITY vol 75 (2013) PARAS 603–606. A person lacks capacity in relation to a matter if at the material time he is unable to make a decision for himself in relation to the matter because of an impairment of, or a disturbance in the functioning of, the mind or the brain, irrespective of whether the disturbance is permanent or temporary: see s 2(1), (2); and MENTAL HEALTH AND CAPACITY vol 75 (2013) PARA 603.

2   As to the Court of Protection see MENTAL HEALTH AND CAPACITY vol 75 (2013) PARA 720 et seq.

3   See the Mental Capacity Act 2005 s 16(1), (2); and MENTAL HEALTH AND CAPACITY vol 75 (2013) PARAS 724, 734. The powers of the court to make such an order or to appoint such a person (a 'deputy') are subject to the provisions of the Act and, in particular, to s 1 ('the principles': see MENTAL HEALTH AND CAPACITY vol 75 (2013) PARA 601) and s 4 ('the best interests: see MENTAL HEALTH AND CAPACITY vol 75 (2013) PARA 606): see s 16(3); and MENTAL HEALTH AND CAPACITY vol 75 (2013) PARA 734. In addition, when deciding whether the appointment of a deputy is in the person's best interests, the court must have regard to the principle that a decision by the court is to be preferred and that the powers of the deputy must be as limited as practicable: see s 16(4); and MENTAL HEALTH AND CAPACITY vol 75 (2013) PARA 734.

4   See the Mental Capacity Act 2005 s 18(1)(i); and MENTAL HEALTH AND CAPACITY vol 75 (2013) PARA 727. Incapacity by reason of minority is not cured by the Act: no will may be made under s 18(1)(i) at a time when the person has not reached the age of 18: see s 18(2).

5   See *Re P* [2009] EWHC 163 (Ch), [2010] Ch 33, [2009] 2 All ER 1198, [2009] All ER (D) 160 (Feb). The Mental Capacity Act 2005 requires the court to ascertain what would be in the person's best interests in all the circumstances of the case, taking into account the matters set out in s 4. Each case turns on its own facts and a factor which is of magnetic importance in one case may be relatively insignificant in another superficially similar case: *Re Peter Jones* [2014] EWCOP 59. For many but not all people it is in their best interests that they be remembered with affection by their family as having done the right thing by their will: *Re M (vulnerable adult) (testamentary capacity)* [2009] EWHC 2525 (Fam), [2010] 3 All ER 682. However the onset of mental incapacity is not an opportunity for moral correction: *Re M (vulnerable adult) (testamentary capacity)* at [65] per Eldergill J. The court can remedy an omission but where a person with capacity has deliberately excluded someone from benefit and then loses capacity, it would, in ordinary circumstances, be inappropriate for the court to make a will including that person simply because it believes the testator 'ought' to have done so: *Re M (vulnerable adult) (testamentary capacity)*.

6   *Scammell v Farmer* [2008] EWHC 1100 (Ch), [2008] WTLR 1261, [2008] All ER (D) 296 (May); *Kicks v Leigh* [2014] EWHC 3926 (Ch), [2014] All ER (D) 295 (Nov); *Simon v Byford* [2014] EWCA Civ 280, 17 ITELR 536, [2014] WTLR 1097.

48. Soundness of mind, memory and understanding.

It is necessary for the validity of a will that the testator should be of sound mind, memory and understanding. These words have consistently been held to mean sound disposing mind, and to import sufficient[1] capacity to deal with and appreciate the various dispositions of property to which the testator is about to affix his signature[2]. Apart from persons who cannot make a valid will through unsoundness of mind[3] in the ordinary sense of that term, a person who is born deaf, dumb and blind has been said to be incapable of so doing[4]. Moreover, a person who is born deaf and dumb, but not blind, is prima facie incapable[5], but he can make a valid will if he is shown to have capacity and to understand what is written down[6]. Dementia arising from advanced age or produced by alcoholism or any other cause may destroy testamentary power[7], although it seems that soundness of mind, memory and understanding, sufficient to give testamentary capacity, as required by the established authorities, can subsist even in circumstances where there is clear evidence of some degree of dementia[8]. There will be cases where the testator will not have sufficient understanding, in the absence of an explanation, but the test is issue-specific and must be considered in the light of the nature and complexity of the particular transaction[9].

1   The question of capacity is almost always one of degree and does not depend solely on scientific or legal definition: see *Boyse v Rossborough* (1857) 6 HL Cas 2 at 45; *Boughton v Knight* (1873) LR 3 P & D 64 at 67; *Burdett v Thompson* (1873) LR 3 P & D 72n.
2   Shep Touch (8th Edn, 1826) p 403; *Marquess of Winchester's Case* (1598) 6 Co Rep 23a; *Hastilow v Stobie* (1865) LR 1 P & D 64 at 68.
        See also *Parker v Felgate* (1883) 8 PD 171, 47 JP 808 and *Clancy v Clancy* [2003] EWHC 1885 (Ch), [2003] 37 LS Gaz R 32, [2003] All ER (D) 536 (Jul) for the situation where there has been some reduction in mental capacity between the testator giving instructions for a will. See also *Perrins v Holland* [2010] EWCA Civ 840, [2011] 2 WLR 1086, [2010] All ER (D) 210 (Jul) (affg *Re Perrins, Perrins v Holland, Perrins v Dooney* [2009] EWHC 1945 (Ch), [2009] WTLR 1387) (testator suffering from multiple sclerosis was held to have had sufficient capacity, knowledge and approval and had validly executed will by use of rubber stamp). As to the power of the Court of Protection to order the execution of a will for a patient see PARA 51 note 4.
3   See Bac Abr, Idiots and Lunatics (F); Bac Abr, Wills (B). As to delusion as the test of insanity see PARA 52.
4   Jarman on Wills (1st Edn) 29; Jarman on Wills (8th Edn) 50; and see Co Litt 42b. Cf, however, the example of Mary Kenny, who was able to write a book although she became deaf, dumb and blind at a very early age. See also PARA 893.
5   Swinburne on Wills (7th Edn) Pt II s 10.
6   *Re Harper* (1843) 6 Man & G 732 (deed); Swinburne on Wills (7th Edn) Pt II s 4 pl 2; s 10 pl 2. As to the evidence required see *Re Owston* (1862) 2 Sw & Tr 461; *Re Geale* (1864) 3 Sw & Tr 431.
7   See *Ridgeway v Darwin* (1802) 8 Ves 65; *Ex p Cranmer* (1806) 12 Ves 445 at 452; *Sherwood v Sanderson* (1815) 19 Ves 280 at 283; *Griffiths v Robins* (1818) 3 Madd 191. As to the effect of alcohol see in particular *Ayrey v Hill* (1824) 2 Add 206 at 209–210; and *Re Heinke, Westminster Bank Ltd v Massey* (1959) Times, 21 January. As to epilepsy see *Foot v Stanton* (1856) Dea & Sw 19. For a discussion of the degree of dementia necessary to render the testator incapable see *Ingram v Wyatt* (1828) 1 Hag Ecc 384 at 400 (revsd on the facts, but not as to capacity, sub nom *Wyatt v Ingram* (1831) 3 Hag Ecc 466). See also PARA 311. As to medical evidence see PARA 893.
8   See *Hoff v Atherton* [2004] EWCA Civ 1554, [2004] All ER (D) 314 (Nov) (the evidence of dementia was sufficient to require the propounder to prove the testatrix's capacity in accordance with the authorities and this burden was discharged on the totality of the evidence) See also PARA 53 note 1 and the cases mentioned therein.
9   *Hoff v Atherton* [2004] EWCA Civ 1554 at [35] [2004] All ER (D) 314 (Nov) per Peter Gibson LJ. See also *Re Beaney* [1978] 2 All ER 595, [1978] 1 WLR 770 (inter vivos transaction, mother giving away almost entire estate to one child and effectively disinheriting the other two; held that she was not aware of that effect and that the degree of understanding for such a gift should be as high as with a will; gift held void). As to the burden of proof see PARA 899 et seq.

49.   Meaning of 'sound disposing mind'. In order to be of sound disposing mind a testator must not only be able to understand that he is by his will giving his property to one or more objects of his regard, but he must also have capacity to comprehend and to recollect the extent[1] of his property and the nature of the claims of others whom by his will he is excluding from participation in that property[2]. Mere forgetfulness to comprehend some property, or to recollect the claims of those excluded, would not seem sufficient to invalidate the will, unless such forgetfulness establishes incapacity to remember sufficient facts to displace illusory notions and beliefs[3]. It is essential that no disorder of the mind should poison his affections, pervert his sense of right or prevent the exercise of his natural faculties, that no delusion should influence his will in disposing of his property and bring about a disposal of it which, if the mind had been sound, would not have been made[4]. Perversion of moral feeling does not constitute unsoundness of mind[5]. Eccentricity alone does not prevent a man from disposing of his property by will[6]; and the extravagance of the provisions of a will is not necessarily in itself conclusive evidence of unsoundness of mind[7]. It is not necessary that a testator should view his will with the eye of a lawyer and comprehend its provisions in their legal form[8]. It may be that certain conditions (including the effects of bereavement) can affect the testator's power to make decisions concerning his dispositions, without necessarily affecting the established recognised indicia of a sound disposing mind, or the general comprehension of the testator; nevertheless, the capacity of the testator to make his own decisions, rather than acquiescing in those of others must be established[9].

Where there is doubt about the testamentary capacity of a testator, this may also raise a question about whether there has been sufficient knowledge and approval of the will, but these are conceptually distinct matters and should be separately considered, on their particular facts[10]. Where such doubts arise, they may affect the incidence of the burden of proof[11].

1   As to a broad summary of the necessary indicia for testamentary capacity see *Banks v Goodfellow* (1870) LR 5 QB 549, per Cockburn CJ at 565. It has been objected that there is not a single case of incapacity decided on the ground that the testator did not understand the extent of the property of which he was disposing (see 35 Conveyancer (NS) (July–August 1971) 303) but the statement of the law set out in the text has stood otherwise unchallenged, and a contrary proposition would seem to conflict with the assumptions behind the former rule that a will disposed only of property existing at the date of the will. This rule was changed by the Wills Act 1837 ss 3, 24 (as originally enacted): see *Re Portal and Lamb* (1885) 30 ChD 50 at 55, CA, per Lindley LJ.

2   Medical evidence is often necessary. The test would seem to be whether there is sufficient capacity in the areas most relevant to making the will. From the authorities these can be listed as: (1) understanding that by the will he is disposing of his property on his death to objects of his regard; (2) knowledge of the probable extent and value of the property being disposed of at the time of the will; (3) appreciation of the possible moral claims of relatives and others not benefited by the will; and (4) sufficient memory at least to react when reminded of facts relevant to these areas. See the analysis of these indicia in *Hoff v Atherton* [2004] EWCA Civ 1554, [2004] All ER (D) 314 (Nov); a further question, arising from (4), whether the inability of the testator to remember matters, without further reminder or explanation, will indicate lack of capacity, seems to remain at large for the particular judge. Capacity is not a memory test and there is no need for the testator to understand the significance of the will on others: *Simon v Byford* [2014] EWCA Civ 280, [2014] All ER (D) 154 (Mar). See also *Allen v Emery* [2005] EWHC 2389 (Ch), 8 ITELR 358, [2005] All ER (D) 175 (Oct) (frail and terminally ill testatrix, instructed solicitor whom she did not know; held: the presence of a doctor to formally assess capacity and understanding was a desirable precaution, but the question of capacity was one for the court on the evidence as a whole; testatrix did have capacity).

   Where the opportunity occurs, a psychiatric examination as to these matters to ascertain the degree of capacity in the proposed testator will reduce the risk that the will may be disputed. As to medical evidence see further PARA 893. It has been said that, if distinctions can be drawn between various degrees of soundness of mind, then whatever is the highest degree of soundness is required to make a will: *Burdett v Thompson* (1873) LR 3 P & D 72n at 73n per Sir J Hannen, explaining dicta by him in *Boughton v Knight* (1873) LR 3 P & D 64 at 72. See also *Re Park, Park v Park* [1954] P 112, [1953] 2 All ER 1411, CA, which disapproves the view that making a will involves a higher degree of mental capacity than marriage as a general proposition, while recognising that different acts may require different levels of mental capacity (eg a complicated as compared with a simple will). It seems that where an inter vivos deed of gift of a testatrix's most valuable asset is made at the same time as her will is executed, the level of understanding required for each transaction is the same: see *Wainwright v Wilson* [2006] All ER (D) 180 (Nov) (after an earlier finding that the testatrix did not have testamentary capacity for the will, the deed of gift was ordered to be set aside for lack of capacity and to fall back into her intestate estate). See also *Re Beaney* [1978] 2 All ER 595, [1978] 1 WLR 770; and PARA 48 note 9.

3   *Harwood v Baker* (1840) 3 Moo PCC 282 at 291; *Banks v Goodfellow* (1870) LR 5 QB 549 at 569; *Burdett v Thompson* (1873) LR 3 P & D 72n; *Re Belliss, Polson v Parrott* (1929) 45 TLR 452 (failure of a testatrix aged 93 to remember past dispositions to her daughters); *Battan Singh v Amirchand* [1948] AC 161 at 170, [1948] 1 All ER 152 at 155–156, PC.

4   *Banks v Goodfellow* (1870) LR 5 QB 549 at 565; and see *Hope v Campbell* [1899] AC 1, HL. The requirement of freedom from influence by mental disorder or delusion was examined in detail by May LJ in *Sharp v Adam* [2006] EWCA Civ 449, 10 ITELR 419, [2006] All ER (D) 277 (Apr), where the court considered it to be as much about mood as about cognition (expert evidence in the case related to cognition but little relevant to questions of mood). It seems that the question of mood as well as cognition must be addressed, when applying the test for capacity, and that modern

neurology and neuro-psychology is to be considered capable of addressing affections of the mood in scientific terms. See also *Kostic v Chaplin* [2007] EWHC 2298 (Ch), 10 ITELR 364, [2007] All ER (D) 203 (Oct) (testator's natural affection for a claimant distorted by delusion, causing new wills to be made by her; held testator lacked capacity for new wills) and PARA 52.

5 *Frere v Peacocke* (1846) 1 Rob Eccl 442 at 456.
6 *Pilkington v Gray* [1899] AC 401 at 407, PC. The mind does not have to be perfectly balanced: *Boughton v Knight* (1873) LR 3 P & D 64 at 66.
7 *Austen v Graham* (1854) 8 Moo PCC 493. However, the rationality of a will, if made without assistance, may be strong evidence that it was executed in a lucid interval: see also PARA 50 note 1. Conversely, the irrationality of a will may suggest that the testator's judgement was impaired: see *Sharp v Adam* [2006] EWCA Civ 449, 10 ITELR 419.
8 *Banks v Goodfellow* (1870) LR 5 QB 549 at 567.
9 See *Key v Key* [2010] EWHC 408 (Ch) at [96], [115], [2010] All ER (D) 155 (Apr) where Briggs J was prepared to make a slight development of the Banks v Goodfellow test (see note 1), to take into account decision-making powers, rather than just comprehension; some affective disorders, such as depression, including that caused by bereavement, are more likely to affect powers of decision-making than comprehension; a person in that condition may have the capacity to understand the scope of his property and the range of the moral claims upon him, without having the mental energy to make any decision of his own about whom to benefit.
10 See PARAS 54, 55; and *Hoff v Atherton* [2004] EWCA Civ 1554, [2004] All ER (D) 314 (Nov).
11 See *Key v Key* [2010] EWHC 408 (Ch) at [97], [2010] All ER (D) 155 (Apr). See also PARA 903.

50. Time at which capacity must exist. The sound disposing mind and memory must exist at the actual moment of execution of the will[1], but the measure of testamentary capacity need not be as complete at the time of execution as it was at the time of giving instructions for the will[2], and it would seem that when a will has been drawn in accordance with the instructions of the testator, while of sound disposing mind, a perfect understanding of all the terms of the will at the time of execution may not be necessary[3]. It also seems that clauses introduced by a solicitor after taking instructions and not subsequently acknowledged or approved will be rejected[4]. Where the testator's understanding of the will at the time of execution is doubtful, proof of mere execution is insufficient[5].

1 See *Billinghurst v Vickers (formerly Leonard)* (1810) 1 Phillim 187; *Wood v Wood* (1811) 1 Phillim 357. See also *Eady v Waring* [1974] 2 OR (2d) 627, Ont CA; *Carr v Beavan* [2008] EWHC 2582 (Ch), [2008[All ER (D) 289 (Oct). As to lucid intervals see *Cartwright v Cartwright* (1793) 1 Phillim 90 at 100; *Banks v Goodfellow* (1870) LR 5 QB 549 at 557; and see PARA 900. See also *Baker v Baker* [2008] EWHC 937 (Ch), [2008] 2 FLR 767; and *Scammell v Farmer* [2008] EWHC 1100 (Ch), [2008] WTLR 1261, [2008] All ER (D) 296 (Mar).
2 It has been said that the principle stated in the text should be applied with the greatest caution when the testator does not himself give instructions to the solicitor but gives them to a lay intermediary who repeats them to the solicitor; in such a case, before presuming validity, the court must be strictly satisfied that there is no ground for suspicion, and that the instructions given to the intermediary were clearly understood and faithfully reported by him and rightly apprehended by the solicitor: *Battan Singh v Amirchand* [1948] AC 161 at 169, [1948] 1 All ER 152 at 155, PC.
3 *Bennet v Duke of Manchester* (1854) 23 LTOS 331; *Parker v Felgate* (1883) 8 PD 171; *Perera v Perera* [1901] AC 354, PC; *Re Wallace, Solicitor of the Duchy of Cornwall v Batten* [1952] 2 TLR 925; and see *Thomas v Jones* [1928] P 162; *Perrins v Holland* [2010] EWCA Civ 840, [2011] 2 WLR 1086, [2010] All ER (D) 210 (Jul). See also *Clancy v Clancy* [2003] EWHC 1885 (Ch), [2003] 37 LS Gaz R 32, [2003] All ER (D) 536 (Jul), where the *Parker v Felgate* principle was applied; *Parker v Felgate* and *Clancy v Clancy* also applied in *Otuka v Alozie* [2006] EWHC 3493 (Ch), [2005] All ER (D) 265 (Dec). See also *Singellos v Singellos; Re Singellos* [2010] EWHC 2353 (Ch), [2011] Ch 324, [2010] All ER (D) 130 (Sep).
4 *Parker v Felgate* (1883) 8 PD 171 at 174 per Hannen P.
5 *Billinghurst v Vickers (formerly Leonard)* (1810) 1 Phillim 187 at 200.

51. Will made while person lacks testamentary capacity. A will made while a person lacks testamentary capacity is void[1], and where a person is handicapped by mental illness to the extent that his estate has been or could have been made subject to the control of the court[2], but nevertheless purports to make a will, letters of administration will be granted as in the case of intestacy[3]. A will executed during incapacity does not become valid by the testator's subsequent recovery[4]. A will may be admitted to probate and a codicil, executed shortly afterwards, refused probate on the ground of a lack of sound disposing mind at the time of execution of the codicil[5].

There is provision for the Court of Protection[6] to inquire whether any person has in his possession or control or has knowledge of any testamentary document executed by a person lacking or having doubtful mental capacity and to direct its production[7].

1   Swinburne on Wills (7th Edn) Pt II ss 3, 4. As to medical evidence of incapacity see PARA 893.
2   It has been said that the need for control of the court is not a good test especially in the case of delusions which can be harmless: see *Re Bohrmann, Caesar and Watmough v Bohrmann* [1938] 1 All ER 271 at 276 per Langton J. As to the Court of Protection see MENTAL HEALTH AND CAPACITY vol 75 (2013) PARA 720 et seq.
3   *Re Rich* [1892] P 143.
4   *Arthur v Bokenham* (1708) 11 Mod Rep 148 at 157; Shep Touch (8th Edn, 1826) p 413. Re-execution alone can validate a will made during incapacity: see *Willock v Noble* (1875) LR 7 HL 580 at 591 per Lord Cairns LC. Where a patient lacks testamentary capacity, a will may, in certain circumstances, be made on his behalf: see PARA 47.
5   *Brouncker v Brouncker* (1812) 2 Phillim 57.
6   As to the Court of Protection see MENTAL HEALTH AND CAPACITY vol 75 (2013) PARA 720.
7   See the wide powers of the Court of Protection under the Mental Capacity Act 2005 Pt 2 (ss 45–61), particularly ss 47–49; the Court of Protection Rules 2007, SI 2007/1744; and MENTAL HEALTH AND CAPACITY vol 75 (2013) PARA 721.

52.   Delusions. Unsoundness of mind exists where there is a defect of reason, consisting in its total or partial absence or in its disturbance. It is frequently marked by the existence of delusion, that is, belief in facts which no rational person could believe[1]. It has been said that delusion is the test of insanity[2] and that the absence or presence of delusion, in the sense of an unreasoned belief in the existence of something extravagant which has no existence save in the patient's heated imagination, forms the true and only test or criterion of the absence or presence of insanity. Delusion in this sense, and insanity are convertible terms[3].

The existence of a delusion compatible with the retention of the general powers and faculties of the mind is not, however, sufficient to overthrow the will, unless the delusion is such as was calculated to influence the testator in making it[4]. Therefore, the mere existence of a delusion in the mind of a person making a disposition is not sufficient to avoid it, even though connected with the subject matter of the disposition, but, once a delusion has been shown to exist, the burden of proving capacity is on the person insisting on the disposition[5]. It is a question of fact whether the delusion affected the disposition[6]. In some cases a testator's natural affection for a person may have become poisoned or distorted by the testator's delusion to such an extent that he has been wholly unable to dispose of his property in the way he would have done, had he been of sound mind[7].

1   *Dew v Clark and Clark* (1826) 3 Add 79 at 90; *Boughton v Knight* (1873) LR 3 P & D 64 at 67; *Sivewright v Sivewright's Trustees* 1920 SC (HL) 63 at 64. See also *Ramsey v Ramsay* [2015] All ER (D) 32 (Sep).
2   See *Dew v Clark and Clark* (1826) 3 Add 79 at 90; *Boughton v Knight* (1873) LR 3 P & D 64 at 67; *Sivewright v Sivewright's Trustees* 1920 SC (HL) 63 at 64.
3   See *Boughton v Knight* (1873) LR 3 P & D 64 at 68–69 per Sir J Hannen, quoting *Dew v Clark and Clark* (1826) 3 Add 79 at 90 per Sir J Nicholl.
4   *Banks v Goodfellow* (1870) LR 5 QB 549 at 571, followed in *Murfett v Smith* (1887) 12 PD 116, DC; *Smee v Smee* (1879) 5 PD 84 at 91.
5   *Waring v Waring* (1848) 6 Moo PCC 341; *Smith v Tebbitt* (1867) LR 1 P & D 398 (delusion that testator was the Holy Ghost); and see *Jenkins v Morris* (1880) 14 ChD 674, CA. It seems that if there is enough evidence to raise the possibility that a defect of mind interfered with a

consideration of the matters which should be taken into account on the making of a will, even if it does not establish that a particular delusion directly affected the terms of the will, that will be enough to place a requirement for positive evidence of capacity on the propounder of the will: *Ledger v Wootton* [2007] EWHC 90 (Ch), [2007] All ER (D) 99 (Oct).

6 See *Dew v Clark and Clark* (1826) 3 Add 79 at 90, where the delusion was held to avoid the will. If a delusion affects only one clause of a will, the will is valid with the exception of that clause: *Re Bohrmann, Caesar and Watmough v Bohrmann* [1938] 1 All ER 271.

7 See *Kostic v Chaplin* [2007] EWHC 2298 (Ch), 10 ITELR 364, [2007] All ER (D) 203 (Oct) (testator made new will leaving everything to political party, while affected by delusions of violent antipathy towards natural beneficiary, for whom he formerly felt affection).

53. Senile incapacity. In cases where unsoundness of mind arises from want of intelligence or memory occasioned by defective organisation, supervening physical infirmity or the decay of advancing age, as distinguished from a functional mental illness, that defect of intelligence or memory is also a cause of incapacity. In these cases, however, although the mental power may be reduced below the ordinary standard, yet if there is sufficient intelligence to understand and appreciate the testamentary act in its different bearings, and sufficient memory to react when prompted, the power to make a will remains[1].

1 *Banks v Goodfellow* (1870) LR 5 QB 549 at 564, 566, 568; *Battan Singh v Amirchand* [1948] AC 161, [1948] 1 All ER 152, PC; *Blackman v Man* [2007] EWHC 3162 (Ch), [2007] All ER (D) 118 (Dec) (where capacity to make a will and knowledge and approval of its contents were established in a testatrix, suffering from mild dementia, who had understood the implications of making the will and had contemplated the claimant's claims to her estate). See *Simon v Byford* [2014] EWCA Civ 280, [2014] All ER (D) 154 (Mar) (capacity is not a memory test and there is no need for the testator to understand the significance of the will on others). See also *Carr v Beavan* [2008] EWHC 2582 (Ch), [2008] All ER (D) 289 (Oct) from which it seems that a diagnosis of mild or even moderate dementia is not of itself an obstacle to satisfying the requirement of testamentary capacity, because a testator may lack capacity upon a particular day but may possess it upon a particular day many months later. Senility involves a global impairment of functions leading to deterioration in personal habits and sensibility as well as intelligence and memory. There is a simple medical rating scale available to show degrees of functional incapacity as well as numerous memory tests. See *Devas v Mackay* [2009] EWHC 1951 (Ch), [2009] All ER (D) 09 (Aug) (ample evidence of advanced degeneration in condition of testatrix to show lack of capacity); see also PARA 55 note 4. See also PARAS 48 note 7, 49 note 2.

(ii) Knowledge and Approval of Testator

54. Testamentary intention necessary for a valid will. It is not necessary that the testator should intend to perform, or be aware that he has performed, a testamentary act[1], provided that he had the clear intention to make a revocable ambulatory disposition of his property which is to take effect on death[2]. Such intention may be proved by extrinsic evidence[3], and, if the formalities of execution have been complied with, the document may be admitted to probate[4]. The intention at the time of execution must be that the document should have immediate and unconditional effect as such revocable ambulatory disposition[5]. Where there is doubt whether a document is testamentary, the burden of proving that it is testamentary is on the person propounding it[6].

1 *Milnes v Foden* (1890) 15 PD 105 at 107 per Hannen P. Thus the following instruments have been held to be testamentary: a deed of gift (*Habergham v Vincent* (1793) 2 Ves 204; *Thorold v Thorold* (1809) 1 Phillim 1; *Re Morgan* (1866) LR 1 P & D 214); articles of agreement (*Green v Froud* (1674) 3 Keb 310); a draft on a banker (*Bartholomew and Brown v Henley* (1820) 3 Phillim 317); a direction for payment by bankers (*Jones v Nicolay* (1850) 2 Rob Eccl 288); an order on a savings bank (*Re Marsden* (1860) 1 Sw & Tr 542); a letter (*Denny v Barton and Rashleigh* (1818) 2 Phillim 575; *Re Mundy* (1860) 2 Sw & Tr 119; cf *Passmore v Passmore* (1811) 1 Phillim 216 at 218); an invalid nomination under the Industrial and Provident Societies Act 1893 (*Re Baxter* [1903] P 12; and see PARA 5 note 3; and FINANCIAL INSTITUTIONS vol 48 (2015) PARA 992). Other informal instruments admitted to probate under the old law are mentioned in *Masterman*

v Maberly (1829) 2 Hag Ecc 235 at 247; and in *Griffin and Amos v Ferard* (1835) 1 Curt 97. See also *Rigden v Vallier* (1751) 2 Ves Sen 252 at 258.

2 *Re Berger* [1990] Ch 118 at 129–130, [1989] 1 All ER 591 at 599. See also *King's Proctor v Daines* (1830) 3 Hag Ecc 218 at 221; *Re Webb* (1864) 3 Sw & Tr 482; *Corbett v Newey* [1998] Ch 57, [1996] 2 All ER 914, CA.

3 *Re English* (1864) 3 Sw & Tr 586; *National Trust for Places of Historic Interest and Natural Beauty v Royal National Institute for the Blind* [1999] All ER (D) 81, sub nom *Re Chapman* (1998–99) 1 ITELR 863. See also PARA 708. Similarly, evidence may be given that the document was not intended to be testamentary, although in form it appears to be so: *Trevelyan v Trevelyan* (1810) 1 Phillim 149; *Nichols v Nichols* (1814) 2 Phillim 180; *Lister v Smith* (1863) 3 Sw & Tr 282; *Re Nosworthy* (1865) 4 Sw & Tr 44. A statement in the document that it is not intended to be a will seems to be conclusive: *Ferguson-Davie v Ferguson-Davie* (1890) 15 PD 109. As to when documents referred to and identified in a will may be incorporated in it and included in the probate see PARA 711.

4 *Cock v Cooke* (1866) LR 1 P & D 241; *Robertson v Smith* (1870) LR 2 P & D 43; *Re Slinn* (1890) 15 PD 156. See also *Cameron's Trustees v Mackenzie* 1915 SC 313, Ct of Sess; *Re Williams, Williams v Ball* [1917] 1 Ch 1, CA; *Warwick v Warwick* (1918) 34 TLR 475, CA. Following the formalities for execution of a will is itself strong evidence of a testamentary intention: *National Trust for Places of Historic Interest and Natural Beauty v Royal National Institute for the Blind* [1999] All ER (D) 81, sub nom *Re Chapman* (1998–99) 1 ITELR 863.

5 The dispositions in a will may be conditional, but its execution may not: see *Corbett v Newey* [1998] Ch 57, [1996] 2 All ER 914, CA; and see PARAS 7, 60.

6 *Griffin and Amos v Ferard* (1835) 1 Curt 97; *Coventry v Williams* (1844) 3 Curt 787; *Napper v Napper* (1846) 10 Jur 342. Before the jurisdiction to rectify wills was conferred (see PARA 187), the probate court would not add a word to the will, but it might omit a word from the probate, if necessary: *Re Swords* [1952] P 368, [1952] 2 All ER 281; *Re Cocke* [1960] 2 All ER 289, [1960] 1 WLR 491; *Re Morris, Lloyds Bank Ltd v Peake* [1971] P 62, [1970] 1 All ER 1057; *Re Phelan* [1972] Fam 33, [1971] 3 All ER 1256. Cf *Re Horrocks, Taylor v Kershaw* [1939] P 198, [1939] 1 All ER 579, CA; and see PARA 739.

55. Effect of want of knowledge or approval. Although knowledge of the contents of a will and approval of it by the testator, at the time of its execution, are essential to the validity of the will[1], this is normally assumed in the case of a competent testator from the fact that he has duly executed it[2]. The burden of proving these facts is assumed by everyone who propounds a will[3]. However, whenever the circumstances under which the will has been prepared raise a well-grounded suspicion that it does not express the testator's mind, the court ought not to pronounce in favour of it unless that suspicion is removed[4]. The question of whether the testator understood what was in the will and what its effect would be is a single issue to be determined by reference to all the relevant evidence and to the appropriate inferences to be drawn from the totality of the evidence available. The single issue approach is generally preferable to considering the issue in two stages, asking first whether the claimant has made out a prima facie case of lack of knowledge and approval and, if so, secondly whether the defendants had rebutted that case[5].

In such suspicious circumstances there will be cases where the court will require, in order to establish knowledge and approval, proof that the testator understood not just the nature of the testamentary provision that he proposed to make, but also its effect[6].

There seems to be a possibility that a testator can have known and approved of a specific part or parts of a will but not of the remainder of it; such circumstances will be rare and it would not be proper for the court to pronounce against part of a will as a means of expressing its disapproval of the propounder[7].

If the circumstances are such as to indicate that the testator may have been impaired, for whatever reason, in his ability to perceive, to be aware of, or comprehend the contents and import of a will, that may raise a suspicion that he does not have knowledge of its contents, approve of it, or both. These circumstances may or may not raise questions about mental or physical inability of the testator; they may or may not raise questions about the participation of other persons in the events leading to the will, or they could raise questions about all of these things. The gravity of the suspicion will vary from serious fraud (which may or may not be expressly pleaded)[8], to questions of mistake as to documents signed[9] or words used[10] that do not raise questions of want of probity. Nevertheless, the circumstances may still indicate a lack of knowledge and approval. The degree of suspicion and the evidence required to satisfy the court of the deceased's knowledge and approval varies according to the circumstances of the particular case[11], but there is no overriding consideration of morality and the standard of proof is only ever the civil standard of the balance of probability[12].

Where it is asserted that there is a lack of knowledge and approval associated with a lack of testamentary capacity, the two matters are conceptually distinct and should not be conflated; testamentary capacity is a prerequisite for a finding of knowledge and approval but it is not necessary to show proof of actual knowledge in every case of doubtful capacity. It is open to a court to infer that a testator who did know what was written in the document that he signed did, in fact understand what he was doing[13] but the court will still need to be satisfied that the testator had intended to make those particular dispositions in order to have approved them[14].

1   See *Hastilow v Stobie* (1865) LR 1 P & D 64; *Guardhouse v Blackburn* (1866) LR 1 P & D 109.
2   *Barry v Butlin* (1838) 2 Moo PCC 480. See also PARA 897.
3   *Cleare v Cleare* (1869) LR 1 P & D 655. The requirement of capacity to understand is a pre-requisite to a finding of knowledge and approval: see *Hoff v Atherton* [2004] EWCA Civ 1554, [2004] All ER (D) 314 (Nov).
4   *Tyrrell v Painton* [1894] P 151 at 159, CA, per Davey LJ; *Wintle v Nye* [1959] 1 All ER 552, [1959] 1 WLR 284, HL; *Gill v Woodall* [2010] EWCA Civ 1430, [2011] 3 WLR 85, [2010] All ER (D) 167 (Dec). The circumstances which are held to excite the suspicions of the court must be limited to circumstances attending, or at least relevant to, the preparation and execution of the will itself: see *Re R* [1951] P 10 at 13, [1950] 2 All ER 117 at 120 per Willmer J. See now *Scammell v Farmer* [2008] EWHC 1100 (Ch), [2008] WTLR 1261, [2008] All ER (D) 296 (May) (undue influence claim not made out despite beneficiary of last will attempting persuasion of testatrix to change will, admitting to destroying earlier will and obstructing investigation by donees under earlier will). See also PARA 901 et seq. For the evidential requirements for proof of knowledge and approval see *Fuller v Strum* [2001] EWCA Civ 1879, [2002] 2 All ER 87, 4 ITELR 454; *Reynolds v Reynolds* [2005] EWHC 6 (Ch), [2005] All ER (D) 70 (Jan). See *Devas v Mackay* [2009] EWHC 1951 (Ch), [2009] All ER (D) 09 (Aug) (testatrix, diagnosed with symptoms of dementia, paralysed and largely unable to communicate was under control of carer at time that she executed a home-made will; the will was witnessed by carer and made carer's son sole beneficiary; held, that there were suspicious circumstances and that testamentary capacity and knowledge and approval had not been established to the satisfaction of the court).
5   *Gill v Woodall* [2010] EWCA Civ 1430 at [22], [64], [71], [2011] 3 WLR 85, [2010] All ER (D) 167 (Dec) per Lord Neuberger MR.
6   See *Re Good, Carapeto v Good* [2002] EWHC 640 (Ch), [2002] All ER (D) 141 (Apr); affd sub nom *Carapeto v Good* [2002] EWCA Civ 944 (suspicious circumstances and assertion of undue influence upon testatrix by housekeeper and her family, in making new will which largely substituted housekeeper's family for her own (who would take under intestacy); held that she knew and approved of will).
7   See *Fuller v Strum* [2001] EWCA Civ 1879, [2002] 2 All ER 87 at 98 per Peter Gibson LJ and at 106–107 per Chadwick LJ.
8   See *Wintle v Nye* [1959] 1 All ER 552, [1959] 1 WLR 284, HL, where in the absence of any express plea of fraud or undue influence a solicitor, having little or no claim upon the testatrix and who had procured a large benefit in her will, was permitted to be cross-examined to the effect that if the testatrix did not know and approve of her will, it was because of fraud. Cf *Boudh v Bodh* [2007] EWCA Civ 1019, [2007] All ER (D) 384 (Oct) (dispute concerning two wills of even date, conflicting evidence and one will found to be fraudulent but both prepared by same persons (who did not benefit) and no real change in gifts).
9   See *Re Hunt* (1875) LR 3 P & D 250, 39 JP 744; *Re Meyer* [1908] P 353, 77 LJP 150.
10   See *Re Horrocks, Taylor v Kershaw* [1939] P 198, [1939] 1 All ER 579.

11 *Boudh v Bodh* [2007] EWCA Civ 1019, [2007] All ER (D) 384 (Oct) per Mummery LJ considering dicta of Viscount Simonds in *Wintle v Nye* [1959] 1 All ER 552, [1959] 1 WLR 284, HL (the circumstances may raise a suspicion that the testator did not know and approve of the contents of the document that is so grave that it can hardly be removed). See also *Wyniczenko v Plucinska-Surowka* [2005] EWHC 2794 (Ch), 8 ITELR 385, [2005] All ER (D) 245 (Nov).

12 *Fuller v Strum* [2001] EWCA Civ 1879, [2002] 2 All ER 87, 4 ITELR 4541. See also *Wyniczenko v Plucinska-Surowka* [2005] EWHC 2794 (Ch), 8 ITELR 385, [2005] All ER (D) 245 (Nov) (assertion of forgery of testatrix's signature not made out, but strong evidence of suspicious circumstances proved want of knowledge and approval of will).

13 *Hoff v Atherton* [2004] EWCA Civ 1554, [2004] All ER (D) 314 (Nov) (Court of Appeal upheld the judge's finding that no further explanation of a straightforward will was needed in the circumstances). Cf *Westendorp v Warwick* [2006] EWHC 915 (Ch), [2006] All ER (D) 248 (Ch).

14 See *Key v Key* [2010] EWHC 408 (Ch) at [116], [2010] All ER (D) 155 (Apr) (testator could not approve will where he lacked the necessary decision-making capacity to make a valid will). See also PARA 49 text and note 9.

(iii) Effect of Undue Influence, Force and Fraud

56. Undue influence and force. A will or part of a will may be set aside as having been obtained by undue influence[1]. If the execution of the will is not in dispute the party alleging undue influence has the right to begin[2], and must discharge the burden of proof[3] by clear evidence that the influence was in fact exercised[4]. It is not enough to prove that the facts are consistent with the hypothesis of undue influence; what must be shown is that the facts are inconsistent with any other hypothesis; the question for the court is whether, in making his disposition, the testator had acted as a free agent[5].

To constitute undue influence there must be coercion[6]; pressure of whatever character, whether acting on the fears or the hopes, if so exerted as to overpower the volition without convincing the judgment, is a species of restraint under which no valid will can be made[7]. The mere fact that the testator was knowingly highly dependent upon the person against whom undue influence is alleged, and possibly even under an awareness that that person may remove their support for the testator, may not be enough to provide evidence of undue influence, by itself; similarly, the fact of such a person taking part in meetings where the testator's affairs were discussed[8].

A person may exercise an unbounded influence over another, which may be a very bad influence, without its being undue influence in the legal sense of the word[9]. Undue influence may be found against a person who had died before the execution of the will, on the ground that the testatrix was under that person's complete control until his death, and was therefore rendered incapable of making a fresh will free from such undue influence[10].

1 As to the allegation of undue influence in probate and the right to cross-examine with the inference of, but without alleging, undue influence see PARA 875. The test of undue influence in probate is very different from the equitable presumption; there is no presumption of undue influence in testamentary matters, per Lord Cranworth in *Boyse v Rossborough* (1857) 6 HL Cas 2, 48 at 51: see PARA 57. If a part only of a will is shown to be obtained by undue influence, that part may be rejected and the remainder pronounced for, providing that the part rejected is severable and distinct: *Rhodes v Rhodes* (1882) 7 App Cas 192, 198.

2 *Hutley v Grimstone* (1879) 5 PD 24; *Craig v Lamoureux* [1920] AC 349, PC. See, however, *Re Parry's Estate, Parry v Fraser* [1977] 1 All ER 309, [1977] 1 WLR 93n.

3 *Craig v Lamoureux* [1920] AC 349, PC; *Boyse v Rossborough* (1857) 6 HL Cas 2 at 49; *Parfitt v Lawless* (1872) LR 2 P & D 462.

4 *Bur Singh v Uttam Singh* (1911) LR 38 Ind App 13, PC. Where a defendant stands accused of having exercised undue influence over a testator, the court ought not to draw adverse inferences from his failure to appear at proceedings or to provide evidence: *Killick v Pountney* [1999] All ER (D) 365, (1999) Times, 30 April.

5   *Re Edwards, Edwards v Edwards* [2007] All ER (D) 46 (May), per Lewison J. See also *Papouis v West* [2004] EWHC 396 (Ch) sub nom *Papouis v Gibson-West* [2004] All ER (D) 98 (Mar) sub nom *Re Bennett, Papouis v Gibson-West* [2004] WTLR 485; and *Scammell v Farmer* [2008] EWHC 1100 (Ch), [2008] WTLR 1261, [2008] All ER (D) 296 (May).

6   *Wingrove v Wingrove* (1885) 11 PD 81 at 82 per Sir J Hannen P ('it is only when the will of the person who becomes a testator is coerced into doing that which he does not desire to do, that it is undue influence'). See also *Williams v Goude* (1828) 1 Hag Ecc 577 at 581 per Sir J Nicholl ('the influence to vitiate an act must amount to force and coercion destroying free agency'); and *Cattermole v Prisk* [2006] 1 FLR 693 at 700 per Judge Norris QC ('the essence of undue influence is coercion, influence or persuasion itself not being illegitimate'); *Re Devillebichot; Brennan v Prior* [2013] EWHC 2867 (Ch), [2013] WTLR 1701, [2013] All ER (D) 243 (Sep) (no evidence of coercion or pressure such as to have overpowered freedom of action); *Schomberg Taylor* [2013] EWHC 2269 Ch, [2013] All ER (D) 74 (Jan) (cogent evidence of persistent unwanted pressure); *Schrader v Schrader* [2013] EWHC 466 Ch, [2013] WTLR 701 (undue influence inferred where vulnerable testatrix dependent on would-be beneficiary and there was no good reason for change in will).

7   *Hall v Hall* (1868) LR 1 P & D 481 at 482 per Sir JP Wilde. See also *Mountain v Bennet* (1787) 1 Cox Eq Cas 353; *Boyse v Rossborough* (1857) 6 HL Cas 2 (actual violence need not be proved, but it must be an influence relating to the making of the will itself and overbearing the mind of the testator); *Baudains v Richardson* [1906] AC 169, PC. 'If there is evidence showing the exertion of improper influence in relation to the execution of a will, it will be easier, and sometimes much easier, where the testator is enfeebled in body or mind, and all the more so if he is enfeebled in both body and mind, to find that such influence was in all the circumstances undue': *Killick v Pountney* [1999] All ER (D) 365, (1999) Times, 30 April per James Munby QC. See also *Re Edwards, Edwards v Edwards* [2007] All ER (D) 46 (May) (deeply distressed elderly testatrix, left hospital and returned home to son, of whom she was frightened; testatrix gave instructions to change will to disinherit other son and only grandson within very short period in favour of son still with her). Cf *Scammell v Farmer* [2008] EWHC 1100 (Ch), [2008] WTLR 1261, [2008] All ER (D) 296 (May) (see PARA 55 note 4). See also *Hubbard v Scott* [2011] EWHC 2750 (Ch), [2012] WTLR 29.

8   See the facts of *Re Good, Carapeto v Good* [2002] EWHC 640 (Ch), (2002) Times, 22 May, [2002] All ER (D) 141 (Apr) (no finding of undue influence, that finding not appealed), order affd, sub nom *Carapeto v Good* [2002] EWCA Civ 944 (testatrix largely dependent, day and night, upon housekeeper); see PARA 57 note 1.

9   In *Wingrove v Wingrove* (1885) 11 PD 81 at 82 Sir J Hannen excluded from the category of undue influence, by way of example, the cases of a young man who succumbs to the fascinations of a woman sufficiently to make a will in her favour, and leaving his relations nothing, and of a man who leaves his property to a man who has encouraged him in evil courses.

10 *Radford v Risdon* (1912) 28 TLR 342, where evidence was allowed of statements by the deceased person not in the presence of the testatrix.

57. Distinction between undue influence and want of knowledge and approval.

A man may approve and know the contents of a will when his volition has been overpowered, and conversely he may of his own free volition execute a document which for some reason he has not approved or which contains matter of which he has no knowledge. These are separate issues, which must be made the subject of separate allegations, although they are often simultaneously alleged in a statement of case[1]. The mere proof of the existence of the relation of parent and child, husband and wife, doctor and patient, solicitor and client, confessor and penitent, guardian and ward or tutor and pupil does not raise a presumption of undue influence sufficient to vitiate a gift by will[2]; but a fiduciary relationship may affect the burden of proof on the issue of knowledge and approval[3].

1   See PARA 875; and as to the relationship between the defences see PARA 891. See also *Re Good, Carapeto v Good* [2002] EWHC 640 (Ch), (2002) Times, 22 May, [2002] All ER (D) 141 (Apr), order affd, sub nom *Carapeto v Good* [2002] EWCA Civ 944 (complications arising from the tax consequences of testatrix's new will and its dispositions may not have been fully clear to her but she was highly intelligent, of full testamentary capacity and well advised; held that she intended to make, knew, and approved the contents of, the will that she made. The undue influence assertion failed; the evidence showed a very close and dependent relationship between testatrix and the principal beneficiaries, her housekeeper and family, but fell short of showing coercion).

2 *Parfitt v Lawless* (1872) LR 2 P & D 462; *Boyse v Rossborough* (1857) 6 HL Cas 2 at 49 per Lord Cranworth LC. As to the relationships which raise a presumption of undue influence see MISREPRESENTATION vol 76 (2013) PARA 836 et seq.
3 See PARA 904.

58. Gift obtained by fraud or fraudulent calumny. Where a legacy is given to a person under a particular character which he has falsely assumed for the purpose of obtaining the bounty[1], and which alone is shown or is inferred to have deceived the testator[2] and to have been the motive of the bounty, the law on the ground of fraud does not permit the donee to avail himself of the legacy[3]; but a false reason given for the legacy is not of itself sufficient to destroy it[4]. In these cases the question must be raised in the probate court[5].

Similarly, a person cannot take an advantage under a will if it is shown that it has been procured by fraudulent calumny, in that a testator has been persuaded against an otherwise natural beneficiary by dishonest or reckless aspersions, cast on that person's character by someone who benefits thereby[6].

1 Such a fraudulent purpose must be alleged in the statement of case and established to defeat the legacy: *Re Posner, Posner v Miller* [1953] P 277, [1953] 1 All ER 1123. See also *M'Kenna v Everitt* (1838) 1 Beav 134; *Giles v Giles, Penfold v Penfold* (1836) 1 Keen 685; *Rishton v Cobb* (1839) 5 My & Cr 145; *Re Pitts* (1859) 29 LJ Ch 168; *Turner v Brittain* (1863) 3 New Rep 21; *Re Boddington, Boddington v Clariat* (1883) 22 ChD 597.
2 *Re Posner, Posner v Miller* [1953] P 277 at 280, [1953] 1 All ER 1123 at 1125.
3 *Kennell v Abbott* (1799) 4 Ves 802 at 809 (explained in *Pratt v Mathew* (1856) 22 Beav 328 at 336; *Re Boddington, Boddington v Clariat* (1883) 22 ChD 597 at 602); *Wilkinson v Joughin* (1866) LR 2 Eq 319.
4 *Kennell v Abbott* (1799) 4 Ves 802 at 808.
5 *Meluish v Milton* (1876) 3 ChD 27, CA, following *Allen v M'Pherson* (1847) 1 HL Cas 191. As to cases where the gift has been obtained on a secret understanding between the testator and the donee see eg *Moss v Cooper* (1861) 1 John & H 352; PARA 169 et seq; and TRUSTS AND POWERS vol 98 (2013) PARA 88 et seq. As to the construction of references to the probate court see PARA 678.
6 The essence of fraudulent calumny is that the person alleged to have been poisoning the testator's mind must either know that the aspersions are false or not care whether they are true or false. If a person believes that he is telling the truth about a potential beneficiary then even if what he tells the testator is objectively untrue, the will is not liable to be set aside on that ground alone: see *Re Edwards* [2007] EWHC 1119 (Ch) at [47], [2007] All ER (D) 46 (May) per Lewison J.

59. Clauses fraudulently introduced excepted from grant. It may be alleged as a defence in a probate claim that the execution of the alleged will was obtained by fraud[1]. Where a clause can be shown to have been introduced into a will by means of fraud practised upon the testator[2], or by forgery after his death[3], it is excepted from the grant. In such a case the court has jurisdiction to declare the executors to be trustees for the person deprived of benefit by the fraud[4]. In the case of an advantage under the will which has been procured by fraudulent calumny, it seems unclear whether the calumny, if established, must inevitably cause the whole will to fail, or only those parts affected where other dispositions remain unaffected[5].

1 See CPR 57.7; and PARA 875. As to the consequence of fraud as affecting the volition see PARA 57. As to the contents of statements of case see PARA 875. As to the right to begin proceedings see PARA 56 note 2.
2 *Guardhouse v Blackburn* (1866) LR 1 P & D 109 (see the fourth rule laid down at 116 per Sir JP Wilde).
3 *Plume v Beale* (1717) 1 P Wms 388. See *Gale v Gale* [2010] EWHC 1575 (Ch), [2010] All ER (D) 234 (Jun) (codicils failed because they had forged signatures, and even if this were not the case, they were executed after testator's mental decline due to Alzheimer's disease and had been backdated). See also PARA 671; and EQUITABLE JURISDICTION vol 47 (2014) PARA 13.
4 *Betts v Doughty* (1879) 5 PD 26. This case was settled, but the principle set out in the text emerged from it. As to evidence in charge of forgery see *Gallagher v Kennedy* [1931] NI 207.
5 *Re Edwards, Edwards v Edwards* [2007] All ER (D) 46 (May); *Allen v M'Pherson* (1847) 1 HL Cas 191 at 207, per Lord Lyndhurst; the deceit must be compared with the capacity or

understanding of the person deceived to decide whether the fraud is such as to nullify the will: *Marsh v Tyrrell and Harding* (1828) 2 Hag Ecc 84, 123. See also *Nesbitt v Nicholson* [2013] EWHC 4027 (Ch), [2014] All ER (D) 102 (Jan).

(5) REQUIREMENTS FOR A VALID WILL: FORMALITIES

(i) Writing

60. Will must be in writing. Every will other than a privileged will[1] must be in writing[2] and signed[3] by or on behalf of[4] the testator[5], and the signature must be made or acknowledged[6] in the presence of two witnesses present at the same time[7]. There are no restrictions as to the materials with which, and upon which, a will may be written[8]. A will may be made[9] or altered in pencil as well as in ink[10], but pencil alterations in a will written in ink are prima facie deliberative[11]. If, however, in a will mainly written in ink, blanks are filled up in pencil before execution, the pencil additions may be included in the probate[12]. A printed or lithographed form may be used, or part of such a form may be utilised[13]. The requirement that a will should be in writing means that a will cannot validly be executed so as to have effect conditionally on the happening of a future event where the condition is not set out in the will itself[14].

1 As to the privileged wills of certain soldiers, sailors and airmen see PARAS 79–81.
2 As to the incorporation of documents referred to in a will in the probate see PARA 711.
3 As to the signature see PARA 62 et seq.
4 As to signature on the testator's behalf see PARA 64.
5 Wills Act 1837 s 9(a) (s 9 substituted by the Administration of Justice Act 1982 s 17).
6 See PARA 68.
7 Wills Act 1837 s 9(c) (as substituted: see note 5). See *Re Devillebichot; Brennan v Prior* [2013] EWHC 2867 (Ch), [2013] WTLR 1701, [2013] All ER (D) 243 (Sep). See also PARAS 70–71.
8 Swinburne on Wills (7th Edn) Pt IV s 25, pl 2. See also *Re Barnes, Hodson v Barnes* (1926) 43 TLR 71 (will written on an eggshell); *Re Slavinskyj's Estate* (1989) 53 SASR 221 (will written in bad Ukrainian on the wall by the testator's bed; photograph of it accepted for probate purposes).
9 *Re Usborne* (1909) 25 TLR 519.
10 *Rymes v Clarkson* (1809) 1 Phillim 22 at 25. See also *Boughton-Knight v Wilson* (1915) 32 TLR 146.
11 *Rymes v Clarkson* (1809) 1 Phillim 22 at 25; *Re Hall* (1871) LR 2 P & D 256; *Re Adams* (1872) LR 2 P & D 367. See also *Re Bellamy* (1866) 14 WR 501.
12 See *Kell v Charmer* (1856) 23 Beav 195. In *Re Tonge* (1891) 66 LT 60, a revocation clause which had been cancelled in pencil was omitted from probate, the court being satisfied on the facts that the deletion was made before execution.
13 See the Interpretation Act 1978 s 5, Sch 1, Sch 2 para 4(1)(b) (meaning of 'writing'); and STATUTES AND LEGISLATIVE PROCESS vol 96 (2012) PARA 1219. See also *Re Moore* [1892] P 378. As to the interpretation of wills made on will forms see *Re Harrison, Turner v Hellard* (1885) 30 ChD 390, CA; *Re Spencer, Hart v Manston* (1886) 54 LT 597; *Re Smithers, Watts v Smithers* [1939] Ch 1015, [1939] 3 All ER 689. See also PARA 200.
14 *Corbett v Newey* [1998] Ch 57, [1996] 2 All ER 914, CA; and see PARA 7.

(ii) Date

61. Date not essential. There is no requirement in law that a will should be dated, and the lack of a date or the inclusion of a wrong one cannot invalidate a will[1]. An exception is that an appointment by will (or other instrument) of a guardian of a minor must be dated[2].

1 *Corbett v Newey* [1998] Ch 57 at 64, 67, 70, [1996] 2 All ER 914 at 920, 923, 926, CA. If a will is dated, the date it should bear is the date of its execution by the testator.
2 See the Children Act 1989 s 5(5); and CHILDREN AND YOUNG PERSONS vol 9 (2012) PARA 166.

(iii) Signature

62. Signature essential. To be valid, a will must be signed by the testator, or by some other person in his presence and by his direction[1]. The signature must be intended by the testator as an act of execution[2], and it must appear that he intended by his signature to give effect to the will[3]. A practical approach is demanded by these words[4]. A normal signature, placed at the foot of a testamentary document, would in most cases carry the implication that the testator intended the signature to give testamentary effect to the document, and affirmative evidence would be needed to rebut it; but if the only appearance of the testator's name leaves it uncertain whether it was intended to authenticate the document as his will, affirmative evidence that that was his intention would be necessary for the will to be valid[5]. It is possible for the Court of Protection, by order, to make arrangements for the execution of a will where a person lacks the capacity to do that for himself[6].

1 Wills Act 1837 s 9(a) (s 9 substituted by the Administration of Justice Act 1982 s 17).
2 *Re Walker* (1862) 2 Sw & Tr 354; *Burke v Moore, Re Moore* (1875) IR 9 Eq 609.
3 Wills Act 1837 s 9(b) (as substituted: see note 1). In the case of the wills of testators dying before 1 January 1983, similar provision was made by the Wills Act Amendment Act 1852 s 1 (repealed); but there was also a requirement that the signature be at or near the end of the will (see PARA 65), such requirement having been abolished in respect of deaths on or after 1 January 1983. See note 4.
4 *Wood v Smith* [1993] Ch 90 at 111, [1992] 3 All ER 556 at 561, CA, per Scott LJ (testator having signed the will at the top, before adding dispositive clauses: if the writing of the will and the appending of the signature are all in one operation it does not matter whereabouts on the document or when in the course of the writing the signature is appended). This approach was applied in *National Trust for Places of Historic Interest and Natural Beauty v Royal National Institute for the Blind* [1999] All ER (D) 81 sub nom *Re Chapman* (1988–99) 1 ITELR 863 to give testamentary effect where a testatrix had signed and had had witnessed a preliminary note from the will draftsman showing 'the probable main provisions' and headed 'Outline Will Provision for Mrs Chapman', in probable anticipation of a formal will. See also *Weatherhill v Pearce* [1995] 2 All ER 492, [1995] 1 WLR 592; *Couser v Couser* [1996] 3 All ER 256 at 261, [1996] 1 WLR 1301 at 1306 (if a will on its face appears to be valid, and the testator's intention is clear, it is a heavy evidential burden on anyone who seeks to disturb that will and the principle that the maxim 'omnia praesumuntur rite et solemniter esse acta' (all things are presumed to be correctly and solemnly done) applies, and one should not search for defects in what occurred). As to the presumption of correctness see STATUTES AND LEGISLATIVE PROCESS vol 96 (2012) PARA 1142.
5 *Wood v Smith* [1993] Ch 90 at 111, [1992] 3 All ER 556 at 561, CA, per Scott LJ. See also PARA 63 text and note 12. In *National Trust for Places of Historic Interest and Natural Beauty v Royal National Institute for the Blind* [1999] All ER (D) 81 sub nom *Re Chapman* (1988–99) 1 ITELR 863, an assertion that Wills Act 1837 s 9(b) limited the court to considering only what was apparent on the face of the document, without recourse to external evidence, failed.
6 See the Mental Capacity Act 2005 ss 1–4, 16(1), (2) and 18(1); PARA 47; and MENTAL HEALTH AND CAPACITY vol 75 (2013) PARA 727.

63. Methods of signature. A mark or initials[1] are sufficient if intended to represent a signature to a will[2], even if the testator's hand is guided in making it[3], and whether the testator can write or not[4], and an incomplete signature is sufficient where there is evidence that he intended it to be the best he could do by way of writing his name[5]. A stamped signature may be sufficient[6], and sealing a will with a seal bearing the testator's initials has been held sufficient where the testator meant it to represent his signature[7], although a mere sealing is not[8]. The signature must have been made with the purpose of authenticating the instrument[9], and accordingly a signature intended merely to guard against other sheets being interpolated in a will is not sufficient[10], nor is a signature made in execution of a previous will (the current document being the previous will with manuscript amendments made after it was originally executed)[11]. The testator's name written by him at the beginning of a will in a phrase such as 'My will by *(name of testator)*', where the will was written out by him as a single operation and there was extrinsic evidence that he intended it to be his signature, can, however, be sufficient[12], as can the writing by the testator of his name in the attestation clause[13]. Passing a dry pen over a signature already written is not a good signature of a will[14], but it may amount to an acknowledgment of his signature by a testator[15].

Signature in an erroneous or assumed name, if intended as the name of the testator, is sufficient[16], as is a description which sufficiently identifies the testator and is intended to represent his name[17]. Where a testator puts his mark to a will in which he is wrongly named, the execution is valid[18].

1   *Re Savory* (1851) 15 Jur 1042; *Re Holtam, Gillett v Rogers* (1913) 108 LT 732. A mark made by the testator's thumb smeared with ink was allowed in *Re Finn* (1935) 105 LJP 36 and conceded to be sufficient in *Borman v Lel* [2001] All ER (D) 94 (Jun), [2002] WTLR 237. A mark of any shape, not necessarily a cross, is sufficient: *Re Kieran* [1933] IR 222.
2   *Re Bryce* (1839) 2 Curt 325; *Re Clarke* (1858) 1 Sw & Tr 22; *Hindmarsh v Charlton* (1861) 8 HL Cas 160; *Re Blewitt* (1880) 5 PD 116; *Re Emerson* (1882) 9 LR Ir 443; *Re Kieran* [1933] IR 222.
3   *Wilson v Beddard* (1841) 12 Sim 28; *Fulton v Kee* [1961] NI 1, CA.
4   *Baker v Dening* (1838) 8 Ad & El 94 (decided on the Statute of Frauds (1677)); *Re Bryce* (1839) 2 Curt 325.
5   *Re Chalcraft, Chalcraft v Giles* [1948] P 222, [1948] 1 All ER 700; cf *Re Maddock* (1874) LR 3 P & D 169 (incomplete signature of attesting witness). See also *Reynolds v Reynolds* [2005] EWHC 6 (Ch), [2005] All ER (D) 70 (Jan) (will validly executed by testatrix's initials even though rest of name, added to initials, may possibly have been added by person unknown).
6   *Jenkins v Gaisford and Thring, Re Jenkins* (1863) 3 Sw & Tr 93.
7   *Re Emerson* (1882) 9 LR Ir 443.
8   *Smith v Evans* (1751) 1 Wils 313; *Grayson v Atkinson* (1752) 2 Ves Sen 454 at 459; *Ellis v Smith* (1754) 1 Ves 11 at 13, 15; *Wright v Wakeford* (1811) 17 Ves 454 at 459 (overruling *Lemayne v Stanley* (1681) 3 Lev 1).
9   See PARA 62 text and notes 3–4. See also *Perrins v Holland* [2010] EWCA Civ 840, [2010] All ER (D) 210 (Jul), [2011] 2 WLR 1086 (affg *Re Perrins, Perrins v Holland, Perrins v Dooney* [2009] EWHC 1945 (Ch), [2009] WTLR 1387) (testator with multiple sclerosis customarily used rubber stamp; will held to be executed by stamp).
10 *Ewen v Franklin* (1855) Dea & Sw 7; *Re Dilkes* (1874) LR 3 P & D 164; *Phipps v Hale* (1874) LR 3 P & D 166. See also *Sweetland v Sweetland* (1865) 4 Sw & Tr 6.
11 *Re White, Barker v Gribble* [1991] Ch 1, [1990] 3 All ER 1 (disapproving *Re Dewell's Goods* (1853) 1 Ecc & Ad 103).
12 *Wood v Smith* [1993] Ch 90, [1992] 3 All ER 556, CA.
13 *Weatherhill v Pearce* [1995] 2 All ER 492, [1995] 1 WLR 592 (following the cases on signatures in attestation clauses cited in PARA 65 note 6).
14 *Playne v Scriven* (1849) 1 Rob Eccl 772; *Kevil v Lynch* (1874) IR 9 Eq 249.
15 *Playne v Scriven* (1849) 1 Rob Eccl 772; *Lewis v Lewis* [1908] P 1 at 5.
16 *Re Glover* (1847) 5 Notes of Cases 553; *Re Redding* (1850) 2 Rob Eccl 339; *Re Clarke* (1858) 1 Sw & Tr 22.
17 *Re Cook, Murison v Cook* [1960] 1 All ER 689, [1960] 1 WLR 353 ('Your loving mother').
18 *Re Douce* (1862) 2 Sw & Tr 593.

64. Signature on behalf of the testator.

A will may be signed on behalf of the testator, but the signature must be made in his presence and by his direction[1]. The person so signing may be one of the attesting witnesses[2], and a signature of that person's own name expressly on behalf of the testator is sufficient[3]. The direction to sign may be implied from the conduct of the deceased and from the accompanying circumstances[4], but the testator must in some way indicate to the two witnesses present that the signature was put there at his request; passive acquiescence is not sufficient[5].

1   Wills Act 1837 s 9(a) (substituted by the Administration of Justice Act 1982 s 17). See *Barrett v Bem* [2012] EWCA Civ 52, [2012] Ch 573, [2012] 2 All ER 920 (testator's sister signed will on

his behalf); and PARA 93. As to wills executed on behalf of patients pursuant to the mental health jurisdiction see PARA 62 note 1.

2 *Re Bailey* (1838) 1 Curt 914; *Smith v Harris* (1845) 1 Rob Eccl 262; *Jenkyns v Gaisford and Thring* (1863) 11 WR 854 (where a facsimile stamp of the testator's name was used).

3 *Re Clark* (1839) 2 Curt 239; *Smith v Harris* (1845) 1 Rob Eccl 262; *Re McLoughlin* [1936] IR 223.

4 *Parker v Parker* (1841) Milw 541.

5 *Re Marshall* (1866) 13 LT 643; *Barrett v Bem* [2012] EWCA Civ 52, [2012] Ch 573, [2012] 2 All ER 920.

65. Position of signature; death before 1983. The will of a testator who died before 1 January 1983[1], as far as regards the position of the signature of the testator or of the person signing for him[2], is deemed valid if the signature is placed at[3] or after, or following[4] or under, or beside[5], or opposite to the end of the will, so that it is apparent on the face of the will that the testator intended to give effect by the signature to the writing signed as his will[6]. No signature is operative, however, to give effect to any disposition which is underneath or which follows it[7], or to any disposition or direction inserted after the signature has been made[8].

1 Ie the date on which the substitution of the Wills Act 1837 s 9 by the Administration of Justice Act 1982 s 17 came into operation: see s 76(11). The Wills Act 1837 s 9 makes no provision as to the position of the signature: see PARA 66. Nothing in the Administration of Justice Act 1982 s 17 affects the will of a testator who died before 1 January 1983: s 73(6)(a).

2 As to a will signed on behalf of the testator see PARA 64.

3 *Re Woodley* (1864) 3 Sw & Tr 429 (signature across last two lines). The name of the testator written as the last word of a holograph will may be a signature: *Trott v Skidmore* (1860) 2 Sw & Tr 12; *Lewis v Lewis* [1908] P 1. A signature or mark in the middle of a will is not sufficient: *Margary v Robinson* (1886) 12 PD 8.

4 *Re Wright* (1865) 4 Sw & Tr 35 (signature across third page of a sheet of notepaper); *Re O'Neill* (1916) 50 ILT 180 (signature of testator below those of the witnesses).

5 *Re Jones* (1865) 4 Sw & Tr 1 (signature at side of attestation clause); *Re Williams* (1865) LR 1 P & D 4 (signature opposite last words of will); *Re Coombs* (1866) LR 1 P & D 302; *Re Ainsworth* (1870) LR 2 P & D 151; *Re Stoakes* (1874) 31 LT 552; *Re Usborne* (1909) 25 TLR 519; *Re Roberts* [1934] P 102 (signature in margin). See, however, *Re Hughes* (1887) 12 PD 107 (where a codicil was executed by a signature in the margin of the will in the mistaken belief that the codicil constituted an alteration of the will, and probate of the codicil was refused).

6 See the Wills Act 1837 s 9 (as originally enacted); and the Wills Act Amendment Act 1852 s 1 (repealed). A signature has been held to be valid where it was placed in the testimonium clause (*Re Mann* (1858) 28 LJP & M 19; *Re Torre* (1862) 8 Jur NS 494); the attestation clause (*Re Walker* (1862) 2 Sw & Tr 354; *Re Huckvale* (1867) LR 1 P & D 375; *Re Casmore* (1869) LR 1 P & D 653; *Re Pearn* (1875) 1 PD 70; *Re Moore* [1901] P 44); following or after or under the clause of attestation (*Re Standley* (1849) 7 Notes of Cases 69), either with or without a blank space intervening; following or after or under or beside the names or one of the names of the attesting witnesses (see *Re Jones* (1865) 4 Sw & Tr 1; *Re Puddephatt* (1870) LR 2 P & D 97 (beneath); *Re Horsford* (1874) LR 3 P & D 211 (following page); *Byles v Cox* (1896) 74 LT 222); and in a box-like space deliberately reserved for the signature but placed among the dispositive words (*Re Hornby* [1946] P 171, [1946] 2 All ER 150). Cf *Re Harris, Murray v Everard* [1952] P 319, [1952] 2 All ER 409 (where the signature was written at the top and towards the right-hand side of the will under the words 'My last will and testament', and probate was refused).

7 *Re Greata* (1856) 2 Jur NS 1172; *Re Dallow* (1866) LR 1 P & D 189; *Re Woods* (1868) LR 1 P & D 556; *Re White* [1896] 1 IR 269; *Re Evans* (1923) 128 LT 669. See also *Re Beadle, Mayes v Beadle* [1974] 1 All ER 493, [1974] 1 WLR 417 (where it was held that a signature on an envelope containing an insufficiently executed will merely identified the document enclosed in it).

8 *Re Arthur* (1871) LR 2 P & D 273; *Re Little, Foster v Cooper* [1960] 1 All ER 387, [1960] 1 WLR 495.

66. Position of signature; death after 1982. In relation to the wills of testators who die on or after 1 January 1983, there is no requirement that the testator's signature should be at the end of the will[1]. The only requirement is that it should appear that the testator intended by his signature to give effect to the will[2].

1   See the Wills Act 1837 s 9 (substituted, as from 1 January 1983, by the Administration of Justice Act 1982 s 17). As to the former rules relating to the position of the signature of a will see the Wills Act 1837 s 9 (as originally enacted); and PARA 65.
2   Wills Act 1837 s 9(b) (as substituted: see note 1). See also PARAS 62–63.

67. Will on several sheets. Where a will consists of several sheets, it is not necessary for the testator to sign all of them, so long as at the time of execution all the sheets are attached in some way[1], even though not necessarily mechanically[2]. Where witnesses saw only the last sheet of the will, it may be presumed that the whole of the will was in the room[3]. Where several sheets constituting a connected disposal of property are found together, the presumption is that they all formed the will of the deceased[4] and that any apparent alteration in their order was made before execution[5]. Probate may be granted of a signed but unattested will enclosed in an envelope both signed by the testator and attested[6], and of a will, attested, but not signed by the testator, enclosed in an envelope signed by him[7].

Declarations by the testator made both before and after execution are admissible to show which parts form the constituent parts of the will[8].

1   *Lewis v Lewis* [1908] P 1 at 5 per Bargrave Deane J. See also *Cook v Lambert* (1863) 3 Sw & Tr 46; *Re West* (1863) 9 Jur NS 1158; *Re Horsford* (1874) LR 3 P & D 211.
2   *Gregory v Queen's Proctor* (1846) 4 Notes of Cases 620 at 639; *Re Little, Foster v Cooper* [1960] 1 All ER 387, [1960] 1 WLR 495 (sheets pressed together on a table by testator).
3   *Bond v Seawell* (1765) 3 Burr 1773.
4   *Marsh v Marsh* (1860) 1 Sw & Tr 528; *Re O'Brien* [1900] P 208; but see *Re M'Key* (1876) IR 11 Eq 220 (where the evidence was insufficient).
5   *Rees v Rees* (1873) LR 3 P & D 84. In *Re Madden* [1905] 2 IR 612, where the sheets were pinned together and the sheet containing the testator's signature and attestation clause came first, the court concluded that that sheet had inadvertently been misplaced either before or after the will was signed, but that at all events the sheet containing the signature was written last.
6   *Re Almosnino* (1859) 29 LJP & M 46; *Re Nicholls, Hunter v Nicholls* [1921] 2 Ch 11.
7   *Re Mann* [1942] P 146, [1942] 2 All ER 193. Where, however, there is no evidence of testamentary intention and the signature on the envelope is merely for identification of its contents, there is no valid will: *Re Bean* [1944] P 83, [1944] 2 All ER 348; *Re Beadle, Mayes v Beadle* [1974] 1 All ER 493, [1974] 1 WLR 417.
8   *Gould v Lakes* (1880) 6 PD 1; *Re Hutchison* (1902) 18 TLR 706.

68. Acknowledgment of signature. A testator must either sign his will or acknowledge his signature in the presence of two or more witnesses present at the same time[1]. It is not necessary for the testator to say, 'This is my signature'; acknowledgment may be by gesture[2], it may be made in answer to a question[3], and production of a will with a signature on it and a request that it be witnessed may be sufficient[4]. The witnesses must, however, see, or have an opportunity of seeing, the signature of the testator[5], and, if what takes place involves an acknowledgment by the testator that the signature is his, that is enough[6]. The signature to be acknowledged may be made either by the testator or by another for him[7], but it must have been intended, at the time when it was made, to authenticate the will in question; thus, on a re-execution of a will with amendments made to it after it was originally executed, acknowledgment of the original signature is not sufficient[8].

In the absence of proof that the witnesses did not see, or could not have seen, the signature of the testator, and in the absence of fraud, the courts presume, where there is a proper attestation clause, or where the evidence shows that the testator knew the law, that the attesting witnesses saw the acknowledged signature[9]. Even where the attestation clause is informal, the presumption of due execution is applied if the attesting witnesses identify their signatures and that of the testator, even though they have no recollection of the circumstances in which the will was executed[10].

1 Wills Act 1837 s 9(c) (s 9 substituted by the Administration of Justice Act 1982 s 17). As to a will signed on behalf of a person under the provisions of the Mental Capacity Act 2005, see PARA 51 note 4; see also PARA 47.
2 *Re Davies* (1850) 2 Rob Eccl 337; but see *Re Owston* (1862) 2 Sw & Tr 461 (where the testator was deaf and dumb).
3 *Kelly v Keatinge* (1871) IR 5 Eq 174.
4 See PARA 69 text and notes 1–2.
5 *Re Harrison* (1841) 2 Curt 863; *Re Claridge* (1879) 39 LT 612; *Re Gunstan, Blake v Blake* (1882) 7 PD 102, CA (following *Hudson v Parker* (1844) 1 Rob Eccl 14; and dissenting from *Gwillim v Gwillim* (1859) 3 Sw & Tr 200 and *Beckett v Howe* (1869) LR 2 P & D 1); *O'Meagher v O'Meagher* (1883) 11 LR Ir 117; *Clery v Barry* (1887) 21 LR Ir 152 at 164, Ir CA; *Pascoe v Smart* (1901) 17 TLR 595; *Couser v Couser* [1996] 3 All ER 256, [1996] 1 WLR 1301; *Sherrington v Sherrington* [2005] EWCA Civ 326, [2005] All ER (D) 359 (Mar). See also PARA 70. As to the incapacity of a blind person to witness a will see PARA 78.
6 *Daintree v Butcher and Fasulo* (1888) 13 PD 102, CA; *Re Hadler, Goodall v Hadler* (1960) Times, 20 October; *Re Staniforth, Gilbert v Heining* (1965) 109 Sol Jo 112. See also *Gillic v Smyth* (1914) 49 ILT 36; *Re White, Barker v Gribble* [1991] Ch 1 at 10, [1990] 3 All ER 1 at 7.
7 *Re Regan* (1838) 1 Curt 908; *Parker v Parker* (1841) Milw 541. A signature pencilled by a third person to show the place of signature cannot, however, be acknowledged: *Reeves v Grainger* (1908) 52 Sol Jo 355. See also PARA 64.
8 *Re White, Barker v Gribble* [1991] Ch 1, [1990] 3 All ER 1 (disapproving *Re Dewell* (1853) 17 Jur 1130). See also *Wood v Smith* [1993] Ch 90, [1992] 3 All ER 556, CA; cf *Re Pattison, Henderson v Priestman* [1918] 2 IR 90 (where a testatrix signed without attesting witnesses, and subsequently signed in the presence of attesting witnesses, but the witnesses signed before her second signature was made; the execution was held valid as an acknowledgment of the earlier signature, but no amendment had been made to the will after the earlier signature).
9 *Wright v Sanderson* (1884) 9 PD 149, CA; *Whiting v Turner* (1903) 89 LT 71; *Kavanagh v Fegan* [1932] IR 566; *Re McLean, Lockhart v McLean* [1950] IR 180; *Sherrington v Sherrington* [2005] EWCA Civ 326, [2005] All ER (D) 359 (Mar). See also *Weatherhill v Pearce* [1995] 2 All ER 492, [1995] 1 WLR 592.
10 *Woodhouse v Balfour* (1887) 13 PD 2; *Re Rees* (1865) 34 LJPM & A 56. As to the presumption of due execution see PARA 77.

69. Presumption that will was already signed by testator. The production of a will by a testator with his signature on it, and a request by him, or by someone acting for him in his presence[1], to the witnesses to attest it, is a sufficient acknowledgment of the signature[2], and the court is not bound to have positive affirmative evidence from the attesting witnesses that the testator's name was signed to the paper before they signed it[3]. The mere circumstance of calling in witnesses who had no opportunity of seeing the testator's signature, without giving them any explanation of the instrument which they are signing, does not, however, amount to an acknowledgment of the signature by a testator[4], especially when there is no evidence that the testator's signature was on the will at the time[5].

1 *Faulds v Jackson* (1845) 6 Notes of Cases, Supp i, PC; *Inglesant v Inglesant* (1874) LR 3 P & D 172; *Re Bishop* (1882) 30 WR 567; *Kavanagh v Fegan* [1932] IR 566; *Cooke v Henry* [1932] IR 574; but see *Morritt v Douglas* (1872) LR 3 P & D 1.
2 Ie for the purpose of the Wills Act 1837 s 9(c) (see PARA 68). See *Gaze v Gaze* (1843) 3 Curt 451; *Keigwin v Keigwin* (1843) 3 Curt 607; *Re Davis* (1843) 3 Curt 748; *Re Dewell* (1853) 17 Jur 1130 (disapproved on another point in *Re White, Barker v Gribble* [1991] Ch 1, [1990] 3 All ER 1: see PARA 63 text and note 11); *Re Claridge* (1879) 39 LT 612; *Re Pattison, Henderson v Priestman* [1918] 2 IR 90; *Weatherhill v Pearce* [1995] 2 All ER 492, [1995] 1 WLR 592; *Couser v Couser* [1996] 3 All ER 256, [1996] 1 WLR 1301; *Re White, Barker v Gribble* above at 10 and 7.
3 *Blake v Knight* (1843) 3 Curt 547. See also PARA 895.
4 *Ilott v Genge* (1842) 3 Curt 160 (affd (1844) 4 Moo PCC 265); *Fischer v Popham* (1875) LR 3 P & D 246; *Wright v Sanderson* (1884) 9 PD 149, CA. For a discussion of the intention that is normally presumed to exist in a witness where there is an attestation clause and the testator's signature is already on the will see *Sherrington v Sherrington* [2005] EWCA Civ 326 at

[42], [2005] All ER (D) 359 (Mar) per Peter Gibson LJ (case concerned attestation but, presumably, the same principles should also follow in an acknowledgement situation). See also PARAS 70, 76.
5   *Re Swinford* (1869) LR 1 P & D 630; *Pearson v Pearson* (1871) LR 2 P & D 451.

(iv) Attestation

70. Requirements for attestation. The testator's signature must be made or acknowledged by him in the presence of two[1] or more witnesses present at the same time[2]. Each witness must then either attest and sign the will or acknowledge his signature[3], in the testator's presence. The testator's complete[4] signature must be made or acknowledged when both the attesting witnesses are actually present at the same time[5], and each witness must attest and sign, or acknowledge, his signature after the testator's signature has been so made or acknowledged[6]. Although it is not essential for the attesting witnesses to sign in the presence of each other[7], it is usual for them to do so. Each witness should be able to say with truth that he knew that the testator had signed the document[8] but it is not necessary that the witness should know that it is the testator's will[9]. To attest, it must be shown that the witness is confirming that he witnessed a person signing his name or acknowledging his prior signature to a document of some sort, rather than the mere fact of having seen that person writing; it is not enough for a witness to sign a will, without an intention to bear witness to what he saw[10]. There is, however, no sufficient acknowledgment unless the witnesses either saw or had the opportunity of seeing the signature, even though the testator expressly states that the paper to be attested is his will or that his signature is inside the will[11].

1   As to superfluous attestation see PARA 44.
2   Wills Act 1837 s 9(c) (s 9 substituted by the Administration of Justice Act 1982 s 17). See *Ahluwalia v Singh* [2012] WTLR 1, [2011] All ER (D) 113 (Sep) (presumption of due execution rebutted as witnesses not present at same time when will signed by testator). The Wills Act 1837 s 9(c) is in the same terms in this respect as the original enactment. Every will duly executed in the manner required by s 9 is valid without any other publication thereof: s 13. 'Publication' is an obsolete procedure whereby the testator made a declaration in the presence of witnesses that the instrument produced to them was his will. This procedure has been superseded by attestation by two witnesses: see s 9(d); and the text to note 3.
3   Wills Act 1837 s 9(d) (as substituted: see note 2). The Wills Act 1837 s 9(d) has effect in relation to wills of persons dying on or after 1 January 1983. Under s 9 (as originally enacted), applying to the wills of persons who died before 1 January 1983, the witnesses were required to attest and sign after the testator signed or acknowledged his signature in their presence, and did not have the alternative of acknowledging their signatures after this had happened. As to wills executed on behalf of patients pursuant to the judge's authorisation under the mental health jurisdiction see PARA 62 note 1. For a case where the witnesses had not signed in the presence of the testator see *Betts v Gannell* (1903) 19 TLR 304. As to the law in Scotland see *Whitworth v Walker* (1915) 32 TLR 195, HL. In an undefended probate action the court allowed the execution of the will to be proved by a person present although not an attesting witness: *Mackay v Rawlinson* (1919) 35 TLR 223. A will duly executed and attested will effect a valid execution of a power of appointment: see TRUSTS AND POWERS vol 98 (2013) PARA 564.
4   See *Re Colling, Lawson v von Winckler* [1972] 3 All ER 729, [1972] 1 WLR 1440 (where one witness was called away in the middle of the testator's signing, so that the full signature was not witnessed; the first witness came back, and the testator and the other witness both acknowledged their signatures in the presence of each other and the first witness, after which the latter signed the will; the attestation was held to be invalid, but, had the will been executed on or after 1 January 1983, it would have been valid (see note 3)).
5   *Wyatt v Berry* [1893] P 5; *Rolleston v Sinclair* [1924] 2 IR 157, Ir CA.
6   *Moore v King* (1842) 3 Curt 243; *Cooper v Bockett* (1843) 3 Curt 648; *Pennant v Kingscote* (1843) 3 Curt 642 at 647; *Hindmarsh v Charlton* (1861) 8 HL Cas 160; *Wyatt v Berry* [1893] P 5; *Brown v Skirrow* [1902] P 3 at 7; *Re Davies, Russell v Delaney* [1951] 1 All ER 920; *Re Colling, Lawson v von Winckler* [1972] 3 All ER 729, [1972] 1 WLR 1440. These decisions must, however,

be read in light of the fact that, since they were decided, it has become permissible for a witness to acknowledge his signature after the testator signs or acknowledges his in the presence of both witnesses: see note 3.

7   Wills Act 1837 s 9(d) (as substituted: see note 2). Section 9(d) confirmed the law on this point in existence prior to 1 January 1983: see *Faulds v Jackson* (1845) 6 Notes of Cases, Supp i, PC; *Re Webb* (1855) Dea & Sw 1 (disapproving the dictum to the contrary in *Casement v Fulton* (1845) 5 Moo PCC 130 at 140); *Sullivan v Sullivan* (1879) 3 LR Ir 299 (followed in *O'Meagher v O'Meagher* (1883) 11 LR Ir 117 and *Re Smythe* (1915) 49 ILT 223); *Brown v Skirrow* [1902] P 3 at 5.

8   *Brown v Skirrow* [1902] P 3 at 5. See also *Casson v Dade* (1781) 1 Bro CC 99; *Couser v Couser* [1996] 3 All ER 256, [1996] 1 WLR 1301; *Sherrington v Sherrington* [2005] EWCA Civ 326, [2005] All ER (D) 359 (Mar).

9   *Smith & Smith v Smith* (1869) LR1 P & D 143; *Re Benjamin* (1934) 150 LT 417; *Re Gibson* [1949] P 434, [1949] 2 All ER 90. As to the capacity of a blind person to witness a will see PARA 78.

10 *Bryan v White* (1850) 2 Rob Eccl 315 at 317; *Griffiths v Griffiths* (1871) LR 2 P & D 300 at 303; *Sherrington v Sherrington* [2005] EWCA Civ 326, [2005] All ER (D) 359 (Mar). See also PARA 76.

11 *Re Gunstan, Blake v Blake* (1882) 7 PD 102, CA (following *Hudson v Parker* (1844) 1 Rob Eccl 14; and dissenting from *Beckett v Howe* (1869) LR 2 P & D 1 and *Gwillim v Gwillim* (1859) 3 Sw & Tr 200); *Daintree v Butcher and Fasulo* (1888) 13 PD 102 at 104 per Cotton J; *Re Swift* (1900) 17 TLR 16; *Re Groffman, Groffman and Block v Groffman* [1969] 2 All ER 108, [1969] 1 WLR 733; *Couser v Couser* [1996] 3 All ER 256, [1996] 1 WLR 1301. As to acknowledgment of signature see PARA 68.

71. Attestation or acknowledgment in the testator's presence. The attestation of a will by the witnesses takes place in the presence of the testator if he might have seen the witnesses sign, had he chosen to look; it is not necessary that he should actually see them sign[1]. He must, however, be mentally capable of recognising the act which is being done, and conscious of the transaction in which the witnesses are engaged, and, if he becomes insensible before the witnesses sign, the attestation is insufficient[2]. The rules for valid acknowledgment by a witness of his signature are the same as for valid acknowledgment by the testator of his signature[3].

1   *Shires v Glascock* (1685) 2 Salk 688; *Davy v Smith* (1693) 3 Salk 395; *Longford v Eyre* (1721) 1 P Wms 740; *Casson v Dade* (1781) 1 Bro CC 99; *Todd v Earl of Winchelsea* (1826) Mood & M 12; *Re Newman* (1838) 1 Curt 914; *Re Ellis* (1840) 2 Curt 395; *Re Colman* (1842) 3 Curt 118; *Tribe v Tribe* (1849) 1 Rob Eccl 775 (testatrix unable to turn in bed to see attestation; will invalid); *Jenner v Ffinch* (1879) 5 PD 106; *Carter v Seaton* (1901) 85 LT 76 (testator could not have had witnesses in sight; will invalid).

2   *Right v Price* (1779) 1 Doug KB 241. See also *Re Chalcraft, Chalcraft v Giles* [1948] P 222, [1948] 1 All ER 700.

3   *Couser v Couser* [1996] 3 All ER 256, [1996] 1 WLR 1301 (witness validly acknowledged her own signature by protesting that the method of execution being adopted was not valid). As to acknowledgment of signature see PARA 68.

72. Form of attestation. Although no form of attestation is necessary[1], it is always desirable to have an attestation clause showing that the statutory requirements have been complied with[2]. In the absence of such a clause an affidavit of due execution must be obtained from one of the attesting witnesses, or from some person who can depose to the facts[3], before probate can be obtained in the usual way on the executor's oath alone[4].

1   See the Wills Act 1837 s 9 (substituted by the Administration of Justice Act 1982 s 17). The Wills Act 1837 s 9 is in the same terms in this respect as the original enactment. This provision means that no clause of attestation stating that the statutory requirements have been carried out need be appended to the will: *Bryan v White* (1850) 14 Jur 919. In *Mason v Bishop* (1883) Cab & El 21, a signature purporting to attest the signatures of the witnesses was held sufficient to attest the execution by the testator. An attestation clause is not strictly part of the testator's will: *Re Atkinson* (1883) 8 PD 165; distinguished in *Re Dowling* [1933] IR 150 (where, on extrinsic evidence, a devise in the attestation clause was admitted as part of the will).

2   See *Re Selby-Bigge* [1950] 1 All ER 1009. The shortest form of attestation clause acceptable to the
    probate registries is 'signed by the testator in our presence and then by us in his'. For a form of
    attestation clause where a blind testator signs by his mark see *Re Sellwood, Heynes v Sellwood*
    (1964) 108 Sol Jo 523.
3   See the Non-Contentious Probate Rules 1987, SI 1987/2024, r 12(1) (amended by SI 1991/1876);
    Belbin v Skeats (1858) 1 Sw & Tr 148; PARAS 733, 894.
4   As to the presumption of due execution see PARA 77. As to the obtaining of probate see PARA 676
    et seq.

73.   Position of attestation. The attesting witnesses are not required to sign their
names on any particular part of the will, so long as the signatures are clearly
intended to attest the testator's signature[1] and it can be shown that their signatures
were affixed at a time after any words in the will below their signatures had been
written in[2]. Where, however, the attestation is not on the same sheet of paper as
the testator's signature, the attestation must be on a paper physically connected
with that sheet[3].

1   *Re Davis* (1843) 3 Curt 748; *Re Chamney* (1849) 1 Rob Eccl 757; *Roberts v Phillips* (1855) 4 E
    & B 450; *Re Braddock* (1876) 1 PD 433; *Re Streatley* [1891] P 172; *Re Fuller* [1892] P 377; *Re
    Ellison* [1907] 2 IR 480 (following *Re Streatley*).
2   *Re Jones* (1842) 1 Notes of Cases 396. See also *Byles v Cox* (1896) 74 LT 222.
3   *Re Braddock* (1876) 1 PD 433. As to a will written on several sheets see PARA 67.

74.   Methods of attestation. To make a valid attestation a witness must either
write his name or make some mark[1] intended to represent his name[2]. A will may
be signed by marks, even though the witnesses are capable of writing[3]. The initials
of an attesting witness may be sufficient[4], unless placed on the will merely for the
purpose of identifying alterations[5].

1   *Harrison v Harrison* (1803) 8 Ves 185; *Addy v Grix* (1803) 8 Ves 504; *Re Ashmore* (1843) 3 Curt
    756; *Clarke v Clarke* (1879) 5 LR Ir 47, Ir CA.
2   *Hindmarsh v Charlton* (1861) 8 HL Cas 160 at 169. In the case of testators dying on or after
    1 January 1983 a witness may acknowledge his signature: see PARA 70.
3   *Re Amiss* (1849) 2 Rob Eccl 116.
4   *Re Christian* (1849) 2 Rob Eccl 110; *Re Blewitt* (1880) 5 PD 116.
5   *Re Martin* (1849) 1 Rob Eccl 712, 714; *Re Cunningham* (1860) 4 Sw & Tr 194; *Re Shearn* (1880)
    50 LJP 15. See also *Re White, Barker v Gribble* [1991] Ch 1, [1990] 3 All ER 1. Attesting
    alterations rather than the will as a whole can, however, be valid if the Wills Act 1837 s 21 is
    complied with: see PARA 84.

75.   Description of witness. A witness may sign a will in any mode which
sufficiently identifies him as the person attesting the will[1]. Thus a sufficient
description of the witness without his name is a valid description[2], and so is a
signature in a wrong name[3], where the signature is intended to represent the
person signing and not some other person as being the actual witness[4]. Signing
part of his name by a witness is not sufficient unless the part signed was intended
to be a complete signature[5]. Formerly, a mere acknowledgment of an existing
signature, as by passing a dry pen over it[6], was also insufficient[7], but, in the case
of the will of a testator who dies on or after 1 January 1983, a witness may
acknowledge his signature[8]. The pen may be guided for a witness unable to write[9].

1   *Re Sperling* (1863) 3 Sw & Tr 272 (followed in *Re Cook, Murison v Cook* [1960] 1 All ER 689,
    [1960] 1 WLR 353, which concerned the testator's signature: see PARA 63 note 17); *Re Eynon*
    (1873) LR 3 P & D 92.
2   *Re Sperling* (1863) 3 Sw & Tr 272 ('servant to' the testator, without any name).
3   *Re Olliver* (1854) 2 Ecc & Ad 57.
4   *Pryor v Pryor* (1860) 29 LJPM & A 114; *Re Leverington* (1886) 11 PD 80. Thus neither a husband
    (*Re White* (1843) 2 Notes of Cases 461) nor a wife (*Re Duggins* (1870) 39 LJP & M 24; *Pryor
    v Pryor*; *Re Leverington*; *Re Cope* (1850) 2 Rob Eccl 335) may sign on behalf of the other in the
    other's name.
5   *Re Maddock* (1874) LR 3 P & D 169.

6 *Re Maddock* (1874) LR 3 P & D 169. See also *Re Cunningham* (1860) 29 LJPM & A 71.
7 *Hindmarsh v Charlton* (1861) 8 HL Cas 160 at 169; *Horne v Featherstone* (1895) 73 LT 32. See also *Playne v Scriven* (1849) 1 Rob Eccl 772. The addition of the date (*Hindmarsh v Charlton*), or of the witness's address (*Re Trevanion* (1850) 2 Rob Eccl 311), or the correction of a letter in the existing signature (*Hindmarsh v Charlton*; *Re Maddock* (1874) LR 3 P & D 169), merely constituted acknowledgments of the existing signature.
8 See PARA 70.
9 *Re Lewis* (1861) 7 Jur NS 688. See also *Harrison v Elvin* (1842) 3 QB 117; *Re Firth* (1858) 4 Jur NS 288.

76. Intention to attest. The court must be satisfied that the names of the witnesses were signed on the will for the purpose of attesting the testator's signature[1]. When the court is satisfied that a signature has been added without any intention to attest the execution, it excludes the signature from the probate (or refuses probate if that leaves the will with insufficient witnesses)[2]. The witness must intend to confirm that he was present when a person signed a document, or acknowledged his signature on it. It is not enough for a witness to sign a will, having a different intention, or having no particular intention behind his act, other than signing his name[3]. It appears also that the strongest evidence is required to show that the witness did not sign with the intention to attest execution by the deceased, where the will contains the signatures of the deceased and the witness and an attestation clause[4].

1 *Re Wilson* (1866) LR 1 P & D 269; *Re Sharman* (1869) LR 1 P & D 661; *Griffiths v Griffiths* (1871) LR 2 P & D 300; *Re Braddock* (1876) 1 PD 433; *Re Streatley* [1891] P 172; *Re Bercovitz, Canning v Enever* [1962] 1 All ER 552, [1962] 1 WLR 321, CA (where the wrong signature was attested). As to the position of attestation see PARA 73. Where a will is amended after it has been executed, re-execution and attestation of the amendments will be sufficient if the Wills Act 1837 s 21 (see PARA 82) is complied with; but, where s 21 does not apply, it is necessary that the witnesses should intend to attest the entire will, not just the amendments: see *Re Martin* (1849) 1 Rob Eccl 712, 714; *Re Shearn* (1880) 29 WR 445; *Re White, Barker v Gribble* [1991] Ch 1, [1990] 3 All ER 1.
2 *Re Sharman* (1869) LR 1 P & D 661; followed in *Re Pursglove* (1872) 26 LT 405 and *Re Murphy* (1873) IR 8 Eq 300. Cf *Mason v Bishop* (1883) Cab & El 21 (where, although the form of attestation was wrong, the testator's signature was in fact attested). As to superfluous attestation see PARA 44.
3 *Bryan v White* (1850) 2 Rob Eccl 315 at 317; *Griffiths v Griffiths* (1871) LR 2 P & D 300 at 303; *Sherrington v Sherrington* [2005] EWCA Civ 326 at [38]–[39], [2005] All ER (D) 359 (Mar) per Peter Gibson LJ. See also PARA 70 text and note 10.
4 See *Sherrington v Sherrington* [2005] EWCA Civ 326 at [42], [2005] All ER (D) 359 (Mar) per Peter Gibson LJ. See also PARA 77.

77. Presumption of due execution. There is a presumption of due execution where there is a proper attestation clause, even though the witnesses have no recollection of having witnessed the will, but this presumption may be rebutted by evidence of the attesting witnesses[1] or otherwise[2]. Where, however, the testator's mental capacity is in question, the evidence of a witness impeaching the will, inasmuch as he is thereby impeaching his own act, is viewed with extreme caution[3], and is not generally accepted without corroboration[4]. Where there is no attestation clause, the presumption of due execution may be applied, usually where no evidence can be produced as to the circumstances of the signing and attestation[5].

The burden of proving due execution, whether by presumption or by positive evidence, rests on the person setting up the will[6]. It may be unnecessary to have recourse to the presumption if the positive evidence of due execution is strong[7].

1 See PARA 895. Clear evidence is needed to rebut the presumption; and the presumption of due execution will still be applied where the evidence shows that the will might not have been duly executed but does not demonstrate that it was not: see *Weatherhill v Pearce* [1995] 2 All ER 492, [1995] 1 WLR 592; *National Trust for Places of Historic Interest and Natural Beauty v Royal*

National Institute for the Blind [1999] All ER (D) 81, sub nom *Re Chapman* (1998–99) 1 ITELR 863; *Sherrington v Sherrington* [2005] EWCA Civ 326, [2005] All ER (D) 359 (Mar); *Kentfield v Wright* [2010] EWHC 1607 (Ch), [2010] All ER (D) 07 (Jul). It seems that, on public policy grounds, 'positive evidence that the witness did not see the testator sign may not be enough to rebut the presumption unless the court is satisfied that it has 'the strongest evidence'' per Peter Gibson LJ in *Sherrington v Sherrington* at [42], citing Lord Penzance in *Wright v Rogers* (1869) LR 1 P & D 678 at 682. In *Wright v Rogers*, at 682, Lord Penzance said that where both witnesses, however, swear that the will was not duly executed and there is no evidence the other way, there is no footing for the court to affirm that the will is duly executed. In *Channon v Perkins* [2005] EWCA Civ 1808 at [45], [2005] All ER (D) 30 (Dec), Arden LJ suggested that there is a sliding scale according to which evidence will constitute the 'strongest' evidence in one case but not in another, depending on the totality of the relevant facts, and the court's evaluation of the probabilities. The more probable it is, from the circumstances, that the will was properly attested, the greater will be the burden on those seeking to displace the presumption as to due execution to which the execution of the will and the attestation clause give rise. In *Channon v Perkins*, evidence from both attesting witnesses that they did not remember witnessing the execution of the will was found, on considering the totality of the evidence in the case, to be based on poor recollection, rather than anything else, and was not strong enough to rebut the presumption. See *Re Whelan* [2015] EWHC 3301 (Ch) where Behrens J found that the evidence was sufficient.

2   *Re Parslow, Parslow v Parslow* (1959) Times, 3 December (evidence of handwriting expert that attestation was forged by testatrix).

3   *Bootle v Blundell* (1815) 19 Ves 494 at 504; *Howard v Braithwaite* (1812) 1 Ves & B 202 at 208.

4   *Kinleside v Harrison* (1818) 2 Phillim 449 at 499. Cf *Burrowes v Lock* (1805) 10 Ves 470 at 473; *Young and Smith v Richards* (1839) 2 Curt 371; *Pennant v Kingscote* (1843) 3 Curt 642. See also *Digg's Case* (circa 1680) cited in Skin at 79; *Hudson's Case* (1682) Skin 79.

5   See PARA 896.

6   See PARA 894.

7   See *Otuka v Alozie* [2006] EWHC 3493 (Ch), [2005] All ER (D) 30 (Dec) (positive evidence in support from three witnesses, including the two attesting witnesses).

78. Capacity of witnesses.

There is no statutory provision which forbids any person from witnessing a will. A blind person, however, is not normally[1] capable of witnessing a will, as mere physical presence without the faculty of sight is not enough to constitute a person a witness to something visible, such as the signature of a will[2]. A child possessing the requisite competence to give evidence[3] is not incompetent to witness a will merely by reason of minority[4], but no person under disability should act as witness to a will unless his mental capacity is such that he is conscious of the act done and unless he will, if required, be able to testify in support of the execution of the will[5]. A will is not invalid because at the time of the execution or at any time afterwards any person attesting the execution is incompetent[6] to be admitted a witness to prove its execution[7]. Executors[8], creditors and their wives or husbands or civil partners[9], and beneficiaries and their wives or husbands or civil partners[10], are all admissible witnesses to prove the execution of a will or its validity or invalidity, but a gift to a non-superfluous attesting witness or to the wife or husband or civil partner of such a witness is void[11].

1   The possibility that a blind person might in very exceptional circumstances be able to witness a will was left open in *Re Gibson* [1949] P 434 at 437, 440, [1949] 2 All ER 90 at 92, 94.

2   *Re Gibson* [1949] P 434, [1949] 2 All ER 90 (citing dicta in *Hudson v Parker* (1844) 1 Rob Eccl 14 at 23, 35, 37, 40 and *Re Gunstan, Blake v Blake* (1882) 7 PD 102 at 107, 113, 116). As to the rule that the witnesses must either have seen or had the opportunity of seeing the testator's signature see PARA 70.

3   As to the competence of minors as witnesses see CIVIL PROCEDURE vol 12 (2015) PARA 793.

4   There is no statutory prohibition, but what is needed in a witness is his mental presence.

5   The object of the legislature was that the witnesses should see and be conscious of the act done and be able to prove it by their own evidence (see *Hudson v Parker* (1844) 1 Rob Eccl 14 at 23); and as to the meaning of 'attest' cf *Bryan v White* (1850) 2 Rob Eccl 315. From this principle in the text follows.

6   As to the competency of witnesses see CIVIL PROCEDURE vol 12 (2015) PARA 793 et seq.

7   Wills Act 1837 s 14. Probate in solemn form has been granted where neither attesting witness could be found: *Re Lemon, Winwood v Lemon* (1961) 105 Sol Jo 1107.

8 See the Wills Act 1837 s 17.
9 Wills Act 1837 s 16 (amended by the Civil Partnership Act 2004 s 71, Sch 4 para 4). As to civil partnerships generally see PARAS 90, 179.
10 Wills Act 1837 s 15 (amended by virtue of the Civil Partnership Act 2004 Sch 4 para 3).
11 See Wills Act 1837 s 15 (as amended: see note 10); and the Wills Act 1968 s 1 (amended by virtue of the Civil Partnership Act 2004 Sch 4 para 3). See further PARAS 41–44.

(v) Privileged Wills

79. Wills of soldiers, sailors and airmen. The will of a soldier[1] in actual military service, a mariner or seaman (including a member of the Royal Navy or marine forces) being either at sea or so circumstanced that, if he were a soldier, he would be in actual military service, or a member of the Royal Air Force similarly circumstanced, is not required to conform to the provisions of the Wills Act 1837[2], either as regards writing, or, if in writing, as regards execution, and is valid, even though the testator is under 18 years of age[3].

'Actual military service' means 'active'[4] military service on the part of a person of either sex[5] and of any rank[6] who is concerned with operations in a war which is or has been in progress or is imminent[7], whether in England and Wales or abroad[8], and whether or not an element of danger exists[9]. The term is the equivalent of the Roman conception of 'in expeditione'[10], if this term is broadly interpreted[11] but it does not import the civil law principle that such a will is valid only for 12 months after discharge[12]. It embraces operations against terrorists[13], clandestine assassins and arsonists[14]. It is enough that the testator has taken some steps towards joining the forces in the field[15], or that his battalion has been ordered to mobilise for active service[16]. Furthermore, a state of war is not essential; and, accordingly, a soldier ordered, before declaration of war, to rejoin his unit to take part in the defence of the realm against external danger is in actual military service[17]. The mere fact that a soldier is in barracks is, however, insufficient[18]. It is not necessary that the service should be in the Queen's forces[19].

Any will so made may be revoked by the maker, notwithstanding that he is still under the age of 18, whether or not the circumstances are then such that he would be entitled to make a similar valid will[20].

1 'Soldier' includes an officer (*Drummond v Parish* (1843) 3 Curt 522), and a civilian in actual military service (*Re Stanley* [1916] P 192).
2 As the will need not be attested, a gift to a witness is valid: see *Re Limond, Limond v Cunliffe* [1915] 2 Ch 240.
3 See the Wills Act 1837 s 11; the Wills (Soldiers and Sailors) Act 1918 ss 1–3, 5(2) (ss 1 3 amended by the Family Law Reform Act 1969 s 3(1)). The Wills (Soldiers and Sailors) Act 1918 s 2, which enlarges the power of sailors to make privileged wills by putting them in the same position as soldiers, applies to a sailor who made his will before, but died after, 6 February 1918 (ie the date on which the Act was passed): *Re Yates* [1919] P 93. The Wills (Soldiers and Sailors) Act 1918 s 4 validated appointments of testamentary guardians by a will within the Wills Act 1837 s 11 (cf *Re Tollemache* [1917] P 246); but by virtue of the Children Act 1989 s 5(5), (13) an appointment of a guardian is now only valid if it is in writing, dated and signed (see CHILDREN AND YOUNG PERSONS vol 9 (2012) PARAS 4, 166). A privileged will suffices to exercise a power of appointment: see TRUSTS AND POWERS vol 98 (2013) PARA 564.
4 *Re Gossage, Wood v Gossage* [1921] P 194, CA; *Re Wingham, Andrews v Wingham* [1949] P 187 at 191, [1948] 2 All ER 908 at 910, CA, per Bucknill LJ.
5 *Re Rowson* [1944] 2 All ER 36.
6 *Re Hayes* (1839) 2 Curt 338; *Re Donaldson* (1840) 2 Curt 386 (surgeon); *Re Cory* (1901) 84 LT 270 at 271 (member of irregular force); *May v May* [1902] P 103n (quartermaster and honorary lieutenant); *Re Stanley* [1916] P 192 (military nurse on leave from hospital ship).
7 *Re Wingham, Andrews v Wingham* [1949] P 187 at 192, [1948] 2 All ER 908 at 911, CA, per Bucknill LJ; and see *Re Rippon* [1943] P 61, [1943] 1 All ER 676.
8 *Re Spark* [1941] P 115, [1941] 2 All ER 782; *Re Rowson* [1944] 2 All ER 36.

9 *Gattward v Knee* [1902] P 99 at 102; *Re Wingham, Andrews v Wingham* [1949] P 187 at 191, [1948] 2 All ER 908 at 910–911, CA, per Bucknill LJ.

10 *Drummond v Parish* (1843) 3 Curt 522, where the history of the privilege is reviewed. See Justinian's Institutes, Lib II, XI (1–4); *Re Phipps* (1840) 2 Curt 368; *Re Limond, Limond v Cunliffe* [1915] 2 Ch 240; *Re Kitchen, Kitchen v Allman* (1919) 35 TLR 612. See also *Godman v Godman* [1920] P 261, CA; *Re Grey* [1922] P 140 (will made in military hospital 18 months after cessation of active service not admitted).

11 *Re Wingham, Andrews v Wingham* [1949] P 187 at 193, [1948] 2 All ER 908 at 911, CA, per Cohen LJ, but see at 195 and at 913 per Denning LJ.

12 *Re Booth, Booth v Booth* [1926] P 118 at 135.

13 *Re Anderson* (1958) 75 WNNSW 334 (service in Malaya).

14 *Re Jones* [1981] Fam 7, [1981] 1 All ER 1 (service in Northern Ireland).

15 *Re Hiscock* [1901] P 78; *Stopford v Stopford* (1903) 19 TLR 185.

16 *Gattward v Knee* [1902] P 99; *Stopford v Stopford* (1903) 19 TLR 185; *Re Booth, Booth v Booth* [1926] P 118.

17 *Re Rippon* [1943] P 61, [1943] 1 All ER 676.

18 *White v Repton* (1844) 3 Curt 818; *Re Hill* (1845) 1 Rob Eccl 276.

19 *Re Donaldson* (1840) 2 Curt 386 (East India Company's private army).

20 Family Law Reform Act 1969 s 3(3), (4).

80. Wills of mariners and seamen. The privilege of a mariner or seaman of being able to make an informal will extends to officers of every rank[1], merchant seamen[2] and marines[3], men or women[4]. For the privilege to apply, it is not necessary that the will should be executed at sea, provided that it is made while on maritime service[5], and it can extend to a mariner or seaman serving on board a vessel permanently stationed in a harbour[6], or on service in a river[7]. The privilege accorded to mariners and seamen of making informal wills is not, it seems, restricted to those who were serving, or had been engaged to serve, on British-registered ships[8].

1 *Re Hayes* (1839) 2 Curt 338; *Re Saunders* (1865) LR 1 P & D 16; *Re Rae* (1891) 27 LR Ir 116. A woman typist in the liner Lusitania, sunk in the 1914-18 war, was included in this category: *Re Hale* [1915] 2 IR 362.

2 *Morrell v Morrell* (1827) 1 Hag Ecc 51; *Re Milligan* (1849) 2 Rob Eccl 108; *Re Parker* (1859) 2 Sw & Tr 375.

3 'Mariner' includes by implication members of the Royal Marines: see the Wills (Soldiers and Sailors) Act 1918 s 2. However, it seems that a marine would also be within the definition of a soldier.

4 See the Wills Act 1837 s 11; the Wills (Soldiers and Sailors) Act 1918; and PARA 79.

5 Ie in the sense that the testator, at the time of making the will, is in post as a ship's officer, or is a member of a particular ship's company serving in that ship, including a member on shore leave or long leave ashore, or is employed by ship owners and having been discharged from one ship is already under orders to join another: see *Re Rapley's Estate, Rapley v Rapley* [1983] 3 All ER 248 at 251, [1983] 1 WLR 1069 at 1073. The unattested will of a seaman who was on leave, having been discharged from one ship and not posted to another, was held not to be valid: *Re Rapley's Estate, Rapley v Rapley*. See also *Re Servoz-Gavin, Ayling v Summers* [2009] EWHC 3168 (Ch), [2010] All ER 410; and note 8.

6 *Re M'Murdo* (1868) LR 1 P & D 540.

7 *Re Austin* (1853) 2 Rob Eccl 611; *Re Patterson* (1898) 79 LT 123. Cf *Re Barnes, Hodson v Barnes* (1926) 136 LT 380, where words written on an eggshell by a Manchester Ship Canal pilot were propounded as a will, and the question whether he could be considered a mariner at sea was considered but not decided.

8 See *Re Servoz-Gavin, Ayling v Summers* [2009] EWHC 3168 (Ch), [2011] Ch 162, [2010] All ER 410 (informal will made by merchant seaman in England, after he had received orders to join foreign-registered vessel in Bombay, was made at a time when he was contemplating and preparing to join the ship; held: there was a valid privileged will).

81. Form of privileged will; revocation. Any form of words, whether written or nuncupative, that is, spoken by the testator in the presence of a credible witness[1], will suffice to constitute a soldier's or sailor's or airman's will, provided that it is a deliberate expression of his wishes[2] and is intended to have testamentary effect[3].

The will, whether formal or informal, may be revoked by a letter or other informal act expressing an intention to revoke, without any new will, provided that the circumstances of the revocation are the same as are required to give validity to a soldier's or sailor's or airman's will[4]. A letter of a testator making erroneous statements as to what he thought that he had done with his estate, but showing no intention to alter his will, is not, however, effective to alter its dispositions[5]. The rule that the subsequent marriage or entry into a civil partnership of the testator revokes his will applies to a privileged will[6]. Return to life as a civilian does not of itself operate as revocation[7]. A privileged will is proved by affidavit showing that the testator, when he made it, was in actual military service or at sea, as the case may be, and that he was domiciled in England or Wales[8].

1 For instances of such wills see *Morrell v Morrell* (1827) 1 Hag Ecc 51; *Re Scott* [1903] P 243; *Re Stable, Dalrymple v Campbell* [1919] P 7; *Re Spicer, Spicer v Richardson* [1949] P 441, [1949] 2 All ER 659. Evidence of statements made by the deceased after executing the will is admissible to prove its contents, but cogent evidence is necessary: *Re MacGillivray* [1946] 2 All ER 301, CA.
2 *Drummond v Parish* (1843) 3 Curt 522; *Re Vernon* (1916) 33 TLR 11 (will and two letters admitted to probate); *Selwood v Selwood* (1920) 125 LT 26. Cf *Boughton-Knight v Wilson* (1915) 32 TLR 146.
3 See *Re Knibbs, Flay v Trueman* [1962] 2 All ER 829, [1962] 1 WLR 852 (words spoken in casual conversation were not testamentary act). See also *Re Donner* (1917) 34 TLR 138; *Re Beech, Beech v Public Trustee* [1923] P 46, CA; *Re MacGillivray* [1946] 2 All ER 301, CA; *Re Knibbs, Flay v Trueman* [1962] 2 All ER 829, [1962] 1 WLR 852.
4 *Re Gossage, Wood v Gossage* [1921] P 194, CA. As to revocation generally see PARA 87 et seq.
5 *Re Beech, Beech v Public Trustee* [1923] P 46, CA. See also *Godman v Godman* [1920] P 261, CA.
6 *Re Wardrop* [1917] P 54. For revocation by entry into a civil partnership see the Wills Act 1837 s 18B; and PARA 90.
7 *Re Coleman* [1920] 2 IR 332.
8 See PARA 710.

(6) ALTERATIONS AND ERASURES IN WILL

82. Effect of unexecuted alterations. No obliteration, interlineation or other alteration made in a will after execution is valid unless duly executed[1], except so far as the words or effect of the will before such alteration are not apparent[2]. It seems that the adding of the dispositive parts of a will after execution may not be seen as invalid, for these purposes, if the writing of the will and the appending of the signature are all one operation[3]. 'Apparent' means apparent on an inspection of the instrument, not apparent by extrinsic evidence[4]. Words are apparent if experts, using magnifying glasses where necessary, can decipher them and satisfy the court that they have done so[5], but, where words are only readable by chemical means[6], or by making a new document, such as an infra-red photograph[7], they are not apparent, and, where there is complete obliteration of a whole legacy, so that the words used are no longer apparent, the obliteration effects a revocation of the legacy in question[8]. Revocation by obliteration may be conditional, and, if the condition in question is unfulfilled, the revocation fails and the will, as made before such revocation, remains operative[9].

1 See *Re White, Barker v Gribble* [1991] Ch 1, [1990] 3 All ER 1. As to the form of execution of alterations see PARAS 84–86. The fact that a testamentary document contains erasures does not necessarily prevent it from being admitted to probate without an action: *Re O'Brien* [1900] P 208.
2 Wills Act 1837 s 21. As to revocation by obliteration of signatures see PARA 105.
3 *Wood v Smith* [1993] Ch 90, [1992] 3 All ER 556, CA (but, on the evidence, the will failed for lack of testamentary capacity).
4 *Townley v Watson* (1844) 3 Curt 761 at 764. See also *Re Ibbetson* (1839) 2 Curt 337; *Re McCabe* (1873) LR 3 P & D 94 at 96; *Re Horsford* (1874) LR 3 P & D 211; *Ffinch v Combe* [1894] P 191.

5 *Ffinch v Combe* [1894] P 191; *Re Brasier* [1899] P 36.
6 *Re Horsford* (1874) LR 3 P & D 211 at 215–216.
7 *Re Itter, Dedman v Godfrey* [1950] P 130, [1950] 1 All ER 68.
8 *Townley v Watson* (1844) 3 Curt 761. See *Re Hamer* (1943) 60 TLR 168 (where part of the words stating the sum given was obliterated and probate passed with the obliteration in blank).
9 As to dependent relative revocation see PARA 108.

83. Time of alteration. In the absence of evidence, the presumption is that alterations, interlineations and erasures were made after execution, and the burden is on the person who seeks to rely on an alteration in a will to adduce some evidence that the alteration was made before the will was executed[1]. Probate is granted in blank as regards such of the original words as are not apparent[2], but, if they are apparent, the probate contains the original words[3]. Very slight affirmative evidence is, however, sufficient[4], at least if the alterations are trifling[5]. Once probate has been granted, the court of construction must accept alterations as having been made before the will was executed[6].

Evidence of declarations of testamentary intention made by the testator before or at the time of execution suffices to displace the above presumption[7], and so does evidence of other persons that the alterations were made before execution[8]. Internal evidence furnished by the document itself may be considered, and the circumstance that a clause would be perfectly meaningless without the interlineation is material[9]. Any evidence which, having regard to the circumstances, reasonably leads to the conclusion that the alterations were made before execution is sufficient[10]. Thus where alterations are necessary to supply blanks left in a will, such as for the names of legatees or the amounts of legacies, and these blanks are afterwards filled in, the presumption is that they were inserted before execution, and an interlineation which appears to have been written with the same ink and the same pen as the rest of the will, and which supplies a blank in the sense, is presumed to have been written before execution[11].

Where the testator indicates, for example by asterisks, the place in the will where matter written before execution is intended to come in, such matter, if proved to be written before the will was executed, may be regarded as a valid interlineation[12]. Words following the executed part of a will cannot, however, be treated as an interlineation merely because they complete an otherwise incomplete sentence in the executed part[13].

1 *Cooper v Bockett* (1846) 4 Moo PCC 419; *Simmons v Rudall* (1851) 1 Sim NS 115 at 137; *Greville v Tylee* (1851) 7 Moo PCC 320; *Doe d Shallcross v Palmer* (1851) 16 QB 747; *Re James* (1858) 1 Sw & Tr 238; *Williams v Ashton* (1860) 1 John & H 115; *Re Benn* [1938] IR 313.
2 *Re Ibbetson* (1839) 2 Curt 337.
3 *Re Beavan* (1840) 2 Curt 369; *Re Martin* (1849) 1 Rob Eccl 712; *Re Gaussen* (1868) 16 WR 212.
4 *Re Duffy* (1871) IR 5 Eq 506.
5 See *Re Hindmarch* (1866) LR 1 P & D 307. Common form probate may be granted of a will including alterations, in the absence of evidence of when the alterations were made, if they appear to the district judge or registrar to be of no practical importance: see the Non-Contentious Probate Rules 1987, SI 1987/2024, r 14(2) (amended by SI 1991/1876); and PARA 735.
6 *Gann v Gregory* (1854) 3 De GM & G 777 at 780; *Cowan v Ball* [1933] NI 173. If, however, an interested party objects to the inclusion of alterations in the probate, it may be possible to bring proceedings for revocation of the grant of probate.
7 *Re Sykes* (1873) LR 3 P & D 26 at 27. See also *Doe d Shallcross v Palmer* (1851) 16 QB 747; *Dench v Dench* (1877) 2 PD 60; *Re Oates, Callow v Sutton* [1946] 2 All ER 735. Declarations as to unattested alterations made after execution of the will are not admissible: *Re Jessop* [1924] P 221.
8 *Tyler v Merchant Taylors' Co* (1890) 15 PD 216; *Re Greenwood* [1892] P 7.
9 *Re Heath* [1892] P 253. See also *Re Cadge* (1868) LR 1 P & D 543; *Re Treeby* (1875) LR 3 P & D 242; *Doherty v Dwyer* (1890) 25 LR Ir 297 (where the attestation clause referred generally to a 'few erasures and alterations'). The mere fact that the alterations are dated earlier than the execution is not enough: *Re Adamson* (1875) LR 3 P & D 253.

10 *Moore v Moore* (1872) IR 6 Eq 166; *Re Tonge* (1891) 66 LT 60.
11 *Re Hindmarch* (1866) LR 1 P & D 307; *Re Cadge* (1868) LR 1 P & D 543; *Re Benn* [1938] IR
     313. A clause inconsistent with the rest of the will, and struck out in pencil, was ignored in *Re
     Tonge* (1891) 66 LT 60. See also *Birch v Birch* (1848) 1 Rob Eccl 675.
12 *Re Birt* (1871) LR 2 P & D 214; *Re Greenwood* [1892] P 7. See also *Re White* (1860) 6 Jur NS
     808.
13 *Re Anstee* [1893] P 283. See also *Re White* [1896] 1 IR 269; *Re Gee* (1898) 78 LT 843.

84. Validity of alteration after signature. If an alteration (other than an
obliteration[1]) is made in a will after it is signed, the will must be signed again by
the testator (and duly witnessed), and it is not sufficient for the testator to
acknowledge his original signature[2]; the testator and the witnesses may sign in the
margin or in some other part of the will opposite or near to the alteration or at the
foot or end or opposite a memorandum referring to the alteration at the end of
some other part of the will[3]. The initials of the testator and the witnesses are
sufficient for this purpose[4], but the initials of the witnesses alone are not[5]. The
testator and witnesses do not, however, fulfil the statutory requirement by merely
going over their signatures with a dry pen; there must be either an execution of the
alteration or a re-execution of the will[6].

1 Ie an obliteration which renders the words no longer apparent (see PARA 82).
2 *Re White, Barker v Gribble* [1991] Ch 1, [1990] 3 All ER 1 (disapproving *Re Dewell* (1853) 17
   Jur 1130).
3 Wills Act 1837 s 21. More than one such alteration may be attested by a single marginal execution:
   see *Re Treeby* (1875) LR 3 P & D 242; *Re Wilkinson* (1881) 6 PD 100. The Wills Act 1837 s 21
   enables alterations to have effect, even though it is the alterations rather than the altered will as a
   whole which are executed and attested. As to this distinction see *Re White, Barker v Gribble*
   [1991] Ch 1, [1990] 3 All ER 1.
4 *Re Blewitt* (1880) 5 PD 116.
5 *Re Cunningham* (1860) 4 Sw & Tr 194; *Re Shearn* (1880) 50 LJP 15.
6 *Re Cunningham* (1860) 4 Sw & Tr 194. Execution of the alteration must conform with the
   Wills Act 1837 s 21 (see the text and note 3), whilst re-execution of the will must conform with
   s 9 (see PARA 60 et seq).

85. Effect of codicil on alterations. Unattested alterations in a will are validated
by a subsequent codicil confirming the will[1], unless it appears from the codicil or
otherwise that the alterations were merely deliberative[2], because a codicil is a
republication of a will and validates it at the time of execution of the codicil[3]. If
the codicil makes no mention of alterations, the presumption is that they were
made after the date of the codicil, but this may be rebutted by evidence[4].

1 *Re Heath* [1892] P 253; *Tyler v Merchant Taylors' Co* (1890) 15 PD 216; *Re Hay, Kerr v Stinnear*
   [1904] 1 Ch 317; *Oldroyd v Harvey* [1907] P 326 (second codicil).
2 *Re Hall* (1871) LR 2 P & D 256 at 257.
3 As to republication see PARAS 113–115.
4 *Lushington v Onslow* (1848) 6 Notes of Cases 183; *Re Sykes* (1873) LR 3 P & D 26 at 27. See
   also *Christmas and Christmas v Whinyates* (1863) 3 Sw & Tr 81 at 89 (where mutilation of a will
   was presumed to have taken place after the execution of a codicil). The evidence may extend to a
   testator's statements, made before the execution of a codicil to a will, which indicate that
   alterations or interlineations in the will were made before the execution of the codicil; see *Re Sykes*
   (1873) LR 3 P & D 26 at 28.

86. Alterations by stranger. A will altered by a stranger after execution by the
testator must, if possible, be restored to the state in which it was at the time of
execution, and probate is given without the alteration[1].

1 *Re Rolfe* (1846) 4 Notes of Cases 406. See also *Re North* (1842) 6 Jur 564; *Re Escott* (1842) 1
   Notes of Cases 571.

(7) REVOCATION OF WILL

(i) Revocation by Marriage

87. General rule as to revocation by marriage. With certain exceptions[1], a will is revoked by the testator's marriage[2], even if the marriage is voidable[3], and whether or not it is in fact avoided[4].

However, a will made in exercise of a power of appointment takes effect notwithstanding the testator's subsequent marriage, unless the property so appointed would in default of appointment pass to his personal representatives[5]. A will comprising property not subject to a power of appointment, and also property subject to appointment by the testator but falling within the above exception, is revoked by the marriage of the testator as to property not subject to the power, but remains valid as an appointment under the power[6]. Under the doctrine of mutual wills, the floating trust, which arises by agreement of the testators, and which crystallizes on the death of the first testator, is irrevocable and is not destroyed by the remarriage of the second testator after the death of the first and the consequent revocation of his will[7].

1   See the text to notes 5–6; and PARAS 88–89.
2   As to wills made on or after 1 January 1983 see the Wills Act 1837 s 18(1) (s 18 substituted by the Administration of Justice Act 1982 s 18(1)). As to wills made before that date see the Wills Act 1837 s 18 (as originally enacted). Section 18 does not affect any will made before 1 January 1983 (ie the date on which the Administration of Justice Act 1982 s 18(1) came into force): ss 73(7), 76(11). The general rule applies to soldiers' wills: *Re Wardrop* [1917] P 54. The marriage must be a lawful marriage: *Mette v Mette* (1859) 1 Sw & Tr 416; *Warter v Warter* (1890) 15 PD 152. As to persons who may lawfully marry see MATRIMONIAL AND CIVIL PARTNERSHIP LAW vol 72 (2015) PARA 33 et seq. 'Marriage' includes marriage of a same sex couple: see the Marriage (Same Sex Couples) Act 2013 Sch 3 para 1(1)(a), (2), (3); and MATRIMONIAL AND CIVIL PARTNERSHIP LAW vol 72 (2015) PARAS 1–2. As to the effect of divorce or annulment of marriage on testamentary provision for the former spouse see PARAS 177–178.
3   Ie voidable under the Matrimonial Causes Act 1973 s 12: see MATRIMONIAL AND CIVIL PARTNERSHIP LAW vol 72 (2015) PARA 387 et seq.
4   *Re Roberts, Roberts v Roberts* [1978] 3 All ER 225, [1978] 1 WLR 653, CA.
5   As to wills made before 1 January 1983 see the Wills Act 1837 s 18 (as originally enacted); and TRUSTS AND POWERS vol 98 (2013) PARA 619. As to wills made after 31 December 1982 see s 18(2) (as substituted: see note 2). As to the nature of the grant of probate in such a case see PARA 749.
6   See *Re Russell* (1890) 15 PD 111; and PARA 749.
7   *Re Goodchild, Goodchild v Goodchild* [1996] 1 All ER 670 at 678, [1997] 1 FCR 45 at 54, per Carnwath J, affd (without addressing this point) [1997] 3 All ER 63, [1997] 1 WLR 1216 (on the facts of the case, the wills were held not to be mutual; that finding upheld on appeal). As to mutual wills, see PARA 10.

88. Will in contemplation of marriage made before 1983. A will made after 31 December 1925 and before 1 January 1983[1] and expressed to be made in contemplation of a marriage is not revoked by the solemnisation of the marriage contemplated[2]. To gain the benefit of this provision the whole[3] will must have been made in contemplation of a particular marriage which was subsequently solemnised; a general statement that it was made in contemplation of marriage is not sufficient[4]. It is enough if on the terms of the will and in the circumstances the will 'practically expressed' that it was made in contemplation of the particular marriage[5].

1   The Law of Property Act 1925 s 177(1), which applied to wills made after 31 December 1925 (s 177(2)), is repealed by the Administration of Justice Act 1982 s 75(1), Sch 9 Pt I, and replaced by provisions of that Act (see PARA 89). The repeal of the Law of Property Act 1925 s 177 does

not, however, affect a will made before 1 January 1983 (ie the date on which the Administration of Justice Act 1982 s 18 came into force): ss 73(7), 76(11).

2   Law of Property Act 1925 s 177(1) (repealed: see note 1). This overruled *Re Cadywold* (1858) 1 Sw & Tr 34 and *Otway v Sadleir* (1858) 4 Ir Jur NS 97.

3   *Re Coleman* [1976] Ch 1, [1975] 1 All ER 675.

4   *Sallis v Jones* [1936] P 43.

5   *Pilot v Gainfort* [1931] P 103 (where the testator referred to the woman whom he shortly afterwards married as 'my wife'); *Re Knight* (1944) unreported but referred to in *Re Langston* [1953] P 100 at 103, [1953] 1 All ER 928 at 930 ('my future wife'); *Re Langston* ('my fiancée').

89.   Will in expectation of marriage made after 1982. Where it appears from a will made on or after 1 January 1983[1] that at the time it was made the testator was expecting to be married to a particular person, and that he intended that the will should not be revoked by the marriage, the will is not revoked by his marriage to that person[2].

Where it appears from a will made on or after 1 January 1983 that at the time it was made the testator was expecting to be married to a particular person, and that he intended that a disposition in the will should not be revoked by his marriage to that person, that disposition takes effect notwithstanding the marriage[3]. Further, any other disposition in the will takes effect also, unless it appears from the will that the testator intended the disposition to be revoked by the marriage[4].

1   The provisions of the Wills Act 1837 s 18 do not apply to any will made before 1 January 1983: see PARA 87 note 2.

2   Wills Act 1837 s 18(3) (substituted by the Administration of Justice Act 1982 s 18(1)). 'Marriage' includes marriage of a same sex couple: see the Marriage (Same Sex Couples) Act 2013 Sch 3 para 1(1)(a), (2), (3); and MATRIMONIAL AND CIVIL PARTNERSHIP LAW vol 72 (2015) PARAS 1–2.

3   Wills Act 1837 s 18(4)(a) (as substituted: see note 2).

4   Wills Act 1837 s 18(4)(b) (as substituted: see note 2).

(ii) Revocation by Civil Partnership

90.   General rule as to revocation by civil partnership. With certain exceptions[1], a will is revoked by the formation of a civil partnership[2] between the testator and another person[3].

However, a will made in exercise of a power of appointment takes effect notwithstanding a subsequent formation of a civil partnership between the testator and another person, unless the property so appointed would in default of appointment pass to the testator's personal representatives[4]. A will comprising property not subject to a power of appointment, and also property subject to appointment by the testator but falling within the above exception, is revoked by the formation of a civil partnership between the testator and another person as to property not subject to the power, but remains valid as an appointment under the power[5].

1   See the text to notes 3–4; and PARA 91.

2   Ie a relationship between two persons of the same sex formed when they register as civil partners of each other under the Civil Partnership Act 2004: see s 1; and MATRIMONIAL AND CIVIL PARTNERSHIP LAW vol 72 (2015) PARA 3. Provision is made for the dissolution or annulment of a civil partnership (see Pt 2 Ch 2 (ss 37–64)) and for property and financial arrangements (see Pt 2 Ch 3 (ss 65–72)). As to the effect of dissolution or annulment of civil partnership on testamentary provision for the former civil partner see PARA 179.

3   Wills Act 1837 s 18B(1) (s 18B added by the Civil Partnership Act 2004 s 71, Sch 4 paras 1, 2).

4   Wills Act 1837 s 18B(2) (added: see note 3).

5   See *Re Russell* (1890) 15 PD 111; and PARA 749.

91. Will in expectation of civil partnership. Where it appears from a will that at the time it was made the testator was expecting to form a civil partnership with a particular person, and that he intended that the will should not be revoked by the formation of the civil partnership, the will is not revoked by its formation[1].

Where it appears from a will that at the time it was made the testator was expecting to form a civil partnership with a particular person, and that he intended that a disposition in the will should not be revoked by the formation of the civil partnership, that disposition takes effect despite the formation of the civil partnership[2]. Further, any other disposition in the will takes effect also, unless it appears from the will that the testator intended the disposition to be revoked by the formation of the civil partnership[3].

1 Wills Act 1837 s 18B(3) (s 18B added by the Civil Partnership Act 2004 s 71, Sch 4 paras 1, 2). As to the meaning of 'civil partnership' see PARA 90 note 2. See further *Court v Despallieres, Re Ikin* [2009] EWHC 3340 (Ch), [2010] 2 All ER 451, [2009] All ER (D) 167 (Dec) (clause that will was intended to survive marriage, civil partnership or adoption did not show that the testator expected to form a civil partnership; will held revoked).
2 Wills Act 1837 s 18B(4), (5) (as added: see note 1).
3 Wills Act 1837 s 18B(4), (6) (as added: see note 1).

(iii) Voluntary Revocation

A. REQUISITES FOR REVOCATION

92. Revocable nature of will. A will is of its own nature revocable, and, even though a testator attempts to make his testament and last will irrevocable by the use of the strongest and most express terms, he may nevertheless revoke it, because his own act and deed cannot alter the judgment of law to make that irrevocable which is of its own nature revocable[1].

1 *Vynior's Case* (1609) 8 Co Rep 81b. See also PARA 2. As to the effect of contracts not to revoke a will see PARA 21; as to the revocation of joint and mutual wills see PARA 23; and as to the revocation of a privileged will see PARAS 79–81.

93. Intention to revoke. To effect a revocation there must be an intention to revoke[1], and a will is not revoked by any presumption of intention based on an alteration of circumstances[2]. If anything is done by the testator or by his direction which, if there were an intention to revoke, would amount to a revocation, the presumption of law from that act is in favour of the existence of the intention to revoke, but this presumption may be rebutted by evidence showing that that intention did not exist[3]. An act done without that intention is wholly ineffectual[4], even if the act results in the destruction of the will[5]. Thus no revocation results where a testator destroys the will through inadvertence[6], or under the belief that it is useless[7] or invalid[8], or has already been revoked[9], or where he is drunk at the time of an alleged revocation[10] or where he is suffering from mental disorder at the time, even though he subsequently recovers[11]. Similarly, an express revocation clause in a subsequent, duly executed, will may be ineffective if it is made under a mistake or in the belief that some other disposition will take effect which in fact does not[12].

There must be an act of revocation accompanying the intention to revoke, and the expression of an intention to revoke at some future time or by some future instrument is not sufficient[13]. The fact that the act and intention of revocation are accompanied by an expression of intention to make a new will which is not in fact made does not prevent the revocation from being effective[14].

The intention to revoke may be evidenced by the declarations of the testator, especially if those declarations were contemporaneous with the act of revocation[15], or that intention may be inferred from the nature of the act done[16].

Once due execution of a will is proved, the burden of showing that it has been revoked lies on those who seek to establish revocation, and, in the absence of proof, revocation is not presumed[17].

1 See the Wills Act 1837 s 20.
2 See the Wills Act 1837 s 19. See also *Re Wells' Trusts, Hardisty v Wells* (1889) 42 ChD 646 (where the will disposed of a fund which the testator afterwards disposed of by deed in such a way that the latter disposition was void as to one-fifth, and it was held that this one-fifth passed under the will).
3 See *Onions v Tyrer* (1716) 1 P Wms 343 at 344; *Burtenshaw v Gilbert* (1774) 1 Cowp 49 at 52; and PARA 397.
4 *Clarkson v Clarkson* (1862) 2 Sw & Tr 497; *Re Thornton* (1889) 14 PD 82.
5 *James v Shrimpton* (1876) 1 PD 431. See also *Clarkson v Clarkson* (1862) 2 Sw & Tr 497; *Cheese v Lovejoy* (1877) 2 PD 251 at 253, CA.
6 *Burtenshaw v Gilbert* (1774) 1 Cowp 49 at 52 per Lord Mansfield CJ.
7 *Beardsley v Lacey* (1897) 78 LT 25. See also *James v Shrimpton* (1876) 1 PD 431.
8 *Giles v Warren* (1872) LR 2 P & D 401; *Re Thornton* (1889) 14 PD 82.
9 *Scott v Scott* (1859) 1 Sw & Tr 258; *Clarkson v Clarkson* (1862) 2 Sw & Tr 497.
10 *Re Brassington* [1902] P 1.
11 *Scruby and Finch v Fordham* (1822) 1 Add 74; *Re Shaw* (1838) 1 Curt 905; *Borlase v Borlase* (1845) 4 Notes of Cases 106 at 139; *Re Downer* (1853) 18 Jur 66; *Brunt v Brunt* (1873) LR 3 P & D 37; *Re Hine* [1893] P 282; *Re Sabatini* (1969) 114 Sol Jo 35 (where it was held that the same standards of mind and memory and degree of understanding are required as for the original making of the will). See also *Re Taylor, National and Provincial and Union Bank of England v Taylor* (1919) 64 Sol Jo 148 (missing will of person of unsound mind made before lunacy). The subsequent mental disorder of a testator does not effect a revocation of a will made when he was of sound mind: Swinburne on Wills (7th Edn) Pt II s 3; *Forest and Hemburg's Case* (1588) 4 Co Rep 606 at 616. Cf *Re Sabatini* above.
12 See PARAS 107–109. See also the unsuccessful attempt to have the court allow a partial revocation only in *Lamothe v Lamothe* [2006] EWHC 1387 (Ch), [2006] WTLR 1431, [2006] All ER (D) 153 (Jun) (wording in a revocation clause concerning property 'where so ever situated'; in a situation where the testatrix's intentions were otherwise unclear about the significance of the clause, she having property both in England and in Dominica, this was held to show intention to completely revoke an earlier will which did not deal expressly with the Dominican property, but did expressly refer to the English property).
13 *Cleoburey v Beckett* (1851) 14 Beav 583. See also *Burton v Gowell* (1593) Cro Eliz 306; *Thomas d Jones v Evans* (1802) 2 East 488.
14 *Toomer v Sobinska* [1907] P 106; *Re Jones, Evans v Harries* [1976] Ch 200, [1976] 1 All ER 593, CA. It is possible, however, in cases of this kind for the revocation to be conditional on the contemplated new will being made, in which case the revocation may not be effective: see PARA 108 text and notes 4, 18.
15 *Clarke v Scripps* (1852) 2 Rob Eccl 563. See also *Stride v Cooper* (1811) 1 Phillim 334 at 338.
16 *Clarke v Scripps* (1852) 2 Rob Eccl 563; *North v North* (1909) 25 TLR 322.
17 *Harris v Berrall* (1858) 1 Sw & Tr 153; *Sprigge v Sprigge* (1868) LR 1 P & D 608; *Benson v Benson* (1870) LR 2 P & D 172; *Re Taylor, National and Provincial and Union Bank of England v Taylor* (1919) 64 Sol Jo 148. Where, however, the testator has had possession of a will (while of sound mind) and it either cannot be found after his death or is found mutilated or destroyed, there is a rebuttable presumption that it has been destroyed with intention to revoke it: see PARA 106.

94. Methods of revocation. Voluntary revocation[1] of a will or codicil can only be effected:

(1) by another later will or codicil duly executed[2];
(2) by some writing declaring an intention to revoke the will or codicil and duly executed as a will[3]; or
(3) by the burning, tearing or otherwise destroying[4] of the will or codicil by the testator, or by some person in his presence and by his direction, with the intention of revoking it[5].

No conveyance or other act made or done subsequently to the execution of a will or codicil of or relating to any real or personal estate comprised in it, except an act by which the will or codicil is revoked, prevents the operation of the will with respect to such estate or interest in the real or personal estate as the testator has power to dispose of by will at the time of his death[6].

As a will speaks from the testator's death[7] and can be revoked only in one or other of the prescribed ways[8], a testator cannot delegate the power to revoke his will after his death[9].

A will is not revoked, nor the construction of it altered, by reason of any subsequent change of domicile of the testator[10].

1   As to revocation by marriage or civil partnership see PARAS 87, 90.
2   As to revocation by later instrument see PARA 95 et seq.
3   See PARA 95 et seq.
4   As to revocation by destruction see PARAS 101–106.
5   Wills Act 1837 s 20. Section 20 does not apply to soldiers' wills: *Re Gossage, Wood v Gossage* [1921] P 194, CA. The manner in which devises in writing of land might be revoked was formerly laid down by the Statute of Frauds (1677) s 6 (repealed).
6   Wills Act 1837 s 23. The result of this provision is that the cases in which it was formerly held that a will was revoked by an alteration of the estate of the testator are no longer law: *Ford v De Pontès* (1861) 30 Beav 572 at 593. The provision refers to an interest of the testator remaining in the property, and does not apply to cases where the thing meant to be given is gone: *Moor v Raisbeck* (1841) 12 Sim 123 at 139; *Blake v Blake* (1880) 15 ChD 481 at 487 (following *Gale v Gale* (1856) 21 Beav 349). As to ademption by alteration of estate see PARA 156; and as to a change in the nature of the property subject to a power exercised by will see TRUSTS AND POWERS vol 98 (2013) PARA 575.
7   See PARAS 1, 282.
8   See the Wills Act 1837 ss 18, 18B, 20; the text and notes 1–6; and PARAS 87–91.
9   *Stockwell v Ritherdon* (1848) 1 Rob Eccl 661.
10 Wills Act 1963 s 4 (repealing and for this purpose replacing the Wills Act 1861 s 3); *Re Reid* (1866) LR 1 P & D 74. See also *Re Groos* [1904] P 269; and CONFLICT OF LAWS vol 19 (2011) PARA 750.

B.   REVOCATION BY LATER INSTRUMENT

95.   Instrument of revocation. To be effectual, an instrument declaring an intention to revoke[1] a will must be executed in the manner in which a will is required to be executed[2]. Such an instrument is not, however, admitted to probate[3] unless it is itself of a testamentary character[4].

An earlier will is revoked by a later will or codicil expressly revoking that earlier will or all former wills[5], and no particular form of words is required for the purpose of effecting the revocation[6]. An express clause of revocation is not essential[7], but, if inserted in general terms, operates as a rule to revoke all testamentary instruments previously executed by the testator[8], including, usually, testamentary appointments[9]. Such a clause is not, however, conclusive evidence of an intention to effect a complete revocation[10], and may be shown to have been inserted by mistake and without the approval of the testator[11], or to have been dependent on another disposition taking effect which has not in fact taken effect[12].

Where there is no express revocation clause, the question of whether an earlier will is revoked depends on whether it has been revoked by implication; that is, whether it was the testator's intention, to be collected from the instrument, that the dispositions of the earlier will should remain in whole or part operative[13]. However, there is a presumption against implied revocation; an implied revocation can only be found from looking at the terms of successive testamentary instruments where there is a logical inconsistency between them[14].

The words 'last will' do not necessarily operate to revoke all previous testamentary instruments[15], nor even the words 'last and only will'[16]; but, where it is clear from the general tenor of the last will that the testator did not intend an earlier will to remain in force, the earlier will is revoked[17]. There is the possibility that a codicil may have the effect of reviving an earlier revoked will and indirectly bring about the revocation of a later will[18].

1 As to what amounts to such a declaration see *Re Gosling* (1886) 11 PD 79.
2 Wills Act 1837 s 20. A privileged will may, however, be revoked by an unattested instrument: *Re Gossage, Wood v Gossage* [1921] P 194, CA; *Re Newland* [1952] P 71, [1952] 1 All ER 841.
3 *Re Fraser* (1869) LR 2 P & D 40; *Re Eyre* [1905] 2 IR 540. As to the form of grant of administration in such a case see PARA 791.
4 *Re Hubbard* (1865) LR 1 P & D 53; *Re Hicks* (1869) LR 1 P & D 683; *Re Durance* (1872) LR 2 P & D 406 (where a letter signed by the testator and duly attested directing his brother to obtain his will and burn it unread was held sufficient to revoke the will); *Re Spracklan's Estate* [1938] 2 All ER 345, CA.
5 Wills Act 1837 s 20.
6 *Birks v Birks* (1865) 4 Sw & Tr 23 at 30; *Cottrell v Cottrell* (1872) LR 2 P & D 397; *Re Brennan* [1932] IR 633. The insertion in the attestation clause of words referring to the revocation of a previous codicil have been held to have no operative effect: *Re Atkinson* (1883) 8 PD 165. See also *Lamothe v Lamothe* [2006] EWHC 1387 (Ch), [2006] WTLR 1431, [2006] All ER (D) 153 (Jun); and see PARA 93 text and note 12.
7 *Dempsey v Lawson* (1877) 2 PD 98 at 107; *Re Brennan* [1932] IR 633. See also *Re Craig, Price v Craig* [2006] EWHC 2561 (Ch), 9 ITELR 393 (testator's true intentions clear from attendance notes of his solicitors; rectification granted).
8 *Sotheran v Dening* (1881) 20 ChD 99, CA. See also *Cottrell v Cottrell* (1872) LR 2 P & D 397.
9 *Sotheran v Dening* (1881) 20 ChD 99, CA; *Re Kingdon, Wilkins v Pryer* (1886) 32 ChD 604 (where a testamentary appointment under a special power was held to be revoked by a general revocatory clause). Although a general clause of revocation does not necessarily revoke an exercise of a power of appointment, it requires cogent evidence to exclude revocation (*Lowthorpe-Lutwidge v Lowthorpe-Lutwidge* [1935] P 151), but such evidence may be supplied by the surrounding circumstances (*Smith v Thompson* (1931) 47 TLR 603). See also *Cadell v Wilcocks* [1898] P 21 at 26. It is open to doubt whether or not a will made in exercise of a power is revoked by a second will made in exercise of another power and containing a general clause of revocation: see *Re Merritt* (1858) 1 Sw & Tr 112; *Re Joys* (1860) 4 Sw & Tr 214 (decisions which were considered unfavourably but not overruled by Jessel MR in *Sotheran v Dening* above at 105–106).
10 *Denny v Barton and Rashleigh* (1818) 2 Phillim 575; *O'Leary v Douglass* (1878) 1 LR Ir 45 at 50. See also *Gladstone v Tempest* (1840) 2 Curt 650; *Dempsey v Lawson* (1877) 2 PD 98 at 107; *Re O'Connor* [1942] 1 All ER 546; *Re Wayland* [1951] 2 All ER 1041. For the wider, probate court approach available to evidence in considering questions of animus revocandi compared to that available in the construction of a will: see *Lamothe v Lamothe* [2006] EWHC 1387 (Ch), [2007] All ER (D) 153 (Jun).
11 *Powell v Mouchett, Lichfield v Mouchett* (1821) Madd & G 216; *Re Oswald* (1874) LR 3 P & D 162; *Re Moore* [1892] P 378; *Marklew v Turner* (1900) 17 TLR 10; *Re Hope Brown* [1942] P 136, [1942] 2 All ER 176; *Re Cocke* [1960] 2 All ER 289, [1960] 1 WLR 491; *Re Phelan* [1972] Fam 33, [1971] 3 All ER 1256. See *Re Wayland* [1951] 2 All ER 1041; *Re Vickers' Estate* 2001 JLR 712, (2001–02) 4 ITELR 584, Royal Ct Jer (where general revocation clauses in wills disposing of property in one country were held not to revoke wills disposing of property elsewhere). See also *Re Chief Edward Iguda Aleyideino's Estate, Aleyideino v Aleyideino* [2003] JRC 018, 2003 JLR Note 7, (2003–04) 6 ITELR 584, Royal Ct Jer (English will and later Nigerian will with conflicting provisions). See further PARAS 398, 400. As to the court's power to rectify a will see PARA 187. It seems that in considering whether there is animus revocandi, the court will not impute knowledge and approval of a draftsman's mistake to the testator, so as to bind the testator to the wording: *Re Morris, Lords Bank Ltd v Peake* [1971] P 62, [1970] 1 All ER 1057; *Lamothe v Lamothe* [2006] EWHC 1387 (Ch), [2006] WTLR 1431, [2006] All ER (D) 153 (Jun).
12 See PARA 108.
13 See *Dempsey v Lawson* (1877) 2 PD 98; and PARAS 96, 98.
14 See *Perdoni v Curati* [2011] EWHC 3442 (Ch), [2012] WTLR 505, 14 ITELR 725; affd on different grounds [2012] EWCA Civ 1381, [2013] WTLR 63, 15 ITELR 480.
15 *Cutto v Gilbert* (1854) 9 Moo PCC 131 (overruling on this point *Plenty v West and Budd* (1845) 1 Rob Eccl 264). See also *Stoddart v Grant* (1852) 1 Macq 163 at 171, HL, per Lord Truro; *Freeman v Freeman* (1854) 5 De GM & G 704; *Lemage v Goodban* (1865) LR 1 P & D 57; *Re Howard* (1869) LR 1 P & D 636; *Leslie v Leslie* (1872) IR 6 Eq 332; *Re de la Saussaye* (1873) LR 3 P & D 42; *Re Petchell* (1874) LR 3 P & D 153 at 156; *Re O'Connor* (1884) 13 LR Ir 406; *Kitcat*

v King [1930] P 266; *Re Hawksley's Settlements, Black v Tidy* [1934] Ch 384. In *Loftus v Stoney* (1867) 17 I Ch R 178, two wills, one described as 'last' and the other 'duplicate', were admitted to probate, and the court of construction held that the will marked 'last' was the real will. The express confirmation in a third codicil of a will and one of two previous codicils does not of itself operate to revoke the other codicil: *Follett v Pettman* (1883) 23 ChD 337.

16 *Simpson v Foxon* [1907] P 54 (following *Lemage v Goodban* (1865) LR 1 P & D 57).

17 *Pepper v Pepper* (1870) IR 5 Eq 85; *Dempsey v Lawson* (1877) 2 PD 98; *Re Brennan* [1932] IR 633. See also PARAS 389–390.

18 See *Hoare Trustees v Jacques* [2008] EWHC 2022 (Ch), [2008] All ER (D) 68 (Feb), where a codicil made subsequent to a second will was held to refer to and to revive an earlier will and a codicil thereto, which had the effect of revoking the second will. See also *Re Chilcott* [1897] P 233, 66 LJP 108. In both these cases, the expressed intention, as shown by the draftsman, was attributed to the testators. See PARA 100, text and note 4. As to the revival of wills see PARA 110 et seq.

96.   Partial revocation. Either the whole or part only of a will may be revoked[1]. The intention to revoke governs the extent and measure of operation to be attributed to an act of revocation which may extend either to the whole or part only of a will[2]. Where revocation of part makes the rest of the will unintelligible, total revocation results[3]. A gift of residue by a will is revoked by a different gift of residue by a codicil, even though the codicil purports to deal with residue of property not disposed of by the will[4]. An interest clearly given by a will must not, however, be treated as taken away by a revocatory clause in a codicil unless that intention is clearly expressed[5]. Such an intention is not expressed merely by the addition of words of construction susceptible of being read as relating to the same subject matter and directing the will to be construed in a particular way[6].

1 See the Wills Act 1837 s 20. See also *Lamothe v Lamothe* [2006] EWHC 1387 (Ch), [2006] WTLR 1431, [2006] All ER (D) 153 (Jun), where the issue between the parties was whether there should be partial or complete revocation.

2 *Clarke v Scripps* (1852) 2 Rob Eccl 563; *Re Woodward* (1871) LR 2 P & D 206; *Re White* (1879) 3 LR Ir 413 at 416, Ir CA. A mere recital of the testator's object in revoking a gift does not, it seems, limit the operation of an absolute revocation: *Holder v Howell* (1803) 8 Ves 97. As to the effect of the revocation of a devise on an accessory gift of chattels see PARA 388. As to a general revocation clause being effective to revoke only parts of an earlier will as a consequence of mistake or the revocation being in part dependent on other dispositions taking effect see *Re Finnemore* [1992] 1 All ER 800, [1991] 1 WLR 793; and PARAS 108–109.

3 *Leonard v Leonard* [1902] P 243.

4 *Earl Hardwicke v Douglas* (1840) 7 Cl & Fin 795, HL; *Re Pereira, Worsley v Society for the Propagation of the Gospel* (1912) 56 Sol Jo 614; *Re Stoodley, Hooson v Locock* [1916] 1 Ch 242, CA. Cf the effect of two residuary clauses in the same will: *Re Gare, Filmer v Carter* [1952] Ch 80, [1951] 2 All ER 863.

5 *Re Wray, Wray v Wray* [1951] Ch 425, [1951] 1 All ER 375, CA (where a codicil which revoked the appointment of the executrix and directed that the will should take effect as if her name were omitted did not prevent her taking a beneficial interest (following *Re Percival, Boote v Dutton* (1888) 59 LT 21, CA, and *Re Freeman, Hope v Freeman* [1910] 1 Ch 681)); *Re Spensley's Will Trusts, Barclays Bank Ltd v Staughton* [1952] Ch 886, [1952] 2 All ER 49 (revsd on another point [1954] Ch 233, [1954] 1 All ER 178, CA) (where a codicil revoking all provisions for B and directing that the will should be read as if her name did not occur revoked a power of appointment conferred on her, but not a trust in default of appointment in favour of B's children). See also *Kellett v Kellett* (1868) LR 3 HL 160 at 167; *Re Brough, Currey v Brough* (1888) 38 ChD 456; *Re Wilcock, Kay v Dewhirst* [1898] 1 Ch 95 at 98; *Pennefather v Lloyd* [1917] 1 IR 337; *Re Nixon, Askew v Briggs* (1965) 109 Sol Jo 757.

6 See *Re Lawrence's Will Trusts, Public Trustee v Lawrence* [1972] Ch 418, [1971] 3 All ER 433 (where a gift by will was revoked by a codicil containing not only words of revocation but also a direction that the will was in all respects to be construed as if the gift had not been made; and it was held that such a direction merely enforced the words of revocation without affecting the remaining provisions of the will).

97.   Later inconsistent will. A later will or codicil may revoke all earlier wills, even though it contains no clause of revocation. It is a question of intention in each case. Where a later unambiguous will deals with the testator's entire property, it revokes all earlier wills[1], and, if the later will practically covers the same ground as an earlier one, it must be taken as being in substitution for it, and probate of the later will alone be granted[2]. Even where the later will does not completely cover the whole subject matter of an earlier one, if it can be gathered from the language of the testator that he intended to dispose of his property in a different manner from that in which he disposed of it by the earlier will, the earlier instrument is revoked[3].

The mere fact of making a subsequent testamentary disposition does not, however, effect a total revocation of a prior will unless the later disposition expressly or in effect revokes the former, or the two are incapable of standing together[4]. The probate court may decide the question for itself and refuse to admit the earlier document to probate or it may admit several documents to probate and leave it to the court of construction to determine the testator's real testamentary intentions. In such a case the court of construction may still decide that a document admitted to probate has been revoked[5]. A later inconsistent disposition which is not valid for any reason does not revoke an earlier disposition[6]. Where a will has been revoked by a later will and then revived by a codicil, then, unless the codicil expressly[7] revokes the later will or impliedly revokes it by reason of the fact that it involves dispositions inconsistent with those contained in the will[8], all three documents are admitted to probate and their effect is left for the court of construction to determine[9]. The mere fact that a codicil is described as a codicil to an earlier will does not impliedly revoke a later will[10], although it may have this effect[11].

If there are two wholly inconsistent testamentary documents of the same date, or undated, and it cannot be ascertained which of them was executed first, neither document may be admitted to probate[12]. They may, however, be effective to revoke all earlier wills[13].

1   *Henfrey v Henfrey* (1842) 4 Moo PCC 29; *Pepper v Pepper* (1870) IR 5 Eq 85; *Re Palmer, Palmer v Peat* (1889) 58 LJP 44; *Cadell v Wilcocks* [1898] P 21; *Re Fawcett* [1941] P 85, [1941] 2 All ER 341. Where some of the clauses in the earlier will are repeated, but otherwise the new will, which covers the whole of the testator's property, is inconsistent with the earlier will, the whole will is revoked and the repeated clauses take effect under the new will: *Re Hawksley's Settlements, Black v Tidy* [1934] Ch 384.

2   *O'Leary v Douglass* (1879) 3 LR Ir 323, Ir CA. See also *Dempsey v Lawson* (1877) 2 PD 98; *Re Turnour* (1886) 56 LT 671; *Re Palmer, Palmer v Peat* (1889) 58 LJP 44; *M'Ara v M'Cay* (1889) 23 LR Ir 138; *Cadell v Wilcocks* [1898] P 21; and see *Chichester v Quatrefages* [1895] P 186 (codicils).

3   *Dempsey v Lawson* (1877) 2 PD 98 at 105; *Re Bryan* [1907] P 125 at 129; *Re Brennan* [1932] IR 633; *Jones v Treasury Solicitor* (1932) 49 TLR 75, CA.

4   *Lemage v Goodban* (1865) LR 1 P & D 57; *Re Petchell* (1874) LR 3 P & D 153; *Re Summers* (1901) 84 LT 271; *Townsend v Moore* [1905] P 66, CA; *Simpson v Foxon* [1907] P 54; *Reeves v Reeves* [1909] 2 IR 521. Where there is no real inconsistency between two wills made by a testator, the second does not revoke the first: *Deakin v Garvie* (1919) 36 TLR 122, CA. See *Perdoni v Curati* [2011] EWHC 3442 (Ch), [2012] WTLR 505, 14 ITELR 725; affd on different grounds [2012] EWCA Civ 1381, [2013] WTLR 63, 15 ITELR 480 (held, applying *Lemage v Goodban*, a later will did not wholly revoke an earlier will as there was no material inconsistency between them hence a substitutional gift contained in the earlier will could take effect).

5   *Re Hawksley's Settlements, Black v Tidy* [1934] Ch 384; approved in *Re Resch's Will Trusts, Le Cras v Perpetual Trustee Co Ltd, Far West Children's Health Scheme v Perpetual Trustee Co Ltd* [1969] 1 AC 514, [1967] 3 All ER 915, PC. Where the revocation of an earlier will is wholly a matter of construction, it is possible for the matter to be determined in construction proceedings instead of probate proceedings as in *Re Finnemore* [1992] 1 All ER 800, [1991] 1 WLR 793. As to the construction of wills by the court see PARA 185 et seq.

6   See PARA 107 note 2.

7   This may occur indirectly: see *Re Pearson, Rowling v Crowther* [1963] 3 All ER 763, [1963] 1 WLR 1358 (codicil made after later will but expressly referred to earlier revoked will and

confirmed it in all other respects; the earlier will had a revocation clause which became incorporated into the codicil, so expressly revoking the later will).

8 *Hoare Trustees v Jacques* [2008] EWHC 2022 (Ch), [2008] All ER (D) 68 (Feb) (codicil expressly referred to earlier will and made dispositions inconsistent with both wills).

9 See *Re Stedham, Re Dyke* (1881) 6 PD 205; *Re Chilcott* [1897] P 223 (all three documents admitted); *Re Lewis* (1860) 25 JP 280 (later will held revoked); and PARA 112 text and note 8.

10 See note 9.

11 *Re Reynolds* (1873) LR 3 P & D 35; *Re Baker, Baker v Baker* [1929] 1 Ch 668; *Re Alford* (1939) 83 Sol Jo 566; *Re Pearson, Rowling v Crowther* [1963] 3 All ER 763, [1963] 1 WLR 1358. See also *Hoare Trustees v Jacques* [2008] EWHC 2022 (Ch), [2008] All ER (D) 68 (Feb).

12 *Phipps v Earl of Anglesey* (1751) 7 Bro Parl Cas 443; *Loftus v Stoney* (1867) 17 I Ch R 178; *Townsend v Moore* [1905] P 66, CA.

13 *Re Howard, Howard v Treasury Solicitor* [1944] P 39.

98. Loss of later will. Where a later will cannot be produced, the burden of showing that it revoked an earlier will is on the person alleging revocation, and there must be either proof that it contained a clause revoking earlier wills[1] or proof of a difference of disposition[2]. Accordingly, where a testator makes two wills and the later one is lost or destroyed, and there is no secondary evidence of its contents showing that it expressly or impliedly revoked the earlier will, the earlier will is admitted to probate[3]. If, however, there is such evidence, probate of the first will may be refused, and intestacy may result[4].

1 For this purpose, secondary evidence, including declarations of the testator made after execution, has always been admissible of the contents of the last will: *Barkwell v Barkwell* [1928] P 91. Such evidence must, however, be stringent and conclusive: *Cutto v Gilbert* (1854) 9 Moo PCC 131; *Re Wyatt* [1952] 1 All ER 1030; *Broadway v Fernandes* [2007] EWHC 684 (Ch), [2007] All ER (D) 485 (Mar) (no firm evidence that later will ever existed and only guesswork as to its terms); *Re Dear* [1975] 2 NZLR 254, NZ CA (not following *Re Hampshire* [1951] WN 174, where less than stringent evidence was accepted). See also the Civil Evidence Act 1995 ss 1–7 (under which hearsay evidence is in general admissible); and CIVIL PROCEDURE vol 12 (2015) PARA 859 et seq. Where a will has been lost or destroyed in such circumstances that it is not revoked, secondary evidence may be given of its contents: see PARA 716; and CIVIL PROCEDURE vol 12 (2015) PARA 938.

2 *Cutto v Gilbert* (1854) 9 Moo PCC 131 at 147. See also *Goodright d Rolfe v Harwood* (1775) 7 Bro Parl Cas 489; *Wood v Wood* (1867) LR 1 P & D 309 (following *Brown v Brown* (1858) 8 E & B 876 at 886); *Re Debac, Sanger v Hart* (1897) 77 LT 374; *Re Wyatt* [1952] 1 All ER 1030.

3 *Hitchins v Basset* (1688) 2 Salk 592 (affd sub nom *Hungerford v Nosworthy* (1694) Show Parl Cas 146); *Goodright d Rolfe v Harwood* (1775) 7 Bro Parl Cas 489; *Dickinson v Stidolph* (1861) 11 CBNS 341 at 357; *Hellier v Hellier* (1884) 9 PD 237; *Re Wyatt* [1952] 1 All ER 1030; *Broadway v Fernandes* [2007] EWHC 684 (Ch), [2007] All ER (D) 485 (Mar). As to probate of the contents of a lost will see PARA 716.

4 *Wood v Wood* (1867) LR 1 P & D 309.

99. Partly inconsistent wills. Where there are several testamentary instruments which are not wholly inconsistent, they are considered, so far as they can be read together, as constituting the last will of the testator[1]. Any number of testamentary instruments, whatever their relative date or in whatever form they may be, may be admitted to probate as together constituting the last will of the deceased[2]. The presumption against implied revocation is strengthened where the testator uses words showing an intention not to alter his testamentary disposition except in certain specific respects[3]. The question is what disposition the testator intended, not which or what numbers of papers he desired or expected to be admitted to probate[4]. Consequently, the presumption of revocation arising from an apparent inconsistency of testamentary instruments may be rebutted by extrinsic evidence that the testator did not intend revocation (including direct evidence of his intention), where there is some ambiguity on the face of the documents as to whether the deceased meant the particular disposition to be part of his will[5], or where some ambiguity in the light of surrounding circumstances is revealed by extrinsic evidence other than evidence of the testator's intention[6]. If, however, there is no ambiguity arising in either of these ways, extrinsic evidence may not be admitted to show that revocation was not intended[7].

1   *Re Budd* (1862) 3 Sw & Tr 196; *Birks v Birks* (1865) 4 Sw & Tr 23; *Lemage v Goodban* (1865) LR 1 P & D 57; *Re Fenwick* (1867) LR 1 P & D 319; *Re Griffith* (1872) LR 2 P & D 457; *Re Petchell* (1874) LR 3 P & D 153; *Re Hartley* (1880) 50 LJP 1; *Deakin v Garvie* (1919) 36 TLR 122, CA. See also *Re Chester, Ryan v Chester* (1914) 49 ILT 97.
2   *Lemage v Goodban* (1865) LR 1 P & D 57; *Townsend v Moore* [1905] P 66, CA; *Deakin v Garvie* (1919) 36 TLR 122, CA.
3   *Follett v Pettman* (1883) 23 ChD 337.
4   *Dempsey v Lawson* (1877) 2 PD 98 at 107.
5   *Blackwood v Damer* (1783) 3 Phillim 458n; *Methuen v Methuen* (1817) 2 Phillim 416; *Greenough v Martin* (1824) 2 Add 239 at 243; *Busteed v Eager* (1834) Milw 345 at 348. See also *Fawcett v Jones, Codrington and Pulteney* (1810) 3 Phillim 434 at 478.
6   In relation to deaths on or after 1 January 1983 see the Administration of Justice Act 1982 s 21; and PARA 195. As to the law on admissibility of evidence in relation to deaths before that date see *Jenner v Ffinch* (1879) 5 PD 106; *Paton v Ormerod* [1892] P 247; *Re Bryan* [1907] P 125; *Re Brennan* [1932] IR 633.
7   In relation to deaths on or after 1 January 1983 see the Administration of Justice Act 1982 s 21; and PARA 195. See also *Thorne v Rooke* (1841) 2 Curt 799.

100. Revocation by codicil. Where a will is revoked by a subsequent codicil, the question whether an intermediate codicil is also revoked is one of construction. If the revoking codicil distinguishes between the will and the intermediate codicil, for example by date, the intermediate codicil is not revoked[1]. The revocation of a will does not revoke a codicil to it by implication[2], as a properly executed testamentary paper may be revoked only by the methods prescribed by statute[3]. There is a possibility to bring about, indirectly, a revocation where the codicil following a will refers to an earlier revoked will, rather than to the later will, subsequent to which it is made. If this occurs this may have the result of bringing about a revival or republication of the earlier will and this revival may cause the revocation of the later will[4].

1   *Farrer v St Catharine's College, Cambridge* (1873) LR 16 Eq 19. See also *Pratt v Pratt* (1844) 14 Sim 129; *Green v Tribe* (1878) 9 ChD 231; *Follett v Pettman* (1883) 23 ChD 337; *Scott's Trustees v Duke* 1916 SC 732, Ct of Sess. Cf *Re Resch's Will Trusts, Le Cras v Perpetual Trustee Co Ltd, Far West Children's Health Scheme v Perpetual Trustee Co Ltd* [1969] 1 AC 514, [1967] 3 All ER 915, PC (where a third codicil confirming only the will and describing itself as a first codicil was held as a matter of construction not to have revoked the two prior codicils by inference).
2   *Re Savage* (1870) LR 2 P & D 78 (following *Black v Jobling* (1869) LR 1 P & D 685; and disapproving *Clogstoun v Walcott* (1848) 5 Notes of Cases 623 and *Grimwood v Cozens* (1860) 2 Sw & Tr 364). See also *Re Coulthard* (1865) 11 Jur NS 184; *Re Turner* (1872) LR 2 P & D 403; *Farrer v St Catharine's College, Cambridge* (1873) LR 16 Eq 19; *Gardiner v Courthope* (1886) 12 PD 14; *Re Clements* [1892] P 254.
3   See the Wills Act 1837 ss 18, 18B, 20; and PARAS 87, 90, 94. In *Re Bleckley* (1883) 8 PD 169, where there was evidence that the testator, by cutting off his signature to his will, intended to revoke a codicil to it written on the same piece of paper, the codicil was held to be revoked, but the point was not argued.
4   See the Wills Act 1837 s 34 (and PARA 110), which has the effect that the revived will is deemed to be made at the time of revival; the revived will may expressly or impliedly revoke wills made between the date of the execution of the revived will and its revival. As to the effect of this see *Re Baker* [1929] 1 Ch 668; *Re Pearson, Rowling v Crowther* [1963] 3 All ER 763, [1963] 1 WLR 1358 and *Hoare Trustees v Jacques* [2008] EWHC 2022 (Ch), [2008] All ER (D) 68 (Feb). See also PARA 95, for revocation by later instrument and PARA 112, for revival by reference to a will by date.

C.   REVOCATION BY DESTRUCTION

101. Destruction with intention to revoke. A will may be revoked by being burnt, torn or otherwise destroyed[1] by the testator, or by some person in his presence and by his direction, with the intention of revoking it[2]. For this purpose, there must be both an act of destruction[3] and an intention to revoke[4]. A symbolical destruction is not sufficient, so that mere abandonment will not suffice[5]. A will is not destroyed by being struck through with a pen[6], even though done with the intention to revoke[7], for cancelling is not one of the modes of revocation[8]. Moreover, a will is not revoked by being destroyed by mistake[9] or in a fit of madness[10], as even the most complete form of destruction without intention does not revoke a will[11]. It seems that a testator must be of sufficient testamentary capacity to make a will, to be able to form the requisite intention to revoke a will[12].

The intention to revoke a will wholly or in part may be evidenced by proof of the testator's expressed intention in doing the act[13], or of circumstances from which the intention may be inferred, or by the state and condition to which the instrument has been reduced by the act itself[14].

Declarations by the testator that he had destroyed his will are now admissible to prove both his intention to revoke it and the fact of destruction[15].

1   This includes 'cutting': *Hobbs v Knight* (1838) 1 Curt 768; *Re Cooke* (1847) 5 Notes of Cases 390.
2   Wills Act 1837 s 20. See PARA 104. See also *Re Gossage, Wood v Gossage* [1921] P 194, CA (where, although the will was burnt by the direction of the testator, this was not done in his presence).
3   *Cheese v Lovejoy* (1877) 2 PD 251 at 253, CA; *Andrew v Motley* (1862) 12 CBNS 514.
4   *Powell v Powell* (1866) LR 1 P & D 209 at 212; *Giles v Warren* (1872) LR 2 P & D 401. An object of the Statute of Frauds (1677) (see PARA 94 note 5) and of the Wills Act 1837 was to prevent the proof of revocation depending on oral evidence: *Doe d Reed v Harris* (1837) 6 Ad & El 209.
5   See the cases cited in note 3.
6   *Stephens v Taprell* (1840) 2 Curt 458 at 465; *Cheese v Lovejoy* (1877) 2 PD 251, CA. As to revocation by destroying signatures see PARA 105.
7   *Re Brewster* (1859) 6 Jur NS 56. See also *Re Rose* (1845) 4 Notes of Cases 101; *Benson v Benson* (1870) LR 2 P & D 172.
8   'Otherwise destroying' in the Wills Act 1837 s 20 means destroying by some method ejusdem generis with those described in s 20: *Stephens v Taprell* (1840) 2 Curt 458. An obliteration of a legacy may, however, effect a revocation of the legacy: see PARA 82. See also PARA 105.
9   *Giles v Warren* (1872) LR 2 P & D 401; *Re Thornton* (1889) 14 PD 82; *Beardsley v Lacey* (1897) 67 LJP 35; *Re Greenstreet* (1930) 74 Sol Jo 188. See also *Re Southerden, Adams v Southerden* [1925] P 177, CA; *Re Carey* (1977) 121 Sol Jo 173; and PARAS 108–109. As to the evidence of the mistake see *Re Templemore* (1925) 69 Sol Jo 382.
10 *Brunt v Brunt* (1873) LR 3 P & D 37. As to the necessary intention see PARA 93.
11 *Cheese v Lovejoy* (1877) 2 PD 251 at 253, CA, per James LJ. See also *Re King* (1851) 2 Rob Eccl 403; *Re Coleman* (1861) 2 Sw & Tr 314; *Clarkson v Clarkson* (1862) 2 Sw & Tr 497; *Re Thornton* (1889) 14 PD 82; *Re Brassington* [1902] P 1.
12 *Brunt v Brunt* (1873) LR 3 P & D 37, 37 JP 312; *Re Sabatini* (1969) 114 Sol Jo 35.
13 See CIVIL PROCEDURE vol 12 (2015) PARA 870 et seq.
14 *Clarke v Scripps* (1852) 2 Rob Eccl 563 at 567; *Christmas and Christmas v Whinyates* (1863) 3 Sw & Tr 81; *Re Maley* (1887) 12 PD 134. Partial tearing which leaves all the words distinct and legible does not necessarily show an intention to revoke the will: *Re Cowling, Jinkin v Cowling* [1924] P 113.
15 *Re Bridgewater* [1965] 1 All ER 717, [1965] 1 WLR 416, applying the Evidence Act 1938 s 1 (repealed: see now the Civil Evidence Act 1995 ss 1–7, under which hearsay evidence is in general admissible; and CIVIL PROCEDURE vol 12 (2015) PARA 859 et seq). As to the previous law see *Keen v Keen* (1873) LR 3 P & D 105 at 107 per Sir J Hannen; *Re Maley* (1887) 12 PD 134.

102.   Destruction of duplicate. The destruction with the intention of revocation of one part of a will executed in duplicate amounts to a revocation, whether only one part or both parts were in the possession of the testator, and the presumption generally is that by such destruction the testator intended complete revocation[1]. Similarly, if the duplicate in the testator's possession cannot be found after his death, the presumption applies[2]. The presumption is not so strong where the testator destroys one of two duplicates both in his own possession, especially if he has previously made alterations on the part so destroyed[3].

1   *Onions v Tyrer* (1716) 1 P Wms 343 at 346; *Boughey v Moreton* (1758) 2 Lee 532; *Burtenshaw v Gilbert* (1774) 1 Cowp 49; *Rickards v Mumford* (1812) 2 Phillim 23; *Colvin v Fraser* (1829) 2 Hag Ecc 266; *Re Slade* (1869) 20 LT 330. See also *Pemberton v Pemberton* (1807) 13 Ves 290.
2   *Jones v Harding* (1887) 58 LT 60; *Paige v Brooks* (1896) 75 LT 455.
3   *Pemberton v Pemberton* (1807) 13 Ves 290 at 310 per Lord Erskine LC; *Re Hains* (1847) 5 Notes of Cases 621.

103. Incomplete destruction. If a testator leaves unfinished the work of destruction which he had commenced, either in consequence of the interference of a third person or by his own voluntary change of purpose, the will is unrevoked, the intention to revoke being itself revoked before the act was complete[1]. Similarly, probate has been granted of a will the signature to which had been partially erased and rewritten, on the basis that there was no intention to revoke[2], and also where the testator had cut out, but replaced, the part containing the signatures of the witnesses[3]. Probate was not, however, granted where the testator's signature had been cut out and pasted on in the previous position[4].

1   *Doe d Perkes v Perkes* (1820) 3 B & Ald 489; *Re Colberg* (1841) 2 Curt 832; *Elms v Elms* (1858) 1 Sw & Tr 155.
2   *Re Kennett* (1863) 2 New Rep 461. See also *Re Baron De Bode* (1847) 5 Notes of Cases 189.
3   *Re Eeles* (1862) 2 Sw & Tr 600 (where probate was granted with the consent of the parties interested on intestacy).
4   *Bell v Fothergill* (1870) LR 2 P & D 148; *Magnesi v Hazelton* (1881) 44 LT 586. See also PARA 105.

104. Destruction by stranger. Destruction by a third person in the presence and by the direction of the testator is effectual[1]. Destruction by the testator's direction, but not in his presence, is, however, ineffectual[2], and the testator cannot revoke his will by subsequent ratification of a previous unauthorised act of destruction by a third person[3]. If a will is accidentally destroyed by fire, the mere acquiescence of the testator does not effect a revocation[4].

1   See the Wills Act 1837 s 20.
2   *Re Dadds* (1857) Dea & Sw 290; *De Kremer, Lundbeck v De Kremer* (1965) 110 Sol Jo 18.
3   *Gill v Gill* [1909] P 157. See also *Mills v Millward* (1889) 15 PD 20.
4   *Re Booth, Booth v Booth* [1926] P 118.

105. Extent of destruction. To effect destruction there must be sufficient damage, with the intention to revoke, to destroy the entirety of the will[1], but it is sufficient if its essence as a will is destroyed, even though the materials of which it is composed are not[2]. Thus cutting off the testator's signature[3] or scratching it out with a knife[4], or obliterating the testator's signature with a ball-point pen so that it is no longer apparent[5], unless done under a mistaken belief as to the effect of the will[6], or the testator's cutting off of the signatures of attesting witnesses[7], or of any part of the will which he has expressly made part of it[8], if done with the intention to revoke, operates as a revocation unless otherwise explained[9]. Erasure by witnesses of their own signatures does not, however, revoke the will[10].

Where a portion of a will not necessary to its validity as a testamentary instrument is destroyed, the question is whether the portion destroyed is so important as to raise the presumption that the rest cannot have been intended to stand without it, or whether it is unimportant and independent of the rest of the will[11]. The intention may, in part, be inferred from extrinsic circumstances: there may have been declarations, not directly as to the revocation, but such as would lead to the inference whether the testator intended to revoke the will or not[12]. Where a testator destroys some sheets of a will and substitutes others, but does not re-execute the whole will, there is a revocation[13], but merely tearing off part of the commencement of a will[14], or a clause containing legacies[15] or appointing executors[16], does not necessarily revoke the rest of the will[17].

1   *Price v Powell* (1858) 3 H & N 341.
2   *Hobbs v Knight* (1838) 1 Curt 768 at 779–780.
3   *Re Gullan* (1858) 1 Sw & Tr 23; *Re Lewis* (1858) 1 Sw & Tr 31; *Re Simpson* (1859) 5 Jur NS 1366. See also *Hobbs v Knight* (1838) 1 Curt 768; *Bell v Fothergill* (1870) LR 2 P & D 148.
4   *Re Morton* (1887) 12 PD 141. Where, however, the signature is legible, the will is valid: *Re Godfrey* (1893) 69 LT 22.
5   *Re Adams* [1990] Ch 601, [1990] 2 All ER 97. The same test applies for the purposes of deciding whether an obliteration constitutes destruction for the purposes of the Wills Act 1837 s 20 (see PARA 101) as applies for deciding whether an obliteration of part of a will has made it no longer apparent for the purposes of s 21 (see PARA 82): *Re Adams* at 607 and 102.
6   *Stamford v White* [1901] P 46. As to mistake see PARA 109.
7   *Evans v Dallow, Re Dallow* (1862) 31 LJPM & A 128. See also *Re Jones, Evans v Harries* [1976] Ch 200, [1976] 1 All ER 593 (all signatures and certain dispositive clauses excised).
8   *Price v Price* (1858) 27 LJ Ex 409; *Williams v Tyley* (1858) John 530.
9   *Re Wheeler* (1879) 49 LJP 29. The accidental cutting through of a witness's signature is not a revocation: *Re Taylor* (1890) 63 LT 230. As to mistake see PARA 109.
10 *Margary v Robinson* (1886) 12 PD 8; *Re Greenwood* [1892] P 7.
11 *Clarke v Scripps* (1852) 2 Rob Eccl 563; *Re White* (1879) 3 LR Ir 413, Ir CA; *Leonard v Leonard* [1902] P 243 at 248 (where the last three sheets of a will were unintelligible without the first two sheets, which had been destroyed, and the whole was held to be revoked); *Re Green, Ward v Bond* (1962) 106 Sol Jo 1034 (where the first two pages had been destroyed and the last page so mutilated that it was unintelligible and unworkable as a testamentary document and the whole will was held to be revoked).
12 *Clarke v Scripps* (1852) 2 Rob Eccl 563 at 567, per Sir John Dodson.
13 *Treloar v Lean* (1889) 14 PD 49; *Leonard v Leonard* [1902] P 243. See also *Gullan v Grove* (1858) 26 Beav 64.
14 *Re Woodward* (1871) LR 2 P & D 206.
15 *Re Nelson* (1872) IR 6 Eq 569. See also *Christmas and Christmas v Whinyates* (1863) 3 Sw & Tr 81.
16 *Re Leach* (1890) 63 LT 111. See also *Re Maley* (1887) 12 PD 134.
17 Probate is granted of a will in its actual form, where a part has been cut out: *Re Nunn* [1936] 1 All ER 555; *Re Everest* [1975] Fam 44, [1975] 1 All ER 672.

106. Presumption of intention.

Where a will is found destroyed or mutilated, in a place in which the testator would naturally put it if he thought he had destroyed it, the presumption is that the testator destroyed it, and that the destruction was done with the intention to revoke[1], and, if there is a codicil, that the destruction took place after the execution of the codicil[2]. This presumption applies, however, only prima facie and may be rebutted[3]. Similarly, if a will was last traced to the possession of the testator and is not forthcoming at his death[4], there is a prima facie presumption, in the absence of circumstances tending to a contrary conclusion, that the testator destroyed it with the intention to revoke it[5]. The presumption may be rebutted by evidence, which, however, must be clear and satisfactory[6]. Recent declarations by a testator of satisfaction at having settled his affairs[7], or of goodwill towards the persons benefited by the will, or of adherence to the will and to the contents of the will itself[8], may be used for this purpose, but a declaration by the testator of adherence to a will may be answered by his declarations to a contrary effect[9]. Evidence that a testator who was very careful with his paperwork had left a copy will in existence may point against the presumption[10]. The presumption may, it seems, also be rebutted by a consideration of the contents of the will itself[11]. The possibility that the will was destroyed without the privity or consent of the testator, or after his death, is a circumstance to be taken into account, but there is a presumption against fraudulent destruction[12]. Where it is asserted that a valid will existed and was destroyed and there are no copies, it seems there must be a firm evidential basis for the assumption that the proper form and attestation required for validity had been carried out[13].

It appears that the presumption that a will has been revoked if it cannot be found on the testator's death does not operate to revoke duly executed codicils which are found, even though they contain references to the will[14], and even where the will is known to have been destroyed by the testator[15].

Where there is proof that the will was duly executed by a testator who afterwards became mentally disordered, and it is mutilated or not forthcoming, the burden of showing that it had been mutilated or destroyed by the testator when of sound mind is on the party alleging revocation, as the presumption of destruction with the intention to revoke does not apply in such a case[16].

1 *Davies v Davies* (1753) 1 Lee 444; *Lambell v Lambell* (1831) 3 Hag Ecc 568; *Re Lewis* (1858) 1 Sw & Tr 31; *Magnesi v Hazelton* (1881) 44 LT 586.
2 *Christmas and Christmas v Whinyates* (1863) 3 Sw & Tr 81.
3 *Patten v Poulton* (1858) 1 Sw & Tr 55.
4 *Patten v Poulton* (1858) 1 Sw & Tr 55. See *Wren v Wren* [2006] EWHC 2243 (Ch), 9 ITELR 223, [2006] All ER (D) 60 (Oct) and note 8. See also *Re Hudson, Nicholls v Hudson* [2006] EWHC 3006 (Ch), 150 Sol Jo LB 1333, [2006] All ER (D) 60 (Oct) (copy wills sent to relatives and testator expressed pleasure that all was in order just before death; presumption rebutted); *Rowe v Clarke* [2005] EWHC 3068 (Ch), 149 Sol Jo LB 1450, [2005] All ER (D) 368 (Oct) (copy will sent by testator to main beneficiary's mother; presumption was weak in the instant case and was rebutted); cf *Broadway v Fernandes* [2007] EWHC 684 (Ch), [2007] All ER (D) 485 (Mar) (mere assertion of existence of new will, without further evidence of its contents; presumption applied).
5 *Lillie v Lillie* (1829) 3 Hag Ecc 184; *Welch v Phillips* (1836) 1 Moo PCC 299; *Re Brown* (1858) 1 Sw & Tr 32; *Eckersley v Platt* (1866) LR 1 P & D 281; *Keen v Keen* (1873) LR 3 P & D 105; *Sugden v Lord St Leonards* (1876) 1 PD 154 at 217, CA; *Allan v Morrison* [1900] AC 604, PC; *Re Sykes, Drake v Sykes* (1907) 23 TLR 747, CA (not following the dictum of Lord Penzance in *Finch v Finch* (1867) LR 1 P & D 371); *Re Paget* (1913) 47 ILT 284. The presumption applies equally to a codicil: *Re Shaw* (1858) 1 Sw & Tr 62; *Re Debac, Sanger v Hart* (1897) 77 LT 374; *Re Donisthorpe, Churchward v Bowden and Churchward* [1947] WN 226. The presumption does not apply where the will is lost but was in the possession of someone other than the testator: *Chana v Chana* [2001] WTLR 205; *d'Eye v Avery* [2001] WTLR 227.
6 *Eckersley v Platt* (1866) LR 1 P & D 281. See also *Battyll v Lyles and Phillips* (1858) 4 Jur NS 718; *Re Yelland, Broadbent v Francis* (1975) 119 Sol Jo 562; *Re Davies, Panton v Jones* (1978) Times, 23 May. See also *Jersey Society for the Prevention of Cruelty to Animals v Rees* (2001) 4 ITELR 294 (will last known to have been in possession of testatrix and evidence of her intention, shortly before death, to benefit principal beneficiary; presumption rebutted).
7 *Whiteley v King* (1864) 17 CBNS 756. See also *Re Hudson, Nicholls v Hudson* [2006] EWHC 3006 (Ch), 150 Sol Jo LB 1333, [2006] All ER (D) 60 (Oct) and note 4.
8 *Keen v Keen* (1873) LR 3 P & D 105 at 107. See also *Saunders v Saunders* (1848) 6 Notes of Cases 518; *Patten v Poulton* (1858) 1 Sw & Tr 55; *Re Mackenzie* [1909] P 305; *Re Dickson, Dickson v Dickson* (1984) [2002] WTLR 1395, CA; *Jersey Society for the Prevention of Cruelty to Animals v Rees* 2001 JLR 506, (2001–02) 4 ITELR 294, Royal Ct Jer. See *Wren v Wren* [2006] EWHC 2243 (Ch) at [94], 9 ITELR 223 per Rimer J (testator's repeated affirmations, following execution of the dispositions made in the will, made it improbable that the maker of a highly elaborate will would decide to substitute for it a disposition of his estate under the laws of intestacy).
9 *Keen v Keen* (1873) LR 3 P & D 105; *Re Sykes, Drake v Sykes* (1907) 23 TLR 747, CA.
10 *Wren v Wren* [2006] EWHC 2243 (Ch), 9 ITELR 223.
11 *Sugden v Lord St Leonards* (1876) 1 PD 154, CA; *Wren v Wren* [2006] EWHC 2243 (Ch), 9 ITELR 223.
12 *Finch v Finch* (1867) LR 1 P & D 371; *Allan v Morrison* [1900] AC 604, PC. See also *Wren v Wren* [2006] EWHC 2243 (Ch), 9 ITELR 223; and *Re Zielinski, Korab-Karpinski v Lucas-Gardiner* [2007] WTLR 1655.
13 *Parks v Clout* [2003] EWCA Civ 982, [2003] All ER (D) 105 (Jun).
14 *Black v Jobling* (1869) LR 1 P & D 685; *Gardiner v Courthope* (1886) 12 PD 14 (where the codicil had not been destroyed by any of the means authorised by the Wills Act 1837 s 20). It is questionable, however, whether, if the will and codicil were closely connected, destruction of the

will might not effect revocation of the codicil on the basis that the will and codicil together constituted one instrument and that destruction of a substantial part effected revocation of the whole.

15 *Re Turner* (1872) LR 2 P & D 403.

16 *Harris v Berrall* (1858) 1 Sw & Tr 153; *Sprigge v Sprigge* (1868) LR 1 P & D 608; *Benson v Benson* (1870) LR 2 P & D 172 at 176; *Re Hine* [1893] P 282; *Allan v Morrison* [1900] AC 604, PC; *Re Taylor, National and Provincial and Union Bank of England v Taylor* (1919) 64 Sol Jo 148.

D.   CONDITIONAL REVOCATION

107. Expressed or implied revocation. Where property has been disposed of in a will and the same property is again disposed of, either in a subsequent will or in a codicil, then, if there can be found, apart from the description of the subject matter of the gift, words expressly or impliedly effecting revocation, that revocation will stand, whatever the fate of the subsequent disposition may be[1]. If, however, the only revocation is that which is to be gathered from the inconsistency of the subsequent disposition with the earlier one, then, if the second disposition fails to be effective for any reason, there will be no revocation[2]. The whole question depends on the intention of the testator. If the will is revoked simply in order to make a gift in favour of another person, or, as it seems, to vary the dispositions under the will[3], and it is clear that there is no intention to revoke it except for that purpose, the revocation is not effective if the gift is not effective[4]. It is immaterial whether the invalidity of the subsequent disposition is due to the want of capacity of the substituted donee or to a defect in the later gift[5].

In all cases of revocation by destruction or obliteration, the question whether revocation is conditional is a question of fact[6], to be considered in connection with the circumstances in which revocation occurred and the declarations of the testator with which it may have been accompanied[7], which are accordingly admissible in evidence[8]. However, in cases of revocation by subsequent will or codicil, the question is one of construction[9]; revocation is not conditional unless it appears to be such on the construction of the subsequent will or codicil in the light of the extrinsic evidence which is admissible for the purposes of construction[10]. Extrinsic evidence of surrounding circumstances is admissible on the 'armchair principle'[11]. Direct extrinsic evidence of the testator's intention is admissible if either the relevant words are ambiguous on their face, or evidence other than evidence of the testator's intention shows that they are ambiguous when considered in the light of the surrounding circumstances[12].

1   *Ward v Van der Loeff, Burnyeat v Van der Loeff* [1924] AC 653 at 671, HL, per Lord Dunedin (applying *Alexander v Kirkpatrick* (1874) LR 2 Sc & Div 397, HL). It was held that there was effective revocation in *Onions v Tyrer* (1716) 1 P Wms 343; *Tupper v Tupper* (1855) 1 K & J 665; *Quinn v Butler* (1868) LR 6 Eq 225; *Baker v Story* (1874) 31 LT 631.

2   *Ward v Van der Loeff, Burnyeat v Van der Loeff* [1924] AC 653 at 671, HL, per Lord Dunedin (applying *Alexander v Kirkpatrick* (1874) LR 2 Sc & Div 397, HL). It was held in those two cases that there was no revocation. In *Watts v Eden* [2001] All ER (D) 261 (Oct), defendant beneficiary of a share of the estate under the will became an attesting witness to a codicil which increased his share. His gift being void under the Wills Act 1837 s 15 (see PARA 78) and as there was no express revocation in the codicil of the earlier gift, any implication of revocation could only arise if the increased gift were valid. The earlier gift was not revoked. See also *Re Fleetwood, Sidgreaves v Brewer* (1880) 15 ChD 594; *Duguid v Fraser* (1886) 31 ChD 449; *Morley v Rennoldson* [1895] 1 Ch 449, CA; *Vencatanarayana Pillay v Subammal* (1915) 32 TLR 118, PC; *Re Davies, Thomas v Thomas-Davies* [1928] Ch 24; *Re Robinson, Lamb v Robinson* [1930] 2 Ch 332; and see *Doe d Murch v Marchant* (1843) 6 Man & G 813. As to the appointment of a guardian see *Ex p Earl of Ilchester* (1803) 7 Ves 348 at 372–373.

3   *Watts v Eden* [2001] All ER (D) 261 (Oct) (defendants' share of residue increased from 7% to 10%).

4   *Quinn v Butler* (1868) LR 6 Eq 225 at 227. As to dependent relative revocation see PARA 108.

5 *Vencatanarayana Pillay v Subammal* (1915) 32 TLR 118, PC; *Ward v Van der Loeff, Burnyeat v Van der Loeff* [1924] AC 653 at 671, HL; *Re Robinson, Lamb v Robinson* [1930] 2 Ch 332. See *Watts v Eden* [2001] All ER (D) 261 (Oct) and note 2: gift invalidated by reason of attestation by donee.

6 See *Dixon v Treasury Solicitor* [1905] P 42.

7 *Powell v Powell* (1866) LR 1 P & D 209 at 212; *Cossey v Cossey* (1900) 82 LT 203 at 204. See also *Brooke v Kent* (1841) 3 Moo PCC 334 at 350.

8 Questions of this kind in the High Court come before the probate court, ie the division of the High Court in which the will is proved. This is the Family Division for non-contentious business and the Chancery Division for contentious business: see PARA 678. As to such evidence in the probate court in ambiguous cases see PARA 8.

9 *A-G v Lloyd* (1747) 1 Ves Sen 32 at 34; *Freel v Robinson* (1909) 18 OLR 651 at 654–655. As to courts of construction and courts of probate see PARAS 97 text and note 5, 185 et seq. See also *Re Hawksley's Settlements, Black v Tidy* [1934] Ch 384; *Re Resch's Will Trusts, Le Cras v Perpetual Trustee Co Ltd, Far West Children's Health Scheme v Perpetual Trustee Co Ltd* [1969] 1 AC 514, [1967] 3 All ER 915, PC. For a case where a question of revocation which was a question of construction was determined in construction proceedings instead of probate proceedings see *Re Finnemore* [1992] 1 All ER 800, [1991] 1 WLR 793.

10 Thus where another donee is substituted, the revoked disposition is not revived by the fact that that donee fails to come into existence (*Nevill v Boddam* (1860) 28 Beav 554 at 558), or has not the capacity to take a benefit, as in the case of a devise to a charity before the Mortmain and Charitable Uses Act 1891 s 5 (repealed) (*French's Case* (1587) 1 Roll Abr 614; *Devise* (O) 4; *Roper v Radcliffe* (1714) 10 Mod Rep 230 at 233, HL; *Tupper v Tupper* (1855) 1 K & J 665 at 669; *Quinn v Butler* (1868) LR 6 Eq 225 at 227). See also *Re Murray, Murray v Murray* [1956] 2 All ER 353, [1956] 1 WLR 605 (where the invalidity of a substitutional name and arms clause in a codicil did not revive the original clause in the will). Where, however, there is no intention to deprive the original donee of benefit, but the codicil only varies the nature of the gift by imposing trusts on it and these trusts fail for perpetuity, the original gift stands: *Re Bernard's Settlement, Bernard v Jones* [1916] 1 Ch 552. Similarly, an earlier gift may remain effective where a subsequent will repeats a valid gift in an earlier will, but the gift in the later will is nullified by the will being witnessed by the beneficiary's spouse: *Re Finnemore* [1992] 1 All ER 800, [1991] 1 WLR 793. See also *Re Feis, Guillaume v Ritz-Remorf* [1964] Ch 106, [1963] 3 All ER 303 (where the revocation of the will as regards German property was held not conditional on separate arrangements made for that property being effective, so that, as those arrangements were ineffective, the property was undisposed of).

11 Ie the will must be construed in its context and in the light of the surrounding circumstances as the testator sat in his armchair: *Re Finnemore* [1992] 1 All ER 800 at 829–830, [1991] 1 WLR 793 at 825 per Judge Micklem sitting as a judge of the High Court. See also PARA 212 note 12. Where a gift is null and void under the Wills Act 1837 s 15 as a result of the will being witnessed by the beneficiary or the beneficiary's spouse (see PARA 41), that does not preclude the court from looking at the words of the gift for the purposes of ascertaining the testator's intention when he made the document in which the gift is contained: *Re Finnemore*.

12 In relation to deaths on or after 1 January 1983 see the Administration of Justice Act 1982 s 21; and PARA 195. See also *Newton v Newton* (1861) 12 I Ch R 118 at 128–130.

108. Dependent relative revocation. The revocation of a will may be relative to another disposition which has already been made or is intended to be made, and is so dependent on it that revocation is not intended unless that other disposition takes effect[1]. Such a revocation is known as a 'dependent relative revocation', and, if from any cause the other disposition fails to take effect, the will remains operative as it was before the revocation[2]. The doctrine also applies where the purported revocation is based on an assumption of fact which is false, the mistaken belief in that fact being the reason for the revocation[3].

The question may thus arise in the case of destruction of a will as part of the act of making a fresh will, which is not in fact made[4] or is ineffectually made for want of due execution[5], or destruction in order to set up a prior will which needs revival[6]. In order to involve the doctrine of dependent relative revocation, it is not necessary that there should be direct evidence of the physical destruction of the will which it is sought to set up[7]. The question may also arise in the case of obliteration of the amount of a legacy, and the substitution, without proper formalities, of a different amount[8], or obliteration and substitution, in a similar manner, of a different donee[9] or other person[10], or of a different event on which the gift is to take effect[11]. If, however, a complete legacy has been obliterated and a new gift has been substituted which does not take effect (for example, for want of execution), there is (in the absence of other admissible evidence) insufficient evidence for the doctrine of dependent relative revocation to apply, and probate will be granted of the will with the parts obliterated blank[12]. Where, however, some words in a legacy, as opposed to the whole legacy, have been obliterated and other words have been substituted for them, it may be possible to infer that the testator had no intention of revoking the original words unless the substituted words were effective, in which case the doctrine of dependent relative revocation applies and evidence outside the will itself will be admissible to show what the original words were[13]. Thus strips of paper covering the amounts of legacies may be removed to show what the original amounts were, in a case where the doctrine of dependent relative revocation applies[14]. Where it is not possible to infer that the testator intended to revoke the original words only if the words substituted were effective, the doctrine of dependent relevant revocation does not apply, and probate will be granted with the words obliterated blank[15].

In all these and other cases, however, the question is whether the disposition revoked is intended not to operate whatever happens[16], or is only to be revoked if the provisions of the substituted instrument operate in its stead[17]. The court must be satisfied that the testator did not intend to revoke the original will except conditionally, in so far as the other disposition could be set up[18]. Thus, if a will containing a general revocation clause on the face of it contains dispositions which are by some error incomplete, the revocation may be considered as conditional and the later will and the earlier will may both be admitted to probate, but with the exclusion of the revocation clause contained in the later will[19]. Again, where a later will containing a general revocation clause contains the same gift to a particular beneficiary as an earlier will, the gift in the earlier will being valid but that in the later one being invalid because the beneficiary's spouse witnessed the will, the revocation clause in the later will may be construed as not intended to revoke the gift in the earlier will in the event of failure of the gift in the later will[20]; in such a case the evidence of the identical gifts appearing in both wills is sufficient to establish the testator's intentions in this regard without additional extrinsic evidence being required, and the revocation clause may be construed distributively as inoperative in relation to the gift which is the same in both wills while being effective in relation to other dispositions in the earlier will which were replaced by different dispositions in the later will[21].

1   See *Ex p Earl of Ilchester* (1803) 7 Ves 348 at 372–373; *Re Irvine* [1919] 2 IR 485; *Re Addison* (1964) 108 Sol Jo 504.

2   In such a case the intention to revoke has only a conditional existence, the condition being the validity of the disposition intended to be substituted: *Powell v Powell* (1866) LR 1 P & D 209 at 212.

3   *Re Southerden, Adams v Southerden* [1925] P 177 (belief that widow would take whole estate on intestacy); *Re Carey* (1977) 121 Sol Jo 173 (belief that testator had nothing to leave); *Re Finnemore* [1992] 1 All ER 800, [1991] 1 WLR 793 (belief that attestation by beneficiary's spouse would not invalidate gift); *Re Feis, Guillaume v Ritz-Remorf* [1964] Ch 106, [1963] 3 All ER 303 (revocation not founded on mistake).

4   *Re Appelbee* (1828) 1 Hag Ecc 143; *Re Eeles* (1862) 2 Sw & Tr 600; *Dixon v Treasury Solicitor* [1905] P 42; *Re Bromham, Wass v Treasury Solicitor* [1952] 1 All ER 110n; *Re Jones, Evans v Harries* [1976] Ch 200, [1976] 1 All ER 593, CA (parts of the will comprising dispositive clauses and signatures of testatrix and witnesses cut off and not to be found and also evidence of clear intention to make a new will two weeks before death, but will not made; testatrix told witness, eight days before death, that she had not made a will; intention to revoke held to be absolute, rather than conditional). See also note 18.

5 *Hyde v Hyde* (1708) 1 Eq Cas Abr 409; *Onions v Tyrer* (1716) 1 P Wms 343 at 345; *Hide v Mason* (1734) 8 Vin Abr 140, Devise (R2) pl 17; *Dancer v Crabb* (1873) LR 3 P & D 98; *Re Irvin* (1908) 25 TLR 41; *Re Irvine* [1919] 2 IR 485; *West v West* [1921] 2 IR 34. Where a will is destroyed by the testator in the belief that he has validly executed another will, and the second will fails for want of due execution, the first will is not revoked, and evidence may be given of its contents: *Re Bunn, Durber v Bunn* (1926) 134 LT 669; *Re Davies, Russell v Delaney* [1951] 1 All ER 920.
6 *Powell v Powell* (1866) LR 1 P & D 209; *Re Weston* (1869) LR 1 P & D 633; *Welch and Freeman v Gardner* (1887) 51 JP 760; *Cossey v Cossey* (1900) 82 LT 203; *Re Bridgewater* [1965] 1 All ER 717, [1965] 1 WLR 416.
7 *Re Botting, Botting v Botting* [1951] 2 All ER 997.
8 *Winsor v Pratt* (1821) 2 Brod & Bing 650; *Kirke v Kirke* (1828) 4 Russ 435; *Brooke v Kent* (1841) 3 Moo PCC 334 at 350; *Soar v Dolman, Re Rippin* (1842) 3 Curt 121; *Locke v James* (1843) 11 M & W 901; *Re Nelson* (1872) IR 6 Eq 569; *Re Horsford* (1874) LR 3 P & D 211. Obliteration of part of the words describing the amount of the legacy may, however, be effectual: see *Re Nelson* (legacy of 'one hundred and fifty pounds', obliteration of 'one hundred and'); *Re Hamer* (1943) 60 TLR 168 (legacy of 'two hundred and fifty pounds'; obliteration of 'two hundred and'). To ascertain the state of the original instrument infra-red photography may be used: *Re Itter, Dedman v Godfrey* [1948] 2 All ER 1052; *Re Itter, Dedman v Godfrey* [1950] P 130, [1950] 1 All ER 68.
9 *Short d Gastrell v Smith* (1803) 4 East 419; *Re McCabe* (1873) LR 3 P & D 94. See also *Re Zimmer* (1924) 40 TLR 502 (where the doctrine was not applied, it not being clear that the testatrix would have allowed an erased word to stand if she had known that a substituted word would fail for want of attestation).
10 Eg where the person changed is the executor: *Re Parr* (1859) 6 Jur NS 56; *Re Harris* (1860) 1 Sw & Tr 536.
11 *Sturton v Whetlock* (1883) 52 LJP 29 (gift to children at 21 changed to gift at 25).
12 *Re Horsford* (1874) LR 3 P & D 211 (where the legacy was obliterated by a piece of paper on which a new, unattested bequest was written).
13 *Brooke v Kent* (1841) 3 Moo PCC 334; *Re McCabe* (1873) LR 3 P & D 94; *Re Horsford* (1874) LR 3 P & D 211; *Re Itter, Dedman v Godfrey* [1950] P 130, [1950] 1 All ER 68.
14 *Re Horsford* (1874) LR 3 P & D 211; *Re Itter, Dedman v Godfrey* [1950] P 130, [1950] 1 All ER 68. In *Re Gilbert* [1893] P 183, the court ordered the removal of blank paper which had been pasted over the back of a testamentary paper to see whether what had been written amounted to a revocation, but this case appears to be anomalous.
15 *Re Zimmer* (1924) 40 TLR 502.
16 See PARA 93.
17 *Dancer v Crabb* (1873) LR 3 P & D 98 at 104; *Welch and Freeman v Gardner* (1887) 51 JP 760; *Ward v Van der Loeff, Burnyeat v Van der Loeff* [1924] AC 653, HL; *Re Hawksley's Settlements, Black v Tidy* [1934] Ch 384 at 401. The question is not determined by the presence or absence of express words of revocation: *Ward v Van der Loeff, Burnyeat v Van der Loeff* at 667, 684.
18 *Dickinson v Swatman* (1860) 6 Jur NS 831 (as explained in *Powell v Powell* (1866) LR 1 P & D 209 at 213); *Re Mitcheson* (1863) 9 Jur NS 360; *Re Jones, Evans v Harries* [1976] Ch 200, [1976] 1 All ER 593, CA (where it was held that the intention to make a new will is not sufficient in itself to make revocation conditional). As to the weight given to the evidence see *Eckersley v Platt* (1866) LR 1 P & D 281 (witness interested in setting up earlier will); *Re Weston* (1869) LR 1 P & D 633 (testator's declarations not made at time of destruction); *Re Zimmer* (1924) 40 TLR 502. See also note 4.
19 *Re Hope Brown* [1942] P 136, [1942] 2 All ER 176; *Re Cocke* [1960] 2 All ER 289, [1960] 1 WLR 491; *Re Allen* (1962) 106 Sol Jo 115.
20 *Re Crannis, Mansell v Crannis* (1978) 122 Sol Jo 489; *Re Finnemore* [1992] 1 All ER 800, [1991] 1 WLR 793.
21 *Re Finnemore* [1992] 1 All ER 800, [1991] 1 WLR 793.

109. Revocation based on mistake. A revocation is inoperative if it is shown[1] to be made on a mistake either of fact[2] or of law[3], and is considered by the court not to be intended by the testator except conditionally on the mistaken assumption being correct[4].

1 As to evidence in such cases cf PARA 107.
2 *Campbell v French* (1797) 3 Ves 321 (belief that donee was dead); *Doe d Evans v Evans* (1839) 10 Ad & El 228 (belief that A died without issue). See, however, *Re Churchill, Taylor v Manchester University* [1917] 1 Ch 206 at 211 (where it was considered that these cases went too far, and a revocation by a codicil was held to be absolute, notwithstanding an erroneous belief of the testator that he had made an effective gift in his lifetime). See also *Re Plunkett Will Trusts,*

McCarthy v Dillon [1964] IR 259 (mistake as to sale of property); *Re Carey* (1977) 121 Sol Jo 173 (mistake as to existence of estate). In *Thomas v Howell* (1874) LR 18 Eq 198, a gift based on an erroneous assumption as to the value of the estate was conditional on that value proving correct and failed.

3   Eg the belief that the prior will destroyed is no longer of use (*Scott v Scott* (1859) 1 Sw & Tr 258; *Beardsley v Lacey* (1897) 67 LJP 35), or is inoperative (*Lord John Thynne v Stanhope* (1822) 1 Add 52 at 53; *Giles v Warren* (1872) LR 2 P & D 401; *James v Shrimpton* (1876) 1 PD 431; *Re Thornton* (1889) 14 PD 82), or has already been revoked (*Clarkson v Clarkson* (1862) 2 Sw & Tr 497 at 500). Cf *Perrott v Perrott* (1811) 14 East 423 at 440 (appointment by deed); *Re Southerden, Adams v Southerden* [1925] P 177, CA (mistake as to effect of intestacy). Where the mistake is that another instrument is substituted for the destroyed instrument, the case falls within the principle of dependent relative revocation: see PARA 108. See *Re Middleton* (1864) 3 Sw & Tr 583; *Re Finnemore* [1992] 1 All ER 800, [1991] 1 WLR 793 (mistake as to substituted will and as to effect of attestation by spouse of beneficiary). See also *Stamford v White* [1901] P 46 (mistake as to effect of earlier settlement).

4   *Re Faris, Goddard v Overend (No 2)* [1911] 1 IR 469. See also *A-G v Lloyd* (1747) 1 Ves Sen 32 (questioned in *Thomas v Howell* (1874) LR 18 Eq 198 at 212 per Malins V-C). In *A-G v Ward* (1797) 3 Ves 327, *Re Faris, Goddard v Overend (No 2)* and *Re Feis, Guillaume v Ritz-Remorf* [1964] Ch 106, [1963] 3 All ER 303, the revocation was held not to be conditional in this respect, but absolute. See also PARA 108 text and note 3.

(8) REVIVAL OF WILL

110. Methods of revival. The only methods prescribed by statute by which a revoked will or codicil can be revived are either re-execution or the execution of a codicil showing an intention to revive, and, where a will or codicil which has been partly revoked, and afterwards wholly revoked, is revived, the revival does not extend to the part first revoked unless an intention to the contrary is shown[1]. It follows that, where a will has been revoked by a later will, the revocation of the second will, whether by destruction or by codicil, does not have the effect of reviving the first will[2], and, where the first will has been partially revoked by the second, either expressly or impliedly in consequence of a different disposition of part of the testator's property, the cancellation of the second will does not revive the revoked part of the first[3].

As the revocation by destruction of a revoking will fails to revive the first will, there is prima facie an intestacy[4], but evidence may be given that the second will was revoked solely with the intention of validating the earlier will; the revocation of the second will is then treated as conditional, and, the condition not having been fulfilled, the doctrine of dependent relative revocation[5] applies, and the second will is not revoked[6]. Where a will confirmed by a codicil is destroyed, but the codicil is left in being, the will cannot be admitted to probate; the codicil can be so admitted but it does not revive the will[7]. Where an earlier will which has been revoked by a later will is revived by a codicil, the later will stands unless expressly revoked or impliedly revoked by reason of dispositions inconsistent with its being contained in the codicil[8]. Express revocation may occur by reason that the codicil has revived an earlier will containing a revocation clause which is statutorily revived to the date of the codicil[9]. A codicil may revive in its altered state a will or previous codicil to which unattested additions have been made[10]. A will or codicil which has been revoked, or a part of it, may, without revival, have validity given to it by incorporation in a subsequent valid testamentary disposition[11].

For the purpose of reviving a will, no precise form of words is necessary, nor need the reviving instrument be annexed to or indorsed on the will[12]. For a will to be revived, however, it must be in existence; hence a will which has been destroyed, with the intention to revoke it, cannot be revived[13].

1   Wills Act 1837 s 22. Under the old law there was a presumption that a revoked will was revived by the revocation of the revoking will: see *Harwood v Goodright* (1774) 1 Cowp 87 at 91; *Usticke v Bawden* (1824) 2 Add 116.

2   *Major and Mundy v Williams and Iles* (1843) 3 Curt 432; *Re Brown* (1858) 1 Sw & Tr 32. See also *Boulcott v Boulcott* (1853) 2 Drew 25 at 33.

3   *Stride v Sandford* (1853) 17 Jur 263; *Re Hodgkinson* [1893] P 339, CA. In *Re Howard, Howard v Treasury Solicitor* [1944] P 39, two wills of the same date, each revoking all former wills, although inconsistent and not admitted to probate, were held effective to revoke all earlier wills.

4   *Re Brown* (1858) 1 Sw & Tr 32.

5   See PARA 108.

6   *Powell v Powell* (1866) LR 1 P & D 209 (overruling a dictum in *Dickinson v Swatman* (1860) 4 Sw & Tr 205).

7   *Re Formaniuk Estate, Pitz v Kasjan* (1963) 42 DLR (2d) 78, 44 WWR 686, Man CA.

8   See PARA 97. See also *Re Mardon* [1944] P 109, [1944] 2 All ER 397 (draftsman of codicil referred to earlier-revoked will by date and certain clauses therein, but did not address revocation clause or residuary clause and no general confirmation clause in codicil; held, that there was no revocation of later will and both wills admitted to probate with the exception of the two clauses of the first which were not revived).

9   See the Wills Act 1837 s 34; PARA 454; and *Re Pearson, Rowling v Crowther* [1963] 3 All ER 763, [1963] 1 WLR 1358 (codicil revived and confirmed earlier will, including its express revocation clause). See also *Hoare Trustees v Jacques* [2008] EWHC 2022 (Ch), [2008] All ER (D) 68 (Feb) (codicil made clear reference to, and increased certain dispositions in, earlier will; inconsistent with any other intention than revival of same). See also PARA 111 text and note 2.

10 *Neate v Pickard* (1843) 2 Notes of Cases 406. The same rule applies in relation to republication: see PARA 113.

11 *Jorden v Jorden* (1843) 2 Notes of Cases 388. See also *Birkhead v Bowdoin* (1842) 2 Notes of Cases 66; *Re Lindsay* (1892) 8 TLR 507. As to probate in such cases see PARA 711.

12 *Potter v Potter* (1750) 1 Ves Sen 437 at 442.

13 *Hale v Tokelove* (1850) 2 Rob Eccl 318 at 328; *Newton v Newton* (1861) 12 I Ch R 118; *Rogers and Andrews v Goodenough and Rogers* (1862) 2 Sw & Tr 342 at 350; *Re Steele* (1868) LR 1 P & D 575 at 576; *Re Reade* [1902] P 75; *Re Mulock* [1933] IR 171 at 191. If the will is lost without any evidence of its having been destroyed animo revocandi (ie with an intention to revoke), it is capable of being revived: *Re Watson* (1887) 13 VLR 599. Evidence of the contents of a destroyed will, if proved to have been duly executed, may, however, be given to show that it contained a clause revoking previous wills: see PARA 98.

111.   Intention to revive. Where a will which has been revoked is re-executed[1], the fact of re-execution shows that the testator intended to revive it. Where it is revived by codicil, the statutory requirement that there must be an intention to revive it must be satisfied. For this purpose, the intention must appear on the face of the codicil, either by express words referring to a will as revoked and importing an intention to revive it, or by a disposition of the testator's property inconsistent with any other intention, or by some other expressions showing, with reasonable certainty, the existence of the intention and such intention may be imputed to the testator by reason of the wording used by the draftsman[2]. The court ought always to receive such evidence of the surrounding circumstances as, by placing it in the position of the testator, will better enable it to read the true sense of the words he has used[3], and is able to admit evidence of the testator's intention if the words used are ambiguous on their face, or evidence other than evidence of his intention shows the words to be ambiguous in the light of surrounding circumstances[4].

If a codicil refers by date to an existing will and expressly confirms it, that sufficiently shows an intention to revive it, the word 'confirm' being an apt word and expressing the meaning and having the operation of the word 'revive' which is used[5] in the Wills Act 1837[6]. This is so even though the codicil itself takes effect on a contingency[7] and the contingency has not happened at the death of the testator[8]. The intention of revival must, however, appear from the contents of the codicil[9] or otherwise be shown by that document[10]. The mere physical annexation of a codicil to a revoked will is not sufficient to revive it[11], nor is a mere reference by a recital in the codicil to such a will by date[12].

1   Where a will has been revoked by cutting out the signature, pasting the signature on it in the original place is not a re-execution so as to revive the will: *Bell v Fothergill* (1870) LR 2 P & D 148. See also PARA 394.

2   *Re Steele* (1868) LR 1 P & D 575 at 578. In *Hoare Trustees v Jacques* [2008] EWHC 2022 (Ch), [2008] All ER (D) 68 (Feb), the certainty of the intention was to be found in the fact that the solicitor drawing up the codicil was unaware of the existence of a later will and the codicil expressly referred to the earlier revoked will, including its date. The intention of the solicitor had to be attributed to the testatrix: see *Re Chilcott* [1897] P 223; *Re Stedham, Re Dyke* (1881) 6 PD 205. See also PARA 112, text and note 8.

3   *Re Steele* (1868) LR 1 P & D 575 at 576; *McLeod v McNab* [1891] AC 471 at 474, PC; *Re Davis* [1952] P 279, [1952] 2 All ER 509. See also *Lothian's Trustees v Back* 1918 SC 401, Ct of Sess; *Stewart v Maclaren* (1920) 57 SLR 148, HL (revocation of codicil not implied by confirmation of will and another codicil); *Re Mulock* [1933] IR 171 (where the cases were reviewed at length and extrinsic evidence was admitted).

4   In relation to deaths on or after 1 January 1983 see the Administration of Justice Act 1982 s 21; and PARA 195.

5   See the Wills Act 1837 s 22; and PARA 110.

6   *McLeod v McNab* [1891] AC 471, PC. See also *Re Dyke* (1881) 6 PD 205; *Re Pearson, Rowling v Crowther* [1963] 3 All ER 763, [1963] 1 WLR 1358. This is especially so where the codicil, in addition to confirming the revoked will, refers expressly to certain of its terms with a view to rendering them effectual: *Re Van Cutsem* (1890) 63 LT 252; *Re Baker, Baker v Baker* [1929] 1 Ch 668; *Re Alford* (1939) 83 Sol Jo 566. 'Ratify' has the same effect, and it is sufficient to ratify the testator's will, without reference to date, where there is no doubt as to the will referred to, eg where the will has been revoked by marriage (*Neate v Pickard* (1843) 2 Notes of Cases 406), or where the codicil treats the will, so revoked, as subsisting (*Re Earl of Caithness* (1891) 7 TLR 354).

7   *Re Da Silva* (1861) 2 Sw & Tr 315; *Re Colley* (1879) 3 LR Ir 243 (where the testator declared that, in the event of the contingency not happening, the codicil was to be destroyed and not form part of the probate, but it was nevertheless admitted to probate).

8   *Re Bangham* (1876) 1 PD 429.

9   *Marsh v Marsh* (1860) 1 Sw & Tr 528, commented on in *Re Steele* (1868) LR 1 P & D 575.

10   *Re Harper* (1849) 7 Notes of Cases 44; *Re Terrible* (1858) 1 Sw & Tr 140 (where a will in favour of the wife was revoked by the testator's second marriage following her death, and was revived by a duly executed memorandum written on the will, substituting the name of the second wife).

11   *Marsh v Marsh* (1860) 1 Sw & Tr 528.

12   *Re Dennis* [1891] P 326. A mere statement in a codicil that it is a codicil to a revoked will is not, it seems, sufficient to revive the will, although it would have had this effect before the Wills Act 1837. That Act requires some further indication of the testator's intention: *Re Steele* (1868) LR 1 P & D 575 at 577–578 (explaining *Payne and Meredith v Trappes* (1847) 1 Rob Eccl 583); *Re Reynolds* (1873) LR 3 P & D 35; *Goldie v Adam* [1938] P 85, [1938] 1 All ER 586.

112. Revival of will referred to by date.

A codicil is part of the testamentary disposition of the testator and, when a will is revived, then, in the absence of a contrary intention, the revival extends to the will with all previous codicils[1]. The mere fact that a testator describes his will by reference to its original date does not exclude the inference that the will thus referred to is the will as modified by a previous codicil[2]. Where, however, a codicil in its original form was ineffectual, it will not be revived and made effectual without distinct reference to it[3].

Where a codicil purports to revive a will without mentioning its date, evidence of facts and circumstances outside the codicil is admissible for the purpose of identifying it[4], and, only if the result is to disclose an ambiguity, is evidence of the testator's intention allowed[5].

Where the will is referred to by date, extrinsic evidence that the date was stated erroneously is inadmissible[6], but, if it appears on a comparison of successive testamentary instruments that the date is a mistake, it will be disregarded[7]. This will not, however, be done where the mind of the draftsman, which must be treated as that of the testator, was actually applied to the provisions of the wrong document, and he based the reviving codicil on it[8].

1   *Crosbie v Macdoual* (1799) 4 Ves 610; *Green v Tribe* (1878) 9 ChD 231; *Stewart v Maclaren* (1920) 57 SLR 531, HL; *Hoare Trustees v Jacques* [2008] EWHC 2022 (Ch), [2008] All ER (D) 68 (Feb). See also *Re M'Cabe* (1862) 2 Sw & Tr 474; *Re De la Saussaye* (1873) LR 3 P & D 42 at 44. As to the effect of confirmation by codicil see PARAS 113–115. As to cases where the revival was confined to the original will see *Re Reynolds* (1873) LR 3 P & D 35; *McLeod v McNab* [1891] AC 471, PC; *French v Hoey* [1899] 2 IR 472. See also *Re Carritt* (1892) 66 LT 379.
2   *McLeod v McNab* [1891] AC 471, PC.
3   *Burton v Newbery* (1875) 1 ChD 234 (donee an attesting witness), explained in *Green v Tribe* (1878) 9 ChD 231.
4   See *Re M'Cabe* (1862) 2 Sw & Tr 474 (where a revoked will which had been revived in a duly attested letter was found after the testator's death, with two codicils in a sealed envelope indorsed by him with date of sealing and his initials).
5   *Paton v Ormerod* [1892] P 247 (where there was no such ambiguity as to admit declarations by the testatrix of her intention). As to the admissibility of evidence of the testator's intention in resolving ambiguity generally see PARAS 218–219.
6   *Re Chapman* (1844) 1 Rob Eccl 1; *Payne and Meredith v Trappes* (1847) 1 Rob Eccl 583. For a review of the cases on admission of extrinsic evidence see *Re Mulock* [1933] IR 171 at 193 et seq.
7   Thus where an earlier will has been revoked by a later will, and afterwards a codicil is made expressed to be a codicil to and to confirm the earlier will, but it is apparent that the reference should have been to the later will, this is treated as a mere error of description; the earlier will is not revived and probate is granted of the later will and of the codicil, with the reference to the earlier will omitted from the codicil: *Re Brown, Quincey v Quincey* (1846) 11 Jur 111; *Re Whatman* (1864) 34 LJPM & A 17; *Re Steele, Re May, Re Wilson* (1868) LR 1 P & D 575; *Re Law* (1869) 21 LT 399; *Re Anderson* (1870) 39 LJP & M 55; *Re Ince* (1877) 2 PD 111; *Re Turner* (1891) 64 LT 805; *Re Lady Isabella Gordon* [1892] P 228; *Jane v Jane* (1917) 33 TLR 389; *Goldie v Adam* [1938] P 85, [1938] 1 All ER 586; *Re Dear* [1975] 2 NZLR 254, NZ CA.
8   *Re Stedham, Re Dyke* (1881) 6 PD 205; *Re Chilcott* [1897] P 223; *Hoare Trustees v Jacques* [2008] EWHC 2022 (Ch), [2008] All ER (D) 68 (Feb). See also *Re Lewis* (1860) 25 JP 280; and PARA 97. The decisions in *Re Stedham, Re Dyke* and *Re Chilcott* were, however, distinguished in *Goldie v Adam* [1938] P 85, [1938] 1 All ER 586 (where the earlier will was held not to be revived, the conclusion in all the circumstances being that the testator did not intend to revive it), and not followed in *Re Dear* [1975] 2 NZLR 254, NZ CA. In *Re Carleton* [1915] 2 IR 9, a duly executed codicil which, by mistake, was indorsed on and referred to an earlier revoked will, instead of a later will, was held to revive it and all three documents were admitted to probate. Cf *Re Snowden* (1896) 75 LT 279 (which was decided in the contrary sense). See also *Stewart v Maclaren* (1920) 57 SLR 531, HL; *Re Mulock* [1933] IR 171. In *Re Mardon* [1944] P 109, [1944] 2 All ER 397, where a codicil showed an intention to revive part of a revoked will but the revocation clause and residuary gift had been forgotten, it was held that only the parts in question had been revived.

(9) REPUBLICATION OF WILL

113.   Nature and methods of republication. The difference between revival and republication[1] is that, whereas revival restores a will or codicil which has been revoked, republication merely confirms an unrevoked testamentary instrument[2]. There can be no republication without re-execution[3]. The re-execution may take the form of actual re-execution of the will with the necessary formalities[4], or be effected by means of a codicil[5]. For a codicil to have the effect of republishing a will it must contain some reference to it, and, if it does not, there will be no republication[6]; but no precise form of words is necessary[7], and the codicil need not expressly republish the will[8]. Thus if the instrument is described as 'codicil to my will' without in terms confirming it[9], or if the codicil is written on the same paper as the will and refers to 'my executors above named', it operates as a republication of the will[10].

1   The term 'republication' derives from 'publication', the now obsolete procedure whereby the testator made a declaration in the presence of witnesses that the instrument produced to them was his will. This procedure has been superseded by attestation by two witnesses; every will executed

in the manner required by the Wills Act 1837 s 9 (see PARA 70) is valid without any other publication: s 13. Republication is not, therefore, a strictly accurate term for what is now the confirming of a will by re-execution of the will or by making a codicil, but it has persisted as the term for it: see *Berkeley v Berkeley* [1946] AC 555 at 575–576, [1946] 2 All ER 154 at 163, HL. As to the effect of republication see PARA 114.

2   In *Re Turner's Estate* [2003] BCSC 1226, [2004] WTLR 1467, BC Sup Ct, it was held, citing *Re Barke* (1845) 4 Notes of Cases 44 (see PARA 114 note 3), that an invalidly executed will could be republished.

3   *Barnes v Crowe* (1792) 1 Ves 485 at 497. As to methods of revival see PARA 110.

4   As to the formalities of execution see PARA 60 et seq.

5   *Duppa v Mayo* (1669) 1 Wms Saund 275; *Barnes v Crowe* (1792) 1 Ves 485; *Re Smith, Bilke v Roper* (1890) 45 ChD 632.

6   *Re Smith, Bilke v Roper* (1890) 45 ChD 632.

7   *Potter v Potter* (1750) 1 Ves Sen 437 at 444.

8   *Barnes v Crowe* (1792) 1 Ves 485; *Pigott v Waller* (1802) 7 Ves 98 at 120; *Grealey v Sampson* [1917] 1 IR 286, Ir CA.

9   *Skinner v Ogle* (1845) 9 Jur 432; *Re Taylor, Whitby v Highton* (1888) 57 LJ Ch 430. See also *Acherley v Vernon* (1725) 3 Bro Parl Cas 85 at 91, HL; *Rowley v Eyton* (1817) 2 Mer 128 (where the codicil referred to the will, although the report does not say so: see *Re Smith, Bilke v Roper* (1890) 45 ChD 632 at 637); *Yarnold v Wallis* (1840) 4 Y & C Ex 160; *Doe d York v Walker* (1844) 12 M & W 591; *Re Champion, Dudley v Champion* [1893] 1 Ch 101, CA (where, however, there was express confirmation).

10 *Serocold v Hemming* (1758) 2 Lee 490 (cited in *Re Smith, Bilke v Roper* (1890) 45 ChD 632 at 637). Cf the case of a codicil executed for a limited purpose only (see PARA 115).

114.   Date of will shifted by republication. The effect of republishing a will is for many purposes to shift its date to the date of the republishing instrument[1], as if the testator at that date had made a will in the words of the will so republished[2], together with any unattested additions to the will or to any intervening codicils, provided that the alterations or additions form part of the former testamentary paper[3], and together with any codicils effecting alterations[4], except such codicils as are inoperative without being themselves expressly confirmed or incorporated[5] or are expressly or impliedly revoked[6]. The will may thus acquire a force or efficiency which it did not previously possess[7]. In particular, where property is given by a generic description, so as to be capable of increase or diminution and not so as to identify a specific thing and that thing only, the description is prima facie referred not to the date of the will[8], but to the date of the codicil[9], so as to pass all the testator's interest in the property then falling within the description[10]. The effect, of moving the date of a will forward, by republication, does not necessarily affect those incidents and consequences of the will which are linked to the actual date of death, particularly where legislative consequences are concerned[11].

1   *Doe d York v Walker* (1844) 12 M & W 591 at 600; *Grealey v Sampson* [1917] 1 IR 286, Ir CA; *Goonewardene v Goonewardene* [1931] AC 647, HL. As to the methods of effecting republication see PARA 62.

2   *Rogers v Pittis* (1822) 1 Add 30 at 38; *Hamilton v Carroll* (1839) 1 I Eq R 175; *Winter v Winter* (1846) 5 Hare 306; *Re Fraser, Lowther v Fraser* [1904] 1 Ch 726, CA; *Re Malcolm, Marjoribanks v Malcolm* (1923) 156 LT Jo 361; *Re Hardyman, Teesdale v McClintock* [1925] Ch 287; *Re Reeves, Reeves v Pawson* [1928] Ch 351. In *Re Mellor, Dodgson v Ashworth* (1912) 28 TLR 473, a legacy given to an executor by the will passed to another executor substituted by a codicil. In *Re Yates, Singleton v Povah* (1922) 128 LT 619, a legacy given by the will was increased to the amount mentioned in the codicil.

3   *Re Barke* (1845) 4 Notes of Cases 44; *Re Tegg* (1846) 4 Notes of Cases 531. See also PARA 110 note 9. It appears that an addition or a separate paper cannot be republished by a later codicil, but see PARA 113 note 2.

4   *Winter v Winter* (1846) 5 Hare 306 at 312; *Re Rayer, Rayer v Rayer* [1903] 1 Ch 685; *Re Fraser, Lowther v Fraser* [1904] 1 Ch 726 at 734, CA; *Re Taylor, Dale v Dale* [1909] WN 59; *Re Picton, Porter v Jones* [1944] Ch 303; *Re Dack's Will Trusts, Barclays Bank Ltd v Tracey* (1964) 114 L Jo 656. See also *Re De la Saussaye* (1783) LR 3 P & D 42; *Crosbie v Macdoual* (1779) 4 Ves 610 at 616; *Green v Tribe* (1878) 9 ChD 231 at 235; *Follett v Pettman* (1883) 23 ChD 337. The

question whether all or some only of a series of testamentary instruments are to be treated as the testator's will is to be decided in accordance with his intention as collected from all the circumstances of the case: see *Smith v Cunningham* (1823) 1 Add 448 (only some codicils ratified with the will, but all admitted to probate); *Greenough v Martin* (1824) 2 Add 239 (three intermediate codicils not admitted); *McLeod v McNab* [1891] AC 471, PC (intermediate codicil held to be revoked). A codicil may incorporate documents not in existence at the date of the will but referred to in the will as if in existence, and actually so at the date of the codicil: *Re Rendle* (1899) 68 LJP 125; and see PARA 711. As to the revival of a revoked will see PARA 110. As to the exercise of a special power conferred after the date of the will see *Cowper v Mantell* (1856) 22 Beav 223 at 230 (power not executed); and as to a power already conferred, but exercisable on an event after the date of the will see *Re Blackburn, Smiles v Blackburn* (1889) 43 ChD 75 (power executed). See also TRUSTS AND POWERS vol 98 (2013) PARA 599 et seq.

5 As to the need for express incorporation see PARA 112 text and note 3.
6 *McLeod v McNab* [1891] AC 471, PC.
7 *Re Tredgold, Midland Bank Executor and Trustee Co Ltd v Tredgold* [1943] Ch 69 at 72, [1943] 1 All ER 120 at 122 (overruled by *Berkeley v Berkeley* [1946] AC 555, [1946] 2 All ER 154, HL, on the construction of the statute in question in that case).
8 It is assumed that the rule of construction in the Wills Act 1837 s 24 (see PARA 282), referring descriptions of property to the death of the testator, is excluded or is otherwise not applicable.
9 *Doe d York v Walker* (1844) 12 M & W 591; *Lady Langdale v Briggs* (1855) 3 Sm & G 246 at 252; *Re Champion, Dudley v Champion* [1893] 1 Ch 101, CA; *Re Fraser, Lowther v Fraser* [1904] 1 Ch 726 at 734, CA.
10 *Emuss v Smith* (1848) 2 De G & Sm 722 (where a codicil was not effective to pass after-acquired freehold); *Re Pyle, Pyle v Pyle* [1895] 1 Ch 724 (where the testator's interest was transferred to the purchase money where an option to purchase was granted after the will but at the same time as the codicil was executed); *Steele v Steele* [1913] 1 IR 292, Ir CA. Cf *Pattinson v Pattinson* (1832) 1 My & K 12; *Macdonald v Irvine* (1878) 8 ChD 101 at 108, CA (where the legacies were adeemed although the descriptions were accurate when the wills were made).
11 *Berkeley v Berkeley* [1946] AC 555, [1946] 2 All ER 154, HL (enactment of tax legislation referring to 'any provision, however worded', between republishing codicil and death, had no effect upon beneficiary of tax-free annuity because, although the codicil post-dated the legislation, the legislative wording, properly construed, referred to the benefit receivable by the operation of the will at death (if not earlier revoked), rather than the testamentary wording that gave it),

115. Purposes for which date of will not shifted. The original effect of the will and the operative intermediate codicils is not prejudiced by republication[1], and republication does not necessarily make the will operate for all purposes as if it had been originally made at the date of the republishing instrument, for a contrary intention may be shown[2]. Whether a codicil is part of a will, or republishes it, or incorporates or reiterates it, or brings up the date of the will to its own date depends on the particular case[3], and the testator's intention is not to be defeated by treating the will as brought up to the date of the codicil[4]. Republication does not revive a legacy which has been revoked[5], or adeemed or satisfied[6], nor does it revive a gift which has lapsed[7], or substitute a new legatee for one named in the will where the description used may apply to different persons at different times[8]; for the codicil can only act on the will as it existed at the time of republication and at that time the legacy revoked, adeemed or satisfied formed no part of it[9]. Moreover, it seems that republication need not affect conditions attached to a gift[10], but it does not give effect to a condition shown to have been dispensed with by the testator before the date of the codicil[11]. Where the purpose of a will is limited to particular property, the mere making of a codicil will not enlarge its scope[12], nor does a codicil executed for a limited purpose only and not purporting to confirm the will or bring its terms up to its own date have the effect of republishing it[13].

The date of original execution of the will remains as a factor for determining the construction of it, as, for example, where it is necessary to determine the date to which expressions of time occurring in the will are referable[14]. The date when a will is 'made' may depend on the construction of a particular statute[15]. It seems that the express reference to an earlier codicil containing a trust clause, by a republishing codicil (made shortly before, and in anticipation of, the impending death of the testatrix) may be used by the court as evidence, in construing the size of the class of beneficiaries under the clause[16].

1   *Stilwell v Mellersh* (1851) 20 LJ Ch 356. In *Re Beirnstein, Barnett v Beirnstein* [1925] Ch 12, republication of the will did not extend the meaning of 'mortgage' as used in it.

2   *Bowes v Bowes* (1801) 2 Bos & P 500, HL; *Goodtitle d Woodhouse v Meredith* (1813) 2 M & S 5 at 14; *Re Farrer's Estate* (1858) 8 ICLR 370; *Hopwood v Hopwood* (1859) 7 HL Cas 728; *Earl of Mountcashell v Smyth* [1895] 1 IR 346, Ir CA.

3   *Re Elcom, Layborn v Grover Wright* [1894] 1 Ch 303 at 309, CA.

4   *Doe d Biddulph v Hole* (1850) 15 QB 848 at 858; *Re Moore, Long v Moore* [1907] 1 IR 315; *Re Heath's Will Trusts, Hamilton v Lloyds Bank Ltd* [1949] Ch 170, [1949] 1 All ER 199. See also *Re Sebag-Montefiore, Sebag-Montefiore v Alliance Assurance Co Ltd* [1944] Ch 331, [1944] 1 All ER 672, CA (overruled on the construction of the statute there in question in *Berkeley v Berkeley* [1946] AC 555, [1946] 2 All ER 154, HL).

5   As to revocation see PARA 95.

6   *Cowper v Mantell* (1856) 22 Beav 223; *Sidney v Sidney* (1873) LR 17 Eq 65. In accordance with this principle a legacy is not revived if it has been adeemed or satisfied under the presumption against double portions: *Izard v Hurst* (1698) Freem Ch 224; *Drinkwater v Falconer* (1755) 2 Ves Sen 623 at 626; *Monck v Lord Monck* (1810) 1 Ball & B 298; *Booker v Allen* (1831) 2 Russ & M 270; *Powys v Mansfield* (1837) 3 My & Cr 359 at 376; *Montague v Montague* (1852) 15 Beav 565; *Hopwood v Hopwood* (1859) 7 HL Cas 728. As to ademption see PARAS 155–159. If it is doubtful whether the doctrine of ademption is to be applied, the existence of a codicil is important: *Re Aynsley, Kyrle v Turner* [1914] 2 Ch 422 (on appeal [1915] Ch 172, CA); *Re Warren, Warren v Warren* [1932] 1 Ch 42 (distinguishing *Powys v Mansfield* (1837) 3 My & Cr 359). See also *Grealey v Sampson* [1917] 1 IR 286, Ir CA. Exceptionally, republication by a codicil executed after 31 December 1925 prevented the ademption of a gift of an undivided share of land in a will executed before 1 January 1926, where the gift was one which might (without the republication) have been adeemed as a result of the Law of Property Act 1925 converting the undivided share into a notional interest in proceeds of sale, the land being still unsold at the testator's death (*Re Warren, Warren v Warren* above); by contrast, republication did not prevent ademption where an actual conversion into cash had occurred when coal mines were nationalised and their place taken by compensation money (*Re Galway's Will Trusts, Lowther v Viscount Galway* [1950] Ch 1, [1949] 2 All ER 419).

7   *Hutcheson v Hammond* (1790) 3 Bro CC 128; *Doe d Turner v Kett* (1792) 4 Term Rep 601; *Winter v Winter* (1846) 5 Hare 306. As to lapse see PARA 160 et seq.

8   *Drinkwater v Falconer* (1755) 2 Ves Sen 623 at 626; *Doe d Turner v Kett* (1792) 4 Term Rep 601; *Stilwell v Mellersh* (1851) 20 LJ Ch 356 at 361–362; *Re Park, Bott v Chester* [1910] 2 Ch 322 at 328. See also *Anon* (undated), cited in 1 My & K at 14 (bequest to testator's six children; one died, but another was born before republication; the last child was held to be excluded). The authorities are not, however, uniform; for decisions to the contrary see *Perkins v Micklethwaite* (1714) 1 P Wms 274 at 275 (gift to 'youngest son J'; J died in testator's lifetime, but another son J was born afterwards and before the date of the codicil and was held entitled to take); *Re Donald, Moore v Somerset* [1909] 2 Ch 410 ('to whom I have given legacies' held to include legatees by codicil), not following *Anon* above. In *Re Hardyman, Teesdale v McClintock* [1925] Ch 287, the testatrix by her will gave an interest in a legacy to her cousin's 'wife'; the wife died and after her death the testatrix made a codicil republishing her will; the cousin then married again and it was held that the second wife was entitled to the interest in the legacy; this case seems to have turned largely on the fact that at the date of the codicil the testatrix knew that the cousin's first wife was dead. It appears doubtful whether the decisions in *Perkins v Micklethwaite*, *Re Donald, Moore v Somerset* and *Re Hardyman, Teesdale v McClintock* are really reconcilable with what it is submitted is the true principle, as stated in the text. See also *Blech v Blech* [2001] All ER (D) 141 (Dec) and note 15.

9   *Powys v Mansfield* (1837) 3 My & Cr 359 at 376 per Lord Cottenham; cited with approval in *Hopwood v Hopwood* (1859) 7 HL Cas 728; and followed in *Re Galway's Will Trusts, Lowther v Viscount Galway* [1950] Ch 1, [1949] 2 All ER 419.

10 *Stilwell v Mellersh* (1851) 20 LJ Ch 356 (advances 'already' made to be brought into hotchpot; advance after date of will not affected); *Re Park, Bott v Chester* [1910] 2 Ch 322 at 327–328 (condition as to marriage with consent); but see *Re Rayer, Rayer v Rayer* [1903] 1 Ch 685 (direction that annuities were to be free of deduction except legacy duty and income tax; held that effect of republication was that annuitants bore duties substituted for legacy duty by an Act passed before the codicil); *Wedgwood v Denton* (1871) LR 12 Eq 290 (condition relating to residence

during specified lease; renewal of lease before republication); *Re Taylor, Dale v Dale* [1909] WN 59 (effect on gift over to issue of deceased children).

11 *Violett v Brookman* (1857) 26 LJ Ch 308; cf *Cooper v Cooper* (1856) 6 I Ch R 217 at 223. See also PARA 144.

12 *Re Taylor, Whitby v Highton* (1888) 57 LJ Ch 430.

13 *Bowes v Bowes* (1801) 2 Bos & P 500, HL; *Monypenny v Bristow* (1832) 2 Russ & M 117; *Hughes v Turner* (1835) 3 My & K 666; *Ashley v Waugh* (1839) 4 Jur 572. As to the conditions necessary for republication see PARA 113.

14 *Earl of Mountcashell v Smyth* [1895] 1 IR 346 at 360, Ir CA; *Re Moore, Long v Moore* [1907] 1 IR 315 at 320; *Re Heath's Will Trusts, Hamilton v Lloyds Bank Ltd* [1949] Ch 170, [1949] 1 All ER 199.

15 The Wills Act 1837 s 34 provides that, for the purposes of that Act, a will made before that Act and republished afterwards is deemed to have been made at the time of republication. A will made before the Married Women's Reversionary Interests Act 1857 and republished by codicil afterwards was, however, held to have been made at the date of the will and not at the date of the codicil (*Re Elcom, Layborn v Grover Wright* [1894] 1 Ch 303); and a charitable devise was held not to have been invalidated under the law of mortmain (repealed: see the Charities Act 1960 s 38; and CHARITIES vol 8 (2015) PARA 84), because the will in which it was contained was republished by a codicil made within 12 months of the testator's death (*Re Moore, Long v Moore* [1907] 1 IR 315). See also *Rolfe v Perry* (1863) 3 De GJ & Sm 481 (will made before the Real Estate Charges Act 1854, but coming into operation after its commencement). The changes made by the Family Law Reform Act 1969 s 15 (repealed) (see PARA 355) and the Family Law Reform Act 1987 s 1(1) (see PARA 356) to the construction of words descriptive of relationship in wills do not apply to wills made before the respective commencement dates of those provisions, including wills made before the commencement date and confirmed by a codicil after it: see the Family Law Reform Act 1969 s 15(8) (repealed); and the Family Law Reform Act 1987 s 19(7).

16 *Blech v Blech* [2001] All ER (D) 141 (Dec). The court construed 'such of the children of my said son . . . as shall survive me' as including children conceived and born after death of the testatrix, she being aware that the class could easily increase after her anticipated death.

2. TYPES OF TESTAMENTARY DISPOSITION

(1) INTERESTS WHICH MAY BE DISPOSED OF BY WILL

116. Power of disposition by will. The power of disposition by will is not at the testator's caprice, but extends only to the creation of those interests which are recognised by law and to no other[1]. The interest created need not necessarily be the interest of a sole donee vesting immediately in the whole of the property which is the subject of the gift; property may be given to persons as joint tenants or as tenants in common[2] or as a class[3], and future and successive interests may be created[4]. A condition may be attached to the gift[5], or the interest may take the form of an option, exercisable only on the giving of consideration[6]. The donee may be given the right to choose between two or more pieces of property[7]; or it is possible to make a gift of a specific quantity out of some larger asset which constitutes a homogeneous mass, such as a bank account or a holding of shares in a company[8]. Incorporeal interests may be created, such as rentcharges[9] and easements[10].

1 *Soulle v Gerrard* (1596) Cro Eliz 525; *Roe d Dodson v Grew* (1767) Wilm 272 at 274 commenting on the phrase 'at his will and pleasure' in 32 Hen 8 c 1 (Wills) (1540); *Egerton v Earl Brownlow* (1853) 4 HL Cas 1 at 24; *Re Elliot, Kelly v Elliot* [1896] 2 Ch 353 at 356. As to property disposable by will see PARA 25 et seq.
2 *Willing v Baine* (1731) 3 P Wms 113 at 115; *Ritchie's Trustees v M'Donald* 1915 SC 501, Ct of Sess (where a gift to two persons equally for their lives, with a gift over on the death of the survivor, was held to be a joint tenancy). As to the creation of joint tenancies and tenancies in common see further PARA 393 et seq; and as to lapse where there is a gift to joint tenants or tenants in common see PARA 173.
3 See PARAS 175, 302 et seq. As to lapse in the case of class gifts see PARA 174; and as to the rules of convenience for ascertaining a class see PARA 304 et seq.
4 See PARAS 117 text and note 4, 121.
5 See PARA 128 et seq.
6 See PARAS 125–126.
7 See PARA 127.
8 *Hunter v Moss* [1993] 1 WLR 934 (affd [1994] 3 All ER 215, [1994] 1 WLR 452, CA), referring to *Re Cheadle, Bishop v Holt* [1900] 2 Ch 620, CA, and *Re Clifford, Mallam v McFie* [1912] 1 Ch 29. It seems that such a gift will not be valid in relation to tangible property such as houses or cases of wine, unless there is a right of selection given to the beneficiary: *Asten v Asten* [1894] 3 Ch 260; *Re London Wine Co (Shippers) Ltd* [1986] PCC 121; *Hunter v Moss* above.
9 See REAL PROPERTY AND REGISTRATION vol 87 (2012) PARA 1124.
10 As to the creation of easements by express grant see generally REAL PROPERTY AND REGISTRATION vol 87 (2012) PARA 851 et seq. The requirement that a conveyance of an interest in land must be by deed in order to create a legal estate (see the Law of Property Act 1925 s 52(1); and REAL PROPERTY AND REGISTRATION vol 87 (2012) PARA 851) does not prevent the creation of a legal easement by will.

117. Successive and future interests. Formerly, successive and future interests could be created by devise in real estate at law or in equity[1].

Since 31 December 1925, however, successive and future interests in real estate and chattels real can be created only as equitable interests[2]. Between 1 January 1926 and 31 December 1996 inclusive it was possible to create an entailed interest in chattels real (that is leaseholds) and chattels personal but only by the like expressions as those by which before 1 January 1926 a similar estate tail could have been created by deed, not being an executory instrument, in freehold land[3]. Entailed interests cannot be created in any property, real or personal, by instruments coming into effect on or after 1 January 1997[4].

Estates pur autre vie may be created by will[5].

1 See REAL PROPERTY AND REGISTRATION vol 87 (2012) PARA 157.

2 See the Law of Property Act 1925 s 1; and REAL PROPERTY AND REGISTRATION vol 87 (2012)
   PARA 160.
3 See the Law of Property Act 1925 s 130(1) (repealed by the Trusts of Land and Appointment of
   Trustees Act 1996 s 25(2), Sch 4); and PERSONAL PROPERTY vol 80 (2013) PARA 815; REAL
   PROPERTY AND REGISTRATION vol 87 (2012) PARA 114; SETTLEMENTS vol 91 (2012)
   PARA 839.
4 See the Trusts of Land and Appointment of Trustees Act 1996 s 2(6), Sch 1 para 5; PARA 387; and
   REAL PROPERTY AND REGISTRATION vol 87 (2012) PARA 114.
5 As to estates pur autre vie see REAL PROPERTY AND REGISTRATION vol 87 (2012) PARA 146 et
   seq. As to life interests generally see REAL PROPERTY AND REGISTRATION vol 87 (2012)
   PARAS 139–143. An interest may be created by will where the cestui que vie or one or more of the
   cestuis que vie are unborn, provided that they are ascertained within the limits allowed by the
   rules against perpetuities: see *Re Amos, Carrier v Price* [1891] 3 Ch 159 at 166–167 (estate for the
   life of the donee and the life of his heir). Cf *Re Ashforth, Sibley v Ashforth* [1905] 1 Ch 535 at 542,
   546 (estate for the lives of unborn grandchildren, and the survivor of them); and see Challis's Real
   Property (3rd Edn, 1911) p 213.

118. Specific legacies. Legacies[1] are ordinarily divided into two classes, specific
legacies and general legacies, general legacies also being described as legacies of
quantity or number[2].

A specific legacy must be of some thing or of some interest, legal or equitable[3],
forming part of the testator's estate; it must be a part as distinguished from the
whole of his personal property or from the whole of the general residue of his
personal estate; it must be identified by a sufficient description, and separated in
favour of the particular legatee from the general mass of the testator's personal
estate[4]. The forgiveness of a debt by will is a specific legacy of the debt[5]. Where a
particular debt is given but afterwards recovered adversarially by the testator, the
legacy may be adeemed[6]. A pecuniary legacy may be a specific legacy (where it is
described as being taken from particular and identified moneys held by or for the
testator or his estate) or a general legacy (where it is not described in such a way)[7].

A further sub-species of pecuniary legacies is that of demonstrative legacies,
which exhibit some aspects of both a specific legacy and a general legacy
according to factual circumstances[8].

1 As to the danger of distributing legacies within six months of probate where a claim under the
   Inheritance (Provision for Families and Dependants) Act 1975 is likely see PARA 1064.
2 Swinburne on Wills (7th Edn) 308n. As to the failure of legacies see PARA 127. As to ademption
   and satisfaction see PARA 155 et seq; and EQUITABLE JURISDICTION vol 47 (2014) PARA 176
   et seq. As to a third class of legacy (demonstrative legacies) see PARA 120.
3 *Re Sherman, Re Walters, Trevenen v Pearce* [1954] Ch 653, [1954] 1 All ER 893.
4 *Bothamley v Sherson* (1875) LR 20 Eq 304 at 308 per Jessel MR; *Robertson v Broadbent* (1883)
   8 App Cas 812 at 815, HL, per Lord Selborne LC; and see *Dawson v Reid* (1915) 113 LT 52, HL;
   Re Rose, Midland Bank Executor and Trustee Co Ltd v Rose [1949] Ch 78, [1948] 2 All ER 971.
   Where a testator makes a bequest of an option to purchase shares forming part of his estate at less
   than market value but does not make any distinct bequest of the beneficial interest represented by
   the difference between the option price and the market value, the beneficial interest in question is
   not property specifically bequeathed: see PARA 1004 note 3. Savings certificates which are
   specifically bequeathed in a will or form part of the residuary estate or which are left by a holder
   who has died intestate may be transferred to the person beneficially entitled and need not be
   encashed: *Note* [1954] 1 All ER 519.
5 *Re Wedmore, Wedmore v Wedmore* [1907] 2 Ch 277. However, the guarantee of a bank overdraft
   would not normally be a 'debt' for this purpose: *Re Mitchell, Freelove v Mitchell* [1913] 1 Ch 201.
6 *Lawson v Stitch* (1738) 1 Atk 507.
7 See *Lawson v Stitch* (1738) 1 Atk 507 at 508 (gift of money in a bag or of money on a particular
   security would be a specific legacy, but gift of £500 out of such securities as testator owned at death
   or which were purchased at election of executors was held to be a general pecuniary legacy).
8 See *Re Webster, Goss v Webster* [1937] 1 All ER 602, CA; and PARA 120.

119. General legacies. A general legacy may or may not be part of the
testator's property: it has no reference to the actual state of his property, and is a
gift of something which, if the testator leaves sufficient assets, must be raised by

his executors out of his general personal estate. Whether or not a particular thing forms part of the testator's personal estate is a pure question of fact; so long as it is the testator's at his death it is capable of being specifically bequeathed[1]. Whether or not it has been separated from the general personal estate depends upon the true construction of the will. In the case of real estate a devise, whether of a specific property or by way of residue has, in most cases, been held to have been specific[2]. There is, however, authority to the contrary where the earlier cases on residuary gifts of realty were not followed[3].

1   *Fontaine v Tyler* (1821) 9 Price 94; *Stephenson v Dowson* (1840) 3 Beav 342. A gift of a sum of stock in round numbers, or even of a sum of stock in pounds and pence, being the exact amount possessed by the testator at the date of his death, is prima facie a general legacy (*Re Willcocks, Warwick v Willcocks* [1921] 2 Ch 327); but there may be clear indications, as gathered from the will and the surrounding circumstances, that the testator intended to dispose of the specific investments which he held: see *Re Hawkins, Public Trustee v Shaw* [1922] 2 Ch 569. See also *Re Gage, Crozier v Gutheridge* [1934] Ch 536; *Re O'Connor, Westminster Bank Ltd v O'Connor* [1948] Ch 628, [1948] 2 All ER 270.

2   *Hensman v Fryer* (1867) 3 Ch App 420; *Lancefield v Iggulden* (1874) 10 Ch App 136; cf PARA 1000.

3   *Re Wilson, Wilson v Mackay* [1967] Ch 53 at 69, [1966] 2 All ER 867 at 873 per Pennycuick J (where 'all my real estate' was held to be a residuary gift). See also *Franguesco v Shaw* [1977] 1 NSWLR 660.

120. Demonstrative legacies. There is a third kind of legacy, called a demonstrative legacy, which consists of a pecuniary legacy payable out of a particular fund[1]. Such a legacy has the following advantages: (1) it is not adeemed by the total or partial failure at the testator's death of the fund out of which it was directed to be paid, but becomes payable out of the general personal estate to the extent of such failure, pari passu with ordinary general legacies[2]; and (2) it does not abate with the general legacies until after the particular fund is exhausted[3].

1   See *Dawson v Reid* (1915) 113 LT 52, HL (where a preference expressed by the testator that a pecuniary legacy given by the will should be taken from his insurance funds was held to make the legacy demonstrative); *Walford v Walford* [1912] AC 658 (legacies payable from a reversionary fund and nothing in will required delay in administration until the reversion fund fell in); *Re Webster, Goss v Webster* [1937] 1 All ER 602, CA. Cf *Russell v IRC* [1988] 2 All ER 405, [1988] 1 WLR 834 (gifts could not be demonstrative as they could only be made by resort to an identified asset).

2   *Roberts v Pocock* (1798) 4 Ves 150; *Mann v Copland* (1817) 2 Madd 223; *Fowler v Willoughby* (1825) 2 Sim & St 354. As to the ademption of legacies by the failure of the subject matter of the gift see PARA 155 et seq; and EQUITABLE JURISDICTION vol 47 (2014) PARA 176 et seq.

3   *Mullins v Smith* (1860) 1 Drew & Sm 204.

(2) INTERESTS WHICH MAY BE COMPLETED BY WILL

121. Chattels given to successive donees. The common law refused to recognise the possibility of creating a remainder in chattels personal[1].

It is now clearly settled that a chattel personal may be bequeathed for successive and future interests both at law and, through the interposition of trustees, in equity so as to confer enforceable rights on the second and subsequent holders[2]. Where the property in the chattels is not vested in trustees, the precise nature of the interest taken by successive holders has not been finally determined[3]. It seems that the life tenant in possession is a quasi-trustee for the remaindermen, or it may be that he holds the chattel under an implied contract as bailee for the benefit of the remaindermen[4]. Whatever the true theory is, it is clear that the court of equity will at the instance of remaindermen restrain by injunction an attempted disposition by the holder in breach of the terms of the will[5]. Security is only required from the first taker in cases of risk. Usually the first taker merely signs an inventory[6].

To be valid, successive and future interests in property must comply with the rule against perpetuities[7], and must not offend against any rule of public policy[8].

1 For an historical account see 2 Fearne's Contingent Remainders (10th Edn) s 168f. See also *Case of the Grail* (1459) YB 37 Hen 6, fo 30, pl 11; *Anon* (1548) Bro NC pl 388; *Welcden v Elkington* (1576) 2 Plowd 516 at 520; *Paramour v Yardley* (1579) 2 Plowd 539 at 541; *Lord Hastings v Douglas* (1634) Cro Car 343. It was said that a devise of the chattel for an hour is forever: *Anon* (1542) Bro NC pl 334; *Welcden v Elkington* (1576) 2 Plowd 516 at 520.
2 *Hoare v Parker* (1788) 2 Term Rep 376 (trover); *Re Swan, Witham v Swan* [1915] 1 Ch 829. The interest of the second legatee pending the contingency may be a transmissible interest (*Doe d Roberts v Polgrean* (1791) 1 Hy Bl 535), and is of the nature of a chose in action within the Bills of Sale Acts (*Re Tritton, ex p Singleton* (1889) 61 LT 301; *Re Thynne, Thynne v Grey* [1911] 1 Ch 282), although not a chose or thing in action in the ordinary sense. As to chattels settled as heirlooms and other settled chattels see the Law of Property Act 1925 s 130 (amended by the Trusts of Land and Appointment of Trustees Act 1996 s 25(2), Sch4); and *D'Abo v Paget* [2000] All ER (D) 944. See also *Re Earl of Strafford, Royal Bank of Scotland Ltd v Byng* [1978] 3 All ER 18, [1978] 3 WLR 223; affd [1980] Ch 28, [1979] 1 All ER 513 (analysis of powers of life tenant and trustees with respect to surrenders of interest and acceptance of compromise arrangements of chattel interests). See also PERSONAL PROPERTY vol 80 (2013) PARAS 814–815. As to the Bills of Sale Acts see FINANCIAL INSTRUMENTS AND TRANSACTIONS vol 49 (2015) PARA 413 et seq.
3 Cf PERSONAL PROPERTY vol 80 (2013) PARA 815.
4 *Re Swan, Witham v Swan* [1915] 1 Ch 829 at 834–835; and see PERSONAL PROPERTY vol 80 (2013) PARA 815.
5 *Re Swan, Witham v Swan* [1915] 1 Ch 829 at 835.
6 See PERSONAL PROPERTY vol 80 (2013) PARA 815.
7 See PERPETUITIES AND ACCUMULATIONS vol 80 (2013) PARA 9 et seq.
8 Where the duration of a limited gift is fixed by reference to an event contrary to public policy, such as the future separation of husband and wife (*Re Moore, Trafford v Maconochie* (1888) 39 ChD 116, CA) or an attempt to fetter the duty of parents to provide for children's education (*Re Blake, Lynch v Lombard* [1955] IR 89), the gift is void. If the words are not part of the limitation, but impose a condition, it may be possible to reject them, leaving the gift absolute: *Re Moore, Trafford v Maconochie*; and see *Re Lovell, Sparks v Southall* [1920] 1 Ch 122. As to conditions attached to gifts see PARA 128 et seq; and as to the construction of gifts to last until indefinitely distant events see PARA 138.

122. Chattels consumed in the use. In the case of specific gifts of chattels which are consumed in the use of them, the use and the property in the chattels can prima facie have no separate existence[1]. Thus the old rule that a gift of a life interest is an absolute gift, and that a limitation over after a life interest is ineffectual, prima facie still applies[2]. The testator may, however, expressly give a right to consume so much of certain consumables as the donee may require during his lifetime; the donee then has an absolute interest only in the chattels actually consumed, and the testator may validly make a gift over of the amount remaining unconsumed[3]. The rule does not apply in a case where, by the terms of the will or by implication from the circumstances of the case, the chattels are given to the successive legatees in the character of money's worth and are not intended for personal use or consumption by the legatee[4]. If they are stock of a farming or other business given in connection with a gift for life of that business, then, at all events where the stock is necessary to carry on the business, and the business and stock are intended to be kept up[5], the first legatee does not take absolutely[6].

Moreover, the old rule does not apply to residuary gifts of personal estate so far as they comprise such chattels in cases where, under the rule in *Howe v Dartmouth*[7], to effectuate a presumed intention that the legatees are successively to enjoy the same subject matter[8], the chattels must be sold and only the interest of the proceeds paid to the legatee for life[9] unless, by the terms of the will, he is given the right to enjoy them in their original form[10]. As from 1 October 2012, the rule in *Howe v Earl of Dartmouth* has been abolished in relation to new trusts, save in certain circumstances[11].

1   *Randall v Russell* (1817) 3 Mer 190 at 195 per Grant MR.
2   *Randall v Russell* (1817) 3 Mer 190 (corn and hay); *Andrew v Andrew* (1845) 1 Coll 686 at 691 (wine, spirits and hay); *Montresor v Montresor* (1845) 1 Coll 693 (wine and provisions); *Bryant v Easterson* (1859) 5 Jur NS 166 (farming stock); *Phillips v Beal* (1862) 32 Beav 25 (wine for household consumption); *Breton v Mockett* (1878) 9 ChD 95. See also GIFTS vol 52 (2014) PARA 224; PERSONAL PROPERTY vol 80 (2013) PARA 815. The fact that the personal estate bequeathed is of a description not likely to be given for limited interests has been considered in the construction of the will: *Porter v Tournay* (1797) 3 Ves 311 at 313; *Manning v Purcell* (1855) 7 De GM & G 55 at 61; *Randfield v Randfield* (1860) 8 HL Cas 225 at 236–237; *Re Moir's Estate, Moir v Warner* [1882] WN 139. Although the rule prima facie applies, it may be excluded by the circumstances: see *Re Hall's Will* (1855) 1 Jur NS 974.
3   *Re Colyer, Millikin v Snelling* (1886) 55 LT 344.
4   A direction for valuation shows an intention that the property given should be considered to pass as money and not in its original form: *Bryant v Easterson* (1859) 5 Jur NS 166 at 167–168 per Stuart V-C. In that case, there being no direction for valuation, farming stock did not pass to the legatees in remainder.
5   Cf *Maynard v Gibson* [1876] WN 204, followed in *Paine v Countess of Warwick* [1914] 2 KB 486 (deer intended to be kept up by tenant for life). As regards severed crops from time to time on a farm, the life tenant takes absolutely, although intended to keep up the business: *Steward v Cotton* (1777) 5 Russ 17n; *Bryant v Easterson* (1859) 5 Jur NS 166; *Re Powell, Dodd v Williams* [1921] 1 Ch 178 at 180–181.
6   *Montresor v Montresor* (1845) 1 Coll 693 (live and dead stock; tenant for life entitled to produce only); *Groves v Wright* (1856) 2 K & J 347 (farming stock); *Phillips v Beal* (1862) 32 Beav 25 (wine used in wine merchant's business); *Cockayne v Harrison* (1872) LR 13 Eq 432; *Myers v Washbrook* [1901] 1 KB 360 (farming stock). See also *Griffin v McCabe* (1918) 52 ILT 134; *Beresford v Preston* (1920) 54 ILT 48 (where an inquiry was directed). The rule that a gift of consumables is an absolute gift to the first legatee does not apply in the case of farming stock, although not given in connection with a business: see *Groves v Wright* above at 351; *Myers v Washbrook* above at 363 per Darling J. Cf, however, *Bryant v Easterson* (1859) 5 Jur NS 166. A provision that the first legatee is not to be liable for depreciation assists a construction giving him an absolute interest: see *Breton v Mockett* (1878) 9 ChD 95. Where the legatee of farming stock was by the will made subject to an obligation to maintain the stock 'at equal value or as near thereto as circumstances will admit', she was held to be entitled to a proportionate part of the increase in value: *Re Powell, Dodd v Williams* [1921] 1 Ch 178.
7   Ie the rule in *Howe v Earl of Dartmouth, Howe v Countess of Aylesbury* (1802) 7 Ves 137: see PARAS 1122–1126. As to the effect of the rule see also SETTLEMENTS vol 91 (2012) PARAS 846–847; TRUSTS AND POWERS vol 98 (2013) PARAS 172–173. A clause excluding the rule does not necessarily exclude the provisions of the Apportionment Act 1870: see SETTLEMENTS vol 91 (2012) PARA 858. As to the abolition of the rule see the text and note 11.
8   As to this presumption as the ground for the rule in *Howe v Earl of Dartmouth, Howe v Countess of Aylesbury* (1802) 7 Ves 137 see PARA 1122; and TRUSTS AND POWERS vol 98 (2013) PARA 173.
9   *Randall v Russell* (1817) 3 Mer 190 at 195; cf *Re Maclachlan, Maclachlan v Campbell* (1900) 26 VLR 548 (where a tenant for life was held liable to account for livestock).
10 See *Re Bagshaw's Trusts* (1877) 46 LJ Ch 567 at 571, CA; and PARA 1124.
11 See the Trusts (Capital and Income) Act 2013 s 1(2)(a), (b), (4); and TRUSTS AND POWERS vol 98 (2013) PARA 172.

123.   Vesting of interests. Where the legatees are given successive interests in the chattels and they are not vested in trustees, the property in the chattels vests at law in the first legatee on the assent of the executor and in the other successive takers on the happening of the respective future contingencies[1]. The assent of the executor to the first is an assent to all[2].

1   *Foley v Burnell* (1789) 4 Bro Parl Cas 34, 319; *Stevenson v Liverpool Corpn* (1874) LR 10 QB 81; Shep Touch (8th Edn, 1826) pp 419–420. Formerly, where the use only of the chattel was devised, the property continued to be vested in the executors: *Case of the Grail* (1459) YB 37 Hen 6, fo 30, pl 11; *Anon* (1692) Freem Ch 137; *Chamberlaine v Chamberlaine* (1674) Freem Ch 141. See also

Re Swan, Witham v Swan [1915] 1 Ch 829 at 834–835, 84 LJ Ch 590 (where, semble, the first legatee held as bailee for the succeeding legatee); and PARA 121 text and notes 4–5.

2 *Manning's Case* (1609) 8 Co Rep 94b at 96a; *Foley v Burnell* (1789) 4 Bro Parl Cas 34, 319; *Stevenson v Liverpool Corpn* (1874) LR 10 QB 81. As to assents generally see PARA 1139 et seq.

124. Conditional gifts and gifts over. A gift may be made as a conditional gift or limitation subject to the rules restricting such conditions and gifts[1]. A further gift to take effect on a condition not being fulfilled may be made subject to the same restrictions[2]; and such a gift is subject also to the qualification that the second gift must fit in sensibly with the previous gift so as to show what is to be done with the property[3].

1 As to conditions attached to gifts see PARA 128 et seq. As to the limits of suspension of vesting see PERPETUITIES AND ACCUMULATIONS vol 80 (2013) PARAS 9, 22 et seq. See *Re Gray, Allardyce v Roebuck* [2004] EWHC 1538 (Ch), [2004] 3 All ER 754 (conditional option to buy testator's property subject to time limits; the option was still exercisable as testator did not intend to make time of completion of the essence in the condition); and PARA 125 notes 1, 3.
2 See generally *Shaw v Ford* (1877) 7 ChD 669 at 673–674.
3 *Re Catt's Trusts* (1864) 2 Hem & M 46 at 53; *Musgrave v Brooke* (1884) 26 ChD 792 at 794. As to the need for certainty in conditions see PARA 138 et seq.

125. Options to purchase. A person may be given the right to purchase property forming part of the testator's estate either at a price fixed by the testator[1] or by some person or persons nominated by him, such as trustees[2], or at a valuation[3]. Whether or not the right to purchase is personal to the donee or is transmissible depends in each case on the construction of the will[4]. While there may be in an option an element of bounty[5], the exercise of the option creates the relationship of vendor and purchaser between the testator's estate and the donee so as to give the donee the right to have the property free from incumbrances[6].

1 *Earl of Radnor v Shafto* (1805) 11 Ves 448 at 454; *Re Eve, National Provincial Bank Ltd v Eve* [1956] Ch 479, [1956] 2 All ER 321. Cf *Re Hammersley, Foster v Hammersley* [1965] Ch 481, [1965] 2 All ER 24 (where the gift of an option was exercisable on the death of the testator's wife; as she predeceased him, the option was not exercisable). See also *Re Gray; Allardyce v Roebuck* [2004] EWHC 1538 (Ch), [2004] 3 All ER 754; and PARA 124 note 1. As to options in leases see LANDLORD AND TENANT vol 62 (2012) PARA 135 et seq; and as to options to purchase generally see CONVEYANCING vol 23 (2016) PARA 35.
2 See *Earl of Radnor v Shafto* (1805) 11 Ves 448; *Edmonds v Millett* (1855) 20 Beav 54. As to directions for taking the price into account on distribution see *Re Dallmeyer, Dallmeyer v Dallmeyer* [1896] 1 Ch 372, CA. In *Smith v Cotton's Trustees* 1956 SC 338, Ct of Sess, trustees had a discretion to sell shares but had first to offer them to S; the company went into liquidation before the trustees decided to sell, so the option was never exercisable.
3 *Edwards v Edwards* (1837) 1 Jur 654; *Waite v Morland* (1866) 12 Jur NS 763; *Re Dowse, Dowse v Dowse* [1951] 1 All ER 558n; *Talbot v Talbot* [1968] Ch 1, [1967] 2 All ER 920, CA ('at a reasonable valuation'; sufficiently certain), applied in *Re Malpass, Lloyds Bank plc v Malpass* [1985] Ch 42, [1984] 2 All ER 313 (option to purchase at value agreed with district valuer for probate purposes; no valuation because estate exempt from capital transfer tax; inquiry directed); *Dutton v Dutton* [2001] WTLR 553 (option to purchase property 'at a price to be determined by a chartered surveyor'; price to be fair and reasonable, not an open market valuation); *Re Bliss, Layton v Newcombe* [2001] 1 WLR 1973, [2002] WTLR 541 (option to purchase property at 80% of full market price; probate valuation not sufficient; valuation to be made as at death in light of what would have been known to valuer at that time disregarding subsequent events). Where an option was conferred to purchase property at the value placed on it for estate duty purposes, the duty of the executors was to consider the interests of the estate as a whole and they were under no duty to consider the effect as between the beneficiaries: *Re Hayes' Will Trusts, Pattinson v Hayes* [1971] 2 All ER 341, [1971] 1 WLR 758. Where an option to be exercised within three months of death to purchase property at the figure agreed by the executors and the Capital Taxes Office was not exercised within that period because no figure had been agreed, it was held (not following *Re Avard, Hook v Parker* [1948] Ch 43, [1947] 2 All ER 548) that the option did not lapse: *Re Bowles, Hayward v Jackson* [2003] EWHC 253 (Ch), [2003] Ch 422, [2003] 2 All ER 387. See also *Re Gray, Allardyce v Roebuck* [2004] EWHC 1538 (Ch), [2004] 3 All ER 754 (option to purchase at set, discounted price; will specifying periods for acceptance and completion; time for

acceptance of the essence but not time for completion; time for completion was, by analogy with ordinary sale and purchase of houses, not of the essence of the condition and the option was still exercisable).

4　*Skelton v Younghouse* [1942] AC 571, [1942] 1 All ER 650, HL. See also *Taylor v Cooper* (1846) 10 Jur 1078; *Re Cousins, Alexander v Cross* (1885) 30 ChD 203, CA; *McKendrick v Lewis* (1889) 15 VLR 450; *Belshaw v Rollins* [1904] 1 IR 284 at 289; *Re Zerny's Will Trusts, Symons v Zerny* [1968] Ch 415, [1968] 1 All ER 686, CA.

5　*Re Fison's Will Trusts, Fison v Fison* [1950] Ch 394, [1950] 1 All ER 501. The element of bounty confers on the donee a beneficial interest in the estate of the testator (*Re Lander, Lander v Lander* [1951] Ch 546, [1951] 1 All ER 622), but such an interest represented by the difference between option price and market value has been held not to be a property specifically bequeathed (*Re Eve, National Provincial Bank Ltd v Eve* [1956] Ch 479, [1956] 2 All ER 321). If there is a condition not only for the exercise of the option but also for the payment of the purchase money within a specified time, the donee is not entitled to an extension of time because he has not received an abstract of title: *Brooke v Garrod* (1857) 2 De G & J 62. See also *Re Davison and Torrens* (1865) 17 I Ch R 7.

6　*Givan v Massey* (1892) 31 LR Ir 126; *Re Wilson, Wilson v Wilson* [1908] 1 Ch 839; *Re Fison's Will Trusts, Fison v Fison* [1950] Ch 394, [1950] 1 All ER 501. It appears that a gift conditional on the giving of any consideration (*Blower v Morret* (1752) 2 Ves Sen 420 at 422), such as a release of an existing right of dower under the former law (see PARA 1087), or of an existing debt due from the testator (see PARA 1089; and EQUITABLE JURISDICTION vol 47 (2014) PARAS 188–190), prima facie constitutes the donee a purchaser so as to give him priority for his legacy.

126. Rights of person exercising option.

The donee of an option to purchase must as a rule strictly comply with any terms of the option, for example as to the time of signifying his exercise of the option[1], or as to the time of payment[2], but possibly not as to all steps to complete the transaction, subsequent to accepting the offer of the option[3]. He is entitled, on exercising the option, to the surplus, after deducting the option price, on any sale after the testator's death made on a compulsory purchase[4], or in an action to administer the testator's estate[5], or by a life tenant[6]. An option to purchase shares may be exercisable in respect of other shares into which they have been converted[7]. Where two or more options to purchase the same property are given to different donees without any priority, and all are exercised concurrently, the effect may be that all options fail to take effect[8].

The question may arise as to what price or value the testator intended should be the consideration required of the grantee for the exercise of the option; this would seem to be a question of construction of the particular disposition[9].

1　*Re Allgood's Will Trusts, Chatfield v Allen* (18 December 1980, unreported), CA (where trustees were directed to offer property to Mr and Mrs A at a valuation, but no formal offer was made and there was no acceptance within the stipulated two months of the death of the testator; the gift over took effect). Where a will confers an option to purchase property exercisable within a stated time, and a direction that the property is to be sold by the executor in default thereof, with completion within a stated time after acceptance, time is of the essence as regards the exercise of the option. This is analogous to a gift over situation (see PARA 124). Nevertheless, strict compliance with the requirements of acceptance of the irrevocable offer in an option does not necessarily compel same conclusion as regards requirements for completion of the transaction, in the absence of clear wording: see *Re Gray, Allardyce v Roebuck* [2004] EWHC 1538 (Ch), [2004] 3 All ER 754. Where an offer has to be made by the trustees, or the price has to be fixed, time may run only from communication of the terms to the donee: *Lord Lilford v Keck* (1862) 30 Beav 295; *Austin v Tawney* (1867) 2 Ch App 143. If time is directed to run from an event actually happening in the testator's lifetime, but assumed by the testator to happen after his death, the direction may be construed so that time will run from his death: *Evans v Stratford* (1864) 2 Hem & M 142. If no time is fixed, the donee is allowed a reasonable time: *Huckstep v Mathews* (1685) 1 Vern 362.

2　*Master v Willoughby* (1705) 2 Bro Parl Cas 244; *Dawson v Dawson* (1837) 8 Sim 346; *Brooke v Garrod* (1857) 2 De G & J 62. In all these cases there was a gift over on non-payment within the time; the mere signification of acceptance was not sufficient to comply with the terms of the will.

3　From *Re Gray, Allardyce v Roebuck* [2004] EWHC 1538 (Ch), [2004] 3 All ER 754 it seems that whether the will gives a testamentary option or a right of pre-emption or a conditional gift, the time and mode of acceptance requires strict compliance with the will; further testamentary requirements as to completion of the transaction may be considered either (1) analogous to ordinary sale and purchase requirements (ie time not of the essence in the absence of express requirements); or (2) as a testamentary condition. Even if the latter, in the absence of an express gift over or a testamentary direction that the executor moves immediately to sell on expiry of the completion period, the matter is for the judge to consider the testator's intentions.

4   *Re Cant's Estate* (1859) 4 De G & J 503.
5   *Re Kerry, Bocock v Kerry, Arnull v Kerry* [1889] WN 3.
6   *Re Armstrong's Will Trusts, Graham v Armstrong* [1943] Ch 400, [1943] 2 All ER 537.
7   *Re Fison's Will Trusts, Fison v Fison* [1950] Ch 394, [1950] 1 All ER 501.
8   See *Huckstep v Mathews* (1685) 1 Vern 362 at 363; *Jeffrey v Scott* (1879) 27 Grant 314 (Ont).
9   See *Re Bliss* [2001] 1 WLR 1973, 145 Sol Jo LB 122 (gift of option to purchase either or both of flats at 80% of 'full market value', one flat to remain occupied by testatrix's husband for as long as he wished; widower left flat six months after her death. Held that a fresh valuation (not the probate valuation) should be made as at date of death, taking into account only those facts known at that time and ignoring subsequent events, such as the departure of the widower).

127. Right of selection. A testator who has several properties, all having the same description, may by his will give one of them to a donee, leaving the choice to the donee[1]; and generally the testator may give rights to select property to any value or amount[2]. Where the testator has several properties of the same description and gives one to each of several devisees, the right of selection is given to those devisees in the order in which they are named, but, if they are collectively referred to (as, for example, where the testator gives one house to each of his nephews and nieces), the right of selection is, failing agreement, to be determined by lot[3]. The fact that the donee is to be able to select may appear either by express words in the will, or by reasonable inference from it[4], and, where no limit is placed on the right of selection, the court treats the donee as entitled to take the whole property to which the right applies, if he duly shows that such is his choice[5]. The precise wording of the gift, unless limited in some way by the rest of the will, will be given its full effect by the court[6].

If, however, the will shows that the testator intends to give a particular property to a legatee, and, owing to the testator having several properties answering the description in the will of the particular property given, the court is unable to say either from the will itself or from extrinsic evidence[7] which of the several properties the testator referred to, the gift fails for uncertainty[8], and the court cannot, in order to avoid an intestacy, change the will or construe it as giving to the legatee the option of choosing one of the properties[9]. Where a right of selection is given to one donee, and the remainder of the property after selection is given to another donee, specifically and not by way of residuary gift, and the right of selection lapses[10] by the death of the first donee in the testator's lifetime, the gift to the second donee also fails[11].

1   *Asten v Asten* [1894] 3 Ch 260 at 262 per Romer J. See also *Harby v Moore* (1860) 6 Jur NS 883; Co Litt 145a. As to this principle in the case of a deed see DEEDS AND OTHER INSTRUMENTS vol 32 (2012) PARAS 415–416.
2   For an example of a right to select land of a certain value see *Earl of Bandon v Moreland* [1910] 1 IR 220. After an unequivocal selection, the donee cannot change and make a fresh selection: *Littledale v Bickersteth* (1876) 24 WR 507. Cf PARA 154.
3   *Re Knapton, Knapton v Hindle* [1941] Ch 428, [1941] 2 All ER 573.
4   *Asten v Asten* [1894] 3 Ch 260 at 263. See also *Marshal's Case* (1598) 3 Dyer 281a n. Thus where a devise is simply of ten acres adjoining or surrounding a house, part of a larger quantity, the choice of the ten acres is in the donee: *Hobson v Blackburn* (1833) 1 My & K 571 at 575; *Tapley v Eagleton* (1879) 12 ChD 683 ('two houses in K street', the testator having three); *Duckmanton v Duckmanton* (1860) 5 H & N 219 ('one close in R field'). In the case of a gift of a number of shares out of a larger number, some of which are fully paid and others only partly paid, the legatee has an absolute right to select the best shares (*Jacques v Chambers* (1846) 2 Coll 435 at 441; *Millard v Bailey* (1866) LR 1 Eq 378; *O'Donnell v Welsh* [1903] 1 IR 115; Shep Touch (8th Edn, 1826) p 251), unless the class of shares referred to by the testator can be ascertained by construction of the will (*Re Cheadle, Bishop v Holt* [1900] 2 Ch 620, CA; and see note 9). In

    Wilson v Wilson (1847) 1 De G & Sm 152, on the words of the will, the right of selection was given not to the donee, but to the other persons interested.

5   *Arthur v Mackinnon* (1879) 11 ChD 385 (where Jessel MR said that, following the words literally, the donee might take the whole with the exception of one article of probably no value, when the maxim de minimis would apply); *Re Sharland, Kemp v Rozey (No 2)* (1896) 74 LT 664, CA; *Re Baron Wavertree of Delamere, Rutherford v Hall-Walker* [1933] Ch 837. See also *Cooke v Farrand* (1816) 7 Taunt 122; *Kennedy v Kennedy* (1853) 10 Hare 438 (not followed in, but distinguished from, *Arthur v Mackinnon* above; and followed in *Re Gillespie, Gillespie v Gillespie* (1902) 22 NZLR 74 at 76, NZ CA (selection after taking possession)).

6   This is particularly significant with chattel gifts: see *Re Baron Wavertree of Delamere, Rutherford v Hall-Walker* [1933] Ch 837 (the right to select 'such of the furniture and household effects which . . . shall be in or about . . . my residences' was held to extend to all furniture and household effects, including cars and other moveable property). See also *Re Collins' Will Trusts, Donne v Hewetson* [1971] 1 All ER 283, [1971] 1 WLR 37 ('such . . . personal effects as she shall select' extended to stamp and coin collections as well as a motor car).

7   Ie including, where admissible, extrinsic evidence of intention: see PARAS 193, 218–219.

8   *Richardson v Watson* (1833) 4 B & Ad 787; *Blundell v Gladstone* (1852) 3 Mac & G 692; and see PARA 194.

9   *Asten v Asten* [1894] 3 Ch 260 at 263; approved in *Re Cheadle, Bishop v Holt* [1900] 2 Ch 620 at 623, CA, per Lord Alverstone MR. Where the property out of which the gift is made is a homogeneous mass, such as money in a bank account or shares in a company, the gift will be valid even though there is no right of selection: *Hunter v Moss* [1993] 1 WLR 934 (affd [1994] 3 All ER 215, [1994] 1 WLR 452, CA), referring to *Re Cheadle, Bishop v Holt* above and *Re Clifford, Mallam v McFie* [1912] 1 Ch 29.

10   Where nothing passes to the donee until selection, the choice must be made during his life; the right of selection does not pass to his executors: *Re Madge, Pridie v Bellamy* (1928) 44 TLR 372; approved in *Skelton v Younghouse* [1942] AC 571 at 577, [1942] 1 All ER 650 at 653, HL, per Viscount Maugham.

11   *Boyce v Boyce* (1849) 16 Sim 476.

(3) CONDITIONS ATTACHED TO GIFTS BY WILL

128. Rules as to conditions. By his will a testator may freely attach conditions to his gifts, provided that they do not conflict with certain recognised restrictions and are not inconsistent with other provisions of the will[1].

    A condition must not be unlawful[2]; it must not be contrary to public policy[3]; it must not be uncertain[4]; it must not be such that the court declines to investigate whether it has been or will be complied with[5]; and it must not be in such terms that the event causing forfeiture may not occur until a date beyond the limits of the rule against perpetuities[6]. A condition amounting to a trust[7] is subject to the restriction that the object for whose benefit the trust is imposed must be capable of taking[8], but there does not appear to be any like restriction where the condition does not amount to a trust, but binds the donee to do acts which may benefit an object incapable of taking[9].

    A condition which is inconsistent with other provisions of the will may be unenforceable, as, for example, when it is repugnant to the interest given to the donee, or is repugnant to other gifts in the will, or is otherwise inconsistent with the rest of the will[10]. It must also be possible for the condition to be complied with[11].

    Where the condition is in itself valid, the donee may nevertheless in some circumstances be excused from performing it[12].

1   As to an estate in fee granted upon condition see REAL PROPERTY AND REGISTRATION vol 87 (2012) PARAS 72–74, 109–111. As to wills entirely conditional in their operation see PARA 7; and as to the construction of conditions generally see PARA 407 et seq.

A condition will fail if it is in a document which cannot be admitted in evidence as part of the will: see *Re Williams, Taylor v University of Wales* (1908) 24 TLR 716; and PARA 201. As to conditions undertaken by the donee by agreement with the testator see PARA 222; and TRUSTS AND POWERS vol 98 (2013) PARA 87 et seq.

A condition may in effect create a trust: see *Re Frame, Edwards v Taylor* [1939] Ch 700, [1939] 2 All ER 865; *Olszanecki v Hillocks* [2002] EWHC 1997 (Ch), [2004] WTLR 975 (gift of property on condition that donees should permit H to continue to reside there created a trust in favour of H). See also PARA 407.

2   See GIFTS vol 52 (2014) PARAS 251, 263 et seq. A condition which in effect delegates to another a testator's testamentary power is void: *Re Neave, Neave v Neave* [1938] Ch 793, [1938] 3 All ER 220. The conferring of a general or wide-ranging power of appointment does not constitute a delegation of the testamentary power: *Re Beatty's Will Trusts, Hinves v Brooke* [1990] 3 All ER 844, [1990] 1 WLR 1503; and see also PARA 11.

3   See PARAS 131–132. See also *Re Harding Gibbs v Harding* [2007] EWHC 3 (Ch), [2008] Ch 235, [2007] 1 All ER 747 (gift to black community of four London boroughs held to be valid charitable bequest; no public policy objection as the reference to colour is removed by the effect of the Race Relations Act 1976 s 34 (repealed: see now the Equality Act 2010 s 193(4); and DISCRIMINATION vol 33 (2013) PARA 61), where charitable gifts are concerned).

4   See PARAS 138–141.

5   *W — v B —* (1849) 11 Beav 621 (condition relating to cohabitation), as explained in *Cooke v Cooke* (1864) 11 Jur NS 533 at 535 per Wood V-C. Cf *Poole v Bott* (1853) 11 Hare 33 at 39; *Potter v Richards* (1855) 1 Jur NS 462 (condition as to illegal cohabitation).

6   *Re Spitzel's Will Trusts, Spitzel v Spitzel* [1939] 2 All ER 266.

7   See note 1; and TRUSTS AND POWERS vol 98 (2013) PARA 1 et seq.

8   See PARA 33; cf TRUSTS AND POWERS vol 98 (2013) PARA 8.

9   See *Lloyd v Lloyd* (1852) 2 Sim NS 255 (repair of a tomb); *Roche v M'Dermott* [1901] 1 IR 394 (donee to give executors bond for repair of a tomb; but it was suggested that the condition was unenforceable). Cf *Goodman v Saltash Corpn* (1882) 7 App Cas 633.

10 See PARA 142.

11 See PARA 143.

12 See PARA 144 et seq.

129.   Conditions precedent and subsequent. According to the construction of the will[1], a condition is either a condition precedent, that is to say such that there is no gift intended at all unless and until the condition is fulfilled[2], or a condition subsequent, that is to say such that non-compliance with the condition is intended to put an end to the gift[3]. Subject to the terms of the will, the date at which a condition precedent must be fulfilled is the date at which the interest, if any, vests in possession[4]. Where it is doubtful whether a condition is precedent or subsequent, the court prima facie treats it as subsequent, for there is a presumption in favour of early vesting[5]. Words expressing a condition may be treated as being words of limitation[6], and a gift expressed in the form of a limitation may be effective, although as a condition subsequent it would be void[7]. In particular, words providing for the divesting of an interest on marriage may be susceptible of construction as words of limitation[8]. Words which import a condition may also be construed as merely creating a trust or charge, or even simply a personal obligation[9].

1   As to construction with regard to conditions generally see PARA 407 et seq.

2   *Wood v Duke of Southampton* (1692) Show Parl Cas 83, HL; *Wood v Webb* (1695) Show Parl Cas 87; *Harvy v Aston* (1740) Com 726 at 744; *Reynish v Martin* (1746) 3 Atk 330 at 332; *Egerton v Earl Brownlow* (1853) 4 HL Cas 1 at 74. See also CHARITIES vol 8 (2015) PARA 136; GIFTS vol 52 (2014) PARA 251.

3   See *Re Boulter, Capital and Counties Bank v Boulter* [1922] 1 Ch 75; *Sifton v Sifton* [1938] AC 656, [1938] 3 All ER 435, PC. See also CHARITIES vol 8 (2015) PARA 137; GIFTS vol 52 (2014) PARA 251; SETTLEMENTS vol 91 (2012) PARA 641 et seq. A condition in a will that a devisee is to take for himself and his heirs the name and arms of the testator is a condition subsequent, since it cannot be complied with at once: *Gulliver d Corrie v Ashby* (1766) 4 Burr 1929. As to name and arms clauses see PARAS 131, 141; and SETTLEMENTS vol 91 (2012) PARA 646 et seq.

4   *Re Allen, Faith v Allen* [1954] Ch 259, [1954] 1 All ER 526.

5   *Sifton v Sifton* [1938] AC 656 at 676, [1938] 3 All ER 435 at 446, PC; and see *Re Tepper's Will Trusts, Kramer v Ruda* [1987] Ch 358, [1987] 1 All ER 970. Where an interest is contingent on any event, it is in effect precedent to the gift that the event should happen. A vested or contingent interest may be subject to be divested or extinguished on any specified event; the gift is then in effect subject to a condition subsequent. As to vested and contingent remainders see REAL PROPERTY AND REGISTRATION vol 87 (2012) PARAS 164–166; and as to the rules of law restricting the suspension of vesting see PERPETUITIES AND ACCUMULATIONS vol 80 (2013) PARAS 9, 22 et seq. A condition the non-fulfilment of which will put an end to a contingent estate is a condition subsequent, even though the event to which the condition refers is not subsequent to the happening of the contingency, so that the condition really prevents the gift from ever taking effect: *Egerton v Earl Brownlow* (1853) 4 HL Cas 1.

6   *Page v Hayward* (1705) 2 Salk 570 (where a condition as to marriage was construed as a gift of an estate in special tail); *Pelham-Clinton v Duke of Newcastle* [1902] 1 Ch 34, CA (affd [1903] AC 111, HL). Such a construction would no longer be possible in the case of a testator dying on or after 1 January 1997 as entailed interests cannot be created by instruments coming into operation on or after that date: see the Trusts of Land and Appointment of Trustees Act 1996 s 2, Sch 1 para 5; PARA 387; and REAL PROPERTY AND REGISTRATION vol 87 (2012) PARA 114. As to the construction of conditions as words of limitation see further PARA 407.

7   *Re Wilkinson, Page v Public Trustee* [1926] Ch 842 at 847; *Re Wolffe's Will Trusts, Shapley v Wolffe* [1953] 2 All ER 697, [1953] 1 WLR 1211.

8   See PARA 137.

9   See PARA 152.

130. Effect on gift of invalid condition. When a condition is void as illegal[1], contrary to public policy[2], repugnant to a prior gift[3], impossible[4] or uncertain[5], the effect on the gift depends on whether it is of realty or personalty, and whether the condition is precedent or subsequent[6]. If the gift is of realty, and the condition is precedent, the gift as well as the condition fails to take effect[7], and this is so even if there is no gift over as the doctrine as to conditions in terrorem does not apply to devises of realty[8]. If the gift is of personalty and the condition is precedent, then, if it is originally impossible, or is made so by the testator's act or default, the bequest is good, but, if the performance of the condition is the sole motive of the bequest, or its impossibility was unknown to the testator, or the condition which was possible in its creation has since become impossible by an act of God, the bequest fails[9]. A gift of personalty takes effect free from a condition precedent which is voidable and is avoided by the donee, or is repugnant to the gift, or fails to operate on the gift as being in terrorem[10]. A gift subject to a void condition subsequent takes effect free from the condition[11].

1   See PARA 128; and GIFTS vol 52 (2014) PARAS 251, 263–266.

2   See PARAS 131–132.

3   See PARA 142.

4   See PARA 143.

5   See PARAS 133, 138–141.

6   It may be material whether the condition involves malum in se, that is an act which is in its nature wrong (eg to kill a person), or malum prohibitum, that is an act which is forbidden by statute: see *Re Piper, Dodd v Piper* [1946] 2 All ER 503; *Re Elliott, Lloyds Bank Ltd v Burton-on-Trent Hospital Management Committee* [1952] Ch 217, [1952] 1 All ER 145; and see Shep Touch (8th Edn, 1826) p 132. In Ireland it has been doubted whether the distinction between conditions involving malum prohibitum and conditions involving malum in se, which is a distinction of the civil law, is properly applicable in the courts of equity: *Re Blake, Lynch v Lombard* [1955] IR 89 at 104.

7   Co Litt 206b; Shep Touch (8th Edn, 1826) p 132; *Harvey v Lady Aston* (1737) 1 Atk 361 at 375; *Egerton v Earl Brownlow* (1853) 4 HL Cas 1; *Re Turton, Whittington v Turton* [1926] Ch 96 (although Astbury J describes this as 'the old rule' and appears to base his decision on the language of the will and the general intention of the testator, rather than on the rule itself).

8   As to conditions in terrorem see PARA 134.

9   See *Reynish v Martin* (1746) 3 Atk 330 at 332; *Re Moore, Trafford v Maconochie* (1888) 39 ChD 116 at 128–129, CA, per Cotton LJ; *Re Wolffe's Will Trusts, Shapley v Wolffe* [1953] 2 All ER 697, [1953] 1 WLR 1211 (condition the sole motive for the gift and impossibility unknown to

testatrix; gift failed). See also Roper on Legacies (4th Edn) p 757; Jarman on Wills (8th Edn) 1457–1458. See also PARA 143. As to what constitutes an act of God see CONTRACT vol 22 (2012) PARA 478.

10 See PARA 134.

11 *Egerton v Earl Brownlow* (1853) 4 HL Cas 1; *Re Gassiot, Fladgate v Vintners' Co* (1901) 70 LJ Ch 242. Dicta in *Jones v Jones* (1876) 1 QBD 279 and in *Bellairs v Bellairs* (1874) LR 18 Eq 510 suggest that a condition subsequent in restraint of marriage, where the estate is for life or in fee, is valid as regards realty; but this seems doubtful.

131. Condition void if against public policy. A condition may be void, or void in part of its application[1], because it is against public policy[2]. Conditions against public policy are those conditions as to which the state has or may have an interest that they should remain unperformed or unfulfilled[3].

Examples of conditions void as contrary to public policy are conditions inciting the donee to commit a crime[4], to use corruption[5] or to do any act prohibited by law[6]; or inciting the donee to exert private or political party influence in any matter or act of state[7], such as obtaining a peerage[8]; or tending to produce a future separation of husband and wife[9], or the separation of parent and child[10]; or interfering with the right of a parent to control the education of his or her children[11] or their religious instruction[12]; or forbidding the service of the donee in the defence of the realm[13]; or unreasonably[14] restraining marriage[15], trade[16] or industry[17]; and any other conditions tending to such result[18]. A condition requiring the assumption of a name and arms is not contrary to public policy merely because it may require a married woman to assume a name different from that of her husband[19]. It seems that a charitable gift to persons defined by colour is not in itself contrary to public policy[20]. A condition is void if it has a tendency towards harm of the public interest, and it is immaterial that compliance with the condition might be achieved without actual mischief[21].

It is not contrary to public policy for a testator to impose a condition requiring the legatee to be of a particular religious faith[22], and a condition against disputing the will, or disputing legitimacy, is not void on this ground[23] unless there is no gift over[24]. Generally, conditions which appear to be attempts at ousting the jurisdiction of the court are seen as against public policy, although provisions that any doubts or difficulties regarding the terms of a will were to be resolved by a third party would not usually be seen as such an attempt[25]. Testamentary restrictions on challenges to the will that might deter applications under the Inheritance (Provision for Family and Dependents) Act 1975 are not void on public policy grounds[26].

1 There may be severance of a condition: see *Re Howard's Will Trusts, Levin v Bradley* [1961] Ch 507 at 524, [1961] 2 All ER 413 at 422; *Re Hepplewhite's Will Trusts* [1977] CLY 2710 (five conditions of which two were invalid; gift took effect subject to remaining three).

2 As to public policy generally see CONTRACT vol 22 (2012) PARA 429 et seq. A similarity between wills and contracts in this respect has been suggested: see *Cooke v Turner* (1846) 15 M & W 727 at 735 per Rolfe B; *Egerton v Earl Brownlow* (1853) 4 HL Cas 1 at 150 per Pollock CB.

3 *Cooke v Turner* (1846) 15 M & W 727 at 735–736. See also *Evanturel v Evanturel* (1874) LR 6 PC 1 at 29.

4 *Mitchel v Reynolds* (1711) 1 P Wms 181 at 189; Shep Touch (8th Edn, 1826) p 132 (to kill a person); 2 Bl Com (14th Edn) 156.

5 *Egerton v Earl Brownlow* (1853) 4 HL Cas 1 at 59, 99, 172.

6 *Mitchel v Reynolds* (1711) 1 P Wms 181.

7 *Egerton v Earl Brownlow* (1853) 4 HL Cas 1 at 142, 150, 163, 196.

8 *Egerton v Earl Brownlow* (1853) 4 HL Cas 1. See also *Earl of Kingston v Lady Pierepont* (1681) 1 Vern 5. However, in *Fender v St John-Mildmay* [1938] AC 1 at 13, [1937] 3 All ER 402 at 407–408, HL, Lord Atkin doubted whether such a condition would now still be held invalid. The principle has been held not to apply in cases where the title involves no duties other than those of every good citizen: *Re Wallace, Champion v Wallace* [1920] 2 Ch 274, CA (condition precedent of acquiring baronetcy). It appears, moreover, that a gift may be made to a person conditionally

on his claim to a title being sustained, or conditionally on his success or failure in a certain suit: *Earl Fingal v Blake* (1829) 2 Mol 50 at 78; cf *Caithness v Sinclair* 1912 SC 79, Ct of Sess (a Scottish case where a condition that, if a person did not succeed to a peerage, the lands should go over, was upheld). Cf the usual shifting clause in settlements on succession to a title or to family estates: see SETTLEMENTS vol 91 (2012) PARA 641 et seq.

9   See *Re Caborne, Hodge and Nabarro v Smith* [1943] Ch 224, [1943] 2 All ER 7 (doubting *Re Thompson, Lloyds Bank Ltd v George* [1939] 1 All ER 681). See also *Re Johnson's Will Trusts, National Provincial Bank Ltd v Jeffrey* [1967] Ch 387, [1967] 1 All ER 553 (words tending to encourage separation or divorce treated as void condition). The condition is valid, however, where it merely refers to the state of circumstances existing at the testator's death and cannot influence the conduct of the persons in question: *Shewell v Dwarris* (1858) John 172. Similarly, a gift limited to a woman already separated from her husband, with a gift over if she rejoins him, may be valid if the intention is to make provision for the donee: *Re Charleton, Bracey v Sherwin* (1911) 55 Sol Jo 330; *Re Lovell, Sparks v Southall* [1920] 1 Ch 122. As to contracts for separation generally see MATRIMONIAL AND CIVIL PARTNERSHIP LAW vol 72 (2015) PARA 343 et seq.

10   *Re Boulter, Capital and Counties Bank v Boulter* [1922] 1 Ch 75 (condition that children should not reside abroad); *Re Piper, Dodd v Piper* [1946] 2 All ER 503 (condition to keep child away from divorced parent). See also *Re Morgan, Dowson v Davey* (1910) 26 TLR 398 (condition requiring children not to live with their father if separated from his wife); *Re Sandbrook, Noel v Sandbrook* [1912] 2 Ch 471 (condition forfeiting benefits if donees should live with or be under the control of their father). Cf *Colston v Morris* (1821) 6 Madd 89 (where a condition not to interfere with a daughter's education was enforced). A condition requiring adult children to keep away from their parent may be valid: *McDonald v Trustees, Executors and Agency Co Ltd* (1902) 28 VLR 442.

11   *Re Tegg, Public Trustee v Bryant* [1936] 2 All ER 878; *Re Burke* [1951] IR 216.

12   *Re Blake, Lynch v Lombard* [1955] IR 89. See also *Re Borwick, Borwick v Borwick* [1933] Ch 657 (settlement).

13   *Re Beard, Reversionary and General Securities Co Ltd v Hall, Re Beard, Beard v Hall* [1908] 1 Ch 383; *Re Edgar, Cohen v Edgar* [1939] 1 All ER 635 (condition against accepting a public office; commission in territorial army is a public office); *Re Reich, Public Trustee v Guthrie* (1924) 40 TLR 398 (condition preventing a woman from adopting a profession void for uncertainty).

14   See generally *Nordenfelt v Maxim Nordenfelt Guns and Ammunition Co Ltd* [1894] AC 535, HL; and PARA 133 text and note 2.

15   See PARAS 132–133. 'Marriage' includes marriage of a same sex couple: see the Marriage (Same Sex Couples) Act 2013 Sch 3 para 1(1)(a), (2), (3); and MATRIMONIAL AND CIVIL PARTNERSHIP LAW vol 72 (2015) PARAS 1–2.

16   *Cooke v Turner* (1846) 15 M & W 727 at 736; *Egerton v Earl Brownlow* (1853) 4 HL Cas 1 at 18n. Cf, however, *Jones v Bromley* (1821) 6 Madd 137 (where only the construction of the condition was considered). As to restraint of trade see EMPLOYMENT vol 39 (2014) PARA 19; COMPETITION vol 18 (2009) PARA 377 et seq.

17   *Cooke v Turner* (1846) 15 M & W 727 at 736 (donee to leave his land uncultivated); *Egerton v Earl Brownlow* (1853) 4 HL Cas 1 at 144, 241.

18   See eg *Re Wood, Walker v Carlile* (1920) 36 TLR 560 (condition against observing summer time). It appears that a condition forbidding two sisters to reside together, if not uncertain, is not in itself illegal: *Ridgway v Woodhouse* (1844) 7 Beav 437 at 443; cf PARA 139. Where under an Order in Council property in the British dominions of German nationals was charged with payment of claims by British nationals with regard to their property in Germany, a direction that life interests given by a will to German nationals should cease on their being precluded from taking by war legislation was not void as being against public policy: *Re Schiff, Henderson v Schiff* [1921] 1 Ch 149.

19   See *Re Neeld, Carpenter v Inigo-Jones* [1962] Ch 643, [1962] 2 All ER 335, CA. In Australia, however, a name clause has been struck down on the grounds that it was anachronistic and infringed an individual's right to use the surname of his own choosing: *Littras v Littras* [1995] 2 VR 283, Vict SC. See also PARA 141.

20   *Re Harding, Gibbs v Harding* [2007] EWHC 3 (Ch), [2008] Ch 235, [2007] 1 All ER 747 (gift for the benefit of the 'black community' of four London boroughs).

21   *Egerton v Earl Brownlow* (1853) 4 HL Cas 1; *Re Wallace, Champion v Wallace* [1920] 2 Ch 274, CA.

22   See *Re Dickson's Trust* (1850) 1 Sim NS 37 (in case daughter became a nun); *Hodgson v Halford* (1879) 11 ChD 959 (forfeiture on marrying a Christian, or forsaking Jewish religion); *Blathwayt v Baron Cawley* [1976] AC 397, [1975] 3 All ER 625, HL (forfeiture if beneficiary should be or become a Roman Catholic); *Re Tuck's Settlement Trusts, Public Trustee v Tuck* [1978] Ch 49, [1978] 1 All ER 1047, CA (condition that beneficiary should be of the Jewish faith and married

to an 'approved wife'). See also *Wainwright v Miller* [1897] 2 Ch 255; *Re May, Eggar v May* [1917] 2 Ch 126; *Patton v Toronto General Trusts Corpn* [1930] AC 629, PC; *Re May, Eggar v May* [1932] 1 Ch 99, CA. Such a condition may, however, be void for uncertainty: see *Re Tepper's Will Trusts, Kramer v Ruda* [1987] Ch 358, [1987] 1 All ER 970 (condition subsequent forfeiting interests of beneficiaries who remained outside 'the Jewish faith' held to be void in the absence of admissible evidence of the Jewish faith as practised by the testator and his family; proceedings adjourned to enable such evidence to be filed); and see PARA 140. As to the period during which a ban as to religion applies see *Re Wright, Public Trustee v Wright* (1837) 158 LT 368.

23 *Cooke v Turner* (1846) 15 M & W 727; *Evanturel v Evanturel* (1874) LR 6 PC 1 at 29; *Nathan v Leonard* [2002] EWHC 1701 (Ch), [2003] 4 All ER 198, [2003] 1 WLR 827 (where, however, the condition was held to be void for uncertainty of wording). A condition against disputing a will is not, however, construed as extending to cases where there is a reasonable cause for litigation: see PARA 191.

24 *Re Dickson's Trust* (1850) 1 Sim NS 37 at 46.

25 See *Re Tuck's Settlement Trusts, Public Trustee v Tuck* [1978] Ch 49, [1978] 1 All ER 1047, CA.

26 *Nathan v Leonard* [2002] EWHC 1701 (Ch), [2003] 4 All ER 198, [2003] 1 WLR 827 (the no-challenge restriction was not against public policy because any forfeiture of benefit under the will was a factor that the court could take into account in considering an application under the Inheritance (Provision for Family and Dependants) Act 1975). Note that it seems that the question whether an application under the Act, without more, comprises a dispute or challenge to the will or not is left open.

132. Condition in general restraint of marriage. A condition in general restraint of marriage[1] can, in the nature of things, only be a condition subsequent, but the words used may be capable of being treated as words of limitation[2]. If the condition shows an intention to restrain marriage, it is void as being contrary to public policy[3], but the condition is only construed as indicating such an intention where the gift is of personalty[4], including the proceeds of realty directed to be converted[5]. Where the gift is of realty for life or in fee simple, or a legacy charged on real estate, it seems that such a condition may be valid[6]. If a testator gives a legacy to personal representatives with a gift over if the donee has married, the condition is valid, for the testator is merely providing that, if the donee has married, then the testator, and not the donee, is to have the disposition of the gift[7]. It seems to make no difference that the testator has used words of futurity, which prima facie are construed as contemplating a marriage from the date of the will and, therefore, possibly before the date of the testator's death[8]. If, however, the condition operates in terrorem[9], the mere fact that the penalty is not inflicted on the person who violates the condition, but on his children or his personal representatives, does not prevent the condition from being void[10].

1 There is, as yet, no indication of the general position with respect to conditions in restraint of civil partnership. 'Marriage' includes marriage of a same sex couple: see the Marriage (Same Sex Couples) Act 2013 Sch 3 para 1(1)(a), (2), (3); and MATRIMONIAL AND CIVIL PARTNERSHIP LAW vol 72 (2015) PARAS 1–2.

2 See PARAS 129, 407.

3 *Morley v Rennoldson, Morley v Linkson* (1843) 2 Hare 570. See also *Long v Dennis* (1767) 4 Burr 2052 at 2055, 2057; *Lloyd v Lloyd* (1852) 2 Sim NS 255 at 263; and PARA 134 note 3.

4 *Morley v Rennoldson, Morley v Linkson* (1843) 2 Hare 570; *Re Bellamy, Pickard v Holroyd* (1883) 48 LT 212; *Re Wright, Mott v Issott* [1907] 1 Ch 231 at 237.

5 *Bellairs v Bellairs* (1874) LR 18 Eq 510 (following *Lloyd v Lloyd* (1852) 2 Sim NS 255). As to a mixed fund without any direction for conversion see PARA 134 note 1.

6 *Jones v Jones* (1876) 1 QBD 279 at 282; *Bellairs v Bellairs* (1874) LR 18 Eq 510 at 513. See also *Fitchet v Adams* (1740) 2 Stra 1128.

7 *Re Fentem, Cockerton v Fentem* [1950] 2 All ER 1073 (applying *Re Hewett, Eldridge v Iles* [1918] 1 Ch 458).

8 *Re Fentem, Cockerton v Fentem* [1950] 2 All ER 1073 ('in case he should have married').

9 See PARA 134.

10 *Re Fentem, Cockerton v Fentem* [1950] 2 All ER 1073.

133. Condition in partial restraint of marriage. A condition in a gift of realty in partial restraint of marriage[1] is valid whether the condition is precedent or subsequent and whether or not there is a gift over[2]. In the case of personalty such a condition is valid where the restraint is in the circumstances reasonable[3] and where there is a gift over so that the condition is not merely in terrorem[4]. A condition in restraint of a second marriage is valid[5], whether of a widow or a widower[6], and whether the testator was the first spouse or a stranger[7]. So is a condition against marrying a particular person[8], or a member of a particular class of persons[9], or a person of a particular religion[10], or forbidding marriage under a specified and reasonable age[11]; and it seems that a condition may validly prescribe the ceremonies and place of a marriage[12]. Further, an interest may be given conditionally on the donee marrying a particular person[13] or one of a class of persons[14]. A condition which is not, on the face of it, in general restraint of marriage, but which is a deterrent to marriage because the person subject to it can never know whether he can safely marry anyone is unreasonable and void[15].

1　There is, as yet, no indication of the general position with respect to conditions in partial restraint of civil partnership. 'Marriage' includes marriage of a same sex couple: see the Marriage (Same Sex Couples) Act 2013 Sch 3 para 1(1)(a), (2), (3); and MATRIMONIAL AND CIVIL PARTNERSHIP LAW vol 72 (2015) PARAS 1–2.

2　*Haughton v Haughton* (1824) 1 Mol 611.

3　*Keily v Monck* (1795) 3 Ridg Parl Rep 205 at 261; *Morley v Rennoldson, Morley v Linkson* (1843) 2 Hare 570 at 579; *Younge v Furse* (1857) 8 De GM & G 756 at 759.

4　See PARA 134.

5　*Barton v Barton* (1693) 2 Vern 308; *Scott v Tyler* (1788) 2 Bro CC 431 at 487; *Morley v Rennoldson, Morley v Linkson* (1843) 2 Hare 570 at 580; *Lloyd v Lloyd* (1852) 2 Sim NS 255 at 263; *Evans v Rosser* (1864) 2 Hem & M 190. See also *Hampden v Brewer* (1666) 1 Cas in Ch 77; *Pyle v Price* (1802) 6 Ves 779; *Re Rutter, Donaldson v Rutter* [1907] 2 Ch 592. Such a restraint is apparently to be considered as partial only, albeit it is directed against any further marriage: see *Leong v Lim Beng Chye* [1955] AC 648, [1955] 2 All ER 903, PC.

6　*Allen v Jackson* (1875) 1 ChD 399 at 404, CA.

7　*Newton v Marsden* (1862) 2 John & H 356.

8　*Jarvis v Duke* (1681) 1 Vern 19; *Scott v Tyler* (1788) 2 Dick 712 at 721; *Re Bathe, Bathe v Public Trustee* [1925] Ch 377; *Re Hanlon, Heads v Hanlon* [1933] Ch 254. See also *Lester v Garland* (1808) 15 Ves 248.

9　*Jenner v Turner* (1880) 16 ChD 188 (domestic servant); *Greene v Kirkwood* [1895] 1 IR 130 at 142 (legatee marrying beneath her). In *Perrin v Lyon* (1807) 9 East 170, a condition prohibiting marriage to a Scotsman was upheld. Such a condition was not avoided by the Race Relations Act 1976 (repealed: see now the Equality Act 2010; and DISCRIMINATION vol 33 (2013) PARA 1 et seq) as that Act did not extend to discrimination in testamentary dispositions or private trusts: cf *Blathwayt v Baron Cawley* [1976] AC 397, [1975] 3 All ER 625, HL.

10　*Duggan v Kelly* (1848) 10 I Eq R 295 at 473 ('Papist'); *Hodgson v Halford* (1879) 11 ChD 959 ('not a Jew'); *Re Knox* (1889) 23 LR Ir 542 ('not a Protestant'). See also note 9; and PARA 140.

11　*Stackpole v Beaumont* (1796) 3 Ves 89 at 97 (age of 21); *Younge v Furse* (1857) 8 De GM & G 756 (age of 28). See also *Scott v Tyler* (1788) 2 Bro CC 431 at 488 per Lord Thurlow LC. As to consent to marriage see PARA 135.

12　*Scott v Tyler* (1788) 2 Bro CC 431; *Haughton v Haughton* (1824) 1 Mol 611 (marriage 'contrary to the order and established rules' of Quakers); *Renaud v Lamothe* (1902) 32 SCR 357 (the laws and rites of the Catholic Church).

13　*Viscount Falkland v Bertie* (1698) 2 Vern 333; *Davis v Angel* (1862) 4 De GF & J 524; *Kiersey v Flahavan* [1905] 1 IR 45.

14　See *Hodgson v Halford* (1879) 11 ChD 959.

15　*Re Lanyon, Lanyon v Lanyon* [1927] 2 Ch 264 (condition against marrying 'relation by blood'). See also *Re Fentem, Cockerton v Fentem* [1950] 2 All ER 1073.

134. Doctrine of in terrorem. A condition in restraint of marriage attached to a gift of personalty or a gift charged on personal estate only may be void against the donee as being made in terrorem[1], that is to say as a mere idle threat to induce the donee to comply with the condition, but not to affect the bequest[2]. It seems that only conditions in partial, as opposed to general, restraint of marriage are subject to the doctrine of in terrorem³. It does not apply to devises of realty⁴, or to bequests charged on real estate⁵, or on personalty directed to be laid out in the purchase of real estate⁶.

A condition is not in terrorem if the testator shows an intention that it is to be effective⁷, as by making a different disposition of the subject matter of the gift in the event of non-compliance with the condition, that is to say when there is a gift over⁸. If the condition is subsequent, a gift over is essential to the validity of the condition⁹, and must either be specific, or effected by a direction that, on non-compliance with the condition, the gift is to fall into residue¹⁰; a mere residuary gift without more is not enough¹¹. Where in the case of a condition precedent the testator shows by a gift over that it is not merely in terrorem¹², it seems that a mere residuary bequest is enough¹³.

1 The rule was derived from the civil law, as administered by the ecclesiastical courts and adopted by the courts of equity with modifications: see *Bellairs v Bellairs* (1874) LR 18 Eq 510 at 515–516 (where the analogy with the rules as to vesting (see PARA 412 et seq) is pointed out); *Re Whiting's Settlement, Whiting v De Rutzen* [1905] 1 Ch 96 at 115, CA, per Vaughan Williams LJ; *Leong v Lim Beng Chye* [1955] AC 648 at 661, [1955] 2 All ER 903 at 907, PC. As to the case of a mixed gift of real and personal estate, without any trust for conversion, and as to the case of a legacy charged on such a mixed fund see *Reynish v Martin* (1746) 3 Atk 330 at 335; *Duddy v Gresham* (1878) 2 LR Ir 442 at 458, Ir CA, per Ball LC; but cf *Duddy v Gresham* at 466–467 per Christian LJ, apparently followed in *Re Pettifer, Pettifer v Pettifer* [1900] WN 182. 'Marriage' includes marriage of a same sex couple: see the Marriage (Same Sex Couples) Act 2013 Sch 3 para 1(1)(a), (2), (3); and MATRIMONIAL AND CIVIL PARTNERSHIP LAW vol 72 (2015) PARAS 1–2.

2 *Re Dickson's Trust* (1850) 1 Sim NS 37 at 43; *Duddy v Gresham* (1878) 2 LR Ir 442 at 464, Ir CA. As to conditions requiring consent to marriage see PARA 135.

3 As to general restraint of marriage see PARA 132; and as to partial restraint see PARA 133. Conditions in general restraint of marriage have been considered as subject to the doctrine of in terrorem (see *Marples v Bainbridge* (1816) 1 Madd 590; *Bellairs v Bellairs* (1874) LR 18 Eq 510), but it seems that these decisions should be related to grounds of public policy (see the criticism in *Duddy v Gresham* (1878) 2 LR Ir 442 at 468, Ir CA, per Christian LJ). Alternatively, cases in which the restraint has been on remarriage (see eg *Marples v Bainbridge* above) may be explained on the basis that, paradoxically, a condition in restraint of remarriage is treated by the courts as a condition in partial restraint of marriage: see *Leong v Lim Beng Chye* [1955] AC 648, [1955] 2 All ER 903, PC. A gift over does not render valid a condition in general restraint of marriage: *Morley v Rennoldson, Morley v Linkson* (1843) 2 Hare 570; *Lloyd v Lloyd* (1852) 2 Sim NS 255. The doctrine also applies to conditions not to dispute a will: see PARA 188. In *Re Dickson's Trust* (1850) 1 Sim NS 37 at 43, 45, the doctrine was explained as based on public policy; conditions against alienation of the life estate were there said to be void as in terrorem unless there was a gift over, but the case is not now accepted as laying down the true rule as to such conditions: see *Rochford v Hackman* (1852) 9 Hare 475 at 481. It appears, at all events, that the doctrine does not ordinarily apply to conditions other than in restraint of marriage or against disputing a will, which do not contravene any rule of public policy (*Re Dickson's Trust* above (forfeiture if donee became a nun)), and such other conditions do not become in terrorem, or otherwise invalid, by the mere want of a gift over (*Re Dickson's Trust* at 43; *Re Catt's Trusts* (1864) 2 Hem & M 46 at 62, followed in *Re Hanlon, Heads v Hanlon* [1933] Ch 254). On the construction of particular wills, however, other conditions may be construed as inducements or threats addressed to the donee personally, and as not affecting the gift, if the context requires it: see *Byng v Lord Strafford* (1843) 5 Beav 558 at 571–572 (affd sub nom *Hoare v Byng* (1844) 10 Cl & Fin 508, HL); *Re Meagher, Trustees, Executors and Agency Co Ltd v Meagher* [1910] VLR 407 (donee to acquire and learn a profession).

4 *Duddy v Gresham* (1878) 2 LR Ir 442 at 457, 465, Ir CA; *Jenner v Turner* (1880) 16 ChD 188 at 196 per Bacon V-C.

5 *Reynish v Martin* (1746) 3 Atk 330 at 335.

6 *Pullen v Ready* (1743) 2 Atk 587 at 590.

7 As to how far the application of the rule depends on construction in this respect see *Harvey v Lady Aston* (1737) 1 Atk 361 at 377–378 per Willes CJ; *Bellairs v Bellairs* (1874) LR 18 Eq 510 at 576 per Jessel MR. As to the ascertainment of the testator's intention see PARA 224 et seq.

8 See *Craven v Brady* (1867) LR 4 Eq 209 at 215; affd (1869) 4 Ch App 296.

9 *Lloyd v Branton* (1817) 3 Mer 108 at 117 (where the effect of the gift over is explained either as an expression of contrary intention, or as making the prior gift a conditional limitation, namely, a limitation to endure until the condition is broken). See also *Jarvis v Duke* (1681) 1 Vern 19 at 20; *Stratton v Grymes* (1698) 2 Vern 357; *Aston v Aston* (1703) 2 Vern 452 at 453; *Hervey v*

Aston (1738) Willes 83; *Wheeler v Bingham* (1746) 3 Atk 364 at 366; *Re Whiting's Settlement, Whiting v De Rutzen* [1905] 1 Ch 96 at 106, CA; *Re Brace, Gurton v Clements* [1954] 2 All ER 354, [1954] 1 WLR 955.

10 *Lloyd v Branton* (1817) 3 Mer 108. Cf, however, *Pullen v Ready* (1743) 2 Atk 587 at 590.
11 *Wheeler v Bingham* (1746) 3 Atk 364.
12 *Malcolm v O'Callaghan* (1817) 2 Madd 349; *Gardiner v Slater* (1858) 25 Beav 509. In the case of a gift conditional on marriage with consent, a gift over on death before 21 or marriage without consent is not sufficient for this purpose: see *Gray v Gray* (1889) 23 LR Ir 399.
13 *Amos v Horner* (1699) 1 Eq Cas Abr 112 pl 9; *Semphill v Bayly* (1721) Prec Ch 562.

135. Conditions as to consent to marriage. A condition may take the form of a requirement that the consent of a named person be obtained to the donee's marriage[1]. If the condition is precedent and is in terrorem[2], the gift takes effect on marriage without consent[3], but not until marriage[4]. The fact that the testator makes separate provision for the donee in the event of non-compliance with the condition shows that it is not in terrorem[5].

A condition, whether precedent or subsequent, requiring consent to marriage is generally construed as operative only during the life of the person whose consent is required[6]. If, therefore, that person dies during the lifetime of the testator, or before any marriage, the gift takes effect free from the condition[7]. Where the gift vests at a specified age, the condition is construed as referring only to a marriage under that age[8]. Where, however, the condition refers to marriage with a consent attached to a certain office, such as that of trustee or guardian, it may be operative at any time while a person holds or can be appointed to that office[9]. The giving of consent in such cases is of a fiduciary nature[10], but the condition is satisfied as well for the purpose of a gift over as for the purpose of seeing who is entitled under the conditional gift[11] by marriage with the testator's own unqualified[12] previous consent to it[13], or by his subsequent approbation of it[14]. Therefore, condition does not, as a rule, apply to a donee who marries with the testator's consent and becomes a widow after the date of the will during the testator's life[15].

1 'Marriage' includes marriage of a same sex couple: see the Marriage (Same Sex Couples) Act 2013 Sch 3 para 1(1)(a), (2), (3); and MATRIMONIAL AND CIVIL PARTNERSHIP LAW vol 72 (2015) PARAS 1–2.
2 As to gifts in terrorem see PARA 134; and as to conditions precedent and subsequent see PARA 129.
3 *Semphill v Bayly* (1721) Prec Ch 562; *Underwood v Morris* (1741) 2 Atk 184. The actual decision in *Underwood v Morris* was dissented from, however, on account of the devise over, in *Hemmings v Munckley* (1783) 1 Bro CC 304 per Lord Loughborough LC, and in *Scott v Tyler* (1788) 2 Bro CC 431 at 488 per Lord Thurlow LC.
4 *Garbut v Hilton* (1739) 1 Atk 381; *Elton v Elton* (1747) 3 Atk 504; *Gray v Gray* (1889) 23 LR Ir 399. There is, as yet, no case law concerning conditions as to consent to civil partnership.
5 *Bellasis v Ermine* (1663) 1 Cas in Ch 22; *Garret v Pritty* (1693) 2 Vern 293; *Creagh v Wilson* (1706) 2 Vern 572; *Gillet v Wray* (1715) 1 P Wms 284; *Re Nourse, Hampton v Nourse* [1899] 1 Ch 63 at 71. See also *Holmes v Lysaght* (1733) 2 Bro Parl Cas 261. As to limitations depending on marriage see PARA 137.
6 *Mercer v Hall* (1793) 4 Bro CC 326; *Green v Green* (1845) 2 Jo & Lat 529 at 539–540; *Curran v Corbet* [1897] 1 IR 343. See also *Booth v Meyer* (1877) 38 LT 125 (explaining *Dawson v Oliver-Massey* (1876) 2 ChD 753, CA). As to the nature of the consent required see PARA 136.
7 *Peyton v Bury* (1731) 2 P Wms 626 (on appeal sub nom *Painton v Berry* (1732) Kel W 36); *Aislabie v Rice* (1818) 3 Madd 256; *Collett v Collett* (1866) 35 Beav 312.
8 *Desbody v Boyville* (1729) 2 P Wms 547; *Pullen v Ready* (1743) 2 Atk 587; *Knapp v Noyes* (1768) Amb 662. As to gifts vesting on attaining a specified age or on marriage with consent cf *Dobbins v Bland* (1730) 2 Eq Cas Abr 545; *Knight v Cameron* (1807) 14 Ves 389; *West v West* (1863) 4 Giff 198. There is no such restriction where no age is expressly or impliedly specified: *Lloyd v Branton* (1817) 3 Mer 108.
9 *Re Brown's Will, Re Brown's Settlement* (1881) 18 ChD 61, CA (guardian who might be appointed by the court). See also *Gardiner v Slater* (1858) 25 Beav 509 at 511 per Romilly MR. Where the consent of executors or trustees is required, the consent of those who renounce is

unnecessary: *Worthington v Evans* (1823) 1 Sim & St 165; *Boyce v Corbally* (1834) L & G *temp*
Plunk 102; *Ewens v Addison* (1858) 4 Jur NS 1034 (doubting *Graydon v Hicks* (1739) 2 Atk 16).
10 All the trustees or persons holding the office must as a rule concur; a consent of a majority is not
   sufficient unless the testator expressly allows it: *Clarke v Parker* (1812) 19 Ves 1 at 17, 22
   (dissenting from *Harvey v Lady Aston* (1737) 1 Atk 361 at 375). The court may interfere if the
   consent is withheld or refused by a trustee from a corrupt, vicious or unreasonable cause (*Clarke
   v Parker* at 18), and may give consent if a trustee refuses either to consent or dissent (*Goldsmid
   v Goldsmid* (1815) 19 Ves 368). As to the control of a trustee's discretion generally see TRUSTS
   AND POWERS vol 98 (2013) PARA 411.
11 *Re Park, Bott v Chester* [1910] 2 Ch 322 at 325–326.
12 See *Lowry v Patterson* (1874) IR 8 Eq 372.
13 *Clarke v Berkeley* (1716) 2 Vern 720; *Parnell v Lyon* (1813) 1 Ves & B 479; *Coventry v Higgins*
   (1844) 14 Sim 30; *Tweedale v Tweedale* (1878) 7 ChD 633; *Re Park, Bott v Chester* [1910] 2 Ch
   322.
14 *Wheeler v Warner* (1823) 1 Sim & St 304.
15 *Crommelin v Crommelin* (1796) 3 Ves 227.

136. Nature of consent to marriage. Where there is a condition requiring consent to the donee's marriage[1], the consent must be a free consent[2], not obtained by duress[3]. A general consent[4], or a consent evidenced by conduct[5] or presumed from the circumstances[6], or a conditional consent where the condition attached is afterwards performed[7], or a subsequent approbation[8], may be considered as a substantial compliance with the condition, even where a consent in writing is required by the will[9].

A consent given unconditionally cannot be withdrawn[10] except on grounds which affect the propriety of giving the consent[11].

1 As to conditions requiring consent to marriage see PARA 135; and as to limitations depending on
   marriage see PARA 137.
2 No reasons need, as a rule, be given for dissent: *Clarke v Parker* (1812) 19 Ves 1 at 22.
3 *Dillon v Harris* (1830) 4 Bli NS 321, HL; *Re Stephenson's Trusts* (1870) 18 WR 1066
   (mother's consent only to save daughter's reputation). See also *NS v MI* [2006] EWHC 1646
   (Fam), [2006] All ER (D) 48 (Jul) (nullity of marriage case; moral blackmail and physical detention
   overseas induced consent by party to marriage).
4 *Mercer v Hall* (1793) 4 Bro CC 326; *Pollock v Croft* (1816) 1 Mer 181.
5 *D'Aguilar v Drinkwater* (1813) 2 Ves & B 225. See also *Burleton v Humphrey* (1755) Amb 256.
6 *Re Birch* (1853) 17 Beav 358 (where the question of consent was not raised until 28 years after the
   marriage).
7 *Le Jeune v Budd* (1834) 6 Sim 441; *Re Smith, Keeling v Smith* (1890) 44 ChD 654.
8 *Burleton v Humfrey* (1755) Amb 256. It is not, however, the general rule that subsequent
   approbation is sufficient, especially if the vesting of an estate is in question: see *Clarke v Parker*
   (1812) 19 Ves 1 at 21. Cf *Reynish v Martin* (1746) 3 Atk 330 at 331; *Malcolm v O'Callaghan*
   (1817) 2 Madd 349.
9 *Worthington v Evans* (1823) 1 Sim & St 165; *Holton v Lloyd* (1827) 1 Mol 30.
10 *Le Jeune v Budd* (1834) 6 Sim 441 at 455.
11 *Lord Strange v Smith* (1755) Amb 263; *Merry v Ryves* (1757) 1 Eden 1; *Dashwood v Lord
   Bulkeley* (1804) 10 Ves 230 at 242; *Re Brown, Ingall v Brown* [1904] 1 Ch 120.

137. Limitations depending on marriage. The considerations as to conditions in restraint of marriage[1] apply only to conditions, and not to words merely describing the interest created. The question in each case is whether the words constitute a limitation or a condition[2]. An interest may be given to endure so long as the donee remains unmarried[3], and, generally, marriage may be made the ground of a gift ceasing or commencing[4]. The ending of the marriage may be the circumstance contemplated by the will, but if such words tend to encourage divorce or separation, they are more likely to be treated as a void condition than as a limitation[5].

1 See PARA 132 et seq.
2 *Heath v Lewis* (1853) 3 De GM & G 954 at 957; *Re Moore, Trafford v Maconochie* (1888) 39
   ChD 116 at 129, 132, CA; *Re King's Trusts* (1892) 29 LR Ir 401 at 408. See also *Re*

Wolffe's Will Trusts, Shapley v Wolffe [1953] 2 All ER 697, [1953] 1 WLR 1211; *Re Johnson's Will Trusts, National Provincial Bank Ltd v Jeffrey* [1967] Ch 387, [1967] 1 All ER 553; and PARA 129.
3   *Godfrey v Hughes* (1847) 1 Rob Eccl 593; *Heath v Lewis* (1853) 3 De GM & G 954; *Potter v Richards* (1855) 24 LJ Ch 488; *Re King's Trusts* (1892) 29 LR Ir 401; *Re Hewett, Eldridge v Iles* [1918] 1 Ch 458. See also *Re M'Loughlin's Estate* (1878) 1 LR Ir 421, Ir CA.
4   *Webb v Grace* (1848) 2 Ph 701 at 702; *Re Mason, Mason v Mason* [1910] 1 Ch 695, CA; *Re Morton, M'Auley v Harvey* (1919) 53 ILT 105.
5   *Re Johnson's Will Trusts, National Provincial Bank Ltd v Jeffrey* [1967] Ch 387, [1967] 1 All ER 553 (daughter not to receive most of residuary income until after death of, divorce or separation from, present husband: held to be a condition by way of defeasance and void). See also *Re Caborne, Hodge v Smith* [1943] Ch 224, [1943] 2 All ER 7 (condition was necessarily to be regarded as a bar to a reconciliation of the spouses and was held void); and PARAS 129, 131.

138. Effect of uncertainty as to meaning of condition. Unless the court can put a clear meaning on a condition, it is unenforceable and, therefore, in effect, void[1]. The question of uncertainty usually arises[2] where it is alleged that a condition subsequent will defeat a vested estate[3]. To be valid the condition must then be such that the court can see from the beginning precisely and distinctly on the happening of what event it was that the preceding vested estate was to determine[4].

There is a clear distinction, however, between uncertainty of expression[5] and uncertainty in operation. It is the duty of the court to endeavour to resolve uncertainty of expression by construing the will in the light of the ordinary canons of construction, while bearing in mind that the law favours vested estates[6]. As an aid to this, the court may use extrinsic evidence, other than direct evidence of the testator's intentions, as to the meaning of the words actually used[7]. Where the death occurs after 1982 and the uncertainty is in the form of ambiguity or because part of the will is meaningless, evidence of the testator's intention may also be admissible[8]. If, when the will is so construed, a meaning cannot be properly ascribed to the language used by the testator, it fails for uncertainty[9]. If, however, a proper meaning can be given to the language, the next step is to consider whether the condition is too uncertain in operation to satisfy the test of validity previously stated[10]. The fact that the decision whether the condition is fulfilled is given to the trustees cannot resolve uncertainty as to the events prescribed by the testator as those in which the condition is to operate, and such uncertainty is, generally speaking, fatal to the validity of such a condition[11]. This may raise a particular difficulty if the condition in question relates to the relationship between the beneficiary and the trustees[12]. Where, however, the event is sufficiently defined by the testator, there may be an advantage and difficulty may be avoided by conferring the power of decision on trustees[13]. If the gift does not give a discretion to trustees to determine the meaning of a condition in itself uncertain but directs them to pay or withhold a legacy on being satisfied that a certain state of affairs exists, no question of discretion arises; it is the trustees' duty to make up their minds whether the state of affairs does or does not exist and to pay or withhold the legacy accordingly[14]. In the case of a condition precedent no such general or academic test is called for as in the case of a condition subsequent. All that the donee must do is to establish, if he can, at the relevant date, that he satisfied the condition, whatever be the appropriate test. Uncertainty which might invalidate a condition if subsequent does not necessarily do so if it is precedent. Thus it is not right for the court to declare a condition precedent void for uncertainty so as thereby to defeat all possible claimants to the gift unless its terms are such that it is impossible to give them any meaning at all, or such that they involve repugnancies or inconsistencies in the possible tests which they postulate, as distinct, for example, from mere problems of degree[15].

1 *Fillingham v Bromley* (1823) Turn & R 530.
2 For an example of uncertainty in relation to a condition precedent or qualification see *Re Tarnpolsk, Barclays Bank Ltd v Hyer* [1958] 3 All ER 479, [1958] 1 WLR 1157 (condition as to marriage to person of 'Jewish race and religion' uncertain as to race). As to uncertainty in the description of the donee see PARA 45; and as to conditions as to race or religion see PARA 140.
3 As to conditions precedent and conditions subsequent see PARA 129.
4 *Clavering v Ellison* (1859) 7 HL Cas 707 at 725 per Lord Cranworth; *Clayton v Ramsden* [1943] AC 320, [1943] 1 All ER 16; *Bromley v Tryon* [1952] AC 265, [1951] 2 All ER 1058, HL. See also *Re Viscount Exmouth, Viscount Exmouth v Praed* (1883) 23 ChD 158 at 164; *Re Sandbrook, Noel v Sandbrook* [1912] 2 Ch 471 at 477; *Re Hanlon, Heads v Hanlon* [1933] Ch 254; *Sifton v Sifton* [1938] AC 656, [1938] 3 All ER 435, PC; *Fawcett Properties Ltd v Buckingham County Council* [1961] AC 636 at 693, [1960] 3 All ER 503 at 526, HL, per Lord Jenkins; *Re Tepper's Will Trusts, Kramer v Ruda* [1987] Ch 358, [1987] 1 All ER 970 (condition of defeasance on 'marriage outside Jewish faith' was not inevitably void for uncertainty; construction summons adjourned to allow further extrinsic evidence of meaning of words). See also *AN v Barclays Private Bank and Trust (Cayman) Ltd* (2006) 9 ITELR 630 Cayman Is GC.
5 'Uncertainty of expression' is now often called 'conceptual uncertainty': see eg *Re Baden's Deed Trusts (No 2)* [1973] Ch 9 at 20, [1972] 2 All ER 1304 at 1309, CA, per Sachs LJ.
6 As to construction in cases of uncertainty see PARA 262 et seq.
7 *Re Tepper's Will Trusts, Kramer v Ruda* [1987] Ch 358, [1987] 1 All ER 970 (evidence of the Jewish faith as practised by the testator and his family).
8 See the Administration of Justice Act 1982 s 21; and *Re Broadbent, Imperial Cancer Research Fund v Bradley* [2001] EWCA Civ 714 at [44], 3 ITELR 787 at [44], [2001] All ER (D) 219 (May) at [44] per Arden LJ.
9 See *Nathan v Leonard* [2002] EWHC 1701 (Ch), [2003] 4 All ER 198, [2003] 1 WLR 827 (words, apparently accidentally omitted, rendered condition too uncertain and therefore invalid).
10 *Re Viscount Exmouth, Viscount Exmouth v Praed* (1883) 23 ChD 158 at 164; *Re Murray, Martins Bank Ltd v Dill* [1955] Ch 69, [1954] 3 All ER 129, CA; *Re Neeld, Carpenter v Inigo-Jones* [1962] Ch 643, [1962] 2 All ER 335, CA. See also *Re De Vere's Will Trusts, Jellett v O'Brien* [1961] IR 224 (name and arms clause uncertain).
11 *Re Jones, Midland Bank Executor and Trustee Co Ltd v Jones* [1953] Ch 125, [1953] 1 All ER 357.
12 *Re Coxen, McCallum v Coxen* [1948] Ch 747, [1948] 2 All ER 492. Cf *Re Tuck's Settlement Trusts, Public Trustee v Tuck* [1978] Ch 49, [1978] 1 All ER 1047, CA (questions of qualification to be referred to Chief Rabbi).
13 See *AN v Barclays Private Bank and Trust (Cayman) Ltd* (2006) 9 ITELR 630 Cayman Is GC (no-contest condition, where the uncertainty was in the meaning of 'the decisions of the trustees').
14 *Dundee General Hospitals Board of Management v Walker* [1952] 1 All ER 896, HL.
15 *Re Allen, Faith v Allen* [1953] Ch 810, [1953] 2 All ER 898, CA. See also *Re Selby's Will Trusts, Donn v Selby* [1965] 3 All ER 386, [1966] 1 WLR 43; *Re Lowry's Will Trusts, Barclays Bank Ltd v United Newcastle upon Tyne Hospitals Board of Governors* [1967] Ch 638 at 648, [1966] 3 All ER 955 at 959; *Re Abraham's Will Trusts, Caplan v Abrahams* [1969] 1 Ch 463, [1967] 2 All ER 1175 (not following *Re Walter's Will Trusts, National Provincial Bank Ltd v Board of Guardians and Trustees for Relief of Jewish Poor, Registered* (1962) 106 Sol Jo 221).

139. Uncertain conditions as to residence. Whether or not a condition as to residence is uncertain seems to depend on whether the testator uses simple words like 'occupy' or 'reside', in which case the condition is uncertain[1], or postulates more complex requirements, such as residence for a fixed period or personal presence, in which case the condition may be sufficiently certain[2]. The absence of a gift over on defeasance points to the condition being precatory only[3]. In conditions as to residence, 'abroad' normally means 'outside the British Isles'[4].

1 *Fillingham v Bromley* (1823) Turn & R 530 ('live and reside'); *Re M'Cleary, Moffat v M'Cleary* [1932] 1 IR 16 ('come to live'); *Sifton v Sifton* [1938] AC 656, [1938] 3 All ER 435, PC ('continue to reside in Canada'); *Re Field's Will Trusts, Parry-Jones v Hillman* [1950] Ch 520, [1950] 2 All ER 188 ('occupy'); but cf *Re Moir, Warner v Moir* (1884) 25 ChD 605 ('reside'; keeping up establishment held to be sufficient compliance). See also SETTLEMENTS vol 91 (2012) PARA 641 et seq.

2   *Walcot v Botfield* (1854) Kay 534 ('reside or keep up a suitable establishment'); *Dunne v Dunne*
    (1855) 7 De GM & G 207 ('principal place of abode'); *Wynne v Fletcher* (1857) 24 Beav 430
    ('usual place of abode'); *Re Wright, Mott v Issott* [1907] 1 Ch 231 ('reside'); *Re Vivian, Vivian v*
    Swansea (1920) 36 TLR 222 ('reside' for fixed period); *Re Coxen, McCallum v Coxen* [1948] Ch
    747, [1948] 2 All ER 492 ('in the opinion of my trustees she shall have ceased permanently to
    reside therein'); *Re Gape, Verey v Gape* [1952] Ch 743, [1952] 2 All ER 579, CA ('take up
    permanent residence in England'). The requirement in *Re Wilkinson, Page v Public Trustee* [1926]
    Ch 842 ('permanent home') was held valid as a limitation. 'Living with a person' implies personal
    association with that person; mere proximity is insufficient: *Re Paskins' Will Trusts, Paskins v*
    Underwood [1948] 2 All ER 156.
3   *Re Brace, Gurton v Clements* [1954] 2 All ER 354, [1954] 1 WLR 955 ('on condition she will
    always provide a home for my daughter at the above address').
4   *Re Boulter, Capital and Counties Bank v Boulter* [1922] 1 Ch 75.

140. Conditions as to race or religion. Conditions referring to race or religion
are not in themselves intrinsically void as being against public policy[1] or under
statute[2]. However, in such cases the distinction between conditions precedent and
conditions subsequent is of importance[3]. In the case of a condition precedent, it is
sufficient for its validity that a beneficiary or intended beneficiary should be able
to show that he, at all events, fulfils the stated requirements[4], whereas, in the case
of a condition subsequent, it is essential for its validity that the person liable to
suffer the forfeiture must be able to understand precisely what act or omission will
incur the forfeiture[5].

Conditions as to race, which are often bound up with conditions as to religion,
are probably void[6], whether precedent or subsequent, as the whole concept of race
is not sufficiently certain[7].

It now appears, however, that conditions relating to membership of the Church
of England[8] or of the Roman Catholic Church[9] are sufficiently certain even when
subsequent, as are conditions concerning membership of the Protestant[10] or
Lutheran religion[11]. The position regarding the Jewish religion was formerly
unclear, there being two cases, both involving conditions subsequent, where the
condition was upheld[12], but also a large number of other cases, all involving
conditions subsequent, where the condition was held uncertain[13]. The authority of
the latter decisions has, however, been undermined[14] and conditions requiring
adherence to the Jewish faith are now more likely to be upheld[15].

If the condition is uncertain, it is not possible for it to be resolved by some
formula provided by the testator (for example 'in the opinion of my trustees')[16],
although it might be possible for him to refer to an arbiter holding the same views
on religious faith as the testator himself[17]. Extrinsic evidence may also be
admissible, including, in some circumstances, direct evidence of the
testator's intentions[18].

Where a minor is involved, the time for choice as to compliance or
non-compliance with any such condition is postponed until majority and a
reasonable time thereafter[19].

1   *Hodgson v Halford* (1879) 11 ChD 959; *Blathwayt v Baron Cawley* [1976] AC 397, [1975]
    3 All ER 625, HL; but see *Trustees of Church Property of the Diocese of Newcastle v Ebbeck*
    (1960) 104 CLR 394, [1961] ALR 339, Aust HC (where a gift after a life estate to the
    testator's sons and their wives 'if they profess the Protestant faith' was held void, not for
    uncertainty but as against public policy as tending to give rise to discord between husband and
    wife). As to conditions in partial restraint of marriage in general not being against public policy see
    PARA 133.
2   The provisions of the Equality Act 2010 (see DISCRIMINATION vol 33 (2013) PARA 1 et seq) do
    not extend to racial discrimination in testamentary dispositions or private trusts. See the discussion
    of racial discrimination and public policy in *Re Harding, Gibbs v Harding* [2007] EWHC 3 (Ch)
    at [23]–[26], [2008] Ch 235, [2007] 1 All ER 747 (although this concerned a charitable gift and
    discusses the Race Relations Act 1976 s 34 (repealed: see now the Equality Act 2010 s 193(4); and
    DISCRIMINATION vol 33 (2013) PARA 61)).

3   See *Re Selby's Will Trusts, Donn v Selby* [1965] 3 All ER 386 at 388, [1966] 1 WLR 43 at 46 per Buckley J. As to conditions precedent and subsequent see PARA 129.
4   *Re Allen, Faith v Allen* [1953] Ch 810, [1953] 2 All ER 898, CA.
5   See *Clavering v Ellison* (1859) 7 HL Cas 707 at 725 per Lord Cranworth.
6   Ie but not under the Equality Act 2010 (see note 2).
7   *Clayton v Ramsden* [1943] AC 320, [1943] 1 All ER 16, HL ('not of Jewish parentage and of the Jewish faith'; all members of the court held the first limb of the condition void, and four also held the second limb void, although on this latter point the decision has been confined to its particular facts (see *Blathwayt v Baron Cawley* [1976] AC 397 at 425, [1975] 3 All ER 625 at 636, HL, per Lord Wilberforce)); *Re Wolffe's Will Trusts, Shapley v Wolffe* [1953] 2 All ER 697, [1953] 1 WLR 1211 (gift on marriage 'to a person of the Jewish faith and the child of Jewish parents' was construed as a limitation which had not taken effect, but, if it was a condition, it was precedent and incapable of fulfilment; this case was decided before *Re Allen, Faith v Allen* [1953] Ch 810, [1953] 2 All ER 898, CA (cited in note 8) had been reported); *Re Tarnpolsk, Barclays Bank Ltd v Hyer* [1958] 3 All ER 479, [1958] 1 WLR 1157 (marriage with 'a person of Jewish race and religion'; religion posed no difficulty but race wholly uncertain). Cf *Re Tuck's Settlement Trusts, Public Trustee v Tuck* [1978] Ch 49, [1978] 1 All ER 1047 (where the condition precedent 'of Jewish blood by one or both parents' was held certain). See also *Re Gott, Glazebrook v University of Leeds* [1944] Ch 193, [1944] 1 All ER 293 (where Uthwatt J declined to decide whether 'of British and Christian parentage' was certain).
8   *Clavering v Ellison* (1859) 7 HL Cas 707 ('educated in the Protestant religion according to the rites of the Church of England'); *Re Allen, Faith v Allen* [1953] Ch 810, [1953] 2 All ER 898, CA ('a member of the Church of England and an adherent to the doctrines of that church'); *Re Mills' Will Trusts, Yorkshire Insurance Co Ltd v Coward* [1967] 2 All ER 193, [1967] 1 WLR 837 ('a member of the Church of England or of some church abroad professing the same tenets'). Cf *Re Tegg, Public Trustee v Bryant* [1936] 2 All ER 878 (where a condition subsequent that the beneficiary 'should conform to and be a member of the Church of England' was held void for uncertainty). Unless this case can be distinguished from *Blathwayt v Baron Cawley* [1976] AC 397, [1975] 3 All ER 625, HL, by reason of the presence of the word 'conform', its authority must be gravely suspect. See also *Re Gott, Glazebrook v University of Leeds* [1944] Ch 193, [1944] 1 All ER 293 (cited in note 7).
9   *Duggan v Kelly* (1848) 10 I Eq R 295 ('intermarry with a Papist'; valid but confined to minority); *Re May, Eggar v May* [1917] 2 Ch 126 ('not be a Roman Catholic at my death or being a Roman Catholic at my death cease to be a Roman Catholic within a year'); *Re May, Eggar v May* [1932] 1 Ch 99, CA (same will); *Re Wright, Public Trustee v Wright* (1937) 158 LT 368 ('have become or become a Roman Catholic or marry or shall have married a Roman Catholic'; valid but confined to testatrix's lifetime); *Re Morrison's Will Trusts, Walsingham v Blathwayt* [1940] Ch 102, [1939] 4 All ER 332 ('become a Roman Catholic'); *Re Evans, Hewitt v Edwards* [1940] Ch 629 ('become a convert to the Roman Catholic religion'); *McKenna's Will Trusts, Re, Higgins v Bank of Ireland and Mckenna* [1947] IR 277 ('marry a Roman Catholic'); *McCausland v Young* [1949] NI 49, Ir CA ('become a Roman Catholic or profess that he or she is of the Roman Catholic religion'); *Blathwayt v Baron Cawley* [1976] AC 397, [1975] 3 All ER 625, HL ('be or become a Roman Catholic'). Cf *Re Borwick, Borwick v Borwick* [1933] Ch 657 ('be or become a Roman Catholic or not be openly or avowedly Protestant').
10 *Carteret v Carteret* (1723) 2 P Wms 132 ('if the eldest son of A turns Protestant, then to such eldest son'); *Re Knox* (1889) 23 LR Ir 542 ('marry a Protestant wife, the daughter of Protestant parents who have always been Protestants'); but see *Trustees of Church Property of the Diocese of Newcastle v Ebbeck* (1960) 104 CLR 394, [1961] ALR 339, Aust HC (cited in note 1).
11 *Patton v Toronto General Trusts Corpn* [1930] AC 629, PC.
12 See *Re Selby's Will Trusts, Donn v Selby* [1965] 3 All ER 386, [1966] 1 WLR 43 (marry 'out of the Jewish faith'); *Re Abrahams' Will Trusts, Caplan v Abrahams* [1969] 1 Ch 463, [1967] 2 All ER 1175 ('profess the Jewish faith'). Cf *Re Wolffe's Will Trusts, Shapley v Wolffe* [1953] 2 All ER 697, [1953] 1 WLR 1211 (where a gift on marriage 'to a person of the Jewish faith and the child of Jewish parents' was construed as a limitation which had not taken effect, but, if it was a condition, it was a condition precedent and incapable of fulfilment).
13 See *Clayton v Ramsden* [1943] AC 320, [1943] 1 All ER 16, HL ('not of Jewish parentage and of the Jewish faith'); *Re Blaiberg, Blaiberg and Public Trustee v De Andia Yrarrazaval* [1940] Ch 385, [1940] 1 All ER 632 ('of the Jewish faith'); *Re Donn, Donn v Moses* [1944] Ch 8, [1943] 2 All ER 564 ('of the Jewish faith'); *Re Moss's Trusts, Moss v Allen* [1945] 1 All ER 207 ('not a member of the Jewish faith'); *Re Krawitz's Will Trusts, Krawitz v Crawford* [1959] 3 All ER 793, [1959] 1 WLR 1192 ('practise the Jewish religion'); *Re Walter's Will Trusts, National Provincial Bank Ltd v Board of Guardians and Trustees for Relief of Jewish Poor, Registered* (1962) 106 Sol Jo 221 ('marry in the Jewish faith'; uncertain whether beliefs or formalities in issue).

14 In particular, *Clayton v Ramsden* [1943] AC 320, [1943] 1 All ER 16, HL, was described by Lord Wilberforce in *Blathwayt v Baron Cawley* [1976] AC 397 at 425, [1975] 3 All ER 625 at 636, HL, as 'a particular decision on a condition expressed in a particular way about one kind of religious belief or profession' and as not laying down any general principle as to the invalidity on the grounds of uncertainty of all conditions subsequent relating to religious belief.

15 *Re Tuck's Settlement Trusts, Public Trustee v Tuck* [1978] Ch 49 at 65, [1978] 1 All ER 1047 at 1056, CA (where Lord Russell of Killowen said: 'I would not . . . destroy a settlement on the supposition that adherence to the Jewish faith is an unintelligible concept'; and Lord Denning MR at 62 and 1054 agreed). See, however, *Re Tepper's Will Trusts, Kramer v Ruda* [1987] Ch 358, [1987] 1 All ER 970 (conditions subsequent that beneficiaries should 'remain within the Jewish faith' and should not 'marry outside the Jewish faith' held to be too uncertain).

16 See *Re Tuck's Settlement Trusts, Public Trustee v Tuck* [1978] Ch 49, [1978] 1 All ER 1047, CA (where Lord Denning MR at 62 and 1054 considered this was possible; Eveleigh LJ at 66 and 1057 held that it was not; and Lord Russell of Killowen at 65 and 1056 refused to decide the point). See also *Dundee General Hospitals Board of Management v Walker* [1952] 1 All ER 896, HL; and PARA 138.

17 *Re Tuck's Settlement Trusts, Public Trustee v Tuck* [1978] Ch 49 at 66, [1978] 1 All ER 1047 at 1057, CA, per Eveleigh LJ. Cf *Re Coxen, McCallum v Coxen* [1948] Ch 747, [1948] 2 All ER 492 (cited in PARA 138 note 12).

18 See *Re Tepper's Will Trusts, Kramer v Ruda* [1987] Ch 358, [1987] 1 All ER 970 (time granted for evidence to be obtained of the Jewish faith as practised by the testator and his family (other than direct evidence of testator's intentions)). See also the Administration of Justice Act 1982 s 21 which permits direct evidence of the testator's intentions in certain circumstances; and see *Re Broadbent, Imperial Cancer Research Fund v Bradley* [2001] EWCA Civ 714 at [44], 3 ITELR 787, [2001] All ER (D) 219 (May) per Arden LJ.

19 *Carteret v Carteret* (1723) 2 P Wms 132; *Re May, Eggar v May* [1917] 2 Ch 126; *Patton v Toronto General Trusts Corpn* [1930] AC 629, PC; *Re May, Eggar v May* [1932] 1 Ch 99. This consideration is sufficient to defeat the suggestion that such clauses in relation to minors may be against public policy by interfering with parental rights and duties, as suggested by Parker J in *Re Sandbrook, Noel v Sandbrook* [1912] 2 Ch 471 at 476–477. See also *Blathwayt v Baron Cawley* [1976] AC 397 at 426–427, [1975] 3 All ER 625 at 636–637, HL, per Lord Wilberforce.

141. Miscellaneous uncertain conditions. Requirements that the donee is not to be educated abroad[1] or is to retire to a convent[2], or is not to associate with certain persons[3], or is not to be under the control of his father[4], or is not to carry on a profession[5], or is to farm the land devised[6], have been held uncertain[7].

Furthermore, conditional future limitations may in truth be conditions subsequent and void for uncertainty if they do not satisfy the rule[8]. There is, however, nothing uncertain in point of operation or contrary to public policy in requiring a person (including a married woman) who is not a peer or, possibly, a peeress[9] to assume the name, or apply for authority to bear the arms, of another within a limited period[10], although the mode of expression may be too uncertain[11]. The following conditions imposed on donees have at one time been held to be not uncertain, but such as the court enforces: to give up low company[12]; to 'follow the paths of virtue'[13]; not to dispute the testator's will[14]; to marry a person of ample fortune[15]; not to marry or live with or misconduct himself with a named person[16]; to make a certain estate his home and not to let a named person set foot on the property[17]; to make a settlement within six months of the testator's death or on reaching full age or within such further period as the testator's trustees think reasonable[18]. A provision that the donee should lose his interest in a certain estate if he became entitled to certain other property or the bulk of it was held to be valid[19]. A gift to trustees on trust for a person if he behaves well, and to their satisfaction, may sometimes be construed as giving them only a discretion to deprive him of the gift as a condition subsequent[20].

1 *Clavering v Ellison* (1859) 7 HL Cas 707.
2 *Duddy v Gresham* (1878) 2 LR Ir 442, Ir CA.
3 *Jeffreys v Jeffreys* (1901) 84 LT 417; *Re Jones, Midland Bank Executor and Trustee Co Ltd v Jones* [1953] Ch 125, [1953] 1 All ER 357.

4 *Re Sandbrook, Noel v Sandbrook* [1912] 2 Ch 471.

5 *Re Reich, Public Trustee v Guthrie* (1924) 40 TLR 398.

6 *Re Hennessy (Richard B)* (1963) 98 ILTR 39.

7 In *Re Burke* [1951] IR 216, a condition that the donee should not leave Ireland failed to operate because he had already done so at the testator's death.

8 *Re Viscount Exmouth, Viscount Exmouth v Praed* (1883) 23 ChD 158. As to conditions subsequent see PARA 129.

9 In *Re Drax, Dunsany v Sawbridge* (1906) 94 LT 611, a peeress was held to be required to comply with a name and arms clause by using the name in formal documents but not required to use the name in private documents where surnames were not used by peeresses.

10 *Re Neeld, Carpenter v Inigo-Jones* [1962] Ch 643, [1962] 2 All ER 335, CA (disapproving *Re Fry, Reynolds v Denne* [1945] Ch 348, [1945] 2 All ER 205; *Re Lewis' Will Trusts, Whitelaw v Beaumont* [1951] WN 591; *Re Kersey, Alington v Alington* [1952] WN 541; *Re Howard's Will Trusts, Levin v Bradley* [1961] Ch 507, [1961] 2 All ER 413, so far as relating to married women). In Australia, however, a name clause has been struck down on the grounds that it was anachronistic and infringed an individual's right to use the surname of his own choosing: *Littras v Littras* [1995] 2 VR 283, Vict SC. A legal restriction on the choice of surname is not, however, a breach of the Convention for the Protection of Human Rights and Fundamental Freedoms (Rome, 4 November 1950; TS71 (1953); Cmd 8969) (see RIGHTS AND FREEDOMS vol 88A (2013) PARA 88): Application 18131/91 *Stjerna v Finland* (1994) 24 EHRR 195, ECtHR. As to name and arms clauses generally see SETTLEMENTS vol 91 (2012) PARA 646 et seq.

11 *Re Murray, Martins Bank Ltd v Dill* [1955] Ch 69, [1954] 3 All ER 129, CA. See also *De Vere's Will Trusts, Jellett v O'Brien* [1961] IR 224 (decided while *Re Neeld, Carpenter v Inigo-Jones* [1962] Ch 643, [1962] 2 All ER 335, CA (see the text and note 10) was under appeal).

12 *Tattersall v Howell* (1816) 2 Mer 26.

13 *Maud v Maud* (1860) 27 Beav 615.

14 *Evanturel v Evanturel* (1874) LR 6 PC 1. As to judicial discretion to grant relief from forfeiture for challenges to will see *AN v Barclays Private Bank and Trust (Cayman) Ltd* (2006) 9 ITELR 630 Cayman Is GC. As to the constructional limits placed on clauses of this description see PARA 188.

15 *Re Moore's Trusts, Lewis v Moore* (1906) 96 LT 44.

16 *Re Hanlon, Heads v Hanlon* [1933] Ch 254.

17 *Re Talbot-Ponsonby's Estate, Talbot-Ponsonby v Talbot-Ponsonby* [1937] 4 All ER 309.

18 *Re Burton's Settlements, Scott v National Provincial Bank Ltd* [1955] Ch 82, [1954] 3 All ER 193.

19 *Bromley v Tyron* [1952] AC 265, [1951] 2 All ER 1058, HL.

20 *Kingsman v Kingsman* (1706) 2 Vern 559; *Re Coe's Trust* (1858) 4 K & J 199.

142. Inconsistent or repugnant conditions.

A condition is said to be repugnant, and is unenforceable, if it is inconsistent with the nature of the interest given to the donee (such as, for as example, a condition that purports to impose restrictions on the alienation of property given absolutely, or that purports to forfeit property in the event of the donee's bankruptcy[1]), or with other gifts in the will[2], or it may be void as a matter of construction by being inconsistent with the rest of the will[3]. If a condition attaches to the whole gift, rather than merely to incidents of the gift, it will not be repugnant or inconsistent with it, but might yet be void for uncertainty[4]. The effect of a partial restriction on alienation, such as a condition not to sell out of the testator's family, is doubtful[5]. Conditions purporting to hold up payment to donees absolutely entitled in possession may be rejected[6]. The fact that a condition could be displaced or varied by the agreement of the beneficiaries under English trust law would not render it repugnant[7].

1 As in *Re Machu* (1882) 21 Ch D 838. See also *Rhodes v Muswell Hill Land Co* (1861) 29 Beav 560 (a condition that any legatee commencing litigation in relation to the inherited property, including suing for rent, would lose his entitlement was held to be void for repugnancy as it purported to deprive the donee of one of the incidents of ownership).

2 *Re Rosher, Rosher v Rosher* (1884) 26 ChD 801; *Re Cockerill, Mackaness v Percival* [1929] 2 Ch 131 (condition requiring sale at less than real value). See also *Muschamp v Bluett* (1617) J Bridg 132; *Gulliver v Vaux* (1746) 8 De GM & G 167n; *Bradley v Piexoto* (1797) 3 Ves 324; *Bull v Kingston* (1816) 1 Mer 314; *Cuthbert v Purrier* (1822) Jac 415; *Ware v Cann* (1830) 10 B & C 433; *Byng v Lord Strafford* (1843) 5 Beav 558 at 567; *Holmes v Godson* (1856) 8 De GM & G 152; *Re Thompson* (1896) 44 WR 582; *Crofts v Beamish* [1905] 2 IR 349, Ir CA; *McGowan v Grimes* (1921) 55 ILT 208; *Re Fry, Reynolds v Denne* [1945] Ch 348, [1945] 2 All ER 205; *Re*

Wenger's Settlement, Wenger v Baldwin (1963) 107 Sol Jo 981 (condition requiring resettlement); *Re Hennessy (Richard B)* (1963) 98 ILTR 39; and GIFTS vol 52 (2014) PARAS 251, 253. A defeasance clause annexed to a fee tail is defeated by disentailing (*Re Knox* [1912] 1 IR 288), although entailed interests cannot be created by instruments coming into operation on or after 1 January 1997 (see the Trusts of Land and Appointment of Trustees Act 1996 s 2, Sch 1 para 5; PARA 387; and REAL PROPERTY AND REGISTRATION vol 87 (2012) PARA 114; SETTLEMENTS vol 91 (2012) PARAS 506, 577). An absolute gift may be read together with the condition and be cut down by it: *Re Sax* (1883) 68 LT 849. A gift over is void if it defeats or abridges an estate in fee by altering the course of its devolution, and is to take effect at the moment of devolution, and at no other time, or is to defeat an estate and to take effect on the exercise of any of the rights incident to that estate: *Shaw v Ford* (1877) 7 ChD 669 at 673–674 per Fry J. Thus a gift over cannot be made to defeat a prior gift on alienation by the prior donee (cf SETTLEMENTS vol 91 (2012) PARA 816 et seq), or on partition between two or more prior donees (*Shaw v Ford*), or on non-alienation (*Shaw v Ford*; *Re Beetlestone, Beetlestone v Hall* (1907) 122 LT Jo 367), such as devolution on intestacy (see eg *Gulliver v Vaux* above; *Cuthbert v Purrier*; *Ware v Cann*; *Holmes v Godson*), or on forfeiture to the Crown (*Re Wilcocks' Settlement* (1875) 1 ChD 229).

3 In *Charles v Barzey* [2002] UKPC 68, [2003] 1 WLR 437, the gift in a will of the right to the use of a storeroom in a property was held not to be repugnant to a gift of the property itself. As to inconsistency in the will see PARAS 251, 382.

4 See *Nathan v Leonard* [2002] EWHC 1701 (Ch), [2003] 4 All ER 198, [2003] 1 WLR 827 (forfeiture of gift on challenge to the will; it made no difference that gifts to others would also be divested).

5 See *Muschamp v Bluett* (1617) J Bridge 132; *Attwater v Attwater* (1853) 18 Beav 330; *Re Rosher, Rosher v Rosher* (1884) 26 ChD 801; *Re Brown, District Bank Ltd v Brown* [1954] Ch 39, [1953] 2 All ER 1342 (void). Cf *Doe d Gill v Pearson* (1805) 6 East 173; *Re Macleay* (1875) LR 20 Eq 186 (valid).

6 See PARA 146.

7 See *Tod v Barton* [2002] EWHC 265 (Ch), [2002] All ER (D) 265 (Feb), 4 ITELR 715 (testator's express choice of English law and other wording of will allowed for the possibility that sui juris beneficiaries of the entire interest could terminate the will trust).

143. Impossible conditions. The law as to impossible conditions is derived, in the case of realty, from the common law and, in the case of personalty, from the civil law. The authorities seem to support the following propositions:

(1) where the condition is a condition precedent and the gift is of realty, and the condition is impossible for whatever reason, the performance of the condition is not excused and the gift does not vest[1];

(2) where the condition is a condition precedent and the gift is of personalty, and the condition is originally impossible[2], or is subsequently made so by the testator's act or default[3], the condition is rejected and the gift is absolute;

(3) where the performance of the condition is the sole motive of the gift[4], or the impossibility was unknown to the testator[5], or the condition which was possible at the time of its creation has since become impossible by an act of God[6], the civil law agrees with the common law in holding both gift and condition void[7];

(4) where the condition is a condition subsequent, then, whether the gift is of realty[8] or personalty[9], the condition is rejected and the gift is absolute[10].

The impossibility in these cases must be in the nature of things[11]. A condition is not void merely because its performance is highly improbable[12], or because it is out of the power of the donee, or even out of any human power[13], to ensure its performance.

1 Shep Touch (8th Edn, 1826) pp 132–133; Roper on Legacies (4th Edn) p 754; *Roundel v Currer* (1786) 2 Bro CC 67; *Re Turton, Whittington v Turton* [1926] Ch 96 (where the impossibility was due to the acts of the testator). As to conditions precedent see PARA 129.

2 *Lowther v Cavendish* (1758) 1 Eden 99 at 117 (affd sub nom *Lord Charles Cavendish v Lowther* (1759) 3 Bro Parl Cas 186); *Re Thomas's Will Trust, Powell v Thomas* [1930] 2 Ch 67; but see *Re Elliott, Lloyds Bank Ltd v Burton-on-Trent Hospital Management Committee* [1952] Ch 217,

[1952] 1 All ER 145 (where *Re Thomas's Will Trust, Powell v Thomas* was doubted on the ground that the impossibility was unknown to the testator). A direction to accumulate income may be void owing to the reason for it not becoming operative: *Re Thornber, Crabtree v Thornber* [1937] Ch 29, [1936] 2 All ER 1594, CA. See also *Re Parrott, Cox v Parrott* [1946] Ch 183, [1946] 1 All ER 321 (where it was held that a condition that a Christian name be assumed by deed poll is impossible).

3 *Darley v Langworthy* (1744) 3 Bro Parl Cas 359; *Gath v Burton* (1839) 1 Beav 478; *Walker v Walker* (1860) 2 De GF & J 255. See also *Yates v University College, London* (1873) 8 Ch App 454 at 461 (affd (1875) LR 7 HL 438, on the ground that there was no condition at all); *Re Williams, Taylor v University of Wales* (1908) 24 TLR 716; *Re Chambers, Watson v National Children's Home* [2001] WTLR 1375 (gift of half of estate to a charity on condition that it would look after the testator's domestic pets with a gift over on default; testator had no pets at death; gift to charity upheld).

4 *Re Wolffe's Will Trusts, Shapley v Wolffe* [1953] 2 All ER 697, [1953] 1 WLR 1211.

5 *Re Wolffe's Will Trusts, Shapley v Wolffe* [1953] 2 All ER 697, [1953] 1 WLR 1211; *Re Elliott, Lloyds Bank Ltd v Burton-on-Trent Hospital Management Committee* [1952] Ch 217, [1952] 1 All ER 145.

6 *Dawson v Oliver-Massey* (1876) 2 ChD 753 at 755 per Jessel MR (revsd on another point (1876) 2 ChD 756, CA); *Priestley v Holgate* (1857) 3 K & J 286. As to what constitutes an act of God see CONTRACT vol 22 (2012) PARA 478.

7 See *Re Moore, Trafford v Maconochie* (1888) 39 ChD 116 at 128, CA (where, however, the condition was illegal).

8 Shep Touch (8th Edn, 1826) pp 132–133; *Thomas v Howell* (1692) 1 Salk 170; *Bunbury v Doran* (1875) IR 9 CL 284 at 286, Ir Ex Ch; *Re Greenwood, Goodhart v Woodhead* [1903] 1 Ch 749, CA; *Re Croxon, Croxon v Ferrers* [1904] 1 Ch 252; *Re Berens, Re Dowdeswell, Berens-Dowdeswell v Holland-Martin* [1926] Ch 596. A condition subsequent (a defeasance clause) was held to fail where it was subject to an overriding condition which could not have been carried out: *Re Jones, Williams v Rowlands* [1948] Ch 67, [1947] 2 All ER 716 (failure of trustees to buy land on which donees were required to build hall).

9 *Collett v Collett* (1866) 35 Beav 312. See also *Graydon v Hicks* (1739) 2 Atk 16; *Dawson v Oliver-Massey* (1876) 2 ChD 753 at 755 per Jessel MR (revsd on another point (1876) 2 ChD 756, CA); *Re Bird, Bird v Cross* (1894) 8 R 326.

10 Ie as in *Watson v National Children's Home* [1995] 37 LS Gaz R 24 (condition that donee should take care of testator's pets impossible of performance because all the testator's pets had predeceased him).

11 *Franco v Alvares* (1746) 3 Atk 342 (to go from London to Rome in three hours). As to the effect of changing circumstances see *Re Hollis' Hospital Trustees and Hague's Contract* [1899] 2 Ch 540 at 533 per Byrne J.

12 *Re Knox, von Scheffler v Shuldham* [1912] 1 IR 288 (where a condition as to naturalisation was not impossible because a private Act of Parliament might have been obtained).

13 See Com Dig, Condition (D2), cited in *Egerton v Earl Brownlow* (1853) 4 HL Cas 1 at 22n.

144. Conditions nullified or dispensed with by testator. Where, by reason of the acts of the testator or other events, subsequent to the date of the will, a condition imposed by the will is substantially performed or is nullified in the testator's lifetime, the donee will not be bound by it[1]. The result is substantially the same where the testator has dispensed with the condition or has put performance out of the power of the donee[2]. It seems, however, that this rule does not apply where the condition is precedent and attached to a gift of realty, and that in that case the gift will fail[3].

1 See *Wedgwood v Denton* (1871) LR 12 Eq 290 at 296.

2 *Darley v Langworthy* (1774) 3 Bro Parl Cas 359 (bequest of chattels at B conditional on residence; and a subsequent conveyance by the testator of B); *Smith v Cowdery* (1825) 2 Sim & St 358 (condition against marrying T; marriage with T by consent of testator); *Gath v Burton* (1839) 1 Beav 478 (condition requiring payment of debt; satisfied by testator accepting composition); *Violett v Brookman* (1857) 5 WR 342 (condition against disputing father's will; acquiescence by testator in his lifetime in revaluation of father's estate); *Walker v Walker* (1860) 2 De GF & J 255 (condition requiring conveyance by donee; purchase by testator of donee's interest); *Re Park, Bott v Chester* [1910] 2 Ch 322 (marriage with testator's consent); *Re Grove, Public Trustee v Dixon* [1919] 1 Ch 249 (condition for transfer of daughter's shares under a settlement to be held on same trusts as trusts of will; condition impracticable to testator's knowledge and, therefore, discharged).

As to a condition requiring a consent to marriage see PARA 135. There are remarks in some cases suggesting that the true principle is not that the condition is considered to have been fulfilled, but that the donees are exempt from the condition altogether, so that the will must be read as if there were no condition (*Re Park, Bott v Chester* above at 327 per Parker J), but this is doubtful. As to subsequent events see PARA 149. Where there was a specific devise on condition of continuing the testator's business, and the testator gave up the business, it was held on the construction of the will that the devise did not take effect and the land fell into residue: *Re Turton, Whittington v Turton* [1926] Ch 96.

3   *Re Turton, Whittington v Turton* [1926] Ch 96. As to conditions precedent see PARA 129.

145. Further grounds on which donee may be excused from performing a condition.

The donee may be excused from performing a condition by the act of the court[1], or on grounds of public policy[2] in some cases where the condition is subsequent and where on account of the minority[3] or marriage[4] of the donee, or of his public duties, he is not free to perform the condition[5]. The donee is not, however, excused by his own ignorance of a condition[6], unless in the circumstances of the case a duty to give him notice is imposed on a person interested[7], or by his own acts rendering it impossible for him to perform the condition[8], or (except as previously mentioned) by his minority or other disability[9].

1   *Croskery v Ritchie* [1901] 1 IR 437 (sale by court order).
2   See *Re Wenger's Settlement, Wenger v Baldwin* (1963) 107 Sol Jo 981 (where it was said that a condition as to resettlement by grandchildren was probably void on the grounds of public policy as being an attempt to circumvent the rule against perpetuities). As to conditions which are void on the grounds of public policy see PARA 131.
3   Eg, in the case of conditions subsequent requiring an act of volition, where the persons to whom a minor's legal custody and care are committed do not choose that he should conform. A minor cannot, therefore, be said to refuse or neglect to reside at a place (*Partridge v Partridge* [1894] 1 Ch 351, following *Parry v Roberts* (1871) 19 WR 1000), or to refuse or neglect to take a name and arms (*Re Edwards, Lloyd v Boyes* [1910] 1 Ch 541). See also note 9. Cf *Bevan v Mahon-Hagan* (1892) 27 LR Ir 399 (condition precedent). It may be open to a minor to comply with a condition relating to religion on reaching his majority: see PARA 140 note 19. As to conditions subsequent see PARA 129.
4   Thus a married woman may be excused from a condition as to her residence, or as to her return to England, if she can comply with the condition only by separating from her husband: *Wilkinson v Wilkinson* (1871) LR 12 Eq 604; *Re Wilkinson, Page v Public Trustee* [1926] Ch 842; and see *Woods v Townley* (1853) 11 Hare 314.
5   *Re Adair* [1909] 1 IR 311 (absence on military service no breach of condition requiring residence); *Brannigan v Murphy* [1896] 1 IR 418 (parish priest's duties).
6   Eg a condition requiring a certain act to be done within a certain time, as claiming the legacy (*Fry v Porter* (1670) 1 Mod Rep 300; *Lady Anne Fry's Case* (1674) 1 Vent 199; *Burgess v Robinson* (1817) 3 Mer 7; *Hawkes v Baldwin* (1838) 9 Sim 355; *Re Hodges' Legacy* (1873) LR 16 Eq 92; *Powell v Rawle* (1874) LR 18 Eq 243; *Astley v Earl of Essex* (1874) LR 18 Eq 290). But see now *Re Bowles, Hayward v Jackson* [2003] EWHC 253 (Ch), [2003] Ch 422,[2003] 2 All ER 387, in which it was held (not following *Re Avard, Hook v Parker* [1948] Ch 43, [1947] 2 All ER 548) that an option to purchase property within three months of the testator's death at the value agreed between the executors and the Capital Taxes Office did not lapse if the value was not agreed within that period. See also *Re Gray, Allardyce v Roebuck* [2004] EWHC 1538 (Ch), [2004] 3 All ER 754,[2004] WTLR 779 (option to purchase; will specifying periods for acceptance and completion; time for acceptance of the essence, but time for completion not of the essence). As to the meaning of 'neglect or refuse' see *Re Quintin Dick, Lord Cloncurry v Fenton* [1926] Ch 992; and as to the meaning of 'neglect' see *Re Hughes, Rea v Black* [1943] Ch 296, [1943] 2 All ER 269.
7   *Lady Anne Fry's Case* (1674) 1 Vent 199 at 201. The executor is under no obligation to disclose the condition, even where he takes a benefit under it by way of gift over: *Re Lewis, Lewis v Lewis* [1904] 2 Ch 656, CA. See also *Chauncy v Graydon* (1743) 2 Atk 616. As to the difference between the duty of disclosure of an executor and that of a trustee of an express trust see PARA 1055; and TRUSTS AND POWERS vol 98 (2013) PARA 402.
8   See *Philips v Walter* (1720) 2 Bro Parl Cas 250.
9   *Lady Anne Fry's Case* (1674) 1 Vent 199 at 200. Thus a minor (except as mentioned in note 3) is bound by a condition, eg as to taking a name and arms: *Whittingham's Case* (1603) 8 Co Rep 42b at 44b; *Bevan v Mahon-Hagan* (1892) 27 LR Ir 399. See also *Doe d Luscombe v Yates* (1822)

5 B & Ald 544 (condition held substantially complied with by a minor); *Ledward v Hassells* (1856) 2 K & J 370 (condition as to giving a discharge). As to performance by or on behalf of a mentally disordered person see *Re Earl of Sefton* [1898] 2 Ch 378; *Re Crumpe, Orpen v Moriarty* [1912] 1 IR 485; and MENTAL HEALTH AND CAPACITY vol 75 (2013) PARA 556 et seq. As to the possible invalidity of name clauses in modern circumstances see PARA 141 note 10.

146. Conditions not binding on donee. A condition may be ineffectual as against the donee. Thus where there is a direction that a donee is not to enjoy a vested gift in full until he attains a particular age, then, unless there is in the will or some codicil to it a clear indication of intention not only that the donee is not to have the enjoyment of the gift until attaining that age, but that some other person is to have that enjoyment, or unless the property is so clearly taken away from the donee up to the time of attaining that age as to induce the court to hold that as to the previous income there is an intestacy, the court, on the application of the donee (if he is entitled to give a discharge for the gift) or the person deriving title under him, will strike that direction out of the will[1]. There is the possibility that the combination of the wording of the will and the effect of English trust law may permit provisions or conditions to be circumvented by the concerted action of donees[2].

The person entitled under a gift over on non-performance of the condition may, it seems, release the donee from the condition[3]. No one who intentionally prevented a condition from being performed may take advantage of the non-performance[4].

If a legacy is given on a valid condition subsequent that the donee does or abstains from doing any specified act, the court may order payment of the legacy to the donee, but may require security for the observance of the condition[5]. If, however, the condition refers to no act or default of the donee, he may be entitled to payment without giving security[6]. In each case, however, the court gives effect to the testator's intentions, which may modify or exclude these rules[7].

1 *Gosling v Gosling* (1859) John 265 at 272 per Wood V-C (adopted in *Wharton v Masterman* [1895] AC 186 at 192, HL, per Lord Herschell LC); *Re Thompson, Griffith v Thompson* (1896) 44 WR 582; *Re Couturier, Couturier v Shea* [1907] 1 Ch 470 at 473; *Re Hendy, Hayes v Hendy* [1913] VLR 559. See also *Saunders v Vautier* (1841) Cr & Ph 240; and PARA 427 et seq. Cf *Berry v Green* [1938] AC 575, sub nom *Re Blake, Berry v Geen* [1938] 2 All ER 362, HL (where *Wharton v Masterman* was distinguished).
2 See *Tod v Barton* [2002] EWHC 265 (Ch), [2002] All ER (D) 265 (Feb), 4 ITELR 715 (rule in *Saunders v Vautier* (1841) Cr & Ph 240 applied to give validity to deed of variation allowing donee (of annuity from age 65) to receive part of trust fund absolutely). See also *Goulding v James* [1997] 2 All ER 239, CA.
3 See *Ex p Palmer* (1852) 5 De G & Sm 649.
4 Co Litt 206b; *Viscount Falkland v Bertie* (1698) 2 Vern 333 at 344; *Simpson v Vickers* (1807) 14 Ves 341 at 346. See also *Mesgrett v Mesgrett* (1706) 2 Vern 580.
5 *Aston v Aston* (1703) 2 Vern 452; *Colston v Morris* (1821) 6 Madd 89.
6 *Griffiths v Smith* (1790) 1 Ves 97; *Fawkes v Gray* (1811) 18 Ves 131. See also *Madill v Madill* (1907) 26 NZLR 737, NZ CA.
7 Thus the testator may expressly direct an undertaking to be given (see eg *Roche v M'Dermott* [1901] 1 IR 394; *Re Lester, Burton v Lester* (1906) 7 SRNSW 58), and the fact that trustees have the legal estate and active duties in relation to the property may prevent the donee from obtaining a transfer (*Polson v Polson* (1900) 21 NSWLR Eq 90).

147. Substantial performance of conditions. Literal compliance with a condition may be necessary, if the terms of the condition are clear, and if it is capable of being literally complied with[1]. However, in many cases, particularly with regard to conditions requiring a consent to marriage, the court may hold a condition satisfied where it has been complied with substantially[2], although not precisely[3], whether the condition is precedent or subsequent[4]; but a condition to operate as a defeasance of a vested estate must be shown to have happened strictly and to the letter[5]. A condition requiring the donee to claim the legacy may be sufficiently complied with by an order in a claim for administration, even though the donee is not a party[6], but not, it seems, by a mere order on a claim form not asking for general administration[7]. A condition requiring the donee to give a good discharge may similarly be sufficiently performed by bringing a claim[8]. It may be that the court will look at the testator's reasoning, in imposing the condition, and consider whether strict compliance was required or whether what was done was enough to satisfy that reasoning[9].

There may be cases where, in the circumstances, an attempted or inchoate performance is sufficient[10], but this is not the general rule, even though the completion of the performance is prevented by the death of the donee or other act of God[11].

1 *Caldwell v Cresswell* (1871) 6 Ch App 278. See also *Brown v Peys* (1594) Cro Eliz 357. Where a gift to a housekeeper was subject to a condition that she should continue in the service of the testatrix's husband until his death, the condition was literally fulfilled, even though the husband married the housekeeper: *Re Kendrew, Hird v Kendrew* [1953] Ch 291, [1953] 1 All ER 551, CA.

2 As to consent to marriage see PARA 135. See generally *Lord Mohun v Duke of Hamilton* (1703) 2 Bro Parl Cas 239, HL (legacy provided that legatee gave no trouble to executor; release by legatee sufficient); *Scarlett v Lord Abinger* (1865) 34 Beav 338 (condition for settlement of the donee's own estates on trusts of doubtful validity and effect; settlement in general terms on intended beneficiaries sufficient); *Galwey v Barden* [1899] 1 IR 508 (entering on a calling). Cf *Schnell v Tyrrell* (1834) 7 Sim 86 (remaining in England); *Re Stone's Trusts* (1866) 12 Jur NS 447 (claim within time made by third person); *Re Arbib and Class's Contract* [1891] 1 Ch 601, CA (return to England; temporary visit sufficient); *Re Macnamara, Hewitt v Jeans* (1911) 104 LT 771 (benefice not to be held in plurality; union of benefices no breach); *Browne v Browne* [1912] 1 IR 272; *Re Grotian, Cox v Grotrian* [1955] Ch 501, [1955] 1 All ER 788 (declaration of peace; termination of state of war sufficient); but see *Re Sax, Barned v Sax* (1893) 68 LT 849 ('cease to carry on the business'; sale to company, donees serving as managing directors, not sufficient). As to what is sufficient compliance with a name and arms clause see SETTLEMENTS vol 91 (2012) PARAS 646–647. As to what is sufficient compliance with a condition as to residence see *Re Moir, Warner v Moir* (1884) 25 ChD 605 (condition as to residence fulfilled by keeping an establishment); and SETTLEMENTS vol 91 (2012) PARA 642.

3 Co Litt 206a; *Popham v Bampfeild* (1682) 1 Vern 79 at 83; *Daley v Desbouverie* (1738) 2 Atk 261; *Clarke v Parker* (1812) 19 Ves 1 at 24; *Re Smith, Keeling v Smith* (1890) 44 ChD 654 (conditions with respect to marriage). See also *Tanner v Tebbutt* (1843) 2 Y & C Ch Cas 225 (establishment of identity of donee).

4 *Popham v Bampfeild* (1682) 1 Vern 79; *Worsley v Wood* (1796) 6 Term Rep 710 at 719, 722; *Dawson v Oliver-Massey* (1876) 2 ChD 753, CA (conditional gift on marriage with consent of parents, one dead). As to conditions precedent and subsequent see PARA 129.

5 *Hervey-Bathurst v Stanley, Craven v Stanley* (1876) 4 ChD 251 at 272, CA.

6 *Tollner v Marriott* (1830) 4 Sim 19.

7 *Re Hartley, Stedman v Dunster* (1887) 34 ChD 742.

8 *Franco v Alvares* (1746) 3 Atk 342; *Ledward v Hassells* (1856) 2 K & J 370.

9 *Re Selinger's Will Trusts, Midland Bank Executor and Trustee Co Ltd v Levy* [1959] 1 All ER 407, [1959] 1 WLR 217 (testatrix's reasoning for time condition was to ensure rapid administration of estate by trustees; delay was not caused by excessive deliberation by trustees so condition not strictly applied).

10 *Re Conington's Will* (1860) 6 Jur NS 992.

11 *Tulk v Houlditch* (1813) 1 Ves & B 248. See also *Roundel v Currer* (1786) 2 Bro CC 67 (and see 1 Swan 383n); *Priestley v Holgate* (1857) 3 K & J 286. As to what constitutes an act of God see CONTRACT vol 22 (2012) PARA 478.

148. Time of performance of condition. Where the testator has prescribed a period within which a condition must be performed, this period must be strictly observed[1], subject to the jurisdiction, if any, of the court to grant relief from forfeiture[2]. If, however, the testator has not prescribed such a period and the condition is one to be performed by the donee personally, not requiring the intervention or concurrence of any other person, the period for the performance of the condition is necessarily the life of the donee and no longer, and the condition is not complied with if the donee dies without having performed it[3]. Where persons other than the donee are to be benefited, the period allowed is, as a rule, a reasonable period[4].

1 *Simpson v Vickers* (1807) 14 Ves 341 (conditions as to giving a release within a fixed time); *Brooke v Garrod* (1857) 2 De G & J 62 (option to purchase); *Re Goldsmith, Brett v Bingham* [1947] Ch 339, [1947] 1 All ER 451 (payment to testator's estate). But see now *Re Bowles, Hayward v Jackson* [2003] EWHC 253 (Ch),[2003] Ch 422, [2003] 2 All ER 387(option to purchase; strict observance of time limit would have defeated testator's intentions; other beneficiaries not prejudiced by time not being of the essence), not following *Re Avard, Hook v Parker* [1948] Ch 43, [1947] 2 All ER 548 (option to purchase). See also *Re Gray, Allardyce v Roebuck* [2004] EWHC 1538 (Ch), [2004] 3 All ER 754,[2004] WTLR 779 (option to purchase; will specifying periods for acceptance and completion; time for acceptance of the essence, but not time for completion). See further *Austin v Tawney* (1867) 2 Ch App 143; *Re Glubb, Bamfield v Rogers* [1900] 1 Ch 354, CA; *Re Knox, Von Scheffler v Shuldham* [1912] 1 IR 288 (naturalisation within two years); and PARA 145 note 6. As to how the time is computed see *Lester v Garland* (1808) 15 Ves 248; *Gorst v Lowndes* (1841) 11 Sim 434; *Miller v Wheatley* (1891) 28 LR Ir 144; *Re Figgis, Roberts v MacLaren* [1969] 1 Ch 123, [1968] 1 All ER 999. In *Re Packard, Packard v Waters* [1920] 1 Ch 596, where there was a condition to settle a legacy within a year of the testator's death, but no gift over on non-compliance, the limit of time was held not to be of the essence of the condition. See also *Re Selinger's Will Trusts, Midland Bank Executor and Trustee Co Ltd v Levy* [1959] 1 All ER 407, [1959] 1 WLR 217 (time limit was to ensure expeditious action by trustee; time held not to be of essence); and PARA 147 note 9.
   As to a condition to assume a name see *Re Finlay, Dinamore v Finlay* [1932] NI 89; *Re Neeld, Carpenter v Inigo-Jones* [1962] Ch 643 at 691, [1962] 2 All ER 335 at 361, CA. The court has to consider, at any rate in the absence of a gift over, what the testator presumably intended to guard against in imposing the condition: *Re Goodwin, Ainslie v Goodwin* [1924] 2 Ch 26; *Re Selinger's Will Trusts, Midland Bank Executor and Trustee Co Ltd v Levy* [1959] 1 All ER 407, [1959] 1 WLR 217.
2 See PARA 149.
3 *Acherley v Vernon* (1739) Willes 153; *Patching v Barnett* (1881) 51 LJ Ch 74, CA; *Re Greenwood, Goodhart v Woodhead* [1902] 2 Ch 198 at 204–205 per Joyce J (revsd on construction [1903] 1 Ch 749, CA). Thus in the case of a gift conditional on marriage with, or with the consent of, a particular person, the donee has his whole life to perform the condition: *Randal v Payne* (1779) 1 Bro CC 55; *Fitzgerald v Ryan* [1899] 2 IR 637 at 652, 654. See also *Beaumont v Squire* (1852) 17 QB 905 at 933, 936 (criticising *Clifford v Beaumont* (1828) 4 Russ 325).
4 *Huckstep v Mathews* (1685) 1 Vern 362; *Davies v Lowndes* (1835) 1 Bing NC 597 at 618. Cf the rules as to time of performance of a contract: see CONTRACT vol 22 (2012) PARA 499 et seq.

149. Relief against conditions. In certain cases the court[1] may grant a donee relief against a condition precedent[2], or against forfeiture under a condition subsequent, as, for example, where performance has been prevented by the contrivance of the executors[3], or other persons interested[4], and by no fault of the donee[5], or where the condition is in the nature of a penalty[6], and also in the case of conditions relating to matters such as the payment of legacies or other sums[7], or the release of claims[8]. The court gives relief where performance has not been made within the time required by the testator but the parties can be placed in the same situation as if the condition had been strictly performed[9]. The court does not, however, give relief, even in the cases mentioned above, where there is a gift over[10] to any person other than the one who would take by operation of law[11], and except in such cases the court cannot give relief at all[12]. It seems that the difference of approach to relief, according to whether the condition is precedent or subsequent, arises because with a condition precedent relief involves divesting the existing owner and creating a new estate in the person who would have taken had the condition been satisfied, whereas with a condition subsequent all that is required is relief against the divesting consequences of the condition[13].

1 Formerly, the jurisdiction of a court of law to hold a condition substantially performed was not so wide as the equitable jurisdiction to give relief against non-performance: *Clarke v Parker* (1812) 19 Ves 1 at 21–22.

2   *Wallis v Crimes* (1667) 1 Cas in Ch 89 at 90; *Hayward v Angell* (1683) 1 Vern 222; *Woodman v Blake* (1691) 2 Vern 222; *Viscount Falkland v Bertie* (1698) 2 Vern 333 at 339. As to the general rule that conditions must be strictly observed see EQUITABLE JURISDICTION vol 47 (2014) PARA 225. See, however, *Re Bowles, Hayward v Jackson* [2003] EWHC 253 (Ch), [2003] Ch 422, [2003] 2 All ER 387 (not following *Re Avard, Hook v Parker* [1948] Ch 43, [1947] 2 All ER 548); *Re Gray, Allardyce v Roebuck* [2004] EWHC 1538 (Ch), [2004] 3 All ER 754, [2004] WTLR 779. As to conditions precedent and subsequent see PARA 129.

3   *Brooke v Garrod* (1857) 2 De G & J 62. Failure by trustees to carry out the terms of the testator's will is not allowed to prejudice the beneficiaries: *Re Jones, Williams v Rowlands* [1948] Ch 67, [1947] 2 All ER 716 (cited in PARA 143 note 8).

4   Eg persons interested under the gift over (*Viscount Falkland v Bertie* (1698) 2 Vern 333 at 343; and see *D'Aguilar v Drinkwater* (1813) 2 Ves & B 225), or under a prior gift (*Hayes v Hayes* (1674) Cas *temp* Finch 231).

5   *Clarke v Parker* (1812) 19 Ves 1 at 17 per Lord Eldon LC.

6   *Wallis v Crimes* (1667) 1 Cas in Ch 89; *Priestley v Holgate* (1857) 3 K & J 286 at 288. But see also *Nathan v Leonard* [2002] EWHC 1701 (Ch) at [30], [2003] 4 All ER 198, [2003] 1 WLR 827 (judge indicated that relief from forfeiture would be unlikely where will showed testator's clear intention that other non-challenging beneficiaries should lose gift on a challenge to will, over which they had no control).

7   *Paine v Hyde* (1841) 4 Beav 468. Where the heir had entered on breach of condition by the devisee to pay a legacy, the court gave relief to the devisee on payment of the legacy: *Underwood v Swain* (1649) 1 Rep Ch 161; *Barnardiston v Fane* (1699) 2 Vern 366; *Grimston v Lord Bruce* (1707) 1 Salk 156. As to the construction of such conditions see PARA 407; and as to persons entitled to take advantage of them see PARA 146. A condition may raise a case of election: see *Re Burton's Settlements, Scott v National Provincial Bank Ltd* [1955] Ch 82 at 101, [1954] 3 All ER 193 at 204; and TRUSTS AND POWERS vol 98 (2013) PARA 635.

8   *Hayward v Angell* (1683) 1 Vern 222; *Taylor v Popham* (1782) 1 Bro CC 168; *Simpson v Vickers* (1807) 14 Ves 341; *Hollinrake v Lister* (1826) 1 Russ 500 at 508.

9   *Hollinrake v Lister* (1826) 1 Russ 500 at 508; *Re Packard, Packard v Waters* [1920] 1 Ch 596 at 603; *Re Selinger's Will Trusts, Midland Bank Executor and Trustee Co Ltd v Levy* [1959] 1 All ER 407, [1959] 1 WLR 217. See also *Re Sage, Lloyds Bank Ltd v Holland* [1946] Ch 332, [1946] 2 All ER 298 (settlement). Cf *Re Goldsmith, Brett v Bingham* [1947] Ch 339, [1947] 1 All ER 451.

10   A mere clause of revocation, it appears, does not amount to a gift over for this purpose (*Simpson v Vickers* (1807) 14 Ves 341), nor does an express revocation of the gift for non-compliance (*Re Selinger's Will Trusts, Midland Bank Executor and Trustee Co Ltd v Levy* [1959] 1 All ER 407, [1959] 1 WLR 217).

11   *Simpson v Vickers* (1807) 14 Ves 341 at 346. See also *Cage v Russel* (1681) 2 Vent 352. It may be that relief could be available where the condition is subsequent, rather than precedent. This possibility was assumed but not decided (relief was said to be unlikely on the facts) in *Nathan v Leonard* [2002] EWHC 1701 (Ch) at [29], [2003] 4 All ER 198, [2003] 1 WLR 827.

12   Eg against forfeiture under a condition as to marriage with consent: *Ashton v Ashton* (1703) Prec Ch 226; *Dashwood v Lord Bulkeley* (1804) 10 Ves 230 at 239; *Clarke v Parker* (1812) 19 Ves 1.

13   *Nathan v Leonard* [2002] EWHC 1701 (Ch) at [29]–[30], [2003] 4 All ER 198, [2003] 1 WLR 827 (distinction drawn between instant case (condition subsequent) and *Simpson v Vickers* (1807) 14 Ves 341 (condition precedent) as to type of relief required; question whether relief available in condition subsequent left open). See *AN v Barclays Private Bank and Trust (Cayman) Ltd* (2006) 9 ITELR 630, Cayman Is GC (where a condition would operate as a condition precedent the court had no power to grant relief as that would have the effect of rewriting the will settlement).

3. FAILURE OF TESTAMENTARY DISPOSITIONS

(1) CIRCUMSTANCES GIVING RISE TO FAILURE

150. Failure of interests. A gift may fail for reasons personal to the donee; if, for example, he does not live to benefit by the gift, the gift lapses[1]. Further, the donee may disclaim the gift[2]. The gift may also fail, for example, by reason of the paramount claims of the personal representatives, who may require the subject matter of the gift for payment of debts or legacies having priority[3]. There may also be situations where property comprised in a gift becomes affected by insolvency legislation, in priority to all concerned[4]. Again, the property given by the testator may not be his own property, but the property of some other person[5], or it may be affected by a trust or an estoppel-based interest[6].

Acts of the testator prior to the date of the will may cause a gift to fail in the sense that the gift takes effect not as a gift but in entire or partial satisfaction of a liability undertaken by the testator prior to and existing at the date of the will[7]. In certain cases a presumption arises as to the satisfaction, wholly or partially, by gifts in a will, of portions already covenanted to be paid, or of debts already owing to creditors at the date of the will, in which cases, unless the presumption is displaced by evidence or the context of the will, the apportioner or creditor is bound to elect[8].

Where the property given is no longer within the testator's power of disposal at the date of his death, the gift is adeemed[9]. Subject to this doctrine of ademption, no conveyance or other subsequent act of the testator relating to property comprised in the will, except an act revoking the will, prevents the will from operating with respect to the estate or interest in property of which the testator has the power of disposing by will at the time of his death[10].

A gift may also fail by reason of the non-performance of a condition precedent[11], or by reason of the disqualification of the donee for benefiting either by reason of his crime or fraud[12], or because he or his spouse or his civil partner was an attesting witness[13], or by reason of the gift being uncertain[14], or infringing the rule against perpetuities[15], or being contrary to public policy[16]. A gift for purposes partly but not exclusively charitable, and prima facie void, for example for uncertainty or perpetuity, may, however, sometimes be saved from failure and vest in the donee for charitable purposes only[17]. A gift for non-charitable purposes which cannot be enforced by individuals is void[18] save in a few exceptional cases[19].

1   As to lapse see PARA 160 et seq.
2   See PARA 151 et seq.
3   See PARA 17. In the course of administration a gift may be subject to abatement or ademption. As to abatement in the case of specific legacies which are expressed to be given not as specific legacies but as general legacies see *Re Compton, Vaughan v Smith* [1914] 2 Ch 119. As to the administration of assets see PARA 956 et seq. As to the abatement of legacies see PARAS 1087–1094; and as to the order of application of assets see PARAS 993–1018. As to ademption see PARA 155 et seq.
4   See *Re Hemming, Raymond Saul & Co (a firm) v Holden* [2008] EWHC 2731 (Ch), [2009] Ch 313, [2009] 2 WLR 1257.
5   In such cases the true owner may sometimes be compelled under the doctrine of election to elect between taking a benefit under the testator's will and insisting on his own title to the property in question: see *Frear v Frear* [2008] EWCA Civ 1320, [2009] 1 FLR 391, [2008] All ER (D) 24 (Dec); and EQUITABLE JURISDICTION vol 47 (2014) PARA 161 et seq.
6   See PARA 20.
7   As to satisfaction see EQUITABLE JURISDICTION vol 47 (2014) PARA 176 et seq.
8   As to the admissibility of evidence for these purposes see PARA 193 et seq; and EQUITABLE JURISDICTION vol 47 (2014) PARA 187.

9 *Moor v Raisbeck* (1841) 12 Sim 123 at 138; *Blake v Blake* (1880) 15 ChD 481; *Re Viscount Galway's Will Trusts, Lowther v Viscount Galway* [1950] Ch 1, [1949] 2 All ER 419. As to ademption see PARAS 18, 155–159.
10 See the Wills Act 1837 s 23; and PARA 94. Before the commencement of the Wills Act 1837 any conveyance under which the testator's interest was altered, with certain exceptions, caused a gift of the property so affected to fail: see *Grant v Bridger* (1866) LR 3 Eq 347.
11 As to conditions precedent see PARA 129. As to illegality of conditions see PARA 128.
12 See PARA 39.
13 See PARA 41.
14 See PARA 262.
15 See PERPETUITIES AND ACCUMULATIONS vol 80 (2013) PARA 9 et seq.
16 See PARA 131.
17 See the Charitable Trusts (Validation) Act 1954 s 1; and CHARITIES vol 8 (2015) PARA 98 et seq. See also *Ulrich v Treasury Solicitor* [2005] EWHC 67 (Ch), [2005] 1 All ER 1059, [2006] 1 WLR 33 (case on the Charitable Trusts (Validation) Act 1954 in which the authorities are reviewed).
18 *Re Astor's Settlement Trusts, Astor v Scholfield* [1952] Ch 534, [1952] 1 All ER 1067. See also PARA 36; and TRUSTS AND POWERS vol 98 (2013) PARAS 8, 70.
19 See eg *Re Hooper, Parker v Ward* [1932] 1 Ch 38 (maintenance of tomb); *Re Hetherington* [1990] Ch 1 [1989] 2 All ER 129 (saying of masses); and TRUSTS AND POWERS vol 98 (2013) PARA 8.

(2) DISCLAIMER

151. Disclaimer. Disclaimer of a gift by will may be made by any person who is sui juris[1]. Similarly, the object of a discretionary trust or power may release the trustees from the duty of considering whether or not to exercise their discretion in his favour, and, if he does so, he will cease to be an object of that trust or power[2]. A disclaimer executed prior to the death of the testator is ineffective[3].

A disclaimer puts a donee, as regards his liabilities, burdens and rights, in the same position as if no gift had been made to him, but does not necessarily render the gift void in regard to all persons and for all purposes[4], as, for example, where the donee is a trustee[5]. One of several joint tenants cannot make a disclaimer, the only disclaimer which joint tenants can make being one made by all of them[6].

A disclaimer does not operate as a disposition of property but as a non-acceptance of it[7]. A disclaimer accordingly operates so as not to divest but to prevent it from vesting[8] and may, therefore, be effected by informal means[9] as well as by record or deed[10], even if the gift confers a legal estate in property[11]. Since acceptance of a gift or any part of it is inconsistent with an intention to renounce or disclaim it, it is not permissible to disclaim part only of a single gift[12], and the right to disclaim it is altogether extinguished as soon as any benefit has been received under it[13].

1 As to what constitutes a disclaimer see *Doe d Wyatt v Stagg* (1839) 5 Bing NC 564; *Doe d Chidgey v Harris* (1847) 16 M & W 517. Disclaimer can be by conduct but there is a presumption in favour of accepting a gift: *Cook v IRC* [2002] STC (SCD) 318; [2002] WTLR 1003. As to disclaimer of the office and estate of trustee see TRUSTS AND POWERS vol 98 (2013) PARA 252 et seq. As to the effect of disclaimer of a particular estate in accelerating subsequent limitations see PARA 181; and as to the relevance of disclaimer to a partial intestacy see PARA 517. A disclaimed legacy falls into residue: *Re Backhouse, Westminster Bank Ltd v Shaftesbury Society and Ragged School Union* [1931] WN 168. On the sale of land, if one executor disclaims, the proving executor may act: see PARA 608.
      The court may order disclaimer on behalf of a person who lacks capacity to make the decision for himself (see the Mental Capacity Act 2005 s 16; and MENTAL HEALTH AND CAPACITY vol 75 (2013) PARA 734) or a minor (see CHILDREN AND YOUNG PERSONS vol 9 (2012) PARA 39).
2 *Re Gulbenkian's Settlement Trusts (No 2), Stephens v Mann* [1970] Ch 408, [1969] 2 All ER 1173.
3 *Re Smith, Smith v Smith* [2001] 3 All ER 552, [2001] 1 WLR 1937.
4 *Mallott v Wilson* [1903] 2 Ch 494 at 501. See also *Wilson v Wilson* (1847) 1 De G & Sm 152 (disclaimer did not prejudice charge). The gift formerly attracted estate duty (*Re Parsons, Parsons v A-G* [1943] Ch 12, [1942] 2 All ER 496, CA; *Re Stratton's Deed of Disclaimer, Stratton v IRC*

[1958] Ch 42, [1957] 2 All ER 594, CA), but now, if the benefit is disclaimed within two years after the death otherwise than for a consideration of money or money's worth, the gift is not a transfer of value for the purposes of inheritance tax, or a disposal for the purposes of capital gains tax, and in either case the beneficiary is treated as not having become entitled to the interest (see the Inheritance Tax Act 1984 s 142; the Taxation of Chargeable Gains Act 1992 s 62(6); and CAPITAL GAINS TAXATION vol 6 (2011) PARA 704; INHERITANCE TAXATION vol 59A (2014) PARA 76). For deaths on or after 1 February 2012 a person who disclaims an entitlement in a will is to be treated as having died immediately before the testator for the purposes of the Wills Act 1837, thus enabling the substitution of issue of the person disclaiming to take place under the Wills Act 1837 s 33: see the Wills Act 1837 s 33A; and PARA 169.

5   See *Robson v Flight* (1865) 4 De GJ & Sm 608 at 613; and TRUSTS AND POWERS vol 98 (2013) PARA 254.
6   *Re Schär, Midland Bank Executor and Trustee Co v Damer* [1951] Ch 280, [1950] 2 All ER 1069.
7   A person 'cannot have an estate put into him in spite of his teeth': see *Townson v Tickell* (1819) 3 B & Ald 31 at 37 per Abott CJ. As to the situation on a partial intestacy see *Re Scott, Widdows v Friends of the Clergy Corpn* [1975] 2 All ER 1033, [1975] 1 WLR 1260 (discussed in *Re DWS, Re EHS, TWGS v JMG* [2000] 2 All ER 83 at 94). It seems that a disclaimer under intestacy operates so as to allow any remaining members of that beneficiary class to take the disclaimed share or, if none, for the gift to go to the next class entitled, rather than directly to bona vacantia. For deaths on or after 1 February 2012 a person who disclaims an entitlement on intestacy is to be treated as having died immediately before the intestate: see the Administration of Estates Act 1925 s 46; and PARA 485. As to intestate succession see PARA 477 et seq.
8   A beneficiary who disclaims a gift cannot, therefore, control the subsequent devolution of that gift. As to the effect of disclaimer generally see PARAS 180–184.
9   See *Cook v IRC* [2002] STC (SCD) 318 (the evidence from conduct of an intention to disclaim a gift was not strong enough to displace the presumption that the gift would be accepted).
10   A deed is sufficient (*Townson v Tickell* (1819) 3 B & Ald 31; *Begbie v Crook* (1835) 2 Bing NC 70), and is advisable particularly in the case of a trustee (cf *Nicloson v Wordsworth* (1818) 2 Swan 365 at 370; and TRUSTS AND POWERS vol 98 (2013) PARA 252). To satisfy the requirements of the Inheritance Tax Act 1984 s 142 and the Taxation of Chargeable Gains Act 1992 s 62(6) (see note 4), the disclaimer must be effected by an instrument in writing. As to the irrevocability of deeds see PARA 154.
11   *Re Birchall, Birchall v Ashton* (1889) 40 ChD 436 at 439; *Re Clout and Frewer's Contract* [1924] 2 Ch 230. A disclaimer not required to be evidenced by writing is excepted from the requirement that a conveyance (which otherwise includes a disclaimer) of a legal estate must be by deed: see the Law of Property Act 1925 ss 52(1), (2)(b), 205(1)(ii); and DEEDS AND OTHER INSTRUMENTS vol 32 (2012) PARAS 214–215. See also *Townson v Tickell* (1819) 3 B & Ald 31 at 39 per Holroyd J; *Bingham v Lord Clanmorris* (1828) 2 Mol 253; *Stacey v Elph* (1833) 1 My & K 195.
12   *Re Joel, Rogerson v Joel* [1943] Ch 311, [1943] 2 All ER 263, CA; and see PARA 153.
13   See eg *Re Wimperis, Wicken v Wilson* [1914] 1 Ch 502; and PARA 154.

152. Acceptance. If the donee of a gift by will accepts the gift, he takes it with all the benefits and burdens which are incident to it by law[1], or which are validly attached to it by the testator, and, in particular, he takes it with the burden of all the conditions and obligations validly attached to it which are intended to be binding on him[2]. It is a question of construction in each case whether the words of the condition create a charge[3] or a personal obligation[4] or both[5]. Unless the conditions are such that only a trust or charge on the property is created[6], or that the donee is entitled to the enjoyment of the gift only during such period as the conditions are performed by him[7], the donee, on accepting the gift, is bound to observe and perform the conditions[8], the obligation which lies on him being the same as if he had entered into a contract to do so[9]. Thus where the condition requires him to do some act involving expense, he is, if he accepts the gift, personally liable for that act being done, even though the gift is insufficient to enable him to do so without loss[10].

In general, and subject to the terms of the will[11], acceptance may be made by or inferred from informal acts or conduct[12], especially if they amount to acts of ownership[13]. The donee need not expressly accept the gift[14]; unless by the will the duty of doing some act to show his election is put on him[15], his acceptance of the gift is presumed, and the property vests in him unless and until he disclaims[16].

1 As to interest and accretions on legacies see PARA 1080 et seq. As to the administration of assets, the payment of debts, and the liability of the donee, see PARA 956 et seq.

2 *Pitman v Crum Ewing* [1911] AC 217, HL; *Messenger v Andrews* (1828) 4 Russ 478 (where the plaintiff claimed to be in possession not by virtue of the bequest but in satisfaction of money advanced, and an inquiry was ordered whether he accepted); *Hickling v Boyer* (1851) 3 Mac & G 635 (covenants and conditions of lease). See also note 9. As to conditions attached to gifts see PARA 128 et seq. As to the burden of incumbrances see PARAS 1006–1010. As to acceptance of office by a trustee see TRUSTS AND POWERS vol 98 (2013) PARAS 248–251. A legatee who, in pursuance of a condition attached to the legacy, conveys his own land to another has no lien for his legacy on the land conveyed: *Barker v Barker* (1870) LR 10 Eq 438. As to a direction attached to an estate tail for assuming a name and arms see *Vandeleur v Sloane* [1919] 1 IR 116, Ir CA. Entailed interests cannot be created by instruments coming into operation on or after 1 January 1997: see the Trusts of Land and Appointment of Trustees Act 1996 s 2(6), Sch 1 para 5; PARA 387; and REAL PROPERTY AND REGISTRATION vol 87 (2012) PARA 114; SETTLEMENTS vol 91 (2012) PARAS 506, 577. As to conditions requiring the assumption of a name or arms see PARA 141.

3 *Jillard v Edgar* (1849) 3 De G & Sm 502; *Re Cowley, Souch v Cowley* (1885) 53 LT 494; *Re Oliver, Newbald v Beckett* (1890) 62 LT 533.

4 *Rees v Engelback* (1871) LR 12 Eq 225; *Re M'Mahon, M'Mahon v M'Mahon* [1901] 1 IR 489, Ir CA; *Re Loom, Fulford v Reversionary Interest Society Ltd* [1910] 2 Ch 230; *Duffy v Duffy* [1920] 1 IR 122, Ir CA; *Re Hodge, Hodge v Griffiths* [1940] Ch 260; *Re Lester, Lester v Lester* [1942] Ch 324, [1942] 1 All ER 646 (where the authorities are reviewed).

5 *Welby v Rockcliffe* (1830) 1 Russ & M 571; *Wright v Wilkin* (1860) 7 Jur NS 441.

6 See the cases cited in note 3.

7 *Re Robinson, Wright v Tugwell* [1892] 1 Ch 95. See also *A-G v Christ's Hospital* (1830) 1 Russ & M 626 at 628 (where the existence of a gift over did not authorise non-performance). Cf, however, *Re Tyler, Tyler v Tyler* [1891] 3 Ch 252, CA; *Re Da Costa, Clarke v Church of England Collegiate School of St Peter* [1912] 1 Ch 337 (devise of absolute interest subject to condition; condition obnoxious to rule against perpetuities).

8 *Earl of Northumberland v Marquis of Granby* (1760) 1 Eden 489 at 499, also reported sub nom *Earl of Northumberland v Earl of Aylesford* Amb 540 (affd sub nom *Duke of Northumberland v Lord Egremont* (1768) Amb 657); *A-G v Christ's Hospital* (1790) 3 Bro CC 165 (condition of maintaining six children; rents insufficient); *Messenger v Andrews* (1828) 4 Russ 478 (in 'consideration of' paying debts etc; property insufficient); *A-G v Christ's Hospital* (1830) 1 Russ & M 626 at 628 (condition of maintaining four children); *Re Skingley* (1851) 3 Mac & G 221 (condition of keeping house in repair); *Gregg v Coates, Hodgson v Coates* (1856) 23 Beav 33; *Woodhouse v Walker* (1880) 5 QBD 404 at 408 (where the decision is based on liability at common law, but is criticised and explained in *Blackmore v White* [1899] 1 QB 293 at 303–304); *Re Williames, Andrew v Williames* (1885) 54 LT 105, CA; *Blackmore v White* above; *Dingle v Coppen, Coppen v Dingle* [1899] 1 Ch 726 at 733; *Jay v Jay* [1924] 1 KB 826 (where the basis of the liability of the estate of a deceased tenant for life for non-repair is discussed). Cf *Joliffe v Twyford* (1858) 26 Beav 227; *Duffy v Duffy* [1920] 1 IR 122, Ir CA (devise of farm; devisee to pay debts; residue exonerated). As to the liability of a life tenant subject to a condition for repair of the settled property see SETTLEMENTS vol 91 (2012) PARA 887. As to observing the scheme of the will as to a charitable legacy where the trustees have a discretion see *Re Harrison, Harrison v A-G* (1915) 85 LJ Ch 77; and CHARITIES vol 8 (2015) PARA 146.

9 *Gregg v Coates, Hodgson v Coates* (1856) 23 Beav 33 at 38; *Blackmore v White* [1899] 1 QB 293 at 304. The acceptance may also operate to bind the donee by way of estoppel in favour of third persons, eg persons to whom by the condition he is bound to give a release: *Egg v Devey* (1847) 10 Beav 444. See also *Robertson v Junkin* (1896) 26 SCR 192 at 195–196.

10 The court will not order specific performance: *Payne v Haine* (1847) 16 M & W 541; *Re Skingley* (1851) 3 Mac & G 221; *Gregg v Coates, Hodgson v Coates* (1856) 23 Beav 33; *Cooke v Cholmondeley* (1858) 4 Drew 326.

11 The will may require a written acceptance: *Evans v Stratford* (1864) 2 Hem & M 142.

12 *Earl of Northumberland v Marquis of Granby* (1760) 1 Eden 489, sub nom *Earl of Northumberland v Earl of Aylesford* Amb 540; affd sub nom *Duke of Northumberland v Lord Egremont* (1768) Amb 657.

13 See *Bence v Gilpin* (1868) LR 3 Exch 76. Acts done by a donee merely to preserve the property and not amounting to acts of ownership need not amount to acceptance: *A-G v Andrew* (1798) 3 Ves 633. See also *Stacey v Elph* (1833) 1 My & K 195.

14 *Thompson v Leach* (1690) 2 Vent 198 (on appeal (1692) 2 Vent 208, HL); *Townson v Tickell* (1819) 3 B & Ald 31 at 37. See also *Stratton's Deed of Disclaimer, Stratton v IRC* [1958] Ch 42, [1957] 2 All ER 594, CA; and GIFTS vol 52 (2014) PARAS 249–250.
15 Eg in the case of options to purchase (see PARA 125).
16 *Townson v Tickell* (1819) 3 B & Ald 31 at 36–37; Shep Touch (8th Edn, 1826) p 284; *Re Arbib and Class's Contract* [1891] 1 Ch 601, CA. See also *Re Defoe* (1882) 2 OR 623; and GIFTS vol 52 (2014) PARA 250. Acceptance is thus presumed for the purpose of the property vesting in the donee, even if he had no knowledge of the will, but in that case, it appears, not for the purpose of his incurring liabilities: *Houghton v Bell* (1892) 23 SCR 498, 508 (liability as trustee). See also *Cook v IRC* [2002] STC (SCD) 318.

153. Acceptance and disclaimer of blended gifts. Where two distinct properties are given to a donee, prima facie he is entitled to take one and disclaim the other[1], even where the two are included under the same words of gift[2]. His right to do so may, however, be rebutted if the intention of the testator is shown that the two gifts should be taken together, or generally that the option to take one and to disclaim the other should not exist[3]. Where, however, there is a single and undivided gift of an aggregate property, such as a residuary estate, prima facie the donee must either take the whole or nothing[4]. The donee cannot evade this by shedding the onerous consequences of part of the gift onto other parts of the estate, designated as carrying the debts of the testator[5]. A bequest of a leasehold house 'together with the contents' constitutes a single gift[6].

1 *Andrew v Trinity Hall, Cambridge* (1804) 9 Ves 525 at 534; *Warren v Rudall, ex p Godfrey* (1860) 1 John & H 1; *Long v Kent* (1865) 11 Jur NS 724; *Aston v Wood* (1874) 43 LJ Ch 715; *Re Loom, Fulford v Reversionary Interest Society* [1910] 2 Ch 230.
2 *Syer v Gladstone* (1885) 30 ChD 614 (discussed and explained in *Frewen v Law Life Assurance Society* [1896] 2 Ch 511 at 516–517). See also *Re Baron Kensington, Earl of Longford v Baron Kensington* [1902] 1 Ch 203 at 210, 211n.
3 *Guthrie v Walrond* (1883) 22 ChD 573 at 577 per Fry J. See also *Moffett v Bates* (1857) 3 Sm & G 468. It appears that it is readily inferred that the donee is not entitled to disclaim where one gift is a leasehold known by the testator to be onerous and bequeathed so as to show that the remainder of the testator's estate was intended to be free from the burden: *Talbot v Earl of Radnor* (1834) 3 My & K 252 (corrected and explained in *Fairtlough v Johnstone* (1865) 16 I Ch R 442). See also *Re Sitwell, Worsley v Sitwell* (1913) 135 LT Jo 323.
4 *A-G v Brackenbury* (1863) 1 H & C 782 at 791; *Green v Britten* (1872) 42 LJ Ch 187; *Hawkins v Hawkins* (1880) 13 ChD 470 at 474, CA; *Guthrie v Walrond* (1883) 22 ChD 573; *Re Hotchkys, Freke v Calmady* (1886) 32 ChD 408 at 417, 419, CA; *Frewen v Law Life Assurance Society* [1896] 2 Ch 511; *Parnell v Boyd* [1896] 2 IR 571 at 602, Ir CA.
5 *Foulkes v Metropolitan District Rly Co* (1880) 5 CPD 157, 44 JP 568, CA (onerous leasehold was part of residue); cf *Re Day's Will Trusts, Lloyds Bank Ltd v Shafe* [1962] 3 All ER 699, [1962] 1 WLR 1419 (devisee of house was entitled to have cost of bringing house into repair, under testatrix's (as landlord) repairing covenant, paid out of residue).
6 *Re Joel, Rogerson v Joel* [1943] Ch 311, [1943] 2 All ER 263, CA.

154. When a disclaimer or acceptance may be retracted. A mere refusal by a life tenant to receive income, where there has been no change of position as regards the other persons claiming under the will and the refusal is made without consideration, may be retracted so far as regards future payments of income[1]. A life tenant who merely refuses to take possession of a leasehold on account of its burdensome nature is nevertheless entitled to the income of the proceeds of sale[2]. Similarly, if the disclaimer is not of any estate in the property but only of the benefit under the will, accompanied by an assertion of a right by a higher and better title, the person disclaiming is not precluded from acting on his better judgment and taking the property as donee[3]. In general a disclaimer or renunciation of gifts or benefits under a will may be retracted if no one has altered his position on the faith of it[4]. A disclaimer by deed is, however, probably irrevocable[5]. Once a gift is unequivocally accepted[6], it cannot as a rule be repudiated subsequently[7] to the prejudice of others.

1　*Re Young, Fraser v Young* [1913] 1 Ch 272.
2　*Earl of Lonsdale v Countess Berchtoldt* (1857) 3 K & J 185.
3　*Doe d Smyth v Smyth* (1826) 6 B & C 112 at 117.
4　*Re Cranstoun, Gibbs v Home of Rest for Horses* [1949] Ch 523, [1949] 1 All ER 871. Cf Shep Touch (8th Edn, 1826) pp 69–70. See, however, *Re Paradise Motor Co Ltd* [1968] 2 All ER 625 at 632, [1968] 1 WLR 1125 at 1143, CA.
5　A deed is ordinarily irrevocable unless a power of revocation is expressly reserved: see *Re Beesty's Will Trusts, Farrar v Royal Alfred Merchant Seamen's Society* [1966] Ch 223 at 232–233, [1964] 3 All ER 82 at 86–87; and DEEDS AND OTHER INSTRUMENTS vol 32 (2012) PARA 267 et seq. See, however, *Re Smith, Smith v Smith* [2001] 3 All ER 552, [2001] 1 WLR 1937 (although in this case the disclaimer was held to be ineffective, being made prior to death of the testatrix, rather than revoked).
6　*Doe d Chidgey v Harris* (1847) 16 M & W 517 at 523–524 (acceptance held equivocal on subsequent disclaimer); *Re Wimperis, Wicken v Wilson* [1914] 1 Ch 502 (mere negotiations).
7　*A-G v Christ's Hospital* (1830) 1 Russ & M 626 (attempted disclaimer by charity); *A-G v Munby* (1858) 3 H & N 826 at 831 (attempted disclaimer by executors of legatee who had accepted); *Bence v Gilpin* (1868) LR 3 Exch 76; *Parnell v Boyd* [1896] 2 IR 571 at 589, 596, Ir CA. Cf *Re Shepherd, Harris v Shepherd* [1943] Ch 8, [1942] 2 All ER 584.

(3) ADEMPTION

155. Methods of ademption. A testamentary gift may be adeemed or taken away from the donee:

(1)　by a subsequent disposition by the testator of the subject matter of the gift[1];

(2)　by a change in the ownership or nature of the property; and

(3)　by the presumption that the testator does not intend to provide double portions for his children or other persons to whom he stands in loco parentis[2].

If, however, in a will there are gifts of two properties settled in trust, one by reference to the trusts of the other (as, for example, where heirlooms are settled to follow the trusts of realty), the subsequent alteration of the trusts of one property by a deed executed by the testator in his lifetime does not affect earlier testamentary limitations relating to the other property[3]. Apart from the presumption as to double portions, there can be no ademption of a residuary gift[4], although it seems that an intention to adeem a testamentary gift of residue, completely or pro tanto, can be identified and given effect to, without needing to resort to the presumption[5].

1　This may involve a disposition by a person exercising power of attorney on behalf of the testator: see *Banks v National Westminster Bank plc* [2005] EWHC 3479 (Ch), [2005] All ER (D) 159 (Apr) (attorney for testatrix sold house which was to be given to her under will, causing gift to adeem).
2　See EQUITABLE JURISDICTION vol 47 (2014) PARA 176 et seq. See also *Re Vaux, Nicholson v Vaux* [1939] Ch 465, [1938] 4 All ER 703, CA; *Re Cameron, Philips v Cameron* [1999] Ch 386, [1999] 2 All ER 924 (presumption against double portions applied); *Casimir v Alexander* [2001] WTLR 939 (presumption rebutted on the evidence); *Aldridge v Turner* [2004] EWHC 2768 (Ch), [2004] All ER (D) 451 (Nov) (miscellaneous transactions insufficient to raise the presumption against double portions, but lifetime sums given to beneficiaries held to be loans and accountable to the estate); *Race v Race* [2002] EWHC 1868 (Ch), [2002] WTLR 1193 (presumption held to apply in relation to an interest in land). As to the effect of change of ownership of property see PARA 156. As to the admissibility of evidence rebutting or supporting the presumption see PARA 197. See also *Re Malcolm, Marjoribanks v Malcolm* (1923) 156 LT Jo 361; and EQUITABLE JURISDICTION vol 47 (2014) PARA 187.
3　*Re Whitburn, Whitburn v Christie* [1923] 1 Ch 332.
4　*Re Walker, Goodwin v Scott* [1921] 2 Ch 63.

5   See *Re Cameron, Philips v Cameron* [1999] Ch 386 at 419–420, [1999] 2 All ER 924 at 952–953
    per Lindsay J; *Re Eardley's Will, Simeon v Freemantle* [1920] 1 Ch 397 at 404 per Sargant J.

156. Effect of change in ownership or form of property. A specific gift[1] may be
adeemed by its subject matter ceasing to be part of the testator's estate or ceasing
to be subject to his right of disposition[2]. If a specific gift is adeemed, a charge on
it is also adeemed[3]. A bequest of a debt is adeemed by the debt being assigned by
or paid to the testator in his lifetime[4]. Where the testator devises a house which he
has contracted to purchase and the vendor repudiates the contract before the
testator's death, the devisee is not entitled to the purchase money, notwithstanding
a direction that it is to be paid out of the personal estate[5]. A devise of a rentcharge
is adeemed if the rentcharge is subsequently merged on the purchase by the
testator of the property out of which it issues[6]. The gift may be adeemed by the
testator's own disposition of it, for example by sale or change of investment[7]. The
disposition may be by way of a conditional sale and the fact that the conditions
are not fulfilled, or the contract is not entered into until after death, will not
prevent ademption[8]. After a sale of specifically devised property the money
produced by the sale, if not otherwise disposed of by the will, passes as part of the
general personal estate[9], and, if the sale is not completed until after the
testator's death, the donee takes the intermediate rents until completion to which
the testator is entitled[10]. A specific gift of chattels in a certain locality is as a
rule adeemed by their permanent removal to another locality[11].

Various subsequent events which result in the property ceasing to conform to
the description by which it is given cause ademption[12]. Even where the change is
effected by Act of Parliament, ademption follows[13] unless the Act contains a
provision which prevents ademption[14], or the change is a change in name or form
only, and the property exists as substantially the same thing although in a different
shape[15]. Whether the property exists as substantially the same thing at the death
of the testator is a question of fact[16].

Where a gift has been adeemed, it will not be set up again by a codicil
confirming the will[17], at least where the ademption has been effected by a
subsequent gift. In the case of ademption effected by a change in the nature of the
property by operation of law, a codicil may prevent ademption[18].

1   As to general, specific and demonstrative legacies see *Re Borrer's Trusts, Dunlop v Borrer* (1909)
    54 Sol Jo 32; *Re Rose, Midland Bank Executor and Trustee Co Ltd v Rose* [1949] Ch 78, [1948]
    2 All ER 971 (gifts adeemed). See also *Bronsdon v Winter* (1738) Amb 57; *Hayes v Hayes* (1836)
    1 Keen 97 (life interest adeemed in part; interest in remainder not adeemed); *Robinson v Addison*
    (1840) 2 Beav 515; *Re Willcocks, Warwick v Willcocks* [1921] 2 Ch 327 (no ademption); and
    PARA 118 et seq. For an example of the subsequent payment off of government stock which had
    been left as a general legacy see *Re Gage, Crozier v Gutheridge* [1934] Ch 536; and as to a general
    legacy of stock compulsorily acquired by the Treasury before the testator's death see *Re Borne,
    Bailey v Bailey* [1944] Ch 190, [1944] 1 All ER 382. See also *Pennington v Waine* [2002] EWCA
    Civ 227, [2002] 4 All ER 215, [2002] 1 WLR 2075 (lifetime gift, not fully dealt with by way of
    formality before date of death; held to be a valid equitable assignment); and PARA 157 note 8.
2   As to the application of the doctrine of ademption to general and special powers of appointment
    see TRUSTS AND POWERS vol 98 (2013) PARA 574.
3   *Cowper v Mantell* (1856) 22 Beav 223. A devise of a house does not carry a mortgage on the house
    taken by the testator on sale (*Re Clowes* [1893] 1 Ch 214, CA; *Re Richards, Jones v Rebbeck*
    [1921] 1 Ch 513), or purchase money deposited with trustees (*Gilfoyle v Wood-Martin* [1921] 1
    IR 105). Cf *Re Carter, Dodds v Pearson* [1900] 1 Ch 801 (where the testator was a mortgagee in
    possession).
4   See PARA 159.
5   *Re Rix, Steward v Lonsdale* (1921) 90 LJ Ch 474.
6   *Re Bick, Edwards v Bush* [1920] 1 Ch 488. As to rentcharges see REAL PROPERTY AND
    REGISTRATION vol 87 (2012) PARA 1104 et seq. As to the statutory extinguishement of

rentcharges under the Rentcharges Act 1977 see REAL PROPERTY AND REGISTRATION vol 87 (2012) PARA 1168.

7   *Humphreys v Humphreys* (1789) 2 Cox Eq Cas 184 (sale); *Moor v Raisbeck* (1841) 12 Sim 123; *Farrar v Earl Winterton* (1842) 5 Beav 1 (sale); *Lee v Lee* (1858) 27 LJ Ch 824 (sale); *Harrison v Jackson* (1887) 7 ChD 339; *Macdonald v Irvine* (1878) 8 ChD 101, CA (change of investment); *Re Lane, Luard v Lane* (1880) 14 ChD 856 (debentures converted into debenture stock; and see the observations of Joyce J in *Re Herring, Murray v Herring* [1908] 2 Ch 493 at 499); *Re Clowes* [1893] 1 Ch 214, CA (property sold by and afterwards mortgaged to testator); *Re Edwards, Macadam v Wright* [1958] Ch 168, [1957] 2 All ER 495 (agreement for valuable consideration to devise to another); *Banks v National Westminster Bank plc* [2005] EWHC 3479 (Ch), [2005] All ER (D) 159 (Apr) (property sold by testatrix's attorney prior to her death); cf *Re Viertel* [1996] QSC 66, [2003] WTLR 1075, Qld SC. A contract for sale by a testator which is unenforceable or rescinded by the purchaser does not cause ademption (*Re Pearce, Roberts v Stephens* (1894) 8 R 805; and see *Re Thomas, Thomas v Howell* (1886) 34 ChD 166), nor does a mere request by the testator to his agents to sell (*Harrison v Asher* (1848) 2 De G & Sm 436).

8   *Re Sweeting, Sweeting v Sweeting* [1988] 1 All ER 1016 (contract was specifically enforceable by or against the testator by the time of death). This rule also extends to ademption by the exercise of an option, granted by the testator, after his death: *Re Carrington, Ralphs v Swithenbank* [1932] 1 Ch 1, 100 LJ Ch 299; see PARA 157.

9   *Moor v Raisbeck* (1841) 12 Sim 123 at 139; *Banks v National Westminster Bank plc* [2005] EWHC 3479 (Ch), [2005] All ER (D) 159 (Apr).

10 *Watts v Watts* (1873) LR 17 Eq 217 at 221.

11 See the cases cited in PARA 285 notes 2, 9.

12 Eg loss or destruction (*Durrant v Friend* (1852) 5 De G & Sm 343 (specific legatee of chattels lost had no right to insurance money); but cf *Re Durling's Application, sub nom Re Clements* [2007] WTLR 1717, SC (NS) (fire substantially damaged cottage and killed testator; evidence that death occurred before substantial damage; legal title passed before damage occurred; no ademption and insurance proceeds held for devisee); *Trustees, Executors and Agency Co Ltd v Scott* (1898) 24 VLR 522 (fire)); and compulsory purchase or notice to treat, even though the purchase is completed after death (*Ex p Hawkins* (1843) 13 Sim 569; *Re Manchester and Southport Rly Co* (1854) 19 Beav 365; *Re Bagot's Settlement* (1862) 31 LJ Ch 772 (where the purchase money was liable to be reinvested in land); *Watts v Watts* (1873) LR 17 Eq 217; *Manton v Tabois* (1885) 30 ChD 92; *Re Viscount Galway's Will Trusts, Lowther v Viscount Galway* [1950] Ch 1, [1949] 2 All ER 419); cf *Re Viertel* [1996] QSC 66, [2003] WTLR 1075, Qld SC (sale by attorney unknown to testator)). No ademption is, as a rule, caused by the transfer of the specifically bequeathed property by trustees into the testator's own name unless described by reference to the trustees' ownership (*Dingwell v Askew* (1788) 1 Cox Eq Cas 427; *Lee v Lee* (1858) 27 LJ Ch 824; *Re Vickers, Vickers v Mellor* (1899) 81 LT 719 (bequest of trust fund afterwards transferred to testator's banking account); *Toole v Hamilton* [1901] 1 IR 383 (bequest of money receivable under will, subsequently paid to testator's banking account); and see *Clough v Clough* (1834) 3 My & K 296; *Jones v Southall (No 2)* (1862) 32 Beav 31; and cf *Ogilvie-Forbes' Trustees v Ogilvie-Forbes* 1955 SC 405 (where a bequest of the life rent of heritable property was adeemed by transfer to a limited company in which the testator remained the controlling shareholder)); or by the unauthorised acts of third persons without the testator's knowledge (*Earl of Shaftesbury v Countess of Shaftesbury* (1716) 2 Vern 747; *Basan v Brandon* (1836) 8 Sim 171 (investment subsequently ratified by testator); *Jenkins v Jones* (1866) LR 2 Eq 323; but see *Banks v National Westminster Bank plc* [2005] EWHC 3479 (Ch), [2005] All ER (D) 159 (Apr) (narrow exception to ademption seen in *Jenkins v Jones* above may arise where subject matter extinguished by fraud or tortious acts without testator's knowledge). Nor can the value of the specifically bequeathed property be increased by such unauthorised acts, as eg where an agent without authority discharges a liability affecting the property: *Re Larking, Larking v Larking* (1887) 37 ChD 310. As to the preservation of interests in property disposed of on behalf of a person lacking mental capacity see the Mental Capacity Act 2005 ss 66(1)(a)(2), 66(4), Sch 5 para 8, Sch 2 para 8; and MENTAL HEALTH AND CAPACITY vol 75 (2013) PARAS 618, 729.

13 *Frewen v Frewen* (1875) 10 Ch App 610 (advowson affected by Irish Church Act 1869); *Re Slater, Slater v Slater* [1907] 1 Ch 665, CA (water company affected by the Metropolis Water Act 1902). Where by a will made before 1 January 1926 an undivided share of real estate had been devised, and the testator died on or after that date, the conversion of the share into personal estate by the Law of Property Act 1925 ss 34(3), 35 (s 35 now repealed) (see *Re Kempthorne, Charles v Kempthorne* [1930] 1 Ch 268, CA) would cause ademption: *Re Newman, Slater v Newman* [1930] 2 Ch 409. Since 1 January 1997 all trusts for sale formerly imposed by statute have become trusts of land (without a duty to sell) and land formerly held on such statutorily imposed trusts for sale is now held in trust for the persons interested in the land, so that the owner of each undivided share

now has an interest in land: see the Trusts of Land and Appointment of Trustees Act 1996 ss 1, 5, Sch 2 paras 2–5, 7 (repealing the Law of Property Act 1925 ss 32 and amending ss 34, 36 and the Administration of Estates Act 1925 s 33); and REAL PROPERTY AND REGISTRATION vol 87 (2012) PARA 105. Where trusts for sale are imposed expressly by the trust instrument, then, unless the trust was created by the will of a testator who died before 1 January 1997, the existence of the duty to sell no longer means that the land is to be regarded as personal property: see the Trusts of Land and Appointment of Trustees Act 1996 s 3; and REAL PROPERTY AND REGISTRATION vol 87 (2012) PARAS 7, 215. The doctrine of conversion is not wholly abolished by s 3 and will still apply to eg uncompleted agreements for the sale of land. As to the doctrine of conversion see further EQUITABLE JURISDICTION vol 47 (2014) PARA 138 et seq. It is possible that in a will made before 1 January 1997 of a testator dying on or after that date a gift of a share of land which is expressed to be a gift of personalty or a gift of a share of the proceeds of sale might, by a reverse application of *Re Newman, Slater v Newman* above, be adeemed: see further PARAS 288, 291.

14 *Re Jenkins, Jenkins v Davies* [1931] 2 Ch 218, CA (reference in any will etc to old stock to be deemed reference to substituted stock). See also *Re Anderson, Public Trustee v Bielby* (1928) 44 TLR 295; *Re Viscount Galway's Will Trusts, Lowther v Viscount Galway* [1950] Ch 1, [1949] 2 All ER 419 (vesting of coal and coal mines under the Coal Act 1938).

15 *Oakes v Oakes* (1852) 9 Hare 666 at 672; approved in *Re Slater, Slater v Slater* [1907] 1 Ch 665 at 672, CA. See also *Partridge v Partridge* (1736) Cas *temp* Talb 226; *Humphreys v Humphreys* (1789) 2 Cox Eq Cas 184 at 185; *Re Pilkington's Trusts* (1865) 6 New Rep 246.

16 In the following cases the subject matter in its altered form passed under the gift: *Backwell v Child* (1755) Amb 260 (share of profits of partnership; articles renewed and altered); *Collison v Curling* (1842) 9 Cl & Fin 88, HL (consols sold and invested on stock mortgage); *Re Clifford, Mallam v McFie* [1912] 1 Ch 29 (shares subdivided); *Re Greenberry, Hops v Daniell* (1911) 55 Sol Jo 633 (shares subdivided); *Re Faris, Goddard v Overend* [1911] 1 IR 165 (conversion into stock); *Re Leeming, Turner v Leeming* [1912] 1 Ch 828 (reconstruction of company under substantially the same constitution with diminished capital); *Re Humphreys, Wren v Ward* (1915) 60 Sol Jo 105 (shares and stock, but not debentures, in a reconstructed company issued in lieu of shares); *Re Kuypers, Kuypers v Kuypers* [1925] Ch 244 (preference shares with reduced rights issued on a reorganisation of capital in lieu of preference shares, but not new preference shares issued as compensation for the reduction of rights); *Re O'Brien, Little v O'Brien* (1946) 175 LT 406 (shares after subdivision, but not bonus shares; not following *Re Faris, Goddard v Overend* above as regards bonus shares; and see *Re Tetsall, Foyster v Tetsall* [1961] 2 All ER 801, [1961] 1 WLR 938); *Re Lewis's Will Trusts, Lewis v Williams* [1984] 3 All ER 930, [1985] 1 WLR 102 (where it was held, applying *Re Tetsall, Foyster v Tetsall*, that a specific gift of 'my freehold farm' was not effective to carry the testator's holding of three-quarters of the issued shares in a farming company which owned a farm and other assets). See also *Re Dorman* [1994] 1 All ER 804, [1994] 1 WLR 282 (gift of credit balance in specifically identified bank deposit account; money transferred during lifetime of testatrix to new account at same bank yielding higher rate of interest and requiring 30 days' notice of withdrawal but otherwise on same terms; gift held on the facts to amount to gift of a fund and the transfer of the money did not adeem the gift). Treasury rules may prevent ademption on an exchange of one government security for another: *Re Macartney, Brookhouse v Barman* (1920) 36 TLR 394.

17 *Powys v Mansfield* (1837) 3 My & Cr 359; *Re Aynsley, Kyrle v Turner* [1914] 2 Ch 422 (on appeal [1915] 1 Ch 172, CA); *Re Viscount Galway's Will Trusts, Lowther v Viscount Galway* [1950] Ch 1, [1949] 2 All ER 419. Where the ademption is doubtful, the confirmation of the will is important: *Re Aynsley, Kyrle v Turner* at 429.

18 See *Re Warren, Warren v Warren* [1932] 1 Ch 42. The devise by a will made before 1 January 1926 of a testator dying on or after that date of an undivided share of real estate, which would otherwise have been adeemed by the imposition of the statutory trust for sale and the resultant conversion of the share into personal estate (see *Re Kempthorne, Charles v Kempthorne* [1930] 1 Ch 268, CA; *Re Newman, Slater v Newman* [1930] 2 Ch 409; and note 13), but which could be construed as passing all the testator's interest in property was saved by a codicil made after 31 December 1925 confirming the will (*Re Wheeler, Jameson v Cotter* [1928] WN 225; *Re Warren, Warren v Warren*; *Re Harvey, Public Trustee v Hosken* [1947] Ch 285, [1947] 1 All ER 349 (where there was no express confirmation of the will)).

157. Effect of sale, exercise of option or assignment.
A specific devise of real property will be adeemed if the testator subsequently sells it[1]. Such a gift will also be adeemed where the testator enters into a specifically enforceable contract to sell it[2]. Anomalously, the doctrine has been extended to specifically devised property over which the testator grants an option to purchase after the date of the will which is not exercised until after his death[3]. There will, however, be no ademption

in such a case if the context of the will or the circumstances of the case show that the testator had the option present to his mind at the date of the will[4], or otherwise that the donee was intended to take the whole interest of the testator[5]. The exercise of an option which is created before the date of the will does not, however, adeem the gift[6], as the property in the state in which it is given is subject to the option and the donee is, therefore, entitled to the purchase money payable on the exercise of the option[7].

An inter vivos transfer of property which is not formally complete before a testator's death may still constitute a valid equitable assignment[8].

1   *Arnald v Arnald* (1784) 1 Bro CC 401; *Whiteway v Fisher* (1861) 9 WR 433; *Manton v Tabois* (1885) 30 ChD 92. The doctrine is unaffected by the Trusts of Land and Appointment of Trustees Act 1996 s 3, which abolished conversion in relation to property held on an express trust for sale: see REAL PROPERTY AND REGISTRATION vol 87 (2012) PARAS 7, 215. As to the doctrine of conversion see further EQUITABLE JURISDICTION vol 47 (2014) PARA 138 et seq. In *Davenport v National Westminster Bank plc* (14 April 2005, unreported), Ch D), it was held that a specific devise of property which was subsequently sold by the testator's attorney under an enduring power was adeemed (not following *Re Viertel* [1996] QSC 66, [2003] WTLR 1075, Qld SC, in which it was held on similar facts that the gift was not adeemed on the grounds that the testator had had no notice of the sale). See also *Banks v National Westminster Bank plc* [2005] EWHC 3479 (Ch), [2005] All ER (D) 159 (Apr) (donee, having power of attorney, sold house given to her under will and caused gift to adeem; reasoning in *Re Viertel* above, based on testator's ignorance as to sale, not followed).
2   *Hillingdon Estates Co v Stonefield Estates Ltd* [1952] Ch 627 at 632, [1952] 1 All ER 853 at 856. For this purpose, an enforceable right conferred by statute to acquire property will adeem a specific gift of that property: *Re Galway's Will Trusts, Lowther v Viscount Galway* [1950] Ch 1, [1949] 2 All ER 419 (vesting of coal and coal mines under the Coal Act 1938). A notice to treat under the Compulsory Purchase Act 1965 will not of itself adeem a specific gift of property as it does not create a contract of which the court would decree specific performance (*Haynes v Haynes* (1861) 1 Drew & Sm 426 (notice to treat under the Lands Clauses Consolidation Act 1845)); aliter if the price has been fixed, whether by agreement, arbitration or otherwise, for then there is an enforceable agreement (*Harding v Metropolitan Rly Co* (1872) 7 Ch App 154). See also *Re Sweeting, Sweeting v Sweeting* [1988] 1 All ER 1016.
3   *Lawes v Bennett* (1785) 1 Cox Eq Cas 167; *Weeding v Weeding* (1861) 1 John & H 424; *Re Carrington, Ralphs v Swithenbank* [1932] 1 Ch 1, CA (where *Lawes v Bennett* and *Weeding v Weeding* were said to have been acted on too long for the court to overrule them); *Re Rose, Midland Bank Executor and Trustee Co v Rose* [1949] Ch 78, [1948] 2 All ER 971. See also *Re Isaacs, Isaacs v Reginall* [1894] 3 Ch 506 (which applies the doctrine to intestacy). Notice to exercise the option effects a conversion, even if not followed up by completion: *Re Blake, Gawthorne v Blake* [1917] 1 Ch 18. However, the determination, after the testator's death, of a lease containing a provision for determination on payment of compensation does not deprive the specific legatee of the right to the compensation: *Coyne v Coyne* (1876) IR 10 Eq 496.
    The rule applies also to a conditional, but specifically enforceable, contract for the sale of specifically devised property where the contract becomes unconditional after the testator's death: *Re Sweeting, Sweeting v Sweeting* [1988] 1 All ER 1016.
4   *Re Pyle, Pyle v Pyle* [1895] 1 Ch 724 at 729.
5   See *Re Calow, Calow v Calow* [1928] Ch 710 (contract). See also *Re Isaacs, Isaacs v Reginall* [1894] 3 Ch 506 at 510, explaining *Emuss v Smith* (1848) 2 De G & Sm 722 (option to be exercisable only after death).
6   Where the question is whether property passes under a general gift of realty or a general gift of personalty, the exercise of an option over land which was granted before the will was made will cause the property to devolve as personalty: *Lawes v Bennett* (1785) 1 Cox Eq Cas 167.
7   *Drant v Vause* (1842) 1 Y & C Ch Cas 580; *Emuss v Smith* (1848) 2 De G & Sm 722 (codicil after date of contract); *Re Pyle, Pyle v Pyle* [1895] 1 Ch 724. As to the creation of options to purchase by will see PARA 125.
8   See *Pennington v Waine* [2002] EWCA Civ 227, [2002] 4 All ER 215, [2002] 1 WLR 2075 (failure to deliver a share transfer before the death of testatrix did not prevent a finding that a valid inter vivos equitable assignment of the shares had taken place).

158.   No ademption where change of investment contemplated. Where the nature of the property has changed, the first consideration, in deciding whether a gift is adeemed, must always be the words used by the testator in describing or dealing with the property bequeathed[1]. From the words of the particular will, construed according to the usual rules in cases of description[2], the court may find that the testator contemplated a change of investment[3], and that the thing bequeathed is the property which for the time being represents the property which the testator formerly had[4]. In such a case the gift is not dependent on the specific investments representing the gift at the date of the will, but includes reinvestments into which they can be traced[5].

1   *Re Bridle* (1879) 4 CPD 336 at 341 per Lindley J; *Re Slater, Slater v Slater* [1906] 2 Ch 480 at 484 per Joyce J. See also *Re Dorman* [1994] 1 All ER 804, [1994] 1 WLR 282 (no ademption caused by transfer between accounts, as reference to money in particular account construed as money in a fund for a particular purpose; construction narrowly restricted to language used, as intention normally plays no part in question of ademption); but see also reference to testamentary intentions in double portions and residuary gift cases in *Re Cameron, Phillips v Cameron* [1999] Ch 386 at 420, [1999] 2 All ER 924 at 953 (see PARA 155 text and note 2).
2   See PARA 282.
3   *Sidebotham v Watson* (1853) 11 Hare 170 at 174. See also *Earl of Thomond v Earl of Suffolk* (1718) 1 P Wms 461.
4   See *Re Moses, Beddington v Beddington* [1902] 1 Ch 100 at 120, CA; affd sub nom *Beddington v Baumann* [1903] AC 13 at 15, HL, per Earl of Halsbury, LC. See also *Bronsdon v Winter* (1738) Amb 57. A bequest of specified securities or investments representing the same will pass money on deposit representing the securities: *Re Lewis's Will Trusts, O'Sullivan v Robbins* [1937] Ch 118, [1937] 1 All ER 227. See also *Re Bancroft, Bancroft v Bancroft* [1928] Ch 577 (where a bequest of 'all my rights' in a play carried the purchase money under a contract by the testator to sell the play and the contract was not completed until after his death).
5   *Le Grice v Finch* (1817) 3 Mer 50; *Clark v Browne* (1854) 2 Sm & G 524 (these cases were, however, doubted, on the question of construction involved, in *Harrison v Jackson* (1877) 7 ChD 339 at 342–343 per Jessel MR); *Lee v Lee* (1858) 27 LJ Ch 824; *Moore v Moore* (1860) 29 Beav 496; *Morgan v Thomas* (1877) 6 ChD 176 (followed in *Re Kenyon's Estate, Mann v Knapp* (1887) 56 LT 626); *Re Johnstone's Settlement* (1880) 14 ChD 162; *Willett v Finlay* (1892) 29 LR Ir 156 (affd 29 LR Ir 497, Ir CA), explained, as decided on the ground stated in the text to note 4, in *Re Moses, Beddington v Beddington* [1902] 1 Ch 100 at 121, CA (on appeal sub nom *Beddington v Baumann* [1903] AC 13, HL). For this purpose, money on deposit may be an investment: *Re Lewis's Will Trusts, O'Sullivan v Robbins* [1937] Ch 118, [1937] 1 All ER 227; cf *Re Dorman* [1994] 1 All ER 804, [1994] 1 WLR 282 (cited in PARA 156 note 16).

159.   Payment of debt. A bequest of a debt is adeemed by the whole debt being paid to the testator in his lifetime, whether the payment is compulsory or voluntary, and whether the sum is expressed in the bequest or the debt is bequeathed generally[1]. It seems that an inter vivos assignment or transfer into a settlement of the debt will bring about the same effect[2]. The bequest is adeemed pro tanto if the testator receives payment of part of the debt[3].

1   *Earl of Thomond v Earl of Suffolk* (1718) 1 P Wms 461; *Rider v Wager* (1752) 2 P Wms 329; *A-G v Parkin* (1769) Amb 566; *Stanley v Potter* (1789) 2 Cox Eq Cas 180; *Badrick v Stevens* (1792) 3 Bro CC 431; *Fryer v Morris* (1804) 9 Ves 360; *Barker v Rayner* (1826) 2 Russ 122; *Gardner v Hatton* (1833) 6 Sim 93; *Sidney v Sidney* (1873) LR 17 Eq 65; *Re Bridle* (1879) 4 CPD 336. See also *Re Shortts* [1954] 2 DLR 817, OWN 481, Ont HC.
2   *Bizzey v Flight* (1876) 3 Ch D 269, 45 LJ Ch 852.
3   *Ashburner v Macquire* (1786) 2 Bro CC 108 (bankruptcy dividends).

(4) DOCTRINE OF LAPSE

(i) Meaning and Application of Lapse

160.   Meaning of 'lapse'. The term 'lapse' is applied to the failure of a testamentary gift owing to the death of the devisee or legatee in the testator's lifetime[1], whether before or after the date of the will[2], but the testator may indicate in his will that he is using the word in a wider sense[3]. As a rule[4] a devisee or legatee must survive the testator[5] in order that he or his estate may have the benefit of the gift[6], and a confirmation by codicil of a gift in a will to a legatee who has died since the date of the will does not prevent a lapse[7].

1 *Elliott v Davenport* (1705) 1 P Wms 83.
2 *Maybank v Brooks* (1780) 1 Bro CC 84 (where it was held that extrinsic evidence was inadmissible to prove that the testator knew at the date of his will that the legatee was dead); *Clarke v Clemmans, Selway v Clemmans* (1866) 36 LJ Ch 171. A provision in a will against lapse of legacies given by 'this my will' extends to legacies given by a codicil: *Re Smith, Prada v Vandroy* [1916] 2 Ch 368, CA. In relation to testators dying on or after 1 January 1983 and before 1 January 1996 there was also a statutory lapse of a gift to a spouse if there had been dissolution or annulment of the marriage under the Wills Act 1837 s 18A but it did not mean the same as lapse in its ordinary meaning: see *Re Sinclair, Lloyds Bank plc v Imperial Cancer Research Fund* [1985] Ch 446, [1985] 1 All ER 1066, CA; and PARA 177. 'Marriage' includes marriage of a same sex couple: see the Marriage (Same Sex Couples) Act 2013 Sch 3 para 1(1)(a), (2), (3); and MATRIMONIAL AND CIVIL PARTNERSHIP LAW vol 72 (2015) PARAS 1–2. As to the position relating to deaths on or after 1 January 1996 see PARA 178; and as to the position relating to the dissolution or annulment of civil partnerships see PARA 179. As to the consequences of lapse and other types of failure of gifts see PARA 180 et seq.
3 See *Re Fox's Estate, Dawes v Druitt* [1937] 4 All ER 664, CA.
4 For exceptions see PARA 163 et seq.
5 As to the burden of proof of survivorship see PARA 33.
6 5 Bac Abr, Legacies and Devises (L) 4, Legacies (E); *Eliott v Davenport* (1705) 1 P Wms 83. The rule applies to a devise by A on the trusts of the will of a deceased person, and the devise fails as regards devisees who predecease A: *Culsha v Cheese* (1849) 7 Hare 236 at 245. See also *Re Currie's Settlement, Re Rooper, Rooper v Williams* [1910] 1 Ch 329; but cf *Re Playfair, Palmer v Playfair* [1951] Ch 4, [1950] 2 All ER 285.
7 *Hutcheson v Hammond* (1790) 3 Bro CC 128. See also *Re Fraser, Lowther v Fraser* [1904] 1 Ch 726, CA.

161. Application of doctrine of lapse to powers. The doctrine of lapse applies to powers created by will, and a power of appointment[1] or of charging settled estates[2] fails if the testator survives the donee of the power, but the death of the donee of a power prior to the testator does not cause the interests of persons taking in default of appointment to lapse[3].

A power to appoint by will to an individual cannot be exercised in favour of his executors if the individual dies before the donee of the power[4], and, therefore, any appointment to the individual lapses if he predeceases the donee[5]. Where, however, a power of appointment among a class or among named individuals is given by will, and all the objects survive the testator, but one or more die in the lifetime of the donee of the power, the power may be exercised in favour of the survivors[6]. Where there is such a power and the trust estate, in default of appointment, is given to the objects as tenants in common, the death of any object during the testator's lifetime defeats pro tanto the power and the devise over, so that they only remain as to the shares of the survivors[7].

1 *Jones v Southall (No 2)* (1862) 32 Beav 31; *Sharpe v M'Call* [1903] 1 IR 179. See also *Re Baker, Steadman v Dicksee* [1934] WN 94, CA.
2 *Griggs v Gibson, Maynard v Gibson (No 2)* (1866) 35 LJ Ch 458. As to the lapse of powers see further TRUSTS AND POWERS vol 98 (2013) PARAS 568–570, 573.
3 *Nichols v Haviland* (1855) 1 K & J 504. See also *Hardwick v Thurston* (1828) 4 Russ 380; *Edwards v Saloway* (1848) 2 Ph 625; *Kellett v Kellett* (1871) IR 5 Eq 298. As to appointment by a donee who outlives the power see TRUSTS AND POWERS vol 98 (2013) PARA 604.
4 *Re Susanni's Trusts* (1877) 47 LJ Ch 65. An appointment under a general power may be saved from lapse by a substitutional appointment to the executors or administrators of the object of the power: see TRUSTS AND POWERS vol 98 (2013) PARA 568.
5 *Duke of Marlborough v Lord Godolphin* (1750) 2 Ves Sen 61; *Freeland v Pearson* (1867) LR 3 Eq 658 (following *Reid v Reid* (1858) 25 Beav 469; *Kennedy v Kingston* (1821) 2 Jac & W 431). See also *Re Brookman's Trust* (1869) 5 Ch App 182 (where there was a covenant in a marriage

settlement to appoint by will, and the object of the power died in the lifetime of the covenantor); *Muir (or Williams) v Muir* [1943] AC 468 at 485, HL, per Lord Romer. As to surviving objects taking by implication, where no appointment is made and there is no gift over: see TRUSTS AND POWERS vol 98 (2013) PARAS 29–31.

6   See TRUSTS AND POWERS vol 98 (2013) PARA 545.
7   It seems that any purported exercise of the power for an amount greater than that for which it is exercisable, will only be good for the correct amount: see *Re Turner, Hudson v Turner* [1932] 1 Ch 31, 101 LJ Ch 49 (widow of testator, having power to appoint between two children, one dying during the testator's lifetime, purported to exercise power in favour of survivor; held that her powers only extended to one half of the trust estate).

162.   Charities ceasing to exist. Legacies to charitable institutions[1] ceasing to exist in the testator's lifetime lapse[2] or are applicable cy-près[3], depending on whether the gift is construed to be for the benefit of the particular institution or to import a general charitable intention[4].

Where a relevant charity merger under the Charities Act 2011[5] takes place before the death of a testator whose will specifies a gift to one of the previous charities, the gift takes effect as a gift to the merged charity[6], unless the will provides otherwise[7].

Where a testator makes a bequest, without any limitation or trust, to a limited company established for charitable purposes, the gift is a beneficial gift; it cannot be implied from the fact that the bequest was made to a company established for charitable purposes that the testator intended the company to take as trustee for charitable purposes[8]. Where such a company is in insolvent liquidation at the date of his death, but has not been formally dissolved, the gift takes effect, unless the terms of the bequest, properly construed, provided otherwise[9].

1   As to gifts to non-charitable societies see PARA 36.
2   See CHARITIES vol 8 (2015) PARA 148 et seq.
3   As to the doctrine of cy-près see CHARITIES vol 8 (2015) PARA 209 et seq.
4   As to the existence of a general charitable intention see CHARITIES vol 8 (2015) PARA 168 et seq.
5   Ie under the Charities Act 2011 s 306; see CHARITIES vol 8 (2015) PARA 322–323.
6   See the Charities Act 2011 s 311 (re-enacting the Charities Act 1993 s 75F); and CHARITIES vol 8 (2015) PARA 323.
7   See, for eg, *Berry v IBS-STL (UK) LTD (in liquidation)* [2012] EWHC 666 (Ch), [2012] All ER (D) 10 (Mar) (gift of residue to be shared by such of six charities as were in existence at the date of the testatrix's death; in the event of any charity having ceased to exist, the trustees were entitled to distribute according to their discretion, and hence they were not required to pay a portion of the residual estate to a successor charity, which had by that time gone into liquidation).
8   *ARMS (Multiple Sclerosis Research) Ltd, Re, Alleyne v A-G* [1997] 2 All ER 679; [1997] 1 WLR 877; followed in *Re Wedgewood Museum Trust Ltd (in Administration); Young v A-G* [2011] EWHC 3782 (Ch). Gifts to such a company are therefore available to its creditors.
9   The company does not cease to exist until it is formally dissolved: *ARMS (Multiple Sclerosis Research) Ltd, Re, Alleyne v A-G* [1997] 2 All ER 679; [1997] 1 WLR 877. Since the bequests in *ARMS (Multiple Sclerosis Research) Ltd, Re, Alleyne v A-G* were intended to be in favour of the company which was in existence at the date of each testator's death, albeit in compulsory liquidation, they were still available to the creditors of the company.

(ii)   Exceptions from Lapse

163.   Gifts in pursuance of moral obligation. The doctrine of lapse does not apply, even though the legatee predeceases the testator, where the legacy is given with the intention of discharging a moral obligation[1], whether legally binding or not, which is recognised by the testator and is existing at his death[2]. The doctrine applies, however, to a settlement by will made in pursuance of a covenant in marriage articles[3]. A bequest of a debt to the debtor or to him, his executors and administrators, coupled with a direction to hand over securities, lapses like an ordinary legacy[4].

1   Eg a statute-barred debt (*Williamson v Naylor* (1838) 3 Y & C Ex 208; *Philips v Philips* (1844) 3 Hare 281 at 290), or a debt barred by a discharge in bankruptcy (*Re Sowerby's Trusts* (1856) 2 K & J 630; *Turner v Martin* (1857) 7 De GM & G 429). See, however, *Coppin v Coppin* (1725) 2 P Wms 291 at 296 (where legacies to creditors of the amounts of debts which had been released were treated as voluntary gifts).
2   *Stevens v King* [1904] 2 Ch 30; *Re Leach, Chatterton v Leach* [1948] Ch 232, [1948] 1 All ER 383 (legacy by testatrix to her deceased son's creditor).
3   *Re Brookman's Trust* (1869) 5 Ch App 182.
4   *Elliott v Davenport* (1705) 1 P Wms 83; *Toplis v Baker* (1787) 2 Cox Eq Cas 118; *Maitland v Adair* (1796) 3 Ves 231; *Izon v Butler* (1815) 2 Price 34. See also *South v Williams* (1842) 12 Sim 566 (where the will was held to express an intention that the legacy should not lapse).

164.   Alternative gifts. Where it is clear that, in the event of the legatee or devisee predeceasing the testator, an alternative bequest is intended to be substituted[1], the alternative gift takes effect notwithstanding the death of the original legatee in the testator's lifetime. Thus a gift to a person or his heirs has been treated as an alternative bequest under which the next of kin surviving the testator might take[2]. If, however, the intention is merely to signify that the legatee is to take a vested and transmissible interest, the legacy lapses in the ordinary way[3], and the mere addition to the name of the devisee[4] or legatee[5] of words of limitation such as 'and his executors', or formerly 'and his heirs', or the like, or a declaration that a devise or legacy is not to lapse, if unaccompanied by a gift by way of substitution[6], or a declaration that a gift is to vest as from the date of the will, even though words of limitation are added to the name of the legatee or devisee[7], does not prevent a lapse. A declaration that, if any of certain named legatees die in the lifetime of the testator leaving issue living at his death, the benefits given to the legatees so dying are not to lapse, but are to take effect as if those legatees had died immediately after the testator, prevents a lapse, and the benefits of those legatees pass to their respective legal personal representatives as part of their estates[8].

1   As to alternative gifts generally see PARA 320 et seq.
2   *Re Porter's Trust* (1857) 4 K & J 188 at 193.
3   *Re Porter's Trust* (1857) 4 K & J 188 at 193; *Corbyn v French* (1799) 4 Ves 418.
4   *Hutton v Simpson* (1716) 2 Vern 722; *Goodright v Wright* (1717) 1 P Wms 397. As to words of limitation being unnecessary in a will to pass an estate of inheritance in realty see PARA 376.
5   *Elliott v Davenport* (1705) 1 P Wms 83; *Stone v Evans* (1740) 2 Atk 86; *Maybank v Brooks* (1780) 1 Bro CC 84; *Re Currie's Settlement, Re Rooper, Rooper v Williams* [1910] 1 Ch 329 at 333–334.
6   *Sibley v Cook* (1747) 3 Atk 572. See also *Underwood v Wing* (1855) 4 De GM & G 633.
7   *Browne v Hope* (1872) LR 14 Eq 343.
8   *Re Greenwood, Greenwood v Sutcliffe* [1912] 1 Ch 392 (following *Re Clunies-Ross, Stubbings v Clunies-Ross* (1912) 106 LT 96; and distinguishing *Re Gresley's Settlement, Willoughby v Drummond* [1911] 1 Ch 358 and *Re Scott* [1901] 1 KB 228, CA). An appointment by a testatrix in favour of her husband, where she directs that the will is to take effect whether she survives or predeceases him, does not, if he predeceases her, operate in favour of his estate, and there is a lapse: *Re Ladd, Henderson v Porter* [1932] 2 Ch 219.

165.   Legacy to executors of deceased legatee. A legacy may be given to the executors or administrators of a deceased person as an original gift[1], or to the executors or administrators of the legatee as a substitutional gift in case he predeceases the testator[2]. Such a substitutional gift prevents a lapse by the death of the legatee in the lifetime of the testator, and, although the gift does not actually become part of the legatee's estate[3], it is held by his personal representatives in trust to administer it as if it were part of his estate[4]. Moreover, while the gift does not lapse by the death before the testator of the persons who were the executors or administrators at the date of the will, it lapses by the death before the testator of the beneficiary who would take it under the legatee's will or on his intestacy[5], including a personal representative who is himself sole beneficiary[6]. A gift to a person or his executors or administrators to take effect, not on the testator's death, but at a future date, fails if the donee dies before the testator[7].

1   *Trethewy v Helyar* (1876) 4 ChD 53. See also *Re Newton's Trusts* (1867) LR 4 Eq 171 (where a gift of personal estate to the heirs and assigns of a deceased person was treated as a gift to her statutory next of kin).
2   In the following cases lapse was prevented: *Sibley v Cook* (1747) 3 Atk 572 (bequest to A and his executors or administrators with declaration against lapse); *Long v Watkinson* (1852) 17 Beav 471 (to A 'and in case of his death to his executors or administrators'); *Hewitson v Todhunter* (1852) 22 LJ Ch 76 (declaration that, if the legatee died in the testator's lifetime, the legacy should not lapse, but should go to his personal representatives); *Re Wilder's Trusts* (1859) 27 Beav 418 (express words of substitution); *Lord Advocate v Bogie* [1894] AC 83, HL (executors and representatives); *Re Bosanquet, Unwin v Petre* (1915) 85 LJ Ch 14 (personal representative or representatives); *Re Cousen's Will Trusts, Wright v Killick* [1937] Ch 381, [1937] 2 All ER 276 ('interest for his or her personal representatives as part of his or her estate'); *Re Wray, Wray v Wray* [1951] Ch 425, [1951] 1 All ER 375, CA ('be transferred and paid to his personal representatives and form part of his estate and be treated as directed by his will'). See also *Bridge v Abbot* (1791) 3 Bro CC 224 (legal representatives); *Hinchliffe v Westwood* (1848) 2 De G & Sm 216 (reversionary bequest to sons, and, in case of the death of any of them in the lifetime of the tenant for life, to their legal personal representatives); *Re Green's Estate* (1860) 1 Drew & Sm 68 (if no claim by legatee within three years after testator's death, gift to his sister and brother; no lapse by death of legatee in lifetime of testator); *Maxwell v Maxwell* (1868) IR 2 Eq 478 (to younger sons or their executors); *Aspinall v Duckworth* (1866) 35 Beav 307 (declaration against lapse with gift to legatee's executors as part of his personal estate); *Re Smith, Prada v Vandroy* [1916] 2 Ch 368, CA (substituted gift to legal personal representatives of legatees; legacies given by 'this my will' held to include those given by codicil).
        In the following cases there was a lapse, the gift being held to fail on the ground that the expression used did not show an intention to substitute an alternative gift on failure of the primary one: *Bone v Cook* (1824) M'Cle 168 (where a distinction was drawn between a gift to children and a gift to executors or administrators in the event of the death of the legatee); *Smith v Oliver* (1848) 11 Beav 494 (gift to legatee, and, in case of his death, 'not having received his legacy', to his children); *Leach v Leach* (1866) 35 Beav 185 (gifts to remaindermen after life interest; shares of two who died in testator's lifetime lapsed); *Re Masterson, Trevanion v Dumas* [1902] WN 192, CA (gift to remaindermen and their 'heirs and assigns' failed on remaindermen all predeceasing testatrix). As to the general rule that a gift to the executors of a deceased person is taken by them as part of the deceased's estate see PARA 363.
3   This appears to be so notwithstanding that the gift is to the executors or administrators as part of his estate: see *Re Seymour's Trusts* (1859) John 472; *Re Bosanquet, Unwin v Petre* (1915) 85 LJ Ch 14; *Re Cousen's Will Trusts, Wright v Killick* [1937] Ch 381, [1937] 2 All ER 276.
4   *Lord Advocate v Bogie* [1894] AC 83, HL; *Re Cousen's Will Trusts, Wright v Killick* [1937] Ch 381, [1937] 2 All ER 276.
5   *Re Bosanquet, Unwin v Petre* (1915) 85 LJ Ch 14.
6   *Re Cousen's Will Trusts, Wright v Killick* [1937] Ch 381, [1937] 2 All ER 276. See also *Re Wray, Wray v Wray* [1951] Ch 425, [1951] 1 All ER 375, CA.
7   *Tidwell v Ariel* (1818) 3 Madd 403 (legacy to be paid one year after testator's death; 'heir' construed as meaning personal representative). Cf *Re Porter's Trust* (1857) 4 K & J 188 (where *Tidwell v Ariel* was explained).

166.   Interests in tail; testator dying before 1997. Where a testator who died before 1 January 1997 gave an entailed interest or an interest in quasi-entail[1] in property, whether real or personal[2], to a beneficiary who predeceased him leaving issue capable of inheriting under the entail, the gift did not lapse but took effect as if the death of the beneficiary had occurred immediately after the death of the testator[3].

1   As to entailed interests generally see REAL PROPERTY AND REGISTRATION vol 87 (2012) PARA 112 et seq. Entailed interests cannot be created by wills of testators dying on or after 1 January 1997; a gift in the will of such a testator purporting to create an entailed interest will not be effective to do so but will operate instead as a declaration that the property is held in trust for such beneficiary absolutely: see the Trusts of Land and Appointment of Trustees Act 1996 s 2, Sch 1 para 5; and REAL PROPERTY AND REGISTRATION vol 87 (2012) PARA 114; SETTLEMENTS vol 91 (2012) PARAS 506, 577.

2   Between 1 January 1926 and 31 December 1996 inclusive entailed interests could be created in
    personal property as well as in real estate: see the Law of Property Act 1925 s 130(1)–(3), (6)
    (repealed); PARA 387; and REAL PROPERTY AND REGISTRATION vol 87 (2012) PARA 114;
    SETTLEMENTS vol 91 (2012) PARAS 506, 577.
3   Wills Act 1837 s 32 (repealed by the Trusts of Land and Appointment of Trustees Act 1996
    s 25(2), Sch 4). The repeal of the Wills Act 1837 s 32 does not, however, affect any entailed
    interests created before 1 January 1997: Trusts of Land and Appointment of Trustees Act 1996
    s 25(4).

167. Gift to testator's issue; testator dying before 1983. Under the will of a
testator who died before 1 January 1983[1], where there is no contrary intention in
the will[2], a devise or bequest of real or personal property to a child or other issue[3]
of the testator, for any estate or interest not determinable at or before the death
of that child or issue, does not lapse if the devisee or legatee predeceased the
testator leaving issue who were living at the testator's death, but takes effect as if
the devisee or legatee had died immediately after the testator[4], and becomes
disposable under the will[5] of the devisee or legatee, or as part of his estate if he dies
intestate[6]. If the testator intended a gift to go over in the event of his child
predeceasing him, he had expressly so to provide[7].

This rule is also applicable in the case of a gift to a child dead at the date of the
will[8], or where the issue surviving the testator was not living at the death of the
devisee or legatee[9].

The gift must, however, be to the legatee as a designated individual[10]. The
rule is not applicable where the gift is to a class not ascertainable until the
testator's death[11], even where there happens to be only one member of the class[12];
nor is it applicable to the lapse of a gift in joint tenancy where both the donees
predecease the testator and one or both of them leave issue[13].

1   Ie the date on which the substitution of the Wills Act 1837 s 33 by the Administration of Justice
    Act 1982 s 19 came into effect: see s 76(11). Nothing in s 19 affects the will of a testator who died
    before that date: s 73(6)(c). As to the position where the testator died or dies on or after 1 January
    1983 see PARA 169.
2   As to the expression of a contrary intention see *Re Morris, Corfield v Waller* (1916) 86 LJ Ch 456;
    Re Meredith, Davies v Davies [1924] 2 Ch 552; and see *Re Wilson, Lothian v Wilson* (1920) 89 LJ
    Ch 216. See now *Ling v Ling* [2001] All ER (D) 322 (Nov); *Rainbird v Smith* [2012] EWHC 4276
    (Ch), [2013] WTLR 1609; and PARA 169 note 3.
3   The Wills Act 1837 s 33 (as originally enacted) does not apply to collateral relations of the testator
    (*Re Gresley's Settlement, Willoughby v Drummond* [1911] 1 Ch 358), and it does not apply to
    death without attaining a specified age where the attainment of such age is a condition of the
    bequest (*Re Wolson, Wolson v Jackson* [1939] Ch 780, [1939] 3 All ER 852).
        In relation to testators who died on or after 1 January 1970 and before 1 January 1983, the
    Wills Act 1837 s 33 (as originally enacted) has effect as if the reference to a child or other issue of
    the testator (ie the intended beneficiary) included a reference to any illegitimate child of the testator
    and to anyone who would rank as such issue if he, or some other person through whom he
    descended from the testator, had been born legitimate; and as if the reference to the issue of the
    intended beneficiary included a reference to anyone who would rank as such issue if he, or some
    other person through whom he is descended from the intended beneficiary, had been born
    legitimate: Family Law Reform Act 1969 ss 16, 28(3) (s 16 repealed); Family Law Reform Act
    1969 (Commencement No 1) Order 1969, SI 1969/1140, art 2. Personal representatives were,
    however, entitled, by virtue of the Family Law Reform Act 1969 s 17, to convey or distribute
    property without having ascertained that there was no person entitled to any interest by virtue of
    provisions of that Act. Section 17 was repealed with effect from 4 April 1988 by the Family Law
    Reform Act 1987 s 20. Personal representatives must now, therefore, protect themselves by eg
    advertisement under the Trustee Act 1925 s 27 (see *Re Aldhous, Noble v Treasury Solicitor* [1955]
    2 All ER 80, [1955] 1 WLR 459; and TRUSTS AND POWERS vol 98 (2013) PARA 355).
4   Wills Act 1837 s 33 (as originally enacted: see note 1).
5   *Johnson v Johnson* (1843) 3 Hare 157; *Re Mason's Will* (1865) 34 Beav 494. If the child of the
    testator dies bankrupt, the share goes to his trustee in bankruptcy: *Re Pearson, Smith v Pearson*
    [1920] 1 Ch 247 (following a dictum of Stirling LJ in *Re Scott* [1901] 1 KB 228 at 240, CA).
6   *Skinner v Ogle* (1845) 9 Jur 432; *Re Peerless, Peerless v Smith* [1901] WN 151.

7   *Re Mores' Trust* (1851) 10 Hare 171 at 178.
8   *Mower v Orr* (1849) 7 Hare 473; *Wisden v Wisden* (1854) 2 Sm & G 396.
9   *Re Parker* (1860) 1 Sw & Tr 523 (where a testatrix gave all her property to her daughter, and the daughter died in her lifetime leaving a child who also predeceased the testatrix, leaving a child who survived the testatrix). The rule was held to apply where the will was made before but republished after the Wills Act 1837 and the legatee or devisee died after that Act came into operation: *Winter v Winter* (1846) 5 Hare 306.
10 *Re Stansfield, Stansfield v Stansfield* (1880) 15 ChD 84. As to a gift to 'my surviving children' see *Fullford v Fullford* (1853) 16 Beav 565.
11 *Olney v Bates* (1855) 3 Drew 319; *Browne v Hammond* (1858) John 210; *Re Jackson, Shiers v Ashworth* (1883) 25 ChD 162 at 164. As to gifts to a class see PARAS 174–175.
12 *Re Harvey's Estate, Harvey v Gillow* [1893] 1 Ch 567; and see PARA 305.
13 *Re Butler, Joyce v Brew* [1918] 1 IR 394.

168. Effect of death of issue; testator dying before 1983. The rule as to the prevention of lapse under the will of a testator who died before 1 January 1983[1] is aimed solely at preserving the gift to the child in the parent's will and does not in any way affect the administration of the estate of the deceased donee, which is administered in accordance with the law in force at the true date of his death[2]. It is with reference to this true date, and not the fictitious date taken for the purpose of preserving the bequest, that the persons entitled on the donee's death are ascertained[3]. In other respects, however, the gift takes effect exactly as if the actual death of the devisee or legatee had happened immediately after the death of the testator, and with all the consequences of such a death[4]. The property devolves subject to any burden[5] or condition which under the will would have been imposed on the devisee or legatee if he had survived the testator[6].

1   As to this rule see PARA 167.
2   *Re Hurd* [1941] Ch 196, [1941] 1 All ER 238.
3   *Re Basioli, McGahey v Depaoli* [1953] Ch 367, [1953] 1 All ER 301 (not following *Re Councell* (1871) LR 2 P & D 314 and *Re Allen's Trusts* [1909] WN 181).
4   *Johnson v Johnson* (1843) 3 Hare 157; *Eager v Furnivall* (1881) 17 ChD 115 at 118. Hence, if the child died a bankrupt, the benefit of the gift vests in the trustee in bankruptcy: see PARA 167 note 5.
5   *Pickersgill v Rodger* (1876) 5 ChD 163 at 172.
6   See further *Kellett v Kellett* (1871) IR 5 Eq 298; *Re Hensler, Jones v Hensler* (1881) 19 ChD 612; and *Re Basioli, McGahey v Depaoli* [1953] Ch 367 at 375, [1953] 1 All ER 301 at 304. See also *Re Hone's Trusts* (1883) 22 ChD 663; *Pearce v Graham* (1863) 9 Jur NS 568; *Re Blundell, Blundell v Blundell* [1906] 2 Ch 222 at 229; *Eager v Furnivall* (1881) 17 ChD 115; *Re Derbyshire, Webb v Derbyshire* [1906] 1 Ch 135.

169. Gift to testator's issue; testator dying after 1982. Where the will of a testator who dies on or after 1 January 1983[1] contains a devise or bequest to a child or remoter descendant of the testator (including members of a class consisting of such persons), and the intended beneficiary dies before the testator, leaving issue[2], and issue of the intended beneficiary are living at the testator's death, then, unless a contrary intention appears by the will[3], the devise or bequest takes effect as a devise or bequest to the issue living at the testator's death[4]. As previously, if the testator intends a gift which would otherwise be subject to these provisions to go over to a different destination on the intended beneficiary's death, he must expressly so provide[5].

Issue are to take under these provisions through all degrees, according to their stock, in equal shares if more than one, any gift or share which their parent would have taken, but no issue may take whose parent is living at the testator's death and so capable of taking[6]. However[7], in the case of a death occurring on or after 1 February 2012[8], where a will contains a devise or bequest to a person who disclaims it[9] or has been precluded by the forfeiture rule[10] from acquiring it[11], he must, unless a contrary intention appears by the will, be treated for the purposes of the Wills Act 1837 as having died immediately before the testator[12].

1   Ie the date on which the substitution of the Wills Act 1837 s 33 by the Administration of Justice Act 1982 s 19 came into effect: see s 76(11). Nothing in s 19 affects the will of a testator who died before that date: s 73(6)(c).

2   For this purpose, the illegitimacy of any person is to be disregarded (Wills Act 1837 s 33(4)(a) (s 33 substituted by the Administration of Justice Act 1982 s 19)); and a person conceived before the testator's death and born living thereafter is to be taken to have been living at the testator's death (Wills Act 1837 s 33(4)(b) (as so substituted)). Since under s 33 the gift devolves on the issue of the deceased child, an unborn child who is en ventre sa mère at the testator's death would, it is thought, be eligible on the general principle of construction established in *Elliott v Lord Joicey* [1935] AC 209, HL. As to class gifts see PARAS 174–175.

3   As to the expression of a contrary intention see the cases cited in PARA 167 note 2. See also *Ling v Ling* [2001] All ER (D) 322 (Nov) (substitutional gift to all or any of testator's children, living at his death who attained the age of 21 did not show contrary intention sufficient to exclude issue of child who predeceased testator, but who had attained the age of 21 before dying) ; but in *Rainbird v Smith* [2012] EWHC 4276 (Ch); [2013] WTLR 1609 the correct construction of the particular will was that the testator had not intended a bequest to her daughter to pass to the daughter's children under s 33. See also *Bush v Jouliac* [2006] EWHC 363 (Ch), [2006] All ER (D) 108 (Jan), where the necessary contrary intention failed to appear on the face of the will by reason of a clerical error, which was ordered to be rectified. As to rectification see PARA 188.

4   Wills Act 1837 s 33(1) (as substituted: see note 2). Where there is a class gift to the testator's children or remoter descendants and any member of the class predeceases the testator leaving surviving issue, then the class is statutorily extended to include such of that issue as are living at the time of the testator's death, subject to contrary intention in the will: see s 33(2) (as so substituted) The prior law did not extend to such child class gifts and the gift accrued to the surviving class members. As to class gifts to children see PARA 175.

5   See *Re Mores' Trust* (1851) 10 Hare 171 at 178.

6   Wills Act 1837 s 33(3) (as substituted: see note 2).

7   The Wills Act 1837 s 33 (see the text and notes 1–6) is subject to s 33A (see the text and notes 8–12): see s 33(3) (as substituted (see note 2); and amended by the Estates of Deceased Persons (Forfeiture Rule and Law of Succession) Act 2011 s 2(1), (3)).

8   Ie the date on which the Wills Act 1837 s 33A (added by the Estates of Deceased Persons (Forfeiture Rule and Law of Succession) Act 2011 s 2(1), (2)) came into effect (see the Estates of Deceased Persons (Forfeiture Rule and Law of Succession) Act 2011 (Commencement) Order 2011, SI 2011/2913, art 2).

9   Wills Act 1837 s 33A(1)(a) (as added: see note 8).

10   As to the meaning of 'forfeiture rule' see PARA 40 note 2; definition applied by the Wills Act 1837 s 33A(4) (as added: see note 8).

11   Wills Act 1837 s 33A(1)(b) (as added: see note 8)

12   See the Wills Act 1837 s 33A(2) (as added: see note 8). In a case where a person has been precluded by the forefeiture rule under s 33A(1)(b) (see the text and notes 10–11), s 33A(2) does not affect the power of the court to modify the forfeiture rule conferred by the Forfeiture Act 1982 s 2 (see PARA 40): Wills Act 1837 s 33A(3) (as so added).

170. Gift to testator's issue; exercise of power of appointment. A gift under a general power of appointment to a child predeceasing the testator and leaving issue is preserved from lapse[1], but not a gift under a special power[2], or a power of charging given under a will to a life tenant who dies before the testator[3].

1   See the Wills Act 1837 ss 27, 33 (s 33 substituted by the Administration of Justice Act 1982 s 19); and *Eccles v Cheyne* (1856) 2 K & J 676. See also TRUSTS AND POWERS vol 98 (2013) PARA 577. As to general powers (ie powers that the donee may exercise in favour of such persons as he chooses) see TRUSTS AND POWERS vol 98 (2013) PARAS 43, 577 et seq. The Wills Act 1837 s 33 as substituted does not materially differ from the wording of s 33 as originally enacted and the principle stated in the text continues to apply.

2   *Griffiths v Gale* (1844) 12 Sim 327, 354; *Freeland v Pearson* (1867) LR 3 Eq 658; *Holyland v Lewin* (1884) 26 ChD 266, CA. See further TRUSTS AND POWERS vol 98 (2013) PARA 570. As to special powers (ie powers which may be exercised in favour of certain persons only) see TRUSTS AND POWERS vol 98 (2013) PARAS 43, 585 et seq.

3   *Griggs v Gibson, Maynard v Gibson (No 2)* (1866) 35 LJ Ch 458.

171. Shares of residue settled on persons in succession. A bequest of an absolute interest in a fixed share of residue to a named person followed by a direction settling the share does not lapse by reason of the legatee's death in the lifetime of the testator[1]. The testator may make it clear that the trusts of shares directed to be settled are to take effect only if the person to whom the gift is given in the first instance survives the testator. If he does not survive, the share may lapse if given to a named individual[2] or, it seems, accrue to other shares if given to a class[3] or where the gift is made to persons as joint tenants[4].

1 *Re Speakman, Unsworth v Speakman* (1876) 4 ChD 620; *Re Pinhorne, Moreton v Hughes* [1894] 2 Ch 276; *Re Powell, Campbell v Campbell* [1900] 2 Ch 525; *Re Harward, Newton v Bankes* [1938] Ch 632, [1938] 2 All ER 804 (where a legacy given absolutely by the will was settled by a codicil). See also *Re Whitmore, Walters v Harrison* [1902] 2 Ch 66, CA; *Re Walter, Turner v Walter (No 2)* (1912) 56 Sol Jo 632, CA; cf *Re Taylor, Taylor v Taylor* [1931] 2 Ch 237 (share to which legatee 'shall become entitled'). See *Re Osoba, Osoba v Osoba* [1979] 2 All ER 393, [1979] 1 WLR 247, CA (held that the predeceased mother's share of a settled gift to the testator's wife, mother and daughter did not lapse but went to the last surviving beneficiary absolutely. The different purposes attaching to each share were treated as no more than an expression of the testator's motive in making the gift; they were treated as absolute gifts but, there being no words of severance in the will, the gift was one made to joint tenants and no act of severance occurred between the two surviving legatees).
2 *Re Roberts, Tarleton v Bruton* (1885) 30 ChD 234, CA.
3 *Stewart v Jones* (1859) 3 De G & J 532. As to class gifts see PARAS 302–314.
4 *Re Osoba, Osoba v Osoba* [1979] 2 All ER 393, [1979] 1 WLR 247, CA.

172. Future gifts. A legacy to a legatee to become vested at the expiration of a specified period from a testator's death apparently fails if the legatee does not survive the period[1]. If, however, a testator directs payment of the income of a fund for a specified period after his death to one person followed by a bequest of the capital to another, the bequest of the capital does not lapse by that other's death prior to the expiration of the period[2], nor does the death of a prospective life tenant in the testator's lifetime cause a gift in remainder[3] or a contingent limitation over[4] to lapse, although the gift over may lapse from other causes[5]. A bequest in remainder following an absolute gift which would otherwise be void for repugnancy may be rendered valid by the lapse of the prior gift[6].

1 *Smell v Dee* (1707) 2 Salk 415; *Bruce v Charlton* (1842) 13 Sim 65; *Re Eve, Belton v Thompson* (1905) 93 LT 235. See also *Re Laing, Laing v Morrison* [1912] 2 Ch 386. As to cases where payment but not vesting is postponed see PARA 415.
2 *Re Bennett's Trust* (1857) 3 K & J 280; *Re Boam, Shorthouse v Annibal* (1911) 56 Sol Jo 142.
3 *Habergham v Ridehalgh* (1870) LR 9 Eq 395 at 400.
4 *Rackham v De La Mare* (1864) 2 De GJ & Sm 74 (where there was a gift to A for life and after her death to her children, with a gift over in case no child attained a vested interest, and A died in the lifetime of the testator). See also *Re Green's Estate* (1860) 1 Drew & Sm 68; and PARA 446.
5 *Williams v Jones* (1826) 1 Russ 517.
6 *Re Lowman, Devenish v Pester* [1895] 2 Ch 348, CA; *Re Dunstan, Dunstan v Dunstan* [1918] 2 Ch 304. See also PERPETUITIES AND ACCUMULATIONS vol 80 (2013) PARA 95. As to the acceleration of subsequent interests on lapse see PARA 181.

173. Gifts to tenants in common or joint tenants. The doctrine of lapse applies to a devise[1] or bequest[2] to persons as tenants in common, not being a gift to a class[3] or group[4], unless a contrary intention is expressed in the will[5], and the result is that the share of any tenant in common dying before the testator lapses[6]. Lapse also occurs when the share of a tenant in common is revoked[7]. The intention that the share of residue is not to lapse, but is to be taken by the others of the named persons, may be shown by a direction that that share is to fall into residue[8] or by other means[9].

Where, however, property is devised or bequeathed to joint tenants and one of them dies in the testator's lifetime, the doctrine of survivorship prevents a lapse occurring, and the survivor or survivors take the whole[10]. Similarly, if the interest of one of the joint tenants is revoked, the others take the whole and there is no lapse[11].

1   *Ackroyd v Smithson* (1780) 1 Bro CC 503. See also *Digby v Legard* (1774) cited in 3 P Wms at 21.

2   *Bagwell v Dry* (1721) 1 P Wms 700; *Page v Page* (1728) 2 P Wms 489; *Peat v Chapman* (1750) 1 Ves Sen 542; *Re Whiston, Whiston v Woolley* [1924] 1 Ch 122, CA. It may, however, appear from the will that the distribution is to be among such of the named persons as are living at the date of the will: *Re Sharp, Maddison v Gill* [1908] 2 Ch 190, CA. In *Re Featherstone's Trusts* (1882) 22 ChD 111, a direction that the shares should be 'vested legacies' at the time of the testator's death was held to confine the gift to legatees living at his death, but that case is not an authority beyond the particular facts: *Re Whiston, Whiston v Woolley* above; and see *Havergal v Harrison* (1843) 7 Beav 49.

3   As to class gifts see PARAS 174–175. A gift to the children of A, adding their names, is not a class gift, and is subject to lapse: see PARA 175 text and note 10.

4   *Re Peacock, Midland Bank Executor and Trustee Co Ltd v Peacock* [1957] Ch 310, [1957] 2 All ER 98.

5   See the cases cited in notes 8–9.

6   The settlement of the share to which a child 'shall become entitled' does not prevent a lapse if the child predeceases the testator: *Re Taylor, Taylor v Taylor* [1931] 2 Ch 237. It seems, however, that, if one of the named persons has been previously referred to in the will as dead, the fund is divisible among the others and there is no lapse: *Clarke v Clemmans, Selway v Clemmans* (1866) 36 LJ Ch 171; and see *Re Sharp, Maddison v Gill* [1908] 1 Ch 372 (affd [1908] 2 Ch 190, CA).

7   *Owen v Owen* (1738) 1 Atk 494; *Creswell v Cheslyn* (1762) 2 Eden 123 (affd (1763) 3 Bro Parl Cas 246) (approved in *Shaw v M'Mahon* (1843) 4 Dr & War 431 at 438 per Sugden LC, in spite of doubts expressed by Serjeant Hill in 2 Eden 125n); *Ramsay v Shelmerdine* (1865) LR 1 Eq 129; *Sykes v Sykes* (1868) 3 Ch App 301; *Re Forrest, Carr v Forrest* [1931] 1 Ch 162; *Re Midgley, Barclays Bank Ltd v Midgley* [1955] Ch 576, [1955] 2 All ER 625.

8   *Re Palmer, Palmer v Answorth* [1893] 3 Ch 369, CA (overruling on this ground *Humble v Shore* (1847) 1 Hem & M 550n); *Re Allan, Dow v Cassaigne* [1903] 1 Ch 276, CA; *Re Wand, Escritt v Wand* [1907] 1 Ch 391. See also PARA 298.

9   *Harris v Davis* (1844) 1 Coll 416; *Vaudrey v Howard* (1853) 2 WR 32; *Re Hornby's Will* (1859) 7 WR 729; *Re Spiller, Spiller v Madge* (1881) 18 ChD 614; *Re Radcliffe, Young v Beale* (1903) 51 WR 409; *Watson v Donaldson* [1915] 1 IR 63, Ir CA; *Re Wilkins, Wilkins v Wilkins* [1920] 2 Ch 63; *Re Clay, Spencer v Clay* (1922) 153 LT Jo 473; *Re Woods, Woods v Creagh* [1931] 2 Ch 138. In *Re Whiting, Ormond v De Launay* [1913] 2 Ch 1, the mere confirmation of the will in other respects was held sufficient to give the revoked share to the other legatees; but cf *Cheslyn v Cresswell* (1763) 3 Bro Parl Cas 246; *Humble v Shore* (1847) 1 Hem & M 550n (apparently not affected on this ground by *Re Palmer, Palmer v Answorth* [1893] 3 Ch 369, CA); *Re Wood's Will* (1861) 29 Beav 236; *Sykes v Sykes* (1868) 3 Ch App 301 (where there were words in the codicil confirming the will: see *Re Whiting, Ormond v De Launay* above at 3). The decision in *Re Whiting, Ormond v De Launay* above was not followed in *Re Wilkins, Wilkins v Wilkins* above, was doubted in *Re Forrest, Carr v Forrest* [1931] 1 Ch 162, and was distinguished in *Re Midgley, Barclays Bank Ltd v Midgley* [1955] Ch 576, [1955] 2 All ER 625.

10 *Davies v Kempe* (1663) 1 Eq Cas Abr 216 pl 7; *Willing v Baine* (1731) 3 P Wms 113; *Buffar v Bradford* (1741) 2 Atk 220; *Morley v Bird* (1798) 3 Ves 629. See *Re Osoba, Osoba v Osoba* [1979] 2 All ER 393 [1979] 1 WLR 247, CA, where the absence of words of severance in the will was held to create a joint tenancy, so as to defeat a claim that the share of a predeceased legatee had lapsed. See also *Re Bourke's Will Trusts, Barclays Bank Trust Co Ltd v Canada Permanent Trust Co* [1980] 1 All ER 219, [1980] 1 WLR 539, where a gift to 'heirs and surviving issue', without words of severance, created a joint tenancy.

11 *Humphrey v Tayleur* (1752) Amb 136 at 137–138; and see *Sykes v Sykes* (1867) LR 4 Eq 200 at 204–205 (affd (1868) 3 Ch App 301) (tenancy in common).

174. Class gifts. In the case of a gift to a fluctuating[1] class[2], or group[3], as tenants in common, to be ascertained at any particular time, no lapse occurs if a member of the class dies before that time, the class being automatically contracted[4]. Similarly, where a member of the class is precluded from participation either expressly by exception or revocation[5], or by his attesting the will[6], or by being debarred from benefiting on public policy grounds[7], there is no lapse, and the property is divided among those members who are capable of taking. This rule is not, however, applicable where an appointment is made under a power to objects and non-objects; in such a case the part invalidly appointed goes as in default of appointment[8].

A proviso in a class gift that the share of any member predeceasing the testator and leaving issue is not to lapse, but is to go to his executors, does not cause the share of a member dying without issue to lapse so as to exclude the other members of the class from taking the share[9]. It seems that the use of the words 'per stirpes' in relation to the members of a class, or a gift to several persons who do not comprise a class, may indicate that the gift is not to be defeated by lapse; prima facie it indicates the substitution of issue of that donee, as taking in place of their parent[10].

1   The rule applies whether the class fluctuates by increase or diminution, or by diminution alone: see *Lee v Pain* (1844) 4 Hare 201 at 250; *Leigh v Leigh* (1854) 17 Beav 605; *Dimond v Bostock* (1875) 10 Ch App 358; *Viner v Francis* (1789) 2 Bro CC 658.
2   As to what constitutes a class gift see PARA 175.
3   *Re Peacock, Midland Bank Executor and Trustee Co Ltd v Peacock* [1957] Ch 310, [1957] 2 All ER 98.
4   *Viner v Francis* (1789) 2 Bro CC 658; *Doe d Stewart v Sheffield* (1811) 13 East 526; *Shuttleworth v Greaves* (1838) 4 My & Cr 35; *M'Kay v M'Kay* [1900] 1 IR 213; *Re Dunster, Brown v Heywood* [1909] 1 Ch 103. See also *Re Maynard, Pearce v Pearce* [1930] WN 127.
5   *Re Dunster, Brown v Heywood* [1909] 1 Ch 103; and see *Shaw v M'Mahon* (1843) 4 Dr & War 431; *Clark v Phillips* (1853) 17 Jur 886; *M'Kay v M'Kay* [1900] 1 IR 213. See also *Re Jackson, Shiers v Ashworth* (1883) 25 ChD 162 (to all testator's children born or to be born except his son A). In the case of a gift to named persons 'or such of them as shall be living at my death', the named persons constitute a quasi-class and there is a right of survivorship: see *Re Woods, Woods v Creagh* [1931] 2 Ch 138. See also *Watson v Donaldson* [1915] 1 IR 63, Ir CA.
6   *Fell v Biddolph* (1875) LR 10 CP 701. See also *Young v Davies* (1863) 2 Drew & Sm 167; *Re Coleman and Jarrom* (1876) 4 ChD 165 at 173. As to the failure of gifts to witnesses see PARA 41.
7   *Re Peacock, Midland Bank Executor and Trustee Co Ltd v Peacock* [1957] Ch 310, [1957] 2 All ER 98 (testator's wife, member of class entitled to residue, convicted of manslaughter of testator; share passed to those class members who were capable of taking at testator's death).
8   *Re Farncombe's Trusts* (1878) 9 ChD 652; *Re Turner, Hudson v Turner* [1932] 1 Ch 31, 101 LJ Ch 49; and see TRUSTS AND POWERS vol 98 (2013) PARA 620.
9   *Aspinall v Duckworth* (1866) 35 Beav 307.
10 *Sammut v Manzi* [2008] UKPC 58 at [28], [2009] 2 All ER 234, [2009] 1 WLR 1834 per Lord Hope of Craighead.

175.   Meaning of 'class gift'. Prima facie a class gift is a gift to a class of persons included and comprehended under some general description and bearing a certain relation to the testator or another person or united by some common tie[1]. Thus where a testator divides his residue into as many equal shares as he shall have children surviving him, or predeceasing him leaving issue, and gives a share to or in trust for each such child, the gift is to a class[2]. There may also be a class compounded of persons answering one or other of alternative descriptions, for example 'the children of A and the children of B'[3], or 'the children of A who attain 21 and the issue of such as die under that age'[4].

There may be circumstances where the court must consider whether the testator intended to make a gift to a contingent class or, by contrast, a gift to a class on a contingency; the distinction can be a very fine one, but on the result may depend whether a person will fall within the statutory provisions preventing the lapse of a gift to the issue of a class member who predeceases the testator[5].

A gift may be nonetheless a gift to a class because some of the members are referred to by name[6], or because a person who would otherwise fall within the class is excluded by name[7]. A gift to one person and the children of another is not, however, regarded as a class gift[8] unless there is something in the context to show that the testator intended to form a class or group[9], and gifts to several persons designated by name[10] or number[11] or by reference[12] are not class gifts, and are liable to lapse unless a joint tenancy is created[13] or words are added implying a contingency[14].

1 *Kingsbury v Walter* [1901] AC 187, HL. See also *Viner v Francis* (1789) 2 Bro CC 658; *Re Chaplin's Trusts* (1863) 33 LJ Ch 183; *Pearks v Moseley* (1880) 5 App Cas 714 at 723, HL, Lord Selbourne LC; *Re Featherstone's Trusts* (1882) 22 ChD 111 (as to the restriction of this case to its particular facts see *Re Whiston, Whiston v Woolley* [1924] 1 Ch 122, CA); *Re Maynard, Pearce v Pearce* [1930] WN 127. As to the application of the rule against perpetuities to class gifts see PERPETUITIES AND ACCUMULATIONS vol 80 (2013) PARA 81 et seq.

2 *Re Dunster, Brown v Heywood* [1909] 1 Ch 103 (not following *Ramsay v Shelmerdine* (1865) LR 1 Eq 129). See also *Shaw v M'Mahon* (1843) 4 Dr & War 431.

3 *Kingsbury v Walter* [1901] AC 187 at 193, HL, per Lord Davey. See also *Best v Stonehewer* (1865) 2 De GJ & Sm 537.

4 *Pearks v Moseley* (1880) 5 App Cas 714 at 722, HL, per Lord Selbourne LC. As to the identification of donees see PARA 45.

5 See *Ling v Ling* [2001] All ER (D) 322 (Nov); and the Wills Act 1837 s 33(2). See also PARA 169.

6 *Kingsbury v Walter* [1901] AC 187, HL. See also *Shaw v M'Mahon* (1843) 4 Dr & War 431 (to all my children, including A and B); *Re Stanhope's Trusts* (1859) 27 Beav 201 (to four named daughters, and 'all my after-born daughters'); *Re Jackson, Shiers v Ashworth* (1883) 25 ChD 162; *Re Mervin, Mervin v Crossman* [1891] 3 Ch 197. A gift to persons all individually named, or all so described as to be fixed at the time of the gift, and so that there is no fluctuation, is not a class gift: *Cruse v Howell* (1858) 4 Drew 215. But see *Sammut v Manzi* [2008] UKPC 58, [2009] 2 All ER 234, [2009] 1 WLR 1834, where the possibility of a gift to five named persons being construed as a class gift was defeated conclusively by the added words 'in equal shares' after the beneficiaries were named and by a final gift over to the other named beneficiaries if any named beneficiary predeceased the testator without issue. It seems that a class could comprise two named beneficiaries and, if one disclaimed benefit, the class could still exist with a membership of one: *Re Scott, Widdows v Friends of the Clergy Corpn* [1975] 2 All ER 1033, [1975] 1 WLR 1260.

7 *Re Jackson, Shiers v Ashworth* (1883) 25 ChD 162. See also *Dimond v Bostock* (1875) 10 Ch App 358.

8 *Re Wood's Will* (1862) 31 Beav 323; *Re Chaplin's Trusts* (1863) 33 LJ Ch 183 (gift to A and all the children of B); *Re Allen, Wilson v Atter* (1881) 44 LT 240; *Re Venn, Lindon v Ingram* [1904] 2 Ch 52 (gift to the brothers and sisters of A living at her decease and B, C and D in equal shares).

9 *Kingsbury v Walter* [1901] AC 187 at 193, HL, per Lord Davey. See also *Drakeford v Drakeford* (1863) 33 Beav 43 at 48; *Aspinall v Duckworth* (1866) 35 Beav 307; *Re Woods, Woods v Creagh* [1931] 2 Ch 138; *Re Peacock, Midland Bank Executor and Trustee Co Ltd v Peacock* [1957] Ch 310, [1957] 2 All ER 98.

10 *Cresswell v Cheslyn* (1762) 2 Eden 123 (to my sons A and B and my daughter C); *Bain v Lescher* (1840) 11 Sim 397 (gift to the children of A, namely B, C and D); *Burrell v Baskerfield* (1849) 11 Beav 525; *Re Hull's Estate* (1855) 21 Beav 314; *Sykes v Sykes* (1867) LR 4 Eq 200; *Spencer v Wilson* (1873) LR 16 Eq 501; *Re Bentley, Podmore v Smith* (1914) 110 LT 623. See also *Cruse v Howell* (1858) 4 Drew 215; *Re Ramadge* [1969] NI 71 (to my four cousins A, B, C and D in equal shares).

11 *Jacob v Catling* [1881] WN 105. See also *Re Smith's Trusts* (1878) 9 ChD 117; *Re Stansfield, Stansfield v Stansfield* (1880) 15 ChD 84.

12 Eg 'to all the before-mentioned legatees in proportion to their legacies': *Re Gibson's Trusts* (1861) 2 John & H 656; *Nicholson v Patrickson* (1861) 3 Giff 209. The same principle applies to a beneficial gift 'to my executors herein named' (*Barber v Barber* (1838) 3 My & Cr 688; *Hoare v Osborne* (1864) 10 Jur NS 383, 694), but not where the gift is to executors in their official capacity (*Knight v Gould* (1833) 2 My & K 295; *Parsons v Saffery* (1821) 9 Price 578).

13 See *Re Osoba, Osoba v Osoba* [1979] 2 All ER 393, [1979] 1 WLR 247, CA; and PARA 173.

14 Eg a gift to a testator's five great-nieces, A, B, C, D and E equally, to be divided between them if more than one: *Sanders v Ashford* (1860) 28 Beav 609. See also *Re Hornby's Will* (1859) 7 WR 729 (to A, B, C and D 'if living'); *Re Spiller, Spiller v Madge* (1881) 18 ChD 614; *Re Woods, Woods v Creagh* [1931] 2 Ch 138; *Re Peacock, Midland Bank Executor and Trustee Co Ltd v Peacock* [1957] Ch 310, [1957] 2 All ER 98. In *Sammut v Manzi* [2008] UKPC 58 at [32], [2009] 2 All ER 234, [2009] 1 WLR 1834 per Lord Hope of Craighead, the words 'in equal shares', following five named persons, were held to be conclusive against a finding of a class gift.

176. Issue of deceased child; testator dying before 1983. Under the will of a testator who died before 1 January 1983[1], where there is a gift to the children of the testator as a class, a child of the testator who died in his lifetime leaving issue living at the testator's death is not, by virtue of the provision saving gifts to children who so die[2], included as a member of the class[3], and the other members of the class who survive the testator take the subject of the gift between them[4]. However, by suitable words the testator might have substituted the issue of a member of the class for their parent so as to make such issue members of the class[5].

1   Ie the date on which the substitution of the Wills Act 1837 s 33 by the Administration of Justice Act 1982 s 19 came into effect: see s 76(11). Nothing in s 19 affects the will of a testator who died before that date: s 73(6)(c). As to the position under the will of a testator dying on or after 1 January 1983 see PARA 177.
2   Ie the Wills Act 1837 s 33 (as originally enacted) (see PARA 167).
3   See PARA 167.
4   *Re Coleman and Jarrom* (1876) 4 ChD 165 at 168.
5   *Aspinall v Duckworth* (1866) 35 Beav 307; *Re Greenwood, Greenwood v Sutcliffe* [1912] 1 Ch 392; *Re Cousen's Will Trusts, Wright v Killick* [1937] Ch 381 at 391, [1937] 2 All ER 276 at 283–284.

(5) DISSOLUTION OR ANNULMENT OF MARRIAGE OR CIVIL PARTNERSHIP

177. Dissolution or annulment of marriage; deaths after 1982 and before 1996. Where, after a testator has made a will, his marriage is dissolved or annulled[1], and he dies on or after 1 January 1983[2] but before 1 January 1996[3]:

(1)   the will takes effect as if any appointment of the former spouse as an executor and trustee of the will were omitted[4]; and

(2)   any devise or bequest to the former spouse lapses[5],

except in so far as a contrary intention appears by the will[6].

For these purposes, 'lapse' does not have its usual meaning[7]; and the use of the term does not have the result that the spouse, if surviving the testator, is treated as having predeceased him for the purposes of determining the rights of succession to his estate[8]. Thus where a testator left his entire estate to his wife with a gift over in favour of charity if his wife should predecease him or fail to survive him by one month and the marriage was subsequently dissolved and the wife survived him by one month, the gift over was held not to take effect and the estate was held to be undisposed of[9].

Where, however, by the terms of a will an interest in remainder is subject to a life interest and the life interest lapses by virtue of head (2) above, the interest in remainder is to be treated as if it had not been subject to the life interest[10] and, if it was contingent on the termination of the life interest, as if it had not been so contingent[11].

Any failure of a devise or bequest by virtue of head (2) above is without prejudice to any right of the former spouse to apply[12] for reasonable financial provision[13].

1   As originally enacted, the Wills Act 1837 s 18A applied only where the marriage had been dissolved, annulled or declared void by a decree of 'a court'; but s 18A was subsequently amended by the Family Law Act 1986 s 53 with effect from 4 April 1988 so as to apply where the marriage has been dissolved or annulled by a decree of a court of civil jurisdiction in England and Wales (see MATRIMONIAL AND CIVIL PARTNERSHIP LAW vol 72 (2015) PARA 375 et seq), or the marriage has been dissolved or annulled and the divorce or annulment is entitled to recognition in England and Wales by virtue of Pt II (ss 44–54) (see CONFLICT OF LAWS vol 19 (2011) PARA 535 et seq).
2   Ie the date on which the Wills Act 1837 s 18A came into force in relation to deaths on or after that date: Administration of Justice Act 1982 s 76(11). Where the death occurs on or after 1 January

1983, the Wills Act 1837 s 18A applies even if the will was made or the marriage dissolved, annulled or declared void on or before that date.

3 Ie the date with effect from which the Wills Act 1837 s 18A was amended by the Law Reform (Succession) Act 1995 ss 3, 5, Schedule in relation to deaths on or after that date (see PARA 178).

4 Wills Act 1837 s 18A(1)(a) (s 18A added by the Administration of Justice Act 1982 s 18(2)).

5 Wills Act 1837 s 18A(1)(b) (as added: see note 4).

6 Wills Act 1837 s 18A(1) (as added: see note 4).

7 The expression 'lapse' usually means the failure of a testamentary gift owing to the death of the donee in the testator's lifetime: see PARA 160 et seq.

8 *Re Sinclair, Lloyds Bank plc v Imperial Cancer Research Fund* [1985] Ch 446, [1985] 1 All ER 1066, CA (overruling *Re Cherrington* [1984] 2 All ER 285, [1984] 1 WLR 772).

9 *Re Sinclair, Lloyds Bank plc v Imperial Cancer Research Fund* [1985] Ch 446, [1985] 1 All ER 1066, CA; but see PARA 178 note 5.

10 As to the acceleration of subsequent interests generally see PARA 181.

11 Wills Act 1837 s 18A(3) (as added: see note 4). This provision has been repealed in respect of deaths on or after 1 January 1996 by the Law Reform (Succession) Act 1995 s 5, Schedule (see the text and note 3).

12 Ie under the Inheritance (Provision for Family and Dependants) Act 1975 (see PARA 565 et seq).

13 Wills Act 1837 s 18A(2) (as added: see note 4).

178. Dissolution or annulment of marriage; deaths after 1995. Where, after a testator has made a will, a decree of a court of civil jurisdiction in England and Wales dissolves or annuls his marriage[1], or his marriage is dissolved or annulled and the divorce or annulment is entitled to recognition in England and Wales[2], and he dies on or after 1 January 1996[3]:

(1) any provisions of the will appointing executors or trustees or conferring a power of appointment, if they appoint as executor or trustee, or confer the power on, the former spouse, take effect as if the former spouse had died on the date of the dissolution or annulment[4]; and

(2) any property which, or an interest in which, is devised or bequeathed to the former spouse passes as if the former spouse had died on that date[5].

Any failure of a devise or bequest by virtue of head (2) above is without prejudice to any right of the former spouse to apply[6] for reasonable financial provision[7].

1 See MATRIMONIAL AND CIVIL PARTNERSHIP LAW vol 72 (2015) PARA 375 et seq.

2 Ie by virtue of the Family Law Act 1986 Pt II (ss 44–54) (see CONFLICT OF LAWS vol 19 (2011) PARA 535 et seq). 'Marriage' includes marriage of a same sex couple: see the Marriage (Same Sex Couples) Act 2013 Sch 3 para 1(1)(a), (2), (3); and MATRIMONIAL AND CIVIL PARTNERSHIP LAW vol 72 (2015) PARAS 1–2.

3 Ie the date with effect from which the Wills Act 1837 s 18A (as originally added) was amended by the Law Reform (Succession) Act 1995 ss 3, 5, Schedule in respect of deaths on or after that date, regardless of the date of the will and the date of the dissolution or annulment: s 3(2).

4 Wills Act 1837 s 18A(1)(a) (s 18A added by the Administration of Justice Act 1982 s 18(2); the Wills Act 1837 s 18A(1) amended by the Family Law Act 1986 s 53; and s 18A(1)(a), (b) substituted by the Law Reform (Succession) Act 1995 s 3).

5 Wills Act 1837 s 18A(1)(b) (s 18A(1) as added and amended (see note 4); and s 18A(1)(b) as substituted (see note 4)). This effectively reverses *Re Sinclair, Lloyds Bank plc v Imperial Cancer Research Fund* [1985] Ch 446, [1985] 1 All ER 1066, CA (cited in PARA 177 note 8) (see PARA 180 note 6).

6 Ie under the Inheritance (Provision for Family and Dependants) Act 1975 (see PARA 565 et seq).

7 Wills Act 1837 s 18A(2) (as added: see note 4). Section 18A(2) remains unaffected by the amendments made by the Law Reform (Succession) Act 1995 ss 3, 5, Schedule.

179. Dissolution or annulment of civil partnership. If, after a testator has made a will, a court of civil jurisdiction in England and Wales dissolves or annuls his civil partnership[1], or his civil partnership is dissolved or annulled and the dissolution or annulment is entitled to recognition in England and Wales[2], except in so far as a contrary intention appears by the will:

(1)   provisions of the will appointing executors or trustees or conferring a power of appointment, if they appoint or confer the power on the former civil partner, take effect as if the former civil partner had died on the date of the dissolution or annulment[3]; and

(2)   any property which, or an interest in which, is devised or bequeathed to the former civil partner passes as if the former civil partner had died on that date[4].

Any failure of a devise or bequest by virtue of head (2) above is without prejudice to any right of the former civil partner to apply[5] for reasonable financial provision[6].

1 See PARA 90; and MATRIMONIAL AND CIVIL PARTNERSHIP LAW vol 72 (2015) PARA 375 et seq.
2 Ie by virtue of Civil Partnership Act 2004 Pt 5 Ch 3 (ss 219–238) (see CONFLICT OF LAWS vol 19 (2011) PARA 537 et seq).
3 Wills Act 1837 s 18C(1), (2)(a) (s 18C added by the Civil Partnership Act 2004 s 71, Sch 4 paras 1, 2).
4 Wills Act 1837 s 18C(1), (2)(b) (as added: see note 3).
5 Ie under the Inheritance (Provision for Family and Dependants) Act 1975 (see PARA 565 et seq).
6 Wills Act 1837 s 18C(3) (as added: see note 3).

(6) EFFECT OF FAILURE AND LAPSE

180. Lapse or failure of gifts. As a general principle, unless the testator provides otherwise, all gifts, other than gifts of shares or interests in the general residue, which lapse or fail fall into the general residue[1]. If there is no residuary devise or bequest, or if the gift which lapses or fails is of a share or interest in the general residue, the gift passes to those entitled on an intestacy[2], although that prima facie consequence may be altered or affected by the rules on administration of estates, concerning provision for expenses, debts, liabilities and pecuniary legacies[3]. There may be a particular residuary gift, or a gift of the residue of a particular description of property, a specific part of which is the subject of a prior gift, and it may appear that on the failure of the prior gift the subject matter is to fall into the particular residue[4]. Surplus income of residue which is not expressly and validly disposed of during the life of an annuitant does not normally pass under a gift of capital after the death of the annuitant, but passes as on an intestacy[5].

Where the will contains an alternative gift which is expressed to have effect in the event of the donee under the failed gift predeceasing the testator, the alternative gift will not normally be construed as operating where the donee survives the testator and the failure of the gift is for some other reason[6].

1 A gift of land 'not hereinbefore devised' (*Green v Dunn* (1855) 20 Beav 6), or of property 'not . . . disposed of' (*Re Duke of Wellington, Glentanar v Wellington* [1947] Ch 506 at 522–523, [1947] 2 All ER 854 at 862–863; affd [1948] 1 Ch 118, [1947] 2 All ER 854 at 864, CA), carries the land or the property, as the case may be, ineffectively disposed of.
2 See further PARA 183. As to residuary estate see PARAS 1113–1116; and as to intestate succession see PARA 477 et seq. A specific legacy passes on disclaimer under a residuary gift: *Re Backhouse, Westminster Bank Ltd v Shaftesbury Society and Ragged School Union* [1931] WN 168. As to undisposed of interests passing on an intestacy in the absence of a residuary gift see *Hughes v McNaull* [1923] 1 IR 78, Ir CA; *Re Galway* [1944] NI 28. As to the destination of income undisposed of where there is a trust to accumulate for a period exceeding that permitted by law see PERPETUITIES AND ACCUMULATIONS vol 80 (2013) PARAS 157, 160. As to the destination of property directed to be converted where the objects of conversion wholly or partially fail see *Re Hopkinson, Dyson v Hopkinson* [1922] 1 Ch 65; *M'Dermott v A-G (No 2)* [1923] 1 IR 142, CA. As to the effect of the failure of objects see EQUITABLE JURISDICTION vol 47 (2014) PARAS 147–148; and as to the limited importance of the doctrine of conversion after 31 December 1925 see EQUITABLE JURISDICTION vol 47 (2014) PARA 149. Where trusts for sale were

imposed expressly by the trust instrument, then, unless the trust was created by the will of a testator who died before 1 January 1997, the existence of the duty to sell no longer means that the land is to be regarded as personal property: see the Trusts of Land and Appointment of Trustees Act 1996 s 3; and REAL PROPERTY AND REGISTRATION vol 87 (2012) PARAS 7, 215. Thus the doctrine of conversion is now of even more limited importance but it is not wholly abolished by s 3 and will still apply to eg uncompleted agreements for the sale of land. As to the doctrine of conversion see further EQUITABLE JURISDICTION vol 47 (2014) PARA 138 et seq.

3   See the Administration of Estates Act 1925 s 33(1), (2); and *Re Berrey's Will Trusts, Greening v Warner (or Waters)* [1959] 1 All ER 15, [1959] 1 WLR 30 (testamentary and administration expenses were charged against the whole of residue, including a lapsed share, but a fund to provide pecuniary legacies fell primarily on the lapsed share). See also note 4.

4   See eg *Malcolm v Taylor* (1831) 2 Russ & M 416; *De Trafford v Tempest* (1856) 21 Beav 564; *Burke Irwin's Trusts, Barrett v Barrett* [1918] 1 IR 350. Any property of which the testator fails to dispose, either because his will does not contain a gift of general residue, or because a gift of residue does not take effect, is resorted to as the first fund available for the discharge of the funeral, testamentary and administration expenses, debts and liabilities payable out of the testator's estate and also as a fund sufficient to provide for any pecuniary legacies bequeathed: see the Administration of Estates Act 1925 s 33(1), (2); *Re Berrey's Will Trusts, Greening v Warner (or Waters)* [1959] 1 All ER 15, [1959] 1 WLR 30; and note 3. As to the persons entitled on intestacy see PARA 477 et seq.

5   *Re Wragg, Hollingsworth v Wragg* [1959] 2 All ER 717, [1959] 1 WLR 922, CA (distinguishing *Re Shuckburgh's Settlement, Robertson v Shuckburgh* [1901] 2 Ch 794); *Re Nash, Miller v Allen* [1965] 1 All ER 51, [1965] 1 WLR 221. See also *Re Geering, Gulliver v Geering* [1964] Ch 136, [1962] 3 All ER 1043. The income passes under the gift of capital only if there is some context which enables 'after the death' of the annuitant to be interpreted as 'subject to the interest' of the annuitant: *Re Wragg, Hollingsworth v Wragg*. For instances where there has been no such context see PARA 422 note 4. As to the destination of income undisposed of where there is a trust to accumulate for a period exceeding that permitted by law see PERPETUITIES AND ACCUMULATIONS vol 80 (2013) PARAS 157–160.

6   *Re Sinclair, Lloyds Bank plc v Imperial Cancer Research Fund* [1985] Ch 446, [1985] 1 All ER 1066, CA (failure of gift as a result of divorce; for this consequence where the testator's death occurs after 1982 but before 1996 see PARA 177); *Re Robertson, Marsden v Marsden* (1963) 107 Sol Jo 318; *Re Hunter's Executors, Petitioners* 1992 SLT 1141; *Re Jones, Jones v Midland Bank Trust Co Ltd* [1997] [1998] 1 FLR 246, (1997) Times, 29 April, CA (in all the last three cases there was failure of a gift as a result of the donee killing the testator: see PARA 39 note 7). An exception, allowing the alternative gift to take effect, is where there has been a dissolution or annulment of the testator's marriage and the testator dies on or after 1 January 1996, in which case the Wills Act 1837 s 18A (as added and amended) treats the former spouse as dead for the purposes of devolution of any property given to the former spouse: see PARA 178. As to the dissolution and annulment of civil partnerships see PARA 179.

Disclaimer (see PARA 151) and forfeiture (see PARA 39) are other examples of failure of a gift where such an alternative gift would normally not be effective. However, for deaths on or after 1 February 2012 the Estates of Deceased Persons (Forfeiture Rule and Law of Succession) Act 2011, s 1(1), (2), s 2(1), (2) introduces exceptions to enable a person disclaiming or forfeiting their entitlement to be treated as having predeceased for the purposes of Administration of Estates Act 1925 s 46 (statutory trusts on intestacy) (see PARA 485) and Wills Act 1837 s 33 (substitution of issue where gift to issue of testator lapses) (see PARA 169).

181. Acceleration of subsequent interests. The effect of failure of a prior life interest or other particular interest through the donee of that interest being dead or prevented by law from taking the gift[1], for example owing to the attestation of the will by him or his spouse or his civil partner[2], or through revocation by codicil[3], disclaimer[4], forfeiture[5] or lapse[6], is ordinarily to accelerate the subsequent interests which are limited to take effect on the regular determination of that prior interest, but the will may expressly or impliedly indicate a contrary intention[7]. Acceleration may take place even though the effect may be to alter the class of persons designated to take by accelerating the time for ascertaining the class[8]. This will, however, be so only where the terms of the will are consistent with an intention to distribute at a moment which may be anterior to the birth of all the members of the class[9]. Where the trusts following the prior interest are not absolutely vested remainders but are vested subject to being divested, the court will not misconstrue the will in order to give effect to the doctrine of acceleration;

and the effect of a disclaimer is that the residuary estate is held on trust for the remaindermen subject to the defeasance clause[10]. The court construes gifts of subsequent interests as intended to take effect on the failure or determination of the prior interest in any manner[11]. A failure of a prior gift does not, however, accelerate a subsequent executory limitation not taking effect merely on the determination of the prior interests[12]; and subsequent gifts cannot be accelerated where the persons who are to take under them are not in existence[13] or their interests are contingent[14].

1   *Anon* (1431) YB 9 Hen 6 fo 24b; Perkins' Profitable Book s 567. As to the acceleration of interests in remainder subject to a life interest to a spouse or civil partner when the marriage or civil partnership is dissolved or annulled see PARAS 177–179.

2   *Jull v Jacobs* (1876) 3 ChD 703; *Re Clark, Clark v Randall* (1885) 31 ChD 72 (explained in *Aplin v Stone* [1904] 1 Ch 543 at 547–548). See also *Burke v Burke* (1899) 18 NZLR 216; *Re Maybee* (1904) 8 OLR 601. As to the effect of such attestation see PARA 41.

3   *Lainson v Lainson* (1854) 5 De GM & G 754; *Eavestaff v Austin* (1854) 19 Beav 591; *Re Love, Green v Tribe* (1878) 47 LJ Ch 783; *Stephenson v Stephenson* (1885) 52 LT 576; *Re Johnson, Danily v Johnson* (1893) 68 LT 20; *Re Whitehorne, Whitehorne v Best* [1906] 2 Ch 121; *Re Salmonsen, National Provincial Bank Ltd v Salmonsen* (1965) 109 Sol Jo 477. As to revocation by codicil see PARA 95.

4   *Anon* (1459) YB 37 Hen 6 fo 35 pl 23; *Re Scott, Scott v Scott* [1911] 2 Ch 374 at 377; *Re Young, Fraser v Young* [1913] 1 Ch 272 at 275; *Re Willis, Crossman v Kirkaldy* [1917] 1 Ch 365; *Re Hodge, Midland Bank Executor and Trustee Co Ltd v Morrison* [1943] Ch 300, [1943] 2 All ER 304; *Re Davies, Davies v Mackintosh* [1957] 3 All ER 52, [1957] 1 WLR 922; *Re Taylor, Lloyds Bank Ltd v Jones* [1957] 3 All ER 56, [1957] 1 WLR 1043; *Re Hatfeild's Will Trusts* [1958] Ch 469, [1957] 2 All ER 261. See also *Toronto General Trusts Co v Irwin* (1896) 27 OLR 491. But see *Re Scott, Widdows v Friends of the Clergy Corpn* [1975] 2 All ER 1033, [1975] 1 WLR 1260. As to disclaimer see PARA 151.

5   *D'Eyncourt v Gregory* (1864) 34 Beav 36; *Craven v Brady* (1869) 4 Ch App 296; *Blathwayt v Baron Cawley* [1976] AC 397, [1975] 3 All ER 625, HL (where a son born after the forfeiture of a life interest by his father nevertheless took an entailed interest at birth), overruling *Re Blathwayt's Will Trusts, Blathwayt v Blathwayt* [1950] 1 All ER 582 (where it was held that acceleration took place in favour of the next successor at the date of forfeiture). As to forfeiture see PARAS 462–465.

6   *Fuller v Fuller* (1595) Cro Eliz 422. As to failure of a gift to a former spouse as a result of the dissolution or annulment of the marriage see PARAS 177–178. As to failure of a gift to a former civil partner as a result of the dissolution or annulment of the civil partnership see PARA 179.

7   This rule applies both to real and to personal estate: see the cases cited in notes 2–5. In *Midland Bank Executor and Trustee Co Ltd v IRC* [1959] Ch 277, [1959] 1 All ER 180, CA, there was no acceleration where income which was subject to certain trusts for a limited period was subjected by deed and court order to the same trusts as would arise on the expiration of that period, as new and separate trusts were thereby created; furthermore, an intervening contingent trust for accumulation prevented acceleration. In two settlement cases, *Re Flower's Settlement Trusts, Flower v IRC* [1957] 1 All ER 462, [1957] 1 WLR 401, CA (failure for uncertainty of life interests) and *Re Young's Settlement Trusts, Royal Exchange Assurance v Taylor-Young* [1959] 2 All ER 74, [1959] 1 WLR 457 (surrender of life interests), there was held to be no acceleration of subsequent interests because the settlor had shown a contrary intention.

8   Ie pursuant to the rule in *Andrews v Partington* (1791) 3 Bro CC 401: see PARA 307. See also *Re Scott, Widdows v Friends of the Clergy Corpn* [1975] 2 All ER 1033, [1975] 1 WLR 1260, where there was no acceleration of the subsequent interest in income in favour of charities because the gifts were genuine alternatives, contingent upon the persons entitled to the prior life interest not having children, a possibility that remained open. The will also showed an intention against accumulation of income pending the contingency.

9   *Re Kebty-Fletcher's Will Trusts, Public Trustee v Swan and Snowden* [1969] 1 Ch 339 at 344, [1967] 3 All ER 1076 at 1079 per Stamp J; *Re Harker's Will Trusts, Kean v Harker* [1969] 3 All ER 1 at 5, [1969] 1 WLR 1124 at 1128 per Goff J (not following *Re Davies, Davies v Mackintosh* [1957] 3 All ER 52, [1957] 1 WLR 922, although it had been approved by Upjohn J in *Re Taylor, Lloyds Bank Ltd v Jones* [1957] 3 All ER 56, [1957] 1 WLR 1043).

10   *Re Taylor, Lloyds Bank Ltd v Jones* [1957] 3 All ER 56, [1957] 1 WLR 1043. Cf *Re Dawson's Settlement, Lloyds Bank Ltd v Dawson* [1966] 3 All ER 68, [1966] 1 WLR 1456 (where the contingency of attaining the age of 21 or marriage did not prevent acceleration on the failure of the prior interest).

11 *Lainson v Lainson* (1854) 5 De GM & G 754; *Jull v Jacobs* (1876) 3 ChD 703 at 712; *Re Johnson, Danily v Johnson* (1893) 68 LT 20. See also *Re Flower's Settlement Trusts, Flower v IRC* [1957] 1 All ER 462 at 465, [1957] 1 WLR 401 at 405–406, CA, per Jenkins LJ. Where a series of equitable limitations is meant to be exhaustive, the failure of a prior interest will accelerate those in remainder: *Re Willis, Crossman v Kirkaldy* [1917] 1 Ch 365; *Re Conyngham, Conyngham v Conyngham* [1921] 1 Ch 491, CA; *Re Brooke, Brooke v Dickson* [1923] 2 Ch 265, CA. The rule applies when the subsequent interest is a partial interest such as an annuity: *Re Hodge, Midland Bank Executor and Trustee Co Ltd v Morrison* [1943] Ch 300, [1943] 2 All ER 304 (annuity subject to life interest which was disclaimed). In *Re Crother's Trusts* [1915] 1 IR 53, a gift over on death was construed as taking effect on death or remarriage. As to interests determinable on bankruptcy see *Re Cooper, Townend v Townend* (1917) 86 LJ Ch 507. The will may, however, show an intention to destroy the interest in remainder as well as the life interest: *Re Jermingham Trusts, Gormanstown v Nicholl* [1922] 1 IR 115. See *Blathwayt v Baron Cawley* [1976] AC 397, [1975] 3 All ER 625, HL (accelerations of interest by reason of persons becoming Roman Catholic and also following baptism in infancy into that faith).

12 *M'Carthy v M'Carthy* (1878) 1 LR Ir 189; *Aplin v Stone* [1904] 1 Ch 543; *Re Scott, Scott v Scott* [1911] 2 Ch 374 (contingent remainder taking effect as an executory limitation under the Contingent Remainders Act 1877); *Kearney v Kearney* [1911] 1 IR 137, Ir CA; *Re Doland's Will Trusts, Westminster Bank Ltd v Phillips* [1970] Ch 267, [1969] 3 All ER 713. In such cases, therefore, the question of construction arises whether the words introducing the subsequent limitations merely denote the order of succession of the limitations or whether they introduce a new contingency: see *Lainson v Lainson* (1854) 5 De GM & G 754 ('after the death').

13 *Re Townsend's Estate, Townsend v Townsend* (1886) 34 ChD 357 at 360; *Re Vernon, Garland v Shaw* (1906) 95 LT 48 at 54; *Re Cooper, Townend v Townend* (1917) 86 LJ Ch 507. See also *Re Love, Green v Tribe* (1878) 47 LJ Ch 783 (where, pending a member of the class of donees under the subsequent gift coming into existence, the intermediate income was held to fall into residue).

14 *Re Scott, Widdows v Friends of the Clergy Corpn* [1975] 2 All ER 1033, [1975] 1 WLR 1260. Cf *Re Dawson's Settlement, Lloyds Bank Ltd v Dawson* [1966] 3 All ER 68, [1966] 1 WLR 1456; *Re Sinclair, Lloyds Bank plc v Imperial Cancer Research Fund* [1985] Ch 446, [1985] 1 All ER 1066, CA.

182. Contingent gifts over. Where a gift is liable to fail on a contingent event[1] and is followed by a gift over, then, on the contingency happening, the prior gift is divested. It seems that this consequence may follow even where occurrence of the contingent event concerning any single donee causes all other gifts under the will to fail, allowing everything to go to the gift over[2]. Where, owing to lapse or some rule of law, the gift over fails to take effect according to its tenor in favour of the donee[3], the residuary donee or the person entitled on intestacy, as the case may be, takes, but the rule does not apply where the gift over is void for remoteness, the result in such a case being that the prior gift remains absolute[4]. The entire contingency suspending the vesting of the gift over must occur in such cases[5]. The prior gift is not divested, however, where it is inferred that the testator intended divesting not to take place unless the gift over were effective, or where the gift over is void for uncertainty[6]. Where the contingency on which the prior gift is to fail may happen in two ways, and there is a gift over only if it happens in one way, there is an implied gift over if it happens in the other way, provided that in the circumstances this is in accordance with the testator's intention[7].

1 The contingency must be such as is allowed by law as a condition precedent to the vesting of the gift over. Thus it must observe the proper limits, otherwise the prior gift is not divested. Although a prior limitation is invalid because it offends against the perpetuities rule, the ultimate trust may be valid if it is not dependent on the earlier limitation: *Re Hay, Leech v Hay* [1932] NI 215; *Re Canning's Will Trusts, Skues v Lyon* [1936] Ch 309; *Re Coleman, Public Trustee v Coleman* [1936] Ch 528, [1936] 2 All ER 225. The doctrine of dependent invalidity was abolished by the Perpetuities and Accumulations Act 1964 s 6 and, in relation to wills coming into operation on or after 16 July 1964 (see s 15(5)), the ultimate trust cannot be invalidated on the ground of dependent invalidity. See further PERPETUITIES AND ACCUMULATIONS vol 80 (2013)

PARAS 93, 95, 99. As to alternative gifts expressed to have effect where the primary donee predeceases the testator but the primary gift fails for a different reason see PARA 180 text and note 6.

2   *Nathan v Leonard* [2002] EWHC 1701 (Ch), [2003] 4 All ER 198, [2003] 1 WLR 827 ('no-challenge to will' clause would have caused all gifts to fail except gifts over, but for the divesting contingency failing for uncertainty of wording). See also PARA 131 note 23.

3   *Doe d Blomfield v Eyre* (1848) 5 CB 713 (gift over by way of appointment to non-object of the power); *Robinson v Wood* (1858) 4 Jur NS 625 (void gift over to a charity under former mortmain law); *O'Mahoney v Burdett* (1874) LR 7 HL 388 at 399, 407 (lapse); *Re Richard B Hennessy* (1963) 98 ILTR 39 (gift to Λ or his issue after life interest, 'if not' to B; A's interest determined on death in lifetime of tenant for life irrespective of whether B took). See also *Hurst v Hurst* (1882) 21 ChD 278 at 293, CA (forfeiture clause independent of gift over); *Re Archer* (1907) 14 OLR 374 (mortmain); *Re Bold, Banks v Hartland* (1926) 95 LJ Ch 201 (death under 21 of donee of gift over). Where a will gave an annuity and directed the appropriation of a fund to meet it, and made a gift over of the fund, then, although the annuitant died before the testatrix so that the gift to the annuitant failed, the gift over was effective: *Re Clarke, Sheldon v Redrup* [1942] Ch 434, [1942] 2 All ER 294.

4   See *Re Brown and Sibley's Contract* (1876) 3 ChD 156; *Re Pratt's Settlement Trusts, McCullum v Phipps-Hornby* [1943] Ch 356, [1943] 2 All ER 458. See also *Re Atkins Will Trusts, National Westminster Bank Ltd v Atkins* [1974] 2 All ER 1, [1974] 1 WLR 761 (gift over not void for perpetuity; the court could not properly consider the bare possibility that vesting might be delayed by a hypothetical breach of trust); and TRUSTS AND POWERS vol 98 (2013) PARA 623.

5   Where the gift over is to a class not in existence, the coming into existence of the class may be part of the contingency on which the gift over is to take effect, and accordingly, where the other events giving rise to the gift over happen but the class fails to come into existence, the original gift is not divested, the combined contingency not having happened: *Jackson v Noble* (1838) 2 Keen 590 (explained in *Robinson v Wood* (1858) 4 Jur NS 625). Similarly, a gift over, on a contingent event which happens, to the survivor of a number of persons is contingent also on the survivor existing to take the gift, and, if he does not exist, the prior gift is not divested: *Jones v Davies* (1880) 28 WR 455; *Re Deacon's Trusts, Deacon v Deacon, Hagger v Heath* (1906) 95 LT 701.

6   *Re Archer* (1907) 14 OLR 374 at 377 per Riddell J (citing *O'Mahoney v Burdett* (1874) LR 7 HL 388 at 407 per Lord Selborne). See also *Hurst v Hurst* (1882) 21 ChD 278 at 293 per Jessel MR; applied in *Re Rooke, Rooke v Rooke* [1953] Ch 716, sub nom *Re Rooke's Will Trusts, Taylor v Rooke* [1953] 2 All ER 110 (substitutionary gifts to children).

7   *Re Fox's Estate, Dawes v Druitt* [1937] 4 All ER 664, CA; *Re Riggall, Wildash v Riggall* [1949] WN 491 (applying the rule in *Jones v Westcomb* (1711) Prec Ch 316). Cf *Re Graham, Graham v Graham* [1929] 2 Ch 127; *Re Bailey, Barrett v Hyder* [1951] Ch 407, [1951] 1 All ER 391, CA (where no such intention could be attributed to the testator and hence the rule did not apply). The rule does not apply to a gift of an option to purchase to be exercised within a specified time from an event which took place before the testator's death: *Re Hammersley, Foster v Hammersley* [1965] Ch 481, [1965] 2 All ER 24. As to gifts in the alternative see PARAS 180, 320.

183. Lapsed devises and bequests. Where a will contains a residuary devise, then, unless a contrary intention appears, real estate, or an interest in real estate, comprised or intended to be comprised in any specific devise which fails or becomes void by reason of the death of the devisee in the lifetime of the testator, or by reason of the devise being contrary to law, or which is otherwise incapable of taking effect, is included in the residuary devise[1]. If the will contains no residuary devise and a specific devise fails, the devised property passes as on an intestacy[2]. Property included in a residuary devise which lapses also passes as on an intestacy[3].

Lapsed bequests of personalty fall into residue and pass under the residuary bequest[4], or, where there is no residuary bequest, pass as on an intestacy, as does a lapsed residue or share of residue[5].

1   Wills Act 1837 s 25 (amended by the Statute Law Revision (No 2) Act 1888). See *Greated v Greated* (1859) 26 Beav 621 at 629. Before the enactment of the Wills Act 1837, a residuary devise did not include lapsed specific devises: *Cambridge v Rous* (1802) 8 Ves 12 at 25. Parliament intended by that enactment to assimilate the law as to residuary devises of real estate to that of residuary gifts of personal property, which had long been held to comprise any legacy which failed by lapse or by being void ab initio: *Carter v Haswell* (1857) 3 Jur NS 788 at 790 per Stuart V-C.

In *Mason v Ogden* [1903] AC 1, HL, a residuary gift of freehold was held to be a residuary devise within the statute; a gift of the whole of the testator's realty (including copyholds) was not necessary; he in fact had no copyholds. But, in *Springett v Jenings* (1871) 6 Ch App 333 and *Re Brown* (1855) 1 K & J 522, a gift of particular residue was held not to be enough. It seems that the bare possibility of reverter on determination of a determinable fee is capable of passing in a residuary devise: see *Bath and Wells Diocesan Board of Finance v Jenkinson* [2002] EWHC 218 (Ch), [2003] Ch 89, [2002] 4 All ER 245. As to what passes under a residuary gift see PARAS 1113–1114; and as to lapse generally see PARA 160 et seq.

2 See PARA 477 et seq.
3 *Ackroyd v Smithson* (1780) 1 Bro CC 503.
4 *Cambridge v Rous* (1802) 8 Ves 12 at 25. As to residuary bequests see further PARA 1113 et seq; and as to whether lapsed legacies fall into a particular or general residuary gift see PARA 180.
5 *Bagwell v Dry* (1721) 1 P Wms 700; *Page v Page* (1728) 2 P Wms 489; *Sykes v Sykes* (1868) 3 Ch App 301; *Re Midgley, Barclays Bank Ltd v Midgley* [1955] Ch 576, [1955] 2 All ER 625.

184. Charge on lapsed property. Where property is given or appointed by will to one person charged with an annual or lump sum in favour of another, the charge is not affected by the death of the donee of the property before the testator[1], although it will fail if the gift to the donee is adeemed[2]. If, however, the chargee dies in the testator's lifetime[3] or the charge fails[4], for example for illegality[5] or because no chargee is identified[6], the charge as a general rule[7] sinks for the benefit of the devisee. Similarly, where personal property, including a particular fund[8], is bequeathed subject to a charge, and the chargee, for example, does not come into existence[9] or is not identified[10], his interest sinks for the benefit of the legatee. The same principle applies where the object for which the charge was created fails for illegality[11].

A distinction must, however, be drawn between a devise subject to a charge and a devise or bequest with an exception out of it. It is a question of construction of the will in each case. The test is whether the testator meant to give the property minus the thing in question, in which case the thing falls into residue, or that the thing should be a charge on the property, in which case the specific devisee or legatee takes[12].

1 *Wigg v Wigg* (1739) 1 Atk 382; *Hills v Wirley* (1743) 2 Atk 605; *Oke v Heath* (1748) 1 Ves Sen 135. See also *Re Kirk, Kirk v Kirk* (1882) 21 ChD 431, CA (where land was devised to a creditor subject to a condition that he should release a debt, and the creditor predeceased the testator).
2 *Cowper v Mantell* (1856) 22 Beav 223. As to ademption see PARAS 155–159.
3 *Sutcliffe v Cole* (1855) 3 Drew 135. See also *A-G v Milner* (1744) 3 Atk 112.
4 *Re Cooper's Trusts, ex p Sparks* (1853) 4 De GM & G 757. See also *Kennell v Abbott* (1799) 4 Ves 802; *Tucker v Kayess* (1858) 4 K & J 339; *King v Denison* (1813) 1 Ves & B 260 at 265. See further the Wills Act 1837 s 25; and PARA 183.
5 *Baker v Hall* (1806) 12 Ves 497; *Cooke v Stationers' Co* (1831) 3 My & K 262; *Re Clulow's Trust* (1859) 1 John & H 639. See also *Jackson v Hurlock* (1764) 2 Eden 263; *Wright v Row* (1779) 1 Bro CC 61; *Blight v Hartnoll* (1883) 23 ChD 218 at 222, CA.
6 *Re Mulcair* [1960] IR 321.
7 The testator may manifest an intention that the money charged be raised in any event: see *Tregonwell v Sydenham* (1815) 3 Dow 194 at 211, HL, per Lord Eldon. Most of the cases on this point are cases not of lapse but of failure, under the former law relating to mortmain, of charges on land in favour of a charity: see *Arnold v Chapman* (1748) 1 Ves Sen 108; *Greavenor v Hallum* (1767) Amb 643; *Bland v Wilkins* (1782) 1 Bro CC 61n. As to the case where the money charged or interest created is not disposed of by the will see *Sidney v Shelley* (1815) 19 Ves 352 (term of years); *Heptinstall v Gott* (1862) 2 John & H 449. See also *Re Gordon, Watts v Rationalist Press Association Ltd* [1940] Ch 769, [1940] 3 All ER 205 (lapsed gift of personalty and residue of fund charged with payment of debts treated as property not disposed of by will; defendant association not identified as residuary legatee and therefore not subject to the charge).
8 *Scott v Salmond* (1833) 1 My & K 363.
9 *Tucker v Kayess* (1858) 4 K & J 339 at 342.
10 *Re Mulcair* [1960] IR 321.
11 *Re Rogerson, Bird v Lee* [1901] 1 Ch 715. See also CHARITIES vol 8 (2015) PARA 61. As to where there is a partial intestacy see further note 7.

12 *Tucker v Kayess* (1858) 4 K & J 339 at 342; *Re Jupp, Gladman v Jupp* (1903) 87 LT 739. See also *Sutcliffe v Cole* (1855) 3 Drew 135; *Heptinstall v Gott* (1862) 2 John & H 449; *Simmons v Pitt* (1873) 8 Ch App 978; *Blight v Hartnoll* (1883) 23 ChD 218 at 222, CA (distinguishing *Wainman v Field* (1854) Kay 507); *Re Tilden, Coubrough v Royal Society of London* (1938) 82 Sol Jo 334; *Re Meldrum's Will Trusts, Swinson v Meldrum* [1952] Ch 208, [1952] 1 All ER 274 (clear indication that testator's debts, owed to family companies, were to be paid out of specifically gifted bank account rather than from residue, although lapse not relevant in this case).

4. CONSTRUCTION OF WILLS

(1) COURTS OF CONSTRUCTION

185. Functions of the court of construction. In this title the term 'court of construction' is used of any court entertaining, within the scope of its jurisdiction, any question as to the meaning and effect of an instrument of a testamentary nature. The determination of such questions is within the jurisdiction of the High Court and is assigned to the Chancery Division[1] or the County Court, in cases where the value of the estate is within the County Court limit[2]. The procedure is governed by Part 64 of the Civil Procedure Rules which requires claims to be made by issuing a Part 8 claim form[3]. The functions of a court of probate and a court of construction are distinct[4]. In the exercise of its administrative jurisdiction the court may authorise personal representatives to act on the basis of counsel's opinion on a matter of construction[5].

1 See the Senior Courts Act 1981 s 61(1), Sch 1para 1(d); and CPR 64.1(3). See generally PARA 1162 et seq; and COURTS AND TRIBUNALS vol 24 (2010) PARA 704. As to the Civil Procedure Rules generally see CIVIL PROCEDURE vol 11 (2015) PARA 12 et seq.
2 See the County Courts Act 1984 s 23(a); and COURTS AND TRIBUNALS vol 24 (2010) PARA 776. The county court limit is currently £30,000: see the High Court and County Courts Jurisdiction Order 1991, SI 1991/724; the County Court Jurisdiction Order 2014, SI 2014/503; and COURTS AND TRIBUNALS vol 24 (2010) PARA 767.
3 CPR 64.3. As to the meaning of a 'Part 8 claim form' see CIVIL PROCEDURE vol 11 (2015) PARA 152. As to issuing a Part 8 claim form see CIVIL PROCEDURE vol 11 (2015) PARA 152. As to costs see PARA 1196 et seq; CIVIL PROCEDURE vol 12A (2015) PARA 1680 et seq; TRUSTS AND POWERS vol 98 (2013) PARA 347 et seq.
4 As to the function of the probate court see PARAS 8, 679. As to the separation of the functions of the probate court and a court of construction see *Townsend v Moore* [1905] P 66 at 84, 86, 88, CA; *Re Resch's Will Trusts, Le Cras v Perpetual Trustee Co Ltd, Far West Children's Health Scheme v Perpetual Trustee Co Ltd* [1969] 1 AC 514 at 547, [1967] 3 All ER 915 at 925, PC (citing Sir John Nicholl in *Methuen v Methuen* (1817) 2 Phillim 416 at 426 and *Greenough v Martin* (1824) 2 Add 239 at 243); *Re Morris* [1971] P 62, [1970] 1 All ER 1057, [1970] 2 WLR 865. See, however, *Re Finnemore* [1992] 1 All ER 800, [1991] 1 WLR 793 (where, before the grant of probate, the question whether a later will revoked an earlier will was determined in construction proceedings rather than in a probate action). See also *Lamothe v Lamothe* [2006] EWHC 1387 (Ch), [2006] All ER (D) 153 (Jun) (where the court performed a similar function to that in *Re Finnemore*) for analysis of the admissibility of evidence in such circumstances.
5 See the Administration of Justice Act 1985 s 48; and PARA 192.

186. Jurisdiction to correct mistake; death before 1983. A mistake in the will of a testator who died before 1 January 1983[1], such as an error in a name or description, or in the insertion or omission of any words, whether by the testator or his draftsman, may be corrected by the court of construction[2], but only on inferences obtained from the whole will, and not on any extrinsic evidence[3] other than such evidence of the material circumstances as is admissible in construing the will[4].

In relation to such wills the court has no jurisdiction to alter the probate[5], and must be satisfied on the construction of the will alone[6] that there is a mistake or omission in the will; whenever the matter is merely doubtful, the court must adhere to the words of the will[7].

1 Ie the date on which the Administration of Justice Act 1982 s 20 (rectification of wills: see PARAS 187, 741) came into force: see s 76(11). Nothing in s 20 affects the will of a testator who died before that date: s 73(6)(c).
2 *Dent v Pepys* (1822) 6 Madd 350; *Re Boehm* [1891] P 247 (cited in *Re Baynham, Hart v Mackenzie* (1891) 7 TLR 587). As to the rules of construction in relation to the alteration of the words of a will see PARA 253.
3 *Shergold v Boone* (1807) 13 Ves 370 at 376; *Earl Newburgh v Countess Dowager Newburgh* (1820) 5 Madd 364; Sugden's Law of Property 196, 367; *Miller v Travers* (1832) 8 Bing 244;

Langston v Langston (1834) 2 Cl & Fin 194 at 238, HL; *Re Chenoweth, Ward v Dwelley* (1901) 17 TLR 515. See *Barclays Bank Trust Co Ltd v Csoti* [2004] EWHC 2769 (Ch) (Transcript), [2004] All ER (D) 88 (Oct) for a more recent example of the construction approach to a pre-1983 will and death. See also PARA 207. As to the admission of extrinsic evidence in the probate court see PARA 8; and as to the rules of construction in such a case see PARAS 268–269.

4   *Bradshaw v Bradshaw* (1836) 2 Y & C Ex 72.

5   *Taylor v Creagh* (1858) 8 I Ch R 281 at 287. Any correction of such a will must be done by the probate court (*Re Bywater, Bywater v Clarke* (1881) 18 ChD 17 at 22, CA; *Re Carlisle, Belfast Bank Executor and Trustee Co v Patterson* [1950] NI 105 at 112–113), except where the correction can be made as a matter of construction of the will taken as a whole. As to the exclusion of part of a will from probate see PARA 892. As to omitting from the probate words introduced in the will by mistake see *Re Boehm* [1891] P 247; and PARA 739. As to revoking a probate containing a mistake see *Brisco v Baillie and Hamilton* [1902] P 234.

6   In certain circumstances the court may look at the original will to explain, but not to contradict, the probate copy: see *Oppenheim v Henry* (1853) 9 Hare 803n; and PARA 200.

7   *Mellish v Mellish* (1798) 4 Ves 45 at 50; *Philipps v Chamberlaine* (1798) 4 Ves 51 at 57; *Thompson v Whitelock* (1859) 4 De G & J 490 at 500–501. As to the character which the context of a will must bear in order to show mistake see *Morgan v Thomas* (1882) 9 QBD 643 at 645–646, CA.

187.   Jurisdiction to rectify will to correct mistake; death after 1982. Prior to 1 January 1983[1] there was no jurisdiction to rectify a will[2], but there was a jurisdiction to omit words from the probate if it was proved that they had been included through fraud or by mistake[3]. If, however, a court is satisfied that the will of a testator who dies on or after that date is so expressed that it fails to carry out his intentions in consequence of a clerical error, or of a failure to understand his instructions, it may order that the will be rectified so as to carry out his intentions[4]. 'Clerical error' means an inadvertent error made in the process of recording the intended words of the testator in the drafting or the transcription of his will[5]. The introduction of a clause which is inconsistent with the testator's instructions in circumstances in which the draftsman has not applied his mind to its significance or effect (in other words a case of failure to understand the testator's instructions), is also a 'clerical error' for this purpose, but the use of words to which the draftsman has applied his mind but which do not achieve the objective that he and the testator intended is not such an error[6]. It may sometimes be easier to identify a matter as a 'clerical error' where words are omitted than where the wrong words are used[7]. It seems that a failure to include words, excluding the application of certain statutory provisions to the will, can also be treated as a clerical error[8].

Although the standard of proof required in a claim for rectification of a will is that the court should be satisfied on the balance of probability, the probability that a will which a testator has executed in circumstances of some formality reflects his intentions is usually of such weight that convincing evidence to the contrary is necessary[9]. The evidence admissible for this purpose will extend to evidence of the testator's intentions as regards the dispositions for which rectification is sought[10]. It seems that a failure to seek rectification of a will, where that remedy might be available, does not prejudice the admissibility of extrinsic evidence of the testator's intention where it is otherwise admissible[11].

No application for an order for rectification may be made after the end of the period of six months from the date on which representation with respect to the estate of the deceased is first taken out[12], except with the permission of the court[13].

1   Ie the date on which the Administration of Justice Act 1982 s 20 came into force: see s 76(11).

2   *Harter v Harter* (1873) LR 3 P & D 11; *Collins v Elstone* [1893] P 1; *Re Bacharach's Will Trusts, Minden v Bacharach* [1959] Ch 245 at 249, [1958] 3 All ER 618 at 620.

3   *Re Horrocks, Taylor v Kershaw* [1939] P 198, [1939] 1 All ER 579, CA; *Re Morris, Lloyds Bank Ltd v Peake* [1971] P 62, [1970] 1 All ER 1057; *Re Phelan* [1972] Fam 33, [1971] 3 All ER

1256; *Re Reynette-James, Wightman v Reynette-James* [1975] 3 All ER 1037, [1976] 1 WLR 161. See also PARA 741. As to correction of mistakes as a matter of construction of the will see PARA 186.

4   Administration of Justice Act 1982 s 20(1). As to the meaning of 'will' for these purposes see *Marley v Rawlings* [2014] UKSC 2, [2015] AC 129, [2014] 1 All ER 807; and PARA 741. As to the general law of rectification of instruments other than wills, much of which is applicable to this statutory jurisdiction see REAL PROPERTY AND REGISTRATION vol 87 (2012) PARA 181; MISTAKE vol 77 (2016) PARA 33. To obtain rectification it is not enough to show that a mistake has been made; it is also necessary to be able to show what would have been intended if the mistake had not been made: *Racal Group Services Ltd v Ashmore* [1995] STC 1151, CA (covenanted payment to charity). See also *Giles v Royal National Institute of Blind People* [2014] EWHC 1373 (Ch), [2014] STC 1631 (rectification ordered where will failed to mitigate inheritance tax as intended). The main difference between the power of rectifying wills and that of rectifying other instruments is that in the case of wills there is no power to rectify where wording was included under a misunderstanding of their legal effect: cf *Re Butlin's Settlement Trusts, Butlin v Butlin* [1976] Ch 251, [1976] 2 All ER 483 (rectification of a non-testamentary instrument in this manner). As to cases where on the facts rectification of a will was granted see eg *Re Munday, Wong v Wong* [2003] WTLR 1161; *Re Vautier's Estate* 2000 JLR 351, (2000–01) 3 IETLR 566, Royal Ct Jer (mistaken signing of wrong will cured by rectification). As to cases where on the facts it was refused see eg *Re Grattan, Grattan v McNaughton* [2001] WTLR 1305; *Bell v Georgiou* [2002] EWHC 1080 (Ch), [2002] All ER (D) 433 (May), [2002] WTLR 1105; *Allnutt v Wilding* [2007] EWCA Civ 412, [2007] WTLR 941 (rectification denied where testator's attempt to mitigate the effect of inheritance tax failed).

5   *Wordingham v Royal Exchange Trust Co Ltd* [1992] Ch 412, [1992] 3 All ER 204 (failure by solicitor to repeat in a later will a clause in an earlier will which the testator intended to have included; will rectified to include it). See also *Marley v Rawlings* [2014] UKSC 2, [2015] AC 129, [2014] 1 All ER 807 (cited in PARA 188) where it was held that the expression 'clerical error' in the Administration of Justice Act 1982 s 20(1)(a) should be given a wide meaning to include a mistake arising out of office work of a relatively routine nature, such as preparing, filing, sending, organising the execution of, a document 'save, possibly, to the extent that the activity involves some special expertise': see *Marley v Rawlings* at [75] per Lord Neuberger. A clerical error for this purpose may be one made by the testator himself, a solicitor preparing the will, the typist of the will, or anyone else involved: see *Re Williams, Wiles v Madgin* [1985] 1 All ER 964 at 969, [1985] 1 WLR 905 at 911–912 per Nicholls J; and *Marley v Rawlings* at [72] per Lord Neuberger. For an example of an error which was not merely clerical see *Reading v Reading* [2015] EWHC 946 (Ch), [2015] WTLR 1245, [2015] All ER (D) 64 (Feb) (where a solicitor drafting a will overlooked the fact that the term 'issue' did not include stepchildren; this involved the exercise of professional judgement and expertise, therefore rectification was refused).

6   *Re Segelman* [1996] Ch 171 at 184–185, [1995] 3 All ER 676 at 685 (will rectified to delete the clause); *Reading v Reading* [2015] EWHC 946 (Ch), [2015] WTLR 1245, [2015] All ER (D) 64 (Feb) (see note 5). See *Clarke v Brothwood* [2006] EWHC 2939 (Ch), [2006] All ER (D) 207 (Nov), where failure of the draftsman to apply his mind to the significance of a provision that left 60% of the estate undisposed of constituted a clerical error within the Administration of Justice Act 1982 s 20(1)(a). See also *Price v Craig* [2006] EWHC 2561 (Ch), 9 ITELR 393, [2006] All ER (D) 249 (Oct) (clear from attendance note that testator intended children to have whole residue, rather than part only; rectification allowed); applied in *Pengelly v Pengelly* [2007] EWHC 3227 (Ch), [2008] Ch 375, [2008] 3 WLR 66 (rectification allowed to add word 'only' to limit valid executory trust to only those persons included in a class).

7   See *Pengelly v Pengelly* [2007] EWHC 3227 (Ch) at [23], [2008] Ch 375, [2008] 3 WLR 66 per Judge Hodge QC, where he analyses the distinctions made between the three different types of case of failure to carry out the testator's instructions which were identified by Chadwick J in *Re Segelman* [1996] Ch 171 at 184–185, [1995] 3 All ER 676 at 685. See also *Brown v Bimson* [2010] All ER (D) 325 (Jul) ('clerical error' was to be construed as an error in reporting the intended words of the trustee, but not a failure of the trustee to be understood).

8   *Bush v Jouliac* [2006] EWHC 363 (Ch), [2006] All ER (D) 108 (Jan) (inadvertent failure to exclude the effect of Wills Act 1837 s 33 amounted to a clerical error in the circumstances of the case).

9   *Re Segelman* [1996] Ch 171 at 184, [1995] 3 All ER 676 at 684 per Chadwick J; approved in *Walker v Geo H Medlicott & Son* [1999] 1 All ER 685 at 690, [1999] 1 WLR 727 at 731, CA, per Sir Christopher Slade; and applied in *Clarke v Brothwood* [2006] EWHC 2939 (Ch), [2006] All ER (D) 207 (Nov).

10 In *Re Segelman* [1996] Ch 171 at 180, [1995] 3 All ER 676 at 681, Chadwick J proposed a three question approach that has been cited and used in several cases since: First, what were the testator's intentions with regard to the [relevant] dispositions. Secondly, whether the will is so expressed that it fails to carry out those intentions. Thirdly, whether the will is expressed as it is in consequence of (1) a clerical error; or (2) a failure on the part of someone to whom the testator

has given his instructions in connection with his will to understand those instructions. In order to answer the first question the court must admit extrinsic evidence of the testator's intentions concerning the relevant dispositions.

11 *Lamothe v Lamothe* [2006] EWHC 1387 (Ch), [2006] All ER (D) 153 (Jun) (nothing in the Administration of Justice Act 1982 s 20 or s 21 (see PARA 195) limited the existing powers of a court of probate to consider extrinsic evidence, including evidence of testator's intentions, in considering which of competing wills should be admitted to probate).

12 In considering when representation was first taken out, the following are to be left out of account:

    (1)   a grant limited to settled land (see PARA 821 et seq) or to trust property (see PARA 819) (Administration of Justice Act 1982 s 20(4)(a) (s 20(4) substituted by the Inheritance and Trustees' Powers Act 2014 Sch 3 para 3));

    (2)   any other grant that does not permit any of the estate to be distributed (Administration of Justice Act 1982 s 20(4)(b) (as so substituted));

    (3)   a grant limited to real estate or to personal estate (see PARA 820), unless a grant limited to the remainder of the estate has previously been made or is made at the same time (s 20(4)(c) (as so substituted));

    (4)   a grant, or its equivalent, made outside the United Kingdom (s 20(4)(d) (as so substituted)) (see PARA 835 et seq). A grant sealed under the Colonial Probates Act 1892 s 2 (see PARA 837) counts as a grant made in the United Kingdom for these purposes, but is to be taken as dated on the date of sealing (Administration of Justice Act 1982 s 20(5) (s 20(5) added by the Inheritance and Trustees' Powers Act 2014 Sch 3 para 3)).

    As to the meaning of 'United Kingdom' see PARA 4 note 7. As to the procedure relating to claims for the rectification of a will see PARA 889.

13 Administration of Justice Act 1982 s 20(2). See *Hobart v Hobart* [2006] EWHC 1784 (Ch), [2006] All ER (D) 295 (May), where an application to rectify was allowed outside the six month limit as no distribution had occurred, no prejudice was caused by the delay and the application was unopposed.

188. The modern approach to the construction of wills. The modern approach to be taken by the court when it comes to interpreting wills is set out in the case of *Marley v Rawlings*[1]. The approach is the same whether the document in question is a commercial contract or a will[2]. The aim is to identify the intention of the party or parties to the document by interpreting the words used in their documentary, factual and commercial context[3].

The court is concerned to find the intention of the party or parties, and it does this by identifying the meaning of the relevant words:

    (1)   in the light of:

        (a)   the natural and ordinary meaning of those words;

        (b)   the overall purpose of the document;

        (c)   any other provisions of the document;

        (d)   the facts known or assumed by the parties at the time that the document was executed; and

        (e)   common sense, but

    (2)   ignoring subjective evidence of any party's intentions[4].

In addition, in relation to a will, or a provision in a will as opposed to a contract, it is possible to assist its interpretation by reference to evidence of the testator's actual intention[5].

The approach set out by the Supreme Court in *Marley v Rawlings* has been followed by the courts in cases involving the construction of wills[6]. There is a limit to what can be achieved by construction. If the words used are clear and do not lead to an absurd result, they will be given their natural meaning[7].

1 See *Marley v Rawlings* [2014] UKSC 2, [2015] AC 129, [2014] 1 All ER 807 (where a husband and wife executed each other's mirror wills by mistake, it was held that the husband's will was capable of rectification under the Administration of Justice Act 1982 s 20 (see PARA 187 note 5)).

2 See *Marley v Rawlings* [2014] UKSC 2 at [20], [2015] AC 129, [2014] 1 All ER 807 per Lord Neuberger. Thus, the court takes the same approach to interpretation of unilateral notices as it takes to interpretation of contracts: see *Marley v Rawlings* [2014] UKSC 2 at [21], [2015] AC 129, [2014] 1 All ER 807 per Lord Neuberger (applying *Mannai Investment Co Ltd v Eagle Star Life Assurance Co Ltd* [1997] AC 749).

3   See *Marley v Rawlings* [2014] UKSC 2 at [20], [2015] AC 129, [2014] 1 All ER 807 per Lord Neuberger.

4   See *Marley v Rawlings* [2014] UKSC 2 at [19], [2015] AC 129, [2014] 1 All ER 807 per Lord Neuberger.

5   See the Administration of Justice Act 1982 s 21; and PARAS 195, 219.

6   See *Burnard v Burnard* [2014] EWHC 340 (Ch), [2014] All ER (D) 51 (Mar); *Brooke v Purton* [2014] EWHC 547 (Ch), [2014] All ER (D) 262 (Mar); *Rawstron v Freud* [2014] EWHC 2577 (Ch), 17 ITELR 479, [2014] WTLR 1453; *Reading v Reading* [2015] EWHC 946 (Ch), [2015] WTLR 1245, [2015] All ER (D) 64 (Feb); *Slattery v Jagger* [2015] EWHC 3976 (Ch), [2016] All ER (D) 102 (Mar).

7   *Gledhill v Arnold* [2015] EWHC 2939 (Ch), [2016] WTLR 653 (no ambiguity but rectification possible). As to rectification see PARA 187.

189. Difference between construction and rectification. Some case law on construction of contracts takes a wide view of what can be achieved as a matter of construction[1], such as suggesting that although words are normally to be given their natural and ordinary meaning, if one would nevertheless conclude from the background that something must have gone wrong with the language, the law does not require the court to attribute to the parties an intention which they plainly could not have had[2]. All that is required is that it should be clear that something has gone wrong with the language and that it should be clear what a reasonable person would have understood the parties to have meant[3]. However, this approach to interpretation has been described as inconsistent with previously established principles[4] and would reduce the difference between construction and rectification almost to vanishing point.

The distinction between interpretation and rectification is not simply an academic issue of categorisation. If it is a question of interpretation, then the document in question has, and has always had, the meaning and effect as determined by the court, and that is the end of the matter. On the other hand, if it is a question of rectification, then the document, as rectified, has a different meaning from that which it appears to have on its face, and the court would have jurisdiction to refuse rectification or to grant it on terms (for example, if there had been delay, change of position, or third party reliance)[5].

More recent case law has proceeded on the basis that there is a distinction between interpretation and rectification[6].

1   See *Investors Compensation Scheme Ltd v West Bromwich Building Society* [1998] 1 All ER 98, [1998] 1 WLR 896, HL; *Antaios Compania Naviera SA v Salen Rederierna AB* [1985] AC 191, [1984] 3 WLR 592, HL.

2   *Investors Compensation Scheme Ltd v West Bromwich Building Society* [1998] 1 All ER 98 at 115, [1998] 1 WLR 896 at 913, HL, per Lord Hoffman. See also *Antaios Compania Naviera SA v Salen Rederierna AB* [1985] AC 191 at 201, [1984] 3 All ER 229 at 233, HL, per Lord Diplock: 'if detailed semantic and syntactical analysis of words in a commercial contract is going to lead to a conclusion that flouts business commonsense, it must be made to yield to business commonsense'.

3   *Chartbrook Ltd v Persimmon Homes Ltd* [2009] UKHL 38 at [25], [2009] AC 1101, [2009] 4 All ER 677 per Lord Hoffman.

4   See Sir Richard Buxton 'Construction' and Rectification after Chartbrook' [2010] CLJ 253.

5   *Marley v Rawlings* [2014] UKSC 2 at [40], [2015] AC 129, [2014] 1 All ER 807 per Lord Neuberger. The Supreme Court declined to rule on the point. Interpretation was not the basis upon which the courts below had decided this case and it was not the principal ground relied upon in the appeal. The Supreme Court proceeded on the basis that the case failed on interpretation.

6   *ING Bank NV v Ros Roca SA* [2011] EWCA Civ 353 at [110], [2012] 1 WLR 472, where Rix LJ said: 'Construction cannot be pushed beyond its proper limits in pursuit of remedying what is perceived to be a flaw in the working of a contract . . . Judges should not see in Chartbrook an open sesame for reconstructing the parties' contract, but an opportunity to remedy by construction a clear error of language which could not have been intended'. See also *Re BCA Pension Trustees Ltd* [2015] EWHC 3492 (Ch), [2016] 4 WLR 5.

190. Attempts to oust the court's jurisdiction. The jurisdiction of the court in the construction of a will is not ousted by the fact that the will is in a foreign language, or has to be construed by foreign rules of construction[1], nor by any direction or recommendation by the testator that questions of construction are to be decided in a different manner, for example by the trustees or executors, or by arbitration[2]. A direction that a beneficiary resorting to litigation for this purpose is to forfeit his interest is inoperative because, in so far as it prevents him from seeking the aid of the court, it is repugnant, being inconsistent with the nature of the interest given to the donee[3]. Any attempt to require the devolution of property, otherwise than in accordance with law, is likely to be seen as an attempt to oust the jurisdiction of the court, whether the purported method of devolution results from contract or under a will[4].

A condition that a beneficiary is not to dispute the validity of the will[5] or of any other instrument[6], or to interfere with the management of the testator's estate, and on breach of the condition is wholly or partially to forfeit his gift, may, however, be valid and operative for the purpose of causing a forfeiture on litigation by the donee[7]. Such a condition is not, however, construed prima facie to extend to cases where there is a reasonable cause for litigation[8], or to defending proceedings taken by persons other than the donee[9], and, if it is couched in language which prevents the donee from resorting to any proceedings whatever concerning his gift, even to secure its enjoyment[10], or if in the case of gifts of personal estate[11] it is merely imposed in terrorem[12] on the legatee, it is repugnant to the gift and void.

1 *Duchess di Sora v Phillipps* (1863) 10 HL Cas 624 at 636, 639–640 per Lord Chelmsford; *Re Bonnefoi, Surrey v Perrin* [1912] P 233, CA. Cf CONFLICT OF LAWS vol 19 (2011) PARAS 749–752. As to the construction of foreign wills see PARA 203.
2 *Massy v Rogers* (1883) 11 LR Ir 409; *Re Walton's Estate* (1856) 8 De GM & G 173; *Re Raven, Spencer v National Association for the Prevention of Consumption and Other Forms of Tuberculosis* [1915] 1 Ch 673 (where a direction that any doubt as to the identity of a legatee should be decided by the trustees, whose decision should be final, was held contrary to public policy and void for repugnancy); *Re Wynn, Public Trustee v Newborough* [1952] Ch 271, [1952] 1 All ER 341 (where a provision that the trustees should determine matters of doubt was held void for repugnancy and as being contrary to public policy); applied in *AN v Barclay's Private Bank and Trust (Cayman) Ltd* (2006) 9 ITELR 630, Cayman Is GC. See also *Philips v Bury* (1694) Skin 447 at 469 per Eyre J. Acts done in good faith, under a determination by the tribunal set up by the testator, are valid, it appears, not only to protect the executors or trustees but for all purposes: *Re Thompson's Will, Brahe v Mason* [1910] VLR 251 at 255.
3 *Rhodes v Muswell Hill Land Co* (1861) 30 LJ Ch 509 at 511, 560 (a condition that any legatee commencing litigation in relation to the inherited property, including suing for rent, would lose his entitlement was held to be void for repugnancy as it purported to deprive the donee of one of the incidents of ownership); *Massy v Rogers* (1883) 11 LR Ir 409. The persons claiming under the testator may agree on arbitration: see *Ridout v Pain* (1747) 3 Atk 486. As to the stay of proceedings after such a submission to arbitration cf ARBITRATION vol 2 (2008) PARA 1221 et seq. As to repugnant conditions see PARA 142.
4 See *Aribisala v St James Homes (Grosvenor Dock) Ltd* [2007] EWHC 1694 (Ch), [2007] All ER (D) 101 (Jun), where the principle seen in *Re Wynn, Public Trustee v Newborough* [1952] Ch 271, [1952] 1 All ER 341 (see note 2) was held to apply to a contractual provision purporting to exclude the operation of the Law of Property Act 1925 s 49(2) (see CONVEYANCING vol 23 (2016) PARAS 452, 470).
5 *Boughton v Boughton* (1750) 2 Ves Sen 12; *Cooke v Turner* (1846) 15 M & W 727. See also *Re Ogilvie, Ogilvie v Ogilvie* [1918] 1 Ch 492 at 496.
6 *Violett v Brookman* (1857) 26 LJ Ch 308.
7 *Adams v Adams* [1892] 1 Ch 369, CA (frivolous actions); applied in *AN v Barclay's Private Bank and Trust (Cayman) Ltd* (2006) 9 ITELR 630, Cayman Is GC. See also *Re Allan, Havelock v Havelock-Allan* (1896) 12 TLR 299 (proceedings in Parliament); and TRUSTS AND POWERS vol 98 (2013) PARA 655. A donee having a vested interest does not dispute a will merely by claiming payment of a legacy the income of which is directed to be accumulated, in respect of which he is entitled to give a discharge and put an end to the accumulation: *Phillips v Phillips*

[1877] WN 260. See *Nathan v Leonard* [2002] EWHC 1701 (Ch), [2003] 4 All ER 198, [2003] 1 WLR 827, where it was assumed, for the purposes of the case, that an application under the Inheritance (Provision for Family and Dependents) Act 1975 was a contest to or disagreement with a will; there was no claim that the no-contest provision ousted the jurisdiction to construe the will, it did not offend public policy, but it failed for uncertainty of wording.

8   *Powell v Morgan* (1688) 2 Vern 90; *Adams v Adams* [1892] 1 Ch 369 at 375, CA, per Lopes LJ, and at 377 per Kay LJ; *Re Williams, Williams v Williams* [1912] 1 Ch 399 at 401. See also *Nutt v Burrell* (1724) Cas *temp* King 1 (frivolous action, but no forfeiture); *Wallace v Wallace* (1898) 24 VLR 859; *Harrison v Harrison* (1904) 7 OLR 297. See also *AN v Barclay's Private Bank and Trust (Cayman) Ltd* (2006) 9 ITELR 630, Cayman Is GC (no-contest clause could not be validly construed so as to entirely shut out challenges based on probable cause or good faith).

9   *Cooke v Cholmondeley* (1849) 2 Mac & G 18 at 28; *Warbrick v Varley (No 2)* (1861) 30 Beav 347; *Wilkinson v Dyson* (1862) 10 WR 681; *Massy v Rogers* (1883) 11 LR Ir 409 at 421.

10 *Rhodes v Muswell Hill Land Co* (1861) 29 Beav 560 at 563; *Re Williams, Williams v Williams* [1912] 1 Ch 399.

11 The rule does not apply to devises of real estate, or legacies charged on real estate (see PARA 134

12 Eg where there is no gift over on forfeiture: *Morris v Burroughs* (1737) 1 Atk 399 at 404. A gift over, or direction that the gift is to fall into residue, on breach of the condition, prevents such a construction: *Cleaver v Spurling* (1729) 2 P Wms 526 at 528; *Warbrick v Varley (No 2)* (1861) 30 Beav 347 at 350; *Stevenson v Abington* (1863) 11 WR 935. As to conditions in terrorem see PARA 134 et seq.

191. Duty of court to construe will. In an ordinary case, where the rights under a will are in dispute and a meaning can be attached to the words, the court is under a duty not to decline the jurisdiction to declare the meaning of the will, subject to the qualification that it is a matter of discretion for the court whether it should answer a question arising on a contingency which has not yet happened[1]. Normally the court will not do so unless some good cause is shown, such as the reasonable desire on the part of some beneficiary to know the limitations of some will or codicil under which he may be interested. The court will not answer a contingent question unless it has before it a representation of every interest which may in any event be affected[2].

1   *Crofts v Beamish* [1905] 2 IR 349 at 362–363, Ir CA. See also *Ashby v White* (1703) 2 Ld Raym 938 at 956 per Holt CJ; *Dormer v Phillips* (1855) 4 De GM & G 855 at 859.
2   As to who can be made a party to a claim see CPR 64.4.

192. Construction of wills; reliance on counsel's opinion. Where:

(1)   any question of construction[1] has arisen out of the terms of a will[2]; and
(2)   an opinion in writing given by a person who has a ten-year High Court qualification[3] (the 'qualified person') has been obtained on that question by the personal representatives under the will,

the High Court may, on the application of the personal representatives and without hearing argument, make an order authorising those persons to take such steps in reliance on that opinion as are specified in the order[4].

The application is by way of Part 8 claim form[5] which must be supported by a witness statement or affidavit to which must be exhibited copies of all documents, instructions to a qualified person, the qualified person's opinion and draft terms of the desired order[6], the contents and details of which are closely prescribed[7].

When the file is placed before the master he will consider whether the evidence is complete and, if it is, whether it is appropriate for him to deal with the matter, or to send the file to the judge[8]. The master or judge will consider the papers and, if necessary, direct service of notices[9] or request further information[10]. If the court is satisfied that the order sought is appropriate, it will be made and sent to the claimant[11].

The High Court must not, however, make such an order if it appears to the court that a dispute exists which would make it inappropriate for the court to make the order without hearing argument[12].

If the judge makes an order without a hearing, an order does not determine the rights of the beneficiaries but merely absolves the personal representatives from liability as a result of acting on the authorised basis[13].

1   Note that the application must be one of construction and not rectification: see *Re BCA Pension Trustees Ltd* [2015] EWHC 3492 (Ch), [2016] 4 WLR 5. As to the distinction between construction and rectification see PARA 189.
2   For these purposes, 'will' includes a nuncupative will and any testamentary document of which probate may be granted: Administration of Justice Act 1985 s 56. As to the meaning of 'nuncupative' see PARA 81.
3   Ie within the meaning of the Courts and Legal Services Act 1990 s 71: see LEGAL PROFESSIONS vol 65 (2015) PARA 540 et seq; and see also COURTS AND TRIBUNALS vol 24 (2010) PARA 755.
4   Administration of Justice Act 1985 s 48(1) (amended by the Courts and Legal Services Act 1990 s 71(2), Sch 10 para 63).
5   See CPR 64.2(d), 64.3. No defendant need be named and no separate application for permission under CPR 8.2A need be made: see the Chancery Guide (2016 Edn) para 29.28. As to the Civil Procedure Rules generally see CIVIL PROCEDURE vol 11 (2015) PARA 12 et seq. As to issuing a Part 8 claim form generally see CIVIL PROCEDURE vol 11 (2015) PARA 152 et seq.
6   *Chancery Guide* (2016 Edn) para 29.29; and see *The Civil Court Practice*.
7   The witness statement or affidavit (or the exhibits to it) must state (see the *Chancery Guide* (2016 Edn) para 29.30; and *The Civil Court Practice*):
    (1)   the reason for the application;
    (2)   the names of all persons who are, or may be, affected by the order sought;
    (3)   all surrounding circumstances admissible and relevant in construing the document;
    (4)   the date of qualification of the qualified person and his or her experience in the construction of trust documents;
    (5)   the approximate value of the fund or property in question;
    (6)   whether it is known to the applicant that a dispute exists and, if so, details of such dispute; and
    (7)   what steps are proposed to be taken in reliance on the opinion.
8   See the *Chancery Guide* (2016 Edn) para 29.31; and *The Civil Court Practice*.
9   See CPR 19.8A.
10 *Chancery Guide* (2016 Edn) para 29.32. See *The Civil Court Practice; and* CIVIL PROCEDURE vol 11 (2015) PARA 495.
11 *Chancery Guide* (2016 Edn) para 29.32; and see *The Civil Court Practice*.
12 Administration of Justice Act 1985 s 48(2). Thus if any acknowledgment of service is received, the applicant must apply to the master (on notice to the parties who have so acknowledged) for directions. If the applicant desires to pursue the application to the court, in the ordinary case the master will direct that the case proceeds as a Part 8 claim: *Chancery Guide* (2016 Edn) para 25.33. If, on the hearing of the claim, the court is of the opinion that any party who has entered an acknowledgment of service has no reasonably tenable argument contrary to the qualified person's opinion, in the exercise of the court's discretion it may order such party to pay any costs thrown away, or part of them: *Chancery Guide* (2016 Edn) para 29.34.
13 Cf *Re Benjamin, Neville v Benjamin* [1902] 1 Ch 723; and PARA 1106. See also *BCA Pension Plan, Re* [2015] EWHC 3492 (Ch), [2015] All ER (D) 38 (Dec), [2016] 4 WLR 5.

(2) ADMISSIBILITY OF EVIDENCE

(i) Evidence of Testator's Intentions

193. Primary evidence of testator's intentions is the will. In a court of construction[1] the primary evidence of the testator's intentions is the will itself[2], properly authenticated, and any codicil to it[3]. For the purpose of construing a codicil, the court may look at the original will or any other codicil to it, and, similarly, the court may look at a codicil for the purpose of construing the original will[4]. The court may look at a recital of a will contained in a codicil and may construe the will by reference to this recital[5], unless it is obviously erroneous[6].

Extrinsic evidence has always been admitted to a limited extent. In order that the will may be properly expounded, the court adopts the general rule that any evidence of the circumstances is admissible which in its nature and effect simply explains what the testator has written[7], but in general[8] no evidence may be admitted which in its nature or effect is applicable to the purpose of showing merely what he intended to have written[9]. Extrinsic evidence may be resorted to for the purpose of proving a fact which makes intelligible something in the will which, without the aid of such evidence, would not be intelligible[10].

In the case of deaths on or after 1 January 1983, the circumstances in which extrinsic evidence, including evidence of the testator's intention, may be admitted to assist in its interpretation have been codified and extended[11].

The general rule is also qualified, in the case of deaths on or after 1 January 1983, by the ability of the courts to rectify wills and the consequent wider scope for the admissibility of extrinsic evidence of intention, the court necessarily having to construe the will to see whether it fails to carry out the testator's intentions, by reason of clerical error or failure to understand instructions[12].

1   As to courts of construction see PARA 185 et seq. See also PARA 8. As to testamentary instruments entitled to probate see PARAS 707, 723. As to probate in common form see PARA 724 et seq; and as to probate in solemn form see PARA 860 et seq. There is a distinction, in the matter of evidence, between an inquiry into the meaning of a will and an inquiry into the existence of such a document or an inquiry to what extent it represents the testamentary intentions of the deceased: *Reffell v Reffell* (1866) LR 1 P & D 139 at 141 (explaining *Guardhouse v Blackburn* (1866) LR 1 P & D 109 at 114). See also *Re Hawksley's Settlements, Black v Tidy* [1934] Ch 384; *Re Resch's Will Trusts, Le Cras v Perpetual Trustee Co Ltd, Far West Children's Health Scheme v Perpetual Trustee Co Ltd* [1969] 1 AC 514 at 547, [1967] 3 All ER 915 at 925, PC (citing Sir John Nicholl in *Methuen v Methuen* (1817) 2 Phillim 416 at 426 and *Greenough v Martin* (1824) 2 Add 239 at 243). As to rectification of the will see PARA 187.
    As to the construction of wills containing a foreign element see CONFLICT OF LAWS vol 19 (2011) PARAS 749–752. See also PARA 190. As to the construction of foreign wills see PARA 203.
2   The court may also look at the original will in order to explain, but not to contradict, the probate copy: see PARA 200.
3   See PARA 224 et seq.
4   *Hartley v Tribber* (1853) 16 Beav 510 at 515; *Re Townley, Townley v Townley* (1884) 50 LT 394 at 396; and see PARA 200.
5   *Re Venn, Lindon v Ingram* [1904] 2 Ch 52 at 55 (following *Darley v Martin* (1853) 13 CB 683). See also *Grover v Raper* (1856) 5 WR 134.
6   *Skerratt v Oakley* (1798) 7 Term Rep 492. See also *Bamfield v Popham* (1703) 1 P Wms 54; *Re Smith* (1862) 2 John & H 594; *Re Arnold's Estate* (1863) 33 Beav 163 at 171.
7   *Hampshire v Peirce* (1751) 2 Ves Sen 216 at 217, as qualified by *Doe d Hiscocks v Hiscocks* (1839) 5 M & W 363 at 371.
8   As to exceptions see PARAS 195, 199, 218–219, 262.
9   See Wigram's Extrinsic Evidence, pl 9 (4th Edn) pp 7–8, cited with approval in *Re Mayo, Chester v Keirl* [1901] 1 Ch 404 at 405–406 per Farwell J. For a discussion of the admissibility of extrinsic evidence of the surrounding circumstances see *Re Hodgson, Nowell v Flannery* [1936] Ch 203. But see PARA 224.
10 *Clementson v Gandy* (1836) 1 Keen 309 at 316; *Re Glassington, Glassington v Follett* [1906] 2 Ch 305 at 314 per Joyce J (explaining *Higgins v Dawson* [1902] AC 1, HL). As to the admissibility of extrinsic evidence of intention see PARAS 195, 218–219.
11 See the Administration of Justice Act 1982 s 21; and PARAS 219, 220.
12 As to rectification of the will see PARA 187.

194.   Difficulties of construction. The court construes the whole will in the light of the knowledge of the meaning of the words and expressions used and of the identity of the persons and things described by the will, and of the nature of the facts and circumstances there mentioned, which has been obtained by the admission of evidence of the material circumstances[1]. Evidence is not, however, admitted to enable the court to construe a will where the words themselves require no interpretation but the difficulty is only in the construction of the sentence in which the words occur[2]. Where, therefore, the matter in doubt does not relate to the persons and things described by the will, then, even though it can be shown by evidence that the testator's intention was different from that shown by the language of the will, the language of the will, if clear, must settle the rights of the parties[3].

The modern approach to the construction of documents, including wills, allows the court to identify the intention of the party or parties to the documents by interpreting the words used in their documentary, factual and commercial context[4].

Events which might possibly have happened after the date of the will are to be considered, as well as those which did happen[5]. The ascertainment of the testator's intention shown by the will cannot, however, be varied according to the actual course of subsequent events[6].

Where a will contains an executory trust, that is, where the testator has left it to the court to make out from general expressions what his intention is and has not defined his intention by means of precise limitations[7], the court is not confined to the language of the will itself in order to discover his intention; it may refer not only to the motives which led to the will and to its general objects and purpose, to be collected from other instruments to which the will itself refers, but also to any circumstances which may have influenced the mind of the testator towards the provisions it contains[8].

1 See PARA 224. Thus a gift 'to A or B', where A and B represent persons ascertained by description, cannot be construed until it is known who A and B respectively are, and in what relation, if any, the persons represented by B stand to those represented by A, so as to be able to supply what is the contingency to be understood as involved in the word 'or': *Re Roberts, Percival v Roberts* [1903] 2 Ch 200 at 203 per Joyce J. See also *Re Sibley's Trusts* (1877) 5 ChD 494 at 499. As to gifts expressed in the alternative see PARA 320.

2 *Higgins v Dawson* [1902] AC 1 at 10–11, HL, per Lord Davey. Thus evidence is not admitted to prove to which of two antecedents a given relative pronoun was intended to refer (*Castledon v Turner* (1745) 3 Atk 257), or to rebut a presumption which arises from the construction of words simply according to their meaning as words (*Coote v Boyd, Coote v Coote* (1789) 2 Bro CC 521 at 526 per Lord Thurlow LC). The law as stated in the text would not appear to have been changed by the Administration of Justice Act 1982 s 21: see PARA 195.

3 *Higgins v Dawson* [1902] AC 1 at 8, HL, per Lord Shand, and at 9–10 per Lord Davey. See also *Merchant Taylors' Co v A-G* (1871) 6 Ch App 512 at 519.

4 See *Marley v Rawlings* [2014] UKSC 2 at [20], [2015] AC 129, [2014] 1 All ER 807 per Lord Neuberger. See also *Kirin-Amgen Inc v Hoechst Marion Roussel Ltd* [2004] UKHL 46 at [64], [2005] 1 All ER 667, [2005] RPC 169 per Lord Hoffman: 'no one has ever made a non-contextual statement. There is always some context to any utterance, however meagre'. See also *Arbuthnott v Fagan* [1995] CLC 1396, [1995] 1 Lloyds Re Insurance Law Reports 135.

5 *Boreham v Bignall* (1850) 8 Hare 131 at 137; *Grey v Pearson* (1857) 6 HL Cas 61 at 109 per Lord Wensleydale; *Harding v Nott* (1857) 7 E & B 650 at 657–658. See *Blech v Blech* [2001] All ER (D) 141 (Dec) (testatrix knew of strong possibility of children being born after date of will and after her death).

6 *Re Clark's Trusts* (1863) 32 LJ Ch 525 at 529 per Wood V-C.

7 See *Egerton v Earl Brownlow* (1853) 4 HL Cas 1 at 210 per Lord St Leonards. See also *Re Flavel's Will Trusts, Coleman v Flavel* [1969] 2 All ER 232, [1969] 1 WLR 444. As to executory trusts see TRUSTS AND POWERS vol 98 (2013) PARAS 84–86.

8 *Sackville-West v Viscount Holmesdale* (1870) LR 4 HL 543 at 561 per Lord Chelmsford. As to the principle that an executory trust is construed so as best to give effect to the apparent intention of the disposer rather than according to the legal effect of the language used see *Leonard v Earl of Sussex* (1705) 2 Vern 526. See also *Pengelly v Pengelly* [2007] EWHC 3227 (Ch), [2008] Ch 375, [2008] 3 WLR 66, (rectification allowed to add word 'only' so as to create a valid executory trust); *Price v Craig* [2006] EWHC 2561 (Ch), 9 ITELR 393, [2006] All ER (D) 249 (Oct) (attendance

note showed clear intention for executory trust of entire residue, rather than part only; rectification permitted to insert necessary words); and TRUSTS AND POWERS vol 98 (2013) PARA 84.

195. Meaningless or ambiguous language in will of testator dying before 1983.

In relation to the will of a testator who died before 1 January 1983[1], where the words of the will, aided by evidence of the material facts of the case, or, in the case of a latent ambiguity in the description of some person or thing, evidence of the testator's intention[2], are insufficient to determine his meaning, the gift in question is void for uncertainty[3]. Where, however, the testator died on or after that date, then, in so far as any part of the will is meaningless, extrinsic evidence, including evidence of the testator's intention, may be admitted in all cases to assist in its interpretation[4].

Where the meaning of the will of a testator who died before 1 January 1983 is ambiguous[5], then, for the purpose of construction, the court generally resorts to the surrounding circumstances as a help in ascertaining the meaning, and places itself in the testator's position, in order to avoid attributing to him a capricious or unreasonable intention[6]. If the evidence of surrounding circumstances discloses an ambiguity, extrinsic evidence of intention is admissible[7], but, where the ambiguity appears on the face of the instrument, no such evidence is admissible[8]. Where, however, the testator died on or after 1 January 1983, then, in so far as the language used in any part of the will is ambiguous on the face of it, or, in so far as evidence, other than evidence of the testator's intention, shows that the language used in any part of it is ambiguous in the light of surrounding circumstances, extrinsic evidence, including evidence of the testator's intention, may be admitted to assist in its interpretation[9]. The court will not lightly find a patent ambiguity in a clearly written will[10]. It seems that evidence admitted for the purpose of dealing with ambiguity is not generally admitted for all purposes[11].

1   Ie the date on which the Administration of Justice Act 1982 s 21 (see the text to notes 4–9) came into force: see s 76(11). Nothing in s 21 affects the will of any testator who died before that date: s 73(6)(c).
2   As to the rules formerly governing the admissibility of evidence of intention in cases of latent ambiguity see PARA 218.
3   Wigram's Extrinsic Evidence (5th Edn) p 91, Proposition VI.
4   Administration of Justice Act 1982 s 21(1)(a), (2). Nevertheless, the lack of meaning may be too great to be overcome: see *Nathan v Leonard* [2002] EWHC 1701 (Ch), [2003] 4 All ER 198, [2003] 1 WLR 827 (obvious that words had been omitted in home-made codicil but impossible to tell what their effects may have been; testamentary condition failed for uncertainty).
5   The meaning of a will is not ambiguous by reason only of difficulties of construction (*Higgins v Dawson* [1902] AC 1 at 10, HL, per Lord Davey); but see PARA 220 note 11.
6   *Belaney v Belaney* (1867) 2 Ch App 138 at 142; *Hensman v Fryer* (1867) 3 Ch App 420 at 424. See also *Roddy v Fitzgerald* (1858) 6 HL Cas 823 at 876; *Gordon v Gordon* (1871) LR 5 HL 254 at 273. In *Lady Langdale v Briggs* (1856) 8 De GM & G 391 at 429, 431 and in *Leslie v Earl of Rothes* [1894] 2 Ch 499 at 514, CA, this principle was applied in construing a shifting clause. See also PARA 191. As to the presumption in ambiguous cases see PARA 259.
7   See note 2.
8   As to the distinction between latent and patent ambiguity see PARA 220.
9   See the Administration of Justice Act 1982 s 21(1)(b), (c), (2); and PARAS 219–220. There will, nevertheless, be cases where the court may admit evidence but will still be unable to use it as an aid to interpretation: see *Re Williams, Wiles v Madgin* [1985] 1 All ER 964, [1985] 1 WLR 905 (letter to solicitor admitted to assist in interpreting home-made will). See also *Harris v The Beneficiaries of the Estate of Margaret Alice Cooper* [2010] All ER (D) 64 (Jan).
10 See *Re Owen, Hodgson v Clare* [2002] WTLR 619, sub nom *Hodgson v Clare* [1999] All ER (D) 359, sub nom (person dying 'together with me' held to raise no ambiguity; court refused to admit extrinsic evidence of intention).
11 See *Re Williams, Wiles v Madgin* [1985] 1 All ER 964, [1985] 1 WLR 905 (where a submission that the extrinsic evidence was available for all purposes, beyond the ambiguities, was abandoned).

196. Usage of persons acting under a will. Although, as a general rule, the interpretations put on a will by those claiming under it are irrelevant[1], in the case of ancient wills the court may consider the usage of persons acting under the will as explaining its terms, on the ground that it is to be presumed that persons who were concerned have not been committing a breach of trust from the commencement of the trusts to the present time[2]. This is, however, done only in cases where the meaning is doubtful[3].

1 As to the effect of mistake on the construction of wills see MISTAKE vol 77 (2016) PARA 33.
2 *A-G v Sidney Sussex College* (1869) 4 Ch App 722 at 732 per Lord Hatherley LC. As to this rule in the case of deeds see DEEDS AND OTHER INSTRUMENTS vol 32 (2012) PARA 395; and as to this rule in the case of gifts to charities see CHARITIES vol 8 (2015) PARAS 111–113.
3 *A-G v Rochester Corpn* (1854) 5 De GM & G 797 at 822.

197. Evidence of intention admissible to rebut certain presumptions. Where according to equitable doctrines a presumption or an inference from the facts of the case is raised[1], as in the case of the presumptions against double portions[2], or with respect to satisfaction of portions by legacies and of legacies by portions[3], extrinsic evidence is admissible to rebut the presumption, and counter-evidence is then admissible to support it[4]. Evidence in support of the presumption is not, however, admissible unless evidence to rebut it has first been admitted; nor is any evidence admissible to raise a presumption not raised by law[5]. Where, however, the presumption simply arises from the construction of the words of the will, no evidence may be admitted to support or rebut it[6]. Evidence, where admitted, is allowed, not to alter the will or prove the testamentary intention, but to prove some personal obligation on the part of the donee binding on his conscience[7], or to explain acts and events taking place outside the will[8].

Evidence is admissible to rebut, or to support when rebutted, resulting or constructive trusts[9], and, in relation to deaths before 1 January 1926, was admissible in respect of the claims of an executor to a residue undisposed of as against the Crown but not as against the next of kin[10].

1 The presumption must arise out of the facts of the case and not out of the words of the will: see note 6.
2 See EQUITABLE JURISDICTION vol 47 (2014) PARAS 176–185.
3 See EQUITABLE JURISDICTION vol 47 (2014) PARAS 177–179.
4 *Trimmer v Bayne* (1802) 7 Ves 508; *Hurst v Beach* (1821) 5 Madd 351 at 500 per Leach V-C; *Re Tussaud's Estate, Tussaud v Tussaud* (1878) 9 ChD 363 at 373, CA, per James LJ and Brett LJ. See *Re Cameron, Phillips v Cameron* [1999] Ch 386, [1999] 2 All ER 924; and *Aldridge v Turner* [2004] EWHC 2768 (Ch), [2004] All ER (D) 451 (Nov) (where the evidence of small gifts and payments fell far short of raising the presumption, in the first place). See also EQUITABLE JURISDICTION vol 47 (2014) PARA 188.
5 *Re Tussaud's Estate, Tussaud v Tussaud* (1878) 9 ChD 363 at 373, CA, per James LJ.
6 *Coote v Boyd, Coote v Coote* (1789) 2 Bro CC 521 at 527 per Lord Thurlow LC; *Hurst v Beach* (1821) 5 Madd 351 at 360–361 per Leach V-C. Thus the question whether legacies are cumulative or substitutional is a question of construction merely, and no evidence is admissible: *Hall v Hill* (1841) 1 Dr & War 94; *Wilson v O'Leary* (1872) 7 Ch App 448 at 456, CA. Such evidence would amount to a contradiction or amplification of the words of the will, and no evidence for this purpose is admissible: *Lee v Pain* (1844) 4 Hare 201 at 216; and see PARA 202. In *Hubbard v Alexander* (1876) 3 ChD 738, however, evidence was admitted to show the duplicate nature of the instruments, but it is doubtful whether this evidence was properly admitted: see PARA 200 note 3.
7 *Re Shields, Corbould-Ellis v Dales* [1912] 1 Ch 591 at 599–600 (explaining *Hall v Hill* (1841) 1 Dr & War 94 and *Kirk v Eddowes* (1844) 3 Hare 509 at 516, 520; and following *Fowkes v Pascoe* (1875) 10 Ch App 343 at 350, CA, per James LJ). As to evidence of personal obligations of the donee see PARA 221.
8 *Hall v Hill* (1841) 1 Dr & War 94 at 117.
9 See *Cook v Hutchinson* (1836) 1 Keen 42 at 50 per Lord Langdale MR; and TRUSTS AND POWERS vol 98 (2013) PARA 134.
10 See *Williams v Arkle* (1875) LR 7 HL 606; *Re Bacon's Will, Camp v Coe* (1886) 31 ChD 460.

198. Evidence of intention admitted in relation to gifts to executor. Where a testator has expressed, outside his will, the intention of releasing a debt owed to him by, or making a gift of personal estate to, a person who on his death becomes his executor[1], the court admits evidence of the intention[2].

1 This rule was extended to the case of an administrator in *Re James, James v James* [1935] Ch 449, but that decision was doubted in *Re Gonin* [1979] Ch 16 at 35, [1977] 2 All ER 720 at 734 per Walton J.
2 *Strong v Bird* (1874) LR 18 Eq 315; *Re Applebee, Leveson v Beales* [1891] 3 Ch 422; *Re Pink, Pink v Pink* [1912] 2 Ch 528, CA; *Re Goff, Featherstonehaugh v Murphy* (1914) 111 LT 34. See also PARA 625.

199. Character of evidence admissible to aid interpretation of will. The instructions of a testator who died before 1 January 1983 for the preparation of his will may not be given in evidence to prove his intentions[1], except in the cases where evidence of intention is admissible[2]. With regard to such a testator, similar considerations apply to revoked wills[3], a draft of the will[4], letters[5] and to papers or sayings of his[6]. As a general rule[7], documents other than the will may not be referred to for the purpose of the construction of the will[8] unless they are expressly referred to in the will[9].

However, in the case of a testator who died on or after 1 January 1983[10], a will which fails to carry out his intentions in consequence of a failure to understand his instructions may be rectified[11], and extrinsic evidence of the testator's intention, which has always been admissible in cases of latent ambiguity[12], may also be admitted to assist in interpreting any part of a will which is meaningless or ambiguous on its face[13].

1 *Towers v Moor* (1689) 2 Vern 98; *Doe d Hubbard v Hubbard* (1850) 15 QB 227; *Drake v Drake* (1860) 8 HL Cas 172.
2 *Re Hubbuck* [1905] P 129 at 135; *Re Bateman, Wallace v Mawdsley* (1911) 27 TLR 313 (where such evidence was excluded). However, in *Re Ofner, Samuel v Ofner* [1909] 1 Ch 60, CA, such evidence was admitted as evidence identifying the donee and not as evidence of intention. As to latent ambiguity see PARAS 218–220.
3 *Richardson v Watson* (1833) 4 B & Ad 787; *Re Feltham's Will Trusts* (1855) 1 K & J 528 at 532; *Re Waller, White v Scoles* (1899) 80 LT 701, CA; *Re Smith, Smith v Johnson* (1904) 20 TLR 287; *Re Nesbitt's Will Trusts, Dr Barnardo's Homes National Incorp Association v United Newcastle-Upon-Tyne Hospitals of the Board of Governors* [1953] 1 All ER 936, [1953] 1 WLR 595; *Re Tetsall, Foyster v Tetsall* [1961] 2 All ER 801, [1961] 1 WLR 938 (where a revoked will was looked at to identify the subject matter of the gift). A provision which is clearly revoked, even though admitted to probate, may not be resorted to as expressing the intention of the testator for any purpose: *Choa Eng Wan v Choa Giang Tee* [1923] AC 469, PC. Cf *Re Northcliffe, Arnholz v Hudson* [1925] Ch 651 at 654 (cited in PARA 2 note 9).
4 *Miller v Travers* (1832) 8 Bing 244; *Bradshaw v Bradshaw* (1836) 2 Y & C Ex 72.
5 *Bernasconi v Atkinson* (1853) 10 Hare 345 at 354.
6 *Bertie v Falkland* (1698) 1 Salk 231 (papers etc). See also *Sir Lytton Strode v Lady Falkland* (1707) 3 Rep Ch 169; *Bennet v Davis* (1725) 2 P Wms 316 at 318; *Herbert v Reid* (1810) 16 Ves 481 at 490; *Duke of Leeds v Earl of Amherst* (1844) 9 Jur 359; *British Home and Hospital for Incurables v Royal Hospital for Incurables* (1904) 90 LT 601, CA; *Re Brady, Wylie v Ratcliff* (1919) 147 LT Jo 235.
7 See, however, PARA 215.
8 *Hughes v Turner* (1835) 3 My & K 666 at 697–698 (revoked will); *Randall v Daniel* (1857) 24 Beav 193 at 206. Cf *Doe d Brown v Brown* (1809) 11 East 441; *Shore v Wilson, Lady Hewley's Charities* (1842) 9 Cl & Fin 355, HL.
9 See PARA 201.
10 Ie the date on which the Administration of Justice Act 1982 s 20 (rectification) (see PARA 187 and s 21 (evidence) (see PARAS 195, 219 came into in force: see s 76(11). Nothing in ss 20, 21 affects the will of a testator who died before that date: s 73(6)(c).
11 See the Administration of Justice Act 1982 s 20; and PARA 187.
12 This rule is now given statutory force by the Administration of Justice Act 1982 s 21(1)(c), (2): see PARA 219.

13 See the Administration of Justice Act 1982 s 21(1)(a), (b), (2); and PARAS 195, 219. As to the necessity for the testamentary wording to be able to carry the meaning contended for from the evidence see *Re Williams, Wiles v Madgin* [1985] 1 All ER 964, [1985] 1 WLR 905; and PARA 195 note 9.

(ii) Evidence of Language and its Meaning

200. Conclusiveness of probate as to form of will. For the purpose of discovering what words the testator used, and what dispositions he made, the court of construction[1] accepts the probate, in the case of all English wills, as conclusively showing the state in which the will was at its execution[2], and containing the whole will to be construed[3]. The court may look at the original will[4] in order to settle questions arising on the punctuation[5], or on the introduction of a capital letter or other mark which may indicate where a sentence or clause was intended to begin and which may affect its sense, or on the effect of blanks in the will, and generally in order to see whether any light is thrown on the construction of the will by its form[6]. The court may take into account, as assisting the construction, the fact that the will was made on a printed form[7]; but, while the court may look at the original will for the purpose of assisting the construction of the probate copy, it may not do so for the purpose of contradicting it[8].

Where under the present practice a photographic copy of the will is annexed to the probate[9], this in effect is equivalent to the original will.

1 As to courts of construction see PARA 185 et seq.
2 *Bernal v Bernal* (1838) 3 My & Cr 559 at 563n. See also *Lynn v Beaver* (1823) Turn & R 63 at 67 per Lord Eldon LC; *Wordsworth v Wood* (1847) 1 HL Cas 129 at 157n; *Oppenheim v Henry* (1853) 9 Hare 803n; *Gann v Gregory* (1854) 3 De GM & G 777 at 781 (crossed lines over part of will, and pencil alterations); *Barnaby v Tassell* (1871) LR 11 Eq 363 at 368; and PARAS 672, 675; but see the text and note 7. As to the omission from the probate of passages and expressions of a malicious or libellous character see PARA 739; and as to the omission of passages inserted by mistake see PARA 186.
3 As to the reception of a probate in evidence see PARA 675. In *Hubbard v Alexander* (1876) 3 ChD 738, a court of construction admitted evidence to show that two codicils were not two distinct instruments, but not for the purpose of construing them in order to determine whether they were cumulative in effect. It appears that this evidence was wrongly admitted. Such evidence is admissible in the probate court: *Jenner v Ffinch* (1879) 5 PD 106.
4 *Re Harrison, Turner v Hellard* (1885) 30 ChD 390 at 393, CA, per Lord Esher MR, and at 394 per Baggallay LJ. The court may look at the original will, even where the probate is in facsimile form: *Shea v Boschetti* (1854) 18 Beav 321. In the case of foreign wills, the court may look at the original, even though only an English translation has been proved: *Re Cliff's Trusts* [1892] 2 Ch 229. As to the construction of foreign wills see PARA 203.
5 *Houston v Burns* [1918] AC 337 at 342, HL, per Lord Finlay; *Re Steel, Public Trustee v Christian Aid Society* [1979] Ch 218, [1978] 2 All ER 1026 (holograph will made on will form; probate copy typed on will form; differences of punctuation and arrangement; held: court of construction entitled to look at original will and give proper weight to punctuation (or its absence), its arrangement and indentation).
6 *Child v Elsworth* (1852) 2 De GM & G 679 at 683; *Oppenheim v Henry* (1853) 9 Hare 803n per Wood V-C. See also *Philipps v Chamberlaine* (1798) 4 Ves 51 at 57; *Thellusson v Woodford* (1799) 4 Ves 227 at 325 (parenthesis); *Lunn v Osborne* (1834) 7 Sim 56 at 61; *Compton v Bloxham* (1845) 2 Coll 201; *Milsome v Long* (1857) 3 Jur NS 1073 (where the court looked at the will, which confirmed the view based on the probate); *Thompson v Whitelock* (1859) 4 De G & J 490; *Re Baynham, Hart v Mackenzie* (1891) 7 TLR 587; *Munro v Henderson* [1907] 1 IR 440 at 443 (affd [1908] 1 IR 260, Ir CA); *Re Jeffrey, Welch v Jeffrey* [1948] 2 All ER 131. For cases where the court considered the effect of erasures in the original will see *Manning v Purcell* (1855) 7 De GM & G 55 at 66; *Re Battie-Wrightson, Cecil v Battie-Wrightson* [1920] 2 Ch 330.
7 *Re Harrison, Turner v Hellard* (1885) 30 ChD 390, CA; *Re Stevens, Pateman v James* [1952] Ch 323, [1952] 1 All ER 674. There is no rule that, in the case of inconsistency between the words of the printed form and those in the testator's own handwriting, the handwritten words must prevail: *Re Gare, Filmer v Carter* [1952] Ch 80, [1951] 2 All ER 863.

8 *Oppenheim v Henry* (1853) 9 Hare 803n. If, however, none of the parties objects and an inaccuracy in a probate is alleged, the court looks at the original will: *Re Cliff's Trusts* [1892] 2 Ch 229. See also *Philipps v Chamberlaine* (1798) 4 Ves 51 at 57 (mistake alleged); *Compton v Bloxham* (1845) 2 Coll 201 at 204 (original will construed).

9 Cf PARA 732.

201. Other documents referred to in the will. Even though a document is not admitted to probate, it may be referred to in a will in such a manner that the court of construction is entitled to look at it, as being virtually incorporated in that which is admitted to probate[1]. For this to be possible, the document must be clearly identified by the description given of it in the will, and it must be shown to have been in existence at the time when the will was executed[2]. If the document is expressly directed not to form part of the will, it is not admissible to explain the will[3].These strict rules on admissibility have lost some of their force by reason of the modern wider approach to evidence of intention when interpreting wills[4] and that permissible by statute for the rectification and interpretation of wills[5].

A testator cannot by his will reserve a power to dispose of his property by an instrument not duly executed as a will or codicil, or orally, and evidence of any such instrument or oral disposition is, therefore, inadmissible to show his testamentary wishes[6]. If a will refers in the alternative to two documents, that is, an existing document or a future substituted document, evidence as to the existence of the future document cannot be admitted and, consequently, evidence of the former document cannot be admitted either as it would not reveal the testator's whole intention; the gift, therefore, fails for uncertainty[7]. A gift on the trusts of an existing settlement may, however, be effective, even though some of the trusts cannot be given effect as testamentary dispositions[8].

1 *Quihampton v Going* (1876) 24 WR 917. See also *Allen v Maddock* (1858) 11 Moo PCC 427 at 445, 461. As to the incorporation of documents for the purpose of being included in the grant of probate see PARA 711.

2 *Dillon v Harris* (1830) 4 Bli NS 321 at 359, HL; *Allen v Maddock* (1858) 11 Moo PCC 427 at 454; *Quihampton v Going* (1876) 24 WR 917 (entries in ledger); *Singleton v Tomlinson* (1878) 3 App Cas 404 at 413–414, HL, per Lord Cairns (schedule of property); *Re Deprez, Henriques v Deprez* [1917] 1 Ch 24 (entries in testator's account books: see PARA 690 note 3); *Re White, Knight v Briggs* [1925] Ch 179. See also *Reading v Reading* [2015] EWHC 946, [2015] WTLR 1245, [2015] All ER (D) 64 (Feb) (Ch) (letter of wishes).

3 *Re Louis, Louis v Treloar* (1916) 32 TLR 313.

4 A document which does not fulfill these conditions may be relevant to the ascertainment of the testator's intention as part of the matrix of fact, known or assumed at the date of execution: see *Investor's Compensation Scheme Ltd v West Bromwich Building Society* [1998] 1 All ER 98 at 114–115, [1998] 1 WLR 896 at 912–913, HL, per Lord Hoffmann; and see *Marley v Rawlings* [2014] UKSC 2 at [19], [2015] AC 129, [2014] 1 All ER 807 per Lord Neuberger.

5 See the Administration of Justice Act 1982 ss 20, 21; and PARAS 187, 224–225.

6 *Habergham v Vincent* (1793) 2 Ves 204; *Johnson v Ball* (1851) 5 De G & Sm 85 at 91; *Re Fane, Fane v Fane* (1886) 2 TLR 510; *Re Hyslop, Hyslop v Chamberlain* [1894] 3 Ch 522. See also *Reynolds v Kortright* (1854) 18 Beav 417; *Re Walsh, Keenan v Brown* (1911) 30 NZLR 1166.

7 *Re Jones, Jones v Jones* [1942] Ch 328, [1942] 1 All ER 642.

8 *Re Edwards' Will Trusts, Dalgleish v Leighton* [1948] Ch 440, [1948] 1 All ER 821, CA; *Re Schintz's Will Trusts, Lloyds Bank Ltd v Moreton* [1951] Ch 870, [1951] 1 All ER 1095. A gift on the trusts of a deed which does not become operative fails: *Re Hurdle, Balkeney v Hurdle* [1936] 3 All ER 810.

202. Evidence admissible to decipher, interpret or understand words used. Where the characters in which a will is written are difficult to decipher[1], or the language of the will is a language not understood by the court[2], or is the language of a trade, business or locality with which the testator was acquainted[3], the evidence of persons who are skilled in deciphering writing or who understand the language in which the will is written is admissible to declare what the words and characters are, and to inform the court of their proper meaning[4]. Evidence may not, however, be admitted to show that the testator understood common words in a special sense[5], or to explain words or symbols which are not the language of any trade, business or locality, and are known only to the testator himself[6], except such evidence as the will itself refers to as the means by which the meaning of the words or symbols used in it is to be ascertained[7].

1 *Masters v Masters* (1718) 1 P Wms 421 at 425 (illegible writing).
2 See PARA 203 note 1.
3 *Kell v Charmer* (1856) 23 Beav 195 (use of business symbols denoting prices). See also *Goblet v Beechey* (1831) 2 Russ & M 624 (handwriting expert and trade expert in conflict); *Shore v Wilson, Lady Hewley's Charities* (1842) 9 Cl & Fin 355 at 525, HL (local language etc); *Re Rayner, Rayner v Rayner* [1904] 1 Ch 176, CA ('securities' in will of a stockbroker).
4 Wigram's Extrinsic Evidence (5th Edn) p 53, Proposition IV. It seems that where a will is in a foreign language, the court must be furnished with an authenticated translation, and the translation (not the text in the foreign language) is admitted to probate: *Re Berger* [1990] Ch 118, [1989] 1 All ER 591, CA. As to the construction of foreign wills see PARA 203.
5 *King v Badeley* (1834) 3 My & K 417 ('contingent interests'; testator meant expectancies); *Shore v Wilson, Lady Hewley's Charities* (1842) 9 Cl & Fin 355 at 558, HL; *Barrow v Methold* (1855) 1 Jur NS 994 ('premium of insurance'; testator meant policy). However, in the case of a testator who died on or after 1 January 1983, extrinsic evidence may be admitted to assist in interpreting a meaningless or ambiguous part of the will: see PARAS 195, 218–219.
6 *Goblet v Beechey* (1831) 2 Russ & M 624; Wigram's Extrinsic Evidence (5th Edn) p 201, Appendix I; *Clayton v Lord Nugent* (1844) 13 M & W 200 at 206 (cited in note 7). As to deaths on or after 1 January 1983, however, see note 5.
7 See *Clayton v Lord Nugent* (1844) 13 M & W 200 at 206, where a will indicated donees by letters or symbols, and referred for their meaning to a card index; the card index mentioned in the will would have been admissible for the purpose of identifying devisees, but a later index, signed but not attested, which had replaced the earlier index, was not admissible for this purpose. The later index was, however, admissible for identifying donees under a gift of personalty, as a gift of personalty, unlike a devise, did not at the date of the will require to be attested: see *East v Twyford* (1853) 4 HL Cas 517. As to the incorporation of documents in wills see PARAS 201, 711.

203. Construing foreign wills. Where a foreign will is to be construed, there must be a translation of the instrument, and evidence may be admitted to prove:

(1)   the translation of the words;

(2)   the technical meaning of words which are of a technical description or which have a peculiar meaning different from that which they would bear when literally translated into English[1]; and

(3)   where the construction of the will is governed by a foreign system of law, any established principle of construction which would be applied to the particular instrument by the corresponding foreign tribunal[2].

The court, in the light of all the admissible evidence, will determine what the testator intended and will give effect to that intention so far as it is valid and effectual by English law[3].

1 In the case of a foreign will containing foreign technical terms the court avails itself of the assistance of foreign lawyers: *Reynolds v Kortright* (1854) 18 Beav 417 at 425; *Re Cliff's Trusts* [1892] 2 Ch 229 at 232; *Re Manners, Manners v Manners* [1923] 1 Ch 220. As to the foreign element in wills see PARAS 12–13.
2 *Duchess di Sora v Phillipps* (1863) 10 HL Cas 624 at 633, 639–640, correcting the report of *Williams v Williams* (1841) 3 Beav 547. Alternatively, the original will may be looked at: *Re Manners, Manners v Manners* [1923] 1 Ch 220. See also CIVIL PROCEDURE vol 12 (2015) PARA 1006; DEEDS AND OTHER INSTRUMENTS vol 32 (2012) PARA 401. As to the construction of foreign wills see further PARA 241; and CONFLICT OF LAWS vol 19 (2011) PARAS 749–752.
3 *Re Berger* [1990] Ch 118 at 133, [1989] 1 All ER 591 at 602, CA, per Sir Denys Buckley.

204. Evidence of meaning of legal technical terms. Evidence may not be admitted to determine the meaning of technical terms of English law. The terms which constitute technical terms in English law, and their technical meanings[1], are determined by the court with the aid, in certain cases, of established rules of construction. In considering a technically drawn will, the court regards the practice of conveyancers as not wholly irrelevant but not binding[2].

1   Examples of technical terms are 'seised' (*Leach v Jay* (1878) 9 ChD 42, CA); 'vested' (see PARA 412); 'plurality' (*Re Macnamara, Hewitt v Jeans* (1911) 104 LT 771). See also *Sammut v Manzi* [2008] UKPC 58 at [25]–[26], [2009] 2 All ER 234, [2009] 1 WLR 1834 per Lord Hope (it seems that the modern usage of 'per stirpes' should be taken to mean 'by family', so that remote descendants do not take in competition with living immediate ancestors who take under the gift). As to technical and quasi-technical words describing property or donees see PARAS 286 et seq, 328 et seq. As to the former use in wills of words appropriate to a conveyance under the Statute of Uses (1535) see *Re Tanqueray-Willaume and Landau* (1882) 20 ChD 465 at 478, CA; Tudor, LC Real Prop (4th Edn) 307 et seq. See also REAL PROPERTY AND REGISTRATION vol 87 (2012) PARA 96. See also *Ross v Perrin Hughes* [2004] EWHC 2559 (Ch), 7 ITELR 405, [2004] All ER (D) 159 (Nov) ('apartment' held not to be a technical legal term of art but, as it created an ambiguity in the will, evidence of intention was allowed).

2   *Re Athill, Athill v Athill* (1880) 16 ChD 211 at 223, CA; *Re Edwards, Edwards v Edwards* [1894] 3 Ch 644. See also *Villar v Sir Walter Gilbey* [1907] AC 139 at 152, HL, per Lord Atkinson. In considering what are 'usual' clauses, the court treats the question as one of fact, on which evidence of the practice of conveyancers is accepted: *Re Maddy's Estate, Maddy v Maddy* [1901] 2 Ch 820 at 822. The practice of conveyancers is not a helpful guide in construing a clause that is not in the precedent books: *Blathwayt v Baron Cawley* [1976] AC 397 at 421–422, [1975] 3 All ER 625 at 632–633; *D'Abo v Paget* [2000] All ER (D) 944.

205. Evidence of the ordinary meaning of words. The ordinary meaning of a word is the meaning given to it by the ordinary usage of society[1], that is, the testator's society, of that class and period in which he lived and moved[2]. Accordingly, in order to discover the ordinary meaning of any word, the court may not only consult dictionaries of good reputation[3], or other contemporary literary sources[4], but may also consider evidence of the meaning customarily given to the word by persons in such society[5], and, in the case of words describing property, by those who deal in such property[6]. In the construction of the will of a testator who died before 1 January 1983[7], such evidence is not admitted where the meaning is plain and unambiguous on the face of the will[8], but, in relation to the will of a testator who died on or after that date, in so far as such evidence shows that the language is ambiguous[9] in the light of surrounding circumstances, it is admissible together with all other relevant extrinsic evidence, including evidence of the testator's intention[10]. The ordinary meaning of a word is not necessarily the etymological meaning[11], but there may be cases where the court refers to the etymological meaning as a guide[12].

However, the court may depart from the ordinary meaning of a word where it is clear from the context or the surrounding circumstances that a different meaning is intended by the testator[13].

1   See generally PARA 224; and see also *Shore v Wilson, Lady Hewley's Charities* (1842) 9 Cl & Fin 355 at 537, HL, per Coleridge J; *Parker v Marchant* (1843) 1 Ph 356 at 360 ('the ordinary acceptation of language in the transactions of mankind'); *Re How, How v How* [1930] 1 Ch 66; *Re Atkinson's Will Trusts, Atkinson v Hall* [1978] 1 All ER 1275, [1978] 1 WLR 586.

2   *M'Hugh v M'Hugh* [1908] 1 IR 155 at 160 (not archaic or obsolete meaning). As to the analysis of the meaning of 'writing under hand' see *Trustee Solutions Ltd v Dubery* [2006] EWHC 1426 (Ch) at [21]–[36], [2007] 1 All ER 308 (partly revsd on other grounds [2007] EWCA Civ 771, [2008] 1 All ER 826).

3   *Re Rayner, Rayner v Rayner* [1904] 1 Ch 176, CA. The court is not bound by the dictionary: see *Grieves v Rawley* (1852) 10 Hare 63 at 65; and CIVIL PROCEDURE vol 12 (2015) PARA 1002.

4   *Re Rayner, Rayner v Rayner* [1904] 1 Ch 176 at 187, CA (the Times newspaper). Cf *A-G v Cast-Plate Glass Co* (1792) 1 Anst 39 at 44 ('dictionaries or books on the particular subject'); *Shore v Wilson, Lady Hewley's Charities* (1842) 9 Cl & Fin 355 at 568–569, HL; *Marquis Camden v IRC* [1914] 1 KB 641, CA ('any literary help they can find, including the consultation of the works of standard authors and authoritative dictionaries').

5   *Barksdale v Morgan* (1693) 4 Mod Rep 185; *Re Steel, Wappett v Robinson* [1903] 1 Ch 135 ('freeholds' by local usage included customary freeholds); *Re Van Lessen, National Provincial Bank Ltd v Beaumont* [1955] 3 All ER 691, [1955] 1 WLR 1326 (usage among philatelists). The

customary meaning prevails, even though the words in their meaning according to general English usage would create no difficulty in applying the instrument to the facts: Underhill and Strahan's Interpretation of Wills and Settlements (3rd Edn) pp 15–16. The question whether a word has a customary meaning is one of fact: *Simpson v Margitson* (1847) 11 QB 23 at 32. As to custom generally see CUSTOM AND USAGE vol 32 (2012) PARA 1 et seq. Where, however, a word has received a statutory definition of general application, evidence of a different local usage is inadmissible: *O'Donnell v O'Donnell* (1878) 1 LR Ir 284. Cf *Church Property Trustees v Public Trustee* (1907) 27 NZLR 354.

6   *Brannigan v Murphy* [1896] 1 IR 418 at 426; *Re Rayner, Rayner v Rayner* [1904] 1 Ch 176 at 188 per Vaughan Williams LJ; *Re Herring, Murray v Herring* [1908] 2 Ch 493; *Re Van Lessen, National Provincial Bank Ltd v Beaumont* [1955] 3 All ER 691, [1955] 1 WLR 1326 (evidence of stamp dealers).
7   As to the significance of this date see PARA 195 note 1.
8   Cf *Earl de la Warr v Miles* (1881) 17 ChD 535 at 588–589.
9   As to the meaning of 'ambiguity' in this context see PARA 219.
10 See PARAS 195, 218–219. See also *Ross v Perrin Hughes* [2004] EWHC 2559 (Ch), 7 ITELR 405, [2004] All ER (D) 159 (Nov) (meaning of word 'apartment').
11 *Shore v Wilson, Lady Hewley's Charities* (1842) 9 Cl & Fin 355 at 527, HL.
12 *Parr v Parr* (1833) 1 My & K 647 at 648 ('devolve'); *Re Alcock, Bonser v Seville* [1945] Ch 264, [1945] 1 All ER 613 ('between').
13 *Blech v Blech* [2001] All ER (D) 141 (Dec) ('as shall survive me' construed so as to include children born after testatrix's death). See also PARA 189.

206. Decisions as to ordinary meaning.

The ordinary meaning, and, therefore, legal interpretation, of words may vary from time to time according to the usages of the community[1], and there are often many meanings applied in common use to any given word[2]. Accordingly, it has often been a matter for judicial decision in the construction of wills and other documents what is, or was, at a given time the ordinary meaning of a particular word, or the secondary meanings which are or were capable of being given to it[3].

The starting point when construing any will is to attempt to deduce the intention of the testator by giving the words of the will the meaning that they naturally bear, having regard to the contents of the will as a whole[4]. When construing a will, little assistance can be gained from considering how other judges construed similar wording in other cases[5].

1   See generally PARA 224; and see also *Shore v Wilson, Lady Hewley's Charities* (1842) 9 Cl & Fin 355 at 527, HL; *Re Rayner, Rayner v Rayner* [1904] 1 Ch 176 at 185, CA; *Perrin v Morgan* [1943] AC 399 at 417, [1943] 1 All ER 187 at 195, HL, per Lord Thankerton. See *Re Harding, Gibbs v Harding* [2007] EWHC 3 (Ch), [2008] Ch 235, [2007] 1 All ER 747 (construction of 'the black community', according to modern usage).
2   See *Cave v Horsell* [1912] 3 KB 533, CA. Examples of this include the words 'family' (see PARA 348) and 'money' (see PARA 293). As to departing from the primary meaning of words see *Pigg v Clarke* (1876) 3 ChD 672 at 674 per Jessel MR. For a discussion of the circumstances justifying the departure from the ordinary meaning of 'survive' see *Blech v Blech* [2001] All ER (D) 141 (Dec); and see further PARA 242.
3   'Writing under hand' imports signature: see *Trustee Solutions Ltd v Dubery* [2006] EWHC 1426 (Ch), [2007] 1 All ER 308 (partly revsd on other grounds [2007] EWCA Civ 771, [2008] 1 All ER 826). See also *Re Koeppler's Will Trusts, Barclays Bank Trust Co plc v Slack* [1984] Ch 243, [1984] 2 All ER 111 ('as long as' has a well-recognised secondary meaning of 'provided that' or 'if'); revsd on other grounds [1986] Ch 423, [1985] 2 All ER 869, CA. As to the reliance to be placed on previous decisions on the construction of other wills see PARA 237.
4   See *Sammut v Manzi* UKPC 58 at [4], [2009] 2 All ER 234, [2009] 1 WLR 1834. As to the modern approach to interpretation of wills see *Marley v Rawlings* [2014] UKSC 2, [2015] AC 129, [2014] 1 All ER 807; and PARA 188.
5   *Sammut v Manzi* UKPC 58 at [6], [2009] 2 All ER 234, [2009] 1 WLR 1834.

207. Evidence to vary terms of will.

Evidence may never be given in a court of construction in order to complete an incomplete will[1], or to add to[2], vary[3] or contradict[4] the terms of a will, or generally to prove any testamentary intentions of the testator not found in the will[5], or even to reconcile two contradictory clauses, and declare which of the two expresses the testator's real intention[6].

1   Thus no evidence can be given for the purpose of filling up a total blank in a will: *Winne v Littleton* (1681) 2 Cas in Ch 51; *Baylis v A-G* (1741) 2 Atk 239; *Hunt v Hort* (1791) 3 Bro CC 311; *Taylor v Richardson* (1853) 2 Drew 16. As to filling up blanks by construction alone see PARA 253.
2   Eg by inserting a devise or bequest omitted by mistake of the draftsman: *Earl of Newburgh v Countess Dowager of Newburgh* (1820) 5 Madd 364. See also *Selwin v Brown* (1735) 3 Bro Parl Cas 607, HL; *Langston v Langston* (1834) 8 Bli NS 167 at 214, HL (where the court arrived at the conclusion that an error in copying had been made on the instrument as it stood). See also *Whitton v Russell* (1739) 1 Atk 448. As to the jurisdiction to correct mistakes see further PARA 186; and as to possible rectification in such circumstances see PARA 187.
3   Eg by changing the name or description of a legatee (*Del Mare v Robello* (1792) 1 Ves 412; *Drake v Drake* (1860) 8 HL Cas 172; *Re Ely, Tottenham v Ely* (1891) 65 LT 452 (but as to this case see PARA 220 note 1)), or by including a legatee among the persons referred to in a condition (*Lord Cheyney's Case* (1591) 5 Co Rep 68a), or by varying the terms of a legacy (*Lowfield v Stoneham* (1746) 2 Stra 1261), or by adding conditions to a legacy (*Vernon's Case* (1572) 4 Co Rep 1a at 4a; *Lawrence v Dodwell* (1699) 1 Ld Raym 438).
4   *Hampshire v Peirce* (1751) 2 Ves Sen 216 at 217 per Strange MR (where the evidence tendered and rejected with respect to one gift was received as evidence of identification with regard to another); *Clementson v Gandy* (1836) 1 Keen 309. See also *Brown v Langley* (1731) 2 Barn KB 118. Thus no evidence can be given to prove a trust when the terms of the will expressly give a beneficial interest, or vice versa (*Langham v Sandford* (1816) 2 Mer 6 at 17 per Lord Eldon LC; *Irvine v Sullivan* (1869) LR 8 Eq 673 at 677; *Re Huxtable, Huxtable v Crawfurd* [1902] 2 Ch 793, CA; *Re Keen, Evershed v Griffiths* [1937] Ch 236 at 247, [1937] 1 All ER 452 at 459, CA; *Re Rees, Williams v Hopkins* [1950] Ch 204, [1949] 2 All ER 1003, CA), except in cases of fraud (*Russell v Jackson* (1852) 10 Hare 204; *Re Spencer's Will* (1887) 57 LT 519, CA). See PARA 221.
5   *Bertie v Falkland* (1698) 1 Salk 231 at 232; *Bennet v Davis* (1725) 2 P Wms 316 at 318. As to the circumstances in which extrinsic evidence of intention is admissible see PARAS 195, 218–219.
6   *Ulrich v Litchfield* (1742) 2 Atk 372; *Re Bywater, Bywater v Clarke* (1881) 18 ChD 17, CA. It is open to question whether it could be said that in such a case the language used 'in any part' of the will was ambiguous on its face so as to bring the Administration of Justice Act 1982 s 21 into operation. Even where the evidence may be technically admissible it might still not be capable of being used for the purpose for which it was admitted: see *Re Williams, Wiles v Madgin* [1985] 1 All ER 964, [1985] 1 WLR 905. See also *Re Steel, Public Trustee v Christian Aid Society* [1979] Ch 218, [1978] 2 All ER 1026 (admissibility of evidence of punctuation and arrangement). See also PARA 195.

208.   Other evidence of the testator's wishes. Although evidence may be admissible to prove matters constituting an obligation accepted by the donee[1], evidence is not in general admissible to establish testamentary wishes of the testator not manifested in the way required by statute[2]. Accordingly, where a mere power, as opposed to a trust[3], is given by the will to the donee to dispose of property in accordance with wishes orally expressed by the testator, evidence may not be admissible to determine the testator's wishes[4].

1   As to such cases see PARA 221.
2   *Irvine v Sullivan* (1869) LR 8 Eq 673 at 678. See also *Briggs v Penny* (1849) 3 De G & Sm 525 (on appeal (1851) 3 Mac & G 546). As to the circumstances in which evidence of the testator's intention is admissible see, however, PARAS 195, 218–219.
3   As to secret trusts see *Blackwell v Blackwell* [1929] AC 318, HL; *Re Young, Young v Young* [1951] Ch 344, [1950] 2 All ER 1245; PARAS 221–222; and TRUSTS AND POWERS vol 98 (2013) PARA 87 et seq.
4   *Re Hetley, Hetley v Hetley* [1902] 2 Ch 866. Cf *Shirinbai v Ratanbai* (1921) LR 48 Ind App 69, PC (where the oral directions to the donee as to disposal by her will did not deprive the donee of her discretion).

(iii) Evidence for Purposes of Identification

209.   Evidence which is necessarily admissible. The words of a testator's will necessarily refer to facts and circumstances respecting his property and his family and other persons and things, and the meaning and application of his words cannot be ascertained without evidence of such facts and circumstances[1]. Evidence is, therefore, necessarily admissible to show facts and circumstances corresponding, as far as possible, with those referred to in the will, for example to show that persons and property actually exist as described[2].

The court must, however, first attempt to construe the words of the will[3]; and the questions whether further evidence is to be considered, and what is the materiality of that evidence, depend on the construction placed on those words and on the existence of any subject matter to which they exactly correspond[4].

1 *Doe d Hiscocks v Hiscocks* (1839) 5 M & W 363 at 367–368 per Lord Abinger CB; Tudor, LC Real Prop (4th Edn) 489; *Re Birkin, Heald v Millership* [1949] 1 All ER 1045 at 1047 per Harman J.

2 See *Sherratt v Mountford* (1873) 8 Ch App 928 at 929 per James LJ. See also *Sanford v Raikes* (1816) 1 Mer 646 at 653; *Doe d Preedy v Holtom* (1835) 4 Ad & El 76 at 82. See also *Pinnel v Anison* [2005] EWHC 1421 (Ch), sub nom *Pinnell v Annison* [2005] All ER (D) 458 (May) (person matching name and address given in will but not fitting other words of description; evidence admitted to show to whom the testator referred).

3 *Re Seal, Seal v Taylor* [1894] 1 Ch 316 at 322–323, CA; *Re Sykes, Skelton and Dyson v Sykes* [1940] 4 All ER 10. See also *Higstrim v Ray* (1895) 16 NSWLR Eq 1. As to the modern approach to the construction of wills see PARA 188.

4 Where the evidence may be material, it is generally admitted in the first instance, reserving the question of its materiality: *Sayer v Sayer, Innes v Sayer* (1849) 7 Hare 377 at 381. The wider admissibility of evidence of intention under the Administration of Justice Act 1982 s 21 (see PARA 195) may mean that the approach to construction of collective descriptions such as 'belongings' or 'personal belongings' (terms not normally used to relate to real property) may change from that seen in *Re Price, Wasley v Price* [1950] Ch 242, [1950] 1 All ER 338, and in *Re Hynes, Knapp v Hynes* [1950] 2 All ER 879, 94 Sol Jo 687.

210. Plain and unambiguous gift. The evidence necessarily admitted may disclose the existence of persons or property exactly answering the description in the will[1], and show that the will contains a plain, unambiguous and effective gift. Where the testator in such a case died before 1 January 1983[2], further evidence of the testator's intention is not admissible[3] to show that he must have meant some person or property different from that which his words plainly and unambiguously described[4], such as evidence of the testator's fuller knowledge of or intimacy with other persons[5], or his want of knowledge of the person so described[6], or his habit of describing any other person in the same terms[7]; or the state or value generally of the testator's property[8], where the will itself does not make that state or value of importance[9]; or his knowledge or management[10], or the history[11], of the property or any part of it; or the testator's habits of describing other property in the same terms[12]. However, in the construction of the will of a testator who died on or after 1 January 1983, such evidence is admissible to raise an ambiguity[13], and extrinsic evidence, including evidence of the testator's intention, may be given to resolve it[14].

Evidence (other than evidence of the testator's intention) was and has always been admissible to raise a latent ambiguity[15], as by showing that there exists some other subject matter to which the same word might equally, or with a negligible variation, apply[16]. Where such an ambiguity is disclosed, extrinsic evidence of intention is and has always been admissible to resolve it[17].

1 *Horwood v Griffith* (1853) 4 De GM & G 700 at 708; *Millard v Bailey* (1866) LR 1 Eq 378; *Re Seal, Seal v Taylor* [1894] 1 Ch 316 at 323; *Re Trimmer, Crundwell v Trimmer* (1904) 91 LT 26.

2 Ie the date on which the Administration of Justice Act 1982 s 21 (see PARAS 195, 219) came into force: see s 76(11). Nothing in s 21 affects the will of a testator who died before that date: s 73(6)(c).

3 See Just Dig lib 32 s 25; *Re Millar, Barnard v Mahoney* (1898) 17 NZLR 160.

4 *Shore v Wilson, Lady Hewley's Charities* (1842) 9 Cl & Fin 355 at 565, HL, per Tindal CJ; *Re Overhill's Trust* (1853) 1 Sm & G 362 at 366; *Horwood v Griffith* (1853) 4 De GM & G 700 at 708 per Turner LJ.

5 *Holmes v Custance* (1806) 12 Ves 279; *Wilson v Squire* (1842) 1 Y & C Ch Cas 654; *Re Williams, Gregory v Muirhead* (1913) 134 LT Jo 619.

6 *Re Corsellis, Freeborn v Napper* [1906] 2 Ch 316.

7 *Green v Howard* (1779) 1 Bro CC 31 ('relations'); *Ellis v Houstoun* (1878) 10 ChD 236 at 245 ('children'); *Re Parker, Bentham v Wilson* (1881) 17 ChD 262, CA ('second cousins'); *Re Fish, Ingham v Rayner* [1894] 2 Ch 83, CA ('niece'; the actual decision in this case would now be different having regard to the Family Law Reform Act 1987 ss 1, 19: see PARA 356).

8 *Brown v Langley* (1731) 2 Barn KB 118; *Lord Inchiquin v French* (1744) Amb 33 at 40; *Kellett v Kellett* (1811) 1 Ball & B 533 at 542; *Hensman v Fryer* (1867) 3 Ch App 420 at 424; *Re Grainger, Dawson v Higgins* [1900] 2 Ch 756 at 768–769, CA, per Rigby LJ (revsd sub nom *Higgins v Dawson* [1902] AC 1, HL, where, however, the question was rather of construction of the will than of identification).

9 Such evidence may become admissible (see PARA 211) where the descriptions are not clear in the will and are unintelligible without receiving such evidence (*Fonnereau v Poyntz* (1785) 1 Bro CC 472 (explained in *Druce v Denison* (1801) 6 Ves 385 at 401); *Colpoys v Colpoys* (1822) Jac 451; *A-G v Grote* (1827) 2 Russ & M 699 (cited in Wigram's Extrinsic Evidence (5th Edn) p 216, Appendix II); *Boys v Williams* (1831) 2 Russ & M 689; *Hensmann v Fryer* (1867) 3 Ch App 420; *Watson v Arundell* (1876) IR 11 Eq 53 at 75, Ir CA), or where the testator expressly makes the gifts by reference to the amount of his property (*Barksdale v Gilliat* (1818) 1 Swan 562; *Druce v Denison* (explained in *Re Grainger, Dawson v Higgins* [1900] 2 Ch 756, CA)). See also *Re Skillen, Charles v Charles* [1916] 1 Ch 518 (evidence admitted as to state of property of testatrix, but not as to intention); *Grealey v Sampson* [1917] 1 IR 286, Ir CA (evidence not admissible where the question was one of construction). As to such evidence for the purpose of proving the exercise of a power see TRUSTS AND POWERS vol 98 (2013) PARA 589.

10 *Horwood v Griffith* (1853) 4 De GM & G 700. The rule applies especially to cases where the property is described by its local description: *Anon* (1567) 3 Dyer 261b; *Woodden v Osbourn* (1599) Cro Eliz 674; *Doe d Browne v Greening* (1814) 3 M & S 171 at 173; *Doe d Tyrrell v Lyford* (1816) 4 M & S 550 at 555; *Miller v Travers* (1832) 8 Bing 244; *Doe d Templeman v Martin* (1833) 4 B & Ad 771; *Homer v Homer* (1878) 8 ChD 758 at 774, CA.

11 *Millard v Bailey* (1866) LR 1 Eq 378 (gift of shares which had been doubled or subdivided).

12 *Doe d Chichester v Oxenden* (1810) 3 Taunt 147; subsequent proceedings sub nom *Doe d Oxenden v Chichester* (1816) 4 Dow 65, HL ('my estate of A'; evidence not admissible to show testator's habit of including outlying property in this estate). See also *Doe d Brown v Brown* (1809) 11 East 441 (devise of 'copyhold estates'; evidence not admissible to show habit of describing certain freeholds as copyhold); *Doe d Tyrrell v Lyford* (1816) 4 M & S 550 at 557–558; *Evans v Angell* (1858) 26 Beav 202 at 207; *King v King* (1885) 13 LR Ir 531.

13 See *Pinnel v Anison* [2005] EWHC 1421 (Ch), sub nom *Pinnell v Annison* [2005] All ER (D) 458 (May) (an existing person described by name and address in will, but further description as testator's sister raised the ambiguity). As to the meaning of 'ambiguity' in this context see PARA 219.

14 See PARAS 195, 218–219.

15 See note 13.

16 *Doe d Templeman v Martin* (1833) 4 B & Ad 771 at 783 (where it was said that almost any evidence would be admissible for showing an ambiguity); *Grant v Grant* (1870) LR 5 CP 380 (on appeal LR 5 CP 727, Ex Ch); *Re Bowman, Bowman v Bowman* (1891) 8 TLR 117; *Marks v Marks* (1908) 40 SCR 210.

17 As to evidence of surrounding circumstances see PARA 211 et seq; and as to evidence of testator's intention see PARA 218. As to ambiguities in the will of a testator who died on or after 1 January 1983 see the Administration of Justice Act 1982 s 21; and PARAS 195, 219.

211. Gift not plain and unambiguous. Where the words of a will do not plainly and unambiguously refer to any subject, or do so only with inaccuracy[1], or where after the admission of extrinsic evidence it is seen that they refer to more than one subject[2], further evidence is then admissible in order to discover the true subject to which the words refer[3]. Where such evidence discloses an ambiguity[4], or, in the case of a testator dying on or after 1 January 1983[5], where the will is meaningless or an ambiguity appears on the face of the will[6], extrinsic evidence of the testator's intention may be given[7]. The fact that there is no person who answers the description in the will does not, however, render evidence that some other person was intended admissible where there are indications that the testator made the gift in spite of his ignorance whether any such person existed[8].

Where the words were plainly and unambiguously satisfied before, but not at, the date of the will, as, for example, where the person described has died[9] or the property described has ceased to conform to the description[10] before that date, further evidence has always been admitted to discover some other subject existing at that date to which the words as understood by the testator may refer.

1   As to inaccuracy of descriptions generally see PARA 268 et seq. See *Ross v Perrin Hughes* [2004] EWHC 2559 (Ch), [2004] All ER (D) 159 (Nov) ('my apartment' construed as comprising a maisonette and the freehold reversion to a building in which the maisonette was situated); *Pinnel v Anison* [2005] EWHC 1421 (Ch), sub nom *Pinnell v Annison* [2005] All ER (D) 458 (May) (gift expressed to be to 'my sister', but further described by name and address of another existing person in same town).
2   *Miller v Travers* (1832) 8 Bing 244 at 248; *Doe d Hiscocks v Hiscocks* (1839) 5 M & W 363 at 368.
3   *Miller v Travers* (1832) 8 Bing 244 at 247–248; *Re Ray, Cant v Johnstone* [1916] 1 Ch 461; *Pinnel v Anison* [2005] EWHC 1421 (Ch), sub nom *Pinnell v Annison* [2005] All ER (D) 458 (May).
4   As to the meaning of 'ambiguity' in this context see PARA 220.
5   Ie the date on which the Administration of Justice Act 1982 s 21 (see PARAS 195, 219) came into force: see s 76(11). Nothing in s 21 affects the will of a testator who died before that date: s 73(6)(c).
6   As to meaninglessness and patent ambiguity see PARAS 195, 219.
7   See PARAS 218–219.
8   *Del Mare v Robello* (1792) 1 Ves 412 (where a gift to the children of one sister who was a nun was not read as a gift to the children of another sister); *Daubeny v Coghlan* (1842) 12 Sim 507 at 518.
9   *Stringer v Gardiner* (1859) 4 De G & J 468; *Re Halston, Ewen v Halston* [1912] 1 Ch 435. See further PARA 278. As to the doctrine of lapse see PARA 160 et seq.
10 *Re Jameson, King v Winn* [1908] 2 Ch 111; *Re Brady, Wylie v Ratcliff* (1919) 147 LT Jo 235 (description of railway stock); but cf *Re Atlay, Atlay v Atlay* (1912) 56 Sol Jo 444 (where the evidence was treated as direct evidence of intention and excluded).

212. Evidence of surrounding circumstances. Where the words of the will have no reasonable application to the circumstances proved, further evidence of the surrounding circumstances, including, in construing the will of a testator who died on or after 1 January 1983[1], evidence of his actual intention[2], is admissible to discover the meaning of the words which give the will full effect[3]. In all such cases, for the purpose of determining the object of the testator's bounty[4], or the subject matter disposed of[5], or the quantity of interest intended to be given[6], or the other persons and things described by the will[7], and the facts and circumstances there referred to, a court of construction may, and must[8], inquire into every material fact relating to the person or thing said to be identified by that description[9].

For this purpose, evidence is admissible to enable the court to ascertain all the persons and facts which were known to the testator at the time when he made his will[10], and thus to place itself in the testator's position[11]. The court, it is said, puts itself into the testator's armchair[12].

The object of admitting evidence of surrounding circumstances is not for the purpose of speculating on what the testator's intention may have been, where no direct evidence is available[13], but of ascertaining whether the circumstances by which he was surrounded afford any certain indication of his intention[14]. Such evidence is not likely to be of assistance where the subject matter in dispute was not in existence at the date of the will[15], or where, on the construction of the will as a whole, it appears that no gift was intended by the words used[16].

1   Ie the date on which the Administration of Justice Act 1982 s 21 (see PARAS 195, 219) came into force: see s 76(11). Nothing in s 21 affects the will of a testator who died before that date: s 73(6)(c). See *Barclays Bank Trust Co Ltd v Csoti* [2004] EWHC 2769 (Ch) (Transcript), [2004] All ER (D) 88 (Oct) for the approach with such a pre-1983 will and death.

2 As to the admissibility of evidence of intention where any part of a will is meaningless see
   PARA 195.
3 *Doe d Hiscocks v Hiscocks* (1839) 5 M & W 363 at 368; *Shore v Wilson, Lady Hewley's Charities*
   (1842) 9 Cl & Fin 355 at 566, HL, per Tindal CJ; *Re Glassington, Glassington v Follett* [1906]
   2 Ch 305 at 313; *Re Ray, Cant v Johnstone* [1916] 1 Ch 461; *Re Vear, Vear v Vear* (1917) 62 Sol
   Jo 159; Wigram's Extrinsic Evidence (5th Edn) p 47, Proposition III. This proposition is not
   affected by *Higgins v Dawson* [1902] AC 1, HL: see *Re Glassington, Glassington v Follett* at 314;
   Re Cain's Will, Linehan v Cain [1913] VLR 50 at 57–58.
4 *Abbot v Massie* (1796) 3 Ves 148 (gifts to 'W G' and 'Mrs G'); *Price v Page* (1799) 4 Ves 680
   (forename left blank); *Doe d Le Chevalier v Huthwaite* (1820) 3 B & Ald 632 ('to S H second son
   of J H', he being the third son); *Lord Camoys v Blundell* (1848) 1 HL Cas 778 ('to second son of
   E W of L', shown by the circumstances to mean second son of J W of L); *Bernasconi v Atkinson*
   (1853) 10 Hare 345; *Re Bowman, Bowman v Bowman* (1891) 8 TLR 117 ('to Edmund', shown
   to mean Edward commonly called Edmund); *Re Waller, White v Scoles* (1899) 80 LT 701, CA
   ('daughters' of S shown to mean sisters of S). As to misdescription of charities, and as to the
   evidence admissible to clarify ambiguity, see CHARITIES vol 8 (2015) PARAS 109–110.
5 *Goodtitle d Radford v Southern* (1813) 1 M & S 299, 301; *Sanford v Raikes* (1816) 1 Mer 646
   at 653; *Okeden v Clifden* (1826) 2 Russ 309 at 318; *Re Glassington, Glassington v Follett* [1906]
   2 Ch 305 ('real estate' where testatrix had only proceeds of sale of real estate); *Ross v Perrin
   Hughes* [2004] EWHC 2559 (Ch), 7 ITELR 405, [2004] All ER (D) 159 (Nov) ('apartment'
   included freehold reversion to building). See also *Sandover v Brown* [2004] EWHC 1307 (Ch),
   [2004] All ER (D) 53 (May) (complex conveyancing history of property admitted into evidence).
6 *Lowe v Lord Huntingtower* (1824) 4 Russ 532n; *Blundell v Gladstone* (1841) 11 Sim 467 at 486;
   Dashwood v Magniac [1891] 3 Ch 306 at 355–356, 366, 372, CA (evidence of local customs of
   cultivation, including cutting of beech trees, and practice with regard to treatment of proceeds as
   income or capital, and rights of limited owners).
7 *Thomson and Baxter v Hempenstall* (1849) 13 Jur 814.
8 *Anstee v Nelms* (1856) 1 H & N 225 at 232–233 per Bramwell B.
9 See Wigram's Extrinsic Evidence (5th Edn) p 57, Proposition V; *Doe d Gore v Langton* (1831) 2
   B & Ad 680 at 689, 694; *Anstee v Nelms* (1856) 1 H & N 225; *Bunbury v Doran* (1874) IR 8 CL
   516 (testator's religious views); *Dashwood v Magniac* [1891] 3 Ch 306, CA. Wigram's Extrinsic
   Evidence (5th Edn) p 57, Proposition V which, so far as it relates to the discovery of the object of
   the testator's bounty and the subject of disposition, was approved in *Anstee v Nelms*, proceeds as
   follows: 'The same (it is conceived) is true of every other disputed point respecting which it can be
   shown that a knowledge of extrinsic facts can in any way be made ancillary to the right
   interpretation of a testator's words'. Cf, however, PARA 195 text and note 6.
10 For this purpose, it is the duty of personal representatives or trustees to lay before the court all
   relevant facts within their knowledge: *Re Herwin, Herwin v Herwin* [1953] Ch 701, [1953]
   2 All ER 782, CA. See also *Harris v The Beneficiaries of the Estate of Margaret Alice Cooper*
   [2010] All ER (D) 64 (Jan).
11 *Re Overhill's Trust* (1853) 1 Sm & G 362 at 366; *Bernasconi v Atkinson* (1853) 10 Hare 345 at
   348 per Wood V-C (adopted in *Charter v Charter* (1874) LR 7 HL 364 at 377 per Lord Cairns LC;
   Kingsbury v Walter [1901] AC 187 at 189, HL, per Lord Halsbury LC); *Slingsby v Grainger*
   (1859) 7 HL Cas 273 at 288 per Lord Kingsdown; *River Wear Comrs v Adamson* (1877) 2 App
   Cas 743 at 763–764, HL, per Lord Blackburn; *Re Gibbs, Martin v Harding* [1907] 1 Ch 465 at
   469; *Re Eve, Edwards v Burns* [1909] 1 Ch 796 at 799. See also *Re Stephen, Stephen v Stephen*
   [1913] WN 210. See now *Blech v Blech* [2001] All ER (D) 141 (Dec) (testatrix aware of terminal
   illness at time of making codicil and that further grandchildren might be born after her death).
12 *Boyes v Cook* (1880) 14 ChD 53 at 56, CA, per James LJ; *Clifford v Koe* (1880) 5 App Cas 447
   at 462, HL, per Lord Hatherley; *Fitzgerald v Ryan* [1899] 2 IR 637 at 658 per O'Brien CJ; *Re
   Vaughan, Scott v British and Foreign School Society* (1901) 17 TLR 278 at 279; *Re Sykes, Sykes
   v Sykes* [1909] 2 Ch 241 at 251, CA, per Farwell LJ; *Re Wills, Wills v Wills* [1909] 1 IR 268 at
   276, Ir CA; *Perrin v Morgan* [1943] AC 399 at 420, [1943] 1 All ER 187 at 197, HL, per Lord
   Romer. See also PARA 107 note 10. As to a distinction between the construction of contracts and
   that of wills in this respect see *Grant v Grant* (1870) LR 5 CP 727 at 728–729, Ex Ch, per
   Blackburn J. See also *Allgood v Blake* (1873) LR 8 Exch 160 at 162 per Blackburn J; *Barclays
   Bank Trust Co Ltd v Csoti* [2004] EWHC 2769 (Ch) (Transcript), [2004] All ER (D) 88 (Oct). As
   to the modern approach to the construction of wills see *Marley v Rawlings* [2014] UKSC 2,
   [2015] AC 129, [2014] 1 All ER 807; and PARA 188.
13 See PARA 195.
14 *Blackwell v Pennant* (1852) 9 Hare 551 at 552 per Turner V-C.
15 *Re Price, Price v Newton* [1905] 2 Ch 55 at 58.
16 *Re Sykes, Skelton and Dyson v Sykes* [1940] 4 All ER 10.

213. Evidence to identify the subject matter disposed of. In order to identify the subject matter disposed of by a will, all facts relating to the subject matter and object of the gift, such as that it was or was not in the testator's possession, the mode of acquiring it, the local situation, and the distribution of the property, are admissible[1]. In the case of a devise of land in a particular parish, evidence of general reputation as to whether the land in question is in that parish is admissible[2].

1 *Doe d Templeman v Martin* (1833) 4 B & Ad 771 at 785; *Re Vear, Vear v Vear* (1917) 62 Sol Jo 159. See *Sandover v Brown* [2004] EWHC 1307 (Ch), [2004] All ER (D) 53 (May) (property having been in testatrix's family, then subdivided and affected by series of acts by testatrix and others); *Barclays Bank Trust Co Ltd v Csoti* [2004] EWHC 2769 (Ch) (Transcript), [2004] All ER (D) 88 (Oct) (ambiguity in scope of 'my house').
2 *Anstee v Nelms* (1856) 1 H & N 225.

214. Evidence of the testator's knowledge. The evidence of the surrounding circumstances which may be admitted in construing a will[1] includes evidence not only of the testator's circumstances and those of his family and affairs[2], but also of his state of knowledge and belief with regard to those circumstances. Thus where the surname of the intended donee is omitted, evidence is admissible of the testator's knowledge of persons having the forename mentioned in the will[3], and, where the forename is omitted, of persons having the surname referred to[4]. Evidence is also admissible of the testator's understanding of what the name of a certain person was[5]; or of his knowledge that a person answering the description in the will was dead[6], or amply provided for[7]; or his knowledge of the state of his own or another family[8]; or his knowledge of or friendship with the persons alleged to be the donees described in the will, or of the degrees of his intimacy with them[9]. On the same principle, in the case of a gift to a charity, evidence is admissible that the testator was interested in or subscribed to a particular charity[10].

1 See PARAS 212–213.
2 Eg that the testator was to his own knowledge incapable of having further issue (*Re Wohlgemuth, Public Trustee v Wohlgemuth* [1949] Ch 12, [1948] 2 All ER 882; *Re Herwin, Herwin v Herwin* [1953] Ch 701, [1953] 2 All ER 782, CA), or that further children may be born to the testator's children or to other persons in the future (*Blech v Blech* [2001] All ER (D) 141 (Dec)). See also PARA 351 text and note 5.
3 *Re De Rosaz* (1877) 2 PD 66.
4 *Re Gregson's Trust* (1864) 2 Hem & M 504 at 509. See also *Gregory v Smith* (1852) 9 Hare 708.
5 *Bradshaw v Bradshaw* (1836) 2 Y & C Ex 72 at 88; *Blundell v Gladstone* (1841) 11 Sim 467 at 486 (on appeal sub nom *Lord Camoys v Blundell* (1848) 1 HL Cas 778 at 785).
6 *Re Whorwood, Ogle v Lord Sherborne* (1887) 34 ChD 446 at 450, CA. See also *Stringer v Gardiner* (1859) 4 De G & J 468 at 471.
7 *Hodgson v Clarke* (1860) 1 De GF & J 394 at 397–398.
8 *Doe d Thomas v Beynon* (1840) 12 Ad & El 431. See also *Goodinge v Goodinge* (1749) 1 Ves Sen 231; *Re Gregory's Settlement and Will* (1865) 34 Beav 600; *Re Taylor, Cloak v Hammond* (1886) 34 ChD 255. Knowledge of the state of the family of a cousin or remoter relative is apparently not presumed: *Crook v Whitley* (1857) 7 De GM & G 490 at 496; *Re Herbert's Trusts* (1860) 1 John & H 121 at 124. See *Blech v Blech* [2001] All ER (D) 141 (Dec) (testatrix confirmed by codicil knowing she was terminally ill and knowing that further grandchildren might be born after her death; 'survive' construed so as to include such issue). See also *Harris v The Beneficiaries of the Estate of Margaret Alice Cooper* [2010] All ER (D) 64 (Jan).
9 *King's College Hospital v Wheildon* (1854) 18 Beav 30; *Re Feltham's Will Trusts* (1855) 1 K & J 528; *Re Gregory's Settlement and Will* (1865) 34 Beav 600; *Re Noble's Trusts* (1870) IR 5 Eq 140; *Re Twohill* (1879) 3 LR Ir 21; *Re Brake* (1881) 6 PD 217; *Phelan v Slattery* (1887) 19 LR Ir 177; *Re Wyatt, Furniss v Phear* (1888) 36 WR 521; *Re Chappell* [1894] P 98; *Re Beale, Beale v Royal Hospital for Incurables* (1890) 6 TLR 308, CA; *Re Jeffery, Nussey v Jeffery* [1914] 1 Ch 375. In such cases the court inclines to construe the gift as being to the person whom the testator knew best: cf PARA W227. See *Pinnel v Anison* [2005] EWHC 1421 (Ch), sub nom *Pinnell v Annison* [2005] All ER (D) 458 (May) (where the testator had known, but had lost contact with his sister, but there was no evidence of his knowing the living person of the name and address

stated in the will and having the same first name as the sister; held that the sister was the intended donee). See also *Harris v The Beneficiaries of the Estate of Margaret Alice Cooper* [2010] All ER (D) 64 (Jan).

10 *Re Briscoe's Trusts* (1872) 20 WR 355. See also *Re Kilvert's Trusts* (1871) 7 Ch App 170; *Re Fearn's Will* (1879) 27 WR 392; *British Home and Hospital for Incurables v Royal Hospital for Incurables* (1904) 90 LT 601, CA; *Re Julian, O'Brien v Missions to Seamen Trust Corpn Ltd* [1950] IR 57 at 64. Such evidence is not admissible where the words of the will correctly refer to one charity, and there is no other charity which can properly be described by the same words: *Wilson v Squire* (1842) 1 Y & C Ch Cas 654. See also *National Society for the Prevention of Cruelty to Children v Scottish National Society for the Prevention of Cruelty to Children* [1915] AC 207, HL; cf CHARITIES vol 8 (2015) PARAS 108–109.

215. Evidence of the testator's habits. Evidence is not admissible in a court of construction directly to prove a mistake in a will in describing property or a donee[1]; but where, on the construction of the words of the will, it is clear that there is a mistake, evidence of surrounding circumstances[2] becomes admissible to prove how the mistake arose, in order to identify the true subject[3].

For this purpose, evidence is admitted of the testator's habits[4], for example his practice of calling a certain person by a nickname[5] or other name by which he was not commonly known[6], but by which he is described in the will. Similarly, with regard to a description of property which is not accurately satisfied as ordinarily understood, evidence may be admitted of the testator's habit of dealing with certain property under that description and of its accuracy as he understood it[7]. The evidence admissible under this head does not, however, extend to direct evidence of the testator's intention[8], or to evidence indicative of an improbability that the testator intended to benefit certain persons[9]. Such evidence is inadmissible except for the purpose of resolving an ambiguity[10].

1 See PARA 186.
2 See *Re Ray, Cant v Johnstone* [1916] 1 Ch 461; *Re Nicholl, Re Perkins, Nicholl v Perkins* (1920) 125 LT 62.
3 *Selwood v Mildmay* (1797) 3 Ves 306; *Lindgren v Lindgren* (1846) 9 Beav 358 (where it is explained that the doubts as to the soundness of *Selwood v Mildmay*, expressed in *Miller v Travers* (1832) 8 Bing 244 and *Doe d Hiscocks v Hiscocks* (1839) 5 M & W 363, were founded on a misapprehension). See also *Findlater v Lowe* [1904] 1 IR 519. In certain circumstances a will may now be rectified: see PARA 187. Exceptionally, the mistake may be such as to create an ambiguity, so that extrinsic evidence, including evidence of the testator's intentions, may be admissible under the Administration of Justice Act 1982 s 21: see PARAS 195, 218–220.
4 *Bernasconi v Atkinson* (1853) 10 Hare 345 at 349.
5 *Edge v Salisbury* (1749) Amb 70 at 71; *Goodinge v Goodinge* (1749) 1 Ves Sen 231; *Dowset v Sweet* (1753) Amb 175; *Thorn v Dickens* [1906] WN 54 (testator habitually referred to wife as 'mother').
6 *Beaumont v Fell* (1723) 2 P Wms 141 (but as to this case see *Mostyn v Mostyn* (1854) 5 HL Cas 155 at 168); *Parsons v Parsons* (1791) 1 Ves 266; *Lee v Pain* (1844) 4 Hare 201 at 251; *Re Feltham's Will Trusts* (1855) 1 K & J 528; *Andrews v Andrews* (1885) 15 LR Ir 199, Ir CA; *Re Ofner, Samuel v Ofner* [1909] 1 Ch 60, CA. See also *Doe d Hiscocks v Hiscocks* (1839) 5 M & W 363 at 368 per Lord Abinger CB. It seems, however, that this type of evidence should not be relied on where there is sufficient evidence of other circumstances to render the will intelligible: see *Blundell v Gladstone* (1841) 11 Sim 467 at 486; on appeal sub nom *Lord Camoys v Blundell* (1848) 1 HL Cas 778 at 785. Cf PARA 209. See *Re Fletcher, Barclays Bank Ltd v Ewing* [1949] Ch 473, [1949] 1 All ER 732 (testator habitually referred to adopted child as 'H's child', in correspondence and same expression used in will; held to describe the same child).
7 *Doe d Beach v Earl of Jersey* (1825) 3 B & C 870, HL; *Ricketts v Turquand* (1848) 1 HL Cas 472; *Webb v Byng* (1855) 1 K & J 580; *Castle v Fox* (1871) LR 11 Eq 542; *Jennings v Jennings* (1877) 1 LR Ir 552; *Re Vear, Vear v Vear* (1917) 62 Sol Jo 159. See *Sandover v Brown* [2004] EWHC 1307 (Ch), [2004] All ER (D) 53 (May) (testatrix's will referred to her bungalow without separate reference to adjoining backland and evidence that she had referred to it as her 'garden'; held: backland included with bungalow).
8 *Sherratt v Mountford* (1873) 8 Ch App 928 at 931, CA, per Mellish LJ.
9 *Sherratt v Mountford* (1873) 8 Ch App 928 at 930, CA, per James LJ.
10 See PARAS 195, 218–220.

216. Effect of satisfactory evidence. Where any subject of a gift is discovered which not only is within the words of the will, but exhausts the whole of those words, then the investigation must stop; the court takes that interpretation and does not go further[1], unless it is shown that another interpretation also exhausts the words[2] and that there is a latent ambiguity, sometimes called an equivocation[3], arising from the circumstances[4].

1 *Webb v Byng* (1855) 1 K & J 580 at 585 per Wood V-C.
2 *Sherratt v Mountford* (1873) 8 Ch App 928 at 930, CA.
3 Bacon's Maxims reg 23.
4 See PARAS 218–220.

217. Effect of inconclusive evidence. Where, after the admission of the evidence of the surrounding circumstances, the language of a testator who died before 1 January 1983[1] remains ambiguous or obscure, then, except in the case of a latent ambiguity[2], no further evidence, such as evidence of the testator's intention, or of declarations by him as to the persons or property he meant to include under a particular description, or of expressions of testamentary intentions in favour of particular persons who might be so described[3], or of a mistake in the description, or of a mistake in copying the will, or otherwise, is admissible[4], and the gift may be void for uncertainty[5]. Thus, as a legacy to a debtor is prima facie not a release to him of his debt[6], extrinsic evidence is not admitted to show that by the legacy the testator intended to release the debt[7].

However, in construing the will of a testator who died on or after 1 January 1983, whether an ambiguity is patent on the face of the testator's language, or whether it is latent[8], being disclosed by evidence (other than evidence of the testator's intention) to be ambiguous in the light of surrounding circumstances, extrinsic evidence, including evidence of the testator's intention, is admissible[9]. Should the ambiguity still remain, even after the admission of extrinsic evidence, the court may be able to find an alternative construction that will save the gift from complete failure[10]. The court will be reluctant to fail the gift for uncertainty of wording or description. Where ambiguity arises from applying a prima facie clear description to the facts, it is the court's duty, if at all possible, to conclude by reference to the facts which of alternative possible donees was intended by the testator[11].

1 Ie the date on which the Administration of Justice Act 1982 s 21 (see PARAS 195, 219) came into force: see s 76(11). Nothing in s 21 affects the will of a testator who died before that date: s 73(6)(c).
2 As to what constitutes an ambiguity, and as to the evidence admissible in the case of latent ambiguity, see PARAS 218–220.
3 *Willis v Lucas* (1718) 10 Mod Rep 416 at 417; *Andrews v Dobson* (1788) 1 Cox Eq Cas 425; *Doe d Preedy v Holtom* (1835) 4 Ad & El 76; *Doe d Hiscocks v Hiscocks* (1839) 5 M & W 363; *Martin v Drinkwater* (1840) 2 Beav 215 at 218; *Doe d Hubbard v Hubbard* (1850) 15 QB 227; *Douglas v Fellows* (1853) Kay 114; *Bernasconi v Atkinson* (1853) 10 Hare 345 at 348; *Drake v Drake* (1860) 8 HL Cas 172 at 177; *M'Clure v Evans* (1861) 29 Beav 422; *Sullivan v Sullivan* (1870) IR 4 Eq 457 at 460; *Re Ingle's Trusts* (1871) LR 11 Eq 578 at 587; *Farrer v St Catharine's College, Cambridge* (1873) LR 16 Eq 19 at 21; *Charter v Charter* (1874) LR 7 HL 364 at 370, 376, 383; *Baker v Ker* (1882) 11 LR Ir 3 at 17; *Re Taylor, Cloak v Hammond* (1886) 34 ChD 255 at 258, CA; *Re Whorwood, Ogle v Lord Sherborne* (1887) 34 ChD 446 at 450, CA; *Re Ely, Tottenham v Ely* (1891) 65 LT 452 (as to this case see PARA 220 note 1); *Paton v Ormerod* [1892] P 247; *Downe v Sheffield* (1894) 71 LT 292; *Re Cheadle, Bishop v Holt* [1900] 2 Ch 620 at 624, CA; *Re Chenoweth, Ward v Dwelley* (1901) 17 TLR 515; *M'Hugh v M'Hugh* [1908] 1 IR 155 at 159.
4 Wigram's Extrinsic Evidence (5th Edn) p 91, Proposition VI. In the probate court, however, where the question relates to the act of making the will, such evidence is admissible in a doubtful or ambiguous case, at all events if the declarations were made before the will: *Doe d Ellis v Hardy* (1836) 1 Mood & R 525; *Doe d Shallcross v Palmer* (1851) 16 QB 747. See also *Re*

Resch's Will Trusts, Le Cras v Perpetual Trustee Co Ltd, Far West Children's Health Scheme v Perpetual Trustee Co Ltd [1969] 1 AC 514 at 547, [1967] 3 All ER 915 at 925, PC; and PARA 83.
5   *Dowset v Sweet* (1753) Amb 175; *Thomas d Evans v Thomas* (1796) 6 Term Rep 671; *Doe d Hayter v Joinville* (1802) 3 East 172; *Richardson v Watson* (1833) 4 B & Ad 787; *Drake v Drake* (1860) 8 HL Cas 172; *Re Stephenson, Donaldson v Bamber* [1897] 1 Ch 75, CA. A charitable gift may not be void, but may be administered by means of a scheme: *Re Clergy Society* (1856) 2 K & J 615; *Re Bateman, Wallace v Mawdsley* (1911) 27 TLR 313. See also CHARITIES vol 8 (2015) PARA 180.
6   *Re Tinline, Elder v Tinline* (1912) 56 Sol Jo 310. See also PARAS 1067–1068.
7   *Re Tinline, Elder v Tinline* (1912) 56 Sol Jo 310. See also *Selwin v Brown* (1735) 3 Bro Parl Cas 607, HL. Such evidence may be admitted, however, not to show intention, but to show some extraneous act constituting a release apart from the will: *Cross v Sprigg* (1849) 6 Hare 552 (on appeal (1850) 2 Mac & G 113); *Peace v Hains* (1853) 11 Hare 151 at 154.
8   As to the distinction between latent and patent ambiguity see PARA 220.
9   See the Administration of Justice Act 1982 s 21; and PARA 195.
10 *Re Steel, Public Trustee v Christian Aid Society* [1979] Ch 218, [1978] 2 All ER 1026; *Re Williams, Wiles v Madgin* [1985] 1 All ER 964, [1985] 1 WLR 905.
11 See *Pinnel v Anison* [2005] EWHC 1421 (Ch), sub nom *Pinnell v Annison* [2005] All ER (D) 458 (May).

218.   Extrinsic evidence of intention; death of testator before 1983. Where, in the will of a testator who died before 1 January 1983[1], there is a latent ambiguity[2] in the description of some person or thing, and evidence of the surrounding circumstances is insufficient to resolve the ambiguity, then, as a last resort[3], evidence is admissible to prove the testator's declarations of his intention as to which of the persons and things so described was meant by him[4]. Such declarations need not be contemporaneous with the will, but may be of a prior or later date, and may have more or less weight according to the time and circumstances under which they were made[5]. In the case of a patent ambiguity no such evidence is admissible[6].

If no such evidence is available, the uncertainty cannot be removed and the gift is void for uncertainty[7].

1   Ie the date on which the Administration of Justice Act 1982 s 21 (see PARAS 195, 219) came into force: see s 76(11). Nothing in s 21 affects the will of any testator dying before that date: s 73(6)(c).
2   As to the meaning of 'latent ambiguity' see PARA 220.
3   *Healy v Healy* (1875) IR 9 Eq 418 at 421 per Sullivan MR. See also Elphinstone's Introduction to Conveyancing (7th Edn) p 35; and PARA 220.
4   *Jones v Newman* (1750) 1 Wm Bl 60; *Doe d Morgan v Morgan* (1832) 1 Cr & M 235; *Doe d Gord v Needs* (1836) 2 M & W 129; *Fleming v Fleming* (1862) 1 H & C 242; *Phelan v Slattery* (1887) 19 LR Ir 177; *Re Ray, Cant v Johnstone* [1916] 1 Ch 461; *Robertson v Flynn* [1920] 1 IR 78, Ir CA (instructions for will looked at); *Re Cruse, Gass v Ingham* [1930] WN 206. See also *A-G v Hudson* (1720) 1 P Wms 674. Cf *Re Jeffery, Nussey v Jeffery* [1914] 1 Ch 375; and the cases in PARA 220 note 2. This former rule as to latent ambiguity is also stated in dicta in the following cases: *Lord Cheyney's Case* (1591) 5 Co Rep 68a at 68b (citing *Peynel v Peynel* (1373) YB 47 Edw 3, 16b, pl 29); *Lord Lansdown's Case* (1712) 10 Mod Rep 96 at 100; *Doe d Hiscocks v Hiscocks* (1839) 5 M & W 363 at 368 per Lord Abinger CB; *Re Kilvert's Trusts* (1871) 7 Ch App 170 at 173 per James LJ; *Charter v Charter* (1874) LR 7 HL 364 at 370 per Lord Chelmsford, and at 377 per Lord Cairns LC. See also *Re Battie-Wrightson, Cecil v Battie-Wrightson* [1920] 2 Ch 330 (bequest of balance at 'the said bank', no bank having been named). As to the cases where the rule has been stated in relation to the interpretation of instruments inter vivos see DEEDS AND OTHER INSTRUMENTS vol 32 (2012) PARA 409.
5   *Doe d Allen v Allen* (1840) 12 Ad & El 451 at 455. See also *Dwyer v Lysaght* (1812) 2 Ball & B 156 at 162; *Langham v Sanford* (1816) 19 Ves 641 at 649–650 per Lord Eldon LC.
6   As to the meaning of 'patent ambiguity' see PARA 220.
7   *Re Jackson, Beattie v Murphy* [1933] Ch 237 at 242.

219.   Extrinsic evidence of intention; death of testator after 1982. In relation to testators who die on or after 1 January 1983[1], the circumstances in which extrinsic evidence of intention may be admitted have been statutorily defined[2]. The position relating to latent ambiguity[3] has been codified[4], and the circumstances in which extrinsic evidence of intention may be admitted have been extended so as to include patent ambiguity[5] and meaninglessness[6]. In so far as such a testator's language in any part of the will is ambiguous on the face of it, or in so far as evidence (other than evidence of the testator's intention) shows that the language used in any part of it is ambiguous in the light of surrounding circumstances, extrinsic evidence, including evidence of the testator's intention, may now be admitted to assist in its interpretation[7].

1 Ie the date on which the Administration of Justice Act 1982 s 21 (see the text and notes 2–7) came into force: see s 76(11). Nothing in s 21 affects the will of any testator dying before that date: s 73(6)(c).
2 Ie by the Administration of Justice Act 1982 s 21 (see the text and notes 2–7). See also the cases cited in PARA 220 note 11.
3 As to the meaning of 'latent ambiguity' see PARA 220.
4 See the Administration of Justice Act 1982 s 21(1)(c), (2); and PARA 220.
5 See the Administration of Justice Act 1982 s 21(1)(b), (2). As to the meaning of 'patent ambiguity' see PARA 220.
6 See the Administration of Justice Act 1982 s 21(1)(a), (2). See also PARA 195.
7 See the Administration of Justice Act 1982 s 21(1)(b), (c), (2). See *Ross v Perrin Hughes* [2004] EWHC 2559 (Ch), 7 ITELR 405, [2004] All ER (D) 159 (Nov); *Baynes v Hedger* [2008] EWHC 1587 (Ch), [2008] 2 FLR 1805, [2008] All ER (D) 175 (Jul) (possible, but doubted, ambiguity considered against extrinsic evidence); affd on other grounds [2009] EWCA Civ 374, [2009] 2 FLR 767, [2009] All ER (D) 50 (May); *Esson v Esson* [2009] EWHC 3045 (Ch), [2009] All ER (D) 325 (Nov) ('should I predecease him' in codicil created ambiguity in the light of the surrounding circumstances, allowing in evidence of intention); and *Reading v Reading* [2015] EWHC 946 (Ch), [2015] WTLR 1245, [2015] All ER (D) 64 (Feb) (cited in PARA 220 note 14). See also PARA 195.

220. Meanings of 'latent ambiguity' and 'patent ambiguity'. For the purpose of determining whether a latent ambiguity arises on the will of a testator dying before 1 January 1983, the following principles apply.

A latent ambiguity arises when the description in the will, considered in the light of the context, is on the face of it apt to describe and determine, without obscurity at the time when the subject is to be ascertained[1], any of two or more different subjects, either accurately, or subject to inaccuracies such as blanks left in the description, or words which have to be rejected as a false description not applying to any one[2], or which are otherwise negligible[3]. Where the donee is described by a forename, and there are found two persons, one having that name only and the other having that name with others, both are treated as answering the description in the will with sufficient accuracy, and a latent ambiguity arises[4]. A latent ambiguity does not arise where part of the description applies to one subject and another part to another subject[5]; or where from the context of the whole will[6] or by the aid of any rule of construction applicable to the will[7], such as the presumption as to repeated words[8] or as to legitimacy[9], or from the circumstances of the case properly admissible in evidence[10], it can be gathered which of the different subjects was intended.

It is not clear whether the above principles apply for the purpose of determining whether the language used in any part of the will of a testator dying on or after 1 January 1983 is ambiguous for the purposes of the new statutory rule[11]. It seems that recent cases have taken a less rigid approach to the precise nature of the ambiguity[12]. Equally, it is clear that the rule will not be applied where there is no real ambiguity[13].

A latent ambiguity must be distinguished from a patent ambiguity, which arises where the description is on the face of it indefinite and insufficiently clear to determine any subject, as, for example, where there is a gift to 'one of the sons' of a named person who has more than one son[14]. In the construction of the will of a testator who died before 1 January 1983[15], extrinsic evidence of intention is not admissible to resolve such an ambiguity[16], but it is admissible in the case of the will of a testator dying on or after that date[17]. It seems likely that the wider admissibility of extrinsic evidence in the case of deaths after 1982 may mean that less significance will attach to the distinction between latent and patent ambiguity and the exact nature of the particular ambiguity[18].

1 As to the rules of construction relating to the time for ascertaining the property given see
   PARA 282; and as to the time for ascertaining the donee see PARA 299 et seq. Where a donee is
   described by name, and there has been a person in existence known to the testator answering to
   the exact description of the donee, while at the date of the will or of the death of the testator there
   is no such person, extrinsic evidence is admissible to prove not only the testator's intimacy with a
   person who exists to whom a sufficient part of the description is applicable, but even his intention
   to make the gift to that person: *Re Halston, Ewen v Halston* [1912] 1 Ch 435, not following *Re
   Ely, Tottenham v Ely* (1891) 65 LT 452 (which had been disapproved by Farwell LJ in *Re Ofner,
   Samuel v Ofner* [1909] 1 Ch 60 at 63, CA), and applying *Re Blackman* (1852) 16 Beav 377. In *Re
   Ely, Tottenham v Ely* the evidence relied on merely went to prove intention, and was held
   inadmissible as such: see *Re Loughlin, Acheson v O'Meara* [1906] VLR 597 at 601, 603 (where
   Re Ely, Tottenham v Ely is explained).
2 *Price v Page* (1799) 4 Ves 680; *Careless v Careless* (1816) 1 Mer 384 ('to Robert C my nephew
   the son of Joseph C', the testator having two nephews Robert, and no brother Joseph); *Still v Hoste*
   (1821) 6 Madd 192 (name wrong). These three cases were explained in *Doe d Hiscocks v Hiscocks*
   (1839) 5 M & W 363 at 370 per Lord Abinger CB as cases where the inaccurate part of the
   description was either a mere blank or applicable to no person at all. See also *Garner v Garner*
   (1860) 29 Beav 114 (a settlement on 'J G of S and E his wife', there being a J G of B whose
   wife's name was E a niece of the settlor, and a J G of S, whose wife was H); *Re Hubbuck* [1905]
   P 129 ('my granddaughter . . .', there being three); *Re Ray, Cant v Johnstone* [1916] 1 Ch 461; *Re
   Brady, Wylie v Radcliffe* (1919) 147 LT Jo 235; *Re Gowenlock, Public Trustee v Gowenlock*
   (1934) 177 LT Jo 95.
3 *Henderson v Henderson* [1905] 1 IR 353.
4 *Bennett v Marshall* (1856) 2 K & J 740; *Re Wolverton Mortgaged Estates* (1877) 7 ChD 197 at
   199 (where, however, the decision is also sufficiently grounded on evidence of surrounding
   circumstances). See also *Re Halston, Ewen v Halston* [1912] 1 Ch 435.
5 *Doe d Hiscocks v Hiscocks* (1839) 5 M & W 363; *Bernasconi v Atkinson* (1853) 10 Hare 345 at
   348–349; *Re Chappell* [1894] P 98. In *Re Brake* (1881) 6 PD 217, the evidence of intention was
   not relied on.
6 *Doe d Westlake v Westlake* (1820) 4 B & Ald 57 (to 'M W my brother and S W my brother's son',
   there being two persons S W, sons of brothers of the testator).
7 See, however, *Re Freeman's Will Trusts* (10 July 1987, unreported) (cited in note 11).
8 *Webber v Corbett* (1873) LR 16 Eq 515. See also PARA 249. Cf *Healy v Healy* (1875) IR 9 Eq 418.
   In *Doe d Morgan v Morgan* (1832) 1 Cr & M 235, a similar case, this presumption was not alluded
   to, and evidence of intention was admitted; and in *Phelan v Slattery* (1887) 19 LR Ir 177, the
   presumption was excluded by the context, and evidence of intention was admitted.
9 *Re Fish, Ingham v Rayner* [1894] 2 Ch 83, CA; distinguished in *Re Jackson, Beattie v Murphy*
   [1933] Ch 237 (where a latent ambiguity arose because two legitimate persons both satisfied the
   description and, extrinsic evidence being then admitted, it could extend to the claim of an
   illegitimate person). In *Re Ashton* [1892] P 83, this presumption was excluded by the terms of the
   will. As to the presumption as to legitimacy see PARA 350. In *Grant v Grant* (1870) LR 5 CP 380
   (on appeal LR 5 CP 727, Ex Ch), where the devise was to 'my nephew J G', and the testator had
   both a nephew and a nephew by affinity of that name, evidence was held admissible to show the
   relation in which they respectively stood to the testator, and that he did not know of the existence
   of the former, but the question of the admissibility of evidence of intention was not decided. In
   Wells v Wells (1874) LR 18 Eq 504 at 506 per Jessel MR, and in *Merrill v Morton* (1881) 17 ChD
   382 at 386 per Malins V-C, the decision in *Grant v Grant* was dissented from on the ground that
   'nephew' in its ordinary meaning includes only a nephew by consanguinity. See, however, *Re
   Ashton* at 86–87 per Jeune J; *Re Fish, Ingham v Rayner* at 87 per AL Smith LJ. As to the general
   rule with regard to the ordinary meaning of words see PARA 241; and as to the general rule with
   regard to relationships see PARA 328. As to the question of legitimacy with regard to dispositions
   after 31 December 1969 see PARAS 355–356.
10 *Douglas v Fellows* (1853) Kay 114 at 120 per Wood V-C, citing *Fox v Collins* (1761) 2 Eden 107
   (bequest to 'the said A C', there being two of the name mentioned in the will); *Re Cheadle, Bishop
   v Holt* [1900] 2 Ch 620, CA (bequest of 'my 140 shares', where the testatrix had 240 partly and
   40 fully paid up).
11 In *Re Freeman's Will Trusts* (10 July 1987, unreported), Sir Nicholas Browne-Wilkinson V-C
   rejected the submission that the Administration of Justice Act 1982 s 21(1)(c), (2) (see PARA 219)

could only apply in a case where it would be impossible otherwise to decide the meaning of the will and expressed the view that extrinsic evidence of intention was admissible both under the old law and under the statute not only in cases where it was otherwise impossible to determine the testator's intention but also in cases where it was difficult to do so. A similarly liberal approach was adopted in *Re Benham's Will Trusts* [1995] STC 210; *Watson v National Children's Homes* [1995] 37 LS Gaz R 24. Cf *Re Williams, Wiles v Madgin* [1985] 1 All ER 964, [1985] 1 WLR 905 (decided under the Administration of Justice Act 1982 s 21(1)(b), (2) (see PARA 219); Nicholls J took a broad view of what constitutes an ambiguity for the purposes of s 21). By contrast, in *Cook v Saxlova* (18 October 1988, unreported), Millett J expressed the view that the admissibility of extrinsic evidence of intention under the Administration of Justice Act 1982 s 21(1)(c), (2) (as under the former law) did not depend on the difficulty of the question to be answered, nor was it enough that the language used might be capable of more than one meaning or that it might be differently construed by different judges; it was essential that the language of the will should still have more than one meaning after the process of construction was complete.

12 The approach of Lewison J in *Baynes v Hedger* [2008] EWHC 1587 (Ch), [2008] 2 FLR 1805, [2008] All ER (D) 175 (Jul) (affd on other grounds [2009] EWCA Civ 374, [2009] 2 FLR 767, [2009] All ER (D) 50 (May)) seems to follow the broad approach to admissibility under the Administration of Justice Act 1982 s 21, in relying upon the section to deal with the bare possibility of a remaining, but doubted, ambiguity. A similarly less rigid approach to the nature of the ambiguity is seen in *Pinnel v Anison* [2005] EWHC 1421 (Ch), sub nom *Pinnell v Annison* [2005] All ER (D) 458 (May) where a latent ambiguity was examined.

13 See *Hodgson v Clare* [1999] All ER (D) 359, sub nom *Re Owen, Hodgson v Clare* [2002] WTLR 619 (extrinsic evidence could not be admitted under the Administration of Justice Act 1982 s 21 until there is an ambiguity, and even then it is to be admitted as an aid to interpretation, not to rectification).

14 The fact that the ambiguity appears on the face of the will, as where the two persons who may answer the description are both named in the will, does not prevent the ambiguity from being latent for this purpose: *Doe d Gord v Needs* (1836) 2 M & W 129 at 141 (following *Doe d Morgan v Morgan* (1832) 1 Cr & M 235). See also *Reading v Reading* [2015] EWHC 946 (Ch), [2015] WTLR 1245, [2015] All ER (D) 64 (Feb) (the fact that the term 'issue' was found to be ambiguous for another reason did not render is ambiguous on its face for all purposes and therefore the Administration of Justice Act 1982 s 21(1)(b) did not apply, but s 21(1)(c) did apply).

15 Ie the date on which the Administration of Justice Act 1982 s 21 (see PARAS 195, 219) came into force: s 76(11). Nothing in s 21 affects the will of any testator dying before that date: s 76(6)(c). As to the wills of testators dying on or after that date see PARA 219.

16 *Sir Litton Strode v Lady Russel and Lady Falkland* (1707) 2 Vern 621 at 624 per Tracy J; and see PARA 265.

17 See the Administration of Justice Act 1982 s 21(1)(b), (2); and PARA 219.

18 Eg in cases where the ambiguity is caused by unexplained grouping, layout or punctuation in the will: see *Sammut v Manzi* [2008] UKPC 58, [2009] 2 All ER 234, [2009] 1 WLR 1834 (although extrinsic evidence was not used in construing meaning of grouping); *Re Steel, Public Trustee v Christian Aid Society* [1979] Ch 218, [1978] 2 All ER 1026 (punctuation and layout questions). Such cases may also raise the question of whether a part of the will is meaningless within the Administration of Justice Act 1982 s 21(1)(a) (see PARA 195).

(iv) Evidence of Secret Trusts

221. Evidence of secret trusts. In certain cases evidence is admissible to prove matters not disclosed by the will which are binding on a donee under an express or implied undertaking on his part made with the testator. In such cases evidence is admitted, not to show the testator's intention, but to prove the existence of an obligation, in the nature of a trust[1], accepted by and binding on the donee[2]. Historically such evidence was only admitted to prevent fraud on the donee's part[3], but nowadays fraud is not an essential element, and in the absence of actual fraud the standard of proof required is no more than the ordinary civil standard of proof required for the establishment of an ordinary trust[4]. Such evidence is admissible, even though the will expressly states that the gift is to the donee beneficially[5]; but where on the construction of the will the gift is a fiduciary one, no evidence is admissible to show that the donee takes any part of the gift beneficially[6].

If the evidence discloses a secret trust, the beneficiaries take under that trust and not under the will[7]; accordingly, the trust does not fail merely because the beneficiary under it is an attesting witness to the will[8], or predeceases the testator[9].

1 Ie certain language in imperative form, certain subject matter and certain objects: *Kasperbauer v Griffith* [2000] WTLR 333, CA; applied in *Margulies v Margulies* [2000] All ER (D) 344, (2000) 2 ITELR 641, CA. See also *Chinn v Hanrieder* 2009 BCSC 635, 11 ITELR 1009, BCSC. As to the creation of secret trusts generally see TRUSTS AND POWERS vol 98 (2013) PARA 87 et seq.
2 *Re Spencer's Will* (1887) 57 LT 519 at 521, CA; *Re Ellis, Owen v Bentley* (1918) 53 ILT 6. See also TRUSTS AND POWERS vol 98 (2013) PARA 87 et seq. The test in such cases is to consider the case as unaffected by the Wills Act 1837, and then to inquire whether a trust or obligation has been imposed by the testator and accepted by the donee such as a court of equity would enforce: *Jones v Badley* (1868) 3 Ch App 362 at 364, CA, per Lord Cairns LC. See also *Gold v Hill* [1999] 1 FLR 54, [1998] Fam Law 664 (in which a person in whose favour a nomination had been made under a life insurance policy was held by analogy with the doctrine of secret trusts to hold the moneys as constructive trustee for the deceased's cohabitant). See *Healey v Brown* [2002] EWHC 1405 (Ch), 4 ITELR 894, [2002] All ER (D) 249 (Apr), where a claim to a constructive trust in a share of a flat was justified by the case law on secret trusts, rather than under cases on mutual wills (although the property passed between spouses by survivorship, rather than under the will, that was held to be without significance).
3 *McCormick v Grogan* (1869) LR 4 HL 82 at 89, 97; *Re Stead, Witham v Andrew* [1900] 1 Ch 237; *Re Pitt Rivers, Scott v Pitt Rivers* [1902] 1 Ch 403 at 407, CA, per Vaughan Williams LJ; *Tharp v Tharp* [1916] 1 Ch 142; *Re Snowden, Smith v Spowage* [1979] Ch 528, [1979] 2 All ER 172. See also TRUSTS AND POWERS vol 98 (2013) PARA 87 et seq.
4 *Re Snowden, Smith v Spowage* [1979] Ch 528, [1979] 2 All ER 172 (not following *Ottaway v Norman* [1972] Ch 698, [1971] 3 All ER 1325 on this point). See also *Rufenack v Hope Mission* 2002 ABQB 1055, (2003–04) 6 ITELR 1.
5 *Russell v Jackson* (1852) 10 Hare 204; *Re Spencer's Will* (1887) 57 LT 519, CA.
6 *Re Rees, Williams v Hopkins* [1950] Ch 204, [1949] 2 All ER 1003, CA; *Re Karsten, Edwards v Moore* [1953] NZLR 456, NZ CA; *Re Pugh's Will Trusts, Marten v Pugh* [1967] 3 All ER 337, [1967] 1 WLR 1262.
7 *O'Brien v Condon* [1905] 1 IR 51; *Re Young, Young v Young* [1951] Ch 344 at 351, [1950] 2 All ER 1245 at 1251. See also *Cullen v A-G for Ireland* (1866) LR 1 HL 190 at 198; and TRUSTS AND POWERS vol 98 (2013) PARA 87 et seq. For the purpose of administration, however, property comprised in a secret trust may fall to be treated in the same manner as if it had been included in a specific bequest in the will: *Re Maddock, Llewellyn v Washington* [1902] 2 Ch 220, CA. See discussion in *Rawstron v Freud* [2014] EWHC 2577 (Ch), [2014] WTLR 1453, 17 ITELR 479.
8 *Re Young, Young v Young* [1951] Ch 344, [1950] 2 All ER 1245 (not following *Re Fleetwood* (1880) 15 ChD 594 on this point). See also *O'Brien v Condon* [1905] 1 IR 51. As the person named in the will as legatee takes no beneficial interest by reason of the existence of the trust, the legacy is not invalidated under the Wills Act 1837 s 15 (see PARA 41), by his attesting the will: see *Re Ray's Will Trusts, Re Ray's Estate, Public Trustee v Barry* [1936] Ch 520, [1936] 2 All ER 93.
9 *Re Gardner, Huey v Cunningham* [1923] 2 Ch 230. As to the effect of the trustee predeceasing the testator see *Re Maddock, Llewellyn v Washington* [1902] 2 Ch 220, CA; and TRUSTS AND POWERS vol 98 (2013) PARA 87.

222. Fully secret trusts. Where on the face of the will the gift is an absolute one[1], but it can be proved[2] that either before[3] or after[4] the date of the will, but during the testator's lifetime[5], the donee received from the testator a communication of certain trusts or conditions to be attached to the gift[6] and to be binding on the donee[7], and that the donee accepted the gift on those trusts and conditions, either by his express agreement or by his silence[8], and thereby induced the testator to make the gift, or to leave the gift already made unrevoked, then evidence of those trusts or conditions may be admissible, except in so far as such evidence would contradict the will[9].

1 *Burney v Macdonald* (1845) 15 Sim 6; *Russell v Jackson* (1852) 10 Hare 204; *Re Spencer's Will* (1887) 57 LT 519, CA.
2 The proof may consist of an admission by the donee (*Re Maddock, Llewellyn v Washington* [1902] 2 Ch 220, CA; *Re Huxtable, Huxtable v Crawfurd* [1902] 2 Ch 793, CA) or evidence from another source (*Podmore v Gunning* (1836) 7 Sim 644), but it must prove acceptance of the trust

by the donee (*French v French* [1902] 1 IR 172, HL; *Le Page v Gardom* (1915) 84 LJ Ch 749, HL; *Re Gardner, Huey v Cunnington* [1920] 2 Ch 523, CA; *Re Pitt Rivers, Scott v Pitt Rivers* [1902] 1 Ch 403; and see *Re Crawshay, Crawshay v Crawshay* (1890) 43 ChD 615 at 625).

3 *Re Applebee, Leveson v Beales* [1891] 3 Ch 422 at 430–431.

4 *Moss v Cooper* (1861) 1 John & H 352 at 366 per Wood V-C ('a bargain before the will is not at all essential'). Cf *Wekett v Raby* (1724) 2 Bro Parl Cas 386, HL; *Morrison v M'Ferran* [1901] 1 IR 360; *French v French* [1902] 1 IR 230; *Re Gardner, Huey v Cunnington* [1920] 2 Ch 523 at 532.

5 Communication after his death is not sufficient: *Re Boyes, Boyes v Carritt* (1884) 26 ChD 531; *Re Shields, Corbould-Ellis v Dales* [1912] 1 Ch 591; *Re Louis, Louis v Treloar* (1916) 32 TLR 313. See also TRUSTS AND POWERS vol 98 (2013) PARA 87.

6 The method by which the testator's intentions are to be carried out is not material: see *Ottaway v Norman* [1972] Ch 698, [1971] 3 All ER 1325 (donee to make will in favour of another).

7 For cases where the communications were not intended to be binding see *Podmore v Gunning* (1836) 7 Sim 644; *Re Pitt Rivers, Scott v Pitt Rivers* [1902] 1 Ch 403, CA; *Sullivan v Sullivan* [1903] 1 IR 193; *Re Falkiner, Mead v Smith* [1924] 1 Ch 88; *Re Barton, Barton v Bourne* (1932) 48 TLR 205; *Re Stirling, Union Bank of Scotland Ltd v Stirling* [1954] 2 All ER 113, [1954] 1 WLR 763; *Re Snowden, Smith v Spowage* [1979] Ch 528, [1979] 2 All ER 172. See also TRUSTS AND POWERS vol 98 (2013) PARAS 87, 91. An important distinction, in deciding whether any communications are intended to be binding, is whether the language used is imperative or merely precatory: see *Margulies v Margulies* [2000] All ER (D) 344, (2000) 2 ITELR 641, CA, per Nourse LJ (appeal against striking out decision failed for inter alia lack of evidence of clear imperative language. This appeal also shows that the court does not take a restrictive attitude towards evidence in such cases, even on interim applications).

8 The acceptance may be made expressly or silently, as where the donee does not dissent on the communication being made to him: see *Russell v Jackson* (1852) 10 Hare 204; *Moss v Cooper* (1861) 1 John & H 352 at 370–371; and TRUSTS AND POWERS vol 98 (2013) PARAS 89–90. In the latter case, however, the evidence of acceptance must leave no doubt in the mind of the court: *French v French* [1902] 1 IR 172 at 213, HL, per Walker LJ; *Re Williams, Williams v All Souls, Hastings (Parochial Church Council)* [1933] Ch 244.

9 *Re Huxtable, Huxtable v Crawfurd* [1902] 2 Ch 793, CA; *Re Ellis, Owen v Bentley* (1918) 53 ILT 6; *Re Keen, Evershed v Griffiths* [1937] Ch 236 at 247, [1937] 1 All ER 452 at 459, CA. See also *Re Rees, Williams v Hopkins* [1950] Ch 204, [1949] 2 All ER 1003; *Re Spence, Quick v Ackner* [1949] WN 237. See discussion in *Rawstron v Freud* [2014] EWHC 2577 (Ch), [2014] WTLR 1453, 17 ITELR 479.

223. Partly secret trusts. Where on the construction of a will a gift to a donee is not absolute, but subject to trusts or conditions which are not disclosed by the will[1], evidence of the trusts or conditions is admissible only if they were declared and communicated to the trustee (or to one at least of the trustees where there are several[2]) and accepted by him before or at the execution of the will[3]. Where by a subsequent will or codicil the testator increases a legacy which is already bound by a secret trust, but does not before executing the subsequent will or codicil communicate the increase to the trustee, the trust is valid as to the amount of the original legacy only[4].

1 *Blackwell v Blackwell* [1929] AC 318, HL. The trusts must be contained in some document in existence at the date of the will, or be declared orally and accepted by the trustee before or at the date of the will: *Crook v Brooking* (1688) 2 Vern 50, 106; *Pring v Pring* (1689) 2 Vern 99; *Smith v Attersoll* (1826) 1 Russ 266; *Re Fleetwood, Sidgreaves v Brewer* (1880) 15 ChD 594; *Re Huxtable, Huxtable v Crawfurd* [1902] 2 Ch 793, CA; *Re Ellis, Owen v Bentley* (1918) 53 ILT 6. See also *Johnson v Ball* (1851) 5 De G & Sm 85 (explained in *Re Fleetwood, Sidgreaves v Brewer* at 603–604); and the text and note 3.

2 See *Re Gardom, Le Page v A-G* [1914] 1 Ch 662 at 673.

3 *Re Keen, Evershed v Griffiths* [1937] Ch 236, [1937] 1 All ER 452, CA. See also *Johnson v Ball* (1851) 5 De G & Sm 85; *Scott v Brownrigg* (1881) 9 LR Ir 246 at 261; *Re Boyes* (1884) 26 ChD 531 at 535; *Balfe v Halpenny* [1904] 1 IR 486; *Re Karsten, Edwards v Moore* [1953] NZLR 456, NZ CA; *Re Bateman's Will Trusts, Brierley v Perry* [1970] 3 All ER 817, [1970] 1 WLR 1463. Cf *Re Hawksley's Settlement, Black v Tidy* [1934] Ch 384 at 399; and TRUSTS AND POWERS vol 98 (2013) PARA 92.

4 *Re Cooper, Le Neve Foster v National Provincial Bank Ltd* [1939] Ch 811, [1939] 3 All ER 586, CA.

(3) PRINCIPLES OF CONSTRUCTION OF WILLS

(i) Application of Principles of Construction

A.   ASCERTAINMENT OF INTENTION

224.   Basic principles of construction. In the 1990s there was a change in the approach to the construction of legal documents. The decisions which introduced this change concerned the construction of commercial agreements but they affect the approach to the construction of legal documents generally[1]. The principles may be briefly stated as follows:

(1)   interpretation is the ascertainment of the meaning which a document would convey to a reasonable person having all the background knowledge which would reasonably have been available at the time the will was made[2];

(2)   the admissible background knowledge includes 'absolutely anything which would have affected the way in which the language of the will would have been understood by a reasonable man'[3], provided that it is relevant[4];

(3)   the law excludes from the admissible background declarations of subjective intent[5];

(4)   the meaning which a will would convey to a reasonable man is not the same thing as the meaning of its words: the meaning of words is a matter of dictionaries and grammars; the meaning of the will is what having regard to the relevant background the testator would reasonably have been understood to mean; the background may not merely enable the reasonable man to choose between the possible meanings of words which are ambiguous but even to conclude that the testator must, for whatever reason, have used the wrong words or syntax[6];

(5)   the 'rule' that words should be given their 'natural and ordinary meaning' reflects the common sense proposition that we do not easily accept that people have made linguistic mistakes, particularly in formal documents; on the other hand, if one would nevertheless conclude from the background that something must have gone wrong with the language[7], the law does not require judges to attribute to the testator an intention which he plainly could not have had[8].

Although the Supreme Court has described the second limb of the proposition in head (5) above as 'controversial'[9], it has stated that the same principles apply to the interpretation of wills[10].

1   See *Mannai Investment Co Ltd v Eagle Star Life Assurance Co Ltd* [1997] AC 749, [1997] 3 All ER 352; *Investors Compensation Scheme Ltd v West Bromwich Building Society* [1998] 1 All ER 98, [1998] 1 WLR 896, HL. In *Mannai Investment Co Ltd v Eagle Star Life Assurance Co Ltd* at 776–777 and 376–377, Lord Hoffmann specifically referred to the cases on the admissibility of extrinsic evidence to construe wills. For an example of the more modern approach to construction in the context of wills see *Blech v Blech* [2001] All ER (D) 141 (Dec). See also the limitations of the new approach as expressed by Park J in *Breadner v Granville Grossman* [2001] Ch 523 at [36], [2000] 4 All ER 705 at 716 ('although . . . the construction of a legal document has loosened . . . it remains the case that the starting point, and usually the finishing point as well, is to identify the natural and ordinary meaning of the words which the draftsman has used').

2   *Investors Compensation Scheme Ltd v West Bromwich Building Society* [1998] 1 All ER 98 at 113, [1998] 1 WLR 896 at 912, HL, per Lord Hoffmann.

3   *Investors Compensation Scheme Ltd v West Bromwich Building Society* [1998] 1 All ER 98 at 113, [1998] 1 WLR 896 at 912–913, HL, per Lord Hoffmann.

4 *Bank of Credit and Commerce International SA v Ali* [2001] UKHL 8 at [39], [2002] 1 AC 251 at [39], [2001] 1 All ER 961 at [39], per Lord Hoffmann.
5 *Investors Compensation Scheme Ltd v West Bromwich Building Society* [1998] 1 All ER 98 at 113–114, [1998] 1 WLR 896 at 913, HL, per Lord Hoffmann.
6 *Investors Compensation Scheme Ltd v West Bromwich Building Society* [1998] 1 All ER 98 at 114, [1998] 1 WLR 896 at 913, HL, per Lord Hoffmann.
7 But see the need to identify the fact of mistake highlighted in *Breadner v Granville Grossman* [2001] Ch 523 at 536, [2000] 4 All ER 705 at 716 ('Lord Hoffmann . . . had particularly in mind cases where it was realistic to acknowledge that the draftsman had made a 'linguistic mistake", per Park J).
8 *Investors Compensation Scheme Ltd v West Bromwich Building Society* [1998] 1 All ER 98 at 114, [1998] 1 WLR 896 at 913, HL, per Lord Hoffmann.
9 See *Marley v Rawlings* [2014] UKSC 2 at [37], [2015] AC 129, [2014] 1 All ER 807 per Lord Neuberger. As to the modern approach to the construction of wills see PARA 188.
10 See *Marley v Rawlings* [2014] UKSC 2 at [19], [2015] AC 129, [2014] 1 All ER 807. See also PARA 188.

225. Ascertaining intention. The first duty[1] of a court of construction is to ascertain the language of the will, to read the words used and to ascertain the testator's intention from them[2]. Unexpressed mental intentions are irrelevant[3]. Where the will must be in writing, the only question is what is the meaning of the words used in that writing[4]. The expressed intention is in all cases taken as the actual intention, whatever the testator in fact intended[5], and as a general rule the court may not give effect to any intention which is not expressed or implied in the language of the will[6].

However, in certain circumstances extrinsic evidence, including extrinsic evidence of intention, is admissible[7].

1 *Ongley v Chambers* (1824) 8 Moore CP 665 at 685 (applying *Hill v Grange* (1556) 1 Plowd 164 at 170 ('the office of the judges')); *Macpherson v Macpherson* (1852) 16 Jur 847 at 848, HL; *Martin v Lee* (1861) 14 Moo PCC 142 at 153 per Turner LJ ('the paramount duty of the courts'); *Enohin v Wylie* (1862) 10 HL Cas 1 at 26; *Comiskey v Bowring-Hanbury* [1905] AC 84 at 91, HL, per Lord Davey. See also PARA 191.
2 See *Marley v Rawlings* [2014] UKSC 2, [2015] AC 129, [2014] 1 All ER 807. As to the modern approach to the construction of wills see PARA 188.
3 *Doe d Gwillim v Gwillim* (1833) 5 B & Ad 122 at 129 per Parke J.
4 *Grey v Pearson* (1857) 6 HL Cas 61 at 106 per Lord Wensleydale; *Abbott v Middleton, Ricketts v Carpenter* (1858) 7 HL Cas 68 at 114 per Lord Wensleydale (cited in *Re Rowland, Smith v Russell* [1963] Ch 1 at 11, [1962] 2 All ER 837 at 842, CA, per Harman LJ). See also *Roddy v Fitzgerald* (1858) 6 HL Cas 823 at 876 per Lord Wensleydale. As to the requirement of writing see PARA 60.
5 *Simpson v Foxon* [1907] P 54 at 57 per Bargrave Deane J.
6 *Scalé v Rawlins* [1892] AC 342 at 343–344, HL, per Lord Halsbury, and at 344 per Lord Watson. See also *Livesey v Livesey* (1849) 2 HL Cas 419 at 438 per Lord Campbell; *Grover v Burningham* (1850) 5 Exch 184 at 193 (cited with approval in *Re James's Will Trusts, Peard v James* [1962] Ch 226 at 235, [1960] 3 All ER 744 at 747); *Wilson v O'Leary* (1872) 7 Ch App 448 at 453, CA; *Re Duke of Cleveland's Settled Estates* [1893] 3 Ch 244 at 251, CA; *Rose v Rose* [1897] 1 IR 9 at 56, Ir CA; *Re Harpur's Will Trusts, Haller v A-G* [1962] Ch 78 at 94, [1961] 3 All ER 588 at 594, CA, per Harman LJ.
7 See PARAS 195, 218–219. See *Re Williams, Wiles v Madgin* [1985] 1 All ER 964, [1985] 1 WLR 905 (the purpose of extrinsic evidence is to show which of two or more meanings the testator attaches to a particular word or phrase; the word or phrase, read in its context, still has to be capable of bearing that meaning otherwise the evidence did not help).

226. Unimportance of form if intention shown. As a rule, a will is generally construed in the same manner as any other document[1], except that, in the case of a will, if the intention is shown, the mode of expression of that intention[2] and the form and language of the will are unimportant[3]. Thus the want of the technical words which are necessary in some instruments for the purpose of giving expression to intention[4], or any error in grammar[5], or the want or inaccuracy of punctuation marks[6], is immaterial; in all such cases a benevolent construction is adopted[7]. Whether the will appears to have been drawn by the testator himself or by a skilled draftsman on his behalf is taken into consideration[8], and this may guide the court as to the force to be given to technical words[9]. In the former case the testator will be supposed to use words in a popular and not in a legal sense[10], although in both cases the same principles of construction are applicable[11].

1   See *Marley v Rawlings* [2014] UKSC 2, [2015] AC 129, [2014] 1 All ER 807; and PARA 188. See also *Ralph v Carrick* (1879) 11 ChD 873 at 876, CA, per Brett LJ. As to the construction of other documents see DEEDS AND OTHER INSTRUMENTS vol 32 (2012) PARA 364 et seq.
2   *Cave v Cave* (1762) 2 Eden 139 at 144. See also PARA 224.
3   For an exception see the Law of Property Act 1925 s 130(1) (repealed); PARA 384 et seq; and REAL PROPERTY AND REGISTRATION vol 87 (2012) PARA 114.
4   *Strong d Cummin v Cummin* (1759) 2 Burr 767 at 770; *Ralph v Carrick* (1879) 11 ChD 873, CA; *Taylor v Shaw, Re Jones* (1920) 89 LJPC 124. See also PARA 375 et seq.
5   See *Jones v Morgan* (1773), cited in 4 Bro CC at 460 (the court must adopt the testator's intent no matter what words the testator has made use of); *Eden v Wilson* (1852) 4 HL Cas 257 at 284; *Re Norman's Trust* (1853) 3 De GM & G 965 at 967–968; *Hall v Warren* (1861) 9 HL Cas 420 at 427. At the same time, one must not divorce language from its ordinary meaning by introducing a suggestion of false grammar: *Gorringe v Mahlstedt* [1907] AC 225 at 227, HL, per Earl of Halsbury.
6   *Gordon v Gordon* (1871) LR 5 HL 254 at 276 (approving *Sanford v Raikes* (1816) 1 Mer 646 at 651). See also *Gauntlett v Carter* (1853) 17 Beav 586; *Re Campbell, M'Cabe v Campbell* [1918] 1 IR 429. The court may consider the punctuation used: see PARA 200.
7   See Co Litt 112a, 112b; *Jones v Price* (1841) 11 Sim 557 at 565; *Lang v Pugh* (1842) 1 Y & C Ch Cas 718 at 725; *Edgeworth v Edgeworth* (1869) LR 4 HL 35 at 41; *Re Speakman, Unsworth v Speakman* (1876) 4 ChD 620 at 625. The testator is considered to have acted without legal advice: see *Lewis v Rees* (1856) 3 K & J 132 at 147 per Page Wood V-C; *Re Warren's Trusts* (1884) 26 ChD 208 at 217 (both cases on deeds and comparing the strict construction in the case of deeds with the more lenient construction of wills). See also SETTLEMENTS vol 91 (2012) PARA 830.
8   *Richards v Davies* (1862) 13 CBNS 69 at 86 (affd 13 CBNS 861, Ex Ch); *Re Dayrell, Hastie v Dayrell* [1904] 2 Ch 496 at 499. See also *Perrin v Morgan* [1943] AC 399 at 405, [1943] 1 All ER 187 at 189, HL, per Viscount Simon LC; and *Esson v Esson* [2009] EWHC 3045 (Ch), [2009] All ER (D) 325 (Nov) (testatrix, writing her own codicil without legal knowledge, created an ambiguity).
9   *Thellusson v Lord Rendlesham, Thellusson v Thellusson, Hare v Robarts* (1859) 7 HL Cas 429 at 486, 490, 498, 504. See also *Re Bourke's Will Trusts, Barclays Bank Trust Co Ltd v Canada Permanent Trust Co* [1980] 1 All ER 219, [1980] 1 WLR 539 (testator with considerable knowledge of legal phraseology drew up own will; court used his obvious knowledge of distinction between 'heirs' and 'surviving issue' to construe gift as creating substitutional gift between two classes).
10 *Forth v Chapman* (1720) 1 P Wms 663 at 666; *Re Taylor, Taylor v Tweedie* [1923] 1 Ch 99 at 105, CA.
11 *Weale v Ollive (No 2)* (1863) 32 Beav 421 at 423.

227. Legal effect of words. The fact that, when the testator desires to produce a particular disposition, he shows himself able to choose words clearly apt by law to produce that result may lead to the conclusion that, where he uses other words of doubtful import, he does not wish to produce that result[1]. The expression of that which, even if not expressed, would be implied by law has no independent legal effect on the interests created, but, as the whole will is considered, such expressions may be of importance in discovering the testator's intention[2]. A testator cannot be understood to say that he approves of the words that he uses only if they have the meaning that he desires[3].

1   *Langston v Langston* (1834) 2 Cl & Fin 194 at 242, HL; *Martin v Welstead* (1848) 18 LJ Ch 1 at 5; *Welland v Townsend* [1910] 1 IR 177, 181 (following *Jury v Jury* (1882) 9 LR Ir 207).
2   See Co Litt 205a; *Lee v Pain* (1844) 4 Hare 201 at 221; *Re Bourke's Will Trusts, Barclays Bank Trust Co Ltd v Canada Permanent Trust Co* [1980] 1 All ER 219, [1980] 1 WLR 539 (testator with considerable knowledge of legal terms, home-made will using expression 'their heirs and surviving issue'; construed as creating separate classes).

3   *Re Beech's Estate, Beech v Public Trustee* [1923] P 46, 92 LJP 33, CA (if testator executes the will
     with knowledge and approval, the court cannot afterwards exclude those words from probate for
     mistake).

228. Effect where words are ambiguous in context. Where a context is found
which is sufficient to control the meaning of the words, but the words in that
context are ambiguous, contradictory or obscure, or where the words have no
special meaning given to them by the context, and have two or more meanings in
ordinary use, the court adopts that construction which it considers most likely
that, in the circumstances, the testator meant by the words of the will[1], taking into
account the general scope of the will and his general purpose[2]. Such
considerations are, however permissible only where it is a question of choice
between two possible interpretations[3]; they are not legitimate where the normal
meaning of the words offers no difficulty[4].

The construction is not decided on mere conjecture or belief[5], but on judicial
persuasion[6] of what is the testator's intention, either expressly declared or
collected by just reasoning on the words of the will or evidenced by the
surrounding circumstances where they can be called in aid[7].

In the case of the will of a testator dying on or after 1 January 1983 any part
of which is ambiguous on the face of it, extrinsic evidence, including evidence of
the testator's intention, is admissible to assist in its interpretation[8].

1   See *Key v Key* (1853) 4 De GM & G 73 at 84; *Tunaley v Roch* (1857) 3 Drew 720 at 724–725;
     Re Doland's Will Trusts, Westminster Bank Ltd v Phillips [1970] Ch 267, [1969] 3 All ER 713.
     Where in a gift there are two sets of technical words, and their technical meanings cannot with
     consistency be given to both sets, so that 'something has to be sacrificed, it is to be seen what is the
     least sacrifice to be made, and what will best effectuate the intention of the testator': *Ashton v
     Adamson* (1841) 1 Dr & War 198 at 208 per Sugden LC.
2   *Blamford v Blamford* (1615) 3 Bulst 98 at 103; *Mellish v Mellish* (1798) 4 Ves 45 at 50; *Coard
     v Holderness* (1855) 20 Beav 147 at 152, 156; *Prescott v Barker* (1874) 9 Ch App 174 at 187; *Re
     Whiteley, Bishop of London v Whiteley* [1910] 1 Ch 600; *Re Macandrew's Will Trusts, Stephens
     v Barclays Bank Ltd* [1964] Ch 704, [1963] 2 All ER 919 (where the words 'or widow' being
     senseless, they were deemed placed in parenthesis and read as indicating a gift over subject to her
     interest). As to this rule in the construction of executory trusts, where the testator has not been his
     own conveyancer see *Sackville-West v Viscount Holmesdale* (1870). See LR 4 HL 543 at 559, 569,
     572. See also *Sammut v Manzi* [2008] UKPC 58, [2009] 2 All ER 234, [2009] 1 WLR 1834 (single
     gift; unexplained division of five named donees into one group of four cousins and one group
     comprising ex-spouse; reference to equal division; gift construed as being intended to allow equal
     division between all five); *Esson v Esson* [2009] EWHC 3045 (Ch), [2009] All ER (D) 325 (Nov);
     Reading v Reading [2015] EWHC 946 (Ch), [2015] WTLR 1245, [2015] All ER (D) 64 (Feb)
     (expression 'issue of mine' and 'such of my issue' construed as including both children and
     stepchildren and their children, rather than descendants of all degrees). See also TRUSTS AND
     POWERS vol 98 (2013) PARA 33.
3   *Giles v Melson* (1873) LR 6 HL 24 at 31 per Lord Selborne LC; *Gibbons v Gibbons* (1881) 6 App
     Cas 471 at 481, PC; *Re Boden, Boden v Boden* [1907] 1 Ch 132 at 145, CA, per Fletcher
     Moulton LJ.
4   See eg *Mitchell's Trustees v Aspin* 1971 SLT 166, HL. An exception exists, perhaps, in an extreme
     case where the language of the will, according to its normal meaning, is of so extravagant and
     fantastic a nature that the court is forced to conclude that it does not represent the testator's true
     intention: *Re Boden, Boden v Boden* [1907] 1 Ch 132 at 145, CA, per Fletcher Moulton LJ.
5   *Foley v Burnell* (1783) 1 Bro CC 274 at 284; *Barksdale v Gilliat* (1818) 1 Swan 562 at 565;
     Morrall v Sutton (1845) 1 Ph 533 at 540–541; *Re Elliot, Kelly v Elliot* [1896] 2 Ch 353 at 356;
     Inderwick v Tatchell [1903] AC 120 at 122, HL, per Earl of Halsbury LC; *Walford v Walford*
     [1912] AC 658 at 664, HL, per Viscount Haldane LC.
6   *A-G v Grote* (1827) 2 Russ & M 699 at 700.
7   *Doe d Brodbelt v Thomson* (1858) 12 Moo PCC 116 at 127 per Turner LJ. See also *Lady Langdale
     v Briggs* (1856) 8 De GM & G 391 at 429–430. As to the evidence admissible see PARAS 193–194.
8   See the Administration of Justice Act 1982 s 21(1)(b), (2); and PARAS 219–220.

229. Inferences from scope of will. The court makes any reasonable inference from a particular passage, comparing that inference with what is apparent in other parts of the will[1]. This power of inference is, however, limited; a general intention not carried out by some appropriate words in the will itself cannot give the court the right to place the words there for the testator[2], and a priori reasoning on what the testator would naturally intend cannot be allowed to weigh against the proper construction of the words used[3]. In particular, the court is not at liberty to conjecture what the testator would have said if a particular state of things had been presented to his mind, which, it is apparent from the language which he has used, had not occurred to him, and for which, therefore, it cannot be supposed that he intended to make any provision[4].

1   *Law Union and Crown Insurance Co v Hill* [1902] AC 263 at 265, HL, per Earl of Halsbury LC. See also *Jenkins v Hughes* (1860) 8 HL Cas 571 at 588.
2   *Hunter v A-G* [1899] AC 309 at 315, 317, HL, per Earl of Halsbury LC; *Re Evans, Public Trustee v Evans* [1920] 2 Ch 304, CA. As to gifts by implication see PARA 466.
3   *Coltsmann v Coltsmann* (1868) LR 3 HL 121 at 130 per Lord Cairns LC. See *Hodgson v Clare* [1999] All ER (D) 359, sub nom *Re Owen, Hodgson v Clare* [2002] WTLR 619 (suggested constructions that did violence to the clear language of the will were not permissible; an apparent intention to favour certain persons might be inferred, but the will could not be rewritten by the court).
4   *Martin v Holgate* (1866) LR 1 HL 175 at 186 per Lord Chelmsford. See also *Earl of Scarborough v Doe d Savile* (1836) 3 Ad & El 897 at 962, Ex Ch; *Inderwick v Tatchell* [1903] AC 120, HL; *Hodgson v Clare* [1999] All ER (D) 359, sub nom *Re Owen, Hodgson v Clare* [2002] WTLR 619.

230. Cy-près doctrine. The important doctrine of cy-près, under which a donor's intention is effectuated as closely as possible, consistently with certain rules of law, is said to be an aspect of the rule as to general and particular intention[1]. As regards charitable gifts, the doctrine is well established[2]. Before 1 January 1926 the doctrine was applied to the construction of limitations of real estate so as to create estates tail, in accordance with the general intention, even though the actual limitations failed or were inappropriate[3]. Technical words of limitation were, however, generally given their normal legal effect, notwithstanding subsequent words which could not take effect, unless these showed very clearly that the testator meant otherwise[4]. Since on and after 1 January 1926 entailed interests could be created only by the like expressions as would have been effectual for the purpose in a deed made before that date[5], this application of the cy-près doctrine probably became obsolete as regards the wills of testators dying on or after that date[6], and, since entailed interests cannot be created by instruments coming into operation on or after 1 January 1997[7], is certainly obsolete as regards the wills of testators dying on or after that date.

1   As to this rule see PARA 231. See *Re Taylor, Martin v Freeman* (1888) 58 LT 538 at 542. See also *Harwood v Harwood* [2005] EWHC 3019 (Ch), [2005] All ER (D) 121 (Nov) (particular intention failed but general intention given effect).
2   See the Charities Act 2011 ss 61–68; and CHARITIES vol 8 (2015) PARA 176 et seq. As to the former application of the doctrine of cy-près in relation to gifts to successive generations of unborn issue see PERPETUITIES AND ACCUMULATIONS vol 80 (2013) PARA 4.
3   See the cases cited in PARA 231 note 4. See also PARA 391; and PERPETUITIES AND ACCUMULATIONS vol 80 (2013) PARA 4. Where there was a devise to several persons in succession in words sufficient to pass to each of them the fee simple or the whole interest of the testator, the court, in order to give effect to the general intention, construed the gift as of successive estates tail: *Studdert v Von Steiglitz* (1889) 23 LR Ir 564 at 573 (following *Ginger d White v White* (1742) Willes 348; *Kershaw v Kershaw* (1854) 3 E & B 845; *Earl of Tyrone v Marquis of Waterford* (1860) 1 De GF & J 613 at 629; *Hennessey v Bray* (1863) 33 Beav 96 at 100; *Watkins v Frederick* (1865) 11 HL Cas 358 at 366; and explaining *Foster v Earl Romney* (1809) 11 East 594; *Purcell v Purcell* (1840) 2 Dr & War 219n; *Bevan v White* (1844) 7 I Eq R 473); *Re Pennefather, Savile v Savile* [1896] 1 IR 249 at 263 (following *Studdert v Von Steiglitz*). A name and arms clause was an important element in ascertaining the general intention in such a case: *Studdert v Von Steiglitz* at 582.

4 *Jesson v Wright* (1820) 2 Bli 1, HL.
5 See the Law of Property Act 1925 s 130(1) (repealed by the Trusts of Land and Appointment of Trustees Act 1996 s 25(2), Sch 4); PARA 387; and REAL PROPERTY AND REGISTRATION vol 87 (2012) PARA 114.
6 The cy-près doctrine was not expressly abolished in this respect, and it may possibly still have applied in certain circumstances: see PERPETUITIES AND ACCUMULATIONS vol 80 (2013) PARA 4. As to the construction of executory trusts see TRUSTS AND POWERS vol 98 (2013) PARA 84.
7 See the Trusts of Land and Appointment of Trustees Act 1996 s 2, Sch 1para5; PARA 387; and REAL PROPERTY AND REGISTRATION vol 87 (2012) PARA 114.

231. Rule in Lassence v Tierney. A rule often applicable is the rule, usually referred to as the rule in *Lassence v Tierney*[1], that, where the will contains an absolute gift to a donee in the first instance[2], and trusts are engrafted or imposed on the absolute interest[3] which fail, either for lapse or invalidity or any other reason, then the absolute gift takes effect, so far as the trusts have failed, to the exclusion of the residuary donee or persons entitled on intestacy, as the case may be[4]. The rule applies both where the original gift is to trustees on trust for the legatee absolutely and where the original gift is to the legatee direct, if the legacy is effectually segregated from the testator's estate[5]. The rule may apply twice in one will and operate on original shares and also on accruing shares[6].

1 See *Lassence v Tierney* (1849) 1 Mac & G 551. See also *A-G v Lloyds Bank Ltd* [1935] AC 382 at 394, HL, per Lord Tomlin; *Re Gatti's Voluntary Settlement Trusts, De Ville v Gatti* [1936] 2 All ER 1489; *Fyfe v Irwin* [1939] 2 All ER 271, HL. The rule applies to real estate as well as to personalty: *Moryoseph v Moryoseph* [1920] 2 Ch 33.
2 See *McKenna v McCarten* [1915] 1 IR 282; *Re Cohen, Cohen v Cohen* (1915) 60 Sol Jo 239. As to examples where the rule could not be applied for want of an absolute gift in the first instance see *Scawin v Watson* (1847) 10 Beav 200; *Lassence v Tierney* (1849) 1 Mac & G 551; *Re Corbett's Trusts* (1860) John 591; *Savage v Tyers* (1872) 7 Ch App 356; *Re Orr, M'Dermott v Anderson* [1915] 1 IR 191; *Re Cohen's Will Trusts, Cullen v Westminster Bank Ltd* [1936] 1 All ER 103; *Re Drought's Will Trusts, Public Trustee v Palmer* (1967) 101 ILTR 1, Eire SC; *Re Goold's Will Trusts, Lloyds Bank Ltd v Goold* [1967] 3 All ER 652; but see *Watson v Holland (Inspector of Taxes)* [1985] 1 All ER 290, [1984] STC 372 (where the rule was followed and the decision in *Re Goold's Will Trusts, Lloyds Bank Ltd v Goold* was doubted). See also *Re Atkinson's Will Trust, Prescott v Child* [1957] Ch 117, [1956] 3 All ER 738.
3 This must be distinguished from a clause not merely modifying the enjoyment under the absolute gift, but diminishing that estate or totally substituting a new gift: *Gompertz v Gompertz* (1846) 2 Ph 107; *Lassence v Tierney* (1849) 1 Mac & G 551 at 561; *Re Richards, Williams v Gorvin* (1883) 50 LT 22 at 23; *Re Wilcock, Kay v Dewhirst* [1898] 1 Ch 95 at 98–99.
4 *Hancock v Watson* [1902] AC 14 at 22 per Lord Davey. See also *Lassence v Tierney* (1849) 1 Mac & G 551 at 561. As to applications of the rule see *Whittell v Dudin* (1820) 2 Jac & W 279; *Hulme v Hulme* (1839) 9 Sim 644; *Mayer v Townsend* (1841) 3 Beav 443; *Campbell v Brownrigg* (1843) 1 Ph 301; *Ridgway v Woodhouse* (1844) 7 Beav 437; *Kellett v Kellett* (1868) LR 3 HL 160; *Bradford v Young* (1885) 29 ChD 617, CA; *FitzGibbon v M'Neill* [1908] 1 IR 1; *Re Currie's Settlement, Re Rooper, Rooper v Williams* [1910] 1 Ch 329 at 334; *Hughes v McNaull* [1923] 1 IR 78, Ir CA; *Re Atkinson, Atkinson v Weightman* [1925] WN 30, CA; *Re Marshall, Graham v Marshall* [1928] Ch 661 (distinguishing *Re Payne, Taylor v Payne* [1927] 2 Ch 1, where the rule was held not to apply); *Re Atkinson's Will Trust, Prescott v Child* [1957] Ch 117, [1956] 3 All ER 738; *Re Leek, Darwen v Leek* [1969] 1 Ch 563, [1968] 1 All ER 793, CA. See also *Re Burton's Settlement Trusts, Public Trustee v Montefiore* [1955] Ch 348, [1955] 1 All ER 433, CA.
As to cases where the trusts are void for remoteness see PERPETUITIES AND ACCUMULATIONS vol 80 (2013) PARAS 25, 100. The rule does not apply to a gift subject to an independent gift over which fails: *Robinson v Wood* (1858) 4 Jur NS 625 (following *Doe d Blomfield v Eyre* (1848) 5 CB 713 at 746, Ex Ch).
5 *Re Connell's Settlement, Re Benett's Trusts, Fair v Connell* [1915] 1 Ch 867; *Re Harrison, Hunter v Bush* [1918] 2 Ch 59.
6 *Re Litt, Parry v Cooper* [1946] Ch 154, [1946] 1 All ER 314, CA.

232. Construction of will containing inconsistent gifts. Where in the same will[1] there are two inconsistent gifts, the court first attempts to reconcile the successive provisions without unduly straining the language, and to make the whole consistent with the apparent general intention of the testator². Where the two gifts are irreconcilable and the court can find nothing else to assist in determining the question³ (including, in the case of the will of a testator who died on or after 1 January 1983, direct evidence of his intention⁴), the later clause prevails as being the last expression of the testator's wishes⁵.

The rule that the later gift prevails is used only as a last resort when all attempts to reconcile the various provisions of the will have failed⁶, and is subject to the rule that a prior gift should not be disturbed further than is necessary for the purpose of giving effect to the later disposition⁷. Accordingly, if there are two absolute gifts, one of all the testator's property or all his property of a certain description, and the other of portions of that property, the more general gift is confined to the residue of that property⁸, and, if there is a clear, unambiguous gift, and a subsequent clause in terms applying to this gift, or to this and other gifts, and, as so applied, inconsistent with the intention taken as a whole, the subsequent clause is neglected, or applied only to other gifts with which it is not inconsistent⁹.

1　Where there is inconsistency between two wills of different dates, revocation may be inferred: see PARA 97. Two wills of the same date, neither of which can be proved to be the last executed, are void for uncertainty, so far as they are irreconcilable: *Phipps v Earl of Anglesey* (1751) 7 Bro Parl Cas 443, HL. As to the situation where two wills, of different dates, have been admitted to probate and there is inconsistency between them, see *Re Plant, Johnson v Hardwicke* [1952] Ch 298, [1952] 1 All ER 78n and *Tuckey v Henderson* (1863) 33 Beav 174, 9 Jur NS 1306 (in both cases revocation was not to be inferred; there was jurisdiction to place both documents side by side and construe the second will provision as substitutionary to that in the first will).
2　*Morrall v Sutton* (1845) 1 Ph 533 at 537; *Glendening v Glendening* (1846) 9 Beav 324 at 326; *Cradock v Cradock* (1858) 4 Jur NS 626 at 627; *Conquest v Conquest* (1868) 16 WR 453; *Re Bedson's Trusts* (1885) 28 ChD 523 at 525, CA; *Taylor v Sturrock, Sturrock v Sturrock* [1900] AC 225 at 232–233, PC; *Shields v Shields* [1910] 1 IR 116 at 120.
3　*Doe d Leicester v Biggs* (1809) 2 Taunt 109 at 113 ('for want of a better reason'); *Re Bywater, Bywater v Clarke* (1881) 18 ChD 17 at 24, CA, per James LJ.
4　See the Administration of Justice Act 1982 s 21(1)(b), (2); and PARAS 195, 219.
5　Co Litt 112b; *Paramour v Yardley* (1579) 2 Plowd 539 at 541; *Fane v Fane* (1681) 1 Vern 30; *Ulrich v Litchfield* (1742) 2 Atk 372; *Sims v Doughty* (1800) 5 Ves 243 at 247; *Constantine v Constantine* (1801) 6 Ves 100 at 102; *Sherratt v Bentley* (1834) 2 My & K 149 at 157; *Morrall v Sutton* (1845) 1 Ph 533 at 536, 545; *Brocklebank v Johnson* (1855) 20 Beav 205 at 212–213; *Re Hammond, Hammond v Treharne* [1938] 3 All ER 308 (legacy stated in words to be £100 and then in figures £500; £500 prevailed). See also *Hopkinson v Ellis* (1846) 10 Beav 169 (inconsistent directions as to payment of debts). As to the converse rule relating to the construction of deeds see DEEDS AND OTHER INSTRUMENTS vol 32 (2012) PARA 413.
6　*Re Gare, Filmer v Carter* [1952] Ch 80 at 83, [1951] 2 All ER 863 at 865 (where the rule was described as 'a counsel of despair'). See also *Press v Parker* (1825) 10 Moore CP 158 at 167; *White v Parker* (1835) 1 Bing NC 573 at 581; *Marks v Solomons* (1850) 19 LJ Ch 555 (revsg (1849) 18 LJ Ch 234 (where the principle of rejecting the first clause had been relied on)); *Chapman v Gilbert* (1853) 4 De GM & G 366; 3 Bl Com (14th Edn) 380.
7　*Munro v Henderson* [1907] 1 IR 440 at 442 per Barton J; affd [1908] 1 IR 260, Ir CA. See also *Kerr v Baroness Clinton* (1869) LR 8 Eq 462 at 465.
8　*Coke v Bullock* (1604) Cro Jac 49; *Roe d Snape v Nevill* (1848) 11 QB 466. If the more general gift is for life, the other gift may take effect at the end of the life interest: *Young v Burdett* (1724) 5 Bro Parl Cas 54.
9　*Adams v Clerke* (1725) 9 Mod Rep 154 (inconsistent directions as to payment of legacies); *Smith v Pybus* (1804) 9 Ves 566 (to three persons or the survivor of them 'in the order they are now mentioned'); *Doe d Spencer v Pedley* (1836) 1 M & W 662; *Baker v Baker* (1847) 6 Hare 269 ('living' applied only to some of donees); *Bickford v Chalker* (1854) 2 Drew 327 (inconsistent directions as to vesting); *Re Bellamy's Trust* (1862) 1 New Rep 191 ('if living' applied to one only of several).

233. Construction of will containing double residuary gifts. Where two gifts of residue are contained in the same will, the practice was not to treat them as irreconcilable so as to bring into operation the rule that the later must prevail, but to construe the second gift as intended to operate on lapsed legacies or shares of residue, and as regards other property to prefer the first gift[1]. In the case of deaths on or after 1 January 1983[2], the admissibility of direct evidence of the testator's intention[3] and the power to rectify wills[4] means that it will rarely be necessary for courts to construe this case law[5]. Where, however, one residuary gift is in the will and the other in a codicil, the gift in the will is revoked[6].

1   *Re Gare, Filmer v Carter* [1952] Ch 80, [1951] 2 All ER 863. See also *Davis v Bennett* (1861) 30 Beav 226; *Kilvington v Parker* (1872) 21 WR 121; *Bristow v Masefield* (1882) 52 LJ Ch 27; *Re Spencer, Hart v Manston* (1886) 54 LT 597; *Johns v Wilson* [1900] 1 IR 342; *Re Isaac, Harrison v Isaac* [1905] 1 Ch 427. It seems that the second residuary gift will include lapsed legacies only where there is a context showing that this was the testator's intention: *Re Jessop* (1859) 11 I Ch R 424, explained in *Re Isaac, Harrison v Isaac*; *Davis v Bennett* (where lapsed legacies were held to fall into the first gift). As to the rule that the later gift prevails see PARA 232.
2   Ie the date the Administration of Justice Act 1982 came into force.
3   See the Administration of Justice Act 1982 s 21: and PARAS 219, 220.
4   See the Administration of Justice Act 1982 s 20; and PARA 187.
5   Ie on treatment of double residuary gifts (see note 1).
6   *Earl Hardwicke v Douglas* (1840) 7 Cl & Fin 795, HL; *Re Stoodley, Hooson v Locock* [1916] 1 Ch 242, CA; *Pennefather v Lloyd* [1917] 1 IR 337. As to revocation by codicil see PARA 100.

234.   Two gifts of the same subject matter. Where an inconsistency arises through a gift to one person and a subsequent gift in the same instrument of the same thing to another person, it has been held, in order to reconcile the gifts, that both the donees take the gift together as joint tenants or tenants in common[1], or in succession[2], according to the nature of the gift.

1   Co Litt 112b note (1), by Hargrave; *Paramour v Yardley* (1579) 2 Plowd 539 at 541n; *Anon* (1582) Cro Eliz 9; *Ridout v Pain* (1747) 3 Atk 486 at 493 per Hardwicke LC; but see *Sherratt v Bentley* (1834) 2 My & K 149 at 161–162 per Lord Brougham LC (where the construction by which each donee takes a moiety is criticised). In *Re Alexander's Will Trusts* [1948] 2 All ER 111, where the gift was of a divisible article, each donee took a moiety.
2   See *Anon* (1582) Cro Eliz 9 per Anderson CJ; *Gravenor v Watkins* (1871) LR 6 CP 500, Ex Ch (where the Court of Common Pleas construed the gift as a life estate and remainder in fee, and the Exchequer Chamber, without deciding on the nature of the first interest, held that the second was an estate in fee subject to the first); *Re Bagshaw's Trusts* (1877) 46 LJ Ch 567, CA (where the second gift was to the children of the first taker).

B.   APPLICATION OF RULES OF CONSTRUCTION

235.   The rules of construction. Where they are appropriate, the court applies certain established rules of construction from which the testator's intention may be discovered. These rules lay down what inferences ought in doubtful cases to be drawn from particular indications of intention[1]; some determine what meaning should in general be given to particular words and expressions which have acquired a technical or quasi-technical nature[2]; and others determine in what manner particular common forms of disposition are to be given effect, where the testator has not fully and unambiguously disclosed his intentions[3].

Well-settled rules of construction are not lightly departed from in cases where they are applicable[4]. If applicable, they are to be observed strictly, but in a reasonable way[5]. They are to be followed only where the testator has not clearly expressed his own intention and has not given any other guide to the court[6]. They are regarded as a dictionary by which all parties, including the court, are bound, but the court does not have recourse to this dictionary to construe a word or phrase until it has ascertained, from an examination of the language of the whole will, whether or not the testator has indicated his intention of using the word or phrase in other than its dictionary meaning[7].

The greater jurisdiction to admit extrinsic evidence of the testator's intentions where the death occurs after 1982, as an aid to interpretation, reduces the extent to which some rules of construction need to be, or may properly be applied; that is because the meaninglessness of some wording or its ambiguity may justify the admission of evidence of testamentary intention at a relatively early stage of construing the will, possibly avoiding the necessity to apply certain rules of construction[8]. Similarly, the modern approach to the construction of wills which requires the court to ascertain the testator's intention, taking into account matters such as the overall purpose of the document and common sense as well as the natural and ordinary meaning of the words used, will reduce the reliance on these rules[9].

1 Eg the rules as to the effect of a gift over on failure of issue, and the rules as to implication of limitations: see PARAS 454, 466. As to the general approach to construction see PARA 224.

2 *Davenport v Coltman* (1842) 12 Sim 588 at 597; *Grey v Pearson* (1857) 6 HL Cas 61 at 79; *Greville v Browne* (1859) 7 HL Cas 689 at 703; *Re Bawden, National Provincial Bank of England v Cresswell, Bawden v Cresswell* [1894] 1 Ch 693 at 697–698 per Kekewich J ('the dictionary is to be found in those decisions'); *Barraclough v Cooper* [1908] 2 Ch 121n at 124n.

3 *Re Jodrell, Jodrell v Seale* (1890) 44 ChD 590 at 610, CA (previous cases useful 'when they put an interpretation on common forms'). As to the evidence admissible in cases of ambiguity see PARAS 195, 219–220.

4 *Ralph v Carrick* (1879) 11 ChD 873 at 878, CA, per Cotton LJ; *Re Bedson's Trusts* (1885) 28 ChD 523 at 525–526, CA; *Kirby-Smith v Parnell* [1903] 1 Ch 483 at 490 per Buckley J. See also *Blann v Bell* (1852) 2 De GM & G 775 at 781; *Wake v Varah* (1876) 2 ChD 348 at 357, CA; *A-G v Jefferys* [1908] AC 411 at 413–414, HL, per Earl of Halsbury LC. The ground on which these rules are followed is either that certainty in judicial decisions is thereby attained (*Jesson v Wright* (1820) 2 Bli 1 at 56, HL, per Lord Redesdale; *Doe d Clarke v Ludlam* (1831) 7 Bing 275 at 279; *Morrall v Sutton* (1845) 1 Ph 533 at 536; *Grey v Pearson* (1857) 6 HL Cas 61 at 108; *Roddy v Fitzgerald* (1858) 6 HL Cas 823 at 884; *Perrin v Morgan* [1943] AC 399 at 420, [1943] 1 All ER 187 at 197, HL, per Lord Romer), or that the rules make it possible to advise confidently on titles (*Roddy v Fitzgerald* at 875), or that it is to be assumed that lawyers draw instruments according to the known state of the law, which includes the rules from time to time adopted by the court in the construction of wills, and the testator must be supposed to have used his words in the sense so fixed (*Re Bawden, National Provincial Bank of England v Cresswell, Bawden v Cresswell* [1894] 1 Ch 693 at 697–698; and see *Greville v Browne* (1859) 7 HL Cas 689 at 703; *Kingsbury v Walter* [1901] AC 187 at 189, HL, per Earl of Halsbury). It has been suggested that they were invented to give effect to what is in average instances the intention of the testator: *Re Inman, Inman v Rolls* [1893] 3 Ch 518 at 520 per Kekewich J.

5 *Perrin v Morgan* [1943] AC 399 at 420, [1943] 1 All ER 187 at 197, HL, per Lord Romer.

6 *Limpus v Arnold* (1884) 15 QBD 300 at 302, CA; *Re Coward, Coward v Larkman* (1887) 57 LT 285 at 287, CA; *Re Hamlet, Stephen v Cunningham* (1888) 39 ChD 426 at 434, CA; *Re Stone, Baker v Stone* [1895] 2 Ch 196 at 200, CA. 'Little assistance in construing a will is likely to be gained by consideration of how other judges have interpreted similar wording in other cases . . . the starting point must be to look at the natural meaning of the wording . . . without reference to other decisions or to prima facie principles of construction': *Sammut v Manzi* [2008] UKPC 58 at [6], [2009] 2 All ER 234, [2009] 1 WLR 1834 per Lord Phillips of Worth Matravers. See also *Hodgson v Clare* [1999] All ER (D) 359, sub nom *Re Owen, Hodgson v Clare* [2002] WTLR 619 (no scope for presumption against intestacy or extrinsic evidence of intention where wording of will was clear).

7 *Perrin v Morgan* [1943] AC 399 at 421, [1943] 1 All ER 187 at 197, HL, per Lord Romer. The rules of construction, therefore, merely denote an inference in favour of a given construction of particular words (*Lee v Pain* (1844) 4 Hare 201 at 216–217 per Wigram V-C), and are subject to any contrary intention disclosed by the will (*Singleton v Tomlinson* (1878) 3 App Cas 404 at 423, HL, per Lord Hatherley). See *Re Manners, Public Trustee v Manners* [1955] 3 All ER 83, [1955] 1 WLR 1096 (rule of construction that where gift is immediate and vested, class is limited to those in esse at time of testator's death; no sufficient contrary intention shown by direction to distribute when youngest member reached 21). In this respect they differ from rules of law, which operate independently of, and even contrary to, the testator's intention. Formerly, a number of technical rules of law were applicable in the case of real estate, whatever was the intention of the testator, but such rules are now obsolete: see eg REAL PROPERTY AND REGISTRATION vol 87 (2012) PARA 169. In the case of personal estate there are no technical rules to prevent effect being given

to the intention of the testator (*Audsley v Horn* (1859) 1 De GF & J 226 at 237 per Lord
Campbell LC), where not otherwise contrary to law; and this is probably now true of real estate
also. Cf *Re Heath, Public Trustee v Heath* [1936] Ch 259 at 265; and PARA 423 note 8.

8 See the words of Lord Phillips of Worth Matravers in *Sammut v Manzi* [2008] UKPC 58, [2009]
2 All ER 234, [2009] 1 WLR 1834 cited in note 6. See also the Administration of Justice Act 1982
s 21; and PARAS 218–220.

9 See *Marley v Rawlings* [2014] UKSC 2, [2015] AC 129, [2014] 1 All ER 807; and PARA 188.

236. Words used in their ordinary sense. If the language of the will can be read
in its ordinary and natural sense[1] so as to make sense with respect to the
surrounding circumstances, no rule of construction is applicable to ascertain the
testator's intention[2], and no reliance may be placed on former decisions of the
court on similar or even identical words in other wills[3].

Previous decisions on the meaning of a word or phrase[4] may assist the court to
determine what its true meaning may be, but they do not prevent the court from
attributing a different meaning to that word or phrase in a different will, at a
different date, and in a different context[5].

1 See PARA 241; and see generally PARA 224. See also *Marley v Rawlings* [2014] UKSC 2,
[2015] AC 129, [2014] 1 All ER 807; and PARA 188.
2 *Leader v Duffey* (1888) 13 App Cas 294 at 301, 303, HL, per Earl of Halsbury; *Inderwick v
Tatchell* [1903] AC 120 at 122, HL, per Earl of Halsbury; *Comiskey v Bowring-Hanbury*
[1905] AC 84 at 88, HL, per Earl of Halsbury. See also *Hodgson v Clare* [1999] All ER (D) 359,
sub nom *Re Owen, Hodgson v Clare* [2002] WTLR 619; *Re Follett, Barclays Bank Ltd v Dovell*
[1955] 2 All ER 22, [1955] 1 WLR 429, CA (inadvertent omission but unclear what was omitted
or what words would correct the error; wording was construed as it stood). See *Gledhill v Arnold*
[2015] EWHC 2939 (Ch), [2016] WTLR 653, where the words used did not create an ambiguity
but, because of a clerical error, the will did not carry out the testator's intention, hence the court
was able to rectify the will. As to rectification see PARA 187.
3 *Gorringe v Mahlstedt* [1907] AC 225 at 226, HL, per Earl of Halsbury. See also *Re Tredwell,
Jeffray v Tredwell* [1891] 2 Ch 640 at 653, CA; *Re Morgan, Morgan v Morgan* [1893] 3 Ch 222
at 228, 232, CA; *Re Palmer, Palmer v Answorth* [1893] 3 Ch 369 at 373, CA; *Macculloch v
Anderson* [1904] AC 55 at 60, HL, per Earl of Halsbury; *Chapman v Perkins* [1905] AC 106 at
108, HL, per Earl of Halsbury; *Re Cope, Cross v Cross* [1908] 2 Ch 1 at 3, CA. See also *Sammut
v Manzi* [2008] UKPC 58, [2009] 2 All ER 234, [2009] 1 WLR 1834; and PARA 235 note 6.
4 For words and expressions which have been judicially defined see PARA 246. See also *Royal
Society v Robinson* [2015] EWHC 3442 (Ch) (reference in will to 'United Kingdom' should be
construed to include the Isle of Man and Jersey).
5 See *Re Rayner, Rayner v Rayner* [1904] 1 Ch 176 at 189, CA. See also *Re Athill, Athill v Athill*
(1880) 16 ChD 211 at 223, CA, per Jessel MR; *Perrin v Morgan* [1943] AC 399 at 417, [1943]
1 All ER 187 at 195, HL, per Lord Thankerton. See also *Re Alcock, Bonser v Seville* [1945] Ch
264, [1945] 1 All ER 613 ('between', in modern usage, is equivalent to 'among' and, prima facie,
implies equal distribution; cf *Re Birkett, Holland v Duncan* [1950] Ch 330, [1950] 1 All ER 316).

237. Weight to be given to previous decisions. Previous cases on the
construction of other wills are considered by the court, particularly where the
question relates to real property[1], but no weight is given to them[2] except in so far
as they lay down some rule of construction[3] applicable to the case before the court
or are based on reasoning which commends itself to the court. The proper way to
construe a will is to form an opinion apart from the cases and then to see whether
the cases require a modification of that opinion, not to begin by considering how
far the will resembles other wills on which decisions have been given[4].

Although the court may follow a previous decision on another will where the
language was identical with, or very similar to, that in the will under
consideration[5], and where no real distinction exists between the cases[6], mere
similarity of language does not bind the court to adopt a similar construction[7].
The surrounding circumstances may be different in every case and may give a
different meaning to the words[8], and it is the principles of construction
exemplified, rather than the particular decisions themselves, which are followed[9].

One judge is not bound to follow another on questions of mere verbal interpretation[10], and, even when the established rules of construction are properly applied, two minds may fairly differ[11].

1   *Miles v Harford* (1879) 12 ChD 691 at 698; *Morgan v Thomas* (1882) 9 QBD 643 at 644, CA; *Re Bright-Smith, Bright-Smith v Bright-Smith* (1886) 31 ChD 314 at 318. The fact that the testator's intention as to a blended gift of real and personal estate was defeated by these rules so far as regards the real estate did not prevent effect being given to his intention as to the personal estate: *Holmes v Prescott* (1864) 10 Jur NS 507.

2   *Roe d Dodson v Grew* (1767) 2 Wils 322 at 324; *Re Masson, Morton v Masson* (1917) 86 LJ Ch 753 at 756, CA. See also the cases cited in PARA 236 note 3. In *Sammut v Manzi* [2008] UKPC 58 at [6], [2009] 2 All ER 234, [2009] 1 WLR 1834, Lord Phillips of Worth Matravers said: 'the starting point must be to look at the natural meaning of the wording of the will to be construed without reference to other decisions or to prima facie principles of construction'.

3   *Doe d Smith v Fleming* (1835) 2 Cr M & R 638 at 651 per Lord Abinger CB; *Re Ingle's Trusts* (1871) LR 11 Eq 578 at 586–587; *Waring v Currey* (1873) 22 WR 150; *Singleton v Tomlinson* (1878) 3 App Cas 404 at 415, 423; *Re Jackson's Will* (1879) 13 ChD 189 at 194; *Re Jodrell, Jodrell v Seale* (1890) 44 ChD 590 at 610, CA; *Re Morgan, Morgan v Morgan* [1893] 3 Ch 222 at 232, CA; *Walford v Walford* [1912] AC 658 at 664, HL, per Viscount Haldane LC.

4   *Re Tredwell, Jeffray v Tredwell* [1891] 2 Ch 640 at 659–660, CA, per Kay LJ; *Re Blantern, Lowe v Cooke* [1891] WN 54, CA (adopted in *Re Sanford, Sanford v Sanford* [1901] 1 Ch 939 at 941 per Joyce J); *Re Williams, Metcalf v Williams* [1914] 1 Ch 219 at 222 (affd [1914] 2 Ch 61, CA); *Stewart v Murdoch* [1969] NI 78 at 89 per Lord MacDermott LCJ. This whole paragraph as set out in a previous edition of this work was cited and approved in *Re Ramadge* [1969] NI 71 at 74 per Lowry J. See also PARA 235 note 6. As to the authority in general of judicial decisions see CIVIL PROCEDURE vol 11 (2015) PARA 25 et seq.

5   Previous cases may be of little use, for the words of one will are seldom the same as those of another: *Rhodes v Rhodes* (1882) 7 App Cas 192 at 206, PC.

6   *Roddy v Fitzgerald* (1858) 6 HL Cas 823 at 875; *Thorpe v Thorpe* (1862) 1 H & C 326 at 336–337; *Lightfoot v Burstall* (1863) 1 Hem & M 546 at 549. See also *Doe d Penwarden v Gilbert* (1821) 6 Moore CP 268 at 281 ('literally and substantially the same').

7   *Cormack v Copous* (1853) 17 Beav 397 at 402; *Hood v Clapham* (1854) 19 Beav 90 at 94; *Slingsby v Grainger* (1859) 7 HL Cas 273 at 284. 'The nonsense of one man cannot be a guide for that of another': *Smith v Coffin* (1795) 2 Hy Bl 444 at 450. See also *Re Nolan, Sheridan v Nolan* [1912] 1 IR 416 at 420; and *Re Birkett, Holland v Duncan* [1950] Ch 330 at 332, [1950] 1 All ER 316 at 318 (where Danckwerts J pointed to authority that indicates that, where there are conflicting authorities, it may almost be a question of guesswork on occasions, although he relied upon inferences drawn, in this case). As to the testator's intention being gathered from the words of the will see *Graves v Bainbrigge* (1792) 1 Ves 562 at 564 per Lord Commissioner Eyre (cf PARA 243 text and note 9); and see PARA 185.

8   See *Grey v Pearson* (1857) 6 HL Cas 61 at 108 per Lord Wensleydale; *Abbott v Middleton* (1858) 7 HL Cas 68 at 119 per Lord Wensleydale (cited with approval in *Walford v Walford* [1912] AC 658 at 664, HL, per Viscount Haldane LC). See also *Doe d Long v Laming* (1760) 2 Burr 1100 at 1112; *Sayer v Bradley* (1856) 5 HL Cas 873 at 894; *River Wear Comrs v Adamson* (1877) 2 App Cas 743 at 764; *Re Coley, Hollinshead v Coley* [1903] 2 Ch 102 at 109, CA; *Perrin v Morgan* [1943] AC 399 at 408, [1943] 1 All ER 187 at 191, HL. Compare eg *Lord Douglas v Chalmer* (1795) 2 Ves 501 with *Hinckley v Simmons* (1798) 4 Ves 160 (both cases commented on by Lord Eldon LC in *Cambridge v Rous* (1802) 8 Ves 12 at 22).

9   See *Waite v Littlewood* (1872) 8 Ch App 70 at 73 per Lord Selborne LC; *Re Booth, Booth v Booth* [1894] 2 Ch 282 at 285.

10 *Re Veale's Trusts* (1876) 4 ChD 61 at 68 per Jessel MR, who described this rule as the rule laid down by the House of Lords in *Jenkins v Hughes* (1860) 8 HL Cas 571. On a question of mere construction, even the decision of the appeal court on similar grounds is not binding on another court, and much less on a court of equal jurisdiction: *Hack v London Provident Building Society* (1883) 23 ChD 103 at 111, CA, per Jessel MR.

11 *Vickers v Pound* (1858) 6 HL Cas 885 at 899 per Lord Wensleydale; *Re Veale's Trusts* (1876) 4 ChD 61 at 65 per Jessel MR (affd (1877) 5 ChD 622, CA); *Selby v Whittaker* (1877) 6 ChD 239 at 245, CA. See further *Re Chapman, Perkins v Chapman* [1904] 1 Ch 431, CA (where the members of the court agreed as to the principles to be applied, but differed as to the result). See also *Roddy v Fitzgerald* (1858) 6 HL Cas 823 at 876; *Rhodes v Rhodes* (1882) 7 App Cas 192 at 204, PC.

238. Citation of Scottish cases. Scottish cases are available as authorities for the general principles of construction of wills, as those principles are the same in both countries[1]. There are also similar rules of construction in particular cases which exist in both systems of jurisprudence[2], but the law of Scotland does not comprise every rule of construction applicable in England[3]. Where the court is construing the will to discern the ordinary meaning of words in the English language as used therein, where there is no particular point of Scottish law raised, the court gives due weight to Scottish cases[4].

1   *Young v Robertson* (1862) 4 Macq 314, HL; *Hickling v Fair* [1899] AC 15 at 26, HL, per Lord Shand. As to the modern approach to the construction of wills see *Marley v Rawlings* [2014] UKSC 2, [2015] AC 129, [2014] 1 All ER 807; and PARA 188.
2   See *Taylor v Graham* (1878) 3 App Cas 1287 at 1293, HL, per Lord Gordon.
3   *Hickling v Fair* [1899] AC 15 at 25, HL, per Lord Herschell. In the construction of English wills, the rules of another system of jurisprudence may be of authority. Thus in many cases, in the construction of wills of personal estate, the court follows the maxims of the civil law, which were sometimes introduced by ecclesiastical courts having jurisdiction in probate matters, including the greater part of the rules as to legacies: *Monkhouse v Holme* (1783) 1 Bro CC 298 at 300; *Hanson v Graham* (1801) 6 Ves 239; Tudor, LC Real Prop (4th Edn) 440; *Leeming v Sherratt* (1842) 2 Hare 14 at 17; *Parker v Marchant* (1842) 1 Y & C Ch Cas 290 at 299; *Key v Key* (1853) 4 De GM & G 73 at 85.
4   See *Trustee Solutions Ltd v Dubery* [2006] EWHC 1426 (Ch) at [24], [2007] 1 All ER 308 at [24], where the court considered the construction of writing 'under my hand' in *Waterson's Trustees v St Giles Boys' Club* 1943 SC 369.

239. Construction of wills containing a foreign element. The general principles of construction appear to apply to all wills, whether English or foreign, as being common to every system of jurisprudence[1]. However, for the purpose of ascertaining the testator's intention, different systems of law may apply different rules of construction, and effect will be given to any direction in the will, whether express or implied, that it is to be construed in accordance with the rules of construction of any particular system[2]. Nevertheless, where the will of a testator domiciled in England is in a foreign language and uses terms inappropriate to English law but appropriate to a foreign system, the English court, when administering the distribution of the testator's movable property, cannot refer questions on the meaning and effect of the foreign law to the foreign court, even if the testator provided that any such question must be dealt with by the foreign court[3]. The use of technical expressions peculiar to a particular system of law[4] and the testator's choice of language[5] are treated as indications, but not conclusive indications[6], of the system to be applied[7].

Where the will is to be construed according to English law but is written in a foreign language, the court looks at the effect of that language only in order to ascertain the equivalent expressions in English[8].

1   Eg the rule that every will is to be construed in accordance with the intention of the testator as discovered by the will: see PARA 224. As to the modern approach to the construction of wills see *Marley v Rawlings* [2014] UKSC 2, [2015] AC 129, [2014] 1 All ER 807; and PARA 188.
2   *Duchess di Sora v Phillips* (1863) 10 HL Cas 624 at 633 per Lord Cranworth (a case of contract, but the principle applies to the construction of wills). Cf *Re Harman, Lloyd v Tardy* [1894] 3 Ch 607 at 611, 613; *Raphael v Boehm, Cockburn v Raphael* (1852) 22 LJ Ch 299; *Re Price, Tomlin v Latter* [1900] 1 Ch 442; *Re Allen's Estate, Prescott v Allen and Beaumont* [1945] 2 All ER 264. See also *Re Sandys' Will Trust, Sandys v Kirton* [1947] 2 All ER 302, CA; and CONFLICT OF LAWS vol 19 (2011) PARAS 750–752.
3   *Re Berger* [1990] Ch 118 at 133–134, [1989] 1 All ER 591 at 602–603, CA (although, here, the testator had never positively indicated that he did not wish the English court to deal with the *zavah*).
4   *Studd v Cook* (1883) 8 App Cas 577, HL; *Re Cliff's Trusts* [1892] 2 Ch 229.

5   See *Studd v Cook* (1883) 8 App Cas 577 at 593, HL, per Earl of Selbourne LC, and at 600–601 per Lord Watson; *Re Baker's Settlement Trusts, Hunt v Baker* [1908] WN 161; *Re Bonnefoi, Surrey v Perrin* [1912] P 233 at 238–239, CA.
6   *Bradford v Young* (1885) 29 ChD 617 at 624, CA.
7   Where the testator's intention is not expressed and cannot be inferred, the court acts on certain presumptions: see CONFLICT OF LAWS vol 19 (2011) PARA 750.
8   *Reynolds v Kortright* (1854) 18 Beav 417 at 426 per Romilly MR. Cf *Baring v Ashburton* (1886) 54 LT 463. As to the evidence admissible in the case of a will in a foreign language see PARA 203.

240. Rules of law to be considered. For the purpose of ascertaining the testator's intention, those rules of law which prevailed when the will was made, and with reference to which the will may be fairly presumed to have been framed, must be observed[1], except where the testator by his will expressly or by implication refers to the law as existing at his death[2].

An Act of Parliament passed subsequent to the date of a will does not usually affect the ascertainment of the testator's intentions[3], although it may affect their legal operation[4].

1   *Re March, Mander v Harris* (1884) 27 ChD 166 at 169, CA. The date at which a will or provision is 'made' may itself come into question for the applicability of statutory provision: see *Berkely v Berkely* [1946] AC 555, sub nom *Countess of Berkely v RGW Berkely* [1946] 2 All ER 154, HL (will or earlier codicil was 'made' at the date of later confirming instrument).
2   See *Re Bridger, Brompton Hospital for Consumption v Lewis* [1894] 1 Ch 297, CA (gift of property by reference to law of mortmain construed as meaning law at the time of death); *Re Turnbull, Skipper v Wade* [1905] 1 Ch 726 ('free from duty' included duties imposed after the will).
3   *Jones v Ogle* (1872) 8 Ch App 192 at 195 per Lord Selborne LC; *Miller v Callender* (1993) Times, 4 February, HL (succession regulated by the law as it stood at time of testator's death, not by law as it stood at time of vesting). Cf the Administration of Justice Act 1982 ss 20–21 (rectification and interpretation of wills), which apply to the will of a testator who died on or after 1 January 1983 regardless of when the will was made: see PARAS 187, 195.
4   *Re Rayer, Rayer v Rayer* [1903] 1 Ch 685 at 688 (citing *Re Bridger, Brompton Hospital for Consumption v Lewis* [1894] 1 Ch 297, CA). See also *Hasluck v Pedley* (1874) LR 19 Eq 271 at 274 (explained in *Re March, Mander v Harris* (1884) 27 ChD 166 at 169, CA; and followed in *Constable v Constable* (1879) 11 ChD 681 at 686); *Re Baroness Llanover, Herbert v Freshfield (No 2)* [1903] 2 Ch 330; *Re Yates* [1919] P 93. See also *Berkely v Berkely* [1946] AC 555, sub nom *Countess of Berkely v RGW Berkely* [1946] 2 All ER 154, HL.

(ii) Context, Meaning and Effect of Words

241. Words prima facie to receive their grammatical and ordinary meaning. It is a general rule[1], applicable to all wills[2], that, unless it appears from the context of the whole will that the testator intended a different meaning to be given to the words[3], ordinary words are to be first read in their grammatical and ordinary sense[4], and legal and technical words in their legal and technical sense[5], and the usual rules of grammar are to be applied[6].

1   *Re Crawford's Trusts* (1854) 2 Drew 230 at 233 per Kindersley V-C; *Gether v Capper* (1855) 24 LJCP 69 at 71; *Southgate v Clinch* (1858) 4 Jur NS 428 at 429. The rule comes from Justinian's Digest: see Just Dig lib 32 s 69, cited in *Hart v Tulk* (1852) 2 De GM & G 300 at 313 and in *Lowe v Thomas* (1854) 5 De GM & G 315 at 316. The rule that words are to be read in their ordinary and grammatical sense has been enunciated in a very large number of cases, and is commonly described as the 'golden' rule; it is applicable to all kinds of instruments: see *Re Levy, ex p Walton* (1881) 17 ChD 746 at 751, CA; *Caledonian Rly Co v North British Rly Co* (1881) 6 App Cas 114 at 131, HL, per Lord Blackburn; *Spencer v Metropolitan Board of Works* (1882) 22 ChD 142 at 148, CA; and DEEDS AND OTHER INSTRUMENTS vol 32 (2012) PARA 369.
2   *Smith v Butcher* (1878) 10 ChD 113 at 116 per Jessel MR.
3   *Hamilton v Ritchie* [1894] AC 310 at 313, HL, per Lord Watson. See also *Gordon v Gordon* (1871) LR 5 HL 254 at 271 per Lord Chelmsford. The rule as to giving the ordinary meaning to a word is thus not a hard and fast rule, since it is entirely subservient to the context of the will: see

Seale-Hayne v Jodrell [1891] AC 304 at 306, HL, per Lord Herschell; *Perrin v Morgan* [1943] AC 399 at 421, [1943] 1 All ER 187 at 197–198, HL, per Lord Romer; and PARA 242.

4 *Thellusson v Woodford, Woodford v Thellusson* (1799) 4 Ves 227 at 329 per Arden MR; adopted in *Villar v Sir Walter Gilbey* [1907] AC 139 at 147 per Lord Atkinson. See *Poole v Poole* (1804) 3 Bos & P 620 at 627; *Church v Mundy* (1808) 15 Ves 396 at 406; *Trevor v Trevor* (1847) 1 HL Cas 239 at 264, 266–267, 270; *Williams v Lewis* (1859) 6 HL Cas 1013 at 1023; *De Windt v De Windt* (1866) LR 1 HL 87 at 92; *Gibbons v Gibbons* (1881) 6 App Cas 471 at 479, PC; *Hamilton v Ritchies* [1894] AC 310 at 313, HL, per Lord Watson; *Higgins v Dawson* [1902] AC 1 at 12, HL, per Lord Davey; *Gorringe v Mahlstedt* [1907] AC 225 at 232, HL, per Earl of Halsbury; *Tarbutt v Nicholson* (1920) 89 LJPC 127; *Perrin v Morgan* [1943] AC 399 at 406, [1943] 1 All ER 187 at 190, HL, per Viscount Simon LC; *D'Abo v Paget* [2000] All ER (D) 944; *Royal Society for the Prevention of Cruelty to Animals v Sharp* [2010] EWCA Civ 1474, [2011] 1 WLR 980, [2010] All ER (D) 253 (Dec). See also *Marley v Rawlings* [2014] UKSC 2, [2015] AC 129, [2014] 1 All ER 807; and PARA 188.

5 *Aumble v Jones* (1709) 1 Salk 238; *Buck d Whalley v Nurton* (1797) 1 Bos & P 53 at 57; *Jesson v Wright* (1820) 2 Bli 1 at 57, HL; *Roddy v Fitzgerald* (1858) 6 HL Cas 823; *Giles v Melsom* (1873) LR 6 HL 24 at 31; *Von Grutten v Foxwell, Foxwell v Van Grutten* [1897] AC 658 at 672, 684, HL, per Lord Macnaghten; *Re Keane's Estate* [1903] 1 IR 215; *Re Simcoe, Vowler-Simcoe v Vowler* [1913] 1 Ch 552 at 557; *Davy v Redington* [1917] 1 IR 250, Ir CA. See also *D'Abo v Paget* [2000] All ER (D) 944 (where 'child or other issue' was given more restricted legal meaning by testator's reference to earlier law, as guide to his meaning).

6 *Re Harrison, Turner v Hellard* (1885) 30 ChD 390 at 393, CA. Thus relative pronouns and other relative expressions are prima facie referable to the last antecedent: *Castledon v Turner* (1745) 3 Atk 257; *Adshead v Willetts* (1861) 29 Beav 358 at 361; *Re Williams, Gregory v Muirhead* (1913) 134 LT Jo 619. For an example to the contrary see *Fox v Collins* (1761) 2 Eden 107. The construction of a will may thus be a question for a grammarian rather than for a lawyer: *Fenny d Collings v Ewestace* (1815) 4 M & S 58 at 60; *Child v Elsworth* (1852) 2 De GM & G 679 at 683.

242. Effect of context and circumstances in excluding rule. Where words interpreted in their ordinary and grammatical sense are consistent with the surrounding circumstances[1], this sense of the words must be adhered to[2]. Where, however, that course would lead to some absurdity[3] or some repugnance or inconsistency with the declared intention of the testator, collected from the whole of the will, the grammatical and ordinary, or the technical, sense of the words may be modified so as to avoid that absurdity or inconsistency, but no further[4]. If the testator's intention can be collected with reasonable certainty from the whole will, with the aid of extrinsic evidence of a kind properly admissible[5], that intention must have effect given to it beyond and even against the literal or ordinary sense of particular words and expressions, and the court is not bound to adhere to the ordinary or legal meaning[6].

In order to deprive words of their appropriate usual sense there must be sufficient to satisfy the judge that they were meant by the testator to be used in some other sense, and to show what that other sense is[7]. The burden of proof lies on those who attribute to the words such other sense[8].

1 *Shore v Wilson, Lady Hewley's Charities* (1842) 9 Cl & Fin 355 at 525, HL. As to the admissibility of evidence of surrounding circumstances see PARA 212 et seq.

2 *Wigram's Extrinsic Evidence* (5th Edn) p 18, Proposition II; adopted in *Croker v Marquess of Hertford* (1844) 4 Moo PCC 339 at 364. See also *Re Cope, Cross v Cross* [1908] 2 Ch 1 at 4, CA; *Livesey v Livesey* (1849) 2 HL Cas 419 at 432. See also *Marley v Rawlings* [2014] UKSC 2, [2015] AC 129, [2014] 1 All ER 807; and PARA 188.

3 An 'absurdity' does not mean merely a result which the court considers ought not to have been the testator's intention: *Rhodes v Rhodes* (1882) 7 App Cas 192 at 205, PC. It may be that the view of what comprises an 'absurdity' may become modified by the passage of time: see *Nathan v Leonard* [2002] EWHC 1701 (Ch) at [8], [2003] 4 All ER 198 at [8], [2003] 1 WLR 827 at [8] discussing the no-contest condition in *Rhodes v Muswell Hill Land Co* (1861) 29 Beav 560.

4 *Warburton v Loveland d Ivie* (1828) 1 Hud & B 623 at 648, Ex Ch, per Burton J (affd (1832) 2 Dow & Cl 480, HL); adopted in *Grey v Pearson* (1857) 6 HL Cas 61 at 106 per Lord Wensleydale. See also *Hicks v Sallitt* (1854) 3 De GM & G 782 at 793–794; *Grey v Pearson* at 78 per Lord

Cranworth LC; *Abbott v Middleton, Ricketts v Carpenter* (1858) 7 HL Cas 68 at 94, 114; *Slingsby v Grainger* (1859) 7 HL Cas 273 at 284; *Thellusson v Lord Rendlesham, Thellusson v Thellusson, Hare v Robarts* (1859) 7 HL Cas 429 at 454, 470, 488, 490, 494, 519; *Long v Lane* (1885) 17 LR Ir 11 at 35, Ir CA; *Vacher & Sons Ltd v London Society of Compositors* [1913] AC 107 at 117, HL, per Lord Macnaghten; *Re Ionides, London County Westminster and Parr's Bank Ltd v Craies* [1922] WN 46. It has been said that the rule that words are to receive their ordinary and grammatical meaning speaks, not of the meaning of a word, but of a sentence, or of a series of limitations in a will: *Cave v Horsell* [1912] 3 KB 533 at 544, CA, per Buckley LJ. It has also been observed that the branch of the rule stated in the text seems to be but a means of showing by the context that the words were not used in their ordinary sense: *Thellusson v Lord Rendlesham, Thellusson v Thellusson, Hare v Robarts* at 494 per Lord Cranworth; *Rhodes v Rhodes* (1882) 7 App Cas 192 at 205, PC. See *Reading v Reading* [2015] EWHC 946 (Ch), [2015] WTLR 1245, [2015] All ER (D) 64 (Feb) (where, in the context of the will and applying common sense, the ordinary and natural meaning of the words 'issue of mine' and 'such of my issue' were found to include children and stepchildren and their children).

5   As to the admissibility of extrinsic evidence see PARA 193 et seq.
6   *Vauchamp v Bell* (1822) 6 Madd 343 at 347; *Key v Key* (1853) 4 De GM & G 73 at 84; *Ware v Watson* (1855) 7 De GM & G 248 at 259; *Grey v Pearson* (1857) 6 HL Cas 61 at 99 per Lord St Leonards; *Roddy v Fitzgerald* (1858) 6 HL Cas 823 at 871 per Lord Cranworth LC; *Pride v Fooks* (1858) 3 De G & J 252 at 266; *Re Redfern, Redfern v Bryning* (1877) 6 ChD 133 at 136.
7   See *Roddy v Fitzgerald* (1858) 6 HL Cas 823 at 877 per Lord Wensleydale; *Van Grutten v Foxwell, Foxwell v Van Grutten* [1897] AC 658 at 672, HL, per Lord Macnaghten. See also *Hodgson v Clare* [1999] All ER (D) 359, sub nom *Re Owen, Hodgson v Clare* [2002] WTLR 619 (reference to the demise of testator's wife 'together with me' could not be construed as extending to the former wife predeceasing the testator); and *Esson v Esson* [2009] EWHC 3045 (Ch), [2009] All ER (D) 325 (Nov) (wording 'should I predecease him' held, in all the circumstances and in the light of extrinsic evidence, that the testatrix's intention was to create an unconditional gift); *Reading v Reading* [2015] EWHC 946 (Ch), [2015] WTLR 1245, [2015] All ER (D) 64 (Feb) (cited in note 4).
8   *Re Crawford's Trusts* (1854) 2 Drew 230 at 233 per Kindersley V-C.

243. Testator's right to be capricious. A testator has a right to be capricious if he chooses[1], and, subject to the statutory jurisdiction to award reasonable financial provision in favour of the testator's spouse, civil partner, former spouse or former civil partner (but not one who has formed a subsequent marriage or civil partnership), cohabitee, child or dependant[2], his bounty is absolute and without control as to motive[3]. Accordingly, if the words used by the testator are unambiguous in the context, the sense given to the words by the context cannot be departed from, nor is the court induced to put a meaning on them different from that which it judicially determines to be their meaning, on account of any difficulty or inconvenience in carrying out the intention[4], or because they lead to consequences which are generally considered capricious[5], unusual[6], unjust[7], harsh, unreasonable[8] or even absurd[9]. Nevertheless, the court retains the right to, and probably should, look into the reasons for the capriciousness where testamentary capacity is called into question[10].

1   *Hart v Tulk* (1852) 2 De GM & G 300 at 313; *Boosey v Gardener* (1854) 5 De GM & G 122 at 124; *Varley v Winn* (1856) 2 K & J 700 at 707; *Jenkins v Hughes* (1860) 8 HL Cas 571 at 589, 592; *Re Hamlet, Stephen v Cunningham* (1888) 39 ChD 426 at 434, CA; *Crawford's Trustees v Fleck* 1910 SC 998 at 1009, Ct of Sess.
2   Ie under the Inheritance (Provision for Family and Dependants) Act 1975 s 1: see PARA 24; and PARA 565 et seq. The category of cohabitee (ie someone who, during the whole of the period of two years ending immediately before the date when the deceased died, was living in the same household as the deceased and as the husband or wife or civil partner of the deceased) was introduced in relation to persons dying on or after 1 January 1996: see the Inheritance (Provision for Family and Dependants) Act 1975 s 1 (amended by the Law Reform (Succession) Act 1995 s 2; the Civil Partnership Act 2004 s 71, Sch 4 para 15; and the Inheritance and Trustees' Powers Act 2014 Sch 2 paras 1, 2); and PARA 567. 'Spouse' includes a person who is married to a person of the same sex: see the Marriage (Same Sex Couples) Act 2013 Sch 3 para 1(1)(a), (2), (3); and MATRIMONIAL AND CIVIL PARTNERSHIP LAW vol 72 (2015) PARAS 1–2.
3   *Occleston v Fullalove* (1874) 9 Ch App 147 at 161.

4   *Driver d Frank v Frank* (1814) 3 M & S 25 at 30–31 per Dampier J (citing authorities to show that,
     even if the court is perfectly aware of the testator's intention, effect cannot be given to it unless it
     appears from the words of the will); affd on appeal (1818) 8 Taunt 468. See also *Gaskell v Harman*
     (1801) 6 Ves 159 (on appeal (1805) 11 Ves 489 at 497); *Elwin v Elwin* (1803) 8 Ves 547 at
     554–555; *Defflis v Goldschmidt* (1816) 1 Mer 417 at 419–420; *Bernard v Mountague* (1816) 1
     Mer 422 at 431; *Smith v Streatfield* (1816) 1 Mer 358 at 360; *Martineau v Briggs* (1875) 45 LJ
     Ch 674, HL; *Re Seal, Seal v Taylor* [1894] 1 Ch 316 at 321, CA. See also *Marley v Rawlings* [2014]
     UKSC 2, [2015] AC 129, [2014] 1 All ER 807; and PARA 188.
5   *Wharton v Barker* (1858) 4 K & J 483 at 503; *Abbott v Middleton, Ricketts v Carpenter* (1858)
     7 HL Cas 68 at 89 per Lord Cranworth (adopted in *Bathurst v Errington* (1877) 2 App Cas 698
     at 709, HL, per Lord Cairns LC); *Selby v Whittaker* (1877) 6 ChD 239 at 245, CA; *Hickling v Fair*
     [1899] AC 15 at 33, HL, per Lord Shane, and at 38 per Lord Davey; *Re Whitmore, Walters v
     Harrison* [1902] 2 Ch 66 at 70, CA.
6   *Van Grutten v Foxwell, Foxwell v Van Grutten* [1897] AC 658 at 678, HL, per Lord Macnaghten.
7   *Inderwick v Tatchell* [1903] AC 120 at 123, HL, per Earl of Halsbury, and at 126 per Lord
     Lindley.
8   *Abbott v Middleton, Ricketts v Carpenter* (1858) 7 HL Cas 68 at 89 per Lord Cranworth; *Bathurst
     v Errington* (1877) 2 App Cas 698. See also *Mason v Robinson* (1825) 2 Sim & St 295 at 299
     (irrational dispositions); *Re Pollard's Estate* (1863) 3 De GJ & Sm 541 at 553 (dispositions in part
     unusual, in part eccentric); *Martin v Holgate* (1866) LR 1 HL 175 at 189.
9   *Graves v Bainbrigge* (1792) 1 Ves 562 at 564; but see *Re Segelman* [1996] Ch 171, [1995] 3 All ER
     676 (where unambiguous words producing an absurd result were construed so as to produce a
     rational result).
10   *Sharp v Adam* [2006] EWCA Civ 449, 10 ITELR 419, [2006] All ER (D) 277 (Apr) (it seems that
     the court should inquire into why a testator disinherited his children where there is a possibility
     that it is due to disease of the mind).

244. Approach to construction in ambiguous cases. Without some clear
expression of intention on a testator's part the court does not attribute to him a
capricious intention[1], or a whimsical or harsh result to his dispositions[2], where the
words of his will can be read otherwise. Accordingly, if, in the absence of direct
evidence of intention[3], the language used in a will admits of two constructions,
according to one of which the property disposed of devolves in a rational,
convenient and ordinary course of succession, and according to another in an
irrational and inconvenient course, so that the court would be driven to the
conclusion that the testator was acting capriciously, without any intelligible
motive and contrary to the ordinary mode in which persons act in similar cases,
the court leans towards the former construction as being that which was intended,
even if this requires a meaning to be given to the words different from their
ordinary meaning[4].

The appearance of caprice can, however, become a warning signal that
something has gone wrong with the testator's true expression of his intention[5].

1   *Hillersdon v Lowe* (1843) 2 Hare 355 at 366; *Hart v Tulk* (1852) 2 De GM & G 300 at 313;
     Thellusson v Lord Rendlesham, Thellusson v Thellusson, Hare v Robarts (1859) 7 HL Cas 429 at
     497–498.
2   *Barraclough v Cooper* [1908] 2 Ch 121n at 125n. See also *Vickers v Pound* (1858) 6 HL Cas 885
     at 897; *Bathurst v Errington* (1877) 2 App Cas 698 at 714, HL, per Lord Hatherley. See *Hodgson
     v Clare* [1999] All ER (D) 359, sub nom *Re Owen, Hodgson v Clare* [2002] WTLR 619, where
     the result of the will (that gift over of the entire estate, on predecease by spouse, should fail unless
     spouse died 'with testator') was not seen as capricious, whimsical or harsh.
3   Ie where there is an ambiguity on the face of the will of a testator who died on or after 1 January
     1983: see the Administration of Justice Act 1982 s 21(1)(b), (2); and PARAS 195, 219–220. See
     also *Marley v Rawlings* [2014] UKSC 2, [2015] AC 129, [2014] 1 All ER 807; and PARA 188.
4   *Abbott v Middleton, Ricketts v Carpenter* (1858) 7 HL Cas 68 at 89 per Lord Cranworth. See also
     Jenkins v Herries (1819) 4 Madd 67 at 82 per Leach V-C; *Jenkins v Hughes* (1860) 8 HL Cas 571
     at 592; *Atkinson v Holtby* (1863) 10 HL Cas 313 at 330; *Sidney v Wilmer* (1863) 4 De GJ & Sm
     84 at 103; *Gordon v Gordon* (1871) LR 5 HL 254 at 279, 284; *Bathurst v Errington* (1877) 2 App
     Cas 698 at 709, 711, HL, per Lord Cairns; *Selby v Whittaker* (1877) 6 ChD 239 at 248, CA; *Re
     Hudson, Hudson v Hudson* (1882) 20 ChD 406 at 417; *Locke v Dunlop* (1888) 39 ChD 387 at
     393, CA; *Bowman v Bowman* [1899] AC 518 at 528, HL, per Lord Watson; *Re Whitmore,*

Walters v Harrison [1902] 2 Ch 66 at 70, CA; *Re Jones, Lewis v Lewis* [1910] 1 Ch 167 at 172–173. As to construction of the meaning of 'survive', to avoid capricious results, see *Re Allsopp, Cardinal v Warr* [1968] Ch 39 at 47, [1967] 2 All ER 1056 at 1058, CA; and *Blech v Blech* [2001] All ER (D) 141 (Dec).

5 'If the consequence of the language used by a testator, read in its primary and natural sense, is to produce a disposition . . . which is so capricious as to be really irrational, the court may, in my judgment, be justified in concluding that the testator has failed to express himself adequately, and in such a case if, but only if, it can discern the true intention of the testator, it will give effect to it': *Re Doland's Will Trusts, Westminster Bank Ltd v Phillips* [1970] Ch 267 at 272, [1969] 3 All ER 713 at 715 per Buckley J.

245. Words having more than one primary meaning. There are few words, if indeed there are any, which bear a meaning so exact that the reader can disregard the surrounding circumstances and the context in ascertaining the sense in which they are employed[1]. Where a word has more than one proper and recognised meaning, the question in which sense it is used in a particular passage must be decided by the context and the surrounding circumstances, and no one meaning can be treated as having a paramount claim to be adopted in preference to any other[2].

1 *Seale-Hayne v Jodrell* [1891] AC 304 at 306, HL, per Lord Herschell; *Cave v Horsell* [1912] 3 KB 533 at 543, CA, per Buckley LJ. See also *Hodgson v Ambrose* (1780) 1 Doug KB 337 at 341; *Doe d Andrew v Lainchbury* (1809) 11 East 290 at 296. Cf *Re Osburn* (1969) 113 Sol Jo 387, CA (where a gift of a house was held not to be included in a 'list of small presents'). See also *Marley v Rawlings* [2014] UKSC 2, [2015] AC 129, [2014] 1 All ER 807; and PARA 188.

2 *Cave v Horsell* [1912] 3 KB 533 at 543, CA; *Perrin v Morgan* [1943] AC 399 at 406, 417, [1943] 1 All ER 187 at 190, 195. A word which is not in its ordinary meaning a technical word may have several senses and be used in one of them in which it is technical: *Clayton v Gregson* (1835) 5 Ad & El 302 at 308.

246. Words judicially defined. The starting point when ascertaining the testator's intentions must be to look at the natural meaning of the wording of the will to be construed without reference to other decisions or to prima facie principles of construction[1]. A court will therefore place little importance on the meaning ascribed to a particular word in another will which necessarily will have a different context. However, there may be cases where the meaning previously ascribed throws light on the testator's intentions.

Among the words and expressions which have been in common use in wills, the meaning of which at large, or as affected by various contexts, has been the subject of judicial determination, are the following[2]: 'business'[3]; 'creditors'[4]; 'entitled'[5]; 'except upon' attaining an age[6]; 'executorship expenses' or 'testamentary expenses'[7]; 'free of duty'[8]; 'gifts or settlements'[9]; 'probate valuation'[10]; 'marriage'[11]; 'unmarried'[12]; 'minority'[13]; 'simultaneous death'[14]; 'per stirpes'[15]; 'survive'[16]; 'belongings'[17]; 'members of my family' or 'relations'[18]; 'friends of mine'[19]; and 'writing under hand'[20]. The expression 'during the present war' has also received judicial consideration[21]. The words 'subject to the provisions of the preceding clause' mean subject to any effective disposition under that clause[22].

1 *Sammut v Manzi* [2008] UKPC 58 at [6], [2009] 2 All ER 234, [2009] 1 WLR 1834 per Lord Phillips of Worth Matravers.

2 For other examples in relation to property and donees see PARAS 286 et seq, 328 et seq.

3 'Business' in a clause containing a power of advancement has been held to include a medical practice: *Re Williams' Will Trusts, Chartered Bank of India, Australia and China v Williams* [1953] Ch 138, [1953] 1 All ER 536. As to the meaning of 'business' see also PARA 287.

4 'Creditors' extends to all creditors, secured as well as unsecured: *Re Leach, Chatterton v Leach* [1948] Ch 232, [1948] 1 All ER 383.

5 'Entitled' may mean entitled in possession, or entitled in interest: *Chorley v Loveband* (1863) 33 Beav 189; *Re Grylls' Trusts* (1868) LR 6 Eq 589; *Umbers v Jaggard* (1870) LR 9 Eq 200; *Abbiss*

v Burney, Re Finch (1880) 17 ChD 211 at 223; *Re Fothergill's Estate, Price-Fothergill v Price*
[1903] 1 Ch 149. As to the meaning of 'entitled as aforesaid' see *Re Whiter, Windsor v Jones*
(1911) 105 LT 749.

6 This means 'not before': *Re Sumner's Will Trusts, Midland Bank Executor and Trustee Co Ltd v
Sumner* [1969] 1 All ER 779, [1969] 1 WLR 373.

7 These terms are ordinarily synonymous, and denote the expenses incident to the proper
performance of the executor's duty: *Sharp v Lush* (1879) 10 ChD 468 at 470; *Re
Matthews's Will Trusts, Bristow v Matthews* [1961] 3 All ER 869, [1961] 1 WLR 1415. As to the
meaning of 'expenses' see *Re Berrey's Will Trusts, Greening v Waters* [1959] 1 All ER 15, [1959]
1 WLR 30. See further PARAS 1014, 1017. 'Expenses' includes inheritance tax (formerly known
as capital transfer tax) attributable to the value of all property (real and personal) in the United
Kingdom vesting in the deceased's personal representatives; such tax is prima facie treated as a
testamentary expense, but not foreign tax or inheritance tax payable in respect of foreign property
or settled property, which is not: see the Inheritance Tax Act 1984 s 211(1), (2); and PARA 1016.
As to the meaning of 'United Kingdom' see PARA 4 note 7.

8 'Free of duty' prima facie refers to duty payable under English law and not to duty payable under
foreign law, and to duty payable on the testator's death and not to future duty: see PARA 1130.
References to estate duty in any instrument whenever executed have effect as if they included
references to inheritance tax (formerly known as capital transfer tax): Inheritance Tax Act 1984
s 273, Sch 6para1; and see INHERITANCE TAXATION vol 59A (2014) PARA 1.

9 See *Re Noad, Midland Bank Executor and Trustee Co Ltd v Noad* [1944] 2 All ER 470, CA
(where, in the context, the words meant any benefaction); *Re Figgis, Roberts v MacLaren* [1969]
1 Ch 123, [1968] 1 All ER 999 (where 'gifts . . . in my lifetime' did not include money placed in
a joint bank account).

10 'Probate valuation' means the value given in the Inland Revenue affidavit leading to probate (*Re
Eumorfopoulos, Ralli v Eumorfopoulos* [1944] Ch 133, [1943] 2 All ER 719), but 'valuation
agreed for probate' means the valuation agreed ultimately with the fiscal authorities (*Re De
Lisle's Will Trusts, White v De Lisle* [1968] 1 All ER 492, [1968] 1 WLR 322).

11 'Marriage' prima facie refers to a marriage valid in law: *Viscount Falkland v Bertie* (1698) 2 Vern
333 at 336; *Allen v Wood* (1834) 1 Bing NC 8; *Re M'Loughlin's Estate* (1878) 1 LR Ir 421, Ir CA.
'Marriage' includes marriage of a same sex couple: see the Marriage (Same Sex Couples) Act 2013
Sch 3 para 1(1)(a), (2), (3); and MATRIMONIAL AND CIVIL PARTNERSHIP LAW vol 72 (2015)
PARAS 1–2.

12 'Unmarried' has no fixed meaning (*Pratt v Mathew* (1856) 22 Beav 328; *Clarke v Colls* (1861) 9
HL Cas 601), but is generally construed to mean 'never having been married' (*Heywood v
Heywood* (1860) 29 Beav 9 at 16; *Re Sanders' Trusts* (1866) LR 1 Eq 675; *Dalrymple v Hall*
(1881) 16 ChD 715; *Re Sergeant, Mertens v Walley* (1884) 26 ChD 575; *Roberts v Bishop of
Kilmore* [1902] 1 IR 333; *Re Collyer, Collyer v Back* (1907) 24 TLR 117; *Re Hall-Dare, Le
Marchant v Lee Warner* [1916] 1 Ch 272). See also *Re Thistlethwayte's Trust* (1855) 24 LJ Ch
712. It may mean 'not having a spouse living': *Clarke v Colls* (1861) 9 HL Cas 601; *Re Chant,
Chant v Lemon* [1900] 2 Ch 345. See also *Re Jones, Last v Dobson* [1915] 1 Ch 246 (where
'unmarried and without leaving lawful issue' was held to mean 'widower', as otherwise the last five
words were superfluous); and SETTLEMENTS vol 91 (2012) PARA 837. As to a gift to unmarried
children see *Jubber v Jubber* (1839) 9 Sim 503; *Hall v Robertson* (1853) 4 De GM & G 781.

13 In a will executed before 1 January 1970 'minority' prima facie refers to the period up to 21 years
of age (the date of death is not material nor is the construction affected by a codicil confirming the
will executed on or after that date); but in wills executed on or after that date 'minority' prima facie
refers to the period up to 18 years of age (see the Family Law Reform Act 1969 s 1; and CHILDREN
AND YOUNG PERSONS vol 9 (2012) PARA 1), but may refer to the traditional minority, ie the
period up to 21 years of age, or the time during which the testator has kept the child out of full
control of his property (*Milroy v Milroy* (1844) 14 Sim 48; *Fraser v Fraser* (1863) 1 New Rep 430).
As to the meaning of 'children' see PARA 331 et seq.

14 'Simultaneous death' does not mean death in such circumstances that a physician would hold that
death at the same moment of time had been proved (*Hickman v Peacey* [1945] AC 304, [1945]
2 All ER 215, HL, where it is doubted whether in this sense simultaneous death is possible), but
death in such circumstances that the ordinary person would infer that death was simultaneous (see
Re Pringle, Baker v Matheson [1946] Ch 124, [1946] 1 All ER 88). The expression is normally to
be construed as a reference to time, and not to death as a result of the same calamity: *Re Rowland,
Smith v Russell* [1963] Ch 1, [1962] 2 All ER 837, CA (death of wife 'preceding or coinciding with'
testator's death). Cf *Re Harmer* (1964) 42 DLR (2d) 321, Ont CA (where a provision relating to
simultaneous deaths was held to apply where the husband's death preceded that of the testatrix).

15 'Per stirpes' indicates a gift 'by family' so that the head of the line takes in preference to descendants: *Sammut v Manzi* [2008] UKPC 58 at [25], [2009] 2 All ER 234, [2009] 1 WLR 1834 per Lord Hope.

16 See *Blech v Blech* [2001] All ER (D) 141 (Dec) (to 'survive' the testator normally means to be alive at his death).

17 It seems that the term 'belongings' is not apt to describe real property: see *Re Price, Wasley v Price* [1950] Ch 242, [1950] 1 All ER 338. Where 'personal belongings' are given by way of residue, a wider construction, that may extend to bank accounts and shares etc, may be appropriate, but not where there is a particular gift: see *Re Hynes, Knapp v Hynes* [1950] 2 All ER 879, 94 Sol Jo 687, CA.

18 In the absence of issue, 'family' prima facie means blood relations: see *Re Barlow's Will Trusts* [1979] 1 All ER 296, [1979] 1 WLR 278. To avoid failure for uncertainty, there is a rule of construction which normally limits gifts 'to relations' to statutory next of kin of the testator where a division of a gift within the class is called for. This rule was not applied in *Re Barlow's Will Trusts* as the gift was a simple option to family members and friends of the testatrix to buy paintings at a valuation. See also *Re Gansloser's Will Trusts, Chartered Bank of India, Australia and China v Chillingworth* [1952] Ch 30 at 46–47, [1951] 2 All ER 936 at 946.

19 *Re Barlow's Will Trusts* [1979] 1 All ER 296, [1979] 1 WLR 278.

20 The expression 'under hand' imports the signing of the document: see *Trustee Solutions Ltd v Dubery* [2006] EWHC 1426 (Ch), [2007] 1 All ER 308.

21 These words may mean 'during the continuance of hostilities': *Re Cooper, Bendall v Cooper* [1946] Ch 109, [1946] 1 All ER 28. See also *Re Orchard, Carpenter v Lauer* [1948] 1 All ER 203 ('armistice').

22 *Re Edwards' Will Trusts, Dalgleish v Leighton* [1948] Ch 440, [1948] 1 All ER 821, CA.

247. Words referring to time. It is a matter of construction of the whole will whether a particular clause is intended to speak from the testator's death, or from the date of the execution of the will[1] or some other time[2].

Where the testator uses words of futurity without clearly showing the time which he contemplates, and where it is not a question of the real and personal estate comprised in the will[3], prima facie those words should be read as speaking from the date of his making the will and not from the date of his death[4]. In such a case, an event which happens before the date of the will is not within the clause in question, and a phrase such as 'persons who shall die in my lifetime' does not prima facie include persons already dead at the date of the will[5].

The court is, however, especially ready to discover that the testator has fallen into the trap of using tenses ungrammatically and making references to time inaccurately[6]. In such cases the words are not construed in their strictly grammatical sense, but as referring to events which, even if they happened before the date of the will, are past at the testator's death[7].

Where the context shows that the testator could not mean the time of making the will as the time contemplated by him, he must prima facie mean the time of his death[8].

1 *Re Chapman, Perkins v Chapman* [1904] 1 Ch 431 at 440, CA, per Cozens-Hardy LJ; affd sub nom *Chapman v Perkins* [1905] AC 106, HL.

2 See *Re Bayliss's Trust* (1849) 17 Sim 178 ('such as are married', meaning 'such as shall be married at the date when the legacies are payable'). Thus a forfeiture clause may be intended to operate only after the testator's death: see *Re Evans, Hewitt v Edwards* [1940] Ch 629 ('ipso facto' showed that the testator contemplated only an act after his death).

3 As to real and personal estate the will generally speaks from death: see PARA 282. Descriptions of donees taking as individuals generally have reference to the date of the will: see PARA 300.

4 *Bullock v Bennett* (1855) 7 De GM & G 283; *Re Chapman, Perkins v Chapman* [1904] 1 Ch 431 at 436, CA, per Vaughan Williams LJ; *Re Fentem, Cockerton v Fentem* [1950] 2 All ER 1073.

5 See *Coulthurst v Carter* (1852) 15 Beav 421 at 430; *Gorringe v Mahlstedt* [1907] AC 225, HL; *Re Cope, Cross v Cross* [1908] 2 Ch 1, CA; *Re Brown, Leeds v Spencer* [1917] 2 Ch 232; *Re Hewitt, Hewitt v Hewitt* [1926] Ch 740; *Re Walker, Walker v Walker* [1930] 1 Ch 469, CA.

6 *Re Donald, Royal Exchange Assurance v Donald* [1947] 1 All ER 764 at 766, CA, per Lord Greene MR ('who shall have died in the lifetime of J' construed as meaning 'who shall not be living at the death of J', allowing in issue of person who had died before J was born).

7 Thus 'persons who shall die in my lifetime' may mean 'persons who shall not be living at my death': *Loring v Thomas* (1861) 1 Drew & Sm 497 at 516; *Re Lambert, Corns v Harrison* [1908] 2 Ch 117 at 120; *Barraclough v Cooper* [1908] 2 Ch 121n at 126n. See also *Re Birchall, Re Valentine, Kennedy v Birchall* [1940] Ch 424, [1940] 1 All ER 545, CA; *Christopherson v Naylor* (1816) 1 Mer 320; *Re Williams, Metcalfe v Williams* [1914] 2 Ch 61, CA; *Re Kirk, Wethey v Kirk* (1915) 85 LJ Ch 182; *Re Rayner, Couch v Warner* (1925) 134 LT 141 ('shall live to attain 21' held to include child who had attained 21 at date of will); *Mackintosh (or Miller) v Gerrard* [1947] AC 461, HL (where the cases were reviewed); *Re Donald, Royal Exchange Assurance v Donald* [1947] 1 All ER 764, CA ('who shall have died in the lifetime of J' held to include persons dead before J was born). As to similar cases on settlements see *Hewet v Ireland* (1718) 1 P Wms 426; *Manning v Chambers* (1847) 1 De G & Sm 282; *Barnes v Jennings* (1866) LR 2 Eq 448. Where the gift is to named individuals and not to a class, it is easier to suppose that the words are not to be taken in their strict sense: *Re Booth's Will Trusts, Robbins v King* (1940) 163 LT 77; affd on other grounds [1940] WN 293, CA.

8 *Lomax v Holmden* (1749) 1 Ves Sen 290 at 296. A devise of the proceeds of sale of such parts of an estate 'as have been sold' refers, in the absence of a contrary intention appearing in the will, to the date of the testator's death, and includes the proceeds received from sales made after the date of the will: *Re Davies, Scourfield v Davies* [1925] Ch 642. As to a contrary intention appearing in a will see PARA 282.

248. Effect to be given to every word. It is a general, but not inflexible[1], canon of construction that the will should be so construed that every word has effect[2] and the court may, in an appropriate case, attach some significance to the punctuation and its effect[3]. A word ought not to be disregarded if it can be given some meaning[4] which is not contrary to the testator's intention plainly expressed in other parts of the will[5], and it is not to be assumed that the testator has used additional words without some additional purpose or without any purpose at all[6].

The rule is not adhered to where its application would defeat the testator's intention as collected from the context of the whole will[7], and in such cases the words may be regarded as merely explanatory, expressing what would otherwise have been true under the will[8]. There is no presumption that testators use the irreducible minimum of words to effect their purpose, or that each word should change the meaning of the sentence, and the objection of surplusage has weight only when the presence of the word or phrase would be unusual or unaccountable if it were not specially inserted for the purpose of altering the meaning of the sentence[9]. In particular, words are not to be given a meaning other than their ordinary meaning merely because they are in their ordinary meaning only surplusage[10], or because other words, inconsistent with their use in that meaning but insufficient to give them a different meaning, may have to be rejected[11].

1 See *Martin v Holgate* (1866) LR 1 HL 175 at 185 per Lord Cranworth LC (where the rule was countered by the rule that a gift should not be construed as contingent unless the context so requires). See also *Clarke v Colls* (1861) 9 HL Cas 601 at 613, 618.

2 See *Re Lawrence's Will Trusts, Public Trustee v Lawrence* [1972] Ch 418, [1971] 3 All ER 433 ('as if' had the effect of cutting back the effects of a codicil).

3 See *Houston v Burns* [1918] AC 337, 87 LJPC 99, HL; and *Sammut v Manzi* [2008] UKPC 58, [2009] 2 All ER 234, [2009] 1 WLR 1834.

4 *Re Croxon, Croxon v Ferrers* [1904] 1 Ch 252 at 258 ('lawfully' assume, in name and arms clause). See also *Heasman v Pearse* (1871) 7 Ch App 275 at 283.

5 *Doe d Baldwin v Rawding* (1819) 2 B & Ald 441 at 448 per Abbott CJ, and at 451 per Holroyd J. See also *Reeves v Brymer* (1799) 4 Ves 692 at 698; *Constantine v Constantine* (1801) 6 Ves 100 at 102.

6 *Oddie v Woodford* (1821) 3 My & Cr 584 at 614 per Lord Cottenham LC; *Quarm v Quarm* [1892] 1 QB 184 at 186. See also *Foxwell v Van Grutten* (1900) 82 LT 272, HL. See *Re Priestley's Will Trusts, Hambros Bank Executor and Trustee Co Ltd v Rabagliati* [1971] Ch 858 at 864, [1971] 2 All ER 817 at 821 per Russell LJ ('cannot treat as prolixity or tautology the introduction into a general power of appointment of a reference to a . . . special power of appointment').

7 *Sayer v Bradly* (1856) 5 HL Cas 873 at 899.
8 *M'Lachlan v Taitt* (1860) 2 De GF & J 449 at 454 per Lord Campbell LC. See also *Hicks v Sallitt* (1854) 3 De GM & G 782 at 794; *Re Walton's Estate* (1856) 8 De GM & G 173 at 175 per Knight Bruce LJ.
9 *Re Boden, Boden v Boden* [1907] 1 Ch 132 at 143, CA, per Fletcher Moulton LJ. See also *Clarke v Colls* (1861) 9 HL Cas 601 at 613 per Lord Cranworth ('the language of conveyancers is proverbially prolix and redundant').
10 *Monk v Mawdsley* (1827) 1 Sim 286 at 290–291; *Taylor v Beverley* (1844) 1 Coll 108 at 116; *Craik v Lamb* (1844) 1 Coll 489 at 493–494; *Re Kirkbride's Trusts* (1866) LR 2 Eq 400; *Giles v Melsom* (1873) LR 6 HL 24 at 33–34; *Palmer v Orpen* [1894] 1 IR 32 at 38; *Roberts v Bishop of Kilmore* [1902] 1 IR 333; *Re Hampton, Hampton v Mawer* (1918) 62 Sol Jo 585.
11 Even technical words may be given a meaning other than their technical meaning where they are inconsistent with the general intention (*Jesson v Wright* (1820) 2 Bli 1, HL; *Roddy v Fitzgerald* (1858) 6 HL Cas 823), but, unless the inconsistency is plain, the rules of construction must prevail (*Roddy v Fitzgerald* at 871 per Lord Cranworth).

249. Presumption as to repeated words. A canon of construction which is far from universal and always requires a good deal of care in its application[1] is that a word used in one part of the will with some clear and definite meaning is intended to have the same meaning in another part of the will where its meaning is not clear[2].

The force of the context may, however, give different meanings to the same word when used in different parts of the will[3]. As the words must be construed with reference to the subject matter[4], different meanings may be given to the same word or phrase when used both with reference to real property and with reference to personal property in the will, even in the same sentence[5].

1 *Clifford v Koe* (1880) 5 App Cas 447 at 459, HL, per Lord Selborne LC.
2 *Re Birks, Kenyon v Birks* [1900] 1 Ch 417 at 418, CA, per Lindley MR. See also *Ridgeway v Munkittrick* (1841) 1 Dr & War 84 at 93 per Sugden LC; *Edwards v Edwards* (1849) 12 Beav 97 at 100 per Romilly MR; *Re Buckle, Williams v Marson* [1894] 1 Ch 286 at 288, CA. See, however, *Leeming v Sherratt* (1842) 2 Hare 14 at 25; *Rhodes v Rhodes* (1859) 27 Beav 413 at 417; *Haws v Haws* (1747) 3 Atk 524 at 526.
3 *Doe d Cock v Cooper* (1801) 1 East 229 at 233; *Right d Compton v Compton* (1808) 9 East 267 at 272–273; *Dalzell v Welch* (1828) 2 Sim 319 (issue); *Carter v Bentall* (1840) 2 Beav 551 at 558; *Head v Randall* (1843) 2 Y & C Ch Cas 231 (issue); *Hedges v Harpur* (1846) 9 Beav 479 (on appeal (1858) 3 De G & J 129) (issue); *Williams v Teale* (1847) 6 Hare 239 at 250 (issue); *Neathway v Reed* (1853) 3 De GM & G 18 at 22 (surviving); *Edyvean v Archer, Re Brooke* [1903] AC 379, PC (issue). See also *Re Warren's Trusts* (1884) 26 ChD 208 at 216 per Pearson J (settlement). In *Gill v Barrett* (1860) 29 Beav 372, 'then' was used twice in one sentence; the first time as pointing to the event, the second as an adverb of time.
4 *Williams v Jekyl, Elliot v Jekyl* (1755) 2 Ves Sen 681 at 683.
5 *Forth v Chapman* (1720) 1 P Wms 663 at 667; *Doe d Chattaway v Smith* (1816) 5 M & S 126 at 132.

250. Ejusdem generis rule. The ejusdem generis rule[1] as to the meaning of general words following a series of specific descriptions applies to wills as to other instruments, and applies to descriptions of persons and things as well as to descriptions of property[2]. The rule readily gives way to any context showing a contrary intention, and may be overridden by the presumption against intestacy[3], so that, where the general words occur in a clause of the nature of a residuary gift, the ordinary, wider meaning of the words is adhered to[4]. This consideration does not, however, assist where the general words would in their wider meaning carry a residuary estate which is dealt with by another clause of the will[5].

1 As to the ejusdem generis rule generally see DEEDS AND OTHER INSTRUMENTS vol 32 (2012) PARA 435. For examples of the application of the rule to wills see *Trafford v Berrige* (1729) 1 Eq Cas Abr 201 pl 14 ('other things'); *Timewell v Perkins* (1740) 2 Atk 102 ('etc, or in any other thing'); *Stuart v Marquis of Bute* (1813) 1 Dow 73, HL ('things'); *Wrench v Jutting* (1841) 3 Beav 521 ('other goods'); *Lamphier v Despard* (1842) 2 Dr & War 59 ('other chattel property'); *Barnaby v Tassell* (1871) LR 11 Eq 363 at 369 ('etc'); *Re Lord Londesborough, Bridgeman v Lord*

Fitzgerald (1880) 43 LT 408 ('objects of vertu or taste'); *Re Layard, Layard v Earl of Bessborough* (1916) 85 LJ Ch 505, CA ('portraits of myself and all my family and other portraits') (appeal withdrawn on terms (1917) 33 TLR 261, HL); *Re Taylor, Barber v Smith* (1919) 147 LT Jo 253 ('jewellery and other articles of personal or domestic use or ornament' held to include furniture); *Malone v Malone* [1925] 1 IR 140, Ir CA ('and effects of every kind'); *Re Resch's Will Trusts, Le Cras v Perpetual Trustee Co Ltd, Far West Children's Health Scheme v Perpetual Trustee Co Ltd* [1969] 1 AC 514, [1967] 3 All ER 915, PC ('other personal jewellery'). As to the construction of 'etc' see further *Steignes v Steignes* (1730) Mos 296; *Marquis of Hertford v Lord Lowther* (1843) 7 Beav 1; *Twining v Powell* (1845) 2 Coll 262; *Chapman v Chapman* (1876) 4 ChD 800; *Re Andrew's Estate, Creasey v Graves* (1902) 50 WR 471 (real estate included). For examples where the general words were held to retain their ordinary significance see *Kendall v Kendall* (1828) 4 Russ 360; *Arnold v Arnold* (1834) 2 My & K 365 ('my wines and property in England'); *Ellis v Selby* (1835) 7 Sim 352 at 364; *Re Kendall's Trusts* (1851) 14 Beav 608 ('everything I die possessed of, namely . . .'); *Fisher v Hepburn* (1851) 14 Beav 626; *Everall v Browne* (1853) 1 Sm & G 368 ('other property, goods, and articles'). As to the effect of a gift of 'effects' see PARA 288. Although it is more difficult to infer that general words are cut down if there is an enumeration of only one species, or a slender enumeration of species of particulars (*Swinfen v Swinfen (No 4)* (1860) 29 Beav 207; *Campbell v M'Grain* (1875) IR 9 Eq 397 at 400 per Sullivan MR), there is no rule that general words cannot be cut down in those circumstances (*Northey v Paxton* (1888) 60 LT 30; *Re O'Brien, O'Brien v O'Brien* [1906] 1 IR 649 at 653, Ir CA). It seems that the ejusdem generis rule may often be at work in identifying general charitable intention and a corresponding genus in residuary gifts, although it will be easier to apply the rule where there are larger numbers of objects from which to identify the genus and the generality of the intention: see *Re Spence, Ogden v Shackleton* [1979] Ch 483, sub nom *Re Spence's Will Trusts, Ogden v Shackleton* [1978] 3 All ER 92.

2   For examples in investment clauses see *Edwards v Thompson* (1868) 38 LJ Ch 65 ('any railway' restricted to United Kingdom railways); *Re Castlehow, Lamonby v Carter* [1903] 1 Ch 352 ('any railway or other public company' restricted to United Kingdom railways). Cf *Re Stanley, Tennant v Stanley* [1906] 1 Ch 131 (where the context excluded any restriction).

3   *Gibbs v Lawrence* (1860) 30 LJ Ch 170 at 171. See also *Re Kendall's Trust* (1851) 14 Beav 608; *Dean v Gibson* (1867) LR 3 Eq 713 (following *Bridges v Bridges* (1729) 8 Vin Abr, Devise (Ob) 295 pl 13; *Chalmers v Storil* (1813) 2 Ves & B 222 (cases of enumeration of particulars, 'viz' or 'consisting of')); *Chapman v Chapman* (1876) 4 ChD 800; *King v George* (1877) 5 ChD 627, CA; *Re Fleetwood, Sidgreaves v Brewer* (1880) 15 ChD 594; *Re Recknell, White v Carter* [1936] 2 All ER 36. As to the presumption against intestacy see PARA 255.

4   *Parker v Marchant* (1842) 1 Y & C Ch Cas 290 at 301; *Hodgson v Jex* (1876) 2 ChD 122; *Re Parrott, Parrott v Parrott* (1885) 53 LT 12.

5   *Woolcomb v Woolcomb* (1731) 3 P Wms 112; *Mullins v Smith* (1860) 1 Drew & Sm 204; *Smith v Davis* (1866) 14 WR 942, CA; *Campbell v M'Grain* (1875) IR 9 Eq 397; *Re Miller, Daniel v Daniel* (1889) 61 LT 365; *MacPhail v Phillips* [1904] 1 IR 155.

251. Clear words not controlled by subsequent ambiguous words. Subject to the intention shown by the whole will[1], it is a leading principle of construction[2] that words clear and unambiguous in themselves[3] cannot be qualified by other words unless those other words show a very clear exposition of the testator's meaning[4]; nor can the effect of such words be set aside because there is a reason to suppose that they do not produce the effect which the testator intended that they should produce[5]. In the endeavour to read the will as a consistent whole and to reconcile the various clauses with each other[6], a prior gift is not disturbed by a later gift in the same or a subsequent testamentary instrument further than is necessary to give effect to the intentions of the testator shown by reading the will, including all codicils, as a whole[7].

However, in the case of a death on or after 1 January 1983[8], if language used in any part of the will is ambiguous on the face of it or is ambiguous in the light of surrounding circumstances, extrinsic evidence, including evidence of the testator's intention, may be admitted to assist in its interpretation[9].

1   See *Re Bagshaw's Trusts* (1877) 46 LJ Ch 567 at 569, CA.

2   *Goodwin v Finlayson* (1858) 25 Beav 65 at 68 per Romilly MR.

3   As to the position where the words are ambiguous see PARAS 195, 218–219.

4   *Broughton v Broughton, Broughton v James* (1848) 1 HL Cas 406 at 434 per Lord Cottenham LC. See also *Doe d Hearle v Hicks* (1832) 8 Bing 475, HL; *Bickford v Chalker* (1854) 2 Drew 327; *Kerr v Baroness Clinton* (1869) LR 8 Eq 462; *Conmy v Cawley* [1910] 2 IR 465, Ir CA.

5   *Earl Hardwicke v Douglas* (1840) 7 Cl & Fin 795 at 815, HL.
6   See PARA 232.
7   *Doe d Hearle v Hicks* (1832) 8 Bing 475 at 480, HL; *Young v Hassard* (1841) 1 Dr & War 638
      at 644; *Doe d Evers v Ward* (1852) 18 QB 197 at 223; *Williams v Evans* (1853) 1 E & B 727 at
      740; *Wallace v Seymour* (1872) IR 6 CL 219 at 343–344, Ir Exch; *Pennefather v Lloyd* [1917] 1
      IR 337; *Re Florence, Lydall v Haberdashers' Co* (1917) 87 LJ Ch 86; *Re Atkinson, Atkinson v
      Weightman* [1925] WN 30, CA; *Re Bund, Cruickshank v Willis* [1929] 2 Ch 455 at 464. See also
      Stewart v Maclaren (1920) 57 SLR 531; *Re Crawshay, Hore-Ruthven v Public Trustee* [1948] Ch
      123, [1948] 1 All ER 107, CA; *Pratt v Pratt* (1844) 14 Sim 129; *Baynes v Hedger* [2008] EWHC
      1587 (Ch), [2008] 2 FLR 1805, [2008] All ER (D) 175 (Jul) (affd on other grounds [2009] EWCA
      Civ 374, [2009] 2 FLR 767, [2009] All ER (D) 50 (May)). This rule appears to be the explanation
      for the limited effect given to the codicil in *Re Lawrence's Will Trusts, Public Trustee v Lawrence*
      [1972] Ch 418, [1971] 3 All ER 433.
8   Ie the date the Administration of Justice Act 1982 came into force.
9   See the Administration of Justice Act 1982 s 21: and PARAS 219, 220.

252. Effect of recitals or other statements. A recital or other statement, unless obviously erroneous, may be referred to by way of explanation of a gift in itself doubtful or ambiguous[1]. Where, however, the operative part is clear, it cannot be cut down by a recital[2]. A recital showing that the testator is under the impression that he has in his will made a certain disposition is evidence of an intention, inadvertently not expressed, to make that gift[3]. In such a case, effect will be given to the intention if the other provisions of the will allow this to be done[4], and the inference from the recital may be sufficient to overcome and correct the terms of an express gift to the person in question[5]. The court must, however, be satisfied that there has been a mistake in carrying out the testator's intention[6], or the recital is treated as erroneous and disregarded[7].

Mere words of erroneous recital or recognition of indebtedness or of affection do not disclose an intention of making a gift[8], and a recital showing that the testator considered that some person possessed a title to property independent of that of the testator prima facie gives rise to the inference that he did not intend to make a disposition in favour of that person[9].

However, in the case of a death on or after 1 January 1983[10], if language used in any part of the will is ambiguous on the face of it or is ambiguous in the light of surrounding circumstances, extrinsic evidence, including evidence of the testator's intention, may be admitted to assist in its interpretation[11].

1   *Pullin v Pullin* (1825) 10 Moore CP 464; *Darley v Martin* (1853) 13 CB 683; *Grover v Raper*
      (1856) 5 WR 134 (followed in *Re Venn, Lindon v Ingram* [1904] 2 Ch 52). As to inaccurate
      recitals of the indebtedness of a donee, and as to the effect of a direction to bring sums into
      hotchpot see PARA 406.
2   *Culsha v Cheese* (1849) 7 Hare 236; *Savile v Kinnaird* (1865) 11 Jur NS 195. As to reference to
      recitals in deeds for purposes of construction see DEEDS AND OTHER INSTRUMENTS vol 32
      (2012) PARA 418 et seq.
3   *Adams v Adams* (1842) 1 Hare 537 at 541; *Re Smith* (1862) 2 John & H 594 at 598–599.
4   *Bibin v Walker* (1768) Amb 661; *Farrer v St Catharine's College, Cambridge* (1873) LR 16 Eq 19
      at 24; *Re Yates, Singleton v Povah* (1922) 128 LT 619. See also *Law's Trustees v Gray* 1921 SC
      455, Ct of Sess (no bequests by implication where contrary to the general scheme).
5   *Jordan v Fortescue* (1847) 10 Beav 259. See also *Milner v Milner* (1748) 1 Ves Sen 106; *Re
      Margitson, Haggard v Haggard* (1882) 48 LT 172, CA.
6   *Thompson v Whitelock* (1859) 4 De G & J 490 at 500. See also *Smith v Fitzgerald* (1814) 3 Ves
      & B 2 at 8 per Grant MR. As to the possibility of rectification of the will see PARA 187.
7   *Gordon v Hoffman* (1834) 7 Sim 29; *Mann v Fuller* (1854) Kay 624; *Re Arnold's Estate* (1863)
      33 Beav 163 at 171; *Mackenzie v Bradbury* (1865) 35 Beav 617 at 620; *Ives v Dodgson* (1870) LR
      9 Eq 401.
8   *Re Rowe, Pike v Hamlyn* [1898] 1 Ch 153 at 160, CA. See also *Dashwood v Peyton* (1811) 18 Ves
      27 at 46; *Murdoch v Brass* (1904) 6 F 841.
9   *Adams v Adams* (1842) 1 Hare 537 at 540–541. See also *Ralph v Watson* (1840) 9 LJ Ch 328; *A-G
      v Dillon* (1862) 13 I Ch R 127 at 133; *Re Bagot, Paton v Ormerod* [1893] 3 Ch 348, CA; *Re Lee,*

Gibbon v Peele (1910) 103 LT 103; *Re Angus's Will Trusts, Hall v Angus* [1960] 3 All ER 835, [1960] 1 WLR 1296. Cf *Poulson v Wellington* (1729) 2 P Wms 533; *Wilson v Piggott* (1794) 2 Ves 351 at 355 (cases of settlements).

10 Ie the date the Administration of Justice Act 1982 came into force.

11 See the Administration of Justice Act 1982 s 21: and PARAS 219, 220.

253. Alteration of the words of the will. Where the testator's main purpose and intention are ascertained to the satisfaction of the court, then, if particular expressions are found in the will which are inconsistent with that intention, although not sufficient to control it, or which indicate an intention which the law does not permit to take effect, the expressions may be discarded or modified by the court[1]. Thus words and limitations[2] may be supplied[3], changed[4], transposed[5] or rejected[6] where this is justified by the immediate context or the general scheme of the will, particularly where it is plain that a mistake has occurred[7]. Before supplying words, however, the court must be satisfied not only that certain words have been omitted, but that it is certain what words have been omitted[8]. It seems that the dispositive effect of any omitted words must have been known of and approved by the testator for the court to add them, no matter how clear the accidental omission[9]. No alteration may be made to the words of the will unless it is necessary[10], nor may an alteration be made merely on a conjectural hypothesis of the testator's intention, however reasonable, in opposition to the plain and obvious sense of the instrument[11]. In identifying the testator's intention, the court may find that it is artificial to assume that a testator must know what he is doing if he uses language, the effect of which cannot be ascertained without a decision of the court[12].

Where the court is satisfied that the will of a testator dying on or after 1 January 1983 is so expressed that it fails to carry out his intentions, in consequence of a clerical error or a failure to understand his instructions, it may order that the words of the will be rectified so as to carry out his intentions; that will necessitate the admission of extrinsic evidence of the testator's intentions[13]. Where any part of the will of a testator dying on or after 1 January 1983 is meaningless or ambiguous, extrinsic evidence, including evidence of the testator's intention, may be admitted to assist in its interpretation[14].

1 *Towns v Wentworth* (1858) 11 Moo PCC 526 at 543. If the circumstances require it, even a forfeiture clause will be remodelled by the court: *Re Neeld, Carpenter v Inigo-Jones* [1962] Ch 643, [1962] 2 All ER 335, CA, explaining *Re Murray, Martins Bank Ltd v Dill* [1955] Ch 69 at 79, [1954] 3 All ER 129 at 134, CA (where this had been doubted).

2 As to gifts by implication arising under this rule see PARA 466.

3 *Spalding v Spalding* (1630) Cro Car 185 (gift over on death of eldest son in life of wife; 'without issue' supplied); *Doe d Leach v Micklem* (1805) 6 East 486; *Langston v Langston* (1834) 2 Cl & Fin 194, HL; *Abbott v Middleton, Ricketts v Carpenter* (1858) 7 HL Cas 68 ('in the event of my son dying'; 'without children' supplied); *Parker v Tootal* (1865) 11 HL Cas 143 ('first son of T severally and successively in tail male'; 'and other sons' introduced); *Re Hunt, Davies v Hetherington* (1890) 62 LT 753 (to sons at 21 and to daughters 'who shall marry under that age'; the words 'shall attain that age or' introduced); *Re Wroe, Frith v Wilson* (1896) 74 LT 302; *Comiskey v Bowring-Hanbury* [1905] AC 84, HL ('in default of any disposition' construed as meaning in default of any disposition in favour of members of particular class); *Munro v Henderson* [1907] 1 IR 440 (affd [1908] 1 IR 260, Ir CA). See also *Newburgh v Newburgh* (1825) Sugden's Law of Property 367, HL; *Re Broadwell, Mackenzie v Readman* (1912) 134 LT Jo 107; *Re Haygarth, Wickham v Haygarth* [1913] 2 Ch 9; *Re Birkin, Heald v Millership* [1949] 1 All ER 1045 (gift to 'all nephews and nieces of my late sister L'; 'children' inserted after 'nephews and nieces'). See also the cases cited in PARA 254 note 4.

4 *Dent v Pepys* (1822) 6 Madd 350 (name of donee changed); *Hart v Tulk* (1852) 2 De GM & G 300 ('fourth' schedule changed to 'fifth'); *Re Northen's Estate, Salt v Pym* (1884) 28 ChD 153 (ultimate limitation changed, 'estate' being read 'C estate'); *Re Dayrell, Hastie v Dayrell* [1904] 2 Ch 496 (in a direction against vesting of settled chattels in a son or any person made tenant for life, 'or' was read 'of').

5 *Luxford v Cheeke* (1683) 3 Lev 125; *Duke of Marlborough v Lord Godolphin* (1750) 2 Ves Sen 61 at 74 per Lord Hardwicke LC; *Marshall v Hopkins* (1812) 15 East 309; *Chambers v Brailsford* (1816) 19 Ves 652 at 653 per Lord Eldon LC (to make sense of a will otherwise meaningless, and to make it take some effect rather than be totally void); *Hudson v Bryant* (1845) 1 Coll 681 at 685; *Re Bacharach's Will Trusts, Minden v Bacharach* [1959] Ch 245, [1958] 3 All ER 618 (transposition of trusts declared of different parts of residuary estate).
6 *Haws v Haws* (1747) 3 Atk 524 at 525; *Smith v Pybus* (1804) 9 Ves 566; *Sherratt v Bentley* (1834) 2 My & K 149 at 157, 166; *Jones v Price* (1841) 11 Sim 557 at 569; *Pasmore v Huggins* (1855) 21 Beav 103; *Smith v Crabtree* (1877) 6 ChD 591; *Smidmore v Smidmore* (1905) 3 CLR 344. See also *Ellard v Phelan* [1914] 1 IR 76 ('hereinbefore').
7 *Sims v Doughty* (1800) 5 Ves 243 at 247; *Re MacAndrew's Will Trusts, Stephens v Barclays Bank Ltd* [1964] Ch 704, [1963] 2 All ER 919 (words 'or widow' in an otherwise plain scheme of disposition rejected as 'a senseless and incongruous insertion'). Where either or any of two or more alterations may be satisfactory, the court has to inquire which in the circumstances is most probably the intention: *Mason v Baker* (1856) 2 K & J 567; *Wills v Wills* (1875) LR 20 Eq 342.
8 *Re Neeld, Carpenter v Inigo-Jones* [1962] Ch 643 at 677–678, [1962] 2 All ER 335 at 353, CA, per Upjohn LJ. See also *Re Follett, Barclays Bank Ltd v Dovell* [1955] 2 All ER 22, [1955] 1 WLR 429, CA; *Re Whitrick, Sutcliffe v Sutcliffe* [1957] 2 All ER 467, [1957] 1 WLR 884, CA.
9 See *Re Reynette-James, Wightman v Renette-James* [1975] 3 All ER 1037, [1976] 1 WLR 161 (evidence that testatrix was clearly mistaken as to effect of disposition in will, following clerical error; court could not add missing words but omitted some of the remaining parts of the affected clause from probate on basis of lack of knowledge and approval). As to the rectification of clerical errors see PARA 187.
10 *Eden v Wilson* (1852) 4 HL Cas 257 at 284; *Peacock v Stockford* (1853) 3 De GM & G 73 at 77; *Abbott v Middleton* (1855) 21 Beav 143 at 149 per Romilly MR (when the change or insertion 'is required to give to the whole sentence one uniform and consistent meaning, which without it would be irrational or repugnant', it must be made) (on appeal (1858) 7 HL Cas 68 at 94 per Lord St Leonards); *Lady Langdale v Briggs, ex p Lady Bacon, ex p Martineau* (1873) 28 LT 467 at 469 (affd sub nom *Martineau v Briggs* (1875) 45 LJ Ch 674, HL). In *Hope v Potter* (1857) 3 K & J 206 at 209, Wood V-C classified the cases of supplying words into two categories: (1) where there is a necessary implication to avoid an intestacy; (2) where a contingent limitation over is curtailed by, or is to be reconciled with, a previous gift, such as cases where 'in default of issue' has been read 'in default of such issue' (see PARA 454).
11 *Abbott v Middleton, Ricketts v Carpenter* (1858) 7 HL Cas 68 at 81, 114; *Mellor v Daintree* (1886) 33 ChD 198 at 205. See also *Hope v Potter* (1857) 3 K & J 206; *Campbell v Bouskell* (1859) 27 Beav 325; *Re Mitchell, Mitchell v Mitchell* (1913) 108 LT 180; *Re Caldwell's Will Trusts, Jenyns v Sackville West* [1971] 1 All ER 780, [1971] 1 WLR 181.
12 See *Re Segelman* [1996] Ch 171 at 183–184, [1995] 3 All ER 676 at 684 per Chadwick J.
13 See the Administration of Justice Act 1982 s 20(1); *Re Segelman* [1996] Ch 171 at 180, [1995] 3 All ER 676 at 681; and PARA 187. See also *Gledhill v Arnold* [2015] EWHC 2939 (Ch), [2016] WTLR 653. See also 2 Bl Com (14th Edn) 379.
14 See the Administration of Justice Act 1982 s 21(1), (2); and PARAS 195, 219.

254. Examples of changing or supplying words. Where two clauses in a will run parallel to each other (as in the case of clauses settling the separate share of the donees), except for a difference which may have been caused by the omission of some words or other mistake in copying, the court may change the wording or supply the missing words[1]. Further, the scheme of the will as a whole may be sufficiently clear for its spirit to overcome the letter of a particular clause, leading to the necessity of making a suitable implication in the language[2]. Even in such a case, however, the court will refuse to make any alteration where the clauses, read as they stand, are clear and unambiguous and the suggestion of mistake rests only on conjecture[3].

Another example is where a power of appointment, or trust in default of appointment, is inadvertently omitted, but the court is able to determine what the omitted words were[4].

There are many cases where 'and' has been changed by the court into 'or'[5], and vice versa[6].

1 *Re Redfern, Redfern v Bryning* (1877) 6 ChD 133; *Re Northen's Estate, Salt v Pym* (1884) 28 ChD 153; *Phillips v Rail* (1906) 54 WR 517. As to the possibility of rectification see PARA 187.

2 *Re Doland's Will Trusts, Westminster Bank Ltd v Phillips* [1970] Ch 267, [1969] 3 All ER 713
   (applying the authorities relating to secondary interpretation of the language used); considered in
   Westland v Lillis [2003] EWHC 1669 (Ch), [2003] All ER (D) 128 (Jun) (the word 'fail' was
   ordered to be read as including a reference to revocation; this approach was supported by the
   presumption against intestacy). See also PARA 242.
3 *Crawford's Trustees v Fleck* 1910 SC 998, Ct of Sess.
4 *Re Cory, Cory v Morel* [1955] 2 All ER 630, [1955] 1 WLR 725; *Re Riley's Will Trusts, Riley v
   Riley* [1962] 1 All ER 513, [1962] 1 WLR 344. As to gifts by implication see PARA 466.
5 *Haws v Haws* (1747) 1 Ves Sen 13; *Jackson v Jackson* (1749) 1 Ves Sen 217; *Burleigh v Pearson*
   (1749) 1 Ves Sen 281; *Stubbs v Sargon* (1837) 2 Keen 255 at 273; *Stapleton v Stapleton* (1852)
   2 Sim NS 212; *Maynard v Wright* (1858) 26 Beav 285 (where the alternative was that the will was
   void for uncertainty). For instances where the court declined to make the change see *Malden v
   Maine* (1855) 2 Jur NS 206; *Grey v Pearson* (1857) 6 HL Cas 61; *Seccombe v Edwards* (1860) 28
   Beav 440; *Earl of Malmesbury v Countess of Malmesbury, Phillipson v Turner* (1862) 31 Beav
   407; *Coates v Hart* (1863) 32 Beav 349 (on appeal 3 De GJ & Sm 504 at 516); *Barker v Young*
   (1864) 33 Beav 353; *Re Sanders' Trusts* (1866) LR 1 Eq 675. See further PARA 443.
6 *Nichols v Tolley* (1700) 2 Vern 388; *Read v Snell* (1743) 2 Atk 642 at 645; *Eccard v Brooke*
   (1790) 2 Cox Eq Cas 213; *Denn d Wilkins v Kemeys* (1808) 8 East 366; *Horridge v Ferguson*
   (1822) Jac 583; *Green v Harvey* (1842) 1 Hare 428; *Parkin v Knight* (1846) 15 Sim 83; *Lachlan
   v Reynolds* (1852) 9 Hare 796 at 798 (to 'children living at that period or their heirs'); *Shand v
   Kidd* (1854) 19 Beav 310 (to a class, or the issue of those then dead); *Maude v Maude* (1856) 22
   Beav 290; *Greenway v Greenway* (1860) 2 De GF & J 128 at 129. For cases of the enumeration
   disjunctively of the objects of a power of appointment see *Brown v Higgs* (1799) 4 Ves 708
   (reheard (1800) 5 Ves 495; affd (1801) 8 Ves 561; (1813) 18 Ves 192, HL); *Longmore v Broom*
   (1802) 7 Ves 124; *Penny v Turner* (1846) 15 Sim 368; *Salusbury v Denton* (1857) 3 Jur NS 740;
   Re White's Trusts (1860) John 656. See also the cases cited in PARA 320 note 5. In *Re Hayden,
   Pask v Perry* [1931] 2 Ch 333, where there was a gift to a class of persons 'or their issue', the
   change of 'or' into 'and' enabled 'their issue' to be read as words of limitation, and, there being
   three members of the class, each took an estate tail in an undivided third part. As it is not possible
   to create entailed interests by wills or other instruments coming into operation on or after
   1 January 1997 (see the Trusts of Land and Appointment of Trustees Act 1996 s 2, Sch 1 para 5;
   and REAL PROPERTY AND REGISTRATION vol 87 (2012) PARA 114), this solution is no longer
   available: see PARA 387.
      For instances where the court refused to change 'or' into 'and' see *Whitcher v Penley* (1846)
   9 Beav 477; *Penley v Penley* (1850) 12 Beav 547; *Blundell v Chapman* (1864) 33 Beav 648 (all
   cases of substitutional gifts to children). See further PARA 320. See also *Hawksworth v
   Hawksworth* (1858) 27 Beav 1; *Re Woolley, Wormald v Woolley* [1903] 2 Ch 206. As to the
   change of 'or' into 'and' in cases of gifts over see PARA 442.

(iii) Presumptions

A.   PRESUMPTION AGAINST INTESTACY

255. Presumption in doubtful cases. A testator may well intend to die partially
intestate, for, when he makes a will, he is testate only so far as he has expressed
himself in his will[1]. Accordingly, there is no reason for the court in all cases to lean
too heavily against a construction which involves a partial intestacy[2]. Where,
however, the construction of the will is doubtful, the court acts on the
presumption that the testator did not intend to die either wholly or even partially
intestate, provided that on a fair and reasonable construction there is no ground
for a contrary conclusion[3]. Where the will shows an intention of the testator to
dispose of the whole of his property, but, as regards the interests created, two
constructions are possible, according to one of which the will effects a complete
disposition of the whole, but according to the other the will leaves a gap, the court
inclines to the former construction[4].

Although the avoidance of intestacy is to be regarded in construing doubtful
expressions, it is not enough to induce the court to give an unnatural meaning to

a word, or to construe plain words otherwise than according to their plain meaning[5].

1   *Re Edwards, Jones v Jones* [1906] 1 Ch 570 at 574, CA, per Romer LJ. See also *Jackson v Craig* (1851) 20 LJ Ch 204 (property wholly undisposed of); *Webber v Stanley* (1864) 16 CBNS 698 at 760. See also *Hodgson v Clare* [1999] All ER (D) 359, sub nom *Re Owen, Hodgson v Clare* [2002] WTLR 619 ('It may well be that if he had decided to provide for his wife predeceasing him, he would have wanted his residuary estate to go to the same persons. However he did not provide for that possibility': at 621 per Stanley Burnton QC, sitting as a deputy judge of the High Court).
2   *Re Wragg, Hollingsworth v Wragg* [1959] 2 All ER 717 at 723, [1959] 1 WLR 922 at 929, CA, per Lord Evershed MR.
3   *Doe d Wall v Langlands* (1811) 14 East 370 at 372–373; *Edgeworth v Edgeworth* (1869) LR 4 HL 35 at 40–41; *Re Redfern, Redfern v Bryning* (1877) 6 ChD 133 at 136; *Re Harrison, Turner v Hellard* (1885) 30 ChD 390 at 393, CA, per Lord Esher MR; *Kirby-Smith v Parnell* [1903] 1 Ch 483 at 489; *Re Messenger's Estate, Chaplin v Ruane* [1937] 1 All ER 355; *Re Turner, Carpenter v Staveley* [1949] 2 All ER 935; *Re Stevens, Pateman v James* [1952] Ch 323, [1952] 1 All ER 674. See also *Re Bassett's Estate, Perkins v Fladgate* (1872) LR 14 Eq 54 at 57. For examples of references to the leaning against intestacy in doubtful cases see *Royle v Hamilton* (1799) 4 Ves 437 at 439; *Vauchamp v Bell* (1822) 6 Madd 343 at 348; *Dobson v Banks* (1863) 32 Beav 259 at 260; *Re Salter, Farrant v Carter* (1881) 44 LT 603 at 604; *Re Henton, Henton v Henton* (1882) 30 WR 702; *Re Bright-Smith, Bright-Smith v Bright-Smith* (1886) 31 ChD 314 at 319; *Re Lady Monck's Will, Monck v Croker* [1900] 1 IR 56, Ir CA.
4   *Ibbetson v Beckwith* (1735) Cas *temp* Talb 157 at 161. See also *Pinney v Marriott* (1863) 32 Beav 643; and *Westland v Lillis* [2003] EWHC 1669 (Ch), [2003] All ER (D) 128 (Jun) and PARA 254 note 2.
5   *Re Benn, Benn v Benn* (1885) 29 ChD 839 at 847, CA; *Re Edwards, Jones v Jones* [1906] 1 Ch 570 at 574, CA; *Re Powell, Bodvel-Roberts v Poole* [1918] 1 Ch 407; *Hodgson v Clare* [1999] All ER (D) 359, sub nom *Re Owen, Hodgson v Clare* [2002] WTLR 619 (contingency of wife dying 'together with' testator could not extend to her predeceasing him by seven years; there was no real doubt or ambiguity as to the meaning of the will).

256. Force of presumption against intestacy. The force of the presumption against intestacy varies according to the context and the circumstances[1]. It applies especially to property which the testator has at the date of the will, but is not so strong as regards property which he has not yet acquired at that date[2]. Introductory statements setting out the testator's intention to dispose of all his worldly estate[3], or the appointment of executors[4], or the fact that the objects of the testator's bounty are his wife and all his children, his eldest son being treated alike with the rest[5], are strong indications in favour of a universal disposition of all the testator's property.

The presumption applies with particular force to the construction of a residuary gift; where the residue is given, every presumption is made that the testator did not die intestate[6]. Nevertheless, the presumption has been judicially referred to as 'an approach of last resort'[7].

Where, according to one of several possible constructions of the words, a gift would be void for illegality[8] and a partial intestacy would arise, then, unless it is possible to resolve the difficulty in reliance on direct evidence of intention[9], the presumption against intestacy is an additional reason for an alternative construction which would avoid the illegality[10].

1   See *Hall v Hall* [1892] 1 Ch 361 at 367, CA. Formerly, in the case of a devise of the whole legal fee simple of freehold land to trustees, there was an inference in favour of a complete disposition of the equitable interest (*Cuthbert v Robinson* (1882) 51 LJ Ch 238; cf PARA 376 note 3), but now the devise of a legal estate must be of the whole fee simple (see REAL PROPERTY AND REGISTRATION vol 87 (2012) PARA 63; SETTLEMENTS vol 91 (2012) PARA 510; TRUSTS AND POWERS vol 98 (2013) PARA 6).
2   *Re Methuen and Blore's Contract* (1881) 16 ChD 696 at 698–699.
3   *Ibbetson v Beckwith* (1735) Cas *temp* Talb 157; *Jackson v Hogan* (1776) 3 Bro Parl Cas 388; *Goodright d Baker v Stocker* (1792) 5 Term Rep 13; *Doe d Bates v Clayton* (1806) 8 East 141 at

147; *Doe d Wall v Langlands* (1811) 14 East 370 at 372; *Pocock v Bishop of Lincoln* (1821) 6 Moore CP 159; *Hughes v Pritchard* (1877) 6 ChD 24 at 27, CA.

4   *Re Bassett's Estate, Perkins v Fladgate* (1872) LR 14 Eq 54 at 57. See also *Re Messenger's Estate, Chaplin v Ruane* [1937] 1 All ER 355; *Re Turner, Carpenter v Staveley* [1949] 2 All ER 935; but see *Re Stevens, Pateman v James* [1952] Ch 323, [1952] 1 All ER 674 ('I give, devise and bequeath unto' three named persons; no reference to property given; testatrix held to have intended to give all her property although no executors were appointed).

5   *Hall v Hall* [1892] 1 Ch 361 at 367, CA. See also *Lachlan v Reynolds* (1852) 9 Hare 796 at 799; *O'Toole v Browne* (1854) 3 E & B 572 at 585.

6   *Philipps v Chamberlaine* (1798) 4 Ves 51 at 59; *Booth v Booth* (1799) 4 Ves 399 at 407; *Milsom v Awdry* (1800) 5 Ves 465 at 466; *Bolger v Mackell* (1800) 5 Ves 509 at 513; *Leake v Robinson* (1817) 2 Mer 363 at 386; *Goodman v Goodman* (1847) 1 De G & Sm 695 at 699; *Wiggins v Wiggins* (1852) 2 Sim NS 226 at 233; *Re Liverpool Dock Acts, Re Colshead's Will Trusts* (1852) 2 De G & J 690 at 692; *Bentley v Oldfield* (1854) 19 Beav 225 at 232; *Gosling v Gosling* (1859) John 265 at 274; *Fay v Fay* (1880) 5 LR Ir 274 at 282. See also *Harris v The Beneficiaries of the Estate of Margaret Alice Cooper* [2010] All ER (D) 64 (Jan).

7   *Re Le Cren Clarke, Funnell v Stewart* [1996] 1 All ER 715 at 722, [1996] 1 WLR 288 at 296 per Hazel Williamson QC, sitting as a Deputy Judge of the High Court.

8   As to the presumption against illegality see PARA 258.

9   As to the admissibility of extrinsic evidence of intention in cases of patent ambiguity see PARAS 195, 219–220.

10 *Montgomerie v Woodley* (1800) 5 Ves 522; *Taylor v Frobisher* (1852) 5 De G & Sm 191 at 199; *Re Edmondson's Estate* (1868) LR 5 Eq 389; *Re Bevan's Trusts* (1887) 34 ChD 716 at 718; *Re Coppard's Estate, Howlett v Hodson* (1887) 35 ChD 350 (as explained in *Re Wenmoth's Estate, Wenmoth v Wenmoth* (1887) 37 ChD 266 at 270).

257.   Limits of presumption against intestacy. The presumption against intestacy gives no assistance to the court where the contest is not between testacy and intestacy, but between two gifts in the same will[1]. Further, it is not enough to satisfy the court that intestacy was not intended; in order to oust the title of the persons claiming on intestacy, it must be shown distinctly that there are words in the will sufficient to constitute a gift of the property in question[2], expressly or by implication, to some particular donee[3], and the burden of proof is on the alleged donee[4]. However, once it is shown that the testator has manifested an intention of making some gift of the property, and thus excluding the persons entitled on intestacy to a certain extent, there is an end of the claim of those persons, except on the construction of the gift[5], and, if the gift prima facie extends to the whole property, the burden of proof is then shifted to those claiming on intestacy to show to what extent the gift is limited[6].

Before 1 January 1926 it was a rule of law, and not merely a rule of construction[7], that the heir-at-law was not to be disinherited, nor were the next of kin to be deprived of their statutory right of succession, except by express words or necessary implication in the will. With the abolition of the concept of descent to the heir-at-law on intestacy, the former rule of law has evolved into an aid to construction, aimed particularly at the question whether the will shows that the testator intended to die partially intestate, allowing the court to construe the language used in the will without the undue restriction of following a legal rule[8].

1   *Re Price, Price v Newton* [1905] 2 Ch 55 at 58 per Farwell J.

2   *Enohin v Wylie* (1862) 10 HL Cas 1 at 18, 21.

3   *Hall v Warren* (1861) 9 HL Cas 420 at 433, 435. See also *Drake v Drake* (1860) 8 HL Cas 172 at 180; *Re Hobson, Barwick v Holt* [1912] 1 Ch 626 at 634; *Re Wynn, Landolt v Wynn* [1983] 3 All ER 310, sub nom *Re Wynn* [1984] 1 WLR 237. As to gifts by implication see PARA 466 et seq. See also *Re Geering, Gulliver v Geering* [1964] Ch 136 at 146–147, [1962] 3 All ER 1043 at 1048–1049 (presumption applied so that surplus income from annuity was ordered to be accumulated for 21 years from death of testator, provided annuitant lived that long).

4   *Wilce v Wilce* (1831) 7 Bing 664 at 672; *Hall v Warren* (1861) 9 HL Cas 420 at 435.

5   *Awse v Melhuish* (1780) 1 Bro CC 519 at 522 (devise prior to the Wills Act 1837 s 28 (see PARA 374)).

6   *Midland Counties Rly Co v Oswin* (1844) 1 Coll 74 at 78 per Knight Bruce V-C.
7   *Doe d Hick v Dring* (1814) 2 M & S 448 at 454 per Lord Ellenborough CJ; *Hall v Warren* (1861)
    9 HL Cas 420 at 436. Regarded as a rule of construction, this rule would be in favour of intestacy,
    whereas the true presumption is against intestacy: see PARA 255.
8   See PARA 255.

B.   PRESUMPTIONS OF LEGALITY AND OF KNOWLEDGE OF THE TESTATOR

258.   No departure from plain words to escape illegality. The construction of the
will is in the first place considered quite apart from the question of the legality of
the provisions of the will[1]. If the words of the will are plain, they may not be
struck out[2], or taken in a sense different from that which they plainly bear[3], for the
purpose of escaping from the consequences of invalidity under some rule of law,
or even because it appears that the testator may have misunderstood the legal
effect of the various species of gifts, and may have used language the legal
interpretation of which may not carry out the intentions he had in his mind[4].
Where the language used creates a combination of legal and illegal aspects of, or
purposes for, a single gift and a general purpose can be consequently identified,
which is illegal, the whole gift may be tainted by the illegality[5].

1   *Pearks v Moseley* (1880) 5 App Cas 714 at 719, HL, per Lord Selbourne. See also *Taylor v
    Frobisher* (1852) 5 De G & Sm 191 at 197; and PARA 227 text and note 1.
2   *Heasman v Pearse* (1871) 7 Ch App 275 at 283; *Re Coyte, Coyte v Coyte* (1887) 56 LT 510 at
    513.
3   *A-G v Williams* (1794) 2 Cox Eq Cas 387 at 388; *Thellusson v Woodford* (1799) 4 Ves 227 at 329;
    Mainwaring v Beevor (1849) 8 Hare 44 at 48; *Speakman v Speakman* (1850) 8 Hare 180 at 186;
    Tatham v Drummond (1864) 4 De GJ & Sm 484 at 486; *Re Hume, Public Trustee v Mabey* [1912]
    1 Ch 693.
4   *Higgins v Dawson* [1902] AC 1 at 11, HL, per Lord Davey. See also *Egerton v Earl Brownlow*
    (1853) 4 HL Cas 1 at 159; *Nunn v Hancock* (1868) 16 WR 818 at 819. As to the circumstances
    in which there is for probate purposes a presumption in favour of knowledge and approval by the
    testator of the contents of his will see PARA 902.
5   *McGovern v A-G* [1982] Ch 321, [1981] 3 All ER 493.

259.   Presumption where wording of will may give rise to illegality. Where the
wording of the will is ambiguous, and appears according to one construction to
offend against some rule of law and to be partially invalid, but is fairly capable of
another construction which avoids the objection, the latter is presumed to be the
testator's intention[1]. The court has an inclination to believe, if reasonably
possible, that the testator did not intend to transgress the law[2]. This is sometimes
assisted by a presumption in favour of construing gifts as charitable, where it is
possible to do so[3], but the presumption will not help if the wording, on its true
construction, is not capable of creating a valid charitable gift[4]. In the case of the
will of a testator dying on or after 1 January 1983 which is ambiguous, extrinsic
evidence, including evidence of intention, may be admitted to assist in its
interpretation[5].

1   *Martelli v Holloway* (1872) LR 5 HL 532 at 548; *Pearks v Moseley* (1880) 5 App Cas 714 at 719;
    Von Brockdorff v Malcolm (1885) 30 ChD 172 at 179; *Re Pounder, Williams v Pounder* (1886)
    56 LJ Ch 113 at 114; *Re Sanford, Sanford v Sanford* [1901] 1 Ch 939 at 943; *Re Mortimer, Gray
    v Gray* [1905] 2 Ch 502 at 506, CA; *Re Earl of Stamford and Warrington, Payne v Grey* [1912]
    1 Ch 343 at 365, CA. It is open to question whether in these circumstances, in relation to the will
    of a testator who died on or after 1 January 1983, the court will receive evidence of his actual
    intention to the contrary: see PARAS 195, 218–219. See *Re Hetherington, Gibbs v McDonnell*
    [1990] Ch 1, [1989] 2 All ER 129 (gift for saying masses for relatives and for testator after her
    death ordered to be construed as gift for public masses only, so as to avoid invalidating charitable
    gift). As to the limits of this principle of construction see *Re Le Cren Clarke, Funnell v Stewart*
    [1996] 1 All ER 715 at 723, [1996] 1 WLR 288 at 297 (if there is one identifiable purpose that
    is plainly not charitable, it cannot be ignored; that would stretch language and the principles of
    construction too far in pursuit of benignancy).

2 *Leach v Leach* (1843) 2 Y & C Ch Cas 495 at 499 per Knight Bruce V-C.
3 See *Re Harding, Gibbs v Harding* [2007] EWHC 3 (Ch) at [13]–[16], [2008] Ch 235 at [13]–[16], [2007] 1 All ER 747 at [13]–[16]; *Re Smith, Public Trustee v Smith* [1932] 1 Ch 153 at 158, [1931] All ER Rep 617 at 619. See also the cases on charitable gifts in note 1.
4 See *McGovern v A-G* [1982] Ch 321, [1981] 3 All ER 493.
5 See the Administration of Justice Act 1982 s 21(1)(b), (1)(c), (2); and PARAS 195, 219–220.

C.   PRESUMPTION FAVOURING RELATIVES OR PERSONS HAVING A CLAIM ON THE TESTATOR

260. No presumptions that children to be provided for. There is no presumption, in the case of a will[1], that the testator's children are intended to be provided for or to have equal benefits[2]. In the construction of a will the only guide is the testator's language, and there is no supposition that any person is intended to take except those who are described as takers[3].

If, however, the language in a will expressly providing for the testator's family is ambiguous[4], then, in the absence of direct evidence of his intention[5], the court, so far as it can, prefers that construction which will most benefit the testator's family generally, on the ground that this must more nearly correspond with his intention[6]. In such cases, the court construes the will so as to include as many children as possible[7], and to vest their interests on attaining majority, and so as not to make the interests of children who attain majority dependent on surviving their parents[8].

1 As to presumptions in the case of marriage articles see SETTLEMENTS vol 91 (2012) PARAS 532–536.
2 *Re Crosse's Will* (1863) 9 Jur NS 429 at 430. See also *Abbott v Middleton, Ricketts v Carpenter* (1858) 7 HL Cas 68 at 93; *Re Jodrell, Jodrell v Seale* (1890) 44 ChD 590 at 605, CA (affd sub nom *Seale-Hayne v Jodrell* [1891] AC 304, HL). However, as to the court's power to order provision to be made for children from the estate of the deceased see PARA 567 et seq.
3 *Abbott v Middleton, Ricketts v Carpenter* (1858) 7 HL Cas 68 at 93 per Lord Cranworth. See also *Tucker v Harris* (1832) 5 Sim 538 at 543. As to the modern approach to the construction of wills see *Marley v Rawlings* [2014] UKSC 2, [2015] AC 129, [2014] 1 All ER 807; and PARA 188.
4 *Bright v Rowe* (1834) 3 My & K 316 at 322.
5 As to the circumstances in which extrinsic evidence is admissible see PARAS 195, 218–219.
6 *Farrant v Nichols* (1846) 9 Beav 327 at 330; *Bythesea v Bythesea* (1854) 23 LJ Ch 1004 at 1006; *Re Hamlet, Stephen v Cunningham* (1888) 39 ChD 426 at 433–434, CA.
7 *Bouverie v Bouverie* (1847) 2 Ph 349 at 351; *Lee v Lee* (1860) 1 Drew & Sm 85 at 87; *White v Hill* (1867) LR 4 Eq 265 at 271; *Williams v Haythorne, Williams v Williams* (1871) 6 Ch App 782 at 785.
8 This presumption is specially applicable to gifts of portions in a settlement (*Emperor v Rolfe* (1748–9) 1 Ves Sen 208; *Howgrave v Cartier* (1814) 3 Ves & B 79 at 91; and see SETTLEMENTS vol 91 (2012) PARA 639), but it applies also to wills (*Hallifax v Wilson* (1809) 16 Ves 168 at 172; *Jackson v Dover* (1864) 2 Hem & M 209 at 215; *Re Knowles, Nottage v Buxton* (1882) 21 ChD 806; *Re Hamlet, Stephen v Cunningham* (1888) 39 ChD 426 at 433, CA; *Re Roberts, Percival v Roberts* [1903] 2 Ch 200 at 204 per Joyce J ('in case of ambiguity or doubt that construction is to be favoured which will allow of a child who takes a vested interest making such provision as is usual for his family'); *Duffield v M'Master* [1906] 1 IR 333, Ir CA). The different character of a will is a circumstance to be weighed in applying the rule: *Farrer v Barker* (1852) 9 Hare 737 at 744; *Tucker v Harris* (1832) 5 Sim 538 at 543. It is not clear whether the rule applies to grandchildren, or other persons to whom the testator is not in loco parentis: see *Re Hamlet, Stephen v Cunningham* (1888) 38 ChD 183 at 190; on appeal 39 ChD 426 at 433–434, CA (where Cotton LJ, differing from the view expressed in the court below, thought that the rule would apply to such persons). See also *Farrer v Barker* (1852) 9 Hare 737 at 744; *Re Hannam, Haddelsey v Hannam* [1897] 2 Ch 39, 66 LJ Ch 471.

261.   Presumptions in favour of other persons. Where the words of the will are ambiguous, then, in the absence of direct evidence of the testator's intention[1], the court may sometimes be assisted by the presumptions that, in the absence of special circumstances, relatives of equal degree are of equal importance to a testator as recipients of his bounty[2], and that, as a rule, a testator does not pass over a near relative for the purpose of benefiting more remote relatives, or over any relative or other person having a claim on him[3], or with whom he was intimate[4], for the purpose of benefiting relatives having no claim or strangers. The latter presumption, however, gives no assistance to the court in a contest between persons related in equal degree to the testator[5], nor are any of these presumptions applicable unless their application accords with the actual words of the will[6].

1   As to the circumstances in which extrinsic evidence is admissible see PARAS 195, 218–219.
2   *Hewet v Ireland* (1718) 1 P Wms 426; *Jenkins v Hughes* (1860) 8 HL Cas 571 at 590; *Swift v Swift* (1863) 32 LJ Ch 479 at 480; *Heasman v Pearse* (1871) 7 Ch App 275 at 284; *Selby v Whittaker* (1877) 6 ChD 239 at 249, CA, per James LJ; *Re Prosser, Prosser v Griffith* [1929] WN 85. The presumption seems to give little assistance where the question is one of whether siblings who were already dead by the date of the will were within the construction of 'my brothers and sisters': see *Thomas v Kent* [2006] EWCA Civ 1485, [2006] All ER (D) 57 (May) (court relied upon a construction in the light of facts known to testator at time of making will).
3   See *Re Gregory's Settlement and Will* (1865) 34 Beav 600 at 602 (where the testator's godson was preferred to his brother, the description applying partly to both). However, it is doubtful whether this decision would now be followed.
4   *Careless v Careless* (1816) 1 Mer 384 at 389. Evidence of the testator's degrees of intimacy with the various claimants is admitted for the purpose of applying this presumption: see PARA 214.
5   *Re Price, Price v Newton* [1905] 2 Ch 55 at 58. See also *Thomas v Kent* [2006] EWCA Civ 1485, [2006] All ER (D) 57 (May).
6   *Beaudry v Barbeau* [1900] AC 569 at 575, PC.

(iv) Uncertainty

262.   Circumstances in which a gift is held void for uncertainty. The absurd or irrational nature of a disposition clearly expressed, or the difficulties in interpreting a disposition ambiguously expressed, are not enough to render the disposition void for uncertainty; to be void for this reason, it must be utterly impossible to put a meaning on it[1]. A gift expressed in language too vague to be enforced cannot be rescued by giving the executor a power of choice[2].

The court has always been reluctant to hold a gift void for uncertainty[3], and has always adopted the benevolent rule that, if there is ever so little reason in favour of one construction of an ambiguous gift more than another, the adoption of the construction favoured is at least nearer the testator's intention than that the whole disposition should be void and the persons entitled on an intestacy let in[4]. In such cases extrinsic evidence has always been admitted to elucidate the testator's meaning[5], and, in so far as any part of the will of a testator who died on or after 1 January 1983 is meaningless, such extrinsic evidence may include evidence of the testator's intention[6]. The court may be willing to assist in overcoming uncertainty by the use of construction, combined with its powers to direct inquiry[7].

1   *Re Roberts, Repington v Roberts-Gawen* (1881) 19 ChD 520 at 529, CA. See also *Mason v Robinson* (1825) 2 Sim & St 295 at 298; *Doe d Winter v Perratt* (1843) 6 Man & G 314 at 361–362, HL; *Anthony v Donges* [1998] 2 FLR 775, [1998] Fam Law 666 (gift to testator's wife of 'such minimal part of my estate as she may be entitled to under English law for maintenance purposes'). See also *Re Thurlow, Riddick v Kennard* [1972] Ch 379, [1972] 1 All ER 10 (impossible to say that, either in ordinary or in legal language, the word 'descendants' could include collateral relatives). In *Nathan v Leonard* [2002] EWHC 1701 (Ch), [2003] 4 All ER 198, [2003] 1 WLR 827 it was obvious that words were missing but impossible to find out what they were.
2   *Re Beatty's Will Trusts, Hinves v Brooke* [1990] 3 All ER 844 at 848, [1990] 1 WLR 1503 at 1507–1508 per Hoffmann J.
3   See *Pinnel v Anison* [2005] EWHC 1421 (Ch), sub nom *Pinnell v Annison* [2005] All ER (D) 458 (May) (ambiguity as to which of two potential donees was intended was resolved by recourse to extrinsic evidence).

4 *Doe d Winter v Perratt* (1843) 6 Man & G 314 at 359, HL, per Lord Brougham. See also *Oddie v Woodford* (1821) 3 My & Cr 584 (followed in *Doe d Angell v Angell* (1846) 9 QB 328 at 354); *Bristow v Bristow* (1842) 5 Beav 289 at 292; *Stephens v Powys* (1857) 1 De G & J 24. As to the presumption against intestacy see PARAS 255–257.

5 As to the avoidance of uncertainty see PARA 263. As to the modern approach to the construction of wills see *Marley v Rawlings* [2014] UKSC 2, [2015] AC 129, [2014] 1 All ER 807; and PARA 188.

6 See the Administration of Justice Act 1982 s 21(1)(a), (2); and PARA 195.

7 *Re Malpass, Lloyds Bank plc v Malpass* [1985] Ch 42, [1984] 2 All ER 313 (will provided ineffective mechanism to ascertain value of property, the subject of a testamentary option; as the machinery was a subsidiary part of the option and provided to protect the other beneficiaries, the court construed the option and directed its own inquiry to the district valuer).

263. Admission of extrinsic evidence to avoid uncertainty. The court will attempt to ascertain the testator's intention as expressed in the will by reference to all admissible matters[1].

Where it is impossible to ascertain the testator's intention in this way, uncertainty may be avoided by the proper admission of extrinsic evidence[2], which in certain circumstances may include evidence of the testator's intention[3], but, if such evidence is insufficient to resolve the ambiguity[4], the gift fails for uncertainty[5].

Uncertainty may also be avoided by reference to the context, or by application of the maxim id certum est quod certum reddi potest[6]. Thus indefinite words added to a gift do not render it uncertain if the gift is substantially ascertained from the nature of the case[7], and no objection can arise where, although the amount of the gift is indefinite, it is stated to be for a particular purpose and the court can by inquiry ascertain what is the sum sufficient or necessary to answer that purpose[8]. Further, a testator may validly appoint persons to select the objects of his bounty, provided that the objects are individual persons or corporations[9], but no delegation of the testamentary power is permitted where the gift is for purposes to be selected[10], unless the purposes from which the selection is to be made are confined to exclusively charitable purposes[11]. If the extent of the testator's bounty is to be measured by a formula, he may leave it to his executors to determine the precise amount, even though without that determination there would be no certainty[12].

1 See *Marley v Rawlings* [2014] UKSC 2, [2015] AC 129, [2014] 1 All ER 807; and PARA 188.

2 As to the admission of extrinsic evidence see PARA 193 et seq. As to the circumstances in which a gift is held void for uncertainty see PARA 262.

3 As to the circumstances in which extrinsic evidence of intention is admissible see PARAS 195, 218–219.

4 *Richardson v Watson* (1833) 4 B & Ad 787; *Blundell v Gladstone* (1844) 14 Sim 83; *Asten v Asten* [1894] 3 Ch 260.

5 *Thomas d Evans v Thomas* (1796) 6 Term Rep 671; *Drake v Drake* (1860) 8 HL Cas 172; *Re Stephenson, Donaldson v Bambler* [1897] 1 Ch 75.

6 Ie that which is capable of being made certain ought to be treated as certain: see eg *Adams v Jones* (1852) 9 Hare 485 at 486. A blank in a description does not make a gift uncertain if certainty is given by the context and circumstances admissible in evidence: *Price v Page* (1799) 4 Ves 680; *Phillips v Barker* (1853) 1 Sm & G 583; *Re Harrison, Turner v Hellard* (1885) 30 ChD 390, CA; *Re Wyatt, Furniss v Phear* (1888) 36 WR 521. See also *Re Tuck's Settlement Trusts, Public Trustee v Tuck* [1978] Ch 49 at 66, [1978] 1 All ER 1047 at 1056, CA, per Eveleigh LJ (meaning of 'Jewish Faith' determined by clear reference to Chief Rabbi's definition).

7 *Oddie v Brown* (1859) 4 De G & J 179 at 186, 194 ('or thereabouts'), explaining *Curtis v Lukin* (1842) 5 Beav 147 (until leases 'nearly' expired). See also *Re Hunter's Settlement Trust, Elliott v Hunter* (1939) 83 Sol Jo 339.

8 *Dundee Magistrates v Morris* (1858) 3 Macq 134, HL. See also *Broad v Bevan* (1823) 1 Russ 511n (considered in *Abraham v Alman* (1826) 1 Russ 509 at 516); *Jackson v Hamilton* (1846) 3 Jo & Lat 702 at 709 (sufficient to remunerate executors for their trouble); *Edwardes v Jones (No 2)* (1866) 35 Beav 474; *Re Mills, Midland Bank Executor and Trustees Co Ltd v United Birmingham*

Hospitals Board of Governors [1953] 1 All ER 835, [1953] 1 WLR 554 ('such sum as shall be
necessary to endow a bed'); *Re Golay, Morris v Bridgewater* [1965] 2 All ER 660, [1965] 1 WLR
969 (bequest of 'reasonable income' valid). As to the court's further powers of inquiry see *Re
Malpass, Lloyds Bank plc v Malpass* [1985] Ch 42, [1984] 2 All ER 313; and PARA 262 note 7.

9 *Re Smith, Johnson v Bright-Smith* [1914] 1 Ch 937 at 948 per Joyce J. The conferment of a general
   or intermediate power is not invalid as a delegation of the testamentary power: *Re
   Beatty's Will Trusts, Hinves v Brooke* [1990] 3 All ER 844, [1990] 1 WLR 1503. See also PARA 3.

10 See eg *Chichester Diocesan Fund and Board of Finance Inc v Simpson* [1944] AC 341, [1944]
   2 All ER 60, HL. See also PARA 11. As to the exclusiveness of gifts for charitable purposes see
   CHARITIES vol 8 (2015) PARA 93; and as to the validation by statute of certain instruments taking
   effect before 16 December 1952 and providing for property to be held for objects partly but not
   exclusively charitable see CHARITIES vol 8 (2015) PARAS 98–103. As to the extent to which equity
   will recognise a trust which is not for the benefit of ascertained or ascertainable beneficiaries
   generally see *Re Endacott, Corpe v Endacott* [1960] Ch 232, [1959] 3 All ER 562, CA; *Re
   Denley's Trust Deed, Holman v HH Martyn & Co Ltd* [1969] 1 Ch 373, [1968] 3 All ER 65; and
   TRUSTS AND POWERS vol 98 (2013) PARA 8.

11 See *Re Le Cren Clarke, Funnell v Stewart* [1996] 1 All ER 715 at 723, [1996] 1 WLR 288 at 297;
   and the cases relating to charitable gifts in PARA 259 note 1. As to the meaning of 'charitable
   purposes' see CHARITIES vol 8 (2015) PARA 2 et seq. As to the meaning of delegation of power
   to determine objects CHARITIES vol 8 (2015) PARA 124 et seq.

12 *Re Conn, Conn v Burns* [1898] 1 IR 337 (where portions were to be determined by the wife and
   executors according to the value of the services the daughters might have rendered the family, and,
   in the case of marriage portions, according to the match made).

264. Construction of gifts stated in the alternative. Where the amount of a gift[1]
is stated in the alternative, the gift may be construed, according to the
construction most favourable to the donee[2], as a gift of the larger amount[3], and a
direction to apply a sum not exceeding a stated amount for a particular purpose
may be similarly construed as a gift of the stated amount, after any discretion
applying to the gift is spent[4].

1 As to alternative donees see PARA 320 et seq.
2 See PARA 368.
3 *Seale v Seale* (1715) 1 P Wms 290.
4 *Thompson v Thompson* (1844) 1 Coll 381 at 395, 397 (following *Cope v Wilmot* (1772) 1 Coll
   396n); *Gough v Bult* (1848) 16 Sim 45.

265. Construction of gift to one of a set of persons. Where the donee is defined
as one of a set of persons satisfying some description (as in the case of a gift to one
of the sons of a named person), and there are in existence several persons in the
set, the gift is void for uncertainty unless there is sufficient evidence[1] to show what
was the testator's intention[2]. Where, however, at the date of the will there are no
persons in existence who are members of the set or who satisfy the description, the
gift may admit of being construed to mean the person who first becomes a
member of the set or satisfies the description[3].

1 As to the circumstances in which extrinsic evidence of intention is admissible see PARAS 195,
   218–219.
2 *Dowset v Sweet* (1753) Amb 175, explained in *Del Mare v Robello* (1792) 1 Ves 412 at 415. See
   also *Hampshire v Peirce* (1751) 2 Ves Sen 216. As to class gifts generally see PARA 302 et seq.
3 *Bate v Amherst* (1663) T Raym 82; *Blackburn v Stables* (1814) 2 Ves & B 367; *Powell v Davies*
   (1839) 1 Beav 532; *Ashburner v Wilson* (1850) 17 Sim 204. As to this rule in construing
   descriptions see PARA 300.

266. Examples of gifts void for uncertainty. Gifts void for uncertainty include:
   (1)   gifts which are wanting in particularity of expression, as to the subject[1]
          or object[2] of the gift, where no person is nominated by the testator or
          other means provided for giving particularity, or such means fail[3], and
          no rule of construction sufficiently assists the court[4];
   (2)   gifts which depend on an infinite number of persons or things[5];

(3)   gifts which may have two or more alternative meanings, where there is
        nothing in the context or the admissible evidence[6], or any rule of
        construction[7], to enable the court to resolve the ambiguity[8];

(4)   gifts which are to be applied in perpetuity for purposes which cannot be
        construed as necessarily charitable[9], and include, without the possibility
        of severance, purposes[10] for which a perpetual gift is not allowed[11];

(5)   gifts in which the testator has purported to give his executors a power
        of choice among objects expressed in language too uncertain to be
        capable of enforcement[12].

1   *Peck v Halsey* (1726) 2 P Wms 387 ('some of my best linen'); *Jubber v Jubber* (1839) 9 Sim 503
    ('a handsome gratuity'). See also *Re Campsill, Reading v Hinde* (1910) 128 LT Jo 548 (where the
    testamentary document consisted of a list of names with sums of money); *Jones d Henry v Hancock*
    (1816) 4 Dow 145, HL; *White v White* (1908) 28 NZLR 129 ('a small portion of what is left');
    Anthony v Donges [1998] 2 FLR 775, [1998] Fam Law 666 (gift to testator's wife of 'such minimal
    part of my estate as she may entitled to under English law for maintenance purposes'); cf *Re Golay,
    Morris v Bridgewater* [1965] 2 All ER 660, 662, [1965] 1 WLR 969 (the words 'reasonable
    income' directed an objective determinant of amount, which the court could, if necessary, apply;
    gift not defeated by uncertainty). The word 'all', used as a noun, is regarded as not uncertain: *Re
    Shepherd, Mitchell v Loram* (1914) 58 Sol Jo 304 (not following *Bowman v Milbanke* (1664) 1
    Lev 130).
2   For cases of uncertainty in relation to donees see PARA 45.
3   *Boyce v Boyce* (1849) 16 Sim 476 (devise to be ascertained by a person who was dead). See also
    Jerningham v Herbert (1828) 4 Russ 388 (devise to be ascertained by future act of testatrix made
    impossible by her mental disorder).
4   In *Re Bassett's Estate, Perkins v Fladgate* (1872) LR 14 Eq 54 at 57 (followed in *Re Byrne, Byrne
    v Byrne* (1898) 24 VLR 832), the presumption against intestacy supplied the omission of any
    description of subject matter. See also PARA 256 note 4. In *Mohun v Mohun* (1818) 1 Swan 201,
    a similar omission made the gift void.
        There are, however, circumstances where the lack of particularity can be overcome by other
    evidence provided by the will itself. The will may, even without particularity, still be clear enough
    to dispose of property: see *Re Messenger's Estate, Chaplin v Ruane* [1937] 1 All ER 355, 81 Sol
    Jo 138 (home-made will appointed EAC (the testator's daughter) as executor; after providing for
    payment of debts and expenses, it followed 'I give and bequeath to EAC' and was then signed; held
    daughter entitled to entire estate). This case was applied in *Re Turner, Carpenter v Stavely* [1949]
    2 All ER 935, 94 Sol Jo 114; and considered in *Re Stevens, Pateman v James* [1952] Ch 323,
    [1952] 1 All ER 674 (will was able to pass the estate, despite absence of particularity of subject
    matter and failure to appoint an executor). As to the extent to which factors other than the
    wording of the will are admissible as an aid to ascertaining the testator's intention see *Marley v
    Rawlings* [2014] UKSC 2 at [19], [2015] AC 129, [2014] 1 All ER 807 per Lord Neuberger; and
    PARA 188.
5   *Re Moore, Prior v Moore* [1901] 1 Ch 936 ('all the persons living at my death'). A gift depending
    for duration on the death of the last survivor of all the lineal descendants of Queen Victoria who
    should be living at the testator's death was not void for uncertainty, at least in the case of a testator
    dying in 1926: *Re Villar, Public Trustee v Villar* [1929] 1 Ch 243, CA; *Re Leverhulme, Cooper v
    Leverhulme (No 2)* [1943] 2 All ER 274; and see PERPETUITIES AND ACCUMULATIONS vol 80
    (2013) PARA 22.
6   As to the admissibility of evidence in such cases, whether for identification or otherwise see
    PARA 193 et seq; and as to the admissibility of extrinsic evidence of intention in cases of ambiguity
    see PARAS 219–220.
7   See PARA 220 text and notes 7–9.
8   Eg where the subject matter is one of a number of things and the testator does not give the choice
    to the donee (*Asten v Asten* [1894] 3 Ch 260, commenting on *Richardson v Watson* (1833) 4 B
    & Ad 787); but such a gift may be valid where the property from which the gift is to be made is
    a homogeneous mass, such as a bank account or a holding of shares (*Hunter v Moss* [1993] 1 WLR
    934 (affd [1994] 3 All ER 215, [1994] 1 WLR 452, CA), referring to *Re Cheadle, Bishop v Holt*
    [1900] 2 Ch 620, CA, and *Re Clifford, Mallam v McFie* [1912] 1 Ch 29). For examples see
    PARA 127 note 4. Where a primary gift payable out of the income of a fund fails, and the extent
    of the gift is not sufficiently defined, a gift of the balance of the income fails for uncertainty: *Re
    Porter, Porter v Porter* [1925] Ch 746.
9   As to the meaning of 'charitable purposes' see CHARITIES vol 8 (2015) PARA 2.

10 Eg 'public' or 'benevolent' purposes: see CHARITIES vol 8 (2015) PARA 46 et seq.
11 See eg *Chichester Diocesan Fund and Board of Finance Inc v Simpson* [1944] AC 341, [1944] 2 All ER 60, HL. See also CHARITIES vol 8 (2015) PARAS 4, 46 et seq; PERPETUITIES AND ACCUMULATIONS vol 80 (2013) PARA 5; TRUSTS AND POWERS vol 98 (2013) PARA 8. As to the validation by statute of certain instruments taking effect before 16 December 1952 and providing for property to be held for objects partly but not exclusively charitable see CHARITIES vol 8 (2015) PARAS 98–103.
12 See *Re Beatty's Will Trusts, Hinves v Brooke* [1990] 3 All ER 844 at 848, [1990] 1 WLR 1503 at 1507–1508 per Hoffmann J, and the cases therein mentioned.

(v) Misdescription of Property or Persons

267. Construction of will where description is accurate. If all the terms of description fit some particular property[1], that property and nothing more passes; the description will not be enlarged so as to include anything which some of those terms do not accurately fit[2], nor will it be restricted so as not to include some part of the property accurately described[3]. Where a description is certain, additional words do not affect it, but, where the first description is uncertain, additional words may remove the uncertainty[4]. The accurate use in a will of the name of an individual or society creates a strong presumption that the person so described is the donee intended by the testator, although it may not exclude further inquiry as to the person intended[5].

1 *Re Seal, Seal v Taylor* [1894] 1 Ch 316, CA.
2 *Webber v Stanley* (1864) 16 CBNS 698 (dissenting from *Stanley v Stanley* (1862) 2 John & H 491); *Hardwick v Hardwick* (1873) LR 16 Eq 168 at 175; *Whitfield v Langdale* (1875) 1 ChD 61 at 74; *Re Seal, Seal v Taylor* [1894] 1 Ch 316 at 323, CA. See also *Doe d Brown v Brown* (1809) 11 East 441; *Doe d Browne v Greening* (1814) 3 M & S 171; *Doe d Tyrrell v Lyford* (1816) 4 M & S 550; *Okeden v Clifden* (1826) 2 Russ 309; *Miller v Travers* (1832) 8 Bing 244; *Doe d Hubbard v Hubbard* (1850) 15 QB 227 at 245; *Slingsby v Grainger* (1859) 7 HL Cas 273; *Homer v Homer* (1878) 8 ChD 758, CA; *Corballis v Corballis* (1882) 9 LR Ir 309.
3 *Down v Down* (1817) 1 Moore CP 80; *Pullin v Pullin* (1825) 10 Moore CP 464; *Doe d Templeman v Martin* (1833) 4 B & Ad 771.
4 See *Doe d Harris v Greathed* (1806) 8 East 91 at 103–104.
5 *National Society for the Prevention of Cruelty to Children v Scottish National Society for the Prevention of Cruelty to Children* [1915] AC 207, HL. Cf *Re Meyers, London Life Association v St George's Hospital* [1951] Ch 534, [1951] 1 All ER 538; *Re Satterthwaite's Will Trusts, Midland Bank Executor and Trustee Co Ltd v Royal Veterinary College* [1966] 1 All ER 919, [1966] 1 WLR 277, CA. See also *Pinnel v Anison* [2005] EWHC 1421 (Ch), sub nom *Pinnell v Annison* [2005] All ER (D) 458 (May); and PARA 268 text and note 2. As to the evidence admissible where the gift is plain and unambiguous see PARA 210.

268. Construction of will where description is inaccurate. If, when examined, the words of description do not fit any subject with accuracy, and if there must be some modification of them[1] in order to place a sensible construction on the will, then the whole must be looked at fairly in order to see what are the leading words of description and what is the subordinate matter, and generally how the subject, whether the property or the donee, intended by the testator can be identified[2]. For this purpose, extrinsic evidence has always been received[3], and this may include evidence of the testator's intention in certain circumstances[4]. In such cases the words are presumed to be a misdescription of a subject existing and with regard to which the will may validly operate[5]. Where, however, the context shows that the testator was not merely misdescribing an actually existing subject, but was under an erroneous impression that the subject actually did exist as described, or that he could dispose of it, the gift may fail[6].

1 As to modifying the words of the will see PARAS 186, 253–254.
2 See eg *Doe d Humphreys v Roberts* (1822) 5 B & Ad 407; *Re Ofner, Samuel v Ofner* [1909] 1 Ch 60, CA; *Re Harte* [2015] EWHC 2351 (Ch), [2015] WTLR 1735. In *Pinnel v Anison* [2005]

EWHC 1421 (Ch), sub nom *Pinnell v Annison* [2005] All ER (D) 458 (May), the approach was to make references to 'my sister' and gifts over to surviving children of 'either my brother or sister' predominant, indicating a gift within the family, rather than to a non-family person who was accurately named.

3   *Hardwick v Hardwick* (1873) LR 16 Eq 168; *Re Bright-Smith, Bright-Smith v Bright-Smith* (1886) 31 ChD 314 at 317. See also PARA 209 et seq.

4   As to when evidence of the testator's intention is admissible see PARAS 195, 218–219.

5   The presumption is that a designation in general words of the property intended to be affected by a will refers prima facie to that property only on which the will is capable of operating (*Maxwell v Maxwell* (1852) 2 De GM & G 705 at 715 (approving *Wentworth v Cox* (1822) 6 Madd 363 at 364); *Baring v Ashburton* (1886) 54 LT 463), and that the testator intended to dispose only of his own property (see EQUITABLE JURISDICTION vol 47 (2014) PARA 167).

6   Eg where the context shows that the testator erroneously believed that he had such property as described, or where he had only the intention of acquiring it (*Evans v Tripp* (1821) 6 Madd 91; *Waters v Wood* (1852) 5 De G & Sm 717; *Millar v Woodside* (1872) IR 6 Eq 546; and see *Re Mulder, Westminster Bank Ltd v Mulder* [1943] 2 All ER 150, CA (testator entitled to a share in a business but purporting to dispose of whole)), or where the testator described persons who he merely imagined were in existence, and who did not exist (*Del Mare v Robello* (1792) 1 Ves 412; *Daubeny v Coghlan* (1842) 12 Sim 507). A similar result may follow where there is a gift for a charitable purpose, which though possible at the date of the will, has ceased to be so before the testator's death and no general charitable intention can be otherwise identified: *Re Spence's Will Trusts, Ogden v Shackleton* [1979] Ch 483 at 495–496, [1978] 3 All ER 92 at 100–101.

269. Falsa demonstratio non nocet. It is a rule of construction, which applies to all written instruments and not to wills alone[1], that, if, of various terms used to describe a subject matter (whether a person or property), some are sufficient to ascertain the subject matter with certainty but others add a description which is not true, these other terms are not allowed to vitiate the gift[2]. The rule in full is 'falsa demonstratio non nocet cum de corpore constat'[3], and the second part of this maxim is an essential part of it[4]. The false description must merely be added onto that which is otherwise clear[5], although it need not come at the end of the sentence[6]. The characteristic of cases within the rule is that the description, so far as it is false, applies to no subject at all, and, so far as it is true, applies to one only[7]. There has been a judicial extension of the rule to cover cases where no accurate description of the property appears at all on the will, but the court is nevertheless clear about what is meant by the words used[8].

1   As to this rule in the case of deeds see DEEDS AND OTHER INSTRUMENTS vol 32 (2012) PARAS 428–429, 432.

2   *Llewellyn v Earl of Jersey* (1843) 11 M & W 183 at 189 per Parke B (deed); *Morrell v Fisher* (1849) 4 Exch 591 at 604 per Alderson B. See also *Goodright d Lamb v Pears* (1809) 11 East 58; *Anderson v Berkley* [1902] 1 Ch 936 at 940.

3   Ie a false description does not vitiate when there is no doubt as to the subject meant. See *Travers v Blundell* (1877) 6 ChD 436 at 442, 444, CA. Other versions are 'nil facit error nominis cum de corpore vel persona constat' (*Re Brocket, Dawes v Miller* [1908] 1 Ch 185 at 194), and 'praesentia corporis tollit errorem nominis' (Bacon's Maxims, reg 25).

4   *Re Brocket, Dawes v Miller* [1908] 1 Ch 185 at 194.

5   *Thomas d Evans v Thomas* (1796) 6 Term Rep 671 at 676 per Lord Kenyon CJ.

6   *Cowen v Truefitt Ltd* [1899] 2 Ch 309 at 311, CA (lease).

7   *Morrell v Fisher* (1849) 4 Exch 591 at 604; *Re Rayer, Rayer v Rayer* [1903] 1 Ch 685.

8   See *Re Gifford, Gifford v Seaman* [1944] Ch 186 at 188, [1944] 1 All ER 268 at 269 per Simonds J (gift of income from testatrix's 'war bonds' was apt, using falsa demonstratio construction, to cover a conversion stock (not named in the will) into which the bonds had been converted, but not savings certificates and defence bonds not owned or contemplated at the date of the will); following Eve J in *Re Price, Trumper v Price* [1932] 2 Ch 54 at 56–57, making the same concession as Eve J, that this carried the falsa demonstratio rule further than it had previously been applied. See PARA 270 notes 16, 21.

270. Description wholly false. Where the description is wholly false, so that no known existing person or thing satisfies the description, but the context of the will and the circumstances of the case[1] show unambiguously whom or what the testator meant, the description is rejected and the testator's intention is given effect[2].

This rule has been applied to false descriptions of donees in cases where one or more of the legatee's names was wrongly given[3]; where a corporation was misdescribed[4]; where the legatee was described as 'rector' instead of 'vicar'[5], or as 'apothecary' instead of 'dispenser'[6]; and where the name of the father[7] or mother[8] of the legatees was wrongly given. In a number of cases a gift to the children of one person has taken effect in favour of the children of another person where the context and circumstances show that they were the persons intended[9].

The rule has most often been applied to false descriptions of property, where no property accurately answering the description given belonged to the testator at the date of the will[10]. In such circumstances 'my money on deposit receipt' in a named bank has passed shares in the bank[11]; 'shares' has passed debenture stock[12]; 'sums owing' has passed sums due under documents which were unenforceable for want of registration[13]; 'real estate' has passed the proceeds of sale of real estate[14]; 'war loans' has passed Exchequer bonds[15], conversion stock and Treasury bonds[16]; 'stocks or shares in the Great Eastern Railway' was held to pass stock substituted on the amalgamation of that company with other companies[17]; a gift of the credit balance in an identified bank deposit account which was paid during the lifetime of the testatrix into a new account which yielded a higher rate of interest but was otherwise on very similar terms has been held to carry the money in the new account[18]; and a gift of property described as 'Lithbridge' has passed a property in fact called 'Silkbridge'[19]. The principle is limited to cases of misdescription of property in the testator's possession at the date of the will; there is no ground for assuming that he was falsely describing property he did not then possess and perhaps did not contemplate possessing[20]. Also, the rule cannot be applied where there is a misapprehension by the testator as to the nature of the property owned by him at the date of the will, as distinct from a case of misdescription[21].

1   As to the reception of evidence in such cases see PARA 209 et seq.
2   See *Re Milner-Gibson-Cullum, Cust v A-G* [1924] 1 Ch 456 (where a portrait was said to be wrongly described, but there was no difficulty in identifying the picture intended to pass).See also *Re Harte* [2015] EWHC 2351 (Ch), [2015] WTLR 1735.
3   *Masters v Masters* (1718) 1 P Wms 421 at 425 (Mrs Swopper described as 'Mrs Sawyer'); *Beaumont v Fell* (1723) 2 P Wms 141 (Gertrude Yardley described as 'Catherine Earnley', there being no such person); *Lee v Pain* (1844) 4 Hare 201 at 253 (Miss F A J described as 'Miss S J', there being a Mrs S J but it being clear that the gift was for an unmarried woman).
4   *A-G v Rye Corpn* (1817) 7 Taunt 546; *Queen's College, Oxford v Sutton* (1842) 12 Sim 521. As to misdescription of charities see CHARITIES vol 8 (2015) PARA 109.
5   *Hopkinson v Ellis* (1842) 5 Beav 34.
6   *Ellis v Bartrum (No 2)* (1857) 25 Beav 109.
7   *Douglas v Fellows* (1853) Kay 114.
8   *Bradwin v Harpur* (1759) Amb 374.
9   *Bradwin v Harpur* (1759) Amb 374; *Douglas v Fellows* (1853) Kay 114; *Re Waller, White v Scoles* (1899) 68 LJ Ch 526, CA (where the father was stated to be dead at the date of the will, the person named was still alive and unmarried, but another, of the same family but with different forenames, was dead leaving three children). See also *Bristow v Bristow* (1842) 5 Beav 289 at 291 (where the donees were the three remaining children of a named uncle, who had no children, but a cousin of the same name had three children answering the description); *Lord Camoys v Blundell* (1848) 1 HL Cas 778 (where a gift to the second son of E W was construed as a gift to the second son of J W, E W being his eldest son).
10 The rule cannot be applied if the testator had property at the date of the will which accurately answered the description: *Re Weeding, Armstrong v Wilkin* [1896] 2 Ch 364; *Re Lamb, Marston v Chauvet* (1933) 49 TLR 541.
11 *Re Cranfield, Mosse v Cranfield* [1895] 1 IR 80. See also *Re Vear, Vear v Vear* (1917) 62 Sol Jo 159.

12 *Re Weeding, Armstrong v Wilkin* [1896] 2 Ch 364.
13 *Re Rowe, Pike v Hamlyn* [1898] 1 Ch 153, CA.
14 *Re Glassington, Glassington v Follett* [1906] 2 Ch 305, not followed in *Re Lewis's Will Trusts, Lewis v Williams* [1984] 3 All ER 930, [1985] 1 WLR 102 (where a gift of 'my freehold farm' was held not to carry the testator's holding of three-quarters of the issued shares in a family farming company which owned a farm and other assets).
15 *Re Ionides, London County Westminster and Parr's Bank Ltd v Craies* (1922) 38 TLR 269.
16 *Re Price, Trumper v Price* [1932] 2 Ch 54; *Re Gifford, Gifford v Seaman* [1944] Ch 186, [1944] 1 All ER 268.
17 *Re Anderson, Public Trustee v Bielby* (1928) 44 TLR 295 (where stock in the company formed on the amalgamation, which the testator had purchased before the date of the will but after the amalgamation, did not, however, pass). In this case the Act which brought about the amalgamation contained provision for the adaptation of references to stock in wills etc: see PARA 156 text and note 12.
18 *Re Dorman* [1994] 1 All ER 804, [1994] 1 WLR 282.
19 *Re Nicholl, Re Perkins, Nicholl v Perkins* (1920) 125 LT 62.
20 *Re Gifford, Gifford v Seaman* [1944] Ch 186 at 189, [1944] 1 All ER 268 at 269 (where a gift of 'war bonds' was held to pass consolidated stock, but not national savings certificates and defence bonds acquired after the date of the will).
21 *Re Lewis's Will Trusts, Lewis v Williams* [1984] 3 All ER 930 at 932, [1985] 1 WLR 102 at 105 (decided by Scott J on the basis that it was not a case of misdescription because the testator really thought that he was leaving a farm, rather than anything else); considering *Re Gifford, Gifford v Seaman* [1944] Ch 186, [1944] 1 All ER 268. See also *Re Mulder, Westminster Bank Ltd v Mulder* [1943] 2 All ER 150 (testator mistaken as to his interest in a business).

271. Limits of the rule. The rule of 'falsa demonstratio non nocet'[1] is limited by a second rule of no less importance, namely that additional words are not rejected as a false description if they are capable of being read as accurate words of restriction[2]. If, therefore, it is doubtful whether the words of the will import a false reference or description, or whether they are words of restriction which limit the generality of former words, the court never presumes error or falsehood, and the latter construction is preferred[3]. Accordingly, where there exists some subject as to which all the descriptions are true, and some subject as to which part is true and part false, the words are considered to be words of true restriction, so that they refer to that subject only as to which all the descriptions are true[4].

Additional words have been construed as words of true restriction where they consisted of references to tenure[5], occupation[6], locality[7], mode of acquisition or title[8], or of descriptions of donees[9].

In order for the words to be so construed, all the words must be wholly true as to the restricted part, and there must be no clear intention that the whole should pass[10].

1 As to this rule see PARA 269.
2 Non accipi debent verba in demonstrationem falsam quae competunt in limitationem veram: Bacon's Maxims reg 13.
3 *Morrell v Fisher* (1849) 4 Exch 591 at 604 per Alderson B. See also *Doe d Ashforth v Bower* (1832) 3 B & Ad 453 at 459; *Nightingall v Smith* (1848) 1 Exch 879 at 886; *Re Brocket, Dawes v Miller* [1908] 1 Ch 185 at 190.
4 *Ridge v Newton* (1842) 2 Dr & War 239; *Morrell v Fisher* (1849) 4 Exch 591; *Slingsby v Grainger* (1859) 7 HL Cas 273 at 283, 287; *Gilliat v Gilliat* (1860) 28 Beav 481; *Pedley v Dodds, Dodds v Pedley* (1866) LR 2 Eq 819; *O'Connor v O'Connor* (1870) IR 4 Eq 483; *Millar v Woodside* (1872) IR 6 Eq 546; *Re Bennett, ex p Kirk* (1877) 5 ChD 800, CA.
5 *Roe d Conolly v Vernon and Vyse* (1804) 5 East 51; *Doe d Brown v Brown* (1809) 11 East 441; *Stone v Greening* (1843) 13 Sim 390; *Hall v Fisher* (1844) 1 Coll 47 (but, as to the last two cases cited see *Re Bright-Smith, Bright-Smith v Bright-Smith* (1886) 31 ChD 314; *Hallett v Hallett* (1898) 14 TLR 420, CA; and the cases cited in PARA 277 note 6); *Quennell v Turner* (1851) 13 Beav 240; *Mathews v Mathews* (1867) LR 4 Eq 278.
6 *Higham v Baker* (1583) Cro Eliz 15. See also *Doe d Parkin v Parkin* (1814) 5 Taunt 321; *Doe d Renow v Ashley* (1847) 10 QB 663; *Morrell v Fisher* (1849) 4 Exch 591; *Doe d Hubbard v*

Hubbard (1850) 15 QB 227; *Whitfield v Langdale* (1875) 1 ChD 61 at 80; *Homer v Homer* (1878) 8 ChD 758, CA; *Re Seal, Seal v Taylor* [1894] 1 Ch 316, CA.

7   *White v Vitty* (1826) 2 Russ 484; *Moser v Platt* (1844) 14 Sim 95; *Attwater v Attwater* (1853) 18 Beav 330; *Evans v Angell* (1858) 26 Beav 202; *Webber v Stanley* (1864) 16 CBNS 698; *Lambert v Overton* (1864) 11 LT 503; *Smith v Ridgway* (1866) LR 1 Exch 331, Ex Ch; *Keogh v Keogh* (1874) IR 8 Eq 179.

8   *Doe d Ryall v Bell* (1800) 8 Term Rep 579; *Roe d Conolly v Vernon and Vyse* (1804) 5 East 51; *Wilkinson v Bewicke* (1853) 3 De GM & G 937; *Cave v Harris, Harris v Cave* (1887) 57 LT 768. Cf *Norman v Norman* [1919] 1 Ch 297.

9   *Wrightson v Calvert* (1860) 1 John & H 250.

10 *Paul v Paul* (1760) 1 Wm Bl 255 at 256; *Hardwick v Hardwick* (1873) LR 16 Eq 168 at 176–177.

272. Description partly true as to each of two or more subjects.

If the description is not strictly applicable to any person or thing, but is applicable partly to one person or thing and partly to another, the court has always inquired into the material circumstances of the case for the purpose of deciding whether the testator intended to make the gift applicable to the one or the other[1], and may in certain circumstances receive evidence of the testator's intention[2]. The court will be reluctant to conclude that the gift fails for uncertainty, particularly in cases of ambiguity in description[3].

1   *Bernasconi v Atkinson* (1853) 10 Hare 345 at 349. See also *Bradshaw v Bradshaw* (1836) 2 Y & C Ex 72; *Adams v Jones* (1852) 9 Hare 485; *Re Hooper, Hooper v Warner* (1902) 88 LT 160. As to criticisms of this rule see *Doe d Hiscocks v Hiscocks* (1839) 5 M & W 363 at 369. As to the names of donees see *British Home and Hospital for Incurables v Royal Hospital for Incurables* (1904) 90 LT 601, CA; and as to the subject matter of the gift see *Rowlatt v Easton* (1863) 2 New Rep 262 (where the court had to decide between two types of stock, neither of which exactly answered the description). For an example where a description of land was capable of several possible applications, see *Sandover v Brown* [2004] EWHC 1307 (Ch), [2004] All ER (D) 53 (May) (conveyancing history of land examined to ascertain meaning).

2   As to the admissibility of evidence of the testator's intention see PARAS 195, 218–219.

3   See *Pinnel v Anison* [2005] EWHC 1421 (Ch), sub nom *Pinnell v Annison* [2005] All ER (D) 458 (May), where the testator left a gift to 'my sister, Doreen H of [address]', but the testator's sister was Doreen A, who did not live at that address. Extrinsic evidence showed no proven connection between the testator and Doreen H, but also, no contact with his sister after 1945. The judge relied on reference to the sister and circumstances indicating an intention to make a gift within the family.

273. General description followed by enumeration of particulars.

Where some subject matter is given under a description applicable to the whole, and then words of enumeration are added which do not completely enumerate and exhaust all the particulars which are included under the previous description, the question is which is the predominant description[1]. There is no rule that, of the two descriptions, the first is to prevail. If the subsequent words are meant to substitute a definite and precise statement for an antecedent generality, they must be read as explanatory and, if necessary, as restrictive of the prior general description[2]; otherwise the general description is given its full effect[3].

1   *West v Lawday* (1865) 11 HL Cas 375 at 384; *Hardwick v Hardwick* (1873) LR 16 Eq 168; *Travers v Blundell* (1877) 6 ChD 436 at 441, 443, CA. See also *Blake v Blake* [1923] 1 IR 88.

2   *Re Brocket, Dawes v Miller* [1908] 1 Ch 185 at 195 per Joyce J (devise of 'all the real estate' to which the testatrix was entitled under a will, 'namely' certain parcels omitting one parcel; that parcel did not pass). Cf *D'Aglie v Fryer* (1841) 12 Sim 1; *Glanville v Glanville* (1863) 33 Beav 302. See also the following cases of donee description: *Re Segelman* [1996] Ch 171, [1995] 3 All ER 676 (subsequent particular description was able to be removed by rectification for clerical error); *Re Scarisbrick, Cockshott v Public Trustee* [1951] Ch 622, [1951] 1 All ER 822, CA (class of donees modified by subsequent requirement to be 'in needy circumstances'; operated as further restriction of class); *Re Allen, Faith v Allen* [1953] Ch 810, [1953] 2 All ER 898 (subsequent reference to membership of, and adherence to, Anglican church and doctrine acted as restriction).

3   *Matthews v Maude* (1830) 1 Russ & M 397; *Reeves v Baker* (1854) 18 Beav 372 ('all my property whether freehold or personal' passed copyholds); *Stanley v Stanley* (1862) 2 John & H 491; *West*

v Lawday (1865) 11 HL Cas 375 at 384; *Re Roberts, Kiff v Roberts* (1886) 55 LT 498, CA ('all my property, leasehold and freehold' passed personalty); *Roberts v Thorp* (1911) 56 Sol Jo 13 ('all my property,' followed by a list of specific chattels, passed realty); *Stapleton v D'Alton* (1914) 49 ILT 62 (gift of remainder of estate consisting of certain described property); *Norman v Norman* [1919] 1 Ch 297; *Moore v Phelan* [1920] 1 IR 232 ('the seven houses I hold in' S Terrace passed the eight houses there to which the testatrix was entitled).

274. Inaccuracy in number of donees. Where there is a gift to a number of persons designated by a class or group description, with a statement of the number of the donees which is either greater or less[1] than the actual number of persons who fit the description at the death of the testator (as in the case of a gift to the four children of a named person, who at the death of the testator is shown to have five children), then, unless it appears that all the persons so designated were intended to take independently of their number[2], the court considers with how many of such persons the testator was acquainted at the date of his will, and, if the number corresponds with the number in the will, may thus be able to identify the particular persons described[3]. For this purpose, direct evidence of the testator's intention was formerly inadmissible[4] but may now be admissible in construing the will of a testator who died on or after 1 January 1983[5].

There are, however, cases where the court may arrive at the conclusion that all the persons satisfying a particular description are intended to be benefited, and, if there has been an inaccurate statement of the number of the persons composing the class, the court rejects the number[6]. Thus if it appears that at the date of the will the fact was, and the testator knew, that the number of persons who then answered the description was greater or less than the number shown by the will[7], or if the number could not then, in fact and to the testator's knowledge, be ascertained[8], or if (where the gift would otherwise be void for uncertainty) there is no evidence at all of the testator's knowledge or other admissible evidence to enable the court to determine who were meant by the description[9], the court may reject the number as a mistake.

1 *Re Sharp, Maddison v Gill* [1908] 2 Ch 190, CA.
2 *Matthews v Foulshaw* (1864) 12 WR 1141.
3 *Sherer v Bishop* (1792) 4 Bro CC 55; *Lord Selsey v Lord Lake* (1839) 1 Beav 146 at 151 ('her five daughters'; there were five sons and one daughter, who alone took); *Lane v Green* (1851) 4 De G & Sm 239 (to the four sons of A; she had three sons and one daughter, who all took); *Newman v Piercey* (1876) 4 ChD 41; *Re Mayo, Chester v Keirl* [1901] 1 Ch 404 at 407. Another child, en ventre sa mère, and not known to the testator, may then be excluded: *Re Emery's Estate, Jones v Emery* (1876) 3 ChD 300; *Re Smiley* (1908) 28 NZLR 1; *Re McNeil, Wright v Johnstone* (1909) 9 SRNSW 220. For cases where the enumeration corrected a mistake in the names see *Garth v Meyrick* (1779) 1 Bro CC 30; *Humphreys v Humphreys* (1789) 2 Cox Eq Cas 184.
4 *Re Mayo, Chester v Keirl* [1901] 1 Ch 404.
5 See PARAS 195, 219.
6 *Re Stephenson, Donaldson v Bamber* [1897] 1 Ch 75 at 81, CA, per Lord Russell of Killowen CJ, and at 85 per Lindley LJ; *Re Sharp, Maddison v Gill* [1908] 2 Ch 190 at 194, CA. See also *Harrison v Harrison* (1829) 1 Russ & M 71 at 72; *Hare v Cartridge* (1842) 13 Sim 165; *Lee v Pain* (1844) 4 Hare 201 at 249 (the last two cases cited were commented on in *Re Stephenson, Donaldson v Bamber*); *Yeats v Yeats* (1852) 16 Beav 170 at 171; *Matthews v Foulshaw* (1864) 12 WR 1141; *Re Dutton, Plunkett v Simeon* [1893] WN 65; *Re Groom, Booty v Groom* [1897] 2 Ch 407; and see *Lord Selsey v Lord Lake* (1839) 1 Beav 146. The rule does not apply where the persons are described by name: see *Re Whiston, Whiston v Woolley* [1924] 1 Ch 122, CA.
7 *Hampshire v Peirce* (1751) 2 Ves Sen 216; *Scott v Fenoulhett* (1784) 1 Cox Eq Cas 79; *Daniell v Daniell* (1849) 3 De G & Sm 337; *Lee v Lee* (1864) 10 Jur NS 1041; *Spencer v Ward* (1870) LR 9 Eq 507.
8 *Sleech v Thorington* (1754) 2 Ves Sen 560 ('to the two servants living with me at my death').
9 *Tomkins v Tomkins* (1743) 19 Ves 126n; *Stebbing v Walkey* (1786) 2 Bro CC 85 at 86 (where, however, Kenyon MR said, 'I yield to the authority of the cases and not to the reason of them'); *Garvey v Hibbert* (1812) 19 Ves 125 (a leading case on this mode of construction); *Harrison v Harrison* (1829) 1 Russ & M 71 at 72; *Lee v Pain* (1844) 4 Hare 201 at 249; *Morrison v Martin*

(1846) 5 Hare 507; *Wrightson v Calvert* (1860) 1 John & H 250 at 251 per Wood V-C (explained in *Newman v Piercey* (1876) 4 ChD 41 at 47 per Jessel MR); *Re Bassett's Estate, Perkins v Fladgate* (1872) LR 14 Eq 54; *McKechnie v Vaughan* (1873) LR 15 Eq 289; *Re Sharp, Maddison v Gill* [1908] 2 Ch 190, CA.

275. Designation by name or description. A donee has often been sufficiently designated by a nickname or erroneous name proved to have been used by the testator, or by a name gained by reputation and known to the testator[1], and property may be sufficiently described by the description the testator was accustomed to use[2].

1   *River's Case* (1737) 1 Atk 410 (illegitimate sons described as 'my sons'; but see now PARAS 355–356). See also *Gynes v Kemsley* (1677) Freem KB 293 ('Margery' described as 'Margaret'); *Baylis v A-G* (1741) 2 Atk 239; *Edge v Salisbury* (1749) Amb 70 at 71; *Goodinge v Goodinge* (1749) 1 Ves Sen 231; *Dowset v Sweet* (1753) Amb 175 ('James' described as 'John'); *Parsons v Parsons* (1791) 1 Ves 266; *Lee v Pain* (1844) 4 Hare 201 at 251–252; *Andrews v Andrews* (1885) 15 LR Ir 199, Ir CA.
2   Cf *Doe d Beach v Earl of Jersey* (1825) 3 B & C 870 ('my Briton Ferry estate'; estate not situated in Briton Ferry). This may extend to a testator's habit of failing to expressly differentiate between adjoining areas of land, but which have a different nature or function: see *Sandover v Brown* [2004] EWHC 1307 (Ch), [2004] All ER (D) 53 (May) (garden and uncultivated backland field were all referred to as testatrix's 'garden'). See also the cases cited in PARA 215 note 7.

276. Discrepancy between name and description. Where a donee is designated by name and description, then, if there is a person who has that name and the description is incorrect for him and all others, the description is ignored, for it is a rule that a name will prevail against an error of description[1] unless the false description is due to the fraud of the alleged donee[2]. The name alone, however, will not prevail unless it appears that the description is mistaken. For the rule to apply, it is necessary first to show that there is an error in the description[3]. Similarly, where a description is correct and sufficient, an incorrect name may be ignored[4].

Where, however, either the name alone or the description alone is sufficient to identify a subject, and they do not identify the same subject, then, according to the circumstances of the case, the description and not the name[5], or the name and not the description[6], may prevail. The name is in fact only a mode of description[7], and the question is to determine which portion of the whole description is to prevail[8]. For this purpose, evidence is admissible of all the facts known to the testator at the date of the will, and in certain circumstances direct evidence of his intention may be received[9]. On the evidence properly admissible, a test often applied is to inquire whether the testator was more likely to err in the name or in the description[10]. Thus if there is a person for whom the name is accurate, but the testator was not intimate with him, and there is also a person for whom the name is inaccurate but the description is sufficient to identify him, and the testator was intimate with him, the latter is the person entitled[11].

If the question cannot be answered, the gift is void for uncertainty[12].

1   See Bacon's Maxims reg 25. See also *Giles v Giles, Penfold v Penfold* (1836) 1 Keen 685; *Doe d Gains v Rouse* (1848) 5 CB 422; *Ford v Batley* (1852) 23 LJ Ch 225; *Ormiston's Executors v Laws* 1966 SLT 110, Ct of Sess (where a gift 'to my fiancée S M', who in fact had never been a fiancée, took effect).
2   *Giles v Giles, Penfold v Penfold* (1836) 1 Keen 685. See also *Kennell v Abbott* (1799) 4 Ves 802; *Wilkinson v Joughin* (1866) LR 2 Eq 319; *Re Posner, Posner v Miller* [1953] P 277, [1953] 1 All ER 1123.
3   See *Drake v Drake* (1860) 8 HL Cas 172 at 179 per Lord Campbell LC; adopted in *Charter v Charter* (1874) LR 7 HL 364 at 380–381 per Lord Cairns LC. As to the difficulties in applying this rule see *Lord Camoys v Blundell* (1848) 1 HL Cas 778; *Garland v Beverley* (1878) 9 ChD 213 at 218–219. The court does not conjecture that an error existed: *Mostyn v Mostyn* (1854) 5 HL Cas 155.

4 *Pitcairne v Brase* (1679) Cas *temp* Finch 403; *Dowset v Sweet* (1753) Amb 175; *Stockdale v Bushby* (1815) Coop G 229.

5 *Garth v Meyrick* (1779) 1 Bro CC 30; *Smith v Coney* (1801) 6 Ves 42; *Doe d Le Chevalier v Huthwaite* (1820) 3 B & Ald 632; *Bradshaw v Bradshaw* (1836) 2 Y & C Ex 72; *Lord Camoys v Blundell* (1848) 1 HL Cas 778; *Adams v Jones* (1852) 9 Hare 485; *Re Blackman* (1852) 16 Beav 377; *Re Feltham's Will Trusts* (1855) 1 K & J 528; *Hodgson v Clarke* (1860) 1 De GF & J 394 at 397; *Re Nunn's Trusts* (1875) LR 19 Eq 331; *Re Hooper, Hooper v Warner* (1902) 88 LT 160. See also *Pinnel v Anison* [2005] EWHC 1421 (Ch), sub nom *Pinnell v Annison* [2005] All ER (D) 458 (May) (testator cited correct name and address of one person, but she did not meet the description of being the testator's sister; the sister had the forename used but not the surname or address; held that the description as sister was the predominant factor).

6 *Newbolt v Pryce* (1844) 14 Sim 354; *Garner v Garner* (1860) 29 Beav 114; *Gillett v Gane* (1870) LR 10 Eq 29; *Farrer v St Catharine's College, Cambridge* (1873) LR 16 Eq 19; *Garland v Beverley* (1878) 9 ChD 213; *Re Taylor, Cloak v Hammond* (1886) 34 ChD 255, CA.

7 A description of legatees as those 'named' in the will, although primarily referring to those mentioned by name, may denote persons merely specified or mentioned by another description: *Bromley v Wright* (1849) 7 Hare 334; *Re Holmes' Trusts* (1853) 1 Drew 321; *Seale-Hayne v Jodrell* [1891] AC 304 at 306, HL, per Lord Herschell, and at 309 per Lord Hannen.

8 *Bernasconi v Atkinson* (1853) 10 Hare 345 at 351.

9 Direct evidence of the intention of a testator who died before 1 January 1983, such as the instructions for his will, is not admissible unless both the name and description are equally, although not necessarily completely, applicable to two persons: *Lord Camoys v Blundell* (1848) 1 HL Cas 778; *Bernasconi v Atkinson* (1853) 10 Hare 345; *Drake v Drake* (1860) 8 HL Cas 172; *Charter v Charter* (1874) LR 7 HL 364 at 377, as explained in *Re Ray, Cant v Johnstone* [1916] 1 Ch 461; and see PARAS 218, 220. In construing the will of a testator who died on or after 1 January 1983, direct evidence of his intention in such cases is more widely admissible: see PARAS 195, 219.

10 *Bernasconi v Atkinson* (1853) 10 Hare 345 at 351–352, approved in *Re Fry, Mathews v Freeman* (1874) 22 WR 813, CA; *Re Lord Blayney's Trusts* (1875) IR 9 Eq 413; *Re Lyon's Trusts* (1879) 48 LJ Ch 245. See also PARA 209 et seq.

11 *Charter v Charter* (1874) LR 7 HL 364; *Re Brake* (1881) 6 PD 217; *Re Chappell* [1894] P 98; *Re Blake's Trusts* [1904] 1 IR 98. See also *Pinnel v Anison* [2005] EWHC 1421 (Ch), sub nom *Pinnell v Annison* [2005] All ER (D) 458 (May) (where there was little evidence of the testator's familiarity or contact with either the named person or the testator's sister who had the same forename).

12 *Drake v Drake* (1860) 8 HL Cas 172. However, there is judicial reluctance to reach such a conclusion: see PARA 272 text and note 3. See also PARA 45.

277. Examples of cases of discrepancy. The rule that, in a case of designation both by name and description, one part of the designation may prevail over the other[1] has been applied both to descriptions of donees[2] and of property[3], and the court has rejected reference to particular parishes, streets or other localities[4], to occupation[5], to a particular tenure, such as freehold or leasehold[6], to a mode of acquisition[7] and to acreage[8].

1 See PARA 276.

2 *Ryall v Hannam* (1847) 10 Beav 536 (to 'E A, a natural daughter of' a named person, where the name and sex of the child were incorrect); *Re Rickit's Trusts* (1853) 11 Hare 299 (to a niece of a named person, where the only child was a nephew); *Ford v Batley* (1853) 17 Beav 303 (to a man living with a woman wrongly named, where evidence of surrounding circumstances was sufficient to identify the donee); *Stringer v Gardiner* (1859) 4 De G & J 468 ('to my niece E S'; a grandniece E J S was held entitled). See also *Doe d Gains v Rouse* (1848) 5 CB 422 ('my wife C', where the testator had a wife M but was living with C with whom he had contracted an invalid marriage); *Re Ingle's Trusts* (1871) LR 11 Eq 578 ('my late nephew M'; a nephew M who was still living was preferred to the testator's deceased brother of the same name); *Thomson v Eastwood* (1877) 2 App Cas 215 (where the legatee was described as 'the son of' a named person, the question whether he was born in lawful wedlock was immaterial; but see now PARAS 355–356); *Re Marquess of Bute, Marquess of Bute v Ryder* (1884) 27 ChD 196 (gift to person entitled under a deed of entail, there being no such deed); *Anderson v Berkley* [1902] 1 Ch 936 ('to A's wife L', where there was no marriage, although the testator was told that there had been one); *Re Hooper, Hooper v Warner* (1902) 88 LT 160 (to 'P H, son of C A H'; B H, one of three sons, held entitled).

3 *Day v Trig* (1715) 1 P Wms 286 (a devise of all freehold houses in a named locality where the testator had only leasehold houses); *Door v Geary* (1749) 1 Ves Sen 255 (stock wrongly named but correct in amount); *Drake v Martin* (1856) 23 Beav 89 (bank stock passed government stock

otherwise sufficiently identified); *Ellis v Eden (No 2)* (1858) 25 Beav 482 (stock 'in my name' passed stock purchased but not transferred to testator); *Rowlatt v Easton* (1863) 2 New Rep 262 (name and amount of stock incorrect); *Burbey v Burbey* (1867) 15 LT 501; *Coltman v Gregory* (1870) 40 LJ Ch 352 (stock stated to be in joint names but actually in testator's name alone); *Norman v Norman* [1919] 1 Ch 297 (devise of land correctly described but wrongly stated to be purchased wholly from a named person). In *Mackinley v Sison* (1837) 8 Sim 561, *Power v Lencham* (1838) 2 Jo Ex Ir 728, and *Quennell v Turner* (1851) 13 Beav 240, stock 'standing in my name' passed stock standing in the name of trustees. See also *Williams v Williams* (1786) 2 Bro CC 87; *Maybery v Brooking* (1855) 7 De GM & G 673; *Wilson v Morley* (1877) 5 ChD 776; *Re Hodgson, Darley v Hodgson* [1899] 1 Ch 666.

4   *Owens v Bean* (1678) Cas *temp* Finch 395 (parish right, county wrong); *Hastead v Searle* (1679) 1 Ld Raym 728; *Brown v Longley* (1732) 2 Eq Cas Abr 416 pl 14; *Doe d Beach v Earl of Jersey* (1818) 1 B & Ald 550 (on appeal (1825) 3 B & C 870); *Newton v Lucas* (1836) 1 My & Cr 391; *Gauntlett v Carter* (1853) 17 Beav 586; *Armstrong v Buckland* (1854) 18 Beav 204; *Tann v Tann* (1863) 2 New Rep 412; *Harman v Gurner* (1866) 35 Beav 478 (where, however, there was evidence of habitual misdescription by the testator); *Homer v Homer* (1878) 8 ChD 758, CA; *Re Mayell, Foley v Wood* [1913] 2 Ch 488.

5   *Blague v Gold* (1637) Cro Car 447, 473; *Goodtitle d Paul v Paul* (1760) 2 Burr 1089; *Marshall v Hopkins* (1812) 15 East 309 (where the words were transposed); *Goodtitle d Radford v Southern* (1813) 1 M & S 299; *Nightingall v Smith* (1848) 1 Exch 879; *Doe d Campton v Carpenter* (1850) 15 Jur 719; *White v Birch* (1867) 36 LJ Ch 174 (dissenting from *Doe d Parkin v Parkin* (1814) 5 Taunt 321); *Hardwick v Hardwick* (1873) LR 16 Eq 168.

6   *Denn d Wilkins v Kemeys* (1808) 8 East 366; *Doe d Dunning v Cranstoun* (1840) 7 M & W 1; *Nelson v Hopkins* (1851) 21 LJ Ch 410; *Re Bright-Smith, Bright-Smith v Bright-Smith* (1886) 31 ChD 314; *Re Steel, Wappett v Robinson* [1903] 1 Ch 135 (where, however, there was evidence of local usage). Cf *Saxton v Saxton* (1879) 13 ChD 359. For instances where references to tenure were construed restrictively see PARA 271.

7   *Hill v St John* (1775) 3 Bro Parl Cas 375; *Welby v Welby* (1813) 2 Ves & B 187 at 191; *Harrison v Hyde* (1859) 4 H & N 805; *Sealy v Stawell* (1868) IR 2 Eq 326 at 348; *Cooch v Walden* (1877) 46 LJ Ch 639. See also *Girdlestone v Creed* (1853) 10 Hare 480 at 487; *Thorp v Tomson* (1588) 2 Leon 120.

8   *Whitfield v Langdale* (1875) 1 ChD 61 at 76–77.

278. Change of circumstances between will and death affecting accuracy of name or description. Although descriptions in a will must be construed according to the usual rules as to the circumstances to be taken into account[1], where a person or body who once satisfied the description no longer exist at the date of the will, another person or body existing at the date of the will, and satisfying the description inaccurately but sufficiently, may be entitled under the gift[2].

An accurate description of a donee by name is not as a rule affected, in the case of a person, by a change of name before the testator's death[3], or, in the case of a society, corporation or body, by a change of name or by reorganization if the donee substantially exists in the same nature as at the date of the will[4]. Accordingly, gifts to or for the purposes of a named hospital were not, in general, affected by the setting up of the National Health Service between the date of the will and the testator's death[5]. There may, however, be circumstances, where the viability of the purposes specified may cease between the dates of will and death, so as to cause the gift to fail[6]. By the terms of the will, the use or adoption of a specified name[7] at the testator's death[8], or at the time of payment or vesting[9], or at some other time[10], may be a condition of the gift taking effect at all.

The principle still remains that clear wording, free of ambiguity, is to be given its ordinary and natural meaning[11].

1   As to property see PARA 282 et seq; and as to donees see PARA 299 et seq.

2   *Dowset v Sweet* (1753) Amb 175 note (2); *Dooley v Mahon* (1877) IR 11 Eq 299; and see the cases cited in PARA 220 note 1. As to a legacy to a non-existing or dissolved charitable institution see CHARITIES vol 8 (2015) PARAS 149–151, 157–159.

3   As to change of name generally see REGISTRATION CONCERNING THE INDIVIDUAL vol 88 (2012) PARAS 326–329.

4   *Re Joy, Purday v Johnson* (1888) 60 LT 175 (amalgamation of two societies); *Re Wedgwood,*
    Sweet v Cotton [1914] 2 Ch 245 (charitable work carried on at same home, although transferred
    from one association to another); *Re Donald, Moore v Somerset* [1909] 2 Ch 410 (gift for benefit
    of volunteer and militia units substantially existing as the Territorial Army). Cf *Re Andrews,*
    Dunedin Corpn v Smyth (1910) 29 NZLR 43 (effect of introduction of compulsory service); and
    see *Re Quibell's Will Trusts, White v Reichert* [1956] 3 All ER 679, [1957] 1 WLR 186 (bequest
    of shares in company to be formed passed shares although company was formed before death).

5   *Re Morgan's Will Trusts, Lewarne v Minister of Health* [1950] Ch 637, [1950] 1 All ER 1097; *Re*
    Glass, Public Trustee v South-West Middlesex Hospital Management Committee [1950] Ch 643n,
    [1950] 2 All ER 953n; *Re Hunter, Lloyds Bank Ltd v Girton College, Cambridge (Mistress and*
    Governors) [1951] Ch 190, [1951] 1 All ER 58; *Re Meyers, London Life Association v St*
    George's Hospital [1951] Ch 534, [1951] 1 All ER 538; *McClement's Trustees v Campbell* 1951
    SC 167, Ct of Sess; *Thomson's Trustees v Leith Hospital* 1951 SC 533, Ct of Sess; *Re Little,*
    Barclays Bank Ltd v Bournemouth and East Dorset Hospital Management Committee [1953]
    2 All ER 852, [1953] 1 WLR 1132. See also *Re Ginger, Wood Roberts v Westminster Hospital*
    Board of Governors [1951] Ch 458, [1951] 1 All ER 422; *Re Mills, Midland Bank Executor and*
    Trustee Co Ltd v United Birmingham Hospitals Board of Governors [1953] 1 All ER 835, [1953]
    1 WLR 554. Cf *Re Buzzacott, Munday v King's College Hospital* [1953] Ch 28, [1952] 2 All ER
    1011; *Re Bawden's Settlement, Besant v Board of Governors of the London Hospital* [1953]
    2 All ER 1235, [1954] 1 WLR 33n; *Re Hayes' Will Trusts, Dobie v Board of Governors of the*
    National Hospital [1953] 2 All ER 1242, [1954] 1 WLR 22; *Connell's Trustees v Milngavie*
    District Nursing Association 1953 SC 230, Ct of Sess; *Mollison's Trustees v Aberdeen General*
    Hospitals Board of Management 1953 SC 264, Ct of Sess; *Re Adams, Gee v Barnet Group*
    Hospital Management Committee [1968] Ch 80, [1967] 3 All ER 285, CA ('endowing beds for
    paying patients' includes providing support for those who occupy the beds); and CHARITIES vol 8
    (2015) PARA 155.

6   *Re Spence, Ogden v Shackleton* [1979] Ch 483, sub nom *Re Spence's Will Trusts, Ogden v*
    Shackleton [1978] 3 All ER 92 (gift to 'old folks home' for specific charitable purpose became
    impossible of performance by date of death; no general charitable intention discernible so gift
    failed).

7   The word 'name' may be used in a figurative sense, as meaning 'stock': *Pyot v Pyot* (1749) 1 Ves
    Sen 335 (where a change of name by marriage did not exclude); *Doe d Wright v Plumptre* (1820)
    3 B & Ald 474 at 482; *Carpenter v Bott* (1847) 15 Sim 606; *Re Maher, Maher v Toppin* [1909]
    1 IR 70, Ir CA.

8   *Bon v Smith* (1596) Cro Eliz 532 (woman, who had changed name by marriage before
    testator's death; not entitled); *Jobson's Case* (1597) Cro Eliz 576 (marriage after testator's death;
    entitled).

9   *Doe d Wright v Plumptre* (1820) 3 B & Ald 474 at 482; *Re Neeld, Inigo-Jones v Inigo-Jones (No*
    3) [1969] 2 All ER 1025, [1969] 1 WLR 988 (person required to adopt name and arms within
    12 months of becoming entitled to certain rents and profits).

10 Eg at birth, so that the name is the family name: *Barlow v Bateman* (1735) 2 Bro Parl Cas 272;
    Leigh v Leigh (1808) 15 Ves 92.

11 See *Re Marryat, Westminster Bank Ltd v Hobcroft* [1948] Ch 298, [1948] 1 All ER 796 (gifts to
    unnamed employees in the service of a named limited company could not be construed as applying
    to service with the predecessor unincorporated business of the same name).

279. Construction of gift of property generically described. A gift which
accurately describes property of a generic nature (that is, property susceptible to
increase or diminution between the date of the will and death[1]) belonging to the
testator at the date of the will does not fail where the description is sufficiently apt
to indicate particular property belonging to the testator at his death, even though
as a description of that property it is inaccurate, and that particular property
accordingly passes under the gift[2], the inaccuracy being then of no importance.
Where, out of several properties alleged to satisfy the description at the death,
only one accurately satisfies it[3], only that property passes under the gift[4]. Where
no property at all is sufficiently described by the words of the will at the
testator's death, the gift fails[5]. Where, however, the testator had neither at the date
of the will nor at his death property accurately described by the words of the will,
the court may from the circumstances be able to infer what was meant to be

described, and the gift does not necessarily fail[6]. In the case of bequests of personal property, the gift may take effect as a general legacy[7].

1 See PARA 282.
2 *Cooch v Walden* (1877) 46 LJ Ch 639; *Saxton v Saxton* (1879) 13 ChD 359 (devise of leasehold house held to carry freehold acquired after the date of the will). Cf *Re Willis, Spencer v Willis* [1911] 2 Ch 563 (plots purchased subsequently to devise of house 'in which I now reside' held to pass); *Re Reeves, Reeves v Pawson* [1928] Ch 351 (where 'my present lease' was held to refer, by virtue of a codicil confirming the will (see PARA 114), to a renewed lease, the renewal being before the date of the codicil); *Re Fleming's Will Trusts, Ennion v Hampstead Old People's Housing Trust Ltd* [1974] 3 All ER 323, [1974] 1 WLR 1552 (devise of leasehold house held to carry freehold acquired after date of will notwithstanding absence of merger). See also *Higgins v Dawson* [1902] AC 1, HL. This approach may not be applicable where it can be shown the particular property had been acquired between the date of the will and the testator's death and had not been within his contemplation at the date of the will: see *Re Gifford, Gifford v Seaman* [1944] Ch 186, [1944] 1 All ER 268.
3 As to the rule of construction in such a case see PARA 271.
4 *Emuss v Smith* (1848) 2 De G & Sm 722; *Re Portal and Lamb* (1885) 30 ChD 50, CA; *Cave v Harris, Harris v Cave* (1887) 57 LT 768; *Re Potter, Stevens v Potter* (1900) 83 LT 405. See also *Webb v Byng* (1855) 1 K & J 580 at 594 (after-acquired property held not to pass under the name testatrix was wont to use as to other property).
5 *Barber v Wood* (1877) 4 ChD 885; *Re Knight, Knight v Burgess* (1887) 34 ChD 518.
6 *Re Jameson, King v Winn* [1908] 2 Ch 111 at 116. See also *King v Wright* (1845) 14 Sim 400; *Flood v Flood* [1902] 1 IR 538; *Re Gifford, Gifford v Seaman* [1944] Ch 186, [1944] 1 All ER 268; *Re Quibell's Will Trusts, White v Reichert* [1956] 3 All ER 679, [1957] 1 WLR 186 (will contemplated gift of future shares in company to be incorporated by will trustees but testator subsequently incorporated business himself; held, a valid gift of shares); but see *Re Lewis's Will Trusts, Lewis v Williams* [1984] 3 All ER 930, [1985] 1 WLR 102 (where a gift of 'my freehold farm' was held not to carry the testator's holding of three-quarters of the issued shares in a family farming company which owned a farm and other assets, even though the testator owned the shares at the date of his will as well as at the date of his death). Where the testator died on or after 1 January 1983, evidence of his intention may be admissible: see PARAS 195, 219.
7 *Selwood v Mildmay* (1797) 3 Ves 306; *Lindgren v Lindgren* (1846) 9 Beav 358; and see PARA 215 note 3. See also *Findlater v Lowe* [1904] 1 IR 519.

280. Construction of gift of property specifically described. Where specific property existing at the date of the will is described, the whole of that property may pass under the gift notwithstanding that at the date of the death the description applies accurately to part only of that property[1]. The question of what property is considered to be comprised within the description at the date of death may be affected by statutory provision[2].

1 *Re Evans, Evans v Powell* [1909] 1 Ch 784; cf Re Willis, Spencer v Willis [1911] 2 Ch 563.
2 See eg *Acheson v Russell* [1951] Ch 67, sub nom *Re Manor Farm, Kytes Hardwick, Acheson v Russell* [1950] 2 All ER 572 (description of 'the family property at K H' came within Law of Property Act 1925 s 176(1) (as to which see REAL PROPERTY AND REGISTRATION vol 87 (2012) PARA 136), so as to pass interest in entail as well as fee simple interest).

5. CONSTRUCTION OF PARTICULAR DISPOSITIONS

(1) APPLICATION OF RULES OF CONSTRUCTION OF PARTICULAR DISPOSITIONS

281. Application of rules of construction in relation to particular dispositions. To modern eyes many of the rules of construction relating to particular dispositions[1] seem highly artificial. They were developed at a time when different rules applied to the devolution of realty and personalty[2]; the courts had no statutory power to rectify wills[3] and the power to admit extrinsic evidence as an aid to construction was more limited than the current statutory power[4]. In addition, there was a medieval horror of a vacuum and therefore courts leant in favour of early vesting[5].

The modern approach to the construction of wills relies on establishing the intention of the testator from the words used in their documentary, factual and commercial context[6]. In the circumstances, it is unlikely that a modern court would feel bound by these rules.

1 See PARAS 282–476.
2 See PARA 1011; and see also PERSONAL PROPERTY vol 80 (2013) PARA 801; SETTLEMENTS vol 91 (2012) PARA 839.
3 See the Administration of Justice Act 1982 s 20; and PARA 187.
4 See the Administration of Justice Act 1982 s 21; and PARAS 119, 220.
5 See, for example, Templeman J in *Re Mallinson Consolidated Trusts, Mallinson v Gooley* [1974] 2 All ER 530 at 533, [1974] 1 WLR 1120 at 1123.
6 See *Marley v Rawlings* [2014] UKSC 2 at [20], [2015] AC 129, [2014] 1 All ER 807 per Lord Neuberger; and PARA 188.

(2) PROPERTY PASSING

(i) General Effect of Property Passing

282. Will speaks from death. Unless a contrary intention appears in it[1], a will[2] must be construed, with reference to the real estate[3] and personal estate[4] comprised in it[5], to speak and take effect as if it had been executed immediately before the testator's death[6], and as if the condition of things to which it refers in this respect is that existing immediately before his death[7]. This provision does not, however, preclude the investigation of circumstances at the date of the will in order to ascertain whether a gift has been adeemed[8].

Where the thing given is generic[9], so that the description may from time to time apply to different amounts of property of like nature or to different objects, the effect of the rule, if applicable, is that the property answering the description at the testator's death passes under the gift[10].

No contrary intention is shown by the mere use of a possessive adjective[11] in the case of such a generic gift[12], or by a description of the property as being that of which the testator is seised or possessed[13]. A description of the property as that which the testator 'now' owns or occupies may according to the circumstances[14], but it appears prima facie does not, show a contrary intention so as to exclude after-acquired property of the generic nature[15]. Particular problems may arise where the will expressly refers to a collection of items or where collections of items are included in more general gifts[16].

The provisions of the Wills Act 1837[17] do not, however, affect a description of some specific thing existing at the date of the will[18].

1 See the text and notes 11–15.

2 As to the meaning of 'will' see PARA 1.

3 For these purposes, 'real estate' includes manors, advowsons, messuages, land, tithes, rents and hereditaments, whether corporeal, incorporeal or personal, and any estate, right or interest (other than a chattel interest) therein: Wills Act 1837 s 1 (amended by the Trusts of Land and Appointment of Trustees Act 1996 s 25(2), Sch 4). As to the abolition of copyhold and customary tenure see CUSTOM AND USAGE vol 32 (2012) PARA 41 et seq. An undivided share in land now only exists in equity: see REAL PROPERTY AND REGISTRATION vol 87 (2012) PARA 215 et seq. As to tithes see ECCLESIASTICAL LAW vol 34 (2011) PARA 975 et seq; and as to devises of 'land' and other general devises see PARA 284.

4 For these purposes, 'personal estate' includes leasehold estates and other chattels real, and also money, shares of government and other funds, securities for money (not being real estates), debts, choses (or things) in action, rights, credits, goods and all other property whatsoever which by law devolves upon the executor or administrator, and any share or interest therein: Wills Act 1837 s 1. So far as this definition of 'personal estate' refers to property which devolves on the executor or administrator, it must be understood as excepting real estate, although by virtue of enactments passed since the Wills Act 1837 real estate in which a deceased had an interest not ceasing on his death now devolves on his personal representative: see PARA 945. As to bequests of 'personal estate' see PARA 288. For the purposes of conflict of laws, the distinction is not between personalty and realty as in the case of wills, but between immovables and movables: see *Re Grassi, Stubberfield v Grassi* [1905] 1 Ch 584 at 590–591; *Re Lyne's Settlement Trusts, Re Gibbs, Lyne v Gibbs* [1919] 1 Ch 80, CA; *Re Cartwright, Cartwright v Smith* [1939] Ch 90, [1948] 4 All ER 209, CA. See also CONFLICT OF LAWS vol 19 (2011) PARAS 676 et seq, 729 et seq.

5 This includes property subject to a general (but not a special) power exercised by the will (see TRUSTS AND POWERS vol 98 (2013) PARAS 577, 585), even where the will purports to exercise a power over property which at the testator's death has become his absolute property (*Re James, Hole v Bethune* [1910] 1 Ch 157). The phrase 'with reference to the real and personal estate comprised in it' only subjects after-purchased and after-acquired estates to the dispositions previously made: *Lady Langdale v Briggs* (1856) 8 De GM & G 391 at 432 per Turner LJ. The Wills Act 1837 does not resolve a doubt which may exist as to whether particular property is passed by a specific or residuary gift: *Re Portal and Lamb* (1885) 30 ChD 50 at 55, CA, per Lindley LJ. A release of debts to a specified person is within the Wills Act 1837 s 24 (*Everett v Everett* (1877) 7 ChD 428, CA); but see *Re Mitchell, Freelove v Mitchell* [1913] 1 Ch 201 (right of surety's executors to indemnity against claims made after his death under his guarantee not included in release of 'all debts'). The question whether the rule that a will speaks from death applies to exceptions from gifts was raised in *Hughes v Jones* (1863) 1 Hem & M 765 at 770. As to descriptions of things not comprised in the will cf *Re Williams, James v Williams* (1910) 26 TLR 307 (direction to pay debts of chapels held to extend to debts incurred and chapels built after testator's death).

6 Wills Act 1837 s 24. Before the Wills Act 1837, a will spoke as regards personal estate from the death (*Re Chapman, Perkins v Chapman* [1904] 1 Ch 431 at 436, CA), and as regards real estate from the date of the will, unless the contrary intention was shown: see PARA 26 note 3. Thus the effect of the Wills Act 1837 was to extend to real estate the rule of construction as to the time from which the will was to be taken to speak which before that Act was applicable to personal estate: *Cole v Scott* (1849) 1 Mac & G 518. See also *Harwood v Harwood* [2005] EWHC 3019 (Ch) at [16], [2005] All ER (D) 121 (Nov) at [16] per Judge Weeks QC (wording 'all my . . . [collection of articles] . . . collected during my lifetime' the possessive adjective 'my' would normally be construed as meaning at the date of death of the testator; further wording 'such of the same as shall still be owned by me and be in my possession at my death' probably displaced that reading; however the wording 'together with any further chattels as additions to . . . such chattels' probably restored effect of the Wills Act 1837 s 24.

7 *Higgins v Dawson* [1902] AC 1 at 7, HL.

8 See *Re Edwards, Macadam v Wright* [1958] Ch 168 at 176, [1957] 2 All ER 495 at 501, CA, per Jenkins LJ. As to ademption see PARAS 155–159.

9 Ie it may increase, diminish or otherwise change during the testator's life: *Goodlad v Burnett* (1855) 1 K & J 341 at 349; *Re Slater, Slater v Slater* [1906] 2 Ch 480 at 485; *Re Gillins, Inglis v Gillins* [1909] 1 Ch 345. The Wills Act 1837 s 24 does not, however, merely apply to a residuary gift; it applies to specific gifts: *Lady Langdale v Briggs* (1856) 8 De GM & G 391 at 436–437; *Re Ord, Dickinson v Dickinson* (1879) 12 ChD 22 at 25, CA. As to the effect of a general devise of the testator's real or personal property in exercising a general power see TRUSTS AND POWERS vol 98 (2013) PARAS 577, 583.

10 Eg where the testator acquired further property of the same kind (*Lady Langdale v Briggs* (1856) 8 De GM & G 391 (where 'all my freehold lands' and 'all my leasehold lands' included those held

at death); *Trinder v Trinder* (1866) LR 1 Eq 695 (where 'my shares in the Great Western Railway' included stock purchased subsequent to the will); *Lysaght v Edwards* (1876) 2 ChD 499 at 505 (general gift of real estate); *Everett v Everett* (1877) 7 ChD 428, CA (where debts released by the will were held to include those contracted after it was made); *Re Russell, Russell v Chell* (1882) 19 ChD 432 (where a bequest of the testator's share in a partnership passed the whole business, the testator having bought out his partners before death)); or where he acquired a further or different interest, but the property still satisfies the description (*Saxton v Saxton* (1879) 13 ChD 359 ('my term and interest in the leasehold dwelling house' specified; purchase of reversion to leasehold); *Re Quibell's Will Trusts, White v Reichert* [1956] 3 All ER 679, [1957] 1 WLR 186 (bequest of shares in company to be formed after the testator's death; bequest carried shares although company was formed before death)). In *Re Gillins, Inglis v Gillins* [1909] 1 Ch 345, a gift of '25 shares' passed only shares as subdivided after the date of the will; but this case was explained as a case of a general legacy in *Re Clifford, Mallam v McFie* [1912] 1 Ch 29 at 31. See also *Re M'Afee, Mack v Quirey* [1909] 1 IR 124. In *Re Davies, Scourfield v Davies* [1925] Ch 642, a gift of the 'proceeds of such parts as have been sold' was held to refer to the parts sold at the testator's death.

A gift of the testator's land in a certain locality thus prima facie passes all the land he has in that locality at the time of his death: *Doe d York v Walker* (1844) 12 M & W 591 ('all . . . lands . . . which I am seised of . . . in the parish or lordship of Great Bowden'); *Re Ord, Dickinson v Dickinson* (1879) 12 ChD 22 at 25, CA ('my leasehold houses situate at C'); *Re Bridger, Brompton Hospital for Consumption v Lewis* [1894] 1 Ch 297 at 302, CA, per Davey LJ. The additional property may pass notwithstanding that it has been specifically devised by a codicil, if the specific devise fails: *Re Davies, Thomas v Thomas-Davies* [1928] Ch 24.

11 *Goodlad v Burnett* (1855) 1 K & J 341; *Ferguson v Ferguson* (1872) IR 6 Eq 199 ('my stock in trade and debts accruing therefrom'); *Re Ord, Dickinson v Dickinson* (1879) 12 ChD 22, CA; *Re Russell, Russell v Chell* (1882) 19 ChD 432; *Re Bancroft, Bancroft v Bancroft* [1928] Ch 577.

12 It is otherwise where the gift is not generic and the possessive pronoun then shows a contrary intention: *Re Sikes, Moxon v Crossley* [1927] 1 Ch 364 ('my piano'). Such a possessive adjective may be an indication that the gift is not generic: see *Goodlad v Burnett* (1855) 1 K & J 341 at 348–349; and note 17.

13 *Doe d York v Walker* (1844) 12 M & W 591; *Re Horton, Lloyd v Hatchett* [1920] 2 Ch 1 (copyholds 'now held by me'); *Re Davies, Scourfield v Davies* [1925] Ch 642; *Re Fleming's Will Trusts, Ennion v Hampstead Old People's Housing Trust Ltd* [1974] 3 All ER 323, [1974] 1 WLR 1552 (where a devise of 'my leasehold house' was held to carry a freehold interest acquired after the date of the will). Cf *Re Fowler, Fowler v Wittingham* (1915) 139 LT Jo 183 (where a devise of 'my house and land known as [R] wherein I now reside' was held to include adjoining fields bought at the same time as the house and let to tenants, but not adjoining land bought after the date of the will).

14 *Cole v Scott* (1849) 1 Mac & G 518 (where, however, the testator distinguished certain property which should be vested in him at his death). See also *A-G v Bury* (1701) 1 Eq Cas Abr 201; *Hutchinson v Barrow* (1861) 6 H & N 583; *Williams v Owen* (1863) 2 New Rep 585; *Re Edwards, Rowland v Edwards* (1890) 63 LT 481. As to *Cole v Scott* see *Re Farrer's Estate* (1858) 8 ICLR 370 at 377–378; and the cases cited in note 15.

15 *Wagstaff v Wagstaff* (1869) LR 8 Eq 229 ('which I now possess'). See also *Hepburn v Skirving* (1858) 4 Jur NS 651 (where it was held that 'now' must be understood to refer to the death); *Re Midland Rly Co* (1865) 34 Beav 525; *Re Ashburnham, Gaby v Ashburnham* (1912) 107 LT 601 ('all my effects at present at A'; no contrary intention). Cf *Lady Langdale v Briggs* (1856) 8 De GM & G 391 at 437 per Turner LJ; *Re Ord, Dickinson v Dickinson* (1879) 12 ChD 22, CA ('subject to the annuity now charged thereon'; no contrary intention). In *Re Champion, Dudley v Champion* [1893] 1 Ch 101 at 107–108, CA, per North J, the words 'and now in my own occupation', and in *Re Willis, Spencer v Willis* [1911] 2 Ch 563 at 568, the words 'and in which I now reside', were treated as a mere additional description of the property, and not a vital or essential part of the description cutting down the earlier words, which were read as applied to the circumstances existing at the testator's death, and, therefore, the words quoted were rejected. Similarly, in *Re Horton, Lloyd v Hatchett* [1920] 2 Ch 1, the words 'now held by me' were treated as mere additional description, not cutting down the earlier part of the devise. As to whether there is any principle on which the court may reject such words cf *Magee v Lavell* (1874) LR 9 CP 107 at 113; and PARA 267 et seq. As to the effect in general of adverbs of time in a will cf PARA 247.

16 See the description of chattels and the consequent construction problems associated with fluctuating collections in *Harwood v Harwood* [2005] EWHC 3019 (Ch), [2005] All ER (D) 121 (Nov).

17 Ie the Wills Act 1837 s 24: see the text and notes 1–6.

18 *Emuss v Smith* (1848) 2 De G & Sm 722 at 733, 736 (where 'all that my freehold estate . . . purchased of B' did not comprise a parcel of leasehold mixed with it, even though the testator subsequently bought the reversion); cf *Re Fleming's Will Trusts, Ennion v Hampstead Old People's Housing Trust Ltd* [1974] 3 All ER 323, [1974] 1 WLR 1552 (cited in note 13); *Douglas v Douglas* (1854) Kay 400 (money 'which has been charged' on certain land); *Re Gibson, Mathews v Foulsham* (1866) LR 2 Eq 669 at 672 ('my 1,000 NBR shares'); *Re Portal and Lamb* (1885) 30 ChD 50, CA ('my cottage and land'); *Cave v Harris, Harris v Cave* (1887) 57 LT 768 at 770; *Re Evans, Evans v Powell* [1909] 1 Ch 784 ('house and effects known as C Villa'); *Re Alexander, Bathurst v Greenwood* [1910] WN 94, CA. As to the ademption of specific gifts see PARAS 155–159.

283. Necessary rights and benefits follow the principal gift.

It is a rule applicable to a gift by will[1], as well as to a grant by deed[2], that all rights and benefits which are necessary and essential[3] elements in the reasonable enjoyment of the subject matter of the gift in the state in which it is given[4] are prima facie included[5]. This result does not necessarily arise from construction, but from the circumstance of necessary dependence shown by the facts of the case; and, when all surrounding circumstances which may legitimately be inquired into are known, there may be no implied gift or the extent of it may be controlled[6].

1 *Pearson v Spencer* (1863) 3 B & S 761, Ex Ch; *Phillips v Low* [1892] 1 Ch 47 at 51; *Milner's Safe Co Ltd v Great Northern and City Rly Co* [1907] 1 Ch 208 at 219. See also *Taws v Knowles* [1891] 2 QB 564, CA.
2 See DEEDS AND OTHER INSTRUMENTS vol 32 (2012) PARA 258.
3 *Palmer v Fletcher* (1663) 1 Lev 122.
4 See *Pheysey v Vicary* (1847) 16 M & W 484 (road to house not included); *Ewart v Cochrane* (1861) 4 Macq 117 at 122, HL, considered in *Moncrieff v Jamieson* [2007] UKHL 42, [2008] 4 All ER 752, [2007] 1 WLR 2620 (it seems that it may not be necessary to show that all rights, claimed as necessary for use and enjoyment of inter vivos grant of access, were actually in use at date of grant, provided they were within reasonable contemplation at the time of the grant).
5 Shep Touch (8th Edn, 1826) p 89. See also *Re Livingstone, Livingstone v Durel* (1917) 61 Sol Jo 384 ('moneys which shall arise from sale of land in Ireland' held to include bonuses paid on statutory sale). Cf DEEDS AND OTHER INSTRUMENTS vol 32 (2012) PARA 258. As to income and capital receipts see SETTLEMENTS vol 91 (2012) PARA 845 et seq.
6 *Phillips v Low* [1892] 1 Ch 47 at 50–51. See also *Birmingham, Dudley and District Banking Co v Ross* (1888) 38 ChD 295 at 308, 311, 315, CA. As to the right to accumulations of income see *Re Woolf, Public Trustee v Lazarus* [1920] 1 Ch 184 (not included); *Re Mellor, Alvarez v Dodgson* [1922] 1 Ch 312, CA (not included); *Re Blackwell, Blackwell v Blackwell* [1926] Ch 223, CA (included). As to the right to a contingent preference dividend see *Re Marjoribanks, Marjoribanks v Dansey* [1923] 2 Ch 307 (included). As to the disposal of surplus income when accumulation stops see *Re Thornber, Crabtree v Thornber* [1937] Ch 29, [1936] 2 All ER 1594, CA (surplus income dealt with as income of undisposed residuary estate); and PERPETUITIES AND ACCUMULATIONS vol 80 (2013) PARAS 160–163. As to the title to repaid income tax on accumulations during minority see *Re Fulford, Fulford v Hyslop* [1930] 1 Ch 71 (beneficiary absolutely entitled). As to the title to accretions to shares in a company see *Re Buxton, Buxton v Buxton* [1930] 1 Ch 648 (included). A gift of national savings certificates includes accretions to them as these are capitalised: *Re Holder's Will Trusts, National Provincial Bank Ltd v Holder* [1953] Ch 468, [1953] 2 All ER 1.

284. General description of property.

A description of property of any kind in a general manner such as 'land', 'personal estate', and the like, not identifying any particular item of such property, prima facie[1] includes all interest, legal or equitable[2], vested or contingent[3], in possession, reversion, remainder or expectancy[4], in property of that kind[5], capable of being so disposed of[6] by the testator's will[7]. Prima facie, general descriptions of property are construed in their general sense[8], but are capable of being controlled by the context, for example under the ejusdem generis rule[9] and, perhaps, by the usage of the testator[10]. The terms 'legacy' and 'bequest' in their ordinary sense are used of a gift of money or a chattel[11], but with a proper controlling context are capable of meaning a devise of land[12]. As a matter of construction, an annuity may be included in the term 'legacy'[13]. The term 'belongings' is not, without more, apt to describe real property[14].

A description of property which in its usual sense is apt to include kinds of property of both a real and personal nature is not restricted to real estate only, or to personal estate only, by reason that the limitations are more applicable to that particular kind of property, or are even inapplicable to any but that particular kind of property[15], although this is an indication to be considered in connection with the whole context[16].

A general description of chattels which is made the subject of a gift for life and other interests in succession may not include consumable chattels or livestock if, on the true construction of the will, the testator evinces an intention only to dispose of chattels having a permanent existence[17].

1   For an example of a contrary intention shown by the will taken as a whole see *Teatt v Strong* (1760) 3 Bro Parl Cas 219, HL. The contrary intention must amount to an intention to exclude such interests, as distinct from an absence of the intention to include them: *Doe d Lord and Lady Cholmondeley v Weatherby* (1809) 11 East 322 at 333; *Doe d Pell v Jeyes* (1830) 1 B & Ad 593 at 600; *Doe d Howell v Thomas* (1840) 1 Man & G 335 at 344.
2   Thus a general devise of the testator's land, or land in a particular locality, includes land contracted to be purchased and not actually conveyed to him (*Greenhill v Greenhill* (1711) 2 Vern 679; *Atcherley v Vernon* (1723) 10 Mod Rep 518; *Holmes v Barker* (1816) 2 Madd 462), and an option to purchase the testator's land includes land contracted to be purchased but not actually conveyed to him (*Re Fison's Will Trusts, Fison v Fison* [1950] Ch 394, [1950] 1 All ER 501). As to other general descriptions of property see *Collison v Girling* (1838) 4 My & Cr 63 at 75 (consols); *Re Stevens, Stevens v Keily* [1888] WN 110 ('my estate share and interest' in a business). A description of stock of, or to, which the testator may 'be possessed or entitled' at his death does not ordinarily include stock purchased on his instructions, but after his death: *Thomas v Thomas* (1859) 27 Beav 537.
3   *Ingilby v Amcotts* (1856) 21 Beav 585.
4   *Wheeler v Walroone* (1647) Aleyn 28; *Ridout v Pain* (1747) 3 Atk 486 at 492; *Re Egan, Mills v Penton* [1899] 1 Ch 688 ('money in my possession' passed reversionary interest; but cf *Re Lucas-Tooth, Lucas-Tooth v Public Trustee* (1923) 156 LT Jo 382 ('die possessed of' is inapplicable to a reversionary aliquot interest in stocks and shares)). See also *Church v Mundy* (1808) 15 Ves 396; *Doe d Howell v Thomas* (1840) 1 Man & G 335; *Tennent v Tennent* (1844) 1 Jo & Lat 379 at 389 (where the fact that property was limited to the same uses as the land under the uses of which the testator's interest arose was not sufficient to exclude that interest); *Alliston v Chapple* (1860) 6 Jur NS 288 (remainder in specific real estate given by the same will). Similarly, an unsettled reversion in settled land passes under a gift of 'lands not settled' (*Cook v Garrard* (1668) 1 Lev 212; *Chester v Chester* (1730) 3 P Wms 56; *Glover v Spendlove* (1793) 4 Bro CC 337; *A-G v Vigor* (1803) 8 Ves 256; *Jones v Skinner* (1835) 5 LJ Ch 87; *Incorporated Society in Dublin v Richards* (1841) 1 Dr & War 258), and 'property not included in' a certain settlement may include an absolute interest under an ultimate trust in that settlement (*O'Reilly v Smith* (1851) 17 LTOS 280; *Re Green, Walsh v Green* (1893) 31 LR Ir 338). Expressions of this kind, however, are ambiguous and capable of meaning either the land not comprised in the settlement, or so much of the land in settlement as is not subject to the trusts of the settlement: *Ford v Ford* (1848) 6 Hare 486 at 494; *Incorporated Society in Dublin v Richards* above at 280–281. See also *Goodtitle d Daniel v Miles* (1805) 6 East 494; *Re Mather, Mather v Mather* [1927] WN 13.
5   As to mortgages and leasehold interests with regard to a gift of 'land' see further PARA 291; and as to growing crops see PARA 291. A devise of real estate may not include charges thereon to which the testator was entitled: *Davy v Redington* [1917] 1 IR 250, Ir CA. In *Re Shepherd, Mitchell v Loram* (1914) 58 Sol Jo 304, a gift and bequest of 'all' was held to include real estate.
6   As to the exercise of an after-acquired power see TRUSTS AND POWERS vol 98 (2013) PARAS 582, 592.
7   A different rule applies where the question is whether the testator is purporting to dispose of the property of another so as to bring the doctrine of election into play. In such a case the intention to dispose of the property of the other person must appear clearly and distinctly, and general words will not usually be construed to include such property: see eg *Re Mengel's Will Trusts, Westminster Bank Ltd v Mengel* [1962] Ch 791, [1962] 2 All ER 490 (where a bequest of 'all the remainder of my property' did not extend to anything which was not the testator's property). See also *Frear v Frear* [2008] EWCA Civ 1320, [2009] 2 FCR 727, [2009] 1 FLR 391 where the issue

arose as to the purported disposal of her house by the testatrix; the Court of Appeal agreed with the judge's finding that the will raised the doctrine of election, but not with his reasoning as to the affected quantum. See EQUITABLE JURISDICTION vol 47 (2014) PARA 161.

8   See PARA 241. See also *Re Masson, Morton v Masson* (1917) 86 LJ Ch 753, 61 Sol Jo 676, CA (long list of household effects and chattels did not extend to stamp collection held apart at bank).

9   As to the ejusdem generis rule see PARA 250.

10 See *Re Van Lessen, National Provincial Bank Ltd v Beamont* [1955] 3 All ER 691, [1955] 1 WLR 1326 (experienced philatelist used expression '. . . stamps of British Colonies . . .'; evidence was given that philatelists would understand the term 'collection of British Colonies' in a wider sense than in general usage; held that the testator had used the language of philatelists and the wider meaning applied).

11 *Windus v Windus* (1856) 6 De GM & G 549; *Ward v Grey* (1859) 26 Beav 485 at 494 (real estate directed to be sold included, but not real estate not to be sold); *White v Lake* (1868) LR 6 Eq 188 at 192 (proceeds of real estate not included); *Re King's Trusts* (1892) 29 LR Ir 401 at 410 (interest in realty not included). A gift of residue, however, is not a 'legacy' in the ordinary sense: *Ward v Grey* above. In *Re Kennedy, Corbould v Kennedy* [1917] 1 Ch 9, CA, a life interest in residue was held to be a bequest within a provision making bequests free of death duties.

12 *Brady v Cubitt* (1778) 1 Doug KB 31 at 40 per Lord Mansfield CJ. See also *Beckley v Newland* (1723) 2 P Wms 182 at 186 per Lord Macclesfield LC; *Hope d Brown v Taylor* (1757) 1 Burr 268; *Whicker v Hume* (1851) 14 Beav 509 at 518; *Gyett v Williams* (1862) 2 John & H 429 at 436. For cases in which the appointment of a 'residuary legatee' will give to the appointee the residuary real estate see PARA 298.

13 *Bromley v Wright* (1849) 7 Hare 334; cf *Re Feather, Harrison v Tapsell* [1945] Ch 343, [1945] 1 All ER 552.

14 *Re Price, Wasley v Price* [1950] Ch 242, [1950] 1 All ER 338 (but see also the discussion of cases on the point).

15 Eg gifts of 'property', or of a residue of estates and effects and similar gifts (*Doe d Burkitt v Chapman* (1789) 1 Hy Bl 223; *Morgan d Surman v Surman* (1808) 1 Taunt 289; *Doe d Wall v Langlands* (1811) 14 East 370; *Thomas v Phelps* (1828) 4 Russ 348 at 351; *Ackers v Phipps* (1835) 3 Cl & Fin 665 at 691, HL; *Hunter v Pugh* (1839) 4 Jur 571; *Morrison v Hoppe* (1851) 4 De G & Sm 234; *D'Almaine v Moseley* (1853) 1 Drew 629; *Fullerton v Martin* (1853) 22 LJ Ch 893; *O'Toole v Browne* (1854) 3 E & B 572; *Re Greenwich Hospital Improvement Act* (1855) 20 Beav 458; *Streatfeild v Cooper* (1859) 27 Beav 338; *Hamilton v Buckmaster* (1866) LR 3 Eq 323; *Stein v Ritherdon* (1868) 37 LJ Ch 369 at 371; *Lloyd v Lloyd* (1869) LR 7 Eq 458; *Cameron v Harper* (1892) 21 SCR 273; *Kirby-Smith v Parnell* [1903] 1 Ch 483); or land with its appurtenances where leasehold land was blended in enjoyment with freehold (*Hobson v Blackburn* (1833) 1 My & K 571); or other gifts where the will shows that the testator had other kinds of property present to his mind and the trusts can be applied to such portion of the blended property as is capable of being so taken (*Saumarez v Saumarez* (1839) 4 My & Cr 331; explained in *Stokes v Salomons* (1851) 9 Hare 75 at 83). In *Re Fetherston-Haugh-Whitney's Estate* [1924] 1 IR 153, Ir CA, 'property' was restricted in the context to personal estate. Gifts to trustees took effect subject to resulting trusts as to parts of the property in *Dunnage v White* (1820) 1 Jac & W 583 and *Longley v Longley* (1871) LR 13 Eq 133.

16 *Fullerton v Martin* (1853) 22 LJ Ch 893; *Prescott v Barker* (1874) 9 Ch App 174; *Kirby-Smith v Parnell* [1903] 1 Ch 483. See also *Newland v Marjoribanks* (1813) 5 Taunt 268; *Doe d Hurrell v Hurrell* (1821) 5 B & Ald 18; *Coard v Holderness* (1855) 20 Beav 147; *Doe d Spearing v Buckner* (1796) 6 Term Rep 610 (which was doubted in *Fullerton v Martin* above); *Pogson v Thomas* (1840) 6 Bing NC 337 (which was doubted in *Stein v Ritherdon* (1868) 37 LJ Ch 369). Such indications, however, become of less weight where there is a direction for sale and distribution: *Dobson v Bowness* (1868) LR 5 Eq 404 at 408. See also *O'Toole v Browne* (1854) 3 E & B 572; *Streatfeild v Cooper* (1859) 27 Beav 338.

17 *Porter v Tournay* (1797) 3 Ves 311 at 313; *Sealy v Stawell* (1868) IR 2 Eq 326 at 348; *Re Moir's Estate, Moir v Warner* [1882] WN 139 (heirlooms). See also PARA 122.

(ii) Effect of Description by Locality

285. Property included in a description of property by its locality. A description of property by its locality[1] does not in general include property in any other locality at the testator's death[2], unless the restriction to that locality is to be rejected on the principle of 'falsa demonstratio non nocet'[3]. There may be difficulties where a house, farm or other land is described by name, in ascertaining the precise limits of what is intended to be given, particularly where the testator has made the gift out of a larger parcel; such difficulties will usually allow recourse to extrinsic evidence[4]. If, however, the property described is movable, the intention is inferred, unless the context is to the contrary[5], that the gift includes property which is usually in that situation and has been removed merely temporarily[6], or of necessity for its preservation[7], or, it seems, wrongly[8], but not in general property otherwise removed for an indefinite length of time[9] or permanently[10]. Further, as choses (or things) in action are not considered as absolutely localised[11], a general description of property in a certain locality prima facie[12] does not include any choses in action due, payable or recoverable there, or represented by documents, other than Bank of England notes or other notes treated as cash[13], which are kept there[14], unless the locality is a place where such documents are usually kept[15]. A description of chattels in a certain receptacle does not ordinarily include articles in that specified place which are mere accessories to any things in another place[16], but may include such sum of money[17] as may ordinarily be found there[18].

1   A restriction to a locality in the light of the context only applied to part of the gift in *Norris v Norris* (1846) 2 Coll 719; *Domvile v Taylor* (1863) 32 Beav 604. A gift of 'the contents' of a leasehold residence ordinarily includes everything which could, as between landlord and tenant, be removed by the testator from the house: *Re Oppenheim, Oppenheim v Oppenheim* (1914) 111 LT 937.

2   *Earl of Shaftesbury v Countess of Shaftesbury* (1716) 2 Vern 747; *Green v Symonds* (1730) 1 Bro CC 129n; *Heseltine v Heseltine* (1818) 3 Madd 276; *Colleton v Garth* (1833) 6 Sim 19; *Houlding v Cross* (1855) 1 Jur NS 250; *Spencer v Spencer* (1856) 21 Beav 548; *Blagrove v Coore* (1859) 27 Beav 138; *Wilkins v Jodrell* (1863) 11 WR 588. This holds good even if the property is acquired, or brought to that locality, after the date of the will: see *Gayre v Gayre* (1705) 2 Vern 538; *Sayer v Sayer* (1714) 2 Vern 688. For examples as to real estate see PARA 271 note 7. Goods in transit to the named locality do not pass (*Duke of Beaufort v Lord Dundonald* (1716) 2 Vern 739; *Lord Brooke v Earl of Warwick* (1848) 2 De G & Sm 425; *Lane v Sewell* (1874) 43 LJ Ch 378), but in *Lord Brooke v Earl of Warwick* pictures temporarily away from the mansion for cleaning passed.

3   Ie a false description does not vitiate when there is no doubt as to the subject meant. See *Land v Devaynes* (1794) 4 Bro CC 537; *Norreys v Franks* (1875) IR 9 Eq 18 at 34; *Re Brimble, Brimble v Brimble* (1918) 144 LT Jo 217. As to the principle of 'falsa demonstratio non nocet' see PARA 269.

4   See eg *Sandover v Brown* [2004] EWHC 1307 (Ch), [2004] All ER (D) 53 (May) (gift of 'my freehold land known as 'L'; testatrix owned large parcel of land, known as 'L' enclosing smaller parcels comprising a bungalow (also known as 'L') with garden and a separate field; held that the bungalow, garden and adjacent field only comprised the gift). See also *Barclays Bank Trust Co Ltd v Csoti* [2004] EWHC 2769 (Ch), [2004] All ER (D) 88 (Oct) (gift of 'my house' where testator owned large piece of land on which he had erected two houses; construed as only the house occupied by testator before his death).

5   *Re Earl of Stamford, Hall v Lambert* (1906) 22 TLR 632, CA.

6   *Lord Brooke v Earl of Warwick* (1848) 2 De G & Sm 425; *Spencer v Spencer* (1856) 21 Beav 548 at 549; *Bruce v Curzon Howe* (1870) 19 WR 116; *Rawlinson v Rawlinson* (1876) 34 LT 848; *Re Lea, Wells v Holt* (1911) 104 LT 253.

7   *Chapman v Hart* (1749) 1 Ves Sen 271 at 273 (goods in a ship; original situation was temporary and precarious); *Moore v Moore* (1781) 1 Bro CC 127 at 129; *Re Johnston, Cockerell v Earl of Essex* (1884) 26 ChD 538 at 553–554; *Re Baxendale, Baxendale v Baxendale* (1919) 148 LT Jo 139 (plate at bank for safety).

8   *Earl of Shaftesbury v Countess of Shaftesbury* (1716) 2 Vern 747 at 748.

9   *Re Baroness Zouche, Dugdale v Baroness Zouche* [1919] 2 Ch 178; *Re Heilbronner, Nathan v Kenny* [1953] 2 All ER 1016, [1953] 1 WLR 1254.

10   Except in such cases as are referred to in notes 7–8, permanent removal adeems the gift (*Green v Symonds* (1730) 1 Bro CC 129n; and see the cases cited in note 2), even if unknown to the testator, but made by an authorised agent (*Earl of Shaftesbury v Countess of Shaftesbury* (1716) 2 Vern 747). As to the meaning of the 'contents' of a house see PARA 296.

11   See CHOSES IN ACTION vol 13 (2009) PARA 2.

12 For cases where sufficient intention to the contrary was shown see *Scorey v Harrison* (1852) 16 Jur 1130; *Earl of Tyrone v Marquis of Waterford* (1860) 1 De GF & J 613; *Guthrie v Walrond* (1883) 22 ChD 573; *Re Prater, Desinge v Beare* (1888) 37 ChD 481, CA ('half of my property at R's bank'); *Re Robson, Robson v Hamilton* [1891] 2 Ch 559; *Re Clark, McKecknie v Clark* [1904] 1 Ch 294 (where of two localities, that of the bond debtor and that of the certificate, the latter was preferred); *Young v Bain, Re Young* (1902) 21 NZLR 503. See also *Re Dorman* [1994] 1 All ER 804, [1994] 1 WLR 282 (specific legacies were given from a particular named deposit account; person having enduring power of attorney, without knowledge of will, closed account and transferred funds into another; held that the will reference to the original account was effectively to a fund and the change was in name and form only, not in substance; the new account was subject to the specific gifts).

13 *Popham v Lady Aylesbury* (1748) Amb 68; *Brooke v Turner* (1836) 7 Sim 671; *Mahony v Donovan* (1863) 14 I Ch R 262 at 388, Ir CA. See also *Re Robson, Robson v Hamilton* [1891] 2 Ch 559 at 560. As to gifts of money see further PARA 293.

14 *Chapman v Hart* (1749) 1 Ves Sen 271; *Moore v Moore* (1781) 1 Bro CC 127 (bond); *Jones v Lord Sefton* (1798) 4 Ves 166; *Nisbett v Murray, Murray v Nisbett* (1799) 5 Ves 149; *Fleming v Brook* (1804) 1 Sch & Lef 318 (where the rule was adhered to in spite of an exception of a specified chose in action); *Stuart v Marquis of Bute* (1806) 11 Ves 657 at 662; *Brooke v Turner* (1836) 7 Sim 671 (promissory notes and mortgage); *Marquis of Hertford v Lord Lowther* (1843) 7 Beav 1; *Rhodes v Rhodes* (1874) 22 WR 835; *Thorne v Thorne* (1903) 33 SCR 309; *Lazarus v Lazarus* (1919) 88 LJ Ch 525, CA (bearer bonds, certificates and share scrip). In *Re O'Brien, O'Brien v O'Brien* [1906] 1 IR 649, Ir CA, an intention excluding even a sum of cash was found in the will.

15 Eg a bureau, desk, box or bank where documents and money are usually kept: *Roberts v Kuffin* (1741) 2 Atk 112; *Re Robson, Robson v Hamilton* [1891] 2 Ch 559, followed in *Speaker's Executor v Spicker* 1969 SLT (Notes) 7, Ct of Sess (where a gift of a bureau and contents passed money in it also, there being nothing to suggest that the testator meant to distinguish between the different types of property). A gift of a 'box' or other receptacle does not ordinarily include securities which it contains: *Re Hunter, Northey v Northey* (1908) 25 TLR 19; *Joseph v Phillips* [1934] AC 348, PC (where a gift of 'personal effects, including desk with contents' was held not to include pass books and promissory notes in the desk). See also *McAfee v Kerr* (1918) 52 ILT 178. As to a bequest of the contents of a room see *Re Neilson, Cumming v Clyde* (1929) 73 Sol Jo 765.

16 Eg title deeds or the key to another receptacle: *Brooke v Turner* (1836) 7 Sim 671 at 681; *Re Robson, Robson v Hamilton* [1891] 2 Ch 559 at 565; *Re Craven, Crewdson v Craven* (1908) 99 LT 390 (affd (1909) 100 LT 284, CA) (gift of a house and its contents; bonds and securities were excluded). See also *McAfee v Kerr* (1918) 52 ILT 178. As to the general rule as to accessories see PARA 283.

17 *Swinfen v Swinfen (No 4)* (1860) 29 Beav 207.

18 *Chapman v Hart* (1749) 1 Ves Sen 271 at 273 per Lord Hardwicke LC ('if not an extraordinary sum, and just received').

(iii) Effect of Particular Words

286. Meaning of 'appurtenances', 'appertaining' etc. Land does not pass under the word 'appurtenances' used with reference to other land and in its strict technical sense, but it does pass if it appears that a wider sense was intended to be given to the word[1], as in the case of a gift of 'land appertaining' to other land[2]. It may be easier to argue for a wider meaning where the 'land appurtaining' falls within the curtilage of the principal piece of land devised[3]. Choses (or things) in action do not ordinarily pass as appertaining to other property[4].

1 *Buck d Whalley v Nurton* (1797) 1 Bos & P 53 at 57.

2 In the following cases land was held to pass under 'appurtenances' in a gift of a house with its appurtenances, or under a gift of a house simply, with a suitable context: *Hardwood and Higham's Case* (1586) Godb 40; *Boocher v Samford* (1588) Cro Eliz 113; *Gennings v Lake* (1629) Cro Car 168 at 169 (Crown grant); *Blackborn v Edgley* (1719) 1 P Wms 600 at 603; *Doe d Lempriere v Martin* (1777) 2 Wm Bl 1148 (copyhold land held for a different term); *Ongley v Chambers* (1824) 8 Moore CP 665; *Hobson v Blackburn* (1833) 1 My & K 571 (leaseholds blended in enjoyment with freeholds); *Leach v Leach* [1878] WN 79; *Cuthbert v Robinson* (1882) 51 LJ Ch 238 (charge of legacies and devise to trustees considered material).

In the following cases land was held not to pass under 'appurtenances': *Bettisworth's Case* (1580) 2 Co Rep 31b at 32a; *Yates v Clincard* (1599) Cro Eliz 704 (devise of copyhold house with the appurtenances where the land in question was freehold); *Hearn v Allen* (1627) Cro Car 57; *Smith v Ridgway* (1866) LR 1 Exch 331, Ex Ch. See also *Hill v Grange* (1556) 1 Plowd 164 at 170; *Doe d Renow v Ashley* (1847) 10 QB 663; *Pheysey v Vicary* (1847) 16 M & W 484 at 494 (where a means of access was held on the facts not to be a way of necessity and not to pass under 'land and appurtenances'); *Evans v Angell* (1858) 26 Beav 202; *Lister v Pickford* (1865) 34 Beav 576. In some of these cases it was said that the land would have passed if the words had been 'with the land appertaining'.

3   See *Methuen-Campbell v Walters* [1979] QB 525, [1979] 1 All ER 606 (although an authority on statutory leasehold enfranchisement, the Court of Appeal examined the meanings of 'appurtenance' and 'appurtaining' extensively: see in particular Buckley LJ at 542 and 620 for this and analysis of 'curtilage' in different contexts). For extensive discussion of the meaning of 'curtilage' see *Sumption v Greenwich London Borough Council* [2007] EWHC 2776 (Admin), [2008] 1 P & CR 336, [2007] All ER (D) 482 (Nov).

4   *Finch v Finch* (1876) 35 LT 235 (where 'appurtenances' of a factory did not include outstanding loans); *Re McCalmont, Rooper v McCalmont* (1903) 19 TLR 490. As to descriptions by locality cf PARA 285.

287. Meaning of 'business'. A bequest of a testator's 'business' or of his share in a business[1] prima facie includes his interest in all the assets, including such interest in the land on which it is carried on as forms part of those assets[2]; but in the context or circumstances it may comprise or exclude various items, such as book debts[3], bank balances[4], the stock in trade[5] or the land on which it is carried on[6], or may be extended to property not part of the assets[7]. A direction to trustees to carry on a business entitles them to carry on business in the premises which the testator was accustomed to use, and a bequest of a business in a suitable context may include the premises where it was carried on[8]. A bequest of goodwill together with specified corporeal assets does not, however, in the absence of a strong indication to the contrary, include freehold premises in which the business is carried on, and a bequest of debts due in respect of the business prima facie carries only debts due from trade debtors, and does not include a credit balance in the account of the business at a bank[9]. 'Business' may include a profession[10].

It is a question of construction of the words of the will whether a bequest of a business subjects the legatee to the obligation to discharge the trade liabilities out of the assets[11], or is free of such an obligation so that the trade liabilities are borne by the testator's residuary estate[12].

1   See *Re Barfield, Goodman v Child* (1901) 84 LT 28 (where, in the circumstances, undrawn profits were included); *Re Lawes-Wittewronge, Maurice v Bennett* [1915] 1 Ch 408 ('one-fifth share of net profits'; one-fifth of shares included but not one-fifth of debentures also held by testator).

2   *Re Rhagg, Easten v Boyd* [1938] Ch 828, [1938] 3 All ER 314. See also *Rogers v Rogers* (1910) 11 SRNSW 38; *Re White, McCann v Hall* [1958] Ch 762, [1958] 1 All ER 379; *Mandeville v Duncan* 1965 SLT 246, Ct of Sess. As to the power of an executor to carry on the testator's business see PARA 1035 et seq.

3   *Stuart v Marquis of Bute* (1806) 11 Ves 657 (on appeal (1813) 1 Dow 73, HL); *Delany v Delany* (1885) 15 LR Ir 55 (explained in *Re Barfield, Goodman v Child* (1901) 84 LT 28). See also *Re Beard, Simpson v Beard* (1888) 57 LJ Ch 887; *Re Deller's Estate, Warman v Greenwood* [1888] WN 62; *Re Stevens, Stevens v Keily* [1888] WN 110 at 116; *Re Hawkins, Hawkins v Argent* (1913) 109 LT 969.

4   *Re Haigh, Haigh v Haigh* (1907) 51 Sol Jo 343 (not included); *Re Hawkins, Hawkins v Argent* (1913) 109 LT 969 (included); *Re Beecham, Woolley v Beecham* (1919) 63 Sol Jo 430 (included).

5   *Blake v Shaw* (1860) John 732 (gift of 'plant and goodwill'; stock in trade excluded); *Delany v Delany* (1885) 15 LR Ir 55 (stock in trade excluded).

6   *Blake v Shaw* (1860) John 732 (interest in land of no value apart from business); *Re Henton, Henton v Henton* (1882) 30 WR 702 (freehold shop excluded); *Re Hawkins, Hawkins v Argent* (1913) 109 LT 969 (house included).

7   *Bevan v A-G* (1863) 4 Giff 361 (debt of partner included); *Re Barfield, Goodman v Child* (1901) 84 LT 28 (share of capital and undrawn profits included); *Re England, England v Bayles* [1906] VLR 94 ('goodwill' meant provision in articles for testator's family).

8 *Hall v Fennell* (1875) IR 9 Eq 615 at 618; *Devitt v Kearney* (1883) 13 LR Ir 45, Ir CA. See also
   Re Martin, Martin v Martin [1892] WN 120 ('rents and profits' of business). A trustee or personal
   representative must account for a new lease which he acquires for the purposes of a business
   bequeathed by the will: *Re Jarvis, Edge v Jarvis* [1958] 2 All ER 336, [1958] 1 WLR 815; and see
   PARA 657; TRUSTS AND POWERS vol 98 (2013) PARA 693.
9 *Re Betts, Burrell v Betts* [1949] 1 All ER 568.
10 *Re Williams' Will Trusts, Chartered Bank of India, Australia and China v Williams* [1953] Ch
   138, [1953] 1 All ER 536 (medical practice). See also PARA 246 note 2.
11 *Re White, McCann v Hull* [1958] Ch 762 at 773, [1958] 1 All ER 379 at 385 per Wynn-Parry J,
   who held the case was one where the business should be regarded as an entity and the substance
   of the bequest as the assets of the business subject to its liabilities (applying dicta in *Re Rhagg,
   Easten v Boyd* [1938] Ch 828 at 836, [1938] 3 All ER 314 at 319).
12 See *Re Timberlake, Archer v Timberlake* (1919) 63 Sol Jo 286; and see the declaration made by
   Farwell J in *Re Harland-Peck, Hercy v Mayglothing* as cited in [1941] Ch 182 at 183, [1940]
   4 All ER 347 at 352, CA. Where a testator's share in real estate forming part of the assets of a
   partnership is devised by him separately from the rest of his interest in the partnership property,
   the devisee prima facie takes the share free from liability for the partnership debts as between the
   beneficiaries, if the other partnership property is sufficient to meet the debts: *Re Holland, Bretell
   v Holland* [1907] 2 Ch 88 (distinguishing *Farquhar v Hadden* (1871) 7 Ch App 1 (where the
   partnership was insolvent)).

288. Meaning of 'effects', 'personal estate', 'goods' etc. A gift of the
testator's 'effects'[1] without a context sufficient to control it may include the whole
of the testator's personal estate where that property is not otherwise disposed of
by the will[2], and is prima facie confined to personal estate[3] unless an inference to
the contrary arises from the context, in which case even real estate may be
comprised in the term[4]. The term may also by the context[5] be restricted to
particular kinds of personal estate[6]. Thus, in a gift of a house with its furniture
and a class of articles which tend to the beneficial occupation and enjoyment of
the house, ending with 'all other effects', the term may, by the ejusdem generis
rule[7], be restricted to other articles of that nature[8]; and 'effects' is often used in a
restricted sense, meaning goods and movables[9], a sense especially applicable
where other parts of the personal estate are separately disposed of[10], or where
there is a subsequent residuary gift of personal estate[11].

'Personal effects' generally means physical chattels having some personal
connection with the testator, such as articles of personal or domestic use or
ornament, clothing and furniture, and so forth, but not money or securities for
money[12]. The expressions 'personal estate', 'personal estate and effects' and
'personal property' are prima facie confined to personal estate in the legal sense[13],
but may, in the context or circumstances, include realty[14]. A gift of 'any other
personal property' may be seen as a residuary gift of personal estate[15] and the
expression 'personal chattels' has been given a wide construction in many cases[16].

In the case of a testator who dies between 1 January 1926 and 31 December
1996 inclusive, personal property in the legal sense includes, by reason of the
doctrine of conversion, land held by trustees subject to a trust for sale, and a share
in the proceeds of sale of land held on trust for sale, but does not include, by
reason of the doctrine of reconversion, personalty held on trust for sale for
investment in land[17]. However, in relation to the wills of testators who die on or
after 1 January 1997, personal property in the legal sense will not include land
held by trustees subject to a trust for sale (except where the trust for sale was
created by the will of a testator who died before 1 January 1997), but will include
personal property subject to a trust for sale in order that the trustees may acquire
land (except where the trust for sale was created by the will of a testator who died
before 1 January 1997)[18]. Where land is subject to a trust for sale which was

created by the will of a testator who died before 1 January 1997, the land or a share in the proceeds of sale of the same will pass under a gift of personal property.

A gift of 'goods' or 'goods and chattels' is prima facie sufficient to include the whole personal estate[19], but may be restricted under the ejusdem generis rule or otherwise[20]. 'Belongings' is capable of carrying the whole of the testator's residuary personalty, but is not an apt expression in relation to realty[21], and it may by its context have a more restricted meaning[22].

1   As to the meaning of 'household effects' see PARA 296.
2   *Hodgson v Jex* (1876) 2 ChD 122. See also *Campbell v Prescott* (1808) 15 Ves 500 at 507; *Michell v Michell* (1820) 5 Madd 69 at 71; *Parker v Marchant* (1842) 1 Y & C Ch Cas 290 at 303; *Malone v Malone* [1925] 1 IR 140, Ir CA ('and effects of every kind'); *Re Fitzpatrick, Deane v De Valera* (1934) 78 Sol Jo 735.
3   *Cave v Cave* (1762) 2 Eden 139; *Camfield v Gilbert* (1803) 3 East 516; *Doe d Hick v Dring* (1814) 2 M & S 448; *Henderson v Farbridge* (1826) 1 Russ 479; *Doe d Haw v Earles* (1846) 15 M & W 450; *Hall v Hall* [1892] 1 Ch 361 at 365, CA, per Lindley LJ (approving Hawkins on Wills (1st Edn) 55). See also *Vertannes v Robinson* (1927) LR 54 Ind App 276, PC. Cf *Smyth v Smyth* (1878) 8 ChD 561 at 564–566 (where Malins V-C dissented from *Camfield v Gilbert* above and *Doe d Hick v Dring* above).
4   *Hogan v Jackson* (1775) 1 Cowp 299 (devise of residue of testator's 'effects, both real and personal') (affd (1776) 3 Bro Parl Cas 388), followed in *Lord Torrington v Bowman* (1852) 22 LJ Ch 236; *Doe d Chillcott v White* (1800) 1 East 33 (after devise of goods and land to A, power to give whatever A thought proper of her 'said effects' to B and C); *Marquis of Tichfield v Horncastle* (1838) 2 Jur 610 (effects defined by references elsewhere in the will to 'real estate' and 'property'); *Milsome v Long* (1857) 3 Jur NS 1073 ('stock in trade, money, book debts and effects' carried a reversion in real estate); *Phillips v Beal* (1858) 25 Beav 25 ('devise'); *Hall v Hall* [1892] 1 Ch 361, CA (intention inferred from the words 'devise', 'wheresoever situate', 'property' etc); *Re Wass, Re Clark* (1906) 95 LT 758 (meaning of 'personal estate and effects' affected by charge of debts, use of 'devise' and words of limitation).
5   *Re O'Loughlin* (1870) LR 2 P & D 102.
6   *Gibbs v Lawrence* (1860) 7 Jur NS 137; *Cross v Wilks* (1866) 35 Beav 562; *Watson v Arundel* (1876) IR 10 Eq 299; *Re Hammersley, Heasman v Hammersley* (1899) 81 LT 150.
7   As to the ejusdem generis rule see PARA 250.
8   *Gibbs v Lawrence* (1860) 7 Jur NS 137; *Campbell v M'Grain* (1875) IR 9 Eq 397; *Re Miller, Daniel v Daniel* (1889) 61 LT 365 (banknotes, securities and jewellery not included); *Re Taylor, Barber v Smith* (1919) 147 LT Jo 253 (car not included) (but see note 12); *Re Curling* [1928] IR 521.
9   *Michell v Michell* (1820) 5 Madd 69 at 72 per Leach V-C.
10   *Rawlings v Jennings* (1806) 13 Ves 39 at 46.
11   *MacPhail v Phillips* [1904] 1 IR 155.
12   *Joseph v Phillips* [1934] AC 348, PC. The express inclusion of a desk does not include articles contained in it which are not personal effects, such as pass books and promissory notes: *Joseph v Phillips* at 352–353 (distinguishing *Re Robson, Robson v Hamilton* [1891] 2 Ch 559); and see PARA 285 note 15. Prima facie the meaning of 'personal effects' is such that it would include stamp and coin collections and cars: *Re Collin's Will Trusts, Donne v Hewetson* [1971] 1 All ER 283, [1971] 1 WLR 37; see also *Re Crispin's Will Trusts, Arkwright v Thurley* [1975] Ch 245, [1974] 3 All ER 772 (clock collection). In the context, 'personal effects' may extend to the residuary personal estate: *Re Wolfe* [1919] 2 IR 491.
13   *Buchanan v Harrison* (1861) 31 LJ Ch 74; *Belaney v Belaney* (1867) 2 Ch App 138; *Ex p Yates* (1869) 20 LT 940; *Re Cook* [1948] Ch 212, [1948] 1 All ER 231 (where it was assumed that 'personal estate' was used as a term of art). See also PARA 282 note 4. As to the meaning of 'estate' see PARA 289; and as to the meaning of 'real estate' see PARA 291. As to the meaning of 'personal chattels' see the Administration of Estates Act 1925 s 55(1)(x); and PARA 488 note 4. In *Re Hey's Settlement Trusts, Hey v Nickell-Lean* [1945] Ch 294, [1945] 1 All ER 618, 'property' in the expression 'income of property actually producing income' was construed as 'property forming part of my estate'.
14   *Doe d Tofield v Tofield* (1809) 11 East 246 at 249 (property over which the testator had an absolute personal power of disposition). See also *Lines v Lines* (1869) 22 LT 400; *Cadman v Cadman* (1872) LR 13 Eq 470 at 474 (freehold rights conferred by navigation shares, if remaining realty, would pass under residuary gift of personal estate); *Re Smalley, Smalley v Smalley* (1883) 49 LT 662; *Re Wass, Re Clarke* (1906) 95 LT 758.

15 *Re Barnes's Will Trusts, Prior v Barnes* [1972] 2 All ER 639, [1972] 1 WLR 587, (the gift was seen as capable of sweeping up a lapsed specific gift of 'any money I may leave').

16 It seems that the expression 'personal chattels' may extend to such diverse objects as a motor yacht: *Re Chaplin, Royal Bank of Scotland v Chaplin* [1950] Ch 507, [1950] 2 All ER 155, and racehorses: *Re Hutchinson, Holt v Hutchinson* [1955] Ch 255, [1955] 1 All ER 689 (applying Administration of Estates Act 1925 s 55(1)(x) in an intestacy). See also *Re Crispin's Will Trusts, Arkwright v Thurley* [1975] Ch 245, [1974] 3 All ER 772. 'Personal chattels' are often expressly given the meaning given by the Administration of estates Act 1925 s 55(1)(x). The definition was amended by the Inheritance and Trustees' Powers Act 2014 s 3(1): see PARA 489 note 4. Unless the will provides otherwise, the amended definition applies where the will was made on or after 1 October 2014: see the Inheritance and Trustees' Powers Act 2014 s 3(2).

17 *Re Kempthorne, Charles v Kempthorne* [1930] 1 Ch 268, CA; *Re Newman, Slater v Newman* [1930] 2 Ch 409; *Re Cook, Beck v Grant* [1948] Ch 212, [1948] 1 All ER 231. As to the doctrines of conversion and reconversion see EQUITABLE JURISDICTION vol 47 (2014) PARA 138 et seq.

18 See the Trusts of Land and Appointment of Trustees Act 1996 ss 3, 25(5); and REAL PROPERTY AND REGISTRATION vol 87 (2012) PARAS 7, 215. Since 1 January 1997 all trusts for sale formerly imposed by statute have become trusts of land (without a duty to sell) and land formerly held on such statutorily imposed trusts for sale is now held in trust for the persons interested in the land, so that the owner of each undivided share now has an interest in land: see the Trusts of Land and Appointment of Trustees Act 1996 ss 1, 5, Sch 2 paras 2–5, 7 (amending the Law of Property Act 1925 ss 32, 34, 36 and the Administration of Estates Act 1925 s 33); and REAL PROPERTY AND REGISTRATION vol 87 (2012) PARA 105.

19 *Stuart v Marquis of Bute* (1806) 11 Ves 657 at 666; *Kendall v Kendall* (1828) 4 Russ 360 at 370; *Parker v Marchant* (1842) 1 Y & C Ch Cas 290 at 303; *Avison v Simpson* (1859) John 43; Shep Touch (8th Edn, 1826) p 447. As to the meaning of 'household goods' see PARA 296.

20 See *Lamphier v Despard* (1842) 2 Dr & War 59 (residuary gift elsewhere in will); *Manton v Tabois* (1885) 30 ChD 92 at 97.

21 *Re Mills' Will Trusts, Marriott v Mills* [1937] 1 All ER 142; *Re Price, Wasley v Price* [1950] Ch 242, [1950] 1 All ER 338 (explaining *Re Bradfield, Bradfield v Bradfield* [1914] WN 423). Cf *Re Schott's Will Trusts* (1968) 206 Estates Gazette 538 ('belongings' comprised the whole of the testatrix's real and personal estate).

22 *Re Hynes, Knapp v Hynes* [1950] 2 All ER 879, CA (particular gift, not carrying stocks and shares and bank balance).

289. Meaning of 'estate' and 'possessions'. 'Estate', as a general description of property[1], is not a technical word[2], and prima facie, when used in a suitable context, is a very wide term[3] being sufficient to include the whole real[4] and personal[5] estate. 'Possessions' has a similar meaning[6].

1 As to the effect of 'estate' in describing the testator's interest cf PARA 377 note 3. As to the meaning of 'personal estate' see PARA 288; and as to the meaning of 'real estate' see PARA 291.

2 *Basset v St Levan* (1894) 13 R 235 at 248, 250.

3 See *Hamilton Corpn v Hodsdon* (1847) 6 Moo PCC 76 at 82.

4 *Countess of Bridgwater v Duke of Bolton* (1704) 1 Salk 236; *Churchill v Dibden* (1754) 9 Sim 447n; *Jongsma v Jongsma* (1787) 1 Cox Eq Cas 362 (copyholds); *Midland Counties Rly Co v Oswin* (1844) 1 Coll 74; *Patterson v Huddart* (1853) 17 Beav 210; *Fullerton v Martin* (1853) 22 LJ Ch 893; *O'Toole v Browne* (1854) 3 E & B 572; *Meeds v Wood* (1854) 19 Beav 215; *Hawksworth v Hawksworth* (1858) 27 Beav 1; *Stein v Ritherdon* (1868) 37 LJ Ch 369. See also *Hounsell v Dunning* [1902] 1 Ch 512 at 520–521 (indications that copyholds were not included).

5 As to the effect of the context in confining 'estate' to personal estate see *Marhant v Twisden* (1711) Gilb Ch 30; *Molyneux v Rowe* (1856) 25 LJ Ch 570.

6 *Re Brigden, Chaytor v Edwin* [1938] Ch 205, [1937] 4 All ER 342. It seems that 'all my substance' also has a similar meaning: *Re Fox's Estate, Dawes v Druitt* [1937] 4 All ER 664, CA.

290. Meaning of house and buildings. Words which prima facie describe only a house or other building may, in suitable contexts and circumstances, include land necessary for the convenient use and occupation of it[1]. A gift of a house 'and premises' is prima facie sufficient to include such land[2] and the appurtenances of the house[3]. Even other land commonly enjoyed with the house may be included in such a description[4]. A gift of a house prima facie includes chattels affixed to and used for the decoration or convenience of the house[5]. A gift of 'my apartment' has been held to include the freehold reversion of the building within which the apartment is situated[6], however, a right to occupy 'my house' was given a restrictive meaning where there were questions about the extent of the use by the testator[7].

1   Co Litt 5b (garden and curtilage); *Smith v Martin* (1672) 2 Wms Saund 394; *Smith v Ridgway* (1866) LR 1 Exch 331 at 333–334, Ex Ch ('land so intimately connected with the use of the building that without it the building would be useless'). See also *Lombe v Stoughton* (1849) 18 LJ Ch 400; *Brown v Brown* (1901) 1 SRNSW Eq 218. Cf the meaning of 'house' in the Lands Clauses Consolidation Act 1845 s 92: see COMPULSORY ACQUISITION OF LAND vol 18 (2009) PARA 626.
2   *Lethbridge v Lethbridge* (1862) 4 De GF & J 35; *Re Willis, Spencer v Willis* [1911] 2 Ch 563 at 569.
3   *Re Seal, Seal v Taylor* [1894] 1 Ch 316 at 320, CA. See also *Read v Read* (1866) 15 WR 165.
4   *Blackborn v Edgley* (1719) 1 P Wms 600 at 603; *Gulliver d Jefferies v Poyntz* (1770) 2 Wm Bl 726; *Doe d Clements v Collins* (1788) 2 Term Rep 498; *Doe d Hemming v Willetts* (1849) 7 CB 709; *Ross v Veal* (1855) 1 Jur NS 751; *Hibon v Hibon* (1863) 9 Jur NS 511 (the gifts, in the last three cases cited, were of a 'house and premises'); *Mocatta v Mocatta* (1883) 49 LT 629; *Re Willis, Spencer v Willis* [1911] 2 Ch 563; *Re Fuller, Arnold v Chandler* (1915) 59 Sol Jo 304 (gift of a house and land, described as 'now in the occupation of' R, held to include separate land leased to R before the making of the will); *Barclays Bank Ltd v Zeitline* (1962) 182 Estates Gazette 291 (gift of home included garage and flat at rear of garden of house held on lease separate from but identical to lease of house). See also *Heach v Prichard* [1882] WN 140. See also *Sandover v Brown* [2004] EWHC 1307 (Ch), [2004] All ER (D) 53 (May) (testatrix's unfenced and unused land adjacent to rear garden of her house, from which she derived pleasure in watching the wildlife, was included along with the house in the description 'my freehold land L').
5   *Re Whaley, Whaley v Roehrich* [1908] 1 Ch 615.
6   *Ross v Perrin-Hughes* [2004] EWHC 2559 (Ch), 7 ITELR 405, [2004] All ER (D) 159 (Nov).
7   See *Bergliter v Cohen* [2006] EWHC 123 (Ch), [2006] All ER (D) 88 (Jan).

291. Meaning of devise of land and other general devises. A devise of the testator's land[1], or of the testator's land in any place[2] or in the occupation of any person mentioned in the will, or otherwise described in a general manner, and any other general devise[3] which would describe a leasehold estate if the testator had no freehold estate which could be described by it, must be construed to include his leasehold estates, or such of those estates or any of them to which such description extends, as the case may be, as well as freehold estates, unless a contrary intention appears by the will[4].

A devise of 'real estate'[5] may be such a general devise as is mentioned above[6], but is more readily given its technical meaning and will not generally pass leaseholds[7], although it may do so where there is no real estate[8], or where the special circumstances or the context so require[9]. Similarly, 'lands and tenements'[10], although prima facie meaning real estate, will pass leaseholds if there is no real estate[11], or if the intention to include leaseholds is clear[12].

A gift of land in a named place is capable of including incorporeal hereditaments, such as an advowson in gross[13], tithes[14] and tithe rentcharges[15], issuing out of land in that locality. A gift of land passes growing crops[16], unless the will shows a contrary intention[17]. A gift, ostensibly of land, might not extend to shares in a family company owning that land[18]. A gift of 'family property' at a named place has been held to extend to both fee simple and entailed interests in land[19].

In the case of a testator who died between 1 January 1926 and 31 December 1996 inclusive, a gift of land or real estate would not include land held on trust for sale or a share in the proceeds of sale of such land by reason of the doctrine of conversion[20], unless there is nothing else the testator could have intended[21]. However, on and after 1 January 1997 the doctrine of conversion has been abolished in respect of all trusts for sale whenever created or arising, except where the trust for sale was created by the will of a testator who died before 1 January

1997[22], so that a gift of land or real estate in the will of a testator who dies on or after 1 January 1997 will now pass land held by trustees subject to a trust for sale (except where the trust for sale was created by the will of a testator who died before 1 January 1997), or an undivided share in the proceeds of sale of land held on trust for sale (except where the trust for sale was created by the will of a testator who died before 1 January 1997); and it will also pass an undivided share in land which is not subject to a trust for sale[23]. Where land is subject to a trust for sale which was created by the will of a testator who died before 1 January 1997, the doctrine of conversion still applies so that such land or a share in the proceeds of sale of the same will not pass under a gift of land.

Formerly, money held on trust for investment in land, as to which no effective election to reconvert the property had been made[24], would ordinarily be included under a description of 'land' or 'real estate' generally[25]. However, the doctrine of reconversion whereby personal property subject to a trust for sale in order that the trustees may acquire land is to be regarded as land has been abolished in respect of all trusts for sale whenever created or arising, except where the trust for sale was created by the will of a testator who died before 1 January 1997[26], so that personal property which is held on trust for sale in order that the trustees may acquire land will not pass under a gift of land or real estate in the will of a testator who dies on or after 1 January 1997 (except where the trust for sale was created by the will of a testator who died before 1 January 1997). Where personal property is subject to a trust for sale which was created by the will of a testator who died before 1 January 1997 in order that the trustees may acquire land, the doctrine of reconversion still applies so that such property should pass under a gift of land.

A gift of a house of which the testator is described as the owner and occupier is satisfied if the testator is the owner and the house is kept ready for his occupation, even though the testator is not himself actually resident there[27].

1   In wills made before the Wills Act 1837, a devise of 'land' prima facie did not include leaseholds where there were freehold estates as to which the gift could be operative: *Rose v Bartlett* (1633) Cro Car 292 ('land and tenements'); *Davis v Gibbs* (1730) 3 P Wms 26; *Chapman v Hart* (1749) 1 Ves Sen 271; *Thompson v Lady Lawley* (1800) 2 Bos & P 303; *Swift v Swift* (1859) 1 De GF & J 160 at 170–171. Leaseholds, however, might pass under the gift, either if there were no freeholds for the gift to operate upon, or if the will showed such an intention: *Day v Trig* (1715) 1 P Wms 286; *Hartley v Hurle* (1800) 5 Ves 540; *Goodman v Edwards* (1833) 2 My & K 759; *Gully v Davis* (1870) LR 10 Eq 562. The object of the Wills Act 1837 was to shift the burden of proof to the persons who deny that in a will 'land' is meant to include leasehold estates in land: *Prescott v Barker* (1874) 9 Ch App 174 at 186.

2   *Wilson v Eden* (1850) 5 Exch 752; on appeal (1852) 16 Beav 153 (land 'at or near' W; a case where the Court of Chancery concurred with the opinions of the courts of common law whose opinions had been taken).

3   As to the purport of this phrase see *Butler v Butler* (1884) 28 ChD 66 at 72.

4   Wills Act 1837 s 26 (amended by the Statute Law (Repeals) Act 1969). See *Wilson v Eden* (1850) 5 Exch 752 (on appeal (1852) 16 Beav 153) (no restriction by addition of 'all other my real estate in the country of D'; nor by the fact that limitations were adapted to real estate only); *Prescott v Barker* (1874) 9 Ch App 174 (provisions of will inconsistent with leaseholds being included). A contrary intention may be shown, eg in a suitable context, by another gift of 'all my leasehold estate' (see *Re Guyton and Rosenberg's Contract* [1901] 2 Ch 591), or of 'all my personal estate wheresoever situated' (*Butler v Butler* (1884) 28 ChD 66); but not by a mere gift of personal estate simply, or by a specific bequest of a specified leasehold (*Re Davison, Greenwell v Davison* (1888) 58 LT 304).

5   As to the technical meaning of 'real estate', apart from the Wills Act 1837 s 26 or a controlling context see REAL PROPERTY AND REGISTRATION vol 87 (2012) PARA 2. In *Evans v Evans* (1849) 17 Sim 86, a special meaning was given to the term, and certain tithes were excluded. See also PARA 282 note 3.

6   *Moase v White* (1876) 3 ChD 763, commented on in *Butler v Butler* (1884) 28 ChD 66 at 75; *Re Davison, Greenwell v Davison* (1888) 58 LT 304; *Re Uttermare, Leeson v Foulis* [1893] WN 158. See also *Hester v Trustees, Executors and Agency Co Ltd* (1892) 18 VLR 509. As to the meaning of 'estate' see PARA 289. As to the meaning of 'personal estate' see PARA 288; and see PARA 282 note 4.

7   See *Butler v Butler* (1884) 28 ChD 66; *Prescott v Barker* (1874) 9 Ch App 174 (applicability of limitations to real estate only). See also *Smith v Baker* (1737) 1 Atk 385 at 386; *Parker v Marchant* (1843) 5 Man & G 498; *Turner v Turner* (1852) 21 LJ Ch 843 (where leasehold ground rents were not included); *Holmes v Milward* (1878) 47 LJ Ch 522.

8   *Re Holt, Holt v Holt* [1921] 2 Ch 17 (where it was held, distinguishing *Butler v Butler* (1884) 28 ChD 66, that the case was not within the Wills Act 1837 s 26; and the principle of *Rose v Bartlett* (1633) Cro Car 292 was applied). See also *Gully v Davis* (1870) LR 10 Eq 562.

9   See *Swift v Swift* (1859) 1 De GF & J 160; *Mathews v Mathews* (1867) LR 4 Eq 278; *Re Guyton and Rosenberg's Contract* [1901] 2 Ch 591 (devise of real estate passed testator's freehold and leasehold interests in the same land).

10   According to 2 Jarman on Wills (8th Edn) 1270, 'tenements' and 'hereditaments' include all real estate.

11   *Rose v Bartlett* (1633) Cro Car 292 at 293.

12   *Swift v Swift* (1859) 1 De GF & J 160.

13   *Re Hodgson, Taylor v Hodgson* [1898] 2 Ch 545. Cf, however, *Westfaling v Westfaling* (1746) 3 Atk 460 at 464; *Crompton v Jarratt* (1885) 30 ChD 298.

14   *Inchley v Robinson* (1587) 3 Leon 165.

15   *Re Lory's Will Trusts, Lambrick v Public Trustee of the Colony and Protectorate of Kenya* [1950] 1 All ER 349; but cf *West v Lawday* (1865) 11 HL Cas 375 at 386–387. As to the commutation of tithes and the general extinguishment of tithe rentcharge see ECCLESIASTICAL LAW vol 34 (2011) PARAS 978–981.

16   *Spencer's Case* (1622) Win 51.

17   A bequest of 'stock' passes growing crops as against the devisee of the land: see *Blake v Gibbs* (1825) 5 Russ 13n; *Rudge v Winnall* (1849) 12 Beav 357. See also PARA 930. It seems that a contrary intention is not shown by a mere residuary bequest of personalty: *Cooper v Woolfitt* (1857) 2 H & N 122.

18   *Re Lewis's Will Trusts, Lewis v Williams* [1984] 3 All ER 930, [1985] 1 WLR 102 (specific gift of 'my freehold farm' not capable of extending to shares comprising 75% holding in family company owning the farm).

19   See *Acheson v Russell* [1951] Ch 67 sub nom *Re Manor Farm, Kytes Hardwick* [1950] 2 All ER 572.

20   *Re Kempthorne, Charles v Kempthorne* [1930] 1 Ch 268, CA; *Re Newman, Slater v Newman* [1930] 2 Ch 409; *Re Cook, Beck v Grant* [1948] Ch 212, [1948] 1 All ER 231. As to the doctrines of conversion and reconversion see EQUITABLE JURISDICTION vol 47 (2014) PARA 138 et seq.

21   *Re Lowman, Devenish v Pester* [1895] 2 Ch 348, CA (a gift of 'land' passed the testator's share of the proceeds of sale of land); *Re Glassington, Glassington v Follett* [1906] 2 Ch 305 (a gift of 'real estate' passed the testator's share of the proceeds of sale of land).

22   See the Trusts of Land and Appointment of Trustees Act 1996 ss 3, 25(5); and REAL PROPERTY AND REGISTRATION vol 87 (2012) PARAS 7, 215. The doctrine of conversion is, however, not wholly abolished by s 3 and will still apply to eg uncompleted agreements for the sale of land.

23   On or after 1 January 1997, an undivided share in land need not subsist behind a trust for sale: see the Trusts of Land and Appointment of Trustees Act 1996 ss 1–5; and REAL PROPERTY AND REGISTRATION vol 87 (2012) PARA 103 et seq. The statutory trusts imposed by the Law of Property Act 1925 ss 34, 36 and the Administration of Estates Act 1925 s 33 are no longer trusts for sale but trusts of land (without a duty to sell): see the Trusts of Land and Appointment of Trustees Act 1996 s 5, Sch 2; and REAL PROPERTY AND REGISTRATION vol 87 (2012) PARA 105.

24   See EQUITABLE JURISDICTION vol 47 (2014) PARAS 155–160.

25   See EQUITABLE JURISDICTION vol 47 (2014) PARA 143.

26   See the Trusts of Land and Appointment of Trustees Act 1996 ss 3, 25(5). The doctrine is, however, not wholly abolished by s 3 and will still apply to eg uncompleted agreements for the purchase of land.

27   *Re Garland, Eve v Garland* [1934] Ch 620. Cf *Re Powell, Public Trustee v Bailey* (1982) 31 SASR 361, S Aust (where the gift of a residence forming the testatrix's principal place of abode at the time of her death was held to refer to her residence before she was admitted as a patient to the mental hospital where she died).

292. Meaning of 'living' of church. A gift of the 'living' of a certain church is ambiguous; it is sufficient to pass the advowson, but may be restricted to a single presentation, as where the will shows an intention that the devisee should have a benefit personal to himself and should himself be presented[1].

1   *Webb v Byng* (1856) 2 K & J 669 at 674 per Wood V-C; on appeal 8 De GM & G 633 (where the decision of the Vice-Chancellor was obiter, as on appeal it was held that he had no jurisdiction for want of parties). As to the modern restrictions on the transfer of advowsons see ECCLESIASTICAL LAW vol 34 (2011) PARA 583 et seq.

293. Meaning of 'money'. 'Money' in a will has no strict technical meaning[1]. It was formerly construed strictly as comprehending only cash under the testator's immediate control unless there was a context to extend its meaning, but it has been judicially recognised that it is a word which in popular usage has a diversity of meanings, and the rule now is that, in construing any particular will, the court must determine the meaning attached to the word by the testator without any presumption that it bears any one of its possible meanings[2]. 'Money' ordinarily includes cash and notes in hand[3], money immediately payable to the testator at call[4] and money at a bank on current or deposit account[5]. It may include money in the hands of trustees awaiting investment[6], and investments readily able to be turned into money[7]; it may also include the whole of the testator's personal estate[8], and even his real estate[9]. The fact that a specific gift comes after the gift in question may, however, prevent it from being residuary, but it is not conclusive against its being a residuary gift[10], and the fact that there is a residuary gift elsewhere in the will may rebut the inference that a gift of money is of a residuary nature[11]. 'Money' has in particular received a wide meaning where the court has been influenced by the presumption against intestacy[12].

Qualifying words may necessitate a stricter construction; thus 'ready money', in its ordinary sense, includes money on current account at a bank[13] or in the hands of an agent acting as banker[14], and money on deposit account at a bank where no notice of withdrawal is required[15]; but it does not ordinarily include money on deposit account where a substantial[16] previous notice of withdrawal is required[17] according to the usual course of business[18], or other choses (or things) in action generally[19]. Similarly, the use of the word 'cash' may have a restrictive effect[20]. 'Cash at my bankers' includes money on deposit, if that money is payable on demand, but not otherwise[21]. A wide construction is, however, permitted by the use of such terms as 'money due and owing'[22], and by the description of money by its investment situation[23].

A gift of money invested in various stocks, if a gift of the particular investments mentioned, is adeemed on a subsequent change of investment by the testator into stocks not coming within the description[24]. The ordinary meaning of 'investments', unaffected by any context, does not include money on deposit at a bank[25]; conversely, a gift of a bank deposit does not carry investments held for the testator by the bank[26].

1   *Re Cadogan, Cadogan v Palagi* (1883) 25 ChD 154 at 157 per Kay J. Its meaning is flexible: *Re Townley, Townley v Townley* (1884) 50 LT 394 at 396 per Pearson J.
2   *Perrin v Morgan* [1943] AC 399, [1943] 1 All ER 187, HL (where the earlier cases to the contrary were disapproved by the majority, but Lord Russell of Killowen (and, it seems, Lord Romer) thought that the old rule was right but had been misapplied); *Re Barnes' Will Trusts, Prior v Barnes* [1972] 2 All ER 639, [1972] 1 WLR 587. Where property not falling within the strict meaning of money is excepted from a gift of money, this is a reason for extending the meaning: *Re White* (1882) 7 PD 65; *Re Buller, Buller v Giberne* (1896) 74 LT 406.
3   *Downing v Townsend* (1755) Amb 280 at 281; *Barrett v White* (1855) 1 Jur NS 652 at 653; *Re Windsor, Public Trustee v Windsor* (1913) 108 LT 947 (where money orders were treated as 'cash').

4   *Byrom v Brandreth* (1873) LR 16 Eq 475 at 479; *Re Friedman, Friedman v Friedman*
    (1908) 8 SRNSW 127.
5   *Manning v Purcell* (1855) 7 De GM & G 55 at 64, 67 (followed in *Re Collings, Jones v Collings*
    [1933] Ch 920); *Harper's Trustee v Bain* (1903) 5 F 716 (money on deposit for four years included
    in 'moneys . . . in any . . . banks'); *Re Glendinning, Steel v Glendinning* (1918) 88 LJ Ch 87 ('all
    my moneys at the bank'); *Perrin v Morgan* [1943] AC 399 at 421, [1943] 1 All ER 187 at 198,
    HL, per Lord Romer; *Re Trundle, Emanuel v Trundle* [1961] 1 All ER 103, [1960] 1 WLR 1388.
    Cf *Masson v Smellie* (1903) 6 F 148 (where 'money in banks' did not pass an unpaid legacy which
    was in fact in a bank); *Re Boorer, Boorer v Boorer* [1908] WN 189 ('cash at bankers'); *Re
    Lowe's Estate, Swann v Rockley* [1938] 2 All ER 774 (where money in which the testator had an
    interest, but which stood to an account over which he had no control, did not pass); *Re Stonham,
    Lloyds Bank Ltd v Maynard* [1963] 1 All ER 377, [1963] 1 WLR 238 (where 'cash in X Bank' was
    in the context held to include money on both current and deposit accounts). 'Money on my current
    account' may pass money on deposit account, where the testator has never had a current account
    (*Re Vear, Vear v Vear* (1917) 62 Sol Jo 159), but money 'to my account' has been held to mean
    money on current account, and not to include money in the hands of trustees (*Re Bradfield,
    Bradfield v Bradfield* [1914] WN 423).
6   *Ogle v Knipe* (1869) LR 8 Eq 434.
7   Eg stock was included in 'money' in the wills considered in *Lynn v Kerridge* (1737) West *temp*
    Hard 172; *Waite v Combes* (1852) 5 De G & Sm 676; *Newman v Newman* (1858) 26 Beav 218;
    Chapman v Reynolds (1860) 28 Beav 221 (where the fact that the state of the property of the
    testatrix rendered it impossible that after payment of debts the bequest could have anything except
    government stock to operate on was considered a reason for extending the meaning); *Hart v
    Hernandez* (1885) 52 LT 217; *Re Smith, Henderson-Roe v Hitchins* (1889) 42 ChD 302 at 303;
    Re Adkins, Solomon v Catchpole (1908) 98 LT 667 (consols). Shares were included in *Re Dutton,
    Herbert v Harrison* (1869) 20 LT 386. In *Lloyd v Lloyd* (1886) 54 LT 841, rents and a bond which
    would naturally come to the executors as money passed. In *O'Connor v O'Connor* [1911] 1 IR
    263, mortgages not able to be called in were excluded. Where the gift is of money after payment
    of debts or legacies, or both debts and legacies, either generally out of the estate or out of certain
    property, the gift is often construed as ejusdem generis with that made subject to the payment, and
    for this reason may pass the residuary personal estate: *Dicks v Lambert* (1799) 4 Ves 725; *Kendall
    v Kendall* (1828) 4 Russ 360; *Rogers v Thomas* (1837) 2 Keen 8; *Dowson v Gaskoin* (1837) 2
    Keen 14; *Barrett v White* (1855) 1 Jur NS 652; *Grosvenor v Durston* (1858) 25 Beav 97 at 99;
    Langdale v Whitfield (1858) 4 K & J 426 at 436; *Stocks v Barre* (1859) John 54; *Re Egan, Mills
    v Penton* [1899] 1 Ch 688.
8   *Perrin v Morgan* [1943] AC 399 at 407, [1943] 1 All ER 187 at 190, HL, per Viscount Simon LC,
    and at 421–422 and 198 per Lord Romer. See also *Legge v Asgill* (1818) Turn & R 265n; *Dowson
    v Gaskoin* (1837) 2 Keen 14; *Cowling v Cowling* (1859) 26 Beav 449 at 451 per Romilly MR;
    Montagu v Earl of Sandwich (1863) 33 Beav 324; *Re Pringle, Walker v Stewart* (1881) 17 ChD
    819; *Re Cadogan, Cadogan v Palagi* (1883) 25 ChD 154; *Re Maclean, Williams v Nelson* (1894)
    11 TLR 82; *Re Bramley* [1902] P 106; *Re Skillen, Charles v Charles* [1916] 1 Ch 518; *Re Woolley,
    Cathcart v Eyskens* [1918] 1 Ch 33 (reversionary interest under settlement); *Re Recknell, White v
    Carter* [1936] 2 All ER 36 (effect of 'all'); *Re Gammon, Shelton v Williams* [1986] CLY 3547
    ('remainder of money'). In *Re Townley, Townley v Townley* (1884) 50 LT 394, personal estate
    except household furniture and effects passed. In *Prichard v Prichard* (1870) LR 11 Eq 232, the
    testator had little money, strictly so called, but large personal estate and some freehold property;
    and the whole of the personal estate, including leaseholds, passed, but not the freehold property.
9   *Perrin v Morgan* [1943] AC 399 at 407, [1943] 1 All ER 187 at 190, HL, per Viscount Simon LC;
    Re Gammon, Shelton v Williams [1986] CLY 3547 ('remainder of money'). Cf *Re Tribe, Tribe v
    Truro Cathedral (Dean and Chapter)* (1915) 85 LJ Ch 79; and as to the effect of 'all' see *Re
    Jennings, Caldbeck v Stafford and Lindemere* [1930] 1 IR 196 at 206. In view of the present
    liability by statute of real and personal estate for payment of debts (see PARAS 998–1006), it may
    be that 'the remainder of any moneys' after payment of debts will carry residuary property, both
    real and personal: *Re Mellor, Porter v Hindsley* [1929] 1 Ch 446; *Re Shaw, Mountain v Mountain*
    [1929] WN 246. Cf *Re Emerson, Morrill v Nutty* [1929] 1 Ch 128 (where 'residue of money at
    the time of my death' carried the residuary general estate, but not freehold ground rents). In *Stooke
    v Stooke* (1866) 35 Beav 396 at 397, Romilly MR gave an instance where he considered that realty
    would be comprised. See also *Ferman v Ryan* [1912] QSR 145.
10 See *Re Pringle, Walker v Stewart* (1881) 17 ChD 819 at 823; *Re Townley, Townley v Townley*
    (1884) 50 LT 394; *Re Maclean, Williams v Nelson* (1894) 11 TLR 82.
11 *Willis v Plaskett* (1841) 4 Beav 208 at 210; *Williams v Williams* (1878) 8 ChD 789, CA; *Re Mann,
    Ford v Ward* [1912] 1 Ch 388 at 391 (distinguishing *Re Adkins, Solomon v Catchpole* (1908) 98

LT 667). In *Re Capel, Arbuthnot v Capel* (1914) 59 Sol Jo 177, however, 'the rest of my money' passed a reversionary interest in personalty, even though there was a further gift in form residuary.

12 See *Lowe v Thomas* (1854) Kay 369 at 377 per Wood V-C (on appeal 5 De GM & G 315); *Boardman v Stanley* (1873) 21 WR 644; *Re Cadogan, Cadogan v Palagi* (1883) 25 ChD 154 at 157 per Kay J.

13 *Taylor v Taylor* (1837) 1 Jur 401; *Fryer v Ranken* (1840) 11 Sim 55; *Parker v Marchant* (1842) 1 Y & C Ch Cas 290 at 305–306 (on appeal (1843) 1 Ph 356); *Re Powell's Trust* (1858) John 49.

14 *Fryer v Ranken* (1840) 11 Sim 55.

15 *Stein v Ritherdon* (1868) 37 LJ Ch 369; *Mayne v Mayne* [1897] 1 IR 324.

16 The opinion has been expressed that, if money on deposit with bankers is subject to more than 24 hours' notice of withdrawal, it is not ready money: *Re Price, Price v Newton* [1905] 2 Ch 55 at 56 per Farwell J.

17 *Mayne v Mayne* [1897] 1 IR 324 (seven or ten days); *Re Wheeler, Hankinson v Hayter* [1904] 2 Ch 66 (14 days).

18 The waiver, by the bank, of the notice required does not make money so deposited 'ready money' (*Mayne v Mayne* [1897] 1 IR 324), unless it is the usual course of business (*Re Rodmell, Safford v Safford* (1913) 108 LT 184). A mere power to require notice for money, according to practice payable on demand, does not, however, prevent money deposited from being ready money: *Re Cosgrove's Estate, Willis v Goddard* (1909) Times, 3 April. A common practice of waiver on terms was not considered sufficient in *Re Friedman, Friedman v Friedman* (1908) 8 SRNSW 127.

19 Eg a sum due on note of hand (*Re Powell's Trust* (1858) John 49); money in the hands of an agent not acting as banker (*Smith v Butler* (1846) 3 Jo & Lat 565; *Cooke v Wagster* (1854) 2 Sm & G 296 at 300 (where, however, the sum in question passed as 'money' generally)); the apportioned parts of unreceived rent, dividends, interest or pension (*Fryer v Ranken* (1840) 11 Sim 55; *May v Grave* (1849) 3 De G & Sm 462; *Stein v Ritherdon* (1868) 37 LJ Ch 369); government or other stock (*Enohin v Wylie* (1862) 10 HL Cas 1; *Bevan v Bevan* (1880) 5 LR Ir 57, Ir CA); or a share of another testator's residue (*Re Andrews, Andrews v O'Mara* (1899) 25 VLR 408). See generally CHOSES IN ACTION.

20 *Beales v Crisford* (1843) 13 Sim 592 (gift of residue 'all but cash or moneys so called'; promissory notes, bonds and long annuities held not to be within the exception); *Nevinson v Lady Lennard* (1865) 34 Beav 487 ('money . . . if any such cash be remaining').

21 See *Re Boorer, Boorer v Boorer* [1908] WN 189, which was stated to lay down no general rule, and not followed, in *Re Stonham, Lloyds Bank Ltd v Maynard* [1963] 1 All ER 377, [1963] 1 WLR 238 (where in the context of the will as a whole 'cash in X Bank' was held to pass money in a deposit as well as in a current account). A sum in the National Savings Bank which cannot, except as to small sums, be withdrawn without notice is not cash: *Re Ashworth, Bent v Thomas* (1942) 86 Sol Jo 134.

22 *Bide v Harrison* (1873) LR 17 Eq 76 (damages on claim enforced by executors). Money received after the testator's death on claims which did not at the testator's death constitute debts (*Stephenson v Dowson* (1840) 3 Beav 342 (freight not yet earned); *Collins v Doyle* (1826) 1 Russ 135; *Martin v Hobson* (1873) 8 Ch App 401), and the apportioned parts, for the testator's lifetime, of dividends not declared until after his death (*Re Burke, Wood v Taylor* [1914] 1 IR 81), have been held not to pass under such words as 'money due or owing'. 'Money due and owing' or 'money owing' may include, as a rule, any sums payable at a future date or on a future contingency: *Brown v Brown* (1858) 6 WR 613 at 614 per Wood V-C (money raisable on request; money left at bank until called for); *Petty v Willson* (1869) 4 Ch App 574 (money receivable by executors under a policy of assurance); *Re Derbyshire, Webb v Derbyshire* [1906] 1 Ch 135 (money on deposit at bank there included, whether notice of withdrawal was required or not; the presumption against intestacy was applied).

23 *Gallini v Noble* (1810) 3 Mer 691 ('money in the Bank of England', testator having no account there); *Reilly v Stoney* (1865) 16 I Ch R 295 ('in the Bank of' I); *Stooke v Stooke* (1866) 35 Beav 396 ('in whatever it may be, in bonds or consols or anything else'); *Wilkes v Collin* (1869) LR 8 Eq 338 ('in real securities'). See also *Brennan v Brennan* (1868) IR 2 Eq 321 ('in the Bank of' I); *Sealy v Stawell* (1868) IR 2 Eq 326 ('in my drawer'); *Re Pringle, Walker v Stewart* (1881) 17 ChD 819 ('however invested'); *Re Harding, Drew v St Thomas' Hospital* (1910) 27 TLR 102 ('moneys invested in any banks or institutions' included consols). Cf *Langdale v Whitfeld* (1858) 4 K & J 426 (money, of or to which the testatrix might be 'possessed or entitled', included money due); *Vaisey v Reynolds* (1828) 5 Russ 12 ('moneys in hand', being contrasted with money out at interest on security, included money due); *Howell v Gayler* (1842) 5 Beav 157 ('money I may have' in books of the bank did not include stock in names of trustees); *Loring v Thomas* (1861) 5 LT 269; *Re Saxby, Saxby v Kiddell* [1890] WN 171 (money in savings bank); *Re Glendinning, Steel v Glendinning* (1918) 88 LJ Ch 87 ('moneys at the bank'); and see *Re Butler, Le Bas v Herbert* [1894] 3 Ch 250 at 251. As to 'money in the funds' see PARA 295.

24 *Harrison v Jackson* (1877) 7 ChD 339; *Re Sayer, McClellan v Clark* (1884) 50 LT 616; *Re Robe, Slade v Walpole* (1889) 61 LT 497; *Re Slater, Slater v Slater* [1907] 1 Ch 665, CA. Where, however, a testator describes property with reference to the source from which he received it, no ademption results from change of investment: *Morgan v Thomas* (1877) 6 ChD 176.

25 *Re Price, Price v Newton* [1905] 2 Ch 55. See also *Archibald v Hartley* (1852) 21 LJ Ch 399; *Re Sudlow, Smith v Sudlow* [1914] WN 424 (money on deposit with employer not 'invested'); but cf *Re Lewis' Will Trusts, O'Sullivan v Robbins* [1937] Ch 118, [1937] 1 All ER 227.

26 *Re Heilbronner, Nathan v Kenny* [1953] 2 All ER 1016, [1953] 1 WLR 1254.

294. Meaning of 'securities'. According to its literal meaning, 'securities' includes such money as is secured either on property[1] or on personal security[2] (including even promissory notes[3] and bills of exchange[4]), and any stock or other investment which, by the terms of its creation, is a security for the payment of money[5]; but it does not include money for which a mere acknowledgment of indebtedness has been given[6], or the ordinary description of stock and shares in a public company[7]. 'Securities' is, however, very commonly used as a synonym for investments, or property dealt with on the Stock Exchange, and this meaning may readily be attributed to the word[8]; and generally other meanings may be given to it, according to the context of the will and the circumstances of the case[9].

1 *Cust v Goring* (1854) 18 Beav 383 (Scottish heritable bond); *Ogle v Knipe* (1869) LR 8 Eq 434 (mortgage). Cf *Robinson v Robinson* (1851) 1 De GM & G 247 at 262 (turnpike bonds). A vendor's lien was not considered a security in *Goold v Teague* (1858) 5 Jur NS 116, but the case was doubted and distinguished in *Callow v Callow* (1889) 42 ChD 550, following the observations in Sugden's Vendors and Purchasers (14th Edn) 684 and Dart's Vendors and Purchasers (6th Edn) 827. As to mortgages see further MORTGAGE.

2 Eg a bond (*Bacchus v Gilbee* (1863) 3 De GJ & Sm 577; *Re Beavan, Beavan v Beavan* (1885) 53 LT 245 at 247 per Kay J) or policy of assurance (*Lawrance v Galsworthy* (1857) 3 Jur NS 1049); but see *Re Lilly's Will Trusts, Public Trustee v Johnstone* [1948] 2 All ER 906 (where policy money was excluded).

3 *Re Beavan, Beavan v Beavan* (1885) 53 LT 245; but see *Stiles v Guy* (1832) 4 Y & C Ex 571 (promissory note would not be security for purposes of direction to trustees to invest in approved securities).

4 *Barry v Harding* (1844) 1 Jo & Lat 475 at 483 per Sugden LC; but see *Southcot v Watson* (1745) 3 Atk 226 at 232 (banknotes).

5 *Bescoby v Pack* (1823) 1 Sim & St 500 (stock in public funds); *Turner v Turner* (1852) 21 LJ Ch 843 (consols, but not insurance company's shares); *Re Beavan, Beavan v Beavan* (1885) 53 LT 245 (consols and railway debenture stocks). Cf *Hudleston v Gouldsbury* (1847) 10 Beav 547 (shares in canal company not security for money).

6 *Vaisey v Reynolds* (1828) 5 Russ 12 (money at bank); *Barry v Harding* (1844) 1 Jo & Lat 475 (IOU); *Hopkins v Abbott* (1875) LR 19 Eq 222 (banker's deposit notes); *Re Beavan, Beavan v Beavan* (1885) 53 LT 245 at 247 per Kay J (IOUs). See also *Re Mason's Will* (1865) 34 Beav 494 (legacy).

7 *Harris v Harris* (1861) 29 Beav 107; *Ogle v Knipe* (1869) LR 8 Eq 434 (bank stock); *M'Donnell v Morrow* (1889) 23 LR Ir 591 (shares in companies); *Re Kavanagh, Murphy v Doyle* (1892) 29 LR Ir 333, Ir CA (partly paid bank shares excluded from trustee investment clause); *Re Maitland, Chitty v Maitland* (1896) 74 LT 274; *Re Smithers, Watts v Smithers* [1939] Ch 1015, [1939] 3 All ER 689. See also *Re Hutchinson, Crispin v Hadden* (1919) 88 LJ Ch 352.

8 *Dicks v Lambert* (1799) 4 Ves 725; *Re Rayner, Rayner v Rayner* [1904] 1 Ch 176, CA. See also *Re Johnson, Greenwood v Greenwood* (1903) 89 LT 520, CA; *Re Mort, Perpetual Trustee Co Ltd v Bisdee* (1904) 4 SRNSW 760; *Re J H* (1911) 25 OLR 132; *Re Scorer, Burtt v Harrison* (1924) 94 LJ Ch 196. A bequest of 'all money, shares and securities at my bankers' does not pass stocks of which only stock receipts and inscription receipts are at the bank: *Re Hay Drummond, Halsey v Pechell* (1922) 128 LT 621. As to the Stock Exchange see FINANCIAL SERVICES REGULATION vol 50 (2016) PARA 96.

9 *Dicks v Lambert* (1799) 4 Ves 725 (stock included); *Re Gent and Eason's Contract* [1905] 1 Ch 386 (where power to vary securities included power to sell real estate); *Re Douglas's Will Trusts, Lloyds Bank Ltd v Nelson* [1959] 2 All ER 620, [1959] 1 WLR 744 (affd on another point [1959] 3 All ER 785, [1959] 1 WLR 1212, CA) (where 'power to invest in securities' was held to include stocks or shares or bonds). As to the meaning of 'securities standing in any name' see *Re Mayne, Stoneham v Woods* [1914] 2 Ch 115.

295. Meaning of 'stocks and shares', 'funds', 'war loan' etc. The natural meaning of 'stocks and shares' is stocks and shares of limited companies[1]. A bequest of 'shares' in a particular company may pass the testator's stock in that company which is of the same nature as, and identical with, shares[2], but prima facie[3] not stock issued as security, such as debentures or debenture stock[4]. For the purposes of an investment clause, 'stock' may include shares[5].

'The funds', standing alone and without a context, has been held to mean the funds established by various Acts of Parliament and forming part of the National Debt of the United Kingdom[6]. Where in a will words of description refer to the funds, as in the case of 'funded property', 'money in the funds' and like expressions, prima facie the reference is to such public funds[7], but the context and the circumstances may require a different construction[8].

'War loan' has been held to apply to any security created for the purpose of the 1914–18 war[9]. 'War bonds' has been held not to include war stock[10].

1   *Re Everett, Prince v Hunt* [1944] Ch 176, [1944] 2 All ER 19. In *Re Purnchard's Will Trusts, Public Trustee v Pelly* [1948] Ch 312, [1948] 1 All ER 790, the phrase was given a wide meaning, there being no residuary gift.

2   *Morrice v Aylmer* (1875) LR 7 HL 717 (overruling *Oakes v Oakes* (1852) 9 Hare 666). Stock issued on a reconstruction of a company may pass under a gift of 'all my shares', but not debentures: *Re Humphreys, Wren v Ward* (1915) 114 LT 230. A bequest of 'my shares in different securities' does not carry an interest which the testator has as next of kin in shares and stock forming part of the unadministered estate of an intestate: *Re Holmes, Villiers v Holmes* [1917] 1 IR 165. But see *Re Leigh's Will Trusts* [1970] Ch 277, [1969] 3 All ER 432, where a bequest of 'all shares which I hold and any other interest or assets which I may have in S Ltd' passed shares in S Ltd and a debt due from S Ltd which formed part of the testatrix's husband's unadministered estate. As to a gift of shares including 'current dividends' see *Re Raven, Spencer v Raven* (1914) 111 LT 938; and as to the apportionment of dividend on cumulative preference shares see *Re Wakley, Wakley v Vachell* [1920] 2 Ch 205, CA. Whether bonus shares will pass to a life tenant under a gift of 'dividends, bonuses and income' depends on whether they are issued as capital or income: *Re Speir, Holt v Speir* [1924] 1 Ch 359, CA. In *Re Quibell's Will Trusts, White v Reichert* [1956] 3 All ER 679, [1957] 1 WLR 186, a bequest of shares in a company to be formed after the testator's death carried shares in the company, even though it was in fact formed by the testator in his lifetime.

3   See, however, *Re Weeding, Armstrong v Wilkin* [1896] 2 Ch 364 (where the testator had no shares).

4   *Dillon v Arkins* (1885) 17 LR Ir 636, Ir CA; *Re Bodman, Bodman v Bodman* [1891] 3 Ch 135; *Re Connolly, Walton v Connolly* (1914) 110 LT 688; *Re Humphreys, Wren v Ward* (1915) 114 LT 230. A direction to invest in stocks, shares or convertible debentures 'in the 'blue chip' category' is too uncertain to be enforceable: *Re Kolb's Will Trusts* [1962] Ch 531, [1961] 3 All ER 811. As to the construction of investment clauses generally see TRUSTS AND POWERS vol 98 (2013) PARA 446 et seq.

5   See *Re Inman, Inman v Inman* [1915] 1 Ch 187. Cf *Re Willis, Spencer v Willis* [1911] 2 Ch 563. As to whether a bequest of stock is general or specific see PARA 119.

6   *Slingsby v Grainger* (1859) 7 HL Cas 273 at 280, 285; cf *Re Hill, Fettes v Hill* [1914] WN 132 ('public stocks of the Bank of England'). As to the National Debt see FINANCIAL INSTRUMENTS AND TRANSACTIONS vol 49 (2015) PARA 112 et seq.

7   *Slingsby v Grainger* (1859) 7 HL Cas 273. See also *Ridge v Newton* (1842) 2 Dr & War 239; *Burnie v Getting* (1845) 2 Coll 324; *Ellis v Eden* (1857) 23 Beav 543; *Howard v Kay* (1858) 27 LJ Ch 448; *Brown v Brown* (1858) 6 WR 613; *Wilday v Sandys* (1869) LR 7 Eq 455.

8   *Mangin v Mangin* (1852) 16 Beav 300; *Ellis v Eden* (1857) 23 Beav 543 (foreign funds); *Slingsby v Grainger* (1859) 7 HL Cas 273; *Cadett v Earle* (1877) 5 ChD 710.

9   *Re Price, Trumper v Price* [1932] 2 Ch 54. See also *Re Ionides, London County Westminster and Parr's Bank Ltd v Craies* [1922] WN 46 (where Exchequer bonds issued under the War Loan Act 1919 were included in 'war loans'); *Re Cruse, Gass v Ingham* [1930] WN 206.

10 *Re Balchin* (1922) 38 TLR 868. In *Re Gifford, Gifford v Seaman* [1944] Ch 186, [1944] 1 All ER 268, consolidated inscribed stock passed under the description of 'War Bonds' on the principle of 'falsa demonstratio non nocet' (see PARA 269), but not national savings certificates and defence

bonds not held by the testatrix at the date of her will. A gift of 'war savings certificates' was held not to include national savings certificates where the testatrix had both: *Re Lamb, Marston v Chauvet* (1933) 49 TLR 541.

296. Meaning of miscellaneous terms. In the construction of wills, the meaning in various contexts of the following terms has been discussed: 'arrears of rent'[1]; 'articles of domestic use or ornament'[2]; 'articles of vertu'[3]; 'bonds'[4]; 'books'[5]; 'carriage'[6]; 'cash'[7]; 'debentures'[8]; 'fortune'[9]; 'furniture'[10]; 'horses'[11] and 'bloodstock'[12]; 'household effects'[13], 'household furniture'[14], 'household furniture and effects'[15], 'household goods'[16], 'personal and household goods and effects'[17], 'contents of my house' or 'home'[18], and similar expressions[19]; 'jewellery'[20]; 'movables'[21]; 'pictures'[22]; 'plate'[23]; and 'private papers'[24]. 'Pensions and allowances' has been held not to include subscriptions and donations which are purely voluntary[25]. 'Wages' has been held to mean fixed cash payments, and not to mean other benefits such as commission[26]. 'All my share and interest' is not, without more, generally capable of applying to the proceeds from the lifetime sale of the subject matter of a specific legacy[27]. 'The right to occupy my house' may raise several different problems of construction in some circumstances[28].

1 *Re Ford, Myers v Molesworth* [1911] 1 Ch 455.
2 *Petre v Ferrers* (1891) 61 LJ Ch 426 (not relics); *Re Owen, Peat v Owen* (1898) 78 LT 643.
3 *Re Baroness Zouche, Dugdale v Baroness Zouche* [1919] 2 Ch 178; *Re Tomline's Will Trusts, Pretyman v Pretyman* [1931] 1 Ch 521. See also *Re Lord Londesborough, Bridgeman v Lord Fitzgerald* (1880) 50 LJ Ch 9.
4 Bonds are instruments under seal, and do not include certificates of stock not sealed: *Re Manners, Manners v Manners* [1923] 1 Ch 220.
5 Manuscript letters bound in volumes may pass as 'books' (*Re Tomline's Will Trusts, Pretyman v Pretyman* [1931] 1 Ch 521 (certain of the 'Paston Letters')); so also may a manuscript log book (*Re Barratt, Barratt v Coates* (1915) 31 TLR 502, CA). See also *Re Masson, Morton v Masson* (1917) 86 LJ Ch 753, CA (stamp collection not included in 'books'), disapproving *Re Fortlage, Ross v Fortlage* (1916) 60 Sol Jo 527.
6 *Denholm's Trustees v Denholm* 1908 SC 43, Ct of Sess (car included).
7 See PARA 293.
8 *Re Herring, Murray v Herring* [1908] 2 Ch 493 (debenture stock included). See also *Phillips v Eastwood* (1835) L & G temp Sugd 270 at 291–292 (policies of assurance included under the particular will). The decision in *Re Lane, Luard v Lane* (1880) 14 ChD 856 (debenture stock not included) has sometimes been doubted: see *Dillon v Arkins* (1885) 17 LR Ir 636, Ir CA. A gift of debenture stock passes debentures if no debenture stock exists to satisfy the gift: *Re Nottage, Jones v Palmer (No 2)* [1895] 2 Ch 657, CA.
9 *Baring v Ashburton* (1886) 54 LT 463. See also *Bacon v Cosby* (1851) 4 De G & Sm 261; *Spearing v Hawkes* (1857) 6 I Ch R 297.
10 *Re Seton-Smith, Burnand v Waite* [1902] 1 Ch 717 (tenant's and trade fixtures there excluded). See also *Hele v Gilbert* (1752) 2 Ves Sen 430 (china); *Cremorne v Antrobus* (1829) 5 Russ 312; *Holden v Ramsbottom* (1863) 4 Giff 205 (plated articles); *Re Lord Londesborough, Bridgeman v Lord Fitzgerald* (1880) 50 LJ Ch 9 (pictures); *Petre v Ferrers* (1891) 61 LJ Ch 426 (not relics); *Re Willey, Goulding v Shirtcliffe* (1929) 45 TLR 327 (cabinet wireless set). Books as a rule are not included, at any rate in an eighteenth-century will (*Bridgeman v Dove* (1744) 3 Atk 201 at 202; *Kelly v Powlet* (1763) Amb 605; *Cremorne v Antrobus* above at 321; *Porter v Tournay* (1797) 3 Ves 311), but it seems that, having regard to modern habits of life, an intention to include books in the term is now readily inferred (see *Re Holden* (1903) 5 OLR 156 at 162), eg in a gift of a house and its furniture, as kept up in the testator's lifetime (*Ouseley v Anstruther* (1847) 10 Beav 453 at 462; *Hutchinson v Smith* (1863) 1 New Rep 513). In *Re Crispin's Will Trusts, Arkwright v Thurley* [1975] Ch 245, [1974] 3 All ER 772, CA, it was held that clocks do not cease to be furniture because they form part of a collection.
11 *Re Sykes, Skelton and Dyson v Sykes* [1940] 4 All ER 10 (where an interest as tenant in common in three horses did not pass).
12 *Re Gillson, Ellis v Leader* [1949] Ch 99, [1948] 2 All ER 990, CA (where a half share in a thoroughbred horse passed but not a fortieth interest in another horse managed by a syndicate, as this interest was in the nature of an investment).
13 *Re Bourne, Bourne v Brandreth* (1888) 58 LT 537 (wine included) (following *Cole v Fitzgerald* (1823) 1 Sim & St 189 (on appeal (1827) 3 Russ 301)); *Re Ashburnham, Gaby v Ashburnham*

(1912) 107 LT 601; *Re White, White v White* [1916] 1 Ch 172; *Re Fortlage, Ross v Fortlage* (1916) 60 Sol Jo 527 (in the last three cases cited a car was included); *Burnside v Burnside* (1921) 56 ILT 20 (furniture and books in college rooms included); *Re Baron Wavertree of Delamere, Rutherford v Hall-Walker* [1933] Ch 837 (cars, consumable stores, garden implements and movable plants included).

14 *Kelly v Powlet* (1763) Amb 605 (plate, pictures etc); *Manning v Purcell* (1855) 7 De GM & G 55 at 68 (such part of tavern furniture as was for domestic or personal use); *Stone v Parker* (1860) 29 LJ Ch 874 (cows, horses and farming stock prima facie excluded); *Finney v Grice* (1878) 10 ChD 13 (tenant's fixtures excluded).

15 *Pratt v Jackson* (1726) 1 Bro Parl Cas 222 (furniture in house let furnished excluded); *Northey v Paxton* (1888) 60 LT 30 (not jewellery). See also *Tempest v Tempest* (1856) 2 K & J 635 (personal ornaments and chattels not for use or ornament in the house excluded); *Field v Peckett (No 2)* (1861) 29 Beav 573 (ornaments); *Stone v Parker* (1860) 1 Drew & Sm 212 (not farming stock); *Re Hammersley, Heasman v Hammersley* (1899) 81 LT 150 (jewellery excluded); *MacPhail v Phillips* [1904] 1 IR 155 (stock in trade excluded); *Re Howe, Ferniehough v Wilkinson* [1908] WN 223 (car included); *Re White, White v White* [1916] 1 Ch 172 (cars included); *Re Fothergill, Horwood v Fothergill* (1916) 51 L Jo 169 (kangaroos and various birds held not to pass under gift of 'articles of household use or ornament').

16 *Pellew v Horsford* (1856) 2 Jur NS 514. See also *Nicholls v Osborn* (1727) 2 P Wms 419; *Stapleton v Conway* (1750) 1 Ves Sen 427; *Re Johnson, Sandy v Reilly* (1905) 92 LT 357 ('household property' shown to mean residue).

17 *Re Mengel's Will Trusts, Westminster Bank Ltd v Mengel* [1962] Ch 791, [1962] 2 All ER 490 (library of books, etchings and mountain photographs shown by context not to be included). As to the meanings of 'effects' and 'personal effects' see PARA 288.

18 *Re Eumorfopoulos, Ralli v Eumorfopoulos* [1944] Ch 133, [1943] 2 All ER 719 (articles normally kept in the house but temporarily sent away included; articles at the bank or occasionally at the house excluded; cf PARA 285); *Re Abbott, Public Trustee v St Dunstan's, British Home and Hospital for Incurables and Trustees of Western Ophthalmic Hospital and Lady Dugan* [1944] 2 All ER 457, CA (choses in action not included).

19 In ascertaining what passes under such a bequest in the will of a tradesman, the court will direct an inquiry, distinguishing articles used for his own domestic or personal use and those used in trade or as merchandise: see the decree in *Le Farrant v Spencer* (1748) 1 Ves Sen 97 (cited in *Manning v Purcell* (1855) 7 De GM & G 55 at 64n).

20 *Re Whitby, Public Trustee v Whitby* [1944] Ch 210, [1944] 1 All ER 299.

21 *Re Walsh, Walsh v Walsh* [1953] Ch 473, [1953] 1 All ER 982 (movable chattels only).

22 *Re Du Maurier, Millar v Coles* (1916) 32 TLR 579; *Re Layard, Layard v Earl of Bessborough* (1916) 85 LJ Ch 505, CA (appeal withdrawn on terms (1917) 33 TLR 261, HL); *Re Lane, Meagher v National Gallery for Ireland* (1917) 33 TLR 418 (right to have portrait painted).

23 *Holden v Ramsbottom* (1863) 4 Giff 205 (plated articles excluded); not followed in *Re Grimwood, Trewhella v Grimwood* [1946] Ch 54, [1945] 2 All ER 686 (Sheffield plate and electro-plate included). See also *Re Lewis, Prothero v Lewis* (1909) 26 TLR 145 (silver-mounted articles excluded); *Field v Peckett (No 2)* (1861) 29 Beav 573 at 574.

24 *Re Dickens, Dickens v Hawkesley* [1935] Ch 267, CA.

25 *Re Scott, Scott v Scott (No 2)* (1915) 31 TLR 505.

26 *Re Smith, Phillips v Smith* [1915] WN 12; *Re Peacock, Public Trustee v Birchenough* (1929) 45 TLR 301. See also *Re Whelan, Doyle v Woodliff* (1922) 153 LT Jo 47.

27 *Banks v National Westminster Bank plc* [2005] EWHC 3479 (Ch), [2005] All ER (D) 159 (Apr) (legatee sold property under enduring power of attorney, without intention to adeem).

28 See *Bergliter v Cohen* [2006] EWHC 123 (Ch), [2006] All ER (D) 88 (Jan) (questions of just what was the subject matter of the gift and the extent of the right, where three adjoining properties were owned and might have been intended).

297. Release of debts.

Where a testator by his will releases all debts owing to him, it depends on the circumstances whether this is confined to personal debts[1], or extends to business or other debts[2], and whether or not both secured and unsecured debts are released[3].

1 *Re Neville, Neville v First Garden City Ltd* [1925] Ch 44.

2 *Midland Bank Executor and Trustee Co Ltd v Yarners Coffee Ltd* [1937] 2 All ER 54. Even on this wider construction the release will not, it seems, extend to money at a bank on current or deposit account: *Midland Bank Executor and Trustee Co Ltd v Yarners Coffee Ltd* at 56–57. Where there is a direction that debts due from a legatee are to be brought into account, and the debts exceed the legacy, there is no release of the excess: *Re Clark, Cross v Hillis* [1924] WN 75.

3   *Re Coghill, Drury v Burgess* [1948] 1 All ER 254 (where unsecured, but not secured, debts were released). As to the effect of legacies to debtors see PARA 217; and as to the time for determining what debts are released see PARA 282 note 5.

298. Residuary gifts. In a suitable context, many words are capable of denoting the whole or the residue of the testator's real and personal estate[1]. A gift of 'the remainder' of the residuary fund may, on the construction of the will, be either a gift of the balance of the fund after a deduction of previous gifts out of it, or a gift of the whole fund subject to the previous gifts; in the latter case, but not the former, the gift of the fund carries with it any previous gift which fails[2].

The appointment of any person to be 'residuary legatee' prima facie[3] gives him only the residue of the personal estate[4]. If, however, the context or the circumstances require, it may also pass the residue of the real estate, as, for example, where the intention to dispose of the whole real and personal estate is shown or to be inferred[5]. The fact that parts of the real estate are specifically devised may be sufficient to give the residuary legatee the residue of the real estate[6], but not where the residuary legatee is one of the specific devisees[7]. The fact that the testator had no real estate at the date of his will[8], or had no real estate other than that of which the will contains specific and complete dispositions[9], is evidence against this extension of the meaning of 'residuary legatee', but not conclusive evidence[10].

The effect of a gift of general residue, and the property comprised in it, are dealt with elsewhere in this title[11]. Similar rules hold good as to particular residuary gifts by way of general descriptions of particular kinds of property belonging to the testator remaining undisposed of[12]. There is a group of anomalous cases where particular residuary gifts (usually charitable) remain following otherwise invalid purpose gifts to maintain mausolea and tombs; these seem to be decided on the basis that the initial purpose gift imposes only a moral obligation and that the cost of providing for the initial purpose is small compared to the residuary gift and can be ascertained with certainty[13]. A direction that, on the failure or determination of the trusts declared concerning a share of residue, the share is to fall into residue prima facie constitutes a gift of that share by way of addition to the other shares of residue[14].

If a testator's residuary estate is given by his will in proportional shares, and one or more of the shares of residue are exempt from inheritance tax (usually because given to the testator's spouse or to a charity) while another or other shares are not so exempt, in the absence of express provision to the contrary the residuary estate is divided in the proportions provided by the will without regard to any inheritance tax attributable to the non-exempt shares, and any such inheritance tax is then borne by those shares[15].

1   *Blight v Hartnoll* (1883) 23 ChD 218 at 222, CA. See also *Huxtep v Brooman* (1785) 1 Bro CC 437 ('all I am worth'); *Doe d Wall v Langlands* (1811) 14 East 370 ('the residue of all my property, goods and chattels'); *Fleming v Burrows* (1826) 1 Russ 276 ('or what else I may then be possessed of at my decease'); *Wilce v Wilce* (1831) 7 Bing 664 ('everything else I die possessed of'); *Cogswell v Armstrong* (1855) 2 K & J 227 ('all other real and personal estate'); *Re Greenwich Hospital Improvement Act* (1855) 20 Beav 458 ('all my . . . other property of every description'); *Attree v Attree* (1871) LR 11 Eq 280 ('all the rest'); *Smyth v Smyth* (1878) 8 ChD 561 ('all the rest, residue . . . and all other my effects'); *Re Johnson, Sandy v Reilly* (1905) 49 Sol Jo 314 ('the remainder of my household property'); *Re Craven, Crewdson v Craven* (1908) 24 TLR 750 ('the rest of my investments'); *Re Brace, Gurton v Clements* [1954] 2 All ER 354, [1954] 1 WLR 955 ('any possessions I may have'); *Re Gammon, Shelton v Williams* [1986] CLY 3547 ('remainder of money'); *Re Barnes's Will Trusts, Prior v Barnes* [1972] 2 All ER 639, [1972] 1 WLR 587 ('any other personal property'); *Re Hetherington, Gibbs v McDonnell* [1990] Ch 1, [1989] 2 All ER 129 ('whatever is left over'). It seems that 'etc' may suffice: *Chapman v Chapman* (1876) 4 ChD 800;

Re Andrew's Estate, Creasey v Graves (1902) 50 WR 471. As to the meaning of 'effects' see PARA 288; and as to the meaning of 'estate' see PARA 289.

2 *Re Parnell, Ranks v Holmes* [1944] Ch 107.

3 Eg when used alone or in a will which appears to make a distinction between real and personal property: *Singleton v Tomlinson* (1878) 3 App Cas 404 at 417. Other words in the will may negative the prima facie beneficial interest of the residuary legatee: *Re Hawksley's Settlements, Black v Tidy* [1934] Ch 384.

4 *Wills v Wills* (1841) 1 Dr & War 439. See also *Kellett v Kellett* (1815) 3 Dow 248, HL (explained in *Windus v Windus* (1856) 6 De GM & G 549 at 557–558); *Lea v Grundy* (1855) 1 Jur NS 951; *Cooney v Nicholls* (1881) 7 LR Ir 107, Ir CA; *Gethin v Allen* (1888) 23 LR Ir 236; *Re Morris, Morris v Atherden* (1894) 71 LT 179.

5 *Pitman v Stevens* (1812) 15 East 505; *Day v Daveron* (1841) 12 Sim 200; *Davenport v Coltman* (1842) 12 Sim 588; *Warren v Newton* (1844) Drury *temp* Sugd 464; *Evans v Crosbie* (1847) 15 Sim 600; *Wildes v Davies* (1853) 1 Sm & G 475; *Re Gyles* (1863) 14 I Ch R 311; *Singleton v Tomlinson* (1878) 3 App Cas 404; *Re Salter, Farrant v Carter* (1881) 44 LT 603; *Re Greally, Travers v O'Donoghue* [1910] 1 IR 239 at 242. See also *Re Pereira, Worsley v Society for the Propagation of the Gospel* (1912) 28 TLR 479.

6 *Hughes v Pritchard* (1877) 6 ChD 24, CA (explained in *Re Methuen and Blore's Contract* (1881) 16 ChD 696 at 700; and followed in *Re Bailey, Barclays Bank Ltd v James* [1945] Ch 191, [1945] 1 All ER 616).

7 *Hillas v Hillas* (1847) 10 I Eq R 134; *Re Morris, Morris v Atherden* (1894) 71 LT 179; *Re Gibbs, Martin v Harding* [1907] 1 Ch 465 at 468.

8 *Re Methuen and Blore's Contract* (1881) 16 ChD 696.

9 *Re Gibbs, Martin v Harding* [1907] 1 Ch 465.

10 *Re Stephen, Stephen v Stephen* [1913] WN 210 (where *Re Gibbs, Martin v Harding* [1907] 1 Ch 465 is distinguished in the context of that case). See also *Re Fetherston-Haugh-Whitney's Estate* [1924] 1 IR 153, Ir CA.

11 See PARA 1113. As to the effect of two residuary gifts see PARA 233; and as to the distinction between a gift of the residue and a gift of the residue of the residuary estate see *Re Whitrod, Burrows v Base* [1926] Ch 118.

12 *M'Kay v M'Kay* [1900] 1 IR 213 at 217 (residue of furniture etc); *Mason v Ogden* [1903] AC 1, HL (residue of freeholds). In *Re Brown* (1855) 1 K & J 522 (hereditaments comprised in a settlement) and *Springett v Jenings* (1871) 6 Ch App 333 (hereditaments in a named parish) the descriptions were specific and not general.

13 See *Re Dalziel, Midland Bank Executor & Trustee Co Ltd v Governors of St Bartholomew's Hospital* [1943] Ch 277, [1943] 2 All ER 656 and the cases and reasoning therein.

14 *Re Palmer, Palmer v Answorth* [1893] 3 Ch 369, CA (life interest substituted for absolute interest by codicil; share to fall into residue on death of life tenant); *Re Allan, Dow v Cassaigne* [1903] 1 Ch 276, CA (share to fall into residue on death of beneficiary without having issue); *Re Wand, Escritt v Wand* [1907] 1 Ch 391 (share to be forfeited and fall into residue if certain event happened during testator's life). See also *Re Ballance, Ballance v Lanphier* (1889) 42 ChD 62; and PARA 173.

15 *Re Ratcliffe, Holmes v McMullan* [1999] STC 262 (not following *Re Benham's Will Trusts, Lockhart v Harker* [1995] STC 210). As to inheritance tax generally see INHERITANCE TAXATION.

(3) PERSONS ENTITLED TO TAKE

(i) Time of Ascertainment of Donees

A.   IDENTIFYING DONEES

299. General considerations when identifying donees. The ascertainment of the donee is an element in ascertaining the vesting of a gift. Accordingly, the presumption in favour of early vesting[1] has been invoked, in doubtful cases, to assist in determining which of various persons was intended by a description capable of denoting any of them[2]; but in general this presumption does no more than suggest the most desirable method of carrying the testator's intention into effect, and does not assist in finding out whom he intended as the objects of his bounty[3]. In a class gift[4] an express direction as to vesting (for example at a specified age), or a gift over, is in general immaterial in ascertaining the class[5], unless it alters the description of the class[6].

1 As to the presumption in favour of early vesting see PARA 413.
2 *Radford v Willis* (1871) 7 Ch App 7 at 10. The 'rules of convenience' (see PARAS 305–308) are sometimes said to be directed to make the property vest as early as possible: *Gimblett v Purton* (1871) LR 12 Eq 427 at 430.
3 *Doe d Smith v Fleming* (1835) 2 Cr M & R 638 at 654 per Lord Abinger CB.
4 See PARAS 174–175.
5 *Williams v Haythorne, Williams v Williams* (1871) 6 Ch App 782. See also *Re Payne* (1858) 25 Beav 556 (vested at 21 or on leaving issue at death before that age).
6 *Williams v Russell* (1863) 10 Jur NS 168; *Re Knowles, Nottage v Buxton* (1882) 21 ChD 806.

300. Identifying individuals. Where the donee is designated by a description which may at different times apply to different individuals, and the context does not point to any specific future time as the time at which the donee is to be ascertained, then prima facie the only person who is entitled to take is the one who satisfies the description at the date of the will[1], provided that there is a person who to the testator's knowledge then satisfies it[2]. Where the context shows that the donee is to be ascertained in the future, but does not show at what specific time, then the first person to satisfy the description is presumed to be intended[3]. The context may, however, show that the donee in each case is to be ascertained at the testator's death[4], or some other definite future time[5]. Where a qualification is required as a condition precedent to the vesting of an interest, the qualification must be satisfied at the date when the interest vests in possession[6].

Donees may be partly designated by gender, for example the eldest son of an individual, or an individual's daughters. The fact that a person has an acquired gender[7] does not affect the disposal or devolution of property under a will made before 4 April 2005[8]. After that day, and after a full gender recognition certificate is issued to a person, the person's gender becomes for all purposes the acquired gender (so that, if the acquired gender is the male gender, the person's sex becomes that of a man and, if it is the female gender, the person's sex becomes that of a woman)[9]. This will not affect things done, or events occurring, before the certificate is issued; but it will operate for the interpretation of wills made on or after 4 April 2005, whether they are made before the certificate is issued or afterwards[10].

1 The provisions of the Wills Act 1837 s 24 (see PARA 282) do not apply with reference to the objects of the testator's bounty: *Bullock v Bennett* (1855) 7 De GM & G 283 at 285–286. As to where the designation is that of the holder of an office see *Re Jones' Estate* (1927) 43 TLR 324; and PARA 367.
2 *Thompson v Thompson* (1844) 1 Coll 381 at 388, 391 (eldest son at date of codicil took); *Re Whorwood, Ogle v Lord Sherborne* (1887) 34 ChD 446, CA (to 'Lord S'); *Amyot v Dwarris* [1904] AC 268, PC ('the eldest son of my sister'). See also *Lomax v Holmden* (1749) 1 Ves Sen 290. As to gifts to the holder of an office see PARA 367; as to gifts to a 'wife' see PARA 346; and as to gifts to servants see PARAS 365–366.
3 *Radford v Willis* (1871) 7 Ch App 7 (gift to future 'husband' of daughter unmarried at date of will); *Re Hickman, Hickman v Hickman* [1948] Ch 624, [1948] 2 All ER 303 (gift to future 'wife' of grandson unmarried at testatrix's death). As to gifts to one of a number of persons see PARA 265; and as to gifts to an 'eldest son' etc see PARA 333.
4 *Re Laffan and Downes' Contract* [1897] 1 IR 469 (superioress of two convents at the testatrix's death); *Re Daniels, London City and Midland Executor and Trustee Co Ltd v Daniels* (1918) 87 LJ Ch 661 (legacy to the Lord Mayor 'for the time being'; the holder of the office at the testator's death held entitled).
5 See *Re Earl of Cathcart* (1912) 56 Sol Jo 271 (gift to a successor to a title); *Re Earl of Caledon, Almander v Earl of Caledon* [1915] 1 Ch 150 (gift of chattels to the person who should become entitled to a house); *Re Drummond's Settlement, Foster v Foster* [1988] 1 All ER 449, [1988] 1

WLR 234, CA (gift to such 'as shall then be living' construed as relating to the time of death of persons alive at the date of the settlement; no perpetuity objection).
6   *Re Allen, Faith v Allen* [1954] Ch 259, [1954] 1 All ER 526.
7   Ie acquired in accordance with the Gender Recognition Act 2004.
8   Gender Recognition Act 2004 s 15.
9   Gender Recognition Act 2004 s 9(1). Section 9(1) is subject to provision made by the Gender Recognition Act 2004 (eg s 15) or any other enactment or any subordinate legislation: s 9(3).
10 Gender Recognition Act 2004 s 9(2). Where a disposition or devolution of any property under a will made on or after 4 April 2005 (ie the appointed day) is different from what it would be but for the fact that a person's gender has become an acquired gender, he may apply to the High Court for an order on the ground of being adversely affected by the different disposition or devolution of the property: s 18(1), (2). The court may then, if it is satisfied that it is just to do so, make in relation to any person benefiting from the different disposition or devolution of the property such order as it considers appropriate, and in particular may make provision for the payment of a lump sum to the applicant, the transfer of property to the applicant, the settlement of property for the benefit of the applicant, or the acquisition of property and either its transfer to the applicant or its settlement for the benefit of the applicant: s 18(3), (4). An order may also contain consequential or supplementary provisions for giving effect to the order or for ensuring that it operates fairly as between the applicant and the other person or persons affected by it, and an order may, in particular, confer powers on trustees: s 18(5).

301. Identifying members of group of individuals. If the gift is immediate and is a separate bequest of a specific amount to each one of a group of certain children who are to take as individuals and not as a class, prima facie only those in existence at the testator's death may take, and those coming into existence afterwards are excluded[1]. The fact that at the date of the will or of the testator's death there are no members of the group in existence does not render future members admissible[2]. If such a gift is postponed, all those who come into existence before the time of distribution are let in[3]. The rule is grounded on the inconvenience of postponing distribution until all the children who might be born and the total amount of their bequests can be ascertained[4], and accordingly it does not apply where by the provisions of the will this inconvenience does not exist[5], or is expressly contemplated by the testator[6].

1   *Garbrand v Mayot* (1689) 2 Vern 105 (child born after date of will); *Ringrose v Bramham* (1794) 2 Cox Eq Cas 384 (a legacy 'to every child he hath by his wife E'); *Storrs v Benbow* (1833) 2 My & K 46 (on appeal (1853) 3 De GM & G 390) (gift to 'each child that may be born to' certain persons; a child en ventre sa mère was held to be included, but other children born after the death of the testator were excluded); *Townsend v Early* (1860) 3 De GF & J 1 ('may be born' covered only those born between the date of the codicil and the testator's death or en ventre leur mères at his death). See also *Butler v Lowe* (1839) 10 Sim 317 (under a gift to each of the children of certain persons, begotten or to be begotten, children born after the death of the testator were excluded); *Peyton v Hughes* (1842) 7 Jur 311; *Mann v Thompson* (1854) Kay 628 ('to all and every the child and children'); *Rogers v Mutch* (1878) 10 ChD 25 ('to each of the children who shall live to attain' 21); *Re Thompson's Will, Brahe v Mason* [1910] VLR 251; *Re Bellville, Westminster Bank Ltd v Walton* [1941] Ch 414, [1941] 2 All ER 629, CA ('any daughter of B born after the date of this my will'). As to gifts to classes and groups see also PARAS 174–175.
2   *Mann v Thompson* (1854) Kay 628 at 644; *Rogers v Mutch* (1878) 10 ChD 25.
3   *A-G v Crispin* (1784) 1 Bro CC 386.
4   *Mann v Thompson* (1854) Kay 628 at 643; *Rogers v Mutch* (1878) 10 ChD 25; *Re Bellville, Westminster Bank Ltd v Walton* [1941] Ch 414 at 418, [1941] 2 All ER 629 at 631, CA.
5   *Re Bellville, Westminster Bank Ltd v Walton* [1941] Ch 414 at 419, [1941] 2 All ER 629 at 632, CA. In *Evans v Harris* (1842) 5 Beav 45, a fund was set apart out of which alone the legacies in question were payable; a child born after the testatrix's death was let in.
6   *Re Bellville, Westminster Bank Ltd v Walton* [1941] Ch 414 at 419, [1941] 2 All ER 629 at 632, CA. See also *Defflis v Goldschmidt* (1816) 1 Mer 417 (postponed gift; all members included).

B.   CLASS GIFTS

302. Time when class ascertained. In class gifts the interests of all the members must vest in interest at the same time; so, for example, if there is a gift to A for life and then to B and the children of C, the class must vest in interest at the testator's death, even though it is capable of enlargement by the birth of subsequent children of C during the lifetime of the life tenant[1]. The class may be ascertained at any particular point of time[2], for example at the death of the testator[3], or of the life tenant[4], or during the testator's lifetime at the date when he made his will[5], and the period of distribution may be postponed to a different and later time[6].

The words of the will may clearly indicate the point of time at which the class is to be ascertained; thus in a gift to children 'now living', only those in existence at the date of the will can take, and all children born after that date are excluded[7]. Similarly, in a gift to children living at the death of the testator or any other person[8], or at any particular future time[9], or to children now born or to be born during the lifetime of their named parent[10], the time of ascertaining the class is fixed by the express words of the will. If what is contemplated actually comprises a compound class and a class closing rule will apply to one part of the class, but is not compatible with the other, that would not of itself prevent the rule applying to the one part or to the gift as a whole[11]. In order to close a class, the court will not presume that a woman is past childbearing[12] or inquire into an individual's capacity to have children[13]. A question may arise as to whether the gift is, on its true construction, a class gift or not; it seems that the fact that some of the donees are named is not necessarily fatal to the gift being to a class[14].

1 *Kingsbury v Walter* [1901] AC 187 at 194 per Lord Davey.
2 *Re Hannam, Haddelsey v Hannam* [1897] 2 Ch 39.
3 *Viner v Francis* (1789) 2 Cox Eq Cas 190; *Leigh v Leigh* (1854) 17 Beav 605; *Sanders v Ashford* (1860) 28 Beav 609.
4 *Smith v Smith* (1837) 8 Sim 353; *Lee v Pain* (1844) 4 Hare 201 at 250.
5 *Re Hornby's Will* (1859) 7 WR 729.
6 *Re Hannam, Haddelsey v Hannam* [1897] 2 Ch 39. There will be cases where the gift may involve different classes of potential donees and possibly considerable delays in distribution: see *Re Bourke's Will Trusts, Barclay's Bank Trust Co Ltd v Canada Permanent Trust Co* [1980] 1 All ER 219, [1980] 1 WLR 539 (construction of contingent gift over to persons 'or their heirs and surviving issue'). See also *Re Barlow's Will Trusts* [1979] 1 All ER 296, [1979] 1 WLR 278 (gift of rights to purchase paintings to 'any members of my family and any friends of mine who wish to do so' was held to be a gift to two distinct classes of person; in neither case was it necessary that all members of the class should be identifiable at the time of distribution, so long as it was possible to determine whether or not applicants fell within one class or the other).
7 *James v Richardson* (1677) 1 Eq Cas Abr 214 pl 11; affd (1678) Freem KB 472n, HL.
8 *Barker v Lea* (1814) 3 Ves & B 113; *Jennings v Newman* (1839) 10 Sim 219 (where the gift was postponed to a life estate to one of the class, who was held to take); *Turner v Hudson* (1847) 10 Beav 222; *Re Helsby, Neate v Bozie* (1914) 84 LJ Ch 682 (where the gift was to the next of kin of the testator at the death of the life tenant); *Re Bulcock, Ingham v Ingham* [1916] 2 Ch 495 (where the gift was to an artificial class of next of kin of a special kind). Where the next of kin are to be ascertained at a specified time subsequent to the death of the testator, the class is ascertained on the hypothesis that the testator dies at the specified time: *Hutchinson v National Refuges for Homeless and Destitute Children* [1920] AC 795, HL. See also *Re Mellish, Day v Withers* [1916] 1 Ch 562; and PARA 313.
9 *Jee v Audley* (1787) 1 Cox Eq Cas 324; *Hughes v Hughes* (1807) 14 Ves 256 (youngest grandchild attaining 21); *Dodd v Wake* (1837) 8 Sim 615; *Boughton v Boughton* (1848) 1 HL Cas 406; *Hodson v Micklethwaite* (1854) 2 Drew 294; *Stuart v Cockerell* (1870) 5 Ch App 713. See also *Re Deighton's Settled Estates* (1876) 2 ChD 783, CA; *Wylie's Trustees v Bruce* 1919 SC 211 (gift to heirs of A after life estate); *Conolly v Brophy* (1920) 54 ILT 41 (bequest to children surviving when youngest attains 21). Where life interests are given to several persons in succession, and on the death of the last-named person there is a gift to a class of persons 'then living', the word 'then' is generally to be taken as referring grammatically to the death of that person, even where his death took place before that of the testator: *Archer v Jegon* (1837) 8 Sim 446; *Re Milne, Grant v Heysham* (1887) 56 LJ Ch 543 (affd (1888) 57 LT 828, CA); *Palmer v Orpen* [1894] 1 IR 32. In *Gaskell v Holmes* (1844) 3 Hare 438, 'then' was referred to the death of the testator; and in *Widdicombe v Muller* (1853) 1 Drew 443, 'then' was referred to the death of an annuitant.

10 *Scott v Earl of Scarborough* (1838) 1 Beav 154.
11 See *Re Clifford's Settlement Trusts, Heaton v Westwater* [1981] Ch 63, [1980] 1 All ER 1013 (one part for grandchildren reaching age 25 before a particular date, one part for other grandchildren who had not). See also *Re Chapman's Settlement Trusts, Jones v Chapman* [1978] 1 All ER 1122, [1977] 1 WLR 1163.
12 *Re Deloitte, Griffiths v Deloitte* [1926] Ch 56 (applying *Jee v Audley* (1787) 1 Cox Eq Cas 324). In *Berry v Green* [1938] AC 575, sub nom *Re Blake, Berry v Geen* [1938] 2 All ER 362, HL, the question was reserved. For the purpose of the rule against perpetuities and of terminating accumulations of income as applied to instruments taking effect on or after 16 July 1964, a woman over 55 is presumed to be past childbearing: see the Perpetuities and Accumulations Act 1964 ss 2, 14; and PERPETUITIES AND ACCUMULATIONS vol 80 (2013) PARAS 76, 130.
13 *Figg v Clarke* [1997] 1 WLR 603. The court might, however, authorise a distribution on the basis that an individual is incapable of having further children: *IRC v Bernstein* [1960] Ch 444 at 454, [1960] 1 All ER 697 at 702; *Re Westminster Bank Ltd's Declaration of Trust* [1963] 2 All ER 400n at 401n, [1963] 1 WLR 820 at 822; *Re Pettifor's Will Trusts, Roberts v Roberts* [1966] Ch 257, [1966] 1 All ER 913; *Figg v Clarke* above at 609–610; *Re Levy Estate Trust* [2000] CLY 5263.
14 The fact that some of the individuals are named does not deprive the gift of its characteristic as a glass gift; the question is whether this is a gift to the body as a whole: see *Sammut v Manzi* [2008] UKPC 58 at [41], [2009] 2 All ER 234 at [41], [2009] 1 WLR 1834 at [47] per Lord Hope citing Lords Davey and Macnaghten in *Kingsbury v Walter* [1901] AC 187 at 191, [1900–3] All ER Rep Ext 1531 at 1533–1534.

303. Gift to class on contingency.

Where there is a gift to a class on a contingent event, the time of happening of the contingency is not imported into the description of the individuals composing the class[1]. The circumstance, however, that the gift is only to take effect on the happening of the contingency is to be taken into consideration in combination with indications of the testator's intention to be found in other parts of his will[2], and, on the whole of the will, the description of the class may be varied and the contingency applied to the class[3]. It seems, though, that the distinction between a gift to a class upon a contingency and a gift to a contingent class may be a difficult one to draw, at times[4].

1 *Boulton v Beard* (1853) 3 De GM & G 608 at 612 per Turner LJ; *Hickling v Fair* [1899] AC 15 at 35, HL, per Lord Davey; *Re Walker, Dunkerly v Hewerdine* [1917] 1 Ch 38; *Re Sutcliffe, Alison v Alison* [1934] Ch 219. Hence the contingency that there are to be issue living at the time of distribution is not imported into the description of the issue who are to take, so as to exclude issue who have died before the date of distribution: *Re Sutcliffe, Alison v Alison*.
2 *Selby v Whittaker* (1877) 6 ChD 239 at 250, CA, per Baggallay LJ.
3 *Selby v Whittaker* (1877) 6 ChD 239, CA. Thus in a gift (if a named person should leave any child) to all his children, the class is not restricted to children whom he leaves at his death: *Boulton v Beard* (1853) 3 De GM & G 608; *M'Lachlan v Taitt* (1860) 2 De GF & J 449. As to the application to wills of the rule in *Emperor v Rolfe* (1748–9) 1 Ves Sen 208 see PARA 260. The context may, however, show the contrary, eg if the gift is to 'such' children (*Re Watson's Trusts* (1870) LR 10 Eq 36; and see *Sheffield v Kennett* (1859) 4 De G & J 593), or is to 'vest' (in the legal sense) at the death of the parent (*Selby v Whittaker*; and see *Wilson v Mount* (1854) 19 Beav 292 (gift over, if no 'such' issue)).
4 See *Ling v Ling* [2001] All ER (D) 322 (Nov) (T left gift over on predecease of wife to 'all or any' of his two children living at his death that attained 21; T's son attained 21 but predeceased T, leaving his own son A; T's daughter claimed to be sole surviving member of contingent class and that the will showed contrary intention to displace Wills Act 1837 s 33(2); held that there was no contrary intention and A fell within the class).

304. Rules of convenience existing to ascertain class membership.

Where it cannot be gathered, from the context and circumstances, what time is referred to for ascertaining a class, the court acts on certain rules of construction[1] which have been framed for the convenience of the donees and the administration of the property, and have accordingly been called rules of convenience[2]. It may be that judicial recourse to the application of these rules may now be affected by more modern approaches to construction of wills, in line with the intention-based approach to construing commercial agreements[3].

1   As to these rules see PARA 305 et seq. They are not overriding rules of law: see *Re Wernher's Settlement Trusts, Lloyds Bank Ltd v Earl Mountbatten* [1961] 1 All ER 184 at 187, [1961] 1 WLR 136 at 139 per Buckley J (citing *Re Bleckly, Bleckly v Bleckly* [1951] Ch 740 at 750, [1951] 1 All ER 1064 at 1070, CA). The testator should, it seems, be taken to have framed his trust with the rule in mind, unless the assumption is conclusively negatived by the words of the will: see *Re Wernher's Settlement Trusts, Lloyds Bank Ltd v Earl Mountbatten* at 189 and 141.
2   *Re Emmet's Estate, Emmet v Emmet* (1880) 13 ChD 484, CA; *Re Powell, Crosland v Holliday* [1898] 1 Ch 227 at 230 per Kekewich J. As to what gifts are subject to the rules see PARAS 310–311. The rules are admittedly 'not founded on any view of the testator's intention' (*Re Emmet's Estate, Emmet v Emmet* at 490 per Jessel MR; *Re Roberts, Repington v Roberts-Gawen* (1881) 19 ChD 520 at 527, CA), and are 'artificial' (*Leake v Robinson* (1817) 2 Mer 363 at 383 per Grant MR; *Re Chartres, Farman v Barrett* [1927] 1 Ch 466). The rules generally for ascertainment of a class, both as to personal property and real property, are said to be founded on the presumption that only persons in being are intended to take: *Ellison v Airey* (1748) 1 Ves Sen 111 at 114; *Crone v Odell* (1811) 1 Ball & B 449 at 459 (affd (1815) 3 Dow 61, HL); *Bartleman v Murchison* (1831) 2 Russ & M 136 at 140. As to implied gifts to the objects of an unexercised power of selection, and as to the rules for ascertaining a class taking in default of appointment under a power see TRUSTS AND POWERS vol 98 (2013) PARAS 29–30.
3   See *Thomas v Kent* [2006] EWCA Civ 1485, [2006] All ER (D) 57 (May); *Investors Compensation Scheme Ltd v West Bromwich Building Society* [1998] 1 All ER 98, [1998] 1 WLR 896. See also PARA 305 text and note 7. More generally, see the judgment of Lord Neuberger in See *Marley v Rawlings* [2014] UKSC 2 at [20], [2015] AC 129, [2014] 1 All ER 807: whether the document in question is a commercial contract or a will, the aim is to identify the intention of the party or parties to the document by interpreting the words used in their documentary, factual and commercial context.

305. The first rule of convenience. The first rule of convenience is as follows: a class[1] is prima facie composed of those members (if any) existing, ascertainable and capable of taking[2] at the date of distribution[3], which is usually at the testator's death[4], but, where the date of distribution is later, the class opens so as to let in all those members coming into existence before the date of distribution[5]. Where, however, the gift is immediate, but at the testator's death no member of the class has yet come into existence, then prima facie all the members of the class who are born at any future period are intended to take under the gift[6].

The class is ascertained independently of those members of it who die before the testator; there is no question of lapse of their shares, and they are not included[7]; nor, formerly, even where they were issue of the testator, did they take by leaving issue living at his death, even if the class consisted of only one person[8]. However, under the will of a testator who dies on or after 1 January 1983, if the class consists of children or remoter descendants of his, and a member of that class dies before him leaving issue, and issue of that member are living at the testator's death, then, unless a contrary intention appears by the will, the devise or bequest takes effect as if the class included the issue of its deceased member living at the testator's death[9].

As regards members of a class taking under a postponed gift, the death of any one of them who has survived the testator but dies before the date of distribution does not defeat his interest[10], provided that the contingency of surviving that date is not part of the description of the class[11]. Thus the objects among whom the property becomes ultimately divisible are those members of the class who may be living at the date of distribution, and the representatives of such as may have died before that date having survived the testator[12].

1   As to what kinds of classes are subject to this rule see PARA 309.
2   See *Fell v Biddolph* (1875) LR 10 CP 701 at 709 (where two of the class had attested the will: see PARA 44); *Re Coleman and Jarrom* (1876) 4 ChD 165 at 169, 173 per Jessel MR.
3   As to the date of distribution see PARA 306.

4 *Re Winn, Brook v Whitton* [1910] 1 Ch 278 at 286, 289 per Parker J. See also *Singleton v Gilbert* (1784) 1 Cox Eq Cas 68; *Viner v Francis* (1789) 2 Cox Eq Cas 190; *Hill v Chapman* (1791) 3 Bro CC 391; *Davidson v Dallas* (1808) 14 Ves 576. This rule applies to an immediate gift to a class 'or so many of them as shall be living' at a postponed period (*Trelawney v Molesworth* (1701) Colles 163), and to a class described as living at the death of a person who died in the lifetime of the testator (*Lee v Pain* (1844) 4 Hare 201 at 250; *Dimond v Bostock* (1875) 10 Ch App 358), or as living at the date of the will (*Leigh v Leigh* (1854) 17 Beav 605). As to a gift to a class of 'unmarried' persons see *Jubber v Jubber* (1839) 9 Sim 503; *Hall v Robertson* (1853) 4 De GM & G 781 ('unmarried daughters' ascertained at date of codicil); *Blagrove v Coore* (1859) 27 Beav 138 (ascertained at death). Where a fund is left to a class contingently on their attaining 21, the eldest of the class on attaining 21 takes a vested interest in possession in his share, and a contingent interest in the shares of the members of the class who are still under 21: *Re Williams' Settlement, Williams v Williams* [1911] 1 Ch 441. Where the gift is revoked as regards some members of the class, the effect is to increase the shares of the other members: *Watson v Donaldson* [1915] 1 IR 63, Ir CA; and see PARA 174.
5 *Ellison v Airey* (1748) 1 Ves Sen 111; *Bartlett v Hollister* (1757) Amb 334; *Congreve v Congreve* (1781) 1 Bro CC 530; *Devisme v Mello* (1782) 1 Bro CC 537; *Simmons v Vallance* (1793) 4 Bro CC 345; *Middleton v Messenger* (1799) 5 Ves 136; *Walker v Shore* (1808) 15 Ves 122 at 125; *Tebbs v Carpenter* (1816) 1 Madd 290; *Marshall v Bousfield* (1817) 2 Madd 166; *Cooke v Bowen* (1840) 4 Y & C Ex 244; *Moffatt v Burnie* (1853) 18 Beav 211 at 214; *Oppenheim v Henry* (1853) 10 Hare 441; *Browne v Hammond* (1858) John 210 at 212n. See also *Hickling v Fair* [1899] AC 15 at 35, HL, per Lord Davey. See also *Marshall v Hill* [2003] All ER (D) 304 (Mar) (testatrix executed deed of variation referring to 'grandchildren' at time when there was only one grandchild; held that this allowed in grandchildren born after her death). Apart from this letting in of additional members, the postponement of the gift does not postpone the time of ascertainment of the class (*Lee v Lee* (1860) 1 Drew & Sm 85 at 87), and other persons who come into existence after the period of distribution are excluded (*Hill v Chapman* (1791) 3 Bro CC 391; *Re Roberts, Repington v Roberts-Gawen* (1881) 19 ChD 520 at 527, CA). Members of the class need not survive the period of distribution: *Re Wood, Moore v Bailey* (1880) 43 LT 730; *Re Walker, Dunkerly v Hewerdine* [1917] 1 Ch 38. As to the meaning of 'period of distribution' see PARA 306 note 1.
6 *Weld v Bradbury* (1715) 2 Vern 705; *Shepherd v Ingram* (1764) Amb 448; *Odell v Crone* (1815) 3 Dow 61, HL ('younger children'); *Leake v Robinson* (1817) 2 Mer 363 at 383; *Hutcheson v Jones* (1817) 2 Madd 124; *Harris v Lloyd* (1823) Turn & R 310 at 314; *Armitage v Williams* (1859) 27 Beav 346.
7 *Christopherson v Naylor* (1816) 1 Mer 320; *Re Hannam, Haddelsey v Hannam* [1897] 2 Ch 39; cf *Gowling v Thompson* (1868) LR 11 Eq 366n (where the general principle was displaced); and see PARAS 174, 322. But see a more modern approach to this type of problem and the construction approach by Chadwick LJ in *Thomas v Kent* [2006] EWCA Civ 1485, [2006] All ER (D) 57 (May) (an ultimate trust, following the failure of three earlier trusts, to the testator's siblings, with gifts over to their children; five siblings were dead by date of will; held that the class included all siblings, regardless of date of death; judicial consideration of approach seen in *Re Hannam*, but general 'armchair principle' approach applied in preference to the rule in *Re Hannam*).
8 *Olney v Bates* (1855) 3 Drew 319; *Browne v Hammond* (1858) John 210 (deciding that the Wills Act 1837 s 33 (see PARA 167) had no application); *Re Harvey's Estate, Harvey v Gillow* [1893] 1 Ch 567; *Re Kinnear, Kinnear v Barnett* (1904) 90 LT 537.
9 Wills Act 1837 s 33(2) (substituted by the Administration of Justice Act 1982 s 19). See further PARAS 169, 177. See also *Ling v Ling* [2001] All ER (D) 322 (Nov).
10 *Devisme v Mello* (1782) 1 Bro CC 537; *Stanley v Wise* (1788) 1 Cox Eq Cas 432; *Cooke v Bowen* (1840) 4 Y & C Ex 244; *Watson v Watson* (1840) 11 Sim 73; *Swan v Bowden* (1842) 11 LJ Ch 155; *Locker v Bradley* (1842) 5 Beav 593; *Salmon v Green* (1849) 11 Beav 453; *Pattison v Pattison* (1855) 19 Beav 638. The interests of such persons are vested but subject to being divested in quantity by the birth of further members of the class: see eg *Stanley v Wise* (1788) 1 Cox Eq Cas 432; *Baldwin v Rogers* (1853) 3 De GM & G 649. A provision in the final limitation requiring a sole beneficiary to survive the life tenant will not be reflected back into the primary limitation: *Re Stephens, Tomalin v Tomalin's Trustee* [1927] 1 Ch 1, CA.
11 *Parr v Parr* (1833) 1 My & K 647 (to 'devolve' on children of life tenant). There may be a gift over or a substitutionary gift defeating a member's interest: *Pope v Whitcombe* (1827) 3 Russ 124; *Re Miles, Miles v Miles* (1889) 61 LT 359. See also *Re Shaw, Williams v Pledger* (1912) 56 Sol Jo 380.
12 *Re Roberts, Percival v Roberts* [1903] 2 Ch 200 at 202 per Joyce J.

306. Date of distribution. The date of distribution[1] may be postponed either by some prior gift, or by the nature of the property given, or by the conditions attached to the gift. Where the gift is postponed to a life estate, the date of distribution is usually, but not necessarily, the determination of the life estate[2]. This can involve long periods of delay and consequent complication in determining the composition of the class entitled to the gift, particularly with successive life interests[3], but the existence of a mere charge on a fund, for example an annuity charged on it, does not necessarily affect the time at which the class is ascertained[4].

If there is a prior life interest determinable on bankruptcy and there is no postponement of payment until the death of the life tenant, the class is fixed at the time of bankruptcy[5]; but, where the limitation over to the class after the life interest postpones payment until the death of the life tenant[6], or expressly directs the property to be applicable in the same manner as if the life tenant were dead[7], this extends the class so as to let in those coming into existence before the death[8].

Where a life interest is determinable on remarriage, and the gift over expressly refers only to the death of the life tenant, but the court construes the gift over as impliedly intended to take effect on the remarriage, it may be that the class of children is to be ascertained at the remarriage, although expressly described as to be ascertained at the death[9].

Where the property is reversionary, the date of distribution may be postponed until it falls into possession[10], but there is no postponement in case of a gift of a residue which includes a reversionary interest with other property[11].

1   An expression such as 'date of distribution' or 'period of distribution' is, strictly speaking, a misnomer; it does not denote the moment when the trustees will distribute the fund, but merely indicates the time when the class of beneficiaries finally closes: see *Re Cockle's Will Trusts, Re Pittaway, Moreland v Draffen, Risdon v Public Trustee* [1967] Ch 690 at 704, [1967] 1 All ER 391 at 394 per Stamp J.

2   *Ayton v Ayton* (1787) 1 Cox Eq Cas 327; *Middleton v Messenger* (1799) 5 Ves 136; *Barnaby v Tassell* (1871) LR 11 Eq 363; *Re Cockle's Will Trusts, Re Pittaway, Moreland v Draffen, Risdon v Public Trustee* [1967] Ch 690, [1967] 1 All ER 391; *Re Deeley's Settlement, Batchelor v Russell* [1974] Ch 454, [1973] 3 All ER 1127. Cf *Re Knapp's Settlement, Knapp v Vassall* [1895] 1 Ch 91 at 96 per North J. As to a gift to the 'descendants' of two successive life tenants see *Re Roberts, Repington v Roberts-Gawen* (1881) 19 ChD 520 at 527, CA, per Jessel MR (see note 3 on this point).

3   See *Thomas v Kent* [2006] EWCA Civ 1485, [2006] All ER (D) 57 (May) (two successive life tenants followed by failed gift to issue of last life tenant, followed by ultimate gift over to testator's siblings with substitutional gifts to their children: distribution delayed by 47 years; the issue of the substitutional gift was remitted to the judge for further representation and consideration).

4   *Singleton v Gilbert* (1784) 1 Cox Eq Cas 68; *Hill v Chapman* (1791) 3 Bro CC 391; *Watson v Watson* (1840) 11 Sim 73; *Bortoft v Wadsworth* (1864) 12 WR 523; *Coventry v Coventry* (1865) 2 Drew & Sm 470; *Re Whiteford, Inglis v Whiteford* [1903] 1 Ch 889; *Re Hiscoe, Hiscoe v Waite* (1883) 48 LT 510; *Gardner v James* (1843) 6 Beav 170 (where there could be no distribution until the death of the surviving annuitant).

5   *Re Smith* (1862) 2 John & H 594 at 600–601; *Re Aylwin's Trusts* (1873) LR 16 Eq 585; *Re Curzon, Martin v Perry* (1912) 56 Sol Jo 362.

6   *Brandon v Aston* (1843) 2 Y & C Ch Cas 24 at 30.

7   *Re Bedson's Trusts* (1885) 28 ChD 523, CA.

8   Where the limitation over is substitutional in nature, it may be that the class is limited to those members still living at the date of distribution, on the assumption that the testator would have been much more likely to intend that the gift would take effect in favour of the living rather than the dead; see *Thomas v Kent* [2006] EWCA Civ 1485 at [24], [2006] All ER (D) 57 (May), per Chadwick LJ.

9   See *Bainbridge v Cream* (1852) 16 Beav 25 (followed in *Stanford v Stanford* (1886) 34 ChD 362 at 366); *Re Tucker, Bowchier v Gordon* (1887) 56 LT 118 at 119 (where Stirling J said that he did not understand *Bainbridge v Cream*); *Re Dear, Helby v Dear* (1889) 61 LT 432 at 434 (where Kay J said that he considered *Bainbridge v Cream* to be a reasonable extension of *Luxford v Cheeke* (1683) 3 Lev 125); *Re Crother's Trusts* [1915] 1 IR 53; *Re Warner, Watts v Silvey* [1918] 1 Ch 368.

10 *Walker v Shore* (1808) 15 Ves 122 at 125 (followed in *Harvey v Stracey* (1852) 1 Drew 73 at 123).
11 *Hagger v Payne* (1857) 23 Beav 474; *Coventry v Coventry* (1865) 2 Drew & Sm 470.

307. The second rule of convenience. The second rule of convenience deals with the determination of the date of distribution[1] where the gift is of the corpus of property[2] and is postponed by reason of the conditions attached to it, as where payment is to be made on the attainment by the donee of a specified age[3], or on his or her marriage[4], or in other cases, it appears, where such conditions are of a nature personal to the donees. The rule is as follows: where the postponement of enjoyment is due to conditions attached to the gift, the date of distribution is considered to be reached as soon as the conditions are so far performed that some one member of the class would be entitled to the enjoyment of his share, if the class were then not susceptible of increase[5], and the class is then closed[6]. Thus where there is an immediate gift to a class, to be paid on the members attaining a specified age, the date of distribution is the date of the testator's death, if any member of the class has then attained that age[7], and, if not, the time of the first occasion when a member attains that age[8]. In applying the rule, the court is careful to distinguish between those provisions which are aimed solely at fixing the time of vesting of interest and provisions which determine the size of the class[9].

1 As to the meaning of 'date of distribution' see PARA 306 note 1.
2 As to gifts of income see PARA 310; and as to real estate see PARA 311.
3 See the text and notes 7–8. Where, however, a class takes at birth, a gift over on the members failing to attain a specified age does not postpone the period of distribution: *Davidson v Dallas* (1808) 14 Ves 576.
4 *Barrington v Tristram* (1801) 6 Ves 345; *Dawson v Oliver-Massey* (1876) 2 ChD 753 at 756, CA.
5 *Re Emmet's Estate, Emmet v Emmet* (1880) 13 ChD 484 at 490, CA; *Re Bedson's Trusts* (1885) 28 ChD 523 at 526, CA; *Re Knapp's Settlement, Knapp v Vassall* [1895] 1 Ch 91 at 96; Underhill and Strahan's Interpretation of Wills and Settlements (3rd Edn) 77.
6 Ie in accordance with the first rule: see PARA 305.
7 *Picken v Matthews* (1878) 10 ChD 264. See also *Gillman v Daunt* (1856) 3 K & J 48.
8 *Andrews v Partington* (1791) 3 Bro CC 401; *Prescott v Long* (1795) 2 Ves 690; *Hoste v Pratt* (1798) 3 Ves 730; *Whitbread v Lord St John* (1804) 10 Ves 152; *Curtis v Curtis* (1821) 6 Madd 14; *Titcomb v Butler* (1830) 3 Sim 417; *Balm v Balm* (1830) 3 Sim 492; *Blease v Burgh* (1840) 2 Beav 221; *Robley v Ridings* (1847) 11 Jur 813; *Re Mervin, Mervin v Crossman* [1891] 3 Ch 197; *Re Knapp's Settlement, Knapp v Vassall* [1895] 1 Ch 91; *Re Chapman's Settlement Trusts, Jones v Chapman* [1978] 1 All ER 1122, [1977] 1 WLR 1163, CA; *Re Clifford's Settlement Trusts, Heaton v Westwater* [1981] Ch 63, [1980] 1 All ER 1013; *Millbank v Millbank* [1982] 79 LS Gaz R 1291; *Re Drummond's Settlement, Foster v Foster* [1988] 1 All ER 449, [1988] 1 WLR 234. See also PERPETUITIES AND ACCUMULATIONS vol 80 (2013) PARA 83. The rule is termed 'the rule in *Andrews v Partington*', but in that case Lord Thurlow LC treated the rule as already established, although, as pointed out in *Prescott v Long* (1795) 2 Ves 690 at 692 per Lord Loughborough, it does not appear in *Andrews v Partington* what are the cases he referred to. The rule seems, however, to have been applied in *Gilmore v Severn* (1785) 1 Bro CC 582. A child en ventre sa mère when the eldest attains the specified age is included in the class: *Trustees, Executors and Agency Co Ltd v Sleeman* (1899) 25 VLR 187; and see PARA 362. Where the gift is to children who attain 21, a child who has attained that age at the date of the will is not excluded (*Re Rayner, Couch v Warner* (1925) 134 LT 141), although in general words of futurity are construed strictly (*Re Walker, Walker v Walker* [1930] 1 Ch 469, CA; and see PARA 247). The rule applies also in the case of settlements: see PARA 308 note 4; and SETTLEMENTS vol 91 (2012) PARA 827.
9 See *Re Chapman's Settlement Trusts, Jones v Chapman* [1978] 1 All ER 1122, [1977] 1 WLR 1163, CA, where the provisions could be separated without difficulty and cf *Re Tom's Settlement, Rose v Evans* [1987] 1 All ER 1081, [1987] 1 WLR 1021, where the words 'living at the closing date' prevented the application of the rule.

308. Application of the second rule of convenience. The second rule of convenience[1] is adopted to reconcile inconsistent directions in a will that all the children or other persons comprising the class[2] are to take, but that the fund is to be divided at a time when the class cannot be ascertained[3]. The rule is not applied unless it is necessary[4], and in substance this will only be where the testator has made his testamentary disposition in such terms that he must, or may, be taken to have intended a distribution at a moment which may be anterior to the birth of all the members of the class[5]. In any event, the rule must give way to language sufficiently clear to displace it[6]. Thus it is not applied where the provisions of the will are inconsistent with any right of the first child attaining the specified age or satisfying the conditions as to payment of his share[7], as, for example, where there is an effective direction, extending beyond the time when a child first attains the specified age or satisfies the conditions, to accumulate income[8], or to allow maintenance or advancement[9].

Where the application of the rule would cause the gift to the class, or any other gift in the will connected with it, to fail as being contrary to law (for example, under the rule against perpetuities), and some other construction, such as that the class is ascertained at the testator's death, is possible under the will[10] by which the gift takes effect, it appears that the rule is not applied but that the alternative construction is adopted[11].

The rule may be applied notwithstanding that there is a previous life interest[12], as, for example, where no child is born until after the expiration of the previous interest[13], unless the testator shows that the expiration of that life interest is intended by him to be the date of distribution[14].

The rule applies both where the gift and direction as to payment are distinct, so that the gift is not contingent[15], and where the gift is contingent on attaining the specified age[16] or other event, or is subject to a gift over in any such event[17].

An analogous rule operates where the date of distribution is the date when the youngest of the class of donees attains a certain age; in such a case the gift is immediate and vested and the class is confined to those in being at the date of the testator's death[18] or, if the gift is subject to intervening life interests, the date of the termination of the last of those life interests[19]. The rule does not apply if there is no one in existence at the date of the testator's death who is entitled to a share absolutely vested in interest and possession[20].

1   As to the second rule see PARA 307.
2   See PARA 309.
3   *Re Stephens, Kilby v Betts* [1904] 1 Ch 322 at 328 per Buckley J; *Re Wernher's Settlement Trusts, Lloyds Bank Ltd v Earl Mountbatten* [1961] 1 All ER 184 at 187, [1961] 1 WLR 136 at 139 per Buckley J; *Re Tom's Settlement, Rose v Evans* [1987] 1 All ER 1081 at 1085, [1987] 1 WLR 1021 at 1025 per Sir Nicholas Browne-Wilkinson V-C. See also *Defflis v Goldschmidt* (1816) 1 Mer 417 at 420 per Grant MR; *Mainwaring v Beevor* (1849) 8 Hare 44 at 49 per Wigram V-C; but see *Mann v Thompson* (1854) Kay 628 at 641 (where Wood V-C appears not to have concurred in this view). The rule has often been criticised. In *Andrews v Partington* (1791) 3 Bro CC 401 at 404, Lord Thurlow LC said that there was no greater inconvenience in the case of a devise than in that of a marriage settlement, where nobody doubted that the same expression meant all the children. See also note 4.
4   *Re Stephens, Kilby v Betts* [1904] 1 Ch 322 at 328 per Buckley J. The rule has been applied to similar gifts to children in a voluntary settlement (*Re Knapp's Settlement, Knapp v Vassall* [1895] 1 Ch 91; *Re Edmondson's Will Trusts, Baron Sandford v Edmondson* [1972] 1 All ER 444, [1972] 1 WLR 183, CA), although by reason of the previous life estate given to the parent it is not normally called into play in the case of a marriage settlement (*Mann v Thompson* (1854) Kay 628 at 642). See SETTLEMENTS vol 91 (2012) PARA 827. The rule may be excluded where the income has been divided between two tenants for life: see *Re Faux, Taylor v Faux* (1915) 84 LJ Ch 873; applied in *Re Paul's Settlement Trusts, Paul v Nelson* [1920] 1 Ch 99. For a discussion of the rule and its origin see *Re Chartres, Farman v Barrett* [1927] 1 Ch 466 (where it was applied, although the condition of attaining the age of 21 had become definite only by the release of a power of appointment).
5   *Re Kebty-Fletcher's Will Trusts, Public Trustee v Swan* [1969] 1 Ch 339 at 344, [1967] 3 All ER 1076 at 1079 per Stamp J; *Re Harker's Will Trusts, Kean v Harker* [1969] 3 All ER 1, [1969] 1 WLR 1124 (in both of which cases *Re Davies, Davies v Mackintosh* [1957] 3 All ER 52, [1957]

1 WLR 922 was doubted); *Re Drummond's Settlement, Foster v Foster* [1988] 1 All ER 449 at 454, [1988] 1 WLR 234 at 239–240 per Sir Denis Buckley.

6 See eg *Re Bleckly, Bleckly v Bleckly* [1951] Ch 740 at 750, [1951] 1 All ER 1064 at 1070, CA, per Sir Raymond Evershed MR; *Re Edmondson's Will Trusts, Baron Sandford v Edmondson* [1972] 1 All ER 444, [1972] 1 WLR 183, CA (where the words 'whenever born' in the deed of appointment were held to exclude the rule); *Re Tom's Settlement, Rose v Evans* [1987] 1 All ER 1081, [1987] 1 WLR 1021 (where a specific reference to the period during which beneficiaries must be born was held to exclude the rule). The rule is not, however, excluded by the fact that the class is described as 'all' or 'all and every' the children of a person (*Andrews v Partington* (1791) 3 Bro CC 401; *Prescott v Long* (1795) 2 Ves 690), nor do words of futurity such as 'hereafter to be born' necessarily exclude the rule (*Re Wernher's Settlement Trusts, Lloyds Bank Ltd v Earl Mountbatten* [1961] 1 All ER 184, [1961] 1 WLR 136 (words related to period between date of deed and date of distribution); *Re Chapman's Settlement Trusts, Jones v Chapman* [1978] 1 All ER 1122, [1977] 1 WLR 1163, CA ('now born or who shall be born hereafter')).

7 Cf *Re Kipping, Kipping v Kipping* [1914] 1 Ch 62; *Macculloch v Anderson* [1904] AC 55 at 61, HL.

8 *Watson v Young* (1885) 28 ChD 436; *Re Pilkington, Pilkington v Pilkington* (1892) 29 LR Ir 370; *Re Stephens, Kilby v Betts* [1904] 1 Ch 322; *Re Stevens, Trustees, Executors and Agency Co Ltd v Teague* [1912] VLR 194 at 201–202; *Re Watt's Will Trusts* [1936] 2 All ER 1555. This may not be the case where the direction for accumulation is ineffective owing to the right of beneficiaries to determine it and take the property free from accumulation: *Curtis v Curtis* (1821) 6 Madd 14; *Coventry v Coventry* (1865) 2 Drew & Sm 470. See also PARA 146.

9 *Gardner v James* (1843) 6 Beav 170; *Bateman v Foster* (1844) 1 Coll 118 at 126; *Mainwaring v Beevor* (1849) 8 Hare 44; *Iredell v Iredell* (1858) 25 Beav 485; *Armitage v Williams* (1859) 27 Beav 346; *Bateman v Gray* (1868) LR 6 Eq 215 (advancement out of 'vested or presumptive shares' relied on) (followed in *Re Courtenay, Pearce v Foxwell* (1905) 74 LJ Ch 654; but doubted and not followed in *Re Deloitte, Griffiths v Allbeury* [1919] 1 Ch 209, CA). See also *Titcomb v Butler* (1830) 3 Sim 417 (power to allow maintenance insufficient); *Mower v Orr* (1849) 7 Hare 473 at 477; *Hagger v Payne* (1857) 23 Beav 474 at 479; *Gimblett v Purton* (1871) LR 12 Eq 427 at 430 (power of advancement relating to presumptive shares only); *Re Henderson's Trusts, Schreiber v Baring* [1969] 3 All ER 769, [1969] 1 WLR 651, CA (power of advancement relating to vested presumptive shares).

10 As to this rule in cases of ambiguous construction see PARA 259; and PERPETUITIES AND ACCUMULATIONS vol 80 (2013) PARA 32.

11 *Elliott v Elliott* (1841) 12 Sim 276 (where there was a gift to children of E, as and when attaining 22, with a provision for interest in the meantime, and Shadwell V-C saw no objection to holding the class to be ascertained at the testator's death). See also PERPETUITIES AND ACCUMULATIONS vol 80 (2013) PARA 83. *Elliott v Elliott* was explained, as decided on the ground stated in the text, in *Mainwaring v Beevor* (1849) 8 Hare 44 at 48 and *Re Wenmoth's Estate, Wenmoth v Wenmoth* (1887) 37 ChD 266 at 270; and it was followed in *Re Coppard's Estate, Howlett v Hodson* (1887) 35 ChD 350. See also *Re Hobson's Will, Hobson v Sharp* [1907] VLR 724 at 730. Cf the cases as to gifts of income cited in PARA 310 note 6. However, *Elliott v Elliott* (1841) 12 Sim 276 has been much criticised: see *Re Pilkington, Pilkington v Pilkington* (1892) 29 LR Ir 370 at 376. See also *Re Mervin, Mervin v Crossman* [1891] 3 Ch 197 at 203–204 (where *Elliott v Elliott* was supported on account of the gift of interest; but this is open to question as the gift of interest would only make the gift of principal a vested and not a contingent gift, and would not alter the date of distribution); *Re Barker, Capon v Flick* (1905) 92 LT 831; *Re Ransome's Will Trusts, Moberley v Ransome* [1957] Ch 348, [1957] 1 All ER 690. *Re Coppard's Estate, Howlett v Hodson* (1887) 35 ChD 350 was not intended to go beyond *Elliott v Elliott* (1841) 12 Sim 276 (*Re Mervin, Mervin v Crossman* [1891] 3 Ch 197), and, in so far as it does so, ought not to be followed (*Re Stevens, Clark v Stevens* (1896) 40 Sol Jo 296).

12 *Clarke v Clarke* (1836) 8 Sim 59; *Re Emmet's Estate, Emmet v Emmet* (1880) 13 ChD 484, CA (in both of which cases no children had attained the specified age at the expiration of the previous interest).

13 *Re Bleckly, Bleckly v Bleckly* [1951] Ch 740, [1951] 1 All ER 1064, CA. See also *Robley v Ridings* (1847) 11 Jur 813.

14 *Kevern v Williams* (1832) 5 Sim 171 (followed in *Berkeley v Swinburne* (1848) 16 Sim 275 at 285–286; and explained in *Re Emmet's Estate, Emmet v Emmet* (1880) 13 ChD 484, CA (cited in PARA 307 note 5)).

15 *Andrews v Partington* (1791) 3 Bro CC 401 (explained in *Re Mervin, Mervin v Crossman* [1891] 3 Ch 197 at 203 per Stirling J).

16 *Whitbread v Lord St John* (1804) 10 Ves 152; *Balm v Balm* (1830) 3 Sim 492; *Locke v Lamb* (1867) LR 4 Eq 372; *Gimblett v Purton* (1871) LR 12 Eq 427.

17 *Barrington v Tristram* (1801) 6 Ves 345.

18   *Re Manners, Public Trustee v Manners* [1955] 3 All ER 83, [1955] 1 WLR 1096.
19   *Smith v Jackson* (1823) 1 LJOS Ch 231.
20   *Re Ransome's Will Trusts, Moberley v Ransome* [1957] Ch 348, [1957] 1 All ER 690 (gift to such of R's children as should be living on the youngest of R's children attaining 21).

309. Classes subject to the rules. The rules of convenience[1] apply to a gift to a class of children whether the parent is the testator or any other person, alive or dead[2], and, it appears, to any other description of a class[3] which, in the context and circumstances, does not point out some other mode of ascertaining the class[4]. The rules are applicable even where the class is described as 'begotten or to be begotten', 'born or to be born' or in like words[5], and no future period is fixed by the will[6], in which case the words in question are held to provide for the birth of children between the making of the will and the testator's death[7]. However it may be otherwise where the expression 'whenever born' is used[8]. The rules are also applicable where the gift is postponed to a life interest given to a named person who by these rules takes as a member of the class[9].

1   As to the rules of convenience see PARAS 304–307.
2   *Viner v Francis* (1789) 2 Cox Eq Cas 190.
3   Eg grandchildren (*Mainwaring v Beevor* (1849) 8 Hare 44; *Wetherell v Wetherell* (1863) 1 De GJ & Sm 134 ('grandchildren and great-grandchildren' of A and B); *Coventry v Coventry* (1865) 2 Drew & Sm 470; *Gimblett v Purton* (1871) LR 12 Eq 427); cousins (*Baldwin v Rogers* (1853) 3 De GM & G 649); issue (*Re Deeley's Settlement, Batchelor v Russell* [1974] Ch 454, [1973] 3 All ER 1127; *Re Edmondson's Will Trusts, Baron Sandford v Edmondson* [1972] 1 All ER 444, [1972] 1 WLR 183, CA; *Re Cockle's Will Trusts, Re Pittaway, Moreland v Draffen, Risdon v Public Trustee* [1967] Ch 690, [1967] 1 All ER 391); descriptions by other grades of relationship (*Baldwin v Rogers* (1853) 3 De GM & G 649 at 656 per Turner LJ); and generally, it appears, descriptions of any fluctuating body (*Re Laffan and Downes' Contract* [1897] 1 IR 469 at 473; *Re Smith, Johnson v Bright-Smith* [1914] 1 Ch 937). See also CHARITIES vol 8 (2015) PARA 62; PERPETUITIES AND ACCUMULATIONS vol 80 (2013) PARA 5.
4   As to gifts to 'next of kin' of any person see PARA 313; and see generally PARAS 300–301.
5   *Sprackling v Ranier* (1761) 1 Dick 344; *Whitbread v Lord St John* (1804) 10 Ves 152; *Gilbert v Boorman* (1805) 11 Ves 238; *Clarke v Clarke* (1836) 8 Sim 59; *Butler v Lowe* (1839) 10 Sim 317; *Dias v De Livera* (1879) 5 App Cas 123 at 134, PC.
6   *Scott v Earl of Scarborough* (1838) 1 Beav 154 at 168 (where, however, the gift was to children born 'during the lifetime of their respective parents' so that children born after the date of distribution were let in); *Re Wernher's Settlement Trusts, Lloyds Bank Ltd v Earl Mountbatten* [1961] 1 All ER 184, [1961] 1 WLR 136. See also PARA 308 note 6.
7   *Storrs v Benbow* (1833) 2 My & K 46 at 48; *Dias v De Livera* (1879) 5 App Cas 123 at 135, PC. Cf PARA 311 note 7 (real estate).
8   The expression 'whenever born' tends to displace the application of these rules where a class is capable of further increase, because it is sufficiently specific in pointing to all future times: see *Re Clifford's Settlement Trusts, Heaton v Westwater* [1981] Ch 63 at 66, [1980] 1 All ER 1013 at 1016 per Sir Robert Megarry V-C; *Re Edmondson's Will Trusts, Baron Sandford of Banbury v Edmondson* [1972] 1 All ER 444, [1972] 1 WLR 183, CA.
9   *Elmsley v Young* (1835) 2 My & K 780; *King v Tootel* (1858) 25 Beav 23; *Reay v Rawlinson* (1860) 29 Beav 88; *Almack v Horn* (1863) 1 Hem & M 630. See also the cases as to next of kin cited in PARA 313 note 2.

310. Gifts subject to the rules. The rules of convenience[1] apply to gifts of the corpus of personal estate[2], or of a mixed fund of real and personal estate[3]. In the case of gifts of income only of such property, or of sums payable at intervals[4], the class taking any particular payment is normally to be ascertained so as to let in all members coming into existence before the time for that payment[5], and the class, it appears, is not to be closed finally for all subsequent payments at the time when the right to receive income first accrues to any member of the class, except in cases where other considerations require it[6].

1   As to the rules of convenience see PARA 304 et seq.
2   Gifts of real estate, or a mixed fund of real and personal estate, held on trust for conversion and investment are subject to the rules, if the doctrine of conversion applies: *Hoste v Pratt* (1798) 3 Ves

730; *Re Mervin, Mervin v Crossman* [1891] 3 Ch 197. The doctrine of conversion, whereby land held by trustees subject to a trust for sale is regarded as personal property, has been abolished, except where the trust for sale was created by the will of a testator who died before 1 January 1997: see the Trusts of Land and Appointment of Trustees Act 1996 ss 3, 25(5); and REAL PROPERTY AND REGISTRATION vol 87 (2012) PARAS 7, 215. The doctrine of conversion is, however, not wholly abolished by s 3 and will still apply to eg uncompleted agreements for the sale of land. As to the doctrine of conversion see further EQUITABLE JURISDICTION vol 47 (2014) PARA 138 et seq.

3   See *Andrews v Partington* (1791) 3 Bro CC 401 (residue); *Dawson v Oliver-Massey* (1876) 2 ChD 753, CA; *Re Emmet's Estate, Emmet v Emmet* (1880) 13 ChD 484, CA.

4   *Re Latham, Seymour v Bolton* [1901] WN 248 (annuity to children attaining 21; two who had attained 21 alone entitled to payment).

5   *Re Wenmoth's Estate, Wenmoth v Wenmoth* (1887) 37 ChD 266 (where Chitty J held that the rule in *Andrews v Partington* (1791) 3 Bro CC 401 (see PARA 307) did not apply to gifts of income). The decision in *Re Wenmoth's Estate, Wenmoth v Wenmoth* was criticised and explained by Buckley J in *Re Stephens, Kilby v Betts* [1904] 1 Ch 322, but these criticisms have, however, been dissented from as unnecessary (*Re Carter, Walker v Litchfield* (1911) 30 NZLR 707 at 723, NZ CA), and *Re Wenmoth's Estate, Wenmoth v Wenmoth* was followed in *Re Ward's Will Trusts, Ward v Ward* [1965] Ch 856, [1964] 3 All ER 442.

6   *Re Stephens, Kilby v Betts* [1904] 1 Ch 322. In *Re Powell, Crosland v Holliday* [1898] 1 Ch 227 (gift of real estate), the class was thus closed, but, if the ordinary rule had been applied, a subsequent gift would have been void under the rule against perpetuities. See the comments made in this case on *Re Wenmoth's Estate, Wenmoth v Wenmoth* (1887) 37 ChD 266. In so far as *Re Powell, Crosland v Holliday* purports to lay down a general rule of construction, it is dissented from in *Re Carter, Walker v Litchfield* (1911) 30 NZLR 707, NZ CA, and in *Re Ward's Will Trusts, Ward v Ward* [1965] Ch 856, [1964] 3 All ER 442 (where *Re Wenmoth's Estate, Wenmoth v Wenmoth* above was followed). See also *Mogg v Mogg* (1815) 1 Mer 654, referred to as an authority as to the difference between gifts of corpus and of income in *Re Wenmoth's Estate, Wenmoth v Wenmoth*.

311. Gifts of real estate alone to a class. If a gift of real estate alone to a class is construed as being immediate on the testator's death, this is the time when the class is ascertained if any members of the class have then come into being[1]. If no members of the class have then come into being, the gift must take effect as an executory devise, and all members, whenever born, will be let in[2]. A devise, not otherwise postponed, to 'all and every' the children of a person is construed as immediate and the class is ascertained at the testator's death[3].

As future interests can be equitable only[4], limitations not taking effect at the testator's death (including limitations to a class which is liable to fluctuate) must take effect, if at all, as equitable executory devises[5]. Where there is an executory devise to a class of children who attain a specified age, the same rule applies to devises as in the case of personalty and, unless the will points plainly to a contrary intention, children who are born after a child attains that age are excluded[6].

In a gift not otherwise postponed, a description of a class of children as 'born and to be born', or 'begotten and to be begotten', may cause the gift to take effect as an executory devise, and accordingly all the children, whether in existence at the testator's death or otherwise, may take under the gift[7].

In an executory devise to a class on the death of any person or on any other postponed event which does not import contingency in the class, the donees are prima facie ascertained so as to let in all who come into existence and satisfy the description before that event[8]. Where, in a gift to a class not postponed otherwise than by the fact that the description may refer to persons yet to come into existence, and that no member of the class has come into existence at the testator's death, all the members of the class coming into existence at any time are let in[9].

1   *Singleton v Gilbert* (1784) 1 Cox Eq Cas 68; *Doe d Thwaites v Over* (1808) 1 Taunt 263; *Crone v Odell* (1811) 1 Ball & B 449 at 458 (affd (1815) 3 Dow 61, HL); *Re Johnson, Danily v Johnson*

   (1893) 68 LT 20 (acceleration of ascertainment by revocation of prior interest); Shep Touch (8th Edn, 1826) p 436. The rule was applied to gifts of income in *Re Powell, Crosland v Holliday* [1898] 1 Ch 227 at 231: see PARA 310 note 6.

2 *Weld v Bradbury* (1715) 2 Vern 705.

3 *Scott v Harwood* (1821) 5 Madd 332.

4 See REAL PROPERTY AND REGISTRATION vol 87 (2012) PARA 160. As to a devise to a parent and his children or issue see PARA 389 et seq.

5 See REAL PROPERTY AND REGISTRATION vol 87 (2012) PARA 168.

6 *Re Canney's Trusts, Mayers v Strover* (1910) 101 LT 905; *Re Curzon, Martin v Perry* (1912) 56 Sol Jo 362; *Re Chapman, Charley v Lewis* (1922) 56 ILT 32; *Re Edmondson's Will Trusts, Baron Sandford v Edmondson* [1972] 1 All ER 444, [1972] 1 WLR 183, CA (rule applicable to a settlement of realty) (disapproving *Blackman v Fysh* [1892] 3 Ch 209, CA).

7 *Mogg v Mogg* (1815) 1 Mer 654 at 690 (explained in 3 Preston's Conveyancing (3rd Edn) 555); *Gooch v Gooch* (1853) 3 De GM & G 366 (where, however, the devises were devises of rents and profits only). It appears that the rule referring such words to the interval between the date of the will and the testator's death, which is applicable to personal estate (see PARA 309 text and note 7), does not apply to gifts of income of real estate: see *Dias v De Livera* (1879) 5 App Cas 123 at 132, PC. See also *Cook v Cook* (1706) 2 Vern 545 (where, it appears, 'begotten' was construed to include 'to be begotten'; as to this construction see PARA 330); *Eddowes v Eddowes* (1862) 30 Beav 603; but see *Woodhouse v Herrick* (1855) 1 K & J 352 at 358, 360.

8 *Crone v Odell* (1811) 1 Ball & B 449 at 459; *Browne v Hammond* (1858) John 210 at 212n; *Holland v Wood* (1870) LR 11 Eq 91 at 96; *Re Canney's Trusts, Mayers v Strover* (1910) 101 LT 905.

9 *Shepherd v Ingram* (1764) Amb 448.

312. Gift carrying intermediate income made to a class. Where a gift carrying intermediate income, such as a gift of residuary personal estate[1], is made to a contingent class, then, if members of the class attain a vested interest on coming into existence, whether subject or not to being diminished in any event, the members for the time being in existence share the income[2]. If, however, members attain a vested interest on attaining a certain age, or on satisfying some other description or condition, a member of the class attaining a vested interest takes only the income of the share to which he would be entitled if the other members of the class for the time being in existence[3] had attained vested interests[4]. Where the class is potentially or actually increased by birth or becomes decreased by the death of a potential member before obtaining a vested interest, there will be an inevitable change in the interests of the members; unless apportionment is clearly excluded, this will require only such income as is attributable to a member's lifetime to be apportioned to him and so that outgoings are, likewise, apportioned equitably[5]. If, however, a gift not carrying intermediate income is made to such a class, the members of the class whose interests are transmissible for the time being take the whole income[6] unless the testator sufficiently indicates that the income is to be divisible equally between all the members of the class, as by including a power of maintenance[7].

1 See PARA 1083.

2 *Shepherd v Ingram* (1764) Amb 448. In *Re Ransome's Will Trusts, Moberley v Ransome* [1957] Ch 348, [1957] 1 All ER 690, a beneficiary with a contingent interest only was not entitled to income after the permitted period of accumulation by virtue of the Trustee Act 1925 s 31(1)(ii) (see CHILDREN AND YOUNG PERSONS vol 9 (2012) PARA 63), because a contrary intention within s 69(2) (see TRUSTS AND POWERS vol 98 (2013) PARA 4) was disclosed by the existence of an express direction to accumulate: see PERPETUITIES AND ACCUMULATIONS vol 80 (2013) PARA 136. Where the law intervenes to prevent further accumulations, the income will in general pass to residue or on an intestacy, as the case may be: *Re Ransome's Will Trusts, Moberley v Ransome*.

3 On the birth of another child, and the consequent probable enlargement of the class, the child is not entitled to participate in income which has arisen prior to his birth: *Mills v Norris* (1800) 5 Ves 335; *Scott v Earl of Scarborough* (1838) 1 Beav 154. See also *Re Joel's Will Trusts, Rogerson v Brudenell-Bruce* [1967] Ch 14, [1966] 2 All ER 482 and text and note 5.

4   *Re Holford, Holford v Holford* [1894] 3 Ch 30, CA; *Re Jeffery, Arnold v Burt* [1895] 2 Ch 577;
    Re Faux, Taylor v Faux, as reported in [1915] WN 135; *Re Maber, Ward v Maber* [1928] Ch 88;
    Re King, Public Trustee v Aldridge [1928] Ch 330.
5   *Re Joel's Will Trusts, Rogerson v Brudenell-Bruce* [1967] Ch 14, [1966] 2 All ER 482
    (Apportionment Act 1870 (see REAL PROPERTY AND REGISTRATION vol 87 (2012) PARA 551)
    held to be generally applicable to this situation unless clearly excluded).
6   *Re Averill, Salsbury v Buckle* [1898] 1 Ch 523; *Re Walmsley's Settled Estates* (1911) 105 LT 332.
    See also *Stone v Harrison* (1846) 2 Coll 715 (sum of consols).
7   *Re Woodiwiss' Will Trusts, Robotham v Burn* (1959) 109 L Jo 154. In *Re Stevens, Stevens
    v Stevens* [1915] 1 Ch 429, there was, after the death of the life tenant, a trust of 'as well the
    income as the corpus' for children attaining 21 or marrying; each child was entitled to a share of
    rents from the death of the life tenant as and when he became entitled to a corresponding share of
    the corpus, with maintenance in the meantime.

313. Gifts to next of kin. Whatever may be the time of distribution, where there
is a gift to a testator's next of kin, without more, the class prima facie has to be
ascertained[1] as at the testator's death[2], and, where there is a gift to the next of kin
of any other person, the class prima facie has to be ascertained at that
person's death, if he survived the testator[3], and, if he did not, the class consists of
those of the next of kin living at the testator's death[4]. The law applied is the law
in force at the date that the disposition came into effect. Hence, where the
disposition pre-dates the statutes introducing equality of treatment for adopted[5]
and illegitimate children[6], such children are not normally[7] included in the class.

In a gift to a class of next of kin of the testator (or his nearest relatives or a
similar class) living at a future date of distribution, the entire class is ascertained
as at the testator's death, but only those of the class who survive to the date of
distribution may take[8]. The exercise, by will, of a special power to distribute
amongst 'relations' or 'relatives' of the donee does not require the application of
the rule of construction limiting such a gift to statutory next of kin[9].

Where the gift was to the testator's next of kin entitled by virtue of the
former Statutes of Distribution[10], even though they were to be so entitled at some
future time[11], the class was prima facie ascertained as at the testator's death[12]. The
context might, however, require them to be ascertained as if the testator had died
at some other date[13]. The same rules appear to apply to the ascertainment of
persons entitled under the provisions as to succession on intestacy[14] now in
force[15].

1   As to the construction of gifts to next of kin generally see PARAS 343–344; and as to the
    ascertainment of a class of next of kin directed to be ascertained on the assumption that a person
    died 'without having been married' see SETTLEMENTS vol 91 (2012) PARA 837.
2   *Wharton v Barker* (1858) 4 K & J 483 at 488 per Wood V-C. See also *Seifferth v Badham* (1846)
    9 Beav 370; *Say v Creed* (1847) 5 Hare 580 at 587; *Ware v Rowland* (1848) 2 Ph 635; *Bird v
    Luckie* (1850) 8 Hare 301 (where the sole next of kin took a prior life estate); *Gorbell v Davison,
    Gorbell v Forrest* (1854) 18 Beav 556 (two of class had prior life interests); *Moss v Dunlop* (1859)
    John 490; *Lee v Lee* (1860) 1 Drew & Sm 85 (one had prior interest); *Harrison v Harrison* (1860)
    28 Beav 21; *Re Ford, Patten v Sparks* (1895) 72 LT 5, CA; *Re Maher, Maher v Toppin* [1909] 1
    IR 70, Ir CA. In *Re Clanchy's Will Trusts, Lynch v Edwards* [1970] 2 All ER 489, CA, the terms
    of the will required that the class be ascertained at a later date, when the nearest in blood to the
    testator then living took. In *Re Shield, Bache v Shield* [1974] Ch 373, [1974] 2 All ER 274, a
    composite class of the testator's and his wife's relations was held to be ascertained at the
    widow's death.
3   *Philps v Evans* (1850) 4 De G & Sm 188; *Gundry v Pinniger* (1852) 1 De GM & G 502. See also
    Jacobs v Jacobs (1853) 16 Beav 557 (criticised in *Re Kilvert, Midland Bank Executor and
    Trustee Co Ltd v Kilvert* [1957] Ch 388, [1957] 2 All ER 146).
4   *Philps v Evans* (1850) 4 De G & Sm 188; *Wharton v Barker* (1858) 4 K & J 483 at 502; *Re Philps'
    Will* (1868) LR 7 Eq 151 ('heirs' construed as next of kin). As to a contrary intention see *Re Rees,
    Williams v Davies* (1890) 44 ChD 484.

5 See for example the Adoption Acts 1950 and 1976, both of which conferred inheritance rights on adopted children but only provided that this did not affect any disposition made before they came into effect. Such limitation has been preserved in later statutes: see PARA 357.

6 See the Family Law Reform Act 1969, the Family Law Reform Act 1988; and PARAS 355–356.

7 See *Gregg v Pigott* [2012] EWHC 732 (Ch), [2012] 3 WLR 913 where a settlement created in 1948 left property to a life tenant and then to her statutory next of kin. Her statutory next of kin would have been her nephews but for the fact that they had been adopted. However, it was held that article 14 of the Convention for the Protection of Human Rights and Fundamental Freedoms (prohibition on discrimination on any ground such as birth or other status: see RIGHTS AND FREEDOMS vol 88A (2013) PARAS 88, 506 et seq) can operate retrospectively to allow the admission of adopted children, provided it does not produce an unfair result.

8 *Spink v Lewis* (1791) 3 Bro CC 355; *Re Nash, Prall v Bevan* (1894) 71 LT 5, CA (followed in *Re Winn, Brook v Whitton* [1910] 1 Ch 278 ('next of kin . . . living at the time of the trusts failing')). See, however, *Re Tuckett's Will Trusts, Williams v National Provincial Bank Ltd* (1967) 111 Sol Jo 811 (where the testatrix's next of kin were determined as at the future date of distribution which was the date of death of the testatrix's only son).

9 *Re Poulton's Will Trusts, Smail v Litchfield* [1987] 1 All ER 1068, [1987] 1 WLR 795 (held that the rule was an artificial one designed to prevent failure of gift for uncertainty; it had no application where the gift was certain and gifts to cousins by donee's will were valid).

10 As to the Statutes of Distribution see PARA 343.

11 See *Re Winn, Brook v Whitton* [1910] 1 Ch 278 at 289 (where Parker J explained that in such cases the ordinary rule which would have ascertained the class at the time referred to is rebutted, because of the necessity for every person who claims under the gift to prove his title by virtue of the statute).

12 *Doe d Garner v Lawson* (1803) 3 East 278; *Markham v Ivatt* (1855) 20 Beav 579; *Bullock v Downes* (1860) 9 HL Cas 1; *Mortimore v Mortimore* (1879) 4 App Cas 448, HL; *Re Wilson, Wilson v Batchelor* [1907] 1 Ch 450 (affd [1907] 2 Ch 572, CA).

13 *Wharton v Barker* (1858) 4 K & J 483; *Clowes v Hilliard* (1876) 4 ChD 413; *Sturge and Great Western Rly Co* (1881) 19 ChD 444; *Re McFee, McFee v Toner* (1910) 103 LT 210; *Re Helsby, Neate v Bozie* (1914) 84 LJ Ch 682; *Re Mellish, Day v Withers* [1916] 1 Ch 562; *Hutchinson v National Refuges for Homeless and Destitute Children* [1920] AC 795, HL; *Re Krawitz's Will Trusts, Krawitz v Crawford* [1959] 3 All ER 793 at 797, [1959] 1 WLR 1192 at 1196.

14 See the Administration of Estates Act 1925 s 46; and PARA 485 et seq.

15 See *Re Bridgen, Chaytor v Edwin* [1938] Ch 205 at 209, [1937] 4 All ER 342 at 344; *Re Krawitz's Will Trusts, Krawitz v Crawford* [1959] 3 All ER 793, [1959] 1 WLR 1192. In *Re Mitchell, Hatton v Jones* [1954] Ch 525, [1954] 2 All ER 246, the Crown took under a gift to the person or persons who would have been entitled on the death of the testator's widow intestate: see PARA 512.

314. Shares in which next of kin take. Where there was a gift to next of kin under or according to the former Statutes of Distribution[1], they took as tenants in common in the shares fixed by the statutes if either the will in terms referred to the statutory mode of distribution[2], or was silent on the subject[3]; but, if, for example, the testator directed that they were to take equally, and did not refer to the Statutes of Distribution, effect was given to the direction[4]. A gift to persons entitled beneficially under the provisions as to succession on intestacy now in force[5] has, it seems, a similar effect[6].

Where the gift is to next of kin excluding certain persons, the next of kin are ascertained as if these persons were dead at the time in question, but without any other difference from the above rule[7].

1 As to the Statutes of Distribution see PARA 343.

2 *Holloway v Radcliffe* (1857) 23 Beav 163 ('equally as if the same had to be paid under the statute'; 'equally' rejected); *Fielden v Ashworth* (1875) LR 20 Eq 410 at 412 ('share and share alike, as the law directs'; 'share and share alike' disregarded). Cf *Re Taylor, Taylor v Ley* (1885) 52 LT 839, CA.

3 A gift to the persons entitled under the statutes gives a description not only of the persons, but of their interests: *Martin v Glover* (1844) 1 Coll 269 at 272.

4 *Re Richards, Davies v Edwards* [1910] 2 Ch 74 at 76 per Swinfen Eady J (following *Mattison v Tanfield* (1840) 3 Beav 131 at 132).

5 See PARA 313 note 11.
6 See *Re Bridgen, Chaytor v Edwin* [1938] Ch 205, [1937] 4 All ER 342 (direction to divide equally among relations). For a case where the persons entitled took equally as named individuals and as joint tenants see *Re Krawitz's Will Trusts, Krawitz v Crawford* [1959] 3 All ER 793, [1959] 1 WLR 1192.
7 *White v Springett* (1869) 4 Ch App 300; *Re Taylor, Taylor v Ley* (1885) 52 LT 839, CA; and see *Lee v Lee* (1860) 1 Drew & Sm 85; *Lindsay v Ellicott* (1876) 46 LJ Ch 878. See also *Re Krawitz's Will Trusts, Krawitz v Crawford* [1959] 3 All ER 793, [1959] 1 WLR 1192.

C.   SURVIVORSHIP

315. Usual meanings of 'survive'. The word 'survive' and its derivatives ordinarily refer to the longest in duration of lives running concurrently[1]; they may, however, refer not to concurrent lives but to the fact of living to and after a named event or death[2]. There is no rule of construction as to the period to which survivorship refers apart from a context[3]. The question must in every case be answered by applying ordinary principles of construction to the particular language used and having regard to any relevant surrounding circumstances[4]. The language used must be construed in its natural sense unless the context shows that this would defeat the testator's intention[5], and the mere fact that, so construed, the will might in certain possible, or even probable, circumstances produce results which seem fanciful or even harsh is not a sufficient ground for adopting another interpretation[6]. Although this fact may raise doubts whether the construction fulfils the testator's intention, doubts are not enough; it must be possible to discover from the language used what the intention was, that is, that the testator intended to use 'survive' in some secondary sense[7].

1   *Re Delany, Delany v Delany* (1895) 39 Sol Jo 468. See also *Gee v Liddell* (1866) LR 2 Eq 341 at 344 per Lord Romilly MR ('the person to survive must be living at the death of the person who is to be survived'); *Re Heath, Jackson v Norman* (1904) 48 Sol Jo 416; *Re Bourke's Will Trusts, Barclays Bank Trust Co Ltd v Canada Permanent Trust Co* [1980] 1 All ER 219, [1980] 1 WLR 539 (where 'surviving issue' meant surviving children, rather than surviving issue of all degrees).
2   *Re Clark's Estate* (1864) 3 De GJ & Sm 111; *Mellor v Daintree* (1886) 33 ChD 198 at 210; *Re Sing, Sing v Mills* [1914] WN 90. For a discussion of the uses of the word 'survive' and of these cases see *Knight v Knight* (1912) 14 CLR 86; *Re Sadler, Furniss v Cooper* (1915) 60 Sol Jo 89 ('with benefit of survivorship in the same family'). 'Surviving' means prima facie 'living both to and after a particular point of time': see *Elliott v Lord Joicey* [1935] AC 209 at 218, HL; *Re Hodgson, Hodgson v Gillett* [1952] 1 All ER 769; *Re Allsop, Cardinal v Warr* [1968] Ch 39 at 45–46, 48, 51, sub nom *Re Alsop, Cardinal v Warr* [1967] 2 All ER 1056 at 1057–1058, 1059, 1061, CA, per curiam. Where two events were specified, 'surviving' was held to mean living at the happening of the last of those two: *Re Castle, Public Trustee v Floud* [1949] Ch 46, [1948] 2 All ER 927; cf *Re Gargan, Governor & Co of Bank of Ireland v A-G* [1962] IR 264 (where it was held that, in order to survive two events, the beneficiary had to be alive at the occurrence of the first). But see also *Blech v Blech* [2001] All ER (D) 141 (Dec), where a gift to such children of the testatrix's son 'as shall survive me' was construed, having regard to the surrounding circumstances and relevant context, so as to include children born after the testatrix's death. For a similar result see *Marshall v Hill* [2003] All ER (D) 304 (Mar) (the use of 'survive' and 'grandchildren' at a date when there was only one grandchild; construed as extending to grandchildren born after testatrix's death and before first grandchild reached age of 25). As to the effect of clauses of accruer see PARA 410.
3   *Re Benn, Benn v Benn* (1885) 29 ChD 839 at 844, CA, per Cotton LJ; *Inderwick v Tatchell* [1903] AC 120 at 123, HL; *Re James's Will Trusts, Peard v James* [1962] Ch 226 at 245, [1960] 3 All ER 744 at 754.
4   *Re James's Will Trusts, Peard v James* [1962] Ch 226 at 245, [1960] 3 All ER 744 at 754. See also *Re Allsop, Cardinal v Warr* [1968] Ch 39, sub nom *Re Alsop, Cardinal v Warr* [1967] 2 All ER 1056, CA (where 'as shall survive me and attain the age of 21 years' was read on the construction of the whole will as 'as shall . . . (in the case of those born in my lifetime) . . . survive me and . . . (in any case) . . . attain the age of 21 years'). Cf *Re Riley's Will Trusts, Barclays Bank Ltd v Riley* (1964) 108 Sol Jo 174, CA (where 'survivors of my said children and their issue' was read on the construction of the whole will not to impose survivorship so far as the issue were concerned). See also *Blech v Blech* [2001] All ER (D) 141 (Dec) and note 2.

5 *Gilmour v MacPhillamy* [1930] AC 712, PC; *Re James's Will Trusts, Peard v James* [1962] Ch 226 at 245, [1960] 3 All ER 744 at 754.
6 *Wake v Varah* (1876) 2 ChD 348, CA; *Auger v Beaudry* [1920] AC 1010, PC; *Gilmour v MacPhillamy* [1930] AC 712, PC; *Re James's Will Trusts, Peard v James* [1962] Ch 226 at 245, [1960] 3 All ER 744 at 754.
7 See the cases cited in note 6.

316. Use of words such as 'survivors' otherwise than in a strict sense. 'Survivor' and similar words may be used in other than the strict sense. Thus, in a set of dispositions in favour of several persons and their children or issue, the words may be used in a sense in which the element of survivorship involves not a survivorship between the named persons, but the subsistence of a line of children or issue, or of vested estates and interests[1]. Alternatively, they may be used as meaning 'others'[2], but, where it is proper to adopt a secondary meaning, a meaning which imports some kind or element of survivorship (for example survival by issue) is to be preferred to construing 'survivors' as equivalent to 'others'[3]. Such words may receive one of the constructions mentioned above[4] where the context requires it, but not otherwise[5]. Thus, after a gift to several children in tail, a gift over on the death of any of them without issue indefinitely to the 'survivors' in tail is construed as to the 'others', creating cross-remainders[6]. Where the gift is to several persons equally for their respective lives and after the death of any to his children, but, if any die without children, to the survivors for life[7], with remainder to their children, without more[8], then as a rule only children of survivors in the ordinary sense can take under the gift over[9]. Where, however, to similar gifts there is added a limitation over if all the tenants for life die without children, then the children of a predeceased life tenant may participate in the share of one who dies without children after their parent[10].

1 *Re Friend's Settlement, Cole v Allcot* [1906] 1 Ch 47 at 54 (case of a deed). This was really the effect of the construction given to the words 'survive me' in *Re Allsop, Cardinal v Warr* [1968] Ch 39, sub nom *Re Alsop, Cardinal v Warr* [1967] 2 All ER 1056 at 1059 per Lord Denning MR, so that it was read as 'live after me' in application to grandchildren (see PARA 315 note 4). *Re Allsop, Cardinal v Warr* was considered in both *Blech v Blech* [2001] All ER (D) 141 (Dec) and *Marshall v Hill* [2003] All ER (D) 304 (Mar).
2 *Wilmot v Wilmot* (1802) 8 Ves 10; *Leake v Robinson* (1817) 2 Mer 363 at 394; *Smith v Osborne* (1857) 6 HL Cas 375 at 393; *O'Brien v O'Brien* [1896] 2 IR 459, Ir CA; *Powell v Hellicar* [1919] 1 Ch 138.
3 *Waite v Littlewood* (1872) 8 Ch App 70; *Re James's Will Trusts, Peard v James* [1962] Ch 226 at 245, [1960] 3 All ER 744 at 755.
4 See the text to notes 1–2.
5 *Davidson v Dallas* (1808) 14 Ves 576 at 578 (where the construction 'others' is described as a forced construction); *Winterton v Crawfurd* (1830) 1 Russ & M 407. See also *Cromek v Lumb* (1839) 3 Y & C Ex 565; *Leeming v Sherratt* (1842) 2 Hare 14 at 24; *Stead v Platt* (1853) 18 Beav 50; *Mann v Thompson* (1854) Kay 628 at 644; *Greenwood v Percy* (1859) 26 Beav 572; *Nevill v Boddam* (1860) 28 Beav 554 at 559; *De Garagnol v Liardet* (1863) 32 Beav 608.
6 *Doe d Watts v Wainewright* (1793) 5 Term Rep 427; *Smith v Osborne* (1857) 6 HL Cas 375. Entailed interests cannot be created by instruments coming into operation on or after 1 January 1997: see the Trusts of Land and Appointment of Trustees Act 1996 s 2(6), Sch 1 para 5; PARA 387; and REAL PROPERTY AND REGISTRATION vol 87 (2012) PARA 114. The position is similar if the limitations prior to the gift over are to a number of persons for life, with remainder to their sons and daughters in strict settlement: *Cole v Sewell* (1848) 2 HL Cas 186 at 227; *Re Tharp's Estate* (1863) 1 De GJ & Sm 453. Subject to certain exceptions, new settlements created on or after 1 January 1997 are not subject to the Settled Land Act 1925: see the Trusts of Land and Appointment of Trustees Act 1996 s 2; REAL PROPERTY AND REGISTRATION vol 87 (2012) PARA 104; and SETTLEMENTS vol 91 (2012) PARA 576.
7 If in such a case the survivors take absolutely, there may be ground for reading 'survivor', in respect of the last, as 'longest liver', as in *Maden v Taylor* (1876) 45 LJ Ch 569, followed in *Davidson v Kimpton* (1881) 18 ChD 213; *Re Roper's Estate, Morrell v Gissing* (1889) 41 ChD 409. Cf *King v Frost* (1890) 15 App Cas 548 at 553; *Re Mortimer, Griffiths v Mortimer* (1885) 54 LJ Ch 414; *Askew v Askew* (1888) 57 LJ Ch 629.

8   Eg a further gift over: see the text to note 10; and PARA 317.
9   *Re Usticke* (1866) 35 Beav 338; *Re Horner's Estate, Pomfret v Graham* (1881) 19 ChD 186; *Re
     Dunlevy's Trusts* (1882) 9 LR Ir 349, Ir CA; *Re Rubbins, Gill v Worrall* (1898) 79 LT 313, CA;
     Olphert v Olphert [1903] 1 IR 325; *Garland v Smyth* [1904] 1 IR 35, Ir CA. See also *Re Bowman,
     Re Lay, Whytehead v Boulton* (1889) 41 ChD 525 at 531. A contrary intention in favour of issue
     may be shown by a substitutional gift, but 'survivors' may nevertheless have its ordinary meaning
     (*Willetts v Willetts* (1848) 7 Hare 38; *Blundell v Chapman* (1864) 33 Beav 648; *Re Hobson,
     Barwick v Holt* [1912] 1 Ch 626 at 633); and without construing 'survivors' as 'others', 'their
     issue' may mean the issue not of surviving children only, but of all the children (*Re Corbett's Trusts*
     (1860) John 591 at 598 per Wood V-C; *Re Bowman, Re Lay, Whytehead v Boulton* (1889) 41
     ChD 525 at 529). In *Hodge v Foot* (1865) 34 Beav 349, 'survivors' was held to mean 'others'.
10   *Re Bowman, Re Lay, Whytehead v Boulton* (1889) 41 ChD 525 at 531 per Kay J; *Harrison v
     Harrison* [1901] 2 Ch 136 at 142 per Cozens-Hardy J; *O'Brien v O'Brien* [1896] 2 IR 459 at 495,
     Ir CA. The inference made from the gift over, in pursuance of the presumption against intestacy
     (see PARAS 255–257), is that the objects of the testator's bounty previously named take between
     them the entire estate in every state of circumstances consistent with the gift over not taking effect:
     O'Brien v O'Brien at 466. Children of predeceased tenants for life do not take merely on account
     of a direction that accruing shares are to be taken in the same manner as original shares: see
     Harrison v Harrison above at 142–144 (disapproving the proposition stated on this point in *Re
     Bowman, Re Lay, Whytehead v Boulton* above at 531); *Inderwick v Tatchell, Tatchell v Tatchell,
     Inderwick v Inderwick* [1901] 2 Ch 738, CA (affd [1903] AC 120, HL). See also *Re Robson,
     Howden v Robson* [1899] WN 260; *Re James's Will Trusts, Peard v James* [1962] Ch 226, [1960]
     3 All ER 744.

317. Stirpital survivorship. If all the shares in the devised property are settled
and there is a general clause of accruer on the death of each life tenant without
children to the survivors of the life tenants, all the accrued shares being settled in
the same way as the original shares, and, if these dispositions are followed by a
gift over in the event of all dying without issue[1], this may show an intention not
to use 'survivors' in its proper sense, but to use it in the sense of those who survive
either in person or figuratively in issue[2]. In general, however, 'survivor' is taken in
its natural sense[3], and the mere fact that a fund is initially given in shares which
are settled on stirpital trusts and that, on failure of the trusts in favour of one
stirps, the share of that stirps is directed to accrue to the shares of the survivors
of the original life tenants to be held on the trusts of their original shares, is an
insufficient ground for holding that the testator intended 'survive' or 'survivors' to
bear a secondary meaning[4].

Similarly, a gift over to the 'others'[5], or to those 'remaining'[6], of a number of
persons after a gift to each or one of them is not read as meaning 'survivors' unless
in the context this is necessary[7].

1   The absence of a gift over is not conclusive to show that 'survivor' is to be taken in the literal sense:
     Powell v Hellicar [1919] 1 Ch 138.
2   *Re Benn, Benn v Benn* (1885) 29 ChD 839 at 844–845, CA, per Cotton LJ, explaining *Waite v
     Littlewood* (1872) 8 Ch App 70; *Wake v Varah* (1876) 2 ChD 348 at 358, CA; *Re Bilham,
     Buchanan v Hill* [1901] 2 Ch 169; *Lamont (or Chearnley) v Millar* [1921] WN 334, sub nom
     Curle's Trustees v Millar 1922 SC (HL) 15. The fact that some only of the shares are settled
     (*Lucena v Lucena* (1877) 7 ChD 255, CA), or that there is an ultimate gift over on the death
     without issue of some of the first takers (*Re Hobson, Barwick v Holt* [1912] 1 Ch 626 at 633),
     is not sufficient to give 'survivors' the meaning of surviving in person or in issue. In older cases
     'survivors' was said to be construed as 'others' (*Holland v Allsop* (1861) 29 Beav 498; *Re
     Keep's Will* (1863) 32 Beav 122; *Hurry v Morgan* (1866) LR 3 Eq 152; *Badger v Gregory* (1869)
     LR 8 Eq 78; *Re Row's Estate* (1874) 43 LJ Ch 347; *Askew v Askew* (1888) 57 LJ Ch 629), but
     in many of these cases all the other stirpes were in fact surviving (*Re Bilham, Buchanan v Hill*
     [1901] 2 Ch 169 at 175 per Joyce J), and, as pointed out in *Waite v Littlewood* (1872) 8 Ch
     App 70 at 73–74 per Lord Selborne LC, it is not necessary to adopt the meaning 'others' in such
     cases; it is sufficient to read 'survivors' as meaning 'surviving in person or in stirps'. See also *Wake
     v Varah* (1876) 2 ChD 348 at 358, CA, per James LJ. This construction has, however, been
     dissented from in Ireland (*O'Brien v O'Brien* [1896] 2 IR 459, Ir CA), and has been described as
     'forced and fanciful' (*King v Frost, Underwood v Frost, Price v Frost, Plomley v Frost* (1890) 15
     App Cas 548 at 553, PC); and it is not clear that 'survivor' can properly be so construed unless the

limitations are expressly framed so as to produce that result (*Re Hobson, Barwick v Holt* [1912] 1 Ch 626 at 632–633 per Parker J). For a case where, in the context of the will, the ordinary meaning of the word was adhered to see *Browne v Rainsford* (1867) IR 1 Eq 384.

3   *Auger v Beaudry* [1920] AC 1010, PC; *Gilmour v MacPhillamy* [1930] AC 712, PC. As to the expression 'benefit of survivorship in the same family' see *Re Sadler, Furniss v Cooper* (1915) 60 Sol Jo 89.

4   *Re James's Will Trusts, Peard v James* [1962] Ch 226 at 245, [1960] 3 All ER 744 at 754. As to distribution per stirpes generally see PARAS 396–397.

5   *Re Chaston, Chaston v Seago* (1881) 18 ChD 218 at 223 (where 'the others and other of my said children' was held to mean 'children other than children who die or have died without leaving lawful issue'); followed in *Re Crosse, Crosse v Crosse* [1933] WN 36. See also *Slade v Parr* (1842) 7 Jur 102 (where the context contained the word 'survivors'). The 'others surviving' of a number of persons may according to the context mean 'then surviving' (*Beckwith v Beckwith* (1876) 36 LT 128, CA), or 'others' (*Re Arnold's Trusts* (1870) LR 10 Eq 252; but as to this case see the cases cited in PARA 316 note 9).

6   *Re Speak, Speak v Speak* (1912) 56 Sol Jo 273 (not following *Sheridan v O'Reilly* [1900] 1 IR 386).

7   *Re Hagen's Trusts* (1877) 46 LJ Ch 665; *Stanley v Bond* [1913] 1 IR 170.

318.   Ascertainment of survivors at date of distribution. Where there is a gift to a number of persons and the survivors[1] and survivor of them, or with benefit of survivorship, or in like words[2], or where there is a postponed gift to persons 'surviving', then, in default of any expressed intention of the testator[3], the survivorship is prima facie referred to the period of distribution[4]. Thus the time in question, where the gift is immediate, is the testator's death[5], and, where the gift is postponed to a life estate, is the death of the life tenant[6] or the death of the testator, whichever last happens[7]; and this applies whether the gift is of real or of personal estate[8]. It seems that the question whether a gift involving the survivor or survivors of a group is immediate or postponed to the distribution period may depend upon whether the gift may be seen as one to joint tenants or as one to tenants in common[9]. There may be cases where the words used have the effect of creating distinct and separate classes rather than a single composite class, so as to guide the court in deciding both the time of ascertainment and the survivors referred to[10].

1   A gift to 'survivors' may vest in a sole survivor: *Hearn v Baker* (1856) 2 K & J 383.

2   *Wiley v Chanteperdrix* [1894] 1 IR 209 at 215. It is assumed that the words are words of gift by way of purchase, and not merely words of limitation. As to the use of such words as words of limitation see PARA 395.

3   *Blackmore v Snee* (1857) 1 De G & J 455 at 460. For examples of a context clearly showing such an intention see *Wordsworth v Wood* (1847) 1 HL Cas 129 at 156; *White v Baker* (1860) 2 De GF & J 55. For an example of a context excluding the rule in the text see *Rogers v Towsey* (1845) 9 Jur 575.

4   *Cripps v Wolcott* (1819) 4 Madd 11 at 15; *Vorley v Richardson* (1856) 8 De GM & G 126 at 129 (when youngest child attained 21); *Wiley v Chanteperdrix* [1894] 1 IR 209 at 215. In certain early cases survivorship was held, even in a postponed gift, to refer to the testator's death (see *Rose d Vere v Hill* (1766) 3 Burr 1881; *Wilson v Bayly* (1760) 3 Bro Parl Cas 195, HL; *Doe d Long v Prigg* (1828) 8 B & C 231), but the rule in *Cripps v Wolcott* (1819) 4 Madd 11 at 15 has been constantly followed in England, and in Scottish cases has been approved by the House of Lords (*Young v Robertson* (1862) 4 Macq 314 at 319, HL (where Lord Westbury LC stated that the rule of construction is the same in the jurisprudence of both England and Scotland); *Bowman v Bowman* [1899] AC 518 at 525–526, HL). See also *Outerbridge v Hollis* [1951] WN 318, PC. As to the meaning of 'period of distribution' see PARA 306 note 1.

5   *Stringer v Phillips* (1730) 1 Eq Cas Abr 292; *Bass v Russell* (1829) Taml 18; *Ashford v Haines* (1851) 21 LJ Ch 496; *Neathway v Reed* (1853) 3 De GM & G 18; *Howard v Howard* (1856) 21 Beav 550; *Re Phillips* (1921) 151 LT Jo 162. The will may show that 'survivor' means survivor inter se, so that if of two persons both die in the lifetime of the life tenant, the executors of the survivor will take: *Re Wood, Hardy v Hull* (1923) 130 LT 408. See also *Young's Trustees v Young* 1927 SC (HL) 6.

6   *Cripps v Wolcott* (1819) 4 Madd 11; *Re Benn, Benn v Benn* (1885) 29 ChD 839 at 844, CA, per Cotton LJ; *Re Poultney, Poultney v Poultney* [1912] 2 Ch 541 at 543, CA,

per Cozens-Hardy MR (stating the rule in *Cripps v Wolcott* as 'where there is a gift to A for life, with remainder to A, B and C and to the survivors or survivor, the survivorship is ascertained at the death of the tenant for life'); *Re Douglas's Will Trusts, Lloyds Bank Ltd v Nelson* [1959] 3 All ER 785, [1959] 1 WLR 1212, CA. See also *Jenour v Jenour* (1805) 10 Ves 562; *Blewitt v Roberts* (1841) Cr & Ph 274 at 283; *Taylor v Beverley* (1844) 1 Coll 108; *Whitton v Field* (1846) 9 Beav 368; *Davies v Thorns* (1849) 3 De G & Sm 347; *M'Donald v Bryce* (1853) 16 Beav 581; *Neathway v Reed* (1853) 3 De GM & G 18; *Re Pritchard's Trusts* (1855) 3 Drew 163; *Hearn v Baker* (1856) 2 K & J 383; *Re Crawhall's Trust* (1856) 8 De GM & G 480; *Hesketh v Magennis* (1859) 27 Beav 395; *Young v Davies* (1863) 2 Drew & Sm 167 at 170; *Naylor v Robson* (1865) 34 Beav 571; *Re Belfast Town Council, ex p Sayers* (1884) 13 LR Ir 169 at 172.

7   *Spurrell v Spurrell* (1853) 11 Hare 54.
8   *Re Gregson's Trust Estate* (1864) 2 De GJ & Sm 428; *Buckle v Fawcett* (1845) 4 Hare 536 at 542 (mixed fund). See also *Howard v Collins* (1868) LR 5 Eq 349. As to doubts as to the application of the rule to real estate see *Taaffe v Conmee* (1862) 10 HL Cas 64 at 77.
9   *Re Douglas's Will Trusts, Lloyds Bank Ltd v Nelson* [1959] 3 All ER 785, 787-8 [1959] 1 WLR 1212, CA (the gift of residue was made to T's three sisters 'or the survivor or survivors of them' as joint tenants; had it been made to them as tenants in common it seems that those words may have been effective to create an immediate vested gift, subject to divestment by the reference to 'survivor(s)', following a rule identified in *Browne v Lord Kenyon* (1813) 3 Madd 410. As it was, the reference to 'survivor' was seen as merely expository of earlier words and the period referred to was that of distribution, ie the death or remarriage of the widow).
10   See *Re Bourke's Will Trusts, Barclays Bank Trust Co Ltd v Canada Permanent Trust Co* [1980] 1 All ER 219, [1980] 1 WLR 539 ('their heirs and surviving issue' held to be two different classes, both to be ascertained at the same time, ie the death of the praepositus).

319. Survivorship on contingent event. Where there is a gift to several persons, followed by an express contingent gift over on any event to the survivors or survivor, the survivorship may be independent of both the contingent event and the period of distribution[1], or alternatively may refer either to the period of distribution[2] or to the contingent event[3], according to the context in the particular case.

1   Ie it may refer only to survivorship between the named persons: *White v Baker* (1860) 2 De GF & J 55; *Re Wood, Hardy v Hull* (1923) 130 LT 408. The court leans against a construction involving a gift of the whole to the last survivor, particularly where there are words indicating a tenancy in common, and it attempts to discover a time to which the survivorship is to be referred: *Cambridge v Rous* (1858) 25 Beav 409 at 415. As to the meaning of 'period of distribution' see PARA 306 note 1.
2   *Cambridge v Rous* (1858) 25 Beav 409; *Re Pickworth, Snaith v Parkinson* [1899] 1 Ch 642, CA.
3   *Crowder v Stone* (1829) 3 Russ 217.

D.   ALTERNATIVE GIFTS

320. Gifts expressed in the alternative. Two or more gifts may be made to take effect alternatively, for example in certain mutually exclusive events[1]; thus a gift to A or B, where A and B are donees described or named and mutually exclusive[2], is an alternative gift. In such a gift there is generally a contingency implied, even if not expressed, on the happening of which the gift is to take effect in favour of the second-named donee, and the circumstances of the gift must be ascertained before the contingency can be determined[3]. Usually it refers to the death of the first-named donee before a particular event, for example the testator's death or some other date of distribution, and it is inferred that the testator's intention is that the first donee is to take if then alive, but that the second donee is to take if the first does not survive the particular event[4].

If such a contingency is not expressed or implied, then, if A and B are mutually exclusive, the gift[5] is void for uncertainty[6] unless either there is a general charitable intent, in which case the court is able to determine the mode in which the gift is to take effect[7], or where there is direct evidence of his intention[8], or the gift is made by way of a power of appointment which is in the nature of a trust[9].

There may be cases where the contingency relates to an earlier limitation that is itself void for perpetuity; in such a case, there arise questions whether the alternative gift is 'dependent upon and expectant upon' the void primary gift and, in turn, whether that should invalidate the alternative gift[10].

Although there are detailed rules relating to alternate gifts which have been developed by the judiciary over the years[11], it is unlikely that today's judges will be aided by such rules given that the modern approach to construction of wills is to ascertain the intention of the testator[12].

1   It has first to be determined in all cases whether the second gift (eg where it is to take effect on the death of the first donee without issue, or leaving issue) takes effect by way of succession to the first gift, or is an alternative to the first gift: *Ware v Watson* (1855) 7 De GM & G 248 at 258. See also *Hatch v Hatch* (1855) 20 Beav 105; *Parsons v Coke* (1858) 4 Drew 296. An executory limitation to take effect on the donee dying under certain circumstances (eg leaving no issue) may take effect on the death of the donee under these circumstances during the life of the testator, and, therefore, as a substitutional gift: see note 10 and see PARA 321. A gift 'to A and/or B' constitutes a joint tenancy: *Re Lewis, Goronway v Richards* [1942] Ch 424, [1942] 2 All ER 364.
2   There may be cases, such as gifts to 'heirs or next of kin', where the terms are used as applying to one class and not as alternative: *Lowndes v Stone* (1799) 4 Ves 649; *Re Thompson's Trusts* (1878) 9 ChD 607. If B is the general term for a large class (namely 'descendants') of which A is an enumeration of members, or a sub-class (namely 'children'), and the gift is to 'each of A or B', the gift is not void but includes all B, and 'or' need not be altered: see *Clay v Pennington* (1835) 7 Sim 370; *Solly v Solly* (1858) 5 Jur NS 36. It may be that the words used create more than one class of beneficiaries to the same gift, but which are not alternative to each other, see *Re Bourke's Will Trusts, Barclays Bank Trust Co Ltd v Canada Permanent Trust Co* [1980] 1 All ER 219, [1980] 1 WLR 539 ('their heirs and surviving issue').
3   See PARA 194 note 1.
4   *Re Sibley's Trusts* (1877) 5 ChD 494 at 499. See also *Turner v Moor* (1801) 6 Ves 557 at 559; *Salisbury v Petty* (1843) 3 Hare 86 at 93; *Carey v Carey* (1857) 6 I Ch R 255; *Walmsley v Foxhall* (1863) 1 De GJ & Sm 605; *Re Pearce, Eastwood v Pearce* (1912) 56 Sol Jo 686, CA. Cf *Bowman v Bowman* [1899] AC 518 at 523, HL (where 'or' was held to mean 'whom failing', and Lord Watson said that the point to be determined was at what period of time the testator must be held to have intended that the right of the donee should come to an end if he was not then alive, and that the right of the conditional donee should arise). Thus a gift to A, with a substitutional gift to his children or to his issue, takes effect in favour of A if he is living at the period of distribution (*Montagu v Nucella* (1826) 1 Russ 165; *Jones v Torin* (1833) 6 Sim 255; *Whitcher v Penley* (1846) 9 Beav 477; *Chipchase v Simpson* (1849) 16 Sim 485; *Penley v Penley* (1850) 12 Beav 547; *Sparks v Restal* (1857) 24 Beav 218; *Margitson v Hall* (1864) 10 Jur NS 89; *Holland v Wood* (1870) LR 11 Eq 91), and in favour of his children or issue if he is not then living (*Davenport v Hanbury* (1796) 3 Ves 257; *Girdlestone v Doe* (1828) 2 Sim 225 (A or his heirs); *Salisbury v Petty* (1843) 3 Hare 86; *Re Porter's Trust* (1857) 4 K & J 188). The contingency of the death of one of the alternate donees in the lifetime of the life tenant may sometimes be implied: see *Re Fisher, Robinson v Eardley* [1915] 1 Ch 302. A gift may be given for alternative purposes and be capable of taking effect for the second purpose without the first being carried out: *Re Sahal's Will Trusts, Alliance Assurance Co Ltd v A-G* [1958] 3 All ER 428, [1958] 1 WLR 1243.
5   Ie if read without alteration, but sometimes words are capable of alteration. Thus 'or' may be changed to 'and' if necessary, and in accordance with the whole will (*Richardson v Spraag* (1718) 1 P Wms 434; *Eccard v Brooke* (1790) 2 Cox Eq Cas 213; *Horridge v Ferguson* (1822) Jac 583; *Parkin v Knight* (1846) 15 Sim 83; *Re Turney, Turney v Turney* [1899] 2 Ch 739 at 745, CA; *Re Hayden, Pask v Perry* [1931] 2 Ch 333; and see generally PARA 254), but this is not done if the gift can be read as a substitutional gift on some contingency (*Speakman v Speakman* (1850) 8 Hare 180). See also note 4.
6   *Richardson v Spraag* (1718) 1 P Wms 434 per Jekyll MR; *Longmore v Broom* (1802) 7 Ves 124 at 128 per Grant MR; *Flint v Warren* (1847) 15 Sim 626 at 629. As to uncertainty generally see PARAS 262–266.
7   See CHARITIES vol 8 (2015) PARA 105 et seq.
8   As to the circumstances in which direct evidence of intention may be admitted to assist in interpretation see PARAS 182, 195, 218–219. See also *Westland v Lillis* [2003] EWHC 1669 (Ch), [2003] All ER (D) 128 (Jun), where considerable difficulties remained, even after admission of extrinsic evidence of intention, concerning the effects of revocation by codicil upon gifts, where provision was made for 'failure'.

9   *Longmore v Broom* (1802) 7 Ves 124. In such a case, where there is no appointment and no gift over in default of appointment, the gift goes to the donees A and B equally: *Penny v Turner* (1848) 2 Ph 493; *Re White's Trusts* (1860) John 656. See generally TRUSTS AND POWERS vol 98 (2013) PARA 2.

10 *Re Hubbard's Will Trusts, Marston v Angier* [1963] Ch 275, [1962] 2 All ER 917 (Buckley J analyses three lines of authority: one line, based upon the presumed intention of the testator, showing circumstances where the alternative gift itself becomes void and two lines of cases which do not have that result). As to alternative limitations one of which is void under the rule against perpetuities see PERPETUITIES AND ACCUMULATIONS vol 80 (2013) PARA 93.

11 See PARAS 321–327.

12 See *Marley v Rawlings* [2014] UKSC 2, [2015] AC 129, [2014] 1 All ER 807; and PARA 188.

321. Original and substitutional gifts. An alternative gift is either original or substitutional[1]. The gift is original where there is a direct gift to the second donee, even though it is only to take effect if the contingency happens[2]; it is substitutional where the second donee takes no direct gift but merely, on the happening of the contingency, the benefit which has been already given to the first donee. Thus the gift is substitutional where the interest which the alternative donee is to take is by a prior clause in the will given to the first donee, so that the second donee merely stands in the place of the first if the first donee is not capable of taking on the particular contingency in contemplation. A gift is original where the interest which the second donee is to take is not by a prior clause given to the first donee[3]. Thus if the gift is to a person for life and after his death to the testator's nephews and nieces then living and the issue of such of them as may be then dead, such issue to take their parent's share only, there is no gift to a nephew who predeceases the life tenant leaving issue, and his issue are the objects of an original gift. Where, however, the gift after the death of the life tenant is to all the testator's nephews and nieces but, if any die before the life tenant leaving issue, then to the issue of that one, the issue taking the parent's share, a nephew who predeceases the life tenant is at first included in the class, and, on his falling out of it, his issue are substituted for him; that is, the gift to the issue is substitutional[4].

The judicial approach to strict application of the rules relating to original and substitutional gifts is likely to change, in line with the more modern, intention-based, 'armchair principle' approach to construction of wills[5].

1   Whether the gift is original or substitutional is a matter of construction. Thus a gift preceded by 'and' is not necessarily original: *Hurry v Hurry* (1870) LR 10 Eq 346 at 348 per James V-C (commenting on *Re Merricks' Trusts* (1866) LR 1 Eq 551 at 558). See also *Maynard v Wright* (1858) 26 Beav 285. In *Re Coulden, Coulden v Coulden* [1908] 1 Ch 320 at 325, there was a direction to sell the real and personal estate on the death of either of two sons who were appointed executors, and to divide the proceeds equally 'amongst my then surviving children and their respective issue'. It was held that 'their issue' were not words of limitation, and that the issue of the surviving children could not compete with their parents and took nothing, while 'issue' was extended to children of deceased children, who took the share which their deceased parent would have taken. Ordinarily, however, in a gift to a person and his issue, the issue take in competition with the named donee: *Re Hammond, Parry v Hammond* [1924] 2 Ch 276.

2   Eg as in *Surridge v Clarkson* (1866) 14 WR 979.

3   *Lanphier v Buck* (1865) 2 Drew & Sm 484 at 494.

4   *Lanphier v Buck* (1865) 2 Drew & Sm 484; *Martin v Holgate* (1866) LR 1 HL 175; *Re Woolley, Wormald v Woolley* [1903] 2 Ch 206 at 209. See also *Attwood v Alford* (1866) LR 2 Eq 479; *Burt v Hellyar* (1872) LR 14 Eq 160; *Re Earle's Settlement Trusts, Reiss v Norrie* [1971] 2 All ER 1188, sub nom *Re Earle's Settlement Trusts, Reiss v Merryweather* [1971] 1 WLR 1118 (where a gift over in a marriage settlement to the issue of the uncles and aunts who might predecease the husband was substitutional, as the original gift to the uncles and aunts was immediately vested but liable to be divested). In the case of a devise to a person and his heirs (*Brett v Rigden* (1568) 1 Plowd 340; *Warner v White* (1782) 3 Bro Parl Cas 435, HL (overruling a dictum of Popham J in *Fuller v Fuller* (1595) Cro Eliz 422)), or to a person and the heirs of his body (*Hartopp's Case* (1591) Cro Eliz 243; *Hutton v Simpson* (1716) 2 Vern 722; *Denn d Radclyffe v Bagshaw* (1796) 6 Term Rep 512; *Doe d Turner v Kett* (1792) 4 Term Rep 601), or of a bequest to a person, his executors or

administrators (*Elliott v Davenport* (1705) 1 P Wms 83), the additional words are words of limitation. The gifts are not substitutional, and the death of the named person in the life of the testator does not enable the heirs or the executors or administrators to take as purchasers under the will. As to 'heirs' as a word of limitation in wills see PARA 384 et seq. As to lapse generally see PARA 160 et seq. In an immediate gift to a person or his personal representatives, the personal representatives take by substitution if the legatee dies in the lifetime of the testator (*Gittings v M'Dermott* (1834) 2 My & K 69), but, where the gift is postponed, expressions such as 'personal representatives' are treated as simply another way of giving the legatee a vested interest on the testator's death, and there is no substitutional gift; and, if the legatee dies in the lifetime of the testator, the personal representatives do not take (*Re Porter's Trust* (1857) 4 K & J 188 at 193, 198 per Wood V-C (explaining *Corbyn v French* (1799) 4 Ves 418); *Thompson v Whitelock* (1859) 4 De G & J 490; *Re Turner* (1865) 2 Drew & Sm 501). The position is similar in a postponed gift to 'A or his heirs', where 'heirs' is used in the sense of 'representatives' (*Tidwell v Ariel* (1818) 3 Madd 403), but not where the word is used in the sense of persons entitled as on intestacy (see *Re Bourke's Will Trusts, Barclays Bank Trust Co Ltd v Canada Permanent Trust Co* [1980] 1 All ER 219, [1980] 1 WLR 539 (gift of residue to 'their heirs and surviving issue' held to be substitutional in nature and given to two distinct classes of donee; 'heirs' held to mean heirs in the strict pre-1926 sense)); in such a case the heirs take as named individuals (*Re Porter's Trust* (1857) 4 K & J 188). Where persons referred to as 'personal representatives' are intended to take beneficially, they take by substitution: *Wingfield v Wingfield* (1878) 9 ChD 658.

5   See *Thomas v Kent* [2006] EWCA Civ 1485 at [17], [2006] All ER (D) 57 (May) per Chadwick LJ (appeal on basis that long-established rules of construction were not followed by judge was dismissed); and *Marley v Rawlings* [2014] UKSC 2 at [20], [2015] AC 129, [2014] 1 All ER 807 per Lord Neuberger: 'whether the document in question is a commercial contract or a will, the aim is to identify the intention of the party or parties to the document by interpreting the words used in their documentary, factual and commercial context'. See also PARA 322 note 6.

322. Effect of time of death of prior donee.

The effect of the time of death of the prior donee in ascertaining the rights of the donees under a substitutional gift varies according as the primary gift is to a named person or group of named persons[1], or to a class, and, if it is to a class, then according as the gift takes effect immediately on the testator's death or is postponed to a subsequent date[2].

If the primary gift is to a named person or group of named persons, the substitutional gift takes effect on the death of the primary donee, whether:

(1)   before the date of the will;

(2)   after the date of the will and before the testator's death[3]; or

(3)   after the testator's death and before the date of distribution[4].

If the substitutional gift is to a class, the class consists in the case of heads (1) and (2) above of those who are living at the testator's death and in the case of head (3) above of those who are living at the death of the primary donee[5].

If the original gift is to a class, a person who was dead at the date of the will may not be included in it[6], and consequently no one can take in his place by way of substitution[7]. Thus if the original donees are a class of parents, and there is a substitutional gift of each parent's share to his children, the children of a parent dead at the date of the will cannot take[8].

A substitutional gift to issue through all degrees is per se contingent. It is a question of construction when the substitution is to take place, but the substituted issue must survive their parents and also the date of substitution (if this is different)[9].

Where the primary gift to a class is immediate, that is, not preceded by any life or other limited interest, a substitutional gift on the death of a member of the class takes effect on the death in the lifetime of the testator of any persons who were living at the date of the will and who, if they had survived, would have taken as members of the class[10].

Where the gift is postponed, the testator is considered to be providing for the death of members of the class between his own death, or the time of ascertainment of the class, and the period of distribution, or the time when the gift is to come into possession[11]. Accordingly, it is prima facie only in respect of persons who are ascertained as members of the class, and capable of taking under the gift, that substitution is effected[12], and the substitutional gift fails as to those who die before the testator or before the time when the class is to be ascertained[13]. If, however, there is no gap between the time of ascertainment of the class and the time of distribution, persons substituted for donees dying in the testator's lifetime, even before the date of the will, may be let in[14].

1 Ie a number of persons taking not as a class, but as individuals: see PARA 301. Cf *Aitken's Trustees v Aitken* 1970 SC 28, HL.

2 See *Ive v King* (1852) 16 Beav 46 at 53–54.

3 Even where the death of the legatee occurs before that of the testator, the gift over takes effect on the presumption that the ulterior legatee was substituted in order to prevent a lapse of the legacy: *Ive v King* (1852) 16 Beav 46 at 54. There is no distinction between a gift to a person known to be alive, and in the event of his death to his children, and a gift to a person who the testator may suppose or believe to be living, but who is in fact dead, with a gift over to his children in case of his death: *Ive v King* at 55–56. As to death of the primary legatee before the date of the will see *Hannam v Sims* (1858) 2 De G & J 151; *Re Booth's Will Trusts, Robbins v King* (1940) 163 LT 77. As to death between the date of the will and the death of the testator see *Le Jeune v Le Jeune* (1837) 2 Keen 701; *Ive v King* above at 54; *Ashling v Knowles* (1856) 3 Drew 593; *Hodgson v Smithson* (1856) 8 De GM & G 604; *Re Faulding's Trust* (1858) 26 Beav 263; *Jones v Frewin* (1864) 3 New Rep 415.

4 *Ive v King* (1852) 16 Beav 46. It makes no difference whether the primary legatee dies before or after the testator, so long as he dies before the death of the life tenant or other date of distribution: *Ashling v Knowles* (1856) 3 Drew 593.

5 *Ive v King* (1852) 16 Beav 46 at 57.

6 The testator is not in this case referring to specific individuals who he believes to be alive (see note 3), and, in referring to a class, he is understood to refer to living persons: *Re Hotchkiss' Trusts* (1869) LR 8 Eq 643 at 649; *Re Musther, Groves v Musther* (1890) 43 ChD 569 at 572, CA; *Re Brown, Leeds v Spencer* [1917] 2 Ch 232. But see *Thomas v Kent* [2006] EWCA Civ 1485, [2006] All ER (D) 57 (May), where an ultimate trust was for a class comprising 'my brothers and sisters'; some brothers had died before the date of the will, two were alive at that date but one was expressly excluded by the will; the judge and the Court of Appeal took the view that the reference to 'brothers', in the plural, showed intention to include brothers who predeceased the date of the will and that all siblings (except the excluded one) should be included, regardless of date of death.

7 In order to claim under the will, the substituted legatees must point out the original legatees in whose place they demand to stand (*Christopherson v Naylor* (1816) 1 Mer 320 at 326); and the substitutional gift fails where the corresponding member of the primary class was dead at the date of the will, and, therefore, could not have taken as a member of the class under the will (*Coulthurst v Carter* (1852) 15 Beav 421 at 427; *Ive v King* (1852) 16 Beav 46 at 53; *Congreve v Palmer* (1853) 16 Beav 435; *Re Wood's Will* (1862) 31 Beav 323); cf *Thomas v Kent* [2006] EWCA Civ 1485,[2006] All ER (D) 57 (May) at note 6, where an intention was discerned to allow the gifts to a primary class (which comprised siblings, including some that were dead by the date of the will) to be given as substitutional gifts to their children; see PARA 324 text and note 2.

8 *Christopherson v Naylor* (1816) 1 Mer 320; *Gray v Garman* (1843) 2 Hare 268; *Re Hotchkiss' Trusts* (1869) LR 8 Eq 643; *Atkinson v Atkinson* (1872) IR 6 Eq 184 at 189; *Kelsey v Ellis* (1878) 38 LT 471; *Re Barker, Asquith v Saville* (1882) 47 LT 38; *Re Webster's Estate, Widgen v Mello* (1883) 23 ChD 737; *Re Chinery, Chinery v Hill* (1888) 39 ChD 614; *Re Musther, Groves v Musther* (1890) 43 ChD 569; *Re Wood, Tullett v Colville* [1894] 3 Ch 381, CA; *Re Offiler, Offiler v Offiler* (1901) 83 LT 758; *Gorringe v Mahlstedt* [1907] AC 225, HL; *Re Cope, Cross v Cross* [1908] 2 Ch 1, CA; *Mackintosh (or Miller) v Gerrard* [1947] AC 461, HL; *Re Brooke's Will Trusts, Jubber v Brooke* [1953] 1 All ER 668, [1953] 1 WLR 439. In *Butter v Ommaney* (1827) 4 Russ 70, children of members of the class who had died in the testator's lifetime were excluded from the substitutional gift. As to certain decisions which were founded on the view that *Christopherson v Naylor* (1816) 1 Mer 320 should not be followed see *Re Hotchkiss' Trusts* (1869) LR 8 Eq 643. It seems that where a gift is substitutional and not original and is made not merely for children but for issue, for any issue to take it must survive its parent: see *Re Manly's Will Trusts, Burton v Williams* [1969] 3 All ER 1011 at 1023, per Ungoed-Thomas J, citing Sir Richard Kindersley V-C in *Lanphier v Buck* (1865) 2 Drew & Sm 484 at 494. See also *Re Earle's Settlement Trusts, Reiss v Norrie* [1971] 2 All ER 1188, sub nom *Re Earle's Settlement Trusts, Reiss v Merryweather* [1971] 1 WLR 1118; see also note 9.

9 *Re Earle's Settlement Trusts, Reiss v Norrie* [1971] 2 All ER 1188, sub nom *Re Earle's Settlement Trusts, Reiss v Merryweather* [1971] 1 WLR 1118.

10 *Re Hayward, Creery v Lingwood* (1882) 19 ChD 470. As to the members of the substituted class see PARA 305 et seq.
11 *Re Gilbert, Daniel v Matthews* (1886) 54 LT 752.
12 See *Re Porter's Trust* (1857) 4 K & J 188 at 191–192 per Wood V-C (citing *Ive v King* (1852) 16 Beav 46). The substitutional gift took effect in *Hilton v Hilton* (1866) 15 WR 193.
13 *Thornhill v Thornhill* (1819) 4 Madd 377; *Neilson v Monro* (1879) 27 WR 936; *Re Hannam, Haddelsey v Hannam* [1897] 2 Ch 39; *Re Ibbetson, Ibbetson v Ibbetson* (1903) 88 LT 461 (to the child or children of J and H 'or their heirs'). See also *Ive v King* (1852) 16 Beav 46 (where the rule is stated but the authorities cited refer to another point); *Ashling v Knowles* (1856) 3 Drew 593 at 595. Cf *Smith v Farr* (1839) 3 Y & C Ex 328.
14 *King v Cleaveland* (1858) 26 Beav 26 (affd (1859) 4 De G & J 477) (to persons 'then living' or their representatives); *Re Philps' Will* (1868) LR 7 Eq 151 (to persons 'then living' or their heirs).

323. Gifts to children defined by reference to the parent's share. The exclusion of children from taking under a gift defined by reference to the parent's share is avoided where the gift can be construed as original and not substitutional. Thus the gift to the children may not be alternative to a gift actually made to the parent; it may be a gift of a share computed on the hypothesis that there had been a gift to the parent. This is an original gift to the children, and does not fail because the parent could not have taken[1].

Further, even where the children are expressed to take only their parent's share, according to the construction of the whole will the class of children may be ascertained, not by reference to those parents only who could take under the original gift to parents, but by reference to all the parents, whether eventually capable of taking or not; this, again, is an original gift to the children[2]. A similar result may follow where the gift is to 'issue' and qualified by reference to their parent's share, although these seem to be mainly substitutional gifts[3]. Such gifts to issue will, it seems, often be construed as per stirpes rather than per capita[4].

1 *Loring v Thomas* (1861) 1 Drew & Sm 497; *Re Chapman's Will* (1863) 32 Beav 382; *Re Woolrich, Harris v Harris* (1879) 11 ChD 663; *Re Chinery, Chinery v Hill* (1888) 39 ChD 614 at 618 per Chitty J; *Re Parsons, Blaber v Parsons* (1894) 8 R 430 at 434; *Re Lambert, Corns v Harrison* [1908] 2 Ch 117; *Re Metcalfe, Metcalfe v Earle* [1909] 1 Ch 424; *Re Stokes, Barlow v Bullock* (1907) 52 Sol Jo 11; *Re Taylor, Taylor v White* (1911) 56 Sol Jo 175; *Re Williams, Metcalf v Williams* [1914] 1 Ch 219 (affd [1914] 2 Ch 61, CA); *Re Kirk, Wethey v Kirk* (1915) 85 LJ Ch 182; *Re Hickey, Beddoes v Hodgson* [1917] 1 Ch 601 (legacy to the descendants of A or their descendants 'living at my death'; words held to govern whole gift). *Loring v Thomas* (1861) 1 Drew & Sm 497 is not affected by *Gorringe v Mahlstedt* [1907] AC 225, and is recognised as an authority in *Barraclough v Cooper* [1908] 2 Ch 121n at 125n. See also *Re Lambert, Corns v Harrison* [1908] 2 Ch 117 at 121 per Eve J.
2 *Jarvis v Pond* (1839) 9 Sim 549 (alternative gift to the children of 'any' sons and daughters 'to have their father's or mother's part'; children of son and daughter dead at date of will entitled to share, even though 'some violence' was done in assigning a share to the parents); *Loring v Thomas* (1861) 1 Drew & Sm 497 ('any' of parents); *Re Sibley's Trusts* (1877) 5 ChD 494 at 501 (where it was said that 'all and every' the parents must mean 'more than two'). In *Re Metcalfe, Metcalfe v Earle* [1909] 1 Ch 424 at 426, Joyce J suggested a distinction between a gift to children and a gift to a class of another description (such as nephews and nieces) where the testator might not have means of knowing the state of the family. As to a postponed alternative gift see *Smith v Smith* (1837) 8 Sim 353; *Habergham v Ridehalgh* (1870) LR 9 Eq 395 (where the gifts were original, being framed on the hypothesis that the person for whom the donees were alternative were ascertained members of the class of first donees, and accordingly it was held that these alternative donees might take in such a case, although the members of the class of first donees predeceased the testator). In *Collins v Johnson* (1835) 8 Sim 356n, the gift was by reference to a prior gift to individuals: see *Re Hannam, Haddelsey v Hannam* [1897] 2 Ch 39 at 45 per North J.
3 *Re Manly's Will Trusts (No 2), Tickle v Manly* [1976] 1 All ER 673 (reference to issue taking 'their deceased parent's share' did not negative the construction of 'issue', on reading the will as a whole, as meaning issue in all degrees without regard to whether their parents could take or not, thus allowing great-grandchildren to take, along with grandchildren).
4 If distributed per capita the situation could arise where child takes a larger share than the deceased parent could have taken: see *Re Manly's Will Trusts (No 2), Tickle v Manly* [1976] 1 All ER 673.

See also *Re Earle's Settlement Trusts, Reiss v Norrie* [1971] 2 All ER 1188, sub nom *Re Earle's Settlement Trusts, Reiss v Merryweather* [1971] 1 WLR 1118; and PARAS 397, 398.

324. Composite class of parents and issue. Where a gift is framed as a gift to a composite class formed of a class of parents living at a certain period and a class of children of parents then dead, there is prima facie an independent and original gift to that class of children[1], and children of parents who were dead before the date of the will may take[2], as well as children of parents who died after that date but before the testator.

1   See *Re Lord's Settlement, Martins Bank Ltd v Lord* [1947] 2 All ER 685 (settlement); *Re Hooper's Settlement Trusts, Bosman v Hooper* [1948] Ch 586, [1948] 2 All ER 261 (settlement). For cases of contrary intention see *Waugh v Waugh* (1833) 2 My & K 41 (where a direction as to the children's share confined the class of children); *Re Thompson's Trusts, ex p Tunstall* (1854) 5 De GM & G 280.
2   *Tytherleigh v Harbin* (1835) 6 Sim 329; *Giles v Giles* (1837) 8 Sim 360; *Rust v Baker* (1837) 8 Sim 443; *Bebb v Beckwith* (1839) 2 Beav 308; *Gaskell v Holmes* (1844) 3 Hare 438; *Coulthurst v Carter* (1852) 15 Beav 421; *Etches v Etches* (1856) 3 Drew 441 at 447 (not followed in *Re Earle's Settlement Trusts, Reiss v Norrie* [1971] 2 All ER 1188, sub nom *Re Earle's Settlement Trusts, Reiss v Merryweather* [1971] 1 WLR 1118 (where a gift over in a marriage settlement to the issue of uncles and aunts who might predecease the husband was substitutional as the original gift was vested and liable to be divested)); *Re Jordan's Trusts* (1863) 2 New Rep 57; *Heasman v Pearse* (1871) 7 Ch App 275; *Re Morrison* [1913] VLR 348. In *Re Faulding's Trusts* (1858) 26 Beav 263, the parent died in the lifetime of the testatrix, but it does not appear whether he died before or after the date of her will. The construction approach used by the Court of Appeal in *Thomas v Kent* [2006] EWCA Civ 1485, [2006] All ER (D) 57 (May) allowed in the children of parents who were already dead by the date of the will, but the court appears to have treated the gifts as substitutional, not original, having discerned a testamentary intention to include a class of parents, regardless of their date of death.

325. Conditions attaching to alternative gift. Conditions attaching to a gift do not prima facie attach to a gift alternative to it, whether original or substitutional[1], although in the case of substitutional gifts it may much more easily be inferred that they attach than in the case of alternative original gifts[2]. Thus unless the testator so provides, it is not in general necessary that an alternative donee should survive the date of distribution in order to take, whether the gift is original[3] or substitutional[4]; nor, in an alternative and original gift, is it in general necessary, unless the testator so provides, that the alternative donee should survive the person for whom he is alternative[5]. In a substitutional gift it is, however, in general necessary that the substituted donee should survive the person for whom he is substituted[6].

1   *Martin v Holgate* (1866) LR 1 HL 175. See also *Lyon v Coward* (1846) 15 Sim 287; *Smith v Palmer* (1848) 7 Hare 225; *Barker v Barker* (1852) 5 De G & Sm 753; *Re Bennett's Trust* (1857) 3 K & J 280 at 285; *Re Wildman's Trusts* (1860) 1 John & H 299; *Re Pell's Trust* (1861) 3 De GF & J 291; *Lanphier v Buck* (1865) 2 Drew & Sm 484 at 496. As to cases where the contingency of the first gift applied to the alternative gift see *Bennett v Merriman* (1843) 6 Beav 360; *Macgregor v Macgregor* (1845) 2 Coll 192; *Re Kirkman's Trust* (1859) 3 De G & J 558. In so far as these latter cases do not depend on the particular contexts of the wills there in question, they are disapproved in *Martin v Holgate* (1866) LR 1 HL 175.
2   *Martin v Holgate* (1866) LR 1 HL 175 at 187 per Lord Chelmsford.
3   *Thompson v Clive* (1857) 23 Beav 282; *Martin v Holgate* (1866) LR 1 HL 175; *Re Woolley, Wormald v Woolley* [1903] 2 Ch 206; *Campbell's Trustee v Dick* 1915 SC 100, Ct of Sess. See also PARAS 322 note 4, 323 text and note 4.
4   *Masters v Scales* (1850) 13 Beav 60; *Re Battersby's Trusts* [1896] 1 IR 600; *Re Bradbury, Wing v Bradbury* (1904) 73 LJ Ch 591, CA; *Re Langlands, Langlands v Langlands* (1917) 87 LJ Ch 1, Ct of Sess. Cf *Todd's Trustees v Todd's Executrix* 1922 SC 1 (substitutional gift, and, therefore, no right vested in the children of H, a son, who predeceased the life renter). The doubt expressed on this point in *Crause v Cooper* (1859) 1 John & H 207 at 213 per Wood V-C was recognised by him as unfounded in *Re Merricks' Trusts* (1886) LR 1 Eq 551 at 558. For a case of a context to the contrary see *Re Kirkman's Trust* (1859) 3 De G & J 558.

5 *Lyon v Coward* (1846) 15 Sim 287; *Lanphier v Buck* (1865) 2 Drew & Sm 484 at 498; *Heasman v Pearse* (1871) 7 Ch App 275; *Re Woolley, Wormald v Woolley* [1903] 2 Ch 206. Cf *Re Jordan's Trusts* (1863) 2 New Rep 57. For a case of a contrary intention shown by the will see *Barker v Barker* (1852) 5 De G & Sm 753.
6 *Thompson v Clive* (1857) 23 Beav 282; *Crause v Cooper* (1859) 1 John & H 207; *Lanphier v Buck* (1865) 2 Drew & Sm 484; *Re Turner* (1865) 2 Drew & Sm 501; *Re Merricks' Trusts* (1866) LR 1 Eq 551 at 560 (explained in *Re Woolley, Wormald v Woolley* [1903] 2 Ch 206 at 209); *Re Manly's Will Trusts, Burton v Williams* [1969] 3 All ER 1011 at 1024, [1969] 1 WLR 1818 at 1831; see PARA 322, text and note 5.

326. Ascertainment of class taking under substituted gift. Subject to the principle that conditions attaching to a gift do not normally attach to a substituted gift[1], the class of substituted donees is ascertained according to the usual rules[2]. Whether the members of classes taking under original and substituted gifts may take concurrently depends on the correspondence between the members of those classes respectively. A gift to a class of parents or their children, or parents or their issue, is construed as substituting for each parent his own children or issue, wherever the context allows that construction[3]. Thus when there are words denoting an intention to divide the property into shares for the purpose of substitution[4], the parents surviving the period of distribution[5] and the children or issue of parents dying before that period[6] then take concurrently[7]. Otherwise, where the original and substitutional gifts are both to classes and there is nothing indicative of a substitution for a member of the original class of a corresponding member of the substituted class[8], the gifts are mutually exclusive, and, if any member of the original class survives the period of distribution, no member of the substituted class can take[9].

In the absence of a contrary intention being shown[10], the substituted donees as between themselves are joint tenants[11], even where the original donees are tenants in common and, therefore, as between original donees and substituted donees taking with them, there is a tenancy in common.

1 As to this principle see PARAS 324–325.
2 As to these rules see PARA 302 et seq. Thus the class is ascertained at the testator's death (*Ive v King* (1852) 16 Beav 46 (children); *Re Philps' Will* (1868) LR 7 Eq 151 at 154 (heirs, in sense of next of kin); *Wingfield v Wingfield* (1878) 9 ChD 658 (heirs)), subject, in the case of a postponed gift, to letting in members of the class coming into existence before the date of distribution (*Re Sibley's Trusts* (1877) 5 ChD 494; *Re Jones's Estate, Hume v Lloyd* (1878) 47 LJ Ch 775 (not following *Hobgen v Neale* (1870) LR 11 Eq 48 on this point)).
3 *Re Coley, Gibson v Gibson* [1901] 1 Ch 40 at 44; *Re Alderton, Hughes v Vanderspar* [1913] WN 129. See PARA 322 text and note 5 and *Thomas v Kent* [2006] EWCA Civ 1485,[2006] All ER (D) 57 (May).
4 *Re Gilbert, Daniel v Matthews* (1886) 54 LT 752 (where it was said that in *Re Dawes' Trusts* (1876) 4 ChD 210 the court's attention had not been drawn to the authorities); *Re Miles, Miles v Miles* (1889) 61 LT 359.
5 As to the meaning of 'period of distribution' see PARA 306 note 1.
6 If all of the original class survive that period, the substituted class are excluded: *Re Coley, Gibson v Gibson* [1901] 1 Ch 40 at 43.
7 See *Re Manly's Will Trusts, Burton v Williams* [1969] 3 All ER 1011, [1969] 1 WLR 1818; *Re Manly's Will Trusts (No 2), Tickle v Manly* [1976] 1 All ER 673; *Re Earle's Settlement Trusts, Reiss v Norrie* [1971] 2 All ER 1188, sub nom *Re Earle's Settlement Trusts, Reiss v Merryweather* [1971] 1 WLR 1118 (gifts to uncles and aunts 'being then dead, leaving issue', where the effect was to create stirpital gifts).
8 Eg gifts to children 'or their heirs': *Finlason v Tatlock* (1870) LR 9 Eq 258.
9 *Re Coley, Gibson v Gibson* [1901] 1 Ch 40.
10 See *Lyon v Coward* (1846) 15 Sim 287 at 290–291; *Hodges v Grant* (1867) LR 4 Eq 140; *A-G v Fletcher* (1871) LR 13 Eq 128; *Re Horner, Eagleton v Horner* (1887) 37 ChD 695 at 711 (where there were double words of severance sufficient to apply to the substituted donees). See also *Re Bourke's Will Trusts, Barclays Bank Trust Co Ltd v Canada Permanent Trust Co* [1980] 1 All ER 219, [1980] 1 WLR 539; and PARA 321 note 4. As to distribution per capita or per stripes in such cases see PARAS 396–400 and the cases at note 7.

11 *Davenport v Hanbury* (1796) 3 Ves 257; *Bridge v Yates* (1842) 12 Sim 645; *Salisbury v Petty*
   (1843) 3 Hare 86 at 93; *Re Hodgson's Trusts* (1854) 1 K & J 178; *M'Gregor v M'Gregor* (1859)
   1 De GF & J 63; *Penny v Clarke* (1860) 1 De GF & J 425 at 431; *Coe v Bigg* (1863) 1 New Rep
   536; *Lanphier v Buck* (1865) 2 Drew & Sm 484; *Heasman v Pearse* (1870) LR 11 Eq 522 at 535
   (on appeal (1871) 7 Ch App 275 at 283); *Re Yates, Bostock v D'Eyncourt* [1891] 3 Ch 53
   (disapproving *Shepherdson v Dale* (1866) 12 Jur NS 156); *Re Battersby's Trusts* [1896] 1 IR 600;
   Re Bourke's Will Trusts, Barclays Bank Trust Co Ltd v Canada Permanent Trust Co [1980]
   1 All ER 219, [1980] 1 WLR 539.

327. Failure of alternative gift. Where an alternative gift fails by reason of the
event not having happened on which it is to take effect, the prior gift to the first
donee may take effect even though he was not living at the period of distribution[1],
because the alternative gift operates as a divesting gift only[2].

In the case of a gift to a group or class, a substitutional gift of the shares of
those who die leaving issue to their issue does not affect the shares of those who
die without leaving issue[3]. That will usually result because such a reference to
issue taking their parent's share, which normally means issue through all degrees,
without more, indicates an intended stirpital distribution to the whole class and to
the substituted issue[4].

1 *Gray v Garman* (1843) 2 Hare 268; *Salisbury v Petty* (1843) 3 Hare 86 at 93.
2 As to divesting generally see PARA 440.
3 *Baldwin v Rogers* (1853) 3 De GM & G 649; *Strother v Dutton* (1857) 1 De G & J 675 at 676.
4 See the analysis of this point in *Re Manly's Will Trusts, Burton v Williams* [1969] 3 All ER 1011
   at 1023 and *Re Manly's Will Trusts (No 2), Tickle v Manly* [1976] 1 All ER 673 at 678-9 per
   Walton J (the fact that a substituted donee can only have his parent's share to the exclusion of that
   parent is a strong indicator of a stirpital distribution; were it a per capita distribution, that could
   possibly see issue taking more than their deceased parent would have done). See also *Baldwin v
   Rogers* (1853) 3 De GM & G 649 (express reference to stirpital gift); and PARA 398.

(ii) Identification of Donees

A.   IDENTIFICATION BY REFERENCE TO RELATIONSHIPS

(A)   General Rule and Particular Descriptions

328. General rule for identifying donees referred to by relationship. Donees may
be identified in a will by reference to relationship[1], or to the holding of an office
or otherwise[2]. A description by relationship prima facie refers only to persons
related by blood[3], including the half-blood[4], and in the exact relationship, if any,
prescribed by the will, for example grandchildren[5], cousins[6] or nephews and
nieces[7]. Prima facie such a description does not refer to persons related by affinity
and not consanguinity[8]; but, by the force of the context of the will[9] or the
circumstances of the case[10], the description may be extended to include persons
related only by affinity[11], or in the same or a different degree of distance in
relationship[12]. The mere fact that in a prior part of the will a person is described
as a relative does not alone admit to a share in a subsequent gift to relatives of that
degree either the named person[13] or other persons of like degree with him[14]; but
this fact is an indication in that direction[15], to be taken into consideration along
with the context of the whole will and the circumstances of the case admissible in
evidence as to identification[16].

1 Where there is a conflict between the description of the relationship and the name and address of
   the legatee, there is a latent ambiguity which the court will attempt to resolve by admitting
   extrinsic evidence to establish which of the alternative possible donees the testator intended to
   benefit: *Pinnel v Anison* [2005] EWHC 1421 (Ch) sub nom *Pinnell v Annison* [2005] All ER (D)
   458 (May) (gift of half share of residue to 'my sister, Doreen Hall' followed by an address;

deceased's sister was called Doreen Anison and lived at a different address; the Doreen Hall living at the specified address was apparently unknown to the deceased).

2   As to gifts by reference to the holding of an office see PARA 367. A reference to a person as a legatee may refer only to an effective legatee, so that a person whose bequest fails is excluded from participating in further benefits given to 'legatees': *Re Feather*, as reported in [1945] 1 All ER 552.

3   As to the question of legitimacy, adoption and assisted fertilisation, see PARA 350 et seq.

4   *Grieves v Rawley* (1852) 10 Hare 63 ('niece'); *Re Hammersley, Kitchen v Myers* (1886) 2 TLR 459; *Re Cozens, Miles v Wilson* [1903] 1 Ch 138 ('my own nephews and nieces'); *Ward v Van Der Loeff* [1924] AC 653, HL ('my brothers and sisters'; not confined to those existing at the date of the will or to those of the whole blood). Cf *Re Reed* (1888) 57 LJ Ch 790; *Re Dowson, Dowson v Beadle* [1909] WN 245 ('my own brothers and sisters'). 'Uterine brothers and sisters' means prima facie brothers and sisters by the same mother, but by a different father: see *Re Vincent, Public Trustee v Vincent* [1926] WN 307 (on the construction of a settlement). Where a gift is made to a beneficiary who leaves issue living at testator's death, the devise or bequest takes effect as if it is to the issue living at the testator's death, unless a contrary intention appears by the will: see the Wills Act 1837 s 33; *Ling v Ling* [2001] All ER (D) 322 (Nov); *Rainbird v Smith* [2012] EWHC 4276 (Ch); and PARA 169. Where a gift is by reference to gender, the fact that a person has acquired a different gender does not affect the disposal or devolution of property under a will made before 4 April 2005 (the coming into force of the Gender Recognition Act 2004) but may affect it under a will made on or after that date: see PARA 329.

5   Where there are persons to satisfy the descriptions taken in their ordinary sense, and there is nothing in the will or the circumstances to give any other sense to the words, 'grandchildren' does not include great-grandchildren (*Lord Orford v Churchill* (1814) 3 Ves & B 59), but 'grandchildren of any degree' will include descendants of any degree other than children (*Re Hall, Hall v Hall* [1932] 1 Ch 262).

6   'First cousins or cousins german' was held not to include the descendants of first cousins: *Sanderson v Bayley* (1838) 4 My & Cr 56. 'First and second cousins' was held to include first cousins once and twice removed in *Re Colahan, Molloy v Hara* [1967] IR 29. Cf *Re Tully, Toolan v Costello* [1941] IR 66 (where 'all my first cousins, first cousins once removed and my second cousins' did not include second cousins once removed). 'Cousins', without further qualification, includes only first cousins: *Stoddart v Nelson, Stanger v Nelson* (1855) 6 De GM & G 68; *Stevenson v Abingdon* (1862) 10 WR 591; *Burbey v Burbey* (1862) 9 Jur NS 96; *Copland's Executors v Milne* 1908 SC 426, Ct of Sess. The dictum in *Caldecott v Harrison* (1840) 9 Sim 457 at 460, that 'cousins' includes cousins of every description, is overruled by the cases previously cited. 'Second cousins' does not normally include first cousins once removed, that is, children or grandchildren of first cousins: *Bridgnorth Corpn v Collins* (1847) 15 Sim 538 at 541; *Re Parker, Bentham v Wilson* (1881) 17 ChD 262, CA (where *Mayott v Mayott* (1786) 2 Bro CC 125, *Silcox v Bell* (1823) 1 Sim & St 301 and *Charge v Goodyear* (1826) 3 Russ 140 (see note 12) are examined). 'Half cousins' includes first cousins, first cousins once removed and second cousins: *Re Chester, Servant v Hills* [1914] 2 Ch 580.

7   As a rule, 'nephews and nieces' does not include grandchildren (*Campbell v Bouskell* (1859) 27 Beav 325; *M'Hugh v M'Hugh* [1908] 1 IR 155 (where the evidence showed that the real nephews and nieces were not the objects of bounty, and there was nothing to show who were those objects)), or great-nephews or great-nieces (*Falkner v Butler* (1765) Amb 514; *Shelley v Bryer* (1821) Jac 207; *Williamson v Moore* (1862) 8 Jur NS 875; *Re Blower's Trusts* (1871) 6 Ch App 351); and 'nieces' does not include great-nieces (*Crook v Whitley* (1857) 7 De GM & G 490). As to acquired gender see note 4; and PARA 329.

8   *Hussey v Berkeley* (1763) 2 Eden 194 at 196 (widow of a grandson, not a grandchild); *Smith v Lidiard* (1857) 3 K & J 252; *Merrill v Morton* (1881) 17 ChD 382.

9   See *Re Cozens, Miles v Wilson* [1903] 1 Ch 138; and the general rule as to construction stated in PARA 224 et seq.

10   See *Re Cozens, Miles v Wilson* [1903] 1 Ch 138. As to the principle of 'falsa demonstratio non nocet' see PARA 269.

11   *Frogley v Phillips* (1861) 3 De GF & J 466; *Re Gue, Smith v Gue* (1892) 61 LJ Ch 510 (affd [1892] WN 132, CA) (where a nephew of the testator's wife took as a 'nephew' and the wife of that nephew took as a 'niece'); *Re Daoust* [1944] 1 All ER 443 (where 'nephews and nieces' included relations by marriage, but not those traced through two marriages, eg husbands of nieces of the testatrix's husband); *Re Davidson, National Provincial Bank Ltd v Davidson* [1949] Ch 670, [1949] 2 All ER 551 (where 'grandchildren' was held to mean grandchildren of the husband of the testatrix by a former wife); *Re Tylor, Barclays Bank Ltd v Norris* (1968) 112 Sol Jo 486 (where 'nephews and nieces' was held to include relations by marriage). In *Re Richards* (1939) 162 LT 47, 'brothers-in-law' and 'sisters-in-law' were construed in the strict sense, ie as persons traced through one marriage. Relatives by affinity are held to take rather than that the gift fail, eg where the

testator has no relatives by consanguinity of the described kind, and none can come into existence to satisfy the description (*Hogg v Cook* (1863) 32 Beav 641; *Adney v Greatrex* (1869) 38 LJ Ch 414; *Sherratt v Mountford* (1873) 8 Ch App 928), or where it is shown that the testator treated the claimant as his own relative, and did not know of the existence of the relative by consanguinity (*Grant v Grant* (1870) LR 5 CP 380; on appeal LR 5 CP 727, Ex Ch). Certain dicta in *Grant v Grant* as to the meaning of 'nephew' were dissented from in *Wells v Wells* (1874) LR 18 Eq 504 at 506 and in *Merrill v Morton* (1881) 17 ChD 382 at 386, and were distinguished in *Re Taylor, Cloak v Hammond* (1886) 34 ChD 255 at 257–258, CA. 'Cousin' may be understood in the circumstances to mean the wife of a cousin: *Re Taylor, Cloak v Hammond*. As to acquired gender see note 4; and PARA 329. In *Reading v Reading* [2015] EWHC 946 (Ch), [2015] All ER (D) 64 (Feb) the ordinary and natural meaning of the word 'issue' was held to connote the actual children of the testator in the biological sense, together with the descendants of those children and so did not in its ordinary and natural meaning include stepchildren; however, factors such as the overall structure of the will indicated that the testator had intended the term to include stepchildren, as well as children, and to limit it to their children, rather than descendants of all degrees.

12 A gift to the testator's 'first and second cousins' has in various contexts been held to include first cousins once or twice removed, and other relations not more remote in degree than second cousins: *Mayott v Mayott* (1786) 2 Bro CC 125 (where a great-niece was also included); *Silcox v Bell* (1823) 1 Sim & St 301; *Charge v Goodyear* (1826) 3 Russ 140; *Wilks v Bannister* (1885) 30 ChD 512. 'Second cousins' has been held to include first cousins once and twice removed, where no true second cousins existed: *Slade v Fooks* (1838) 9 Sim 386; *Re Bonner, Tucker v Good* (1881) 19 ChD 201. See also *Re Rickit's Trusts* (1853) 11 Hare 299 (where 'niece' was held to mean 'nephew'); *Stringer v Gardiner* (1859) 4 De G & J 468 (where a gift to 'my niece E S' went to a great-great-niece of similar name); *Weeds v Bristow* (1866) LR 2 Eq 333 (where 'nephews' included great-nephews). As to the meanings of 'children', 'issue' etc see PARA 330 et seq.

13 Thus where a husband's niece or wife's niece is described as 'my niece A', she does not necessarily take under a subsequent gift to 'my nephews and nieces': *Smith v Lidiard* (1857) 3 K & J 252; *Wells v Wells* (1874) LR 18 Eq 504; *Merrill v Morton* (1881) 17 ChD 382; *Re Green, Bath v Cannon* [1914] 1 Ch 134. Where a grand-nephew is described as 'my nephew J', he does not necessarily take under a gift to 'my nephews and nieces': *Thompson v Robinson* (1859) 27 Beav 486. See also *Re Blower's Trusts* (1871) 6 Ch App 351.

14 *Re Winn, Burgess v Winn* (1916) 86 LJ Ch 124 (where the description of certain of a wife's nieces as 'my nieces' did not bring them all into a residuary gift to 'all my nephews and nieces'); *Re Ridge, Hancock v Dutton* (1933) 149 LT 266, CA (where the description of a grand-nephew as 'nephew' did not entitle grand-nephews to share a gift to 'nephews').

15 *Hussey v Berkeley* (1763) 2 Eden 194 (where a great-granddaughter was described as 'my granddaughter'); *James v Smith* (1844) 14 Sim 214 (where 'my niece M daughter of my nephew T' was admitted to share in a gift to 'my nephews and nieces') (distinguished in *Re Ridge, Hancock v Dutton* (1933) 149 LT 266, CA).

16 *Re Cozens, Miles v Wilson* [1903] 1 Ch 138 at 142–143 (where 'my own nephews and nieces' excluded nephews by affinity previously called 'my nephew A' etc). See further PARAS 209 et seq, 224.

329. Effect of gender recognition certificate. Where a full[1] gender recognition certificate is issued[2] by a Gender Recognition Panel[3] to a person, the person's gender becomes for all purposes the acquired gender (so that, if the acquired gender is the male gender, the person's sex becomes that of a man and, if it is the female gender, the person's sex becomes that of a woman)[4]. The fact that a person's gender has become the acquired gender does not affect the status of the person as the father or mother of a child[5] nor does it affect the disposal or devolution of property under a will or other instrument made before 4 April 2005[6].

Trustees and personal representatives are not under a duty to inquire before conveying or distributing property whether a full gender recognition certificate has been issued to any person or revoked[7] and are not liable to any person by reason of a conveyance or distribution of property made without regard to the issue or revocation of such a certificate provided they had no notice before the conveyance or distribution[8].

Where the disposition or devolution of any property under a will or other instrument (made on or after 4 April 2005) is different from what it would be but for the fact that a person's gender has become the acquired gender, a person may apply to the High Court for an order on the ground of being adversely affected by the different disposition or devolution of the property[9].

1   A full gender recognition certificate will be issued if:
     (1)   the applicant is neither a civil partner nor married (Gender Recognition Act 2004 s 4(2)(a) (s 4(2)(a) substituted by the Marriage (Same Sex Couples) Act 2013 Sch 5 para 3));
     (2)   the applicant is a party to a protected marriage and the applicant's spouse consents to the marriage continuing after the issue of a full gender recognition certificate (Gender Recognition Act 2004 s 4(2)(b) (as so substituted)); or
     (3)   the applicant is a party to a protected civil partnership and the Gender Recognition Panel has decided to issue a full gender recognition certificate to the other party to the civil partnership (Gender Recognition Act 2004 s 4(2)(c) (as so substituted)).
   'Protected marriage' means a marriage under the law of England and Wales or a marriage under the law of a country or territory outside the United Kingdom; 'protected civil partnership' means a civil partnership under the law of England and Wales: see s 25(1) (definitions added by the Marriage (Same Sex Couples) Act 2013 Sch 5 para 14).
   As to circumstances where an interim gender recognition certificate will be issued see s 4(3); and REGISTRATION CONCERNING THE INDIVIDUAL vol 88 (2012) PARA 268).
2   Ie under the Gender Recognition Act 2004 s 4 (see REGISTRATION CONCERNING THE INDIVIDUAL vol 88 (2012) PARA 268).
3   'Gender Recognition Panel' is to be construed in accordance with the Gender Recognition Act 2004 Sch 1 (see REGISTRATION CONCERNING THE INDIVIDUAL vol 88 (2012) PARA 267): s 25.
4   Gender Recognition Act 2004 s 9(1). The Panel must grant the application if the applicant provides the reports and declarations required by s 3 and it is satisfied that the applicant has or has had gender dysphoria (as defined in s 25), has lived in the acquired gender (to be construed in accordance with s 1(2)) throughout the period of two years ending with the date on which the application is made and intends to continue to live in the acquired gender until death: see s 1; and REGISTRATION CONCERNING THE INDIVIDUAL vol 88 (2012) PARA 267.
5   Gender Recognition Act 2004 s 12. See also CHILDREN AND YOUNG PERSONS vol 9 (2012) PARA 93.
6   See the Gender Recognition Act 2004 s 15; the Gender Recognition Act 2004 (Commencement) Order 2005, SI 2005/54; and PARA 300.
7   Gender Recognition Act 2004 s 17(1).
8   Gender Recognition Act 2004 s 17(2). A person prejudiced has the right to follow the property or any property representing it into the hands of another person who has received it unless that person has purchased it for value in good faith and without notice: s 17(3).
9   See the Gender Recognition Act 2004 s 18(1), (2); and the Gender Recognition Act 2004 (Commencement) Order 2005, SI 2005/54. The court may, if it is satisfied that it is just to do so, make in relation to any person benefiting from the different disposition or devolution of the property such order as it considers appropriate: Gender Recognition Act 2004 s 18(3). An order may, in particular, make provision for: the payment of a lump sum or the transfer of property to the applicant, the settlement of property for the benefit of the applicant, the acquisition of property and either its transfer to the applicant or its settlement for the benefit of the applicant: s 18(4). An order may contain consequential or supplementary provisions for giving effect to the order or for ensuring that it operates fairly as between the applicant and the other person or persons affected by it; and an order may, in particular, confer powers on trustees: s 18(5).

330. Gift to children or issue begotten and to be begotten.
A description of children[1] or issue as 'begotten' prima facie includes children or issue to be begotten in the future; and a description of children or issue as 'to be begotten' prima facie includes children or issue already begotten[2]. However, by the context of the will these special meanings may be displaced, and the words may be taken to have their strictly grammatical meaning[3].

1   In general, in wills made on or after 1 January 1970, 'children' includes illegitimate children: see PARAS 355–356.
2   Co Litt 20b; *Cook v Cook* (1706) 2 Vern 545; *Hewet v Ireland* (1718) 1 P Wms 426; *Hebblethwaite v Cartwright* (1734) Cas *temp* Talb 31; *Doe d James v Hallett* (1813) 1 M & S 124; *Almack v Horn* (1863) 1 Hem & M 630 at 633.
3   *Locke v Dunlop* (1888) 39 ChD 387, CA. See also *Anon* (1584) 3 Leon 87.

331. Gift to children. In a will, 'children', with reference to the children of a named person[1], in its ordinary sense[2] refers to the first generation only of descendants by any marriage[3], and does not include any grandchildren[4] or remoter descendants[5], but by the context and the circumstances admissible in evidence[6] it may be extended to such other generations of descendants[7], to the whole line capable of inheriting from the named person[8], or to stepchildren[9]. In a will made on or after 1 January 1970, 'children' includes illegitimate children (unless the contrary intention appears)[10]; and, in wills made before that date, 'children' may be extended to include illegitimate children by the context and the circumstances admissible in evidence[11]. Where a testator dies on or after 1 January 1976, 'children' includes adopted and legitimated children (subject to any contrary intention) and may include such children where the testator dies before that date[12]. There is no fixed rule of construction that, where a legacy is given to 'children' of a person known by the testator to be dead at the date of the will and to have no child then living, grandchildren will take[13].

'Child' does not mean children, and 'child or other issue' does not mean 'child or children'[14].

Where the will of a testator who dies on or after 1 January 1983[15] contains a devise or bequest to a child (or remoter descendant) of the testator, and the intended beneficiary dies before the testator, leaving issue who are living at the testator's death, unless a contrary intention appears by the will, the devise or bequest shall take effect as a devise or bequest to the issue living at the testator's death[16].

1　As to the time of ascertainment of a class of children see PARA 302.
2　As to the general rule of construction see PARA 236; and as to children born as a result of artificial insemination or in vitro fertilisation see PARA 358 et seq.
3　This is so even though a second marriage is not in the testator's contemplation: *Champion v Pickax* (1737) 1 Atk 472; *Barrington v Tristram* (1801) 6 Ves 345; *Ex p Earl of Ilchester* (1803) 7 Ves 348 at 380; *Critchett v Taynton* (1830) 1 Russ & M 541; *Nash v Allen* (1889) 42 ChD 54 at 59. A reference to a present or future husband did not exclude a deceased husband's children in *Pasmore v Huggins* (1855) 21 Beav 103; *Re Pickup's Trusts* (1861) 1 John & H 389. The children of a prior marriage were excluded by the context in *Stavers v Barnard* (1843) 2 Y & C Ch Cas 539 (certain children of a prior marriage specially named); *Stopford v Chaworth* (1845) 8 Beav 331; *Lovejoy v Crafter* (1865) 35 Beav 149; *Re Parrott, Walter v Parrott* (1886) 33 ChD 274, CA; *Re Baynham, Hart v Mackenzie* (1891) 7 TLR 587 ('our children' in will in favour of second wife). In *Re Potter's Will Trusts* [1944] Ch 70, [1943] 1 All ER 805, CA, 'any child' included children of a second marriage.
4　*Reeves v Brymer* (1799) 4 Ves 692 at 697; *Radcliffe v Buckley* (1804) 10 Ves 195; *Thellusson v Woodford* (1829) 5 Russ 100 at 106; *Stavers v Barnard* (1843) 2 Y & C Ch Cas 539 at 540; *Loring v Thomas* (1861) 1 Drew & Sm 497 at 508.
5　*Pride v Fooks* (1858) 3 De G & J 252 at 275; *Re Atkinson, Pybus v Boyd* [1918] 2 Ch 138.
6　As to evidence for identification purposes generally see PARA 209 et seq.
7　Thus 'children' may be construed as 'grandchildren' where the context shows that the testator has used the word in an extended sense (*Royle v Hamilton* (1799) 4 Ves 437; *Radcliffe v Buckley* (1804) 10 Ves 195 at 201; *Re Blackman* (1852) 16 Beav 377 (name added); *Re Crawhall's Trust* (1856) 8 De GM & G 480 at 487), or where the circumstances admissible in evidence give rise to a similar inference, eg in the case of a legacy to the children of a deceased person, where at the date of the will there are, to the testator's knowledge, no children, but only grandchildren alive (*Re Smith, Lord v Hayward* (1887) 35 ChD 558 at 559 per Kay J). See also *Fenn v Death* (1856) 23 Beav 73; *Berry v Berry* (1861) 3 Giff 134; *Gale v Bennett* (1768) Amb 681 (explained in *Pride v Fooks* (1858) 3 De G & J 252 at 275–279). In *Reading v Reading* [2015] EWHC 946 (Ch), [2015] All ER (D) 64 (Feb), 'issue of mine' included both the deceased's children, stepchildren and their children.
　　'Grandchildren of any degree' may include all lawful descendants except children: *Re Hall, Hall v Hall* [1932] 1 Ch 262. 'Children' cannot, it appears, be construed as 'grandchildren' where the parent of the children is alive but has no children at the date of the will (see Hawkins on Wills (3rd Edn) 110, citing *Moor v Raisbeck* (1841) 12 Sim 123 (where, however, the context only

was relied on)), or where the context of the will draws a distinction between children and grandchildren (*Loring v Thomas* (1861) 1 Drew & Sm 497 at 509); and there would be more difficulty in giving 'children' that meaning in case of a gift to the children of several persons, some of whom had children but others grandchildren only, as the court would be disinclined to give different meanings to the same word (*Radcliffe v Buckley* (1804) 10 Ves 195 at 201; *Re Smith, Lord v Hayward* (1887) 35 ChD 558 at 560 per Kay J). As to whether, if there are no children but grandchildren and great-grandchildren, the grandchildren may take to the exclusion of great-grandchildren see *Fenn v Death* (1856) 23 Beav 73 (where it was so held). Cf, however, *Pride v Fooks* (1858) 3 De G & J 252 at 275–279 per Turner LJ; *Re Kirk, Nicholson v Kirk* (1885) 52 LT 346 at 348.

8   Eg in direct gifts (*Brown v Lewis* (1884) 9 App Cas 890, HL) and in gifts over (*Doe d Smith v Webber* (1818) 1 B & Ald 713; *Re Synge's Trusts* (1854) 3 I Ch R 379; *Re Milward's Estate* [1940] Ch 698). As to 'children' as a word of limitation see PARA 384; and as to limitations to a person and his children see PARAS 389–390.

9   Eg where the testator has no children and is accustomed to call his stepchildren by the name 'children': *Re Jeans, Upton v Jeans* (1895) 72 LT 835.

10   See PARAS 355–356. See also note 7.

11   See PARA 350 et seq.

12   See PARA 357. An English testator cannot be supposed to have included children adopted under foreign legislation which conferred only limited rights: see *Re Marshall, Barclays Bank Ltd v Marshall* [1957] Ch 507, [1957] 3 All ER 172, CA; and CONFLICT OF LAWS vol 19 (2011) PARA 742. As to adopted children see also *Re Fletcher, Barclays Bank Ltd v Ewing* [1949] Ch 473, [1949] 1 All ER 732; *Re Gilpin, Hutchinson v Gilpin* [1954] Ch 1, [1953] 2 All ER 1218; *Re Jones's Will Trusts, Jones v Hawtin Squire* [1965] Ch 1124, [1965] 2 All ER 828; *Re Jebb, Ward-Smith v Jebb* [1966] Ch 666, [1965] 3 All ER 358, CA; *Re Brinkley's Will Trusts, Westminster Bank Ltd v Brinkley* [1968] Ch 407, [1967] 3 All ER 805; *Upton v National Westminster Bank plc* [2004] EWHC 1962 (Ch), [2004] WTLR 1339; and CHILDREN AND YOUNG PERSONS vol 9 (2012) PARA 360 et seq.

13   *Re Kirk, Nicholson v Kirk* (1885) 52 LT 346; *Re Atkinson, Pybus v Boyd* [1918] 2 Ch 138.

14   *D'Abo v Paget* [2000] All ER (D) 944 (a will left property on trust to M for life and after his death 'for the child or other issue of the said M . . . who if the devolution of the said property . . . had been subject to limitations in strict settlement in favour of the said M . . . and his issue would on the death of M . . . first have become entitled as tenant in tail in possession to the said property'; M had two daughters; held that the property passed to the eldest daughter alone and not to both daughters as tenants in common).

15   Ie the date on which the substitution of the Wills Act 1837 s 33 by the Administration of Justice Act 1982 s 19 came into effect: see s 76(11). See PARA 169.

16   Wills Act 1837 s 33(1) (as substituted: see note 15). As to 'contrary intention' see *Ling v Ling* [2001] All ER (D) 322 (Nov); *Rainbird v Smith* [2012] EWHC 4276 (Ch).

332. Gift to children of two named persons. A gift to 'the children of A and B', where A and B are two named persons, are married to each other and have children, does not include children of one of them by a former marriage[1]. Where A and B have not, and are not capable of having, children together[2], such a gift has been held to mean grammatically a gift to B and the children of A, and prima facie is construed accordingly[3]. The strict rule has been applied, however, only where the particular circumstances have admitted of no doubt that the strict construction was in complete accordance with the context and the testator's intention[4], and it is rejected where the context or surrounding circumstances require a different construction[5]. Where both classes of children exist, it may be that the gift is to the children of A and the children of B[6]; and the fact that either A or B had no children[7], or that A was dead and B alive at the date of the will[8] or at the date contemplated by the gift[9], or that A and B were relatives of the testator of the same degree[10], or that there are special reasons for B personally being a beneficiary and not his children[11], or that the dispositions of the will point to provision being made for the children of B[12], may affect the construction of the gift[13]. The division will usually be between all the donees per capita[14].

Where there was a gift to the named persons and on the death of either to the children of each, the children of one of the named persons were held on her death to take her share to the exclusion of the children of the other[15].

1 *Re Lewis's Will Trusts, Phillips v Bowkett* [1937] 1 All ER 556.
2 See *Re Walbran, Milner v Walbran* [1906] 1 Ch 64 at 66.
3 *Lugar v Harman* (1786) 1 Cox Eq Cas 250; *Peacock v Stockford* (1853) 3 De GM & G 73 at 78; *Hawes v Hawes* (1880) 14 ChD 614; *Re Featherstone's Trusts* (1882) 22 ChD 111; *Re Walbran, Milner v Walbran* [1906] 1 Ch 64; *Re Cossentine, Philp v Wesleyan Methodist Local Preachers' Mutual Aid Association Trustees* [1933] Ch 119 at 123; *Re Foster's Will Trusts, Smith v Foster* (1967) 111 Sol Jo 685. See also *Re Harper, Plowman v Harper* [1914] 1 Ch 70 at 73; *Re Dale, Mayer v Wood* [1931] 1 Ch 357 at 367; *Re Birkett, Holland v Duncan* [1950] Ch 330, [1950] 1 All ER 316.
4 *Re Dale, Mayer v Wood* [1931] 1 Ch 357 at 367.
5 *Stummvoli v Hales* (1864) 34 Beav 124 at 126 per Romilly MR; *Re Walbran, Milner v Walbran* [1906] 1 Ch 64 at 66.
6 *Mason v Baker* (1856) 2 K & J 567; *Re Davies' Will* (1860) 29 Beav 93.
7 *Wicker v Mitford* (1782) 3 Bro Parl Cas 442; *Stummvoli v Hales* (1864) 34 Beav 124.
8 In such a case B takes: *Lugar v Harman* (1786) 1 Cox Eq Cas 250 (where it was considered that 'of' should have been prefixed to 'B', if his children had been intended). See also *Re Walbran, Milner v Walbran* [1906] 1 Ch 64 for the same view.
9 *Peacock v Stockford* (1853) 3 De GM & G 73 at 78.
10 *Re Walbran, Milner v Walbran* [1906] 1 Ch 64; *Re Prosser, Prosser v Griffith* [1929] WN 85.
11 *Re Harper, Plowman v Harper* [1914] 1 Ch 70.
12 *Re Dale, Mayer v Wood* [1931] 1 Ch 357.
13 See also *Re Ingle's Trusts* (1871) LR 11 Eq 578 (reference in codicil to the legacy left to B).
14 *Butler v Stratton* (1791) 3 Bro CC 367; *Lugar v Harman* (1786) 1Cox Eq Cas 250; *Mason v Baker* (1856) 2 K & J 567; *Re Davies' Will* (1860) 29 Beav 93; *Re Harper, Plowman v Harper* [1914] 1 Ch 70 (notwithstanding the word 'equally'); *Re Dale, Mayer v Wood* [1931] 1 Ch 357; *Re Cossentine, Philp v Wesleyan Methodist Local Preachers' Mutual Aid Association Trustees* [1933] Ch 119; *Re Jeffery, Welch v Jeffery* [1948] 2 All ER 131. However, this is merely a prima facie presumption which can be rebutted. A stirpital distribution was made in *Re Hall, Parker v Knight* [1948] Ch 437; *Re Birkett, Holland v Duncan* [1950] Ch 330, [1950] 1 All ER 316; *Re Jeeves, Morris-Williams v Haylett* [1949] Ch 49, [1948] 2 All ER 961; *Re Daniel, Jones v Michael* [1945] 2 All ER 101, 173 LT 315. In *Re Walbran, Milner v Walbran* [1906] 1 Ch 64 (followed in *Re Prosser, Prosser v Griffith* [1929] WN 85) a share of the estate was to be equally divided between a nephew and the children of another nephew the will was held to direct a division into moieties; but *Re Walbran, Milner v Walbran* was distinguished in *Re Harper, Plowman v Harper* [1914] 1 Ch 70; *Re Dale, Mayer v Wood* [1931] 1 Ch 357; *Re Cossentine, Philp v Wesleyan Methodist Local Preachers' Mutual Aid Association Trustees* [1933] Ch 119; *Re Alcock, Bonser v Alcock* [1945] Ch 264 sub nom *Re Alcock, Bonser v Seville* [1945] 1 All ER 613. See also *Cobban's Executors v Cobban* 1915 SC 82, Ct of Sess and *Campbell's Trustee v Welsh* 1952 SC 343, 1952 SLT 352, Ct of Sess in both of which it was accepted that 'between' could be used colloquially with reference to a division into more than two shares. As to distribution per capita or per stirpes see PARA 396.
15 *England v England* (1869) 20 LT 648.

333. Gift to first son, eldest son etc. The description 'first son' or 'eldest son' of a certain person in the strict sense means the first-born son[1], and similarly for other sons[2]. The circumstances of the case and the context of the will may, however, show that the testator intended the eldest son of the person at the date of the will (which is prima facie the sense of the words where the strict sense is inapplicable[3]), or his eldest son for the time being at some future time[4], or the son taking a family estate[5]. This last sense is normally the sense where the provision made by the will is for portions for younger children[6] and the eldest son is excluded, 'younger children' in such a case prima facie being taken to mean children other than a child taking the estate[7]. It is possible that an eldest son may take under a limitation to, for example, 'second and other sons'[8], but not where by the context of the will he is excluded[9]. Where a first or second son is dead at the date of the will, the will is construed as meaning first or second son at the testator's death[10].

The fact that a person has an acquired gender does not affect the disposal or devolution or property under a will made before 4 April 2005[11].

1 *Bathurst v Errington* (1877) 2 App Cas 698 at 709 per Lord Cairns LC. See also *Bennett v Bennett* (1864) 2 Drew & Sm 266; *Meredith v Treffry* (1879) 12 ChD 170.
2 *Trafford v Ashton* (1710) 2 Vern 660 (second son); *Wilbraham v Scarisbrick* (1847) 1 HL Cas 167; *Lyddon v Ellison* (1854) 19 Beav 565 (where 'younger children' meant children other than the eldest). See also *Crofts v Beamish* [1905] 2 IR 349, Ir CA ('next eldest brother').
3 See *Amyot v Dwarris* [1904] AC 268, PC (treating *Re Harris's Trust* (1854) 2 WR 689 as incorrect). See also PARA 300.
4 *Matthews v Paul* (1819) 3 Swan 328 (eldest at time of distribution); *Stevens v Pyle* (1861) 30 Beav 284 (eldest surviving life tenant); *Caldbeck v Caldbeck* [1911] 1 IR 144.
5 *Ellison v Thomas* (1862) 1 De GJ & Sm 18 (settlement); *Collingwood v Stanhope* (1869) LR 4 HL 43 (settlement). 'Eldest' means eldest in right in primogeniture: *Thellusson v Lord Rendlesham, Thellusson v Thellusson, Hare v Robarts* (1859) 7 HL Cas 429.
6 See SETTLEMENTS vol 91 (2012) PARA 628 et seq.
7 *Chadwick v Doleman* (1705) 2 Vern 528 (settlement). The eldest daughter is a younger child for this purpose: *Beale v Beale* (1713) 1 P Wms 244; *Pierson v Garnet* (1786) 2 Bro CC 38.
8 *Clements v Paske* (1784) 2 Cl & Fin 230n; *Langston v Langston* (1834) 2 Cl & Fin 194, HL; *Re Blake's Estate* (1871) 19 WR 765 (settlement); *Tavernor v Grindley* (1875) 32 LT 424; *Grattan v Langdale* (1883) 11 LR Ir 473.
9 *Locke v Dunlop* (1888) 39 ChD 387, CA. In *Tuite v Bermingham* (1875) LR 7 HL 634, the eldest was expressly excluded from the limitation.
10 *King v Bennett* (1838) 4 M & W 36.
11 See PARA 329.

334. Gift to issue. 'Issue', in its usual legal sense, includes descendants[1] of every degree[2], but 'issue of our marriage' means children only[3]. In a devise of real estate to a person 'and his issue', especially where at the date of the will he has no issue[4], prima facie 'issue' is a word of limitation[5], and the gift formerly created an estate tail in the devisee[6]. The word was treated as equivalent to 'heir of the body'[7], but the context of the will might show that 'issue' was a word of description and not of limitation; the word was of flexible meaning[8]. Between 1 January 1926 and 31 December 1996 inclusive, an interest in tail could only be created by will in the same manner as by deed[9], and the above rules apply only to wills of testators who died before 1 January 1926.

In direct gifts to issue[10] as purchasers, 'issue' may mean either lineal descendants[11], in accordance with its ordinary meaning, or children or some particular class of descendants ascertained by reference to some particular time or event[12]. The meaning is not necessarily restricted to children by a context containing a gift to children couched in similar terms[13], or by gifts referring to issue in the sense of children[14].

1 In general, in any disposition made on or after 1 January 1970, 'issue' includes illegitimate descendants: see PARAS 355–356.
2 *Reading v Reading* [2015] EWHC 946 (Ch), [2015] All ER (D) 64 (Feb) (however, factors such as the overall structure of the will in question and the precise wording used ('issue of mine' and 'such of my issue') were held to demonstrate that the testator had intended to limit the gift to first and second generation descendants (and to include step children: see PARA 328)); *Wythe v Thurlston* (1749) Amb 555; *Hockley v Mawbey* (1790) 1 Ves 143 at 150; *Davenport v Hanbury* (1796) 3 Ves 257 at 258 per Arden MR; *Freeman v Parsley* (1797) 3 Ves 421; *Leigh v Norbury* (1807) 13 Ves 340 at 344; *Bernard v Mountague* (1816) 1 Mer 422 at 434; *Head v Randall* (1843) 2 Y & C Ch Cas 231 at 235; *Hall v Nalder* (1852) 22 LJ Ch 242; *Ross v Ross* (1855) 20 Beav 645 at 648; *Rhodes v Rhodes* (1859) 27 Beav 413 at 416; *Surridge v Clarkson* (1866) 14 WR 979; *Re Corlass* (1875) 1 ChD 460; *Edyvean v Archer, Re Brooke* [1903] AC 379 at 384, PC; *Re Burnham, Carrick v Carrick* [1918] 2 Ch 196; *Re Sutcliffe, Alison v Alison* [1934] Ch 219. See also *Ralph v Carrick* (1879) 11 ChD 873 at 883, CA, per James LJ. Cf *Haydon v Wilshire* (1789) 3 Term Rep 372 at 373; and see note 8.

3	*Re Noad, Noad v Noad* [1951] Ch 553, [1951] 1 All ER 467. See also *Re Earle's Settlement Trusts, Reiss v Norrie* [1971] 2 All ER 1188, sub nom *Re Earle's Settlement Trusts, Reiss v Merryweather* [1971] 1 WLR 1118.
4	As to the rule in *Wild's Case* (1599) 6 Co Rep 16b see PARA 389.
5	See *Roddy v Fitzgerald* (1858) 6 HL Cas 823 at 878; and PARA 391. When qualified, however, as in 'eldest issue male', the word is prima facie a word of purchase: *Lovelace v Lovelace* (1585) Cro Eliz 40 (decided as to freehold lands); *Sheridan v O'Reilly* [1900] 1 IR 386 (distinguished in *Re Cosby's Estate* [1922] 1 IR 120, CA, where 'eldest issue male' gave an estate tail). See also *Re Hobbs, Hobbs v Hobbs* [1917] 1 Ch 569, CA (estates limited to sons and their sons successively); and REAL PROPERTY AND REGISTRATION vol 87 (2012) PARA 167.
6	*Campbell v Bouskell* (1859) 27 Beav 325 at 329; *Walsh v Johnston* [1899] 1 IR 501; *Re Simcoe, Vowler-Simcoe v Vowler* [1913] 1 Ch 552. For cases where 'or' was changed into 'and' see *Re Clerke, Clowes v Clerke* [1915] 2 Ch 301; *Re Hayden, Pask v Perry* [1931] 2 Ch 333. Cf *W Gardiner & Co Ltd v Dessaix* [1915] AC 1096, PC (where on the construction of the will the children took estates in fee simple).
7	*Kavanagh v Morland* (1853) Kay 16 at 24; *Roddy v Fitzgerald* (1858) 6 HL Cas 823 at 871–872; *Re Adams, Adams v Adams* (1906) 94 LT 720 at 722, CA, per Romer LJ. Similarly, in a series of limitations by will of real estate, where after a particular estate in any person a remainder was limited to his issue, 'issue' was prima facie a word of limitation (*King v Melling* (1671) 1 Vent 225), and the rule in *Shelley's Case* (1581) 1 Co Rep 93b applied. As to this rule, which is now abolished, see REAL PROPERTY AND REGISTRATION vol 87 (2012) PARA 167.
8	See *M'Gregor v M'Gregor* (1859) 1 De GF & J 63 at 76 per Lord Campbell LC; *Bradley v Cartwright* (1867) LR 2 CP 511; *Re Birks, Kenyon v Birks* [1900] 1 Ch 417 at 418, CA, per Lindley LJ. 'Issue' is more flexible than 'heirs of the body': *Slater v Dangerfield* (1846) 15 M & W 263 at 273; *Kavanagh v Morland* (1853) Kay 16; *Roddy v Fitzgerald* (1858) 6 HL Cas 823 at 881. See *Reading v Reading* [2015] EWHC 946 (Ch), [2015] All ER (D) 64 (Feb) ('issue of mine' included both the deceased's children, stepchildren and their children).
9	See the Law of Property Act 1925 s 130(1), (2) (repealed by the Trusts of Land and Appointment of Trustees Act 1996 s 25(2), Sch 4, with effect from 1 January 1997); and PARA 387. Entailed interests cannot be created by instruments coming into operation on or after 1 January 1997: see the Trusts of Land and Appointment of Trustees Act 1996 s 2(6), Sch 1 para 5; PARA 387; and REAL PROPERTY AND REGISTRATION vol 87 (2012) PARA 114. The provisions of the Family Law Reform Act 1987 ss 1, 19(1) apply to words purporting to create an entailed interest (see s 19(2) (amended by the Trusts of Land and Appointment of Trustees Act 1996 s 25(1), Sch 3 para 25, with effect from 1 January 1997); and PARA 356), but the provisions of the Family Law Reform Act 1969 s 15 (repealed) do not (see s 15(2) (repealed by the Family Law Reform Act 1987 s 33(4), Sch 4, with effect from 4 April 1988); and PARA 355).
10	As to gifts over in default of issue see PARA 420.
11	See note 1.
12	*Slater v Dangerfield* (1846) 15 M & W 263 at 272; *Sandes v Cooke* (1888) 21 LR Ir 445 at 448; *Re Burnham, Carrick v Carrick* [1918] 2 Ch 196; *Re Bourke's Will Trusts, Barclays Bank Trust Co Ltd v Canada Permanent Trust Co* [1980] 1 All ER 219, [1980] 1 WLR 539. For examples where the usual meaning, namely all descendants, was adhered to see *Dodsworth v Addy* (1842) 11 LJ Ch 382; *Re Jones' Trusts* (1857) 23 Beav 242.
13	*Waldron v Boulter* (1856) 22 Beav 284.
14	For cases where 'issue' was used in different passages in different senses see *Carter v Bentall* (1840) 2 Beav 551; *Louis v Louis* (1863) 9 Jur NS 244; *Re Warren's Trusts* (1884) 26 ChD 208; and PARA 249.

335. Gift to male issue; offspring. Under a gift to 'issue male'[1], or 'male issue'[2], or 'male descendants', or 'male heirs'[3] as purchasers, prima facie[4] only males claiming as descendants of males, and not of females, can take. 'Male descendants' is, however, not a term of art, and males descended from the common ancestor through females are also entitled to share[5]. In deciding who is 'male', the fact that a person has an acquired gender does not affect the disposal or devolution or property under a will made before 4 April 2005, but may affect it under a will made on or after that date[6].

'Offspring' similarly extends prima facie to any degree of lineal descendant[7], but may be restricted or varied in meaning[8].

1	*Lywood v Kimber* (1860) 29 Beav 38.
2	*Re Du Cros' Settlement Trusts, Du Cros Family Trustee Co Ltd v Du Cros* [1961] 3 All ER 193, [1961] 1 WLR 1252.

3   *Doe d Angell v Angell* (1846) 9 QB 328.
4   For an example where 'in the male line' was inconsistent with the donees taking as descendants of
    males only see *Sayer v Bradly* (1856) 5 HL Cas 873 ('nearest of kin in the male line'). In a gift to
    A for life and after his death to his issue 'in tail male', daughters may take, the words 'in tail male'
    being a description of the estate taken: *Trevor v Trevor* (1847) 1 HL Cas 239.
5   *Re Drake, Drake v Drake* [1971] Ch 179, [1970] 3 All ER 32, CA (overruling *Bernal v Bernal*
    (1838) 3 My & Cr 559; and not following *Allen v Crane* (1953) 89 CLR 152). In *Oddie v
    Woodford* (1825) 3 My & Cr 584, where the relevant words were 'male lineal descendant', it was
    held to the contrary, although it was recognised that, apart from the presence of the word 'lineal',
    the result stated in the text would follow.
6   See PARA 329.
7   *Thompson v Beasley* (1854) 3 Drew 7; *Young v Davies* (1863) 2 Drew & Sm 167; *Bradshaw v
    Bradshaw* [1908] 1 IR 288.
8   *Lister v Tidd* (1861) 29 Beav 618 (restricted to children by a direction to settle); *Tabuteau v Nixon*
    (1899) 15 TLR 485.

336. Contexts confining issue to children. The following are examples of
contexts from which the court has inferred that 'issue' has been used by the
testator as meaning 'children'[1]:

(1)   where the testator in a later part of the will or a codicil speaks of the gift
        in question as a gift to children[2], or otherwise defines the issue taking
        under the gift as children[3];

(2)   where the testator expressly or impliedly limits 'issue' in other clauses of
        the same will to mean 'children', and the restriction, in the opinion of
        the court, applies throughout the will[4];

(3)   where in an original gift to issue the person whose issue is designated, or
        in a substitutional gift the first taker, is spoken of as the 'parent', 'father'
        or 'mother' of the issue[5] (as, for example, where the gift to the issue is
        contained in a direction that they are to take the share their parent
        would have taken if living at the time of distribution, and the reference
        to the parent is construed as a reference to the first taker); the use of this
        principle as a rule of construction has been strongly criticised[6] and
        described as dead[7]. To the extent that it may still exist it is easily
        displaced by a context (as, for example, by the use of 'issue' in other
        parts of the will in such a sense as to enlarge this construction and
        restore the word to its original comprehensive meaning[8]), and the court
        is disinclined to apply the rule where there is a gift over on general
        failure of the issue[9] or where the result of its application would in certain
        events be an entire or partial intestacy[10];

(4)   where the testator speaks of the issue of such issue, or uses other phrases
        showing that he contemplated issue of yet further degrees of remoteness
        not included in the 'issue' in question[11].

1   See *Bennett v Houldsworth* [1911] WN 47. The mere fact that 'issue' of a named person is
    described as begotten by him is not sufficient to narrow it down to 'children': *Caulfield v Maguire*
    (1845) 2 Jo & Lat 141 at 178 per Sugden LC. See also *Haydon v Wilshire* (1789) 3 Term Rep 372;
    Evans v Jones (1846) 2 Coll 516 at 523; *Maddock v Legg* (1858) 25 Beav 531. Cf *Hampson v
    Brandwood* (1816) 1 Madd 381 (male issue, with limitation over to daughters).
2   *Goldie v Greaves* (1844) 14 Sim 348; *M'Gregor v M'Gregor* (1859) 1 De GF & J 63; *Baker v
    Bayldon* (1862) 31 Beav 209; *Re Hobbs, Hobbs v Hobbs* [1917] 1 Ch 569, CA. As to the general
    rule that the testator's will is taken as the dictionary showing his meaning see PARA 227.
3   *Peel v Catlow* (1838) 9 Sim 372 (to issue 'in like manner' to previous gift to children); *Farrant v
    Nichols* (1846) 9 Beav 327; *Re Dean, Wollard v Dickinson* [1923] WN 227. A similar result
    followed where the gift was to the 'issue' in equal shares if more than one, and, if only one, the
    whole 'to such one child': *Bryden v Willett* (1869) LR 7 Eq 472; *Re Birks, Kenyon v Birks* [1900]
    1 Ch 417 at 419, CA, per Lindley MR. See also *Re Hopkins' Trusts* (1878) 9 ChD 131.
4   *Cursham v Newland* (1838) 4 M & W 101; *Ridgeway v Munkittrick* (1841) 1 Dr & War 84;
    Edwards v Edwards (1849) 12 Beav 97; *Re Harrison's Estate* (1879) 3 LR Ir 114; *Re Birks,*

Kenyon v Birks [1900] 1 Ch 417, CA; *Re Bourke's Will Trusts, Barclays Bank Trust Co Ltd v Canada Permanent Trust Co* [1980] 1 All ER 219, [1980] 1 WLR 539. See also *Reed v Braithwaite* (1870) LR 11 Eq 514; *Re Noad, Noad v Noad* [1951] Ch 553, [1951] 1 All ER 467 (where 'issue of a marriage' was confined to children).

5 This rule is known as the rule in *Sibley v Perry* (1802) 7 Ves 522, although in this case, as explained by James LJ in *Ralph v Carrick* (1879) 11 ChD 873 at 882, CA, Lord Eldon LC did not intend to lay down any general rule of construction, but was dealing only with the peculiar language of a particular will, and the case is, therefore, an example of the inference under head (2) in the text. The construction mentioned in head (3) in the text became commonly applied as a rule: see *Pruen v Osborne* (1840) 11 Sim 132; *Pope v Pope* (1851) 14 Beav 591; *Bradshaw v Melling* (1853) 19 Beav 417; *Parsons v Coke* (1858) 4 Drew 296; *Smith v Horsfall* (1858) 25 Beav 628; *Tatham v Vernon* (1861) 29 Beav 604; *Stevenson v Abingdon* (1862) 31 Beav 305; *Lanphier v Buck* (1865) 2 Drew & Sm 484 at 492; *Martin v Holgate* (1866) LR 1 HL 175 at 184, 186; *Heasman v Pearse* (1871) 7 Ch App 275 at 282, 284; *Re Judd's Trusts* [1884] WN 206; *Re Birks, Kenyon v Birks* [1900] 1 Ch 417 at 418–419, CA (where it was not necessary to refer to *Sibley v Perry* above to see that 'issue' meant children); *Re Timson, Smiles v Timson* [1916] 2 Ch 362, CA. The rule has been applied to settlements inter vivos as well as wills: *Barraclough v Shillito* [1884] WN 158.

6 *Ralph v Carrick* (1879) 11 ChD 873; *Re Hipwell, Hipwell v Hewitt* [1945] 2 All ER 476, CA; *Re Manly's Will Trusts, Burton v Williams* [1969] 3 All ER 1011, [1969] 1 WLR 1818; *Re Manly's Will Trusts (No 2), Tickle v Manly* [1976] 1 All ER 673.

7 *Re Manly's Will Trusts, Burton v Williams* [1969] 3 All ER 1011 at p 1021, [1969] 1 WLR 1818. In *Re Manly's Will Trusts (No 2), Tickle v Manly* [1976] 1 All ER 673 at 677 Walton J declined to decide whether the rule was merely dying or whether Ungoed-Thomas J had presided over its obsequies in *Re Manly's Will Trusts*.

8 *Maynard v Wright* (1858) 26 Beav 285 at 289 per Romilly MR; *Berry v Fisher* [1903] 1 IR 484 at 488; *Re Embury, Page v Bowyer* (1913) 109 LT 511; *Re Johnson, Pitt v Johnson* (1913) 30 TLR 200 (affd (1914) 30 TLR 505, CA); *Re Langlands, Langlands v Langlands* (1917) 87 LJ Ch 1; *Re Swain, Brett v Ward* [1918] 1 Ch 399; *Re Hipwell, Hipwell v Hewitt* [1945] 2 All ER 476, CA (where 'issue' and 'children' were used in the same clause); *Re Manly's Will Trusts, Burton v Williams* [1969] 3 All ER 1011, [1969] 1 WLR 1818; *Re Manly's Will Trusts (No 2), Tickle v Manly* [1976] 1 All ER 673.

9 *Ross v Ross* (1855) 20 Beav 645 at 651; *Ralph v Carrick* (1879) 11 ChD 873 at 884, CA.

10 *Ross v Ross* (1855) 20 Beav 645 at 652–653. See also *Ralph v Carrick* (1879) 11 ChD 873 at 882, CA, per James LJ, instancing a case where a donee's children predeceased him, leaving his grandchildren alive. In *Birdsall v York* (1859) 5 Jur NS 1237, where the circumstances were similar, it was not argued that there was an intestacy. In *Smith v Horsfall* (1858) 25 Beav 628 at 630, Romilly MR explained his decision in *Ross v Ross* by saying that in the latter case issue was confined to the children of the 'parent', but that the 'parent' might be a grandchild.

11 *Pope v Pope* (1851) 14 Beav 591 at 594 per Romilly MR; *Fairfield v Bushell* (1863) 32 Beav 158.

337. Ascertainment of class of issue. The class of issue is ascertained according to the testator's declared intention[1], and, where this is not otherwise shown, then, according to the ordinary rules, at his death[2], letting in issue coming into existence before the period of distribution[3], and every degree of issue taking concurrently with their descendants. Prima facie they take per capita[4], and, in the absence of words of severance or other inconsistent context[5], as joint tenants[6].

1 *Waldron v Boulter* (1856) 22 Beav 284 (issue of each grandchild ascertained at his death).
2 See PARA 302.
3 *Butter v Ommaney* (1827) 4 Russ 70; *Clay v Pennington* (1835) 7 Sim 370; *Weldon v Hoyland* (1862) 4 De GF & J 564; *Hobgen v Neale* (1870) LR 11 Eq 48; *Surridge v Clarkson* (1866) 14 WR 979; *Re Corlass* (1875) 1 ChD 460; *Berry v Fisher* [1903] 1 IR 484; *Re Taylor's Trusts, Taylor v Blake* [1912] 1 IR 1.
4 *Davenport v Hanbury* (1796) 3 Ves 257; *Re Jones' Trusts* (1857) 23 Beav 242; *Weldon v Hoyland* (1862) 4 De GF & J 564. As to distribution per capita see PARA 396.
5 *Law v Thorp* (1858) 4 Jur NS 447 (with 'benefit of survivorship and accruer of surviving shares').
6 *Davenport v Hanbury* (1796) 3 Ves 257; *Surridge v Clarkson* (1866) 14 WR 979. See PARA 393 note 4 for gifts to several persons without words of severance generally.

338. Gifts to descendants. Whatever may have been its meaning in earlier times[1], 'descendants' now ordinarily refers to children, grandchildren and other issue[2] of every degree of remoteness[3] in descent. Although the word may be confined to mean children by a sufficiently strong context[4], the court does not restrict the word to that sense merely because the testator speaks of the descendants taking their parents' share[5]. The class of descendants taking under a gift is ascertained according to the ordinary rules for ascertaining a class[6]. When ascertained, the descendants prima facie take per capita and not per stirpes[7]; but, in a gift to a group of persons or their descendants, the descendants prima facie take by way of substitution only, and not in competition with their parents, if living at the time of distribution[8].

1 Over a century ago 'descendants' was apparently apt, not merely in legal language but even in popular parlance, to include collateral relations (see *Best v Stonehewer* (1864) 34 Beav 66; affd (1865) 2 De GJ & Sm 537), but not now (see *Re Thurlow, Riddick v Kennard* [1972] Ch 379 at 383, [1972] 1 All ER 10 at 13).
2 *Oddie v Woodford* (1821) 3 My & Cr 584 at 617 ('posterity of all kinds'). A gift to the donee and descendants of his branch of the family did not before 1 January 1926 create an entailed interest (*Re Brownlie, Brownlie v Muaux* [1938] 4 All ER 54), and between 1 January 1926 and 31 December 1996 inclusive could not do so (see PARA 384 et seq). In general, in any disposition made on or after 1 January 1970, 'descendants' includes illegitimate descendants: see PARAS 355–356. In dispositions made before that date, 'descendants' excluded illegitimate persons: *Sydall v Castings Ltd* [1967] 1 QB 302, [1966] 3 All ER 770, CA. See further PARA 350 et seq.
3 Such a description, the members being ascertained according to the ordinary rules, is not void for uncertainty: *Pierson v Garnet* (1786) 2 Bro CC 38, 226. See *Re Hickey, Beddoes v Hodgson* [1917] 1 Ch 601 where the expression was said to include descendants of all degrees.
4 *Smith v Pepper* (1859) 27 Beav 86 ('in proportions . . . under the Statute of Distribution'); *Williamson v Moore* (1862) 8 Jur NS 875 ('my nephews and nieces being descendants of my brothers and sisters'). Cf *Legard v Haworth* (1800) 1 East 120 at 130 (restricted to children and grandchildren); *Re Hickey, Beddoes v Hodgson* [1917] 1 Ch 601 ('descendants' or 'their descendants').
5 *Ralph v Carrick* (1879) 11 ChD 873, CA (where the court refused to apply the so-called 'rule' in *Sibley v Perry* (1802) 7 Ves 522 (see PARA 336 note 5)); *Re Manly's Will Trusts (No 2), Tickle v Manly* [1976] 1 All ER 673.
6 *Tucker v Billing* (1856) 2 Jur NS 483; *Re Roberts, Repington v Roberts-Gawen* (1881) 19 ChD 520, CA. As to gifts to classes see PARAS 174, 302 et seq.
7 *Crosley v Clare* (1761) 3 Swan 320n; *Butler v Stratton* (1791) 3 Bro CC 367; *Re Flower, Matheson v Goodwyn* (1890) 62 LT 216 (revsd on another point 63 LT 201, CA). See also *Rowland v Gorsuch, Price v Gorsuch* (1789) 2 Cox Eq Cas 187 (where the context required a stirpital distribution). Cf *Re Rawlinson, Hill v Withall* [1909] 2 Ch 36. As to distribution per capita and per stirpes see PARA 396 et seq.
8 *Jones v Torin* (1833) 6 Sim 255; *Dick v Lacy* (1845) 8 Beav 214; *Re Flower, Matheson v Goodwyn* (1890) 62 LT 216; *Re Morgan, Morgan v Morgan* [1893] 3 Ch 222 at 227, 231, CA; *Re Manly's Will Trusts (No 2), Tickle v Manly* [1976] 1 All ER 673. The position is similar in the case of a gift to a group of individuals and their descendants: *Tucker v Billing* (1856) 2 Jur NS 483.

339. Gifts to heir or heirs. A gift to the 'heir' or 'heirs'[1] of any person takes effect in favour of the person or persons who satisfy that description at some particular time[2]. The words 'the heir of the body' or 'heirs of the body' of any person have corresponding meanings[3].

In a direct gift to the heir where the ancestor is living, as no one can be the heir of a living person, the technical meaning may be displaced, and the person who is heir presumptive may be designated[4]. Otherwise the heir is prima facie ascertained at the ancestor's death, whether the ancestor is the testator or any other person, and whether the gift is immediate or future[5].

1 Descent to the heir has in general been abolished: see PARAS 478, 538. References to the 'heir' were effective to create interests in tail between 1 January 1926 and 31 December 1996 inclusive (see the Law of Property Act 1925 s 130(1), (2) (repealed); and PARA 387), or to confer equitable interests on an heir taking by purchase, that is, otherwise than by descent (see s 132; the Administration of Estates Act 1925 s 51(1); PARA 341; and PARAS 531–532). By virtue of the Law of Property (Amendment) Act 1924 s 9, Sch 9, the Inheritance Act 1833 (as amended by the Law of Property Amendment Act 1859 s 19) (see PARA 538 et seq) remains in force (although otherwise

repealed) for the purpose of ascertaining the devolution of entailed interests and persons taking as heirs by purchase under such limitations. As to the circumstances in which before 1 January 1926 an heir was construed as taking by purchase see eg *Re Hussey and Green's Contract* [1921] 1 Ch 566; and REAL PROPERTY AND REGISTRATION vol 87 (2012) PARA 167. Before 1 January 1926 a person who was at once the devisee of land under the will of a testator and the heir of the testator took the land as purchaser: see the Inheritance Act 1833 s 3 (repealed); and PARA 540. As to the meaning of 'heir' in bequests of personal estate or a mixed fund see PARA 341.

2   *Archer's Case, Baldwin v Smith* (1597) 1 Co Rep 66b; *Evans v Evans* [1892] 2 Ch 173, CA (conveyance); *Skinner v Gumbleton* [1903] 1 IR 36. A donee's husband does not take under an alternative gift to her 'heir': *Re Boyer, Neathercoat v Lawrence* [1935] Ch 382.

3   See *Van Grutten v Foxwell, Foxwell v Van Grutten* [1897] AC 658, HL; *Wesselenyi v Jamieson* [1907] AC 440, HL (heir in entail under a settlement, the entail in which had been destroyed). A devise to the heirs of the body of a deceased person formerly created an estate tail, the first of such heirs who becomes entitled taking by purchase: see *Mandeville's Case* (1328) Co Litt 26b; and REAL PROPERTY AND REGISTRATION vol 87 (2012) PARA 115. The form of the limitation seems to show a contrary intention so as to prevent the fee simple passing under the Wills Act 1837 s 28 (see PARA 376), but the point has not been decided. A devise to 'my own right heirs except' A (where A is in fact the heir) is ineffectual: *Re Smith, Bull v Smith* [1933] Ch 847 (following *Pugh v Goodtitle* (1787) 3 Bro Parl Cas 454).

4   *Doe d Winter v Perratt* (1843) 6 Man & G 314 at 363, HL, per Lord Brougham LC; *Dormer v Phillips* (1855) 4 De GM & G 855. See also *James v Richardson* (1677) 2 Lev 232; T J 99 (affd (1678) Freem KB 472n, HL); *Darbison v Beaumont* (1714) 1 P Wms 229; *Goodright d Brooking v White* (1775) 2 Wm Bl 1010; *Re Hooper, Hooper v Carpenter* [1936] Ch 442, [1936] 1 All ER 277, CA.

5   *Danvers v Earl of Clarendon* (1681) 1 Vern 35; *Doe d Pilkington v Spratt* (1833) 5 B & Ad 731; *Rawlinson v Wass* (1852) 9 Hare 673; *Re Frith, Hindson v Wood* (1901) 85 LT 455; *Re Maher, Maher v Toppin* [1909] 1 IR 70 at 76, Ir CA. In *Lightfoot v Maybery* [1914] AC 782, HL, the heir was, in the context, held to be ascertainable on the death of the life tenant. As to the heir being ascertainable on an event which gives rise to an executory devise over in his favour see *Doe d King v Frost* (1820) 3 B & Ald 546. In *Re Hooper, Hooper v Carpenter* [1936] Ch 442, [1936] 1 All ER 277, CA, where the gift was to 'such person as shall at the death of my wife be my heir' and the testator's wife predeceased him, the heir was ascertained as if the testator had died at the same time as his wife. See also *Lucas-Tooth v Lucas-Tooth* [1921] 1 AC 594, HL (bequest of stock to the testator's two brothers for life only, and then 'to the heir to the baronetcy at present held by Sir R L'; heir to be ascertained on the death of the survivor of the two brothers).

340.   Devise to heir of particular character. 'Heir' prima facie refers to descent at common law[1], but there may be a devise to heirs of a particular character[2], which, if not referring merely to the descent of an estate tail[3], takes effect only in favour of the heirs general conditionally on their possessing that character, unless the testator's intention is shown to the contrary[4].

1   This was so under the former law, even where copyhold, gavelkind or borough English land was given to the heir of the testator, and prima facie the common law heir, according to the general course of descent, was entitled: *Thorp v Owen* (1854) 2 Sm & G 90; *Davis v Kirk* (1856) 2 K & J 391; *Polley v Polley (No 2)* (1862) 31 Beav 363; *Sladen v Sladen* (1862) 2 John & H 369; *Garland v Beverley* (1878) 9 ChD 213; *Re Smith, Bull v Smith* [1933] Ch 847. See also Co Litt 10a. As all special customs of descent are abolished (see the Administration of Estates Act 1925 s 45(1); and PARAS 477–479), the 'heir' is the heir ascertained under the Inheritance Act 1833 (see PARA 339 note 1), unless some other form of heirship is specified in the will. Cf *Re Higham, Higham v Higham* [1937] 2 All ER 17.

2   Eg to the testator's heirs of his name: *Counden v Clerke* (1612) Hob 29; *Wrightson v Macaulay* (1845) 14 M & W 214; *Thorpe v Thorpe* (1862) 1 H & C 326.

3   Eg in a devise to 'heirs male' construed in the context to mean 'heirs male of the body': see PARA 387.

4   In Co Litt 24b it is said that under a devise to 'heirs female of the body' the person to take by purchase under the gift must be heir general as well as heir female, but this was not considered correct: see *Newcoman v Bethlem Hospital* (1741) Amb 8 App 785; *Goodtitle d Weston v Burtenshaw* (1772) 1 Fearne on Contingent Remainders (10th Edn) 570–573; *Marquis of Cholmondeley v Lord Clinton* (1820) 2 Jac & W 1 at 106–107; *Doe d Angell v Angell* (1846) 9 QB 328 at 351; *Wrightson v Macaulay* (1845) 14 M & W 214 at 231; *Doe d Winter v Perratt* (1826) 5 B & C 48 at 93 (affd (1843) 9 Cl & Fin 606 at 617, 625, HL). See also Hargrave notes to Co Litt 24b (note (3)), 164a (note (2)); *Chambers v Taylor* (1837) 2 My & Cr 376 at 386. As to a devise to the 'heirs male of the body', where these are words of description and not of limitation

(see PARA 387) see *Wills v Palmer* (1770) 5 Burr 2615; *Doe d Angell v Angell* above. See also *Baker v Wall* (1697) 1 Ld Raym 185; *Brown v Barkham* (1717) 1 Stra 35 (on a bill of review in *Newcoman v Bethlem Hospital* above); *Dawes v Ferrers* (1722) 2 P Wms 1; *Re Watkins, Maybery v Lightfoot* [1912] 2 Ch 430 at 436 (ultimately reversed sub nom *Lightfoot v Maybery* [1914] AC 782, HL, where it was held that the expression 'my nearest male heir' was not used in a technical sense, but meant the testator's nearest male relative).

341. Bequest of personalty or mixed fund to heir. Where a gift is of personal estate or of a mixed fund of real and personal estate, 'heir' prima facie retains its usual meaning, and, unless there is something in the will to show a contrary intention, the particular person filling the description of heir-at-law takes the property as a designated person[1]. In a gift of personal estate alone, 'heirs' has been construed as meaning either next of kin[2], the widow taking her share[3], or executors and administrators[4]. The context may, however, give other meanings to the word[5]. In a will coming into operation after 31 December 1925 a limitation of personal estate in favour of the heir of a deceased person operates in favour of the person who, under the law in force before 1 January 1926, would have answered the description of the heir of the deceased in respect of his freehold land[6]. 'Heirs' could properly be used for limitations of entailed interests in personal as well as in real property[7].

1   *Gwynne v Muddock* (1808) 14 Ves 488; *Mounsey v Blamire* (1828) 4 Russ 384; *Tetlow v Ashton* (1850) 15 Jur 213; *De Beauvoir v De Beauvoir* (1852) 3 HL Cas 524 at 557, HL, per Lord St Leonards LC; *Southgate v Clinch* (1858) 4 Jur NS 428; *Re Rootes* (1860) 1 Drew & Sm 228; *Hamilton v Mills* (1861) 29 Beav 193; *Smith v Butcher* (1878) 10 ChD 113; *Keay v Boulton* (1883) 25 ChD 212 at 215 per Pearson J; *Skinner v Gumbleton* [1903] 1 IR 36. See also *Boydell v Golightly* (1844) 14 Sim 327 at 346–347 (where the heir was also next of kin). As to a gift to 'my successors to the titles' see *Re Earl Cathcart* (1912) 56 Sol Jo 271. As to severing the meaning under the former law so that 'heirs' might mean heirs-at-law as to real estate and next of kin as to personal estate see *Vaux v Henderson* (1806) 1 Jac & W 388; *Gittings v M'Dermott* (1834) 2 My & K 69; *Mounsey v Blamire* above at 387; *Wingfield v Wingfield* (1878) 9 ChD 658. Cf *Lowndes v Stone* (1799) 4 Ves 649 (gift of residue to 'next of kin or heir-at-law'); *Re Thompson's Trusts* (1878) 9 ChD 607 (to 'heirs or next of kin'). In *De Beauvoir v De Beauvoir* above the context showed that the person who was to take the real estate was intended also to take the personal estate.
2   *Low v Smith* (1856) 2 Jur NS 344; *Doody v Higgins* (1856) 2 K & J 729; *Re Gamboa's Trusts* (1858) 4 K & J 756; *Re Newton's Trusts* (1867) LR 4 Eq 171 (gift to 'heirs and assigns'); *Re Philps' Will* (1868) LR 7 Eq 151.
3   *Re Steevens' Trusts* (1872) LR 15 Eq 110.
4   *Lachlan v Reynolds* (1852) 9 Hare 796 at 798.
5   Eg children (*Loveday v Hopkins* (1755) Amb 273; *Wilson v Vansittart* (1770) Amb 562; *Symers v Jobson* (1848) 16 Sim 267 ('the heirs of her body'); *Bull v Comberbach* (1858) 25 Beav 540) or issue (*Speakman v Speakman* (1850) 8 Hare 180 at 185).
6   See the Law of Property Act 1925 s 132; and PARAS 531–534. See also *Re Bourke's Will Trusts, Barclays Bank Trust Co Ltd v Canada Permanent Trust Co* [1980] 1 All ER 219, [1980] 1 WLR 539.
7   See the Law of Property Act 1925 s 130(1), (2) (repealed by the Trusts of Land and Appointment of Trustees Act 1996 s 25(2), Sch 4, with effect from 1 January 1997); PARA 387; and REAL PROPERTY AND REGISTRATION vol 87 (2012) PARA 114. Entailed interests cannot be created by instruments coming into operation on or after 1 January 1997: see the Trusts of Land and Appointment of Trustees Act 1996 s 2(6), Sch 1 para 5; PARA 387; and REAL PROPERTY AND REGISTRATION vol 87 (2012) PARA 114.

342. Gift to a person or his heirs. A gift to a named person or his heirs is prima facie substitutional in the case of personal estate, 'heirs' being read as next of kin[1]. If the subject of the gift consists both of real and personal estate[2], 'heirs' is construed according to the nature of the property; the heirs of realty take the real estate, and the heirs of personalty, that is the next of kin, the personalty[3]. In wills before the Wills Act 1837 in a devise to a named person or his heirs, 'or' was changed into 'and', and 'heirs' was treated as a word of limitation, so that the devisee took an estate in fee[4]. This construction has been followed in regard to wills since that Act[5].

1   *Hamilton v Mills* (1861) 29 Beav 193 at 198 per Romilly MR; *Re Ibbetson, Ibbetson v Ibbetson* (1903) 88 LT 461 at 462; *Re Whitehead, Whitehead v Hemsley* [1920] 1 Ch 298 at 304. See also *Girdlestone v Doe* (1828) 2 Sim 225; *Doody v Higgins* (1852) 8 Hare App I, xxxii; *Jacobs v Jacobs* (1853) 16 Beav 557; *Re Craven* (1857) 23 Beav 333; *Re Philps' Will* (1868) LR 7 Eq 151; *Finlason v Tatlock* (1870) LR 9 Eq 258. The husband of a married woman did not take under 'or her heirs' as, before 1 January 1926, he took by reason of his marital right and not as next of kin: *Re Boyer, Neathercoat v Lawrence* [1935] Ch 382 (following *Doody v Higgins* (1856) 2 K & J 729 at 738; and not *Walker v Cusin* [1917] 1 IR 63). As to substitutional gifts generally see PARA 321.
2   *Wingfield v Wingfield* (1878) 9 ChD 658; *Re Whitehead, Whitehead v Hemsley* [1920] 1 Ch 298.
3   *Wingfield v Wingfield* (1878) 9 ChD 658.
4   *Read v Snell* (1743) 2 Atk 642 at 645; *Wright v Wright* (1750) 1 Ves Sen 409 at 411.
5   *Harris v Davis* (1844) 1 Coll 416 (where 'or to their lawful heirs' was construed to mean 'heirs of the body'); *Greenway v Greenway* (1860) 2 De GF & J 128 ('or the heirs of their bodies'). See also *Lachlan v Reynolds* (1852) 9 Hare 796; *Re Walton's Estate* (1856) 8 De GM & G 173; *Polley v Polley* (1861) 29 Beav 134; *Re Boyer, Neathercoat v Lawrence* [1935] Ch 382. Cf *Adshead v Willetts* (1861) 29 Beav 358 (change not made because not necessary). In *Re Walton's Estate* above there was a gift (after a life estate) of proceeds of sale among the testator's five named children 'or their heirs and assigns', and the children took absolutely on his death. See also *Re Masterton, Trevanion v Dumas* [1902] WN 192, CA. On the question whether the Wills Act 1837 s 29 (see PARA 454) altered the construction, changing 'or' into 'and' see *Re Clerke, Clowes v Clerke* [1915] 2 Ch 301; *Re Whitehead, Whitehead v Hemsley* [1920] 1 Ch 298; *Re Hayden, Pask v Perry* [1931] 2 Ch 333. In a gift over of a leasehold farm on the death of the devisee without lawful heirs, it was held in the context that this meant without next of kin being children or descendants: *Gray v Gray* [1915] 1 IR 261.

343. Gift to next of kin. Under a gift to the next of kin[1] of any person[2], simply and without reference either to intestacy or to the Administration of Estates Act 1925[3], replacing the provisions on intestacy contained in the Statutes of Distribution[4], the donees are considered to be the nearest kindred in blood[5], including the half-blood[6], and not to be the statutory next of kin; and prima facie they take as joint tenants. The same meaning is attached prima facie to descriptions similar to next of kin[7]. In a gift to the next of kin of two persons, prima facie the donees are a class composed of the next of kin of one together with the next of kin of the other[8], but, according to the context, may be such persons as are common to the two classes of next of kin[9].

1   Cf generally the cases as to the construction of settlements, and particularly as to gifts to the next of kin of a married woman as if she had died unmarried, cited in SETTLEMENTS vol 91 (2012) PARA 833 et seq. As to the time of ascertaining the class of next of kin see PARA 261.
2   See *Robson v Ibbs* (1837) 6 LJ Ch 213 (where the context supplied the want of mention of the person in question).
3   Ie the Administration of Estates Act 1925 Pt IV (ss 45–52): see PARA 477 et seq.
4   As to the former Statutes of Distribution, which were in force for deaths occurring before 1 January 1926 see PARA 535 et seq. As to what is a sufficient reference to the statutes see *Harris v Newton* (1877) 46 LJ Ch 268. A gift to persons entitled under the former Statutes of Distribution did not include benefits under the Intestates' Estates Act 1890: *Re Morgan, Morgan v Morgan* [1920] 1 Ch 196.
5   *Brandon v Brandon* (1819) 3 Swan 312 (settlement); *Elmsley v Young* (1835) 2 My & K 780 (settlement); *Withy v Mangles* (1843) 10 Cl & Fin 215, HL (settlement) (applied to wills in *Avison v Simpson* (1859) John 43); *Halton v Foster* (1868) 3 Ch App 505; *Re Bulcock, Ingham v Ingham* [1916] 2 Ch 495 ('nearest of kin to myself'); *Re Tuckett's Will Trusts, Williams v National Provincial Bank Ltd* (1967) 111 Sol Jo 811.
6   *Cotton v Scarancke* (1815) 1 Madd 45 (explained in *Halton v Foster* (1868) 3 Ch App 505); *Brigg v Brigg* (1885) 33 WR 454; *Re Fergusson's Will* [1902] 1 Ch 483.
7   *Harris v Newton* (1877) 46 LJ Ch 268 ('legal or next of kin').
8   *Re Soper, Naylor v Kettle* [1912] 2 Ch 467.

9   *Pycroft v Gregory* (1829) 4 Russ 526. As to the effect of the context see *Williams v Ashton* (1860) 1 John & H 115 at 119–120 ('nearest of kin by kinship'; heir held entitled). See also *Sayer v Bradly* (1856) 5 HL Cas 873.

344. Gift to statutory next of kin. If a will describes the donees by reference to the statutory rules, either expressly or impliedly (as, for example, where the distribution is to be as on an intestacy), the distribution may be under either the former law or the current law. References to any Statutes of Distribution in a will coming into operation after 31 December 1925 are to be construed as references to the provisions for the distribution of residuary estates of intestates[1], and references in such a will to statutory next of kin are to be construed, unless the context otherwise requires, as referring to the persons who would take beneficially under those provisions[2]. Trusts declared in a will which came into operation before 1 January 1926 by reference to the former Statutes of Distribution are, unless the contrary thereby appears, to be construed by reference to those former statutes[3]. Hence, in general, the former Statutes of Distribution apply where the trust is created by the will of a testator who died before 1 January 1926, even though the event which brings the trust into effect occurs after 31 December 1925[4]; and also where the will, although coming into operation after 31 December 1925, declares trusts by reference to a settlement made before 1 January 1926[5]. Prima facie[6], a wife[7] or husband[8] was not included in 'next of kin', either apart from the Statutes of Distribution or under them, but it is otherwise for the purposes of the present legislation[9].

Where the disposition came into effect before the legislation removing restrictions on inheritance by adopted or illegitimate relatives, such relatives will normally be excluded from the class[10].

1   Ie the Administration of Estates Act 1925 Pt IV (ss 45–52): see PARA 477 et seq. In a suitable context 'statutory next of kin' may designate a hypothetical class: *Re Krawitz's Will Trusts, Krawitz v Crawford* [1959] 3 All ER 793 at 797, [1959] 1 WLR 1192 at 1196.
2   Administration of Estates Act 1925 s 50(1). In relation to a will coming into operation after 31 December 1952, references to Pt IV are to be construed as including references to the Intestates' Estates Act 1952 Pt I (ss 1–6), Schs 1, 2 (s 6(2)) and, in relation to a will coming into operation on or after 1 January 1996, references to Pt IV are to be construed as including references to the Law Reform (Succession) Act 1995 s 1 (s 1(4)). See PARA 535.
3   Administration of Estates Act 1925 s 50(2). As to the former Statutes of Distribution see PARA 343.
4   *Re Sutcliffe, Sutcliffe v Robertshaw* [1929] 1 Ch 123; *Re Sutton, Evans v Oliver* [1934] Ch 209. Cf *Re Vander Byl, Fladgate v Gore* [1931] 1 Ch 216. There is no contrary intention where there is nothing more than a declaration of trust by reference to the statutes: *Re Hooper's Settlement, Phillips v Lake* [1943] Ch 116, [1943] 1 All ER 173, CA. Cf SETTLEMENTS vol 91 (2012) PARA 836.
5   *Re Walsh, Public Trustee v Walsh* [1936] 1 All ER 327, CA.
6   See *Re Collins' Trust* [1877] WN 87 (widow included in the context).
7   *Garrick v Lord Camden, Patton v Jones* (1807) 14 Ves 372 at 385; *Lee v Lee* (1860) 1 Drew & Sm 85; *Re Parry, Leak v Scott* [1888] WN 179; *Re Fitzgerald's Trusts* (1889) 61 LT 221 ('next of kin in blood'; a case of a settlement). See also SETTLEMENTS vol 91 (2012) PARA 836. Where, however, the donees are the persons who by virtue of the statute would be entitled to the testator's estate, the widow is included: *Martin v Glover* (1844) 1 Coll 269; *Jenkins v Gower* (1846) 2 Coll 537.
8   *Milne v Gilbart, Milne v Milne, Milne v Walker* (1852) 2 De GM & G 715; *Walker v Cusin* [1917] 1 IR 63.
9   See SETTLEMENTS vol 91 (2012) PARA 836; and *Re Gilligan* [1950] P 32 at 37, [1949] 2 All ER 401 at 405.
10 *Gregg v Pigott* [2012] EWHC 732 (Ch), [2012] 3 WLR 913 (where article 14 of the Convention for the Protection of Human Rights and Fundamental Freedoms (prohibition on discrimination on any ground such as birth or other status: see RIGHTS AND FREEDOMS vol 88A (2013) PARAS 88, 506 et seq) was applied retrospectively: see PARA 313 note 7).

345. Gift per stirpes. The Latin word stirps can be translated as meaning 'stock'. However, in modern usage the phrase as a whole can be taken to mean 'by family'[1]. As to how the gift is to be distributed among the members of the family, it is a characteristic of distribution per stirpes that remote descendants do not take in competition with a living immediate ancestor of their own who takes under the gift[2].

1 *Sammut v Manzi* [2008] UKPC 58 at [25], [2009] 2 All ER 234, [2009] 1 WLR 1834 per Lord Hope.
2 *Gibson v Fisher* (1867) LR 5 Eq 51, 37 LJ Ch 67; *Ralph v Carrick* (1879) 11 ChD 873, 884, 48 LJ Ch 801; *Re Rawlinson, Hill v Withall* [1909] 2 Ch 36, 38, 78 LJ Ch 443 cited with approval by Lord Hope in *Sammut v Manzi* [2008] UKPC 58 at [27], [2009] 2 All ER 234, [2009] 1 WLR 1834.

346. Gift to wife or husband. Where a donee is described as the wife of a person, and that person is married at the date of the will, then, in the absence of a context to the contrary, the wife existing at the date of the will prima facie is intended to take, and not any subsequent wife[1]. The fact that the interest conferred is only during widowhood, after a life estate to the husband[2], or that it is expressed to be given for the support of the wife and her husband and his children[3], does not of itself show any contrary intention. If the context shows that intention, or the circumstances so indicate, 'wife' may include a subsequent wife[4], a person not married to the testator or other person whose wife she is said to be[5], or a woman living with a man as his wife[6].

Similar rules apply to 'husband'[7].

Since 5 December 2005 it has been possible for persons of the same sex to form a civil partnership by registering as civil partners[8]. Statutory provisions are amended to ensure that civil partners are treated in the same way as spouses[9]. However, there is no provision which allows the term 'wife', 'husband' or 'spouse' to be interpreted in a will or settlement as including civil partners. Similarly there is no provision which allows 'marriage' to be interpreted as including the formation of a civil partnership.

Since 13 March 2014, marriage now has the same effect in relation to same sex couples as it has in relation to opposite sex couples[10].

1 *Garratt v Niblock* (1830) 1 Russ & M 629; *Re Drew, Drew v Drew* [1899] 1 Ch 336 at 339 per Stirling J (followed in *Re Coley, Hollinshead v Coley* [1903] 2 Ch 102 at 104, 109, CA); *Re D'Oyley, Swayne v D'Oyley* (1921) 152 LT Jo 259. See also *Re Hancock, Malcolm v Burford-Hancock* [1896] 2 Ch 173, CA (settlement). As to a gift to the 'widow' of any person cf *Re Lory* (1891) 7 TLR 419. Where there is no wife at the date of the will or at the testator's death, the first person to answer the description is presumed to be intended: see *Re Hickman, Hickman v Hickman* [1948] Ch 624, [1948] 2 All ER 303.
2 *Re Coley, Hollinshead v Coley* [1903] 2 Ch 102 at 104 per Kekewich J. See also the cases cited in note 3.
3 *Boreham v Bignall* (1850) 8 Hare 131 (followed in *Re Burrow's Trusts* (1864) 10 LT 184; *Firth v Fielden* (1874) 22 WR 622). Cf *Re Lyne's Trust* (1869) LR 8 Eq 65 (which, although followed in *Re Lory* (1891) 7 TLR 419, was not followed in *Firth v Fielden* and was disapproved in *Re Griffiths' Policy* [1903] 1 Ch 739); *Re Coley, Hollinshead v Coley* [1903] 2 Ch 102.
4 *Longworth v Bellamy* (1871) 40 LJ Ch 513; *Re Drew, Drew v Drew* [1899] 1 Ch 336 (in both cases a discretionary trust, after a determinable life interest, for the benefit of the donee, his wife and children was relied on as excluding the rule). See also *Peppin v Bickford* (1797) 3 Ves 570 (person not married until after death of testator; second wife included); *Re Hardyman, Teesdale v McClintock* [1925] Ch 287. In such cases, prima facie no one can take who is not at the death of the named person in the position of his legal wife, and a divorce disentitles her: *Re Morrieson, Hitchens v Morrieson* (1888) 40 ChD 30; *Re Williams' Settlement, Greenwell v Humphries* [1929] 2 Ch 361, CA; *Re Slaughter, Trustees Corpn Ltd v Slaughter* [1945] Ch 355, [1945] 2 All ER 214. Cf *Bullmore v Wynter* (1883) 22 ChD 619. See also *Bosworthick v Clegg* (1929) 45 TLR 438; *Re Allan, Allan v Midland Bank Executor and Trustee Co Ltd* [1954] Ch 295, [1954] 1 All ER 646, CA.

5   In the following cases, the circumstances showed that a mistress or partner in an invalid marriage was denoted by the term 'wife': *Giles v Giles, Penfold v Penfold* (1836) 1 Keen 685; *Doe d Gains v Rouse* (1848) 5 CB 422 (cases where the name of the so-called wife was added); *Pratt v Mathew* (1856) 22 Beav 328 at 337; *Re Petts* (1859) 27 Beav 576; *Turner v Brittain* (1863) 3 New Rep 21; *Re Boddington, Boddington v Clairat* (1884) 25 ChD 685, CA; *Anderson v Berkley* [1902] 1 Ch 936; *Re Wagstaff, Wagstaff v Jalland* [1908] 1 Ch 162, CA; *Re Hammond, Burniston v White* [1911] 2 Ch 342; *Re Smalley, Smalley v Scotton* [1929] 2 Ch 112, CA (where the lawful wife was living); *Re Lynch, Lynch v Lynch* [1943] 1 All ER 168 ('wife', 'widowhood' and 'remarriage' made applicable to spinster by testator's own dictionary).

6   *Re Brown, Golding v Brady* (1910) 26 TLR 257.

7   *Franks v Brooker* (1860) 27 Beav 635; *Radford v Willis* (1871) 7 Ch App 7; *Peasley v Governors of Haileybury and Imperial Service College* [2001] WTLR 1365. In *Re Bryan's Trust* (1851) 2 Sim NS 103, the context referred to a named husband. In *Nash v Allen* (1889) 42 ChD 54, by the context the description meant 'husband surviving her'. A gift to the husband of an unmarried woman, if there is no such person either at the date of the will or at the testator's death, takes effect in favour of her husband if and when she marries: *Blount v Crozier* [1917] 1 IR 461. A divorced husband was held not to be a 'surviving husband' in *Bosworthick v Clegg* (1929) 45 TLR 438; approved in *Re Williams' Settlement, Greenwell v Humphries* [1929] 2 Ch 361, CA.

8   See the Civil Partnership Act 2004 s 1 (which came into force on 5 December 2005); and MATRIMONIAL AND CIVIL PARTNERSHIP LAW vol 72 (2015) PARA 3.

9   As to civil partnership generally see MATRIMONIAL AND CIVIL PARTNERSHIP LAW vol 72 (2015) PARA 3.

10   As to the marriage of same sex couples see MATRIMONIAL AND CIVIL PARTNERSHIP LAW vol 72 (2015) PARAS 1–2.

347. Gift expressed to be during widowhood. If a gift is to the wife, who is accurately so described, expressly 'during widowhood', those words form a condition as to the beginning and ending of her interest, so that the effect of a subsequent divorce before the gift takes effect is that she is disentitled to the gift, as she does not then become a widow[1]. If she is not accurately so described, the words may be read as meaning 'until death or remarriage'[2].

1   *Re Boddington, Boddington v Clairat* (1884) 25 ChD 685, CA; *Re Kettlewell, Jones v Kettlewell* (1907) 98 LT 23.

2   *Re Wagstaff, Wagstaff v Jalland* [1908] 1 Ch 162, CA; *Re Hammond, Burniston v White* [1911] 2 Ch 342. Cf *Re Gale* [1941] Ch 209, [1941] 1 All ER 329 (following *Re Boddington, Boddington v Clairat* (1884) 25 ChD 685, CA). As to marriages or remarriages which are subsequently annulled see PARA 380.

348. Gift to family, friends or dependants. A gift in the will of a married man to his family, or a gift of personalty alone[1] to the family of any person, is prima facie a gift to his children[2], who prima facie take as joint tenants[3], or, if there are no children, to all such persons as would in the case of his intestacy be entitled to take his personal estate[4].

In differing circumstances[5], 'family' may also mean a man's household consisting of himself, his wife, children and servants[6]; or his wife and children[7]; or his next of kin[8]; or his genealogical stock[9]. The word may include any relative whatever, where used to denote the objects of a power of appointment[10] or the grantees of an option[11], or descendants of every degree[12].

In a devise of realty to any named family or the family of any person, the head of the family, or the eldest son and heir presumptive of that person, is prima facie designated, according to the circumstances[13].

Where the family is defined merely by a surname, the court may ascertain from the circumstances of the case what family of that surname was best known to the testator, and the persons to take may be determined accordingly[14].

Where none of these meanings can be given consistently with the will, then, in default of evidence as to the testator's intention[15], the gift may be void for uncertainty[16].

So long as it is not necessary, in order to ascertain the quantum of the intended benefit, to establish the totality of the members of the class, a gift to 'friends' is valid[17]. For this purpose, the relationship must have been a long-standing one, must have been a social as opposed to a business or professional relationship, and, when and if circumstances permitted, there must have been frequent meetings[18].

'Dependants' in a will has been held too uncertain in meaning for the court to give effect to it[19].

1   For this purpose, 'personalty' includes the proceeds of sale of real estate held on trust for sale, if the doctrine of conversion applies: *Woods v Woods* (1836) 1 My & Cr 401 at 408. The doctrine of conversion, whereby land held by trustees subject to a trust for sale is regarded as personal property, has been abolished, except where the trust for sale was created by the will of a testator who died before 1 January 1997: see the Trusts of Land and Appointment of Trustees Act 1996 ss 3, 25(5); and REAL PROPERTY AND REGISTRATION vol 87 (2012) PARAS 7, 215. The doctrine of conversion is, however, not wholly abolished by s 3 and will still apply to eg uncompleted agreements for the sale of land. As to the doctrine of conversion see further EQUITABLE JURISDICTION vol 47 (2014) PARA 138 et seq. The same rule may be applicable to a mixed fund of real and personal estate (*Barnes v Patch* (1803) 8 Ves 604), or to real estate devised alone (*Reay v Rawlinson* (1860) 29 Beav 88; *Burt v Hellyar* (1872) LR 14 Eq 160).

2   *Beales v Crisford* (1843) 13 Sim 592; *Wood v Wood* (1843) 3 Hare 65; *Re Parkinson's Trust* (1851) 1 Sim NS 242 at 245; *Gregory v Smith* (1852) 9 Hare 708; *Re Terry's Will* (1854) 19 Beav 580; *Pigg v Clarke* (1876) 3 ChD 672; *Re Hutchinson and Tenant* (1878) 8 ChD 540 at 541 per Jessel MR; *Re Muffett, Jones v Mason* (1886) 55 LT 671. See also *Barnes v Patch* (1803) 8 Ves 604; *Re Mulqueen's Trusts* (1881) 7 LR Ir 127; *Harkness v Harkness* (1905) 9 OLR 705; *Re M'Cann, Donnelly v Moore* [1916] 1 IR 255. Other relatives are prima facie excluded: *Wood v Wood* above; *Burt v Hellyar* (1872) LR 14 Eq 160; *Re Battersby's Trusts* [1896] 1 IR 600. As to the ascertainment of the class see *Re Parkinson's Trust, ex p Thompson* (1851) 1 Sim NS 242.

3   *Beales v Crisford* (1843) 13 Sim 592; *Gregory v Smith* (1852) 9 Hare 708 at 712. For a case where the children were held to take as tenants in common see *Owen v Penny* (1850) 14 Jur 359.

4   *Doe d Chattaway v Smith* (1816) 5 M & S 126 at 130 per Lord Ellenborough CJ; *Grant v Lynam* (1828) 4 Russ 292 at 297; *Re Maxton* (1858) 4 Jur NS 407. As to the persons entitled on an intestacy see PARA 485 et seq. In a gift of a mixed fund of realty and personalty, 'family' might formerly be used to denote persons entitled by legal succession according to the nature of the property, and to mean the heir as regards the real estate and the next of kin as regards the personal estate: *White v Briggs* (1848) 2 Ph 583. As to the present use of the word 'heir' see PARA 339 note 1.

5   *Blackwell v Bull* (1836) 1 Keen 176 at 181 per Lord Langdale MR; *Sinnott v Walsh* (1880) 5 LR Ir 27 at 41, Ir CA. 'Family' is 'a word of most loose and flexible description': *Green v Marsden* (1853) 1 Drew 646 at 651 per Kindersley V-C. See also *Morton v Tewart* (1842) 2 Y & C Ch Cas 67 at 81.

6   See *Blackwell v Bull* (1836) 1 Keen 176; *Pigg v Clarke* (1876) 3 ChD 672 at 674 per Jessel MR.

7   *Blackwell v Bull* (1836) 1 Keen 176; *Re Drew, Drew v Drew* [1899] 1 Ch 336 at 342. See also *MacLeroth v Bacon* (1799) 5 Ves 159 (husband there included, although not so as a general rule); *James v Lord Wynford* (1854) 2 Sm & G 350.

8   *Cruwys v Colman* (1804) 9 Ves 319. See also note 10.

9   *Lucas v Goldsmid* (1861) 29 Beav 657 at 660 per Romilly MR. See also *Re Macleay* (1875) LR 20 Eq 186 at 187.

10 *Grant v Lynam* (1828) 4 Russ 292; *Snow v Teed* (1870) LR 9 Eq 622 (in power of appointment). See also *Re Keighley, Keighley v Keighley* [1919] 2 Ch 388 (appointment among 'my people'). A disposition in favour of an illegitimate descendant was held valid in *Lambe v Eames* (1871) 6 Ch App 597; but see now PARA 355. If the donee does not exercise the power, in a gift to the family in default of appointment, 'family' is construed to mean next of kin: *Grant v Lynam* at 297.

11 *Re Barlow's Will Trusts* [1979] 1 All ER 296, [1979] 1 WLR 278.

12 *Williams v Williams* (1851) 1 Sim NS 358 at 371. See also *Doe d King v Frost* (1820) 3 B & Ald 546 (to 'younger branches of the family'). Cf *Doe d Smith v Fleming* (1835) 2 Cr M & R 638 (where a similar gift was in the circumstances void for uncertainty); *Armstrong v Armstrong* (1888) 21 LR Ir 114, Ir CA.

13 *Chapman's Case* (1574) 3 Dyer 333b (where 'to remain to the house' was construed to mean 'family', and 'family' meant the 'chief and most worthy and eldest person of the family'; recognised as binding in *Counden v Clerke* (1612) Hob 29 at 33 and in *Crossly v Clare* (1761) Amb 397); *Wright v Atkyns* (1810) 17 Ves 255 at 262 (on appeal (1814) Coop G 111 at 122; revsd, however,

on the words of the will (1823) Turn & R 143 at 145, 155, HL); *Doe d Chattaway v Smith* (1816) 5 M & S 126; *Griffiths v Evan* (1842) 5 Beav 241. As to the use of 'family' as a word of limitation see PARA 384 note 11.

14 *Gregory v Smith* (1852) 9 Hare 708; *Charitable Donations and Bequests Comrs v Deey* (1891) 27 LR Ir 289.

15 As to the admissibility of such evidence see PARAS 195, 218–219.

16 *Harland v Trigg* (1782) 1 Bro CC 142; *Doe d Hayter v Joinville* (1802) 3 East 172; *Yeap Cheah Neo v Ong Cheng Neo* (1875) LR 6 PC 381 at 395; *Re Cullimore's Trusts* (1891) 27 LR Ir 18. See also *Robinson v Waddelow* (1836) 8 Sim 134 (where a gift to daughters 'and their husbands and families' was rejected); but see *Re Parkinson's Trust, ex p Thompson* (1851) 1 Sim NS 242 at 245–246.

17 *Re Coates, Ramsden v Coates* [1955] Ch 495, [1955] 1 All ER 26; *Re Gibbard, Public Trustee v Davis* [1966] 1 All ER 273, [1967] 1 WLR 42; *Re Barlow's Will Trusts* [1979] 1 All ER 296, [1979] 1 WLR 278. For cases where 'friends and relations' has been read as 'relations' see PARA 349 note 1.

18 *Re Barlow's Will Trusts* [1979] 1 All ER 296, [1979] 1 WLR 278.

19 *Re Ball, Hand v Ball* [1947] Ch 228, [1947] 1 All ER 458 (where there was a gift to the son 'or his dependants equally', and the son took absolutely); doubted in *Re Baden's Deed Trusts (No 2)* [1973] Ch 9 at 21, [1972] 2 All ER 1304 at 1311, CA, per Sachs LJ. Cf *Re Sayer, MacGregor v Sayer* [1957] Ch 423, [1956] 3 All ER 600; *Re Saxone Shoe Co Ltd's Trust Deed, Re Abbott's Will Trusts, Abbott v Pearson* [1962] 2 All ER 904, [1962] 1 WLR 943; *Re Baden's Deed Trusts (No 2)* above (cases where 'dependants' was held not so uncertain in meaning as to invalidate provisions in company trust deeds for the benefit of employees, where there was a power of selection). Cf *Re Leek, Darwen v Leek* [1969] 1 Ch 563, [1968] 1 All ER 793, CA (where, if it had not been necessary to ascertain the whole class, the court would have held that a gift to persons who, in the trustees' opinion, had moral claims on a certain person was certain).

349. Gift to relations and relatives. In its primary sense 'relations'[1] extends to relations of every degree of relationship[2], however remote; and, where donees are thus described, this effect is given to the word wherever possible, as for example where the gift is a power of selection and appointment among relations[3], or is to poor relations by way of perpetual charity[4]. In general, however, this meaning cannot be given to the word in a direct gift to relations, or in a gift to them under a power of distribution, on account of the uncertainty[5] in the number of persons designated[6]. In such a case, therefore, the court formerly presumed that the testator intended his next of kin according to the Statutes of Distribution[7], and there is the like presumption now in favour of the persons, other than husband or wife, entitled on intestacy[8].

A gift to 'nearest relations' is confined to those next in blood[9]. This is so even where a charitable intention is shown[10].

The class of relations is as a rule ascertained as if they were described as next of kin[11], and prima facie they take per capita[12] and as joint tenants[13].

The meaning of each set of words has to be decided by reference to the precise verbal and factual context in which the words have been used; further the court will strive to give effect to a gift rather than declare the words meaningless and resort to a partial intestacy[14].

1 In *Gower v Mainwaring* (1750) 2 Ves Sen 87 ('friends and relations'), and in *Re Caplin's Will* (1865) 2 Drew & Sm 527 ('relations or friends'), 'friends' was treated as synonymous with relations, because of the uncertainty of any other construction. See also *Crichton v Grierson* (1828) 3 Bli NS 424, HL, where the same assumption was made; *Coogan v Hayden* (1879) 4 LR Ir 585, where the heir was held entitled (citing *Hensloe's Case* (1600) 9 Co Rep 36b at 39b). Cf *Re Baden's Deed Trusts (No 2)* [1973] Ch 9, [1972] 2 All ER 1304, where 'relations' was held certain in meaning in a company trust deed for the benefit of employees with a power of selection.

2 'Kin' has a similar meaning: see *Re Chapman, Ellick v Cox* (1883) 49 LT 673 at 674 (where 'next male kin' meant next of kin who were males).

3 *Re Poulton's Will Trusts, Smail v Litchfield* [1987] 1 All ER 1068, [1987] 1 WLR 795 (daughter of testatrix empowered to divide estate among her own 'relatives' at her discretion); *Supple v Lowson* (1773) Amb 729.

4 See CHARITIES vol 8 (2015) PARA 17.

5 As to uncertainty see PARAS 262–266.

6 *Brandon v Brandon* (1819) 3 Swan 312 at 319.

7 *Thomas v Hole* (1728) Cas temp Talb 251; *Whithorne v Harris* (1754) 2 Ves Sen 527; *Green v Howard* (1779) 1 Bro CC 31; *Rayner v Mowbray* (1791) 3 Bro CC 234 (persons 'who shall appear to be related to me'); *Masters v Hooper* (1793) 4 Bro CC 207; *Devisme v Mellish* (1800) 5 Ves 529; *Walter v Maunde* (1815) 19 Ves 424 (real estate); *Cracklow v Norie* (1838) 7 LJ Ch 278; *Hibbert v Hibbert* (1873) LR 15 Eq 372 (where an illegitimate relative, described in another gift as if legitimate, was not included). As to the Statutes of Distribution see PARA 343; and as to powers of appointment in favour of relations see TRUSTS AND POWERS vol 98 (2013) PARA 211.

8 See *Re Brigden, Chaytor v Edwin* [1938] Ch 205, [1937] 4 All ER 342 ('all my' relatives does not enlarge the class). As to the persons entitled on intestacy see PARA 485 et seq.

9 *Smith v Campbell* (1815) 19 Ves 400.

10 *Edge v Salisbury* (1749) Amb 70; *Goodinge v Goodinge* (1749) 1 Ves Sen 231.

11 See PARA 343. See also *Pearce v Vincent* (1836) 2 Keen 230; *Bishop v Cappel* (1847) 1 De G & Sm 411; *Eagles v Le Breton* (1873) LR 15 Eq 148; *Re Gansloser's Will Trusts, Chartered Bank of India, Australia and China v Chillingworth* [1952] Ch 30, [1951] 2 All ER 936, CA. Cf *Tiffin v Longman* (1855) 15 Beav 275.

12 *Thomas v Hole* (1728) Cas temp Talb 251; *Tiffin v Longman* (1855) 15 Beav 275; *Re Gansloser's Will Trusts, Chartered Bank of India, Australia and China v Chillingworth* [1952] Ch 30, [1951] 2 All ER 936, CA. For a case of a context to the contrary see *Fielden v Ashworth* (1875) LR 20 Eq 410. As to distribution per capita see PARA 396.

13 *Eagles v Le Breton* (1873) LR 15 Eq 148; *Re Gansloser's Will Trusts, Chartered Bank of India, Australia and China v Chillingworth* [1952] Ch 30, [1951] 2 All ER 936, CA. See also *Re Kilvert, Midland Bank Executor and Trustee Co Ltd v Kilvert* [1957] Ch 388, [1957] 2 All ER 196.

14 *Harris v The Beneficiaries of the Estate of Margaret Alice Cooper* [2010] All ER (D) 64 (Jan) (extrinsic evidence admitted under the Administration of Justice Act 1982 s 21 to determine who were the objects of a gift to 'my surviving relatives' and the extent of their respective interests). As to admission of extrinsic evidence after 1982 see PARA 219.

(B) *Relations through Illegitimacy; Dispositions made before 1970*

350. Relations through illegitimacy generally not included in gift. In a disposition made before 1 January 1970[1] a description of a donee by reference to relationship to the testator or other person (as in gifts to children, issue and the like) prima facie refers only to legitimate children[2] and their descendants, and does not include illegitimate children and their descendants[3]. This rule applies to all descriptions of donees, including the children[4], nephews[5], nieces[6] or relations generally[7] of the person concerned. A person born illegitimate who is subsequently legitimated by the marriage of his parents[8] is, from the date of legitimation, entitled to take an interest under a disposition by will coming thereafter into operation[9] in the same way as if he had been born legitimate, but he cannot do so in such a way as to necessitate severance from a dignity or title of honour of property settled with it, and can do so only in so far as any contrary intention is not expressed in the disposition[10]. A person born illegitimate but subsequently legitimated is not, however, legitimate for the purposes of the will of a testator who was dead before the date of legitimation[11].

The ordinary meaning of 'illegitimate' is adhered to[12], and relations through illegitimacy do not satisfy a description by reference to relationship[13] unless either, from the circumstances at the date of the will[14], it is impossible that any legitimate relation could satisfy it[15] or there appears in the will an intention to include relations through illegitimacy[16]. The question of legitimacy is in all cases decided according to the law of the domicile of the person by reference to whom the relationship of the donees is described, whether the gift is a bequest of personalty[17], a specific devise of real estate[18] or a devise of land on trust to sell and to apply the proceeds of sale as personalty[19].

1 Ie the date of the coming into force of the Family Law Reform Act 1969 s 15 (presumption that references to relations include references to relations through illegitimacy), replaced by the Family Law Reform Act 1987 s 1 in respect of dispositions made on or after 4 April 1988: see

PARAS 355–356. For the purposes of either Act, 'disposition' means a disposition, including an oral disposition, of real or personal property whether inter vivos or by will or codicil; and, notwithstanding any rule of law, a disposition made by will or codicil executed before the coming into force of either Act is not to be treated as made on or after that date by reason only that the will or codicil is confirmed by a codicil executed on or after that date: Family Law Reform Act 1969 s 15(8) (repealed by the Family Law Reform Act 1987 s 33(4), Sch 4, as from 4 April 1988); Family Law Reform Act 1987 s 19(7).

2 As to the rights of legitimated persons see the text and notes 8–11.

3 *Cartwright v Vawdry* (1800) 5 Ves 530; *Wilkinson v Adam* (1813) 1 Ves & B 422 at 462; *Warner v Warner* (1850) 15 Jur 141; *Hill v Crook* (1873) LR 6 HL 265 at 283; *Dorin v Dorin* (1875) LR 7 HL 568; *Re Ayles' Trusts* (1875) 1 ChD 282; *Ellis v Houstoun* (1878) 10 ChD 236 at 241; *Re Eve, Edwards v Burns* [1909] 1 Ch 796 at 800. See also *Re Fish, Ingham v Rayner* [1894] 2 Ch 83, CA ('niece'; legitimate grand-niece preferred to illegitimate grand-niece, where she sufficiently answered the description); *Re Deakin, Starkey v Eyres* [1894] 3 Ch 565 (power to appoint to 'relations' of donee of power, who was illegitimate; appointments to her natural relatives held good except to a person himself illegitimate, there being nothing to enable the court to draw the inference that the testator included him among the 'relations'); *Re Pearce, Alliance Assurance Co Ltd v Francis* [1914] 1 Ch 254, CA (no exception to the rule where the testator wrongly believes the donees to be legitimate) (overruling *Re Du Bochet, Mansell v Allen* [1901] 2 Ch 441); *Re Upton, Upton v National Westminster Bank plc* [2004] EWHC 1962 (Ch), [2004] WTLR 1339 (the exclusion of illegitimate children in pre-1970 dispositions is not a breach of the Human Rights Act 1998). In *Smith v Jobson* (1888) 59 LT 397, it was held that a share given to an illegitimate daughter went over in accordance with a clause providing for the death of 'any of my children'.

4 *Swaine v Kennerley* (1813) 1 Ves & B 469; *Re Wells' Estate* (1868) LR 6 Eq 599; *Hill v Crook* (1873) LR 6 HL 265; *Dorin v Dorin* (1875) LR 7 HL 568 at 574 per Lord Hatherley; *Re Pearce, Alliance Assurance Co Ltd v Francis* [1914] 1 Ch 254, CA; *Re Hall, Hall v Hall* [1932] 1 Ch 262; *Re Dicker, Crallan v Tomlinson* [1947] Ch 248, [1947] 1 All ER 317.

5 *Re Jackson, Beattie v Murphy* [1933] Ch 237 at 241.

6 *Re Fish, Ingham v Rayner* [1894] 2 Ch 83, CA (distinguishing *Re Jackson, Beattie v Murphy* [1933] Ch 237).

7 *Re Deakin, Starkey v Eyres* [1894] 3 Ch 565 at 572; *Sydall v Castings Ltd* [1967] 1 QB 302, [1966] 3 All ER 770, CA (descendant).

8 As to legitimation by marriage see now the Legitimacy Act 1976 ss 2, 3; and CHILDREN AND YOUNG PERSONS vol 9 (2012) PARA 145.

9 As to gifts to legitimated children under the will of a testator who dies after 31 December 1975 see PARA 357.

10 See, as appropriate, the Legitimacy Act 1926 ss 3, 11 (repealed); the Children Act 1975 s 8(9), Sch 1 paras 12, 16 (repealed); and, with effect from 22 August 1976, the Legitimacy Act 1976 ss 5, 11(1), Sch 1 para 4. See also CHILDREN AND YOUNG PERSONS vol 9 (2012) PARA 148. As to the legitimacy of children of voidable marriages which are annulled see the Matrimonial Causes Act 1973 s 16, Sch 1 para 12; and MATRIMONIAL AND CIVIL PARTNERSHIP LAW vol 72 (2015) PARA 381. As to the legitimacy of children of void marriages see now the Legitimacy Act 1976 s 1; *Re Spence, Spence v Dennis* [1990] Ch 197, [1989] 2 All ER 679; affd [1990] Ch 652, [1990] 2 All ER 827, CA; and CHILDREN AND YOUNG PERSONS vol 9 (2012) PARA 144. As a legitimated person is in the same position for all purposes as a person born legitimate in relation to a disposition coming into operation after the date of his legitimation, a residuary bequest to a legitimated son is saved from lapse by the Wills Act 1837 s 33 (as originally enacted) (deaths before 1 January 1983: see PARA 167) or, as the case may be, s 33 (deaths after 31 December 1982: see PARA 169). As to the status of adopted children see PARA 331.

11 *Re Hepworth, Rastall v Hepworth* [1936] Ch 750, [1936] 2 All ER 1159.

12 No mere conjecture, however probable, based on the testator's knowledge of or intimacy with the illegitimate persons can exclude the rule: *Hill v Crook* (1873) LR 6 HL 265 at 276; *Re Pearce, Alliance Assurance Co Ltd v Francis* [1914] 1 Ch 254, CA (overruling *Re Du Bochet, Mansell v Allen* [1901] 2 Ch 441).

13 There is, however, no rule that illegitimate children cannot in any circumstances participate with legitimate children in the benefit of a gift to children generally: *Owen v Bryant* (1852) 2 De GM & G 697. See also *Evans v Davies* (1849) 18 LJ Ch 180; *Hill v Crook* (1873) LR 6 HL 265; *Ebbern v Fowler* [1909] 1 Ch 578, CA; *Re Pearce, Alliance Insurance Co Ltd v Francis* [1914] 1 Ch 254 at 267, CA.

14 If the circumstances at the date of the will show an intention to include illegitimate children, the construction is not varied by subsequent events, such as the circumstances existing at the date of a confirmatory codicil: *Wilkinson v Adam* (1823) 12 Price 470, HL. Ambiguity as to the legitimate

relations may, however, make extrinsic evidence admissible as to the family and as to the person intended: *Re Jackson, Beattie v Murphy* [1933] Ch 237.

15 See the text and notes 17–19; and PARA 352.
16 See PARAS 352–353.
17 *Re Andros, Andros v Andros* (1883) 24 ChD 637; *Re Bischoffsheim, Cassel v Grant* [1948] Ch 79, [1947] 2 All ER 830.
18 *Re Grey's Trusts, Grey v Stamford* [1892] 3 Ch 88.
19 See *Skottowe v Young* (1871) LR 11 Eq 474 (legacy duty), discussed in *Re Goodman's Trusts* (1881) 17 ChD 266, CA (disapproving *Boyes v Bedale* (1863) 1 Hem & M 798, where it was held that legitimacy was decided by the law of the testator's domicile). The doctrine of conversion, whereby land held by trustees subject to a trust for sale is regarded as personal property, has been abolished, except where the trust for sale was created by the will of a testator who died before 1 January 1997: see the Trusts of Land and Appointment of Trustees Act 1996 ss 3, 25(5); and REAL PROPERTY AND REGISTRATION vol 87 (2012) PARAS 7, 215. The doctrine of conversion is, however, not wholly abolished by s 3 and will still apply to eg uncompleted agreements for the sale of land. As to the doctrine of conversion see further EQUITABLE JURISDICTION vol 47 (2014) PARA 138 et seq.

351. Effect of absence of legitimate relations. If there were no legitimate relations answering the description in existence at the date of a will made before 1 January 1970[1], the testator must be presumed to have contemplated the relations through illegitimacy answering the description and being able to take under an immediate gift[2]. There is, however, no such inference where, although there were no legitimate relations in existence at the date of the will, the testator may have contemplated such relations coming into existence in the future[3]. The impossibility of legitimate children coming into existence when a woman is past child-bearing may be sufficient to include illegitimate children in the case of an immediate gift[4]. Similarly, the incapacity of a man to beget children may enable illegitimate children to take[5].

1 Ie the date of the coming into force of the Family Law Reform Act 1969 s 15 (presumption that references to relations include references to relations through illegitimacy), replaced by the Family Law Reform Act 1987 s 1 in respect of dispositions made on or after 4 April 1988: see PARAS 355–356.
2 *Hill v Crook* (1873) LR 6 HL 265 at 282; *Dorin v Dorin* (1875) LR 7 HL 568 at 573, 575. See also *Beachcroft v Beachcroft* (1816) 1 Madd 430; *Lord Woodhouselee v Dalrymple* (1817) 2 Mer 419 (children of a deceased person); *Dilley v Matthews* (1865) 11 Jur NS 425; *Savage v Robertson* (1868) LR 7 Eq 176 (description of mother by her maiden name); *Laker v Hordern* (1876) 1 ChD 644; *Re Haseldine, Grange v Sturdy* (1886) 31 ChD 511, CA; *Re Frogley* [1905] P 137; *O'Loughlin v Bellew* [1906] 1 IR 487.
3 *Dorin v Dorin* (1875) LR 7 HL 568. See also *Dover v Alexander* (1843) 2 Hare 275; *Durrant v Friend* (1852) 5 De G & Sm 343; *Re Brown, Penrose v Manning* (1890) 63 LT 159 (approved in *Re Pearce, Alliance Assurance Co Ltd v Francis* [1914] 1 Ch 254, CA); *Re Dieppe, Millard v Dieppe* (1915) 138 LT Jo 564.
4 *Re Eve, Edwards v Burns* [1909] 1 Ch 796 (immediate gift; existing illegitimate children held entitled). Cf *Paul v Children* (1871) LR 12 Eq 16 (future gift to her child or children; existing illegitimate children not entitled); *Re Brown, Penrose v Manning* (1890) 63 LT 159 (woman 50 years of age, but her illegitimate children excluded).
5 *Re Wohlgemuth, Public Trustee v Wohlgemuth* [1949] Ch 12, [1948] 2 All ER 882 (where evidence was admitted to prove the father's incapacity at the date of the will); *Re Herwin, Herwin v Herwin* [1953] Ch 701, [1953] 2 All ER 782, CA (where fresh evidence of the father's impotence was allowed on appeal).

352. Indications that illegitimate persons are included. In a will made before 1 January 1970[1] the testator may show his intention to include illegitimate children and their descendants in a description by referring to them, or to relations of theirs, elsewhere in his will in terms showing that he treats them as legitimate[2], particularly where it is apparent that the testator knew of the illegitimacy and, therefore, could not be using his language in its ordinary sense[3]. The existence of such an intention may, however, be rebutted by a special and distinct provision for the relations through illegitimacy, or other similar indications that the testator drew a distinction between them and the legitimate relations[4]. Moreover, indications that other illegitimate persons are treated as legitimate are not enough[5], and may even be the ground of the inference against an illegitimate person who claims to be included[6]. Where the testator uses a word in the plural (such as 'children') when to his knowledge there is only a single legitimate person who could take under the gift, an illegitimate child may be included so as to make sense of the description[7], but the use of a plural word is not sufficient to include illegitimate persons if there are legitimate persons sufficient to satisfy the description in its ordinary sense and there are no other indications of an intention to include illegitimate persons[8], or if, supposing them to be included, the words of the will would still remain unsatisfied[9]. It appears that there is no hard and fast rule of construction that the mere description of a person as a relation in an earlier part of a will shows that that person is included in a general description of relations in a later part of the will, but that in all such cases the context of the will and the evidence properly admissible must be considered[10].

1 Ie the date of the coming into force of the Family Law Reform Act 1969 s 15 (presumption that references to relations include references to relations through illegitimacy), replaced by the Family Law Reform Act 1987 s 1 in respect of dispositions made on or after 4 April 1988: see PARAS 355–356.
2 Eg where the parents are spoken of in the will as husband and wife, or the illegitimate person is mentioned as 'son', 'daughter' or 'child' of his or her natural parent, or is otherwise considered as having relations (who in the strict legal sense could not exist) in such a way as impliedly to include the illegitimate person in the description in question: Hill v Crook (1873) LR 6 HL 265 at 285. See also Meredith v Farr (1843) 2 Y & C Ch Cas 525; Worts v Cubitt (1854) 19 Beav 421; Clifton v Goodbun (1868) LR 6 Eq 278; Holt v Sindrey (1868) LR 7 Eq 170 (as explained in Re Pearce, Alliance Assurance Co Ltd v Francis [1913] 2 Ch 674 at 687; affd [1914] 1 Ch 254, CA); Savage v Robertson (1868) LR 7 Eq 176; Lepine v Bean (1870) LR 10 Eq 160; Re Humphries, Smith v Millidge (1883) 24 ChD 691; Re Bryon, Drummond v Leigh (1885) 30 ChD 110; Re Horner, Eagleton v Horner (1887) 37 ChD 695; Re Hastie's Trusts (1887) 35 ChD 728; Seale-Hayne v Jodrell [1891] AC 304, HL (where illegitimate persons previously described as 'cousins' were entitled to take under a gift to 'relatives hereinbefore named'); Re Harrison, Harrison v Higson [1894] 1 Ch 561; Re Walker, Walker v Lutyens [1897] 2 Ch 238; Re Plant, Griffith v Hill (1898) 47 WR 183; Re Wood, Wood v Wood [1902] 2 Ch 542, CA; Re Smilter, Bedford v Hughes [1903] 1 Ch 198; Re Kiddle, Gent v Kiddle (1905) 92 LT 724; Re Corsellis, Freeborn v Napper [1906] 2 Ch 316; Re Helliwell, Pickles v Helliwell [1916] 2 Ch 580 (where nephews and nieces and their children were held to include legitimate descendants of the testator's natural sister); Re B, O v D [1916] 1 IR 364 (where 'children' was held to include an illegitimate child described as 'my daughter' elsewhere in the will); Re Bleckley, Sidebotham v Bleckley [1920] 1 Ch 450 at 460–461, CA.
   Such indications were not considered conclusive in Bagley v Mollard (1830) 1 Russ & M 581; Megson v Hindle (1880) 15 ChD 198, CA (where there were other indications: see the text and note 4); Re Humphries, Smith v Millidge (1883) 24 ChD 691 at 696 per North J (where a reference to 'shares' of daughters was meaningless unless the illegitimate child took); Re Hall, Branston v Weightman (1887) 35 ChD 551 (where the description as 'nephew' was not sufficient to include the person in a gift to the testator's sister's children). As to these cases see Re Parker, Parker v Osborne [1897] 2 Ch 208 at 211 et seq; Re Walker, Walker v Lutyens [1897] 2 Ch 238 at 242. See also Re Dicker [1947] Ch 248, [1947] 1 All ER 317 (where a reference to 'my nephew' in one clause did not entitle him to take as 'child' in another clause), following Re Hall, Branston v Weightman above.
3 As to the importance of showing what knowledge the testator had of the facts giving rise to the illegitimacy see Re Herbert's Trusts (1860) 1 John & H 121 at 124; Hill v Crook (1873) LR 6 HL 265 at 277, 283; Re Horner, Eagleton v Horner (1887) 37 ChD 695 at 707 (commenting on Re Ayles' Trusts (1875) 1 ChD 282); Re Cullum, Mercer v Flood [1924] 1 Ch 540 ('right heirs'; no evidence that testatrix knew of her illegitimacy); Re Taylor, Hockley v O'Neal [1925] Ch 739 (ignorance of illegitimacy). The testator's knowledge of the illegitimacy is not material where his words make sense in their ordinary meaning: see Godfrey v Davis (1801) 6 Ves 43 at 48; Warner v Warner (1850) 15 Jur 141 at 142 per Knight Bruce V-C. The testator's ignorance of the illegitimacy and his belief that the parents of the illegitimate person were married may negative the

inference that that person was intended to take: *Re Pearce, Alliance Assurance Co Ltd v Francis* [1914] 1 Ch 254 at 263, CA. A gift by an unmarried person to his or her own children takes effect (apart from the question of revival after marriage) in favour of illegitimate children: *Clifton v Goodbun* (1868) LR 6 Eq 278. As to the revocation of a will by marriage see PARA 87; and as to revival see PARAS 110–111.

4 *Megson v Hindle* (1880) 15 ChD 198, CA; *Re Hall, Branston v Weightman* (1887) 35 ChD 551 at 557.

5 *Mortimer v West* (1827) 3 Russ 370; *Re Well's Estate* (1868) LR 6 Eq 599; *Re Warden, Midland Bank Executor and Trustee Co Ltd v Warden* (1962) Times, 12 December (cases of particular children being mentioned and treated as 'children'; no inference in favour of illegitimate child not expressly mentioned).

6 *Kelly v Hammond* (1858) 26 Beav 36.

7 *Gill v Shelley* (1831) 2 Russ & M 336; *Leigh v Byron* (1853) 1 Sm & G 486; *Tugwell v Scott* (1857) 24 Beav 141; *Re Embury, Bowyer v Page (No 2)* [1914] WN 220.

8 *Edmunds v Fessey* (1861) 29 Beav 233.

9 *Hart v Durand* (1796) 3 Anst 684. The fact that the property is divided by the testator into a number of shares corresponding with the whole number of legitimate or illegitimate claimants was considered not a sufficient indication in *Cartwright v Vawdry* (1800) 5 Ves 530; *Re Wells' Estate* (1868) LR 6 Eq 599.

10 *Re Cozens, Miles v Wilson* [1903] 1 Ch 138 at 142–143 (following *Re Jodrell, Jodrell v Searle* (1890) 44 ChD 590, CA; affd sub nom *Seale-Hayne v Jodrell* [1891] AC 304, HL).

353. Gifts to illegitimate children of a named person.

Where a gift in a will made before 1 January 1970[1] is to the children of a named person[2], or the children of a named man by a certain woman[3], and is such that in the circumstances existing illegitimate children are denoted, the gift is construed as referring to those who at the date of the will have acquired the reputation[4] of being the named person's children.

1 Ie the date of the coming into force of the Family Law Reform Act 1969 s 15 (presumption that references to relations include references to relations through illegitimacy), replaced by the Family Law Reform Act 1987 s 1 in respect of dispositions made on or after 4 April 1988: see PARAS 355–356.

2 *Laker v Hordern* (1876) 1 ChD 644 at 650.

3 *Wilkinson v Adam* (1813) 1 Ves & B 422; affd (1823) 12 Price 470, HL. This case has been considered to go to the extreme verge of the law: see *Warner v Warner* (1850) 15 Jur 141 at 142.

4 As to the meaning of 'reputation' for this purpose see PARA 354 note 10.

354. Future illegitimate children.

Although, in a will made before 1 January 1970[1], a gift to a sufficiently designated illegitimate child who was alive[2] or en ventre sa mère[3] at the date of the will, or is alive[4] or en ventre sa mère[5] at the date of the testator's death, is valid[6], it was before that date a rule of law grounded on public policy that gifts could not be made by will to illegitimate children not born or begotten at the testator's death by a description expressly or impliedly referring to them as such[7]. The fact that all the intended donees, including those excluded by this rule, were to take as a class does not prevent the gift from taking effect in favour of those who are not excluded[8].

Furthermore, in a will made before 1 January 1970, there cannot be a valid gift to an illegitimate child not alive at the date of the will and described only by reference to the fact of its paternity, as the law did not in such a case permit an inquiry as to paternity[9]. Where, however, the child is described expressly or impliedly by reference to the reputation of its paternity (as in the case of a gift to the children whom a particular woman is reputed to have by a particular man), the gift is valid so long as the child in question has acquired the reputation[10] of that paternity at the testator's death[11]. In the case of a gift to the future illegitimate children of a woman, without further description, there is no difficulty of proof but the gift is subject to the rule that only children born or begotten at the testator's death may take[12].

1   Ie the date of the coming into force of the Family Law Reform Act 1969 s 15 (presumption that references to relations include references to relations through illegitimacy), replaced by the Family Law Reform Act 1987 s 1 in respect of dispositions made on or after 4 April 1988: see PARAS 355–356.

2   See *Metham v Duke of Devon* (1718) 1 P Wms 529; *Barnett v Tugwell* (1862) 31 Beav 232; *Bentley v Blizard* (1858) 4 Jur NS 652. Thus illegitimate children living at the date of the will may take under a gift to children 'legitimate or otherwise' (*Howarth v Mills* (1866) LR 2 Eq 389), or to 'the children of A by her putative husband or any other person she might marry' (*Re Brown's Trust* (1873) LR 16 Eq 239). It is sufficient if the children are referred to by name: *Rivers' Case* (1737) 1 Atk 410; *Re B, O v D* [1916] 1 IR 364.

3   *Gordon v Gordon* (1816) 1 Mer 141; *Evans v Massey* (1819) 8 Price 22 (cases of express gifts to child of whom a woman was pregnant); *Occleston v Fullalove* (1874) 9 Ch App 147 (gift to children of woman which should be reputed to be testator's); *Re Loveland, Loveland v Loveland* [1906] 1 Ch 542 (gift to children of a woman living at the testator's death). Cf *Metham v Duke of Devon* (1718) 1 P Wms 529. As to the rights of a person en ventre sa mère generally see PARA 362.

4   *Occleston v Fullalove* (1874) 9 Ch App 147 (overruling on this point *Medworth v Pope* (1859) 27 Beav 71; *Howarth v Mills* (1866) LR 2 Eq 389); *Perkins v Goodwin* [1877] WN 111.

5   *Crook v Hill* (1876) 3 ChD 773. It has been said that such a child may acquire the reputation of a certain paternity: *Re Connor* (1845) 2 Jo & Lat 456 at 460 per Sugden LC; *Pratt v Mathew* (1856) 22 Beav 328 at 339 per Romilly MR. Cf *Occleston v Fullalove* (1874) 9 Ch App 147 at 153 per Lord Selborne LC, at 158 per James LJ, and at 169 per Mellish LJ; *Re Bolton, Brown v Bolton* (1886) 31 ChD 542 at 549, 553, CA, per Fry LJ (where the child was considered to be described by reference to the fact of paternity, and, therefore, could not take).

6   So long as the provision is limited to children in being when the document takes effect, it is more in accordance with the former rule of public policy that provision should be made for them than that such a provision should be beyond the scope of the law and the offspring should become a burden on public funds: see *Re Loveland, Loveland v Loveland* [1906] 1 Ch 542 at 548 per Swinfen Eady J; *O'Loughlin v Bellew* [1906] 1 IR 487 at 493.

7   *Hill v Crook* (1873) LR 6 HL 265 at 278, 280; *Crook v Hill* (1876) 3 ChD 773; *Holt v Sindrey* (1868) LR 7 Eq 170. As to the abolition of this rule in relation to dispositions of property made on or after 1 January 1970 see PARA 355.

8   *Holt v Sindrey* (1868), as reported in 38 LJ Ch 126; *Hill v Crook* (1873) LR 6 HL 265 at 278; *Crook v Hill* (1876) 3 ChD 773. See also *Ebbern v Fowler* [1909] 1 Ch 578, CA (settlement) (overruling *Re Shaw, Robinson v Shaw* [1894] 2 Ch 573).

9   *Re Bolton, Brown v Bolton* (1886) 31 ChD 542, CA; *Re Du Bochet, Mansell v Allen* [1901] 2 Ch 441 (overruled, but on the question of construction only, in *Re Pearce, Alliance Assurance Co Ltd v Francis* [1914] 1 Ch 254, CA); *Re Homer, Cowlishaw v Rendell* (1916) 86 LJ Ch 324. A child en ventre sa mère is excluded where the description refers to the paternity: *Earle v Wilson* (1811) 17 Ves 528; *Pratt v Matthew* (1856) 22 Beav 328. See also *Re Homer, Cowlishaw v Rendell* (1916) 86 LJ Ch 324.

10   'Reputation' in such cases, it appears, means not that of rumour or fame spread by gossip, but that which springs from acknowledgment, conduct and life: *Occleston v Fullalove* (1874) 9 Ch App 147 at 164. A power for the donee to appoint to his reputed children is valid: *Re Hyde, Smith v Jack* [1932] 1 Ch 95.

11   *Metham v Duke of Devon* (1718) 1 P Wms 529; *Occleston v Fullalove* (1874) 9 Ch App 147. Evidence may be admitted only for the purpose of ascertaining who had acquired such reputation: *Wilkinson v Adam* (1813) 1 Ves & B 442 at 466–467 (affd (1823) 12 Price 470, HL); *Swaine v Kennerley* (1813) 1 Ves & B 469.

12   *Re Hastie's Trusts* (1887) 35 ChD 728; *Re Loveland, Loveland v Loveland* [1906] 1 Ch 542.

(C)   Relations through Illegitimacy; Dispositions made after 31 December 1969 and before 4 April 1988

355. Presumption in favour of illegitimate children and descendants. In any disposition[1] made[2] between 1 January 1970 and 3 April 1988 inclusive, any reference (whether express or implied) to the child or children of any person is, unless the contrary intention appears, to be construed as, or as including, a reference to any illegitimate child of that person[3]; and any reference (whether express or implied) to a person or persons related in some other manner to any person is, unless the contrary intention appears, to be construed as, or as including, a reference to anyone who would be so related if he, or some other person through whom the relationship is deduced, had been born legitimate[4]. These provisions apply only where the reference in question is to a person who is to benefit or to be capable of benefiting under the disposition or, for the purpose of designating such a person, to someone else to or through whom that person is related[5]; but they do not affect the construction of the word 'heir' or 'heirs' or of any expression which is used to create an entailed interest[6] in real or personal property[7].

Any rule of law that a disposition in favour of illegitimate children not in being when the disposition takes effect is void as contrary to public policy[8] is abolished as respects dispositions made on or after 1 January 1970[9].

Where under any disposition any real or personal property or any interest in such property is limited (whether subject to any preceding limitation or charge or not), in such a way that it would, apart from this provision, devolve (as nearly as the law permits) along with a dignity or title of honour, then, whether or not the disposition contains an express reference to the dignity or title of honour, and whether or not the property or some interest in the property may in some event become severed from it, nothing in the above provisions[10] is to operate to sever the property or any interest in it from the dignity or title, but the property or interest is to devolve in all respects as if those provisions had not been enacted[11].

1 As to the meaning of 'disposition' see PARA 350 note 1.
2 For these purposes, a disposition by will or codicil is 'made' when the will or codicil is executed; and, notwithstanding any rule of law, a disposition made by will or codicil executed before 1 January 1970 is not treated as made on or after that date by reason only that the will or codicil is confirmed by a codicil executed on or after that date: Family Law Reform Act 1969 s 15(8) (repealed). Section 15 is repealed by the Family Law Reform Act 1987 s 25(2), Sch 4, in relation to dispositions made on or after 4 April 1988.
3 Family Law Reform Act 1969 s 15(1)(a) (repealed); Family Law Reform Act 1969 (Commencement No 1) Order 1969, SI 1969/1140, art 2.
4 Family Law Reform Act 1969 s 15(1)(b) (repealed). As to the statutory protection of trustees and personal representatives see s 17 (repealed); and PARA 484.
5 Family Law Reform Act 1969 s 15(2) (repealed). Thus s 15(1) (repealed) has no application eg to a gift 'to A but, if he predeceases me without leaving issue, then to B'; the gift to B takes effect even if A left illegitimate issue.
6 Entailed interests cannot be created by instruments coming into operation on or after 1 January 1997: see the Trusts of Land and Appointment of Trustees Act 1996 s 2(6), Sch 1 para 5; PARA 387; and REAL PROPERTY AND REGISTRATION vol 87 (2012) PARA 114.
7 Family Law Reform Act 1969 s 15(2) (repealed).
8 As to the former rule of law see PARA 354.
9 Family Law Reform Act 1969 s 15(7) (repealed).
10 Ie the Family Law Reform Act 1969 s 15 (repealed): see the text and notes 1–9.
11 Family Law Reform Act 1969 s 15(5) (repealed).

(D) Relations through Illegitimacy; Dispositions made on or after 4 April 1988

356. Presumption in favour of illegitimate children and descendants. In dispositions, whether of real or personal property, by will or codicil where the will or codicil is made[1] on or after 4 April 1988, references (whether express or implied) to any relationship between two persons are to be construed, unless the contrary intention appears, without regard to whether or not the father and mother of either of them, or the father or mother of any person through whom the relationship is deduced, have or had been married to each other at any time[2]. The use, without more, of the word 'heir' or 'heirs' or any expression purporting to create an entailed interest[3] in real or personal property does not show a contrary intention[4].

Where under any such disposition of real or personal property by will or codicil, any interest in such property is limited (whether subject to any preceding limitation or charge or not) in such a way that it would, apart from these provisions[5], devolve (as nearly as the law permits) along with a dignity or title of honour, then, whether or not the disposition contains an express reference to the dignity or title of honour, and whether or not the property or some interest in the property may in some event become severed from it, nothing in the above provisions[6] is to operate to sever the property or any interest in it from the dignity or title, but the property or interest is to devolve in all respects as if those provisions had not been enacted[7].

1   Notwithstanding any rule of law, a disposition made by will or codicil executed before 4 April 1988 is not treated as made on or after that date by reason only that the will or codicil is confirmed by a codicil executed on or after that date: Family Law Reform Act 1987 s 19(7).
2   Family Law Reform Act 1987 ss 1(1), 19(1), (6). Nothing restricts these provisions to cases where the reference in question is a reference to a person who is to benefit or who is to be capable of benefiting under the disposition or, for the purpose of designating such a person, to someone else to or through whom that person is related, as is the case with the Family Law Reform Act 1969 s 15 (repealed) (see PARA 355). The Family Law Reform Act 1987 s 19 is without prejudice to the Adoption Act 1976 s 42 (construction of dispositions in cases of adoption: see PARA 357) or the Adoption and Children Act 2002 s 69: Family Law Reform Act 1987 s 19(5) (amended by the Adoption and Children Act 2002 Sch 3 para 52).
3   Entailed interests cannot be created by instruments coming into operation on or after 1 January 1997: see the Trusts of Land and Appointment of Trustees Act 1996 s 2(6), Sch 1 para 5; PARA 387; and REAL PROPERTY AND REGISTRATION vol 87 (2012) PARA 114.
4   Family Law Reform Act 1987 s 19(2) (amended by the Trusts of Land and Appointment of Trustees Act 1996 s 25(1), Sch 3 para 25).
5   Ie the Family Law Reform Act 1987 s 19: see the text and notes 1–4.
6   See note 5.
7   Family Law Reform Act 1987 s 19(4), (6).

(E)   Adopted and Legitimated Children; Testator dying after 1975

357. Dispositions in favour of adopted children. As from 1 January 1976[1], or the date of adoption[2] if later, an adopted child is to be treated in law as the child of the adopters[3] and not the child of any other person[4].

In the case of adoptions before 30 December 2005[5] where the adopters are a married couple, the child is treated as if he had been born as a child of the marriage (whether or not he was in fact born after the marriage was solemnised) and, in any other case, as if he had been born to the adopter in wedlock (but not as a child of any actual marriage of the adopter)[6].

The provision that an adopted child is to be treated as the child of no other person[7] is, however, without prejudice to any interest vested in possession in the adopted child before the adoption, or any interest expectant (whether immediately or not) on an interest so vested[8]. Subject to any contrary indication, any disposition[9] of property contained in the will of a testator who dies on or after 1 January 1976 and before 30 December 2005 is to be construed accordingly[10].

In the case of adoptions after 30 December 2005 where the child is adopted by a couple, or by one of a couple[11], the child is to be treated as the child of the relationship of the couple in question[12].

The provision that an adopted child is to be treated as the child of no other[13] does not prejudice any qualifying interest[14], any interest expectant (whether immediately or not) upon a qualifying interest or any contingent interest (other than a contingent interest in remainder) which the adopted person has immediately before the adoption in the estate of a deceased parent, whether testate or intestate[15]. Subject to any contrary indication, any disposition[16] of property contained in the will of a testator who dies on or after 30 December 2005 is to be construed accordingly[17].

Where a disposition contained in a will made on or after 1 January 1976 depends on the date of birth of a child or children of the adoptive[18] parent or parents, the disposition is to be construed as if the adopted child had been born on the date of adoption, and two or more children adopted on the same date had been born on that date in order of their actual births, but this does not affect any reference to a child's age[19].

Dispositions contained in the will of a testator who dies on or after 1 January 1976 are to be construed on the footing that a legitimated person[20], and any other person, is entitled to take any interest under the will as if he had been born legitimate[21]. A disposition which depends on the date of birth of a child or children of the parent or parents is to be construed as if a legitimated child had been born on the date of legitimation, and two or more children legitimated on the same date had been born on that date in the order of their actual births, but this does not affect any reference to a child's age[22].

If an illegitimate person, or a person adopted by one of his natural parents, dies (at any time) and:

(1)   his parents subsequently marry; and

(2)   the deceased would, if living at the time of the marriage, have become a legitimated person,

the will is to be construed, so far as it relates to the taking of interests by, or in succession to, his spouse, children and remoter issue, as if he had been legitimated by virtue of the marriage[23].

Where a disposition depends on the date of birth of a child who was born illegitimate and who either is adopted by one of the natural parents as sole adoptive parent, or is legitimated (or, if deceased, is treated as legitimated), the above provisions as to the construction of dispositions depending on the date of birth[24] do not affect his rights under the Family Law Reform Act 1969[25] or the Family Law Reform Act 1987[26]. Where a disposition depends on the date of birth of an adopted child who is legitimated (or, if deceased, is treated as legitimated), the provisions relating to the dates of birth of legitimated persons[27] do not affect his entitlement under the similar provisions[28] relating to adoption[29].

None of the above provisions affects the devolution of any property limited (expressly or not) to devolve (as nearly as the law permits) along with any peerage or dignity or title of honour; but this provision applies only if and so far as a contrary intention is not expressed in the will, and has effect subject to the terms of the will[30].

1   Ie the date on which the Adoption Act 1976 came into force (see note 3). Under earlier adoption legislation, the Adoption of Children Act 1926 had no effect either to confer property or inheritance rights on adopted children or to remove such rights from them: see s 5 (repealed); the Adoption Act 1950 did confer inheritance rights by providing in principle that the expression 'child' included an adopted child, but this did not affect a disposition made before 1950: see Sch 5 para 4 (repealed).

2   As to the meaning of 'adoption' see CHILDREN AND YOUNG PERSONS vol 9 (2012) PARA 413.

3   Adoption Act 1976 s 39(1), (5); Adoption and Children Act 2002 s 66(2), 67(1), (5). The Adoption Act 1976 s 73(3), Sch 4 repealed the Children Act 1975 Sch 1 paras 1–11, 14–17, and these provisions were replaced by the Adoption Act 1976 Pt IV (ss 38–49), which was brought into force on 1 January 1988 (see the Children Act 1975 and the Adoption Act 1976 (Commencement No 2) Order 1987, SI 1987/1242, art 2(2), Sch 2). As from 30 December 2005, the Adoption Act 1976 s 39 is replaced by the Adoption and Children Act 2002 s 67 (status conferred by adoption) in

relation to wills of testators dying on or after 1 January 1976: see the Adoption and Children Act 2002 s 73(4), Sch 4 para 17. As to adoption generally see CHILDREN AND YOUNG PERSONS vol 9 (2012) PARA 360 et seq.

4   Adoption Act 1976 s 39(2) (amended by Adoption (Intercountry Aspects) Act 1999 ss 4(2), 17); Adoption and Children Act 2002 s 67(3)(b). See CHILDREN AND YOUNG PERSONS vol 9 (2012) PARAS 414, 415. See *Re Erskine Trust Gregg v Pigot* [2012] EWHC 732 (Ch), [2013] Ch 135, [2012] 3 All ER 532 (adopted sons of the sister of a beneficiary of an English trust made in 1948 were the beneficiary's statutory next of kin; exclusion of adopted children under relevant statute was discriminatory). See also note 3. The Adoption Act 1976 s 39(2) is subject to s 39(3A): see CHILDREN AND YOUNG PERSONS vol 9 (2012) PARA 414.

5   Ie the date as from which the provisions of the Adoption and Children Act 2002 take effect. See note 3.

6   Adoption Act 1976 s 39(1), (5). In the case of a child adopted by one of its natural parents as sole adoptive parent s 39(2) (adopted child to be treated in law as if not the child of any person other than the adopter(s), see note 4) has no effect as respects entitlement to property depending on relationship to that parent, or as respects anything else depending on that relationship: s 39(3).

7   Ie the Adoption Act 1976 s 39(2).

8   Adoption Act 1976 s 42(4). See *Staffordshire County Council v B* [1999] 2 FCR 333, [1998] 1 FLR 261 (a child's contingent interest expectant upon his natural mother's life interest was held to be an interest expectant upon an interest in possession and so was not prejudiced by the child's adoption). See also *S v T1* [2006] WTLR 1461 where Etherton J accepted that there was a real risk that the effect of the Adoption Act 1976 s 39(2) would be to disinherit a minor with a contingent interest in property held on the statutory trusts arising on intestacy. For the purposes of the inheritance tax residence nil-rate band, adopted children are treated as children of their natural parents as well as of their adoptive parents: see the Inheritance Tax Act 1984 s 8K(4); and INHERITANCE TAXATION.

9   As to the meaning of 'disposition' see CHILDREN AND YOUNG PERSONS vol 9 (2012) PARA 417.

10   See the Adoption Act 1976 ss 39(6), 42(1), 46(3). See also note 3.

11   An adoption order may be made on the application of one person who has attained the age of 21 years if the court is satisfied that the person is the partner of a parent of the person to be adopted: see the Adoption and Children Act 2002 s 51(2); and CHILDREN AND YOUNG PERSONS vol 9 (2012) PARA 401.

12   Adoption and Children Act 2002 s 67(3)(a). In the case of a child adopted by one of its natural parents as sole adoptive parent, s 67(3)(b) (child to be treated in law as not being the child of any person other than the adopter(s): see note 4) has no effect as respects entitlement to property depending on relationship to that parent, or as respects anything else depending on that relationship: s 67(4).

13   Ie the Adoption and Children Act 2002 s 67(3).

14   'Qualifying interest' is expressed to mean an interest vested in possession in the adopted person before the adoption: s 69(4). Hence, the interpretation given to the equivalent provision in Adoption Act 1976 in *Staffordshire County Council v B* [1999] 2 FCR 333, [1998] 1 FLR 261 (see note 8) is no longer possible.

15   Adoption and Children Act 2002 s 69(4)(c) (added by the Inheritance and Trustees' Powers Act 2014 s 4).

16   As to the meaning of 'disposition' see CHILDREN AND YOUNG PERSONS vol 9 (2012) PARA 417.

17   See the Adoption and Children Act 2002 ss 66(2), 69(1), 73(4). See notes 2 and 4.

18   As to the meaning of 'adoptive parent' see CHILDREN AND YOUNG PERSONS vol 9 (2012) PARA 414.

19   Adoption Act 1976 s 42(2); Adoption and Children Act 2002 s 69(2). See note 3. Examples of phrases in wills on which this provision can operate are: (1) children of A 'living at my death or born afterwards'; (2) children of A 'living at my death or born afterwards before any one of such children for the time being in existence attains a vested interest and who attain the age of 21 years'; (3) as in head (1) or head (2), but referring to grandchildren of A instead of children of A; (4) A for life 'until he has a child', and then to his child or children: Adoption Act 1976 s 42(3); Adoption and Children Act 2002 s 69(3). Neither the Adoption Act 1976 s 42(2) not the Adoption and Children Act 2002 s 69(2) will affect the reference to the age of 21 years in head (2): Adoption Act 1976 s 42(3) note; Adoption and Children Act 2002 s 69(3) note.

20   For these purposes, 'legitimated person' means a person legitimated or recognised as legitimated under the Legitimacy Act 1976 s 2, s 2A or s 3, or under the Legitimacy Act 1926 s 1 or s 8 (repealed), or (except in s 8) by a legitimation (whether or not by virtue of the subsequent marriage of his parents) recognised by the law of England and Wales and effected under the law of any other country: Legitimacy Act 1976 s 10(1) (amended by the Human Fertilisation and Embryology Act 2008 Sch 6 para 19).

21 See the Legitimacy Act 1976 ss 5(1), (3), 10(1), (3).
22 Legitimacy Act 1976 s 5(4). For examples of phrases in wills on which these provisions can operate see s 5(5) (which sets out examples identical to those set out in note 19).
23 Legitimacy Act 1976 s 5(6).
24 Ie the Adoption Act 1976 s 42(2), the Legitimacy Act 1976 s 5(4) and the Adoption and Children Act 2002 s 69(2).
25 See ie the Family Law Reform Act 1987 ss 14–19 (ss 14–18 repealed).
26 Adoption Act 1976 s 43(1); Legitimacy Act 1976 s 6(1); Adoption and Children Act 2002 s 70(1); and see note 3. These provisions apply in relation to the Adoption and Children Act 2002 where:
    (1)   a testator dies in 2001 bequeathing a legacy to his eldest grandchild living at a specified time;
    (2)   his unmarried daughter has a child in 2002 who is the first grandchild;
    (3)   his married son has a child in 2003;
    (4)   subsequently his unmarried daughter's child is legitimated (or adopted by the mother as sole adoptive parent),
and in all those cases the daughter's child remains the eldest grandchild of the testator throughout: Adoption and Children Act 2002 s 70(2). Similar provisions apply in relation the Legitimacy Act 1976 and the Adoption Act 1976 but in reference to earlier years: see the Legitimacy Act 1976 s 6(3); and the Adoption Act 1976 s 43(2). As to the rights of an illegitimate child with regard to dispositions by will on and after 1 January 1970 see PARA 355.
27 Ie the Legitimacy Act 1976 s 5(4).
28 Ie the Adoption Act 1976 s 42(2) or the Adoption and Children Act 2002 s 69(2).
29 Legitimacy Act 1976 s 6(2) (amended by the Adoption Act 1976 Sch 3 para 24 and the Adoption and Children Act 2002 Sch 3 para 18).
30 Adoption Act 1976 s 44(2), (3); Legitimacy Act 1976 s 11, Sch 1 para 4(3); Adoption and Children Act 2002 s 71(2), (3); and see note 3.

(F)   Artificial Insemination and In Vitro Fertilisation

358.   Children born as a result of artificial insemination before 1 August 1991. A child born in England and Wales between 4 April 1988[1] and 1 August 1991[2] as a result of artificial insemination of a woman who was married[3] at the time of the insemination with the semen of some person other than her husband is, unless it is proved that the husband did not consent to the insemination, treated in law as the child of the parties to that marriage[4]. These provisions[5] do not affect the succession to any dignity or title of honour or render any person capable of succeeding to or transmitting a right to succeed to any such dignity or title[6].

1 Ie the date on which the Family Law Reform Act 1987 s 27 was brought into force: see s 34(2); and the Family Law Reform Act 1987 (Commencement No 1) Order 1988, SI 1988/425, art 2, Schedule.
2 The Family Law Reform Act 1987 s 27 has no effect in relation to children carried by women as the result of their artificial insemination after the date on which the Human Fertilisation and Embryology Act 1990 ss 27–29 (see PARA 358) were brought into force (ie 1 August 1991): see s 49(2); and the Human Fertilisation and Embryology Act 1990 (Commencement No 3 and Transitional Provisions) Order 1991, SI 1991/1400, art 2(2). The Human Fertilisation and Embryology Act 1990 ss 27–29 do not apply children carried by women as a result of the placing in them of embryos or of sperm and eggs, or their artificial insemination, after 6 April 2009 but continue to be relevant to children carried as a result of such treatment before that date: see PARA 359. It is the date of the artificial insemination not the date of birth of child which determines which statute is to apply: *Re C (children) (parent: purported marriage between two women: artificial insemination by donor)* [2006] EWCA Civ 551 sub nom *J v C* [2007] Fam 1, [2006] 3 WLR 876.
3 The marriage must not at that time be a marriage that had not been annulled or dissolved at the time of insemination. As to the meaning of 'marriage' see the Family Law Reform Act 1987 s 27(2); and CHILDREN AND YOUNG PERSONS vol 9 (2012) PARA 113.
4 See the Family Law Reform Act 1987 s 27(1); and CHILDREN AND YOUNG PERSONS vol 9 (2012) PARA 113.
5 Ie the Family Law Reform Act 1987 s 27: see the text and notes 1–4.
6 See the Family Law Reform Act 1987 s 27(3); and CHILDREN AND YOUNG PERSONS vol 9 (2012) PARA 113.

359. Children born as a result of assisted reproduction taking place on or after 1 August 1991 and before 6 April 2009. Provision is made by the Human Fertilisation and Embryology Act 1990[1] in relation to who is to be regarded as the mother and father of a child carried by a woman as a result of the placing in her of embryos or of sperm and eggs, or of her artificial insemination, as the case may be, on or after 1 August 1991[2] but before 6 April 2009[3].

The woman who is carrying or has carried[4] the child as a result of the placing in her of an embryo[5] or of sperm and eggs[6], and no other woman, is the mother of the child[7], unless the child is adopted[8].

Where the woman was a party to a marriage and the creation of the embryo was not brought about with the sperm of the husband, then the husband is treated as the father[9]. If no man is so treated[10] as the father of the child but the embryo or the sperm and eggs were placed in the woman, or she was artificially inseminated in the course of treatment services[11] provided for her and a man together[12] by a person to whom a licence applies[13] and the creation of the embryo carried by her was not brought about with the sperm of that man, that man is to be treated as the father of the child[14]. However where the sperm of a man who had given consent for the use of gametes for treatment of others[15] was used for such a purpose, or the sperm of a man or any embryo the creation of which was brought about with his sperm was used after his death, he is not to be treated as the father of the child[16].

Where by virtue of the provisions described above[17] a person is to be treated as the mother or father of a child, that person is to be treated in law as the mother or, as the case may be, father of the child for all purposes[18], and, where a person is not to be treated as the mother or father of a child, that person is to be treated in law as not being the mother or, as the case may be, father of the child for any purpose[19], so that references to any relationship between two people in any enactment, deed or other instrument or document (whenever passed or made) are to be read accordingly[20]. Nothing in these provisions[21] affects the succession to any dignity or title of honour or renders any person capable of succeeding to or transmitting a right to succeed to any such dignity or title, or the devolution of any property limited (expressly or not) to devolve (as nearly as the law permits) along with any dignity or title of honour[22].

Certain provisions relating to adoption have effect with modifications in relation to parental orders[23].

1　Ie by the Human Fertilisation and Embryology Act 1990 ss 27–29.
2　Ie the date on which the Human Fertilisation and Embryology Act 1990 was brought into force: see s 49(2); and the Human Fertilisation and Embryology Act 1990 (Commencement No 3 and Transitional Provisions) Order 1991, SI 1991/1400, art 2(2).
3　Human Fertilisation and Embryology Act 1990 s 49(3). Sections 27–59 do not apply to children carried by women as a result of the placing in them of embryos or of sperm and eggs, or their artificial insemination after the commencement of the Human Fertilisation and Embryology Act 2008 ss 33–48 (ie 6 April 2009) but they will continue to be relevant to children carried as a result of such treatment before that date: see s 57(2); and the Human Fertilisation and Embryology Act 2008 (Commencement No 1 and Transitional Provisions) Order 2009, SI 2009/479, art 6(1)(a). It is the date of the artificial insemination not the date of birth of child which determines which statute is to apply: *Re C (children) (parent: purported marriage between two women: artificial insemination by donor)* [2006] EWCA Civ 551 sub nom *J v C* [2007] Fam 1, [2006] 3 WLR 876.
4　For these purposes, a woman is not to be treated as carrying a child until the embryo has become implanted: Human Fertilisation and Embryology Act 1990 s 2(3). As to the meaning of 'embryo' see note 5.
5　As to the meaning of 'embryo' see the Human Fertilisation and Embryology Act 1990 s 1(1); and CHILDREN AND YOUNG PERSONS vol 9 (2012) PARA 115.

6   For these purposes, references to eggs are to live human eggs, including cells of the female germ line at any stage of maturity, but not eggs that are in the process of fertilisation or are undergoing any other process capable of resulting in an embryo and references to sperm include cells of the male germ line at any stage of maturity, and references to gametes are to be read accordingly: Human Fertilisation and Embryology Act 1990 s 1(4) (substituted by the Human Fertilisation and Embryology Act 2008 s 1(4)). Sperm is to be treated as partner-donated sperm if the donor of the sperm and the recipient of the sperm declare that they have an intimate physical relationship: Human Fertilisation and Embryology Act 1990 s 1(5) (added by SI 2007/1522).

7   See the Human Fertilisation and Embryology Act 1990 s 27(1), (3); and CHILDREN AND YOUNG PERSONS vol 9 (2012) PARA 115.

8   See the Human Fertilisation and Embryology Act 1990 s 27(2); and CHILDREN AND YOUNG PERSONS vol 9 (2012) PARA 115.

9   See the Human Fertilisation and Embryology Act 1990 s 28(1), (2), (8); and CHILDREN AND YOUNG PERSONS vol 9 (2012) PARA 116. For these purposes, the references to the parties to a marriage at the time referred to in s 28(2) are references to the parties to a marriage subsisting at that time, unless a judicial separation was then in force, but includes the parties to a void marriage if either or both of them reasonably believed at that time that the marriage was valid, and it is presumed, unless the contrary is shown, that one of them reasonably believed at that time that the marriage was valid: s 28(7). 'Judicial separation' includes a legal separation obtained in a country outside the British Islands and recognised in the United Kingdom: s 28(9). As to the meaning of 'British Islands' see STATUTES AND LEGISLATIVE PROCESS vol 96 (2012) PARA 1208. Section 28(2) does not apply to any child who, by virtue of the rules of common law, is treated as the legitimate child of the parties to the marriage, or to any child to the extent that the child is treated by virtue of adoption as not being the man's child: s 28(5)(a), (c) (amended by the Adoption and Children Act 2002 Sch 3 para 78). Where the Human Fertilisation and Embryology Act 1990 s 28(2) applies, no other person is to be treated as the father of the child: s 28(4).

10   Ie by virtue of the Human Fertilisation and Embryology Act 1990 s 28(2): see the text and note 9.

11   For these purposes, 'treatment services' means medical, surgical or obstetric services provided to the public or a section of the public for the purpose of assisting women to carry children: Human Fertilisation and Embryology Act 1990 s 2(1).

12   As to the meaning of 'together' see *Re D* [2005] UKHL 33 sub nom *Re R (a child) (IVF: paternity of child)* [2005] 2 AC 621, [2005] 4 All ER 433; *Evans v Amicus Healthcare Ltd* [2004] EWCA Civ 727, [2005] Fam 1, [2004] 3 All ER 1025.

13   As to the meaning of references to the persons to whom a licence applies see the Human Fertilisation and Embryology Act 1990 s 17(2); and MEDICAL PROFESSIONS vol 74 (2011) PARA 150.

14   See the Human Fertilisation and Embryology Act 1990 s 28(3), (8); and CHILDREN AND YOUNG PERSONS vol 9 (2012) PARA 116. Section 28(3) does not apply to any child who, by virtue of the rules of common law, is treated as the legitimate child of the parties to the marriage, or to any child to the extent that the child is treated by virtue of adoption as not being the man's child: s 28(5)(a), (c) (as amended: see note 9). Where s 28(3) applies, no other person is to be treated as the father of the child: s 28(4).

15   Ie such consent as is required by Human Fertilisation and Embryology Act 1990 Sch 3 para 5: see MEDICAL PROFESSIONS vol 74 (2011) PARA 141. As to the meaning of 'gametes' see the Human Fertilisation and Embryology Act 1990 s 1(1); and CHILDREN AND YOUNG PERSONS vol 9 (2012) PARA 115.

16   See the Human Fertilisation and Embryology Act 1990 s 28(6); and CHILDREN AND YOUNG PERSONS vol 9 (2012) PARA 116. However, the Human Fertilisation and Embryology Act 1990 s 28(6) is subject to s 28(5A), (5B) (see CHILDREN AND YOUNG PERSONS vol 9 (2012) PARA 116). In certain circumstances a deceased man may be treated as the father of a child born as a result of the use of his sperm after his death but only for the purpose of entering his name as the child's father on the appropriate Register of Births and for no other purpose: see ss 28(5I), 29(3A); and CHILDREN AND YOUNG PERSONS vol 9 (2012) PARA 116. As to circumstances where a deceased man may be treated for this limited purpose as the father of a child born after his death without the use of his sperm see the Human Fertilisation and Embryology Act 1990 ss 28(5C), (5D), (5I), 29(3A); and CHILDREN AND YOUNG PERSONS vol 9 (2012) PARA 116.

17   Ie the Human Fertilisation and Embryology Act 1990 ss 27, 28 (see the text and notes 7–16).

18   See the Human Fertilisation and Embryology Act 1990 s 29(1); and CHILDREN AND YOUNG PERSONS vol 9 (2012) PARA 115–116.

19   See the Human Fertilisation and Embryology Act 1990 s 29(2); and CHILDREN AND YOUNG PERSONS vol 9 (2012) PARA 115–116.

20   See the Human Fertilisation and Embryology Act 1990 s 29(3); and CHILDREN AND YOUNG PERSONS vol 9 (2012) PARA 115–116. Thus these provisions, unusually, have retrospective force.

21 Ie the Human Fertilisation and Embryology Act 1990 s 27(1) or s 28(2)–(4), read with s 29.
22 See the Human Fertilisation and Embryology Act 1990 s 29(4); and CHILDREN AND YOUNG
     PERSONS vol 9 (2012) PARA 115–116.
23 See PARA 361 note 1.

**360. Children born as a result of assisted reproduction taking place on or after
6 April 2009.** Provision is made by the Human Fertilisation and Embryology Act
2008[1] in relation to who are to be regarded as the parents of a child carried by a
woman as a result of the placing in her of embryos or of sperm and eggs, or of her
artificial insemination, as the case may be, on or after 6 April 2009[2].

The woman who is carrying or has carried[3] a child as a result of the placing in
her of an embryo[4] or of sperm and eggs[5], and no other woman, is to be treated as
the mother of the child[6], unless that child is adopted[7].

If, at the time of the placing in her of the embryo or the sperm and eggs or of
her insemination, the woman was married[8], and the creation of the embryo
carried by her was not brought about with the sperm of her husband, then the
husband is to be treated as the father of the child unless it is shown that he did not
consent to the placing in her of the embryo or the sperm and eggs or to her
insemination, as the case may be[9].

If, at the time of the placing in her of the embryo or the sperm and eggs or of
her insemination, whether within the United Kingdom or elsewhere, the woman
was a party to a civil partnership[10] or a marriage with another woman, then the
other party to the civil partnership or a marriage is to be treated as a parent of the
child unless it is shown that that party did not consent to the placing in the woman
of the embryo or the sperm and eggs or to her insemination, as the case may be[11].

Where no party to a marriage is treated as the father[12] of the child and no party
to a civil partnership is treated as a parent[13] of the child but the embryo or the
sperm and eggs were placed in the woman, or she was artificially inseminated, in
the course of treatment services[14] provided in the United Kingdom by a person to
whom a licence applies[15] and at the time when the embryo or the sperm and eggs
were placed in her, or she was artificially inseminated the agreed fatherhood
conditions[16] were satisfied in relation to a man, whose sperm did not bring about
the creation of the embryo and who remained alive at that time, the man is to be
treated as the father of the child[17].

Where the same conditions[18] are satisfied and at the time when the embryo or
the sperm and eggs were placed in W, or she was artificially inseminated the
agreed female parenthood conditions[19] were met in relation to another woman,
and the other woman remained alive at that time, the other woman is to be treated
as a parent of the child[20].

Where the sperm of a man who had given consent for the use of gametes for
treatment services or non-medical fertility services[21] is used for such a purpose or
the sperm of a man or any embryo the creation of which was brought about with
his sperm is used after his death, he is not to be treated as the father of the child[22].

A woman is not to be treated as the parent of a child whom she is not carrying
and has not carried[23] merely because of egg donation[24].

Where by virtue of the provisions described above[25] a person is to be treated as
the mother, father or parent of a child, that person is to be treated in law as the
mother or, as the case may be, father of the child for all purposes[26], and, where by
virtue of the provisions described above[27] a person is not to be treated as a parent
of a child, that person is to be treated in law as not being the parent of the child
for any purpose[28], so that references to any relationship between two people in
any enactment, deed or other instrument or document (whenever passed or made)

are to be read accordingly[29]. Where by virtue of the provisions described above[30] a party to a civil partnership is treated as a parent of a child, the child is a legitimate child of its parents[31]. Nothing in these provisions[32] affects the succession to any dignity or title of honour or renders any person capable of succeeding to or transmitting a right to succeed to any such dignity or title, or the devolution of any property limited (expressly or not) to devolve (as nearly as the law permits) along with any dignity or title of honour[33].

Certain provisions relating to adoption have effect with modifications in relation to parental orders[34].

1   Ie by the Human Fertilisation and Embryology Act 2008 ss 33–58.
2   See the Human Fertilisation and Embryology Act 2008 s 68(2); and the Human Fertilisation and Embryology Act (Commencement No 1 and Transitional Provisions) Order 2009, SI 2009/479.
3   As to the meaning of 'carrying a child' see the Human Fertilisation and Embryology Act 1990 s 2(3); and PARA 359 note 4 (definition applied by the Human Fertilisation and Embryology Act 2008 s 58(3)). As to the meaning of 'embryo' see note 4.
4   As to the meaning of 'embryo' see the Human Fertilisation and Embryology Act 1990 s 1(1); and PARA 359 note 5 (definition applied by the Human Fertilisation and Embryology Act 2008 s 58(3)).
5   As to the meanings of 'eggs' and 'sperm' see the Human Fertilisation and Embryology Act 1990 s 1(4); and PARA 359 note 6 (definition applied by the Human Fertilisation and Embryology Act 2008 s 58(3)).
6   See the Human Fertilisation and Embryology Act 2008 s 33(1), (3); and CHILDREN AND YOUNG PERSONS.
7   See the Human Fertilisation and Embryology Act 2008 s 33(2); and CHILDREN AND YOUNG PERSONS.
8   See further the Human Fertilisation and Embryology Act 2008 s 49(1); and CHILDREN AND YOUNG PERSONS.
9   See the Human Fertilisation and Embryology Act 2008 s 35(1), (2); and CHILDREN AND YOUNG PERSONS. This does not affect any common law presumption that a child is the legitimate child of the parties to the marriage, or apply to any child to the extent that the child is treated by virtue of adoption as not being the man's: see s 38(2), (4); and CHILDREN AND YOUNG PERSONS. Where s 35(1) applies, no other person is to be treated as the father of the child: s 38(1).
10 See further the Human Fertilisation and Embryology Act 2008 s 50; and CHILDREN AND YOUNG PERSONS.
11 See the Human Fertilisation and Embryology Act 2008 s 42(1), (2); and CHILDREN AND YOUNG PERSONS. This does not affect any common law presumption that a child is the legitimate child of the parties to a marriage or apply to any child to the extent that the child is treated by virtue of adoption as not being the woman's: see s 45(2), (4); and CHILDREN AND YOUNG PERSONS. Where s 42(1) applies, no man is to be treated as the father of the child: s 45(1).
12 Ie by virtue of the Human Fertilisation and Embryology Act 2008 s 35(1): see the text and note 9.
13 Ie by virtue of the Human Fertilisation and Embryology Act 2008 s 42(1): see the text and note 11.
14 As to the meaning of 'treatment services' see the Human Fertilisation and Embryology Act 1990 s 2(1); and PARA 359 note 11 (definition applied by the Human Fertilisation and Embryology Act 2008 s 58(3)).
15 As to the meaning of references to the persons to whom a licence applies see the Human Fertilisation and Embryology Act 1990; and PARA 359 note 13 (definition applied by the Human Fertilisation and Embryology Act 2008 s 58(3)).
16 As to the agreed fatherhood conditions see the Human Fertilisation and Embryology Act 2008 s 37; and CHILDREN AND YOUNG PERSONS.
17 See the Human Fertilisation and Embryology Act 2008 s 36; and CHILDREN AND YOUNG PERSONS. This does not affect any common law presumption that a child is the legitimate child of the parties to the marriage, or apply to any child to the extent that the child is treated by virtue of adoption as not being the man's child: see s 38(2), (4); and CHILDREN AND YOUNG PERSONS. Where s 36 applies, no other person is to be treated as the father of the child: s 38(1).
18 See notes 14–17.
19 As to the 'agreed female parenthood conditions' see the Human Fertilisation and Embryology Act 2008 s 44(1); and CHILDREN AND YOUNG PERSONS. For the form of such notices and the meaning of 'prohibited degrees of relationship' see note 17.

20 See the Human Fertilisation and Embryology Act 2008 s 43; and CHILDREN AND YOUNG PERSONS. This does not affect any common law presumption that a child is the legitimate child of the parties to the marriage, or apply to any child to the extent that the child is treated by virtue of adoption as not being the woman's child: see s 45(2), (4); CHILDREN AND YOUNG PERSONS. Where s 43 applies, no man is to be treated as the father of the child: s 45(1).

21 Ie such consent as is required by Human Fertilisation and Embryology Act 1990 Sch 3 para 5: see MEDICAL PROFESSIONS vol 74 (2011) PARA 141.

22 See the Human Fertilisation and Embryology Act 2008 ss 39, 41; and CHILDREN AND YOUNG PERSONS.

23 For meaning see note 3.

24 See the Human Fertilisation and Embryology Act 2008 s 47; and CHILDREN AND YOUNG PERSONS.

25 Ie by virtue of the Human Fertilisation and Embryology Act 2008 s 33, 35, 36, 42 or 43.

26 See the Human Fertilisation and Embryology Act 2008 s 48(1); and CHILDREN AND YOUNG PERSONS.

27 Human Fertilisation and Embryology Act 2008 s 33, 38, 41, 45 or 47.

28 See the Human Fertilisation and Embryology Act 2008 s 48(2); and CHILDREN AND YOUNG PERSONS.

29 See the Human Fertilisation and Embryology Act 2008 s 48(5); and CHILDREN AND YOUNG PERSONS. Thus, unusually, these provisions, like those of Human Fertilisation and Embryology Act 1990, have retrospective force.

30 Ie by virtue of the Human Fertilisation and Embryology Act 2008 s 42 and s 43.

31 See the Human Fertilisation and Embryology Act 2008 s 48(6); and CHILDREN AND YOUNG PERSONS.

32 Ie the Human Fertilisation and Embryology Act 2008 s 33(1) or ss 35–47 read with s 48.

33 See the Human Fertilisation and Embryology Act 2008 s 48(7); and CHILDREN AND YOUNG PERSONS.

34 See PARA 361 note 1.

361. Surrogacy and parental orders. On an application made by two people[1] the court[2] may make an order[3] providing for a child to be treated in law as the child of the two parties if:

(1)   the child has been carried[4] by a woman, who is not one of the two people, as the result of the placing in her of an embryo[5] or sperm and eggs[6] or her artificial insemination[7]; and

(2)   the gametes[8] of at least one of the two people were used to bring about the creation of the embryo[9]; and

(3)   certain conditions are satisfied[10].

1   In the case of applications made on or after 6 April 2010 (ie the coming into force of the Human Fertilisation and Embryology Act 2008 s 54(2)) the two people must be husband and wife, civil partners of each other or two persons who are living as partners in an enduring family relationship and are not within prohibited degrees of relationship in relation to each other: see s 54(2); and CHILDREN AND YOUNG PERSONS vol 9 (2012) PARA 129. Before that date applications could only be made by a married couple: see the Human Fertilisation and Embryology Act 1990 s 30 (now repealed). However the repeal of s 30 does not affect the validity of any order made under that provision before it was repealed: see the Human Fertilisation and Embryology Act 2008 s 57(4). Certain provisions relating to adoption have effect with modifications in relation to applications for parental orders under the Human Fertilisation and Embryology Act 1990 s 30 that were made but not disposed of before 6 April 2010: see the Parental Orders (Human Fertilisation and Embryology) Regulations 1994, SI 1994/2767, reg 2, Sch 1 (now repealed); Human Fertilisation and Embryology (Parental Orders) (Consequential, Transitional and Saving Provisions) Order 2010, SI 2010/986, art 3.

2   As to the meaning of 'court' see CHILDREN AND YOUNG PERSONS vol 9 (2012) PARA 145 (definition applied by Human Fertilisation and Embryology Act 2008 s 54(9)).

3   Ie under the Human Fertilisation and Embryology Act 2008 s 54 (see CHILDREN AND YOUNG PERSONS vol 9 (2012) PARA 129).

4   As to the meaning of 'carrying' see PARA 359 note 4.

5   As to the meaning of 'embryo' see PARA 359 note 5.

6   As to the meaning of 'eggs and sperm' see PARA 359 note 6.

7   See the Human Fertilisation and Embryology Act 2008 s 54(1)(a); and CHILDREN AND YOUNG PERSONS vol 9 (2012) PARA 129.

8   As to the meaning of 'gametes' see the Human Fertilisation and Embryology Act 1990 s 1(1); and
    CHILDREN AND YOUNG PERSONS vol 9 (2012) PARA 115.
9   See the Human Fertilisation and Embryology Act 2008 s 54(1)(b); and CHILDREN AND YOUNG
    PERSONS vol 9 (2012) PARA 129.
10 See the Human Fertilisation and Embryology Act 2008 s 54(1)(c); and CHILDREN AND YOUNG
    PERSONS vol 9 (2012) PARA 129. As to the conditions see the Human Fertilisation and
    Embryology Act 2008 s 54(3)–(8); and CHILDREN AND YOUNG PERSONS vol 9 (2012)
    PARA 129.

(G)   Rights of a Person en Ventre sa Mère

362.   Circumstances in which person not yet born is treated as born. Words
referring to children or issue 'born' before or 'living' at or 'surviving' a particular
point of time or event do not in their ordinary or natural meaning include a child
en ventre sa mère at the relevant date[1]. It has, however, been adopted as a rule of
construction[2] for giving effect to a presumed intention[3] that, in a gift or condition
referring to persons of named relationship who are born at or living at a particular
time[4], the description includes a person who is then en ventre sa mère and is
afterwards born alive, and would have come under the description if he had been
then actually born or living, provided that this construction is for the benefit of the
unborn person[5], and, it seems, provided that there is no context in the will
negativing the presumed intention[6]. The rule is commonly stated with respect to
gifts to children[7]; but it also applies to other descriptions of relatives[8], and to
descriptions of persons in conditions as well as in gifts[9]. In order, however, to be
capable of taking under this rule, the person must be capable of having been
begotten, and in dispositions made before 1 January 1970[10], legitimately begotten,
before the period of distribution[11]. The rule has been applied in relation to an
interest appointed in exercise of a power[12].

The proviso that the rule is applied only where it is for the benefit of the unborn
child is subject to an exception in certain cases where there is a question of
applying the rule against perpetuities[13]. Moreover, for the purpose of the rule by
which a devise of real estate to a person and his children was, before 1 January
1926, construed as giving him an estate tail if he had no child in existence at the
death of the testator[14], a child en ventre sa mère was not, it seems, regarded as in
existence[15].

1   See *Elliott v Lord Joicey* [1935] AC 209 at 233, HL.
2   Apart from the construction of a will, a child en ventre sa mère is treated as born for certain other
    purposes, eg for the purpose of taking under the former Statutes of Distribution (see PARA 343)
    or the legislation now governing succession on intestacy (see PARA 567). As to the capacity of a
    person en ventre sa mère to take by devise see PARA 45; and as to his capacity for being a life in
    being for the purpose of the rule against perpetuities see PERPETUITIES AND ACCUMULATIONS
    vol 80 (2013) PARAS 12, 21. In *Re Watson, Culme-Seymour v Brand* [1930] 2 Ch 344, 'within due
    time after my death' was held to refer to the period of gestation. As to this period see CHILDREN
    AND YOUNG PERSONS vol 9 (2012) PARA 94. In the Administration of Estates Act 1925,
    references to a child or issue living at the death of any person include a child or issue en ventre sa
    mère at the death: s 55(2).
3   *Clarke v Blake* (1788) 2 Bro CC 319 at 320 per Lord Thurlow LC; *Trower v Butts* (1823) 1 Sim
    & St 181 at 184 per Leach V-C. The only justification for such a fictional construction is that,
    where a person makes a gift to a class of children or issue described as 'born' before or 'living' at
    or 'surviving' a particular point of time or event, a child en ventre sa mère at the time must
    necessarily be within the reason and motive of the gift: *Elliott v Lord Joicey* [1935] AC 209 at
    233–234, HL, per Lord Russell of Killowen. This construction is not confined to class gifts:
    Re Stern's Will Trusts, Bartlett v Stern [1962] Ch 732 at 735, [1961] 3 All ER 1129 at 1132. In
    Doe d Clarke v Clarke (1795) 2 Hy Bl 399, Eyre CJ said that independently of intention a child
    en ventre sa mère was 'living', and this view was followed in *Re Burrows, Cleghorn v Burrows*
    [1895] 2 Ch 497, but it can no longer be supported in view of *Elliott v Lord Joicey* above (where
    Re Burrows, Cleghorn v Burrows above was overruled).

4   The qualification 'born at' or 'living at' the particular time may be expressly made by the words of the will, or impliedly made under the rules for the ascertainment of the class. Thus the rule applies where the gift is to 'children' simply, where the class is ascertained during the gestation of the unborn person: *Northey v Strange* (1716) 1 P Wms 340 at 342 (where the gift was to children and grandchildren, and a grandchild en ventre sa mère at the testator's death was held not entitled to take). Cf *Storrs v Benbow* (1833) 2 My & K 46 (revsd on appeal (1853) 3 De GM & G 390) (where the gift was 'to each child that may be born' to certain persons); *Mogg v Mogg* (1815) 1 Mer 654; *Re Hallett, Hallett v Hallett* [1892] WN 148.

5   *Villar v Sir Walter Gilbey* [1907] AC 139, HL (where the rule was not applied to a condition reducing the interest of a tenant in tail to a life estate); *Elliott v Lord Joicey* [1935] AC 209, HL (where the rule was not applied where the result would have been to benefit the parent's estate and not the child directly): see PARA 167 note 9. See also *Trower v Butts* (1823) 1 Sim & St 181; *Blasson v Blasson* (1864) 2 De GJ & Sm 665 (where the words in question were used for the purpose only of ascertaining a period of time); *Pearce v Carrington* (1873) 8 Ch App 969 (where the benefit was that the divesting of the unborn person's interest under another clause was prevented). In *Blasson v Blasson* at 670, Lord Westbury LC said that the rule applied only for the purpose of enabling the unborn child to take a benefit to which, if born, the child would be entitled.

6   It seems that the context of the will, as applied to the circumstances, may show that by the description in the will the testator meant to describe persons actually known to him (see *Millar v Turner* (1748) 1 Ves Sen 85 at 86 per Lord Hardwicke LC), or that he had no thought of the child en ventre sa mère as an immediate recipient of his bounty (see *Roper v Roper* (1867) LR 3 CP 32 at 35; *Re Emery's Estate, Jones v Emery* (1876) 3 ChD 300; and PARA 274 note 3). The early equity decisions are not easily reconcilable. According to Buller J in *Doe d Clarke v Clarke* (1795) 2 Hy Bl 399 at 401, there were two classes of cases: the first, where the gift was in the nature of a portion or provision for children, an afterborn child took his share with the rest (see *Millar v Turner* above); the second, where the gift arose from some motives of personal affection, it was confined to children actually in existence (see *Cooper v Forbes* (1786) 2 Bro CC 63 (where Lord Kenyon MR, following *Ellison v Airey* (1748) 1 Ves Sen 111 and *Pierson v Garnet* (1786) 2 Bro CC 38, held that a child en ventre sa mère could not take under a bequest to the children of A living at the testator's death)). See also *Freemantle v Freemantle* (1786) 1 Cox Eq Cas 248; *Musgrave v Parry* (1715) 2 Vern 710.

7   *Hale v Hale* (1692) Prec Ch 50; *Clarke v Blake* (1788) 2 Bro CC 319 (on appeal (1795) 2 Ves 673); *Doe d Clarke v Clarke* (1795) 2 Hy Bl 399; *Rawlins v Rawlins* (1796) 2 Cox Eq Cas 425; *Whitelock v Heddon* (1798) 1 Bos & P 243 ('to any son . . . begotten and born' at a certain time); *Trower v Butts* (1823) 1 Sim & St 181; *Re Salaman, De Pass v Sonnenthal* [1908] 1 Ch 4 at 6, 8, CA.

8   *Storrs v Benbow* (1853) 3 De GM & G 390; *Re Salaman, De Pass v Sonnenthal* [1908] 1 Ch 4, CA (great-nephews and great-nieces); *Re Hallett, Hallett v Hallett* [1892] WN 148. In *Bennett v Honywood* (1772) Amb 708 at 712, the court declined to extend the rule to a gift to 'relations by consanguinity', but the ratio decidendi, that the rule applied only to the case of a devise to children, is contrary to the authorities: see the passages cited from the civil law relating both to lineal and collateral relatives in *Wallis v Hodson* (1740) 2 Atk 114 at 118 per Lord Hardwicke LC.

9   *Burdet v Hopegood* (1718) 1 P Wms 486 (devise in case testator had no son at the time of his death); *Pearce v Carrington* (1873) 8 Ch App 969 (if daughter should be living five years after death of wife and should not then have had any child or children). In *Villar v Sir Walter Gilbey* [1907] AC 139, HL, also a case of a condition, the rule was excluded on the ground of want of benefit.

10   See PARA 350.

11   *Re Corlass* (1875) 1 ChD 460 (where one of the testator's daughters was pregnant, although unmarried, at the date of distribution but married before the child was born, thus rendering it legitimate; but, as this was not its status at the date of distribution, the child did not take).

12   *Re Stern's Will Trusts, Bartlett v Stern* [1962] Ch 732, [1961] 3 All ER 1129 (appointment, under power contained in will, to any widow of W born in testator's lifetime; widow en ventre sa mère at testator's death entitled as being within reason and motive of testator's gift).

13   See PERPETUITIES AND ACCUMULATIONS vol 80 (2013) PARA 21.

14   See PARA 389.

15   *Roper v Roper* (1867) LR 3 CP 32 (where the parent was held to take an estate of inheritance solely); but see *Mason v Clarke* (1853) 17 Beav 126 at 130 (bequest).

B.   IDENTIFICATION BY REFERENCE TO OFFICE OR EMPLOYMENT

363. Gifts to executors. The question whether a disposition by a testator in favour of his executor is to be considered as taken by him by virtue of his office or beneficially is considered elsewhere in this title[1]. Under a gift to the executors of another person, whether directly or by way of substitution for him, prima facie they take the gift as part of his estate[2], but the will may show that they were intended to take beneficially[3].

1   As to the presumption that a legacy is given to an executor as such see PARAS 1069–1070; and as to the effect of a provision that residue is to be at the disposal of the executor see PARAS 479, 517, 537.
2   *Stocks v Dodsley* (1836) 1 Keen 325; *Long v Watkinson* (1852) 17 Beav 471; *Leak v Macdowall (No 2)* (1863) 33 Beav 238; *Trethewy v Helyar* (1876) 4 ChD 53; *Re Valdez' Trusts* (1888) 40 ChD 159 at 162.
3   *Sanders v Franks* (1817) 2 Madd 147; *Wallis v Taylor* (1836) 8 Sim 241.

364.   Effect of bequest to a person's representatives. In a bequest of personal estate to the 'representatives' of any person, whether simply or with the added qualification of 'legal' or 'personal' or 'legal personal', the description is taken in its ordinary sense and prima facie designates the executors or administrators of that person[1]. 'Representatives' is, however, capable of being interpreted in any sense required by the context[2], and this may show that the description means descendants[3], or next of kin[4], as, for example, where it is shown that the donees were to take beneficially and not in any fiduciary capacity[5]. The circumstance that the gift is to the person or his representatives immediately on the testator's death, and not after a life interest, is not a reason for giving to personal representatives the meaning of next of kin[6].

1   *Re Brooks, Public Trustee v White* [1928] Ch 214, CA. A gift to a person for life, and after his death to his personal representatives, gives him an absolute interest: see *Re Brooks, Public Trustee v White*; and PARA 377. For cases establishing this construction of 'representatives' see *Corbyn v French* (1799) 4 Ves 418 at 434–435; *Price v Strange* (1820) 6 Madd 159; *Saberton v Skeels* (1830) 1 Russ & M 587; *Hinchcliffe v Westwood* (1848) 2 De G & Sm 216; *Re Crawford's Trusts* (1854) 2 Drew 230 ('to my cousins german now existing, or their representatives'); *Re Wyndham's Trusts* (1865) LR 1 Eq 290 (husband, as general administrator, preferred to executor of will); *Re Ware, Cumberlege v Cumberlege-Ware* (1890) 45 ChD 269. Cf *Re Best's Settlement Trusts* (1874) LR 18 Eq 686 (settlement).
2   *Re Crawford's Trusts* (1854) 2 Drew 230 at 233 per Kindersley V-C. The mere appointment of executors, or references to executors and administrators, showing that they are distinguished from personal representatives, may, but will not necessarily, give a different sense to the words: *Re Ware, Cumberlege v Cumberlege-Ware* (1890) 45 ChD 269 at 278. See also *Walter v Makin* (1833) 6 Sim 148; *Walker v Marquis of Camden* (1848) 16 Sim 329 (doubted in *Re Crawford's Trusts* above at 241); *Alger v Parrott* (1866) LR 3 Eq 328; *Re Thompson, Machell v Newman* (1886) 55 LT 85. See also *Briggs v Upton* (1872) 7 Ch App 376 (settlement).
3   *Horsepool v Watson* (1797) 3 Ves 383 at 384 ('children and their representatives, being issue'); *Styth v Monro* (1834) 6 Sim 49 (construed 'descendants'); *Atherton v Crowther, Deudon v De Massals* (1854) 19 Beav 448; *Re Horner, Eagleton v Horner* (1887) 37 ChD 695 at 710, 712; *Re Knowles, Rainford v Knowles* (1888) 59 LT 359; *Re Bromley, Wilson v Bromley* (1900) 83 LT 315 ('natural representatives').
4   See *Long v Blackall* (1797) 3 Ves 486 ('legal personal representatives', referring to a future time); *Robinson v Smith* (1833) 6 Sim 47 (husband being a trustee, next of kin apart from husband entitled) (considered in *Stockdale v Nicholson* (1867) LR 4 Eq 359 at 368); *Booth v Vicars* (1844) 1 Coll 6 at 12 ('next legal personal representatives'); *Smith v Palmer* (1848) 7 Hare 225 (division intended); *Atherton v Crowther, Deudon v De Massals* (1854) 19 Beav 448 (to take per stirpes). These cases were decided at a time when the next of kin were determined according to the Statutes of Distribution (see PARA 343). As to the enactments now governing the succession to real and personal estate on intestacy see PARA 485 et seq. In *Holloway v Radcliffe* (1857) 23 Beav 163, there was an express reference to the Statutes of Distribution.
5   *King v Cleaveland* (1859) 4 De G & J 477 at 481.
6   *Re Brooks, Public Trustee v White* [1928] Ch 214, CA (following *Re Crawford's Trusts* (1854) 2 Drew 230; and overruling *Bridge v Abbot* (1791) 3 Bro CC 224 and *Cotton v Cotton* (1839) 2 Beav 67). See also *Hinchcliffe v Westwood* (1848) 2 De G & Sm 216; *Chapman v Chapman* (1864) 33 Beav 556; *Re Turner* (1865) 2 Drew & Sm 501; *Re Thompson, Machell v Newman* (1886) 55 LT 85.

365. Gifts to servants or employees. Gifts to the testator's 'servants' or other donees described by their employment[1] and not by name, taking as individuals, prima facie refer to persons filling the character at the date of the will, and do not import that the employment and character must continue to the testator's death[2]. It may appear, however, that the donees are regarded as a class to be ascertained in accordance with the ordinary rules[3], and generally the context of the will may show that persons filling the character at the date of the will[4], or at the testator's death[5] or at any other time[6], are designated.

1 In *Re Jones, Williams v A-G* (1912) 106 LT 941, CA, a gift to 'clerks' in the employment of a shipping company was held not to include pursers on ships which the company managed. Service in a business is continuous so as to qualify for a legacy where the testator has transferred the business, but remains manager: *Re Howell's Trusts, Barclays Bank Ltd v Simmons* [1937] 3 All ER 647.
2 *Parker v Marchant* (1842) 1 Y & C Ch Cas 290 at 299 per Knight Bruce V-C; *Re Miller, Galloway v Miller* (1913) 135 LT Jo 10. For a similar rule with regard to descriptions generally see PARA 300. The presumption is that legacies to servants are in satisfaction of wages due, if any: *Richardson v Greese* (1743) 3 Atk 65; *Ellard v Phelan* [1914] 1 IR 76.
3 See *Re Marcus, Marcus v Marcus* (1887) 57 LT 399 at 400; and PARA 302 et seq.
4 *Parker v Marchant* (1842) 1 Y & C Ch Cas 290 (distinguished in *Re Marcus, Marcus v Marcus* (1887) 57 LT 399, on the ground of a preceding gift to three named persons who were servants at the date of the codicil); *Jones v Henley* (1685) 2 Rep Ch 361 (where the gift was construed to be to servants at the date of the will who continued as such until the death of the testator).
5 *Re Marcus, Marcus v Marcus* (1887) 57 LT 399; *Re Bell, Wright v Scrivener* (1914) 58 Sol Jo 517 (chauffeur entitled as a 'man servant').
6 *Re Sharland, Kemp v Rozey* [1896] 1 Ch 517; *Re Miller, Galloway v Miller* (1913) 135 LT Jo 10. As to a gift of a year's wages to a servant see *Blackwell v Pennant* (1852) 9 Hare 551 at 554; *Re Ravensworth, Ravensworth v Tindale* [1905] 2 Ch 1, CA; *Re Earl of Sheffield, Ryde v Bristow* [1911] 2 Ch 267, CA.

366. Persons who may benefit under gift to servants. Whether persons are included in the description 'servants' or 'employees' depends on the context and the circumstances[1]. Thus a gift to 'servants living with me at the time of my death' or 'servants in my service at the time of my death' is not confined to persons actually living in the same house with the testator, but, in the ordinary sense of the words, includes persons who are wholly in his service and not free to serve others[2]. A servant or employee who before the testator's death leaves his service, either voluntarily[3] or even on a wrongful dismissal[4], is not entitled to share in such a gift, but a temporary absence while the relationship of service continues is immaterial[5]. Gifts to 'domestic' or 'household' servants are as a rule restricted to indoor servants[6], but there is no fixed rule that outdoor servants not boarded by the testator must be excluded, and it is a question of intention to be determined on an examination of all the circumstances[7]. The question whether 'servants' includes persons ranking above servants depends on the circumstances[8].

1 In *Sleech v Thorington* (1754) 2 Ves Sen 560 at 564, a gift to 'the two servants that shall live with me at the time of my death' was held to include a third taken into service afterwards, the number being rejected (see PARA 271). An annuity to a servant so long as she continues in the service of a person, who in fact predeceases the testator, may take effect as a life annuity: *Burchett v Woolward* (1823) Turn & R 442.
2 *Blackwell v Pennant* (1852) 9 Hare 551 at 553 per Turner V-C (following *Townshend v Windham* (1706) 12 Vern 546 and *Howard v Wilson* (1832) 4 Hag Ecc 107). See also *Chilcot v Bromley* (1806) 12 Ves 114 (coachman provided by agent excluded); *Bulling v Ellice* (1845) 9 Jur 936 (salaried farm bailiff included); *Thrupp v Collett (No 2)* (1858) 26 Beav 147 (servants living off the premises included; but a boy not continuously employed excluded, and, it seems, a charwoman would have been excluded); *Armstrong v Clavering* (1859) 27 Beav 226 (land agent and house steward devoting unemployed time to agency for other landowners included); *Re Lawson, Wardley v Bringloe* [1914] 1 Ch 682 (male nurse); *Re Travers, Hurmson v Carr* (1916) 86 LJ Ch 123 (nurse). Where the testatrix had become mentally disordered, servants appointed by her

receiver were entitled: *Re Silverston, Westminster Bank Ltd v Kohler* [1949] Ch 270, [1949] 1 All ER 641. Cf *Re King, Jackson v A-G* [1917] 2 Ch 420 (servants employed by committee of person mentally disordered not entitled).

3 *Re Serres's Estate, Venes v Marriott* (1862) 8 Jur NS 882; *Re Benyon, Benyon v Grieve* (1884) 51 LT 116.

4 *Darlow v Edwards* (1862) 1 H & C 547, Ex Ch; *Re Hartley's Trusts* (1878) 47 LJ Ch 610.

5 *Herbert v Reid* (1810) 16 Ves 481 at 489 (where Lord Eldon LC, discussing evidence of the servant leaving service, said that the master must explain whether he sent her from the house as putting an end to the relation entirely, or only suspending her services); *Re Lawson, Wardley v Bringlow* [1914] 1 Ch 682; *Re Cole, Cole v Cole* [1919] 1 Ch 218 (military service) (distinguished in *Re Drake, Drake v Green* [1921] 2 Ch 99); *Re Feather, Harrison v Tapsell* [1945] Ch 343, [1945] 1 All ER 552 (on the evidence a contract of employment continued although the employee was on military service); *Re Marryat, Westminster Bank Ltd v Hobcroft* [1948] Ch 298, [1948] 1 All ER 796 (employee to have been in service of company 'at my death for a period of five years'; the period must be continuous, and, on the facts, military service could not be counted); *Re Bedford, National Provincial Bank Ltd v Aulton* [1951] Ch 905, [1951] 1 All ER 1093 ('not less than five years' service'; period need not be continuous but military service could not be counted).

6 *Ogle v Morgan* (1852) 1 De GM & G 359 (indoor servants not receiving board wages) (followed in *Vaughan v Booth* (1852) 16 Jur 808; *Re Drax, Savile v Yeatman* (1887) 57 LT 475); *Re Ogilby, Cochrane v Ogilby* [1903] 1 IR 525; *Re Lawson, Wardley v Bringloe* [1914] 1 Ch 682; *Re Forrest, Bubb v Newcomb* [1916] 2 Ch 386 (farm labourers excluded). 'Indoor and outdoor servants' does not include a resident land agent (*Re Countess of Rosse, Parsons v Earl of Rosse* (1923) 93 LJ Ch 8, CA), or an estate manager (*Re Earl Brownlow, Tower v Sedgewick* (1924) 69 Sol Jo 176); but includes the various persons, gardeners, carpenters, woodmen, farm hands etc employed in the management of a large estate (*Re Drake, Drake v Green* [1921] 2 Ch 99).

7 *Re Jackson, Jackson v Hamilton* [1923] 2 Ch 365, CA; *Re Forbes, Public Trustee v Hadlow* (1934) 78 Sol Jo 336.

8 *Re Cassel, Public Trustee v Ashley* (1922) 39 TLR 75. In *Re Marryat, Westminster Bank Ltd v Hobcroft* [1948] Ch 298, [1948] 1 All ER 796, an apprentice was held to be an 'employee'.

367. Gift to holder of office. The mere description of a donee as the holder of an office is not of itself sufficient to raise the inference that the gift is for the benefit of the office and not of the holder personally[1], unless the context and circumstances show that the holder for the time being was intended[2]. However, a gift to a person either described as, or known to the testator as, the holder of an office, 'or his successors', or a gift to the holder of an office for the time being, is for the benefit of the office or of the association or body in which the office is held[3].

1 *Doe d Phillips v Aldridge* (1791) 4 Term Rep 264; *Donnellan v O'Neill* (1870) IR 5 Eq 523. As to a gift to 'the superior' of a religious order see *Re Barclay, Gardner v Barclay, Steuart v Barclay* [1929] 2 Ch 173, CA; and as to gifts to vicars etc see CHARITIES vol 8 (2015) PARA 119.

2 *Re Corcoran, Corcoran v O'Kane* [1913] 1 IR 1.

3 *Smart v Prujean* (1801) 6 Ves 560 at 567; *Re Fowler, Fowler v Booth* (1914) 31 TLR 102, CA; *Re Ray's Will Trusts, Re Ray's Estate, Public Trustee v Barry* [1936] Ch 520, [1936] 2 All ER 93. As to whether a gift to an executor is annexed to the office see PARA 363. Cf *Re Mellor, Dodgeson v Ashworth* (1912) 56 Sol Jo 596 (testatrix appointed two trustees of will and gave to each legacy of £500; she also gave an annuity to each of the trustees for the time being of her will; by a codicil she revoked the appointment of one of the trustees and appointed another, to whom she gave £50; substituted trustee entitled to an annuity, but not to a legacy of £500).

(4) QUANTITY OF INTEREST TAKEN

(i) General Principles as to Quantity of Interest Taken

368. No presumption as to quantity of interest. A testator is free to give such estate as he thinks fit, consistently with law[1]. There is no presumption that he means one quantity of interest rather than another; and the intended extent of the benefit can be known only from the words in which it is given[2]. If an intention of benefit towards a particular donee is apparent on the face of the will, and the will is ambiguous as to the manner in which the gift is to take effect with regard to the property given or the interest created in it, then, in the absence of all other means of ascertaining the intention[3], the court leans to the construction which is most favourable to the donee[4].

1   As to the extent of the right of disposition see PARA 25 et seq.
2   *Blackburn v Stables* (1814) 2 Ves & B 367 at 370 per Grant MR. See also *Coward v Larkman* (1888) 60 LT 1 at 2, HL. As to the rules of construction of ambiguous words in wills see PARA 228.
3   There is thus no room for the application of the rule where the ordinary principles of construction as to giving effect to every word (*Patching v Dubbins* (1853) Kay 1 at 13–14 per Wood V-C), and as to giving their ordinary meaning to the words (*Taylor v St Helens Corpn* (1877) 6 ChD 264 at 270, CA, per Jessel MR), sufficiently indicate the intention: see PARA 241 et seq. Where the testator dies on or after 1 January 1983, extrinsic evidence, including evidence of his intention, may be admissible to assist in the interpretation of ambiguous language: see the Administration of Justice Act 1982 s 21; and PARAS 195, 218–219.
4   Bac Abr, Wills and Testaments (G) 483. 'Being a grant, a devise must be taken most strongly against the grantor': *Cooper v Woolfitt* (1827) 2 H & N 122 at 125 per Pollock CB. As to the similar rule in the case of deeds see DEEDS AND OTHER INSTRUMENTS vol 32 (2012) PARA 378. As to rights of selection given to the donee see PARA 127; as to a devise of an option of purchase of the testator's land at a fixed price see PARA 125; and as to the devolution of emblements see PARA 930.

369.   Reduction or extension of interest. An interest apparently in fee simple in real estate, or an interest in personal estate, may be made subject to defeasance[1], or may, in the context of the whole will, be reduced to a life interest[2]. Similarly, a life interest may be extended to an absolute interest[3], or may be reduced by the context to an estate until remarriage or other event[4].

If a beneficiary in tail does not fall within the true scope of a provision in the will reducing estates tail to life estates, because he is born outside the period referred to in that provision, his estate tail is not reduced and can validly be barred by a disentailing deed[5]; and an absolute interest[6] subject to an executory gift over on a contingency remains absolute if the contingency does not happen[7].

It is, however, a settled rule of construction that a clear gift is not reduced by anything subsequent in the will which does not with reasonable certainty indicate the testator's intention to reduce it[8]. Moreover, if a testator[9] devises or bequeaths property to his spouse or civil partner in terms which in themselves would give an absolute interest to the spouse or civil partner, but by the same instrument purports to give his issue an interest in the same property, the gift to the spouse or civil partner is presumed to be absolute, notwithstanding the purported gift to the issue, except where a contrary intention is shown[10].

1   *Bird v Webster* (1853) 1 Drew 338.
2   *Sherratt v Bentley* (1834) 2 My & K 149; *Joslin v Hammond* (1834) 3 My & K 110; *Hayes v Hayes* (1836) 1 Keen 97; *Morrall v Sutton* (1842) 5 Beav 100 (on appeal (1845) 1 Ph 533); *Earl of Lonsdale v Countess Barchtoldt* (1854) Kay 646; *Johnston v Antrobus* (1856) 21 Beav 556; *Re Bagshaw's Trusts* (1877) 46 LJ Ch 567, CA; *Re Houghton, Houghton v Brown* (1884) 53 LJ Ch 1018; *Re Russell* (1885) 52 LT 559, CA; *Re Sanford, Sanford v Sanford* [1901] 1 Ch 939 at 942; *Re Lupton* [1905] P 321. See also *Goodtitle d Cross v Wodhull* (1745) Willes 592. An interest may be so reduced even though the gift over is of 'whatever remains' or in similar terms: see PARA 382. If the prior interest is not so reduced, such a gift over is void: see PARAS 381–382.
3   A gift of personal estate to a person for his life, and after his death to his executors, confers an absolute interest: see *Re Brooks, Public Trustee v White* [1928] Ch 214, CA; and PARA 364. As to such gifts with an intervening general power of appointment see TRUSTS AND POWERS vol 98 (2013) PARA 107; and as to unlimited gifts of income being gifts of capital see PARA 375.
4   *Meeds v Wood* (1854) 19 Beav 215 at 222. See also *Lancaster v Varty* (1826) 5 LJOS Ch 41. Conversely, an estate may be extended. Thus a devise to a wife for life provided that she remains a widow, but in case she remarries, then to J S when he attains 23, gives an estate until

J S attains 23, even if she remarries before: *Doe d Dean and Chapter of Westminster v Freeman* (1786) 1 Term Rep 389. See also *Re Cabburn, Gage v Rutland* (1882) 46 LT 848.

5   *Re Watson, Culme-Seymour v Brand* [1930] 2 Ch 344.

6   There must first be an absolute gift: *Re Cohen's Will Trusts, Cullen v Westminster Bank Ltd* [1936] 1 All ER 103. As to the rule in *Lassence v Tierney* (1849) 1 Mac & G 551 see PARA 231.

7   *Watkins v Weston* (1863) 3 De GJ & Sm 434; *Re Bourke's Trusts* (1891) 27 LR Ir 573; *Parnell v Boyd* [1896] 2 IR 571, Ir CA. See also *Re Lady Monck's Will, Monck v Croker* [1900] 1 IR 56, Ir CA.

8   *Thornhill v Hall* (1834) 2 Cl & Fin 22 at 36, HL; *Fetherston v Fetherston* (1835) 3 Cl & Fin 67 at 73, 75, HL; *Re Roberts, Percival v Roberts* [1903] 2 Ch 200 at 204; *Re Freeman, Hope v Freeman* [1910] 1 Ch 681 at 691, CA. This rule does not mean, however, that the court is to make a comparison between the two clauses in question as to lucidity: *Randfield v Randfield* (1860) 8 HL Cas 225 at 235 per Lord Campbell. The rule has, however, often been stated as requiring the subsequent clause to be 'equally' clear with the first, eg as meaning that words which cut down a gift clearly given should be as clear as the words which confer it: see *Doe d Hearle v Hicks* (1832) 8 Bing 475, HL; *Kiver v Oldfield* (1859) 4 De G & J 30 at 37; *Leslie v Earl of Rothes* [1894] 2 Ch 499 at 516, CA. The rule applies not only where the question is one of the revocation of a legacy, but also as between one donee and another person claiming to be donee under the same will: *Re Freeman, Hope v Freeman* [1910] 1 Ch 681 at 687, CA.

9   In relation to a spouse this applies to a testator who dies on or after 1 January 1983 (ie the date on which the Administration of Justice Act 1982 s 22 came into force): see s 76(11). Nothing in s 22 affects the will of a testator who died before 1 January 1983: s 73(6)(c). In relation to a civil partner this applies to a testator who dies as from 5 December 2005 (ie the date on which the relevant provision of the Civil Partnership Act 2004 came into force): Civil Partnership Act 2004 (Commencement No 2) Order 2005, SI 2005/3175.

10 See the Administration of Justice Act 1982 s 22; and the Civil Partnership Act 2004 s 71, Sch 4 para 5. As to clear absolute gifts in the first instance see generally PARA 382.

370. Effect on gift of stated purpose.

If, when making a gift by will, a testator expresses in it a purpose, one of two alternative constructions may be applicable: the gift may be a devise or bequest to a donee either for the particular purpose but not for that purpose only, in which case a beneficial interest is conferred subject to the particular purpose, or for the particular purpose and nothing more, in which case (apart from the particular purpose) no beneficial interest is conferred on the immediate donee[1]. Thus a gift may be subject to a trust extending either to the whole of it[2], or to part of it[3] or to a personal obligation for maintenance of children[4], in which case an inquiry may be directed as to the proper amount to be applied[5]. If, however, the context allows[6], the purpose is treated merely as the testator's motive in making the gift, which is intended to increase the donee's funds to enable him to accomplish that purpose[7], and the donee takes an unfettered interest[8].

1   See the principle adopted by Sir Raymond Evershed MR in *Re Rees, Williams v Hopkins* [1950] Ch 204 at 207–208, [1949] 2 All ER 1003 at 1005, CA (citing *King v Denison* (1813) 1 Ves & B 260 at 272 per Lord Eldon). See also *Irvine v Sullivan* (1869) LR 8 Eq 673; *Croome v Croome* (1889) 61 LT 814, HL; *Re West, George v Grose* [1900] 1 Ch 84; *Re Foord, Foord v Conder* [1922] 2 Ch 519. As to where phrases such as 'subject to' or 'on condition that' are used see PARA 407. See also *Re Gardner, Huey v Cunnington* [1920] 2 Ch 523, CA ('knowing that he will carry out my wishes'); *Re Dulson* (1929) 45 TLR 228 ('in trust on the understanding that'); *Re Williams, Williams v All Souls, Hastings, Parochial Church Council* [1933] Ch 244 ('knowing that he is fully aware of my intention') (distinguishing *Re Falkiner, Mead v Smith* [1924] 1 Ch 88). As to precatory trusts see TRUSTS AND POWERS vol 98 (2013) PARA 34. As to secret trusts see PARAS 221–223; and TRUSTS AND POWERS vol 98 (2013) PARA 87 et seq.

2   *Re Rees, Williams v Hopkins* [1950] Ch 204, [1949] 2 All ER 1003, CA. See also *Cooper v Thornton* (1790) 3 Bro CC 96; *Robinson v Tickell* (1803) 8 Ves 142; *Blakeney v Blakeney* (1833) 6 Sim 52; *Wetherell v Wilson* (1836) 1 Keen 80; *Wood v Richardson* (1840) 4 Beav 174; *Ford v Fowler* (1840) 3 Beav 146; *Hodgson v Green* (1842) 11 LJ Ch 312; *Inderwick v Inderwick* (1844) 13 Sim 652; *Barnes v Grant* (1856) 26 LJ Ch 92; *Wainford v Heyl* (1875) LR 20 Eq 321; *McIsaac v Beaton* (1905) 37 SCR 143; *Re De la Hunty, O'Connor v Butler* [1907] 1 IR 507 at 511; *Re Hickey, Hickey v Hickey* [1913] 1 IR 390, Ir CA.

3 *Raikes v Ward* (1842) 1 Hare 445 at 450; *Longmore v Elcum* (1843) 2 Y & C Ch Cas 363; *Crockett v Crockett* (1848) 2 Ph 553; *Costabadie v Costabadie* (1847) 6 Hare 410 at 414; *Hart v Tribe* (1854) 18 Beav 215. Where children take beneficially, they take, according to the context, either concurrently with the donee (*Jubber v Jubber* (1839) 9 Sim 503; *Wilson v Maddison* (1843) 2 Y & C Ch Cas 372; *Re Nolan, Sheridan v Nolan* [1912] 1 IR 416; *Re Campbell, McCabe v Campbell* [1918] 1 IR 429) or in succession to him (*Chambers v Atkins* (1823) 1 Sim & St 382; *Re Whitty, Evans v Evans* (1881) 43 LT 692).

4 *Hadow v Hadow* (1838) 9 Sim 438; *Leach v Leach* (1843) 13 Sim 304; *Browne v Paull, Hoggins v Paull* (1850) 1 Sim NS 92 at 104; *Re Robertson's Trusts* (1858) 6 WR 405; *Scott v Key* (1865) 11 Jur NS 819; *Lambe v Eames* (1871) 6 Ch App 597.

5 *Hamley v Gilbert* (1821) Jac 354. Cf, however, *Thurston v Essington* (1727) Jac 361n, HL; *Re Booth, Booth v Booth* [1894] 2 Ch 282; *K'Eogh v K'Eogh* [1911] 1 IR 396.

6 In such cases the inference that an unfettered interest is intended may be drawn from the absence of any expression excluding the donee from taking beneficially (*Thorp v Owen* (1843) 2 Hare 607 at 615–616), or from the difficulty in ascertaining the amount intended to be applied for the purposes specified in every possible state of circumstances (*Thorp v Owen* at 615; *Cowman v Harrison* (1852) 10 Hare 234 at 239), or from the fact that the specified object necessarily depends on the choice of the named person, although he may desire it for his own convenience (*Barrs v Fewkes* (1864) 2 Hem & M 60 at 65; and see TRUSTS AND POWERS vol 98 (2013) PARA 153), or that, apart from the will, the donee is already under an obligation to the specified object (*Byne v Blackburn* (1858) 26 Beav 41).

7 *Thorp v Owen* (1843) 2 Hare 607 at 614; *Benson v Whittam, Hemming v Whittam* (1831) 5 Sim 22 at 32. See also *Re Lord Llangattock, Johnson v Church of England Central Board of Finance* (1918) 34 TLR 341 (intention as affecting date of payment).

8 *Thorp v Owen* (1843) 2 Hare 607; *Ward v Biddles* (1847) 16 LJ Ch 455; *Leigh v Leigh* (1848) 12 Jur 907; *Mackett v Mackett* (1872) LR 14 Eq 49 at 53; *Farr v Hennis* (1881) 44 LT 202, CA; *Re Adams and Kensington Vestry* (1884) 27 ChD 394, CA; *Re Hill, Public Trustee v O'Donnell* [1923] 2 Ch 259 ('for the benefit of themselves and their respective families' held to be an absolute gift); *Re Stirling, Union Bank of Scotland Ltd v Stirling* [1954] 2 All ER 113, [1954] 1 WLR 763 (gift to executor with request to dispose of it in accordance with memorandum; no communication of memorandum during lifetime). Cf *Re Rees, Williams v Hopkins* [1950] Ch 204, [1949] 2 All ER 1003, CA. As to a gift to a charity where changes have taken place in the management of the charity, but without interfering with its continuity see *Re Wedgwood, Sweet v Cotton* [1914] 2 Ch 245.

371. Purpose of gift to benefit a donee in a particular manner. If a gift is of a specified amount and the purpose is to benefit the donee personally in a particular manner, it is a question of construction of the particular will whether the testator's primary object is to make the specified gift to the donee, or to have the specified purpose accomplished[1]. Prima facie, in a gift otherwise unconditional, the primary object is to make the specified gift; and, where on the true construction of the will a gift has this primary object and there is also an expression of some secondary purpose, then, if this purpose is satisfied and does not exhaust the gift[2], or, if it becomes impossible (otherwise than through the donee's act or default)[3], the gift takes effect according to the primary purpose. In such a case the donee, if sui juris, is, or his representatives after his death[4] are, prima facie entitled to payment, without the testator's executors being bound to see to the application of the gift[5]. Where, however, the specified purpose is the primary object, the donee is entitled to the gift, but only so far as applicable to that purpose[6] and for no other purpose[7]; and the gift may be so expressed that the cost of accomplishing that purpose may have to be paid out of the testator's estate, even though the primary fund is sufficient[8]. In such cases, so far as the purpose cannot be accomplished or becomes impossible, the gift fails[9].

1 As to legacies made in satisfaction of a moral obligation see EQUITABLE JURISDICTION vol 47 (2014) PARA 176 et seq. A bequest for such purposes as the donee thinks fit is a gift to him: *Paice v Archbishop of Canterbury* (1807) 14 Ves 364 at 370 per Lord Eldon LC. Likewise, in *Isherwood v Payne* (1800) 5 Ves 677 (gift to provide furniture or 'for any other purpose she should think proper') and *Re Harbison, Morris v Larkin* [1902] 1 IR 103 ('for whatever purposes he pleases'), the donee took an unfettered gift. See also *Dowling v Dowling* [1902] 1 IR 79 at 83.

2   *Cope v Wilmot* (1772) Amb 704 (gift not exceeding £3,000 for advancement in business; £1,000 refunded on advancement; donee entitled to balance). As to legacies to buy an annuity see PERSONAL AND OCCUPATIONAL PENSIONS vol 80 (2013) PARA 683.

3   See eg *Barlow v Grant* (1684) 1 Vern 255 (gift for apprenticeship; donee died before requisite age); *Hammond v Neame* (1818) 1 Swan 35 (maintenance of children who did not exist); *Lord Amhurst v Duchess of Leeds* (1842) 12 Sim 476 (gift to pay rent of any residence donee might choose; donee living rent free with son; unconditional gift); *Lockhart v Hardy* (1846) 9 Beav 379 (gift to pay off a mortgage which was foreclosed during the testator's lifetime); *Gough v Bult* (1848) 16 Sim 45 at 54 (gift not exceeding £2,000 for advancement; donee died before advance made; donee's executors entitled to £2,000); *Parsons v Coke* (1858) 27 LJ Ch 828 (gift to carry on testator's business; business subsequently sold by testator); *Palmer v Flower* (1871) LR 13 Eq 250 (gift for purchase of army commission; right of purchase abolished); *Hutchinson v Rough* (1879) 40 LT 289 (gift to establish donee in profession; donee not adopting profession); *Adams v Lopdell* (1890) 25 LR Ir 311; *Re Segelcke, Ziegler v Nicol* [1906] 2 Ch 301 (gift of legacy to make donee's gifts up to an amount already exceeded); *Re Osoba, Osoba v Osoba* [1979] 2 All ER 393, [1979] 1 WLR 247, CA (where a gift of residue on trust for the benefit of a widow, an aged mother (maintenance) and a daughter (training up to university grade) was held to be an absolute trust for all three as joint tenants so that the daughter was absolutely entitled after the death of the others). A gift to a minor for a particular purpose is effectual notwithstanding the failure of the purpose: see CHILDREN AND YOUNG PERSONS vol 9 (2012) PARA 43.

4   *Barlow v Grant* (1684) 1 Vern 255; *Lewes v Lewes* (1848) 16 Sim 266.

5   *Apreece v Apreece* (1813) 1 Ves & B 364 (gift to buy a ring); *Re Skinner's Trusts* (1860) 1 John & H 102 (printing a book). See also *Knox v Lord Hotham* (1845) 15 Sim 82 (purchase of house); *Noel v Jones* (1848) 16 Sim 309 (education of minor); *Dowling v Dowling* [1902] 1 IR 79 (purchase of house). The mere fact that a third person would benefit if the legacy were applied for the specified purpose does not affect the legatee's right: *Adams v Lopdell* (1890) 25 LR Ir 311; *Earl of Mexborough v Savile* (1903) 88 LT 131 (gift to pay estate duty).

6   This applies to capital as well as to income: *Re Black, Falls v Alford* [1907] 1 IR 486, Ir CA.

7   *Dick's Trustees v Dick* (1911) 48 SLR 325 (gift for education of donee in his profession; special diploma there held not included).

8   *Milner v Milner* (1748) 1 Ves Sen 106 (gift of miscalculated sum to make up daughter's fortune to named amount); *Re Sanderson's Trusts* (1857) 3 K & J 497.

9   *Re De Crespigny, De Crespigny v De Crespigny* [1886] WN 24, CA; cf *Re Ward's Trusts* (1872) 7 Ch App 727.

372.   No fetters on the enjoyment of a person with an absolute entitlement. A testator cannot fetter the mode of enjoyment of persons absolutely entitled to a fund, as, for example, where the testator has attempted to postpone the payment of a sum of money to which a person is absolutely entitled to a later date than the attaining of his majority[1]. The court will not insist on the benefit intended for the legatee being taken by him in the form the testator prescribes[2].

1   *Saunders v Vautier* (1841) 4 Beav 115, affd Cr & Ph 240 approved in *Gosling v Gosling* (1859) Johns 265; *Re Johnston, Mills v Johnston* [1894] 3 Ch 204.

2   *Re Skinner's Trusts* (1860) 1 John & H 102; *Re Johnston, Mills v Johnston* [1894] 3 Ch 204.

373.   Gift at discretion of named person. Where a clear gift is made and the application of the gift is left to the discretion of another person, on the true construction of the gift the discretion given may be ineffective[1]. The donee is not, however, so entitled where the discretion extends to deciding what is the amount of the gift and whether it is to be given at all[2].

1   *Gough v Bult* (1848) 16 Sim 45 at 54 per Lord Cottenham LC. See also *Beevor v Partridge* (1840) 11 Sim 229; *Re Johnston, Mills v Johnston* [1894] 3 Ch 204. Cf *Gude v Worthington* (1849) 3 De G & Sm 389.

2   *Re Johnston, Mills v Johnston* [1894] 3 Ch 204 at 208. See also *Cowper v Mantell (No 2)* (1856) 22 Beav 231; *Re Sanderson's Trust* (1857) 3 K & J 497.

374.   Gift to benefit particular property. Where a sum of money is directed to be laid out for particular purposes in connection with certain property and, although no donee is specified, it is clear that the testator's intention was to benefit the persons entitled to the property, those persons are entitled to that money even though the particular purposes fail[1]. Where they are absolutely entitled to the property, those persons are entitled to the money, whether it is actually laid out for the purposes or not[2].

1 *Earl of Lonsdale v Countess Berchtoldt* (1857) 3 K & J 185.
2 *Re Bowes, Earl of Strathmore v Vane* [1896] 1 Ch 507. Cf *Re Colson's Trusts* (1853) Kay 133; *Cox v Sutton* (1856) 2 Jur NS 733 (gift as a repairing fund for the benefit of the persons in possession of an estate); *Kennedy v Kennedy* [1914] AC 215, PC.

(ii) Absolute and Life Interests

A. ABSOLUTE INTERESTS

375. Unlimited gifts of rents or income. An unlimited devise[1] of the rents and profits of land is prima facie a gift of the land itself[2], and an unlimited bequest of dividends, interest, income or produce of personal property, or of a mixed fund, is prima facie a gift of the capital or corpus of the property or fund[3]. This rule does not, however, apply to a gift of income to a charity, as a charity continues in perpetuity and effect can validly be given to a perpetual trust of income for its purposes[4]. Moreover, the rule may be excluded where the will shows an intention not to dispose of the corpus of the property[5], as where the donee is to take an interest of the same nature as another donee who expressly takes a life interest only[6]; and it does not apply where the gift of income is not unlimited[7], or where the gift is not of all the benefits arising from the property[8], but merely of a particular benefit[9], or a benefit to be enjoyed by the donee personally[10]. Thus a gift of an annuity not previously existing is prima facie for the donee's life only[11], but the testator's intention to give a larger interest to the donee, or to render the annuity perpetual, may be inferred from the language of the will[12]; and a distinction is to be drawn between a gift of an annuity charged on property and a gift of a share of the income of property unlimited in point of time[13]. It makes no difference whether the income is given to the donee directly or through the intervention of trustees[14]. A charge on the rents, dividends and income of property indefinitely may in similar cases be a charge on the property itself[15].

If, being entitled to land subject to a lease, a testator devises the 'rent' or 'ground rent' of the land without expressly disposing of his reversion, the devise prima facie includes not only the rent payable during the lease, but also the testator's whole interest in the land[16].

A gift of income to a spinster so long as she continues single and unmarried may[17] be construed as a gift of the income for a period indefinite in point of time and not ceasing with her death unmarried, and thus may amount to a gift of the capital in that event[18]. Where, however, there is a gift of income until marriage followed by a gift over on marriage, the donee of income is not entitled to the corpus[19], even though the gift over takes the form of a trust to settle the corpus for her benefit on her marriage[20].

1 Apart from the Wills Act 1837 s 28 (see PARA 376), the gift would itself, and without any assistance from the context, create merely an estate for life: *Hodson v Ball* (1845) 14 Sim 558 at 571.
2 *Rayman v Gold* (1591) Moore KB 635; *Johnson v Arnold* (1748) 1 Ves Sen 169 at 171; *Murthwaite v Jenkinson* (1824) 2 B & C 357; *Stewart v Garnett* (1830) 3 Sim 398 (where it was held that the words would pass everything that was necessary to the enjoyment of the estate); *Doe d Goldin v Lakeman* (1831) 2 B & Ad 30 (where the estate was conditional); *Harvey v Harvey* (1842) 5 Beav 134; *Plenty v West* (1848) 6 CB 201; *Bignall v Rose* (1854) 24 LJ Ch 27; *Mannox v Greener* (1872) LR 14 Eq 456; Co Litt 4b; *Re Martin, Martin v Martin* [1892] WN 120; *Bates v Taylor* (1893) 19 VLR 120. See also *Charitable Donations and Bequests Comrs v De Clifford* (1841) 1 Dr & War 245; *Adshead v Willetts* (1861) 29 Beav 358; *Shacklock v Jarvis* (1872) 26 LT

682; *Baker v Blount* [1917] 1 IR 316, Ir CA. In *Mannox v Greener* above it was held that the rule was not confined to a devise of 'rents and profits', the rents in that case being described as 'income'. Where, however, a gift of property (eg 'hereditaments') to trustees is sufficient to include an advowson with other property, a trust of the 'rents and annual income' of that property, expressly for life, is not ordinarily sufficient to include the right of new presentation to that advowson (*Martin v Martin* (1842) 12 Sim 579), although a trust of the 'rents and profits' would be sufficient to include that right (*Sherrard v Lord Harborough* (1753) Amb 165 at 167; *Earl of Albemarle v Rogers* (1796) 7 Bro Parl Cas 522, HL; *Cooke v Cholmondeley* (1854) 3 Drew 1; *Cust v Middleton* (1864) 34 LJ Ch 185). See also ECCLESIASTICAL LAW vol 34 (2011) PARA 550.

3　*Elton v Shephard* (1781) 1 Bro CC 532; *Philipps v Chamberlaine* (1798) 4 Ves 51 at 58; *Page v Leapingwell* (1812) 18 Ves 463; *Adamson v Armitage* (1815) 19 Ves 416 at 418; *Stretch v Watkins* (1816) 1 Madd 253; *Clough v Wynne* (1817) 2 Madd 188; *Haig v Swiney* (1823) 1 Sim & St 487; *Benson v Whittam, Hemming v Whittam* (1831) 5 Sim 22; *Phillips v Eastwood* (1835) L & G temp Sugd 270 at 296; *Mackworth v Hinxman* (1836) 2 Keen 658; *Stephenson v Dowson* (1840) 3 Beav 342; *Humphrey v Humphrey* (1851) 1 Sim NS 536 (where other gifts were given 'absolutely'); *Southouse v Bate* (1851) 16 Beav 132; *Jenings v Baily* (1853) 17 Beav 118 (where legacies given at the death of the donee did not exclude the rule); *Tyrell v Clark* (1854) 2 Drew 86; *Boosey v Gardner* (1854) 18 Beav 471 (on appeal on another point 5 De GM & G 122); *Dowling v Dowling* (1866) 1 Ch App 612; *Cooney v Nicholls* (1881) 7 LR Ir 107 at 115, Ir CA; *Davidson v Kimpton* (1881) 18 ChD 213 at 217; *Re L'Herminier, Mounsey v Buston* [1894] 1 Ch 675 at 676 (where the rule was applied to a power to appoint the income of a fund); *Wiley v Chanteperdrix* [1894] 1 IR 209 at 214; *Tredennick v Tredennick* [1900] 1 IR 354; *Sheridan v O'Reilly* [1900] 1 IR 386 at 388, 397; *Re Lawes-Wittewronge, Maurice v Bennett* [1915] 1 Ch 408 (where a gift of net profits was held to carry the capital of shares in companies but not of debentures); *Baker v Blount* [1917] 1 IR 316, Ir CA (where the rule was applied to a gift of part of the income).

4　*Re Levy, Barclays Bank Ltd v Board of Guardians and Trustees for the Relief of the Jewish Poor* [1960] Ch 346, [1960] 1 All ER 42, CA.

5　See *Re Morgan, Morgan v Morgan* [1893] 3 Ch 222 at 227, CA, per Lindley LJ. See also *Re Rawlins' Trusts* (1890) 45 ChD 299, CA; affd sub nom *Scalé v Rawlins* [1892] AC 342, HL.

6　See *Re Morgan, Morgan v Morgan* [1893] 3 Ch 222 at 228, CA, per Lindley LJ. See also *Wynne v Wynne* (1837) 2 Keen 778 at 791; *Blann v Bell* (1852) 2 De GM & G 775 at 781 (sum of bank annuities).

7　*Buchanan v Harrison* (1861) as reported in 31 LJ Ch 74 at 79. See also *Sansbury v Read* (1805) 12 Ves 75; *Re Mason, Mason v Mason* [1910] 1 Ch 695 at 700, CA; *Re Orr, M'Dermott v Anderson* [1915] 1 IR 191 (so long as widow should remain unmarried, but in case she should remarry, then the interest on half the amount).

8　Shep Touch (8th Edn, 1826) p 89.

9　Co Litt 4b; and see REAL PROPERTY AND REGISTRATION vol 87 (2012) PARA 6. As to devises of a right of use and occupation of land see PARA 379.

10　The fact that the donee was a married woman, and that the income was given to her for her separate use, was not sufficient to exclude the rule: *South v Alleine* (1695) 1 Salk 228; *Elton v Shephard* (1781) 1 Bro CC 532; *Adamson v Armitage* (1815) 19 Ves 416; *Tawney v Ward* (1839) 1 Beav 563; *Humphrey v Humphrey* (1851) 1 Sim NS 536; *Watkins v Weston* (1863) 3 De GJ & Sm 434; *Epple v Stone* (1906) 3 CLR 412, Aust HC.

11　See PARA 376 text and note 9.

12　As to the duration of gifts of income generally see REAL PROPERTY AND REGISTRATION vol 87 (2012) PARA 1132 et seq; TRUSTS AND POWERS vol 98 (2013) PARA 171 et seq. As to whether an annuity is payable out of capital or income see TRUSTS AND POWERS vol 98 (2013) PARA 62.

13　See eg *Re Morgan, Morgan v Morgan* [1893] 3 Ch 222 at 228, 230, CA, per Lindley LJ.

14　*Haig v Swiney* (1823) 1 Sim & St 487 at 490.

15　*Baines v Dixon* (1747) 1 Ves Sen 41; *Allan v Backhouse* (1813) 2 Ves & B 65 (affd (1821) Jac 631); *Phillips v Gutteridge* (1862) 3 De GJ & Sm 332 at 336; *Metcalfe v Hutchinson* (1875) 1 ChD 591 at 594; *Re Green, Baldock v Green* (1888) 40 ChD 610 (where the rule was excluded); *Re Young, Brown v Hodgson* [1912] 2 Ch 479 at 482, 486 (referring to *Hambro v Hambro* [1894] 2 Ch 564 (terminable annuity)); *Ramsay v Lowther* (1912) 16 CLR 1 at 18–19 (gift of rents; not indefinite). See also PERSONAL AND OCCUPATIONAL PENSIONS.

16　*Kerry v Derrick* (1605) Cro Jac 104; *Maundy v Maundy* (1735) 2 Stra 1020; *Kaye v Laxon* (1780) 1 Bro CC 76; *Walker v Shore* (1815) 19 Ves 387; *Ashton v Adamson* (1841) 1 Dr & War 198. See also *Cuthbert v Lemprière* (1814) 3 M & S 158. As to the power to devise the rent apart from the reversion see PARA 27.

17　The decision first cited in note 18 has been much criticised: see *Re Henry Will Trust, Mussett v Smith* [1953] 1 All ER 531, [1953] 1 WLR 376 (citing *Re Boddington, Boddington v Clairat* (1884) 25 ChD 685 at 689, CA, and *Re Mason, Mason v Mason* [1910] 1 Ch 695).

18 *Rishton v Cobb* (1839) 5 My & Cr 145 at 152 (followed in *Re Howard, Taylor v Howard* [1901] 1 Ch 412 at 413 (annuity to testator's wife 'so long as she remains unmarried')). Cf *Re Boddington, Boddington v Clairat* (1884) 25 ChD 685, CA (where the donee did not satisfy the requirement of being the testator's 'widow'). See also *Stewart v Murdoch* [1969] NI 78 (where there was a devise and bequest of a farm and chattels to the testator's two daughters so long as they remained unmarried with a gift over on the marriage of the second daughter; neither daughter married, and the interest was held to continue). Where a testator bequeathed his residue to his wife so long as she continued his widow, and, if she married again, the balance, not to exceed £400, was given over, the widow on remarriage took everything, except the sum of £400, absolutely: *Re Rowland, Jones v Rowland* (1902) 86 LT 78 (but as to the absolute interest there held to have been taken see the criticisms of the case in *Re Johnson* (1912) 27 OLR 472 at 477).
19 *Re Mason, Mason v Mason* [1910] 1 Ch 695, CA; *Re Barklie, M'Calmont v Barklie* [1917] 1 IR 1.
20 *Re Henry Will Trust, Mussett v Smith* [1953] 1 All ER 531, [1953] 1 WLR 376.

376. Devise of realty. Before the Wills Act 1837, a limitation to the devisee 'and his heirs' was in general required in order to give him an estate in fee simple, but this rule was not applied with the same strictness as in a grant by deed[1], and it was sufficient if the testator used words such as 'for ever'[2], or gave other indications of an intention that the entire fee should pass[3]. If, however, 'his heirs' was omitted, and there were no words or circumstances showing such an intention, the devisee took only an estate for his life[4].

This rule for the construction of the interest taken under a devise was altered by the Wills Act 1837, which provides that, where any real estate[5] has been devised to any person without any words of limitation, the devise is to be construed to pass the fee simple or other the whole estate or interest which the testator had power to dispose of by will in such real estate[6], unless a contrary intention[7] appears by the will[8]. This rule is applicable only to real estate which exists and belongs to the testator at the time of his death and over which he has then a disposing power, and does not apply to a particular interest in real estate, or an annuity or rentcharge, which the testator is about to create for the first time by his will[9].

1 See REAL PROPERTY AND REGISTRATION vol 87 (2012) PARA 68. In a will 'executor' was as good as 'heir' as a word of limitation to pass the fee simple in real estate (*Rose d Vere v Hill* (1766) 3 Burr 1881 at 1885 (to survivors 'and their representatives'); *Stein v Ritherdon* (1868) 37 LJ Ch 369 at 371), but 'assigns' showed a power of alienation and nothing more (*Milman v Lane* [1901] 2 KB 745 at 750, CA).
2 Co Litt 9b; *Chamberlaine v Turner* (1628) Cro Car 129; *Timewell v Perkins* (1740) 2 Atk 102; *Eastman v Baker* (1808) 1 Taunt 174 at 182; *Doe d Lady Dacre v Roper* (1809) 11 East 518 (referring to the rule as settled without question from 1348 (YB 22 Edw 3, Mich 16) to that day, with the exception of a doubt in Perkins's Laws of England s 557); *Evans v Evans* (1865) 33 LJ Ch 662. Such words did not enlarge an express estate tail into a fee simple: *Vernon v Wright* (1858) 7 HL Cas 35.
3 Thus an intention to give a fee simple might be inferred: (1) from the fact that the donee was required personally to undertake charges on or to pay a sum of money out of the estate (*Doe d Witley v Holmes* (1798) 8 Term Rep 1; *Good v Good* (1857) 7 E & B 295; *Lloyd v Jackson* (1867) LR 2 QB 269 at 273–274; *Bolton v Bolton* (1870) LR 5 Exch 145), but not where the money was charged merely on the estate given, and not on the donee personally (*Denn d Moor v Mellor* (1794) 5 Term Rep 558; affd sub nom *Moor v Denn d Mellor* (1800) 2 Bos & P 247, HL); (2) from the use by the testator in the operative part of the gift of the word 'estate', 'property', or any equivalent expression capable of describing the extent and sum of the testator's interest as well as the substance of the gift, unless used merely by way of reference (*Bailis v Gale* (1750) 2 Ves Sen 48; *Doe d Burton v White* (1847) 1 Exch 526 (affd (1848) 2 Exch 797, Ex Ch); *Re Pollard's Estate* (1863) 3 De GJ & Sm 541 at 556; *Coltsmann v Coltsmann* (1868) LR 3 HL 121 at 129; *Hill v Brown* [1894] AC 125 at 127–128, PC); (3) in certain circumstances from gifts over, which were inconsistent with the donee taking only a life estate (*Burke v Annis* (1853) 11 Hare 232 at 237; *Andrew v Andrew* (1875) 1 ChD 410 at 418, CA); or (4) where this construction was required in order to make the estates of trustees and beneficiaries commensurate (*Challenger v Shephard* (1800) 8 Term Rep 597; *Yarrow v Knightly* (1878) 8 ChD 736 at 739, 743, CA; and see *Smith v Smith* (1861) 8 Jur NS 459).

4 *Doe d Brodbelt v Thomson* (1858) 12 Moo PCC 116; *Bolton v Bolton* (1870) LR 5 Exch 145.
5 As to the meaning of 'real estate' see PARA 282 note 3.
6 As to the interests which a general devise passes apart from this rule see PARA 284.
7 The contrary intention must be gathered from the whole will: *Crumpe v Crumpe* [1900] AC 127
   at 131, HL, per Earl of Halsbury LC; *Pelham-Clinton v Duke of Newcastle* [1902] 1 Ch 34 at 37
   per Buckley J (affd [1903] AC 111, HL). A contrary intention appeared in: *Gravenor v Watkins*
   (1871) LR 6 CP 500; *Quarm v Quarm* [1892] 1 QB 184 (devise to several 'as joint tenants and
   not as tenants in common, and to the survivor or longest liver of them, his or her heirs and
   assigns'); *Re Gannon, Spence v Martin* [1914] 1 IR 86 (interest described as a tenancy). In the
   following cases a contrary intention was held not to be shown: *Wisden v Wisden* (1854) 2 Sm &
   G 396 (use of words of limitation in other gifts); *Brook v Brook* (1856) 3 Sm & G 280 (gift to
   married woman for her separate property with power to appoint the same to her husband and
   children). The creation of successive estates after the gift in question is an indication of contrary
   intention, but not necessarily of an intention to create only life estates: *Re Pennefather, Savile v
   Savile* [1896] 1 IR 249 at 260. Restrictions on alienation (see PARA 381) may be such an indication
   of contrary intention: *Re Sanford, Sanford v Sanford* [1901] 1 Ch 939 at 942.
8 Wills Act 1837 s 28.
9 *Nichols v Hawkes* (1853) 10 Hare 342 at 343–344 per Turner V-C. See also REAL PROPERTY
   AND REGISTRATION vol 87 (2012) PARA 1133.

377. Bequest of personalty. Whatever the date of a will, a gift of personal estate
to a donee without any context restricting his interest confers on him an absolute
interest[1]. When personal property is bequeathed by will to a person for his life and
after his death to his personal representatives, the bequest is ordinarily construed
as an absolute gift to him, as, unless the will shows the contrary, the testator is
assumed to have intended the personal representatives to take in their official
capacity[2]. The gift is so construed even though the life interest is liable to
forfeiture on bankruptcy and the contingency has not happened[3], or a power to
appoint by will is inserted between the life interest and the gift to the personal
representatives[4].

1 *Powell v Boggis* (1866) 35 Beav 535 at 541; *Re Russell* (1885) 52 LT 559, CA. A bequest of
   personalty to a person and his heirs gives him an absolute interest: *Re McElligott, Grant v
   McElligott* [1944] Ch 216, [1944] 1 All ER 441 (residuary bequest to testator's wife and her heirs
   for her and their use and benefit absolutely and forever, the Law of Property Act 1925 s 131 having
   no application).
2 Co Litt 54b; *Holloway v Clarkson* (1843) 2 Hare 521; *Alger v Parrott* (1866) LR 3 Eq 328; *Avern
   v Lloyd* (1868) LR 5 Eq 383; *Wing v Wing* (1876) 24 WR 878; *Re Brooks, Public Trustee v White*
   [1928] Ch 214, CA. The same rule has been applied to settlements inter vivos: see *Re
   Best's Settlement Trusts* (1874) LR 18 Eq 686; and SETTLEMENTS vol 91 (2012) PARA 834. As
   to the construction of gifts to personal representatives see also PARA 364.
3 *Webb v Sadler* (1873) 8 Ch App 419 (where the next beneficial interest was for the life
   tenant's representatives as part of his personal estate). If, however, interests (although contingent)
   of third persons intervene between his determinable life interest and the gift to his representatives,
   they are not prejudiced, as no merger occurs: *Re Chance's Settlement Trusts, Chance v Billing*
   (1918) 62 Sol Jo 349.
4 *Devall v Dickens* (1845) 9 Jur 550. See also *Saberton v Skeels* (1830) 1 Russ & M 587; *A-G v
   Malkin* (1846) 2 Ph 64; *Page v Soper* (1853) 11 Hare 321.

378. Effect of conferring powers of disposition. The interest to be taken by a
donee may be defined by the powers of disposition or rights of enjoyment
conferred on him. A power of disposition may itself be equivalent to the property
in the subject matter of the power, or it may be merely a power of appointment[1].
Independently of the context, there is nothing in the word 'disposal' essentially
indicating power rather than property[2]; and where real or personal estate is given
to a person to be at his own disposal, or in words to the like effect[3], and where the
context does not refer to a power or trust[4], the effect is to create a fee simple in
the case of real estate, and an absolute interest in the case of personal estate[5]. An
absolute interest has been similarly inferred even where the testator contemplated

dispositions made only by the donee's will[6], or subject to other restrictions[7], or where the gift is of a sum of money to be paid at the donee's death[8].

1   As to the construction of such gifts in relation to the creation of powers of appointment see generally TRUSTS AND POWERS vol 98 (2013) PARA 104 et seq.
2   *Nowlan v Walsh, Nowlan v Wilde* (1851) 4 De G & Sm 584 at 586. Power is a restraint on property and is never to be implied from the word 'disposal': *Hixon v Oliver* (1806) 13 Ves 108 at 114. As to the distinction between power and property see *Re Armstrong, ex p Gilchrist* (1886) 17 QBD 521.
3   *Hixon v Oliver* (1806) 13 Ves 108; *Nowlan v Walsh, Nowlan v Wilde* (1851) 4 De G & Sm 584; *Re Maxwell's Will* (1857) 24 Beav 246 ('to be disposed of as my son shall think proper'); *Parnell v Boyd* [1896] 2 IR 571, Ir CA; *Re Bogle, Bogle v Yorstoun* (1898) 78 LT 457; *Reid v Carleton* [1905] 1 IR 147.
4   As to a gift to be disposed of at the discretion of trustees see *Re Booth, Hattersley v Cowgill* (1917) 86 LJ Ch 270. See also *Metcalf v O'Kennedy* (1904) 4 SRNSW 175, Aust HC; *Re Bourk's Will, Cunningham v Rubenach* [1907] VLR 171. As to gifts to executors see PARA 363.
5   *Anon* (1553) Bro NC 62; *Whiskon and Cleytons Case* (1588) 1 Leon 156; *Goodtitle d Pearson v Otway* (1753) 2 Wils 6; *Nowland v Walsh, Nowlan v Wilde* (1851) 4 De G & Sm 584; *Alexander v Alexander* (1856) 6 De GM & G 593; *Re Maxwell's Will* (1857) 24 Beav 246. See also *Kellett v Kellett* (1868) LR 3 HL 160 at 164, 166 (where the principle of *Lassence v Tierney* (1849) 1 Mac & G 551 (see PARA 231) was confirmed).
6   *Robinson v Dusgate* (1690) 2 Vern 181; *Glover v Hall* (1849) 16 Sim 568 at 571 per Shadwell V-C ('a testamentary power of disposition is one of the incidents of the estate given'). Cf *Johnston v Rowlands* (1848) 2 De G & Sm 356; *Evans v Evans* (1865) 33 LJ Ch 662; *Weale v Ollive (No 2)* (1863) 32 Beav 421 at 424–425; *Reigh v Kearney* [1936] 1 IR 138.
7   Eg where dispositions in favour of specified persons are prohibited: *Bull v Kingston* (1815) 1 Mer 314. See also *Comber v Graham* (1830) 1 Russ & M 450.
8   *Hixon v Oliver* (1806) 13 Ves 108.

B.   LIFE INTERESTS

379.   Definition by rights of enjoyment. The interest taken by a donee may be defined by rights of enjoyment attached to it. Thus prima facie a gift of the use[1] or of the free use and occupation[2] of a house or land is a gift of the rents and profits, at all events during the donee's life[3], and prima facie the donee under such a gift need not personally reside in the house or on the land, but may let or dispose of the property during his life[4]. Similarly, prima facie a gift of the 'possession' or 'use and enjoyment' of chattels gives the donee a life interest[5], and the donee may let the goods on hire[6].

1   *Cook v Gerrard* (1668) 1 Saund 180 at 186. Even before the Wills Act 1837 a devise of land 'freely to be enjoyed and possessed' might give the fee: *Loveacres d Mudge v Blight* (1775) 1 Cowp 352; *Thomas v Phelps* (1828) 4 Russ 348. Cf *Bromitt v Moor* (1851) 9 Hare 374 at 378.
2   *Mannox v Greener* (1872) LR 14 Eq 456; *Coward v Larkman* (1888) 60 LT 1, HL. See also *Paramour v Yardley* (1579) 2 Plowd 539 at 542; *Welcden v Elkington* (1576) 2 Plowd 516 at 524; *R v Eatington Inhabitants* (1791) 4 Term Rep 177; *Doe d Chillcott v White* (1800) 1 East 33 (the income of a cottage 'and her living in it').
3   See *Coward v Larkman* (1888) 60 LT 1, HL (whether a gift in perpetuity can be inferred); *Public Trustee v Edmund* (1912) 32 NZLR 202. In *Whittome v Lamb* (1844) 12 M & W 813 at 820–821, a chattel interest only was inferred. Cf *Reay v Rawlinson* (1860) 29 Beav 88 (where a gift of 'grass for a cow' in a field created a profit à prendre).
4   *Clive v Clive* (1854) 2 Eq Rep 913; *Rabbeth v Squire* (1859) 4 De G & J 406 at 413; *Mannox v Greener* (1872) LR 14 Eq 456 at 461; *National Trustees, Executors and Agency Co Ltd v Keast* (1896) 22 VLR 447. An intention that occupation is intended to be personal may be shown by a gift over on ceasing to occupy (*Maclaren v Stainton* (1858) 27 LJ Ch 442; *Stone v Parker* (1860) 29 LJ Ch 874), or by other circumstances (see *Re Varley, Thornton v Varley* (1893) 62 LJ Ch 652; *Re Stewart, Stewart v Hislop* (1904) 23 NZLR 797). Even in such a case, however, there is a right of disposition conferred by the Settled Land Act 1925, provided that the donee exercises his right to occupy the house: *Re Anderson, Halligey v Kirkley* [1920] 1 Ch 175; *Re Gibbons, Gibbons v Gibbons* [1920] 1 Ch 372, CA. See SETTLEMENTS vol 91 (2012) PARA 728 et seq. A personal right of residence, rent free, does not entitle the donee to rents and profits in case of his non-residence: *Parker v Parker* (1863) 1 New Rep 508; *May v May* (1881) 44 LT 412; nor to a

right in case of a sale to receive the income of the proceeds of sale as an equivalent or substitution for the right of personal occupation: *Re Anderson, Halligey v Kirkley*. As to conditions of residence imposed on tenants for life see SETTLEMENTS vol 91 (2012) PARAS 642, 683.

5   *Low v Carter* (1839) 1 Beav 426 at 430; *Espinasse v Luffingham* (1846) 3 Jo & Lat 186 (plate). As to circumstances showing a contrary intention see *Terry v Terry* (1862) 33 Beav 232 (use of book debts and capital). In the case of consumables, an absolute interest is created: *Montresor v Montresor* (1845) 1 Coll 693. See also PARA 122.
6   *Re Williamson, Murray v Williamson* (1906) 94 LT 813 (following *Marshall v Blew* (1741) 2 Atk 217 and *Rabbeth v Squire* (1859) 4 De G & J 406).

380. Determinable interest. A gift until bankruptcy, alienation, marriage or other event which must happen, if at all, during the life of a donee prima facie creates a determinable life interest only[1]; but such a gift, or a gift 'so long as' certain circumstances continue[2] (even, for example, a gift so long as the donee remains unmarried[3]), may create an estate in fee simple or absolute interest determinable only on those circumstances ceasing to exist.

1   *Jordan v Holkham* (1753) Amb 209 (during widowhood); *Banks v Braithwaite* (1863) 32 LJ Ch 198 (alienation); *Re Boddington, Boddington v Clairat* (1884) 25 ChD 685, CA (so long as she continues my widow and unmarried); *Re Mason, Mason v Mason* [1910] 1 Ch 695, CA (marriage); *Re Wiltshire, Eldred v Comport* (1916) 142 LT Jo 57. A gift during widowhood determines on remarriage but is restored on the annulment of the marriage (*Re Dewhirst, Flower v Dewhirst* [1948] Ch 198, [1948] 1 All ER 147; *Re D'Altroy's Will Trusts, Crane v Lowman* [1968] 1 All ER 181, [1968] 1 WLR 120), although transactions completed during the subsistence of the remarriage and on the footing that it subsists cannot be undone (*Re Eaves, Eaves v Eaves* [1940] Ch 109, [1939] 4 All ER 260, CA). Cf PARA 377 text and note 3.
2   See *Sutcliffe v Richardson* (1872) LR 13 Eq 606 (gift of an annuity 'so long as she and my son should live together').
3   See discussion and cases cited at PARA 375 notes 17–20.

C.   ABSOLUTE INTEREST REDUCED TO LIFE INTEREST

381. Absolute or life interest. It has been stated previously that a gift which is apparently absolute may be made subject to defeasance, or may be reduced to a life interest[1]. Thus a gift of real property in fee simple, or of personal property for an interest which prima facie is absolute, may be made subject to an executory gift over; but a gift over which conflicts with the right of disposition attached to the gift is not permitted[2]. Thus a restriction on the donee's right of alienation of an interest clearly given to him is repugnant to the gift and void[3], and a gift over on breach of the restrictions cannot take effect[4]. A gift over if the donee dies without having disposed of the property[5], or of so much as the donee does not dispose of[6], is also void, if, on the construction of the will as a whole, the donee's interest is an absolute interest[7].

1   See PARA 369.
2   See PERSONAL PROPERTY vol 80 (2013) PARAS 869–870; REAL PROPERTY AND REGISTRATION vol 87 (2012) PARAS 94, 110, 172.
3   See GIFTS vol 52 (2014) PARA 253; PERSONAL PROPERTY vol 80 (2013) PARA 869.
4   It is the same where the gift over interferes with the devolution of the property on death: *Shaw v Ford* (1877) 7 ChD 669; *Re Ashton, Ballard v Ashton* [1920] 2 Ch 481 (gift over in the event of the donee dying mentally unfit).
5   *Gulliver v Vaux* (1746) 8 De GM & G 167n; *Lightburne v Gill* (1764) 3 Bro Parl Cas 250, HL; *Ross v Ross* (1819) 1 Jac & W 154; *Bourn v Gibbs* (1831) 1 Russ & M 614; *Re Yalden* (1851) 1 De GM & G 53; *Holmes v Godson* (1856) 8 De GM & G 152; *Bowes v Goslett* (1857) 6 WR 8; *Henderson v Cross* (1861) 29 Beav 216; *Re Dixon, Dixon v Charlesworth* [1903] 2 Ch 458. Cf *Doe d Stevenson v Glover* (1845) 1 CB 448 (doubted in *Holmes v Godson* above); *Re O'Hare, Madden v M'Givern* [1918] 1 IR 160.
6   *Watkins v Williams, Haverd v Church* (1851) 3 Mac & G 622; *Perry v Merritt* (1874) LR 18 Eq 152; *Re Jones, Richards v Jones* [1898] 1 Ch 438 at 441; *Lloyd v Tweedy* [1898] 1 IR 5. If the donee predeceases the testator, the doctrine of repugnancy does not apply, and the gift over takes effect: *Re Dunstan, Dunstan v Dunstan* [1918] 2 Ch 304.

7   An interest in terms absolute may be reduced by the context to a life interest (see PARA 369), even
where the gift over is of property undisposed of (see PARA 382).

382. Clear absolute gift in the first instance. Where there is a clear absolute gift
followed by words purporting to confer a power of disposition[1] with a gift over
if the power is not exercised, the absolute gift takes effect, and the gift over is
inconsistent with it and is void[2].

Thus where personal estate is given to a named donee in terms which confer an
absolute estate, and then further interests are given merely after or on the
termination of that donee's interest, and not in defeasance of it, his absolute
interest is not reduced and the further interests fail[3]. An absolute interest is not cut
down by precatory words unless those words create an imperative obligation[4].

Where there is an absolute gift of property followed by a gift over of the
property after the death of the donee[5] or after his death without issue[6] or without
leaving children[7], or of that part of the property of which he has not disposed, the
absolute gift prevails and the ultimate gift is repugnant and void[8]. It may, however,
appear sufficiently clearly on the construction of the will as a whole that a gift
which is in terms absolute is in fact intended as a gift of a life interest only[9], and
this construction is not prevented merely by the fact that the gift over is of
'whatever remains' or in similar terms[10]. Where a will conferring an absolute
interest is varied by codicil, an intention may appear that the donee is to take a life
interest or a life interest with a power of disposition[11]. If there is a doubt as to
what interest the donee takes, other provisions inconsistent with an absolute gift,
such as a restriction on alienation[12], or a gift over on the donee disposing[13], or
failing to dispose[14], of the property, may show that he is to take a life interest only.

If a testator[15] devises or bequeaths property to his spouse or civil partner in
terms which in themselves would give an absolute interest to the spouse or civil
partner[16], but by the same instrument purports to give his issue an interest in the
same property, the gift to the spouse or civil partner is presumed to be absolute,
notwithstanding the purported gift to the issue, except where a contrary intention
is shown[17].

1   *Comber v Graham* (1830) 1 Russ & M 450; *Brook v Brook* (1856) 3 Sm & G 280; *Howorth v
Dewell* (1860) 29 Beav 18; *McKenna v McCarten* [1915] 1 IR 282. 'To be at her own disposal in
any way she may think best for the benefit of herself and family' is an absolute gift: *Lambe v Eames*
(1871) 6 Ch App 597. See also *Re Hutchinson and Tenant* (1878) 8 ChD 540. A devise to the
testator's wife, her heirs and assigns with the intention that she might enjoy the same during her
life, and by her will dispose of the same as she thought proper, gave her a fee simple estate: *Doe
d Herbert v Thomas* (1835) 3 Ad & El 123. An absolute gift is not reduced by the expression of
a wish as to how the donee is to dispose of the property (*Re Humphrey's Estate* [1916] 1 IR 21),
nor is it necessarily reduced by a direction for settlement (*Re Bannister, Heys-Jones v Bannister*
(1921) 90 LJ Ch 415).
2   *Maskelyn v Maskelyn* (1775) Amb 750; *Hales v Margerum* (1796) 3 Ves 299; *Re
Mortlock's Trusts* (1857) 3 K & J 456 at 457; *Doe d Herbert v Thomas* (1835) 3 Ad & El 123.
See also PARA 369. A gift over in default of disposition by an absolute owner is void: see GIFTS
vol 52 (2014) PARA 253; PERSONAL PROPERTY vol 80 (2013) PARA 869.
3   *Hoare v Byng* (1844) 10 Cl & Fin 508, HL (to B 'and afterwards' to others); *Re Percy, Percy v
Percy* (1883) 24 ChD 616 ('afterwards') (followed in *Hyndman v Hyndman* [1895] 1 IR 179 ('at
their death')); *Re Gouk, Allen v Allen* [1957] 1 All ER 469, [1957] 1 WLR 493 (residuary bequest
to A 'and thereafter' to her issue). It is otherwise where the interests are such that the interests other
than the last can be treated as successive life interests: *Earl of Lonsdale v Countess Berchtoldt*
(1854) Kay 646 ('remainder to B, remainder to C'). As to gifts with power of disposal see
PARA 378.
4   *Re Johnson, Public Trustee v Calvert* [1939] 2 All ER 458. As to precatory words generally see
TRUSTS AND POWERS vol 98 (2013) PARA 66.
5   *Thornhill v Hall* (1834) 2 Cl & Fin 22, HL; *Crozier v Crozier* (1873) LR 15 Eq 282. Cf *Abbott
v Middleton, Ricketts v Carpenter* (1858) 7 HL Cas 68 (gift over on death of third person); *Waters
v Waters* (1857) 3 Jur NS 654.

6 *Randfield v Randfield* (1860) 8 HL Cas 225; *Ley v Ley* (1841) 2 Man & G 780; *Re Mitchell, Mitchell v Mitchell* (1913) 108 LT 180. See also *Fetherston v Fetherston* (1835) 3 Cl & Fin 67, HL.

7 *Home v Pillans* (1833) 2 My & K 15; approved in *Abbott v Middleton, Ricketts v Carpenter* (1858) 7 HL Cas 68.

8 See the cases cited in PARA 381 note 6.

9 See PARA 369.

10 *Constable v Bull* (1849) 3 De G & Sm 411 (on further consideration (1852) 22 LJ Ch 182); *Re Thomson's Estate, Herring v Barrow* (1880) 14 ChD 263, CA; *Re Sheldon and Kemble* (1885) 53 LT 527; *Re Last* [1958] P 137, [1958] 1 All ER 316. See also *Upwell v Halsey* (1720) 1 P Wms 651; *Re Brooks' Will* (1865) 2 Drew & Sm 362; *Re Holden, Holden v Smith* (1888) 57 LJ Ch 648; *Roberts v Thorp* (1911) 56 Sol Jo 13 (no absolute gift in terms); *Re Dixon, Dixon v Dixon* (1912) 56 Sol Jo 445; *Re Wilson, Wilson v Wilson* (1916) 142 LT Jo 41; *Re Cammell, Public Trustee v A-G* (1925) 69 Sol Jo 345. Cf *Re Minchell's Will Trusts* [1964] 2 All ER 47 (where a gift 'for her lifetime, and after her death if anything should be left over . . .' was held to be an absolute gift).

11 *Re Adam's Trusts* (1865) 13 LT 347; *Bibbens v Potter* (1879) 10 ChD 733; *Re Pounder, Williams v Pounder* (1886) 56 LJ Ch 113 (power of disposition inter vivos); *Re Sanford, Sanford v Sanford* [1901] 1 Ch 939 (general power). In *Borton v Borton* (1849) 16 Sim 552, an absolute gift was reduced by a later clause in the will to a life estate, with a power of disposition by will.

12 *Muschamp v Bluett* (1617) J Bridg 132; *Proctor v Upton* (1739) 5 De GM & G 199n; *Mortimer v Hartley* (1851) 6 Exch 47; *Re Banks' Trusts, ex p Hovill* (1855) 2 K & J 387; *Magee v Martin* [1902] 1 IR 367, Ir CA. However, the fact that the testator conceived that he could make the property perpetually inalienable does not alter the force of his words in describing the donees and their interests: *Britton v Twining* (1817) 3 Mer 176 at 183.

13 *Crumpe v Crumpe* [1900] AC 127, HL.

14 *Re Stringer's Estate, Shaw v Jones-Ford* (1877) 6 ChD 1, CA (where, although there was first an absolute gift, it was held that, on the whole will, the donee took an estate for life only, with a power of appointment by deed or will, and, since this power had not been exercised, the limitations over took effect). See also *Comiskey v Bowring-Hanbury* [1905] AC 84, HL (where an absolute gift to the testator's wife was held to be subject to an executory gift over at her death to nieces so far as she should not dispose of the estate by will in their favour); *Shearer v Hogg* (1912) 46 SCR 492, Can SC.

15 In relation to a spouse this applies to a testator who dies on or after 1 January 1983 (ie the date on which the Administration of Justice Act 1982 s 22 came into force): see s 76(11). Nothing in s 22 affects the will of a testator who died before 1 January 1983: s 73(6)(c). In relation to a civil partner this applies to a testator who dies as from 5 December 2005 (ie the date on which the relevant provision of the Civil Partnership Act 2004 came into force): Civil Partnership Act 2004 (Commencement No 2) Order 2005, SI 2005/3175.

16 When deciding whether or not the gift is in terms which in themselves would give an absolute interest, it is permissible to look at the words in the context of the will as a whole: *Re Harrison, Harrison v Gibson* [2005] EWHC 2957 (Ch),[2006] 1 All ER 858, [2006] 1 WLR 1212.

17 Administration of Justice Act 1982 s 22; and the Civil Partnership Act 2004 s 71, Sch 4 para 5. As to reduction or extension of interest see PARA 369.

D.   LIFE INTEREST ENLARGED TO ABSOLUTE INTEREST

383.   Clear gift for life in the first instance. Where a gift is made to a person expressly for life, and after his death to be at his disposal, he does not in general take a greater beneficial interest himself than a life interest[1], and even the addition of a right of absolute disposal during his life may not enlarge his interest to an absolute interest[2]. If, however, the words of disposition can be referred to property rather than merely to power[3], they may have the effect of enlarging the interest to an absolute interest[4].

A bequest to a donee for his absolute enjoyment during his life, and to be disposed of as he thinks fit after his death, is equivalent to a gift for life with general power of appointment by deed or will, and, on the power being exercised in his own favour[5], the donee is entitled to the bequest absolutely[6]. If there is no right of disposition on death, the donee has a general power of appointment inter vivos[7], and the unappointed part passes under a gift over[8].

1   *Nowlan v Walsh, Nowlan v Wilde* (1851) 4 De G & Sm 584 at 585 per Knight Bruce V-C. See also *Anon* (1578) 3 Leon 71 pl 108. Cf *Re Minchell's Will Trusts* [1964] 2 All ER 47 (cited in PARA 382 note 10).

2   *Bradly v Westcott* (1807) 13 Ves 445 (where the distinction between property and power was discussed; the gift was to the donee for life, to be at his full, free and absolute disposal during his life); *Reith v Seymour* (1828) 4 Russ 263 (although the power of disposal was 'either by will or otherwise'); *Re Burkitt, Handcock v Studdert* [1915] 1 IR 205 (life interest, and 'at her death to be disposed of as she so wishes'). In these cases the donee took an interest for life only, with power of disposition. See also *Scott v Josselyn* (1859) 26 Beav 174 (where the donee for life had power to dispose of the capital during her life and to appoint by will); *Pennock v Pennock* (1871) LR 13 Eq 144 (where the donee for life had power to apply the capital for his own benefit). In each case there was a life estate only, with power of disposition. See also *Re Thomson's Estate, Herring v Barrow* (1880) 14 ChD 263, CA. In *Henderson v Cross* (1861) 29 Beav 216, a gift of residue with power for the donee to spend principal and interest, or any part of it, during his life was an absolute gift, and a gift over of what he did not spend was repugnant and void. See also PARA 381.

3   See PARA 378.

4   *Nowlan v Walsh, Nowlan v Wilde* (1851) 4 De G & Sm 584 at 586. See also *Hoy v Master* (1834) 6 Sim 568; *Reid v Carleton* [1905] 1 IR 147 (where the principle was stated by Barton J). This view has been adopted in cases where the life interest has been given for the purpose of introducing other limitations, such as to children, and the power of disposition is to take effect on the failure of these limitations: *Goodtitle d Pearson v Otway* (1753) 2 Wils 6; *Re Maxwell's Will* (1857) 24 Beav 246 at 251.

5   See *Re Stringer's Estate, Shaw v Jones-Ford* (1877) 6 ChD 1, CA.

6   *Re David's Trusts* (1859) John 495 at 500 (where the fund was in court, and a petition for payment out was equivalent to an appointment). See also *Harvey v Harvey* (1842) 5 Beav 134 (full and entire enjoyment of a leasehold held for life to the cestui que vie).

7   *Re Ryder, Burton v Kearsley* [1914] 1 Ch 865, CA (following *Re Richards, Uglow v Richards* [1902] 1 Ch 76; and not adopting the dictum of James LJ in *Re Thomson's Estate, Herring v Barrow* (1880) 14 ChD 263, CA, that the donee had only a right to enjoyment in specie). See also *Bradley v Westcott* (1807) 13 Ves 445.

8   *Re Thomson's Estate, Herring v Barrow* (1880) 14 ChD 263, CA. See also *Pennock v Pennock* (1871) LR 13 Eq 144; *Re Rowland, Jones v Rowland* (1902) 86 LT 78 (as to the £400 see PARA 375 note 18); *Rosenburg v Scraggs* (1900) 19 NZLR 196; *Yates v Yates* (1905) 25 NZLR 263.

(iii) Estates Tail

384. Estates tail before 1926. Before 1 January 1926[1] an estate tail could exist in real estate only; it could be created by will by the same words which were effective for this purpose in a deed, namely by the words heirs 'of the body' or other words expressly or impliedly denoting heirs issuing from the body of the donee, or by the expression 'in tail' which was allowed as an alternative by statute[2]. In a will, however, greater latitude was allowed than in a deed, and an estate tail might also be created by words, such as 'sons' or 'issue', indicating descent from the body of the donee[3]. Accordingly, a devise by the owner in fee simple to the donee and his 'heirs male', or to him and his 'heirs female'[4], or to him and his 'heirs lawfully begotten'[5], formerly created an estate in fee tail special (male or female), or general, respectively[6]; and many words descriptive of descendants were capable in a will of being words of limitation. Thus 'first and every other son' or 'children' might be taken as words of limitation if it was necessary to give them that construction in order to give effect to the testator's intention[7], although ordinarily speaking they were words of purchase[8]; and similarly in the case of 'son', 'eldest son'[9], 'eldest male issue'[10] or 'family'[11]. 'Issue'[12], 'descendants'[13] and 'posterity'[14] were more easily susceptible of such a meaning. If such words included not only persons who were heirs by lineal descent but also persons who could only be collateral heirs, the estate was a fee simple; but if they comprised only persons who were heirs by lineal descent, the estate taken was an estate tail[15], the stock of descent being chosen so as to include all the members of the family intended to take[16].

1   For the rule where the testator's death occurs after 31 December 1925 see PARA 387.

2   See REAL PROPERTY AND REGISTRATION vol 87 (2012) PARAS 114–115. As to the rule in *Mandeville's Case* (1328) Co Litt 26b (limitation to the heirs of the body of a deceased person created an estate tail) see REAL PROPERTY AND REGISTRATION vol 87 (2012) PARA 115. That rule did not apply if the limitation was to heirs general, not special: *Moore v Simkin* (1885) 31 ChD 95.

3   See the text and notes 4–16; and PARA 117. Initial words might be only introductory to the effective limitations which followed, as in *Re Lord Lawrence, Lawrence v Lawrence* [1915] 1 Ch 129, CA, and *Re Elton, Elton v Elton* [1917] 2 Ch 413 (where the initial words of the devise were in each case suggestions of an estate tail, but were held to be merely introductory to later words which conferred life estates, and, therefore, did not govern those later words). As to the circumstances in which an estate tail might be implied see PARA 473.

4   Co Litt 27a; *Anon* (1535) YB 27 Hen 8 fo 27 pl 11; *Baker v Wall* (1697) 1 Ld Raym 185. See also *Blaxton v Stone* (1687) 3 Mod Rep 123; *Lord Ossulston's Case* (1708) 3 Salk 336; *Doe d Earl of Lindsey v Colyear* (1809) 11 East 548; *Doe d Tremewen v Permewen* (1840) 11 Ad & El 431 at 436 (to A and his heir male living to attain 21); *Doe d Angell v Angell* (1846) 9 QB 328; *Good v Good* (1857) 7 E & B 295 at 300 per Lord Campbell CJ. See also *Crumpe v Crumpe* [1900] AC 127, HL (where an intention to create an estate tail was assumed); *Silcocks v Silcocks* [1916] 2 Ch 161. Cf *Re Howarth, Macqueen v Kirby* (1916) 60 Sol Jo 307 (where, under a direction for settlement to A for life and his 'heirs male in tail in the usual way', A took only an estate for life). See also *Tufnell v Borrell* (1875) LR 20 Eq 194 (where a devise to all 'my grandchildren, their heirs male and the heirs male of the survivors and survivor of them' created joint tenancies in the grandchildren for lives with inheritances in tail and cross-remainders in tail).

5   Co Litt 20b; *Turke v Frencham* (1559) 2 Dyer 171a; *Pierson v Vickers* (1804) 5 East 548; *Nanfan v Legh* (1816) 7 Taunt 85; *Good v Good* (1857) 7 E & B 295 at 300 per Lord Campbell CJ. See also *Beresford's Case* (1607) 7 Co Rep 41a. In a devise to A and his 'lawful heirs', prima facie the word 'lawful' did not restrict the sense of the words: *Mathews v Gardiner* (1853) 17 Beav 254 at 257. See also *Simpson v Ashworth* (1843) 6 Beav 412 at 416.

6   See the cases cited in notes 4–5. The addition of 'for ever' did not enlarge the estate tail to an estate in fee simple: *Vernon v Wright* (1858) 7 HL Cas 35. In a gift to a child and his heirs, 'male taking before female', these words only indicated the course of descent, and the child had an estate in fee simple: *Finucane v Daly* [1919] 1 IR 284.

7   For the rule in *Wild's Case* (1599) 6 Co Rep 16b, where there was a devise of real estate to a person, who had no child, 'and his children' see PARA 389. As to the rule in *Shelley's Case* (1581) 1 Co Rep 93b (abolished by statute in relation to wills taking effect after 31 December 1925) see *Van Grutten v Foxwell, Foxwell v Van Grutten* [1897] AC 658, HL; and REAL PROPERTY AND REGISTRATION vol 87 (2012) PARA 167. In *Re Hammond, Parry v Hammond* [1924] 2 Ch 276, *Bowen v Lewis* (1884) 9 App Cas 890 (where Lord Cairns said at 905 that it was clear that, under a gift to children with words of division or inheritance, they took as purchasers), *Coles v Witt* (1856) 2 Jur NS 1226, and *Voller v Carter* (1854) 4 E & B 173, estates tail were created by the particular devises contained in the wills under consideration, those in the last two cases cited being prior to the Wills Act 1837. The gift might be explained by a subsequent gift over on default of issue generally (*Wight v Leigh* (1809) 15 Ves 564; *Herbert v Blunden* (1837) 1 Dr & Wal 78; *Re Childe* [1883] WN 48, explained in *Re Pennefather, Savile v Savile* [1896] 1 IR 249 at 262), or even by a gift over on default of some particular kind of issue, or of issue restricted in some manner (*Foord v Foord* (1730) 3 Bro Parl Cas 124 (without sons); *Wyld v Lewis* (1738) 1 Atk 432 at 434; *Robinson v Hicks* (1758) 3 Bro Parl Cas 180 (without such issue); *Doe d Jones v Davies* (1832) 4 B & Ad 43; *Lewis v Puxley* (1847) 16 M & W 733). There was no rule of construction governing when such words were words of limitation (*East v Twyford* (1851) 9 Hare 713 at 730 per Turner V-C; affd (1853) 4 HL Cas 517), and in all these cases the testator's intention was to be gathered from the whole will and governed the meaning and effect of the gift (*Mandeville v Carrick* (1795) 3 Ridg Parl Rep 352 at 365).

8   *Doe d Phipps v Lord Mulgrave* (1793) 5 Term Rep 320 at 323 per Lord Kenyon CJ; adopted in *Earl Tyrone v Marquis of Waterford* (1860) 1 De GF & J 613 at 624 per Lord Campbell CJ. See also *Doe d Burrin v Charlton* (1840) 1 Man & G 429; *Malcolm v Malcolm* (1856) 21 Beav 225; *Bennett v Bennett* (1864) 2 Drew & Sm 266; *Re Bishop and Richardson's Contract* [1899] 1 IR 71.

9   *Bifield's Case* (1600), cited in 1 Vent 231 per Lord Hale; *Sonday's Case* (1611) 9 Co Rep 127b; *Robinson v Robinson* (1756) 1 Burr 38 (affd sub nom *Robinson v Hicks* (1758) 3 Bro Parl Cas 180); *Lewis v Puxley* (1847) 16 M & W 733. See also *Mellish v Mellish* (1824) 2 B & C 520

(property 'to go to daughter C as follows; if she had a son, to that son'; C took estate in tail male); *Forsbrook v Forsbrook* (1867) 3 Ch App 93. As to gifts over on death without 'children' see PARA 461.

10 *Re Finlay's Estate* [1913] 1 IR 143 (distinguishing the cases cited in PARA 334 note 5). Cf *Re Hobbs, Hobbs v Hobbs* [1917] 1 Ch 569, CA.

11 *Lucas v Goldsmid* (1861) 29 Beav 657; *W Gardiner & Co Ltd v Dessaix* [1915] AC 1096, PC (where, under 'family', children took absolute interests; and see *Wright v Atkyns* (1814) Coop G 111 at 122–123); *Re Taylor, Shaw v Shaw* [1914] 1 IR 111 (devise of leaseholds to A for life and at her death to descend to her next of kin; life interest only in A); *Gray v Gray* [1915] 1 IR 261 (where a leasehold farm went under 'aires' to the next of kin leaving children or descendants).

12 *Harvey v Towell* (1847) 7 Hare 231 (personal estate); *Re Wynch's Trusts, ex p Wynch* (1854) 5 De GM & G 188 at 211, 225. See also PARA 334.

13 *Bird v Webster* (1853) 1 Drew 338 at 340; *Re Sleeman, Cragoe v Goodman* [1929] WN 16 (devise to daughter and her descendants; estate tail).

14 *A-G v Bamfield* (1703) Freem Ch 268; *Young v Davies* (1863) 2 Drew & Sm 167 at 172 (to 'my surviving daughters and their lawful offspring'). Cf *Shannon v Good* (1884) 15 LR Ir 284 at 298, Ir CA. See also REAL PROPERTY AND REGISTRATION vol 87 (2012) PARA 167.

15 Co Litt 9b.

16 *Doe d Gallini v Gallini* (1833) 5 B & Ad 621 at 642; affd (1835) 3 Ad & El 340 at 353, Ex Ch (approved in *Forsbrook v Forsbrook* (1867) 3 Ch App 93 at 98).

385. Quasi-inheritable gifts of personal estate.

Before 1 January 1926[1] a disposition by will of personal estate by words which showed an intention to give an inheritable estate in it to a donee gave him an absolute interest[2]. Thus a donee took an absolute interest under a bequest of personal estate to him and 'his heirs'[3], or to him and the 'heirs of his body'[4], or to him and the 'heirs male of his body'[5], or by virtue of other expressions showing an intention that his issue throughout the whole of their line should take after him by descent[6]. The intention might be inferred by implication from a gift over on failure of his heirs of the body or failure of his issue generally[7].

This rule of construction was applied even in cases where the donee himself was expressly given only a life estate[8] and the inheritable interest arose by virtue of, or by analogy to, the application of the rule in Shelley's Case[9], in spite of the fact that the rule in Shelley's Case was not strictly applicable to personal estate[10].

1 As to estates tail since 31 December 1925 see PARA 387.

2 *Re Hope's Will Trust* [1929] 2 Ch 136 at 141. The rule was often stated in the form 'words which create an estate tail in realty will give an absolute interest in personalty': see *Tothill v Pitt* (1766) 1 Madd 488 at 509 per Sewell MR; *Elton v Eason* (1812) 19 Ves 73 at 78 per Grant MR; *Heron v Stokes* (1842) 2 Dr & War 89 at 106; *Audsley v Horn* (1859) 1 De GF & J 226 at 236; *Williams v Lewis* (1859) 6 HL Cas 1013 at 1020 per Lord Cottenham LC; *Re Lowman, Devenish v Pester* [1895] 2 Ch 348 at 361, CA. The rule was not to be applied too rigidly in every case, for it might contradict the rule in *Forth v Chapman* (1720) 1 P Wms 663 (see PARA 386 text and note 5): *Re Jeaffreson's Trusts* (1866) LR 2 Eq 276 at 280.

3 *Anstruther v Chalmer* (1826) 2 Sim 1; *Re Banks' Trusts, ex p Hovill* (1855) 2 K & J 387. See also *Bigge v Bensley* (1783) 1 Bro CC 187. In these cases there was a preliminary question whether, regard being had to the whole will and considering that the property was personal and not real estate, the words were used in their usual sense as meaning persons to take in succession: *Re Jeaffreson's Trusts* (1866) LR 2 Eq 276 at 280 per Wood V-C. On a consideration of the whole will it might appear that the words 'heirs of the body', and the like, described particular persons: see eg *Dakin v Nicholson* (1837) 6 LJ Ch 329; and PARA 340. The question in the first place, therefore, was not whether the testator intended the donee to have an absolute interest or not (cf *Garth v Baldwin* (1755) 2 Ves Sen 646 at 661 per Lord Hardwicke LC ('it is a limitation of personal estate to one for life and the heirs of his body; which vests absolutely, whether so intended by the testator or not')), but whether the words 'heirs' etc were used in a sense different from their usual sense.

4 *Whitmore v Weld* (1685) 1 Vern 326 at 347; *Garth v Baldwin* (1755) 2 Ves Sen 646; *Crooke v De Vandes* (1803) 9 Ves 197; *Crawford v Trotter* (1819) 4 Madd 361; *Widdison v Hodgkin* (1823) 2 LJOS Ch 9 ('heirs', meaning in the context 'heirs of the body'). See also *A-G v Hird* (1782) 1 Bro CC 170; *Wilkinson v South* (1798) 7 Term Rep 555 at 557.

5   *Leventhorpe v Ashbie* (1635) 1 Roll Abr 831 pl 1; Tudor, LC Real Prop (4th Edn) 382; *Seale v Seale* (1715) 1 P Wms 290. See also *Bennet v Lewknor* (1616) 1 Roll Rep 356 (to A and his heirs male). Cf *Doncaster v Doncaster* (1856) 3 K & J 26 (a gift in a settlement); and see SETTLEMENTS vol 91 (2012) PARA 839.

6   *Re Wynch's Trusts, ex p Wynch* (1854) 5 De GM & G 188 at 206; *Re Barker's Trusts* (1883) 48 LT 573. See, accordingly, *Earl Tyrone v Marquis of Waterford* (1860) 1 De GF & J 613 ('to my brother Lord J B, and to his children in succession'). See also *Britton v Twining* (1817) 3 Mer 176 (to A during his life, and 'after his decease to the heir male of his body, and so on in succession to the heir-at-law, male or female'); *Re Commercial Railway Act, ex p Harrison* (1838) 3 Y & C Ex 275; *Beaver v Nowell* (1845) 25 Beav 551; *Young v Davies* (1863) 2 Drew & Sm 167 ('to my surviving daughters and their lawful offspring'); *Atkinson v l'Estrange* (1885) 15 LR Ir 340 (to A for life and to her heirs after her). As to gifts to a person and his children see further PARAS 389–390.

7   *Chandless v Price* (1796) 3 Ves 99; *Campbell v Harding* (1831) 2 Russ & M 390 at 401–402 (affd sub nom *Candy v Campbell* (1834) 8 Bli NS 469 at 491, HL). See also *Dunk v Fenner* (1831) 2 Russ & M 557; *Simmons v Simmons* (1836) 8 Sim 22; *Re Wynch's Trusts, ex p Wynch* (1854) 5 De GM & G 188 at 208; *Webster v Parr* (1858) 26 Beav 236; *Re Andrew's Will* (1859), as reported in 29 LJ Ch 291 at 292 (where Romilly MR said that the rule was analogous to the cy-près doctrine (see PARAS 230, 391) applicable to similar gifts of realty); *Re Sallery* (1861) 11 I Ch R 236. In earlier cases the rule that the interest was to be construed as an absolute interest had been held not to apply where the words used would, as to freeholds, create an estate tail by implication only: *Atkinson v Hutchinson* (1734) 3 P Wms 258; *Doe v Lyde* (1787) 1 Term Rep 593 at 596. See also *Knight v Ellis* (1789) 2 Bro CC 570 at 578. Where the rule applied, a gift over after failure of issue was void, but, if the failure of issue was restricted to the time of the death of the first taker, the implication corresponding to an estate tail did not arise; the first taker, unless the limitation was to him for life only, took absolutely in the first instance, but subject to a valid executory gift over if he died without leaving issue: *Campbell v Harding* (1831) 2 Russ & M 390 at 401–402. As to the restricted construction of references to death without issue in wills after 31 December 1837 see PARAS 454, 458.

8   *Garth v Baldwin* (1755) 2 Ves Sen 646; *Earl of Chatham v Tothill* (1771) 7 Bro Parl Cas 453; *Britton v Twining* (1817) 3 Mer 176; *Atkinson v l'Estrange* (1885) 15 LR Ir 340; *Re Score, Tolman v Score* (1887) 57 LT 40. Cf *Theebridge v Kilburne* (1751) 2 Ves Sen 233; *Turner v Turner* (1783) 1 Bro CC 316.

9   In the following cases limitations of personal estate took effect as if the rule in *Shelley's Case* (1581) 1 Co Rep 93b (now abolished in relation to instruments coming into operation after 31 December 1925: see PARA 334 note 7) applied to them: *Richards v Lady Bergavenny* (1695) 2 Vern 324; *Stratton v Payne* (1726) 3 Bro Parl Cas 99; *Butterfield v Butterfield* (1748) 1 Ves Sen 133; *Glover v Strothoff* (1786) 2 Bro CC 33; *Robinson v Fitzherbert* (1786) 2 Bro CC 127; *Kinch v Ward* (1825) 2 Sim & St 409; *Earl of Verulam v Bathurst* (1843) 13 Sim 374; *Douglas v Congreve* (1838) 1 Beav 59; *Harvey v Towell* (1847) 7 Hare 231 at 234 (applying the argument of Fearne's Contingent Remainders (7th Edn) 190); *Ousby v Harvey* (1848) 17 LJ Ch 160; *Williams v Lewis* (1859) 6 HL Cas 1013; *Comfort v Brown* (1878) 10 ChD 146; *Re Score, Tolman v Score* (1887) 57 LT 40. In the following cases personalty was settled by reference to realty, to the limitations of which the rule in *Shelley's Case* (1581) 1 Co Rep 93b was applicable: *Brouncker v Bagot* (1816) 1 Mer 271; *Tate v Clarke* (1838) 1 Beav 100. See also the other cases cited in note 8.

10   Cf *Re McElligott, Grant v McElligott* [1944] Ch 216, [1944] 1 All ER 441; and see REAL PROPERTY AND REGISTRATION vol 87 (2012) PARA 81. The rule was not applied if the result would be to defeat entirely the testator's intention appearing from the whole will and capable, without violation of the rules of law, of being carried into effect: *Audsley v Horn* (1859) 1 De GF & J 226 at 236 per Lord Campbell LC; *Dodds v Dodds* (1860) 11 I Ch R 374. For example, 'heirs' might describe particular persons intended to take by purchase: *Sands v Dixwell* (1738), cited in 2 Ves Sen at 652, 661 (reported sub nom *Roberts v Dixwell* 1 Atk 607 (real estate)); *Hodgeson v Bussey* (1740) 2 Atk 89; *Wilson v Vansittart* (1770) Amb 562; *Britton v Twining* (1817) 3 Mer 176 at 182 per Grant MR; *Symers v Jobson* (1848) 16 Sim 267; *Bull v Comberbach* (1858) 25 Beav 540 at 543. If the gift was to the donee for his life and then to his issue, prima facie the donee took for life only, and the issue took on his death: *Knight v Ellis* (1789) 2 Bro CC 570, followed in *Re Wynch's Trusts, ex p Wynch* (1854) 5 De GM & G 188 at 209, 222; *Goldney v Crabb* (1854) 19 Beav 338; *Waldron v Boulter* (1856) 22 Beav 284; *Jackson v Calvert* (1860) 1 John & H 235; *Bannister v Lang* (1867) 17 LT 137; *Foster v Wybrants* (1874) IR 11 Eq 40; *Re Cullen's Estate* [1907] 1 IR 73. In such a gift of blended real and personal estate the donee might take an estate tail in the real estate, and a life interest in the personal estate: *Jackson v Calvert* (1860) 1 John & H 235; *Re Longworth, Longworth v Campbell* [1910] 1 IR 23.

386. Gifts by reference to limitations of real estate. Before 1 January 1926[1], where real and personal estate were blended together in one gift, or where the

personal estate was directed to be enjoyed with the real estate, and the limitations in each case were framed in the usual technical terms creating successive estates tail in respect of real estate, the personal estate went to the person having the first vested estate tail in the real estate[2], subject to being defeated by a donee under a prior estate tail coming into existence and taking a vested interest[3]. This was not a necessary result where, for example, in a will made before 1 January 1838, the estate tail as to the real estate was created by implication from a gift over on failure of issue[4], which as to the personal estate might be construed to mean a failure of issue at the death of the first taker[5].

1   As to estates tail after 31 December 1925 see PARA 387.
2   *Foley v Burnell* (1783) 1 Bro CC 274; *Vaughan v Burslem* (1790) 3 Bro CC 101; *Fordyce v Ford* (1795) 2 Ves 536; *Re Johnson's Trusts* (1866) LR 2 Eq 716. See also *Re Hobbs, Hobbs v Hobbs* [1917] 1 Ch 569, CA; *Re Loughhead, Hamilton v Loughhead* [1918] 1 IR 227; PERSONAL PROPERTY vol 80 (2013) PARAS 814–815; SETTLEMENTS vol 91 (2012) PARA 839.
3   *Re Lowman, Devenish v Pester* [1895] 2 Ch 348, CA.
4   As to the restricted statutory construction of references to death without issue in wills after 31 December 1837 see PARA 454 et seq; and as to the creation of an estate tail by implication where the restricted construction does not apply see PARA 473.
5   *Forth v Chapman* (1720) 1 P Wms 663; Tudor LC Real Prop (4th Edn) 371; *Atkinson v Hutchinson* (1734) 3 P Wms 258 at 260–261. The reason was that the implication in favour of the issue drawn from such a gift over could not be supposed to exist in the case of personal property, since they could not by any construction take under such an implied gift: *Forth v Chapman* above at 667 per Lord Parker LC; but see *Re Andrew's Will* (1859) 27 Beav 608. This explanation was not in fact required where the gift was of personalty alone: see *Re Wynch's Trusts, ex p Wynch* (1854) 5 De GM & G 188 at 208; and PARA 385.

387. Estates tail after 1925. Between 1 January 1926 and 31 December 1996 inclusive it was possible to create an entailed interest in any property, real or personal, but only by way of trust[1], and only by the like expressions as those by which before 1 January 1926 a similar estate could have been created by deed, not being an executory instrument[2]. Informal expressions occurring in a will coming into operation between 1 January 1926 and 31 December 1996 inclusive which formerly would have created an estate tail no longer had that effect, but operated in equity to create absolute, fee simple or other interests corresponding to the interests which would before 1 January 1926 have been created by similar expressions in regard to personal estate[3].

Although, in order to create an entailed interest by will, it was thus necessary to use the same expressions as were required for that purpose in a deed, it was not essential to use the words 'heirs of the body'; 'heirs'[4] alone was sufficient if on the construction of the will it meant 'heirs of the body'[5]. Thus while a devise to a person and his heirs usually gave a fee simple[6], the context may have shown that by heirs was meant 'heirs of the body'[7], so that an entailed interest only was created; and a devise over on the donee's death without heirs of his body[8] may have had the effect of reducing the fee simple to an entailed interest[9]. In such cases, as the gift in the will was, on its construction, to the heirs of the body, it seems that an entailed interest will still have been created.

Clauses reducing estates tail to life interests in the case of persons born in the testator's lifetime fall to be construed with some strictness[10].

Where a person purports by an instrument coming into operation on or after 1 January 1997 to grant to another person an entailed interest in real or personal property, the instrument is not effective to grant an entailed interest but operates instead as a declaration that the property is held in trust absolutely for the person to whom an entailed interest in the property was purportedly granted[11]. Entailed interests created before 1 January 1997 will continue until barred or the property is disposed of[12].

1 See REAL PROPERTY AND REGISTRATION vol 87 (2012) PARA 101; SETTLEMENTS vol 91 (2012) PARA 840.
2 See the Law of Property Act 1925 s 130(1) (repealed by the Trusts of Land and Appointment of Trustees Act 1996 s 25(2), Sch 4); and REAL PROPERTY AND REGISTRATION vol 87 (2012) PARA 114. An entailed interest cannot be created by an instrument coming into operation on or after 1 January 1997: see the text and note 11.
3 See the Law of Property Act 1925 s 130(2) (repealed by the Trusts of Land and Appointment of Trustees Act 1996 Sch 4); and PARAS 390–391. As to an estate tail conferred by implication see PARA 473.
4 'Heirs' might before 1 January 1926, and may before 1 January 1997 to a more restricted extent, be a word of limitation, ie a word defining the quantity of interest which a donee previously mentioned takes (*Harvey v Towell* (1847) 7 Hare 231 at 234), or the word may be a word of purchase, ie it may be descriptive of persons who are themselves to take as donees. As to the use of 'heir' now to confer an equitable interest by purchase, and as to the saving of certain enactments for the purpose of ascertaining the devolution of entailed interests and persons taking as heirs by purchase see PARA 339 note 1.
5 Cf PARA 384; and REAL PROPERTY AND REGISTRATION vol 87 (2012) PARA 115.
6 This might be assisted by the rule in *Shelley's Case* (1581) 1 Co Rep 93b (now abolished: see PARA 385): *Re Norrington, Norrington v Norrington* (1923) 40 TLR 96; *Re Hack, Beadman v Beadman* [1925] Ch 633. However, a word defining the interest the heir was to take gave him a separate interest and made him a new stock of descent: *Re Hussey and Green's Contract, Re Hussey, Hussey v Simper* [1921] 1 Ch 566.
7 Co Litt 21b; *Cowper v Scott* (1731) 3 P Wms 119 at 122 per Jekyll MR; *Roe d James v Avis* (1792) 4 Term Rep 605; *Doe d Jearrad v Bannister* (1840) 10 LJ Ex 33; *Biddulph v Lees* (1859) 28 LJQB 211 at 213, Ex Ch (clause showing that there is some ulterior estate to be taken under the will by way of remainder); *Re Thompson, ex p Thompson* (1864) 16 I Ch R 228, Ir CA ('always to go in the male line'); *O'Hanlon v Unthank* (1872) IR 7 Eq 68 ('heirs being issue').
8 *Wallop v Darby* (1612) Yelv 209; *Jenkins v Herries* (1819) 4 Madd 67; *Jenkins v Hughes* (1860) 8 HL Cas 571. See PARA 473; and REAL PROPERTY AND REGISTRATION vol 87 (2012) PARA 115. It seems that a gift over on failure of issue may have had the same effect where it could be construed as importing an indefinite failure of issue (see PARA 473); but as to the construction of references to failure of issue see PARA 454 et seq.
9 A devise over on default of heirs had the like effect of cutting down the fee simple to an estate tail, if the devisee over was the right heir of the testator, and the first devisee was the testator's child, as, unless the first devise was restricted to an estate tail, the devise over could not take effect (*Nottingham v Jennings* (1700) 1 P Wms 23, 1 Ld Raym 568, Willes 166n; Fearne's Contingent Remainders (10th Edn) 467); and, similarly, if the devisee over was capable of being a collateral heir of the first devisee (*Tyte v Willis* (1733) Cas temp Talb 1; *Pickering v Towers* (1758) Amb 363; *Morgan v Griffiths* (1775) 1 Cowp 234; *Doe d Bean v Halley* (1798) 8 Term Rep 5 at 10; *Doe d Hatch v Bluck* (1816) 6 Taunt 485; *Simpson v Ashworth* (1843) 6 Beav 412; *Hancock v Clavey* (1871) 25 LT 323; Fearne's Contingent Remainders (10th Edn) 466 (Butler note (i)); *Ernst v Zwicker* (1897) 27 SCR 594; *Re McDonald* (1903) 6 OLR 478), or the event on which the gift over was made was necessarily dependent on the existence of a collateral heir (see *Re Waugh, Waugh v Cripps* [1903] 1 Ch 744 at 747). In *Harris v Davis* (1844) 1 Coll 416 at 423, the rule was applied where some, but not all, of the devisees were capable of being collateral heirs. The rule was confined to these cases: see *A-G v Gill* (1726) 2 P Wms 369 (devise over to a charity); *Preston d Eagle v Funnell* (1739) Willes 164 (testator's nearest of kindred, who were not necessarily capable of inheriting from the donee, his son); *Tilburgh v Barbut* (1748) 1 Ves Sen 89 (devise over to first devisee's half-brother, who could not at that time inherit). In *Jenkins v Hughes* (1860) 8 HL Cas 571, the context showed that the 'heir' took an estate tail: see SETTLEMENTS vol 91 (2012) PARA 839. The appointment or acknowledgment of a person as the testator's heir, although he is not the real heir, may give him an inheritable estate: *Parker v Nickson* (1863) 1 De GJ & Sm 177 at 183. As to gifts of real estate to a person and his 'executors' etc see PARA 376 note 1; and as to the appointment of a residuary legatee see PARA 298.
10 *Re Caldwell's Will Trusts, Jenyns v Sackville West* [1971] 1 All ER 780, [1971] 1 WLR 181.
11 Trusts of Land and Appointment of Trustees Act 1996 s 2(6), Sch 1 para 5(1). See also REAL PROPERTY AND REGISTRATION vol 87 (2012) PARA 136.
12 Ie under the Law of Property Act 1925 s 176: see REAL PROPERTY AND REGISTRATION vol 87 (2012) PARA 136.

388. Accessory gift of chattels to go with realty. If a bequest of chattels is accessory to a devise of real estate, and the devise is rendered inoperative by the testator's voluntary act, for example by a voluntary deed settling the land to uses in his lifetime but after the date of his will, it is a question of construction of the bequest whether the chattels are to go with the land as settled by the deeds or whether the bequest stands; but the bequest is not necessarily revoked merely because the devise has been rendered inoperative[1]. If, however, revocation of the devise has been effected by codicil, an alteration of the trusts of the bequest is more likely to be inferred[2].

1   *Re Whitburn, Whitburn v Christie* [1923] 1 Ch 332 (applying *Darley v Langworthy* (1774) 3 Bro Parl Cas 359). Cf *Martineau v Briggs* (1875) 23 WR 889, HL (alteration of freehold devise by codicil but no corresponding alteration of bequest of leaseholds).
2   *Re Towry's Settled Estates, Dallas v Towry* (1889) 41 ChD 64; *Re Whitburn, Whitburn v Christie* [1923] 1 Ch 332 at 338.

(iv) Gifts to a Person and his Children or Issue

389. Devise to person and his children. Before 1 January 1926[1], in a gift to a donee 'and his children'[2], whether 'and his children' were construed as words of limitation, or as words of description of persons to take either concurrently with or in succession to the named donee[3], or in substitution for him[4], was determined by the rule in Wild's Case[5]. This rule, which is not applicable to wills coming into operation after 31 December 1925, was that, in an immediate devise of real estate to a person and his children, prima facie 'children', if the donee had no child at the date of the will[6], was taken to be a word of limitation and the named person had an estate tail[7]. The context might show, however, that the unborn children were to take as purchasers[8]. If, however, he had a child or children at the time of the devise, the will was prima facie construed as giving a joint estate to him and his children as purchasers[9]; even here, however, the context might show that 'children' was a word of limitation and that an estate tail was intended[10], or that the children took in succession to their parents and as purchasers[11]. It seems that, for the purposes of the rule, an only child en ventre sa mère was not regarded as in existence[12]. The rule applied only where the testator had not sufficiently indicated his intention[13], and the court always considered itself at liberty to disregard the rule in both its branches where an adherence to it would have defeated the testator's intention as collected from other passages of his will[14].

1   The effect of the rule in *Wild's Case* (1599) 6 Co Rep 16b was abrogated in relation to devises in wills coming into operation after 31 December 1925 by virtue of the Law of Property Act 1925 s 130(1), (2) (repealed). It is not possible to create entailed interests by instruments coming into operation on or after 1 January 1997: see PARA 387.
2   As to gifts to a donee and his issue see PARA 391.
3   *Lampley v Blower* (1746) 3 Atk 396 at 397 per Lord Hardwicke LC.
4   See PARA 321.
5   *Wild's Case* (1599) 6 Co Rep 16b at 17a.
6   *Seale v Barter* (1801) 2 Bos & P 485; *Clifford v Koe* (1880) 5 App Cas 447 at 453, 463, 469, 471, HL. The Wills Act 1837 did not affect the rule in this respect: *Grieve v Grieve* (1867) 36 LJ Ch 932 at 933.
7   *Wild's Case* (1599) 6 Co Rep 16b at 17a (as stated in *Byng v Byng* (1862) 10 HL Cas 171 at 178 per Lord Cranworth LC); *Sweetapple v Bindon* (1705) 2 Vern 536; *Cook v Cook* (1706) 2 Vern 545; *Wharton v Gresham* (1776) 2 Wm Bl 1083 (where 'to A and his sons in tail male' gave A an estate tail); *Campbell v Bouskell* (1859) 27 Beav 325; *Underhill v Roden* (1876) 2 ChD 494 at 499. Cf *Stevens v Lawton* (1588) Cro Eliz 121; *Trevor v Trevor* (1847) 1 HL Cas 239 (a case of executory trust where the issue took as purchasers). The rule in *Wild's Case* above was inapplicable unless the interests of the parent and children were both concurrent. Thus it did not apply to gifts to the parent for life and after his death to his children: *Chandler v Gibson* (1901)

2 OLR 442; *Grant v Fuller* (1902) 33 SCR 34, Can SC at 37; *Re Sharon and Stuart* (1906) 12 OLR 605 at 609–610. See also *Broadhurst v Morris* (1831) 2 B & Ad 1. As to the interest now created see PARA 391.

8　*Re Moyles' Estate* (1878) 1 LR Ir 155, Ir CA (words of limitation applying to children's interest). The addition of words of limitation did not affect the rule where they could be read as referring to the first donee himself and as describing his interest: *Wharton v Gresham* (1776) 2 Wm Bl 1083; *Cormack v Copous* (1853) 17 Beav 397 at 401. As to the application of the rule see also *Seale v Barter* (1801) 2 Bos & P 485; *Clifford v Koe* (1880) 5 App Cas 447 at 457–458, 469, HL. Where there was a devise to a named person and after his decease to his children, even though he had no children at the time of the devise, every child whom he had might take under the limitation by way of remainder: *Wild's Case* (1599) 6 Co Rep 16b; *Ginger d White v White* (1742) Willes 348 ('to the children of J successively . . . and to their heirs'); *Doe d Liversage v Vaughan* (1822) 5 B & Ald 464.

9　*Wild's Case* (1599) 6 Co Rep 16b; *Oates d Hatterley v Jackson* (1742) 2 Stra 1172.

10　*Wood v Baron* (1801) 1 East 259; *Webb v Byng* (1856) 2 K & J 669 at 673 (affd sub nom *Byng v Byng* (1862) 10 HL Cas 171 at 181–182) (inferences against joint estate drawn from name and arms clause and the fact that heirlooms would be enjoyed jointly if joint estate conferred); *Earl of Tyrone v Marquis of Waterford* (1860) 1 De GF & J 613 at 624 ('children in succession'); *Ward v Ward* [1921] 1 IR 117, Ir CA (devise to J 'with remainder to her and her children for ever'; 'children' was a word of limitation, and J took an estate tail general).

11　*Jeffery v Honywood* (1819) 4 Madd 398 (where words of limitation were added to the limitation to the issue); *Bowen v Scowcroft* (1837) 2 Y & C Ex 640 at 661. See also *Webb v Byng* (1856) 2 K & J 669.

12　*Roper v Roper* (1867) LR 3 CP 32; and see PARA 362.

13　*Re Jones, Lewis v Lewis* [1910] 1 Ch 167 at 175 per Joyce J; *Re Buckmaster's Estate* (1882) 47 LT 514.

14　*Byng v Byng* (1862) 10 HL Cas 171 at 178 per Lord Cranworth LC; *Clifford v Koe* (1880) 5 App Cas 447 at 453, HL, per Lord Selborne LC, and at 471 per Lord Watson. As to the exclusion of the rule in a gift of furniture with real estate see *Grieve v Grieve* (1867) LR 4 Eq 180 (doubted in *Clifford v Koe* at 461–462).

390.　Bequest to a person and his children. The rule in Wild's Case[1] had strictly no application to personal estate[2], and, if in a bequest to a named person and his children 'children' was used as a word of limitation, the named person took, and still takes, an absolute interest[3]. In general, the word is not one of limitation[4], and under such a bequest prima facie the parent and the children take concurrently[5], as joint tenants[6]. The context may, however, point to a different conclusion[7], and slight circumstances have been sufficient to enable the court[8] to come to the conclusion that a gift for life to the named person and after his death to his children was intended[9]. The interests are presumed to be successive where all the children of the donee, whether born before or after the testator's death, are intended to take[10], or where there is a gift over on failure of issue of the parent or other provision showing that the property is contemplated as still subsisting undivided at the parent's death[11], or otherwise inconsistent with the parent taking an interest in the capital together with the children[12].

1　See *Wild's Case* (1599) 6 Co Rep 16b at 17a; and PARA 389.

2　*Audsley v Horn* (1859) 1 De GF & J 226 at 236 per Lord Campbell LC (where, however, a gift over assisted the construction of the gift as creating successive interests); *Re Jones, Lewis v Lewis* [1910] 1 Ch 167. See also the opinions expressed in *Stokes v Heron* (1845) 12 Cl & Fin 161 at 183, 198, HL.

3　*Doe d Gigg v Bradley* (1812) 16 East 399 (where a later child existed at the date of the will); *Cape v Cape* (1837) 2 Y & C Ex 543.

4　*Buffar v Bradford* (1741) 2 Atk 220.

5　*Alcock v Ellen* (1692) Freem Ch 186; *Buffar v Bradford* (1741) 2 Atk 220; *Pyne v Franklin* (1832) 5 Sim 458; *De Witte v De Witte* (1840) 11 Sim 41; *Sutton v Torre* (1842) 6 Jur 234 (cf *Cator v Cator* (1851) 14 Beav 463 on the same will); *Beales v Crisford* (1843) 13 Sim 592 (B and 'his family' construed to mean 'children'); *Bustard v Saunders* (1843) 7 Beav 92; *Mason v Clarke* (1853) 17 Beav 126; *Newill v Newill* (1872) 7 Ch App 253. See also *Jubber v Jubber* (1839) 9 Sim 503; *Salmon v Tidmarsh* (1859) 5 Jur NS 1380 (where the children took at 21); *Re Sproule, Chambers v Chambers* (1915) 49 ILT 96; *Re Astbury, Astbury v Godson* [1926] WN 336. The class of children is ascertained according to the usual rules (see PARA 302 et seq), and, therefore, no child born after the death of the testator, in the case of an immediate gift, can be let in (*De Witte v De Witte* (1840) 11 Sim 41); but in the case of a postponed gift after-born children may be let in (*Cook v Cook* (1706) 2 Vern 545; *Read v Willis* (1844) 1 Coll 86; *Lenden v Blackmore* (1840) 10 Sim 626; but see *Scott v Scott* (1845) 15 Sim 47).

6   See the cases cited in note 5. The context showed that the donees took as tenants in common in *Eccard v Brooke* (1790) 2 Cox Eq Cas 213; *Lenden v Blackmore* (1840) 10 Sim 626; *Paine v Wagner* (1841) 12 Sim 184; *Cunningham v Murray* (1847) 1 De G & Sm 366 (on appeal on another point (1848) 17 LJ Ch 407); *Salmon v Tidmarsh* (1859) 5 Jur NS 1380.

7   *Caffary v Caffary* (1844) 8 Jur 329 (subsequent gift showing that parent took absolutely). The fact that the gift is to the testator's wife and his children does not exclude the ordinary rule that they take concurrently: *Newill v Newill* (1872) 7 Ch App 253 at 259. Cf *Re Seyton, Seyton v Satterthwaite* (1887) 34 ChD 511; *Re Davies' Policy Trusts* [1892] 1 Ch 90 (not following *Re Adam's Policy Trusts* (1883) 23 ChD 525). In a gift to a person, his wife and children, the rule applies, although formerly this was subject to the rule as to the effect of gifts to a person and his wife with other persons: *Gordon v Whieldon* (1848) 11 Beav 170; and see PARA 393. Formerly, when the gift was to a married woman for her separate use and her children, a succession of interests was indicated, for otherwise the separate use could not be applied to the whole fund: *French v French* (1840) 11 Sim 257; *Bain v Lescher* (1840) 11 Sim 397; *Froggatt v Wardell* (1850) 3 De G & Sm 685; *Jeffery v De Vitre* (1857) 24 Beav 296. Cf *Re Seyton, Seyton v Satterthwaite* (1887) 34 ChD 511 (statutory provision for the benefit of 'his wife for her separate use and of his children').

8   *Re Wilmot, Wilmot v Betterton* (1897) 76 LT 415 at 417 per Stirling J. See also *Crockett v Crockett* (1848) 2 Ph 553 at 555 per Lord Cottenham LC; *Newill v Newill* (1872) 7 Ch App 253 at 256; *Re Jones, Lewis v Lewis* [1910] 1 Ch 167 at 172 per Joyce J.

9   *Newman v Nightingale* (1787) 1 Cox Eq Cas 341 (to A or her children for ever); *Crawford v Trotter* (1819) 4 Madd 361; *Cator v Cator* (1851) 14 Beav 463 (addition to previous settled legacy). A direction that the fund is 'to be secure for their use' or similar direction has been considered to show an intention to settle (*Vaughan v Marquis of Headfort* (1840) 10 Sim 639; *French v French* (1840) 11 Sim 257 ('in trust as aforesaid'); *Combe v Hughes* (1872) LR 14 Eq 415; *Re Mills, Mills v Mills* (1902) 22 NZLR 425), although a gift to the named person as a trustee for himself and children, without more, is not sufficient (*Newill v Newill* (1872) 7 Ch App 253 at 258; *Young v Young* (1918) 52 ILT 40). A separate gift to two of the children affected the decision in *Re Owen's Trusts* (1871) LR 12 Eq 316. As to whether or in what cases a power of appointment among the children may be held to be created see *Ward v Grey* (1859) 26 Beav 485 at 494 (commented on in *Hart v Tribe* (1863) 32 Beav 279 at 280); *Bradshaw v Bradshaw* [1908] 1 IR 288.

10 *Morse v Morse* (1829) 2 Sim 485; *Froggatt v Wardell* (1850) 3 De G & Sm 685; *Jeffery v De Vitre* (1857) 24 Beav 296; *Audsley v Horn* (1858) 26 Beav 195 (affd (1859) 1 De GF & J 226); *Ward v Grey* (1859) 26 Beav 485 ('A and her children' spoken of as 'A and her family' in another codicil).

11 *Gawler v Cadby* (1821) Jac 346; *Dawson v Bourne* (1852) 16 Beav 29; *Audsley v Horn* (1858) 26 Beav 195 at 235 (gift over if 'they' (meaning the children) died without issue); *Re Jones, Lewis v Lewis* [1910] 1 Ch 167 at 173; *Conyngham v Tripp* [1925] 1 IR 27.

12 *Garden v Pulteney, Southcote v Earl of Bath* (1765) 2 Eden 323 (if there should be but one younger son, the whole to him); *Parsons v Coke* (1858) 4 Drew 296 (issue to take parents' share); *Newill v Newill* (1872) 7 Ch App 253 at 257–258 (direction that children should take shares in whole fund), approving *Armstrong v Armstrong* (1869) LR 7 Eq 518 at 522.

391. Devise to a person and his issue. In a devise of real property to a person 'and his issue', prima facie 'issue' is used as a word of limitation[1], but it may be a description of the persons to take[2]. Before 1 January 1926, a devise to a person and his issue was treated as equivalent to a devise to the donee and the heirs of his body, and he took an estate tail, as it was presumed that the testator intended the whole line of his issue to benefit[3].

    In such a gift 'issue' was certainly a word of limitation if there were no issue at the date of the will[4]. 'Issue' does not now, however, create an entail, and under such a gift the donee takes the fee simple[5]. Where, however, the context shows that the issue are to take under the gift as purchasers, then prima facie they take as joint tenants with the named person[6].

    Formerly a gift of a succession of interests in real estate to donees, some of whom were not allowed by law to take as purchasers, might be construed under the cy-près doctrine to be a gift of an estate tail in one of them, where that estate, if allowed to descend unbarred, would carry the property to the donees and no others[7]; and words referring to successive generations have been held to be descriptive of the descent of an estate tail and used as words of limitation[8]. This construction is, however, not now normally possible[9].

1　*Tate v Clarke* (1838) 1 Beav 100 at 105; *Slater v Dangerfield* (1846) 15 M & W 263 at 272.
2　See PARA 334.
3　*Roddy v Fitzgerald* (1858) 6 HL Cas 823 at 872 per Lord Cranworth LC. See also *Martin v Swannell* (1840) 2 Beav 249; *Re Coulden, Coulden v Coulden* [1908] 1 Ch 320 at 324 per Parker J; *Re Hammond, Parry v Hammond* [1924] 2 Ch 276 at 280 (where the rule stated in the text was applied to the specific devise). Cf REAL PROPERTY AND REGISTRATION vol 87 (2012) PARA 167. In a gift to A or his issue, 'or' might be changed into 'and', so that A took an estate tail (*Re Clerke, Clowes v Clerke* [1915] 2 Ch 301; *Re Hayden, Pask v Perry* [1931] 2 Ch 333), or, on the construction of the whole will, a fee simple estate (*W Gardiner & Co Ltd v Dessaix* [1915] AC 1096, PC). See also PARA 342.
4　In such a case the rule in *Wild's Case* (1599) 6 Co Rep 16b at 17a applied: *Campbell v Bouskell* (1859) 27 Beav 325; *Underhill v Roden* (1876) 2 ChD 494. See further PARA 389.
5　See the Law of Property Act 1925 s 130(1), (2) (repealed); and PARA 387. It is not possible to create entailed interests by instruments coming into operation on or after 1 January 1997: see PARA 387.
6　*Re Wilmot, Wilmot v Betterton* (1897) 76 LT 415 (where the second branch of the rule in *Wild's Case* (1599) 6 Co Rep 16b was applied, although there were no issue in existence). By force of the context the issue may take in succession to their ancestor: *Doe d Gilman v Elvey* (1803) 4 East 313 (to A and his issue as tenants in common if more than one), following *Doe d Davy v Burnsall* (1794) 6 Term Rep 30; *Trevor v Trevor* (1847) 1 HL Cas 239 (to A and her issue in tail male in strict settlement); *Re Lord Lawrence, Lawrence v Lawrence* [1915] 1 Ch 129, CA.
7　As to the cy-près doctrine in this connection see PARA 230; PERPETUITIES AND ACCUMULATIONS vol 80 (2013) PARA 4.
8　*Wollen v Andrewes* (1824) 2 Bing 126; *Fetherston v Fetherston* (1835) 3 Cl & Fin 67, HL ('heirs male, according to their seniority'); *Trash v Wood* (1839) 4 My & Cr 324 (to 'T's children and so on for ever'); *Snowball v Procter* (1843) 2 Y & C Ch Cas 478 (to children 'and their children after them respectively'); *Jenkins v Hughes* (1860) 8 HL Cas 571; *Forsbrook v Forsbrook* (1867) 3 Ch App 93; *Re Buckton, Buckton v Buckton* [1907] 2 Ch 406. See PARA 384.
9　An entailed interest could not be created by informal expressions: see the Law of Property Act 1925 s 130(1) (repealed); and PARA 387. It is not possible to create entailed interests by instruments coming into operation on or after 1 January 1997: see PARA 387. As to the possibility that the cy-près doctrine may in certain cases still apply see PARA 230 note 6.

392. Bequest to a person and his issue. In a gift of personalty to a person 'and his issue'[1], prima facie all take by purchase[2], and concurrently as joint tenants[3], but the context and the circumstances may show a contrary intention. Thus gifts of personal estate to a person and his issue have in several cases conferred an absolute interest on him[4], particularly where there was a gift over on failure of issue generally[5]; in such cases the context showed that the words were used as words of limitation, whether or not they were so used being a question of construction in each particular case[6]. The result would be the same now, as 'issue' does not create an entailed interest after 31 December 1925[7]. In other cases, under a gift to a person and his issue, the issue have taken alternatively (that is to say, only if their ancestor was not in existence at the time of distribution), either by way of substitution[8] or by way of original gift[9], or have taken in succession to their parent[10].

1　As to bequests to a person for his life and after his death to his issue see PARA 385 note 10.
2　*Re Longworth, Longworth v Campbell* [1910] 1 IR 23 at 35; *Re Taylor's Trusts, Taylor v Blake* [1912] 1 IR 1 at 9. The reason for the rule in relation to devises of realty (see PARA 391 text and note 3) does not apply to personalty: see *Re Hammond, Parry v Hammond* [1924] 2 Ch 276 at 280–281 per Tomlin J (decision on the second question, which concerned personalty not realty), approving the statement in *Re Coulden, Coulden v Coulden* [1908] 1 Ch 320 at 324 per Parker J.

3 *Re Wilmot, Wilmot v Betterton* (1897) 76 LT 415 at 417 (issue). In *Law v Thorp* (1858) 4 Jur NS 447, in the context the donees took as tenants in common with benefit of survivorship between them.

4 *Fereyes v Robertson* (1731) Bunb 301; *Howston v Ives* (1746) 2 Eden 216; *Donn v Penny* (1815) 1 Mer 20; *Lyon v Mitchell* (1816) 1 Madd 467; *Samuel v Samuel* (1845) 9 Jur 222; *Parkin v Knight* (1846) 15 Sim 83. See also *A-G v Bright* (1836) 2 Keen 57; *Tate v Clarke* (1838) 1 Beav 100; *Jordan v Lowe* (1843) 6 Beav 350 (commented on in *Re Wynch's Trusts, ex p Wynch* (1854) 5 De GM & G 188 at 209).

5 *Donn v Penny* (1815) 1 Mer 20; *Beaver v Nowell* (1858) 25 Beav 551; *Re Andrew's Will* (1859) 27 Beav 608.

6 *Re Coulden, Coulden v Coulden* [1908] 1 Ch 320 at 324 per Parker J. See also *Re Hammond, Parry v Hammond* [1924] 2 Ch 276.

7 See PARA 387.

8 *Butter v Ommaney* (1827) 4 Russ 70 (residue); *Pearson v Stephen* (1831) 5 Bli NS 203, HL; *Dick v Lacy* (1845) 8 Beav 214; *Re Stanhope's Trusts* (1859) 27 Beav 201.

9 *Re Coulden, Coulden v Coulden* [1908] 1 Ch 320 at 325.

10 *Parsons v Coke* (1858) 4 Drew 296.

(v) Concurrent Gifts

A.   JOINT TENANCY AND TENANCY IN COMMON

393. General rules where property is given to several persons concurrently. Where property is given to several persons concurrently, the questions whether these persons take as joint tenants or tenants in common[1], and, if as tenants in common, what shares they take[2], depend on the testator's intention to be ascertained from the words of his will as a whole[3], but prima facie a gift to several persons, without words of severance, is a gift to them as joint tenants[4]. Slight indications of an intention to divide the property may negative the idea of a joint tenancy[5], and in a case of ambiguity the court leans to the construction which creates a tenancy in common in preference to that which creates a joint tenancy[6]. If there is to be a sharing, prima facie the shares must be equal[7]. Where a gift comprises original and substitutional shares, a single set of words of severance can properly be applied not only to the original but also to the substituted shares[8].

1 As to joint tenancy and tenancy in common see PERSONAL PROPERTY vol 80 (2013) PARAS 828–830; REAL PROPERTY AND REGISTRATION vol 87 (2012) PARAS 192 et seq, 215 et seq. A tenancy in common or joint tenancy in land can exist in equity either behind a trust for sale or in a trust of land (without a duty to sell): see the Trusts of Land and Appointment of Trustees Act 1996 ss 1–5; and REAL PROPERTY AND REGISTRATION vol 87 (2012) PARAS 103 et seq, 198 et seq. As to gifts to corporations and others see CORPORATIONS vol 24 (2010) PARA 447 et seq.

2 A husband and wife, when taking with other persons, formerly took one share between them (*Re Jeffery, Nussey v Jeffery* [1914] 1 Ch 375), but under a disposition made or coming into operation after 31 December 1925 they are treated as two persons (Law of Property Act 1925 s 37). As to tenancy by entireties, and as to its abolition by s 39(6), Sch 1 Pt VI, see REAL PROPERTY AND REGISTRATION vol 87 (2012) PARAS 196–197. As to a devise to 'heirs' who are co-heiresses see PARA 540. See also *Re Baker, Pursey v Holloway* (1898) 79 LT 343.

3 For this general principle of construction see PARA 224.

4 *Lady Shore v Billingsly* (1687) 1 Vern 482; *Morley v Bird* (1798) 3 Ves 629 at 630; *Stuart v Bruce* (1798) 3 Ves 632; *Crooke v De Vandes* (1803) 9 Ves 197 at 204; *Ritchie's Trustees v M'Donald* 1915 SC 501; *Re Clarkson, Public Trustee v Clarkson* [1915] 2 Ch 216; *Re Brooke's Will Trusts, Jubber v Brooke* [1953] 1 All ER 668 at 674, [1953] 1 WLR 439 at 448; *Re Osoba, Osoba v Osoba* [1979] 2 All ER 393, [1979] 1 WLR 247. Thus under a gift of personalty to A and his children, prima facie they take as joint tenants: *Re Wilmot, Wilmot v Betterton* (1897) 76 LT 415 at 417. The gift may be either specific or residuary (*Morley v Bird* (1798) 3 Ves 628; *Crooke v De Vandes* (1803) 9 Ves 197 at 204; *Walmsley v Foxhall* (1863) 1 De GJ & Sm 605; *M'Donnell v Jebb* (1865) 16 I Ch R 359), and either direct or made through the medium of a trust (*Aston v Smallman* (1706) 2 Vern 556; *Bustard v Saunders* (1843) 7 Beav 92; *Re Clarkson, Public Trustee v Clarkson* [1915] 2 Ch 216 at 220). The addition of words directing 'payment' of the legacy to named

individuals does not mean they take as tenants in common: *Re Clarkson* above despite obiter to
the contrary in *Re Atkinson* [1892] 3 Ch 52 at 54.

5   *Robertson v Fraser* (1871) 6 Ch App 696 at 699 per Lord Hatherley LC (followed in *Re Woolley,
    Wormald v Woolley* [1903] 2 Ch 206 at 211); *Re North, North v Cusden* [1952] Ch 397, [1952]
    1 All ER 609. See also *Re Wilmot, Wilmot v Betterton* (1897) 76 LT 415 at 417. The mere fact
    that the interest is to be divided is not sufficient to make a tenancy in common of the capital:
    Crooke v De Vandes (1803) 9 Ves 197 at 206. A description of the donees as 'joint tenants',
    although a technical description, is not necessarily fatal to a tenancy in common: *Booth v Alington*
    (1857) 3 Jur NS 835. Where a trust is implied, in default of the exercise of a power, for the
    members of the class in whose favour the power might have been exercised, the implied trust,
    subject to any indication of the donor's intention to the contrary, is for distribution equally as
    tenants in common: see TRUSTS AND POWERS vol 98 (2013) PARA 28. As to the inconsistency
    between a power of advancement and a joint tenancy see *Bennett v Houldsworth* (1911) 104 LT
    304; and TRUSTS AND POWERS vol 98 (2013) PARA 510. For discussion of the effect of a power
    to apply income from an interest see *Re Gardner, Ellis v Ellis* [1924] 2 Ch 243, 93 LJ Ch 486.
6   *Jollife v East* (1789) 3 Bro CC 25; *Re Woolley, Wormald v Woolley* [1903] 2 Ch 206 at 211 per
    Joyce J; *Bennett v Houldsworth* [1911] WN 47; *Re Fisher, Robinson v Eardley* [1915] 1 Ch 302.
    Nevertheless, in a grant to two persons jointly and severally, 'severally' was rejected and they took
    as joint tenants: *Slingsby's Case* (1587) 5 Co Rep 18b at 19a.
7   *Robertson v Fraser* (1871) 6 Ch App 696 at 700; *Fisher v Anderson* (1880) 4 SCR 406 at 419.
8   *Crosthwaite v Dean* (1879) 40 LT 837; *Re Froy, Froy v Froy* [1938] Ch 566, [1938] 2 All ER 316.
    In *Re Sibley's Trusts* (1877) 5 ChD 494, there was a gift to 'all and every the children of F or their
    issue in equal shares per capita'; four of the six children were dead at the date of the will, and it
    was held that their issue took the shares of their deceased ancestors between themselves as tenants
    in common; *Penny v Clarke* (1860) 1 De GF & J 425, 29 LJ Ch 370; *Lanphier v Buck* (1865) 2
    Drew & Sm 484 at 498. Cf *Amies v Skillern* (1845) 14 Sim 428. See also *Bridge v Yates* (1842)
    12 Sim 645 (where the issue or children took as joint tenants, prior words of severance not
    extending to their shares); *Re Brook's Will Trusts, Jubber v Brooke* [1953] 1 All ER 668 at 674,
    [1953] 1 WLR 439 at 448 per Upjohn J.

394. Words creating a joint tenancy.

A limitation made to next of kin[1] (whether
described as such or referred to as 'relatives'[2]), or to issue[3], or to legal personal
representatives[4], or to next personal representatives[5], or to children described as
'families'[6], 'family'[7] or simply as 'children'[8], may constitute the donees joint
tenants. A gift may create a joint tenancy between parents and children[9].

1   *Baker v Gibson* (1849) 12 Beav 101.
2   *Eagles v Le Breton* (1873) LR 15 Eq 148.
3   *Hill v Nalder* (1852) 17 Jur 224; *Hobgen v Neale* (1870) LR 11 Eq 48.
4   *Walker v Marquis of Camden* (1848) 16 Sim 329.
5   *Stockdale v Nicholson* (1867) LR 4 Eq 359; *Booth v Vicars* (1844) 1 Coll 6; *Re Kilvert, Midland
    Bank Executor and Trustee Co Ltd v Kilvert* [1957] Ch 388 at 398, [1957] 2 All ER 196 at 203.
6   *Burt v Hellyar* (1872) LR 14 Eq 160.
7   *Wood v Wood* (1843) 3 Hare 65; *Gregory v Smith* (1852) 9 Hare 708.
8   *Oates d Hatterley v Jackson* (1742) 2 Stra 1172; *Binning v Binning* [1895] WN 116. See also
    Mence v Bagster (1850) 4 De G & Sm 162; *Kenworthy v Ward* (1853) 11 Hare 196; *Noble v Stow*
    (1859) 29 Beav 409.
9   *Mason v Clarke* (1853) 17 Beav 126; *Jury v Jury* (1882) 9 LR Ir 207. See also *Armstrong v
    Armstrong* (1869) LR 7 Eq 518. As to a gift to two persons for their joint lives with a contingent
    remainder over to the survivor in fee see *Vick v Edwards* (1735) 3 P Wms 372; *Re Harrison* (1796)
    3 Anst 836. See also *Barker v Gyles* (1727) 3 Bro Parl Cas 104; *Doe d Young v Sotheron* (1831)
    2 B & Ad 628; *Quarm v Quarm* [1892] 1 QB 184.

395. Words creating a tenancy in common.

A conveyance of property to two
persons in moieties creates a tenancy in common[1] between them, and a grant of
a moiety creates a tenancy in common between the grantor and the grantee[2]. If,
therefore, a will directs that property is to be divided[3], or to be equally divided[4],
or to be distributed in joint and equal proportions[5], or that the parties are to
participate[6], or if the gift is among persons equally[7], or share and share alike[8], or
in equal shares and proportions[9], or in moieties[10], or among[11] or between[12] the
donees, or is given to them respectively[13], or to each of them[14], a tenancy in
common is created[15]. Further, a reference to shares (for example the imposing of

an obligation on donees to make payments in equal shares) will convert what would otherwise be a joint tenancy into a tenancy in common[16]. As a matter of construction, expressions apparently indicating a joint tenancy may be controlled by other expressions conferring a tenancy in common[17]. Expressions indicating a tenancy in common may be modified by a subsequent clear expression of intention to create a joint tenancy[18].

In certain cases, to give effect to the whole will, the severance in interest is made to commence at a future time; thus joint estates for life and separate remainders may be created[19], for example by gifts of real estate to several persons, who cannot all marry, and the heirs of their bodies[20], or in other cases in a sufficient context[21].

There is no necessity, in a gift by will, for the application of the rule affecting conveyances operating at common law[22] that there can be no joint tenancy where the co-tenants come into existence at different times, or their interests vest at different times[23], although in both cases the joint tenant must take the same quantity of interest[24]. However, the fact that the vesting of a gift in a will must take place at different times otherwise than by the donees coming into being at different times has been treated as an indication of a tenancy in common[25].

In a gift to a number of persons and the 'survivors' of them or 'with benefit of survivorship', these words may be used as words of limitation to indicate that, even though the named persons take originally as tenants in common, on the death of any of them the survivors are to take the whole estate[26].

1   Tenancy in common of land no longer subsists at law, but can exist in equity either behind a trust for sale or in a trust of land (without a duty to sell): see the Trusts of Land and Appointment of Trustees Act 1996 ss 1–5; and REAL PROPERTY AND REGISTRATION vol 87 (2012) PARAS 103 et seq, 215 et seq. Accordingly, in relation to land, references to tenancy in common are now applicable only in relation to equitable interests: cf eg *Re North, North v Cusden* [1952] Ch 397, [1952] 1 All ER 609.
2   Co Litt 190b, 198b; 2 Bl Com (14th Edn) 193, 399.
3   *Peat v Chapman* (1750) 1 Ves Sen 542; *Ackerman v Burrows* (1814) 3 Ves & B 54.
4   *Phillips v Phillips* (1701) 1 P Wms 34; *Barker v Giles* (1725) 2 P Wms 280; *Jolliffe v East* (1789) 3 Bro CC 25; *Turner v Whittaker* (1856) 23 Beav 196; *Lucas v Goldsmid* (1861) 29 Beav 657; *Davis v Bennett* (1862) 4 De GF & J 327.
5   *Ettricke v Ettricke* (1767) Amb 656; *Gibbon v Warner* (1585) 14 Vin Abr 484 at 485.
6   *Robertson v Fraser* (1871) 6 Ch App 696.
7   *Lewen v Dodd* (1599) Cro Eliz 443; *Denn d Gaskin v Gaskin* (1777) 2 Cowp 657.
8   *Heathe v Heathe* (1741) 2 Atk 121; *Perry v Woods* (1796) 3 Ves 204.
9   *Payne v Webb* (1874) LR 19 Eq 26.
10 *Harrison v Foreman* (1800) 5 Ves 207.
11 *Richardson v Richardson* (1845) 14 Sim 526.
12 *Lashbrook v Cock* (1816) 2 Mer 70; *A-G v Fletcher* (1871) LR 13 Eq 128.
13 *Stephens v Hide* (1734) Cas *temp* Talb 27; *Haws v Haws* (1747) 1 Ves Sen 13; *Marryat v Townly* (1748) 1 Ves Sen 102; *Folkes v Western* (1804) 9 Ves 456; *Davis v Bennett* (1862) 4 De GF & J 327. See also *Vanderplank v King* (1842) 3 Hare 1; *Re Moore's Settlement Trusts* (1862) 31 LJ Ch 368; but see *Re Hodgson's Trust* (1854) 1 K & J 178; *Hobgen v Neale* (1870) LR 11 Eq 48.
14 *Hatton v Finch* (1841) 4 Beav 186.
15 See *Thorowgood v Collins* (1672) Cro Car 75; *Sheppard v Gibbons* (1742) 2 Atk 441; *Loveacres d Mudge v Blight* (1775) 1 Cowp 352. A gift to 'next of kin according to the Statute of Distribution' created a tenancy in common (*Fielden v Ashworth* (1875) LR 20 Eq 410; *Re Richards, Davies v Edwards* [1910] 2 Ch 74; and see *Horn v Coleman* (1853) 1 Sm & G 169; *Bullock v Downes* (1860) 9 HL Cas 1; *Re Ranking's Settlement Trusts* (1868) LR 6 Eq 601 (not following *Horn v Coleman* above and *Re Greenwood's Will* (1861) 8 Jur NS 907)); but it was otherwise if the reference to the statute was merely for the purpose of indicating the beneficiaries (*Withy v Mangles* (1843) 10 Cl & Fin 215, HL). See also *Elmsley v Young* (1835) 2 My & K 780; *Tiffin v Longman* (1852) 15 Beav 275; *Eagles v Le Breton* (1873) LR 15 Eq 148. Cf *Re Gray's Settlement, Akers v Sears* [1896] 2 Ch 802.

16 *Re North, North v Cusden* [1952] Ch 397, [1952] 1 All ER 609. See also *Kew v Rouse* (1685) 1 Vern 353; *Gant v Lawrence* (1811) Wight 395; *Alloway v Alloway* (1843) 4 Dr & War 380; *Ive v King* (1852) 16 Beav 46; *Jones v Jones* (1881) 44 LT 642; *Re Ward, Partridge v Hoare-Ward* [1920] 1 Ch 334 (advancement clause).

17 *Booth v Alington* (1857) 3 Jur NS 835; *Re Wilder's Trusts* (1859) 27 Beav 418; *Paterson v Rolland* (1860) 28 Beav 347; *Oakley v Wood* (1867) 16 LT 450; *Ryves v Ryves* (1871) LR 11 Eq 539. See, however, *Barker v Gyles* (1727) 3 Bro Parl Cas 104; *Jolliffe v East* (1789) 3 Bro CC 25; *Cookson v Bingham* (1853) 17 Beav 262 (affd 3 De GM & G 668); *Edwardes v Jones* (1864) 33 Beav 348; *Yarrow v Knightly* (1878) 8 ChD 736, CA; *Jury v Jury* (1882) 9 LR Ir 207. As to the effect of words of survivorship in a gift see *Lord Bindon v Earl of Suffolk* (1707) 1 P Wms 96; *Perry v Woods* (1796) 3 Ves 204; *Russell v Long* (1799) 4 Ves 551; *Ashford v Haines* (1851) 21 LJ Ch 496. Cf *Moore v Cleghorn* (1847) 10 Beav 423; *Haddelsey v Adams* (1856) 22 Beav 266.

18 *Hurd v Lenthall* (1649) Sty 211; *Stephens v Hide* (1734) Cas temp Talb 27; *Malcolm v Martin* (1790) 3 Bro CC 50; *Armstrong v Eldridge* (1791) 3 Bro CC 215; *Townley v Bolton* (1832) 1 My & K 148; *Ashley v Ashley* (1833) 6 Sim 358; *Pearce v Edmeades* (1838) 3 Y & C Ex 246; *M'Dermott v Wallace* (1842) 5 Beav 142; *Begley v Cook* (1856) 3 Drew 662; *Alt v Gregory* (1856) 8 De GM & G 221; *Cranswick v Pearson, Pearson v Cranswick* (1862) 31 Beav 624; *Daly v Aldworth* (1863) 15 I Ch R 69. Cf *Willes v Douglas* (1847) 10 Beav 47; *Arrow v Mellish* (1847) 1 De G & Sm 355; *Hawkins v Hamerton* (1848) 16 Sim 410; *Ewington v Fenn* (1852) 16 Jur 398; *Re Laverick's Estate* (1853) 18 Jur 304; *Abrey v Newman* (1853) 16 Beav 431; *Re Drakeley's Estate* (1854) 19 Beav 395; *Swan v Holmes* (1854) 19 Beav 471; *Sarel v Sarel* (1856) 23 Beav 87; *Turner v Whittaker* (1856) 23 Beav 196; *Lill v Lill* (1857) 23 Beav 446; *Brown v Jarvis* (1860) 2 De GF & J 168; *Archer v Legg* (1862) 10 WR 703; *Wills v Wills* (1875) LR 20 Eq 342; *Re Hutchinson's Trusts* (1882) 21 ChD 811.

19 Ie created in equity by way of trust, not as legal estates.

20 Littleton's Tenures s 283; *Huntley's Case* (1574) 3 Dyer 326a; *Cook v Cook* (1706) 2 Vern 545 at 546; *Barker v Gyles* (1727) 3 Bro Parl Cas 104; *Forrest v Whiteway* (1849) 3 Exch 367; *Edwards v Champion* (1853) 3 De GM & G 202 at 216; Shep Touch (8th Edn, 1826) p 442. The rule appears to have been recognised in the House of Lords: *Wilkinson v Spearman* (undated), cited in 2 Vern at 545 (limitation by deed); and see *Edwards v Champion* (1847) 1 De G & Sm 75 at 79 note (d). As to the use under the present law of 'heir' as a word of purchase in equitable limitations see PARA 339 note 1.

21 See *Doe d Littlewood v Green* (1838) 4 M & W 229; *Re Atkinson, Wilson v Atkinson* [1892] 3 Ch 52 (following *Re Tiverton Market Act, ex p Tanner* (1855) 20 Beav 374 and *Doe d Littlewood v Green*; and distinguishing *Gordon v Atkinson* (1847) 1 De G & Sm 478, where an initial tenancy in common was created). See REAL PROPERTY AND REGISTRATION vol 87 (2012) PARA 218.

22 See REAL PROPERTY AND REGISTRATION vol 87 (2012) PARA 201.

23 See REAL PROPERTY AND REGISTRATION vol 87 (2012) PARA 201. See also *M'Gregor v M'Gregor* (1859) 1 De GF & J 63 at 73.

24 *Woodgate v Unwin* (1831) 4 Sim 129 (explained in *M'Gregor v M'Gregor* (1859) 1 De GF & J 63 at 73). See REAL PROPERTY AND REGISTRATION vol 87 (2012) PARA 201.

25 *Hand v North* (1863) 10 Jur NS 7 (gift to two persons 'as they attain 21'), explaining *Woodgate v Unwin* (1831) 4 Sim 129 as decided on this ground; followed in *Re Manly's Will Trusts, Burton v Williams* [1969] 3 All ER 1011, [1969] 1 WLR 1818; *Re Manley's Will Trusts (No 2), Tickle v Manley* [1976] 1 All ER 673.

26 *Doe d Borwell v Abey* (1813) 1 M & S 428; *Hatton v Finch* (1841) 4 Beav 186; *Haddelsey v Adams* (1856) 22 Beav 266 (approved in *Taaffe v Conmee* (1862) 10 HL Cas 64 at 83). Cf *Re Drakeley's Estate* (1854) 19 Beav 395; *Wisden v Wisden* (1854) 2 Sm & G 396; *Wiley v Chanteperdrix* [1894] 1 IR 209 at 220. As to the effect of limitations to joint tenants and the survivor of them see Challis's Law of Real Property (3rd Edn) 368.

B.   DISTRIBUTION PER CAPITA AND PER STIRPES

396. Distribution prima facie per capita. In a gift to a number of donees the distribution between them may be intended to be made per capita, in which case each donee takes a share equal in amount to the share of each other donee, or per stirpes, in which each family or stock takes an equal share with every other family or stock, and the share is then subdivided equally between the members of the family or stock. This is the case whether the donees take as a class[1], or as a combination of classes[2], or whether the gift is to named persons and a class taking together as a single class[3], or to named persons, taking as individuals, together with a class[4], or to a number of persons as individuals and not as a class[5]. Prima facie the distribution is made per capita and not per stirpes[6], but the context may easily displace that rule; it is easier to infer a stirpital distribution in what are called cases of family distribution[7]. The prima facie rule is applied even where the bequest is to persons who, under the statutory rules of distribution on intestacy, would take per stirpes[8], and the fact that the donees are living relations of the testator and the children of deceased relations of the same relationship does not ordinarily take the case out of the rule[9].

1   *Weld v Bradbury* (1715) 2 Vern 705 (the children of J S and J N); *Butler v Stratton* (1791) 3 Bro CC 367 (descendants of A and B); *Lady Lincoln v Pelham* (1804) 10 Ves 166 at 175; *Tomlin v Hatfield* (1841) 12 Sim 167; *Turner v Hudson* (1847) 10 Beav 222 (parents and children 'to be classed together'); *Pattison v Pattison* (1855) 19 Beav 638 ('their said children'); *Re Lloyd's Estate, Baker v Mason* (1856) 2 Jur NS 539; *Armitage v Williams* (1859) 27 Beav 346; *Rook v A-G* (1862) 31 Beav 313; *Weldon v Hoyland* (1862) 4 De GF & J 564 (issue); *Re Stone, Baker v Stone* [1895] 2 Ch 196, CA ('children of the aforesaid share and share alike').
2   *Northey v Strange* (1716) 1 P Wms 340 at 343 (children and grandchildren); *Barnes v Patch* (1803) 8 Ves 604; *Dugdale v Dugdale* (1849) 11 Beav 402; *Cancellor v Cancellor* (1862) 2 Drew & Sm 194 (children and issue); *Re Fox's Will* (1865) 35 Beav 163 (surviving brothers and sister and their children).
3   *Kekewich v Barker* (1903) 88 LT 130, HL.
4   *Blackler v Webb* (1726) 2 P Wms 383; *Butler v Stratton* (1791) 3 Bro CC 367; *Lenden v Blackmore* (1840) 10 Sim 626; *Dowding v Smith* (1841) 3 Beav 541; *Paine v Wagner* (1841) 12 Sim 184; *Rickabe v Garwood* (1845) 8 Beav 579; *Cunningham v Murray* (1847) 1 De G & Sm 366; *Baker v Baker* (1847) 6 Hare 269; *Amson v Harris* (1854) 19 Beav 210; *Tyndale v Wilkinson* (1856) 23 Beav 74; *Re Harper, Plowman v Harper* [1914] 1 Ch 70 at 75 where Sargant J described such decisions as 'necessarily rather in the nature of guesswork'.
5   *Cooke v Bowen* (1840) 4 Y & C Ex 244. Cf *Re Upton, Barclays Bank Ltd v Upton* (1965) 109 Sol Jo 236, CA (where there was a gift to named grand-nephews and grand-nieces of the testator's husband per stirpes).
6   *Butler v Stratton* (1791) 3 Bro C C 367; *Lugar v Harman* (1786) 1 Cox Eq Cas 250; *Re Harper, Plowman v Harper* [1914] 1 Ch 70 (notwithstanding the word 'equally'); *Re Cossentine, Philp v Wesleyan Methodist Local Preachers' Mutual Aid Association Trustees* [1933] Ch 119; *Re Alcock, Bonser v Alcock* [1945] Ch 264 sub nom *Re Alcock, Bonser v Seville* [1945] 1 All ER 613; *Re Hall, Parker v Knight* [1948] Ch 437 at 440 per Harman J; *Re Birkett, Holland v Duncan* [1950] Ch 330, [1950] 1 All ER 316.
7   *Re Hall, Parker v Knight* [1948] Ch 437 at 440; *Re Birkett, Holland v Duncan* [1950] Ch 330, [1950] 1 All ER 316.
8   *Lady Lincoln v Pelham* (1804) 10 Ves 166 at 176.
9   *Blackler v Webb* (1726) 2 P Wms 383; *Amson v Harris* (1854) 19 Beav 210; *Payne v Webb* (1874) 31 LT 637; *Evans v Turner* (1904) 23 NZLR 825. As to cases considering basis of distribution where property is left to the children of A and B see PARA 332.

397. Inference from context in favour of distribution per stirpes. Although prima facie a distribution is made per capita[1], the context of the whole will may require a stirpital distribution[2]. Such a construction has been adopted where the number of shares was mentioned and was equal to the number of parents[3], where the words used implied a further subdivision of a share[4], where there was a reference to the Statutes of Distribution[5], and where the gift was to a number of parents and their children in such a manner that the children were substituted for[6], or took on the death of, their respective parents[7]. Gifts to several parents and at, or after, their deaths to their children, or to their issue, have received this construction as meaning at or after their respective deaths[8].

If a stirpital division is once clearly indicated, the court leans to a stirpital division throughout[9]. Where, however, the children of all the parents are mentioned together as forming a single group or class to take under a single gift without any other indication of distribution per stirpes, the children take per capita[10]. If the gift is postponed to the death of all the parents, then, where the intermediate income after the death of any parent is given to or is to be applied for the benefit of his children per stirpes, this fact is an element to be considered in favour of distribution of the capital per stirpes[11], but does not rebut a clear direction that the distribution is to be per capita[12].

1   See PARA 396.
2   *Brett v Horton* (1841) 4 Beav 239 at 242; *Nettleton v Stephenson* (1849) 18 LJ Ch 191 (gift over to others of the class per stirpes); *Archer v Legg* (1862) 31 Beav 187 at 193 (gift over to others of the class per stirpes); *Re Sibley's Trusts* (1877) 5 ChD 494; *Campbell's Trustee v Dick* 1915 SC 100, Ct of Sess; *Re Hickey, Beddoes v Hodgson* [1917] 1 Ch 601 (legacy 'to the descendants' of A 'or their descendants living at my death').
3   *Overton v Banister* (1841) 4 Beav 205.
4   *Davis v Bennett* (1862) 4 De GF & J 327 at 329; *Capes v Dalton* (1902) 86 LT 129, CA (revsd sub nom *Kekewich v Barker* (1903) 88 LT 130, HL).
5   *Mattison v Tanfield* (1840) 3 Beav 131; *Lewis v Morris* (1854) 19 Beav 34. Where there is no express reference to the Statutes of Distribution there is nothing to prevent the normal rule applying that without words of severance all members of a class take as joint tenants: *Eagles v Le Breton* (1873) LR (15) Eq 148, 42 LJ Ch 362; *Re Gransloser's Will Trusts, Chartered Bank of India, Australia and China v Chillingworth* [1952] Ch 30, [1951] 2 All ER 936; *Re Kilvert, Midland Bank Executor and Trustee Co Ltd v Kilvert* [1957] Ch 388, [1957] 2 All ER 196 (criticising *Rowland v Gorsuch, Price v Gorsuch* (1798) 2 Cox Eq Cas 187). As to the Statutes of Distribution see PARA 343.
6   *Alker v Barton* (1842) 12 LJ Ch 16; *Congreve v Palmer* (1853) 16 Beav 435; *Timins v Stackhouse* (1858) 27 Beav 434; *Palmer v Crutwell* (1862) 8 Jur NS 479; *Gowling v Thompson* (1868) LR 11 Eq 366n; *Re Alchorne, Eade v Bourner* (1911) 130 LT Jo 528; *Re Daniel, Jones v Michael* [1945] 2 All ER 101. Cf *Atkinson v Bartrum* (1860) 28 Beav 219. As to substitutional gifts see PARA 321. No presumption in favour of distribution per stirpes arises in case of an original alternative gift to issue (*Abbay v Howe* (1847) 1 De G & Sm 470), but the description of issue by reference to their 'respective' parents (*Re Coulden, Coulden v Coulden* [1908] 1 Ch 320 at 326), or a direction that the issue are to take their parents' share (*Shand v Kidd* (1854) 19 Beav 310), are indications of distribution per stirpes.
7   'Respective' in such cases points to a stirpital distribution: *Re Campbell's Trusts* (1886) 31 ChD 685 (affd 33 ChD 98, CA). See also *Hunt v Dorsett* (1855) 5 De GM & G 570; *Archer v Legg* (1862) 31 Beav 187 at 191; *Booth v Vicars* (1844) 1 Coll 6. Cf *Smith v Streatfield* (1816) 1 Mer 358 at 361; *Ayscough v Savage* (1865) 13 WR 373.
8   *Re Hutchinson's Trusts* (1882) 21 ChD 811. See also *Taniere v Pearkes* (1825) 2 Sim & St 383; *Flinn v Jenkins* (1844) 1 Coll 365; *Arrow v Mellish* (1847) 1 De G & Sm 355; *Willes v Douglas* (1847) 10 Beav 47; *Waldron v Boulter* (1856) 22 Beav 284; *Turner v Whittaker* (1856) 23 Beav 196; *Wills v Wills* (1875) LR 20 Eq 342; *Barnaby v Tassell* (1871) LR 11 Eq 363; *Re Browne's Will Trusts, Landon v Brown* [1915] 1 Ch 690; *McDonnell v Neil* [1951] AC 342, PC; *Re Errington, Gibbs v Lassam* [1927] 1 Ch 421 (where the rule that deaths means respective deaths is stated and was held to apply to substituted gifts). Cf *Re Telfair, Garrioch v Barclay* (1902) 86 LT 496; *Re Ragdale, Public Trustee v Tuffill* [1934] Ch 352; *Re Foster* [1946] Ch 135, [1946] 1 All ER 333.
9   *Re Smythe, Guinness v Smythe* [1932] IR 136.
10 *Stephens v Hide* (1734) Cas *temp* Talb 27; *Pearce v Edmeades* (1838) 3 Y & C Ex 246; *Abrey v Newman* (1853) 16 Beav 431; *Stevenson v Gullan* (1854) 18 Beav 590 (surviving children); *Swabey v Goldie* (1875) 1 ChD 380, CA (where the inconvenience of keeping intermediate income in suspense did not prevent per capita distribution).
11 *Brett v Horton* (1841) 4 Beav 239 at 242; *Re Campbell's Trusts* (1886) 31 ChD 685 (affd 33 ChD 98, CA). See also *Bradshaw v Melling* (1853) 23 LJ Ch 603 (express reference to trust of income). It appears, however, that such a fact is of itself insufficient to raise a presumption in favour of distribution per stirpes: *Re Stone, Baker v Stone* [1895] 2 Ch 196 at 200, CA, per Lopes LJ. A mere discretionary trust is insufficient: *Nockolds v Locke* (1856) 3 K & J 6.
12 *Re Stone, Baker v Stone* [1895] 2 Ch 196, CA (where property was to be divided 'share and share alike').

398. Substitution of issue. Where in a gift issue are substituted for or take after their respective ancestors, the members of each set of issue prima facie take per capita as between themselves the share which is distributed per stirpes to them[1], but the context may show that the substitution is distributive throughout and a distribution per stirpes intended². A characteristic of distribution per stirpes is that remote descendants do not take in competition with a living immediate ancestor of their own who takes under the gift³.

1   *Armstrong v Stockham* (1843) 7 Jur 230; *Birdsall v York* (1859) 5 Jur NS 1237; *Gowling v Thompson* (1868) LR 11 Eq 366n; *Barnaby v Tassell* (1871) LR 11 Eq 363; *Re Sibley's Trusts* (1877) 5 ChD 494. See also *Re Cockle's Will Trusts, Re Pittaway, Moreland v Draffen, Risdon v Public Trustee* [1967] Ch 690, [1967] 1 All ER 391. As to the shares of substituted donees see PARAS 321, 326.
2   *Ross v Ross* (1855) 20 Beav 645; *Re Orton's Trust* (1866) LR 3 Eq 375; *Gibson v Fisher* (1867) LR 5 Eq 51.
3   *Pearson v Stephen* (1831) 2 Dow & Cl 328; *Dick v Lacy* (1845) 8 Beav 214; *Amson v Harris* (1854) 19 Beav 210; *Re Bennett's Trust* (1857) 3 K & J 280 at 284; *Gibson v Fisher* (1867) LR 5 Eq 51; *Re Rawlinson, Hill v Withall* [1909] 2 Ch 36 at 38.

399. Determination of stocks. The determination of the persons forming the stocks from which the stirpes are to spring is a matter of construction of each will. Sometimes it may appear from the terms of the gift that the stocks should be persons who might themselves take under the gift, for example the original takers for whom the stirpes are substituted¹, and not ancestors of such takers², but there is no rule of construction which requires that the stocks of descent are to be found among the takers and not among the ancestors³.

1   *Robinson v Shepherd* (1863) 4 De GJ & Sm 129; *Re Wilson, Parker v Winder* (1883) 24 ChD 664; *Re Dering, Neall v Beale* (1911) 105 LT 404; *Re Alexander, Alexander v Alexander* [1919] 1 Ch 371.
2   See *Gibson v Fisher* (1867) LR 5 Eq 51 (where the context required such a determination of the stocks).
3   *Sidney v Perpetual Trustees Estates and Agency Co of New Zealand Ltd* [1944] AC 194 at 202, [1944] 2 All ER 225 at 228, PC; *Re Upton, Barclays Bank Ltd v Upton* (1965) 109 Sol Jo 236, CA.

400. Presumption as to interests of donees named together. The context of a will may show that persons named together as donees are intended to take successively¹, either in the order of their names² or according to seniority in age³, whichever is appropriate to the context and the circumstances of the case. Without such a context, prima facie a gift to persons named together as donees is not construed to give them estates in succession⁴.

1   See eg *Re Green, Fitzwilliam v Green* (1916) 50 ILT 179 (bequest to widow 'during her lifetime to be held by her in the interest of my grandson'; interest given to widow for life, remainder to grandson). As to successive interests in consumables see PARA 122; and as to the rule with regard to the construction of successive interests in real estate see REAL PROPERTY AND REGISTRATION vol 87 (2012) PARA 157 et seq. As to the construction of successive interests in settled property generally see SETTLEMENTS vol 91 (2012) PARA 501 et seq.
2   *Stratford v Powell* (1807) 1 Ball & B 1. Similarly, if the testator gives one of a number of like things to each of several donees, prima facie it appears that the legatees exercise their rights of selection according to the priority of the gifts: *Duckmanton v Duckmanton* (1860) 5 H & N 219 at 222; *Asten v Asten* [1894] 3 Ch 260 at 263 per Romer J (though the gifts here were void for uncertainty); and see PARA 127 note 4.
3   *Ongley v Peale* (1712) 2 Ld Raym 1312; *Lewis d Ormond v Waters* (1805) 6 East 336 (first and other sons); *Young v Sheppard* (1847) 10 Beav 207 ('to devolve in succession upon my remaining children'); *Honywood v Honywood* (1905) 92 LT 814, HL (first and other son); *Re Harcourt, Fitzwilliam v Portman* [1920] 1 Ch 492 (devise on death of eldest son without issue to every other son, other than a son entitled to the barony, every such son to take for life with remainder to his sons in tail). See also *Cradock v Cradock* (1858) 4 Jur NS 626. In the case of real estate, a direction for settlement on children in succession may be 'an epitome of a strict settlement': *Doe d Phipps v Lord Mulgrave* (1793) 5 Term Rep 320 at 324; *Earl of Tyrone v Marquis of Waterford* (1860) 1 De GF & J 613 at 623. There is a general rule of construction, not confined to wills, that 'first and other sons' imports successive interests: see *Re Gosset's Settlement, Gribble v Lloyds Bank* [1943] Ch 351 at 354, [1943] 2 All ER 515 at 516; *Lewis d Ormond v Waters* (1805) 6 East 336. Cf SETTLEMENTS vol 91 (2012) PARA 618.

4 *De Windt v De Windt* (1866) LR 1 HL 87; *Surtees v Surtees* (1871) LR 12 Eq 400; *Allgood v Blake* (1873) LR 8 Exch 160 at 169–170; *Re Roberts, Repington v Roberts-Gawen* (1881) 19 ChD 520 at 529–530, CA (in a gift to a class for life 'we have no right to import the word 'successive' or the word 'successively' or the words 'for the time being' or any words of that sort').

(vi) Cumulative and Substitutional Gifts

401. Gifts clearly cumulative. A testator may well intend to give two or more gifts, of equal or unequal amounts, to the same donee, and, where the intention to do so is clear, effect is given to it[1]. The question in each case is what is the intention collected from the whole will[2], and, although rules of construction of wills have been laid down for assisting in determining whether several legacies to the same person are cumulative or substitutional, they are applicable only where there is no internal evidence of intention in the testamentary instrument as, if there is such evidence, it must prevail[3].

1 *Burkinshaw v Hodge* (1874) 22 WR 484. See also *Re Dyke, Dyke v Dyke* (1881) 44 LT 568 at 570; *Re Segelcke, Ziegler v Nicol* [1906] 2 Ch 301 (where the additional gift was held not to be reduced by the expression of an intention to make up the earlier gift to a certain amount, in fact less than the earlier gift).

2 *Guy v Sharp* (1833) 1 My & K 589 at 603. In treating a plurality of writings as constituting a single testamentary instrument or separate testamentary instruments, the probate is binding on the court of construction: *Baillie v Butterfield* (1787) 1 Cox Eq Cas 392; *Brine v Ferrier* (1835) 7 Sim 549; and see PARA 200. As to the presumption against double portions in the case of a child and a parent or person in loco parentis, where one gift is non-testamentary see EQUITABLE JURISDICTION vol 47 (2014) PARA 177. As to when a subsequent gift is subject to conditions imposed with respect to the first gift see PARA 408.

3 *Kidd v North* (1846) 2 Ph 91 at 97 per Lord Cottenham LC. Thus where eg two wills are admitted to probate, the court of construction is entitled to look at both and draw conclusions from internal evidence so provided that a gift in the second will is substitutional, although the court is not entitled to regard the first will as revoked by the second in toto: *Re Plant, Johnson v Hardwicke*, as reported in [1952] Ch 298 at 301. As to a plurality of wills see note 2.

402. Presumptions in case of two gifts to the same person in one instrument. Where two legacies are given by the same testamentary instrument[1] to the same person described in the same terms in each case, and are of the same specific thing or of the same specified amount, the second is presumed to be merely a repetition of the first[2], and prima facie the legatee takes only one such legacy. If, however, such legacies are of different specified amounts[3], or have substantially different incidents[4], or if one is a residuary gift and the other a specific or pecuniary legacy[5], the second legacy is presumed to be cumulative, and prima facie the legatee takes both[6].

1 As to the treatment of several instruments as a single will see PARA 401 note 2.

2 *Garth v Meyrick* (1779) 1 Bro CC 30; *Holford v Wood* (1798) 4 Ves 76 at 86, 91; *Heming v Clutterbuck* (1827) 1 Bli NS 479, HL (where the judgment is based on an alleged finding of the ecclesiastical court that the two instruments were one will); *Brine v Ferrier* (1835) 7 Sim 549.

3 *Hooley v Hatton* (1773) 1 Bro CC 390n; *Curry v Pile* (1787) 2 Bro CC 225.

4 *Mackinnon v Peach* (1838) 2 Keen 555; *Ford v Ruxton* (1844) 1 Coll 403; *Inglefield v Coghlan* (1845) 2 Coll 247; *Thompson v Teulon, Teulon v Teulon* (1852) 22 LJ Ch 243; *Wildes v Davies* (1853) 22 LJ Ch 495 at 497; *Strong v Ingram* (1833) 6 Sim 197. See also *Whyte v Kearney* (1827) 3 Russ 208. In *Manning v Thesiger* (1835) 3 My & K 29 (where the times of payment were different) and *Greenwood v Greenwood* (1776) 1 Bro CC 31n (one legacy to legatee's separate use), the differences were not sufficient to render the legacies cumulative.

5 *Kirkpatrick v Bedford, Bedford v Kirkpatrick* (1878) 4 App Cas 96 at 103, 109, HL; *Gordon v Alexander* (1858) 4 Jur NS 1097.

6 For a case of context to the contrary see *Yockney v Hansard* (1844) 3 Hare 620 (second annuity in substitution for first).

403. Presumptions in case of two gifts to the same person in different instruments. If the same specific thing is given by two different testamentary instruments[1] to the same person, the second gift is presumed to be a mere repetition of the first[2]. Apart from such repeated specific gifts, the general principle is[3] that if by different testamentary instruments two legacies, whether of the same or different amounts, are given to the same person, they are presumed to be additional to each other[4]. The presumption is strengthened by any substantial difference between the gifts[5].

The context of the instruments may, however, lead to a contrary inference[6]. Thus where the later gift is of the same specified amount as the earlier[7], and is expressed to be given for the same cause or motive[8], prima facie the later gift is merely a repetition of the first[9], and generally, whatever the amounts of the legacies, where the later instrument purports to explain[10], repeat[11] or be in substitution for[12] the earlier instrument in respect of the gift, or otherwise to be the final declaration of the testator's intentions[13], the later gift supersedes the earlier[14].

1 As to what are separate instruments see PARA 401 note 2.
2 *Duke of St Albans v Beauclerk* (1743) 2 Atk 636 at 640 per Lord Hardwicke LC; *Hooley v Hatton* (1773) 1 Bro CC 390n per Ashton J (in each case discussing the authorities in the civil law).
3 See the rule briefly stated in *Re Davies, Davies v Mackintosh* [1957] 3 All ER 52 at 54, [1957] 1 WLR 922 at 925.
4 *Foy v Foy* (1758) 1 Cox Eq Cas 163; *Ridges v Morrison* (1784) 1 Bro CC 389; *Baillie v Butterfield* (1787) 1 Cox Eq Cas 392; *Benyon v Benyon* (1810) 17 Ves 34 at 43; *Wray v Field* (1822) 6 Madd 300 (affd (1826) 2 Russ 257); *Mackenzie v Mackenzie* (1826) 2 Russ 262; *Lord v Sutcliffe* (1828) 2 Sim 273; *Robley v Robley* (1839) 2 Beav 95 at 101; *Tweedale v Tweedale* (1840) 10 Sim 453; *Radburn v Jervis, Hare v Hill* (1840) 3 Beav 450; *Forbes v Lawrence* (1844) 1 Coll 495; *Marquis of Hertford v Lord Lowther* (1844) 4 LTOS 450; *Lee v Pain* (1844) 4 Hare 201 at 215, 231; *Lobley v Stocks* (1854) 19 Beav 392; *Townshend v Mostyn* (1858) 26 Beav 72; *Johnstone v Earl of Harrowby* (1859) 1 De GF & J 183; *Cresswell v Cresswell* (1868) LR 6 Eq 69 at 76; *Re Davies, Davies v Mackintosh* [1957] 3 All ER 52, [1957] 1 WLR 922.
5 *Masters v Masters* (1718) 1 P Wms 421 at 423; *Suisse v Lord Lowther* (1843) 2 Hare 424 at 433; *Lee v Pain* (1844) 4 Hare 201 at 223–224 (legacies carrying interest from different dates and to legatee by different descriptions).
6 The fact that other legacies to other donees in the same will are given in terms expressly making them cumulative is some indication that legacies not so described are substitutional (*Allen v Callow* (1796) 3 Ves 289; *Barclay v Wainwright* (1797) 3 Ves 462; *Russell v Dickson* (1842) 2 Dr & War 133 at 139 (affd (1853) 4 HL Cas 293)), but is of slight importance in rebutting a presumption applicable to the case (*Mackenzie v Mackenzie* (1826) 2 Russ 262 at 273; *Suisse v Lord Lowther* (1843) 2 Hare 424 at 430). See also *Wray v Field* (1822) 6 Madd 300. Cf *Re Nixon, Askew v Briggs* (1965) 109 Sol Jo 757 (where in a home-made codicil the intention to substitute was inferred); *Re Resch's Will Trusts, Le Cras v Perpetual Trustee Co Ltd, Far West Children's Health Scheme v Perpetual Trustee Co Ltd* [1969] 1 AC 514, [1967] 3 All ER 915, PC (where a consistent scheme of benefits disclosed by the instruments rebutted the presumption that the legacies were cumulative). The fact that legacies are given in terms making them substitutional does not make other legacies not so described substitutional, where the presumption that they are cumulative is otherwise applicable: *Re Armstrong, Ayne v Woodward* (1893) 31 LR Ir 154.
7 There is no presumption of repetition raised if in either instrument there is no motive or no motive other than the testator's own bounty (*Suisse v Lord Lowther* (1843) 2 Hare 424 at 432), or a different motive expressed, although the sums are the same, or where the same motive is expressed in both and the legacies are of different amounts (*Hurst v Beach* (1821) 5 Madd 351 at 358–359).
8 *Duke of St Albans v Beauclerk* (1743) 2 Atk 636; *Ridges v Morrison* (1784) 1 Bro CC 389; *Hurst v Beach* (1821) 5 Madd 351; *Wray v Field* (1822) 6 Madd 300 at 303 per Leach V-C; *Suisse v Lord Lowther* (1843) 2 Hare 424 at 432 per Wood V-C. As to the meaning of 'the same cause' see *Wilson v O'Leary* (1872) 7 Ch App 448 at 455, CA. Where the gift in each case is to a person by description, for example to 'my servant', the descriptive words are not an expression of motive: *Roch v Callen* (1847) 6 Hare 531 at 534. See also *Suisse v Lord Lowther* above.
9 *Duke of St Albans v Beauclerk* (1743) 2 Atk 636 at 640 per Lord Hardwicke LC (adopting the rule of the civil law); *Benyon v Benyon* (1810) 17 Ves 34 (to executor for his trouble); *Hurst v Beach* (1821) 5 Madd 351 at 358–359.

10 *Moggridge v Thackwell* (1792) 1 Ves 464 at 473 per Lord Thurlow LC.
11 *Moggridge v Thackwell* (1792) 1 Ves 464 ('simple repetition, where it is exact and punctual, has been regarded as sufficient proof' that the legacies were not cumulative); *Tatham v Drummond* (1864) 33 LJ Ch 438. See also *Benyon v Benyon* (1810) 17 Ves 34 at 42 (gift of income of trust legacy altered); *Hubbard v Alexander* (1876) 3 ChD 738. Thus many legacies may be given to the same donees in the same or nearly the same terms as in the prior instrument: *Coote v Boyd* (1789) 2 Bro CC 521; *Barclay v Wainwright* (1797) 3 Ves 462; *Whyte v Whyte* (1873) LR 17 Eq 50 (instruments of same date and contents). See also the cases cited in note 12. In *Wilson v O'Leary* (1872) 7 Ch App 448, CA, this was not sufficient in the context and circumstances of that case to rebut the presumption that the legacies were cumulative.
12 *Duke of St Albans v Beauclerk* (1743) 2 Atk 636; *Jackson v Jackson* (1788) 2 Cox Eq Cas 35; *Osborne v Duke of Leeds* (1800) 5 Ves 369 at 382; *A-G v Harley* (1819) 4 Madd 263; *Gillespie v Alexander* (1824) 2 Sim & St 145; *Simon v Barber* (1829) Taml 14; *Fraser v Byng* (1829) 1 Russ & M 90 at 101–102; *Robley v Robley* (1839) 2 Beav 95; *A-G v George* (1843) 12 LJ Ch 165; *Suisse v Lord Lowther* (1843) 2 Hare 424 at 437; *Kidd v North* (1846) 2 Ph 91; *Duncan v Duncan (No 2)* (1859) 27 Beav 392; *Tuckey v Henderson* (1863) 33 Beav 174 (gifts of legacies by different instruments substitutional); *Bell v Park* [1914] 1 IR 158, Ir CA; *Grealey v Sampson* [1917] 1 IR 286, Ir CA; *Re Michell, Thomas v Hoskins* [1929] 1 Ch 552 (where two codicils of the same date were held to be duplicates of the same instrument); *Re Bagnall, Scale v Willett* [1948] WN 324; *Re Plant, Johnson v Hardwicke* [1952] Ch 298, [1952] 1 All ER 78n (gifts substitutional).
13 *Russell v Dickson* (1853) 4 HL Cas 293 (recital that testator had not time to alter will); cf *Sawrey v Rumney* (1852) 5 De G & Sm 698 (alteration as to a legacy in a will already altered by a previous codicil).
14 As to conditions attaching to cumulative and substituted legacies see PARA 409.

(vii) Hotchpot Clauses

404. Hotchpot of prior advances. A hotchpot clause[1] directing past advances or other sums or property[2] to be brought into account is construed so as to give effect to the whole will[3] and, as in the case of other divesting provisions[4], is in general construed strictly[5]. Such a clause is not, of itself, a release from the personal liability, if any, of the donees to repay such advances, at all events where the gift to the donee is settled on him for life[6]. A hotchpot clause as between members of a class cannot be used to enlarge the share of a beneficiary who is not a member of the class[7].

'Advances' primarily means advances of money, whether by way of loan or by payment at the legatee's request[8], and ordinarily does not include payments made after the testator's death, even in discharge of liabilities undertaken during his lifetime on the legatee's behalf[9], or other kinds of property given during life[10]; but it may include all gifts during life, and advances made by the trustees or executors of the testator after his death are included where those advances are contemplated in the will[11].

If the clause relates to advances made by any person in his lifetime, without more, a gift by the will of that person[12], or an interest taken under his intestacy[13], is not within the clause.

1 As to the nature and purpose of a hotchpot clause see SETTLEMENTS vol 91 (2012) PARA 825. The object of such a clause is in general to produce equality as between the donees, taking into consideration past gifts. As to the effect of such clauses generally see *Fox v Fox* (1870) LR 11 Eq 142 (effect as notional increase of testator's estate); *Smith v Crabtree* (1877) 6 ChD 591 (exclusion of set-off of debt against specific legacy); *Wheeler v Humphreys* [1898] AC 506, HL. An advance to the life tenant of a settled share may have to be brought into account against the stirps: *Re Sparkes, Kemp-Welch v Kemp-Welch* (1911) 56 Sol Jo 90. A child is not liable to bring into account his parent's debt to the estate: *Re Binns, Public Trustee v Ingle* [1929] 1 Ch 677. A clause directing loans to a son, to be taken 'in and towards satisfaction' of his share of residue and 'to be brought into hotchpot and accounted for accordingly', was held to be a mere hotchpot clause adapted to loans instead of advances and not to operate as a release or gift: *Re Horn, Westminster Bank Ltd v Horn* [1946] Ch 254, [1946] 2 All ER 118, CA.
2 An appropriate hotchpot clause requiring appointed shares to be brought into account may result in life interests appointed having to be brought into account, but is prima facie confined to interests

which are vested and not contingent and, as regards reversionary interests, to those which are absolutely and indefeasibly vested: *Re Gordon, Public Trustee v Bland* [1942] Ch 131, [1942] 1 All ER 59 (applying *Re West, Denton v West* [1921] 1 Ch 533 at 540 per Astbury J). A life interest is brought into account at its actuarial value determined at the date it falls into possession: see *Re Westropp* (1903) 37 ILT 183; *Re Thomson Settlement Trusts, Robertson v Makepeace* [1953] Ch 414, [1953] 1 All ER 1139; and SETTLEMENTS vol 91 (2012) PARA 825.

3   *Brocklehurst v Flint* (1852) 16 Beav 100; *Stares v Penton* (1867) LR 4 Eq 40 (where the clause ceased to operate after one member of the class became entitled to payment); *Stewart v Stewart* (1880) 15 ChD 539. See also *Re Arbuthnot, Arbuthnot v Arbuthnot* [1915] 1 Ch 422. A clause merely requiring hotchpot will not, without more, amount to a direction to release a debt owing to the estate: *Re Horn, Westminster Bank Ltd v Horn* [1946] Ch 254, [1946] 2 All ER 118, CA (disapproving *Re Trollope, Game v Trollope* [1915] 1 Ch 853). A hotchpot clause may fail as being conditional on a circumstance which has not come to pass: *Nugee v Chapman* (1860) 29 Beav 288.

4   As to divesting provisions generally see PARAS 440–444.

5   Thus even where the person directed to account has obtained a benefit, the clause is not extended to advances to persons other than those contemplated by the clause: *M'Clure v Evans* (1861) 29 Beav 422 (husband of legatee). See also *White v Turner* (1858) 25 Beav 505. As to advances to a married woman legatee during coverture under the law before the Married Women's Property Act 1882 see *Douglas v Willes* (1849) 7 Hare 318 (assignees of legatee, under assignment before advance); *Silverside v Silverside* (1858) 25 Beav 340 (children of legatee); *Poole v Poole* (1871) 7 Ch App 17 at 19; *Hewitt v Jardine* (1872) LR 14 Eq 58; *Re Haygarth, Wickham v Haygarth* [1913] 2 Ch 9.

6   *Re Warde, Warde v Ridgway* (1914) 111 LT 35; *Re Young, Young v Young* [1914] 1 Ch 581 (affd [1914] 1 Ch 976, CA); *Re Barker, Gilbey v Barker* [1918] 1 Ch 128.

7   *Stewart v Stewart* (1880) 15 ChD 539. See also *Meinertzagen v Walters* (1872) 7 Ch App 670, CA.

8   *Re Jaques, Hodgson v Braisby* [1903] 1 Ch 267 at 274, CA per Stirling LJ (land conveyed by testator did not have to be accounted for as 'advances or money lent'). 'Advances' may include sums which as debts have become statute-barred (*Poole v Poole* (1871) 7 Ch App 17), or the balance of a debt after deducting the dividends received by the testator in the legatee's bankruptcy (*Auster v Powell* (1863) 1 De GJ & Sm 99; *Re Ainsworth, Millington v Ainsworth* [1922] 1 Ch 22). Where, however, the clause directs hotchpot, not of the sums advanced, but of the debts owing, the effect of a composition or bankruptcy (*Golds v Greenfield* (1854) 2 Sm & G 476) or of the statutes of limitation (*Re Jolly, Gathercole v Norfolk* [1900] 2 Ch 616, CA) is to render the clause inoperative as to those debts.

9   *Auster v Powell* (1863) 1 De GJ & Sm 99; *Re Whitehouse, Whitehouse v Edwards* (1887) 37 ChD 683.

10 Eg a gift of leaseholds: *Douglas v Willes* (1849) 7 Hare 318; or land: *Re Jaques, Hodgson v Braisby* [1903] 1 Ch 267. As to advances in distribution on intestacy see further PARA 502.

11 *Re Whiteford, Inglis v Whiteford* [1903] 1 Ch 889 (where the report of *Hilton v Hilton* (1872) LR 14 Eq 468 is corrected). The payment by the testator of a premium for a son is not an 'advancement' to be accounted for: *Re Watney, Watney v Gold* (1911) 56 Sol Jo 109 (fee paid to an architect for son to learn his business).

12 *Cooper v Cooper* (1873) 8 Ch App 813. Dicta in *Leake v Leake* (1805) 10 Ves 477, and decisions in *Onslow v Michell* (1812) 18 Ves 490, and *Goolding v Haverfield* (1824) 13 Price 593 (see also *Fazakerley v Gillibrand* (1834) 6 Sim 591), to the effect that a provision by will is an advancement in the lifetime of the testator, were criticised in *Cooper v Cooper* above at 825–828. For criticism of *Onslow v Michell* see also *Re Livesey's Settlement Trusts, Livesey v Livesey* [1953] 2 All ER 723 at 726, [1953] 1 WLR 1114 at 1117–1118 (testamentary gift mere bounty to which clause providing for sums provided for 'advancement or preferment in the world' to be taken in satisfaction pro tanto of portions did not apply). As to the extent of advancement clauses see CHILDREN AND YOUNG PERSONS vol 9 (2012) PARA 73 et seq.

13 *Twisden v Twisden* (1804) 9 Ves 413 at 427.

405.   Method of bringing advances into account. Apart from a special direction[1], there are two methods of bringing advances into account[2].

The first method is to value the estate at the testator's death[3], if the will shows that he contemplated immediate division, or at the time fixed by the will for distribution[4] if, for example, there is a prior life interest[5]; to that value is added for computation the amount of the advances; the total is then divided into the required number of shares and the advances are deducted from the advanced beneficiaries' shares respectively. The income is then divided on the footing that these shares represent the shares of the persons interested in the residuary estate[6].

The second method[7] is to defer the valuation until the period of actual distribution[8]. Meanwhile to the actual income of the estate there is added for the purpose of computation a sum for interest on the amount of the advances[9]. The income thus notionally arrived at is divided into the required number of shares, and interest[10] on the advances is deducted from the shares of that income of the advanced beneficiaries respectively[11]. When the time for distribution of the capital arrives, the amount of the advances is added to the sum actually in hand to be divided; the total is then divided between beneficiaries and the beneficiaries are debited with their advances[12]. The second method has been adopted where, from the nature of the estate or a substantial part of it, it is not practicable to make a fair and proper valuation at the time fixed for distribution[13], or where it appears from the will as a whole that the testator did not contemplate that there would in fact be an actual distribution at that time[14]; and it seems that this is the rule which should be generally adopted[15]. It appears, however, that each donee bears a share of any annuities charged on the estate, according to his aliquot share as determined by the will apart from hotchpot[16].

1   See *Re Willoughby, Willoughby v Decies* [1911] 2 Ch 581 at 594, 600, 602, CA (where a direction securing equality of portions was held to refer only to capital).
2   See *Re Slee, Midland Bank Executor and Trustee Co Ltd v Slee* [1962] 1 All ER 542 at 549, [1962] 1 WLR 496 at 507 per Cross J (where the court considered that it was free to decide to adopt whichever of the two methods seemed the more appropriate).
3   See *Re Mansel, Smith v Mansel* [1930] 1 Ch 352 at 355–356, 362; *Re Gunther's Will Trusts, Alexander v Gunther* [1939] Ch 985, [1939] 3 All ER 291. See also *Re Oram, Oram v Oram* [1940] Ch 1001, [1940] 4 All ER 161.
4   Ie whether at the testator's death (*Hilton v Hilton* (1872) LR 14 Eq 468; *Field v Seward* (1877) 5 ChD 538 at 539; *Re Lambert, Middleton v Moore* [1897] 2 Ch 169; *Re Whiteford, Inglis v Whiteford* [1903] 1 Ch 889) or other later time (*Andrewes v George* (1830) 3 Sim 393 at 394; *Re Rees, Rees v George* (1881) 17 ChD 701; *Re Dallmeyer, Dallmeyer v Dallmeyer* [1896] 1 Ch 372, CA). The effect of a charge on the fund, such as a life annuity secured by a part of the fund being set apart to meet it, does not alter the period for distribution for this purpose: *Re Whiteford, Inglis v Whiteford* [1903] 1 Ch 889; *Re Willoughby, Willoughby v Decies* [1911] 2 Ch 581 at 597, CA. Settled funds must be brought into hotchpot at the value at the date of the settlement: *Re Crocker, Crocker v Crocker* [1916] 1 Ch 25.
5   Eg as in *Re Rees, Rees v George* (1881) 17 ChD 701. See also *Re Dallmeyer, Dallmeyer v Dallmeyer* [1896] 1 Ch 372 at 393–394, CA.
6   *Re Hargreaves, Hargreaves v Hargreaves* (1903) 88 LT 100, CA; *Re Gilbert, Gilbert v Gilbert* [1908] WN 63; *Re Hart, Hart v Arnold* (1912) 107 LT 759; *Re Mansel, Smith v Mansel* [1930] 1 Ch 352.
7   This method was adopted in *Re Wills, Dulverton v Macleod* [1939] Ch 705, [1939] 2 All ER 775 (income), *Re Hillas-Drake, National Provincial Bank Ltd v Liddell* [1944] Ch 235, [1944] 1 All ER 375 (capital), and *Re Slee, Midland Bank Executor and Trustee Co Ltd v Slee* [1962] 1 All ER 542, [1962] 1 WLR 496.
8   See *Re Slee, Midland Bank Executor and Trustee Co Ltd v Slee* [1962] 1 All ER 542, [1962] 1 WLR 496.
9   *Re Slee, Midland Bank Executor and Trustee Co Ltd v Slee* [1962] 1 All ER 542, [1962] 1 WLR 496.
10 Under neither method is interest charged up to the testator's death (*Re Willoughby, Willoughby v Decies* [1911] 2 Ch 581, CA; and see *Re Whiteford, Inglis v Whiteford* [1903] 1 Ch 889), or other time fixed for distribution (*Re Dallmeyer, Dallmeyer v Dallmeyer* [1896] 1 Ch 372, CA; *Re Willoughby, Willoughby v Decies* above; *Re Forster-Brown, Barry v Forster-Brown* [1914] 2 Ch 584). Interest, however, runs from that time to the date of actual distribution: *Re Dallmeyer, Dallmeyer v Dallmeyer* above. The rate of interest has usually been 4% per annum when that was the rate of interest laid down by court rules for an account of legacies directed by judgment: *Re Davy, Hollingsworth v Davy* [1908] 1 Ch 61, CA (approving in this respect *Stewart v Stewart* (1880) 15 ChD 539, *Re Rees, Rees v George* (1881) 17 ChD 701 and *Re Hargreaves, Hargreaves v Hargreaves* (1902) 86 LT 43 (varied on appeal (1903) 88 LT 100, CA, where calculation of

interest was held unnecessary); and disapproving in this respect *Re Lambert, Middleton v Moore* [1897] 2 Ch 169 and *Re Whiteford, Inglis v Whiteford* [1903] 1 Ch 889); *Re Cooke, Randall v Cooke* [1916] 1 Ch 480. The rate of interest applicable to an account of legacies directed by judgment is currently the basic rate payable for the time being on funds in court: CPR PD 40A*Accounts, Inquiries etc* PD 40A para 15. The current basic rate of interest on funds in court is 0.1% with effect from 6 June 2016. The rate was previously 0.3% with effect from 1 July 2009, 1% with effect from 1 June 2009, 2% with effect from 1 February 2009 and 4% with effect from 1 February 2002. As to court fund rates generally see the Government website. As to the CPR see CIVIL PROCEDURE vol 11 (2015) PARA 12 et seq.

11 *Re Mansel, Smith v Mansel* [1930] 1 Ch 352; *Re Slee, Midland Bank Executor and Trustee Co Ltd v Slee* [1962] 1 All ER 542, [1962] 1 WLR 496. As to deducting income tax see *Re Foster, Hunt v Foster* [1920] 1 Ch 391.

12 See *Re Slee, Midland Bank Executor and Trustee Co Ltd v Slee* [1962] 1 All ER 542 at 549, [1962] 1 WLR 496 at 506–507 per Cross J. This case illustrates the second method being applied where the problem was complicated by the existence of several funds and the incidence of legacy duty and estate duty. As to the incidence of duty see also *Re Tollemache, Forbes v Public Trustee* [1930] WN 138; *Re Beddington, Micholls v Samuel* [1900] 1 Ch 771; *Re Crocker, Crocker v Crocker* [1916] 1 Ch 25.

13 *Re Craven, Watson v Craven* [1914] 1 Ch 358; *Re Forster-Brown, Barry v Forster-Brown* [1914] 2 Ch 584; *Re Cooke, Randall v Cooke* [1916] 1 Ch 480. See also *Re Tod, Bradshaw v Turner* [1916] 1 Ch 567, discussing the decision in *Re Hargreaves, Hargreaves v Hargreaves* (1903) 88 LT 100, CA, which was distinguished in the three cases previously cited. The second method was applied in *Re Rees, Rees v George* (1881) 17 ChD 701, but without noting the distinction between the two methods.

14 *Re Poyser, Landon v Poyser* [1908] 1 Ch 828.

15 *Re Wills, Dulverton v Macleod* [1939] Ch 705 (where the subject was reviewed by Simonds J); *Re Hillas-Drake, National Provincial Bank Ltd v Liddell* [1944] Ch 235, [1944] 1 All ER 375 (not following *Re Gunther's Will Trusts, Alexander v Gunther* [1939] Ch 985, [1939] 3 All ER 291, and *Re Oram, Oram v Oram* [1940] Ch 1001, [1940] 4 All ER 161, as contrary to previous practice); *Re Slee, Midland Bank Executor and Trustee Co Ltd v Slee* [1962] 1 All ER 542, [1962] 1 WLR 496 (not adopting the method followed in *Re Mansel, Smith v Mansel* [1930] 1 Ch 352).

16 *Re Hargreaves, Hargreaves v Hargreaves* (1903) 88 LT 100, CA. In *Re Poyser, Landon v Poyser* (1908) as reported in 99 LT 50, Warrington J at 53 thought that there must have been some slip in *Re Hargreaves, Hargreaves v Hargreaves* in drawing up the order or otherwise with regard to this point. The rule is, however, regarded as 'undoubted' in *Re Hargreaves, Hargreaves v Hargreaves* at 101 per Romer LJ.

406. Effect on hotchpot where testator recites amounts of advances. Where a testator states by recital in his will the sum advanced, a mistake in amount cannot be corrected if the hotchpot clause clearly directs hotchpot of the sum recited to have been advanced[1]; but if the clause directs hotchpot of that sum, or so much of it as remains unpaid, the intention is inferred that only the amount actually owing is to be brought into account, and the mistake may be corrected[2].

The testator may refer to non-testamentary documents, even those made subsequent to the date of his will; such documents may be referred to as evidence of the advances made[3], but may not be used for the purpose of varying the terms of the will[4].

1 *Re Wood, Ward v Wood* (1886) 32 ChD 517. But a will which fails to carry out the testator's intention because of a clerical error or a failure to understand his instructions can be rectified under the Administration of Justice Act 1982 s 20(1): see PARA 187.

2 *Re Taylor's Estate, Tomlin v Underhay* (1882) 22 ChD 495 at 500, CA; *Re Kelsey, Woolley v Kelsey, Kelsey v Kelsey* [1905] 2 Ch 465 at 470 (not following *Re Aird's Estate, Aird v Quick* (1879) 12 ChD 291).

3 *Whateley v Spooner* (1857) 3 K & J 542. In *Smith v Conder* (1878) 9 ChD 170 and *Re Coyte, Coyte v Coyte* (1887) 56 LT 510, it was said that subsequent unattested letters or entries in a book could not be referred to, on account of the Wills Act 1837. It appears, however, that this is so only for the purpose of admitting them to probate. In *Quihampton v Going* (1876) 24 WR 917, the entries were made previously to the date of the will. See also *Kirk v Eddowes* (1844) 3 Hare 509 at 518 (testator's declarations at time of advance, made after date of will). In *Re Deprez, Henriques v Deprez* [1917] 1 Ch 24, however, where there was a direction in a codicil that

advances appearing in the testator's books of account should be brought into hotchpot, entries after the date of the codicil were not receivable as evidence of advances.

4　*Whateley v Spooner* (1857) 3 K & J 542; *Smith v Conder* (1878) 9 ChD 170.

(5) CONDITIONAL GIFTS

(i) General Provisions relating to Conditional Gifts

407. Clarity and effect of conditions or obligations. Where a testator has by any language[1] clearly attached conditions[2] or obligations to his gifts, his expressed intention is paramount. Where, however, the will is not clear, it is a settled rule of construction that words are not construed as importing a condition (particularly a condition of forfeiture) if they are fairly capable of another interpretation[3].

Words expressing a condition may be treated as being words of limitation[4] or as creating merely a trust[5] or charge[6]. A gift on condition that the donee makes certain payments for the benefit of other persons[7] or a gift subject to such payments[8] is generally construed as constituting those payments a charge on the property given where, in the circumstances existing at the date of the will, some surplus could remain out of the property after making the payments[9], and as constituting the donee a trustee of the property where no substantial surplus could remain after making the payments at the date of the will[10]. When the surplus is appropriated to a purpose which may or may not require the whole of it to be applied, the question is one of construction of the particular will[11].

As in other provisions[12] in a will, words may be rejected or supplied or the natural sense of conditions varied where this is required by the context[13], but the court does this with reluctance and words are not readily inserted which will prevent vesting[14].

1　*Re Williams, Williams v Williams* [1897] 2 Ch 12 at 18, CA, per Lindley LJ. As to uncertainty in a condition see PARAS 138–141.
2　As to conditions generally see PARA 128 et seq.
3　*Edgeworth v Edgeworth* (1869) LR 4 HL 35 at 41 per Lord Westbury. See also *Wright v Wilkin* (1860) 31 LJQB 7 (affd (1862) 31 LJQB 196, Ex Ch); *Re Gregory, How v Charrington* (1935) 52 TLR 130 (where there was a gift to a charity on condition that the charity was not subsidised by the state or by a public or local authority). As to divesting generally see PARA 440 et seq; and as to imposing a condition when a power of appointment is exercised see *Re Neave, Neave v Neave* [1938] Ch 793, [1938] 3 All ER 220.
4　*Page v Hayward* (1705) 2 Salk 570; *Pelham-Clinton v Duke of Newcastle* [1902] 1 Ch 34, CA (affd [1903] AC 111, HL).
5　*Oddie v Brown* (1859) 4 De G & J 179 at 194; *Wright v Wilkin* (1860) 31 LJQB 7 (affd (1862) 31 LJQB 196, Ex Ch); *Re Hall* (1918) 53 ILT 11. In *Re Frame, Edwards v Taylor* [1939] Ch 700, [1939] 2 All ER 865, it was held that a gift on condition that the donee adopted the testator's daughter involved that the donee should receive the property on trust to provide maintenance, and this was a trust which would be enforced. In *Olszanecki v Hillocks* [2002] EWHC 1997 (Ch), [2002] All ER (D) 68 (Aug), [2004] WTLR 975, a gift of a share in a property to donees on condition that they allow another to occupy the property was held to create a trust.
6　It is a question of construction in each case whether a charge or a personal obligation is created or whether both are created: *Re Lester, Lester v Lester* [1942] Ch 324 at 325, [1942] 1 All ER 646 at 647 per Simonds J.
7　*Hodge v Churchward* (1847) 16 Sim 71; *Cunningham v Foot* (1878) 3 App Cas 974, HL; *Re Oliver, Newbald v Beckitt* (1890) 62 LT 533; *Re Hazlette* [1915] 1 IR 285, Ir CA.
8　*Hughes v Kelly* (1843) 3 Dr & War 482 (settlement); *Jacquet v Jacquet* (1859) 27 Beav 332; *Proud v Proud* (1862) 32 Beav 234; *Re Cowley, Souch v Cowley* (1885) 53 LT 494; *Re Scott, Scott v Scott (No 2)* (1915) 31 TLR 505 (devise subject to payment of pensions and allowances).
9　As to where there is a direction to pay an annuity out of the income of a fund see PERSONAL AND OCCUPATIONAL PENSIONS vol 80 (2013) PARA 675 et seq.

10 *Wright v Wilkin* (1860) 2 B & S 232 (affd (1862) 2 B & S 259); *A-G v Wax Chandlers' Co* (1873) LR 6 HL 1; *Re Corcoran, Corcoran v O'Kane* [1913] 1 IR 1 at 7. But see *Bird v Harris* (1870) LR 9 Eq 204 where a gift to executors to pay the income to the testator's wife for life with no disposition of the reversion was held to create a trust. The refusal to perform the condition or the death of the donee does not disappoint those entitled under the condition: *Re Kirk, Kirk v Kirk* (1882) 21 ChD 431, CA. The question has arisen chiefly in cases of charitable gifts of sums payable out of income: see *Thetford School Case* (1609) 8 Co Rep 130b; and CHARITIES vol 8 (2015) PARA 131 et seq.
11 *A-G v Wax Chandlers' Co* (1873) LR 6 HL 1 at 9–10.
12 As to the general principle in regard to rejecting or adding words see PARA 253.
13 *Lunn v Osborne, Pruen v Osborne* (1834) 7 Sim 56. See also *Doe d Leach v Micklem* (1805) 6 East 486; *Perrin v Lyon, Lyon v Geddes* (1807) 9 East 170; *Re Lowry's Will Trusts, Barclays Bank Ltd v United Newcastle-upon-Tyne Hospitals Board of Governors* [1967] Ch 638, [1966] 3 All ER 955 (where 'as equivalent charities' was added to make sense of the words in the will). As to changing 'and' to 'or' and vice versa see PARA 442 et seq. A condition relating to religion may be varied as respects a minor so as to enable the donee to make a considered choice: see *Re May, Eggar v May* [1917] 2 Ch 126; *Re May, Eggar v May* [1932] 1 Ch 99, CA. See also *Patton v Toronto General Trusts Corpn* [1930] AC 629, PC.
14 *Walker v Mower* (1852) 16 Beav 365; *Hope v Potter* (1857) 3 K & J 206; *Re Litchfield, Horton v Jones* (1911) 104 LT 631 at 632.

408. Whether conditions attach to a series of gifts. A condition attached to the first of a series of gifts may attach only to that one or generally throughout the series[1].

In a gift expressly made 'in the same manner' as another gift, the reference may be to the conditions attached by the testator[2] to the mode in which a class is to take only[3], and not to the mode of settlement, if any, of that gift[4], or other restrictions[5]; or the words may refer to all the interests, including gifts over, into which, under the principal gift, the absolute interest was to be divided[6].

1 For examples where the application of a condition to several gifts was in question see *Cockrill v Pitchforth* (1845) 1 Coll 626; *Doe d Bailey v Sloggett* (1850) 5 Exch 107; *Paylor v Pegg* (1857) 24 Beav 105 (gifts commencing with 'likewise') (distinguishing *Boosey v Gardener* (1854) 5 De GM & G 122); *Gordon v Gordon* (1871) LR 5 HL 254; *Rhodes v Rhodes* (1882) 7 App Cas 192 at 209, PC; *Re M'Garrity, Ballance and Benson v M'Garrity* (1912) 46 ILT 175. As to examples concerning the question of vesting see PARA 417.
2 The true rule of construction is not to look out for any conditions which may be affixed by law to the donees' interests, but to give effect, as far as possible, to the words of the will: *Ord v Ord* (1866) LR 2 Eq 393 at 396.
3 Eg the separate use (*Shanley v Baker* (1799) 4 Ves 732), or tenancy in common (*Lumley v Robbins* (1853) 10 Hare 621 at 629; *Re Wilder's Trusts* (1859) 27 Beav 418), or condition as to marriage, if valid (*Younge v Furse* (1857) 8 De GM & G 756), attached to the gift referred to.
4 *Eames v Anstee* (1863) 33 Beav 264 at 267; *Re Green, Crowson v Wild* [1907] VLR 284.
5 Eg a restriction on the class of persons taking may not be imported: *Yardley v Yardley* (1858) 26 Beav 38; *Pigott v Wilder* (1858) 26 Beav 90; *Re Wilder's Trusts* (1859) 27 Beav 418. See, however, *Swift v Swift* (1863) 32 LJ Ch 479.
6 *Ross v Ross* (1845) 2 Coll 269 at 272 per Knight Bruce V-C; *Re Liverpool Dock Acts, Re Colshead's Will Trusts* (1852) 2 De G & J 690; *Auldjo v Wallace* (1862) 31 Beav 193; *Re Shirley's Trusts* (1863) 32 Beav 394; *Ord v Ord* (1866) LR 2 Eq 393. See also *Milsom v Awdry* (1800) 5 Ves 465 at 467. There is no inflexible rule on the subject: *Pigott v Wilder* (1858) 26 Beav 90. As to the multiplication of charges in gifts by reference see SETTLEMENTS vol 91 (2012) PARA 624.

409. Conditions applying to cumulative and substituted legacies. Legacies given expressly[1] or impliedly[2] in addition to or in substitution for a legacy previously given so as to vary the amount of that legacy[3] are prima facie subject to the like conditions, if any, in respect of the mode of enjoyment of that legacy as are imposed on the original legacy[4]. The context or the circumstances may, however, exclude this rule[5], and it does not apply, unless the context so requires[6], where its application would turn an apparently absolute gift into a life interest[7], or alter the interests in the property[8], or where the character of the gifts is entirely different[9], or, in general, where the legatee of a substituted legacy is not the same as the legatee of the original legacy[10], although it may apply in this case[11].

1 The rule applies especially to cases of an express declaration, the presumption being that the testator merely intended to alter the amount of the legacy: *Re Boden, Boden v Boden* [1907] 1 Ch 132 at 149–150, CA. As to whether a gift is cumulative or substituted see PARA 401 et seq.
2 *Johnstone v Earl of Harrowby* (1859) 1 De GF & J 183. See, however, *Re Boden, Boden v Boden* [1907] 1 Ch 132 at 149–150.
3 It seems that the rule is not confined to questions of amount and may apply to cases where the substituted legatee is different from the original legatee: *Re Backhouse, Salmon v Backhouse* [1916] 1 Ch 65. See also *Re Joseph, Pain v Joseph* [1908] 2 Ch 507 at 512, CA, per Farwell LJ. In *Barry v Crundall* (1835) 7 Sim 430, trustees only were changed, and there was no change in the beneficial interest, notwithstanding an imperfect allusion to the original gift. See also *Fenton v Farington* (1856) 2 Jur NS 1120.
4 *Leacroft v Maynard* (1791) 3 Bro CC 233 (charged on same fund); *Crowder v Clowes* (1794) 2 Ves 449 (raisable out of same property); *Cooper v Day* (1817) 3 Mer 154; *Earl of Shaftesbury v Duke of Marlborough* (1835) 7 Sim 237 (cases as to legacy duty); *Martin v Drinkwater* (1840) 2 Beav 215; *Day v Croft* (1842) 4 Beav 561 (separate use); *Bristow v Bristow* (1842) 5 Beav 289 (charged on same fund); *Warwick v Hawkins* (1852) 5 De G & Sm 481 (separate use); *Giesler v Jones* (1858) 25 Beav 418 (payment postponed to death of life tenant of original legacy); *Duncan v Duncan (No 2)* (1859) 25 Beav 392 (provision for increase not applying to original legacy); *Duffield v Currie* (1860) 29 Beav 284 (same time of payment); *Re Smith* (1862) 2 John & H 594 at 600 (determination on insolvency); *Re Boddington, Boddington v Clairat* (1884) 25 ChD 685, CA (condition as to widowhood); *Re Benyon, Benyon v Grieve* (1884) 51 LT 116 (condition as to remaining in testator's service); *Re Colyer, Millikin v Snelling* (1886) 55 LT 344 (payment deferred to death of life tenant of original legacy); *Re Boden, Boden v Boden* [1907] 1 Ch 132, CA (annuities charged alike on income alone); *Re Crichton's Settlement, Sweetman v Batty* (1912) 106 LT 588 (limitation of gift during spinsterhood). As to cases where one legacy was given free of legacy duty (now abolished: see INHERITANCE TAXATION vol 59A (2014) PARA 1) cf *Burrows v Cottrell* (1830) 3 Sim 375; *Re Boden, Boden v Boden* above at 150 per Fletcher Moulton LJ. See also *Johnstone v Earl of Harrowby* (1859) 1 De GF & J 183 at 191 (legacy out of same fund, free of legacy duty). As to conditions attaching to alternate gifts, whether original or substitutional, see PARA 325.
5 *Re Mores' Trust* (1851) 10 Hare 171. See also *Overend v Gurney* (1834) 7 Sim 128; *Goodman v Goodman* (1847) 1 De G & Sm 695; *King v Tootel* (1858) 25 Beav 23.
6 See *Re Freme's Contract* [1895] 2 Ch 778, CA.
7 The rule is, in general, only applied where the original legacy is given absolutely or subject to defeasance: *Re Mores' Trust* (1851) 10 Hare 171 at 176 per Turner V-C; *Mann v Fuller* (1854) Kay 624 at 626 per Wood V-C; *Cooney v Nicholls* (1881) 7 LR Ir 107 at 115, Ir CA (cases where the original legacy was settled and the donee was life tenant); *Re Joseph, Pain v Joseph* [1908] 2 Ch 507 at 511, CA. See also note 1.
8 *Alexander v Alexander* (1842) 5 Beav 518; *Re Mores' Trust* (1851) 10 Hare 171 at 176; *Re Gibson's Trusts* (1861) 2 John & H 656 at 673; *Hargreaves v Pennington* (1864) 34 LJ Ch 180; *Hill v Jones* (1868) 37 LJ Ch 465; *Re Joseph, Pain v Joseph* [1908] 2 Ch 507 at 511, CA. In *Cookson v Hancock* (1836) 2 My & Cr 606, the trusts of the original legacy attached to the substituted legacy in the context of the will and codicil.
9 *Alexander v Alexander* (1842) 5 Beav 518 (pecuniary legacy substituted for residue); *Tibbs v Elliott* (1865) 34 Beav 424 (where a provision that the issue were to succeed to the parents' shares in property specifically devised did not extend to the parents' shares in residue); *Re Howe, Wilkinson v Ferniehough* (1910) 103 LT 185.
10 *Chatteris v Young* (1827) 2 Russ 183; *Haley v Bannister* (1857) 23 Beav 336; *Re Joseph, Pain v Joseph* [1908] 2 Ch 507, CA.
11 *Re Backhouse, Salmon v Backhouse* [1916] 1 Ch 65 at 72; *Leacroft v Maynard* (1791) 1 Ves 280; *Re MacCarthy's Will Trusts* [1958] IR 311.

410. Whether conditions apply to shares received under accruer clauses. A clause of accruer which divests and disposes of the share of a donee dying before a particular time, or in particular circumstances, prima facie refers only to the original share of that donee, and does not extend to shares which have accrued under the clause[1]. A similar construction applies where the description of the property subject to the clause of accruer is not necessarily comprehensive both of the donee's original share and of his other shares, or of his whole interest under the gifts in question, including the clauses of accruer[2]; but this construction does not apply where the clause clearly refers to the donee's whole interest in the fund[3], or to a plurality of shares of a single donee[4]. The word 'share' alone, or a similar word, may also be explained by the context to mean the donee's whole interest[5], for example by any expression directing the accrued shares to devolve in a similar way to the original shares[6], or by a context treating the accrued and original shares as blended, or as devolving together[7], or by the will showing an intention to create one aggregate fund and dispose of that absolutely[8], or by a context treating the whole property as subject to a gift over in an aggregate mass[9].

In general, the conditions applicable to an original share are not applicable to the share accrued to it under a clause of accruer[10] unless an intention that they are to apply is shown or can be inferred[11]. In the absence of a contrary intention, an accruing share accrues to other shares in equal proportions[12].

1   *Rudge v Barker* (1735) Cas *temp* Talb 124; *Re Scaife, ex p West* (1784) 1 Bro CC 575; *Crowder v Stone* (1829) 3 Russ 217 at 223; *Rickett v Guillemard* (1841) 12 Sim 88; *Re Lybbe's Will Trusts, Kildahl v Bowker* [1954] 1 All ER 487, [1954] 1 WLR 573 (where it was held that there was insufficient indication to justify departure from the ordinary meaning of 'share' which meant 'original share' and did not include 'accrued share'). As to the operation of an accruer clause in relation to a share to which the doctrine of *Lassence v Tierney* (1849) 1 Mac & G 551 (see PARA 231) was applied see *Re Atkinson's Will Trusts, Prescott v Child* [1957] Ch 117, [1956] 3 All ER 738.

2   *Woodward v Glasbrook* (1700) 2 Vern 388 (his part or share); *Perkins v Micklethwaite* (1714) 1 P Wms 274 (portion); *Bright v Rowe* (1834) 3 My & K 316 (her, his or their portion or portions); *Rickett v Guillemard* (1841) 12 Sim 88 (his, her or their shares); *Maddison v Chapman* (1858) 4 K & J 709 at 716 (the part of the deceased); *Goodwin v Finlayson* (1858) 25 Beav 65 (his or her part); *Evans v Evans* (1858) 25 Beav 81 at 88 (his or her share). There has been adverse criticism of *Pain v Benson* (1744) 3 Atk 78 (his, her or their shares), and it has not been followed: *Goodwin v Finlayson* above. A description of the property subject to the clause of accruer in terms such as 'his, her or their share or shares' may be read as if 'shares' corresponded to 'their', and, therefore, as not denoting a plurality of the shares of a single donee: *Bright v Rowe* (1834) 3 My & K 316; *Rickett v Guillemard* (1841) 12 Sim 88; *Wilmot v Flewitt* (1865) 11 Jur NS 820 at 821; *Sutton v Sutton* (1892) 30 LR Ir 251 at 268, Ir CA (deed); *Ganapathy Pillay v Alamaloo* [1929] AC 462, PC.

3   *Goodman v Goodman* (1847) 1 De G & Sm 695 (the interest and capital of child dying); *Douglas v Andrews* (1851) 14 Beav 347 at 353 (the part and parts, share and shares and interest of him, her or them); *Re Crawhall's Trust* (1856) 8 De GM & G 480 (with benefit of survivorship); *Re Henriques' Trusts* [1875] WN 187 (part share and interest); *Re Sadler, Furniss v Cooper* (1915) 60 Sol Jo 89; *Re Morris, Corfield v Waller* (1916) 86 LJ Ch 456.

4   *Re Chaston, Chaston v Seago* (1881) 18 ChD 218 at 224; *Clifton v Crawford* (1900) 27 AR 315 at 319.

5   *Doe d Clift v Birkhead* (1849) 4 Exch 110.

6   *Giles v Melsom* (1873) LR 6 HL 24. See also *Eyre v Marsden* (1839) 4 My & Cr 231; *Leeming v Sherratt* (1842) 2 Hare 14 at 25.

7   *Milsom v Awdry* (1800) 5 Ves 465; *Douglas v Andrews* (1851) 14 Beav 347 at 351–352. As to directions that a share of residue given under a previous gift is to fall into residue either generally or in certain events see PARA 298.

8   *Re Allan, Dow v Cassaigne* [1903] 1 Ch 276 at 284, CA, per Vaughan-Williams LJ; discussed in *Re Lybbe's Will Trusts, Kildahl v Bowker* [1954] 1 All ER 487, [1954] 1 WLR 573.

9   *Worlidge v Churchill* (1792) 3 Bro CC 465; *Barker v Lea* (1823) Turn & R 413 at 415; *Eyre v Marsden* (1838) 2 Keen 564 at 575; *Sillick v Booth* (1841) 1 Y & C Ch Cas 117 at 121; *Doe d Clift v Birkhead* (1849) 4 Exch 110; *Dutton v Crowdy* (1863) 33 LJ Ch 241; *Re Henriques' Trusts* [1875] WN 187. Where a share was to accrue to the shares of daughters, the accruer was held to operate independently of survivorship of the daughters taking accruing shares: *Re Walter's Will Trusts, Stuart v Pitman* [1949] Ch 91, [1948] 2 All ER 955.

10   *Gibbons v Langdon* (1833) 6 Sim 260; *Ranelagh v Ranelagh* (1841) 4 Beav 419 (original gift for life); *Jones v Hall* (1849) 16 Sim 500; *Leigh v Mosley* (1851) 14 Beav 605 (no tenancy in common in accrued shares); *Ware v Watson* (1855) 7 De GM & G 248 (direction for settlement of daughter's share applied to original share only).

11 *Milsom v Awdry* (1800) 5 Ves 465; *Cursham v Newland* (1839) 2 Beav 145; *Re Jarman's Trusts* (1865) LR 1 Eq 71 (separate use attaching to the 'share or shares'); *Giles v Melsom* (1873) LR 6 HL 24; *Sutton v Sutton* (1892) 30 LR Ir 251 at 260, Ir CA. See also *Trickey v Trickey* (1832) 3 My & K 560 at 565; *Hayes v Hayes* [1917] 1 IR 194.

12 See *Re Bower's Settlement Trusts, Bower v Ridley-Thompson* [1942] Ch 197, [1942] 1 All ER 278; *Re Steel, Public Trustee v Christian Aid Society* [1979] Ch 218, [1978] 2 All ER 1026. In *Re Huntington's Settlement Trusts, Struthers v Mayne* [1949] Ch 414, [1949] 1 All ER 674, it was held that, under an accruer clause adding accruing shares to those whose trusts had not failed or determined, a share which had vested absolutely and been paid out to a beneficiary was entitled to participate in accruing shares, since the trusts of the paid-out share had not failed or determined.

411. Contingency happening in testator's lifetime. Whenever there is an interest validly limited by will, either by way of remainder or by way of executory interest, and all the preceding estates have failed or determined, and the events on which the interest is limited have taken effect, it is in general immaterial whether this has happened in the testator's lifetime or after his death[1]. Thus in the case of a gift over on a prior named individual donee dying in any contingent circumstances[2], or dying before any specified time or event[3], the gift over as a rule takes effect if the prior donee so dies during the testator's lifetime[4]. A gift over on a prior donee dying without having attained a vested interest takes effect if that prior donee dies in the testator's lifetime, even if he otherwise satisfies the conditions of the prior gift[5]. However, on its true construction, a will may be held to refer only to events taking place after the testator's death or other time[6].

1 *Varley v Winn* (1856) 2 K & J 700 at 705.
2 Eg where the gift over is on death before 21 and the prior donee dies during the testator's lifetime not having attained 21 (*Ledsome v Hickman* (1708) 2 Vern 611; *Perkins v Micklethwaite* (1714) 1 P Wms 274 (death before 21 or marriage); *Northey v Strange* (1716) 1 P Wms 340 at 343; *Willing v Baine* (1731) 3 P Wms 113), or if the gift over is on death without issue (*Mackinnon v Peach* (1838) 2 Keen 555 at 560; *Varley v Winn* (1856) 2 K & J 700), or on death without issue who become entitled under an intermediate gift (*Rackham v De La Mare* (1864) 2 De GJ & Sm 74), or on death leaving issue (*Rheeder v Ower* (1791) 3 Bro CC 240).
3 Eg on death before payment (*Ive v King* (1852) 16 Beav 46 at 54), or before division of the estate (*Bretton v Lethulier* (1710) 2 Vern 653), or before the legacy becomes payable (*Darrel v Molesworth* (1700) 2 Vern 378; *Walker v Main* (1819) 1 Jac & W 1; *Humphreys v Howes* (1830) 1 Russ & M 639).
4 If, however, the prior donee dies before the testator but not before the specified event, the gift over does not normally take effect: see PARA 445. As to the general rule in cases of failure of a prior interest see PARA 180.
5 *Re Gaitskell's Trust* (1873) LR 15 Eq 386.
6 *Chapman v Perkins* [1905] AC 106, HL.

(ii) Vesting

A. PRESUMPTION AS TO VESTING

412. Meaning of 'vest'. The proper legal meaning of 'vest' is vest in interest[1]. Where a testator uses this word, as, for example, by directing that the gift is to vest on a certain event, prima facie it must be given its proper legal meaning, and the gift is then contingent until the happening of the event[2], whether the gift is of real or personal estate[3]. The context may, however, show, by indications that the donee is to take a vested interest before the specified event, that 'vest' is used in another sense, for example in the sense of 'fall into possession'[4], or 'become payable'[5] or 'be indefeasibly vested'[6]. Where 'vested' means 'indefeasibly vested', the gift may be vested before the specified event, subject only to being divested if the event does not happen[7]. A direction with regard to vesting of a gift to a class may, on the construction of a particular will, even introduce a new category of persons to share in the gift[8].

1   *Re Baxter's Trusts* (1864) 10 Jur NS 845 at 847; *Hale v Hale* (1876) 3 ChD 643 at 646. See also PERPETUITIES AND ACCUMULATIONS vol 80 (2013) PARA 27; REAL PROPERTY AND REGISTRATION vol 87 (2012) PARA 161. As to the general rule of construction of words see PARA 241.
2   *Glanvill v Glanvill* (1816) 2 Mer 38; *Russel v Buchanan* (1836) 7 Sim 628; *Ring v Hardwick* (1840) 2 Beav 352; *Griffith v Blunt* (1841) 4 Beav 248; *Comport v Austen* (1841) 12 Sim 218; *Re Thruston's Will Trusts* (1849) 17 Sim 21; *Re Blakemore's Settlement* (1855) 20 Beav 214; *Re Morse's Settlement* (1855) 21 Beav 174; *Rowland v Tawney* (1858) 26 Beav 67; *Wakefield v Dyott* (1858) 4 Jur NS 1098; *Sheffield v Kennett* (1859) 27 Beav 207 (affd 4 De G & J 593); *Draycott v Wood* (1856) 5 WR 158; *Re Arnold's Estate* (1863) 33 Beav 163 at 173; *Richardson v Power* (1865) 19 CBNS 780, Ex Ch; *Lushington v Penrice, Penrice v Lushington* (1868) 18 LT 597; *Creeth v Wilson* (1882) 9 LR Ir 216 at 223; *Re Whiston, Whiston v Woolley* [1924] 1 Ch 122, CA, distinguishing *Re Featherstone's Trusts* (1882) 22 ChD 111. See also *Re Wrightson, Battie-Wrightson v Thomas* [1904] 2 Ch 95, CA (where the testator directed that no beneficiary was to have a vested interest or be entitled to the possession); *Parkes (or Keswick) v Parkes (or Keswick)* [1936] 3 All ER 653, HL. A provision for maintenance out of 'vested or expectant' shares in such a case does not alter the meaning of 'vest': *Bull v Pritchard* (1847) 5 Hare 567 at 572; *Re Thatcher's Trusts* (1859) 26 Beav 365 at 369. See also *Pickford v Brown, Brown v Brown* (1856) 2 K & J 426.
3   *Re Featherstone's Trusts* (1882) 22 ChD 111 at 114 per Kay J.
4   *Simpson v Peach* (1873) LR 16 Eq 208.
5   *Williams v Haythorne, Williams v Williams* (1871) 6 Ch App 782 at 788. For a case where a distinction was expressly drawn between vesting and payment in the will see *Ellis v Maxwell* (1841) 3 Beav 587.
6   *Berkeley v Swinburne* (1848) 16 Sim 275 at 281–282; *Taylor v Frobisher* (1852) 5 De G & Sm 191; *Poole v Bott* (1853) 11 Hare 33 at 37–38; *Barnet v Barnet* (1861) 29 Beav 239; *Re Baxter's Trusts* (1864) 10 Jur NS 845; *Re Edmondson's Estate* (1868) LR 5 Eq 389; *Re Parr's Trusts* (1871) 41 LJ Ch 170; *Armytage v Wilkinson* (1878) 3 App Cas 355 at 372–373, PC; *Best v Williams* [1890] WN 189.
7   See the cases cited in note 6. As to divesting generally see PARA 440 et seq.
8   *Williams v Russell* (1863) 10 Jur NS 168. See also *Bickford v Chalker* (1854) 2 Drew 327 (where a direction as to vesting was rejected). As to a gift to a class on contingency generally see PARA 303.

413. Early vesting favoured. Where there is a doubt as to the time of vesting, the presumption is in favour of the early vesting[1] of the gift and, accordingly, it vests at the testator's death[2] or at the earliest moment after that date which is possible in the context[3], whether it is of real[4] or personal[5] estate. It is presumed that the testator intended the gift to be vested, subject to being divested, rather than to remain in suspense[6]. The presumption is especially applicable where the interest created is a remainder, the reason being that keeping the remainder contingent might in many cases exclude the issue of a person intended to take in tail by the parent's dying before the remainder became vested[7]. It is also especially applicable where the donees are the children of a named person as a class[8], and where the gift is of a residuary personal estate or residuary real and personal estate so as to avoid intestacy[9].

1   The policy of the law favouring early vesting does not justify a contingent gift being misconstrued to make it vest earlier than the time contemplated by the testator: *Re Ransome's Will Trusts, Moberley v Ransome* [1957] Ch 348 at 361, [1957] 1 All ER 690 at 696 per Upjohn J. As to the rules of convenience, which rest on the policy favouring early vesting see PARA 305 et seq.
2   A bequest making no reference to time takes effect at the testator's death unless this date would disturb provisions already made in the will, or unless an intention that the bequest is to operate at a later date clearly appears: *Hamilton v Ritchie* [1894] AC 310, HL; *Bernard v Walker* (1921) 55 ILT 73, HL.
3   *Re Blakemore's Settlement* (1855) 20 Beav 214 at 217 (where the gifts were nevertheless held void for remoteness); *Darley v Perceval* [1900] 1 IR 129 at 135–136; *Ward v Brown* [1916] 2 AC 121, PC. As a will is ambulatory until death (see PARA 2), the testator cannot make a legacy vest at the

date of the will, and a provision to that effect does not prevent lapse: *Browne v Hope* (1872) LR 14 Eq 343. As to the meaning of 'lapse' see PARA 160.

4   *Driver d Frank v Frank* (1818) 8 Taunt 468, Ex Ch; *Duffield v Duffield* (1829) 3 Bli NS 260 at 311, 331, HL (in construing devises there is a presumption in favour of vesting although the presumption will not apply where a condition precedent to the vesting is so clearly expressed that the court cannot treat the gift as vested without deciding in direct opposition to the terms of the will); *Re Wrightson, Battie-Wrightson v Thomas* [1904] 2 Ch 95 at 103, CA; *Re Blackwell, Blackwell v Blackwell* [1926] Ch 223 at 233–234, CA; *Bickersteth v Shanu* [1936] AC 290, [1936] 1 All ER 227, PC.

5   *Brocklebank v Johnson* (1855) 20 Beav 205 at 215; *Re Merricks' Trusts* (1866) LR 1 Eq 551 at 557; *Rhodes v Rhodes* (1882) 7 App Cas 192 at 211, PC; *Parkes (or Keswick) v Parkes (or Keswick)* [1936] 3 All ER 653, HL (the intention of the testator as expressed in the will must have effect given to it, beyond and even against, the literal sense of particular expressions per Lord Maughan at 669).

6   *Taylor v Graham* (1878) 3 App Cas 1287 at 1297, HL, per Lord Blackburn; *Hickling v Fair* [1899] AC 15 at 30, 36, HL; *Yule's Trustees v Deans* 1919 SC 570, Ct of Sess.

7   *Driver d Frank v Frank* (1814) 3 M & S 25 at 36 (affd (1818) 8 Taunt 488, Ex Ch), following *Doe d Comberbach v Perryn* (1789) 3 Term Rep 484 at 494. See also *Ives v Legge* (1743) 3 Term Rep 448n; *Re Watkins, Maybery v Lightfoot* (1913), as reported in 108 LT 237 at 240, CA, per Buckley LJ, who dissented, and whose decision was upheld on appeal sub nom *Lightfoot v Maybery* [1914] AC 782, HL. Contingent remainders failed if the contingency had not been fulfilled when the previous interest determined: see PARA 418. To modify the hardship of the rule, it is an established rule of construction that in doubtful cases a remainder, if possible, should be construed as vested rather than contingent. This rule is the foundation of a long series of decisions from *Boraston's Case* (1587) 3 Co Rep 16a onwards: *Browne v Browne* (1857) 3 Sm & G 568 at 588. See PARA 419 et seq. See also *Pearks v Moseley* (1880) 5 App Cas 714, HL at 721. As to remainders in general see REAL PROPERTY AND REGISTRATION vol 87 (2012) PARA 162 et seq. Entailed interests cannot be created by instruments coming into operation on or after 1 January 1997: see the Trusts of Land and Appointment of Trustees Act 1996 s 2(6), Sch 1 para 5; PARA 387; and REAL PROPERTY AND REGISTRATION vol 87 (2012) PARA 114.

8   *M'Lachlan v Taitt* (1860) 2 De GF & J 449 at 454 per Lord Campbell LC. But see *Selby v Whittaker* (1877) 6 ChD 239 at 249, CA, per James LJ, and at 251 per Cotton LJ. There may be no reason for the application of the presumption in the case of a child if all the testator's descendants living at the period of distribution are provided for: *Re Deighton's Settled Estates* (1876) 2 ChD 783, CA.

9   *Love v l'Estrange* (1727) 5 Bro Parl Cas 59; *Booth v Booth* (1799) 4 Ves 399; *Oddie v Brown* (1859) 4 De G & J 179 at 194; *Pearman v Pearman* (1864) 33 Beav 394 at 396; *West v West* (1863) 4 Giff 198. As to gifts carrying the intermediate interest see PARA 430 et seq.

414.   Effect of presumption of early vesting on determining whether condition is precedent or subsequent.

The presumption in favour of early vesting[1] may assist in determining whether a condition is to be construed as precedent or subsequent[2]. On the construction of the particular will it may be plain that a condition is or is not a condition precedent[3], and the same condition may in one case be precedent and in another be subsequent[4]. In the first instance the context of the whole will must be considered[5], but, if on construction it is doubtful whether the condition is precedent or subsequent, the presumption in favour of early vesting applies[6] and the condition is treated as subsequent[7].

1   As to the presumption in favour of early vesting see PARA 413.

2   See *Re Lowry's Will Trusts, Barclays Bank Ltd v United Newcastle-upon-Tyne Hospitals Board of Governors* [1967] Ch 638 at 650, [1966] 3 All ER 955 at 960 per Cross J (where, however, interests conferred on three charities were held to be future contingent interests and not vested interests in remainder liable to be divested by an event occurring before they vested in possession).

3   Eg 'provided A marry B', which is clearly a condition precedent: *Davis v Angel* (1862) 4 De GF & J 524; *Fitzgerald v Ryan* [1899] 2 IR 637 at 647, 663, Ir CA; *Kiersey v Flahavan* [1905] 1 IR 45. See also *Re Welstead* (1858) 25 Beav 612 (bequest for purchase of nomination not a condition at all); *Re Emson, Grain v Grain* (1905) 93 LT 104 ('subject to' trustees being appointed as governors). As to the meaning of and distinction between conditions precedent and conditions subsequent see PARA 129.

4   *Robinson v Comyns* (1736) Cas *temp* Talb 164 at 166; *Doe d Planner v Scuddamore* (1800) 2 Bos & P 289 at 295 per Lord Eldon CJ, and at 297 per Heath J (where it was held that a condition is to be construed as precedent or subsequent according to the testator's intention); *Egerton v Earl*

Brownlow (1853) 4 HL Cas 1 at 157, 183; *Re Kavanagh, Murphy v Broder* (1874) IR 9 CL 123 at 130. It has been suggested that a condition is likely to be a condition precedent, eg where the condition involves anything in the nature of consideration (*Acherley v Vernon* (1739) Willes 153 per Willes CJ), such as a release of dower (*Wheddon v Oxenham* (1731) 2 Eq Cas Abr 546 pl 24), or where the nature of the interest is such as to allow time for the performance of the act before enjoyment, or where the condition is capable of being performed instantly (Jarman on Wills (8th Edn) 1459). These suggestions are considered in *Fitzgerald v Ryan* [1899] 2 IR 637 at 646–647. For cases where the allowance of a period of time for the performance of the condition, extending to the life of the donee, did not prevent the condition being precedent see also *Randal v Payne* (1779) 1 Bro CC 55; *Re M'Mahon, M'Mahon v M'Mahon* [1901] 1 IR 489, CA; *Horrigan v Horrigan* [1904] 1 IR 29 (on appeal [1904] 1 IR 271, Ir CA); *Kiersey v Flahavan* [1905] 1 IR 45 (cases of devises conditional on marriage with a named person or into a named family).

5　*Egerton v Earl Brownlow* (1853) 4 HL Cas 1 at 132, 157; cf *Carlton v Thompson* (1867) LR 1 Sc & Div 232 at 235, HL.

6　It applies only where the matter is not clear: *Hickling v Fair* [1899] AC 15 at 27, HL.

7　*Egerton v Earl Brownlow* (1853) 4 HL Cas 1 at 157, 182–183, 189; *Woodhouse v Herrick* (1855) 1 K & J 352 at 359–360; *Lady Langdale v Briggs* (1856) 8 De GM & G 391; *Re Greenwood, Goodhart v Woodhead* [1903] 1 Ch 749 at 755, CA; *Re Blackwell, Blackwell v Blackwell* [1926] Ch 223; *Bickersteth v Shanu* [1936] AC 290, [1936] 1 All ER 227, PC; *Sifton v Sifton* [1938] AC 656 at 676, [1938] 3 All ER 435 at 446, PC.

B.　CIRCUMSTANCES AFFECTING VESTING

415. Postponement of enjoyment only. In addition to the general presumption in favour of early vesting[1], particular circumstances may affect the question whether a gift is vested. Thus where a condition can be fairly read as postponing merely the right of possession or of obtaining payment, transfer or conveyance, so that there is an express or implied distinction between the time of vesting and time of enjoyment, the gift is held to be vested at the earlier date if the rest of the context allows[2]. This construction is particularly applicable where the postponement is for the convenience of the testator's estate[3] or is occasioned by the gift of some prior interest filling up the interval[4].

Thus where the testator suspends the enjoyment until payment of his debts[5] or other incident of administration of his estate[6], prima facie the vesting is not suspended until that payment or other event; the nature of the provision shows that it is merely the enjoyment which is postponed. There may, however, be an intention clearly expressed[7] to suspend vesting until such an event[8], and effect must be given to this intention, however inconvenient the result may be[9]. Similarly, although vesting of a legacy (whether pecuniary or residuary) may be postponed until actual payment if the context is clear[10], in case of doubt the court interprets a gift apparently vesting on payment as vesting when the legacy becomes payable[11].

1　As to the presumption in favour of early vesting see PARA 413.

2　As to real estate see *Montgomerie v Woodley* (1800) 5 Ves 522 at 526; *Bingley v Broadhead* (1803) 8 Ves 415; *Duffield v Duffield* (1829) 1 Dow & Cl 268 at 311, HL, per Best CJ; *Snow v Poulden* (1836) 1 Keen 186; *Peard v Kekewich* (1852) 15 Beav 166 at 171; *Dennis v Frend* (1863) 14 I Ch R 271 (donee 'not to become entitled to or take the estate' until 23). See also *Boraston's Case* (1587) 3 Co Rep 16a, 19; and PARA 419. As to personal estate see *Dodson v Hay* (1791) 3 Bro CC 405 at 410; *Re Panter, Panter-Downs v Bally* (1906) 22 TLR 431; and PARAS 425–426. As to a mixed fund see *M'Lachlan v Taitt* (1860) 2 De GF & J 449 (where the children became beneficially interested on the death of the parent). Cf *Re McGeorge, Ratcliff v McGeorge* [1963] Ch 544, [1963] 1 All ER 519 (where a separate devise and bequest were directed not to 'take effect until after the death of my wife', and it was held that this direction deferred the vesting in possession (but not its vesting in interest) until the death of the testator's widow).

3　See the text and notes 5–6. As to legacies payable out of personal estate see PARA 425; and as to legacies charged on real estate see PARA 438.

4　See PARAS 422, 429, 440.

5   *Barnardiston v Carter* (1717) 3 Bro Parl Cas 64; *Tewart v Lawson* (1874) LR 18 Eq 490. See also
    Marshall v Holloway (1820) 2 Swan 432 at 446 per Lord Eldon LC (direction to accumulate did
    not prevent a vested interest); *Bacon v Proctor* (1822) Turn & R 31 at 40.

6   Eg investment as directed (*Sitwell v Bernard* (1801) 6 Ves 520) or performance of trusts (*Birds v
    Askey* (1857) 24 Beav 615). A trust for sale of real estate, and for payment of the proceeds to
    certain donees, ascertained without reference to the time or other features of the sale, the sale being
    merely for the purpose of division and for the convenience of the estate, does not make the sale a
    condition precedent to vesting of their interests: *Parker v Sowerby* (1853) 1 Drew 488 (affd on
    another point (1854) 4 De GM & G 321). See also *Re Raw, Morris v Griffiths* (1884) 26 ChD 601
    at 602. As to the effect of trusts void for remoteness see PERPETUITIES AND ACCUMULATIONS
    vol 80 (2013) PARA 42; and as to the rules applicable to gifts of the proceeds of sale of real estate
    see PARA 425. Since 1 January 1997 all trusts for sale formerly imposed by statute have become
    trusts of land (without a duty to sell) and land formerly held on such statutorily imposed trusts for
    sale is now held in trust for the persons interested in the land, so that the owner of each undivided
    share now has an interest in land: see the Trusts of Land and Appointment of Trustees Act 1996
    ss 1, 5, Sch 2 paras 2–5, 7 (amending the Law of Property Act 1925 ss 32, 34, 36 and the
    Administration of Estates Act 1925 s 33); and REAL PROPERTY AND REGISTRATION vol 87
    (2012) PARA 105.

7   In such a case the court does not allow the legatees to be prejudiced by the delay of the executors
    or trustees: *Small v Wing* (1730) 5 Bro Parl Cas 66; *Gaskell v Harman* (1805) 11 Ves 489 at 507;
    Bernard v Mountague (1816) 1 Mer 422 at 433; *Astley v Earl of Essex* (1871) 6 Ch App 898.

8   Eg until payment of debts or discharge of incumbrances (*Bagshaw v Spencer* (1748) 1 Ves Sen 142
    at 144; *Bernard v Mountague* (1816) 1 Mer 422; *Tewart v Lawson* (1874) LR 18 Eq 490 at 495;
    Re Bewick, Ryle v Ryle [1911] 1 Ch 116), or until discharge of mortgage and sale (*Elwin v Elwin*
    (1803) 8 Ves 547 (to named persons, if living at time of sale); *Blight v Hartnoll* (1881) 19 ChD 294
    (to class of grandchildren living at time of sale)).

9   *Gaskell v Harman* (1801) 6 Ves 159; on appeal (1805) 11 Ves 489 at 497; *Bernard v Mountague*
    (1816) 1 Mer 422 at 433.

10 *Gaskell v Harman* (1801) 6 Ves 159; on appeal (1805) 11 Ves 489 at 497.

11 *Stapleton v Palmer* (1794) 4 Bro CC 490; *Gaskell v Harman* (1801) 6 Ves 159; *Re Kirkley,
    Halligey v Kirkley* (1918) 87 LJ Ch 247. As to gifts over on death before payment cf PARA 451.

416. Contingency in description of donee or subject matter of gift. An estate or
interest must remain contingent until there is a person having all the qualifications
which the testator requires and completely answering the description of the object
of his bounty given in the will[1]. Where the postponement of the gift is on account
of some qualification attached to the donee, the gift is prima facie contingent on
his qualification being acquired[2]. Thus a gift to a person 'at', 'if', 'as soon as',
'when' or 'provided' he attains a certain age, without further context to govern the
meaning of the words, is contingent and vests only on the attainment[3] of the
required age[4], this being a quality or description which the donee must in general
possess in order to claim under the gift[5]. In a similar gift to a class[6], the specified
age in general determines the persons who may claim as members of the class[7].
Such words have, however, in various contexts been held not really to import
contingency in the sense of a condition precedent to the vesting, but to have the
effect of a proviso or condition subsequent operating as a defeasance of a vested
interest[8].

1   *Proctor v Bishop of Bath and Wells* (1794) 2 Hy Bl 358 (the first son of A that should be bred a
    clergyman); *Leake v Robinson* (1817) 2 Mer 363 at 385; *Duffield v Duffield* (1829) 1 Dow & Cl
    268 at 311, HL, per Best CJ (such children as should attain 21) (following *Stephens v Stephens*
    (1736) Cas *temp* Talb 228 (such son as should attain 21)); *Re Laing, Laing v Morrison* [1912] 2
    Ch 386 at 392; *Re Astor, Astor v Astor* [1922] 1 Ch 364, CA; *Re Lowry's Will Trusts, Barclays
    Bank Ltd v United Newcastle-upon-Tyne Hospitals Board of Governors* [1967] Ch 638, [1966]
    3 All ER 995 (where, on the failure of certain trusts, there was a gift to such specified charities as
    should then remain as independent charities). As to the ascertainment of the donee see the
    rules stated in PARA 299 et seq, which may determine the vesting (see *Driver d Frank v Frank*
    (1818) 8 Taunt 468, Ex Ch (remainders to second and other sons, vested as they came into
    existence)).

2   As to persons 'living' at a particular time see *Cooper v Macdonald* (1873) LR 16 Eq 258 (where
    'then living' was held to mean 'who or whose issue may then be living'; cf PARA 315 et seq); and

PARA 300. As to gifts to survivors see *Jones v Davies* (1880) 28 WR 455 (where the testator gave all his real and personal estate to his two sons and daughter in equal shares absolutely, and, if his daughter should die without leaving issue, to the survivors of his sons, and it was held that the survival of the sons was part of the contingency raising the gifts over, and, therefore, the sons having predeceased the daughter, the daughter's estate became indefeasible, although she died without leaving issue). As to survivorship generally see PARA 315 et seq. A gift to a survivor itself imports a contingency: *Whitby v Von Luedecke* [1906] 1 Ch 783; *Re Legh's Settlement Trusts, Public Trustee v Legh* [1938] Ch 39, [1937] 3 All ER 823, CA. Cf PERPETUITIES AND ACCUMULATIONS vol 80 (2013) PARA 30.

3   As to the time at which a person attains a particular age see the Family Law Reform Act 1969 s 9 for anniversaries occurring on or after 1 January 1970; for anniversaries before that date see *Re Shurey, Savory v Shurey* [1918] 1 Ch 263; and CHILDREN AND YOUNG PERSONS vol 9 (2012) PARA 2.

4   As to real estate see *Re Francis, Francis v Francis* [1905] 2 Ch 295 (following *Johnson v Gabriel and Bellamy* (1588) Cro Eliz 122, cited as *Grant's Case* in 10 Co Rep at 50a; and explained in *Lampet's Case* (1612) 10 Co Rep 46b at 50a); *Love v Love* (1881) 7 LR Ir 306 ('on his attaining' 23); *Phipps v Ackers* (1842) 9 Cl & Fin 583 at 590–591, HL, per Tindal CJ; *Doe d Wheedon v Lea* (1789) 3 Term Rep 41 at 43 per Ashurst J. As to personal estate see *Stapleton v Cheales* (1711) Prec Ch 317; Tudor, LC Real Prop (4th Edn) 438, 440; *Atkinson v Turner* (1740) 2 Atk 41; *Hanson v Graham* (1801) 6 Ves 239 at 243–245; *Butcher v Leach* (1843) 5 Beav 392; *Mair v Quilter* (1843) 2 Y & C Ch Cas 465; *Re Edwards, Jones v Jones* [1906] 1 Ch 570 at 573, CA; *Re Kirkley, Halligey v Kirkley* (1918) 87 LJ Ch 247 (where a bequest to members of a class to be paid if and when they respectively attained the age of 21 was held contingent); *Re Blackwell, Blackwell v Blackwell* [1926] Ch 223, CA ('absolutely upon his attaining the age of twenty-one years').

5   *Leake v Robinson* (1817) 2 Mer 363 at 385–386. Where the will contains a direction to pay, transfer or assign to the donee on his attaining a specified age, the gift does not vest until that age is attained: *Walker v Mower* (1852) 16 Beav 365.

6   *Judd v Judd* (1830) 3 Sim 525; *Hunter v Judd* (1833) 4 Sim 455. Where there is a gift to a class conditional on attainment of a specified age and, if there should be only one member of the class, to him, no condition being stated, with a gift over, the condition applying to the class is not imported into the gift to the single child: see *Walker v Mower* (1852) 16 Beav 365; *Johnson v Foulds* (1868) LR 5 Eq 268; *Re Fletcher, Doré v Fletcher* (1885) 53 LT 813.

7   As to real estate see *Duffield v Duffield* (1829) 1 Dow & Cl 268, HL; *Newman v Newman* (1839) 10 Sim 51; *Kennedy v Sedgwick* (1857) 3 K & J 540; *Re Astor, Astor v Astor* [1922] 1 Ch 364, CA. As to personal estate see *Leake v Robinson* (1817) 2 Mer 363; *Bull v Pritchard* (1826) 1 Russ 213; *Porter v Fox* (1834) 6 Sim 485 (mixed fund); *Chance v Chance* (1853) 16 Beav 572; *Merlin v Blagrave* (1858) 25 Beav 125; *Thomas v Wilberforce* (1862) 31 Beav 299; *Bowyer v West* (1871) 24 LT 414; *Re Williams, Spencer v Brighouse* (1886) 54 LT 831. As to the ascertainment of classes see PARA 302.

8   *Andrew v Andrew* (1875) 1 ChD 410 at 417–418, CA, per James LJ; *Re James' Settled Estates* (1884) 51 LT 596 at 597; *Re Campbell, Cooper v Campbell* (1919) 88 LJ Ch 239, 120 LT 562; *Bickersteth v Shanu* [1936] AC 290, [1936] 1 All ER 227, PC. Cf *Re McGeorge, Ratcliff v McGeorge* [1963] Ch 544, [1963] 1 All ER 519 (where the words 'shall not take effect until after the death of my wife' merely postponed the vesting in possession). As to the position where there is a gift over on a devise of real estate see PARA 423.

417. Contingencies in successive gifts.

A contingency which is a condition precedent to vesting of a particular estate or interest prima facie applies to all interests dependent on that estate or interest or limited in immediate succession to that estate or interest as a continuous series[1], but not to other limitations[2]. Further, even if gifts follow other gifts, and, for example, all are contingent on a certain event[3], the court may infer from the will, taken as a whole, that it is a mere inaccuracy of expression, and that the contingency is really meant to apply only to such of the subsequent trusts and limitations as necessarily depend for their existence on the happening of the event in question[4].

1   *Davis v Norton* (1726) 2 P Wms 390; *Doe d Watson v Shipphard* (1779) 1 Doug KB 75; *Toldervy v Colt* (1836) 1 Y & C Ex 621; *Cattley v Vincent* (1852) 15 Beav 198; *Paylor v Pegg* (1857) 24 Beav 105 (words misplaced within will); *Hill v Hill* (1860) 8 WR 536. See also *Gray v Golding* (1860) 6 Jur NS 474, HL; *Crosse v Eldridge* (1918) 53 L Jo 52. For instances of contrary intention generally, inferred from the will as a whole see *Sheffield v Earl of Coventry* (1852) 2 De GM & G 551; *Boosey v Gardener* (1854) 5 De GM & G 122.

2 *Partridge v Foster (No 2)* (1866) 35 Beav 545.

3 *Pearson v Rutter* (1853) 3 De GM & G 398 at 406 (affd, without affecting this point, sub nom *Grey v Pearson* (1857) 6 HL Cas 61). See also *Sheffield v Earl of Coventry* (1852) 2 De GM & G 551; *Boosey v Gardener* (1854) 5 De GM & G 122; *Duffield v M'Master* [1906] 1 IR 333, Ir CA.

4 *Quicke v Leach* (1844) 13 M & W 218. See also *Napper v Sanders* (1632) Hut 118, approved in *Lethieullier v Tracy* (1753) 3 Atk 774 at 781–782 per Lord Hardwicke LC; *Horton v Whittaker* (1786) 1 Term Rep 346; *Doe d Lees v Ford* (1853) 2 E & B 970 at 974, 983; *Eaton v Hewitt* (1862) 2 Drew & Sm 184; *Re Blight, Blight v Hartnoll* (1880) 13 ChD 858.

C. VESTING OF REMAINDERS

418. Former rule as to contingent remainders. Until statute intervened[1] a contingent remainder created in a will which fulfilled the requisites of a valid common law remainder, took effect as a legal remainder and could not be construed as an executory devise[2]. Legal remainders failed if they did not comply with the common law rules[3]. The common law rules did not apply to equitable limitations, and, as future interests have ceased to be capable of subsisting at law[4] these rules cannot apply to contingent remainders created since the change.

1 See the Contingent Remainders Act 1877 s 1 (repealed) which saved contingent remainders which would have failed under the common law rules, but been valid if created by means of a trust: the Real Property Act 1845 s 8 (repealed); and REAL PROPERTY AND REGISTRATION vol 87 (2012) PARA 166.

2 This rule was known as the rule in *Purefoy v Rogers* (1671) 2 Wms Saund 380: see REAL PROPERTY AND REGISTRATION vol 87 (2012) PARA 169.

3 Contingent legal remainders failed if the contingency had not occurred by the time of the determination of the preceding estate. This was because at common law it was not possible to have an abeyance of seisin: see REAL PROPERTY AND REGISTRATION vol 87 (2012) PARA 166;; Preston on Estates (2nd Edn, 1820) Vol 1 pp 17, 249.

4 Ie by virtue of the Law of Property Act 1925 s 1: see REAL PROPERTY AND REGISTRATION. All future interests in land which were formerly capable of being created as legal interests are now capable of being created as equitable interests: see s 4(1); and REAL PROPERTY AND REGISTRATION vol 87 (2012) PARA 101. As to the rule in *Purefoy v Rogers* (1671) 2 Wms Saund 380 see *Cole v Sewell* (1843) 4 Dr & War 1 at 27; *White v Summers* [1908] 2 Ch 256. As to future interests see *Pearks v Moseley* (1880) 5 App Cas 714 at 721, HL; Challis's Law of Real Property (3rd Edn) p 74 et seq, p 119 et seq, p 168 et seq; and REAL PROPERTY AND REGISTRATION vol 87 (2012) PARAS 164 et seq, 168 et seq.

419. Boraston's Case; Phipps v Ackers. Even if it is expressed to take effect on a contingent event, a future interest may be construed to be a vested interest, taking effect in its natural order on the determination of the previous interest[1]. Thus where real estate is devised to a devisee in fee when[2] he attains a specified age, and a prior interest is limited to endure pending his attainment of that age, the subsequent gift is vested in interest, and takes effect in possession on the attainment of that age; and, even if the devisee dies without attaining that age, the gift is not divested, but the property devolves as part of his estate[3]. A devise, after a prior gift for life, to a child of the life tenant or other donee if attaining a specified age is not, however, made vested merely by the fact that it is expressed to take effect 'from and after'[4] the death of the life tenant[5], although this expression may be of importance if there are other indications that the child's interest is vested[6].

It is essential that a prior interest should be limited. If it is not, the rule in Boraston's Case[7] does not apply and words of contingency then have their natural effect and create only a contingent interest[8]. The prior interest may be given to some person, either for the benefit of the donee himself, for example for his education and maintenance[9], or for the benefit of the prior donee or other persons[10].

1   *Phipps v Ackers* (1842) 9 Cl & Fin 583 at 591 per Tindal CJ. The happening of the event in such a case 'no more imports a condition precedent than any other words indicating that a remainderman is not to take until after the determination of the particular estate': *Phipps v Ackers*.

2   In *Boraston's Case* (1587) 3 Co Rep 16a, 19, the words chiefly considered were 'when' and 'then'. In *Phipps v Ackers* (1842) 9 Cl & Fin 583 at 591, Tindal CJ included 'if' as attracting the rule. See, however, *Doe d Wheedon v Lea* (1789) 3 Term Rep 41 at 43.

3   *Boraston's Case* (1587) 3 Co Rep 16a, 19 (where it seems to have been considered as a certainty that, if there was a devise to executors for payment of debts and performance of the will until a son should come of full age, the son would likewise have taken a vested, not a contingent, remainder); Tudor, LC Real Prop (4th Edn) 427; *Doe d Wheedon v Lea* (1789) 3 Term Rep 41. As to vested and contingent remainders see REAL PROPERTY AND REGISTRATION vol 87 (2012) PARAS 164–166; and as to the effect of a gift over in the event of failure to attain the specified age see PARA 423.

4   The ordinary meaning of 'after the death of' occurring in a clause in a will disposing of capital of residue is not equivalent to 'subject to' prior interests, so as to carry surplus income before the death occurs: see *Re Wragg, Hollingsworth v Wragg* [1959] 2 All ER 717, [1959] 1 WLR 922, CA; and PARA 180.

5   *Alexander v Alexander* (1855) 16 CB 59; *Re Williams, Spencer v Brighouse* (1886) 54 LT 831; *Re Jobson, Jobson v Richardson* (1889) 44 ChD 154.

6   *Andrew v Andrew* (1875) 1 ChD 410, CA (where, as pointed out in *Re Jobson, Jobson v Richardson* (1889) 44 ChD 154 at 158 per North J, there was a gift over in default of the life tenant having a son); *Re James* (1884) 51 LT 596. Cf *Tatham v Vernon* (1861) 29 Beav 604 at 617. In *Simmonds v Cock* (1861) 29 Beav 455, the condition as to age was held to be, in the particular context, a condition subsequent.

7   See the text to notes 2–3.

8   *Phipps v Ackers* (1842) 9 Cl & Fin 583 at 590 per Tindal CJ; *Re Blackwell, Blackwell v Blackwell* [1926] Ch 223, CA (where an immediate gift for the eldest of the testator's sons, if any, 'who shall be living at the time of my death absolutely upon his attaining the age of 21 years', was held to be contingent on his attaining that age). In such a case no distinction can be drawn between 'when' and 'if': *Re Francis, Francis v Francis* [1905] 2 Ch 295 at 298.

9   *Goodtitle d Hayward v Whitby* (1757) 1 Burr 228; *Denn d Satterthwaite v Satterthwaite* (1764) 1 Wm Bl 519; *Stanley v Stanley* (1809) 16 Ves 491; *Goodright d Revell v Parker* (1813) 1 M & S 692 (renewable leaseholds); *Warter v Hutchinson* (1823) 1 B & C 721; *Warter v Hutchinson* (1820) 5 Moore CP 143; *Doe d Cadogan v Ewart* (1838) 7 Ad & El 636 at 663, 665; *Jackson v Marjoribanks* (1841) 12 Sim 93; *Bird v Bird* (1842) 6 Jur 1030; *Greene v Potter* (1843) 2 Y & C Ch Cas 517 at 522; *Milroy v Milroy* (1844) 14 Sim 48 (blended fund); *Re Mottram* (1864) 10 Jur NS 915.

10   *Boraston's Case* (1587) 3 Co Rep 16a, 19; *Taylor d Smith v Biddall* (1677) 2 Mod Rep 289; *Mansfield v Dugard* (1713) 1 Eq Cas Abr 195 pl 4; *Doe d Morris v Underdown* (1741) Willes 293; *Doe d Wheedon v Lea* (1789) 3 Term Rep 41; *Parkin v Knight* (1846) 15 Sim 83 at 86; *James v Lord Wynford* (1852) 1 Sm & G 40; *Re Radford, Jones v Radford* (1918) 62 Sol Jo 604. Cf *Hook v Taylor* (1706) 2 Vern 561 (maintenance until placed out as an apprentice).

420. Gifts in default of issue. The words 'in default of issue' or 'in default of such issue' introducing a gift after an estate tail are not words of contingency, but have been held to be appropriate words to use for introducing a remainder[1], and the gift may take effect even though issue have come into existence and failed[2].

1   *White v Summers* [1908] 2 Ch 256 at 271 per Parker J. See also *Leadbeater v Cross* (1876) 2 QBD 18. Similarly, the words 'in default of such issue' or 'for want of such issue' have been held to introduce a vested remainder and not a contingent limitation, where the prior gift was for life only: *Goodright d Lloyd v Jones* (1815) 4 M & S 88; *White v Summers* [1908] 2 Ch 256 at 272.

2   *Doe d Baroness Dacre v Dowager Lady Dacre* (1798) 1 Bos & P 250; *Lewis d Ormond v Waters* (1805) 6 East 336; *Ashley v Ashley* (1833) 6 Sim 358 at 363. Entailed interests cannot be created by instruments coming into operation on or after 1 January 1997: see the Trusts of Land and Appointment of Trustees Act 1996 s 2(6), Sch 1 para 5; PARA 387; and REAL PROPERTY AND REGISTRATION vol 87 (2012) PARA 114.

421. Application of the rule in *Boraston's Case* to personalty. The rule in Boraston's Case[1] is applicable to real estate and to equitable interests in it[2], but it applies also to personal estate which is directed to be converted into real estate[3]. Where land and personalty are devised together, with a direction to invest the personalty in the purchase of land, the rule applies to the personalty[4]. The rule has subsequently been applied where the gift is a gift of both personalty and realty[5] and also to a gift of personalty alone[6].

1 As to the rule in *Boraston's Case* (1587) 3 Co Rep 16a, 19 see PARA 419.
2 *Phipps v Ackers* (1842) 9 Cl & Fin 583, HL.
3 See *Snow v Poulden* (1836) 1 Keen 186. Although this case was said in argument to be within the principle of *Boraston's Case* (1587) 3 Co Rep 16a, 19, there was no prior estate (see PARA 419), and the vested estate, an estate tail, was subject to be divested if the donee did not attain 25. See also *Attwater v Attwater* (1853) 18 Beav 330.
4 *Jackson v Marjoribanks* (1841) 12 Sim 93 at 98.
5 *Whitter v Bremridge* (1866) LR 2 Eq 736; *Finch v Lane* (1870) LR 10 Eq 501, 503.
6 *Re Heath, Public Trustee v Heath* [1936] Ch 259 at 265 per Farwell J.

422. Gifts subject to prior interests. With regard to both real and personal estate there is a rule, analogous to the rule in *Boraston's Case*[1], under which words apparently of condition do not prevent vesting. Thus words which, although in the form of a condition, merely denote that the gift is to come into possession on the failure or at the determination of prior interests do not as a general rule form a condition precedent to vesting[2]. However, in order that a gift in such terms may be vested, the condition on which the gift is dependent must involve no incident but such as is essential to the failure or determination of the interests previously limited[3], and must be equivalent to 'subject to the interests previously given'[4]. If any additional condition, not connected with the previous limitation, is imposed by the testator, that condition must be fulfilled prior to vesting[5].

1 As to the rule in *Boraston's Case* (1587) 3 Co Rep 16a, 19 see PARA 419.
2 See *Pearsall v Simpson* (1808) 15 Ves 29 (where there was a gift to A for life, then the capital for her children; if no child, for her husband for life; and after his death, in case he should become entitled, to other persons; there was no child, and, as the husband died in the lifetime of A, he never became entitled, yet the ultimate gift to other persons took effect); *Maddison v Chapman* (1858) 4 K & J 709 at 719 per Page Wood V-C (affd (1859) 3 De G & J 536); *Edgeworth v Edgeworth* (1869) LR 4 HL 35 at 41 per Lord Westbury; *Webb v Hearing* (1617) Cro Jac 415. See also *Massey v Hudson* (1817) 2 Mer 130 at 131; *Hillersdon v Lowe* (1843) 2 Hare 355 at 369, 371; *Key v Key* (1853) 4 De GM & G 73 at 79 ('in case annuitants or any of them shall survive K'); *Re Smith's Trusts* (1865) LR 1 Eq 79 ('in case of the death of E during the life of J'); *Chellew v Martin* (1873) 28 LT 662 at 664; *Leadbeater v Cross* (1876) 2 QBD 18 at 22; *Yule's Trustees v Deans* 1919 SC 570. Cf *Franks v Price* (1838) 5 Bing NC 37; *Re Blight, Blight v Hartnoll* (1880) 13 ChD 858; *Re Lowry's Will Trusts, Barclays Bank Ltd v United Newcastle-upon-Tyne Hospitals Board of Governors* [1967] Ch 638, [1966] 3 All ER 955. The principle may be applied not only where the contingency is a condition subsequent for the determination of the previous gift, but where it is a condition precedent to that gift: *Re Sanforth's Will* [1901] WN 152. A gift in default of appointment under a power is not of itself contingent until the exercise of that power; it is vested subject to being divested by appointments under the power: see TRUSTS AND POWERS vol 98 (2013) PARA 549.
3 *Maddison v Chapman* (1858) 4 K & J 709 at 719 per Wood V-C; *M'Kay v M'Kay* [1901] 1 IR 109 at 120.
4 *Maddison v Chapman* (1858) 4 K & J 709 at 719 per Wood V-C (affd (1859) 3 De G & J 536); *Re Martin, Smith v Martin* (1885) 53 LT 34 at 35 per Kay J; *Re Shuckburgh's Settlement, Robertson v Shuckburgh* [1901] 2 Ch 794 at 798; *Re Burden, Mitchell v St Luke's Hostel Trustees* [1948] Ch 160, [1948] 1 All ER 31. Cf *Birds v Askey* (1857) 24 Beav 615. However, in order to interpret 'after the death of my wife' as equivalent to 'subject to my wife's interests', some special context is needed: see *Re Browne's Will Trusts, Landon v Brown* [1915] 1 Ch 690; *Re Wragg, Hollingsworth v Wragg* [1959] 2 All ER 717, [1959] 1 WLR 922, CA; and PARAS 180, 420 note 4. For instances where the natural construction was given to such words see *Weatherall v Thornburgh* (1878) 8 ChD 261, CA; *Berry v Green* [1938] AC 575 at 582, sub nom *Re Blake, Berry v Geen* [1938] 2 All ER 362 at 365, HL; *Re Gillett's Will Trusts* [1950] Ch 102, [1949] 2 All ER 893; *Re Robb's Will Trusts, Marshall v Marshall* [1953] Ch 459, [1953] 1 All ER 920;

Re Nash, Miller v Allen [1965] 1 All ER 51, [1965] 1 WLR 221. As to the construction of 'after the death of' an annuitant see *Re Geering, Gulliver v Geering* [1964] Ch 136, [1962] 3 All ER 1043.
5   *Maddison v Chapman* (1858) 4 K & J 709 at 720; *Edgeworth v Edgeworth* (1869) LR 4 HL 35 at 40 per Lord Hatherley LC; *Merchants Bank of Canada v Keefer* (1885) 13 SCR 515 (where it was held that the words 'if then living' added a contingency because they were otherwise redundant).

423. Contingent gift over. Where real estate is devised to a devisee 'if' or 'when' he attains a specified age and there is a gift over[1] in the event of his failing to attain that age, with or without other contingencies, the attainment of the age is held to be a condition subsequent and not precedent, and the estate is vested immediately subject to its being divested if the devisee dies under that age[2]. For this rule to apply, there must be an express gift over which sets out the conditions on which the gift over will take place and which includes among those conditions the counterparts, although not necessarily the identical counterparts, of the conditions applicable to the prior gift[3]. The rule is based on the principle that in the event of the devisee dying under that age the subsequent gift over sufficiently shows the testator's meaning to have been that the first devisee should take whatever interest the party claiming under the devise over is not entitled to, which gives him the immediate interest subject only to the chance of its being divested on a future contingency[4]. The rule does not apply where there is an express direction as to vesting[5], and it is not required where vesting is implied from a trust for maintenance out of the intermediate income[6]. There is no difference in this respect between devises to individuals and devises to classes where, for example, there is a gift to children as they respectively attain a specified age but, if they all die under that age, a gift over[7]; and the rule applies to personal as well as to real estate[8]. The rule has been applied where the original gift was apparently contingent on surviving a life tenant but there was a gift over if the donee should die in the lifetime of the life tenant without leaving issue[9]. However, a gift over on the death of the donee before the life tenant, simply and without any further contingency, does not raise the same inference as to vesting[10].

1   As to gifts over by necessary implication see PARA 466.
2   *Phipps v Ackers* (1842) 9 Cl & Fin 583 at 591–592, HL (cited in PARA 419); *McGredy v IRC* [1951] NI 155; *Re Penton's Settlements, Humphrey v Birch-Reynardson* [1968] 1 All ER 36, [1968] 1 WLR 248; *Re Kilpatrick's Policies Trusts, Kilpatrick v IRC* [1966] Ch 730, [1966] 2 All ER 149, CA; *Brotherton v IRC* [1978] 2 All ER 267, [1978] 1 WLR 610, CA. See also PARAS 435–436, 448.
3   *Re Mallinson Consolidated Trusts, Mallinson v Gooley* [1974] 2 All ER 530 at 534, [1974] 1 WLR 1120 at 1124 per Templeman J: 'faced with a prior gift which creates a condition precedent followed by a gift over which creates a condition subsequent in relation to the same events, the court being in favour of early vesting resolves the dilemma by accepting the condition subsequent which achieves early vesting'. See also *Re Penton's Settlements, Humphreys v Birch-Reynardson* [1968] 1 All ER 36 at 43, [1968] 1 WLR 248 at 256 per Ungoed-Thomas J.
4   *Phipps v Ackers* (1842) 9 Cl & Fin 583 at 592, HL; *Bull v Pritchard* (1847) 5 Hare 567 at 571 per Wigram V-C (adopted in *Boulton v Beard* (1853) 3 De GM & G 608 at 613 per Turner LJ). This rule dates from and is sometimes called the rule in *Edwards v Hammond* (1684) 3 Lev 132, and instances of its application before *Phipps v Ackers* above are *Bromfield v Crowder* (1805) 1 Bos & PNR 313 (affd (1811) cited in 14 East at 604, HL); *Doe d Hunt v Moore* (1811) 14 East 601. The judges were consulted in *Phipps v Ackers* (1842) 9 Cl & Fin 583 at 592, HL in order to review these last two cases; *Doe d Hunt v Moore* above had been doubted by Lord Brougham at an earlier stage (*Phipps v Ackers* (1835) 3 Cl & Fin 702, HL). Lord St Leonards referred with approval to *Bromfield v Crowder* above, *Doe d Hunt v Moore* above and *Phipps v Ackers* above in *Egerton v Earl Brownlow* (1853) 4 HL Cas 1 at 224–226. See also *Hepworth v Scale* (1855) 1 Jur NS 698; *Re Dennis* (1903) 5 OLR 46. The rule was described by Templeman J in *Re*

Mallinson Consolidated Trusts, Mallinson v Gooley [1974] 2 All ER 530 at 532, [1974] 1 WLR 1120 at 1121 as having 'outlived its usefulness'.

5　*Russel v Buchanan* (1836) 7 Sim 628.

6　*Re Astor, Astor v Astor* [1922] 1 Ch 364 at 368, CA, per Russell J.

7　*Doe d Roake v Nowell* (1813) 1 M & S 327 (affd sub nom *Randoll v Doe d Roake* (1817) 5 Dow 202, HL); *Farmer v Francis* (1824) 2 Bing 151 (subsequent proceedings (1826) 2 Sim & St 505); *Doe d Dolley v Ward* (1839) 9 Ad & El 582. Cf *Blagrove v Hancock* (1848) 16 Sim 371 (which seems not to be in accordance with other decisions).

8　The rule appears to have been established with a view to preventing gifts in remainder being liable to destruction as contingent remainders owing to there being no legal estate to support them before they fell into possession, and, for this purpose, the language of the will was strained: *Pearks v Moseley* (1880) 5 App Cas 714 at 721, HL, per Lord Selborne LC; *Re Astor, Astor v Astor* [1922] 1 Ch 364 at 385, CA, per Warrington LJ. On this view the rule should have been confined to legal remainders but it applied to equitable remainders (*Phipps v Ackers* (1842) 9 Cl & Fin 583 at 594, 599, HL), to executory trusts (*Phipps v Ackers* at 600; *Stanley v Stanley* (1809) 16 Ves 491), to gifts of residuary real and personal estate (*Whitter v Bemridge* (1866) LR 2 Eq 736), and to personalty alone (*Re Heath, Public Trustee v Heath* [1936] Ch 259, which at 265 also makes it plain that the rule does not apply where there is no gift over). See also *McGredy and McGredy's Trustees v IRC* [1951] NI 155; *Re Kilpatrick's Policies Trusts, Kilpatrick v IRC* [1966] Ch 730, [1966] 2 All ER 149, CA.

9　*Finch v Lane* (1870) LR 10 Eq 501.

10　*Doe d Planner v Scudamore* (1800) 2 Bos & P 289. As to the effects of gifts at a specified age followed by a gift over on death under the specified age without issue see the text and note 7. See also PARA 424.

424. Contingency part of description of donee.

The rule as to contingent gifts over[1] does not apply where the contingency is part of the description of the donee, as, for example, where the devise is to such children as attain or shall attain the specified age[2]. The difference is to be noted[3] between a gift in this form, which is contingent, and a gift to certain persons at the specified age, which is vested, there being in each case a gift over[4]. The rule does not apply where the gift over is contingent on an event which either cannot happen until after the death of the first taker[5] or has no relation to the first taker's interest[6].

1　As to this rule see PARA 423 text and notes 1–4.

2　*Duffield v Duffield* (1829) 3 Bli NS 260 at 333, HL; *Festing v Allen* (1843) 12 M & W 279; *Re Astor, Astor v Astor* [1922] 1 Ch 364, CA. See also *Bull v Pritchard* (1847) 5 Hare 567 at 571–572; *Holmes v Prescott* (1864) 10 Jur NS 507; *Rhodes v Whitehead* (1865) 2 Drew & Sm 532 at 536; *Price v Hall* (1868) LR 5 Eq 399 at 402; *Re Murphy, Murphy v Murphy and Byrne* [1964] IR 308 (gift over conditional). The decisions in *Riley v Garnett* (1849) 3 De G & Sm 629 and *Browne v Browne* (1857) 26 LJ Ch 635 (see *Best v Donmall* (1871) 40 LJ Ch 160 at 162–163) were overruled: see *Holmes v Prescott* above; *Re Williams, Spencer v Brighouse* (1886) 54 LT 831. Decisions on the disposition of realty in which words were given an unnatural construction to prevent gifts being found invalid as a result of the common law rules on contingent remainders (see PARA 418) have no application to the construction of gifts of personal property: *Pearks v Moseley* (1880) 5 App Cas 714 at 721 and 730, HL. A devise to donees where the contingency of attaining a specified age was part of the description has been held to be contingent on attaining the age in limitations construed as operating as contingent remainders (see *Brackenbury v Gibbons* (1876) 2 ChD 417; *Symes v Symes* [1896] 1 Ch 272; *White v Summers* [1908] 2 Ch 256), and in gifts operating as executory limitations (see *Abbiss v Burney, Re Finch* (1880) 17 ChD 211, CA (equitable estate); *Re Lechmere and Lloyd* (1881) 18 ChD 524; *Miles v Jarvis* (1883) 24 ChD 633; *Dean v Dean* [1891] 3 Ch 150; *Re Bourne, Rymer v Harpley* (1887) 56 LT 388); but the distinction between contingent remainders and executory limitations has lost its importance (see PARA 418). See also *Muskett v Eaton* (1875) 1 ChD 435 (where a reference to children born in due time after the death of the life tenant showed that attainment of a specified age was not part of the description); *Perceval v Perceval* (1870) LR 9 Eq 386; *Re Eddels' Trusts* (1871) LR 11 Eq 559; *Pearks v Moseley* (1880) 5 App Cas 714 at 730, HL; *Ferguson v Ferguson* (1886) 17 LR Ir 552 at 559–560; *Webster v Boddington* (1858) 26 Beav 128.

3　*Doe d Dolley v Ward* (1839) 9 Ad & El 582 at 605–606; *Holmes v Prescott* (1864) 10 Jur NS 507 at 513 per Wood V-C; *Re Hume, Public Trustee v Mabey* [1912] 1 Ch 693 at 699 per Parker J. See, however, *Re Mid Kent Railway Act 1856, ex p Styan* (1859) John 387 at 396.

4   See *Farmer v Francis* (1824) 2 Bing 151; *Farmer v Francis* (1826) 2 Sim & St 505; *Doe d Dolley v Ward* (1839) 9 Ad & El 582 at 605–606; *Attwater v Attwater* (1853) 18 Beav 330; and PARA 423.
5   *L'Estrange v L'Estrange* (1890) 25 LR Ir 399 at 417, Ir CA.
6   *Price v Hall* (1868) LR 5 Eq 399 at 403.

E.   GIFTS OUT OF PERSONAL ESTATE

(A)   In general

425. Property to which the rules apply. The following rules apply to specific legacies of personal estate, including leaseholds[1] and the proceeds of real estate held on trust for sale[2], and to general legacies so far as they are charged on personal estate or the proceeds of sale of real estate held on trust for sale; but in the case of trusts for sale, where the testator dies on or after 1 January 1997, the rules only apply where the trust for sale was created by the will of another testator who died before that date[3]. If freeholds are given together with leaseholds or other personal estate under a single description in terms such that a vested estate in the freeholds is given[4], the interests in the leaseholds or other personal estate may also be considered as vested even though, according to the rules, they would be regarded as contingent[5].

1   *Re Hudson's Minors* (1843) Drury *temp* Sug 6; *Ingram v Suckling* (1859) 7 WR 386.
2   *Re Hart's Trusts, ex p Block* (1858) 3 De G & J 195; *Bellairs v Bellairs* (1874) LR 18 Eq 510 at 514.
3   In relation to all other trusts for sale, the doctrine of conversion whereby land held by trustees subject to a trust for sale is to be regarded as personal property has been abolished: see the Trusts of Land and Appointment of Trustees Act 1996 ss 3, 25(5); and REAL PROPERTY AND REGISTRATION vol 87 (2012) PARAS 7, 215. The doctrine of conversion is not wholly abolished by s 3 and will still apply to eg uncompleted agreements for the sale of land. As to the doctrine of conversion see further EQUITABLE JURISDICTION vol 47 (2014) PARA 138 et seq.
4   Ie under the rules described in PARA 412 et seq.
5   *Farmer v Francis* (1826) 2 Sim & St 505 (residue); *Tapscott v Newcombe* (1842) 6 Jur 755; *James v Lord Wynford* (1852) 1 Sm & G 40 at 59–60. The rules of law as to contingent remainders in real estate did not prevent effect being given to the intention as to the personal estate: *Holmes v Prescott* (1864) 10 Jur NS 507; *White v Summers* [1908] 2 Ch 256 at 264. See also PARA 418 note 2.

426. Distinction between vesting and payment. In all cases of legacies given on any future event, whether certain to happen or not, where the gift is wholly dependent on that event[1] so that it must have happened before any part of the testator's bounty can attach to the legatee, the time of vesting is the occurrence of that event, but, where the gift is not so dependent, the time of payment only is postponed to that event[2]. Where the gift is not wholly dependent on the event, the legatee may take a vested interest at once subject to such postponed payment[3].

1   In such cases 'the time is annexed to the substance of the gift': *Monkhouse v Holme* (1783) 1 Bro CC 298 at 300.
2   *May v Wood* (1792) 3 Bro CC 471 at 473 (but see *Hanson v Graham* (1801) 6 Ves 239; *Booth v Booth* (1799) 4 Ves 399 at 405); *Leeming v Sherratt* (1842) 2 Hare 14 at 19.
3   The court adopts the view of the civil law that such a legacy is owed at the present time but payable in the future: *Maddison v Andrew* (1747) 1 Ves Sen 57 at 59; *Monkhouse v Holme* (1783) 1 Bro CC 298 at 300; *Crickett v Dolby* (1795) 3 Ves 10 at 13; *Re Crother's Trusts (No 2)* [1917] 1 IR 356. Accordingly, if the legatee has a vested interest but he dies before the date of payment, his representatives are entitled: *Bateman v Roach* (1724) 9 Mod Rep 104. See also PARA 415.

(B)   Direction as to Payment

427. Gift contained wholly in direction to pay. Where a gift is a simple gift on a future event, or from and after a future event or is contained wholly in a direction to pay, or to divide or to transfer, at or from and after a future event, so that there is no gift except in the direction to pay or transfer, prima facie the vesting is postponed until that event happens; and, consequently, if the legatee dies before that event, prima facie his representatives are not entitled to payment[1]. Thus a legacy to a named person at a certain definite future time, without more, prima facie is contingent and he or his representatives take no interest if he dies before that time[2]. A gift to a class on a contingency prima facie does not, however, render the contingency applicable to the description of the class[3].

1   *Stapleton v Cheales* (1711) Prec Ch 317 (the second rule in this case); *Leake v Robinson* (1817) 2 Mer 363 at 387 per Grant MR; *Webber v Webber* (1823) 1 Sim & St 311 (marriage); *Murray v Tancred* (1840) 10 Sim 465; *Leeming v Sherratt* (1842) 2 Hare 14 at 18; *Bruce v Charlton* (1842) 13 Sim 65; *Chevaux v Aislabie* (1842) 13 Sim 71; *Lang v Pugh* (1842) 1 Y & C Ch Cas 718; *Beck v Burn* (1844) 7 Beav 492 (which, however, should have been decided otherwise because of the intervening life estate: see *Adams v Robarts* (1858) 25 Beav 658 at 661); *Morgan v Morgan* (1851) 4 De G & Sm 164 (marriage); *Chance v Chance* (1853) 16 Beav 572; *Gardiner v Slater* (1858) 25 Beav 509; *Re Wrangham's Trust* (1860) 1 Drew & Sm 358; *Locke v Lamb* (1867) LR 4 Eq 372; *Johnston v O'Neill* (1879) 3 LR Ir 476 at 482.
2   *Smell v Dee* (1707) 2 Salk 415 (criticised on other grounds in *King v Withers* (1735) Cas temp Talb 117 at 124); *Bruce v Charlton* (1842) 13 Sim 65 at 68; *Re Eve, Belton v Thompson* (1905) 93 LT 235. As to cases where there was a distinction between the gift and the direction to pay see PARA 428 note 4. As to a direction for payment within a certain time see *Edmunds v Waugh* (1858) 4 Drew 275; on appeal (1863) 2 New Rep 408.
3   As to a gift to a class on contingency see PARA 303.

428. Express distinction between gift and time of payment. If the words of a gift express a distinction between the gift itself and the event denoting the time of payment, division or transfer[1], and this time is the attainment by the donee of the age of 21 years[2] or other age[3] or is any other event which, assuming the requisite duration of life, must necessarily happen at a determinable time[4], then prima facie[5] the gift is not contingent in respect of that event[6]. The donee's personal representative is accordingly entitled to the gift, even if the donee dies before attaining the specified age or before the named event, but prima facie he is not entitled to payment before the donee himself would have been so entitled[7]. This presumption as to vesting does not arise where the gift is on an event, such as the donee's marriage, which will not necessarily happen at all, however long the donee or other person concerned lives[8]. However, in such a case, other indications may be present to show that the vesting is independent of the named event[9].

Even where the gift and direction to pay are distinct, the context may show that the gift is contingent[10]. A mere direction for accumulation until payment, however, is not sufficient[11], and even an express contingency attached to payment may not be sufficient to make the vesting contingent[12].

1   As to what is sufficient distinction between the gift and the direction to pay see *Re Bartholomew's Trust* (1849) 1 Mac & G 354 (commented on in *Locke v Lamb* (1867) LR 4 Eq 372 at 380); *Williams v Clark* (1851) 4 De G & Sm 472 (where a distinction was considered to exist); *Shum v Hobbs* (1855) 3 Drew 93; *Merry v Hill* (1869) LR 8 Eq 619 (where no distinction existed). See also *Cooney v Nicholls* (1881) 7 LR Ir 107, Ir CA.
2   *Chambers v Jeoffrey* (1709) 2 Eq Cas Abr 541 pl 9; *Skey v Barnes* (1816) 3 Mer 335; *Vivian v Mills* (1839) 1 Beav 315; *Lister v Bradley* (1841) 1 Hare 10 at 12 ('to my four children, to be paid them when or if they attain 21'); *Williams v Clark* (1851) 4 De G & Sm 472; *Shrimpton v Shrimpton* (1862) 31 Beav 425.
3   *Farmer v Francis* (1826) 2 Sim & St 505; *Blease v Burgh* (1840) 2 Beav 221; *Saumarez v Saumarez* (1865) 34 Beav 432. Such postponement of enjoyment after his majority may be ineffectual against the donee: see PARA 146.
4   *Sidney v Vaughan* (1721) 2 Bro Parl Cas 254 (six months after serving apprenticeship); *Chaffers v Abell* (1839) 3 Jur 577 (when youngest 21). As to a gift with a direction to pay at a certain fixed time after the testator's death see *Sheldon v Sheldon* (1739) 9 Mod Rep 211; *Jackson v Jackson* (1749) 1 Ves Sen 217; *Lucas v Carline* (1840) 2 Beav 367; *Leeming v Sherratt* (1842) 2 Hare 14 at 19–20; *Bromley v Wright* (1849) 7 Hare 334 at 344; *Oppenheim v Henry* (1853) 10 Hare 441.

5 For instances where the context displaced the presumption see *Oseland v Oseland* (1795) 3 Anst 628; *Knight v Cameron* (1807) 14 Ves 389 (where the gift was also contingent on the donee being then living).

6 This is the first rule in *Stapleton v Cheales* (1711) Prec Ch 317: Tudor, LC Real Prop (4th Edn) 438, 459. See *Jackson v Jackson* (1749) 1 Ves Sen 217 (gifts to R, 'to be paid' at various times); *Wadley v North* (1797) 3 Ves 364 (gift to children of A, 'each receiving' his share at 21); *Bolger v Mackell* (1800) 5 Ves 509 ('to be paid' at 21 or marriage); *Clutterbuck v Edwards* (1832) 2 Russ & M 577. The rule arose in the ecclesiastical courts and was adopted by courts of law and of equity as to personal legacies but not as to real estate or legacies charged on real estate: see *Maddison v Andrew* (1747) 1 Ves Sen 57 at 59; *Mackell v Winter* (1797) 3 Ves 536 at 543 per Lord Loughborough LC; and PARA 724.

7 *Chester v Painter* (1725) 2 P Wms 335 at 337; *Roden v Smith* (1744) Amb 588; *Maher v Maher* (1877) 1 LR Ir 22. The effect on an apparent contingent gift of a direction for payment of the whole interest of the legacy to the donee in the meantime will, however, entitle the personal representative to immediate payment on the death of the donee, even before the donee himself would have been entitled to payment: see PARA 430 et seq.

8 *Atkins v Hiccocks* (1737) 1 Atk 500; *Ellis v Ellis* (1802) 1 Sch & Lef 1; *Morgan v Morgan* (1851) 4 De G & Sm 164 at 167; *Re Cantillon's Minors* (1864) 16 I Ch R 301 at 308. In *Maher v Maher* (1877) 1 LR Ir 22, the testator bequeathed £1,500 to each of his younger children surviving him, which was to be paid as they should respectively attain 21 or marry with consent; and it was held that the legacies were vested but that the personal representative of a child dying a spinster under 21 was not entitled to payment until the time at which that child would have attained that age.

9 See eg *Booth v Booth* (1799) 4 Ves 399 (whole interest given in the meantime); *Vize v Stoney* (1841) 1 Dr & War 337 at 349–350 (legacy carrying interest); *Corr v Corr* (1873) IR 7 Eq 397; *M'Cutcheon v Allen* (1880) 5 LR Ir 268; *Re Wrey, Stuart v Wrey* (1885) 30 ChD 507 (legacy carrying interest); and PARA 430 et seq.

10 *Knight v Cameron* (1807) 14 Ves 389; *Judd v Judd* (1830) 3 Sim 525 (reconsidered in *Hunter v Judd* (1833) 4 Sim 455); *Chevaux v Aislabie* (1842) 13 Sim 71; *Merry v Hill* (1869) LR 8 Eq 619. See also *Heath v Perry* (1744) 3 Atk 101.

11 *Stretch v Watkins* (1816) 1 Madd 253; *Bull v Johns* (1830) Taml 513; *Josselyn v Josselyn* (1837) 9 Sim 63; *Blease v Burgh* (1840) 2 Beav 221 at 226; *Saunders v Vautier* (1841) Cr & Ph 240; *Oppenheim v Henry* (1853) 10 Hare 441; *Re Bragger, Bragger v Bragger* (1887) 56 LT 521; *Re Thompson, Griffith v Thompson* (1896) 44 WR 582; *Re Couturier, Couturier v Shea* [1907] 1 Ch 470. A donee having a vested interest, subject to postponement by such accumulation, may put an end to such accumulation and claim payment on attaining majority: *Re Couturier, Couturier v Shea* above at 473.

12 *Massey v Hudson* (1817) 2 Mer 130 ('12 months from death of B in case B shall happen to survive my wife'); *Clutterbuck v Edwards* (1832) 2 Russ & M 577 ('on decease of wife if he shall then have attained 21'); *Wright v Wright* (1852) 21 LJ Ch 775 (if donees were of competent understanding).

429. Implied distinction between gift and time of payment. The context may show that a gift is vested, even where there is no express distinction between the gift and a direction as to the time of payment. Thus it may appear that the reason for the postponement of the gift is on account of prior interests given in the meantime, or on account of the nature of the property and the convenience of administration[1]. In such a case, the gift prima facie vests independently of the postponement of enjoyment[2].

Accordingly, prima facie no contingency is imported by the fact that the legacy is given after a life interest in the property bequeathed[3]. Where a legacy is given to a donee contingently on attaining a specified age, the fact that the legacy is also postponed to a life interest prima facie does not render it contingent on the donee's surviving the life tenant[4], and the fact that the interest is given to another person pending his attaining that age may be an indication of a vested gift[5].

A gift to a class of children when the youngest attains a specified age confers a vested interest on all who attain that age, whether they are living or dead at the time of payment[6]. There is, however, no general principle of construction applicable to gifts when the youngest attains a specified age that the child must attain that age in order to take a vested interest[7]. The question must always turn on the actual words of the will under consideration[8]. A contrary inference may be drawn from other provisions in the will[9]. In the case of a similar gift to individuals, and not to a class, prima facie they take vested interests, even though they die before the specified age[10].

1 See the rule, which is applicable generally to the vesting of any gift, stated at PARA 382.

2 *Packham v Gregory* (1845) 4 Hare 396 at 398; *Bromley v Wright* (1849) 7 Hare 334 at 339; *Re Bennett's Trust* (1857) 3 K & J 280 at 283; *Adams v Robarts* (1858) 25 Beav 658 at 661; *Re Couturier, Couturier v Shea* [1907] 1 Ch 470 at 472; *Browne v Moody* [1936] AC 635, [1936] 2 All ER 1695, PC; *Greenwood v Greenwood* [1939] 2 All ER 150n, PC; *Re Brooke's Will Trusts, Jubber v Brooke* [1953] 1 All ER 668, [1953] 1 WLR 439.

3 *Corbett v Palmer* (1735) 2 Eq Cas Abr 548 pl 24; *Medlicot v Bowes* (1749) 1 Ves Sen 207; *Hatch v Mills* (1759) 1 Eden 342; *Barnes v Allen* (1782) 1 Bro CC 181; *Monkhouse v Holme* (1783) 1 Bro CC 298; *A-G v Crispin* (1784) 1 Bro CC 386; *Benyon v Maddison* (1786) 2 Bro CC 75; *Roebuck v Dean* (1793) 4 Bro CC 403; *Molesworth v Molesworth* (1793) 4 Bro CC 408; *Bayley v Bishop* (1803) 9 Ves 6; *Hallifax v Wilson* (1809) 16 Ves 168; *Blamire v Geldart* (1809) 16 Ves 314; *Burton v Hodsoll* (1827) 2 Sim 24; *Cousins v Schroder* (1830) 4 Sim 23; *Cochrane v Wiltshire* (1847) 16 LJ Ch 366; *Re Bright's Trusts* (1855) 21 Beav 67; *Strother v Dutton* (1857) 1 De G & J 675; *Adams v Robarts* (1858) 25 Beav 658; *Hickling v Fair* [1899] AC 15, HL; *Re Crother's Trusts (No 2)* [1917] 1 IR 356. For an example of a context to the contrary see *Willis v Plaskett* (1841) 4 Beav 208.

4 *Hallifax v Wilson* (1809) 16 Ves 168; *Walker v Main* (1819) 1 Jac & W 1; *Cousins v Schroder* (1830) 4 Sim 23; *Jones v Jones* (1843) 13 Sim 561; *Mendham v Williams* (1866) LR 2 Eq 396; *Re Cohn, National Westminster Bank Ltd v Cohn* [1974] 3 All ER 928, [1974] 1 WLR 1378, CA. For an example of a context to the contrary see *Billingsley v Wills* (1745) 3 Atk 219.

5 *Lane v Goudge* (1803) 9 Ves 225; *Re Cohn, National Westminster Bank Ltd v Cohn* [1974] 3 All ER 928, [1974] 1 WLR 1378, CA.

6 *Leeming v Sherratt* (1842) 2 Hare 14; *Re Smith's Will* (1855) 20 Beav 197; *Brocklebank v Johnson* (1855) 20 Beav 205; *Kennedy v Sedgwick* (1857) 3 K & J 540. As to cases where the children were expressly required to survive distribution see *Castle v Eate* (1844) 7 Beav 296; *Re Hunter's Trusts* (1865) LR 1 Eq 295. As to special cases regarding the time of payment see *Beckton v Barton* (1859) 5 Jur NS 349; *Evans v Pilkington* (1839) 10 Sim 412. See also *Re Nicholson, Stace v Nicholson* (1904) 24 NZLR 633; *Re Osmond, Cummings v Galaway* (1910) 30 NZLR 65.

7 *Re Lodwig, Lodwig v Evans* [1916] 2 Ch 26, CA (disapproving the dictum in *Leeming v Sherratt* (1842) 2 Hare 14 at 23, that, where a testator postpones the division of residue until his youngest child attains a particular age, no child who does not attain that age can be intended to take; and disapproving *Lloyd v Lloyd* (1856) 3 K & J 20 and *Parker v Sowerby* (1853) 1 Drew 488, so far as the decisions in those cases were based on the dictum in *Leeming v Sherratt* above). See also *Cooper v Cooper* (1861) 29 Beav 229 (where the gift was not to a class but to individuals).

8 *Re Lodwig, Lodwig v Evans* [1916] 2 Ch 26 at 36, CA (where the interests of the children were held not to be contingent on attaining the age). As to other cases where the interests of the children have been held not to be contingent on attaining the age see *Re Grove's Trusts* (1862) 3 Giff 575; *Boulton v Pilcher* (1861) 29 Beav 633 (where the court relied on a trust for maintenance which appears to have been treated as a trust to maintain each beneficiary with the income of his expectant share; cf PARA 431); *Knox v Wells* (1864) 2 Hem & M 674 (where there was a distinction between the gift and the direction as to time of payment; cf PARA 428). As to cases where the interests of the children have been held to be contingent see *Lloyd v Lloyd* (1856) 3 K & J 20; *Coldicott v Best* [1881] WN 150; cf *Ford v Rawlins* (1823) 1 Sim & St 328 (where there was a discretionary power to distribute among children when the youngest attained 21).

9 See the cases cited in note 8.

10 *Cooper v Cooper* (1861) 29 Beav 229; *Re Radford, Jones v Radford* (1918) 62 Sol Jo 604.

(C) Direction as to Maintenance

430. Postponed gift accompanied by gift of interim interest. Unless the context is to the contrary[1], where a postponed gift is accompanied by a gift of the whole interim interest of the fund to the donee[2], it is presumed that the testator meant a single immediate vested gift[3]. In order to raise this presumption, the gift of interim income must be free from contingency[4], but it may be dependent on the non-occurrence of the event on which the gift of capital is to take effect[5]. Accordingly, the presumption does not arise where the capital and income of the legacy are given in a single gift[6] so that the same contingency applies to them both.

Where the presumption applies, it applies whatever the nature of the contingent event denoting the time of payment of the capital of the legacy[7].

The fact that the income and capital of the subject matter are given subject to annuities or life interests is immaterial; however the capital given may be charged, if the income of that capital less the charges is given, then the rule is satisfied[8]. It has been held insufficient, however, that the income of property equal in amount to the property which is to be the subject of the gift should be directed to be paid to the legatee, if the severance of the particular property given from the rest of the testator's property is only to take place at the future time of payment[9]; or that an annuity equal to the interest on the sum given should be given to the donee pending the event, but not as interest on the capital[10].

1   For cases where in the context the gift of capital was nevertheless held contingent see *Vawdrey v Geddes* (1830) 1 Russ & M 203 at 208 (where there was a gift over (see PARA 435) in the case of death before a particular time, although the case has been criticised in this respect); *Mills v Robarts* (1830) Taml 476; *Re Bulley's Trust Estate* (1865) 11 Jur NS 847. See also *Harrison v Tucker* [2003] EWHC 1168 (Ch), [2003] WTLR 883.

2   A postponed legacy may in certain cases carry interest from the testator's death, but this may be independent of the question whether the legacy is vested or not: see eg *Wynch v Wynch* (1788) 1 Cox Eq Cas 433; *Re Rouse's Estate* (1852) 9 Hare 649. As to the question of interest on legacies see *Re Palfreeman, Public Trustee v Palfreeman* [1914] 1 Ch 877 (criticising *Pickwick v Gibbes* (1839) 1 Beav 271 and *Coventry v Higgins* (1844) 14 Sim 30; and holding that legacies payable to a legatee on attaining a specific age carried interest on the expiration of one year from the testator's death if the legatee had attained the age in the testator's lifetime). See generally PARA 1080 et seq.

3   *Cloberry v Lampen* (1677) 2 Eq Cas Abr 539; *Fonnereau v Fonnereau* (1748) 1 Ves Sen 118; *Green v Pigot* (1781) 1 Bro CC 103; *May v Wood* (1792) 3 Bro CC 471 at 474; *Keily v Monck* (1795) 3 Ridg Parl Rep 205 at 256; *Hanson v Graham* (1801) 6 Ves 239 at 249; *Gardiner v But* (1818) 3 Madd 425; *Rose v Sowerby* (1830) Taml 376; *Vawdry v Geddes* (1830) 1 Russ & M 203 at 208 per Leach MR; *Saunders v Vautier* (1841) Cr & Ph 240 at 248; *Re Jacob's Will* (1861) 29 Beav 402; *Dundas v Wolfe Murray* (1863) 1 Hem & M 425; *Re Bunn, Isaacson v Webster* (1880) 16 ChD 47 at 48; *Re Wrey, Stuart v Wrey* (1885) 30 ChD 507 at 510, 512; *Scotney v Lomer* (1886) 31 ChD 380, CA; *Brennan v Brennan* [1894] 1 IR 69 at 73 per Chatterton V-C. In so far as *Batsford v Kebbell* (1797) 3 Ves 363, and *Spencer v Wilson* (1873) LR 16 Eq 501 at 514, depend on treating the gifts of capital and of income of the property as separate gifts, they are not followed: see eg *Re Holt's Estate, Bolding v Strugnell* (1876) 45 LJ Ch 208 at 209; and note 9. An intention to make such separate gifts may, however, be shown: see *Re Peek's Trusts* (1873) LR 16 Eq 221. A mere direction to allow maintenance not amounting to a gift of the interest does not render the legacy payable before the legatee would be entitled: *Harrison v Buckle* (1719) 1 Stra 238. See also *Hanson v Graham* at 249.

4   See *Hubert v Parsons* (1751) 2 Ves Sen 261 at 263; *Re Thruston's Will Trusts* (1849) 17 Sim 21.

5   *Hammond v Maule* (1844) 1 Coll 281.

6   *Knight v Knight* (1826) 2 Sim & St 490. See also *Morgan v Morgan* (1851) 4 De G & Sm 164 at 167; *Re Kirkley, Halligey v Kirkley* (1918) 87 LJ Ch 247. For a contrary decision see *Collins v Metcalfe* (1687) 1 Vern 462. Cf *Locke v Lamb* (1867) LR 4 Eq 372 (where the interest was directed to be accumulated); *Breedon v Tugman* (1834) 3 My & K 289 (where the construction making the same contingency apply to both was avoided).

7   *Booth v Booth* (1799) 4 Ves 399; *Vize v Stoney* (1841) 1 Dr & War 337 at 350; *Re Wrey, Stuart v Wrey* (1885) 30 ChD 507 (marriage).

8   *Potts v Atherton* (1859) 28 LJ Ch 486 (life annuity); *Jones v Mackilwain* (1862) 1 Russ 220. See also *Lane v Goudge* (1803) 9 Ves 225.

9   *Batsford v Kebbell* (1797) 3 Ves 363 (where the testatrix gave to A the dividends of a £500 stock until he should attain the age of 32, at which time she directed her executors to transfer the principal to him; and it was held that the legacy did not vest until A was 32). See also *Re Hart's Trusts, ex p Block* (1858) 3 De G & J 195 at 202; *Re Wrey, Stuart v Wrey* (1885) 30 ChD 507 (where the testatrix by her will, after specific bequests of bonds, gave all the rest of her stocks and shares on trust to pay the income to G until his marriage, and at the time of his marriage to hand over the stocks and shares to him; and it was held that G took a vested interest under the gift and, being of age, was entitled to have the stocks and shares comprised in the gift transferred to him, even though he had not married). In *Re Wrey, Stuart v Wrey* at 510, Kay J said that *Batsford*

v Kebbell above, where the essential point was that the gifts of dividends and capital were distinct, would not be followed except in a case on all fours with it.

10 *Watson v Hayes* (1839) 5 My & Cr 125 at 134; *Merlin v Blagrave* (1858) 25 Beav 125.

431. Distinct gift of interim maintenance. A distinct gift for maintenance does not in itself make vested a legacy which would otherwise be contingent[1]. The giving of maintenance is not equivalent to giving the whole interest on a legacy[2].

Where the donee is an individual or one of a group of persons taking as individuals and not as a class, the fact that the gift is to carry interest, and that the whole interest or income of the gift is directed to be applied for the donee's maintenance, or in some other manner for his benefit, until the contingent event on which the legacy itself is given, is an indication[3] that vesting is independent of the contingency[4]. This inference in favour of vesting is not necessarily excluded by the fact that the mode of application of the interest may come to an end before the specified event, as, for example, where the interest is to be applied for education alone[5], or where interest is payable only during minority but payment of capital is to be at some greater age[6]. In general, however, if there necessarily occurs an interval or gap which separates the gift of income from the gift of capital, the gift of capital is not vested[7] unless there are other indications to that effect[8].

A legacy may be vested even though the gift of interest includes a direction that the trustees are to pay the whole or such part of that interest as they think fit for the donee's maintenance[9]. A similar rule applies to gifts to a number of persons as a group and not as a class if the direction applies to their respective shares or interests[10].

1 *Watson v Hayes* (1839) 5 My & Cr 125 at 133 per Lord Cottenham LC.
2 *Pulsford v Hunter* (1792) 3 Bro CC 416 at 419; *Leake v Robinson* (1817) 2 Mer 363 at 386; *Watson v Hayes* (1839) 5 My & Cr 125 at 133 per Lord Cottenham LC. As to the effect of gift of interest on contingent legacies see PARA 430. As to gifts which were held to be mere maintenance as opposed to gifts of interest see *Watson v Hayes*; *Boughton v Boughton* (1848) 1 HL Cas 406 at 434; *Rudge v Winnall* (1849) 12 Beav 357. The doubt thrown on the observations in *Pulsford v Hunter* above in *Fox v Fox* (1875) LR 19 Eq 286 at 289 per Jessel MR does not appear to be well founded: see *Wilson v Knox* (1884) 13 LR Ir 349 at 356 per Porter MR.
3 A gift of interim maintenance does not make vested a gift which in the whole context is clearly contingent: *Butcher v Leach* (1843) 5 Beav 392; *Re Coleman, Henry v Strong* (1888) 39 ChD 443, CA.
4 *Hoath v Hoath* (1785) 2 Bro CC 3; *Walcott v Hall* (1788) 2 Bro CC 305; *Hanson v Graham* (1801) 6 Ves 239; *Branstrom v Wilkinson* (1802) 7 Ves 421 (father appointed trustee during minority); *Lane v Goudge* (1803) 9 Ves 225; *Rose v Sowerby* (1830) Taml 376; *Lister v Bradley* (1841) 1 Hare 10 at 13 (interest payable to mother of legatees for their support and education); *Brocklebank v Johnson* (1855) 20 Beav 205 at 211; *Re Hart's Trust, ex p Block* (1858) 3 De G & J 195; *Shrimpton v Shrimpton* (1862) 31 Beav 425 at 427; *Re Holt's Estate, Bolding v Strugnell* (1876) 45 LJ Ch 208; *Re Bunn, Isaacson v Webster* (1880) 16 ChD 47; *Re Byrne, Byrne v Kenny* (1889) 23 LR Ir 260 (gift to each of a group); *Brennan v Brennan* [1894] 1 IR 69 at 73; *Re Williams, Williams v Williams* [1907] 1 Ch 180 at 183.
5 *Dodson v Hay* (1791) 3 Bro CC 405 at 409–410.
6 See *Davies v Fisher* (1842) 5 Beav 201 at 211, 212; *Milroy v Milroy* (1844) 14 Sim 48 at 55; *Harrison v Grimwood* (1849) 12 Beav 192; *Tatham v Vernon* (1861) 29 Beav 604. See generally PARA 246.
7 *Hanson v Graham* (1801) 6 Ves 239 at 250; *Tawney v Ward* (1849) 1 Beav 563; *Thomas v Wilberforce* (1862) 31 Beav 299 at 302 per Lord Romilly MR; *Pearson v Dolman* (1866) LR 3 Eq 315 at 321 per Wood V-C (gift defeasible on alienation).
8 *Pearman v Pearman* (1864) 33 Beav 394 at 396.
9 *Re Rouse's Estate* (1852) 9 Hare 649; *Re Sanderson's Trust* (1857) 3 K & J 497 at 507; *Re Parker, Barker v Barker* (1880) 16 ChD 44 at 46 per Jessel MR; *Re Williams, Williams v Williams* [1907] 1 Ch 180 at 183 per Neville J; *Re Ussher, Foster v Ussher* [1922] 2 Ch 321 at 329–331. See also *Re Woolf, Public Trustee v Lazarus* [1920] 1 Ch 184 at 189.
10 *Re Gossling, Gossling v Elcock* [1903] 1 Ch 448, CA; *Re Livingston* (1907) 14 OLR 161. Cf *Re Barnshaw's Trusts* (1867) 15 WR 378.

432. Class gift with direction to apply income. Where there is a gift to a class at a specified age, with a direction to apply the whole income of each presumptive share for the maintenance or benefit of the corresponding member of the class, the members of the class in general take vested interests irrespective of their attaining the age[1], even if the trustees have a discretion as to the mode of application of such share of the interest[2]. This rule does not apply where the gift for maintenance is not out of each share of the fund for the benefit of the corresponding member of the class, but is a general gift for maintenance of the whole class out of the whole undivided interest of the fund[3].

Where the direction accompanying a gift to a class at a specified age is to apply the income of the presumptive share of each member, or so much of that income as the trustees think proper, for his maintenance until payment, it may be possible[4] to draw the inference that the members take vested interests independently of attaining that age[5], at all events if the context does not show the contrary[6] and assists that inference[7]. A trust that at the discretion of the trustees a sufficient part of the income of the presumptive shares should be applied in maintenance has been considered insufficient to render the gift of capital a vested gift[8]. In general the distinction for this purpose between gifts to named individuals and a gift to a class appears to be that a gift to a named person, although in terms contingent, is vested if there is a direction to pay the interest to him in the meantime, even if there is an additional direction that the trustees are to pay the whole or such part of the interest as they think fit. However, in the case of a gift to a class which in terms is contingent on the attaining of a specified age, a direction to apply the whole or part of the income of the fund in the meantime for the maintenance of the whole class does not vest an interest in a member of the class who does not attain a specified age[9].

1   *Dodson v Hay* (1791) 3 Bro CC 405; *Bell v Cade* (1861) 2 John & H 122.
2   *Perrott v Davies* (1877) 38 LT 52 (where a direction to apply the income for the respective maintenance of the children as the trustees should think proper was construed as referring to respective shares).
3   *Taylor v Bacon* (1836) 8 Sim 100; *Southern v Wollaston* (1852) 16 Beav 166; *Tracy v Butcher* (1857) 24 Beav 438; *Lloyd v Lloyd* (1856) 3 K & J 20 (explaining *Jones v Mackilwain* (1826) 1 Russ 220); *Re Hunter's Trusts* (1865) LR 1 Eq 295 at 298; *Re Ashmore's Trusts* (1869) LR 9 Eq 99 (not affected on this point by *Fox v Fox* (1875) LR 19 Eq 286); *Re Morris, Salter v A-G* (1885) 52 LT 840; *Re Martin, Tuke v Gilbert* (1887) 57 LT 471. Cf *Parker v Golding* (1843) 13 Sim 418.
4   *Re Hume, Public Trustee v Mabey* [1912] 1 Ch 693 at 699 per Parker J.
5   *Fox v Fox* (1875) LR 19 Eq 286 at 290–291 (dissenting in this respect from *Re Ashmore's Trusts* (1869) LR 9 Eq 99; and following *Harrison v Grimwood* (1849) 12 Beav 192, 18 LJ Ch 485). It was pointed out in *Wilson v Knox* (1884) 13 LR Ir 349, that no such question arose for decision in *Fox v Fox* above, since the gift of income was by reference to the presumptive shares of the donees; but that case (although doubted in *Dewar v Brooke* (1880) 14 ChD 529 at 532; *Re Martin, Tuke v Gilbert* (1887) 57 LT 471 at 474; *Brennan v Brennan* [1894] 1 IR 69 at 73; *Re Wintle, Tucker v Wintle* [1896] 2 Ch 711 at 715, 719) was considered by Lindley MR and Jeune P in *Re Turney, Turney v Turney* [1899] 2 Ch 739 at 747–748, CA, to be good sense and good law; and it was followed, as laying down the rule described in the text, in *Re Eichardt, Brebner v O'Meara* (1905) 25 NZLR 374, *Re Levy, Cohen v Cohen* (1907) 7 SRNSW 885 and *Re Ussher, Foster v Ussher* [1922] 2 Ch 321. See also *Re Campbell, Cooper v Campbell* (1919) 88 LJ Ch 239, 120 LT 562 (reference to maintenance from 'his expectant share or interest'); and note 7.
6   Thus the inference is excluded where the class is clearly a contingent class, with the specified age forming part of the description of the class: *Re Ricketts, Ricketts v Ricketts* (1910) 103 LT 278; *Re Hume, Public Trustee v Mabey* [1912] 1 Ch 693.
7   *Re Campbell, Cooper v Campbell* (1919) 88 LJ Ch 239, 120 LT 562. In *Fox v Fox* (1875) LR 19 Eq 286, the construction in favour of vesting was also indicated by a gift over (see PARA 436).
8   See *Vawdry v Geddes* (1830) 1 Russ & M 203 at 207 (where there was also an alternative trust for accumulation); *Boreham v Bignall* (1850) 8 Hare 131 (where the will contained an

advancement clause relating to presumptive shares); *Hardcastle v Hardcastle* (1862) 1 Hem & M 405 at 410 per Wood V-C.

9   *Re Grimshaw's Trusts* (1879) 11 ChD 406; *Re Parker, Barker v Barker* (1880) 16 ChD 44; *Re Mervin, Mervin v Crossman* [1891] 3 Ch 197 at 202. See also *Bowyer v West* (1871) 24 LT 414; *Re Hume, Public Trustee v Mabey* [1912] 1 Ch 693.

433.   Where gift remains contingent. A mere discretionary power to apply income for maintenance is not sufficient to vest a gift, whether the donee is a class[1], an individual[2] or a group of persons taking not as a class[3], and whether there is[4] or is not[5] a direction to accumulate the income not so applied for the benefit of persons who ultimately attain a vested interest. Moreover, where the gift is a specific or general legacy and interest is given for maintenance pending the donee reaching a specified age, but under the other provisions of the will there is no possibility of the separation of the subject matter of the gift from the rest of the testator's estate, the inference is that the gift remains contingent[6].

1   *Leake v Robinson* (1817) 2 Mer 363; *Marquis of Bute v Harman* (1846) 9 Beav 320 (but see *Southern v Wollaston* (1852) 16 Beav 166 at 168n); *Re Thatcher's Trusts* (1859) 26 Beav 365 at 369; *Dewar v Brooke* (1880) 14 ChD 529; *Re Wintle, Tucker v Wintle* [1896] 2 Ch 711; *Re Ricketts, Ricketts v Ricketts* (1910) 103 LT 278; *Re Hume, Public Trustee v Mabey* [1912] 1 Ch 693 at 699.

2   *Russell v Russell* [1903] 1 IR 168. The decision to the contrary in *Eccles v Birkett* (1850) 4 De G & Sm 105, where no reasons were given, was explained in *Locke v Lamb* (1867) LR 4 Eq 372 at 379, on the ground of the gift being a gift of interest. Cf *Re Jobson, Jobson v Richardson* (1889) 44 ChD 154 at 157; *Re Rogers, Lloyds Bank Ltd v Lory* [1944] Ch 297, [1944] 2 All ER 1, CA. See also *Harrison v Tucker* [2003] EWHC 1168 (Ch), [2003] All ER (D) 341 (May), [2003] WTLR 883.

3   *Wilson v Knox* (1884) 13 LR Ir 349.

4   See *Pickford v Brown, Brown v Brown* (1856) 2 K & J 426; *Merry v Hill* (1869) LR 8 Eq 619; *Re Hume, Public Trustee v Mabey* [1912] 1 Ch 693.

5   *Re Wintle, Tucker v Wintle* [1896] 2 Ch 711.

6   *Re Lord Nunburnholme, Wilson v Nunburnholme* [1912] 1 Ch 489, CA. See also *Cromek v Lumb* (1839) 3 Y & C Ex 565 at 576 per Alderson B, approving 1 Roper on Legacies (3rd Edn) 500, which explained *Batsford v Kebbell* (1797) 3 Ves 363 (cited in PARA 430 note 9).

(D)   Severance from the Estate

434.   Direction for severance from testator's estate. Prima facie, the circumstance that a testator has expressly or impliedly directed that, for the purpose of the gift, the legacy fund is to be severed, either immediately or on any intermediate event, from his general estate is sufficient to show that the further postponement of enjoyment is not for the purpose of making the gift contingent[1]. For this purpose, it is a sufficient separation if, as a matter of bookkeeping or physically, the trustees properly set apart the property as being property to which no one but the donee has any right to look, subject, if necessary, to the right to resort to it to satisfy the testator's debts[2].

1   *Branstrom v Wilkinson* (1802) 7 Ves 421 (appointment of separate trustee); *Saunders v Vautier* (1841) Cr & Ph 240 at 248; *Lister v Bradley* (1841) 1 Hare 10 at 13; *Greet v Greet* (1842) 5 Beav 123; *Strother v Dutton* (1857) 1 De G & J 675 at 676; *Dundas v Wolfe Murray* (1863) 1 Hem & M 425 at 431–432 per Wood V-C (where it was said that the mere fact of the fund being severed is not the essential point but rather that it must be a severance connected with the legacy itself); *Parsons v Peters* (1864) 13 WR 214; *Re Wrey, Stuart v Wrey* (1885) 30 ChD 507 at 509; *Re Bevan's Trusts* (1887) 34 ChD 716 at 718; *Brennan v Brennan* [1894] 1 IR 69 at 72.

2   *Re Lord Nunburnholme, Wilson v Nunburnholme* [1912] 1 Ch 489 at 497, CA, per Buckley LJ.

(E)   Effect of Gift Over

435.   Gifts over. The circumstance of a gift of property being followed by a gift over[1] to another donee on a certain contingency does not alone prevent the first gift from vesting in the meantime, and, although it may be called in aid of other circumstances for that purpose[2], the effect of the gift over may be to vest the first gift[3]. This result does not, however, follow irrespective of other contingencies attached to the original gift[4].

1   As to gifts over by necessary implication see PARA 466.
2   *Shepherd v Ingram* (1764) Amb 448; *Skey v Barnes* (1816) 3 Mer 335 at 340 per Grant MR (criticising *Scott v Bargeman* (1722) 2 P Wms 68); *Davies v Fisher* (1842) 5 Beav 201 at 214; *Hardcastle v Hardcastle* (1862) 1 Hem & M 405 at 412; *Re M'Garrity, Ballance v M'Garrity* (1912) 46 ILT 175; *Re Campbell, Cooper v Campbell* (1919) 88 LJ Ch 239, 120 LT 562.
3   As to contingent gifts over generally see PARA 423.
4   See *Malcolm v O'Callaghan* (1817) 2 Madd 349 at 354; *Malcolm v O'Callaghan* (1833) Coop temp Brough 73; *Re Thomson's Trusts* (1870) LR 11 Eq 146; *Re Gunning's Estate* (1884) 13 LR Ir 203.

436. Failure to attain specified age. Where a gift is made to an individual donee if he attains a specified age and a gift over is made in the event of the donee failing to attain that age, the gift over is treated as showing that the first gift is vested[1]. Where there are indications in favour of the original gift being vested independently of the specified age, this confirms that the mere gift over does not prevent the vesting[2]. Thus a gift over on death under the specified age without issue does not prevent vesting[3]; and if the original gift is to a class and the gift over refers to the shares of those dying under that age, the inference is that the original gift is vested[4].

In a gift to a class, the gift over may show that a person not attaining the specified age is nevertheless to take or to be treated as taking a share as a member of the class, and that that share is given over in the specified events; accordingly, the attainment of the specified age is not then a condition precedent to vesting[5].

1   See *Re Heath, Public Trustee v Heath* [1936] Ch 259; and PARA 423. See also *O'Reilly v Walsh* (1872) IR 6 Eq 555; *Re Bateman's Trusts* (1873) LR 15 Eq 355. Distinguish, however, *Re Edwards, Jones v Jones* [1906] 1 Ch 570 (where the gift was to a child who attained 21 and that condition was thus part of the description of the donee); *Re Mallinson's Consolidated Trusts, Mallinson v Gooley* [1974] 2 All ER 530, [1974] 1 WLR 1120 (where the gift over was in the terms 'subject as aforesaid' and the initial gift was held to be contingent). See also PARA 437. At one time a different view from that stated in the text was taken: see *Vawdry v Geddes* (1830) 1 Russ & M 203 at 208 per Leach MR; *Bland v Williams* (1834) 3 My & K 411 at 417 per Leach MR; *Festing v Allen* (1844) 5 Hare 573 at 577 per Wood V-C.
2   *Davies v Fisher* (1842) 5 Beav 201 at 214; *Hardcastle v Hardcastle* (1862) 1 Hem & M 405 at 412; *Re Baxter's Trusts* (1864) 4 New Rep 131. In *Ridgway v Ridgway* (1851) 4 De G & Sm 271, the question was not the vesting of the gift but the application of the intermediate income.
3   *Bland v Williams* (1834) 3 My & K 411; *Harrison v Grimwood* (1849) 12 Beav 192 (see PARA 423); *Mytton v Boodle* (1834) 6 Sim 457; *Phipps v Ackers* (1842) 9 Cl & Fin 583, HL (see PARA 419) (where the question addressed to the judges omitted the words 'without leaving issue' in order, apparently, to have the case of *Doe d Hunt v Moore* (1811) 14 East 601 (real estate: see PARA 423) reconsidered); *Wetherell v Wetherell* (1863) 1 De GJ & Sm 134; *Whitter v Bremridge* (1866) LR 2 Eq 736 (where there was a gift of residuary real and personal estate on trust to sell and invest, and pay 'the property and interest arising therefrom to A on his attaining the age of 24; but in case of his not attaining that age, or leaving male issue, I give, devise and bequeath the properties to other persons'; and it was held that A took an absolute vested interest in the testator's estate which was liable to be divested in the events mentioned in the will).
4   If the gift over is to a stranger and not to the other members of the class, the inference is that the person not attaining the specified age is nevertheless to take a share as a member of the class (see the cases cited in note 5); and if the gift over is an accruer clause in favour of the other members of the class, the inference is the same in order that the accruer clause may not be useless (see *Re Edmondson's Estate* (1868) LR 5 Eq 389; *Re Gunning's Estate* (1884) 13 LR Ir 203).
5   *Berkeley v Swinburne* (1848) 16 Sim 275 at 284; *Taylor v Frobisher* (1852) 5 De G & Sm 191 at 199; *Fox v Fox* (1875) LR 19 Eq 286 at 291; *Re Turney, Turney v Turney* [1899] 2 Ch 739 at 746, 748, CA.

437. Gift over on parent's death without issue. Where a gift is made to the children generally of a named person at a specified age (and, therefore, prima facie contingently on attaining that age), a gift over on the parent's death without issue does not of itself render the gift vested without regard to the attainment of that age[1]. However, in gifts to a class of children surviving their parent at such an age, a similar gift over has sometimes given rise to the inference that the attainment of that age was not a condition precedent[2].

1   *Walker v Mower* (1852) 16 Beav 365; *Re Wrangham's Trust* (1860) 1 Drew & Sm 358; *Kidman v Kidman* (1871) 40 LJ Ch 359; *Re Edwards, Jones v Jones* [1906] 1 Ch 570 at 573, CA; *Re Ricketts, Ricketts v Ricketts* (1910) 103 LT 278; *Re Campbell, Cooper v Campbell* (1919) 88 LJ Ch 239, 120 LT 562.
2   *Bree v Perfect* (1844) 1 Coll 128 (followed in *Ingram v Suckling* (1859) 7 WR 386; *Re Bevan's Trusts* (1887) 34 ChD 716 at 719). *Bree v Perfect* has not, however, always been accepted as correct: see *Re Edwards, Jones v Jones* [1906] 1 Ch 570 at 572, CA, per Romer LJ.

F.   LEGACIES CHARGED ON REAL ESTATE OR A MIXED FUND

438.   Vesting of legacy charged on real estate. So far as they are charged on real estate, legacies prima facie[1] do not vest until the time fixed for payment[2] and fail if the donee dies before that time, even though interest is given in the meantime[3]. If, however, the payment is clearly postponed, not for reasons personal to the donee but for the benefit of the estate[4] or merely in order to let in a prior life or other limited interest[5], then the legacies vest at once. This rule applies generally, whether the land is the primary or the auxiliary fund and whether the gift is for a portion or is merely a general legacy, and whether the donee is a child or a stranger[6].

1   For cases where the context showed an intention excluding this presumption see *Watkins v Cheek* (1825) 2 Sim & St 199; *Hudson v Forster* (1841) 2 Mont D & De G 177; *Brown v Wooler* (1843) 2 Y & C Ch Cas 134.
2   *Lady Poulet v Lord Poulet* (1685) 1 Vern 204 at 321; *Smith v Smith* (1688) 2 Vern 92; *Yates v Phettiplace* (1700) 2 Vern 416; *Carter v Bletsoe* (1708) 2 Vern 617; *Langley v Oates* (1708) 2 Eq Cas Abr 541 pl 7; *Jennings v Looks* (1725) 2 P Wms 276; *Rich v Wilson* (1728) Mos 68; *Duke of Chandos v Talbot* (1731) 2 P Wms 601 at 610; *Hall v Terry* (1738) 1 Atk 502; *Re Hudson's Minors* (1843) Drury temp Sug 6; *Davidson v Proctor* (1849) 19 LJ Ch 395; *Bolton v Bolton* (1861) 12 I Ch R 233; *Taylor v Lambert* (1876) 2 ChD 177. See also Tudor, LC Real Prop (4th Edn) 434. Cf *Gordon v Raynes* (1732) 3 P Wms 134.
3   *Gawler v Standerwick* (1788) 2 Cox Eq Cas 15; *Harrison v Naylor* (1790) 2 Cox Eq Cas 247; *Pearce v Loman, Pearce v Taylor* (1796) 3 Ves 135; *Parker v Hodgson* (1861) 1 Drew & Sm 568. See also *Smith v Smith* (1688) 2 Vern 92; *Boycot v Cotton* (1738) 1 Atk 552 at 555. Cf *Phipps v Lord Mulgrave* (1798) 3 Ves 613.
4   *Lowther v Condon* (1741) 2 Atk 127 at 128; *Manning v Herbert* (1769) Amb 575 at 576; *Clark v Ross* (1773) 2 Dick 529; *Kemp v Davy* (1774) 1 Bro CC 120n; *Murkin v Phillipson* (1834) 3 My & K 257 at 261; *Goulbourn v Brooks* (1837) 2 Y & C Ex 539 at 543; *Evans v Scott* (1847) 1 HL Cas 43 at 57; *Goodman v Drury* (1852) 21 LJ Ch 680 (where, however, the context excluded the presumption arising from the prior life estate); *Remnant v Hood* (1860) 2 De GF & J 396 at 410–411; *Haverty v Curtis* [1895] 1 IR 23 at 34.
5   *King v Withers* (1735) Cas temp Talb 117; *Tunstall v Brachen* (1753) Amb 167; *Embrey v Martin* (1754) Amb 230; *Jeale v Titchener* (1771) Amb 703; *Dawson v Killet* (1781) 1 Bro CC 119; *Godwin v Munday* (1783) 1 Bro CC 191; *Bayley v Bishop* (1803) 9 Ves 6; *Poole v Terry* (1831) 4 Sim 294.
6   *Duke of Chandos v Talbot* (1731) 2 P Wms 601 at 612n. As to portions generally see SETTLEMENTS vol 91 (2012) PARA 628 et seq.

439.   Vesting of legacy charged on mixed fund. Formerly, where legacies were charged both on real and on personal estate, the personal estate prima facie was applied first towards payment and the real estate only in aid of it. So far as the personal estate was applied towards payment, the vesting of the legacies was governed by the ordinary rules[1] applying to bequests of pure personal estate alone[2]; and, so far as it was necessary to resort to the real estate, the vesting was governed by the rules[3] applying to legacies charged on real estate alone[4]. Now, however, where the testator's real and personal estate have been given as a mixed fund for payment of legacies, these are, in the absence of a contrary intention, borne by the real and personal estate rateably, and the rules as to vesting in the case of personal estate probably apply to the whole[5].

1 As to these rules see PARA 425.
2 *Re Hudson's Minors* (1843) Drury *temp* Sug 6.
3 As to these rules see PARA 438.
4 *Duke of Chandos v Talbot* (1731) 2 P Wms 601 at 612n; *Prowse v Abingdon* (1738) 1 Atk 482; *Van v Clark* (1739) 1 Atk 510; *Parker v Hodgson* (1861) 1 Drew & Sm 568. Where the legatee died before the time of payment, his personal representatives might be entitled so far as the personal estate was concerned: *Richardson v Greese* (1743) 3 Atk 65 at 69; *Anon* (1744) 2 Eq Cas Abr 551 pl 33.
5 As to the order of application of assets, and as to the exclusion of the statutory order by the creation of a mixed fund see PARAS 993, 998 et seq.

(iii) Divesting

440. General principle that court leans against the divesting of vested interests. In a doubtful case[1] the court leans against the divesting of vested interests[2] and favours that construction which leads to the vesting indefeasibly of the property as early as possible[3]. In general, therefore, subject to the intention shown by the will as a whole[4], divesting conditions are construed strictly[5], and, where there is a prior vested gift and then a clause divesting the gift in a specified contingency, the court does not hold the gift divested unless the precise contingency referred to occurs, and does not introduce other contingencies unless the context requires that course[6].

1 The rule is inapplicable where the intention as to divesting is plainly shown: see *Re Ball, Slattery v Ball* (1888) 40 ChD 11 at 13, CA; and PARA 441 note 11.
2 *Maddison v Chapman* (1858) 4 K & J 709 at 721, 723; *Re Wood, Moore v Bailey* (1880) 43 LT 730 at 732; *Re Roberts, Percival v Roberts* [1903] 2 Ch 200 at 204.
3 *Minors v Battison* (1876) 1 App Cas 428, HL; *Re Teale, Teale v Teale* (1885) 53 LT 936 at 937.
4 *Lady Langdale v Briggs* (1856) 8 De GM & G 391 at 429–430. As to shifting clauses (otherwise known as forfeiture or defeasance clauses) see SETTLEMENTS vol 91 (2012) PARA 641; and as to miscellaneous uncertain conditions attached to gifts see PARA 141.
5 *Fraunces' Case* (1609) 8 Co Rep 89b at 90b; *Kiallmark v Kiallmark* (1856) 26 LJ Ch 1 at 4; *Blagrove v Bradshaw* (1858) 4 Drew 230 at 235. The principle applies not only to the divesting of vested estates but also to the defeating of contingent estates: *Kiallmark v Kiallmark* at 4. Accordingly, in cases of gifts to children of a named parent followed by a gift over if all the children die in the lifetime of their parent, where some but not all survive their parent, all take: *Bromhead v Hunt* (1821) 2 Jac & W 459; *Gordon v Hope* (1849) 3 De G & Sm 351 (settlement); *Templeman v Warrington* (1842) 13 Sim 267 at 270 (gift over, if but one child at parent's decease, to that one); *Re Firth, Loveridge v Firth* [1914] 2 Ch 386; *Re Stephens, Tomalin v Tomalin's Trustee* [1927] 1 Ch 1, CA. As to divesting in the case of a condition subsequent see PARAS 414, 423.
6 *Tarbuck v Tarbuck* (1835) 4 LJ Ch 129; *Cox v Parker* (1856) 22 Beav 168; *Potts v Atherton* (1859) 28 LJ Ch 486 at 488; *Re Kirkbride's Trusts* (1866) LR 2 Eq 400 at 402; *Re Pickworth, Snaith v Parkinson* [1899] 1 Ch 642, CA; *Re Searle, Searle v Searle* [1905] WN 86. As to the change of conjunctions in particular cases see PARA 442.

441. Gift over on death 'without leaving children'. Where there is a gift to a named person for life and after his death to his children, either generally or on attaining any age or on any other event[1], in terms which give the children a vested absolute interest independently of whether the children survive their parent or not[2], followed by a gift over if the parent dies 'without leaving children', these words are construed so as not to destroy any prior vested interest[3], and are read as 'without having children'[4], or 'without having had children'[5], or 'without having had a child who attained a vested interest'[6], according to the context.

The rule is not confined to a case in which the life tenant is the parent of or stands in loco parentis to the donee in remainder, but extends to a case in which the life tenant is a complete stranger[7], and, it seems, to a case in which the children mentioned in the gift over take no interest but there is an interest in their parent[8], or in any one else[9], independent of the children surviving their parent, and where the result of reading the words in their ordinary sense would be to divest interests which the testator apparently intended to remain vested. The rule is not affected by the circumstances that the testator knew of the existence of a child of the named person, and that such knowledge appears on the face of the will itself[10]. The rule is inapplicable where the context shows that the prior vested interests were intended to be destroyed in accordance with the plain meaning of the words[11], or where the subject matter of the gift is an annuity bequeathed so as to involve the notion of personal enjoyment by each of the successive donees[12]. Moreover, the rule does not necessarily apply where there is a disposition in a settlement in default of appointment and the subsequent provision in the event of death without having children is in a will or codicil exercising the power of appointment[13].

1 Eg in cases where the interest of the children is to vest at birth (*Treharne v Layton* (1875) LR 10 QB 459, Ex Ch; *Re Bradbury, Wing v Bradbury* (1904) 73 LJ Ch 591, CA; *Re Goldney, Re Dighton, Clarke v Dighton* (1911) 130 LT Jo 484), or at the age of majority (*Maitland v Chalie* (1822) 6 Madd 243; *Re Thompson's Trust, ex p Oliver* (1852) 5 De G & Sm 667), or at that age or marriage (*Casamajor v Strode* (1843) 8 Jur 14), or when the youngest attains the age of majority (*Kennedy v Sedgwick* (1857) 3 K & J 540), or any similar event if only the vesting is without reference to the surviving of the parent (*Barkworth v Barkworth* (1906) 75 LJ Ch 754 at 756 per Joyce J).

2 The rule is, therefore, inapplicable where the interests of the children are contingent on their surviving their parents: *Bythesea v Bythesea* (1854) 23 LJ Ch 1004; *Sheffield v Kennett* (1859) 4 De G & J 593; *Re Watson's Trusts* (1870) LR 10 Eq 36 (where *Bryden v Willett* (1869) LR 7 Eq 472 is criticised). See also *Re Heath's Settlement* (1856) 23 Beav 193; *Pride v Fooks* (1858) 3 De G & J 252; *Chadwick v Greenall* (1861) 7 Jur NS 959; *Young v Turner* (1861) 1 B & S 550; *Jeyes v Savage* (1875) 10 Ch App 555 (settlement). A non-exclusive power of appointment by the parent does not, however, exclude the rule: see *Re Jackson's Will* (1879) 13 ChD 189.

3 *Re Cobbold, Cobbold v Lawton* [1903] 2 Ch 299, CA (report corrected in *Re Davey, Prisk v Mitchell* [1915] 1 Ch 837 at 847n, CA); *Chunilal Parvatishankar v Bai Samrath* (1914) 30 TLR 407, PC; *Re MacAndrew's Will Trusts, Stephens v Barclays Bank Ltd* [1964] Ch 704, [1963] 2 All ER 919.

4 *Re Buckinghamshire Rly Co, Re Tookey's Trusts, ex p Hooper* (1852) 1 Drew 264; *Kennedy v Sedgwick* (1857) 3 K & J 540; *White v Hill* (1867) LR 4 Eq 265; *Re Brown's Trust* (1873) LR 16 Eq 239; *Re Jackson's Will* (1879) 13 ChD 189 at 194 per Jessel MR.

5 *Marshall v Hill* (1814) 2 M & S 608 at 615; *Bryden v Willett* (1869) LR 7 Eq 472 at 476; *Treharne v Layton* (1875) LR 10 QB 459 at 461, Ex Ch.

6 See *Re Milling's Settlement, Peake v Thom* [1944] Ch 263 at 268, [1944] 1 All ER 541 at 544, stating the rule in *Maitland v Chalie* (1822) 6 Madd 243 in the amended form as formulated in *Re Cobbold, Cobbold v Lawton* [1903] 2 Ch 299, CA (see the text and note 3).

7 *Casamajor v Strode* (1843) 8 Jur 14.

8 *Re Bogle, Bogle v Yorstoun* (1898) 78 LT 457 (where the gift was to the parent for life and afterwards to his executors and administrators contingently on the parent having two or more children attaining 21 years).

9 *Re Jackson's Will* (1879) 13 ChD 189 at 194 per Jessel MR. See, however, *Armstrong v Armstrong* (1888) 21 LR Ir 114, Ir CA (where it was held that the words 'without leaving' may be read 'without having had' where the result of so doing is to make the whole instrument consistent and where the contrary construction would have the effect of divesting a previously vested gift in a manner inconsistent with the expressed intention of the testator; but they will not be so read for the purpose of altering the event on which the divesting of a gift previously vested is to take place).

10 *Re Cobbold, Cobbold v Lawton* [1903] 2 Ch 299, CA at 304 per Romer LJ (see note 3).

11 *Hedges v Harpur, Hedges v Blick* (1858) 3 De G & J 129 at 141; *Re Hamlet, Stephen v Cunningham* (1888) 39 ChD 426, CA; *Clay v Coles* (1887) 57 LT 682 at 683–684 per Stirling J; *Re Ball, Slattery v Ball* (1888) 40 ChD 11 at 13, CA. See, however, *Barkworth v Barkworth* (1906) 75 LJ Ch 754 at 756 (where it is suggested that the relevant sentence properly should not appear in the report of *Re Ball, Slattery v Ball*). Thus, the rule does not generally apply to a gift to a person absolutely followed by a gift over on his death without leaving issue: *Armstrong v Armstrong*

(1888) 21 LR Ir 114, Ir CA; *Re Ball, Slattery v Ball,* disapproving *White v Hight* (1879) 12 ChD 751. See also *Re Hambleton, Hamilton v Hambleton* [1884] WN 157; but cf *Re Bogle, Bogle v Yorstoun* (1898) 78 LT 457.

12 *Re Hemingway, James v Dawson* (1890) 45 ChD 453 at 456.

13 *Re Milling's Settlement, Peake v Thom* [1944] Ch 263 at 269, [1944] 1 All ER 541 at 544 per Morton J.

442. Construction of 'or' as 'and'. If there is a devise to a named person in fee simple[1] or a bequest to a named person absolutely[2] with a gift over in either case if he dies without children or under the age of majority to other donees, 'or' is read as 'and', and the gift over does not take effect unless both events happen. This rule of construction depends on the testator's presumed intention to benefit the children of the devisee directly or indirectly, an intention which would be defeated if the devisee were to die under the age of majority leaving children and 'or' were construed disjunctively[3]. The alteration is made even if the sentence as altered contains a condition repugnant to the character of the estate given[4]. A similar rule holds good as to gifts over if the donee in question dies before a life tenant under a previous gift or without issue[5].

This rule of construction is also applicable where the prior devise or bequest is contingent on the donee leaving issue[6], or on his attaining majority[7], if he takes absolutely.

Where, however, a prior donee takes for life only and his issue take express absolute interests and there is a similar gift over, this alteration cannot be adopted so as to defeat the interests of subsequent takers[8]. Where a prior donee takes in tail[9] or takes for life only with remainder to his issue as purchasers in tail[10], a gift over on his death under age or on the failure of his issue may be read without the alteration of 'or' to 'and'; but even in this case a death under the specified age does not in general carry the estate over unless there is also a failure of issue, as the gift over would not be read so as to defeat any issue in tail[11]. A death without issue, although after attaining that age, may, however, carry the estate over by way of remainder[12] or otherwise.

On the same principle[13], or to avoid inconsistency[14], where a prior gift is absolute, or contingent on attaining a specified age or on marriage or on a specified age or marriage as alternative events, a gift over on the donee's death before attaining that age or marriage is read as if 'or' were 'and'.

Where the interest of a donee is postponed to a life interest but is contingent only on his attaining a certain age and not on his surviving the life tenant, a gift over on his death before the life tenant or under the specified age is construed as if 'or' were 'and'[15].

1 *Price v Hunt* (1684) Poll 645; *Fairfield v Morgan* (1805) 2 Bos & PNR 38; *Eastman v Baker* (1808) 1 Taunt 174 at 182; *Right d Day v Day* (1812) 16 East 67; *Doe d Herbert v Selby* (1824) 2 B & C 926 at 932; *Morris v Morris* (1853) 17 Beav 198; *Mahaffy v Rooney* (1853) 5 Ir Jur 245; *Imray v Imeson* (1872) 26 LT 93. *Sowell v Garret* (1596) Moore KB 422 (accepted as an authority on this point in *Wright d Burrill v Kemp* (1789) 3 Term Rep 470 at 474 per Buller J and in *Denn d Wilkins v Kemeys* (1808) 8 East 366 at 367 per Le Blanc J) is referable to other grounds: see the decision as reported sub nom *Soulle v Gerrard* Cro Eliz 525; and note 11.

2 The rule applies both to real and to personal estate: *Wright v Marsom* [1895] WN 148. See also *Weddell v Mundy* (1801) 6 Ves 341; *Mytton v Boodle* (1834) 6 Sim 457.

3 *Re Crutchley, Kidson v Marsden* [1912] 2 Ch 335 at 337 per Parker J. See, however, the doubts expressed in *Grey v Pearson* (1857) 6 HL Cas 61 at 80 per Lord Cranworth LC, who nevertheless approved of the rule as being an established rule. According to the structure of the sentence, if 'without' is used followed by two events both governed by 'without', the use of 'or' is correct (see *Stretton v Fitzgerald* (1889) 23 LR Ir 466 at 472–473 per Fitzgibbon LJ), and in such a case it is not necessary to alter the words.

4 Eg gifts over on the donee dying without issue or intestate: see *Incorporated Society in Dublin v Richards* (1841) 1 Dr & War 258 at 283; *Green v Harvey* (1842) 1 Hare 428; *Greated v Greated*

(1859) 26 Beav 621 at 627 (gift over in event of 'any of them dying before having heirs of their body or making a particular disposition of his or her property'); *Re Crutchley, Kidson v Marsden* [1912] 2 Ch 335. Cf *Beachcroft v Broome* (1791) 4 Term Rep 441; *Cuthbert v Purrier* (1822) Jac 415; *Stretton v Fitzgerald* (1889) 23 LR Ir 466.

5   *Wright d Burrill v Kemp* (1789) 3 Term Rep 470; *Denn d Wilkins v Kemeys* (1808) 8 East 366.
6   *Johnson v Simcock* (1861) 7 H & N 344, Ex Ch.
7   *Mytton v Boodle* (1834) 6 Sim 457; *Wright v Marsom* [1895] WN 148.
8   *Cooke v Mirehouse* (1864) 34 Beav 27.
9   *Woodward v Glasbrook* (1700) 2 Vern 388; *Brownswood v Edwards* (1751) 2 Ves Sen 243 at 249 per Lord Hardwicke LC; *Mortimer v Hartley* (1848) 6 CB 819, (1851) 6 Exch 47, (1851) 3 De G & Sm 316 (where the Court of Chancery adopted the opinion of the Court of Exchequer and not that of the Court of Common Pleas after sending cases for the opinion of those courts); *Grey v Pearson* (1857) 6 HL Cas 61 at 93 per Lord St Leonards. Entailed interests cannot be created by instruments coming into operation on or after 1 January 1997: see the Trusts of Land and Appointment of Trustees Act 1996 s 2(6), Sch 1 para 5; PARA 387; and REAL PROPERTY AND REGISTRATION vol 87 (2012) PARA 114.
10 *Hasker v Sutton* (1824) 9 Moore CP 2. See also note 9.
11 *Soulle v Gerrard* (1596) Cro Eliz 525 (where the estate tail was implied from the gift over, and the subsequent limitation could not then have taken effect by way of executory devise). However, this case would now be decided otherwise. See also *Grey v Pearson* (1857) 6 HL Cas 61. The effect, so far as death under age is concerned, is, therefore, the same as if 'or' were read as 'and': cf *Monkhouse v Monkhouse* (1829) 3 Sim 119 at 126 (gift over on death or want of issue construed as on death and want of issue).
12 *Brownsword v Edwards* (1751) 2 Ves Sen 243; *Hasker v Sutton* (1824) 9 Moore CP 2 (where the remainder was held to be contingent). This appears to be the case also referred to in *Grey v Pearson* (1857) 6 HL Cas 61 at 93 per Lord St Leonards, but there described as the case of death 'under age leaving issue'.
13 This was the ground for the rule stated in *Re Clegg's Estate, ex p Evans* (1862) 14 I Ch R 70, Ir CA; *Re Cantillon's Minors* (1864) 16 I Ch R 301 at 311 (contingent on marriage); *Butler v Trustees, Executors and Agency Co Ltd* (1906) 3 CLR 435 at 443 (gift over on death before 21 unmarried and without issue).
14 This was the ground for the rule stated in *Grant v Dyer* (1813) 2 Dow 73 at 88, HL; *Malcolm v O'Callaghan* (1833) Coop *temp* Brough 73 at 76 (contingent on marriage with consent). See also *Thackeray v Hampson* (1825) 2 Sim & St 214; *Grimshawe v Pickup* (1839) 9 Sim 591; *Thompson v Teulon, Teulon v Teulon* (1852) 22 LJ Ch 243 (alternative events); *Collett v Collett* (1866) 35 Beav 312.
15 *Miles v Dyer* (1832) 5 Sim 435 (subsequent proceedings (1837) 8 Sim 330); followed, as laying down an established rule of construction, in *Bentley v Meech* (1858) 25 Beav 197.

443. Construction of 'and' as 'or'.

In general, the court is unwilling to change 'and' into 'or' in a gift over on several events connected by 'and' where the words may be given their ordinary sense, as the effect would be to divest the prior gift in events other than the compound event which the testator has provided for[1]. Thus after a gift to a donee absolutely[2] or in tail[3], or for life with remainder to his children[4], a gift over on the donee dying under the age of majority and without issue is read in its ordinary sense, and is not read as if 'and' were 'or' merely for the possible benefit of the issue.

'And' may be construed as 'or' where one member of the sentence includes the other, so that, by construing the words literally, one member of the sentence would be rendered unnecessary, and the change is made in order to give effect to each member of the sentence[5]. The majority of the cases have also been cases in which 'and' has been construed disjunctively in order to favour the vesting of a legacy and not in order to divest it[6]. The alteration is not, however, made if, by giving to one member of the sentence some less usual meaning, effect can be given to every word[7]. Thus if, after a gift to a person absolutely or for life and afterwards to his children, there is a gift over on his death 'unmarried and without issue', 'and' may be read as 'or' where 'unmarried' is necessarily given its ordinary meaning of 'never having been married'[8]; but as a rule, if in such a gift over 'unmarried' can be given the meaning 'without leaving a spouse'[9], so as to give effect to all the words without altering the conjunctions, this construction is adopted rather than the words being altered[10].

There is an additional objection to the change of 'and' to 'or' if, as a result, any part of the sentence becomes inoperative[11].

1   *Doe d Usher v Jessep* (1810) 12 East 288 at 293; *Key v Key* (1855) 1 Jur NS 372 (where *Brown v Walker* (1824) 2 LJOS Ch 82 is commented on); *Reed v Braithwaite* (1871) LR 11 Eq 514; *Lillie v Willis* (1899) 31 OR 198; *Re Metcalfe, Metcalfe v Metcalfe* (1900) 32 OR 103.
2   *Coates v Hart* (1863) 32 Beav 349.
3   *Doe d Usher v Jessep* (1810) 12 East 288; approved in *Grey v Pearson* (1857) 6 HL Cas 61 (where *Brownsword v Edwards* (1751) 2 Ves Sen 243 is explained and the construction there adopted by Lord Hardwicke LC, which was similar to that where 'or' is used (see PARA 442), was disapproved). Entailed interests cannot be created by instruments coming into operation on or after 1 January 1997: see the Trusts of Land and Appointment of Trustees Act 1996 s 2(6), Sch 1 para 5; PARA 387; and REAL PROPERTY AND REGISTRATION vol 87 (2012) PARA 114.
4   *Malcolm v Malcolm* (1856) 21 Beav 225.
5   *Day v Day* (1854) Kay 703 at 708 per Wood V-C.
6   *Day v Day* (1854) Kay 703 at 708 per Wood V-C.
7   As to the general rule to this effect see PARA 248.
8   *Maberly v Strode* (1797) 3 Ves 450 at 454; *Bell v Phyn* (1802) 7 Ves 453 at 459 per Grant MR; *Carolin v Carolin* (1881) 17 LR Ir 25n; *Long v Lane* (1885) 17 LR Ir 24, Ir CA; *Roberts v Bishop of Kilmore* [1902] 1 IR 333 (where 'unmarried' was held to be used in this sense throughout the will). Cf *Mackenzie v King* (1848) 12 Jur 787 (where 'nor' was read 'or not').
9   As to this meaning see PARA 246 note 11.
10 *Re Sanders' Trusts* (1866) LR 1 Eq 675; *Re King, Salisbury v Ridley* (1890) 62 LT 789; *Re Chant, Chant v Lemon* [1900] 2 Ch 345 at 348; *Re Jones, Last v Dobson* [1915] 1 Ch 246 (where 'unmarried and without lawful issue' was held to mean 'without leaving a widow'). Cf *Dillon v Harris* (1830) 4 Bli NS 321 at 365, 369, HL ('and' not to be read in the disjunctive as 'or,' where it will tend to frustrate and not to further the general intent). After a gift of realty in fee simple or an absolute gift of personalty, or a gift for life followed by a gift to the donee's children, a gift over on a prior donee dying a minor unmarried and without issue prima facie is construed as given on a single contingency attended with two qualifications (dying an infant and either without leaving a wife surviving him, or, without children) and the words are not to be read disjunctively unless the context requires: *Doe d Everett v Cooke* (1806) 7 East 269 at 272 (where 'unmarried' was taken to mean 'without leaving a spouse'). Cf *Framlingham v Brand* (1746) 3 Atk 390 where it was taken to mean 'without having married'. Such a word as 'unmarried' in such a context cannot be struck out or left inoperative: *Doe d Baldwin v Rawding* (1819) 2 B & Ald 441. See also PARA 248.
11 *Key v Key* (1855) 1 Jur NS 372; *Re Kirkbride's Trusts* (1866) LR 2 Eq 400 at 403.

444. Survivorship clauses after a life interest construed as merely divesting. If there is a gift after a life estate to a number of persons as tenants in common[1] or alternatively to such of them as survive the life tenant, the survivorship clause prima facie is a divesting clause only, and, if none of the donees survives the life tenant, their representatives take[2]. A similar rule applies where, after a gift to a number of persons as tenants in common, there is a gift on any contingency to the survivor of them; this is construed as conditional on his surviving the life tenant or some specified event[3]. This rule does not, however, apply where, in the context of the will, a gift to the survivor of a number of persons is construed as referring to survivorship among themselves and not as conditional on his surviving the life tenant; in such a case the longest liver takes the gift, even if all die in the lifetime of the life tenant[4]; nor does the rule apply where the condition as to surviving the life tenant applies to the original gift[5].

The time of operation of a divesting provision may be limited by the context, for example by a direction for payment, transfer or conveyance to the donee or for the doing of any such act on any specified event[6]. The court considers that the trustees or executors could not conveniently obey such a direction if divesting were intended to take place after that event[7].

1 Where the gift is to a number of persons as joint tenants and the words referable to survivorship are merely expansive or expository of the previous words so as to make the right to obtain anything under the gift contingent on surviving the life tenant, there will be an intestacy if all the joint tenants predecease the life tenant: *Re Douglas's Will Trusts, Lloyds Bank Ltd v Nelson* [1959] 3 All ER 785, [1959] 1 WLR 1212, CA.

2 *Browne v Lord Kenyon* (1818) 3 Madd 410; *Sturgess v Pearson* (1819) 4 Madd 411 (where there was a bequest to A of interest and dividends of personal property for life, and then to be equally divided among her three children or such of them as were living at her death; the children all died in the lifetime of the life tenant, and it was held that they took vested interests, transmissible to their representatives); *Belk v Slack* (1836) 1 Keen 238; *Wagstaff v Crosby* (1846) 2 Coll 746; *Page v May* (1857) 24 Beav 323; *Wiley v Chanteperdrix* [1894] 1 IR 209; *Re Pickworth, Snaith v Parkinson* [1899] 1 Ch 642, CA; *Penny v Railways Comr* [1900] AC 628 at 634, PC; *Ward v Brown* [1916] 2 AC 121, PC; *Re Douglas's Will Trusts, Lloyds Bank Ltd v Nelson* [1959] 3 All ER 785, [1959] 1 WLR 1212, CA. As to the meaning and ascertainment of survivors see PARAS 315, 318.

3 *Harrison v Foreman* (1800) 5 Ves 207; *Peters v Dipple* (1841) 12 Sim 101; *Clarke v Lubbock* (1842) 1 Y & C Ch Cas 492 (surviving testator); *Eaton v Barker* (1845) 2 Coll 124; *Littlejohns v Household* (1855) 21 Beav 29; *Cambridge v Rous* (1858) 25 Beav 409; *Maddison v Chapman* (1861) 1 John & H 470; *Marriott v Abell* (1869) LR 7 Eq 478; *Re Deacon's Trusts, Deacon v Deacon, Hagger v Heath* (1906) 95 LT 701. See also *Benn v Dixon, Dixon v Nicholson, Dixon v Priestley* (1847) 16 Sim 21; *Re Clark's Trusts* (1870) LR 9 Eq 378; *Jones v Davies* (1880) 28 WR 455; *Young's Trustees v Young* 1927 SC (HL) 6.

4 *Scurfield v Howes* (1790) 3 Bro CC 90; *White v Baker* (1860) 2 De GF & J 55 (commented on, although accepted as correct, in *Re Pickworth, Snaith v Parkinson* [1899] 1 Ch 642, CA); *Re Wood, Hodge v Hull* (1923) 68 Sol Jo 186.

5 *Willis v Plaskett* (1841) 4 Beav 208.

6 See *Vulliamy v Huskisson* (1838) 3 Y & C Ex 80; *Doe d Lloyd v Davies* (1854) 23 LJCP 169. Subject to such a context, the operation of a divesting clause operates whenever the contingency happens on which it is to take effect: see eg *Witham v Witham* (1861) 3 De GF & J 758. As to particular gifts over see PARA 449 et seq.

7 *Woodburne v Woodburne* (1850) 3 De G & Sm 643; *Glyn v Glyn* (1857) 26 LJ Ch 409; *O'Mahoney v Burdett* (1874) LR 7 HL 388 at 403, 406; *Re Luddy, Peard v Morton* (1883) 25 ChD 394 at 397; *Re Kerr's Estate* [1913] 1 IR 214. This indication of intention may be overborne: see *Martineau v Rogers* (1856) 8 De GM & G 328 at 333.

(iv) Gifts over by Inference

445. Gift over by necessary implication. Where a testator has provided for the determination of an estate in any of two or more events and has then given a gift over expressly to take place in one only of those events, then, in the absence of any indication to the contrary[1], the court may necessarily imply an intention on the testator's part that the gift over is to take effect not merely on the specified event but on the happening of any of the events determining the previous estate[2].

The principle is applicable only where, after looking at all the relevant circumstances (including the will itself), the court comes to the conclusion that the testator must certainly have intended the disposition over to take effect in the event which has actually happened[3]. Accordingly, where the prior gift is conditional, for example on the donee attaining a particular age, and the condition is satisfied during the testator's lifetime, a gift over on non-fulfilment of the condition does not normally take effect, even though the prior donee dies before the testator causing the prior gift to lapse[4].

1 An indication to the contrary was found in *Re Tredwell, Jeffray v Tredwell* [1891] 2 Ch 640, CA; *Chia Khwee Eng v Chia Poh Choon* [1923] AC 424, PC (explained in *Stewart v Murdoch* [1969] NI 78, on the basis of a gift of more than a life interest in the first instance).

2 *Jones v Westcomb* (1711) Prec Ch 316; *Re Fox's Estate, Dawes v Druitt* [1937] 4 All ER 664 at 666, CA. See also *Prestwidge v Groombridge* (1833) 6 Sim 171; *Lenox v Lenox* (1839) 10 Sim 400

at 409; *Wing v Angrave* (1860) 8 HL Cas 183 at 200; *Pride v Fooks* (1858) 3 De G & J 252 at 267; *Re Chappell's Trusts* (1862) 10 WR 573; *Re Tredwell, Jeffray v Tredwell* [1891] 2 Ch 640 at 656, CA, per Bowen LJ; *Re Bowen, Treasury Solicitor v Bowen* [1949] Ch 67, [1948] 2 All ER 979; *Re Riggall, Wildash v Riggall* [1949] WN 491; *Re Koeppler's Will Trusts, Barclays Bank Trust Co Ltd v Slack* [1984] Ch 243 at 263 et seq, [1984] 2 All ER 111 at 126 et seq per Peter Gibson J (revsd on other grounds [1986] Ch 423, [1985] 2 All ER 869, CA). The first-known case on this point is that of *Curius and Coponius* (BC 68) (Cicero, Oratio pro Cæcina, c 18), cited in *Wing v Angrave* (1860) 8 HL Cas 183 at 200 per Lord Campbell LC and *Hall v Warren* (1861) 9 HL Cas 420 at 429–430 (affg *Warren v Rudall, Hall v Warren* (1858) 4 K & J 603 at 610, where the case of *Curius and Coponius* is fully quoted). As to the destination of accumulation of income prior to the vesting see *Re Woolf, Public Trustee v Lazarus* [1920] 1 Ch 184; *Re Ussher, Foster v Ussher* [1922] 2 Ch 321.

3   *Re Bailey, Barrett v Hyder* [1951] Ch 407 at 420, [1951] 1 All ER 391 at 397, CA (approving dicta of Romer LJ in *Re Fox's Estate, Dawes v Druitt* [1937] 4 All ER 664 at 669); *Re Robertson, Marsden v Marsden* (1963) 107 Sol Jo 318; *Re Koeppler's Will Trusts, Barclays Bank Trust Co Ltd v Slack* [1984] Ch 243 at 265, [1984] 2 All ER 111 at 128 per Peter Gibson J (revsd on other grounds [1986] Ch 423, [1985] 2 All ER 869, CA) (the principle is not applicable where it would involve contradicting the express terms of the condition precedent for the gift over); *Re Sinclair, Lloyds Bank plc v Imperial Cancer Research Fund* [1985] Ch 446 at 455, [1985] 1 All ER 1066 at 1072, CA; *Re Hunter's Executors, Petitioners* 1992 SLT 1141; *Re Jones, Jones v Midland Bank Trust Co Ltd* [1998] 1 FLR 246, CA. In none of these cases was the principle held applicable.

4   *Calthorpe v Gough* (1789) 3 Bro CC 395n; *Doo v Brabant* (1792) 3 Bro CC 393; *Humberstone v Stanton* (1813) 1 Ves & B 385; *Cox v Parker* (1856) 22 Beav 168; *Re Graham, Graham v Graham* [1929] 2 Ch 127 (distinguished in *Re Bowen, Treasury Solicitor v Bowen* [1949] Ch 67 at 72, [1948] 2 All ER 979 at 982); *Re Bailey, Barrett v Hyder* [1951] Ch 407, [1951] 1 All ER 391, CA. In *Williams v Chitty, Chitty v Chitty* (1797) 3 Ves 545, the contrary contention was abandoned. The cases were explained in *Kellett v Kellett* (1871) IR 5 Eq 298 at 305. The same rule applies in a case where the prior donees are a class: *Brookman v Smith* (1872) LR 7 Exch 271, Ex Ch (approving *Tarbuck v Tarbuck* (1835) 4 LJ Ch 129). Cf, however, *Re May, Cockerton v Jones* [1944] Ch 1, [1943] 2 All ER 604 (where there was a gift over if no child attained 21; one child attained that age, but died between the date of the will and the date of a codicil which confirmed it; and it was held that the gift over took effect). It appears that the rule applies to a gift by way of substitution (see PARA 321), where the events giving rise to the substitutional gift do not happen: see *Hannam v Sims* (1858) 2 De G & J 151 at 154 per Turner LJ. The fact that the prior gift fails by reason of some rule of law may not, however, prevent the gift over from taking effect: *Hall v Warren* (1861) 9 HL Cas 420 (disapproving *A-G v Hodgson* (1846) 15 Sim 146 and *Philpott v St George's Hospital* (1855) 21 Beav 134 (which was revsd on another point (1857) 6 HL Cas 338)). As to where the event giving rise to the gift over happens, and the prior donee dies during the testator's lifetime see PARA 411.

446.   Examples of cases where testator must have intended gift over to take effect. If there is a conditional limitation over of an estate defeating a prior absolute interest, and the prior gift by any means whatever is taken out of the case, the subsequent limitation may take effect[1]. Similarly, where there is a prior particular interest given, with remainder to a person unborn and on the death of the donee in remainder, or on his death under age a gift over, then, even if the unborn person never came into existence[2] and so could not fulfil the condition of dying or dying under age, it is inferred that the gift over is to take effect[3] whenever it can do so in immediate succession to the prior limitation in the manner of a remainder[4]. Where a gift is made with an obligation imposed on the donee to do some act, with a gift over in default of performance, it is inferred that the gift over is also to take effect if the donee dies in the testator's lifetime without having performed the condition[5] or fails to come into existence[6].

Where the testator makes a gift to a woman for her life so long as she remains unmarried, and then directs that, in the event of her marrying, the property is to go over to another, without more, then the gift over takes effect on the determination of her estate, that is on her marriage, if she marries, and on her death, if she does not[7]. Conversely, where the first gift is during widowhood and the gift over is on death, the court infers that the gift over is to take effect also on remarriage[8].

Similarly, where, after a gift to one person for his life or until some event such as bankruptcy, there is a gift over on some of such events, but the other events are ignored by the testator, the court infers that the gift over is also to take effect on death or on the other events, where the inference is consistent with the whole will[9].

1 *Avelyn v Ward* (1750) 1 Ves Sen 420; *Re Sheppard's Trusts* (1855) 1 K & J 269 at 276; *Barnes v Jennings* (1866) LR 2 Eq 448 at 451; *Edgeworth v Edgeworth* (1869) LR 4 HL 35 at 40. See also *Re Green's Estate* (1860) 1 Drew & Sm 68; *Re Smith's Trusts* (1865) LR 1 Eq 79 at 83.

2 See *Foster v Cook* (1791) 3 Bro CC 347 (child still-born; gift over took effect).

3 *Jones v Westcomb* (1711) Prec Ch 316; *Re Fox's Estate, Dawes v Druitt* [1937] 4 All ER 664, CA (where the rule in *Jones v Westcomb* is stated); *Re Riggall, Wildash v Riggall* [1949] WN 491. See also *Andrews d Jones v Fulham* (1738) 2 Stra 1092; *Gulliver v Wickett* (1745) 1 Wils 105 (contrary to the opinion of the Court of Common Pleas on the same will in *Roe d Fulham v Wickett* (1741) Willes 303; as to these cases see *Frogmorton d Bramstone v Holyday* (1765) 3 Burr 1618 at 1624 per Lord Mansfield CJ; and note 4); *Fonnereau v Fonnereau* (1745) 3 Atk 315; *Statham v Bell* (1774) 1 Cowp 40; *Underwood v Wing* (1855) 4 De GM & G 633 at 662. The rule applies also where the prior donees are a class: *Meadows v Parry* (1812) 1 Ves & B 124; *Murray v Jones, Fawcett v Jones* (1813) 2 Ves & B 313; *Mackinnon v Peach* (1833) 2 My & K 202; *Wilson v Mount* (1840) 2 Beav 397; *Evers v Challis* (1859) 7 HL Cas 531; *Lanphier v Buck* (1865) 2 Drew & Sm 484; *Beardsley v Beynon* (1865) 13 WR 831.

4 In *Evers v Challis* (1859) 7 HL Cas 531 at 549, 555, *Gulliver v Wickett* (1745) 1 Wils 105 is explained as based on the doctrines relating to contingent remainders; and the gift in *Evers v Challis* was held valid and able to take effect as a contingent remainder. The doctrine does not apply to a gift over by way of executory devise the contingencies in which cannot be split so as accurately to correspond with the events which have happened: *Hancock v Watson* [1902] AC 14, HL. However, it applies to limitations of personal estate which may take effect immediately on the termination of prior limitations in the manner of a remainder: *Jones v Westcomb* (1711) Prec Ch 316.

5 *Avelyn v Ward* (1750) 1 Ves Sen 420; *Doe d Wells v Scott* (1814) 3 M & S 300; *Underwood v Wing* (1855) 4 De GM & G 633 at 662–663.

6 *Scatterwood v Edge* (1699) 1 Salk 229.

7 *Luxford v Cheeke* (1683) 3 Lev 125; *Jordan v Holkham* (1753) Amb 209; *Gordon v Adolphus* (1769) 3 Bro Parl Cas 306; *Meeds v Wood* (1854) 19 Beav 215; *Browne v Hammond* (1858) John 210; *Brown v Jarvis* (1860) 2 De GF & J 168; *Walpole v Laslett* (1862) 1 New Rep 180; *Eaton v Hewitt* (1862) 2 Drew & Sm 184; *Wardroper v Cutfield* (1864) 10 Jur NS 194; *Underhill v Roden* (1876) 2 ChD 494 at 497; *Re Mason, Mason v Mason* [1910] 1 Ch 695, CA. See also *Re Cane, Ruff v Sivers* (1890) 63 LT 746; *O'Donoghue v O'Donoghue* [1906] 1 IR 482 (settlement); *Re Griffiths* [1917] P 59. In *Pile v Salter* (1832) 5 Sim 411, this doctrine was held not to extend to a gift over to the woman with other persons on her remarriage, so as to make it take effect on her death; but this case was said to be wrongly decided in *Underhill v Roden* above, and was not followed in *Wardroper v Cutfield* (1864) 10 Jur NS 194 and *Scarborough v Scarborough* (1888) 58 LT 851. In *Stewart v Murdoch* [1969] NI 78, it was pointed out that this line of authorities depends on the preceding interest being truly one for life, and not in the first instance absolute, when the gift over will take effect only on the happening of the specified contingency. Cf PARA 375.

8 *Bainbridge v Cream* (1852) 16 Beav 25; *Stanford v Stanford* (1886) 34 ChD 362; *Re Dear, Helby v Dear* (1889) 58 LJ Ch 659; *Stanier v Hodgkinson* (1903) 73 LJ Ch 179 at 183n; *Re Warner, Watts v Silvey* [1918] 1 Ch 368. However, the will may make it clear that the gift over is not to take effect before death: *Re Tredwell, Jeffray v Tredwell* [1891] 2 Ch 640, CA. See also *Re Carleton* (1909) 28 NZLR 1066. As to the ascertainment of a class on such events cf PARA 306. The contrary has been decided as to a settlement inter vivos: see *Re Wyatt, Gowan v Wyatt* (1889) 60 LT 920. Where in relation to a gift the express mention of only one of two relevant events is due to carelessness, a corresponding gift in the other event may be implied to give effect to the testator's intention: *Re Akeroyd's Settlement, Roberts v Akeroyd* [1893] 3 Ch 363, CA; *Re Main, Official Solicitor v Main* [1947] 1 All ER 255.

9 *Etches v Etches* (1856) 3 Drew 441 (gift until bankruptcy; gift over on death implied); *Re Seaton, Ellis v Seaton* [1913] 2 Ch 614 (gift until she should receive a legacy). Cf *Re Akeroyd's Settlement, Roberts v Akeroyd* [1893] 3 Ch 363, CA (gift over on bankruptcy implied), distinguishing *Re*

Tredwell, Jeffray v Tredwell [1891] 2 Ch 640, CA. There is a distinction between a limitation for a definite period with a gift over on some of the events defining that period, when the rules stated in the text may apply, and a limitation followed by an executory gift over on any collateral contingency, which is to determine the first estate sooner than it would otherwise be determined: see *Sheffield v Lord Orrery* (1745) 3 Atk 282 at 285; *Walpole v Laslett* (1862) 1 New Rep 180.

447. Inferences from gifts over or other clauses. The presence of a gift over as an indication of intention may be more or less valuable according to the context and the circumstances[1]. Ambiguous words in an original gift may be explained by unambiguous words in a gift over[2] or other subsequent clause[3]; but where the words in an original gift are plain and unambiguous taken by themselves, a gift over confined to one particular event does not compel the court to place a forced construction on the original gift[4].

A gift to a donee at a specified age, followed by a gift over on his death before that age without leaving issue, confers a vested interest subject to an executory gift over, for the gift over is not to take effect on death under the specified age if issue is left[5].

1 *Boughton v James* (1844) 1 Coll 26 at 44 per Knight Bruce V-C.
2 *Ralph v Carrick* (1879) 11 ChD 873 at 884, CA. See also *Judd v Judd* (1830) 3 Sim 525 (reconsidered in *Hunter v Judd* (1833) 4 Sim 455); *Re Swain, Brett v Ward* [1918] 1 Ch 399 (settled on appeal [1918] 1 Ch 574, CA); *Re Rawson, Rigby v Rawson* (1920) 124 LT 498.
3 Eg an advancement clause or hotchpot clause, as in *Vivian v Mills* (1839) 1 Beav 315; *Harrison v Grimwood* (1849), as reported in 12 Beav 192 at 199; *Walker v Simpson* (1855) 1 K & J 713 at 720. See also *Re Jacob's Will* (1861) 7 Jur NS 302; *Re Turney, Turney v Turney* [1899] 2 Ch 739 at 746, 748 (where there was provision for interest on the 'respective portions' of children until they attained 25, and a gift over of the 'share' of a child not attaining 25 to a stranger).
4 *Re Rawlinson, Hill v Withall* [1909] 2 Ch 36 at 39. See also *Walker v Mower* (1852) 16 Beav 365.
5 *Bland v Williams* (1834) 3 My & K 411 at 417 per Leach MR. As to failure to attain a specified age generally see PARA 436.

448. Exclusion of persons entitled on intestacy. Where a will shows an intention that persons claiming under the testator as on intestacy are not to take in any event but the testator has expressly provided for other persons to take in certain contingencies, the restriction as to such contingencies may sometimes be disregarded and the gift in the will may take effect in all events[1]. However, except in such cases, the title of the persons claiming on a failure of the gift or for want of disposition by the testator is not excluded merely by reason that he has not contemplated all contingencies; such persons take on every event for which the testator has not provided[2].

1 See *Bradford v Foley* (1779) 1 Doug KB 63; *Harman v Dickenson* (1781) 1 Bro CC 91; *Horton v Whittaker* (1786) 1 Term Rep 346; and the cases cited in PARA 257 note 7.
2 *Lord Amherst v Lytton* (1729) 5 Bro Parl Cas 254; *Sheffield v Lord Orrery* (1745) 3 Atk 282 at 285–286; *Doe d Vessey v Wilkinson* (1788) 2 Term Rep 209 at 218; *Shuldham v Smith* (1818) 6 Dow 22, HL; *Dicken v Clarke* (1837) 2 Y & C Ex 572.

(v) Particular Conditions

A. GIFTS OVER IN THE EVENT OF DEATH

449. General rule that death is not a contingency. The event of death being inevitable, a gift to one person in the event of the death of another is only treated as a gift in remainder where the first taker takes for life only. A gift over of property given to a person absolutely in the event of his death is always construed as a gift over in the event of his death before the period of distribution[1] or vesting unless some other period is indicated by the context[2].

The rule is based on the ground that, as death is inevitable, it cannot be deemed a contingency; the testator could not have intended merely to provide for the possibility of the donee dying. It is also based on the presumption in favour of vesting[3].

If, therefore, the gift is immediate and there is a gift over in the event of the donee's death, without any suggestion of succession, prima facie the gift over takes effect only where the donee dies in the testator's lifetime, as an alternative gift[4], and, if the gift is postponed to a life interest, prima facie the gift over takes effect only on death before the life tenant, as an alternative gift[5]. Alternatively, if the context so requires, the gift over may be construed as referring to death before vesting[6].

In some cases, however, the context of the will shows that the first donee takes not an absolute interest but a life interest only, or that the gift in case of death is to take effect not as a contingent gift but by way of succession in any event; the second donee then takes on the death of the first donee at any time[7]. A gift to one person in the event of the death of another is treated as a gift in remainder or succession only where the interest of the first taker is a mere life interest[8]. Where an indefinite gift to one person is followed by a gift over 'at' or 'after' his death, then prima facie the gift over takes effect, if at all, by way of succession not contingency[9]. In such a case it depends on the construction of the will as a whole whether the prior gift is to be treated as absolute and the gift over as void, or whether the prior gift is reduced to a life interest[10].

Death is regarded as a contingent event only from necessity and where the words import no other contingency[11].

1   As to the meaning of 'period of distribution' see PARA 306 note 1.
2   *Penny v Railways Comr* [1900] AC 628 at 634, PC. See also *Hodgson v Smithson* (1856) 8 De GM & G 604; *O'Mahoney v Burdett* (1874) LR 7 HL 388 at 395 per Lord Cairns LC.
3   *Home v Pillans* (1833) 2 My & K 15 at 20–21. As to the presumption as to vesting see PARAS 412–414.
4   *Lord Bindon v Earl of Suffolk* (1707) 1 P Wms 96 at 97; *Hinckley v Simmons* (1798) 4 Ves 160; *King v Taylor* (1801) 5 Ves 806; *Turner v Moor* (1801) 6 Ves 557; *Cambridge v Rous* (1802) 8 Ves 12 at 21; *Webster v Hale* (1803) 8 Ves 410; *Ommaney v Bevan* (1811) 18 Ves 291; *Slade v Milner* (1819) 4 Madd 144; *Crigan v Baines* (1834) 7 Sim 40; *Clarke v Lubbock* (1842) 1 Y & C Ch Cas 492; *Howard v Howard* (1856) 21 Beav 550; *Taylor v Stainton* (1856) 2 Jur NS 634; *Schenk v Agnew* (1858) 4 K & J 405; *Re Neary's Estate* (1881) 7 LR Ir 311; *Elliott v Smith* (1882) 22 ChD 236; *Re Valdez's Trusts* (1888) 40 ChD 159 at 162; *Re Reeves, Edwards v Reeves-Hughes* (1907) 51 Sol Jo 325; *Re Fisher, Robinson v Eardley* [1915] 1 Ch 302 (following *Howard v Howard* (1856) 21 Beav 550). As to alternative gifts see PARA 320 et seq.
5   *Hervey v M'Laughlin* (1815) 1 Price 264; *Edwards v Edwards* (1852) 15 Beav 357 at 363–364 (the third rule there stated is not affected on this point by *O'Mahoney v Burdett* (1874) LR 7 HL 388: see PARA 450 note 6); *Green v Barrow* (1853) 10 Hare 459 at 461; *Bolitho v Hillyar* (1865) 11 Jur NS 556. See also *Galland v Leonard* (1818) 1 Swan 161; *Le Jeune v Le Jeune* (1837) 2 Keen 701.
6   *Penny v Railways Comr* [1900] AC 628, PC; *Re Kerr's Estate* [1913] 1 IR 214.
7   *Billings v Sandom* (1784) 1 Bro CC 393; *Nowland v Nelligan* (1785) 1 Bro CC 489; *Lord Douglas v Chalmer* (1795) 2 Ves 501; *Smart v Clark* (1827) 3 Russ 365; *Tilson v Jones, Tilson v Thornton* (1830) 1 Russ & M 553; *Jones v Morris* (1922) 91 LJ Ch 495. Cf *Wilkins v Jodrell* (1879) 13 ChD 564 at 569; *Watson v Watson* (1881) 7 PD 10. As to the weight to be given to various circumstances see *Taylor v Stainton* (1856) 2 Jur NS 634.
8   *Penny v Railways Comr* [1900] AC 628 at 634, PC.
9   *Re Adam's Trusts* (1865) 13 LT 347.
10 *Lloyd v Tweedy* [1898] 1 IR 5 at 17. See also *Lady Monck's Will, Monck v Croker* [1900] 1 IR 56 at 66, Ir CA; and PARAS 381–382. If the later gift contains no reference to death but is introduced merely by words such as 'thereafter', the prior gift is not reduced: *Re Gouk, Allen v Allen* [1957] 1 All ER 469, [1957] 1 WLR 493.
11 *Gawler v Cadby* (1821) Jac 346 at 348; *Woodroofe v Woodroofe* [1894] 1 IR 299 at 302. As to gifts on death coupled with a contingency see PARA 450.

450. Gift over on death with contingency. Where a gift over is on death coupled with some contingency, such as on the death of the donee without leaving issue or without leaving issue living at the time of his death, then prima facie the gift over takes effect on the donee's death at any time[1], and not merely on his death before the date of distribution[2], if the rest of the contingency is fulfilled at his death[3]. It is immaterial that the donees under the gift over are the children of the first taker[4], and the rule is the same for real and personal estate[5] and whether there is a previous life interest[6] or not[7].

However, in the context of the will, the contingency may be confined to a death during the lifetime of a life tenant[8] or during the testator's lifetime[9] or before distribution or some other event[10]. Thus where on a particular event the fund is directed to be divided or the donee's receipt is directed to be a good discharge, the death without issue is confined to the period prior to division or payment, as otherwise the direction could not be carried out[11].

It may sometimes appear that the gift over is not an executory limitation defeating the prior gift at any time but a substitutional gift, and the death with a contingency is confined to the period within which substitution takes place[12]; or there may be alternative gifts over, whether the death takes place with or without a failure of issue or other contingent event[13].

1   As to contingencies happening in the testator's lifetime see PARA 411.
2   As to the meaning of 'date of distribution' see PARA 306 note 1.
3   *Ingram v Soutten* (1874) LR 7 HL 408 (dying without issue living at her death); *O'Mahoney v Burdett* (1874) LR 7 HL 388 (dying unmarried or without children); *Woodroofe v Woodroofe* [1894] 1 IR 299 at 302 (dying without issue surviving him); *Re Richardson's Trusts* [1896] 1 IR 295, Ir CA (dying leaving children fatherless); *Re Schnadhorst, Sandkuhl v Schnadhorst* [1902] 2 Ch 234, CA (dying leaving issue); *Duffill v Duffill* [1903] AC 491, PC (dying before his brother); *Re Williams' Will Trusts, Rees v Williams* [1949] 2 All ER 11 (dying without issue surviving her); *Re McGrane, McGrane v McGrane* (1964) 98 ILTR 95 (dying before his brother). See also *Smith v Stewart* (1851) 4 De G & Sm 253, 15 Jur 834; *Smith v Spencer* (1856) 6 De GM & G 631 (where the original donee took at 21 but the gift over was not restricted to a death under that age); *Drake v Collins* (1869) 20 LT 970; *Re Parry and Daggs* (1885) 31 ChD 130, CA.
4   *Home v Pillans* (1833) 2 My & K 15 at 22; *Re Schnadhorst, Sandkuhl v Schnadhorst* [1901] 2 Ch 338 at 343 (affd [1902] 2 Ch 234, CA).
5   *Slaney v Slaney* (1864) 33 Beav 631.
6   The fourth rule in *Edwards v Edwards* (1852) 15 Beav 357 at 364 et seq, enunciated by Romilly MR, to the effect that, where such a gift is postponed, prima facie the gift over refers to a death without issue before the period of distribution, was disapproved in *O'Mahoney v Burdett* (1874) LR 7 HL 388, and was not applied in *Re Schnadhorst, Sandkuhl v Schnadhorst* [1902] 2 Ch 234, CA, or *Re Williams' Will Trusts, Rees v Williams* [1949] 2 All ER 11. The following cases, where the fourth rule in *Edwards v Edwards* above was followed, may perhaps be supported on the contexts of the wills in question: *Barker v Cocks* (1843) 6 Beav 82; *Beckton v Barton* (1859) 27 Beav 99; *Slaney v Slaney* (1864) 33 Beav 631; *Wood v Wood* (1866) 35 Beav 587.
7   *Child v Giblett* (1834) 3 My & K 71; *Smith v Stewart* (1851) 4 De G & Sm 253; *Edwards v Edwards* (1852) 15 Beav 357 at 363; *Cotton v Cotton* (1854) 23 LJ Ch 489; *Randfield v Randfield* (1860) 8 HL Cas 225; *Bowers v Bowers* (1870) 5 Ch App 244.
8   *Besant v Cox* (1877) 6 ChD 604 (gift over to survivors of a class leaving issue) (following *Olivant v Wright* (1875) 1 ChD 346, CA, and distinguishing *O'Mahoney v Burdett* (1874) LR 7 HL 388); *McCormick v Simpson* [1907] AC 494, PC; *Re Mitchell, Mitchell v Mitchell* (1913) 108 LT 180; *Re Roberts, Roberts v Morgan* [1916] 2 Ch 42; *Christian v Taylor* [1926] AC 773, PC. However, *Besant v Cox* above and *Re Smaling, Johnson v Smaling* (1877) 26 WR 231 are of doubtful authority, having regard to the rule previously laid down in *O'Mahoney v Burdett* above: see *Woodroofe v Woodroofe* [1894] 1 IR 299 at 302.
9   *Re Luddy, Peard v Morton* (1883) 25 ChD 394.
10   *Brotherton v Bury* (1853) 18 Beav 65 (before attaining 21); *Clark v Henry* (1871) 6 Ch App 588; *Hordern v Hordern* [1909] AC 210 at 216, PC.
11   *Galland v Leonard* (1818) 1 Swan 161; *Barker v Cocks* (1843) 6 Beav 82; *Wheable v Withers* (1849) 16 Sim 505; *Johnston v Antrobus* (1856) 21 Beav 556; *Re Anstice* (1856) 23 Beav 135;

O'Mahoney v Burdett (1874) LR 7 HL 388 at 403, 406; *Lewin v Killey* (1888) 13 App Cas 783, PC; *Re Mackinlay, Scrimgeour v Mackinlay* (1911) 56 Sol Jo 142; *Re Mitchell, Mitchell v Mitchell* (1913) 108 LT 180.

12 *Re Hayward, Creery v Lingwood* (1882) 19 ChD 470. As to substitutional gifts see PARA 321.

13 *Clayton v Lowe* (1822) 5 B & Ald 636 (gifts over both on death without children and on death leaving children); *Gee v Manchester Corpn* (1852) 17 QB 737 at 745. The ratio decidendi of these cases, that the addition of all the contingencies amounted to certainty, was dissented from in *Gosling v Townshend* (1853) 17 Beav 245, 2 WR 23; *Cooper v Cooper* (1855) 1 K & J 658 at 662; *Bowers v Bowers* (1870) 5 Ch App 244 at 248. However, it appears to have been approved in *O'Mahoney v Burdett* (1874) LR 7 HL 388 at 397 per Lord Cairns LC (explaining *Da Costa v Keir* (1827) 3 Russ 360 as decided on this and other grounds). See also *Galland v Leonard* (1818) 1 Swan 161; *Woodburne v Woodburne* (1853) 23 LJ Ch 336; *Re Brailsford, Holmes v Crompton and Evans' Union Bank* [1916] 2 Ch 536 (following *Gee v Manchester Corpn* (1852) 17 QB 737); *Re Colles' Estate* [1918] 1 IR 1 (settlement).

451. Gift over on death before actual receipts. As a rule, a gift over may be made on the donee dying before he actually receives his legacy or on his becoming disentitled to receive it before actual payment. If expressed with sufficient certainty, such a gift is valid[1], as also is any gift where the gift over is of the part of the property which has not been received[2]. A gift over on death during the continuance of the trusts of the will may be valid, at least in the case of a specific gift[3].

Such a gift over in the case of a residuary gift, and applying to the whole fund, referring to the time when the fund is 'receivable' or 'de jure receivable' may be void for uncertainty[4]. There is no objection to postponing the vesting of a residuary gift until actual receipt[5], and there appears to be no sufficient reason for a different rule in postponing the divesting where the intention is clearly shown[6].

The court inclines to construe such gifts over so that the period during which the operation of the gift over is to extend may not continue beyond the time at which the legacy is by law receivable[7], that is, in general, where the gift is not otherwise postponed, at a year from the testator's death[8], and in other cases at the death of the life tenant or other period of distribution[9]. This construction cannot be adopted, however, where the language of the will is precise and refers to actual receipt[10].

1 *Johnson v Crook* (1879) 12 ChD 639 (approved in *Re Chaston, Chaston v Seago* (1881) 18 ChD 218); *Re Wilkins, Spencer v Duckworth* (1881) 18 ChD 634; *Re Goulder, Goulder v Goulder* [1905] 2 Ch 100 (not following *Martin v Martin* (1866) LR 2 Eq 404; dicta in *Minors v Battison* (1876) 1 App Cas 428 at 437, 443, 446, HL; and *Bubb v Padwick* (1880) 13 ChD 517). These cases were considered in *Re Petrie, Lloyds Bank Ltd v Royal National Institute for the Blind* [1962] Ch 355 at 365–366, [1961] 3 All ER 1067 at 1071, CA. See also *Faulkner v Hollingsworth* (1784), cited in 8 Ves at 558 (where there was a gift over if the legatee died before certain real estate was sold and the money was received; explained as involving an inquiry on an ascertainable matter in *Re Chaston, Chaston v Seago* (1881) 18 ChD 218).

2 *Re Chaston, Chaston v Seago* (1881) 18 ChD 218; *Re Goulder, Goulder v Goulder* [1905] 2 Ch 100 (explained in *Re Petrie, Lloyds Bank Ltd v Royal National Institute for the Blind* [1962] Ch 355, [1961] 3 All ER 1067, CA).

3 *Re Teale, Teale v Teale* (1885) 53 LT 936.

4 *Hutcheon v Mannington* (1791) 1 Ves 366 (as explained by Jessel MR in *Johnson v Crook* (1879) 12 ChD 639) (where on the construction adopted the gift over was on death before the gift was receivable); *Martin v Martin* (1866) LR 2 Eq 404; *Minors v Battison* (1876) 1 App Cas 428, HL; *Bubb v Padwick* (1880) 13 ChD 517; *Roberts v Youle* (1880) 49 LJ Ch 744 at 745; *Re Hudson* [1912] VLR 140.

5 *Gaskell v Harman* (1801) 6 Ves 159; on appeal (1805) 11 Ves 489 at 497 per Lord Eldon LC (explaining *Hutcheon v Mannington* (1791) 1 Ves 366).

6 Notwithstanding the inconvenience, effect may be given to such an intention: see PARA 243; cf *Ditmas v Robertson* (1840) 4 Jur 957 (where arrival in England was held to be certain).

7 *Re Sampson, Sampson v Sampson* [1896] 1 Ch 630 at 635–636. See also *Whiting v Force* (1840) 2 Beav 571 (where 'receiving' was construed with its correlative 'pay' in the original gift); *Rammell v Gillow* (1845) 15 LJ Ch 35 at 39; and the cases in notes 8–9. In particular cases an inquiry may

be directed as to when the property could have been got in (*Law v Thompson* (1827) 4 Russ 92; *Re Arrowsmith's Trust* (1860) 2 De GF & J 474, 29 LJ Ch 774), although in *Hutcheon v Mannington* (1791) 1 Ves 366 at 367, Lord Thurlow considered such an inquiry impracticable and the gift over void for uncertainty.

8   *Re Arrowsmith's Trust* (1860) 2 De GF & J 474, 29 LJ Ch 774; *Re Collison, Collison v Barber* (1879) 12 ChD 834; *Re Wilkins, Spencer v Duckworth* (1881) 18 ChD 634 (residue; gift over before final division of testator's estate); *Barnes v Whittaker* (1893) 14 NSW Eq 148; *Hunt v Hunt* (1902) 2 SRNSW Eq 72; *Re Petrie, Lloyds Bank Ltd v Royal National Institute for the Blind* [1962] Ch 355, [1961] 3 All ER 1067, CA. See also *Re Jones, Midland Bank Executor and Trustee Co Ltd v League of Welldoers* [1950] 2 All ER 239 (explained in *Re Petrie, Lloyds Bank Ltd v Royal National Institute for the Blind* above); and PERPETUITIES AND ACCUMULATIONS vol 80 (2013) PARAS 27, 30.

9   *Re Dodgson's Trusts* (1853) 1 Drew 440; *Minors v Battison* (1876) 1 App Cas 428, HL; *Re Chaston, Chaston v Seago* (1881) 18 ChD 218; *Wilks v Bannister* (1885) 30 ChD 512. Cf *Re Byrne's Will Trusts, Dowling v Lawler* [1967] IR 304 (death before 'residue of my estate has been ascertained and disposed of'; no longer applicable after change of character from executrix to trustee).

10   *Johnson v Crook* (1879) 12 ChD 639; *Re Goulder, Goulder v Goulder* [1905] 2 Ch 100; *Re Petrie, Lloyds Bank Ltd v Royal National Institute for the Blind* [1962] Ch 355, [1961] 3 All ER 1067, CA.

452. Gift over on death before legacy is due. A gift over on the death of a donee before the gift becomes due or payable is valid and may take effect on the death of the donee in the testator's lifetime[1]. The time at which the gift becomes due or payable for the purposes of the gift over depends on the date of distribution contemplated by the will[2], but is susceptible of a variety of interpretations according to the context[3]. In a gift to children, where the time for payment is after a life interest on their attaining a certain age or other qualification, for example in the case of sons at the age of 21 and in the case of daughters at 21 or marriage, the gift is not read as making the provision for a child contingent on surviving both or either of its parents unless the intention is clearly so expressed[4]. In such a case a gift over on death before the gift becomes payable is confined to a death before attaining the age of 21 or other qualification, 'payable' being construed to mean 'vested'; and accordingly the share of a child who attains 21 and dies in the lifetime of his parent is not divested[5].

1   *Willing v Baine* (1731) 3 P Wms 113; *Humberstone v Stanton* (1813) 1 Ves & B 385; *Walker v Main* (1819) 1 Jac & W 1; *Humphreys v Howes* (1830) 1 Russ & M 639. See also *Miller v Warren* (1690) 2 Vern 207; *Darrel v Molesworth* (1700) 2 Vern 378 (accepted as an authority on this point in *Ive v King* (1852) 16 Beav 46 at 54). See, however, the notes to *Miller v Warren* and *Darrel v Molesworth* in the reports cited.

2   Eg the death of the life tenant, where the legacy is given after a life interest: *Crowder v Stone* (1829) 3 Russ 217 at 222; *Creswick v Gaskell* (1853) 16 Beav 577. In the case of immediate legacies, the death of the testator was considered to be denoted in *Collins v Macpherson* (1827) 2 Sim 87; *Cort v Winder* (1844) 1 Coll 320; *Whitman v Aitken* (1866) LR 2 Eq 414 at 417. The expiration of a year from the testator's death may be adopted in particular cases where the context does not otherwise provide: cf the cases cited in PARA 451 note 8.

3   *Cort v Winder* (1844) 1 Coll 320 at 322 per Knight Bruce V-C.

4   As to presumptions in favour of children see PARA 260.

5   *Emperor v Rolfe* (1748–9) 1 Ves Sen 208; *Cholmondeley v Meyrick* (1758) 1 Eden 77; *Earl of Salisbury v Lambe* (1759) 1 Eden 465; *Willis v Willis* (1796) 3 Ves 51; *Hope v Lord Clifden* (1801) 6 Ves 499; *Schenck v Legh* (1803) 9 Ves 300; *Powis v Burdett* (1804) 9 Ves 428 (in spite of expressions referring to 'leaving' children); *Hallifax v Wilson* (1809) 16 Ves 168; *Walker v Main* (1819) 1 Jac & W 1 (death before legacy 'due and payable'); *Hayward v James* (1860) 28 Beav 523; *Haydon v Rose* (1870) LR 10 Eq 224; *Partridge v Baylis* (1881) 17 ChD 835; *Wakefield v Maffet* (1885) 10 App Cas 422 at 433, 435, HL. Cf, however, *Re Williams* (1849) 12 Beav 317. The doctrine of these cases should not be extended: *Rammell v Gillow* (1845) 15 LJ Ch 35 at 38 per Wigram V-C (following *Whatford v Moore* (1837) 3 My & Cr 270 at 289).

453. Gift over on death before becoming entitled. In a gift over on the death of the donee before becoming entitled, 'entitled' has no definite legal meaning and may mean either entitled in interest[1] or entitled in possession[2], according to the context. A gift over on death before being 'entitled in possession' is, in a context requiring it, capable of being construed as 'entitled in interest'[3].

A gift over on the donee's death before attaining a vested interest prima facie refers to death before vesting in the technical sense[4]. If, however, the context so requires, it may refer to death before taking possession[5] or before having the right to possession[6].

1 *Re Crosland, Craig v Midgley* (1886) 54 LT 238; *Re MacAndrew's Will Trusts, Stephens v Barclays Bank Ltd* [1964] Ch 704, [1963] 2 All ER 919. See also PARA 197 note 4.
2 *Re Maunder, Maunder v Maunder* [1902] 2 Ch 875 (affd [1903] 1 Ch 451, CA), following *Turner v Gosset* (1865) 34 Beav 593 at 594. See also *Jopp v Wood* (1865) 2 De GJ & Sm 323 (settlement; prior donee unborn and entitled at birth); *Re Noyce, Brown v Rigg* (1885) 31 ChD 75; *Re Whiter, Windsor v Jones* (1911) 105 LT 749.
3 *Re Yates' Trusts* (1851) 16 Jur 78.
4 *Parkin v Hodgkinson* (1846) 15 Sim 293; *Bull v Jones* (1862) 31 LJ Ch 858 at 861; *Richardson v Power* (1865) 19 CBNS 780 at 802, Ex Ch (remainder in fee simple). See also *Re Arnold's Estate* (1863) 33 Beav 163 at 173 (on the same will). The gift over took effect on a class of prior donees failing to come into existence in *Beardsley v Beynon* (1865) 12 LT 698.
5 *King v Cullen* (1848) 2 De G & Sm 252 at 254 (where the will showed that a death after vesting, in the technical sense, was within the testator's meaning); *Re Morris* (1857) 26 LJ Ch 688; *Young v Robertson* (1862) 4 Macq 314, HL (gift over to survivors).
6 *Sillick v Booth* (1841) 1 Y & C Ch Cas 117 at 121, 124.

B.   LIMITATIONS ON FAILURE OF ISSUE

454.   Statutory rule as to the effect of gifts where person dies without issue. In the case of wills made after 31 December 1837[1], the words 'die without issue', or 'die without leaving issue', or 'have no issue', or any other words which may import either a want or failure of issue of any person in his lifetime or at the time of his death, or an indefinite failure of his issue, are construed to mean a want or failure of issue in the lifetime or at the time of the death of that person, and not an indefinite failure of issue, unless a contrary intention appears by the will[2].

This rule has been applied to gifts on death 'without leaving male issue'[3] but not to like gifts in terms of 'heirs of the body' or 'heirs' even though coupled with words of procreation[4]. It has been doubted whether the rule applies to words such as 'in default of issue' or 'on failure of issue' of a named person not containing, in themselves or by inference from the context, any reference to the death of that person[5]; but the fact that the rule contemplates words which may import a failure of issue in the lifetime of the named person appears to be inconsistent with the doubt. The rule has been held not to apply where the words referring to dying without issue are combined with other words, such as 'dying under 21'[6], and it has been questioned whether it applies to any but an entire failure of issue[7].

1 See the Wills Act 1837 s 34. Restrictions were placed on the creation of executory interests to take effect on failure of issue by the Law of Property Act 1925 s 134: see REAL PROPERTY AND REGISTRATION vol 87 (2012) PARA 173.
2 Wills Act 1837 s 29. See *O'Neill v Montgomery* (1861) 12 I Ch R 163; *Re Mid-Kent Railway Act 1856, ex p Bate* (1863) 11 WR 417; *Dowling v Dowling* (1866) 1 Ch App 612 at 616; *Gwynne v Berry* (1875) IR 9 CL 494; *Re Chinnery's Estate* (1877) 1 LR Ir 296; *Re Davey, Prisk v Mitchell* [1915] 1 Ch 837, CA (where it was held on the facts that 'dying without leaving lawful issue' must be ascertained within a life in being at the testator's death).
3 *Re Edwards, Edwards v Edwards* [1894] 3 Ch 644 (following *Upton v Hardman* (1874) IR 9 Eq 157). Cf *Neville v Thacker* (1888) 23 LR Ir 344.
4 *Harris v Davis* (1844) 1 Coll 416 at 424 (in case of there being no heir); *Re Sallery* (1861) 11 I Ch R 236 ('without heirs or issue'); *Dawson v Small* (1874) 9 Ch App 651 ('without heirs male of his body lawfully begot'); *Re Brown and Campbell* (1898) 29 OR 402 ('without lawful heirs by him begotten'); *Re Ross* (1901) 1 SRNSW 1 ('without lawful heirs'); *Re Leach, Leach v Leach* [1912]

2 Ch 422 at 428 ('without leaving a male heir'); *Re Conboy's Estate* [1916] 1 IR 51 ('heir or issue'). Cf *Dodds v Dodds* (1860) 10 I Ch R 476 ('without lawful male heir').

5 Hawkins on Wills (1st Edn) 177, (3rd Edn) 213; *Shand v Robinson* (1898) 19 NSW Eq 85 at 88. However, for the contrary view see *Neville v Thacker* (1888) 23 LR Ir 344 at 357; *Green v Green* (1849) 3 De G & Sm 480 (where the contrary appears to have been assumed).

6 *Morris v Morris* (1853) 17 Beav 198 at 202.

7 *Re Thomas, Thomas v Thomas* [1921] 1 Ch 306 at 310.

455. Statutory rule as to death without issue varied by contrary intention. A contrary intention excluding the statutory rule[1] may be shown by the fact that the person whose failure of issue is contemplated has a prior entailed interest, or that a preceding gift is, without any implication arising from the words in question[2], a limitation of an entailed interest to that person or issue[3], or otherwise, generally, by the context of the will[4].

1 As to the statutory rule see PARA 454.

2 *Re O'Bierne* (1844) 1 Jo & Lat 352.

3 See the Wills Act 1837 s 29. As to possible constructions of s 29, as applied to real and personal estate respectively see *Greenway v Greenway* (1860) 2 De GF & J 128 at 136–137 per Lord Campbell LC. For an example of such a contrary intention see *Fay v Fay* (1880) 5 LR Ir 274. See also *Re Clerke, Clowes v Clerke* [1915] 2 Ch 301. Entailed interests cannot be created by instruments coming into operation on or after 1 January 1997 (see the Trusts of Land and Appointment of Trustees Act 1996 s 2(6), Sch 1 para 5; PARA 387; and REAL PROPERTY AND REGISTRATION vol 87 (2012) PARA 114), but between 1 January 1926 and 31 December 1996 inclusive could have been created by will (although only by words which would have that effect in a deed (see PARAS 387, 473)).

4 *Green v Green* (1849) 3 De G & Sm 480; *Green v Giles* (1855) 5 I Ch R 25; *Neville v Thacker* (1888) 23 LR Ir 344; *Weldon v Weldon* [1911] 1 IR 177, Ir CA (followed in *Cowan v Ball* [1933] NI 173). See also *Re Thomas, Thomas v Thomas* [1921] 1 Ch 306.

456. Reference to issue taking under prior gifts. The statutory rule[1] does not apply where the words of limitation refer to the contingency that no issue described in a preceding gift should be born or that there should be no issue who should live to attain the age or otherwise answer the description required for obtaining a vested interest by a preceding gift to such issue[2].

Where, after gifts to particular descriptions of issue, the gift over is 'in default of such issue', the word 'such' cannot, as a general rule, be rejected, and the statutory rule is excluded[3]. Where, however, the particular descriptions of issue are to take in tail, especially if their interests are shown to be interests in tail to each of them successively, 'such issue' may be construed as 'their issue', so that the subsequent limitations take effect as remainders[4]. In other cases, on the will taken as a whole the word 'such' was rejected in order to give the first son an entailed interest[5]. Words referring to failure of issue of a person in a gift over following a devise to the children of that person, or other special class of his issue, not being a contingent class, either in fee simple or in fee tail, prima facie mean in default of such children or other special class of issue, and the gift takes effect only on failure of the previous gifts[6]. A similar rule operates in cases of bequests of personalty or of a mixed fund where the prior bequest is an absolute bequest to children or other special class of issue, not being a contingent class[7].

The statutory rule is also excluded if the failure of issue, expressly or by inference from the will taken as a whole, is ascertained at a specified death[8] or is indefinite[9].

1 As to the statutory rule see PARA 454.

2 Wills Act 1837 s 29 proviso. See also *Re Bence, Smith v Bence* [1891] 3 Ch 242 at 249, CA.

3 *Staines v Maddock* (1728) 3 Bro Parl Cas 108; *Denne d Briddon v Page* (1783) 11 East 603n; *Hay v Earl of Coventry* (1789) 3 Term Rep 83; *Doe d Comberbach v Perryn* (1789) 3 Term Rep 484; *Goodtitle d Sweet v Herring* (1801) 1 East 264; *R v Marquis of Stafford* (1806) 7 East 521; *Foster v Earl of Romney* (1809) 11 East 594; *Ryan v Cowley* (1835) L & G temp Sugd 7; *Boydell v*

Golightly, Boydell v Stanton, Boydell v Morland (1844) 14 Sim 327 at 344; *Ashburner v Wilson* (1850) 17 Sim 204; *Bridger v Ramsay* (1853) 10 Hare 320.

4 *Lewis d Ormond v Waters* (1805) 6 East 336; *Biddulph v Lees* (1858) EB & E 289, Ex Ch.

5 *Evans d Brooke v Astley* (1764) 3 Burr 1570; *Parker v Tootal* (1865) 11 HL Cas 143. See also PARA 473. The same construction may be adopted where the gift over is in default of issue 'as aforesaid': *Malcolm v Taylor* (1831) 2 Russ & M 416; *Walker v Petchell* (1845) 1 CB 652. As to cases of implied reference to previous gifts see PARA 457. Entailed interests cannot be created by instruments coming into operation on or after 1 January 1997: see the Trusts of Land and Appointment of Trustees Act 1996 s 2(6), Sch 1 para 5; PARA 387; and REAL PROPERTY AND REGISTRATION vol 87 (2012) PARA 114.

6 *Bamfield v Popham* (1703) 1 P Wms 54 (see the comments on this case at 1 P Wms 760); *Blackborn v Edgley* (1719) 1 P Wms 600; *Goodright v Dunham* (1779) 1 Doug KB 264; *Baker v Tucker* (1850) 3 HL Cas 106; *Cormack v Copous* (1853) 17 Beav 397 at 402; *Foster v Hayes* (1855) 4 E & B 717 at 734, Ex Ch; *Towns v Wentworth* (1858) 11 Moo PCC 526 at 547; *Smyth v Power* (1876) IR 10 Eq 192 at 199.

7 *Salkeld v Vernon, Salkeld v Salkeld* (1758) 1 Eden 64; *Vandergucht v Blake* (1795) 2 Ves 534; *Ellicombe v Gompertz* (1837) 3 My & Cr 127; *Robinson v Hunt* (1841) 4 Beav 450; *Leeming v Sherratt* (1842) 2 Hare 14 at 17; *Pride v Fooks* (1858) 3 De G & J 252 at 280 per Turner LJ; *Re Wyndham's Trusts* (1865) LR 1 Eq 290; *Re Sanders' Trusts* (1866) LR 1 Eq 675; *Re Merceron's Trusts, Davies v Merceron* (1876) 4 ChD 182; *Re Carr* (1902) 2 SRNSW 1.

8 *Westwood v Southey* (1852) 2 Sim NS 192 at 203; *Re Edwards, Jones v Jones* [1906] 1 Ch 570, CA (disapproving *Kidman v Kidman* (1871) 40 LJ Ch 359 at 360).

9 *Bowen v Lewis* (1884) 9 App Cas 890.

457. Where the prior gift is contingent. It is more difficult, although not impossible[1], to apply a reference to 'issue' to those taking under the prior gifts where the prior limitation is on contingent events[2], or is to a contingent class, such as sons attaining 21 or surviving a life tenant, so that there may be issue who may not take under it[3], or where the prior limitation is to a definite number of the children[4], or if the issue taking under previous gifts take for life only[5]. The fact that the issue take merely as objects of a power of appointment does not, however, prevent the construction of a reference to 'issue' from being construed as a reference to such issue, objects of the power, as are living at the death of the appointor[6].

1 *Bryan v Mansion* (1852) 5 De G & Sm 737 at 742 (where, however, in the context, 'issue' meant 'children'); *Sanders v Ashford* (1860) 28 Beav 609 (where the gift over was in default of issue attaining 21); *Re Merceron's Trusts, Davies v Merceron* (1876) 4 ChD 182 (where there was a gift to children living at the parent's death and a gift over if the parent were to 'die without issue'); *Hutchinson v Tottenham* [1898] 1 IR 403 (affd [1899] 1 IR 344, Ir CA) (children born in testatrix's lifetime).

2 *Andree v Ward* (1826) 1 Russ 260 (if ancestor married a woman of specified fortune); *Campbell v Harding* (1831) 2 Russ & M 390 (if ancestor married) (affd sub nom *Candy v Campbell* (1834) 2 Cl & Fin 421, HL); *Franks v Price* (1838) 5 Bing NC 37; *Franks v Price* (1840) 3 Beav 182.

3 *Doe d Rew v Lucraft* (1832) 1 Moo & S 573 (prior issue taking at 21); *Pride v Fooks* (1858) 3 De G & J 252 at 280–281 per Turner LJ.

4 *Langley v Baldwin* (1707) 1 Eq Cas Abr 185 pl 29 (first six sons only); *A-G v Sutton* (1721) 1 P Wms 754, HL (first and second sons only); *Stanley v Lennard* (1758) 1 Eden 87 (eldest son only); *Key v Key* (1853) 4 De GM & G 73 at 80 (eldest surviving son).

5 *Parr v Swindels* (1828) 4 Russ 283.

6 *Target v Gaunt* (1718) 1 P Wms 432; *Hockley v Mawbey* (1790) 3 Bro CC 82; *Ryan v Cowley* (1835) L & G temp Sugd 7; *Leeming v Sherratt* (1842) 2 Hare 14; *Eastwood v Avison* (1869) LR 4 Exch 141.

458. Gift over to apply when interest vests in possession. If a person predeceases a life tenant without leaving issue, a gift over (whether of real or personal estate) which is to take place when the interest given will vest in possession[1] extends to the event of the person and his issue dying in the lifetime of the life tenant[2].

1   Cf *Dunn v Morgan* (1915) 84 LJ Ch 812 (where 'die without issue' meant without leaving issue surviving him; and, as the interests had previously vested in possession and the gift over would divest them, a construction was adopted which would avoid the uncertainty of divesting).
2   *Crowder v Stone* (1829) 3 Russ 217; *Jarman v Vye* (1866) LR 2 Eq 784.

459.   Interpretation where the statutory rule as to death without issue does not apply. In general[1], in gifts not within the statutory rule[2] (whether the gift is of real estate[3] or personal estate[4] or both together[5]), words importing failure of issue import an indefinite failure of issue at any time, however remote[6], unless the context of the will or the nature of the gift[7] shows an intention to the contrary. A contrary intention is shown, for example, where the issue is referred to as surviving a living person[8], or where the context shows that 'issue' means 'children'[9]. Similarly, if the gift over is directed to take effect 'at the death' of the ancestor (a prior donee under the will), this is some indication, but not a conclusive indication[10], that the failure of issue is confined to the death of the prior donee[11]. If the gift over could not reasonably be meant to depend on a general failure of issue, the inference is that a failure at the death of the named ancestor is intended[12].

1   As to the exceptions see PARA 460.
2   Ie not within the Wills Act 1837 s 29 (see PARA 454), either as being prior to it or as being within s 29 proviso (see PARA 456): see *Re Bence, Smith v Bence* [1891] 3 Ch 242, CA.
3   *Lee's Case* (1584) 1 Leon 285; *Newton v Barnardine* (1587) Moore KB 127; *Lady Lanesborough v Fox* (1733) Cas *temp* Talb 262, HL; *Cole v Goble* (1853) 13 CB 445. See also the cases as to death 'without leaving issue' cited in PARA 460 note 4. As to the implication of an estate tail under the old law in such a case see PARA 473.
4   *Beauclerk v Dormer* (1742) 2 Atk 308; *Gray v Shawne* (1758) 1 Eden 153; *Destouches v Walker* (1764) 2 Eden 261; *Howston v Ives* (1764) 2 Eden 216; *Grey v Montagu* (1770) 3 Bro Parl Cas 314; *Bigge v Bensley* (1783) 1 Bro CC 187; *Glover v Strothoff* (1786) 2 Bro CC 33; *Everest v Gell* (1791) 1 Ves 286; *Chandless v Price* (1796) 3 Ves 99 at 101; *Rawlins v Goldfrap* (1800) 5 Ves 440, (1809) 1 Ves 520; *Lepine v Ferard* (1831) 2 Russ & M 378; *Candy v Campbell* (1834) 2 Cl & Fin 421, HL; *Falkiner v Hornidge* (1858) 8 I Ch R 184; *Re Johnson's Trusts* (1866) LR 2 Eq 716 at 720; *Fisher v Webster* (1872) LR 14 Eq 283.
5   *Salkeld v Vernon, Salkeld v Salkeld* (1758) 1 Eden 64; *Jeffery v Sprigge* (1784) 1 Cox Eq Cas 62; *Boehm v Clarke* (1804) 9 Ves 580; *Barlow v Salter* (1810) 17 Ves 479; *Donn v Penny* (1815) 1 Mer 20.
6   As to the possible objection as regards remoteness in such cases see PERPETUITIES AND ACCUMULATIONS vol 80 (2013) PARA 32.
7   *King v Withers* (1735) Cas *temp* Talb 117 at 121; *Campbell v Harding* (1831) 2 Russ & M 390 at 406. Thus in cases where the property is a leasehold for lives, the failure must occur within the lives of the cestuis que vie: *Low v Burron* (1734) 3 P Wms 262; *Campbell v Harding* at 406. Where, however, the leasehold was renewable for ever, the effect in a case under the law prior to the Wills Act 1837 was that the failure might be indefinitely remote, and in such cases an estate in quasi-entail was created: *Croly v Croly* (1825) Batt 1; *Manning v Moore* (1832) Alc & N 96; *Lee v Flinn* (1833) Alc & N 418.
8   *Baker v Lucas* (1828) 1 Mol 481; *Gee v Liddell* (1866) LR 2 Eq 341.
9   *Doe d Lyde v Lyde* (1787) 1 Term Rep 593; *Carter v Bentall* (1840) 2 Beav 551; *Bryan v Mansion* (1852) 5 De G & Sm 737.
10 *Walter v Drew* (1723) 1 Com 373; *Theebridge v Kilburne* (1751) 2 Ves Sen 233 at 236; *Doe d Cock v Cooper* (1801) 1 East 229.
11 *Pinbury v Elkin* (1719) 1 P Wms 563; *Trotter v Oswald* (1787) 1 Cox Eq Cas 317; *Wilkinson v South* (1798) 7 Term Rep 555; *Gawler v Cadby* (1821) Jac 346 at 348; *Rackstraw v Vile* (1824) 1 Sim & St 604, following *Doe d King v Frost* (1820) 3 B & Ald 546 (commented on in Lewis's Law of Perpetuity 234–235); *Ex p Davies* (1851) 2 Sim NS 114. As to the use of the word 'then' see *Campbell v Harding* (1831) 2 Russ & M 390 at 410; *Pye v Linwood* (1842) 6 Jur 618.
12 *Re Rye's Settlement* (1852) 10 Hare 106 at 111.

460. Exceptions to the statutory rule as to death without issue. There are recognised exceptions to the statutory rule, and rules have been adopted as to wills not subject to the statutory rule[1], as follows:

(1)   where the subject matter is personal estate, a gift on a death 'without leaving issue' is prima facie confined to a failure of issue at death[2], but, where the subject matter is real estate, the gift prima facie[3] extends to an indefinite failure of issue[4]; where real estate and personal estate are comprised in the same gift, the words are construed differently, according to the subject matter[5];

(2)   a gift of property to which the testator is entitled in possession, to take effect on failure of his own issue, not preceded by any other gift, is not a future gift but is a gift in possession at the testator's death in the event of there being at that time a failure of his issue[6];

(3)   where the testator under the limitations of another instrument is entitled in remainder or reversion on failure of the issue, or the issue male or female, of any person, and the testator makes a gift of the property, not preceded by any other limitation, on failure of that issue, these words do not make the gift a future gift but are merely a description of the testator's interest[7]; the question in such cases is whether the issue referred to in the will is the same as or is different from the issue capable of taking under the other instrument[8];

(4)   where the court finds an intention that the persons entitled under the gift over are to enjoy the benefits of their gift as a personal provision during their lives, and are not merely to take interests which are not vested in possession but vested in right, the inference may be drawn that the failure of issue is confined to the lives of those persons[9]; this is so, for example, where the gift over provides for a charge of a legacy, intended as a personal provision[10], or where the gift over is to such of a number of named or described persons as are living at the time of failure[11]; the inference also arises in a gift over to the survivors of the persons, failure of whose issue is contemplated, where 'survivors' is used in its ordinary sense of surviving the failure of issue[12], but not where 'survivor' means 'the longest liver'[13] or 'surviving stirps' or 'other'[14]; similarly, where the only interest taken under the gift over is a life interest, or succession of life interests, it can be inferred that the failure of issue is confined to the lives of the donees under the gift over[15];

(5)   where, after a devise to a person and his heirs[16], or after a bequest to a person absolutely[17], there is a gift over on his dying under or over a certain age without issue, the compound event is restricted to his dying under or over that age without issue living at his death.

1   For the statutory rule see the Wills Act 1837 s 29; and PARA 454. As to the interpretation adopted where s 29 does not apply see PARA 459.
2   *Forth v Chapman* (1720) 1 P Wms 663; *Atkinson v Hutchinson* (1734) 3 P Wms 258; *Sabbarton v Sabbarton* (1738) Cas *temp* Talb 55, 245; *Sheffield v Lord Orrery* (1745) 3 Atk 282 at 287; *Lampley v Blower* (1746) 3 Atk 396; *Sheppard v Lessingham* (1751) Amb 122; *Taylor v Clarke* (1763) 2 Eden 202; *Gordon v Adolphus* (1769) 3 Bro Parl Cas 306; *Goodtitle d Peake v Pegden* (1788) 2 Term Rep 721; *Radford v Radford* (1836) 1 Keen 486; *Daniel v Warren* (1843) 2 Y & C Ch Cas 290; *Mansell v Grove* (1843) 2 Y & C Ch Cas 484; *Hawkins v Hamerton* (1848) 16 Sim 410; *Re Synge's Trusts* (1854) 3 I Ch R 379; *Sealy v Stawell* (1868) IR 2 Eq 326 at 353; *Auger v Beaudry* [1920] AC 1010, PC.
3   For instances of a context to the contrary see *Porter v Bradley* (1789) 3 Term Rep 143 (leaving . . . behind him); *Roe d Sheers v Jeffery* (1798) 7 Term Rep 589, following *Pells v Brown* (1620) Cro

Jac 590 (gift over of life estates to living persons). Although these cases have been criticised, they do not appear to be overruled: see *Van Tassel v Frederick* (1896) 27 OR 646 at 648. Cf head (4) in the text.

4 *Walter v Drew* (1723) 1 Com 373; *Denn d Geering v Shenton* (1776) 1 Cowp 410; *Tenny d Agar v Agar* (1810) 12 East 253; *Dansey v Griffiths* (1815) 4 M & S 61; *Franklin v Lay* (1820) 6 Madd 258; *Wollen v Andrewes* (1824) 2 Bing 126; *Heather v Winder* (1835) 5 LJ Ch 41; *Doe d Cadogan v Ewart* (1838) 7 Ad & El 636; *Bamford v Lord* (1854) 14 CB 708; *Feakes v Standley* (1857) 24 Beav 485; *Biss v Smith* (1857) 2 H & N 105; *Richards v Davies* (1862) 13 CBNS 69 (affd 13 CBNS 861, Ex Ch); *Re Thomas, Thomas v Thomas* [1921] 1 Ch 306. In such cases an implied estate tail might formerly have arisen: see PARA 473.

5 *Forth v Chapman* (1720) 1 P Wms 663; *Sheffield v Lord Orrery* (1745) 3 Atk 282 at 287; *Radford v Radford* (1836) 1 Keen 486; *Bamford v Lord* (1854) 14 CB 708; *Greenway v Greenway* (1860) 2 De GF & J 128 at 137.

6 *French v Caddell* (1765) 3 Bro Parl Cas 257, HL; *Wellington v Wellington* (1768) 4 Burr 2165; *Lytton v Lytton* (1793) 4 Bro CC 441; *Sanford v Irby* (1820) 3 B & Ald 654.

7 *Badger v Lloyd* (1699) 1 Ld Raym 523; *Lytton v Lytton* (1793) 4 Bro CC 441; *Egerton v Jones* (1830) 3 Sim 409.

8 *Sanford v Irby* (1820) 3 B & Ald 654; *Morse v Lord Ormonde* (1826) 1 Russ 382; *Eno v Eno* (1847) 6 Hare 171; *Lewis v Templer* (1864) 33 Beav 625 (in these cases the issue was the same); *Lady Lanesborough v Fox* (1733) Cas *temp* Talb 262, HL; *Jones v Morgan* (1774) 3 Bro Parl Cas 323; *Bankes v Holme* (1821) 1 Russ 394n, HL (in these cases the issue was different).

9 *Doe d Smith v Webber* (1818) 1 B & Ald 713 at 721.

10 *Nichols v Hooper* (1712) 1 P Wms 198; *Doe d Smith v Webber* (1818) 1 B & Ald 713 at 721. The mere fact of a legacy given on failure of issue is insufficient: see *Doe d Todd v Duesbury* (1841) 8 M & W 514.

11 *Murray v Addenbrook* (1830) 4 Russ 407 at 419; *Greenwood v Verdon* (1854) 1 K & J 74 at 81.

12 *Hughes v Sayer* (1718) 1 P Wms 534; *Ranelagh v Ranelagh* (1834) 2 My & K 441 at 448; *Turner v Frampton* (1846) 2 Coll 331; *Westwood v Southey* (1852) 2 Sim NS 192 at 201. See also *Massey v Hudson* (1817) 2 Mer 130 (where a substitutional gift to the personal representatives of the survivor excluded the presumption).

13 *Chadock v Cowley* (1624) Cro Jac 695.

14 As to the usual meanings of 'survive', and as to the use of words such as 'survivors' see PARAS 315–316.

15 *Trafford v Boehm* (1746) 3 Atk 440 at 494; *Roe d Sheers v Jeffery* (1798) 7 Term Rep 589 (where the failure was said to be confined to the life of the prior donee). Cf *Lepine v Ferard* (1831) 2 Russ & M 378 at 398 per Lord Brougham. This is not the case where life interests are not the only interests arising under the gift over; the mere fact that the next interest under the gift over is for life is insufficient: *Boehm v Clarke* (1804) 9 Ves 580 at 582; *Barlow v Salter* (1810) 17 Ves 479 at 482; *Doe d Jones v Owens* (1830) 1 B & Ad 318 at 320–321.

16 *Toovey v Bassett* (1809) 10 East 460; *Right d Day v Day* (1812) 16 East 67; *Glover v Monckton* (1825) 3 Bing 13; *Doe d Johnson v Johnson* (1852) 8 Exch 81; *Gwynne v Berry* (1875) IR 9 CL 494.

17 *Pawlet v Dogget* (1688) 2 Vern 86; *Martin v Long* (1690) 2 Vern 151 (leaseholds). See also *Morris v Morris* (1853) 17 Beav 198 (where there was a gift over if the prior donee should die without issue or before 21, and where 'or' was construed as 'and' as it would have been before the Wills Act 1837); *Re Morgan* (1883) 24 ChD 114.

461. Interpretation of other gifts over. A devise over on death without having or leaving an heir or male heir or heirs of the body[1] prima facie[2] refers to a failure of such heirs at any time[3].

In order not to disappoint more remote generations of issue, a devise over of real property on a death without children, either after a prior gift in fee or generally without words of limitation, may be construed as taking effect on death and failure of issue either indefinitely[4] or within a limited time, for example before the death of the named ancestor[5], according to the context. Prima facie the words 'child or children' mean what they say, but it is open to the court to give them a wider meaning, as synonymous with 'issue'[6]. A similar gift over of personal property prima facie refers to a failure of children at the death of the named parent[7]. The words are not considered to mean a failure of issue indefinitely if the effect is to defeat the testator's intention, and, especially in bequests of personal property, the ordinary meaning of 'children' is adhered to[8], but in some cases a similar rule to that in the case of real property may be applied to personal property[9].

A gift over on death 'without having children' is construed as on death 'without having had children', and fails to take effect if the parent has had a child, even though no child survives him[10].

1 Such an expression is not subject to the Wills Act 1837 s 29: see PARA 454 note 4.
2 For instances where the context showed an intention to the contrary see *Polley v Polley* (1861) 29 Beav 134; *Coltsmann v Coltsmann* (1868) LR 3 HL 121; *Re Leach, Leach v Leach* [1912] 2 Ch 422.
3 *Nottingham v Jennings* (1700) 1 P Wms 23; *A-G v Hird* (1782) 1 Bro CC 170; *Crooke v De Vandes* (1803) 9 Ves 197.
4 *Milliner v Robinson* (1600) Moore KB 682 (sub nom *Bifield's Case* cited in 1 Vent at 231) (devise to A with a gift over on his death not leaving a son); *Doe d Blesard v Simpson* (1842) 3 Man & G 929 at 954, Ex Ch; *Bacon v Cosby* (1851) 4 De G & Sm 261; *Re Milward's Estate, ex p Midland Rly Co* [1940] Ch 698 at 703.
5 *Doe d Smith v Webber* (1818) 1 B & Ald 713; *Re Milward's Estate, ex p Midland Rly Co* [1940] Ch 698. See also *Parker v Birks* (1854) 1 K & J 156; *Richards v Davies* (1862) 13 CBNS 69 at 87 per Byles J (affd (1863) 13 CBNS 861); *Re Thomas, Vivian v Vivian* [1920] 1 Ch 515.
6 *Re Milward's Estate, ex p Midland Rly Co* [1940] Ch 698 at 705.
7 *Hughes v Sayer* (1718) 1 P Wms 534; *Pleydell v Pleydell* (1721) 1 P Wms 748; *Thicknesse v Liege* (1775) 3 Bro Parl Cas 365; *Re Booth, Pickard v Booth* [1900] 1 Ch 768 (where *Jeffreys v Conner* (1860) 28 Beav 328 is explained); *Re Raphael, Permanent Trustee Co of New South Wales Ltd v Lee* (1903) 3 SRNSW 196.
8 *Studholme v Hodgson* (1734) 3 P Wms 300 at 304; *Stone v Maule* (1829) 2 Sim 490; *Mathews v Gardiner* (1853) 17 Beav 254; *Jeffreys v Conner* (1860) 28 Beav 328.
9 *Re Synge's Trusts* (1854) 3 I Ch R 379.
10 *Weakley d Knight v Rugg* (1797) 7 Term Rep 322; *Bell v Phyn* (1802) 7 Ves 453; *Wall v Tomlinson* (1810) 16 Ves 413; *Jeffreys v Conner* (1860) 28 Beav 328. See also *Re Johnston and Smith* (1906) 12 OLR 262; *M'Kay v M'Allister* (1912) 46 ILT 88, Ir CA; *Chunilal Parvatishankar v Bai Samrath* (1914) 30 TLR 407, PC (cases of gifts over on death without having 'issue').

C. FORFEITURE ON ALIENATION

462. Validity and interpretation of forfeiture clauses. A life or other limited interest can be validly given subject to a forfeiture clause on bankruptcy or alienation or on similar events[1]. Such clauses are construed strictly[2]. Words may, however, be used which compel the court to hold that in the circumstances a forfeiture has been incurred, even though, apart from the forfeiture clause, the interest has been preserved[3]. Even in the absence of express words to that effect, forfeiture is not incurred by a consent to an advance, whether the advance is made under an express power contained in the will[4] or under the statutory power[5] of advancement[6].

In all cases the burden lies on those who assert that forfeiture has taken place[7].

1 As to what interests may validly be made subject to such forfeiture clauses see GIFTS vol 52 (2014) PARA 254; PERSONAL PROPERTY vol 80 (2013) PARA 869 et seq. As to the construction of forfeiture clauses with respect to references to bankruptcy see BANKRUPTCY AND INDIVIDUAL INSOLVENCY vol 5 (2013) PARAS 418–422. As to a forfeiture clause on alienation except an alienation by way of settlement see *Re Galsworthy, Galsworthy v Galsworthy* [1922] 2 Ch 558.
2 *Re Mair, Williamson v French* [1909] 2 Ch 280 at 282 (charge withdrawn before dividends accrued; no forfeiture). See also *Re Sheward, Sheward v Brown* [1893] 3 Ch 502 (document on the face of it a charge, but not intended as such; no forfeiture); *Re Evans, Public Trustee v Evans* [1920] 2 Ch 304, CA; *Re Bell, Bell v Agnew* (1931) 47 TLR 401; *Re Walker, Public Trustee v Walker* [1939] Ch 974, [1939] 3 All ER 902.
3 *Hurst v Hurst* (1882) 21 ChD 278, CA (disclaimer by chargee); *Re Porter, Coulson v Capper* [1892] 3 Ch 481 (assignment inoperative under Australian law); *Re Baker, Baker v Baker* [1904] 1 Ch 157 (charges, even though cancelled by creditors before distribution).
4 *Re Hodgson, Weston v Hodgson* [1913] 1 Ch 34; *Re Shaw's Settlement Trusts, Shaw v Shaw* [1951] Ch 833, [1951] 1 All ER 656.

5   As to this statutory power see the Trustee Act 1925 s 32; and CHILDREN AND YOUNG PERSONS vol 9 (2012) PARA 76 et seq; TRUSTS AND POWERS vol 98 (2013) PARA 516.

6   *Re Rees, Lloyds Bank Ltd v Rees* [1954] Ch 202, [1954] 1 All ER 7. *Re Stimpson's Trusts* [1931] 2 Ch 77, to the contrary, was doubted in *Re Shaw's Settlement Trusts, Shaw v Shaw* [1951] Ch 833 at 840, [1951] 1 All ER 656 at 659 and *Re Rees, Lloyds Bank Ltd v Rees* at 209 and 10. See CHILDREN AND YOUNG PERSONS vol 9 (2012) PARA 76 et seq; SETTLEMENTS vol 91 (2012) PARA 818.

7   *Cox v Bockett* (1865) 35 Beav 48 at 51.

463. Effect of forfeiture clauses. Whether an act or event causes a forfeiture[1] depends on the true construction of the forfeiture clause, for example whether a definite act on the donee's part is required or whether the clause goes further and contemplates events where he is passive[2]. There is, however, no forfeiture if there is no loss of the beneficial right to enjoy the property[3] as the payments of income accrue due[4], and there is no vesting of the right in another person[5]. Forfeiture clauses on alienation prima facie refer to alienation by way of anticipation and do not, unless so expressed[6], refer to dispositions of income already accrued due or already vested in the donee[7]. If a doubt arises whether a document of alienation is intended to deal with income already accrued due or with future income only, the court favours the construction which prevents a forfeiture[8].

No forfeiture is caused where the donee, in good faith and not as a contrivance to evade the clause[9], gives a power of attorney or authority to receive the income.

A power of attorney given for value as a colourable assignment or for the express purpose of passing the property to a creditor may, however, cause forfeiture[10].

1   As to the events causing forfeiture in relation to protective trusts under the Trustee Act 1925 s 33 see SETTLEMENTS vol 91 (2012) PARA 819.

2   *Re Pozot's Settlement Trusts, Westminster Bank Ltd v Guerbois* [1952] Ch 427 at 445, [1952] 1 All ER 1107 at 1117, CA. See also PARA 465.

3   *Lockwood v Sikes* (1884) 51 LT 562; *Re Selby, Church v Tancred* [1903] 1 Ch 715.

4   *Re Sampson, Sampson v Sampson* [1896] 1 Ch 630, followed in *Re Jenkins, Williams v Jenkins* [1915] 1 Ch 46. As to the effect of such a clause on income accruing due during a conditional discharge in bankruptcy see *Re Clark, Clark v Clark* [1926] Ch 833.

5   *Re Brewer's Settlement, Morton v Blackmore* [1896] 2 Ch 503 (loan of trust fund to life tenant, who spent it; income payable to him did not become 'vested in' another person). As to a petition in bankruptcy not followed by a bankruptcy order see SETTLEMENTS vol 91 (2012) PARA 820. Cf *Re Broughton, Peat v Broughton* (1887) 57 LT 8. See also *Craven v Brady* (1869) 4 Ch App 296 (forfeiture on being deprived of control of rents; marriage under law before 1883 caused forfeiture); *Re Dash, Darley v King, King v Darley* (1887) 57 LT 219 (conviction; no administrator appointed; no forfeiture); *Re Beaumont, Woods v Beaumont* (1910) 79 LJ Ch 744 (appointment of receiver caused no vesting in another person); *Re Mordaunt, Mordaunt v Mordaunt* (1914) 49 L Jo 225 (debt, although postponed to capital falling into possession, also charged on present income); *Re Crother's Trusts* [1915] 1 IR 53. Cf *Bonfield v Hassell* (1863) 32 LJ Ch 475 (marriage caused no forfeiture of annuity). As to the effect of a clause of forfeiture on the interest being taken in execution see *Blackman v Fysh* [1892] 3 Ch 209, CA (receiver).

6   *Bates v Bates* [1884] WN 129; dissented from, however, in *Re Greenwood, Sutcliffe v Gledhill* [1901] 1 Ch 887 at 893.

7   *Re Stulz's Trusts, ex p Kingsford* (1853) 4 De GM & G 404 at 409 (where the testator even provided for attempts 'to anticipate or otherwise assign or incumber' the bequest); *Sutton, Carden & Co v Goodrich* (1899) 80 LT 765; *Re Greenwood, Sutcliffe v Gledhill* [1901] 1 Ch 887.

8   *Cox v Bockett* (1865) 35 Beav 48; *Durran v Durran* (1904) 91 LT 819 at 820, CA.

9   *Croft v Lumley* (1858) 6 HL Cas 672 (covenant in lease); *Avison v Holmes, Penny v Avison* (1861) 1 John & H 530; *Re Swannell, Morice v Swannell* (1909) 101 LT 76; *Smith v Perpetual Trustee Co Ltd* (1910) 11 CLR 148.

10   *Doe d Mitchinson v Carter* (1799) 8 Term Rep 300; *Doe d Duke of Norfolk v Hawke* (1802) 2 East 481; *Wilkinson v Wilkinson* (1819) 3 Swan 515; *Oldham v Oldham* (1867) LR 3 Eq 404.

464. Forfeiture on alienation. Where a forfeiture clause provides for forfeiture on alienation only, no forfeiture is caused by events in which the beneficiary plays a purely passive role[1] or by acts done by other persons against the donee's will, such as a charging order[2], or appointment of a receiver[3], or an alienation by order of the court under its power[4] to authorise dealings with trust property[5], or by any proceedings in bankruptcy commenced by creditors without the concurrence of the donee[6]. A charge by a life tenant after a receiver for him had been appointed in lunacy was void and did not give rise to a forfeiture[7].

Unless the clause extends to an attempted assignment, it is not brought into operation by a mere attempt to assign or by an assignment which is nugatory[8]. Even where the clause extends to an attempt to assign, mere negotiations for an assignment[9] or the giving of an authority to receive the income[10] are insufficient to bring the clause into operation; but a settlement, although invalid, may give rise to a forfeiture in such a case[11].

1 *Re Pozot's Settlement Trusts, Westminster Bank Ltd v Guerbois* [1952] Ch 427 at 445, [1952] 1 All ER 1107 at 1117, CA.
2 *Re Kelly's Settlement, West v Turner* (1888) 59 LT 494.
3 *Campbell v Campbell and Davis* (1895) 72 LT 294.
4 See the Trustee Act 1925 s 57; and TRUSTS AND POWERS vol 98 (2013) PARA 646.
5 *Re Mair, Richards v Doxat* [1935] Ch 562. See also *Re Salting, Baillie-Hamilton v Morgan* [1932] 2 Ch 57.
6 See *Whitfield v Prickett* (1838) 2 Keen 608; *Graham v Lee* (1857) 23 Beav 388; and SETTLEMENTS vol 91 (2012) PARA 820. It is otherwise where the clause provides for forfeiture on bankruptcy: see BANKRUPTCY AND INDIVIDUAL INSOLVENCY vol 5 (2013) PARAS 418–419. Cf *Doe d Mitchinson v Carter* (1798) 8 Term Rep 57 at 61.
7 *Re Marshall, Marshall v Whateley* [1920] 1 Ch 284. A charge after the appointment of a deputy under the Mental Capacity Act 2005 s 16 (replacing the Mental Health Act 1989 s 99 (repealed)) would probably also be void: see MENTAL HEALTH AND CAPACITY vol 75 (2013) PARAS 724, 734.
8 *Re Wormald, Frank v Muzeen* (1890) 43 ChD 630; *Re Adamson, Public Trustee v Billing* (1913) 109 LT 25 (cases where a restraint on anticipation made the assignment nugatory).
9 *Graham v Lee* (1857) 23 Beav 388.
10 *Wilkinson v Wilkinson* (1819) 3 Swan 515. See also the cases cited in PARA 463 note 10.
11 *Re Porter, Coulson v Capper* [1892] 3 Ch 481. But see *Re Sheward, Sheward v Brown* [1893] 3 Ch 502 (where no forfeiture was caused by a document amounting to, but not intended to be, an equitable assignment and which could have been set aside in proceedings for that purpose).

465. Forfeiture where the donee is a passive or unwilling party. The forfeiture clause may go further and provide for forfeiture if the donee does or suffers any act by which the income would, but for the provisions of the forfeiture clause, become payable to another[1]. In such cases, the use of expressions such as 'suffer' or 'permit' indicate that even a passive attitude of the donee may suffice to cause forfeiture[2]. If the clause is restricted to cases where the income would become payable to or vested in another, no forfeiture is caused by any proceedings which do not have that effect[3]; but on the wording of the clause it may in some cases be sufficient if the donee is deprived of personal enjoyment of the income[4]. Whether an order made under trading with the enemy legislation[5] causes a forfeiture depends on the wording of the clause; such an order is an event causing the income to become payable to[6] but not vested in[7] another, but it is not an act permitted or suffered by the beneficiary[8].

Where the clause provided for forfeiture if the beneficiary should be unable to give a personal discharge, no forfeiture was incurred by the appointment of a receiver in lunacy[9].

1 This is so where the income is directed to be held on the statutory protective trusts: see SETTLEMENTS vol 91 (2012) PARA 818. These also provide for forfeiture if any event happens by which the beneficiary would be deprived of his right to receive capital or income: see *Re Richardson's Will Trusts, Public Trustee v Llewellyn Evans' Trustee* [1958] Ch 504, [1958] 1 All ER 538; *Edmonds v Edmonds* [1965] 1 All ER 379n, [1965] 1 WLR 58.
2 *Roffey v Bent* (1867) LR 3 Eq 759 (charging order); *Re Throckmorton, ex p Eyston* (1877) 7 ChD 145, CA (hostile bankruptcy); *Re Moore* (1885) 17 LR Ir 549 (registration of a judgment); *Re*

Detmold, *Detmold v Detmold* (1889) 40 ChD 585 (insolvency); *Re Sartoris's Estate, Sartoris v Sartoris* [1892] 1 Ch 11, CA (receiving order) (followed in *Re Laye, Turnbull v Laye* [1913] 1 Ch 298). See also BANKRUPTCY AND INDIVIDUAL INSOLVENCY vol 5 (2013) PARAS 418–419. As to the meaning of 'suffer any process' see note 8.

3   *Re James, Clutterbuck v James* (1890) 62 LT 545 (Scottish sequestration; no vesting of property in another); *Re Ryan* (1887) 19 LR Ir 24 (execution on cattle); *Re Moon, ex p Dawes* (1886) 17 QBD 275 (filing of bankruptcy petition, not followed by adjudication). There was no forfeiture where the beneficiary authorised payment to another of a dividend which he expected, but the authority was rendered nugatory by the company failing to declare the dividend: *Re Longman, Westminster Bank Ltd v Hatton* [1955] 1 All ER 455, [1955] 1 WLR 197.

4   *Re Baring's Settlement Trusts, Baring Bros & Co Ltd v Liddell* [1940] Ch 737, [1940] 3 All ER 20 (sequestration); *Re Hatch, Public Trustee v Hatch* [1948] Ch 592, [1948] 2 All ER 288 (beneficiary residing in enemy territory); *Re Richardson's Will Trusts, Public Trustee v Llewellyn Evans' Trustee* [1958] Ch 504, [1958] 1 All ER 538 (equitable charge created by court order in divorce proceedings); *Edmonds v Edmonds* [1965] 1 All ER 379n, [1965] 1 WLR 58 (attachment of earnings order in divorce proceedings).

5   Eg the Trading with the Enemy Act 1939: see ARMED CONFLICT AND EMERGENCY vol 3 (2011) PARA 197 et seq.

6   *Re Gourju's Will Trusts, Starling v Custodian of Enemy Property* [1943] Ch 24, [1942] 2 All ER 605. See also *Re Pozot's Settlement Trusts, Westminster Bank Ltd v Guerbois* [1952] Ch 427 at 450–451, 453, [1952] 1 All ER 1107 at 1121–1122, CA.

7   *Re Pozot's Settlement Trusts, Westminster Bank Ltd v Guerbois* [1952] Ch 427, [1952] 1 All ER 1107, CA. As to the effect of an order under earlier legislation see *Re Levinstein, Levinstein v Levinstein* [1921] 2 Ch 251; *Re Biedermann, Best v Wertheim* [1922] 2 Ch 771, CA (both cases of charges under the Treaty of Peace (Austria) Order 1920, SR & O 1920/1613).

8   *Re Hall, Public Trustee v Montgomery* [1944] Ch 46, [1943] 2 All ER 753; *Re Harris, Cope v Evans* [1945] Ch 316, [1945] 1 All ER 702 (where it was also held that the words 'suffer any process' in the forfeiture clause meant some form of legal process and could not refer to the passing of an Act of Parliament or the making of an Order in Council or the giving of any direction under any such order).

9   *Re Oppenheim's Will Trusts, Westminster Bank Ltd v Oppenheim* [1950] Ch 633, [1950] 2 All ER 86. On the ratio of that decision, that the clause was not intended to operate where the income would remain for the benefit of the donee (cf PARA 462), it seems that no forfeiture should be incurred under such a clause on the appointment of a deputy under the Mental Capacity Act 2005 s 16 (replacing the Mental Health Act 1983 s 99 (repealed)) (see MENTAL HEALTH AND CAPACITY vol 75 (2013) PARAS 724, 734).

(6) IMPLIED GIFTS

466. Gifts by implication. Until receiving statutory power to rectify wills[1] the court had no jurisdiction to grant rectification of a will. It could omit words included as a result of fraud or inadvertence or which were offensive in character[2] and in very limited circumstances could imply them. The ability to rectify wills together with the court's extended powers to admit extrinsic evidence[3] to aid construction of a will have together rendered the old rules on implication much less important.

The reading of words into a will as a matter of necessary implication is a measure which will be applied only with the greatest caution, and is legitimate only where the court can gather from the will as a whole that something has been omitted and, with sufficient precision, the nature of the omission[4]. Accordingly, limitations and gifts will arise by necessary implication only where there is so strong a probability of intention shown by the words of the will that a contrary intention cannot be supposed[5].

Implication may be founded on two grounds. It may either arise from an elliptical form of expression which involves and implies something else as contemplated by the person using the expression, or the implication may be founded on the form of gift, or on a direction to do something which cannot be carried into effect without, of necessity, involving something else in order to give effect to that direction, or something else which is a consequence necessarily resulting from that direction[6]. Thus if the will shows that the testator must necessarily have intended an interest to be given which there are no words in the will expressly to create, the court will supply the defect by implication and thus mould his language so as to carry into effect, as far as possible, the intention which it considers the testator has sufficiently declared in the will as a whole[7]. The doctrine arises where, in order to fulfil the testator's intentions which are manifest from the words of the will, there is a gap to be filled up in the dispositions[8]. A construction which leads to an intestacy should be avoided unless the language necessarily leads to this result[9].

An interest will not be implied in favour of any person for whom it cannot be said that the testator intended to provide[10].

1   For statutory power to rectify see the Administration of Justice Act 1982 s 20; and PARA 889.
2   For exclusion of part of a will see PARA 739.
3   For statutory power to admit extrinsic evidence see the Administration of Justice Act 1982 s 21; and PARA 219.
4   *Re Whitrick, Sutcliffe v Sutcliffe* [1957] 2 All ER 467 at 469, [1957] 1 WLR 884 at 887–888, CA. See also *Re Follett, Barclays Bank Ltd v Dovell* [1955] 2 All ER 22, [1955] 1 WLR 429, CA. As to implied gifts to a class in default of the exercise of a power of appointment see TRUSTS AND POWERS vol 98 (2013) PARAS 30–31; and as to reading in words in a clause of defeasance see PARA 440 et seq.
5   *Wilkinson v Adam* (1813) 1 Ves & B 422 at 466 per Lord Eldon LC; *Crook v Hill* (1871) 6 Ch App 311 at 315 per James LJ. See also *Roe d Bendale v Summerset* (1770) 5 Burr 2608 at 2609; *Upton v Lord Ferrers* (1801) 5 Ves 801 at 806; *R v Ringstead Inhabitants* (1829) 9 B & C 218 at 224; *Scalé v Rawlins* [1892] AC 342, HL.
6   *Parker v Tootal* (1865) 11 HL Cas 143 at 161 per Lord Westbury LC.
7   *Towns v Wentworth* (1858) 11 Moo PCC 526 at 543 per Lord Kingsdown (followed in *Sweeting v Prideaux* (1876) 2 ChD 413 at 416); *Re Redfern, Redfern v Bryning* (1877) 6 ChD 133; *Mellor v Daintree* (1886) 33 ChD 198 at 206; *Re Smith, Veasey v Smith* [1948] Ch 49, [1947] 2 All ER 708; *Re Segelman* [1996] Ch 171 at 193–194, [1995] 3 All ER 676 at 693.
8   *Watkins v Frederick* (1865) 11 HL Cas 358 at 374. See eg *Saunders v Lowe* (1775) 2 Wm Bl 1014 (where there was a gift to trustees during the lives of four daughters and the survivor, on trust for the survivor and the child or children of such daughters who should first die); *Re Morton, M'Auley v Harvey* (1919) 53 ILT 105.
9   *Re Ragdale, Public Trustee v Tuffill* [1934] Ch 352; *Re Geering, Gulliver v Geering* [1964] Ch 136 at 147, [1962] 3 All ER 1043 at 1049 per Cross J. As to the presumption against intestacy see PARAS 255–257.
10 *Monypenny v Dering* (1852) 2 De GM & G 145 at 174; *Re Rising, Rising v Rising* [1904] 1 Ch 533; *Re Mortimer, Gray v Gray* [1905] 2 Ch 502, CA.

467. When a gift is implied. Gifts may be given by implication to persons not mentioned in the will[1], to persons so mentioned but not as objects of the testator's bounty[2] and, by the extension of the words of the express gift to cover interests which those words, taken alone, would not create, to persons mentioned as objects of the testator's bounty[3].

Gifts are not implied where the only question is the manner in which the words are to be read, and no interest is inferred which the words of the gift taken in some sense or other would not create[4]; nor are gifts implied where words are altered or supplied as being erroneously written or omitted, so long as the quantum of interest conferred on the donees under the will is unchanged[5]. An interest cannot be raised by implication in a gift of another person's property under the doctrine of election[6], nor, in general, by a mere erroneous recital of a right which the testator considers to belong to the person claiming the implied estate[7].

1   See the cases cited in PARA 468 notes 3–5.

2   See PARA 468. As to the effect of recitals that a certain person is entitled to a certain interest either as constituting a gift to that person of that interest or otherwise see PARA 252.

3   See PARA 471.

4   *Tunaley v Roch* (1857) 3 Drew 720 at 725; *Crumpe v Crumpe* [1900] AC 127 at 132–133, HL, per Lord Ashbourne. See also *Ramsden v Hassard* (1791) 3 Bro CC 236; *Acheson v Fair* (1843) 3 Dr & War 512 at 527; *Greenwood v Greenwood* (1877) 5 ChD 954, CA.

5   As to the alteration of words see PARAS 253–254. As to examples where whole limitations were inserted see *Mellor v Daintree* (1886) 33 ChD 198; *Phillips v Rail* (1906) 54 WR 517.

6   *Dashwood v Peyton* (1811) 18 Ves 27 at 48. As to the doctrine of election see EQUITABLE JURISDICTION vol 47 (2014) PARA 161 et seq.

7   *Dashwood v Peyton* (1811) 18 Ves 27 at 41, 48 (discussing *Tilly v Tilly* (1743) (unreported), cited in *Dashwood v Peyton* at 43). As to recitals showing an intended gift see PARA 252.

468. Examples of implied gifts.

A life estate has been held to be impliedly conferred on a person where the will contains a gift after the death of that person, and the court has from the context of the will inferred an intention on the testator's part that that person should enjoy the property in the meantime[1]. In general, however, a gift after the death of any person does not by implication confer on him any interest[2]. From a declared intention to provide for posthumous children, it may in some instances be inferred that the testator intended to provide for children born in his lifetime after the date of his will[3], but this is not an inference to be drawn in all cases[4]. Words of exclusion, for example a direction that certain of a specified class of persons are not to take any benefit, may imply a gift to the other members of the class[5]. Similarly, a declaration excluding some of those who would be entitled on an intestacy may imply a gift to those not so excluded[6]. Where the testatrix provided only for her husband's death before or within one month after her decease, an absolute gift to him in the event of his surviving that period was implied[7]. In some cases, where the omission is clear, a power of appointment[8] or trust in default of appointment[9] has been implied.

1   *Roe d Bendall v Summerset* (1770) 2 Wm Bl 692; *Bird v Hunsdon* (1818) 3 Swan 342; *Townley v Bolton* (1832) 1 My & K 148; *Re Smith's Trusts* (1865) LR 1 Eq 79; *Re Blake's Trust* (1867) LR 3 Eq 799. See also *Blackwell v Bull* (1836) 1 Keen 176; *Cockshott v Cockshott* (1846) 2 Coll 432; *Allin v Crawshay* (1851) 9 Hare 382. All these cases rest on the context of the instruments in question (see *Barnet v Barnet* (1861) 29 Beav 239 at 244) and are regarded as special in character (see *Ralph v Carrick* (1877) 5 ChD 984 at 995 (affd on this point (1879) 11 ChD 873, CA); *Re Stanley's Settlement, Maddocks v Andrews* [1916] 2 Ch 50).

2   *Dyer v Dyer* (1816) 1 Mer 414; *Re Drakeley's Estate* (1854) 19 Beav 395; *Swan v Holmes* (1854) 19 Beav 471; *Cranley v Dixon* (1857) 23 Beav 512; *Barnet v Barnet* (1861) 29 Beav 239; *Isaacson v Van Goor* (1872) 42 LJ Ch 193; *Round v Pickett* (1878) 47 LJ Ch 631; *Ralph v Carrick* (1879) 11 ChD 873, CA.

3   *White v Barber* (1771) 5 Burr 2703; *Re Lindsay* (1852) 5 Ir Jur 97; *Goodfellow v Goodfellow* (1854) 18 Beav 356 (where the effect of a subsequent codicil was not relied on).

4   *Doe d Blakiston v Haslewood* (1851) 10 CB 544 (where *White v Barber* (1771) 5 Burr 2703 was emphatically dissented from). However, see also *Re Lindsay* (1852) 5 Ir Jur 97.

5   As to such an implication see PARA 257 note 8. In the case of next of kin, it was not sufficient to exclude them from any benefits under the will; as they claimed outside the will, they had to be excluded from any benefit in the testator's estate: *Re Holmes, Holmes v Holmes* (1890) 62 LT 383.

6   *Lett v Randall* (1855) 3 Sm & G 83; *Bund v Green* (1879) 12 ChD 819; *Re Wynn, Landolt v Wynn* [1983] 3 All ER 310, [1984] 1 WLR 237 (doubting *Johnson v Johnson* (1841) 4 Beav 318). See also *Re Holmes, Holmes v Holmes* (1890) 62 LT 383 (where the direction excluded named next of kin from taking under the will of the testator, not from taking on his intestacy).

7   *Re Smith, Veasey v Smith* [1948] Ch 49, [1947] 2 All ER 708.

8   *Re Cory, Cory v Morel* [1955] 2 All ER 630, [1955] 1 WLR 725; *Re Riley's Will Trusts, Riley v Riley* [1962] 1 All ER 513, [1962] 1 WLR 344.

9   *Re Riley's Will Trusts, Riley v Riley* [1962] 1 All ER 513, [1962] 1 WLR 344. See also *Re Van Den Bok Will Trusts* (1960) unreported, but referred to in *Re Riley's Will Trusts, Riley v Riley*. See also TRUSTS AND POWERS vol 98 (2013) PARA 29.

469. Gift over on death to testator's successor on intestacy.

Before 1 January 1926, where a will contained a devise of real estate after the death of a named person A to the heir-at-law of the testator, but there was no express disposition of the property during A's life, a gift to A for his life was implied. In view of the future gift to the heir-at-law it was not to be supposed that he was also to take an immediate estate by descent[1]. Similarly, a bequest of personal estate after the death of a named person A to the person or persons at the date of the will[2] presumptively entitled in the event of the testator's intestacy gave to A a life interest, where the will contained no express disposition of the property during A's life[3]. It appears that, if the named person was one of the persons presumptively entitled on an intestacy, and the gift was to the rest of such persons, the same implication arose[4].

The rule did not apply where the donee under the gift (in the case of realty) was a stranger and not the heir[5], or was only one of several co-heirs[6], or (in the case of personalty) was a stranger; nor did it apply where the gift was to some only of the persons presumptively entitled on intestacy[7]; nor where the donee (although the sole heir or next of kin, as the case might be) had someone else taking with him[8].

There was no implied gift under this rule of construction where the person in whose favour the implication would arise took an express beneficial interest in the property or any part of it[9]; nor where there was an immediate residuary clause[10]. Apparently, the implication did not arise where the property was subject to a covenant against alienation which was not infringed as the will stood, but which would be infringed if the doctrine were applied[11].

As descent to the heir has been abolished, the rule in its original form cannot apply to real estate. Real estate and personal estate undisposed of by will become subject to a power of sale[12], and the net residue after payment of debts and expenses goes to the persons entitled under the modern rules as to succession on intestacy[13]. Where property, real or personal, is given after the death of A to the persons actually or presumptively entitled under the modern rules, the reasoning of the old rule would seem still to apply, and a life interest to be implied in favour of A.

1   *Gardner v Sheldon* (1671) Vaugh 259 at 263 per Vaughan CJ. See also *Anon* (1498) YB 13 Hen 7, fo 17, pl 22; *Horton v Horton* (1604) Cro Jac 74 at 75; *City of London v Garway* (1706) 2 Vern 571 per Wright, Lord Keeper; *Dashwood v Peyton* (1811) 18 Ves 27 at 40, 48 per Lord Eldon LC; *Denn d Franklin v Trout* (1812) 15 East 394; *Doe d Driver v Bowling* (1822) 5 B & Ald 722 at 727; Tudor, LC Real Prop (4th Edn) 388.
2   *Stevens v Hale* (1862) 2 Drew & Sm 22 at 28.
3   *Blackwell v Bull* (1836) 1 Keen 176 at 182; *Stevens v Hale* (1862) 2 Drew & Sm 22 at 27.
4   *Cock v Cock* (1873) 21 WR 807 (gift to children after death of mother).
5   *Rayman v Gold* (1591) Moore KB 635 (adversely commented on in *Roe d Bendall v Summerset* (1770) 2 Wm Bl 692, as reported 5 Burr 2608); *Gardner v Sheldon* (1671) Vaugh 259 (overruling Bro Abr, Devise, pl 48); *Fawlkner v Fawlkner* (1681) 1 Vern 21 at 22; *City of London v Garway* (1706) 2 Vern 571; *Aspinall v Petvin* (1824) 1 Sim & St 544; *R v Ringstead Inhabitants* (1829) 9 B & C 218 at 224–225; *Cranley v Dixon* (1857) 23 Beav 512 at 516.
6   *Barnet v Barnet* (1861) 29 Beav 239; *Re Willatts, Willatts v Artley* [1905] 1 Ch 378 (revsd on another point [1905] 2 Ch 135, CA).
7   *Re Springfield, Chamberlin v Springfield* [1894] 3 Ch 603. See also *Stevens v Hale* (1862) 2 Drew & Sm 22 at 28 (contingent class); *Woodhouse v Spurgeon* (1883) 49 LT 97; *Greene v Flood* (1885) 15 LR Ir 450. In *Cockshott v Cockshott* (1846) 2 Coll 432, the point was not raised.
8   *Ralph v Carrick* (1879) 11 ChD 873, CA, disapproving *Humphreys v Humphreys* (1867) LR 4 Eq 475 (where the gift was to a contingent class living at the death of the wife). The title of the heir was not necessarily excluded by the fact that he was expressly given a partial interest: *Camfield v Gilbert* (1803) 3 East 516. In *Willis v Lucas* (1718) 1 P Wms 472, Parker LC strongly inclined to the contrary view.
9   *Higham v Baker* (1583) Cro Eliz 15 (where the wife took express interests: (1) beneficially in part of the first property; and (2) for payment of debts in the second property, in which alone she was

held entitled to an interest by implication); *Boon v Cornforth* (1751) 2 Ves Sen 277; *Aspinall v Petvin* (1824) 1 Sim & St 544 (express interest in a moiety).
10 *Stevens v Hale* (1862) 2 Drew & Sm 22 at 28.
11 *Horton v Horton* (1604) Cro Jac 74; *Dyer v Dyer* (1816) 1 Mer 414.
12 See the Administration of Estates Act 1925 s 33 (amended by the Trusts of Land and Appointment of Trustees Act 1996 s 5, Sch 2 para 5(1)–(5); and the Trustee Act 2000 s 40(1), Sch 2 Pt II para 27); and PARAS 1135–1138.
13 As to these rules see PARA 485 et seq.

470. Effect on income entitlement of gift over after death of survivor of life tenants. Where there is a gift equally between A, B and C for their respective lives and on the death of the survivor of them[1] the whole property is given over, the court has implied an intention on the part of the testator that the survivor or survivors of A, B and C must after the death of one or more of them[2] be entitled to all the income right up to the period of distribution, subject to any contrary intention shown by the context[3]. The rule is founded either on the ground that the gift over modifies the prior words, showing that a joint tenancy was intended, or on the ground of implication in order to carry the testator's evident intention into effect[4]. The rule has been applied notwithstanding the presence of a clause substituting issue for their deceased parents[5]. There is no corresponding implication in the case of a gift, on the death of a life tenant, to two persons, with a gift over if neither of them is then living[6].

1 See *Tuckerman v Jefferies* (1706) 11 Mod Rep 108; *Armstrong v Eldridge* (1791) 3 Bro CC 215; *Doe d Borwell v Abey* (1813) 1 M & S 428; *Pearce v Edmeades* (1838) 3 Y & C Ex 246; *Smyth v Smyth* (1855) 3 WR 189; *Begley v Cook* (1856) 3 Drew 662 at 666; *Cranswick v Pearson, Pearson v Cranswick* (1862) 31 Beav 624; *Re Richerson, Scales v Heyhoe (No 2)* [1893] 3 Ch 146 at 150; *Re Buller, Buller v Giberne* (1896) 74 LT 406 at 408; *Re Telfair, Garrioch v Barclay* (1902) 86 LT 496; *Jennings v Hanna* [1904] 1 IR 540; *Re Hobson, Barwick v Holt* [1912] 1 Ch 626 at 631; *Re Stanley's Settlement, Maddocks v Andrews* [1916] 2 Ch 50. As to gifts 'at their death' see further *Malcolm v Martin* (1790) 3 Bro CC 50; *Townley v Bolton* (1832) 1 My & K 148; *Alt v Gregory* (1856) 8 De GM & G 221. Cf *Moffatt v Burnie* (1853) 18 Beav 211. As to interests in annuities limited for the lives of two or more persons see PERSONAL AND OCCUPATIONAL PENSIONS vol 80 (2013) PARA 699. As to the distributive construction where different properties are given and the gift over is on the death of all see PARA 476; and as to gifts of shares in the same property see especially *Round v Pickett* (1878) 47 LJ Ch 631.
2 *Re Ragdale, Public Trustee v Tuffill* [1934] Ch 352; *Re Pringle, Baker v Matheson* [1946] Ch 124, [1946] 1 All ER 88; *Re Foster* [1946] Ch 135, [1946] 1 All ER 333.
3 *Hawkins v Hamerton* (1848) 16 Sim 410 (express gift in one contingency to survivors and their issue); *Doe d Patrick v Royle* (1849) 13 QB 100 (after the death of either of them); *Re Hobson, Barwick v Holt* [1912] 1 Ch 626 (provision for some of ultimate takers during lives of first takers).
4 See the cases cited in note 1.
5 *Re Tate, Williamson v Gilpin* [1914] 2 Ch 182; followed in *Re Hey's Settlement Trusts, Hey v Nickell-Lean* [1945] Ch 294, [1945] 1 All ER 618.
6 *Baxter v Losh* (1851) 14 Beav 612.

471. Implication of absolute interests from gifts over. Implication of an absolute interest often arises from a gift over where after a prior gift[1] the property given is directed to go over in a particular event and it is taken to have been intended that it was not to go over in any other event[2]. Thus where there is a gift to the donee until he attains a certain age, followed by a gift over to other persons on his failure to attain that age, the donee takes by implication absolutely if he attains the age[3]. Such a gift is not implied where the gift over and the period for which the property is held in suspense do not correspond[4]. A gift to trustees for a person until he attains a certain age, without any gift over, does not always give that person the absolute interest[5], but it may do so if there are other indications that such is the intention[6] and that the trust is only to point out the mode of taking[7].

1 There is no such implication where there is no prior gift: *James v Shannon* (1868) IR 2 Eq 118.

2 See *Re Harrison's Estate* (1870) 5 Ch App 408 at 411 per Giffard LJ; *Re Thomson's Trusts* (1870)
   LR 11 Eq 146; *Re Lane's Estate, Meagher v Governors and Guardians of the National Gallery of
   Ireland and Heaven* [1946] 1 All ER 735 (where there was a gift of a life interest which was to go
   over if the donee did not remarry, and this was held to give an absolute interest on remarriage).
   See also *Spence v Handford* (1858) 4 Jur NS 987 (where a gift of a life interest was construed as
   a gift of an absolute interest subject to an executory gift over in certain events).
3 *Tomkins v Tomkins* (1743) cited in 1 Burr at 234; *Wainewright v Wainewright* (1797) 3 Ves 558;
   Goodright d Hoskins v Hoskins (1808) 9 East 306; *Doe d Wright v Cundall* (1808) 9 East 400;
   Gardiner v Stevens (1860) 7 Jur NS 307; *Cropton v Davies* (1869) LR 4 CP 159. See also *Paylor
   v Pegg* (1857) 24 Beav 105 (where the donee took as heir-at-law).
4 *Savage v Tyers* (1872) 7 Ch App 356 at 364 (first gift a life estate). See also *Fitzhenry v Bonner*
   (1853) 2 Drew 36.
5 *Re Hedley's Trusts* (1877) 25 WR 529; *Re Arnould, Arnould v Lloyd* [1955] 2 All ER 316, [1955]
   1 WLR 539. Neither of these cases was followed in *McClymont v Hooper* (1973) 47 ALJR 222,
   Aust HC. See also *Re Vickers* [1912] VLR 385.
6 Such a gift was held to give the absolute interest in *Newland v Shephard* (1723) 2 P Wms 194
   (where no gift over occurred); disapproved in *Fonnereau v Fonnereau* (1745) 3 Atk 315 at 317 per
   Lord Hardwicke LC and in *Peat v Powell* (1760) Amb 387 (where on majority attained the trust
   was to cease). See, however, Jarman on Wills (8th Edn) 682–683; *Cropton v Davies* (1869) LR 4
   CP 159 at 167; *Wilks v Williams* (1861) 2 John & H 125 at 128 per Wood V-C.
7 *Hale v Beck* (1764) 2 Eden 229; *Atkinson v Paice* (1781) 1 Bro CC 91; *McClymont v Hooper*
   (1973) 47 ALJR 222, Aust HC (not following *Re Hedley's Trusts* (1877) 25 WR 529; *Re Arnould,
   Arnould v Lloyd* [1955] 2 All ER 316, [1955] 1 WLR 539).

472. Bequest over on failure of children. Where there is a bequest to a parent,
either indefinitely or for life, followed by a bequest over if he dies without having
or leaving children, or by a like bequest over referring to issue, then, on the
parent's death leaving children, the court does not imply any gift to those children[1]
unless there are other matters in the will raising an inference in their favour[2].

1 *Scalé v Rawlins* [1892] AC 342, HL (affg *Re Rawlins' Trusts* (1890) 45 ChD 299 at 304, 306, 308,
   CA; and approving *Kinsella v Caffrey* (1860) 11 I Ch R 154 at 160). See also *Cooper v Pitcher*
   (1846) 16 LJ Ch 24; *Ranelagh v Ranelagh* (1849) 12 Beav 200; *Lee v Busk* (1852) 2 De GM &
   G 810; *Sparks v Restal* (1857) 24 Beav 218; *Neighbour v Thurlow* (1860) 28 Beav 33; *Re
   Hayton's Trusts* (1864) 4 New Rep 55; *Dowling v Dowling* (1866) 1 Ch App 612; *Seymour v
   Kilbee* (1879) 3 LR Ir 33; *Champ v Champ* (1892) 30 LR Ir 72 (where the rule was applied to a
   deed). The contrary decision in *Ex p Rogers* (1816) 2 Madd 449 has been doubted (see *Lee v Busk*
   (1852) 2 De GM & G 810; *Neighbour v Thurlow* (1860) 28 Beav 33; *Webster v Parr* (1858) 26
   Beav 236), but can, perhaps, be explained by the special circumstances.
2 *Kinsella v Caffrey* (1860) 11 I Ch R 154; *Wetherell v Wetherell* (1862) 4 Giff 51 (on appeal (1863)
   1 De GJ & Sm 134); *M'Clean v Simpson* (1887) 19 LR Ir 528.

473. Estate tail by implication. In a will coming into operation before 1 January
1926, an estate tail was conferred by a devise of real estate capable of being
entailed[1] to a person and his heirs[2], followed by a devise over on his death without
heirs of the body or on a general failure of his issue where the statutory
presumption as to gifts on failure of issue is inapplicable or excluded by the
context[3]. The estate tail in such a case was, however, conferred as a question of
construction, 'heirs' being equivalent to heirs of the body, and the same effect
would, it seems, be given to such a gift in a will coming into operation between
1 January 1926 and 31 December 1996 inclusive[4].

Similarly, in a will coming into operation before 1 January 1926, an estate tail
was conferred where there was a devise to a person without words of limitation
or to him for life followed by a devise over on his death without heirs of his body
or on failure of issue[5]. This was, however, an implication designed to carry out the
testator's intention, and did not apply to deeds[6]. There was a presumption that the
issue were intended to be benefited and the only way to give effect to that
intention was to treat the first taker's interest as an estate tail[7]. A devise over on
the death of a prior donee without having or leaving a son might in the same way

create an estate tail by implication[8], and, where between the interest of the prior donee and the devise over there was a devise to the eldest son of the prior donee, the effect might be to give an estate tail to the prior donee in remainder on the estate of his eldest son[9].

There was in general no enlargement of the estate of a person by a gift over on failure of his issue where the later gift merely referred to issue taking under previous gifts, either by purchase or by descent of an estate tail; nor in general where the failure of issue was limited to a particular period[10].

In all such cases between 1 January 1926 and 31 December 1996 inclusive, where before 1 January 1926 an estate tail would have been implied, the gifts take effect as gifts of the fee simple[11].

Entailed interests cannot be created by instruments coming into operation on or after 1 January 1997; and any entailed interest purportedly granted on or after that date will take effect as an absolute interest[12].

1 Where the property was not capable of being entailed, as in the case of copyholds in a manor in which there was no custom to entail, the effect was in general a fee simple conditional: *Doe d Simpson v Simpson* (1838) 4 Bing NC 333; affd sub nom *Doe d Blesard v Simpson* (1842) 3 Man & G 929, Ex Ch.

2 *Soulle v Gerrard* (1596) Cro Eliz 525; *Tuttesham v Roberts* (1603) Cro Jac 22; *Brown v Jervas* (1611) Cro Jac 290; *Webb v Hearing* (1617) Cro Jac 415; *Chadock v Cowley* (1624) Cro Jac 695; *Holmes v Willett* (1681) Freem KB 483, sub nom *Holmes v Meynel* (1681) T Raym 452; *Brice v Smith* (1737) Willes 1; *Roe v Scott and Smart* (1787), cited in 1 Fearne's Contingent Remainders (10th Edn) 473n; *Denn d Geering v Shenton* (1776) 1 Cowp 410; *Doe d Ellis v Ellis* (1808) 9 East 382; *Tenny d Agar v Agar* (1810) 12 East 253; *Dansey v Griffiths* (1815) 4 M & S 61; *Doe d Jones v Owens* (1830) 1 B & Ad 318.

3 A gift over may be construed as a gift over on general failure of issue only where the general statutory rule that failure of issue is to be construed as meaning failure in the lifetime of the prior donee is inapplicable or excluded by the context: see PARA 454 et seq.

4 In this respect the same construction is applied to limitations in deeds: *Anon* (1341) 35 Lib Ass, pl 14; *Anon* (1441) YB 19 Hen 6, fo 73, pl 2. See also *Fisher v Wigg* (1701) 1 P Wms 14 at 15; *Bamfield v Popham* (1703) 1 P Wms 54 at 57n; *Morgan v Morgan* (1870) LR 10 Eq 99 (followed in *Arthur v Walker* [1897] 1 IR 68, where *Olivant v Wright* (1878) 9 ChD 646 is explained); and REAL PROPERTY AND REGISTRATION vol 87 (2012) PARA 115. Consequently, these limitations were not affected by the Law of Property Act 1925 s 130(2) (repealed by the Trusts of Land and Appointment of Trustees Act 1996 s 25(2), Sch 4, with effect from 1 January 1997): see PARA 387. An entailed interest cannot be created by an instrument coming into operation on or after 1 January 1997: see the text and note 12.

5 *Sonday's Case* (1611) 9 Co Rep 127b; *Langley v Baldwin* (1707) 1 Eq Cas Abr 185 pl 29; *A-G v Sutton* (1721) 3 Bro Parl Cas 75, 1 P Wms 754, HL; *Allanson v Clitherow* (1747) 1 Ves Sen 24; *Stanley v Lennard* (1758) 1 Eden 87; *Daintry v Daintry* (1795) 6 Term Rep 307; *Wight v Leigh* (1809) 15 Ves 564; *Parr v Swindels* (1828) 4 Russ 283; *Briscoe v Briscoe* (1830) Hayes 34 (quasi-entail in lease for lives); *Machell v Weeding* (1836) 8 Sim 4; *Simmons v Simmons* (1836) 8 Sim 22; *Franks v Price* (1840) 3 Beav 182; *Stanhouse v Gaskell* (1852) 17 Jur 157; *Key v Key* (1853) 4 De GM & G 73; *Butt v Thomas* (1855) 11 Exch 235; *Eastwood v Avison* (1869) LR 4 Exch 141 (where a contrary intention was shown and the prior donee took for life only); *Re Waugh, Waugh v Cripps* [1903] 1 Ch 744 (on death 'without an heir'). As to limiting intermediate estates to certain of the issue see *Key v Key* (1853) 4 De GM & G 73 at 81–82; *Parker v Tootal* (1865) 11 HL Cas 143 at 169–170; *Neville v Thacker* (1888) 23 LR Ir 344 at 364.

6 *Seagood v Hone* (1634) Cro Car 366 at 367; Lewis's Law of Perpetuity 180–181; 2 Preston's Estates 484; *Olivant v Wright* (1878) 9 ChD 646 at 650; *Arthur v Walker* [1897] 1 IR 68 at 76.

7 See the grounds of the rule stated in *Foster v Hayes* (1855) 4 E & B 717 at 734. It was said to be made for the purpose of giving effect to the testator's general intention: *Mathews v Gardiner* (1853) 17 Beav 254 at 257 per Romilly MR. As to estates tail which were formerly implied see *Parker v Tootal* (1865) 11 HL Cas 143.

8 *Milliner v Robinson* (1600) Moore KB 682 (sub nom *Bifield's Case* cited in 1 Vent at 231). See also *Wyld v Lewis* (1738) 1 Atk 432; *Raggett v Beaty* (1828) 5 Bing 243; *Bacon v Cosby* (1851) 4 De G & Sm 261; *Re Bird and Barnard's Contract* (1888) 59 LT 166.

9 *Bell v Bell* (1864) 15 I Ch R 517; *Andrew v Andrew* (1875) 1 ChD 410, CA.

10 *Lethieullier v Tracy* (1754) 3 Atk 784; *Bradshaw v Skilbeck* (1835) 2 Bing NC 182; *Jenkins v Hughes* (1860) 8 HL Cas 571 at 593. See also *Bamfield v Popham* (1703) 1 P Wms 54; *Robinson v Hunt* (1841) 4 Beav 450; *Baker v Tucker* (1850) 3 HL Cas 106; *Hamilton v West* (1846) 10 I Eq R 75; *Bridger v Ramsey* (1853) 10 Hare 320; *Foster v Hayes* (1855) 4 E & B 717 at 734, Ex Ch; *Towns v Wentworth* (1858) 11 Moo PCC 526; *Peyton v Lambert* (1858) 8 ICLR 485 at 504; *Sanders v Ashford* (1860) 28 Beav 609; *Smyth v Power* (1876) IR 10 Eq 192 at 199. Cf *Doe d Harris v Taylor* (1847) 10 QB 718 (dissenting from *Barnacle v Nightingale* (1845) 14 Sim 456, on the same will; but not followed in *Re Arnold's Estate* (1863) 33 Beav 163).

11 See the Law of Property Act 1925 s 130(2) (repealed by the Trusts of Land and Appointment of Trustees Act 1996 s 25(2), Sch 4, with effect from 1 January 1997); and PARA 387.

12 See the Trusts of Land and Appointment of Trustees Act 1996 s 2(6), Sch 1 para 5; PARA 387; and REAL PROPERTY AND REGISTRATION vol 87 (2012) PARA 114.

474. Implication of cross-remainders. Before 1 January 1926 cross-remainders between a number of donees[1] might be implied where they or they and their issue in tail took shares in the property and the testator intended that the whole estate should go over together and only on failure of all the donees taking under the previous gifts. This intention could be carried out only by not letting any part of the estate pass as on an intestacy in the meantime and, therefore, by implying the cross-remainders[2]. That the testator had himself provided for the mode in which the donees took after each other, such as by expressly giving them cross-remainders in particular events, was a circumstance to be weighed as showing an intention negativing implied remainders[3], but was not decisive[4].

Thus a gift to a number of persons as tenants in common in tail or to a number of persons for life with remainder as to each share to their respective issue in tail, with a gift over on failure of the issue generally of all the group of persons, might give rise to implied cross-remainders in tail[5], although a gift over on failure of the issue of each of them had no such effect but took effect as to each share on failure of the issue concerned[6]. The same inference in favour of cross-limitations was made where the property was subject as a whole to a gift over on failure of issue confined to the life of the ancestor[7].

As cross-remainders in tail would not before 1 January 1926 have been implied in a deed[8], they cannot be implied in a will where the testator has died after 31 December 1925[9]. However, before 1 January 1997[10] they could be created by express limitation, and, whether arising by implication under the former law or by express limitation, they would, if there is a tenancy in common, now subsist under a trust of land with a power of sale[11] or under an express trust for sale[12].

1 The suggestion in some old cases (collected in Tudor, LC Real Prop (4th Edn) 410–411) that cross-remainders might be implied between two, but not so readily between three or more, is no longer tenable: see the cases cited in notes 2–5. As to the different rule with respect to implication of cross-remainders in the case of settlements see SETTLEMENTS vol 91 (2012) PARA 619.

2 *Doe d Gorges v Webb* (1808) 1 Taunt 234; *Atkinson v Holtby* (1863) 10 HL Cas 313; *Powell v Howells* (1868) LR 3 QB 654; *Hannaford v Hannaford* (1871) LR 7 QB 116; *Maden v Taylor* (1876) 45 LJ Ch 569 at 573 per Jessel MR; *Van Grutten v Foxwell, Foxwell v Van Grutten* [1897] AC 658 at 680, HL, per Lord Macnaghten; *Re Parker, Stephenson v Parker* [1901] 1 Ch 408. See also *Ashley v Ashley* (1833) 6 Sim 358; *Taaffe v Conmee* (1862) 10 HL Cas 64. The fact that the gift over is expressed to be 'in remainder' does not defeat the implication (*Doe d Burden v Burville* (1801) 2 East 47n), although it was decided otherwise where the words were 'in reversion' (*Pery v White* (1778) 2 Cowp 777), but the decision appears to have turned mainly on the supposition that 'respectively' must be inserted in the previous limitations. Cf *Doe d Patrick v Royle* (1849) 13 QB 100 at 114.

3 *Clache's Case* (1572) 3 Dyer 330b; *Rabbeth v Squire (No 2)* (1854) 19 Beav 77 (on appeal (1859) 4 De G & J 406).

4 *Atkinson v Barton* (1861) 3 De GF & J 339 at 349 per Turner LJ; revsd sub nom *Atkinson v Holtby* (1863) 10 HL Cas 313 (but without relying on the application of *Clache's Case* (1572) 3 Dyer 330b). See also *Vanderplank v King* (1843) 3 Hare 1 at 20 per Wigram V-C; *Re Clark's Trusts* (1863) 32 LJ Ch 525 at 528 per Wood V-C.

5   *Anon* (1572) 3 Dyer 303b, pl 49; *Anon* (1590) 4 Leon 14, pl 51; *Holmes v Willett* (1681) Freem KB 483, sub nom *Holmes v Meynel* (1681) T Raym 452; *Wright v Lord Cadogan* (1764) 2 Eden 239 at 250; *Wright v Holford* (1774) 1 Cowp 31; *Phipard v Mansfield* (1778) 1 Doug KB 53n; *Atherton v Pye* (1792) 4 Term Rep 710; *Burnaby v Griffin* (1796) 3 Ves 266 at 274; *Watson v Foxon* (1801) 2 East 36; *Green v Stephens* (1810) 17 Ves 64; *Skey v Barnes* (1816) 3 Mer 335 at 343 per Grant MR; *Doe d Southouse v Jenkins* (1829) 5 Bing 469; *Livesey v Harding* (1830) 1 Russ & M 636; *Brooke v Turner* (1836) 2 Bing NC 422; *Taaffe v Conmee* (1862) 10 HL Cas 64; *Powell v Howells* (1868) LR 3 QB 654 at 655. See also the cases cited in note 2.

6   *Comber v Hill* (1734) 2 Stra 699; *Williams v Browne* (1734) 2 Stra 996; *Davenport v Oldis* (1738) 1 Atk 579 (in which cases a gift over in default of 'such' issue was considered to mean such issue respectively; but these cases are criticised in *Watson v Foxon* (1801) 2 East 36 and might now be decided otherwise); *Re Tharp's Estate* (1863) 1 De GJ & Sm 453; *Dutton v Crowdy* (1863) 33 Beav 272. See also *Huntley's Case* (1574) 3 Dyer 326a.

7   *Maden v Taylor* (1876) 45 LJ Ch 569. It does not appear that the Wills Act 1837 s 29 affects gifts of real estate on failure of issue in cases where, apart from s 29, cross-remainders would be implied, inasmuch as in all such cases there is a preceding gift in tail to the issue or the ancestor: see PARA 456.

8   *Edwards v Alliston* (1827) 4 Russ 78; *Doe d Clift v Birkhead* (1849) 4 Exch 110 at 124.

9   As to estates tail after 31 December 1925 see PARA 387.

10 Entailed interests cannot be created by instruments coming into operation on or after 1 January 1997: see the Trusts of Land and Appointment of Trustees Act 1996 s 2(6), Sch 1 para 5; PARA 387; and REAL PROPERTY AND REGISTRATION vol 87 (2012) PARA 114.

11 Ie in accordance with the Law of Property Act 1925 s 34(3) (amended by the Trusts of Land and Appointment of Trustees Act 1996 s 5, Sch 2 para 3(1), (3), in relation to dispositions to persons in undivided shares whenever made) (see REAL PROPERTY AND REGISTRATION vol 87 (2012) PARA 219) and the Trusts of Land and Appointment of Trustees Act 1996 s 6(1) (see SETTLEMENTS vol 91 (2012) PARA 804; TRUSTS AND POWERS vol 98 (2013) PARA 476).

12 As to tenancies in common generally see REAL PROPERTY AND REGISTRATION vol 87 (2012) PARA 215 et seq. Entailed interests could between 1 January 1926 and 31 December 1996 inclusive be created in personal property (see PARA 387), but cannot be created by instruments coming into operation on or after 1 January 1997 (see note 10). Since 1 January 1997 all trusts for sale formerly imposed by statute have become trusts of land (without a duty to sell) and land formerly held on such statutorily imposed trusts for sale is now held in trust for the persons interested in the land, so that the owner of each undivided share now has an interest in land: see the Trusts of Land and Appointment of Trustees Act 1996 ss 1, 5, Sch 2 paras 2–5, 7 (amending the Law of Property Act 1925 ss 32, 34, 36 and the Administration of Estates Act 1925 s 33); and REAL PROPERTY AND REGISTRATION vol 87 (2012) PARA 105.

475. Implication of executory cross-limitations. Executory cross-limitations[1] are implied to fill up a hiatus in the limitations which seems from the context to have been contrary to the testator's intention[2], but they cannot be implied to divest an interest given by the will[3]. Thus in a gift to several persons contingently on satisfying a specified condition or description as tenants in common, with a gift over on all failing to satisfy that condition or description, cross-limitations are implied on the death of each of them failing to attain that description[4]. Depending on the context, the persons between whom the cross-limitations are implied in such a case may be the original stocks, or their respective issues taking under the will[5], or both[6].

Although the existence of other cross-limitations between different persons does not prevent the implication[7], where those express cross-limitations are in favour of the very persons to whom the implied cross-limitations would convey the property, that circumstance is of weight in determining the intention[8].

1   The rules as to implication are stated in *Re Hudson, Hudson v Hudson* (1882) 20 ChD 406 at 415 per Kay J. As to implication of gifts for life to survivors see PARA 470.

2   *Coates v Hart, Borrett v Hart* (1863) 3 De GJ & Sm 504 at 516–517; *Re Ridge's Trusts* (1872) 7 Ch App 665. However, the court declined to find an implied gift of capital in *Re Mears, Parker v Mears* [1914] 1 Ch 694. See also *Re Riall, Westminster Bank Ltd v Harrison* [1939] 3 All ER 657; *Re Hart's Will Trusts, Public Trustee v Barclays Bank Ltd* [1950] Ch 84, [1949] 2 All ER 898.

3   *Skey v Barnes* (1816) 3 Mer 335 at 343 per Grant MR; *Bromhead v Hunt* (1821) 2 Jac & W 459; *Baxter v Losh* (1851) 14 Beav 612; *Beaver v Nowell* (1858) 25 Beav 551; *Re Clark's Trusts* (1863) 32 LJ Ch 525.

4   Eg contingently on attaining 21 (*Scott v Bargeman* (1722) 2 P Wms 68 (gift over on death before legacies payable); *Mackell v Winter* (1797) 3 Ves 236, 536), or 21 or marriage (*Re Clark's Trusts* (1863) 32 LJ Ch 525; followed in *Re Bickerton's Settlement, Shaw v Bickerton* [1942] Ch 84, [1942] 1 All ER 217), or in the event of surviving a named person (*Graves v Waters* (1847) 10 I Eq R 234). In *Skey v Barnes* (1816) 3 Mer 335, *Scott v Bargeman* above was criticised on another ground by Grant MR, who, however, said that he considered the decision correct. See also *Vize v Stoney* (1841) 1 Dr & War 337 at 348.

5   *Atkinson v Holtby* (1863) 10 HL Cas 313 (revsg *Atkinson v Barton* (1861) 3 De GF & J 339).

6   *Roe d Wren v Clayton* (1805) 6 East 628. See also *Burnaby v Griffin* (1796) 3 Ves 266; *Horne v Barton* (1815) 19 Ves 398 (where an express direction for cross-remainders was so construed).

7   *Re Clark's Trusts* (1863) 32 LJ Ch 525.

8   *Rabbeth v Squire* (1859) 4 De G & J 406 at 413–414. Cf *Sutton v Sutton* (1892) 30 LR Ir 251, Ir CA.

476. Distributive construction. Cases where particular property is given to one person for life and after his death that property with other property not expressly disposed of during his life is given to other persons, and the question is what happens to that other property during the first person's life, are to be distinguished from cases of implication, where the question is rather whether the words alluding to the time of death are to be referred distributively[1] and to be confined to the property given to the life tenant, in which event the ultimate donees will take an immediate estate in the remainder of the property[2]. Instead of implying cross-remainders, a similar construction may be adopted where a fund is given to each of several donees for life and there is a general gift over of the whole fund on the deaths of all the donees so as to carry each portion of the fund to the remainderman on the death of the life tenant of that portion[3]. If the words cannot be read distributively, the persons entitled as on intestacy cannot be excluded[4].

1   See *Rhodes v Rhodes* (1882) 7 App Cas 192, PC (where it was held that words are to be construed according to their plain, ordinary meaning unless the context shows them to have been used in a different sense or unless the rule, if acted on, would lead to some manifest absurdity or incongruity). The testator must be presumed not to have intended an absurdity; nevertheless, if he is shown by the context or by the whole will to have so intended, the intention, if not illegal, must be carried out.

2   *Doe d Annandale v Brazier* (1821) 5 B & Ald 64. See also *Cook v Gerrard* (1668) 1 Saund 180; *Simpson v Hornby* (1716) Gilb Ch 115 at 120, sub nom *Sympson v Hornsby* Prec Ch 439 at 452; *Lill v Lill* (1857) 23 Beav 446 (distinguished in *Jennings v Hanna* [1904] 1 IR 540); *Rhodes v Rhodes* (1882) 7 App Cas 192, PC.

3   *Re Browne's Will Trusts, Landon v Brown* [1915] 1 Ch 690. See also *Drew v Killick* (1847) 1 De G & Sm 266; *Swan v Holmes* (1854) 19 Beav 471; *Sarel v Sarel* (1856) 23 Beav 87; *Re Motherwell, Keane v Motherwell* [1910] 1 IR 249.

4   *R v Ringstead Inhabitants* (1829) 9 B & C 218 at 233; *Attwater v Attwater* (1853) 18 Beav 330 at 338. See *Davenport v Coltman* (1842) 9 M & W 481; and subsequent proceedings 12 Sim 588 (where the Court of Chancery approved the judgment of the Court of Exchequer). See also *Stevens v Pyle* (1860) 28 Beav 388; *Round v Pickett* (1878) 47 LJ Ch 631.

6. INTESTATE SUCCESSION

(1) LEGAL FRAMEWORK RELATING TO INTESTATE SUCCESSION

477. Rules of intestate succession. The rules of intestate succession[1] are laid down by statute[2], and govern the distribution of the residuary estate of intestates[3], subject to the court's overriding power in relation to family provision[4]. They apply to all property[5] of which the deceased owner[6] died intestate[7], subject to certain savings[8].

The old rules of distribution and descent still apply where the deceased died intestate before 1926[9]; where the death intestate occurred after 1925[10] intestate succession is governed by the rules enacted in the Administration of Estates Act 1925 as amended from time to time[11].

1 The term 'rules of intestate succession' is used to describe the distributive provisions or trusts established by the Administration of Estates Act 1925 Pt IV (ss 45–52) because, since the assimilation of the rules applicable to real estate and personalty, the distinction between 'distribution' and 'descent' is in the great majority of cases obsolete.

Before 1926 'distribution' was confined to the division of the personal estate of a deceased person among his next of kin. 'Descent' was used to describe the passing of real estate (which in this connection did not include leaseholds or chattels real) by inheritance to the heir: see *Bickley v Bickley* (1867) LR 4 Eq 216 at 220; and Co Litt 237a. 'A descent is a means whereby one doth derive his title to certain lands as heir to some of his ancestors': Co Litt 13b. The Inheritance Act 1833 s 1, now superseded as regards deaths after 1925 but preserved as regards the devolution of entailed interests and for certain other purposes (see PARA 538 et seq), defines 'descent' as meaning the title to inherit land by reason of consanguinity, as well where the heir is an ancestor or collateral relation as where he is a child or other issue. It is no longer possible to create entailed interests but existing entailed interests are unaffected: see the Trusts of Land and Appointment of Trustees Act 1996 s 2(6), Sch 1 para 5; and REAL PROPERTY AND REGISTRATION vol 87 (2012) PARA 114. As to the meaning of 'heir' in a modern will see PARAS 339–342.

2 Ie in the Administration of Estates Act 1925 Pt IV (which had the effect of greatly restricting the class of next of kin who could take under an intestacy), amended, as regards deaths intestate after 1952, by the Intestates' Estates Act 1952 (which further reduced the class of relatives who can take where there is a surviving spouse and no issue); and the Inheritance and Trustees' Powers Act 2014 (which reduced those who can take when the estate leaves no issue but there is a surviving spouse or civil partner); and further amended:
   (1) as regards deaths intestate after 1966, by the Family Provision Act 1966 ss 1, 9, 10(2);
   (2) as regards the illegitimate children of a person dying intestate after 1969, by the Family Law Reform Act 1969 ss 3(2), 14(3), (6), which is replaced as regards the illegitimate relations of a person dying on or after 4 July 1988 by the more comprehensive provisions of the Family Law Reform Act 1987 (see further PARA 482);
   (3) as regards deaths intestate after 1995 by the Law Reform (Succession) Act 1995 (which introduced a 28 day survivorship condition for the spouse of an intestate);
   (4) as from 5 December 2005 by the Civil Partnership Act 2004 Sch 4 (Sch 4 amends enactments relating to wills, administration of estates and family provision so that they apply to civil partnerships in the same way they apply to marriage); and
   (5) as from 1 February 2012 by the Estates of Deceased Persons (Forfeiture Rule and Law of Succession) Act 2011 (overcoming the requirement a child cannot inherit in place of his parent if that parent is still alive (see PARA 507).
The Intestates' Estates Act 1952 increased the amount of the lump sum to which the surviving spouse of a person dying intestate after 1952 was entitled; this was further increased as regards spouses dying intestate after 1966 by the Family Law Reform Act 1966. The Lord Chancellor was then given power to vary the fixed net sum (as it became called) and exercised that power as regards spouses dying intestate on or after 1 July 1972 by the Family Provision (Intestate Succession) Order 1972, SI 1972/916; as regards spouses dying intestate on or after 16 March 1977 by the Family Provision (Intestate Succession) Order 1977, SI 1977/415; as regards spouses dying intestate on or after 1 March 1981 by the Family Provision (Intestate Succession) Order 1981, SI 1981/255; as regards spouses dying on or after 1 December 1993 by the Family Provision (Intestate Succession) Order 1993, SI 1993/2906; as regards spouses and civil partners dying on or

after 1 February 2009 by the Family Provision (Intestate Succession) Order 2009, SI 2009/135. For the amounts of the lump sum or fixed net sum during the periods to which the provisions apply see PARAS 485 note 18, 488 note 4, 521.

The statutory code creates a sort of statutory will for the intestate (*Cooper v Cooper* (1874) LR 7 HL 53 at 66). As regards the question what system of law applies to intestate succession to immovable property and movable property see CONFLICT OF LAWS vol 19 (2011) PARA 729 et seq.

3 As regards the meaning of the 'residuary estate' of intestates see PARA 1137 text and note 2.

4 See the Inheritance (Provision for Family and Dependants) Act 1975 s 1(1), which applies to deaths on or after 1 April 1976 (ss 1(1), 27(3)); and PARA 565 et seq. The Inheritance (Family Provision) Act 1938 (repealed) was applied to intestacies as from 1 January 1953 by the Intestates' Estates Act 1952 s 7(a) (repealed). As to the dangers of distributing an estate within six months of the grant see PARA 1064.

5 *Re Ford, Ford v Ford* [1902] 2 Ch 605, CA. The rules of intestate succession do not, however, govern the descent of entailed interests: see PARA 531. See also note 1.

6 A person entitled to exercise a general power of appointment by will is not treated for this purpose as an owner of the property subject to the power, and if he fails to exercise his power the property devolves in accordance with the provisions of the instrument creating the power: see TRUSTS AND POWERS vol 98 (2013) PARA 105. If the power is exercised by will the property becomes part of the estate: Administration of Estates Act 1925 s 55(3).

7 See the Administration of Estates Act 1925 s 33 (see PARA 1135 et seq), and the definition of 'intestate' in s 55(1)(vi) by which intestate includes a person who leaves a will but dies intestate as to some beneficial interest in his real or personal estate: see PARA 1135 note 1. As to the application of the Administration of Estates Act 1925 to partial intestacies see PARAS 479, 514 et seq.

8 The cases in which former rules may still apply are stated in PARAS 293, 342–348.

9 See the Administration of Estates Act 1925 ss 54, 58(2) (repealed).

10 See the Administration of Estates Act 1925 s 58(2) (repealed).

11 See note 2.

478. Extent of operation of the old law of intestacy.

The old rules of descent were in general abolished as regards deaths after 1925[1] but have been indefinitely retained for certain purposes by means of statutory savings[2]. Accordingly, an entailed interest created before 1997[3] devolves in the same manner as an estate tail of the same kind descended before 1926, except that in all cases the entailed interest devolves as an equitable interest[4]. A person entitled to take beneficially as an heir, either general or special, of a deceased person may be ascertained by reference to the old law[5].

The old rules may still apply to the descent of the freehold estate of a person of unsound mind or defective living and of full age on 1 January 1926[6], and for determining the devolution of property of a minor dying after 1925 unmarried where the minor had or was deemed to have had an entailed interest[7]. Moreover, partial intestacy may occur after 1925 in respect of the estate of a person who died before 1926, and in such cases the old rules of descent and distribution will still apply[8].

1 Administration of Estates Act 1925 s 45(1)(a). As to the abolition of escheat see s 45(1)(d); as to the abolition of tenancy by the curtesy and of dower and freebench see s 45(1)(b), (c). See further REAL PROPERTY AND REGISTRATION vol 87 (2012) PARAS 157 et seq, 267. Nothing in s 45 affects the descent or devolution of an entailed interest: s 45(2). Entailed interests cannot be created after 1996: see PARA 477 note 1.

2 See the Administration of Estates Act 1925 s 51.

3 As to entailed interests see note 1.

4 See the Law of Property (Amendment) Act 1924 s 9, Sch 9 (preserving, in relation to the devolution of entailed interests as equitable interests, the Inheritance Act 1833, as amended by the Law of Property Amendment Act 1859 s 19; for the enactments preserved see PARA 538 et seq); Law of Property Act 1925 s 130(4); Administration of Estates Act 1925 ss 45(2), 51(4) (s 51(4) is repealed by the Trusts of Land and Appointment of Trustees Act 1996, but the repeal does not affect existing entailed interests; see further PARA 531). As to descent of an estate tail before 1926 see PARA 560. As to the operation of the legislation of 1925 upon an estate tail in an undivided share in land to turn it into an absolute interest in personalty see *Re Price* [1928] Ch 579. Apparently where land is subject to custom, upon a death after 1925, the descent must be traced to the heir

at common law of the last purchaser, the custom being totally ignored, and not by following the custom up to 1926 and then the common law: *Re Price*. As to the abolition of customary descent on 1 January 1926 see PARA 561 et seq.

5   Administration of Estates Act 1925 s 51(1). See PARA 532. As to the construction of the word 'heir' in a will PARAS 339–342.

6   Administration of Estates Act 1925 s 51(2) (amended by the Mental Treatment Act 1930 s 20(5); the Mental Health Act 1959 s 149(2), Sch 8). See also PARA 533. Although, as such a person would be aged 111 on 1 January 2016, it is unlikely that this provision will ever now take effect.

7   Administration of Estates Act 1925 s 51(3) (as originally enacted). See PARA 534. The effect of this provision is that the property in question reverted to the settlor if the minor died without having been married and without having attained his majority. If the minor died before 4 April 1988 this would be so even if he had illegitimate children: see the Family Law Reform Act 1969 s 14(5) (as originally enacted). If the minor died on or after 4 April 1988 the illegitimate issue of the minor would be entitled under the entail: see the Family Law Reform Act 1987 ss 1, 18; and PARAS 482, 535. In the case of a minor dying on or after 1 January 1997 the Administration of Estates Act 1925 s 51(3) does not apply unless the minor dies not only without having been married or having formed a civil partnership but also without issue; in such a case the minor is deemed to have had a life interest in the property in question instead of an entailed interest: see s 51(3) (amended by the Trusts of Land and Appointment of Trustees Act 1996 s 25, Sch 3 para 6, Sch 4). Since 5 December 2005 the Administration of Estates Act 1925 s 51(3) refers to civil partnership as well as marriage: see s 51(3) (amended by the Civil Partnership Act 2004 s 71, Sch 4 para 11).

8   See *Re McKee, Public Trustee v McKee* [1931] 2 Ch 145 at 147, CA. For an example of a partial intestacy occurring after the termination of a trust for accumulation see *Re Walpole, Public Trustee v Canterbury* [1933] Ch 431, where the testatrix died in 1901. See also the Intestates Estates Act 1884 s 7 (repealed as respects deaths after 1925); and PARA 555.

479. Intestacy may be either total or partial. Intestacy may be either total or partial[1]. Total intestacy occurs where a person makes no effective[2] testamentary disposition of any of the property[3] of which he is competent to dispose by will. Partial intestacy[4] occurs where the testator's will, though partly effective, either:

(1)   altogether fails to dispose of some specific property of his; or

(2)   having purported to dispose of all his property, has failed to dispose effectively of some interest which has arisen in consequence of the will, as for instance a reversionary interest[5] or a life interest[6].

In the first case the failure occurs at the date of death, whereas in the second it may occur at the date of death or at some later date. In the first case where the testator died after 1925 and before 1997[7] the undisposed of estate was held (subject to the provisions of the will[8]) on the statutory trust for sale[9]; in the case of a testator dying after 1996 his undisposed estate is held in trust by his personal representatives with power to sell it[10]. This is not so, however, in the second case, where (subject to the provisions of the will) certain special statutory provisions[11] applicable only to such a case govern the administration[12].

1   For the general meaning of 'intestate' for the purposes of the Administration of Estates Act 1925 see PARA 1135 note 1.

2   Accordingly a person dies intestate even if he has left a will where the will is ineffective: *Re Ford, Ford v Ford* [1902] 2 Ch 605, CA; *Re Cuffe, Fooks v Cuffe* [1908] 2 Ch 500. Where the will makes no disposition of any beneficial interest, the mere appointment of an executor does not constitute a disposition of the estate, for the repeal of the Executors Act 1830 has not revived the old rule by which an executor was treated in such a case as taking the testator's personal estate beneficially: *Re Skeats, Thain v Gibbs* [1936] Ch 683, [1936] 2 All ER 298.

3   As to entailed property see PARA 531.

4   The Statute of Distribution (1670) (repealed as respects deaths after 1925) did not apply to a partial intestacy nor even where the only effective part of the will was the appointment of executors (*Re Roby, Howlett v Newington* [1908] 1 Ch 71, CA), but the courts of equity applied the statute by analogy (*Vachell v Jefferys* (1701) Prec Ch 170; revsd on appeal sub nom *Vachell v Breton* (1706) 5 Bro Parl Cas 51, HL; *Re Roby, Howlett v Newington*). Nor did the Intestates' Estates Act 1890 (repealed as respects deaths after 1925), apply to a partial intestacy. For the Intestates Estates Act 1884 s 7 (repealed as respects deaths after 1925) see PARA 555.

5   See *Re McKee, Public Trustee v McKee* [1931] 2 Ch 145, CA. It seems that if an estate were given upon trust to convert and to stand possessed of the net proceeds upon trust for two persons in

equal shares and one of the beneficiaries predeceased the testator, the case would also fall within the second category mentioned in the text: *Re McKee, Public Trustee v McKee* at 165–166.

6   See *Re Plowman, Westminster Bank Ltd v Plowman* [1943] Ch 269, [1943] 2 All ER 532. See also *Re Thornber, Crabtree v Thornber* [1937] Ch 29, [1936] 2 All ER 1594, CA; and PARA 517 note 6.

7   See PARA 478 text and note 7.

8   See the Administration of Estates Act 1925 s 33(7), which provides that, where the deceased leaves a will s 33 is to have effect subject to the provisions contained in the will. As to the provisions which are to be taken into account cf PARA 517 text and note 5.

9   See the Administration of Estates Act 1925 s 33 (as originally enacted); and PARAS 1135–1136. See also *Re McKee, Public Trustee v McKee* [1931] 2 Ch 145 at 160, 165, CA; *Re Plowman, Westminster Bank Ltd v Plowman* [1943] Ch 269 at 274, [1943] 2 All ER 532 at 535.

10   See the Administration of Estates Act 1925 s 33(1) (substituted by the Trusts of Land and Appointment of Trustees Act 1996 s 5(1), Sch 2 para 5).

11   Ie those contained in the Administration of Estates Act 1925 s 49 (as amended (in relation to deaths after 1952) by the Intestates' Estates Act 1952 ss 3, 4, and (in relation to deaths after 1995) by the Law Reform (Succession) Act 1995): see PARA 514 et seq. These provisions are expressly to apply where any person dies leaving a will effectively disposing of part of his property (see the Administration of Estates Act 1925 s 49(1)); 'property' is, however, defined to include any interest in real or personal property (see s 55(1)(xvii); and PARA 608 note 4); and see *Re McKee, Public Trustee v McKee* [1931] 2 Ch 145 at 166, CA.

12   See *Re McKee, Public Trustee v McKee* [1931] 2 Ch 145, CA; *Re Plowman, Westminster Bank Ltd v Plowman* [1943] Ch 269, [1943] 2 All ER 532.

(2) CAPACITY TO TAKE UNDER AN INTESTACY

480.   A person who unlawfully kills an intestate forfeits entitlement. A person who is shown to the satisfaction of the court[1] to be guilty of murder or manslaughter[2], or of any other serious criminal act[3] which resulted in death, cannot take any benefit under the will or intestacy of his victim[4]. A person who is found 'not guilty by reason of insanity' is not precluded from benefit as this special verdict amounts to an acquittal[5]. The disposition of the share which a killer who is precluded from benefit would otherwise have taken depends on the date of the killing. Where the killing occurs before 1 February 2012[6] the person who is precluded from benefit by the forfeiture rule is to be struck out[7]. Where the killing occurs on or after that date the person who is precluded from benefit by the forfeiture rule is to be treated for the purposes of intestacy as having died immediately before the intestate[8]. It is possible to obtain relief from forfeiture where the unlawful killing was the result of manslaughter as opposed to murder[9].

1   As to the burden of proof see PARA 39 note 2.

2   It is irrelevant that the manslaughter is on the basis of diminished responsibility under the Homicide Act 1957 s 2(see CRIMINAL LAW vol 25 (2016) PARA 109); the principle of public policy that a criminal cannot benefit from his crime is not dependent on the degree of his moral culpability for the offence: *Re Giles, Giles v Giles* [1972] Ch 544 at 552, [1971] 3 All ER 1141 at 1145 per Pennycuick V-C; *Dunbar v Plant* [1998] Ch 412; [1997] 4 All ER 289, CA. See also PARA 756. See further PARAS 39–40.

3   Such as aiding and abetting suicide contrary to the Suicide Act 1961 s 2(1) (see CRIMINAL LAW vol 25 (2016) PARA 122).

4   See PARAS 39–40.

5   See CRIMINAL LAW vol 25 (2016) PARA 122.

6   Ie the date on which the Administration of Estates Act 1925 s 46A came into force (see the text and note 8; and PARA 488).

7   *Re Callaway, Callaway v Treasury Solicitor* [1956] Ch 559, [1956] 2 All ER 451 (daughter killed mother; daughter sole beneficiary under mother's will; daughter and son would normally have been entitled on mother's intestacy; son took beneficial interest in whole estate to the exclusion of any claim by the Crown to bona vacantia). As to the right to a grant see PARA 756.
     As to who should take the estate where the person primarily entitled under the intestacy rules is disqualified see *Re Scott, Widdows v Friends of the Clergy Corpn* [1975] 2 All ER 1033, [1975] 1 WLR 1260 (where both members of the class primarily entitled disclaimed and it was held that

the estate went to the next following class under the Administration of Estates Act 1925 s 46); and *Re DWS and EHS, TWGS (a child) v JMG* [2001] Ch 568, [2001] 1 All ER 97 (in which a father died intestate having been murdered by his only son; he was survived by the son, his son's son and a sister; it was held that the son's son did not take because the Administration of Estates Act 1925 s 47(1)(i) (see PARA 499) provided that no issue could take if the parent was living at the death of the intestate. The provision was unambiguous and should be given its literal meaning. Since the issue of the intestate had failed to attain an absolute vested interest the effect of s 47(2) (Sedley LJ dissenting) was that the residuary estate of the intestate would devolve as if the intestate had died without leaving issue living at the death to the next class entitled: brothers and sisters of the whole blood). The position is the same whether the surviving parent is prevented from taking by disclaimer or disqualification: per Aldous LJ at [23].

8   See the Administration of Estates Act 1925 s 46A; and PARA 488. The effect is that issue of the killer are able to take their parents' share under s 47(1), which provision similarly provides that a person who disclaims is to be treated as having predeceased the intestate: see PARA 499 et seq.

9   See the Forfeiture Act 1982 ss 2, 5; and PARAS 39, 40.

481. The concept of legitimacy. At common law a person is in principle entitled to take under the rules of intestacy only if he is legitimate and is able to establish kinship with the intestate exclusively through persons who are legitimate. The common law rule has now been largely negatived by statute[1]. The concept of legitimacy has itself, however, been modified and extended by statute.

In the case of a person dying intestate on or after 29 October 1959[2] the child of a void marriage whenever born is treated as the legitimate child of his parents if they or either of them reasonably believed that they were validly married at the date of conception or at the time of the celebration of the marriage, if later[3]. This rule applied only if the father of the child was domiciled in England and Wales at time of the birth or, if he dies before the birth, if he was so domiciled immediately before his death[4]. However, as from 13 March 2014 it also applies where, if a woman is treated as the female parent of a child[5], that female parent was domiciled in England and Wales at the time of the birth, or if she died before the birth, was so domiciled immediately before her death[6].

A person born on or after 4 April 1988[7] to a married woman as the result of artificial insemination with the semen of a person other than the husband is also now treated as the legitimate child of the marriage unless it is proved to the satisfaction of the court that the husband did not consent[8]. These provisions were replaced with effect from 1 August 1991 by similar but more comprehensive provisions catering for children born on or after that date as a result of artificial insemination or in vitro fertilisation[9]. In the case of births as a result of assisted reproduction on or after 6 April 2009[10] the rules remain the same for married couples but new rules are introduced to apply to opposite sex unmarried couples, female civil partners and female unmarried couples[11].

1   As to illegitimate and legitimated children see PARA 482; and as to adopted children see PARA 485.
2   Ie the commencement date of the Legitimacy Act 1959: see s 6(3) (repealed).
3   See the Legitimacy Act 1959 s 2(1), (4) (repealed); replaced by the Legitimacy Act 1976 s 1 with effect from 22 August 1976 (see s 12(2)); and CHILDREN AND YOUNG PERSONS vol 9 (2012) PARA 144. Any relationship between two persons must now be construed in accordance with the Family Law Reform Act 1987 s 1: see PARA 482; and CHILDREN AND YOUNG PERSONS vol 9 (2012) PARA 144. Marriage includes marriage of a same sex couple (see PARA 87) and the Legitimacy Act 1976 s 1(1) also applies in relation to the child of a void marriage which has resulted from the purported conversion of a civil partnership under the Marriage (Same Sex Couples) Act 2013 s 9 (see MATRIMONIAL AND CIVIL PARTNERSHIP LAW vol 72 (2015) PARA 61): see the Legitimacy Act 1976 s 1(5); and PARA 87.
4   See the Legitimacy Act 1976 s 1(2) (replacing the identical provisions of the Legitimacy Act 1959 s 2(2) (repealed)); and CHILDREN AND YOUNG PERSONS vol 9 (2012) PARA 144. As to domicile generally see CONFLICT OF LAWS vol 19 (2011) PARA 336 et seq.
5   Ie by virtue of the Human Fertilisation and Embryology Act 2008 s 42 or 43 (see CHILDREN AND YOUNG PERSONS vol 9 (2012) PARA 126).

6 See the Legitimacy Act 1976 s 1(2) (substituted by SI 2014/560); and CHILDREN AND YOUNG
   PERSONS vol 9 (2012) PARA 144.
7 Ie the commencement date of the Family Law Reform Act 1987 s 27: see s 34(2); the Family Law
   Reform Act 1987 (Commencement No 1) Order 1988, SI 1988/425; and PARA 358.
8 See the Family Law Reform Act 1987 s 27(1); and PARA 358. For this purpose a void marriage is
   treated as valid if both or either of the parties reasonably believed that the marriage was valid, it
   being presumed unless the contrary is shown that one of the parties so believed at the time that the
   marriage was valid: see s 27(2); and PARA 358.
9 See the Human Fertilisation and Embryology Act 1990 ss 27, 28, 29; and PARA 359.
10 Ie the commencement date of the Human Fertilisation and Embryology Act 2008: see Human
   Fertilisation and Embryology Act 2008 (Commencement No 1 and Transitional Provisions) Order
   2009, SI 2009/479; and PARA 360.
11 See the Human Fertilisation and Embryology Act 2008 Pt 2 (ss 33–58); and PARA 360.

482. Position on intestacy of illegitimate and legitimated children. In the case of
a death before 1970[1] illegitimate children were not 'issue' within the meaning of
the statutory provisions relating to succession on intestacy[2] and were in general
precluded from taking as such under an intestacy[3].

Legitimated children might share in the estate of an intestate dying after the
date of legitimation if they had been legitimated under English law or (except in
the case of real property where the old law of descent still applied) if their
legitimation under foreign law was recognised in England[4].

In the case of a death after 1969[5] and before 4 April 1988, the provisions as to
intestate succession[6] had effect as if any reference to the issue of the intestate
included a reference to any illegitimate child of his and to the issue of any such
child; any reference to the child or children of the intestate included a reference to
any illegitimate child or children of his; and in relation to an intestate who was an
illegitimate child any reference to the parent, parents, father or mother of the
intestate were a reference to his natural parent, parents, father or mother[7]. The
parents of an illegitimate child were given the same rights of succession as they
would have had if the child had been born legitimate save that the father was
presumed to have predeceased the child unless the contrary was shown[8]. The
statutory trusts were not, however, varied so as to include all persons who, but for
their own ancestor's illegitimacy, would have been included in the next of kin. The
only change was to include in the next of kin of an intestate his own illegitimate
children and their legitimate issue[9].

In the case of a death on or after 4 April 1988 the foregoing rules do not apply
and have been replaced by the general principle of construction contained in the
Family Law Reform Act 1987[10], which provides that in enactments passed and
instruments made after that date[11] references (however expressed) to any
relationship between two persons are, unless the contrary intention appears, to be
construed without regard to whether or not the father and mother of either of
them, or the father and mother of any person through whom the relationship is
deduced, have or had been married to each other at any time[12]. This general
principle of construction is expressly extended to the statutory provisions relating
to succession on intestacy[13]. For this purpose, however, an illegitimate child is
presumed not to have been survived by his father or by any person related to him
only through his father unless the contrary is shown[14]. Similar provisions also
exist in relation to a woman who is a parent of a child where another woman,
who was treated by artificial insemination, has agreed to her being a parent by
virtue of certain provisions[15] of the Human Fertilisation and Embryology Act
2008[16].

The fact that the legislation conferring rights on illegitimate children was not made retrospective is not in breach of provisions[17] of the Convention for the Protection of Human Rights and Fundamental Freedoms[18].

1   See the Family Law Reform Act 1969 s 14(9) (repealed).
2   Ie the Administration of Estates Act 1925 s 46 (amended by the Intestates' Estates Act 1952 s 1, and reproduced in amended form in Sch 1 (see s 4); and amended by the Family Provision Act 1966 s 1): see PARA 485 et seq. After 1926, however, an illegitimate child or his issue could take on the death of his mother intestate and without leaving legitimate issue, and the mother of an illegitimate child who died intestate and without having been legitimated was entitled to take as if the child had been born legitimate if she was his only surviving parent: see the Legitimacy Act 1926 s 9(1), (2) (repealed); and the Legitimacy Act 1959 s 1(2) (repealed).
3   See *Re Makein, Makein v Makein* [1955] Ch 194 at 201, [1955] 1 All ER 57 at 59 per Harman J; and cf PARA 300. As to the principle that references to 'children' in a will prima facie refer to legitimate children see *Hill v Crook* (1873) LR 6 HL 265; and PARA 350. As to the principle that an illegitimate child was not entitled to claim under the Inheritance (Family Provision) Act 1938 (repealed), as extended by the Intestates' Estates Act 1952 (repealed) see *Re Makein, Makein v Makein*. As to the provisions of the Inheritance (Provision for Family and Dependants) Act 1975 see PARA 565 et seq.
4   See CONFLICT OF LAWS vol 19 (2011) PARA 618 et seq.
5   See note 1.
6   Ie the Administration of Estates Act 1925 Pt IV (ss 45–52).
7   See the Family Law Reform Act 1969 s 14(3) (repealed).
8   See the Family Law Reform Act 1969 s 14(2), (4) (repealed).
9   See PARA 768 note 6. As to succession by illegitimate persons generally see PARA 350 et seq.
10 See the Family Law Reform Act 1987 s 1; and CHILDREN AND YOUNG PERSONS vol 9 (2012) PARA 142.
11 Ie the date of the coming into force of the Family Law Reform Act 1969 s 1: see the Family Law Reform Act 1987 (Commencement No 1) Order 1988, SI 1988/425; and CHILDREN AND YOUNG PERSONS vol 9 (2012) PARA 142.
12 Family Law Reform Act 1987 s 1(1).
13 Family Law Reform Act 1987 s 18(1).
14 Family Law Reform Act 1987 s 18(2). However this does not apply if a person is recorded as the intestate's father, or as a parent (other than the mother) of the intestate in a register of births kept (or having effect as if kept) under the Births and Deaths Registration Act 1953 or in a record of a birth included in an index kept under s 30(1) (indexes relating to certain other registers etc): Family Law Reform Act 1987 s 18(2ZA) (added by the Inheritance and Trustees' Powers Act 2014 s 5).
15 Ie by virtue of the Human Fertilisation and Embryology Act 2008 s 43 (see CHILDREN AND YOUNG PERSONS vol 9 (2012) PARA 126).
16 See the Family Law Reform Act 1987 s 18(2A) (added by the Human Fertilisation and Embryology Act 2008 Sch 6 para 25(2)).
17 Ie the Convention for the Protection of Human Rights and Fundamental Freedoms (Rome, 4 November 1950; TS 71 (1953; Cmd 8969) arts 1, 8 and 14 as contained in the Human Rights Act 1998 Sch 1 (see RIGHTS AND FREEDOMS vol 88A (2013) PARA 14).
18 *Upton v National Westminster Bank plc* [2004] EWHC 1962 (Ch), [2004] WTLR 1339. There are sound reasons (such as certainty) for not making such legislation retrospective. In any event the litigation was between private individuals.

483.   Position on intestacy of adopted children. Where an adoption order was made in England or Wales before 30 December 2005[1] and the adopter or the adopted person or any other person dies intestate at any time after the making of the order, his property devolves as if, where the adopters are a married couple, the adopted person had been born as a child of the marriage (whether or not he was in fact born after the marriage was solemnised), and, in any other case, as if he had been born to the adopter in wedlock (but not as a child of any actual marriage of the adopter)[2].

Where an adoption order was made in England or Wales on or after 30 December 2005[3] the child is to be treated as if born as the legitimate child of the adopters or adopter[4]. Where the adopter or the adopted person or any other person dies intestate at any time after the making of the order, his property devolves as if, where the adopters are a couple[5] or the adopter is a partner of one of his parents, he was a child of the relationship of the couple in question[6].

Apart from certain statutory exceptions[7], a person adopted is to be treated as not being the child of any person other than the adopters or adopter[8]. However in the case of a person adopted by one of his natural parents as sole adoptive parent this has no effect as respects entitlement to property depending on relationship to that parent, or as respects anything else depending on that relationship[9].

Any relative of any degree (other than the adoptive father and adoptive mother) under an adoptive relationship may be referred to as an adoptive of that degree[10].

1   See the Adoption Act 1976 ss 39, 42, 46(4), replacing in relation to deaths after 1975 the identical provisions of the Children Act 1975 s 8(9), (10), Schs 1, 2 (all repealed); and CHILDREN AND YOUNG PERSONS vol 9 (2012) PARA 414 et seq. The corresponding provisions of the Adoption Act 1958 s 16(4) were repealed in relation to dispositions of property after 1975 by the Children Act 1975 s 108(1)(b), Sch 4 Pt I save in relation to Northern Ireland: see s 109(2) (repealed). Where a child is adopted under a foreign order which is recognised in England, his succession rights would seem to be those which he would have enjoyed had the adoption taken place in England: *Re Valentine's Settlement, Valentine v Valentine* [1965] Ch 831, [1965] 2 All ER 226, CA. Different principles may apply if succession is governed by foreign law: see CONFLICT OF LAWS vol 19 (2011) PARA 729 et seq.

2   See the Adoption Act 1976 s 39(1); and CHILDREN AND YOUNG PERSONS vol 9 (2012) PARA 414. An adopted child is not prevented by s 39 from being legitimated under the Legitimacy Act 1976 s 2 or 3 if either parent is the sole adoptive parent: s 4(1) (amended by the Adoption Act 1976 Sch 23 para 23).

3   See the Adoption and Children Act 2002 s 66; and CHILDREN AND YOUNG PERSONS vol 9 (2012) PARA 413.

4   See the Adoption and Children Act 2002 s 67(1), (2); and CHILDREN AND YOUNG PERSONS vol 9 (2012) PARA 415. An adopted child is not prevented by s 67 from being legitimated under the Legitimacy Act 1976 s 2 or s 3 if either natural parent is the sole adoptive parent: s 4(1) (amended by the Adoption and Children Act 2002 Sch 3 para 17).

5   As to the meaning of 'couple' see the Adoption and Children Act 2002 ss 144(4), 147, Sch 6; and CHILDREN AND YOUNG PERSONS vol 9 (2012) PARA 393.

6   See the Adoption and Children Act 2002 s 67(2); and CHILDREN AND YOUNG PERSONS vol 9 (2012) PARA 415.

7   In the will of a testator who dies on or after 30 December 2005, subject to contrary indication, the general rule does not apply to prejudice any qualifying interest, any interest expectant (whether immediately or not) upon a qualifying interest or, in the case of adoptions on or after 1 October 2014, any contingent interest (other than a contingent interest in remainder) which the adopted person had immediately before the adoption in the estate of a deceased parent: see the Adoption and Children Act 2002 s 69(4); and CHILDREN AND YOUNG PERSONS vol 9 (2012) PARA 417. A child adopted by others is also treated as the child of the natural parents for the purposes of the inheritance tax residence nil band rate :see the Inheritance Tax Act 1984 ss 8E, 8K; and INHERITANCE TAXATION vol 59A (2014) PARA 23.

8   See the Adoption Act 1976 s 39(1), (2); Adoption and Children Act 2002 s 67(3)(b); and CHILDREN AND YOUNG PERSONS vol 9 (2012) PARAS 414–415. See *S v T* [2006] WTLR 1461, where an order was made under the Variation of Trusts Act 1958 to vary the terms of the statutory trusts applying on intestacy to prevent the possibility of an adoption order ending a child's beneficial entitlement to his father's estate.

    Before 1 January 1997, references to dispositions of property included references to a disposition by the creation of an entailed interest: see the Adoption Act 1976 s 46(5) (repealed as from that date by the Trusts of Land and Appointment of Trustees Act 1996 s 25, Sch 4). Entailed interests can no longer be created: see PARA 477 note 1. The Adoption Act 1958 s 16(1) (repealed) formerly applied to exclude property subject to an entailed interest under a disposition made before the adoption order, and that application is not affected in relation to dispositions of property made before 1976: see the Adoption Act 1976 s 42(1).

9   See the Adoption and Children Act 2002 s 67(4); and CHILDREN AND YOUNG PERSONS vol 9 (2012) PARA 415.

10 See the Adoption Act 1976 s 41; the Adoption and Children Act 2002 s 68(1); and CHILDREN AND YOUNG PERSONS vol 9 (2012) PARA 415.

484.   Protection of personal representatives for misdistribution on intestacy in certain cases. Personal representatives are under a strict duty under the general law to distribute the estate to the persons entitled to it and if they mistakenly pay away trust moneys to the wrong party they are accountable to the party entitled, whether or not the mistake was made in good faith[1]. The strict rule has been modified by statute. If the personal representatives of a person dying after 1969 at any time before 4 April 1988[2] distribute property among persons entitled without having ascertained that there is no person who is or may be entitled by virtue of the provisions of the Family Law Reform Act 1969 relating to the property rights of illegitimate children[3], they were not liable to any such person of whose claim they had no notice at the time of the distribution, but this provision did not prejudice the right of any such person to follow the property or any property representing it, into the hands of any person, other than a purchaser, who might have received it[4]. A similar exception from the general rule has been introduced in relation to adopted and legitimated children. The personal representatives of a person dying on or after 1 January 1976 and before 4 April 1988 are relieved from any duty on distributing property to make inquiries whether any person is adopted or is illegitimate or has been adopted by one of his natural parents and could be legitimated (or if deceased be treated as legitimated)[5].

The exception for illegitimate children has, however, now been abolished. Personal representatives who distribute property on or after 4 April 1988 are no longer free from liability if they distribute without having ascertained that no person whose parents were not married to each other at the time of his birth, or who claims through such a person, is or may be entitled to an interest in the property[6].

1 See PARA 1256. Personal representatives may protect themselves by seeking an order of the court authorising a distribution on a certain footing (*Re Benjamin, Neville v Benjamin* [1902] 1 Ch 723) or they may protect themselves by advertisement (see the Trustee Act 1925 s 27 (see PARAS 964–965); and see *Re Aldhous* [1955] 2 All ER 80, [1955] 1 WLR 459). A personal representative who acts honestly and reasonably and who fairly ought to be excused for breach of trust and for omitting to obtain the directions of the court in the matter in which he has committed such breach may be relieved either wholly or partly from personal liability: see the Trustee Act 1925 ss 61, 68(1) para (17); and TRUSTS AND POWERS vol 98 (2013) PARA 707.

2 See notes 3, 5.

3 Ie by virtue of the Family Law Reform Act 1969 s 14 (repealed with respect to persons dying on or after 4 April 1988) (which provided for succession to and from illegitimate persons on an intestacy: see PARA 482) and ss 15, 16 (repealed) (see PARA 300).

4 See the Children Act 1975 s 8, Sch 1 para 15(1) (repealed), which was replaced by the Adoption Act 1976 s 45(1) and the Legitimacy Act 1976 s 7(1); and, in relation to adoptions on or after 30 December 2005, the Adoption and Children Act 2002 s 72(2): see PARA 1063. There is, however, a presumption that a child is predeceased by its father or second female parent where the parents were not married or in a civil partnership unless the father or second female parent is registered as the child's parent: see the Family Law Reform Act 1987 s 18(2), (2ZA), (2A); and PARA 482.

5 See the Children Act 1975 Sch 1 para 15(1) (repealed); the Adoption and Children Act 2002 s 72(2); and note 4.

6 The Family Law Reform Act 1969 s 17 was repealed with effect from 4 April 1988 by the Family Law Reform Act 1987 s 20. Since this repeal does not extend to persons who are adopted or legitimated or claim through persons who are adopted or legitimated, persons who are illegitimate or claim through persons who are illegitimate are better protected than they are in cases where trust assets are misdistributed.

(3) DEATHS INTESTATE AFTER 1952

(i) Right of Surviving Spouse or Civil Partner

485. Rights of surviving spouse or civil partner where there is no issue. If the intestate[1] dies on or after 1 October 2014[2] and leaves a spouse or civil partner[3] who survives the intestate by the period of 28 days[4] and leaves no issue[5] the residuary estate[6] is held in trust for the surviving spouse or civil partner absolutely[7].

If the intestate dies on or after 1 January 1996[8] but before 1 October 2014[9] and leaves a spouse or civil partner who survives the intestate by the period of 28 days[10] and leaves no issue and no parent[11], brother or sister of the whole blood or issue of a brother or sister of the whole blood[12], the whole residuary estate is held in trust for the surviving spouse or civil partner absolutely[13]. In the case of an intestate dying before 1 January 1996 the surviving spouse's entitlement is contingent merely on having survived the intestate[14].

If the intestate dies before 1 October 2014[15] and leaves no issue but leaves a parent, brother or sister of the whole blood or issue of a brother or sister of the whole blood the surviving spouse or civil partner takes (regardless of their value[16]) the personal chattels[17], a fixed net sum[18] absolutely[19], subject (in the case of an intestate dying on or after 1 January 1996)[20] to surviving the intestate by the period of 28 days beginning with the day on which the intestate died[21], free of inheritance tax and costs, and with interest primarily payable out of income[22] at 6 per cent per annum[23] until paid or appropriated and, subject to providing for that sum and the interest on it, the residuary estate is held as to one-half in trust for the surviving spouse or civil partner absolutely[24]. The other half is held for the parents equally if more than one[25] and, if none, for the brothers and sisters of the whole blood on the statutory trusts[26].

1 As to the meaning of 'intestate' see PARA 1135 note 1.
2 Ie the date on which the Administration of Estates Act 1925 s 46(1)(i), Table para (1) was substituted by the Inheritance Trustees' Powers Act 2014 s 1(2), (2): see the Inheritance Trustees' Powers Act 2014 s 12(4); and the Inheritance and Trustees' Powers Act 2014 (Commencement) Order 2014, SI 2014/2039, art 2. The provisions in this paragraph deal with the law relating to deaths after 1952 (ie the date at which the Administration of Estates Act 1925 was amended by the Intestates' Estates Act 1952) (see PARA 477).
3 Spouse includes a person who is married to a person of the same sex: see Marriage (Same Sex Couples) Act 2013 Sch 3 para 1(1)(c), (2), (3); and MATRIMONIAL AND CIVIL PARTNERSHIP LAW vol 72 (2015) PARAS 1–2. Spouses, and civil partners, are for all purposes of distribution or division under the Administration of Estates Act 1925 s 46(1)–(1A) treated as two persons: s 46(2) (amended by the Civil Partnership Act 2004 Sch 4 Pt 2 para 7).
4 See the Administration of Estates Act 1925 s 46(2A) (added by the Law Reform (Succession) Act 1995 s 1(1); and amended by the Civil Partnership Act 2004 s 71, Sch 4 para 7). Where the intestate's spouse or civil partner survived the intestate but died before the end of the period of 28 days beginning with the day on which the intestate died, the Administration of Estates Act 1925 s 46 has effect as respects the intestate as if the spouse or civil partner had not survived the intestate: s 46(2A) (as so added and amended).
5 As to the meaning of 'issue' see PARA 482. It seems necessary that 'no issue' must here be read, in the first instance, as an absolute failure of issue at the death of the intestate, and not as 'no issue who attain an absolutely vested interest' under the statutory trusts set out in PARAS 500–499; cf PARA 506 text and note 1. See also the Administration of Estates Act 1925 s 47(2).
6 The residuary estate consists of the real and personal estate of the intestate. 'Real and personal estate' means every beneficial interest (including rights of entry and reverter) of the intestate in real and personal estate which (otherwise than in right of a power of appointment or of the testamentary power conferred by statute to dispose of entailed interests) he could, if of full age and capacity, have disposed of by his will and references (however expressed) to any relationship between two persons is construed in accordance with the Family Law Reform Act 1987 s 1 (see

    CHILDREN AND YOUNG PERSONS vol 9 (2012) PARA 142): Administration of Estates Act 1925 s 52 (amended by the Family Law Reform Act 1987 s 33(1), Sch 2 para 4).

7 Administration of Estates Act 1925 s 46(1)(i), Table para (1) (substituted by the Inheritance Trustees' Powers Act 2014 s 1(2), (2)).

8 Ie the date on which the Administration of Estates Act 1925 s 46(2A) was added by the Law Reform (Succession) Act 1995 s 1(1): see s 1(2).

9 See note 2.

10 See the Administration of Estates Act 1925 s 46(2A) (added by the Law Reform (Succession) Act 1995 s 1(1); and amended by the Civil Partnership Act 2004 s 71, Sch 4 para 7).

11 Since the Family Law Reform Act 1969 the old presumptions against the inclusion of illegitimate relationships on an intestacy have been reversed. See generally CHILDREN AND YOUNG PERSONS vol 9 (2012) PARA 142 et seq. As to the presumption on death before 1970 and as to legitimation see PARA 482. As to adoption see PARA 483; and CHILDREN AND YOUNG PERSONS vol 9 (2012) PARA 360 et seq. As references to any relationship between two persons is to be construed, for the purposes of the Administration of Estates Act 1925 Pt IV (ss 45–52), in accordance with the Family Law Reform Act 1987 s 1 (see CHILDREN AND YOUNG PERSONS vol 9 (2012) PARA 142), 'parent' does not of itself include step-parents or parents by marriage: see the Administration of Estates Act 1925 s 52; and note 6.

12 References to the intestate leaving or not leaving a member of the class consisting of brothers or sisters of the whole blood of the intestate and issue of such brothers or sisters are construed as references to the intestate leaving or not leaving a member of that class who attains an absolutely vested interest: Administration of Estates Act 1925 s 47(4) (added by the Intestates' Estates Act 1952 s 1(3)(c)).

13 See the Administration of Estates Act 1925 s 46(1)(i), Table para (1) (as substituted (see note 7); and amended by the Civil Partnership Act 2004 s 71, Sch 4 para 7).

14 See the Administration of Estates Act 1925 s 46(1)(i), Table para (1) (as substituted: see note 7).

15 See note 2.

16 See *Crispin's Will Trusts, Arkwright v Thurley* [1975] Ch 245 at 248, [1974] 3 All ER 772, CA.

17 As to the meaning of 'personal chattels' see PARA 488 note 4.

18 The fixed net sum is of the amount provided by or under the Family Provision Act 1966 s 1: Administration of Estates Act 1925 s 46(1) (amended by the Family Provision Act 1966 s 1) (now repealed). The sum may be increased by order: see the Family Provision Act 1966 s 1(1), (3), (4) (repealed). The sum has changed from time to time as follows: death on or after 1 January 1953: £20,000 (Intestates' Estates Act 1952 s 1); death on or after 1 January 1967: £30,000 (Family Provision Act 1966 s 1); death on or after 1 July 1972: £40,000 (Family Provision (Intestate Succession) Order 1972, SI 1972/916); death on or after 15 March 1977: £55,000 (Family Provision (Intestate Succession) Order 1977, SI 1977/415); death on or after 1 March 1981: £85,000 (Family Provision (Intestate Succession) Order 1981, SI 1981/255); death on or after 1 June 1987: £125,000 (Family Provision (Intestate Succession) Order 1987, SI 1987/799); death on or after 1 December 1993: £200,000 (Family Provision (Intestate Succession) Order 1993, SI 1993/2906); death on or after 1 February 2009: £450,000 (Family Provision (Intestate Succession) Order 2009, SI 2009/135). As to the fixed net sum after 1 October 2014 and where the deceased leaves issue see PARA 488 note 4. As to the powers of personal representatives to raise the fixed net sum see PARA 495.

19 By the Administration of Estates Act 1925 the sum is charged on the residuary estate of the intestate other than the personal chattels (see s 46(1)(i), Table para (3)), but it amounts to an absolute gift, and in practice is always treated as such, and where the estate does not exceed the relevant sum after payment of testamentary expenses, debts and tax, the surviving spouse or civil partner takes all.

20 See note 8.

21 See note 10.

22 Administration of Estates Act 1925 s 46(4) (added by the Intestates' Estates Act 1952 s 1(4); and amended by the Family Provision Act 1966 s 1(2)(b), as regards deaths after 1 January 1967); Inheritance Tax Act 1984 s 273, Sch 6 para 1. This altered the law as laid down in *Re Saunders, Public Trustee v Saunders* [1929] 1 Ch 674 where the interest was held to be primarily payable out of capital. See note 2.

23 Interest is payable at such rate as may be specified by order: see the Administration of Estates Act 1925 s 46(1)(i) (substituted by the Intestates' Estates Act 1952 s 1(2); and amended by the Administration of Justice Act 1977 s 28).

    Since 1 October 1983 interest is payable at the rate of 6% per annum: Intestate Succession (Interest and Capitalisation) Order 1977, SI 1977/1491, art 2 (amended by SI 1983/1374).

24　Administration of Estates Act 1925 s 46(1)(i), Table para (3)(a) (substituted by the Intestates'
　　Estates Act 1952 s 1(2); and amended by the Family Provision Act 1966 s 1(2)(a) and the Civil
　　Partnership Act 2004 s 71, Sch 4 para 7).

25　As to the entitlement of parents to share with a surviving spouse or civil partner in the case of
　　deaths before 1 October 2014 see PARA 508.

26　As to the entitlement of brothers and sisters of the whole blood to share with a surviving spouse
　　or civil partner in the case of deaths before 1 October 2014 see PARA 510.

**486.　Rights of surviving spouse or civil partner where the deceased dies before
October 2014 leaving issue.** If the intestate dies before 1 October 2014 leaving
issue[1], the surviving spouse[2] or civil partner, if surviving the intestate by the period
of 28 days beginning with the day on which the intestate died[3], takes the personal
chattels[4], a fixed net sum[5] absolutely[6], free of inheritance tax and costs, and with
interest primarily payable out of income[7] at 6 per cent per annum[8] until paid or
appropriated, and a life interest in half the remainder[9]. If the trusts in favour of the
intestate's issue fail because no child or other issue attains an absolutely vested
interest, the residuary estate devolves as if the intestate had died without leaving
issue[10].

1　The provisions in this paragraph deal with the law relating to deaths after 1952 (ie the date at
　　which the Administration of Estates Act 1925 was amended by the Intestates' Estates Act 1952)
　　(see PARA 477) but before 1 October 2014 (ie the date on which the Administration of Estates Act
　　1925 s 46(1)(i), Table para (1) was substituted by the Inheritance Trustees' Powers Act 2014
　　s 1(2), (2)) (see PARA 485 note 2). As to the meaning of 'intestate' see PARA 1137 note 1. As to
　　the meaning of 'issue' see PARA 482. This applies whether or not the intestate also leaves a parent,
　　a brother or sister of the whole blood or issue of a brother or sister of the whole blood: see the
　　Administration of Estates Act 1925 s 46(1)(i), Table para (2) (substituted by the Intestates' Estates
　　Act 1952 s 1(2); and amended by the Family Provision Act 1966 s 1(2)(a); and the Civil
　　Partnership Act 2004 s 71, Sch 4 para 7).

2　'Spouse' includes a person who is married to a person of the same sex: see the Marriage (Same
　　Sex Couples) Act 2013 Sch 3 para 1(1)(a), (2), (3); and MATRIMONIAL AND CIVIL
　　PARTNERSHIP LAW vol 72 (2015) PARAS 1–2.

3　Administration of Estates Act 1925 s 46(2A) (added with effect from 1 January 1996 by the Law
　　Reform (Succession) Act 1995 s 1(1), (3)): see PARA 485 note 4.

4　As to the meaning of 'personal chattels' see PARA 488 note 4.

5　The fixed net sum is of the amount provided by or under the Family Provision Act 1966 s 1:
　　Administration of Estates Act 1925 s 46(1) (amended by the Family Provision Act 1966 s 1). The
　　sum may be increased by order of the Lord Chancellor: see the Family Provision Act 1966 s 1(1),
　　(3), (4). The sum has changed from time to time as follows: death on or after 1 January 1953:
　　£5,000 (Intestates' Estates Act 1952 s 1); death on or after 1 January 1967: £8,750 (Family
　　Provision Act 1966 s 1); death on or after 1 July 1972: £15,000 (Family Provision (Intestate
　　Succession) Order 1972, SI 1972/916); death on or after 15 March 1977: £25,000 (Family
　　Provision (Intestate Succession) Order 1977, SI 1977/415); death on or after 1 March 1981:
　　£40,000 (Family Provision (Intestate Succession) Order 1981, SI 1981/255); death on or after
　　1 June 1987: £75,000 (Family Provision (Intestate Succession) Order 1987, SI 1987/799); death on
　　or after 1 December 1993: £125,000 (Family Provision (Intestate Succession) Order 1993, SI
　　1993/2906) death on or after 1 February 2009: £250,000 (Family Provision (Intestate Succession)
　　Order 2009, SI 2009/135). As to the fixed net sum where the deceased leaves no issue see
　　PARA 485 note 11.

6　See PARA 485 note 19.

7　See PARA 485 note 22.

8　See PARA 485 note 23.

9　Administration of Estates Act 1925 s 46(1)(i), Table para (2) (as substituted and amended: see note
　　1); Inheritance Tax Act 1984 s 273, Sch 6 para 1.

10　See the Administration of Estates Act 1925 s 47(2). As from 1 February 2012 this provision is
　　subject to s 46A (see PARA 488): s 47(4A) (added by the Estates of Deceased Persons (Forfeiture
　　Rule and Law of Succession) Act 2011 s 1(1), (4)). See also PARA 505.

**487.　Rights of surviving spouse or civil partner before October 2014 to require
capitalisation of life interest.** Before 1 October 2014[1] the life interest of a surviving
spouse[2] or civil partner in part of the residuary estate[3], while it is in possession[4],
must, if the surviving spouse or civil partner so elects[5], be purchased or redeemed

by the personal representative⁶ by paying its capital value⁷ to the tenant for life or the persons deriving title under the tenant for life⁸, and the costs of the transaction and the residuary estate may then be dealt with and distributed free from the life interest⁹.

1   The provisions in this paragraph deal with the law relating to deaths after 1952 (ie the date at which the Administration of Estates Act 1925 was amended by the Intestates' Estates Act 1952) (see PARA 477) but before 1 October 2014 (ie the date on which the Administration of Estates Act 1925 ss 47A, 48(2)(b) were repealed by the Inheritance Trustees' Powers Act 2014 Sch 4 para 1(3), (4)).
2   Ie, where the intestate dies on or after 1 January 1996, a spouse who survives the intestate by the period of 28 days beginning with the date on which the intestate dies: see PARA 486.
3   See PARA 486.
4   Where a will of a person who dies partially intestate (see PARAS 479, 514 et seq) creates a life interest in property in possession and the remaining interest in that property forms part of the residuary estate, that remaining interest is, until the life interest determines, property not in possession and the interest of the surviving spouse or civil partner in it is, therefore, not redeemable: see the Administration of Estates Act 1925 s 49(4) (added by the Intestates' Estates Act 1952 ss 3(3), 4). As to the meaning of 'will' see PARA 607 note 1; as to the meaning of 'intestate' see PARA 1137 note 1; and as to the meaning of 'property' see PARA 608 note 4.The life interest vests immediately on the intestate's death: *Cooper v Cooper* (1874) LR 7 HL 53.
5   An election to redeem a life interest is only exercisable if at the time of the election the whole of the part of the residuary estate concerned consists of property in possession: Administration of Estates Act 1925 s 47A(3) (s 47A added by the Intestates' Estates Act 1952 s 2). A life interest in property partly in possession and partly not is treated as consisting of two separate life interests in those respective parts of the property: Administration of Estates Act 1925 s 47A(3) (as so added). An election must be exercised within 12 months from the date on which a general grant (see s 47A(9) (as so added)) of representation is first taken out unless the court extends this period (s 47A(5) (as so added; amended by the Civil Partnership Act 2004 s 71, Sch 4 para 9)). The court may extend the period if it is satisfied by the surviving spouse or civil partner that the limitation to 12 months would operate unfairly in consequence of (Administration of Estates Act 1925 s 47A(5) proviso (as so added and amended):
     (1)   the representation first taken out being probate of a will subsequently revoked on the ground that the will was invalid;
     (2)   a question whether a person had an interest in the estate, or as to the nature of an interest in the estate, not having been determined at the time when representation was first taken out; or
     (3)   some other circumstances affecting the administration or distribution of the estate.
     In considering for this purpose when representation was first taken out, a grant limited to settled land or to trust property must be left out of account and a grant limited to real estate or to personal estate must also be left out of account unless a grant limited to the remainder of the estate has previously been made or is made at the same time: s 47A(9) (as so added). As to the meaning of 'court' see PARA 957 note 2. As to the meaning of 'settled land' see PARA 821 note 2; and as to the meaning of 'real estate' see PARA 607 note 1.
     The election, which is irrevocable except with the consent of the personal representative and can be effectively made by a tenant for life who is a minor (s 47A(8) (as so added)), must be notified in writing to the personal representative (s 47A(6) (as so added)), except where the tenant for life is the sole personal representative (s 47A(1) (as so added; amended by the Civil Partnership Act 2004 s 71, Sch 4 para 9)), when written notice must be given to the senior registrar (Administration of Estates Act 1925 s 47A(7) (as so added; amended by the Administration of Justice Act 1970 s 1(6), Sch 2 para 4 and the Senior Courts Act 1981 s 152(1), Sch 5)). Where there are two or more personal representatives of whom one is the tenant for life, the written notice must be given to all of them except the tenant for life: Administration of Estates Act 1925 s 47A(6) (as so added) An election by a tenant for life who is a minor is as valid and binding as it would be if the tenant for life were of age, but the personal representative must, instead of paying the capital value of the life interest to the tenant for life, deal with it in the same manner as with any other part of the residuary estate to which he is entitled absolutely: 47A(8) (as so added). As to the meaning of 'tenant for life' see PARA 828 note 5. As to the meaning of 'personal representative' see PARA 608.
6   Where there is a life interest, administration can be granted only to two or more persons, except where the grant is to a trust corporation (see the Senior Courts Act 1981 s 114(2); and PARA 775); but 'personal representative' is in general used in the singular in the Administration of Estates Act

1925 s 47A, and a sole surviving administrator, as well as a sole executor, can therefore act for this purpose subject to the special provision set out in note 5.

7   Where the surviving spouse or civil partner of an intestate exercises the right to redeem the life interest in his residuary estate, the capital value of the interest is reckoned in such manner as the Lord Chancellor may by order direct: Administration of Estates Act 1925 s 47A(3A) (s 47A(3A), (3B) added by the Administration of Justice Act 1977 s 28(3); and amended by Civil Partnership Act 2004 s 71, Sch 4 para 9). Where an election is exercised in accordance with the Administration of Estates Act 1925 s 47A(6), (7) (see note 5) the capital value of the life interest of the surviving spouse or civil partner must be reckoned in accordance with the Intestate Succession (Interest and Capitalisation) Order 1977, SI 1977/1491, art 3(2), (3): art 3(1) (amended by SI 2005/2114). The Intestate Succession (Interest and Capitalisation) Order 1977, SI 1977/1491, applies where the right to redeem is exercised on or after 15 September 1977 (see arts 1, 3(1)) and replaces the rules contained in the Administration of Estates Act 1925 s 47A(2), (4) (repealed with effect from the same date by the Administration of Justice Act 1977 s 32, Sch 5 Pt VI). As to the rules which applied to elections made before 15 September 1977 see the Administration of Estates Act 1925 s 47A(2), (4) (added by the Intestates' Estates Act 1952 s 2).

The capital sum (including the costs) required for the purchase or redemption of the life interest of a surviving spouse or civil partner of an intestate may be raised by charging the residuary estate or any part of it (other than the personal chattels), so far as the sum has not been satisfied by the application of any part of the residuary estate: Administration of Estates Act 1925 s 48(2)(b) (amended by the Civil Partnership Act 2004 s 71, Sch 4 para 10). As to powers of personal representatives in respect of the fixed net sum see the Administration of Estates Act 1925 s 48(2); and PARA 495. As to the meaning of 'personal chattels' see PARA 488 note 4.

8   Since the life interest is to be redeemed while in possession, these persons can only be assignees or chargees.

9   Administration of Estates Act 1925 s 47A(1) (as so added and amended: see note 5). This power to redeem is given for the purpose of facilitating the distribution of the estate. It would seem that the whole costs of the transaction are thrown upon the residuary estate.

488.   Rights of surviving spouse or civil partner where the deceased dies on or after 1 October 2014 leaving issue. If the intestate dies on or after 1 October 2014[1] leaving issue[2], the surviving spouse or civil partner, if surviving the intestate by the period of 28 days beginning with the day on which the intestate died[3], takes the personal chattels[4] absolutely, a fixed net sum[5] free of inheritance tax and costs[6], together with simple interest on it primarily payable out of income[7] until paid or appropriated[8]. Subject to providing for this sum and interest, the residuary estate (other than the personal chattels) is held as to one half in trust for the surviving spouse or civil partner absolutely[9]. The other half is held for the issue on the statutory trusts[10].

Where a person is entitled to an interest in the residuary estate in accordance with the above provisions[11] but disclaims it or is precluded by the forfeiture rule[12] from acquiring it, he is treated for the purposes of the distribution of the residuary estate[13] as having died immediately before the intestate[14].

If the trusts in favour of the intestate's issue fail because no child or other issue attains an absolutely vested interest, the residuary estate devolves as if the intestate had died without leaving issue[15].

1   Ie the date on which the Inheritance and Trustees Powers Act 2014 came into force.

2   As to the meaning of 'intestate' see PARA 1135 note 1. As to the meaning of 'issue' see PARA 482. In relation to deaths prior to 1 October 2014, this applies whether or not the intestate also leaves a parent, a brother or sister of the whole blood or issue of a brother or sister of the whole blood: see the Administration of Estates Act 1925 s 46(1)(i), Table para (2) (as substituted by the Intestates' Estates Act 1952 s 1(2); and amended by the Civil Partnership Act 2004 s 71, Sch 4 para 7 (see PARA 485 text and notes 15–26)).

3   Administration of Estates Act 1925 s 46(2A) (added with effect from 1 January 1996 by the Law Reform (Succession) Act 1995 s 1(1), (3)): see PARA 485 note 8. Spouse includes a person who is married to a person of the same sex: see Marriage (Same Sex Couples) Act 2013 Sch 3 para 1(1)(c), (2), (3); and MATRIMONIAL AND CIVIL PARTNERSHIP LAW vol 72 (2015) PARA 1 et seq.

4   'Personal chattels' means tangible movable property, other than any such property which consists of money or securities for money, or was used at the death of the intestate solely or mainly for

business purposes, or was held at the death of the intestate solely as an investment: Administration of Estates Act 1925 s 55(1)(x) (substituted by the Inheritance and Trustees' Powers Act 2014 s 3(1)).

5   The fixed net sum is the sum to be determined in accordance with the Administration of Estates Act 1925 Sch 1A: see s 46(1), Sch 1A para 1 (s 46(1) as substituted (see note 1); Sch 1A added by the Inheritance and Trustees' Powers Act 2014 Sch 1). As from 1 October 2014 (ie the coming into force of the substituted Administration of Estates Act 1925 Sch 1A), the amount of the fixed sum is the amount fixed by order under the Family Provision Act 1966 immediately before that date: see the Administration of Estates Act 1925 Sch 1A para 2 (as so added). The fixed net sum provided by order under the Family Provision Act 1966 in force at that time was £250,000 (see the Family Provision (Intestate Succession) Order 2009, SI 2009/135). The fixed net sum may be specified by order made by statutory instrument: see the Administration of Estates Act 1925 Sch 1A paras 2–7 (as so added). At the date at which this volume states the law no orders had been made under Sch 1A. As to the fixed net sum before 1 October 2014 where the deceased leaves no issue see PARA 485 note 18. As to the power of the personal representatives to raise the fixed sum see PARA 495.

6   As to inheritance tax on death generally see INHERITANCE TAXATION vol 59A (2014) PARA 58 et seq.

7   See the Administration of Estates Act 1925 s 46(4) (added by the Intestates' Estates Act 1952 s 1(4), and amended by the Family Provision Act 1966 s 1, the Civil Partnership Act 2004 Sch 4 para 7). The interest rate applicable where the intestate died on or after 1 October 2014 is the Bank of England rate that had effect at the end of the day on which the intestate died: see the Administration of Estates Act 1925 s 46(1A) (added by the Administration of Justice Act 1977 s 28(1); and substituted by the Inheritance and Trustees' Powers Act 2014 s 1(1)). For these purposes 'Bank of England rate' means the rate announced by the Monetary Police Committee of the Bank of England as the official bank rate or where an order under the Bank of England Act 1998 s 19 (reserve powers: see FINANCIAL INSTITUTIONS vol 48 (2015) PARA 107) is in force, any equivalent rate determined by the Treasury under that provision: Administration of Estates Act 1925 s 46(5) (s 46(5)–(9) added by the Inheritance and Trustees' Powers Act 2014 s 1(1)). The definition of Bank of England and the interest provided by the Administration of Estates Act 1925 s 46(1A) may be amended by order made by statutory instrument: see s 46(6)–(9) (as so added). At the date at which this volume states the law no such order had been made. As to interest rates applicable before this date see PARA 486 text and note 8.

     The Administration of Estates Act 1925 s 47(2), (4) are subject to s 46A (see text and note 14): Administration of Estates Act 1925 s 47(4A) (added by Estates of Deceased Persons (Forfeiture Rule and Law of Succession) Act 2011 s 1(4)).

8   Administration of Estates Act 1925 s 46(1)(i), Table para (2) (substituted by the Inheritance and Trustees' Powers Act 2014 s 1(1)).

9   Administration of Estates Act 1925 s 46(1)(i), Table para (3) (as substituted: see note 7).

10   As to the statutory trusts see PARA 499.

11   Ie in accordance with the Administration of Estates Act 1925 s 46.

12   As to the meaning of the 'forfeiture rule' see the Forfeiture Act 1982; and PARA 39. But in a case to which the forfeiture rule applies this does not affect the power conferred by the Forfeiture Act 1982 s 2 (power of court to modify the forfeiture rule: see PARA 40): see the Administration of Estates Act 1925 s 46A(3); and PARA 507.

13   Ie for the purposes of the Administration of Estates Act 1925 Pt IV (ss 45–52).

14   See the Administration of Estates Act 1925 s 46A; and PARA 507.

15   See the Administration of Estates Act 1925 s 47(2). See also PARA 505.

489. Rights of surviving spouse or civil partner to require appropriation of dwelling house comprised in the estate.

Where the residuary estate of the intestate[1] comprises an interest[2] in a dwelling house[3] in which the surviving spouse or civil partner[4] was resident[5] at the time of the intestate's death, the surviving spouse or civil partner may (except if he or she is sole personal representative) by written notice[6] within twelve months[7] of the date of the first taking out of representation[8] require the personal representative to appropriate[9] the intestate's interest[10] in the dwelling house in or towards satisfaction of any absolute interest[11] of the surviving spouse or civil partner in the intestate's real or personal estate[12]. The appropriation is made at the value of the house at the time of appropriation and not as at the date of death[13].

1 As to the meaning of 'intestate' see PARA 1135 note 1; definition applied by virtue of the Intestates' Estates Act 1952 s 6(1).
2 The intestate's interest in the dwelling house must not, if the right is to be exercised, have been a tenancy which would determine or could by notice given after the date of death be determined within two years of that date (Intestates' Estates Act 1952 s 5, Sch 2 para 1(2) (amended by the Civil Partnership Act 2004 s 71, Sch 4 para 13)). This condition does not apply (no matter when the death occurred) if:
    (1)   the surviving spouse or civil partner would in consequence of such an appropriation become entitled under the Leasehold Reform Act 1967 to acquire the freehold or an extended leasehold either immediately on the appropriation or before the tenancy determines (s 7(8)(a), (9) (amended by the Civil Partnership Act 2004 s 71, Sch 4 para 6)); or
    (2)   the intestate had given notice under that Act and the benefit of the notice is appropriated with the tenancy (Leasehold Reform Act 1967 s 7(8)(b), (9)).
3 Where part of a building was, at the date of the death of the intestate, occupied as a separate dwelling, that dwelling is treated as a dwelling house: Intestates' Estates Act 1952 Sch 2 para 1(5). Except where the context otherwise requires, references to a dwelling house include references to any garden or portion of ground attached to and usually occupied with, or otherwise required for the amenity or convenience of, the dwelling house: Sch 2 para 7(1).
4 Where the surviving spouse or civil partner lacks capacity (within the meaning of the Mental Capacity Act 2005) to make a requirement or give a consent under the Intestates' Estates Act 1952 Sch 2, the requirement or consent may be made or given by a deputy appointed by the Court of Protection with power in that respect or, if no deputy has that power, by that court: Sch 2 para 6(1) (substituted by the Mental Capacity Act 2005 Sch 6 para 8). A requirement or consent made or given under the Intestates' Estates Act 1952 Sch 2 by a surviving spouse or civil partner who is an infant is valid and binding as it would be if he or she were of age and, as respects an appropriation in pursuance of Sch 2 para 1, the provisions of the Administration of Estates Act 1925 s 41 (see PARA 1153) as to obtaining the consent of the infant's parent or guardian, or of the court on behalf of the infant, do not apply: Intestates' Estates Act 1952 Sch 2 para 6(2) (amended by the Civil Partnership Act 2004 s 71, Sch 4 para 13(2)). The right to acquire the dwelling house is not exercisable after the death of the surviving spouse or civil partner: Intestates' Estates Act 1952 Sch 2 para 3(1)(b) (amended by Civil Partnership Act 2004 s 71, Sch 4 Part 2 para 13).
5 'Was resident' is not defined within the Intestates' Estates Act 1952 but must mean 'had his home', that is, it is not necessary that the surviving spouse or civil partner should be physically present there at the moment of the intestate's death. The capital gains tax cases on the meaning of 'resident' may be helpful: see *Goodwin v Curtiss* [1998] STC 475; 70 TC 478; *Dutton-Forshaw v HMRC* [2015] UKFTT 478 (TC), [2016] STI 146. As to capital gains tax generally see CAPITAL GAINS TAXATION vol 6 (2011) PARA 601 et seq.
6 See the Intestates' Estates Act 1952 Sch 2 para 3(1)(c) (amended by the Civil Partnership Act 2004 s 71, Sch 4 para 13(2)). The notice is revocable only with the consent of the personal representative: see the Intestates' Estates Act 1952 s 3(2).
7 The court may extend the period of 12 months referred to in the text if the surviving spouse or civil partner applies for it to be extended and satisfies the court that a period limited to 12 months would operate unfairly:
    (1)   in consequence of the representation first taken out being probate of a will subsequently revoked on the ground that the will was invalid (Intestates' Estates Act 1952 Sch 2 para 3(3)(a) (Sch 2 para 3(3)(a) substituted and Sch 2 para 3(4), (5) added by the Inheritance and Trustees' Powers Act 20914 Sch 4 para 2(3))); or
    (2)   in consequence of a question whether a person had an interest in the estate, or as to the nature of an interest in the estate, not having been determined at the time when representation was first taken out (Intestates' Estates Act 1952 Sch 2 para 3(3)(b) (as so substituted)); or
    (3)   in consequence of some other circumstances affecting the administration or distribution of the estate (Sch 2 para 3(3)(c) (as so substituted)).
8 See the Intestates' Estates Act 1952 Sch 2 para 3(1)(a). For the purposes of the construction of the references in Sch 2 para 3 to the first taking out of representation, there must be left out of account:
    (1)   a grant limited to settled land or to trust property (Sch 2 para 3(4)(a) (as added: see note 7));
    (2)   any other grant that does not permit any of the estate to be distributed (Sch 2 para 3(4)(b) (as so added));

(3)   a grant limited to real estate or to personal estate, unless a grant limited to the remainder of the estate has previously been made or is made at the same time (Sch 2 para 3(4)(c) (as so added));

(4)   a grant, or its equivalent, made outside the United Kingdom (but see Sch 2 para 3(5)) (Sch 2 para 3(4)(d) (as so added)).

A grant sealed under the Colonial Probates Act 1892 s 2 (see PARA 837) counts as a grant made in the United Kingdom for the purposes of the Intestates' Estates Act 1952 Sch 2 para 3(4), but is to be taken as dated on the date of sealing: Sch 2 para 3(5) (as so added).

9   The appropriation is made under the Administration of Estates Act 1925 s 41 (see PARAS 1153–1154), and may be made in part consideration of a money payment: see the Intestates' Estates Act 1952 Sch 2 paras 1(1), 5(2) (Sch 2 para 5(2) amended by the Civil Partnership Act 2004 s 71, Sch 4 para 13(2)). Hence, where the absolute interest of the surviving spouse or civil partner in the estate is less than the value of the dwelling house, the surviving spouse or civil partner is nevertheless entitled to pay the difference and require the dwelling house to be appropriated. See also *Re Phelps, Wells v Phelps* [1980] Ch 275, [1979] 3 All ER 373, CA.

An appropriation in or towards satisfaction of entitlement on intestacy, is exempt from stamp duty land tax: Finance Act 2003 Sch 3 para 3A(1) (added by the Finance Act 2004 s 300(1)). However if the spouse or civil partner acquiring the property gives any consideration for it, other than the assumption of secured debt, the transaction is not exempt and the chargeable consideration for the transaction is determined in accordance with the Finance Act 2003 Sch 4 para 8A(1) (see STAMP TAXES vol 96 (2012) PARA 443): Sch 3 para 3A(2), (3) (as so added).

Where the surviving spouse or civil partner is one of two or more personal representatives, the rule that a trustee may not be a purchaser of trust property does not prevent the surviving spouse or civil partner from purchasing out of the estate an interest in a dwelling house in which he or she was resident at the time of the intestate's death: Intestates' Estates Act 1952 Sch 2 para 5(1) (amended by Civil Partnership Act 2004 s 71, Sch 4 Part 2 para 13). Where:

(1)   the dwelling-house forms part of a building and an interest in the whole of the building is comprised in the residuary estate;

(2)   the dwelling-house is held with agricultural land and an interest in the agricultural land is comprised in the residuary estate;

(3)   the whole or part of the dwelling-house was at the time of the intestate's death used as a hotel or lodging house; or

(4)   a part of the dwelling-house was at the time of the intestate's death used for purposes other than domestic purposes,

the right conferred by Sch 2 para 1 is not exercisable unless the court, on being satisfied that the exercise of that right is not likely to diminish the value of assets in the residuary estate (other than the said interest in the dwelling-house) or make them more difficult to dispose of, so orders: Sch 2 para 2. See also PARA 490.

10   See note 2.

11   In the case of deaths before 1 October 2014, 'absolute interest' will include any entitlement to a capitalised life interest under the Administration of Estates Act 1925 s 47A which was added by the Intestates' Estates Act 1952 and repealed for deaths on or after 1 October 2014 by the Inheritance and Trustees' Powers Act 2014 s 11, Sch 4 para 1(1) (see PARA 487).

12   Intestates' Estates Act 1952 Sch 2 para 1(1) (amended by the Civil Partnership Act 2004 s 71, Sch 4 para 13). Nothing in the Administration of Estates Act 1925 s 41(5) (see PARA 1153) prevents the personal representative from giving effect to this right: Intestates' Estates Act 1952 Sch 2 para 1(3) (amended by the Civil Partnership Act 2004 s 71, Sch 4 para 13). The surviving spouse or civil partner may require the personal representative to have the interest in the dwelling house valued in accordance with the Administration of Estates Act 1925 s 41 (see PARA 1153), and to inform him or her of the result of the valuation before he or she decides whether to exercise the right: Intestates' Estates Act 1952 Sch 2 para 3(2) (amended by the Civil Partnership Act 2004 s 71, Sch 4 para 13).

13   *Robinson v Collins* [1975] 1 All ER 321, sub nom *Re Collins, Robinson v Collins* [1975] 1 WLR 309. See also PARA 1157.

490. Restriction on sale of dwelling house comprised in the estate. During the twelve months within which the written notice must be served[1] the personal representative may only sell or otherwise dispose of the dwelling house[2] with the written consent of the surviving spouse or civil partner, or in the course of administration owing to want of other assets, or by the authority of the court to which he can apply at any time to have the matter determined[3]. These provisions[4] do not confer any right on the surviving spouse or civil partner as against a purchaser from the personal representative[5].

The right of the surviving spouse or civil partner of a tenant of a house subject to the rent restriction legislation to remain in occupation[6] and the right of a spouse or civil partner without a beneficial interest in a property to occupy property in the beneficial ownership of the other spouse or civil partner[7] are considered elsewhere in this work.

1 Where the court extends this period, it may direct that the Intestates' Estates Act 1952 Sch 2 para 4 is to apply in relation to the extended period as it applied in relation to the original period of 12 months: Sch 2 para 4(3).
2 As to the meaning of 'dwelling house' see PARA 489 note 3.
3 Intestates' Estates Act 1952 Sch 2 para 4(1), (2) (Sch 2 para 4 amended by the Civil Partnership Act 2004 s 71, Sch 4 para 13). The personal representatives as well as the surviving spouse or civil partner may apply to the court in the circumstances in which a court order is necessary (see PARA 489 note 9), and if the court is satisfied that the exercise of the right to acquire the dwelling house is likely to diminish the value of the residuary estate (other than the interest in the dwelling house in question) or make it more difficult to dispose of, the court may authorise the personal representative to dispose of that interest within the period of 12 months: see the Intestates' Estates Act 1952 Sch 2 paras 2, 4(2) (as so amended). Schedule 2 para 4 does not apply where the surviving spouse or civil partner is the sole personal representative or one of two or more personal representatives: Sch 2 para 4(4) (as so amended). Spouse includes a person who is married to a person of the same sex: see Marriage (Same Sex Couples) Act 2013 Sch 3 para 1(1)(c), (2), (3); and MATRIMONIAL AND CIVIL PARTNERSHIP LAW vol 72 (2015) PARAS 1–2 et seq.
4 Ie the Intestates' Estates Act 1952 Sch 2 para 4: see Sch 2 para 4(5).
5 Intestates' Estates Act 1952 Sch 2 para 4(5) (amended by the Civil Partnership Act 2004 s 71, Sch 4 para 13).
6 See the Rent Act 1977 s 2, Sch 1 para 2; and LANDLORD AND TENANT vol 63 (2012) PARA 956 et seq.
7 See eg *Westminster Bank Ltd v Lee* [1956] Ch 7, [1955] 2 All ER 883; and the Family Law Act 1996 Pt IV (ss 30–63).

491. Entitlement of spouse on intestacy when death occurs after judicial separation. If, on the death of one of the parties to a marriage, a decree of judicial separation is in force, the property of the deceased spouse passes on intestacy as if the other party to the marriage had then been dead[1]. An order that one party to a marriage be no longer bound to cohabit[2] does not for this purpose have effect as a decree of judicial separation[3]. This, however, is only the position where the death occurred on or after 1 August 1970[4]. Before that date, and now in the case of intestate distribution by reference to a death before 1 August 1970[5], only property of a wife acquired since the date of decree passes on intestacy in this manner[6]. On the other hand, a wife who had been judicially separated from her husband was entitled on his death intestate to her interests in his property under the ordinary rules[7].

A covenant by a wife in a separation deed that she would accept an annuity in lieu of her rights at common law or by custom in her husband's estate on his death did not necessarily bar her claim to her interest on an intestacy[8]. A separation deed in ordinary form did not normally affect the right of a surviving spouse on intestacy[9].

1 See the Matrimonial Causes Act 1973 s 18(2); PARA 770; and MATRIMONIAL AND CIVIL PARTNERSHIP LAW vol 72 (2015) PARA 257. Spouse includes a person who is married to a person of the same sex: see Marriage (Same Sex Couples) Act 2013 Sch 3 para 1(1)(c), (2), (3); and MATRIMONIAL AND CIVIL PARTNERSHIP LAW vol 72 (2015) PARA 1 et seq.
2 Ie under the Matrimonial Proceedings (Magistrates' Courts) Act 1960 s 2(1)(a) (repealed): see the Matrimonial Causes Act 1973 s 18(3).
3 Matrimonial Causes Act 1973 s 18(3).
4 See the Matrimonial Causes Act 1973 Sch 1 para 13 (derived from the Matrimonial Proceedings and Property Act 1970 ss 29, 40 (repealed)).
5 See the Matrimonial Causes Act 1973 Sch 1 para 13, saving the application of the Matrimonial Causes Act 1965 s 20(3) (otherwise repealed), in relation to the death of a wife intestate before 1 August 1970. See text and note 4.

6 Matrimonial Causes Act 1973 s 20(3) (repealed); Matrimonial Proceedings and Property Act 1970 s 40(3) (repealed). Such property includes future interests to which she was entitled at the date of the decree of judicial separation: see the Matrimonial Causes Act 1965 s 20(3) (repealed). As to the grant in such a case see PARA 770.

7 See *Rolfe v Perry* (1863) 1 New Rep 428, where a woman who had been divorced a *mensa et thoro* from her husband who died intestate was held entitled to share in his estate. Any ground on which a decree of divorce a *mensa et thoro* might have been pronounced immediately before the commencement of the Matrimonial Causes Act 1857 ceased to be a ground on which a petition for judicial separation might be presented, as from 1 January 1971: see the Divorce Reform Act 1969 ss 8(1), 11(1) (repealed); cf *Re Ihler* (1873) LR 3 P & D 50.

8 *Slatter v Slatter* (1834) 1 Y & C Ex 28. This case may also be explained on the ground that an annuity is not a satisfaction of the wife's rights on an intestacy (cf *Couch v Stratton* (1799) 4 Ves 391; *Salisbury v Salisbury* (1848) 6 Hare 526), and it does not necessarily follow that the rights under an intestacy cannot in such a deed be barred by apt words. See also PARA 498; and EQUITABLE JURISDICTION vol 47 (2014) PARA 193.

9 The surviving spouse's right could be barred by the use of apt words: see *Wilcocks v Wilcocks* (1706) 2 Vern 558; *Blandy v Widmore* (1715) 2 Vern 709; *Garthshore v Chalie* (1804) 10 Ves 1.

492. Entitlement of civil partner on intestacy when death occurs whilst separation order in force.

If, on the death of one of the parties to a civil partnership[1], a separation order[2] is in force, and the separation is continuing, the property of the deceased civil partner passes on intestacy as if the other civil partner had then been dead[3].

1 As to declarations of presumed death where a missing person is presumed dead see MATRIMONIAL AND CIVIL PARTNERSHIP LAW vol 72 (2015) PARA 459.

2 As to separation orders see the Civil Partnership Act 2004 s 56; and MATRIMONIAL AND CIVIL PARTNERSHIP LAW vol 72 (2015) PARA 396.

3 See the Civil Partnership Act 2004 s 57; and MATRIMONIAL AND CIVIL PARTNERSHIP LAW vol 72 (2015) PARA 257. Where there is no surviving civil partner the issue of an intestate takes the residuary estate upon the statutory trusts see PARA 500. As to the inheritance by parents where there is no surviving issue, spouse or civil partner see PARA 509. As to the inheritance of other relatives were there is no surviving parent, issue, spouse or civil partner see PARA 511.

493. No entitlement on intestacy for former spouse.

Where a marriage[1] is null or has been annulled[2] or dissolved by a decree absolute of divorce, on the death intestate of one party to the marriage the other is not a surviving husband or wife and therefore takes no interest in the estate[3].

1 Marriage includes marriage of a same sex couple: see Marriage (Same Sex Couples) Act 2013 Sch 3 para 1(1)(a), (2), (3); and MATRIMONIAL AND CIVIL PARTNERSHIP LAW vol 72 (2015) PARAS 1–2.

2 As to the powers of annulment of a marriage see MATRIMONIAL AND CIVIL PARTNERSHIP LAW vol 72 (2015) PARA 375 et seq.

3 Cf *Re Morrieson, Hitchins v Morrieson* (1888) 40 ChD 30; *Bosworthwick v Clegg* (1929) 45 TLR 438; *Re Williams' Settlement, Greenwell v Humphries* [1929] 2 Ch 361, CA; *Re Slaughter, Trustees Corpn Ltd v Slaughter* [1945] Ch 355, [1945] 2 All ER 214; *Re Allan, Allan v Midland Bank Executor and Trustee Co Ltd* [1954] Ch 295, [1954] 1 All ER 646, CA (decisions as to the meaning of 'husband' and 'wife' in wills and settlements). See also *Re Seaford, Seaford v Seifert* [1968] P 53, [1968] 1 All ER 482 (filing of application for decree absolute later on same day that intestate died; the death destroyed the cause of action so there was no longer any subject-matter to which the purported decree absolute could apply; wife remained married to the intestate at his death). See also PARAS 125–126; and TRUSTS AND POWERS vol 98 (2013) PARA 188. It seems clear that these decisions must govern the construction of the words of the Administration of Estates Act 1925 s 46(1)(i) (substituted by the Intestates' Estates Act 1952 s 1(1)(2); and amended by the Family Provision Act 1966 s 1; and by the Statute Law (Repeals) Act 1981). As to recognition of foreign divorces in non-contentious probate proceedings see PARA 771.

494. No entitlement on intestacy for former civil partner.

Where a civil partnership is void[1] or has been declared voidable[2] or dissolved by a decree of dissolution[3] on the death intestate of one party to the partnership the other is not a surviving civil partner and therefore takes no interest in the estate[4].

1 As to when a civil partnership is void see the Civil Partnership Act 2004 s 49; and MATRIMONIAL AND CIVIL PARTNERSHIP LAW vol 72 (2015) PARA 386.
2 As to when a civil partnership is voidable see Civil Partnership Act 2004 s 50; and MATRIMONIAL AND CIVIL PARTNERSHIP LAW vol 72 (2015) PARA 387 et seq.
3 As to the dissolution of a civil partnership see the Civil Partnership Act 2004 s 44; and MATRIMONIAL AND CIVIL PARTNERSHIP LAW vol 72 (2015) PARA 396 et seq.
4 See the Civil Partnership Act 2004 s 71 and Sch 4 (which amend enactments relating to wills, administration of estates and family provision so that they apply in relation to civil partnerships as they apply in relation to marriage); and see, in particular, the Wills Act 1837, ss 18B, 18C; and PARAS 90, 179.

495. Powers of personal representative to raise fixed sum. The personal representatives[1] may raise the fixed net sum[2] or any part thereof and the interest thereon payable to the surviving spouse or civil partner of the intestate[3] on the security of the whole or any part of the residuary estate of the intestate (other than the personal chattels)[4], so far as that estate may be sufficient for the purpose of the said sum and interest may not have been satisfied by an appropriation[5] under the statutory power available in that behalf, and the amount, if any, properly required for the payment of the costs of the transaction[6].

1 As to the meaning of 'personal representative' see PARA 608. As to the duty and the protection of personal representatives see PARA 484.
2 As to the fixed net sum see PARAS 485 note 18, 488 note 4.
3 As to the meaning of 'intestate' see PARA 1135 note 1. Spouse includes a person who is married to a person of the same sex: see Marriage (Same Sex Couples) Act 2013 Sch 3 para 1(1)(c), (2), (3); and MATRIMONIAL AND CIVIL PARTNERSHIP LAW vol 72 (2015) PARA 1 et seq.
4 As to the meaning of 'personal chattels' see PARA 488 note 4.
5 As to the personal representative's power of appropriation see PARA 1153.
6 Administration of Estates Act 1925 s 48(2) (amended by the Intestates' Estates Act 1952 s 2, the Family Provision Act 1966 s 1, the Civil Partnership Act 2004 Sch 4 para 10, and the Inheritance and Trustees' Powers Act 2014 Sch 4 para 1(1), (4)).

496. Right of surviving spouse or civil partner to income where the deceased dies before October 2014 leaving issue. Before 1 October 2014 the income[1] of so much of the real and personal estate of the deceased as may not be disposed of by his will[2], if any, or may not be required for administration purposes[3], may, however such estate is invested, as from the death of the deceased, be treated and applied as income, and for that purpose any necessary apportionment may be made between tenant for life and remainderman[4], that is, the surviving spouse or civil partner and issue[5].

1 The income includes net rents and profits of real estate and chattels real after payment of rates, taxes, rent, costs of insurance, repairs and other outgoings properly attributable to income: Administration of Estates Act 1925 s 33(5). As to the meaning of 'real estate' see PARA 607 note 1.
2 As to the meaning of 'will' see PARA 607 note 1.
3 See PARAS 1135–1136.
4 Administration of Estates Act 1925 s 33(5). This will, it seems, exclude the rule in *Howe v Earl of Dartmouth* (see *Re Sullivan, Dunkley v Sullivan* [1930] 1 Ch 84; and PARAS 1122–1127), so that half the entire income is payable to the surviving spouse or civil partner; but see *Re Fisher, Harris v Fisher* [1943] Ch 377, [1943] 2 All ER 615 (rule in Re Earl of Chesterfield's Trusts, excluded as to reversionary interests by the Administration of Estates Act 1925 s 33(1) (as originally enacted), but not excluded as to other property not producing income unless the property has been retained by a proper exercise of the discretion to postpone sale). The amendment to the Administration of Estates Act 1925 s 33(1) made by the Trusts of Land and Appointment of Trustees Act 1996 s 5, Sch 2 para 5 (see PARA 1135) by which with effect from 1 January 1997 a power of sale was substituted for the former trust for sale of an intestate's estate, may further reduce the chances of the rule in *Howe v Earl of Dartmouth* applying: see PARA 1124.

The reference to apportionment seems to import the rule in *Allhusen v Whittell* as to administration expenses and debts being payable partly out of capital and partly out of income for the first year after the intestate's death: see *Re Wills, Wills v Hamilton* [1915] 1 Ch 769; *Re Ullswater, Barclays Bank Ltd v Lowther* [1952] Ch 105, [1951] 2 All ER 989. As to these rules and their application in detail see PARA 1118 et seq.

5   As to the meaning of 'issue' see PARA 482. Spouse includes a person who is married to a person of the same sex: see Marriage (Same Sex Couples) Act 2013 Sch 3 para 1(1)(c), (2), (3); and MATRIMONIAL AND CIVIL PARTNERSHIP LAW vol 72 (2015) PARA 1 et seq.

497. Intestacy and doctrine of performance. Where a person dies intestate having covenanted to provide money at or after his death and a share of the estate devolves on the covenantee, this may operate as performance of the covenant[1]. The principle does not apply where the money has become due in the covenantor's lifetime so that a claim could have been brought for breach of covenant[2].

1   See *Blandy v Widmore* (1715) 1 P Wms 324; 2 White & Tud LC (9th Edn) 357 and EQUITABLE JURISDICTION vol 47 (2014) PARA 193.
2   *Oliver v Brickland* (1732) cited in 3 Atk 419 at 420; *Lee v Cox and D'Aranda* (1747) 3 Atk 419, sub nom *Lee v D'Aranda* (1747) 1 Ves Sen 1; *Lang v Lang* (1837) 8 Sim 451. See EQUITABLE JURISDICTION vol 47 (2014) PARA 193.

498. Barring a widow's claim to benefit on intestacy by covenant or settlement. A widow's claim[1] to benefit in her husband's estate on his intestacy may be barred wholly or partially by the terms of a covenant or settlement if provision is made by it for the wife upon the husband's death[2] or by the terms of his will where he has died partially intestate.

If a man by his will gives property to his wife and declares that it is to be taken in satisfaction of her rights under his intestacy, and dies partially intestate, her rights in respect of the property as to which he has died intestate are determined by considering whether the intestacy appears to have been accidental or intentional. If the husband has on the face of his will disposed of all his property, but in the events which have happened part of it does not pass by his will, it is considered that he did not intend his wife to be in any worse position than his next of kin, and she takes her share of the property which is undisposed of[3]. Where, however, the intestacy is apparent on the face of the will, it is considered that he deliberately left the property to pass to his statutory next of kin in reliance on the exclusion of his wife by the declaration contained in his will, and she is therefore barred of her share under the intestacy[4].

1   It is submitted that the same principles apply to civil partnerships and to same sex marriages.
2   See EQUITABLE JURISDICTION vol 47 (2014) PARA 193. The widow's claim is not barred where the provision has been made to take effect before the husband's death: *Lang v Lang* (1837) 8 Sim 451. It seems that the widow would be entitled by disclaiming the provision made by covenant or settlement to claim her full rights under the intestacy and if these do not make reasonable provision she is now entitled to claim further provision under the Inheritance (Provision for Family and Dependants) Act 1975: see PARA 565 et seq.
3   *Pickering v Lord Stamford* (1797) 3 Ves 332 (on appeal 3 Ves 492); *Garthshore v Chalie* (1804) 10 Ves 1.
4   *Lett v Randall* (1855) 3 Sm & G 83 at 87–90.

(ii) Rights of Issue under the Statutory Trusts

499. The statutory trusts. Where any part of the residuary estate of an intestate[1] is directed to be held on the statutory trusts for the issue[2] of the intestate it is held in trust, in equal shares if more than one, for all or any of the children or child of the intestate, living at his death, who attain the age of 18 or marry[3] or form a civil partnership under that age, and for all or any of the issue living at the death of the intestate who attain the age of 18 or marry or form a civil partnership under that age of any child of the intestate who predeceases the intestate[4]. Such issue is to take through all degrees, according to their stocks, in equal shares if more than one, the share which their parent would have taken if living at the death of the intestate, and so that, subject to the following provisions[5], no issue can take, whose parent is living at the death of the intestate, and so capable of taking[6]. A posthumous child or issue can take under these provisions[7].

Where a person disclaims[8] his inheritance under the intestacy rules or is disqualified by the forfeiture rule[9] from acquiring it, he is treated as immediately having died and the inheritance passes to the next person entitled to inherit[10].

1   As to the meaning of 'intestate' see PARA 1135 note 1.
2   As to the meaning of 'issue' see PARA 482. As to when the residuary estate is held to be on statutory trusts for the issue see PARAS 500, 501.
3   Marriage includes marriage of a same sex couple: see Marriage (Same Sex Couples) Act 2013 Sch 3 para 1(1)(a), (2), (3); and MATRIMONIAL AND CIVIL PARTNERSHIP LAW vol 72 (2015) PARAS 1–2.
4   Administration of Estates Act 1925 s 47(1)(i) (amended by the Family Law Reform Act 1969 s 3(2); the Civil Partnership Act 2004 s 71, Sch 4 para 8; and the Estates of Deceased Persons (Forfeiture Rule and Law of Succession) Act 2011 s 1(1), (3)). For the analogous provision by which a lapse is prevented in will cases see the Wills Act 1837 s 33; and PARA 176.
5   Ie subject to the Administration of Estates Act 1925 s 46A (see PARA 507).
6   Administration of Estates Act 1925 s 47(1)(i) (as amended: see note 4). The issue of the intestate's issue therefore take per stirpes, ie by their stocks, and so if the intestate has two children, A and B, and B predeceases him leaving two surviving children, C and D, A will take half and C and D a quarter each.
7   References to a child or issue living at the death of any person include a child or issue en ventre sa mere at the death: Administration of Estates Act 1925 s 55(2). See also *Wallis v Hodson* (1740) 2 Atk 114.
8   As to disclaimer see PARA 151.
9   As to the meaning of the 'forfeiture rule' see the Forfeiture Act 1982; and PARA 39.
10 See the Administration of Estates Act 1925 s 46A; and PARA 507.

500. Rights of Issue where there is no surviving spouse or civil partner. Where the intestate[1] does not leave a surviving spouse or civil partner[2] or, in the case of an intestate dying on or after 1 January 1996, the intestate's spouse or civil partner survives but dies before the end of the period of 28 days beginning with the day on which the intestate died[3], the issue[4] of an intestate take the whole of his residuary estate upon the statutory trusts[5].

1   As to the meaning of 'intestate' see PARA 1135 note 1.
2   Spouse includes a person who is married to a person of the same sex: see Marriage (Same Sex Couples) Act 2013 Sch 3 para 1(1)(c), (2), (3); and MATRIMONIAL AND CIVIL PARTNERSHIP LAW vol 72 (2015) PARAS 1–2.
3   Administration of Estates Act 1925 s 46(2A) (added by the Law Reform (Succession) Act 1995 s 1(1), (3); and amended by Civil Partnership Act 2004 s 71, Sch 4 para 7).
4   As to the meaning of 'issue' see PARA 482.
5   Administration of Estates Act 1925 s 46(1)(ii) (amended by the Civil Partnership Act 2004 s 71, Sch 4 para 7). As to the statutory trusts see PARA 499. They are very conveniently stated thus: (1) all members of a class take equally; (2) shares of members under 18 are contingent on the attaining of that age or marrying or forming a civil partnership under that age; (3) the share of any member who predeceases the testator is taken by his children or remoter issue equally among them per stirpes, but contingently upon attaining 18 or marrying or forming a civil partnership under that age: see PARA 499.

501. Rights of Issue where there is a surviving spouse or civil partner. Where the intestate[1] leaves a spouse or civil partner who survives for 28 days[2], or, in the case of deaths before 1996, a surviving spouse or civil partner[3], the issue[4] take upon the statutory trusts[5] subject to his or her interests; accordingly, they take immediately one-half of the residuary estate less the personal chattels[6], and the fixed net sum[7].

Where the intestate dies before 1 October 2014, the issue take the half of the residuary estate in which the surviving spouse or civil partner has a life interest upon the death of the surviving spouse or civil partner[8].

1   As to the meaning of 'intestate' see PARA 1135 note 1.
2   Spouse includes a person who is married to a person of the same sex: see Marriage (Same Sex Couples) Act 2013 Sch 3 para 1(1)(c), (2), (3); and MATRIMONIAL AND CIVIL PARTNERSHIP LAW vol 72 (2015) PARAS 1–2.
3   'Spouse' includes a person who is married to a person of the same sex: see the Marriage (Same Sex Couples) Act 2013 Sch 3 para 1(1)(a), (2), (3); and MATRIMONIAL AND CIVIL PARTNERSHIP LAW vol 72 (2015) PARAS 1–2.
4   As to the meaning of 'issue' see PARA 482.
5   As to the statutory trusts see PARA 499 (and see PARA 500 note 5).
6   As to the meaning of 'chattels' see PARA 488 note 3.
7   See the Administration of Estates Act 1925 s 46(1)(i), Table para (2) (substituted by the Inheritance and Trustees' Powers Act 2014 s 1(2)). As to the fixed net sum see PARA 488 note 5.
8   See the Administration of Estates Act 1925 s 46(1)(i), Table para (2); and PARA 486.

502. Former requirement for issue to account for advancements. The statutory power of advancement[1] and the statutory provisions for maintenance and accumulation of surplus income[2] apply to the shares of minor beneficiaries[3].

Where, in the case of an intestate dying before 1996[4], any part of the residuary estate held on the statutory trusts for issue[5] was divisible into shares, then any money or property which, by way of advancement or on the marriage of a child of the intestate[6] had been paid to the child by the intestate[7] or settled by the intestate for the benefit of the child (including any life or less interest and including property covenanted to be paid or settled) had, subject to any contrary intention expressed or appearing from the circumstances of the case, to be taken as being so paid or settled in or towards satisfaction of the share of the child or the share which the child would have taken if living at the death of the intestate and had to be brought into account at a valuation (the value to be reckoned as at the death of the intestate) in accordance with the requirements of the personal representatives[8]. Advances by the personal representatives under the statutory power might also have to be brought into hotchpot[9]. These provisions are abolished in relation to deaths on or after 1 January 1996[10].

1   See the Trustee Act 1925 s 32; and CHILDREN AND YOUNG PERSONS vol 9 (2012) PARA 76 et seq.
2   See the Trustee Act 1925 s 31; and CHILDREN AND YOUNG PERSONS vol 9 (2012) PARA 63 et seq.
3   Administration of Estates Act 1925 s 47(1)(ii). When an infant marries or forms a civil partnership such infant is entitled to give valid receipts for the income of the infant's share or interest: s 47(1)(ii) (amended by the Civil Partnership Act 2004 s 71, Sch 4 para 8(4)).
4   The hotchpot provisions contained in the Administration of Estates Act 1925 s 47(1)(iii) were repealed with effect from 1 January 1996 by the Law Reform (Succession) Act 1995 ss 1(2)(a), (3), 5, Schedule.
5   The hotchpot provisions (see note 4) were confined to the issue of the intestate: see the Administration of Estates Act 1925 s 49(1)(a) (repealed with effect from 1 January 1996 by the Law Reform (Succession) Act 1995 s 1(2)(b), 5, Schedule).
6   These words confined the rule to settlements made either by way of advancement or on the marriage of the child concerned, so that benefits under other settlements did not have to be brought into account: *Re Hayward, Kerrod v Hayward* [1957] Ch 528, [1957] 2 All ER 474, CA.
7   An advance by trustees in pursuance of an appointment made by the intestate in exercise of a power was not an advance within the meaning of the Administration of Estates Act 1925 s 47(1)(iii) (repealed: see note 4): *Re Reeve, Reeve v Reeve* [1935] Ch 110.
8   Administration of Estates Act 1925 s 47(1)(iii) (repealed: see note 4). Cf valuation for hotchpot where a testator has directed in his will that advances in his lifetime are to be brought into account: see PARA 1117; and PARA 536 et seq. See also, in relation to partial intestacies *Re Grover's Will Trust, National Provincial Bank Ltd v Clarke* [1971] Ch 168 at 179, [1970] 1 All ER 1185 at 1190 per Pennycuick J; and PARA 515 note 10.

9 See the Trustee Act 1925 s 32(1) proviso (b); and CHILDREN AND YOUNG PERSONS vol 9 (2012) PARA 77. As to valuation for the purposes of hotchpot in cases of testacy, cf PARAS 1117, 349; and in relation to partial intestacies see note 8.
10 See notes 4–5.

503. What payments constituted advancements. In the case of an intestate dying before 1996[1] it may still be necessary to determine what payments were made by way of advancement. For the purpose of determining whether a payment is made by way of advancement a distinction is drawn between sums given as casual payments or to relieve a child from temporary difficulties, and sums given to start a child in life or make a provision for him. The latter only are deemed advances by way of portion, but if the gift made by the intestate was of a large amount there is a prima facie presumption that it was given by way of portion[2]. No general rule can be laid down as to what is and what is not to be considered a portion, for the time and manner of the gift have in every case to be considered[3], as must any intention expressed or appearing from the circumstances of the case[4]. Payments for education or maintenance[5], or apprenticeship[6], or gifts of jewellery or clothing[7], or small allowances[8], are not advances. The payment which is made as a provision for a child is nonetheless a portion because it will not necessarily be permanent, or because it is not paid directly or entirely to him; accordingly, where a father makes a provision for a son on his marriage, or a daughter's portion is paid to her husband who covenants to lay it out in land to be settled, these are advances, and the whole sum paid, not merely the value of the child's life interest, is to be brought into account[9].

1 The hotchpot provisions contained in the Administration of Estates Act 1925 ss 47(1)(iii), 49(1)(a) were repealed in relation to deaths on or after 1 January 1996 by the Law Reform (Succession) Act 1995 s 1(2)(a), (b), (3), 5, Schedule.
2 *Re Scott, Langton v Scott* [1903] 1 Ch 1, CA, where *Taylor v Taylor* (1875) LR 20 Eq 155 was followed in preference to *Boyd v Boyd* (1867) LR 4 Eq 305 and *Re Blockley, Blockley v Blockley* (1885) 29 ChD 250. Cf *Watson v Watson* (1864) 33 Beav 574. See also PARA 348 et seq.
3 *Re Scott, Langton v Scott* [1903] 1 Ch 1, CA; *Re Hayward, Kerrod v Hayward* [1957] Ch 528, [1957] 2 All ER 474, CA (nominations of £507 National Savings Certificates held not to be advancements in relation to an estate of £1,780).
4 See PARA 502 note 8.
5 *Pusey v Desbouvrie* (1734) 3 P Wms 315 at 317 note (o); *Re Cameron* [1999] Ch 386, [1999] 2 All ER 924.
6 *Hender v Rose* (1718) 2 Eq Cas Abr 265.
7 *Elliot v Collier* (1747) 3 Atk 526 at 528.
8 *Hatfeild v Minet* (1878) 8 ChD 136 at 144, CA, per James LJ, where the payments of an annuity to a child under a deed of covenant during the father's life were not ordered to be brought into hotchpot, but the value of the annuity at the death was treated as an advancement.
9 *Weyland v Weyland* (1742) 2 Atk 632; *Lord Kircudbright v Lady Kircudbright* (1802) 8 Ves 51; *Taylor v Taylor* (1875) LR 20 Eq 155; *Re Scott, Langton v Scott* [1903] 1 Ch 1, CA. See the Administration of Estates Act 1925 s 47(1)(iii) (reprinted in the Intestates' Estates Act 1952 Sch 1; and repealed as regards deaths after 1995: see note 1), under which property settled for the benefit of the child includes any life or less interest and property covenanted to be paid or settled: see PARA 502.

504. Extent of the doctrine of advancement. The doctrine relating to advances applies on the partial intestacy of a person dying before 1996[1], and in such a case benefits taken by children or remoter issue under the will have to be brought into account[2]. Advances by a mother, where she is the intestate, must be brought into account[3]. A widow is not entitled to the benefit of the doctrine for the purpose of ascertaining the amount of her share of her intestate husband's estate, for the intention is merely to secure equality among the children[4]. Children of the intestate bring into account all advances made by him at a value determined as at his death in accordance with the requirements of the personal representative[5].

These provisions apply where all the provisions of a will, including the appointment of an executor, fail, for that is a total intestacy[6].

Advances are taken without interest up to the date of the intestate's death, but from the death (in as much as the distribution is referred back to the actual date of the death) interest is allowed[7].

1 See PARA 503 note 1.
2 See PARA 514.
3 See the Administration of Estates Act 1925 s 47(1)(iii) (reprinted in the Intestates' Estates Act 1952 s 4, Sch 1; and repealed as regards deaths after 1995: see PARA 503 note 1). This appears to overrule *Holt v Frederick* (1726) 2 P Wms 356.
4 *Lord Kircudbright v Lady Kircudbright* (1802) 8 Ves 51. As to valuation see PARA 502 note 9.
5 See the Administration of Estates Act 1925 s 47(1)(iii) (repealed: see note 3); and cf the Trustee Act 1925 s 22(3) (see TRUSTS AND POWERS vol 98 (2013) PARA 520). Remoter issue taking in substitution for a child bring into account advances made to their parent: see the Administration of Estates Act 1925 s 47(1)(i), (iii) (repealed: see note 3). As to collaterals see PARA 511.
6 See *Re Ford, Ford v Ford* [1902] 2 Ch 605, CA.
7 *Stewart v Stewart* (1880) 15 ChD 539 at 545 per Jessel MR. As to valuation see PARA 502 text to note 8.

505. Receipts by minors for income from their share or interest on intestacy. A minor who is married[1] or a party to a civil partnership has power to give valid receipts for the income of his or her share or interest[2], and personal representatives[3] may permit any minor contingently interested to have the use and enjoyment of any personal chattels[4] in such manner and subject to such conditions, if any, as they may consider reasonable, and without being liable to account for any consequential loss[5].

1 Marriage includes marriage of a same sex couple: see Marriage (Same Sex Couples) Act 2013 Sch 3 para 1(1)(a), (2), (3); and MATRIMONIAL AND CIVIL PARTNERSHIP LAW vol 72 (2015) PARAS 1–2.
2 Administration of Estates Act 1925 s 47(1)(ii) (amended by the Civil Partnership Act 2004 s 71, Sch 4 para 8(2)). Cf the Law of Property Act 1925 s 21. See further CHILDREN AND YOUNG PERSONS vol 9 (2012) PARA A 40.
3 As to the meaning of 'personal representative' see PARA 608.
4 As to the meaning of 'chattels' see PARA 488 note 3.
5 Administration of Estates Act 1925 s 47(1)(iv).

506. Failure of statutory trusts for issue. Where the trusts for the issue fail by the death of all before attaining an absolutely vested interest, the residuary estate together with all accumulations of income, or so much of it as has not been paid or applied under any power affecting it, is distributed as if the intestate left no issue surviving him[1].

1 Administration of Estates Act 1925 s 47(2)(a). In these circumstances, in Pt IV (ss 45–52), references to the intestate 'leaving no issue' must be construed as 'leaving no issue who attain an absolutely vested interest' (s 47(2)(b)); and references to the intestate 'leaving issue' or 'leaving a child or other issue' must be construed as 'leaving issue who attain an absolutely vested interest' (s 47(2)(c)). The Administration of Estates Act 1925 s 47(2), (4) are subject to s 46A (see PARA 507): Administration of Estates Act 1925 s 47(4A) (added by Estates of Deceased Persons (Forfeiture Rule and Law of Succession) Act 2011 s 1(4)).

(iii) Rights of Relatives Other than Issue, Spouse or Civil Partner of Deceased

507. Application of statutory trusts to relatives other than issue. Where the residuary estate of an intestate or part thereof is held on the statutory trusts for any class of relatives of the intestate, other than issue of the intestate, the same are to be held on trusts corresponding to the statutory trusts for the issue of the intestate with the substitution of references to the members or member of that class for references to the children or child of the intestate[1].

1   As to the statutory trusts in relation to issue see PARA 499.

508. Rights of parents on intestacy where there is a surviving spouse or civil partner. Where the intestate[1] dies on or after 1 October 2014[2], and his spouse[3] or civil partner survived him but died before the end of the period of 28 days beginning with the day on which the intestate died, the intestate rules of intestate succession[4] have effect as respects the intestate as if the spouse or civil partner had not survived the intestate[5] and the residuary estate will be held on the statutory trusts for the issue of the intestate or, where there is no issue, to his parents[6].

Where the intestate died before 1 October 2014[7] leaving a spouse or civil partner who survives the intestate by the period of 28 days beginning with the date on which the intestate died[8] or, as regards deaths before 1995, where the intestate leaves a surviving spouse or civil partner[9] and no issue, but leaves parents or a parent[10] (whether or not brothers or sisters of the intestate or their issue also survive), the parent or parents take half the residuary estate, less the personal chattels[11] and the fixed net sum[12], if there are two parents, in equal shares, absolutely[13].

1   As to the meaning of 'intestate' see PARA 1135 note 1.
2   Ie the date on which the Administration of Estates Act 1925 s 46(1)(i), Table was substituted by the Inheritance Trustees' Powers Act 2014 s 1(2), (2): see the Inheritance Trustees' Powers Act 2014 s 12(4); and the Inheritance and Trustees' Powers Act 2014 (Commencement) Order 2014, SI 2014/2039, art 2.
3   Spouse includes a person who is married to a person of the same sex: see Marriage (Same Sex Couples) Act 2013 Sch 3 para 1(1)(c), (2), (3); and MATRIMONIAL AND CIVIL PARTNERSHIP LAW vol 72 (2015) PARAS 1–2 et seq.
4   Ie the Administration of Estates Act 1925 s 46.
5   Administration of Estates Act 1925 s 46(2A) (added by the Law Reform (Succession) Act 1995 s 1(1); and amended by the Civil Partnership Act 2004 s 71, Sch 4 para 7).
6   See the Administration of Estates Act 1925 s 46(1)(ii), (iii), (iv); and PARA 509. A person who disclaims or forfeits his interest is treated as having died: see s 46A; and PARA 488.
7   See note 2.
8   See the Administration of Estates Act 1925 s 46(2A) (as added in relation to deaths on or after 1 January 1996); and PARA 485.
9   Where the intestate and the intestate's spouse or civil partner have died in circumstances rendering it uncertain which of them survived the other, the spouse or civil partner will not be deemed to have survived, even if younger than the intestate: see PARA 485 text and note 14.
10 See PARA 485 note 4.
11 As to the meaning of 'chattels' see PARA 488 note 3.
12 As to the fixed net sum see PARA 485 note 18.
13 Administration of Estates Act 1925 s 46(1)(i), Table para (3)(b)(i) (substituted by the Intestates' Estates Act 1952 s 1(2); and amended by the Family Provision Act 1966 s 1(2)(a) and the Civil Partnership Act 2004 s 71, Sch 4 para 7).

509. Rights of parents on intestacy where there is no surviving spouse or civil partner. Where the intestate[1] leaves no spouse[2] or civil partner who survives the intestate by the period of 28 days[3] or, in the case of deaths before 1996 where the intestate leaves no surviving spouse or civil partner[4] and leaves a parent or parents[5] but no issue, the parents take the residuary estate in equal shares absolutely; or if there is only one that parent takes the whole absolutely[6]. The parents to take must be relations in blood and therefore step-parents and parents by marriage are excluded. The rights of succession to a legitimated person dying intestate and the rights of the mother of an illegitimate child dying intestate are considered elsewhere[7].

1   As to the meaning of 'intestate' see PARA 1135 note 1.

2 Spouse includes a person who is married to a person of the same sex: see Marriage (Same Sex Couples) Act 2013 Sch 3 para 1(1)(c), (2), (3); and MATRIMONIAL AND CIVIL PARTNERSHIP LAW vol 72 (2015) PARAS 1–2 et seq.
3 See the Administration of Estates Act 1925 s 46(2A) (as added in relation to deaths on or after 1 January 1996); and PARA 485. A person who disclaims or forfeits his interest is treated as having died: see s 46A; and PARA 488.
4 See PARAS 485, 508.
5 See PARA 485 note 11.
6 Administration of Estates Act 1925 s 46(1)(iii), (iv) (amended by the Intestates' Estates Act 1952 s 1(3)(a); and the Civil Partnership Act 2004 s 71, Sch 4 para 7).
7 See PARA 482; and CHILDREN AND YOUNG PERSONS vol 9 (2012) PARA 142.

510. Rights of other relatives on intestacy where there is a surviving spouse or civil partner. Where a person dies intestate[1] on or after 1 October 2014[2], his spouse[3], or civil partner, take the residuary estate absolutely providing they survive him by 28 days[4]. Where the spouse or civil partner die before the end of that period the intestate rules of intestate succession[5] have effect as respects the intestate as if the spouse or civil partner had not survived[6] and the residuary estate will be held on the statutory trusts for the issue[7] of the intestate[8] or, where there is no issue, to his parents[9] or, where the intestate leaves no issue or parents, the residuary estate goes to certain relatives living at the intestate's death and in a set order and manner[10]. Similar provision is made where the beneficiary disclaims, or is precluded by the forfeiture rules from acquiring, an interest in the estate[11] and particular provision is made for the issue of a beneficiary under the statutory trusts where the beneficiary dies without having reached 18 or having married or formed a civil partnership[12].

Where a person dies intestate before 1 October 2014[13] and, leaves a spouse or civil partner who survives the intestate by the period of 28 days[14] or, in the case of deaths before 1996 where the intestate leaves a surviving spouse or civil partner[15] and neither issue nor parent[16] but leaves a brother or sister of the whole blood or issue of a brother or sister of the whole blood[17], half the residuary estate, less the personal chattels[18] and the fixed net sum[19], is held on the statutory trusts[20] for the brothers and sisters of the whole blood[21]. Where the intestate leaves no issue and no parent or brother or sister of the whole blood, or issue of such a brother or sister, any surviving spouse or civil partner takes to the exclusion of any of the intestate's relations[22].

1 As to the meaning of 'intestate' see PARA 1135 note 1.
2 Ie the date on which the Administration of Estates Act 1925 s 46(1)(i), Table was substituted by the Inheritance Trustees' Powers Act 2014 s 1(2), (2)): see the Inheritance and Trustees' Powers Act 2014 s 12(4); and the Inheritance and Trustees' Powers Act (Commencement) Order 2014, SI 2014/2039.
3 Spouse includes a person who is married to a person of the same sex: see Marriage (Same Sex Couples) Act 2013 Sch 3 para 1(1)(c), (2), (3); and MATRIMONIAL AND CIVIL PARTNERSHIP LAW vol 72 (2015) PARAS 1–2 et seq.
4 See the Administration of Estates Act 1925 s 46(1)(i)(1), (2A); and PARA 485. A person who disclaims or forfeits his interest is treated as having died: see s 46A; and PARA 488.
5 Ie the Administration of Estates Act 1925 s 46.
6 Administration of Estates Act 1925 s 46(2A) (added by the Law Reform (Succession) Act 1995 s 1(1); and amended by the Civil Partnership Act 2004 s 71, Sch 4 para 7).
7 As to the meaning of 'issue' see PARA 482.
8 See the Administration of Estates Act 1925 s 46(1)(ii); and PARA 500.
9 See the Administration of Estates Act 1925 s 46(1)(iii), (iv); and PARA 509.
10 See the Administration of Estates Act 1925 s 46(1)(v); and PARA 511.
11 See the Administration of Estates Act 1925 s 46A; and PARA 507.
12 See the Administration of Estates Act 1925 s 47(4A)–(4D); and PARA 507.
13 See note 2.

14 See the Administration of Estates Act 1925 s 46(2A) (as added in relation to deaths on or after 1 January 1996); and PARA 485.
15 See PARAS 485, 508.
16 See PARA 485 note 12.
17 See PARA 485 note 12.
18 As to the meaning of 'chattels' see PARA 488 note 3.
19 As to the fixed net sum see PARA 485 note 18.
20 See PARA 511.
21 Administration of Estates Act 1925 s 46(1)(i), Table para (3)(b)(ii) (substituted by the Intestates' Estates Act 1952 s 1(2); and amended by the Family Provision Act 1966 s 1(2)(a) and the Civil Partnership Act 2004 s 71, Sch 4 para 7).
22 See PARA 485.

511. Rights of other relatives on intestacy where there is no surviving spouse or civil partner. Where the intestate does not leave a spouse or civil partner who survives by the period of 28 days beginning with the date of the intestate's death[1] and leaves neither issue nor parent then the residuary estate goes to the following persons living at the intestate's death and in the following order and manner:

(1) brothers and sisters of the whole blood;
(2) brothers and sisters of the half blood;
(3) grandparents;
(4) uncles and aunts of the whole blood;
(5) uncles and aunts of the half blood[2].

With the exception of grandparents who, like parents, must take absolutely, these classes of relatives take upon trusts[3] corresponding to the statutory trusts for the issue of the intestate as if such classes of relatives were substituted for issue in those trusts[4]. Accordingly, if there survive the intestate members of any one of the classes, or (except in the case of grandparents) descendants, however remote, of members who have predeceased the intestate, they take per stirpes[5] to the exclusion of every class later in the list[6].

Throughout these provisions spouses and civil partners are to be treated as two persons[7]. A direction by a testator that his estate is not to go to any of the persons entitled under the foregoing provisions is ineffective if he died intestate, for he cannot override the law[8], but he may direct that, in case of his dying intestate, some persons included are not to take[9].

1 See the Administration of Estates Act 1925 s 46(2A) (as added in relation to deaths on or after 1 January 1996); and PARA 485. A person who disclaims or forfeits his interest is treated as having died: see s 46A; and PARA 485. Where the intestate died before 1996 there is no survival contingency and a spouse who merely survives the intestate by however short a period is entitled under the intestacy rules: see PARA 485. As to the meaning of 'intestate' see PARA 1135 note 1. Spouse includes a person who is married to a person of the same sex: see Marriage (Same Sex Couples) Act 2013 Sch 3 para 1(1)(c), (2), (3); and MATRIMONIAL AND CIVIL PARTNERSHIP LAW vol 72 (2015) PARAS 1–2 et seq.
2 Administration of Estates Act 1925 s 46(1)(v) (amended by the Intestates' Estates Act 1952 s 1(3)(b); and the Civil Partnership Act 2004 s 71, Sch 4 para 7).
3 For the statutory trusts for issue see PARA 500 et seq.
4 Administration of Estates Act 1925 s 47(3). Where the residuary estate of an intestate or any part of it is directed to be held on the statutory trusts for any class of relatives of the intestate, other than issue of the intestate, it must be held on trusts corresponding to the statutory trusts for the issue of the intestate (other than the provision for bringing any money or property into account) as if such trusts were repeated with the substitution of references to the members or member of that class for references to the children or child of the intestate: s 47(3). An additional subsection (s 47(5)) added by the Intestates' Estates Act 1952 ss 1(3)(c), 4, was repealed by the Family Provision Act 1966 s 9. The classes and the issue in these trusts include illegitimate, legitimate and adopted persons: see PARAS 482–483. As to a posthumous child see PARA 499; as to the power of children after marriage to give receipts see PARA 505; and as to the power of personal representatives to put a minor in possession of personal chattels see PARA 505.
5 As to the meaning of 'per stirpes' see PARA 345.

6   The effect of the foregoing provisions is shown in PARA 518. Even where the intestate died before 1996, the provisions requiring the issue of the intestate to bring advances into hotchpot or, in the case of partial intestacy, to bring benefits under the will into account did not apply to collaterals: see the Administration of Estates Act 1925 ss 47(3), 49(1)(a) (amended by the Intestates' Estates Act 1952 s 3, and set out as amended in Sch 1). The Administration of Estates Act 1925 s 49(1)(a) was abolished in relation to the issue of an intestate dying after 1995: see PARA 502.

7   Administration of Estates Act 1925 s 46(2) (amended by the Civil Partnership Act 2004 Sch 4 para 7). At common law a husband and wife were regarded as one person, but from 1883 to 1925 this was a rule of construction only and readily gave way to any contrary intention, and from 1 January 1926 it was abolished: see the Law of Property Act 1925 s 37; and REAL PROPERTY AND REGISTRATION vol 87 (2012) PARA 197.

8   *Johnson v Johnson* (1841) 4 Beav 318.

9   *Bund v Green* (1879) 12 ChD 819, such a direction being construed as an implied gift to the others. However, it may be construed otherwise and the question is purely one of construction of the will: see *Re Holmes, Holmes v Holmes* (1890) 62 LT 383.

(iv) Rights of the Crown and the Duchies

512. Bona vacantia. If no person takes an absolute interest the Crown or the Duchy of Lancaster or the Duke of Cornwall for the time being, as the case may be, takes the intestate's residuary estate as bona vacantia, and in lieu of any right to escheat[1], and does so by statutory and not by prerogative right[2]. Power is reserved to the Crown or the Duchy or the Duke to provide for the intestate's dependants, whether kindred or not, and other persons for whom the intestate might reasonably have been expected to make provision, according to the existing practice[3].

1   Administration of Estates Act 1925 s 46(1)(vi). See also PARA 552 et seq. Bona vacantia are jura regalia, and the right to them within the Duchy of Lancaster is vested in the Crown by a separate title and within the Duchy of Cornwall is vested in the Duke of Cornwall: see CROWN AND CROWN PROCEEDINGS vol 29 (2014) PARA 145 et seq. The jura regalia relating to property in the County Palatine of Durham have been revested in the Crown: see CROWN AND CROWN PROCEEDINGS vol 29 (2014) PARA 212. As to proceedings by the Crown to get in an estate passing to it as bona vacantia, and as to the procedure in obtaining a grant to the Treasury Solicitor or other Crown nominee on behalf of the Crown see PARA 778 et seq. As to the rights of next of kin who subsequently establish their claim see PARA 780.

2   *Re Mitchell, Hatton v Jones* [1954] Ch 525, [1954] 2 All ER 246. As to what are bona vacantia within the Crown's prerogative right see *A-G of Ontario v Mercer* (1883) 8 App Cas 767 at 778, PC; CROWN AND CROWN PROCEEDINGS vol 29 (2014) PARA 145 et seq.

3   Administration of Estates Act 1925 s 46(1)(vi). Cf PARA 557. The Inheritance (Provision for Family and Dependants) Act 1975 (see PARA 565 et seq) applies to claims against the Crown in some cases where, in the nature of things, its predecessor legislation could not have applied.

513. When right to bona vacantia arises. Prior to 13 October 2004[1] the Crown's right to claim title to land taken as bona vacantia was defeated if the personal representatives or any other person succeeded after the intestate's death in obtaining a first registration of land forming part of the intestate's estate[2]. Similarly, a transfer of registered land for valuable consideration defeated the Crown's right to take as bona vacantia[3]. The equivalent provision in the Land Registration Act 2002 does not refer expressly to the position of the Crown. However, it provides that if the proprietor is not entitled to the estate for his own benefit, or not entitled solely for his own benefit, then, as between himself and the persons beneficially entitled to the estate, the estate is vested in him subject to such of their interests as he has notice of[4].

There is provision for rules as to the passing of a registered estate or charge as bona vacantia for the purposes of the Land Registration Act 2002[5].

1   Ie the date on which the Land Registration Act 1925 was repealed by the Land Registration Act 2002 Sch 13: see the Land Registration Act 2002 (Commencement No 4) Order 2003, SI 2003/1725, art 2.

2 See the Land Registration Act 1925 s 5 (repealed: see note 1). See also *Re Suarez (No 2)* [1924] 2 Ch 19; *Morelle Ltd v Wakeling* [1955] 2 QB 379 at 409–411, [1955] 1 All ER 708 at 719–721, CA (overruled but not on this point in *A-G v Parsons* [1956] AC 421, [1956] 1 All ER 65, HL).
3 See the Land Registration Act 1925 s 20 (repealed: see note 1).
4 Land Registration Act 2002 s 11(5). This accords with the fundamental objective of the Act that the register should be a complete and accurate reflection of the state of the title of the land at any given time to allow investigation of title to land on line, with the absolute minimum of additional inquiries and inspections: see *Land Registration for the Twenty-First Century: A Conveyancing Revolution* (Law Com No 271) (2001) para 1.5.
5 See the Land Registration Act 2002 s 85; and REAL PROPERTY AND REGISTRATION vol 87 (2012) PARA 403. At the date at which this volume states the law no such rules had been made.

(v) Partial Intestacy

514. Modification of rules applying on total intestacy where there is a will dealing with part of the estate. Before 1926 there was no provision for persons taking under the will to bring their benefits into account when claiming under a partial intestacy[1]. This led to anomalies which it is thought were intended to be corrected in 1925[2]. It was then provided that where any person died leaving a will effectively disposing of part of his property the part of the Administration of Estates Act 1925 concerned with the distribution of the residuary estate[3] should have effect as respects the part of his property not so disposed of[4], subject to the provisions contained in the will and subject to modifications[5]. The first modification[6] has given rise to trouble in its application of the hotchpot principle[7]. The second modification provided that the personal representative should, subject to his rights and powers for the purposes of administration, be a trustee for the persons entitled under that part of the Act[8] in respect of the part of the estate not expressly disposed of unless it appeared by the will that the personal representative was intended to take that part beneficially[9].

1 See *Re Young, Young v Young* [1951] Ch 185 at 189, [1950] 2 All ER 1040 at 1042; *Re Roby, Howlett v Newington* [1908] 1 Ch 71, CA.
2 See the Administration of Estates Act 1925 s 49, criticised by Danckwerts J in *Re Morton, Morton v Warham* [1956] Ch 644 at 647, [1956] 3 All ER 259 at 260.
3 Ie the Administration of Estates Act 1925 Pt IV (ss 45–52) (as originally enacted). See further PARA 517.
4 See PARA 479.
5 See the Administration of Estates Act 1925 s 49.
6 See PARA 515.
7 The hotchpot provisions in the intestacy rules have been abolished in relation to deaths on or after 1 January 1996: see PARA 502 note 4.
8 Ie under the Administration of Estates Act 1925 Pt IV (as originally enacted).
9 See the Administration of Estates Act 1925 s 49(1)(b); and PARA 517. As to a third modification see PARA 516.

515. The hotchpot modification. The hotchpot modification[1] provides that the requirements as to bringing property into account should apply to any beneficial interests acquired by any issue[2] of the deceased under the deceased's will, but not to beneficial interests so acquired by any other persons[3]. 'The requirements' in question are those referring[4] to money or property paid by way of advancement or on marriage[5]. The provision does not require legacies or shares of residue to be brought into account[6]. However, it has always been construed as if it had that effect[7] so that all beneficial interests taken by issue under the will have to be brought into account[8], and if a gift to a beneficiary and his children has to be brought into account that is to be treated as a gift of the capital of the interest in which the beneficiary and his children have successive interests[9]. Where, however, a life or less interest has to be brought into account and the remaining beneficial interests in the fund do not together amount to an entire interest of a beneficiary and his issue, the life or less interest has to be brought into account at its actuarial value[10].

1   The hotchpot provisions in the intestacy rules have been abolished in relation to deaths on or after 1 January 1996: see PARA 502 note 4.
2   'Issue' is to be contrasted with 'child' in the Administration of Estates Act 1925 s 47(1)(iii) (repealed in relation to deaths on or after 1 January 1996) (see PARA 502): *Re Morton, Morton v Warham* [1956] Ch 644 at 648, [1956] 3 All ER 259 at 261 per Danckwerts J.
3   See the Administration of Estates Act 1925 s 49(1)(a) (amended by the Intestates' Estates Act 1952 s 3, and set out in amended form in Sch 1 (see s 4); and repealed in relation to deaths on or after 1 January 1996 by the Law Reform (Succession) Act 1995 s 1(2)(b), (3), 5, Schedule).
4   There were no such requirements before the Administration of Estates Act 1925, and no others in it: see PARA 514; and note 8.
5   See the Administration of Estates Act 1925 s 47(1)(iii) (repealed in relation to deaths on or after 1 January 1996); and PARA 502.
6   See *Re Grover's Will Trusts, National Provincial Bank Ltd v Clarke* [1971] Ch 168 at 174, [1970] 1 All ER 1185 at 1187 per Pennycuick J.
7   The limitation suggested in the first part of the judgment in *Re Grover's Will Trusts, National Provincial Bank Ltd v Clarke* [1971] Ch 168, [1970] 1 All ER 1185, namely that issue do not have to bring into account legacies or shares of residue, was not applied in that case, and does not seem ever to have been argued, presumably because of the effect of the earlier decisions.
8   *Re Young, Young v Young* [1951] Ch 185, [1950] 2 All ER 1040; *Re Grover's Will Trusts, National Provincial Bank Ltd v Clarke* [1971] Ch 168, [1970] 1 All ER 1185. The Administration of Estates Act 1925 s 49(1)(a) (repealed: see note 3) was amended by the Intestates' Estates Act 1952 s 3(2) so as expressly to confine the requirements to those in the Administration of Estates Act 1925 s 47, but this must always have been the effect of s 49(1)(a). See note 4.
9   See note 8.
10 *Re Morton, Morton v Warham* [1956] Ch 644, [1956] 3 All ER 259, explained in *Re Grover's Will Trusts, National Provincial Bank Ltd v Clarke* [1971] Ch 168 at 178, [1970] 1 All ER 1185 at 1190 per Pennycuick J. The date of such valuation is unclear: *Re Grover's Will Trusts, National Provincial Bank Ltd v Clarke* at 179 and at 1191. See also PARA 1117, and cf PARA 502.

516. Future interests. Similar difficulties attend the application of the provisions of the Administration of Estates Act 1925 relating to partial intestacies[1], to future interests created by the will which fall to be distributed under a partial intestacy. Such a case has to be distinguished from the case where a testator fails altogether to dispose of some specific property of his, not arising in consequence of the will[2]. In the latter case, subject to the provisions of the will, the statutory trusts for sale[3] will apply[4]. In the former case the statutory trusts for sale do not apply, and the interest does not have to be sold, for it cannot necessarily be asserted at the date of testator's death that he is partially intestate, nor did the legislature contemplate the payment or recoupment of testamentary expenses out of an item of future property or intend to refer[5] to reversionary interests other than those properly so called forming part of the intestate's estate[6]. Where, however, the testator's will gives a life interest in residue without providing for what is to happen afterwards, and there is a partial intestacy of the remainder on the widow's life interest, she is entitled immediately to the statutory legacy, because the provisions relating to partial intestacy[7], when read with the provisions as to the distribution of residue on an intestacy[8], do not provide for this to be payable to her personal representatives as part of her estate on her death, but to her, and the statutory charge is not merely a charge on the reversion as a separate asset[9].

In relation to deaths after 1952 and before 1996 the fixed net sum payable to a surviving spouse under a partial intestacy is payable less the value of any beneficial interests taken under the will, and no fixed net sum is payable if the value of these exceeds the amount of the fixed net sum[10]. After 1952 references to beneficial interests acquired under a will are construed as including a beneficial interest acquired under a general but not a special power of appointment[11].

1 Ie the Administration of Estates Act 1925 s 49. As to the difficulties relating to hotchpot see PARA 515.
2 See PARAS 479, 514.
3 Ie under the Administration of Estates Act 1925 s 33: see PARAS 1135–1136.
4 As to the respective application of the Administration of Estates Act 1925 s 33 and s 49 see PARA 479.
5 Ie in the Administration of Estates Act 1925 s 33.
6 *Re McKee Public Trustee v McKee* [1931] 2 Ch 145 at 148, 150, 160, CA. The terms of an express trust for sale, if there is one, override any statutory trusts for sale in any event: *Re McKee, Public Trustee v McKee* at 149, 159.
7 See note 1.
8 Ie the Administration of Estates Act 1925 s 46.
9 See *Re Bowen-Buscarlet's Will Trusts, Nathan v Bowen-Buscarlet* [1972] Ch 463 at 467–468, [1971] 3 All ER 636 at 638–639 per Goff J, following *Re Douglas' Will Trusts, Lloyds Bank Ltd v Nelson* [1959] 2 All ER 620, [1959] 1 WLR 744 (affd on another point [1959] 3 All ER 785, [1959] 1 WLR 1212, CA), and not following *Re McKee, Public Trustee v McKee* [1931] 2 Ch 145 on this point. The amendments of the Administration of Estates Act 1925 s 49 by the Intestates' Estates Act 1952 ss 1, 3, may also have affected the position.
10 Administration of Estates Act 1925 s 49(1)(aa) (added by the Intestates' Estates Act 1952 s 3(2), and set out in amended form in Sch 1; amended by the Family Provision Act 1966 s 1; and repealed in relation to deaths on or after 1 January 1996 by the Law Reform (Succession) Act 1995 ss 1(2)(b), (3), 5, Schedule).
11 Administration of Estates Act 1925 s 49(2) (added by the Intestates' Estates Act 1952 s 3(3), and set out in amended form in Sch 1; and repealed in relation to deaths on or after 1 January 1996 by the Law Reform (Succession) Act 1995 ss 1(2)(b), (3), 5, Schedule). As to general powers (ie powers that the donee may exercise in favour of such persons as he chooses) see TRUSTS AND POWERS vol 98 (2013) PARAS 188, 577 et seq. As to special powers (ie powers which may be exercised in favour of certain persons only) see TRUSTS AND POWERS vol 98 (2013) PARAS 188, 585 et seq.

517. Trusteeship. The personal representative[1] holds the undisposed of estate, subject to his rights and powers for purposes of administration, in trust for the persons entitled on an intestacy under the statutory provisions already set out[2] unless it appears from the will[3] that he was to take beneficially[4]. The onus is on the personal representative to show that he is so entitled, and this appears to be so even when the Crown is entitled under the partial intestacy.

These provisions take effect subject to the provisions contained in the will[5]; but this means the provisions which remain operative and effective and does not include any provisions which become inoperative by virtue of a disclaimer[6].

1 As to the meaning of 'personal representative' see PARA 608.
2 See PARA 485 et seq.
3 As to the meaning of 'will' see PARA 607 note 1. See *Re Carville, Shone v Walthamstow Borough Council* [1937] 4 All ER 464 ('residue to be disposed of as my executors shall think fit'; executors did not take beneficially); and see also *Re Skeats, Thain v Gibbs* [1936] Ch 683, [1936] 2 All ER 298. Cf the cases cited in PARA 539, with reference to the law before 1926.
4 Administration of Estates Act 1925 s 49(1)(b).
5 See PARA 514; and the Administration of Estates Act 1925 s 49(1).
6 *Re Sullivan, Dunkley v Sullivan* [1930] 1 Ch 84 (where, by disclaiming a life interest under the will, the widow avoided the effect of a provision that royalties should be treated as capital, and was held entitled to receive them as income under her life interest as on an intestacy). See also *Re Thornber, Crabtree v Thornber* [1937] Ch 29, [1936] 2 All ER 1594, CA (gift of annuity out of income of residue to testator's widow; trust for accumulation of surplus income for 21 years or her life; gift of capital and accumulated income at expiration of that period to testator's children; testator died without issue: trust for accumulation inoperative).

(vi) Summary of Distribution on Intestacy

518. Distribution on death on or after 1 October 2014 where there is a surviving spouse or civil partner. Where a person dies intestate[1] on or after 1 October 2014[2] his estate is to be distributed or held on trusts in the following manner[3].

The surviving spouse[4] or civil partner takes the interests described below, but in the case of the death of a person intestate on or after 1 January 1996 such rights are contingent on surviving the intestate by the period of 28 days[5].

When the intestate leaves issue or relatives of any of the classes described below the surviving spouse or civil partner takes the following interests:

(1) the surviving spouse or civil partner takes the personal chattels absolutely[6];

(2) the residuary estate of the intestate (other than the personal chattels) stands charged with the payment of a fixed net sum[7], free of death duties and costs, to the surviving spouse or civil partner, together with simple interest on it from the date of the death at the prescribed rate[8] until paid or appropriated[9];

(3) subject to the above, the residuary estate (other than the personal chattels) is held, as to one half, in trust for the surviving spouse or civil partner absolutely and, as to the other half, on the statutory trusts for the issue of the intestate[10].

1 As to the meaning of 'intestate' see PARA 1135 note 1.
2 Ie the date on which the Administration of Estates Act 1925 s 46(1)(i), Table was substituted by the Inheritance Trustees' Powers Act 2014 s 1(1), (2): see the Inheritance Trustees' Powers Act 2014 s 12(4); and the Inheritance and Trustees' Powers Act 2014 (Commencement) Order 2014, SI 2014/2039, art 2. As to distribution before 1 October 2014 see PARA 519.
3 The estate is also to be distributed in this manner following the disclaimer or forfeiture on intestacy by the spouse or civil partner: see the Administration of Estates Act 1925 s 46A; and PARA 488.
4 Spouse includes a person who is married to a person of the same sex: see Marriage (Same Sex Couples) Act 2013 Sch 3 para 1(1)(c), (2), (3); and MATRIMONIAL AND CIVIL PARTNERSHIP LAW vol 72 (2015) PARAS 1–2 et seq.
5 See the Administration of Estates Act 1925 s 46(2A) (as added in relation to deaths on or after 1 January 1996); and PARA 485. As to commorientes see also PARA 746.
6 Administration of Estates Act 1925 s 46(1)(i) Table, (2)(A) (s 46(1)(i) Table substituted by the Inheritance and Trustees' Powers Act 2014 s 1(1), (2)): see PARAS 485–488. As to the meaning of 'personal chattels' see PARA 488 note 4.
7 As to the fixed net sum see PARA 488 note 4.
8 Ie the Bank of England rate that had effect at the end of the day on which the intestate died: Administration of Estates Act 1925 s 46(1A) (added by the Administration of Justice Act 1977 s 28(1); and substituted by the Inheritance and Trustees' Powers Act 2014 s 1(1), (3)). For these purposes the 'Bank of England rate' means the rate announced by the Monetary Policy Committee of the Bank of England as the official bank rate or, where an order under the Bank of England Act 1998 s 19 (reserve powers) is in force, any equivalent rate determined by the Treasury under provision: Administration of Estates Act 1925 s 46(5) (s 46(5)–(9) added by the Inheritance and Trustees' Powers Act 2014 s 1(1), (4)). This definition and the Administration of Estates Act 1925 s 46(1A) may be amended by order made by statutory instruments: see s 46(6), (7) (as so added).
9 Administration of Estates Act 1925 s 46(1)(i), Table para (2)(B) (as substituted: see note 6). See PARAS 485–488.
10 Administration of Estates Act 1925 s 46(1)(i), Table para (2)(C) (as substituted: see note 6): see PARA 488. As to the statutory trusts see PARA 500.

519. Distribution on death after 1952 but before 1 October 2014 where there is a surviving spouse or civil partner. Where a person dies intestate[1] on or after 1 January 1953 but before 1 October 2014[2] his estate is to be distributed or held on trusts in the following manner.

The surviving spouse[3] or civil partner takes the interests described below, but in the case of the death of a person intestate on or after 1 January 1996 such rights are contingent on surviving the intestate by the period of 28 days[4].

When the intestate leaves issue or relatives of any of the classes described below the surviving spouse or civil partner takes the following interests:

(1)   the surviving spouse or civil partner takes the personal chattels absolutely[5];

(2)   the surviving spouse or civil partner takes the fixed net sum[6] absolutely[7];

(3)   subject to the above, the estate is distributed or held on trust as follows (note that if there are relatives of any class there is no need to proceed to a subsequent class):

    (a)   issue: one-half to the surviving spouse or civil partner for life and then to the issue on the statutory trusts[8]; other half to the issue on the statutory trusts[9];

    (b)   parent or parents: one-half to the surviving spouse or civil partner absolutely[10]; other half to the parent (or parents equally) absolutely[11];

    (c)   brothers and sisters of the whole blood (including issue of deceased ones, that is to say, nephews and nieces): one-half to the surviving spouse or civil partner absolutely[12]; other half to the brothers and sisters on the statutory trusts[13];

    (d)   brothers and sisters of the half blood (including issue of deceased ones): all to the surviving spouse or civil partner absolutely[14];

    (e)   grandparents: all to the surviving spouse or civil partner absolutely[15];

    (f)   uncles and aunts of the whole blood (including issue of deceased ones): all to the surviving spouse or civil partner absolutely[16];

    (g)   uncles and aunts of the half blood (including issue of deceased ones): all to the surviving spouse or civil partner absolutely[17].

Where the intestate does not leave issue or relatives of any of the classes described above the surviving spouse or civil partner takes the entire estate[18].

1   As to the meaning of 'intestate' see PARA 1135 note 1.

2   Ie the date on which the Administration of Estates Act 1925 s 46(1)(i), Table para (1) was substituted by the Inheritance Trustees' Powers Act 2014 s 1(2), (2): see the Inheritance Trustees' Powers Act 2014 s 12(4); and the Inheritance and Trustees' Powers Act 2014 (Commencement) Order 2014, SI 2014/2039, art 2. As to succession after 1 October 2014 see PARA 518.

3   Spouse includes a person who is married to a person of the same sex: see Marriage (Same Sex Couples) Act 2013 Sch 3 para 1(1)(c), (2), (3); and MATRIMONIAL AND CIVIL PARTNERSHIP LAW vol 72 (2015) PARAS 1–2 et seq.

4   See the Administration of Estates Act 1925 s 46(2A) (as added in relation to deaths on or after 1 January 1996); and PARA 485. As to commorientes see also PARA 746.

5   Administration of Estates Act 1925 s 46(1)(i) (substituted by the Intestates' Estates Act 1952 s 1), Administration of Estates Act 1925 s 46(1), Table paras (2), (3) (Table paras (2), (3) amended by the Family Provision Act 1966 s 1; the Administration of Justice Act 1977 s 28(1)(a); the Statute Law (Repeals) Act 1981; and the Civil Partnership Act 2004 s 71, Sch 4 para 7): see PARAS 485–488. As to the meaning of 'personal chattels' see PARA 488 note 4.

6   As to the fixed net sum see PARAS 485 note 18, 488 note 4.

7   Administration of Estates Act 1925 s 46(1)(i), Table paras (2), (3) (as substituted and amended: see note 3). See PARAS 485–488.

8   Administration of Estates Act 1925 s 46(1)(i), Table para (2)(a) (as substituted and amended: see note 3): see PARA 488. As to the statutory trusts see PARA 500.

9   Administration of Estates Act 1925 s 46(1)(i), Table para (2)(b) (as substituted and amended: see note 3): see PARA 488. If the trusts for the issue fail in the lifetime of the surviving spouse of civil partner, the residuary estate devolves as if the intestate had died without leaving issue: see s 47(2)(a); and PARA 488.

10 Administration of Estates Act 1925 s 47(1)(i), Table para (3)(a) (as substituted and amended: see note 3): see PARA 485.
11 Administration of Estates Act 1925 s 47(1)(i), Table para (3)(b)(i) (as substituted and amended: see note 3): see PARA 508. The parents do not take on the statutory trusts.
12 Administration of Estates Act 1925 s 46(1)(i), Table para (3)(a) (as substituted and amended: see note 3): see PARA 485.
13 Administration of Estates Act 1925 s 46(1)(i), Table para (3)(b)(ii) (as amended: see note 3): see PARA 510. Nephews or nieces take deceased parent's share. If all brothers and sisters are dead, nephews and nieces take per stirpes. As to the meaning of 'per stirpes' see PARA 345.
14 Administration of Estates Act 1925 s 46(1)(i), Table para (1) (as substituted: see note 3): see PARA 485.
15 Administration of Estates Act 1925 s 46(1)(i), Table para (1) (as substituted: see note 3): see PARA 485. Grandparents do not take on the statutory trusts.
16 Administration of Estates Act 1925 s 46(1)(i), Table para (1) (as substituted: see note 3): see PARA 485.
17 Administration of Estates Act 1925 s 46(1)(i), Table para (1) (as substituted: see note 3): see PARA 485.
18 Administration of Estates Act 1925 s 46(1)(i), Table para (1) (as substituted: see note 3): see PARA 485. Second or more remote cousins have no rights.

520. Distribution on death after 1952 where there is no surviving spouse or civil partner. Where a person dies intestate on or after 1 January 1953 with no surviving[1] spouse or civil partner his estate is to be distributed or held on trusts as follows (note that if there are relatives of any class there is no need to proceed to a subsequent class):

(1)   issue: all to the issue on the statutory trusts[2];
(2)   parents: all to the parent (or parents equally) absolutely[3];
(3)   brothers and sisters of the whole blood (including issue of deceased ones, that is to say, nephews and nieces): all to the brothers and sisters on the statutory trusts[4];
(4)   brothers and sisters of the half blood (including issue of deceased ones): all to the brothers and sisters on the statutory trusts[5];
(5)   grandparents: all to the grandparent (or grandparents equally) absolutely[6];
(6)   uncles and aunts of the whole blood (including issue of deceased ones): all to the uncles and aunts on the statutory trusts[7];
(7)   uncles and aunts of the half blood (including issue of deceased ones): all to the uncles and aunts on the statutory trusts[8];
(8)   no relative of the above classes: all to the Crown, the Duchy of Lancaster or the Duke of Cornwall[9].

1   In the case of the death of a person intestate on or after 1 January 1996 the spouse or civil partner must survive the intestate by the period of 28 days: see the Administration of Estates Act 1925 s 46(2A) (as added in relation to deaths on or after 1 January 1996); and PARA 485. As to distribution where there is a surviving spouse or civil partner see PARA 518. As to commorientes see also PARA 746.
2   Administration of Estates Act 1925 s 46(1)(ii) (amended by the Civil Partnership Act 2004 s 71, Sch 4 para 7): see PARA 500.
3   Administration of Estates Act 1925 s 46(1)(iii), (iv) (amended by the Intestates' Estates Act 1952 s 1; and the Civil Partnership Act 2004 s 71, Sch 4 para 7): see PARA 509. The parents do not take on the statutory trusts.
4   Administration of Estates Act 1925 s 46(1)(v), first head (amended by the Civil Partnership Act 2004 s 71, Sch 4 para 7): see PARA 511. Nephews or nieces take their deceased parent's share. If all brothers and sisters are dead, nephews and nieces take per stirpes. As to the meaning of 'per stirpes' see PARA 345.
5   Administration of Estates Act 1925 s 46(1)(v), second head (amended by the Civil Partnership Act 2004 s 71, Sch 4 para 7): see PARA 511.
6   Administration of Estates Act 1925 s 46(1)(v), third head (amended by the Civil Partnership Act 2004 s 71, Sch 4 para 7): see PARA 511. Grandparents do not take on the statutory trusts.

7 Administration of Estates Act 1925 s 46(1)(v), fourth head (amended by the Civil Partnership Act 2004 s 71, Sch 4 para 7): see PARA 511. Cousins take their deceased parent's share. If all uncles and aunts are dead, the cousins take per stirpes.
8 Administration of Estates Act 1925 s 46(1)(v), fifth head (amended by the Intestates' Estates Act 1925 s 1; and the Civil Partnership Act 2004 s 71, Sch 4 para 7): see PARA 511.
9 Administration of Estates Act 1925 s 46(1)(vi): see PARA 512. Second or more remote cousins have no rights.

(4) DEATHS INTESTATE AFTER 1925 AND BEFORE 1953

521. Surviving spouse's absolute interests. Where an intestate dying after 1925 but before 1953 left a husband or wife, whether there were issue or not, the surviving spouse took all personal chattels[1] absolutely and a sum of £1,000 absolutely[2] free of death duties and costs and with interest[3] at 5 per cent per annum from the date of death until payment or appropriation[4]. The surviving spouse took an absolute interest in the whole estate where under the provisions in favour of the relatives of the deceased[5] no person took an absolute vested interest[6].

1 As to the meaning of 'personal chattels' see PARA 488 note 4.
2 By the Administration of Estates Act 1925 s 46(1)(i) (as originally enacted) this sum is expressed to be charged on the residuary estate, but is in effect an absolute gift: cf PARA 485 note 19.
3 Such interest is a charge on the corpus of the estate and not upon income: *Re Saunders, Public Trustee v Saunders* [1929] 1 Ch 674. As to the position as regards interest on the corresponding sums payable in the case of deaths after 1952 see PARA 485 text and note 23.
4 Administration of Estates Act 1925 s 46(1)(i) (as originally enacted). As to commorientes see PARA 746.
5 As to these provisions see PARA 526.
6 See the Administration of Estates Act 1925 s 46(1)(v) (as originally enacted).

522. Surviving spouse's life interest. Where an intestate dying after 1925 but before 1953 left no issue[1] the surviving spouse was entitled (in addition to the absolute rights as to personal chattels and the capital sum of £1,000[2]) to a life interest in the whole residuary estate[3]. If the intestate left issue the surviving spouse took a life interest in half only, but if the trusts of the other half failed in the lifetime of the surviving spouse, he took that other half for the residue of his life[4].

1 See PARAS 482–483, 485 note 3.
2 See PARA 521. As to the meaning of 'personal chattels' see PARA 488 note 4.
3 Administration of Estates Act 1925 s 46(1)(i)(a) (as originally enacted). See also note 4. As to commorientes see PARA 746.
4 Administration of Estates Act 1925 s 46(1)(i)(b) (as originally enacted). Shortly stated, the trusts of the other half are for the issue who attain 21 or marry: see s 47(1) (as originally enacted). The position under s 46(1)(i)(a), (b) (as originally enacted), where the trusts for the issue fail, is curious. On the one hand, the definition of 'no issue' in s 47(2)(b) brings the position within s 46(1)(i)(a) (as originally enacted), and the surviving spouse takes a life interest in the whole residuary estate less the personal chattels and the £1,000. On the other hand, by s 46(1)(i)(b) (as originally enacted), he or she is expressly given a life interest in the half which the issue would have taken for the residue of his or her life and, as he or she already has a life interest in half under s 46(1)(i)(a) (as originally enacted), it follows that he or she takes half the net income until the trusts for the issue fail, and the whole net income from that time till death, together with (by s 47(2)(a)) the income for the period from death to the time of the failure of the trusts for issue and the accumulations of it, less any money paid or applied by way of advancement or maintenance. Of these two constructions it is submitted the latter must prevail.

523. Personal representative's power to redeem life interest. While the life interest of a surviving spouse[1] was in possession[2], it could, with his consent where he was not the sole personal representative, or, where he was the sole personal representative[3], with the leave of the court, be redeemed[4] by the personal representative paying its capital value, reckoned according to tables[5] selected by the personal representative, and the costs of the transaction, and the residuary estate might then be dealt with or distributed free from the life interest[6]. The capital sum had to be paid to the surviving spouse or persons deriving title under him[7]. The capital sum (including costs) could be raised by charging the residuary estate or any part of it (other than the personal chattels[8]) so far as it was not satisfied by the application of any part of the residuary estate[9]. The sum of £1,000[10] or any part of it could be similarly raised or satisfied by appropriation[11].

1   See PARA 522. As to commorientes see PARA 746.
2   The life interest vests immediately on the death of the intestate: *Cooper v Cooper* (1874) LR 7 HL 53.
3   Where there is a life interest, the appointment of two administrators or a trust corporation as administrators is necessary (Supreme Court of Judicature (Consolidation) Act 1925 s 160(1) (repealed)). The Administration of Estates Act 1925 s 48(1) (as originally enacted) referred to 'personal representative' in the singular, so as to cover a sole executor or sole surviving administrator. As to the office of representative see PARA 605 et seq.
4   Administration of Estates Act 1925 s 48(1) (as originally enacted).
5   Reference could be made to the tables in the Succession Duty Act 1853, Schedule (repealed), and to the tables of life insurance societies.
6   Administration of Estates Act 1925 s 48(1) (as originally enacted).
7   Administration of Estates Act 1925 s 48(1) (as originally enacted).
8   As to the meaning of 'chattels' see PARA 488 note 3.
9   Administration of Estates Act 1925 s 48(2)(b) (as originally enacted: now repealed by the Inheritance and Trustees' Powers Act 2014 Sch 4 para 1(4)(b)). As to the statutory powers of appropriation see PARA 1153 et seq.
10   See PARA 521.
11   Administration of Estates Act 1925 s 48(2)(a) (as originally enacted).

524. Issue. The interests taken by issue upon the statutory trusts in the case of an intestate dying after 1925 but before 1953 were the same as are taken in the case of a death after 1952[1], except that the capital sum payable to any surviving spouse was only £1,000[2].

1   See PARA 500 et seq.
2   See the Administration of Estates Act 1925 s 46(1)(i), (ii) (as originally enacted).

525. Parents. Where an intestate dying after 1925 but before 1953 left no issue but parents or a parent[1] then, subject to the interests of a surviving spouse, if any[2], the parents shared the residuary estate equally between them or, if there was only one, that one took the whole[3]. These were absolute interests[4], since the statutory trusts could not be applicable to them. The parents to take had to be related by blood, so excluding step parents and parents by marriage[5]. The rights of the parents of a legitimated person dying intestate are considered elsewhere[6].

1   As to the meaning of 'parent' see PARA 485 note 11.
2   See PARA 522. As to commorientes see PARA 746.
3   Administration of Estates Act 1925 s 46(1)(iii), (iv) (as originally enacted).
4   See the Administration of Estates Act 1925 s 46(1)(iii), (iv) (as originally enacted).
5   See PARA 482.
6   See further PARA 482 note 2.

526. Other relations. Where an intestate dying after 1925 but before 1953 left no issue or parent then, subject to the interests of the surviving spouse, if any[1], the residuary estate went to the same persons and in the same order and on the same trusts (where applicable) as apply in the case of a death after 1952 where the intestate leaves neither spouse, issue nor parent[2].

1   See PARA 522. As to commorientes see PARA 746.
2   See the Administration of Estates Act 1925 s 46(1)(v) (as originally enacted), by which an order of succession applied similar to that set out in PARA 511.

527. Rights of the Crown. The rights of the Crown, which have not been affected by the Intestates' Estates Act 1952, are as already stated in relation to deaths after 1952[1].

1 See the Administration of Estates Act 1925 s 46(1)(vi); and PARAS 512–513.

528. Partial intestacy. On the partial intestacy of a person dying after 1925 and before 1953 there is no provision for a surviving spouse to bring into account any beneficial interest under the will[1]; nor was the requirement as to the bringing into account of the beneficial interests of issue under the will expressly extended to beneficial interests acquired by virtue of the exercise of a general power of appointment[2]. The hotchpot provisions have been abolished altogether in relation to deaths after 1995[3]. Subject to these differences similar provisions apply in the case of deaths throughout the period since 1925[4].

1 See PARA 514 et seq. As to commorientes see PARA 746.
2 Ie there is no provision corresponding to that set out in PARA 516 text and note 11.
3 Ie by the Law Reform (Succession) Act 1995 s 1(1): see PARA 514 et seq. As to hotchpot see PARA 404 et seq.
4 See the Administration of Estates Act 1925 s 49 (as originally enacted). As to the position where a surviving spouse takes a life interest under a will see PARA 516.

529. Distribution on death after 1925 but before 1953 where there is a surviving spouse. Where a person died intestate on or after 1 January 1926 and before 1 January 1953 his estate is to be distributed or held on trust in the following manner.

Where the intestate leaves issue or relatives of any of the classes described below the surviving spouse takes the following interests:
(1)   the surviving spouse takes the personal chattels[1] absolutely[2];
(2)   the surviving spouse takes £1,000 absolutely[3];
(3)   subject to the above, the estate is distributed or held on trust as follows (note that if there are relatives of any class there is no need to proceed to a subsequent class):
    (a)   issue: one-half to the surviving spouse for life and then to the issue on the statutory trusts; other half to the issue on the statutory trusts[4];
    (b)   parent or parents: all to the surviving spouse for life[5] and then to the parent (or parents equally) absolutely[6];
    (c)   brothers and sisters of the whole blood (including issue of deceased ones, that is to say, nephews and nieces): all to the surviving spouse for life[7] and then to the brothers and sisters on the statutory trusts[8];
    (d)   brothers and sisters of the half blood (including issue of deceased ones): all to the surviving spouse for life[9] and then to the brothers and sisters on the statutory trusts[10];
    (e)   grandparents: all to the surviving spouse for life[11] and then to the grandparent (or grandparents equally) absolutely[12];
    (f)   uncles and aunts of the whole blood (including issue of deceased ones): all to the surviving spouse for life[13] and then to the uncles and aunts on the statutory trusts[14];
    (g)   uncles and aunts of the half blood (including issue of deceased ones): all to the surviving spouse for life[15] and then to the uncles and aunts on the statutory trusts[16].

Where the intestate does not leave issue or relatives of any of the classes described above the surviving spouse takes the entire estate[17].

1   As to the meaning of 'chattels' see PARA 488 note 3.
2   Administration of Estates Act 1925 s 46(1)(i). Throughout this paragraph references to this Act are to the Act as originally enacted. See PARA 521. As to commorientes see PARA 746.
3   Administration of Estates Act 1925 s 46(1)(i).
4   Administration of Estates Act 1925 s 46(1)(i)(b): see PARA 524. If the trusts for issue fail in the lifetime of the spouse, he or she takes their half for the residue of his or her life: s 46(1)(i)(b).
5   Administration of Estates Act 1925 s 46(1)(i)(a).
6   Administration of Estates Act 1925 s 46(1)(iii), (iv): see PARA 525. The parents do not take on the statutory trusts.
7   Administration of Estates Act 1925 s 46(1)(i)(a).
8   Administration of Estates Act 1925 s 46(1)(v), first head: see PARA 526. Nephews or nieces take their deceased parent's share. If all brothers and sisters are dead, nephews and nieces take per stirpes. As to the meaning of 'per stirpes' see PARA 345.
9   Administration of Estates Act 1925 s 46(1)(i)(a).
10 Administration of Estates Act 1925 s 46(1)(v), second head: see PARA 526.
11 Administration of Estates Act 1925 s 46(1)(i)(a).
12 Administration of Estates Act 1925 s 46(1)(v), third head: see PARA 526. Grandparents do not take on the statutory trusts.
13 Administration of Estates Act 1925 s 46(1)(i)(a).
14 Administration of Estates Act 1925 s 46(1)(v), fourth head: see PARA 526. Cousins take their deceased parent's share. If all the uncles and aunts are dead, the cousins take per stirpes.
15 Administration of Estates Act 1925 s 46(1)(i)(a).
16 Administration of Estates Act 1925 s 46(1)(v), fifth head: see PARA 526.
17 Administration of Estates Act 1925 s 46(1)(v), sixth head: see PARA 521. Second or more remote cousins have no rights.

530. Distribution on death after 1925 but before 1953 where there is no surviving spouse. Where a person died intestate on or after 1 January 1926 and before 1 January 1953 with no surviving spouse[1] his estate is to be distributed or held on trust as follows (note that if there are relatives of any class there is no need to proceed to a subsequent class):

(1)   issue: all to the issue on statutory trusts[2];
(2)   parents: all to the parent (or parents equally) absolutely[3];
(3)   brothers and sisters of the whole blood (including issue of deceased ones, that is to say, nephews and nieces): all to the brothers and sisters on the statutory trusts[4];
(4)   brothers and sisters of the half blood (including issue of deceased ones): all to the brothers and sisters on the statutory trusts[5];
(5)   grandparents: all to the grandparent (or grandparents equally) absolutely[6];
(6)   uncles and aunts of the whole blood (including issue of deceased ones): all to the uncles and aunts on the statutory trusts[7];
(7)   uncles and aunts of the half blood (including issue of deceased ones): all to the uncles and aunts on the statutory trusts[8];
(8)   no relative of the above classes: all to the Crown, the Duchy of Lancaster or the Duke of Cornwall[9].

1   As to distribution where there is a surviving spouse see PARA 529. As to commorientes see PARA 746.
2   Administration of Estates Act 1925 s 46(1)(ii). Throughout this paragraph references to this Act are to the Act as originally enacted. See PARA 524.
3   Administration of Estates Act 1925 s 46(1)(iii), (iv): see PARA 525. The parents do not take on the statutory trusts.
4   Administration of Estates Act 1925 s 46(1)(v), first head: see PARA 526. Nephews or nieces take deceased parent's share. If all brothers and sisters are dead, nephews and nieces take per stirpes. As to the meaning of 'per stirpes' see PARA 345.
5   Administration of Estates Act 1925 s 46(1)(v), second head: see PARA 526.

6   Administration of Estates Act 1925 s 46(1)(v), third head: see PARA 526. Grandparents do not
    take on statutory trusts.
7   Administration of Estates Act 1925 s 46(1)(v), fourth head: see PARA 526. Cousins take their
    deceased parent's share. If all the uncles and aunts are dead, the cousins take per stirpes.
8   Administration of Estates Act 1925 s 46(1)(v), fifth head: see PARA 526.
9   Administration of Estates Act 1925 s 46(1)(vi): see PARA 527. Second or more remote cousins have
    no rights.

(5) DEATHS INTESTATE BEFORE 1926

(i) Application of Old Rules in respect of Deaths after 1926

531. Entailed interests. The rules of intestate succession, as enacted by the
amended Administration of Estates Act 1925[1] do not affect the devolution of an
entailed interest[2] as an equitable interest[3]; and accordingly the pre-1926 rules of
descent continue to apply[4]. Entailed interests cannot be created after 1996[5], but
this does not affect the devolution of existing entailed interests[6].

    An entailed interest, like the former estate tail, is in certain circumstances liable
to be barred by the execution of a disentailing assurance, which will defeat all
subsequent interests in tail[7]. The same result may now be achieved under similar
circumstances by the will of the tenant in tail in possession under the statutory
power of disposing of an entailed interest by will[8]. On the failure of issue under
the entail, the entailed interest will revert to the owner of the reversion expectant
on the determination of the entailed interest and not to the Crown[9]. The owner of
the reversion will be traced by the rules relating to deaths after 1925[10].

1   See the Administration of Estates Act 1925 Pt IV (ss 45–52); and as to amendments see PARA 477
    note 2.
2   See PARA 478 text and notes 3, 6. An interest in tail or in tail male or in tail female or in tail special
    could be created by way of trust in any property, real or personal, and is known as an entailed
    interest: see the Law of Property Act 1925 s 130(1) (repealed); and REAL PROPERTY AND
    REGISTRATION vol 87 (2012) PARA 112 et seq.
3   Administration of Estates Act 1925 ss 45(2), 51(4) (repealed with savings by the Trusts of Land
    and Appointment of Trustees Act 1996 s 25(2), Sch 4).
4   See PARA 478. See, however, PARA 483.
5   See the Trusts of land and Appointment of Trustees Act 1996 s 2(6), Sch 1 para 5; and REAL
    PROPERTY AND REGISTRATION vol 87 (2012) PARA 114.
6   See the Trusts of land and Appointment of Trustees Act 1996 Sch 1 para 5; and REAL PROPERTY
    AND REGISTRATION vol 87 (2012) PARA 114.
7   See REAL PROPERTY AND REGISTRATION vol 87 (2012) PARA 121 et seq.
8   See the Law of Property Act 1925 s 176; and PARA328.
9   Com Dig, Escheat (A 1); Fitz Nat Brev 144. Before 1926 failure of an estate tail did not lead to an
    escheat. As to escheat see PARA 552.
10 There may be exceptional cases, eg where the estate tail is in freeholds and the owner of the
    reversion is a person of unsound mind and comes within the provisions of the Administration of
    Estates Act 1925 s 51(2) (see PARA 533), or is a minor who dies without ever having been married
    or formed a civil partnership (see s 51(3); and PARA 534).

532. Heirs by purchase. Under a limitation of real or personal property which
before 1926 would, in the case of freehold land, have conferred on the heir an
estate by purchase, the property devolves upon the person who would have been
entitled as heir in respect of freehold land under the rules in force before 1926[1].
This rule applies both to an heir general and an heir special[2], but only to
limitations or trusts created by an instrument coming into operation after 1925,
although the date of the deceased's death is immaterial[3].

1   See the Law of Property Act 1925 s 132; the Administration of Estates Act 1925 s 51(1); the Law
    of Property (Amendment) Act 1924 s 9, Sch 9 (preserving, as regards the ascertainment of persons

who are to take equitable interests as heirs by purchase, the Inheritance Act 1833, as amended by the Law of Property Amendment Act 1859 s 19; for the enactments preserved see PARA 539 et seq). As to the distinction between taking by descent and by purchase see PARA 539.

2   Law of Property Act 1925 s 132(1). As to the meaning of 'heir' see PARAS 339–342.
3   Law of Property Act 1925 s 132(2).

533. Mental disorder continuing from 1925 until death. Where a person of unsound mind or defective living[1] and of full age on 1 January 1926 was before that date[2] entitled to a beneficial interest in freehold property[3], and dies thereafter without having recovered his testamentary capacity and therefore has been unable since 1925 to make a will, the beneficial interest (not being an interest ceasing on his death)[4] devolves without prejudice to any will of his[5], in accordance with the general law[6] in force before 1926[7]. This rule has been applied to exclude the rights of a person legitimated since 1926[8] in spite of the express statutory provisions as to the rights of legitimated persons[9]. A person of unsound mind or defective living is not deemed to have recovered his testamentary capacity unless his receiver has been discharged[10]. It is not, however, necessary in order to receive the benefit of this provision that a receiver be appointed, but the provision only relates to the descent of the beneficial interest to the heir, and the real estate must now bear its rateable share of the funeral and testamentary expenses, debts and liabilities[11].

1   'Person of unsound mind' includes a person of unsound mind whether so found or not, and in relation to a person of unsound mind not so found; and 'defective' includes every person affected by the provisions of the Lunacy Act 1890 s 116, as extended by the Mental Deficiency Act 1913 s 64 (both repealed by the Mental Health Act 1983 which applied to a person 'incapable, by reason of mental disorder, of managing and administering his property and affairs' (see ss 94(2) and 95 and itself repealed): see now the Mental Capacity Act 2005; and MENTAL HEALTH AND CAPACITY vol 75 (2013) PARA 606 et seq), and for whose benefit a receiver has been appointed: Administration of Estates Act 1925 s 55(1)(viii) (now repealed).
2   *Re Bradshaw, Bradshaw v Bradshaw* [1950] Ch 582, [1950] 1 All ER 643, CA.
3   The exemption from the new provisions is confined to freehold property; leaseholds are expressly excluded: see the Administration of Estates Act 1925 s 51(2).
4   This is the wording of the Administration of Estates Act 1925 s 1: see PARA 945. The wording of the Land Transfer Act 1897 s 1(1) (repealed as to deaths after 1925), to which the land is virtually made subject was rather different: 'real estate is vested in any person without a right in any other person to take by survivorship'.
5   The person suffering from a mental disorder may have made an effective will before his illness or during a lucid interval before 1926.
6   General law means the general law of intestacy before 1926, so that the special custom of gavelkind which would in fact have applied before 1926 ceases to do so under these provisions, and the land devolves under the common law as at that date: *Re Higham, Higham v Higham* [1937] 2 All ER 17. As to gavelkind see PARA 563.
7   Law of Property (Amendment) Act 1924 s 9, Sch 9 (preserving in relation to lunatics and defectives the Inheritance Act 1833, as amended by the Law of Property Amendment Act 1859 s 19; for the enactments preserved see PARA 539 et seq); Administration of Estates Act 1925 s 51(2) (amended by the Mental Treatment Act 1930 s 20(5); and the Mental Health Act 1959 s 149(2), Sch 8). The rule applied even if, by reason of the transitional provisions of the Law of Property Act 1925, the interest became after 1925 only an interest in the proceeds of sale of the real estate: *Re Bradshaw, Bradshaw v Bradshaw* [1950] Ch 582, [1950] 1 All ER 643, CA. As to real property sold before 1926 see also *Re Harding, Westminster Bank Ltd v Laver* [1934] Ch 271.
8   *Re Berrey, Lewis v Berrey* [1936] Ch 274.
9   See CHILDREN AND YOUNG PERSONS vol 9 (2012) PARA 142 et seq.
10   Administration of Estates Act 1925 s 51(2) (as amended: see note 7).
11   *Re Gates, Gates v Gates* [1930] 1 Ch 199.

534. Minors dying without having married. If after 1925 and before 1997 a minor who is equitably entitled under a settlement or will to a vested estate in fee simple or absolute interest in freehold land or in any property settled to devolve with it or as freehold land dies without having been married, the land or property devolves as if the minor's interest in it was an entailed interest[1]. The provision applies to a minor entitled under an intestacy since in such a case there is a notional settlement. Upon the death of such a minor the land devolves on the person who would have been heir in tail under the old law if the minor's interest had been an estate in tail. If the heir in tail is a minor his interest is an entailed one until he attains full age or marries[2].

1 Administration of Estates Act 1925 s 51(3) (amended in respect of deaths on or after 1 January 1997 by the Trusts of Land and Appointment of Trustees Act 1996 s 25(1), Schs 3, 4). As to the effect of this provision see PARA 478 note 7.
2 *Re Taylor, Pullan v Taylor* [1931] 2 Ch 242. As to entailed interests see PARA 531.

535. Reference to Statutes of Distribution. In an instrument inter vivos made or in a will coming into operation after 1925, references to any Statutes of Distribution are to be construed as references to the rules of distribution enacted by the Administration of Estates Act 1925[1], and, in the case of an instrument inter vivos made or a will coming into operation after 1952, to the same rules as amended by the Intestates' Estates Act 1952[2], and references to statutory next of kin[3], unless the context otherwise requires, as references to the persons who would take under those rules[4]. Trusts declared in an instrument inter vivos made or a will coming into operation before 1926 by reference to the Statutes of Distribution are, unless the contrary appears[5], to be construed as referring to the enactments (other than the Intestates' Estates Act 1890[6]) in force relating to the distribution on an intestacy immediately before 1926[7].

The presumption is that the rules to be applied are to be applied at the death of the deceased[8], and that the shares in which and trusts upon which the beneficiaries indicated by the rules are to take are those prescribed in the case of an intestacy[9]. The rules are to be applied in the same way in respect of all limitations in wills which the law may construe as limitations in favour of the next of kin according to the Statutes of Distribution[10].

1 See PARAS 521–530. This includes, in relation to an instrument inter vivos made or a will coming into operation after 1 January 1953, references to the Intestates' Estates Act 1952 Pt I (ss 1–6), Schs 1, 2; and in relation to an instrument inter vivos made or a will or codicil coming into operation after 4 April 1988, references to the Family Law Reform Act 1987 s 18: Administration of Estates Act 1925 s 50(3) (added by the Family Law Reform Act 1987 Sch 2 para 3); Intestates' Estates Act 1952 s 6(2); Family Law Reform Act 1987 s 18(3), (4) (amended by the Human Fertilisation and Embryology Act 2008 Sch 6 para 25(3)).
2 See PARA 485 et seq.
3 A mere reference to 'next of kin' has been construed as an implied reference to the Statutes of Distribution: *Re Jackson, Holliday v Jackson* [1944] WN 26.
4 Administration of Estates Act 1925 s 50(1); Intestates' Estates Act 1952 s 6(2).
5 For instances where wills have been construed as showing no contrary intention see *Re Sutcliffe, Sutcliffe v Robertshaw* [1929] 1 Ch 123; *Re Sutton, Evans v Oliver* [1934] Ch 209; *Re Walsh, Public Trustee v Walsh* [1936] 1 All ER 327, CA.
6 As to the Intestates' Estates Act 1890 see PARA 538. It was held in *Re Morgan, Morgan v Morgan* [1920] 1 Ch 196 that the Intestates' Estates Act 1890 was not included in the phrase 'Statutes of Distribution' or in the phrase 'statutes for the distribution of the personal estate of intestates'. As to the meaning of 'statute for the distribution of the estates of intestate persons' see *Re Hughes, Loddiges v Jones* [1916] 1 Ch 493.
7 Administration of Estates Act 1925 s 50(2). See PARA537. See also *Re Sutcliffe, Sutcliffe v Robertshaw* [1929] 1 Ch 123; *Re Sutton, Evans v Oliver* [1934] Ch 209.
8 See eg *Re Gansloser's Will Trusts, Chartered Bank of India, Australia and China v Chillingworth* [1952] Ch 30, [1951] 2 All ER 936, CA, and the cases there cited.
9 *Re Nightingale, Bowden v Griffiths* [1909] 1 Ch 385; but see *Re Gansloser's Will Trusts, Chartered Bank of India, Australia and China v Chillingworth* [1952] Ch 30, [1951] 2 All ER 936, CA, for the basis of distribution where a gift to 'relations' is construed as a gift to those entitled on intestacy.
10 There are several such, eg a bequest of personalty to 'the heirs of A' or 'to A or his heirs'; 'the nearest relatives of A'. The question is one of construction: see PARA172 et seq.

(ii) The Old Rules: Distribution of Personal Estate

536. Rules for distribution of personal estate. Although in theory it is still possible, it is in practice now highly improbable that the pre-1926 rules for distribution of personal estate will be needed at the present day. The rules for descent of real estate are marginally more likely to be relevant in the cases indicated previously[1] since title can in rare instances still depend on these.

The rules for distribution of personal estate are therefore only briefly summarised[2].

1   See PARAS 531–534.
2   See PARA 537.

537. The old rules. After administration[1] the personal estate was distributed in the following order[2]. First a surviving husband took his wife's whole estate[3]. Secondly, a widow took one-third of her husband's personal estate if he left issue and half if he left no issue[4]. If he died totally intestate after 1 September 1890 without issue the widow took absolutely all his real and personal estate up to a value of £500[5]. Thirdly, if there were no next of kin the widow took £500 and half the residue[6]. Fourthly, subject to the rights of the surviving spouse as indicated previously, the children took in equal portions and if any children were then dead such persons as legally represented those children took[7], being their descendants, and not their next of kin[8]. Descendants to the remotest degree stood in the place of their parent or other ancestor and took by their stocks the share which he or she would have taken[9]. The heir at law took equally with other children and accounted equally with them for advance of personalty but not for land or improvements of land inherited[10]. Subsequent entitlements were the father[11], the mother, brothers or sister, sharing equally[12], grandparents (if there were no brothers or sisters), nephews and nieces, and other relations ascertained in accordance with the civil law[13]. Subject to this the Crown took the personal estate as bona vacantia but any executors might take as against the Crown[14].

1   As to administration see PARA 956 et seq. As to the distinction between administration and distribution see PARA 1107.
2   See the Statute of Distribution (1670) (repealed as respects deaths after 1925). The interests vested immediately on the death: *Cooper v Cooper* (1874) LR 7 HL 53.
3   However, property acquired by a wife after decree of judicial separation passed as if the husband had predeceased her: Matrimonial Causes Act 1857 s 25 (repealed and replaced by the Supreme Court of Judicature (Consolidation) Act 1925 s 194(1)(a) (repealed); see now the Matrimonial Causes Act 1973 s 18(2); and PARAS 491, 770).
4   Statute of Distribution (1670) s 3 (repealed as regards deaths after 1925).
5   Intestates' Estates Act 1890 ss 1, 2, 4 (repealed as regards deaths after 1925). These rights might be barred by a marriage settlement.
6   The other half went to the Crown. Separation or divorce had the same effect as under current law: see PARAS 491–493. As to other bars see PARA 498.
7   Children other than the heir at law had to bring into account any estates by settlement of the intestate and any advancements. A posthumous child was treated as if born in the father's lifetime: see PARA 499.
8   *Bridge v Abbot* (1791) 3 Bro CC 224 at 226; *Evans v Charles* (1794) 1 Anst 128 at 132; *Price v Strange* (1820) 6 Madd 159.
9   *Re Ross' Trusts* (1871) LR 13 Eq 286; *Re Natt, Walker v Gammage* (1888) 37 ChD 517.
10   *Smith v Smith* (1801) 5 Ves 721.
11   Ie subject to the widow's rights if there were no descendants.
12   Children but not grandchildren of brothers or sisters could take their parents' share.
13   Quot personae tot gradus applied, by which the degrees of relationship were ascertained by counting up the number of generations to the common ancestor and then counting down the number of generations to the claimant. Relatives of a higher degree (ie separated by a smaller number of steps) took to the exclusion of those of a lower degree and relatives of the same degree took equally.

14 The Executors Act 1830 did not alter the position in this respect. As to bona vacantia see
PARAS 512–513.

(iii) The Old Rules: Descent of Real Estate

538. Descent to the heir of real estate. Real estate descended to the heir in
accordance with the following rules which are still applicable in the cases
mentioned previously[1] and may, in increasingly rare cases, still be of relevance in
matters of title[2]. The heir to freehold property was ascertained according to the
following rules, which applied only in cases of death before 1926 and on or after
1 January 1834[3]. The descent of equitable estates was governed by the same
rules as the descent of legal estates[4]. Dower and curtesy are discussed elsewhere in
this work[5].

1 See PARA 531.
2 See PARA 536.
3 This is the date on which the Inheritance Act 1833 came into force. The rules according to which
the heir was ascertained before that date have still to be observed in cases where the death in
question occurred before 1 January 1834, and, in so far as they differ from that Act, they are stated
in the notes to this title. For the general supersession as regards deaths after 1925 of previously
existing rules of descent by the Administration of Estates Act 1925 see s 45(1); and PARA 478. For
the preservation for certain purposes of the operation of the Inheritance Act 1833, amended by the
Law of Property Amendment Act 1859 s 19, see PARAS 480 note 4, 532 note 1, 533 note 7.
4 *Banks v Sutton* (1732) 2 P Wms 700 at 713; *Trash v Wood* (1839) 4 My & Cr 324.
5 See REAL PROPERTY AND REGISTRATION vol 87 (2012) PARA 152 et seq.

539. Rule 1: descent traced from the purchaser. In every case descent was traced
from the purchaser[1]. The person who last acquired the land otherwise than by
descent, or than by any escheat, partition or inclosure by the effect of which the
land became part of or descendible in the same manner as other land acquired by
descent, was the purchaser[2]. The person last entitled to or who had a right to the
land, whether he did or did not obtain the possession or receipt of its rents and
profits, was considered to have been the purchaser of it, unless it was proved that
he inherited it, and in like manner the last person from whom the land was proved
to have been inherited was in every case considered to have been the purchaser
unless it was proved that he inherited it[3].

The intention of the Inheritance Act 1833 was only to lay down rules where
there was any doubt[4]. Therefore, where a woman took as a coparcener by descent,
and died intestate leaving a son, the whole of her share vested in the son, and it
was not necessary to trace the descent as to that share from the purchaser from
whom the coparcener derived her title[5].

1 Inheritance Act 1833 s 2. Where there was a total failure of the purchaser's heirs, or where any
land was descendible as if an ancestor had been its purchaser, and there was a total failure of the
heirs of that ancestor, the land descended and the descent was then traced from the person last
entitled to the land as if he had been its purchaser: Law of Property Amendment Act 1859 s 19.
2 Inheritance Act 1833 s 1. As to escheat see PARA 552.
3 Inheritance Act 1833 ss 1, 2. The rule in cases where the death took place before 1834 was that
inheritances lineally descend to the issue in infinitum of the person last actually seised, but never
lineally ascend: 2 Bl Com (14th Edn) 208. As to what constituted actual seisin for the purpose of
this rule see *R v Sutton* (1835) 5 Nev & MKB 353; *Goodtitle d Newman v Newman* (1774) 3 Wils
516; and Watkins' Law of Descents (4th Edn) 52.
4 *Cooper v France* (1850) 19 LJ Ch 313 at 314 per Shadwell V-C.
5 *Cooper v France* (1850) 19 LJ Ch 313; *Re Matson, James v Dickinson* [1897] 2 Ch 509. It is
difficult to reconcile these decisions with the Inheritance Act 1833 s 2, but *Cooper v France* has
never been questioned. As to coparceners see PARA 546.

540. Limitation to heirs. Where by an assurance land was limited to the grantor
or to the heirs of the grantor, and, similarly, where by a will land was devised to

the person who was in fact the testator's heir, the grantor or his heir, or the testator's heir (as the case might be), took as purchaser[1], and was deemed to be the purchaser for all purposes[2]. This rule applied to a devise to or in trust for the testator's right heirs, or to any other form of words where the devise was in effect to the heir or to the person who should be the heir of the testator at the time of the testator's death, and was not confined to a devise to the testator's heir simply[3]. The quality of the estate taken was altered, so that where a man devised land to his own right heirs and left coheiresses, they took as joint tenants and not as coparceners or tenants in common[4].

1 Inheritance Act 1833 s 3. This reversed the old rule under which the grantor or his heir or the testator's heir was considered to be entitled as of his former estate, or part of it: see *Pibus v Mitford* (1674) 1 Vent 372; *Chaplin v Leroux* (1816) 5 M & S 14; *Biederman v Seymour* (1841) 3 Beav 368.
2 *Strickland v Strickland* (1839) 10 Sim 374; *Owen v Gibbons* [1902] 1 Ch 636, CA.
3 *Owen v Gibbons* [1902] 1 Ch 636, CA.
4 *Owens v Gibbons* [1902] 1 Ch 636, CA. As to coparceners see PARA 546. As to tenancy in common see REAL PROPERTY AND REGISTRATION vol 87 (2012) PARA 215 et seq.

541. Devise to trustees. Where the descent was broken by a devise to trustees on trust to convey to the testator's heir, they were bound to convey to the heir according to the common law, that is, the heir of the paternal line, even if it came to the testator from the maternal line[1]. A mere devise, however, to trustees for a purpose which failed (such as a devise on a trust for conversion which was void for remoteness) did not affect the quality of the interest undisposed of, so that the heir took the land in the character in which the testator had it, and if it came to the testator ex parte materna, his heir ex parte materna would take, and not his heir according to the common law[2].

This rule applied only to cases where the land was limited to the person or to the 'heirs' of the person conveying the land; it did not apply where there was a limitation to a person designate, even though such persona designata was in fact the heir[3].

1 *Davis v Kirk* (1856) 2 K & J 391.
2 *Buchanan v Harrison* (1861) 1 John & H 662.
3 *Heywood v Heywood* (1865) 34 Beav 317.

542. When descent was traced from an ancestor. Where a person had become entitled to land under a limitation or devise to his ancestor's heirs, the land descended and the descent was traced as if the ancestor had been the purchaser[1].

1 Inheritance Act 1833 s 4. Eg if B, being the only child of A, settled land by a settlement in which the ultimate limitation was to A's right heirs and all the previous limitations failed, the descent was to be traced from A, and not from B. This was contrary to the former rule, under which such a grant or devise was treated as a restoration to the grantor or testator or part of his original estate, so that the line of descent was not broken: *Moore v Simkin* (1885) 31 ChD 95. The object of the Inheritance Act 1833 s 4 was only to provide how the land was to descend in case the purchaser did not dispose of it, not to alter the estate which he himself took. Accordingly, where land was limited to the right heirs of X (who took no interest in it), and his right heirs at the date of his death were three sisters and five daughters of a deceased sister, although for the purpose of ascertaining who were the personae designatae it was necessary to trace the descent from X, yet such persons did not take by descent from him, but under the direct gift to them, and therefore they took as joint tenants and not as coparceners: *Berens v Fellowes* (1887) 56 LT 391. As to coparceners see PARA 546.

543. Failure of purchaser's heirs. Where there was a total failure of heirs of the purchaser, or where any land was descendible as if an ancestor had been the purchaser of it, and there was a total failure of the heirs of that ancestor, the land descended and the descent was traced from the person last entitled as if he had been its purchaser[1].

1 Law of Property Amendment Act 1859 ss 19, 20. The Inheritance Act 1833 failed to provide for this case, with the result that in the case of deaths between 1 January 1834 and 13 August 1859, where there was a total failure of heirs of the purchaser, the heirs of the person last seised were not entitled to the land by descent, eg where an illegitimate person purchased land which descended to his son who died intestate and a bachelor, the persons claiming through the son's mother were not entitled to take as his heirs: *Doe d Blackburn v Blackburn* (1836) 1 Mood & R 547.

544. Merger of equitable and legal estates. The equitable estate merged in the legal estate if they united in the same person and were co-extensive and commensurate, and the legal estate then governed the descent. Therefore, if the intestate held the equitable estate as purchaser but the legal estate by descent, the descent was traced from the last purchaser of the legal estate[1].

1 *Brydges v Brydges, Philips v Brydges* (1796) 3 Ves 120; *Re Douglas, Wood v Douglas* (1884) 28 ChD 327.

545. Rule 2: priority of males. The descent on a death intestate before 1926 was in the first place to the issue of the purchaser lineally, the male issue being admitted before the female[1].

1 2 Bl Com (14th Edn) 212.

546. Rule 3: coparceners. The eldest only of two or more males of equal degree inherited, but females of equal degree all inherited together[1]. Females or heirs of females who inherited together were called coparceners[2]; coparceners were said to be one heir to their ancestor[3], but on the death of a coparcener intestate her share descended to her heirs[4], and was subject to her husband's right of curtesy[5]. Even after a partition each coparcener continued entitled to her share by descent and not by purchase[6].

1 2 Bl Com (14th Edn) 214.
2 Bac Abr, Coparceners; Littleton's Tenures ss 241, 254.
3 Littleton's Tenures s 24; Co Litt 163b.
4 Littleton's Tenures s 280; *Paterson v Mills* (1850) 19 LJ Ch 310; *Cooper v France* (1850) 19 LJ Ch 313; *Re Matson, James v Dickinson* [1897] 2 Ch 509.
5 Co Litt 174b. As to curtesy see REAL PROPERTY AND REGISTRATION vol 87 (2012) PARA 152 et seq.
6 *Doe d Crosthwaite v Dixon* (1836) 5 Ad & El 834.

547. Rule 4: lineal descendants. On a death intestate before 1926 the lineal descendants in infinitum of any deceased person represented their ancestor[1]; in other words they occupied the same position as he would have occupied if he had been alive[2].

1 2 Bl Com (14th Edn) 216.
2 Eg if A died having had an elder son, B, who predeceased his father, but leaving a son D, and a younger son C, who survived A, A's heir was his grandson D.

548. Rule 5: lineal ancestors. On failure of lineal descendants or issue of the purchaser, the nearest lineal ancestor inherited[1]. Accordingly a father was heir to his intestate son, in preference to the intestate's brother. This rule was, however, read as meaning that every lineal ancestor should be capable of being heir to any of his issue who were capable of inheriting from him. It did not do away with the rule that, in order to claim as heir, the claimant must be a son born in wedlock, and it was not sufficient that he should be legitimate in the country of his birth. Therefore, a son born in Scotland before wedlock, although legitimated by the subsequent marriage of his parents, could not take land in England as heir of his father, neither could his father inherit land from him under this rule[2].

1 Inheritance Act 1833 s 6. The rule in cases where the death took place before 1 January 1834 was that on failure of lineal descendants or issue of the person last seised the inheritance descended to the blood of the first purchaser (2 Bl Com (14th Edn) 220), which was based on the feudal rule that a fief could not ascend. This rule was subject to an apparent exception, called the doctrine of possessio fratris, under which the descent between brothers and sisters was immediate, so that in making out their title it was not necessary to name the common father, even if living (*Collingwood v Pace* (1664) 1 Vent 413), and although the father was in fact unable to hold the fief, eg by reason of being an alien; for, it was said, although the fief is not antiquum, still it descends 'ut antiquum', and, the ancestor for this purpose being an assumed person, he must further be assumed to have been a capable ancestor (*Kynnaird v Leslie* (1866) LR 1 CP 389). However, the Inheritance Act 1833 s 5 provided that no brother or sister should be considered to inherit immediately from his or her brother or sister, but every such descent should be traced through the parent.
2 *Re Don's Estate* (1857) 4 Drew 194; cf *Doe d Birtwhistle v Vardill* (1835) 2 Cl & Fin 571, HL.

549. Rule 6: priority of paternal line. The paternal ancestor was preferred to the maternal ancestor. Accordingly no male maternal ancestor or any of his descendants was capable of inheriting until all the paternal ancestors and their descendants had failed; nor was any female paternal ancestor, or any of her descendants, until all the male paternal ancestors and their descendants had failed; nor was any female maternal ancestor, or any of her descendants, until all the male maternal ancestors and their descendants had failed[1].

Under this rule the descendants of the maternal ancestors had to be sought for, and taken as heirs when it had been shown after due inquiry that there was no reasonable probability of discovering descendants of a paternal ancestor. It was not necessary to show positively that there were no descendants of a male paternal ancestor[2]. Where there was a failure of male paternal ancestors and their descendants, the mother of a more remote male paternal ancestor and her descendants were preferred to the mother of a less remote male paternal ancestor and her descendants; and where there was a failure of male maternal ancestors and their descendants, the mother of a more remote male maternal ancestor and her descendants were preferred to the mother of a less remote male maternal ancestor and her descendants[3].

1 Inheritance Act 1833 s 7.
2 *Greaves v Greenwood* (1877) 2 Ex D 289, CA. As to the absence of any presumption of death without issue see CIVIL PROCEDURE vol 12 (2015) PARA 760.
3 Inheritance Act 1833 s 8.

550. Rule 7: half blood. Any person related by the half blood was on a death intestate before 1926 capable of being the heir, and stood in the order of inheritance next after any relation in the same degree of the whole blood and his issue where the common ancestor was a male, and next after the common ancestor where the common ancestor was a female; so that the brother of the half blood on the part of the father inherited next after the sisters of the whole blood on the part of the father and their issue, and the brother of the half blood on the part of the mother inherited next after the mother[1].

1 Inheritance Act 1833 s 9. The rule in cases where the death took place before 1 January 1834 was that the collateral heir of the person last seised must be his next collateral kinsman of the whole blood; kinsmen of the half blood could not inherit: 2 Bl Com (14th Edn) 224, 227.

551. Qualified heir. Where an owner of freeholds died intestate before 1926 leaving his wife pregnant, the qualified heir (the person who would be the heir if no child were subsequently born ranking before him in accordance with the rules of descent) was entitled to go into possession of the property and receive and retain the rents for his own benefit[1]. Possibly this was not the case where the legal estate was outstanding in trustees[2].

1 This applied both to rents actually received, and also to those accrued due before the birth of the posthumous child: *Richards v Richards* (1860) John 754; *Re Mowlem* (1874) LR 18 Eq 9; and see *Re Wilmer's Trusts, Moore v Wingfield* [1903] 1 Ch 874 at 888 per Buckley J.

   In order to prevent the supplanting of the heir by a suppositious child of a deceased person, the heir presumptive was entitled to obtain, on petition (*Ex p Bellet* (1786) 1 Cox Eq Cas 297), a writ de ventre inspiciendo, to examine whether the widow claiming to be pregnant by the deceased husband was pregnant or not (Co Litt, 19th Edn by Hargrave (1832), 8b). This writ was addressed to the sheriff commanding him to impanel a jury of 12 knights and 12 matrons to examine the widow. If the jury found she was pregnant she could be detained in safe custody until after delivery, or the expiration of 40 weeks from the death of the husband (see *Willoughby's Case* (1597) Cro Eliz 566; *Theaker's Case* (1624) Cro Jac 686), but the practice in the more modern cases was to give a right of access to persons representing the petitioner, rather than to order the strict detention of the woman (*Ex p Aiscough* (1731) 2 P Wms 591; *Re Brown, ex p Wallop* (1792) 4 Bro CC 90, and the cases cited in the judgment). The grant was also extended to devisees: *Re Brown, ex p Wallop*.

2 *Goodale v Gawthorne* (1854) 2 Sm & G 375, which was criticised, but not definitely dissented from, in *Richards v Richards* (1860) John 754.

552. Escheat. Where on an intestacy before 1926 there was no heir, real property was subject to a right of escheat. Escheat was the right whereby land of which there was no longer any tenant returned, by reason of tenure, to the lord by whom, or by whose predecessors in title, the tenure was created[1]. It was not strictly a reversion, as there could not and cannot be a reversion expectant upon an estate in fee simple, nor did the lord take the land by way of succession or inheritance as if from the tenant. The tenant's estate, subject to any charges upon it which he may have created, had come to an end, and the lord was in by his own right[2]. Escheat was an incident of feudal tenure, and was based on the want of a tenant to perform the feudal services[3].

1 *A-G of Ontario v Mercer* (1883) 8 App Cas 767 at 772, PC, per Lord Selborne LC. 'Escheate is a term of art and derived from the French word escheate that is cadere, excidere or accidere and signifyeth properly when by accident the lands fall to the lord of whom they are holden': Co Litt 13a. See also Co Litt 92b; Termes de la Ley sv Escheate; Com Dig, Escheat (A 1); *May and Bannister v Street* (1588) Cro Eliz 120. As to escheat and its abolition see REAL PROPERTY AND REGISTRATION vol 87 (2012) PARA 267.

2 *A-G of Ontario v Mercer* (1883) 8 App Cas 767 at 772, PC.

3 See *A-G v Sands* (1670) Hard 488; Tudor, LC Real Prop (4th Edn) 211; *Burgess v Wheate* (1759)1 Eden 177 at 201 per Clarke MR.

553. Land subject to escheat. Land held in socage, whether of the Crown or a mesne lord, was always liable to escheat in the case of death intestate before 1926; but the interest which escheated could only be the whole fee[1]. On the failure of issue under an estate tail, the land entailed did not escheat, but reverted to the owner of the reversion in fee expectant on the determination of the estate tail[2].

1 Before the passing of the Intestates' Estates Act 1884 things which did not lie in tenure were not subject to escheat. Accordingly a rentcharge did not escheat on the death of the owner intestate and without heirs, but ceased for the benefit of the owner of the land charged: *A-G v Sands* (1670) Hard 488 per Hale CB; Tudor, LC Real Prop (4th Edn) 211; and see *Dean and Canons of Windsor and Webb's Case* (1613) Godb 211. As to escheat see PARA 552.

2 Com Dig, Escheat (A 1); Fitz Nat Brev 144.

554. Escheat for want of a tenant. Escheat propter defectum tenentis[1] occurred in the case of a death intestate before 1926 where the last owner died intestate as to the land and without any heir. In this event (which most commonly occurred where an illegitimate child[2] became possessed of lands as purchaser, and died intestate without issue) the lord or the Crown, as the case may be, re-entered in right of his or its former ownership, the estate which was granted having come to an end[3].

1   Ie escheat for want of a tenant. There was also an escheat propter delictum tenentis (on account of the crime of the tenant) which practically became obsolete in 1870. Escheat for want of a tenant also occurred on the dissolution of a corporation or company: see REAL PROPERTY AND REGISTRATION vol 87 (2012) PARA 267. As to escheat see PARA 552.
2   Under the former law an illegitimate child is nullius filius (Co Litt 3b). See also CHILDREN AND YOUNG PERSONS vol 9 (2012) PARA 142.
3   *Burgess v Wheate* (1759) 1 Eden 177; 2 Co Inst 64.

555. Intestates' Estates Act 1884.

Before the passing of the Intestates' Estates Act 1884[1], the legal owner of the estate was entitled to retain it for his own benefit notwithstanding that the equitable owner had died intestate and without heirs, for there could not be an escheat where the Crown or the lord had a tenant[2]. In the case of the death intestate and without heirs on or after 14 August 1884 and before 1926 of a person entitled to any estate or interest, legal or equitable, in any corporeal hereditament, or to any equitable estate or interest in any corporeal hereditament, whether devised or not devised to trustees by that person's will, the law of escheat applied as if his estate or interest were a legal estate in corporeal hereditaments[3]; and where any beneficial interest in the real estate of any deceased person, whether legal or equitable, was, owing to the failure of the objects of the devise or other circumstances happening either before or after that person's death, in whole or in part not effectually disposed of, that person was deemed for the purposes of the Intestates' Estates Act 1884 to have died intestate in respect of such part of the said beneficial interest as was ineffectually disposed of[4].

1   The Intestates' Estates Act 1884 is repealed as respects deaths after 1925.
2   This principle was applied to the case of a trustee of freeholds who had no beneficiary (*Burgess v Wheate* (1759) 1 Eden 177; *Cox v Parker* (1856) 22 Beav 168); a trustee of copyholds (*Taylor v Haygarth* (1844) 14 Sim 8); a trustee of shares in the New River Company (*Davall v New River Co* (1849) 3 De G & Sm 394); and a legal mortgagee (*Beale v Symonds* (1853) 16 Beav 406). An equitable mortgagee, or a mortgagee of a term, however, was not entitled to the estate on failure of the mortgagor's heirs. Subject to the mortgage debt the estate escheated to the Crown: *Rogers v Maule* (1841) 1 Y & C Ch Cas 4; *Prescott v Tyler* (1837) 1 Jur 470. The Crown was not entitled to call on a trustee to whom personalty had been bequeathed upon trust for conversion to convert it in order to raise a title in the Crown by way of escheat (*Walker v Denne* (1793) 2 Ves 170); nor was the Crown entitled to call upon a trustee to whom land had been devised on condition that he paid a certain sum to charity, the gift to the charity being void under the Statutes of Mortmain, to raise that sum and pay it to the Crown (*Henchman v A-G* (1834) 3 My & K 485). The equitable doctrine of notional conversion was, however, no bar to the Crown: *Talbot v Jevers* [1917] 2 Ch 363, CA. As to escheat see PARA 552.
3   Intestates' Estates Act 1884 s 4 (repealed as respects deaths after 1925). For a more recent decision on the doctrine of escheat see *Re Lowe's Will Trusts, More v A-G* [1973] 2 All ER 1136, [1973] 1 WLR 882, CA.
4   Intestates' Estates Act 1884 s 7 (repealed as respects deaths after 1925). Sections 4 and 7 are to be read together, so that where a testatrix who left no heir devised a house to trustees in trust to sell and pay debts and legacies, and the will contained no gift of the residue of the proceeds of sale, it was held under s 7 that she had died intestate as regards the residue, and that under s 4 it escheated to the Crown: *Re Wood, A-G v Anderson* [1896] 2 Ch 596.

556. To whom land escheated.

Escheat in the case of death intestate before 1926 was to the mesne lord if he could be found but, as since 1290 sub-infeudation has been forbidden[1], in the great majority of cases there was no record of the mesne tenure, and the escheat was to the Crown as the lord paramount of the whole soil of the country, or to the Duchy of Lancaster in cases within the Duchy[2]. Copyhold land could not escheat to the Crown unless the Crown was lord of the manor of which the copyholds were held[3].

As the Land Transfer Act 1897[4] did not bind the Crown, it would appear that escheated real estate vested in the Crown and not in the legal personal representative, so that where the Treasury Solicitor applied for a grant to him, as the representative of the Crown, of administration of the estate of a person who had died without issue illegitimate and intestate, the proper form was to grant letters of administration of the personal estate only[5].

The Crown's right to an escheat could be barred by adverse possession[6] or first registration with absolute title[7].

1 18 Edw 1 (Quia Emptores) (1289) c 1; *Re Holliday* [1922] 2 Ch 698. As to escheat see PARA 552.
2 *Dyke v Walford* (1848) 5 Moo PCC 434; *Megit v Johnson* (1780) 2 Doug KB 542 at 548 per Lord Mansfield CJ. As to the Duchy of Lancaster see the Intestates' Estates Act 1884 s 8 (repealed as regards deaths after 1925); and CROWN AND CROWN PROCEEDINGS vol 29 (2014) PARA 214 et seq. As to escheat in the Duchy of Cornwall, cf *Re Canning, Solicitor to the Duchy of Cornwall v Canning* (1880) 5 PD 114.
3 *Walker v Denne* (1793) 2 Ves 170. As to land formerly copyhold see CUSTOM AND USAGE vol 32 (2012) PARA 42; REAL PROPERTY AND REGISTRATION vol 87 (2012) PARA 36 et seq. See also PARA 562.
4 For provisions as to the devolution of real estate see the Land Transfer Act 1897 s 1 (repealed as respects deaths after 1925). The first registration of any person as proprietor of freehold land with an absolute title had the effect, under the Land Transfer Act 1875 s 7 (repealed), of barring any claim to the land already accrued to the Crown by way of escheat. Escheat subsequent to such first registration was preserved by s 105 (repealed): *Re Suarez (No 2)* [1924] 2 Ch 19. As to the effect of registration on the Crown's right to bona vacantia under the modern law see PARA 513.
5 *Re Hartley* [1899] P 40. Where, on the other hand, a creditor of the intestate applied for administration, the grant was made 'in respect of all the estate of the deceased, which by law devolves to and vests in the legal personal representative' leaving the question open: *Re Ball* (1902) 47 Sol Jo 129.
6 *Tuthill v Rogers* (1844) 6 I Eq R 429. As to adverse possession see LIMITATION PERIODS vol 68 (2016) PARA 1076 et seq; REAL PROPERTY AND REGISTRATION vol 87 (2012) PARA 1049.
7 *Re Suarez (No 2)* [1924] 2 Ch 19; Land Transfer Act 1875 s 7 (repealed). Escheat subsequent to such first registration was preserved by s 105 (repealed).

557. Regrant of escheated land. Property which had escheated to the Crown on a death intestate before 1926 might in certain cases be granted to the family of, or to persons adopted as part of the family of, the person whose estate it had been, or to the person discovering the escheat[1], and on application being duly made this might be done by way of waiver of the Crown's rights[2]; but, subject as above, the Crown could not grant any real estate alleged to be escheated until after an inquisition finding the title to it had been returned to the Central Office of the Supreme Court[3]. Such inquisition should have found of whom the estate was held, and if it did not so find, any person aggrieved was entitled to obtain from the High Court an order for the taking of another inquisition[4], but no inquisition could prejudice any rights which at the time of the death leading to the inquisition were vested in some other person[5].

1 Crown Private Estate Act 1800; Crown Lands Act 1819; Intestates' Estates Act 1884 s 6 (repealed as regards deaths after 1925); and cf *Moggridge v Thackwell* (1803) 7 Ves 36 at 71; *Mason v A-G of Jamaica* (1843) 4 Moo PCC 228.
2 Intestates' Estates Act 1884 s 6 (repealed as regards deaths after 1925).
3 Escheat (Procedure) Act 1887 s 2(3).
4 Escheat (Procedure) Act 1887 s 2(5).
5 Escheat (Procedure) Act 1887 s 2(4). For the rules made under this Act see the Escheat Procedure Rules 1889, SR & O Rev 1903, IV p 1, and the Escheat Procedure (Duchy of Lancaster) Rules 1910, SR & O 1913, p 235. As to the inquisition of escheat see CROWN AND CROWN PROCEEDINGS vol 29 (2014) PARA 145 et seq.

558. Escheat to mesne lord. The rights of a mesne lord taking by escheat before 1926 were similar to those of the Crown[1], but some act of the lord was necessary to perfect his title; the actual possession of the land could not be gained until he entered or brought his action to recover the land[2]. His right to escheat for want of a tenant[3] was after 29 August 1833[4] subject to the payment of the debts of his tenant, even though those debts were not charged by the tenant on his land[5]. The Intestates' Estates Act 1884[6] appears to have been as much in favour of the mesne lord, if any, as of the Crown[7].

1   See PARA 552 et seq.
2   3 Cru Dig (4th Edn) 398.
3   See PARA 554.
4   See the Administration of Estates Act 1833 (repealed as respects deaths after 1925).
5   *Evans v Brown* (1842) 5 Beav 114; *Hughes v Wells* (1852) 9 Hare 749.
6   See PARA 555 note 1.
7   See PARA 555. The commonest case of escheat to a mesne lord arose in the case of copyholds. As to land formerly copyhold see CUSTOM AND USAGE vol 32 (2012) PARA 42; REAL PROPERTY AND REGISTRATION vol 87 (2012) PARA 36 et seq. See also PARA 562.

559. Estate tail. An estate tail before 1926 was such an estate as was limited to a succession of owners in a descending line only[1], and on a failure of such owners reverted to the grantor, unless barred. On the death of an owner of an estate tail the heirs in tail were entitled per formam doni[2].

1   As to entailed interests after 1925 see PARA 531; and as to the devolution of the legal estate in settled land since that date see PARA 949.
2   13 Edw 1 (Statute of Westminster the Second) (1285) c 1. The language of the Land Transfer Act 1897 s 1(1) (repealed as respects deaths after 1925) was wide enough to include these estates, but it seems that s 1(1) did not in fact include such estates.

560. Descent of estate tail. Within the limits marked out by the original grant, the descent of an estate tail on a death before 1926 was the same, and the rules for ascertaining the heir were the same as those of an estate in fee simple[1]; but the limitation of the grant to the heirs of the donee's body rendered it impossible that any of those rules subsequent to rule 4[2] should apply; and if the estate was limited in tail male or in tail female, rules 2 and 3[3] were so far unnecessary. In cases, however, where there was a special custom of descent, that custom was to be taken into account in ascertaining the heir in tail; accordingly an estate tail in gavelkind land descended to all the donee's sons in equal shares, while borough english land granted to a man and the heirs of his body descended to his youngest son (or youngest brother by special custom)[4], and copyhold land granted to a man and the heirs of his body descended to his heir according to the custom of the manor[5].

On the failure of issue under an estate tail the land did not escheat, but reverted to the owner of the reversion in fee expectant on the determination of the estate tail[6].

1   See PARA 538 et seq.
2   See PARA 547.
3   See PARAS 545–546.
4   As to gavelkind see PARA 563; and as to borough english see PARA 564.
5   Copyhold land was only entailable by custom: *Doe d Wightwick v Truby* (1774) 2 Wm Bl 944 at 946. Where there was no custom to entail, a grant of copyhold in words which, in the case of freehold would create an estate tail, created a fee simple conditional on birth of issue: *Doe d Spencer v Clark* (1822) 5 B & Ald 458; *Doe d Blesard v Simpson* (1842) 3 Man & G 929, Ex Ch; *Hardcastle v Dennison* (1861) 10 CBNS 606. As to land formerly copyhold see CUSTOM AND USAGE vol 32 (2012) PARA 42; REAL PROPERTY AND REGISTRATION vol 87 (2012) PARA 36 et seq. See also PARA 562.
6   Com Dig, Escheat (A 1); Fitz Nat Brev 144.

561. Customary land. Customary land of all kinds[1] descended on a death before 1926 to the heir according to the custom, but, subject to the custom, the rules for ascertaining the heir already set out[2] applied to customary land as if it was freehold[3].

An equitable estate, where the trust was executed (for example in the case of an equity of redemption or of a resulting trust) descended in the same way as if the estate were legal[4], except in the cases where the customary descent was only applicable to the case of 'a tenant dying seised'[5]. An executory interest, however, descended to the heir according to the common law[6].

The descent of customary land was not broken unless the owner conveyed away all his interest and, on another transaction and by another conveyance, took back the estate as a new estate, and so as to take it by purchase. It was not sufficient to convey it to a trustee for the owner[7]. Customary freehold ceased to exist as such on 1 January 1926, and is now subject to the same rules as ordinary freehold[8].

1 'Customary land' includes customary freehold, gavelkind land, borough english land and copyholds: see PARAS 562–564.
2 See PARA 536 et seq.
3 In the Inheritance Act 1833 s 1, 'land' includes manors, advowsons, messuages, and all other hereditaments, whether corporeal or incorporeal, and whether freehold, copyhold (see PARA 562), or of any other tenure, and whether descendible according to the common law or according to the custom of gavelkind (see PARA 563) or borough english (see PARA 564), or any other custom. See also *Brown's Case* (1581) 4 Co Rep 21a at 22a; *Hook v Hook* (1862) 1 Hem & M 43.
4 *Blunt v Clark* (1658) 2 Sid 61; *Roberts v Dixwell* (1738) 1 Atk 607; *Starkey v Starkey* (1746) 8 Bac Abr 302; *Fawcet v Lowther* (1751) 2 Ves Sen 300; *Re Hudson, Cassels v Hudson* [1908] 1 Ch 655.
5 Elton on Copyholds (2nd Edn) 139; *Payne v Barker* (1662) O Bridg 18; *Rider v Wood* (1855) 1 K & J 644 at 657. In *Trash v Wood* (1839) 4 My & Cr 324, the custom as proved was that on the death of a tenant seised of copyhold it should go to the younger son, but it was held that, despite the word 'seised', the customary heir in tail was entitled to land vested in a trustee in trust for the intestate and his heirs in tail, 'for it is not to be expected that the court rolls should furnish evidence of a custom immediately applicable to trust estates, because all the transactions recorded in the court rolls are of transfers of the legal estate': *Trash v Wood* at 329 per Lord Cottenham LC.
6 *Payne v Barker* (1662) O Bridg 18; *Mallinson v Siddle* (1870) 18 WR 569; *Trash v Wood* (1839) 4 My & Cr 324; *Re Hudson, Cassels v Hudson* [1908] 1 Ch 655.
7 *Nanson v Barnes* (1869) LR 7 Eq 250.
8 See REAL PROPERTY AND REGISTRATION vol 87 (2012) PARA 41. See also the Administration of Estates Act 1925 s 45(1)(a).

562. Copyholds. Copyholds[1] descended according to the custom of the manor of which they were held[2]. In deciding questions as to the custom of a manor, the court would not depart from the literal meaning of the words of the custom as proved, or supply other words in their place, and in cases to which the custom as proved did not extend, the land descended to the heir at common law[3]. Copyholds were compulsorily enfranchised on 1 January 1926, and former copyholds are now subject to the same rules as freeholds[4].

1 Copyhold land was land held by copy of court roll, held at the will of the lord according to the custom of the manor. As to the nature of manors and manorial customs see CUSTOM AND USAGE vol 32 (2012) PARA 41 et seq. As to copyhold see REAL PROPERTY AND REGISTRATION vol 87 (2012) PARA 36 et seq.
2 As to customs of the manor see CUSTOM AND USAGE vol 32 (2012) PARA 41 et seq.
3 *Denn v Spray* (1786) 1 Term Rep 466; *Muggleton v Barnett* (1857) 2 H & N 653, Ex Ch. Where the custom was for the land to descend to the youngest son or daughter, brother or sister, uncle or aunt, and a tenant died leaving none of these but sons of a deceased uncle, it was held that the heir at common law was entitled to the land, and not the youngest son of the youngest uncle: *Re Smart, Smart v Smart* (1881) 18 ChD 165.
4 See REAL PROPERTY AND REGISTRATION vol 87 (2012) PARA 36 et seq.

563. Descent of gavelkind land. In Kent gavelkind[1] was, before 1926, the common law and a matter of judicial knowledge which did not need to be proved by evidence[2]. The descent was among all the sons or their representatives; where one brother died without issue, all his brothers inherited[3], but if a brother died leaving issue, such issue stood in their father's place per stirpes[4].

In default of sons and their issue, land subject to the custom of gavelkind descended to daughters[5]. The partibility among heirs of the same degree extended to all degrees of remoteness[6]. Females took after males of the same degree; but jure representationis they might inherit together with males[7].

It seems that under a devise to the right heirs of the testator or of a stranger the heir at common law and not the gavelkind heirs took the devised estate[8]. This form of descent has been abolished with regard to the estate of any person dying after 1925[9].

1 As to the custom of gavelkind generally see REAL PROPERTY AND REGISTRATION vol 87 (2012) PARA 32.
2 *Re Chenoweth, Ward v Dwelley* [1902] 2 Ch 488. 'In the county of Kent, where lands and tenements are holden in gavelkind, there by the custom and use the issues male ought equally to inherit': Littleton's Tenures s 210.
3 *Re Chenoweth, Ward v Dwelley* [1902] 2 Ch 488.
4 Co Litt 140a; *Crump d Woolley v Norwood* (1815) 7 Taunt 362.
5 Statute Prerogativa Regis (temp incert) c 18 (repealed).
6 *Re Chenoweth, Ward v Dwelley* [1902] 2 Ch 488; *Hook v Hook* (1862) 1 Hem & M 43.
7 *Clements v Scudamore* (1703) 1 P Wms 63.
8 *Thorp v Owen* (1854) 2 Sm & G 90; *Garland v Beverley* (1878) 9 ChD 213; and cf *Polley v Polley (No 2)* (1862) 31 Beav 363 (borough english); and Co Litt 10a. But see contra *Sladen v Sladen* (1862) 2 John & H 369 at 373 per Page Wood V-C; and *Hawes v Hawes* (1880) 14 ChD 614 (limitation in a deed). As to borough english see PARA 564.
9 Administration of Estates Act 1925 s 45(1)(a). See also *Re Price* [1928] Ch 579. As to the statutory exceptions in cases of incapacity see PARAS 533–534. Apparently the descent must be traced to the heir at law of the last purchaser and not to the gavelkind heir on a death after 1925 (*Re Price*); see also PARA 478 note 4.

564. Descent of borough english land. Land which was subject to the custom of borough english[1] descended to the youngest son of the deceased owner[2]. By special custom land might descend to the youngest brother, the youngest daughter or sister, or the youngest in any other degree[3]. The daughter of a youngest son (who had died in the lifetime of his father) took *jure representationis* in preference to the next younger son who had survived the father[4].

A devise of borough english land to the heir or heirs of a deceased person might be read as a devise to the heir or heirs at common law, who took as personae designatae, and not to the borough english heir or heirs[5]. A younger son who took land by the custom of borough english was nevertheless entitled to his full share of the intestate's personalty[6].

The custom of borough english was abolished with regard to the estate of any person dying after 1925[7].

1 As to the custom of borough english generally see REAL PROPERTY AND REGISTRATION vol 87 (2012) PARA 33.
2 Littleton's Tenures s 165: 'For some boroughs have such a custom that if a man have issue many sonnes and dyeth the youngest son shall inherit all the tenements which were his father's within the same borough as heire unto his father by force of the custome: the which is called borough english'.
3 1 Roll Abr 624, pl 2; *Bayly v Stevens* (1607) Cro Jac 198; *Reve v Malster and Barrow* (1635) Cro Car 410; *Rapley and Chaplein's Case* (1610) Godb 166; *Denn v Spray* (1786) 1 Term Rep 466; *Re Smart, Smart v Smart* (1881) 18 ChD 165; cf *Muggleton v Barnett* (1857) 2 H & N 653 Ex Ch.
4 *Clements v Scudamore* (1703) 1 P Wms 63.
5 *Polley v Polley (No 2)* (1862) 31 Beav 363. See also PARA 563 note 8.
6 *Lutwyche v Lutwyche* (1735) Cas *temp* Talb 276.
7 Administration of Estates Act 1925 s 45(1)(a). As to the statutory exceptions in cases of incapacity see PARAS 533–534.

INDEX

Wills and Intestacy

ADMINISTRATION CLAIM
accounts, order for 1181
Chancery Masters, powers of 1180
common account, liability on 1184
concurrent, stay of proceedings after judgment in 1177
conduct of 1175
consolidation 1175
costs—
  administration proceedings, of 1197
  appeal against order for 1211
  creditors' entitlement on indemnity basis 1205
  default, in 1201
  delay or mistake, effect of 1202
  fund for payment of 1199
  general rule 1196
  improper litigation, of 1209
  inquiries, of 1208
  liability for 1200
  overpaid beneficiary, of 1206
  parties other than personal representatives, of 1203
  personal representative in default, of 1201
  personal representative, liability of 1200
  prospective costs orders 1198
  unpaid residuary legatees, proceedings by 1207
  unsuccessful claims and appeals, of 1210
creditor's—
  generally 1173
  proceedings and judgment, effect of 1191
  right to indemnity by 1204
debts and legacies, interest on 1187
decision, notice of 1195
examination of 1193
existing interest, power having 1174
institution of 1171

ADMINISTRATION CLAIM—*continued*
judgment—
  personal representative's powers, effect on 1190
  time for payment, order fixing 1189
kin inquiries 1194
limitation of liability defence 1185
order of application. *See*
  ADMINISTRATION OF ASSETS
  OF DECEASED'S ESTATE
order to lodge money in court 1186
parties to 1172
payment into court, enforcement of order for 1188
personal representative's right to indemnity by creditor 1204
proceedings under judgment—
  decision, notice of 1195
  directions 1192
  examination of claims 1193
  kin inquiries 1194
requirements for making 1174
stay, conduct of proceedings after 1178
wilful default, order for account on footing of 1183

ADMINISTRATION OF ASSETS OF DECEASED'S ESTATE
See also EXECUTOR; LETTERS OF
  ADMINISTRATION; PERSONAL
  REPRESENTATIVE; PROBATE
body, disposal of 956
cash, investment of 962
debts, payment of—
  insolvent estate—
    available assets 988
    bankruptcy rules, application of 981
    creditors having disappeared, retention of sum to pay 986

ADMINISTRATION OF ASSETS OF
DECEASED'S ESTATE—*continued*
debts, payment of—*continued*
insolvent estate—*continued*
doubtful solvency, cases of 982
interest on debts 984
personal representative paying
debts in full, protection of
983
secured creditors 987
time for proving 985
solvent estate—
acknowledgement of debt 976
assets properly applicable for 969
beneficiary, creditor's statutory
rights against 970
charge for payment 979
duty as to 966
foreign assets, equality of
payment 968
foreign currency, payable in 967
part payment 977
pending administration action,
effect of registration 971
registration of judgment, effect
of 972
Statute of Frauds, debts barred
by 975
statute-barred debts 974
statutory preferences 973
time running against creditor 978
trust for 980
entry into deceased's house 958
estate, getting in 959
family provision, distribution pending
proceedings for 1064
foreign assets, getting in 960
inventory 957
liabilities not presently due, discharge
of—
contingent liabilities 989
court order, protection under 991
leasehold etc, protection in regard
to 990
rentcharge, protection in regard to
990
notices for claims—
advertisements, issue of 964
effect of advertising 965
order of application—
debts and liabilities, payment of—
charge, what constituted 1007

ADMINISTRATION OF ASSETS OF
DECEASED'S ESTATE—*continued*
order of application—*continued*
debts and liabilities, payment
of—*continued*
contrary intention, what
constituted 1008
death after 1925 998
interests charged with payment of
debts 1006
one charge, several properties
comprised in 1009
particular property, liabilities
incident to 1011
payment of debts, property
charged with 1002
pecuniary legacies, fund for 1003
property appointed 1005
property specifically devised or
bequeathed 1004
property undisposed of by will
999
residuary gift, property included
in 1000
separate mortgages, several
properties comprised in 1010
specific gifts, property subject of
1001
will made before 31 December
1925 1012
exonerated gift, lapse of 995
marshalling, principle of 997
secured and unsecured debts 996
statutory—
displacement of 994
mixed fund, exclusion by creation
of 993
presumed intention of testator,
based on 992
testamentary and administrative
expenses—
capital gains tax 1016
costs of proceedings 1017
general costs of administration
1014
general principle 1013
indemnity, right of 1018
inheritance tax 1016
Public Trustee, fees of 1015
trust corporations, fees of 1015
personal security, lending money on
963

References are to paragraph numbers; superior figures refer to notes

ADMINISTRATION OF ASSETS OF
  DECEASED'S ESTATE—*continued*
powers—
  agents, nominees and custodians,
    employment and payment of
    1049, 1050
  alienate and charge, to—
    additional powers 1022
    creditor or surviving partner, sale
      to 1029
    depreciatory conditions 1032
    himself, representative not to sell
      to 1030
    impeachable, transaction being
      1028
    land, alienation of 1024
    manner of sale 1031
    particular powers 1021
    personalty, alienation of 1023
    power to insure 1033
    power to recover rent 1034
    purchaser, common law
      protection of 1025
    purchaser, statutory protection
      of—
      notice and receipt 1026
      revocation or variation of
        probate, etc 1027
      statements from representative
        1027
  compromise of claims—
    co-executor's claim 1044
    generally 1043
  deceased's business, carrying on—
    administration order, right to
      1042
    borrowing powers 1037
    creditors' right of subrogation
      1041
    express power, need for 1035
    funds employed for 1036
    indemnity—
      extent of 1040
      right to 1039
    liability of representative 1039
    limited company, conversion to
      1038
  duties in exercising 1020
  payment into court—
    costs, deduction of 1048
    lodgement justifiable, where 1047
    practice 1046

ADMINISTRATION OF ASSETS OF
  DECEASED'S ESTATE—*continued*
powers—*continued*
  payment into court—*continued*
    statutory right 1045
  statutory powers 1019
  survivorship—
    personal or annexed to office,
      powers being 1052
    statutory 1051
realisation of assets, year allowed for
  961
refunding—
  creditor and legatees, between 1101
  estate administered out of court,
    creditor's right on 1103
  fund in court, creditor's right
    against 1102
  future payments, right to equalise
    out of 1098
  intestacy, on 1100
  legatees, at instance of 1099
  one or more beneficiaries insolvent,
    contribution where 1104
  order or enactment protecting
    representatives, effect of 1106
  personal representative and legatee,
    between 1096
  personal representative and
    residuary legatee, between
    1097
  purchasers, right of creditors
    against 1105
  right to follow assets 1095
retention or postponement of
  conversion of securities, discretion
  as to 961
ADMINISTRATION OF DECEASED'S
  ESTATE
meaning 607n[1]
administration order—
  application for 1166
  assets within jurisdiction, not
    limited to 1182
  discretion of court 1179
  transfer of proceedings 1176
annuity, abatement 1090
appropriation, power of 1153
assignable, office not being 642
common law power of
  appropriation—
  contingent legacies 1159
  effect of 1161
  extent of 1161
  settled legacies 1160

References are to paragraph numbers; superior figures refer to notes

ADMINISTRATION OF DECEASED'S
  ESTATE—*continued*
common law power of
  appropriation—*continued*
  vested legacies 1158
determination of questions by court—
  administration order, application
    for 1166
  costs 1197
  guidance of court, personal
    representative's right to 1168
  jurisdiction 1162
  service of documents out of
    jurisdiction 1167
  without administration 1169
Lloyd's Name, directions as to estate
  of 1170
refunding—
  creditor and legatees, between 1101
  estate administered out of court,
    creditor's right on 1103
  fund in court, creditor's right
    against 1102
  future payments, right to equalise
    out of 1098
  intestacy, on 1100
  legatees, at instance of 1099
  one or more beneficiaries insolvent,
    contribution where 1104
  order or enactment protecting
    representatives, effect of 1106
  personal representative and legatee,
    between 1096
  personal representative and
    residuary legatee, between
    1097
  purchasers, right of creditors
    against 1105
  right to follow assets 1095
solvent small estates, by Public
  Trustee—
  application for order 1164
  order of court 1165
statutory power of appropriation—
  consents required—
    absolute interests, for 1154
    minor, on behalf of 1154
    settled legacies 1155
  effect of 1156
  fund, setting apart 1153
  persons bound by 1156
  valuation 1157
ADMINISTRATOR OF ESTATE
See also PERSONAL REPRESENTATIVE

ADMINISTRATOR OF
  ESTATE—*continued*
meaning 607
acts before grant—
  property, vesting of 644
  title, source of 643
appointment, discretionary powers of
  court 758
foreign, grant to 845
minority or life interest, two required
  for 799
number of 757
relation back of title—
  doctrine of 645
  limitation of time, effect on 647
  proceedings begun before grant 647
  validation of disposition 646
title, source of 643
ADOPTION
intestacy, capacity of adopted child to
  take on 483
testamentary disposition in favour of
  adopted child 357, 1063
ANNUITY
abatement of 1090
arrears, no interest on 1084
defeasible annuity 1091
gift over of fund after death of
  annuitant 1092
inheritance tax 1133
payment of 1058
residuary estate, payment out of 1121
reversionary, valuation 1094
valuation of 1093
APPEAL
death of appellant in criminal matter
  1286
probate claim, in 890
ARBITRATION
deceased's estate, claim against 1299
ASSISTED HUMAN REPRODUCTION
child born as result of, as donee under
  will 358–360
BANKRUPT
See also BANKRUPTCY
executor, appointment as 624
legacy paid to 1065
BANKRUPTCY
legatee, of 1068
personal representative, of 923
BENEFICE
right of presentation, exercise by
  personal representative 944

References are to paragraph numbers; superior figures refer to notes

BENEFICIARY
administration claim. *See*
    ADMINISTRATION CLAIM
donee under will. *See* DONEE UNDER
    WILL
probate claim. *See* PROBATE CLAIM
selection by executor 11
testator and, fiduciary relationship
    between 904
BEQUEST
See also GIFT BY WILL; LEGACY
meaning 17n³
personal property 377
BILL OF EXCHANGE
devolution on personal representative
    935
endorsement by personal
    representative 1241
BODY
disposal of 31
BODY CORPORATE
See also CORPORATION
testamentary gift to 35
BONA VACANTIA
administration, grant of 778
defeating right 513
when right arising 512
BOROUGH ENGLISH
descent of land 564
BREACH OF TRUST
deceased trustee's liability 1238
personal representative's liability 1238
BUILDING CONTRACT
death of contractor, effect of 1216
death of employer, effect of 1215
BURDEN OF PROOF
testamentary capacity 899
will made in lucid interval 900
CAPITAL GAINS TAX
deceased, due from 1016
CASE MANAGEMENT
probate claim 877
CAUSE OF ACTION
survival on death—
    act or omission causing death, for
        1280
    action against representative 1278
    action by representative 1277
    criminal appeal 1286
    death of party to claim, effect of
        1283
    dissolution of civil partnership
        proceedings 1285
    divorce proceedings 1285

CAUSE OF ACTION—*continued*
survival on death—*continued*
    exemplary damages, no recovery
        1281
    generally 940
    land covenant, relating to 1282
    nature of cases surviving 1279
    payment out of court 1284
CAVEAT
appearance by caveator 692
caveator: meaning 690
entry of 690
non-appearance by caveator 693
subsequent proceedings, remaining in
    force for 694
summons for directions 692
warnings, issue of 691
CHANCERY DIVISION
probate jurisdiction 605, 678
CHARGE
mixed fund, legacy charged on 439
real estate, legacy charged on 438
CHARITABLE GIFT
charity ceasing to exist 162
cy-près doctrine 230
receipt for 37
CHATTELS
devise of 121
devolution on personal representative
    928
successive donees, given to 121
use, consumed in 122
CHEQUE
devolution on personal representative
    935
CHILD
See also MINOR
donee under will. *See* DONEE UNDER
    WILL
financial provision from
    deceased's estate. *See* FAMILY
    PROVISION
legacy to. *See* LEGACY
CHOSE IN ACTION
will, not disposable by 32
CHURCH
gift of 'living' 292
CIVIL PARTNERSHIP
death, effect on dissolution or
    annulment proceedings 1285
will, effect of dissolution or annulment
    on 179
CODICIL
meaning 1

References are to paragraph numbers; superior figures refer to notes

CODICIL—*continued*
  alterations in will, effect on 85
  legatee confirming, effect of 43
  probate of 712
  revival of will, effect of 112
  revocation of will by 1, 100
  validity of 862
CO-EXECUTOR
  duty to take care 1253
  liability for acts of 1252
COMMORIENTES
  presumption after 1925 746
CONDITIONAL GIFT
  alienation, forfeiture on—
    forfeiture clause—
      burden of proof 462
      effect of 463
      object of 462
      order of court, alienation by 464
      passive or unwilling party, donee
        as 465
      passive role, events in which
        beneficiary playing 464
      void charge by life tenant, exclusion
        of 464
  conditions—
    consent to marriage, as to—
      death of named person 135
      named person, of 135
      nature of 136
    donee, not binding on 146
    excuse, grounds of 145
    general rules 128
    impossible 143
    inconsistent 128, 142
    invalidity, effect of 130
    nullified or dispensed with by
      testator 144
    precedent 129
    public policy, contrary to 128, 131
    race or religion, as to 140
    relief against 149
    repugnant 142
    restraint of marriage—
      general 132
      in terrorem, doctrine of 134
      limitations depending on 137
      partial 133
    subsequent 129
    substantial performance of 147
    time of performance 148
    uncertainty—
      conditional future limitations 141
      effect of 138

CONDITIONAL GIFT—*continued*
  conditions—*continued*
    uncertainty—*continued*
      examples of 141
      expression, of 138
      operation, of 138
      residence, as to 139
    unlawful, not to be 128
  construction—
    accruer clause 410
    clarity and effect 407
    contingency happening in
      testator's lifetime, where 411
    cumulative and substituted legacies
      409
    series of gifts 408
  divesting—
    construction of 'and' as 'or' 443
    construction of 'or' as 'and' 442
    court leaning against 440
    doubtful case, in 440
    gift over on death without leaving
      child 441
    survivorship clause 444
  failure of issue, limitations on—
    construction 461
    contingency of prior gift 457
    life tenant, person predeceasing 458
    other gifts over on 461
    prior gifts, reference to issue taking
      under 456
    statutory rule—
      contrary indication excluding
        455, 459
      exceptions to 460
      generally 454
      not applying, rules applying in
        case of 459
  inference, gifts over by—
    application of rule 446
    conditional limitation 446
    intention, indication of 447
    necessary implication 445
    other clauses, inference from 447
    persons entitled on intestacy,
      exclusion of 448
  vesting—
    circumstances affecting 415
    donee, contingency in description
      of 416
    mixed fund, charge on 439
    personal estate, gifts out of—
      direction to pay, gifts contained
        wholly in 427

CONDITIONAL GIFT—*continued*
vesting—*continued*
personal estate, gifts out
of—*continued*
gift and time of payment
expressly distinguished 428
gift and time of payment
implicdly distinguished 429
gift over—
first gift, vesting of 435
parent's death without issue,
on 437
specified age, failure to attain
436
maintenance, direction as to—
class gift with direction to
apply income 432
gift remaining contingent 433
interim interest, gift of 430
interim maintenance, gift of
431
property to which rules apply
425
severance from estate, direction
for 434
vesting and payment
distinguished 426
postponement of enjoyment only
415
presumption—
early vesting, in favour of 413
precedent or subsequent
condition 414
prior gift, effect of gift over on—
contingent gift over 423
description of donees, contingency
as part of 424
real estate, charge on 438
remainder, of—
Boraston's Case 419, 421
former rule 418
future interest, construction of
419
gifts subject to prior interests 422
issue, gifts in default of 420
personalty, of 421
Phipps v Ackers 419
prior interest, limited 419
subject matter of gift, contingency
in description of 416
successive gifts, contingency in 417
vest: meaning 412

CONSTRUCTION OF WILL
alteration of words, effect of 253
ambiguous cases, presumption in 244
changing or supplying words, effect
of 254
conditional gifts. *See* CONDITIONAL
GIFT
court of construction—
meaning 185
counsel's opinion, reliance on 192
duty to construe 191
functions of 185
jurisdiction, attempts to oust 190
mistake, jurisdiction to correct—
death after 1982 187
death before 1983 186
Part 8 claim form, application by
192
difficulties of 194
ejusdem generis rule 250
every word, effect to be given to 248
evidence, admissibility of—
character of 199
executory trust, will containing 194
general rule 193
gift to executor, as to 198
identification, for purposes of—
evidence necessarily admissible
209
extrinsic evidence of intention—
testator dying after 1982 219
testator dying before 1983 218
gift not plain and unambiguous
211
gift plain and unambiguous 210
inconclusive evidence, effect of
217
latent ambiguity: meaning 220
patent ambiguity: meaning 220
satisfactory evidence, effect of
216
subject matter disposed of, of
213
surrounding circumstances, of
212
testator's habits, of 215
testator's knowledge, of 214
instructions of testator 199
language and meaning, of—
characters, deciphering 202
documents referred to in will 201
foreign wills 203
interpretation of 202

CONSTRUCTION OF
  WILL—*continued*
  evidence, admissibility of—*continued*
    language and meaning,
      of—*continued*
      legal technical terms, meaning
        of 204
      ordinary meaning of words, of
        205, 206
      probate, conclusiveness of 200
      variation of terms, as to 207
    meaningless or ambiguous language,
      as to 195
    persons acting under will, usage of
      196
    photographic copy of will 200
    presumptions, as to 197
    secret trust, of—
      fully secret 222
      generally 221
      partly secret 223
    testator's wishes, of 208
    will itself, of 193
    words and expression, as to 194
  foreign element, will with 239
  grammatical and ordinary meaning of
    words—
    context and circumstances, effect in
      excluding rule 242
    general rule 241
  implied gift. *See* GIFT BY WILL
  intention, ascertainment of—
    ambiguous context, words used in
      228
    basic principles 224
    change in approach to 224
    clear, general or paramount
      intention 253
    cy-près doctrine 230
    double residuary gifts 233
    duty of court 225
    expressed, as 225
    form, unimportance of 226
    inconsistent gifts 232
    language, ascertaining 225
    Lassence v Tierney, rule in 231
    legal effect of words 227
    scope of will, inferences from 229
    two gifts of same subject matter
      234
  modern approach to 188
  more than one primary meaning,
    words having 245
  ordinary sense, words used in 236

CONSTRUCTION OF
  WILL—*continued*
  particular dispositions, application of
    rules to 281
  persons entitled to take. *See* DONEE
    UNDER WILL
  presumptions—
    children, in favour of 260
    intention of testator, of 259
    intestacy, against—
      doubtful cases, in 255
      force of 256
      limits of 257
      two gifts in same will, contest
        between 257
    legality, of—
      ambiguous cases, in 259
      plain words, no departure from
        258
    relatives of equal degree, in favour
      of 261
  previous decisions, weight given to
    237
  property or persons, misdescription
    of—
    accurate description, effect of 267
    additional words resolving 267
    change of circumstances between
      will and death 278
    falsa demonstratio non nocet 269
    general description followed by
      enumeration of particulars 273
    generic description, accuracy of 279
    inaccurate description, effect of 268
    limits of rule 271
    name and description, designation
      by—
      application of rule 277
      generally 276
    name or description, designation
      by 275
    nickname or erroneous name, donee
      designated by 275
    number of donees, inaccuracy in
      274
    specific description, accuracy of 280
    two or more subjects, description
      partly true as to 272
    wholly false, description being 270
  property passing, construction of—
    appertaining: meaning 286
    appurtenances: meaning 286
    business: meaning 287
    death, will speaking from 282
    debts, release of 297

References are to paragraph numbers; superior figures refer to notes

CONSTRUCTION OF
  WILL—*continued*
property passing, construction
  of—*continued*
  effects, gift of 288
  estate: meaning 289
  funds: meaning 295
  general description of 284
  general devises 291
  generic, thing being 282
  goods: meaning 288
  house and buildings 290
  land, devise of 291
  living of church 292
  locality, effect of description by 285
  miscellaneous terms 296
  money: meaning 293
  personal estate: meaning 288
  possessions: meaning 289
  principal gift, accessories following
    283
  real estate: meaning 282n^3
  residuary gifts 298
  right to occupy house: meaning 296
  securities: meaning 294
  stocks and shares: meaning 295
  war loan: meaning 295
quantity of interest taken—
  absolute interest—
    personalty, bequest of 377
    powers of disposition, effect of
      conferring 378
    realty, devise of 376
    rent or income, unlimited gift of
      375
  absolute interest reduced to life
    interest—
    clear absolute gift in first
      instance 382
    generally 381
  benefit to donee in particular
    manner 371
  concurrent gifts—
    distribution per stirpes, inference
      in favour of 397
    distribution prima facie per
      capita 396
    general rules 393
    interests of donees names
      together, presumption as to
      400
    issue, substitution of 398
    joint tenancy, words creating 394
    stocks, determination of 399

CONSTRUCTION OF
  WILL—*continued*
quantity of interest taken—*continued*
  concurrent gifts—*continued*
    tenancy in common, words
      creating 395
  cumulative or substitutional gifts—
    gifts clearly cumulative 401
    gifts in different instruments,
      presumption in case of 403
    gifts in same instrument,
      presumption in case of 402
  hotchpot clause—
    advances recited 406
    method of bringing advances into
      account 405
    prior advances 404
  life interest—
    determinable interest 380
    right of enjoyment, definition by
      379
  life interest enlarged to absolute
    interest 383
  named person, gift at discretion of
    373
  no presumption as to 368
  particular property, gift to benefit
    374
  person and children, bequest to 390
  person and children, devise to 389
  person and issue, bequest to 392
  person and issue, devise to 391
  person with absolute entitlement, no
    fetters on 372
  reduction or extension of 369
  stated purpose, effect of 370
recitals or other statements, effect of
  252
repeated words, presumption as to
  249
rules of construction 235
rules of law, consideration of 240
Scottish cases, citation of 238
subsequent ambiguous words, clear
  words not controlled by 251
testator's right to be capricious 243
time, words referring to 247
uncertainty—
  alternative, gifts stated in 264
  avoidance of 263
  examples of void gifts 266
  extrinsic evidence, admission of 263
  gift held void for 262
  one of a set of persons, gift to 265
words judicially defined 246

References are to paragraph numbers; superior figures refer to notes

CONSULAR OFFICER
grant of administration to 802
grant of representation to 719
property, powers over 667

CONTRACT
freedom of testamentary disposition,
  restricting 20
personal representative, by 1288

COPYHOLD
descent of 562

COPYRIGHT
devolution on personal representative
  939

CORPORATION
executor, appointment as 622

CORPORATION SOLE
lease, devolution to 943

COSTS
administration claim. *See*
  ADMINISTRATION CLAIM (costs)
executor's liability for 910
personal representative, claim by 1276
probate claim. *See* PROBATE CLAIM
  (costs)

COUNTERCLAIM
probate proceedings 873

COUNTY COURT
probate jurisdiction 866
transfer of probate proceedings to and
  from 867

COURT OF PROBATE
derivation of jurisdiction 676
transfer of jurisdiction to High Court
  677

COVENANT
breach of, action by personal
  representative 1282
family provision, making 22

CREDITOR
meaning 787
administration claim—
  costs on indemnity basis,
    entitlement to 1205
  effect of registration of 971
  institution of 1171
  personal representative's right to
    indemnity 1204
  proceedings, taking 1173
beneficiary, statutory rights against
  970
letters of administration, grant to 786
refunding—
  creditor and legatees, between 1101
  estate administered out of court,
    right on 1103

CREDITOR—*continued*
refunding—*continued*
  fund in court, right against 1102
  purchasers, right against 1105
time running against 978

CROPS
devolution on personal representative
  930

CROSS-EXAMINATION
probate proceedings 874

CUSTOMARY LAND
meaning 561n[1]
descent of 561

CY-PRÈS
doctrine 230

DEATH
criminal appeal, effect on 1286
devolution of property on 917
dissolution of civil partnership, effect
  on 1285
divorce, effect on 1285
intestate. *See* INTESTACY
personal representative, of 1289
testamentary disposition. *See*
  TESTAMENTARY DISPOSITION;
  WILL (TESTAMENT)

DEBT
testator, release by 297

DEBTOR
executor, appointment as 625

DEED
will in form of 3

DEPENDANT
meaning 348

DEVASTAVIT
meaning 1244
bankruptcy of representative, proof
  in 1248
concurrence of party in 1250
devolution of liability 1249
gratuitous bailee, unremunerated
  representative as 1247
maladministration, committed on
  1245
nature of 1244
negligence, by 1246

DEVISE
meaning 17n[3]

DIGITAL ASSET
devolution on personal representative
  941

DISCLOSURE AND INSPECTION OF
  DOCUMENTS
probate claim 880

DISPOSITION INTER VIVOS
  will distinguished 2
DISSOLUTION OF CIVIL
    PARTNERSHIP
  death, effect of 1285
  will, effect on 179
DISTRICT PROBATE REGISTRY
  court, co-operation with 682
  jurisdiction of district registrar 683
DIVORCE
  death, effect of 1285
DONATIO MORTIS CAUSA
  will distinguished 2
DONEE UNDER WILL
  See also GIFT BY WILL
  alternative gifts—
    children, to 323
    class, ascertainment of 326
    conditions attaching to 325
    contingency 320
    expression of 320
    failure of 327
    original and substitutional 321
    parents and issue, composite class
      of 324
    time of death of prior donee, effect
      of 322
    uncertainty 320
  ascertainable, to be 33
  capacity to benefit—
    corporate body 35
    general rule 33
    inability to give receipt 33
    lack of 34
    non-charitable society 36
  certainty, described with 33
  change of name between will and
    death 278
  class gift—
    contingency, on 303
    intermediate income, of 312
    next of kin—
      ascertainment of 314
      gifts to 313
      shares in which taking 314
    parents and issue, composite class
      of 324
    real estate alone, of 311
    rules of convenience—
      classes subject to 309
      conditions attached to property,
        postponement of gift by
        reason of 307, 308
      date of distribution 306
      gifts subject to 310

DONEE UNDER WILL—*continued*
  class gift—*continued*
    rules of convenience—*continued*
      inconsistent directions,
        reconciliation of 308
      judicial recourse to 304
      members ascertainable and
        capable of taking at date of
        distribution 305
    time when class ascertained 302
  disqualification from benefiting—
    forfeiture rule—
      effect of 39
      modification of 40
    fraud, for 38
    legatee attesting codicil, effect of 43
    murder or manslaughter 39, 40
    undue influence, for 38
    witness, gift to—
      exceptions to general rule 42
      legatee attesting codicil, effect of
        43
      superfluous attestation 44
  gender, designated by 300
  identifiable, to be 45
  identification of—
    adopted child, disposition in favour
      of 357
    artificial insemination, child born as
      result of 358
    assisted reproduction, child born as
      result of—
      on or after 1 August 1991 and
        before 6 April 2009 359
      on or after 6 April 2009 360
    legitimated child, disposition in
      favour of 357
    office or employment, by reference
      to—
      executors, gifts to 363
      office holder, gift to 367
      representatives, bequest to 364
      servants or employees, gifts to
        365, 366
    parental order, effect of 361
    person en ventre sa mère, treatment
      of 362
    relationship, by reference to—
      adopted child, disposition in
        favour of 357
      affinity, by 328
      artificial insemination, child born
        as result of 358

DONEE UNDER WILL—*continued*
  identification of—*continued*
    relationship, by reference
        to—*continued*
      assisted reproduction, child born
          as result of 359, 360
      blood, by 328
      children or issue begotten and to
          be begotten 330
      children, meaning of issue
          confined to 336
      children, reference to 331
      civil partner 346
      class of issue, ascertainment of
          337
      descendants: meaning 338
      eldest son 333
      family, friends and dependants,
          gift to 348
      first son 333
      gender recognition certificate,
          effect of 329
      general rule 328
      heir of particular character 340
      heir or heirs: meaning 339
      issue: meaning 334
      legitimated child, disposition in
          favour of 357
      male issue: meaning 335
      next of kin, gift to 343
      offspring: meaning 335
      parental order, effect of 361
      per stirpes: meaning 345
      person en ventre sa mere,
          treatment of 362
      person or heirs, gift to 342
      personalty or mixed fund
          bequeathed to heir 341
      relations: meaning 349
      rules of distribution, reference
          to 344
      surrogacy order, effect of 361
      two named persons, children of
          332
      widowhood, gift during 347
      wife or husband, description as
          346
    surrogacy order, effect of 361
  inability to give receipt 33
  mental disorder, suffering from 37
  name and description, designation
      by—

DONEE UNDER WILL—*continued*
  name and description, designation
      by—*continued*
    application of rule 277
    generally 276
  nickname or erroneous name,
      designated by 275
  persons incapable of taking 34
  power of disposition, effect of
      conferring 378
  receipt by 37
  time of ascertainment—
    general considerations 299
    groups, gifts to 301
    individuals, gifts to 300
    uncertainty as to 45
EJUSDEM GENERIS
  will, application to 250
EMBLEMENT
  devolution on personal representative
      930
ENTAILED INTEREST
  accessory gift of chattels with realty
      388
  after 1925 387
  before 1926 384
  creation of 384
  gift by reference to limitation of real
      estate 386
  implication, by 473
  quasi-inheritable gift of personal
      estate 385
  real estate, existing in 384
EQUITABLE INTEREST
  will, disposable by 27
ESTOPPEL
  freedom of testamentary disposition,
      restriction 20
EVIDENCE
  due execution of will 894
EXECUTION OF WILL
  evidence of 894
  presumption of due execution 895
  testamentary form unnecessary 5
EXECUTOR
  See also PERSONAL REPRESENTATIVE
  meaning 606
  acceptance of office—
    effect of 629
    generally 610
    grant of probate, obtaining 627
    methods of 627
    no renunciation after 628
    trusts, accepting 629

EXECUTOR—*continued*
  acts before probate—
    examples of 634
    liability for 636
    powers 634
  appointment—
    acceptance of office 610
    conditional 617
    court, power of 614
    different properties, for 616
    dissolution or annulment of
        marriage or civil partnership,
        failure as result of 618
    ecclesiastical court of
        administrators, by 605
    express nomination by testator 611
    implication, by 610, 613
    means of 610
    person other than testator,
        nomination by 612
    persons eligible for—
      corporation 622
      debtor 625
      incomplete gifts, donees of 626
      insolvent person 624
      lack of restrictions on 619
      mental capacity, person lacking
          621
      minor 620
      partnership 623
    renunciation of office 610
    right of, derivation 605
    statutory 614
    substituted 617
    will, by 2, 4
  assignable, office not being 642
  beneficiaries, power to select 11
  chain of representation, break in 640
  choice of 619
  citation of 698
  costs, liability for 910
  de son tort. *See* EXECUTOR DE SON
      TORT
  devolution of office—
    death, on—
      chain of representation, break in
          640
      executor of sole survivor, on 637
      full executor and limited executor,
          powers of 639
      power to prove, reservation of
          638
      powers and liabilities 641
      survivor, on 637

EXECUTOR—*continued*
  devolution of office—*continued*
    other than on death 642
    different properties, for 616
    duties of—
      body, disposal of 956
      entry into deceased's house 958
      inventory 957
    general executor 615
    gift to, by reference to office 363
    identity, question as to 611
    legacy to—
      defaulting executor, lien on interest
          of 1071
      entitlement to 1070
      presumption as to 1069
    misdescription of 738
    non-proving, powers reserved to 729
    number of 611
    oath 728
    probate, right to 725
    proceedings before probate 635
    property abroad, for 616
    propound a will, no need for 861
    renunciation of office—
      acceptance of office, effect of 628
      effect of 631
      final 630
      generally 610
      grant, before 627
      power to renounce 630
      withdrawal of 632
    special executor 615, 747
    special or general powers conferred
        on 11
    tenor, according to 610, 613
    title, source of 633
    universal 615n[1]
    year 961
EXECUTOR DE SON TORT
  meaning 606
  citation of 699
  civil liability 1269
  creditor's action, answer to 1268
  execution against chattels taken by
      1267
  inheritance lax, liability for 1267
  intermeddling with estate—
    charity, acts of 1263
    determination of liability 1265
    foreign assets, taking possession of
        1264
    fraudulently obtaining or retaining
        estate 1261
    necessity, acts of 1263

EXECUTOR DE SON
   TORT—*continued*
  intermeddling with estate—*continued*
   receipt of property 1264
   slight acts of interference 1262
  lawful acts binding estate 1266
  liability to be sued 1267
  person chargeable as 1261
  representative of, liability of 1270
FAMILY DIVISION
  probate jurisdiction 605, 678
FAMILY PROVISION
  application for—
   acknowledgement of service 599
   case management 602
   claim for 599
   contract to leave property by will
    intended to defeat—
    application in relation to 588
    general considerations 589
    trustees and personal
     representatives, protection
     of 590
   costs 604
   county court jurisdiction 599
   disclosure 602
   disposition intended to defeat—
    application in relation to 586
    general considerations 589
    subsidiary applications 587
    trustees and personal
     representatives, protection
     of 590
   extension of time, application for
    598
   generally 4
   High Court jurisdiction 599
   mode of 599
   parties to 600
   persons entitled to make 567
   procedure subsequent to 602
   statutory provisions 566
   time for 597
   transfer between courts 601
   written evidence, filing 602
  freedom of testamentary disposition,
   restriction on 21
  matters taken into account—
   child of deceased or person treated
    as, in relation to 580
   cohabitees, in relation to 579
   common statutory guidelines 571
   conduct of applicant or other
    person 576

FAMILY PROVISION—*continued*
  matters taken into account—*continued*
   deceased's reason for not making
    provision 576
   estate, size and nature of 574
   financial resources and financial
    needs 572
   former spouse or civil partner, in
    relation to 578
   obligations and responsibilities of
    deceased 573
   person being maintained by
    deceased, in relation to 581
   physical or mental disability of
    applicant or beneficiary 575
   spouse or civil partner, in relation
    to 577
  order for—
   consequential provisions in 592
   discharge of 594
   effect of 593
   entry and filing 602
   interim 603
   lump sum, for 591
   maintenance agreement, variation
    and revocation of 596
   orders in divorce or dissolution
    proceedings, variation and
    discharge of 595
   periodical payments, for 591
   revival of 594
   suspension of 594
   types of 591
   variation of 594
  particular covenants making, effect
   of 22
  pending proceedings, effect on
   distribution of estate 1064
  persons for whom made 567
  property available for financial
   provision—
   contract to leave property by will
    intended to defeat, in respect
    of—
    general considerations 589
    generally 588
    trustees and personal
     representatives, protection
     of 590
   disposition intended to defeat
    application, made in respect
    of—
    general considerations 589
    generally 586
    subsidiary applications 587

FAMILY PROVISION—*continued*
property available for financial
provision—*continued*
disposition intended to defeat
application, made in respect
of—*continued*
trustees and personal
representatives, protection
of 590
gifts mortis causa 584
joint tenancy, property held on 585
net estate: meaning 582
nominees, money payable to 583
trustees and personal
representatives, protection of
590
reasonable financial provision—
application by non-spouse, in case
of 570
application by spouse or civil
partner, in case of 569
test of 568
testamentary disposition, restrictions
on 565
FIDUCIARY
testator and beneficiary, relationship
between 904
FIXTURES
devolution on personal representative
932
FORGERY
will, of 671
FRAUD
clause in will introduced by 59
legacy obtained by 38, 58
probate obtained by 671
GAVELKIND
meaning 563
descent of 563
GENDER RECOGNITION
CERTIFICATE
disposition or devolution under will,
effect on 329
GIFT BY WILL
meaning 17n^3
alternative, stated in 264
class—
meaning 175
lapse, doctrine of 174
conditional gift. *See* CONDITIONAL
GIFT
corporate body, to 35
donee. *See* DONEE UNDER WILL
double residuary 233

GIFT BY WILL—*continued*
fraud, obtained by 58
gift over. *See* GIFT OVER
heir, to—
meaning 339
next of kin, as 342
particular character, of 340
personalty or mixed fund
bequeathed to 341
hotchpot clause—
advances recited 406
members of class, between 404
method of bringing advances into
account 405
prior advances, of 404
implied gift—
absolute interests, implication from
gifts over 471
cross-remainders, implication of
474
distributive construction 476
estate tail by implication 473
examples of 469
executory cross-limitations,
implication of 475
failure of children, bequest on 472
grounds for implication 466
life estate 468
nature of implication 467
power of court 466
survivor of life tenants, gift over on
death of 470
testator's successor in intestacy, gift
over on death to 469
incomplete, donee of as executor 626
inconsistent 232
non-charitable purposes, for 36
non-charitable society, to 36
one of a set of persons, to 265
preconditions necessary for taking
effect 19
receipt for 37
residuary, construction 298
restraint of marriage, condition in—
consent to marriage, as to—
death of named person 135
named person, of 135
nature of 136
general 132
in terrorem, doctrine of 134
limitations depending on 137
partial 133
two, of same subject matter 234
unincorporated association, to 36

References are to paragraph numbers; superior figures refer to notes

GIFT BY WILL—*continued*
  witness, to—
    exceptions to general rule 42
    generally 41
    legatee attesting codicil, effect of 43
    superfluous attestation 44
GIFT OVER
  meaning 17n^3
  actual receipts, before 451
  construction 449
  contingency, with 450
  death before becoming entitled 453
  death before legacy due 452
  substitutional gift, as 450
  time of fund being receivable 451
GRANT OF PROBATE OR
  ADMINISTRATION
  caveat—
    appearance by caveator 692
    caveator: meaning 690
    entry of 690
    non-appearance by caveator 693
    subsequent proceedings, remaining
      in force for 694
    warnings, issue of 691
  citation—
    meaning 695
    accept or refuse grant, to 698
    executor de son tort, of 699
    non-contentious business 695
    person cited, appearance by 697
    service of 696
    will, to propound 700
  Commonwealth or colonial grant,
    resealing—
    applicable territories 837
    application for 841
    cancellation 843
    Colonial Probates Act 1892,
      countries in which applying
      838
    estate in England and Wales, effect
      on 839
    evidence required 840
    general effect of 835
    practice and procedure 841
    Republic of Ireland, from 836
    requirements for 840
    sureties, requirement of 840
  Commonwealth, resealing English
    grant in 842
  effect of—
    collateral matters, not conclusive as
      to 670
    evidence, receipt in 675

GRANT OF PROBATE OR
  ADMINISTRATION—*continued*
  effect of—*continued*
    execution and validity of will,
      evidence of 669
    forgery and fraud, powers as to 671
    generally 669
    non-proving executors, on 673
    original will, court looking at 672
    real estate, on 674
  English grant, recognition in Scotland
    and Northern Ireland 833
  estate exempt from necessity for—
    consular officer, powers of 667
    foreign convention, under 664
    funds in court, payment of 666
    investment or insurance, payment
      of 663
    life policy effected abroad, right to
      receive money from 665
    Monarch, of 660
    personal effects and pension,
      disposition of 662
    small estate 661
    statute, by 661
  failure to take out, civil remedy 659,
    668
  foreign domicile grant—
    foreign administrator, to 845
    procedure for 846
    right to 844
  foreign law, evidence of 706
  grant within United Kingdom,
    recognition of—
    effect of 834
    generally 830
  High Court—
    contentious and non-contentious
      business 684
    ex parte applications 703
    fees 686
    foreign law, evidence of 706
    jurisdiction—
      Chancery Division 679
      contentious and non-contentious
        business 684
      Court of Probate jurisdiction 677
      derivation of 676
      district judge, of 681
      district registrar, of 683
      Family Division and Chancery
        Division, distribution of
        business between 678
      master, of 681
      probate court functions 679

References are to paragraph numbers; superior figures refer to notes

GRANT OF PROBATE OR
  ADMINISTRATION—*continued*
High Court—*continued*
  jurisdiction—*continued*
    probate registries, co-operation
      with 682
    testamentary papers, powers
      over 680
  summons—
    accept probate, to 689
    appeal by 705
    application by 701
    ex parte application, not required
      for 703
    procedure by 702
    refuse probate, to 689
    service of 704
  instruments entitled to probate—
  England and Wales, will in—
    burnt, faded or torn will 717
    codicil 712
    conflict of laws 709
    documents, incorporation of 711
    duplicate will 715
    form of, immaterial 708
    generally 707
    joint will 714
    lost will, contents of 716
    privileged will 710
    requirements 708
    several testamentary instruments,
      where 713
    soldier's, sailor's or airman's will
      710
  foreigner's will—
    consular officer, powers of 719
    duly authenticated copy,
      admission to proof 721
    English grant following foreign
      grant, extent of 720
    person dying domiciled abroad
      718
  property abroad, will disposing of—
    separate will of English property
      723
    solely of property abroad 722
  need for 659
  Northern Irish grant 832
  probate court, functions of 679
  revocation of—
    better administration, for purpose
      of 850

GRANT OF PROBATE OR
  ADMINISTRATION—*continued*
  revocation of—*continued*
    effect of—
      generally 855
      legal proceedings, on 857
      payment made in good faith, on
        856
      validity of conveyance, on 858
    executor, no application by 853
    false suggestion, on ground of 848
    instance of court, at 851
    jurisdiction 847
    limited grant, of 852
    non-contentious matter, in 854
    procedure for 854
    stay after 859
    subsequent will, on discovery of
      849
    want of due execution, for 849
  revocation, claim for 888
  Scottish confirmations 831
GUARDIAN OF CHILD
  appointment by will 2, 4
  cohabitee, application by $4n^9$
HIGH COURT OF JUSTICE
  grant of probate or administration.
    See GRANT OF PROBATE OR
      ADMINISTRATION (High Court)
  probate jurisdiction 865
  transfer of probate proceedings to and
    from 867
HOTCHPOT
  partial intestacy, on 515
  valuation of estate for purposes of
    1117
ILLEGITIMACY
  meaning 350
  capacity to take under intestacy, effect
    on 481, 482
  donee under will, identification of—
    disposition after 31 December 1969
      and before 4 April 1988 355
    disposition before 1970—
      future illegitimate child 354
      illegitimate child of named
        person, gift to 353
      inclusion of illegitimate person,
        indication of 352
      legitimate relations, effect of
        absence of 351
      relations not generally included in
        gift 350

ILLEGITIMACY—*continued*
  donee under will, identification
    of—*continued*
      disposition on or after 4 April
        1988 356
      subsequent legitimation, effect of 350,
        357
INCOME
  unlimited gift of 375
INHERITANCE
  family provision. *See* FAMILY
    PROVISION
  intestacy. *See* INTESTACY
  personal representative, liability of
    1217
  tax. *See* INHERITANCE TAX
  will, under. *See* GIFT BY WILL
INHERITANCE TAX
  alteration of rules in will 4
  annuity 1133
  burden of 1128
  deceased's estate, payment on 1016
  executor de son tort, liability of 1267
  free of duty provisions 1129
  incidence of—
    partially exempt residue 1134
    words affecting 1131
    words not affecting 1132
  provision for, from testator's estate 4
  residue, paid from 4n[7]
INSPECTION OF DOCUMENT
  probate proceedings 881
INSURANCE
  payment to personal representative
    938
  personal representative's power to
    insure 1033
INTERNATIONAL WILL
  requirements for 14
INTESTACY
  capacity to take under—
    adopted child, of 483
    artificial insemination, child born
      through 481
    illegitimate child, of 482
    kinship, establishment of 481
    legitimate child, of 481
    legitimated child, of 482
    personal representative, protection
      of 484
    unlawful killing, on 480
  death intestate after 1925 and before
    1953—
    Crown, rights of 527
    issue 524

INTESTACY—*continued*
  death intestate after 1925 and before
    1953—*continued*
    no surviving spouse, summary of
      distributions 530
    parents, rights of 525
    partial intestacy 528
    personal representative, power to
      redeem life interest 523
    relatives, rights of 526
    statutory trusts, rights of issue
      under 525
    summary of distributions 529
    surviving spouse—
      absolute interests of 521
      life interests of 522
  death intestate after 1952—
    bona vacantia—
      defeating 513
      foreigner dying aboard, property
        in United Kingdom of 513
      where arising 512
    no surviving spouse or partner,
      where—
      rights of issue 500
      rights of parents 509
      rights of relatives 511
      summary of distributions 520
    parents, rights of—
      no surviving spouse or partner,
        where 509
      surviving spouse or partner,
        where 508
    partial intestacy—
      future interests, application of
        provisions to 516
      history of 514
      hotchpot modification 515
      personal representative, estate
        held by 517
      trusteeship 517
    relatives, rights of—
      no surviving spouse or partner,
        where 511
      surviving spouse or partner,
        where 510
    statutory trusts, rights of issue
      under—
      advancement—
        excluded payments 503
        extent of doctrine 504
        payments constituting 503
        power of 502

INTESTACY—*continued*
　death intestate after 1952—*continued*
　　statutory trusts, rights of issue
　　　under—*continued*
　　　beneficiary 507
　　　failure of trusts 506
　　　maintenance and accumulation of
　　　　income, provision for 502
　　　minor, receipts by 505
　　　no surviving spouse or civil
　　　　partner 500
　　　posthumous child 499
　　　rules for 499
　　　surviving spouse or civil partner
　　　　501
　　surviving spouse or civil partner,
　　　rights of—
　　　covenant, performance of 497
　　　dissolution of civil partnership,
　　　　effect of 494
　　　divorce, effect of 493
　　　dwelling house comprised in
　　　　estate—
　　　　appropriation of 489
　　　　sale, restriction on 490
　　　income, to 496
　　　issue, deceased leaving 486, 488
　　　judicial separated spouse, death
　　　　of 491
　　　life interest, capitalisation of 487
　　　no issue, where 485
　　　nullity, effect of 493
　　　performance, doctrine of 497
　　　personal representative, powers
　　　　of 495
　　　separation order in force, death of
　　　　civil partner 492
　　　widow's right to benefit, barring
　　　　498
　　surviving spouse or partner, where—
　　　death after 2014, distribution on
　　　　518
　　　rights of issue 501
　　　rights of parents 508
　　　rights of relatives 510
　　　summary of distributions 519
　death intestate before 1926—
　　entailed interests, devolution of 531
　　old rules, application to death after
　　　1926—
　　　entailed interests, devolution of
　　　　531

INTESTACY—*continued*
　death intestate before
　　1926—*continued*
　　old rules, application to death after
　　　1926—*continued*
　　　heirs by purchase, position of
　　　　532
　　　mental disorder continuing from
　　　　1925 533
　　　minor dying without having
　　　　married 534
　　　Statutes of Distribution, reference
　　　　to 535
　　personal estate, distribution of—
　　　old rules 537
　　　order of 537
　　　rules for 536
　　real estate, descent of—
　　　borough English land 564
　　　child unborn, where 551
　　　coparceners, rule for 546
　　　copyhold 562
　　　customary land 561
　　　escheat—
　　　　meaning 552
　　　　land subject to 553
　　　　mesne lord, to 558
　　　　regrant of land 557
　　　　right of 552
　　　　statutory provisions 555
　　　　tenant, for want of 554
　　　　to whom land escheated 556
　　　estate tail—
　　　　descent of 560
　　　　failure of owners on 559
　　　female heirs, inheritance by 546
　　　gavelkind land 563
　　　half blood, persons related by
　　　　550
　　　heir, to 538
　　　lineal ancestors, position of 548
　　　lineal descendants, position of
　　　　547
　　　males, priority of 545
　　　paternal line, priority of 549
　　　purchaser, descent traced from—
　　　　ancestor, descent traced to 542
　　　　equitable and legal estates,
　　　　　merger of 544
　　　　limitation to heirs 540
　　　　purchaser's heirs, failure of 543
　　　　rule 539

References are to paragraph numbers; superior figures refer to notes

INTESTACY—*continued*
　death intestate before
　　1926—*continued*
　　real estate, descent of—*continued*
　　　purchaser, descent traced
　　　　from—*continued*
　　　　trustees, devise to 541
　　　　qualified heir, position of 551
　ineffective will, on 479n²
　interest actions 777
　partial: meaning 479
　presumption against—
　　doubtful cases, in 255
　　force of 256
　　limits of 257
　　two gifts in same will, contest
　　　between 257
　Public Trustee, estate vesting in 644
　refunding on 1100
　residuary estate—
　　distribution 1137
　　income pending distribution 1138
　　investment, powers of 1136
　　trusts 1135
　succession—
　　old rules, operation of 477, 478
　　rules of 477
　testator's successor, gift over on death
　　469
　total: meaning 479
JOINT TENANCY
　See also JOINT TENANT
　family provision from property held
　　on 585
　gift by will of share in property 29
　words in will creating 394
JOINT TENANT
　See also JOINT TENANCY
　gift to, doctrine of lapse 173
JOINT WILL
　meaning 9, 714
　grant of probate or administration 9,
　　714
JUDGMENT
　personal representative, against—
　　claimant succeeding on claim only
　　　1292
　　default, by 1294
　　enforcement of 1295
　　failure of personal representative,
　　　on 1293
　　future assets, against 1291
JUDICIAL TRUSTEE
　appointment of 642

JURISDICTION
　probate jurisdiction 605, 678
LEASEHOLD
　devolution on death 942
LEGACY
　See also BEQUEST; GIFT BY WILL
　abatement—
　　debt, legacy in satisfaction of 1089
　　defeasible annuity 1091
　　demonstrative legacy 1088
　　general legacy 1087
　　specific legacy 1088
　absolute bequest with directions as to
　　application 1061
　admission of assets 1298
　adopted child, entitlement of 1063
　bankrupt, payment to 1065
　child subject to parental order,
　　entitlement of 1063
　contingent legacy—
　　generally 1059
　　intermediate income, carrying 1083
　debtor, to—
　　general legatee bringing debt into
　　　account 1067
　　legatee's bankruptcy, effect of 1068
　demonstrative legacy 120
　distribution—
　　beneficiaries, no duty to notify
　　　1055
　　executor's year, within 1054
　　obligation of 1053
　executor of deceased legatee, to 165
　executor, to—
　　defaulting executor, lien on interest
　　　of 1071
　　entitlement to 1070
　　presumption as to 1069
　family provision, pending proceedings
　　for 1064
　formal deed of release, execution of
　　1057
　future gifts 172
　general legacy 118, 119
　illegitimate child, entitlement of 1063
　interest and accretions—
　　account, direction for 1080
　　account, on 1187
　　appropriation of payments 1086
　　arrears of annuity 1084
　　contingent legacy 1083
　　date from which interest payable
　　　1081
　　dividends and rents 1085
　　future date, legacy payable at 1082

LEGACY—*continued*
  interest and accretions—*continued*
    general principles 1080
    non-residuary 1080
  payment of—
    admission of assets, as 1300
    machinery of 1056
    receipts 1056
  pecuniary legacy—
    generally 118
    order of application of assets on
      payment of—
      first fund for payment 1108
      general rules before 1926 1109
      land specifically devised, where
        1110
      mixed fund, where 1111
      realty as primary or exclusive
        fund for 1112
      statutory interpretation,
        difficulties of 1107
  person under disability, payment to
    1065
  proceedings for recovery, limitation
    of 1066
  specific legacy—
    generally 118
    preservation of 1060
  vested gift, payment of 1062
LEGAL AID
  personal representative, action by or
    against 1275
  probate claim 864
LETTERS OF ADMINISTRATION
  See also ADMINISTRATION OF
    DECEASED'S ESTATE
  action, grant limited to 817
  administration simple—
    bona vacantia 778
    creditor—
      meaning 787
      entitlement to grant 786
    Crown, right of 778
    foreign representative, grant to 767
    next of kin—
      contest between 773
      interest actions 777
      joint grant 775
      order of priority 768
      personal representative, procedure
        to add 776
      procedure 776
      right of preference, circumstances
        affecting 774

LETTERS OF
  ADMINISTRATION—*continued*
  administration simple—*continued*
    person having prior right to
      administer 768
    personal representative handing
      property to Crown, proceedings
      against 781
    persons entitled in default 769
    Public Trustee, grant to—
      entitlement 784
      limitation of powers 785
    solicitor of Duchies of Lancaster
      and Cornwall, grant to 782
    surviving spouse or civil partner—
      foreign divorce, etc, recognition
        of 771
      right to grant 770
      sole and joint grant 772
    Treasury Solicitor—
      grant to 779
      proceedings by or against 780
    trust corporation, grant to 783
  attorney, grant to—
    application for 800
    concurrent grant, seeking 800
    consular officer as attorney 802
    requirements for 801
    status of 803
  consular officer, grant to 802
  general grant of—
    beneficiary under trust, application
      by 762
    discretionary, notice to parties 763
    evidence required 765
    grounds other than intestacy, on
      755
    guarantees 766
    jurisdiction, foundation of 754
    oath 765
    order of priority 768
    person entitled to, passing over—
      consent, by 760
      person with prior right presumed
        dead, where 761
      special circumstances, in 759
    receiver, to 759
    sureties 766
    time for issue of 764
    unlawful killing, refusal in case of
      756
  grant ad colligenda bona 815
  incapacity of person entitled,
    administration during—

LETTERS OF
    ADMINISTRATION—*continued*
incapacity of person entitled,
    administration during—*continued*
    grant of 804
    person to whom grant made 805
    representative lacking mental
        capacity after grant 807
    stranger or creditor, grant to 806
limited grant, examples of 820
minority of person entitled,
    administration during—
    administrator's liability to account
        797
    co-executor as minor 798
    grant of 795
    limit of grant 796
    two administrators, necessity for
        799
mortgagees, exercise of jurisdiction
    by 818
non-trust corporation grant to 813
probate claim, pending determination
    of—
    administrator's liability to account
        812
    application for 810
    determination of office 811
    exercise of jurisdiction 809
    grant of 808
    procedure 810
representative, power of court to
    dispense with 818
specific property, grant limited to 819
unadministered estate—
    grant de bonis non 793
    rights of preference, observing 794
unincorporated body, grant to 814
will abroad or mislaid, grant in case
    of 816
will annexed—
    circumstances for 788
    de bonis non 788
    grant of 755
    person to whom made 790
    second grant, necessity for 792
    special cases 789
    testamentary instrument revoking
        former will, where 791
LIFE INTEREST
    gift by will 381
LLOYD'S
    deceased Name, directions relating to
        estate 1170

MAINTENANCE AGREEMENT
    meaning 596n[3]
    financial provision order, variation or
        revocation following 596
MANSLAUGHTER
    disqualification from benefit under
        will—
    forfeiture rule 39
    modification of rule 40
    intestacy, effect on capacity to take
        under 480
MARRIAGE
    dissolution or annulment, effect on
        will 177, 178
MARSHALLING
    principle generally 997
MENTALLY DISORDERED PERSON
    OR PATIENT
    administration of estate on behalf of
        807
    executor, appointment as 621
    legacy to, payment of 1065
MERGER
    estate held by personal representative,
        of 925
MINOR
    See also CHILD
    appropriation, consent to 1154
    executor, appointment as 620
    financial provision from
        deceased's estate. *See* FAMILY
        PROVISION
    legacy to—
    entitlement to income not applied in
        maintenance 1078
    parent or guardian, payment to
        1073
    payment of 1065, 1072
    personal representative, discharge
        of 1074
    statutory power of maintenance,
        application of 1079
    testator as parent or in loco
        parentis, maintenance out of
        income 1076
    testator's child, not 1077
    trustees, appointment of 1075
MONEY
    meaning 293
MORTGAGE
    devolution of mortgage estate on
        personal representative 953
    separate mortgages, several properties
        comprised in 1010

References are to paragraph numbers; superior figures refer to notes

MURDER
See also MANSLAUGHTER
disqualification from benefit under
  will—
  forfeiture rule 39
  modification of rule 40
intestacy, effect on capacity to take
  under 480
MUTUAL WILL
meaning 10
doctrine of 10
freedom of testamentary disposition,
  restriction on 23
mutual intention required 23
remarriage of second testator, effect
  of 87
NEXT-OF-KIN
meaning 343
NULLITY OF MARRIAGE
will, effect on 177, 178
OMISSION
death, cause of 1280
PARENT
intestate succession rights 508, 509,
  525
PARTICULARS OF CLAIM
probate claim 872
PARTNERSHIP
debts, personal
    representative's liability for—
    debts contracted after death 1235
    debts incurred while deceased
      partner 1232
    discharge of partnership liability
      1233
executor, appointment as 623
wrongful act of co-partner, personal
    representative's liability 1234
PARTNERSHIP PROPERTY
devolution on personal representative
  919, 920
PATENT (INVENTION)
devolution on personal representative
  939
PERPETUITIES, RULE AGAINST
freedom of testamentary disposition,
  restriction on 24
PERSONAL ESTATE
meaning 288
bequest of 377
conditional gift, vesting of. *See*
  CONDITIONAL GIFT
intestacy, distribution on. *See*
  INTESTACY

PERSONAL ESTATE—*continued*
quasi-inheritable gift of 385
PERSONAL REPRESENTATIVE
See also ADMINISTRATION OF
    DECEASED'S ESTATE; EXECUTOR
meaning 608
account, liability to—
  generally 1254
  order of court 1254
  tax purposes, for 1255
action against—
  admission of assets—
    arbitration, agreement for 1299
    conduct, by 1298
    effect of 1301
    express acknowledgement, by
      1298
    extent of 1300
    legacy, payment of 1300
    statutory demand, setting aside
      1301
  claim form, indorsement on 1271
  costs claimed by personal
    representative 1276
  defences 1290
  future assets, judgment against
    1291
  joinder of representative and
    personal claims 1273
  judgment—
    claimant succeeding on claim
      only 1292
    default, by 1294
    enforcement of 1295
    personal representative failing,
      where 1293
  legal aid 1275
  non-parties, notice of claim to 1272
  parties 1271
  permission to defend proceedings
    1274
  plene administravit, defence of
    1290
  plene administravit praeter, defence
    of 1290
  protection of personal
    representative 1300
  set-off, right of 1296
  survival of cause of action 1278,
    1279
action by—
  claim form, indorsement on 1271
  costs claimed by personal
    representative 1276

PERSONAL
   REPRESENTATIVE—*continued*
  action by—*continued*
    joinder of representative and
      personal claims 1273
    legal aid 1275
    non-parties, notice of claim to 1272
    parties 1271
    permission to bring proceedings
      1274
    survival of cause of action 1277,
      1279
  advertisements, issue of 964
  agent, liability for 1251
  assent—
    ad valorem stamp duty, previously
      attracting 1151
    costs of transfer 1152
    irrevocability 1146
    personalty, of—
      condition attached to 1140
      executor, gift to 1142
      implication, by 1141
      necessity for 1139
      one of several representatives, of
        1139
    purchaser, protection of—
      charge by way of legal mortgage,
        subject to 1145
      duties, debts or liabilities, security
        for 1145
      effect of 1146
      form of 1144
      legal estate, subject to 1145
      person in favour of whom
        executed 1143
      power of 1143
    relation back 1146
    trustee, personal representative
      becoming—
      assent or severance of property,
        on 1149
      effect of 1150
    trusteeship, in relation to 1148
  balances due from, interest on 1257
  balances due to, interest on 1258
  breach of trust 1238
  co-executor—
    duty to take care 1253
    liability for 1252
  common account, liability on 1184
  custodian, liability for 1251

PERSONAL
   REPRESENTATIVE—*continued*
  deceased's obligations, liability for—
    agreement for lease, specific
      performance of 1227
    assignee of term, representative of
      1223
    bankrupt testator 1219
    breach of trust, for 1238
    building contract—
      contractor's death, effect of 1216
      employer's death, effect on 1215
    contract to leave property by will
      1221
    contributories 1230
    distress, remedy by 1226
    entry upon deceased's leasehold,
      effect of 1224
    fines and penalties, for 1218
    general rule 1212
    guarantee, contract of 1236
    implied obligations 1237
    incomplete gifts, completion of
      1220
    joint obligations 1231
    land contracted to be sold,
      conveyance of 1214
    lifetime disposition of assets 1221
    original lessee 1222
    partnership debts—
      debts contracted after death 1235
      debts incurred while partner
        1232
      discharge of liability 1233
    personal considerations, contract
      founded on 1213
    personal liability, limitation of 1225
    settled freehold, as to 1229
    settled leasehold, as to 1228
    shares, devolution of title to 1230
    statutory obligations 1218
    tax, for 1217
    trustee in bankruptcy, property
      vested in 1219
    underwriting agreements 1230
    wrongful acts of co-partner 1234
  devolution of property on—
    meaning 916, 947
    benefice, presentation of 944
    causes of action, survival of 940
    chattels—
      crops 930

PERSONAL
  REPRESENTATIVE—*continued*
  devolution of property on—*continued*
    chattels—*continued*
      deceased's power of election,
        exercise of 933
      emblements 930
      natural products of soil 931
      ornamental fixtures 932
      payments to representatives 938
      personal property 928
      shares in company 929
      trade fixtures 932
    chose in action—
      bill of exchange 935
      compensation 937
      copyright 939
      covenant 934
      digital asset 941
      generally 934
      insurance policy 938
      option to take shares 936
      patent 939
    constructive conversion 918
    corporation sole, lease to 943
    death, on 917
    general power of appointment,
      subject to—
      personal estate 955
      real estate 954
    gift mortis causa, exception for 921
    interest in devolved property—
      apportionment 927
      beneficiary, of 922
      joint representation 926
      merger of estates 925
      nature of 922
      representative's bankruptcy, effect
        of 923
      representative's judgment creditor,
        right of 924
    leasehold 942
    mortgage estate 953
    partnership property 919
    personal estate—
      meaning 917
      death, on 917
      general power of appointment,
        subject to 955
    real estate—
      meaning 946
      death, on 917

PERSONAL
  REPRESENTATIVE—*continued*
  devolution of property on—*continued*
    real estate—*continued*
      deeming provisions 948
      general power of appointment,
        subject to 954
      settled land 949
      statutory devolution 945
      vesting 947
      surplus partnership assets, lien on
        920
    trust—
      exercise of powers 952
      personalty held on 950
      realty 951
  disposition preceding financial
    provision application, protection
    of 590
  distribution of assets, protection on
    484
  even hand between beneficiaries, duty
    of 1020
  goods, supply to testator's business
    657
  guidance of court, right to 1168
  indemnity, right of 1018
  limitation of liability defence 1185
  nominee, liability for 1251
  order to lodge money in court 1186
  own acts, liability for—
    devastavit, to beneficiaries on—
      bankruptcy of representative,
        proof in 1248
      concurrence of party in 1250
      devolution of liability 1249
      gratuitous bailee, unremunerated
        representative as 1247
      maladministration, for 1245
      nature of devastavit 1244
      negligence, for 1246
    third party, to—
      bill of exchange, endorsement of
        1241
      own contract, on 1239
      powers of intervention 1243
      promise to answer damages 1240
      tort, for 1242
      undue delay, for 1243
  own business, employment of estate
    assets in 658
  paramount title of 17

References are to paragraph numbers; superior figures refer to notes

PERSONAL
REPRESENTATIVE—*continued*
payment into court, enforcement of
    order for 1188
powers—
    agent, nominee or custodian,
        employment and payment of
        1049, 1050
    alienation and charge, to—
        additional powers 1022
        creditor or surviving partner, sale
            to 1029
        depreciatory conditions 1032
        impeachable transaction 1028
        land, alienation of 1024
        manner of sale 1031
        particular powers 1021
        personalty, alienation of 1023
        power to insure 1033
        power to recover rent 1034
        purchaser, common law
            protection of 1025
        purchaser, statutory protection
            of—
            notice and receipt 1026
            revocation or variation of
                probate, etc 1027
            statements from representative
                1027
        self, representative not to sell to
            1030
    compromise of claims—
        co-executor's claim 1044
        generally 1043
    deceased's business, carrying on—
        administration order, right to
            1042
        borrowing powers 1037
        creditor's right of subrogation
            1041
        express power, need for 1035
        funds employed for 1036
        indemnity—
            extent of 1040
            right to 1039
        liability of representative 1039
        limited company, conversion to
            1038
    duties in exercising 1020
    payment into court—
        costs, deduction of 1048
        lodgement justifiable, where 1047

PERSONAL
REPRESENTATIVE—*continued*
powers—*continued*
    payment into court—*continued*
        practice 1046
        statutory right 1045
    statutory powers 1019
    survivorship—
        personal or annexed to office,
            powers being 1052
        statutory 1051
profit, prohibition on making 657
protection of 1297
refunding—
    order or enactment protecting
        representative, effect of 1106
    representative and legatee, between
        1096
    representative and residuary legatee,
        between 1097
relief from liability—
    beneficiary's interest, indemnity for
        1260
    jurisdiction to grant 1259
remuneration—
    acting for beneficiary, costs of 655
    court allowing 648, 656
    direction in will for 648, 652
    general principle 648
    litigation costs 654
    professional personal
        representative—
        charging clause in will 650
        no charging clause in will 651
        unavailability under statute or
            will 653
    statute, authorised by 648
    time and trouble, for 649
special executor as 615, 747
substitution or removal, power of
    High Court 1163
trust property, purchase of 657
trustee, becoming—
    assent or severance of property, on
        1149
    effect of 1150
    generally 609
unauthorised payment by 1256
wilful default, order for account on
    footing of 1183
year, realisation of investments within
    961
POSSESSIONS
meaning 289

References are to paragraph numbers; superior figures refer to notes

POWER OF APPOINTMENT
devolution of property subject to 954, 955
PRIVILEGED WILL
actual military service: meaning 79
execution of 79
form of 81
mariner or seaman 80
proof of 81, 710
revocation 79, 81
PROBATE
common form business. *See* PROBATE IN COMMON FORM
contentious business. *See* PROBATE CLAIM
court. *See* PROBATE COURT
rules of court 685
PROBATE CLAIM
appeal 890
case management 877
claim form—
failure to acknowledge service 869
issue of 868
rules governing 868
service out of jurisdiction 868
commencement, effect of 868
compromise of 885
costs—
assessment, allowable on 913
certain portions of estate, payable from 914
default of defence, in 912
discretion of court 908
executor, liability of 910
generally 908
security for 915
successful party, of 909
unsuccessful party, of 911
counterclaim 873
defence 873
directions questionnaire 877
disclosure of documents 880
discontinuance of 883
dismissal of 883
evidence, directions as to 882
further information, court order for 879
inspection of documents 881
judgment in default not available in 876
judgment, effect of 887
jurisdiction—
County Court 866
High Court 865
non-parties, notice to 878

PROBATE CLAIM—*continued*
notice of intention to cross-examine only, limitation of costs on 874
opposing probate—
grounds for 891
medical evidence, value and function of 893
part of will, as to 892
statement of case 891
want of due execution, on ground of—
death of witness, effect of 896
evidence of execution 894
faulty memory of witness, effect of 896
presumption 895
want of knowledge and approval, on ground of—
circumstances rebutting presumption 903
fiduciary relationship, proof of existence of 904
partial exclusion 906
presumption 902
probate court, issue raised in 907
requirement of 901
will prepared by person in own favour, where 905
want of sound disposing, on ground of—
burden of proof—
generally 899
lucid interval, will made in 900
immaturity 898
learning difficulties, adult having 898
person of full age and sound mind, testamentary capacity 897
particulars of claim 872
parties 878
privilege 882
probate action 885n[1]
proof in solemn form—
legal aid 864
no need for, where 861
persons entitled to call for 863
pre-action protocol, observing 860
validity of codicil in doubt, where 862
rectification of will, for 889
reply 873
revocation of grant, for 888
settlement 885

References are to paragraph numbers; superior figures refer to notes

PROBATE CLAIM—*continued*
  statement of case, contents of 875
  striking out 884
  summary judgment 884
  testamentary capacity, medical
    evidence 893
  testamentary documents—
    meaning 870
    evidence of 870
    transmission of 871
    verification 871
  transfer of proceedings 867
  trial 886
  withdrawal of proceedings 883
PROBATE COURT
  meaning 8n², 678
  administration claim. *See*
    ADMINISTRATION CLAIM
  functions 679
  grant of probate or administration.
    See GRANT OF PROBATE OR
    ADMINISTRATION
  jurisdiction 8n², 678
  powers over testamentary papers 680
  probate claim. *See* PROBATE CLAIM
PROBATE IN COMMON FORM
  account from holder of original grant
    753
  application for—
    executor's oath 728
    nuncupative wills and copies, on
      730
    personal application 727
    place of 724
    probate practitioner, through 726
    solicitor, through 726
  blind or illiterate testator, will of 734
  cessate grant—
    account from holder of original
      grant 753
    generally 752
  commorientes 746
  date, doubt as to 737
  death—
    commorientes 746
    leave to swear to 744
    presumption of 745
    proof of 743
  documents attached to or incorporated
    in will, production of 736
  double grant 751
  due execution, proof of 733
  engrossment of documents 732
  executor, misdescription of 738
  executor's right to 725

PROBATE IN COMMON
  FORM—*continued*
  general grant 747
  High Court, in—
    appeal 705
    citation 695
    contentious business, and 684
    costs 687
    notices, service of 704
    probate rules 685
    standing searches 688
    summons, application by 701
  inheritance tax account 731
  issue of grant, time for 742
  limited grant—
    property appointed, limited to 749
    special executor, appointment of
      747
    time, limited to 750
    types of 748
  non-proving executor, powers reserved
    to 729
  obliteration, interlineation or
    alteration, evidence as to 735
  original will and documents, deposit
    of 732
  record, completing 732
  rectification of will 741
  revocation, doubt as to 737
  words excluded from probate—
    application, practice on 740
    examples of 739
    jurisdiction 739
PROBATE RULES
  making of 685
PROMISSORY NOTE
  devolution on death 935
PROPERTY
  not disposable by will—
    chose in action 32
    testator, not belonging to 30
    testator's body 31
  will, disposition by 18, 26
PUBLIC TRUSTEE
  directions by 644n⁶
  fees payable to 1015
  intestacy, estate vesting on 644
  letters of administration, grant to—
    entitlement 784
    limitation of powers 785
  solvent small estate, administration
    of—
    application for order 1164
    order of court 1165

RACE
  gift by will, condition as to 140
REAL ESTATE
  devise of 376
  devolution on personal representative.
    See PERSONAL REPRESENTATIVE
  entailed estate 386
  grant of probate or administration,
    effect of 674
RECTIFICATION
  will 466, 741, 889
RELATIONS
  meaning 349
RELIGION
  gift by will, condition as to 140
RENT
  devise of 375
RESIDUARY ESTATE
  absolutely, given—
    general power of appointment,
      property subject to 1114
    hotchpot, valuation of estate for
      1117
    legatee's right to have residue
      ascertained 1116
    scope of gift 1113
    share of residue, failure of 1115
  disposition of property, presumptions
    1130
  inheritance tax—
    burden of 1128
    disposition of property,
      presumptions 1130
    free of duty provisions 1129
    incidence of—
      words affecting 1131
      words not affecting 1132
    partially exempt residue 1134
  settled estate—
    Allhusen v Whittel, rule in 1118
    annuities, payment of 1121
    debts, real estate charged with 1120
    Howe v Earl of Dartmouth,
      rule in—
        exceptions 1123
        no trust for conversion, effect of
          1125
        trust for conversion, effect of
          1124
    income of residue, ascertaining
      1118
    income-producing property,
      retention of 1126
    interest on legacies 1119

RESIDUARY ESTATE—*continued*
  settled estate—*continued*
    retention of reversionary property,
      adjustment on 1127
    trust for conversion, effect of 1124
REVOCATION OF WILL
  act of 93
  civil partnership, by—
    general rule 90
    power of appointment, will in
      exercise of 90
    will in expectation of partnership,
      exception for 91
  codicil, by 100
  codicil, effect on 1
  conditional—
    dependent relative 108
    express or implied revocation 107
    intention 108
    mistake as to 109
    question of fact 107
    same property subsequently
      disposed of 107
  covenant against, enforceability 21
  dependent relative 108
  destruction, by—
    duplicate, of 102
    extent of 105
    incomplete 103
    intention 101
    presumption of intention 106
    stranger, by 104
    sufficient damage 105
    testator later becoming mentally
      disordered 106
  doubt as to, evidence relating to 737
  intention to revoke 93
  international will 14
  later instrument, by—
    codicil 100
    execution of 95
    gift of residue, of 96
    later inconsistent will 97
    loss of later will, effect of 98
    partial 96
    partly inconsistent will 99
  marriage, by—
    general rule 87
    power of appointment, will in
      exercise of 87
    will in contemplation of marriage
      pre-1983, exception for 88
    will in expectation of marriage post
      1982, exception for 89
  methods of 94

REVOCATION OF WILL—*continued*
  partial 96
  privileged will 79, 81
  revival—
    execution of codicil, by 110
    form of 110
    intention 111
    methods of 110
    previous codicils, extending to 112
    re-execution, by 110
    reference to will by date 112
  voluntary—
    after death, no delegation of power 94
    intention to revoke 93
    methods of 94
    revocable nature 92
RULES OF COURT
  probate rules 685
SALE OF LAND
  will as memorandum of contract 6
SECRET TRUST
  evidence establishing 221
  fully secret 222
  partly secret 223
SECURITIES
  meaning 294
  share in company. *See* SHARE IN COMPANY
SECURITY FOR COSTS
  probate proceedings 915
SET-OFF
  personal representative, claim by or against 1296
SETTLED LAND
  meaning 821n^2
  devolution on personal representative 949
  grant of probate or administration. *See* SETTLED LAND GRANT
  tenant for life, obligations of—
    settled freehold 1229
    settled leasehold 1228
SETTLED LAND GRANT
  disposal of settled land 829
  general grant including 826
  land ceasing to be settled, limited grant on 827
  legal estate, devolution of 823
  order of priority 822
  representative, renunciation by 828
  revocation, application for 828
  separate, requirement of 826
  special executor 821

SETTLED LAND GRANT—*continued*
  special or additional personal representative, application for 828
  tenant for life, on death of 825
  where required 824
SHARE IN COMPANY
  See also SECURITIES
  devolution on personal representative 929
  option to take. *See* SHARE OPTION
  transfer by personal representative 1230
SHARE OPTION
  devolution on personal representative 936
SIGNATURE
  will, of. *See* WILL (TESTAMENT) (signature)
SOCIETY
  non-charitable, gift to 36, 37
SOIL
  natural products of, devolution on personal representative 931
SOLICITORS REGULATION AUTHORITY
  undue delay by personal representative, intervention powers 1243
SPECIFIC PERFORMANCE
  gift by will 21
STAMP DUTY
  abolition of 1151
STAMP DUTY LAND TAX
  will or intestacy, acquisition of property under 1151
STATEMENT OF CASE
  probate claim, in 875
STOCKS AND SHARES
  See also SECURITIES; SHARE IN COMPANY
  meaning 295
SURETY
  death of, effect 1236
SURROGACY
  child born as result, as donee under will 361
SURVIVORSHIP
  contingent event, on 319
  date of distribution, ascertainment of survivors at 318
  period to which referring 315
  stirpital 317
  survive: meaning 315

SURVIVORSHIP—*continued*
  use of words other than in strict
    sense 316
TENANCY IN COMMON
  See also TENANT IN COMMON
  gift by will of share in property 29
  words in will creating 395
TENANT IN COMMON
  See also TENANCY IN COMMON
  gift to, doctrine of lapse 173
TESTAMENT
  See also WILL (TESTAMENT)
  meaning 1
  civil law, at 1n[1]
TESTAMENTARY CAPACITY
  blind, deaf or dumb person 48
  dementia, effect of 48
  generally 46
  knowledge or approval, lack of 55
  medical evidence 49n[2]
  mental disability, person suffering—
    Court of Protection, inquiry by 51
    delusions, evidence of 52
    provision for 47
    senile incapacity 53
    sound disposing mind—
      meaning 49
      time at which existing 50
    soundness of mind, memory and
      understanding 48
    unsoundness of mind, existence of
      52
    will made during incapacity, status
      of 51
  proof of 4
  senile incapacity 53
  sound disposing mind—
    meaning 49
    time at which existing 50
  soundness of mind, memory and
    understanding, need for 48
  summary of indicia 49n[1]
TESTAMENTARY DISPOSITION
  acceptance of—
    benefits and burdens, of 152
    blended gifts, of 153
    making of 152
    retraction of 154
  ademption—
    assignment, effect of 157
    change of investment, contemplation
      of 158
    debt, payment of 159
    exercise of option, effect of 157
    methods of 155

TESTAMENTARY
  DISPOSITION—*continued*
  ademption—*continued*
    ownership or form of property,
      change in 156
    sale, effect of 157
  disclaimer—
    blended gifts, of 153
    effect of 151
    person making 151
    retraction of 154
  failure of—
    acts of testator prior to date of will
      150
    condition precedent, non-
      performance of 150
    disposal of property before death,
      on 150
    dissolution or annulment of civil
      partnership 179
    effect of—
      contingent gift over 182
      general rule 180
      residuary devise, inclusion in 183
      subsequent interests, acceleration
        of 181
    marriage, dissolution or annulment
      of—
      death after 1982 and before
        1996 177
      death after 1995 178
    personal representatives, paramount
      claims of 150
    reasons for 150
  freedom, restrictions on—
    agreement to make mutual wills,
      under 23
    agreement, by 26
    contract, by 20
    enforceability 21
    estoppel, by 20
    family provision, effect of 21
    generally 565
    rule against perpetuities, under 24
    statute, by 24
    trust, by 20
  interests, creation of—
    chattels consumed in use 122
    chattels given to successive donees
      121
    conditional gifts 124
    equitable 117
    estate pur autre vie 117
    gift over 124
    law, recognised by 116

References are to paragraph numbers; superior figures refer to notes

TESTAMENTARY
   DISPOSITION—*continued*
  interests, creation of—*continued*
    option to purchase—
     generally 125
     rights of person exercising 126
    selection, right of 127
    successive and future 117
    vesting 123
  lapse—
   meaning 160
   charitable legacy, of 162
   effect of—
    contingent gift over 182
    general rule 180
    intestacy, lapsed demise passing
     on 183
    residuary devise, inclusion in 183
    subsequent interests, acceleration
     of 181
   exceptions—
    alternative gift 164
    class gift 174, 175
    death of issue, testator dying
     before 1983 168
    executor of deceased legatee,
     legacy to 165
    future gift 172
    gift to testator's issue—
     exercise of appointment 170
     testator dying after 1983 169
     testator dying before 1983 167
    interests in tail, testator dying
     before 1997 166
    issue of deceased child, testator
     dying before 1983 176
    joint tenants, gift to 173
    moral obligation, gift in
     pursuance of 163
    settled shares 171
    tenants in common, gift to 173
   lapsed property, charge on 184
   powers, application of doctrine to
    161
  property, of—
    co-ownership 29
    equitable interests 27
    examples of 27
    immovables and movables 25
    real and personal estate 26

TESTAMENTARY
   DISPOSITION—*continued*
  property, of—*continued*
    testator's title, state of 28
    purpose forbidden by law, for 34
TESTATOR
  beneficiary and, fiduciary relationship
   between 904
  capacity. *See* TESTAMENTARY
   CAPACITY
  will. *See* WILL (TESTAMENT)
TITLE (RIGHT)
  personal representative, of 17
  testator, of 28
TRIAL
  probate claim, of 886
TRUST
  See also TRUSTEE
  conversion, for 1124
  corporation. *See* TRUST
   CORPORATION
  devolution on personal
   representative—
    exercise of trustee's powers 952
    personalty held on trust 950
    realty held on trust 951
  execution, determination of questions
   by court—
    jurisdiction 1162
    parties to proceedings 1172
  freedom of testamentary disposition,
   restriction on 20
  intestacy, on 1135
  new: meaning 1123n^{12}
  payment of debts, for 980
TRUST CORPORATION
  fees, payment out of deceased's estate
   1015
  letters of administration, grant of 783
TRUSTEE
  See also TRUST
  assent of personal representative to
   trusteeship 1148
  disposition preceding financial
   provision application, protection
   on 590
  personal representative as 609, 1149,
   1150
  probate, grant of 613
UNDUE INFLUENCE
  donee under will, by 38

UNDUE INFLUENCE—*continued*
  validity of will, effect on 56
  want of knowledge and approval
    distinguished 57
UNINCORPORATED ASSOCIATION
  gift to 36
VALIDITY OF WILL
  formalities—
    attestation—
      capacity of witness 78
      due execution, presumption of 77
      form of 72
      intention 76
      methods of 74
      position of 73
      requirements for 70
      testator's presence, in 71
      witness, description of 75
    date, no requirement for 61
    signature—
      acknowledgement of 68, 71
      act of execution, as 62
      attestation 70
      erroneous or assumed name, in
        63
      methods of 63
      on behalf of testator 64
      position of 65, 66
      presumption as to 69
      requirement 62
      several sheets, will on 67
      witnesses, in presence of 68
    writing 60
  mental element—
    clause fraudulently introduced,
      exception from grant 59
    force, effect of 56
    knowledge or approval, lack of—
      generally 55
      undue influence, and 57
    testamentary capacity. *See*
      TESTAMENTARY CAPACITY
    testamentary intention, need for 54
    undue influence—
      effect of 56
      want of knowledge or approval,
        and 57
  privileged will—
    actual military service: meaning 79
    execution of 79
    form of 81
    mariner or seaman 80
    proof of 81

VALIDITY OF WILL—*continued*
  privileged will—*continued*
    revocation 79, 81
VALUE ADDED TAX
  personal representative, liability to
    pay 1217
WILL (TESTAMENT)
  admissibility of evidence. *See*
    CONSTRUCTION OF WILL
    (evidence, admissibility of)
  alteration—
    codicil, effect of 85
    due execution of 82
    signature, after 84
    stranger, by 86
    time of 83
  ambiguous cases, presumption in 244
  attestation—
    due execution, presumption of 77
    form of 72
    intention 76
    methods of 74
    position of 73
    requirements for 70
    testator's presence, in 71
    witness, description of 75
  beneficiary. *See* BENEFICIARY
  concealing 671
  conditional revocation. *See*
    REVOCATION OF WILL
    (conditional)
  conditionally testamentary instrument
    7
  construction of. *See* CONSTRUCTION
    OF WILL
  contingency, reference to 7
  date of 61
  death, gift over on. *See* GIFT OVER
  declaration of intention, as 2
  deed, in form of 3
  delegation of power to make 11
  disposition by. *See* TESTAMENTARY
    DISPOSITION
  disposition inter vivos distinguished 2
  donee—
    capacity to benefit. *See* DONEE
    UNDER WILL
    gift by will, of. *See* GIFT BY WILL
  effectual gift by, preconditions 19
  erasures—
    due execution of 82
    time of 83
  essential characteristics 2
  execution, form of 5
  executor. *See* EXECUTOR

WILL (TESTAMENT)—*continued*
  foreign element in—
    essential validity 13
    European Union legislation 13
    formal validity 12
  forgery of 671
  formalities. *See* VALIDITY OF WILL
    (formalities)
  heir, gift to. *See* GIFT BY WILL
  hotchpot clause. *See* GIFT BY WILL
  implied words 466
  incapacity, ground of opposition to
    probate claim. *See* PROBATE
    CLAIM (opposing probate)
  instructions of testator, evidence as
    to 199
  intention of testator—
    need for testamentary intention 54
    principles of construction. *See*
      CONSTRUCTION OF WILL
  interlineations 83
  international will 14
  intestacy. *See* INTESTACY
  irrevocable, declared to be 2
  joint will 9, 714
  legacy. *See* LEGACY
  life interest. *See* LIFE INTEREST
  matters dealt with by 4
  mutual will. *See* MUTUAL WILL
  nature of instrument, evidence of 8
  omission of words from 466
  particular dispositions, construction
    of. *See* CONSTRUCTION OF WILL
  partly testamentary instrument 6
  personalty bequeathed by 17
  power of appointment. *See* POWER
    OF APPOINTMENT
  preparation, evidence of instructions
    199
  presumptions. *See* CONSTRUCTION
    OF WILL (presumptions)
  privileged will. *See* PRIVILEGED WILL
  probate. *See* PROBATE; PROBATE
    CLAIM; PROBATE IN COMMON
    FORM
  property disposable by. *See*
    TESTAMENTARY DISPOSITION
  property, effect on 18
  realty devised by 17
  rectification—
    application for 889
    powers of court 466, 741
  republication—
    meaning 113n[1]

WILL (TESTAMENT)—*continued*
  republication—*continued*
    date of will, shifting—
      excepted purposes 115
      generally 114
    effect of 113
    methods of 113
    nature of 113
    original effect, not prejudicing 115
  residuary estate. *See* RESIDUARY
    ESTATE
  revocation. *See* REVOCATION OF
    WILL
  rules of convenience. *See* DONEE
    UNDER WILL (class gift)
  safe-keeping 15, 16
  signature—
    acknowledgement of 68, 71
    act of execution, as 62
    attestation 70
    erroneous or assumed name, in 63
    methods of 63
    on behalf of testator 64
    position of 65, 66
    presumption as to 69
    requirement 62
    several sheets, will on 67
    witnesses, in presence of 68
  statutory declaration to support 4n[13]
  testamentary capacity. *See*
    TESTAMENTARY CAPACITY
  testamentary disposition. *See*
    TESTAMENTARY DISPOSITION
  testamentary form 5
  uncertainty. *See* CONSTRUCTION OF
    WILL
  unsoundness of mind. *See*
    TESTAMENTARY CAPACITY
  validity. *See* VALIDITY OF WILL
  witness—
    capacity of 78
    child as 78
    gift to—
      exceptions to general rule 42
      generally 41
      legatee attesting codicil, effect of
        43
      superfluous attestation 44
    gift to spouse or civil partner of 78
    signature of testator, to 68
  writing 60
WITNESS
  summons. *See* WITNESS SUMMONS
  will, to. *See* WILL (TESTAMENT)

References are to paragraph numbers; superior figures refer to notes

WITNESS SUMMONS
   testamentary documents, as to 680

Words and Phrases

abroad 139
absurdity 242n^3
action 885n^1
actual military service 79
administration—
 (Administration of Estates Act 1925)
  607n^1
 (Senior Courts Act 1981) 622n^8
administrator 607
advances 404
annuities 927n^2
apparent 82
appeal court 890n^{14}
appurtenances 286
authorised court officer 687n^8
authorised officer 727n^{11}
Bank of England rate 488n^6, 518n^8
begotten 330
beneficiary—
 (Administration of Justice Act 1985)
  1163n^2
 (Inheritance (Provision for Family and
  Dependants) Act 1975) 572n^6
bequest 284
business 287
caeterorum grant 748
caveator 690
child—
 (Inheritance (Provision for Family and
  Dependants) Act 1975) 567n^9
 (Wills Act 1837) 331n^3
child or children 461
children 330n^1, 331
citation 695
class gift 175
clerical error 187
codicil 1
confirmation 831n^1
conveyance 858n^1
costs 687n^1
court 888n^2, 957n^2
court of construction 185
cousins 328n^6
creditor 787

Crown—
 (Administration of Estates Act 1925)
  782n^1
 (Non-Contentious Probate Rules
  1987) 769n^2
customary land 561n^1
debt—
 (Administration of Estates Act 1925)
  643n^5
 (County Courts (Interest on Judgment
  Debts) Order 1991 1187n^1
decision 890n^5
deposit schedule 1046n^3
descendants 338
descent 477n^1
devolution 916
die without issue 458n^1
disposal 378
disposition—
 (Administration of Estates Act 1925)
  969n^7
 (Family Law Reform Act 1987) 350n^1
 (Inheritance (Provision for Family and
  Dependants) Act 1975) 586n^6
district judge—
 (Administration of Estates Act 1925)
  631n^6
 (Non-Contentious Probate Rules
  1987) 687n^7
dividends 927n^3
document 880n^1
donee—
 (Inheritance (Provision for Family and
  Dependants) Act) 1975 586n^8,
  587n^2, 588n^{10}, 589n^6
 (Law of Property Act 1925) 17n^3
eldest 333n^5
employees 366
entitled 246n^4, 453
equitable interests 969n^2
escheat 552
estate 289, 620n^5
executor 606, 608n^3, 831n^1
expenses 246n^6
fairly 1259n^2

family 246n[17], 348
first cousins or cousins german 328n[6]
first son or eldest son 333
former civil partner 567
former spouse 567n[6]
free of duty 246n[8]
general law 533n[6]
general power 955n[2]
gift 17n[3]
grandchildren 328n[5]
grant—
   (Administration of Estates Act 1925)
     631n[7]
   (Non-Contentious Probate Fees Order
     2004) 686n[4]
   (Senior Courts Act 1981) 683n[2]
grantee 990n[8]
Great Britain 4n[7], 622n[4]
half cousins 328n[6]
heir 341
hereditaments 291n[10]
husband 41n[3]
illegitimate 350
income 1138n[1]
internal law 12n[3]
intestate 1135n[1]
investments 293
issue 334, 457n[1], 459
joint grant 772
judge 890n[13]
judicial separation 359n[9]
kin 349n[2]
land 561n[3]
lapse 160, 177n[7]
latent ambiguity 220
lease 990n[2]
legacy 284
legal estates 969n[2]
legitimated person 357n[19]
letters of administration 728n[2]
limitation 17n[3]
living with a person 139n[2]
lower court 890n[14]
maintenance agreement 596n[3]
mariner 80n[3]
marriage 42n[2], 87n[2], 89n[2], 131n[15],
   132n[1], 133n[1], 134n[1], 135n[1], 160n[2],
   178n[2], 246n[10], 591n[15], 596n[3],
   770n[1]
minority 246n[12]
money 293

nephews and nieces 328n[7, 11]
net estate 582
new trust 1118n[7], 1123n[12], 1127n[2]
nominated registry 691n[2]
non-contentious or common form
   probate business 678n[5]
oath 728n[2]
parent's share 327
partner 623
patent ambiguity 220
pecuniary legacy 1003
per stirpes 204n[1], 246n[14], 345
person of unsound mind 533n[1]
personal applicant 727n[1]
personal chattels 488n[3]
personal effects 288
personal estate 282n[4], 288, 917
personal representative—
   (Administration of Estates Act 1925)
     608, 947
   (Inheritance Tax Act 1984) 1266n[3]
   (Public Trustee Act 1906) 642
personalty 348n[1]
possession 1022n[8]
prescribed—
   (Administration of Justice Act 1982)
     16n[5]
   (Senior Courts Act 1981) 808n[7]
probate 8n[2]
probate action 885n[1]
probate claim 680n[2]
probate counterclaim 873n[9]
probate court 8n[2]
probate practitioner 688n[5]
probate rules—
   (Administration of Estates Act 1971)
     840n[2]
   (Senior Courts Act 1981) 620n[6]
probate valuation 246n[9]
property—
   (Administration of Estates Act 1925)
     608n[4]
   (Forfeiture Act 1982) 40n[6]
   (Inheritance (Provision for Family and
     Dependants) Act 1975) 582n[2],
     586n[15], 588n[5]
   (Law of Property Act 1925) 943n[1]
protected civil partnership 329n[1]
protected marriage 329n[1]
purchaser 858n[4], 1147n[4]
qualifying interest 357n[13]
ready money 293

References are to paragraph numbers; superior figures refer to notes

real and personal estate 485n^6
real estate—
  (Administration of Estates Act 1925)
    607n^1, 917, 946
  (Senior Courts Act 1981) 620n^5
  (Wills Act 1837) 282n^3
registrar 631n^7
registration convention 16n^7
registry 680n^2
relations 349
relevant beneficiary 885n^3
relevant document 843n^1
relevant office 680n^2
rent 927n^1
rentcharge 927n^1
representation 608n^2
representatives 364
reputation 354n^{10}
Secretary of State 14n^1
secured debt 1151n^4
securities 294
senior district judge 691n^2
servants 366
settled land 629n^2, 821n^2, 822n^1
settled legacy, share or interest 1155n^2
simultaneous death 246n^{13}
soldier 79n^1
sole grant 772
sole solicitor 1243n^3
solicitor 687n^1
sound disposing mind 49
special personal representatives 829n^1
specified 644
spouse—
  (generally) 4n^9, 24n^1, 26n^4, 243n^2
  (Inheritance (Provision for Family and
    Dependants) Act 1975) 567n^4,
    593n^7
state 12n^6
statement of case 875n^4
stocks and shares 295

successor 976n^5
survive 246n^{15}, 315
survivor—
  (generally) 318n^5, 460
  (Insolvency Act 1986) 988n^9
tenements 291n^{10}
testamentary document 870
treasury solicitor—
  (Administration of Estates Act 1925)
    782n^1
  (Non-Contentious Probate Rules
    1987) 769n^1
  (Senior Courts Act 1981) 622
treatment services 359n^{11}
trust corporation 622n^4
trustee—
  (generally) 1259n^3
  (Inheritance (Provision for Family and
    Dependants) Act 1975) 590n^1
undertaker 787n^{10}
United Kingdom 4n^7, 622n^4
unmarried 246n^{11}, 4443n^{10}
uterine brothers and sisters 328n^4
valuable consideration 858n^4
value lost to the estate 988n^8
vest 412
vested 412
wages 296
wife 41n^3
will—
  (generally) 870n^1
  (Administration of Justice Act 1985)
    192n^1, 607n^1, 885n^1
  (Inheritance (Provision for Family and
    Dependants) Act 1975) 566n^8
  (Senior Courts Act 1981) 620n^4
  (Wills Act 1963) 1, 12n^7
witness statement 882n^2
written request 1046n^6
younger children 333n^2